THE
ALL ENGLAND
LAW REPORTS

1974
VOLUME 2

EDITOR
R N G Harrison BA
of Lincoln's Inn, Barrister

ASSISTANT EDITOR
Christine Ivamy MA
of Gray's Inn, Barrister

LONDON
BUTTERWORTHS

ENGLAND: Butterworth & Co (Publishers) Ltd
London: 88 Kingsway, WC2B 6AB

AUSTRALIA: Butterworths Pty Ltd
Sydney: 586 Pacific Highway, Chatswood, NSW 2067
Melbourne: 343 Little Collins Street, 3000
Brisbane: 240 Queen Street, 4000

CANADA: Butterworth & Co (Canada) Ltd
Toronto: 2265 Midland Avenue, Scarborough, M1P 4S1

NEW ZEALAND: Butterworths of New Zealand Ltd
Wellington: 26–28 Waring Taylor Street 1

SOUTH AFRICA: Butterworth & Co (South Africa) (Pty) Ltd
Durban: 152–154 Gale Street

ISBN 0 406 85109 3

Printed in Great Britain by R J Acford Ltd, Industrial Estate, Chichester, Sussex

REPORTERS

House of Lords

Christine Ivamy Barrister

Privy Council

Christine Ivamy Barrister

Court of Appeal, Civil Division

Wendy Shockett Barrister
L J Kovats Esq Barrister

Mary Rose Plummer Barrister
A S Virdi Esq Barrister

Court of Appeal, Criminal Division

N P Metcalfe Esq Barrister

Courts-Martial Appeals

N P Metcalfe Esq Barrister

Chancery Division

Jacqueline Metcalfe Barrister
Evelyn Budd Barrister

R W Farrin Esq Barrister
Susan Corbett Barrister

Queen's Bench Division

F K Anklesaria Esq Barrister
Jacqueline Charles Barrister
M Denise Chorlton Barrister
J M Collins Esq Barrister
Janet Harding Barrister

E H Hunter Esq Barrister
Lea Josse Barrister
Gwynedd Lewis Barrister
Deirdre McKinney Barrister
Gerald Price Esq Barrister

Family Division

R C T Habesch Esq Barrister

National Industrial Relations Court

Gordon H Scott Esq Barrister

Revenue Cases

Rengan Krishnan Esq Barrister

Admiralty

N P Metcalfe Esq Barrister

MANAGER

John W Wilkes Esq

House of Lords

The Lord High Chancellor: Lord Elwyn-Jones

Lords of Appeal in Ordinary

Lord Reid
Lord Morris of Borth-y-Gest
Viscount Dilhorne
Lord Wilberforce
Lord Pearson

Lord Diplock
Lord Simon of Glaisdale
Lord Cross of Chelsea
Lord Kilbrandon
Lord Salmon

Court of Appeal

The Lord High Chancellor

The Lord Chief Justice of England: Lord Widgery

The Master of the Rolls: Lord Denning

The President of the Family Division: Sir George Gillespie Baker

Lords Justices of Appeal

Sir William Arthian Davies
Sir Charles Ritchie Russell
Sir Herbert Edmund Davies
Sir Henry Josceline Phillimore
    (died 5th June 1974)
Sir John Megaw
Sir Denys Burton Buckley
Sir David Arnold Scott Cairns

Sir Edward Blanshard Stamp
Sir John Frederick Eustace Stephenson
Sir Alan Stewart Orr
Sir Eustace Wentworth Roskill
Sir Frederick Horace Lawton
Sir Leslie George Scarman
Sir Arthur Evan James
Sir Roger Fray Greenwood Ormrod
    (appointed 22nd April 1974)

Chancery Division

The Lord High Chancellor
The Vice-Chancellor: Sir John Pennycuick

Sir John Anthony Plowman
Sir Reginald William Goff
Sir Robert Edgar Megarry
Sir John Patrick Graham
Sir Peter Harry Batson Woodroffe Foster

Sir John Norman Keates Whitford
Sir John Anson Brightman
Sir Ernest Irvine Goulding
Sir Sydney William Templeman
Sir Raymond Henry Walton

Queen's Bench Division

The Lord Chief Justice of England

Sir John Percy Ashworth
Sir Aubrey Melford Steed Stevenson
Sir Gerald Alfred Thesiger
Sir Basil Nield
Sir Bernard Joseph Maxwell MacKenna
Sir Alan Abraham Mocatta
Sir John Thompson
Sir Daniel James Brabin
Sir Helenus Patrick Joseph Milmo
Sir Joseph Donaldson Cantley
Sir Patrick Reginald Evelyn Browne
Sir George Stanley Waller
Sir Hugh Eames Park
Sir Ralph Vincent Cusack
Sir Stephen Chapman
Sir John Ramsay Willis
Sir Graham Russell Swanwick
Sir Patrick McCarthy O'Connor
Sir John Francis Donaldson
Sir Geoffrey Dawson Lane
Sir John Robertson Dunn Crichton
Sir Samuel Burgess Ridgway Cooke

Sir Bernard Caulfield
Sir Nigel Cyprian Bridge
Sir Sebag Shaw
Sir Hilary Gwynne Talbot
Sir Edward Walter Eveleigh
Sir William Lloyd Mars-Jones
Sir Ralph Kilner Brown
Sir Phillip Wien
Sir Peter Henry Rowley Bristow
Sir Hugh Harry Valentine Forbes
Sir Desmond James Conrad Ackner
Sir William Hugh Griffiths
Sir Robert Hugh Mais
Sir Neil Lawson
Sir David Powell Croom-Johnson
Sir John Raymond Phillips
Sir Leslie Kenneth Edward Boreham
Sir John Douglas May
Sir Michael Robert Emanuel Kerr
Sir Alfred William Michael Davies
Sir John Dexter Stocker
Sir Kenneth George Illtyd Jones

Family Division

The President of the Family Division

Sir Roger Fray Greenwood Ormrod
(appointed Lord Justice of Appeal,
22nd April 1974)
Sir Charles William Stanley Rees
Sir Reginald Withers Payne
Sir Neville Major Ginner Faulks
Sir James Roualeyn Hovell-Thurlow
Cumming-Bruce
Sir John Brinsmead Latey
Dame Elizabeth Kathleen Lane
Sir Henry Vivian Brandon

Sir Robin Horace Walford Dunn
Sir William Arthur Bagnall
Sir Alfred Kenneth Hollings
Sir Tasker Watkins VC
Sir John Lewis Arnold
Sir Charles Trevor Reeve
Sir Morris Finer
Sir Francis Brooks Purchas
(appointed 22nd April 1974)
Sir Haydn Tudor Evans
(appointed 21st June 1974)

CITATION

These Reports are cited thus:

[1974] 2 All ER

REFERENCES

These reports contain references, which follow after the headnotes, to the following major works of legal reference described in the manner indicated below—

Halsbury's Laws of England

The reference 2 Halsbury's Laws (3rd Edn) 20, para 48, refers to paragraph 48 on page 20 of volume 2 of the third edition, and the reference 2 Halsbury's Laws (4th Edn) 708, para 1535, refers to paragraph 1535 on page 708 of volume 2 of the fourth edition of Halsbury's Laws of England.

Halsbury's Statutes of England

The reference 5 Halsbury's Statutes (3rd Edn) 302 refers to page 302 of volume 5 of the third edition of Halsbury's Statutes of England.

English and Empire Digest

References are to the replacement volumes (including reissue volumes) of the Digest, and to the continuation volumes of the replacement volumes.

The reference 31 Digest (Repl) 244, 3794, refers to case numbers 3794 on page 244 of Digest Replacement Volume 31.

The reference Digest (Cont Vol B) 287, 7540b, refers to case number 7540b on page 287 of Digest Continuation Volume B.

The reference 28(1) Digest (Reissue) 167, 507, refers to case number 507 on page 167 of Digest Replacement Volume 28(1) Reissue.

Halsbury's Statutory Instruments

The reference 12 Halsbury's Statutory Instruments (Second Reissue) 124, refers to page 124 of the second reissue of volume 12 of Halsbury's Statutory Instruments; references to subsequent reissues are similar.

Encyclopaedia of Forms and Precedents

The reference 7 Ency Forms & Precedents (4th Edn) 247, Form 12, refers to Form 12 on page 247 of volume 7 of the fourth edition of the Encyclopaedia of Forms and Precedents.

Cases reported in volume 2

Index

CHARACTER
Evidence of. *See* **Criminal Law** (Evidence).

CHARGE
Legal aid – Costs – Charge on property recovered for deficiency of costs. *See* **Legal Aid (Costs).**

CHARITY
Rates. *See* **Rates** (Relief).

CHARTERPARTY
See **Shipping.**

CHEQUE
Consideration. *See* **Bill of Exchange** (Cheque).

CHILD
Child boarded out with foster parents – Discrimination on ground of colour. *See* **Race Relations** (Discrimination – Unlawful discrimination – Provision of goods facilities and services – Discrimination by person concerned with goods etc to a section of the public – Section of the public – Local authority – Children in care of local authority).
Criminal offence – Compensation. *See* **Criminal Law** (Compensation – Compensation order – Children and young persons).
Income tax – Relief. *See* **Income Tax** (Relief).

CHILDREN AND YOUNG PERSONS
Compensation order – Power of court to order parent or guardian to pay compensation instead of child or young person. *See* **Criminal Law** (Compensation – Compensation order – Children and young persons).

CLASS GIFT
Will. *See* **Will** (Class gift).

COLLISION
At sea – Fatal accident – Action by alien. *See* **Fatal Accident** (Action – Competency – Alien – Action by alien against another alien – Collision between foreign vessels on high seas).

COLOUR
Trade mark. *See* **Trade Mark** (Mark – Meaning – Representation or description of external appearance of goods – Colour scheme).

COMMISSION
Estate agent. *See* **Estate Agent.**

COMMONS

COMMONWEALTH IMMIGRANT
Appeal – Appeal to tribunal from adjudicator. *See* **Immigration** (Appeal).

COMPANY
Contempt of court. *See* **Contempt of Court** (Company).
Director – Duty – Bailment of goods to company – Duty of care. *See* **Negligence** (Duty to take care – Circumstances in which duty arising – Bailment of goods – Assumption of duty of care by third party – Bailment of goods to company).
Execution against. *See* **Execution.**

CRIMINAL LAW—*continued*

Dangerous drugs. *See* **Drugs** (Dangerous drugs).

Discharge of oil into prohibited sea areas. *See* **Shipping** (Oil in navigable waters — Discharge of oil from ship into prohibited sea areas).

False trade description. *See* **Trade Description.**

Food. *See* **Food and Drugs.**

Fraud — Conspiracy to defraud. *See* Conspiracy — Conspiracy to defraud, *ante.*

Fraudulent evasion of restriction on importation of certain goods. *See* **Customs** (Importation of prohibited goods — Knowingly concerned in fraudulent evasion).

Immigration — Offences — Statute — Retrospective operation. *See* **Immigration** (Statute controlling operation — Retrospective operation).

Legal aid. *See* **Legal Aid.**

Practice — Evidence — Husband or wife. *See* Evidence — Admissibility — Evidence of husband or wife, *ante.*

Probation order. *See* Sentence — Probation order, *post.*

DEAD BODY
  Coroner – Power to detain. *See* **Coroner** (Inquest – Custody of body).

DECREE NISI
  See **Divorce.**

DEFENCE
  Statutory – Food and Drugs Act 1955. *See* **Food and Drugs** (Sale – Food).

DEFERRED SENTENCE
  Location of Crown Court – Conviction of further offence before different location. *See* **Crown Court** (Transfer of proceedings between locations – Sentence – Deferred sentence passed on offender).

DEVELOPMENT
  Development scheme. *See* **Compulsory Purchase** (Compensation).
  Land – Generally. *See* **Town and Country Planning.**

DIRECTIONS
  Summons – Hearing. *See* **Practice** (Summons for directions).
  Surtax. *See* **Surtax.**

DIRECTOR
  Company. *See* **Company** (Director).

DISABLEMENT BENEFIT
  Industrial injury. *See* **Industrial Injury.**

DISCOVERY
  Marine insurance actions – Order for ship's papers – Order before delivery of defence – Scuttling cases – When order should be made – Factors to be considered by judge – Factors to be considered in deciding whether to order stay pending compliance with order for ship's papers – RSC Ord 72, r 10(1)(2). **Probatina Shipping Co Ltd v Sun Insurance Office Ltd** 478
  Production of documents – Document – Meaning – Tape recording – Tape recording of conversation between parties – Whether tape recording a 'document' – RSC Ord 24, r 10(1). **Grant v Southwestern and County Properties Ltd** 465
  Inspection of documents to which reference made in pleadings or affidavits – Reference to document – Record of conversation – Tape recording – Allegation in pleading that conversation between parties 'was being recorded' – Whether tape recording a document to which 'reference is made' in pleading. RSC Ord 24, r 10. **Grant v Southwestern and County Properties Ltd** 465
  Parties – Order for discovery against person not a party to proceedings – Claim in respect of personal injuries or death – Meaning of 'in respect of' – Claim for personal injuries against hospital – Plaintiff's solicitors allowing claim to become statute-barred – Action against solicitors for breach of duty – Documents relating to injury in possession of hospital – Application for order for discovery against hospital – Whether claim against solicitors claim 'in respect of' personal injuries – Administration of Justice Act 1970, s 32(1). **Paterson v Chadwick** 772
  Privilege – Legal professional privilege – Document brought into existence when litigation contemplated – Document for purpose of litigation – Document prepared by plaintiff for purpose of instructing solicitor and obtaining advice – Tape recording by plaintiff of conversation with defendant – Whether tape recording a document prepared by plaintiff for solicitor. **Grant v Southwestern and County Properties Ltd** 465
  Production before commencement of proceedings – Claim in respect of personal injuries – Discretion – Circumstances in which discovery should be ordered – Duty of proposed plaintiff to set out in writing nature of allegation so as to show documents might be material to claim – Legally aided plaintiff – Desirability of early disclosure which might affect continuance of claim – Likelihood of documents showing whether substantial prospect of success – Discovery likely to assist in disposing fairly of dispute or result in saving of costs – Administration of Justice Act 1970, s 31 – RSC Ord 24, r 8. **Shaw v Vauxhall Motors Ltd** .. 1185
  Similar transactions – Relevance – Discovery directed solely to credit – Passing-off action – Allegation in statement of claim that defendant supplied Scotch whisky to importers in specified countries for admixture with local spirits – Admixture passed off in those countries as genuine Scotch whisky – Application by plaintiffs for discovery of other documents alleged to relate to similar transactions in other countries and in connection with other spirits – Evidence of defendants' knowledge of and complicity in activities of foreign importers – Whether discovery should be ordered. **Ballantine (George) & Son Ltd v F E R Dixon & Son Ltd** 503

DISCRIMINATION
  Colour, race or ethnic or national origins – Discrimination on ground of. *See* **Race Relations** (Discrimination).

DISMISSAL
  Generally. *See* **Industrial Relations** (Unfair dismissal).
  Unfair – Compensation. *See* **Industrial Relations** (Unfair industrial practice – Compensation).

INJURY
Industrial. *See* **Industrial Injury.**

INQUEST
See **Coroner.**

INSPECTION
Document – Inspection of documents to which reference is made in pleadings or affidavits. *See* **Discovery** (Production of documents – Inspection of documents to which reference is made in pleadings or affidavits).

INSURANCE
Marine insurance – Order for ship's papers. *See* **Discovery** (Marine insurance actions).

INTENTION
Murder – Foresight. *See* **Criminal Law** (Murder – Mens rea – Foresight).

INTEREST
Contingent interest – Settlement. *See* **Settlement** (Contingent interest).

INTERLOCUTORY INJUNCTION
Generally. *See* **Injunction.**

INTERNATIONAL LAW
Municipal law – Relationship – Right of individual under international law – Enforcement of right in English courts – Necessity of showing rule of international law has been adopted by English law – Duty of country to receive back nationals expelled by foreign state – British protected person – Whether British protected person having right to enter United Kingdom on being expelled from country of residence – Whether right enforceable by individual in English courts. **Thakrar v Secretary of State for the Home Department**

INTOXICATING LIQUOR
Licensing. *See* **Licensing.**

INTOXICATION
Manslaughter. *See* **Criminal Law** (Manslaughter – Mens rea – Causing death by unlawful act – Intoxication).

ISSUE ESTOPPEL
Criminal law. *See* **Criminal Law** (Estoppel – Issue estoppel).

JOINT TENANCY
Matrimonial home – Home jointly owned by spouses. *See* **Husband and Wife** (Property).

JUDGE
Crown Court – Justices. *See* **Crown Court** (Justices as judges).
Discretion – Reference to European Court. *See* **European Economic Community** (European Court – Reference to court).

JUDGMENT
Execution of. *See* **Execution.**
Foreign. *See* **Conflict of Laws** (Foreign judgment).
Judicial decision as authority – Ratio decidendi – House of Lords – Majority decision of House of Lords – No discernible ratio decidendi common to majority speeches – Reasoning of House of Lords not binding – Court of Appeal free to adopt reasoning which appears to it to be correct – Court of Appeal bound to adopt reasoning which supports House of Lords decision. **Harper v National Coal Board.** .. ..

JURISDICTION
Certiorari. *See* **Certiorari** (Jurisdiction).
Court – Jurisdiction to grant relief from forfeiture – Extent of jurisdiction. *See* **Equity** (Forfeiture – Relief).
Court of Appeal – Appeal against conviction. *See* **Criminal Law** (Appeal – Court of Appeal).
Injunction. *See* **Injunction.**
Mortgagee – Action for possession. *See* **Mortgage** (Possession of mortgaged premises – Jurisdiction).

JURY
Direction to jury – Corroboration – Accomplice – Duty of judge. *See* **Criminal Law** (Evidence – Corroboration).

JUSTICES
Crown Court. *See* **Crown Court.**
Generally. *See* **Magistrates.**

LAND
Compulsory purchase. *See* **Compulsory Purchase.**
Restrictive covenant affecting. *See* **Restrictive Covenant** (Restrictive covenant affecting land).
Sale. *See* **Sale of Land.**
Water supply. *See* **Water Supply.**

NUISANCE

Statutory nuisance – Nuisance order – Duty of justices – Justices bound to make order on finding that nuisance exists – Discretion as to implementation of order – Power to delay operation of order – Duty of justices to take into account surrounding circumstances – House constituting nuisance subject to unconfirmed compulsory purchase order under slum clearance programme – Power of justices to delay operation of order in view of prospective demolition of house – Public Health Act 1936, s 94(2). **Nottingham Corpn v Newton**   760

OBSTRUCTION

Highway, on. *See* **Highway.**

OFFICIAL RECEIVER

Winding-up – Powers – Sale of land. *See* **Company** (Winding-up – Liquidator – Powers).

OFFICIAL REFEREE

Reference to – Procedure. *See* **Practice** (Reference to referee).

OIL IN NAVIGABLE WATERS

See **Shipping.**

ON-LICENCE

Intoxicating liquor – Grant subject to condition. *See* **Licensing** (Licence – Condition – Grant of licence subject to condition – On-licence)

ORDER

Compensation. *See* **Criminal Law** (Compensation).

Criminal proceedings in. *See* **Criminal Law** (Compensation).

Legal aid. *See* **Legal Aid.**

Probation – Right of appeal against order. *See* **Criminal Law** (Appeal – Sentence – Probation order).

ORIGINATING SUMMONS

Summons to which appearance not required – Procedure – Insertion of particulars of hearing by master – RSC Appendix A, Form 10. **Practice Direction**   566

OVERSEAS SECURITIES

Income arising from – Tax – Domicile. *See* **Income Tax** (Domicile – Income arising from overseas securities and possessions).

PART PERFORMANCE

Sale of land – Contract. *See* **Sale of Land** (Contract – Part performance).

PAYMENT

Guarantee. *See* **Guarantee.**

PERMITTED DEVELOPMENT

See **Town and Country Planning** (Development).

PERPETUITIES

Rule against perpetuities – Possibility of gift vesting outside perpetuity period – Delay in vesting involving breach of trust – Trust for sale – Vesting of gift on completion of sale – Devise in will of life interest in real property – Trust to sell farm on death of life tenant – Proceeds of sale to be divided among class of beneficiaries living at date of completion of sale – No express or implied power to postpone sale – Duty of trustees to sell property within year of life tenant's death – Possibility that trustees might delay completing sale for more than 21 years – Whether possibility to be taken into account. **Re Atkins's Will Trusts** ..   1

PERSONAL INJURIES

Action – Discovery – Order for discovery against person not a party to proceedings. *See* **Discovery** (Production of documents – Parties – Order for discovery against person not a party to proceedings – Claim in respect of personal injuries or death).

Production of documents before commencement of proceedings. *See* **Discovery** (Production of documents – Production before commencement of proceedings).

Limitation of time. *See* **Limitation of Action.**

Damages. *See* **Damages.**

PICKETING

Peaceful picketing – Immunity from prosecution or civil action in certain circumstances. *See* **Trade Dispute** (Picketing – Right of peaceful picketing).

PLANNING PERMISSION

Land. *See* **Town and Country Planning** (Development).

PLEADING

Divorce. *See* **Divorce** (Practice).

POLICE

Road traffic – Direction by constable engaged in regulation of traffic – Failure to comply with direction. *See* **Road Traffic** (Direction – Failure to comply with direction).

POLLUTION

Oil in navigable waters. *See* **Shipping** (Oil in navigable waters).

POSSESSION

Dangerous drugs. *See* **Drugs** (Dangerous drugs).

Mortgaged property, of. *See* **Mortgage** (Possession of mortgaged premises).

POWER

PRACTICE

PRECEDENT

PREROGATIVE ORDERS

PRESCRIPTION

PRIVILEGE

PRIVY COUNCIL

PROBATE

ROAD TRAFFIC—*continued*

SALE

SALE OF GOODS

SALE OF LAND

SECURITY

SECURITY FOR COSTS

SENTENCE

SEPARATE TRIAL

Cases noted

Statutes, etc, noted

Words and Phrases

Corrigenda

[1974] 1 All ER

p 662. Horrocks v Lowe. Line *d* 5: for 'the chairman' substitute 'a member'. Lines *d* 6 and *e* 1: delete the words 'which had been responsible for leasing the land'.

[1974] 2 All ER

p 207. R v Scott. Line *b* 2: delete line beginning 'of a misdemeanour. Section 84 provided . . .' and in its place substitute: 'of the 1956 Act. There is no justification for seeking to invoke the offence of conspiracy'.

p 275. Re Shield's Will Trusts. Counsel for the widow: read '*J P Whittaker*' instead of as printed.

p 762. Nottingham Corporation v Newton. Counsel for the respondent: for '*James Harper*' read '*Joseph Harper*'.

Re Atkins's Will Trusts
National Westminster Bank Ltd v Atkins
and others

CHANCERY DIVISION
PENNYCUICK V-C
21st, 22nd JANUARY 1974

Perpetuities – Rule against perpetuities – Possibility of gift vesting outside perpetuity period – Delay in vesting involving breach of trust – Trust for sale – Vesting of gift on completion of sale – Devise in will of life interest in real property – Trust to sell farm on death of life tenant – Proceeds of sale to be divided among class of beneficiaries living at date of completion of sale – No express or implied power to postpone sale – Duty of trustees to sell property within year of life tenant's death – Possibility that trustees might delay completing sale for more than 21 years – Whether possibility to be taken into account.

Will – Construction – Trust for sale – Direction to divide proceeds of sale amongst such beneficiaries 'as shall be living at the date of the completion of the . . . sale' – Meaning of 'completion'.

By his will the testator appointed the bank to be his executor and trustee. By cl 4 of the will he devised his farm to the bank on trust to allow his stepson to have the full use and enjoyment thereof and, on the stepson's death or when he ceased to work the farm, the bank was directed to sell the farm and to divide the net proceeds of sale equally and per capita amongst such of the following: (i) the grandchildren of his deceased brother, (ii) a named beneficiary and (iii) 'the four children' of his niece, 'as shall be living at the date of the completion of the said sale'. No time for sale was mentioned in the will and no express power to postpone sale was included. Clause 6 of the will contained a residuary gift to the bank on trust to sell, call in or convert into money 'such parts . . . as shall not consist of ready money with power to postpone such sale calling in and conversion'. The testator died in 1957. The bank vested the farm in the stepson who occupied and worked it until his death in March 1972. Nine grandchildren of the deceased brother as well as the other beneficiaries named in cl 4 were living at the date of the stepson's death and were living at all material times thereafter. The bank sold the farm, save for a small plot of 1·242 acres, in September 1972. On a summons by the bank seeking the determination (i) of the proper construction of the words 'at the date of the completion of the . . . sale' in cl 4 and (ii) of the question whether the clause was void for perpetuity, it was contended by those interested in the residuary estate that the gift over on the stepson's death was void in that the gift might have failed to vest within 21 years of his death, since the sale of the farm might not have been completed within that period.

Held – (1) The expression 'at the date of the completion of the . . . sale' in cl 4 denoted the date at which the sale was completed in accordance with the ordinary meaning of that word in the language of conveyancing, i e the execution of a conveyance and the payment of the purchase price (see p 5 *b*, post).

B

(2) The gift over on the stepson's death was not void for perpetuity for the following *a*
reasons—

(i) No power to postpone sale could be implied under s 25(1)ᵃ of the Law of Property Act 1925 in relation to the direction in cl 4 to sell the farm on the stepson's death,
for a contrary intention was apparent from the terms of the will in that (a) the testator could not have contemplated the bank retaining and continuing to work the land
and there could be no question of the beneficiaries doing so, (b) the beneficiaries' *b*
shares were limited to arise on completion of the sale, and (c) in relation to the residuary estate there was an express power to postpone sale (see pp 5 *h* to 6 *d*, post).

(ii) Accordingly the bank was bound to sell the farm immediately on the stepson's
death, i e as soon as would be convenient in the proper course of realisation. By
analogy with the executor's year that amounted to a duty to sell within one year of
the stepson's death (see p 6 *d* and *e*, post).

(iii) Although in determining whether a gift was void for perpetuity the court had to *c*
take into account the possibility of delay in consequence of physical causes, it could
not properly take into account the possibility that a breach of trust by the bank might
delay the vesting of the beneficiaries' interests beyond the perpetuity period.   Since
the sale had to be completed within one year of the stepson's death, the vesting
would take effect within that year and there could be no question of perpetuity (see
p 7 *a b* and *j* to p 8 *a*, post); *Re Wood* [1894] 3 Ch 381 distinguished; *Re Petrie* [1961] *d*
3 All ER 1067 applied.

Notes

For determination of the time of vesting under the perpetuities rule, see 29 Halsbury's
Laws (3rd Edn) 284-287, paras 572-577, and for cases on the subject, see 37 Digest
(Repl) 56-61, *14-50*.   *e*

For the Law of Property Act 1925, s 25, see 27 Halsbury's Statutes (3rd Edn) 375.

Cases referred to in judgment

Petrie (deceased), Re, Lloyds Bank Ltd v Royal National Institute for the Blind [1961] 3 All
    ER 1067, [1962] Ch 355, [1961] 3 WLR 1348, CA, Digest (Cont Vol A) 108, *1313a*.
Rooke's Will Trusts, Re, Taylor v Rooke [1953] 2 All ER 110, [1953] Ch 716, [1953] 2 WLR *f*
    716, 47 Digest (Repl) 370, *3315*.
Wood, Re, Tullett v Colville [1894] 3 Ch 381, 63 LJCh 790, 71 LT 413, CA, 37 Digest (Repl)
    96, *306*.

Cases also cited

Elwin v Elwin (1803) 8 Ves Jun 547.   *g*
Inland Revenue Comrs v Bernstein [1961] 1 All ER 320, [1961] Ch 399, CA.
Johnson v Crook (1879) 12 Ch D 639.
Jones (deceased), Re, Midland Bank Executor and Trustee Co Ltd v League of Welldoers
    [1950] 2 All ER 239.

Adjourned summons

By an originating summons dated 26th March 1973 the plaintiff, the National West- *h*
minster Bank Ltd ('the bank'), the executor of Charles Edward Atkins, deceased
('the testator'), sought the determination of the court of a question arising on the
construction of the testator's will and in the events which had happened.   The defendants were (1) Michael John Atkins, (2) Paul Atkins, (3) Andrew John Hardy, (4)
Rodney Arthur Hardy, (5) Teresa Jane Collins, (6) Marion Elizabeth Bee, (6) Sandra *i*
Jayne Atkins, (8) David Robert Atkins, (9) Robin James Atkins, (10) Suzette Helene
Harrad, (11) Andrew Stevenson, (12) Mary Stevenson, (13) Ian Bruce Stevenson and
(14) Elizabeth Ann McQuire (all of whom claimed to be beneficially entitled to a

*a   Section 25(1) is set out at p 5 *f*, post

a
share in the proceeds of sale of the testator's property under cl 4(a) of the will);
(15) Helene Lydia Atkins (the testator's widow); and (16) Phyllis Eileen Russell
(who claimed to be beneficially interested in the testator's residuary estate). The
facts are set out in the judgment.

Nathaniel Micklem for the bank.
Roger A Cooke for the first to fourteenth defendants.
b *G M Shillingford* for the fifteenth and sixteenth defendants.

PENNYCUICK V-C. This originating summons is concerned with the trusts of the
will of one Charles Edward Atkins (to whom I will refer as 'the testator'). The testator made his will on 1st February 1956. He was then, and remained until his death, a
c married man but having no child. By his will he appointed National Provincial Bank
Ltd to be the executor and trustee of his will. He made certain specific bequests and
devises. Then, by cl 4(a), he made the following disposition:

> 'I GIVE AND DEVISE Unto the Bank free of duty my freehold Farm with the
> Farm House and buildings known as Church Farm Newton Flotman UPON TRUST
> *d* that the Bank shall allow my Step-Son Ernest Alexander Double to have the
> full use and enjoyment thereof free of rent for so long as he shall continue to
> work the farm in good and husbandlike manner he keeping the said Farm and
> the House and buildings thereof in good order and repair and insured against
> loss or damage by fire in the name of the Bank with such Insurance Office and for
> such sums as the Bank shall nominate and upon the death of the said Ernest
> *e* Alexander Double or upon his ceasing to work the said farm as aforesaid I DIRECT
> the Bank to sell the same with the Farm House and buildings and to divide
> the net proceeds of sale thereof equally and per capita amongst such of the
> following as shall be living at the date of the completion of the said sale namely,
> the Grandchildren of my late Brother Thomas William Atkins, the said Suzette
> Russell and the four children of my Niece Phyllis Stevenson'.

f
There follow certain further specific pecuniary gifts. Then in cl 6 there is a residuary
gift to the bank—

> 'UPON TRUST to sell call in and convert into money all such parts thereof as shall
> not consist of ready money with power to postpone such sale calling in and con-
> version for such period as the Bank in its discretion shall think fit without being
> *g* liable for any loss occasioned thereby ...'

Then it constitutes a residuary trust fund and directs the bank to hold that trust
fund on trust to pay to the wife during her life the sum of £3 per week out of income,
with power to resort to capital. Clause 7 contains a direction to convert the residuary
trust fund and out of the proceeds of such conversion gives a number of further lega-
h cies. Finally, there is an ultimate residuary gift to Phyllis Eileen Russell and Ernest
Alexander Double 'or to such one of them as shall survive me and my said Wife
and if both shall so survive then in equal shares.'
    The testator died on 18th October 1957 and his will was proved by the bank on
17th December 1957. The bank proceeded to vest Church Farm in the stepson,
Ernest Alexander Double and he in fact continued to occupy and farm Church Farm
j throughout the remainder of his life. Ernest Alexander Double died on 30th March
1972. On the death of Ernest Alexander Double, according to the terms of cl 4,
there came into effect the direction which I have already read, namely—

> 'I DIRECT the Bank to sell the same ... and to divide the net proceeds of sale
> thereof equally and per capita amongst [certain classes of persons, naming
> them] as shall be living at the date of the completion of the said sale ...'

So far as the classes of persons are concerned, the brother, Thomas William Atkins, *a*
had nine grandchildren, all of whom were living at the death of Ernest Alexander
Double, and are still living. Suzette Russell was living at the death of Ernest Alexander
Double, and is still living; she is now Mrs Suzette Helene Harrad. Finally, the
niece, Phyllis Stevenson, had four children. Once again, they all survived the
testator and Ernest Alexander Double, and are all still living.

In case it is material so to state, the testator's residuary estate is extremely small, *b*
and unless on the proper construction of the will and by operation of law Church Farm
is thrown into the residuary estate, the residuary estate is entirely insufficient to pay
the widow, who is still living, the weekly sum of £3.

On those facts, the question has arisen as to the construction of the direction to the
bank to sell Church Farm and divide the proceeds amongst such of the named
beneficiaries 'as shall be living at the date of the completion of the said sale'. The *c*
first question is on the construction of the clause. Then, if the clause is construed in a
certain way, the question arises whether the clause is void for perpetuity, in which
case Church Farm would fall into residue.

The present summons was issued by the National Westminster Bank Ltd, which is
the successor of the bank named in the testator's will. The first nine defendants
are the grandchildren of Thomas William Atkins. The tenth is Suzette Harrad, form- *d*
erly Suzette Russell. The next four are the children of Phyllis Stevenson. Finally,
there is the widow, Mrs Helene Lydia Atkins, and Mrs Phyllis Eileen Russell, the
surviving residuary legatee. It will be remembered that the residuary gift is to her
and Ernest Alexander Double 'or to such one of them as shall survive me and
my said Wife.'

The questions raised by the originating summons are as follows: *e*

'1. Whether upon the true construction of the Will of the above-named Testator
. . . and in the events which have happened the Plaintiff hold the proceeds of the
sale of (A) the Testator's freehold property known as Church Farm Newton Flot-
man (save and except a parcel thereof containing 1.242 acres or thereabouts
hereinafter called "the retained plot") and (B) the retained plot (1) on trust to divide
the same in equal shares between the grandchildren of the Testator's brother *f*
Thomas William Atkins deceased living on the Thirtieth day of November [1972]
being the date of the completion of the sale of Church Farm aforesaid (except
the retained plot) the Defendant Suzette Helene Harrad and the Defendants
Andrew Stevenson, Mary Stevenson, Ian Bruce Stevenson and Elizabeth Anne
McQuire (being the four children of the Testator's niece Phyllis Stevenson hereinafter called "the primary class") (2) on the trusts declared by the Testator *g*
concerning his residuary estate (3) on trust in equal shares for such of the primary
class as shall be living at the date of the completion of a contract for sale of the
retained plot (4) on some other and what trusts.'

The question is not quite self-explanatory, having regard to the reference to
the retained plot. The position is this, that on 7th September 1972—that is, something *h*
under six months from the death of Ernest Alexander Double—the bank, in its
capacity of personal representative of Ernest Alexander Double, sold Church Farm
save for a small plot of 1.242 acres, that contract being completed on 30th November
1972. The purchase price was £34,000. However, acting on professional advice, the
bank kept out of the auction a small parcel containing 1·242 acres (that is, the retained
plot), the reason being that an appeal against the refusal of planning application
was pending at the date of the sale of Church Farm itself. In the end, since the evi- *j*
dence in this case was completed, that appeal has been dismissed, and it is now the
intention of the bank to sell the retained plot, the price expected to be realised
being £500. It will be seen that the retained plot is a very small part of the entire
acreage and the price expected to be realised on it is a very small part of the total
proceeds of sale of Church Farm. On the other hand, on one construction of the

testator's will, the retention and subsequent sale of the retained plot would be of practical importance should one of the beneficiaries happen to die before the completion of the sale of the retained plot.

The first question which arises in logical sequence is what is meant by the expression 'at the date of the completion of the said sale' in cl 4 of the testator's will. I will leave out of account, in answering that and the subsequent question, any complication introduced by the retained plot. It seems to me that those words are themselves quite unambiguous and can only denote the date at which the sale of Church Farm is completed, in accordance with the ordinary meaning of that word in the language of conveyancing, namely, the execution of a conveyance and the payment of the purchase price. Counsel for the first to fourteenth defendants invited me (rather as a second string and I think without much optimism) to hold that this expression 'the completion of the said sale' ought to be construed as referring not to the completion of the sale but to the event which gave rise to the direction to sell, namely, the death of Ernest Alexander Double. I find it quite impossible so to construe that expression. That would no doubt be a perfectly sensible disposition for the testator to have made: but it is not the disposition which he has expressed himself to make, and there is nothing in the nature of the direction to divide amongst beneficiaries living at the date of completion of a sale which is either impossible or so extravagant that one should distort words from their natural meaning in order to avoid such a result. Such a provision is unfamiliar to me. It appears, however, from the textbooks that testators do sometimes make such a disposition in order to avoid the inconvenience and perhaps additional liability to duty which would arise in the event of one of the class of beneficiaries dying during the interval between the death of the testator himself and completion of a sale of property pursuant to a direction in his will.

So one has in this will a life interest followed by a direction to sell, no time for sale being mentioned and no express power to postpone sale being included, followed by a direction for division of the proceeds of sale amongst a class of beneficiaries living at the completion of the sale.

I turn next to consider whether a power to postpone sale must be implied in relation to the direction contained in cl 4 of the will to sell the farm on the death of Ernest Alexander Double. Section 25(1) of the Law of Property Act 1925 is in these terms: 'A power to postpone sale shall, in the case of every trust for sale of land, be implied unless a contrary intention appears'; and, as is stated in the note[1], whenever a trust for sale is imposed by statute there is (unless a contrary intention appears) an implied power to postpone sale. Section 25(2) provides:

> 'Where there is a power to postpone the sale, then (subject to any express direction to the contrary in the instrument, if any, creating the trust for sale) the trustees for sale shall not be liable in any way for postponing the sale, in the exercise of their discretion, for any indefinite period . . .'

That is a new provision; and, as pointed out by Harman J in *Re Rooke's Will Trusts*[2]: 'I am, however, left with this question of construction: Is there here apparent a contrary intention?' It seems to me that in the case of this will there is indeed apparent a contrary intention.

First, looking at the matter in broad terms by way of background, it will be remembered that the subject-matter of the direction is a farm which would have been worked by Ernest Alexander Double during his lifetime. Then the testator appoints the bank as his executor and trustee and directs the bank to sell the farm and divide the proceeds amongst no less than 14 persons. It is clear to demonstration that, given those circumstances, the testator could not have contemplated that the bank would retain and continue to work this farm, nor would there be any question of any of the beneficiaries doing so. The testator then, I think, contemplated an immediate

1   Halsbury's Statutes of England (3rd Edn), vol 27, p 375
2   [1953] 2 All ER 110 at 113, [1953] Ch 716 at 723

sale and distribution of the proceeds. That background may well not of itself be
sufficient to amount to the appearance of a contrary intention. One must, I think,
find something more within the four corners of the will. That, it seems to me, one
does indeed find. In the first place, and most important, the vesting of the shares
of the beneficiaries in the proceeds of sale is limited to arise on completion of the sale.
If the trustee had a power to postpone and could properly exercise that power for
an indefinite period, then the result would be that the vesting of the beneficial
interests would depend on the manner in which the trustee exercised an administrative direction. The court will strain against putting a construction on a testamentary
provision which leads to this highly undesirable and inequitable consequence. That
circumstance would, I think, be sufficient against the background to involve the
appearance of a contrary intention. However, the matter does not end there, because
in cl 6 of the will, in his residuary gift, the testator introduces an express power to
postpone the sale of his residuary estate for such period as the bank shall think fit.
The introduction of that express power to postpone sale in relation to residue is a
strong ground for saying that the testator had a contrary intention in relation to the
farm where no such express provision appeared. I conclude, therefore, that a
contrary intention does indeed appear.

The effect of that is that the trustee was bound to sell the farm immediately on
the death of Ernest Alexander Double. By 'immediately' is of course meant not the
day after his death, but as soon as would be convenient in a proper course of realisation. I deliberately use rather general words, because the duty of the bank to effect
immediate sale would depend, as regards a matter of days or months, on certain
particular circumstances; for example, I imagine, the time of year when the farm
can best be sold. However that may be, I am content to say, by analogy with the
executor's year which was adopted in *Re Petrie*[1], to which I will refer in a moment,
that the duty of the bank was to sell this farm within one year of the death of Ernest
Alexander Double.

Having reached the conclusion which I have expressed on the first two points—
namely, that the proceeds of sale of the farm became divisible amongst the beneficiaries living at the date of completion of the sale, and that the duty of the bank was
to sell within the year, at latest, from the death of Ernest Alexander Double—then
one comes to the question: was such a disposition void on the ground of perpetuity,
namely, that the interests of the beneficiaries might not vest within 21 years from the
death of Ernest Alexander Double, who was a life in being at the death of the testator?

Counsel for the fifteenth and sixteenth defendants stressed, as is undoubtedly true,
that in applying the rule against perpetuities as it stood before the Perpetuities and
Accumulations Act 1964, one must look at possible and not actual events (see, for
instance, Theobald on Wills[2]), and there is no doubt that the court over the years has
sometimes taken into account some very remote possibilities. Counsel relied in
particular on *Re Wood*[3], a decision of the Court of Appeal which has come in for a good
deal of textbook criticism since, but which I suppose in comparable circumstances
I should be bound to follow. It seems to me, however, that there is a critical distinction to be made between the possibility of delay owing to physical causes such
as were considered in *Re Wood*[3], and the possibility of delay owing to breach of trust
on the part of the trustee concerned. In the former case one must, I suppose, take
into account anything physically capable of happening. I should myself wish to
reserve consideration on that matter in relation to certain highly improbable events.
On the other hand, where delay can only arise should there be a breach of trust,
that is a possibility which it seems to me the court must clearly disregard. The court
will go on the basis that equity regards that as done which ought to be done, and it
will treat the trustees as having done whatever they were bound to do. It will not

1   [1961] 3 All ER 1067, [1962] Ch 355
2   13th Edn (1963), p 532, para 1483
3   [1894] 3 Ch 381

allow the rights of beneficiaries to be defeated because the trustees fail to carry out their fiduciary duties.

So, in the present case, the duty of the trustee was to sell this farm immediately, and that means at the latest, as I have held, within one year of the death of Ernest Alexander Double, and the court should not and cannot properly take into account the possibility that the bank, in breach of trust, might fail to realise within the time in which it was bound to realise. The result is that one must treat the sale as something which must be completed within, at the most, 12 months from the death of Ernest Alexander Double, and accordingly the vesting of the interests of the beneficiaries would take effect within one year of the death of Ernest Alexander Double, and there can be no question of perpetuity.

The view that I have expressed derives considerable support from the decision of the Court of Appeal in Re Petrie[1], in which that court reversed a decision of my own and reached (if I may respectfully say so) what appears to be an eminently fair and sensible result. It will be sufficient to read the headnote, which accurately summarises for the present purposes what was said by Lord Evershed MR[2]:

'A testatrix, who died on January 5, 1959, directed her trustees "to realise and divide the residue of my estate as follows:" after directing the payment of a pecuniary charitable legacy she gave, in the events which happened, to the "following charitable institutions the remainder of the said residue equally among them as follows . . . (fourth) any national appeal to the public which may exist in the United Kingdom at the time when the residue of my estate is realised as aforesaid, for contributions for research into the substances, such as cortisone, that are essential to the treatment of rheumatoid arthritis [and then there is a gift over]." The will contained no power to postpone realisation. The estate of the testatrix at her death, in addition to cash and money on deposit with a building society, consisted of Government securities or securities of which there was a regular Stock Exchange quotation. Pennycuick J. held that the fourth disposition was void, since the "national appeal" might not have to be ascertained until a date after the expiration of 21 years from the death of the testatrix, and the gift over . . . was equally void as being dependent on the happening of too remote an event. On appeal:—Held, that the formula "when the residue of my estate is realised as aforesaid" did not require the court to introduce the inconvenience of a literal construction and postpone the relevant date until the sale of the last asset of the estate of the testatrix had been completed, but that the words must be construed as referring to the date when the shares of residue should be "receivable or de jure receivable", that was, on the completion in fact of the administration of the estate in the ordinary course, or the expiration of the executor's year, whichever should first happen; and that, having regard to the application to the court, the administration could not be regarded as completed, so that the relevant date was January 5, 1960, the expiration of the executor's year.'

Lord Evershed MR in his judgment reviewed a number of cases and expressed the conclusion which is I think accurately summarised in the headnote. So, in that case the Court of Appeal adopted a broad approach to this matter and treated a reference to 'completion of the realisation of the residue of my estate' as meaning the date when the shares of residue should be receivable or would be receivable in the ordinary course of administration. The present case is, I think, considerably a fortiori because in that case the executors in proper course of administration could have retained, in special circumstances, certain particular assets for more than the executor's year. On the other hand, in the present case it would have been a breach of trust for the

1 [1961] 3 All ER 1067, [1962] Ch 355
2 [1962] Ch at 355, 356

bank not to have sold the farm immediately—meaning, as I have held, within a
year from the death.

I conclude, then, that this gift is not open to objection on the ground of perpetuity,
with the result that on completion of the sale of the farm the interests of the 14
beneficiaries vested in possession.

There remains the odd question resulting from the retention of a small plot out
of the main bulk of this farm. I have already read the alternative contentions which
are advanced in the summons. In fact, this question is now an academic one, since
not only has the main body been sold well within the year, but the year has elapsed,
and accordingly, on any possible basis, the 14 beneficiaries have now taken a vested
interest in the retained plot, as well as in the proceeds of the bulk of the farm. I
need not, therefore, express a view on what I think is a difficult question of negligible
practical importance.

The conclusion which I have reached involves a reformulation of the answer to the
questions, but the result, I think, is simply that, on the true construction of the will
and in the events which have happened, the bank holds the proceeds of sale of the
whole farm, including the retained plot, on trust to divide the same in equal shares
between all the 14 beneficiaries.

Judgment accordingly.

Solicitors: *Sharpe, Pritchard & Co*, agents for *Mills & Reeve*, Norwich (for the bank);
Asshetons, agents for *Hill & Perks*, Norwich (for the first to fourteenth defendants);
Field, Fisher & Martineau (for the fifteenth and sixteenth defendants).

Evelyn Budd Barrister.

Smirk v Lyndale Developments Ltd

Reversed in part CA [1975] 1 All ER
690

CHANCERY DIVISION

PENNYCUICK V-C

6th, 7th, 8th, 28th, 29th NOVEMBER, 5th DECEMBER 1973

*Landlord and tenant – Encroachment – Encroachment by tenant – Encroachment on other
land owned by landlord and not included in tenancy – Title of tenant to land taken – Failure
to communicate to landlord any disclaimer of landlord's title – Presumption that land taken
as part of holding comprised in tenancy.*

Behind two adjoining houses, 191 and 193 Victoria Road, lay a strip of land some 75
feet in depth. The part of the strip ('the blue plot') that was behind no 191 was some 15
feet wide and the part ('the pink plot') behind no 193 somewhat narrower. At all
material times until 1966 the houses and the strip were owned by the British Railways
Board. The houses were occupied by servants or former servants of the board. In
1955 the plaintiff went into possession of no 191 under a service tenancy; no 193
had been for many years in the possession of T under a similar service tenancy.
Neither tenancy included the blue or pink plots. The board, however, made no
use of the plots and the plaintiff did not know for certain whether the board owned
the plots. The plaintiff and his wife took effective possession of the blue plot not
later than 1960, thereafter cultivating and enjoying it as a garden. T used the pink
plot to grow vegetables, and after T's death in 1958 the plaintiff began to use it for
the same purpose, taking effective possession of it in about 1968. The plaintiff had
no communication of any kind directly or indirectly with any officer of the board
concerning the blue plot, nor was there any evidence that any officer of the board

had ever become aware of the plaintiff's activities on the blue plot. In 1966 the defendant acquired from the board the freehold interest in nos 191 and 193 and, subject to a claim by the defendant, in the blue and pink plots. The existing tenancy of no 191 was terminated in 1967 and a new tenancy was then created between the plaintiff and the defendant. There was no suggestion that the new tenancy included the blue plot. In June 1973 it appeared that the defendant was about to develop both the blue and the pink plots, and the plaintiff thereupon issued a writ seeking a declaration that he had a good possessory title to the blue plot and/or the pink plot or, alternatively, a declaration that he held the blue plot and/or pink plot as an extension of the locus of his tenancy of no 191.

Held – (i) The plaintiff did not have a good possessory title to either plot. Where a tenant, during the currency of his tenancy, took possession of land, whether or not immediately adjacent to the demised premises, and whether or not the land was waste or belonged to the landlord or a third person, there was a presumption that the land so taken was part of the holding unless the tenant, during the term, communicated to his landlord some disclaimer of his landlord's title. There was nothing on the facts which could in any way rebut the presumption that P was occupying the blue and pink plots by way of an addition to land comprised in his tenancy and not otherwise adversely to the landlord (see p 12 *f* to *h*, p 13 *a* to *c*, p 14 *h* and *j* and p 20 *a* and *b*, post); *Kingsmill v Millard* (1855) 11 Exch 313 and *Tabor v Godfrey* (1895) 64 LJQB 245 followed; *Whitmore v Humphries* (1871) LR 7 CP 1, *J F Perrott & Co Ltd v Cohen* [1950] 2 All ER 939 and *Williams Brothers Direct Supply Stores Ltd v Raftery* [1957] 3 All ER 593 explained; *Lord Hastings v Saddler* (1898) 79 LT 355 not followed.

(ii) The plaintiff held neither plot as an extension of the locus of his tenancy of no 191. Although he would have been entitled to a declaration that he so held the blue plot if the tenancy from the board were still subsisting, the break in the tenancy necessarily negated that claim, for no new right could have accrued against the defendant during the period of the new tenancy (see p 20 *b* to *d*, post).

Notes
For encroachments, see 23 Halsbury's Laws (3rd Edn) 503-505, paras 1146-1149, and for cases on encroachments and accretions, see 31(2) Digest (Reissue) 925-927, 7634-7643.

Cases referred to in judgment
Hastings (Lord) v Saddler (1898) 79 LT 355, DC, 31(2) Digest (Reissue) 926, 7639.
Kingsmill v Millard (1855) 11 Exch 313, 19 JP 661, 3 CLR 1022, 156 ER 849, 11 Digest (Repl) 57, 850.
Leigh v Jack (1879) 5 Ex D 264, 49 LJQB 220, 42 LT 463, 44 JP 488, CA, 26 Digest (Repl) 336, 553.
Lissenden v C A V Bosch Ltd [1940] 1 All ER 425, [1940] AC 412, HL.
Marshall v Taylor [1895] 1 Ch 641, 64 LJCh 416, 72 LT 670, 12 R 310, CA, 7 Digest (Repl) 283, 108.
Perrott (J F) & Co Ltd v Cohen [1950] 2 All ER 939, [1951] 1 KB 705, CA, 31(2) Digest (Reissue) 926, 7638.
Tabor v Godfrey (1895) 64 LJQB 245, 31(2) Digest (Reissue) 925, 7637.
Whitmore v Humphries (1871) LR 7 CP 1, 41 LJCP 43, 25 LT 496, 35 JP 807, 11 Digest (Repl) 57, 852.
Williams Brothers Direct Supply Stores Ltd v Raftery [1957] 3 All ER 593, [1958] 1 QB 159, [1957] 3 WLR 931, CA, 32 Digest (Repl) 508, 1132.

Cases also cited
Andrews v Hailes (1853) 2 E & B 349, 118 ER 797.
Attorney-General v Tomline (1880) 15 Ch D 150, CA.

Hayward v Challoner (or Chaloner) [1967] 3 All ER 122, [1968] 1 QB 107.
Lewis (Doe d) v Rees (1834) 6 C & P 610, 172 ER 1386.
Lisburne (Earl) v Davies (1866) LR 1 CP 259.
Seddon v Smith (1877) 36 LT 168, CA.

Action

By a writ issued on 14th June 1973, the plaintiff, George Frederick Smirk, brought an
action against the defendant, Lyndale Developments Ltd, in which he claimed, inter
alia, (i) a declaration that the plaintiff had a good possessory title to certain land at
the rear of 191 Victoria Road, Woolston, and further or alternatively certain land
at the rear of 193 Victoria Road; (ii) alternatively, a declaration that the plaintiff held
the land at the rear of no 191 and further or alternatively the land at the rear of no 193
as an extension of the locus of his tenancy of no 191; (iii) an injunction to restrain
the defendant from doing (by its directors, servants or agents or any of them
otherwise howsoever) the following acts or any of them, namely, entering on, or
interfering with the occupation, use or enjoyment by the plaintiff of the land at the
rear of no 191 and further or alternatively the land at the rear of no 193. The facts
are set out in the judgment.

David Ritchie for the plaintiff.
Roger A Cooke for the defendants.

Cur adv vult

5th December. **PENNYCUICK V-C.** In this action the plaintiff is Mr George
Frederick Smirk; the defendant is Lyndale Developments Ltd. The plaintiff is
the tenant of a house known as 191 Victoria Road, Woolston in the county borough
and city of Southampton, and claims to have acquired a possessory title to two plots
of land, one behind no 191 and one behind the adjoining house, no 193. The defendant acquired the freehold interest in both the houses and also, subject to the plaintiff's claim, to both the plots behind in 1966. I will set out the facts as I find them.

Victoria Road runs in approximately a southerly direction towards Southampton
Water—to be precise it runs south south-west. On its east side stands a row of
houses, including no 191 and no 193 to the south of it. The houses are fenced at the
back; beyond the fence, that is, on the east side, runs a path parallel with Victoria
Road, which is freely accessible to the public. Then across that path runs a strip of
land some 75 feet in depth opposite to nos 191 and 193. The strip opposite no 191
is approximately 15 feet wide but that opposite no 193 rather narrower. These two
plots, i e the plots behind nos 191 and 193 respectively, are coloured blue and pink
respectively on a plan annexed to the statement of claim, and form the subject-matter
of the action.

At all material times up to the year 1966 the central stretch of Victoria Road including nos 191 and 193 and also a strip including the blue and pink plots behind
belonged to the British Railways Board. The houses were occupied by servants or
former servants of the board. The strip itself, or parts of it, had been used for allotments in the 1939-45 war, but the strip appears to have become more or less derelict
thereafter. British Railways made no use of the strip. In November 1955 the
plaintiff went into possession of no 191 under a service tenancy, the terms of which
are recorded in his rent book. That book is headed 'Service Tenancy'. No 193 had
been in possession of a Mr Tully for many years under a similar service tenancy.
The tenancies did not include the blue and pink plots. It will be convenient at this
stage to set out the relevant history of the two plots separately.

Number 191

Very soon after taking possession of the house, the plaintiff and his wife set about
turning the blue plot to account. In 1956 they began to lay out the ground and in
1958 began to cultivate it as a flower garden. In 1956 they began, and by 1959 they
had completed, a rough but adequate fence along the north, west and east side of

the plot.   There was a path, but no fence, along the south side between the blue plot
and the pink plot.   By 1959 they had brought the blue plot into some sort of cultivation and effectively fenced it except where it adjoins the pink plot.   They have ever
since continued to cultivate and enjoy it as a flower and ornamental garden.

The plaintiff did not know for certain that British Railways was the owner of the
strip, although he had heard talk to that effect.   He had no communication of any
kind directly or indirectly with any officer of British Railways concerning the blue
plot, nor is there any evidence that any officer of British Railways ever became aware
of the plaintiff's activities on the blue plot.   I am satisfied that at some date not later
than the year 1960 the plaintiff had taken and has thenceforward retained exclusive
possession of the blue plot.

Number 193

Mr Tully started to grow vegetables on the pink plot as far back as 1940 and for a
short while paid 6d a quarter to British Railways for this privilege.   The payments
were soon dropped but Mr Tully continued, in the plaintiff's words, to cultivate the
plot 'after a style' until his death in 1958.   Mr Tully erected a rough fence on three
sides to keep the children out, leaving the north side, that side between the pink and
blue plot, unfenced. I am not satisfied, on the evidence before me, that Mr Tully's
activities on the pink plot were of a character sufficiently extensive and continuous
to constitute possession of the plot.   The proper view I think, on the very meagre
evidence, is rather that he continued to use parts of the plot in a rather desultory
manner for the purpose of growing some vegetables.   After the death of Mr Tully,
his widow more or less let the plot go to rack and ruin and the fence was broken down
by children.   At some date, as to which there was an acute conflict of evidence,
the plaintiff began to grow vegetables on the pink plot and built, or rather rebuilt, a
rough but effective fence round it on the same three sides, thus converting the blue and
pink plots into a single enclosed flower and vegetable garden.   I will return to the
evidence on this point later.   At this stage I will confine myself to the fact that the
plaintiff did not take possession of the pink plot earlier than 1966 or thereabouts.

To return to the history of both plots.   Towards the end of 1966 the defendant
purchased from British Railways at a public auction the whole central strip in Victoria
Road, including nos 191 and 193, and also the strip to the east, including the blue and
pink plots.   By conveyance dated 10th January 1967 the whole of the land comprised in this purchase was conveyed to the defendant.   Shortly afterwards the defendant gave each of the tenants, including the plaintiff, a new rent book described as
'Rent Book for freehold tenancy' in substitution for the old rent book described as
'Service Tenancy'.   The terms of the new tenancy, as set out in the rent book, are
quite different from those of the old tenancy, and I think it is clear that the old tenancy
of no 191 must be regarded as having been terminated in 1967 and a new tenancy
then created.   It is not suggested that the new tenancy comprised the blue plot unless
the blue plot had somehow become annexed to the house by operation of law.   The
defendant purchased the strip to the east of Victoria Road, including the blue and
pink plots, with a view to development and, after some rebuffs, obtained planning
permission to build houses on the strip.   In June 1973 the approach of a bulldozer
gave warning of an imminent invasion of the blue and pink plots, and on 14th June
1973 the plaintiff issued the writ in this action and he obtained interim relief pending
the trial of the action.

The statement of claim was delivered on 29th June.   I need not, I think, read it
in detail, but it sets out a possessory title to the freehold or alternatively the leasehold
of both plots.   I think it will be sufficient to read the claim:

> '(1) A declaration that the Plaintiff has a good possessory title to [the blue plot]
> and further or alternatively [the pink plot]. (2) Alternatively a declaration that
> the Plaintiff holds [the blue plot] and further or alternatively [the pink plot] as
> an extension of the locus of his tenancy of 191 Victoria Road aforesaid.'

I need not read the defence and counterclaim which were delivered on 16th August.

[His Lordship then reviewed the evidence, finding that the plaintiff and his wife had taken effective possession of the blue plot not later than 1960 and that the plaintiff had not taken possession of the pink plot before about 1968. His Lordship then continued:] I must mention one further point. The plaintiff was asked a set of questions as to his intentions. He said it never occurred to him this land would come to belong to him 'so that I could sell it'. Then he was asked: 'If you had moved from the house, what would have happened then?' and he said: 'If I had moved from the house I would not have expected to get it. I have no right to it'; and the plaintiff's wife said something of the same effect. She was asked: 'If you had moved from the house, what would have happened?' and she answered: 'It depends on the distance, not if far away. I thought it was only to accommodate us when we were there.'

I turn now the the law applicable where a tenant, during the currency of his tenancy, takes possession of adjoining land belonging to his landlord. The law on this point, if I may respectfully say so, has got into something of a tangle. I will refer first to *Kingsmill v Millard*[1]. The sidenote is as follows[2]:

'Where a tenant incloses land, whether adjacent to, or distant from, the demised premises, and whether the land be part of a waste, or belong to the landlord or a third person, it is a presumption of fact, that the inclosure is part of the holding, unless the tenant, during the term, does some act disclaiming his landlord's title . . .'

In the course of argument Alderson B made this comment[3]:

'It seems to me, that the acts of the tenant to rebut the presumption should be such acts as in a manner set the landlord at defiance; for instance, if the tenant gave the landlord notice of a conveyance, and he did not interfere: but if the landlord has no knowledge of it, what is there to undeceive him in supposing that the tenant occupies the waste as part of the holding?'

Then Parke B gave judgment in these terms[4]:

'It is laid down in all the cases—whether the inclosed land is part of the waste, or belongs to the landlord or a third person—that the presumption is, that the tenant has inclosed it for the benefit of his landlord, unless he has done some act disclaiming the landlord's title. I am disposed to discard the definition, that the encroachment is made "for the benefit of the landlord," and to adopt that of Lord Campbell, viz. that the encroachment must be considered as annexed to the holding, unless it clearly appears that the tenant made it for his own benefit. It is not necessary that the land inclosed should be adjacent to the demised premises; the same rule prevails when the encroachment is at a distance. That is now the law; and I must add, that even though at the time of making the encroachment there is nothing to rebut the presumption that the tenant intended to hold it as a portion of his farm, yet circumstances may afterwards occur by which it may be severed from the farm: for instance, if the tenant conveys it to another person, and the conveyance is communicated to the landlord, then it can no longer be considered as part of the holding. But if the landlord is allowed to remain under the belief that the encroachment is part of the farm, the tenant is estopped from denying it, and must render it up at the end of the term as a portion of the holding.'

1 (1855) 11 Exch 313
2 (1855) 11 Exch at 313
3 (1855) 11 Exch at 316
4 (1855) 11 Exch at 318, 319

a   Then both other barons agreed.

It will be observed that in his judgment Parke B in terms states that the presumption that the tenant has inclosed for the benefit of the landlord applies, irrespective of whether the inclosed land is part of the waste or belongs to the landlord; and indeed he uses the word 'encroachment' as appropriate in either case. He then goes on to state in terms, following and agreeing with what Alderson B said in the course of argument, that in order to displace the presumption there must be com-

b   munication to the landlord. That decision of high authority seems to me to be in accordance with justice and common sense and, unless I were compelled to do otherwise by subsequent authority, I would certainly adopt it. I should add, as is perhaps obvious, as appears in some of the later cases, that the presumption may be rebutted by any form of express or implied agreement or in some cases, as Parke B

c   says, by estoppel.

The next case is *Whitmore v Humphries*[1], where Willes J says:

d   'This case raises a question upon a branch of the law which involves considerations of some nicety. By the rule of law applicable to this subject the landlord is entitled at the determination of the tenancy to recover from the tenant, not only the land originally demised, but also any land which the tenant may have added to it by encroachment from the waste, such encroachment being deemed to be made by him as tenant as an addition to his holding, and consequently for the benefit of his landlord, unless it is made under circumstances which shew an intention to hold it for his own benefit alone, and not as part of his holding under the landlord. This rule undoubtedly applies when the encroachment is made over land belonging to the landlord, and no inquiry appears ever to have been

e   made in such cases, whether it was made with the consent of the landlord or not. In such cases the reasonableness of the rule is very obvious; it only gives back to the landlord that which is rightly his, and prevents the tenant, who has taken advantage of his tenancy to encroach, from keeping that which it would be a breach of the duty arising from the relation of landlord and tenant not to give up. The rule, however, goes further than this. It is not confined to cases where the

f   encroachment is upon land to which the landlord is entitled, it applies to cases where the land encroached upon does not belong to the landlord.'

And he then goes on to deal with the position where the encroachment is on land to which the landlord is not entitled. He continues[2]:

g   'The rule is based upon the obligation of the tenant to protect his landlord's rights, and to deliver up the subject of his tenancy in the same condition, fair wear and tear excepted, as that in which he enjoyed it. There is often great temptation and opportunity afforded to the tenant to take in adjoining land which may or may not be his landlord's, and it is considered more convenient and more in accordance with the rights of property that the tenant who has availed himself of the opportunity afforded him by his tenancy to make encroachments,

h   should be presumed to have intended to make them for the benefit of the reversioner, except under circumstances pointing to an intention to take the land for his own benefit exclusively. The result is to avoid questions which would otherwise frequently arise as to the property in land, and to exclude persons who have come in as tenants, and who are likely to encroach, from raising such questions. The reason of the rule appears on the one hand to be

j   entirely independent of any notice of encroachment being a wrong done, and so also on the other hand it appears to be quite independent of the question, whether the encroachment was made with the assent of the landlord. [Then, I do not

1   (1871) LR 7 CP 1 at 4, 5
2   (1871) LR 7 CP at 5, 6

think I need read the next passage, but read on further.] For these reasons *a*
I come to the conclusion that the meaning of the word "encroachment" is quite
apart from any question of assent or dissent on the part of the landlord, and
signifies something taken in by the tenant by reason of his being tenant without
anything to shew that it was so taken otherwise than for the benefit of the landlord, to be held as part of the demised premises, and given up accordingly at
the end of the term.'
b

That decision is, I think, generally in accordance with the decision in *Kingsmill v
Millard*[1], but I should perhaps mention that the learned judge appears to be addressing himself exclusively to encroachment on waste; and again in one or two other
sentences he appears to fasten on the tenant's intention without raising the further
critical point of communication of the intention to a landlord. There is nothing in *c*
that case which in any way shakes the authority of *Kingsmill v Millard*[1].
    Then comes *Tabor v Godfrey*[2]. The headnote runs as follows:

'The tenant under a lease for years encroached upon and occupied a piece of
land belonging to his landlord and adjoining the demised premises for a period of
more than twelve years. The landlord during the term brought an action for *d*
an injunction and damages for trespass:—*Held*, that the action would not lie.
The tenant must be deemed to have occupied the piece of ground as part of the
holding, and he was entitled so to occupy it during the remainder of his lease.'

It appears from the next paragraph that the point was tried by Charles J without
a jury. Charles J, after holding that 12 years of occupation had elapsed, proceeds as *e*
follows[3]:

'... and I should, apart from the legal question here, have to hold, certainly
as to the strip, that the defendant had acquired a right to the freehold under
the statute. But that is not the true inference, nor do I think the Statute of
Limitations has anything to do with the case. But I do think that in the events *f*
which have happened, both the landlord and the tenant have treated this strip
as part of the land demised. At the end of the lease the tenant could not have
set up that the strip was his own, or said that it was not part of the land included
in the lease. A tenant who enters under one title cannot turn round and say he
entered under another. I remember a case of a lease under a tenant by the
curtesy and the lessee saying that no such lease could be granted—and in vain.
The principle is that a man who gets in by reason of being tenant must take land *g*
as under his original take. That is the reason why it is said that a tenant who
has occupied an encroachment has occupied it for the benefit of his landlord.
It is said that that principle cannot be applied during the currency of the
tenancy, but I believe it has been so applied, and I think that it does apply to a
tenant who so occupies during the currency of his tenancy.'
h

That judgment is entirely in accordance with the principle laid down in *Kingsmill
v Millard*[1]. The effect is that the tenant in the case before the learned judge did not
acquire a freehold title as against his landlord; what he did acquire was a leasehold
interest in the land encroached on—that land being treated as an addition to the
original subject-matter of the tenancy. It is worth noticing that this was not 'waste' *j*
land, but that the learned judge uses the word 'encroachment' and treats the
presumption as applicable to the land, although it was not 'waste'.

---

1   (1855) 11 Exch 313
2   (1895) 64 LJQB 245
3   (1895) 64 LJQB at 247

a
So far there is no difficulty on the authorities. The next case, however, does introduce a difficulty, and it seems to me is quite inconsistent with what was said in *Kingsmill v Millard*[1] and the other cases. The case is *Lord Hastings v Saddler*[2]. The
headnote runs as follows:

b
'H. demised an island to E. Subsequently E. occupied two other plots of H.'s
land. These plots were situate on the mainland, and were something between
half a mile and a mile from the island demised to E. They were inclosed land.
There was no evidence that they were occupied by E. as an addition to his holding
under H., and no rent was paid in respect of them. After more than twelve
years had elapsed, when E.'s tenancy of the island had determined, H. brought
an action against E.'s successor in title to obtain possession of the two plots.

c
The County Court judge held that there was a presumption that E. had occupied
them as H.'s tenant, and in the absence of evidence to rebut this presumption
H. was entitled to recover possession. On appeal: Held, that there was no such
presumption. *Semble*: The presumption that a tenant who occupies more
land than is demised to him occupies it for the benefit of his landlord is confined
to encroachment on waste.'

d
In the course of argument[4] *Kingsmill v Millard*[1] was cited, as was *Whitmore v Humphries*[4], and Lord Russell CJ, after stating what had happened in the county court,
said[4]:

'The judge began by telling the jury that there was a presumption in favour
of the plaintiff—that they should assume that the gardens occupied by the

e
defendant's predecessors in title were occupied by them not for their own benefit
but were merely an addition to the land originally let to them by the plaintiff,
and therefore part of their holding, unless the defendant could prove that this
was not in fact the case. I see no ground in point of law for saying that this
presumption of fact has ever been applied to anything but one limited class of
cases—cases of encroachment in its well understood meaning. It is a doctrine

f
that I do not think should be extended. It has been argued that the case of
[*Tabor*] v. *Godfrey*[5] shows that it is not confined to encroachment merely. In
that case undoubtedly the land occupied by the tenant was not waste, and the
case was not therefore one of encroachment. Neither was it a case where the
doctrine of presumption in favour of the landlord was applied. I have read the
judgment of the learned and most careful judge who tried the case—Charles, J.—

g
and I can find not the faintest reference to any presumption in the matter. He
appears to have decided the case simply on the ground that the conclusion to
be come to was the one suggested by all the circumstances of the case. If he had
thought the doctrine applicable to other cases than those of encroachment, the
learned judge would certainly have applied it, as the circumstances there were
more proper for its application than they are here—the land occupied having

h
been immediately adjoining the demised premises. But the learned judge said
nothing about the presumption. He put the true point to the jury. What was the
proper inference from all the facts of the case? What do you think? he asked.
Do you think the land was occupied by the tenant as a mere extension of the *locus*
of his tenancy? If you do you should find a verdict for the landlord. If you
think the tenant took possession not as tenant, but with the object or desire

i

___

1   (1855) 11 Exch 313
2   (1898) 79 LT 355
3   (1898) 79 LT at 356
4   (1871) LR 7 CP 1
5   (1895) 64 LJQB 245

simply of benefiting him himself, and so as to acquire the ownership of the
land occupied under the Statute of Limitations, you should find for the tenant.   *a*
That is precisely what should have been done here. There must be a new
trial.'

Then Wills J said[1]:

'I am entirely of the same opinion. The doctrine that land occupied by a
tenant in addition to his holding is to be regarded *primâ facie* as an encroachment   *b*
for the benefit of his landlord, has hitherto been confined to cases fulfilling two
conditions—cases where the land occupied is waste, and where it is adjoining or,
at any rate adjacent, to the land demised. There is no case where it has been
applied where either of these conditions was absent. In this state of the reports
it is a strong thing to say that the same doctrine has all along applied to cases
such as this. Similar cases in past centuries must have occurred again and again.   *c*
Yet there is not a single decision reported where the doctrine has been held
applicable . . . I think it is too late now to say that in principle it should apply.'

I mention in passing that this case might well have been decided on the simple
ground that the plots on the mainland were too far away from the demised land for
the presumption to apply. Both the learned judges, however, made a number of   *d*
statements of law which I find quite impossible to reconcile with the principle laid
down in *Kingsmill v Millard*[2], and the judgment of Lord Russell CJ, as reported, is
singularly unsatisfactory in other respects. In the first place both learned judges
say that the presumption has never been applied except to the one limited class of
cases, namely, cases of encroachment in its well understood meaning, that is to say
an encroachment on the waste; that statement is I think, with all due respect, flatly   *e*
contrary to what was said by the Court of Exchequer in *Kingsmill v Millard*[3], where
Parke B said:

'. . . whether the inclosed land is part of the waste, or belongs to the landlord
or a third person . . . the presumption is, that the tenant has inclosed it for the
benefit of his landlord . . .'
                                                                                    f

But then, when one comes to the way in which Lord Russell CJ deals with *Tabor v
Godfrey*[4], something has gone very seriously amiss either in his judgment or possibly
in the report. Lord Russell CJ says that the learned judge put the issues to the jury
but it would appear from the report of *Tabor v Godfrey*[4] that that case was tried by
Charles J without a jury, and there never was a charge to the jury. Lord Russell CJ
then goes on in his account of this, with respect, fictitious address to the jury, to pose   *g*
two alternatives, namely: was the land occupied by the tenant as a mere extension
of the locus of his tenancy? or did he take possession, not as tenant, but with the
object or desire simply of benefiting himself so as to acquire the ownership of the land
under the Statute of Limitations? Those alternatives do not correspond to anything
which Charles J said in *Tabor v Godfrey*[4]; nor are they true alternatives. Finally,
the second alternative is, it seems to me, a singularly capricious and illogical one,   *h*
indicating that the tenant's right to acquire the freehold of the property encroached
on by him depends on his uncommunicated intention. That would be a very strange
state of the law. I will mention in a moment something which was said by Cohen
LJ[5] on that case but, subject to that, it seems to me that that case does not bind me,
and I am certainly free to choose between it and *Kingsmill v Millard*[2], and I prefer,
and propose to apply, *Kingsmill v Millard*[2].
                                                                                    j

---

1   (1898) 79 LT at 356
2   (1855) 11 Exch 313
3   (1855) 11 Exch at 318
4   (1895) 64 LJQB 245
5   In *J F Perrott & Co Ltd v Cohen* [1950] 2 All ER 939, [1951] 1 KB 705

a   The next case I would refer to is *J F Perrott & Co Ltd v Cohen*[1], in the Court of Appeal. The headnote runs as follows[2]:

'A tenant of premises under a lease from 1936 to 1948 entered into occupation of land of the landlords, on which there were lavatories, which adjoined the demised premises. This was discovered by the landlords who, in 1943, by their solicitor protested. The tenant claimed that the land was included in the lease.

b   The landlords' solicitor (who had repudiated the claim and proposed that the landlords and tenant should come to some arrangement about the future use of lavatories on the land) asked the tenant to withdraw his claim and said that when he was in a position to make any proposition with regard to the lavatories he would communicate with the tenant. The solicitor did not make any such proposition, the tenant did not withdraw his claim, and he continued in occupa-

c   tion of the land with the lavatories for five years until the end of the lease. At the termination of the tenancy the landlords claimed for repairs to the lavatories on the land as being subject to the tenant's covenants for repair contained in the lease:—*Held*, following *Tabor* v. *Godfrey*[3], as explained by the Divisional Court in *Lord Hastings* v. *Saddler*[4], that the tenant could not deny that the land was included in his lease and he was therefore liable under his covenant to repair

d   the lavatories.'

Kingsmill v Millard[5] was apparently not cited. Somervell LJ based himself on the principle laid down by Charles J in *Tabor v Godfrey*[3]; I do not think it would be useful to read his judgment on the facts, but he said[6]:

'That being so, it is right to treat the lavatories as part of the demised premises;

e   and the tenant—who of course at one time wanted the lavatories so treated—cannot now adopt the other position and say: "Although I have occupied them, although I have treated them as part of the demised premises as against my landlords when their solicitor suggested they were not part of the demised premises, I shall now change my position and claim that they were not included in the demise".'

f   Then Denning LJ said[7]:

'I fully agree with the judgment of Somervell, L.J., and I too only wish to say a few words on the question of the lavatories. It raises a question which has not hitherto been before this court, and it is this: if a tenant encroaches upon property of the lessor which adjoins the demised premises [and it is to be observed that Denning LJ uses the word 'encroachment' as most people would do today

g   without any specific connotation of waste], does the tenant become liable to repair the property on which he has encroached, just as if it were included under the covenants to repair contained in the lease? The principle underlying the cases on encroachment is not perhaps strictly an estoppel, but it is akin to it. If a tenant takes possession of adjoining property and by his conduct represents that he is holding it under the demise, then, if the landlord acts on that representation by

h   allowing the tenant to remain in possession, the tenant cannot afterwards assert that he is holding it on any other footing. The tenant cannot, for instance, claim that he is holding it adversely to the landlord so as to acquire a title under the Limitation Act of 1939; nor can he claim that he is only a licensee, who has all the benefits of occupation but none of the burdens of the lease. The reason

j   1   [1950] 2 All ER 939, [1951] 1 KB 705
2   [1951] 1 KB at 705
3   (1895) 64 LJQB 245
4   (1898) 79 LT 355
5   (1855) 11 Exch 313
6   [1951] 1 KB at 708, cf [1950] 2 All ER at 942
7   [1951] 1 KB at 709, 710, cf [1950] 2 All ER at 942, 943

is not because of any doctrine of "blowing hot and cold"; for that, as Lord Atkin once said, is merely a descriptive phrase which does not express any precise legal concept: see *Lissenden* v. *C. A. V. Bosch Ltd*[1]. The reason is because the tenant has by his conduct made a representation that was intended to be binding, was intended to be acted on, and was in fact acted on; and he cannot be allowed to go back on it.'

Then he elaborates that. So both Somervell and Denning LJJ base their judgments on estoppel; both refer to *Tabor v Godfrey*[2]. Those judgments appear to me in conformity with the principles laid down in *Kingsmill v Millard*[3], and in particular the requirement laid down in that case of communication between the landlord and the tenant. Here, the result of the communication was an estoppel; it might have been another case of express or implied agreement.

The difficulty in this case lies with the judgment of Cohen LJ, who says this[4]:

'At one time I felt great doubt on the question of the lavatories. My doubt was whether the equitable principle on which the judge arrived at his decision was really applicable to the facts as he found them. Fortunately I am not compelled to reach a conclusion on that point because [counsel for the landlords] called our attention to *Tabor* v. *Godfrey*[2], which was explained in *Hastings (Lord)* v. *Saddler*[5]. As thus explained, *Tabor's* case[2] seems to amount to this: that where a tenant has occupied land of the landlord's not included in the demised premises, according to the terms of the demise, but adjoining them, and, after the tenancy has determined, the landlord seeks to eject this former tenant, therefrom, but the tenant relies on the Statute of Limitations, the proper question for the judge to put to the jury, or to decide himself if there is no jury, is: "Do you think . . ." [and he there sets out the words put by Lord Russell CJ in *Lord Hastings v Saddler*[5] into the mouth of Charles J in *Tabor v Godfrey*[2]. Then he says:] If that be so, it seems to me that, on the facts of this case, the proper conclusion must be that the tenant was purporting to occupy the lavatories as part of the demised premises; he says so in his letter of August 18, 1943; and though it is true, as [Somervell LJ] has pointed out, that his right to do so was disputed in writing by the solicitor for the landlords, none the less, it is common ground that he continued to occupy the lavatories in exactly the same way as before, allowing the secretary of the landlords to use one of the lavatories down to the end of the tenancy. In those circumstances it seems to me that the only proper answer to the question is that the occupation of the defendant was on the basis that the lavatories were part of the demised premises.'

Then he concludes[4]:

'For these reasons, as well as for the reasons given by [Somervell LJ], I think that the decision of the judge was right on all points and that the appeal should be dismissed.'

I have, naturally, very great regard for anything that was said by Cohen LJ. In this case, however, what he says of *Lord Hastings v Saddler*[5], the case having been decided on another point, and he alone of the three Lords Justices mentioning *Lord Hastings v Saddler*[5], is obiter; and *Kingsmill v Millard*[3] was apparently not cited at all. I think, in spite of what Cohen LJ said in *Lord Hastings v Saddler*[5], I still

1   [1940] 1 All ER 425 at 436, [1940] AC 412 at 429
2   (1895) 64 LJQB 245
3   (1855) 11 Exch 313
4   [1951] 1 KB 709, cf [1950] 2 All ER at 942
5   (1898) 79 LT 355

a ought not to follow that case. I should add that I am not at all clear that this second ground in Cohen LJ's judgment is really consistent with the ground based on estoppel on which the other two Lords Justices decided the case.

I must mention, finally, *Williams Brothers Direct Supply Ltd v Raftery*[1]. The headnote runs as follows[2]:

b   'The plaintiffs, the registered owners of land at the rear of a row of shops with flats above, brought an action in the county court against the defendant, the tenant of one of the flats, for possession of the strip of land at the rear of his premises, an order for removal of certain fencing and sheds on the land, and damages for trespass. The defendant claimed that he was the owner of the land, having been in uninterrupted occupation of it for over 12 years, and that he had thereby acquired a squatter's title under the provisions of the Limitation Act, c   1939. At the hearing it was shown that the plaintiffs had bought the land in 1937 and intended to develop it, but were prevented, in 1939 by the outbreak of war, and in 1948—after their representative had gone onto the land to prepare plans for building—by the refusal of planning permission, but that they had never abandoned their intention to develop it when opportunity arose. For the defendant it was shown that in 1940 the tenants of the flats had begun cultivating d   the land at the rear of their premises as part of the war effort, some of them obtaining oral permission from the owners to do so. One H. had cultivated the land behind flat No. 367a and marked off a boundary to it with old bricks. In 1943 the defendant became tenant of No. 367a, took over the land previously cultivated by H., without the owner's permission and without paying rent for it, and continued to grow food on it until 1949, when he abandoned cultivation and e   turned part of the land over to the purposes of rearing greyhounds, putting up sheds and a fence to keep the dogs in. He had had no idea of taking over the land and had not kept the plaintiffs out, but had thought that he was exercising rights over the land to which he was entitled as tenant of No. 367a:—*Held*, (1) that, on the evidence, the plaintiffs had never discontinued their possession. (2) That having regard to the nature of the property, the acts of user by the f   defendant did not interfere and were consistent with the purpose to which the owners intended to devote it, and were not sufficient to amount to a dispossession of them within the meaning of section 5(1) of the Limitation Act, 1939; and that the owners were accordingly entitled to orders for possession and for the removal of the fencing and sheds, and to nominal damages for trespass. *Leigh* v. *Jack*[3] applied. *Marshall* v. *Taylor*[4] distinguished.'

g
That was a case between landlord and tenant, but apparently the circumstance that a different principle might apply where encroachment was by the tenant on his landlord's ground, rather than as between strangers, was never put in argument or brought to the minds of the Court of Appeal. *Whitmore v Humphries*[5] was mentioned in argument as setting out a parallel principle in relation to encroachment h   by a tenant, but otherwise the cases as between landlord and tenant are not referred to, either in argument, or in the judgments, and the judgments proceed entirely on the principles applicable as between strangers. It seems to me that, that being so, the case is of no real assistance where one is concerned to apply the principles applicable as between landlord and tenant. Indeed, if their Lordships' attention had been directed to that principle, which is quite a different one from that applicable j   as between strangers, the decision would, I think, have been a much simpler one and

1   [1957] 3 All ER 593, [1958] 1 QB 159
2   [1958] 1 QB at 159, 160
3   (1879) 5 Ex D 264
4   [1895] 1 Ch 641
5   (1871) LR 7 CP 1

in very different terms.   Having been through the authorities, I propose as I said   *a*
earlier, to adopt and apply the principle laid down in *Kingsmill v Millard*[1].

To return to the present case, there is nothing on the facts which could in anyway
rebut the presumption, which it seems to me is applicable in this case, namely that
the tenant, the plaintiff, was occupying the plots by way of an addition to land comprised in his tenancy, and not otherwise adversely to the landlord. I need only add
on this point that if, contrary to my view, the unilateral intention of the plaintiff   *b*
was relevant, the plaintiff's very candid evidence of intention would be fatal to his
own case.

I should next mention the alternative claim that the plaintiff holds the blue plot
or alternatively the pink plot as an extension of the locus of his tenancy
of 191 Victoria Road.   On the facts the plaintiff would it seems to me be entitled to
that relief as regards the blue plot if the tenancy under British Railways were still   *c*
subsisting: that is to say, the presumption would be that he had taken possession
of the blue plot by way of addition to the subject-matter comprised in the tenancy
under British Railways—that is the actual decision in *Tabor v Godfrey*[2]. It seems to
me, however, that the break in the tenancy necessarily negates this claim. Whatever
accrued or accruing right the plaintiff may have had to include the blue plot in his
tenancy from British Railways, this right must have determined with his tenancy   *d*
under British Railways, and obviously no new right can have accrued against the
defendant during the short time in which the defendant has been his landlord.
There can be no ground for treating a period of two different tenancies as continuous
for the present purposes. Contrast the position where a possessory title is
acquired by successive squatters or against successive freeholders. The tenant, so
long as the presumption applies, can do no more than acquire an addition to the   *e*
subject-matter of the tenancy and his interest in that additional subject-matter
must necessarily determine together with his interest in the original subject-matter.

I was taken at some length through a series of cases of discontinuance and dispossession as between strangers.   Those cases show that in a case of land not admitting of continuous occupation, as here with these two plots, discontinuance and
dispossession may involve some highly complex factors, including intention.   Prob-   *f*
lems of this kind do not, however, arise here, and it would not be useful for me to
go into them.

For the reasons I have given, I propose to dismiss this action.

Action dismissed.

Solicitors: *Lovell, Son & Pitfield*, agents for *Paris, Smith & Randall*, Southampton (for   *g*
the plaintiff); *Riders*, agents for *G H Fowler, Shaw & Holloway*, Brighton (for the
defendant).

Susan Corbett   Barrister.

---

1   (1855) 11 Exch 313   *h*
2   (1895) 64 LJQB 245

a

Smedleys Ltd v Breed

HOUSE OF LORDS

LORD HAILSHAM OF ST MARYLEBONE, VISCOUNT DILHORNE, LORD DIPLOCK, LORD CROSS OF CHELSEA AND LORD KILBRANDON

22nd JANUARY, 21st MARCH 1974

b

Food and drugs – Sale – Food – Not of substance demanded – Extraneous matter – Defence – Presence of extraneous matter unavoidable consequence of process of collection or preparation – Reasonable care taken by defendant to avoid presence of extraneous matter – Whether sufficient to establish defence – Food and Drugs Act 1955, ss 2(1), 3(3).

c *Food and drugs – Offence — Prosecution – Food and drugs authority – Discretion whether to prosecute – Public interest – Duty to consider whether prosecution in public interest.*

The defendants manufactured tins of peas. They had installed a satisfactory system of manufacturing and spot checking the peas which they canned. It included a mech-anical screening process which eliminated waste matter of markedly higher or lower

d specific gravity than the peas, and a further process of visual inspection of all the peas as they passed on their way along a white conveyor belt towards their final destination. The inspection was made by a team of properly trained and experienced women sorters who removed any extraneous material which they saw. In the 1971 canning season the defendants produced some 3½ million tins of peas and only four complaints were received concerning the presence of extraneous matter in the

e tins. One of those complaints was made by a customer who, on opening a tin of the defendants' peas which she had bought at a supermarket, discovered that, in addition to the peas, it contained a caterpillar. It appeared that, because the cater-pillar was of a similar density, diameter and weight to the peas, it had escaped the defendants' mechanical screening process and, because it was of a similar colour to the peas, it had not been noticed by the visual inspectors. The food and drugs auth-

f ority laid an information against the defendants under ss 2(1)*ᵃ* and 113(3)*ᵇ* of the Food and Drugs Act 1955 alleging that food which was not of the substance and quality demanded by the customer had been sold to her to her prejudice and the authority were reasonably satisfied that the offence was due to the act or default of the de-fendants. The defendants contended that they were entitled to rely on the defence under s 3(3)*ᶜ* of the 1955 Act in that they had taken all reasonable care to avoid the

g presence of extraneous matter in the food.

Held – (i) In order to establish a defence under s 3(3) it was necessary to show that the presence of the extraneous matter was a consequence of the process of collection or preparation of the food and that that consequence could not have been avoided by any human agency; it was not sufficient for the defendant to show that he had taken

h all reasonable care to avoid the presence of the extraneous matter. Accordingly, even if it were accepted that the presence of the caterpillar was a consequence of the process of collection or preparation rather than something which had occurred despite those processes, the defendants were not entitled to rely on s 3(3) since the caterpillar could have been removed from the peas during the process of collection or preparation and its presence could thereby have been avoided (see p 26 *d e* and *j*

j to p 27 *b* and *e* to *g*, p 28 *a* and *b*, p 30 *e g* and *h*, p 32 *c*, p 35 *b*, p 36 *c* to *f* and p 37 *f*, post).

(ii) Even if it were possible to establish a defence under s 3(3) by showing that the

---

a Section 2(1), so far as material, is set out at p 24 *g*, post
b Section 113(3) is set out at p 25 *d* and *e*, post
c Section 3(3), so far as material, is set out at p 24 *j*, post

presence of the extraneous matter was unavoidable by the exercise of reasonable
care, it would be necessary for the defendants to show that, not only they themselves, *a*
but everybody engaged in the processes of collection and preparation had exercised
reasonable care to avoid the presence of the extraneous matter, and that the defendants had failed to do so (see p 28 *d e g* and *h*, p 31 *g* to p 32 *a*, p 35 *f* and p 37 *f*, post).

Lindley v George W Horner & Co Ltd [1950] 1 All ER 234 approved.

Per Viscount Dilhorne, Lord Cross of Chelsea and Lord Kilbrandon. Food and *b*
drugs authorities are not bound to commence a prosecution in every case in which
they think that an offence under the Food and Drugs Act 1955 has been committed.
Before doing so they should consider whether a prosecution is desirable to protect
the general interests of consumers. In cases where it is apparent that a prosecution
does not serve the general interests of consumers, the justices may think fit, if they
find that the Act has been contravened, to grant an absolute discharge (see p 33 *d e* *c*
and *h* and p 37 *e* and *g*, post).

Decision of the Divisional Court of the Queen's Bench Division [1973] 3 All ER 339
affirmed.

Notes

For the sale of food or drugs not of the nature, substance or quality demanded, see *d*
17 Halsbury's Laws (3rd Edn) 484, 485, para 900; for the statutory defences available,
see ibid 489, 490, para 907; for cases on the subject, see 25 Digest (Repl) 91-96, *165-197*,
122, *332*.

For the Food and Drugs Act 1955, ss 2, 3, 113, see 14 Halsbury's Statutes (3rd Edn)
21, 23, 108.

Cases referred to in opinions *e*

Alphacell Ltd v Woodward [1972] 2 All ER 475, [1972] AC 824, [1972] 2 WLR 1320,
    [1972] Crim LR 41, HL.
Bibby-Cheshire v Golden Wonder Ltd [1972] 3 All ER 738, [1972] 1 WLR 1487, DC.
Edwards v Llaethdy Meirion Ltd (1957) 107 LJo 138, [1957] Crim LR 402, DC.
Hacking v Brooks (1961) unreported.
Kenny v Cox [1920] All ER Rep 620, 89 LJKB 1258, 124 LT 221, 85 JP 70, 26 Cox CC 659, *f*
    DC, 25 Digest (Repl) 148, *614*.
Lindley v George W Horner & Co Ltd [1950] 1 All ER 234, 114 JP 124, 48 LGR 174, DC,
    25 Digest (Repl) 112, *332*.
Sherras v De Rutzen [1895] 1 QB 918, [1895-99] All ER Rep 1167, 64 LJMC 218, 72 LT
    839, 59 JP 440, 18 Cox CC 157, 15 R 388, DC, 14 Digest (Repl) 39, 90.
Shortt v Robinson (1899) 68 LJQB 352, 80 LT 261, 63 JP 295, DC, 25 Digest (Repl) 91, *167*. *g*
Sweet v Parsley [1969] 1 All ER 347, [1970] AC 132, [1969] 2 WLR 470, 133 JP 188, 53
    Cr App Rep 221, HL.
Warnock v Johnstone (1881) 8 R (J) 55, 25 Digest (Repl) 97, **59*.

Appeal

On 6th June 1972 an information was preferred before the justices for the county of *h*
Dorset acting in and for the petty sessional division of Dorchester, by the respondent,
William Roger Breed, against the appellants, Smedleys Ltd. The information alleged
that on 25th February 1972 Tesco Stores Ltd, Tesco House, Delamere Road, Cheshunt,
Hertfordshire, sold to the prejudice of Winifred Maud Voss ('Mrs Voss') of 205 Damers
Road, Dorchester, the purchaser thereof, certain food called garden peas which was
not of the substance demanded by the purchaser in that the food contained a cater- *j*
pillar, the larva of one of the hawk moths, contrary to s 2(1) of the Food and Drugs
Act 1955, and the Dorset County Council, being the food and drugs authority concerned, by the respondent were reasonably satisfied that the offence was due to the
act or default of the appellants and that Tesco Stores Ltd could establish a defence
under s 113(1) of the 1955 Act.

a
The justices heard the information on 30th August 1972 and found the following facts:

'(a) Mrs. Voss had bought a tin of garden peas with other articles from Tesco Stores Limited, Dorchester, on the 25th February 1972. The tin had been supplied to Tesco Stores Limited by the appellant. (b) On opening the tin on the 29th February 1972, she found a caterpillar in the tin among the peas. (c) The cater-pillar, which was the larva of a hawk moth, had been canned with the peas.

b
(d) The caterpillar was of a size, colour, density and weight similar to that of the peas in the tin. (3) The tin of peas had been canned by the appellants at their factory in Dundee, Scotland, on the 19th August, 1971, and was one of the 3,500,000 similar tins produced by that Factory during the 6 to 7 week canning season in 1971. Each tin contained between 150 and 200 peas. (f) The appellant had con-stituted and maintained a system whereby the peas were subject to visual

c
examination by properly trained and experienced employees who were not permitted to remain on the inspection line for long periods and who were paid a bonus if they detected and removed extraneous matter. (g) The canning pro-cess involved the contents of the tins being pressure-cooked for 22 minutes at 250°F. (h) The appellants had instituted and maintained a satisfactory system for the random sampling of tins of peas at the end of the canning process so that

d
they could be checked for quality control. (i) Apart from the present case the appellant had received only three other complaints involving extraneous matter found in tins canned at the factory during the 1971 canning season. (j) The cater-pillar found in the tin in this case was sterile, harmless and would not have con-stituted a danger to health if it had been consumed, and it did not affect the substance of the peas. (k) It would have been possible but impracticable for

e
the peas to have been collected in such a way as to avoid the possibility of a cater-pillar being present in the can of peas.'

The appellants contended that the presence of the caterpillar in the tin was an unavoidable consequence of the process of collection or preparation and that they had therefore established a defence under s 3(3) of the 1955 Act since the Act did not

f
impose a standard which called for a system of canning which was 100 per cent fool-proof and the defence under s 3(3) imported a standard of reasonable care. The decision of the justices was as follows:

'We were of the opinion that the offence charged against the appellant was an absolute offence and that although the appellant had satisfied us that they had taken all reasonable care to prevent the presence of the caterpillar in the tin,

g
this was not an unavoidable consequence of the process of collection or prepara-tion of the peas. We considered that we were bound by the decision in *Lindley v Horner*[1]. Accordingly we convicted the appellant.'

The appellants appealed against that decision by way of a case stated for the opinion of the High Court. On 23rd May 1973 the Divisional Court of the Queen's Bench

h
Division[2] (Lord Widgery CJ, MacKenna and Bean JJ) dismissed the appeal. The court certified that the decision involved a question of law of general public importance but refused leave to appeal. On 15th October 1973 the House of Lords on report from the appeal committee gave leave to appeal.

E F Jowitt QC and *Colin Colston* for the appellants.
Ian Hill QC and *Giles Best* for the respondent.

j
Their Lordships took time for consideration.

21st March. The following opinions were delivered.

1 [1950] 1 All ER 234
2 [1973] 3 All ER 339, [1973] QB 977

LORD HAILSHAM OF ST MARYLEBONE. My Lords, on 25th February *a*
1972 Mrs Voss, a Dorset housewife, entered a supermarket belonging to Tesco Stores
Ltd and bought a tin of Smedleys' peas. It goes without saying that both Tesco
Stores Ltd and Smedleys Ltd are firms of the highest reputation, and no one who has
read this case or heard it argued could possibly conceive that what has occurred here
reflects in any way on the quality of their products, still less on their commercial
reputations.

Unfortunately, and without any fault or negligence on the part of the manage- *b*
ment of either company, when Mrs Voss got home, she discovered that the tin, in
addition to something more than 150 peas, contained a green caterpillar, the larva
of one of the species of hawk moth. This innocent insect, thus deprived of its natural
destiny, was in fact entirely harmless, since, prior to its entry into the tin, it had been
subjected to a cooking process of 20 minutes duration at 250°F, and, had she
cared to do so, Mrs Voss could have consumed the caterpillar without injury to her- *c*
self, and even, perhaps, with benefit. She was not, however, to know this, and with
commendable civic zeal, she felt it her duty to report the matter to the local authority,
and in consequence, grinding slow, but exceeding small, the machinery of the law was
set in inexorable motion.

Thereafter, the caterpillar achieved a sort of posthumous apotheosis. From local *d*
authority to the Dorchester magistrates, from the Dorchester magistrates to a Divisional Court presided over by the Lord Chief Justice of England[1], from the Lord Chief
Justice to the House of Lords, the immolated insect has at length plodded its metho-
dical way to the highest tribunal in the land. It now falls to me to deliver my opinion
on its case.

The Food and Drugs Act 1955, s 113, provides a means whereby, if prosecuted for *e*
an offence under the Act, a defendant can seek to cast the blame on a third party
and exonerate himself, and, in order to save the needless expense of an unnecessary
prosecution, the local authority is empowered, when it is reasonably satisfied that a
defence of this kind could be established, to short-circuit proceedings by prosecuting
the third party direct. Thus it was that Smedleys Ltd, the present appellants, and
not Tesco Stores Ltd, found themselves defendants to a summons which alleged *f*
that the sale by Tesco Stores Ltd was of peas which were not of the substance
demanded by Mrs Voss since they included the caterpillar and that was due to
the act or default of the appellants.

The relevant sections of the 1955 Act are as follows: s 2(1) provides:

'If a person sells to the prejudice of the purchaser any food . . . which is not
. . . of the substance . . . of the food . . . demanded by the purchaser, he shall, *g*
subject to the provisions of the next following section, be guilty of an offence.'

Although the contrary had been contended below, it was conceded before your
Lordships that the peas, with the caterpillar among them, were not of the substance
demanded by Mrs Voss.

Despite what has been said by my noble and learned friend, Viscount Dilhorne, to
the contrary, I think this concession to have been right. I believe a housewife who *h*
orders peas is entitled to complain if, instead of peas, she gets a mixture of peas
and caterpillars, and that she is not bound to treat the caterpillar as a kind of
uncovenanted blessing.

Section 3(3) of the Act provides:

'In proceedings under section two of this Act in respect of any food . . . containing some extraneous matter, it shall be a defence for the defendant to prove *j*
that the presence of that matter was an unavoidable consequence of the process
of collection or preparation.'

The principal contention of the appellants before your Lordships was that, on the true
construction of this subsection, and on the facts found by the magistrates, the presence

a of the caterpillar amongst the peas was an unavoidable consequence of the process of collection or preparation.

Section 113 of the Act provides the means of defence of the original vendor referred to above, and the power of the local authority to short-circuit the prosecution. It reads (so far as material) as follows:

b '(1) A person against whom proceedings are brought under this Act shall, upon information duly laid by him and on giving to the prosecution not less than three clear days' notice of his intention, be entitled to have any person to whose act or default he alleges that the contravention of the provisions in question was due brought before the court in the proceedings; and if, after the contravention has been proved, the original defendant proves that the contravention was due to the act or default of that other person, that other person may be convicted of the c offence, and, if the original defendant further proves that he has used all due diligence to secure that the provisions in question were complied with, he shall be acquitted of the offence.

'(2) [Immaterial for this purpose].

'(3) Where it appears to the authority concerned that an offence has been committed in respect of which proceedings might be taken under this Act against d some person and the authority are reasonably satisfied that the offence of which complaint is made was due to the act or default of some other person and that the first-mentioned person could establish a defence under subsection (1) of this section, they may cause proceedings to be taken against that other person without first causing proceedings to be taken against the first-mentioned person.

'In any such proceedings the defendant may be charged with, and, on proof e that the contravention was due to his act or default, be convicted of, the offence with which the first-mentioned person might have been charged.'

The appellants did not seek themselves to make use of this procedure as regards any third party, and thus the case before the magistrates turned (a) on the ability of the prosecution to prove the contravention by Tesco Stores Ltd, and the act or default f of the appellants and (b) on the ability of the appellants to establish a defence under s 3(3) of the Act.

In the event, the magistrates convicted the appellants and subjected them to a fine of £25, but, on the application of the appellants, stated a case for the Divisional Court raising the following questions, viz:

g '1(a) Whether section 2(1) of the Food and Drugs Act, 1955, creates an absolute offence; (b) whether a defence under section 3(3) of the said Act is established if the defendant proves that he took all reasonable care to avoid the presence of extraneous matters in the food; 2. Whether we were right, on the facts found by us, to convict the appellant in this case.'

After expressing a good deal of sympathy with the appellants, the Divisional Court[1] h (Lord Widgery CJ, MacKenna and Bean JJ) dismissed the appeal and affirmed the conviction. But they certified that a point of law of general public importance was involved in their decision, namely:

'Is a defence established under section 3(3) of the Food and Drugs Act 1955 if a Defendant proves that he took all reasonable care to avoid the presence of extraneous matter in the food he manufactures?'

j
Leave to appeal was subsequently given by the appeal committee of your Lordships' House.

My Lords, I do not think that I need discuss the actual terms of the case stated by the magistrates. Though the contrary was argued in the Divisional Court[1], it was

1 [1973] 3 All ER 339, [1973] QB 977

accepted in this House that the substance of the peas and caterpillar taken together
were not of the substance demanded by the purchaser. On the other hand, the appellants gave the fullest and most candid account of their processes which led the magistrates to conclude that they 'had taken all reasonable care to prevent the presence of
the caterpillar in the tin'. Thus, if the question certified by the Divisional Court[1]
were to be answered affirmatively, it would be clear that the conviction could not be
sustained. The appellants established that they had a satisfactory system of manufacture and spot checking for quality, that they had a screening process which eliminated waste matter of markedly higher or lower specific gravity than the peas, and a
system of visual inspection of all the peas as they passed on their way along a white
conveyor belt towards their final destinations by which a team of women sorters under
a supervisor inspected them and removed any extraneous material they might see.
Unfortunately, the caterpillar was of the same or similar density, diameter and weight
as the peas, and so escaped the mechanical screening processes, and, being of a green
colour similar to that of the peas, appears to have been missed by the visual inspectors.

It is clear that it was the failure of the visual inspectors to detect and remove the
caterpillar from the peas along the conveyor belt which led to its continued presence
when it reached the cooking and canning stages. There was no finding by the magistrates to the effect that it was unavoidable that the caterpillar should have escaped
detection at this stage nor even that it was not due to some momentary act of careless-
ness, or negligence, on the part of the inspectors. It is clear that this was no accidental
omission on the magistrates' part. It was an inescapable inference from the evidence.
Whilst I accept that the system was as good as reasonable skill and diligence on the
part of management could make it, on the construction which I am constrained to
place on the relevant provisions of the Act, the absence of any finding that the failure
to eliminate the caterpillar was unavoidable is, in my opinion, fatal to the appeal.

My Lords, as has been pointed out by my noble and learned friend, Lord Diplock,
the expression 'absolute offence' is imprecise (see *Sweet v Parsley*[2]). Clearly the offence
contemplated in s 2(1) of the Food and Drugs Act 1955 is an absolute offence if all that
is meant by that is an absence of mens rea. It is one of those offences described by
Wright J in *Sherras v De Rutzen*[3] which 'are not criminal in any real sense, but are
acts which in the public interest are prohibited under a penalty'. (See also *Alphacell
Ltd v Woodward*[4], per Viscount Dilhorne and per Lord Salmon.) But clearly it is not an
absolute offence in the sense that no defence is possible once the prohibited act is
proved. There is such a defence under s 113, and, at any rate in theory, there is such
a defence under s 3(3), though it is fair to add that the combined ingenuity of counsel and
the House failed to produce a convincing instance, short of the construction sought
to be placed on it by the appellants, where, if sufficient facts were proved to satisfy
s 2(1), a defence under s 3(3) would be convincingly available. Indeed, in the one
case where the subject seems to have been discussed under the original 1875 Act
(viz *Warnock v Johnstone*[5]), two members of the court reached their destination by
way of what was then the exception, and one by way of the substantive definition.

In theory at least, therefore, it is a defence to a charge under s 2(1) if a defendant can
establish that, on the balance of probabilities, notwithstanding that facts are proved
bringing the case within s 2(1) the presence of any extraneous matter was an unavoidable consequence of the process of collection or distribution. This involves at
least three elements: (1) a process of collection or distribution, (2) of which the presence of the extraneous matter was a consequence, and, (3) that that consequence
was unavoidable. I am by no means convinced in the present case that the appellants
have made any sort of case that the failure to eliminate extraneous matter which was

1   [1973] 3 All ER 339, [1973] QB 977
2   [1969] 1 All ER 347 at 360, [1970] AC 132 at 162
3   [1895] 1 QB 918 at 922, [1895-99] All ER Rep 1167 at 1169
4   [1972] 2 All ER 475 at 483, 491, [1972] AC 824 at 839, 848
5   (1881) 8 R (J) 55

a always there can, on the ordinary use of language, be described as a consequence of the process of collection or preparation, and I do not regard the process of dealing with the peas after vining and podding as part of any process of collection. I agree with those of my noble and learned friends who have said that it would be more natural to describe the presence of the caterpillar to have occurred despite the processes rather than because of them.   But, on any view of the case, I do not think that, if

b consequence it were, it was an 'unavoidable' consequence.

In construing the word 'unavoidable' in this context I must have regard (1) to the ordinary and natural meaning of the word, and (2) to the context in which it occurs in the Act. In applying it I must remember that the case finds that:

> 'It would have been possible but impracticable for the peas to have been
> collected [sic] in such a way as to avoid the possibility of a caterpillar being present
c > in the can of peas.'

I doubt myself whether the omission of any reference to the expression 'preparation' is altogether accidental in this finding. But, on the assumption, which favours the appellants, that such might be the case, I consider that this somewhat cryptic finding refers to an argument by the appellants based on the fact that in any commercial

d process, manual or mechanical, some failures, human or mechanical, will take place and that statistically, out of an output by the appellants of 3,500,000 tins for 1971, there had only been four complaints involving extraneous matter, including the present case. If so, I regard the contention as irrelevant. What has to be shown in order to constitute a defence under s 3(3) of the Act is not that *some* failures are unavoidable and that, owing to the excellence of the system, statistically the failures have been

e few. This is matter in mitigation. What has to be shown under s 3(3) is that the 'presence of *that* matter' (i e the particular piece of extraneous matter) in the particular parcel of food the subject of the charge was 'the unavoidable consequence of the process'. As I ventured to point out in argument, over a long enough run any sort of process, however excellent, will statistically result in some failures, human or otherwise, and these are statistically predictable in the light of experience. But that will

f not necessarily be a defence under s 3(3). What is required is the proof, on the balance of probabilities, that the particular piece of extraneous matter was present in the particular parcel of food as the unavoidable consequence of the process itself. Thus in *Warnock v Johnstone*[1] it was established that added water in buttermilk was, at least at that time, an unavoidable consequence of the process by which buttermilk is produced, and, incidentally, was always found to a greater or lesser extent in any

g samples of buttermilk.

At this stage, I think it might be convenient if I made, as it were, a footnote on the disjunctive use in s 3(3) of the nouns 'collection' and 'preparation'. It was pointed out, in the course of argument, that if the words were to be interpreted in one sense, the effect would be extraordinary and unreasonable. Were it the case that a defendant could argue that it was a sufficient defence to establish that the presence of the extraneous matter could not have been avoided in the collection, though it could have

h been avoided in the later process of preparation, the result would be ridiculous. I believe that the clue to this absurdity was pointed out in argument by my noble and learned friend, Lord Diplock.

There are foods (for instance field cabbage) which are subjected to a process in collection, but suffer no process of preparation before being sold to the housewife.

j There are also foods, which, although collected in their natural state, are subjected to processes of preparation before being sold to the housewife. An example would be tinned peas. Section 3(3) of the Act is concerned with contamination by extraneous matters. If the consequence of one of the two processes is the presence of extraneous matter it is for the defendant to show that its presence is unavoidable. In the case of field cabbages the nature of the process of collection, whatever process is adopted,

1 (1881) 8 R (J) 55

may be such that the presence in the heart of the cabbage of a certain amount of   *a*
extraneous matter (eg dust or grit) is 'unavoidable'. As there is no subsequent process of preparation, there is a defence, if, in the particular case, there is a certain
amount of extraneous matter which can be said to be the unavoidable consequence
of the process of collection. On the other hand, in the case of tinned peas there is a
process of preparation as well as a process of collection. In that case the consequences
of the processes of collection are not unavoidable unless they cannot be removed in   *b*
the course of preparation.

  This, however, does not beg the question how one should construe 'unavoidable'.
I must read the word as being contrasted with 'avoidable', and this must mean that
some human act or omission could have avoided the consequence. The only question
is the standard of precaution to be exacted in deciding whether a consequence is
'unavoidable'. Obviously any consequence is avoidable by the simple expedient of not   *c*
engaging in the process at all. But that clearly is not what is meant unless the process
itself is open to serious criticism as unnecessary or inefficient. I do not think the words
'avoidable' or 'unavoidable' are to be construed in any strained metaphysical or
absolute sense. I believe they are to be construed with common sense in the way that
a jury might construe them. This, in my view, means no more, and no less, than this.
If any human agency in any way concerned in a proper process could have avoided   *d*
the consequence by the exercise of a high standard of reasonable care, then the
consequence is avoidable. On the other hand, if no human agency concerned with
the process could, by the exercise of a high standard of reasonable care have avoided
the contamination, the consequence, if a consequence of the process, is unavoidable
within the meaning of s 3(3).

  It will be seen that this construction falls short of absolute liability. But it does not   *e*
save a defendant who can only show that he himself has exercised every possible
diligence, where he cannot also show that the consequence could never have been
avoided by any other human agency connected with the process using the requisite
degree of care and diligence. In that event to escape liability he must establish a
defence under s 113, and to do so he must (1) identify the third party (who may, or
may not, be, his own employee) whose act or default had as its consequence the pre-   *f*
sence of the extraneous matter, (2) adopt the prescribed procedures, and (3) exonerate
himself by showing that he had used all diligence. There may be many cases where
he does not choose to lay the blame on another. There may be others where he
cannot do so. Indeed, if the appellants here could not identify the visual inspectors
whose vigilance this caterpillar escaped, this case would be one. But if he cannot or
will not avail himself of s 113, a defendant must be convicted if he cannot show that   *g*
the presence of the particular extraneous matter in the particular parcel of food was a
consequence of the process of collection or preparation (as the case may be) which
was unavoidable by any human agency provided that all concerned exercised a high
standard of reasonable care in what they were supposed to do. In other words, he
must suffer conviction unless the consequence was, in the ordinary sense of the
word, 'unavoidable', whether or not he could have avoided it by reasonable diligence   *h*
of his own.

  I find myself quite unable to construe the word 'unavoidable' by inserting any reference to the care or diligence of the defendant. It would have been perfectly simple for
the draftsman to insert such a reference, had he wished to do so, and in fact, apart
from s 113, to the language of which MacKenna J[1] drew attention, the draftsman
did insert such a reference in s 8(3)(*b*) of the Act.

  The Divisional Court[1] in the present case felt itself bound by the decision in *Lindley*   *j*
v Horner[2], and in truth it has been accepted that the facts of that case are indistinguishable from the present. It follows from what I have said that, in my view, that

---

1 [1973] 3 All ER at 346, [1973] QB at 978
2 [1950] 1 All ER 234

a case was rightly decided, and I only desire to add with Lord Widgery CJ in the present case that, sympathise as one may with a manufacturer with a reputation and record as excellent as that of the appellants, to construe the Food and Drugs Act 1955 in a sense less strict than that which I have adopted would make a serious inroad on the legislation for consumer protection which Parliament has adopted and by successive Acts extended, over a period, now, of more than a century. I think it

b would be unwise on the present occasion to say anything about *Bibby-Cheshire v Golden Wonder Ltd*[1] to which we were referred. I do not think there is anything in that decision with which what I have said is at variance. But it was based on the slightly different provisions of the Weights and Measures Act 1963, and, though I believe that I would have concurred in the result, as did Lord Widgery CJ, who was a party both to that and the present case, I do not think it desirable to express a concluded view on it.

c In my view, the appeal fails and should be dismissed.

VISCOUNT DILHORNE. My Lords, the tin of peas bought by Mrs Voss on 25th February 1972 from Tesco Stores Ltd at Dorchester in Dorset when opened was was found to contain a caterpillar. The tin was one of $3\frac{1}{2}$ million tins of peas produced

d in the appellants' factory in Dundee. The peas and the caterpillar were in the course of the canning process pressure cooked for 22 minutes at 250°F with the result that the caterpillar was, so the justices found, 'sterile, harmless and would not have constituted a danger to health if it had been consumed'.

Proceedings under the Food and Drugs Act 1955 might have been instituted against Tesco Stores Ltd for an offence under that Act. If they had been, Tesco Stores Ltd

e might have sought to rely on s 113(1) of that Act and to prove that the contravention of the Act was due to the act or default of the appellants in which case the appellants might have been convicted of an offence and Tesco Stores Ltd have secured their acquittal if they had proved that they had used all due diligence to secure that the provisions of the Act were complied with.

Under s 113(3) when it appears to the authority concerned, in this case the Dorset

f County Council, that an offence has been committed in respect of which proceedings could be taken against some person and the authority is reasonably satisfied that the offence was due to the act or default of some other person and the first-mentioned person could establish a defence under s 113(1), the authority may cause proceedings to be instituted against the person whose act or default was responsible without prosecuting the first-mentioned person. If such proceedings are instituted, a conviction

g may ensue if the contravention of the Act was due to the accused's act or default.

In reliance on this provision, the chief inspector of weights and measures of the Dorset County Council, on 6th June 1972, laid an information charging the appellants with having sold to the prejudice of Mrs Voss—

h 'certain food called Garden Peas which was not of the substance demanded by the purchaser in that the said food contained a caterpillar the larva of one of the hawk moths, contrary to Section 2 of the Food and Drugs Act 1955 . . .'

The magistrates on 30th August 1972 convicted the appellants. The case they stated includes no finding by them that the peas were not of the substance demanded by the purchaser. Indeed, they expressly found as a fact that the caterpillar did not affect the substance of the peas. In view of this finding, I must confess to difficulty in

j understanding how the justices came to convict the appellants. Mrs Voss no doubt did not expect to find a caterpillar in the tin of peas she bought. If she had bought peas at a market stall and with the peas there were bits of pea pods or pea leaves or even a caterpillar their presence would not affect the substance of the peas: and the

---

1   [1972] 3 All ER 738, [1972] 1 WLR 1487

charge the appellants had to meet was of selling peas not of the substance demanded
and the justices found that the substance of the peas was not affected.

The case stated does not, however, record any contention by the appellants that the
peas were of the substance demanded. Their contention as recorded in the case stated
appears to have related only to the defence under s 3(3) of the 1955 Act which they
sought to establish. It may be that it was not contended in the magistrates' court that
the peas were of the substance demanded but in the Divisional Court[1] counsel for
the appellants put this contention forward without success and in this House has
refrained from doing so. In these circumstances, one must consider the case on the
basis that the garden peas were not of the substance demanded, even though the
justices found that their substance was unaffected by the caterpillar.

Section 3(3) of the 1955 Act reads as follows:

'In proceedings under section two of this Act in respect of any food or drug
containing some extraneous matter, it shall be a defence for the defendant to
prove that the presence of that matter was an unavoidable consequence of the
process of collection or preparation.'

So the question the justices had to decide was, had the appellants proved that the
presence of the caterpillar in the tin was the unavoidable consequence of their process of collection or preparation. They came to the conclusion that it was not; and
the Divisional Court[1] came to the same conclusion.

The unavoidable consequence of a process is, in my opinion, something that is
bound to result from that process. It is something that cannot be prevented. That it
should be there as a result of the process is inevitable. To succeed on this defence
the appellants had to show that as a result of their process there would be a caterpillar in every tin of peas they produced. That they could not and would not want to
do. The caterpillar was there not in consequence of but despite their process and so,
in my opinion, their defence failed. In the process of canning the peas we were told
that hot brine was added so brine was in every tin of peas. The presence of the brine
was the inevitable and unavoidable consequence of the appellants' process, so if they
were prosecuted under s 2(1) of the 1955 Act for selling to the prejudice of the purchaser
peas not of the nature or substance or quality demanded on account of the presence
of the brine, s 3(3) would provide them with a good defence.

On this view of the meaning of s 3(3) the question whether the appellants had or
had not taken reasonable care to exclude the caterpillar is irrelevant. The justices
found as a fact that it would have been possible but impracticable for the peas to be
collected in such a way as to avoid the possibility of the caterpillar being present
in the can and held that the appellants had taken all reasonable care to prevent
its inclusion but s 3(3) does not say that it shall be a defence to prove that all reasonable care has been taken to prevent that, but that the presence of the extraneous
matter must be the unavoidable consequence of the process. It does not say, but
could have said, that it must be the consequence of the process which was unavoidable
by the exercise of reasonable care and so to construe the subsection would, in my
opinion, be to put an impermissible gloss on it.

To establish an offence under s 2(1) in relation to food, it must be proved that there
has been a sale of food for human consumption which was not the nature, substance
or quality demanded to the prejudice of the purchaser. It is not necessary to show that
there was any intent to sell food not of the nature, substance or quality demanded.
It suffices to establish that such a sale took place. If it did, then the vendor can be
prosecuted. He may avoid conviction by reliance on s 113(1) and the food and drugs
authority for the purposes of the Act (see s 83) may, instead of prosecuting the vendor,
prosecute the person whose act or default was, in their opinion, the cause of the
contravention. Such a person may himself rely on s 113(1).

---

1 [1973] 3 All ER 339, [1973] QB 977

a Section 3 specifies various defences an accused person may rely on. In the light of these provisions it is misleading to speak of the offence created by s 2 as an absolute offence save in the sense that it is not necessary to prove an intent to sell food inferior to that demanded to the prejudice of the purchaser. It is not absolute in the sense that proof of such a sale must necessarily result in a conviction.

b The presence of extraneous matter does not necessarily prove that the food sold was not of the nature, substance or quality demanded. If, for instance, a cabbage bought on a market stall was found to contain a caterpillar it would be difficult to contend that the cabbage was not of the nature, substance or quality demanded. The fact that buttermilk contained water was held by two members of the court in *Warnock v Johnstone*[1] not to make the buttermilk not of the nature, substance or quality demanded. The third member of the court based his conclusion that no offence *c* had been committed on the defence provided by s 6(4) of the Food and Drugs Act 1875. Section 6 made it an offence to sell to the prejudice of the purchaser any article of food or any drug which was not of the nature, substance and quality demanded—

> 'provided that an offence shall not be deemed to be committed under this section . . . (4) Where the food or drug is unavoidably mixed with some extraneous matter in the process of collection or preparation.'

d The justices who have to determine these questions of fact, may decide that despite the presence of extraneous matter the food was of the nature, substance and quality demanded (see, for instance, *Edwards v Llaethdy Meirion Ltd*[2]; *Kenny v Cox*[3]; *Shortt v Robinson*[4]). If, however, it appears that on account of the presence of such matter the food was not of the nature, substance or quality demanded, then the question *e* whether the defence under s 3(3) is established may arise. It is not easy to relate this defence to the substantive offence. It may have been enacted to make it clear beyond all doubt that a conviction should not result if the matter was there as the unavoidable consequence of the process. Whatever the reason for its enactment may have been, it is our task to give effect to the words of the subsection. I do not find them ambiguous. Just as it is not the inevitable consequence of the making of ice cream *f* that it should contain human hair (*Hacking v Brooks*[5]), so it was not the unavoidable consequence of the process of canning peas that a tin should contain a caterpillar.

In Bell and O'Keefe's Sale of Food and Drugs[6] it is stated in relation to 'Unavoidable consequence' that 'The Act implies reasonable care'. No authority is cited and I see nothing in the 1955 Act or in s 3(3) to justify the implication.

g If, contrary to my view, such an impliction falls to be made and the subsection has to be read as if it ran 'the consequences unavoidable by the exercise of reasonable care', then, in my opinion, the result would be the same and this appeal should be dismissed. Then the question is not whether the appellants had instituted and maintained a satisfactory system for the prevention of the inclusion of caterpillars in their tins of peas but whether the presence of this caterpillar in this tin could have been avoided by the exercise of reasonable care. I do not think that its inclusion was *h* the consequence of the appellants' process but, assuming it was, I cannot myself come to the conclusion that it was proved by the appellants—and the onus lay on them to prove it—that its presence was unavoidable by the exercise of reasonable care, even though, as the justices found, it was of the same size, colour, density and weight as a pea. It was detected by Mrs Voss when she opened the can. It should have been detected in the course of the visual inspection to which the peas were subjected before

j
1   (1881) 8 R (J) 55
2   (1957) 107 LJo 138
3   [1920] All ER Rep 620
4   (1899) 68 LJQB 352
5   (1961) unreported
6   14th Edn (1968), p 58

they were canned. It was not. If reasonable care had been taken, I cannot believe that
the caterpillar would have been in the tin.

In this connection the words of Lord Goddard CJ in *Lindley v George W Horner &
Co Ltd*[1] are relevant.   In that case a nail was found in a sweet.   In this case the caterpillar was not found in a pea.   Lord Goddard CJ held that the presence of the nail
was not the unavoidable consequence of the process of collection or preparation,
saying[2]:

'The manufacturer or his servant did not notice the nail. If it had been noticed,
its presence could have been avoided and it could have been taken out.'

Here those employed on visual inspection of the peas did not notice the caterpillar.
If they had done so it would have been taken out.   Its presence was not therefore
unavoidable.

I cannot conclude this opinion without making some observations with regard to
the propriety of instituting a prosecution in this case. Section 97(1) and Sch 6 to the 1955
Act impose on food and drugs authorities as defined in s 83, i e the Common Council
of the City of London, county borough and metropolitan borough councils, some
non-county borough and urban district councils, and the county council for every
area in the county for which there is no other food and drugs authority, the duty to
prosecute for offences against s 2. It was in performance of this duty that the prosecution was started in this case by an officer authorised by the Dorset County Council.
True it is that the Act does not prohibit prosecutions by private individuals but the
Act clearly contemplates they will ordinarily be instituted by food and drugs authorities who are responsible bodies.   In this case it was not suggested that the slightest
harm was or could have been suffered by Mrs Voss.   On 4th May 1972, before the
information was laid, the appellants wrote to the chief inspector of weights and measures for the county of Dorset describing in very considerable detail the system
followed by the appellants in the processing of peas, their mechanical methods of
cleaning the crop and their system of visual inspection before the peas were canned.
The justices found that out of the 3½ million tins of peas canned in the 1971 season,
the appellants had received only three other complaints. At the end of their letter
the appellants asked permission to contact the customer to offer their apology and
to explain the care taken. If they had done so, it is unlikely that Mrs Voss would not
have been satisfied.

It was not suggested that there were any other practicable steps that the appellants
should or could have taken to secure the exclusion of the caterpillar.   Their process
was not criticised.   Its presence must have been due to human failure in the course of
the visual inspection.   The chances of it happening again were, if this was the only
caterpillar found in a tin, 3,499,999 to 1 or, if all four complaints related to caterpillars
in tins 874,999 to 1.

In these circumstances what useful purpose was served by the prosecution of the
appellants? Why, despite the full disclosure made by the appellants was one instituted? It may have been the view that, in every case where an offence was known
or suspected, it was the duty of a food and drugs authority to institute a prosecution,
that if the evidence sufficed a prosecution should automatically be started.

In 1951 the question was raised whether it was not a basic principle of the rule of
law that the operation of the law is automatic where an offence is known or suspected.
The then Attorney-General, Sir Hartley Shawcross, said:

'It has never been the rule of this country—I hope it never will be—that criminal
offences must automatically be the subject of prosecution'.

---

1   [1950] 1 All ER 234
2   [1950] 1 All ER at 235

a He pointed out that the Attorney-General and the Director of Public Prosecutions only intervene to direct a prosecution when they consider it in the public interest to do so and he cited a statement made by Lord Simon in 1925 when he said:

'. . . there is no greater nonsense talked about the Attorney-General's duty than the suggestion that in all cases the Attorney-General ought to decide to prosecute merely because he thinks there is what the lawyers call a case. It is not true and
b no one who has held the office of Attorney-General supposes it is.'

Sir Hartley Shawcross's statement was endorsed, I think, by more than one of his successors.

Section 109(1) of the Food and Drugs Act 1955 provides that certain government departments may institute proceedings 'where they are of opinion that the general
c interests of consumers are affected' and s 127(1) gives the Minister of Agriculture power to authorise a prosecution if he is of opinion that the failure of a food and drugs authority to prosecute 'affects the general interests of consumers'. In other words, these departments and the Minister may prosecute where they consider it to be in the public interest.

Does a different rule apply in relation to prosecutions by food and drug authorities
d under the Food and Drugs Act? In deciding whether or not to prosecute are they not to have regard to the general interests of consumers? I do not find anything in the Act imposing on them the duty to prosecute automatically whenever an offence is known or suspected and I cannot believe that they should not consider whether the general interests of consumers were likely to be affected when deciding whether or not to institute proceedings. In this case when full information was given by the appellants
e before the information was laid, I am, I must confess, entirely at a loss to see on what grounds it could have been thought that a prosecution was desirable to protect the general interests of consumers.

The exercise by food and drugs authorities of discretion in the institution of criminal proceedings and the omission to do so where they consider that a prosecution will serve no useful purpose is no more the exercise of a dispensing power than the
f omission of the law officers, the Director of Public Prosecutions and the police to prosecute for an offence. I have never heard it suggested that the failure of the police to prosecute for every traffic offence which comes to their notice is an exercise by them of a dispensing power. No duty is imposed on them to prosecute in every single case and although this Act imposes on the food and drugs authorities the duty of prosecuting for offences under s 2, it does not say—and I would find it surprising if it had—that they
g must prosecute in every case without regard to whether the public interest will be served by a prosecution. What this litigation has cost I dread to think. A great deal of the time of the courts has been occupied. I cannot see that any advantage to the general body of consumers has or will result, apart, perhaps, from the exposition of the law. In cases where it is apparent that a prosecution does not serve the general interests of consumers, the justices may think fit, if they find that the Act has been contravened,
h to grant an absolute discharge.

In this case, for the reasons I have stated, in my opinion this appeal should be dismissed.

j **LORD DIPLOCK.** My Lords, s 2 of the Food and Drugs Act 1955 is not concerned with health or hygiene but with breaches of contracts for the sale of food or drugs. It makes it a criminal offence to sell to the prejudice of the purchaser any food or drug which is not of the nature or not of the substance or not of the quality demanded. So if the purchaser gets what he contracted to buy there is no contravention of this section, though if the food is injurious to health there may be an offence under some other section even though there is no breach of the contract of sale.

If the purchaser does not get what he contracted to buy but gets something different in nature or in substance or in quality, this constitutes a contravention of the section by the seller and an offence under the Act, unless the person charged can prove facts which constitute one of the special defences under s 3 or s 115. The only person who can contravene s 2 is the seller who is the actual party to the contract of sale. Prima facie he is the person who is guilty of the offence; but if he can identify some other person to whose act or default his own contravention of the section was due and can also prove that he himself used all due diligence to prevent the contravention, the liability for the offence is by s 113 transferred from the actual seller to that other person.

Although ss 2 and 3 relate to all sales of food for human consumption, the kind of sale primarily contemplated by these sections is a sale by retail to the consumer. The purchaser on such a sale cannot be taken to know the technical meaning of trade descriptions applied to articles of food where these differ from the ordinary meaning of the words used in the description. So in determining what was 'the food or drug demanded by the purchaser', the words by which the goods that he purchased were described must be understood in their popular sense.

In 1875 when a provision similar to s 2(1) was first enacted retail sales in shops were conducted orally. The modern system of self-service was unknown. The purchaser asked for what he wanted. The food or drug sold to him had to comply with the words of description that he used. It was this kind of sale that Parliament had in mind when in 1938 it provided for defences available to the seller substantially to the same effect as those now contained in s 3 of the present Act. In a self-service store, however, where the customer himself selects the goods which are to be the subject-matter of the contract of sale, the 'food or drug demanded by the purchaser', within the meaning of s 2, is that which is represented by the seller to be offered for sale, whether the representation is by the description under which it is displayed or which appears on the outside of the package or container in which it is offered or, if there is no other description, by what it appears to be on visual inspection.

The raw material of many articles of food is subject to some process in preparing it for retail sale. The process may involve the addition of some other substance to the principal constituent of the finished product. If all articles sold under a particular description contain the same additive, as 'strawberry jam' contains sugar in addition to strawberries and 'buttermilk', at any rate in 1881, contained water in addition to milk, no offence is committed under s 2(1) by selling under that description an article of food which contains that additive. Indeed, an offence is committed by selling under that description an article which does not.

Where, however, the article of food which has been subjected to a process in preparing it for retail sale contains a substance the presence of which is not implicit in the particular description under which it is sold, there is a prima facie contravention of s 2(1). To such a prima facie contravention there may be one or other of two defences available to the seller under s 3.

If the substance has been intentionally added, and does not render the food injurious to health, it is a defence under s 3(1) for the person charged to prove—

'that the operation in question was not carried out fraudulently, and that the article was sold having attached thereto a notice of adequate size, distinctly and legibly printed and conspicuously visible, stating explicitly the nature of the operation, or was sold in a wrapper or container displaying such a notice.'

The other defence is under s 3(3). The subsection, which has already been cited by your Lordships, relates to food containing 'extraneous matter' in contrast to food to which 'any substance has been added' referred to in s 3(1). In the context of the section I should myself construe 'extraneous matter' as meaning some substance that was not intended to be present. It can hardly be supposed that sub-ss (1) and (3) were meant to cover the same ground; since if sub-s (3) as well as sub-s (1) were *a* dealing with a substance which was intentionally added in the process of preparation of the food, there would be a defence without its being necessary to prove that the notice that is expressly required under sub-s (1) was attached to the article sold or displayed on its wrapper or container.

b A majority of your Lordships, however, are of opinion that the presence of 'extraneous matter' in an article of food which is the product of a process of preparation can only be the 'consequence' of that process if every article of food produced by it contains similar extraneous matter. I find myself unable to accept this, but no useful purpose would be served by my elaborating the reasons for what would only be a minority opinion; for this appeal comes before your Lordships' House in order to obtain an authoritative ruling as to what must be proved by a defendant to establish a defence under s 3(3) of the Food and Drugs Act 1955.

c The responsibility for enforcing the provisions of the Act lies with numerous local authorities throughout England and Wales. Prosecutions for offences under the Act are dealt with by magistrates' courts all over the country. What matters is that a majority of your Lordships should agree as to the meaning of s 3(3) and should express that meaning in terms that are not liable to be misunderstood and are easy to apply to the circumstances of particular cases.

d The only point on which it would appear that those of your Lordships who form the majority are not of the same opinion is as to whether the defence under s 3(3) is available where some substance, such as brine in the instant case, has been added as part of the process of preparation and no notice of this has been given as is required to constitute a defence under s 3(1). For the reason I have already given I am of opinion that it is not.

e I understand this to be also the opinion of my noble and learned friends, Lord Hailsham of St Marylebone and Lord Cross of Chelsea. So my concurrence gives a majority for this view.

In the result no one has been able to think of any circumstances in which the defence under s 3(3) could be applicable. So local authorities and magistrates can in practice ignore the subsection altogether. This has the merit of simplicity.

f I nevertheless would also have dismissed the appeal though for a different reason. I should have dismissed it on the ground that the appellants, though they proved that the presence of the caterpillar in the can of peas was a 'consequence of the process of preparation' failed to prove that this consequence was 'unavoidable'. This I think means that it could not have been avoided by the exercise of reasonable care by anyone engaged in operating the process—not only those responsible for management and supervision of the work people but also the work people themselves.

g

LORD CROSS OF CHELSEA.   My Lords, s 2(1) of the Food and Drugs Act, 1955 provides:

h
> 'If a person sells to the prejudice of the purchaser any food . . . which is not . . . of the substance . . . of the food . . . demanded by the purchaser, he shall, subject to the provisions of the next following section, be guilty of an offence.'

And s 3(3) provides:

j
> 'In proceedings under section 2 of this Act in respect of any food or drug containing some extraneous matter, it shall be a defence for the defendant to prove that the presence of that matter was an unavoidable consequence of the process of collection or preparation.'

The food in question here was the tin of peas bought by Mrs Voss and the extraneous matter of the presence of which complaint is made was the caterpillar contained in it. The question to be decided is whether its presence was the unavoidable

consequence of the process of collection and preparation.   I begin by asking
myself, 'Why was the caterpillar there?'   It was there because it had been on a   *a*
pea pod before the process of collection or preparation began and because it was not
eliminated in the course of the process.   As it was about the same size and shape
as the peas it passed through the screening machinery with them and those employed
by the appellants to examine the peas as they came along the inspection line failed to
detect and remove it.   It is said with truth that in the process of tinning peas, however   *b*
good your system and however carefully you operate it, it is inevitable that from time
to time a caterpillar or some other similar 'extraneous matter' will slip through the
net.   But it is not, to my mind, a natural use of language to say that the presence of
such extraneous matter is a 'consequence of the process'.   Those words appear to
me to relate to extraneous matter (such as, in this case, brine and salt) which is normally found with the food at the end of the process rather than to extraneous matter   *c*
(such as, in this case, pods, earth and caterpillars) which is found with the food at the
beginning of the process and is not eliminated by any of the parts of the process
designed to eliminate it.   The presence of such extraneous matter at the end of the
process would, I think, more naturally be said to be 'despite' the process than
'in consequence' of it.   But if this be too narrow an approach and one accepts
that the presence of this caterpillar in this tin was a consequence of the process,   I   *d*
cannot see how the fact that it is inevitable that, however good their system and
however high the standard of care which they exercise, caterpillars or similar extraneous matter will find their way into a few of the millions of tins of peas produced
by the appellants involves the consequence that the presence of this caterpillar in
this tin was 'unavoidable'.   Although it resembled a pea this caterpillar cannot have
been indistinguishable from a pea or Mrs Voss would not have noticed it.   So if one of   *e*
the employees working on the inspection line had noticed it she would have removed
it and its presence in the tin would have been avoided—nor can I see why, in this
connection, it should make any difference whether the employee who failed to spot
this caterpillar was or was not guilty of negligence.   I appreciate that to construe the
subsection in this way means that it has no practical effect since the sort of extraneous
matter the presence of which could, in my view, properly be said to be an 'unavoid-   *f*
able consequence of the process' would not prevent the food in question from being
of the substance demanded by the purchaser and so there could be no prima facie
offence under s 2 to which the subsection would have to be invoked as a defence.
But this argument loses much of its force if one pays regard to the ancestry of the
subsection.   Section 6 of the Sale of Food and Drugs Act 1875 provided:

'No person shall sell to the prejudice of the purchaser any article of food or   *g*
any drug which is not of the nature, substance, and quality of the article
demanded . . . provided that an offence shall not be deemed to be committed
under this section in the following cases; that is to say . . .
'(4) Where the food or drug is unavoidably mixed with some extraneous
matter in the process of collection or preparation.'
                                                                                        h
In that—its original—form the subsection was, as I read it, inserted 'ex abundanti
cautela' to make it clear that an article of food was not to be held to be not of the
'substance' demanded by the purchaser simply because some extraneous matter was
necessarily mixed with it in the course of its collection or preparation.   It is interesting
to observe that in *Warnock v Johnstone*[1], a case concerning 'buttermilk' which could
not be produced without the addition of water to the milk in the churning, the   *j*
Lord Justice-Clerk and Lord Craighill thought that the case fell under the proviso,
while Lord Young thought that it was not necessary for the seller to rely on the
proviso since there was no prima facie contravention of the section apart from the
proviso.   The appellants conceded that if the statutory provisions had remained in

1 (1881) 8 R (J) 55

a the form in which they were enacted in 1875 they would not have been able to bring themselves within the subsection. They submitted, however, that when they took their present form in ss 3(1) and 4(4) of the Food and Drugs Act 1938—which were repeated in ss 2(1) and 3(4) of the 1955 Act—they began to cover a case such as this where it is not as a practical matter possible to ensure that extraneous matter not intended to be included with the food will never on any occasion be contained in it but the seller has taken all reasonable steps to avoid its presence. It is true that in *b* 1938 the relevant provisions were altered in two ways—first the subsection came to be expressed as a defence to proceedings brought under the earlier section instead of as a proviso negativing the existence of any offence; secondly instead of applying only where it could be said that the food had been 'mixed' with some extraneous matter in the process it was made to apply wherever the food contains some extraneous matter but it is proved that its presence was an unavoidable consequence of *c* the process. I cannot, however, bring myself to think that Parliament intended these comparatively minor changes to have the far-reaching effect for which the appellants contend. In ss 8(3)(*b*) and 113(1) of the 1955 Act (which repeat provisions which were contained in the 1938 Act) Parliament has expressly provided that proof of the exercise of reasonable diligence shall in certain circumstances be a defence to proceedings brought under the Act, and if it had meant that proof of the exercise *d* of due diligence was to be a defence to proceedings under s 2(1) it would surely have said so in terms   It follows that I think that *Lindley v Horner*[1] was rightly decided and that this appeal should be dismissed. The statutory provisions which had to be construed in the *Bibby-Cheshire* case[2] were quite different from those to be construed here and that case, whether it was rightly or wrongly decided, throws no light on this. I would add in conclusion that I agree with what has been said by my *e* noble and learned friend, Viscount Dilhorne, as to the propriety of a prosecution being brought in a case such as this.

LORD KILBRANDON. My Lords, I had prepared a speech expressing my concurrence with the opinion of my noble and learned friend, Lord Diplock. For *f* the reason which he gives, namely, the undesirability of elaborating minority opinions in a judgment which is primarily concerned to give guidance to those concerned with the administration of a statutory code, I will content myself with a formal expression of that concurrence.

I wish to add, however, that I entirely agree with what my noble and learned friend, Viscount Dilhorne, has said as to the policy which ought to govern the institution of *g* prosecutions in complaints under the Food and Drugs Act 1955.

Appeal dismissed.

Solicitors: *Batchelor, Street, Longstaffe*, agents for *Wilkin & Chapman*, Grimsby (for the appellants); *Sharpe, Pritchard & Co*, agents for *K A Abel*, Clerk to the Dorset County *h* Council (for the respondent).

Christine Ivamy Barrister.

---

1   [1950] 1 All ER 234
2   [1972] 3 All ER 738, [1972] 1 WLR 1487

R v Dudley Justices, ex parte Curlett   a

QUEEN'S BENCH DIVISION
LORD WIDGERY CJ, MACKENNA AND MAY JJ
1st FEBRUARY 1974

                                                               b
Licensing – Licence – Condition – Grant of licence subject to condition – On-licence – Condition restricting use of licence to off-sales and for obtaining occasional licences – Power of justices to impose condition – Validity of licence – Licensing Act 1964, ss 1(2), 4(1) (as amended by the Finance Act 1967, ss 5(1), 45(8), Sch 16, Part I).

Licensing justices granted the respondent an 'on-licence' in respect of certain premises,   c
the grant being subject to the condition, imposed under s 4(1)^a of the Licensing Act
1964, 'that except for "off" sales the licence shall not be used in any way whatsoever
for any purpose other than that of obtaining occasional licences under the Licensing
Act 1964 or any enactment thereof'. The applicant, who had objected to the grant
of the licence, applied for an order of certiorari to quash the licence.

                                                               d
Held – Although the justices had wide powers under s 4 to attach conditions to a
licence granted by them, under s 1(2)(a)^b of the 1964 Act the essential requirement of
an on-licence was that it should permit the sale of intoxicating liquor for consumption
on the premises. Since the effect of the condition which the justices had imposed was
to prohibit on-sales the licence granted was not an on-licence nor was it any other form
of licence known to the law. Accordingly the application would be granted (see   e
p 40 *a b e h* and *j* and p 41 *a* and *b*, post).
    Dictum of Lord Goddard CJ in *R v Brighton Justices, ex parte Jarvis* [1954] 1 All ER
at 200 applied.

Notes
For justices licences and conditions attached thereto, see 22 Halsbury's Laws (3rd Edn)   f
539, 540, paras 1066-1068, and for cases on the subject, see 30 Digest (Reissue) 38, 39,
281-291.
    For the Licensing Act 1964, ss 1, 4, see 17 Halsbury's Statutes (3rd Edn) 1059.

Cases referred to in judgment
R v Brighton Justices, ex parte Jarvis [1954] 1 All ER 197, [1954] 1 WLR 203, 118 JP 117,   g
    52 LGR 148, DC, 30 Digest (Reissue) 86, 648.
R v Sussex Confirming Authority, ex parte Tamplin & Sons' Brewery (Brighton) Ltd [1937]
    4 All ER 106, 157 LT 590, 101 JP 562, 35 LGR 593, DC.

Motions for certiorari and prohibition
This was an application by way of motion on behalf of Donald Stuart Curlett for an   h
order of certiorari to bring up and quash the grant to the respondent, Paul Bye, by the
Dudley licensing justices on 21st June 1973 of a justices' on-licence, subject to a condition, in respect of premises known as 120, Brettell Lane, Amblecote in the county
of Stafford, and/or for an order of prohibition to prohibit the justices from granting
justices' on-licences subject to the condition that except for off-sales the licence should
not be used in any way whatsoever for any purpose other than the obtaining of   j

---

a   Section 4(1), as amended and so far as material, provides: '. . . licensing justices granting
    a new justices' on-licence, other than a licence for the sale of wine alone, may attach to
    it such conditions governing the tenure of the licence and any other matters as they think
    proper in the interests of the public . . .'
b   Section 1(2), as amended and so far as material, is set out at p 40 *a*, post

a occasional licences under the Licensing Act 1964 or any re-enactment thereof. At the hearing the application for an order of prohibition was not pursued. The facts are set out in the judgment of Lord Widgery CJ.

M G M Morse for the applicant
R G Beckett for the respondent.
The justices did not appear and were not represented.

b

LORD WIDGERY CJ. In these proceedings counsel moves for an order of certiorari to bring up and quash a decision of the licensing justices for the county borough of Dudley, a decision given on 21st June 1973 the effect of which was to grant to one Paul Bye a justices' on-licence in respect of premises at 120 Brettell Lane, Amblecote, *c* Staffordshire.

The applicant is a Mr Donald Stuart Curlett, who is amongst other things a licensee in the area, and treasurer of the Brierley Hill Licensed Trade Association. He attended before the justices and objected to the grant of the licence now in issue. It has not been suggested before us that the applicant lacks authority to apply for certiorari to quash the licence.

d The licence was, as I say, an on-licence, and it contained on its face the usual provision which is to be found in a non-licence, that the licensee could sell liquor for consumption either on or off the premises. That of course is merely a reference to the definition of 'Justices' on-licence' in s 1(2) of the Licensing Act 1964, which maintained the principle which has been in force for many years, namely that on obtaining an on-licence, the licensee may sell either on or off the premises.

e A condition however was attached to the licence, and it reads thus:

'This licence is granted subject to the condition endorsed hereon and shall have effect from the date hereof until the 4th day of April 1974.'

The condition said—

f 'This licence is granted subject to the condition that except for "off" sales the licence shall not be used in any way whatsoever for any purpose other than that of obtaining occasional licences under the Licensing Act 1964 or any enactment thereof.'

What is submitted on behalf of the applicant is that the attachment of that condition rendered the licence a nullity because it rendered the licence a form of licence *g* unknown to the law.

The background of this dispute is easily understood. Under the 1964 Act an occasional licence to set up a bar and sell liquor in premises not normally licensed and on a special occasion is authorised by s 180, but the only person to whom an occasional licence can be issued is the holder of a justices' on-licence. It is in a sense the perquisite of the licensees who hold on-licences that it is from their ranks that anyone who is to *h* be granted an occasional licence to sell liquor from a special place is to be drawn. One can well understand that many holders of off-licences who have no ambition to run premises in which liquor is sold on the premises, would nevertheless find it convenient to apply for and obtain occasional licences from time to time. But, as I have said, it seems clear to me that the privilege of applying for an occasional licence is quite deliberately restricted to those who hold a justices' on-licence.

j It is not really disputed that the form of the licence with the condition imposed in this case is put forward as a means of circumventing that restriction, because the licence with that restriction, taken on its face, would mean that the respondent was the holder of an on-licence and thus entitled to apply for occasional licences, even though the condition prevented him from ever selling liquor for consumption on his own premises at all.

It is said by the applicant that that is a form of licence not known to the law, and for my part I entirely agree with that. Section 1(2) of the 1964 Act, as I have already said, sets out the two basic forms of licence available for the sale of liquor. A justices' on-licence means '(a) a justices' licence authorising sale for consumption either on or off the premises for which the licence is granted . . .' A justices' off-licence means '(b) a justices' licence authorising sale for consumption off those premises only.'

An application for a licence and the grant of a licence must fall within one or other of those categories, and the law as I understand it knows no third.

I am supported in that view to some extent at any rate by the observations of Lord Goddard CJ in *R v Brighton Justices, ex parte Jarvis*[1]. A somewhat similar device was being attacked in that case, although the purpose of the applicant was there to curtail an occasional licence so as to restrict it to off-sales, in other words to curtail what was on its face an on-licence to a sphere of operation in which only off-sales were possible. Lord Goddard CJ said[2]:

> 'The justices can grant only a full on-licence. That is what an occasional licence must be. Whether or not they can impose any conditions I do not know. But what they have done here is to say: "We will give you an occasional licence, that is to say, a full licence, on the terms that you use it only as an off-licence and sell at places where you have got an off-licence." In fact, however, the justices have no power to consent to the grant of such a licence. There is no power to turn an off-licence into an on-licence in this way, and no power to restrict an on-licence into an off-licence.'

What is being attacked there is the grant of a licence which is in name an on-licence, but to restrict its operation to off-sales. I take the *Brighton Justices'* case[1] as authority in support of the proposition that that cannot be done within the law.

Counsel for the respondent, who has argued persuasively on the other side, would have us say that all that happened in the present instance is that the justices have lawfully exercised the discretion given to them by s 4 (1) of the 1964 Act when granting an on-licence to attach a condition to the licence. He cites *R v Sussex Confirming Authority, ex parte Tamplin & Sons' Brewery (Brighton) Ltd*[3] for certain dicta of Humphreys J indicating how wide that discretion can be. I would not for a moment seek to depart from what Humphreys J has said[4] about the width of the power of attaching conditions under s 4, but fundamental to the whole question is that you cannot attach conditions unless you are granting an on-licence, and in my judgment this hybrid animal which the justices sought to create in the present proceedings was not an on-licence, indeed it was not a form of licence known to the law at all. Accordingly, I think it was irregularly granted, and I would allow certiorari to go to quash it.

MACKENNA J. I do not read s 1(2) of the 1964 Act as meaning that there can be an on-licence which is restricted to sales for consumption off the premises. The sub-section uses the two expressions 'on-licence' and 'off-licence'. It follows from this that an on-licence is something different from an off-licence. If words mean anything, it must be an essential difference between the two kinds of licence that the on-licence permits consumption on the premises, and that the off-licence does not. It defines the two expressions. There is nothing in the two definitions which forces me to decide otherwise than according to the plain meaning of the words that an on-licence must contain at least a permission to sell on the premises. It may be true that an on-licence can be restricted by conditions or in some other way to sales on the premises and may

---

1 [1954] 1 All ER 197, [1954] 1 WLR 203
2 [1954] 1 All ER at 200, [1954] 1 WLR at 207
3 [1937] 4 All ER 106
4 [1937] 4 All ER at 110-112

a   not also permit sales off the premises; but it does not follow from this that if the
licence does not permit on-sales, it will still be an on-licence. I do not read s 4 as permitting a condition to be attached to an on-licence which prohibits sales for consumption on the premises and turns the on-licence into something different. An on-licence
restricted to sales for consumption off the premises is something which the 1964 Act
does not recognise or sanction. I agree with the order proposed by Lord Widgery CJ.

b   **MAY J.** I also agree.

Certiorari granted; licence quashed.

Solicitors: *Sharpe, Pritchard & Co*, agents for *Woolley, Beavon & Littleford*, Wolverhampton (for the applicant); *Lee, Bolton & Lee*, agents for *Bannister & King*, Stourbridge
c   (for the respondent).

N P Metcalfe Esq   Barrister.

Hyam v Director of Public Prosecutions

d

Distinguished in R v BELFON [1976]
3 All ER 46

HOUSE OF LORDS
LORD HAILSHAM OF ST MARYLEBONE, VISCOUNT DILHORNE, LORD DIPLOCK, LORD CROSS OF
CHELSEA AND LORD KILBRANDON
15th, 16th, 17th JANUARY, 21st MARCH 1974

e   *Criminal law – Murder – Mens rea – Foresight – Probable consequences – Proof that accused
had foreseen death or grievous bodily harm as a probable consequence of his act – Not accused's
motive or desire to cause death or grievous bodily harm – Whether foresight of probable
consequences sufficient mens rea.*

*Criminal law – Murder – Mens rea – Intent to cause grievous bodily harm – Meaning of
f   'grievous bodily harm' – Serious bodily harm – Whether limited to harm likely to endanger
life.*

For some time the appellant had been J's mistress but their relationship ceased in
consequence of the appellant suffering from some gynaecological trouble. Thereafter the appellant became suspicious of J's relationship with a Mrs B; she made
attempts to break up that relationship by writing anonymous letters. Eventually
g   one night she drove to the house where Mrs B was living with her son and two
daughters, and set fire to it. She did nothing to alert the occupants of the house to
the danger she had put them in, or the fire brigade, but drove back to her home some
five miles away. As a result of the fire Mrs B's two daughters were killed. The appellant was charged with their murder. She admitted that she realised that what she
had done was very dangerous to anyone living in the house but said that she did not
h   intend to cause death or grievous bodily harm; she was jealous of Mrs B, whom she
believed to be about to marry J, and her motive in starting the fire was to frighten Mrs
B into leaving the neighbourhood. The judge directed the jury that the prosecution
had to prove beyond reasonable doubt that the appellant intended to kill or do
serious bodily harm to Mrs B. They were told that, if they were satisfied that 'when
j   the [appellant] set fire to the house she knew that it was highly probable that this
would cause . . . serious bodily harm', then the prosecution had established the necessary intent, and it was immaterial that the appellant's motive was merely to frighten
Mrs B. The appellant was convicted of murder and her appeal to the Court of Appeal*a*
was dismissed. She appealed to the House of Lords, contending (i) that the knowledge

a   [1973] 3 All ER 842

that a certain consequence was a highly probable consequence did not establish an intent to produce that result, and (ii) that in order to sustain a conviction for murder it was necessary to prove an intent to kill or to endanger life and therefore intent to do serious bodily harm did not suffice.

Held (Lord Diplock and Lord Kilbrandon dissenting) – The appeal would be dismissed for the following reasons—

(i) (Lord Diplock and Lord Kilbrandon concurring) In order to establish the mens rea of murder it was sufficient to prove that, when the accused performed the relevant acts, he knew that it was probable that those acts would result in grievous bodily harm to somebody, even though he did not desire to bring that result about. However (per Lord Hailsham of St Marylebone) it was necessary to show that the accused intended to expose a potential victim to the risk of grievous bodily harm in that the accused's acts had been performed deliberately and without lawful excuse (see p 52 *a* to *c e* and *h* to p 53 *a*, p 54 *g* and *j* to p 55 *e*, p 56 *d* to *f*, p 59 *d* to *f*, p 61 *a* to *d*, p 62 *d* and *e*, p 63 *a* to *c*, p 71 *b* to *f* and p 72 *c* to *f*, post).

(ii) For that purpose 'grievous bodily harm' meant 'really serious bodily harm' and was not limited to harm of such a nature as to endanger life (see p 47 *b* to *d*, p 56 *d*, p 61 *f* and *h* to p 62 *a* and *d* and p 71 *d* and *f*, post).

(iii) It followed that the appellant was guilty of murder for, on the direction given to them by the judge, the jury must have been satisfied that, when the appellant set fire to the house, she realised that it was highly probable that one or more of the inmates would suffer serious bodily harm in consequence of her acts but nevertheless she had deliberately chosen to expose them to that danger (see p 56 *b* and *c*, p 57 *e*, p 59 *g* and p 71 *g*, post)

Per Lord Diplock.   In murder and crimes of that class no distinction is to be drawn between the state of mind of one who does an act because he desires it to produce a particular evil consequence, and the state of mind of one who does an act knowing that it is likely to produce that consequence, although it may not be the object he was seeking to achieve by doing the act.   What is common to both those states of mind is willingness to produce the particular evil consequence and that is the mens rea needed to satisfy a requirement that in order to constitute the offence with which the accused is charged he must have acted with 'intent' to produce a particular evil consequence (see p 63 *a* to *c*, post).

R v Vickers [1957] 2 All ER 741 and *Director of Public Prosecutions v Smith* [1960] 3 All ER 161 applied.

Decision of the Court of Appeal, Criminal Division, sub nom *R v Hyam* [1973] 3 All ER 842 affirmed.

Notes

For the mens rea of murder, see 10 Halsbury's Laws (3rd Edn) 707, para 1354, and for cases on the subject, see 15 Digest (Repl) 930, 931, 8913, 8914.

Cases referred to in opinions

Cunliffe v Goodman [1950] 1 All ER 720, [1950] 2 KB 237, CA, 31(2) Digest (Reissue) 61, 5217.

Director of Public Prosecutions v Beard [1920] AC 479, [1920] All ER Rep 21, sub nom *R v Beard* 89 LJKB 437, 122 LT 625, 84 JP 129, 26 Cox CC 573, 14 Cr App Rep 159, HL, 14 Digest (Repl) 71, 332.

Director of Public Prosecutions v Smith [1960] 3 All ER 161, [1961] AC 290, [1960] 3 WLR 546, 124 JP 473, 44 Cr App Rep 261, HL; rvsg sub nom *R v Smith* [1960] 2 All ER 450, [1960] 3 WLR 92, CCA, Digest (Cont Vol A) 428, 9145a.

Hardy v Motor Insurers' Bureau [1964] 2 All ER 742, [1964] 2 QB 745, [1964] 3 WLR 433, [1964] 1 Lloyd's Rep 397, CA, Digest (Cont Vol B) 462, 3703a.

a   Holmes v Director of Public Prosecutions [1946] 2 All ER 124, [1946] AC 588, 115 LJKB 417,
    175 LT 327, HL; affg sub nom R v Holmes [1946] 1 All ER 524, CCA, 15 Digest
    (Repl) 941, 9021.
    Hosegood v Hosegood (1950) 66 TLR 735, 48 LGR 253, CA, 27(1) Digest (Reissue) 431, 3160.
    Lang v Lang [1954] 3 All ER 571, [1955] AC 402, [1954] 3 WLR 762, 119 JP 368, PC, 27(1)
    Digest (Reissue) 451, 3286.
b   Parker v R (1963) 111 CLR 610.
    R v Ashman (1858) 1 F & F 88, 175 ER 638, 15 Digest (Repl) 986, 9645.
    R v Bubb, R v Hook (1850) 14 JP 562, 4 Cox CC 455, 15 Digest (Repl) 957, 9254.
    R v Cox (1818) Russ & Ry 362, 15 Digest (Repl) 985, 9644.
    R v Desmond (1868) The Times, 28th April.
    R v Doherty (1887) 16 Cox CC 306, 14 Digest (Repl) 71, 327.
c   R v Gibbins and Procter (1918) 82 JP 287, 13 Cr App Rep 134, CCA, 14 Digest (Repl)
    254, 2216.
    R v Jakac [1961] VR 367, Digest (Cont Vol A) 430, *5841b.
    R v Lumley (1911) 76 JP 208, 22 Cox CC 625, 15 Digest (Repl) 951, 9195.
    R v Porter (1873) 12 Cox CC 444, 15 Digest (Repl) 947, 9131.
    R v Vickers [1957] 2 All ER 741, [1957] 2 QB 664, [1957] 3 WLR 326, 121 JP 510, 41 Cr
    App Rep 189, CCA, Digest (Cont Vol A) 427, 8914a.
d   R v Wallett [1968] 2 All ER 296, [1968] 2 QB 367, [1968] 2 WLR 1199, 132 JP 318, 52 Cr
    App Rep 271, CA, Digest (Cont Vol C) 255, 9145b.
    R v Ward [1956] 1 All ER 565, [1956] 1 QB 351, [1956] 2 WLR 423, 40 Cr App Rep 1,
    CCA, Digest (Cont Vol A) 417, 8507a.
    Southern Portland Cement Ltd v Cooper [1974] 1 All ER 87, [1974] 2 WLR 152, PC.
e   Woolmington v Director of Public Prosecutions [1935] AC 462, [1935] All ER Rep 1, 104
    LJKB 443, 153 LT 232, 25 Cr App Rep 72, 30 Cox CC 234, HL, 14 Digest (Repl) 493,
    4768.

Appeal

f   On 24th November 1972 in the Crown Court at Warwick before Ackner J the appellant, Pearl Kathleen Hyam, was convicted (by a majority verdict of 11 to 1) on two
counts charging her with murder. She was sentenced to life imprisonment. She
appealed against conviction by leave of the trial judge. On 18th June 1973 the Court of
Appeal, Criminal Division[1] (Cairns LJ, Browne and Shaw JJ) dismissed the appeal but
certified that the decision involved a point of law of general public importance and
gave leave to appeal to the House of Lords. The facts are set out in the opinion of
g   Lord Hailsham of St Marylebone.

Charles McCullough QC and B A Farrer for the appellant.
Sir Michael Havers QC, L S Shields QC and Bruce Laughland for the Crown.

Their Lordships took time for consideration.

h   21st March. The following opinions were delivered.

LORD HAILSHAM OF ST MARYLEBONE. My Lords, in my view the one
point in this case is the intention which it is necessary to impute to an accused person
in order to find him guilty of the crime of murder. Is it simply the intention to kill or
cause grievous bodily harm (in the sense of really serious injury) as is commonly
assumed, or is it enough that he intends wilfully to expose another to the risk of death
j   or grievous bodily harm in the sense of really serious injury? I do not believe that
knowledge or any degree of foresight is enough. Knowledge or foresight is at the best
material which entitles or compels a jury to draw the necessary inference as to intention. But what is that intention? It is acknowledged that intention to achieve the
result of death or grievous bodily harm in the sense of really serious injury is enough

1   [1973] 3 All ER 842, [1973] 3 WLR 475

to convict. But may the intention wilfully to expose a victim to the serious risk of death or really serious injury also be enough? It is on the answer to this question that, in my view, depends the outcome of the present appeal.

On an indictment containing two counts alleging the murder of two female children, the appellant in this case pleaded guilty to manslaughter, but after a trial lasting three days was convicted of murder by a majority verdict of 11 to one. The question in the appeal is whether the verdicts of murder can stand or whether verdicts of manslaughter should be substituted for them.

The facts are simple, and not in dispute. In the early hours of Saturday, 15th July 1972, the appellant set fire to a dwelling-house in Coventry by deliberately pouring about a half gallon of petrol through the letterbox and igniting it by means of a newspaper and a match. The house contained four persons, presumably asleep. They were a Mrs Booth and her three children, a boy and the two young girls who were the subjects of the charges. Mrs Booth and the boy escaped alive through a window. The two girls died as the result of asphyxia by the fumes generated by the fire. The appellant's motive (in the sense in which I shall use the word 'motive') was jealously of Mrs Booth whom the appellant believed was likely to marry a Mr Jones of whom the appellant herself was the discarded, or partly discarded, mistress. Her account of her actions, and her defence, was that she had started the fire only with the intention of frightening Mrs Booth into leaving the neighbourhood, and that she did not intend to cause death or grievous bodily harm. The judge directed the jury:

'The prosecution must prove, beyond all reasonable doubt, that the accused intended to (kill or) do serious bodily harm to Mrs Booth, the mother of the deceased girls. If you are satisfied that when the accused set fire to the house she knew that it was highly probable that this would cause (death or) serious bodily harm then the prosecution will have established the necessary intent. It matters not if her motive was, as she says, to frighten Mrs Booth.'

The judge explained that he had put brackets round the words 'kill or' and 'death or' because he advised the jury to concentrate on the intent to do serious bodily harm rather than the intent to kill.

There were other passages in the summing-up to the same effect, but this was the vital passage, and the judge reduced it to writing and caused the jury to retire with it into the jury room. As the case proceeded, it is the only passage in the judge's summing-up to which I need draw attention, and gives rise to the only point which was argued before your Lordships' House. The Court of Appeal[1] dismissed the appeal 'not without some reluctance', and, in giving leave to appeal to the House of Lords, certified that it involved the following point of law of general public importance, namely, the question:

'Is malice aforethought in the crime of murder established by proof beyond reasonable doubt that when doing the act which led to the death of another the accused knew that it was highly probable that that act would result in death or serious bodily harm?'

This is the only question which, in my view, it is necessary to consider and the whole appeal is, therefore, within a fairly narrow compass. Both in the Court of Appeal and in your Lordships' House the Crown disclaimed, in my view rightly, any argument based on the so called 'proviso' (now s 2(1) of the Criminal Appeal Act 1968), and accordingly the question certified remains to be considered solely on its merits.

Before directing my mind to the simple point involved there are two general topics I desire to discuss. The first is as to the historical context in which the point falls to be decided, and the second is as to the precise senses in which I shall endeavour to use certain common words such as 'motive', 'intention', 'purpose', 'object', 'desire'.

---

1 [1973] 3 All ER 842, [1973] 3 WLR 475

a My Lords, the distinction between murder and manslaughter, both felonies at common law, appears to derive from the statutes of Henry VIII[1] and Edward VI[2] by which benefit of clergy was withdrawn from murder committed ex malitia praecogitata, which in the form 'malice prepense' or 'prepensed' and 'malice afore-thought' has continued in common use in legal circles to the present date. (See on this topic Bacon's Abridgment, sv Murder.)

b The precise value of this phrase is open to doubt. As long ago as 1883 Stephen[3] described it as 'a phrase which is never used except to mislead or to be explained away' and advised its abolition as a term of art and the substitution for it of a 'definite enumeration of the states of mind intended to be taken as constitutent elements of murder.' In the present case Cairns LJ[4] in delivering the judgment now appealed from said:

c   'There is no doubt that murder is killing "with malice aforethought", and there is no doubt that neither the word "malice" nor the word "aforethought" is to be construed in any ordinary sense.'

I agree with this latter observation, and would myself think that the sooner the phrase is consigned to the limbo of legal history the better for precision and lucidity d in the interpretation of our criminal law.

  However, 'malice aforethought' was and is part of our criminal jurisprudence and by the beginning of the 20th century (and for long before that) had come by judicial interpretation to cover a number of states of mind which rendered guilty of murder men and women whose conviction of a capital offence would not be considered acceptable today even by the most convinced adherents of the death penalty. In the e first place, until the decision in *Woolmington v Director of Public Prosecutions*[5] it was commonly held[6]:

    'Every person who kills another is presumed to have wilfully murdered him, unless the circumstances are such as to raise a contrary presumption.

    'The burden of proving circumstances of excuse, justification, or extenuation f is upon the person who is shown to have killed another.'

In the second place, by a doctrine known as that of 'constructive malice' a person was deemed to have committed murder ex malitia praecogitata if he had either of the following states of mind:

g   'An intent to commit any felony whatever;

    'An intent to oppose by force any officer of justice on his way to, in, or returning from the execution of the duty of arresting, keeping in custody, or imprisoning any person whom he is lawfully entitled to arrest, keep in custody, or imprison, or the duty of keeping the peace or dispersing an unlawful assembly, provided that the offender has notice that the person killed is such an officer so employed',

h and the expression 'officer of justice' could be held to include not merely a constable, but any private person who happened in the given circumstances to have the right to do any of the acts concerned[7]. This remained the law until 1957, when, by s 1 of the Homicide Act of that year, the doctrine of constructive malice in the above sense was abolished and a man was said not to be guilty of murder unless the killing were—

j 1 23 Hen 8 c 1, 25 Hen 8 c 3
   2 1 Ed 6 c 12, 5 & 6 Ed 6 c 10
   3 History of the Criminal Law (1883), vol 3, p 83
   4 [1973] 3 All ER at 845, [1973] 3 WLR at 479
   5 [1935] AC 462, [1935] All ER Rep 1
   6 See Stephen's Digest of the Criminal Law (1877), p 152, art 230
   7 See Stephen's Digest of the Criminal Law (1877), pp 144, 145, art 223

'done with the same malice aforethought (express or implied) as is required
for a killing to amount to murder when not done in the course or furtherance of
another offence.'

Incidentally, in my view this section clearly recognises a state of affairs described as
'implied malice' which is distinguished both from 'express malice' and from 'constructive malice'.   This may be an inconvenient terminology but no account of the law
which fails to recognise it can be considered accurate.

Further, the same Act of Parliament also reduced the number of cases of murder
ex malitia praecogitata by inaugurating the defence of 'diminished responsibility'
(Homicide Act 1957, s 2).   In approaching the question which I am asked to decide
today, insofar as I am a free agent, I cannot ignore the repeatedly evinced intention of
Parliament (soon afterwards, as I shall proceed to show, added to by s 8 of the Criminal
Justice Act 1967) to mitigate the severity of the law as it developed under the
successive interpretations of malice aforethought by judicial decision.

The abolition of the doctrine of constructive malice laid the way open for the
decision in R v Vickers[1] reargued before a particularly strong full Court of Criminal
Appeal.   Technically this decision only rejected the ingenious argument of some
academic lawyers that, by enacting s 1 of the Homicide Act 1957, Parliament, despite
the express words of the section, had inadvertently got rid of the doctrine of implied
malice as well as constructive malice.   But, in giving the judgment of the court,
Lord Goddard CJ took the opportunity to define the doctrine of implied malice so
retained, and to give what has since become the classical definition of murder, repeatedly employed ever since, as killing 'with the intention [either] to kill or to do
some grievous bodily harm' (see per Lord Goddard CJ[2], quoting from the summing-
up of the trial judge).   It will be noticed that in this definition the reference is to intention and there is no reference to foresight of the consequences as such either as equivalent to intention in murder or as an alternative to the requisite intention, or to a
'high degree of probability' to describe the degree of certainty of what has to be
foreseen, although both the foresight and the degree of probability must be at least
material which the jury may and, on occasion, must use as the basis on which an
adverse inference is drawn as to the intention of the killer.   Not unnaturally counsel
for the appellant in this case strongly stressed this circumstance in his argument before
their Lordships.   I have to remark that if at this stage we were to overthrow the
decision in R v Vickers[1] a very high proportion of those now in prison for convictions
of murder must necessarily have their convictions set aside and verdicts of manslaughter substituted.   This consideration ought not perhaps logically to affect our
decision, but I am personally relieved to find that I find myself in agreement with
the decision in R v Vickers[1].

I now pause to say a word about the expression 'grievous bodily harm', another
term of art in English criminal law of respectable pedigree (cf statute 43 Geo 3 c 58
and R v Cox[3]) but uncertain meaning.   In the context of murder, the Commissioners
on the Criminal Law in their report of 1839[4] used the expression 'great harm' as
opposed to 'slight harm' in connection with murder, but, apart from the context of
murder, 'grievous bodily harm' has been used in connection with various statutory
offences under various Acts including the Offences against the Person Act 1861 and
other statutes and, shortly before that Act, Willes J in R v Ashman[5] defined 'grievous
bodily harm' as not necessarily involving injury which is 'permanent or dangerous,
if it be such as seriously to interfere with comfort or health', and for many years

---

1   [1957] 2 All ER 741, [1957] 2 QB 664
2   [1957] 2 All ER at 744, [1957] 2 QB at 672
3   (1818) Russ & Ry 362
4   Fourth Report of Her Majesty's Commissioners on Criminal Law (8th March 1839)
5   (1858) 1 F & F 88 at 89

a Willes J's opinion was cited as the authoritative definition. But this led Lord Devlin[1] in a moment of extra-judicial levity to conclude that, if this were right, it would open the door in murder to a verdict of 'murder by pin prick', since it could not be denied that constantly pricking a man on the stomach with a pin would certainly seriously interfere with his comfort, and in certain cases by some misadventure might cause death. In *Director of Public Prosecutions v Smith*[2], to which I will turn in a moment, the late Viscount Kilmuir LC put an end to the strange doctrine with the words:

'...I can find no warrant for giving the words "grievous bodily harm" a meaning other than that which the words convey in their ordinary and natural meaning. "Bodily harm" needs no explanation and "grievous" means no more and no less than "really serious".'

Since that date, if not before, it has been the practice to direct juries on the authority of *R v Vickers*[3] and this passage in *Director of Public Prosecutions v Smith*[2] that murder means that a man causes the death of another 'with the intent to cause death or really serious injury'. What injuries are 'really serious' within the meaning of this definition is a question left for the jury to decide for themselves. Obviously it would include any injury likely to endanger life, but, speaking for myself, I would also consider it obvious that there are many injuries which a jury would call really serious which in the ordinary course would not be likely to endanger life. I think it would be difficult by a purely judicial interpretation to restrict the definition further. In particular, if it were desired to restrict the definition of murder by defining it as killing with intent to cause death or endanger life, I would think that an Act of Parliament would be necessary, and, before passing legislation it would be desirable for Parliament to investigate policy considerations more widely than is desirable or possible in the course of a judicial investigation based on a single case. In particular I would hope that Parliament would consider whether the substitution in effect of the phrase 'intent to endanger life' for 'to inflict really serious injury' as the mental element of intention in murder would not impose on juries a task unnecessarily onerous or would be morally justifiable. One can visualise a situation in which a defendant said, 'True I intended to inflict really serious injury on my victim, but it is most unfortunate that he died. I did not really intend to endanger his life'. I am not as clear myself as some of my colleagues that this defence should be permitted to avail him as a valid defence to a charge of murder.

The next stage in my historical summary must necessarily be the much discussed case of *Director of Public Prosecutions v Smith*[4] to which I have just referred in a limited context. One of the questions much canvassed in the hearing of this appeal was how much if anything in this decision has survived the enactment of s 8 of the Criminal Justice Act 1967 and whether, on the assumption that anything relevant to this appeal survived, this House should yield to the invitation expressed in the current edition of Smith and Hogan[5] to 'overrule that case by virtue of the House's newly assumed power to reverse its previous decisions'.

I will not rehearse the facts in *Director of Public Prosecutions v Smith*[4] since they are sufficiently well known. A criminal seeking to escape killed a police officer who tried to stop him by sitting on the bonnet of his car. The criminal accelerated and threw the officer off in the path of oncoming traffic and this caused him fatal injuries. The defendant's own account of the matter in court was that he lacked the necessary

1 See Criminal Responsibility and Punishment: Functions of Judge and Jury [1954] Crim LR 661 at 669
2 [1960] 3 All ER 161 at 171, [1961] AC 290 at 334
3 [1957] 2 All ER 741, [1957] 2 QB 367
4 [1960] 3 All ER 161, [1961] AC 290
5 Criminal Law (3rd Edn, 1973), p 229

criminal intention because he had become frightened. There was a good deal of
very powerful evidence that this defence was untrue in fact, but the judge in effect
directed the jury, which convicted him, that this was not material, because they
should convict of (capital) murder if satisfied that the accused 'as a reasonable man
must have contemplated that grievous bodily harm to the officer was likely to result
as the consequence of what he did'. Here there is a clear indication of foresight of
the consequences as a possible ingredient of malice aforethought, and that likelihood
and not certainty of the consequences is enough. A strong Court of Criminal Appeal[1]
(Byrne, Winn and Sachs JJ) quashed the conviction on the ground that this was a
misdirection. Byrne J, in delivering a judgment of the court which personally I
find in the main persuasive, lucid and coherent, said[2]:

> 'The law on this point as it stands today is ... that, as a man is usually able to
> foresee what are the natural consequences of his acts, so it is, as a rule, reasonable
> to infer that he did foresee them and intend them. Although, however, that
> is an inference which may be drawn, and on the facts in certain circumstances
> must inevitably be drawn, yet if on all the facts of the particular case it is not the
> correct inference, then it should not be drawn.'

And later[3]:

> 'The final question for the jury must always be whether on the facts as a whole
> an actual intent to do grievous bodily harm was established, remembering of
> course that intent and desire are different things and that, once it is proved that
> an accused man knows that a result is certain, the fact that he does not desire that
> result is irrelevant.'

The House of Lords[4], consisting of Viscount Kilmuir LC and Lords Goddard, Tucker,
Denning, and Parker of Waddington, reversed the decision of the Court of Criminal
Appeal[1], and it is the opinion of Viscount Kilmuir LC, speaking with the agreement
of the rest, that we have read in extenso and discussed in considerable detail.

My Lords, I do not wish to say anything which is not deeply respectful of my learned
and greatly admired predecessor as Lord Chancellor with whom I was for many years
on terms of intimate friendship, nor of the extremely strong House which followed
the lead of his speech in this case. But it would be affectation in me not to recognise
that the decision of this House in *Director of Public Prosecutions v Smith*[4] has proved at
all times highly controversial, has given rise to an extensive body of literature both
here and in the Commonwealth, and has proved unusually difficult to interpret (see,
for instance, Smith and Hogan[5], Glanville Williams Criminal Law[6]). It was
unequivocally dissented from by the Australian High Court (*Parker v R*[7]). It
was exhaustively criticised by the Law Commission (1967), and the Law Commission's criticisms formed the basis, in part, of the action of Parliament in passing
the Criminal Justice Act 1967, s 8, which was believed at the time to have reversed

---

1   [1960] 2 All ER 450, [1961] AC 290
2   [1960] 2 All ER at 453, [1961] AC at 300
3   [1960] 2 All ER at 455, [1961] AC at 302
4   [1960] 3 All ER 161, [1961] AC 290
5   Criminal Law (3rd Edn, 1973), p 227
6   2nd Edn (1961), p 94 ff. See also Glanville Williams 'Constructive Malice Revived' 23
     MLR 605; Salmon 'The Criminal Law Relating to Intent' 14 CLP 1; Cross 'The Need
     for a Re-definition of Murder' [1960] Crim LR 728; Lord MacDermott 'Murder in 1963',
     Birmingham University Press; Lord Denning 'Responsibility before the Law' (1961),
     Hebrew University Press; Prevezer 'Recent Developments in the Law of Murder' 14
     CLP 16; *DPP v Smith* [1960] Crim LR 765; Travers and Morris 'Imputed Intent in Murder
     or *Smith* v. *Smyth*' 35 ALJ 154; Buxton 'The Retreat from *Smith*' [1966] Crim LR 195
7   (1963) 111 CLR 610

a it (see Smith and Hogan[1]), and the learned authors of that work, whilst not accepting that this is the true effect of the section, reach the conclusion that[2] 'It would have been most unfortunate if Smith[3] had been held still to be law after all' and owing to the interpretation they themselves put on the case they invited this House to make use of the Practice Direction of 1966[4] to overrule it as 'the only right course'.   These are weighty criticisms by responsible persons, and, in spite of the

b distinction of the House, and the reverence and affection with which I regard the memory of my predecessor, I feel bound to examine them seriously. Indeed, in a provocative article amongst those cited above one author has done extensive research which appears to conclude that, in actual practice, judges, in directing juries, are in fact ignoring the House of Lords and following R v Vickers[5] and Byrne J in R v Smith (see The Retreat from Smith[6]).

c   However this may be, it is beyond question that the actual decision in Director of Public Prosecutions v Smith[3] has given rise to a series of wholly irreconcilable interpretations. There have been maximalising interpretations, notably from its critics, and minimalising interpretations, usually from its defenders, e g per Lord Denning MR and Pearson LJ in Hardy v Motor Insurers' Bureau[7]. It has been interpreted as importing an irrebuttable presumption of evidence (Law Commission Report

d 1967), and as deciding a new rule of substantive criminal law (Glanville Williams[8] and Smith and Hogan[1]).   It has been interpreted as being of general application, or limited to the crime of murder, or to 'such a case as the present' (per Lord Denning MR and Pearson LJ)[9]. It has been interpreted as importing an objective criterion into the essentially subjective question of intent, as re-introducing the repealed doctrine of constructive malice[10], or, alternatively, as upholding the subjective test of intention, but sticking an objective label on the nature and quality of the act

e done. I am not going to endeavour to decide between these rival and wholly irreconcilable interpretations for the very good reason that I believe that each can be justified by particular phrases to be found in the report. What is beyond question is that an attempt to revive the decision in toto without interpreting it de novo would be to introduce confusion and not lucidity into the law. Far better to recognise that

f Parliament in 1967, after considering a report by the Law Commission[11], decided that it was better to turn its back on what was rightly or wrongly taken as the main argumentation of Director of Public Prosecutions v Smith[3], and to impose the rule of a subjective test both as to foresight of the consequences and as to intention, as s 8 of the Criminal Justice Act 1967 appears to do, while yet retaining the intention to cause grievous bodily harm (in the sense explained) as a possible alternative to intent to kill as the essential mental element in the crime of murder. Such at least is the proper

g inference to be drawn from the decision of Parliament to enact the first and the failure of Parliament to enact the second of the two draft clauses in the Law Commission's recommendations[12], and such at least appears to have been the view of the Court of Appeal in R v Wallett[13] which is the last of the citations I wish to make in this historical survey of the subject.

h _____

1   Criminal Law (3rd Edn, 1973), p 228
2   Criminal Law (3rd Edn, 1973), p 229
3   [1960] 3 All ER 161, [1961] AC 290
4   [1966] 3 All ER 77, [1966] 1 WLR 1234
5   [1957] 2 All ER 741, [1957] 2 QB 664
6   [1966] Crim LR 195
j 7   [1964] 2 All ER 742 at 745, 747, 748, [1964] 2 QB 745 at 758, 762
8   Criminal Law (2nd Edn, 1961), p 94
9   [1964] 2 All ER at 745, 748, [1964] 2 QB at 759, 764
10 (1960) 23 MLR 605
11 'Imputed Criminal Intent (Director of Public Prosecutions v. Smith)' (12th December 1966)
12 The draft clauses appear in the appendix to the report
13 [1968] 2 All ER 296, [1968] 2 QB 367

In that case a male defendant of less than average intelligence shook a little girl a
so savagely that she died. The trial judge directed the jury impeccably if the above
view of the effect of the Criminal Justice Act 1967, s 8, be accepted, but, when they
returned for further guidance as to the difference between murder and manslaughter,
concluded his additional advice by saying that what the jury had to consider was
whether the defendant knew 'quite well at the time he was doing something *any
ordinary person like himself* [emphasis mine] would know it was doing her really serious b
bodily harm'. The Court of Appeal[1] held that it would not be safe to allow the
resulting verdict of guilty to stand. I do not believe that they could have done so if
they had not accepted the general approach which I have indicated as the true view
of the effect of s 8 of the Criminal Justice Act 1967 on *Director of Public Prosecutions v
Smith*[2].

The judgment of Winn LJ in *R v Wallett*[1] was referred to in the Court of Appeal in c
the present case[3] as supporting their own view of the 1967 Act. With respect this
carries exactly the opposite implication to that attached to it by the Court of Appeal.
Winn LJ was saying that so long as the judge was telling the jury that if they were
sure that the accused with all his defects did intend grievous bodily harm, that is
murder, but that the moment he suggested or might be taken as suggesting that the
test was objective his charge fell on the wrong side of the line laid down by the 1967 d
Act.

At the end of the day there are, I think, two reasons against formally overruling
Director of Public Prosecutions v Smith[2] in virtue of our Practice Direction[4] as suggested
by the authors of Smith and Hogan. The first is that in view of the diversity of
interpretation it is difficult to know exactly what one is overruling. Indeed, if the
extreme minimalising interpretations be adopted, there is little or nothing to overrule e
or indeed little enough to require the intervention of Parliament in 1967. The second
is that there are at least two passages in *Director of Public Prosecutions v Smith*[2] of
permanent value which on any view ought not to be overruled. The first is the
passage at the end of Viscount Kilmuir LC's opinion[5] which disposes at least in this
context of the doctrine of *R v Ashman*[6] regarding the nature of grievous bodily harm,
and thus excludes the possibility of 'murder by pinprick'. The second is the earlier f
passage[7] where Viscount Kilmuir LC says:

'The unlawful and voluntary act must clearly be aimed at someone in order
to eliminate cases of negligence or of careless or dangerous driving.'

There is also a more important third element latent in the decision to which I will
return later, and which seems to justify the result, if not all the reasoning. g

The view taken above of *Director of Public Prosecutions v Smith*[2] and of the 1967 Act
is not enough to dispose of the present appeal. For, whatever may be said by way of
criticism of the crucial passage in the judge's direction, it was impeccable at least in
this, that it applied the jury's mind to a subjective test of what was the state of the
mind of the accused. The question raised by Ackner J's charge to the jury is not
whether he revived the passages in *Director of Public Prosecutions v Smith*[2] which seem h
to suggest an objective test, but (i) whether, on the assumption that the test is subjective, foresight of the probable consequences is an alternative species of malice afore-

1   [1968] 2 All ER 296, [1968] 2 QB 367
2   [1960] 3 All ER 161, [1961] AC 290   j
3   [1973] 3 All ER at 848, [1973] 3 WLR at 482, quoting Winn LJ [1968] 2 All ER at 298, [1968]
      2 QB at 370
4   [1966] 3 All ER 77, [1966] 1 WLR 1234
5   [1960] 3 All ER at 172, [1961] AC at 335
6   (1858) 1 F & F 88
7   [1960] 3 All ER at 167, [1961] AC at 327

a thought to intention, or, as Pearson LJ clearly suggests in *Hardy v Motor Insurers' Bureau*[1], whether foresight of the probable consequence is only another way of describing intention and (ii) on the assumption that foresight can be used as an alternative or equivalent of intention whether a high degree of probability in that which is foreseen is enough.   This seems to me the point in this case, and I do not find it altogether easy to decide.   In order to equip myself to do so, I must embark
b on a brief enquiry into the meaning of some ordinary words. It has been pointed out more than once that 'motive' has two distinct but related meanings.   I do not claim to say which sense is correct. Both are used but it is important to realise that they are not the same. In the first sense 'motive' means an emotion prompting an act. This is the sense in which I used the term when I said that the admitted motive of the appellant was jealousy of Mrs Booth. The motive for murder in this sense may be jealousy, fear,
c hatred, desire for money, perverted lust, or even, as in so called 'mercy killings', compassion or love. In this sense motive is entirely distinct from intention or purpose. It is the emotion which gives rise to the intention and it is the latter and not the former which converts an actus reus into a criminal act.   Thus as Smith and Hogan point out[2], 'The mother who kills her imbecile and suffering child . . . is just as guilty of murder as is the man who kills for gain.'   (See also the discussion on this used
d by Viscount Maugham[3]).   On the other hand 'motive' can mean a 'kind of intention' (see Glanville Williams[4]). In this sense, in his direction to the jury, the judge (quoted above, and in the judgment of the Court of Appeal[5]) has said: 'It matters not if her motive was . . . to frighten Mrs Booth.' See also the discussion of this sense by Lord Wright[6].   I agree with the Court of Appeal that it is desirable, to avoid confusion, to use the word 'motive' in this context always in the first sense, and I have attempted so to do.
e It is, however, important to realise that in the second sense too, motive, which in that sense is to be equated with the ultimate 'end' of a course of action, often described as its 'purpose' or 'object', although 'a kind of intention', is not co-extensive with intention, which embraces, in addition to the end, all the necessary consequences of an action including the means to the end and any consequences intended along with
f the end.   In the present case the appellant's 'motive'—in the second sense—may have been to frighten Mrs Booth. This does not exclude, and the jury must have affirmed, the intention to expose the sleepers in the house to the high probability of grievous bodily harm and in many cases it may involve an actual intention to kill or cause grievous bodily harm.   Thus, also, in a Victorian melodrama the villain's motive—in the second sense—or his 'end', his 'purpose', 'object' or 'intention' may have been to acquire an inheritance.   But this does not exclude, and may involve,
g the intention to slay the rightful heir, or abduct his sister.   Or again, in the Law Commission's report[7] on *Director of Public Prosecutions v Smith*[8] the example is given where the end is to be paid insurance moneys, the means is to blow up an aircraft in flight, and the inseparable consequence is the death of passengers and crew.
I know of no better judicial interpretation of 'intention' or 'intent' than that given
h in a civil case by Asquith LJ (*Cunliffe v Goodman*[9]) when he said:

---

1 [1964] 2 All ER at 749, [1964] 2 QB at 764
2 Criminal Law (3rd Edn, 1973), p 53
3 In *Crofter Hand Woven Harris Tweed Co Ltd v Veitch* [1942] 1 All ER 142 at 152, 153, [1942] AC 435 at 452
4 Criminal Law (2nd Edn, 1961), p 48
j 5 [1973] 3 All ER at 845, [1973] 3 WLR at 479
6 In *Crofter Hand Woven Harris Tweed Co Ltd v Veitch* [1942] 1 All ER at 161, 162, [1942] AC at 469
7 'Imputed Criminal Intent (*Director of Public Prosecutions v. Smith*)' pp 14, 15, para 18 (12th December 1966)
8 [1960] 3 All ER 161, [1961] AC 290
9 [1950] 1 All ER 720 at 724, [1950] 2 KB 237 at 253

'An "intention," to my mind, connotes a state of affairs which the party "intending"—I will call him X.—does more than merely contemplate. It connotes a
state of affairs which, on the contrary, he decides, so far as in him lies, to bring
about, and which, in point of possibility, he has a reasonable prospect of being
able to bring about, by his own act of volition.'

If this be a good definition of 'intention' for the purposes of the criminal law of murder,
and so long as it is held to include the means as well as the end and the inseparable
consequences of the end as well as the means, I think it is clear that 'intention' is clearly
to be distinguished alike from 'desire' and from foresight of the probable consequences. As the Law Commission pointed out in their disquisition[1] on *Director of
Public Prosecutions v Smith*[2], a man may desire to blow up an aircraft in flight in order
to obtain insurance moneys. But if any passengers are killed he is guilty of murder,
as their death will be a moral certainty if he carries out his intention. There is no
difference between blowing up the aircraft and intending the death of some or all of
the passengers. On the other hand, the surgeon in a heart transplant operation may
intend to save his patient's life, but he may recognise that there is at least a high degree
of probability that his action will kill the patient. In that case he intends his patient's
life, but he foresees as a high degree of probability that he will cause his death, which
he neither intends nor desires, since he regards the operation not as a means to killing
his patient, but as the best, and possibly the only, means of ensuring his survival.

If this be the right view of the meaning of words, the question certified in this case
must, strictly speaking, be answered in the negative. No doubt foresight and the
degree of likelihood with which the consequences are foreseen are essential factors
which should be placed before a jury in directing them whether the consequences
are intended. But the true view is that put forward by Byrne J in *Director of Public
Prosecutions v Smith*[2]:

'While that is an inference which may be drawn, and on the facts in certain
circumstances must inevitably be drawn, yet if on all the facts of the particular
case it is not the correct inference, then it should not be drawn.'

This is in accordance with the views of Denning LJ in *Hosegood v Hosegood*[3] when he
says:

'When people say that a man must be taken to intend the natural consequences of his acts, they fall into error: there is no "must" about it. It is only
"may".'

This passage was cited by Lord Porter in *Lang v Lang*[4], where the perfectly proper
distinction, noted above, that a consequence may be intended though it is not desired,
is also drawn, and should be taken as established.

I do not, therefore, consider, as was suggested in argument, that the fact that a
state of affairs is correctly foreseen as a highly probable consequence of what is done
is the same thing as the fact that the state of affairs is intended. The highest that can
be put in the context of the present set of facts is that what was intended was to expose
the inhabitants of the house to the serious risk of death or grievous bodily harm and
not actually to cause death or grievous bodily harm. I do not think that these
propositions are identical.

But this, again, does not dispose of the matter. Another way of putting the case
for the Crown was that, even if it be conceded that foresight of the probable consequences is not the same thing as intention, it can, nevertheless, be an alternative

1 'Imputed Criminal Intent (*Director of Public Prosecution v. Smith*)', pp 14, 15, para 18 (12th
  December 1966)
2 [1960] 3 All ER 161, [1961] AC 290
3 (1950) TLR 735 at 738
4 [1954] 3 All ER 571 at 578, [1955] AC 402 at 425

type of malice aforethought, equally effective as intention to convert an unlawful killing into murder. This view, which is inconsistent with the view that foresight of a high degree of probability is only another way of describing intention, derives some support from the way in which the proposition is put in Stephen's Digest[1] where it is said that malice aforethought for the purpose of the law of murder includes a state of mind in which there is—

> 'Knowledge that the act which causes death will probably cause the death of, or grievous bodily harm to, some person, whether such person is the person actually killed or not, although such knowledge is accompanied by indifference whether death or grievous bodily harm is caused or not, or by a wish that it may not be caused'.

If this be right, Ackner J's direction can be justified on the grounds that such knowledge is itself a separate species of malice aforethought, and not simply another way of describing intention. Apart from *Director of Public Prosecutions v Smith*[2] (if and insofar as it may be regarded as authority for this proposition) the diligence of counsel was unable to discover an English case directly supporting this view, but persuasive authority for it exists in *R v Jakac*[3] where the Supreme Court of Victoria expressly adopted the passage from Stephen's Digest cited above and said: 'We do not think that the passage cited from *Stephen's Digest* has ever been seriously challenged as a correct statement of the law'. Further support for the view of the law embodied in this proposition can be derived from the direction of Avory J to the jury in *R v Lumley*[4] and perhaps from the direction in *R v Ward*[5], described in the Court of Criminal Appeal in *Director of Public Prosecutions v Smith*[6] as the 'high water-mark' and not to be relied on now as a fair direction in other respects in the light of the Criminal Justice Act 1967, s 8. Reference was also made to the 19th century case of *R v Desmond*[7] in which Cockburn CJ after expounding the doctrine of constructive malice, which then applied, said:

> 'There was another and larger view of the case. If a man did an act, more especially if that were an illegal act, although its immediate purpose might not be to take life, yet if it were such that life was necessarily endangered by it,—if a man did such an act, not with the purpose of taking life, but with the knowledge or belief that life was likely to be sacrificed by it, that was not only murder by the law of England, but by the law of probably every other country.'

This clearly applies the test of foresight, and the criterion of probability and not certainty, but the foresight described is of danger to life, and not grievous bodily harm even in the sense defined in *Director of Public Prosecutions v Smith*[2]. Like other 19th century cases, the direction given was at a time when no jury could have the prisoner's sworn testimony to consider, and when there was no adequate system of criminal appeal. Moreover, it is not really satisfactory to charge a jury on two parallel legal theories each leading to the same result and leave them with no means of saying which of the two their verdict is intended to follow. The jury itself may well have founded their verdict in *R v Desmond*[7] entirely on the doctrine of constructive malice to which, at the time, the defence had, it would seem, no possible answer.

At this point counsel on both sides addressed a number of arguments to the

1 Digest of the Criminal Law (1877), p 144, art 223
2 [1960] 3 All ER 161, [1961] AC 290
3 [1961] VR 367 at 372
4 (1911) 76 JP 208
5 [1956] 1 All ER 565, [1956] 1 QB 351
6 [1960] 2 All ER at 454, [1961] AC at 301
7 (1868) The Times, 28th April

House based on principle and public policy. Of these the most notable were as _a follows:

(1) Counsel for the Crown urged the necessity of treating deaths such as any arising from the recent bomb outrages as murder. Reference was made to the 19th century case of *R v Desmond*[1]. These cases, however, must surely be judged like any other on their facts. If murder consists, and consists only, in slaying with intent to kill, or intent to cause grievous harm to some person, a jury must decide the matter _b after taking into account all relevant circumstances including any warnings given, and any evidence tendered on behalf of the accused, and come to the appropriate conclusion. There should be no difficulty in securing convictions in appropriate cases. If, on the other hand, the mental ingredients in murder may consist in the deliberate exposure of potential victims to the substantial risk of death or grievous bodily harm, in the actual knowledge that such risk is being incurred, then an appro- _c priate direction to that effect can be made. I do not think that it is appropriate for this House in its judicial capacity to be unduly swayed by motives of public policy in defining crimes which have been so long before the courts as have murder and manslaughter.

(2) Counsel for the defence argued that actual foresight of a high decree of pro- bability was too indefinite a phrase to enable juries consistently to administer this _d important branch of the law. Reference was made to an observation of Lord Reid in a recent civil case (*Southern Portland Cement v Cooper*[2]) with which I respectfully agree. Lord Reid said:

'Chance probability or likelihood is always a matter of degree. It is rarely capable of precise assessment. Many different expressions are in common use. It can be said that the occurrence of a future event is very likely, rather likely, _e more probable than not, not unlikely, quite likely, not improbable, more than a mere possibility etc. It is neither practicable nor reasonable to draw a line at extreme probability.'

If I were to accept the direction of Ackner J as correct in the present case for all pur- poses, or to answer without qualification the question certified in the affirmative, _f I should, I think, be driven to draw the line in a criminal case of high importance at precisely the point at which it was said to be neither practicable nor reasonable to do so.

I must, however, qualify the negative answer I have proposed to the question certified as of general public importance. For the reasons I have given, I do not think that foresight as such of a high degree of probability is at all the same thing as _g intention, and, in my view, it is not foresight but intention which constitutes the mental element in murder. It is the absence of intention to kill or cause grievous bodily harm which absolves the heart surgeon in the case of the transplant, notwith- standing that he foresees as a matter of high probability that his action will probably actually kill the patient. It is the presence of an actual intention to kill or cause grievous bodily harm which convicts the murderer who takes a very long shot at _h his victim and kills him notwithstanding that he thinks correctly as he takes his aim that the odds are very much against his hitting him at all.

But what are we to say of the state of mind of a defendant who knows that a pro- posed course of conduct exposes a third party to a serious risk of death or grievous bodily harm, without actually intending those consequences, but nevertheless and without lawful excuse deliberately pursues that course of conduct regardless whether the consequences to his potential victim take place or not? In that case, if my analysis be correct, there is not merely actual foresight of the probable consequences, but actual intention to expose his victim to the risk of those consequences whether they

1   (1868) The Times, 28th April
2   [1974] 1 All ER 87 at 94, [1974] 2 WLR 152 at 160

in fact occur or not. Is that intention sufficient to reduce the crime to manslaughter notwithstanding a jury's finding that they are sure that it was the intention with which the act was done? In my opinion, it is not, and in this my opinion corresponds with the opinion of the Commissioners on the Criminal Law[1] when they said, 'Again, it appears to us that it ought to make no difference in point of legal distinction whether death results from a direct intention to kill, or from wilfully doing an act of which death is the probable consequence'. And again in a later passage[2], 'It is the *wilful exposure* of life to peril that constitutes the crime'. The heart surgeon exposes his patient to the risk, but does everything he can to save his life, regarding his actions as the best or only means of securing the patient's survival. He is, therefore, not exposing his patient to the risk without lawful excuse or regardless of the consequences. The reckless motorist who is guilty of manslaughter, but not murder, is not at least ordinarily aiming his actions at anyone in the sense explained in *Director of Public Prosecutions v Smith*[3]. If he were, it is quite possible that, as in *Director of Public Prosecutions v Smith*[4], he might be convicted of murder. In the field of guilty knowledge it has long been accepted both for the purposes of criminal and civil law that 'a man who deliberately shuts his eyes to the truth will not be heard to say that he did not know it'. (See per Lord Reid in *Southern Portland Cement v Cooper*[5].) Cannot the same be said of the state of intention of a man who, with actual appreciation of the risks and without lawful excuse, wilfully decides to expose potential victims to the risk of death or really serious injury regardless of whether the consequences take place or not? This seems to me to be the truth underlying the statement of the law in Stephen's Digest, the summing-up of Cockburn CJ in *R v Desmond*[6], and of Avory J in *R v Lumley*[7] and of those phrases in *Director of Public Prosecutions v Smith*[4] in which it seems to be said that a rational man must be taken to intend the consequences of his acts. It is not a revival of the doctrine of constructive malice or the substitution of an objective for a subjective test of knowledge or intention. It is the man's actual state of knowledge and intent which, as in all other cases, determines his criminal responsibility. Nor, for the like reason, does this set up an irrebuttable presumption. It simply proclaims the moral truth that if a man, in full knowledge of the danger involved, and without lawful excuse, deliberately does that which exposes a victim to the risk of the probable grievous bodily harm (in the sense explained) or death, and the victim dies, the perpetrator of the crime is guilty of murder and not manslaughter to the same extent as if he had actually intended the consequence to follow, and irrespective of whether he wishes it. That is because the two types of intention are morally indistinguishable, although factually and logically distinct, and because it is therefore just that they should bear the same consequences to the perpetrator as they have the same consequences for the victim if death ensues.

This is not very far from the situation in this case. The jury appear to have taken this as a carefully premeditated case and that this was so can hardly be disputed, and, though it was disputed, the jury clearly rejected this view. The appellant had made her way to the house in a van in the early hours of the morning. She took with her a jerry can containing at least half a gallon of petrol. As she passed Mr Jones's house she carefully made sure that he was in his own home and not with Mrs Booth, because, as she said, she did not want to do Mr Jones any harm. She

---

1 See Fourth Report of Her Majesty's Commissioners on Criminal Law (8th March 1839), p xx
2 Ibid, p xxiv
3 [1960] 3 All ER at 167, [1961] AC at 327
4 [1960] 3 All ER 161, [1961] AC 290
5 [1974] 1 All ER at 93, [1974] 2 WLR at 158
6 (1868) The Times, 28th April
7 (1911) 76 JP 208

parked the van at a distance from Mrs Booth's house, and when she got to the front
door she carefully removed a milk bottle from the step in case she might knock it
over and arouse somebody by the noise. And when she had started the fire she crept
back to her van and made off home without arousing anyone or giving the alarm.
Once it is conceded that she was actually and subjectively aware of the danger to
the sleeping occupants of the house in what she did, and that was the point which
the judge brought to the jury's attention, it must surely follow naturally that she
did what she did with the intention of exposing them to the danger of death or
really serious injury regardless of whether such consequences actually ensued or
not. Obviously in theory, a further logical step is involved after actual foresight
of the probability of danger is established. But in practice and in the context of
this case the step is not one which, given the facts, can be seriously debated. For
this reason I do not think the summing-up can be faulted, since the judge drew the
jury's attention to the only debatable question in the case, and gave them a correct
direction in regard to it.

I therefore propose the following propositions in answer to the question of general
public importance.

(1) Before an act can be murder it must be 'aimed at someone' as explained in
Director of Public Prosecutions v Smith[1], and must in addition be an act committed
with one of the following intentions, the test of which is always subjective to the
actual defendant: (i) The intention to cause death; (ii) The intention to cause grievous
bodily harm in the sense of that term explained in *Director of Public Prosecutions v
Smith*[2], i e really serious injury; (iii) Where the defendant knows that there is a
serious risk that death or grievous bodily harm will ensue from his acts, and commits
those acts deliberately and without lawful excuse, the intention to expose a potential
victim to that risk as the result of those acts. It does not matter in such circumstances
whether the defendant desires those consequences to ensue or not and in none of
these cases does it matter that the act and the intention were aimed at a potential
victim other than the one who succumbed.

(2) Without an intention of one of these three types the mere fact that the defendant's conduct is done in the knowledge that grievous bodily harm is likely or highly
likely to ensue from his conduct is not by itself enough to convert a homicide into
the crime of murder. Nevertheless, for the reasons I have given in my opinion the
appeal fails and should be dismissed.

VISCOUNT DILHORNE. My Lords, for some considerable time the appellant
had had regular sexual relations with a Mr Jones. In consequence of her having
some gynaecological trouble those relations ceased and were not resumed after she
had had an operation in 1968. She became suspicious of Mr Jones's relations with
a Mrs Booth and very jealous of her. She tried to break up that association by the
writing of anonymous letters. In May 1972 Mrs Booth obtained a decree nisi for
divorce from her husband. That decree was due to be made absolute towards the
end of July 1972 and then Mrs Booth would have been free to marry Mr Jones.

On 15th July 1972 at about 2 a m the appellant drove a van to the house where Mrs
Booth lived with her son and two daughters aged, we were told, 17 and 11. On her
way there she went past Mr Jones's house to see if he was there. The lights were
on so she decided that he was. She did that, she said, because she did not want to
do any harm to Mr Jones. She parked the van round the corner from Mrs Booth's
house. She took a gallon can of petrol from the van and poured petrol through
the letterbox in Mrs Booth's front door. She then put newspaper in the letterbox
and lit it. The petrol ignited and the appellant said that she realised that what she

---

1   [1960] 3 All ER at 167, [1961] AC at 327
2   [1960] 3 All ER at 172, [1961] AC at 335

had done was tremendously dangerous to anyone living in the house. She, however, did nothing to alert the occupants of the house to the danger she had put them in or the fire brigade. She just drove to her home some five miles away. Mrs Booth and her son succeeded in escaping from the house. Her two daughters did not and were killed. The appellant was charged with, and convicted of, their murder.

At the beginning of his summing-up Ackner J told the jury that a person who unlawfully and deliberately causes the death of another intending either to kill or to do serious bodily harm is guilty of murder. He said that there was no dispute that the appellant had killed the two children and that it was not suggested that the setting fire to the house was other than a deliberate act. He told the jury that the only question on which they had to focus their attention was the appellant's intent.

He had written down, and he had handed to the jury, his direction with regard to intent. It was in the following terms:

'The prosecution must prove, beyond all reasonable doubt, that the accused intended to (kill or) do serious bodily harm to Mrs Booth, the mother of the deceased girls. If you are satisfied that when the accused set fire to the house she knew that it was highly probable that this would cause (death or) serious bodily harm then the prosecution will have established the necessary intent. It matters not if her motive was, as she says, to frighten Mrs Booth.'

In the light of that direction and their verdict one must take it that the jury were satisfied that the appellant knew that, when she set fire to the house, it was highly probable that she would cause serious bodily harm.

The appellant's appeal to the Court of Appeal (Criminal Division)[1] on the ground that this was a misdirection was dismissed, but that court granted leave to appeal to this House, certifying that the following point of law was of general public importance:

'Is malice aforethought in the crime of murder established by proof beyond reasonable doubt that when doing the act which led to the death of another the accused knew that it was highly probable that that act would result in death or serious bodily harm?'

It is to be observed that Ackner J in his direction to the jury said that such knowledge established the necessary intent. The question certified asked whether it constituted malice aforethought. If it did, it does not follow that it established an intent to do grievous bodily harm.

In this House counsel for the appellant contended that the question certified should be answered in the negative. He submitted that knowledge that a certain consequence was a highly probable consequence does not establish an intent to produce that result. 'All consequences that are foreseen are not', he said, 'necessarily intended'.

He also contended that the direction given by Ackner J was erroneous in another respect, namely, that, despite the decision in R v Vickers[2] and the decision of this House in Director of Public Prosecutions v Smith[3] to the contrary, intent to do grievous bodily harm did not, nor did knowledge that such harm was the probable result, suffice to make a killing murder. For it to be murder, he contended that the intent must be to kill or to endanger life or, if knowledge was enough, knowledge that the act would kill or endanger life.

---

1   [1973] 3 All ER 842, [1973] 3 WLR 475
2   [1957] 3 All ER 741, [1957] 2 QB 664
3   [1960] 3 All ER 161, [1961] AC 290

With regard to his first contention, so long ago as 1868 Cockburn CJ at the Central Criminal Court in the Fenian trials, *R v Desmond*[1], directed the jury that if a man did an act—

'not with the purpose of taking life, but with the knowledge or belief that life was likely to be sacrificed by it, that was not only murder by the law of England, but by the law of probably every other country.'

In his Digest of the Criminal Law[2] Sir James Stephen defined 'malice aforethought' as involving the following states of mind:

'(*a*) An intention to cause the death of, or grievous bodily harm to, any person, whether such person is the person actually killed or not;

'(*b*) Knowledge that the act which causes death will probably cause the death of, or grievous bodily harm to, some other person, whether such person is the person actually killed or not, although such knowledge is accompanied by indifference whether death or grievous bodily harm is caused or not, or by a wish that it may not be caused;

'(*c*) An intent to commit any felony whatever;

'(*d*) An intent to oppose by force any officer of justice on his way to, in, or returning from the execution of the duty of arresting, keeping in custody, or imprisoning any person whom he is lawfully entitled to arrest, keep in custody, or imprison, or the duty of keeping the peace or dispersing an unlawful assembly, provided that the offender has notice that the person killed is such an officer so employed.'

The Royal Commission on Capital Punishment[3] in their report said that this was the statement of the modern law most commonly cited as authoritative. The Royal Commission did not dissent from but endorsed Stephen's statement that such knowledge amounted to malice aforethought. In para 76[4] five propositions were stated which, the report said, were commonly accepted. The fifth proposition was:

'(v) It is murder if one person kills another by an intentional act which he knows to be likely to kill or to cause grievous bodily harm . . . and may either be recklessly indifferent as to the results of his act or may even desire that no harm should be caused by it.'

The propositions, the report said[5], fell within paragraph (*a*) and (*b*) of the article of Stephen's Digest and 'it has been generally agreed that they are properly included in the category of murder' and in para 473[6] it is stated:

'Under the existing law as stated by Stephen, the question the jury have to consider in such a case is whether the accused knew or was aware of the likely consequences of his act: and we think that the law is sound.'

In *R v Jakac*[7] the Full Court of the Supreme Court of Victoria delivered a judgment in which it was said that the Royal Commission's fifth proposition was clearly the law.

Stephen in his Digest treated such knowledge as a separate head of malice aforethought and distinct from those in which intent is necessary. The Royal Commission

1   (1868) The Times, 28th April
2   (1877), pp 144, 145, art 223
3   (1953) Cmd 8932, p 27, para 74
4   At p 28
5   At p 29, para 77
6   At p 163
7   [1961] VR 367

treated it as justifying a conviction of murder even if the accused did not intend
to kill or to do grievous bodily harm. If this view is right, then Ackner J was wrong
in telling the jury that proof of such knowledge established the neccessary intent.

On the other hand, Lord Devlin in a lecture he gave in 1954[1] said that where a
man has decided that certain consequences would probably happen, then—

> 'for the purposes of the law he intended them to happen, and it does not
> matter whether he wanted them to happen or not . . . it is criminal intent in
> the strict sense.'

Pearson LJ appears to have been of the same opinion for in *Hardy v Motor Insurers'
Bureau*[2] he said:

> 'Then this is the syllogism. No reasonable man doing such an act could fail to
> foresee that it would in all probability injure the other person. The accused
> is a reasonable man. Therefore, he must have foreseen, when he did the act,
> that it would in all probability injure the other person. Therefore, he had the
> intent to injure the other person.'

Whether or not it be that the doing of the act with the knowledge that certain
consequences are highly probable is to be treated as establishing the intent to bring
about those consequences, I think it is clear that for at least 100 years such knowledge
has been recognised as amounting to malice aforethought. In my opinion, it follows
if the second contention advanced on behalf of the appellant is rejected, that the
question certified should be answered in the affirmative.

While I do not think that it is strictly necessary in this case to decide whether such
knowledge establishes the necessary intent, for, if Ackner J was wrong about that, it
is not such a misdirection as would warrant the quashing of the conviction as, even
if it did not establish intent, it was correct in that such knowledge amounted to malice
aforethought, I am inclined to the view that Ackner J was correct. A man may
do an act with a number of intentions. If he does it deliberately and intentionally,
knowing when he does it that it is highly probable that grievous bodily harm will
result, I think most people would say and be justified in saying that whatever other
intentions he may have had as well, he at least intended grievous bodily harm.

I think, too, that if Ackner J had left the question of intent in the way in which it is
left in the vast majority of cases, namely, was it proved that the accused had intended
to kill or to do grievous bodily harm, no reasonable jury could on the facts of this
case have come to any other conclusion than that she had intended to do grievous
bodily harm, bearing in mind her knowledge and the fact that, before she set fire to
the house, she took steps to make sure that Mr Jones was not in it as she did not want
to harm him. If the normal direction had been given, much litigation would have
been avoided.

I now turn to the second contention advanced on behalf of the appellant. This has
two facets; first, that the reference to the intent to cause grievous bodily harm has
been based on the law that killing in the course or furtherance of a felony is murder,
and that when the Homicide Act 1957 was enacted abolishing constructive malice
it meant that it no longer sufficed to establish intent to do grievous bodily harm;
and, secondly, that, if intent to do grievous bodily harm still made a killing murder,
it must be intent to do grievous bodily harm of such a character that life was likely
to be endangered.

Committing grievous bodily harm was for many, many years, and until all felonies
were abolished, a felony. Consequently so long as the doctrine of constructive
malice was part of the law of England, to secure a conviction for murder, it was only

---

1 Criminal Responsibility and Punishment: Functions of Judge and Jury [1954] Crim LR
   661 at 667
2 [1964] 2 All ER 742 at 748, [1964] 2 QB 745 at 763, 764

necessary to prove that the death resulted from an act committed in the course of
or in furtherance of the commission of grievous bodily harm. But when one looks
at the cases and the old textbooks, one does not find any indication that proof of
intent to do grievous bodily harm was an ingredient of murder only on account of
the doctrine of constructive malice. Indeed, one finds the contrary.

Coke in his Institutes throws no light on this though he went so far as to say[1] that,
if death resulted from an unlawful act, it was murder. In Hale's Pleas of the Crown[2]
it is said that it is murder 'If a man doe an act that apparently must introduce harm,
and death ensue', and in his History of the Pleas of the Crown[3] it is said that malice
which makes a killing murder is of two kinds, malice in fact and malice in law, and
that—

> 'Malice in fact is a deliberate intention of doing some corporal harm to the
> person of another . . . It must be a compassing or designing to do some bodily
> harm.'

Hale[4] gave as one instance where murder was to be implied by law the case where
the killing was done by a person that intends a theft or burglary. He thus distinguished constructive malice implied from a killing in the course of or in furtherance
of another offence from malice in fact; and, for there to be malice in fact, it was
enough that there should be an intention to do some bodily harm.

Stephen in his Digest also distinguished between intent to kill or to do grievous
bodily harm and knowledge that death or bodily harm was likely to result (paras
(a) and (b)) from constructive malice (paras (c) and (d)), and I can find no case to
support the contention that a direction that an intent to do grievous bodily harm
was regarded and treated as a direction based on constructive malice.

In R v Bubb, R v Hook[5] the jury was directed that there must be an intention to
cause death or some serious bodily injury. In R v Porter[6] Brett J told the jury that
'if the prisoner kicked the man, intending to inflict grievous harm, and death ensued
from it, he was guilty of murder'. In R v Doherty[7] Stephens J said:

> 'What, then, is the intention necessary to constitute murder? Several inten-
> tions would have this effect; but I need mention only two in this case, namely,
> an intention to kill and an intention to do grievous bodily harm.'

In R v Lumley[8] Avory J told a jury that if the accused had contemplated that grievous
bodily harm was likely to result, it was murder. In R v Gibbins and Procter[9] the Court
of Criminal Appeal dismissed an appeal where the judge had directed the jury that it
would be murder if the accused wilfully and deliberately withheld food from a child
'so as to cause her to weaken and to cause her grievous bodily injury as a result of
which she died'. In Director of Public Prosecutions v Beard[10] Lord Birkenhead LC
referred to a charge of murder 'based upon intention to kill or to do grievous bodily
harm' and in Holmes v Director of Public Prosecutions[11] Lord Simon, with whose speech
the other Members of the House agreed, referred to malice as the intention to kill or
to inflict grievous bodily harm.

---

1   3 Instit, p 56
2   (1685), p 44
3   (1800), vol I, p 451
4   (1800), vol I, p 465
5   (1850) 14 JP 562
6   (1873) 12 Cox CC 444
7   (1887) 16 Cox CC 306
8   (1911) 76 JP 208
9   (1918) 82 JP 287
10 [1920] AC 479 at 499, [1920] All ER Rep 21 at 28
11 [1946] 2 All ER 124 at 127, [1946] AC 588 at 598

a   Killing with intent to do grievous bodily harm has thus for many years been regarded as murder, quite apart from the doctrine of constructive malice. This was recognised in the Report of the Royal Commission on Capital Punishment[1]. Their five propositions stated in para 76[2] which were, so the report said[3], generally accepted to be properly included in the category of murder, were—

b   'all cases where the accused either *intended* to cause death or grievous bodily harm or *knew* that his act was likely to cause death or grievous bodily harm.'

The Royal Commission went on to recommend the abolition of constructive malice, and in para 123[4] suggested a clause for inclusion in a Bill to bring that about.

   Section 1 of the Homicide Act 1957 is in all material respects similar to the clause proposed. It would, indeed, be odd if the Royal Commission by recommending *c* the abolition of constructive malice had in fact proposed the abolition of intent to do grievous bodily harm as an ingredient of murder when the commission had not intended and did not recommend that. Parliament may, of course, do more by an Act than it intends but if, as in my opinion was the case, intent to do grievous bodily harm was entirely distinct from constructive malice, then the conclusion that Parliament did so by the Homicide Act 1957 must be rejected. In my opinion *R v Vickers*[5] *d* was rightly decided and this House was right in saying that was so in *Director of Public Prosecutions v Smith*[6].

   I now turn to the second facet of the appellant's contention, namely, that the words 'grievous bodily harm' are to be interpreted as meaning harm of such a character as is likely to endanger life. In *R v Desmond*[7] Cockburn CJ said that 'knowledge or belief that life was likely to be sacrificed' made a death murder. This may have been *e* unduly favourable to the accused. Stephen in his Digest did not limit grievous bodily harm to harm likely to endanger life, though, as counsel for the appellant pointed out, in his History of the Criminal Law[8] Stephen said that paras (*a*) and (*b*) of his Article in his Digest and para 174 of the draft Criminal Code produced by the Criminal Law Commission 1878-79 exactly corresponded. The draft Code did not use the words 'grievous bodily harm' but proposed that it would be murder if 'the *f* offender means to cause the person killed any bodily injury which is known to the offender to be likely to cause death'. Therefore, counsel for the appellant contended, when Stephen referred to grievous bodily harm he meant harm likely to cause death. This inference was the sole foundation for this part of his argument.

   In *R v Ashman*[9] Willes J said in a case where a man was charged with shooting with intent to do grievous bodily harm, that it was—

g   'not necessary that such harm should have been actually done, or that it should be either permanent or dangerous, if it be such as seriously to interfere with comfort or health, it is sufficient.'

Since then that interpretation has in a number of cases been placed on the words 'grievous bodily harm' in murder and other cases. Donovan J in *Director of Public h Prosecutions v Smith*[6] used it. So far from grievous bodily harm being limited to harm likely to endanger life, since *R v Ashman*[9] its meaning has been extended. This extension was terminated by the decision in *Director of Public Prosecutions v Smith*[6],

1   (1953) Cmd 8932
2   At p 28
j   3   At p 29, para 77
4   Page 45
5   [1957] 2 All ER 741, [1957] 2 QB 664
6   [1960] 3 All ER 161, [1961] AC 290
7   (1868) The Times, 28th April
8   (1883), vol 3, p 80
9   (1858) 1 F & F 88 at 89

Viscount Kilmuir LC saying that there was no warrant for giving the words a meaning
other than that which the words convey in their ordinary and natural meaning.

If the words bore the meaning now contended for, there must have been many
murder cases in which that was not explained to the jury and in which there was
consequently a substantial misdirection. The Royal Commission on Capital Punishment[1] in their review of the law did not suggest that the words had this limited
meaning. Indeed, in para 472[2] of the report the following appears:

> 'We should therefore prefer to limit murder to cases where the act by which
> death is caused is intended to kill or to 'endanger life' or is known to be likely
> to kill or endanger life. But we do not believe that, if this change were made, it
> would lead to any great difference in the day-to-day administration of the law.'

In the same paragraph it is stated that Stephen expressed the opinion that to substitute 'bodily injury known to the offender to be likely to cause death' would to
some extent narrow the definition. So little weight can be attached to the inference
which we are asked to draw from the comparison of the Article in his Digest with the
provisions of the draft Criminal Code.

Our task is to say what, in our opinion, the law is, not what it should be. In the
light of what I have said, in my opinion, the words 'grievous bodily harm' must, as
Viscount Kilmuir LC said, be given their ordinary and natural meaning and not have
the gloss put on them for which the appellant contends. The House can, it is now
recognised, review its previous decisions. I see no reason to review its decision in
Director of Public Prosecutions v Smith[3] on the questions raised in this case. No
question here arises of any objective or subjective test, for the jury must be taken
to have found that the appellant knew it was highly probable that serious bodily
harm would be caused.

To change the law to substitute 'bodily injury known to the offender to be likely
to cause death' for 'grievous bodily harm' is a task that should, in my opinion, be left
to Parliament if it thinks such a change expedient. If it is made, an accused will be
able to say: true it is that I intended grievous bodily harm or that I knew such harm
was likely to result but I never intended to kill the dead man or to put his life in
danger and I did not know that by doing him serious bodily harm I would put his life
in danger. But I share the view of the majority of the Royal Commission[1] that such a
change would not lead to any great difference in the day to day administration
of the law.

For these reasons in my opinion this appeal should be dismissed.

LORD DIPLOCK. My Lords, what distinguishes murder from manslaughter
today is that murder now falls within the class of crime in which the mental element
or mens rea necessary to constitute the offence in English law includes the attitude of
mind of the accused not only towards his physical act itself, which is the actus rea of
the offence, as is the case with manslaughter, but also towards a particular evil
consequence of that act. As I shall endeavour to show, this was not always so. That
it is so now is the consequence of the enactment of s 1 of the Homicide Act 1957 and (if
the decision of this House in *Director of Public Prosecutions v Smith*[3] was right) of the
enactment of s 8 of the Criminal Justice Act 1967.

This appeal raises two separate questions. The first is common to all crimes of
this class. It is: what is the attitude of mind of the accused towards the particular
evil consequence of his physical act that must be proved in order to constitute the
offence? The second is special to the crime of murder. It is: what is the relevant

---

1 (1953) Cmd 8932
2 At p 162
3 [1960] 3 All ER 161, [1961] AC 290

a evil consequence of his physical act which causes death, towards which the attitude of mind of the accused must be determined on a charge of murder?

On the first question I do not desire to say more than that I agree with those of your Lordships who take the uncomplicated view that in crimes of this class no distinction is to be drawn in English law between the state of mind of one who does an act because he desires it to produce a particular evil consequence, and the state of

b mind of one who does the act knowing full well that it is likely to produce that consequence although it may not be the object he was seeking to achieve by doing the act. What is common to both these states of mind is willingness to produce the particular evil consequence: and this, in my view, is the mens rea needed to satisfy a requirement, whether imposed by statute or existing at common law, that in order to constitute the offence with which the accused is charged he must have acted with 'intent' to produce a particular evil consequence or, in the ancient phrase which still

c survives in crimes of homicide, with 'malice aforethought'.

I turn then to the second question. I believe that all your Lordships are agreed that if the English law of homicide were based on concepts that are satisfactory, both intellectually and morally, the crime of murder ought to be distinguished from less heinous forms of homicide by restricting it to cases where the consequence of his act, which the accused desired or foresaw as likely, was the death of a human being.

d Where we differ is whether it is still open to this House to declare in its judicial capacity that this is now the law of England, or whether to define the law of murder thus would involve so basic a change in the existing law that it could only properly be made by Act of Parliament. For my part I think that Parliament itself has, by the Homicide Act 1957, made it constitutionally permissible for this House so to declare, and I believe that this House ought to do so.

e Any discussion of the historical development of the law of homicide is complicated by the varying ways in which those who wrote on this subject from the 17th century onwards have differentiated between malice that is 'express' and malice that is 'implied'. In the interests of clarity I shall endeavour to avoid these terms and speak instead of 'actual malice' and 'constructive malice'. By 'actual malice' I mean the attitude of mind of the killer towards the infliction of bodily injury on another

f person at the time he did the act that caused the death; by 'constructive malice' I mean those circumstances which until the passing of the Homicide Act 1957 rendered killing murder without its being necessary to enquire into the attitude of mind of the killer towards the infliction of bodily injury on another person. For the purposes of the present case the relevant example of 'constructive malice' is where the killing was done in the course or furtherance of some felony other than homicide.

g I readily concede that prior to 1957 it had become commonplace for judges (myself included) to define the 'intent' which must be proved to justify a conviction for murder as an intent 'to kill *or to do grievous bodily harm*', and that this practice has continued since the passing of the Homicide Act 1957 during which period it has received the approval of the Court of Criminal Appeal in *R v Vickers*[1] and of this House itself in *Director of Public Prosecutions v Smith*[2].

h My Lords, the now familiar expression 'grievous bodily harm' appears to owe its place in the development of the English law of homicide to its use in 1803 in Lord Ellenborough's Act[3], which made it a felony to shoot at, stab or cut any other person 'with intent to murder, maim, disfigure . . . or do some other grievous bodily harm'. There was a proviso that if the act were committed 'under such circumstances as that if death had ensued therefrom the same would not in law have

j amounted to the crime of murder' the accused was to be acquitted of the felony. In this context the 'intent' with which the act was committed appears to be distinguished from the 'circumstances' under which it was committed and the

1   [1957] 2 All ER 741, [1957] 2 QB 664
2   [1960] 3 All ER 161, [1961] AC 290
3   43 Geo 3 c 58

latter to refer to such surrounding circumstances as self-defence, a sudden falling out, provocation or preventing an escape from lawful custody or apprehension.

I have found no trace of the actual expression 'grievous bodily harm' being used before 1803, by writers on the law of homicide or by judges, to describe what was a sufficient evil intention to constitute that 'malice aforethought' that was the badge of murder. Apart from minor piecemeal exceptions of assaults in particular circumstances which had been made felonies by earlier statutes, until the passing of Lord Ellenborough's Act, assaults, however serious their physical consequences, were classified as no more than misdemeanours unless they resulted in death. So if intention to cause physical injury short of death was sufficient 'malice aforethought' for the crime of murder, this must at that time have been because it was 'actual malice' and not 'constructive malice' implied by law when the act that caused the death was done in the course of furtherance of some other felony.

The felony created by Lord Ellenborough's Act was one in which the intent with which the physical act was done was a necessary ingredient of the offence; but the intent here, unlike that needed to constitute actual malice in the offence of murder, was defined in the statute itself. Consequently after the passing of Lord Ellenborough's Act, wherever the act that caused the death was shooting, stabbing or cutting, it became constructive malice and so made the killing murder if the intent with which the act was done was to do any 'grievous bodily harm' within the meaning of the statute. This provision was re-enacted in 1828[1] and remained in force until it was replaced by s 18 of the Offences against the Person Act 1861 which extended the felonious offence to causing grievous bodily harm by any means if done 'with intent to maim, disfigure or disable . . . or to do some other grievous bodily harm', and omitted the proviso.

The expression 'grievous bodily harm' in the earlier statutes had been construed by Graham B in *R v Cox*[2] and Willes J in *R v Ashman*[3]. In the words of Willes J[4]:

'It is not necessary that such harm . . . should be either permanent or dangerous, if it be such as seriously to interfere with comfort or health, it is sufficient.'

Until the decision of this House in *Director of Public Prosecutions v Smith*[5] this statement of Willes J had been accepted as authoritative on the meaning of this expression in the Offences Against the Person Act 1861 which was passed shortly after it.

Neither *R v Cox*[2] nor *R v Ashman*[3] was concerned with a charge of murder: but the effect of the acceptance of Willes J's definition was to make it constructive malice sufficient to support a charge of murder if the act that caused the death was done with the intent seriously to interfere with the comfort or health of any person, even though that act was not one foreseen as being in the least likely to endanger life.

In the result, so long as the doctrine of constructive malice continued to be part of the English law of murder, it ceased to matter whether the actual intent with which the act that caused the death was done was an intent to do 'grievous bodily harm' within the meaning of the successive statutes or some more heinous intent that might have had to be proved in order to show actual malice sufficient to constitute the crime of murder at common law. So where, as in the generality of murder charges, the prosecution did not rely on the intent of the accused to commit some other felony such as robbery, rape or abortion, but relied solely on his intent to do physical harm to any person, the distinction between constructive malice and actual malice had no practical consequences and in course of time came to be overlooked.

1   9 Geo 4 c 31
2   (1818) Russ & Ry 362
3   (1858) 1 F & F 88
4   (1858) 1 F & F at 88, 89
5   [1960] 3 All ER 161, [1961] AC 290

In 1957 all this was altered. The doctrine of constructive malice was abolished by s 1 of the Homicide Act 1957. So it was no longer sufficient on a charge of murder to prove that the accused had killed another person in the course or in furtherance of the statutory offence under s 18 of the Offences against the Person Act 1861 for which the only intent necessary was an intent to 'do grievous bodily harm' as that expression in the statute had been construed by the courts. It became necessary to prove that his intent was such as would have amounted to actual malice at common law if none of the statutes from Lord Ellenborough's Act onwards had been passed.

The passing of the Homicide Act 1957 thus required the courts to embark on an enquiry in which the first step was to ascertain in what terms judges were directing juries at the close of the 18th century as to the state of mind of the accused which had to be proved to sustain a charge of murder on the ground of actual malice. If that were the end of the enquiry, however, and judges were again to direct juries in the same terms as their 18th century predecessors, the effect of the passing of the Homicide Act 1957 would have been to set back the clock 200 years. To do this would frustrate the underlying principle which is the justification for retaining the common law as a living source of rules binding on all members of contemporary society in England. The rules of which it is the source, cannot be unchanging. In the field of crime their purpose is to discourage conduct which is commonly accepted by Englishmen to be harmful to society in the circumstances in which men and women live today; not in the circumstances of two centuries ago. They must reflect contemporary views of what is just, what is moral, what is humane, and not those current in an earlier and more primitive or violent age. For unless they do, the system of criminal justice will break down. The unique combination of the functions of judge and jury in a criminal trial, the absence of any means of impugning a jury's verdict of acquittal, or of questioning a direction by the judge which states the law in a way unduly favourable to the accused, have the practical consequence that effect is not given to a criminal law if it outrages the instinctive sense of justice of judges and of juries alike.

So with the passing of the Homicide Act 1957 the courts were faced with a dual task: first, to discover as a matter of historical research what state of mind of the accused was regarded by the 18th century judges as constituting actual malice for the purposes of the crime of murder; and, secondly, to decide in what respects the views on this matter of subsequent generations of judges, if all of them were wise, would have been modified to take account of the way in which material circumstances and social concepts had been developed throughout the 19th and 20th centuries —a task which presents a challenge without precedent to the wisdom of those on whom this decision rests.

The material for the task of historical research is scanty. There was no systematic contemporaneous reporting of criminal trials before the 19th century. There was no check on how individual judges directed juries on the criminal law, unless the judge himself chose to reserve a point of law for the informal consideration of his brother judges at Serjeant's Inn—and even such reports as there are of the opinions expressed by all the judges on points of law which were reserved, are sparse and haphazard. The major sources of information are the works of institutional writers on the subject, starting with Coke in 1612, followed by Hale in 1685, by Foster J in 1762 and finishing with East in 1803. They were the subject of detailed critical analysis by Sir James Stephen in the 19th century in his Digest of the Criminal Law written in 1877 and History of Criminal Law written in 1883.

If what was written before the 19th century about the degree of violence that must have been intended by the accused in order to support a charge of murder is to be properly understood, there are several matters to be borne in mind.

(1) It must be remembered that, judged by present-day standards, we are dealing with a violent age. Men were used to carry deadly weapons and not slow to resort to them. So, at the beginning of the period Coke did not classify as murder a killing

on 'a sudden falling out'. Later when this defence became merged in the general doctrine of provocation most of the cases with which the writers were preoccupied involved the use of deadly weapons and it is not without significance that Lord Ellenborough's Act itself was concerned only with shooting, stabbing and cutting.

(2) Medical and surgical science were in a very primitive state. Any bodily injury, particularly if it involved risk of sepsis through an open wound, might well prove mortal although today the likelihood of its resulting in death would be insignificant. It was not until the last quarter of the 19th century that antiseptics came into general use.

(3) Until the 19th century the common law did not recognise unconsummated attempts to commit a crime as being criminal offences in themselves. So in relation to the crime of murder judges were dealing with bodily injuries which had in fact been fatal, and so demonstrated to have been of a kind which could endanger life.

(4) As stated by Sir Michael Foster it was accepted law in the 18th century that once the fact of killing was proved the onus lay on the prisoner to prove facts negativing malice aforethought unless such facts arose out of the evidence produced against him.

(5) Until as late as 1898 persons accused of murder were incompetent to give evidence in their own defence. So the actual intent with which they had done the act which had in fact caused death could only be a matter of inference from the evidence of other witnesses as to what the accused had done or said. In drawing this inference from what he had done it was necessary to assume that the accused was gifted with the foresight and reasoning capacity of a 'reasonable man' and, as such, must have foreseen as a possible consequence of his act, and this within his intention, anything which, in the ordinary course of events, might result from it.

Bearing these considerations in mind, I, for my part, find it impossible to say with confidence whether or not by the close of this period judges, when in connection with malice aforethought they used various expressions connoting physical injuries, did so with the unexpressed major premise in mind: 'All physical injuries at any rate if they are serious, are likely to 'endanger life' and so equated intent to cause serious physical injuries with intent to endanger life. Probably they did not at the beginning of the period. Hale thought that an intent to do *any* bodily harm to another was sufficient. The rigour of this doctrine had, however, been modified by the time of Foster. He considered that there must be an intent to do *great* bodily harm, and some light on what he meant by this may perhaps be found in his explanation of a verdict of manslaughter as being justified because the death resulted from a stroke by a cudgel *not likely to kill*. Stephen in his Digest of the Criminal Law[1] regards this as a landmark. He says of Foster that he—

'may be regarded as having laid down the foundation of the modern doctrine on the subject, which has since his time been recognised in a vast number of cases, that the general presumption of malice which arises from the fact of killing is rebutted *if it appear that the means used were not likely to cause death*.'

East[2], writing in the year that Lord Ellenborough's Act was passed, defines 'malice aforethought express' as 'where the deliberate Purpose of the Perpetrator was to deprive another of Life, or do him some great bodily Harm'. But in discussing the relevance of the manner of procuring the death, which under the then existing law would constitute the principal material from which the inference of malice would be drawn, he says[3]: 'But he who wilfully and deliberately does *any act which apparently endangers another's life*, and thereby occasions his death, shall, unless he clearly prove the contrary, be adjudged to kill him of malice prepense.' So East,

1 (1877), p 360
2 Pleas of the Crown (1803), vol 1, p 223
3 Ibid, p 225

a whether consciously or not, appears to treat inflicting 'great bodily harm' as the same thing as doing an act which endangers life.

In their Fourth Report the Commissioners on Criminal Law writing in 1839 treated as self-evident the proposition that all serious physical injuries are likely to endanger life. In their prefatory remarks on homicide they wrote[1]:

b 'Neither is there any difference between the direct intention to kill and the intention to do some great bodily harm short of death . . . as no one can wilfully do great bodily harm without placing life in jeopardy.'

This led them to conclude[2]: 'It is the *wilful exposure* of life to peril that constitutes the crime [sc murder]'. And even as late as 1883 Stephen in his History of the Criminal Law, when comparing his own previous digest with the draft code, proposed by the Criminal Code Commissioners, of whom he himself was one, felt able to say[3] 'that *c* the two exactly correspond', although in the Digest he had defined the relevant intention as an intention '. . . to cause grievous bodily harm' whereas in the draft code it was defined as an intention 'to cause . . . any bodily injury which is known to the offender to be likely to cause death.'

As a final footnote bringing the matter into the 20th century, it appears from para *d* 106 of the Report of the Royal Commission on Capital Punishment[4] published in 1953, that Lord Goddard CJ and Humphreys J, who supported the proposal that a person ought not to be liable to be convicted of murder unless he had intentionally or knowingly endangered life, had 'suggested a definition in terms of the infliction of grievous bodily harm because they held that a *person who wittingly inflicts grievous bodily harm must know that he is endangering life* . . .' Lord Goddard CJ is reported *e* (para 472[5]) as having told the commission that under the existing law he would direct a jury to that effect.

My Lords, even if the first step towards the solution of the problem with which the courts were confronted by the statutory abolition of the doctrine of constructive malice does not lead to a confident conclusion that judges at the close of the 18th century would only have regarded as sufficient to constitute the actual malice needed *f* for the crime of murder an intention to inflict bodily injury if the intended injury was such as in the existing state of medical skill and science it was likely to endanger life, any difficulty created by this is, I think, resolved when one proceeds to the second step, viz a consideration of how the law in this matter would have developed in the 19th and 20th centuries if there had been no doctrine of constructive malice.

Since the first Commissioners on the Criminal Law issued their Fourth Report in *g* 1839, it has been the uniform view of those who have assumed or been charged with the task of codifying the law of homicide that the relevant intention on a charge of murder should be an intention to kill or to cause any bodily injury which is known to the offender to be likely to endanger life. Such was the view expressed by the Criminal Code Commissioners in 1879, by Stephen in 1877 and 1883, by the Royal Commission on Capital Punishment in 1953 and by the Law Commission in 1966. The significance of the citations that I have already made from all but the last of *h* these is that they show that it was the opinion of these eminent lawyers at the various dates when they were writing that this would involve a rationalisation of the existing common law rather than any change in it. I have no doubt that the judges in the course of the 19th and 20th centuries would have held this to be the law as to express malice had they not been diverted from doing so by the doctrine of constructive malice.

j The opportunity of doing so, however, did not arise until the Homicide Act 1957

---

1 Fourth Report of Her Majesty's Commission on Criminal Law, p xx
2 At p xxiv
3 At p 83
4 (1953) Cmd 8932, p 39
5 At p 162

was passed and *R v Vickers*[1] came before the Court of Criminal Appeal. The judge had directed the jury in the same terms as he would have done before the passing of the 1957 Act, viz that murder is killing with the intent to kill or to do grievous bodily harm. In dismissing the appeal Lord Goddard CJ said that killing with that intention had always been malice aforethought in English law. As I have endeavoured to show this is historically inaccurate. The actual expression 'grievous bodily harm' did not come into use until the passing of Lord Ellenborough's Act, when under the doctrine of constructive malice a killing in the course of committing an offence under that Act or any of its successors became murder. On the other hand, if 'grievous bodily harm' meant, as Lord Goddard CJ appears to have thought it did when he gave evidence before the Royal Commission on Capital Punishment a few years before, 'bodily harm likely to endanger life', this statement of the law is accurate. Where it is liable to be misleading, however, is that it uses a phrase taken from a statutory definition of a different offence which, in cases relating to that different offence, had been construed in accordance with the direction of Willes J in *R v Ashman*[2] as including bodily harm which temporarily, albeit seriously, interfered with comfort or health, although as a result of the advance of medical skill and knowledge it was not in the least likely to endanger life.

It proved to be misleading when the matter came before this House in *Director of Public Prosecutions v Smith*[3]. That case is best remembered and most criticised for its apparent acceptance of what has come to be known as the objective test of that element in mens rea which involves intending or foreseeing the consequences of an act done voluntarily. This part of the judgment has been overruled by s 8 of the Criminal Justice Act 1967; but in *Director of Public Prosecutions v Smith*[3] this House also approved as a definition of the intention required to constitute the crime of murder 'an intention to kill or to cause 'grievous bodily harm', giving to 'grievous bodily harm' the same meaning in this definition as it bears in s 18 of the Offences against the Person Act 1861.

In his speech Viscount Kilmuir LC rejected the submission that in cases of murder the expression 'grievous bodily harm', if used in the definition of the relevant intent, should be understood in the restricted sense of bodily harm 'obviously dangerous to life' or 'likely to kill', though he acknowledged that it had been used in this restricted sense in many of the cases. While rejecting this restricted construction he also rejected the wide construction propounded by Willes J in *R v Ashman*[2]. 'Grievous bodily harm' in his view meant 'really serious bodily harm'—neither more nor less.

My Lords, this House in *Director of Public Prosecutions v Smith*[3] considered, in my view rightly, that it was still open to it in 1961 in its judicial capacity to define the mens rea required to constitute the common law crime of murder after the doctrine of constructive malice had been abolished by Act of Parliament. If that be so, it has in my opinion been open to this House since it assumed the power in 1966 to overrule its previous decisions, to refuse to follow this part of Viscount Kilmuir LC's speech in *Director of Public Prosecutions v Smith*[3], if we are satisfied that it is wrong in law, is liable to cause injustice and offends concepts of what is right and what is wrong that command general acceptance in contemporary society.

For my part, I am satisfied that the decision of this House in *Director of Public Prosecutions v Smith*[3] was wrong insofar as it rejected the submission that in order to amount to the crime of murder the offender, if he did not intend to kill, must have intended or foreseen as a likely consequence of his act that human life would be endangered. I have already given at some length the reasons why I think so. I will not repeat them. I think the reason why this House fell into error was because it failed

1 [1957] 2 All ER 741, [1957] 2 QB 664
2 (1858) 1 F & F 88
3 [1960] 3 All ER 161, [1961] AC 290

a to appreciate that the concept of 'intention to do grievous bodily harm' only became relevant to the common law crime of murder as a result of the passing of Lord Ellenborough's Act in 1803 and the application to the new felony thereby created of the then current common law doctrine of constructive malice. This led this House to approach the problem as one of the proper construction of the words 'grievous bodily harm' which because, though *only* because, of the doctrine of constructive

b malice had over the past 100 years become part of the standard definition of mens rea in murder, as well as part of the statutory definition of mens rea in the statutory felony of causing grievous bodily harm with intent to cause grievous bodily harm. I do not question that in the statutory offence 'grievous bodily harm' bears the meaning ascribed to it by this House in *Director of Public Prosecutions v Smith*[1] but the actual problem which confronted this House in *Director of Public Prosecutions v Smith*[1] and the Court of Criminal Appeal in *R v Vickers*[2] was a much more complex one. What

c it involved, I have endeavoured to analyse earlier in my speech.

It was, I venture to think, a comparable failure to appreciate the significance of the accidents of history in the development of English criminal law that led this House in the same case to adopt the objective test of intention as to the consequences of a voluntary act, i e that part of the decision that is now overruled by the Criminal Justice Act 1967. Intention can only be subjective. It was the actual intention of the

d offender himself that the objective test was designed to ascertain. So long as the offender was not permitted to give evidence of what his actual intention was, the objective test provided the only way, imperfect though it might be, of ascertaining this. The Criminal Evidence Act 1898 changed all this. A defendant to a charge of felony became entitled to give evidence in his own defence. The objective test no longer provided the only means available in a criminal trial of ascertaining the actual

e intention of the offender: but it had been so for so long, that this House overlooked the historical fact that the objective test did not define the relevant intention as to the consequences of a voluntary act. It was no more than one means of ascertaining the relevant intention, to which the Criminal Evidence Act 1898 added another— the defendant's own evidence of what his actual intention was.

f My Lords, if a decision of this House is founded on a proposition of law which is erroneous in a respect which makes it bear too harshly on a defendant to a criminal charge, particularly where that charge is one of murder, I have no doubt that your Lordships are entitled to correct that proposition and to apply it in its corrected form. I think that your Lordships ought to do so. That all your Lordships are agreed that the law as to the relevant intent in the common law crime of murder ought to be as I have endeavoured to state it; that that was also the view of successive Commissions

g who have considered this topic between 1839 and 1966 and of Sir James Stephen, satisfies me that to leave this error uncorrected would offend concepts of what is right and what is wrong that command general acceptance in contemporary society.

If your Lordships were to take this course it would involve allowing this appeal; for although Ackner J's direction to the jury was correct as respects the attitude of

h mind of the appellant towards the particular evil consequences of her physical act that must be proved in order to constitute the crime of murder, he followed the decision of this House in *Director of Public Prosecutions v Smith*[1] in his direction as to the nature of those particular evil consequences. So he stated them too broadly. The respondent does not invite this House to apply the proviso to s 2(1) of the Criminal Appeal Act 1968, and your Lordships have heard no argument about it.

j For my part I would allow the appeal and substitute a verdict of guilty of manslaughter for the verdict of guilty of murder.

1   [1960] 3 All ER 161, [1961] AC 290
2   [1957] 2 All ER 741, [1957] 2 QB 664

LORD CROSS OF CHELSEA. My Lords, Ackner J directed the jury in the *a*
following terms:

'The prosecution must prove, beyond all reasonable doubt, that the accused
intended to (kill or) do serious bodily harm to Mrs Booth, the mother of the
deceased girls. If you are satisfied that when the accused set fire to the house
she knew that it was highly probable that this would cause (death or) serious
bodily harm then the prosecution will have established the necessary intent. It *b*
matters not if her motive was, as she says, to frighten Mrs Booth.'

As the jury returned a verdict of guilty they must have been satisfied that the appellant when she set fire to the house realised at the least that it was highly probable that
one or more of the inmates would suffer serious bodily harm. On the other hand, it
must be assumed in her favour that they thought that her motive—in the sense of the *c*
object which she wished to achieve by her act—may not have been to inflict serious
bodily harm on Mrs Booth or anyone else but simply to frighten her away from
Coventry. It is conceded that the judge did not fall into the error of inviting the jury
to consider the appellant's state of mind 'objectively'. He told them to ask themselves
what '*she*' realised, not what a normal woman would have realised, would be the likely
result of her act. Further, there is no question of her having acted 'recklessly' in the *d*
sense of not having reflected on the probable consequences of her act. The verdict
negatives 'recklessness' in this sense. The question which we are asked to answer is,
therefore, as I see it, whether subpara (*b*) of art 223 of Stephen's Digest of the Criminal Law[1] states the law correctly. That article—so far as relevant for present purposes—runs as follows:

'Murder is unlawful homicide with malice aforethought. Malice aforethought *e*
means . . . (*a*) an intention to cause the death of, or grievous bodily harm to, any
person, whether such person is the person actually killed or not; (*b*) Knowledge
that the act which causes death will probably cause the death of, or grievous bodily
harm to, some person, whether such person is the person actually killed or not,
although such knowledge is accompanied by indifference whether death or *f*
grievous bodily harm is caused or not, or by a wish that it may not be caused . . .'

I agree with my noble and learned friend, Lord Kilbrandon, that now that murder
no longer attracts the death penalty it would be logical to replace the two crimes of
murder and manslaughter by a single offence of unlawful homicide; but there are
considerations, in which logic plays little part, which tell against the making of such
a change—and as long as one has the two separate crimes one has to decide on which *g*
side of the line any given state of mind falls. Stephen's definition covers four states of
mind. A(1) an intent to kill, (2) knowledge that the act in question will probably
cause death. B(1) an intent to cause grievous bodily harm, (2) knowledge that the
act in question will probably cause grievous bodily harm. Counsel for the appellant
argued strenuously that there was a great gulf fixed between A(1) and B(1) on the
one hand, and A(2) and B(2) on the other, and that unless the accused believed *h*
that the consequences in question were certain to ensue one ought not to equate mere
foresight of consequences with an intention to produce them. Even if one views the
matter simply from the point of view of linguistics I am not sure that the ordinary
man would agree. If, for example, someone parks a car in a city street with a time
bomb in it which explodes and injures a number of people I think that the ordinary
man might well argue as follows: 'The man responsible for this outrage did not injure *j*
these people unintentionally; he injured them intentionally. So he can fairly be
said to have intentionally injured them—that is to say, to have intended to injure
them. The fact that he was not certain that anyone would be injured is quite irrele-

_____

1   (1877) p 144

a vant;—(after all, how could he possibly be certain that anyone would be injured?)—
and the fact that, although he foresaw that it was likely that some people would be
injured, it was a matter of indifference to him whether they were injured or not
(his object being simply to call attention to Irish grievances and to demonstrate the
power of the IRA) is equally irrelevant.' But I can see that a logician might object that
the ordinary man was using the word 'intentionally' with two different shades of
meaning, and I am prepared to assume that as a matter of the correct use of language
b the man in question did not intend to injure those who were in fact injured by his
act. But we are not debating a problem of linguistics; we are asking ourselves whether
Stephen was right in saying that the states of mind labelled A(2) and B(2) constitute
'malice aforethought'. The first question to be answered is whether if an intention
to kill—using intention in the strict sense of the word—is murder—as it plainly is—
doing an unlawful act with knowledge that it may well cause death ought also to be
c murder. I have no doubt whatever that it ought to be. On this point I agree entirely
with the view expressed by Cockburn CJ in the passage in his summing-up in *R v
Desmond*[1] which is quoted by my noble and learned friend, Lord Hailsham of St
Marylebone. Turning now to the states of mind labelled B(1) and (2)—if it is the
law that an intention to cause grievous bodily harm—using intention in the strict sense
of the word—is 'malice aforethought', whether or not one realises that one's act may
d endanger life, then I think that it is right that the doing of an act which one realises
may well cause grievous bodily harm should also constitute malice aforethought
whether or not one realises that one's act may endanger life. No doubt many people
think that Stephen's four categories ought to be reduced to two (namely, an intention
to kill and a willingness to endanger life), and my noble and learned friend, Lord Diplock, whose speech I have had the advantage of reading, thinks that since the passing
e of the Homicide Act 1957 it has been open to the courts to declare that this is in fact
the law. But to achieve that result it would be necessary for us to overrule *R v
Vickers*[2] and that part of the decision in *Director of Public Prosecutions v Smith*[3]
which approved *R v Vickers*[2]. For the reasons which I give in the second part of this
opinion, I do not think that we ought to consider doing that in this case and so I think
that we should for present purposes accept Stephen's art 223(a) and (b) as a correct
f statement of the law. Although judges have generally only used subpara (a) in their
directions to juries, subpara (b) has been sometimes used, as for example, by Avory J
in *R v Lumley*[4]. Counsel did not refer us to any case in which any doubt has been
thrown on its correctness and it was accepted as correct in the Supreme Court of
Victoria in *R v Jakac*[5]. In the result, therefore, I think that the only criticism which
can be directed against Ackner J's summing-up is that by the insertion of the word
g 'highly' before 'probable' it was unduly favourable to the appellant.
      It was not until counsel for the appellant was in the middle of his reply that I appreci-
ated that he was contending as an alternative to his main argument that *R v Vickers*[2]
had been wrongly decided. My failure to appreciate this may well have been partly
due to the fact that I have never before had to grapple with this obscure and highly
h technical branch of the law, but the fact that counsel for the Crown did not deal with
this point at all in his argument is some indication that counsel, if he was intending
to make it in his opening, did not lay much stress on it at that stage. Moreover, although by the close of the argument I could see that it was a serious point it was only
when I read the speech of my noble and learned friend, Lord Diplock, that I fully
appreciated the historical and logical basis for it. Briefly the argument as I understand
j it, runs as follow—that the Court of Criminal Appeal was wrong when it said in *R v
Vickers*[2] that an intention to inflict grievous bodily harm had itself *'always'* supplied

1 (1868) The Times, 28th April
2 [1957] 2 All ER 741, [1957] 2 QB 664
3 [1960] 3 All ER 161, [1961] AC 290
4 (1911) 76 JP 208
5 [1961] VR 367

the necessary 'malice' to support a conviction for murder whether or not the accused
realised that what he was doing was likely to endanger life; that such an intention
only came to supply the necessary malice after the intentional infliction of grievous
bodily harm had been made a felony by Lord Ellenborough's Act; that accordingly
what came to be the common form direction that an intention to do grievous bodily
harm constituted 'malice aforethought' was, whether those who used it realised the
fact or not, only justified by the doctrine of constructive malice and that, whether or
not it realised what it was doing, Parliament when it abolished constructive malice
by the Homicide Act 1957 in effect swept away the existing law of 'malice aforethought'
in cases in which an intent to kill could not be proved and left it to the courts to re-
define the mental element requisite in such cases to support a conviction for murder.
My noble and learned friend may be right. On the other hand, my noble and learned
friend, Viscount Dilhorne, whose speech I have also had the advantage of reading,
thinks that he is wrong—and he may be right in so thinking. All that I am certain of is
that I am not prepared to decide between them without having heard the fullest
possible argument on the point from counsel on both sides—especially as a decision
that *R v Vickers*[1] was wrongly decided might have serious repercussions since the
direction approved in that case must have been given in many homicide cases in the
last 17 years. For my part, therefore, I shall content myself with saying that *on the
footing that R v Vickers*[1] *was rightly decided* the answer to the question put to us should
be 'Yes' and that this appeal should be dismissed.

LORD KILBRANDON. My Lords, having had the advantage of reading the
speech of my noble and learned friend, Lord Diplock, I have no difficulty in coming
to the conclusion that to kill with the intention of causing grievous bodily harm is
murder only if grievous bodily harm means some injury which is likely to cause death:
if murder is to be found proved in the absence of an intention to kill, the jury must
be satisfied from the nature of the act itself or from other evidence that the accused
knew that death was a likely consequence of the act and was indifferent whether that
consequence followed or not. It is because I regard the adoption of a fresh definition
of the intention, beyond an intention to kill, necessary to support a charge of murder
as inevitably called for by the passing into law of the Homicide Act 1957 that I have
come to the conclusion that this House is entitled to declare the common law basis on
which the rule laid down by Parliament rests, rather than leaving it to Parliament
itself to do so. It is a satisfaction to me to be able to say that in my opinion such a declaration would be in conformity with the common law of Scotland, where constructive
malice has never formed part of the law of murder.

My Lords, it is not so easy to feel satisfaction at the doubts and difficulties which
seem to surround the crime of murder and the distinguishing from it of the crime of
manslaughter. There is something wrong when crimes of such gravity, and I will
say of such familiarity, call for the display of so formidable a degree of forensic and
judicial learning as the present case has given rise to. I believe this to show that a
more radical look at the problem is called for, and was called for immediately on the
passing of the Murder (Abolition of Death Penalty) Act 1965. Until that time the
content of murder—and I am not talking about the definition of murder—was
that form of homicide which is punishable with death. (It is not necessary to notice
the experimental period during which capital murder and non-capital murder
existed side-by-side.) Since no homicides are now punishable with death, these many
hours and days have been occupied in trying to adjust a definition of that which has
no content. There does not appear to be any good reason why the crimes of murder
and manslaughter should not both be abolished, and the single crime of unlawful
homicide substituted; one case will differ from another in gravity, and that can
be taken care of by variation of sentences downwards from life imprisonment. It is

1   [1957] 2 All ER 741, [1957] 2 QB 664

a   no longer true, if it was ever true, to say that murder, as we now define it, is necessarily the most heinous example of unlawful homicide.   The present case could form
an excellent example exhibiting as it does, assuming it to be capable of classification
as manslaughter, a degree of cold-blooded cruelty exceeding that to be found in many
an impulsive crime which could never, on our present law, be so classified.

My Lords, since the passage in the summing-up of the learned judge which was
particularly noticed is not consistent with the common law as it has now, as I agree,
b   been shown to be, and the proviso was not relied on, it follows that this appeal
should be allowed.

Appeal dismissed.

Solicitors: *Callingham, Tucker & Co*, agents for *Varley, Hibbs & Co*, Coventry (for the
c   appellant); *Director of Public Prosecutions.*

Christine Ivamy   Barrister.

Applin v Race Relations Board

d   HOUSE OF LORDS
LORD REID, LORD MORRIS OF BORTH-Y-GEST, LORD WILBERFORCE, LORD SIMON OF
GLAISDALE AND LORD SALMON
28th, 29th, 30th JANUARY, 27th MARCH 1974

Race relations – Discrimination – Unlawful discrimination – Provision of goods, facilities and
e   *services – Discrimination by person concerned with provision of goods etc to a section of the*
public – Section of the public – Persons seeking to obtain or use goods etc – Children in care
of local authority – Local authority in exercise of statutory duty placing children with foster
parents – Foster parents undertaking to care for each child and bring him up as they would
a child of their own – Whether children in care a 'section of the public' – Whether children
persons seeking to obtain or use facilities and services provided by foster parents – Whether
f   *unlawful for foster parents to refuse to accept coloured children – Race Relations Act 1968, s 2(1).*

For many years Mr and Mrs Watson had, without reward and as a public service,
received into their home for a period children whom local authorities, acting under
their statutory duty, had taken into care.   In 1970 the Watsons moved to a new house
and asked certain local authorities how they could best help with child care work.   It
was arranged that they would take in children in emergencies at any hour and give
g   them temporary accommodation.   They generally had four or five children in their
home and the average duration of the stay of each child was about three weeks.
Under the Boarding-Out of Children Regulations 1955[a] the Watsons were required
to sign a form in which they undertook to care for each child and to bring him up
as they would a child of their own.   The Watsons' home was open to all children in
care subject to the limitation of numbers imposed by the available accommodation.
h   About 60 per cent of the children who stayed with them were coloured.   The defendant objected to the Watsons taking in coloured children and by means of a circular
letter distributed to local residents incited the Watsons to refuse to accept coloured
children into their home.   The Watsons reported the matter to the Race Relations
Board.   In proceedings by the board for a declaration that the defendant's action
was unlawful under s 12[b] of the Race Relations Act 1968 in that he had incited the
j   Watsons unlawfully to discriminate against the coloured children under s 2(1)[c] of

---

a   SI 1955 No 1377
b   Section 12 provides: 'Any person who deliberately aids, induces or incites another person
to do an act which is unlawful by virtue of any provision of this Part of this Act shall
be treated for the purposes of this Act as doing that act.'
c   Section 2(1) is set out at p 76 g, post

the 1968 Act, the defendant contended that a refusal to take in such children would
not be unlawful under s 2(1) since the children were to be treated as members of
the Watsons' family, and therefore, did not constitute 'a section of the public', and
furthermore that it was not the children but the local authorities who were seeking
to obtain and use the facilities and services provided by the Watsons.

Held (Lord Wilberforce dissenting) – The Watsons were providing facilities and
services to 'a section of the public', i e children in the care of the local authorities,
and, by refusing to take in coloured children sent to them by the local authorities,
they would have been discriminating against persons 'seeking to obtain or use those
. . . facilities or services', within the meaning of s 2(1). The situation was not one of
a purely domestic character since the Watsons had made a practice of taking in any
child for whom a home was required; although they undertook to treat the children,
and did treat them, as members of their own family, they were not in fact members
of the family; nor were they in the same situation as guests since there was no real
element of personal selection of the children who came to the Watsons. Furthermore,
although the children were not themselves able to seek to obtain or use facilities
or services, those who were sent to the Watsons' home were, within s 2(1), persons
seeking, through the agency of the local authorities, to obtain or use the facilities
and services which the Watsons provided. It followed that the action of the defendant
in inciting the Watsons to refuse to take in coloured children was unlawful under
s 12 of the 1968 Act (see p 77 *a* to *f*, p 78 *c* to *f*, p 79 *f* and *g*, p 80 *h* to p 81 *a c* and *d*,
p 91 *f g* and *j*, p 92 *a* and *g*, p 93 *c*, p 94 *j*, p 95 *a g* and *h* and p 96 *a c* and *e*, post).

Quaere.   Whether it is possible to discriminate against local authorities, as a
'section of the public', on the ground of colour (see p 77 *d*, p 92 *c e* and *f* and p 96 *d*,
post).

Decision of the Court of Appeal sub nom *Race Relations Board v Applin* [1973]
2 All ER 1190 affirmed.

Notes
For discrimination on racial grounds in the provision of goods, facilities and services,
see Supplement to 7 Halsbury's Laws (3rd Edn) para 1280, 1, 2.

For the Race Relations Act 1968, ss 2, 12, see 40 Halsbury's Statutes (3rd Edn)
105, 112.

Cases referred to in opinions
Charter v Race Relations Board [1973] 1 All ER 512, [1973] AC 868, [1973] 2 WLR 299,
HL.
Heydon's Case (1584) 3 Co Rep 7a, Moore KB 128, 76 ER 637, 21 Digest (Repl) 652, 1424.
Rugby Joint Water Board v Foottit, Rugby Joint Water Board v Shaw-Fox [1972] 1 All
ER 1057, [1973] AC 202, [1972] 2 WLR 757, 71 LGR 339, 24 P & CR 256, HL.
Tzu-Tsai Cheng v Governor of Pentonville Prison [1973] 2 All ER 204, [1973] AC 931,
[1973] 2 WLR 746, HL.

Appeal
At all material times Mr and Mrs Watson, who lived at 61 Oakroyd Avenue, Potters
Bar, Hertfordshire, had, as foster parents, taken into their home children who were
in the care of Barnet Borough Council, Haringey Borough Council and Hertfordshire
County Council. Although the Watsons were entitled to refuse to accept any child
offered by the local authorities they had never done so except when they had no
accommodation available. About 60 per cent of the children whom the Watsons
took into their home were coloured. The children generally stayed about three
weeks. On average the Watsons had four or five children in their home at any one
time.

The Race Relations Board ('the board') brought proceedings in the Westminster
County Court against the appellant, Peter W Applin, and against Kenneth Walker,

a claiming (i) a declaration that the acts referred to in para 4 of the particulars of claim were unlawful by virtue of ss 2 and 12 of the Race Relations Act 1968, and (ii) an injunction restraining the appellant and Mr Taylor, their servants or agents from deliberately inducing or inciting any other person to do an act which was unlawful by virtue of any provision in Part I of the 1968 Act. Paragraph 4 of the particulars of claim alleged that during August 1971 the appellant and Mr Taylor had repeatedly

b acted in breach of s 12 of the 1968 Act by deliberately inducing and/or inciting Mr and Mrs Watson to act unlawfully, contrary to s 2 of the 1968 Act, by refusing or deliberately omitting, on the ground of colour, race or ethnic or national origins, to provide the facilities and services of child fostering at their home to persons seeking to obtain or use those facilities or services. The particulars of inducement or incitement given in para 4 were, as to the appellant, that he, his servants or agents had published and distributed to the residents of Oakroyd Avenue a circular dated 5th

c August 1971, signed by him as branch organiser of the South Hertfordshire branch of the National Front organisation, deliberately inducing or inciting Mr and Mrs Watson to act unlawfully as aforesaid; that he, his servants or agents had organised and advertised a public meeting, held on 26th August 1971 at Oakmere House, High Street, Potters Bar, with the purpose of deliberately inducing or inciting Mr

d and Mrs Watson to act unlawfully as aforesaid; that he, his servants or agents on or about 25th August 1971 had published and distributed to the residents of Oakroyd Avenue an undated open letter, signed by him, so as deliberately to induce or incite Mr and Mrs Watson to act unlawfully as aforesaid. The particulars given in para 4 as to Mr Taylor were that he had written and sent two letters, dated 9th and 16th August 1971, deliberately inducing or inciting Mr and Mrs Watson to act as aforesaid;

e that he had participated in organising and advertising the meeting of 26th August and at that meeting had made a speech deliberately inducing or inciting Mr and Mrs Watson to act as aforesaid. His Honour Judge Ruttle, in a reserved judgment given on 25th July 1972, gave judgment for the appellant and Mr Taylor holding that there was incitement within the meaning of s 12 of the 1968 Act in respect of the circular dated 5th August but not in respect of the meeting of 26th August; but that the

f incitement proved against the appellant and Mr Taylor was not incitement of Mr and Mrs Watson to do an unlawful act since Mr and Mrs Watson were not concerned with the provision of facilities or services to a section of the public within s 2 of the 1968 Act. On 13th April 1973 the Court of Appeal[1] (Lord Denning MR, Buckley and Stephenson LJJ) allowed an appeal by the board and ordered that judgment be entered for the board against both the appellant and Mr Taylor for a declaration

g that the acts referred to in para 4 of the particulars of claim were unlawful by virtue of ss 2 and 12 of the 1968 Act. The court refused the appellant leave to appeal but on 14th June the appeal committee of the House of Lords granted leave. The facts are set out in the opinion of Lord Reid.

John Vinelott QC and *Mark Potter* for the appellant.
J P Comyn QC and *M J Beloff* for the board.

h
Their Lordships took time for consideration.

27th March. The following opinions were delivered.

LORD REID. My Lords, for many years Mr and Mrs Watson, have, without reward
j and as a public service, taken into their home for a period children in care of local authorities. In January 1970 they moved to a house in Potters Bar more suitable for the purpose. They asked the borough of Haringey how best they could help in child care work and it was arranged that they would take in children in emergencies at any hour and give them temporary accommodation. They generally had four or

---

1   [1973] 2 All ER 1190, [1973] QB 815

five of these children in their home and the average duration of stay of each child   *a*
was about three weeks. About 60 per cent of these children were coloured.

This attracted some notice from neighbours and some publicity. Criticism by
neighbours died away but the matter was taken up by the appellant and another
man who wished to stop the Watsons from taking in coloured children. This caused
the Watsons to get in touch with the Race Relations Board. The board took action
against the appellant and the other man in Westminster County Court claiming a   *b*
declaration that these actions were unlawful by virtue of ss 12 and 2 of the Race
Relations Act 1968.

Section 12 provides that any person who deliberately incites another person to do
an act made unlawful by the Act shall be treated as doing that act. It is admitted
by the appellant that his acts amounted to incitement. The question in the appeal
is whether he was inciting the Watsons to do an unlawful act; would it have been   *c*
unlawful for the Watsons, while being willing to take in white children, to refuse to
take in coloured children? If so, the appellant was inciting them to do an unlawful
act and this appeal must fail.

This is not an easy question. The board say that the Act must not be given a narrow
interpretation, and that, on a fair reading of its terms, they cover the present case.
The appellant denies this and says that the Act was never intended to apply to domes-   *d*
tic situations. So it is necessary to make a careful examination of the terms of the
Act. Section 1 defines discrimination. It provides:

'(1) For the purposes of this Act a person discriminates against another if on
the ground of colour, race or ethnic or national origins he treats that other, in
any situation to which section 2, 3, 4 or 5 below applies, less favourably than he
treats or would treat other persons, and in this Act references to discrimination   *e*
are references to discrimination on any of those grounds.

'(2) It is hereby declared that for those purposes segregating a person from
other persons on any of those grounds is treating him less favourably than they
are treated.'

We have in this case to determine whether the facts constitute a situation to which   *f*
s 2 applies. It is in these terms:

'(1) It shall be unlawful for any person concerned with the provision to the
public or a section of the public (whether on payment or otherwise) of any goods,
facilities or services to discriminate against any person seeking to obtain or use
those goods, facilities or services by refusing or deliberately omitting to provide
him with any of them or to provide him with goods, services or facilities of the   *g*
like quality, in the like manner and on the like terms in and on which the former
normally makes them available to other members of the public.

'(2) The following are examples of the facilities and services mentioned in subsection (1) above, that is to say—access to and use of any place which members
of the public are permitted to enter; accommodation in a hotel, boarding house
or other similar establishment; facilities by way of banking or insurance or for   *h*
grants, loans, credit or finance; facilities for education, instruction or training;
facilities for entertainment, recreation or refreshment; facilities for transport or
travel; the services of any business profession or trade or local or other public
authority.'

I see neither need nor justification for reading into this section any implied exclusion   *j*
of domestic situations. The head of a household is concerned with the provision of
goods, facilities and services to members of the household including his family,
guests and servants. But no one suggests that that is covered by this section. The
reason is that the members of a private household are not a section of the public.
Servants are expressly excluded by s 8(6). No doubt it was desirable to make this
clear but I do not think it was necessary.

a On the other hand, if a household ceases to be a private household then the Act may apply. Section 2(2) expressly mentions a boarding-house. It was said that the Watsons in effect keep a boarding-house. I do not think that that is so. Their establishment falls somewhere between a private household and a boarding-house.

The householder selects his guests. The Watsons do not select the children whom they take in. No doubt they could refuse a child if they considered him obviously unsuitable; but that does not mean that they select the children whom they do take.
b The importance of selection is explained in *Charter v Race Relations Board*[1].

Before dealing further with the main argument it may be well to dispose of an argument that the phraseology of s 2 will not cover this case. Discrimination must be against the person seeking to obtain goods, facilities or services. The appellant argues that here the only person seeking to obtain the facility is the local authority: the child neither does nor can seek them. Then he argues that there could not be dis-
c crimination against the local authority because it is not a member of the public. But there is nothing novel in a person in charge of a child acting on the child's behalf. I do not think that the local authority is seeking any facilities for itself. It is seeking facilities for the child and in doing so acting on behalf of the child.

So it is unnecessary to decide whether there can be discrimination against a local authority. I am inclined to think not. I doubt whether in this context a local authority
d is a member of the public. If a local authority sought facilities for two children, one white and the other coloured, I do not think that it fits the terms of this section to say that a person who agrees to take in the white child but refused to take in the coloured child thereby discriminates against the local authority.

Returning to the main argument, I think that the proper approach is to see whether, taking the natural meaning of the words of s 2(1), the Watsons do or do not come
e within the scope of the provision. First, they are concerned with the provision of goods, facilities and services: they make a practice of providing them. It may be doubted whether the section applies to an isolated transaction but here there is a course of conduct. Secondly, the children in care are a section of the public. I do not attach importance to the children being in care of the local authority. If the Watsons made a practice of receiving children without any real selection from parents who
f wished to have their children cared for for a short period, the case would be exactly the same.

The difficult question is whether the Watsons' establishment can be regarded as a private household. I take the words 'private household' from s 8(6) which provides that s 2 shall not apply to the employment of any person for the purposes of a private household. It cannot have been intended that discrimination with regard to ser-
g vants in a private household should be permissible, but that discrimination with regard to other members of a private household should be unlawful. I have already said that in my view an ordinary family is not within the scope of s 2 and I think that the words 'private household' in s 8(6) afford a good guide in drawing the line between an ordinary family and an establishment to which s 2 does apply.

A private household includes parents, their children, guests and it may be servants.
h It must also include children such as adopted children, illegitimate children of one parent who have been taken into the family and other children who, though not legally adopted, have been made at least semi-permanent members of the family. And guests will include children whom the parents have selected and chosen to invite to stay with them for a time. But there must come a stage when the household has been so expanded that it can no longer be regarded as a private household.
j The appellant argues that the Watsons' establishment should be regarded as a private household. The number of children in their care at any one time is small and the Watsons have undertaken to treat them and do in fact treat them as members of their family.

---

1 [1973] 1 All ER 512, [1973] AC 868

The Watsons take in these children under regulations[1] made under the Children
Act 1948. That Act by s 13 provides for the local authority boarding out children in
care subject to the provision of regulations. The regulations apply to 'the boarding
of a child . . . with foster parents to live in their dwelling as a member of their
family' (reg 1). Regulation 30 deals with a child remaining for more than eight
weeks 'in the household of which he is already a member' and the regulations require
'foster parents' to give an undertaking to 'bring up' the child as they would a child
of their own, to consult a doctor when necessary, to permit authorised persons to
visit their house, and to allow the council to remove the child.

    I do not regard the fact that the Watsons are acting under this Act and these
regulations, or the fact that they have given these undertakings as of primary importance. If they had had a similar practice of receiving unselected children for short
periods from some other source and had given somewhat similar undertakings I
think that that case would have been indistinguishable from the present case.

    Nor do I regard it as of primary importance that the Watsons treat the children
while they are with them as members of their family. People who invite the children
of friends to stay with them will generally treat them as members of their family.
But that does not mean that for their short stay such children become members of
the host's family; they are guests. There is a world of difference between treating
a child as if he were a member of the family and in fact making him a member of
the family.

    If the Watsons generally have four or five children with them for periods of about
three weeks each, they must take in more than 50 children each year, and we know
that in all they have taken in over 300 children over a long period. I regard it as
quite unreal to suppose that each of these children became in any true sense part of
the Watsons' family. In my view, in their laudable desire to be of service to a section
of the public, children in care, they have expanded their establishment well beyond
anything that could properly be called a private household. It is clear that they
would never discriminate on the ground of colour. But they were being incited to
do so and we must consider what the position would have been if they had given
way to the incitement. In my judgment if they had either refused to take in coloured
children while accepting others or had discriminated against coloured children while
under their care they would have come well within the scope of s 2 of the 1968 Act.

    I would therefore dismiss the appeal.

LORD MORRIS OF BORTH-Y-GEST. My Lords, it is the duty of a local
authority to receive certain children into their care. Some children have neither
parent nor guardian and some children have been or continue to be abandoned by
parents or guardian. In some cases the parents or guardian of a child are either
temporarily or permanently prevented from providing for a child's accommodation,
maintenance and upbringing. This may result from ill-health or from infirmity.
It may result from a variety of other circumstances. The intervention of the local
authority may, therefore, in all such cases be necessary in the interests of the welfare
of the child. The local authority have a statutory duty to act. They must when
necessary take children into their care. They clearly must not discriminate on the
ground of colour or race or ethnic or national origins.

    At any given time there are probably many tens of thousands of such children in
care. Particulars as to their number and as to the manner of their accommodation
are presented to Parliament and are published in a command paper. Local authorities
have statutory authority enabling them to discharge in various ways their duty to
provide accommodation and maintenance for a child. One way which is widely
adopted is to board children out. Another way is to maintain children in local
authority children's homes.

---

1   The Boarding-Out of Children Regulations 1955 (SI 1955 No 1377)

a   Among those with whom the local authorities for Haringey, Barnet and Hertfordshire have for many years boarded out children have been a Mr and Mrs Watson.
Since 1970 this has been at the house in Oakroyd Avenue, Potters Bar, to which in
that year Mr and Mrs Watson moved. The boarding out was not for long periods.
Usually the length of stay of a child accepted by Mr and Mrs Watson was two to
three weeks. About four or five were taken at a time, but exceptionally the number
b   could be seven. Some 60 per cent of the children accepted by Mr and Mrs Watson
were coloured children.

The appellant was in 1971 the branch organiser of the South Hertfordshire branch
of an organisation called the National Front. He was the signatory of a circular letter
dated 5th August 1971, which was distributed to those, including Mr and Mrs
Watson, who resided in Oakroyd Avenue. For present purposes it suffices to say
that it is not now in contest that the appellant 'incited' Mr and Mrs Watson to refuse to
c   include coloured children amongst those whom they took as boarders. Though the
efforts of the appellant were not only unwelcome to and were spurned by Mr and
Mrs Watson the question which is raised is whether the incitement was to do an
unlawful act (see s 12 of the Race Relations Act 1968). If Mr and Mrs Watson had
refused to accept coloured children, would they have been guilty of unlawful
discrimination contrary to s 2 of the Act?

d   To deal with this question it is necessary to consider first whether Mr and Mrs
Watson were 'concerned with the provision to the public or a section of the public
(whether on payment or otherwise) of any goods, facilities or services' and if so,
secondly, whether if they had refused to accept a child on the ground of colour or
race or ethnic or national origins they would have been discriminating—

e   'against any person seeking to obtain or use those goods, facilities or services
by refusing or deliberately omitting to provide him with any of them or to
provide him with goods, services or facilities of the like quality, in the like manner
and on the like terms in and on which the former normally makes them available
to other members of the public.'

f   As to the first of these my firm conclusion is that Mr and Mrs Watson were concerned with the provision of facilities or services to a section of the public. I regard
children in the care of local authorities as a section of the public. In the present case
the section comprised the children in the care of three particular local authorities.
Mr and Mrs Watson were concerned to provide facilities or services to such children.
Section 2(2) gives examples of the kinds of facilities and services which are denoted in
the section. The range and sweep of them is very wide. Included within the many
g   varieties of examples there are set out: accommodation in a boarding-house or other
similar establishment; facilities for education, instruction or training; and facilities
for entertainment, recreation or refreshment.

The exercise by local authorities of their statutory power of boarding out children
in their care is, as would be expected, carefully regulated. Elaborate provisions are
contained in the Boarding-Out of Children Regulations 1955. The persons with whom
h   children may be boarded out are prescribed. It is essential that those to whom a public
authority is by statute entitled to delegate its public duty of looking after children
in care should be persons who can be trusted to discharge so important a duty.
There are (inter alia) provisions relating to medical examinations of children before
and during boarding out and provisions relating to reports by visitors and provisions
relating to registers kept by local authorities. The persons with whom a child is for
j   the time being 'boarded out' (who in the regulations are by definition called 'foster
parents' even in cases where the boarding out is for a period expected not to exceed
eight weeks in all) are required to sign an undertaking. By the first of seven clauses
in the undertaking the 'foster parents' undertake to care for a child and bring him
up as they would a child of their own. A child is boarded with 'foster parents' to
live in their dwelling as a member of their family.

The facility or service provided by Mr and Mrs Watson was that of receiving
young boarders for short periods and of looking after them with the same tender
care as they (Mr and Mrs Watson) would have bestowed on children of their own.
Mr and Mrs Watson were in fact content only to receive reimbursement of what it
cost them to look after the children without asking for payment as such. They
undertook their responsibilities from the most commendable of motives.

On behalf of the appellant much reliance was placed on the fact that the above-
mentioned undertaking had to be given. It was contended that in the context of s 2
the otherwise wide and indeterminate meaning of the words 'facilities or services' must
be restricted. The words should be read as applying to facilities and services which
have an impersonal quality but not as applying to a facility such as 'fostering' which
necessarily involves the creation of a personal bond or relationship. In line with this
submission it was said that the facilities and services denoted by s 2 exclude those
which depend on a family relationship or those which bring people into a domestic
relationship. So it was said that s 2 does not cover facilities or services which are
rendered within a family circle and that the children received by Mr and Mrs Watson
became and should be regarded as having been within their family circle. Reference
was made to certain exceptions laid down in the Act (e g in ss 7, 8(6) and (10)) and
it was submitted that Parliament could not have intended to permit discrimination
in regard to shared residential accommodation but to prohibit it in the case of child
fostering where the relationship is very close.

Persuasively as these submissions were developed and amplified I am not persuaded
that the facilities and services provided by Mr and Mrs Watson were outside those
designated by s 2. Very many of those which are indicated by s 2(2) are far from being
impersonal. Many of them involve the creation of bonds and relationships which
are essentially personal. Many of them involve relationships which have 'domestic'
features—though it is to be noted that the Act does not introduce the word 'domestic'
as a description or as a criterion.

Within schools which provide 'facilities for education, instruction or training' there
are essentially personal relationships. Within schools large or small where children
board there are relationships marked by 'domestic' features. Those in charge may
be in loco parentis. So also 'a boarding house or other similar establishment' may
pride itself on having created and maintained such personal relationships with and
between guests that the recurrent visits of returning guests have many of the features
of a family reunion or of re-entry to a domestic hearth.

It is further to be noted that the early sections of the Act which begin with the
words 'it shall be unlawful' are followed by sections beginning with the words 'it shall
not be unlawful'. It has not been suggested that anywhere within those latter sections is there a provision which would make discrimination (as defined in the Act)
not unlawful on the part of those with whom children under care are boarded out.

The provision of facilities or services within a home to the members of a family
does not fall within s 2. For one thing such facilities or services are only available to
and for the members of the family or for those who may be voluntarily invited to
share in them. It may be otherwise if the facilities or services of a home are thrown
open and are made available so that others outside the family may seek to obtain
or use them. In the present case Mr and Mrs Watson decided to open their home
and to make its facilities and services available—and available under specially favourable conditions—to children in the care of certain local authorities.

I consider therefore that Mr and Mrs Watson were concerned with the provision
of facilities and services to a section of the public. The second question which arises is
whether if they had refused to accept a child on the ground of colour (or race or
ethnic or national origins) they would have discriminated 'against any person seeking
to obtain or use' the facilities or services. In my view, they clearly would. Mr and
Mrs Watson were not under any obligation to receive children in care as boarders
at all and they could at any time have said that they would discontinue receiving

a them. But they could not say that they were willing to accept children and then discriminate on the ground of colour.

After they had intimated to three local authorities that they were willing to open their home to receive children, the procedure was that the three local authorities would from time to time ask if certain children could be accepted. There might have been reasons why Mr and Mrs Watson did not wish to receive certain children,
b though in fact there was no occasion when they were in fact unwilling to receive a child for whom they had room. A refusal to accept some children would have been fully open to them always provided that it was not 'on the ground of colour, race or ethnic or national origins'. So also if they received children some of whom were coloured, the coloured children could not be segregated nor in any of the ways referred to in the Act be treated differently from the others.
c When the local authorities required Mr and Mrs Watson to receive the children, they did so, in my view, on behalf of the children and in the interests of the children so that it could fairly and properly be said that the children were seeking to obtain and use the facilities and services which Mr and Mrs Watson were concerned to provide. If there had been a refusal on the ground of colour to take a child, that would have been, within s 2 of the 1968 Act, an unlawful discrimination against a
d coloured child seeking to obtain or use the facilities or services. The circumstance that children in care do not in the nature of things personally order their affairs is immaterial. It is because they are in care that others must make arrangements on their behalf.

I would dismiss the appeal.

e **LORD WILBERFORCE.** My Lords, the proceedings in this appeal have become largely academic, but they raise an issue of general importance. That is whether the Race Relations Act 1968 enables proceedings to be brought against a married couple who express unwillingness to receive into their home a child in the care of a local authority on grounds of colour, race, ethnic or national origin. The actual question in the case is whether the appellant, Peter W Applin, was guilty of unlawful action
f in inciting Mr and Mrs Watson to discriminate, as regards acceptance into their home, against coloured children. The test of illegality under s 12 is whether the incited act is unlawful by virtue of any provision in Part I of the Act. Mr and Mrs Watson did not in fact yield to the incitement and had no intention of doing so. There is no question of their having done, or doing, any act of discrimination on racial grounds. For years, from the best of motives, they have received into their home children in
g care, the majority of whom have been coloured children. So the question becomes the hypothetical one: whether, if Mr and Mrs Watson were to refuse to accept coloured children, they would be guilty of an act of discrimination within the meaning of the Act—and so liable to proceedings under the Act.

The Race Relations Act 1968 is an Act of very wide and general scope; its policy is to prevent discrimination on grounds of colour, race or ethnic or national origin
h (which I shall refer to as 'colour etc'), over as wide a field as possible. But, as the Act itself shows, Parliament was conscious that this is a difficult area in which to legislate: there are limits to the possibility of changing people's conduct and prejudices by statute. So it was recognised that there were certain areas which it would be wise to leave out of the general prohibition. Broadly speaking, the separation is between acts in the public sphere, to which the statute is to apply, and acts in the
j private sphere, which are to be exempted.

The Act does not lay down any very definite line of separation. It gives some indications. In s 2(1) it refers to provision to the public or a section of the public: in s 2(2) it gives an illustrative list of the kind of facilities and services which are to be within the Act. Moreover there are to be found in other sections exceptions from the general application of the Act, the common character of which is that they relate to situations of a private, or household, or intimate character.

There are evidently a number of situations which are not explicitly dealt with: one   *a*
such is that of clubs, an important social area in which discrimination on one of the
stated grounds is quite likely to be found. Another situation is that of relations of a
familial or quasi-familial character. Both of these are common enough, and likely
enough to be exposed to possible discrimination. Absence of specific mention of
these leads one to suppose that Parliament intended to leave it to the courts to apply
the Act, in the light of its general policy. This House had to do this, in relation to   *b*
clubs, in *Charter v Race Relations Board*[1]. In my opinion, it has to do the same in the
present situation.

I look first, then, for such indication as can be found of the Act's general scope.
The 'public' character of the situation with which the Act is concerned is emphasised
in s 2(1) first by the words 'the public or a section of the public'. I understand these
words as referring to what is often called the public at large, or the general public.   *c*
The phrase 'section of the public' has been much debated and one view is that it
covers any members, however few, so long as they are not selected for personal
reasons. It has been argued that a local authority is a section of the public. But I do
not think that the phrase does more than to include cases where less than the whole
of the public may seek the goods, facilities or services, for example, a public library
which caters for residents: the public, of which a section is involved, is still the public   *d*
at large. This is confirmed by the rest of the section. Though the words used are
very general, so general indeed, that they can be made to cover operations of almost
any scale, they do suggest, to my mind, something which is generally available to
whoever wants it, a suggestion strengthened by 'normally makes them available to
other members of the public'. And this impression is greatly strengthened by sub-s
(2) which I quote for convenience: *e*

> 'The following are examples of the facilities and services mentioned in sub-
> section (1) above, that is to say—access to and use of any place which members
> of the public are permitted to enter; accommodation in a hotel, boarding house
> or other similar establishment; facilities by way of banking or insurance or for
> grants, loans, credit or finance; facilities for education, instruction or training;
> facilities for entertainment, recreation or refreshment; facilities for transport or   *f*
> travel; the services of any business, profession or trade or local or other public
> authority.'

Now I am aware, that these are stated as examples, non-exhaustive no doubt.
But they are very comprehensive examples; and I regard it as both legitimate and
necessary to use a list such as this for the purpose of gathering the general philosophy   *g*
and flavour of the Act. It is difficult, indeed, to see for what other purpose the list
could have been given, for most of the examples are quite obviously within any
normal meaning of facilities and services. It may help to eliminate some doubts, but
it must also have been intended as a guide to the character of facilities and services
in mind. What it suggests, in combination with s 2(1), is that the area in which
discrimination is forbidden is that in which a person is concerned to provide some-   *h*
thing which in its nature is generally offered to and needed by the public at large,
or a section of it, which is offered impersonally to all who choose to go through the
doors or approach the counter: things which, in their nature, would be provided to
anyone, and the refusal of which to persons of different colour etc could only be
ascribed to discrimination on grounds of colour etc. Conversely, they do not extend
to matters, the provision of which is a private matter, as to which the motives of the   *j*
refusing provider may reasonably have nothing to do with colour etc at all.

Then there are the exceptions. Those of particular interest are: Section 7(1)(2)—
dealing with lodgers in small premises. Section 7(6)—dealing with sharing of cabins.
Section 7(7)—dealing with private disposals of owner occupied premises not through

---

1   [1973] 1 All ER 512, [1973] AC 868

a an estate agent. Section 8(6)—dealing with the employment of any person for the purposes of a private household. Section 8(10)—dealing with the sharing of accommodation on a ship by employed persons.

I regard these exceptions as very significant; but I would not use them, as we were invited to do, just to construct arguments based on anomalies, though it is difficult to avoid the force of an argument that if Mrs Watson could refuse to employ a *b* coloured nurse or a coloured charwoman or to accept a coloured lodger it seems strange that she could not refuse to accept a coloured child. But arguments based on anomalies are liable to be dangerous in an Act such as this, for on any view many must exist. I prefer to regard the exceptions as yet further signposts directing one away from situations of a private or intimate or domestic character. And an expressio unius argument seems to me, in such an Act as this, where 'purpose' and 'policy' *c* are all important, with respect, to be pedantic and misplaced.

I have so far attempted to extract the meaning of s 2 of the Act by considerations of a general and purposive character. A process of word by word analysis may suggest, as the careful judgments in the Court of Appeal[1] show, that such a case as the present comes within it: the Watsons are 'concerned', because they habitually do what they do; the local authorities are 'a section of the public', or the children are *d* 'a section of the public'. The 'seeking' is done by the local authorities either for themselves or as agents for the children: what the Watsons offer are 'facilities' or 'services' or both. So it all adds up to a total application of this section. No doubt each of these steps can be forcefully argued, though I must say that some of them seem to me rather strained, but there remain two questions: would the ordinary man regard the subsection as a whole as applying to decisions to take children into *e* his home: is the end result consistent with the purpose of the Act?

I have so far spoken of admission to the home, but I must now analyse more carefully what exactly it is that Mr and Mrs Watson do. They are acting in accordance with the provisions of the Children Act 1948. This Act is only one of many which relate to the taking by householders of other people's children into their home or family. Most important, and closely related, is the adoption legislation, and the *f* Children Act 1958, which deals with fostering. I should regard it as inconceivable that the Race Relations Act 1968 should apply in either of these two areas; the case of the 1958 Act is, I understand, one as to which doubts are thought to exist, but, with respect, I cannot share them. I should therefore expect that a consistent policy would place the Children Act 1948, so far as it relates to the reception of children and cases covered by it, in the same category.

g The basic provision, relevant here, is s 1 of the 1948 Act. I quote sub-ss (1) and (2):

'(1) Where it appears to a local authority with respect to a child in their area appearing to them to be under the age of seventeen—(a) that he has neither parent nor guardian or has been and remains abandoned by his parents or guardian or is lost; or (b) that his parents or guardian are, for the time being *h* or permanently, prevented by reason of mental or bodily disease or infirmity or other incapacity or any other circumstances from providing for his proper accommodation, maintenance and upbringing; and (c) in either case, that the intervention of the local authority under this section is necessary in the interests of the welfare of the child, it shall be the duty of the local authority to receive the child into their care under this section.

j '(2) Where a local authority have received a child into their care under this section, it shall, subject to the provisions of this Part of this Act, be their duty to keep the child in their care so long as the welfare of the child appears to them to require it and the child has not attained the age of eighteen.'

Then follow ss 12 and 13:

---

1   [1973] 2 All ER 1190, [1973] QB 815

'12.—(1) Where a child is in the care of a local authority, it shall be the duty of
that authority to exercise their powers with respect to him so as to further his
best interests, and to afford him opportunity for the proper development of
his character and abilities.

'(2) In providing for a child in their care, a local authority shall make such use
of facilities and services available for children in the care of their own parents as
appears to the local authority reasonable in his case.

'13[1].—(1) A local authority shall discharge their duty to provide accommodation
and maintenance for a child in their care in such one of the following ways as
they think fit, namely,—(a) by boarding him out on such terms as to payment
by the authority and otherwise as the authority may, subject to the provisions
of this Act and regulations thereunder, determine; or (b) by maintaining him in a
community home or in any such home as is referred to in section 64 of the
Children and Young Persons Act 1969; or (c) by maintaining him in a voluntary
home (other than a community home) the managers of which are willing to
receive him; or by making such other arrangements as seem appropriate to the
local authority . . .'

Regulations have been made under s 14[2]. Their general scope is defined in reg 1
as follows:

'(1) Subject to the provisions of paragraphs (2) and (3) of this Regulation, these
Regulations shall apply to the boarding of a child—(a) by a local authority in
whose care the child is, or (b) by a voluntary organisation in whose charge the
child is otherwise than under an approved school order, with foster parents to
live in their dwelling as a member of their family, and the boarding of a child
to which these Regulations apply as aforesaid is hereinafter referred to as
"boarding-out", and "boarded out" and "boarded out" shall be construed
accordingly.'

Then there are somewhat different regulations, according as the child is expected
to remain more or less than eight weeks, but I do not think that the details matter.
In either case an undertaking has to be signed by the 'foster parents'. This recites
that the named child has been received into their home 'as a member of our family',
and para 1 contains an undertaking that 'we will care for (the child) and bring him
up as we would a child of our own'. Various other obligations are specified.

What is the effect of this, and what relationship is established? First, we must not
be confused by labels. The label 'foster parent' may or may not be strictly appropriate, or bear the sense that it bears elsewhere. Here it means no more or less than a
person who undertakes the responsibilities defined by the Act and regulations. The
label 'boarding-out' again is purely shorthand for what happens under the Act and
regulations; it has no independent meaning, and to point to the use of the same words
among the list of facilities in the 1968 Act, s 2(2), is an argument of pure verbalism.

In truth, to describe the Watsons as providing 'board' or 'board and lodging' is to
ignore what the Children Act 1948, Part I, is setting out to achieve. This is not merely
to provide shelter, or a bed, for children who have nowhere to sleep. It is to provide
a substitute for the child's parents when the child has lost its parents or when its
parents, for some reason, become incapable of performing their parental duties.
Section 1 of the Children Act 1948 is quite explicit as to this. Equally explicit are the
regulations, insisting as they do, that the child shall be received as a member of the
family and brought up as such.

To suggest that all persons such as the Watsons provide is board and lodging of a
superior kind is to misrepresent, and indeed to degrade, what is expected of them.

1   As amended by the Children and Young Persons Act 1969, s 49
2   The Boarding-Out of Children Regulations 1955 (SI 1955 No 1377)

a   And certainly Mr and Mrs Watson do not look at the matter in this way. This is what Mr Watson said:

'Yes. We try and take them into our family as such, so that from whatever disturbed circumstances they have come, they come into an immediate family atmosphere and become one of the family. We try and provide play facilities, toys, for them and interests for them and my wife is keen on this, an established

b   routine which they can enter and forget their immediate worries and troubles in the joy of playing with other children and having facilities for playing in both the nursery and our garden.'

And again:

c   'Q Would it be right to say that in relation to these children you quite simply take them into your family to live as your own child for the period for which you have them? A I would hope it was rather more than that because we seek to take a child in a disturbed state and bring it into an environment that will assist it at a particular crisis in his life.

'Q You certainly agree that you give it the care and attention that you would your own child and because it is often in a disturbed state, often more than you

d   would your own child? A Yes.

'Q You may think these are silly questions but they have a purpose. You certainly do not consider yourself in the nature of an hotel or boarding house keeper in relation to them? A No, I do not.

'Q You certainly do not consider yourself simply to be a schoolmaster or an instructor for the period? A No, I do not.

e   'Q The point being that you and your wife give, or your wife when you are not there, endeavour to give them your whole time and care in every aspect of their life as a child, and you regard yourself, I am sure you do it anyway, you regard yourself as under an obligation to the council to do that so far as the children are concerned. A Yes I do.'

f   All of this is what one would expect, or at least hope for, from people offering their service. It underlines the essentially personal, domestic and familial nature of the relationship.

There are two arguments which I must deal with. First, it is said that the local authority, in taking children into care, is performing a public service and so, therefore, must the 'foster parents'. But this does not follow. The public character of the local

g   authority's work does not determine the character of that of private persons whom the authority asks to help. The local authority is under a statutory duty to take children into care and it cannot turn anyone away. But the foster parents are volunteers: they need not accept anyone. The local authority takes children into care: the foster parents take them into their home. Their position is quite different from that of 'community homes' which can be regarded as an adjunct of the local authority.

h   Mr and Mrs Watson are helping the local authority in its public duty, but in a personal and private way, as the regulations show.

Secondly, it is said that the Watsons only take children for short periods, so that the familial aspect is slight or non-existent. There are two answers to this. First, the 'incitement' was quite general: it was not against taking children for two to three weeks, but against taking them at all. The actual period hitherto taken is irrelevant.

j   Secondly, I cannot accept that, in the case of a child, possibly itself disturbed and of an impressionable age, whose parents have suddenly become unable to act, the need for immediate substitute parenthood, and appropriate care and affection, is not real and significant. Even three weeks in such conditions may be critical. I add that I can see no relevance in the total number of children in care. The nature of Mr and Mrs Watson's relationship to the children cannot depend on how many other people act as they do.

My Lords, I cannot bring myself to agree that the Race Relations Act 1968, with the
possibility of proceedings in court, can ever have been intended to apply to a situation
so essentially private, domestic and familial as this. To say otherwise means that a
woman maintaining a household, with perhaps her own children and others taken
in from care, may not say: 'I am very sorry, I have nothing against coloured children,
or white children, or children from far off countries about which I know nothing,
but I cannot take the responsibility of caring for them as my own.' To say this, represents an undesirable and impractical intrusion in the spheres of private decision and
one which is not likely to advance the cause of improving race relations. It is not,
in my opinion, called for by the Act.
    I would allow the appeal.

LORD SIMON OF GLAISDALE.

I

My Lords, by Part I of the Children Act 1948, it is the duty of local authorities to assume
care of children in certain cases. Of section 1 I need cite only sub-ss (1) and (2) and
part of sub-s (3):

    '(1) Where it appears to a local authority with respect to a child in their area
    appearing to them to be under the age of seventeen—(a) that he has neither
    parent nor guardian or has been and remains abandoned by his parents or
    guardian or is lost; or (b) that his parents or guardian are, for the time being or
    permanently, prevented by reason of mental or bodily disease or infirmity or
    other incapacity or any other circumstances from providing for his proper
    accommodation, maintenance and upbringing; and (c) in either case, that the
    intervention of the local authority under this section is necessary in the interests
    of the welfare of the child, it shall be the duty of the local authority to receive
    the child into their care under this section.
    '(2) Where a local authority have received a child into their care under this
    section, it shall, subject to the provisions of this Part of this Act, be their duty to
    keep the child in their care so long as the welfare of the child appears to them to
    require it and the child has not attained the age of eighteen.
    '(3) Nothing in this section shall authorise a local authority to keep a child in
    their care under this section if any parent or guardian desires to take over the
    care of the child . . .'

Section 2 provides for the local authority by resolution in certain circumstances to
assume parental care. The treatment of the children of whom the local authorities
have assumed care under Part I of the Act is dealt with under Part II. I set out only
s 12, which deals with the general duty of the local authority in respect of a child
in its care, and part of s 13, which stipulates the mode of provision of accommodation
and maintenance for such child:

    '12.—(1) Where a child is in the care of a local authority, it shall be the duty of
    that authority to exercise their powers with respect to him so as to further his
    best interests, and to afford him opportunity for the proper development of his
    character and abilities.
    '(2) In providing for a child in their care, a local authority shall make such use
    of facilities and services available for children in the care of their own parents as
    appears to the local authority reasonable in his case.
    '13.—(1) A local authority shall discharge their duty to provide accommodation
    and maintenance for a child in their care in such one of the following ways as
    they think fit, namely,—(a) by boarding him out on such terms as to payment by
    the authority and otherwise as the authority may, subject to the provisions of this
    Act and regulations thereunder, determine; or (b) by maintaining him in a
    community home or in any such home as is referred to in section 64 of the

Children and Young Persons Act 1969; or (c) by maintaining him in a voluntary home (other than a community home) the managers of which are willing to receive him; or by making such other arrangements as seem appropriate to the local authority . . .'

It will be noted that the statute does not refer to 'fostering' (with its concomitant 'foster-parent' and 'foster-child'), but to 'boarding-out'. The former terms do, however, appear in the regulations which the Secretary of State may, by s 14, make for the provision of children boarded-out by local authorities under s 13(1); and I shall for convenience sometimes here use the word 'foster' etc. The regulations are the Boarding-Out of Children Regulations 1955. Regulation 2 imposes limitations on the status of persons with whom children may be boarded out (e g a husband and wife jointly). Regulation 4 imposes a duty on the placing authority to terminate the boarding-out if it appears the boarding-out is no longer in the child's best interests. Regulation 5 gives power to a supervising visitor under the regulations to remove a child forthwith from the foster-parents if that visitor considers that the conditions in which the child is boarded out endanger his health, safety or morals. Regulation 7 provides for medical examination of the child during boarding out; reg 9 for reports by visitors on the child; reg 10 for case records to be kept ; and reg 11 for registers to be kept by local authorities, in which must be entered in respect of every boarded out child various personal details of the child and of each foster-parent. (In addition, your Lordships were told, the local authorities keep a non-statutory register of persons who are willing to accept for fostering children in local authority care.) Scheduled to the regulations is a form of undertaking to be signed by the foster-parents. The relevant part is as follows:

'We/I, A.B. [and B.B.] . . . having . . . received from [the council of the county/ county borough of   (hereinafter called "the Council")] . . . C.D. . . . into our/my home as a member of our/my family undertake that—1. We/I will care for C.D. and bring him/her up as we /I would a child of our/my own . . .'

Then follow a number of undertakings relating to the religious upbringing of the child, to medical consultation and examination 'at such times and places as[the council] . . . may require', to informing the council immediately of any serious occurrence affecting the child, to permitting any authorised visitor to see the child and visit the house, to allowing the child to be removed when so requested by a person authorised by the council, and to prior notification to the council of any change of address.

It appears from the command paper Children in Care in England and Wales[1], Table I, that the total number of children in care of local authorities in March 1972 in England and Wales was 90,586, of whom 29,901 (about one-third) were boarded out and 1,860 were in lodgings (by virtue of an amendment to the 1948 Act, which it is unnecessary to set out). Table I also tabulates the circumstances in which children came into care during the 12 months to 31st March 1972: by far the most frequent circumstances was the short-term illness of the parent or guardian. Table II gives the breakdown by local authorities. Of the three with which your Lordships are concerned in the instant appeal, Hertfordshire had 1,309 children in care, constituting 4·5 per 1,000 of its estimated population under the age of 18; Barnet had 274 children in care (3·8 per 1,000); Haringey 856 (12·6 per 1,000).

Mr and Mrs Watson have for 23 years been fostering children in local authority care. During that time they have taken in over 300 children, of whom about 60 per cent were coloured. They do it as the practical expression of their Christian faith. Normally they take four or five children at a time, but it may rise to seven in emergencies. The length of stay was generally two or three weeks. At the end of

---

1 Cmnd 5434

January 1970 the Watsons moved from Finchley to a house in Potters Bar, Hertfordshire; the move was partly prompted by a desire for improved amenities for
the children taken in. In evidence at the Westminster County Court in these
proceedings Mr Watson said:

'When we moved to Potters Bar we approached the borough of Haringey, with
whom we had had dealings before, and from whom most of our children had
come, to ask what was the way in which we could most help them in their
child care work. They said that the most helpful thing we could do, if we were
prepared to do it, was to be willing to take children in emergency at any hour
of the night or day and give them temporary accommodation in our home
and in our family, until they were able to sort out their immediate problems.'

I draw attention to the words 'in emergency' and 'temporary'. Similar arrangements
were made with the authorities of the borough of Barnet and the Hertford County
Council.

The activities of Mr and Mrs Watson to which I have referred aroused the resentment of the appellant, Mr Applin, and of Mr Taylor (who has not been represented
before your Lordships), respectively the branch organiser and the area organiser of
an organisation called the 'National Front'; they objected to coloured children being
among the Watsons' beneficiaries. In pursuance of this objection the appellant
and Mr Taylor started locally a public agitation against Mr and Mrs Watson. Their
aim was admittedly to procure that the Watsons confined their beneficence to white
children.

Mr Watson made a complaint to the Race Relations Board (see the Race Relations
Act 1968, s 15), and in due course the Race Relations Board started proceedings in
the county court, claiming that the actions of the appellant and Mr Taylor amounted
to unlawful incitement under the 1968 Act and also seeking an injunction against
them (see ss 12 and 19). Before the learned county court judge it was contended
on behalf of the appellant and Mr Taylor that, even if the course of action that they
were urging on Mr and Mrs Watson would have been unlawful under the 1968
Act, their own conduct did not nevertheless amount to unlawful incitement under
s 12. That contention has, however, now been abandoned. The sole issue before your
Lordships is therefore whether, if Mr and Mrs Watson had acceded to the agitation
of the appellant and Mr Taylor and refused to foster any other than white children
in care, that would have been unlawful action under the Act. In a careful judgment
the learned county court judge decided that issue in favour of the appellant and
Mr Taylor. His decision was reversed by the Court of Appeal[1], who granted a declaration that the acts of the appellant and Mr Taylor were unlawful by virtue of ss 12
and 2 of the 1968 Act; though they refrained from granting an injunction, on the
ground that there was no threat of repetition of the action complained of. The
appellant now appeals to your Lordships' House.

The following are the key provisions of the 1968 Act:

'1.—(1) For the purposes of this Act a person discriminates against another if
on the ground of colour, race or ethnic or national origins he treats that other,
in any situation to which section 2, 3, 4 or 5 below applies, less favourably than
he treats or would treat other persons, and in this Act references to discrimination are references to discrimination on any of those grounds . . .

'2.—(1) It shall be unlawful for any person concerned with the provision to
the public or a section of the public (whether on payment or otherwise) of any
goods, facilities or services to discriminate against any person seeking to obtain
or use those goods, facilities or services by refusing or deliberately omitting
to provide him with any of them or to provide him with goods, services or

---

1   [1973] 2 All ER 1190, [1973] QB 815

a facilities of the like quality, in the like manner and on the like terms in and on
   which the former normally makes them available to other members of the
   public.
   '(2) The following are examples of the facilities and services mentioned in
   subsection (1) above, that is to say—access to and use of any place which members
   of the public are permitted to enter; accommodation in a hotel, boarding house
b or other similar establishment; facilities by way of banking or insurance or
   for grants, loans, credit or finance; facilities for education, instruction or training;
   facilities for entertainment, recreation or refreshment; facilities for transport
   or travel; the services of any business, profession or trade or local or other
   public authority.'

                                    II

c In *Heydon's Case*[1] it was resolved by the Barons of the Exchequer:

   '... for the sure and true ... interpretation of all statutes in general (be they
   penal ... or beneficial, restrictive or enlarging of the common law,) four things
   are to be discerned and considered: ... 1st. What was the common law before
   the making of the Act ... 2nd. What was the mischief and defect for which the
   common law did not provide. 3rd. What remedy the Parliament hath resolved
d and appointed to cure the disease of the commonwealth. And, 4th. The true
   reason of the remedy; and then the office of all the Judges is always to make
   such ... construction as shall suppress the mischief, and advance the remedy,
   and to suppress subtle inventions and evasions for continuance of the mischief,
   and *pro privato commodo*, and to add force and life to the cure and remedy,
   according to the true intent of the makers of the Act, *pro bono publico*.'

e This approach has frequently been adopted: see Maxwell on the Interpretation of
   Statutes[2].
   The common law before the making of the first Race Relations Act (1965) was
   that people could discriminate against others on the ground of colour etc to their
   hearts' content. This unbridled capacity to discriminate was the mischief and defect
   for which common law did not provide. The remedy Parliament resolved and
f appointed was to make certain acts of discrimination unlawful. The reason for
   the remedy must have been that discrimination was thought to be socially divisive
   (indeed, s 6 of the 1965 Act suggests, potentially subversive of public order) and
   derogatory to human dignity. The 1968 Act widens and strengthens the provisions
   of the 1965 Act, the latter having been apparently thought to be inadequate remedy
   for the mischief.
g Did the matter rest there, thus simply stated, this appeal would present little
   difficulty. The appellant was plainly inciting the Watsons to discriminate in their
   fostering facilities and services in favour of white children in care and against
   coloured. The difficulty arises by reason of the fact that Parliament did not make
   discrimination on the ground of colour universally unlawful. In *Charter v Race
   Relations Board*[3] I gratefully adopted the language used by my noble and learned
h friend, Lord Reid, for the final impression which the 1968 Act made:

   'I would infer from the Act as a whole that the legislature thought all
   discrimination on racial grounds to be deplorable but thought it unwise or
   impracticable to attempt to apply legal sanctions in situations of a purely private
   character.'

j The hesitations about applying the general provision to situations of a purely private
   character appear partly from the words 'person concerned with the provision *to the
   public or a section of the public*' (which fell for construction in *Charter's* case[4]), partly

1 (1584) 3 Co Rep 7a at 7b
2 12th Edn (1969), pp 40-43
3 [1973] 1 All ER 512 at 527, [1973] AC 868 at 900
4 [1973] 1 All ER 512, [1973] AC 868

from the provisions of ss 7 and 8. The result of Parliament's hesitation to legislate
against every act of racial discrimination means that there must be a number of   *a*
borderline situations which Parliament either did not envisage, or else preferred not
to deal with by specific statutory regulation, rather leaving them to the courts.
In consequence, though there can be no doubt what is the paramount purpose of
the Act—namely, the discouragement of racial discrimination by various deterrents
and other remedies—room was left for the powerful argument for the appellant   *b*
to the following effect. Parliament undoubtedly refrained from making all situations
of racial discrimination unlawful; in particular, Parliament refrained from carrying
its sanctions into the family circle. For example, it would not be unlawful for a
stepfather to discriminate on the ground of colour in favour of a white stepson and
against a coloured stepson. Nor even (as the board agrees) would it be an offence
for a proposed adopter of a child to discriminate in his act of adoption on the ground   *c*
of colour: since, in taking the child into his family, he is not a person concerned with
the provision *to the public or a section of the public* of any goods, facilities or services.
So too, it was argued, with a foster-parent under the Children Act 1948: look at
the very opening of the form of undertaking. 'We ... having ... received ... C.D.
... into our ... home as a member of our ... family undertake that ... we ... will
care for ... and bring him ... up as we ... would a child of our ... own'. Counsel   *d*
adds, for good measure, that it would be odd for Parliament to allow discrimination
on the ground of colour in relation to the employment of, say, a nurse for the children
(see s 8(6)), but not in relation to the children themselves, who are received into the
much more intimate role of members of the family.

Where the paramount statutory purpose is palpable, the fact that it has not been
carried through into every conceivable situation does not, in my view, mean that   *e*
'the mischief rule' (*Heydon's Case*[1]) ceases to have any value. At the very least it
should operate, where Parliament has stipulated express exemptions in derogation
of its paramount statutory purpose, to cause the courts to hesitate in going on to
imply further exemptions in added derogation.

Moreover, the appellant's argument which I have just rehearsed presupposes
that the facilities and services with which your Lordships are concerned are those   *f*
provided by the Watsons to the children—and provided in the Watsons' home after
the children's entry there. But the appellant and Mr Taylor were not inciting the
Watsons to discriminate against the coloured children once they had had entry to
the house: they were inciting the Watsons to deny entry to coloured children.
It is therefore necessary to examine the words used in the statute to see whether they
extend to such conduct. If they do, such conduct lies more obviously in the public
domain (to apply a test I ventured to propose to your Lordships in *Charter's* case[2])   *g*
than discrimination within the household.

Furthermore, if the statute extends to the relationship, not between the Watsons
and the children, but to that between the Watsons and the local authorities—if,
in other words, it extends to what (if anything) the Watsons provided for the local
authorities, and the Watsons could have been regarded as discriminating in that   *h*
respect if they had yielded to the incitement—the situation would be entirely in
the public domain and plainly be within the mischief of the statute. This, too, calls
for a close examination of the language of the statute.

A linguistic examination is in any event called for as a check against interpretation
in the light of statutory purpose.

III

In examining the language of a statute which affects people in their ordinary,
unspecialised lives, there is a 'golden' rule that the words are presumptively intended

1 (1584) 3 Co Rep 7a
2 [1973] 1 All ER at 527, [1973] AC at 901

a in their natural, ordinary and grammatical meaning. This canon of construction, always potent, is particularly so if there are forensic situations which Parliament seemingly either did not envisage or preferred not to deal with (rather leaving them to the courts): see *Tzu-Tsai Cheng v Governor of Pentonville Prison*[1]. This 'golden' rule has, however, a rider: the Interpretation Act 1889 is a code assisting the drafts-man to signal the legislative intention to the courts; so that the natural, ordinary and grammatical language may be extended by the provisions of the Interpretation
b Act. With these aids I turn to analyse s 2(1) of the 1968 Act.

'It shall be unlawful for any person . . .'

By the Interpretation Act 1889, s 1(1)(*b*), words in the singular include the plural, unless the contrary intention appears. No contrary intention appears here; so
c 'any person' extends to Mr or Mrs Watson or both of them together. By s 19 of the 1889 Act 'person' includes any body of persons corporate or unincorporate, unless the contrary intention appears (see also s 2). 'Person' therefore extends to the local authorities in the absence of a contrary intention appearing. Not only does no such contrary intention appear, but the references in s 2(2) of the Race Relations Act 1968 to 'facilities for education' and 'the services of any . . . local . . . authority' reinforce
d the Interpretation Act, and make it clear that the reference to 'person' in the opening line of s 2(1), as also in s 1, includes the three local authorities with which your Lordships are concerned. This conclusion will be important to the interpretation of 'person' when it appears later in s 2(1).

'. . . concerned with the provision . . . of any goods, facilities or services . . .'

e In pursuance of their duty under Part II of the Children Act 1948, the local authorities were concerned with the provision of goods, facilities and services to the children whom they had taken into care in pursuance of their duty under Part I of the Act—including the provision of accommodation and maintenance by boarding-out (s 13(1)(*a*)).

The Watsons were concerned with the provision of boarding-out facilities to the
f local authorities, whereby they could discharge their duty to provide accommodation and maintenance for the children in their care. The Watsons were also concerned with the provisions of goods, facilities and services to the children themselves—not only once the children had entered their home, but also in permitting their entry. I do not say that 'provision of facilities' extends to 'provision of facilities to obtain facilities'. But it seems to me to be a natural use of the words 'provision of facilities'
g to include a right to enter a home provided for homeless children. In this respect the instant case differs from *Charter's* case[2], where the facilities and services in question were those within the club itself.

' . . . to the public or a section of the public . . .'

It was not disputed on behalf of the appellant that the children fell within this
h description before they entered the Watsons' home. But it was claimed that on entry they ceased to be a section of the public and became members of the Watsons' family; reliance being particularly placed on the opening words of the form of undertaking to be signed by foster-parents. I cannot agree that the children ceased to be a section of the public on their entry into the Watsons' home. The opening words of the form of undertaking must be read together with the regulations and
j the remaining provisions of the undertaking, which differentiate these children significantly from normal members of a family. Moreover, there were over 300 of them in 25 years. They only stayed for short periods. Though I am not convinced

1 [1973] 2 All ER 204 at 213, 214, [1973] AC 931 at 950, 951
2 [1973] 1 All ER 512, [1973] AC 868

that a process of screening or selection which was held in *Charter's* case[1] to be the
criterion differentiating the members of a club from a section of the public is a *a*
touchstone in all circumstances, for what it is worth the Watsons did not pick and
choose among the children they were asked to take—it was the children's need
alone which was their recommendation. Most important of all, the children did not,
on being boarded out, cease to be in the care of the local authority. If I may again
venture to apply a test which I proposed in *Charter's* case[2] the provision was made *b*
by the Watsons to persons aggregated in a public role. Or, to apply the words of
my noble and learned friend, Lord Reid[3], which I have already cited, this was not
a situation 'of a purely private character'. In any cases, the incited action was to
prevent the coloured children's very entry into the Watsons' household so that they
would remain outside, in the public domain.

I also respectfully agree with Buckley LJ[4] that the local authorities too constituted *c*
a section of the public. Their own role is by definition wholly in the public domain.

'*. . . to discriminate . . .*'

This term is defined in s 1(1). The word 'would' ('would treat') is important.
If the Watsons had declared that they would accept white children but not coloured
children, they would be treating the latter less favourably than the former in allowing *d*
the former, but not the latter, entry to their home; and also treating the latter
less favourably than they *would* treat the former *after* entry to their home.

Moreover, I respectfully agree with Lord Denning MR[5] that by insisting on white
children only the Watsons would be, within the statutory definition, discriminating
against the local authorities themselves on the ground of colour. It is inadmissible
to read s 1(1) as if it read 'on the ground of *his* colour'. Not only would this involve *e*
reading into the subsection a word which is not there; it would also mean that some
conduct which is plainly within the 'mischief' would escape—for example, discriminating against a white woman on the ground that she had married a coloured man.
It would therefore, in my view, be discrimination if the Watsons had treated local
authorities seeking boarding-out facilities for coloured children less favourably than
they *would* treat local authorities who either had no coloured children in care or who *f*
proffered none for boarding-out.

'*. . . against any person seeking to obtain or use those facilities [etc] . . .*'

The children were persons seeking (through the local authorities) to obtain and
use boarding-out facilities.

The local authorities were seeking to obtain and use boarding-out facilities on *g*
behalf of the children (white and coloured) and also to obtain such facilities on their
own behalf in order to fulfil their statutory duties. 'Person' would include the
local authorities by virtue of the Interpretation Act 1889, in the absence of a contrary
intention appearing. It was argued on behalf of the appellant that the use of the word
'him' ('to provide *him* with any of them or to provide *him* with goods [etc] of the like
quality [etc]') showed a contrary intention, the pronoun being inappropriate to a *h*
local authority. But where the draftsman uses the same word twice within four
lines there is a strong presumption against a change of usage; and I have already
ventured to point out why 'person' in the opening line of s 2(1) must include local
authorities. Furthermore, once the draftsman has used the shorthand of the Interpretation Act ('person' for 'persons or persons, including bodies corporate or *j*

1 [1973] 1 All ER 512, [1973] AC 868
2 [1973] 1 All ER at 527, [1973] AC at 901
3 [1973] 1 All ER at 516, [1973] AC at 887
4 [1973] 2 All ER at 1197, [1973] QB at 829
5 [1973] 2 All ER at 1196, [1973] QB at 828

a unincorporate') it is natural and quite neutral for him to use the pronoun 'him' (rather than 'him or them'). I therefore think that 'any person seeking to obtain' includes the local authorities.

'... by refusing ... to provide him with any of them ...'

b This phrase is complete in itself, the following words being alternative (starting with the word 'or'). If the Watsons had refused to take coloured children, they would have been refusing boarding-out facilities to the coloured children seeking (through the local authorities) to obtain and to use them. If they refused the local authority boarding-out facilities for their coloured children, they would be refusing to provide the local authorities with *some* of their boarding-out facilities ('any of them').

c I am, therefore, of opinion that the conduct to which the Watsons were incited by the appellant would have been unlawful in the terms of ss 1 and 2 of the 1968 Act, without straining them, but with the aid of the Interpretation Act 1889. Linguistic scrutiny, therefore, reinforces interpretation in accordance with the rule in *Heydon's Case*[1].

d   IV

I turn, finally, to consider other matters that were canvassed during the argument.

The examples in s 2(2)

I think that counsel for the appellant was justified in claiming that these on balance
e tell in favour of his client, all the facilities and services which are there exemplified being *to the public at large*. But I do not think much weight can be put on this sub-section. First giving examples merely, it is self-evidently not intended to be exhaustive. Secondly, it seems to be setting out some of the most easily envisagable and most derogatory forms of discrimination. Thirdly, in view of this and of the fact that the s 2(1) facilities and services are limited to those provided to the public
f or a section of the public, it is not surprising that the leading examples are those provided to the public at large. Fourthly, I have already pointed out the significance of the express inclusion of local authority facilities and services among the examples. Fifthly, accommodation in a boarding-house and facilities for education and recreation are not so very different in kind from the facilities and services which the Watsons provide for the children. In sum, there is nothing in s 2(2) which leads me to
g think that the conduct incited to is other than within the plain mischief of the Act and falls within the natural meaning of the words of ss 1(1) and 2(1).

Anomalies

Courts will try to construe an Act of Parliament in such a way as to avoid anomaly; since anomalies involve injustice—treating A and B differently in essentially comparable
h circumstances—and Parliament is to be presumed to intend justice: Maxwell on the Interpretation of Statutes[2].   The presumption against anomaly and injustice will have special force where it seems probable that Parliament has not envisaged the actual forensic situation: see *Rugby Joint Water Board v Foottit*[3].   Counsel for the appellant was able to point to a number of anomalies which would arise from the respondents' interpretation of the Act—the most stiking arising out of s 8(6),
j to which I have already referred. But construction to avoid anomaly is a secondary

1 (1584) 3 Co Rep 7a
2 12th Edn (1969), ch 10, pp 199 et seq
3 [1972] 1 All ER 1057 at 1077, [1973] AC 202 at 231

canon, subordinate to the 'mischief' rule and the 'golden' rule: see *Tzu-Tsai Cheng v Governor of Pentonville Prison*[1]. There are bound to be anomalous borderline cases in view of the hesitation of the legislature to carry its predominant policy into situations of a purely private character. No doubt the interpretation contended for on behalf of the appellant would minimise some of the anomalies (though at the cost of derogation from the paramount parliamentary purpose); but anomalies would still remain, even on the appellant's case. For example, on their case it would be lawful to discriminate as regards children in care whom the local authorities seek to board out; but it would be unlawful to discriminate in relation to the (presumably older) children in care whom the local authorities seek to place in lodgings (other than premises falling within s 7). Then, on the appellant's argument, a corporation sole (e g a bishop) can be a 'person seeking ...' within s 2(1), but not a corporation aggregate (e g a dean and chapter). Since anomalies are inherent in an Act of this sort, and since even the appellant's construction (in derogation of the paramount parliamentary purpose) would not avoid them, I do not think that the presumption against anomaly operates to prevent your Lordships from applying the major canons of construction.

The children when in the Watsons' household

It follows from the view I have already expressed that the children did not, on entering the Watsons' household, cease to be a section of the public, so that it would have been unlawful to have discriminated amongst the children within the household on the ground of colour—though what the appellant and Mr Taylor were inciting was a discrimination prior thereto, namely, at the entry of the children to the house: nor would the Watsons themselves have considered for a moment discriminating in this way amongst the children boarded out with them.

Adoption and private fostering

It was conceded on behalf of the board that discrimination in adoption would not be unlawful under the Race Relations Act. This seems to me to be unquestionable; an adoptive parent is, no more than a natural parent, as such concerned with the provision of goods, facilities or services to a section of the public, but rather to members of his legal family (i e to persons aggregated in their private roles: see *Charter's* case[2]).

It was conceded on behalf of the board that the Race Relations Act 1968 did not apply to children privately fostered under the Children Act 1958. Counsel for the appellant seized on the concession to emphasise the common features between 1948 Act children and 1958 Act children—in particular in relation to local authority responsibility and control. But your Lordships are not called on to say whether the board's concession was rightly made—some private fostering, e g with a view to adoption, is obviously outside the 1968 Act; and the board has in any event a wide discretion under s 15(4) of the 1968 Act. But no concession in point of law especially on a point not directly in question, could constrain your Lordships in the proper interpretation of the 1968 Act with regard to 1948 Act children.

I would dismiss the appeal.

LORD SALMON. My Lords, I have come to the conclusion, not without considerable doubt, that this appeal should be dismissed. All the relevant arguments have been so fully canvassed by your Lordships that I need add only a few observations of my own.

The appeal seems to me to turn on whether or not Mr and Mrs Watson were concerned with the provision to the 'public or a section of the public ... of any ...

---

1 [1973] 2 All ER at 219, [1973] AC at 957
2 [1973] 1 All ER at 527, [1973] AC at 901

a facilities or services' within the meaning of those words in s 2(1) of the Race Relations Act 1968. The difficulty lies in deciding whether that section excludes the provision of facilities or services to a section of the public within the private or domestic sphere, for example in a private household. As a rule no doubt it does, but after some hesitation I have come to the conclusion that it does not always do so; not, for example, in the special circumstances of the present case.

b I find it impossible, on the uncontradicted evidence, to hold that the Watsons' establishment was not a private household in which they treated the children whom they took in exactly as if those children had been members of their own family. This, of course, does not mean that the children in reality became members of the Watsons' family. A stay of three or four weeks is too transient to establish a relationship which is essentially of a much more permanent character. As a general rule a householder is not concerned in providing any facilities or services to the public, c or to a section of the public, in his own home. I cannot, however, accept that he may never be concerned in doing so. I recognise that it would be absurd to consider that the members of his family or his guests or servants are, in their respective capacities, 'the public or a section of the public' for the purposes of the Act. Section 2 does not touch the employment of any person for the purposes of a private household. Discrimination against such persons could, however, be prohibited by s 3 d were it not for the express exception contained in s 8(6) of the Act. A householder is entitled to choose which members of his family he will allow to live with him, whom he will adopt as a member of his family, whom he will employ and whom he will invite as a guest in his own home. There is nothing in the Act to prevent him discriminating between any of these on any ground he pleases. The Act, clearly, does not interfere with freedom of choice in these spheres. Were it to do so, it would e not help, but might well hinder race relations. Suppose A has a large number of acquaintances, black and white, and he gives a private party to which he invites only those who are white, or, for that matter, only those who are black, he would not be infringing the Act. He would be concerned in providing facilities only to his invited guests who cannot, in my view, sensibly be regarded as 'a section of the public'. f Suppose, however, that A throws his stately home open to the public and excludes those who are black, he would clearly be infringing the Act for, in such a case, he would be concerned with the provision of facilities or services to the public.

Children in care are undoubtedly a section of the public, unfortunately quite a large section, in dire need of special facilities and services which the Watsons are and have for so long been conscientiously concerned to provide. It is, I think, important to remember that this is not a case of foster parents who are prepared to foster g only such children as they may select; still less is it a case of fostering with a view to adoption. Such fostering would not, in my view, constitute the provision of facilities or services to any section of the public, but only to personally selected individuals. The Watsons, on the other hand, have for upwards of 20 years let it be known to the three local authorities concerned that, subject only to a limitation of numbers imposed by their available accommodation, their home is open to all h comers amongst children in care. They have in a very real sense been concerned with the provision of facilities and services to a section of the public in their own private household. This no doubt is an unusual situation. It may seem strange that any prospective foster parents, more selective, less humane, charitable and public spirited than the Watsons, might be entitled to say 'no black children', but that the Watsons, j because of their past generosity, would be precluded from saying so. This, however, would impose no hardship on the Watsons. They have courageously resisted the highly improper pressure and incitement to discriminate which they have suffered at the hands of the appellant. The last thing that the Watsons would willingly do is to discriminate against any child on the ground of his colour, race or ethnic or national origins; nor do I believe that it is in the least likely that anyone else who has acted as the Watsons have done would feel otherwise. There could, however, be nothing to prevent them from deciding to discontinue or curtail the provision of the facilities and services which they have been concerned to provide in the past. They could *a* not, however, lawfully discriminate between black and white children in taking such a decision. This is because they are and have for long past been concerned with the provision of facilities and services to a section of the public in their own private household. They therefore come within the sphere of s 2(1) and not, to my mind, within any of the express or implied exceptions to that section contained in any of *b* the other provisions of the Act.

I entertain no doubt at all but that the children sent by the local authorities to the Watsons were persons seeking, through the local authorities, to obtain or use facilities or services. Had the Watsons, on account of the appellant's behaviour, turned them away because of their colour, they would have been refusing to provide facilities and services to a section of the public for whom they were concerned *c* to supply such facilities and services.

I am by no means sure that local authorities are a section of the public. No doubt the members of any local authority are a section of the public but each local authority has a separate identity just as a company is a different entity from its corporators. Even if local authorities may be regarded as a section of the public and as seeking to obtain facilities or services for themselves, I doubt whether the *d* Watsons, if they refused to foster coloured children in the care of those local authorities, would be discriminating against them unless it could be shown that they were willing to foster coloured children in the care of other local authorities. It is, however, unnecessary to express a concluded view on this point because I am satisfied that the local authorities were seeking facilities and services on behalf of the children in their care. Accordingly, the appellant was inciting the Watsons to refuse facilities or services to any coloured child seeking such facilities or services through the local *e* authority which had him in care. And this, in the special circumstances of this case, is something which, in my view, the Watsons could not lawfully have done.

My Lords, for these reasons, I would dismiss the appeal.

Appeal dismissed.   *f*

Solicitors: *A E Hamlin & Co* (for the appellant); *Lawford & Co* (for the board).

Christine Ivamy Barrister.

a # Federal Steam Navigation Co Ltd and another v Department of Trade and Industry

HOUSE OF LORDS

LORD REID, LORD MORRIS OF BORTH-Y-GEST, LORD WILBERFORCE, LORD SIMON OF GLAISDALE

b AND LORD SALMON

1st, 4th, 5th, 6th FEBRUARY, 27th MARCH 1974

Shipping – Oil in navigable waters – Discharge of oil from ship into prohibited sea area – Offence – 'Owner or master' guilty of offence – Whether 'or' used in alternative and exclusionary sense – Whether owner and master may both be convicted of offence in respect of the
c *same discharge – Oil in Navigable Waters Act 1955, s 1(1) (as amended by the Oil in Navigable Waters Act 1963, s 3, Schs 1, 2).*

A British ship on the high seas discharged a mixture of oil and water into the sea in an area that was a prohibited sea area under the Oil in Navigable Waters Act 1955. The owner of the ship and the master were prosecuted and both were convicted of
d an offence under s 1(1)[a] of the 1955 Act. They appealed, contending that they could not both be charged with and convicted of the offence since s 1(1) provided that 'the owner or master' should be guilty of the offence.

Held – (Lord Reid and Lord Morris of Borth-y-Gest dissenting) – The appeal would be dismissed since the word 'or' in s 1(1) was used conjunctively and not in an alterna-
e tive and exclusionary sense. Accordingly the owner and the master could each be convicted of an offence (see p 110 *e* to *g*, p 111 *h*, p 112 *b f* and *h* and p 113 *d* and *h*, post).

Decision of the Court of Appeal sub nom *R v Federal Steam Navigation Co Ltd, R v Moran* [1973] 3 All ER 849 affirmed.

f ## Notes

For the discharge of certain oils into prohibited sea areas, see 35 Halsbury's Laws (3rd Edn) 841, para 1324.

For the Oil in Navigable Waters Act 1955, s 1, see 31 Halsbury's Statutes (3rd Edn) 616.

A new subsection was substituted for s 1(1) of the 1955 Act by the Oil in Navigable
g Waters Act 1971, s 1, which came into force on 1st March 1973.

Cases referred to in opinions

Attorney-General v Beauchamp [1920] 1 KB 650, 89 LJKB 219, 122 LT 527, 84 JP 41, 26 Cox CC 563, DC, 44 Digest (Repl) 323, *1575*.

Blakeley, The (1916) 234 Fed 959.

h *Brown & Co v T & J Harrison* (1927) 96 LJKB 1025, [1927] All ER Rep 195, sub nom *Brown & Co Ltd v Harrison, Hourani v Harrison* 137 LT 549, 17 Asp MLC 294, 32 Com Cas 305, CA; *affg* (1927) 43 TLR 394, 41 Digest (Repl) 313, *1189*.

Heydon's Case (1584) 3 Co Rep 7a, Moore KB 128, 76 ER 637, 21 Digest (Repl) 652, *1424*.

Morgan v Thomas (1882) 9 QBD 643, 51 LJQB 556, 47 LT 281, CA, 48 Digest (Repl) 423, *3714*.

j *Prim v Smith* (1888) 20 QBD 643, 57 LJQB 336, 58 LT 606, CA, 16 Digest (Repl) 500, *3254*.

R v Oakes [1959] 2 All ER 92, [1959] 2 QB 350, [1959] 2 WLR 694, 123 JP 290, 43 Cr App Rep 114, CCA, Digest (Cont Vol A) 413, *7655a*.

---

a Section 1(1), as amended, is set out at p 99 *e*, post

F

River Wear Comrs, The v Adamson (1877) 2 App Cas 743, [1874-80] All ER Rep 1, 47
LJQB 193, 37 LT 543, 42 JP 244, 3 Asp MLC 521, HL; *affg* (1876) 1 QBD 546, CA,
42 Digest (Repl) 1135, 9450.
Sutherland Publishing Co Ltd v Caxton Publishing Co Ltd [1937] 4 All ER 405, [1938] Ch
174, CA; *affd* [1938] 4 All ER 389, [1939] AC 178, 108 LJCh 5, 160 LT 17, HL, 13
Digest (Repl) 128, 680.

Appeal
On 25th October 1972 at the Central Criminal Court before his Honour Judge King-
Hamilton QC, on a prosecution brought by the respondents, the Department of
Trade and Industry, on behalf of the Crown, the appellants, the Federal Steam
Navigation Co Ltd, the owner of the motor vessel Huntingdon, and Derek Ernest
Moran, the master of the vessel, were charged on an indictment containing four
counts. Count 2 charged the first appellant with being the owner of a British ship
registered in the United Kingdom from which a mixture containing fuel oil was
discharged into a prohibited sea area, contrary to s 1(1) of the Oil in Navigable Waters
Act 1955. Count 4 charged the second appellant with being the master of a British
ship registered in the United Kingdom from which a mixture containing fuel oil was
discharged into a prohibited sea area, contrary to s 1(1) of the 1955 Act. Both counts
related to the same discharge. Counts 1 and 3 charged the appellants respectively with
similar offences. On arraignment counsel for the appellants submitted that, under
s 1(1), the Crown had to elect whether to prosecute the first or the second appellant
and could not prosecute both. That submission was rejected by the judge and, on
26th October, the appellants pleaded guilty to counts 2 and 4. Counts 1 and 3 were
not proceeded with. The first appellant was fined £2,500 and the second appellant
£250. They appealed against conviction with leave of the judge. On 9th July 1973
the Court of Appeal, Criminal Division[1] (Lawton, James LJJ and Mocatta J) dismissed the appeal but certified that the following point of law of general public
importance was involved in the decision:

'Whether both the owner and master of a ship to which section 1(1) of the
Oil in Navigable Waters Act 1955 (as amended) applies or, alternatively, only
one or other of them can be convicted of an offence under that subsection in
respect of one and the same discharge of oil or a mixture containing oil.'

The court refused leave to appeal but on 15th November 1973 the appeal committee
of the House of Lords gave leave. The facts are set out in the opinion of Lord Reid.

J G Le Quesne QC and *J D W Hayman* for the appellants.
Sir Elwyn Jones QC and *Robin Auld* for the respondents.

Their Lordships took time for consideration.

27th March. The following judgments were delivered.

LORD REID. My Lords, in August 1970 the Huntingdon, a British ship registered
in the United Kingdom, while on a voyage from Port Arthur in Quebec to New York
discharged a quantity of a mixture of oil and water into the sea at a point off Nova
Scotia.
In 1955 the United Kingdom accepted an International Convention for the Prevention of Pollution of the Sea by Oil[2]. It created certain prohibited zones. The point
of this discharge was within such a zone. It prohibited discharge in terms which

---

1   [1973] 3 All ER 849, [1973] 1 WLR 1373
2   Cmd 9197

a admittedly include the present case and provided that any contravention should be an offence punishable under the laws of the territory in which the ship is registered. Then it provided by art X:

b
'(1) Any Contracting Government may furnish to the Contracting Government in the territory of which a ship is registered particulars in writing of evidence that any provision of the Convention has been contravened in respect of that ship, wheresoever the alleged contravention may have taken place. If it is practicable to do so, the competent authorities of the former Government shall notify the master of the ship of the alleged contravention.

c
'(2) Upon receiving such particulars the latter Government shall investigate the matter, and may request the former Government to furnish further or better particulars of the alleged contravention. If the Government in the territory of which the ship is registered is satisfied that sufficient evidence is available in the form required by law to enable proceedings against the owner or master of the ship to be taken in respect of the alleged contravention, it shall cause such proceedings to be taken as soon as possible, and shall inform the other Contracting Government and the Bureau of the result of such proceedings.'

d Thereafter there was passed the Oil in Navigable Waters Act 1955. This Act was passed to give effect to the convention and also to cover all cases of discharge into any navigable waters within the territory of the United Kingdom. The relevant part of s 1, as amended by the Oil in Navigable Waters Act 1963, provides:

e
'(1) If any oil to which this section applies is discharged from a British ship registered in the United Kingdom into a part of the sea which is a prohibited sea area, or if any mixture containing not less than one hundred parts of oil to which this section applies in a million parts of the mixture is discharged from such a ship into such a part of the sea, the owner or master of the ship shall, subject to the provisions of this Act, be guilty of an offence under this section.'

f The owners and master of the Huntingdon were each charged with an offence against s 1(1). Despite objection both were committed for trial. At the trial further objections were taken that since the Act provides that the 'owner or master' shall be guilty of an offence, both could not be found guilty. These objections were overruled and both were found guilty. The Court of Appeal[1] upheld the convictions and your Lordships now have to decide the true construction of s 1(1) of the 1955 Act.

g The respondents contend that the provision should be read as if it had provided that 'the owner and master of the ship shall . . . each be guilty of an offence'. The appellants contend that the words of the statute are perfectly plain and there is no sufficient reason for putting other words in their place.

There are many cases where an ordinary English word or phrase is capable of having more than one meaning, either in ordinary or technical usage. Then, on well recognised principles of construction it is right, in circumstances which I need not stop
h to reformulate, to reject the more natural meaning and adopt a secondary meaning of that word or phrase. But that would not help the respondents. 'Or' can never mean 'and'. The dictionaries have been searched in vain for any trace of any usage by which 'or' has a conjunctive meaning. It is true that in some authorities it has been stated that 'or' can be held or construed to mean 'and'. In my judgment that is quite wrong.

j There is, however, another principle of construction. In very limited classes of circumstances, which I must later examine, it has been held proper to strike out a word from a statute or other writing and to substitute one or more other words for the word struck out. That is something much more drastic than giving a secondary meaning to a word as a matter of construction.

1 [1973] 3 All ER 849, [1973] 1 WLR 1373

In my judgment the question here is whether there is anything in the Act or in surrounding circumstances which it is permissible to consider, which could justify striking out the word 'or' and substituting the words 'and . . . each'. It would be necessary to put in the word each because otherwise 'owner and master' would suggest a joint offence—a result for which no one contends.

There is a multitude of cases where courts have considered whether it is proper to substitute one word for another, and in particular whether it is proper to substitute 'and' for 'or' or vice versa. There may be some difference between commercial or informal writings, on the one hand, and deeds and statutes on the other hand. One is entitled to expect greater skill in drafting deeds and statutes. A great number of different words have been used in stating the criteria, and I do not think that it would be useful or indeed possible to examine them all.

Cases where it has properly been held that a word can be struck out of a deed or statute and another substituted can as far as I am aware be grouped under three heads: where without such substitution the provision is unintelligible or absurd or totally unreasonable; where it is unworkable; and where it is totally irreconcilable with the plain intention shewn by the rest of the deed or statute. I do not say that in all such cases it is proper to strike out a word and substitute another. What I do say is that I cannot discover or recall any case outside these three classes where such substitution would be permissible.

In this Act the phrase 'owner or master' is used in six sections. In ss 4, 10 and 13 there can be no doubt that the word 'or' is intended. In ss 1 and 3 it is argued for the respondents that 'or' was not intended and that 'and' should be substituted for it. In s 5(5) the wording is the same as in ss 1 and 3 but even if the respondents were right about these sections it would not follow that a similar substitution should be made in s 5(5). This subsection deals with offences to be created by regulations made under the section. Some of the matters to be covered by these regulations have nothing to do with the master or with the conduct of the ship while at sea and it cannot have been intended to make the master responsible for such matters. On the other hand, there are matters where it would be appropriate to hold the master responsible. So if the respondents are right about ss 1 and 3 the amendment here would have to be to add the words 'or both' so as to make the provision read: 'the owner or master of the ship or both as the case may be' shall be guilty of an offence. So we would have the curious result that in three sections the word 'or' must stand unaltered, in two sections it must be altered in one way and in another section it must be altered in a different way. If the appellants are right there is no need to make any alteration in any of these sections.

Section 1 is taken from the convention[1] to which I have already referred. There in art X which I have quoted the phrase used is 'owner or master' and it was not argued that the convention was wrongly drafted. Section 3 is taken from the Oil in Navigable Waters Act 1922. There again the phrase used is 'owner or master'. The respondents argue that the 1922 Act was wrongly drafted. But there again the phrase is used several times in that Act and in most cases the use of the disjunctive 'or' is plainly correct.

So one thing at least is clear. The use of the disjunctive 'or' in s 1 of the 1955 Act was not a clerical error. The draftsman not unnaturally took the phrase which he found in the convention. He might have altered it. Perhaps it would have been better if he had altered it. But that is not a good reason for the court refusing to accept the Act as it stands.

There is nothing unintelligible or absurd or even unreasonable in enacting that each contravention shall give rise to one offence and only one, but that the prosecution shall have a choice as to who is to be prosecuted. This may be a novelty in English law but novelties are not always unreasonable. The reason why it is necessary to

1 The International Convention for the Prevention of Pollution of the Sea by Oil, 1954 (Cmd 9197)

a have a choice is plain.   No one can be prosecuted unless our courts have jurisdiction over him and neither the convention nor the 1955 Act creates any fresh ground of jurisdiction.   There can be cases when a ship can be registered in the United Kingdom although the owner has neither residence nor a place of business here.   In such cases the owner could not be prosecuted but there would be jurisdiction against the master if found in this country.   So it was proper to have an alternative.   In the other cases

b covered by the Act, discharge from a place on land or discharge in the course of transfer of oil from or to a vessel, there was no need for an alternative.   In the first of these the occupier of the place is made responsible however guiltless he might be and there is no provision for prosecuting the persons actually responsible.   And in the second the person in charge is made responsible.

It was, however, strenuously argued that to give such a choice to the prosecution was not only novel but unworkable under our English system.   Here I think that the

c Court of Appeal[1] have been misled by some ill-advised concessions made by counsel for the present appellants—concessions withdrawn in this House.   There is no difficulty about who is to make the choice.   Section 12 sets out those who may prosecute and if a choice has to be made it must be made at an early stage: if only one can be convicted then two must not be put in jeopardy at the same time.   I think that the

d appellants were right in objecting to both being committed for trial and they were certainly right in objecting to both being charged in the same indictment.   The choice is not final because if proceedings against one miscarry and he is not convicted, then the other can be prosecuted.   But, looking to the nature of the statutory defence in s 4, it is very unlikely that if one is acquitted the other can be convicted.

There would be little to be gained by prosecuting both owner and master.   If the

e offence warrants a large fine it would have to be imposed on the owner because on ordinary principles any fine imposed on the master would have to be related to his ability to pay it.

So it certainly cannot be said that the general intention or policy of the Act, which as regards s 1 is to give effect to the convention, requires that both shall be liable to prosecution.   And I am by no means sure that if the draftsman had given more

f thought to the matter he would have done other than he did.   In my judgment to alter the words of the Act in the way the argument for the respondents requires would go very much farther than would be warranted by any exacting principle or authority and is quite unnecessary.

I would therefore allow this appeal.

g **LORD MORRIS OF BORTH-Y-GEST.**   My Lords, on 13th August 1970 the motor vessel Huntingdon, a British ship registered in the United Kingdom, was on a voyage from Port Arthur in the Province of Quebec to New York.   When at a point some 85 miles from the south-east coast of Nova Scotia a mixture containing fuel oil was discharged from the ship into the sea.   The ship was owned by the Federal Steam Navigation Co Ltd.   The master was Mr Derek Ernest Moran.

h It is provided by s 1(1) of the Oil in Navigable Waters Act 1955 (as amended by the Oil in Navigable Waters Act 1963) as follows:

'If any oil to which this section applies is discharged from a British ship registered in the United Kingdom into a part of the sea which is a prohibited sea area, or if a mixture containing not less than one hundred parts of oil to which this section applies in a million parts of the mixture is discharged from such a ship

j into such a part of the sea, the owner or master of the ship shall, subject to the provisions of this Act, be guilty of an offence under this section.'

The section applied (see sub-s (2)) inter alia to fuel oil.   The part of the sea into which the mixture containing fuel oil was discharged from the Huntingdon was in

1   [1973] 3 All ER 849, [1973] 1 WLR 1373

fact a prohibited sea area (see s 3 of the 1955 Act). The statutory words therefore
became applicable, viz the words—'the owner or master of the ship shall, subject to *a*
the provisions of this Act, be guilty of an offence under this section.' The reference
to the conditioning effect of the provisions of the Act directed attention, inter alia,
to the provisions of s 4 of the Act which enabled certain special defences to be proved.

Section 3 of the Act relates to what may be called United Kingdom waters and
sub-s (1) provides as follows: *b*

'If any oil or mixture containing oil is discharged into waters to which this
section applies from any vessel, or from any place on land, or from any apparatus
used for transferring oil from or to any vessel (whether to or from a place on
land or to or from another vessel), then subject to the provisions of this Act—
(a) if the discharge is from a vessel, the owner or master of the vessel, or (b) if the
discharge is from a place on land, the occupier of that place, or (c) if the discharge *c*
is from apparatus used for transferring oil from or to a vessel, the person in charge
of the apparatus, shall be guilty of an offence under this section.'

By s 5 of the Act power is given to make regulations requiring British ships registered
in the United Kingdom to be fitted with certain equipment for the purpose of preventing or reducing discharges of oil and mixtures containing oil into the sea. By sub-s (5) *d*
of that section it is provided as follows:

'If, in the case of any ship, the provisions of any regulations under this section
which apply to that ship are contravened, the owner or master of the ship shall
be guilty of an offence under this section.'

The 1955 Act was an Act— *e*

'to enable effect to be given to the International Convention for the Prevention
of Pollution of the Sea by Oil, 1954[1], and otherwise to make new provision for
preventing the pollution of navigable waters by oil.'

After the discharge from the Huntingdon on 13th August 1970 had been observed
(as it was from a patrol aircraft of the Canadian armed services) the Canadian govern- *f*
ment (a contracting government to the convention) furnished particulars to the
United Kingdom government (also a contracting government). Article X of the
convention is in the following terms:

'(1) Any Contracting Government may furnish to the Contracting Government
in the territory of which a ship is registered particulars in writing of evidence *g*
that any provision of the Convention has been contravened in respect of that
ship, wheresoever the alleged contravention may have taken place. If it is
practicable to do so, the competent authorities of the former Government shall
notify the master of the ship of the alleged contravention.
'(2) Upon receiving such particulars the latter Government shall investigate
the matter, and may request the former Government to furnish further or better *h*
particulars of the alleged contravention. If the Government in the territory of
which the ship is registered is satisfied that sufficient evidence is available in
the form required by law to enable proceedings against the owner or master of
the ship to be taken in respect of the alleged contravention, it shall cause such
proceedings to be taken as soon as possible, and shall inform the other
Contracting Government and the Bureau of the result of such proceedings.' *j*

For some reason or other the investigation seems to have taken much time, but
eventually proceedings were taken. By s 12 of the Act certain proceedings can only
be brought by persons designated or by or with the consent of the Attorney-General.

1 Cmd 9197

a   The present proceedings could only be brought by or with the consent of the Attorney-General or by the appropriate Minister or a person authorised by any general or special directions of the Minister. The present proceedings were presumably brought either by the Minister of Trade and Industry or by someone authorised by him.

b   The passage of time made summary proceedings impossible and after committal an indictment was preferred charging the owners (who were first named) and the master with offences under s 1(1) of the Act. There were four counts: the first and second were against the owners: the third and fourth against the master. The first and third alleged a discharge of fuel oil: the second and fourth alleged a discharge of a mixture containing fuel oil. Effectively consideration was given to the second and fourth counts (i e those which alleged that the discharge was of a mixture).

c   When the case came on at the Central Criminal Court on 25th October 1972 counsel (who appeared both for the owners and also for the master) made a submission to the learned judge (before arraignment) that the proceedings ought only at that stage to continue against one of the accused and that it was then for the prosecution to elect as between the two. The submission was that if a conviction followed of the one against whom the prosecution elected in the first place to proceed then no conviction of the other would be possible. In substance the submission was that only d   one or the other of the two accused could ever be convicted but not both. The ruling of the learned judge was that in s 1(1) of the Act the word 'or' had to be construed in a conjunctive sense and that the indictment had been properly framed.

The moment then came for the charges to be put to the accused. To the second count against the owners counsel put in a plea in writing by the company—a plea of guilty. On behalf of his other client (Captain Moran) counsel then formally moved e   (before the charges against Captain Moran were put to him) that the indictment should be quashed insofar as it related to Captain Moran. The motion was based on (but without the need for a repetition of) the submissions previously made. The contention was that 'there being a conviction recorded against the company, as a matter of law Captain Moran should not be convicted'. The learned judge rejected the motion. Captain Moran then pleaded guilty to the fourth count. As counts 1 and 2 f   were alternative, and as counts 3 and 4 were likewise alternative, the pleas of guilty by the company and by Captain Moran to pleas 2 and 4 respectively made it unnecessary to proceed on counts 1 and 3 in respect of which there were pleas of not guilty. In pleading guilty to count 4, Captain Moran, through his counsel, preserved his right to appeal on the points of law raised.

After the facts had been fully outlined by counsel for the prosecution and after g   circumstances in mitigation (which seem mainly to have been referable to the events on the ship and the circumstances of the discharge) had been explained by counsel for the defence the learned judge imposed a fine of £2,500 on the company and a fine of £250 on Captain Moran and ordered that the taxed costs of the prosecution be paid by the defendants jointly and severally.

The defendants appealed to the Court of Appeal[1] (Lawton, James LJJ and Mocatta h   J). The appeals were dismissed. The court certified that a point of law of general public importance was involved—i e whether both owner and master or, alternatively, only one or other of them could be convicted in respect of one and the same discharge.

In giving the judgment of the Court of Appeal Lawton LJ while recognising that in ordinary contexts the word 'or' is to be read disjunctively pointed to some of the 'odd' or 'absurd' results that would follow if in s 1 it were so to be read. The i   court concluded that the intention of Parliament (discernible from s 1(1) itself) was that the word was to be read conjunctively. In argument it was conceded in the Court of Appeal that both owner and master were liable to prosecution. That, the court concluded, could only be on the basis that Parliament made both owner and master responsible for the discharge of oil or a mixture: it could not have been the intention

---

1   [1973] 3 All ER 849, [1973] 1 WLR 1373

of Parliament that one of the two so responsible should be freed from responsibility   *a*
immediately a conviction was recorded against the other.

    There are many cases which illustrate that the words 'or' and 'and' often appear
in a masquerading role. On occasion one of the two words might be used in circumstances which suggest that it must have been used by mistake: see *Morgan v Thomas*[1]
per Jessel MR.   On occasion one of the two words might be used in circumstances
which suggest that had there been further thought it would have been clear that the   *b*
other word would better express intention.

    In *The River Wear Commissioners v Adamson*[2] a question arose as to the construction
and effect of an Act of Parliament. In his speech Lord Blackburn said:

    'As long ago as *Heydon's Case*[3] Lord *Coke* says that it was resolved "that for the
    sure and true interpretation of all statutes in general (be they penal or beneficial,
    restrictive or enlarging of the Common Law) four things are to be discerned and   *c*
    considered; 1st. What was the Common Law before the Act? 2nd. What was
    the mischief and effect for which the Common Law did not provide? 3rd. What
    remedy the Parliament hath resolved and appointed to cure the disease of the
    Commonwealth? And 4th.   The true reason of the remedy;   and then the
    office of all the Judges is always to make such construction as shall suppress the
    mischief and advance the remedy." But it is to be borne in mind that the office   *d*
    of the Judges is not to legislate, but to declare the expressed intention of the
    Legislature, even if that intention appears to the Court injudicious; and I believe
    that it is not disputed that what Lord *Wensleydale* used to call the golden rule is
    right, viz., that we are to take the whole statute together, and construe it all to-
    gether, giving the words their ordinary signification, unless when so applied
    they produce an inconsistency, or an absurdity or inconvenience so great as to   *e*
    convince the Court that the intention could not have been to use them in their
    ordinary signification, and to justify the Court in putting on them some other
    signification, which, though less proper, is one which the Court thinks the words
    will bear.'

    In *Prim v Smith*[4] a question arose as to the interpretation of a section of an Act of   *f*
Parliament. Lopes LJ said:

    'We are asked to read "or" as if it were "and". No doubt there are cases where
    this should be done, but they are cases where the natural meaning would give
    rise to an interpretation unreasonable, inconsistent or unjust.'

He held that in the particular case no such result followed from reading the word   *g*
'or' in its natural sense.

    In *Brown & Co v T & J Harrison*[5] the Court of Appeal held that in art IV, r 2(q) of
the Schedule to the Carriage of Goods by Sea Act 1924 the word 'or' should be read
as 'and'. Atkin LJ said:

    'Again, I disagree with the learned Judge in his view that the word "or" can
    never have a conjunctive sense. I think it quite commonly and grammatically   *h*
    can have a conjunctive sense. It is generally disjunctive, but it may be plain from
    the collocation of the words that it is meant in a conjunctive sense, and certainly
    where the use of the word as a disjunctive leads to repugnance or absurdity it is
    quite plain within the ordinary principles of construction adopted by the Court
    to give the word a conjunctive use. Here it is quite plain that the use of the   *j*
    word as a disjunctive leads to an absurdity . . .'

1   (1882) 9 QBD 643 at 645, 646
2   (1877) 2 App Cas 743 at 764, 765, [1874-80] All ER Rep 1 at 12
3   (1584) 3 Co Rep 7a
4   (1888) 2 QB 643 at 645
5   (1927) 96 LJKB 1025 at 1034, [1927] All ER Rep 195 at 203, 204

a   In *R v Oakes*[1] it was held that the word 'and' in s 7 of the Official Secrets Act 1920 should be read as 'or'. Lord Parker CJ said[2]:

> 'It seems to this court that, where the literal reading of a statute, and a penal statute, produces an intelligible result, clearly there is no ground for reading in words or changing words according to what may be the supposed intention of Parliament. Here, however, we venture to think that the result is unintelligible.
> *b*   LORD COLERIDGE, J., in *A.-G. v. Beauchamp*[3] put it quite shortly in these words: "Inquestionably, when one is construing a penal statute, the first thing is to construe it according to the ordinary rules of grammar, and if a construction which satisfies those rules makes the enactment intelligible, and especially if it carries out the obvious intention of the legislature as gathered from a general perusal of the whole statute, that grammatical construction ought not to be
> *c*   departed from." '

Lord Parker CJ went on to hold that the literal construction of s 7 produced an unintelligible result.

The problem which this appeal raises is one of considerable difficulty. In considering it my mind has wavered. The offence created by s 1 of the Act is of a very special
d nature. Most offences in our criminal law are defined by relation to what a person does. Under s 1 of this Act guilt of an offence results from the occurrence of an event. If oil or a mixture containing oil is discharged from a ship then, subject only to certain special defences (see s 4) guilt in a person or persons arises. Guilt may result without any question of mens rea. If the case of the owner of the ship is considered then the section says that, subject to the provisions of the Act, he 'shall' be guilty. If the case
e of the master of the ship is considered then he, subject to the provisions of the Act, 'shall' be guilty. So that whichever one in turn is considered he is guilty of an offence under s 1. Does this have the result that they are both guilty? Yet can they both be guilty when the section says that 'the owner or master' shall be guilty?

In s 12 of the Act there are provisions relating to the initiation of proceedings. In respect of any offence under s 1 no proceedings can be brought except by or with
f the consent of the Attorney-General or by the appropriate Minister or a person authorised by any general or special directions of the Minister. It clearly appears, therefore, that the draftsman had well in mind the distinction between being guilty of an offence and the initiation of proceedings. Had it been decided to enact that as between two persons in each one of whom guilt could at least alternatively have been shown to rest only one was to be selected as the subject of proceedings it would have
g been possible to enact that proceedings could only be brought against one. That was not done. The initiation of proceedings against both owner and master is not prohibited. Furthermore, though there are the elusive words 'owner or master . . . shall . . . be guilty' there is no express provision enacting that only one shall be convicted. The question is raised whether that is implicit in or results from the use of the words 'owner or master'.

h   It can properly be inferred that Parliament intended not only to give effect to the international convention[4] but furthermore to make new provision for preventing pollution. Does this indicate that with a realisation of the harm caused by pollution of the sea and with a view to preventing it Parliament intended that enforcement should be by a widely drawn net? Did Parliament intend that the owner as well as the master should be guilty of an offence, but wished to ensure that if one of them
j was not amenable to the jurisdiction the absence of that one would not be a bar to the conviction of the other?

---

1   [1959] 2 All ER 92, [1959] 2 QB 350
2   [1959] 2 All ER at 94, [1959] 2 QB at 354, 355
3   [1920] 1 KB 650 at 655
4   The International Convention for the Prevention of Pollution of the Sea by Oil, 1954 (Cmd 9197)

It is in many situations and circumstances desirable that certain criminal proceedings should only be commenced after obtaining some consent such as that of the
Attorney-General. It may be unusual to give a choice to the prosecution to select
the person to be prosecuted as between two people, in each of whom, if each is separately considered, guilt can be shown to rest. Did Parliament intend that in regard to
one of two such persons the prosecution would have to make a choice? Is that the
inherent result of what Parliament has enacted? If the prosecution must decide
against whom to proceed no special guidance is given as to how to select.

From a procedural point of view the present case illustrates certain problems
which may arise. In the Court of Appeal[1] it was conceded, as is stated in the judgment, that there was no impediment in law to the starting by the Department of
Trade and Industry of a prosecution against both the owner and the master. In
argument in this House an alternative submission was developed to the effect that
the department or the Minister was wrong in so starting the proceedings and that
it would have been possible by some appropriate proceedings at an early stage to
compel the department or the Minister to elect as between the owner and the
master and to make only one of them a defendant. As a variant of this submission it
was suggested that at the committal stage there was error in allowing the case to go
forward against more than one.

The procedural position that was created at the hearing of the case at the Central
Criminal Court was at least unusual. Of course it could have been avoided had the
prosecution only been initiated against one party. But as matters proceeded the
moment came when it was suggested that the prosecution had to make an election
and that the result of the election would be or could be that an accused person, in
whom, if separately considered, guilt rested, was to be absolved. It is not usually
the function of the prosecution to make such a decision. Equally it is not usually
within the power of two accused persons to arrange between themselves that one
only will be convicted and that the other must be exonerated. That would be the
result if a plea of guilty by one must have the consequence that proceedings against
the other must abate. Again, of course, this situation could be avoided if a prosecution
were only initiated against one.

If, however, both owner and master were before the trial court and both pleaded
not guilty, difficulties would result if the trial proceeded against both. For present
purposes I assume that if one of the special defences denoted in s 4 were proved it
would avail in favour of both accused. If a trial proceeded against both and if the
prosecution gave evidence in regard to all the facts which it would be for them to
prove, the jury would have to be told that if they were fully satisfied as to these and
if they did not consider that there was proof of any special defence there could be a
conviction but that they could convict one but one only of the two accused. But that
would be to entrust a jury with a duty of selection which surely is not and ought not
ever to be any part of their function. This I think shows that unless both owner and
master can be convicted it would not be right to allow a trial against them both to
continue. The prosecution would have to decide to proceed only against one while
reserving the right, if the prosecution failed, to proceed against the other.

It was submitted that a consideration of the provisions of s 3(1) gave support to the
view that the words 'owner or master' must be read disjunctively. Under (b) guilt
rests in one person only, i e the occupier. Under (c) guilt rests in one person only, i e
the person in charge of the apparatus. Why—under (a) should guilt rest in two persons?
But s 3(1) follows, as does s 5(5), on the words in s 1(1) and if under s 1(1) there could
be guilt in both owner and master, so should there be under the other sections. It
has also to be remembered that there will be no difficulty in bringing 'the occupier of
the place' before the court and similarly no difficulty in respect of 'the person in charge

1   [1973] 3 All ER 849, [1973] 1 WLR 1373

a   of the apparatus' while there may be difficulty in bringing one or other of the master and the owner. The phrase 'owner or master' may therefore have been used to make it clear that while each was guilty there would be no bar to a prosecution of one or the other. Therefore, I do not think that a consideration of s 3(1) gives positive assistance in reaching a conclusion.

b   It was contended that the intention of Parliament was that the imposition of a fine on a master could be or should be the means of penalising the owner and reliance was placed on the provisions of s 13(1). A reference to that subsection does not bear out that contention. If a fine is imposed on a master and is unpaid the power in the court to direct a levy by distress or poinding and sale of the vessel may be quite unavailing if it is no longer possible for the vessel to be the subject of any such order. The penalty imposed on a master (which must only be the penalty which the court considers to be appropriate in his case) will remain. Accordingly, I do not think that a consideration

c   of the question of penalties much assists in reaching a conclusion, though there is some force in the contention that if both owner and master are liable to be convicted there could be the risk of a double penalty in respect of the one event.

In my view, the present problem must be solved by considering the meaning in their context of the words which Parliament has used. It might have been expected that there would have been some judicial consideration of some words comparable

d   to the words 'the owner or master of the ship shall . . . be guilty of an offence' but rather surprisingly the researches of counsel have not found any closely relevant authority.   I do not propose to enlarge the enquiry by considering the meanings of other sections in other Acts of Parliament, but it is relevant to note that the words 'master or owner' or 'owner or master' often appear in the Merchant Shipping Act

e   1894. By way of illustration s 113(2) provides as follows:

'If a master of a ship carries any seaman to sea without entering into an agreement with him in accordance with this Act, the master in the case of a foreign going ship, and the master or owner in the case of a home trade ship, shall for each offence be liable to a fine not exceeding five pounds.'

f   Section 16 contains a provision in different form as follows:

'If the master or owner of a ship uses or attempts to use for her navigation a certificate of registry not legally granted in respect of the ship, he shall, in respect of each offence, be guilty of a misdemeanor, and the ship shall be subject to forfeiture under this Act.'

g   Section 200 refers to regulations respecting medicines and anti-scorbutics and sub-s (4) provides as follows:

'If any requirement of this section with respect to the provision of medicines, medical stores, book of instruction, or anti-scorbutics is not complied with in the

h   case of any ship, the owner or master of that ship shall, for each offence, be liable to a fine not exceeding twenty pounds, unless he can prove that the non-compliance was not caused through his inattention, neglect, or wilful default.'

A different provision in s 58 is to be noted:

i   'Where any person is beneficially interested, otherwise than by way of mortgage, in any ship or share in a ship registered in the name of some other person as owner, the person so interested shall, as well as the registered owner, be subject to all pecuniary penalties imposed by this or any other Act on the owners of ships or shares therein, so nevertheless that proceedings may be taken for the enforecment of any such penalties against both or either of the aforesaid parties, with or without joining the other of them.'

In s 281, sub-ss (1) and (2) are as follows:

a

'(1) The owner or master of every passenger steamer required to have a passenger steamer's certificate shall forthwith on the receipt of the certificate by him or his agent cause one of the duplicates to be put up in some conspicuous place on board the steamer, so as to be legible to all persons on board, and to be kept so put up and legible while the certificate remains in force, and the steamer is in use.

b

'(2) If the owner or master fails without reasonable cause to comply with this section, he shall for each offence be liable to a fine not exceeding ten pounds.'

Section 432 provides as follows:

'(1) Every British sea-going steamship if employed to carry passengers, shall have her compasses properly adjusted from time to time; and every British sea-going steamship not used wholly as a tug shall be provided with a hose capable of being connected with the engines of the ship, and adapted for extinguishing fire in any part of the ship.

c

'(2) If any such British sea-going steamship plies or goes to sea from any port in the United Kingdom and any requirement of this section is not complied with, then for each matter in which default is made, the owner (if in fault) shall be liable to a fine not exceeding one hundred pounds, and the master (if in fault) shall be liable to a fine not exceeding fifty pounds.'

d

I note (while indicating no view as to meaning) that in regard to Part III of the Act it is provided by s 359(1) as follows:

'In the absence of any agreement to the contrary, the owner of a ship shall be the person ultimately responsible as between himself and the other persons by this Part of this Act made liable in respect of any default in complying with any requirement thereof.'

e

It is also to be noted that some sections of the Act use the words 'if any person'. In s 289 (sub-s (4)), it is provided:

f

'If any requirement of this section is not complied with in the case of any emigrant ship, the owner charterer or master of the ship or any of them shall for each offence be liable to a fine not exceeding one hundred pounds.'

In s 1(1) of the Oil in Navigable Waters Act 1922 the wording was as follows:

g

'If any oil is discharged, or allowed to escape whether directly or indirectly, into any waters to which this Act applies from any vessel or from any place on land or from any apparatus used for the purpose of transferring oil from or to any vessel to or from any other vessel (whether a vessel to which this Act applies or not) or to or from any place, the owner or master of the vessel, from which the oil is discharged or allowed to escape, the occupier of the land, or the person having charge of the apparatus, as the case may be, shall be guilty of an offence and shall, in respect of each such offence, be liable on summary conviction to a fine not exceeding one hundred pounds:'

h

There followed a proviso in these terms:

j

'Provided that it shall be a good defence to proceedings for an offence under this section to prove—(a) if the proceedings are against the owner or master of a vessel, that the escape of the oil was due to, or that it was necessary to discharge the oil by reason of, the vessel being in collision or the happening to the vessel of some damage or accident, and also, if the proceedings are in respect of an escape of oil, that all reasonable means were taken by the master to prevent the a   escape; and (b) if the proceedings are against any other person and are in respect of an escape of oil, that all reasonable means were taken by that person to prevent the escape.'

The Merchant Shipping (Safety and Load Line Conventions) Act 1932 was passed to give effect to an international convention, and there are provisions to the effect that for contraventions the 'owner or master' of a ship shall be liable to be fined.

b   In a different Act, the Rivers (Prevention of Pollution) Act 1951, the first part of sub-s (8) of s 2 is as follows:

'Where an offence punishable under this section which has been committed by a body corporate is proved to have been committed with the consent or connivance of or to be attributable to any neglect on the part of any director, manager,
c   secretary or other similar officer of the body corporate, or any person purporting to act in any such capacity, he as well as the body corporate shall be deemed to be guilty of that offence and shall be liable to be proceeded against and punished accordingly . . .'

In the Merchant Shipping Act 1964, s 5(2) provides as follows:

d   'If any ship proceeds, or attempts to proceed, to sea in contravention of this section the owner or master of the ship shall be liable to a fine not exceeding one hundred pounds.'

And s 7(1) provides as follows:

e   'If the cargo ship construction and survey rules are contravened in any respect in relation to a ship, the owner or master of the ship shall be liable on conviction on indictment to a fine not exceeding five hundred pounds, or on summary conviction to a fine not exceeding one hundred pounds.'

The Oil in Navigable Waters Act 1955 has an interpretation section, i e s 22, and it is relevant to note that by s 22(6) it is provided:

f   'Subject to the preceding subsections, expressions used in this Act and in the Merchant Shipping Act, 1894, have the same meanings in this Act as in that Act.'

To that extent there is a link between the two Acts.

I refer to the above provisions (and references could very considerably be extended) solely to illustrate some of the variations of forms of words that have been used, but
g   my decision in this case must relate only to the sections now calling for interpretation. I have rehearsed a number of considerations which are relevant and I have referred to some problems that may arise in practice. But I return to the words 'owner or master'. The word 'or' denotes an alternative. The phrase 'owner or master' suggests one or the other. The conception of 'owner or master' is different from the conception of 'owner and master'. In the context of the three sections I am not prepared to say
h   that to read 'or' as having its ordinary and natural and perfectly intelligible meaning leads either to repugnancy or absurdity or inconsistency. I cannot say that there will be either unreasonable or inconvenient or unjust results if the word 'or' is given its normal meaning and ordinary signification. I cannot say that I am sure that Parliament intended the word 'or' to be read as 'and'. If I am wrong in this, then Parliament can easily legislate to make its intention clear. It would have been so easy to
j   use some appropriate form of words to provide that an owner and a master should each be liable. Particularly in a penal provision a word ought not to be given a meaning other than its normal meaning unless it is quite clear that some other meaning was intended and that the word was used by mistake. In a proper case this may be inferred if the result of giving a word its normal meaning would be inconsistency or absurdity or repugnancy.

For the reasons which I have set out I have been driven to the conclusion that in the
context now being considered the word 'or' must be given a disjunctive meaning.
A decision ought to be reached at the outset as to the person against whom proceedings
are to be started; but an acquittal of that person will not inevitably or automatically
preclude the initiation of proceedings against the other if, while having regard to the
acquittal, there are nevertheless any reasons which warrant further action.

It was submitted on behalf of the appellants that the success of their contention as
to the meaning of the subsection should lead to the result that both convictions should
be quashed. I cannot think that that is right. The result of my view is that at the hearing
after the owners pleaded guilty the master could not have been convicted. I consider
that the case should be remitted to the Court of Appeal so as to bring it about that
while the conviction of the owners will stand the conviction of the master should be
set aside.

I would allow the appeal accordingly.

LORD WILBERFORCE.   My Lords, it is important to state precisely what we
are asked to decide in this appeal. It is to determine the meaning of the following
phrase—extracted from s 1(1) of the Oil in Navigable Waters Act 1955:

> 'If any oil . . . is discharged from a British ship . . . the owner or master of
> the ship shall . . . be guilty of an offence under this section.'

To say that what we have to decide is whether 'or' is conjunctive or disjunctive or,
putting it more bluntly, whether 'or' means 'and', appears to me, with respect, to be a
dangerous simplification. It is the meaning of the phrase as a whole that concerns us.

The appellants ask us to say that, in this context, 'or' has an alternative and exclusionary sense, so that either the master or the owner is guilty but not both. Thus,
once either one or the other has pleaded or been found guilty or, maybe, has been
proceeded against, proceedings against the other cannot be brought. This strange
result—modus ponendo tollens—

> ' See how the fates their gifts allot,
>   If A is guilty, B is not,'

was rejected by the judge at the trial, and rejected unanimously by the Court of
Appeal (Criminal Division)[1] which court pungently pointed out anomalies and
absurdities to which it would give rise. I agree with these courts: for myself, indeed,
to give the phrase this signification is to make it legally meaningless.

In logic, there is no rule which requires that 'or' should carry an exclusive force.
Whether it does so depends on the context. So one must ask what, in a legal context,
is the meaning of an assertion that 'A or B' is to be guilty of an offence? The law is
supposed to be certain: the subject is entitled, and presumptively bound, to know
what laws, particularly what criminal laws, apply to him. To say that a law which
fails to satisfy these demands is void for uncertainty, is certainly a last resort, but if that
conclusion is to be avoided, some intelligible meaning must be found by supplying,
or substituting, words within the limits of what courts may legitimately do. It seems
clear enough that where the law says that something is to happen to 'A or B', if what
is intended is an exclusionary alternative (i e one, but not the other), the law must
state either some qualification by which the affected person may be determined,
or must name a third person by whom the choice may be made. The Act does
neither of these expressly; so on any view some addition to the statutory words is
required.

The following seem to be the only possibilities:

1. The words might mean 'the owner or the master whichever is responsible for
causing the discharge'. This would be intelligible; but it cannot be the meaning

---

1   [1973] 3 All ER 849, [1973] 1 WLR 1373

a   here, because the Act evidently creates an absolute offence. In many, if not most, cases it is impossible to find out who caused, or was responsible for, the discharge of the oil: that is why the section is written in the form 'if any oil is discharged'. There is absolute liability, subject only to certain statutory defences. So liability cannot depend on responsibility.

2. The words might mean 'the owner or failing him (i e if he cannot be found or
b   proceeded against) the master'. This would be intelligible though perhaps difficult to apply. It would have the result of letting the master escape if the owner could be found. There seems no sound policy reason for this: often, indeed usually, the master would be the person who discharged or ordered the discharge of the oil and sanctions against him would seem of primary importance. Nobody has contended that the section should bear this second meaning.

3. The words might mean something like: 'the owner or master at the option
c   of the prosecution'. This is, in substance, what the appellants contend for. But I find this less acceptable even than the other two. (a) To say that either A or B—neither of whom may have caused the discharge, or possess any mens rea—is liable to be prosecuted at the choice of the Attorney-General or of a government department, with the consequence that once the choice is made the other is innocent, appears to
d   to me to introduce a novel and offensive principle of law. No discrimen is stated, or suggested, according to which the choice is to be made: it is left as a naked, as well as an unexpressed, discretion. I cannot believe that this is constitutional. It is said that prosecutors, including the police and the Director of Public Prosecutions, have a discretionary right not to proceed against persons, or all of the persons, against whom a case has been or could be made and that the interpretation contended for here goes
e   no further. But whatever the constitutional limits of the former discretion may be, and some limits there certainly are, there is a world of difference between it and a discretion quite uncontrolled, to fix an offence on one of two persons to the exclusion of the other. Apart from this, (b) it is impossible, at least for me, to discern what legislative policy there could be for forcing the prosecution into a choice between these two persons (cf The Blakeley[1]).   (c) To accept that such an election must be made
f   involves a number of procedural difficulties, if not absurdities, which are well pointed out by the Court of Appeal which I need not repeat. In spite of some extensive shifting of ground in this House, these difficulties remain. (d) To achieve this meaning some considerable rewriting of the subsection is required. At the very least it is necessary to insert: 'at the option of the prosecution (or perhaps the Attorney-General, or perhaps the Minister—which?)'. And even this will not really do: the expanded phrase
g   'guilty at the option of . . .' remains difficult to understand. If the option is to relate to the commencement of proceedings, it should say so; similarly if it is to relate to the obtaining of a conviction some addition is certainly needed: what addition is uncertain. So I cannot accept this as a reasonable, or indeed possible, interpretation of the phrase.

If all these meanings are rejected, there remains the course of treating 'or' as ex-
h   pressing a non-exclusionary alternative—in modern logic symbolised by 'v'. In lawyers' terms this may be described as the course of substituting 'and' for 'or', or, rather the course of redrafting the phrase so as to read: 'the owner and the master shall each be guilty', or, if the phrase of convenience were permitted, 'the owner and/or the master'. To substitute 'and' for 'or' is a strong and exceptional interference with a legislative text, and in a penal statute one must be even more convinced of its necessity.
j   It is surgery rather than therapeutics. But there are sound precedents for so doing: my noble and learned friend, Lord Morris of Borth-y-Gest, has mentioned some of the best known; they are sufficient illustrations and I need not restate them. I would add, however, one United States case[2], a civil case, on an Act concerning seamen of 1915. This contained the words: 'Any failure on the part of [the] master . .

---

1   (1916) 234 Fed 959
2   The Blakeley (1916) Fed 959

shall render the master or vessel or the owner of the vessel liable in damages'. A district Court in Washington DC read 'or' as 'and' saying that there could not have been any purpose or intention on the part of Congress to compel the seaman to elect as to which to pursue and thereby exempt the others from liability. Although this was a civil, not a criminal case, I find the conclusion and the reasoning reassuring.

So the power is undoubted, and the only question is whether the necessity for so drastic a change has been made out. In my opinion, it has, since the only alternative contended for leads to results so arbitrary and contrary to legal principle, and itself requires such a degree of rewriting, as not merely to commend but to impose the change. The reading in question, on the other hand, produces a normal and satisfactory result. Two further observations:

1. It is pointed out that the combination 'owner or master' appears in other places in the Act and it is said, first, that it must bear the same meaning throughout and, secondly, that in some places at least, it must carry the normal alternative, exclusionary, sense. The short answer to this is that we are not construing 'or', or even 'owner or master', but the whole phrase in which these words appear. Whether the words bear the same, or a different, meaning in other phrase-contexts, can only be decided by an analysis of the latter. For my part, some of these contexts require 'or' to be read as 'and' just as firmly as does s 1(1).

2. Some argument was drawn from the 1954 convention[1] to give effect to which this Act was passed. It is true that art X of that convention contains the words 'owner or master' and historically it is possible that the draftsman of s 1(1) of the Act took them, unreflectingly, from this source. But I do not think that any conclusion follows from this. Even if the convention uses the words 'disjunctively', which is not certain, there is no rule or principle which requires us to assume that the Act does the same. The only presumption is that the Act complies with the obligations assumed under the convention: this it does whether it uses 'or' or 'and': in the latter case the United Kingdom has merely gone further than the convention. This it is entitled to do.

My Lords, I regret to express an opinion differing from that so strongly held by those who have preceded me in this House. The revelation of this difference of opinion may perhaps be salutary, if the draftsmen are encouraged to care in the use of 'or', 'and' or even, if I dare to say so, 'and/or'.

In my opinion, the Court of Appeal's decision was right and I would dismiss the appeal.

LORD SIMON OF GLAISDALE. My Lords, when your Lordships adjourned consideration of this appeal at the conclusion of the argument, I was of opinion that the course urged on your Lordships by the respondents went beyond the permissible limits of judicial law-making in a matter of statutory construction. But I have now had the advantage of reading in draft the speeches prepared by my noble and learned friends, Lord Wilberforce and Lord Salmon; and I have been convinced that s 1(1) makes no sense, in the light of constitutional and legal usage, as it now stands—so that it is necessary to conclude that the draftsman used 'or' in error for 'and', and that as a matter of construction 'and' should be substituted. No doubt it would be necessary to make similar substitutions in ss 3(1)(a) and 5(5).

I would, therefore, dismiss the appeal.

LORD SALMON. My Lords, I do not suppose that any two words in the English language have more often been used interchangeably than 'and' and 'or'. However unfortunate or incorrect this practice may be, many examples of it are to be found in all manner of documents and statutes. There are many reported cases which turn on whether, in its particular context, the word 'or' is to be read conjunctively or the word 'and' disjunctively.

1 The International Convention for the Prevention of Pollution of the Sea by Oil, 1954 (Cmd 9197)

a There is high authority for the view that the word 'or' can never mean 'and' although it is sometimes used by mistake when 'and' is intended: see Jessel MR in *Morgan v Thomas*[1] and MacKinnon J in *Brown & Co v T & J Harrison*[2]. On the other hand, there is also the high authority of Bankes and Atkin LJJ, on appeal in *Brown & Co v T & J Harrison*[3], that 'or' is quite commonly and grammatically used in a conjunctive sense. In *Sutherland Publishing Co Ltd v Caxton Publishing Co Ltd*[4] MacKinnon

b LJ was able pungently to restate the contrary view which he had expressed 11 years previously. The Oxford dictionary seems to support Jessel MR and MacKinnon LJ.

I do not, however, attach any real importance as to whether the one school of thought or the other is right on this interesting grammatical point. In *Brown & Co v T & J Harrison*[3] the Court of Appeal agreed with MacKinnon J as to the effect of the relevant statutory provision. MacKinnon J reached his conclusion by holding

c that the word 'and' should be substituted for the word 'or'. The Court of Appeal reached their conclusion by holding that the word 'or', on its true construction, meant 'and'. The result was the same.

There is certainly no doubt that generally it is assumed that 'or' is intended to be used disjunctively and the word 'and' conjunctively. Nevertheless, it is equally well settled that if so to construe those words leads to an intelligible or absurd result, the

d courts will read the word 'or' conjunctively and 'and' disjunctively as the case may be; or to put it another way, substitute the one word for the other. This principle has been applied time and again even in penal statutes: see for example *R v Oakes*[5]. The present appeal turns on whether it would be possible to make any sense of s 1 (sub-s (1)) or s 3 (sub-s (1)) or s 5 (sub-s (5)) of the Oil in Navigable Waters Act 1955 if this House were to reverse the Court of Appeal[6] and hold that the word 'or' is

e used disjunctively in its context in those sections, namely, 'The owner or master of the vessel shall be guilty of an offence under this section.'

Section 1 deals with pollution of the sea in a prohibited area by oil from a British ship registered in the United Kingdom. Section 3 deals (amongst other things) with the pollution by oil of United Kingdom waters from any ship. Section 5 provides for regulations being made by the Minister requiring British ships registered in the

f United Kingdom to be fitted with certain equipment for the prevention or reduction of pollution of the sea by oil. These sections all create offences. If a ship pollutes the sea with oil under ss 1 or 3 or puts to sea without the equipment prescribed by regulations made under s 5, then the 'owner or master of the vessel shall be guilty of an offence'. These offences are absolute in the sense that they are committed without any mens rea being necessary, if the events postulated in the sections occur.

g Section 4 provides for certain special defences under ss 1 and 3 which are available alike to the owner and the master.

If 'or' in those sections is to be treated as disjunctive, it is, in my view, quite impossible to give the sections any intelligible meaning. The sections would be unintelligible and absurd for they would be providing that the owner or the master is guilty, but not both, without giving any indication to show which is guilty. If either or both

h were prosecuted, neither could, in any circumstances, be convicted. Each, to my mind, would have the unanswerable defence 'It is true that on the facts which have been proved, one or other of us must be guilty but both of us cannot be guilty. Since the Act does not give any indication as to which of us is guilty, the prosecution has embarked on the impossible task of attempting to prove beyond reasonable doubt that it is I who am guilty.' The appellants seek to escape from this insuperable

j

1   (1882) 9 QBD 643 at 645
2   (1927) 43 TLR 394
3   (1927) 96 LJKB 1025, [1927] All ER Rep 195
4   [1937] 4 All ER 405, [1938] Ch 174
5   [1959] 2 All ER 92, [1959] 2 QB 350
6   [1973] 3 All ER 849, [1973] 1 WLR 1373

difficulty by arguing that the Act gives an option to the prosecutor to elect which *a* of the two is guilty. This argument is, however, impossible to accept unless words can be read into the relevant sections which are not there. It would be necessary to insert after the words 'the owner or master of the vessel' some such words as 'at the option of the prosecutor'. This might make the sections intelligible but they would remain absurd and also become otherwise objectionable. It is conceded that no offence has ever before been created the existence of which depends on the exer- *b* cise of such an option or indeed of any option. It would be repugnant to our law that the question whether A or B is guilty of an offence should depend on the whim of the prosecutor. It is only very rarely that words can be read into a statute, and then only if it is necessary to do so for the purpose of making the statute comply with the obvious intention of Parliament. There is no precedent for implying words into a statute in order to give it the bizarre meaning for which the appellants contend and *c* which, in my view, Parliament cannot possibly have intended. On the other hand, there are ample precedents of the highest authority for reading the word 'or' for 'and' or substituting the word 'and' for 'or' when otherwise, as here, the statute would be unintelligible and absurd.

It has always been the invariable constitutional practice of Parliament to enact who shall be guilty of the offences which it creates. It would be a sad day for this *d* country were Parliament to abdicate those functions by writing words into a statute giving a Minister, or anyone else, the power to choose who is to be guilty of a statutory offence.

Parliament has written no such words in the 1955 Act. The learned trial judge and the Court of Appeal have not done so. The courts have interpreted the language of the Act by giving it an intelligible and sensible meaning in accordance with authority. *e* The niceties of grammar are no doubt of great importance. But there are things of even greater importance—as our courts have always recognised.

My Lords, it would surely be a catastrophe if this House were to compel the courts to read words into the statute which are not there in order to confer on the Minister a power which he expressly disclaims and which would be offensive both to long established constitutional practice and the whole spirit of the common law. This is *f* what, in my view, lends a real importance to this appeal which otherwise would turn solely on a narrow point of construction.

The fact that the words 'owner or master', used disjunctively, make sense, and indeed if used conjunctively, would not make sense in a different context in other sections of the statute, does not seem to me to be significant of anything except of an indifferent standard of draftsmanship. Nor am I impressed by the argument on *g* behalf of the appellants founded on s 6 which provides that an offence shall not be punishable on summary conviction by a fine exceeding £1,000. It does not surprise me that if, in the events postulated in ss 1, 3 and 5 the owner and the master is each, as I think, guilty of an offence, each should be liable to the maximum fine. This of course, does not mean that the maximum fine would always be imposed.

I recognise that a prosecutor is sometimes in possession of evidence which, if accepted, *h* shows that A and B are each guilty of an offence. He could prosecute them both but he is not bound necessarily to do so. He has a discretion which, in certain circumstances, he might properly exercise, to prosecute A and not B. This discretion is, however, fundamentally different from the power of deciding whether, given certain facts, the statute means that A and not B is guilty of an offence.

I do not consider that any help in construing s 1 can be derived from the International *j* Convention for the Prevention of Pollution of the Sea by Oil 1954[1]. I recognise that s 1 springs from art X just as s 5 of the Act springs from art VII of that convention. I am prepared to assume (without deciding the point) that s 1 could have kept within

1 Cmd 9197

a the letter of art X if it had laid down that in the circumstances postulated the owner alone should be guilty of an offence or if it had laid down that the master alone should be guilty of an offence. It would, I recognise, follow that, on my construction of s 1, Parliament went further than required by art X just as it obviously went much further in s 5 than required by art VII of the convention. I do not find this strange or unusual. Australia, for example, took the same course as I think we did, although in somewhat

b more elegant language, by enacting s 7 of their Pollution of the Sea by Oil Act 1960. Clearly, if the spirit of the convention was to ensure that all reasonable steps should be taken to discourage pollution of the sea, it would be clear to Parliament that the most effective means of attaining those ends would be to make the owner and the master each guilty of an offence whenever pollution occurred, or a ship put to sea without complying with some such requirement in respect of equipment as

c is laid down in s 5 of the Act. It has not been suggested that ss 1 and 3 are unfair in making the owner guilty in the event of pollution occurring, although it is obvious that the master is more likely to be directly responsible. The object of making the owners liable is to discourage them from taking a tolerant attitude towards a master who causes pollution. The object of making the master personally liable is to ensure that he will do everything he can to avoid pollution. I can see nothing unfair in making

d the master guilty for any contravention of s 5. If the vessel is not fitted with the proper equipment and the master knows it, he should refuse to put to sea until the vessel is properly equipped. If he puts to sea when there has been some contravention of s 5 of which he could not have known, no court, were he to be prosecuted, would do more than impose a nominal fine, or give him an absolute discharge.

The legislature rightly regarded pollution of the sea as one of the serious evils of

e modern times. That, in my view, is why it considered that the owner and the master should each, irrespective of mens rea, be guilty of an offence in the circumstances referred to in ss 1, 3 and 5 of the Act. What I am quite certain Parliament could not have intended is to have provided that either the master or the owner should be guilty of an offence—but not both—without giving any clues as to which was to be guilty.

There are many serious procedural difficulties referred to in the powerful judgment

f of the Court of Appeal[1], and other difficulties canvassed in argument which would arise if the construction for which counsel on behalf of the appellants contended were to be accepted. If the prosecutor has the unique right of electing whether the owner or master is guilty of an offence, when and how is the election to be made? At one time it was conceded by the appellants that the owners and the master could both be indicted and tried together and the prosecutor could elect at any time before verdict

g which of the two might be found guilty of the offence. In the present case no election was made so presumably neither could properly be convicted unless the power of election passed to the jury by default. At a very late stage in the argument before your Lordships, the original concession had to be withdrawn and a fresh one substituted. It was then conceded that the election had to be made at the committal proceedings and only the owner or master could be sent for trial. This would, I think, mean that

h in the present case there has been a mistrial. Whilst these, and other serious procedural difficulties which would arise on the appellants' construction, point strongly to that construction being wrong, I prefer to rely chiefly on the grounds which I have already indicated for rejecting it.

My Lords, I would dismiss this appeal.

j *Appeal dismissed.*

Solicitors: *Norton, Rose, Botterell & Roche* (for the appellants); *Solicitor, Department of Trade and Industry.*

Christine Ivamy   Barrister.

1 [1973] 3 All ER 849, [1973] 1 WLR 1373

R v Rugby Justices, ex parte Prince

QUEEN'S BENCH DIVISION
LORD WIDGERY CJ, MACKENNA AND MAY JJ
29th, 30th JANUARY 1974

Magistrates – Committal – Committal for sentence – Summary trial of indictable offence – Court of opinion that greater punishment should be inflicted for offence than court has power to inflict – Conviction of three offences – Court of opinion suspended sentence exceeding six months appropriate if coupled with supervision order – Court having no power to impose that sentence – Supervision order only possible if suspended sentence for any one offence exceeding six months – Court having power to impose consecutive sentences of up to 12 months – Whether court of opinion that greater punishment should be inflicted than court having power to inflict – Whether committal ultra vires – Magistrates' Courts Act 1952, s 29.

The applicant was charged with two offences of burglary and one offence of deception. He asked for a summary trial and pleaded guilty. Having heard his antecedents the justices were of opinion that a prison sentence was appropriate but that the case was a suitable one for a suspended sentence provided that it could be coupled with a supervision order under s 12(1)ᵃ of the Criminal Justice Act 1972. Since, however, a supervision order could only be made if the suspended sentence for any one offence exceeded six months, the maximum which the justices could impose for each offence, they decided to commit the applicant to the Crown Court for sentence under s 29ᵇ of the Magistrates' Courts Act 1952. The Crown Court, however, imposed an immediate sentence of 12 months imprisonment. The applicant moved for, inter alia, an order of certiorari to quash the order committing him to the Crown Court, contending that the justices had no power to make the order under s 29 of the 1952 Act, since (i) they had power to impose immediate consecutive sentences of up to 12 months imprisonment for the offences of which he had been convicted, (ii) they were of opinion that a suspended sentence exceeding 6 months imprisonment was appropriate, and (iii) therefore they were not, within s 29, 'of opinion ... that greater punishment should be inflicted for the offence than [they had] power to inflict'.

Held (MacKenna J dissenting) – The word 'offence' in s 29 could not be construed as including the plural and therefore it was sufficient for the purposes of s 29 if the justices were of opinion that a greater punishment should be inflicted than they had power to inflict for each offence of which the applicant had been convicted. Since a suspended sentence exceeding six months imprisonment was a 'greater punishment' than a sentence, whether immediate or suspended, of six months imprisonment, the maximum which the justices had power to inflict for each offence, they had power under s 29 to commit the applicant for sentence. The motion would therefore be dismissed (see p 119 c to h and j to p 120 a and p 121 a, post).

Notes
For committal to Crown Court for sentence for indictable offences triable summarily, see 25 Halsbury's Laws (3rd Edn) 226, 227, para 421.

---

a   Section 12(1) provides: 'Where a court sentences an offender for a single offence to imprisonment for a term of more than six months and makes an order suspending the sentence under section 39(1) of the Criminal Justice Act 1967, the court may make a suspended sentence supervision order (in this Act referred to as "a supervision order") placing the offender under the supervision of a supervising officer for a period specified in the order not exceeding the period which under the said section 39(1) is the operational period in relation to the suspended sentence.'

b   Section 29, so far as material, is set out at p 118 h, post

For the Magistrates' Courts Act 1952, s 29, see 21 Halsbury's Statutes (3rd Edn) 215.
For the Criminal Justice Act 1972, s 12, see 42 Halsbury's Statutes (3rd Edn) 111.

Cases cited

R v Richards (Isabelle) [1973] 3 All ER 1088, [1973] 3 WLR 888, CA.
R v Tower Bridge Magistrate, ex parte Osman [1971] 2 All ER 1018, [1971] 1 WLR 1109, DC.

Motions for certiorari and mandamus

These were applications by way of motion by William John Prince for (1) an order of
certiorari to bring up and quash an order made by the Rugby justices dated 30th
November 1973 whereby they committed the applicant to the Crown Court at Warwick
for sentence under s 29 of the Magistrates' Courts Act 1952; (2) an order of certiorari
to quash the order made by the Crown Court on 13th December 1973 committing
the applicant to prison for a total of 12 months; and (3) for an order of mandamus
directed to the Rugby Magistrates' Court directing the justices to pass sentence on
the applicant. The facts are set out in the judgment of Lord Widgery CJ.

A J Engel for the applicant.
The respondents did not appear and were not represented.

LORD WIDGERY CJ. In these proceedings counsel moves on behalf of one
William John Prince for an order of certiorari to remove into this court and quash
an order of the Rugby justices made on 30th November 1973 whereby they committed
the applicant to the Crown Court for sentence in purported exercise of their powers
under s 29 of the Magistrates' Courts Act 1952. There is a further application for
certiorari to remove and quash an order of the Warwick Crown Court made pursuant
to the purported committal by the justices under s 29. Finally relief is asked in the
form of an order of mandamus directed to the Rugby justices to start again, in other
words to rehear the matter which was originally before them.

The case arises in this way. On 9th November 1973 the applicant was before the
Rugby justices charged with three offences. They were not particularly serious offences
as these things go. The first was a charge of burglary, entering a shop as a trespasser
and stealing a coat-hanger worth 5p; the second was a charge of burglary, entering a
restaurant as a trespasser and stealing £20 in money; and finally obtaining by deception a meal to the value of 44p. Following on those charges before the Rugby justices
on 9th November the applicant pleaded guilty; he asked for summary trial, which
was agreeable to the court, and his antecedents were then produced for the consideration of the court.

The antecedents disclose a rather sad state of affairs. The applicant has a substantial
criminal record and has served a number of terms of imprisonment. The justices,
to whom I would like to pay a tribute for the extreme care which they took in this
case, decided in the light of those antecedents that they wanted a social inquiry
report and an adjournment was granted in order that that might be done. When
the matter eventually came back before the justices for decision, it is quite clear,
as their affidavit shows, that they were immediately of the opinion that this was a
proper case for prison.

Again I comment that this was the correct question posed at this stage, namely
to ask whether their subsidiary powers of putting on probation and the like could be
appropriate. But they rejected these and decided it was a proper matter for prison.
Their own powers were confined to a sentence of imprisonment, either immediate
or suspended, for a maximum of six months for each offence with the power, if they
thought fit, to make two such sentences consecutive thus making a total period of
imprisonment of 12 months.

It is quite evident the justices did not think that within those powers this matter
could be properly disposed of. What they had in mind, and they were frank about

it, was that this was potentially a case for a suspended sentence, but they were not
going to have a suspended sentence unless it could be coupled with a supervision
order under s 12(1) of the Criminal Justice Act 1972. That they could not do, because
under the terms of s 12 a supervision order can be attached to a suspended sentence
only if the suspended sentence exceeds a period of six months in respect of any one
offence, and for the reasons which I have already given, it was not possible for the
justices to impose a sentence of more than six months in respect of any one of these
offences; hence if they chose to impose a sentence within their powers and suspend
it, they would not be able to attach a supervision order to it.

Very wisely they were not disposed to try the experiment of a suspended sentence
without the reinforcement of a supervision order. All these matters seem to have
been discussed very openly in court, and the applicant, who was represented by a
solicitor, was clearly favouring the possibility of a suspended sentence.

Faced with the dilemma in which the justices found themselves, someone had the
idea, and it is not quite clear who had it first, that the way out of the difficulty was
to commit the applicant to the Crown Court under s 29 of the 1952 Act because, once
in the Crown Court on such a committal, the Crown Court could impose a sentence
in excess of six months imprisonment for any one offence and thus open the door to
the making of a suspended sentence with a supervision order.

This suggestion when it was raised and canvassed, was welcomed by the applicant
and his advisers, and I think fairly one can say encouraged by them. To make quite
sure that the point should not be missed, the applicant's solicitor asked the court if a
letter could be sent to the Crown Court explaining that the purpose of the committal
was to enable a suspended sentence to be passed with a supervision order in respect
of it. So the matter came to the Crown Court.

In fact in the Crown Court, the learned presiding judge took the view, as he was
perfectly entitled to do, that this was not a case for a suspended sentence at all, and
he passed an immediate sentence of 12 months imprisonment, which was in fact
within the powers of the justices themselves. If the Crown Court had adopted the
justices' suggestion, we should have heard no more about this case, but as in fact the
ultimate result was not that which the applicant hoped to achieve, inquiry was made
whether there was any defect in the procedure which had produced this unwelcome
result.

It is finally contended before us today that the committal to the Crown Court
was in excess of the justices' jurisdiction, and that it should be quashed, and it would
follow from that that the disposal of the case in the Crown Court would also be
quashed, and we should be back, as I said at the very beginning, with the justices in
a position to try again.

The basis on which the application for certiorari is made is that on the facts which
I have outlined at some little length, the justices had no jurisdiction to make a
committal to the Crown Court at all. What s 29 of the 1952 Act says is this:

> 'Where on the summary trial under subsection (3) of section eighteen or sec-
> tion nineteen of this Act of an indictable offence a person who is not less than
> seventeen years old is convicted of the offence, then, if on obtaining information
> about his character and antecedents the court is of opinion that they are such that
> greater punishment should be inflicted for the offence than the court has power
> to inflict, the court may, in accordance with section 56 of the Criminal Justice
> Act 1967, commit him in custody or on bail to the Crown Court for sentence ...'

What is said here is that the justices were not of the opinion, having heard the antecedents and character of the applicant, that greater punishment should be inflicted for
the offence than the justices themselves had power to inflict. What is argued is
that the justices came to the conclusion that a different form of punishment was
appropriate than that which they had power to inflict, and it is pressed on us that
that is not enough to justify a committal under s 29 and the language of the section

a requires the justices to form the conclusion that greater punishment is required than that which lies within their own powers.

Counsel for the applicant puts the matter very clearly and we are indebted to him for his argument. He says on the one hand the maximum powers of the justices were to send the applicant to prison for an immediate prison sentence of 12 months. The justices' assessment of the case was that it required a suspended sent-
b ence plus a supervision order. Counsel says: if you look at those two alternatives, it cannot be said that a suspended sentence plus a supervision order is greater punishment than immediate 12 months imprisonment, therefore he says it is clear on the justices' own assessment of the offence it did not show that a greater punishment was required than they could inflict. It is a very attractive argument, very attractively put before us, and at first blush it impressed me with its common sense, but having thought about the matter overnight, I have come to the conclusion that the argument
c cannot be sustained.

To begin with, I think it is wrong when making a comparison between the justices' powers and the justices' assessment of the offences to put the three offences all together and talk in terms of a possible sentence in the magistrates' court of 12 months immediate imprisonment. It is trite that when several charges are before the court,
d the charges are dealt with separately, the justices have to impose a separate sentence for each, and I think under s 29 of the 1952 Act one has to take the charges individu-
ally. I do not overlook the fact that under the Interpretation Act 1889 it would be possible to regard a reference to an offence in the singular under s 29 as a reference to 'offences' in the plural, but for my part, having regard to the traditional background and approach to sentencing for multiple offences, the context of s 29 excludes the reading of 'an offence' as being 'some offences'. Accordingly I start with the proposi-
e tion that one looks at the offences individually. The justices' powers in respect of one of these offences tried individually would have been to impose a sentence of imprisonment for up to six months, either immediate or suspended.

Why did not they use those powers? Why did they regard those powers as inadequate? The answer is perfectly clear. They regarded those powers as inadequate
f because the maximum period of imprisonment which those powers enabled them to impose for a single offence was insufficient to enable the term to be suspended and a supervision order added. Fundamentally, when one gets down to the nub of the problem here, the justices were saying: we cannot deal with the offences because the maximum possible sentence is insufficient to allow this case to be properly dealt with. Accordingly they committed the matter to the Crown Court to exercise their
g extended powers of imprisonment—extended when compared with the powers of the justices.

Having reached that point, I ask myself why this is not a case where the justices were of the opinion that the offences required greater punishment than they could inflict. In my judgment this is exactly what it was, the offence required a longer term than six months and the justices could not inflict a longer term than six months.
h Accordingly, approaching the matter in this way, it appears to me this is a case within the provisions of s 29. But, says counsel for the applicant, one must not over-
look the fact that what the justices had in mind was a suspended sentence, and he says a suspended sentence is not a greater punishment than an immediate sentence. If one is thinking in terms of imprisonment of an equal length, it may very well be right to say that a suspended sentence is not more severe than an immediate sent-
j ence; indeed the situation may well be the other way. But here we are not dealing with competition, as it were, with two terms of equal length; we are considering a term of six months in the magistrates' court and a longer term imposed by the Crown Court. We do not know what longer term the justices had in mind. It must have been less than two years because they were thinking of a suspended sentence. It might have been as little as nine months, they do not tell us, but what is clear is that it was contemplated that the sentence imposed by the Crown Court should be

longer than six months, and that being so in my judgment this constitutes greater *a* punishment for present purposes. For those reasons I have come to the conclusion that the justices' committal was within the terms of s 29 of the 1952 Act and any attack on it on the basis of jurisdiction fails.

I would add one other word, that is to say that we had argument on one side only, and there has been no one in this case interested to contend that this was not a case for certiorari at all. I approach the matter on the basis that certiorari should have *b* gone had the substantive matter been established, but I wish it to be clearly understood by those who may refer to this case in future that we have not decided that this was a case in which certiorari could properly be sought, and had the application been opposed on that ground, it may be, I do not know, that we should have based our conclusion on a different footing. For myself I would refuse the present application for the reasons I have advanced. *c*

MACKENNA J. The justices had power to impose a sentence not exceeding six months for each of the applicant's three offences, and sentences which did not exceed in the aggregate 12 months. They had power to suspend any such sentences, but no power to attach a supervision order to any sentence that suspended. This last limitation is the designed effect of s 12 of the Criminal Justice Act 1972, which prevents *d* the court from making such an order unless the sentence which it passes for a single offence exceeds six months. I read the justices' findings to mean (1) that they were of opinion that the applicant's offences merited punishment exceeding six months, which would have been met by sentences aggregating nine or 12 months, or indeed any other period of more than six months; and (2) that they would have given him such a sentence themselves and suspended it if they could also have made a super- *e* vision order. Because they could not make a supervision order they sent the case to the Crown Court, which had that power but as it happens did not exercise it.

On these facts the question is whether the case falls within s 29 of the Magistrates' Courts Act 1952. This section provides that where on the summary trial of a person of 17 years or more that person is convicted and the court is of opinion that his character and antecedents are such that greater punishment should be inflicted for *f* the offence than the court has power to inflict, the court may send the case to the Crown Court.

On these provisions the first question is whether the words 'an indictable offence' and the words 'the offence' are limited to an offence in the singular, or whether they include 'offences' in the plural. Section 1 of the Interpretation Act 1889 directs us to read singular words as including the plural unless the context otherwise requires. *g* In my opinion the context of s 29 does *not* otherwise require; on the contrary I think that it makes better sense if the words are read as including the plural. Where there are several offences, what matters is the total effect of the sentence which the justices have power to impose, in other words the aggregate of the sentences for all the indictable offences tried by them.

If that is the right reading of s 29, the justices had no power to send this case to the *h* Crown Court unless they were of opinion that a greater punishment should be imposed than one of 12 months, which they themselves had the power to inflict. I do not think that a suspended sentence of nine or 12 months with a supervision order attached is a greater punishment than an unsuspended sentence of 12 months which, as I say, the justices themselves had the power to inflict.

For this reason I would have held that the order under s 29 was wrongly made with *i* whatever consequences follow from that conclusion, but as Lord Widgery CJ and May J think otherwise, the case will be dealt with as they direct.

MAY J. For my part, having regard to the context of s 29 and to the general principles applicable to sentencing, I agree respectfully with the view expressed by *a* Lord Widgery CJ that in s 29 the words 'an indictable offence' and 'the offence' must be read in the singular and cannot be read as 'offences' or 'the offences'. In the circumstances I agree with the judgment of Lord Widgery CJ and for the reasons that he has given would dismiss this application.

Application refused. Leave to appeal to the House of Lords refused.

b Solicitors: *Prime & Co*, Rugby (for the applicant).

N P Metcalfe Esq   Barrister.

c

Practice Direction

d CROWN COURT

Crown Court – Transfer of proceedings between locations – Sentence – Deferred sentence passed on offender – Conviction of further offence before different location of court during period of deferment – Sentence for original offence – Criminal Justice Act 1972, s 22(1)(4).

e With the concurrence of the Lord Chancellor and pursuant to s 4(5)[1] of the Courts Act 1971, I direct that the following addition shall be made at the end of para 14 of the directions on the distribution of crown court business given by me on 14th October 1971[2]:

f 'Where the Crown Court has deferred passing sentence under s 22(1)[3] of the Criminal Justice Act 1972, and before the expiration of the period of deferment the offender is convicted in a different location of the Crown Court of another offence, the power to pass sentence for the original offence under s 22(4) may be exercised in the location of the Crown Court where he was convicted of the subsequent offence.'

g 22nd March 1974   WIDGERY CJ

---

1   See 41 Halsbury's Statutes (3rd Edn) 291
2   [1971] 3 All ER 829, [1971] 1 WLR 1535
3   See 42 Halsbury's Statutes (3rd Edn) 123

Maxwell v Department of Trade and Industry and others

COURT OF APPEAL, CIVIL DIVISION

LORD DENNING MR, ORR AND LAWTON LJJ

14th, 15th, 16th, 17th, 18th, 21st, 25th JANUARY 1974

Company – Investigation by Board of Trade – Proceedings before inspectors – Natural justice – Duty to hear parties – Party liable to criticism – Opportunity to answer tentative conclusions of inspectors critical of him before report signed – Opportunity to answer evidence from other witnesses which might be basis for criticism – Companies Act 1948, s 165(b) (as amended by the Companies Act 1967, s 38).

The plaintiff was the chairman and chief executive of a public company. The Department of Trade and Industry, in exercise of its powers under the Companies Act 1948, s 165(b)[a], appointed inspectors to investigate and report on the affairs of the company; in particular the inspectors were instructed to report whether, in their opinion, the company's shareholders had been given all the information they might have expected with regard to the company's relations with certain other companies. The plaintiff, among others, gave evidence to the inspectors who put questions to him about the matters with which they were concerned. Once it had become apparent to the inspectors that the plaintiff might be open to criticism in their report, they put to him on a number of occasions the substance of what other witnesses had said about him which could, if accepted, be the basis of criticism; on other occasions, however, they did not do so. Having heard the evidence the inspectors drafted and signed an interim report which was subsequently published by the department. The report was very critical of the plaintiff, who brought an action against the inspectors and the department claiming a declaration that the inspectors had acted in breach of the rules of natural justice in that, having formulated their tentative criticisms of him, they had failed to give him an opportunity of answering those criticisms before signing their report, and further that they had failed to put to the plaintiff all relevant statements made by other witnesses, or in documents, which were prejudicial to him so as to give him an opportunity of answering them.

Held – The plaintiff was not entitled to the relief sought for the following reasons—

(i) A clear distinction was to be drawn between an inquiry based on a charge or accusation and one such as that on which the inspectors had been engaged in which they were asked to establish what had happened and, in the course of so doing, to form certain views or conclusions. Having heard the evidence and reached their conclusions the inspectors were under no obligation to put to a witness such of those conclusions as might be critical of him. All that was necessary was that the inspectors

---

[a] Section 165, as amended, provides: 'Without prejudice to their powers under the last foregoing section, the Board of Trade—(a) shall appoint one or more competent inspectors to investigate the affairs of a company and to report thereon in such manner as the Board direct, if—(i) the company by special resolution; or (ii) the court by order; declares that its affairs ought to be investigated by an inspector appointed by the Board; and (b) may do so if it appears to the Board that there are circumstances suggesting—(i) that its business is being or has been conducted with intent to defraud its creditors or the creditors of any other person or otherwise for a fraudulent or unlawful purpose or in a manner oppressive of any part of its members or that it was formed for any fraudulent or unlawful purpose; or (ii) that persons concerned with its formation or the management of its affairs have in connection therewith been guilty of fraud, misfeasance or other misconduct towards it or towards its members; or (iii) that its members have not been given all the information with respect to its affairs which they might reasonably expect.'

a should put to the witness the points that they proposed to consider when he first came to give evidence. Once the inspectors had heard the evidence they were entitled to come to the final conclusions which would be embodied in their report. The inspectors had conducted the enquiry fairly; the fact that certain matters of detail had not been put to the plaintiff when he was giving evidence was not a ground for impugning the report (see p 127 *e* and *g*, p 129 *b* to *d* and *h*, p 131 *b* to *e*, p 132 *h* to
b p 133 *a* and *c* and p 134 *a* and *b*, post).

(ii) Even if the inspectors had failed to observe the rules of natural justice the bare declaration sought by the plaintiff was one that the court would only make in exceptional circumstances and was not appropriate in the instant case (see p 128 *f*, p 131 *f* and p 134 *f* and *g*, post).

Notes

c For the investigation of a company's affairs, see 6 Halsbury's Laws (3rd Edn) 388-393, paras 753-760.

For the right to be heard, see 1 Halsbury's Laws (4th Edn) 90, para 74.

For the Companies Act 1948, s 165, see 5 Halsbury's Statutes (3rd Edn) 243.

Cases referred to in judgments

d *Board of Education v Rice* [1911] AC 179, [1911-13] All ER Rep 36, 80 LJKB 796, 104 LT 689, 75 JP 393, 9 LGR 652, HL, 19 Digest (Repl) 630, 206.

Kanda (B Surinder Singh) v Government of the Federation of Malaya [1962] AC 322, [1962] 2 WLR 1153, PC.

Local Government Board v Arlidge [1915] AC 120, [1914-15] All ER Rep 1, 84 LJKB 72, 111 LT 905, 79 JP 97, 12 LGR 1109, HL, 22 Digest (Reissue) 327, 3083.

e *Pergamon Press Ltd, Re* [1970] 3 All ER 535, [1971] Ch 388, [1970] 3 WLR 792, CA, Digest (Cont Vol C) 107, 4188e.

Russell v Duke of Norfolk [1949] 1 All ER 109, 32 Digest (Repl) 31, 187.

University of Ceylon v Fernando [1960] 1 All ER 631, [1960] 1 WLR 223, PC, 19 Digest (Repl) 655, *362.

Appeal

f The plaintiff, Ian Robert Maxwell, was at all material times the chairman of Pergamon Press Ltd ('Pergamon') and of International Learning Systems Corporation Ltd ('ILSC'), a company which was jointly owned by Pergamon and British Printing Corporation Ltd. On 17th June 1969 Leasco Data Processing Corporation ('Leasco'), an American company, agreed in writing with the plaintiff in his personal capacity to make an offer to acquire the issued shares of Pergamon. The plaintiff gave Leasco
g certain warranties. On 21st August 1969 Leasco announced that it did not intend to proceed with the proposed offer. One of the reasons for that decision was a report by auditors on the position of ILSC which stated:

'. . . there have been shortcomings in the accounting systems for [ILSC and its subsidiaries] and there are uncertainties as to the values to be attributed to goodwill, origination and publishing costs and the position in respect of claims under
h insurance policies. In our opinion, the books have not been properly kept, and in addition proper returns have not been received from overseas branches. As a result we have not received the information that we require to satisfy ourselves as to the amounts at which a substantial part of the assets and liabilities both in the United Kingdom and overseas have been entered in the accounts or as to the results shown therein. Accordingly we are not able to report that the accounts
j together show a true and fair view of the state of affairs of the company and of the group at the 28th December 1968 and of the results of the group for the eighteen months ended on that date, or comply with the Companies Acts 1948 and 1967.'

Following the report various press statements were released and a number of meetings took place. The matter was investigated by the Panel on Takeovers and Mergers and on 27th August the panel issued a statement which read in part:

'In the opinion of the Panel, however, there are substantial grounds for questioning whether the shareholders of Pergamon were in fact given at the appropriate times all the information about the affairs of their company which, in the circumstances, they would reasonably be entitled to expect . . .'

The panel concluded that it was a question for further inquiry whether the shareholders of Pergamon had received such information. The panel also expressed misgivings regarding ILSC. They felt that shareholders might well have been led to believe that ILSC would make very substantial profits whereas it was doubtful whether ILSC would make any profits at all. The plaintiff appealed against the findings of the panel to an appellate panel presided over by Lord Pearson but the appeal was dismissed.

On 9th September 1969 the first defendant, the Board of Trade, subsequently the Department of Trade and Industry ('the department'), pursuant to its powers under the Companies Act 1948, s 165(b), as amended by the Companies Act 1967, s 38, appointed the second and third defendants, Rondle Owen Charles Stable and Ronald George Leach ('the inspectors'), as inspectors to investigate and report on the affairs of ILSC and Pergamon; in particular the inspectors were expressly instructed to report whether, in their opinion, shareholders of Pergamon had been given all the information they might reasonably have expected with regard to (a) Pergamon's interest in and relation to ILSC and (b) Pergamon's transactions with Maxwell Scientific Incorporated.

The inspectors were anxious to start their investigation as early as possible but in December 1969 they were confronted by the refusal of certain witnesses, including the plaintiff, to answer any questions at all in relation to the affairs of Pergamon unless they were given certain assurances which they claimed to be entitled to receive if the rules of natural justice were to be observed; in particular they claimed the right to cross-examine any witness whose evidence was or tended to be adverse. The inspectors refused to give those assurances and applied to the court for orders pursuant to s 167(3) of the 1948 Act, making the plaintiff and five other directors of Pergamon respondents to the application. On 24th April 1970 Plowman J held that the directors were not justified in refusing to answer the inspectors' questions. Three of the directors, including the plaintiff, appealed against that order. On 13th July 1970 the appeal was dismissed[1]. Thereafter the plaintiff was recalled on nine separate occasions to give evidence before the inspectors.

On 2nd June 1971 the inspectors signed their report, consisting of a final report on the affairs of ILSC and an interim report on the affairs of Pergamon. The report was published by the department on 13th July 1971. Paragraph 127 of the report was as follows:

'It should perhaps be stated at this stage that having seen Mr Clark and Mr Kerman [who were former directors of Pergamon] before seeing [the plaintiff] and having permitted every witness to have a transcript of his own evidence, [the plaintiff], by consulting with Mr Clark and Mr Kerman, could have become aware of the principal matters to which his attention was to be drawn in the course of his questioning by us. Certainly it was never our intention to spring matters on him or take him by surprise. If he wished to defer dealing with a topic until a later date, he had only to ask. As far as practicable we told him in advance what topics we proposed to touch on at any given hearing, and he told us that he did in fact keep in close touch with Mr Clark to ascertain the questions we had asked Mr Clark on any given topic prior to coming to give evidence to us on the same topic, and it is a fact that throughout our inquiry Mr Clark and [the plaintiff] instructed the same firm of solicitors to act for them . . . It is also a fact that there

---

1   *Re Pergamon Press Ltd* [1970] 3 All ER 535, [1971] Ch 388

a was no occasion when either [the plaintiff] or Mr Clark saw us to give evidence
without [their solicitor] being present.'

By a writ issued on 13th July 1971 the plaintiff brought an action against the department and the inspectors and by a writ issued on 5th August 1971 he brought a further
action against the inspectors. The actions were consolidated by an order of Master
Bickford Smith made on 19th August 1971. On 30th September 1971 Forbes J refused
b a motion by the plaintiff for certain injunctions against the defendants. In the actions
the plaintiff claimed (i) against the defendants and each of them declarations that (a)
the purported report by the inspectors (alternatively all of the contents thereof so
far as they touched and concerned the plaintiff or any of his affairs) had been made
in breach of duty and unlawfully and was null and void; (b) any or any further printing or publication or communication by or on behalf of the defendants to any person
c whatsoever of either of the purported report (or any of the aforesaid contents thereof)
or any copies, extracts or summaries therefrom or thereof was or would be an abuse
of and beyond the powers of the defendants and unlawful; (c) the department was
not entitled to bring or to cause or permit or assist any other person to bring any
action or proceedings in consequence of or in any way or to any extent in reliance on
the purported report (or any of the aforesaid contents thereof) or on the investigation
d (or any part of the investigation which touched and concerned the plaintiff or any of
his affairs); (ii) against the inspectors injunctions restraining each of them by themselves their servants or agents or otherwise howsoever from (a) in any way further
proceeding with the investigation under s 165(b) of the 1948 Act, as amended, into the
affairs of ILSC and Pergamon insofar as any such investigation might be concerned
with any act or omission on the part of the plaintiff; (b) drafting, completing or
e delivering to the department any report or reports whether interim or final on the
matters aforesaid or any part of them; (c) informing the department other than by
way of an interim or final report of matters coming to their knowledge as a result
of the aforesaid investigation tending to show that an offence has been committed by
the plaintiff.

On 20th December 1972 Wien J dismissed the plaintiff's action and the plaintiff
f appealed on the ground that the judge had misdirected himself, decided wrongly in
law and wrongly exercised his discretion in the following respects: (i) in holding that
the inspectors had in all the circumstances satisfied the requirements of natural justice
so far as the plaintiff was concerned in their conduct of the investigation and in making
their reports; (ii) in holding that the plaintiff had been given proper and sufficient
notice of what had been said against him by other witnesses or what allegations he had
g to meet, alternatively in holding that the plaintiff had been told by the inspectors the
substance of the evidence which had been given against him and/or what statements
had been made affecting him; (iii) in holding that the Court of Appeal in *Re Pergamon
Press Ltd*[1] had rejected the submission that inspectors appointed by the department
pursuant to the Companies Acts 1948 to 1967 were never under a duty to put the
substance of their proposed or provisional conclusions to a witness whose conduct was
h likely to be severely criticised in those conclusions in the event of their becoming
final conclusions; (iv) in failing to hold that in the circumstances of the particular
case the rules of natural justice required the inspectors to put their proposed criticisms
of the plaintiff or the substance thereof to the plaintiff for his comments or explanations before permitting such criticisms to become final conclusions in their reports;
and (v) in holding that in all the circumstances the inspectors had acted fairly towards
j the plaintiff and that the plaintiff had no just cause to complain about the procedure
adopted by the inspectors in their preparation and making of the reports.

Michael Ogden QC and *Anthony Grabiner* for the plaintiff.
J G Le Quesne QC, Gordon Slynn, Peter Gibson and *D R N Hunt* for the department.
Raymond Kidwell QC, Gordon Slynn, Peter Gibson and *D R N Hunt* for the inspectors.

1 [1970] 3 All ER 535, [1971] Ch 388

Cur adv vult   *a*

25th January. The following judgments were read.

LORD DENNING MR. The Pergamon Press affair still goes on. Three and a half years ago we laid down some guidelines for the inspectors to follow: see *Re Pergamon Press Ltd*[1]. The inspectors have since then held their investigation. They have made two interim reports and a final report. Their reports are very critical of the plaintiff, Mr Robert Maxwell. He is very upset by these criticisms. So much so that he has launched attacks against all of the reports and against the inspectors themselves. Today we are concerned with his attack on the first interim report. Mr Maxwell says that many of the criticisms were made in disregard of the rules of natural justice. He asks us to declare accordingly.   *b*

The matter has already been considered by two of the judges of the High Court. The first interim report was signed on 2nd June 1971. Mr Maxwell applied to Forbes J for an interim injunction to restrain the inspectors from proceeding with their investigation. After a hearing which lasted several days, on 30th September 1971 Forbes J refused the injunction; but in the course of his judgment he expressed the view that the inspectors had failed in their duty. He said: *c*

> 'At no time did they formulate their tentative criticisms and give Mr Maxwell an opportunity of dealing with them. It follows that, in my judgment, the probability is that the trial judge would find a failure by the inspectors to direct themselves properly as to the rules of natural justice which should govern their investigations.'   *d*

He went on to say in that event the trial judge might hold the report to be a nullity. But, although he expressed that interim view, Forbes J thought that the investigation should go on; because the inspectors could still remedy their failure by putting their criticisms to Mr Maxwell. So the judge refused an injunction. Mr Maxwell did not appeal from that refusal. Encouraged, no doubt, by the opinion that the judge expressed, he took the case on to trial.   *e*

In December 1972 the case was tried before Wien J. It lasted several days. At first Mr S C Silkin QC appeared for Mr Maxwell. Next Mr Maxwell conducted it himself. Afterwards he instructed Mr Michael Ogden QC. Eventually Wien J came to a conclusion which was entirely opposite to the opinion reached by Forbes J. Wien J said: *f*

> 'I am quite satisfied that in every instance the inspectors gave proper and sufficient notice to Mr Maxwell of what was said against him or what it was that he had to meet . . . I consider that they succeeded in being eminently fair and that the plaintiff has no just cause for complaint.'   *g*

Each of the judges had substantially the same material before him. The difference between them is this. Forbes J thought that, at the inquiry before inspectors, there were three stages: First, the hearing of the evidence (including Mr Maxwell's) and the study of documents; secondly, the inspectors coming to a conclusion (necessarily tentative in the circumstances); and thirdly, putting the substance of that conclusion to the witness. Wien J held that natural justice did not require those three stages. In particular, it did not require the third stage. All that was required was that the inspectors should give Mr Maxwell 'a fair opportunity of correcting what is said against him. An outline of the case is enough.'   *h*

In view of this difference between the judges, I will try to state the considerations which are to be borne in mind in respect of an inquiry under the Companies Act 1948. First and foremost, when a matter is referred to an inspector for investigation and report, it is a very special kind of inquiry. It must not be confused with other inquiries   *j*

---

1 [1970] 3 All ER 535, [1971] Ch 388

which we have had to consider. Remember what it is *not*. It is *not* a trial of anyone, nor anything like it. There is no accused person. There is no prosecutor. There is no charge. It is not like a disciplinary proceeding before a professional body. Nor is it like an application to expel a man from a trade union or a club, or anything of that kind. It is not even like a committee which considers whether there is a prima facie case against a person. It is simply an investigation, without anyone being accused.

Second, there is no one to present a case to the inspector. There is no 'counsel for the commission'. The inspector has to do it all himself. He has himself to seek out the relevant documents and to gather the witnesses. He has himself to study the documents, to examine the witnesses and to have their evidence recorded. He has himself to direct the witnesses to the relevant matters. He has himself to cross-examine them to test their accuracy or their veracity. No one else is there to cross-examine them. Even if a witness says things prejudicial to someone else, that other does not hear it and is not there to cross-examine him.

Third, the investigation is in private. This is necessary because witnesses may say something defamatory of someone else; and it would be quite wrong for it to be published without the party affected being able to challenge it. The only persons present are the inspectors and their staff, the shorthand writer, the witness and his lawyers, if he desires them.

Fourth, the inspectors have to make their report. They should state their findings on the evidence and their opinions on the matters referred to them. If their report is to be of value, they should make it with courage and frankness, keeping nothing back. The public interest demands it. It may on occasion be necessary for them to condemn or criticise a man. Before doing so, they must act fairly by him. But what does fairness demand? That is the question.

Forbes J thought that, in order to do what was fair, after hearing the evidence and studying the documents, the inspectors ought to come to a conclusion (*which was necessarily tentative*) and put the substance of that conclusion to the witness. He was led to that view by the observation of Sachs LJ in *Re Pergamon Press Ltd*[1]. I do not think that is right. Just think what it means. After hearing all the evidence inspectors have to sit down and come to *tentative* conclusions. If these are such as to be critical of any of the witnesses, they have to re-open the inquiry, recall those witnesses, and put to them the criticisms which they are disposed to make. What will be the response of those witnesses? They will at once want to refute the *tentative* conclusions by calling other witnesses, or by asking for further investigations. In short, the inquiry will develop into a series of minor trials in which a witness will be accused of misconduct and seek to answer it. That would hold up the inquiry indefinitely. I do not think it is necessary. It is sufficient for the inspectors to put the points to the witnesses as and when they come in the first place. After hearing the evidence, the inspectors have to come to their conclusions. These need not be tentative in the least. They can be final and definite, ready for their report.

Counsel for Mr Maxwell realised that we might not accept the view of Forbes J. So he put a lesser alternative. He submitted that, in order to do what was fair to a witness, the inspectors ought to take all the relevant statements made by other witnesses—or contained in documents—which were prejudicial to the man and put them to him, so as to give him an opportunity of answering them. If the inspectors failed to do this on matters of substance, they failed to observe the rules of natural justice and the court should declare accordingly.

In support of this submission, counsel treated us to a detailed analysis of the voluminous documents in the case. On the one hand he took the report of the inspectors with all the many criticisms they made of Mr Maxwell. On the other hand he took the transcripts of the evidence given by Mr Maxwell before the inspectors. The report was long and detailed. It covered 209 pages of close type. The transcripts were even

---

1   [1970] 3 All ER at 544, [1971] Ch at 405

longer. They covered 12 days of evidence and contained 366 pages of closely typed
questions and answers. Counsel for Mr Maxwell took each of the criticisms in the report,
one by one. He then went to the transcripts of evidence to see if each criticism had
been put to Mr Maxwell. In all he took us through some 30 criticisms contained in
the report and the transcripts. He asserted that in about three-fourths of the cases
the criticisms had not been put—or not fully put—to Mr Maxwell. In answer counsel
for the department followed the same course. He took us through the criticisms. He
showed that in nearly every one the inspectors had put the point to Mr Maxwell or
had indicated it in such a way that he must have known what was troubling them.
Counsel acknowledged that there were a few criticisms in which the precise point
had not been put to Mr Maxwell; but he asserted that these were covered by the
general line of questions put to him. I will give two or three illustrations to show the
sort of criticisms which were made of the report.
  Conclusion (a) was:

> 'Mr Maxwell obtained information which was confidential to Caxton Holdings
> from a former secretary of Caxton Holdings and used the information to damage
> Caxton Publishing's business in South Africa, so as to strengthen his position in
> the negotiations which he was about to open with the object of acquiring Caxton
> Holdings for Pergamon.'

The transcript of evidence shows that the inspectors put it fairly and squarely to
Mr Maxwell that he employed the former secretary of Caxton Holdings and sent him
and another man to South Africa so as to depress the business of Caxton Holdings
in South Africa, and succeeded to such an extent that Caxton in South Africa lost the
entirety of their sales force as the result of the activities of Pergamon. The only part
which was not put in terms was that Mr Maxwell obtained from the former secretary
information that was confidential. The inspectors appear to have got that from the
former secretary himself, who gave evidence before them.
  Conclusion (c) was:

> '... the offer document containing the offers which Ansbacher, on behalf of
> Pergamon, made for the preference and ordinary shares of Caxton Holdings
> contained this false statement:—"There is no agreement or arrangement where-
> by any share of Caxton acquired pursuant to the offers will or may be transferred
> to any other person" which was false to the knowledge of Mr Ormrod of
> Ansbachers and Mr Maxwell.'

The evidence shows that the inspectors put it fairly and squarely to Mr Maxwell
that that statement was false. He answered that it was true, and argued about the
meaning of it. The inspectors did not in terms put it to him that he *knew* it was
false, but it was clearly to be implied from the way they questioned him.
  Conclusion (h) was:

> '... there were irregularities in the procedures surrounding the increasing of
> the capital of I.L.S.C. from £1,000,000 to £2,000,000, including the creation of
> minutes signed by Mr Maxwell purporting to be minutes of a meeting of
> the board of I.L.S.C. which never took place ... We think that the minutes were
> brought into existence to clothe with some semblance of formality a decision
> between Mr Maxwell, whose signature appears on the minutes, taken without
> regard to the restrictions on the powers of the directors of I.L.S.C. as set out in
> the Memorandum of Association and without regard to the method of altering
> the capital as set out in the Articles of Association and without regard to the
> views of other members of the Board of I.L.S.C.'

The evidence shows that the inspectors put it fairly and squarely to Mr Maxwell
that the minute book was not properly kept and that a minute might be prepared

a purely for the record without there having been a meeting. But this particular minute for this particular meeting was not put to him. It would not seem to be necessary to put this particular minute to him, seeing that there were the questions relating to the minutes in general.

I am not going further into all the details to which we have been subjected for this reason: I think this line of attack is entirely misconceived. It must be remembered

b that the inspectors are doing a public duty in the public interest. They must do what is fair to the best of their ability. They will, of course, put to a witness the points of substance which occur to them—so as to give him the chance to explain or correct any relevant statement which is prejudicial to him. They may even recall him to do so. But they are not to be criticised because they may on occasion overlook something or other. Even the most skilled advocate, expert in cross-examination, forgets

c now and again to put this or that point to a witness. And we all excuse him, knowing how difficult it is to remember everything. The inspector is entitled to at least as much consideration as the advocate. To borrow from Shakespeare[1], he is not to have 'All his faults observ'd, Set in a note-book, learn'd, and conn'd by rote', to make a lawyers' holiday. His task is burdensome and thankless enough as it is. It would be intolerable if he were liable to be pilloried afterwards for doing it. No one of

d standing would ever be found to undertake it. The public interest demands that, so long as he acts honestly and does what is fair to the best of his ability, his report is not to be impugned in the courts of law.

This disposes also of counsel for Mr Maxwell's other complaint. He said that, early on in the inquiry, the inspectors gave an assurance that they would put their tentative conclusions to the witness—and nevertheless failed in the later stages to do

e so, without giving any warning. But counsel for the department pointed out that, when the passages were read at large in their context, the inspectors gave no such assurance. In any case, any failure to do so was an oversight which did not result in any unfairness.

I would only say one word about the relief asked. Counsel for Mr Maxwell recognised that the court could not set aside the report, in whole or in part. It could

f not declare it, or any part of it, to be null and void. At most he asked for a declaration that natural justice had not been observed in the making of it. Whilst I would not restrict it in any way the court's jurisdiction to grant a declaration, the case must be very rare in which it would be right to make such a bare declaration in the air. This is certainly not a case for it.

In conclusion, I would say this. I have studied all the points of detail which have

g been put to us. And I have read the judgment of Wien J on them. I would like to express my appreciation of it and endorse all that he said. This is nothing more or less than an attempt by Mr Maxwell to appeal from the findings of the inspectors to the courts. But Parliament has given no appeal. So Mr Maxwell has tried to get round it by attacking the conduct of the inspectors themselves. In this he has failed utterly. To my mind the inspectors did their work with conspicuous fairness. They

h investigated all the matters with the greatest care. They went meticulously into the details of these complicated transactions. They put to Mr Maxwell all the points which appeared to call for an explanation or an answer. They gave him every opportunity of dealing with them. If there were one or two points which they overlooked, these were as nothing in relation to the wide field which they covered. I regret that, having done their work so well, they should now be harassed by this attack on them.

j It has never been done before in all the many inquiries under the Companies Acts. And I hope it will never happen again. I would dismiss the appeal.

ORR LJ. I agree with the judgment delivered by Lord Denning MR and only add a brief judgment of my own because of the very different views expressed by Forbes J,

---

1   Julius Caesar, IV. iii. 96

F

who heard the application for an interim injunction, and Wien J, who tried the
action, as to the extent of the obligations which natural justice imposes on inspectors
conducting an investigation under s 165 of the Companies Act 1948 and as to the
allegation that the inspectors in this case, having said they would follow a certain
course, later failed to do so.

As to the first of these matters, Forbes J took the view that natural justice, as
applied to such an investigation, requires the adoption of a three stage procedure of
which the third stage is that the inspectors, having heard the evidence and studied
the documents, and having come to tentative conclusions, should, if any of those
conclusions involves a criticism of anyone, put the substance of it to him. On the
second question he took the view, on the evidence before him, that the inspectors in
the present case had announced that they would follow this procedure but in the
event failed to do so. Wien J, however, held that natural justice does not in this
form of investigation require that a three stage procedure should be followed, and
further that the inspectors had never said that they would follow such a procedure.

In holding that natural justice required a three stage procedure, Forbes J founded
his conclusion on two short passages, one in the judgment of Sachs LJ and the other
in that of Buckley LJ in *Re Pergamon Press Ltd*[1]. But these passages in my judgment,
even if considered in isolation, by no means unambiguously support the alleged
three stage procedure. Buckley LJ says that[2]—

> 'the inspectors should give him, if he has not already had it, such information
> of the complaint or criticism which they may make of him in their report
> and of their reasons for doing so . . .'

which seems to me to imply that it is sufficient if he has been given the relevant information as it emerged from the evidence of witnesses or the study of documents before the inspectors formed their tentative conclusion, and the same qualification
may well, as it appears to me, be implied in the corresponding passage from the judgment of Sachs LJ[3]. Moreover both passages must be considered in the context of the
judgments as a whole, in which there is no indication that the other members of the
court disagreed with the conclusion of Lord Denning MR who had firmly rejected, as
going too far, submissions on behalf of different appellants that, whenever the inspectors
thought of making adverse criticisms of someone they should draft the proposed
passage of their report and put it before the party for his comments, or alternatively
that those concerned ought to see any proposed finding against them before it was
included in the report. Finally, the statement of Lord Denning MR that[4]:

> 'The inspectors can obtain information in any way which they think best, but
> before they condemn or criticise a man, they must give him a fair opportunity
> for correcting or contradicting what is said against him. They need not quote
> chapter and verse . . .'

follows closely the language used by Lord Loreburn LC in *Board of Education v Rice*[5]
and quoted with approval in subsequent cases; and we have been referred to no
authority, apart from the above passages, which indicates that in a procedure such as
that with which we are here concerned, which has been in existence since the Companies Act 1862, any higher duty is laid on the inspectors. As Tucker LJ, also quoted
with approval in subsequent cases, pointed out in *Russell v Duke of Norfolk*[6]:

---

1 [1970] 3 All ER 535 at 544, 545, [1971] Ch 388 at 405, 407
2 [1970] 3 All ER at 545, [1971] Ch at 407
3 [1970] 3 All ER at 544, [1971] Ch at 405
4 [1970] 3 All ER at 539, [1971] Ch at 399, 400
5 [1911] AC 179 at 182, [1911-13] All ER Rep 36 at 38
6 [1949] 1 All ER 109 at 118

a
'The requirements of natural justice must depend on the circumstances of the case, the nature of the inquiry, the rules under which the tribunal is acting, the subject-matter that is being dealt with, and so forth.'

In my judgment a clear distinction exists for the present purpose between an inquiry based on a charge or accusation and an investigation such as the present in which the inspectors are required in the public interest to find out what has hap-

b
pened, and in the course of so doing form certain views or conclusions. In the former case it is essential that the person against whom the accusation or charge is made should know its terms. In the latter, on the authority to which I have referred, the only requirement is, in my judgment, as stated by Lord Denning MR in the passage quoted above.

For these reasons I am satisfied that Wien J was right in his conclusion on this issue

c
and in my judgment he was also right, considering the matter on rather fuller material than had been before Forbes J, in finding that the inspectors had throughout the investigation consistently and carefully stopped short of saying that they would adopt the three stage procedure. In this, for the reasons I have given, they were fully justified and I would only add that if they had acceded to some of the requests made to them at different stages the investigation would have been prolonged indefinitely and a

d
procedure which Parliament has considered necessary in the public interest might well have been frustrated.

The remaining issue in the appeal is whether the inspectors fairly put to the plain-tiff the substance of the evidence on the basis of which various criticisms were made of him in the interim report. These matters were considered carefully and in detail by Wien J but in the end the question to be answered was whether in this respect the

e
plaintiff was fairly treated. For the reasons given by the judge I am satisfied that he was.

In the result the question of relief does not arise. Counsel for the plaintiff did not in any event pursue the claim for an injunction or for a declaration that the report was a nullity, but argued that if there had been a failure of natural justice there should be a declaration in some limited form. I accept that this court would have jurisdiction to

f
grant relief by way of a bare declaration, but agree with Lord Denning MR that the circumstances which would justify the grant of such relief in the context of an investi-gation under s 165 would have to be of a very exceptional kind.

I also would dismiss this appeal.

g
LAWTON LJ.   For many decades now the British public have become accustomed to reading about inquiries started by the government of the day or a Minister. Some-times the inquiries are held, as was the one in this case, under powers given by a statute; others are held because a Minister wants to find out something. The subject-matter of inquiry may range from questions touching the integrity of Ministers (the Lynskey Inquiry), and national security (the Vassall Inquiry), to questions whether a

h
youth was assaulted by two police officers (the Thurso Inquiry). Some inquiries are held in public and a few take on some of the characteristics of a state trial; others are held in private. Whenever inquiries are held the British public expects them to be conducted fairly; and on many occasions in the past 60 years the courts have said that they must be conducted fairly.

j
From time to time during that period lawyers and judges have tried to define what constitutes fairness. Like defining an elephant, it is not easy to do, although fairness in practice has the elephantine quality of being easy to recognise. As a result of these efforts a word in common usage has acquired the trappings of legalism: 'acting fairly' has become 'acting in accordance with the rules of natural justice', and on occasion has been dressed up with Latin tags. This phrase in my opinion serves no useful purpose and in recent years it has encouraged lawyers to try to put those who

hold inquiries into legal straitjackets. It is pertinent in this connection to recall what   *a*
Lord Shaw of Dunfermline said in *Local Government Board v Arlidge*[1]:

> 'And the assumption that the methods of natural justice are ex necessitate those
> of courts of justice is wholly unfounded . . . In so far as the term "natural justice"
> means that a result or process should be just, it is a harmless though it may be a
> high-sounding expression; in so far as it attempts to reflect the old jus naturale it
> is a confused and unwarranted transfer into the ethical sphere of a term employed   *b*
> for other distinctions; and, in so far as it is resorted to for other purposes, it is
> vacuous.'

For the purposes of my judgment I intend to ask myself this simple question: did
the inspector act fairly towards the plaintiff?

This question cannot be answered without knowledge of what the inspectors were   *c*
inquiring into. They had been appointed by the Department of Trade and Industry
to investigate the affairs of International Learning Systems Corporation Ltd and Pergamon Press Ltd and to report thereon (see s 165(*a*) of the Companies Act 1948). The
department made the appointment not because there were circumstances suggesting
that the businesses of these companies were being conducted dishonestly or that those
connected with their management had been guilty of fraud (see s 165(*b*)(i) and (ii)),   *d*
but because it had been suggested by the Takeover Panel that Pergamon Press Ltd's
shareholders might not have been given all the information with respect to its affairs
which they might reasonably have expected (see s 165(*b*)(iii)).

In their terms of reference the inspectors were specifically instructed to report on
this matter of information. It followed that they had to find out first what information
had been given and then to express their opinion whether enough had been given.   *e*
What was to be done if they were of the opinion that not enough information had been
given, or the affairs of the two companies were in disorder, was not for them to decide.
The inspectors were not instructed to investigate any charge against the plaintiff
or any other officer of these companies; their duty was to find out what had happened,
and to report their opinion. This was a very different task from that which is sometimes imposed on those holding inquiries when they are asked to decide whether   *f*
allegations of specific misconduct have been made out. For examples, see *University
of Ceylon v Fernando*[2] and *Kanda v Government of Malaya*[3]. That which fairness calls
for in one kind of inquiry may not be called for in another. Those conducting an
inquiry are in the best position to decide what fairness calls for.

In all these cases there are, in my judgment, two facets of fairness: what is done
and how it is done. Doing what is right may still result in unfairness if it is done in   *g*
the wrong way.

As to what was done, once it became apparent to the inspectors that the plaintiff
might be open to criticism in their report, on many occasions they put to him the
substance of what other witnesses had said about him which could, if they accepted
the evidence, be the basis for criticism. On a few occasions they did not, and by the
standards of perfection it might have been better if they had. In putting the sub-   *h*
stance of what had been said by other witnesses the inspectors were, no doubt, trying
to do what those holding inquiries had been enjoined to do by Lord Loreburn LC
in *Board of Education v Rice*[4], namely to give any one in the plaintiff's position a fair
opportunity for correcting or contradicting any relevant statement prejudicial to his
view.

What they did not do was to give the plaintiff an opportunity of correcting or   *j*
contradicting the opinions which they were minded to report to the department

---

1   [1915] AC 120 at 138, [1914-15] All ER Rep 1 at 10
2   [1960] 1 All ER 631, [1960] 1 WLR 223
3   [1962] AC 322, [1962] 2 WLR 1153
4   [1911] AC 179 at 182, [1911-13] All ER Rep 36 at 38

a as to what evidence they thought credible and what inferences they should draw from such evidence. The plaintiff submits they should have done so, and that their omission constituted unfairness. I do not agree. The plaintiff's submission was founded on some observations made by Sachs LJ during the hearing of what was the first of a series of proceedings which have been started by the plaintiff in respect of this inquiry: see *Re Pergamon Press Ltd*[1]. The learned Lord Justice was there commenting

b on what the court, of which he was a member, had been told the inspectors had promised to do. The inspectors had said more than what had been reported and that which had not been reported altered the sense. Further, endorsing with his approval what the inspectors were reported to have said was not necessary for the purpose of deciding the appeal. The researches of counsel have not produced any other case which has suggested that at the end of an inquiry those likely to be criticised in a

c report should be given an opportunity of refuting the tentative conclusions of whoever is making it. Those who conduct inquiries have to base their decisions, findings, conclusions or opinions (whichever is the appropriate word to describe what they have a duty to do) on the evidence. In my judgment they are no more bound to tell a witness likely to be criticised in their report what they have in mind to say about him than has a judge sitting alone who has to decide which of two conflicting witnesses

d is telling the truth. The judge must ensure that the witness whose credibility is suspected has a fair opportunity of correcting or contradicting the substance of what other witnesses have said or are expected to say which is in conflict with his testimony. Inspectors should do the same but I can see no reason why they should do any more.

There was little criticism of the way the inspectors had done what they did. It was submitted, however, that when putting to the plaintiff for his comments the sub-

e stance of what witnesses had said they did not make plain what was the sting of their questions, with the result that the plaintiff was deprived of an opportunity of refuting any injurious criticism which was founded on his answers. An example was said to be provided by conclusion (c) in para 319 of the inspectors' report which was to the effect that the plaintiff knew that an offer document contained a false statement. In order to deal with this kind of criticism it is necessary to consider how the inquiry

f was conducted. Both the inspectors were distinguished professional men. The plaintiff is clearly intelligent and quick witted; he has had an exceptionally wide experience of life and when the inquiry started he was a member of Parliament. He did not have to have spelt out to him the relevance and point of every question he was asked. The inspectors must have appreciated this. It is manifest from the transcript that they treated him throughout with courtesy and patience; and Mr

g Owen Stable QC, who asked nearly all the questions, was clearly most anxious to avoid any kind of aggressive, hectoring cross-examination. For my own part I can but admire the way he dealt with a witness who tended to be verbose and irrelevant. I am satisfied that the plaintiff was able to appreciate, and nearly always did appreciate, what was the point of the questions put to him.

I come now to what, in my judgment, should be the approach of the court to the

h criticisms which have been made of the conduct of the inspectors. The plaintiff submitted that many, but not all, of the specific criticisms of him which they put into their report were made unfairly. This was enough, it was submitted, to justify the court finding and declaring that the inquiry had been conducted unfairly. Alternatively, it was submitted that the court could find that some of the criticisms were unfair and specify in the declaration which they were. If a declaration is an appropriate remedy

j in a case of this kind, and I am doubtful whether it is for reasons which I will state later, the proper approach, so it seems to me, is that which is followed in the Criminal Division of this court when exercising its jurisdiction under s 2 of the Criminal Appeal Act 1968. When it is submitted that a verdict should be quashed because of alleged irregularities in the course of a trial the proceedings have to be considered as a whole

---

1 [1970] 3 All ER 535 at 544, [1971] Ch 388 at 405

and the question asked whether the verdict was unsafe or unsatisfactory. In this case *a* the question is whether this inquiry, considered as a whole, was conducted fairly. It would be wrong to treat the inquiry as raising a series of issues, some of which could be said to have been fairly determined, some not. To do anything of the kind would get close to giving dissatisfied witnesses a right of appeal when Parliament has not done so. For my part, I have no hesitation in finding that it was conducted fairly. I would adopt the detailed reasoning set out in Wien J's judgment. *b*

I should say in conclusion that I am doubtful whether, even if I had found on the merits in favour of the plaintiff, I would have adjudged that he was entitled to a declaration that the inquiry had been conducted unfairly or that specified criticisms had been made unfairly. That was the only relief he asked for from this court. Below he had asked for an injunction against the department to restrain further publication of the report, but this he could not get because the department represents the Crown. *c* He had also asked for a declaration that the report was null and void; but before this court, without abandoning this, his counsel did not ask for such a declaration. For my part I cannot see how any such declaration could ever be made in respect of a report made to the Minister under s 165. The courts cannot declare null and void events which have happened. What they can do is to declare that the making of a report shall have no legal consequences, as was done in *Kanda's* case[1]. The report in *d* this case itself neither produced, nor could directly produce, any legal consequences. On receiving it the Minister had to decide what action to take; and even if the inquiry had been conducted unfairly the report might have contained information which the Minister would be under a duty to consider for the purpose of performing his statutory duty to safeguard the interests of shareholders. The fact is that a declaration to the effect that the inquiry had been conducted unfairly or that specified criticisms had *e* been made unfairly would produce no practical result. The Minister would not be stopped from initiating proceedings if he thought that the facts justified such a course. It was submitted that such a declaration would protect the plaintiff's reputation. It might; but the protection would only be temporary if the Minister initiated proceedings; and in any proceedings the fact that the inquiry had been conducted unfairly would be irrelevant. In my judgment a man who has been unfairly criticised in a *f* report made under s 165 is in the same position as one who had been unfairly criticised in a speech made in Parliament. He has suffered 'damnum' but not 'injuria'. Cases may occur (although they are unlikely to do so as long as the Minister appoints competent and experienced professional men as inspectors) in which the inspectors had behaved so unfairly that the public interest requires a court to say so. In my judgment, even if there had been unfairness in the conduct of this inquiry, which *g* there was not, this is not such a case.

I would dismiss the appeal.

Appeal dismissed. Leave to appeal to the House of Lords refused.

Solicitors: *Lewis Silkin & Partners* (for the plaintiff); *Treasury Solicitor* (for the depart- *h* ment and the inspectors).

L J Kovats Esq   Barrister.

1   [1962] AC 322, [1962] 2 WLR 1153

a

Brown v Allied Ironfounders Ltd

HOUSE OF LORDS

LORD REID, LORD MORRIS OF BORTH-Y-GEST, VISCOUNT DILHORNE, LORD SIMON OF GLAISDALE AND LORD KILBRANDON

11th, 12th FEBRUARY, 27th MARCH 1974

b

Factories – Lifting excessive weights – Person not to be employed to lift, carry or move excessive weight – Meaning of 'employed to . . . move' – Employee instructed to paint stillages – Necessary to turn stillages to paint underneath – Stillages too heavy for one person to turn safely – Employers knowing stillages had been turned single-handed on previous occasions – Employee not instructed to seek help in turning stillages – Help available if asked for – Whether employee

c *'employed to . . . move' stillages single-handed – Factories Act 1961, s 72(1).*

The defendants employed the plaintiff in their factory. Her usual work having come to an end temporarily, the plaintiff was asked to help in another department. The chargehand in that department told her to paint stillages, i e wire mesh cages each weighing one to 1¼ cwt. In order to paint the bottom of a stillage it was necessary to

d turn it on its side. It was the normal practice for two women to turn the stillages. The plaintiff had worked on painting stillages two years previously with two or three other women and they had then helped each other to turn them over. The chargehand knew, however, that some women did turn stillages single-handed. The plaintiff was working alone on painting the stillages and, although she could have obtained assistance, she turned them without doing so. As a result she suffered injury

e to her back. She instituted proceedings against the defendants claiming that they were in breach of the duty imposed on them by s 72(1)[a] of the Factories Act 1961 in that she had been 'employed to . . . move [a] load so heavy as to be likely to cause injury to [her]'. The defendants admitted that turning the stillages was work too heavy for a woman to do on her own.

f **Held** – Since the plaintiff had been employed to paint the stillages, and since, in order to paint them, it was necessary to turn them, it followed that she had been employed to turn them. As the stillages were too heavy to be turned by one woman and as (per Lord Simon of Glaisdale and Lord Kilbrandon) the defendants knew that stillages had in the past been moved by women on their own, s 72(1) imposed a duty on the defendants to instruct the plaintiff not to turn the stillages without assistance. It was immaterial that the plaintiff could have obtained assistance. Since the defendants had

g not instructed her to do so it followed that the plaintiff had been employed to turn the stillages single-handed and the defendants were therefore in breach of their statutory duty (see p 136 *d*, p 137 *a d g* and *j*, p 139 *b f* and *g*, p 140 *f* and *g* and p 141 *c* to *g*, post).

Notes

h For provisions as to lifting excessive weights, see 17 Halsbury's Laws (3rd Edn) 122, para 203.

     For the Factories Act 1961, s 72, see 13 Halsbury's Statutes (3rd Edn) 473.

Cases referred to in opinions

Kinsella v Harris Lebus Ltd (17th December 1963) unreported; [1963] Bar Library

j   transcript 327; noted 108 Sol Jo 14, CA.

Peat v N J Muschamp & Co Ltd (1969) 7 KIR 469, CA.

Appeal

This was an appeal by Christina Brown against an interlocutor of the First Division of

---

a   Section 72(1) is set out at p 138 *e*, post

the Court of Session dated 18th May 1973 reversing an interlocutor of the Lord
Ordinary (Lord Wheatley) pronounced on 16th June 1971. The action was an action of
damages in which the appellant sought reparation from the respondents, Allied Iron-
founders Ltd, in respect of an injury to her back which she claimed to have sustained
on 2nd September 1966 while in the employment of the respondents. The Lord
Ordinary found the respondents liable in damages to the appellant. The respondents
reclaimed to the Inner House and the First Division unanimously allowed the reclaiming motion and assoilzied the respondents. The facts are set out in the opinion
of Viscount Dilhorne.

T W F O'Brien QC and *J F Wheatley* for the appellant.
D M Ross QC and *J A D Hope* for the respondents.

Their Lordships took time for consideration.

27th March. The following opinions were delivered.

LORD REID. My Lords, for the reasons given by my noble and learned friend,
Viscount Dilhorne, I would allow the appeal.

LORD MORRIS OF BORTH-Y-GEST. My Lords, I have found this case more
difficult than I think have other of your Lordships. Common law fault in the respondents having been negatived, the appellant's success in her action depended on her
showing that there was a breach of statutory duty. Though s 72(1) of the Factories
Act 1961 begins with the words 'A person shall not be employed to . . .' it is clear, as is
pointed out in the opinion of the First Division, that the effect is to impose a prohibition on an employer. So what the section provides is that no employer shall employ a
person to lift, carry or move any load so heavy as to be likely to cause any injury to
him. Accordingly, it was for the appellant at the trial to prove that the respondents
did employ her to do just that.

Both sides accept the findings of fact of the learned Lord Ordinary (Lord Wheatley).
No issue in relation to contributory negligence has been raised by the appellant so we
have not been faced with any problem nor asked to deal with any question whether
difficulty was presented by a finding that the appellant was herself contributorily
negligent if what she did was only what she was (in breach of statute) employed to do.

In the result I think that the decision in the case depends on the question whether
the very careful findings of fact of the learned Lord Ordinary justified his conclusion.
Without rehearsing all those findings it is to be noted that the appellant had once or
twice (though apparently some two years previously) been employed in the department to which, on 2nd September 1966, she was invited to go when she was held up in
her own work (which consisted of stud welding) in her own department. The findings
include a finding that on those other occasions she had always worked in association
with other women employees; that she knew that it was the 'normal' practice to have
the assistance of another employee to turn a stillage; that it was a reasonable assumption that when she had first worked in that department she would have been told that
she could always invoke help when stillages had to be moved. But on the day in
question she was not told by Mr Leishman that she should get help or could get help if
she desired it. On that day there were, in fact, two employees who, though engaged
on somewhat different tasks, were reasonably close to where the appellant was sent to
work, and who knew of the practice to give help when it was required. Though they
had not actually been told to give such help it would have been in order for them to
give it. The evidence was that they would have been willing to help the appellant had
she asked them to help her in moving or lifting on the day in question.

The appellant was told by Mr Leishman to paint stillages. In order that the painting
should be properly done the stillages would at some time have to be lifted or moved.

a Such lifting or moving was therefore something that was inherently a part of what the appellant was employed to do. Furthermore, stillages were not of varying but of constant and recognisable size, pattern and weight. She was sent to do the work alone. But if she did the lifting or moving alone it was likely (though not inevitable) that injury would be caused to her. Though she was (inferentially) employed to lift or move the stillages she was not expressly told to do the lifting or moving alone and, on *b* the other hand, she was not expressly told that she must not do it alone.

The position was, therefore, that on the day in question the appellant became obliged to leave the department where she was then working and to go to another. She was told by Mr Leishman to do the work of painting stillages. That work was not unfamiliar to her. There was a finding of the learned Lord Ordinary that she was displeased with the way in which she was told to get on with the work. Though there *c* was evidence that in connection with the painting of the stillages there was what was said to be a 'general' practice to seek help when stillages had to be moved there was contrary evidence to the effect that some women did not follow that practice but lifted or moved them without asking for help. That was known to Mr Leishman.

In all the circumstances, did the giving of a direction to proceed with the work of painting stillages involve and include a direction to lift or move them? To that question *d* I think that the answer must be, Yes. The work necessarily involved that in the course of painting a stillage it would have to be moved or lifted. But did the direction involve or include a direction to lift or move them unaided? If the lifting or moving of them unaided was to be excluded, should that have been a matter for specific instruction and specific exclusion? Should such a specific instruction and exclusion have been given, having regard to the special circumstances that the appellant was *e* not doing what was at the time her normal work (even though she had done such work some two years previously) and was (in what she either rightly or wrongly thought was rather an abrupt and unsympathetic manner), just sent to do the work of painting and sent to do it alone and in a place where no others were then doing that work and without any word to her or to others as to the seeking or giving of help?

That she should have been given a specific instruction was the conclusion of the *f* learned Lord Ordinary. He expressed it as follows:

'Leishman on his own admission knew that some women carried out this operation without asking for his assistance. When, on behalf of the [respondents], he employed the [appellant] to do this job, he ought to have instructed her that she was not to lift or move the stillages without assistance. She was sent to do the job alone, and she might be one of the women who would attempt to do it all *g* without assistance. The failure to instruct her not to lift or move the stillages without assistance and leaving it to her own individual decision whether to ask for assistance or not resulted in her doing the job alone and so constituted a breach of s 72(1).'

The question arising in this appeal is whether the decision of the Lord Ordinary can *h* be supported and whether it ought to have been reversed. I do not find any assistance in any authority. That is for the reason that, in my view, a question whether a person was or was not employed to lift, carry or move a load so heavy as to be likely to cause any injury to him is a question of fact which calls for decision having regard to the particular circumstances of each particular case. After considerable hesitation I have reached the conclusions that the special facts of the case did warrant the finding of the *j* learned Lord Ordinary that there had been a breach of statutory duty.

Accordingly I would allow the appeal.

VISCOUNT DILHORNE. My Lords, the appellant was employed as a stud welder by the respondents in their factory at Falkirk. When on 2nd September 1966 she required more materials for her work, she was told by her chargehand that they

were not available and that she would have to wait seven to ten days for them. He
asked her if she would work in another department in the factory to help out and she
agreed to do so. He saw a Mr Leishman, the chargehand in the blackening shop, and
then told the appellant that there was a job for her there. When the appellant saw
Mr Leishman, he seemed to have had some doubt about how to employ her, but in
the end told her to paint stillages. They are wire mesh cages used for transporting
metal from one department to another and measured about three feet six inches in
length, two feet to two feet six inches in width and between three and four feet in
height. Each weighed in the region of one to $1\frac{1}{4}$ cwt.

To paint the bottom of the stillage, it had to be turned on its side. Then when the
painting was finished, it had to be raised on to its legs again. It was admitted by the
respondents that the stillages were too heavy to be turned by one woman working
alone.

The appellant, who was working alone when she was painting the stillages, turned
them on that day without assistance. As a result she hurt her back. She instituted
these proceedings claiming damages alleging negligence and breach of statutory duty
by the respondents. The Lord Ordinary (Lord Wheatley) rejected the claim based on
negligence but found that there had been a breach of statutory duty. He also held that
she had been guilty of contributory negligence, which he assessed at 50 per cent.

In the reclaiming motion of the respondents, the only issue raised was whether the
finding that there had been a breach of statutory duty was right. Both parties accepted
the Lord Ordinary's assessment of the damages and the appellant did not challenge
his finding of negligence on her part and his rejection of her claim at common law.
The Inner House held that there had been no breach of statutory duty and from their
decision the appellant now appeals.

Section 72(1) of the Factories Act 1961 is in the following terms:

'A person shall not be employed to lift, carry or move any load so heavy as to
be likely to cause injury to him.'

In the light of the admission that turning the stillages was work too heavy for a
woman to do alone, the only question for decision in this appeal is whether the
appellant was employed to turn them single-handed, or, as the respondents contended,
only employed to turn them with assistance.

In their answer to condescendence II the respondents admitted that it was normal
practice for women painting stillages to have assistance in turning them over. The
appellant had worked on painting stillages, she said, two years before. She had then
worked on painting them with two or three other women and they had helped each
other in turning them over. She admitted that that was the normal practice. She did
not say that she knew women had done it single-handed. Mr Leishman said in evidence that he knew that some women did turn the stillages single-handed. On 2nd
September 1966 the appellant was sent to paint stillages by herself but she could have
had assistance in turning them over if she had asked for it.

The fact that it was normal practice for two women to turn the stillages does not
mean that if a woman did it by herself she was doing what she was not employed to do.
To say that that was the normal practice does not mean that it was the invariable practice. The appellant was not told on 2nd September 1966 that she must not move stillages
by herself and it was not established that when previously employed on painting stillages she had been told that. She knew that turning them by herself was a departure from the normal practice but there was no finding that she knew that she must
not do so.

Section 72(1) is the first of four sections in the Act dealing with employment.
Section 73 provides that a female person shall not be employed in a part of a factory
in which certain processes are carried on; s 74 that a woman or young person shall not
be employed in certain operations, one of which is the cleaning of workrooms where
certain work is carried on, and s 75 prohibits the employment of a woman or young

person on certain processes save under certain conditions. So in relation to s 73, it is the place where a female young person is employed and in relation to ss 74 and 75 it is the work a woman or young person was employed to do that has to be considered. In relation to s 72(1) there are two questions to be considered: first, was the load so heavy as to be likely to cause injury, and, secondly, was a person employed to lift, carry or move it. The first does not arise in this case in view of the respondents' admission. As to the second, a person employed, as the appellant was, to paint stillages, has in order to do that to turn them. So she was employed to turn them and not having been told not to turn them by herself, either on 2nd September 1966, or previously, she cannot, in my opinion, be said to have been doing something she was not employed to do when she turned them single-handed.

We were told that only two cases on the construction of s 72(1) and its predecessor, s 56(1), of the Factories Act 1937, could be traced. One was *Kinsella v Harris Lebus Ltd*[1], the other *Peat v N J Muschamp & Co Ltd*[2]. The transcript[3] of the judgments in the Court of Appeal in the *Kinsella* case[1] show that the plaintiff had claimed damages for negligence and for breach of s 56(1) of the Factories Act 1937, as amended by the Factories Act 1959. As amended, s 56(1) was in the same terms as s 72(1) of the 1961 Act. Judge Lane had held that there was negligence but no breach of statutory duty. The defendants appealed and the plaintiff appealed against the finding that there had been no breach of statutory duty. The plaintiff had suffered a hernia as a result of lifting a jig weighing 145 lbs on to a press. The Court of Appeal appear to have based their conclusion that there was no breach of statutory duty on the ground that the weight of the jig was not such as likely to cause injury to the plaintiff, but Willmer LJ went on to say:

'Moreover, it is to be borne in mind that it would be difficult to prove that this plaintiff "was employed to lift, carry or move" any such load as the statute is aimed at; for the evidence shows that facilities were available to him for obtaining assistance if he required it. In such circumstances, it seems to me that a prosecution under the Act would be doomed to failure.'

I take it that by this observation Willmer LJ meant that the fact that the defendants had made arrangements to enable the plaintiff to obtain assistance supported the contention that he was not employed to lift the jig by himself; but if he meant—and I do not think he can have—that the fact that the plaintiff could have had help, showed that he was not employed to lift the jig by himself, I cannot agree with him. If it is left to a workman to decide whether to lift, move or carry heavy objects and he carries one which is too heavy for him and suffers injury, in my view he cannot be said to have been doing something he was not employed to do when he carried it.

In *Peat v N J Muschamp & Co Ltd*[2] the Court of Appeal dismissed an appeal from Blain J who had rejected a claim based on negligence and on breach of s 72(1). There the plaintiff had suffered injury as a result of lifting a piece of chain of some 65 lbs in weight a distance of three feet from the ground. He was a one-legged man who had suffered some back strain in the past and he was one of a gang of four men all of whom were invalided to some extent or physically handicapped. Blain J held that the plaintiff was employed to do his work 'with such assistance from fellow members of the gang as he might on occasions need if and when he needed it'. Davies LJ in the course of his judgment is reported as having said[4]:

'... it is beyond question that the plaintiff had been told by the foreman that he must ask for help and assistance if he ever wanted it to lift anything'

---

1   (1963) 108 Sol Jo 14
2   (1969) 7 KIR 469
3   [1963] Bar Library transcript 327
4   (1969) 7 KIR at 473

and that when the plaintiff told the foreman that the chain was too heavy for him, the plaintiff admitted that the foreman 'told him to get somebody to help him'. Davies LJ thought that the case was much stronger in favour of the defendants that the *Kinsella* case[1] for a number of reasons, one of them being that help was more readily available. He cited a passage from Willmer LJ's judgment which included the passage cited above and dismissed the appeal. Widgery LJ was also in favour of dismissing the appeal, saying[2]:

> 'The only approach to this matter which even begins to fit the section is to say that he was employed to lift this 65 pound load from the ground by himself, but the judge's finding, properly understood, is that he was not so employed and that, if this load had to be taken from the ground, it was open to him, and he was expected, if he thought it right, to get assistance from another member of the gang.'

Later he said[2] that the only question which had troubled him was whether the employers were wrong in leaving to this plaintiff the decision whether or not he should ask for assistance. He accepted[3] that a man who had to lift articles of different weights and different sizes and shape might well expect his employers to give him guidance as to when he should and when he should not seek assistance.

> 'An employer in such a case cannot wash his hands of the whole problem by simply telling the employee to ask for help when he thinks he needs it.'

Karminski LJ agreed that the appeal should be dismissed.

If the ratio decidendi of that case was that it was left to the plaintiff to decide whether or not to lift the chain by himself and if he decided to lift it by himself, he was not employed to do that, then, in my opinion, the decision was wrong. On the other hand, if in fact the plaintiff had been told that he must not lift the chain without assistance, then when he lifted it he did something that he was not employed to do and the decision was right. The question whether or not assistance was readily available if required appears to me irrelevant to the vital question, what was the employee employed to do?

For these reasons, in my opinion, this appeal should be allowed.

LORD SIMON OF GLAISDALE. My Lords, I have had the advantage of reading in draft the speeches prepared by my noble and learned friends, Viscount Dilhorne and Lord Kilbrandon. I agree with them, and I would allow the appeal.

LORD KILBRANDON. My Lords, it is agreed that the question in this appeal is to be decided on the facts as they were found by the Lord Ordinary. They have been summarised by my noble and learned friend, Viscount Dilhorne, in his speech, and I do not need to state them for myself. We have to decide whether the appellant was employed to lift, carry or move a load so heavy as to be likely to cause injury to her. If she was, her employers were in breach of s 72 of the Factories Act 1961.

In the course of day-to-day operation of a factory the employees are constantly moving weights as part of their duties under their contracts. Employers are not required or expected to be on constant watch to see that no one moves a weight which is too heavy for him, nor would such solicitude be well received, however

---

1   (1963) 108 Sol Jo 14
2   (1969) 7 KIR at 476
3   (1969) 7 KIR at 476, 477

a kindly intentioned. It is clearly not called for by the terms of s 72. Often it must be left to the employee to make up the load he is to move; if the work does not necessarily involve the moving of injuriously heavy weights, but is quite compatible with the selection by the employee of a safe load for individual movement, the employer cannot be said to have employed him to move a weight which was not safe. Again, some movements obviously require, and must be allotted, more than one man.

b Take a length of railway track weighing 600 lbs, and suppose that a gang of five men is normally detailed to lift it. Then each man is employed to lift a load of 120 lbs. But if two members of the gang elect to leave the job for some purpose of their own, and the three remaining decide to lift the rail by themselves, then each is lifting 200 lbs, which may be a weight likely to cause him injury, although each is only employed to lift 120 lbs. The employer is not in breach of the section.

c I give these instances for two reasons. First, they show what, with all respect, seems to me to be the inadequacy of the test suggested by learned counsel for the appellant, namely, that unless a person is prohibited from doing a particular act in the course of his employment, he is employed to do that act. There may possibly be fields, other than the present, in which such a test would be useful. But I cannot believe that s 72 involves this, that whenever a man in the course of his employment lifts a load

d which is too heavy for him, then unless he has been forbidden to lift that load, he has been employed to lift that load.

Secondly, the instances provide a marked contrast to the circumstances of the present appeal. The appellant was sent to paint, and therefore incidentally to move, stillages. To move a stillage is a two-woman job. The foreman set her to painting it by herself. He knew that from time to time stillages were moved as a one-woman

e job, and that so to do subjected the woman concerned to a load so heavy as to be likely to cause her injury. He did not detail anyone to help the appellant, and he did not order her to apply for help when she wanted to move a stillage. It was left to her to ask for help when she wanted it. In these circumstances I would hold that the foreman selected the load, namely, about $1\frac{1}{4}$ cwt, for the appellant to move, in the sense that, in the knowledge that that load was accepted by some of the women who painted

f stillages, he took the risk of the appellant treating it as a one-woman load. I confess that the case seems to me to be a narrow one, but in my opinion the knowledge of the past dangerous practice imposed here a duty to order help to stand by or to insist definitely on the appellant applying for help. Not having taken either of these steps, he must be held to have employed the appellant to move a load of $1\frac{1}{4}$ cwt. To compare this job with my previous instances, if the foreman had taken either of these

g steps, and the appellant had nevertheless decided to move the stillage alone, she would have been employed to move half the weight, not the whole weight, of the stillage, and s 72 would not have been contravened.

We were referred to *Kinsella v Harris Lebus Ltd*[1] and *Peat v N J Muschamp & Co Ltd*[2]. For my part I find the reports of these decisions, as also the facts on which they depended, to be of some obscurity, and I do not think that, although they appear to be

h the only authorities on s 72, they are helpful in this case. I am to some extent confirmed in the general view I have taken about the duties of employers under the section by the fact that there should be such unusual paucity of decisions about a process which is of the essence of all industrial work—the lifting and moving of loads. The employer will not normally order dangerous loads to be handled, and the employee is too skilled and sensible to do it off his own bat. In any event, this is not

j the class of case in which the multiplication of citations is profitable.

I would accordingly agree with my noble and learned friend, Viscount Dilhorne, that this appeal should be allowed.

---

1 (1963) 108 Sol Jo 14
2 (1969) 7 KIR 469

Appeal allowed.   **a**

Solicitors: *Grant, Saw & Sons*, agents for *T Allison Gray & Sutherland*, Falkirk, and
Thos J Addly, Son & Co, Edinburgh (for the appellant); *Blount, Petre & Co*, agents
for *Mackintosh & Co*, Glasgow, and *Simpson & Marwick WS*, Edinburgh (for the
respondents).

b

Christine Ivamy Barrister.

R v Hogan

Overruled in DPP v HUMPHRYS
[1976] 2 All ER 497

c

CROWN COURT AT LEEDS

LAWSON J

19th, 20th, 21st, 22nd NOVEMBER 1973

Dictum of LAWSON J at 154 approved
in R v HUMPHRYS [1975] 2 All ER
1023

Criminal law – Estoppel – Issue estoppel – Application to criminal proceedings – Operation in **d**
favour of prosecution as well as defendant – Circumstances in which issue estoppel applicable –
Defendant convicted of causing grievous bodily harm with intent – Victim subsequently dying
– Defendant charged with murder – Issues of grievous bodily harm, intent, and absence of
lawful excuse determined by verdict of jury in earlier proceedings – Whether defendant
precluded from raising those issues at trial for murder.

In the course of an incident on the night of 15th June 1972 the defendant injured **e**
another man. He was charged with causing that man grievous bodily harm with
intent to do so, contrary to s 18 of the Offences against the Person Act 1861. He
pleaded not guilty and raised the issue of self-defence but on 12th October he was
found guilty by a jury. He did not appeal against his conviction. On 9th November
the injured man died. The defendant was charged with his murder and pleaded not
guilty. Before the trial the judge was invited to rule whether it was open to the **f**
defendant to rehearse before the jury at his trial for murder any of the matters in
issue before the jury at the trial in October 1972.

Held – (i) The doctrine of 'issue estoppel' applied in criminal as well as in civil proceedings. Furthermore it operated not only in favour of the defendant but also in
favour of the prosecution. The doctrine applied where there had been earlier pro- **g**
ceedings involving the same defendant in which issues had arisen and been established
which could be determined with precision and certainty by referring to the earlier
record and by what had transpired in the course of the earlier proceedings in relation
to those issues (see p 154 g and h and p 155 b, post).

(ii) In order to have convicted the defendant in the earlier proceedings of causing **h**
grievous bodily harm with intent the jury must have found it proved (a) that the
injured man had suffered grievous bodily harm; (b) that the grievous bodily harm
had been inflicted deliberately by the defendant; (c) that it had been inflicted without
lawful excuse and not in self-defence, and (d) that at the time when it was so inflicted
the defendant had intended to cause grievous bodily harm to the injured man. It
followed that the jury in the second trial were precluded from reconsidering those
four issues which had been determined by the first jury's verdict of guilty, but could **j**
consider such questions as the causation of the death and provocation, neither of
which had been in issue at the first trial (see p 145 h to p 146 c and p 155 h and j, post).

R v Wilkes (1948) 77 CLR 511, dictum of Lord MacDermott in *Sambasivam v Public
Prosecutor, Federation of Malaya* [1950] AC at 479, *Mraz v The Queen (No 2)* (1956) 96
CLR 62 and *Brown v Robinson* (1960) 60 SRNSW 297 applied.

a Dicta of Lord Devlin in *Connelly v DPP* [1964] 2 All ER at 437, and of Lord Parker CJ and Diplock LJ in *Mills v Cooper* [1967] 2 All ER at 103, 104, 105, not followed.

Note
For estoppel by record, see 15 Halsbury's Laws (3rd Edn) 176-178, paras 346-348; for estoppel by judgments inter partes and res judicata, see ibid 181-187, paras 354-
b 362.

Cases referred to in judgment
Brown v Robinson (1960) 60 SRNSW 297.
Connelly v Director of Public Prosecutions [1964] 2 All ER 401, [1964] AC 1254, [1964] 2 WLR 1145, 128 JP 418, 48 Cr App Rep 183, HL; *affg* sub nom *R v Connelly* [1963] 3
c   All ER 510, [1963] 3 WLR 839, CCA, Digest (Cont Vol B) 250, *472a*.
Harris v State of Georgia (1941) 17 SE 2d 573.
Kemp v The King (1951) 83 CLR 341.
Mills v Cooper [1967] 2 All ER 100, [1967] 2 QB 459, [1967] 2 WLR 1343, 131 JP 349, 65 LGR 275, DC, Digest (Cont Vol C) 337, *472b*.
Mraz v R (No 2) (1956) 96 CLR 62, 30 ALJ 604.
d *R v Clift* (1952) 52 SRNSW 213, 69 WNNSW 87.
R v Maskell (1970) 54 Cr App Rep 429, CA.
R v Ollis [1900] 2 QB 758, [1900-3] All ER Rep 733, 69 LJQB 918, 83 LT 251, 64 JP 518, CCR, 14 Digest (Repl) 422, *4104*.
R v Thomas [1949] 2 All ER 662, [1950] 1 KB 26, 33 Cr App Rep 200, CCA, 14 Digest (Repl) 383, *3735*.
e *R v Wilkes* (1948) 77 CLR 511.
Sambasivam v Public Prosecutor, Federation of Malaya [1950] AC 458, 66 (pt 2) TLR 254, PC, 15 Digest (Repl) 784, **4912*.
Sealfon v United States (1948) 332 US 575, 68 S Ct 237.

Ruling
f On 19th November 1973 the defendant, James Faulkner Hogan, was arraigned in the Crown Court at Leeds and pleaded not guilty to the murder of David Moroney on 9th November 1972. Before the jury were empanelled counsel for the Crown, with the assent of counsel for the defendant, invited Lawson J to rule whether it was open for the defendant to put in issue before the jury any matters which the Crown submitted could be taken as concluded against him and in favour of the Crown in rela-
g tion to the events which occurred on the night of 15th-16th June 1972, on which night Moroney received injuries which the Crown contended, but the defendant did not admit, had caused the death of Moroney on 9th November 1972, by reason that on 12th October 1972 the defendant had been convicted by a jury of causing grievous bodily harm to Moroney on that night with intent to cause him grievous bodily harm, contrary to s 18 of the Offences against the Person Act 1861. After hearing
h argument Lawson J gave his ruling in favour of the Crown and the trial thereafter proceeded. At the conclusion of the trial Lawson J gave a considered judgment on the issues raised. The facts are set out in the judgment.

H H Ognall QC and *Brian Walsh* for the Crown.
Humphrey Potts QC and *David Wagstaff* for the defendant.
j
                                                                    Cur adv vult

22nd November. **LAWSON J.** On the night of 15th-16th June 1972 an incident occurred in Huddersfield in which the defendant, James Faulkner Hogan, and Daniel Moroney were involved; in the course of this Moroney received injuries. Following this incident the defendant was arrested and charged with causing grievous bodily harm to Moroney with intent to cause him grievous bodily harm, contrary to s 18 of the Offences against the Person Act 1861. In due course the defendant was committed for trial on this charge on which, on arraignment, he pleaded not guilty. At his trial by jury at this Crown Court in October 1972 he was, on 12th October, found guilty of the offence charged and thereafter duly sentenced to imprisonment He did not appeal and has not appealed against this conviction.

On 9th November 1972 Moroney died and the defendant was subsequently committed for trial charged with the murder of Moroney on 9th November 1972, to which, on arraignment, he pleaded not guilty. It is appropriate to mention that, from the time of his arrest on 19th June 1972 until the present trial, he has been in custody either awaiting trial on the first charge or serving the sentence of imprisonment which was imposed on him on 12th October.

I was informed by counsel for the prosecution, which is being conducted by the Director of Public Prosecutions, that he proposed at the appropriate stage to seek my ruling whether it was open for the defendant at this trial to rehearse before the jury to be empanelled any of those matters which could be taken as concluded against him and in favour of the Crown in relation to the events of the night of 15th-16th June 1972, as a result of the verdict of guilty to the s 18 charge which was returned by the jury on 12th October.

Counsel for the defendant, whilst reserving all rights and contentions in the matter, agreed that it would be proper for me to hear arguments affecting the ruling requested, in the absence of the jury panel and before a jury was formed for the present trial. This was clearly an appropriate and convenient course, as counsel's opening and the leading and cross-examination of prosecution and defence evidence would necessarily have to be conducted within the framework of such ruling as I might give; and the matter proceeded in this way, I having given my ruling on the first day of the trial, before the jury were empanelled.

On the short history of the facts of this case which I have recounted, it is clear that it would not have been open for the defendant to rely on his present arraignment for murder on the plea of autrefois convict in relation to the s 18 offence. This is plain from reference to R v Thomas[1]. The headnote reads as follows[2]:

'Where a person has been convicted of wounding with intent to murder and the person wounded subsequently dies of the wounds inflicted, a plea of autrefois convict is not a good answer by the person who inflicted the wound to an indictment for murder.'

The facts are slightly different because in that case the first conviction was of wounding with intent to murder, which is a s 18 offence, whereas here the first conviction is a conviction for doing grievous bodily harm with intent to do grievous bodily harm, also a s 18 offence but, of course, intent to do grievous bodily harm is one of the alternative mental elements in the offence of murder.

The judgment of the court in R v Thomas[1] contains a fairly full citation of the earlier relevant authority to which it is unnecessary for me to refer. The points on which my ruling must turn, briefly, are first, whether or not the doctrine which is known conveniently as 'issue estoppel' applies as between the prosecution and defendant in criminal proceedings. I shall refer later to authorities which utter opinions both ways; opinions of Lord Devlin and Lord Parker CJ that it does not: other opinions suggest that it does. Secondly, if this doctrine does so apply, does it operate only in favour of the defendant, as Diplock LJ suggested in Mills v Cooper[3], a case to which I will later refer, or has it, as when applied in civil proceedings, a mutual

---

1　[1949] 2 All ER 662, [1950] 1 KB 26
2　[1950] 1 KB at 26
3　[1967] 2 All ER 100, [1967] 2 QB 459

a operation? Does it operate in favour of the prosecution as well as in favour of the defence? Thirdly, how are the matters to which issue estoppel relates to be identified when a case arises in which the application of the doctrine is to be considered? This involves two enquiries, first the isolation of the relevant issues and, secondly, the materials to be used for that purpose.

b Issue estoppel can be said to exist when there is a judicial establishment of a proposition of law or fact between parties to earlier litigation and when the same question arises in later litigation between the same parties. In the latter litigation the established proposition is treated as conclusive between those same parties. It can also be described as a situation when, between the same parties to current litigation, there has been an issue or issues distinctly raised and found in earlier litigation between the same parties. I take the essence of these descriptions of issue estoppel

c from observations in judgments of Dixon CJ in two Australian cases, *R v Wilkes*[1] and *Mraz v The Queen (No 2)*[2], to which I will later refer. Issue estoppel as I described it is based on a general principle of finality, subject to appeal, of judicial decisions between the parties to them.

The present state of the law on this point may, I find, be appropriately summarised as follows. (1) There is no direct English authority concluding the question

d whether issue estoppel applies or does not apply in criminal proceedings. There are in English cases dicta pointing in both directions. (2) Issue estoppel is a principle quite different from 'res judicata' and from the principles of the criminal law against double jeopardy—the latter of which relates only to the protection of the defendant in criminal proceedings and which, as I have indicated, would have no application in the present case. (3) There is substantial and, to my mind, highly persuasive

e Australian and American authority which supports the application of issue estoppel to criminal proceedings when, but only when, a defendant relies on its application against a further prosecution. Until the present case it does not seem to have been argued that the doctrine applies also against the defence. Again no case appears in which that argument could relevantly have been made. (4) Owing to the way in which verdicts in criminal proceedings in this country are normally taken and

f recorded, that is in the form of general verdicts of guilty or not guilty and not in the form of special verdicts, it must be a rare case when it is possible to use Dixon J's tests of 'judicial establishment of a proposition' or 'an issue distinctly raised and found', in such a way as precisely and certainly to identify the matter which can form the subject of issue estoppel.

Most offences under English law involve a consideration of a number of different

g questions of fact which are related to the elements which the Crown has proved in order to establish guilt of that offence. This can be illustrated by the offence under s 18 of the Offences against the Person Act 1861, of which the defendant was found guilty on 12th October 1972. The elements of this offence which the Crown must prove to the appropriate degree are: (1) that the victim suffered grievous bodily harm, (2) that this grievous bodily harm was inflicted deliberately by the defendant,

h (3) that it was so inflicted without lawful excuse, and (4) that at the time when grievous bodily harm was deliberately inflicted the defendant intended to cause grievous bodily harm to the victim, and the defendant's intention has to be ascertained, bearing in mind the provisions of s 8 of the Criminal Justice Act 1967.

A verdict of guilty of this offence involves that the prosecution have proved all these four factors. Proof of the third factor, that is infliction of grievous bodily harm

j without lawful excuse, eliminates lawful excuse and thus demonstrates that against the defendant the Crown have negatived self-defence. Proof of the fourth factor, the necessary intent, demonstrates that the prosecution have proved the specific intent which is a common element between a s 18 offence and the offence of murder

---

1 (1948) 77 CLR 511
2 (1956) 96 CLR 62

although, of course, intent to kill, into the refinements of which it is unnecessary to
enter, is an alternative intent in the offence of murder. Thus, in my judgment, it
can be said quite emphatically that in the defendant's case the proceedings which
terminated on 12th October 1972 enable one precisely to identify what were then
judicially established as propositions of fact or what issues were distinctly raised and
found. This would be the case if all that was seen in the present case was the record of
the court which, in my judgment, is clearly admissible and which is in evidence; but
here the matter goes further because it is undisputed that the issue of self-defence
was clearly raised and determined. The authorities do suggest that when the question
arises of identifying issues determined it is right for the court, if necessary, to ascertain
what those issues were by reference to what emerged in the course of the earlier
proceedings.

I now turn to the authorities which are, in fact, listed in Archbold[1]. Not all of these
authorities are of assistance in the present case but I will deal with those to which
counsel have drawn my attention and which I agree with them are authorities at
which one should look. It is useful, I think, to take the authorities chronologically,
bearing in mind the persuasive value of American, in the sense of Anglo-Saxon
American and Australian authority.

In point of time the first case to which it is useful to make reference is *Sealfon v
United States*[2], which was decided early in January 1948 in the Supreme Court of the
United States. The headnote reads[3]:

'1. Petitioner was tried and acquitted on a charge of conspiracy to defraud
the United States by presenting false invoices and making false representations
to a ration board to the effect that certain sales of sugar products were made to
exempt agencies. Thereafter, he was tried and convicted for aiding and abetting
the uttering and publishing of the false invoices introduced in the conspiracy
trial. The crux of the prosecutor's case at the second trial was an alleged agreement necessarily found in the first trial to be nonexistent. *Held*: In the unique
circumstances of this case, the jury's verdict in the conspiracy trial was a determination favorable to petitioner of the facts essential to the conviction of the
substantive offense; and *res judicata* was a valid defense to the second prosecution. 2. The doctrine of *res judicata* is applicable to criminal as well as civil
proceedings, and operates to conclude those matters in issue which have been
determined by a previous verdict, even though the offenses be different.'

There are certain passages in the opinion of the court delivered by a well-known
American judge, Douglas J, and it is not necessary for me to read a great deal but
what he says in one passage is as follows[4]:

'Thus the only question in this case is whether the jury's verdict in the conspiracy trial was a determination favorable to petitioner of the facts essential
to conviction of the substantive offense. This depends upon the facts adduced
at each trial and the instructions under which the jury arrived at its verdict at
the first trial.'

And then he goes on to deal with the detail in the context of the facts adduced and
the instruction given, and later he says[5]:

'Viewed in this setting, the verdict [that is the verdict of the trial where the
petitioner admittedly wrote and sent the letter which was in issue at his trial]

1 Criminal Pleading, Evidence and Practice (38th Edn, 1973), pp 166–168, paras 388, 388a
2 (1948) 332 US 575
3 (1948) 332 US at 575
4 (1948) 332 US at 578, 579
5 (1948) 332 US at 580

is a determination that petitioner ... did not do so pursuant to an agreement with Greenberg to defraud. So interpreted [proceeds the learned judge], the earlier verdict precludes a later conviction of the substantive offense. The basic facts in each trial were identical. As we read the records of the two trials, the petitioner could be convicted of either offense only on proof that he wrote the letter pursuant to an agreement with Greenberg. Under the evidence introduced, petitioner could have aided and abetted Greenberg in no other way. Indeed, respondent does not urge that he could. Thus the core of the prosecutor's case was in each case the same: the letter, and the circumstances surrounding it and to be inferred from it, and the false invoices.'

That, I think, is sufficient of that case.

The next case in point of time is an Australian case, *R v Wilkes*[1] in the High Court of Australia. The court there consisted of eminent judges. Latham CJ dissented from the others and the ruling judgment of the majority of that court was delivered by that well-known and highly regarded Australian judge, Dixon J. The facts as appear from the headnote are as follows[2]:

'An information against W. and his wife charged three offences: (1) manslaughter of B.; (2) conspiracy with B. and P. to procure the unlawful miscarriage of B.; and (3) conspiracy with P. to defeat the course of public justice. The case for the prosecution rested largely on the evidence of P., an alleged accomplice who had been pardoned, and who deposed that he had arranged with W. and his wife to procure the miscarriage of B., that B. had died whilst in W.'s house, and that, after removing B.'s body to another place, W. had told him to give to the police an untrue account of B.'s death. The jury found both accused not guilty on the first two counts [that is the counts of manslaughter and conspiracy to procure miscarriage], but guilty on the third count. On appeal, the Court of Criminal Appeal quashed the conviction on the ground of inconsistency between the verdicts.'

And that was upheld by the High Court of Australia:

'*Held*, by Rich, Dixon and McTiernan JJ (*Latham* C.J. dissenting,) that special leave to appeal to the High Court should be refused. *Per Dixon* J. (and *semble per McTiernan* J.): Although the High Court has jurisdiction to grant special leave to appeal from judgments of acquittal, this is an exceptional power, to be carefully exercised in that it is not in accordance with the general principles of English law . . .'

And then issue estoppel in criminal trials is discussed.

What Dixon J said on the question of issue estoppel in criminal trials was as follows[3]:

'Whilst there is not a great deal of authority upon the subject, it appears to me that there is nothing wrong in the view that there is an issue estoppel, if it appears by record of itself or as explained by proper evidence, that the same point was determined in favour of the prisoner in a previous criminal trial which is brought in issue on a second criminal trial of the same prisoner. That seems to be implied in the language used by *Wright* J. in *R. v. Ollis*[4] ... Such a question must rarely arise because the conditions can seldom be fulfilled which are necessary before

---

1   (1948) 77 CLR 511
2   (1948) 77 CLR at 511
3   (1948) 77 CLR at 518, 519
4   [1900] 2 QB 758, [1900–3] All ER Rep 733

an issue estoppel in favour of a prisoner and against the Crown can occur. There must be a prior proceeding determined against the Crown necessarily involving an issue which again arises in a subsequent proceeding by the Crown against the same prisoner. The allegation of the Crown in the subsequent proceeding must itself be inconsistent with the acquittal of the prisoner in the previous proceeding. But if such a condition of affairs arises I see no reason why the ordinary rules of issue estoppel should not apply. Such rules are not to be confused with those of *res judicata*, which in criminal proceedings are expressed in the pleas of *autrefois acquit* and *autrefois convict.*'

I interpose there. That statement of Dixon J is mentioned in an observation by Diplock LJ in *Mills v Cooper*[1] to which I will later refer. Dixon J continued[2]:

'They are pleas which are concerned with the judicial determination of an alleged criminal liability and in the case of conviction with the substitution of a new liability. Issue estoppel is concerned with the judicial establishment of a proposition of law or fact between parties. It depends upon well-known doctrines which control the relitigation of issues which are settled by prior litigation. However, it is not necessary for us to determine any such question upon the present application. It is a question, as I have said, about which in criminal matters there is little authority.'

The next case to be referred to is *R v Thomas*[3], which I have already mentioned. In that case the question of issue estoppel was not argued and indeed it seems fair to say that the court in its judgment seems to have approached the matter of the murder trial, which was the second trial in that case, on the assumption that all the elements in murder would be open for consideration. It does not subsequently appear in the course of the judgment but I think that is a fair way of dealing with the matter.

The next case to which I must refer is *Sambasivam v Public Prosecutor, Federation of Malaya*[4], which is a Privy Council case. The facts of the case are somewhat long and complicated and set out adequately in the headnote and I do not think it is necessary for me to read that. In delivering the opinion of the Privy Council, Lord MacDermott in a passage dealing with the question of issue estoppel—at least it seems to me that it refers to the question of issue estoppel, although he is dealing with it under the rubric of res judicata—says[5]:

'The effect of a verdict of acquittal pronounced by a competent court on a lawful charge and after a lawful trial is not completely stated by saying that the person acquitted cannot be tried again for the same offence. To that it must be added that the verdict is binding and conclusive in all subsequent proceedings between the parties to the adjudication. The maxim "Res judicata pro veritate accipitur" is no less applicable to criminal than to civil proceedings. Here, the appellant having been acquitted at the first trial on the charge of having ammunition in his possession, the prosecution was bound to accept the correctness of that verdict and was precluded from taking any step to challenge it at the second trial. And the appellant was no less entitled to rely on his acquittal in so far as it might be relevant in his defence.'

That, I think, is the only relevant passage in that case.

---

1   [1967] 2 All ER at 105, [1967] 2 QB at 469
2   (1948) 77 CLR at 519
3   [1949] 2 All ER 662, [1950] 1 KB 26
4   [1950] AC 458
5   [1950] AC at 479

a I turn now to another case in the High Court of Australia, *Mraz v The Queen (No 2)*[1], the headnote of which reads as follows:

'M. was indicted on a charge of murder of a woman, the Crown case being that the death of the woman had been caused during or immediately after the commission of an act of rape upon her by M. At the trial it was not disputed that there had been sexual intercourse between M. and the woman and that
b at the time, or shortly afterwards, the woman had died, but the real issue contested was whether or not such intercourse had taken place against the woman's will. The jury found M. not guilty of murder but guilty of manslaughter. The conviction for manslaughter was quashed on appeal by the High Court. M. was subsequently indicted for rape on the same facts and to such indictment, in addition to pleading not guilty, he entered a special plea of issue estoppel
c in reliance on the verdict in the earlier proceedings. Both pleas were found against M. His appeal to the Court of Criminal Appeal in relation to the special plea was dismissed, and he applied for special leave to appeal against such dismissal. *Held*, (1) that a consideration of the indictment and the verdict of not guilty of murder but guilty of manslaughter understood by reference to the law of homicide established that the jury had found that an act of M. had
d caused the death of the woman but involved as a matter of law a finding either (a) that M. did not commit rape or (b) that though his act caused death it was not during or immediately after the commission of rape; (2) that in order to exclude the possibility of alternative (b) being the ground of the verdict it was open to the appellant to rely on the fact that there was no issue taken at the trial that sexual intercourse had not taken place between M. and the woman
e and at that time or shortly afterwards she had died; (3) that, on that footing, the verdict must be taken to cover the issue of rape and to negative its commission by M.; (4) that the order of the High Court vacating the finding of manslaughter did not prevent consideration of the jury's verdict upon the foregoing basis; (5) that it followed that the verdict of the jury of not guilty of murder involved as a matter of law a finding that the appellant did not
f commit rape and a plea of issue estoppel was accordingly made out.'

Here again the judgment of the court is one in which Dixon CJ took part, and the relevant passages, to my mind, in this judgment are as follows. Dealing with what the verdicts involved, he says[2]:

g '... so long as the verdict stood in its entirety, the applicant was entitled to rely as creating an issue estoppel against the Crown. He was entitled so to rely upon it because when he pleaded not guilty to the indictment of murder the issues which were thereby joined between him and the Crown necessarily raised for determination the existence of the three elements we have mentioned and the verdict upon those issues must, for the reasons we have given, be taken
h to have affirmed the existence of the third and to have denied the existence of one or other of the other two elements.'

I interpose to say that why earlier on I analysed the ingredients of the s 18 offence was precisely for the reason indicated in the last passage from this judgment of the High Court of Australia. Then the judgment proceeds[3]:

j 'It is nothing to the point that the verdict may have been the result of a misdirection of the judge and that owing to the misdirection the jury may have found the verdict without understanding or intending what as a matter of

---

1 (1956) 96 CLR at 62, 63
2 (1956) 96 CLR at 68
3 (1956) 96 CLR at 68, 69

law is its necessary meaning or its legal consequences. The law which gives effect to issue estoppels is not concerned with the correctness or incorrectness of the finding which amounts to an estoppel, still less with the process of reasoning by which the finding was reached in fact; it does not matter that the finding may be thought to be due to the jury having been put upon the wrong track by some direction of the presiding judge or to the jury having got on the wrong track unaided.'

I interpose. The facts in *Mraz v The Queen (No 2)*[1] clearly indicated that the jury got on the wrong track probably as a result of a misdirection by the trial judge which appears in the report of the case. Continuing the judgment[2]:

'It is enough that an issue or issues have been distinctly raised and found. Once that is done, then, so long as the finding stands, if there be any subsequent litigation between the same parties, no allegations legally inconsistent with the finding may be made by one of them against the other. *Res judicata pro veritate accipitur.*'

Dixon CJ then referred to earlier decisions and concluded that paragraph[2]: 'And as, has already been said, this applies in pleas of the Crown'. Again, I think there is nothing more I need read of that, except this passage[2]: 'Now in ascertaining what were the issues determined judicially it is proper to look beyond the record'. Of course, in this case, I have referred to it not being disputed that self-defence was an issue in the earlier case.

I will now come to the case in the English House of Lords which is perhaps the first English authority on the subject, *Connelly v Director of Public Prosecutions*[3]. Again the facts of this case are accurately summarised in the headnote and for present purposes it seems to me to be unnecessary to refer to them. The question was whether the defendant, Connelly, who had been convicted of manslaughter at a first trial, which conviction was quashed by the Court of Appeal[4], could be tried again at a second trial on a further indictment on a charge of robbery related to the same incident which formed the subject of the murder charge on which he had been found guilty of manslaughter at the first trial. The House of Lords[3] held that he was liable to stand his second trial. I will put it that way.

In the course of the case the question of issue estoppel was discussed and debated amongst many other issues and it is not altogether easy to isolate from a long report the particular passages which are of importance, but I will use my best endeavours to do so.

The matter is first referred to in the course of argument of counsel for the appellant in the Court of Criminal Appeal and it seems to me that one can usefully point to two passages, two interventions by Lawton J when this question of issue estoppel was being argued. He said[5]:

'No: he has not been acquitted on the charge of murder [that is the first trial]. It is astonishing that if issue estoppel exists as a plea in bar the lawyers of the nineteenth century never raised it and that the textbooks have no reference to it.'

Well, that is a position which has now been cured because since *Connelly's* case[3] the textbooks do have a reference to it.

1 (1956) 96 CLR 62
2 (1956) 96 CLR at 69
3 [1964] 2 All ER 401, [1964] AC 1254
4 [1963] 3 All ER 510, [1964] AC 1254
5 [1964] AC at 1262

a   There is a later intervention by Lawton J, in the course of argument for the Crown, where he says[1]:

'I am worried about issue estoppel, for two reasons: (1) This doctrine arises commonly in civil cases, and it would be deplorable that a defence available in civil cases would not be available in identical circumstances in a criminal matter; and (2) it would also be deplorable if there were divergences between countries *b*   under the common law system, and if English law lagged behind because of a strict rule of pleading.'

The matter is dealt with in the judgment of the court delivered by Edmund Davies J, in a passage where he started by saying[2]:

'The submission as to "issue estoppel", which was the second matter advanced *c*   on the appellant's behalf, is a somewhat novel one in the criminal courts of this country, although it is being increasingly raised both in the Commonwealth and in the United States.'

And then he refers to a United States case[3], and to an article in the Melbourne University Law Review[4]. Then he refers to a passage in *Mraz v The Queen (No 2)*[5], *d*   which I have cited. He mentions *Brown v Robinson*[6], a case to which I will shortly come. He says[7]:

'Does issue estoppel avail an accused person in this country? We do not find ourselves, in the circumstances of the present case, called on to give a definite answer to that question.'

e   And then he refers to the second observation of Lawton J[1]. He cites other authorities and he then says[8]: 'Assuming, without deciding, that such a plea may validly be raised in the criminal courts of this country . . .' And then he cites from Herron J in a case from New South Wales *R v Clift*[9]:

'. . . the situation would not often arise in a criminal court, where the very issue of fact upon which the decision rests can be so isolated as to be capable of *f*   decision that such issue had been already determined in another previous criminal trial.'

The decision went by way of appeal to the House of Lords[10]. There are a large number of passages in the report and I do not propose to read them all. I refer to passages from the speech of Lord Morris of Borth-y-Gest[11], and to a further passage[12] *g*   where he quotes *Sambasivam*[13], *Mraz*[14] and two other cases *Brown v Robinson*[6] and *Sealfon v United States*[15]. I have referred to three of those cases. I will come in a moment to *Brown v Robinson*[6]. I refer also to the final passages[16] in Lord Morris of Borth-y-Gest's speech.

1   [1964] AC at 1267
2   [1963] 3 All ER at 516, 517, [1964] AC at 1273, 1274
h   3   *Harris v State of Georgia* (1941) 17 SE 2d 573
4   (1961), vol 3, pp 101 et seq
5   (1956) 96 CLR at 68
6   (1960) 60 SRNSW 297
7   [1963] 3 All ER at 517, [1964] AC at 1274
8   [1963] 3 All ER at 518, [1964] AC at 1275
9   (1952) 52 SRNSW 213 at 217
j 10   [1964] 2 All ER 401, [1964] AC 1254
11   [1964] 2 All ER at 418, 420, 421, [1964] AC at 1314, 1315, 1317, 1318, 1319
12   [1964] 2 All ER at 422, [1964] AC at 1321
13   [1950] AC 458
14   (1956) 96 CLR 62
15   (1948) 332 US 575
16   [1964] 2 All ER at 427, 428, [1964] AC at 1329, 1330

In Lord Hodson's speech there are passages[1] bearing on this matter where he   *a*
specifically deals with looking beyond the record in order to determine what questions
had been decided. Then in Lord Devlin's speech there are important passages, the
purport of which is that issue estoppel has no place in the English criminal law.
Lord Devlin starts dealing specifically with this matter and I point to the ruling
passage[2], which contains a reference to *Sambasivam*[3]. He comes back to the point
in the passage beginning[4]: 'I turn now to consider the doctrine of issue estoppel'   *b*
and he makes references to *Mraz*[5] and *Sealfon*[6]. And then he goes on[7]:

> 'In my opinion, therefore, if issue estoppel is applicable in criminal trials,
> it does not assist the appellant here ... Altogether there seems to me to be a
> number of difficulties about the introduction of issue estoppel into the criminal
> law. The first, the necessity for analysis, I have already mentioned. It introduces
> an element of chance. Assume that the appellant was actually acquitted of   *c*
> murder and that he had been tried alone. Analysis would then have shown
> nothing.'

This is the point about identifying the issues. Then he says[8]:

> 'It is only the fact that he was tried with others that enables the appellant   *d*
> to put forward an analysis in this case. The truth is that for estoppel on issues
> to work satisfactorily, the issues need to be formulated with some precision.
> In civil suits this is usually done as a matter of record: in the criminal process
> it is not. If issue estoppel is going to be introduced into the criminal law, the
> proper basis for it is a system of special verdicts on separate issues; but that
> would be to introduce a profound change into the working of our law which   *e*
> I am not prepared at present to countenance. Then, since estoppel is available
> to both parties in civil law there is the question whether it should be made
> available to the prosecution in criminal law. No one so far has advocated that
> it should; but is it necessary in the interests of justice to give the defence this
> unreciprocated advantage? The defence rightly enjoys the privilege of not
> having to prove anything; it has only to raise a reasonable doubt. Is it also   *f*
> to have the right to say that a fact which it has raised a reasonable doubt about
> is to be treated as conclusively established in its favour?'

I say no more about this question which does not arise in the present case.

Finally in his speech Lord Pearce[9] deals with the matter concerning double
jeopardy and the general question of res judicata and referring also to the article
in the Melbourne University Law Review[10], to *Sealfon*[6], the American case, and   *g*
to *Wilkes*[11] and *Mraz*[5], to both of which I have referred, and to *Kemp v The King*[12].

Kemp v The King[12] is another Australian case referred to in Archbold[13]. I have looked
at it and I think counsel have looked at it too and it is of no assistance in this case. Lord

h

---

1   [1964] 2 All ER at 428, 429, 430, [1964] AC at 1231, 1332, 1333, 1334
2   [1964] 2 All ER at 434, [1964] AC at 1340, 1341
3   [1950] AC 458
4   [1964] 2 All ER at 436, [1964] AC at 1343
5   (1956) 96 CLR 62
6   (1948) 332 US 575
7   [1964] 2 All ER at 437, [1964] AC at 1345
8   [1964] 2 All ER at 437, [1964] AC at 1345, 1346
9   [1964] 2 All ER at 449, 450, [1964] AC at 1365, 1366
10 (1961), vol 3, pp 101 et seq
11 (1948) 77 CLR 511
12 (1951) 83 CLR 341
13 Criminal Pleading, Evidence and Practice (38th Edn, 1973), p 166, para 388

i

a Pearce also refers to *Brown v Robinson*[1] and then, finally, towards the end of his speech, he says[2]:

'I agree with the opinion of my noble and learned friend LORD DEVLIN, save in so far as I am not in accord with his more general criticism of issue estoppel.'

Well, that is *Connelly*[3]. It is very bad to count heads and not very profitable to do so. Lord Reid seems to have expressed no opinion on issue estoppel at all, if one
b may say so, with the greatest respect, perhaps prudently, because it really did not arise on the facts of the case.

The impression one gets from Lord Morris of Borth-y-Gest, Lord Hodson and Lord Pearce is that they think probably issue estoppel does apply to criminal proceedings but the question of the difficulty of establishing the issues which are to be the subject-matter—this difficulty and the problems of reciprocity—seemed to be
c worrying all of them. Finally, Lord Devlin quite clearly is of the opposite opinion.

The next case to which I turn is *Brown v Robinson*[1]. The headnote reads as follows[4]:

'R. was tried on an indictment for manslaughter arising out of the death of a passenger in the vehicle which he was driving. There was some evidence given at the trial that he was at the time of the accident under the influence of intoxi-
d cating liquor. He was acquitted of manslaughter and later prosecuted on a charge of driving under the influence of intoxicating liquor, to which charge he pleaded issue estoppel. *Held, per curiam*, before issue estoppel can apply against the Crown in a criminal case there must be a prior proceeding determined against the Crown necessarily involving an issue distinctly raised and found in such proceeding which again arises in a subsequent proceeding by the Crown against
e the same prisoner. In ascertaining what issues were judicially determined in a former proceeding the court should look beyond the formal record of the proceedings; pleas of *res judicata* and *autrefois acquit* compared with issue estoppel.'

The matter is dealt with in the judgment of the court delivered by Herron and Maguire JJ, and the relevant passages begin[5]:
f
'Before issue estoppel can succeed in a case such as this there must be a prior proceeding determined against the Crown necessarily involving an issue which again arises in a subsequent proceeding by the Crown against the same prisoner. The allegation of the Crown in the subsequent proceeding must itself be inconsistent with the acquittal of the prisoner in the previous proceeding. It depends
g upon an issue or issues having been distinctly raised and found in the former proceeding. Once this is done, then, so long as the finding stands if there be any subsequent litigation between the same parties no allegations legally inconsistent with the same finding may be made by one of them against the other. In other words the principle of the issue as to estoppel is to treat an issue of fact or law as settled once and for all between the parties if it is distinctly raised and
h if the judgment pronounced implies its determination necessarily as a matter of law.'

Then there is a futher passage[6] which I think it is unnecessary for me to read. It is dealing with difference between res judicata, the double jeopardy doctrine, and issue estoppel and indicating that in issue estoppel it is proper for the court to look at the transcript of the earlier proceeding.

j
1 (1960) 60 SRNSW 297
2 [1964] 2 All ER at 451, [1964] AC at 1368
3 [1964] 2 All ER 401, [1964] CA 1254
4 (1960) 60 SRNSW at 297
5 (1960) 60 SRNSW at 301
6 (1960) 60 SRNSW at 302

Then Hardie J deals with the point of issue estoppel and says[1]:

'Issue estoppel, as was said in R. v. Wilkes[2] is rarely available in a criminal case "because the conditions can seldom be fulfilled which are necessary before an issue estoppel in favour of a prisoner and against the Crown can occur". The problem is one of identifying and segregating the particular issue of fact which the jury's verdict must necessarily be taken to have determined in favour of the accused. To enable such an issue to be identified, recourse is invariably had to the summing-up of the trial judge. Where—as in this case—there was no summing-up and apparently no direction or instruction given by the trial judge as to the ingredients of the crime of manslaughter, I see the greatest difficulty in arriving at the conclusion that any particular issue of fact has necessarily been determined by the jury's verdict of not guilty.'

There are two more cases, first, *Mills v Cooper*[3]. It is unnecessary to deal with the facts of that case in which the gist was accurately set out in the headnote. In the course of his judgment Lord Parker CJ doubted whether issue estoppel had any place in the criminal law at all.

Diplock LJ[4] took the view—at least I think this is a fair summary of this passage of his judgment—that issue estoppel did, in fact, apply to criminal proceedings but it operated only within the framework of autrefois acquit and autrefois convict. I find that very difficult to reconcile with the Commonwealth and United States authorities to which I have referred where the difference between the double jeopardy position and the issue estoppel position is pointed out. One of the important matters in relation to the difference is that with double jeopardy one is, in a sense, bound by the record, but so far as the authorities go when one is concerned with issue estoppel it is legitimate to travel into territory which is beyond the record in order to ascertain what actually happened in the course of the earlier proceedings.

The matter was again canvassed in argument, finally, in *R v Maskell*[5]. This is referred to in Archbold[6]. I have looked at the authority, but in my judgment it provides no help in this case. Eveleigh J, delivering the judgment of the court in that case, indicated that the court did not propose to deal with the argued point of issue estoppel, which they did not think arose on the facts of that case. One of the problems was that the parties to the then current proceedings were different from the parties to the earlier proceedings. Eveleigh J also indicated that the approach the court was going to make to the case was through application of the better known and well established principles of double jeopardy.

Now, all those authorities seem to me to support my summary of the law as I found it. The authorities lead me to the conclusion that the answer to the three questions which I earlier posed are as follows: first, that issue estoppel does apply between the Crown and the defendant in criminal proceedings. Secondly, that it applies with mutuality. I found it difficult to conceive of any principle of estoppel between the parties which only operates unilaterally—that is, of course, the distinction between issue estoppel and the double jeopardy principles. Thirdly, when, as in the present case—which admittedly may be an exceptional one—one can determine the relevant issues with precision and certainty by referring to the earlier record and by what has transpired in the course of the earlier proceedings in relation to these issues, it seems to me that issue estoppel can clearly operate.

Counsel for the defence has put forward what I think are three main arguments. His first argument is a forceful one, but I have been confronted with the task of

---

1 (1960) 60 SRNSW at 307
2 (1948) 77 CLR 511 at 518
3 [1967] 2 All ER 100, [1967] 2 QB 459
4 [1967] 2 All ER at 104, 105, [1967] 2 QB at 468, 469
5 (1970) 54 Cr App Rep 429
6 Criminal Pleading, Evidence and Practice (38th Edn, 1973), pp 167, 168, para 388a

making a decision and there is some kind of proverb about places where angels fear to tread. His first argument is that the application of issue estoppel as such in criminal proceedings, at least against a defendant, has never been part of the law of England. He submits that the double jeopardy principle is the only method with which a doctrine of that kind can be applied.

For the reasons which I have endeavoured to give I do not accept that argument. In my judgment issue estoppel is part of the law of England and applies as part of the law of England to criminal proceedings, subject to its necessary limitations and provided its difficulties can be overcome.

Secondly, counsel submits that one must have regard—and this may be a very good argument—to the difficulties which would arise if one applied the doctrine of issue estoppel in favour of the Crown against the defendant. The first question is, 'How do you really determine what issues have been decided in earlier proceedings?' This is a case, it may be a rare one, where, in my judgment and for the reasons that I have indicated, it is possible to do this with precision and certainty.

Thirdly, as a difficulty counsel suggests that the jury involved in the second trial, the trial which was going to take place at the time when I announced the effect of my ruling, could only try part of the case, and he suggested perhaps it was really the most important part of the case because what the jury, on my ruling, were precluded from doing was to reconsider the issues on the four factors involved in the s 18 offence which were determined by the earlier jury's verdict of guilty. The most important, perhaps, of those factors was that of intent, having regard also to s 8 of the Criminal Justice Act 1967. But, I ask where, as in the present case, the Crown has once proved the necessary intent of murder to the satisfaction of a jury, what is really the position of the second jury? If counsel is right they would be, so to speak, sitting on appeal from the verdict of their predecessors, and if they were to reach a contrary result the position would, at least, be extremely confused.

Finally in his arguments counsel submitted that to allow issue estoppel to operate in this case would be to erode the principle that the prosecution has got to prove its case to the appropriate standard. But I ask, how often has the prosecution got to do that? If they do it once and do it to the satisfaction of the jury, whom one must assume in the defendant's first trial were appropriately directed and arrived at a correct verdict because that conviction has not been subjected to an appeal, have the Crown done all that is required of them to do? The problem has not arisen here, but one can envisage cases of witnesses who were available to give evidence at a first trial, and whose evidence was vital on issues then determined, who might not be available at a second trial. As I say, it has not happened here, but unless issue estoppel were operative, subject to its proper limits and satisfying the proper conditions, there could be grave problems in a case of that kind.

Then counsel also submits that where in the second proceedings—this trial, the trial which took place after I had given my ruling—there is a defence which could not have been an issue in the earlier proceedings, the defence is placed in a difficulty. Now, it is quite clear that there were two matters open to the defence in this case which could not have been in issue in the earlier proceedings. The defence of provocation could not have arisen in the proceedings under s 18 because provocation was only a factor to be considered on sentence. Provocation is only a matter to be considered so far as guilt is concerned in murder cases where its effect is well known. Furthermore, of course, at the earlier trial, because Moroney had not at that time died, no question of causation of death was involved. Now, I can see no difficulty arising in this situation. The defence can obviously raise provocation and the prosecution cannot obtain a murder conviction unless they negative provocation. It is true that this involves going into the whole incident in which the injury was received in the event of the injury proving to be the cause of death, but is it not—I put this rhetorically—simplifying the jury's task if they do not at the same time have to grapple with the equally difficult subject of self-defence? I think reference to authorities does indicate that juries do find it extremely difficult when these two issues—self-defence and provocation—are run, so to speak, in harness. From that point of view I would suggest it is a consideration—to the extent that the jury at the second trial are relieved of reconsidering an issue already determined—that makes their task, difficult enough as it is in a murder case, perhaps a little easier to fulfil and perhaps enables them a little more happily to reach an acceptable verdict.

For those reasons I reject counsel's submissions, helpful and forceful as they were, and I uphold counsel for the Crown's submission. I did so in a very few words on 19th November but I have tried to give my reasons more extensively today.

Ruling accordingly.

The defendant was acquitted.

Solicitors: *Director of Public Prosecutions*; *Armitage, Sykes & Hinchcliffe*, Huddersfield (for the defendant).

John M Collins Esq Barrister.

Asher and others v Secretary of State for the Environment and another

COURT OF APPEAL, CIVIL DIVISION
LORD DENNING MR, ORR AND LAWTON LJJ
23rd, 24th, 25th, 31st JANUARY 1974

Housing – Housing authority dwellings – Fair rent – Duty of authority to charge fair rent – Local authority – Default – Remedy of Secretary of State – Power to direct district auditor to make extraordinary audit of housing revenue account – Power exercised instead of appointing housing commissioner to discharge authority's functions – Validity of exercise of power – Motive of Minister – Relevance – Minister having in mind that surcharge consequent on audit would disqualify members of local authority – Audit directed before determination of fair rents and therefore before ultimate deficiency to housing revenue account ascertainable – Whether direction of Minister ultra vires – Local Government Act 1933, s 236(1) – Housing Finance Act 1972, s 95(1)(7).

Practice – Striking out – Action – Vexatious proceedings – Attempt to relitigate issue determined in earlier proceedings – Parties – Different parties in subsequent proceedings – Local authority – Extraordinary audit – Secretary of State directing audit – Auditor surcharging amount of deficiency in accounts on councillors – Appeal of councillors to High Court dismissed – Secretary of State not party to appeal – Subsequent proceedings by councillors against Secretary of State and auditor – Allegation that direction to hold audit invalid – Whether allegation could have been raised in earlier proceedings.

The Housing Finance Act 1972, which came into force in August 1972, placed a duty on local authorities to determine fair rents for council houses; meanwhile to make progressive increases towards fair rents by increasing rents by £1 a week for the first year, 1st October 1972 to 30th September 1973, and by further increases in subsequent years; on determintaion of the fair rents to repay any amount in excess of the fair rents which had been collected, and to introduce a rent rebate scheme for council tenants by reference to their needs and resources. The members of an urban district council refused to bring the 1972 Act into operation on the ground that they had made a pledge to the electors not to do so. They did not increase council house rents in the district by £1 from 1st October 1972. On 13th November 1972 the Secretary of State made a default order under s 95(1)^a of the 1972 Act declaring the council to be in default in bringing the Act into operation and directing the council to remedy the default within 16 days of the order. On the expiry of those 16 days the Minister could have appointed a housing commissioner, under s 95(7) of the 1972 Act, to carry out the council's functions under the Act but instead, on 16th November 1972, the Minister in exercise of his powers under s 236(1)^b of the Local Government Act 1933, directed the district auditor to hold an extraordinary audit of the council's housing revenue account for the period from 1st April to 16th November 1972. The district auditor having heard submissions from the councillors decided, by making estimates, that a loss of £6,985 had been incurred to the housing revenue account by the negligence and misconduct of the councillors in failing to bring the 1972 Act into operation. The auditor issued a certificate under s 228 of the 1933 Act surcharging that amount on the councillors jointly and severally. The councillors appealed against the surcharge to the High Court pursuant to s 229 of the 1933 Act, the district auditor being the respondent to the appeal. In that appeal the councillors did not contend that the Minister's direction to hold the extraordinary audit was invalid and the Minister was not a party to the appeal. The High Court^c upheld the surcharge. The councillors did not appeal against that decision and on expiry of the time for appealing the certificate of surcharge became final and the sum surcharged on the councillors became due from them. They also became disqualified from being members of the council because of the surcharge on them. On 9th October 1973 the Minister made an order appointing a housing commissioner to carry out the council's functions under the 1972 Act. On 29th October 1973 the councillors commenced proceedings against the Minister and the then district auditor claiming, against the Minister, a declaration that his direction to hold the extraordinary audit was ultra vires because it was punitive in intent and was made to secure some object, not specified, other than the proper object of recoupment of moneys lost by the councillors' default; the particulars alleged that the Minister ought to have appointed a housing commissioner before October 1973 and that his failure to do so had prejudiced the councillors

---

a Section 95, so far as material, provides:
    '(1) Where the Secretary of State is of opinion, whether on representations made to him or otherwise, that a local authority—(a) have failed effectively to discharge any of their functions under Part I, II, V or VI of this Act; or (b) have failed so to discharge any function conferred on them by this Act or any other enactment as to secure the effective discharge of any of their functions under those Parts of this Act ... he may after such inquiry as he may think fit make an order declaring the authority to be in default ...
    '(7) If the Secretary of State is satisfied, after such inquiry as he may think fit, that an authority with respect to whom an order has been made under subsection (1) above have failed to comply with any requirement of the order within the time limited by it for compliance with that requirement, he may by order, without prejudice to any other means of enforcing the order, appoint a person (hereafter referred to as a "Housing Commissioner")—(a) to discharge in the name of the authority and at their expense, subject to such limitations, conditions or exceptions (if any) as may be specified in the order—(i) such functions of the authority under Part I, II, V or VI of this Act as are so specified; (ii) such other functions of the authority as are so specified as being functions which the Secretary of State considers necessary or expedient for the discharge of those functions; (b) to discharge at the expense of the authority any incidental or supplementary functions the discharge of which the Secretary of State considers necessary or expedient, and may direct that the authority shall not during such time as the Commissioner's appointment continues perform any function conferred by the order on the Commissioner ...'
b Section 236(1) provides: 'The Minister may at any time direct a district auditor to hold an extraordinary audit of any accounts which are subject to audit by a district auditor.'
c [1973] 3 All ER 1008

by increasing the amount of their liability to surcharge; and that it was wrong to order an extraordinary audit before the fair rents had been finally determined because until such determination there was uncertainty as to the ultimate loss or deficiency to the housing revenue account. As against the district auditor the councillors claimed a declaration that he could not lawfully enforce the surcharge on the councillors. The defendants applied to strike out the statement of claim as disclosing no reasonable cause of action against either defendant and as being vexatious or otherwise an abuse of the process of the court.

Held – (i) The statement of claim disclosed no cause of action against the defendants. The Minister in exercising his power to direct an extraordinary audit under the 1933 Act in preference to appointing a housing commissioner under the 1972 Act had acted lawfully and had not exercised his power for improper motives for the following reasons—

(a) It was for the Minister to decide which of several courses open to him was the best course to take, and, so long as he acted in good faith and not frivolously or vexatiously, his decision could not be questioned. Even if, when directing the audit, the Minister had had in mind that a surcharge consequent on the audit would result in the disqualification of the councillors he had not thereby exercised his power for an improper purpose (see p 165 *a* to *c* and *j*, p 166 *e* and *f* and p 169 *d* to *j*, post); *R v Barnet and Camden Rent Tribunal, ex parte Frey Investments Ltd* [1972] 1 All ER 1185 applied.

(b) It was lawful for the Minister to direct an extraordinary audit before the fair rents had been determined even though it necessitated the auditor making estimates in deciding the amount of the loss or deficiency incurred to the housing revenue account. District auditors often had to deal with contingencies and uncertainties and to make estimates; at the time the audit was directed to be made a loss or deficiency in the accounts had already been incurred, due to the councillors' failure to implement the 1972 Act, and the Minister was entitled to take steps by directing the audit to find out the amount of the loss or deficiency (see p 165 *d e* and *j*, p 167 *e* and p 170 *c*, post).

(ii) The claim against the district auditor was vexatious because it was an attempt to relitigate the matter of the surcharge which had already been decided in the previous appeal to the High Court; in that appeal it had been open to the councillors to challenge the validity of the Minister's direction to hold the audit; that matter had not been raised then and could not be raised in the present proceedings (see p 165 *f g* and *j*, p 167 *g* and *h* and p 170 *d* to *g*, post).

(iii) Accordingly, the statement of claim should be struck out.

Notes

For power of Secretary of State where default by local authority in performance of functions under the Housing Finance Act 1972, see Supplement to 19 Halsbury's Laws (3rd Edn) para 956A.

For power of Minister to direct holding of extraordinary audit, see 24 Halsbury's Laws (3rd Edn) 591, para 1087; for powers and duties of district auditor, see ibid, 586, 587, para 1078, and for cases on the subject, see 33 Digest (Repl) 21-26, 97-120.

For the Local Government Act 1933, ss 228, 229, 236, see 19 Halsbury's Statutes (3rd Edn) 528, 529, 533.

For the Housing Finance Act 1972, s 95, see 42 Halsbury's Statutes (3rd Edn) 643.

Cases referred to in judgments

Asher v Lacey [1973] 3 All ER 1008, [1973] 1 WLR 1412, DC.

Associated Provincial Picture Houses Ltd v Wednesbury Corpn [1947] 2 All ER 680, [1948] 1 KB 223, [1948] LJR 190, 177 LT 641, 112 JP 55, CA, 45 Digest (Repl) 215, *189*.

Belcher v Reading Corpn [1949] 2 All ER 969, [1950] Ch 380, 114 JP 21, 26 Digest (Repl) 704, *141*.

Gerrard (Thomas) & Son Ltd, Re [1967] 2 All ER 525, [1968] Ch 455, [1967] 3 WLR 84, Digest (Cont Vol C) 104, *3881a.*

Henderson v Henderson (1843) 3 Hare 100, [1843-60] All ER Rep 378, 1 LTOS 410, 67 ER 313, 21 Digest (Repl) 244, *306.*

Kingston Cotton Mill Co (No 2), Re [1896] 2 Ch 279, 65 LJCh 673, 74 LT 568, 3 Mans 171, CA, 9 Digest (Repl) 569, *3754.*

Padfield v Minister of Agriculture, Fisheries and Food [1968] 1 All ER 694, [1968] AC 997, [1968] 2 WLR 924, HL, Digest (Cont Vol C) 388, *569a.*

Pooley v District Auditor, No 8 Audit District, Middlesex (1965) 63 LGR 236, CA; *affg* (1964) 63 LGR 60, Digest (Cont Vol B) 503, *112a.*

R v Barnet and Camden Rent Tribunal, ex parte Frey Investments Ltd [1972] 1 All ER 1185, [1972] 2 QB 342, [1972] 2 WLR 619, 136 JP 367, 24 P & CR 202, CA.

R v Brixton Prison (Governor), ex parte Soblen [1962] 3 All ER 641, [1963] 2 QB 243, [1962] 3 WLR 1154, CA, Digest (Cont Vol A) 24, *149a.*

Roberts v Hopwood [1925] AC 578, [1925] All ER Rep 24, 94 LJKB 542, 133 LT 289, 89 JP 105, HL, 33 Digest (Repl) 23, *107.*

Sydney Municipal Council v Campbell [1925] AC 338, 94 LJPC 65, 133 LT 63, PC, 11 Digest (Repl) 119, *120.*

Cases also cited

R v Drury [1894] 2 IR 489.

R v Paddington and St Marylebone Rent Tribunal, ex parte Bell London and Provincial Properties Ltd [1949] 1 All ER 720, [1949] 1 KB 666, DC.

Interlocutory appeal

By an amended statement of claim the plaintiffs, Terry William Asher and ten others, who at all material times were the elected members of the urban district council of Clay Cross in Derbyshire, claimed (1) against the first defendant, the Secretary of State for the Environment, a declaration that his direction to the former district auditor for Clay Cross urban district, Cyril Dickson Lacey, to hold an extraordinary audit of the council's housing revenue account for the period from 1st April 1972 to 16th November 1972 was ultra vires and of no effect in law because the direction was punitive in intent and/or was made solely or principally to secure some object (which the plaintiffs could not specify) other than the recoupment of moneys lost by the plaintiffs' default; and (2) against the second defendant, H Harrison ('the district auditor') the district auditor for the time being of Clay Cross urban district, a declaration that he might not lawfully make complaint or take action or direct action to be taken to recover from the plaintiffs or any of them the sum or any part of the sum which the former district auditor had purported to surcharge on the plaintiffs. In relation to the claim against the Secretary of State, para 5 of the statement of claim alleged (i) that he, well knowing that the plaintiffs had resolved not to implement the material provisions of the Housing Finance Act 1972, at no time before 9th October 1973 took any steps to exercise his default powers under the 1972 Act so as to enable fair rents to be fixed and rent rebates and allowances to be calculated; (ii) that the Secretary of State, by failing to take those steps, had made it impossible or unnecessarily difficult for the audit to be undertaken with any certainty or reasonable certainty as to the sums involved; (iii) that the Secretary of State for Wales, in respect of two other urban districts, Bedwas and Machen, and Merthyr Tydfil, had promptly appointed housing commissioners by orders made in or about November 1972 notwithstanding that the councils of those urban districts had been in like default in their obligations under the 1972 Act as the plaintiffs had been, and had not then or at any time directed that an extraordinary audit be held of the accounts of those two councils. Paragraph 6 of the statement of claim alleged that further and in the alternative that the Secretary of State's direction was ultra vires on the following grounds, i e that the audit and surcharge (consequent thereon) were based on the failure of the plaintiffs to make an

increase towards fair rents in the year 1972-73 in an amount which in the first week *a*
produced additional rental income of an amount equal to £1 times the number of
Clay Cross urban district council's qualifying dwellings on 1st October 1972; the
sum of £1 per dwelling however distributed among the dwellings was not a certain
rent increase under the 1972 Act but was a payment on account of any additional
rent which might be found due when fair rents were fixed pursuant to Part V of the
1972 Act, and was subject to an express provision in s 67 of the Act for reduction of *b*
rent and repayment to the tenant of all excess sums charged if the fair rent when
determined fell below the contractual rent as increased; in the premises, the Secretary of State by his direction had obliged the district auditor to calculate as if it were a
loss or deficiency potential revenue which by statute might not eventually be due
on balance to Clay Cross Urban District Council. In relation to the claim against the
district auditor the particulars alleged that pursuant to the Secretary of State's direc- *c*
tion to hold an extraordinary audit the former district auditor had purported to
surcharge on the plaintiffs jointly and severally the sum of £6,985·00 and to certify
such sum as being due and that the district auditor proposed, unless the court declared that to do so would be unlawful, to make complaint or to take action or direct
action to be taken to recover from the plaintiffs or some of them the sum or part of
the sum which the former district auditor had purported to surcharge on the plaintiffs. *d*
By notice of motion dated 13th December 1973 the Secretary of State and the district
auditor applied for an order under RSC Ord 18, r 19, or under the inherent jurisdiction
of the court, that the statement of claim be struck out as against him on the ground
that it disclosed no reasonable cause of action or was frivolous or vexatious or otherwise
an abuse of the process of the court, and that the action be dismissed. By order dated
21st December 1973, Megarry J ordered that the amended statement of claim be *e*
struck out as against both defendants on the ground that it disclosed no reasonable
cause of action. Pursuant to leave of Megarry J the plaintiffs appealed against that
order. The grounds of the appeal were (i) that the judge had erred in holding that
the amended statement of claim and in particular the matters set out in paras 5 and
6 thereof disclosed no reasonable cause of action; (ii) that in particular the judge ought
to have held that the only proper consideration to which the Secretary of State should *f*
have had regard when directing the holding of an extraordinary audit under s 236(1)
of the Local Government Act 1933 was the protection of the ratepayers of the district,
and (iii) that the judge had erred in stating in obiter dicta that the district auditor
was probably entitled to rely on res judicata and that the proceedings against the
district auditor were vexatious. The Secretary of State and the district auditor served
respondent's notices under RSC Ord 59, r 6(2), which respectively gave notice that *g*
on the hearing of the appeal the Secretary of State would contend that the judge's
judgment should be affirmed on the additional grounds that the amended statement
of claim as against the Secretary of State was frivolous or vexatious and otherwise
an abuse of the process of the court and should be struck out accordingly, and that
the district auditor would contend that the judgment should be affirmed on the
additional grounds that the amended statement of claim disclosed no reasonable cause *h*
of action and was otherwise an abuse of the process of the court and should be struck
out accordingly. The facts are set out in the judgment of Lord Denning MR.

Lord Gifford for the plaintiffs.
Peter Gibson for the Secretary of State.
G H FitzGerald and G R G Roots for the district auditor.

Cur adv vult

31st January. The following judgments were read.

LORD DENNING MR. In Clay Cross in Derbyshire there are 1,340 council
houses. The local council let them to tenants at very low rents. The average was

£1·50 a week. Many other councils also let their houses at very low rents. Parliament decided that this could not continue. It said that council tenants were to pay fair rents. It laid down a procedure for ascertaining what was a fair rent for every council house. But this procedure might take some little time to implement. And it might be hard on the tenants to make a big increase in one big jump. So, by the Housing Finance Act 1972, Parliament enacted that there should be a gradual progression towards fair rents. In particular, the low rents were to be increased by £1 a week from 1st October 1972. That would bring the Clay Cross rents up to £2·50 a week for the year 1st October 1972 to 30th September 1973. During the next year there was to be an increase of 50p a week. And so on until the fair rents were ascertained. If it turned out, when the fair rents were ascertained, that the increases had been too much—that is, more than the fair rents—then the councils had to repay to the tenants the excess amount which they had collected.

But, whilst providing for those increases, Parliament also sought to prevent hardship on those tenants who could not afford to pay. It enacted that the council could grant rebates to tenants according to 'their needs and resources'. The cost of these rebates was to be borne, almost entirely, by the central government. They would pay 90 per cent of the rent rebates. The local council would only pay 10 per cent. So only 10 per cent would fall on the local ratepayers. The 90 per cent fell on the general body of taxpayers.

In order to carry out the 1972 Act, Parliament placed a duty on the local council: (i) to determine fair rents, subject to the scrutiny of rent scrutiny boards: see ss 49 to 60; (ii) meanwhile to make progressive increases towards fair rents by increases of £1 a week for the first year (see ss 62, 63(4), 65(1)) and other increases in subsequent years; (iii) when the fair rent was ascertained, to repay any excess: see s 67; (iv) to make rebate from rents to tenants by reference to their needs and resources: see s 18.

But the councillors of Clay Cross flatly refused to carry out the duties laid on them by Parliament. Each of them on taking office had made this solemn declaration[1]:

> 'I [giving his name], having been elected to the office of Councillor for the Urban District of Clay Cross in Derbyshire, hereby declare that I take the said office upon myself and will duly and faithfully fulfil the duties thereof according to the best of my judgment and ability.'

Each one of the councillors deliberately broke that promise. Each of them refused to carry out the duties laid on him by Parliament. Both before the 1972 Act was passed, and after it, they repeatedly said that the council would not under any circumstances operate it. The clerk to the council and the chief financial officer warned them of the consequences. The Secretary of State himself warned them. Yet they persisted in defying the law. They actually instructed the officers to take no steps to put the Act into operation. The result was to benefit the well-to-do tenants (whose rents were not increased) and to injure the poor tenants (who did not get any rebates).

The councillors made this excuse. They claimed that they had been elected mainly on their housing policies and had pledged not to carry out any measures such as were contained in the 1972 Act. They considered, therefore, that they had a clear moral obligation to carry out their pledges.

Let me examine for a moment this supposed moral obligation. According to them, they went to the electors, saying: 'If you elect us to be your councillors, we will not increase your rents, nor will we charge you the *fair rents* which the statute prescribes.' They said that in respect of *rents*. But test it by supposing that they said it in respect of *rates*. Suppose they went to the electors saying: 'We will not charge you the *rates* which the statute prescribes.' After the election, the council would not have the money to pay the outgoings. They could not pay the dustmen. The refuse would not be

---

1 As required by s 61(1) of the Local Government Act 1933 and Sch 2 to the Urban District Council Election Rules 1969 (SI 1969 No 756)

collected. The place would wither for lack of sustenance—unless help came from outside. Would they then be so bold as to say that they had a moral obligation not to charge the rates? To my mind their plain obligation, moral as well as legal, was to carry out the duties imposed on them by law. They do not escape this obligation by saying that they were elected for the purpose—by electors to whom they gave false pledges—pledges which they knew or ought to have known they could not fulfil. They could not validly promise that they would not increase the rents when they were in duty bound to do so.

Faced with this open defiance of the law, what were those in authority to do? There were four courses open.

1. *Mandamus*

One way undoubtedly would be to apply to the High Court for a writ of mandamus to order the councillors to carry out their statutory duty. But what would be the consequence? In their stubborn frame of mind, they would disobey the order of the court. They would be fined or sent to prison. But what would happen then? If recent experience is anything to go by, they would become martyrs. That does no good to anyone.

2. *Housing commissioner*

Another way would be to take a special course provided by the 1972 Act itself. Under s 95 the Secretary of State is enabled to make a 'default order' declaring the council to be in default and ordering them to take specified steps to remedy the default. If the council fails to take those steps, the Secretary of State is authorised to appoint a 'Housing Commissioner' to discharge the duties of increasing the rents, and so forth. The housing commissioner would be authorised to appoint his own staff and conduct all the business relating to the rents. The expense would all fall on the local authority, that is, the ratepayers.

This course would seem to have considerable advantages. But it would also have this grave disadvantage. The housing commissioner would have to operate in a hostile territory with no knowledge of the terrain. He might meet with opposition on all sides. The councillors would still be the elected representatives of the town. They would still be responsible for the conduct of its affairs, save only for this housing finance. They would still be attending the council offices. They might make things very difficult for the housing commissioner. True it is that, if they wilfully obstructed him, they could be taken to court and fined up to £400: see s 98. But, short of wilful obstruction, the housing commissioner could be put into a very embarrassing position.

3. *Reduction of housing subsidy*

The 1972 Act itself contains another way. It authorises the Secretary of State to withdraw any housing subsidy which is being paid to the council. He can reduce it, suspend it, or even discontinue it: see s 99. But what good would this do? It would not help in the least to get the duties fulfilled.

4. *Extraordinary audit*

This is the course which is in controversy. There is nothing in the 1972 Act which points to this course of action; and the councillors say that it is not legitimate. To this I will return in a moment. But, meanwhile, I will state what it is.

Every year the accounts of a local authority are subject to audit by a district auditor. But, in addition, the Minister may at any time direct a district auditor to hold an extraordinary audit. This is conducted on the same principles as the annual audit. These must be noted.

The district auditor holds a position of much responsibility. In some respects he is like a company auditor. He is a watchdog to see that the accounts are properly kept and that no one is making off with the funds. He is not bound to be of a suspicious a turn of mind: see *Re Kingston Cotton Mill Co (No 2)*[1]; but, if anything suspicious does turn up, it is his duty to take care to follow it up: see *Re Thomas Gerrard & Son Ltd*[2]. In other respects, however, the duties of a district auditor go far beyond those of a company auditor. He must see whether, on the financial side, the councillors and their officers have discharged their duties according to law. He must listen to any elector who makes objection to the accounts. He must make his own investigation

b also. If he finds that the councillors or the officers, or any of them, have expended money improperly or unreasonably, or allowed it to be so expended, it is his duty to surcharge them: see *Roberts v Hopwood*[3]; *Pooley v District Auditor, No 8 Audit District, Middlesex*[4]. If he finds that they have failed to get in money which they ought to have done, and thus brought about a loss or deficiency—owing to their negligence or misconduct—it is his duty to surcharge them so as to make it good: see s 228(1)(d)

c of the Local Government Act 1933. In making the surcharge, he must, of course, act fairly. Whenever he proposes to surcharge anyone, he must let him know the case against him and give him a fair opportunity of answering it, and of calling witnessses, if desired. At the end he must issue his certificate of surcharge. If called on, he must give in writing the reasons for his decision. The party surcharged can appeal to the High Court both on law and on fact; and the High Court can, in a proper case, grant

d relief. But, if he does not appeal, or if he appeals and his appeal is dismissed, then the sum certified is payable by him and can be recovered as a civil debt. The district auditor is bound to enforce it—by levying execution or by taking proceedings in bankruptcy—unless the party surcharged has no money and it would be unreasonable to incur the expense of enforcement. But, whether he pays the debt or not, if the amount surcharged exceeds £500, he is automatically disqualified from being a

e councillor.

Those were the four courses open. The 1972 Act came into force in August 1972. The council ought to have increased the rents by £1 a week from 1st October 1972. But they did not do so. On 13th November 1972 the Secretary of State, after considering their representations, made a default order[5] against them. He directed them to take steps within 16 days to remedy their default. On the expiry of those 16 days he

f could have appointed a housing commissioner. But he did not choose to do so. Instead he decided to direct an extraordinary audit.

By a letter dated 16th November 1972 the Secretary of State directed the district auditor to hold an extraordinary audit for the period from 1st April to 16th November 1972. The district auditor considered everything. He heard the submissions of the councillors. He came to the conclusion that a loss of £6,985 had been incurred by

g their negligence and misconduct. He surcharged them in that sum. They asked him to state his reasons in writing. He did so. He said:

'This was no accidental omission to carry out their statutory duties, but a deliberate flouting of the law in furtherance of their political views. This was a clear breach of their duty as members to act reasonably and to do their duty to the ratepayers according to law, and amounted to negligence [and] also to mis-

h conduct.'

The councillors appealed to the High Court. On 30th July 1973 their appeal was dismissed: see *Asher v Lacey*[6]. They could have appealed to this court, but they did not do so. Their time for appeal expired on 5th October 1973. Thereupon the certificate of the district auditor became final. The councillors were bound to pay the

j ───────────────────────────────

1 [1896] 2 Ch 279
2 [1967] 2 All ER 525, [1968] Ch 455
3 [1925] AC 578, [1925] All ER Rep 24
4 (1965) 63 LGR 236
5 The Clay Cross Urban District Council (Housing Default) Order 1972 (SI 1972 No 1713)
6 [1973] 3 All ER 1008, [1973] 1 WLR 1412

sum of £6,985 for the period to 16th November 1972. They became disqualified from being members of the council then or for the following five years: see s 59(1)(d) of the 1933 Act.

Seeing that the councillors were disqualified, they had no longer any authority to act. Something had to be done. So four days later the Secretary of State took action. He took another course open to him. He appointed a housing commissioner. He had already made a default order on 13th November 1972 which the council had disobeyed. So he was able to, and did, on 9th October 1973, make an order[1] appointing Mr W P D Skillington CB to be the housing commissioner to carry out the functions under the 1972 Act, in lieu of the council.

The housing commissioner had hardly started, however, when the councillors tried to stop it all. On 29th October 1973 they took out an originating summons in the Chancery Division (which was afterwards amended so as to become a statement of claim) against the Secretary of State and the district auditor. They claimed that the Secretary of State was wrong to direct an extraordinary audit and that his direction was of no effect in law. The defendants applied to strike it out. On 21st December 1973 Megarry J did strike it out. The councillors appeal to this court.

The first ground of attack was that the direction for an extraordinary audit—

'was punitive in intent and/or was made solely or principally to secure some object . . . other than the recoupment of moneys lost by the [councillors'] default and was ultra vires the [Secretary of State]'.

Counsel for the councillors put it before us in this way. The 1972 Act provided a clear and specific way in which the Secretary of State could proceed, namely, by appointing a housing commissioner. He could have done this at the beginning of December 1972. Instead of doing so, he waited over ten months until 9th October 1973 before he appointed a housing commissioner. This long delay was extremely pre-judicial to the councillors because it meant that their liability to surcharge was mounting up every week. In the six weeks or so from 1st October 1972 to 16th November 1972 it had to come to a net sum of £6,985. In ten months it would come to £50,000.

Furthermore, said counsel, instead of appointing a housing commissioner, the Secretary of State had chosen to take a course not stated in the 1972 Act at all. He directed an extraordinary audit. He must have known that the councillors had no means and were unable to pay. So his purpose must have been to punish them, or at any rate to get them disqualified. It was not lawful, said counsel, for the Secretary of State to use an extraordinary audit for such a purpose. It was an ulterior object which rendered his direction invalid and of no effect. He relied on *R v Brixton Prison (Governor), ex parte Soblen*[2], which was founded on *Sydney Municipal Council v Campbell*[3]. At any rate, said counsel, if the Secretary of State had such thoughts in his mind, he was being influenced by irrelevant considerations and had exercised his discretion wrongly. He relied on *Associated Provincial Picture Houses Ltd v Wednesbury Corpn*[4] and *Padfield v Minister of Agriculture, Fisheries and Food*[5].

It lies ill in the mouth of these councillors to say that the Secretary of State has acted unlawfully. Here they are, the 11 councillors of Clay Cross. Each of them deliberately broke the solemn promise which he gave when he accepted office. Each of them has flagrantly defied the law. Each of them is determined to continue to defy it. Yet they come to the court and complain that the Secretary of State has acted unlawfully. If he has done so, we would not hesitate to say so. We will not tolerate

1 The Clay Cross Urban District Council (Housing Commissioner) Order 1973 (SI 1973 No 1675)
2 [1962] 3 All ER 641 at 661, [1963] 2 QB 243 at 302
3 [1925] AC 338
4 [1947] 2 All ER 680, [1948] 1 KB 223
5 [1968] 1 All ER 694, [1968] AC 997

a any abuse of power by the executive arm of government. But here there is none. These 11 councillors, by their conduct, have presented a grave problem to all concerned in the good government of this country. The Secretary of State is the one person who can take action to see that the law is obeyed. He is the one to decide which of several courses open is the best one to take. So long as he acts in good faith, his decision is not to be questioned: see *R v Barnet and Camden Rent Tribunal, ex parte Frey Investments Ltd*[1]. In the case of two towns in Wales, Bedwas and Machen and Merthyr

b Tydfil, the Secretary of State for Wales appointed a housing commissioner. In the case of Clay Cross in Derbyshire, the Secretary of State for the Environment directed an extraordinary audit. In every case it is for him to decide. It may be that in this case he did have, at the back of his mind, that if he directed an extraordinary audit the result would be that these 11 councillors would be disqualified. Even if he did think

c so, there was nothing wrong in it. These men were flagrantly defying the law. They were not fit to be councillors. The sooner they were disqualified the better. If the only means of doing it was by an extraordinary audit, then let it be done that way. It is a lawful means to a legitimate end.

The second ground of attack was on the ground that the sum of £1 per dwelling was not a certain rent increase but was provisional only. It might have to be repaid

d if the fair rent turned out to be quite low. A direction for an extraordinary audit (leading to a surcharge) ought not to be made for a loss or deficiency which might never occur.

I do not think there is anything in this point. District auditors have often to deal with contingencies and uncertainties. They do so by making assessments and estimates as best they can, doing their calculations on the cautious side. In this very case

e the rents were so low that the district auditor could well say that when increased by £1 a week no part of that £1 would ever be repayable. But, whether that be so or not, there was at the time of the audit clearly a deficiency in the accounts. The district auditor was quite justified in surcharging the councillors with that deficiency. They ought to make it good, whatever way the ultimate balance might turn out to be. In my opinion, therefore, the attack made by the councillors against the Secretary of

f State is entirely without foundation. The statement of claim disclosed no reasonable cause of action. I go further. I think these proceedings are vexatious. The councillors have already had their full say against the surcharge. They appealed to the Divisional Court[2], who upheld it. On that appeal the Divisional Court could and would have considered any points which the councillors wished to make, including any which went to the validity of the extraordinary audit. The councillors could then have

g attacked the direction made by the Secretary of State, alleging that it was improper. If they had done so, the court would no doubt have made the Secretary of State a party and had the matter thrashed out. But the councillors did not attack it then. They could have appealed to this court and raised it here. But they did not do so. Not having raised it in those proceedings, I do not think they should be allowed to raise it now in these proceedings. Strictly the matter is not res judicata, but these courts have

h ample power to prevent any abuse of their process. These proceedings are, in my opinion, an abuse. These councillors are seeking, by one shift or another, to escape the consequences of their own wrongdoing. The time had come when they must be told quite firmly that the law must be obeyed. Their disobedience cannot be tolerated. They are disqualified. They must stand down. Others must be elected in their place —others who will fulfil the duties which these 11 have failed to do. I trust that there

j are good men to be found in Clay Cross ready to take over. I would dismiss the appeal.

ORR LJ. I agree with the judgment of Lord Denning MR and wish to add only a few words as to the the three major issues which arise in this appeal.

1   [1972] 1 All ER 1185, [1972] 2 QB 342
2   [1973] 3 All ER 1008, [1973] 1 WLR 1412

The first two issues are whether the statement of claim discloses a possible cause of
action on the basis, first, that the Secretary of State in ordering an extraordinary
audit in November 1972, and in failing to appoint a housing commissioner until nearly
a year later could be held to have exercised his powers from wrong motives; and,
secondly, that he ought not to have ordered the extraordinary audit at a time when
the amounts of the fair rents had not been finally determined. The third issue is
whether the judge was right in holding that as regards the second defendant, the
present district auditor, the claim was vexatious on the ground that it is an endeavour
to relitigate a matter which had already been decided by the Divisional Court[1].

As to the first issue, it was accepted for the plaintiffs that the Minister had power
do what he did and it was not suggested that he acted in bad faith; but it was claimed
that his decision to order the extraordinary audit was governed by a desire, not to
obtain recoupment to the local authority of moneys lost, but to punish the plaintiffs;
and it was further claimed that the purpose as well as the effect of postponing the
appointment of a housing commissioner was to make the plaintiffs liable to further
surcharges in the future. One of the complaints made for the plaintiffs before the
learned judge was that the Secretary of State had not, before ordering the audit, endeavoured to make any appraisal as to the likelihood or otherwise of such an audit and
its consequential surcharge producing any recoupment to the council; and I agree with
the judge that this argument, so far as it went, tended to refute rather than support the
allegation of punitive intent. For myself I can see, on the material before us, no
reason to suppose that the Minister in ordering the audit had assumed that the
plaintiffs would be unable to make good any part of the deficiency which might be
surcharged on them; and if he had in mind the disqualification consequent on a surcharge, from holding office as a local government councillor, I consider that he was
fully justified in doing so. The instrument of surcharge is and has long been the
means adopted by Parliament of maintaining the observance of proper standards
both by councillors and by council officials in the financial administration of local
government, and in my view it has a remedial rather than a punitive object, but
in any event, I have no doubt that it was rightly applied; for it is not in dispute that
the plaintiffs had been given repeated warnings as to the consequence which might
follow from their defiance of the law, and had deliberately chosen to persevere in
that defiance.

As to the postponement of the appointment of a housing commissioner, it is accepted
that the Secretary of State could not, in view of the time limits for compliance allowed
in the default order of 13th November 1972, have made the appointment before the
end of November or early December of that year. From 28th February 1973,
the date of the plaintiffs' notice of appeal against the surcharge, until 5th October
1973, when the surcharge became final, the fact that an appeal was being pursued
might well in itself have been a sufficient reason why the appointment should be
delayed, but apart from this, the Secretary of State was in my view entitled to take
into account that the plaintiffs might yet repent of their defiance of the law, as other
councillors elsewhere apparently did, and also the problem with which a housing
commissioner would be faced in a local government area of which the councillors
had repeatedly expressed and publicised their antagonism to the 1972 Act, with the
result that there would be obvious difficulties in collecting increased rents. Moreover, the appointment of a housing commissioner is, as counsel for the Secretary of
State pointed out, a negation of local government, or at least an acceptance of its
failure, and this to my mind was a good reason why the Secretary of State should hesitate before taking such a step. I would add that the only other possible courses open
to him were mandamus, which is enforceable in the last resort by committal to
prison, and a reduction in government subsidies which would impose an additional

---

1 [1973] 3 All ER 1008, [1973] 1 WLR 1412

burden on the ratepayers; and for those reasons I do not consider that the Secretary of State can be criticised for not adopting either of these courses.

It was argued that, whereas in the present case the Secretary of State ordered an extraordinary audit but did not appoint a housing commissioner, in certain cases arising in Wales the Minister responsible had appointed a housing commissioner and had not ordered an audit, and this fact, it was claimed, in some way exhibited that the Secretary of State's decisions in the present case were wrong. I cannot see why. It is true that both Ministers belonged to the same government, but it does not follow that the same course ought to have been taken regardless of any differences in the particular circumstances. Moreover, as the judge pointed out, even if the same action ought to have been taken, it does not follow that what was done in Wales was right and what was done at Clay Cross was wrong.

For these reasons I can find no substance in the first ground of appeal. The second ground is whether it was wrong to order an extraordinary audit before the fair rents were finally determined, and it is claimed that this action caused prejudice to the plaintiffs. If, however, no extraordinary audit had been ordered, the annual audit would in the ordinary course have been due to take place before final determination of the rents, and this argument therefore involves that the audits provided for in the Local Government Act 1933, and in no way curtailed by any express provision of the 1972 Act, should be suspended during the substantial period which would elapse before the determination: but I can find in the legislation no warrant for any such suspension. There must inevitably, as it seems to me, be cases where an audit has to deal with uncertainties and in the present case I am satisfied that the amount of the surcharge was, having regard to the low level of the existing rents in the district, entirely fair to the plaintiffs. For these reasons I am unable to find any substance in the second ground of appeal.

The judge was therefore, in my view, fully justified in concluding that the statement of claim disclosed no cause of action against either the Secretary of State or the district auditor, and in these circumstances the third ground of appeal is of no practical importance, but in my judgment it is also without foundation. The argument for the plaintiffs was that it was not open to them on the appeal to the Divisional Court[1] against the surcharge to allege that, for the reasons since advanced in this appeal, the Secretary of State's direction to Mr Lacey, the then district auditor, to conduct an extraordinary audit was invalid, and that Megarry J was therefore wrong in holding that in the present proceedings the plaintiffs were seeking to relitigate as against the present district auditor an issue which could have been raised against his predecessor in the Divisional Court. I am unable to accept this argument. In my judgment it was open to the plaintiffs to allege in the appeal against the surcharge the invalidity of the Secretary of State's order for the extraordinary audit. The effect of their doing so would, no doubt, have been that the Divisional Court would have had at least to hear submissions from counsel on behalf of the Secretary of State, and, it may be, to allow the Secretary of State to be joined in the appeal; but I can see no reason why that, if it were necessary, could not have been done. Accordingly in my judgment the judge was right in holding that the present appeal is vexatious as respects the second defendant, the district auditor, and I would only add that, for this purpose, it has been accepted for the plaintiffs that nothing turns on the defendant in the Divisional Court (Mr Lacey) and the second defendant in the present proceedings (Mr Harrison) being different individuals.

For these reasons, as well as those given by Lord Denning MR, I would dismiss this appeal.

LAWTON LJ. All the plaintiffs, after being elected as councillors to the Clay Cross Urban District Council, made declarations of acceptance of office as required by s 61

---

1   [1973] 3 All ER 1008, [1973] 1 WLR 1412

of the Local Government Act 1933 and the Urban District Council Election Rules
1969[1]. Each declared that he would duly and faithfully fulfil the duties of his office.
Those duties required them to carry out the provisions of any Acts of Parliament
which applied to their district. One such Act was the Housing Finance Act 1972. All
refused to apply this Act and made their refusal known to all. Faced with this contumacy the Secretary of State, who had the constitutional duty of seeing that the Act
was put into operation, had to take some action.

What was he to do? He thought he had four options open to him; first, he could
appoint a housing commissioner to do what the council refused to do, because of the
contumacy of the plaintiffs as councillors (see s 95(7) of the 1972 Act); secondly, he
could apply to the High Court for an order of mandamus against the plaintiffs;
thirdly, he could reduce or suspend the subsidies payable under the 1972 Act or any
other subsidy in respect of housing (see s 99(1)); and, fourthly, he could safeguard the
council's housing revenue account and indirectly put pressure on the plaintiffs to
carry out their duties by means of the financial control provisions of the Local
Government Act 1933 (see Part X of that Act).

Each of these courses had advantages and disadvantages. The appointment of a
housing commissioner would have ensured that the 1972 Act was applied in Clay Cross.
The main disadvantage of this course was that it would have taken a considerable
amount of control over council housing away from those who had been elected to
exercise that control. Further, the statutory requirements of giving notice of default
and time for representations to be made by a council subject to a default order
would have resulted in some delay in making the appointment of a housing commissioner with consequential loss to the housing revenue account meanwhile. Counsel
for the plaintiffs accepted that a housing commissioner could not have been appointed
before 16th November 1972, the date on which the Secretary of State directed the
district auditor to hold an extraordinary audit of the housing revenue account. The
disadvantages of making orders of mandamus against persons who have convinced
themselves (as these plaintiffs have) that they are entitled in conscience to defy the
law are so well known that I need not specify them. The reduction or suspension of
subsidies would bear hardly on the ratepayers generally rather than on those who
had caused the difficulty. Finally, the financial control provisions of the 1933 Act have
proved to be a most effective way of safeguarding local authority finances and of dis-
couraging misconduct and negligence in the conduct of local government because
those who are guilty have to make good any financial loss which may have resulted
from what they did or failed to do. It is significant that when the clerk of the council,
in a report circulated amongst the plaintiffs, advised them that they were bound in
law to apply the 1972 Act, he warned them of the likely financial consequences of
their not doing so.

The Secretary of State decided to use this last option. If in law it was open to him,
he was justified in doing what he did. Balancing the advantages and disadvantages of
one possible course of action against another and making a decision is what Secretaries
of State have to do: it is the very stuff of government and the courts should not
interfere save for good reason and disagreeing with the decision is not in itself a good
reason.

The plaintiffs do not suggest in their reamended statement of claim that the
Secretary of State had no power to direct an extraordinary audit, and once directed,
on the admitted facts in this case, it was bound to result in their being surcharged by
the district auditor in a sum estimated to be the amount of the loss to the housing
revenue account resulting from their contumacy in refusing to implement the Act.
What they do allege is that he exercised his power to give this direction for a purpose
which was outside the objects and policy of the 1933 Act. They say that the proper

1   SI 1969 No 756, Sch 2

a purpose was the recoupment of moneys lost by the plaintiffs' default. They do not
specify what his improper purpose was but they do allege that the direction was punitive in intent. They submit that an improper purpose can be inferred from the following: first, the Secretary of State did not appoint a housing commissioner; secondly,
because he did not do so there was no one to set in motion the procedures for fixing
fair rents and rent rebates with the result, as the Secretary of State must have
b appreciated, that the district auditor would find it impossible or unnecessarily difficult
to assess the sums lost to the housing revenue account; and thirdly, the Secretary of
State for Wales had acted differently: he had appointed housing commissioners
in two local government areas.

These being proceedings to strike out the reamended statement of claim, I have
reminded myself that this court is not concerned to discover whether the Secretary
of State had an improper purpose, but whether the particulars pleaded could be a
c reasonable foundation for that allegation. In my judgment they could not be.

By 13th November 1972 the Secretary of State knew that the plaintiffs had failed
to discharge their duties under the 1972 Act and had no intention of doing so: he
made a default order[1] on that date. It followed that the council's housing revenue
account must have already incurred a loss or deficiency by reason of the plaintiffs'
d contumacy. In my judgment the Secretary of State was entitled to take the steps
necessary to find out what was the amount of this loss or deficiency. This he did by
giving a direction for an extraordinary audit. When held the amount of the loss or
deficiency could be ascertained, and the 1933 Act contained provisions for its recovery
by the district auditor from those responsible. It is pertinent to bear in mind that the
Secretary of State was concerned solely with directing the audit. What happened
e afterwards if a loss or deficiency was found was prescribed by the 1933 Act: see ss 228,
232 and 233. The Secretary of State himself took no step which required any of the
plaintiffs to pay any sum certified by the district auditor to be due by way of surcharge.
He set the financial control machinery in motion; but it was the operation of that
machinery by the district auditor which produced the surcharge. This being so, in
my judgment, the decision of the Secretary of State to direct an extraordinary audit
f cannot be challenged unless it was made in bad faith or was frivolous or vexatious;
and nothing of the kind has been suggested. See R v Barnet and Camden Rent Tribunal,
ex parte Frey Investments Ltd[2]. But even if the Secretary of State's intention was punitive and coercive, that, in my judgment, could not signify that he gave the direction
for a purpose which was outside the objects and policy of the 1933 Act. Part X of that
Act provided for financial control over local government; and s 228 makes clear to all
g engaged in local government, whether as councillors or employees, what will be the
consequences of any misconduct or negligence causing financial loss. In my judgment
the objects of the financial control provisions of the 1933 Act include punitive and
coercive ones.

If it was not improper for the Secretary of State to have in mind the punitive and
coercive objects of the 1933 Act and he had powers to direct an extraordinary audit
h (which is not challenged) his choice of one course of action rather than another cannot
possibly be a reasonable foundation for an inference that he had some, wholly unspecified, improper purpose in doing what he did. It may well be that the appointment of a housing commissioner is usually the most appropriate way of implementing the 1972 Act when a local authority is in default: but there is nothing in the 1972
Act which excludes the power to direct an extraordinary audit given by the 1933 Act.
j If the Secretary of State has a choice of powers (as I adjudge he has) the fact that the
Secretary of State for Wales, being possessed of the same powers, chose differently
is wholly incapable of proving the existence of an improper motive.

---

1 SI 1972 No 1713
2 [1972] 1 All ER 1185, [1972] QB 342

I come now to the allegation that the Secretary of State's failure to appoint a housing *a* commissioner made the ascertainment of a loss or deficiency impossible or unnecessarily difficult. The fact is that the district auditor did make a finding as to the loss sustained by the council. It was an assessment arrived at after making an estimate as to what the rent rebates might have been had that Act been brought into operation. No estimate was made by him as to what might have to be repaid by the council if the fair rents to be assessed later by the rent scrutiny board were *b* less than the increases in rent which the Act ordered local authorities to make as from 1st October 1972. The reason for this is clear: the plaintiffs, who were represented by their member of Parliament (who showed that he had a grasp of all the points which could arise), never suggested that this was a possibility. The making of estimates is part of a district auditor's work and the courts have recognised this: see *Roberts v Hopwood*[1] and *Pooley v District Auditor, No 8 Audit District, Middlesex*[2]. *c* In my judgment giving a district auditor directions to hold an audit which would necessitate his making estimates cannot be a foundation from which it could be inferred, reasonably or otherwise, that the Secretary of State had some improper motive. It follows that the reamended statement of claim discloses no reasonable cause of action. It should be struck out.

There is another reason why this claim should be struck out. In my judgment the *d* plaintiffs had exhausted their rights of appeal against the surcharge before the issue of the writ in this action. They are now trying to get the court to reconsider contentions which they put forward, or could have put forward, in their appeal to the Divisional Court[3] against the surcharge. That appeal was made pursuant to s 229 of the 1933 Act. The plaintiffs were persons aggrieved by the surcharge made on them; and on the hearing of the appeal the Divisional Court had *e* power 'to confirm, vary or quash' it (see s 229(2)). According to the Concise Oxford Dictionary the word 'quash' means to 'annul, make void, reject as not valid, put an end to (especially by legal procedure or authority)'. It follows, so it seems to me, that any contention, which, if valid on the facts, would have justified the Divisional Court quashing the surcharge could have been put forward in the appeal. This would have included a contention that the direction to hold the extraordinary audit which resulted *f* in the surcharge was invalid because the Secretary of State gave it for a purpose outside the objects and policy of the 1933 Act. No such contention was put forward in the appeal. As it could have been, the plaintiffs cannot now bring another action so as to get a second chance to do what they omitted to do in the appeal. See *Henderson v Henderson*[4]. Counsel for the plaintiffs submitted that it would have been impracticable to argue this contention before the Divisional Court as the Secretary of State *g* was not a party to the appeal. This difficulty could easily have been overcome by the court asking him to appear. This was done in *Belcher v Reading Corpn*[5].

There is a good practical reason why those who have used their statutory right of appeal against surcharges should not be allowed to start another action raising contentions which could have been put forward in the appeal. Once an appeal has been finally determined, a person surcharged to an amount exceeding £500 is disqualified *h* from being a member of a local authority: see s 59(1)(d). These plaintiffs became disqualified on 5th October 1973 when the time expired within which they could have appealed to this court. The Clay Cross Urban District Council continues to exist as a body corporate (see s 31(2) of the 1933 Act), but until the vacancies created by the plaintiffs' disqualification are filled by elections it cannot do anything which requires a resolution of the council. It is like a ship abandoned by the crew; it can float and *j*

1   [1925] AC 578, [1925] All ER Rep 24
2   (1965) 63 LGR 236
3   [1973] 3 All ER 1008, [1973] 1 WLR 1412
4   (1843) 3 Hare 100 at 114, 115, [1843-60] All ER Rep 378 at 381, 382, per Wigram V-C
5   [1949] 2 All ER 969 at 984, 985, [1950] Ch 380 at 394

keep on the course last set, but it cannot alter course to meet new circumstances, and it will stop when its fuel runs out; and the fuel which keeps councils going is money raised by rates or borrowed. It would be an intolerable situation if disqualified councillors at any time during the six years allowed by the Limitation Act 1939, as amended, could raise doubts about their own status and that of the persons elected to replace them by issuing a writ challenging the validity of the Secretary of State's exercise of his powers to direct an extraordinary audit. The law will not allow any such doubt to be raised.

I too would dimiss the appeal.

Appeal dismissed.

Solicitors: *Seifert, Sedley & Co* (for the plaintiffs); *Treasury Solicitor; Clifford-Turner & Co* (for the district auditor).

Wendy Shockett   Barrister.

R v Immigration Appeal Tribunal, ex parte Samaraweera

QUEEN'S BENCH DIVISION
LORD WIDGERY CJ, MACKENNA AND MAY JJ
25th JANUARY 1974

Immigration – Appeal – Appeal to tribunal from adjudicator – Time limit for appealing – Appeal to tribunal within prescribed period – Leave to appeal granted by adjudicator on oral application – Notice of appeal to be served on tribunal as soon as practicable thereafter – Whether time limit applicable where leave given on oral application – Whether notice of appeal to be served as soon as practicable and in any event within prescribed period – Immigration Appeals (Procedure) Rules 1970 (SI 1970 No 794), rr 13(1)(2), 14(1)(2).

The applicant, who was an immigrant, sought a decision from an adjudicator in order to secure his right to remain in the United Kingdom. On 27th October 1972 the adjudicator decided against him. The applicant forthwith made an oral application to the adjudicator under rr 13(1)[a] and 14(2)[b] of the Immigration Appeals (Procedure) Rules 1970 for leave to appeal to the Immigration Appeal Tribunal. The applicant did not, however, serve his written notice of appeal on the tribunal under r 14(1)[c] of the 1970 rules until 19th March 1973. The tribunal declined jurisdiction on the ground that the notice had not been given within seven days of the adjudicator's decision in accordance with r 13(2)[d] of the 1970 rules. The applicant moved for an order of mandamus directed to the tribunal requiring it to hear his appeal, contending that, where leave had been given by an adjudicator on an oral application, r 14(2) required that notice of appeal should be given 'as soon as practicable thereafter' and accordingly the time limit provided for in r 13(2) had no application.

---

a   Rule 13(1) is set out at p 173 *d*, post
b   Rule 14(2) is set out at p 174 *a*, post
c   Rule 14(1), so far as material, provides: 'Subject to the provisions of paragraph (2) below, notice of appeal ... shall be given ... by completing [the prescribed form] and serving it on ... the Tribunal ...'
d   Rule 13(2) is set out at p 173 *e*, post

Held (May J dissenting) – The requirement in r 14(2) that notice of appeal should be given 'as soon as practicable' was additional to the requirement in r 13(2) that it should be given within seven days. Accordingly, where an adjudicator had granted leave to appeal on an oral application, notice of appeal had to be given as soon as practicable thereafter and, in any event, within seven days. It followed that the applicant's notice of appeal was out of time and the motion would therefore be dismissed (see p 174 *h* to p 175 *a* and *d*, post).

Notes

For appeals to the Immigration Appeal Tribunal, see 4 Halsbury's Laws (4th Edn) 515, 516, para 1025.

The Immigration Appeals (Procedure) Rules 1970 lapsed on the repeal of the enabling powers contained in the Immigration Appeals Act 1969 by the Immigration Act 1971, s 34, Sch 6 ,which came into force on 1st January 1973. For provisions corresponding to rr 13, 14 of the 1970 rules, see the Immigration Appeals (Procedure) Rules 1972 (SI 1972 No 1684), rr 15, 16 (2 Halsbury's Statutory Instruments (3rd Reissue) 40, 41).

Motion for mandamus

By notice of motion dated 5th July 1973, Basil Jayanatha Samaraweera, applied for an order of mandamus directed to the Immigration Appeal Tribunal to hear and determine the appeal of the applicant against the determination, dated 27th October 1972 made by J K Brownlees Esq, an adjudicator appointed under s 1 of the Immigration Appeals Act 1969. The grounds on which relief was sought were that, as a successful application for leave to appeal had been made to the adjudicator, the tribunal had been wrong in law in the decision expressed in a letter to the applicant's solicitors dated 12th April 1973, wherein it was stated that the applicant's notice of appeal was out of time, and in refusing to hear and determine the appeal. The facts are set out in the judgment of Lord Widgery CJ.

Nigel Murray for the applicant.
Gordon Slynn for the tribunal.

LORD WIDGERY CJ. In these proceedings counsel moves on behalf of one Samaraweera for an order of mandamus directed to the Immigration Appeal Tribunal requiring it to hear and determine an appeal by the applicant against the determination of an adjudicator appointed under the Immigration Appeals Act 1969, that decision being dated 27th October 1972.

The issue which this court is required to determine is purely a matter of interpretation of the Immigration Appeals (Procedure) Rules 1970[1], and it is therefore unnecessary to go into the factual background at this stage beyond saying that the applicant, being in danger of being deported from this country, sought a decision from an adjudicator appointed under the Immigration Appeals Act 1969, the purpose of his appeal being to secure his right to remain in this country. The adjudicator found against him and, as I have already said, the decision of the adjudicator was given on 27th October 1972. The applicant thereupon wished to appeal from the adjudicator's conclusion to the Immigration Appeal Tribunal. In due course—indeed it was after a considerable lapse of time—namely, on 19th March 1973, the applicant's advisers sought to lodge on his behalf an appeal against the adjudicator's decision. The attitude of the tribunal was that the application was out of time and out of time in a manner which the tribunal had no power to rectify; in other words that the time limit said to have been breached was one that the tribunal had no power to extend. Accordingly the tribunal declined jurisdiction and that resulted in the present application for mandamus.

---

1   SI 1970 No 794

a   In deciding within what time the applicant was required to move in order to bring his appeal before the tribunal we have to consider rr 12, 13 and 14 of the Immigration Appeals (Procedure) Rules 1970[1].

Rule 12 provides that an appeal shall lie only with the leave of the adjudicator or the tribunal in every case, with certain exceptions there specified, which I do not find relevant to the applicant. I notice in passing that there are exceptions; in other words there are cases where leave is not required at all, but the general rule under *b*   r 12 is that an appeal shall lie only with the leave of the adjudicator or the tribunal in every case.

When one passes to r 13 the cross-heading for that rule is 'Time limit for appealing'. I should say, before I look at the terms of r 13, that it is agreed between counsel, and I think rightly agreed, that a would-be appellant who seeks to go to the tribunal, and who requires leave for that purpose, can in the first instance either ask for leave *c*   from the adjudicator or ask for leave direct from the tribunal itself. If he asks for leave from the adjudicator first, then he can on a refusal, and provided he acts within the appropriate time, apply again to the tribunal for leave to appeal.

Rule 13 then deals with the time for appealing. Rule 13(1) provides: 'Application to an adjudicator for leave to appeal shall be made forthwith after the making of *d*   the determination in question.' It is there clear, and no doubt for very good reasons, that the whole of these procedures contemplate a speedy determination of the issue, and one finds, therefore, that a would-be applicant who chooses to ask the adjudicator for leave to appeal must make his application forthwith after the making of the determination in question. On the other hand r 13(2) provides:

e   'Application to the Tribunal for leave to appeal or notice of appeal may be made or given not later than 7 days after the making of the determination in question.'

Seven days is thus to be compared with 'forthwith' in the case of an application direct to the adjudicator.

Rule 14(1) is concerned with the form in which these appeals and applications may *f*   be made. I say 'appeals and applications' because r 14(5) in effect provides that if one uses a form of application for leave when it should be a notice of appeal, or vice versa, the document can be treated as having the function which it ought to have. Rule 14(1) specifies the form in which an application for leave to appeal, or a notice of appeal, shall appear. It is in fact a perfectly simple form, comparable perhaps to the sort of form one completes when applying for a driving licence.

g   Thus taking the matter so far the would-be applicant must decide first of all whether to go to the adjudicator or the tribunal in the first instance. If he decides to go to the adjudicator he must apply forthwith and he must use the form in r 14(1), subject to an exemption in r 14(2) to which I will come in a moment. If he is successful in his application to the adjudicator we are told, and I have no reason to doubt it, that the form which he used in applying for leave goes forward to the tribunal and *h*   serves the purpose of a notice of appeal; in other words no further document is required from a successful applicant who succeeds in obtaining leave from the adjudicator.

On the other hand, if the applicant fails to obtain leave from the adjudicator, he must then apply to the tribunal if he wishes to pursue the matter, and he must then, I think clearly, bear in mind the time limit in r 13(2) because I think that his appli- *j*   cation to the tribunal following his failure before the adjudicator must be made within seven days after the initial determination by the adjudicator of the issue.

So far so good. It is in r 14(2) that the problems with which we are faced arise. That provides:

---

1   SI 1970 No 794

'Notwithstanding the provisions of paragraph (1) above, an application to an
adjudicator for leave to appeal may be made orally by the applicant or by a person duly authorised by him in that behalf or, in the case of an applicant who
is a minor or who is for any reason incapable of acting, by any person acting on
his behalf; but in that event the requirements of paragraph (1) above shall be
complied with as soon as practicable thereafter.'

What happened in the present case was that following the adjudicator's judgment
an oral application for leave to appeal was made to the adjudicator and it was granted,
precisely the kind of procedure contemplated by r 14(2), and the whole dispute turns
on the period within which in those events the formal application under r 14(2) must
be made.

One argument is that r 14(2) in a sense stands on its own, that it is intended to deal
with a specific instance in which the application is made orally and disposed of
orally, and that the time limit, if time limit it be, in r 14(2), namely, that the form shall
be filled up as soon as practicable, is the only time limit which applies in cases of
this kind.

In other words, it is argued by counsel for the applicant that the successful oral
application means that the appeal is on foot, there is no reason why in those circumstances the time limits in r 13 should be applied and it suffices if the formal matter
of completing the form of application follows in an indeterminate time provided
that it is as soon as practicable after the adjudicator's decision.

Counsel for the tribunal on the other hand contends that the requirement that
an application for leave to appeal or notice of appeal to the tribunal should be made
within seven days under r 13(2) applied to the follow-up formal document under
r 14(2) as well. He says that the reference in r 14(2) to that document following 'as
soon as practicable thereafter' is in effect an additional restriction on the freedom of
movement of the would-be appellant who, he says, must comply with both requirements. He must in other words produce his form as soon as is reasonably practicable
and in any event, counsel would say, within seven days after the initial determination.

I have not found this an easy case at all because the rules are not particularly clearly
drafted and problems have arisen in argument. But I think in the end that what
counsel for the tribunal says is right. I think that the underlying purpose of these
rules is that the appropriate application should be made speedily and that there shall
be produced by the applicant a form which sets out the terms on which he is seeking to support his appeal. It sets out amongst other things, his name and address,
his grounds of appeal and such like. This form must appear at some stage in order
that it may be the foundation of the application to the tribunal. Among the examples
I have already given, if the application to the adjudicator is made accompanied
by the form, as it may be, and the application is granted, then the form goes forward
and is the notice of appeal. Equally, if the adjudicator refuses an application made
on the form and the applicant wishes to apply to the tribunal, the same form can
be used, and if he is successful with the tribunal, then that form goes forward as the
notice of appeal. Again I think that where under r 14(2) the oral application is refused by the adjudicator, then the applicant, who goes to the tribunal, is going there
for leave to appeal and I think that the restriction in r 13(2) applies to him. If
he is successful in his oral application for leave to appeal to the adjudicator, then he
no longer requires leave, but the form has to be filled up and in this instance it is
fairly to be described as the notice of appeal.

One asks oneself what else it is? If leave is obtained, a document is produced. The
document is properly described as the notice of appeal, and so again one finds that it
comes within the terms of r 13(2).

In a sentence, I have come to the conclusion that counsel for the tribunal's argument is right and that the restrictions imposed by rr 13(2) and 14(2) are in the present
type of case in effect cumulative. The applicant must comply with both, and as this

a applicant clearly did not comply with that imposed by r 13(2), that is sufficient to justify the conclusion of the tribunal and thus to defeat the application for mandamus, which I would refuse.

MACKENNA J. The closing words of r 14(2) provide that if an oral application is
b made to the adjudicator, the requirements of r 14(1) shall be complied with as soon as practicable. That means that the appellant must file his application to the tribunal for leave to appeal, as soon as practicable, if he has been refused leave by the adjudicator and must file his notice of appeal as soon as practicable if he has been given leave.

I read r 13(2) as applying among others to cases where the appellant applies for leave to the adjudicator and gets it. In that case he must file his notice of appeal
c within seven days.

The question is whether these words in r 14(2) 'as soon as practicable' supersede in cases covered by that paragraph the provisions of r 13(2), which say that the application or the notice of appeal may be given not later than seven days after the determination in question, meaning, I think, that they must be given or made within that period.

d I accept counsel for the tribunal's argument that the two rules are to be read together and that in the cases covered by r 14(2) the appellant must make his application or give his notice of appeal as soon as practicable and in any event within seven days. I do not read r 14(2) as providing a longer period for the notice of appeal in the case of an oral application for leave to appeal made to the adjudicator. If this had been intended I should have expected r 14(2) to have contained the words 'notwithstanding
e r 13(2)'. Nobody can suggest any reason why a different, and a longer, period should be prescribed where an oral application under the later rule is made.

Speaking for myself, I regret that these important provisions should be so obscurely worded and I have no great confidence that my conclusion is the right one. A possible alternative construction might be that r 13(2) applies only to cases where the application has been made in the first instance to the tribunal, but that construction too
f would have its difficulties. I agree with Lord Widgery CJ that the application fails.

MAY J. It is with diffidence that I have reached a firm conclusion on the proper construction of the relevant regulations contrary to that expressed by Lord Widgery CJ and MacKenna J. In construing them I would draw attention, first, to r 12 and point out that appeals under the rules may be of two types: one requiring the leave
g of either the adjudicator or the tribunal; the other as of right requiring the leave of neither. Secondly, I notice the headings to rr 13 and 14 respectively: r 13 'Time for appealing'; r 14 'Notice of appeal and application for leave to appeal'. Thirdly, I notice para (5) of r 14, which as I see it in every case equates an application for leave to appeal with a notice of appeal. Fourthly, I agree with what has fallen from Mac-
h Kenna J that these regulations are badly drafted and accordingly I have no doubt that if they can be construed in favour of a would-be appellant, then they should be so construed.

It is, I think, unnecessary for me to go through the regulations in detail but enough for me to state the scheme of procedure which in my view they lay down. In cases where leave to appeal is not required, then by r 13(2) notice of appeal must be given to the tribunal within seven days, and must be given on the appropriate form,
j form 2 in the schedule to the rules, which, be it noted in passing, is headed 'Notice of appeal or application for leave to appeal from adjudicator' and has two parts: the first part a notice of appeal containing grounds of appeal and stating whether or not a hearing of the appeal is requested; the second part being relevant only when the form is used as an application for leave to appeal. So much then for cases where leave is not required.

Where leave is required the application may be made either to the adjudicator or to the tribunal. If it is made to the adjudicator, it must by r 13(1) be made forthwith after the making of the determination. It may be made to the adjudicator either in writing or orally. If in writing, then it must be made on the form to which I have already referred. If the application is granted, that is enough. The written application stands as the notice of appeal and the appeal goes forward. If the application on the form is refused, then the applicant still has the further opportunity of going to the tribunal and seeking leave from the tribunal. That must be done within the seven days laid down by r 13(2) and on the form which has already been put before the adjudicator. If the tribunal grant leave to appeal, then the appeal goes forward in the normal way. If the tribunal refuse leave, that is the end of the matter.

However, if the application to the adjudicator for leave is made orally and is refused, then again the applicant has a second opportunity of seeking leave, from the tribunal. He must go to the tribunal within seven days as laid down by r 13(2) and he must apply to the tribunal on the form. He cannot apply to the tribunal orally. If the application is oral and is granted by the adjudicator, then in my judgment the applicant does not have to go to the tribunal at all, save for the substantive hearing of the appeal. All that has to be done is, as it were, to fill out the application for leave by giving the formal grounds of appeal, which will be apparent to the adjudicator in any event because he has just been hearing the application against which it is sought to appeal. The staff sitting with the adjudicator will know that leave has been granted and that the appeal is on foot. All that is required is for the applicant to fill out his granted application by giving his formal grounds which he must give on the form, and he must give them as soon as practicable thereafter. That may well be outside the period of seven days for persons within the country, or the period of 28 days in respect of persons outside the country, particularly, for instance, if the applicant happens to be a minor.

Finally, if the application is in the first place to the tribunal, then that has to be made within seven days on the form under r 13(2).

In my judgment the underlying purpose of the rules is not so much to get the form completed and before the tribunal within the time limited, but to get an appeal started or refused within the time limited by r 13(2). For my part, therefore, I would accept counsel for the applicant's argument as to the proper construction of the rules and pass to consider whether or not in the circumstances of this case r 14(2) was in fact complied with. But having regard to the different view taken by Lord Widgery CJ and MacKenna J that question does not now arise.

Mandamus refused.

Solicitors: *Emerson Mott*, Basingstoke (for the applicant); *Treasury Solicitor*.

N P Metcalfe Esq   Barrister.

a

Kavanagh v Hiscock and another

QUEEN'S BENCH DIVISION
LORD WIDGERY CJ, BOREHAM AND MAY JJ
4th, 5th, 7th FEBRUARY 1974

b

*Trade dispute – Picketing – Right of peaceful picketing – Nature of right – Immunity from
prosecution or civil action in certain circumstances – Picketer asserting right to communicate
with driver of vehicle – Picketer one of large crowd – Police apprehending likelihood of disorder
– Police forming cordon to enable vehicle to pass freely – Effect of cordon to prevent picketer
communicating with driver – Picketer assaulting constable in attempt to break through cordon*
c *– Whether police infringing right of picketer to communicate with driver – Whether constable
assaulted in execution of his duty – Industrial Relations Act 1971, s 134(1)(2).*

During a strike of electricians at a building site, some 30 or 40 people, including the
appellant, assembled outside the site gates. Four of them, not including the appellant,
wore armbands signifying that they were 'official pickets'. There were also present
d some 24 police officers under the command of a superintendent. The superintendent
knew that the number of people present was very much higher than the number
of people usually present. It was expected that at about 5 p m a coach would leave
the site carrying electrical workers who had been employed to do the work usually
done by the strikers. The general purpose of those who had assembled was to dissuade
the people in the coach from continuing their work and the driver from continuing
e to carry them.   On the instructions of the superintendent a cordon of police was
formed on each side of the gate in order to keep those who had assembled away
from the path of the coach.   Only the four official pickets remained by the gate
and inside the cordon.   However, just before the coach appeared, those four were
also cleared from the gateway.   The purpose of the superintendent was to prevent
disorder and to enable the coach to leave the site without disorder.   The effect of
f the police action was, however, that no one was able to speak to the coach driver
or the occupants of the coach.   The appellant, seeing that, with the removal of the
four pickets, there was no one to speak to the driver or passengers, and, taking
the view that the rights of the pickets were being infringed, attempted to break
through the cordon and in doing so struck one of the police officers a blow. The
appellant was convicted of assaulting a police officer when in the execution of his duty,
g contrary to s 51(1) of the Police Act 1964. He appealed, contending that the police
officer was not acting in the execution of his duty since the pickets, on behalf of those
assembled, had a right under s 134[a] of the Industrial Relations Act 1971 to approach
the coach driver in an attempt peacefully to persuade him not to carry the strike-
breaking workers and accordingly the police were not acting lawfully by forming
cordons so as to prevent the pickets from exercising that right.

h

Held – Section 134(2) of the 1971 Act did not confer on a picket a positive right which
was capable of being infringed; its sole effect was to confer, in specified circumstances,
an immunity from prosecution or civil proceedings to which the picket might otherwise be liable. In particular the pickets had no right to stop the coach for the purpose
of peaceful persuasion.   Accordingly, by preventing the pickets from approaching
i the coach the police were not infringing any right conferred on the pickets by statute
but were fulfilling their own duty to prevent a breach of the peace.   The appeal would
therefore be dismissed (see p 183 *e f* and *h*, p 184 *a g* and *h*, p 185 *e* to *j* and p 186 *b*, post)
   Broome v Director of Public Prosecutions [1974] 1 All ER 314 applied.

---

a   Section 134, so far as material, is set out at p 183 *b* and *d*, post

Notes

For peaceful picketing, see 38 Halsbury's Laws (3rd Edn) 361, para 625, and for cases
on the subject, see 45 Digest (Repl) 588, *700-*704.

For the Police Act 1964, s 51, see 25 Halsbury's Statutes (3rd Edn) 364.

For the Industrial Relations Act 1971, s 134, see 41 Halsbury's Statutes (3rd Edn)
2157.

Cases referred to in judgments

Broome v Director of Public Prosecutions [1974] 1 All ER 314, [1974] 2 WLR 58, HL.

Piddington v Bates, Robson v Ribton-Turner [1960] 3 All ER 660, [1961] 1 WLR 162,
DC, Digest (Cont Vol A) 411, 7369c.

Tynan v Balmer [1966] 2 All ER 133, [1967] 1 QB 91, [1966] 2 WLR 1181, DC, Digest
(Cont Vol B) 330, 1586b.

Case stated

This was an appeal by way of case stated by David Prys Jones Esq, metropolitan
stipendiary magistrate, sitting at Lambeth Magistrates' Court on 9th July 1973.

On 28th March 1973 two charges were preferred against the appellant, Peter
Roger Kavanagh, by the first respondent, Alan Hiscock, a police constable, namely (i)
that the appellant assaulted the respondent when in the execution of his duty at
Lambeth Palace Road, London, SE1, on 28th March 1973, contrary to s 51(1) of the
Police Act 1964; (ii) that the appellant wilfully obstructed the respondent when
in the execution of his duty as aforesaid, contrary to s 51(3) of the Police Act 1964.

On 9th July 1973 a further charge was preferred against the appellant by the second
respondent, John David Richardson, a police constable, that the appellant wilfully
obstructed the respondent when in the execution of his duty at Lambeth Palace Road,
London, SE1, on 28th March 1973, contrary to s 51(3) of the Police Act 1964.

The magistrate found the following facts. (a) On 28th March 1973 there was in
progress a strike of electricians at St Thomas's Hospital building site in Lambeth
Palace Road, London, SE1. The strike had been going on for several weeks prior
to that date. At about 5 p m on 28th March 1973 there were between 30 and 40
people including the appellant assembled outside the site gates. Four men, not including the appellant, who were described as official pickets, wore armbands.
There were also present 24 police officers, including the two respondents, under
the command of Superintendent Brooks. (b) The number of demonstrators present
on that day was, and was known to Superintendent Brooks to be, very much higher
than the number of people, usually about six or eight, found demonstrating at
that site on most earlier occasions. Of that large number of demonstrators many
—the appellant estimated between 40 and 50—had no direct connection with the
particular strike and had come from lobbying their members of Parliament at
Westminster. That fact was known to both the appellant and to Superintendent
Brooks. (c) It was expected that at around 5 p m a coach carrying electrical workers
who had been employed to do the work formerly done by strikers would depart
through the site gates. The general purpose of the demonstrators was to seek to
dissuade those people in the coach from continuing their work and to dissuade the
driver of the coach from continuing to carry them. (d) Under the instructions of
the superintendent a cordon of police officers was formed on each side of the entrance
in order to keep those who had assembled away from the path of the coach. After
the cordons were formed four official pickets remained inside the cordons by the gate.
Just before the departure of the coach the superintendent also cleared those four
men from the gateway. The purpose of the superintendent's actions was to prevent
disorder and to enable the coach to leave the site without disorder; one of the effects
of the superintendent's actions was that none of the persons assembled was
permitted to speak to the driver of the coach. (e) Up to that point there had been
no disorder or violence threatened or offered by the four official pickets or any of

a the other persons assembled. The superintendent arrived at his view that cordons should be formed and that no person should be permitted to approach the driver on the grounds that on previous occasions when larger than normal numbers had been present pickets at that site had abused the driver and workers in the coach by calling them scabs and phrases of that nature, and from the numbers of those attending he was of the opinion that if the coach had stopped in the gateway there *b* would have been similar abuse from the crowd and that therefore the action which he took was necessary to prevent disorder amounting to a breach of the peace. (f) On 28th March 1973 the appellant was not an official of any union. He had recently been an official of the Transport and General Workers Union of which he was still both a member and—at another place of work—a shop steward. On the day in question he had been requested by a representative of the strikers to approach *c* the coach driver who, it was presumed, was also a member of the TGWU. At about 4.45 p m the appellant entered the site through another gate without any difficulty. He had three or four minutes conversation with the coach driver and requested him not to pass the picket. He did not ask the driver of what union, if any, he was a member. The appellant formed the view that further persuasion might induce the driver not to return to the site. The appellant rejoined the demonstrators gathered *d* outside the gate behind the police cordon. (g) The appellant, who knew some of the police officers by sight, did not tell any of them that he wanted to speak to the coach driver when the coach came out, and only formed that desire when the four official pickets moved from the gateway. (h) After the four official pickets had been cleared from the gateway and the coach began to emerge, the appellant pushed forward against the respondent Pc Hiscock. Pc Hiscock said, 'Keep moving and stop pushing'. *e* The appellant said, 'You can't tell me what to do, you little squirt' and punched Pc Hiscock in the back. The respondent Pc Richardson said to the appellant, 'Cut that out, keep moving'. The appellant said, 'You can't fucking move me, I am a union official and I want to talk to the driver of that coach'. Pc Richardson said, 'You can't speak to him, so keep moving'. The appellant said, 'You can't fucking move me, I want to speak to him' and tried to push past Pc Richardson who again told *f* the appellant that he could not speak to the driver. The appellant continued to try and push past the officer shouting and swearing as he did so. Pc Richardson then arrested the appellant. At that time the coach passed through unimpeded. When the coach had arrived at the exit there was a lot of pushing from the crowd against the police cordons and remarks such as 'scabs' and 'blacklegs' were made to the driver and passengers.

g It was contended on behalf of the appellant that while it was not objectionable for all save four of the crowd to be kept away from the gate, the moving-away of the four official pickets rendered the police actions unlawful. The persons assembled, including the appellant, were exercising their right under s 134 of the Industrial Relations Act 1971 peacefully to persuade the driver not to carry the strike-breaking workers. While it might be proper for police officers to require that that right be *h* exercised through the agency of a limited number of pickets, the action taken amounted to a complete denial of that right. The four official pickets could lawfully have pushed forward and the appellant at the time he pushed forward was in no worse position. The respondents in restraining him were not acting in the execution of their duty.

It was contended on behalf of the respondents that the superintendent was *j* entitled to take the steps which he had taken, and that those steps did not conflict with such right as was conferred by statute. Further as the respondents were acting in the execution of their duty when they formed the cordon, they could not cease to be so acting by reason of actions taken by a superior officer of which they were unaware. So far as the appellant was concerned the officers were fully justified in preventing him from interfering with the progress of the coach and at all times were acting in the execution of their duty.

The magistrate was of the opinion that the superintendent was justified in taking
the action he thought right to prevent disorder, and that it was within his discretion
to get the official pickets to move away. The appellant wanted to come forward,
and the fact that the four official pickets had been moved away did not justify him
in doing so. He concluded that the respondent police officers were at the material
time acting in the execution of their duty and accordingly convicted the appellant
on all three charges fining him £10 for the assault and £5 on each of the obstruction
charges together with £10 costs.

Lord Gifford for the appellant.
John Hazan QC and *Geoffrey Nice* for the respondents.

LORD WIDGERY CJ. This is an appeal by case stated by one of Her Majesty's
metropolitan stipendiary magistrates sitting at Lambeth. He had to deal with two
charges laid on 28th March 1973 preferred against the appellant, Mr Kavanagh, by
the respondent Alan Hiscock, a police constable. The first charge was that the appellant assaulted the respondent police constable when in the execution of his duty at
Lambeth Palace Road, Lambeth, on 28th March 1973 contrary to s 51(1) of the Police
Act 1964; and secondly that the appellant wilfully obstructed the said respondent
when in the execution of his duty at the same time and place. A further information
was later preferred in similar terms by the second respondent, John David Richardson.

This is a case in which the facts are important, and I shall have to spend a little
time in going into them. On the date when all this happened, 28th March 1973,
there was a strike of electricians at St Thomas's Hospital in Lambeth Palace Road.
The strike had been going on for several weeks, and at about 5 p m on 28th March
there were between 30 and 40 people, including the appellant, assembled outside
the site gates. There were four men, of whom the appellant was not one, who were
described as official pickets, and who wore armbands. The remainder wore no
armbands, and many of them had no interest in the particular trade dispute at St
Thomas's Hospital, but happened to be in the vicinity because they had been lobbying
their members of Parliament. The number of people, 30 to 40, was greater than
those present normally at this time of the evening; the normal practice was for
six or eight people to be picketing or demonstrating outside the gates when the
workers were leaving. The police were obviously alerted to the fact that something
unusual might happen and they were there in what I suspect was a great deal more
than usual strength. There were in fact about 24 police officers present. At about
5 p m a coach left from the site. The coach was carrying electrical workers who had
been employed inside the site to do the work which was normally done by those
who were on strike. The magistrate finds that the general purpose of the 30 or 40
demonstrators, as he calls them, who had assembled was to dissuade the people
in the coach from continuing to work on the site.

Going on with the recital of the facts which the magistrate has stated, the superintendent of police who was in charge of the police officers, gave instructions that a
cordon was to be formed on each side of the entrance in order to keep those who had
assembled away from the path of the coach. The picture that that presents I think
is perfectly simple; one sees, as it were, two cordons one on each side of the entrance
preventing the group on the pavement from getting into what was the intended
path of the coach.

After the cordons had been formed, the four official pickets remained inside the
cordons by the gate. In other words they, unlike the 30 odd others, were not restricted
initially in standing where they chose in the gateway through which the coach would
pass. However, just before the coach appeared, these four men were also cleared
from the gateway. It is not clear from the case exactly where they went, but the
police officer, in the words of the magistrate, cleared them from the gateway, so
that at the very least they were made to stand to one side.

a   The purpose of the superintendent, according to the magistrate's finding, was
to prevent disorder and to enable the coach to leave the site without disorder. But
one of the effects of the superintendent's action was that none of the persons assembled
was permitted to speak to the driver of the coach. I pause to stress that, because
much of counsel for the appellant's argument turns on that last finding. What
it means is that by the time the coach actually appeared, there was no one within
b   the police cordon who was in the position to go up and speak to the driver.
   Up to this point there had been no disorder or violence threatened or offered by
the pickets. I interpolate that up to this point there had been no occasion for that
anyway, because the workers leaving the hospital had not yet appeared:

>   'The Superintendent arrived at his view that cordons should be formed and
>   that no person should be permitted to approach the driver on the grounds
c >   that on previous occasions when larger than normal numbers had been present
>   pickets at that site had abused the driver and workers in the coach be calling
>   them scabs and phrases of that nature, and from the numbers of those attending
>   he was of the opinion that if the coach had stopped in the gateway there would
>   have been similar abuse from the crowd and that therefore the action which he
>   took was necessary to prevent disorder amounting to a breach of the peace.'
d

The magistrate then goes on to deal with the appellant's own actions on that afternoon, and I do not think I need read then in quite the same detail. He was not
directly concerned with the strike at the hospital; he had been a union official in
another union not concerned in the strike, the Transport and General Workers
Union, and it had been suggested to him that he should approach the driver of the
e   coach, because the driver of the coach was probably a member of the TGWU, and
it might be that the appellant would have more influence with the driver of the
coach in persuading him not to continue driving these workers.
   So there was the appellant outside the site at about 4.45 p m. He was wily enough,
if I may say so, to realise that he might be able to have a word with the driver if
he got into the site by the back way, which he did. It is an interesting sidelight,
f   though I think no more in this case, that the appellant himself had full opportunity
to talk to the driver of the coach, because he got into the site and had three or four
minutes with the driver before the coach came out.
   When the coach attempted to come out, the appellant was back on the pavement
behind the police cordon together with the other demonstrators to whom I have
referred. The appellant was not offended by the presence of the police cordon so
g   long as the four official pickets were still in the gateway and were in a position to
approach the driver of the coach. His reasoning, no doubt, was that he could not
expect the police to allow everybody to come in, but so long as there were four
people there, picketing in the accepted sense could take place. But as soon as he saw
the four official pickets removed and realised there was no one inside the cordon who
could approach the coach driver and the passengers, it was then he felt the rights of
h   the pickets were being infringed, and it was then he began to push against Pc Hiscock
in his position in the police cordon in front. It suffices to say that after an exchange of
observations between the police officer and the appellant, the appellant tried to push
through the cordon and eventually he struck one of the police officers a blow with his
fist.
   That is the picture presented by the facts, and, leaving aside for the moment the
j   contentions in the court below, I pass to the last paragraph of the case which gives
the magistrate's conclusions. He said:

>   'I was of the opinion that the Superintendent was justified in taking the action
>   he thought right to prevent disorder, and that it was within his discretion to get
>   the official pickets to move away. The appellant wanted to come forward, and
>   the fact that the four official pickets had been moved away did not justify him

in doing so. I concluded that the Respondent police officers were at the material
time acting in the execution of their duty and accordingly convicted the
appellant . . .'

The issue before us is whether, on those facts, it was right as a matter of law to conclude that the respondent police officers were at the material time acting in the
execution of their duty.

Taking the respondents' argument in this case first, it can, I think, be put quite
simply. This stated case has the disadvantages inherent in this form of procedure
that it does not find all the facts (that is almost impossible) and of course unless there
is a special request, it does not contain the evidence. But bearing those difficulties
in mind, I find no difficulty when I read the case as a whole in reconstructing the
picture and the motives on the police side. It seems to me perfectly clear that the
concern of the police superintendent was that if nothing was done, the coach would be
stopped at the gates, there would then be a shouting match, if one may so describe it,
between the pickets and the passengers in the coach, that having been the sort of
conduct which occurred before, and there might be worse than that; there might be
actual violence used, and in any case the right of the coach driver to drive his coach
out would be interfered with. I think that the only purpose of the police officers was
to prescribe a path through which the coach could pass without there being any
prospect of its being held up on its way.

Was that on its face a lawful and proper act for a responsible police officer in the
circumstances? On its face, and ignoring for the moment counsel for the appellant's
argument, it seems to me that it was. There are in fact two, indeed perhaps three,
ways in which the police officer could justify the conclusion that he ought to use his
men to clear a path through the crowd for the coach to reach the highway. In the
first place he had reasonable apprehension that otherwise the coach would be stopped,
and it is now clear that even pickets cannot stop a vehicle unless the driver wishes to
stop. The police officer had reasonable apprehension that the rights of the coach
driver and the passengers would be interfered with by being forced to stop. He had
reasonable apprehension that there would be disorder, as the magistrate finds, and
certainly there might be such language as might amount to the offence of using
threatening words and behaviour.

Furthermore, police officers have the general duty to regulate the use of the highway by competing users, and to make sure everybody gets a fair share. If the driver
of a vehicle wants to drive down the highway and is obstructed by others in his
path, the police are within their rights, if they can, to make a path for the vehicle.

Looking at the matter from the police side, it seems there was ample justification
for the police officer thinking it right in the course of his duty to prescribe these
cordons and to clear everybody away from within the cordons. I say 'everybody'
because one man alone standing in front of a motor vehicle can stop it as effectively
as 40. I have no doubt that the four pickets were moved out of the path of the vehicle
to make sure it was not impeded.

What is the case on the other side? The case on the other side eloquently urged on
us by counsel for the appellant is really based on s 134 of the Industrial Relations Act
1971, which is the most modern piece of legislation dealing with pickets and their
rights and duties. In a sentence, what counsel contends is that under this section, to
which I must refer in detail in a moment, the individual pickets had a right to
approach the coach driver with a view to persuading him not to drive the coach on
future occasions. He says that that right having been conferred on the pickets by
statute, it was not lawful for the police to take it away by drawing up these cordons
in the circumstances which were prevailing at that time.

Counsel for the appellant, I feel sure, would not seek to contend that the rights of
the pickets would always override the actions of police officers in maintaining order,
but he says that in the circumstances of this case the police adopted methods which

a were too draconian, having regard to the pickets' rights, to be justified by the facts found by the magistrate.

What s 134(1) says is this:

b 'The provisions of this section shall have effect where one or more persons (in this section referred to as "pickets"), in contemplation or furtherance of an industrial dispute, attend at or near—(a) a place where a person works or carries on business, or (b) any other place where a person happens to be, not being a place where he resides, and do so only for the purpose of peacefully obtaining information from him or peacefully communicating information to him or peacefully persuading him to work or not to work.'

c So far I see no reason to think that any of these pickets, if that is the right way to describe them, failed to qualify under s 134(1). They were attending at or near the place where these people worked, and certainly in the first instance, one would accept that they did so only for the purpose of peacefully obtaining information from the workers or peacefully communicating information to them.

What happens if a person gets himself within s 134(1)? What are the consequences? We find them in s 134(2) which provides:

d 'In the circumstances specified in the preceding subsection, the attendance of the pickets at that place for that purpose—(a) shall not of itself constitute an offence under section 7 of the Conspiracy, and Protection of Property Act 1875 (penalty for intimidation or annoyance by violence or otherwise) or under any other enactment or rule of law, and (b) shall not of itself constitute a tort.'

e There has been considerable debate, not only in this court today but in other courts on other days, as to precisely what is the effect of s 134(2). It is put forward by counsel for the appellant, as it has been put forward in argument before, as creating a positive right for a person who comes within s 134(1) to approach and persuade the worker to whom his attentions are directed. It is described as a right, and it is on that footing *f* that the action of the police is said to be an infringement of the right of the picket under s 134(2).

I venture to think, in common I believe with their Lordships in the House of Lords in *Broome v Director of Public Prosecutions*[1], that it is inapt to describe that which is conferred by s 134(2) as a right. I think it is misleading, and I think the word used by Lord Salmon[2], 'immunity', is a very much better word, because when one looks at the wording of s 134(2) again, it is quite clear that what is being conferred is *g* immunity from proceedings in certain circumstances. It is an immunity from being prosecuted under the criminal law, and an immunity from being sued in tort. But if in fact a picket has so behaved himself that he is in no danger of being prosecuted for a criminal offence or sued in tort, he does not need immunity, and so the sub-section has no effect on him. Up to the moment when cross words developed between the appellant and the police officer, I see no reason why he was in danger *h* of prosecution or being sued in tort. Indeed he was in a position in which s 134 was an irrelevance to him.

I am of the opinion that the true view of this subsection is that it is one creating immunities where required, and not one creating positive rights capable of being infringed by the police officers in this case.

In the House of Lords in *Broome v Director of Public Prosecutions*[1] there are references *j* to this matter, because as is now well known, in that case it was established for the first time in the House of Lords that the provisions of s 134 confer no right on a picket of stopping a vehicle against the driver's will. It had, I am sure, been widely

---

1 [1974] 1 All ER 314, [1974] 2 WLR 58
2 [1974] 1 All ER at 325, [1974] 2 WLR at 70

believed in trade union circles and perhaps in other circles before, that any picket   *a*
seeking to persuade the driver of a vehicle, could stop the vehicle first for the purpose;
that is in order to be effective in his persuasion. But the House of Lords has stated in
Broome v Director of Public Prosecutions[1] that that is not so. It is fundamental to a
proper understanding of the present case that there was no right in any of these
pickets to stop the progress of the vehicle unless the driver wished to stop.

In the speech of Lord Reid there was a paragraph which has given counsel for the   *b*
appellant great comfort, and is again in a substantial way the basis of his argument.
Lord Reid, having read s 134 and referred to an earlier case, *Tynan v Balmer*[2], said[3]:

> 'His attendance [i e the picket's attendance] there is only made lawful by
> sub-s (2) if he attended only for the purpose of obtaining or communicating
> information or "peacefully persuading" the lorry driver. Attendance for that
> purpose must I think include the right to try to persuade anyone who chooses   *c*
> to stop and listen, at least insofar as this is done in a reasonable way with due
> consideration for the rights of others. A right to attend for the purpose of
> peaceful persuasion would be meaningless unless this were implied.'

This suggestion that a picket enjoys a right in those terms does not appear in the
other speeches; indeed there are instances in the speeches of the other Law Lords   *d*
adopting an approach which I, with deference, adopt, that it is a matter of immunity
and not a matter of right. In my judgment Lord Reid is not to be construed in that
passage[3] as indicating the existence of the kind of positive right for which counsel
for the appellant contends.

As I see Lord Reid's observations[3], he is accepting that attendance is the only privilege which is conferred by the section—attendance with a view peacefully to persuade   *e*
—and I think what he is saying is that a picket who attends within the terms of the
immunity conferred by the section does not lose his immunity simply because he
tries to persuade anyone who chooses to stop and listen, to listen to him. What
Lord Reid is saying is that it would be absurd to grant immunities for attendance
if one did not also extend the immunity to the act of peaceful persuasion whilst
attending. For my part I do not believe the dictum goes beyond that, and when one   *f*
refers to the speeches of the other Law Lords, it is I think clear that they regard the
section as creating an immunity and not a right.

For those reasons I find myself unable to support counsel for the appellant in his
argument. On many occasions in the course of the hearing, perhaps too often, I
invited him to explain just exactly what a picket could lawfully do in regard to this
coach as it approached. He maintained that the picket could approach the coach   *g*
and endeavour to make his voice heard. But if one recognises, as one now must,
that there was no right to stop the coach, I find it very difficult to see just what it
was that any of these pickets was deprived of doing. For the reasons which I have
given, it seems to me that prima facie the police action was within the law as being
within the execution of their duty, and the supposed existence of a conflicting right
in the picket is not well-founded, because s 134(2) gives no such right. For those   *h*
reasons I would dismiss the appeal.

BOREHAM J. I agree, but out of deference to the argument put before us by
counsel for the appellant I add a few comments of my own. I agree, if I may say so,
entirely with the comments of Lord Widgery CJ so far as the actions of the police
are concerned. I am entirely convinced that they were acting lawfully, that they   *j*
were doing no more than was reasonably necessary in order to prevent what they

1 [1974] 1 All ER 314, [1974] 2 WLR 58
2 [1966] 2 All ER 133, [1967] 1 QB 91
3 [1974] 1 All ER at 319, [1974] 2 WLR at 63

a apprehended and reasonably apprehended, namely a breach of the peace and/or an obstruction so far as the vehicle was concerned. That, in my judgment, was the duty of overriding importance in circumstances such as this, and the police in my judgment behaved properly and lawfully.

I too agree that there is a basic fallacy in the argument put forward on behalf of the appellant in this case so far as what is called his rights are concerned. I venture
b to doubt whether it is helpful to use in this context the expression 'the rights of pickets', at least if it is not made clear that it is a right which is very strictly circumscribed. Certainly, as Lord Reid[1] has said in his speech in the House of Lords, it can only be exercised with due regard to the rights of other people, and in my judgment it would follow from that, that it must be exercised also with due regard to the duties of other people.

c For my part I rely on the approach of Lord Salmon[2] at the end of his speech. Having set out the relevant and essential parts of s 134 of the 1971 Act, he continues thus:

> 'These words [i e the words of the section] make it plain that it is nothing but the attendance of the pickets at the places specified which is protected; and then only if their attendance is for one of the specified purposes. The section gives no
d protection in respect of anything the pickets may say or do whilst they are attending if what they say or do is itself unlawful. But for the section, the mere attendance of pickets might constitute an offence under s 7(2) and (4) of the 1875 Act or under the Highways Act 1959, or constitute a tort, for example, nuisance. [These in my judgment are the important words:] The section, therefore, gives a narrow but nevertheless real immunity to pickets. It clearly does no more.'

e Certainly in my view there is nothing in s 134 which can possibly impinge on the undoubted right and the undoubted duty of police officers to take sensible preventive action where they reasonably apprehend a breach of the peace or an obstruction. It may be, as counsel for the appellant has said, that the rights of pickets are in fact much more restricted than some have thought in days gone by. But that in my
f view is the result of a fair and proper reading of s 134. For those reasons and for those given by Lord Widgery CJ I too would dismiss the appeal.

MAY J. Both before the learned stipendiary magistrate and in this court the appellant contended that s 134 of the Industrial Relations Act 1971 gave him a right, in the sense of a positive entitlement, to picket peacefully, that is to seek peacefully
g to persuade the driver of the coach to cease carrying the electricians who were not on strike. In my judgment this is not the effect of s 134(1) nor what, by its plain terms, it enacts. Section 134 merely provides, as did its statutory predecessors, that the activity specified in s 134(1), which may loosely be described as peaceful picketing, shall not of itself, and those words require to be stressed, constitute a criminal offence
h of a civil wrong. I think that this appears quite clearly from the speeches of Lord Morris of Borth-y-Gest, Viscount Dilhorne and Lord Salmon in the recent case of *Broome v Director of Public Prosecutions*[3]. Where, however, a police officer reasonably anticipates that in the circumstances obtaining in the particular case the consequence of any peaceful picketing may well be a breach of the peace, either by the pickets or by spectators, whether supporters of the pickets or not, then it is the duty of that police officer to take such steps as are reasonably necessary to prevent that anticipated
j breach of the peace. Those steps may include requiring would-be pickets to desist, for so long as the police officer may reasonably deem necessary to prevent the breach

---

1 [1974] 1 All ER 314 at 319, [1974] 2 WLR 58 at 63
2 [1974] 1 All ER 325, [1974] 2 WLR at 69, 70
3 [1974] 1 All ER 314, [1974] 2 WLR 58

of that peace, from any attempt to picket at that place.   If authority were needed
for this proposition, it may in my view be found in the judgment of Lord Parker CJ
in this court in *Piddington v Bates*[1].

In the present case the learned stipendiary magistrate, as I think rightly, found
that the police superintendent was of the justified opinion that the action which he
took was necessary to prevent disorder amounting to a breach of the peace. In these
circumstances, for these reasons and for those expressed by Lord Widgery CJ and
Boreham J, I think the respondent police officers were acting in the execution of their
duty at the relevant time and I agree that this appeal should be dismissed.

7th February 1974. **LORD WIDGERY CJ.** Counsel for the appellant asks this court
to certify the following as a point of law of public general importance arising in the
course of the proceedings:

> 'Whether s 134(2) of the Industrial Relations Act 1971 had the effect of con-
> ferring, on a person who attends at premises for the purposes set out in s 134(1)
> of the said Act, a positive right to approach the driver of a vehicle leaving those
> premises with a view to persuading him not to work, if such approach would
> be in disobedience of an otherwise lawful order of a police officer.'

The view of this court, as appears from the judgments already delivered, is that
this point is already covered by the authority of the House of Lords in *Broome v
Director of Public Prosecutions*[2]. If this is the correct view, then logic would require
us to refuse a certificate on the present occasion. We recognise, however, in due
humility, that others may take a different view and may be able to distinguish the
present case from *Broome's* case[2]. We are also of course impressed by the fact that
there is no appeal from the refusal of a certificate on our part, and at the present time
this is an extremely important subject in the public interest.

For these reasons we will certify the point proposed, and would respectfully welcome any guidance from their Lordships' House as to whether this is the appropriate
approach to the question of granting a certificate or refusing it.

It must follow from the view I have already taken that this is not a case for leave,
although I have already expressed our view about the certificate.

Appeal dismissed.   Point of law of general public importance certified.   Leave to appeal refused.

27th February.   *The appeal committee of the House of Lords refused leave to appeal, stating
that the case was completely covered by* Broome v Director of Public Prosecutions[2].

Solicitors: *Gaster, Vowles, Turner & Loeffler* (for the appellant); *Solicitor, Metropolitan
Police* (for the respondents).

N P Metcalfe Esq   Barrister.

1   [1960] 3 All ER 660, [1961] 1 WLR 162
2   [1974] 1 All ER 314, [1974] 2 WLR 58

Murphy v Ingram (Inspector of Taxes)

COURT OF APPEAL, CIVIL DIVISION
RUSSELL, BUCKLEY AND ORR LJJ
27th, 28th FEBRUARY, 12th MARCH 1974

Income tax – Relief – Children – Income of child – Reduction or disallowance of relief – Child entitled in his own right to an income exceeding prescribed amount – Daughter – Marriage during year of assessment – Post-nuptial income of daughter – Income deemed for income tax purposes to be husband's income and not to be her income – Whether daughter entitled to post-nuptial income in her own right – Whether post-nuptial income to be disregarded for purposes of child relief – Income Tax Act 1952, ss 212(4) (as substituted by the Finance Act 1963, s 13), 354(1).

Income tax – Relief – Children – Income of child – Reduction or disallowance of relief – Child entitled in his own right to an income exceeding prescribed amount – Earnings of child – Whether earnings 'income' to which child 'entitled in his own right' – Income Tax Act 1952, s 212(4) (as substituted by the Finance Act 1963, s 13).

The taxpayer's daughter was born on 9th May 1946. During the first 2½ months of the fiscal year 1969-70 she was receiving full-time instruction at a university. On 19th July 1969 she married and in October of the same year she began employment as a teacher. For the fiscal year in question, her income prior to her marriage was only £10, whereas her income after marriage was not less than £270. The taxpayer claimed child allowance under s 212[a] of the Income Tax Act 1952 for the year 1969-70 contending (a) that since the daughter's income consisted of earnings it was not 'income' to which she was 'entitled in [her] own right' within s 212(4), and (b), alternatively,

---

[a] Section 212, so far as material, and as amended by the Finance Act 1957, s 12, the Finance Act 1963, ss 12, 13, and the Finance Act 1969, s 11, provides:
    '(1) If the claimant proves—(a) that there is living at any time within the year of assessment a child of his with respect to whom one of the conditions in subsection (2) of this section is fulfilled . . . he shall, subject to the provisions of this and the next following section, be entitled in respect of each such child to a deduction from the amount of income tax with which he is chargeable equal to tax at the standard rate on the appropriate amount for the child. In this provision "child" includes a stepchild and an illegitimate child whose parents have married each other after his birth.
    '(1A) The appropriate amount for the child shall vary according to the age of the child at the commencement of the year of assessment, and subject to subsection (4) of this section—(a) for a child shown by the claimant to have been then over the age of sixteen, shall be one hundred and sixty-five pounds . . .
    '(2) The conditions referred to in subsection (1) of this section are—(a) that the child is born in, or is under the age of sixteen years at the commencement of, the year of assessment referred to in that subsection; or (b) that the child is over the age of sixteen years at the commencement of that year of assessment but is receiving full-time instruction at any university, college, school or other educational establishment . . .
    '(4) In the case of a child who is entitled in his own right to an income exceeding £115 a year the appropriate amount for the child shall be reduced by the amount of the excess, and accordingly no relief shall be allowed under this section where the excess is equal to or greater than the amount which apart from this subsection would be the appropriate amount for the child: Provided that in calculating the income of the child for the purpose of this subsection no account shall be taken of any income to which the child is entitled as the holder of a scholarship, bursary, or other similar educational endowment . . .'

that by virtue of s 354(1)[b] of the 1952 Act her post-nuptial income was 'deemed for income tax purposes to be [her husband's] income and not to be her income' and accordingly the only income to which she was 'entitled in [her] own right' was the income of £10.

Held – (i) The reference to 'income' to which a child was 'entitled in his own right' in s 212 included earnings and was not limited to unearned income such as income under a trust (see p 190 b and d, post); *Miles (Inspector of Taxes) v Morrow* (1940) 23 Tax Cas 465 and *Williams v Doulton (Inspector of Taxes)* [1948] 1 All ER 603 approved.

(ii) The deeming provisions of s 354(1) operated only in the context of the system of assessment, liability and collection applied to the particular situation of a wife and husband living together; the words 'for income tax purposes' in s 354(1) did not extend the operation of that subsection to the tax liability of a third person. Accordingly for the purposes of s 212, the taxpayer's daughter was entitled in her own right to her post-nuptial income with the result that her earnings for the fiscal year were more than enough to negative the taxpayer's claim to child allowance (see p 191 g and h and p 192 f and g, post).

Decision of Megarry J [1973] 2 All ER 523 reversed.

Notes

For the reduction and disallowance of relief in relation to children entitled to income in their own right, see 20 Halsbury's Laws (3rd Edn) 441, 442, para 824, and for cases on the subject, see 28(1) Digest (Reissue) 448, *1603-1606*.

For the Income Tax Act 1952, ss 212, 354, see 31 Halsbury's Statutes (2nd Edn) 202, 342.

For 1970-71 and subsequent years of assessment ss 212 and 354 of the 1952 Act have been replaced by ss 10 and 37 of the Income and Corporation Taxes Act 1970.

Cases referred to in judgment

Cameron (decd), Re, Kingsley v Inland Revenue Comrs [1965] 3 All ER 474, [1967] Ch 1, 42 Tax Cas 539, [1966] 2 WLR 243, sub nom *Cameron's Executors v Inland Revenue Comrs* 44 ATC 259, [1965] TR 271, 28(1) Digest (Reissue) 387, *1420*.

Hill (Arthur) v The East and West India Dock Co (1884) 9 App Cas 448, 53 LJCh 842, 51 LT 163, 48 JP 788, HL, 44 Digest (Repl) 225, *424*.

Leitch v Emmott [1929] 2 KB 236, 14 Tax Cas 633, [1929] All ER Rep 638, 98 LJKB 673, 141 LT 311, CA, 28(1) Digest (Reissue) 385, *1411*.

Mapp (Inspector of Taxes) v Oram [1969] 3 All ER 215, [1970] AC 362, 45 Tax Cas 651, [1969] 3 WLR 557, sub nom *Oram v Mapp* 48 ATC 270, [1969] TR 269, HL; *affg in part, rvsg in part* [1968] 3 All ER 1, [1969] 1 Ch 293, [1968] 3 WLR 442, [1968] TR 163, CA, 28(1) Digest (Reissue) 448, *1606*.

Miles (Inspector of Taxes) v Morrow (1940) 23 Tax Cas 465, DC (NI), 28(1) Digest (Reissue) 449, **1181*.

Walton, Ex parte, Re Levy (1881) 17 Ch D 746, [1881-85] All ER Rep 548, 50 LJCh 657 45 LT 1, CA, 4 Digest (Repl) 11, *4*.

Williams v Doulton (Inspector of Taxes) [1948] 1 All ER 603, 28 Tax Cas 522, [1948] TR 173, 41 R & IT 486, 28(1) Digest (Reissue) 448, *1604*.

---

b   Section 354(1) provides: 'Subject to the provisions of this Part of this Act, a woman's income chargeable to income tax shall, so far as it is income for a year of assessment or part of a year of assessment during which she is a married woman living with her husband, be deemed for income tax purposes to be his income and not to be her income: Provided that the question whether there is any income of hers chargeable to income tax for any year of assessment, and, if so, what is to be taken to be the amount thereof for income tax purposes, shall not be affected by the provisions of this subsection.'

Cases also cited

Luke v Inland Revenue Comrs [1963] 1 All ER 655, [1963] AC 557, 40 Tax Cas 630, HL.
Nugent-Head v Jacob (Inspector of Taxes) [1948] 1 All ER 414, [1948] AC 321, 30 Tax Cas 83. HL.

Appeal and cross-appeal

The taxpayer, George Henry Murphy, had a daughter, Eileen, born on 9th May 1946. The daughter was receiving full-time instruction at the University of York until 19th June 1969. A month later she married and in October of the same year she started work as a teacher. Her income between 6th April 1969 and the date of her marriage was £10. Her total income between the date of her marriage and 5th April 1970 was not less than £270. The taxpayer claimed child allowance in respect of his daughter for the year 1969-70. The inspector of taxes disallowed the claim. The General Commissioners affirmed that decision but at the request of the taxpayer stated a case[1] for the opinion of the High Court.   On 9th April 1973 Megarry J[2] allowed the taxpayer's appeal holding that the income to which the daughter was entitled in her own right under s 212(4) of the Income Tax Act 1952 was only £10, her post-nuptial income of £270 plus being 'deemed for income tax purposes' (which included the claim to child relief under s 212(4)) to be her husband's income, under s 354(1) of the 1952 Act. His Lordship, however, rejected the taxpayer's further contention that when the daughter married, she ceased to be a child for the purposes of s 212(4) with the result that there was no child who was entitled in his or her own right to an income exceeding £115 a year within the section. The Crown appealed on the grounds, inter alia: (a) that the daughter's income after her marriage was income to which she was entitled in her own right, and (b) that the deeming provision contained in s 354(1) of the 1952 Act, whereby the income of a married woman living with her husband was deemed for income tax purposes to be his income and not to be her income, applied only between the daughter and her husband and not between the daughter and the taxpayer.   The taxpayer cross-appealed seeking, inter alia, a ruling that earnings were not 'income' within the meaning of s 212(4) of the Income Tax Act 1952.

Patrick Medd QC and *Harry Woolf* for the Crown.
The taxpayer appeared in person.

Cur adv vult

12th March.   **RUSSELL LJ** read the following judgment of the court.   This case at first instance before Megarry J is reported below[2] and reference may be made to the reports for detail.   He held that the taxpayer was, contrary to the views of the General Commissioners, entitled to claim in respect of the fiscal year 1969-70 child allowance for his daughter, under s 212 of the Income Tax Act 1952, notwithstanding that her earnings in respect of that year, if relevant, were more than enough to negative any claim to child allowance.

The judge reached his decision in favour of the taxpayer because he concluded that the daughter's earnings after her marriage of £270 plus were an income to which she was not entitled in her own right, a conclusion based on s 354(1) of the same Act, which provides that a woman's income chargeable to tax, so far as it is income for any part of a year of assessment during which she is a married woman living with her husband, is to be 'deemed for income tax purposes to be his income and not to be her income'.   It is that conclusion which is attacked by the Crown in this appeal.

Before reaching that point, it is convenient to deal briefly with certain other grounds on which the taxpayer sought in the alternative to support the reversal of the determination of the General Commissioners.   First, he argued that when the daughter

---

1 The case stated is set out at [1973] 2 All ER 524-526
2 [1973] 2 All ER 523, [1973] Ch 434, [1973] STC 309

married she ceased to be relevantly his child, and her earnings after marriage were not her earnings as a child; in those circumstances her only earnings as a child were £10 before marriage. This is a point in no way related to s 354. We are unable to find any cogency at all in this argument. Second, he argued that when the daughter ceased to be in full-time education at the university she ceased to be relevantly his child, with the same result. Our comment on this argument is the same. Third, he argued that, since the daughter's income was earnings, it was not income to which she was entitled in her own right, a phrase, it was said, more apt to refer to, for example, income under a trust. In two cases the phrase has been held to cover earnings: *Miles (Inspector of Taxes) v Morrow*[1], in the Northern Ireland Divisional Court, and *Williams v Doulton (Inspector of Taxes)*[2] at first instance, following the former case. In *Mapp (Inspector of Taxes) v Oram*[3], the point was conceded by experienced leading counsel in the Court of Appeal[4]: see the judgment of Dankwerts LJ. It seems likely that the discussion of the point in the speeches in the House of Lords[3] was initiated by one of their Lordships. Some of them expressed tentative views on the point, which were of course obiter dicta, since the decision in the case was that, the earnings of the relevant child being in France and spent there, the child had no relevant income because the income to which the child has to be entitled in his own right under s 212 is income chargeable to tax under United Kingdom tax legislation. We prefer the views on this point of Lords Hodson and Pearson to those of Lord Upjohn, and consider that earnings of a child are relevant to s 212.

The taxpayer suggested a number of other points: but, after listening to comments from this court, he very properly did not press them, and we need not mention them. They had no validity for the purposes of this appeal.

We turn therefore to the point on the Crown's appeal. Initially the question is whether the deeming provision in s 354(1) is properly to be considered as extending in its operation beyond the scope of a system dealing with the application of the charge to tax on income of a married couple while living together, by force of the words 'for income tax purposes'; for we apprehend that without those words it could scarcely be thought that the subsection could have any relevance to the question whether for s 212 a female child's income chargeable to tax was something to which she was entitled in her own right.

The group of sections forming Part XIV of the 1952 Act is headed 'Special provisions as to Married Persons' and is concerned exclusively with adjustment of the methods of assessment and collection of tax in the situation of a man and wife living together and no other situation, unless the decision of the judge is correct. This group of sections first appeared in the Finance Act 1950, not with that cross-heading, but quite recognisably, as the language of s 30 shows, as a group dealing comprehensively with the particular situation above-mentioned. The fact mentioned by the judge that the Finance Act 1950, as is normal, dealt with other matters does not, with respect, alter that. The provision in s 354(1) is a deeming provision. It has been remarked on high authority that in considering 'deeming' provisions in statutes it is important to have in mind what appears to be the purpose of their enactment: see, for example, *Hill v The East and West India Dock Co*[5], and the passage quoted from James LJ in another case[6] in *Leitch v Emmott*[7].

As was argued for the Crown, it would not be expected that in any way the deeming provisions of the 1950 equivalent of s 354 were intended to alter anywhere in the fiscal legislation the total charge to or liability for income tax that previously obtained,

1   (1940) 23 Tax Cas 465
2   [1948] 1 All ER 603, 28 Tax Cas 522
3   [1969] 3 All ER 215, [1970] AC 362, 45 Tax Cas 651
4   [1968] 3 All ER 1, [1969] 1 Ch 293, 45 Tax Cas 651
5   (1884) 9 App Cas 448 at 454-456
6   *Ex parte Walton, Re Levy* (1881) 17 Ch D 746 at 756, [1881-85] All ER Rep 548 at 553
7   [1929] 2 KB 236 at 248, 14 Tax Cas 633 at 643, 644, [1929] All ER Rep 638 at 642, 643

a which would be the result if the decision of the judge on the language introduced in 1950 is correct. In this connection we note that the judge placed reliance on the fact that the deeming provision here is apparently double: it is not only that the income is deemed to be that of the husband; it is also deemed not to be that of the wife. This, in our view, is to attribute to the latter phrase an undue significance, when it may very well be referable to an anxiety to make clear that for relevant purposes the income is not to be treated as hers as well as his.

b We now turn to the anomalies which would result from the judge's interpretation. Now it is true that anomalies are to be expected in a complicated fiscal system, and do not necessarily solve a question of construction. But there are anomalies and anomalies. Some are the outcome of an attempt at simplification of administration. One such is that a total child allowance can be claimed for a fiscal year even when the

c child is born on 5th April at the end of that year, a practical exercise in legitimate tax avoidance in which one member of the court (albeit with assistance) successfully indulged: though, of course, that was counter-productive at the other end.

Equally, a result of administrative convenience is that, provided that a child manages to avoid being sent down from a university until 7th April in any year, his father is entitled to a child allowance for the whole of the current fiscal year, save in the event

d of the failed student sufficiently succeeding financially in the immediate future. But these anomalies and inequalities in a family and between families are readily explained on grounds of administrative convenience. But the anomalies which may result from the decision under appeal are susceptible of no such acceptable explanation. We indicate only a few.

Suppose twin sisters, with the same history as the taxpayer's daughter Eileen in

e this case; but Eileen 'A' marries and Eileen 'B' does not. The taxpayer would be entitled to child allowance for Eileen 'A' but not Eileen 'B'. Suppose two fathers, one of Eileen 'A' and the other of Eileen 'B': the former gets the child allowance; the latter does not.

Suppose that in the present case either Eileen or her husband had asked for separate assessment under this group of sections. In that case it is plain that on no footing could

f the taxpayer have relied on s 354 as entitling him to child allowance. And hereunder it is to be observed that if Eileen's husband (if there were no separate assessment) had failed to pay the tax, the Crown could have required Eileen directly to pay the tax which would have been chargeable in respect of her income had there been separate assessment. Again, if Eileen had separated from her husband after a disastrous week's honeymoon, the allowance could not have been claimed by the

g taxpayer.

All these matters go to demonstrate, in our judgment, not only anomalies but absurdities which follow if the deeming provisions of s 354(1) are extended in their operation beyond the context of the system of assessment, liability and collection applied by Part XIV of the 1952 Act to the particular situation of a wife and husband living together (and only while living together), and in particular to the operation of

h s 212 on the final tax liability of a third person. It is in the highest degree improbable that Part XIV was designed to affect the amount of anybody's tax liability save that of the happy couple, replacing as it did previous statutory provisions which were so limited.

The learned judge found himself in a position of difficulty, which can also be a position of danger, of having before him a litigant in person. We say a position of

j danger because in such circumstances a judge must in some sense don the wig and gown of advocate for the untutored litigant in person; and no man or advocate is human who does not tend to be persuaded in some sort by his own advocacy.

Basically the learned judge founded his decision on the change in language between that of the former provisions dealing with the tax situation of a woman and a married women contained in r 16 of the All Schedules Rules[1] of the Income Tax

---

1 See the Income Tax Act 1918, Sch 1, 'General Rules applicable to Schedules A, B, C, D, and E'

Act 1918 and the provisions introduced in their place in the Finance Act 1950. In effect he found that in the language of the former there was that which well justified the decision in this court in *Leitch v Emmott*[1] confining it to a question of assessment and collection in the particular situation of married couples living together; but that in 1950 there was a marked change in language which must be assumed to have intended the introduction of a change, the new language ('for income tax purposes') being quite general and sufficient in its literal scope to affect s 212.

In this connection he distinguished the decision of Harman LJ, sitting at first instance in *Re Cameron (decd)*[2], as being a decision not for income tax purposes but for estate duty purposes. This distinction was perfectly valid on the question of the decision. The learned judge also inferred that *Leitch v Emmott*[1] had not been cited to Harman LJ but had been discovered by the judge during reservation of his judgment. It was shown to us by reference to counsel's notes that this was a wrong inference; but it appeared that it was not there argued that the change from r 16 to s 354 had produced any relevant change. Harman LJ obviously thought that it had not; and counsel engaged did not suggest that it had. To that extent alone the case is of value to us, but it is not without some value.

The rewriting in 1950 of that part of the tax code special to the situation of spouses living together included a belated recognition of the fact that all property and therefore income of a married woman was now her own. It was no longer necessary to refer to her trading income or income of her separate property in this context: that went without saying. That which had been a proviso to an enactment limited to such separate property (for purposes of assessment and collection) could in effect be elevated to the substantive part of s 354(1).

In our judgment, the error into which the learned judge fell was to assume that, because there was a change in language in a general rewriting and up-dating of a group of sections designed to cover a particular and limited situation, the change in language must be taken at, so to speak, its full stretch as indicating an extension—and, as we have sought to show, an improbable one—into a quite different and unrelated sphere, by the artificial process of deeming. In this, in our judgment, he erred. In our view, 'for income tax purposes' in s 354(1) is to be confined in its meaning to the triangular relationship of Crown, husband and wife—a fiscal ménage à trois. The quoted words are sufficiently explained by a desire to negative a suggestion that beneficial entitlement of a wife to her own income was intended to be transferred to the husband. For these reasons, we allow the appeal of the Crown.

There is another possible approach to the same result, which may be sound and by which we were at one time certainly much attracted. That is by the direct application of the proviso to s 354(1) to s 212. Hereunder the argument for the Crown is as follows. In order to find the answers to two questions, you are directed by the proviso to ignore the deeming provisions of s 354(1): the first question is whether there is any income of the wife chargeable to income tax: the second question is how much is it for income tax purposes: under s 212 these are the only questions to be asked of a daughter child: quod est demonstrandum. We are not altogether sure that is really a different question. For it might be said that, the questions having been answered, the first part of s 354(1) still bites on the answer.

However this may be, in our judgment, for the reasons that we have given, the decision of the learned judge was erroneous, and the appeal must be allowed.

Appeal allowed; cross-appeal dismissed. Decision of General Commissioners restored.

Solicitor: *Solicitor of Inland Revenue.*

Rengan Krishnan Esq   Barrister.

---

1   [1929] 2 KB 236, 14 Tax Cas 633, [1929] All ER Rep 638
2   [1965] 3 All ER 474, [1967] Ch 1, 43 Tax Cas 539

Re Hastings-Bass (deceased)
Hastings and others v Inland Revenue Commissioners

COURT OF APPEAL, CIVIL DIVISION

MEGAW, BUCKLEY AND ROSKILL LJJ

28th, 29th, 30th, 31st JANUARY, 1st FEBRUARY, 14th MARCH 1974

Settlement – Advancement – Power of advancement – Exercise of power by trustees – Validity – Understanding of trustees – Trustees failing to have proper understanding of effect of advancement – Advancement of funds of settlement to son of life tenant – Advanced funds to be held on trusts of sub-settlement – Trust for son for life with certain other powers and trusts – All powers and trusts other than life interest void for perpetuity – Whether advancement for benefit of son – Whether advancement effective to create a life interest in possession in son.

Trust and trustee – Powers of trustee – Advancement – Application of capital money for advancement of beneficiary – Advancement creating no interest in capital – Validity – Funds advanced to trustees of sub-settlement – Life interest with certain trusts and powers over – Trusts and powers over void for perpetuity – Whether capital money 'applied' – Whether advancement within powers of trustees – Trustee Act 1925, s 32(1).

By a settlement made in 1947 ('the 1947 settlement') property was settled on trusts under which the beneficial interests were: (a) a protected life interest for A, (b) after A's death on trust for such of his sons or remoter male issue as A should by deed revocable or irrevocable or by will or codicil appoint; (c) on specified trusts in default of and subject to any such appointment; (d) certain remainders over, and (e) a power for A to appoint a life interest in half the settled fund in favour of any wife that might survive him. A had four children. The first was a son, W, born on 30th January 1948. By a revocable deed of appointment dated 2nd January 1958 A appointed that the trustees of the settlement should from and after his death (and subject to any interest appointed in favour of his widow) stand possessed of the trust fund in trust for W, if and when he should attain the age of 25 years, absolutely.   In 1957 A's sister had made a settlement ('the 1957 settlement') of a sum of £500 on trust under which she gave a life interest to W, and created certain powers and other interests.   The rate of estate duty prospectively payable on property passing on A's death was high. Accordingly, a scheme was devised whereby estate duty might be reduced.   The scheme took the form of an advancement by the trustees of the 1947 settlement, under the powers conferred on them by the Trustee Act 1925, s 32(1)^a, of a fund valued at £50,000 to the trustees of the 1957 settlement to be held on the trusts of the 1957 settlement.   Since W was not a life in being at the date of the 1947 settlement it followed that the powers and beneficial trusts of the advanced fund declared by reference to the 1957 settlement, other than W's life interest, were void for perpetuity, although, in the existing state of the law, the trustees did not appreciate

---

a   Section 32(1), so far as material, provides: 'Trustees may at any time or times pay or apply any capital money subject to a trust, for the advancement or benefit, in such manner as they may, in their absolute discretion, think fit, of any person entitled to the capital of the trust property or of any share thereof, whether absolutely or contingently on his attaining any specified age or on the occurrence of any other event, or subject to a gift over on his death under any specified age or on the occurrence of any other event, and whether in possession or in remainder or reversion, and such payment or application may be made notwithstanding that the interest of such person is liable to be defeated by the exercise of a power of appointment or revocation, or to be diminished by the increase of the class to which he belongs . . .'

H

that at the time of the advancement. A died on 4th June 1964. On a summons by the trustees to determine whether or not estate duty was payable on the advanced fund on A's death, the Inland Revenue Commissioners contended that the advancement was ineffective to create a life interest in possession in W in the advanced fund, which therefore remained subject to the trusts of the 1947 settlement, on the grounds (a) that trustees making an advancement by way of a sub-settlement must have a proper understanding of the effect of the sub-settlement for otherwise they could not take into account all the relevant circumstances, or give due consideration and weight to the benefit to be conferred on the person advanced; and (b) that in any event the advancement was in excess of the powers conferred on the trustees by s 32 of the 1925 Act which did not authorise a sub-settlement creating no interest at all in capital. It was common ground that if the advancement was effective to create a life interest in possession in W no estate duty was payable on the advanced fund on A's death.

Held – The advancement was effective to create a life interest in possession in W for the following reasons—

(1) Where, by the terms of a trust (as under s 32 of the 1925 Act), a trustee was given a discretion as to some matter under which he acted in good faith, the court should not interfere with his action, notwithstanding that it did not have the full effect which he intended, unless (i) what he had achieved was unauthorised by the power conferred on him or (ii) it was clear that he would not have acted as he did (a) had he not taken into account considerations which he should not have taken into account, or (b) had he not failed to take into account considerations which he ought to have taken into account (see p 203 f, post).

(2) If the advancement were effective W thereupon became entitled to an indefeasible life interest in possession in a fund of £50,000. Because of the incidence of estate duty, if the advancement were ineffective his interest in that £50,000 would remain a contingent interest, dependent on his attaining the age of 25, in a net sum of 27 per cent of £50,000, i e £13,500. Although the trusts of the sub-settlement intended to take effect on W's death would also have benefited W indirectly those benefits were of far less significance than the major benefits of the saving of death duties coupled with an acceleration of W's interest; in the circumstances there could be no doubt that the duty-saving aspect of the scheme was the primary consideration in the minds of the trustees. The commissioners had, therefore, failed to establish that, had the trustees realised that the ulterior trusts would fail for perpetuity, they would not have acted as they did, for the trustees could not reasonably have thought that failure would mean that the scheme could not be regarded as being for the benefit of W (see p 201 e to j and p 202 b e and j to p 203 b and e g, post); *Re Abrahams' Will Trusts* [1967] 2 All ER 1175 distinguished.

(3) Although the sub-settlement was ineffective to create any beneficial interests in the capital of the advanced fund it did not follow that the trustees had acted in excess of the power conferred on them by s 32 of the 1925 Act. The trustees had 'applied' part of the capital of the trust fund, within s 32(1), when they transferred the investments to the trustees of the 1957 settlement for that was manifestly a disposition of a part of the capital assets of the trust (see p 203 j to p 204 c, post).

Notes

For powers of advancement, see 21 Halsbury's Laws (3rd Edn) 177-180, paras 384-391, and for cases on the subject, see 28(2) Digest (Reissue) 781-788, 1107-1164.

For the Trustee Act 1925, s 32, see 38 Halsbury's Statutes (3rd Edn) 143.

Cases referred to in judgment

Abrahams' Will Trusts, Re, Caplan v Abrahams [1967] 2 All ER 1175, [1969] 1 Ch 463, [1967] 3 WLR 1198, Digest (Cont Vol C) 797, 4606.

Pauling's Settlement Trusts, Re, Younghusband v Coutts & Co [1963] 3 All ER 1, [1964] Ch 303, [1963] 3 WLR 742, CA, 47 Digest (Repl) 513, *4656*.

Pilkington v Inland Revenue Comrs [1962] 3 All ER 622, [1964] AC 612, 40 Tax Cas 416, [1962] 3 WLR 1051, 41 ATC 285, [1962] TR 265, HL; *rvsg sub nom Re Pilkington's Will Trusts, Pilkington v Pilkington* [1961] 2 All ER 330, [1961] Ch 466, [1961] 2 WLR 776, CA; *affg* [1959] 2 All ER 623, [1959] Ch 699, [1959] 3 WLR 116, 28(2) Digest (Reissue) 785, *1139*.

Cases also cited

Allan's Will Trusts, Re, Curtis v Nalder [1958] 1 All ER 401, [1958] 1 WLR 220.

Bristow v Warde (1794) 2 Ves 336, 30 ER 660, LC.

Dean v Prince [1953] 2 All ER 636, [1953] Ch 590; *rvsd* [1954] 1 All ER 749, [1954] Ch 409, CA.

Dundee General Hospitals Board of Management v Walker [1952] 1 All ER 896, sub nom *Dundee General Hospitals v Bell's Trustees* 1952 SC (HL) 78, HL.

Gisborne v Gisborne (1877) 2 App Cas 300, HL.

Gresham's Settlement, Re, Lloyds Bank Ltd v Gresham [1956] 2 All ER 193, [1956] 1 WLR 573.

Gulbenkian's Settlement Trusts, Re, Whishaw v Stephens [1968] 3 All ER 785, [1970] AC 508, HL.

Morgan v Gronow (1873) LR 16 Eq 1.

Roper-Curzon v Roper-Curzon (1871) LR 11 Eq 452.

Ropner's Settlement Trusts, Re, Ropner v Ropner [1956] 3 All ER 332, [1956] 1 WLR 902.

Turner, Re, Hudson v Turner [1932] 1 Ch 31, [1931] All ER Rep 782.

Vestey's Settlement, Re, Lloyds Bank Ltd v O'Meara [1950] 2 All ER 891, [1951] Ch 209, CA.

Wollasten v King (1869) LR 8 Eq 165.

Appeal

By an originating summons dated 18th April 1972 the plaintiffs, (1) Robin Hood William Stewart Hastings, (2) Martin Wakefield Jacomb (the trustees of a settlement dated 1st April 1947 ('the 1947 settlement') and made between Sir William Arthur Hamar Bass of the first part, Peter Robin Hood Hastings of the second part and others of the third part) and (3) Francis Bellett Cockburn (with the first plaintiff a trustee of a settlement dated 29th October 1957 ('the 1957 settlement') and made between Diana Wilmot Hastings and others) sought the determination of the court on a question arising on the construction of the 1947 and 1957 settlements and a deed of appointment made on 2nd January 1957 by Peter Robin Hood Hastings-Bass, formerly Peter Robin Hood Hastings ('the deceased'). The defendants were the Inland Revenue Commissioners. By an order made on 2nd November 1972 Plowman J, in answer to the question raised in the summons, declared that, on the true construction of the settlements, the deed of appointment and the Finance Act 1894, as amended, and in the events which had happened, estate duty became payable on the death of the deceased under ss 1 and 2(1)(b) of the Finance Act 1894 in respect of the investments and property then representing the investments transferred out of the 1947 settlement on 21st March 1958 by the trustees of the 1947 settlement to the trustees of the 1957 settlement as an advancement for the benefit of William Edward Robin Hood Hastings-Bass ('William'). The plaintiffs appealed against that order on the grounds (1) that the judge had been wrong in holding (a) that the case was on all fours with *Re Abrahams' Will Trusts*[1] and that no distinction in principle could be drawn between the two cases; (b) that the decision in *Re Abrahams' Will Trusts*[1] was correct; (c) that the decision in that case was binding on him, and (d) that in view of that decision he was bound to hold that estate duty became payable on the death of the deceased in respect of the investments and property then representing the advanced funds; (2) that, even if the relevant advance did no more than create a valid life interest in

1 [1967] 2 All ER 1175, [1969] 1 Ch 463

favour of William in respect of the advanced funds, it was still for his 'benefit', within the meaning of s 32(1) of the Trustee Act 1925, and still fell within the statutory powers of advancement possessed by the trustees of the 1947 settlement; and (3) that the relevant advance, being made in good faith and within the statutory powers possessed by the trustees of the 1947 settlement, was a valid advance and was not invalidated merely because the other beneficial interests and powers which the trustees believed that they were creating in relation to the advanced funds, in addition to the life interest in favour of William, were, contrary to their understanding of the law, perpetuitous. The facts are set out in the judgment of the court.

Christopher Slade QC and *H Hillaby* for the plaintiffs.
N C H Browne-Wilkinson QC and *Peter Gibson* for the commissioners.

Cur adv vult

14th March. **BUCKLEY LJ** read the following judgment of the court. This appeal raises a difficult question relating to an advancement under the Trustee Act 1925, s 32, by way of sub-settlement, some of the beneficial trusts of which are void for perpetuity. The appeal is from a judgment of Plowman J delivered on 2nd November 1972.

By a settlement dated 1st April 1947 (which we will call 'the 1947 settlement'), made on the marriage of Peter Robin Hood Hastings (who later assumed the additional surname of Bass and whom we will call 'Captain Hastings-Bass'), his uncle, Sir William Bass, settled property on trusts under which the beneficial interests were as follows: (a) a protected life interest for Captain Hastings-Bass; (b) after his death on trust for such of his sons or remoter male issue as Captain Hastings-Bass should by deed revocable or irrevocable or by will or codicil appoint; (c) in default of and subject to any such appointment on trust for such son of Captain Hastings-Bass as should first attain the age of 25 years before the expiration of 21 years after the death of Captain Hastings-Bass and, if there should be no such son, on trust for such son of Captain Hastings-Bass as should first attain the age of 21 years; (d) with remainders on similar trusts to two other nephews of the settlor and their respective male issue and an ultimate trust in favour of a named person; (e) with power for Captain Hastings-Bass by deed revocable or irrevocable executed prior to and in contemplation of any marriage or by will or codicil to appoint a life or less interest in not exceeding one-half of the trust fund in favour of any wife who might survive him. Captain Hastings-Bass had four children, a son (William) born on 30th January 1948, a son (Simon) born on 2nd May 1950, a son (John) born on 5th June 1954, and a daughter.

By a revocable deed of appointment dated 2nd January 1958, Captain Hastings-Bass in exercise of his power in that behalf under the 1947 settlement appointed that the trustees should from and after his death (and subject to any interest appointed in favour of his widow) stand possessed of the trust fund in trust for his son William, if and when he should attain the age of 25 years absolutely. William was then nearly ten years old, and he was bound to attain the age of 25 years, if at all, within 21 years of his father's death. The appointment appears to have had no significant effect on his contingent interest.

In the preceding year, on 29th October 1957, Miss Diana Hastings, a sister of Captain Hastings-Bass, had made a settlement of a sum of £500 on trusts under which the beneficial interests were as follows: (a) a life interest for William; (b) after his death in trust for such of his issue as he without transgressing the rule against perpetuities should by deed revocable or irrevocable or by will or codicil appoint; (c) in default of and subject to any such appointment in trust for his children who should attain the age of 21 years and if more than one in equal shares subject to hotchpot; (d) if there should be no such child of William in trust for such of the issue of Captain Hastings-Bass living at the date of the failure of the foregoing trusts as the trustees without transgressing the rule against perpetuities should by deed appoint; (e) in default of and subject to any such appointment in trust for Captain Hastings-Bass's youngest son John absolutely; (f) with power for William by deed made in contemplation of marriage or by will or codicil to appoint to any wife who might survive him a life or lesser interest in the whole or any part of the trust fund. This settlement (which we will call 'the 1957 settlement') contained a power for the trustees in their absolute discretion from time to time and at any time after William should have attained 21 to hand over the whole or such part of the capital of the trust fund to him free from the trusts of the settlement as they might think fit. It also contained a power for the trustees at their discretion with the consent in writing of William to revoke by deed all or any of the trusts therein contained concerning the whole of the trust fund or any part or parts thereof and to declare such new or other trusts for the benefit of William or any child or remoter issue of his as the trustees might think proper.

The rate of estate duty prospectively payable on property passing on the death of Captain Hastings-Bass was high, and accordingly the solicitor to the 1947 settlement trustees devised a scheme which was described by Captain Hastings-Bass in a contemporary letter as 'a scheme whereby some of the enormous death duties may be reduced on the settlement'. This scheme took the form of a transfer by the 1947 settlement trustees under the statutory power of advancement to the 1957 settlement trustees on the trusts of the 1957 settlement of a fund valued at £50,000. On 21st March 1958 the 1947 settlement trustees with the consent of Captain Hastings-Bass and in exercise of the statutory power of advancement transferred out of the 1947 settlement to the trustees of the 1957 settlement investments to the value of £50,000 by way of advancement for the benefit of William to be held on the trusts of the latter settlement. The trusts of the 1957 settlement, as applied to the trust fund settled by that settlement, were innocent of any offence against the perpetuity rule. It is evident that the trustees' solicitor conceived that the trusts of the 1957 settlement as applicable to the funds transferred out of the 1947 settlement would also escape infringing the perpetuity rule. This view was consistent with the subsequent decision of Danckwerts J, dated 14th May 1959, in *Re Pilkington's Will Trusts*[1]. But the Inland Revenue Commissioners appealed from that decision and eventually in the House of Lords[2] it was held that a power of advancement was a special power and that accordingly trusts called into existence by its exercise must be written into the instrument creating the power for the purposes of applying the perpetuity rule.

William was not a life in being at the date of the 1947 settlement, and accordingly it is now common ground that all the powers and beneficial trusts of the advanced fund declared by reference to the 1957 settlement other than the life interest of William are void for perpetuity.

It is also common ground that, if the transaction of 21st March 1958 was effective to create a life interest in possession in William in the advanced fund, no estate duty became payable on that fund on the death of Captain Hastings-Bass, which occurred on 4th June 1964. The Inland Revenue Commissioners, however, contend that the effect of the transaction was not to create any new beneficial interests in the £50,000 fund, but that this fund at all times remained subject to the trusts of the 1947 settlement. On this footing it is clear that estate duty would have become payable on the fund on Captain Hastings-Bass's death.

In these circumstances, the plaintiffs, who are the present trustees of the 1947 settlement, applied by originating summons in the Chancery Division for the determination of the question whether estate duty did or did not become payable on the death of Captain Hastings-Bass in respect of the advanced fund. The only defendants to these proceedings are the Inland Revenue Commissioners. William attained the age of 25 years on 30th January 1973 and accordingly no one but he has any interest in the capital of the 1947 settlement fund, and the only persons interested in the

---

1 [1959] 2 All ER 623, [1959] Ch 699, 40 Tax Cas 416
2 *Pilkington v Inland Revenue Comrs* [1962] 3 All ER 622, [1964] AC 612, 40 Tax Cas 416

income of that fund are himself and his mother, who is at present entitled under a testamentary appointment made by Captain Hastings-Bass to half the income of the fund. She does not, however, seek to assert that the 1958 advancement was not effective to create a life interest in possession in William in the advanced fund.

The case came in due course before Plowman J for decision, and, following an earlier decision of Cross J in *Re Abrahams' Will Trusts*[1], the learned judge held that the result actually produced by the 1958 advance was substantially or essentially different from the intentions of the 1947 settlement trustees when they made it. Following Cross J, Plowman J took the view that the 1947 settlement trustees never effectively exercised the power of advancement, and that accordingly the £50,000 fund at all times remained subject to the trusts of the 1947 settlement. He therefore decided that estate duty did become payable on that fund on the death of Captain Hastings-Bass. From that decision the plaintiffs appeal.

We have had the advantage of excellently clear arguments on both sides in the appeal. The contentions can be shortly stated in this way. The plaintiffs contend, first, that, notwithstanding that the 1958 advancement did no more than create a valid life interest for William, it was nevertheless for his benefit and fell within the terms of the trustees' statutory power of advancement; secondly, that in these circumstances, the advancement having been made in good faith, it was valid and was not invalidated by reason of the fact that the beneficial interests intended to take effect after William's death were, contrary to the trustees' understanding, void for perpetuity; thirdly, that *Re Abrahams' Will Trusts*[1] was wrongly decided; and fourthly, that if this was not the case, *Re Abrahams' Will Trusts*[1] is distinguishable on its facts from the present case. We add parenthetically that counsel for the plaintiffs reserved the right to argue in the House of Lords that *Pilkington v Inland Revenue Comrs*[2] had been wrongly decided in their Lordships' House. The commissioners contend, first, that *Re Abrahams' Will Trusts*[1] was rightly decided and cannot be distinguished from the present case; secondly, that the statutory power of advancement confers a fiduciary discretion which can only be properly exercised after giving due consideration to all relevant factors and, in particular, the benefit proposed to be conferred on the person advanced; thirdly, that the essential features of a power of advancement are (a) that it is a power to pay or apply capital, and (b) that it is exercisable for the benefit of one person only, namely, the person advanced, and that beneficial interests for other persons can only be conferred as incidental to and part and parcel of the benefit to him; fourthly, that consequently trustees making an advancement by way of a sub-settlement must have a proper understanding of the effect of that sub-settlement, for, if they do not, they have not exercised it validly; fifthly, that in the present case the trustees never directed their minds to an advancement which merely gave William a life interest in income; sixthly, that the court cannot retrospectively substitute its own discretion for that of the trustees by determining that the advancement in its attenuated form of a mere life interest for William was for his benefit, since the discretion was conferred on the trustees; finally, that s 32 does not authorise either (a) an advancement by way of sub-settlement under which all capital interests are void for perpetuity or (b) a sub-settlement creating no interest at all in capital.

The facts in *Re Abrahams' Will Trusts*[1] were in many respects similar to those in the present case. By the combined effect of the will of a testator and of a settlement made on the occasion of the marriage of his son, Gerald, under a power in that behalf contained in the will the residuary estate of the testator was at the relevant time held on trust for Gerald for life (in part protected) and thereafter on trust for Gerald's children or remoter issue as he should appoint and in default of and subject to such appointment in trust for any or all of his children who should attain the age of 21 years or, being female, marry under that age, and if more than one in equal shares

---

1   [1967] 2 All ER 1175, [1969] 1 Ch 463
2   [1962] 3 All ER 622, [1964] AC 612, 40 Tax Cas 416

absolutely, with remainder on trust for the children and remoter issue of another son of the testator and an ultimate remainder in favour of nephews and nieces of the testator living at his death. Gerald had two children only, daughters born after the death of the testator. In 1957, when these two children were aged respectively nine and six years, the trustees with Gerald's consent purported to make an advancement of £25,000 for the benefit of each of them by way of sub-settlement under the trusts of which in each case the daughter took a protected life interest with trusts in remainder for the benefit of her children and remoter issue and otherwise which were all void for perpetuity. If the advancements were effective, they operated to create valid defeasible life interests in favour of the daughters respectively but created no other valid powers or beneficial interests. Counsel for the Inland Revenue Commissioners there contended that the trustees had exercised the power of advancement on the footing that they were producing a certain result and that in fact they produced a totally different result and so could not be rightly said to have exercised the power at all. Cross J dealt with this argument as follows[1]:

'The power which the trustees purported to exercise by setting up Carole's fund (to take her as an example) and declaring the trusts of it which are contained in the 1957 settlement was a power exercisable for the benefit of Carole, and for nobody else. The various other persons to whom the settlement purported to give benefits were not objects of that power of advancement. The position was that the trustees had a discretion as to the manner in which they would benefit Carole, and they considered that an appropriate way to benefit her would be to create this settlement under which beneficial interests were given to other members of her family besides herself. If one looks at the matter in that way it seems to me reasonable to hold that the effect of the invalidity of some of the limitations in the 1957 settlement by reason of the rule against perpetuities may not be the same as it would have been had the 1957 settlement been created by the exercise of a special power of appointment under which all the supposed beneficiaries were objects. It is one thing to say that if a trustee has power to appoint a fund to all or any of a class of objects and he appoints a life interest to one object which is not void for perpetuity and remainders to other objects which are void, then the life interest survives the invalidity of the remainders; but it is another thing to say that if a trustee has power to benefit A in a number of different ways and he chooses to benefit him by making a settlement on him for life with remainders to his issue, which remainders are void for perpetuity, then A can claim to obtain that part of the benefit intended for him which is represented by the life interest. The interests given to separate objects of an ordinary special power are separate interests, but all the interests created in Carole's fund were intended as part and parcel of a single benefit to her.'

The learned judge went on to say that, if the invalidity caused by the operation of the rule against perpetuities were quite small as compared with the parts of the sub-settlement which were unaffected by the rule, the court might be prepared to say that the valid parts of the sub-settlement would survive intact; but he went on to say that on the facts of the case before him there was no doubt that the effect of the operation of the rule was wholly to alter the character of the sub-settlement, and accordingly he held that the trustees had never validly exercised the power of advancement. As we understand him, Cross J decided this question on the basis of what we have called the fourth submission of the commissioners in the present case. We must therefore consider whether that submission is sound in principle.

Counsel for the commissioners supports the submission on the following grounds. The power of advancement is, he says, a fiduciary power, and as to this we think there is really no dispute. He says that the trustees can only properly exercise such a power

1   [1967] 2 All ER at 1191, [1969] 1 Ch at 484, 485

after giving due consideration and weight to all relevant circumstances. As they must weigh the benefit which the advancement will confer on the person advanced against those interests under the settlement which will be adversely affected by the advancement, they cannot give due consideration and weight to the benefit to be conferred on the person advanced unless they appreciate the true nature of that benefit. Counsel for the commissioners contends that, if in the present case when the trustees made the advancement they believed that all the trusts of the sub-settlement would take effect, they cannot have applied their minds to the right question.

In support of these contentions he relies on what was said in this court in *Re Pauling's Settlement Trusts*[1]:

> 'Being a fiduciary power, it seems to us quite clear that the power can be exercised only if it is for the benefit of the child or remoter issue to be advanced or, as was said during argument, it is thought to be "a good thing" for the advanced person to have a share of capital before his or her due time. That this must be so, we think, follows from a consideration of the fact that the parties to a settlement intend the normal trusts to take effect, and that a power of advancement be exercised only if there is some good reason for it. That good reason must be beneficial to the person to be advanced; the power cannot be exercised capriciously or with some other benefit in view. The trustees, before exercising the power, have to weigh on the one side the benefit to the proposed advancee, and on the other hand the rights of those who are or may hereafter become interested under the trusts of the settlement.'

He also relied on observations made by Upjohn LJ[2] and Lord Radcliffe in *Pilkington v Inland Revenue Comrs*[3]. That case related to a testamentary settlement to which the statutory power of advancement was applicable. The trustees, being minded to make an advancement under the statutory power on the terms of a sub-settlement, applied to the court for directions whether they could lawfully so exercise the power. The trusts of the proposed sub-settlement were such that, as in the present case, they would have been to a considerable extent void for perpetuity, although this fact was not realised by the trustees. In the Court of Appeal[2] the case was decided on the basis that the statutory power did not enable the trustees to make a sub-settlement. Of the judges who constituted the court, only Upjohn LJ dealt with the perpetuity point, on which he disagreed with the view which had been expressed by Danckwerts J[4], referred to earlier. Having held that all the trusts proposed to be declared in respect of the period after the date when the child advanced should have attained the age of 30 were void for perpetuity, Upjohn LJ said[5]:

> 'The effect, therefore, of the rule against perpetuities on the proposed settlement is basic; it entirely alters the settlement, and that seems to me to be fatal to this case, for the trustees have never been asked to express any opinion as to whether they would think the proposed settlement, modified by reason of the rule against perpetuities in the manner I have mentioned, is for the benefit of Penelope. That is a matter to which they have never addressed their minds, and, therefore, it cannot possibly be justified under s. 32, for it has not been shown that the trustees think that the settlement, as so modified, is for the advancement or benefit of Penelope.'

---

1   [1963] 3 All ER 1 at 9, [1964] Ch 303 at 303
2   [1961] 2 All ER 330, [1961] Ch 466, 40 Tax Cas 416
3   [1962] 3 All ER 622, [1964] AC 612, 40 Tax Cas 416
4   [1959] 2 All ER 623, [1959] Ch 699, 40 Tax Cas 416
5   [1961] 2 All ER at 341, [1961] Ch at 489, 490, 40 Tax Cas at 430

a   The House of Lords[1] differed from the Court of Appeal[2] on the main ground of decision, holding that it is within the powers of trustees to make an advancement under the statutory power by way of sub-settlement, but they agreed with the view of Upjohn LJ on the perpetuity point. They accordingly reached the conclusion that there were legal objections to the proposed sub-settlement which the trustees had placed before the court, which, as Lord Radcliffe[3] said, went to the root of what

b   was proposed.

It is, in our opinion, important to bear in mind that in *Pilkington v Inland Revenue Comrs*[1] the trustees were seeking the directions of the court before taking action. The court would of course not authorise trustees to set up a sub-settlement many of the trusts of which would be void. The trustees were not asking the court to consider any other form of sub-settlement, nor had they presumably applied their own minds

c   to that question at all.

It is at this point relevant, we think, to state that at the death of Captain Hastings-Bass the value of the advanced fund was £57,318 and that there were investments representing accumulations of income of that fund which were then of the value of £8,373. If Captain Hastings-Bass were liable for surtax in respect of the income of the advanced fund this liability amounted at the time of his death to £7,500. Accordingly,

d   at his death the estimated net value of the fund and accumulations (if surtax was payable) was £58,191. If duty became payable on his death in respect of that fund, it would have amounted to £42,318, and the total additional liability in the event of the funds becoming aggregable for estate duty purposes, including the surtax liability, would have been £59,588. The rate of duty payable on Captain Hastings-Bass's death in respect of the aggregable assets which were liable to duty at the full

e   rate was 75 per cent with the benefit of marginal relief. Accordingly, the duty on the advanced fund would have been at the rate of, say, 73 per cent.

If the advancement was effective, William thereupon became entitled to an indefeasible life interest in possession in a fund of £50,000. If the advancement was ineffective his interest in that £50,000 remained a contingent interest, dependent on his attaining the age of 25, in a net sum of 27 per cent of £50,000 or £13,500. There can

f   be no doubt that the capitalised value of an indefeasible life interest in possession in £50,000 for a boy of ten would greatly exceed the value of a right for the same boy to receive a capital sum of £13,500 in the event of his attaining the age of 25. In this respect, apart from other considerations, the advancement was calculated to benefit William very greatly.

We can feel no doubt that in such circumstances the duty-saving aspect of the

g   scheme was a primary consideration in the minds of the trustees. The trusts of the sub-settlement which were intended to take effect after William's death in favour of his issue could also (had they been capable of taking effect) legitimately be regarded as beneficial to him as making some provision for any issue he might have for whom he would otherwise be expected to wish to make provision out of his free estate, and as securing the fund for that end. The intended power for William to make

h   provision for a widow under the sub-settlement could also legitimately be regarded as benefiting William indirectly in a similar manner, and the power for the trustees to pay capital to him for his own use could also clearly be regarded as conferring a contingent benefit on him. But, in our opinion, these indirect or contingent benefits (had they been capable of taking effect) should be regarded as mere make-weights which might be treated as enhancing the benefit to William of the scheme as a whole,

j   but which were of far less significance than the major benefits of the saving of death duties coupled with an acceleration of William's interest.

In these circumstances, to what considerations is it reasonable to suppose that the trustees addressed their minds before making the advancement? No doubt it is right to say that they should and would have considered whether the aggregate of all *a* the provisions of the sub-settlement (if fully effective) would be for William's benefit, but in doing so they could not, we think, have failed to consider to what extent each of those provisions could properly be regarded as contributing to the aggregate benefit, and in particular they could not have failed to consider to what extent the conferring on William of an immediate and indefeasible life interest in possession would benefit him. The circumstances of the case, in our view, make it clear that *b* this aspect of the arrangement must have been the prime consideration in the minds of the trustees, and this is, we think, borne out by the terms of Captain Hastings-Bass's contemporary letter to which we have already referred.

The fact that the ulterior trusts of the sub-settlement failed for perpetuity cannot decrease the element of direct benefit to William in the scheme. Moreover, the effect of the failure of those trusts was to leave William's contingent interest in *c* capital under the 1947 settlement intact. He was consequently left with a greater prospect of securing the ownership of the capital of the fund than would have been the case had the trusts of the sub-settlement taken effect in full.

As regards weighing the benefit to William of the intended sub-settlement against the expectant interests of others under the 1947 settlement, the true effect of the sub-settlement necessarily affected those expectant interests less adversely than the *d* sub-settlement would have done, had it taken effect as intended. Instead of those expectant interests being entirely displaced, so that, for instance, Simon would have been cut out entirely, they were left intact with the benefit of the saving of estate duty at a high rate on the death of Captain Hastings-Bass. Had it occurred to the trustees that the ulterior trusts might all fail for perpetuity, they could not reasonably have thought that this could tip the scales in the weighing operation against the *e* scheme. The law cannot, in our judgment, require the trustees' exercise of their discretion to be treated as a nullity on the basis of an absurd assumption that, had they realised its true legal effect, they would have reached an unreasonable conclusion as the result of the weighing operation.

In these circumstances, can it be said that the trustees have never exercised their discretion under s 32? There can be no doubt that the transfer of investments to the *f* 1957 settlement trustees was an exercise of some kind of discretion. What the 1947 settlement trustees did was not obligatory; they chose to do it. If one asks what discretion they exercised, there can be no doubt that they believed themselves to be acting under s 32. They made the transfer to the 1957 settlement trustees because they considered that it would benefit William. Can the fact that they believed their action would have a different legal effect from the limited effect which alone it *g* could have result in the transfer not having been an exercise of their discretion under that subsection? There is no reason to suppose that, in the light of their own understanding or advice as to the law, they failed to ask themselves the right questions or to arrive in good faith at a reasonable conclusion. Amongst the questions they must have asked themselves was the question whether a sub-settlement limiting William's interest in the advanced fund to a life interest would be for his benefit. *h* For reasons which we have already indicated, the only answer which they could reasonably have given themselves to that question would have been affirmative, even without regard to any indirect or contingent benefits intended to be conferred on William by the other provisions of the sub-settlement. They may not have asked themselves whether to give William an immediate life interest without any further variation of the trusts of the 1947 settlement would benefit William, but the *j* consequence would not, in our opinion, be that their action should be regarded as something other than an exercise of their discretion under s 32.

Where trustees intend to make an advancement by way of sub-settlement, they must no doubt genuinely apply their minds to the question whether the sub-settlement as a whole will operate for the benefit of the person advanced; but this does not, we think, involve regarding this benefit as a benefit of a monolithic character,

a It is, in our opinion, more naturally and logically to be regarded as a bundle of benefits of distinct characters. Each and all of those benefits is conferred, or is intended to be conferred, by a single exercise of the discretion under s 32. If by operation of law one or more of those benefits cannot take effect, it does not seem to us to follow that those which survive should not be regarded as having been brought into being by an exercise of the discretion. If the resultant effect of the intended advancement
b were such that it could not reasonably be regarded as being beneficial to the person intended to be advanced, the advancement could not stand, for it would not be within the powers of the trustees under s 32. In any other case, however, the advancement should, in our judgment, be permitted to take effect in the manner and to the extent that it is capable of doing so.

In *Re Abrahams' Will Trusts*[1] the beneficial interest of each daughter in her advanced
c fund was a protected life interest only, not, as in the present case, an indefeasible one. This was the only beneficial interest under the sub-settlement in that case which was capable of taking effect; and the interest of each daughter under the head settlement —that is, the combined effect of the will and marriage settlement—in the capital of her advanced fund was a right to one-half only of the capital contingently on her attaining the age of 21 or marrying. Cross J might well have been justified in that
d case in considering that the intended sub-settlement in its attenuated form could not reasonably be regarded as beneficial to the daughter intended to be advanced and so could not be treated as an exercise of discretion falling within the terms of s 32. If so, we think he reached the right conclusion. His decision should not, in our judgment, be regarded as authority for the fourth contention of the commissioners in the present case. It should not, we think, be treated as laying down any principle applic-
e able in any case other than one in which the effect of the perpetuity rule has been to alter the intended consequences of an advancement so drastically that the trustees cannot reasonably be supposed to have addressed their minds to the questions relevant to the true effect of the transaction. We do not consider that the operation of the rule has produced such a drastic effect in the present case.

To sum up the preceding observations, in our judgment, where by the terms of a
f trust (as under s 32) a trustee is given a discretion as to some matter under which he acts in good faith, the court should not interfere with his action notwithstanding that it does not have the full effect which he intended, unless (1) what he has achieved is unauthorised by the power conferred on him, or (2) it is clear that he would not have acted as he did (a) had he not taken into account considerations which he should not have taken into account, or (b) had he not failed to take into account considera-
g tions which he ought to have taken into account. In the present case (2) above has not, in our judgment, been established; but the commissioners contend that for reasons stated in their third submission, sub-head (a), and their final submission what the trustees achieved in the present case was in excess of their power.

Before dealing with that point we should say one word about the commissioners' sixth contention. In our judgment, the court is not being asked to exercise any
h discretion, but only to determine whether the trustees have validly exercised their discretion. Accordingly, we think that there is nothing in this submission.

The commissioners' third submission, sub-head (a), and their last submission can be conveniently considered together and amount in the present case to this: that since the sub-settlement was ineffective to create any beneficial interest in the capital of the advanced fund, there was no payment or application of capital within the con-
j templation of s 32. In our judgment, the 1947 settlement trustees did 'apply' part of the capital of the trust fund within the meaning of the section when they transferred the investments to the 1957 settlement trustees. This was manifestly a disposition of a part of the capital assets of their trust. The fact that the sub-settlement declared no effective beneficial trusts of capital but created only a limited beneficial interest

---

1   [1967] 2 All ER 1175, [1969] 1 Ch 463

in income does not, in our judgment, deprive the transaction of that character. Its *a*
effect was that the 1957 settlement trustees held the transferred assets on an express
trust for William for life and subject thereto on constructive trusts for the persons
beneficially interested therein under the 1947 settlement with the powers and
subject to the provisions conferred by and contained in the latter settlement. The
position is, we think, no different from what it would have been had the sub-settlement expressly declared such constructive trusts. The 1947 settlement trustees *b*
parted with the transferred assets and could not, we think, have recovered them
even after William's death. They parted with the legal ownership and had no
equitable interest in the transferred assets which would have enabled them to assert
any claim to them at any time thereafter. We consequently feel unable to accept
these submissions of the commissioners. In *Pilkington v Inland Revenue Comrs*[1] Lord
Radcliffe said that he had been unable to find in the words of s 32 anything which in *c*
terms or by implication restricted the width of the manner or purpose of advancement. We also can find nothing in the language of the section to limit the power of
trustees thereunder to making an advancement in a manner which creates new beneficial interests in capital.

For these reasons, we allow this appeal and substitute for the order of the learned
judge a declaration that estate duty did not become payable on the death of Captain *d*
Hastings-Bass.

Appeal allowed.   Leave to appeal to the House of Lords.

Solicitors: *Bircham & Co* (for the plaintiffs); *Solicitor of Inland Revenue.*

A S Virdi Esq   Barrister. *e*

R v Scott

f

COURT OF APPEAL, CRIMINAL DIVISION
ROSKILL, JAMES LJJ AND MICHAEL DAVIES J
19th, 20th DECEMBER 1973, 29th JANUARY 1974

Affirmed HL sub nom SCOTT v COMR
OF POLICE [1974] 3 All ER 1032

Criminal law – Conspiracy – Conspiracy to defraud – Fraud – Elements of fraud – Deceit – *g*
Whether deceit a necessary ingredient of fraud – Whether necessary to prove that accused
had agreed to deceive intended victim and by such deceit to defraud him.

The appellant was charged with conspiracy to defraud, the particulars of the count
alleging that he and others had 'conspired together and with other persons unknown
to defraud such companies and persons as might be caused loss by the unlawful *h*
copying and distribution of films the copyright in which and the distribution rights
of which belonged to companies and persons other than the said persons so conspiring
and by divers subtle, crafty and fraudulent means and devices'. The appellant
admitted agreeing with employees of cinema owners that, in return for payment,
those employees would, without their employers' consent, temporarily abstract
cinematograph films for the purpose of enabling him to make and distribute copies
of those films on a commercial basis, the abstraction, copying and distribution being
made without the knowledge or consent of the owners of the copyright in, or distribution rights of, those films. The appellant was convicted and appealed, contending

---

1   [1962] 3 All ER at 628, [1964] AC at 636, 40 Tax Cas at 438

a that the count was bad in law in that the offence charged did not include any ingredient of deceit, of intent to deceive or of an agreement to deceive the persons and companies alleged to have been defrauded.

Held – The common law offence of conspiracy to defraud was not limited to an agreement between two or more persons to deceive the intended victim and by such
b deceit to defraud him. Conspiracy to defraud might, but did not necessarily, involve an agreement to defraud by deceit. The appeal would therefore be dismissed (see p 210 *a* and *b*, post).

Dictum of James J in *R v Sinclair* [1968] 3 All ER at 246 applied.
Dictum of Buckley J in *Re London and Globe Finance Corpn Ltd* [1900-3] All ER Rep at 893 explained.

c

Notes

For conspiracy to defraud, see 10 Halsbury's Laws (3rd Edn) 834, 835, para 1610, and for cases on the subject, see 15 Digest (Repl) 1199-1204, *12,181-12,239*.

d **Cases referred to in judgment**

London and Globe Finance Corpn Ltd, Re [1903] 1 Ch 728, [1900-3] All ER Rep 891, 72 LJCh 368, 88 LT 194, 10 Mans 198, 10 Digest (Repl) 1042, *7218*.
R v Sinclair [1968] 3 All ER 241, [1968] 1 WLR 1246, 132 JP 527, 52 Cr App Rep 618, CA, Digest (Cont Vol C) 185, *869a*.
R v Willetts (1906) 70 JP 127, 15 Digest (Repl) 1202, *12,210*.
e *R v Williams* [1953] 1 All ER 1068, [1953] 1 QB 660, [1953] 2 WLR 937, 117 JP 251, 37 Cr App Rep 71, CCA, 15 Digest (Repl) 1058, *10,429*.
Welham v Director of Public Prosecutions [1960] 1 All ER 805, [1961] AC 103, [1960] 2 WLR 669, 124 JP 280, 44 Cr App Rep 124, HL, Digest (Cont Vol A) 452, *12,915b*.

Cases also cited
f *Director of Public Prosecutions v Ray* [1973] 3 All ER 131, [1973] 3 WLR 359, HL.
R v Blake (1844) 6 QB 126.
R v Bokenham [1910] The Times, 22nd July.
R v Kylsant [1932] 1 KB 442, CCA.
R v Mitchell [1964] Crim LR 297, CCA.
R v O'Connell (1844) 11 Cl & Fin 155.
g *R v Warburton* (1870) LR 1 CCR 274.
R v Whiteley (1907) 148 CC Ct Cas 267.
R v Whittaker [1914] 3 KB 1283, CCA.

Appeal
h Anthony Peter James Scott appealed against his conviction on 23rd October 1973 at the Central Criminal Court before his Honour Judge Hines on two counts (counts 1 and 7) of an indictment containing 36 counts in all. Count 1 charged the appellant with conspiracy to defraud. Count 7 charged him with conspiracy to contravene the provisions of s 21(1)(*a*) of the Copyright Act 1956. After the judge had rejected a submission on behalf of the appellant that count 1 was bad in law the appellant
j pleaded guilty to counts 1 and 7 whereupon the Crown chose not to proceed against him on the other counts with which he was charged. He was sentenced to two years imprisonment on count 1 and one year imprisonment on count 7 to run concurrently. The facts are set out in the judgment of the court.

L J Blom-Cooper QC and *Brian Warner* for the appellant.
Michael Worsley and *Christopher Hilliard* for the Crown.

20th December. At the conclusion of argument the court dismissed the appeal and   *a*
stated that it would give its reasons for doing so at a later date.

29th January. **ROSKILL LJ.** The reasons for judgment of the court which I am
about to read have been agreed by Michael Davies J, who is unable to be here today.
In October 1973 at the Central Criminal Court before his Honour Judge Hines the
appellant Anthony Scott and nine others were arraigned on an indictment which   *b*
contained 36 counts. The appellant pleaded not guilty to all the counts with which
he was charged. During the long opening of the case for the prosecution counsel for
the appellant informed the judge that the appellant was prepared to admit certain
facts alleged by the Crown. Those facts were that the appellant had agreed with
employees of cinema owners that in return for payment those employees would,
without their employers' consent, temporarily abstract cinematograph films for the   *c*
purpose of enabling the appellant to make and distribute copies of the films on a
commercial basis, such abstraction, copying and distribution being made without the
knowledge and consent of the owners of the copyright in or distribution rights of
such films. Counsel invited the judge to hear submissions that, on the basis of those
admitted facts, count 1 of the indictment was bad in law. Count 1 alleged a conspiracy to defraud. The particulars of the offence were that the appellant and others—   *d*

> 'conspired together and with other persons unknown to defraud such com-
> panies and persons as might be caused loss by the unlawful copying and distri-
> bution of films the copyright in which and the distribution rights of which
> belonged to companies and persons other than the said persons so conspiring
> and by divers subtle, crafty and fraudulent means and devices.'   *e*

It was clear that if counsel's submissions failed the appellant would on the admitted
facts have no defence to count 1 and would, reasonably, have no option but to plead
guilty to that count. It was further indicated that the appellant would in that event
also be prepared to plead guilty to count 7. That count alleged conspiracy by the
appellant and his two co-accused to contravene the provisions of the Copyright Act
1956, s 21(1)(a), the particulars of the offence being that they—   *f*

> 'conspired together and with other persons unlawfully to make for sale or
> hire films which they knew to be infringing copies of works in which copyright
> then existed.'

Although the several offences created by s 21 of the 1956 Act are summary offences
carrying comparatively minor penalties prescribed by sub-ss (7) and (8) of that   *g*
section, it was not contended in relation to count 7—nor could it be contended
successfully—that an agreement between two or more persons to commit such
summary offences or any of them could not constitute a criminal conspiracy.
    The submission of counsel for the appellant in relation to count 1 was and is that
the offences charged did not include any ingredient of deceit, of intent to deceive or
of an agreement to deceive the persons and companies allegedly defrauded, and   *h*
that in the absence of that ingedient in the charge, and in the absence of evidence
supporting that ingredient, the count was bad in law. The judge heard, as this court
has heard, the careful and detailed argument of counsel. But he overruled the
submission. The appellant then changed his pleas to 'guilty' on counts 1 and 7.
The Crown were content not to proceed further on the other counts with which the
appellant was charged. The conviction of the appellant on his own confession in   *j*
these circumstances in no way prejudices his right of appeal against conviction
because the appellant's argument involves a question of law, namely, that on the
admitted facts no charge of conspiracy to defraud properly lay.
    There is no need to recite in this judgment the detailed facts which gave rise to the
charges. It is frankly admitted on behalf of the appellant that his conduct was

a dishonest and involved the deliberate and planned pirating of copyright. It is argued
that for such conduct the law provides remedies both civil and criminal without
resorting to the criminal offence of conspiracy to defraud. There exist the usual civil
remedies for infringement of copyright. There exist the appropriate criminal
remedies under s 21 of the 1956 Act. Therefore there is no necessity to seek another
remedy. Further it is wrong to resort to the common law offence of conspiring to
b defraud to meet a situation for which the law already provides sufficient remedies.
On the facts admitted the appellant was clearly guilty of an offence against s 21(1)(a)
of a misdemeanour. Section 84 provided that any director who 'with intent to deceive
spiracy to defraud as the remedy for his actions. The argument for the appellant is
that the Crown, by resorting to a charge of conspiracy to defraud, is seeking to
enlarge the law relating to conspiracy to defraud by applying it to circumstances
c for which statutory provisions are already made.

The foundation of counsel's argument is the well-known passage in the judgment
of Buckley J in *Re London and Globe Finance Corpn Ltd*[1]. It is well to bear in mind the
background to that decision. The company, of which Mr Whittaker Wright had
been managing director, was in liquidation. The Official Receiver was appointed
provisional liquidator. As the result of the public examination of Mr Wright, criminal
d proceedings were contemplated but the Director of Public Prosecutions, on advice
from the then law officers of the Crown, declined to prosecute. A member of the
committee of inspection then took out a summons for an order that the Official
Receiver be directed to take proceedings, the costs of proceedings to be paid out of
the assets of the company. The summons was opposed by one substantial creditor.
It was suggested that proceedings might be taken under ss 83 and 84 of the Larceny
e Act 1861 and under s 166 of the Companies Act 1862. Section 83 provided that any
director who 'with intent to defraud', inter alia, made or concurred in the making of
any false entry in any book of any body corporate or public company should be guilty
of a misdemeanor. Section 84 provided that any director who 'with intent to deceive
or defraud', inter alia, made any written statement or account which he knew to be
false in any material particular should be guilty of a misdemeanour. It is important to
f observe at this juncture that, in the group of sections numbered 80 to 84 in the Larceny
Act 1861, it is only in s 84 that the concept of deception or deceit appears. Sections 80,
82 and 83 speak of 'intent to defraud'. Section 81 speaks of 'fraudulently'. Section 84
alone speaks of 'intent to deceive or defraud'.

Buckley J said[2]:

g 'In both ss. 83 and 84 of the Larceny Act of 1861 . . . the offence is that making of
or publishing a false statement or account, or a false or fraudulent entry with
intent to deceive or defraud.'

Pausing there, that sentence does not distinguish between the ingedients of the two
sections, 'intent to defraud' in s 83 and 'intent to deceive or defraud' in s 84. Then
h follows the passage relied on in the present case[1]:

'To deceive is, I apprehend, to induce a man to believe that a thing is true which
is false, and which the person practising the deceit knows or believes to be false.
To defraud is to deprive by deceit: it is by deceit to induce a man to act to his
injury. More tersely it may be put, that to deceive is by falsehood to induce a
j state of mind; to defraud is by deceit to induce a course of action.'

This passage, it is said, has often been approved and is an exhaustive definition of
both 'to deceive' and 'to defraud'. It is argued that the language used shows that at

1 [1903] 1 Ch 728 at 732, 733, [1900-3] All ER Rep 891 at 893
2 [1903] 1 Ch at 732, [1900-3] All ER Rep at 893

common law there cannot be an intent to defraud without also the essential element of deceit. The words 'to defraud is by deceit to induce' demonstrate that defrauding is the consequence of deceit, and that deceit is a prerequisite of defrauding. Counsel conceded, or went far towards conceding, that in relation to certain offences created by statute 'fraud' and 'to defraud' have been used as synonymous with 'dishonesty' and 'to induce a result by dishonesty'. This is said to be explicable on the basis that the element of mens rea in the statutory offence is satisfied if the actus reus is accompanied by dishonest intention. But, it is argued, whatever may be the position in relation to statutory offences, at common law there cannot be an intent to defraud without also an intent to deceive and there cannot be an agreement to defraud without also an agreement to deceive.

Support for this argument was sought by counsel for the appellant in the speeches in the House of Lords in *Welham v Director of Public Prosecutions*[1]. He argued that in that case the House of Lords expressly approved of the passage in the judgment of Buckley J[2]. Lord Radcliffe[3] cited a number of cases in which the passage had been approved in the Court of Criminal Appeal. Lord Denning[4] said the passage was one from which 'much valuable guidance is to be obtained'. Counsel pointed out, rightly as we think, that the decision in *Welham's* case[1] was as to the meaning of the words 'intent to defraud' in s 4(1) of the Forgery Act 1913, and that their Lordships were not concerned with the meaning of those words in relation to the common law offence of conspiracy to defraud.

It is to be observed however that Lord Radcliffe[5] declined to accept either the submission for the appellant or for the Crown as to the meaning of Buckley J's statement[2]. He pointed out that the question the learned judge was deciding was whether to sanction the prosecution of Mr Wright under ss 83 and 84 of the Larceny Act 1861 at the expense of the company's funds, and that the passage was obiter. Lord Radcliffe made it plain that he did not consider the passage to contain 'an exhaustive account of the legal significance of deceit and fraud'. There is no suggestion in the speech of Lord Denning that he regarded the statement of Buckley J as an exhaustive definition.

In the present appeal counsel for the Crown invited our attention to the report of the argument of Mr John Buzzard, following the Solicitor General for the Crown in *Welham's* case[1]. Counsel said[6]:

'There is one element of Buckley J.'s definition of "intent to defraud" which is wrong, and which could cause confusion . . . if acted upon. Plainly, "to deceive is . . . to induce a man to believe that a thing is true which is false . . .," but deceit is not an essential element of fraud, for one can defraud without the use of deceit: see section 80 of the Larceny Act, 1861. Conversion of trust property with intent to defraud, which is the subject of that section, is quite inconsistent with Buckley J.'s definition, because a person converting property to his own use and benefit does not intend by deceit to induce another to act or refrain from acting; he simply pockets, for example, the funds in question.'

This criticism of the statement of Buckley J is highly relevant to the present issue. Counsel for the Crown carried the argument a stage further by pointing out that Mr Buzzard could have supported his argument with a reference to s 81 of the 1861 Act. He added that a person who with intent to defraud destroys documents contrary to

---

1   [1960] 1 All ER 805, [1961] AC 103
2   [1903] 1 Ch at 732 [1900-3] All ER Rep at 893
3   [1960] 1 All ER at 810, 811, [1961] AC at 127, 128
4   [1960] 1 All ER at 814, [1961] AC at 131
5   [1960] 1 All ER at 809, 810, [1961] AC at 125, 126
6   [1961] AC at 118, 119

a s 83 might well do so without any intent to deceive. It appears that a somewhat similar argument had been advanced by Mr Buzzard in *R v Williams*[1].

Their Lordships in *Welham's* case[2] did not deal with Mr Buzzard's argument, no doubt for the reason that in considering the meaning of the words in the Forgery Act 1913, s 4(1), the matter did not arise for decision. But the argument was certainly not rejected for it was expressly stated that the statement in question was not
b exhaustive.

We were also referred to *R v Sinclair*[3]. The charge there was of conspiracy to cheat and defraud a company, its shareholders and creditors by fraudulent use of the company's assets and fraudulent concealment of such use. The trial judge directed the jury that in order to prove fraud the prosecution has to show that the conduct was 'deliberately dishonest'. This court, in a reserved judgment, upheld that direc-
c tion. In that case it was not suggested that in order to prove the offence charged, the prosecution had to prove an intent to deceive or an agreement to deceive the shareholders and creditors of the company.

Counsel for the appellant sought to distinguish the present case from *R v Sinclair*[3] which, he argued, involved an 'inbuilt' element of deception by the directors of the shareholders and creditors to whom the directors owed a duty in relation to the use
d of the company's assets; the very acts complained of were both dishonest and deceitful; therefore the question whether 'deceit' was a prerequisite of 'to defraud' did not arise in that case. We are unable to accept the argument that *Sinclair*[3] can be distinguished on that ground. If the ingredient of 'agreement to deceive' is always an essential ingredient of 'agreement to defraud' the jury in *Sinclair*[3] ought to have been so directed and the judgment of this court, in that case delivered by James J,
e would not and indeed ought not to have been phrased as it was. The highest counsel for the appellant can legitimately put his submission is that *Sinclair*[3] is not against his present argument because that argument was not there advanced and therefore was not considered by this court. Nonetheless the statement in the judgment of James J[4] 'To cheat and defraud is to act with deliberate dishonesty to the prejudice of another person's proprietary right' is contrary to counsel's argument. We can
f decline to follow that statement only if we are satisfied in the light of the present argument that had it been advanced in *Sinclair*[3], that part of the judgment at least would have been differently expressed. We are not so satisfied.

Counsel for the Crown invited our attention to a number of cases in which conspiracy to defraud had been charged in relation to the pirating of musical and other copyrights. It is no discourtesy to his detailed argument that we do not refer to all
g the authorities he cited. The point in issue, as both he and counsel for the appellant agreed, albeit important, is short. The most interesting of the cases cited by counsel for the Crown is *R v Willetts*[5]. In that case an argument akin to that of counsel for the appellant appears to have been advanced—apparently unsuccessfully. But the short point in the present case is whether the passage in the judgment of Buckley J[6] is to be treated as an exhaustive definition of 'to defraud'. If it is, then there can be
h no common law conspiracy to defraud unless it is alleged and proved that there was an intention to deceive which resulted in the victim being defrauded. We do not say anything in derogation of the help and guidance which, as has been said in earlier cases, is to be derived from that passage. But it must be understood in the context in which it appears and in the light of the question for decision in that case. We venture to think that no one would be more surprised than Buckley J if it had
j been suggested to him that, 70 years hence, his words would be construed as an

1 [1953] 1 QB 660 at 662
2 [1960] 1 All ER 805, [1961] AC 103
3 [1968] 3 All ER 241, [1968] 1 WLR 1246
4 [1968] 3 All ER at 246, [1968] 1 WLR at 1250
5 (1906) 70 JP 127
6 [1903] 1 Ch at 732, 733, [1900-3] All ER Rep at 893

exhaustive definition of 'to defraud' in relation to the common law offence of *a*
conspiracy to defraud.

In our judgment neither principle nor authority drives us to the conclusion that
the common law offence of conspiracy to defraud is limited to an agreement between
two or more persons to deceive the intended victim and by such deceit to defraud
him. We find no reason to depart from what was said in *R v Sinclair*[1]. Conspiracy to
defraud may involve, but does not necessarily involve, an agreement to defraud by *b*
deceit. This is, with respect to the argument of counsel, the short answer to the
question raised by this appeal. It was for this reason that we dismissed the appeal
against conviction.

*Appeal dismissed. Leave to appeal to the House of Lords granted, the court certifying
that the following point of law of general public importance was involved: 'Whether, on a
charge of conspiracy to defraud, the Crown must establish an agreement to deprive the* *c*
*owners of their property by deception; or whether it is sufficient to prove an agreement to
prejudice the rights of another or others without lawful justification and in circumstances
of dishonesty?'*

Solicitors: *Registrar of Criminal Appeals* (for the appellant); *Solicitor, Metropolitan
Police.* *d*

A S Virdi Esq   Barrister.

Practice Direction

e

CHANCERY DIVISION

*Practice – Chambers – Chancery Division– Applications – Powers of principal clerks – Ex
parte applications – RSC Ord 12, r 7 – RSC Ord 15, r 7 – RSC Ord 48, r 1 – RSC Ord 49,
rr 1, 2 – RSC Ord 65, r 4.*

1. It has been decided that the principal clerks in Chancery chambers, of the grade *f*
of principal and senior executive officer, may assist the masters in the making of the
following orders on ex parte application: (a) for leave to enter conditional appearance
(RSC Ord 12, r 7), (b) to carry on proceedings (Ord 15, r 7), (c) for examination of
judgment debtors (Ord 48, r 1), (d) garnishee orders nisi (Ord 49, rr 1 and 2) and
(e) for substituted service within the jurisdiction, by post only (Ord 65, r 4).

2. The evidence in support of any such application will be lodged with the master's *g*
summons clerk and normally considered by his principal clerk, who will deal provisionally with the application. The master will initial the draft or note of any such
order (or, in the case of leave to enter conditional appearance, sign the appropriate
fiat) before the order takes effect.

3. Principal clerks may also, without reference to the master: (a) give leave to file
affidavits notwithstanding any irregularity in their form, (b) sign fiats to amend *h*
when a judge or master has already authorised the amendment and (c) sign certificates
of attendances in chambers for the purpose of taxation of costs.

4. Any applicant dissatisfied with a principal clerk's refusal of an order, leave, fiat
or certificate or with the terms thereof may apply ex parte to the master, who will
consider the matter afresh.

5. Nothing shall prevent a master from dealing in the first instance with any of the *j*
matters listed above if it is more convenient for him to do so.

By the direction of the Vice-Chancellor.

R E BALL
Chief Master

3rd April 1974

---

1   [1968] 3 All ER 241, [1968] 1 WLR 1246

R v Jackson (Alan Victor)

COURT OF APPEAL, CRIMINAL DIVISION
SCARMAN LJ, THESIGER AND BRISTOW JJ
22nd, 28th JANUARY 1974

Applied in R v WEHNER [1977]
3 All ER 553

Criminal law – Incorrigible rogue – Sentence – Probation – Committal to Crown Court – Power of Crown Court – Power of court by or before which person convicted of offence to make probation order – Whether Crown Court having power to make probation order in respect of person committed as incorrigible rogue – Vagrancy Act 1824, ss 5, 10 (as amended by the Courts Act 1971, s 56(1), Sch 8, para 5) – Criminal Justice Act 1948, s 3(1).

Where a person, on conviction of an offence by justices, is deemed to be an incorrigible rogue and is accordingly committed to the Crown Court under s 5[a] of the Vagrancy Act 1824, that court has no power under s 3(1)[b] of the Criminal Justice Act 1948 to make a probation order, instead of ordering a term of imprisonment under s 10[c] of the 1824 Act, since the Crown Court is not, within s 3(1), the 'court by or before which [that] person is convicted of an offence' (see p 212 j to p 213 c and f and p 214 b, post).

R v Thomas Evans [1915] 2 KB 762 and *R v Walters* [1968] 3 All ER 863 applied.

Notes

For incorrigible rogues, see 10 Halsbury's Laws (3rd Edn) 701, 702, paras 1341, 1342, and for cases on the subject, see 14 Digest (Repl) 142, 143, *1060-1062*, and 15 Digest (Repl) 929, 8896.

For the Vagrancy Act 1824, ss 5, 10, see 8 Halsbury's Statutes (3rd Edn) 75, 77.

For the Criminal Justice Act 1948, s 3, see ibid 339.

For the Courts Act 1971, s 56, Sch 8, para 5, see 41 Halsbury's Statutes (3rd Edn) 320, 343.

Cases referred to in judgment

R v Thomas Evans [1915] 2 KB 762, 84 LJKB 1603, 113 LT 508, 79 JP 415, 25 Cox CC 72, 11 Cr App Rep 178, CCA, 14 Digest (Repl) 142, *1061*.

R v Walters [1968] 3 All ER 863, [1969] 1 QB 255, [1968] 3 WLR 987, 133 JP 73, 53 Cr App Rep 9, CA, Digest (Cont Vol C) 187, *1062a*.

Appeal

On 30th March 1973 in the Crown Court at Maidstone the appellant, Alan Victor Jackson, having been convicted before justices on three charges of indecent exposure, and committed to the court as an incorrigible rogue pursuant to s 5 of the Vagrancy Act 1824, was put on probation for three years. On 14th May 1973 the appellant pleaded guilty at Sheerness Magistrates' Court to an offence of indecent assault and was committed under s 29 of the Magistrates' Court Act 1952 to the Crown Court at Maidstone for sentence, where, on 14th September 1973, he was sentenced by his Honour Judge Gower QC to nine months imprisonment, and to a further consecutive sentence of nine months imprisonment in respect of the breach of the probation order made on 30th March 1973. He appealed against that sentence

---

a   Section 5, as amended and so far as material, provides: ' . . . every person committing any offence against this Act which shall subject him or her to be dealt with as a rogue and vagabond, such person having been at some former time adjudged so to be, and duly convicted thereof . . . shall be deemed an incorrigible rogue within the true intent and meaning of this Act; and it shall be lawful for any justice of the peace to commit such offender (being thereof convicted before him . . .) to the Crown Court . . .'

b   Section 3(1), so far as material, is set out at p 212 *j*, post

c   Section 10, as amended and so far as material, is set out at p 212 *g*, post

(especially that relating to the breach of the probation order) with leave of the single *a*
judge. The matter first came before the court on 22nd January 1974 when the court
gave the appellant leave to appeal out of time against the probation order made on
30th March 1973 and adjourned the hearing of the appeal against sentence. The
hearing of both appeals came before the court (similarly constituted) on 28th January
1974. The facts are set out in the judgment of the court.
                                                                                        b
David C Humphreys for the appellant.
Michael Lewer for the Crown.

SCARMAN LJ delivered the following judgment of the court. On 14th September
1973 at Maidstone Crown Court the appellant was sentenced to nine months im- *c*
prisonment for an offence of indecent assault to which he had pleaded guilty. He
was in breach of a probation order and for that breach he was sentenced to a further
nine months imprisonment consecutive on the term imposed in respect of the
indecent assault. He appealed against the total sentence of 18 months imprisonment
to the full court, with the leave of the single judge. The appeal came before the full
court on 22nd January 1974 and in the course of the hearing it became evident to *d*
the court that it was possible to argue that the probation order in respect of which
it was said he was in breach ought never to have been made.
    In order that one may understand the point that arises on the application it is
necessary to go a little into the past history. On 28th June 1972 he was dealt with by
justices acting pursuant to their powers contained in the Vagrancy Act 1824. He was
found to have committed one of the offences specified in s 4 of the Act; convicted *e*
of that offence, he was deemed to be a rogue and vagabond within the true intent
and meaning of the Act. In 1973 he committed another offence, an offence also
specified in the 1824 Act; being convicted on 5th February of that offence, he was
deemed an incorrigible rogue pursuant to s 5 of the Act and committed by the
justices to the Crown Court for sentence. On 30th March 1973 the Crown Court
made a probation order.   *f*
    When a person is deemed an incorrigible rogue within the intent and meaning
of the Act, s 5 provides that it shall be lawful for any justice of the peace to commit
such an offender to quarter sessions (now the Crown Court). The Crown Court's
jurisdiction is to be found in s 10 of the 1824 Act which reads as follows:

> 'When any incorrigible rogue shall have been committed to the Crown Court, *g*
> it shall be lawful for the Crown Court to examine into the circumstances of the
> case, and to order, if they think fit, that such offender be . . . imprisoned . . . for
> any time not exceeding one year from the time of making such order . . .'

The question we have to decide is whether the Crown Court has the power to make
any order other than a term of imprisonment.
    The jurisdiction of a court to make a probation order is to be found in s 3 of the *h*
Criminal Justice Act 1948, a section reproduced in the Powers of the Criminal Courts
Act 1973, s 2. Since the 1973 Act, though enacted, has not yet been brought into
force, I will read the section as it appears in the 1948 Act. Section 3(1), so far as is
relevant to the point now under consideration, provides as follows:

> 'Where a court by or before which a person is convicted of an offence . . . is *j*
> of opinion that having regard to the circumstances, including the nature of the
> offence and the character of the offender, it is expedient to do so, the court may,
> instead of sentencing him, make a probation order . . .'

The question arises whether the Crown Court, when on 30th March it made the
probation order, was in fact a court by or before which the appellant had been

convicted of an offence. If it were not, then it had no power to make the probation order. One is, therefore, obliged to return to a consideration of the Vagrancy Act 1824. It is clear that the Crown Court, acting pursuant to s 10 of the 1824 Act, did not convict the offender. The conviction had been effected by the justices, who, acting pursuant to s 5 of the 1824 Act, deemed him to be an incorrigible rogue and committed him to the Crown Court for sentence. Thus it was already established, before the offender reached the Crown Court, that he was an incorrigible rogue. All that the Crown Court had power to do was to examine the circumstances of the case; and to order, if they thought fit, a term of imprisonment.

This general view of the 1824 Act is one that is supported by authority and I would refer to two cases to which we have had our attention drawn in the course of argument. The first is *R v Evans*[1]. That case shows that the offence which makes a man an incorrigible rogue has to be established before and by the justices. If for any reason they have not done so it is not open to quarter sessions, or now the Crown Court, to make a finding that the offender is an incorrigible rogue. Thus *R v Evans*[1] shows that conviction and the deeming of the man to be an incorrigible rogue are matters which occur, and can only occur, in the magistrates' court.

The other case is *R v Walters*[2]. That was a case in which quarter sessions purported to pass two sentences, each of nine months, consecutively in respect of the two offences which led to the man being deemed an incorrigible rogue. The Court of Appeal allowed the appeal against the order of quarter sessions and I quote the headnote[3]:

> 'Held ... that the defendant's committal to quarter sessions under section 5 was as an incorrigible rogue, which he was deemed to be as a result of the two offences, and it was for that state, and not for the two offences, for which the sentence under section 10 was to be imposed; and that, accordingly, quarter sessions had power to impose a single sentence only, for a maximum of 12 months ...'

That being the meaning, as this court understands it, of the relevant provision of the 1824 Act, namely, that a man is established as an incorrigible rogue in the course of the proceedings before the justices, it is clear that, unless there be some statutory modification of the words of s 3(1) of the 1948 Act, the Crown Court has no power to make a probation order; for it is not the court by or before which he was convicted.

This is a difficulty which has been considered in other contexts by the legislature. It has been expressly provided (s 29(3) of the Criminal Justice Act 1948) that quarter sessions, and now the Crown Court, should have all the powers for dealing with an offender committed for sentence as they would have, had he been convicted before them.

More directly, Parliament has considered the matter in relation to the 1824 Act. Section 67(5) of the Mental Health Act 1959 provides that the power of the court of quarter sessions to make a hospital order in the case of a person convicted by that court of an offence may in the like circumstances and subject to the like conditions be exercised by such a court in the case of a person committed to the court under s 5 of the Vagrancy Act 1824.

Thus it is possible to say that Parliament has become aware since 1824, if it were not aware of it in 1824, that the powers of quarter sessions to deal with an incorrigible rogue are limited to the powers set out in s 10 of the 1824 Act and that, if it be desired to widen those powers, express statutory provision is needed. Parliament clearly thought it was needed in matters of mental health and made provision in s 67(5)

---

1 [1915] 2 KB 762
2 [1968] 3 All ER 863, [1969] 1 QB 255
3 [1969] 1 QB at 255

of the 1959 Act. Furthermore when in 1948 Parliament had to consider how to handle the problem of committal from magistrates' courts to quarter sessions for the purpose of sentence, care was taken to ensure that the words 'by or before the court which convicted of the offence' in s 3 were to be interpreted as including, in that particular case, quarter sessions to whom the offender was committed.

With those considerations in mind this court thinks it cannot do other than to say that the words of s 3 mean precisely what they say; that, when an incorrigible rogue is committed by justices to the Crown Court, the Crown Court is not the convicting court, it is the sentencing court only, and that it has no power to make a probation order. For those reasons the probation order, in our judgment, cannot stand.

That, however, is not the end of the matter. There is still in being the committal of an incorrigible rogue, namely this appellant, to the Crown Court and that committal might be said not to have been dealt with finally now that the probation order has been quashed. In accordance with well accepted principles when an order of the court is quashed this court has power within certain limits to substitute the order that it thinks just.

This takes me back to s 10 of the Vagrancy Act 1824. It may be said that this is a very antique piece of law. So it is, but it contains a very relevant provision to the task that we now have in hand. Quarter sessions (now the Crown Court) are not obliged when an incorrigible rogue is committed by justices to make any order for imprisonment. The section provides that it shall be lawful for them to examine the circumstances of the case and to order, if they think fit, that such offender be imprisoned for a term not exceeding 12 months. First it will be observed that they are to examine the facts of the case. They do so with a view to sentence, not with a view to the establishment of liability; and then they are to order, if they think fit, imprisonment. Thus it would be open, and it is open, to the Crown Court to make no order and it now falls to this court to decide whether no order should be made or, if an order should be made, what order would be appropriate. That leads, by a natural process, to the appeal against sentence.

When one bears in mind that the Court of Appeal under s 11 of the Criminal Appeal Act 1968 has the overall task of looking at the totality of the terms of imprisonment imposed, it seems to the court to be reasonable to have regard to what was done on the other offence in determining what ought to be done on the Vagrancy Act 1824 finding. On the other offence the appellant was sentenced to nine months imprisonment. It has not been suggested to this court that there was anything wrong in principle with that sentence and in our judgment it was a sentence that was correct in principle and fully justified in all the circumstances. Should the appellant also be sentenced to a term of imprisonment because at that time he was an incorrigible rogue in respect of whom a probation order had been made which ought not to have been made?

The view that this court takes is that there was no need at the stage at which this matter came before the Crown Court dealing with the charge of indecent assault to add anything to the term of imprisonment—whether it be thought of as something added because there had been a breach of a probation order or whether it be thought of as something to be imposed because he was an incorrigible rogue.

In our judgment, and I need not go into any detail, nine months was a term which was fully justified and if anything further was to be done by way of imprisonment it should have been done concurrently. In our view there was no need to have visited this incorrigible rogue in the circumstances with a term of imprisonment additional to that of nine months. Of course the Crown Court believed it was faced with a breach of a probation order. We, on our view of the law, have found that there was no lawful probation order in being, but that he was in fact an incorrigible rogue who had not been effectively dealt with. Accordingly, insofar as sentence is concerned, we do not think that justice requires us to impose any penalty in respect of the finding that he was an incorrigible rogue. There was clearly under the statute a discretion whether *a* to impose any imprisonment, and we think that had the matter been properly before the Crown Court it would have been wrong in principle to have imposed any penalty in the circumstances of this case.

We are aware that the 1824 Act, even though it is antiquated law not fitted to the modern apparatus of the administration of criminal justice, is nevertheless often used by the police, who find it a very useful statute to deal with certain circumstances

b frequently arising particularly in our industrialised urban centres, but this really is in our view no reason for continuing on the statute book in its present form a statute so out of touch with modern developments in the administration of the criminal law and we express the hope that a look will be taken at this Act so that a modern version more attune with present methods may be evolved and passed into law.

Finally one may express the hope that such picturesque phrases as 'rogue' and 'vagabond' and 'incorrigible rogue' pass right out of the vocabulary of current law.

c Look at the ridiculous situation in this case. How can one, as a matter of grammatical logic, make a probation order which assumes the possibility of rehabilitation in respect of a man who by statute is deemed incorrigible. That verbal infelicity is enough to indicate an urgent need for rewriting the 1824 Act. Moreover it is obvious that the sort of petty offender who finds himself in front of justices and deemed to be, because of his record, an incorrigible rogue is, in fact, just the sort of person who

d may be prevented from lapsing into a career of crime by the well-timed intervention of a probation officer. The ancient and out-of-date law prevents that happening unless, as I understand it, justices can somehow or other manoeuvre the proceedings before them into a situation in which they can avail themselves of s 56 of the Criminal Justice Act 1967.

I say no more of s 56. The magistrates' courts did not act under this section and it is

e not always applicable: there are bound to be many cases in which a man is deemed to be an incorrigible rogue to which it would be quite impossible to apply s 56 of the 1967 Act.

For those reasons, we decide as follows. The appellant is given leave out of time to appeal against the making of the probation order of 30th March 1973, the

f appeal succeeds and the probation order is quashed. On the appeal against sentence this court takes the view that justice does not require the imposition of any penalty under the Vagrancy Act 1824.

The result, therefore, will be as follows. The sentence of nine months imprisonment, which has already been served, in respect of the indecent assault stands, but that is the only sentence of the court that does stand. The probation order is quashed

g and no other order is made in its place.

Appeal against probation order allowed.   Appeal against sentence allowed in part; sentence varied.

Solicitors: *Winch, Greensted & Winch*, Sittingbourne, Kent (for the appellant); *A C*
h *Staples*, Maidstone (for the Crown).

N P Metcalfe Esq   Barrister.

Hammertons Cars Ltd v London Borough of Redbridge

QUEEN'S BENCH DIVISION

LORD WIDGERY CJ, BOREHAM AND MAY JJ

4th FEBRUARY 1974

Criminal law – Compensation – Loss or damage resulting from offence – Costs incurred in civil proceedings against accused – Civil proceedings taken by victim in respect of matters constituting offence – Victim not recovering costs of civil proceedings – Whether victim entitled to compensation in respect of costs following conviction of accused – Criminal Justice Act 1972, s 1(1).

Car dealers sold a car to U. They described the car as being in 'perfect condition' and made certain other representations about it. Those representations were false and U brought a civil action against the dealers. That action was settled to U's satisfaction but U was left to pay his own legal costs of £170 and a fee of £25 for an engineer's inspection of the car. Three informations were preferred against the dealers in consequence of the sale. The first alleged that the dealers had applied a false trade description 'perfect condition' to the car, contrary to s 1(1)(a) of the Trade Descriptions Act 1968. The second and third also alleged offences against s 1(1)(a) and (b) of the 1968 Act. The dealers pleaded guilty and were fined. Following the imposition of the fines U applied for compensation. The justices considered that U had been left with a loss of £195 incurred in the civil proceedings in consequence of the offence referred to in the first information. Accordingly, they made an order under s 1(1)[a] of the Criminal Justice Act 1972 requiring the dealers to pay U £195. The dealers appealed against that order.

Held – If a victim brought civil proceedings, and those proceedings were brought to an end, they should be regarded as quite independent of the criminal proceedings and no compensation order should be made in the criminal proceedings in respect of liabilities which arose, or might have arisen, in the civil proceedings. Accordingly the appeal would be allowed and the compensation order quashed (see p 219 *a* to *d*, post).

Quaere. Whether an obligation to pay costs in independent civil proceedings can ever come within the phrase 'loss or damage resulting from [the] offence' in s 1(1) of the 1972 Act (see p 218 *j*, post).

Notes

For compensation orders, see Supplement to 10 Halsbury's Laws (3rd Edn) para 1020B.

For the Trade Descriptions Act 1968, s 1, see 37 Halsbury's Statutes (3rd Edn) 949.

For the Criminal Justice Act 1972, s 1, see 42 Halsbury's Statutes (3rd Edn) 102.

Case cited

R v Daly [1974] 1 All ER 290, [1974] 1 WLR 133, CA.

---

a Section 1(1), so far as material, provides: 'Subject to the provisions of this Part of this Act, a court by or before which a person is convicted of an offence, in addition to dealing with him in any other way, may, on application or otherwise, make an order (in this Act referred to as " a compensation order") requiring him to pay compensation for any . . . loss or damage resulting from that offence or any other offence which is taken into consideration by the court in determining sentence.'

Case stated

a

This was an appeal by way of a case stated by justices for the North-East London Area, acting in and for the petty sessional division of Beacontree, in respect of their adjudication as a magistrates' court sitting at Stratford, London, on 25th July 1973.

On 23rd May 1973 three informations were preferred by the first respondent, the London Borough of Redbridge, against the appellants, Hammertons Cars Ltd,

b

that they (i) at 330 Eastern Avenue, Ilford, in the London Borough of Redbridge, on 27th January 1973 in the course of a trade or business did apply a false trade description 'perfect condition' to certain goods, namely a Daimler Sovereign motor car, registration mark UTL 856K, contrary to s 1(1)(a) of the Trade Descriptions Act 1968; (ii) at 330 Eastern Avenue, Ilford, in the London Borough of Redbridge, on 27th January 1973 in the course of a trade or business did apply a false trade description

c

to the effect that certain goods, namely a Daimler Sovereign motor car, registration mark UTL 856K, had sustained only slight damage to the front wing, contrary to s 1(1)(a) of the Trade Descriptions Act 1968; and (iii) at 330 Eastern Avenue, Ilford, in the London Borough of Redbridge, on 27th January 1973 in the course of a trade or business did supply certain goods, namely a Daimler Sovereign motor car, registration mark UTL 856K, to which a false trade description had been applied as

d

to its fitness for purpose, by means of major structural alterations to the motor car subsequent to its having sustained extensive impact damage, contrary to s 1(1)(b) or the Trade Descriptions Act 1968.

The appellants pleaded guilty to each of the three informations. The justices fined the appellants £100 for the offence referred to in the first mentioned information and £25 for each of the other two offences, and ordered the appellants to pay a total of £30 for costs, being £10 in each case.

e

Following the imposition of those sentences the justices entertained an application for compensation by the second respondent, Kenneth Underhill, the purchaser from the appellants of the Daimler Sovereign motor car, registration mark UTL 856K, to which the informations related. Mr Underhill stated that he was seeking compensation of £195 which sum he had lost in consequence of his purchase of the car. In

f

his evidence, he agreed that the appellants had taken back the car and that the sum that he was claiming was in respect of £170 legal costs incurred by his solicitors, Tringhams, of 46 Crawford Street, London, on his behalf in an attempted settlement of a possible civil claim to be brought by Mr Underhill against the appellants, and £25 for an engineer's fee for inspecting the car. There was produced and shown to Mr Underhill a letter dated 12th April 1973 from his solicitors, Tringhams, to

g

solicitors for the appellants, H Montlake & Co, 197 High Road, Ilford, Essex, in which it was said, inter alia:

'We acknowledge receipt of your clients' cheque for £2,800. Once your clients have collected the car from Mrs Underhill and the arrangements are complete for releasing our client from his liability to the finance company, this matter will have reached a satisfactory conclusion.'

h

In evidence Mr Underhill stated:

'My solicitors advised me not to press the costs because it could take up to eighteen months and one has got to accept the advice of one's solicitors so I agreed that we should not claim costs.'

j

It was contended by counsel for the appellants that letter of 12th April 1973, coupled with the evidence of Mr Underhill, showed that there had been accord and satisfaction in respect of the proposed civil claim to be brought by Mr Underhill against the appellants and that accordingly it would be wrong in law and in fact to award compensation.

Apart from Mr Underhill's claim for £195 compensation no contentions were made by either respondent, and the justices were not referred to reported cases.

The justices were of opinion that the sum of £195 was an expense properly
incurred by Mr Underhill in connection with his civil claim and although, to avoid
delay, he had made no claim for costs, it was their view that he had nevertheless been
left with a loss of £195 resulting from the offence referred to in the first mentioned
information. They accordingly made a compensation order under s 1 of the
Criminal Justice Act 1972 requiring the appellants to pay Mr Underhill the sum of
£195, the compensation to be paid in 21 days.

Richard Rains for the appellants.
Mr Underhill appeared in person.
The London Borough of Redbridge did not appear and were not represented.

LORD WIDGERY CJ. This is an appeal by case stated by justices for the North-
East London Area sitting at Beacontree on 25th July 1973. On that occasion they had
before them three informations laid by the London Borough of Redbridge against
the appellants, alleging that the appellants had committed three offences under the
Trade Descriptions Act 1968; in particular, that they had applied three false trade
descriptions to a Daimler Sovereign motor car which was sold at about this time
by the appellants to Mr Underhill, the second respondent.

The appellants pleaded guilty. They were fined for the offences. Then the question
was raised whether a compensation order should not also be made under s 1(1) of
the Criminal Justice Act 1972.

Mr Underhill, who has appeared in court today, tells us that he has incurred a
great deal of expense arising out of buying this defective car, and one can well understand that this might be so. But the particular order requested of the justices was
in the amount of £195, which was money said by Mr Underhill to have been lost
in the following circumstances.

In parallel as it were, or slightly in advance of the proceedings before the justices,
civil proceedings had been instituted by Mr Underhill against the appellants. Those
civil proceedings were eventually settled. We are not given the full details of settlement in the case stated, but that they were settled is perfectly clear. The settlement
did not involve the appellants paying Mr Underhill's costs in the civil proceedings
and it did not involve the appellants paying for an inspection fee of an expert, which
I think was another £25, although the civil proceedings were settled, one must
assume, to Mr Underhill's satisfaction. No application for his costs had been made in
those proceedings and the justices find that Mr Underhill himself knew he was not
going to get any costs because he had been advised by his solicitors not to press for
them because it would take up to 18 months. So it seemed he took his solicitors'
advice and regarded the civil proceedings as concluded, although in fact they contained
no provision for payment of costs to him.

Then the justices were invited to make a compensation order under s 1 of the 1972
Act in the sum of £195 and did so, thinking that the costs in the civil proceedings
could properly be described as loss or damage resulting from the offence under the
Trade Descriptions Act 1968.

As I have had occasion to say more than once in the last few weeks, the Trade
Descriptions Act 1968 is still a relatively new statute and there is a great deal to learn
about it. The Criminal Justice Act 1972 is even newer and there is a great deal which
we shall have to learn about the practice affecting compensation orders under Part I.

But I am quite clear that the justices were wrong in making this order in favour
of Mr Underhill. It may be, although I do not think it is necessary to decide this
today, that the phrase 'loss or damage resulting from [the] offence' is quite inappropriate to cover a liability for costs in civil proceedings independent of the criminal
proceedings in which the compensation order is made. I would like to hear it argued
another day whether an obligation to pay costs in independent civil proceedings
can ever come within the phrase 'loss or damage resulting from [the] offence'. Also

a it may have one day to be considered whether the loss, if loss it be, is not too remote. But I think the principle on which the present case should be determined is this. It seems to me to be abundantly clear that if the victim brings civil proceedings, and those civil proceedings are brought to an end, then they should be regarded as quite independent of the criminal proceedings and no compensation order should be made in the criminal proceedings in respect of liabilities which arose, or might *b* have arisen, in the civil proceedings. As I said in argument, if in the civil proceedings the judge had been asked to make an order for costs and had refused, it would be almost ludicrous to suggest that the dissatisfied party could come to the justices and get them to countermand the High Court judge's order in the civil case. That of course is an extreme example, but I think the principle applies here, and I do not, therefore, think the justices should make compensation orders in respect of obligations *c* arising out of civil proceedings which have themselves been determined, as were these.

Accordingly I would allow this appeal and quash the compensation order.

BOREHAM J. I agree.

MAY J. I also agree.

d *Appeal allowed. Compensation order set aside.*

Solicitors: *H Montlake & Co*, Ilford (for the appellants).

N P Metcalfe Esq Barrister.

e

Re Cement Makers' Federation's Agreement (No 2)

f
RESTRICTIVE PRACTICES COURT
MOCATTA P, MR P A DELAFIELD, MR W R BOOTH AND MR N L SALMON
29th, 30th, 31st OCTOBER, 1st, 2nd, 5th NOVEMBER 1973, 14th JANUARY 1974

g *Restrictive trade practices – Application – Variation of decision of court – Leave to make application – Leave granted where prima facie evidence of a material change in the relevant circumstances – Meaning of 'relevant circumstances' – Restrictive Trade Practices Act 1956, s 22(4).*

h *Restrictive trade practices – Application – Variation of decision of court – Leave to make application – Leave granted where prima facie evidence of a material change in the relevant circumstances – Evidence – Applicant making submission as to economic consequences of course of action – Applicant not adducing evidence of economist – Whether evidence of economist essential – Restrictive Trade Practices Act 1956, s 22(4).*

j From 1934 onwards the Cement Makers' Federation ('the federation') controlled the price of cement manufactured in the United Kingdom. The arrangements whereby the price was fixed were contained in the federation's 'White Book' ('the agreement'). The price structure was founded on 'basing points' and 'distance zones'. Each cement works, or group of adjacent works, was treated as a 'basing point' and a 'base price' was fixed for cement delivered within a five mile radius of the basing point. Concentric circles of radii increasing by successive five miles were drawn delimiting zones within which the delivered price increased by specific amounts and those concentric circles from each basing point continued until one intersected a corresponding circle bounding a similar zone from another basing point. The price structure was approved by an independent costs committee. As a result of the price structure the price of cement included an element of transport subsidy, for cement, being a heavy substance, was expensive to transport. Nevertheless the general effect of the price structure was to make it unattractive to a cement manufacturer to deliver cement beyond the area in which the distance zones were based on the works from which delivery was made. In 1961 when the agreement was referred to the Restrictive Practices Court[a] by the Registrar of Restrictive Trading Agreements under s 20(2)(a) of the Restrictive Trade Practices Act 1956, the federation succeeded in justifying, under s 21(1)(b)[b] of the Act, the main price fixing restrictions in the agreement. The court found that the cement industry was an expanding industry working to full capacity and that the federation's scheme had resulted in substantially lower overall prices for cement than would have prevailed under conditions of open competition, that that was a substantial benefit to the public, that there were no detriments outweighing that advantage and that therefore the general price restriction was not unreasonable within the balancing provisions of s 21(1). Accordingly the court declared that the price restriction was not contrary to the public interest. In 1973 the registrar applied to the court under s 22[c] of the 1956 Act for leave to apply for the discharge of the 1961 declaration in respect of the restrictions on the grounds that (1) the cement industry was not in 1973, and had not been for a number of years, an expanding industry working to full capacity; (ii) that prices were no longer fixed under the agreement at a level lower than that which would be required under free competition to attract investment of capital in new works; (iii) that accordingly the reasoning

---

a   [1961] 2 All ER 75

b   Section 21, so far as material, provides:

'(1) For the purposes of any proceedings before the Court under the last foregoing section, a restriction accepted in pursuance of any agreement shall be deemed to be contrary to the public interest unless the Court is satisfied of any one or more of the following circumstances, that is to say— . . . (b) that the removal of the restriction would deny to the public as purchasers, consumers or users of any goods other specific and substantial benefits or advantages enjoyed or likely to be enjoyed by them as such, whether by virtue of the restriction itself or of any arrangements or operations resulting therefrom; . . . and is further satisfied (in any such case) that the restriction is not unreasonable having regard to the balance between those circumstances and any detriment to the public or to persons not parties to the agreement (being purchasers, consumers or users of goods produced or sold by such parties, or persons engaged or seeking to become engaged in the trade or business of selling such goods or of producing or selling similar goods) resulting or likely to result from the operation of the restriction.

'(2) In this section "purchasers", "consumers" and "users" include persons purchasing, consuming or using for the purpose or in the course of trade or business or for public purposes; and references in this section to any one person include references to any two or more persons being inter-connected bodies corporate or individuals carrying on business in partnership with each other.'

c   Section 22, so far as material, provides:

'(1) The Court may, upon application made in accordance with this section, discharge any previous declaration of the Court in respect of any restriction and any order made by the Court in pursuance thereof and substitute such other declaration, and make such order in pursuance thereof, as appears to the Court to be proper at the time of the hearing of the application.

'(2) The provisions of section twenty-one of this Act shall apply with the necessary modifications in relation to proceedings on an application under this section as they apply in relation to the proceedings therein mentioned.

'(3) An application under this section may be made by the Registrar . . .

'(4) No application shall be made under this section except with the leave of the Court, and such leave shall not be granted except upon prima facie evidence of a material change in the relevant circumstances.'

a   by which the court had concluded that the agreement operated to keep down the overall price of cement lower than it would have been under free competition was no
longer applicable; (iv) that there had, since 1961, been important improvements in
the methods of distribution of cement but the agreement was not so operated as to
take any or any substantial account of them; (v) that there had, in general, been
no significant change in base prices and distance circles since 1961 except where
b   necessitated by the opening of new works; (vi) that it was no longer correct that in
view of the infrequency and small scale of changes in the price of cement the terms
of the agreement preventing members from quoting a fixed price for cement delivered
throughout the period of a long-term contract did not result in any serious financial
disadvantage to purchasers of cement; (vii) that the federation had in making a price
increase which came into operation in May 1971 departed from the principles on which
c   prices had been fixed in the past and that the increase was accordingly substantially
greater. The federation contended (a) that as s 21(1) applied to s 22(4) by virtue of
s 22(2), the court could only exercise its discretion to give leave where there was, within
s 22(4), prima facie evidence of a material change in 'the relevant circumstances'
i e where there were one or more than one set of circumstances contained in the
gateways set out in s 21(1); and (b) that the registrar could not make submissions
d   as to the economic consequence of a course of action without the support of
evidence of an economist.

Held – (i) On the true construction of s 22(4) the words 'material change in the
relevant circumstances' meant a change in an essential part of the reasoning by which
the court had reached its previous conclusion (see p 226 *d* and *g*, post); dicta of Dip-
e   lock J in *Re Black Bolt and Nut Association of Great Britain's Agreement* [1960] 3 All ER at
142 and in *Re The Cement Makers' Federation's Agreement* [1961] 2 All ER at 93 applied.

   (ii) It was not essential, for the success of an application for leave under s 22(4),
for the applicant's case to be supported by the evidence of an economist or a merchant
banker (see p 226 *h*, post).

   (iii) The registrar's application would be refused for it had not been shown in
f   respect of any of the grounds on which he relied that there was prima facie evidence
of a material change in the relevant circumstances within the meaning of s 22(4)
(see p 228 *b* and *g*, p 229 *b*, p 230 *a*, p 231 *e* and *h* and p 232 *b* and *d*, post).

Notes

For applications to vary decisions of the Restrictive Practices Court, see 38 Halsbury's
g   Laws (3rd Edn) 126, para 170.

   For the Restrictive Trade Practices Act 1956, ss 20, 21, 22, see 37 Halsbury's Statutes
(3rd Edn) 99, 101, 102.

Cases referred to in judgment

h   *Black Bolt and Nut Association of Great Britain's Agreement, Re* [1960] 3 All ER 122, LR
2 RP 50, [1960] 1 WLR 884, 45 Digest (Repl) 413, 174.
*British Iron and Steel Federation and National Federation of Scrap Iron, Steel and Metal
Merchants' Agreement, Re* (1964) LR 4 RP 299, 45 Digest (Repl) 419, 179.
Cement Makers' Federation's Agreement, Re [1961] 2 All ER 75, LR 2 RP 241, [1961]
1 WLR 581, 45 Digest (Repl) 416, 176.
Permanent Magnet Association's Agreement, Re [1962] 2 All ER 775, LR 3 RP 119, [1962]
j   1 WLR 781, 45 Digest (Repl) 433, 201.

Cases also cited

Cozens v North Devon Hospital Management Committee [1966] 2 All ER 799, [1966] 2
QB 330, CA.
Evans Marshall & Co Ltd v Bertola SA [1973] 1 All ER 992, [1973] 1 WLR 349, CA.

Inland Revenue Comrs v Littlewoods Mail Order Stores, Littlewoods Mail Order Stores v   a
    Inland Revenue Comrs [1962] 2 All ER 279, [1963] AC 135, HL.
Locked Coil Ropemakers' Association's, Mining Rope Association's and Wire Rope Manu-
    facturers' Association's Agreements, Re [1965] 1 All ER 382, LR 5 RP 146.
National Sulphuric Acid Association Ltd's Agreement, Re [1963] 3 All ER 73, LR 4 RP 169.
National Sulphuric Acid Associations' Agreement (No 2), Re (1966) LR 6 RP 210.
Vitkovice Horni a Hutni Tezirstvo v Korner [1951] 2 All ER 334, [1951] AC 869, HL.   b
Wiseman v Borneman [1969] 3 All ER 275, [1971] AC 297, HL.
Yarn Spinners' Agreement, Re [1959] 1 All ER 299, LR 1 RP 118.

Application

By a notice of reference, dated 25th November 1957, the Registrar of Restrictive
Trading Agreements, pursuant to s 20(2)(a) of the Restrictive Trade Practices Act   c
1956, referred to the Restrictive Practices Court an agreement made between the
respondents, the members of the Cement Makers' Federation ('the federation'),
and contained in the federation's constitution stated to be effective on 1st January
1953, and the declarations and undertakings of members to be bound by and observe
the constitution, a document entitled 'Common Price and Marketing Arrangements'
and known as the 'White Book', a document entitled 'Statement of Prices' setting   d
out regradings and other price revisions for operation from 1st July 1957, the schedule
of Merchants' Terms number 12 and Price schedules numbered 1 to 11, resolutions
of the council of the federation, and in two sets of maps of the London District,
England and Wales and of Northern Ireland showing the basis of the price structure
and prices operative from 1st July 1956 and 1957 respectively. On 16th March 1961
the court[1] (Diplock P, Mr W L Heywood, Mr W G Campbell and Sir Gilbert   e
Flemming) declared that most of the restrictions contained in the agreement were
not contrary to the public interest. By a notice, dated 18th April 1973, the registrar[2]
applied to the court for leave to apply under s 22 of the 1956 Act for the discharge
of the declaration contained in the court's order of 16th March 1961 insofar as the
declaration was to the effect that the restrictions were not contrary to the public
interest. The facts are set out in the judgment of the court.   f

Christopher Staughton QC and *F M Ferris* for the registrar.
Roger Parker QC and *R C Southwell* for the federation.

                                                    Cur adv vult

14th January.   **MOCATTA P** read the following judgment of the court. The
court has before it an application made on behalf of the Registrar of Restrictive   g
Trading Agreements for leave under s 22 of the Restrictive Trade Practices Act 1956.
This is only the second occasion on which the jurisdiction of the court under that
section has been invoked.

In 1961, after a 15 day hearing in the reference, the court[1] made declarations to the
effect that the major restrictions contained in the price agreement or 'White Book'
of the respondents, the Cement Makers' Federation ('the federation'), were not   h
contrary to the public interest. The federation had succeeded in justifying their
main restrictions under s 21(1)(b) in that the court accepted that their scheme had
resulted in substantially lower overall prices for cement than would have prevailed
under conditions of open competition, that this was a substantial benefit to the public,
that there were no detriments outweighing that advantage and that, therefore,
the general price restriction was not unreasonable within the balancing provisions   j
of s 21(1).

---

1   [1961] 2 All ER 75, LR 2 RP 241
2   On 1st November 1973 the functions of the registrar were transferred to the Director
    General of Fair Trading and the office of Registrar of Restrictive Trading Agreements was
    abolished (see ss 94 and 140(3) of the Fair Trading Act 1973 and the Fair Trading Act
    1973 (Commencement No 2) Order 1973 (SI 1973 No 1652))

a   Section 22(1) provides that the court may, on application being made in accordance with the section, discharge any previous declaration of the court in respect of any restriction. Subsection (4) provides:

'No application shall be made under this section except with the leave of the Court, and such leave shall not be granted except upon prima facie evidence
b   of a material change in the relevant circumstances.'

In order that the grounds on which this application for leave is made can be understood, it is necessary to set out in summary form the reasoning which led the court in 1961 to come to its conclusion in favour of the federation. We cannot improve on the summary of this reasoning contained in para 4 of the first affidavit of the registrar
c   in support of this application as follows:

'(1) Cement was, at the time of the hearing, delivered either in cwt. paper bags or in bulk in special pressurised vehicles. The use of the latter method had expanded considerably in recent years before the hearing and then accounted for some 40% of deliveries. Cement is a heavy material and, at the date of the hearing, transport costs on the average represented about 18% of the total
d   cost of the delivered product. (2) Cement making is a continuous process and there is considerable economy in working to capacity. The available calculations suggested that to work "only" at 90% capacity at a modern works would increase the cost per ton of cement by a figure of the order of 3 to $3\frac{1}{2}$%, and at 1959 costs and prices would reduce the annual profit earned by the works by some 20 to 25%. (3) In practice the method by which prices are fixed by the Federation
e   is as follows. In England and Wales each cement works or group of adjacent works is treated as a 'basing point' and a 'base price' is fixed for cement delivered within a 5 miles radius of the basing point. Concentric circles of radii increasing by successive 5 miles are drawn delimiting zones within which the delivered price increases by specified amounts. The concentric circles from each basing point continue until one intersects a corresponding circle bounding a similar
f   zone price from another basing point. (4) The price structure applied under the Agreement was approved by an Independent Costs Committee whose functions and methods of operation are described at pages 251-253 of the report.   (5) The general effect of the price structure was to make it unattractive to a cement manufacturer to deliver cement beyond the area in which the distance zones are based on the works from which delivery is made since the price which he
g   can obtain grows less as the point of delivery approaches another works. But the existence of a transport subsidy under the scheme created an economic inducement to him not merely to restrict his deliveries of cement to the distance zones based on his works but to deliver as much as he could as near to his own works as possible. (6) Taking one year with another the overall demand for cement would continue to expand at about the same rate as it had done in the
h   past, namely, some $3\frac{1}{2}$% to 4% per annum; the overall demand for cement would not be materially affected by rises or falls in the price level of the order of 5% to 10%; and the industry was working to full capacity at the date of the hearing and any increase in demand could only be met by the creation of new capacity. (7) In an expanding industry in the long term the price level under free competition would be at or around the level at which there is sufficient
j   return on cement produced at new works (after providing sufficient depreciation) to attract the investment of capital in a new works. (8) That in the future supply would keep in step with demand except for short periods at particular times and places. (9) The minimum return which would attract investment in a new works was higher under free competition than under the common price agreement because the risk was greater. (10) The return required upon new capital invested

in the cement industry under free competition would be in the range of 15% to *a*
20%. (11) To obtain a return of 15% on capital invested would require either an
increase in price or reduction in costs, or a combination of the two, of the order of
25s. per ton and to obtain a return of 20% would require a similar increase in
price or reduction in costs of the order of 40s. per ton; there was no evidence to
suggest that economies in costs either of manufacture or delivery of anything
like the order of 25s. would be attained at any new works and the Court concluded *b*
that the postulated return could only be achieved by an increase in the price of
cement which could properly be described as 'substantial'. (12) The evidence as to
the return obtained upon the capital invested in the two most recently constructed works showed that at one the return was 9% and at the other it was 7·1%.
(13) The members of the Federation, following the advice of the Independent
Costs Committee, had been content in the past eight years before the hearing to *c*
fix the price of cement at a level which showed a return of under 10% on capital
invested in new works despite the fact that collectively they had had a monopoly
of the trade in what had been almost continuously a seller's market. (14) Any
change in policy in the fixing of prices which involved a departure from the
principles on which prices had been fixed in the past either in relation to method
or in relation to the profit margin allowed would be a material change in relevant *d*
circumstances entitling the Registrar to apply to the Court under sec. 22 of the
Act of 1956.'

The grounds on which the registrar applied to the court under s 22, as set out in his
notice, were as follows:

'(1) The Cement industry is not at present, and has not been for a number of *e*
years, an expanding industry working to full capacity
'(2) Prices are no longer fixed under the above-mentioned agreement at a level
lower than that which would be required under free competition to attract
investment of capital in new works
'(3) Accordingly the reasoning by which the Court concluded that the agree- *f*
ment is so operated as to keep down the overall price of cement to a level substantially lower than it would have been under free competition is no longer
applicable
'(4) Since 1961 there have been important improvements in the methods of distribution of cement but the agreement is not so operated as to take any or any
substantial account of them; in particular purchasers consumers and users of
cement who require cement at places near to bulk depots are deprived of the *g*
opportunity to purchase cement at prices which take into account the savings in
costs resulting from the delivery of cement from low cost works to such depots
in bulk and by modern means of transport
'(5)There have been no significant changes in base prices and distance circles
since 1961 except where necessitated by the opening of new works and the clo- *h*
sure of old ones; base prices at new works have in most cases been fixed substantially above normal and have not been reduced to take account of efficient and
low-cost production at such works; and in the result purchasers consumers and
users of cement who require cement at places supplied from a works for which the
base price is fixed substantially above the normal are deprived of the opportunity
to purchase cement at a price which takes due account of the costs of production *j*
at those works
'(6) It is no longer correct that in view of the infrequency and small scale of
changes in the price of cement the terms of the agreement preventing members
of the Cement Makers' Federation ("the Federation") from quoting a fixed price
for cement delivered throughout the period of a long term contract do not result
in any serious financial disadvantage to purchasers of cement

'(7) The Federation has in making the price increase which came into operation on the 10th May 1971 departed from the principles on which prices have been fixed in the past and that increase was accordingly substantially greater.'

The registrar's original affidavit in support of his application necessarily dealt with what was alleged to be the new factual situation at some length and exhibited a considerable volume of documents. There were also before the court three affidavits by Mr Alan James Peech who, since 1st September 1970, has been the independent chairman of the federation and a member of the federation's independent costs committee. These affidavits, together with a substantial number of supporting tables exhibited thereto, were filed on behalf of the federation. No objections were taken to this course on behalf of the registrar, whilst reserving his position on the question whether, under s 22 of the 1956 Act and r 65 of the Restrictive Practices Court Rules[1], a respondent to an application for leave under s 22 was entitled not only to be heard on the application but also to file evidence on his own behalf.

There was considerable difference between the submissions of counsel as to the construction of the words 'except upon prima facie evidence of a material change in the relevant circumstances' in s 22(4). It was common ground that the court had a discretion under the section even if the words just quoted were satisfied. There was, however, an acute difference between the arguments as to the meaning of the words 'relevant circumstances'.

The submission of counsel for the federation, stated broadly, was that the court should not exercise its discretion in favour of a rehearing, with the immense expenditure of time, labour and money that that would involve, unless there was, in the judgment of the court, a real likelihood, on the prima facie evidence before it, that the court would, on a second hearing, reverse the decision it had reached on the first hearing. Counsel for the federation drew attention to s 22(2), which reads:

'The provisions of section twenty-one of this Act shall apply with the necessary modifications in relation to proceedings on an application under this section as they apply in relation to the proceedings therein mentioned.'

Section 21(1), which introduces what are called the 'gateways', provides:

'. . . a restriction accepted in pursuance of any agreement shall be deemed to be contrary to the public interest unless the Court is satisfied of any one or more of the following circumstances . . .'

Since s 21(1) applied to s 22(4) by reason of the provisions of s 22(2), counsel for the federation argued that the 'relevant circumstances' in s 22(4) were one, or more than one, of the sets of circumstances contained in one or more of the gateways set out in s 21(1). He admitted, however, that there were remarks in the judgments of the court delivered by Diplock J in *Re Black Bolt and Nut Association of Great Britain's Agreement*[2] and in this reference[3], which were contrary to his submission as to the true construction of s 22(4). He submitted that these remarks were obiter and had been made without the benefit of due consideration of the arguments and submissions of counsel. He further criticised the registrar's evidence in that in his submission it was insufficient for the registrar to make submissions as to the economic consequences of a course of action without the support, even on an application for leave under s 22, of the evidence of an economist.

Counsel for the registrar submitted that counsel for the federation's argument as to the meaning of 'relevant circumstances' in s 22(4) must be wrong. It would not be right to refer back to s 21(1) in relation to what were there described as 'circumstances' without further taking into account the balancing provisions at the end of

---

1   SI 1957 No 603
2   [1960] 3 All ER 122 at 142, LR 2 RP 50 at 102
     [1961] 2 All ER at 93, LR 2 RP at 287

that section, where they appear after the tabulation of the gateways. The argument for the federation would preclude as irrelevant prima facie evidence, however strong, of a material change in a detriment, which might have been the basis of a previous declaration of the court in favour of the registrar.

Counsel for the registrar very properly drew the attention of the court to the provisions of s 10 of the amending Act of 1968. Subsection (1) of that section added a new gateway on which a respondent might rely. Subsection (3) reads as follows:

> 'Notwithstanding anything in subsection (4) of section 22 of the Act of 1956, leave to make an application under that section for the discharge of a declaration or order of the Restrictive Practices Court made before the commencement of this Act may, if the applicant proposes to rely on the amendment of section 21 of that Act effected by subsection 1 of this section, be granted upon prima facie evidence of the relevance of that amendment to the application.'

This is, of course, a special provision to deal with an alteration of the law made since s 22 of the 1956 Act was enacted. It certainly affords no support for counsel for the federation's argument and appears to be consistent with the view advanced on behalf of the registrar.

Shortly stated, the submission made by counsel for the registrar was that the meaning of the words in question in s 22(4) referred to a change in an essential part of the reasoning by which the court had reached its previous conclusion. This view was consistent with the passages in two earlier judgments of this court delivered by Diplock J, referred to and sought to be distinguished by counsel for the federation. Moreover, those statements had been applied in two subsequent cases: see *Re Permanent Magnet Association's Agreement*[1] and *Re British Iron and Steel Federation and National Federation of Scrap Iron, Steel and Metal Merchants' Agreement*[2]. There, after referring to *Re Black Bolt and Nut Association's Agreement*[3], the court said[4]:

> 'A departure from the general principle that the prices fixed should be sufficient but no more to bring forward for use by the steelmakers all scrap arising in the country would be a material change in the relevant circumstances. So also might be a radical change in the method of arriving at steel prices or in the supervision of the levy-remission scheme by the Iron and Steel Board or any successor statutory or other body that may be charged with its present duties.'

We accept the construction of the disputed words in s 22(4) submitted on behalf of the registrar and proceed to consider the evidence in this case with a view to assessing whether it amounts to prima facie evidence of a change in an essential part of the reasoning by which the court arrived at its previous conclusion in favour of the federation. We also accept that, on an application for leave of this nature, which is preliminary in character, it is not essential to success on behalf of the applicant, whether he be the registrar or a respondent, that his case should be supported by the evidence of an economist or merchant banker, though it may well be, depending on the facts in any particular case, that success would be difficult to achieve without such evidence.

Before considering in detail the grounds on which the registrar bases his application, it is right that we should mention one further preliminary matter arising out of counsel's speech on behalf of the federation. The federation was formed in 1918, but its control over the price of cement manufactured in this country dates from 1934. The system of control then initiated is substantially, as regards its main principles, the same as is in operation today. In 1947 the Minister of Works appointed the fforde Committee to examine the price structure of the industry. The committee

---

1   [1962] 2 All ER 775 at 800, 801, LR 3 RP 119 at 177
2   (1964) LR 4 RP 299 at 359
3   [1960] 3 All ER 122, LR 2 RP 50
4   (1964) LR 4 RP at 359, 360

reported that in their view the prices fixed up to that date had not been unreasonable, but recommended improvements in the method of fixing prices. As a result of these recommendations the federation appointed an independent costs committee consisting of the then independent chairman of the federation and the independent accountant. That committee worked with the representative of the Minister of Works until government control was withdrawn in 1951. From the inception of the committee down to the present time the same gentleman has acted as independent accountant, and there have been but three holders of the office of independent chairman.

The notice of reference in this case was served in November 1957. It was followed by a detailed cost investigation. In January 1961 the hearing began, and the court's decision[1] in favour of the federation was delivered on 16th March. Certain further improvements suggested in the judgment of the court have since been adopted by the federation. In view of this very creditable history, it was submitted for the federation that the registrar's application should be examined most critically before it was granted and the enormous expense incurred of a further full hearing.

Notwithstanding that the history of the activities of the federation as just briefly outlined is correct, we cannot attach much weight to this line of reasoning. No doubt, as we have said, the section gives the court a discretion, but, notwithstanding a creditable past history of an industry and its price agreement, effect must be given to the statutory right in s 22 for a variation of a previous decision of the court. If prima facie evidence be given of a change in an essential part of the reasoning by which the court arrived at its previous decision, it would, we apprehend, require quite exceptional circumstances to induce the court to exercise its discretion against the granting of leave under s 22(4).

Of the grounds relied on by the registrar as providing prima facie evidence of a material change in the relevant circumstances the first three are the most important and, taken together, are said to be evidence that prices are not now lower overall than would be the case under free competition or not substantially lower, or, if they are lower, they are no longer sufficiently lower to be reasonable having regard to the alleged detriments covered by grounds (4), (5) and (6).

The first matter to be considered is whether the cement industry is at present an expanding industry as the court in 1961 found it to have been, or whether the contrary has been the case for a number of years, as is submitted for the registrar. The court has had to consider a number of tables as to available capacity and the use of such capacity in the years from 1961 down to today. The figures can be looked at in a number of different ways to suggest very different conclusions. Thus from the registrar's point of view perhaps the most striking fact to emerge was that the total production of common price cements, i e cements subject to the prices fixed under the price agreement, was the same in the year 1964 as for the year 1971, namely, 15·6 million metric tonnes. On the other hand, the total home production of cement for all purposes—and this would seem the more important comparison—was 16·78 million metric tonnes in 1964 as against the higher figure of 18·23 in 1971. As regards the capacity of the industry, in 1960, the last completed year before the court's decision[1] on the reference, the capacity was 13·75 million metric tonnes, whereas in 1972 it was 19·58.

There are no doubt bound to be some variations up and down in production in particular years due to fluctuations in the state of the national economy and the imposition and raising of government controls. We thought it might be more useful, therefore, to consider five year moving averages rather than pick on comparisons between selected couples of years. The five year average down to and including 1960 for total production was 12·78 million metric tonnes; since then the moving average has shown an increase each year down to and including the latest figures

---

1   [1961] 2 All ER 75, LR 2 RP 241

available or estimated for 1973 of 18·52. The five year average for the capacity of the industry down to and including 1960 was 13·34 million metric tonnes; there has again been a steady increase year by year in the moving five year average down to and including the latest available or estimated figures for 1973 of 20·24.

We think it also useful to bear in mind the evidence about plans for increasing capacity dealt with in the first affidavit of Mr Peech, the independent chairman of the federation and member of the independent costs committee. Thus by 1977 it is planned to increase the capacity as existing at the end of 1973 of 21,131,000 metric tonnes by 2,369,000, and this at a high and increasing capital cost.

Having regard to the figures mentioned we do not think it right to conclude that, taking an overall view of the industry since the court's judgment[1] in 1961, it has not continued to expand as was then forecast. Whilst it cannot be said that, with the exception of 1964 and 1973, the industry has been working to 100 per cent of capacity throughout, the percentage of capacity used has overall been high. Certainly there has been no lack of new investment in the industry, as the increase in capacity demonstrates.

The court accepted in its judgment in 1961 that the return required on new capital invested in the cement industry under free competition would be in the range of 15 to 20 per cent. On the basis of certain figures obtained from the federation in respect of the return on capital employed in the six most recently constructed works, it was submitted that the agreement prices are no longer being fixed at a level lower than that which would be required to attract investment of capital in new works under conditions of free competition. The relevant figures for the purposes of this submission were contained in table 12 of an exhibit to Mr Peech's affidavit and there was much debate about the correct conclusions to draw from them. It is to be noted in the first place that these new works are all works of existing members of the federation; there has been no new entrant to the industry. Secondly, as was demonstrated in relation to perhaps the most successful of the six on the figures in the table, it can be misleading to consider only the return on capital of one of the new works taken by itself since, owing to the zoning system, the new works may take away custom from existing works of the same member and reduce the return on the capital employed in those works. Thirdly, the figures given for each of the six new works covered a considerable number of years; the average returns on capital employed at four of the works was 10·7, 9·81, 9·88 and 13·31 per cent. Fourthly, the largest new works of all had for each of the first three years of operation shown substantial losses. If the return on capital for all six works, taken together, be taken as shown in the last column of table 12, the highest figure for any year since 1962 was 8·97 per cent, and for 1972 the figure was 6·82 per cent. We are unable to draw from the figures in this table, which were all based on depreciated replacement values, the conclusion that a prima facie case has been shown to the effect of the second ground on which the registrar based his application. Apart from this, we are impressed by the low returns on capital employed in the cement industry as compared with the 15 to 20 per cent figures mentioned above and with the average figures in other industries as shown in table 8 of Mr Peech's affidavit.

Before leaving this ground of the registrar's application, we should add that the independent accountant has done recalculations similar to the assessments discussed[2] in the report of the judgment of the court in 1961. The first sought to assess the position facing a new entrant to the industry desiring initial yields of 15 or 20 per cent on his initial investment and calculated in relation to the experiences of (a) the lowest cost works in the industry and (b) the second newest works. These figures showed that the new entrant could not achieve initial yields of 15 or 20 per cent on his initial investment without effecting substantial economies as compared with the lowest cost works or the second newest works in the industry. Put in another way, if the new

---

1   [1961] 2 All ER 75, LR 2 RP 241
2   (1961) LR 2 RP at 261

entrant had costs of the lowest cost works and secured the gross realised price of that works, his return on capital would be 9·16 per cent. The comparable figure for a comparison with the costs and realised price of the second newest works would be 6·80 per cent. We would add that in our view the cost of construction of a new works has, for the purposes of the calculations, been taken at an unrealistically low figure. In our opinion these figures confirm the conclusion we had reached based on the figures in relation to the six most recently constructed works.

Having reached the above conclusions on the first two and most important of the grounds relied on by the registrar in support of his application, it follows that we are unable to accept that he has made out a prima facie case to the effect of his third ground, namely, that the court's previous reasoning that the agreement was so operated as to keep the overall price of cement at a level substantially lower than it would have been under free competition is no longer applicable.

The fourth ground on which the registrar relies concerns a new detriment. The ground is based on the greatly increased use of bulk depots all over the country in comparison with the use of such depots in 1961. The use of depots is not mentioned in the judgment of the court[1] on the reference. Despite the greatly increased use of depots, 52 in 1972 as against 23 by 1961, which appear for the most part to be fed by special trains consisting of 100 ton bogie cement wagons in which the cement is carried under pressure so that it can be blown out on discharge, the price of cement supplied from such depots is, under the zoning system, calculated by reference to the nearest producing works. The registrar suggested that it might well be that the actual cost of manufacturing the cement delivered from a depot was considerably lower than the cost of cement ascertained by reference to the nearest producing works. The latter might have a higher base price than the works, often far distant, producing the cement deposited at the depot. The registrar was unable to suggest what was the precise significance of the establishment of so many bulk depots without an accountancy investigation of the relevant figures. He suggested, however, that substantial savings of costs were likely to have resulted from the establishment of bulk depots. The common price scheme had not been adjusted to these new circumstances. In particular no cost savings accrued to purchasers near bulk depots.

On the evidence before us it appears that there are a variety of reasons for the greatly extended use of depots, of which perhaps the most important has been the growth in the demand for bulk cement deliveries from suppliers of ready mixed concrete, manufacturers of concrete blocks and others. The proportion of cement delivered in bulk has grown from 40 per cent in 1961 to 73 per cent in 1973 of all despatches. Of this about one-third passes through depots. The existence of depots facilitates prompt deliveries, enables users to dispense with storage capacity and, since the depots are in the main fed by rail, reduces the numbers of vehicles on the roads in the vicinity of a works. Further, depots can be and are fed by works left with a surplus of supply after the needs of their local area have been satisfied. For example, delivery in bulk by train to depots in the special wagons mentioned is now a more efficient and cheaper method of distribution from the Thames concentration of cement works than the older method of sea transport in bags.

As regards the effect of the increased use of depots on costs, Mr Peech's evidence showed that, as a proportion of the overall total costs of manufacturing and selling, delivery and depot expenses were 18·9 per cent in 1960 and 20·2 per cent in 1972. The increase in the use of depots has not, therefore, overall reduced the proportion of total costs attributable to delivery expenses. Figures prepared specially by two members and contained in tables 15 and 16 exhibited by Mr Peech compared the respective costs of delivery of bags and bulk to a variety of sites as between deliveries ex-works and ex-depots. The results varied considerably and showed no general reduction in costs of delivery in favour of depots.

---

1 [1961] 2 All ER 75, LR 2 RP 241

Interesting though the increased use of depots since 1961 and the reasons therefor no doubt are, we are quite unable, on the evidence before us, to draw any inference that the failure to depart from the previously agreed system of prices by reference to base prices at works and increases in prices by zones radiating outwards from such works has, by reason of the increased use of depots, become a detriment.

We now pass to the fifth ground set out in the registrar's notice of application, which complains of the lack of significant changes in base prices and distance circles since 1961 save where necessitated by the opening of new works and the closure of old ones: in the case of new works it is alleged that base prices have in most cases been fixed substantially above normal and have not been reduced to take account of efficient and low-cost production at such works. Apart from the specific allegation about base prices at new works the suggestion was that the system had been allowed to ossify.

The present position is that of the 29 works in England and Wales no less than 20 have the same base price—sometimes referred to as the normal base price; it is also, at £8·72 per metric tonne, the lowest base price, though in the past this has not always been the case. The remaining nine base prices range up to the figure of £9·27.

As regards the six new works, we have already discussed these at some length in considering the registrar's second ground. We add that, where a new works is erected on the site of an old one, the practice under the agreement is that the previous base price applies to the new works. Of the six new works three have the normal base price. The other three have higher ones which are calculated so as to give a modest return on the capital employed. We have already discussed the returns on the capital employed in the new works and it is unnecessary to add to this.

As regards other base prices and the general charge of ossification, the history of price changes generally since the previous judgment of the court is as follows. As regards base prices for existing works, these were reviewed in 1961 and 1963. Two changes were made in the former and eight in the latter year. Of the ten changes, four were reductions to the normal base price. In 1961 there were also substantial changes in the distance circles or zoning variations. In each of 1964 and 1965 the independent costs committee reviewed base prices and recommended that no changes should be made.

Apart from the changes in base prices mentioned there have, from 1961 onwards, from time to time been rises of so much per tonne on basic prices, the last being a very substantial increase of £1.40 per tonne in May 1971. It is unnecessary to go into all the detail of these changes. It is, however, important to remember that in April 1965 the Prices and Incomes Board was set up by royal warrant, and that in August 1966 the Prices and Incomes Act was passed. A price increase of 31p per tonne was, in July 1965, agreed by the government without reference to the board, whilst in August 1967 and November 1969 price increases were approved by the board, though they were smaller than the federation had requested. In April 1970 a price increase was approved by the government without reference to the board which, after the change of government in June of that year, seems to have ceased to function after August. There was a price increase in October 1970, and the final increase of £1·40 already mentioned took place in May 1971. At that time the federation said they would not increase prices for 12 months.

It will be remembered that the Confederation of British Industry took the initiative in the third quarter of 1971 to secure a voluntary price freeze. This lasted for approximately a year, by which time stage I of the government's counter-inflationary policy came into effect for 90 days from 30th November 1972. This was extended to the end of April 1973, when stage II began. Despite the creation of a new Prices Commission, the change is more than a change in name, since it might be difficult for the commission to find it possible to approve a change in price applicable to all works of all members of the federation. No special virtue can therefore be claimed on behalf of the federation in having made no change in price since May 1971. It is further to be appreciated that since the Counter-Inflation Act 1972, even if the base price of a particular works had been reduced, it would not have been possible to have secured a counterbalancing increase in the base price of another works, whereas since the federation's price structure and the stewardship of the independent costs committee depend on an overall return on capital there could, within the price agreement, be no room for significant downward alterations in base prices unless there were upward compensatory alterations elsewhere. We have already commented on the relatively low overall return on capital employed in the industry by reference to table 8 in Mr Peech's affidavit. More particularly we may mention that in 1969 the figure was 2·5 per cent and in 1970 5·9 per cent, against 9·9 per cent and 8·5 per cent respectively for all manufacturing industry according to figures printed in Hansard. The price increase in April and October 1970 and May 1971 were, therefore, not surprising in view of the low returns on capital prevailing in the industry in 1969 and 1970.

We add, in relation to prices in general in the cement industry, a reference to the table of annual average price indices derived from government statistical sources and set out in table 18 in Mr Peech's affidavit. Until 1970 the cement price index rose less above the base price taken as 1963 than did the indices for construction materials, house building materials, consumer retail sale prices and brick prices. In 1970 and 1971 by reason of the price increases made in those two years the cement index was higher than the others, but for July 1973 the cement index was again below the other indices, and significantly so.

It is intrinsic in any price agreement in an industry that, if it ceased to exist, some prices would fall below the previously mentioned agreement prices, whilst others might rise. It is right that this should be borne in mind, but if the overall range of prices is lower during the operation of a price agreement than would be the case under a system of free competition, very definite and considerable detriments would have to be shown to outweigh the consequential benefit to the public. From what has been said it will have appeared that we can find no evidence supporting the submission that there is any substance in the fifth ground relied on by the registrar.

As regards the ancillary restriction, justified in the previous judgment under s 21 (1)(g), preventing members of the federation from quoting a fixed price for cement delivered during the period of a long-term contract, it was argued for the registrar that the substantial increase in price since August 1966 and the inability to obtain long-term fixed-price contracts for the supply of cement were considered to be severe disadvantages to contractors in the public sector.

Brief references to the evidence will indicate the restricted character of this detriment, to which the court gave consideration in 1961. Cement constitutes only about 3 per cent of the total value of all building and civil engineering contracts. The biggest rise in cement prices—that of May 1971—was an increase of 17 per cent on the previous figure. Applied to 3 per cent of a contract's value, this would result in an overall increase of 0·51 per cent. Apart from these overall figures, if a contractor cannot get a fixed price for his cement for say a two year contract, he can cover himself by including a margin to meet the contingency of a rise in cement prices during the two years. On the other hand, if a cement maker were permitted to quote a fixed price for deliveries over two years, he would probably likewise add an element to his quotation to cover himself against rising costs. We are unable, on the evidence before us, to find any suggestion of a material change in the circumstances relative to this restriction apart or different from those adduced and debated before the court in 1961.

Finally we must consider the submission for the registrar that the federation, when making the price increase that came into operation on 10th May 1971, departed from the principles on which prices had been fixed in the past. That substantial price increase was effective from the date mentioned, but the increase of £1·40 per tonne was intended to produce a return of 10 per cent on capital employed for the whole of 1971. It therefore had a retrospective element in its objective. The independent costs committee, in reporting on this to the council of the federation, stated that this involved a different approach to price increases from that hitherto adopted and raised a substantial point of principle which the council would wish to consider. The registrar submitted that in conditions of free competition no company would be likely to attempt to recoup past losses or make up for inadequate past profits, with the result that under such conditions the price increase in May 1971 would have been substantially less. No evidence was advanced in support of this submission, and it suffices to say that the court is unable to accept it.

During the previous hearing before the court the federation offered an assurance that if the registrar at any time represented to the federation that he had reason to suppose that there might have been a material change in the relevant circumstances, the federation would supply him with such information relative to prices and costs as was in the possession of the independent costs committee for the purpose of enabling him to decide whether he should make an application under s 22. Further, if, having seen such information, the registrar considered it to be his duty to make an application under that section, the federation was willing that the information so supplied should be placed before the court for the purpose of such application. Such assurance to the court was fully implemented by the federation from the date of our previous judgment: counsel for the federation repeated it as to the future should the court dismiss the registrar's application for leave under s 22(4).

For the reasons set out in this judgment the court is of the opinion that prima facie evidence has not been adduced of a material change in the relevant circumstances. The leave sought by the registrar is therefore refused and the federation's assurance once again becomes operative.

We have, throughout this judgment, referred to the registrar. In fact, by reason of the provisions of the Fair Trading Act 1973 the office of Registrar of Restrictive Trading Agreements became merged in that of the Director-General of Fair Trading on 31st October 1973, during the hearing of the application. The distinguished and creative tenure by Sir Ralph Sich of his onerous office, which began in 1956 after the passing into law of the Act of Parliament setting up this court, then came to an end. We wish, in taking leave today of the last piece of the court's work with which Sir Rupert has been associated, to record the gratitude of all those who have adjudicated here for the unfailing, fair-minded and utterly conscientious devotion to duty shown by him over the years in the conduct by him of the various proceedings before the court to which he has been a party.

Application dismissed.

Solicitors: *Treasury Solicitor; Sydney Morse & Co* (for the federation).

Christine Ivamy Barrister.

Hoffman v Thomas

QUEEN'S BENCH DIVISION
LORD WIDGERY CJ, ASHWORTH AND MELFORD STEVENSON JJ
13th DECEMBER 1973

Road traffic – Directions – Failure to comply with direction – Direction by constable engaged in regulation of traffic – Direction given by constable in execution of duty – Power at common law of constable to direct traffic derived from duty to protect life and property – Accused driving car on motorway – Constable directing accused to leave carriageway in order to take part in traffic census – Accused refusing to comply with constable's direction – Whether direction given by constable in execution of duty – Road Traffic Act 1972, s 22(1).

The appellant was driving along a motorway when he was directed by a police constable to drive on to the hard shoulder in order to take part in a traffic census. The constable was selecting vehicles at random from the stream of traffic to take part in the census. The appellant stopped in response to the constable's signal. He declined however to take part in the census and drove on. The appellant was convicted on an information which alleged that he, being a person driving a motor vehicle, did, on the direction of a police constable engaged for the time being in the regulation of traffic, refuse to proceed in a particular line of traffic when directed to do so by the constable in the execution of his duty, contrary to s 22(1)^a of the Road Traffic Act 1972. On appeal,

Held – The right of a police constable at common law to regulate traffic derived from his duty to protect life and property. It arose because of the danger that unregulated traffic could present. The right did not therefore include a right to direct a motorist to take part in a traffic census. Since neither at common law nor by statute did the constable have any right to direct the appellant to leave the motorway and go into the census area it followed that the direction given by the constable had not been given in the execution of his duty. The appeal should therefore be allowed and the conviction quashed (see p 238 *j* to p 239 *b*, post).

Quaere. Whether, in arbitrarily selecting vehicles from a stream of traffic and causing those vehicles to enter the census point, the constable could be described as being 'engaged in the regulation of traffic' within s 22(1) of the 1972 Act (see p 236 *j* to p 237 *b* and p 239 *a*, post).

Notes
For the duty of motorists to comply with the directions of constables engaged in regulating traffic, see 33 Halsbury's Laws (3rd Edn) 559, para 949.

For the Road Traffic Act 1972, s 22, see 42 Halsbury's Statutes (3rd Edn) 1667.

Case referred to in judgment
R v Waterfield, R v Lynn [1963] 3 All ER 659, [1964] 1 QB 164, [1963] 3 WLR 946, 128 JP 48, 48 Cr App Rep 42, CCA, Digest (Cont Vol A) 416, 8201a.

Case stated
This was an appeal by way of a case stated by justices for the county of Kent in respect of their adjudication as a magistrates' court sitting at West Malling, Kent, on 13th February 1973.

On 20th October 1972 an information was preferred by the respondent, Roy Percy Thomas, an inspector of police, against the appellant, Anthony Edward Hoffman, that

---

a Section 22(1) is set out at p 236 *f*, post

he on 29th September 1972 on the M20 motorway, Wrotham, being a person driving a
motor vehicle, did, on the direction of a police constable, engaged for the time being
in the regulation of traffic on a road, refuse to proceed in a particular line of traffic,
when directed to do so by the police constable in the execution of his duty, contrary to
s 22 of the Road Traffic Act 1972.

The following facts were found. On 29th September 1972 Pc Hayward was engaged
in controlling traffic at a census point on the southbound carriageway of the M20
motorway near Wrotham in Kent about 400 yards from its junction with the A20.
The census was a random sample census for which vehicles were being extracted at
random by the constable in small groups from the flow of traffic to pass through a
census point situated on the hard shoulder of the road adjacent to the carriageway and
slightly beyond the point where the constable was standing in the carriageway.
There were warning boards placed on the approach to the census, the last one being
'Stop at Census Point', placed on the central reservation shortly before the census
point. At that point the southbound carriageway of the M20 consisted of two lanes
but, from the junction of the M20 and the A20, traffic flow on the southbound
carriageway of the M20 was restricted to the offside lane by a line of cones placed
down the centre of the carriageway. At the point where the constable was standing
the line of cones dividing the carriageway ceased, save for a single one in the nearside
lane beyond the police officer so that vehicles could be extracted from the flow of
traffic and could then pass through the gap in the cones, across the nearside lane and
on to the census point on the hard shoulder. At the census point there was a line of
cones on the outside edge of the hard shoulder behind which vehicles taking part in
the census were to pass. From the point where the constable was standing, with the
exception of the single cone set out in the nearside lane just behind the constable,
both lanes of the southbound carriageway were clear. The appellant was driving in a
line of traffic in the offside lane of the southbound carriageway of the M20. The
constable gave one combined signal, which he demonstrated to the justices, directing
the appellant not to proceed down the main carriageway but to go into the census
lane. The appellant did not comply with that instruction but stopped in the main
carriageway. The constable went to the appellant who said that he refused to enter
the census and then drove forward in the offside lane of the carriageway continuing on
his journey. The intention of the constable in stopping the appellant and then directing him on to the hard shoulder was so that he should comply with the request on the
sign which said 'Stop at Census Point'.

It was contended by the appellant: (i) that he accepted that the constable was for
the time being engaged in the regulation of traffic, but submitted that in directing the
appellant to pass through or stop at the census point and to proceed in a particular
line of traffic for that purpose he was not acting in the execution of his duty; (ii) that
the powers and duties of a constable to regulate road traffic arose from, and were
limited by, his general duty to preserve law and order and to protect life and property
save insofar as statute extended that duty or authorised his powers to be exercised for
additional purposes; if a constable, sought to stop or direct a motorist from his lawful
course on the highway, otherwise than in the exercise of such duties or for such
purposes, his acts amounted to an obstruction; (iii) that the wording of s 22 of the Road
Traffic Act 1972 contemplated that a constable while engaged in the regulation of
traffic, might yet give a signal or direction which was outside the scope of his duty; if
the constable did so then the citizen was not obliged to obey the signal or direction;
(iv) that no provision in any statute confered any power or duty on a constable to
require a citizen to participate in a traffic census or to give him directions for that
purpose; the direction of the constable, which on the evidence was given to the
appellant for that purpose, was not a direction with which the appellant was obliged
to comply.

It was contended by the respondent that whatever the appellant's obligations in
relation to the census might have been, Pc Hayward was engaged in the regulation of

traffic on a motorway on which the maximum permissible speed was 70 m p h and acting in the execution of his duty for the protection of life and property and was entitled to direct the appellant to proceed from the offside lane into the nearside lane.

The justices were of the opinion that the respondent was correct in his submission that the constable was in fact protecting life and property and as no argument had been advanced that the informatory signs were other than lawfully erected, they came to the conclusion that the officer was acting in the execution of his duty in requesting traffic to comply with those signs and to go to the census point whether or not the driver agreed to take part in the census or not. Accordingly they convicted the appellant, fined him the sum of £10, and ordered that his driving licence be endorsed with the conviction.

Mark Potter for the appellant.
Michael Lewer for the respondent.

LORD WIDGERY CJ. This is an appeal by case stated by justices for the county of Kent sitting at West Malling as a magistrates' court. On 13th February 1973 they convicted the present appellant of an offence laid in these terms:

> '. . . that he on the 29th September 1972 at M.20 motorway, Wrotham in the County of Kent, being a person driving a motor vehicle, did, on the direction of a Police Constable engaged for the time being in the regulation of traffic on a road, refuse to proceed in a particular line of traffic, when directed to do so by the Police Constable in the execution of his duty, contrary to Section 22 of the Road Traffic Act, 1972.'

The circumstances on the day in question were these, that the highway authority was holding a traffic census. The persons conducting the census had set up tables and the like on the hard shoulder of the motorway, and the police officer, Pc Hayward, had been stationed on the motorway to assist in the conduct of the census in the manner which I will describe in a moment. Physically the traffic had been controlled by a number of cones of a familiar kind; the effect of which was first of all to deflect oncoming traffic into the outer of the two lanes of the motorway. At this point the motorway consisted only of two lanes and the hard shoulder, and the cones were laid out in such a way that all approaching traffic was canalised into the outer of the two lanes. Then just before the census point was reached a line of cones was laid down so as to separate the hard shoulder from the nearside lane of the motorway, and traffic at that point was thus able to proceed in two directions; one direction would be to continue down the motorway itself, both carriageways being free of obstruction once the police officer was passed; the alternative was for the driver to bear to his left and on to the hard shoulder, and present himself for the purposes of the census. What Pc Hayward undoubtedly was doing was making a random selection of vehicles as they came along the motorway, directing some to the census point and allowing others to go on their way.

At the moment when the appellant appeared in the line of traffic he was signalled by the police officer to go into the census area. Some acute controversy arose earlier in the history of this case as to the precise nature of the signal given by the police officer, but it is clear by the amendment of the case that he gave a single signal which he demonstrated to the justices, the effect of which was to direct the appellant to leave the motorway, go on to the hard shoulder and thence to the census point.

The appellant did not want to do that; he stopped on seeing the signal by the police officer, and discovering that he was required to go to the census point he declined to do so. He just drove straight on down the motorway and hence was prosecuted in the terms I have already given for having refused to proceed in a particular line of traffic when asked to do so by a police constable.

There is one other factor in this case which I think can be got out of the way at quite
an early point. The justices found that in addition to the presence of Pc Hayward,
whose functions I hope I have already adequately described, there was on or near the
motorway on the approach side, that is to say the side from which one would approach
coming to this census point, a sign which bore the words 'Stop at Census Point'. This
sign I find a very odd one in the circumstances, because it is common ground between
counsel that there is no statutory power in the highway authority or anybody else to
conduct a compulsory census; in other words there is no authority whereby motorists
can be compelled to leave the highway and take part in a census exercise. Yet this
sign, which was exhibited and which is peremptory in its terms is an authorised sign.
We have been referred to the appropriate regulations, which are the Traffic Signs
Regulations and General Directions 1964[1]; when one goes through the various pictures of various signs which the schedules contain, one finds above no 830 a sign in
precisely the form which I have described. However, it comes under the general
heading of 'Informatory Signs' as opposed to mandatory signs, and so it is. I am quite
satisfied, without going into details, that this is not one of those signs, non-compliance
with which immediately gives rise to an offence. Despite its peremptory language it is
informatory, and it seems to me that in those circumstances the presence of this sign is
neither here nor there so far as the present issue is concerned.

The way the issue arises in this case is on the submission of counsel for the appellant
that the police officer was not acting in the execution of his duty in the degree and
manner necessary in order that a disobeyance of his order should amount to an
offence.

I turn, therefore, to the section on which this prosecution was based; it is s 22 of the
Road Traffic Act 1972. Subsection (1) says:

> 'Where a constable is for the time being engaged in the regulation of traffic in a
> road, or where a traffic sign, being a sign of the prescribed size, colour and type, or
> of another character authorised by the Secretary of State under the provisions in
> that behalf of the Road Traffic Regulation Act 1967, has been lawfully placed on
> or near a road, a person driving or propelling a vehicle who—(a) neglects or re-
> fuses to stop the vehicle or to make it proceed in, or keep to, a particular line of
> traffic when directed so to do by the constable in the execution of his duty, or (b)
> fails to comply with the indication given by the sign, shall be guilty of an offence.'

One has to look carefully, therefore, at the constituents of this section to see what it
is which makes up the offence charged. It is to be observed that, leaving aside irrelevant factors, the section contemplates that there shall be a constable for the time
being engaged in the regulation of traffic in a road. One of the matters, therefore, for
consideration is whether Pc Hayward satisfied that condition first of all. Assuming for
the moment that he did, the next feature is that he shall direct the vehicle to proceed
in a particular line of traffic, and that the vehicle's driver shall have declined to accept
the invitation and refused to go into the particular line of traffic, and thirdly that the
direction given by the constable shall be a direction issued in the execution of his duty.

There is some doubt in my mind whether it is proper to describe the officer involved in this particular exercise as regulating traffic for present purposes at all. That a
police officer has a duty to regulate traffic is unquestioned where the traffic requires
regulation, and if this were an instance in which there was a possibility of collision
between vehicles, or confusion of vehicles or anything else which required regulation
for the conduct of those vehicles in that sense then I would have had no hesitation in
saying that the first requirement of s 22 had been complied with. But I have some
doubts, although I do not find it necessary to express a final conclusion on this point,
whether it was right to describe this officer as regulating the traffic at all, when all

---

1   SI 1964 No 1857

QBD Hoffman v Thomas (Lord Widgery CJ) 237

that he was doing was arbitrarily abstracting or selecting certain vehicles from a
stream of traffic proceeding along its lawful course and causing those vehicles to enter
the census point in order that their drivers may answer questions.

I will assume for the moment for the purposes of this judgment that that was a
regulation of traffic but I express some considerable doubts whether that really is the
case. The real issue here is whether the direction given by the police constable in the
circumstances which I have described was a direction given by him in the execution of
his duty. If his duty empowered or authorised him to order the appellant to go into
the census point, so be it; then I would have no doubt that the police officer was acting
in the execution of his duty. But underlying all the argument in this case is the
accepted fact that there was no power to hold a compulsory census, and no power
existed to order the appellant to subject himself to that census.

In deciding whether that circumstance prevents the direction from being a direction
given in the execution of the constable's duty, I obtain the greatest assistance from the
decision of this court in *R v Waterfield*[1]. It is a case in which a reserved judgment of the
court was delivered by Ashworth J. In that case a suspect motor car was in a car park
and two police officers were watching it. It was suspect because there was suspicion
that it had been involved in a serious crime. Along came the two appellants in that
case, Lynn and Waterfield, and they made to enter the car, whereupon the police
officers approached and told them that they could not remove the car. One of the
police officers gave the customary sign to stop which police officers use, by standing in
front of the car and holding up his right hand. Section 223 of the Road Traffic Act
1960, which was then the relevant authority, provided:

'A person driving a motor vehicle on a road and a person riding on a road a
bicycle or tricycle, not being a motor vehicle, shall stop the same on being so
required by a police constable in uniform . . .'

The approach to the present problem is, if I may say so with respect, well exemplified
in Ashworth J's judgment. He said[2]:

'In most cases it is probably more convenient to consider what the police
constable was actually doing and in particular whether such conduct was prima
facie an unlawful interference with a person's liberty or property. If so, it is then
relevant to consider whether (a) such conduct falls within the general scope of any
duty imposed by statute or recognised at common law and (b) whether such conduct, albeit within the general scope of such a duty, involved an unjustifiable use
of powers associated with the duty.'

Looking at that approach, it is perfectly clear that the police constable's action in the
instant case did amount to an interference with the appellant's personal liberty or
property; therefore one has to go on and consider its justification under the heads to
which Ashworth J refers. In *R v Waterfield*[1] the court, for reasons that I do not go
into, came to the conclusion that in that particular instance the police officers had no
power to prevent the removal of the car, and the court went on to decide that in
those circumstances the signal to stop given by the police officer was of no materiality,
because if he had no power to prevent the removal of the car, he had no power to
give a signal to stop, and no offence was committed merely because that signal was
not observed. However, it is for the approach as stated by Ashworth J that I refer
primarily to *R v Waterfield*[1].

---

1 [1963] 3 All ER 659, [1964] 1 QB 164
2 [1963] 3 All ER at 661, [1964] 1 QB at 170, 171

What then is the general duty of a police constable in these matters? In Halsbury's Laws of England[1] there is this statement:

'The first duty of a constable is always to prevent the commission of a crime. If a constable reasonably apprehends that the action of any person may result in a breach of the peace it is his duty to prevent that action. It is his general duty to protect life and property, and the general function of controlling traffic on the roads is derived from this duty.'

In the present instance there is nothing in the case which I can find to suggest that any life or property was endangered at all. There is no reason why the proceedings which were being conducted should give rise to such a danger, and nothing in the facts found to indicate that there was in this case any such danger. So the conception that the police officer was acting in the protection of life and property seems to me not to be supported on the facts of this case, and although the right to regulate traffic must necessarily be a very wide one, as I have already indicated, that right does stem from the general duty to protect life and property.

It is not a right to regulate traffic for the police officer's own personal motives or entertainment; it is fundamentally a right to regulate traffic because of the dangers to life and limb which unregulated traffic can present. Accordingly it seems to me that neither at common law, nor by any statutory provisions to which we have been referred, had this police officer any right to direct the appellant to leave the motorway and go into the census area.

This judgment has been much shortened, as has the argument, by the consensus of agreement that no such statutory right exists. I have come to the conclusion that when the police officer made this signal directing the appellant to leave the motorway and go into the census area, he made a signal which he had no power to make either at common law or by virtue of statute, and consequently it seems to me in my judgment that the giving of that signal cannot have been an act in the execution of his duty, and on that ground alone it seems to me that the appellant's argument is successful and should be sustained.

But before leaving the case I would draw attention to the fact that this problem has not wholly escaped the authorities, because as long ago as 1948 there was a circular issued by the Minister of Transport to highway authorities making recommendations as to the methods by which a census of this kind should be performed. In that circular one finds these words[2]:

'There are no statutory powers to stop or slow down vehicles for the purpose of taking a census. It is, therefore, essential that any survey undertaken should be made with the full co-operation of the police, and a constable should be present to stop or slow down the traffic at each census point.'

Those words seem to me to be a recognition by the Minister of Transport that the highway authority has no power to conduct a census, and the suggestion that the assistance of the police should be enlisted in consequence in order that power and authority should exist.

For the reasons which I have already given I do not think that the police have the power to issue a direction of the kind which was issued in this case, and since the taking of censuses is no doubt a desirable practice, it may well be that the proper course is for the appropriate government department to see that appropriate powers are obtained to enable an activity of this kind to be conducted whether the individual driver wishes it or not.

But returning to the facts of this case, in my opinion the action of the police officer was not an action done in the execution of his duty; that vital factor is missing from the

1   3rd Edn, vol 30, p 129, para 206
2   Ministry of Transport Circular 612, para 13

constituents of the offence charged, I think he was wrongly convicted, I would allow the appeal and quash the conviction.

ASHWORTH J. I agree.

MELFORD STEVENSON J. So do I.

Appeal allowed.

Solicitors: *A E Hamlin & Co* (for the appellant); *Sharpe, Pritchard & Co*, agents for *A C Staples*, Maidstone (for the respondent).

Jacqueline Charles Barrister.

English Clays Lovering Pochin & Co Ltd v Plymouth Corporation

COURT OF APPEAL, CIVIL DIVISION
RUSSELL, STAMP LJJ AND BRIGHTMAN J
5th, 6th, 7th, 8th, 11th, 22nd FEBRUARY 1974

Town and country planning – Development – Permitted development — Development by mineral undertakers – Erection, alteration or extension of building, plant or machinery – Development on land in or adjacent to and belonging to a quarry or mine – Mine – Site on which mining operations are carried out – Mining operations –Winning and working of minerals –Adjacent – Belonging to – Meaning – Plaintiffs engaged in production of china clay – Crude slurry extracted from ground and partly treated on site – Slurry conveyed by pipeline to second site two miles distant – Process of drying clay completed on second site – Whether second site part of larger site on which 'mining operations are carried on' – Whether second site 'land in or adjacent to and belonging to a . . . mine' – Town and Country Planning General Development Order 1963 (SI 1963 No 709), arts 2, 3, Sch 1, class XVIII, para 2.

The plaintiff was a mineral undertaker engaged in the production of china clay. The china clay was extracted from the ground on land ('Lee Moor') owned by the plaintiff. That was done by a process of detaching, by high pressure water jets, the mechanical combination of china clay and associates and subsequently, by a system of refinement, driving off or abstracting from the slurry substantially all but the china clay. The slurry was passed from Lee Moor through a pipeline some three or four miles to another site ('Marsh Mills') owned by the plaintiff. Between the nearest points of the land belonging to the plaintiff at Lee Moor and Marsh Mills the distance was about two miles. At Marsh Mills the slurry was subjected to further treatment whereby the final water content was removed leaving a marketable cake or powder. The plaintiff wished to erect new buildings and plant at Marsh Mills. It sought a declaration that the proposed development was permitted by art 3(1)[a] of, and Sch 1,

---

a   Article 3(1) provides: 'Subject to the subsequent provisions of this order, development of any class specified in schedule 1 to this order is permitted by this order and may be undertaken upon land to which this order applies, without the permission of the local planning authority or the Minister: Provided that the permission granted by this Order in respect of any such class of development shall be subject to any condition or limitation imposed in the said schedule 1 in relation to that class.'

class XVIII to, the Town and Country Planning General Development Order 1963, contending that, by virtue of the definitions in art 2(1)[b] of the 1963 order, the Marsh Mills site was 'land in or adjacent to and belonging to a quarry or mine comprised in [the plaintiff's] undertaking' within para 2[c] of class XVIII.

Held – The plaintiff was not entitled to the declaration sought for the following reasons—

(i) Marsh Mills was not, within art 2(1), a site on which 'mining operations', i e the 'winning and working' of minerals, took place since the winning and working of the china clay, i e its extraction from the land, took place at Lee Moor and it was impossible to regard Lee Moor, the pipeline and Marsh Mills together as a single site. Accordingly the land at Marsh Mills on which it was proposed to erect the building was not 'land in . . . a mine' within class XVIII, para 2 (see p 242 h and j and p 243 e and f, post).

(ii) Neither was Marsh Mills land 'adjacent to' a mine. The word 'adjacent' meant close to or nearby or lying by, its significance or application in point of distance depending on the circumstances in which the word was used. The word as used in class XVIII, para 2, had to be understood in the planning context of permission to erect buildings and plant for purposes connected with operations at the site of a mine either on that site or very near to that site so that they would not appear to be other than a growth of that site. In that sense Marsh Mills could not be considered as 'adjacent to' the site at Lee Moor (see p 243 a to c, post).

Per Curiam. The words 'and belonging to' in para 2 of class XVIII relate both to a case when the particular land is in a mine and to a case where it is adjacent to a mine. The words indicate that the land on which the building is to be erected is or is to be dedicated to the service of the mine in, or adjacent to which it is, and not to the service of some distant mine (see p 244 d f and g, post).

Decision of Goulding J [1973] 2 All ER 730 affirmed.

Notes

For permitted development by mineral undertakers, see 37 Halsbury's Laws (3rd Edn) 296, para 406.

For the Town and Country Planning General Development Order 1963 (SI 1963 No 709), arts 2, 3, Sch 1, class XVIII, see 21 Halsbury's Statutory Instruments (2nd Reissue) 107, 111, 130. The 1963 order was revoked and replaced as from 1st March 1973 by the Town and Country Planning General Development Order 1973 (SI 1973 No 31).

---

b   Article 2(1), so far as material, provides: 'In this order, unless the context otherwise requires— . . . "mine" includes any site on which mining operations are carried on; . . . "mining operations" means the winning and working of minerals in, on or under land, whether by surface or underground working; . . .'

c   Paragraph 2 reads: 'The erection, alteration or extension by mineral undertakers on land in or adjacent to and belonging to a quarry or mine comprised in their undertaking of any building, plant or machinery, or structure or erection in the nature of plant or machinery, which is required in connection with the winning or working of minerals, including coal won or worked by virtue of section 36(1) of the Coal Industry Nationalisation Act 1946, but not any other coal, in pursuance of permission granted or deemed to be granted under Part III of the Act, or which is required in connection with the treatment or disposal of such minerals: Provided that permission shall be required for the erection, alteration or extension of a building, but the local planning authority shall not refuse permission and shall not impose conditions upon the grant thereof, unless they are satisfied that it is expedient so to do on the ground that: (a) the erection, alteration or extension of such building would injure the amenity of the neighbourhood and modifications can reasonably be made or conditions can reasonably be imposed in order to avoid or reduce the injury; or (b) the proposed building or extension ought to be, and can reasonably be, sited elsewhere.'

a **Case referred to in judgment**
English Clays Lovering Pochin & Co Ltd v Davis, Watts, Blake Bearne & Co Ltd v Davis
(1966) 12 RRC 307, [1967] JPL 223, [1966] RVR 607, [1966] RA 475, LT.

Appeal
By a summons dated 25th May 1972 the appellant, English Clays Lovering Pochin &
b Co Ltd, claimed against the respondent, Plymouth Corporation, a declaration that the
erection of a clay drier building and store building together with necessary conveyor
and two chimneys at Marsh Mills, Plymouth, as proposed by the appellant in a planning
application dated 11th February 1972, would be development by a mineral undertaker
permitted by art 3 and class XVIII of Sch 1 to the Town and Country Planning General
Development Orders 1963 to 1969[1], subject to the conditions and limitations imposed
c in Sch 1 in relation to that class.   On 1st December 1972 Goulding J[2] dismissed the
summons and the appellant appealed.   By a respondent's notice the respondent
sought to affirm the decision of the judge on, inter alia, the additional ground that the
land at Marsh Mills was not land 'belonging to' any quarry or mine. The facts are set
out in the judgment of the court.

d *Charles Sparrow QC* and *Guy Seward* for the appellant.
Jeremiah Harman QC and *Elizabeth Appleby* for the respondent.

Cur adv vult

22nd February.   **RUSSELL LJ** delivered the following judgment of the court.
This appeal from Goulding J[2] raises the question whether the proposed erection of
e certain buildings and plant by the appellant at the site known as Marsh Mills comes
within the permission to develop conferred by art 3 and Sch 1, class XVIII, para 2, of
the Town and Country Planning General Development Order 1963[3]. Class XVIII,
para 2, refers to:

'The erection . . . by mineral undertakers on land in or adjacent to and belong-
f ing to a quarry or mine comprised in their undertaking of any building, plant or
machinery . . . which is required in connection with the winning or working of
minerals . . . or which is required in connection with the treatment or disposal of
such minerals . . .'

The general development order contains, either directly or by force of s 31 of the
Interpretation Act 1889, certain definitions. (1) ' "Minerals" includes all minerals and
g substances in or under land of a kind ordinarily worked for removal by underground
or surface working . . .': see the Town and Country Planning Act 1962, s 221. (2)
' "Mining operations" means the winning and working of minerals in, on or under
land, whether by surface or underground working'. (3) ' "Mine" includes any site
on which mining operations are carried on'. (4) ' "Mineral undertakers" means
undertakers engaged in mining operations'.
h The mineral with which we are concerned in this case is china clay. It is a substance
which is found in some granite measures taking the place of the decomposed felspar
constituent of the granite. It is therefore mechanically associated in the ground with
much else, and requires, if it is to be put to industrial and merchantable use, to be
separated out. This is done by first detaching, by high pressure water jet, the mechanical combination of china clay and its associates, and subsequently by a system of refine-
j ment of the resultant slurry (that is to say, water with china clay and impurities in
suspension) driving off or abstracting from the slurry substantially all but china clay.

---

1   SI 1963 No 709, as amended by SI 1964 No 1239, SI 1965 No 498, SI 1967 No 1076, SI 1968 No
      1623 and SI 1969 No 276
2   [1973] 2 All ER 730, [1973] 1 WLR 1346
3   SI 1963 No 709

The resultant slurry is then passed through fine filters which separate the china clay
from the water vehicle, leaving in effect a substance (china clay) from which the final
water content may be driven by heating, leaving a marketable cake or powder.
This is a very rough, but we think adequate, description of the process. We state in
advance that the process which we have described takes place at the property of the
appellant high up at Lee Moor up to the point where the slurry is to be regarded as
china clay in suspension in the residue of the water originally used in the first detaching.
From there the slurry continues in a pipe some three or four miles along a narrow
strip of land, the site of an old tramway, to the site called Marsh Mills in the valley of
the Plym, and at Marsh Mills the rest of the process described takes place, Marsh
Mills being conveniently sited as a point of distribution of the merchantable china
clay. The appellant wishes, by the erection of modern buildings and plant at Marsh
Mills, to improve its output of china clay in the market, which without doubt is a
praiseworthy object.

If the definitions that have been mentioned are applied to class XVIII, para 2, and to
the mineral now in question, the requirements for inclusion in the general development order permission may be thus stated: (1) the building (for example) proposed to
be erected on the particular land at Marsh Mills must be proposed to be erected by an
undertaker engaged in the winning and working of a mineral (china clay) in, on or
under land whether by surface or underground working, china clay in this case
qualifying as a mineral in the context of a definition of a mineral as including substances in or under land of a kind ordinarily worked for removal by underground or
surface working. (2) The particular land at Marsh Mills on which it is proposed to
erect the building must be shown to be in or adjacent to and belonging to a site on
which the winning and working of china clay in, on or under land whether by surface
or underground working is carried on. (3) The site last mentioned must be comprised
in the undertaker's undertaking. (4) The building on the particular land must be
required in connection with the winning or working of china clay, or required in
connection with the treatment or disposal of china clay. The crucial question in this
appeal turns on the second of these requirements for inclusion in the general development order permission.

It is first argued that Marsh Mills is a mine and therefore land in a mine in the sense
that it is a site on which the working of china clay on land by surface working is carried
on. This argument reads 'winning and working' as 'winning or working', and asserts
that working of the mineral continues until the merchantable china clay in cake or
powder form is produced by final filtration and drying at Marsh Mills. It is secondly
argued that Marsh Mills is land in a mine because there is one site constituting a mine
(as defined) which consists of Lee Moor, the pipeline, and Marsh Mills, in the whole of
which the operation of winning and working china clay is carried out, and of which site
Marsh Mills is a part. It is thirdly and alternatively argued that if the land at Marsh
Mills is not land in a mine as being itself a mine or part of a mine, it is adjacent to and
belonging to a mine at Lee Moor.

We entirely reject the first argument. No one, in our view, would describe the land
at Marsh Mills as a mine. It is simply a place where china clay is separated out from
the water that has carried it there from Lee Moor down the pipe. There is no china
clay to be found in nature at Marsh Mills. Does the definition of 'mine' as including a
site on which the winning and working of china clay, whether by surface or underground working, are carried on carry the matter any further? Not in our judgment.
The comprehensive phrase 'winning and working' simply does not take place at
Marsh Mills: and contrast the phrase 'winning or working' in class XVIII, para 2.

The second argument we also reject: that is, that there is a mine consisting of Lee
Moor, the pipeline strip and Marsh Mills. It is quite fanciful, in our view, to describe
these three aspects of the appellant's undertaking as 'a site' on which mining operations as defined are carried on. Rather are they three sites on only one of which such
operations are carried on.

a   The third argument is that the land at Marsh Mills is 'adjacent to and belonging to' the Lee Moor mine. As the crow flies, between the nearest points of the land belonging to the appellant at Lee Moor and Marsh Mills the distance is some two miles. 'Adjacent' means close to or nearby or lying by: its significance or application in point of distance depends on the circumstances in which the word is used. The particular circumstances here are that the general development order is concerned with plan-
b   ning. It is easy to understand a general permission to erect buildings and plant, for purposes connected with operations at the site of a mine, *on* that site; or if not on that site (a word of somewhat loose import) very near to that site so that it would not appear to be other than a growth of the site; and this we believe to be the significance of the words 'adjacent to' in this paragraph of the general development order. On that footing, Marsh Mills cannot be regarded as adjacent to the site of the mine at Lee
c   Moor, separated as it is by not less than two miles of agricultural country, woodland, and parkland descending steeply from Lee Moor.

In connection with the phrase 'adjacent to' some reliance was placed on the joining of the Lee Moor land to the Marsh Mills land by the narrow strip of land (the old tramway) carrying the pipe, and the fact that there was one continuous process starting with the removal of relevant soil etc containing china clay by high pressure
d   water jet and finishing with the drying out at Marsh Mills. We think this reliance is not justifiable. If it were relevant, it would make Marsh Mills adjacent—or, for that matter, part of one site of a mine—however many miles might separate it from Lee Moor, which cannot be right. The same objection may be made to what was contended for the appellant to be the test of adjacency, the operational test.

It is perhaps not necessary to be dogmatic on the point in this case; but our present
e   view is that to 'win' a mineral is to make it available or accessible to be removed from the land, and to 'work' a mineral is (at least initially) to remove it from its position in the land: in the present case the china clay is 'won' when the overburden is taken away, and 'worked' (at least initially) when the water jets remove the china clay together with its mechanically associated other substances from their position in the earth or land to a situation of suspension in water. Thereafter it may be that the pro-
f   cesses of separation out are more aptly described as treatment. Hereunder we draw attention to the definition of 'minerals' (already noticed) and in particular to the words 'in or under land . . . ordinarily worked for removal', which suggest to us removal from the land—that is to say, the corporeal hereditament. It was contended for the appellant that 'working' of the china clay continues until there is a merchantable substance: and an argument to that effect was based on a comparison of class XVIII, para 2, with the definition in the general development order of 'industrial
g   process'. That is in the following terms:

'. . . "industrial process" means any process for or incidental to any of the following purposes, namely:— (*a*) the making of any article or of part of any article, or (*b*) the altering, repairing, ornamenting, finishing, cleaning, washing, packing or canning, or adapting for sale, or breaking up or demolition, of any
h   article, or (*c*) without prejudice to the foregoing paragraphs, the getting, dressing or treatment of minerals, being a process carried on in the course of trade or business . . .'

The words 'the getting, dressing or treatment of minerals' are, it was suggested, to be taken as synonymous with 'winning', 'working' and 'treatment' in class XVIII, para 2: 'dressing', it was said, embraces separating out of the china clay (see an article
j   on Ore Dressing in the Encyclopaedia Britannica): 'treatment' must be something, it is said, which is *not* 'dressing' in the definition of 'industrial process': 'treatment' must mean the same in class XVIII, para 2, and therefore does not include 'dressing': if therefore 'working' in class XVIII, para 2, does not include the process of separating out, there is a serious defect or lacuna, in that erection of plant etc for separating out (for example) china clay *cannot* come within the general development order: therefore

'working' must be taken to include separation out. This argument appears to us to be over-refined, and to be based on a false premise; that is to say, that in the definition of 'industrial process', 'treatment' is something which cannot be or include 'dressing'.

An argument for the appellant was based on the language of a Ministerial decision on a planning appeal by the appellant in 1958. This related primarily to activities at Lee Moor and Wotter (which is in the Lee Moor area), but the application and appeal extended also to Marsh Mills. The decision letter was headed '*Winning and working of china clay and allied minerals Lee Moor, Wotter and Marsh Mills . . .*' The appeal was described as an appeal 'against conditions imposed by the [local planning authority] in granting permission for the winning and working of minerals from part of an area of land at Lee Moor, Wotter and Marsh Mills'. Marsh Mills was among the lands indicated on the plan as relevantly outlined and in respect of which the Minister 'grants permission for the winning and working of china clay and minerals overlying china clay'. We observe these phrases, but they do nothing to persuade us that the land at Marsh Mills is either the site of a mine or part of the site of a mine. We note that reference is made to minerals other than china clay; and there has never been any suggestion that Marsh Mills deals in any way with any other mineral.

So far as the requirement of 'belonging to' a mine in class XVIII, para 2, is concerned, it is not necessary to our decision to express a view on its significance. We think that as a matter of grammar the words 'and belonging to' relate both to a case where the particular land is in a mine and to a case where it is adjacent to a mine. If the words 'and belonging to' were absent, the situation would be that the site of the proposed (for example) building must be in or adjacent to a mine which is comprised in the undertaking of the person who proposes to erect the building; and the building must be required in connection with the winning or working or treatment or disposal of minerals. Thus far it would, we apprehend, be supposed that this would refer to, for example, the treatment of minerals extracted from *that* mine. But it might have been arguable that the reference being to, for example, the treatment of minerals generally, the permission enabled the erection of a building in or adjacent to mine A when it was not required in relation to minerals extracted from mine A but was required in relation to minerals extracted from mine B many miles away: hence 'and belonging to' as indicating that the land on which the building is to be erected is or is to be dedicated to the service of mine A—the mine in or adjacent to which it is—and not to the service of some distant mine B. If that be the right approach, 'belonging to' has some effect: and if the Marsh Mills activities as hitherto conducted were in, so to speak, the heart of the Lee Moor operations, so that what is proposed would be on land in or adjacent to the mine, the site or sites of the proposed building and plant would be land 'belonging to' the mine.

We only add that we entirely agree with the comments of Goulding J[1] on the rating case of *English Clays Lovering Pochin & Co Ltd v Davis Ltd*[2], which simply demonstrates that in the context of legislation of differing characters or purposes the words 'adjacent to' may have different applications.

Accordingly, we dismiss the appeal.

Appeal dismissed. Leave to appeal to the House of Lords refused.

Solicitors: *Robbins, Olivey & Lake*, agents for *Stephens & Scown*, St Austell (for the appellant); *H R Haydon*, Town Clerk, Plymouth Corporation (for the respondent).

S A Hatteea Esq Barrister.

---

1 [1973] 2 All ER at 739, 740, [1973] 1 WLR at 1356, 1357
2 (1966) 12 RRC 307

R v Wall

COURT OF APPEAL, CRIMINAL DIVISION
CAIRNS LJ, GRIFFITHS AND MAIS JJ
5th MARCH 1974

Customs – Importation of prohibited goods – Knowingly concerned in fraudulent evasion – Jurisdiction – Acts performed abroad – Accused and others charged with being concerned in fraudulent evasion on specified date – Accused having taken steps abroad on earlier date for purpose of fraudulent evasion – Whether accused 'knowingly concerned' in fraudulent evasion on date specified – Whether jurisdiction to try accused – Customs and Excise Act 1952, s 304.

The appellant was charged with two others that on 17th February 1972 he had been knowingly concerned in the fraudulent evasion of the restriction imposed on the importation of cannabis by s 2^a of the Dangerous Drugs Act 1965, contrary to s 304^b of the Customs and Excise Act 1952. He admitted that, at a date earlier than 17th February, he had been with the other defendants in Afghanistan but denied any association with the importation of cannabis. However it was shown that his finger-prints had been found on a wrapper of cannabis in a van belonging to one of the co-defendants. He was convicted and appealed, contending that the jury might have believed that the only part played by him had been his handling of the goods abroad for the purpose of their being transmitted to the United Kingdom; it was argued that, on that basis, the conviction could not stand since he had been charged with the others that on 17th February he had been knowingly concerned in the fraudulent evasion whereas he had done nothing on that date and what he had done earlier had been done abroad.

Held – Although in general an act committed abroad could not be the subject of criminal proceedings in England, the fraudulent evasion which was the subject of the charge had taken place in England on 17th February and, because of the steps which the appellant had taken earlier for the purpose of the fraudulent evasion, it followed he had been 'knowingly concerned' in it, within the meaning of s 304. Accordingly the appellant had been properly convicted and the appeal would be dismissed (see p 248 *b* and *g*, p 249 *g* and p 250 *b*, post).

R v Robert Millar (Contractors) Ltd [1970] 1 All ER 577, *R v Baxter* [1971] 2 All ER 359 and dictum of Willis J in *R v Smith (Donald)* [1973] 2 All ER at 1167 applied.

Notes

For the offence of being knowingly concerned in the fraudulent evasion of the restrictions on the importation of goods, see 33 Halsbury's Laws (3rd Edn) 42, 43, para 81.

For the Customs and Excise Act 1952, s 304, see 9 Halsbury's Statutes (3rd Edn) 201.

For the Dangerous Drugs Act 1965, s 2, see 21 Halsbury's Statutes (3rd Edn) 953.

Cases referred to in judgment

Director of Public Prosecutions v Doot [1973] 1 All ER 940, [1973] AC 807, [1973] 2 WLR 532, 57 Cr App Rep 600, HL; *rvsg sub nom R v Doot* [1972] 2 All ER 1046, [1973] QB 73, [1972] 3 WLR 33, 57 Cr App Rep 13, CA.

R v Baxter [1971] 2 All ER 359, [1972] 1 QB 1, [1971] 2 WLR 1138, [1971] Crim LR 281, sub nom *R v Baxter (Robert)* 55 Cr App Rep 214, CA.

R v Robert Millar (Contractors) Ltd [1970] 1 All ER 577, [1970] 2 QB 54, [1970] 2 WLR 541, 54 Cr App Rep 158, CA.

R v Smith (Donald) [1973] 2 All ER 1161, [1973] QB 924, [1973] 3 WLR 88, CA.

---

a Section 2 is set out at p 246 *f*, post
b Section 304, so far as material, is set out at p 246 *e*, post

Treacy v Director of Public Prosecutions [1971] 1 All ER 110, [1971] AC 537, [1971] 2 WLR 112, 55 Cr App Rep 113, HL; *affg* sub nom *R v Treacy* [1970] 3 All ER 205, [1970] 3 WLR 592, CA.

Appeal

Geoffrey David Wall appealed against his conviction in the Crown Court at Maidstone on 19th July 1973 before his Honour Judge Gower QC on a charge of being knowingly concerned in the fraudulent evasion of the restriction imposed by s 2 of the Dangerous Drugs Act 1965 on the importation of a dangerous drug, contrary to s 304 of the Customs and Excise Act 1952. The appellant was sentenced to four years imprisonment. He appealed by leave of the full court. The facts are set out in the judgment of the court.

Michael Parker QC and *Michael Gale* for the appellant.
Anthony Hidden for the Crown.

CAIRNS LJ delivered the judgment of the court. On 19th July 1973, before the Crown Court at Maidstone, this appellant was convicted of being knowingly concerned in the fraudulent evasion of the restriction imposed on the importation of a dangerous drug. The charge was laid under s 304 of the Customs and Excise Act 1952 which provides:

'Without prejudice to any other provision of this Act, if any person . . . (*b*) is, in relation to any goods, in any way knowingly concerned in any fraudulent evasion or attempt at evasion of any duty chargeable thereon or of any such prohibition or restriction as aforesaid [i e a restriction on importation] or of any provision of this Act applicable to those goods, [he shall be guilty of an offence].'

The Dangerous Drugs Act 1965, s 2, provides:

'It shall not be lawful for a person to import into the United Kingdom a drug to which this Part of this Act applies except under a licence granted by a Secretary of State.'

Cannabis is one of the drugs to which that Part of the Act applies (see s 1). The appellant was sentenced to four years imprisonment. He appeals against conviction by leave of the full court, the full court having taken the view that a substantial point of law arises in the case.

On 15th February 1973 one Robin Brettell came to the house of one Ian Metcalf and his wife Linda in Stourbridge. Of these three, who were co-defendants with the appellant, the two men pleaded guilty, the woman pleaded not guilty and was acquitted. On 16th February 1973 the Metcalfs together with Brettell went down to Dover in their car, which was left in the town, crossed to Calais and the next day they met one Bushell, another co-defendant who was convicted. He had a Commer van. Later in the day Metcalf brought the van to Folkestone. It was searched by customs officers and was found to contain some three hundredweight of cannabis; some of it wrapped and some of it in loose packages. The value on the 'pushers' market' was said to be in the neighbourhood of £100,000. At about 8 o'clock that evening, while the Metcalfs were still being seen by customs officers, other officers went in a car patrolling the area round about the examination shed. They reached some parked vehicles including the Metcalfs' car. The driver was one Costello, another defendant who was convicted. There were two passengers, Bushell and Brettell. Costello denied that he had just disembarked. The officer making the enquiry noticed some French cigarettes in the vehicle. The officer moved away but returned after ten minutes to find that the car had gone. At 12.45 the following morning some police officers made a search of the Metcalfs' home. About a quarter of a mile from it they found the Metcalfs' car with Costello driving and Bushell and Brettell as passengers, and all three were arrested.

On 30th March police and customs officers went to a farm where the appellant was living with a Mrs Skidmore. The appellant was arrested and when told this was on suspicion of being concerned with the importation of cannabis he made no reply. Correspondence was found at the farm addressed to Costello. Later the appellant said that he had left the United Kingdom in December. It was pointed out that his passport suggested that he had been out of the country from June to September 1972, and again from December 1972 to January 1973. He said that that was right, that he did leave in June with Costello. The December trip was intended to buy some clothes because he had made money out of clothes on the previous trip. He said that he went by car on the December trip. He was asked if it was Bushell's car. He agreed and said there was a 'bird' with them. They went across Europe and to Iran. He left Bushell at Meshed. He himself went to Afghanistan and Kabul. He flew back to the United Kingdom arriving in the first or second week of January 1973. It was put to him that he went out with Bushell and Mrs Skidmore in a Commer van and he said Yes. He said that he had seen Bushell briefly in Kandahar. Mrs Skidmore had left Bushell in France. He said he had nothing more to do with Bushell after seeing him in Kandahar. He was then told his finger-prints appeared on a wrapper of cannabis in the van and he replied that he handled a lot of 'shit' in Kandahar. (The word 'shit' is used by some people as meaning cannabis.) He said that he went to one of the farms where they grew it and saw some hundreds of slabs and had seen slabs covered by polythene. He said his reason for going out in the van was because he knew the roads and could help with the driving. He had known Costello for four years and Bushell for a short time; Bushell's finger-prints had also been found on a wrapper.

The appellant agreed that they had talked about 'shit' on the way out and the price of it had been mentioned. He said he did not know how his finger-prints got there. He gave evidence and said that he had known Mrs Skidmore for about two years and Costello for about three weeks. He did not know Brettell or the Metcalfs. In the summer of 1972 he went with Costello on a trip to the Middle East. When he found that there were shirts on sale he brought 300 back for resale. In December, when staying with Mrs Skidmore, he decided to go out again on another trip. He met a man called Bosworth who was taking people out to Afghanistan and he volunteered to help Bosworth with the driving. Mrs Skidmore and the children came with him and there was another couple too. By the time they got to Iran he and Mrs Skidmore were arguing. At Meshed it was decided it would be best for him to leave them. He went out looking for contacts for shirts and met the party again at Kandahar. When he was going around there was cannabis in the shops, which he was asked to buy. He smoked it there and went to a farm where it was cultivated. He said he used to handle cannabis when shown it in shops. There were polythene bags in the van in which he had travelled out and he could well have touched a polythene bag containing food or clothes. He said he flew back to England on his own. About a month later he got a telephone call from Mrs Skidmore asking him to pick her up at Dover. He brought her back to the farmhouse and denied being a party to loading the cannabis on the van. He said he had no idea it was going to be used for that purpose. Clearly that evidence as a whole was rejected by the jury.

The basis of this appeal is that the jury may have believed that the only part played by the appellant in this business was his handling of the goods abroad for the purposes of their being transmitted to this country and on that basis the conviction cannot stand because the appellant was charged with the others that on 17th February 1973 he was knowingly concerned in the fraudulent evasion of the restriction on importation. It is said that if he did nothing relevant on that day and if what he did do earlier was not done in England then he was wrongly convicted. Counsel for the appellant relied on the proposition that in general an act committed abroad cannot be the subject of criminal proceedings in this country. To that proposition there are admittedly exceptions, but it was contended that none of them apply to s 304 of the 1952 Act.

The court was referred to *Director of Public Prosecutions v Doot*[1], *Treacy v Director of Public Prosecutions*[2], *R v Baxter*[3] and *R v Millar*[4] for the purposes of distinguishing them. In the view of this court acts done abroad in order to further the fraudulent evasion of a restriction on importation into this country are punishable under s 304 of the 1952 Act. If it were not so a person abroad who slipped a package containing a dangerous drug into the luggage of an innocent passenger who then brought it into this country would not be punishable under this section, nor, so far as we are aware, under any other.

In our judgment the view that we take is supported by passages in the judgments in the cases to which we were referred. In *R v Baxter*[3] a person had despatched from Northern Ireland letters addressed to firms in Liverpool containing fraudulent football pool claims and was charged with attempting to obtain moneys by deception. Sachs LJ, delivering the judgment of the court, said[5]:

> 'An alternative but no less effective way of expressing the matter is to say that he who despatches a missile or a missive arranges for its transport and delivery (essential parts of the attempt) and is thus committing part of the crime within the jurisdiction by the means which he has arranged. The physical personal presence of an offender within this country is not, according to our law, an essential element of offences committed here.'

Then Sachs LJ went on[6]:

> 'Up to this point only passing reference has been made to the decision in *Treacy v Director of Public Prosecutions*[2] (which concerned a demand with menaces posted in this country to someone in Germany) because the court today has so far been dealing with the issue before it on broad grounds. It is appropriate, however, to say, first, that there is nothing in the above decision which in any way militates against the views so far expressed in this judgment; secondly, there is much in it to support them. Indeed on a narrower ground it might be said to conclude the issue against the appellant. The attempt to obtain the money by deception in the shape of a letter can be likened to the demand by letter which was under consideration in the House of Lords; and it appears that all their Lordships were disposed to hold that had it been a case of a demand despatched abroad which had arrived in England, there would have been jurisdiction here to try the offence— indeed three of their Lordships specifically so stated.'

If despatching in a letter from a foreign place to England containing false pretences or a blackmailing threat can be regarded as constituting an offence punishable here we do not see why taking part in the despatch of drugs from abroad to England with a view to evading the restriction on import should not be punishable here as being concerned in such evasion of restriction on import into the United Kingdom.

R v Millar[4] was a case concerning death by dangerous driving of a vehicle in England; the vehicle had been despatched by its owners, who were a Scottish company, from Scotland and the owners of the vehicle as well as the driver were charged with causing death by dangerous driving. Fenton Atkinson LJ said[7]:

---

1   [1973] 1 All ER 940, [1973] AC 807
2   [1971] 1 All ER 110, [1971] AC 537
3   [1971] 2 All ER 359, [1972] 1 QB 1
4   [1970] 1 All ER 577, [1970] 2 QB 54
5   [1971] 2 All ER at 362, [1972] 1 QB at 12
6   [1971] 2 All ER at 363, [1972] 1 QB at 13
7   [1970] 1 All ER at 580, [1970] 2 QB at 72

a   'We turn now to counsel for the appellants' second point. He has assembled
     with very great industry a mass of authorities going back 200 years or more; but,
     in our view, he has been unable to find any case which establishes his proposition.
     He has against him at least two statements of the law by very learned authors. I
     refer first to Russell on Crime[1] where the law is stated in this way: "A simple
     but important point is sometimes overlooked, namely, that when the law
b   relating to principals and accessories as such is under consideration there is
     only one crime, although there may be more than one person . . . then the
     question arises as to the category in which each one is to be placed, that is, whether
     he is accessory before the fact, or principal in the first or second degree or an
     accessory after the fact. There is one crime, and that it has been committed
     must be established before there can be any question of criminal guilt or
c   participation in it." '

Fenton Atkinson LJ goes on quoting[2] from Russell[1]:

     ' "To make a man responsible for a crime, whether felony or misdemeanour, it
     is not essential that he should be present at the place where the crime takes effect,
     if he had, in fact, set in motion the agencies by which the crime is effected. But in
d   case of absence from the scene of the crime, to make a man responsible as a
     principal offender, he must have set in force physical agencies or have employed
     an innocent agent." It seems to us that in this case the company and Mr Robert
     Millar set in motion on the road this vehicle with the known dangerous tyre. The
     other statement of law to which one would refer is by Professor Glanville Will-
     iams which appears in an article in the Law Quarterly Review[3] where he dealt
e   with secondary parties, accessories and abettors. He wrote: "Where a crime
     is committed in England, a secondary party (accessory or abettor) can be pun-
     ished even though he was not within British territorial jurisdiction at the time
     when the crime was committed or when he gave his assistance—at least if he is a
     citizen of the United Kingdom. [These are the important words.] This is an applica-
     tion of the principle that secondary parties are guilty not of self-subsisting crimes
f   on their own account but of participation in a crime committed by another."
     We think that the law is correctly stated in the passages that I have read, and here
     the offence of causing death by dangerous driving was committed in England by
     Mr Hart; but the appellants are guilty of participating in that crime and not of
     some self-subsisting crime on their own account and, therefore, they are in the
     same position as the principal offender and they are liable to be tried in this
g   country.'

So here there is one offence, that of being knowingly concerned in fraudulent
evasion on 17th February 1973, and just as in R v Millar[4] the part played by the company was played earlier and in another country, so here if that was the only part played
by the appellant he was indictable here for it. Further support for our view is to be
h   found in R v Smith (Donald)[5]. That was a case, concerning cannabis, under s 304 of the
1952 Act, and though the issues there were quite different from those here, counsel for
the appellant very properly drew our attention to this sentence[6] in the judgment of
the court delivered by Willis J: 'It was quite unnecessary to prove that the applicant
did anything to further the transaction in this country.'

j
1   12th Edn (1964), pp 128, 129
2   [1970] 1 All ER at 580, [1970] 2 QB at 73
3   Venue and the Ambit of Criminal Law (1965) 81 LQR 530
4   [1970] 1 All ER 577, [1970] 2 QB 54
5   [1973] 2 All ER 1161, [1973] QB 924
6   [1973] 2 All ER at 1167, [1973] QB at 936

Finally it was contended that because s 62 of the 1952 Act expressly makes punishable acts committed abroad, s 304 must be confined to acts done in this country. We cannot accept that argument. Section 62 is concerned with the doing of something which of its nature is done at sea or in a foreign port. Section 304 is concerned with importation into this country (as in *R v Millar*[1] the death by dangerous driving was concerned with driving in this country) but that does not rule out criminal liability for a person whose participation consisted in acts done elsewhere. For these reasons the appeal is dismissed.

Appeal dismissed.

Solicitors: *Registrar of Criminal Appeals* (for the appellant); *Solicitor, Customs and Excise.*

Jacqueline Charles Barrister.

Maunsell v Olins and another

COURT OF APPEAL, CIVIL DIVISION   Affirmed HL [1975] 1 All ER 16
EDMUND DAVIES, CAIRNS AND LAWTON LJJ
21st FEBRUARY 1974

Rent restriction – Sub-tenancy – Determination of superior tenancy – Sub-tenancy of dwelling-house forming part of premises let as a whole on superior letting – Premises as a whole not constituting dwelling-house let on protected tenancy – Farm – Cottage adjoining farmhouse – Tenant of farm sub-letting cottage – Sub-tenancy protected as between tenant and sub-tenant – Termination of tenancy of farm – Whether farm 'premises' of which cottage 'forming part' – Whether sub-tenancy of cottage protected as against landlord of farm – Rent Act 1968, s 18(5).

The plaintiff owned the freehold of a farm which comprised about 106 acres and which included a farmhouse, two cottages and other farm buildings. B was the head tenant of the farm. The tenancy was protected under the Agricultural Holdings Act 1948. The tenancy agreement provided for a tenancy from year to year and contained a provision that the tenant should not sublet except for the cottages. In 1959 B sublet one of the cottages, which adjoined the farmhouse, to the defendant on an unfurnished letting which, as between the defendant and B, was protected by the Rent Acts. B died in 1971 and his tenancy was terminated by the plaintiff on 25th March 1973. The plaintiff brought proceedings for possession of the cottage. The defendant contended that he was entitled to the protection of the Rent Acts by virtue of s 18(5)[a] of the Rent Act 1968 since the cottage was 'a dwelling-house' forming 'part of premises' (i e the farm) which had been let as a whole on a superior letting and which did not constitute a dwelling-house let on a protected tenancy.

Held – The farm was not 'premises' of which the cottage formed part, within the meaning of s 18(5); the mere fact that the cottage was physically attached to or adjacent to the farmhouse did not make it 'part of the premises' in the sense intended by the section (see p 255 *b e* and *f* and p 256 *a* to *d*, post).
Hobhouse v Wall [1963] 1 All ER 701 followed.

---

1   [1970] 1 All ER 577, [1970] 2 QB 54
a   Section 18(5) is set out at p 251 *j* to p 252 *a*, post

Notes

For protection under the Rent Acts of a sub-tenant of premises forming part of a superior letting, see 23 Halsbury's Laws (3rd Edn) 826-829, para 1611, and for cases on the subject, see 31(2) Digest (Reissue) 1100-1105, 8551-8580.

For the Rent Act 1968, s 18, see 18 Halsbury's Statutes (3rd Edn) 808.

Cases referred to in judgments

Cow v Casey [1949] 1 All ER 197, [1949] 1 KB 474, [1949] LJR 565, CA, 31(2) Digest (Reissue) 1102, 8562.

Hobhouse v Wall [1963] 1 All ER 701, [1963] 2 QB 124, [1963] 2 WLR 604, CA, 31(2) Digest (Reissue) 1102, 8565.

Lethbridge v Lethbridge (1861) 3 De GF & J 523, 30 LJCh 388, 4 LT 127, 45 ER 981, 47 Digest (Repl) 421, 3771.

Whitley v Stumbles [1930] AC 544, 99 LJKB 518, 143 LT 441, HL, 31(2) Digest (Reissue) 933, 7675.

Cases also cited

Bracey v Read [1962] 3 All ER 472, [1963] Ch 88, DC.

Gardiner v Sevenoaks Rural District Council [1950] 2 All ER 84.

Appeal

The plaintiff, Nesta Gwendoline Maunsell, owned the freehold of Hallsannery Farm, Bideford, Devon. The farm included two cottages, 1 and 2 Hallsannery Cottages. In about 1924 the plaintiff let the farm to Ernest Beer who continued to farm it until his death on 15th March 1971. The tenancy was protected under the Agricultural Holdings Act 1948. For some years the first defendant, Ilmars Olins, was employed by Mr Beer on the farm as a farm labourer and, with his wife, the second defendant, he occupied 2 Hallsannery Cottages as a service occupant. In 1955 the first defendant left the employment of Mr Beer and obtained employment with a firm of agricultural engineers but he stayed in the cottage. Subsequently, when 1 Hallsannery Cottages, which adjoined the farmhouse, became vacant, Mr Beer granted the defendants a tenancy of that cottage unfurnished at a rent of £1 a week. The tenancy was, as between the defendants and Mr Beer, protected under the Rent Acts. On the death of Mr Beer the plaintiff served a notice to quit on his estate and in consequence the tenancy of the farm came to an end on 25th March 1973. The plaintiff, taking the view that the sub-tenancy of the defendants came to an end with the termination of the tenancy of Mr Beer, brought proceedings in the Bideford County Court for possession of 1 Hallsannery Cottages and mesne profits. On 26th July 1973 his Honour Judge Stansfield dismissed the claim holding that the defendants were entitled to the protection of the Rent Act 1968 by virtue of s 18(5) of that Act. The plaintiff appealed.

Derek Wood for the plaintiff.
Simon Tuckey for the defendants.

CAIRNS LJ delivered the first judgment at the invitation of Edmund Davies LJ. This is an appeal from a judgment of his Honour Judge Stansfield delivered at the Bideford County Court on 26th July 1973. He dismissed the plaintiff's claim for possession of a cottage and mesne profits, holding that the defendants were entitled to the protection of the Rent Act 1968. The issue arose under s 18(5) of that Act which provides:

'Where a dwelling-house—(a) forms part of premises which have been let as a whole on a superior letting but do not constitute a dwelling-house let on a protected tenancy; and (b) is itself let on a protected tenancy . . . this Act shall apply in relation to the dwelling-house as if, in lieu of the superior letting, there *a* had been separate lettings of the dwelling-house and of the remainder of the premises, for the like purposes as under the superior letting, and at rents equal to the just proportion of the rent under the superior letting.'

It was agreed in the court below—and neither party has sought to resile from these agreements—that the cottage which was the subject-matter of the action stands on land which forms part of a farm which was the subject of a superior letting, that letting *b* not being a protected letting, and that the cottage itself was sublet to the defendants on a letting which was a protected letting as between those sub-tenants and the tenant of the farm who sublet to them. The whole issue before the learned county court judge and in this court has been whether that cottage is 'part of [the] premises' within the meaning of s 18(5) of the 1968 Act.

The facts can be quite shortly stated, because they are not in any way in dispute. The plaintiff is the freeholder of a farm of 106 acres called Hallsannery Farm, which *c* includes a farmhouse, two cottages and other farm buildings. The cottage, the subject-matter of the action, is one of those two and is attached to the farmhouse. The head tenant of the farm for many years was a Mr Beer. On 30th April 1963 the tenancy agreement between him and the plaintiff was reduced to writing. It provided for a tenancy from year to year from Lady Day, and there was a provision that the tenant was not to sublet except for the cottages. *d*

The cottage in question was sublet by Mr Beer to the defendants in 1959. It was an unfurnished letting. The first defendant was not then working on the farm, but worked somewhere quite separately. But, as I have already said, it was common ground that the tenancy as between the defendants and Mr Beer was a protected tenancy. The tenancy which Mr Beer held from the plaintiff, on the other hand, was protected by the Agricultural Holdings Act 1948, and the Rent Acts did not apply *e* thereto. On 15th March 1971 Mr Beer died. On 26th April 1971 notice to quit was served by the plaintiff on Mr Beer's estate, but as a full year's notice expiring on 25th March was required, the notice had to be for 25th March 1973, and at that date Mr Beer's tenancy came to an end.

The plaintiff's case was that the sub-tenancy of the defendants died with the tenancy of Mr Beer. The defendants in answer to the plaintiff's claim relied solely on s 18(5) of *f* the Rent Act 1968. That subsection has a history to which it is convenient to refer. Under the earlier Rent Acts, when the tenancy of a house was protected and when part of that house was sublet, the sub-tenant was protected as against the freeholder. But in *Cow v Casey*[1] it was held that where the superior letting was not a protected one, the sub-tenancy was not protected. It was principally in consequence of that decision that in the Housing Repairs and Rents Act 1954 a section was introduced, *g* s 41 of that Act, which provided protection in terms which appear to me to be in substance identical with s 18(5) of the 1968 Act.

Counsel for the defendants has sought to persuade this court that there is a difference of meaning between the two enactments, because s 41 of the 1954 Act refers to 'a dwelling-house to which the [Increase of Rent and Mortgage Interest (Restrictions) Act 1920] applies [which] forms part of premises, not being such a dwelling-house, *h* which have been let as a whole on a superior letting' whereas s 18(5) of the 1968 Act refers to 'a dwelling-house [which] forms part of premises which have been let as a whole on a superior letting but do not constitute a dwelling-house let on a protected tenancy . . .' I can only say that, to my mind, the difference in wording conveys no difference of meaning. It is not to be expected that it would, having regard to the fact that the 1968 Act was a consolidating Act. *j*

That is a point of some importance, because the main authority that has to be considered in this case, *Hobhouse v Wall*[2], was a case which was decided under s 41 of the Act of 1954. In that case, as appears from the headnote[3]:

---

1 [1949] 1 All ER 197, [1949] 1 KB 474
2 [1963] 1 All ER 701, [1963] 2 QB 124
3 [1963] 2 QB at 124, 125

'The plaintiffs were the owners of a large farm which they let to C. At all material times a cottage on the farm had been sub-let by C.'s predecessors and by C. to the defendant, who was not employed on the farm. C. determined the defendant's contractual tenancy in 1959 by a notice to quit and thereafter the defendant remained in possession of the cottage as a statutory tenant vis-à-vis C. under the Rent Restriction Acts. In 1961, C. surrendered his tenancy to the plaintiffs who let the farm two months later to H. No rent was accepted from the defendant by the plaintiffs or by H. after the surrender of C.'s tenancy, and they treated the defendant as a trespasser from the date of the surrender. On a claim for possession of the cottage by the plaintiffs, to which they joined H. as co-plaintiff, the defendant relied on the protection given by section 41 of the Housing Repairs and Rents Act, 1954:—*Held*, that, on its true construction, section 41 of the Housing Repairs and Rents Act, 1954, contemplated that the superior letting should be a letting of a residential dwelling-house, and a sub-letting was not within the section unless it formed part of "premises" in the sense of something in the nature of buildings comprised in the superior letting. The section, therefore, did not apply to the sub-letting of a cottage on a large farm and, accordingly, the plaintiffs' claim for possession succeeded.'

I have read that holding as it appears in the headnote, but, as will appear from a passage in the leading judgment, which I shall read, that is not quite accurate, insofar as it refers to the superior letting being a letting of a residential dwelling-house. I propose to read a substantial passage from the judgment of Upjohn LJ, where, after reading the section, he went on as follows[1]:

'It is quite clear that if a large dwelling-house, which is not subject to the Rent Acts, is divided into a number of dwelling-houses, which are subject to the Rent Acts, that section alters the previous law as laid down in *Cow* v. *Casey*[2], and that, when a superior letting of the whole dwelling-house comes to an end for any reason, the occupants of the dwelling-houses within the larger dwelling-house become entitled to maintain the protection of the Rent Acts as against the head landlord. That seems plain.

'The whole question that we have to consider is whether s. 41 of the Act of 1954 covers this case; and I do not find it an easy question to answer. The submissions on each side have been short, but to the point, because, indeed, the matter is not susceptible of prolonged exposition. I think that the argument of counsel for the defendant comes to this: that a literal meaning must be given to the word "premises"; that is to say, as was pointed out by Viscount Hailsham in *Whitley* v. *Stumbles*[3]: ". . . in strict conveyancing language the word 'premises' is used as meaning the subject-matter of the habendum in a lease . . ." So here what is the position? Counsel for the defendant rightly points out that here there is a lease of Holly Tree Farm and some eighty-seven acres, and those are the premises. Part of those premises are Ivy Cottage and some ten acres. Therefore, he says, s. 41 applies. He further points out that there is a contrast between the word "premises" and "a dwelling-house" in that section; and he points out that it would have been possible to use the words "forms part of a dwelling-house" instead of "premises", but, for my part, I think that would lead to considerable difficulties of drafting and would produce an inelegant result.

'We were very properly referred to a number of authorities on the meaning of the word "premises", and, indeed, there is a long list to be found set out in Stroud's Judicial Dictionary[4] where the definitions continue for three and a half

1   [1963] 1 All ER at 703, 704, [1963] 2 QB at 130-132
2   [1949] 1 All ER 197, [1949] 1 KB 474
3   [1930] AC 544 at 546
4   3rd Edn (1953), vol 3, pp 2272 et seq

pages. As TURNER, L.J., pointed out in *Lethbridge* v. *Lethbridge*[1]: ". . . there is no doubt . . . that the word admits of a limited as well as an enlarged sense, and that the context and surrounding circumstances must determine whether it was used in an enlarged or in a limited sense." I do not think that one is really assisted by authorities on wills or on other statutes. We must construe the words of the section and, as I have already said, I do not think it is one which is easy of solution.

'My approach to the construction of the section is this: the Rent Acts are dealing with what are essentially dwelling-houses and protecting the rights of occupants in certain cases. The Rent Acts do not in general deal with large farms which are the subject-matter of the Agricultural Holdings Acts. So when one sees that the section is dealing with a dwelling-house which forms part of premises not being such a dwelling-house, which have been let as a whole on a superior letting, I think, without attempting any definition, that the draftsman or Parliament is here thinking of premises as something in the nature of buildings. Again, however, I am not going to lay down any rule, because there is such an infinite variety of circumstances which may arise under the Rent Acts that it would be most unwise to try and fetter courts in their construction of s. 41 of the Housing Repairs and Rents Act, 1954, and in their application of that section to the particular facts of a particular case. However, to my way of thinking, the draftsman never intended, and did not envisage, a case such as we have here; that is to say, a case where there is a large farm with seventy or eighty acres of land, and as part of it a labourer's cottage, or something of that sort; and I do not think that it would be right, on the construction of s. 41, to describe Ivy Cottage as part of the premises of Holly Tree Farm. I cannot think that the section meant that. Although it may be, as counsel for the defendant has said, that the word "premises" has a strict conveyancing sense, yet I do not think that "premises" is used in s. 41 in its strict conveyancing sense, but in a more popular sense. I do not think that the word "premises" in s. 41 includes Ivy Cottage as part of the premises of Holly Tree Farm. Ivy Cottage is a cottage standing on the land and within the farm of Holly Tree Farm, but for the purposes of s. 41 it would not be proper, I think, to describe it as part of the premises of Holly Tree Farm. I think that the learned county court judge, who delivered a careful reserved judgment, reached a correct conclusion on the section and I would dismiss the appeal.'

Davies LJ agreed without adding anything, and Ormerod LJ, having dealt with a point to which I need not refer, said at the end of his judgment[2]:

'I agree with UPJOHN, L.J., that this is a difficult matter to determine. It is a short point of construction and, in a sense, it is a point that depends largely on first impressions, particularly as the word "premises" is a word which is capable of such a wide and infinite variety of meanings, according to the particular circumstances in which it is used. Like UPJOHN, L.J., without attempting any exhaustive definition of the word "premises", which might be embarrassing to other people in future cases, I have come to the conclusion that it is not intended to apply to the circumstances of this case, and I, too, would dismiss the appeal.'

The learned county court judge distinguished *Hobhouse* v *Wall*[3] on these grounds. He said at the end of his judgment:

'I held that 1 Hallsannery Cottages did form part of the premises, Hallsannery Farm, for the purposes of s 18(5), thereby distinguishing *Hobhouse* v *Wall*[3] on the facts and gave judgment for the defendant accordingly. My reasons

---

1   (1861) 3 De G F & J 523 at 531
2   [1963] 1 All ER at 704, [1963] 2 QB at 133
3   [1963] 1 All ER 701, [1963] 2 QB 124

were that 1 Hallsannery Cottages was let out without any land and that it did physically form part of the farm buildings as evidenced by the photographs. In those circumstances I formed the opinion that the farmhouse and its nexus of adjacent farm buildings were effectively "premises" of which 1 Hallsannery Cottages formed part for the purposes of the subsection and that *Hobhouse v Wall*[1] would have been decided differently if the facts in that case had been such as obtained here.'

With all respect to the learned county court judge, I do not consider that this is a sufficient ground for distinction. In principle, if a farm cottage standing separately is not to be regarded as part of the premises of the farm, it would be unreasonable to consider that merely because the cottage adjoins the farmhouse it should make any difference to the result. I do not propose to investigate questions which might arise as to what would be the position if instead of being a separate cottage it were part of the farmhouse that was sublet, or anything of that kind.

We were invited by counsel for the plaintiff to answer separately two questions: first, whether or not the farm as a whole constitutes premises within the meaning of the subsection; and second, whether or not the cottage is part of the premises in the sense intended by that subsection As counsel for the plaintiff said, Upjohn LJ in his judgment[2] seems rather to have interwoven the two questions, and I do not propose to attempt to unweave them. I prefer to say that, just as Upjohn LJ said in that case[3]:

'... the draftsman never intended, and did not envisage, a case such as we have here; that is to say, a case where there is a large farm with seventy or eighty acres of land, and as part of it a labourer's cottage, or something of that sort; and I do not think it would be right, on the construction of s. 41, to describe Ivy Cottage as part of the premises [as were there farmed].'

I have reached the conclusion in this case that the draftsman never intended, and did not envisage, that a farm cottage such as 1 Hallsannery Cottages should be regarded as part of the premises merely because physically it was attached to or adjacent to the farmhouse.

Counsel for the defendants has contended that in many contexts 'premises' has a wider meaning, and invites us to apply that wider meaning here. As to what conclusion I should have reached if *Hobhouse v Wall*[1] had not been decided in the way it was decided, I express no opinion; but having regard to the decision of the Court of Appeal in that case, I feel bound to say that the learned judge in this case came to the wrong conclusion, and that the appeal should be allowed.

LAWTON LJ. In my judgment, the key to the construction of the words in s 18(5) of the Rent Act 1968, 'forms part of premises which have been let as a whole on a superior letting', lies in the legislative history and policy of the section. This history begins with the decision of this court in *Cow v Casey*[4]. The effect of that decision was to remove from the protection of the Rent Acts many flats which had been made out of large Victorian houses on leases to developers. Parliament decided that tenants of this kind of dwelling-house should have the protection given by the Rent Acts, and accordingly gave protection by s 41 of the Housing Repairs and Rents Act 1954.

This section reappeared with a slight change in wording as s 18(5) of the Rent Act 1968. It is relevant to note that the 1968 Act was a consolidating statute. It follows,

---

1   [1963] 1 All ER 701, [1963] 2 QB 124
2   [1963] 1 All ER at 703, [1963] 2 QB at 130
3   [1963] 1 All ER at 704, [1963] 2 QB at 132
4   [1949] 1 All ER 197, [1949] 1 KB 474

so it seems to me, that s 18(5) must be construed in the light of the policy shown by the legislative history. That policy is not concerned with giving protection to the tenants of agricultural holdings. Such tenants had their own protection under the Agricultural Holdings Act 1948. If this be right, then the word 'premises' must be construed against the background of the Rent Act legislation and not in any other way; and if construed against that background, then in my judgment the word 'premises' will not cover a farm. In this case the letting (and I quote from the lease) was 'of the holding or farm, including the cottages'. The cottage with which this appeal is concerned formed part of the farm, and the policy of the Rent Act 1968 was not to give protection to the tenants of farms, or parts thereof. For my part, I accept the reasoning of Upjohn LJ in his judgment in *Hobhouse v Wall*[1].

I would allow the appeal.

EDMUND DAVIES LJ. I think I have experienced greater difficulty than Cairns and Lawton LJJ in coming to a conclusion about this case. But ultimately I have come to the conclusion that the proper approach was that adopted in *Hobhouse v Wall*[1] by Upjohn LJ, and I do not consider that the facts of the two cases are so distinguishable as to lead to the diametrically opposed conclusion contended for on behalf of the plaintiff. I therefore respectfully agree with the reasons given by Cairns and Lawton LJJ for allowing the appeal and in the order proposed.

Appeal allowed. Leave to appeal refused.

Solicitors: *Macfarlanes*, agents for *Seldon, Ward & Nuttall*, Bideford (for the plaintiff); *T A Goaman & Wright*, Bideford (for the defendants).

Mary Rose Plummer Barrister.

---

1 [1963] 1 All ER 701 at 704, [1963] 2 QB 124 at 132

R v MacDonagh

COURT OF APPEAL, CRIMINAL DIVISION
LORD WIDGERY CJ, SCARMAN LJ, THESIGER, BRISTOW AND MAY JJ
1st, 20th FEBRUARY 1974

Road traffic – Driving while disqualified for holding licence – Driving – Meaning – Using driver's controls for purpose of directing movement of car – Accused pushing car with both feet on road and occasionally adjusting steering wheel – Whether 'driving' – Road Traffic Act 1972, s 99(b).

A police officer told the appellant, who was then disqualified from driving, to move his car as it was causing an obstruction on the road. Some ten minutes later the officer found the appellant manoeuvring it. The appellant's version was that he was pushing the car with his shoulder against the door pillar and both feet on the road, and was controlling that movement by his hand on the steering wheel. He was charged with driving the car while disqualified, contrary to s 99(b)[a] of the Road Traffic Act 1972. The jury were directed that even if the appellant's version was correct it would still be proper to describe the appellant as driving the car and thus guilty of the offence if he was 'in a substantial sense controlling the movement and direction of the car'. The appellant was convicted. On appeal,

Held – Although the word 'drive' meant, essentially, to use the driver's controls for the purpose of directing the movement of the car, the activity in question had to fall within the ordinary meaning of the word 'drive'. The word could not extend to the activity of a person who was not in the car, had both feet in the road, and was making no use of the controls apart from an occasional adjustment of the steering wheel; accordingly, the jury should have been directed that, if the appellant's version of the facts was, or might be, correct, he should be acquitted. The appeal would therefore be allowed and the conviction quashed (see p 258 *j* and p 260 *c d* and *f*, post).

Dictum of Lord Parker CJ in *R v Roberts* [1964] 2 All ER at 542 applied.

Wallace v Major [1946] 2 All ER 87 doubted.

Notes

For the meaning of driving in the road traffic legislation, see 33 Halsbury's Laws (3rd Edn) 450, 451, para 768, and for cases on the subject, see 45 Digest (Repl) 103, 331-337.

For the Road Traffic Act 1972, s 99, see 42 Halsbury's Statutes (3rd Edn) 1751.

Cases referred to in judgment

Ames v MacLeod 1969 JC 1.

R v Roberts [1964] 2 All ER 541, [1965] 1 QB 85, [1964] 3 WLR 180, 128 JP 395, 48 Cr App Rep 296, CCA, 45 Digest (Repl) 103, *337*.

Saycell v Bool [1948] 2 All ER 83, 112 JP 341, 46 LGR 447, DC, 45 Digest (Repl) 118, *411*.

Wallace v Major [1946] 2 All ER 87, [1946] KB 473, 115 LJKB 402, 175 LT 84, 110 JP 231, 44 LGR 237, DC, 45 Digest (Repl) 87, *289*.

Cases also cited

R v Manning [1961] Crim LR 561, CCA.

Shimmell v Fisher [1951] 2 All ER 672, 115 JP 526, DC.

---

a Section 99, so far as material, is set out at p 258 *h*, post

K

Appeal

On 15th August 1973 in the Crown Court at St James's Square, London, SW1, before Mr Recorder Barker QC, the appellant, Brian MacDonagh, was convicted by a majority verdict of ten to two of driving a motor vehicle on a road while disqualified. He was fined £20, with one month's imprisonment in default, his licence was endorsed and he was ordered to pay £10 costs. He appealed against his conviction with leave of the single judge. The case first came before the court (Scarman LJ Thesiger and Bristow JJ) on 21st January 1974 when it was adjourned for the hearing before a full court of five judges. The facts are set out in the judgment of the court.

P J Martin for the appellant.
James Rant for the Crown.

Cur adv vult

20th February. **LORD WIDGERY CJ** read the following judgment of the court. On 15th August 1973 at the Inner London Crown Court, the appellant was convicted by a majority of ten to two of driving a motor vehicle whilst disqualified. He was fined £20 with one month's imprisonment in default and his licence was endorsed. He was also ordered to pay £10 costs. He now appeals against his conviction by leave of the single judge.

It was not disputed that on 6th September 1972, at a time when the appellant was disqualified from driving, his motor car, a Triumph 2000, was in Cornford Grove, London, SW12. A police officer had told him to move it as it was causing an obstruction, and some ten minutes later when the police officer returned to the scene he found the appellant in the process of manoeuvring the car. There was a conflict of evidence whether the engine was running, the police officer maintaining that it was, at all events for part of the time, whereas the appellant contended that it was not. If the police officer's version of the facts was right there seems little doubt that this man was properly convicted, but the recorder left to the jury, as he was bound to do, the issue whether the police officer or the appellant had correctly stated the facts.

The appellant's version was that he had pushed the car standing with his two feet on the road putting his shoulder against the door pillar and putting one hand inside the car on the steering wheel in order to control its movement. The recorder directed the jury that even if they found that the facts were, or might have been, as thus described by the appellant, it would still be proper to describe him as driving the car and thus guilty of the offence if he was 'in a substantial sense controlling the movement and direction of the car'. The matter now comes before this court on a short but important issue, namely, whether the recorder should have directed the jury that if they thought the facts were, or might have been, as stated by the appellant, then he was not driving and therefore entitled to an acquittal.

By s 99 of the Road Traffic Act 1972 it is provided:

'If a person disqualified for holding or obtaining a licence . . . (b) while he is so disqualified drives on a road a motor vehicle . . . he shall be guilty of an offence.'

Numerous other provisions of the same Act make it an offence to drive a motor vehicle when lacking some necessary qualification. Thus, under s 84, a person may not drive unless he has the appropriate driving licence. The Act does not define the word 'drive' and in its simplest meaning we think that it refers to a person using the driver's controls for the purpose of directing the movement of the vehicle. It matters not that the vehicle is not moving under its own power, or is being driven by the force of gravity, or even that it is being pushed by other well-wishers. The essence of driving is the use of the driver's controls in order to direct the movement, however that movement is produced.

There are an infinite number of ways in which a person may control the movement of a motor vehicle, apart from the orthodox one of sitting in the driving seat and using the engine for propulsion. He may be coasting down a hill with the gears in neutral and the engine switched off; he may be steering a vehicle which is being towed by another. As has already been pointed out, he may be sitting in the driving seat whilst others push, or half sitting in the driving seat but keeping one foot on the road in order to induce the car to move. Finally, as in the present case, he may be standing in the road and himself pushing the car with or without using the steering wheel to direct it. Although the word 'drive' must be given a wide meaning, the courts must be alert to see that the net is not thrown so widely that it includes activities which cannot be said to be driving a motor vehicle in any ordinary use of that word in the English language. Unless this is done, absurdity may result by requiring the obtaining of a driving licence and third party insurance in circumstances which cannot have been contemplated by Parliament.

This approach to the problem which we have outlined is, we think, supported by the authorities. In *Wallace v Major*[1] the headnote reads:

'A person who is at the wheel of a disabled motor vehicle for the purpose of steering it while it is being towed by another motor vehicle is not a driver and is not driving a mechanically propelled vehicle within the meaning of s. 11 of the Road Traffic Act, 1930.'

In reaching this decision, Lord Goddard CJ said[2]:

'After all, we have to remember that this is a penal Act, and we are bound to construe the Act strictly and ought not to stretch the language in any way; and, in my judgment, it is impossible to say that a person who is merely steering a vehicle which is being drawn by another vehicle is driving that vehicle.'

Whilst we adopt Lord Goddard CJ's approach to penal legislation, we respectfully doubt whether the correct conclusion was reached on the facts of that case. The court seems to have regarded the defendant as merely a steersman, and to have ignored his responsibility for the use of brakes. Treating him as a mere steersman, the court found support in what is now s 196 of the 1972 Act for saying that he could not be a driver.

In *Saycell v Bool*[3] the owner of a lorry which had run out of petrol released the handbrake and whilst sitting in the driving seat steered the vehicle down an incline for a distance of 100 yards, and Lord Goddard CJ said[4]: '. . . it seems impossible to say that in those circumstances he was not driving the vehicle.'

In *R v Roberts*[5] the Court of Criminal Appeal declined to say that the appellant was 'driving' when he had maliciously released the handbrake of a motor vehicle and thus allowed it to run down a hill unattended. Lord Parker CJ said[6]:

'. . . a man cannot be said to be a driver on the authorities unless he is in the driving seat or in control of the steering wheel and also has something to do with the propulsion . . . There is no case, so far as this court knows, where a man has been held to be guilty of taking and driving away if, though he has something to do with the movement and the propulsion, he is not driving in any ordinary sense of the word.'

We would draw attention to the two factors to which Lord Parker CJ refers: first, that the alleged driver must be in the driving seat, or in control of the steering wheel, and,

1 [1946] KB 473
2 [1946] 2 All ER 87 at 88, [1946] KB 473 at 477
3 [1948] 2 All ER 83
4 [1948] 2 All ER at 84
5 [1964] 2 All ER 541, [1965] 1 QB 85
6 [1964] 2 All ER at 542, [1965] 1 QB at 88

secondly, that his activities are nevertheless not to be held to amount to driving unless they come within the ordinary meaning of that word.

The last case to which we would refer is *Ames v MacLeod*[1], where the facts were very close to those of the instant case. The accused, who was alleged to have been driving a motor car, had been walking beside it as it ran down a slight incline, and had steered it by placing his hand on the wheel. The car had run out of petrol. The Lord Justice-General (Clyde) thought[2] that the question turned on whether the defendant was 'in a substantial sense contolling the movement and direction of the car', and held that this test was satisfied. The other judges concurred.

We respectfully agree that a person cannot be driving unless he satisfies the test adopted by the Court of Session, and we recognise the importance that this legislation should be given the same meaning in England as in Scotland. But we do not think that the test is exhaustive. It is still necessary to consider whether the activity in question can fall within the ordinary meaning of the word 'driving'. Giving the words their ordinary meaning there must be a distinction between driving a car and pushing it. The dividing line will not always be easy to draw, and the distinction will often turn on the extent and degree to which the defendant was relying on the use of the driver's controls. Where, however, the defendant was walking beside a vehicle which was being pushed or moving under gravity, we do not think that the mere fact that he had his hand on the steering wheel is enough to say that he was driving in any ordinary sense of the word.

The view that such a defendant is not driving for the purposes of the Road Traffic Act 1972 is reinforced by a consideration of the consequences which would flow under that Act if a different view were taken. Some of the motor vehicles to which the Act applies, notably motor-cycles, must from their nature be manhandled from time to time. Suppose a man pushes a broken down motor-cycle by walking beside it and holding the handlebars; such activity would bring him within any of the definitions of 'driving' suggested by the Crown because he is in full control of the vehicle and is using the steering (and possibly the braking) controls. Can it possibly have been intended by Parliament to require such a person to hold a driving licence? We think not. So in the present case we do not think that any ordinary meaning of the word 'drive' could extend to a man who is not in the motor car, who has both feet on the road, and who is making no use of the controls apart from an occasional adjustment of the steering wheel.

Cases such as these are near the borderline, and a different conclusion might well be open to the tribunal of fact if the accused had one foot in the car in order to make more effective use of the controls. In the present case, however, the jury should have been directed that if the appellant's version of the facts was, or might be, correct, he should be acquitted. The appeal will accordingly be allowed and the conviction quashed.

Appeal allowed. Conviction quashed.

Solicitors: *Registrar of Criminal Appeals* (for the appellant); *Solicitor, Metropolitan Police* (for the Crown).

N P Metcalfe Esq   Barrister.

---

1   1969 JC 1
2   1969 JC at 3

a Thakrar v Secretary of State for the Home Department

COURT OF APPEAL, CIVIL DIVISION

LORD DENNING MR, ORR AND LAWTON LJJ

30th, 31st JANUARY, 1st, 4th FEBRUARY 1974

b *Immigration – Leave – Non-patrial – Right of entry – Expellee – Obligation of country under international law to receive back its nationals expelled from other countries – British protected person – Non-patrial expelled from normal country of residence – Expellee claiming to be British protected person – Right of British protected person to enter United Kingdom – Expellee refused leave to enter United Kingdom – Whether expellee entitled to enter United Kingdom as of right for purpose of settling there permanently – Immigration Act 1971, s 3(1).*

c *International law – Municipal law – Relationship – Right of individual under international law – Enforcement of right in English courts – Necessity of showing rule of international law has been adopted by English law – Duty of country to receive back nationals expelled by foreign state – British protected person – Whether British protected person having right to enter United Kingdom on being expelled from country of residence – Whether right enforce-*
d *able by individual in English courts.*

The applicant, who was of Asian origin, was born in Uganda in 1939. Uganda was then a British protectorate and, after the passing of the British Nationality Act 1948, the applicant was a British protected person within the meaning of that Act. In 1962, under the Uganda Independence Act 1962, Uganda ceased to be a protectorate and became an independent country. Individuals who had formerly been British protected
e persons within the meaning of the 1948 Act retained that status unless they became Ugandan citizens. In March 1967, on the registration of birth of the elder of his two children, the applicant's nationality was stated to be 'Citizen of Uganda'. In 1969 the applicant obtained a trading licence available only to Ugandan citizens. In August 1972 the government of Uganda ordered the removal from the country of all non-Ugandan Asians. The applicant left Uganda and came to England in September 1973.
f He did not have an entry certificate and on his arrival at Heathrow airport he was re-fused leave to enter the United Kingdom by an immigration officer. The applicant moved the Divisional Court for an order quashing that decision. The matter was further considered by the Home Office. The Home Office authorities concluded that on the evidence the applicant had at some time applied for and obtained Uganda citizen-ship. The Secretary of State decided therefore that the applicant had failed to satisfy
g him that he was a British protected person. Following that decision the Divisional Court[a] dismissed the applicant's motion and the applicant appealed, contending, inter alia, (i) that as a British protected person he was as much a British national as a citizen of the United Kingdom and colonies and accordingly, if he was expelled from the country where he was living, under the rules of international law he was entitled as of right to come to the United Kingdom, and (ii) that he remained in English law
h a British protected person since he had never submitted to the High Commission in Uganda a declaration renouncing his status as a British protected person in accord-ance with art 20(1)[b] of the British Protectorates, Protected States and Protected Persons Order 1969[c].

---

a [1947] 1 All ER 415

j b Article 20(1), so far as material, provides: '... any person of full age and capacity who is a British protected person by or under any provision ... of this Order and—(a) is also a citizen of any country mentioned in section 1(3) of the [British Nationality Act 1948] or of the Republic of Ireland or a national of a foreign country as defined in section 32(1) of the [1948] Act; or (b) satisfies the authority to whom the declaration of renunciation is submitted that after registration of the declaration he will become such a citizen or national, may by declaration renounce his status as a British protected person.'

c SI 1969 No 1832

Held – The appeal would be dismissed for the following reasons—

    (i) There was no rule of public international law that a British protected person who had never lived in the United Kingdom was entitled to settle in the United Kingdom on being expelled from his own country. Even if there were such a rule the applicant could not rely on it since (a) not having been adopted by English municipal law it would not be enforced by the English courts; rules of international law only had validity to the extent that they were accepted and adopted by domestic law; (b) the rules of international law only governed the relations between states and could not therefore be relied on by the applicant for his own benefit (see p 266 b and d to g, p 272 c and d and p 273 f and g, post); *Chung Chi Cheung v R* [1938] 4 All ER 786 applied.

    (ii) Even if the applicant were a British protected person, he required leave under s 3(1)^d of the Immigration Act 1971 as a non-patrial to enter the United Kingdom. The 1971 Act was a comprehensive code and could not be construed as preserving any right the applicant might have had under international law. Accordingly, although the fact that an entrant was a British protected person would assist his claim for leave to enter, it did not give him a right to do so (see p 267 f and g, p 271 e g and h and p 272 f, post).

    (iii) The applicant was not in any event entitled to be treated as a British protected person. Under s 2(1)^e of the Uganda Independence Act 1962 and art 18(2)^f of the 1969 order a British protected person ceased to be such on becoming a citizen of Uganda under the law of that country. It was therefore immaterial that the applicant had never submitted a declaration to the British High Commission renouncing his status as a British protected person. On the evidence submitted to him the Secretary of State was justified in concluding that the applicant had registered as a Ugandan citizen under Ugandan law and thus ceased to be a British protected person (see p 268 h, p 269 b to d and f, p 270 g and j, p 271 b and p 272 e, post).

    Decision of the Divisional Court of the Queen's Bench Division sub nom *R v An Immigration Officer at Heathrow Airport, ex parte Thakrar* [1974] 1 All ER 415 affirmed.

Notes

For the rules governing the entry to the United Kingdom of persons born outside the United Kingdom, see 4 Halsbury's Laws (4th Edn) 470-472, paras 974-976.

    For the Uganda Independence Act 1962, s 2, see 4 Halsbury's Statutes (3rd Edn) 441.

    For the Immigration Act 1971, s 3, see 41 Halsbury's Statutes (3rd Edn) 20.

    For the British Protectorates, Protected States and Protected Persons Order 1969, arts 18, 20, see 2 Halsbury's Statutory Instruments (3rd Reissue) 19.

Cases referred to in judgments

A (an infant), Re, Hanif v The Secretary of State for Home Affairs, Re S (N) (an infant), Singh v The Secretary of State for Home Affairs [1968] 2 All ER 145, sub nom *Re Mohamed Arif (an infant), Re Nirbhai Singh (an infant)* [1968] Ch 643, [1968] 2 WLR 1290, CA, Digest (Cont Vol C) 19, *157ra*.

Chung Chi Cheung v R [1938] 4 All ER 786, [1939] AC 160, 108 LJPC 17, 160 LT 148, 19 Asp MLC 243 PC, 14 Digest (Repl) 153, *1164*.

Heathfield v Chilton (1767) 4 Burr 2015, 98 ER 50, 11 Digest (Repl) 632, *551*.

K (H) (an infant), Re [1967] 1 All ER 226, sub nom *Re H K (Infant)* [1967] 2 QB 617, [1967] 2 WLR 962, DC, Digest (Cont Vol C) 18, *157qa*.

Mwenya, Re [1959] 3 All ER 525, [1960] 1 QB 241, [1959] 3 WLR 767, CA, 16 Digest (Repl) 282, *517*.

Nyali Ltd v Attorney-General [1955] 1 All ER 646, [1956] 1 QB 1, [1955] 2 WLR 649, CA; affd [1956] 2 All ER 689, [1957] AC 253, [1956] 3 WLR 341, HL, Digest (Cont Vol A) 267, *879a*.

---

d Section 3(1), so far as material, is set out at p 271 f, post

e Section 2(1), so far as material, is set out at p 268 j, post

f Article 18(2), so far as material, is set out at p 269 a, post

Ol le Njogo v Attorney-General (1913) 5 EALR 70.

R v Secretary of State for Home Affairs, ex parte Soblen [1962] 3 All ER 373, [1963] 1 QB 829, [1962] 3 WLR 1145, DC, Digest (Cont Vol A) 22, 99a.

R v Secretary of State for the Home Department, ex parte Mughal [1973] 1 WLR 1133, DC; affd [1973] 3 All ER 796, [1973] 3 WLR 647, CA.

Sobhuza II v Miller [1926] AC 518, 95 LJPC 137, 135 LT 215, PC, 8 Digest (Repl) 686, 12.

Appeal

The applicant, Pravinlal Amarshi Thakrar, applied to the Divisional Court of the Queen's Bench Division (i) for an order of certiorari to remove into the court with a view to its being quashed a refusal of leave to enter the United Kingdom, which refusal was made by an immigration officer to the applicant at Heathrow airport on 5th September 1973, (ii) for an order of mandamus directed to the immigration officer and to the Secretary of State for the Home Department to give the applicant leave to enter the United Kingdom, or otherwise to admit him into the United Kingdom, and (iii) for an order that a writ of habeas corpus be issued directed to the Secretary of State for Home Affairs and the chief immigration officer to have the applicant brought before the court immediately after the receipt of the writ to undergo and receive all and singular such matters and things as the court should then consider concerning him. The motion came on for hearing before the Divisional Court[1] (Lord Widgery CJ, Bridge and May JJ) on 9th October 1973. The court had before it an affidavit sworn by Mr A E Corben, an assistant secretary at the Home Office in charge of B2 Division of the Immigration and Nationality Department, in which he stated that, although he was not satisfied that the applicant was a British protected person, on the assumption that he was, the applicant should in any event be refused leave to enter the United Kingdom for settlement, under s 3(2) of the Immigration Act 1971 and r 38 of the Statement of Immigration Rules for Control on Entry: Commonwealth Citizens[2], since he had no special voucher or entry certificate. The court adjourned the hearing for further consideration by the Home Office. The hearing was resumed on 23rd October when the court had before it (i) a second affidavit sworn by Mr Corben, containing the decision of the Secretary of State, which made it clear that he had not been satisfied by the applicant that the applicant was a British protected person and accordingly was required to treat the applicant as not being of that status; and (ii) an affidavit sworn by Mr Robert Calder, a member of HM Diplomatic Service who was serving as Uganda Desk Officer in the Nationality and Treaty Department of the Foreign and Commonwealth Office, which had been placed before the Secretary of State and had formed the basis of his decision; in the affidavit Mr Calder gave in detail all the factors which had been put before him on the question whether the applicant had applied for and obtained Uganda citizenship and which had led to his own conclusion that the applicant had not retained British status. Much of that material had been supplied by the applicant. The court concluded that there were no grounds for interfering with the Secretary of State's decision and accordingly dismissed the motion for orders of certiorari and mandamus but granted the applicant bail pending an appeal to the Court of Appeal. The applicant appealed on the grounds: (i) that the court was wrong in holding that the applicant was not a British protected person; (ii) that the court had wrongly held that the Secretary of State had dealt with the matter fairly in arriving at the conclusion that the applicant had lost his status as a British protected person and had acquired Uganda citizenship; (iii) that the court had wrongly held that there was no error in law in the Secretary of State's failure to deal with the issue of renunciation; in particular that the court was wrong in holding that a renunciation of status as a British protected

---

1   [1974] 1 All ER 415, [1974] 2 WLR 34
2   HC 79, laid before Parliament on 25th January 1973 under s 3(2) of the Immigration Act 1971

person need not be registered with the British authorities; (iv) that the court was
wrong in holding that the legal obligation to admit British nationals who were expelled from other countries had not survived after the passing of the Immigration
Act 1971; (v) that the court had failed to take into account that the duty to admit
expellees from Uganda had been recognised by the British Government and by the
Secretary of State.   The facts are set out in the judgment of Lord Denning MR.

Sir Dingle Foot QC and *Eugene Cotran* for the applicant.
Gordon Slynn and *J W Priest* for the Secretary of State.

Cur adv vult

4th February.   The following judgments were read.

LORD DENNING MR. In 1972 a sword fell on the Asians living in Uganda.   It
was the sword of the President, General Amin.   He declared that all Asians who were
not citizens of Uganda must leave the country within 90 days.   The declaration placed
thousands in sore plight.   This is the story of one of them.

Pravinlal Amarshi Thakrar is 33 years of age.   He was born in Uganda.   He had
lived there all his life save for four years as a student in Bombay.   He had married a
Tanzanian girl, and they had two little daughters, aged five and two. He was engaged
in the family business in Masaka.   His father and mother lived there too.   They
had come originally from India and had been in Uganda for over 40 years.   They
had six sons and two daughters, all born in Uganda.   The father and mother, having
been born in India, had always been British subjects.   They had been registered,
ever since 1953, as citizens of the United Kingdom and colonies.   But their sons and
daughters, having been born in Uganda whilst it was a protectorate, were British
protected persons.

After Uganda became independent in 1962, all the members of the family were
able, if they chose, to apply to become citizens of Uganda.   The father and mother
remained British subjects.   They held British passports.   Some of the others of the
family remained British protected persons.   Others became Ugandan citizens.   But
what did Pravinlal do?   Did he become a Uganda citizen or not?   That is the
question.

But before I go into it, I must say what happened to the family after President
Amin's sword fell.   Quite a number of the family went to Bombay. These were
the father and the mother, two of the sons and a daughter. In addition, Pravinlal's
wife and two children went to Bombay, but Pravinlal himself did not go with them.
Two other sons went to England.   But Pravinlal and one of his brothers stayed on
for a time in Uganda.

Pravinlal himself had at one time held a passport as a British protected person.   He
had held it from 1954 to 1964.   He had used it when he went for four years as a
student to Bombay.   But he had not renewed it after 1964. When Amin's sword fell
in October 1972 he tried to renew it.   He went to the British High Commission in
Kampala, but found it difficult to get there.   There were queues a mile long.   Everything was in confusion.   Eventually he was seen.   The High Commission gave him
a letter to take to the Uganda Immigration Department to get their remarks on him.
He took it there.   The Uganda authorities wrote on it: 'Subject has never been
registered as citizen of Uganda.   No previous Uganda passport.'

Seeing that that document said he was not a Uganda citizen, Pravinlal hoped to claim
that he was a British protected person.   He hoped to get a passport from the British
High Commission.   For that purpose he was travelling from Masaka to Kampala.
He was stopped at a road block.   He was kicked and punched by the soldiers.   They
took from him all his money and his case with all his papers.   So he never got a

passport from the British High Commission.   He went to the Red Cross office in
Kampala. They issued him with a United Nations document which authorised him to
travel to Austria. His brother did the same.

On 7th November 1972 Pravinlal went to Austria. He stayed there in the United
Nations camp. He worked for a time on a farm.   In March 1973 his brother got to
England. So Pravinlal determined also to get to England himself if he could.

On 4th September 1973 Pravinlal went by air to Zurich and thence to London. He
arrived at 6.30 p m. He told the immigration officer that he wished to spend ten
days in the United Kingdom to visit his brother and that he then intended to travel
on to India to spend a short holiday with the family; he produced an Austrian passport for aliens; but it did not have a visa for the United Kingdom, nor a visa for India.
It described his nationality as 'not established'.   He produced a ticket for India which
was out of date.   The immigration officer made careful enquiries.   He was not
satisfied with his story and refused to admit him.   He served him with this notice:

'To Pravinlal Thakrar
'You have asked for leave to enter the United Kingdom as a visitor but you do
not have a United Kingdom visa.   You have also asked for leave to enter as a
visitor for ten days, but I am not satisfied that you intend to stay only for this
period. I therefore refuse you leave to enter the United Kingdom. I have
given/propose to give directions for your removal on 5 Sept, 1973 . . . by flight
. . . to Zurich.'

That notice was served on Pravinlal at 8 p m.   He was detained overnight pending
his departure next day.   Meanwhile one of his brothers got into touch with the
Joint Council for the Welfare of Immigrants.   Next day at 10.45 a m Pravinlal told a
different story to the immigration authorities. He said that he had come to England
to settle here and that he had a right to be here.   He said he had £30,000 in England.
He gave the immigration officer particulars of his father and mother and the rest of
the family.   He claimed that he was a British protected person and not a citizen of
Uganda. He said that Her Majesty's Government had, through the Secretary of State
for Home Affairs, accepted moral and legal responsibility to allow entry into England
of all British Ugandan Asians, i e Asians who are either citizens of the United Kingdom
and colonies or British protected persons who had not acquired Ugandan citizenship.
In view of this assertion, Pravinlal was not sent off straightaway. He was detained
pending further enquiries.

On 14th September 1973 Pravinlal by his solicitor applied for a writ of habeas
corpus.   On 5th October 1973 he applied for certiorari and mandamus.   These were
refused[1].   He appeals to this court.

International law
Counsel for Pravinlal raises this fundamental point: let us assume for the time
being that Pravinlal is, as he asserts, a British protected person.   Counsel says that
as such he is a British national just as much as a citizen of the United Kingdom
and colonies. As a British national, if he is expelled from the land where he is living,
he is entitled as of right to come into the United Kingdom.   This right, says counsel,
is given by international law; and international law, he says, is part of the law of the
land.   It is incorporated into it and is to be enforced by the courts unless it is excluded
by Parliament. To support this claim in international law, counsel quoted
Oppenheim[2]: 'The home State of expelled persons is bound to receive them on the
home territory.'

To support his assertion that international law is part of the law of the land, counsel

---

1   [1974] 1 All ER 415, [1974] 2 WLR 34
2   International Law (8th Edn, 1955), vol 1, p 646

quoted Sir William Blackstone in his Commentaries[1], and Lord Mansfield in *Heath-field v Chilton*[2]. They said that the law of nations is 'part of the law of the land'. But they were speaking of the law of nations, and then only of that part of it which was universally accepted and known for certain, such as the immunity of ambassadors. They were not speaking of rules which were not universally accepted nor known for certain. In my opinion, the rules of international law only become part of our law insofar as they are accepted and adopted by us. I would follow the words of Lord Atkin in *Chung Chi Cheung v R*[3]:

> 'It must be always remembered that, so far, at any rate, as the courts of this country are concerned, international law has no validity save in so far as its principles are accepted and adopted by our own domestic law.'

Test it by reference to the very point we have to consider here: the mass expulsion of Asians from Uganda. International law has never had to cope with such a problem. None of the jurists, so far as I can discover, has considered it. The statement of Oppenheim[4] is all very well when one is considering a home state which is a *self-contained* country with no overseas territories or protectorates. If one of its citizens goes to a foreign country and is expelled from it, the home state may well be bound to accept him on his home territory if he has nowhere else to go. But that rule does not apply when the home state is an outgoing country with far-flung commitments abroad, such as the United Kingdom has or recently did have. Take the class of persons with whom we are here concerned—British protected persons. They are said to be British nationals, but they are not British subjects. These number, or used to number, many millions. They were not born here. They have never lived here. They live thousands of miles away in countries which have no connection with England except that they were once a British protectorate. Is it to be said that by international law every one of them has a right if expelled to come into these small islands? Surely not. This country would not have room for them. It is not as if it was only one or two coming. They come not as single files but in battalions. Mass expulsions on this scale have never hitherto come within the cognisance of international law. To my mind, there is no rule of international law to which we may have recourse. There is no rule by which we are bound to receive them.

Even in regard to self-contained countries, however, the rule of international law is only a rule as between two states. It is not a rule as between an individual and a state. The expelling state—if it had a good case—might call on the home state to receive the person whom it expelled. But the individual could not pray the rule in aid for his own benefit. Moreover, the rule would only apply if he had nowhere else to go. If he went to Austria, as Pravinlal did, the rule would not apply to him; or, if he could go to India, where his wife and children are, the rule would not apply to him. So, even that rule of international law would not avail Pravinlal here.

Domestic law

So I turn to our domestic law. To understand it, I must first describe the legal position of Uganda. It has never been part of Her Majesty's Dominions. It was a British protectorate from 1894 to 1962, when it became independent. In strict international law, the sovereignty over Uganda was not in the Queen of England, but in the local rulers, the Kabake of Buganda and the kings of Toro, Ankoli and Bunyoro. The defence and external affairs were under the control of the government of the United Kingdom and much of the internal administration also: see the

---

1   Volume IV, p 67
    (1767) 4 Burr 2015 at 2016
    [1938] 4 All ER 786 at 790, [1937] AC 160 at 167, 168
    International Law (8th Edn, 1955), vol 1, p 646

qualities of a protectorate described in *Sobhuza II v Miller*[1]; *Nyali Ltd v Attorney-General*[2]; *Re Mwenya*[3]. The people born there and living there were not British subjects, but they were British protected persons. As such they were under the protection of the British Crown, but they had not the same rights as British subjects. They had never, so far as I can discover, the right of entry, without leave, into the United Kingdom. So far as our courts were concerned, they were until 1949 classified as *aliens*: see Mervyn Jones on British Nationality Law and Practice[4] and Halsbury's Laws of England[5]. This was altered by ss 3(3) and 32(1) of the British Nationality Act 1948. Those sections said that in that Act and the Aliens Restriction Acts 1914 and 1919, the expression 'alien' shall not include a British protected person. But those Acts did not deal with the right of entry into the United Kingdom. It seems that in that respect the position remained unchanged. That is to say, a British protected person had not an absolute right to enter the United Kingdom; he could only come by leave. The issue to him of a passport by the governor of a protectorate would, no doubt, import leave. So every British protected person, on getting a passport, could enter. But without a passport, he had no right at all. Such was the position until Uganda became independent in 1962.

In 1962 the Commonwealth Immigrants Act 1962 was passed. In 1968 it was amended. It put British protected persons on a par with Commonwealth citizens generally: see s 1(4). They had no right to come without leave. They were subject to examination by an immigration officer, who would admit or refuse admission according to the rules.

In 1971 there was the Immigration Act 1971. It is a new code which comprehends all persons who wish to enter into or stay in the United Kingdom. It divides them into two broad classes: (1) those who have a right of abode in the United Kingdom; these are called patrials; (2) those who have not the right of abode in the United Kingdom; these are not patrials.

Pravinlal Thakrar was not a patrial. He was, he says, a British protected person. Assume that he was. He would come within the governing provision in s 3(1):

'. . . where a person is not patrial . . . he shall not enter the United Kingdom unless given leave to do so in accordance with this Act . . .'

Section 3(2) authorises the Secretary of State to make rules. He has done so in a statement[6] which governs Commonwealth citizens and British protected persons alike (see para 1). The position since the 1971 Act is clear. Although Pravinlal was expelled from Uganda, he would by our law require leave to enter. He had no right whatever to enter without leave. No doubt if he was a British protected person, the immigration authorities would take it as a point in his favour. But it would give him no right to enter.

The question was raised before us as to the jurisdiction of the immigration officer. In a case where a man is undoubtedly a Commonwealth citizen or a British protected person, the immigration officer, of course, enquires into the facts of a case so as to see whether the man should be given leave to enter or not. In so doing he must act fairly: see *Re K (H) (an infant)*[7] and *Re A (an infant)*[8]. But a question may arise as to the status of the man who wishes to enter. Suppose he claims to be a patrial; or a citizen of the United Kingdom and colonies; or a British protected person.

1 [1926] AC 518 at 528
2 [1955] 1 All ER 646, [1956] 1 QB 1
3 [1959] 3 All ER 525, [1960] 1 QB 241
4 (1947), p 289
5 4th Edn, vol 4, p 457, para 948
6 Statement of Immigration Rules for Control on Entry: Commonwealth Citizens, laid before Parliament on 25th January 1973 (HC 79)
7 [1967] 1 All ER 226 at 231, [1967] 2 QB 617 at 630, per Lord Parker CJ
8 [1968] 2 All ER 145 at 151, 152, [1968] Ch 643 at 661

The immigration officer may have doubts about his claim.   In such a case I am clearly of opinion that the immigration officer has jurisdiction to enquire into it.   In doing so, he must of course act fairly.   He is to be guided by s 3(8) of the 1971 Act, which says:

> 'When any question arises under this Act whether or not a person is patrial, or is entitled to any exemption under this Act, it shall lie on the person asserting it to prove that he is.'

If the immigration officer decides against his claim and refuses him leave to enter, the man can appeal to an adjudicator and thence to the Immigration Appeal Tribunal under ss 12 to 23 of the 1971 Act.   Alternatively he can, in a proper case, move for certiorari to quash the immigration officer's decision on the ground that it is bad in law, and mandamus.   But he cannot do anything else.   I agree with Lord Widgery CJ in *R v Secretary of State for the Home Department, ex parte Mughal*[1], that in a case where any immigrant is coming into England for the first time and is refused admission, he can choose to go away if he pleases.   If he opposes, and is detained, or is sent back, his detention or removal is not unlawful.   So it is not a case for habeas corpus: see *R v Secretary of State for Home Affairs, ex parte Soblen*[2].

The point of law

Counsel for Pravinlal said that Pravinlal was in point of law a British protected person and should be treated as such.   Even though he had no right to enter without leave, yet he should be given special consideration.   Counsel submitted that after 1962 a British protected person living in Uganda—who wished to become a Ugandan citizen—did not lose his status unless three things happened.   (1) He applied to the Ugandan Government to be registered as a Ugandan citizen and made a declaration of his willingness to renounce his status as a British protected person: see s 3 of the Uganda Citizenship Ordinance 1962.   (2) He submitted to the British High Commission in Uganda a declaration renouncing his status as a British protected person: see arts 20 and 22 of the British Protectorates, Protected States and Protected Persons Order 1969[3].   (3) He produced evidence to the Uganda government that he had renounced his status as a British protected person: see s 6(2) of the Uganda Citizenship Ordinance 1962.

Counsel for Pravinlal said that there was no evidence that Pravinlal had ever satisfied the second requirement.   He had never submitted to the British High Commission in Uganda a declaration renouncing his status as a British protected person.   Accordingly under Uganda law he was never a citizen of Uganda.

Counsel for the Secretary of State admitted that Pravinlal had never submitted to the British High Commission any declaration of renunciation.   But he said that counsel for Pravinlal was wrong in his law.   Those three requirements would only be necessary if a British protected person in Uganda wanted to become a citizen of another country, such as Kenya.   But those three requirements were not necessary if he wanted to become a citizen of Uganda itself.   I think counsel for the Secretary of State is right.   The present case is governed by art 18 of the British Protectorates, Protected States and Protected Persons Order 1969, which is to be read with art 13 of that order and s 1(3) of the British Nationality Act 1948 and s 2(1) of the Uganda Independence Act 1962.   The most material sections are these.   Section 2(1) of the Uganda Independence Act 1962 says that a British protected person in Uganda shall cease to be such 'upon his becoming a citizen of Uganda under the law thereof'.   Article 18(2) of the 1969 order (as applied here) reads:

---

1   [1973] 1 WLR 1133 at 1136
2   [1962] 3 All ER 373, [1963] 1 QB 829
3   SI 1969 No 1832

'A person who, by virtue of his connection with [the former protectorate of Uganda] is a British protected person ... shall cease to be such if he becomes a [citizen of the former protectorate of Uganda].'

The sole question is, therefore: did Pravinlal become a citizen of Uganda under the law thereof? The law of Uganda is to be found in the Uganda Citizenship Ordinance 1962. The relevant sections are s 3(1)(3), especially the form of declaration in Sch 3, and s 6(2). As I read those provisions, in order to become a Uganda citizen, Pravinlal would only have to go to the Uganda authorities and make a declaration there in the prescribed form. That would be enough. As soon as that was done, he would become a Ugandan citizen.

The result is this. When Uganda attained independence in 1962 Pravinlal was a British protected person in that country. After independence he would cease to be a British protected person as soon as he became a Ugandan citizen. In order to become a Ugandan citizen he only had to register with the Ugandan government and make a declaration in the specified form to that government. Thereupon he automatically became a citizen of Uganda. There is no need for him to renounce his status as a British protected person, seeing that he automatically lost that status by reason of s 2(1) of the Uganda Independence Act 1962. It is satisfactory to find that the British High Commission in Uganda acted on that footing. Mr Calder in his affidavit says:

'To my knowledge the British High Commission only registered renunciations of status of British protected persons where such persons had become or wished to become a citizen of a country other than Uganda. To my knowledge it was not the practice of the British High Commission to accept registration of renunciations by British protected persons who had become or wished to become Ugandan citizens because it was considered that such persons automatically ceased to be a British protected person by virtue of the above-mentioned provisions when they became citizens of Uganda.'

In my opinion the practice of the British High Commission was and is correct. If a British protected person in Uganda wished to become a Ugandan citizen, it was only necessary for him to register himself as a Ugandan citizen with the Ugandan government and make the required declaration of allegiance and so forth to that government.

The facts

Finally I turn to the facts in this case. Counsel for Pravinlal recognised that he could not seek to reverse the immigration officer's decision on a point of fact; but he submitted that Pravinlal had not been treated fairly, at any rate in the later stages, because he was not given an opportunity of dealing with a point about the business in Masaka. I must say that I think the immigration officers acted with the utmost fairness. But the matter is of such moment to Pravinlal himself that I would state the points which go to show that he was not a British protected person. There is good ground for thinking that he had registered himself as a citizen of Uganda at any rate by 1967.

(1) In March 1967 when the birth of the elder child was registered at the registry office in Masaka. The mother gave the information of the nationality of the parents. The register says: 'Father: Citizen of Uganda. Mother: Citizen of Tanzania.'

(2) After 2nd April 1969 it was necessary for every person who was not a citizen of Uganda to obtain a valid passport from his own country. Otherwise his presence in Uganda would be unlawful: see s 8 of the Uganda Immigration Act 1969. Pravinlal never obtained a passport from the British High Commission. So his presence would have been unlawful unless he had taken Ugandan citizenship.

(3) In March 1969 it was necessary for anybody carrying on business in Uganda to have a trading licence. These licences were issued in two different forms: one for

citizens of Uganda; the other for non-citizens. Pravinlal was issued with trade
licences for the years 1970, 1971 and 1972, which were all in the form issued to citizens
of Uganda and not to non-citizens. They were issued for the carrying on of a wholesale and retail business at plot 5, shop 2, Kampala Road, Masaka.

(4) Under the Trade (Licensing) Act 1969 of Uganda the Minister was authorised to,
and did, divide the trading areas into two categories: (i) general licence areas where
anyone could trade; (ii) special areas where only Ugandan citizens were allowed to
trade and non-citizens were prohibited. One of the special areas (for Ugandan
citizens only) was Kampala Road, Masaka. So Pravinlal would not have been allowed
to trade there unless he was a Ugandan citizen. At a very late stage Pravinlal said
he was given special permission to trade there by the town clerk of Masaka; but
this cannot be regarded as very reliable.

(5) Pravinlal relied on the registration of the younger child, a daughter, who was
born on 3rd March 1970. But the registration of the birth was not made until 11th
September 1972—2½ years later—after President Amin had ordered the expulsion
of immigrants. The grandfather gave the information and gave the nationality
of the father then as: 'Father: British protected person. Mother: a citizen of
Tanzania.' I am afraid that at that time such an entry cannot be regarded as reliable.

(6) The statement made by the Ugandan authorities in October 1972 that the
'subject has never been registered as a citizen of Uganda'; and in January 1974 that
he was not a Uganda citizen. Mr Calder, an expert at the Foreign Office here, says
that such statements could not be relied on. They were often put out by the immigration authorities in Uganda during or since the exodus, without regard to the
provisions of Ugandan law concerning citizenship and in order to deny Ugandan
citizenship to those who had acquired it.

(7) Finally, in June 1973, when Pravinlal was in Austria, his case was taken up by
the Joint Council for the Welfare of Immigrants. They submitted that he was
entitled to passport facilities. That submission was not accepted. He did not wait
to see if he could get a passsport. On the contrary, he came on 4th September 1973.
On arrival, he said he came on a ten day visit. That was not true. Telling a lie is
no passport to favour.

It is quite plain to me that the immigration officers acted fairly. They took
everything into account. Even while these proceedings have been in progress, they
have considered all additional information which has been put forward. Right up
to the hearing of the court, new affidavits have been put in. In the result the immigration officers are not satisfied that Pravinlal was a British protected person; and
I must say there is ample material for them to so hold. I would commend the care
and consideration which they gave to this case. There is no ground whatever for
interfering with their decision.

Conclusion

In conclusion, I would say this. Pravinlal Thakrar has asserted that he is a British
protected person, and that, on being expelled from Uganda, he has a legal right to
enter this country. I am satisfied that he has no such right. There is no legal right
in him to enter this country. If he had been a British protected person, that would be
a factor in his favour which would be given serious consideration by the immigration
officers and by the Secretary of State. It might tip the scale and he might be allowed
to enter. But Pravinlal never got anywhere near showing that he was a British protected person. So he is not entitled to any special consideration. Everyone will be
sorry for the plight in which he finds himself. He is a man of standing, intelligence
and ability. But, he ought to consider this. His father and mother are in India.
His wife and two children are in India. It might be better for him to join them in
that great country, where there may be more scope for him than here. This country
is not large enough to take in all those whom we would gladly accept. I would
dismiss the appeal.

ORR LJ. It would not have been possible to listen to the arguments in this case without feeling great sympathy for the sufferings of the Ugandan Asians, but I have come to the clear conclusion that the appeal must fail on each of the issues raised on the applicant's behalf. As to the questions whether the immigration officer treated the applicant unfairly and whether he fell into an error of law by misconstruing the relevant provisions of the British Protectorates, Protected States and Protected Persons Order 1969 or the Uganda Citizenship Ordinance 1962 (re-enacted, after Ugandan independence, in the Uganda Citizenship (Amendment) Act 1963, there is nothing I wish to add to the reasons given by Lord Denning MR; but I would add a brief reference to Sir Dingle Foot's submission based on international law.

His submission was that there existed prior to the enactment of the Immigration Act 1971 a rule of international law whereby the applicant, so long as he retained the status of a British protected person, had a right, in the event of his being expelled from Uganda, to come to this country, and that the Immigration Act 1971 should not be construed as depriving him of that right.

This submission raises two questions. One is whether assuming that the applicant remained a British protected person and enjoyed before the enactment of the 1971 Act the right under international law which is claimed on his behalf, that Act should be construed as preserving such a right. The other is whether the applicant, again assuming that he remained a British protected person, enjoyed before the enactment of the 1971 Act the right which is claimed on his behalf.

On the first of these questions we have been referred to conflicting theories in textbooks as to the circumstances in which a rule of international law may become a rule of municipal law; but I need not pause on this controversy since it is common ground (see per Lord Atkin in *Chung Chi Cheung v R*[1]) that a rule of international law cannot be treated as incorporated into English municipal law where to do so would be inconsistent with the provisions of a statute. In the present case it is, in my judgment, clear beyond any doubt that the right which the applicant claims under international law is in conflict with the opening words of s 3(1) of the Immigration Act 1971, which provides as follows:

> 'Except as otherwise provided by or under this Act, where a person is not patrial—(a) he shall not enter the United Kingdom unless given leave to do so . . .

The Act is there saying that any exception to the rule that a non-patrial requires leave to enter the United Kingdom is to be found in the Act itself or in the regulations made under the Act, and it would plainly, in my judgment, be inconsistent with this provision to recognise any further exception based on international law. For this reason alone in my judgment the 1971 Act cannot be construed as preserving any such right under international law as the applicant claims; but I would add that, quite apart from the opening words of s 3(1), I should have reached the same conclusion on the basis of the first object of the Act, as declared in its long title, 'to amend and replace the present immigration laws', coupled with a consideration of the provisions of the Act as a whole, which introduced in this context a wholly novel distinction between 'patrial' and 'non-patrial' persons and was plainly intended to be a comprehensive code. In these circumstances, if it had been intended to preserve any rule of international law not embraced in the code, it is in my judgment clear that express reference would have been made to the rule in question.

Having reached this conclusion as to the first question raised in this part of the case, I do not find it strictly necessary to consider the second; but, having heard a full argument, I think it right to express my conclusion on it. In his judgment in the Divisional Court Lord Widgery CJ said[2]:

---

1   [1938] 4 All ER 786 at 790, [1939] AC 160 at 167, 168
2   [1974] 1 All ER 415 at 418, [1974] 2 WLR 34 at 37

'. . . there clearly is authority that in international law an obligation on a
country exists to receive back its nationals if those nationals are expelled from
other countries in the world.'

Before this court counsel for the Secretary of State, while accepting that there is a
rule of international law whereby a country is under an obligation in certain circumstances to receive its nationals expelled from another country, and while not for this
purpose seeking to draw any distinction between British citizens and British protected
persons, made it clear that he did not accept that there is any such obligation owed to
the individual concerned or that the obligation applies in every case of expulsion of a
national from a foreign territory. He claimed that the obligation is owed, not to the
individual expelled, but towards all other states and is restricted to the receiving of a
national who has nowhere else to go. These limitations on the obligation are in my
judgment supported by the relevant passage in Oppenheim[1] and by views expressed
in certain other textbooks. On the whole of the argument I have not been satisfied
that the obligation under international law goes beyond these limits and I am inclined, although it is unnecessary to decide the point, to accept counsel's contention
that the rule came into being as a necessary corollary of the recognition by international law of a state's right not to accept aliens into its territory if it does not wish
to do so.

For these reasons, in addition to those given by Lord Denning MR, I would dismiss
this appeal.

LAWTON LJ (read by Orr LJ). I too agree that this appeal should be dismissed.
In my opinion there was ample evidence before the immigration officers to justify
their refusal of leave to enter the United Kingdom; and had the issue in this appeal
been whether the applicant had proved that he was a British protected person (which
it was not), I would have adjudged that he had not done so. Further, for the reasons
already given, I am satisfied that the immigration officers treated the applicant
fairly and that they did not misconstrue the relevant statutory instruments and
ordinances.

Even if I had not come to the conclusion I have on the evidence, I should have
adjudged that the Immigration Act 1971 applies to him even if he was a British protected person with nowhere else to go who has been expelled from Uganda. I appreciate that the civilised states have for a very long time accepted that there is an
obligation on them to receive back into their territories their subjects who have been
expelled from other states and who have nowhere else to go. This is part of the
comity of nations and has come to be recognised as a rule of public international law.
But who is to define the limits of the rule? How is it to be enforced between states?
And who, if anyone, can enforce it against a state? In this sphere of jurisprudence
there has been no Moses to bring the law of nations down from Mount Sinai. As with
the Mosaic Law, there have been many learned doctors to comment on it, but without a Moses there is something lacking. Blackstone[2] seemed to think that the law
of nations resulted 'from those principles of natural justice, in which all the learned of
every nation agree'. But when anyone in the United Kingdom seeks to enforce against
the Crown what he alleges is a right arising under public international law, the courts
have to decide what is the nature and extent of the right and whether there are any
limitations imposed on it by statute. This was the opinion of the Privy Council in
Chung Chi Cheung v R[3], per Lord Atkin. I would follow it.

When deciding the nature and extent of the rule of public international law which
is under consideration in this appeal, it is, I think, pertinent to keep in mind the
historical background which produced it. It is probable that it arose out of the medieval concept of allegiance. The King was under a duty to protect his liege subjects.

1 International Law (8th Edn, 1955), vol 1, p 646
2 Commentaries vol IV, p 67
3 [1938] 4 All ER 786 at 790, [1939] AC 160 at 167, 168

Until the British Nationality Act 1948 the status of a British subject was based on allegiance. The right to come to the United Kingdom was enjoyed by those who owed allegiance. Those who lived overseas in territories which had been settled as colonies, ceded or acquired by conquest, did owe allegiance; but those who lived in territories which the Crown for various reasons found it convenient to administer without annexation probably did not owe allegiance. This was the opinion of the law officers given in 1855 in relation to the Ionian Islands (see McNair International Law Opinions[1]). A similar view was expressed in relation to those living in what used to be called the East African Protectorate: see *Ol le Njogo v Attorney-General*[2].   The source of law in these territories was derived from divers Acts which were consolidated in the Foreign Jurisdiction Act 1890.   The very title of that Act reveals the attitude of the Crown to those territories and to those who lived in them.

The second half of the 19th century saw a vast increase in the number and size of the territories which the Crown administered without annexation. They came to be called protectorates. Uganda became one in 1894. Millions of people were affected.   One of the benefits which they obtained was protection by the Crown.   But they did not become British subjects and the places where they lived were not part of the Crown's dominions. Until the passing of the British Nationality Act 1948 they were in law aliens; and, until the Aliens Order 1943[3], when in the United Kingdom they had to comply with the Aliens Order 1920. Before 1948, in my judgment, it could not have been argued that such persons were British subjects, or, to use a loose expression which is not used in the 1948 Act, British nationals for the purpose of the rule of public international law which is under consideration. The 1948 Act swept away the long established concept of allegiance as the basis of British citizenship and replaced it by new concepts. Citizens of specified self-governing countries were given the status of British subjects (see s 1(3)) and as more and more countries, which in the past had come under British administration, even if they were not British dominions, became independent, they were added to list in s 1(3). Uganda was added in 1963. The result was that by 1971 millions of people in different parts of the world who before 1948 were not British subjects although under British protection acquired the status of British subjects; and even if they had not acquired that status, they had ceased to be aliens (see s 32(1)). Did a rule of public international law which was probably based on allegiance apply to those millions who had acquired this status not under an international convention but by a municipal statute? In my judgment it did not. The rule is so vague and imprecise that it is difficult to know to whom it does apply. Those who owe allegiance to the Crown may be within its ambit.   I am confident that British protected persons, which is what the applicant claims to be, are not.

Whatever may be the nature and extent of the rule, I am satisfied that Parliament can decide whether it should be accepted and adopted within the realm; and by implication it has made its decision in the Immigration Act 1971 which regulates all entry into and stay in the United Kingdom. No person has any right of entry which is not given by that Act. Such rights as may be given by public international law to individuals are not rights given by the Act. It follows that they are of no value in municipal law. That does not mean that the Crown should disregard its duties under public international law. The fact that a British protected person has been expelled by another state and has nowhere else to go is, in my judgment, a factor, but no more than a factor, to be taken into account when the giving of leave is being considered.

Appeal dismissed. Applicant to surrender to his bail. Leave to appeal to the House of Lords refused.

Solicitors: *Jaques & Co* (for the applicant); *Treasury Solicitor*.

L J Kovats Esq Barrister.

---

1   (1956) Vol 1, p 40
2   (1913) 5 EALR 70 at 77
3   SR & O 1943 No 1378

Re Shield's Will Trusts
Bache v Shield and others

CHANCERY DIVISION
PENNYCUICK V-C
25th, 30th JANUARY 1974

Will – Class gift – Time of ascertainment of class – Gift to wife for life with remainder to relations of testator and wife – Date for ascertaining relations – Shares – Gift to be 'shared to my relations also my wife's relations' – Whether testator's relations and wife's relations to be ascertained at testator's death or wife's death – Whether testator contemplated single class of his own and wife's relations amongst whom gift to be shared equally.

The testator made a bequest in his will in the following terms: 'I GIVE AND BEQUEATH unto my wife . . . all my money and investments until her death then after that it will be shared to my relations also my wife's relations'. The testator died and letters of administration were granted to his widow and to the plaintiff. The plaintiff took out a summons seeking the determination of the court whether, on the true construction of the will and in the events that had happened, (i) the testator's relations and the widow's relations were to be ascertained as at the date of the testator's death or as at the date of his widow's death, and (ii) the testator's relations and his widow's relations each shared per capita one moiety of the trust or shared equally per capita the entire trust fund.

Held – (i) Where a gift was made to the relations of two different persons, it depended on the terms of the particular will which of three possible alternatives as to the date or dates at which the class or classes of the relations were to be ascertained, was adopted. Since it seemed much more likely that the testator would have contemplated an immediate distribution of the estate between living relations than the vesting of reversionary interests, the most probable intention to be ascribed to the testator was that his relations, as well as the widow's relations, should be ascertained at the widow's death. The order of the wording of the bequest, the gift to the widow being followed by a direction that the estate should on her death be 'shared to my relations also my wife's relations', accorded with that view (see p 277 *a* to *c* and p 279 *d* and *e*, post); *Re Gansloser's Will Trusts* [1951] 2 All ER 936 distinguished.

(ii) The word 'shares' imported a distribution per capita. On the true construction of the words used by the testator, he had contemplated a single composite class consisting of his relations and his widow's relations amongst whom the whole trust fund was to be shared equally. Accordingly each of the testator's relations and the widow's relations shared equally in the trust fund (see p 279 *h* and *j*, post).

Notes

For the time when the class of next-of-kin to whom a gift is given by will is ascertained, see 39 Halsbury's Laws (3rd Edn) 1042, 1043, para 1564, and for cases on the subject, see 49 Digest (Repl) 794-796, 7467-7484.

For the general principles of construction governing ascertainment of testator's intention, see 39 Halsbury's Laws (3rd Edn) 973-975, para 1474, and for cases on the subject, see 48 Digest (Repl) 397-399, 3447-3479.

Cases referred to in judgment

Clanchy's Will Trusts, Re, Lynch v Edwards [1970] 2 All ER 489, CA, Digest (Cont Vol C) 1069, 7528a.

Gansloser's Will Trusts, Re, Chartered Bank of India, Australia and China v Chillingworth [1951] 2 All ER 936, [1952] Ch 30, CA; *affg* [1951] 2 All ER 321, [1951] Ch 864, 49 Digest (Repl) 797, 7492.

Gundry v Pinniger (1852) 14 Beav 94, [1843-60] All ER Rep 403, 1 De GM & G 502, 21 LJCh 405, 18 LTOS 325, 16 Jur 488, 42 ER 647, 49 Digest (Repl) 794, 7467.

Cases also cited

Alcock v Sloper (1833) 2 My & K 699.

Barratt, Re, National Provincial Bank Ltd v Barratt [1925] Ch 550, [1925] All ER Rep 193.

Bridgen, Re, Chaytor v Edwin [1937] 4 All ER 342, [1938] 1 Ch 205.

Collins v Collins (1833) 2 My & K 703.

Evans' Will Trusts, Re, Pickering v Evans [1921] 2 Ch 309.

Howe v Earl of Dartmouth, Howe v Countess of Aylesbury (1802) 7 Ves 137, [1775-1802] All ER Rep 24.

Jones, Re, Richards v Jones [1898] 1 Ch 438.

Pickering v Pickering (1839) 4 My & Cr 289, [1835-42] All ER Rep 534.

Adjourned summons

By his will dated 24th June 1968 Charles Edwin Shield deceased ('the testator') did not appoint any executors. After declaring the will to be his last will and revoking all previous wills made by him the testator declared:

> 'I GIVE AND BEQUEATH unto my wife Mary Victoria Shield ['the widow'] all my money and investments until her death then after that it will be shared to my relations also [the widow's] relations.'

The testator then went on to give 23 pecuniary legacies. The testator died on 14th April 1972 and on 15th November letters of administration to his estate with the will annexed were granted to the widow and to the plaintiff, Nigel William Bache. By a summons dated 4th April 1973 the plaintiff sought the determination of the court whether, on the true construction of the will and in the events that had happened, the gift and bequest by the testator in his will of 'all my money and investments' (a) comprised (i) his entire net estate, (ii) his entire net estate subject to the payment of pecuniary legacies contained in the will, (iii) all or any of the assets of the estate specified in para 7 of an affidavit sworn by the plaintiff; (b) operated (i) to make an absolute gift to the widow, (ii) to create a valid trust for life for the widow with remainder for the relations of the testator and of the widow, (iii) to create some other and if so what trust; (c) if it were held under (b) that the gift and bequest created a valid trust for the benefit of the relations of the testator and of the widow, whether (i) such relations were to be ascertained as at the date of the testator's death or as at the date of the widow's death, (ii) the relations of the testator and the relations of the widow each shared per capita one moiety of the trust fund or shared equally per capita the entire trust fund. The defendants were: (1) the widow, (2) Benjamin Edgar Shield, the testator's brother, (3) Martha Elizabeth Bache, and (4) the vicar and churchwardens of St Peter's Church, Cookley. The second and third defendants both claimed to be beneficially entitled under the will and the fourth defendants were the legatees of a monetary bequest in the will. On 25th January 1974 Pennycuick V-C determined, in answer to questions (a) and (b), that the bequest comprised the testator's entire net estate, subject to the payment of pecuniary legacies contained in the will, and operated to create a valid trust for life for the widow with remainder for the relations of the testator and widow. His Lordship reserved judgment on question (c). The facts are set out in the judgment.

Gavin Lightman for the plaintiff.

J S Whitaker for the widow.

P J Talbot for the second defendant.

A G Boyle for the third defendant.

K J Farrow for the fourth defendants.

Cur adv vult

30th January. **PENNYCUICK V-C** delivered the following judgment. When this summons came before me a week or so ago, I answered the first two questions raised in it and I reserved judgment on the last question because it raised certain matters of law which I wished to consider further.

In a home-made will the testator made a bequest in the following terms: 'I GIVE AND BEQUEATH unto my wife Mary Victoria all my money and investments until her death then after that it will be shared to my relations also my wife's relations.' I have already held that the effect of those words was that they operated as a residuary gift on trust for the widow for life. Then on her death come these words: '. . . it will be shared to my relations also my wife's relations.' It is not dispute that in the absence of some indication of different intention a gift to relations, in order to save its validity, is construed as a gift to the statutory next-of-kin of whoever is the person concerned. Moreover, it is well-established that, always in the absence of any indication of different intention, the next-of-kin of a person will normally be ascertained as at the death of that person.

However, an obvious difficulty arises in the case which occasionally occurs where the gift is to the relations of two different persons, here the relations of the testator himself and the relations of the widow. When one finds such a disposition, there are three possible alternatives as to the date or dates at which the class or classes of the relations are to be ascertained. The first is to ascertain the relations of the testator at his death and then ascertain the relations of the widow at her death. The second is to ascertain the relations of both the testator and the widow at his death. The third is to ascertain the relations of both the testator and the widow at the death of the widow. Obviously it depends on the terms of the particular will which of those alternatives is to be adopted. The summons in the present case only puts before the court the second and third alternatives, namely whether such relations are to be ascertained as at the date of death of the testator, or as at the date of death of the widow.

So far as the first alternative is concerned, that involves this: that at the death of the testator one ascertains his relations, that is to say, his statutory next-of-kin; then those relations take a vested interest in reversion on the widow's life interest, the amount of their respective shares being dependent on the number of relations of the widow who come into the class at her death; on the death of the widow one ascertains her relations, that is to say, her statutory next-of-kin; and then one has a composite class amongst whom the fund is to be distributed. That is a perfectly lawful and effective disposition and I do not myself find it quite as absurd as from time to time has been suggested. However, it is, I think, one which would be unlikely to have been in contemplation of this rather simple testator. This alternative found no favour with the Court of Appeal in *Re Gansloser's Will Trusts*[1], where the terms of the will were more favourable to it than are those here. I do not think I ought to adopt that alternative.

The second alternative is that the relations of each class shall be ascertained at the death of the testator, that is to say, you then ascertain who are the relations of the testator, that is to say his statutory next-of-kin, and you also then ascertain who are the relations of the widow, that is to say the persons who would be her statutory next-of-kin if she had died on the same day as the testator. The relations of the testator and the widow respectively then take a vested interest in reversion on the life interest of the widow. That is the view which commended itself to the Court of Appeal in *Re Gansloser's Will Trusts*[1] on somewhat similar words to the words used here, but when one looks at the words used in that case and the judgments in that case, one finds a critical difference between those words and the words in the

---

1 [1951] 2 All ER 936, [1952] Ch 30

present case. It seems to me rather improbable that this testator should have contemplated the ascertainment of the whole class on his own death and that the members of the class should then take a vested reversionary interest.

The third alternative is that the relations of the testator and the relations of the widow should be ascertained at the death of the widow; that is to say, on the death of the widow one ascertains who would be the statutory next-of-kin of the testator if he had died on the same day as the widow, and one ascertains who are in fact the statutory next-of-kin of the widow. It seems to me that that is altogether the more probable intention to ascribe to the testator. It is, I think, much more likely that the testator would have contemplated an immediate distribution of his estate between the living than that he should have contemplated the vesting of reversionary interests. Unless I am constrained by authority to hold otherwise, I reach that conclusion with very little hesitation.

I turn now to *Re Gansloser's Will Trusts*[1]. The headnote in that case runs as follows[2]:

'A testator by his will dated April 15, 1929, gave the residue of his estate which consisted wholly of personalty, "... to be divided ... one half to my wife's relations one half to my own relations but not till the death of my wife ..." The testator died in 1929 and was survived by his wife who died in 1949. Neither the testator nor his wife had issue, but both had several collateral relations. The construction of the testator's will depended upon the law in force in the Straits Settlements at the time of his death. Under that law the law in force in England before 1926 was applicable, and it was conceded that under that law the term "relations" must be construed as those persons who would have taken under the Statutes of Distribution. On the two further questions on what date the class was to be ascertained and how the estate was to be distributed among the class so ascertained:—*Held*, (1) that on the true construction of the will the rule in *Gundry* v. *Pinniger*[3], that the date at which the class was to be ascertained was the date of the death of the propositus, was excluded, and the date for that purpose was the date of the death of the testator, and (2) that the class so ascertained took as joint tenants, for although where there is in the will an express reference to the Statutes of Distribution, those statutes determine not only the persons who are to take but also the shares and manner in which they are to take, where there is no such reference, the ordinary rule applies that where there is a gift to a class without words of severance, the members of the class take as joint tenants.'

That was an appeal from a decision of Vaisey J[4] who had held[5]—

'that the term "relations" must be construed as meaning those persons who would have taken under the Statutes of Distribution on intestacy; and that those persons formed an artificial class to be ascertained as at the death of the testator, and, in the case of the wife's relations, on the hypothetical footing that she had died intestate at the date of his death ...'

And, secondly, that the members of the two classes, so ascertained took as joint tenants and not in the shares prescribed by the statutes. There was no appeal as to the half-share of the estate given to the testator's own relations. The three children of the wife's deceased brother Frank appealed.

So, in the Court of Appeal[1], there being no appeal on the half-share given to the testator's own relations, the choice lay between the date which Vaisey J had selected,

1 [1951] 2 All ER 936, [1952] Ch 30
2 [1952] Ch at 30, 31
3 (1852) 14 Beav 94, [1843-60] All ER Rep 403
4 [1951] 2 All ER 231, [1951] Ch 864
5 [1951] Ch at 864

namely the death of the testator, and the two dates contended for by the appellants, namely, as regards the testator's relations, his death, and as regards the wife's relations, her death.

Evershed MR said[1]:

'... but the questions which we have to consider are: (i) whether the class so restricted is to be ascertained at the date of the wife's death or at the date of the coming into operation of the will, *viz.*, the [testator's] death; and (ii) having answered question (i), how, among the class so ascertained, is the estate to be distributed?'

Then later he said[2]:

'The first point to note is that the testator "desires" his estate "to be divided as follows," and then the two halves are designated ... *Prima facie* it would be, I think, surprising to suppose that the testator intended the executors to set to work at once to find out the class of persons entitled to one half, but to wait for a long time—twenty years—before they started to discover who was entitled to the other half. It seems to me that the language contemplates the ascertainment once and for all, at his death, of the persons who will constitute the classes ultimately entitled to his estate. That ... is supported by the next few words which follow, "... but not till the death of my wife." I think, if the idea had been that, as regards part of the residue, the persons to take were not to be, and could not be, discovered until the wife's death, that is a very remarkable way of giving effect to the intention. The testator ... contemplates an immediate operation of discovering the classes, and then he adds that, although those are the classes to take, they are not to enjoy the property until the death of his wife and until that event she is to have the unrestricted use of the income.'

Then Jenkins LJ said[3]:

'In the present case, I agree with Sir Raymond Evershed, M.R., that the language and scheme of the will make it sufficiently plain that the testator's intention was that both his wife's relations and his own relations should be ascertained at one and the same time, namely, as at the testator's death. My reasons for that view are these. The testator's direction is: "... I desire [the remainder of my estate] to be divided as follows *viz.*: one half to my wife's relations one half to my own relations ..." That, on the face of it, is a direction for an immediate division to be effected at the testator's death and to be effected once and for all. It is a division to be made as to one half to his wife's relations and as to one half to his own relations—that is to say, to the next of kin according to the statutes of two different people, the testator himself and his wife, who may or may not survive him. In view of this direction for immediate distribution, it seems to me that *prima facie* the proper conclusion must be that those persons, the objects of the distribution, are to be ascertained at one and the same time, namely, the testator's own death. I think that that conclusion is reinforced by what follows. The testator continues: "... but not till the death of my wife." Those words were relied on in argument as equivalent to a gift of a life interest to the wife preceding the direction to divide which should, it was said, be regarded as if it had been expressed as a gift in remainder expectant on the wife's death. In my view, however, there is for the present purpose a real distinction between a disposition in

1   [1951] 2 All ER at 939, [1952] Ch at 35
2   [1951] 2 All ER at 941, [1952] Ch at 38
3   [1951] 2 All ER at 945, [1952] Ch at 44, 45

that form and the language actually used by this testator. I regard the word "but" as highly significant. The testator, having directed a division which, according to its terms, is capable of being immediately carried out, goes on to say that this operation is to be postponed until a certain date. That he does by the words: "... but not till the death of my wife." Moreover, if the gift of "one half to my wife's relations" is to be construed as a gift "to my wife's next-of-kin according to the statutes ascertained as at her death," the words "... but not till the death of my wife," though not on that construction deprived of all meaning, would not, as it seems to me, be wholly appropriate.'

It will be seen that in those judgments—and it is particularly clear from the judgment of Jenkins LJ—the greatest reliance is placed on the order of the words in the gift, that is to say, first there is a direction that 'the remainder of my estate is to be divided as follows'; then that is followed by the words 'but not till the death of my wife'. Given that order of wording, the testator was held to have contemplated the immediate ascertainment of both classes.

In the present case the order of the words is reversed, that is to say, there is first a gift to the widow of 'all my money and investments until her death', and that is followed by a direction that the estate 'will be shared to my relations also my wife's relations'. I am not much enamoured of distinctions based on mere differences in the order of words, but there is no doubt that in *Re Gansloser's Will Trusts*[1] the Court of Appeal treated the order of the words as of critical importance, and it seems to me that with the order of words inverted, I am not only entitled but rather encouraged by the decision in *Re Gansloser's Will Trusts*[1] to reach the view which seems to me to be most likely to carry out the intention of the testator, namely, that the date for ascertainment of both classes is the death of the widow. I propose so to construe this will.

I was also referred to *Re Clanchy's Will Trusts*[2], which was a case in the Court of Appeal relating to next-of-kin. It was there held that the date for ascertainment of the next-of-kin was the death of someone with a life interest, but the case turned on entirely special considerations under the will.

It remains to consider a secondary question raised by the summons, namely whether the relations of the testator and the relations of the widow each share per capita one moiety of the trust fund or share equally per capita the entire trust fund, or otherwise how and on what trusts the trust fund is to be held. I have called that a secondary question, but it is in fact bound up with the first question. On the first question I have assumed that the second question should be answered on the basis that the relations of both constituted a single class. This is a question of great practical importance to the beneficiaries concerned, bearing in mind that there are nine members of the class of the testator's relations and only two members of the class of the widow's relations. It seems to me that on the words used by the testator there is no real doubt that the testator contemplated a single class consisting of his own relations and the widow's relations amongst whom the whole trust fund was to be shared, that is to say, each member of a composite class should take an equal share of the whole trust fund. The word 'shares' imports a distribution per capita. I do not think it is legitimate to construe the words used by the testator as a direction that the whole trust fund shall be shared in the sense of dividing between two classes, one 'my relations' and two, 'my wife's relations'. If that were so, the result would be, I suppose, each class would take half the fund as joint tenants, but that is not a legitimate view of the words used by the testator.

I propose accordingly to declare in answer to question (c) of the summons that the

---

1   [1951] 2 All ER 936, [1952] Ch 30
2   [1970] 2 All ER 489

relations are to be ascertained as at the date of death of the widow and that the
relations of the testator and the relations of the widow share equally per capita in
the entire trust fund.

Declaration accordingly.

Solicitors: *Routh, Stacey, Pengelly & Boulton*, agents for *Talbot & Talbot*, Kidderminster
(for the plaintiff and the defendants).

Evelyn Budd Barrister.

Fountain Forestry Ltd v Edwards and another

CHANCERY DIVISION
BRIGHTMAN J
21st, 22nd, 23rd NOVEMBER, 13th DECEMBER 1973

*Executor and administrator – Dealings with assets of estate – Power of one of two or more
personal representatives to bind estate – Contract to sell asset – Contract made by one administrator – Contract expressed to be between purchaser and both administrators – Administrator signing on behalf of himself and as agent for other administrator – Other administrator
ignorant of contract – Whether contract binding on estate.*

*Executor and administrator – Dealings with assets of estate – Real property – Administra-
tors – Power of one of two or more administrators to deal with real property – Contract by one
of two administrators to sell real property – Whether contract binding on estate – Administration of Estates Act 1925, s 2.*

At the time of his death the deceased was the owner of certain freehold property. He
died intestate and letters of administration were granted to his widow and son. The
plaintiffs negotiated with the son for the purchase of the property and a contract was
signed which was expressed to be made between the son and widow of the one part
and the plaintiffs of the other, whereby the son and widow agreed to sell and the
plaintiffs to purchase the property. The son was expressed to sign the contract 'for
self and [the widow]'. In fact the son had not consulted the widow prior to the signing
of the contract and she had not expressly ratified the contract since. The widow
proved reluctant to execute an engrossment of the contract and the plaintiffs brought
proceedings for specific performance contending that the contract was binding on the
deceased's estate since one of two or more personal representatives was entitled to
enter into a contract for the sale of an asset so as to bind the estate without the consent
of the other personal representative or representatives.

Held – On the assumption that, by virtue of s 2^a of the Administration of Estates Act
1925, one of two executors had power to enter into a contract binding on the deceased's
estate to sell freehold land, and that an administrator had the same power of disposition as an executor, nonetheless the plaintiffs were not entitled to specific performance,
since the son had not bound himself to sell the property without the concurrence of
the widow but had bound the estate on the assumption, which he warranted to be
correct, that he had authority to sign as agent for her. That assumption having been

---

a Section 2, so far as material, is set out at p 283 *f* and *g*, post

falsified there was no contract to be enforced; all that could be sued on was the warranty of authority given by the son (see p 283 *h*, p 285 *f* and *g* and p 287 *a* to *c*, post).
Sneesby v Thorne (1855) 7 De GM & G 399 applied.

Notes

For the power of personal representatives to deal with the estate, see 16 Halsbury's Laws (3rd Edn) 357-366, paras 691-706, and for cases on the subject, see 24 Digest (Repl) 618-639, 6138-6303.

For the Administration of Estates Act 1925, s 2, see 13 Halsbury's Statutes (3rd Edn) 40.

Cases referred to in judgment

Anon (1536) 1 Dyer 23b, 73 ER 49, 24 Digest (Repl) 619, 6141.

Herbert v Pigott (1834) 2 Cr & M 384, 4 Tyr 285, 2 Dowl PC 392, 3 LJEx 79, 149 ER 809.

Hudson v Hudson (1737) 1 Atk 460, West temp Hard 155, 26 ER 292, LC, 24 Digest (Repl) 667, 6552.

Jacomb v Harwood (1751) 2 Ves Sen 265, 28 ER 172, 24 Digest (Repl) 619, 6142.

Simpson v Gutteridge (1816) 1 Madd 609, 56 ER 224, 24 Digest (Repl) 619, 6143.

Smith v Everett (1859) 29 LJCh 236, 27 Beav 446, 34 LTOS 58, 5 Jur NS 1332, 54 ER 175, 24 Digest (Repl) 640, 6316.

Sneesby v Thorne (1855) 3 Eq Rep 662, 25 LTOS 125, 1 Jur NS 536, 44 Digest (Repl) 48, *333*; affd on other grounds (1885) 7 De GM & G 399, 3 Eq Rep 849, 25 LTOS 250, 1 Jur NS 1058, 44 ER 156, LJJ, 24 Digest (Repl) 619, 6144.

Stanley v Bernes (1828) 1 Hag Ecc 221, 162 ER 564, 23 Digest (Repl) 226, 2714.

Turner v Hardey (1842) 9 M & W 770, 1 Dowl NS 954, 11 LJEx 277, 152 ER 326, 24 Digest (Repl) 785, 7750.

Warwick (Earl of) v Greville (1809) 1 Phillim 123, 161 ER 934, 23 Digest (Repl) 144, 1503.

Willand v Fenn (circa 1743) cited 2 Ves Sen at 267, 28 ER 173, 24 Digest (Repl) 619, 6147.

Cases also cited

Beswick v Beswick [1967] 2 All ER 1197, [1968] AC 58, HL.

Godwin v Francis (1870) LR 5 CP 295.

Ingham, Re, Jones v Ingham [1893] 1 Ch 352.

Johnson v Clarke [1928] Ch 847.

Trollope's Will Trusts, Re, Public Trustee v Trollope [1927] 1 Ch 596, [1927] All ER Rep 365.

Warner v Sampson [1958] 1 All ER 44, [1958] 1 QB 404.

Summons

By a writ issued on 26th January 1973 the plaintiff company, Fountain Forestry Ltd, brought an action against Robert Ieuan Edwards and Mary Jones Edwards, the personal representatives of Hugh Robert Edwards, deceased, claiming specific performance of a contract for the sale of certain land. By a summons issued on 9th May the plaintiff company applied for summary judgment. The facts are set out in the judgment.

John Mummery for the plaintiff company.
Patrick Talbot for the defendants.

Cur adv vult

13th December. **BRIGHTMAN J** read the following judgment. This is a summons under RSC Ord 86 for a summary order for specific performance of a contract for the sale of land.

On 6th May 1965 Hugh Robert Edwards died. He was at his death the owner in fee simple of 107 acres of mountain land and sheep-walk in the county of Montgomery, to which I shall refer as 'the second property' since it is the land secondly described in the agreement sought to be enforced. The deceased died intestate and letters of administration were granted to his widow, Mary Jones Edwards, whom I shall call 'the widow', and his son, Robert Ieuan Edwards, whom I shall call 'the son'. The son was the owner in his own right, in fee simple, of an adjoining area of mountain land and sheep-walk of similar acreage to which I will refer as 'the first property'.

The plaintiff company, Fountain Forestry Ltd, negotiated with the son for the purchase of the first and second properties. On 25th February 1971 a contract was signed. The contract is expressed to be made between the son and the widow of the one part and the plaintiff company of the other part. Thereby the son and the widow agreed to sell and the plaintiff company to purchase the first and second properties at the price of £5,992. The son was expressed to sign the contract 'for self and Mary Jones Edwards'. The son and the widow are the defendants to this action.

Prior to the signing of the contract it was agreed by correspondence that the son was selling the first property as beneficial owner and that the widow and the son were selling the second property as personal representatives of the deceased. The purchase price was apportioned as to £3,000 to the first property and £2,992 to the second property.

On 15th March 1971 the plaintiff company's solicitors submitted a draft conveyance to the defendants' solicitors. This was returned approved on 2nd April and on 19th April the plaintiff company's solicitors submitted an engrossment of the conveyance for execution by the defendants. Many letters passed. Finally on 26th January 1972 it became apparent that the engrossment had not been returned executed by the defendants because the widow was reluctant to execute it. On 26th January 1973 a writ was issued by the plaintiff company for specific performance of the agreement and on 9th May a summons was issued under RSC Ord 86.

According to the affidavit evidence of the widow and the son, the son did not in fact consult the widow prior to the signing of the contract and the contract has not been expressly ratified by her since. I must accept these facts as correct for the purposes of the summons but if the action comes to trial it is, of course, possible that the position will be shown to be quite otherwise.

Counsel for the plaintiff company submitted that where there are two or more personal representatives, any one of them is entitled to enter into a contract for the sale of an asset so as to bind the estate of the deceased without the concurrence of the other personal representative or representatives, and that therefore the contract in the present case is binding on the deceased's estate, notwithstanding that the widow did not sign it and did not authorise the son to sign on her behalf. Counsel for the defendants submitted first that, although that may be the law in the case of executors, it is not the law in the case of administrators since they are bound to act jointly. But, even if it is the law in the case of administrators, it does not apply to the present case because the son erroneously believed he had, or would receive, the authority of the widow, whereas in fact he did not have that authority and could not get it. In those circumstances, submitted counsel, the court will not decree specific performance. In support of the second proposition counsel relied on *Sneesby v Thorne*[1] to which I shall have to refer in detail later.

I deal first with the submission that one administrator has power to bind the estate of the deceased without the concurrence of his co-administrator. On this aspect of the case I have had able arguments from counsel on both sides which have been the product of considerable research undertaken by them. As early as 1536 it was held[2] that one of two executors could make a valid disposition of the entire

1 (1855) 7 De GM & G 399
2 See *Anon* 1 Dyer 23b

interest in a term of years which had been vested in the deceased, without the concurrence of his co-executor. There are numerous later cases to the like effect. In 1751 Strange MR said[1]:

> 'Nothing is clearer than this, and I never knew it questioned in the case of executors, that each executor has the entire controul of the personal estate of [the] testator, may release, or pay a debt, or transfer any part of [the] testator's property, without [the] concurrence of the other executor.'

In 1816 Plumer V-C said[2]: '. . . a Gift, Sale, Surrender, Payment, Release, or Judgment confessed by one Executor, is as effectual as if all of them had joined.' The point could not, I think, have arisen before 1898 in relation to freeholds since these vested in the devisee or heir-at-law and not in the executors unless also devisees.

Until 1898, therefore, I am satisfied that it was competent for one of two executors to sell or contract to sell an asset forming part of the personal estate of the deceased at his death, although probably it would not have been competent for a single executor to have varied the terms of a contract for sale which both executors had previously made: compare *Turner v Hardey*[3].

Section 2(2) of the Land Transfer Act 1897 provided that the powers, rights, duties, and liabilities of personal representatives, in respect of personal estate, should apply to real estate as if that real estate were a chattel real vested in them. If the subsection had stopped there, one of two executors would have been able to contract to sell and to convey the deceased's real estate. But a proviso to the subsection said that it should not be lawful for some or one only of joint personal representatives, without the authority of the court, *to sell or transfer real estate*. In that Act real estate does not include leaseholds. In the result, between 1898 and 1925, one of two executors could contract to sell and could convey leaseholds and pure personalty but could not contract to sell or convey freehold land.

Section 2(1) of the Administration of Estates Act 1925, which replaced with amendments s 2(1) and (2) of the 1897 Act provides:

> '. . . all powers, duties, rights, equities, obligations, and liabilities of a personal representative in force at the commencement of this Act with respect to chattels real, shall apply and attach to the personal representative and shall have effect with respect to real estate vested in him . . .'

save that s 2(2) of the 1925 Act does not permit one of two or more personal representatives *to convey real estate* 'without the concurrence therein of all such representatives or an order of the court . . .' There are two departures from the 1897 Act. Under s 3, 'real estate' includes leaseholds; and, as I have indicated, the restriction in s 2(2) is expressed only to apply to a conveyance; the wording in s 2(2) of the 1897 Act was 'sell or transfer'. It seems to me that the likely effect of the 1925 Act is, and for the purposes of this judgment I am prepared to assume, that one of two executors is now able to enter into a contract binding on a deceased's estate to sell freehold as well as leasehold land and pure personalty belonging to the deceased at his death, although he cannot implement that contract in relation to freeholds without the concurrence of his co-executor or co-executors or a court order.

I turn to the difficult question whether administrators are in the same position as executors. In 1737 Lord Hardwicke LC decided *Hudson v Hudson*[4]. On the death of John Hudson intestate letters of administration were granted to Benjamin Hudson

---

1 *Jacomb v Harwood* 2 Ves Sen 265 at 267
2 *Simpson v Gutteridge* 1 Madd 609 at 616
3 (1842) 9 M & W 770
4 (1737) 1 Atk 460

senior and William Hudson. The administrators appointed Benjamin Hudson junior and Joseph Hudson to be their attorneys for the purpose of getting in certain assets. William, as administrator, without the concurrence of his co-administrator, settled accounts with the attorneys and granted them a general release. William thereafter died. In a suit by Benjamin senior, the surviving administrator, against the attorneys for an account, the attorneys relied on the accounts settled with William and the release which he had granted. Lord Hardwicke LC said[1]:

'... I am of opinion that one administrator cannot release a debt, or convey an interest, so as to bind the other, and that the case of an administrator differs from that of an executor.'

This observation was, in strictness, obiter, because Lord Hardwicke LC went on to decide first, that the attorneys were accountable to the administrators in their personal capacity and not in their representative capacity and that therefore a release by one principal was sufficient, as in the case of joint creditors; secondly, that the release was unfair and collusive and ought to be set aside in equity.

In *Jacomb v Harwood*[2], to which I have already referred, Strange MR mentioned with approval an unreported case, *Willand v Fenn*[3], decided in the Court of King's Bench in 1738 or a little later, where *Hudson v Hudson*[4] was not followed, and it was held, after apparently much protracted argument, that there was no distinction in this respect between executors and administrators. The reference to the case is extremely brief. A footnote in Selwyn's Nisi Prius[5] suggests that *Willand v Fenn*[3] may perhaps not have proceeded in quite the manner recounted by Strange MR. The authority of *Willand v Fenn*[3] is, I think, limited.

The next two cases on this topic to which I was referred were decisions of Sir John Nicholl in the Prerogative Court in 1809 and 1828. In *Warwick v Greville*[6] there were competing claims to the administration of an intestate's estate on the part of Lord Warwick, his brother, his sister and the son of a deceased sister. The decision to whom the grant should be given rested with the discretion of the court. In decreeing administration to the younger brother, Sir John Nicholl said[7]:

'Assuming, however, that Lord Warwick and his sister did unite in praying for a joint administration, the interests indeed would be even, but it would be an application for a joint, opposed to an application for a sole, administration. It has been correctly stated that the Court never forces a joint administration because, if the administrators were at variance, it almost put an end to the administration. Further, the Court prefers ceteris paribus a sole to a joint administration, because it is infinitely better for the estate; administrators must join and be joined in every act, which would not only be inconvenient to themselves, but, what is of more consequence, must be inconvenient to those who have demands on the estate either as creditor or as entitled in distribution.'

In *Stanley v Bernes*[8], on an application for administration pendente lite, limited to the recovery of debts amounting to £14,800, the two administrators sought leave to

1 (1737) 1 Atk at 460
2 (1751) 2 Ves Sen 265
3 Unreported; cited 2 Ves Sen at 267
4 (1737) 1 Atk 460
5 13th Edn, 1869, p 692, footnote (v)
6 (1809) 1 Phillim 123
7 1 Phillim at 126
8 (1828) 1 Hag Ecc 221

enter into separate administration bonds each for half £14,800 instead of a joint bond for the whole. This proposal did not appeal to Sir John Nicholl who said[1]:

> 'The prayer that the administrators may give separate bonds is quite a novel application—I can see no necessity for it, nor would any advantage result, because administrators must always act jointly; they cannot, like executors, act independently.'

Finally, I come to *Smith v Everett*[2]. This was a decision of Romilly MR in 1859. William Smith and Everett were partners in a country bank. Smith died. Probate of his will was granted to his widow and two others. Everett settled accounts with the widow's co-executors but the widow herself was not a party to such settlement. The widow then instituted a suit to establish the right of the estate to a moiety of the goodwill and profits of the banking business notwithstanding the settled accounts. Everett relied on the accounts which he had settled with the plaintiff's co-executors. Romilly MR said[3]:

> 'It is a settled principle with respect to executors, that any two may settle an account; in fact, one may settle an account, and it binds the others, though it may be a question as between co-executors whether they are liable to each other, or whether they are liable to their *cestuis que trust* for acting improperly. In *Herbert v. Pigott*[4] two out of four executors brought an action in respect of the testator's estate; the other two executors released the debt: it was held to be binding on those bringing the action. There was, then, a question whether the same principle extended to administrators, and later authorities have held that it does; still there is no question that executors have that power.'

Counsel have shown me that there is a report[5] of this case which omits the vital words 'and later authorities have held that it does', but they appear in a third report[6]. The remark about administrators was, of course, obiter.

It appears to me that there is no decisive authority which answers the question whether one administrator, acting without his co-administrator, has the same power of disposition as an executor acting without the concurrence of his co-executor. But having regard to the statement of Romilly MR that the question was settled by 1859 in favour of the administrator who acts alone, I am content to assume for present purposes that the view which he expressed was a correct interpretation of the law with the result that an administrator has power, at the present day, to bind the intestate's estate by his own act without the concurrence of his co-administrator.

I turn therefore, on the basis of that assumption, to the second defence. This, as I have said, is founded on *Sneesby v Thorne*[7] to the effect that specific performance ought not to be decreed since the contract was based on the supposition that the widow, as co-administrator, concurred. In the *Sneesby* case[7] the testator died in 1845. His will was proved by his executors, Thorne and Smith. The executors had retained certain leasehold properties in their hands unsold. In 1851 Thorne, who was about to set off for a journey abroad, received a communication from Smith to the effect that he proposed to sublease the property. Thorne objected and advocated a sale with vacant possession. In April 1852 Smith made an attempt at a sale which was unsuccessful. Thorne, when he learned of this, expressed his satisfaction because he considered

1 (1828) 1 Hag Ecc at 221, 222
2 (1859) 29 LJCh 236
3 29 LJCh at 239, 240
4 (1834) 2 Cr & Mee 384
5 27 Beav 446 at 454
6 34 LTOS 58 at 59
7 (1855) 7 De GM & G 399

that the proposed price was too low. However, Smith pressed ahead, and on 18th August 1852 an agreement was expressed to be made between Thorne and Smith as executors of the testator of the one part, and the plaintiff, Sneesby, of the other part, for the sale of the property at a certain price. The agreement was signed by Smith on behalf of himself and Thorne. As soon as Thorne learned of the sale he objected on the ground that it was at an under value and on his return to England he declined to implement it. Thereupon the plaintiff sued Thorne and Smith for specific performance. The suit came before Page Wood V-C[1]. Page Wood V-C seems to have dismissed the suit principally on the ground that it would, or might, leave the executors exposed to an action for breach of trust for selling at less than the full value. The action then went to the Court of Appeal in Chancery. Knight Bruce LJ commenced his judgment by assuming, without deciding, that the sale was not at an under value and that the terms were proper and that Smith had, at the time when he signed the contract, power as one of two executors without the concurrence of his co-executor, to enter into a contract effectual at law and in equity for the sale of the property at a sufficient price and on proper terms. He then said[2]:

'... I am of opinion, that Mr. Smith never intended to exercise such a power by entering into the contract independently of his co-executor. The form of the contract and the circumstances satisfy me that Smith, when he signed the contract, considered that he had Mr. Thorne's concurrence, and would not have signed it if he had believed that Mr. Thorne would not sanction his act. Thorne had not, in fact, given authority to enter into the contract, and has refused to adopt it. It is, therefore, inoperative as against him personally. To enforce it against Smith and the testator's estate, would be to enforce a contract different from that into which Smith intended to enter.'

Turner LJ said[3]:

'It is plain that Smith would never have entered into this contract, had he not supposed that Thorne would ratify it. A decree for specific performance would, therefore, place him in a position in which he never intended to place himself.'

Turner LJ went on to observe that he would have dismissed the suit on the ground of a sale at a possible under value but I am not concerned in this judgment with that part of his decision.

In my view the ratio decidendi of the decision on appeal was this. On the assumption that one of two executors had power in 1852 to sell and transfer leaseholds without the concurrence of his co-executor, the court might well have ordered specific performance if Smith had in fact purported to contract as executor without the concurrence of Thorne. But in fact that was not the contract which Smith purported to make. He purported to contract with the concurrence of Thorne. The contract was expressed to be made by both Thorne and Smith. Smith signed, not only on his own behalf but also as agent for Thorne. On the face of the contract, therefore, it was an agreement the validity of which depended on Smith having Thorne's authority. If Smith had Thorne's authority, well and good. The contract would then have been effectively made by both executors. If he did not have Thorne's authority and Thorne did not ratify the act of his supposed agent, there would be no enforceable contract except that Smith would be liable to Sneesby in damages for breach of warranty of authority. One thing which was plain for all to see was that Smith did not purport to enter into a contract without the concurrence of his co-executor; that would have been an entirely different contract. To put the matter shortly, a contract purporting to be

1　(1855) 3 Eq Rep 662
2　7 De GM & G at 402
3　7 De GM & G at 402, 403

made by two executors jointly cannot be enforced as if it were a contract by one executor severally when it transpires that the other executor did not contract.

In my judgment the decision in *Sneesby v Thorne*[1] completely covers the present case. The son did not purport to bind the estate of the deceased without the concurrence of the widow. He purported to bind the estate for himself, as one administrator, and as the authorised agent of the widow as his co-administrator. He bound himself as one of two administrators and he warranted that he had authority to bind the other administrator, the widow. He did not bind himself to sell without the concurrence of the widow. It was really the reverse. He bound the estate of the deceased only on the assumption, which he warranted to be correct, that he had authority to sign as agent for the widow. That assumption having been falsified, there is no contract to be enforced in relation to the second property. All that may be sued on is the warranty of authority given by the son. I say nothing about the enforcement of the contract in relation to the first property as that is not an isssue before me.

In the circumstances the summons is dismissed.

Summons dismissed.

Solicitors: *Vizards* (for the plaintiff company); *Robbins, Olivey & Lake* (for the defendants).

Susan Corbett Barrister.

Ross Hillman Ltd v Bond

QUEEN'S BENCH DIVISION
LORD WIDGERY CJ, MACKENNA AND MAY JJ
21st, 22nd JANUARY, 8th FEBRUARY 1974

Road traffic – Construction, weight, equipment and use of vehicles – Regulations – Causing vehicle to be used on road in breach of regulations – Mens rea of offence – Driver employed by company overloading one of company's vehicles – Company having forbidden drivers to overload vehicles – Knowledge of overloading – Knowledge of company required to be that of someone exercising control over company's affairs – Company having no knowledge of overloading – Whether company having 'caused' vehicle to be used in contravention of regulations – Whether offence absolute – Road Traffic Act 1972, s 40(5)(b).

The appellants, a limited company, owned a number of goods vehicles including a tipper lorry. Under the Goods Vehicles (Testing and Plating) Regulations 1971[a] the lorry carried a plating certificate restricting its rear axle weight to ten tons. The appellants expressly warned their drivers not to overload their vehicles in breach of the respective plating certificates. One of the appellants' drivers took the tipper lorry from their premises unloaded. He drove it to a quarry and loaded it with tarmac. Subsequently the lorry was stopped by the police and it was found that its rear axle weight so loaded was 11 tons 1¾ cwts. The appellants were charged on an information alleging that they had caused to be used on a road a goods vehicle to which the 1971 regulations applied and for which the rear axle weight of the vehicle exceeded

---

1   (1855) 7 De G M & G 399
a   SI 1971 No 352

that shown on the plating certificate, contrary to reg 121(1)[b] of the Motor Vehicles (Construction and Use) Regulations 1969[c] and s 40(5)[d] of the Road Traffic Act 1972. The justices convicted the appellants, holding that the offence created by s 40(5)(b) of the 1972 Act of 'causing' a vehicle to be used on a road which did not comply with the regulations was an absolute one and therefore it was immaterial that they had no knowledge of the overloading by their driver. On appeal,

Held – On the true construction of s 40(5)(b) a person could not be convicted of causing or permitting an unlawful user of a vehicle without proof that he had knowledge of the facts rendering the user unlawful. Furthermore if the defendant was a limited company the knowledge had to be that of someone exercising a directing mind over the company's affairs and not someone in the position of the appellants' driver. The appeal would therefore be allowed (see p 297 *d* to *f* and p 298 *e* and *f*, post).

Dictum of Lord Wright in *McLeod (or Houston) v Buchanan* [1940] 2 All ER at 187, *James & Son Ltd v Smee* [1954] 3 All ER 273 and *Lovelace v Director of Public Prosecutions* [1954] 3 All ER 481 applied.

Sopp v Long [1969] 1 All ER 855 distinguished.

Hunter v Clark 1956 JC 59 not followed.

Notes

For causing or permitting an offence, see 10 Halsbury's Laws (3rd Edn) 279, 280, para 519.

For penalty for contravention of regulations governing use of motor vehicles, see 33 Halsbury's Laws (3rd Edn) 487, 488, para 832, and for cases on the subject, see 45 Digest (Repl) 70-71, *205-214*.

For the Road Traffic Act 1972, s 40, see 42 Halsbury's Statutes (3rd Edn) 1680.

As from 13th February 1973 the Motor Vehicles (Construction and Use) Regulations 1969, reg 121, has been replaced by the Motor Vehicles (Construction and Use) Regulations 1973 (SI 1973 No 24), reg 142.

Cases referred to in judgment

Austin (F) Leyton Ltd v East [1961] Crim LR 119, DC.

Carmichael & Sons (Worcester) Ltd v Cottle [1971] RTR 11, 114 Sol Jo 867, DC.

Crawford v Haughton [1972] 1 All ER 535, [1972] 1 WLR 572, [1972] RTR 125, [1973] Crim LR 788, DC.

Hill and Sons (Botley and Denmead) Ltd v Hampshire Chief Constable [1972] RTR 29, 115 Sol Jo 675, DC.

Houston v Buchanan. See *McLeod (or Houston) v Buchanan*, infra.

Hunter v Clark 1956 JC 59, sub nom *Clark v Hunter* 1956 SLT 188, 45 Digest (Repl) 74, *792.

James & Son Ltd v Smee, Green v Burnett [1954] 3 All ER 273, [1955] 1 QB 78, [1954] 3 WLR 631, 118 JP 536, 52 LGR 545, DC, 45 Digest (Repl) 70, *208*.

Lovelace v Director of Public Prosecutions [1954] 3 All ER 481, [1954] 1 WLR 1468, 119 JP 21, DC, 45 Digest (Repl) 194, *25*.

McLeod (or Houston) v Buchanan [1940] 2 All ER 179, 1940 SC(HL) 17, 1940 SLT 232, HL, 29 Digest (Repl) 538, *3693*.

Magna Plant Ltd v Mitchell [1966] Crim LR 394, 110 Sol Jo 349, DC, Digest (Cont Vol B) 671, *211a*.

---

b Regulation 121(1), so far as material, provides: 'As respects a goods vehicle to which this Part of the Regulations applies, whether laden or unladen and whether or not drawing or being drawn by another vehicle, the following provisions of this paragraph shall apply . . . namely . . . (b) the axle weight for each axle shown in column (2) of the plating certificate for that vehicle shall not be exceeded . . .'

c SI 1969 No 321

d Section 40(5), so far as material, is set out at p 290 *h*, post

Mitchell v Morrison 1938 JC 64, 45 Digest (Repl) 138, *1190.

Rushton v Martin [1952] WN 258, 96 Sol Jo 345, DC, 45 Digest (Repl) 136, 49a.

Shave v Rosner [1954] 2 All ER 280, [1954] 2 QB 113, [1954] 2 WLR 1057, 118 JP 364, 52 LGR 337, DC, 45 Digest (Repl) 71, 210.

Sopp v Long [1969] 1 All ER 855, [1970] 1 QB 518, [1969] 2 WLR 587, 133 JP 261, 67 LGR 389, DC, Digest (Cont Vol C) 1058, 148a.

Windle v Dunning & Son Ltd [1968] 2 All ER 46, [1968] 1 WLR 552, 132 JP 284, 66 LGR 516, DC, Digest (Cont Vol C) 921, 205a.

Cases also cited

Cobb v Williams [1973] RTR 113, DC.

Garrett v Hooper [1973] RTR 1, DC.

Case stated

This was an appeal by way of a case stated by justices for the borough of Devizes, in respect of their adjudication as a magistrates' court sitting at Devizes on 16th April 1973.

On 1st February 1973 at a court of summary jurisdiction sitting at Devizes an information was preferred by the respondent, Percy J Bond, against the appellants, Ross Hillman Ltd, that they on 12th December 1972, in the borough of Devizes, did cause to be used on a road called New Park Street a motor lorry, being a goods vehicle to which the plating and testing regulations applied and for which a plating certificate had been issued, the axle weight for the rear axle of which exceeded the axle weight shown on the plating certificate, contrary to reg 121 of the Motor Vehicles (Construction and Use) Regulations 1969 and s 40 of the Road Traffic Act 1972.

The justices found the following facts. (a) At 11.18 a m on 12th December 1972 Pc Box was on duty in New Park Street, Devizes, when he directed a Dodge tipper motor lorry being driven by Mr A E Huntley to the public weighbridge at The Wharf, Devizes. The vehicle was laden with tarmac. Pc Box found that the gross weight of the vehicle was 16 tons 8 cwt. The weight of the rear axle was 11 tons 1¾ cwts. The plating certificate showed the weight of the rear axle as ten tons and the gross plated weight as 16 tons. The vehicle was owned by the appellants and on 21st December 1972 Mr K Hillman, a director, was interviewed by Pc May. The offence was pointed out to him and he was told that the appellants would be reported. (b) The motor lorry had left the appellants' premises on 12th December unladen and had been driven by the appellants' employee, Mr A E Huntley, to Whatley Quarry where it was loaded with tarmac. The quarry ticket was produced showing 16·26 tonne which is the metric equivalent of 16 imperial tons. At the time of the check in Devizes the vehicle was on its way from Whatley Quarry to Henley-on-Thames. The appellants' drivers had been warned about overloading both by notices in their pay packets and also by a large notice displayed in the appellants' premises. The appellants owned 14 lorries engaged primarily in quarry work and delivered some 5,000 tons per week. Thay had no previous convictions for overloading.

There had been no dispute concerning the facts and the appellants based their defence on the interpretation of the word 'cause'. It was contended on behalf of the appellants that 'to cause' involved some express or positive mandate from the person 'causing' to the other person or some authority from the former to the latter arising in the circumstances of the case. Reference was made to Wilkinson's Road Traffic Offences[1] and in particular to *McLeod v Buchanan*[2]. Reference was also made on behalf of the appellants to the term 'to permit' and to *James & Son Ltd v Smee*[3] and to other

---

1 7th Edn (1973), p 28

2 [1940] 2 All ER 179

3 [1954] 3 All ER 273, [1955] 1 QB 78

passages in Wilkinson[1]. It was argued that since 'to permit' was a vaguer term than   a
'to cause' there was an even greater burden on the prosecution to prove that the
appellants 'caused' the use of the vehicle in contravention of the construction and
use regulations, ie some knowledge on the part of the appellants. It was further
contended on behalf of the appellants that since the vehicle had left their premises
unladen and they had taken all steps to ensure that their employees did not overload their vehicles the act of their employee overloading their vehicle at Whatley   b
Quarry was a 'novus actus interveniens'.

The respondent contended that the appellants had caused their vehicle to be
used on the road in that it was on company business and that the offence of overloading
contrary to the construction and use regulations was an absolute offence and that
the appellants were therefore guilty of causing their vehicle to be used in contravention of the regulations. The respondent relied on certain passages in Wilkinson[2] and   c
in particular *Hunter v Clark*[3] and *F Austin (Leyton) Ltd v East*[4].

The justices were of the opinion that the appellants had caused the vehicle to be
used on their business and that under the construction and use regulations 'cause'
imported an absolute obligation. The appellants were convicted and fined £15.

J P M Phillips for the appellants.   d
Nicholas Medawar for the respondent.

Cur adv vult

8th February. **MAY J** read the first judgment at the invitation of Lord Widgery CJ.
I have the authority of MacKenna J to say that he agrees with the judgment which I am   e
about to deliver. This is an appeal by way of a case stated from the conviction by the
Devizes borough justices of the appellants on 16th April 1973 on an information
alleging that they on 12th December 1972 caused to be used on the roads a goods
vehicle to which the Goods Vehicles (Plating and Testing) Regulations 1971[5] applied
and for which a plating certificate had been issued in circumstances in which the rear
axle weight of that vehicle exceeded the rear axle weight shown in that certificate,   f
contrary to reg 121 of the Motor Vehicles (Construction and Use) Regulations 1969[6]
and s 40 of the Road Traffic Act 1972.

Insofar as is material in the present case, reg 121 of the 1969 regulations provides that
as respects a vehicle to which the plating and testing regulations apply the axle
weight for each axle shown in the plating certificate for the vehicle shall not be exceeded. The Motor Vehicles (Construction and Use) Regulations 1969 in their turn   g
were made pursuant to powers given to the Secretary of State by the predecessor of
s 40 of the Road Traffic Act 1972. Section 40(5) provides:

'... a person ... (b) who uses on a road a motor vehicle which does not comply
with any such regulations or causes or permits a vehicle to be so used, shall be
guilty of an offence.'   h

The brief facts of the present case are that the appellants owned a number of
vehicles, including the Dodge tipper lorry with which we are particularly concerned.
This was a vehicle to which the plating and testing regulations applied and its plating
certificate restricted its rear axle weight to ten tons. There was evidence before the

---

1   7th Edn (1973), pp 29, 30
2   7th Edn (1973), pp 28, 29
3   1956 SLT 188
4   [1961] Crim LR 119
5   SI 1971 No 352
6   SI 1969 No 321

justices, which they accepted, that the appellants warned their employed drivers by
notices in their pay packets and displayed at the appellants' premises to be very careful not to overload their vehicles in breach of their respective plating certificates.

On 12th December 1972 one of the appellants' drivers in the course of his employment took the tipper lorry to which I have referred out from their premises unloaded.
He drove it from there to a quarry where it was loaded with tarmac. On its journey
from the quarry it was stopped by a police officer and taken to a weighbridge where it
was found that its rear axle weight so loaded was 11 tons 1¾cwts, or more than a ton
in excess of the permitted loading shown on its plating certificate.

Now it is common ground that the provisions of s 40(5)(b) of the Road Traffic Act
1972 create three distinct types of offence, namely: (1) that of using a motor vehicle
on a road which does not comply with a requirement of the 1969 regulations; (2) that
of causing a vehicle to be so used; and (3) that of permitting a vehicle to be so used.

As I have said, these appellants were charged with an offence of the second type,
that of causing the material tipper lorry to be overloaded in contravention of reg 121.

At the hearings before both the justices and this court the appellants contended that
they could not be convicted of this offence unless and until some prior knowledge on
their part of the unlawful condition of the vehicle was shown; and that as the appellants were a limited company that knowledge had to be the knowledge of someone
exercising a directing mind in and about the company's affairs and not, for instance,
merely that of the driver of the material lorry at the relevant time.

The respondent's contention throughout has been that the offence of causing the
use of a vehicle in contravention of reg 121 is an absolute offence, not requiring proof
of mens rea or knowledge on the part of anyone. Consequently, since the vehicle was
on the road on the appellants' business when it was stopped by the police officer they
had caused it to be there in its overloaded condition and should thus be convicted,
knowledge or no knowledge.

The justices preferred the respondent's contentions, and the question for this court
is whether they were right to do so. The answer to this question is essentially a matter
of construction of the relevant statutory provision, namely, s 40(5)(b) of the 1972 Act.
This being so, one may obtain some help from cases in which the construction of similar
words in other statutes has had to be considered, but as Edmund Davies LJ pointed
out in *Sopp v Long*[1], a case to which I shall have to return later, particular care must be
taken.

With this in mind, but in anticipation of the comparison which will have to be made
between the terms of s 40(5)(b) and those of certain other statutes, it is to be stressed
that the former does create the three separate offences already referred to; it is not
limited, for instance, to creating only two offences comprising an unlawful user on the
one hand and causing that user; and, for what it is worth, by its actual phraseology
seems to separate the offence of user from the two other offences of causing the user
and permitting the user.

It might have been thought reasonable in the past, when the provisions now contained in s 40(5)(b) were first considered, to have construed the three types of offence
in the same way, holding that proof of knowledge was either necessary in each or
unnecessary in all. However, a full court decided otherwise in *James & Son Ltd v
Smee*[2]. There the relevant statutory provision was reg 101 of the Motor Vehicles
(Construction and Use) Regulations 1951, which was in these terms[3]:

'If any person uses or causes or permits to be used on a road a motor vehicle
. . . in contravention of or fails to comply with any of the preceding regulations
. . . he shall for each offence, be liable to a fine . . .'

1 [1969] 1 All ER 855 at 859, [1970] 1 QB 518 at 524
2 [1954] 3 All ER 273, [1955] 1 QB 78
3 SI 1951 No 2101

It was held that although the 'using' type of offence was an absolute one and could be committed without proof of knowledge, nevertheless the 'permitting' type of offence required proof of knowledge in some responsible officer of the defendant limited company.

At this stage two comments may be made. First, where the defendant who is alleged to have permitted the unlawful user is a company, the state of mind or knowledge of the mere driver is not enough. Support for that proposition can be found in *Hill and Sons (Botley and Denmead) Ltd v Hampshire Chief Constable*[1], where, after quoting a passage from the judgment of Lord Parker CJ in *Magna Plant Ltd v Mitchell*[2], Lord Widgery CJ said:

'I find that judgment valuable for two reasons, first of all it reminds one of the undoubted principle that, when the accused person alleged to have permitted a wrongful act is a company, one must look to the mind of those officers of the company who can fairly be described as its brains rather than its hands. In the present case, therefore, one must look to the mind of Mr Hill, the director, and not to the individual workman. Furthermore that case emphasises that, even if an individual is guilty of reckless conduct, that is not sufficient to impute knowledge to the employer unless the recklessness is the act of someone who can fairly be described as the brains of the company.'

Secondly, if the class of person who can properly be said to be using a vehicle within s 40(5)(*b*) extends beyond the actual driver, and beyond the owner of the vehicle present in it controlling or having the power to control the driver, and includes any owner-employer when his vehicle is being driven by his servant on his business, then this would be a reason for holding that proof of knowledge was not required when the offence was one of causing the unlawful user. Otherwise the unknowing employer's liability would depend on whether he was charged as one using the vehicle, when ignorance would be no answer, or as one causing it to be used, when proof of knowledge would be essential.

In this connection, however, and on the basic question as to the proper construction of what I may describe as the 'causing' type of offence, it is necessary to refer to *Lovelace v Director of Public Prosecutions*[3]. In that case the appellant presented at a theatre, of which he was the licensee and manager, a play the script of which had been authorised by the Lord Chamberlain under s 15 of the Theatres Act 1843 which was in these terms:

'. . . Every person who for hire shall act or present, or cause to be acted or presented, any new stage play, or any act, scene, or part thereof . . . until the same shall have been allowed by the lord chamberlain [shall incur a penalty].'

Before the performance the appellant told his actors that they were to adhere strictly to the script. One of them did not and acted in an indecent manner. The appellant was charged with causing a part of the play to be presented without the approval of the Lord Chamberlain and was convicted by the stipendiary magistrate. In the course of his judgment allowing the appeal Lord Goddard CJ said[4]:

'We are asked in the present case to say that the conviction was wrong because the charge was "causing" and there was no evidence of any causation, as the facts found by the magistrate show that the appellant took every precaution to prevent that being done which was done. It has been held repeatedly that, although the prohibition of doing an act is absolute so that scienter or mens rea is not necessary,

1   [1972] RTR 29 at 34
2   (1966) 110 Sol Jo 349
3   [1954] 3 All ER 481, [1954] 1 WLR 1468
4   [1954] 3 All ER at 483, [1954] 1 WLR at 1471

different considerations apply where a person is charged with "causing" or "permitting" the act to be done, because one cannot "cause" or "permit" an act to be done unless one has knowledge of the facts. LORD WRIGHT put it in this way in *Houston* v. *Buchanan*[1]: "To 'cause' the user involves some express or positive mandate from the person 'causing' to the other person, or some authority from the former to the latter, arising in the circumstances of the case." In the present case counsel for the prosecution contended that, as the appellant undoubtedly caused the presentation of the play, he caused the presentation of that part of the play which was unauthorised. I think it would be unreal to hold that. However much one may dislike deciding these cases on whether the prosecution, in framing the charge, chose the word "present" or the words "cause to be presented", the fact is that, if a defendant is to be convicted of "causing" something, there must be some act of his which is equivalent to causing, that is to say, a command or direction to do the wrongful act. There was no "causing" in the present case.'

In my opinion three points should be made on this authority. First, although the statutory provision created no offence of 'permitting' the presentation of a play without the approval of the Lord Chamberlain, but spoke only of presenting or causing a play to be so presented, nevertheless this court held that the offence of causing the play to be presented without approval was not an absolute offence but required proof of knowledge, of mens rea. Secondly, Lord Goddard CJ quoted with approval, and in my opinion founded himself on the quotation from Lord Wright's speech in *Houston v Buchanan*[1] which dealt with the meaning of the word 'cause'. Thirdly, Lord Goddard CJ pointed out that although one may dislike making the decision of a case of this nature dependant on the precise part of the statute which the prosecution chooses in framing the charge, nevertheless this is a matter for the prosecution and not for the court.

Although I keep firmly in mind the warning given by Edmund Davies LJ in *Sopp v Long*[2] to which I have referred, I think that at the least Lord Wright's dictum in *Houston v Buchanan*[1] and the decision in *Lovelace v Director of Public Prosecutions*[3] are strong persuasive authority that where a statute creates an offence of causing something to be done this is not to be construed as an absolute offence but as one requiring proof of the appropriate mens rea.

Further, bearing in mind the third point which I have made on the passage quoted from Lord Goddard CJ's judgment in *Lovelace v Director of Public Prosecutions*[4], I do not find that my present opinion that the ambit of the 'user' offence under s 40(5)(b) is not limited to the actual driver only but extends to catch the employer of the driver acting in the course of his employment (see *Windle v Dunning & Son Ltd*[5], *Carmichael & Sons Ltd v Cottle*[6] and *Crawford v Haughton*[7]) lessens the persuasive effect of the decision in *Lovelace's* case[3]. It may be that had the appellants been charged here with the mere user in contravention of the regulation they would have been properly convicted. However, they were not so charged and we have to consider, as did the court in *Lovelace v Director of Public Prosecutions*[3], the offence with which they were in fact charged.

We were also referred to the decision in *Shave v Rosner*[8] in support of the appellants' argument in the instant case. In my opinion, however, that case was concerned not

1 [1940] 2 All ER 179 at 187
2 [1969] 1 All ER at 859, [1970] 1 QB at 524
3 [1954] 3 All ER 481, [1954] 1 WLR 1468
4 [1954] 3 All ER at 483, [1954] 1 WLR at 1471
5 [1968] 2 All ER 46, [1968] 1 WLR 552
6 [1971] RTR 11
7 [1972] 1 All ER 535, [1972] 1 WLR 572
8 [1954] 2 All ER 280, [1954] 2 QB 113

with knowledge or mens rea but with whether there was in truth a sufficient chain of causation to render the defendant liable.

Secondly, in general I find it difficult as a matter of ordinary English to appreciate how someone can be said to have caused another to do or omit to do something unless he either knows or deliberately chooses not to know what it is that that other is doing or failing to do.

Thirdly, since the two words 'causes' and 'permits' are placed in such close juxta-position in s 40(5)(b) and separate from the word 'uses', I would myself tend towards a construction of the section which treated the offence of causing the unlawful user in the same way as the offence of permitting the unlawful user has to be treated. If the latter requires some mens rea, for which proposition *James & Son Ltd v Smee*[1] is author-ity, then it would seem logical that the former should do so also.

This last is the argument which commended itself to Lord Sorn in his dissenting judgment in the Scottish case of *Hunter v Clark*[2] to which I must now refer. That was a case under the Motor Vehicles (Construction and Use) Regulations 1955[3], of which reg 104 was materially in the same terms as reg 101 of the 1951 regulations which fell to be considered in *James & Son Ltd v Smee*[1]. The defendant was apparently originally charged with causing or permitting a motor vehicle to be used on a road on which the brakes were not maintained in good and efficient working order, contrary to the provisions of reg 76 of the 1955 regulations and the sheriff-substitute convicted him of that offence. No duplicity argument appears to have been taken at any time. On the defendant's appeal by way of case stated to the High Court of Justiciary the Crown conceded that the offence of permitting the use of the vehicle, in contravention of reg 76, required proof of knowledge of the relevant circumstances, that this had not been proved and that in consequence this part of the conviction could not stand. However the prosecution went on to contend that the offence of causing the use of the vehicle in contravention of reg 76 was an absolute offence requiring no proof of knowledge or mens rea and that therefore the defendant had been rightly convicted.

This contention the Lord Justice-General (Lord Clyde) accepted. He agreed[4], as indeed the Crown had conceded, that: 'Permission to use in contravention of a Regulation necessarily involves knowledge of the fact that there is a contravention ...' quoting in support of this proposition the second part of Lord Wright's dictum in *Houston v Buchanan*[5] which dealt with the meaning of the word 'permit'. He did not, however, refer to the immediately preceding passage from Lord Wright's speech dealing with the meaning of the word 'cause', even though the two dicta did so follow each other and were in my opinion spoken to all intents in the same breath. Cf *Lovelace v Director of Public Prosecutions*[6] to which I have already referred.

The learned Lord Justice-General considered the case before him analogous to that of *Mitchell v Morrison*[7], which was apparently the decision of a full court of seven judges. In that earlier case the relevant regulation laid on the defendant who was the holder of a goods vehicle licence the duty 'of causing to be kept a current record' of all the prescribed details of his drivers' working hours.

Counsel for the appellants in our case contended that the regulation construed in *Mitchell v Morrison*[7] could and should be distinguished from the requirements of s 40(5)(b). In *Mitchell v Morrison*[7] the obligation under consideration was a personal obligation laid on the licence-holder to cause proper records to be kept, and if they

1 [1954] 3 All ER 273, [1955] 1 QB 78
2 1956 JC 59
3 SI 1955 No 482
4 1956 JC at 63
5 [1940] 2 All ER at 187
6 [1954] 3 All ER 481, [1954] 1 WLR 1468
7 1938 JC 64

were not kept then he had failed in that personal obligation whether he knew they had been properly kept or not. Neither in *Hunter v Clark*[1] nor in our case was there any personal duty imposed on the defendant to cause anything; the question was indeed the very different one, namely, 'Did he cause the relevant contravention?' Counsel, therefore, suggested that the ratio of the Lord Justice-General's judgment proceeded on two false premises. Unassisted by any other authority I would very respectfully agree.

The judgment of the second member of the court in *Hunter v Clark*[1], Lord Russell, proceeded on what, with hesitation, he considered to be the proper construction of the relevant regulation. He did not deal with what I may describe as the juxtaposition argument, which was the one which Lord Sorn favoured. Lord Russell based his decision on the fact that in some of the other substantive regulations, that is to say regulations other than regs 76 and 104, absence of knowledge or the exercise of proper care was expressly stated to be a defence, whereas in the substantive regulation then under consideration, the braking system reg 76, the obligation to maintain was absolute. In my opinion Lord Russell's approach was in truth merely to construe the substantive braking system regulation and not the regulation which created the actual offence, in which the words 'causes or permits' appeared.

For my part, and subject to later authority, to which I shall refer, I prefer Lord Sorn's dissenting judgment. He held that the offence committed by 'user' was absolute. It having been conceded by the Crown that under a charge of 'permitting' knowledge had to be proved, then one ought to construe that part of the regulation that dealt with 'causing' in the same way—and he said[2]:

'. . . I think we must similarly read the words "causes to be used . . . in contravention" as denoting a person who causes not only use but use in contravention.'

And Lord Sorn then went on to refer to the 'causing' part of Lord Wright's dictum in *Houston v Buchanan*[3]. I confess that I find the logic of the reasoning of Lord Sorn more convincing than that of the majority of the court.

However, *Hunter v Clark*[1] was considered with approval by the court in *Sopp v Long*[4], a decision to which I have already referred. That was a case under s 24(1) of the Weights and Measures Act 1963, which provided:

'. . . any person who, in selling . . . any goods by weight or other measurement . . . delivers or causes to be delivered to the buyer a lesser quantity than that purported to be sold . . . shall be guilty of an offence.'

The facts were that the barmaid, who was also the manageress of the refreshment room at Windsor railway station, sold a short measure of whisky. Senior to her in the chain of command was a district manager; above him a general manager; above him the defendant appellant who was the secretary of British Transport Hotels Ltd, and as such held the liquor licence for the station refreshment room. He was convicted of 'causing to be delivered' the short measure of whisky. He appealed successfully to quarter sessions, but the Divisional Court reversed quarter sessions on a case stated.

In giving the leading judgment Edmund Davies LJ pointed out[5], as I have already said, that the citation of authority on the construction of other statutes calls for particular care. I, therefore, remind myself that s 24 of the Weights and Measures Act 1963 did not contain the word 'permits'; the relevant offence was committed only by one who 'delivers or causes to be delivered'. I also remind myself that ss 26 and 27 of

---

1   1956 JC 59
2   1956 JC at 68
3   [1940] 2 All ER at 187
4   [1969] 1 All ER 855, [1970] 1 QB 518
5   [1969] 1 All ER at 859, [1970] 1 QB at 524

the 1963 Act provide possible statutory defences for someone causing something to be done but who can show that he has no guilty knowledge or mens rea.

Edmund Davies LJ went on to suggest that because there was no master-servant relationship involved in the facts of either *Lovelace v Director of Public Prosecutions*[1] or *Houston v Buchanan*[2] these cases could be distinguished from the case before the court in *Sopp v Long*[3]. I respectfully comment, first, that neither was there any real master-servant relationship in *Sopp v Long*[3], and secondly, that I doubt whether these factual considerations are really material on the basic question of the construction of the relevant statutory provisions. Nevertheless I agree with Edmund Davies LJ that *Houston v Buchanan*[2] was a 'permitting' case, and thus that Lord Wright's dictum[4] in his speech on 'causing' was obiter. I have, however, already expressed the view that both dicta were, as it were, spoken by Lord Wright in the same breath.

Be this as it may, Edmund Davies LJ then went on to cite the Lord-Justice General in *Hunter v Clark*[5] with approval and expressed what I believe to be the real ratio of his own judgment in *Sopp v Long*[6] in this way:

'Only the licensee can sell—that is common ground—and he alone sold. Being absent from the premises he sold through his servant, the barmaid; by every sale he conducted through her, he thereby "caused" to be delivered that which was sold; and that he did, whether that which was delivered was a short measure or a full measure.'

On the facts such reasoning cannot be applied to the instant case. Indeed counsel for the appellants before us submitted, I think with some force, that *Sopp v Long*[3] was a case dealing in effect with licensing matters and had therefore to be considered a special case in the light of the distinctive nature of the whole tenor of licensing legislation, with the emphasis which it places on the situation and responsibility of the relevant licensee.

Counsel for the appellants also referred us to *Rushton v Martin*[7]. In that case the general manager of a group of five road haulage executive depots was charged and convicted by justices of causing the use of a motor vehicle and trailer on a road in contravention of reg 67 of the Motor Vehicles (Construction and Use) Regulations 1947[8], in that the locking pin of the towing bar was in a dangerous condition. A maintenance superintendent was employed at each of the five depots answerable to the defendant, as well as mechanics and drivers, but as in *Sopp v Long*[3] it was the defendant who was generally responsible for the operation of the vehicles and the management of his group. On appeal to this court the conviction was set aside. The report of the judgment of Oliver J contained this passage[9]:

'There was no vicarious responsibility; the defendant had not been negligent and could not possibly have known that there was anything wrong with the vehicle. As that was so, the appeal would be allowed.'

In my opinion, however, the issue in *Rushton v Martin*[7], as in *Shave v Rosner*[10], was really whether or not the necessary chain of causation existed, and thus the decision

---

1   [1954] 3 All ER 481, [1954] 1 WLR 1468
2   [1940] 2 All ER 179
3   [1969] 1 All ER 855, [1970] 1 QB 518
4   [1940] 2 All ER at 187
5   1956 JC 59
6   [1969] 1 All ER at 860, [1970] 1 QB at 526
7   [1952] WN 258
8   SR & O 1947 No 670
9   [1952] WN at 258
10 [1954] 2 All ER 280, [1954] 2 QB 113

is not directly in point in the instant case. Nevertheless the reference in the short passage from the judgment quoted above to the defendant's knowledge may be noted.

Finally, counsel for the respondent referred us to *F Austin (Leyton) Ltd v East*[1]. In that case justices had convicted a limited company of unlawfully causing a motor vehicle to be on a road in a dangerous condition, contrary to regs 73 and 104 of the Motor Vehicles (Construction and Use) Regulations 1955. The company appealed to the Divisional Court on the ground that on the evidence before the justices it was impossible to say that the vehicle had not been properly maintained and thus that the breach of reg 73 must have been due to the existence of a latent defect. This court dismissed the appeal, holding that reg 73 created an absolute obligation and that therefore the question of latent defect was irrelevant.

It does not appear, however, that the point in issue in the present case was ever argued in *F Austin (Leyton) Ltd v East*[1]; it seems to have been assumed before the justices that if there had been a breach of reg 73 then this had been caused by the company, and thus the contrary argument was not open to the latter on appeal. In these circumstances I do not think that this is an authority which helps us one way or the other.

What then is the result? Unassisted by any authority I would as a matter of ordinary English construe both the word 'causes' and the word 'permits' in s 40(5)(b) of the 1972 Act as requiring prior knowledge of the facts constituting the unlawful user. Secondly, I am averse to adding to the catalogue of absolute offences unless that is the clear intention of Parliament. Thirdly, if, as I think and as is supported by authority, actual user of a vehicle in contravention of the regulations is an absolute offence, and if, as I also think, a master 'uses' the vehicle which his servant is driving on that master's business, then I think that the mischief against which the regulations are directed, that of having unsafe vehicles on the roads, is adequately dealt with. Having regard to the ordinary meaning of 'causes' I do not find it surprising that whereas on given facts a master charged with using will be convicted, on the same facts a master charged with causing that use will be acquitted. Prosecutors must use the correct offence in law with which to charge defendants; if they are genuinely in doubt they can always lay informations in the alternative.

Do the relevant authorities require me to take a different view on the basic issue in the instant case? I do not think that they do. In *James & Son Ltd v Smee*[2] the offence of mere 'user' was held to be an absolute one; the 'permits' type of offence, however, was held to require proof of knowledge. In *Lovelace v Director of Public Prosecutions*[3] the word 'causes' in a state which did not include the word 'permits' was held to require proof of knowledge and this court relied on the dictum of Lord Wright in *Houston v Buchanan*[4] insofar as it dealt with the word 'causes'. On the other hand, in *Hunter v Clark*[5] two members of the court held that 'causes' in the Motor Vehicles (Construction and Use) Regulations 1955 did not require proof of knowledge. However, I think that the reasoning in the judgment of the Lord Justice-General is open to question: so also, in my opinion as I have indicated, can that be said of the judgment of Lord Russell. I prefer Lord Sorn's dissenting judgment, which referred to Lord Wright's dictum in *Houston v Buchanan*[4] on the meaning of 'causing' and held that the use of the phrase 'causes or permits' required one to treat both offences in the same way—thus, since use of the word 'permits' required proof of knowledge, so also did the use of the word 'causes'.

1 [1961] Crim LR 119
2 [1954] 3 All ER 273, [1955] 1 QB 78
3 [1954] 3 All ER 481, [1954] 1 WLR 1468
4 [1940] 2 All ER at 187
5 1956 JC 59

Nevertheless I face the fact that in *Sopp v Long*[1], this court effectively approved the view of the majority in *Hunter v Clark*[2]. But the relevant statute in *Sopp v Long*[1] only referred to a person who 'causes', and it must be remembered that the defendant in *Sopp v Long*[1] was the licensee and thus technically the only person authorised by licensing law to sell the whisky. It is, in my opinion, only on this last ground that the ratio of the decision in *Sopp v Long*[1] can be supported in the light of the other decisions to which I have referred.

For instance, apart from this special feature of *Sopp v Long*[1] I do not think that the respective decisions in it and in *Lovelace v Director of Public Prosecutions*[3] can properly be reconciled. I am not, with respect, impressed with the argument that because *Houston v Buchanan*[4] was a permitting case Lord Wright's dictum[5] on the meaning of 'permits' is in the circumstances any more relevant than his reference to the meaning of the word 'causes'. In my opinion the position on the authorities is in law this. If the true ratio of the decision in *Sopp v Long*[1] was that which I have indicated that I think it was, then despite the approval of *Hunter v Clark*[2] which it contained in my view, we can and should distinguish it from the instant case, and decide the latter on the basis of the decision in *James & Son Ltd v Smee*[6] and the argument contained in Lord Sorn's judgment in *Hunter v Clark*[2]. If *Sopp v Long*[1] was not in reality decided on the ground of the special individual position of the licensee of licensed premises, then with respect I do not think that its decision can be reconciled with that in *Lovelace v Director of Public Prosecutions*[3], and of the two I prefer the latter for the reasons which will have become apparent.

In either event I am of the opinion that one must construe both the two types of offence created by s 40(5)(b), the one of causing and the other of permitting the unlawful user, as requiring proof of mens rea, of knowledge of the facts rendering the user unlawful. I would also hold that if the defendant in a given case is a limited company, then such knowledge must be the knowledge of someone exercising a directing mind over the company's affairs.

In the result I would allow this appeal and quash the conviction.

LORD WIDGERY CJ. I also agree and the appeal will be allowed and the conviction quashed.

Appeal allowed. Conviction quashed.

Solicitors: *E P Rugg & Co* (for the appellants); *Sharpe, Pritchard & Co*, agents for *Farnfield & Nicholls*, Trowbridge (for the respondent).

N P Metcalfe Esq   Barrister.

---

1   [1969] 1 All ER 855, [1970] 1 QB 518
2   1956 JC 59
3   [1954] 3 All ER 481, [1954] 1 WLR 1468
4   [1940] 2 All ER 179
5   [1940] 2 All ER at 187
6   [1954] 3 All ER 273, [1955] 1 QB 78

Hanstead Investments Ltd v Inland Revenue Commissioners

CHANCERY DIVISION   Reversed CA [1975] 2 All ER 1066

BRIGHTMAN J

7th, 8th MARCH 1974

Surtax – Company – Undistributed income – Direction – Income available for distribution – Income not applied or applicable to current requirements of company's business – Income applied in or towards payment for business, undertaking or property – Payment for stock-in-trade as distinct from capital asset – Property-dealing company – Sum expended on first acquisition of property – Property resold at profit exceeding sum paid – Whether sum paid part of income or gross receipts of company – Whether expenditure on stock-in-trade expenditure on 'business, undertaking or property' – Income Tax Act 1952, s 246(2).

H Ltd was a private company incorporated in May 1959 with a nominal capital of £1,000 divided into 1,000 ordinary shares of £1 each. The issued share capital of the company was £2 which was held by H and his brother P. At all material times when the company was not dormant, it carried on the business of dealing in land. About six months before the company was incorporated, H had bought an estate comprising a mansion house, cottages and surrounding land for £120,000. On 17th May 1961 the mansion house and some cottages were conveyed to the company for £6,000. Two days later the company conveyed the property to A at a price of £49,000. The company took £11,250 on completion and the balance of £37,750 was left on mortgage to be paid by instalments over five years. The instalments were all duly paid. It was not clear from what source the company had obtained the £6,000 to pay H. The Inland Revenue Commissioners made a surtax direction in respect of the £6,000 for the accounting period 21st August 1959 to 30th April 1962 under ss 245[a] and 246(2)[b] of the Income Tax Act 1952. The company contended that the £6,000 was not, within s 246(2), 'income available for distribution to the members of the company' since it had not been paid out of the income, i e the profits, of the company but out of the company's gross receipts, and furthermore it was not a sum expended or applied in or towards payment for a 'business, undertaking or property', within s 246(2)(a)(i) but in or towards payment for stock-in-trade as distinct from a capital asset.

Held – The purchase price of £6,000 paid to H by the company was 'income available for distribution' within the meaning of s 246(2) since it was a sum 'applied . . . out of the income of the company'; the £6,000 was to be regarded as income of the company available for distribution since the profit made by the company in the relevant period exceeded the figure of £6,000. Furthermore, the fact that the subject-matter of the acquisition was stock-in-trade as distinct from a capital asset did not preclude the application of s 246 as the words 'business, undertaking or property' in s 246(2)(a)(i) were wide enough to include stock-in-trade (see p 310 h to p 311 a, post).

Morris Securities Ltd v Inland Revenue Comrs (1940) 23 Tax Cas 525 followed.

Notes

For the power to make surtax directions in relation to the undistributed income of a company, see 20 Halsbury's Laws (3rd Edn) 551-553, paras 1073-1075.

The provisions for apportioning the undistributed income of a company among members of the company for the purposes of assessment to surtax were abolished on the introduction of corporation tax on 6th April 1966. The special provisions for determining whether income is to be regarded as income available for distribution

---

a   Section 245 is set out at p 307 *c* to *e*, post

b   Section 246(2), so far as material, is set out at p 308 *b* to *d* and *h*, post and not as having been applied or as being applicable to the current requirements of the company's business, were preserved for the purpose of determining the shortfall in the distributions of a close company and, in relation to accounting periods ending after 5th April 1973, for the purpose of determining the 'relevant income' of a close company. For the power to apportion the excess of a close company's relevant income over its distributions, see Supplement to 20 Halsbury's Laws (3rd Edn), para 2044, and for cases on the subject, see 28(1) Digest (Reissue) 406-418, 1481-1518.

For the Income Tax Act 1952, ss 245, 246, see 31 Halsbury's Statutes (2nd Edn) 232, 233.

Sections 245 and 246(1) and the proviso to s 246(2) of the 1952 Act were repealed by the Finance Act 1965, s 97(5), Sch 22, Part IV. Section 246(2) of the 1952 Act was replaced by the Income and Corporation Taxes Act 1970, s 293(1) in relation to accounting periods ending after 5th April 1970. Section 293(1) of the 1970 Act was replaced by the Finance Act 1972, Sch 16, para 12(1), in relation to accounting periods ending after 5th April 1973.

Case referred to in judgment

Morris Securities Ltd v Inland Revenue Comrs (1940) 23 Tax Cas 525, 28(1) Digest (Reissue) 410, 1494.

Case stated

1. At a meeting of the Commissioners for the Special Purposes of the Income Tax Acts held on 27th, 28th and 29th March 1972 Hanstead Investments Ltd ('the company') appealed against the direction made by the Crown under s 245 of the Income Tax Act 1952 in respect of the period 21st August 1959 to 30th April 1962 and the following apportionments made under s 248(1) of the 1952 Act: Henry J Pelham, £23,961; Paul N D Pelham, £23,961.

2. Shortly stated the question for the commissioners' decision was whether or not, having regard to the provisions of Chapter III of Part IX of the 1952 Act, the company failed to distribute a reasonable part of its income from all sources for the period 21st August 1959 to 30th April 1962.

[Paragraphs 3 and 4 referred to the evidence given and the documents proved or admitted before the commissioners.]

5. As a result of the evidence both oral and documentary adduced before them, the commissioners found the following facts proved or admitted: (1) The company was incorporated on 7th May 1959 as a private company limited by shares, having as its main object the acquisition and holding of property for the purposes of investment only, any proceeds of realisation not being available for payment of dividends. At all material times, however, the company carried on the business of dealing in land and had been assessed to tax on that footing. (2) The company's nominal capital was £1,000, divided into 1,000 ordinary shares of £1 each, and the issued share capital was £2. Mr Henry Pelham and a Mr Heritage (as nominee for Mr Paul Pelham during minority) were the original shareholders, each being the owner of one £1 share. The directors of the company were Mr Henry Pelham from its incorporation in 1959 until March 1966, Mr Paul Pelham from June 1963 to March 1966 and Mr Heritage during some of those years. (3) At a sale by public auction in October 1958 Mr Henry Pelham purchased the Hanstead Estate (comprising Hanstead House, various buildings and many acres of land) for £120,000 with the intention (which was subsequently carried out) that the beneficial ownership of the whole or parts should eventually be transferred to one of the property dealing or investment companies (there were then about 15 to 20) controlled by the Pelham family ('the Pelham companies'). At that time the mother of Mr Henry Pelham and Mr Paul Pelham ('the brothers') was relieving herself of her interests in the family business with the object that the brothers should carry it on and share equally in its profits and assets. It was the family intention (which was subsequently carried out) that the Hanstead Estate should go into a company or companies owned by the brothers. The bulk of the purchase money was borrowed

a from the bank and others, with the intention (which was subsequently carried out) that the borrowings should be repaid out of sales of parts of the estate. Accordingly Mr Henry Pelham did not himself take any conveyance until a sub-purchaser was found. (4) After its incorporation in 1959 the company was dormant until 1961, when it was selected to be the company to take part of the estate remaining unsold. By a conveyance dated 17th May 1961 and made between (1) Sir John Henry Swain

b Richardson, Baronet, and others (vendors) (2) Mr Henry Pelham (purchaser) and (3) the company (sub-purchaser), Hanstead House and five adjoining cottages were conveyed by the vendors at the direction of Mr Henry Pelham as trustee to the company in consideration of the sum of £6,000 paid by the company to Mr Henry Pelham. The source of that purchase money was not established before the commissioners, but it was presumed by Mr Henry Pelham to have been a loan from the bank. The figure of £6,000 was arrived at by an apportionment of the original price of £120,000 by the

c solicitors who were instructed to deal with the conveyance. (5) By a conveyance dated 19th May 1961 and made between (1) the company and (2) Ambassador College (UK) Ltd ('the college') Hanstead House and the five adjoining cottages were conveyed to the college in consideration of the sum of £49,000 paid to the company by the college. The company received £11,250 in cash and the balance of £37,750 was left outstanding

d on mortgage, repayable with interest at the rate of 6½ per cent in 20 quarterly instalments and secured by a legal charge dated 19th May 1961 and made between (1) the college (2) Herbert Armstrong (surety) and (3) the company. (6) Prior to the conveyance of 19th May 1961 Mr Henry Pelham had received some low offers for the purchase of Hanstead House alone, without its guest house, a large summer house, the adjoining cottages and remaining land. In about the spring of 1959 two serious

e offers for the purchase of Hanstead House were made, one by British European Airways for £15,000 (to include the guest and summer houses and about four or five acres of land), and another by the Rosegrowers Association for £13,000 (to include the guest and summer houses). The Admiralty also became interested in the property, but made no offer. After the sale by the company of Hanstead House to the college the guest and summer houses together with 20 to 25 acres of land were sold by Mr

f Henry Pelham for £10,000 to other purchasers. (7) At that time (early 1959) it was difficult to dispose of a house of the size and nature of Hanstead House. There were the problems and expense of division and modernisation. The company was understandably reluctant not to clinch the deal with the college, although the security was viewed with some apprehension. Hanstead House was purchased by the college to serve as the headquarters in England of an American religious organisation called 'the

g Radio Church of God Incorporated'. The organisation, which did not apparently fit into any known sect, devoted much time to broadcasting on the radio religious messages and appeals to listeners to write to the Radio Church for booklets and information. Hanstead House was required partly as a church or assembly place and partly as a school for children of members of the congregation, and the organisation appeared to entertain grandiose and expensive plans for the adaptation of Hanstead

h House, adaptation which might well affect the saleability of the property if it became necessary to realise any security. Little was known of the organisation's financial position, except that its income was derived from its members. Mr Henry Pelham had introduced the college to a building society but the latter had after some investigations declined to advance any money for the purchase. The company was therefore forced to lend the balance of the purchase price or lose the deal. In the event the college paid all instalments and interest as the same became due under the legal

j charge. (8) From 19th May 1961 until October 1964 the company was again dormant. During that period the company had little or no liquid assets after setting aside sufficient funds to meet its estimated liabilities including income and profits tax. According to the company's balance sheet as at 30th April 1962 it had liquid assets amounting to £65; as at 30th April 1963 liquid assets amounting to £7,475; and as at 30th April 1964 liquid assets amounting to £14,622. A reference to liability to

profits tax did not appear in the company's accounts until those for the year ended
30th April 1965 signed on 8th March 1967. Until the company restarted in October
1964 with the purchase of a property in Hartswood Road, Shepherds Bush, the company's moneys had been left in the hands of another of the Pelham companies, the
management company, Henry Pelham and Partners Ltd. Between October 1964 and
30th April 1965 the company purchased various properties at a total cost of £238,360
6s 7d, which sum was greatly in excess of the cash available and was raised by extensive borrowing. (9) The company's draft accounts for the period ended 30th April 1962
and for the two years ended 30th April 1963 and 1964 ('the 1962, the 1963 and the 1964
accounts' respectively) were delivered by hand to the company's directors on 15th
January 1965 and were duly certified by the company's accountants on 1st February
1965. The 1962 accounts contained a profit and loss appropriation account which appropriated £16,000 to 'Income Tax Schedule D 1961/62'. The balance sheets in the three
sets of accounts revealed the following surpluses of 'Sundry Debtors' over 'Current
Liabilities':

	1962	1963	1964
Sundry debtors	£17,078 15s 1d	£23,269 15s 4d	£31,293 10s 0d
Current liabilities	£17,012 15s 9d	£15,794 3s 0d	£16,670 15s 7d
Excess of sundry debtors over current liabilities	£65 19s 4d	£7,475 12s 4d	£14,622 14s 5d

In the 1962 balance sheet the current liability was to normal creditors consisting
almost entirely of the estimated income tax liability. (10) The company's accounts
for the year ended 30th April 1965 ('the 1965 accounts') were certified on 8th March
1967. Those accounts included the following items:

Balance sheet	£	s	d
Current assets	243,910	17	11
Current liabilities	227,930	8	3
	15,980	9	8

Included in the current liabilities were the following:

Taxation Sch D 1961-62 to 1964-65	£16,064 19s 6d
Profits tax 1961-62 to 1964-65	£7,210 19s 0d
Appropriation account	
Profits tax 1961-62 to 1963-64	£7,188 12s 0d
Profits tax 1964-65	£22 7s 0d

The £7,188 12s (which was eventually agreed with the Inland Revenue at some date
after 30th April 1965) was 15 per cent of £47,923 8s 9d which was the total of:

(a) £42,612 11s 3d profit on sale of Hanstead House
(b) £5,310 17s 6d   balance transferred to appropriation account

See profit and loss appropriation account 1962

(11) The delay in the preparation of the company's 1962, 1963 and 1964 accounts was attributed to the following factors: (a) The number of Pelham companies had increased to about 30 and there was a general backlog of accounts, about which the directors were very concerned. (b) The accounts of the Pelham companies had for many years been audited by a small suburban firm of accountants, but the work was becoming too much for them. Rather than terminate their services, the company had in 1963 appointed Messrs Barton, Mayhew & Co as consultants to advise (inter alia) on a more efficient book-keeping system and to select book-keepers who might assist the accountants by providing draft accounts and trial balances. (c) Meantime the accountants found it easier to prepare accounts for two or three years together. (d) There was no evidence before the commissioners that the preparation of accounts had been deliberately delayed with any tax objective. (12) The company's policy was to plough back its profit and trade with it and, after October 1964, to expand. A surplus of £7,000, for instance, enabled the company to put down a deposit on a purchase of property at £70,000, and to obtain a contract, without which it was more difficult to raise money for completion. The directors themselves were not in favour of recommending dividends during the relevant periods and were never advised to do so by their accountants or consultants. In any event they would not have been prepared to consider any dividend in the absence of draft accounts. They were aware of the strange implications on the payment of dividends, and of the risk of surtax directions if sufficient dividends were not declared. In the circumstances they took the view that the position of the company did not warrant any declaration of dividends, even when draft accounts threw up a substantial surplus for the first time (the 1964 accounts), because by that date (January 1965) the company had committed itself to large purchases. Even if the surplus had been considerably larger the directors were of the opinion that they still would not have recommended a dividend. (13) Mr Hamilton gave evidence on accountancy matters (which the commissioners accepted) to the effect that it was the normal practice for companies to wait for accounts to be drawn up before deciding whether to pay dividends, even if the position of the company in question was fairly simple or straightforward. He himself did not see the company's 1962, 1963 and 1964 accounts until some time in January 1965. Later, having seen the draft 1965 accounts, he realised that the earlier accounts did not include any reference to profits tax liability. In his opinion such a reference ought clearly to have been included. Had references to profits tax been included in the accounts, the figures for 'Sundry Debtors' less 'Current Liabilities' (see (9) above) would have shown the position more correctly as follows:

	1962			1963			1964		
	£	s	d	£	s	d	£	s	d
Excess of sundry debtors over current liabilities per balance sheets	65	19	4	7,475	12	4	14,622	14	5
Profits tax liability 1961-62 to 1963-64	7,188	12	0	7,188	12	0	7,188	12	0
	(—) 7,122	12	8	(+) 287	0	4	(+) 7,434	2	5

(14) On 31st March 1967 the company was put into voluntary liquidation. The reason for that step was that the Pelham family had been advised by their solicitors to liquidate the Pelham companies and to create trading settlements, so as to avoid certain effects of the operation of the Finance Act 1965 on close companies.

6. It was contended on behalf of the company: (a) that it was for the Crown to establish that the company had not within a reasonable time after 30th April 1962 distributed a reasonable part of its income for the period ended 30th April 1962;

(b) that it was not enough for the Crown to show that it would have been reasonable for the company to have made a distribution, if at the same time it could be said (as it was submitted was indeed the case) that it would be equally reasonable to withhold a distribution; (c) that any requirements advisable for the development of the company's business should be taken into account; (d) that the proper time for deciding whether a distribution should have been made was the date when the accounts for the period were available for consideration by the directors, that is, during January 1965; (e) that in all the circumstances it was not unreasonable for the company not to have declared a dividend for the period even if (contrary to contention (d) above) the proper time for considering the matter was at some time before January 1965; (f) that s 246(2)(a)(i) of the Income Tax Act 1952 had no application to the case, because the £6,000 paid by the company under the conveyance dated 17th May 1961 was not paid out of 'the income' of the company; alternatively, if the £6,000 fell to be treated as available for distribution, the tribunal was still required to be satisfied (under the proviso to s 246(2)) that the company did not in fact make a reasonable distribution; (g) that the appeal should be upheld and that the direction and consequential apportionments should be cancelled.

7. It was contended on behalf of the Crown: (a) that in all the circumstances the company had not within a reasonable time after the period ended 30th April 1962 distributed a reasonable part of its income from all sources for the period within the meaning of s 245 of the 1952 Act; (b) that a reasonable time (after that period) elapsed on or about 30th April 1963, alternatively long before 1st February 1965 when the accounts for the period were certified; in the alternative, (c) that the question in issue fell to be decided on the company's accounts certified by the auditors and adopted by the company after Mr Hamilton had seen the company's 1962, 1963 and 1964 accounts in January 1965, which accounts had been submitted to the Revenue; (d) that it was unreasonable to claim that it was essential to retain the whole of the company's profit for the purposes of its trade. There could have been no requirement for the maintenance and development during the years to 30th April 1963 or 1964 as in those years the company had no trading activity of any sort; (e) that because the company had been dormant from May 1961 until October 1964 its financial position could easily have been ascertained at any time in that period; (f) that with regard to the payment of £6,000 made by the company under the conveyance dated 17th May 1961, £5,998 should be regarded as income available for distribution by virtue of s 246(2)(a) of the 1952 Act; (g) that the appeal should be dismissed and the direction and consequential apportionments confirmed.

[Paragraph 8 noted the cases[1] referred to.]

9. The commissioners took time to consider their decision and gave it in writing on 22nd May 1972 as follows:

'In these appeals against directions and apportionments made under Sections 245 and 248 of the Income Tax Act, 1952, two questions remain for determination: first, whether the Crown has established that the Company unreasonably withheld from distribution its income for the period 21 August 1959 to 30 April 1962; and second, whether the sum of £6,000 ought in any event to have been distributed as deemed income of that period.

'The main facts on which we base our decision are as follows: The Company's accounts for the period ended 30 April 1962 were prepared by the Company's Auditors towards the end of the year 1964, delivered by hand to the Company's Directors on 15 January 1965 and certified by the Auditors on 1 February 1965.

---

1 *Burton (Montague) Ltd v Inland Revenue Comrs* (1936) 20 Tax Cas 48, [1934] All ER Rep 829, HL; *Fattorini (Thomas) (Lancashire) Ltd v Inland Revenue Comrs* [1942] 1 All ER 619, [1942] AC 643, 24 Tax Cas 328, HL; *Morris Securities Ltd v Inland Revenue Comrs* (1940) 23 Tax Cas 525; *Mucklow (A & J) Ltd v Inland Revenue Comrs* [1954] 2 All ER 508, [1954] Ch 615, 35 Tax Cas 251, CA

Examination of those accounts and the accounts for the succeeding years reveal surpluses or deficits (making allowance for Profits Tax liability) in the following approximate figures:

Period ended	30 April 1962	Deficit	£7,000
Year ended	30 April 1963	Surplus	£288
Year ended	30 April 1964	Surplus	£7,000.

'Delay in preparation of the accounts was attributed to the Auditors, although the Directors were anxious to know the true financial position. The question of payment of dividends was never considered by the Directors. Payment of the £6,000 in question for the purchase of land was repaid out of the £42,613 11s 3d., being the proceeds of the resale within two days of the bulk of the land. Prior to the purchase of the land and for some time after its resale the Company had no surplus cash Part of the proceeds of sale was received in cash and the remainder was left on mortgage, the value of which as a security was somewhat uncertain for a few years.

'The first question arises under the general impact of Section 245 and in particular with regard to the construction and application of the words "within a reasonable time after the end of any year or other period for which accounts have been made up". Having considered the arguments and the authorities addressed to us, we conclude that in all the circumstances a reasonable time for the making of a distribution (if any) would have been within a year or so, i e until 30 April 1963 or thereabout. While there is no evidence of premeditated delay in the preparation of the Company's accounts, we think that a delay of nearly three years was not reasonable and that it should not now be allowed to operate to the possible advantage of the Company's members and to the possible disadvantage of the Crown. If we are right in our conclusion thus far it follows, from the fact that as there was only a small surplus (£288) building up during the year ended 30 April 1963, that it was not unreasonable for the Company not to have declared any dividend.

'The second question turns on the construction and application of Section 246(2)(a)(i), subject to the effect of the proviso to that subsection. This aspect, in the absence of any guiding authority, has caused us some difficulty. Having considered the arguments addressed to us, we think that the key to the application of the subsection lies in the words "out of the income of the company". It seems to us that if the sum to be considered has not in fact been paid out of capital, it must be taken to have been paid out of income so as to call into operation that subsection. Having found that the £6,000 in question was paid otherwise than out of capital, we think that such amount was caught by the subsection and must therefore be regarded prima facie as having been available for distribution, unless exempted by the proviso, as being payment for the first property of a substantial character in fact acquired by the Company.

'Before Section 246(2) can operate so as to make Section 245 apply, the proviso to Section 246(2) requires us to be satisfied as to two matters, the first of which we have just dealt with. The second is "that the company has not in fact distributed a reasonable part of its actual income in such manner as to render the amount distributed liable to be included in the statements to be made by the members of the company of their total income for the purposes of surtax". In our opinion, for the proviso to operate there must in fact have been a distribution, and such distribution must have formed part of the members' total incomes. These conditions were not satisfied by the Company in the present case and consequently the Company cannot in our view avail itself of the proviso. Upon that footing we confirm the direction and dismiss the appeal in principle, leaving figures to be agreed between the parties.'

10. Figures were agreed between the parties on 4th July 1972 and on 10th August the commissioners accordingly reduced the apportionments for the period 21st August 1959 to 30th April 1962 as follows: H J Pelham, £18,092·50; P N D Pelham, £18,092·50.

11. Immediately after the determination of the appeal the company declared its dissatisfaction therewith as being erroneous in point of law and on 15th August 1972 required the commissioners to state a case for the opinion of the High Court pursuant to the Taxes Management Act 1970, s 56.

Michael Fox QC and *A E W Park* for the company.
Leonard Bromley QC and *Harry Woolf* for the Crown.

BRIGHTMAN J. The taxpayer in this case is a company called Hanstead Investments Ltd, which was incorporated on 7th May 1959 with a capital of 1,000 ordinary shares of £1 each. At all material times when not dormant, the company carried on the business of dealing in land. The issued capital of the company was at all times two fully paid shares of £1, which were severally held by, or on behalf of, two brothers called Mr Henry Pelham and Mr Paul Pelham.

A surtax direction was made against the company under s 245 of the Income Tax Act 1952 in respect of an accounting period from 21st August 1959 to 30th April 1962, as a result of which the actual income from all sources of the company was apportioned equally between the two brothers, the apportionment amounting to just under £24,000 in each case.

The facts proved or admitted before the Special Commissioners are set out in para 5 of the stated case. A summary will be sufficient for the purposes of this judgment. About six months before the incorporation of the company, Mr Henry Pelham bought at auction the Hanstead Estate in Hertfordshire, comprising a mansion house, some cottages and a considerable area of surrounding land. The price was £120,000. Most of the purchase price was borrowed from a bank and from others with the intention that the borrowings should be repaid out of the proceeds of various sales to sub-purchasers. On 17th May 1961, that is to say 2½ years after the auction sale, and about two years after the incorporation of the company, the mansion house and some cottages were conveyed to the company in consideration of the sum of £6,000 said to have been paid by the company to Mr Henry Pelham. The £6,000 was apparently an apportionment of the £120,000, made by the solicitors who were dealing with the conveyancing. By a conveyance dated two days later, the same property was to be conveyed to a company called Ambassador College (UK) Ltd in consideration of £49,000. The sum of £11,250 out of the £49,000 was paid in cash. The balance of £37,750 was left outstanding on a five year instalment mortgage. There is no actual finding as to the source of the £6,000 paid by the company to Mr Henry Pelham and it must, I think, either have been a loan from someone or perhaps the amount was left outstanding until the £11,250 cash had been received. The net profit to the company on the sale, after deducting the purchase price and various expenses, was £42,612.

The first accounts of the company consisted of a balance sheet as at 30th April 1962, an income and expenditure account for the period 21st August 1959—by a typing error put as '31st August'—to 30th April 1962, and a profit and loss (appropriation) account for the like period. The balance sheet showed a revenue reserve of £29,463 at 30th April 1962 which represented the profit on the sale of Hanstead House and the cottages, after deducting certain preliminary expenses and tax. The balance sheet also showed liabilities of some £17,000, corrected to £24,200 after taking £7,188 profits tax into account, and assets consisting of £29,400 due on the mortgage, and sundry debts due to the company of £17,078. The balance sheet as at 30th April 1963 showed a slightly increased revenue reserve, liabilities of some £23,000 and assets consisting of £22,050 due under the instalment mortgage, and £23,269 sundry debts due to the company. The balance sheet at 30th April 1964 showed a minimally reduced revenue reserve, liabilities of some £23,800 and assets consisting of £14,700 due under the instalment mortgage and £31,293 sundry debts due to the company. I should have mentioned that the liabilities I indicated as at 30th April 1963 and 1964 are adjusted for the missing profits tax of £7,188.

On these figures, treating the instalment mortgage as unrealisable in the sense of being illiquid, and the other debts due to the company as readily realisable, there was a deficiency in liquid assets as at 30th April 1962 of about £7,000, a sufficiency as at 30th April 1963 of some £300, and a sufficiency as at 30th April 1964 of about £7,000. In March 1967 the company was placed in voluntary liquidation. The three sets of accounts to which I have referred were delivered to the directors in mid-January 1965, and certified by the auditors on 1st February.

I think at this stage it will be convenient to read the relevant parts of ss 245 and 246. Section 245 is as follows:

> 'With a view to preventing the avoidance of the payment of surtax through the withholding from distribution of income of a company which would otherwise be distributed, it is hereby enacted that where it appears to the Special Commissioners that any company to which this section applies has not, within a reasonable time after the end of any year or other period for which accounts have been made up, distributed to its members, in such manner as to render the amount distributed liable to be included in the statements to be made by the members of the company of their total income for the purposes of surtax, a reasonable part of its actual income from all sources for the said year or other period, the Commissioners may, by notice in writing to the company, direct that, for purposes of assessment to surtax, the said income of the company shall, for the year or other period specified in the notice, be deemed to be the income of the members, and the amount thereof shall be apportioned among the members.'

The decision of the Special Commissioners, after setting out the facts and the contentions was this:

> 'The first question arises under the general impact of Section 245 and in particular with regard to the construction and application of the words "within a reasonable time after the end of any year or other period for which accounts have been made up". Having considered the arguments and the authorities addressed to us, we conclude that in all the circumstances a reasonable time for the making of a distribution (if any) would have been within a year or so, i e until 30th April 1963 or thereabouts. [They mean, of course, a year or so after 30th April 1962 which ends the period with which the direction is dealing.] While there is no evidence of premeditated delay in the preparation of the Company's accounts, we think that a delay of nearly three years was not reasonable and that it should not now be allowed to operate to the possible advantage of the Company's members and to the possible disadvantage of the Crown. If we are right in our conclusion thus far it follows, from the fact that as there was only a small surplus (£288) building up during the year ended 30th April 1963, that it was not unreasonable for the Company not to have declared any dividend.'

The Special Commissioners, therefore, were finding that as the surplus liquid assets amounted to only £288 by 30th April 1963 it was not unreasonable, so far as s 245 was concerned, for the company to have distributed to its members no part of its actual income from all sources for the period ending 30th April 1962.

The Special Commissioners then directed their attention to s 246 of the Act, which is dealing with—I quote the sidenote—'Tests of adequacy of distribution of income'. Subsection (1) reads:

> 'In determining under the last preceding section whether any company has or has not made such a distribution of its actual income as is therein mentioned,

the Special Commissioners shall have regard not only to the current requirements of the company's business but also to such other requirements as may be necessary or advisable for the maintenance and development of that business.'

Then there is a gloss on sub-s (1) imposed by sub-s (2), the relevant part of which reads as follows:

'For the purposes of the said last preceding section [s 245] any such sum as is hereinafter described shall be regarded as income available for distribution among the members of the company and not as having been applied or being applicable to the current requirements of the company's business or to such other require-ments as may be necessary or advisable for the maintenance and development of that business, that is to say—(a) any sum expended or applied, or intended to be expended or applied, out of the income of the company . . .—(i) in or towards payment for the business, undertaking or property which the company was formed to acquire or which was the first business undertaking or property of a substantial character in fact acquired by the company; or (ii) in . . . repayment of any . . . debt . . . incurred in or towards payment for any such business, under-taking or property . . . or incurred for the purpose of raising money applied or to be applied in or towards payment therefor; or (iii) in meeting any obligations of the company in respect of the acquisition of any such business, undertaking or property.'

The Special Commissioners dealt with this section in two parts. They started as follows:

'The second question turns on the construction and application of Section 246(2)(a)(i) [but I think that para (ii) and (iii) may also be material], subject to the effect of the proviso to that subsection [which I have not yet read]. This aspect, in the absence of any guiding authority, has caused us some difficulty. Having considered the arguments addressed to us, we think that the key to the applica-tion of the subsection lies in the words "out of the income of the company". It seems to us that if the sum to be considered has not in fact been paid out of capital, it must be taken to have been paid out of income so as to call into opera-tion that subsection. Having found that the £6,000 in question was paid otherwise than out of capital, we think that such amount was caught by the subsection and must therefore be regarded prima facie as having been available for distri-bution, unless exempted by the proviso, as being payment for the first property of a substantial character in fact acquired by the Company.'

This part of the decision of the Special Commissioners is a live issue before me.
I will now read the proviso to s 246(2) which I have not yet read. It says:

'Provided that this subsection shall not operate so as to make the said last preceding section apply as respects any company unless it appears to the Special Commissioners, not only that income of the company has been or is to be expended or applied for one or more of the purposes mentioned in this sub-section, but also that the company has not in fact distributed a reasonable part of its actual income in such manner as to render the amount distributed liable to be included in the statements to be made by the members of the company of their total income for the purposes of surtax.'

The Special Commissioners continue as follows:

'Before Section 246(2) can operate so as to make Section 245 apply, the proviso to Section 246(2) requires us to be satisfied as to two matters, the first of which we have just dealt with. The second is "that the company has not in fact distri-buted a reasonable part of its actual income in such manner as to render the

amount distributed liable to be included in the statements to be made by the
members of the company of their total income for the purposes of surtax". In
our opinion, for the proviso to operate there must in fact have been a distribution,
and such distribution must have formed part of the members' total incomes.
These conditions were not satisfied by the Company in the present case and consequently the Company cannot in our view avail itself of the proviso. Upon that
footing we confirm the direction and dismiss the appeal in principle, leaving
figures to be agreed between the parties [as, in fact, they were].'

This part of the decision of the Special Commissioners is not supported by the
Crown. In other words, it is conceded before me that the proviso is capable of applying
although there has not, in fact, been any distribution at all by the company to its
members in respect of the period in question.

The general scheme of ss 245 and 246 seems to have been as follows. The object
was to prevent surtax being avoided through non-distribution of income by certain
companies. If a reasonable part of the company's actual income from all sources
for an accounting period was not distributed within a reasonable time, then a surtax
direction might follow. Section 246 deals with what might roughly be called the
availability of income. The first subsection adumbrates permissible excuses for non-
distribution. They are, or include, the current requirements of the company's
business and other requirements necessary, or advisable, for the maintenance and
development of the company's business. Subsection (2) enumerates excuses for non-
distribution which are not permissible. It does this by saying that certain specified
sums, which are therein described, are to be regarded as available for distribution
and not as applied, or as applicable, for current or future requirements of the business
if certain conditions are satisfied. The conditions (so far as relevant for present
purposes) are, first, that the sum which is to be deemed available must be a sum spent
or intended to be spent out of the income of the company; clearly, it would be unjust
to penalise a company in relation to non-distribution of income merely because capital
had been used in order to acquire assets; secondly, the subject-matter acquired by
the expenditure of such sum must be the business or undertaking or property which
the company was formed to acquire, or it must be the first business or the first undertaking, or the first property of a substantial character in fact acquired by the company.

Counsel for the company submitted that the £6,000 purchase price for Hanstead
House and the cottages was not paid, or discharged, out of the income of the company.
It was, he submitted, paid out of the gross receipts of the company. This is a trading
company, and in the case of a trading company, he said, the income of the company
is the balance which is left after deducting from gross receipts the company's various trading expenses, of which this £6,000 was one. Therefore, as a matter of accounting logic, he said, the £6,000 was not paid out of the company's income because
the company's income did not fall to be ascertained until the £6,000 had already
been deducted.

The Special Commissioners, it was said, fell into two errors. They prefaced
their decision on what they described as the first question, with this sentence:

'Payment of the £6,000 in question for the purchase of land was repaid out of
the £42,613 11s 3d., being the proceeds of the resale within two days of the bulk
of the land.'

That, submitted counsel, was manifestly wrong because, quite clearly, the £42,613
was a figure struck after taking off the £6,000 purchase money. I accept that submission as a valid criticism of the manner in which the Special Commissioners formulated their reasons.

The second error, submitted counsel, into which the Special Commissioners
stumbled, was the conclusion that the £6,000 was paid out of income merely because
there was no capital from which it could possibly have been wholly paid. The only

capital ever received by the company was the sum of £2. The commissioners' process
of reasoning ignores the distinction, it was submitted, between gross receipts and net
profits. Only the net profits are distributable to members of the company, not gross
receipts. If one looks at the balance sheet it is clear that the £6,000, though not paid
out of capital, was not paid out of profits either, but out of the £49,000 consideration
money payable to the company.

Although I see the force of counsel's argument, I do not feel able to accept it. It
seems to me that a similar point arose in *Morris Securities Ltd v Inland Revenue Comrs*[1].
In that case the company dealt in land. It was incorporated in 1933. The first property
acquired by the company was bought for some £31,000. A surtax direction was made
in respect of the year to 5th July 1935. That was a year in which the company made
a trading profit of about £6,000, and a further profit in the form of the share of
net profits of a firm with which it was in partnership of about £15,000, making a
net profit of some £21,000 in all. In the same year the company applied about
£13,000 in repayment of a debt incurred by the company in respect of the acquisition of the property that I have mentioned. A surtax direction was made under
the enactment which preceded s 245. Lawrence J said this in the course of his
judgment[2]:

> 'Mr. Tucker on behalf of the Appellant Company has submitted that, in view
> of the findings of fact of the Board of Referees, they have gone wrong in law, and
> their conclusions cannot be supported. The points that I understood him to raise
> were these. One point that he made (I will call it the first point) was that the
> £13,000 which was repaid to Mr. Wheeler by the Company during the year in
> question was not paid out of income within the meaning of Section 31, Sub-
> section (1), of the Finance Act, 1926, and that therefore the Board of Referees
> were wrong in their holding in paragraph 10 of the Case. The Attorney-General,
> in answer to that argument, pointed out that the Company having made a
> profit of £21,000 in the year in question, and the £13,000 having been a sum
> expended or applied towards the payment for the first property of a substantial
> character in fact acquired by the Company, the sum of £13,000 must be regarded
> as income available for distribution, because it must be treated as paid out of
> income, having regard to the fact that the Company had in that year made a
> profit of £21,000. I am of opinion that the argument on behalf of the Crown is
> right on this point, and it is impossible to say that when a company has in fact
> made a *bona fide* profit of £21,000, and has discharged a liability of a less sum
> than the amount of that profit, that liability has not been discharged out of
> income.'

It might, perhaps, be correct to add 'at any rate in the case of a company, such as this,
with a paid up capital of £100'.

This conclusion of the learned judge appears to me to be sound logic and I am not
prepared to depart from it in the present case. *Morris Securities Ltd*[1] has, I am told,
gone unchallenged so far as any reported decisions are concerned. Accordingly, I
think it is correct to say that the £6,000 was applied out of the income of the company
within the meaning of s 246(2)(*a*).

Counsel for the company then submitted that s 246 had no application where the
subject-matter of the expenditure is stock-in-trade as distinct from a capital asset. In
my judgment, the words 'business, undertaking or property' are clearly wide enough
to comprehend stock-in-trade and, as I have said, the subject-matter of the acquisition
in *Morris Securities Ltd*[1] was also stock-in-trade. I should not, therefore, be able to
accede to this submission of counsel even if I felt tempted to by the wording of the

---

1 (1940) Tax Cas 525
2 (1940) Tax Cas at 532, 533

paragraph, without differing from Lawrence J, which I am not prepared to do. I
therefore, reject the argument.

In the result, I am of the opinion that the Special Commissioners did not err in law
in relation to any part of their decision that has been the subject-matter of argument
before me.

*Appeal dismissed. Case remitted to the Special Commissioners for determination on the basis
that the proviso to s 246(2) is applicable, that the £6,000 falls within s 246(2)(a) and that they
do not disturb the finding that a reasonable time for the making of a distribution had expired
on or about 30th April 1963. Application of company for repayment of tax pending
determination of commissioners adjourned with liberty to apply.*

Solicitors: *Geo & Wm Webb* (for the company); *Solicitor of Inland Revenue.*

Rengan Krishnan Esq Barrister.

Christie Owen & Davies Ltd v Rapacioli

COURT OF APPEAL, CIVIL DIVISION
CAIRNS, ORR AND JAMES LJJ
11th, 12th FEBRUARY 1974

*Estate agent – Commission – Agreement to pay commission on introduction of a person' ready
able and willing' to purchase at price acceptable to vendor – Introduction of person willing
to purchase on terms agreed by vendor – Prospective purchaser's offer accepted by vendor –
Draft contract prepared by vendor's solicitors and approved by purchaser's solicitors–Contract
engrossed and signed by purchaser – Vendor thereafter refusing to proceed with contract –
Whether estate agents entitled to commission.*

The defendant instructed estate agents to assist him in the sale of the lease and goodwill of a restaurant and to quote a price of £20,000. It was agreed that the estate
agents would be entitled to a commission if they effected 'an introduction either
directly or indirectly of a person ready able and willing to purchase' at £20,000 or for
any other price acceptable to the defendant. The agents introduced A as a prospective purchaser. A offered £17,700 and the defendant agreed to accept that offer.
Solicitors were accordingly instructed on both sides. The defendant's solicitors prepared a draft contract and sent it to A's solicitors who approved it on his behalf.
The contract was then engrossed and signed by A. A's solicitors sent it to the defendant's solicitors for the defendant's signature together with a cheque for the balance
of the deposit. The defendant, however, had in the meantime received a better offer
and so declined to proceed with the contract. The estate agents claimed that in the
circumstances they were entitled to their commission.

Held – The question whether an estate agent's commission was payable depended on
the terms of the contract between the agent and the vendor and on the ordinary
rules of construction. Where the commission was payable on the introduction of a
person 'ready able and willing to purchase' it would be payable, even though the
transaction proved abortive, if the agent had introduced a person who was able to
purchase and who expressed his readiness and willingness to do so by an unqualified
offer, provided that the offer was one which was within the terms that the agent had

been authorised to invite and it was the vendor and not the prospective purchaser
who withdrew before contract. It followed that in the circumstances the agents *a*
were ¡entitled to their commission (see p 318 *g* to p 319 *b d e* and *j* to p 320 *a d* and
e, post).

Luxor *(Eastbourne) Ltd v Cooper* [1941] 1 All ER 33, and dicta of Cohen LJ in *Graham
and Scott (Southgate) Ltd v Oxlade* [1950] 1 All ER at 861, of Hodson J in *McCullum v
Hicks* [1950] 1 All ER at 867, of Bucknill LJ in *Dennis Reed Ltd v Goody* [1950] 1 All ER
at 922 and of Sellers LJ in *Ackroyd & Sons v Hasan* [1960] 2 All ER at 265 applied. *b*

Dicta of Denning LJ in *McCallum v Hicks* [1950] 1 All ER at 866 and in *Dennis Reed
Ltd v Goody* [1950] 1 All ER at 924 disapproved.

Notes
For estate agents' commission, see 1 Halsbury's Laws (4th Edn) 479, para 801, and for
cases on the subject, see 1 Digest (Repl) 594-596, *1909-1925*. *c*

Cases referred to in judgments
Ackroyd & Sons v Hasan [1960] 2 All ER 254, [1960] 2 QB 144, [1960] 2 WLR 810, CA, 1
   Digest (Repl) 589, *1893*.
Bennett (E H) and Partners v Millett [1948] 2 All ER 929, [1949] 1 KB 362, [1949] LJR 1050,
   1 Digest (Repl) 587, *1885*. *d*
Dellafiora v Lester, Lester v Adrian Barr & Co Ltd [1962] 3 All ER 393, [1962] 1 WLR
   1208, CA, Digest (Cont Vol A) 8, *1925a*.
Giddys v Horsfall [1947] 1 All ER 460, 63 TLR 160, 1 Digest (Repl) 587, *1884*.
Graham and Scott (Southgate) Ltd v Oxlade [1950] 1 All ER 856, [1950] 2 KB 257, CA;
   affg [1950] 1 All ER 91, 1 Digest (Repl) 588, *1888*.
Lee (John) & Son (Grantham) Ltd v Railway Executive [1949] 2 All ER 581, 65 TLR 604, CA, *e*
   38 Digest (Repl) 402, *624*.
Long (Peter) & Partners v Burns [1956] 3 All ER 207, [1956] 1 WLR 1083, CA; *affg* [1956]
   2 All ER 25, [1956] 1 WLR 413, 1 Digest (Repl) 596, *1925*.
Luxor (Eastbourne) Ltd (in liquidation) v Cooper [1941] 1 All ER 33, [1941] AC 108, 110
   LJKB 131, 164 LT 313, HL, 1 Digest (Repl) 587, *1881*.
McCallum v Hicks [1950] 1 All ER 864, [1950] 2 KB 271, CA, 1 Digest (Repl) 588, *1889*. *f*
Martin Gale & Wright v Buswell (1961) 178 Estates Gazette 709, 105 Sol Jo 466, CA.
Nelson (E P) & Co v Rolfe [1949] 2 All ER 584, [1950] 1 KB 139, CA, 1 Digest (Repl) 571
   1816.
Reed (Dennis) Ltd v Goody [1950] 1 All ER 919, [1950] 2 KB 277, CA, 1 Digest (Repl) 594,
   1911.
Wilkinson (A L) Ltd v Brown [1966] 1 All ER 509, [1966] 1 WLR 194, CA, Digest (Cont *g*
   Vol B) 10, *1914b*.
Wilkinson (A L) Ltd v O'Neil (1961) 181 Estates Gazette 137, CA.

Appeal
This was an appeal by the plaintiffs, Christie Owen & Davies Ltd, against the judgment of his Honour Deputy Judge Ellison given at Westminster County Court on 6th *h*
July 1973 whereby he dismissed the plaintiffs' action against the defendant, Renzo
Rapacioli, for £835 commission which the plaintiffs claimed to be entitled to under
an agreement contained in a letter dated 1st June 1971. The facts are set out in the
judgment of Cairns LJ.

Adrian Hamilton QC for the plaintiffs.
Roland Watt for the defendant. *j*

CAIRNS LJ. This is an appeal from the judgment of Deputy Judge Ellison given
at Westminster County Court on 6th July 1973. The action was by estate agents
for commission. Their claim was dismissed, and they appealed. The defendant

a   is a restauranteur. In June 1971 he instructed the plaintiffs to assist him in the sale of the lease and goodwill of his restaurant at 113 High Holborn, and to quote a price of £20,000, stock at valuation. The terms as to commission set out in a letter dated 1st June 1971 from the plaintiffs to the defendant were that in the event of the plaintiffs 'effecting an introduction either directly or indirectly of a person ready able and willing to purchase at the above price'—that is the £20,000—or for any other

b   price the defendant might agree to accept, the plaintiffs could look to the defendant and his company jointly and severally for the commission in accordance with an attached scale. It was admitted that the defendant agreed to these terms.

The plaintiffs did introduce a prospective purchaser, a Mr Abbas. On 15th June he telephoned to Mr Bristow, a director of the plaintiffs, and offered £17,700 for the lease and goodwill, plus the stock at valuation. Mr Bristow spoke to the defendant about this offer, and he agreed to accept this lower price. Solicitors were instructed on

c   both sides. The defendant's solicitors prepared the draft contract and sent it to Messrs Pollard Thomas & Co, solicitors for Mr Abbas, the partner of that firm who dealt with the matter being Mr Goldberg. The draft contract was approved by Mr Goldberg on behalf of Mr Abbas and returned to the defendant's solicitors with a letter of 16th July. The contract was then engrossed, and Mr Abbas signed it. On 20th July Mr

d   Goldberg sent it to G H Moss & Co, the defendant's solicitors, for signature by the defendant. The contract provided for a deposit of £1,850. A £500 deposit had already been paid, and with the letter of 20th July Mr Goldberg sent a cheque for the balance of £1,350. Then the defendant, having apparently got a better offer, declined to go on with the transaction. The whole question in the action was whether Mr Abbas was a person 'ready able and willing to purchase'. The learned judge held that he was

e   not, because no binding contract had been entered into between him and the defendant. If he was a person ready, able and willing to purchase, then the plaintiffs had earned their commission, which, according to the scale, would be £835.

This appeal, therefore, raises once again the question of how the words 'ready able and willing to purchase' are to be construed, and we have had interesting and helpful arguments from counsel on both sides with regard to that matter. It is conceded on

f   behalf of the defendant that Mr Abbas was *able* to purchase at the price mentioned, £17,700. So it is on the words 'ready and willing' that we have to concentrate.

I start, as one inevitably does in a case about estate agents' commission, with the decision of the House of Lords in *Luxor (Eastbourne) Ltd v Cooper*[1], but bearing in mind that in that case the contract was for commission to be paid on completion of sale. I quote from Viscount Simon LC. He said[2]:

g   'There is, I think, considerable difficulty, and no little danger, in trying to formulate general propositions on such a subject, for contracts with commission agents do not follow a single pattern, and the primary necessity in each instance is to ascertain with precision what are the express terms of the particular contract under discussion, and then to consider whether these express terms necessitate the addition, by implication, of other terms.'

h   In that case, the agents could only succeed if a term could be implied. In the present case, no implied term is relied on. Viscount Simon LC said[3]:

'It may be useful to point out that contracts under which an agent may be occupied in endeavouring to dispose of the property of a principal fall into several obvious classes. There is the class in which the agent is promised a commission by

j   his principal if he succeeds in introducing to his principal a person who makes an adequate offer, usually an offer of not less than the stipulated amount. If that is all that is needed in order to earn his reward, it is obvious that he is entitled to be

1   [1941] 1 All ER 33, [1941] AC 108
2   [1941] 1 All ER at 40, [1941] AC at 119
3   [1941] 1 All ER at 40, 41, [1941] AC at 120

paid when this has been done, whether his principal accepts the offer and carries through the bargain or not.'

Then Lord Russell of Killowen said[1]:

'A few preliminary observations occur to me. (1) Commission contracts are subject to no peculiar rules or principles of their own. The law which governs them is the law which governs all contracts and all questions of agency. (2) No general rule can be laid down by which the rights of the agent or the liabilities of the principal under commission contracts are to be determined. In each case, these must depend upon the exact terms of the contract in question, and upon the true construction of those terms.'

The third proposition is one that is not relevant here. In a later passage Lord Russell of Killowen said this[2]:

'I have already expressed my view as to the true meaning of a contract to pay a commission for the introduction of a purchaser at a specified or minimum price. It is possible that an owner may be willing to bind himself to pay a commission for the mere introduction of one who offers to purchase at the specified or minimum price, but such a construction of the contract would, in my opinion, require clear and unequivocal language.'

Then in 1949 and 1950 there was a clutch of cases in the Court of Appeal dealing with this topic. The first of them was *E P Nelson & Co v Rolfe*[3]. There the terms were for payment of commission on the introduction of a person able, ready and willing to purchase on the principal's terms. A person was introduced who offered to buy on those terms, but by then an option had been given to another prospective purchaser and the principal refused to sell to the person introduced by the agent. The agent was held to be entitled to commission. The value of the decision for us is, however, reduced by the fact that the defendant admitted that the person introduced was able, ready and willing to purchase.

The next case was *Graham and Scott (Southgate) Ltd v Oxlade*[4]. The words to be construed there were 'willing and able to purchase', and Roxburgh J's decision[5] in favour of the defendant was affirmed by the Court of Appeal[4] because the person introduced had merely made an offer 'subject to survey'. It is useful to quote a sentence or two from the judgment of Cohen LJ[6]:

'I think that the agent may prove that a person he has introduced is willing to purchase the property by showing that that person has made an unqualified offer or expressed an unqualified intention to make an offer notwithstanding that such an offer until accepted could be withdrawn. On the other hand, if the evidence shows that the offer is qualified by a condition inserted to prevent the other party turning the offer into a contract by acceptance, I think it is impossible to say that the agent has discharged the onus which rests on him of proving that the person he has introduced was willing to purchase the property.'

The first sentence of that passage is strongly in favour of the plaintiffs' contention here.

The next case is *McCallum v Hicks*[7]. There the defendant instructed the plaintiffs

---

1 [1941] 1 All ER at 43, 44, [1941] AC at 124
2 [1941] 1 All ER at 47, [1941] AC at 129
3 [1949] 2 All ER 584, [1950] 1 KB 139
4 [1950] 1 All ER 856, [1950] 2 KB 257
5 [1950] 1 All ER 91
6 [1950] 1 All ER at 861, [1950] 2 KB at 266
7 [1950] 1 All ER 864, [1950] 2 KB 271

to 'find someone to buy my house'. A person was introduced, and he and the defendant signed a provisional agreement 'subject to contract'. Later the defendant resiled from the transaction. The Court of Appeal, Bucknill, Denning LJJ, and Hodson J, unanimously held that 'find someone to buy' meant 'find a purchaser', and that commission was only payable when at least a binding contract for sale had been entered into. Denning LJ made some observations of wide significance. He said[1]:

> 'Some agents recently have been endeavouring to alter the ordinary understanding of the expressions "find a purchaser" or "introduce a purchaser" by getting a house owner to sign a document which makes him liable for commission if the agent introduces "a person able, ready and willing to purchase". Once such a form is signed, they say they are entitled to commission if they introduce a person who makes an offer but does not sign a binding contract. If this is correct, it means, that where a number of house agents induce a house owner to let them put his house on their books the owner may find himself liable to pay commission, not only on the sale which is completed through one agent, but also on offers which have been made through other agents and have never reached a binding contract: see, for instance, *Giddys* v. *Horsfall*[2], *E. H. Bennett & Partners* v. *Millett*[3], and *E. P. Nelson & Co.* v. *Rolfe*[4]. This is so contrary to the common understanding of men, and also to common fairness that the courts will endeavour to interpret the contract so as to avoid such a result. As I pointed out in *John Lee & Son (Grantham), Ltd.* v. *Railway Executive*[5], the common law is vigilant to prevent any abuse of freedom of contract, and, rather than permit any abuse, it will assume that the party intended to be reasonable and will give the contract a reasonable interpretation. This is especially so in the case of forms which the public are invited to sign without legal advice. So, recently, in the notable decision of *Graham & Scott (Southgate), Ltd.* v. *Oxlade*[6], this court held that a person could not be said to be "willing" to purchase if all that he had done was to sign "subject to contract" or "subject to survey". This shakes the authority of previous cases, and opens the way to an interpretation of the new form of words so as to give them the same effect as "find a purchaser". A person may not properly be said to be "willing" to purchase, so as to entitle an agent to commission unless he is irrevocably willing, that is, unless he has given irrevocable proof of his willingness by entering into a binding contract to purchase.'

Hodson J said[7]:

> 'There was in this case no contract for sale, as has been admitted. In those circumstances, I think it unnecessary to consider further whether, if the learned county court judge had been justified in interpreting the words as being willing, able and ready to buy at the figure named, there was evidence in this case which would justify a judgment in favour of the plaintiff.'

It appears to me that those words suggest an approach closer to that of Cohen LJ in *Graham and Scott (Southgate) Ltd v Oxlade*[6] than to that of Denning LJ.

The next case is *Dennis Reed Ltd v Goody*[8]. There the words were 'ready, able and willing'. The plaintiffs introduced a person who signed an agreement to buy at the

---

1 [1950] 1 All ER at 866, [1950] 2 KB at 275, 276
2 [1947] 1 All ER 460
3 [1948] 2 All ER 929, [1949] 1 KB 362
4 [1949] 2 All ER 584, [1950] 1 KB 139
5 [1949] 2 All ER 581
6 [1950] 1 All ER 856, [1950] 2 KB 257
7 [1950] 1 All ER at 867, [1950] 2 KB at 276, 277
8 [1950] 1 All ER 919, [1950] 2 KB 277

defendant's price, but subject to an indemnity against road charges. The defendant consulted solicitors about this proposed condition, and before they had made up their minds the prospective purchaser withdrew. The same Court of Appeal as in *McCallum v Hicks*[1] held that the plaintiffs were not entitled to commission. Bucknill LJ said[2]:

> 'Counsel for the plaintiffs argued that the decision of the learned judge was based on an erroneous interpretation of the critical words in the agreement sued on and the correct interpretation was that the commission was payable as soon as the agents had found Mr. Himsley, who was on May 20 a person ready and willing to purchase the property as proved by his signature to the agreement, and was, in fact, ready and able to purchase it because he owned assets sufficient to enable him to produce the purchase money at the time of completion of the contract of purchase. I think there is considerable weight in this argument. It seems to me that the plaintiffs place an interpretation on the words which would, in effect, make them equivalent to words such as, "on introduction of a purchaser". I think the words of this clause which are in question are intended to give to the agents a claim to commission in circumstances which fall short of the execution of an enforceable contract on both sides. I do not think it unreasonable that house agents should try to arrange for their claim to commission to be earned in some cases where a sale through their introduction of a person willing to purchase is not in fact effected. In my opinion, if subsequently to May 20, the defendants had refused to sell, while the purchaser remained willing and able to purchase, the commission would have been payable. The fatal defect in the plaintiffs' claim in this case, in my opinion, is that it was the purchaser, and not the defendants, who withdrew from the negotiations. On the other hand, the plaintiffs' claim to commission is, in my opinion, not established merely by showing that Mr. Himsley, the person whom they introduced, was able and willing to purchase the property at any one particular moment of time. They must prove that he was ready, able and willing to purchase up to the time when an enforceable contract for the purchase of the house was made between the parties, or, alternatively, up to a time when the defendants refused to enter into such a contract on terms on which Mr. Himsley was willing to purchase and the defendants were at one time willing to sell.'

The whole of that passage supports the plaintiffs' case here.

Denning LJ reiterated and elaborated the views he had expressed in *McCallum v Hicks*[1], and I quote only a short passage. He quoted the words of the agreement between the agents and their principal, and then said[3]:

> 'On consideration of this clause, I am satisfied that it is capable of a reasonable construction. The words "upon your introducing" do not mean that commission becomes due at the moment of introduction. The introduction takes place when the order to view is given, and no one knows then whether the person introduced will like the house or not. The words "upon your introducing" cannot, therefore, signify the time when an agent becomes entitled to commission, but can only signify the services to be rendered by the agent. They mean "In consideration of your introducing." Now, whom must the agent introduce? He must introduce: " . . . a person ready, able and willing to purchase the above property for the sum of £2,825 or such other price to which I shall assent." These words do not mean a person ready, able and willing "to make an offer", or even "to enter into a contract." They mean a person ready, able and willing "to purchase", i.e., to complete the purchase. He must be a person who is "able"

1   [1950] 1 All ER 864, [1950] 2 KB 271
2   [1950] 1 All ER at 922, [1950] 2 KB at 282, 283
3   [1950] 1 All ER at 924, 925, [1950] 2 KB at 287, 288

at the proper time to complete; *i.e.*., he must then have the necessary financial resources. He must also be "ready," *i.e.*, he must have made all necessary preparations by having the cash or a banker's draft ready to hand over. He must also be "willing," *i.e.*, he must be willing to hand over the money in return for the conveyance. This interpretation means that the special clause has practically the same effect as the usual terms on which an estate agent is employed. This is just as it should be, for, having regard to what took place when the housewife was asked to sign the document, I should not expect it to go beyond the ordinary understanding on these matters. So far I have considered this particular clause only. I would, however, like to add that the various new clauses that have appeared seem to be capable of a similar interpretation. I can see no sensible distinction between instructions to "find a purchaser", "find a party prepared to purchase," "find a purchaser able and willing to complete the transaction,"' and "find a person ready, willing and able to purchase".'

With the utmost respect to the present Master of the Rolls, that appears to me to be contrary to the views expressed in the House of Lords in *Luxor (Eastbourne) Ltd v Cooper*[1], that the exact terms of the contract are of great importance. Counsel for the defendant here, naturally relied heavily on the opinions expressed by Denning LJ in those two cases.

The next case is *Peter Long & Partners v Burns*[2], where Lord Goddard CJ held that where commission was payable on the introduction of a person ready and willing to enter into a binding contract, and an agreement was entered into from which the intending purchaser resiled because he found that he had been induced to enter into it by an innocent misrepresentation, the agent was not entitled to commission. That decision was upheld by the Court of Appeal[3]. This is merely an illustration of the principle formerly enunciated that if the *purchaser* changes his mind before a binding contract has been made, no commission is payable.

In *Ackroyd & Sons v Hason*[4] commission was to be paid on the introduction of a party prepared to enter into a contract to purchase on terms to which the defendant might assent. The plaintiffs introduced applicants and, after some negotiations which were 'subject to contract', a contract was prepared which the applicants signed, but the defendant refused to sign. It was held by the Court of Appeal (Sellers, Ormerod and Upjohn LJJ) that as the defendant had not assented to the terms, the commission was not payable. Sellers LJ said[5]:

> 'I am not at present satisfied that he was wrong in his conclusions and that circumstances could arise, under such an agreement as this, where commission would be payable where the assent of the vendors, which the agreement requires, could be an assent which fell short of concluding a bargain with the proposed purchasers.'

Neither of the other two Lords Justices expressed a view on that point, and the basis of the decison was that the defendant had never assented to the terms. In the present case, the defendant *had* agreed to reduce his price from £20,000 to £17,700.

In *Martin Gale & Wright v Buswell*[6] commission was payable on the agents' introducing anyone prepared to purchase on terms acceptable to the principal. A person was introduced who, after an agreement 'subject to contract', signed an agreement the terms of which had been approved by both parties' solicitors. It was held that the agents were not entitled to commission. Holroyd Pearce LJ seems to have based his judgment on the view that 'prepared' was equivalent to 'willing and able', and

1 [1941] 1 All ER 33, [1941] AC 108
2 [1956] 2 All ER 25, [1956] 1 WLR 413
3 [1956] 3 All ER 207, [1956] 1 WLR 1083
4 [1960] 2 All ER 254, [1960] 2 QB 144
5 [1960] 2 All ER at 265, [1960] 2 QB at 167
6 (1961) 178 Estates Gazette 709

while it was shown that the prospective purchaser was 'willing', it was not shown
that he was 'able'. Upjohn LJ took the view that it was not established that the terms
were acceptable to the vendor. Donovan LJ considered that the term 'subject to
contract' remained operative. Because of the differing grounds of the decision,
I do not find this a helpful authority.

Dellafiora v Lester[1] is a decision on the meaning of 'able to purchase'. It was held
that on the proposed sale of the leasehold, where the landlord's consent to an assignment was required, and was refused, it could not be said that the proposed assignee
was able to purchase. A deposit had been paid, and a contract drawn up, but not
signed. It is worthy of note that Lord Denning MR said[2]:' Was the purchaser here a
person willing and able to purchase the business? Willing, certainly. Able?' The
second question Lord Denning MR answered, 'No'. But his answer to the first question seems more consistent with the views expressed by other members of the
Court of Appeal in earlier cases than with his own statements in *McCallum v Hicks*[3]
and in *Dennis Reed Ltd v Goody*[4].

In *A L Wilkinson Ltd v O'Neil*[5] the Court of Appeal (Holyroyd Pearce, Willmer and
Davies LJJ) upheld the decision of a county court judge that agents were entitled to
commission which was payable on the introduction of an applicant 'willing and able
to sign a contract'. I read these words from the headnote:

> 'An applicant was introduced who agreed to purchase at the price asked, and
> the preparation of the contract proceeded, in due course reaching a point where
> the purchaser's solicitors had returned a draft with a few suggested amendments,
> most of which were verbal. Evidence was given that the purchaser would have
> met the vendor's wishes with regard to those amendments which were substan-
> tial. The vendor's solicitors wrote suggesting a postponement of the completion
> date, without adverting to the amendments proposed. Subsequently the vendor
> withdrew, apparently because he had had a better offer.'

This is the case nearest to the present one on the facts, and counsel for the defendant
does not seek to distinguish it, though he rightly points out that many of the earlier
authorities, and particularly *Martin Gale & Wright v Buswell*[6], were not cited.

In *A L Wilkinson Ltd v Brown*[7] the words were 'prepared to enter into a contract',
and the Court of Appeal (Harman, Diplock and Salmon LJJ) construed those words
as being equivalent to 'ready and willing to enter into a contract'. There was, however,
never more than an expectancy that the person introduced would enter into a contract,
and the agents failed. The only assistance which that case can afford to us is that there
is no suggestion in any of the judgments that the signature of a binding contract was
a precondition of commission being paid.

It seems to me that the trend of the authorities supports the three propositions
enunciated by counsel for the plaintiffs. (1) The decision whether the commission
is payable depends on the terms of the contract and on ordinary rules of construction.
(2) When the agreement between principal and agent is for commission to be payable on the introduction of a person ready, able and willing to purchase, the commission is payable if a sale actually results, but may become payable when the transaction becomes abortive. (3) Commission is payable when a person who is able to
purchase is introduced and expresses readiness and willingness by an unqualified

---

1   [1962] 3 All ER 393, [1962] 1 WLR 1208
2   [1962] 3 All ER at 396, [1962] 1 WLR at 1213
3   [1950] 1 All ER 864, [1950] 2 KB 271
4   [1950] 1 All ER 919, [1950] 2 KB 277
5   (1961) 181 Estates Gazette 137
6   (1961) 178 Estates Gazette 709
7   [1966] 1 All ER 509, [1966] 1 WLR 194

offer to purchase, though such offer has not been accepted and could be withdrawn.

In connection with the third proposition, it is to be assumed that the offer is one within the terms that the agent has been authorised to invite; also, that the offer is not withdrawn by the applicant, but is refused by the vendor. In my judgment, on the facts in this case, the plaintiffs bring themselves within that proposition and are entitled to the commission claimed.

I would therefore allow the appeal, and direct judgment to be entered for the plaintiffs for £835.

ORR LJ. I agree. The contract in this case was that commission should be payable in the event of the plaintiffs effecting an introduction of a person ready, able and willing to purchase at the named price, or at any other price that the defendant might agree to accept. It is not a case in which an offer made by a person so introduced was later withdrawn (*Dennis Reed Ltd v Goody*[1]), or in which the offer was expressed to be 'subject to contract' (*Martin Gale & Wright v Buswell*[2]), or qualified by some condition (*Graham and Scott (Southgate) Ltd v Oxlade*[3]). In those circumstances, in my judgment, on the authorities to which Cairns LJ has referred, the entitlement to commission arose when the person introduced by the plaintiffs made a firm offer for the purchase of the property in question on terms acceptable to the vendor. The views expressed by Denning LJ in *McCallum v Hicks*[4] and *Dennis Reed Ltd v Goody*[1] and by Hodson J in the latter case, that the entitlement does not arise until some later date, whether it be the signing of a contract or the completion of a sale, cannot, with great respect, be accepted as correct.

The result is that where a prospective vendor binds himself, on the terms with which we are here concerned, to more than one estate agent, he may find himself liable to pay more than one commission. This consideration clearly influenced Denning LJ in expressing the views to which I have referred. But, in my judgment, the authorities to which Cairns LJ has referred, going back for a quarter of a century or more, are clear, and the remedy of the prospective vendor, if he wishes to avoid paying more than one commission, is not to enter into a contract on such terms as those with which we are here concerned.

I, too, would allow the appeal.

JAMES LJ. The defendant argues that the learned judge was right in law in holding that:

'. . . the defendant did not go to the extent of binding himself to anybody at all in this matter even though we are not dealing with a case of completed purchase and think that on all the law we can find, and keeping a close eye on the exact terms of this contract, I would not think that the plaintiffs can recover damages at all for this episode.'

That somewhat curiously expressed finding is said by the defendant to be consistent with the authorities, save for *A L Wilkinson Ltd v O'Neil*[5], and that case, it is suggested, would have been differently decided had the court been referred to the earlier decision of *Martin Gale & Wright v Buswell*[2]. I cannot accept that argument. The authorities are quite clear that each case must be decided on the terms of the contract. It is not for the court to rewrite the contract in terms in which it is considered that the

1 [1950] 1 All ER 919, [1950] 2 KB 277
2 (1961) 178 Estates Gazette 709
3 [1950] 1 All ER 856, [1950] 2 KB 257
4 [1950] 1 All ER 864, [1950] 2 KB 271
5 (1961) 181 Estates Gazette 137

parties ought, or, in common understanding are to be expected, to have contracted.

To ascertain whether an agent is entitled to commission one must look to see what is the event on the happening of which commission is payable. If the event has happened, the commission is due; otherwise it is not: see *Luxor (Eastbourne) Ltd v Cooper*[1], per Viscount Simon LC in the passage cited by Cairns LJ; see also in the same case, Lord Russell of Killowen[2] and Lord Wright[3].

I will not add to the length of this judgment by citations from cases already referred to by Cairns LJ in his judgment. I find in the judgment of Cohen LJ in *Graham and Scott (Southgate) Ltd v Oxlade*[4], in the judgments of Bucknill LJ and Hodson J in *McCallum v Hicks*[5], of Bucknill LJ and Hodson J again in *Dennis Reed Ltd v Goody*[6], of Upjohn and Ormerod LJJ in *Ackroyd & Sons v Hasan*[7], a consistent body of judicial opinion, consistent with, and in certain passages, in favour of, the plaintiffs' contention—see particularly Bucknill LJ in *Dennis Reed Ltd v Goody*[8]. I pay great respect to the observations of Denning LJ in *McCallum v Hicks*[5] and in *Dennis Reed Ltd v Goody*[6], but I find them out of line with the body of opinion to which I have referred, and contrary to the speeches in the House of Lords in the *Luxor* case[9].

In relation to the passages relied on by counsel for the defendant in the *Dennis Reed* case[10], these are clearly obiter. There is no dispute in this case that Mr Abbas was a person able to purchase. He expressed readiness and willingness to purchase by making this unqualified offer to purchase. The price was agreed by the defendant. The contract was engrossed and executed by Mr Abbas in the presence of the defendant's solicitors. There was nothing more for Mr Abbas to do. Then the defendant withdrew. In those circumstances, on the terms of this agreement between the parties, the commission became payable because Mr Abbas was indeed a person ready, able and willing to purchase.

I agree with the order proposed by Cairns LJ.

Appeal allowed. Leave to appeal to House of Lords refused.

Solicitors: *Lake, Parry & Treadwell* (for the plaintiffs); *G H Moss & Co* (for the defendant).

Mary Rose Plummer   Barrister.

1   [1941] 1 All ER 33 at 40, 41, [1941] AC 108 at 120
2   [1941] 1 All ER at 46, [1941] AC at 128
3   [1941] 1 All ER at 48, [1941] AC at 130
4   [1950] 1 All ER 856, [1950] 2 KB 257
5   [1950] 1 All ER 864, [1950] 2 KB 271
6   [1950] 1 All ER 919, [1950] 2 KB 277
7   [1960] 2 All ER 254, [1960] 2 QB 144
8   [1950] 1 All ER at 922, [1950] 2 KB at 283
9   [1941] 1 All ER 33, [1941] AC 108
10 [1950] 1 All ER at 925, [1940] 2 KB at 288

Wrotham Park Estate Company v Parkside Homes Ltd and others
Wrotham Park Estate Company v Parkside Homes Ltd

CHANCERY DIVISION
BRIGHTMAN J
9th, 10th, 11th, 12th, 13th, 16th, 17th, 18th, 19th, 20th, 23rd, 24th JULY, 19th OCTOBER
1973

Restrictive covenant – Restrictive covenant affecting land – Benefit of covenant – Covenant capable of benefiting land – Estate owner reasonably taking view that covenant for benefit of his land – Others reasonably taking view that benefit of covenant spent – Whether covenant should be upheld.

Injunction – Mandatory injunction – Discretion over grant of remedy – Principles on which exercised – Breach after issue of writ – Houses built in breach of restrictive covenant – No interlocutory relief claimed – Whether plaintiff entitled to injunction requiring demolition of houses.

Injunction – Damages in lieu of injunction – Measure of damages – Breach of restrictive covenant affecting land – Breach not diminishing value of retained land – Defendant making profit from breach – Plaintiff not limited to nominal damages – Damages representing a percentage of profit anticipated from activity constituting breach – Calculation of percentage.

Certain land, which was mainly agricultural, consisted of three fragmented blocks, the area in the middle of the main block being known as Wrotham Park with its mansion house and home farm.   Outer portions of the land had from time to time been sold off for development.   In April 1935 the owner of the land sold part of it ('area 14') to a developer. By cl 3 of the conveyance the purchaser covenanted with 'the Vendor and his assigns owner or owners for the time being of the Vendor's Wrotham Park Estate using that term in the broad and popular sense' that he and his successors in title would observe and perform the restrictive covenants contained in the second schedule to the conveyance.   Clause 5 provided that the vendor might release any stipulations.   The second schedule included a covenant ('the layout stipulation') not to develop the land conveyed for building purposes 'except in strict accordance with a lay-out plan to be first submitted to and approved in writing by the Vendor or his Surveyors such plan to indicate thereon the roads sewers and drains to be constructed'.   The restrictive covenants were registered against the purchaser under the Land Charges Act 1925.   The development of area 14, approved by the vendor, consisted exclusively of private houses with gardens; in the centre was a triangle of land on which there were no buildings;   the only access to the triangle was by a path some ten feet wide running alongside a property known as 11 Brooklands Gardens.   In about 1955 the local authority bought the triangle and in 1969 decided to sell off a part of it as building land.   They bought 11 Brooklands Gardens and obtained planning consent to the demolition of no 11, to the driving of a road through the space thus made available, and to the erection of 13 houses and garages on the greater part of the triangle ('the site').   In 1971 the local authority offered the site for sale by public auction as freehold building land.   The particulars of sale stated that the property was sold subject to certain restrictive covenants and rights referred to in the charges register in which the stipulations in the 1935 conveyance were fully set out. A development company ('Parkside') were interested in purchasing the property. Prior to the auction sale their solicitors neither made enquiries into the nature of the restrictive covenants in the 1935 conveyance nor drew Parkside's attention to the existence of the covenants. At the auction sale Parkside were the successful bidders. Parkside applied for and received planning consent to build an additional house on the site. In October 1971 the site was transferred to Parkside and demolition of no 11 began; Parkside began to accept holding deposits from prospective purchasers who were intending to enter into building and purchase agreements with them. By a letter dated 5th January 1972 managing agents for the plaintiffs, who were the successors in title to the original vendor, drew Parkside's attention to the layout stipulation in the 1935 conveyance, asserting that any further development on the site would be in contravention of it, and seeking an assurance that no building would take place. Parkside's solicitors replied the next day confirming that they were aware of the stipulation but stating that they were advised that it was not enforceable. By the end of January some preliminary building work on one or more houses had begun. On 14th February 1972 the plaintiffs issued a writ against Parkside, seeking an injunction to restrain them from building on the development site other than in accordance with a layout plan approved by the plaintiffs, and a mandatory injunction for the demolition of any buildings erected in breach of the stipulation. The plaintiffs made no application for interlocutory relief. Holding deposits had been accepted in respect of all 14 houses, and building work proceeded. An arrangement was made with an insurance company for the provision of indemnities and, for premiums totalling £700, backed by a counter-indemnity from Parkside, each prospective purchaser was insured against loss up to £20,000; on that basis contracts were exchanged with purchasers of all 14 houses between the beginning of October and the end of November 1972. Parkside parted with the entire site with the exception of the road. The houses were completed in about January 1973 and the purchasers moved in. In April and May the purchasers and their mortgagees were added as co-defendants to the plaintiffs' action.

Held – (i) The layout stipulation was enforceable as between the plaintiffs and the defendants because (a) it had clearly been entered into for the benefit of land belonging to the covenantee; (b) that land was sufficiently defined or ascertainable; (c) the Wrotham Park estate had been and still was capable of being benefited by the stipulations; if a restriction was bargained for at the time of sale with the intention of giving the vendor a protection which he desired for the land he retained and the restriction was expressed to be imposed for the benefit of the estate so that both sides were apparently accepting that the restriction was of value to the retained land, the validity of the restriction should be upheld so long as an estate owner might reasonably take the view that the restriction remained of value to his estate; the restriction should not be discarded merely because others might reasonably argue that the restriction was spent (see p 331 g to p 332 a, p 333 f and p 335 c to h, post); *Lord Northbourne v Johnston & Son* [1922] 2 Ch 309 and *Marten v Flight Refuelling Ltd* [1961] 2 All ER 696 applied.

(ii) The development carried out by Parkside was a clear and material breach of the layout stipulation, but the plaintiffs were not entitled to relief by way of a mandatory injunction. Although it was not fatal to the plaintiffs' case that interim relief had not been sought, a plaintiff was not entitled as of course to have everything pulled down that had been built after the issue of the writ. In the circumstances it would be an unpardonable waste of much needed houses to direct their demolition; furthermore it was unnecessary to demolish the houses in order to preserve the integrity of the restrictive covenants imposed on the rest of area 14 (see p 330 j, p 331 f and p 337 g to j, post); *Isenberg v East India House Estate Co Ltd* (1863) 3 De GJ & Sm 263 and *Redland Bricks Ltd v Morris* [1969] 2 All ER 576 applied.

(iii) The court had jurisdiction to grant mandatory injunctions against Parkside to remove the road and against the subsequent purchasers, and therefore had

a power to award damages against each of them in lieu of an injunction. Although the breach of the layout stipulation was a once and for all breach which had occurred in or about October 1971, i e before any of the subsequent purchasers had completed their purchases, they had aided and abetted the breach by contributing their deposits and entering into contracts to purchase and building contracts with Parkside while the development was still in progress (see p 338 b c g and h, post); *Powell v Hemsley*
b [1909] 2 Ch 252 distinguished.

(iv) Although the value of Wrotham Park estate had not been diminished by the breach of the layout stipulation it did not follow that the plaintiffs were only entitled to nominal damages, for that would mean that the defendants would be left in undisturbed possession of the fruits of their wrongdoing. A just substitute for mandatory injunctions would be such a sum of money as might reasonably have been demanded by the plaintiffs from Parkside as a quid pro quo for relaxing the
c covenants. A developer would have expected to make about £50,000 profit on the development and in all the circumstances a sum equal to five per cent of the anticipated profit would be a reasonable sum. Accordingly the plaintiffs were entitled to damages of £2,500 to be apportioned equally between the defendants (see p 339 b to e, p 341 e g and h and p 342 a to e, post); *Whitwham v Westminster Brymbo Coal &*
d *Coke Co* [1896] 2 Ch 538, *Watson, Laidlaw & Co Ltd v Pott, Cassels and Williamson* (1914) 31 RPC 104, dictum of Lord Sumner in *Leeds Industrial Co-operative Society Ltd v Slack* [1924] AC at 870, *Strand Electric & Engineering Co Ltd v Brisford Entertainments Ltd* [1952] 1 All ER 796, and *Penarth Dock Engineering Co Ltd v Pounds* [1963] 1 Lloyd's Rep 359 applied.

Notes
e For restrictive covenants, see 34 Halsbury's Laws (3rd Edn) 198, para 330, and for cases on the subject, see 40 Digest (Repl) 337-367, 2751-2936.

For mandatory injunctions, see 21 Halsbury's Laws (3rd Edn) 361-364, paras 757-762, and for cases on the subject, see 28(2) Digest (Reissue) 994-1003, 247-333.

For damages in lieu of injunction, see 21 Halsbury's Laws (3rd Edn) 357-360, paras
f 747-753, and for cases on damages in lieu of or in addition to injunction, see 28(2) Digest (Reissue) 1013-1021, 397-469.

Cases referred to in judgment
Achilli v Tovell [1927] 2 Ch 243, 96 LJCh 493, 137 LT 805, 28(2) Digest (Reissue) 1052, 718.
g *Durell v Pritchard* (1865) 1 Ch App 244, 35 LJCh 223, 13 LT 545, sub nom *Darrell v Pritchard* 12 Jur NS 16, LJJ, 28(2) Digest (Reissue) 1002, 319.
Everett v Remington [1892] 3 Ch 148, 61 LJCh 574, 67 LT 80, 40 Digest (Repl) 346, 2798.
Hubbard v Vosper [1972] 1 All ER 1023, [1972] 2 QB 84, [1972] 2 WLR 389, CA.
Isenberg v East India House Estate Co Ltd (1863) 3 De GJ & Sm 263, 3 New Rep 345, 33 LJCh 392, 9 LT 625, 28 JP 228, 10 Jur NS 221, 46 ER 637, LC, 28(2) Digest (Reissue)
h 1001, 312.
Kilbey v Haviland (1871) 24 LT 353, 28(2) Digest (Reissue) 1032, 572.
Krehl v Burrell (1879) 11 Ch D 146, 40 LT 637, CA, 28(2) Digest (Reissue) 1001, 310.
Leeds Industrial Co-operative Society Ltd v Slack [1924] AC 851, [1924] All ER Rep 259, 93 LJCh 436, 131 LT 710, HL, 28(2) Digest (Reissue) 1012, 396.
Leicester (Earl of) v Wells-next-the-Sea Urban District Council [1972] 3 All ER 77, [1973]
j Ch 110, [1972] 3 WLR 486, 24 P & CR 72.
Manners (Lord) v Johnson (1875) 1 Ch D 673, 45 LJCh 404, 40 JP 345, 28(2) Digest (Reissue) 1052, 710.
Marten v Flight Refuelling Ltd [1961] 2 All ER 696, [1962] Ch 115, [1961] 2 WLR 1018, Digest (Cont Vol A) 1315, 2885a.
Northbourne (Lord) v Johnston & Son [1922] 2 Ch 309, [1922] All ER Rep 144, 92 LJCh 12, 128 LT 496, 40 Digest (Repl) 352, 2834.

Penarth Dock Engineering Co Ltd v Pounds [1963] 1 Lloyd's Rep 359.
Powell v Hemsley [1909] 2 Ch 252, 78 LJCh 741, 101 LT 262, CA; *affg* [1909] 1 Ch 680, 78 LJCh 337, 12 Digest (Reissue) 774, 5517.
Redland Bricks Ltd v Morris [1969] 2 All ER 576, [1970] AC 652, [1969] 2 WLR 1437, HL, Digest (Cont Vol C) 560, 271a.
Rogers v Hosegood [1900] 2 Ch 388, [1900-3] All ER Rep 915, 69 LJCh 652, 83 LT 186, CA, 40 Digest (Repl) 340, 2769.
Sharp v Harrison [1922] 1 Ch 502, 91 LJCh 442, 28(2) Digest (Reissue) 1053, 723.
Smith v Day (1880) 13 Ch D 651, CA, 28(2) Digest (Reissue) 1001, 311.
Stevens v Willing & Co Ltd (1929) 167 LT Jo 178, 67 L Jo 223, 40 Digest (Repl) 345, 2792.
Strand Electric and Engineering Co Ltd v Brisford Entertainments Ltd [1952] 1 All ER 796, [1952] 2 QB 246, CA, 46 Digest (Repl) 485, 330.
Watson, Laidlaw & Co Ltd v Pott, Cassels and Williamson (1914) 31 RPC 104, HL, 36 Digest (Repl) 1010, 3580.
Whitwham v Westminster Brymbo Coal and Coke Co [1896] 2 Ch 538, 65 LJCh 741, 74 LT 804, CA; *affg* [1896] 1 Ch 894, 33 Digest (Repl) 858, 1094.

Cases also cited

Addis v Gramophone Co Ltd [1909] AC 488, HL.
Ambler (Doe d) v Woodbridge (1829) 9 B & C 376.
Ballard's Conveyance, Re [1937] 2 All ER 691, [1937] Ch 473.
Baxter v Four Oaks Properties Ltd [1965] 1 All ER 906, [1965] Ch 816.
Brunner v Greenslade [1970] 3 All ER 833, [1971] Ch 993.
Charrington v Simons & Co Ltd [1971] 2 All ER 588, [1971] 1 WLR 598, CA.
Coleshill and District Investment Co Ltd v Minister of Housing and Local Government [1969] 2 All ER 525, [1969] 1 WLR 746, HL.
Colls v Home & Colonial Stores Ltd [1904] AC 179, [1904-7] All ER Rep 5, HL.
Congleton Corpn v Pattison (1808) 10 East 130.
Doherty v Allman (or Allen) (1878) 3 App Cas 709, HL.
Dolphin's Conveyance, Re, Birmingham Corpn v Boden [1970] 2 All ER 664, [1970] 1 Ch 654.
Donmar Productions Ltd v Bart [1967] 2 All ER 338n, [1967] 1 WLR 740.
Drake v Gray [1936] 1 All ER 363, [1936] Ch 451, CA.
Flureau v Thornhill (1776) 2 Wm Bl 1078, [1775-1802] All ER Rep 91.
Freeman-Thomas Indenture, Re, Eastbourne Corpn v Tilley [1957] 1 All ER 532, [1957] 1 WLR 560.
Gadd's Land Transfer, Re, Cornmill Developments Ltd v Bridle Lane (Estates) Ltd [1965] 2 All ER 800, [1966] Ch 56.
Gaskin v Balls (1879) 13 Ch D 324, CA.
Hadley v Baxendale (1854) 9 Exch 341, [1843-60] All ER Rep 461.
Hanning v Gable-Jeffreys Properties Ltd [1965] 1 All ER 924, [1965] 1 WLR 1390.
Harman Pictures NV v Osborne [1967] 2 All ER 324, [1967] 1 WLR 723.
Holland v Worley (1884) 26 Ch D 578.
Jeffkins' Indentures, Re [1965] 1 All ER 608, [1965] 1 WLR 375.
Kelly v Barrett [1924] 2 Ch 379, [1924] All ER Rep 503, CA.
Kenny v Preen [1962] 3 All ER 814, [1963] 1 QB 499, CA.
Krehl v Burrell (1878) 7 Ch D 551.
London County Council v Allen [1914] 3 KB 642, [1914-15] All ER Rep 1008, CA.
Long Eaton Recreation Grounds Co v Midland Railway Co [1902] 2 KB 574, CA.
Lowe v Partridge (11th July 1973) unreported.
National Trust for Places of Historic Interest or Natural Beauty v Midlands Electricity Board [1952] 1 All ER 298, [1952] Ch 380.
Newton Abbot Co-operative Society Ltd v Williamson & Treadgold Ltd [1952] 1 All ER 279, [1952] Ch 286.
Oriental Steamship Co v Tylor [1893] 2 QB 518, CA.
Page v Kings Parade Properties Ltd (1967) 20 P & CR 710.

a

Perera v Vandiyar [1953] 1 All ER 1109, [1953] 1 WLR 672, CA.
Powell v Hemsley [1909] 1 Ch 680.
Pride of Derby & Derbyshire Angling Association Ltd v British Celanese Ltd [1953] 1 All ER 179, [1953] Ch 149, CA.
Reading Industrial Co-operative Society Ltd v Palmer [1912] 2 Ch 42.
Reid v Bickerstaff [1909] 2 Ch 305, [1908-10] All ER Rep 298, CA.

b

Richards v Revitt (1877) 7 Ch D 224.
Rookes v Barnard [1964] 1 All ER 367, [1964] AC 1129, HL.
Sayers v Collyer (1884) 28 Ch D 103, [1881-5] All ER Rep 385, CA.
Seager v Copydex Ltd [1967] 2 All ER 415, [1967] 1 WLR 923, CA.
Seager v Copydex Ltd (No 2) [1969] 2 All ER 718, [1969] 1 WLR 809, CA.
Selwyn's Conveyance, Re, Hayman v Soole [1967] 1 All ER 339, [1967] Ch 674.

c

Shepherd Homes Ltd v Sandham [1970] 3 All ER 402, [1971] Ch 340.
Stilwell v Blackman [1967] 3 All ER 514, [1968] Ch 508.
Tulk v Moxhay (1848) 18 LJCh 83, [1843-60] All ER Rep 9, LC.
Wroth v Tyler [1973] 1 All ER 897, [1973] 2 WLR 405.
Zetland (Marquess) v Driver [1937] 3 All ER 795, [1937] Ch 651; *rvsd* [1938] 2 All ER 158, [1939] Ch 1, CA.

d

Actions

By their writ, issued on 14th February 1972, and statement of claim, served on 1st March 1972, the plaintiffs, the Wrotham Park Estate Company, sought against the defendant Parkside Homes Ltd ('Parkside'):

e

'1. An injunction restraining [Parkside] by itself, its employees or agents or otherwise howsoever from building on or developing for building purposes the land at the rear of Brooklands Gardens, Sherwood Avenue and Elmscroft Road, Potters Bar, Hertfordshire, otherwise than in accordance with a lay-out plan approved in writing by or on behalf of the Plaintiffs in breach of the restrictions contained in a Conveyance dated 10th April 1935 and made between The Right Honourable Edmund Henry Earl of Strafford of the one part and Aubrey Aston Blake of the other part ['the Blake conveyance']. 2. An order that [Parkside] demolish any building or buildings erected on the said land in breach of the said restrictions . . . 4. Further or other relief.'

f

By an order of Foster J, dated 12th April 1973 (i) 26 persons who during 1972 and 1973 had purchased from Parkside dwelling-houses erected on the land, and a building society as the mortgagee of certain of those properties, were added as co-defendants; (ii) the writ and the statement of claim were amended (a) by the deletion from para 2 of the words '[Parkside] demolish any building or' and (b) by the addition at the end of para 2 of the words 'be demolished by the respective owners thereof'. By an order of Pennycuick V-C dated 23rd May 1973, five building societies and a bank, as mortgagees, and Keith John Pilcher and Jane Pilcher, as purchasers of dwelling-houses erected on the land, were added as co-defendants. By a writ issued on 13th July 1972 the plaintiffs claimed against Parkside (1) an injunction restraining Parkside by itself, its employees or agents or otherwise howsoever from building on or developing for building purposes any of the land forming the rear gardens of premises known as 5, 7, 9, 13, 15 and 17 Brooklands Gardens, Potters Bar, Hertfordshire, in breach of the restrictions contained in the Blake conveyance; (2) further or other relief. The facts are set out in the judgment.

g

h

j

G H Newsom QC and *Richard Scott* for the plaintiffs.
H E Francis QC and *Brian Morcom* for Parkside.
H E Francis QC and *R A Cooke* for the subsequent purchasers.
R A Cooke for the mortgagees.

Cur adv vult   a

19th October.   **BRIGHTMAN J** read the following judgment.   These actions
relate to the enforcement of a restrictive covenant imposed on land at Potters Bar in
Hertfordshire.   The Strafford family has for many years owned an extensive area of
land lying within and on the edge of a quadrilateral formed by Potters Bar, South
Mimms, Elstree and Barnet.   The village of South Mimms is a mile to the west of   b
Potters Bar; Barnet begins about two miles south of Potters Bar; Elstree is about
three miles west of Barnet.   The countryside within this quadrilateral is at present
mainly agricultural.   That which belongs to the Strafford family consists of three fragmented blocks.   The main block lies between Potters Bar and Barnet.   In the middle of
this block is Wrotham Park, with the mansion house and home farm.   The second
and smaller block is on the north-east or Potters Bar side of Elstree.   The two blocks   c
just fail to meet.   The third block is relatively small and lies outside the quadrilateral, a short distance to the north-west of South Mimms.   The land still enjoyed
by the Strafford family is now vested in a family company, the Wrotham Park Estate
Company, the plaintiffs in this action, except for a small part which belongs to the
trustees of a marriage settlement.   The whole of the land falls under the general
description of the Wrotham Park estate, according to the plaintiffs.   d
   Outer portions of the estate have from time to time been sold off for development.
The development which is relevant for the purposes of this action has taken place
at Potters Bar.   Potters Bar is now a town of some 25,000 or more inhabitants.   It
is intersected by a railway line which runs north-west and south-east, and by a road
running north-east and south-west.   I will call this road 'Baker Street' although
the name strictly applies only to the southern part of it.   Fringes of the estate adjacent   e
to the town of Potters Bar have been sold off for development since early this century.
There were a few small sales before the first world war.   Sales were more frequent
between the wars.   The areas sold off are numbered on an agreed plan and I will use
the same numbering in this judgment.
   There were some 13 important sales between the wars.   The areas so sold form an
irregularly shaped block of land that could be contained within a circle of half a mile   f
radius.   The development consisted mainly of the building of detached and semi-
detached private houses, with a few shops and offices.   It is unnecessary to refer to
every sale but I will mention enough to indicate the general pattern.   Areas 3, 5, 7
and 8 lie north of the railway line and east of Baker Street.   They were sold in the
period 1927-1930 to a developer named Mr King.   The conveyances did not impose
restrictive covenants but the areas were in fact laid out in the familiar pattern of a   g
building estate.   In 1931 area 9, lying to the south of the railway line and to the west
of Baker Street, was sold to another developer, Mr Warboys.   The conveyance included a somewhat haphazard series of stipulations.   There was a restriction against
the erection of any buildings except private dwelling-houses or a shop for the sale
of building requisites; a building line was imposed; there were stipulations directed
against offensive types of user.   Area 11, also south of the railway line but east of   h
Baker Street, was sold to a developer named Mr Hicks in 1934.   Restrictions were
again imposed but these were directed only against offensive types of user.   Area 2,
to the south of area 11, had been sold for development ten years earlier.
   Area 12, adjacent to and south of area 9, was sold to the same purchaser, Mr Warboys, in 1934.   On this occasion a stipulation relating to the design of buildings was
imposed.   There was also a covenant not to develop the land except in accordance   j
with the layout shown on the plan to the conveyance itself, save with the consent of
the vendor or his agent. This was the first layout stipulation imposed. In the event,
the development differed from the specified layout, but that is immaterial to these
actions.   In 1934 area 13, on the opposite (i e east) side of Baker Street, was sold to a
developer called Mr Blake.   The restrictions imposed were limited to stipulations
against offensive user.

In April 1935 Mr Blake acquired from the sixth earl area 14, which is the area with which this section is concerned. It lies to the west of areas 9 and 12. I will refer to the covenants in more detail later. At this stage it is sufficient to say that the conveyance contained a layout stipulation but no design stipulation. The remaining restrictions were directed against offensive user.

The last important pre-war sale for building purposes was the sale of area 10 in November 1935 to a developer called Mr Read. This lies to the south of area 14. Like the conveyance of area 14, but not exactly similar, the conveyance contained a layout stipulation but no design stipulation. The remaining restrictions were directed against offensive user. In 1938 and 1940 the sixth earl sold extensive areas of land to the Middlesex County Council, subject to restrictions designed to preserve the land as 'green belt'. One area was to the west and the other to the east of Wrotham Park.

In general terms the tide of development at Potters Bar to the south and west of the railway flowed as far as areas 10, 11 and 2 before the last war, perhaps also including land to the west of area 2 which seems not to have been derived from the estate. It will be necessary to descend into a little detail, for it is part of the defendants' case that later development has destroyed the utility of the layout stipulation imposed on area 14. It is therefore necessary to have the scale of such development in the mind's eye. Working from west to east the position on the Potters Bar fringe of the estate is now as follows. Area 16, to the south-west of area 10, has been used for council housing to a depth of 300 yards. There is then some marriage settlement land to the south of part of area 10 which is a housing estate with a depth of 200 yards. This is followed by a belt of land of similar depth with three rows of houses to the south of the remainder of area 10. This land seems never to have been part of the estate. There is then another stretch of land, never apparently part of the estate, which is residential. It is south of part of area 11 and is mostly 200 yards in depth. Between part of this stretch of land and the estate there is a school with playing-fields. Next comes area 2 with a depth of 175 yards and two rows of houses, to the south of the remainder of area 11. Finally, there is the south-eastern extremity of area 13 which was developed for housing after the war; between one end of this extremity and the estate there is another school with large playing-fields; at the other end is area 43, about 150 yards deep with four rows of houses, which was developed some time after 1957. There is one additional factor. The construction of a motorway, described as a ring-road, has just begun which will cut in half the open land lying between Wrotham Park and Potters Bar. There is also a scheme on foot whereby the plaintiffs may sell land north of the ring-road for carefully controlled development, and a conditional contract of great complexity has been concluded. The project is at present uncertain and the requisite planning permission has so far been withheld.

I turn to a more detailed description of the conveyance of area 14. The conveyance was dated 10th April 1935. At that time the land was described as in the parish of South Mimms. By cl 3 the purchaser, Mr Blake, covenanted in the following terms with the sixth earl:

'The purchaser hereby covenants with the Vendor and his assigns owner or owners for the time being of the Vendor's Wrotham Park Estate using that term in the broad and popular sense so as to bind the owner or owners for the time being of the property hereby conveyed and to the intent that the restrictions and stipulations hereinafter referred to shall run with the land and be for the benefit of the Vendor's said Wrotham Park Estate that he the purchaser and all persons deriving title under him the owner and occupiers for the time being of the property hereby conveyed will observe and perform the restrictive covenants and provisions contained in the Second Schedule hereto PROVIDED that the said covenant shall bind the purchaser or other the owner or owners for the time being of the property hereby conveyed only so long as he or they shall be the owner or owners thereof.'

Clause 5 provided that a purchaser of a part of the Wrotham Park estate should not be entitled to enforce any covenant unless the benefit had been expressly assigned to him. It also provided that the vendor might release any stipulations, it being declared that no general building scheme affected the estate. The restrictive covenants and provisions referred to in the second schedule were as follows: stipulation (1) related to the erection of fences. Stipulations (3) to (7) contained restrictions against types of user considered offensive or undesirable. Stipulation (2) is the important one and reads as follows:

'Not to develop the said land for building purposes except in strict accordance with a lay-out plan to be first submitted to and approved in writing by the Vendor or his Surveyors such plan to indicate thereon the roads sewers and drains to be constructed.'

Two days later the vendor caused the restrictive covenants to be duly registered against Mr Blake under the Land Charges Act 1925.

The layout stipulation in the conveyance of area 10 to Mr Read was in the same terms with an addition to the effect that approval should not be unreasonably withheld; this qualification would have been implied if not expressed, as was conceded before me. The layout stipulation in the conveyance of area 12 to Mr Warboys was linked with a design stipulation but was to the same general effect.

Area 14 comprised 47 acres. The development consists exclusively of private houses, mostly semi-detached, and all initially with gardens appropriate to that type of property. The layout of the plots, as the land was first developed, may be described as roughly based on a design of concentric semi-circles. The heart of the development consisted of some 65 detached or semi-detached houses enclosed by Sherwood Avenue to the west, Brooklands Gardens to the north, Aberdale Gardens to the east and Elmscroft Gardens to the south. In the centre there was an isosceles triangle of land with a base of 100 yards and sides of 170 yards on which there were no buildings. This triangle of land seems originally to have been used as allotments. The only access to it was by a path some ten feet in width running down the side of 11 Brooklands Gardens.

In or before 1955 the Potters Bar Urban District Council bought the triangle for £225. At the time when the present story starts the apex of the triangle was used as a children's playground and the remainder was waste land with vestiges of allotments still visible. It was not a rubbish dump, but overgrown and untended and used by adjoining householders as a convenient place for bonfires of garden refuse. In 1969 the urban district council decided to turn their purchase to account by selling off a part as building land. They bought 11 Brooklands Gardens for £6,500. They obtained from Hertfordshire County Council planning consent to demolish no 11, to the driving of a road through the space thus made available and to the erection of 13 detached houses and garages on the greater part of the triangle, leaving out, however, the apex which was in use as a playground. I will for convenience refer to the land in respect of which planning consent was given, including the means of access replacing no 11, as 'the allotment site'.

I turn back to the title of the covenantee. The sixth earl died in 1951. In 1954 his executor assented to the vesting of the estate in his daughter, Lady Elizabeth Byng, as a tenant for life. In 1964 Lady Elizabeth sold and transferred the estate to the plaintiffs (then with a different name). The total area of the three blocks of land at the time of the Blake conveyance was about 4,000 acres. It is now about 2,400 acres. The managing director of the plaintiffs is Lady Elizabeth's son, Mr Byng.

On 9th September 1971 the Potters Bar Urban District Council offered the allotment site for sale by public auction as freehold building land. The sale was extensively advertised. Mr Byng came to hear of the offer and obtained a copy of the particulars of sale. He was concerned to see that the existence of the covenants had not been overlooked, as indeed they had not. The particulars of sale referred to the planning permission for 13 houses. The special conditions contained this:

'6. The property is sold subject to certain restrictive covenants and rights referred to in the respective Charges Registers of the said titles and a copy of the same having been supplied to the Purchaser he shall be deemed to purchase with full knowledge thereof and shall raise no requisition or objection in relation thereto.'

The stipulations in the Blake conveyance were set out in full in the charges register. The allotment site was knocked down to a company called Parkside Homes Ltd ('Parkside') for £90,000. It is said to have been a record price. Before buying, neither Parkside nor its solicitors were provided with or requested a copy of the restrictive covenants entered on the charges register. Twelve days after the contract Parkside's solicitors submitted so-called enquiries before contract and also requisitions on title. Enquiry 7 was as follows:

'Consents. Have all consents required under any covenant affecting the property been obtained? If not, please give details. [Reply:] None necessary.'

Requisition 10 was as follows:

'Please supply evidence that the lay-out has been approved in accordance with the covenants in the Conveyance 10th April 1935 or indicate why such approval is not required in accordance with the first stipulation in that Conveyance. [Reply:] No approval has been necessary as any lay-out will be that of your clients who will no doubt comply with any requirements in due course.'

At the same time, as happens on these occasions, Parkside sought to improve on the existing planning consent. It applied for and received consent to insert (I am tempted to say squeeze) one additional house onto the allotment site.

On 12th October the allotment site was transferred to Parkside which was duly registered as owner. In the same month the demolition of no 11 began, and shortly afterwards building plans were approved. In December road works were begun.

By a letter dated 5th January 1972 Messrs Berry Brothers & Legge, the managing agents for the plaintiffs, drew Parkside's attention to the layout stipulation in the Blake conveyance, and asserted that any further development on the allotment site would be in contravention of it. They sought an assurance that no building would take place. Parkside's solicitors replied the next day confirming that they were aware of the stipulation but saying that they were advised by counsel that it was not enforceable. In fact what had happened was this. Prior to the auction sale Parkside's solicitors neither made enquiries into the nature of the restrictive covenants in the Blake conveyance nor drew the attention of their client to the existence of the covenants. After the purchase, when the solicitors obtained a copy of the restrictions, they saw counsel in conference. Counsel expressed the opinion that the stipulation was not enforceable, principally on the ground, according to a letter which is in evidence, that the requirement for approval was personal to the sixth earl and died with him. The conference took place on 6th October, that is to say six days before completion. Parkside's solicitors did not tell their client that they were seeking advice, nor did they report to their client the purport of the advice which they had received until some three months later.

Since October 1971 Parkside had been receiving holding deposits from prospective purchasers who were intending to enter into building and purchase agreements with Parkside. Parkside continued to accept such deposits. By the end of January some preliminary building work on one or more houses had commenced, but this had not, I think, gone beyond simple matters like footings.

On 14th February the plaintiffs issued a writ against Parkside. The relief sought *a* was an injunction to restrain Parkside from building on the allotment site other than in accordance with a layout plan approved by the plaintiffs and a mandatory injunction for the demolition of any buildings erected in breach of the stipulation. The issue of the writ and the service of the statement of claim a fortnight later did not deter Parkside. Holding deposits had been accepted in respect of all 14 houses (although no contracts had been signed) and building works proceeded. By mid- *b* July, according to a letter from Parkside's solicitors, the access road had been largely constructed and the various houses were all in various stages of erection, some being quite well advanced. Prospective purchasers were keen to exchange contracts and Parkside itself was anxious to proceed with sales and thus realise its investment. However, it was obvious that purchasers' solicitors would hesitate to advise their clients to exchange contracts with an action of this sort pending. Accordingly, an *c* approach was made to the Eagle Star Insurance Co Ltd for the provision of indemnities. For premiums which totalled £700, backed by a counter-indemnity from Parkside, each purchaser was insured against loss up to £20,000. On that basis contracts were exchanged with purchasers of all 14 houses between the beginning of October and the end of November 1972. The houses were completed in or after January 1973 and the new owners moved in. In April and May the purchasers and their *d* mortgagees were added as co-defendants. Difficulty was experienced by the plaintiffs in learning from Parkside the names of the various purchasers. This caused the plaintiffs great indignation and led to interlocutory proceedings. Although ventilated at the hearing of this action, such obstruction is not material to anything I have to decide.

I turn first to the nature, scope and purpose of the layout covenant. In terms it is *e* an absolute prohibition against development for building purposes except in strict accordance with a layout plan approved by the vendor, the sixth earl, or his surveyors. No point was taken before me that the stipulation was personal to the sixth earl and died with him. Counsel on both sides accepted that the word 'vendor' in the stipulation must, as a matter of construction, be capable of including successors in title. Counsel for the plaintiffs submitted that a layout plan was one which indicated the *f* position of houses, that is to say density and arrangement of buildings and the position of roads, and also in the context of this particular stipulation, the line of sewers and drains. He conceded that the covenantee would have no right under such a stipulation to refuse approval unreasonably, and in particular, that the stipulation could not lawfully have been used as a bargaining counter in order to demand money from Mr Blake as the price for allowing him to develop. The plaintiffs were not able to *g* produce any application by Mr Blake for approval of a layout plan or any copy of an approval granted to him. However, counsel for the plaintiffs submitted that I ought to infer that written approval, pursuant to the stipulation, was granted to the layout of area 14 in the form of the layout as it existed prior to the activities of Parkside. He asked me to infer that the layout plan must have been approved on the basis that the triangle, including the allotment site, was deliberately left open *h* and unbuilt on, since the sole access thereto was a path or track about ten feet wide; it was not disputed that this was too narrow for access by trade and other vehicles. In the result, submitted counsel for the plaintiffs, Parkside's operations on the allotment site were (1) a development thereof for building purposes not in accordance with a layout plan first submitted to and approved by the plaintiffs; (2) a development which conflicted with the layout plan which I ought to infer had been approved when *j* area 14 was originally developed; (3) a development which, on the evidence of Mr Byng, the plaintiffs would certainly not have approved if a layout plan thereof had been submitted; and (4) a development which the plaintiffs could reasonably have declined to approve. In these circumstances, counsel for the plaintiffs submitted that the development perpetrated by Parkside on the allotment site was a clear breach, and a material breach, of the layout stipulation, assuming it to be an enforceable restriction.

Counsel for Parkside and the subsequent purchasers, supported by counsel for the mortgagees, submitted that the only purpose of the layout covenant was to facilitate the development of adjoining areas by leading to a co-ordinated system of roads and drainage. He remarked on the fact that the plaintiffs could not produce a single layout approval, although some of the development of areas 10, 12, and 14 took place after the last war. He submitted that the stipulation ought to be construed as if it merely required the purchaser 'not to lay out roads sewers and drains except in strict accordance with a layout plan to be first submitted to and approved in writing by the vendor or his surveyors'.

In my judgment the stipulation does not bear the restricted interpretation which the defendants seek to place on it. I can see no reason for confining the stipulation to roads, sewers and drains. It would, in my view, be an unnatural construction of the language of the stipulation. It seems to me that a layout plan of a proposed building estate means a plan which at least shows building plots, as well as the roads giving access thereto. Indeed, Parkside's solicitors in correspondence with others in relation to the allotment site constantly used the expression 'layout plan' to mean, as I would expect, a plan indicating the building plots; see for example their letter of 13th July 1972 to Eagle Star: 'I enclose herewith a copy of the layout plan. You will see that it shows 14 houses and an access road'. There are several similar letters.

I also think it right to infer that Mr Blake did not act in breach of covenant but duly submitted a layout plan or plans for approval before building operations began, and that these were approved. It is hardly credible that the sixth earl, having taken layout covenants in respect of areas 10, 12 and 14 within a few months of each other, should not have troubled to exact compliance or that Mr Blake should have ignored or defied the stipulation. Lack of suitable access to the triangle leads to the inevitable inference that the layout of area 14 was approved on the basis that the triangle should remain free from buildings. This is consistent with the marking on a plan approved by the planning officer of the Hertfordshire County Council which was compiled in 1936 as part of a draft planning resolution under the then planning legislation. The absence of a layout plan in respect of the original development may well be accounted for by the fact that the offices of the managing agents were destroyed during the last war. Accordingly I accept counsel for the plaintiffs' submissions on the nature, scope and purpose of the layout covenant and as to the inferences which ought to be drawn.

The next issue is whether the stipulation in question is enforceable as between the plaintiffs and the defendants or any of them, having regard to the fact that they are respectively the assigns of the original covenantee and the original covenantor. This issue can appropriately be broken down into the questions posed in the judgment of Wilberforce J in *Marten v Flight Refuelling Ltd*[1]: (a) Whether the covenant was entered into for the benefit of any land of the covenantee. The answer to that question is clearly affirmative because the covenant so states. (b) Whether that land is sufficiently defined or ascertainable. The intended identification is expressed in the conveyance as the earl's Wrotham Park estate 'using that term in the broad and popular sense'. The latter words are a reflection of the judgment of Romer J in *Everett v Remington*[2]. Their purpose seems to be to restrict the right to enforce the covenant to the person who is properly to be regarded from time to time as the owner of, in substance, the Wrotham Park estate, as distinct from lessees and purchasers of parts thereof, and to annex the benefit of the covenant to such estate. The defendants dispute that the description 'Wrotham Park Estate' embraced more than the mansion house, the park and the home farm. I am however satisfied from the evidence that the expression included, in 1935, the three blocks of land near Potters Bar, Elstree and South Mimms, and that the land now held by the plaintiffs is still in substance the Wrotham Park estate. The whole of such land has, at all material times, been administered as a

1   [1961] 2 All ER 696, [1962] Ch 115
2   [1892] 3 Ch 148 at 157, 158

single agricultural estate and all of it went by local repute under the name of the Wrotham Park estate. I see no reason to doubt that the description was used in that sense by the parties to the 1935 conveyance and ought to be interpreted in the same sense for the purposes of this action. (c) Whether the Wrotham Park estate was and still is capable of being benefited by the stipulations. This is the point against which the defendants concentrated their attack when challenging enforceability. Before I examine the evidence it will be helpful to refer, on matters of principle, to certain previous cases. *Lord Northbourne v Johnston & Son*[1] was a decision of Sargant J on a covenant imposed in 1881 on the sale of land at Gateshead in Northumberland which formed part of the Shipcote estate. The covenant restricted the land to user for private dwelling-houses. The defendants bought a house in 1920 for conversion into a shop. The learned judge found that the restrictions[2]—

'were aimed in general at preserving the amenities and character of the neighbourhood both for the convenience of the residents in the houses that were from time to time built and for the beneficial development of the portions of the estate that were for the time being unsold.'

He added:

'It is obvious that these two results are closely connected, and that while the second object might be the only one in which the vendor on each successive occasion might be directly concerned, a considerable indirect effect would ordinarily be produced on the reputation and saleability of the unsold portions of the estate for the time being by the preservation or abandonment of those amenities of the developed portions of the estate which were secured or stipulated for by the various restrictive covenants introduced on the occasion of their being built upon.'

Among the defences raised by the defendants was a submission ('the second defence') that the land still belonging to the plaintiff was not land which would be damaged by the breach of the covenant and that accordingly the covenant could not be enforced against an assignee of the covenantor. The learned judge said[3]:

'The second defence, if well founded, would entirely or almost entirely destroy at a very early date the enforceability of the restrictive covenants on any considerable building estate that was being developed on the freehold system. When once a building plot or house had passed from the hands of the original purchasers to those of a third party, it would be incumbent on the owner of the estate to show, as a condition precedent to the enforcement of the covenant, first, that he had intended the covenant to be for the benefit of such portions of the estate as he still retained, and secondly, that it was in fact for their benefit at the time when enforcement was sought. In the case of a building estate of any size it would be impossible to define and point out precisely those portions of it which the owner was seeking to protect or benefit by the restrictive covenants on any particular plot. To enter on every sale into such a precise arrangement as in *Rogers* v. *Hosegood*[4] would be impracticable and absurd, and, indeed, would not produce the result required. The practical and usual course is for the vendor to impose covenants the benefit of which will not be attached to any particular parcel of land, but will be enforceable by the vendor for the general benefit of his unsold estate for the time being. Nor do I think that the vendor must on each occasion of enforcement show that the result will in fact be to benefit his

---

1 [1922] 2 Ch 309, [1922] All ER Rep 144
2 [1922] 2 Ch at 315, 316, [1922] All ER Rep at 147
3 [1922] 2 Ch at 318, 319, cf [1922] All ER Rep at 148
4 [1900] 2 Ch 388, [1900-3] All ER Rep 915

remaining estate. Benefit or detriment is often a question of opinion on which there may be the greatest divergence of view, and the greatest difficulty in arriving at a clear conclusion. It is, in my judgment, sufficient for the vendor to say, at any rate in the first instance, that the bargain was that he should be protected against certain acts which were recognized as being likely to prove noxious or detrimental to his building estate treated as a whole. The covenantor, being then, in my judgment, bound at the very least to show that the estate remaining to the covenantee at the date of the action was not intended to be protected by the covenants, or that the breach of the covenants could not possibly hurt such remaining estate, the question arises whether this onus has been discharged in the present case.'

Wilberforce J dealing in the *Marten*[1] case with a covenant restricting land to agricultural user said:

'If an owner of land, on selling part of it, thinks fit to impose a restriction on user, and the restriction was imposed for the purpose of benefiting the land retained, the court would normally assume that it is capable of doing so. There might, of course, be exceptional cases where the covenant was, on the face of it, taken capriciously or not bona fide, but a covenant taken by the owner of an agricultural estate not to use a sold-off portion for other than agricultural purposes could hardly fall within either of these categories.'

He then picked up Sargant J's observations[2] about benefit or detriment being matters of opinion on which views might greatly diverge and added[3]:

'Why, indeed, should the court seek to substitute its own standard for those of the parties—and on what basis can it do so?'

These words were echoed by Plowman J in *Earl of Leicester v Wells-next-the-Sea Urban District Council*[4].

In these circumstances I commence my review of the evidence with an inclination towards concluding that at the time when the stipulation was imposed responsible persons believed or accepted that the stipulation was capable of performing a service which would benefit and continue to benefit the Wrotham Park estate.

On this aspect of the case I have had the evidence of Mr Byng and also of two experienced surveyors, Mr Parker and Mr Eve. My Byng recognised the social necessity for allowing development to take place on the fringes of the estate. He stressed, however, the importance to the landowner of confining it to the right sort of development. He considered that the restrictions imposed by the sixth earl were of great importance for this purpose, both for visual and amenity reasons. He said it was crucial to the estate that only high class development should be permitted. It was important to exclude extremes such as high-rise blocks of flats which might be seen from the estate and were offensive to the eye. It was also important to control density. High density overloaded the local services and also brought social evils in its train which might affect the estate. Mr Byng, for his part, desired to preserve the integrity of the covenants, not only for the protection of the estate but also in the interests of existing residents who were already housed on land sold off by the estate. He felt that the estate owed a moral responsibility to such persons to protect their amenities as well as its own.

Mr Parker was the expert witness called on behalf of the plaintiffs. He had graduated from Cambridge University, is a Fellow of the Royal Institution of Chartered

---

1   [1961] 2 All ER at 706, [1962] Ch at 136, 137
2   In *Lord Northbourne v Johnston & Son* [1922] 2 Ch at 319, cf [1922] All ER Rep at 148
3   [1961] 2 All ER at 706, [1962] Ch at 137
4   [1972] 3 All ER 77 at 89, [1973] Ch 110 at 125

Surveyors and for 13 years has been a partner in a firm of surveyors, land agents and auctioneers with a wide general practice. His firm acts for certain Cambridge colleges as well as other corporate and individual clients and currently has full management of, or supervises, something over a quarter of a million acres of land. I will endeavour to summarise his evidence. Urban development, although it must be accepted, is an alien intrusion on agricultural land. A landowner whose estate is sandwiched between two growing towns—in this case Potters Bar and Barnet— has much anxiety over what is happening on his boundaries. Restrictive covenants imposed on a sale of land for development afford the landowner a powerful tool to ensure that the development is carried out harmoniously and coherently. Mr Parker was asked whether the layout covenant imposed on area 14 was of value to the estate at the time when it was imposed and whether it still retained a value to the estate. He said that the covenant was a very valuable benefit to the estate in 1935 because it enabled the sixth earl to control the type of development which could take place on the land affected. Mr Parker emphasised the environmental importance of open spaces within a development. He considered that the layout covenant still remained of latent value to the estate. The estate owner would be able to control redevelopment, if and when it should take place. It also enabled him to control undue exploitation of land already developed. Given freedom of action a resourceful developer can still exploit previously developed areas, including area 14, by forming a new access road, if necessary demolishing a house for this purpose, and thereby opening up back gardens and existing open spaces for the construction of further houses, as indeed has happened in area 14. The layout covenant is therefore still of value to the estate owner if it requires his approval to this type of in-filling; for it will enable the estate owner to prevent deterioration of the neighbourhood as a result of undue exploitation. Put broadly, the layout covenant enabled, and still enables, the estate owner to ensure that the development which takes place on the periphery of his estate is pleasing to him and not out of character with the neighbourhood and the estate. It is not a sufficient protection for the landowner to rely on the planning authorities. Therefore, Mr Parker would say that the layout covenant imposed on area 14 still benefits the estate.

Mr Parker expressed two other reasons for taking the view that the layout covenant on area 14 was still of value to the estate. He said that if the layout covenants imposed on areas 14, 12 and 10 did not, as he put it, stand up, then this would affect the validity of, or at any rate the respect accorded to, other restrictive covenants such as those intended to be imposed if development should take place on the estate to the north of the ring-road. Thirdly, he said that the erection of the 14 extra houses on the allotment site would mean that there were 14 fewer potential buyers who might seek to buy houses on parts of the estate which came to be developed at a later date. I found neither of these propositions convincing and I exclude them from further consideration.

Mr Parker conceded in cross-examination that the building of the houses on the allotment site had not affected the market value of the estate. That, in my judgment, is clearly a correct view and the concession was rightly made.

Mr Eve gave evidence on behalf of the defendants. He also is a Fellow of the Royal Institution of Chartered Surveyors, and is a partner in a London firm of surveyors and valuers concerned to a considerable extent with town and country planning matters. He has practised as a surveyor since 1954, although he gained his professional qualification at some later date. He described the development in and around area 14 as low in terms of height and density. He conceded, as I understood his evidence, that the layout covenant imposed on area 14 benefited the estate at the time when the covenant was given. But he expressed the view that the covenant ceased to benefit the estate when area 10 to the south was developed. Without being too precise, the benefit of the layout covenant ran out, in his view, when the land to the south had been developed to a depth of 200 yards or so. He conceded, however, that *a* a layout covenant, although imposed on land at a greater distance than 200 yards, might benefit the estate if it could have the effect of excluding certain extreme forms of development that would depreciate the estate, by which I think he had in mind development that was visually offensive to the estate owner. But, speaking generally, Mr Eve took the view that the benefit to the estate of the layout convenants on areas 14, 10 and 12 was really exhausted as a result of other development between

b those areas and the estate. In other words, a layout covenant and, indeed, other restrictive covenants taken for the benefit of an estate owner and intended to control the nature of a development, die off as the tide of development advances.

There was evidence by two householders, whose homes backed on to the allotment site, of the prejudice to their amenities resulting from the new development. Both experts were in agreement that these householders had lost something of value to them. Mr Parker described the development as thoroughly misplaced and, in his

c view, the planning authority should never have assented to it.

There can be obvious cases where a restrictive covenant clearly is, or clearly is not, of benefit to an estate. Between these two extremes there is inevitably an area where the benefit to the estate is a matter of personal opinion, where responsible and reasonable persons can have divergent views sincerely and reasonably held. In my judgment,

d in such cases, it is not for the court to pronounce which is the correct view. I think that the court can only decide whether a particular view is one which can reasonably be held. If a restriction is bargained for at the time of sale with the intention of giving the vendor a protection which he desires for the land he retains, and the restriction is expressed to be imposed for the benefit of the estate so that both sides are apparently accepting that the restriction is of value to the retained land, I think that the validity of the restriction should be upheld so long as an estate owner may

e reasonably take the view that the restriction remains of value to his estate, and that the restriction should not be discarded merely because others may reasonably argue that the restriction is spent. I think that this accords with the judgment of Sargant J in the *Northbourne* case[1] and of Wilberforce J in the *Marten* case[2]. The view expressed by Mr Byng and by Mr Parker is, in my judgment, a reasonable one, although it may

f be a matter of opinion whether it is correct or not. My own opinion is that it is correct, and I would so hold. For it seems to me that an estate owner, living on a residential and agricultural estate sandwiched between two developing towns, is properly interested in the standard of development of those towns. To take an extreme case, which is not this case, a Wrotham Park estate lying between two overcrowded slum districts would be a less desirable and less marketable property than a Wrotham Park estate lying between two carefully developed and uncrowded districts. If

g the rest of areas 14, 10 and 12 were subjected to the same kind of exploitation that the allotment site has suffered, it seems to me that a reasonable owner of the Wrotham Park estate might well fear that the quality of the development on the periphery of his estate was deteriorating to his disadvantage. I therefore conclude that the layout covenant imposed on area 14 is still capable of benefiting the Wrotham Park estate, or,

h at any rate, that the contrary has not been proved.

On the issue of enforceability there remains only the question whether the allotment site is subject to the burden of the restrictive covenant. That question is to be answered affirmatively. The covenant was duly registered in 1935 as a class D (ii) land charge under the Land Charges Act 1925; therefore purchasers took with notice of it and are bound by it.

j I must now consider the relief to which the plaintiffs are entitled, that is to say a mandatory injunction or damages (both are not sought); if damages, whether substantial or nominal; or a declaration of the plaintiffs' rights as the sole relief. The plaintiffs made it abundantly clear at the outset of the case that the relief they

---

1 [1922] 2 Ch 309, [1922] All ER Rep 144
2 [1961] 2 All ER 696, [1962] Ch 115

primarily sought was a mandatory injunction. This did not stem from outraged feelings or from indifference to the welfare of those who have made the offending houses their homes. It sprang from the belief, sincerely held, that there was no other effective way of preserving the integrity of the planning restrictions imposed by the terms of the Blake conveyance. Quite apart from the benefit to the Wrotham Park estate, the plaintiffs, as I have already said, take the view that they have a moral obligation towards the residents of the building estates to enforce the restrictive covenants so far as they are lawfully entitled to do so. I agree. The plaintiffs do not seek to bulldoze the occupiers out of their homes but are content that they shall have a period of two years in which to acquire other homes with the help of the £20,000 or so that will come to each of them under the indemnity assurance that has been arranged.

The plaintiffs concede that they are not entitled to a mandatory injunction 'as of course'. Every case must depend essentially on its own particular circumstances. This has been said in case after case and was reaffirmed in *Redland Bricks Ltd v Morris*[1]. The plaintiffs rely in this particular case on the fact that Parkside was warned of the plaintiffs' rights by the letter dated 5th January 1972 and that a writ claiming a mandatory injunction was served in the middle of February before any substantial construction had taken place; that Parkside deliberately chanced its arm and continued with the building of the houses; and that the present occupiers bought with full knowledge of the legal claims advanced by the plaintiffs and completed their purchases with the security of large insurance policies which they believed were adequate to protect them from all loss. In such circumstances, it was said, those concerned proceeded at their own risk and must now take the consequences.

Undoubtedly it is a highly material factor that Parkside, aided and abetted by those who entered into contracts with it, continued building operations in the face of the clear and early protest by the plaintiffs and the issue of proceedings. In such circumstances a defendant proceeds at his own peril and in such or similar circumstances the court made mandatory orders to demolish bay windows in *Lord Manners v Johnson*[2]; to remove buildings that obstructed easements of way and of light in *Krehl v Burrell*[3] and *Achilli v Tovell*[4]; and to demolish an advertisement hoarding in *Stevens v Willing & Co Ltd*[5]. See also as to the attitude of the court *Smith v Day*[6]. But even where the defendant has continued in the face of protest or writ, there is no rule that the plaintiff will be granted a mandatory injunction if he succeeds at the trial. Such relief was refused in *Isenberg v East India House Estate Co Ltd*[7] although the defendants had accelerated building operations between the date of the plaintiff's warning and the filing of the bill; and in *Kilbey v Haviland*[8] and *Sharp v Harrison*[9], where the defendant continued to build in defiance of a warning that proceedings would be taken.

In the *Isenberg* case[10] Lord Westbury LC said:

'Every one of this class of cases must depend upon its own peculiar circumstances. The common law remedy for a grievance of this description is an action for damages; an action liable to be resorted to as long as the cause of damage continues. Upon that ground, and by reason also of the damage in many cases

---

1   [1969] 2 All ER 576 at 579, [1970] AC 652 at 665
2   (1875) 1 Ch D 673
3   (1879) 11 Ch D 146
4   [1927] 2 Ch 243
5   (1929) 167 LT Jo 178
6   (1880) 13 Ch D 651
7   (1863) 3 De GJ & Sm 263
8   (1871) 24 LT 353
9   [1922] 1 Ch 502
10 (1863) 3 De GJ & Sm 263 at 271, 272

not admitting of being estimated in money, this Court has assumed jurisdiction. This jurisdiction of this Court, so far as it partakes of the nature of a preventive remedy, that is, prohibition of further damage or an intended damage, is a jurisdiction that may be exercised without difficulty, and rests upon the clearest principles. But there has been superadded to that the power of the Court to grant what has been denominated a mandatory injunction, that is, an order compelling a Defendant to restore things to the condition in which they were at the time when the Plaintiff's complaint was made. The exercise of that power is one that must be attended with the greatest possible caution. I think, without intending to lay down any rule, that it is confined to cases where the injury done to the Plaintiff cannot be estimated and sufficiently compensated by a pecuniary sum. Where it admits of being so estimated, and where the evil sustained by the Plaintiff may be abundantly compensated in money there appears to me to be no necessity to superadd the exercise of that extraordinary power by this Court.'

In *Durell v Pritchard*[1], where a mandatory injunction was refused, Turner LJ said that the court would not interfere by way of mandatory injunction except where extreme or, at all events, very serious damage will ensue from withholding an injunction. In *Kilbey v Haviland*[2], where the defendant had transgressed a building line, Bacon V-C found that the covenant-breaker had built in defiance of regulations which he was bound to observe and placed a house where it was certain to be injurious to the adjoining lots. He described the defendant's conduct as inexcusable; it was another question whether he should be compelled to pull the house down. A mandatory injunction was refused.

One naturally asks why in the present case the plaintiffs did not seek interim relief to prevent the houses being erected before the trial of the action. The reasons were threefold. In the first place the plaintiffs candidly admitted that they did not wish to accept the risk of having to pay compensation pursuant to the cross-undertaking in damages which they would have been required to give. Secondly, the plaintiffs assumed, wrongly in view of the decision of the Court of Appeal in *Hubbard v Vosper*[3], that they would need to establish a strong prima facie case that they were entitled to enforce the stipulation before interim relief would be granted, and the plaintiffs were not, at that stage, equipped with the requisite evidence. Thirdly, on previous occasions the mere issue of a writ had proved sufficient.

Counsel for the plaintiffs submitted, and I accept, that it is no answer to a claim for a mandatory injunction that the plaintiffs, having issued proceedings, deliberately held their hand and did not seek the assistance of the court for the purpose of preserving the status quo. On the other hand, it is, in my view, equally true that a plaintiff is not entitled 'as of course' to have everything pulled down that was built after the issue of the writ. The erection of the houses, whether one likes it or not, is a fait accompli and the houses are now the homes of people. I accept that this particular fait accompli is reversible and could be undone. But I cannot close my eyes to the fact that the houses now exist. It would, in my opinion, be an unpardonable waste of much needed houses to direct that they now be pulled down and I have never had a moment's doubt during the hearing of this case that such an order ought to be refused. No damage of a financial nature has been done to the plaintiffs by the breach of the lay-out stipulation. The plaintiffs' use of the Wrotham Park estate has not been and will not be impeded. It is totally unnecessary to demolish the houses in order to preserve the integrity of the restrictive covenants imposed on the rest of area 14. Without hesitation I decline to grant a mandatory injunction. But the fact that these houses will remain does not spell out a charter entitling others to despoil adjacent areas of

1 (1865) 1 Ch App 244 at 250
2 (1871) 24 LT 353
3 [1972] 1 All ER 1023, [1972] 2 QB 84

land in breach of valid restrictions imposed by the conveyances. A developer who
tries that course may be in for a rude awakening.

I now consider the question what damages, if any, should be awarded to the plaintiffs. I am able, under the jurisdiction which originated with the Chancery Amendment Act 1858 (Lord Cairns's Act), to award damages in substitution for an injunction. But before I discuss quantum of damages I must answer the question, damages
against whom? For I apprehend that I am not able to award damages against a defendant except as a substitute for an injunction that I could have granted against the
same defendant. Parkside has parted with the ownership of the allotment site except
the road. I am able to grant a mandatory injunction to compel Parkside to remove
the road, at any rate once the houses have gone. I can therefore award damages
against Parkside in substitution for that injunction. I am not able to award damages
against Parkside as a substitute for an injunction to remove the houses because I
cannot order Parkside to demolish them. But I can award damages against each of
the purchasers in substitution for any mandatory injunction that I could have granted
against the same purchaser. Counsel for Parkside and the subsequent purchasers
submitted that I would have no jurisdiction to grant an injunction against a purchaser
because, he said, the layout stipulation was breached once and for all when Parkside
commenced the development of the allotment site, i e in or about October 1971. The
covenant is not, he said, a continuing one which has been breached day by day by
the purchasers who now own the plots. He relied on *Powell v Hemsley*[1]. In that case
there were two covenants: (1) a covenant to erect no buildings except private houses
and outbuildings at the rear of such houses, and (2) a covenant before erecting any
building to submit a plan for approval. Lessees of the defendant convenantor breached
the first covenant by erecting an outbuilding at the front, and the second covenant
by putting up a house without submitting plans for approval. The plaintiff took a
conveyance of the covenantee's land after these breaches had taken place. Subsequently, the lessees' trustee in bankruptcy disclaimed so that the defendant convenantor resumed possession. It was held by Eve J and the Court of Appeal[1] that the
defendant was not liable. The two breaches of covenant had taken place once and for
all before the plaintiff became the owner of the covenantee's land. The defendant
had not instigated or been associated with the breaches. The first covenant did not
imply a continuing obligation not to permit an offending outbuilding to remain on
the land; the second covenant did not imply a continuing obligation not to permit
a building to remain on the land which the covenantee had not approved and could
reasonably have rejected.

In my view *Powell v Hemsley*[1] does not assist the purchasers. The plaintiffs were
the owners of the benefit of the covenant at the time when it was first breached.
Although the development started before any of the individual defendants purchased, i e in late 1971, the process of development was still continuing down to
the end of 1972. All the individual defendants, except two, aided and abetted the
breach by contributing their deposits and entering into contracts to purchase and
building contracts with Parkside while the development was still in progress. In
these circumstances it seems to me that I have jurisdiction to grant mandatory injunctions against all such individual defendants and I am therefore able to award
damages against them in substitution.

I must, however, say one word concerning the position of the last two defendants,
Mr and Mrs Pilcher. Their home is on plot 4. They do not appear to have been in
direct contractual relationship with Parkside so far as I am aware. What apparently
happened was that a Mr Newman entered into purchase and building agreements
with Parkside on 17th October 1972, for a total consideration of £17,400. On 29th
December 1972 Mr Newman agreed to sell plot 4 to Mr and Mrs Pilcher for the sum
of £7,500 and he assigned to them the benefit of the building agreement for £9,785.

[1909] 2 Ch 252, CA; *affg* [1909] 1 Ch 680

No submission has been made to me that Mr and Mrs Pilcher ought, on these facts, to be treated differently from the other defendants. I infer that, at the time when the Pilchers bought, the development of plot 4 was still incomplete. In these circumstances I regard the Pilchers as being in the same position as the other individual defendants so far as liability in damages is concerned.

I turn to the consideration of the quantum of damages. I was asked by the parties to assess the damages myself, should the question arise, rather than to direct an enquiry. The basic rule in contract is to measure damages by that sum of money which will put the plaintiff in the same same position as he would have been in if the contract had not been broken. From that basis, the defendants argue that the damages are nil or purely nominal, because the value of the Wrotham Park estate (as the plaintiffs concede) is not diminished by one farthing in consequence of the construction of a road and the erection of 14 houses on the allotment site. If, therefore (the defendants submit), I refuse an injunction I ought to award no damages in lieu. That would seem, on the face of it, a result of questionable fairness on the facts of this case. Had the offending development been the erection of an advertisement hoarding in defiance of protests and writs, I apprehend (assuming my conclusions on other points to be correct) that the court would not have hesitated to grant a mandatory injunction for its removal. If, for social and economic reasons, the court does not see fit in the exercise of its discretion, to order demolition of the 14 houses, is it just that the plaintiffs should receive no compensation and that the defendants should be left in undisturbed possession of the fruits of their wrongdoing? Common sense would seem to demand a negative answer to this question. A comparable prolem arose in wayleave cases where the defendant had trespassed by making use of the plaintiff's underground ways to the defendant's profit but without diminishing the value of the plaintiff's property. The plaintiff in such cases received damages assessed by reference to a reasonable wayleave rent. This principle was considered and extended in *Whitwham v Westminster Brymbo Coal and Coke Co*[1]. For six years the defendants wrongfully tipped colliery waste on to the plaintiff's land. At the trial the defendants were directed to cease tipping and to give up possession. The question then arose what damages should be awarded for the wrongful act done to the plaintiff during the period of the defendants' unauthorised user of the land. The official referee found that the diminution in the value of the plaintiff's land was only £200, but that the value of the plaintiff's land to the defendants in 1888 for tipping purposes for six years was some £900. It was held that the proper scale of damages was the higher sum on the ground that a trespasser should not be allowed to make use of another person's land without in some way compensating that other person for that user.

A like principle was applied by the House of Lords in a Scottish case, *Watson, Laidlaw & Co Ltd v Pott, Cassels and Williamson*[2]. A patentee elected to sue an infringer for damages rather than for an account of profits. Part of the infringement had taken place in Java. There was evidence that the patentee could not have competed successfully in that island. It was submitted that no damages ought to be awarded in respect of the Java infringement. Lord Shaw said[3]:

'It is at this stage of the case . . . that a second principle comes into play. It is not exactly the principle of restoration, either directly or expressed through compensation, but it is the principle underlying price or hire. It plainly extends— and I am inclined to think not infrequently extends—to Patent cases. But, indeed, it is not confined to them. For wherever an abstraction or invasion of property has occurred, then, unless such abstraction or invasion were to be sanctioned by law,

1   [1896] 2 Ch 538
2   (1914) 31 RPC 104
3   (1914) 31 RPC at 119

the law ought to yield a recompense under the category or principle, as I say, either of price or of hire. If A, being a liveryman, keeps his horse standing idle in the stable, and B, against his wish or without his knowledge, rides or drives it out, it is no answer to A for B to say: "Against what loss do you want to be restored? I restore the horse. There is no loss. The horse is none the worse; it is the better for the exercise." I confess to your Lordships that this seems to me to be precisely in principle the kind of question and retort which underlay the argument of the learned Counsel for the Appellants about the Java trade.'

He continued[1]:

'. . . in such cases it appears to me that the correct and full measure is only reached by adding that a patentee is also entitled, on the principle of price or hire, to a royalty for the unauthorised sale or use of every one of the infringing machines in a market which the infringer, if left to himself, might not have reached. Otherwise, that property which consists in the monopoly of the patented articles granted to the patentee has been invaded, and indeed abstracted, and the law, when appealed to, would be standing by and allowing the invader or abstractor to go free.'

The same principle was applied to detinue in *Strand Electric and Engineering Co Ltd v Brisford Entertainments Ltd*[2]. The defendants came into possession of portable switchboards which were part of the stock-in-trade of the plaintiffs. The defendants used them for their own profit for 43 weeks. The trial judge ordered the return of the switchboards and awarded damages. The damages took into account the fact that if the defendants had not wrongfully retained the switchboards the plaintiffs would be unlikely to have hired out every one for the full period of 43 weeks. It was held by the Court of Appeal that the plaintiffs were entitled to recover as damages the full market rate of hire for the whole period of detention. It will be sufficient to read these extracts from the judgment of Denning LJ[3]:

'In assessing damages, whether for a breach of contract or for a tort, the general rule is that the plaintiff recovers the loss he has suffered, no more and no less. This rule is, however, often departed from.'

He then gave examples and continued[3]:

'The question in this case is: What is the proper measure of damages for the wrongful detention of goods? Does it fall within the general rule that the plaintiff only recovers for the loss he has suffered, or within some other, and, if so, what rule? It is strange that there is no authority on this point in English law, but there is plenty on the analogous case of detention of land. The rule there is that a wrongdoer who keeps the owner out of his land must pay a fair rental value for it, even though the owner would not have been able to use it himself or to let it to anyone else. So, also, a wrongdoer who uses land for his own purposes without the owner's consent, as, for instance, for a fair ground or as a way-leave, must pay a reasonable hire for it even though he has done no damage to the land at all: *Whitwham v. Westminster Brymbo Coal & Coke Co.*[4] I see no reason why the same principle should not apply to detention of goods. If a wrongdoer has made use of goods for his own purposes, then he must pay a reasonable hire for them even though the owner has, in fact, suffered no loss. It may be that the owner would not have used the goods himself, or that he had a substitute readily available which he used without extra cost to himself. Nevertheless, the owner is

1　(1914) 31 RPC at 120
2　[1952] 1 All ER 796, [1952] 2 QB 246
3　[1952] 1 All ER at 800, [1952] 2 QB at 253
4　[1896] 2 Ch 538

entitled to a reasonable hire. If the wrongdoer had asked the owner for permission to use the goods the owner would be entitled to ask for a reasonable remuneration as the price of his permission. The wrongdoer cannot be better off because he did not ask permission. He cannot be better off by doing wrong than he would be by doing right. He must, therefore, pay a reasonable hire.'

The point was further considered in *Penarth Dock Engineering Co Ltd v Pounds*[1] by Lord Denning MR sitting as a judge of the Queen's Bench Division. The defendant had contracted to buy a floating dock and to remove it from the plaintiffs' dock premises. The defendant defaulted in the removal of the purchase. The plaintiffs, however, had suffered no damage, since the dock premises had become disused. The plaintiffs claimed a mandatory injunction and damages. It was held that the plaintiffs were entitled to damages at a rate per week representing a reasonable berthing charge.

The facts of the cases I have mentioned are a long way from the facts of the case before me. Should I, as invited by the plaintiffs, apply a like principle to a case where the defendant Parkside, in defiance of protest and writ, has invaded the plaintiffs' rights in order to reap a financial profit for itself? In *Leeds Industrial Co-operative Society Ltd v Slack*[2] Lord Sumner said:

'. . . no money awarded in substitution can be justly awarded, unless it is at any rate designed to be a preferable equivalent for an injunction and therefore an adequate substitute for it . . .'

This was said in a dissenting speech but his dissent did not arise in the context of that observation. In the present case I am faced with the problem what damages ought to be awarded to the plaintiffs in the place of mandatory injunctions which would have restored the plaintiffs' rights. If the plaintiffs are merely given a nominal sum, or no sum, in substitution for injunctions, it seems to me that justice will manifestly not have been done.

As I have said, the general rule would be to measure damages by reference to that sum which would place the plaintiffs in the same position as if the covenant had not been broken. The defendant Parkside and the individual purchasers could have avoided breaking the covenant in two ways. One course would have been not to develop the allotment site. The other course would have been for Parkside to have sought from the plaintiffs a relaxation of the covenant. On the facts of this particular case the plaintiffs, rightly conscious of their obligations towards existing residents, would clearly not have granted any relaxation, but for present purposes I must assume that they would have been induced to do so. In my judgment a just substitute for a mandatory injunction would be such a sum of money as might reasonably have been demanded by the plaintiffs from Parkside as a quid pro quo for relaxing the covenant. The plaintiffs submitted that that sum should be a substantial proportion of the development value of the land. This is currently put at no less than £10,000 per plot, i e £140,000 on the assumption that the plots are undeveloped. Mr Parker gave evidence that a half or a third of the development value was commonly demanded by a landowner whose property stood in the way of a development. I do not agree with that approach to damages in this type of case. I bear in mind the following factors: (1) The layout covenant is not an asset which the estate owner ever contemplated he would have either the opportunity or the desire to turn to account. It has no commercial or even nuisance value. For it cannot be turned to account except to the detriment of the existing residents who are people the estate owner professes to protect. (2) The breach of covenant which has actually taken place is over a very small area and the impact of this particular breach on the Wrotham Park estate is insignificant. The validity of the covenant over the rest of area 14 is unaffected. I think that in a

1 [1963] 1 Lloyd's Rep 359
2 [1924] AC 851 at 870, [1924] All ER Rep 259 at 268

case such as the present a landowner faced with a request from a developer which, it must be assumed, he feels reluctantly obliged to grant, would have first asked the developer what profit he expected to make from his operations. With the benefit of foresight the developer would, in the present case, have said about £50,000, for that is the profit which Parkside concedes it made from the development. I think that the landowner would then reasonably have required a certain percentage of that anticipated profit as a price for the relaxation of the covenant, assuming, as I must, that he feels obliged to relax it. In assessing what would be a fair percentage I think that the court ought, on the particular facts of this case, to act with great moderation. For it is to be borne in mind that the plaintiffs were aware, before the auction took place, that the land was being offered for sale as freehold building land for 13 houses, and the plaintiffs knew that they were not going to consent to any such development. The plaintiffs could have informed the urban district council of their attitude in advance of the auction or could have given the like information to Parkside prior to completion of the contract for sale. In either event it seems highly unlikely that Parkside would have parted with its £90,000, at any rate unconditionally. I think that damages must be assessed in such a case on a basis which is fair and, in all the circumstances, in my judgment a sum equal to 5 per cent of Parkside's anticipated profit is the most that is fair. I accordingly award the sum of £2,500 in substitution for mandatory injunctions. I think that this amount should be treated as apportioned between the 14 respective owners or joint owners of the plots and Parkside (as the owner of the road) in 1/15th shares, so that the damages awarded will be £166 odd in each case. In fact, I apprehend that by virtue of the arrangement between Parkside and the insurance office the entirety of the £2,500 will ultimately be recoverable from Parkside, so that the apportionment does not have any real significance. I will also grant a declaration in appropriate terms after I have heard submissions from counsel as to such terms.

There is a second action before me. This relates to the back gardens of nos 5, 7 and 9 Brooklands Gardens and to the back gardens of nos 13, 15 and 17. Parkside has entered into contracts to purchase parts of these six gardens and has obtained planning permission to erect two houses thereon, each of which would straddle three gardens. The only difference between the two cases is that, in this case, fortunately, no building works have been begun. The appropriate remedies are therefore a declaration and an injunction restraining Parkside from building in breach of the layout covenant. I will hear argument as to the form of the declaration and injunction. No question of damages arises.

Declaration in first action that plaintiffs entitled to benefit of restrictive covenant in cl 3 of 1935 conveyance and that the burden of the stipulation in para (2) of the second schedule to the conveyance burdens the land and that plaintiffs entitled to enforce stipulation against defendants and each of them; damages of £2,500 awarded to the plaintiffs to be paid in equal shares by Parkside and each of the purchasers. Declaration in similar terms in second action; injunction granted restraining Parkside from building on or developing land for building purposes.

Solicitors: *Farrer & Co* (for the plaintiffs); *Breeze & Wyles*, Enfield (for Parkside and the subsequent purchasers); *Breeze & Wyles; Wedlake Bell; Wild, Sapte & Co* (for the mortgagees).

Susan Corbett Barrister.

Ord v Maidstone and District Hospital Management Committee

NATIONAL INDUSTRIAL RELATIONS COURT

SIR JOHN DONALDSON P, MR R BOYFIELD AND SIR REGINALD GRIFFITHS

12th, 26th FEBRUARY 1974

Industrial relations – Unfair dismissal – Right of employee not to be unfairly dismissed – Restriction on right to complain of unfair dismissal where employee reaches normal retiring age or 65 – Normal retiring age – Meaning – Employee in undertaking where 60 regarded as pensionable age – Employees retained in undertaking after age of 60 at discretion of employers – Employee dismissed when aged 61 – Whether employee having right to present complaint of unfair dismissal – Industrial Relations Act 1971, s 28(b).

The employee, a mental health officer in the employment of the National Health Service, was dismissed after he had attained the age of 61. Mental health officers were regarded as having reached 'pensionable age' when aged 60. From that time onwards it was within the discretion of the employers whether or not such officers were retained in service. An officer who could still give effective service was not in normal circumstances denied the opportunity of continuing to work solely on the grounds of his age. Officers did not usually retire on reaching the age of 60 and there was no usual age at which the employers decided that an officer should be retired. An industrial tribunal held that it could not investigate a complaint of unfair dismissal by the employee under s 22[a] of the Industrial Relations Act 1971 on the ground that, since the employee was over 60, he had attained the 'normal retiring age' for an employee holding the position which he held, within s 28(b)[b] of the 1971 Act. The employee appealed.

Held – The tribunal had erred in concluding that the concept of 'pensionable age' inevitably carried with it the notion that that was the 'normal retiring age' for the purposes of s 28(b). The words 'normal retiring age' in s 28(b) meant 'the age at which the employees concerned usually retire' and were not concerned with the entitlement of an employee to a pension. It followed that, since there was no usual age at which officers retired and the employee was under 65 at the time of his dismissal, he was not excluded from presenting a complaint under s 22. Accordingly the appeal would be allowed and the complaint remitted to the tribunal to be determined on its merits (see p 345 h and p 346 a and d, post).

Notes

For unfair dismissal and the upper age limit restrictions on complaints of unfair dismissal, see Supplement to 38 Halsbury's Laws (3rd Edn) para 677B, 18, 24.

For the Industrial Relations Act 1971, ss 22, 28, see 41 Halsbury's Statutes (3rd Edn) 2088, 2094.

---

a   Section 22, so far as material, provides:

'(1) In every employment to which this section applies every employee shall have the right not to be unfairly dismissed by his employer; and accordingly, in any such employment, it shall be an unfair industrial practice for an employer to dismiss an employee unfairly.

'(2) This section applies to every employment except in so far as its application is excluded by or under any of sections 27 to 31 of this Act . . .'

b   Section 28, so far as material, is set out at p 344 e and f, post

Appeal

This was an appeal by John Walter Ord against the decision of an industrial tribunal (chairman J W Cronin Esq) sitting at Ashford, Kent, dated 19th November 1973, that it was precluded from hearing a complaint of unfair dismissal by the appellant against the respondents, the Maidstone and District Hospital Management Committee, on the ground that at the date on which he was dismissed by the respondents the appellant had attained 'normal retiring age' within s 28(b) of the Industrial Relations Act 1971. The facts are set out in the judgment of the court.

James Mitchell for the appellant.
Mr D Lawrence Jones, group secretary, Maidstone and District Hospital Management Committee, for the respondents.

Cur adv vult

26th February. **SIR JOHN DONALDSON P** read the following judgment of the court. The unfair dismissal provisions of the Industrial Relations Act 1971 do not apply to employees who have attained normal retiring age. The appellant was a mental health officer employed by the respondents, Maidstone and District Hospital Management Committee, from April 1954 until September 1973. He complained that he was unfairly dismissed. The industrial tribunal sitting at Ashford, Kent, unanimously held that it could not investigate his complaint because he had reached the normal retiring age at the time at which he was dismissed. He now appeals from this decision.

This is the first occasion on which this court has had to consider the meaning of s 28(b) of the 1971 Act. Section 28 provides:

'... section 22 of this Act does not apply to the dismissal of an employee from any employment if the employee—(a) was not continuously employed for a period of not less than 104 weeks ending with the effective date of termination, or (b) on or before the effective date of termination attained the age which, in the undertaking in which he was employed, was the normal retiring age for an employee holding the position which he held, or, if a man, attained the age of sixty-five, or, if a woman, attained the age of sixty.'

The essence of the problem is what is meant by 'normal retiring age'?

There are two important birthdays in the life of a mental health officer in the employment of the National Health Service. The first is his 55th birthday. If he has then been in the service for a minimum period (ten years in September 1973, but now only five years), he thereupon becomes entitled to retire on pension. The second is his 60th birthday. This, for mental health officers and some other special classes of officer who need a degree of physical fitness and patience which tends to disappear with increasing years, is known as 'pensionable age'. Subject to good health and conduct, a mental health officer is automatically retained in the service until he reaches 'pensionable age'. But at and from that age employing authorities, such as hospital management committees, review the position of individual officers and decide whether or not to allow them to continue in the service.

The Ministry of Health issued a circular HM (54) 21, dated 12th March 1954, which gave guidance to employing authorities on the action which they should take. In substance it was that (a) officers should be given at least six months notice that they would be retired; (b) subject to special considerations, such as a redundancy situation or the need to make room for the promotion of younger officers, an officer who could continue to give effective service should not in normal circumstances be denied, solely on grounds of age, the opportunity of continuing to work if he so wished; (c) it would only be in very exceptional circumstances that an officer's fitness to perform his duties would extend beyond the age of 70.

The appellant's 60th birthday fell on 8th May 1972. In accordance with the respondents' policy, which was based on the Ministry's circular, the appellant's position was reviewed before that date. In consequence he received a letter dated 24th January 1972 in the following terms:

'*Retention of Staff Beyond Pensionable Age.*

'In accordance with advice received from the Department of Health, the Management Committee require that the position of all staff who are nearing or have passed normal pensionable age be reviewed and your position has therefore been considered.

'I have to inform you that they decided to continue your engagement in your present post, if you so desire, subject to a review in six months' time.'

A similar letter dated 27th July 1972 was sent to the appellant. The appellant's position was again reviewed at the end of 1972, but on this occasion the decision was different. In due course he received a letter dated 2nd January 1973 reading:

'In reference to my letter of the 27th July, 1972, your position has again been reviewed and it has been decided that we are unable to continue your employment and I have therefore to give you six months' notice to terminate your engagement on the 2nd July, 1973.'

For reasons which are not material, the appellant's service was in fact extended until September 1973, but it then came to an end.

In proceedings before the tribunal, the appellant was represented by Mrs R Lambie, of the Confederation of Health Service Employees, and the tribunal paid tribute to her keenness and enthusiasm in promoting his interests. In this court, the appellant was represented by counsel. We mention this change of representation because it may be that the arguments addressed to us were not identical with those addressed to the tribunal. On both occasions the respondent management committee was represented by Mr Lawrence Jones, the group secretary.

It was common ground before us that mental health officers do not usually retire before they have attained the age of 60 or on attaining that age. At some time thereafter, unless the employee himself takes the initiative, the employing authority decides that he should be retired and gives him the appropriate notice. But there is no usual age at which this step is taken, although as time goes on it becomes more and more likely that any particular officer will be retired following the next review of his position.

It is also common ground that the age of 60 is known in the health service as the pensionable age for mental health officers and that whereas before that age the initiative for retirement will almost always come from the employee, after that age it is at least as likely—and probably more likely—to come from the employing authority. Furthermore, service after the age of 60 is regarded by all concerned as 'retention beyond pensionable age' (see the heading to the committee's letters) or 'retention on extended service' (a phrase used by Mrs Lambie before the tribunal).

The tribunal concluded that the concept of pensionable age inevitably carried with it the notion that this was the 'normal retiring age' for the purposes of s 28 of the 1971 Act. In this we think that the tribunal erred.

In the light of some of the arguments of Mr Lawrence Jones, we think that it is of importance to stress that s 28 of the 1971 Act is not intended to have, and does not have, any effect on the pension scheme applicable to employees of the health service or on the age at which they should be compulsorily retired. The purpose of the section is simply to limit the range of employees who enjoy the right not to be unfairly dismissed. This it does by excluding short-term employees and those who are beyond a certain age. Bearing in mind that the Secretary of State has power under s 29(2) of the 1971 Act to vary or remove these limitations we infer that the intention of Parliament was to ensure that industrial tribunals were not flooded with complaints in the initial stages of the operation of the 1971 Act rather than to declare that short-term and older employees were not entitled to fair treatment.

In our judgment, counsel for the appellant is right when he submits that the words 'normal retiring age' should be given their ordinary meaning. The ordinary meaning is 'the age at which the employees concerned usually retire'. It has nothing to do with whether the employees are or are not then entitled to a pension. Still less has it anything to do with a notional chronological landmark indicating the beginning of a period during which it is the policy of the employer to consider whether and when to compulsorily retire the employee. This view of the meaning of the words is supported by a consideration of the mischief at which s 22 of the 1971 Act is aimed, namely unfair dismissal. If members of a group of employees are usually retired at a given age, retirement at that age is unlikely to give rise to a sense of grievance. Still less is it likely to be in fact unfair. But compulsory retirement short of this age, even if a full pension has been earned, may greatly aggrieve the employee, whether or not it is in fact unfair. The appellant had not in fact earned a full pension and was about to enter a period of service which, for pension purposes, counted as double time—hence, in part, his grievance.

Mr Lawrence Jones very fairly admitted that if 'normal retiring age' was not the same as pensionable age there was no normal retiring age in the case of mental health officers, since these officers are retired at different ages depending on individual circumstances. It follows that as the appellant was under 65 at the time of his dismissal, he is not excluded from presenting a complaint under s 22 of the 1971 Act. His complaint will therefore be remitted to the tribunal for a hearing and determination on its merits, of which we know nothing.

We should be sorry if anyone concluded from the terms of this judgment that in our view the operation of a retirement policy based on the Ministry of Health circular HM 54(21) is likely to lead to unfair dismissals. All that we are saying is that, on the facts of this case, the appellant is entitled to ask an industrial tribunal to decide whether or not he has been unfairly dismissed. In reaching a conclusion on that matter, the tribunal will be able to consider all the circumstances of the appellant's case, including the needs of the health service in the district.

Clearly there is a need for compulsory retirement of all employees at some age or in some circumstances and such a retirement at the appropriate time will be both fair and reasonable. However, it is a fact that, for many, retirement is most unwelcome. For them its very finality breeds discontent. From this it is but a short step to a deep-seated conviction that they have been unfairly treated. The existence of a right to complain to an industrial tribunal might well make employers more sensitive to the feelings of their employees and at the same time remove the sense of injustice which comes from nursing an imagined wrong for which there is no remedy.

Parliament therefore may wish at some stage to consider whether it would not be better to treat the attainment of retiring age as a circumstance capable of justifying a dismissal rather than as a reason for denying an employee the right to complain of having been unfairly dismissed.

Appeal allowed.

Solicitors: *Gillhams* (for the appellant).

Gordon H Scott Esq Barrister.

a

R v Royce-Bentley

COURT OF APPEAL, CRIMINAL DIVISION
LORD WIDGERY CJ, MEGAW LJ AND KERR J
18th FEBRUARY 1974

b

Criminal law – Evidence – Corroboration – Accomplice – Duty of judge – Prosecution witness giving evidence partly favourable to prosecution and partly favourable to defence – Evidence indicating witness might be accomplice of defendant – Whether judge bound to give jury accomplice direction.

c When a prosecution witness gives evidence that is partly favourable to the prosecution and partly favourable to the defence, and the evidence indicates that the witness might be an accomplice, the judge, before deciding whether he should give the jury a direction that the witness might be an accomplice and a warning as to the danger of convicting on an accomplice's uncorroborated evidence, should first consult counsel in the absence of the jury. Having done that, he should consider whether on *d* the whole more harm to the defence would be done by giving the direction than by not giving it. If he then concludes that no accomplice direction or warning should be given to the jury, no irregularity is committed by him (see p 350 *a* and *d*, post).

Notes

e For corroboration of evidence by accomplices and the effect of absence of corroboration, see 10 Halsbury's Laws (3rd Edn) 459, 461, 462, paras 844, 848, and for cases on corroboration, see 14 Digest (Repl) 533-545, 5177-5304.

Case referred to in judgment

R v Peach (14th January 1974) unreported, CA.

f ### Case also cited

Davies v Director of Public Prosecutions [1954] 1 All ER 507, [1954] AC 378, HL.

Appeal

On 9th May 1973 in the Crown Court at Bedford before his Honour Judge Lymbery QC the appellant, John William Royce-Bentley, was convicted of the theft of a motor *g* car transporter and was sentenced to 18 months imprisonment. He appealed against his conviction by leave of the single judge. The facts are set out in the judgment of the court.

J P Wadsworth (who did not appear in the court below) for the appellant.
R G Marshall-Andrews for the Crown.

h

LORD WIDGERY CJ delivered the following judgment of the court. At the Bedford Crown Court on 9th May 1973 before Judge Lymbery and a jury, the appellant was convicted of the theft of a motor car transporter trailer, and sentenced to *j* 18 months imprisonment. He appeals to this court against his conviction by leave of the single judge, and as will appear in a moment, it is a somewhat unusual case in a number of respects.

The offence alleged arose out of the fact that when on 31st March the service manager of a company in Dunstable arrived at his firm's premises, he found that the perimeter wire fence at the rear of the car park had been cut, and a car transporter trailer belonging to the firm and valued at about £250 had been moved from the position in which it had been left that night. It was still within the confines of the car park, but had been moved from its position. Further evidence was given that on the previous evening at about 9.40 pm two men called Hammond and Pegg, who had been working in the area, when they left their place of employment and walked along a lane near the point in the lane where the wire had been cut, saw a Rover motor car parked in the lane; in the driver's seat they saw a young boy and further along the lane they saw a man struggling to manoeuvre a trailer towards the Rover car. They also noticed the hole in the fence. They became suspicious, and driving off they reported the matter to the police.

The police evidence was that at about midnight that same night the appellant and a 15 year old boy called Potts walked into the police station, and the appellant said:

'We came in because I thought you might want to see us. We were behind Hawthorn Bakers when a man came out and I thought he took the number of my car. I thought I had better explain to the police just in case.'

Then there was told a story which was repeated at the trial. The substance of the defence was that the appellant and the young boy had gone out in the appellant's car that night in order that the appellant could give Potts a driving lesson on this private lane running beside the company's car park. Their account was that reversing the car down the lane preparatory to giving Potts a driving lesson, the appellant had noticed some obstruction in the lane, and going back to investigate what it was, had found the fence cut and had found the car transporter trailer in question partly in and partly outside the car park, and to that extent blocking the path. The appellant's story was that he had done no more than try to move the trailer out of his way in the lane, but having been seen by these two men and thinking they had suspicions of his conduct, he thought it right to go to the police and explain the situation. Notwithstanding that explanation which was spoken to by the appellant and, as will appear in a moment, in some measure by Potts, the jury convicted, and the matter comes before us. The first and perhaps principal difficulty in this case is that the shorthand writer who took the shorthand note at the trial was not able to make a transcript; we need not go into the reasons for that, but it meant some other shorthand writer had to do his or her best with the shorthand notes, and the judge had to be consulted to see what light could be thrown on the matter. One approaches the matter in this court conscious of the fact that we have not got in full supply the normal material on which this appeal would be argued.

The only point raised before us is that the boy Potts was called as a witness for the Crown, and the trial judge did not give the jury any direction in regard to the possibility of his being an accomplice, or in regard to the necessity for his evidence being corroborated if he was an accomplice: everything in argument before us has turned on that. So one must look a little closer at just what happened at the trial. Potts, the young boy, was undoubtedly called for the prosecution. We are told he gave evidence in accordance with his statement for the major part of his period in the witness box. In the statement which he gave to the police, although he begins by recounting the intention of the appellant and himself to go out on a driving lesson, he does include in his original statement at least one or two remarks which might be said to support the view that the appellant had tried to pull the trailer out and steal it. In particular the boy in his statement said that when they had left the scene and had gone back to the appellant's garage and had a cup of coffee, the appellant had said to Potts, 'I would have had that if it was more convenient', meaning the trailer. That statement was an extremely important feature in the case for the prosecution, the prosecution seeking to show he had tried to extract the trailer and take it away.

The boy when he gave evidence stuck to his proof over a considerable area, but he did not quite satisfy counsel for the prosecution in his answers on a vital part of *a*   the case, and according to the transcript which we have of this part of the boy's evidence, it ran something like this: 'Q Can you remember him [the appellant] saying anything about what had happened? A Only that it was a struggle to get it in.' That by itself was not adverse to the appellant; it might merely mean that the trailer had been found part out of the compound and the appellant tried to get it in. The trial judge asked him to repeat that, and then the witness said: 'He said I would have

b   had it, if it had been more convenient in a funny sort of way, it was the way he said it.' Pausing there, again the vital prosecution words, 'I would have had it, if it had been more convenient' appear in the evidence but qualified by the boy saying, 'He said it in a funny sort of way.' Further on in the transcript: 'Q Did you know what he was talking about? A Yes, the trailer, he said he had struggled to get it and I said you should have called and I would have given you a hand.' Importance is attached to

c   that answer as showing that the boy was potentially a party to the alleged charge of theft laid against the appellant. And further on again, '. . . [the appellant] said we had best report that and I said it was a good idea'. The judge said, 'We had best report what?' The boy said, 'to cover him I think he said'. On those somewhat fragile foundations the submission is made today first that the boy was giving evidence which in a measure at any rate was adverse to the appellant's case, and secondly that the boy

d   was disclosing that he might be a party to any criminal design on the part of the appellant, and thus might potentially be considered an accomplice. The matter had troubled both counsel and judge throughout this short trial, which lasted just over a day, and the judge at quite an early stage had shown he was considering whether he would have to give the jury an accomplice direction in regard to Potts. But at the end of the case, and before the summing-up was begun, the judge consulted both counsel

e   whether this was a case in which Potts ought to be put before the jury as a potential accomplice. The judge had obviously very much in mind all the relevant factors, but after discussion counsel for the defendant said: 'I would prefer there not to be a warning in the very special circumstances of this case.' The judge accepted that situation and he gave no warning in regard to Potts.

    To turn to the principle to be applied, a relevant decision is in this court in *R v*

f   *Peach*[1]. This again was an unusual case because here again the prosecution had called a witness who was intended to give evidence adverse to the defence, and who would on any view have been an accomplice in the sense of his implication in the offence if the case against the defendant was a sound case at all. But in the event the so-called accomplice in *R v Peach*[1], when he gave his evidence for the Crown, not only failed to come up to proof but failed to give any evidence which was adverse to the

g   defence. In this court it was held that in those circumstances there was no obligation on the judge to give an accomplice warning, because the supposed accomplice having said nothing injurious to the defendant, there was no danger of the jury convicting on the evidence of that accomplice whether it was corroborated or not.

    In giving the judgment of the court I said:

h   'But of course the real point here, and one only has to think about the case for a few minutes, is that if Griffin [that is the accomplice] was not giving evidence adverse to the accused, the ordinary reason for giving a direction on accomplices and corroboration did not arise. The whole purpose of the well-known requirement for directing juries in this sense in a criminal case is that one is normally concerned with an accomplice who has given adverse evidence.

j   If there was no such evidence, then no such direction was necessary because the law does not require a direction on corroboration unless the evidence is adverse.'

  We start today with that proposition, that if the so-called accomplice does not in fact give evidence adverse to the accused, no warning is required for the reason there

---

1 (14th January 1974) unreported

given. Today we have to move on to the slightly different situation in which the *a* alleged accomplice has given some evidence which is favourable to the defence and some evidence which is potentially favourable to the prosecution as well. It seems we have to face up, perhaps for the first time, to laying down a principle as to the conduct of the trial judge in that situation. We approach it on the footing that in this case there was in the extract from the transcript which I have read some evidence given by the boy which could be treated as adverse to the appellant, and also some *b* evidence given by the boy which might entitle the jury to hold him to be an accomplice, but there was also, as I have said, a good deal of other evidence given by the boy which was favourable to the defence. Cases will obviously arise in which a witness who gives evidence of these two different characters may wish to be upheld by the defence because, on the whole, he is more favourable to them, and cases will therefore arise where the defence do not want the credibility of the witness *c* attacked by an accomplice direction because they attach too much importance to that evidence themselves.

In our judgment, where a trial judge is faced with the situation which arises here, he should of course consult counsel in the absence of the jury before taking any final decision, but having done that, he ought to consider whether on the whole, more harm to the defence would be done by giving the accomplice direction than by not *d* giving it, and if he comes to the conclusion that on the whole more harm would be done in that way, then it is no irregularity on his part in the conduct of the trial if he decides not to give the accomplice direction. It may still, of course, be possible to attack a conviction thus obtained on other general grounds, that it was unsafe or unsatisfactory, but we do not regard the judge as committing an irregularity for the purposes of the Criminal Appeal Act 1968 if, having considered both aspects of the *e* alleged accomplice evidence, he comes to the conclusion on balance that more harm would be done by giving the direction than by refraining from giving it. It follows that if he comes to that conclusion with the active encouragement of counsel for the defence, the more clear is it that no irregularity has taken place. We have come to the conclusion that the only point taken in this case on the appeal against conviction is not upheld, and accordingly the appeal against conviction is dismissed. *f*

This man did not appeal against his sentence, the reason being that he was advised, and no doubt rightly advised, that, against the background of his prior criminal record, it was not really easy to contend that a sentence of 18 months imprisonment was in any way out of scale with his case. However, the case has taken an unusual turn; there has been a very considerable delay and additional anxiety resting on him owing to the difficulties of obtaining the transcript to which I have already referred. We *g* think that on the whole justice might be done if, having served the equivalent of 12 months imprisonment, the appellant is not required to return to prison. In order to achieve that result it is necessary first of all for him to apply for leave to appeal against sentence; that has been done by counsel for the appellant this morning. The court then gives him an extension of time in which to appeal against sentence and then gives him leave to appeal against sentence, and having treated this application *h* as the hearing of the ultimate substantive appeal, the court allows the appeal against sentence to the extent of reducing the sentence to such a term as will enable him to return home today and not go back to prison.

Appeal against conviction dismissed. Leave to appeal against sentence; appeal allowed; sentence varied. *j*

Solicitors: *Williams & Co*, Dunstable (for the appellant); *Clayton & Co*, Luton (for the Crown).

N P Metcalfe Esq Barrister.

Cuzner (formerly Underdown) v Underdown

COURT OF APPEAL, CIVIL DIVISION
DAVIES LJ AND WALTON J
23rd MAY 1973

Divorce – Financial provision – Conduct of parties – Duty of court to have regard to conduct – Circumstances in which regard should be had to conduct – Conduct obvious and gross – Party wholly responsible for breakdown of marriage – Matrimonial home conveyed in joint names – House entirely paid for by husband – Wife accepting half share in house while unknown to husband having adulterous relationship – Wife solely to blame for breakdown of marriage – Husband entitled to transfer of wife's share in house.

The parties were married in August 1958 and had three children, born between 1959 and 1965. Until 1962 the wife worked full-time earning between £7·50 and £10 a week. Thereafter she worked part-time and never earned more than £5 a week. The money which she earned was spent for her own purposes and on extra clothes for the children. In 1964 the husband bought the council house in which they were living. The wife made no financial contribution to that purchase. In 1969 they decided to sell the house and buy a larger one. The husband paid the deposit on the new house and all the charges including mortgage payments were paid by him. It was intended that the house should be conveyed into the husband's name alone but he was advised that it might be advantageous from the point of view of estate duty for the house to be conveyed into the joint names of himself and the wife. On 2nd May 1970, six days before the transfer was due to take place, the wife admitted to the husband that since about Christmas 1969, when the move to the new house was in contemplation, she had been committing adultery with the co-respondent. Despite her confession the husband did not want her to leave him and on 8th May the new house was conveyed into their joint names. However, six weeks after they moved into the new house, the wife left. The husband subsequently divorced her on the ground of her adultery and the wife married the co-respondent. The wife applied under s 17 of the Married Women's Property Act 1882 for a declaration that the house was jointly owned by the husband and herself and for an order that it be sold and the proceeds divided equally between them. The judge found that the wife had been entirely to blame for the breakdown of the marriage. He refused her application and made an order under s 4 of the Matrimonial Proceedings and Property 1970 that her interest in the property be transferred to the husband. The wife appealed.

Held – The conduct of the wife in taking a half share of the house while she was committing adultery with the co-respondent was 'obvious and gross' misconduct and, even allowing for the fact that she had brought up the children and that a portion of her earnings had been used in the home, it would not be just that she should have a share in it, particularly (per Walton J) in view of the finding that she was entirely to blame for the breakdown of the marriage. The appeal would therefore be dismissed (see p 354 *f* to *j* and p 355 *b* to *g*, post).

Notes
For financial provision on granting a decree of divorce and the matters to be considered by the court in exercising its powers, see Supplement to 12 Halsbury's Laws (3rd Edn) para 987A, 1-4.

For the Married Women's Property Act 1882, s 17, see 17 Halsbury's Statutes (3rd Edn) 120.

For the Matrimonial Proceedings and Property Act 1970, s 4, see 40 Halsbury's Statutes (3rd Edn) 802. As from 1st January 1974, s 4 of the 1970 Act has been replaced by the Matrimonial Causes Act 1973, s 24.

Cases referred to in judgments
Wachtel v Wachtel [1973] 1 All ER 829, [1973] Fam 72, [1973] 2 WLR 366, CA.
White v White and King (1972) 116 Sol Jo 219, CA.

Cases also cited
Mesher v Mesher [1973] The Times, 13th February, [1973] Bar Library transcript 59, CA.
Trippas v Trippas [1973] 2 All ER 1, [1973] Fam 134, [1973] 2 WLR 585, CA.

Appeal
The wife, Shirley Ann Cuzner (formerly Underdown), and the husband, Derrick
Reginald Underdown, were married on 5th August 1958. They had three children,
born between 1959 and 1965. The parties first lived at 166 Berry Green Road, Cheshunt, which was a council house of which the husband was the tenant. In 1964 the
husband bought the house from the council and it was transferred into his sole name.
The wife made no direct contributions to the purchase money or the mortgage
repayments. The husband paid all the outgoings of the house. The wife worked
full-time until 1962, earning between £7·50 and £10 a week. Thereafter she worked
part-time until 1969, never earning more than £5 a week. She did not save any of
those earnings for family purposes, but used them for her own purposes and for extra
clothes for the children. In 1969 the parties decided to move to a larger house and the
husband signed a contract in his own name for the purchase of 30 Bellamy Road,
Cheshunt. His solicitor, however, advised him that the home should be conveyed
into the joint names of himself and the wife so that, in the event of his predeceasing
the wife, she would be protected in her occupation. The husband explained that
to the wife and she signed the necessary documents for the house to be transferred
into their joint names. Unknown to the husband, however, the wife had formed
an association with the co-respondent. Shortly before Christmas 1969 the wife
and the co-respondent committed adultery and continued to do so thereafter. The
husband learnt of the wife's relationship with the co-respondent on 2nd May 1970,
six days before they were due to move into the new house. The wife was initially
undecided whether to stay with the husband but, two days after the original disclosure, she said that she would stay with him and would move with the children
to the new house. Accordingly on 8th May they moved and 30 Bellamy Road
was transferred into their joint names by a formal document of transfer. Six weeks
later the wife left the husband taking the children with her, and went to live with the
co-respondent. The eldest child subsequently returned to live with the husband.
   On 3rd December 1970 the husband filed a petition for divorce on the ground of the
wife's adultery. The suit was undefended and the husband was granted a decree nisi
which was made absolute on 30th March 1972. The husband applied for an order,
under s 4 of the Matrimonial Proceedings and Property Act 1970, that the wife transfer
her interest in 30 Bellamy Road to him or, alternatively, that she should settle her
interest for the benefit of the children. The wife applied under s 17 of the Married
Women's Property Act 1882 for a declaration that 30 Bellamy Road was owned jointly
by the husband and wife and for an order that the property be sold and the proceeds
of sale divided between them. By an order dated 1st March 1973 Dunn J dismissed
the wife's application and granted that of the husband, ordering that the wife transfer
all her interest in 30 Bellamy Road to the husband absolutely. The wife appealed.

Paul Focke for the wife.
Mathew Thorpe for the husband.

DAVIES LJ. This is an appeal by a wife, who was the respondent in the main suit,
from an order made by Dunn J on 1st March 1973. It is to be observed that the learned

a   judge gave leave to appeal to the wife, as I shall call her. Her application was with regard to what had been the last matrimonial home, 30 Bellamy Road, Cheshunt, though for only a short time, some six weeks, did they live there together. The house was in joint names, in circumstances which I shall explain in a moment. The wife applied under s 17 of the Married Women's Property Act 1882 for a declaration that the house was jointly owned and for an order for its sale and for the proceeds to be

b   equally divided. The judge refused to accede to that application and on the contrary made an order against her to transfer to the husband her interest in the property.

    The parties were married in August 1958, and have had three children. The parties were very young when they were married, 18 and 16. There is a daughter aged 14 who is now living with the husband; and another daughter, aged nine, and a son, aged eight, now living with the wife. Originally (I do not quite know when) they lived in a

c   rented council house, of which the husband was the tenant. In 1964 he bought the house from the council. It is to be observed that the wife made no contribution to the purchase of the house, either to the deposit or in the nature of payments of the mortgage interest. In 1969 they were going to move to a bigger and better house, the one that I mentioned just now, 30 Bellamy Road. They sold the ex-council house, and that sale produced, after the payment of all encumbrances, a total sum of £1,950.

d   I come now to the purchase of 30 Bellamy Road. The deposit in respect of that house was paid by the husband, and all charges have been paid by him. We were told that the monthly mortgage payments amount to some £35. The documents originally were all going to be in the husband's name, but apparently, after some discussion with his solicitor, he was advised that it might be advantageous, from the point of view of estate duty, to have it conveyed into joint names; and on 8th May 1970

e   the house was transferred to these two people in their joint names.

    But something else had been happening behind the scenes. Apparently round about Christmas 1969, when the move to this house was in contemplation, the wife started to have an adulterous affair with the man who subsequently became the co-respondent. Six days before the transfer of the house, namely, on 2nd May 1970, they had been celebrating the birthday of the daughter Deborah, and as a result of an incident

f   that took place then the wife admitted to her husband that she had been committing adultery behind his back with the co-respondent for some five months from round about Christmas. Six days later, on 8th May, they moved into the house and lived there only about six weeks when the wife left. The husband at first apparently did not believe the wife when she told him that she had committed adultery and despite her confession did not want her to go; he tried to persuade her to stay. But she went.

g   Now he is living in the house—the matrimonial home as it was for this short period— with the eldest child and a Mrs Peacock, whom he wishes to marry and who has a daughter some 14 years old. He earns about £1,800 a year.

    The two younger children are with their mother living in a maisonette, also at Cheshunt, 154 Bury Green Road, which is in the joint names of the co-respondent and his former wife. That apparently is to be sold and the proceeds divided equally

h   between the co-respondent and his former wife, which might fetch him some £3,000. They have only two bedrooms there, and the accommodation is insufficient because, in addition to these two children, the wife has another child by the co-respondent.

    The reasons for the proposal of the wife that the house should be sold and that the proceeds should be equally divided between the parties are clearly stated in the judgment, and I think that, although it is a longish passage, I should read it. It forms part

j   of a very full and clear judgment of Dunn J:

    'The wife and the two younger children and the co-respondent and a baby born to the wife by the co-respondent in May 1971, are living at 154 Bury Green Road, Cheshunt. This is a two-bedroomed [maisonette], and all three children have to share a bedroom. It is owned jointly by the co-respondent and his former wife who has divorced him, the co-respondent having remarried the wife. It had

apparently been agreed between the co-respondent and his wife that 154 Bury   *a*
Green Road should be sold and the proceeds of sale split equally between them.
The wife in this case says that the equity in that [maisonette] is about £6,000, so
that if and when the [maisonette] is sold, the co-respondent will receive about
£3,000. She says that a new house large enough for the co-respondent, herself
and the three children, will cost about £13,000. The co-respondent earns about
£2,000 a year; he is an engineer. So on the basis that he would not be able to   *b*
obtain a mortgage in excess of three times his annual income, the maximum
mortgage which he could obtain would be about £6,000. So that if the £3,000,
his share of the proceeds of sale of 154 Bury Green Road, is added to that, there is
still a shortfall of some £4,000 to enable the co-respondent and the wife to buy a
suitable house for £13,000. Therefore, the wife asks that 30 Bellamy Road should
be sold and that her half-share should be paid out of the proceeds. The value of 30   *c*
Bellamy Road, I was told, is between £13,000 and £14,000. The husband said that
a house opposite had been sold for £13,000, and I prefer the lower figure. There is
outstanding still a first mortgage of about £4,400, and a second mortgage of
somewhere about £600 which was raised in order that central heating should be
put in, so that the total mortgage is about £5,000. Therefore, the equity in that
house if it were sold is about £8,000, and if the house were sold and each of the   *d*
parties were to receive his and her half share, which is what the wife asks, each
would receive something under £4,000 when the normal legal and other charges
are deducted. The wife says that this would be sufficient for her to enable her and
the co-respondent to buy the larger house . . .'

But, as the judge goes on to point out, if that were done the husband (a) would be
deprived of the use and occupation of the former matrimonial home, which he, so far   *e*
as money is concerned, entirely paid for, and (b) would, in all the circumstances,
probably have insufficient money to arrange to acquire a house suitable for himself,
Mrs Peacock, her daughter and his own eldest daughter.

I do not think that I need refer in detail to the submissions made in the notice of
appeal and so clearly argued and presented in this court by learned counsel for the
wife. I confess that, despite the authorities, with which we are very familiar and to   *f*
which we have been referred this morning, the wife's proposition is an astonishing
one. Even allowing for the fact that this wife brought up the children and for some
years was earning £10 a week and subsequently £5 a week and, no doubt, using it to
some extent in the home, considering that the half share in this house was transferred
to her when she was actually carrying on this clandestine association with the co-
respondent, it is really quite amazing to me, despite the fundamental changes in the   *g*
law that have been made by recent legislation, that she should now seek to have half
the beneficial interest in it.

As the wife admitted and the husband said before the learned judge, it is quite
certain that if the husband had known at the time when this house was acquired that
she was committing adultery with the co-respondent, the house would never have
been put into joint names; it would have been put into the husband's name. I   *h*
suppose learned counsel would say: well, even if that were so, it would not have
stopped her coming along and asking for a half share or some share in the house. That
is no doubt true. But here is the case of a house entirely paid for by the husband, and
transferred into joint names simply with the idea that that transfer would advantage
the wife in some respect in the future when they had no doubt been looking forward
to living in the house for the rest of their lives so far as could be reasonably foreseen.   *j*
I think that this application by the wife was almost an impudent application. What
she was doing was seeking to turn the husband out of this house so that she might have
some share of it in order to contribute to the purchase of a house for herself and the
co-respondent. Under the Matrimonial Proceedings and Property Act 1970 the court
has to do, insofar as it can, what is just. I cannot see any justice in such an order as
is asked for by the wife in the present case.

It is a short point. It was very fully dealt with by the learned judge. He referred among other cases to *White v White and King*[1]. There are, as the learned judge says, certain distinctions between *White v White and King*[1] and the present case. But, apart from two matters, namely, that the co-respondent's house in that case provided better accommodation and that the only child of the marriage was with the husband, that case is extraordinarily close to the present one. I do not think it is necessary for me to repeat the quotation which the judge made from the judgment of Lord Denning MR in *White v White and King*[1], but it seems to me that this case is very close indeed to it. Following the observations that Lord Denning MR made in that case I think that it would be quite wrong that the husband should be turned out of the house which he himself has provided in this case. In relation to *Wachtel v Wachtel*[2] (to which, of course, we were referred once more) the learned judge took the view that in this case, though conduct, as we all know, does not often matter now, the wife's conduct in taking a half share in the house while she was committing adultery with the co-respondent was, within the words that Lord Denning MR used in that case, 'obvious and gross' misconduct. For myself, I would not dream of interfering with the learned judge's order, which I think, in all the circumstances, was the only right and proper one.

WALTON J. I entirely agree with everything that has fallen from Davies LJ. Like Davies LJ, I think that the judgment of Dunn J is absolutely impeccable. I would only add one word in regard to *Wachtel v Wachtel*[2] and that is this. The general principles which are there enunciated—and they are only general principles—are principles which govern the normal situation in 99 per cent of divorce cases; that is to say, cases in which some blame can be attached to both parties for the breakdown of the marriage. To my mind, it is an important point here that the whole of the blame was placed by the learned judge on the wife. He said:

'It is true that in many cases when a marriage breaks down both parties have contributed to that breakdown, but it is remarkable in this case that no allegation of any kind has been made against the conduct of the husband.'

Pausing there, that *is* a most remarkable circumstance. The learned judge went on:

'In my judgment, this marriage broke down entirely because of the wife's adultery with the co-respondent and because of her subsequent desertion without just cause or excuse.'

In the light of that finding, like Davies LJ, I think that the wife's proposals in this matter are impudent.

I would dismiss this appeal.

Appeal dismissed.

Solicitors: *Batchelor Street Longstaffe*, agents for *Smith & Harrison*, Waltham Cross, Herts (for the wife); *H E Aston & Co* (for the husband).

Mary Rose Plummer   Barrister.

1   (1972) 116 Sol Jo 219
2   [1973] 1 All ER 829, [1973] Fam 72

R v Oxford City Justices, ex parte H

QUEEN'S BENCH DIVISION

LORD WIDGERY CJ, BRIDGE AND BAGNALL JJ

15th MARCH 1974

Child – Care – Local authority – Assumption by authority of parental rights – Illegitimate child – Custody – Right of putative father – Authority having assumed parental rights of mother – Application by putative father for custody of child – Whether justices having jurisdiction to entertain application – Children Act 1948, s 2(1) – Guardianship of Minors Act 1971, ss 9(1), 14(1).

A local authority passed a resolution under s 2 (1)(b)[a] of the Children Act 1948 in respect of an illegitimate child in their care on the ground that it appeared to them that the child's mother, who suffered from mental illness, was incapable of caring for the child. The effect of the resolution was that the parental rights of the mother vested in the authority. The putative father of the child sought to issue a complaint before the justices addressed to the mother asking for an order under ss 9(1)[b] and 14(1)[c] of the Guardianship of Minors Act 1971 that the custody of the child be committed to him. The justices held that, in view of the resolution passed by the local authority, they had no jurisdiction to entertain the complaint. The father applied for an order of mandamus against the justices.

Held – The parental rights which the local authority had assumed were the parental rights of the mother; the resolution left the parental rights of the putative father, and in particular his rights under the 1971 Act, entirely untouched. Accordingly the justices not only had jurisdiction to hear the father's complaint but ought to do so, having in mind as the first and paramount consideration the welfare of the child in the light of all the relevant circumstances, including the existence of the authority's resolution and the scheme of the 1948 Act. An order of mandamus should be granted accordingly (see p 360 g and j to p 361 c, post).

Re K (an infant) [1972] 3 All ER 769 explained.

Notes

For assumption of parental rights by a local authority, see 21 Halsbury's Laws (3rd Edn) 277-279, paras 592-594, and for cases on the subject, see 28(2) Digest (Reissue) 942, 943, 2440, 2441.

For the custody of illegitimate children, see 1 Halsbury's Laws (4th Edn) 348, para 613, and for cases on the subject, see 3 Digest (Repl) 432-434, 268-287.

For the Children Act 1948, s 2, see 17 Halsbury's Statutes (3rd Edn) 542.

For the Guardianship of Minors Act 1971, ss 9 and 14, see 41 Halsbury's Statutes (3rd Edn) 766, 771.

Cases referred to in judgment

K (an infant), Re, M (an infant), Re, Hertfordshire County Council v H [1972] 3 All ER 769, 70 LGR 560, DC.

M (an infant), Re [1961] 1 All ER 788, [1961] Ch 328, [1961] 2 WLR 350, 125 JP 278, CA, 28(2) Digest (Reissue) 940, 2433.

---

a   Section 2(1) is set out at p 357 f and g, post
b   Section 9(1) is set out at p 358 d, post
c   Section 14(1) is set out at p 358 e, post

Motion for mandamus

This was an application by way of motion for an order of mandamus directed to the respondents, the Oxford City Justices, requiring them to issue a summons under ss 9(1) and 14(1) of the Guardianship of Minors Act 1971 to determine the issue of the custody of the applicant's daughter, who was in the care of the Royal Borough of Kensington and Chelsea ('the local authority'). The grounds of the application were that the respondent justices had erred in law in holding that the resolution passed by the local authority inder s 2(1)(b) of the Children Act 1948, vesting parental rights in respect of the daughter in the local authority, precluded the applicant from proceeding under the 1971 Act. The facts are set out in the judgment of Bagnall J.

C F Fletcher-Cooke QC and *David MacKenzie Ross* for the applicant.
Gordon Slynn as amicus curiae.
The respondent justices and the local authority did not appear and were not represented.

BAGNALL J delivered the first judgment at the invitation of Lord Widgery CJ. Counsel moves on behalf of the applicant for an order of mandamus to issue to the justices of the city of Oxford. The applicant seeks that order to enjoin those justices, in effect, to hear the complaint which he seeks to make as the father of an illegitimate child for an order that the custody of that child be committed to him under the Guardianship of Minors Act 1971.

The mother of the child regrettably suffers from a mental illness and because of that the council of the Royal Borough of Kensington and Chelsea passed an appropriate resolution in exercise of their powers under the Children Act 1948 whereby certain parental rights in respect of the child were committed to them.

The relevant sections of the 1948 Act are few and I should refer to them. Section 2(1) of the Children Act 1948 is in the following terms:

> 'Subject to the provisions of this Part of this Act, a local authority may resolve with respect to any child in their care under the foregoing section [and I interpose that the child in question was in such care at the relevant time] in whose case it appears to them—(a) that his parents are dead and that he has no guardian; or (b) that a parent of guardian of his (hereinafter referred to as the person on whose account the resolution was passed) has abandoned him or suffers from some permanent disability rendering the said person incapable of caring for the child, or is of such habits or mode of life as to be unfit to have the care of the child, that all the rights and powers which the deceased parents would have if they were still living, or, as the case may be, all the rights and powers of the person on whose account the resolution was passed, shall vest in the local authority.'

It was such a resolution which the council of the royal borough passed in the instant case. There follow in s 2(2) powers designed to give the person described as the person on whose account the resolution was passed certain rights of protest, and in the last resort of invoking the jurisdiction of the juvenile court on the question whether the resolution so passed should remain in force.

By s 4(1) it is provided:

> 'Subject to the provisions of this Part of this Act, a resolution under section two of this Act shall continue in force until the child with respect to whom it was passed attains the age of eighteen.'

Section 4(2) empowers the local authority to rescind the existing resolution by a subsequent resolution, and s 4(3) gives power, in the circumstances relevant in this case, to the person on whose account the resolution was passed once more to invoke the jurisdiction of the juvenile court to determine whether the resolution should continue in effect.

By s 59 of the 1948 Act, which is a definition section, it is made clear that the expression 'parent' in relation to a child who is illegitimate means his mother, to the exclusion of his father.

It will be observed from those sections that a resolution may be passed, for example, because one parent suffers from a permanent disability, notwithstanding the situation of the other parent, and that the parental rights which vest in the local authority are those rights of the person on whose account the resolution was passed. Section 2 and the subsequent sections have no impact on a parent not being the parent on whose account the resolution was passed.

The Guardianship of Minors Act 1971, the provisions of which are sought to be invoked in the present case, by s 9(1) provides as follows:

> 'The court may, on the application of the mother or father of a minor (who may apply without next friend), make such order regarding—(a) the custody of the minor; and (b) the right of access to the minor of his mother or father, as the court thinks fit having regard to the welfare of the minor and to the conduct and wishes of the mother and father.'

By s 14(1) it is provided, re-enacting legislation contained in the Legitimacy Act 1959, as follows:

> 'Subject to the provisions of this section, subsection (1) of section 9 of this Act shall apply in relation to a minor who is illegitimate as it applies in relation to a minor who is legitimate, and references in that subsection, and in any other provision of this Act so far as it relates to proceedings under that subsection, to the father or mother or parent of a minor shall be construed accordingly.'

Section 14(3), so far as material, is in the following terms:

> 'For the purposes of section ... 5 ... of this Act, a person being the natural father of an illegitimate child and being entitled to his custody by virtue of an order in force under section 9 of this Act, as applied by this section, shall be treated as if he were the lawful father of the minor ...'

Finally s 5 provides:

> '(1) Where a minor has no parent, no guardian of the person, and no other person having parental rights with respect to him, the court, on the application of any person, may, if it thinks fit, appoint the applicant to be the guardian of the minor.
>
> '(2) A court may entertain an application under this section to appoint a guardian of a minor notwithstanding that, by virtue of a resolution under section 2 of the Children Act 1948, a local authority have parental rights with respect to him; but where on such an application the court appoints a guardian the resolution shall cease to have effect.'

Two observations may be made on those sections. First, whereas under the Children Act 1948 the father of an illegitimate child is not, and is not to be treated as, a parent of that child, yet for purposes of applications for custody under the 1971 Act, the father of an illegitimate child has, in effect, all the rights of the father of a legitimate child. Secondly, whereas the appointment of a guardian under s 5 of that Act is seen to be inconsistent with the continuance of parental rights in a local authority, no such inconsistency is seen in s 9 of the Act because there is no reference, as there is in s 5, to the effect of an order for custody on an existing resolution under the 1948 Act.

a Armed with the power conferred by the 1971 Act the applicant sought to issue a complaint before the justices addressed to the mother asking for an order for custody. The justices decided that they had no jurisdiction to entertain the complaint, and, after an abortive attempt to appeal that decision to a Divisional Court of the Family Division, the applicant now moves for his order of mandamus in this court.

b The justices felt that they were constrained to reach their decision refusing jurisdiction by a decision of a Divisional Court of the Family Division, in *Re K (an infant)*, *Re M (an infant)*, *Hertfordshire County Council v H*[1]. The headnote in that case is in the following terms[2]:

c 'In March 1971, with the consent of the mother, a local authority made an order under s 2(1)(*b*) of the Children Act 1948, vesting in themselves the rights and powers of the mother in respect of her two illegitimate children. In June of the same year, H, the putative father, applied to the justices under ss 9(1) and 14(1) of the Guardianship of Minors Act 1971 for an order granting him access to the children. About a month later, the justices, having heard the application, granted him reasonable access to the infants by appointment but no taking out access. The local authority appealed, contending that while they had no objection to the father having access, the discretion to grant access was

d theirs and not that of the court. *Held* – While H, as the putative father, had a right under ss 9(1) and 14(1) of the 1971 Act to make an application to the justices for an order granting access, the fact that at the material time the local authority had already assumed parental rights by virtue of an order under s 2(1)(*b*) of the Children Act 1948, left the justices no alternative but to decline the application and leave the discretion with regard to access to the local authority; accordingly

e the appeal would be allowed and the order of the justices rescinded.'

The ratio decidendi of the decision of the Divisional Court is to be found in a passage[3] at the end of the judgment of Payne J. After referring to a decision in *Re M*[4] in the Court of Appeal in which that court had considered in relation to the inherent wardship jurisdiction a possible conflict between the exercise of powers under the Children

f Act 1948 by a local authority and the inherent jurisdiction of the court, Payne J[3] cited a passage from the judgment of Lord Evershed MR[5] in these terms:

'What then is the effect of this statute to which I have made such references as occur to me to be necessary? [That was of course the Children Act 1948.] I think that the effect may be stated in two propositions. First, the enactment is such that in a case like the present there is in the Act a clear and comprehensive

g scheme laid down, (what LORD SUMNER called a modus operandi[6]) involving positive duties imposed by Parliament on the local authority and a precise formulation of the way in which the consequent powers are to be exercised, and, secondly, that as regards these duties and powers the discretion is conferred on the authority by the words—"appears to them"—which have occurred in the citations that I have made ... On those premises, that is to say in the absence

h of any challenge as to the propriety of what the local authority or its officers have done as distinct from their wisdom, I feel compelled, by the clear indication of the language to which I have alluded in the statute, to conclude that this matter of judging the present best interests of the child in the circumstances

---

j 1 [1972] 3 All ER 769
2 [1972] 3 All ER at 769
3 [1972] 3 All ER at 772
4 [1961] 1 All ER 788, [1961] Ch 328
5 [1961] 1 All ER at 792, 793, [1961] Ch at 341, 342
6 In *Attorney-General v De Keyser's Royal Hotel Ltd* [1920] AC 508 at 561, [1920] All ER Rep 80 at 103

of this case has been placed by Parliament in the exclusive jurisdiction of the local authority.'

It is apparent from that citation that the Court of Appeal concluded that the statute did not oust the inherent jurisdiction of the court over its wards but that that jurisdiction had to be exercised consistently with what Lord Evershed MR called the scheme or modus operandi of the statute.

After that citation Payne J went on as follows[1]:

'Speaking for myself, that is the way in which I would approach the present case. There is no challenge to the propriety of what the local authority have done. Their resolution was passed under s 2 with the concurrence of the mother, and, although the father of the illegitimate child has the right given him by the Guardianship of Minors Act 1971 to apply to the court for an order for custody or access, the court must then apply s 9 under which it may, on the application of the father or mother, make such order as the court thinks fit. Bearing in mind the existence of the order under s 2 of the Children Act 1948, it seems to me that the justices in the circumstances of this case had no alternative but to decline the application of the father and to leave the discretion with regard to access to the local authority. It may be—argument has been addressed to us on this basis—that one could go further and say that the justices had no power to make an order on such an application in any event. For myself I would prefer to leave that second limb of the argument until some later occasion, should it arise, when full argument on both sides may be addressed to the court.'

It is to be observed that the attitude which the justices in the present case had taken is to answer what Payne J called the second limb of the argument in the affirmative. But in that case itself it seems to me to be clear that the Divisional Court held that there was jurisdiction but that the jurisdiction had to be exercised in the light of the statutory scheme contained in the 1948 Act, and that when Payne J observed that the justices had no alternative but to decline the application in front of them, his reference to no alternative existing in the circumstances of that case was consistent only with a view that the justices had jurisdiction to determine the case but had to take all circumstances, including the statute, into account.

I think that that was a right view for this reason, that relating the statute to the facts of the present case the parental rights which the local authority has assumed are the parental rights of the mother, the person on whose account the resolution was passed, leaving entirely untouched the parental rights of the father, in this case the putative father, and in particular his rights under the 1971 Act.

I am fortified in that view first by the absence of any reference in s 9 of that Act to a 1948 Act resolution in contradistinction to the reference to such a resolution in s 5, indicating that the existence of such a resolution would not be inconsistent with the exercise of the jurisdiction under s 9. I am no less fortified in that conclusion by the very helpful arguments which counsel presented to us, for which I am indebted, in his capacity as amicus curiae, indicating that for his part he could not advance any argument why in this particular case the order sought on behalf of the applicant should not be made.

In my judgment the justices have jurisdiction to hear the case and I would only add this; that Re K[2] in the Divisional Court of the Family Division, from which I have cited, was concerned only with access, a matter which must necessarily be under the day-to-day and continuing control and discretion of the local authority. It may well be that a question of custody falls within a quite different category, though I am anxious to express no opinion of my own on it.

1   [1972] 3 All ER at 772
2   [1972] 3 All ER 769

I think that the justices ought to hear the complaint, and, as in every other case concerning the custody and upbringing of minors, ought to determine it having in their minds as the first and paramount consideration the welfare of the minor, but looking at the welfare of the minor in the light of all relevant circumstances including the existence of the resolution and the scheme of the 1948 Act. In my view the order should be granted.

BRIDGE J. I find myself in complete agreement not only with the conclusion expressed in the judgment just delivered but also with its reasoning, and I would only add that I have great sympathy with the justices and the course which they took here in a difficult field of matrimonial law.

LORD WIDGERY CJ. I also agree. Accordingly the order of mandamus will go directing the justices to hear and determine the application.

Order accordingly.

Solicitors: *Field, Fisher & Martineau*, agents for *Sims & Co*, Oxford (for the applicant); *Treasury Solicitor.*

N P Metcalfe Esq   Barrister.

Rogers v Rogers

COURT OF APPEAL, CIVIL DIVISION
DAVIES LJ AND SIR GORDON WILLMER
15th FEBRUARY 1974

Divorce – Practice – Pleading – Time – Leave to file answer out of time – Conduct – Relevance of conduct in main suit – Leave to file answer containing cross-prayer alleging desertion and adultery – Petition by wife alleging intolerable behaviour – Acknowledgment by husband that he would defend suit and oppose applications for ancillary relief – Delay in filing answer caused by attempted reconciliation by husband and time taken to obtain sufficient evidence of adultery – Husband applying for leave to file answer – Application supported by affidavit exhibiting draft answer – Refusal of application liable to prejudice husband in ancillary proceedings and in relation to costs of main suit.

The husband and wife were married in July 1967 and had a child shortly afterwards. In January 1973, after some trouble between them, the wife left the husband and petitioned for divorce alleging that the husband had behaved in such a way that she could not reasonably be expected to live with him. The husband acknowledged service of the petition and indicated his intention to defend the suit and oppose the wife's applications for ancillary relief. During the next six months the husband made attempts to achieve a reconciliation with the wife. Meanwhile he lodged an application for a legal aid certificate to defend the suit. After some correspondence the legal aid authorities refused the application. On 31st August the petition was set down for hearing on 7th December. The husband had meanwhile failed to file his answer. However, he suspected that the wife had been committing adultery for some time and on 15th and 20th November he obtained satisfactory evidence of her adultery. Therefore, on 7th December, he applied for leave to file an answer out of time. The application was supported by an affidavit sworn by the husband relating to the merits of the application and exhibiting a draft answer which denied the allegations concerning his behaviour and contained a cross-prayer based on allegations of desertion and adultery on the part of the wife. The judge refused the application on the ground that questions of conduct were irrelevant in the main suit and could be investigated in the ancillary proceedings.

Held – Although conduct was generally irrelevant, it was not irrelevant in every case; each case had to be considered on its own individual facts. In the circumstances the husband's application should be allowed since he had indicated in his acknowledgment of service that he intended to defend and, although he had not done very much since then, the evidence to support his allegation of adultery had only come to hand shortly before the hearing; furthermore, if the suit were allowed to proceed undefended he would be estopped from denying in the ancillary proceedings the allegations concerning his behaviour and he would not be able to avoid an order to pay the costs of the suit. Accordingly the appeal would be allowed (see p 363 h and p 364 a to f, post).

Collins v Collins [1972] 2 All ER 658 and Spill v Spill [1972] 3 All ER 9 distinguished.

Dictum of Lord Denning MR in Wachtel v Wachtel [1973] 1 All ER at 835, 836 explained.

Note
For the time for filing and delivery of an answer, see 12 Halsbury's Laws (3rd Edn) 338, 339, para 703.

Cases referred to in judgments
Collins v Collins [1972] 2 All ER 658, [1972] 1 WLR 689, CA.
Spill v Spill [1972] 3 All ER 9, [1972] 1 WLR 793, CA.
Wachtel v Wachtel [1973] 1 All ER 829, [1973] Fam 72, [1973] 2 WLR 366, CA.

Case also cited
Huxford v Huxford [1972] 1 All ER 330, [1972] 1 WLR 210.

Interlocutory appeal
The husband, John Leslie Rogers, appealed against an order of his Honour Judge Ifor Lloyd QC made on 7th December 1973 refusing his application for leave to file out of time an answer to the petition by the wife, Dorothy Margaret Rogers, for a decree of divorce. The facts are set out in the judgment of Davies LJ.

T A C Coningsby for the husband.
Henry Palmer for the wife.

DAVIES LJ. This is an appeal by a respondent husband from an order made by his Honour Judge Ifor Lloyd on 7th December 1973, when he refused an application made on behalf of the husband to file an answer out of time. The facts are very short. The parties were married in July 1967 and had a child very shortly afterwards. In January 1973 the wife left, after trouble between them. Her departure was swiftly followed by her petition, dated 26th January 1973, alleging the breakdown of the marriage owing to intolerable conduct on the part of the husband. The husband went to solicitors, and on 26th February they filed an acknowledgment of service, indicating the husband's intention to defend the suit and also to oppose her applications on all the ancillary matters referred to in the form. According to an affidavit which was not before the learned judge but of which the substance, we are told, was communicated to him by learned counsel for the husband, he was attempting during the next six months to achieve a reconciliation with his wife. Meanwhile an application was made by solicitors on his behalf for a legal aid certificate, and after some correspondence that was eventually turned down by the local committee (in Cambridge, I think) and in a turning it down they said that the observations made by this court in the well-known case of *Wachtel v Wachtel*[1] in effect prevented them from granting a legal aid certificate.

Nothing more was done. It is suggested by counsel for the wife that the husband could have appealed to the area committee, or indeed he could have appeared in person, though I can see difficulties about the latter course. So the husband did nothing more in the proceedings and on 31st August the case was set down; and, of course, according to the rules even though he was out of strict time in filing an answer he

b could nevertheless have filed an answer up until that date. Nothing was done then, and the hearing was fixed for 7th December, the date on which the learned judge made this order.

The husband had had his suspicions for some time that his wife was associating with a man or men and eventually, according to the evidence now filed on his behalf, on 15th and 20th November he obtained satisfactory evidence to show that his wife

c was indeed committing adultery. That being so, the application was made to Judge Lloyd.

Among the authorities cited to us was a case in this court, *Spill v Spill*[2], which indicated that in support of an application of this kind there should be a satisfactory explanation of the husband's change of mind (in that case he had not indicated an intention to defend in the first instance whereas of course this man had); the husband had

d not sworn an affidavit relating to the merits of his application (in the present case we have such an affidavit); nor was there a draft answer before the court (in the present case we have a draft answer exhibited). It seems to me that, quite apart from what counsel has told us, the husband here has got his tackle in proper order. The draft answer contains a denial of intolerable conduct; it contains an allegation of desertion; and, perhaps more importantly, it contains an allegation of adultery.

e As I have said, when the matter was before the legal aid authorities there was no suggestion of any cross-prayer but merely an indication that the husband was defending the charge of intolerable conduct. Before the county court, however, as I have just indicated, there was the draft answer, which contained, in addition to the husband's denial, this allegation of adultery. When the matter came before Judge

f Lloyd the case was argued by counsel on both sides, and the judge, like the legal aid authorities, took the view, in the light of the decision in *Wachtel v Watchtel*[1] that conduct was irrelevant, that whoever was right and whoever was wrong about the intolerable conduct made no difference and, it would appear, whether adultery against the wife was proved would make no difference either. The passage on which, it would appear, both the legal aid authorities and the learned judge relied was in *Wachtel v Wachtel*[3]. It is so well known and has been discussed so often that I do

g not think it necessary to read it. In effect, what Lord Denning MR was saying was that, in the light of the change in the law on a main suit, allegations of conduct or misconduct were really irrelevant and that those matters could be investigated in ancillary proceedings. But I do not think that Lord Denning MR could possibly have meant that in any and every case conduct was quite irrelevant unless (to use his words) it was 'obvious and gross'. I think he could not have meant that in the light of the

h wording of s 5(1) of the Matrimonial Proceedings and Property Act 1970, which expressly provides, in the last few lines of the section, after sub-paras (a) to (g), dealing with ancillary proceedings:

'... and so to exercise those powers as to place the parties, so far as it is practicable and, having regard to their conduct, just to do so ...'

j And it does seem to me that in ancillary proceedings it is right that by and large the court should, in the words of the statute, have regard to their conduct.

---

1   [1973] 1 All ER 829, [1973] Fam 72
2   [1972] 3 All ER 9, [1972] 1 WLR 793
3   [1973] 1 All ER at 835, 836, [1973] Fam at 90

It is pointed out by counsel for the husband, quite apart from the cross-allegation of adultery, that if this suit as it stands at the moment were allowed to go undefended without an answer the husband would be estopped from alleging in ancillary proceedings that his conduct had not been intolerable. It seems to me that, in all the circumstances of this case, in the light of the efforts that the husband made from shortly after the filing of the petition to put his case forward, it would be wrong to debar him from defending the suit. It is perfectly true that he has not done very much since the acknowledgment of service and did not take any opportunity of filing an answer; but the evidence that would justify him in making a cross-charge only came into his possession, as I have indicated, towards the end of November, and there was really not much time to do anything between then and 7th December, when the case was down for hearing and he applied to file an answer.

We have had other authorities cited to us. The facts in each are different from each other, and I think it is a truism to say that applications of this kind should be dealt with and decided on their individual facts. I cannot myself see that the husband could really have done very much more than he did. It is suggested that he stands to gain nothing by defending the suit. Well, his counsel made for him what I thought was a good point, and I think this is valid: he said that, if the case goes on as it stands at present and if the wife succeeds, as she might, the husband would be ordered to pay the costs. Counsel for the wife frankly says that he would be under a duty to ask on behalf of the legal aid fund that the husband be ordered to pay the costs. The husband says that if he wins he would not be ordered to pay the costs, and also that he might have a chance of getting the alleged adulterer ordered to pay the costs. I think there is substance in both of those matters.

In all the circumstances of this case, realising as I do that of course it is not a matter of right that the husband should be allowed to file an answer out of time at this stage but is a matter of grace, in my opinion the learned judge ought to have made, and this court ought to make, the order prayed for; and I would allow the appeal and give leave to file an answer out of time.

SIR GORDON WILLMER. I agree and I venture to add only a very few words on one aspect of the case. We were in the course of the argument very properly referred to the decision of this court in *Collins v Collins*[1]. It so happens that on that occasion this court was constituted in the same way as the court today, and the appeal was from the same learned judge, against a similar order. I only refer to the case to point out the difference. That was a case in which the learned judge, as here, had refused leave to file an answer; and we upheld the learned judge's refusal. But that was a case where the petition was presented on the ground of s 2(1)(e) of the Act, that is to say a simple allegation of five years separation. It was pointed out by Davies LJ in delivering the leading judgment that such an allegation in these days carries no stigma, whereas it would be quite different, and different considerations would apply, if there were an allegation of, for instance, adultery. Here we have just such a case, where there are allegations of misconduct by the wife and a proposed allegation of adultery by the husband. It seems to me that in those circumstances different considerations do apply as compared with those in *Collins v Collins*,[1] and that for that reason it is proper to come to a conclusion opposite to that to which we came in that case.

Appeal allowed. Answer to be filed within seven days.

Solicitors: *Ellis & Fairbairn*, agents for *Claude Barker & Partners*, Watford (for the husband); *Nicholls, Christie & Crocker*, Harrow (for the wife).

A S Virdi Esq   Barrister.

---

1   [1972] 2 All ER 658, [1972] 1 WLR 689

Allen and others v Distillers Co (Biochemicals) Ltd
Albrice and others v Distillers Co (Biochemicals) Ltd

QUEEN'S BENCH DIVISION

EVELEIGH J

20th NOVEMBER, 19th DECEMBER 1973, 16th JANUARY, 1st, 26th FEBRUARY, 20th MARCH 1974

Damages – Infant – Claim by infant plaintiff – Entitlement of infant on majority to money recovered – Compromise of action – Approval of court – Money paid into court – Terms of settlement providing for payment and transfer of money 'in such manner as the judge may direct to or for the benefit of' infant – Application for approval of draft deed providing for postponement of date of infant's entitlement until date after attainment of majority – Whether court having inherent jurisdiction to approve terms postponing infant's entitlement – Whether court having jurisdiction under terms of compromise.

Variation of trusts – Jurisdiction – Damages recovered by infant – Payment to trustees to hold for benefit of infant until attaining majority – Variation of trust by adding term postponing infant's entitlement until date after attainment of majority – Whether court having jurisdiction to add term – Variation of Trusts Act 1958, s 1(1).

Actions brought by infant plaintiffs in the Queen's Bench Division were compromised. It was ordered by the court that the terms of settlement arrived at between the parties be approved, that a sum of money standing in a joint account be paid into court, that effect be given to the terms of settlement and that the actions be dismissed save for the purpose of carrying the terms into effect with liberty to apply for that purpose. The settlement provided that there should be paid and transferred out of the sum in court 'in such manner as the judge may direct to or for the benefit of each child' a specified amount. Applications were made for payment out to trustees on the terms of a draft deed submitted for the court's approval which empowered the trustees to defer the date on which the infant would be entitled to receive the sum paid out beyond the age of majority. It was contended, inter alia, that, even if the court had no inherent jurisdiction to make such an order, it had power under s 1(1)[a] of the Variation of Trusts Act 1958 to vary the terms on which the sum paid out was held by the trustees so as to accord with the terms of the draft deed; alternatively that the court had jurisdiction to make the order under the terms on which the actions had been settled.

Held – (i) The court had no inherent jurisdiction to order the payment to trustees of a sum recovered by way of damages by an infant on terms that would defer the infant's entitlement beyond the age of majority (see p 371 c and p 373 b, post); *Isaac v Gompertz* (1789) 1 Ves Jun 44, dicta of Turner LJ in *Field v Moore* (1855) 7 De GM & G at 713, 720, 721, of Cotton and Lindley LJJ in *Re Leigh* (1888) 40 Ch D at 294, 296, *Re Embleton* [1946] 2 All ER 542, and *Chapman v Chapman* [1954] 1 All ER 798 applied.

(ii) Furthermore the court had no power to make such an order by virtue of the 1958 Act for the payment out to trustees of sums in court did not give rise to the kind of trust contemplated by the 1958 Act and, in any event, the suggested variation would not constitute a variation at all but would be a new trust made on behalf of an absolute owner (see p 373 h and p 374 b, post).

---

a   Section 1(1), so far as material, is set out at p 373 d and e, post

(iii) However the terms of the settlement approved by the court were so wide   *a*
that, if they were found in a deed of settlement, they would give the trustees power
to postpone entitlement. Since the court had approved the compromise in the
exercise of its ordinary jurisdiction founded by the issue of the original writs, the
terms of the settlement gave power to postpone entitlement in each appropriate
case (see p 376 c and j to p 377 a, post); *Warren v King* [1963] 3 All ER 993 applied; *Re
Hooker's Settlement* [1954] 3 All ER 321 distinguished.   *b*

Notes

For money recovered on the compromise of an action brought by an infant, see
11 Halsbury's Laws (3rd Edn) 313, 314, para 509.

    For the jurisdiction of the courts to vary trusts, see 38 ibid 1029-1031, para 1772.

    For the Variation of Trusts Act 1958, s 1, see 38 Halsbury's Statutes (3rd Edn) 220.   *c*

Cases referred to in judgment

Buckmaster v Buckmaster (1887) 35 Ch D 21, CA; *affd* sub nom *Seaton v Seaton* (1888)
    13 App Cas 61, 57 LJCh 661, 58 LT 565, HL, 24 Digest (Repl) 942, 9535.

Chapman v Chapman [1954] 1 All ER 798, [1954] AC 429, [1954] 2 WLR 723 33 ATC 84,   *d*
    47 R & IT 310, HL, 47 Digest (Repl) 329, 2973.

Collins v Brook (1859) H & N 270, 28 LJEx 143, 32 LTOS 357, 157 ER 842, 43 Digest
    (Repl) 144, 1292.

Embleton, Re [1946] 2 All ER 542, [1947] KB 142, [1947] LJR 423, 175 LT 451, CA, 13
    Digest (Repl) 431, 568.

Field v Moore, Field v Brown (1855) 7 De G M & G 691, 25 LJCh 66, 26 LTOS 207, 2 Jur   *e*
    NS 145, 44 ER 269, 40 Digest (Repl) 669, 1628.

Hooker's Settlement, Re, Heron v Public Trustee [1954] 3 All ER 321, [1955] Ch 55, [1954]
    3 WLR 606, 40 Digest (Repl) 590, 942.

Isaac v Gompertz (1789) 1 Ves Jun 44, 30 ER 222, LC.

Leigh, Re, Leigh v Leigh (1888) 40 Ch D 290, 58 LJCh 306, 60 LT 404, CA, 51 Digest
    (Repl) 777, 3447.

Rook v Worth (1750) 1 Ves Sen 460, [1558-1774] All ER Rep 586, 27 ER 1142, LC, 40   *f*
    Digest (Repl) 742, 2285.

Smith v Brown (1871) LR 6 QB 729, 40 LJQB 214, 24 LT 808, 36 JP 264, 1 Asp MLC 56,
    1 Digest (Repl) 169, 555.

Taylor (formerly Ryan) v Cheltenham & Hereford Breweries Ltd [1952] 1 All ER 1135,
    [1952] 2 QB 493, CA, 36 Digest (Repl) 227, 1208.

Towler's Settlement Trusts, Re [1963] 3 All ER 759, sub nom *Re T's Settlement Trusts*   *g*
    [1964] Ch 158. [1963] 3 WLR 987, 47 Digest (Repl) 337, 3014.

Warren v King [1963] 3 All ER 993, [1964] 1 WLR 122, CA, Digest (Cont Vol A) 1196,
    1070d.

Summonses

By summonses dated 19th November 1973 and in identical terms, the infant plaintiffs,   *h*
suing by their next friends, and other plaintiffs named in the schedule to the writs
in the actions against the defendants, Distillers Co (Biochemicals) Ltd, applied to the
court pursuant to the terms of a settlement approved by Geoffrey Lane J on 30th July
1973, for an order that the draft trust deeds in respect of the infant plaintiffs listed
in the schedule annexed to the summonses be approved by the court, that certain   *j*
sums listed in the schedule be paid for the benefit of the infant plaintiffs to trustees
as an interim payment on account of the total sum to be paid to the infant plaintiffs
on the final assessment and for approval by the court of the infant plaintiffs' damages
under the terms of the settlement agreed to by the defendants, that those sums be
paid to the next friend or guardian of each infant plaintiff for the infant's immediate
benefit, and that further sums specified in the schedule be paid to the respective

trustees of each infant plaintiff. The summonses were heard in chambers but judgment was delivered in open court.

F B Purchas QC, James Miskin QC, John Balcombe QC and *J P Harris* for the plaintiffs.
John Vinelott QC and *John Waite* as amici curiae.
The defendants did not appear and were not represented.

Cur adv vult

16th January. **EVELEIGH J** read the following judgment. On 30th July 1973 Geoffrey Lane J ordered that terms of settlement arrived at between the parties in these two actions be approved, that the sum of £5,929,800 then standing in a joint account with a bank be paid into court on 28th August 1973, that effect be given to the terms of settlement and that the actions be dismissed save for the purpose of carrying the terms into effect. It was ordered that there be liberty to apply for such purpose.

The relevant terms can be summarised as follows. Out of the sum in court there should be paid and transferred—

'in such manner as the judge may direct to or for the benefit of each child . . . an amount equal to 40 per cent of the final assessment of such child's disability.'

Solicitors for the plaintiffs and counsel instructed by them were to form an assessment panel appointed by the court. An assessment made by the assessment panel was to become the final assessment on approval by a judge of the High Court. If in any particular case the Distillers Co Ltd and the Distillers Co (Biochemicals) Ltd did not agree the assessment of the panel or if such assessment was not approved then the assessment should be made by the judge himself. It was provided:

'On such assessment the child concerned, by his Next Friend, shall be the plaintiff and the Distillers Company Ltd. and the Distillers Company (Bio-chemicals) Ltd. shall be defendants and the ordinary rules of evidence and procedure shall apply thereto, the assessment being treated as a contested issue.'

The judge's approval or his assessment, as the case might be, was to be the final assessment and there should be no appeal therefrom. It was provided that the method of assessment should not 'Deprive a child (by his Next Friend) of the right to object to the provisional assessment by the Assessment panel'.

The matter first came before me on 20th November, when applications were made by summons in each action in identical terms. The object of the summonses was to obtain an interim payment out of court for the children in varying sums all being considerably less than the probable final assessment. Application was made for payment out to trustees on the terms of draft deeds submitted for the court's approval. I was told by counsel that in some of the cases then before me and in a number of others to be dealt with in the future the parents were and would be asking 'That the date when the infant should be entitled to receive the sum paid out should be deferred beyond the age of eighteen'. To secure this object the following clause had been drafted:

'5. (a) The trustees shall hold the Trust Fund upon trust to raise and pay there-out to the Infant for the Infant's own benefit absolutely the sum of   when the infant attains the age of   years and to hold the remainder of the Trust Fund upon trust for the Infant when the Infant attains the age of   years abso-lutely. (b) The Trusts aforesaid shall carry the intermediate income and section 31 of the Trustee Act 1925 (as amended by the Family Law Reform Act 1969) shall apply in relation thereto as if in sub-section 1 thereof the words "As the

Trustees think fit" were substituted for the words "As may in all the circumstances be reasonable" and as if the proviso to that sub-section were omitted
and section 32 of the Trustee Act 1925 shall apply as if the proviso to sub-section 1
thereof were omitted.   (c) If the Infant shall die under the said age of   years
the Trustees shall (subject to the trusts and powers hereinbefore contained and
to any exercise thereof) hold the Trust Fund upon trust for such person or
persons and in such shares and with and subject to such trusts powers and provisions and generally in such manner as the Infant may by will or codicil appoint
and in default of and subject to any such appointment the Trustees shall hold
the Trust Fund upon trust for such persons (other than the Crown) and in
such proportions if any as would be entitled thereto as next of kin of the Infant
under the laws relating to intestacy in force at the death of the infant if the
Infant had died solvent domiciled in England and the Trust Fund comprised
the Infant's entire estate.   (d) Subject as aforesaid the Trustees shall hold the
Trust Fund upon trust to pay the same to the Trustees of the Thalidomide
Children's Trust for the purposes of the said Trust.'

I was informed by counsel of some of the reasons likely to be advanced by the parents
for the insertion of this clause. In some cases it might be possible to bring the infant
within s 101 of the Mental Health Act 1959 and thus invoke the assistance of the Court
of Protection but some parents felt, unfortunately, that some social stigma would
be attracted. In the case of a child unable to hear and unable to communicate there
would be an inability to manage or administer its property or affairs yet it might be
impossible to satisfy the judge nominated for the purposes of Part VIII of the Mental
Health Act 1959 that the infant was incapable 'by reason of mental disorder' as
required by s 101 of the 1959 Act. At the other extreme were children with high
academic potential whose physical disabilities made it vital that they should receive
university education and/or professional training but who (so it was feared) might be
diverted by the possession of a large sum of money. In other cases there was the
danger that a young disabled person of 18 years of age might be an easy victim of a
fortune seeker.
As I had doubts as to the power of the court to order payment to trustees on the
terms proposed or to make any order that would effectively achieve the intended
object without the assistance of the Court of Protection where appropriate, I adjourned
the applications so that the question of the court's jurisdiction could be fully argued.
For this purpose the court has had the additional assistance of counsel as amicus
curiae instructed by the Official Solicitor.
I would like to emphasise that I have listened to the arguments and reached my
decision on an isolated question of law. I have not considered in any particular case
whether the court ought or ought not to defer the child's entitlement if empowered
to do so and, indeed, I have not yet heard any evidence directed to that issue.
Counsel for the plaintiffs submitted that the court has always had, as part of its
inherent jurisdiction, the widest powers of dealing with an infant's money in any
way which was for the infant's benefit. It was conceded that there was no statutory
authority for the jurisdiction but it was said that the wording of the rules of the Supreme Court under RSC Ord 80 and the wording of s 205 of the Supreme Court of
Judicature (Consolidation) Act 1925, coupled with s 174 of the County Courts Act
1959, recognised the existence of the widest powers. It was also submitted that if
the money in court were ordered to be paid out to trustees until the infant attained
majority, which clearly could be done, application could then be made to the court
to vary the trust under the Variation of Trusts Act 1958 by incorporating the clause
now asked for. The court, it was said, would avoid a circuity of actions and do in
one step that which could in any event be done in two. Finally it was submitted,
but without enthusiasm, that there has been no settlement in these actions and that
the court is being asked to sanction a compromise in which a figure for damages is

now being agreed with a term of the compromise that the money should be paid to trustees on the trusts provided for in cl 5. In this case the court would be sanctioning a compromise under RSC Ord 80, r 11. Order 80, r 12 (3), provides:

> 'Without prejudice to the foregoing provisions of this rule, directions given under this rule may include any general or special directions that the Court thinks fit to give and, in particular, directions as to how the money is to be applied or dealt with and as to any payment to be made, either directly or out of the amount paid into court and whether before or after the money is transferred to or paid into a county court, to the plaintiff, or to the next friend in respect of moneys paid or expenses incurred for or on behalf or for the benefit of the person under disability or for his maintenance or otherwise for his benefit or to the plaintiff's solicitor in respect of costs.'

Section 205(1) of the Supreme Court of Judicature (Consolidation) Act 1925 empowers the High Court to transfer an infant's money to the county court where, as the subsection provides, it—

> 'shall, subject to any special order or direction of the High Court or a judge and to county court rules, be invested, applied or otherwise dealt with for the benefit of that person in such manner as the county court in its discretion thinks fit.'

Section 174(2) of the County Courts Act 1959 provides that money transferred from the High Court—

> 'shall . . . be invested, applied or otherwise dealt with for the benefit of the person to whom the order relates in such manner as the county court in its discretion thinks fit.'

It is argued that these provisions give to a county court judge complete discretion in dealing with an infant's money provided it is for the benefit of the infant. (Reference was made to *Re Towler's Settlement Trusts*[1] where it was recognised that to defer entitlement could be for the infant's benefit.) It was said that it would be strange for Parliament to confer on the county court judge a power wider than that possessed by a judge of the High Court. The statutory provisions referred to do not confer the wide power on a judge of the High Court for it is well recognised that the jurisdiction of the superior courts is not enlarged, nor ousted, except by express enactment (*Smith v Brown*[2]). However, it is submitted that Parliament must have proceeded on the assumption that the High Court had the widest powers and Parliament is presumed to know the law.

When seeking to discover whether or not the court has certain powers by virtue of its inherent jurisdiction I do not find it helpful to try to discover what assumption, if any, Parliament was making when these statutes were enacted. It is for the court to decide what is the law and when interpreting a statute the court will assume that Parliament understood the law to be that which the court has decided it was. Therefore, if I come to the conclusion, apart from consideration of these statutes, that the High Court lacked the power claimed for it, I would have to construe the statutory provisions in a manner consistent with that premise. It is not difficult so to do. Section 205(1) is, in my judgment, empowering the county court to exercise the powers of the High Court in its discretion, that is to say without further reference to the High Court, save insofar as the High Court has not otherwise ordered or directed. The provisions of CCR Ord 5, r 19, are significant in this connection. That rule deals with damages recovered initially in the county court itself. Paragraph (6) of r 19 reads:

1   [1963] 3 All ER 759, [1964] Ch 158
2   (1871) LR 6 QB 729

o

'The money and any interest thereon shall be invested applied or otherwise dealt with for the benefit of the person under disability as the judge or, with the leave of the judge, the registrar shall from time to time direct.'

The word 'discretion' on which counsel placed reliance does not appear. It surely would not be contended that s 205(1) gives the county court a greater power in relation to money transferred from the High Court than it has when dealing with money recovered in the county court. I do not think it right to regard the use of the word 'discretion' in s 205(1) as indicating unlimited jurisdiction. I regard that word as indicating only the freedom with which the court may act in exercising such powers as are within its jurisdiction without further reference to the High Court. Order 16, r 13 governs the control of the money received from the High Court in terms similar to those contained in Ord 5, r 19. If there is any wider jurisdiction conferred by the use of the word 'discretion' in s 205(1), those responsible for the rules have failed to bring it out. In determining the extent of the court's jurisdiction the proper approach is to look at the authorities and discover it from them.

Counsel have been unable to discover a single case in the Court of Chancery or in the common law courts where power has been exercised to maintain control over an infant's property after attaining the age of majority except where specifically authorised by statute, for example the Infant Settlements Act 1855. In an action at law an infant sued by his prochein amy. The prochein amy was an officer of the court. He was appointed to protect the infant and to prosecute the action after the infant had initiated proceedings by issuing the writ. The prochein amy could receive the damages and a receipt from him was a valid discharge protecting the defendant. The money, however, belonged to the infant (see *Collins v Brook*[1]). The prochein amy had no power to deal with the money but simply held it to pay over to the plaintiff when he attained 21. In the Court of Chancery a suit was instituted by a next friend filing the bill on the infant's behalf. The institution of the suit made the infant a ward of court. The infant's money would thus be in the control of the court which exercised its control by the appointment of a guardian.

While the prochein amy's only power was to retain the money received, application could be made to the Court of Chancery for the appointment of a guardian who could give a valid receipt and relieve the prochein amy of his responsibility.

The Supreme Court of Judicature Act 1873, which combined the powers and jurisdiction previously possessed by the separate courts, provided that in questions relating to the custody and education of infants the rules of equity should prevail and generally in all matters in which there was any conflict or variance between the rules of equity and the rules of the common law with reference to the same matter the rules of equity should prevail. No case has been cited to me to suggest that any other court had a greater power of control over an infant or his property than had the Court of Chancery. Rule 15 of the rules of procedure contained in the schedule to the 1873 Act provided:

'Married women and infants may respectively sue as plaintiffs by their next friends, in the manner practised in the Court of Chancery before the passing of this Act ...'

The schedule contained no rule relating to the control of an infant's damages or other property. Section 73 of the 1873 Act, however, provided that existing forms and methods of procedure should continue to be used and practised in the High Court of Justice in the manner applicable in the respective courts whose jurisdiction had been transferred to the High Court. The earliest rule dealing with money recovered by an infant in the Queen's Bench Division was RSC Ord 22, r 15. That rule provided:

---

1   (1859) H & N 270

'... the court or a judge may at or after the trial order that the whole or any part of such sum shall be paid into court to the credit of an account intituled in the cause or matter; and any sum so paid into court, and any dividends or interest thereon, shall be subject to such orders as may from time to time be made by the court or a judge concerning the same, and may either be invested or be paid out of court, or transferred to such persons, to be held and applied upon and for such trusts and in such manner as the court or judge shall direct.'

This rule does not purport to confer on the court a jurisdiction it did not already have. No rule could do that. There is nothing in the wording of the rule which suggests that there was in one of the several old courts jurisdiction wider than that of the Court of Chancery. I therefore have no reason to suppose that there somewhere exists authority for a wider jurisdiction in the courts of common law when counsel's researches have been unable to find it.

It seems to me therefore that if there is an inherent jurisdiction in the High Court to defer beyond majority an infant's entitlement that power must be found to exist in Chancery and if in the Chancery courts such a power is disclaimed it is not possible to conclude that it exists in some other division of the High Court.

Romer LJ said in *Taylor (formerly Ryan) v Cheltenham & Hereford Breweries Ltd*[1]:

'It is well settled that, if the capital and income of a legacy is given to an infant and the gift is followed by a direction that the capital is not to be paid to the infant until he attains the age of, say, thirty, and there is no gift over in the event of his dying under that age, he can claim payment of the legacy when he attains his majority, the principle being that a man is entitled to possession of property in which no one but he has an interest.'

In *Re Embleton*[2] it was held that the discretionary control of the fund in court terminates on the infant's coming of age and the whole fund must be paid out to him on his application. The Court of Chancery would not allow an infant being entitled absolutely to a fund to leave the fund in court and receive payment of the dividends once he had attained 21: *Isaac v Gompertz*[3].

If the court were to order payment out to trustees to hold for the infant at a given age without the creation of a minority interest in someone else the infant would be able to claim the property on attaining majority. The trustee could have no greater power to retain the money than that possessed by the court itself if the money had remained in court.

Seeing that the money recovered as damages is the infant's money absolutely the creation of a minority interest would diminish the interest of the infant. Has the court power to do this? It was a rule of the Court of Chancery not to allow conversion of an infant's property. This was so not merely in relation to conversion of real property into personal but even of personal into real (*Rook v Worth*[4]). An infant of 17 could make a will of personalty but if the property were converted into realty the infant would have lost his power of disposition. In *Re Towler's Settlements Trusts*[5] Wilberforce J said:

'The Court of Chancery has never claimed for itself a power to direct a settlement of an infant's property. Indeed, it has more than once been stated authoritatively that it cannot do so (see, for example, *Re Leigh, Leigh v. Leigh*[6]). It acquired

---

1   [1952] 1 All ER 1135 at 1141, [1952] 2 QB 493 at 505
2   [1946] 2 All ER 542, [1947] 1 KB 142
3   (1789) 1 Ves Jun 44
4   (1750) 1 Ves Sen 460
5   [1963] 3 All ER at 761, [1964] Ch at 161
6   (1888) 40 Ch D 290

under the Infant Settlements Act, 1855, a limited jurisdiction to settle an infant's property on marriage, but this has not been extended to other cases.'

It was also recognised that the court had no power to compel a settlement of the personal estate of an infant ward even when in contempt. In *Field v Moore*[1] Turner LJ referred to a case in which he had appeared as counsel and said:

'My recollection of this case enables me to state, that, upon the hearing of the petition first presented by the guardian, it was very much considered, on behalf of the infant ward and of her infant husband ... and by the then Lord Chancellor, whether any valid settlement of the infant's property could be made, it being desired by all parties that there should be such a settlement, but it was thought that it could not be done. Independently of my own recollection, the orders which were made prove, I think, most clearly, that this was the opinion of the Court. The property of this ward was wholly personal. By far the greater part of it was actually in Court, and if it had been thought that a valid settlement could be made, the Court would of course have, in the first instance, directed that upon the infant attaining twenty-one, the funds should be transferred to the trustees upon the trusts of the settlement, and have thus bound the funds by those trusts.'

Later he said[2]:

'That this Court has no power to change the character of an infant's estate, upon the notion of the change being beneficial to the infant, is now too well settled to admit of its being disputed.'

A number of cases in which the court refused to alter beneficial rights might appear to rest on a refusal to act in a manner which would seem to interfere with the wishes of the settlor or testator. However, no such consideration appears to underlie the reasoning in *Field v Moore*[3] and a number of other cases prominent among which is that of *Re Leigh*[4]. An infant ward of court was guilty of contempt in marrying without leave. A managing clerk of the solicitors of the infant's family spoke to him as to his contempt of court and explained that the proper course would be for him to submit to the judgment of the court and execute such settlement as the judge might direct. The court ordered the infant to execute a settlement and he did so. As soon as he attained 21 the infant brought his action to set aside the settlement and he also appealed against the order directing it. Cotton LJ said[5]:

'Now was the order right? I think not, looking upon it as an order made by the Judge against the infant *in invitum* ordering him to deprive himself of a considerable interest in his property. In my opinion, however good it might be for the parties, the Court of Chancery has no jurisdiction or power to make any such order.'

Lindley LJ said[6]:

'It is quite obvious from the note taken of Mr. Justice *Kay's* judgment that this point about the jurisdiction of the Court was passed over *sub silentio*: it was assumed, and not argued or discussed. The decision of this Court in *Buckmaster v. Buckmaster*[7] had not then been pronounced, and it seems to me to have been

---

1   (1855) 7 De GM & G 691 at 713
2   (1855) 7 De GM & G at 720, 721
3   (1855) 7 De GM & G 691
4   (1888) 40 Ch D 290
5   (1888) 40 Ch D at 294
6   (1888) 40 Ch D at 296
7   (1887) 35 Ch D 21

a taken for granted that if a ward of Court married, the Court had power to make him execute a settlement. I confess that that erroneous idea was more or less prevalent till it was carefully examined in this court[1] and in the House of Lords in *Buckmaster* v. *Buckmaster*[2], but it is now well settled that the Court has no jurisdiction to compel an infant ward to make a settlement of his property.'

b   In *Chapman* v *Chapman*[3] the House of Lords made it clear that there was no un-limited inherent jurisdiction in the court to deal with an infant's property. The authorities to which I have referred in my opinion establish that the court has no inherent jurisdiction to postpone beyond the age of majority the infant's entitlement to damages recovered in the Queen's Bench Division. Consequently, there is no such power in the court to authorise cl 5 of the trust deed proposed in these cases.

c   Counsel for the plaintiffs has contended that, whatever the position might have been before 1958, the Variation of Trusts Act 1958 has had the effect of giving the court wider powers. Section 1(1) of that Act provides:

'Where property, whether real or personal, is held on trusts arising, whether before or after the passing of this Act, under any will, settlement or other dis-position, the court may if it thinks fit by order approve on behalf of—(*a*) any per-
d son having, directly or indirectly, an interest, whether vested or contingent, under the trusts who by reason of infancy or other incapacity is incapable of assenting . . . any arrangement (by whomsoever proposed, and whether or not there is any other person beneficially interested who is capable of assenting thereto) varying or revoking all or any of the trusts . . . Provided that except by virtue of paragraph (*d*) of this subsection the court shall not approve an arrange-
e ment on behalf of any person unless the carrying out thereof would be for the benefit of that person.'

f   In *Re Towler's Settlement Trusts*[4] there was a settlement, the effect of which was that subject to a life interest in one-half of the trust fund for the applicant (a mother), the whole of the trust fund was held on trust for two infants (one being the respondent to the application) on attaining the age of 21 years. At that age the infant respondent would become entitled absolutely to one-fourth of the trust fund in possession. The infant was said to be irresponsible and immature and it was alleged that the immedi-ate possession of a large sum of money would be detrimental to her. Wilberforce J authorised a variation which deferred the infant's right to capital for a period during which she was given a protected life interest. The learned judge said that on the evidence it appeared to him to be a definite benefit for the infant to be protected for a
g period against creditors. Counsel for the plaintiffs argues that if the money is paid out to trustees to hold for the infant until the age of majority (which undoubtedly can be done) then application could be made to the court to vary the trust by the addition of the proposed cl 5 if the court considered that a deferment of the infant's right to possession of the fund would be beneficial. It is said that as this could be done in two stages I ought to approve the clause and do it in one.

h   In my judgment this argument fails in limine. For I do not think that the payment out to the trustees in the first instance gives rise to the kind of trust contemplated by the 1958 Act. As a common lawyer struggling with this problem I am reminded of the first sentence in the chapter on Trusts contained in Snell's Equity[5]: 'No one has yet succeeded in giving an entirely satisfactory definition of a Trust.' An agent may hold and deal with property of his principal in such circumstances as to constitute him a trustee for his principal but leaving aside the manner in which the trust is

---

1 (1887) 35 Ch D 21
2 Sub nom *Seaton v Seaton* (1888) 13 App Cas 61
3 [1954] 1 All ER 798, [1954] AC 429
4 [1963] 3 All ER 759, [1964] Ch 158
5 27th Edn (1973), p 87

created no one would contemplate the possibility of there being a trust of the kind referred to in the 1958 Act. The Act contemplates a situation where a beneficial interest is created which did not previously exist and probably one which is related to at least one other beneficial interest. Moreover, the Act is designed to deal with a situation where the original disposition was intended to endure according to its terms but which in the light of changed attitudes and circumstances it is fair and reasonable to vary.

In any event, I do not think that the so-called variation would be a variation at all. It would be a new trust made on behalf of an absolute owner.

If the court were to attempt to participate in the device suggested it would be making use of the 1958 Act to give it a jurisdiction not previously possessed and for a purpose not contemplated by the Act. In *Re Towler's Settlement Trusts*[1], after referring to the limited jurisdiction of the Court of Chancery, Wilberforce J said[2]:

'There is no reason to suppose that the absence of the wider jurisdiction was part of the mischief which the Act of 1958 was intended to remedy, and, in view of the well-accepted limits on the court's jurisdiction laid down by statute or authority, it seems unlikely that it was. I am certainly reluctant to suppose that a whole new jurisdiction has been incidentally conferred by the use of general words.'

I arrive at my conclusion with mixed feelings. It may well be that the wider jurisdiction contended for would be useful in some cases. I am speaking generally now for I emphasise that I have not investigated the facts of the cases of the thalidomide children for this purpose. It should not be assumed that the court would face an easy task in deciding whether or not to postpone entitlement but that should not deter it. If the court possessed the jurisdiction it would also be conferred on the county court by virtue of s 205 of the Supreme Court of Judicature (Consolidation) Act 1925 unless the High Court otherwise ordered. An argument based on the Variation of Trusts Act 1958 might equally apply to the original jurisdiction of the county court for sums within its limits. As Wilberforce J said[2], following on the passage I have last quoted:

'There are obvious difficulties in attributing so wide a meaning to the Act of 1958. For example, is the court to consult the wishes of the infant? That is, as has been found here, a matter of considerable difficulty, and where, as here, the infant is nearly twenty-one, it seems preferable, if her wishes can be taken into account, to leave the matter over until she can decide for herself. Or can the court impose a settlement against the infant's wishes? To do this would involve going much further than the court goes under the [Infant Settlements Act] 1855 and would place on the court a heavy responsibility (which it does not have generally in variation of trusts applications) of considering and estimating the views of other persons (often including parents and medical and psychological experts) as to what is for the infant's benefit.'

I do not suggest that an investigation into the desirability of postponing entitlement is one which the High Court in any one of its divisions is unable or even reluctant to undertake, and I do not read the above quoted passage as so saying. It does, however, emphasise the need to consider a possible conflict of interests, and to consider how the court is to be assisted in detecting it.

It is not an easy matter to decide in relation to a ten year old child, in spite of tragic physical deformities, whether or not that child would be better or worse off if in control of its money when it reaches majority. Now that that age is 18 years one has a sneaking feeling that to postpone would be advantageous but Parliament has

1   [1963] 3 All ER 759, [1964] Ch 158
2   [1963] 3 All ER at 761, [1964] Ch at 161

determined the age and perhaps the sneaking feeling is simply a prejudice due to my own age. Let us assume that at 18 a deformed child is mentally normal or even of superior mental ability and fully capable of managing its own affairs, and yet the entitlement has been postponed. It would not be possible by an application under the Variation of Trusts Act 1958 to reverse the position without infringing the rights of the intestacy inheritors. While the trustees would have a power of advancement the extent to which they might exercise it would be a possible source of conflict between parent and child.   Insofar as incapacity to manage and administer his affairs is by reason of mental disorder application can be made when the infant is 17 by which time the position may be much clearer.

The final submission which I have to consider is that the court is not being asked itself to deal with the infants' money under RSC Ord 80, r 12, but is being asked to approve a compromise under r 11. It is said that until the precise figure is determined there has been no final settlement. There are several difficulties in the way of this view. The parties had already arrived at a compromise which was sanctioned when Geoffrey Lane J approved the settlement. Compromise involves two parties, a plaintiff and a defendant. There is no suggestion that the defendants have taken or wish to take any part in suggesting a postponement of the individual infant's entitlement. While counsel wish to keep this point open it is not one that has been strongly argued before me.

There is no doubt that the court could sanction a postponement of the infants' entitlement as part of a compromise where that is made a term of the compromise (see *Warren v King*[1]). There, at the suggestion of the Court of Appeal, a clause was inserted in a trust deed deferring the infant's entitlement. The parties themselves, however, reached agreement on the matter and it came before the court for approval as a term of the compromise. What ultimately happened, however, is not reported. No one in argument before me has cast any doubt on the court's power to approve such a compromise where an infant is concerned. The court must clearly possess the power to do so. A son might sue his father in a property dispute and the father might well be prepared to give way on terms including one which postpones the vesting of the absolute interest. Clearly such an agreement could be made an order of the court. In the present cases, however, cl 5 of the proposed trust deed forms no part of the agreement between the parties.

There is another possible aspect of this case that has occurred to me, and that is this. Clause 6(ii) of the agreement, in dealing with the role of the judge, says that—

> 'out of the sum standing to the credit of the said account there shall be paid and transferred in such manner as the judge may direct, to or for the benefit of each child, an amount equal to 40 per cent of the final assessment of such child's disability determined in accordance with the procedure set out in paragraphs 3-6 below, together with such part of the interest which shall have accrued to such account as may be attributable to the said amount.'

I ask myself whether those words are of themselves wide enough to cover a payment out which defers entitlement, or any arrangement which defers entitlement. If they do, then it seems to me that it may be argued that the compromise placed before the court for its approval and approved by Geoffrey Lane J, was one which contained the power that is sought in this case.

I would be very grateful for any help that counsel could either now or at some other time give me on that point. I am reluctant to impose further on the help of the Official Solicitor and counsel instructed by him, to whom I am extremely grateful, but on the whole I think the adversary procedure is the best way of getting to the truth of many problems, and I would be grateful if the amicus would be prepared to help the court in this matter also.

No order on applications. Summonses adjourned into chambers.

---

1 [1963] 3 All ER 993, [1964] 1 WLR 122

20th March. **EVELEIGH J** read the following judgment in open court. I have now heard argument on the question whether the terms of settlement approved by Geoffrey Lane J themselves give the court the power to postpone entitlement when there is no inherent jurisdiction so to do.

It has been agreed on all sides that the words used are themselves so wide that if they were found in a deed of settlement they would certainly give power to trustees to postpone entitlement, and I so decide. The question is whether they give power to the court when incorporated in the terms of settlement approved by the court.

Counsel as amicus curiae has submitted that the words used do not empower the court to postpone entitlement on two grounds. The first contention was that the parties must not be taken to have intended to give the court a greater power than it exercised by virtue of its inherent jurisdiction and the words used must be construed in that light. When the words themselves are unambiguous I see no reason to make any assumption as to the parties' intentions other than that which the words themselves disclose. If, however, it is permissible to look beyond the words it is right that I should take note of the fact that before the offer of the defendants was accepted very many parents sought an assurance that there would be power to postpone and they were advised that there would be. Moreover, the defendants set up a separate trust with the widest powers being given to persons of distinction as trustees. In those circumstances I see no reason to assume that the parties contracted on the basis that the powers of the court should be limited to inherent jurisdiction.

The second contention was that the parties could not give to the court a jurisdiction wider than that which it already has. Reliance was placed on *Re Hooker's Settlement*[1]. In that case, however, the matter the court was asked to decide whether it should give its consent to a deed revoking a settlement which contained a clause by which the settlor could revoke the trusts of the settlement with the consent of a judge of the Chancery Division. The matter came before the court only on a summons asking the court for such consent. The court was not otherwise seised of the case. The present cases have come before the court as actions commenced by writs claiming damages for negligence. In actions of this kind the court may adjudicate fully on the claim or approve a compromise. In either case it may administer the money paid into court as damages. It may also approve a compromise which specifically postpones the entitlement of the plaintiffs as I have stated in the judgment already delivered.

When the parties address the court on the terms of a proposed compromise of an infant's action, the views of the judge are frequently invited and given. I can see no reason why there should not be a compromise which, instead of specifying the period for postponement of entitlement, agrees to such a period as the court may decide is beneficial to the infant. Such an agreement does not give the court a power beyond its jurisdiction, for the court has power to approve a compromise which postpones entitlement. It merely invokes the assistance of the court in determining to what extent postponement is beneficial when the parties seek to compromise a matter of which the court is already seised.

In *Re Hooker's Settlement*[2] Danckwerts J said: 'This is an attempt to make the judge an arbitrator without his consent.' This cannot be said of the present case, for in dealing with actions for personal injuries properly commenced by writ the court itself has approved a compromise and has itself accepted the task of deciding how the money should be dealt with.

The actions with which I am concerned have been compromised. The court has approved the terms. This it has power to do in the ordinary exercise of its jurisdiction. The fact that the court has a role to play in carrying out the terms of the compromise does not mean that it is being asked to act without jurisdiction. The issue of the original

---

1 [1954] 3 All ER 321, [1955] Ch 55
2 [1954] 3 All ER at 323, [1955] Ch at 59

writs founded the jurisdiction of the court. I therefore hold that the terms of settlement give the court the power to postpone entitlement in each appropriate case.

Order accordingly.

Solicitors: *Kimber, Bull & Co* (for the plaintiffs); *Official Solicitor.*

E H Hunter Esq   Barrister.

Waddington v Miah

HOUSE OF LORDS
LORD REID, LORD MORRIS OF BORTH-Y-GEST, VISCOUNT DILHORNE, LORD SIMON OF GLAISDALE AND LORD SALMON
18th, 19th MARCH, 1st MAY 1974

Immigration – Statute controlling immigration – Retrospective operation – Penal provisions – Illegal entry – Possession of false passport – Whether statute creating offences in respect of acts performed before it came into force – Immigration Act 1971, ss 24(1)(a), 26(1)(d).

The penal provisions of the Immigration Act 1971, in particular ss 24(1)(a)[a] and 26(1)(d)[b], are not retrospective and accordingly a person cannot be convicted of an offence under the 1971 Act in respect of anything done by him before 1st January 1973, the date when the 1971 Act came into force (see p 379 b c g and h, p 380 f g and j and p 381 a to c, post).

Decision of the Court of Appeal, Criminal Division, sub nom *R v Miah* [1974] 1 All ER 1110 affirmed.

Notes
For offences under the Immigration Act 1971, see 4 Halsbury's Laws (4th Edn) 518-522, paras 1027-1030.

For the presumption against the retrospective operation of statutes, see 36 Halsbury's Laws (3rd Edn) 423-426, paras 644, 645, and for cases on the subject, see 44 Digest (Repl) 285, 1136-1145.

For the Immigration Act 1971, ss 24, 26, see 41 Halsbury's Statutes (3rd Edn) 43, 47.

Appeal
This was an appeal by Geoffrey Waddington, Acting Chief Superintendent of the Lincolnshire constabulary, against the order of the Court of Appeal, Criminal Division[1] (Stephenson LJ, Chapman and Forbes JJ) dated 20th December 1973 allowing an appeal by the respondent, Moyna Miah alias Abid Ullah, against his conviction in the Crown Court at Grimsby on 10th October 1973 on two counts of an indictment

---

a Section 24(1), so far as material, provides: 'A person who is not patrial shall be guilty of an offence . . . in any of the following cases:—(a) if contrary to this Act he knowingly enters the United Kingdon in breach of a deportation order or without leave . . .'
b Section 26(1), so far as material, provides: 'A person shall be guilty of an offence . . . in any of the following cases . . . (d) if, without lawful authority, he alters any certificate of patriality, entry clearance, work permit or other document issued or made under or for the purposes of this Act, or uses for the purposes of this Act, or has in his possession for such use, any passport, certificate of patriality, entry clearance, work permit or other document which he knows or has reasonable cause to believe to be false . . .'
1 [1974] 1 All ER 1110

charging him with offences against ss 24 and 26 of the Immigration Act 1971. The facts are set out in the opinion of Lord Reid.

Charles McCullough QC and *David Farrer* for the appellant.
E F Jowitt QC and *C G Young* for the respondent.

Their Lordships took time for consideration.

1st May. The following opinions were delivered.

LORD REID. My Lords, the respondent was tried in the Crown Court at Grimsby on an indictment which contained two counts. Count 1 stated the offence charged as 'Illegal Immigrant, contrary to Section 24 of the Immigration Act 1971' and count 2 stated the offence as 'Possession of False Passport, contrary to Section 26 of the Immigration Act 1971'. That Act was passed on 28th October 1971 but the greater part of it, including ss 24 and 26, did not come into force until 1st January 1973. But the particulars given under count 1 were that the respondent—

'on a day unknown between the 22nd day of October 1970 and the 29th day of September 1972, being a person who was not patrial within the meaning of the Immigration Act 1971, knowingly entered the United Kingdom without leave.'

And the particulars given under count 2 were that the respondent—

'on the 29th day of September 1972, had in his possession for the purposes of the Immigration Act 1971, a Passport No. AC386290 which he had reasonable cause to believe to be false.'

Despite objection that the Act is not retrospective the respondent was convicted. His conviction was quashed by the Court of Appeal[1]. That court in granting leave to the prosecution to appeal certified the following question:

'Whether the appellant could be convicted of offences against the Immigration Act 1971 in respect of things done by him before the Act came into force, and in particular offences against ss 24(1)(a) and 26(1)(d) of the Act.'

The facts are conveniently set out in an agreed statement as follows:

'The Respondent, an (unidentified) non-patrial for the purposes of the Immigra-Act, 1971, and probably a native of Bangladesh, entered the United Kingdom at Heathrow airport on 28th October, 1971. He passed himself off to the Immigration Officer as one Abid Ullah, a non-patrial Pakistani who had come to the United Kingdom in 1957 and had returned on a visit to Bangladesh in October, 1970. For this purpose the Respondent presented a passport originally issued to the true Abid Ullah and subsequently altered by the substitition of a photograph of the Respondent. The Respondent subsequently took various employments in the United Kingdom, finally working in a foundry at Scunthorpe. He was seen by police officers on 29th September, 1972 and questioned as to his true identity. In his possession were found the passport used to obtain entry and an earlier passport issued to Abid Ullah. The police took possession of them immediately. Throughout subsequent questioning he maintained that he was Abid Ullah and recited details of his life and produced documents in support of his claim. Forensic examination of the passport showed that this was not so. On 11th May, 1973, the Chief Constable of the Lincolnshire Constabulary issued a certificate for the purposes of Section 28 of the Immigration Act, 1971. Informations were laid on 28th June, 1973.'

The law with regard to immigrants such as the respondent was previously contained in the Commonwealth Immigrants Acts of 1962 and 1968 These Acts were repealed by the 1971 Act. It has I think been generally understood that, when provisions in an earlier Act are replaced by provisions in a later Act which repeals the earlier Act, and in the absence of special provisions in the later Act, offenders against the earlier Act before the date of its repeal can still be prosecuted under the earlier Act after its repeal and the later Act has no application.

Counsel informed us that he had examined a number of recent Acts which repealed earlier Acts and had found that in some there were special transitional provisions which substantially achieved that result, in others there were no such provisions so that the ordinary rule would apply, but that he had found none which authorised proceedings for an offence under the later Act in respect of acts committed before it came into force. That is what I would have expected because there has for a very long time been a strong feeling against making legislation, and particularly criminal legislation, retrospective.

It is also I think important to bear in mind that the Declaration of Human Rights of the United Nations[1] provides in art 11(2):

> 'No one shall be held guilty of any penal offence on account of any act or omission which did not constitute a penal offence, under national or international law, at the time when it was committed. Nor shall a heavier penalty be imposed than the one that was applicable at the time the penal offence was committed.'

And the Convention for the Protection of Human Rights and Fundamental Freedoms[2] ratified by the United Kingdom in 1951 provides by art 7:

> '(1) No one shall be held guilty of any criminal offence on account of any act or omission which did not constitute a criminal offence under national or international law at the time when it was committed. Nor shall a heavier penalty be imposed than the one that was applicable at the time the criminal offence was committed.
>
> '(2) This Article shall not prejudice the trial and punishment of any person for any act or omission which, at the time when it was committed, was criminal according to the general principles of law recognised by civilised nations.'

So it is hardly credible that any government department would promote or that Parliament would pass retrospective criminal legislation.

Yet whoever authorised this prosecution must somehow have formed an opinion that Parliament had made ss 24 and 26 of the 1971 Act retrospective. That contention was strongly urged in the Crown Court and in the Court of Appeal[3], but when this case was opened before your Lordships, counsel said that he had been unable to find any argument which he thought he could properly submit to the House. In so doing I think that he acted with complete propriety. But nevertheless he drew our attention to every possible aspect of the matter and in view of the importance of the general principle we spent two days on a full investigation.

In the courts below the prosecution relied chiefly on s 34(1) of the 1971 Act but also relied to some extent on s 35(3). These provisions are as follows:

> '34.—(1) Subject to the following provisions of this section, the enactments mentioned in Schedule 6 to this Act are hereby repealed, as from the coming into force of this Act, to the extent mentioned in column 3 of the Schedule; and—(a) this Act, as from its coming into force, shall apply in relation to entrants or others arriving in the United Kingdom at whatever date before or after it comes into

1   (1949) Cmd 7662
2   (1953) Cmd 8969
3   [1974] 1 All ER 1110

force; and (*b*) after this Act comes into force anything done under or for the purposes of the former immigration laws shall have effect, in so far as any corresponding action could be taken under or for the purposes of this Act, as if done by way of action so taken, and in relation to anything so done this Act shall apply accordingly . . .

'35.—. . . (3) The provisions of section 28(1) and (2) above shall have effect, as from the passing of this Act, in relation to offences under section 4A (unauthorised landing) of the Commonwealth Immigrants Act 1962 as amended by the Commonwealth Immigrants Act 1968, other than offences committed six months or more before the passing of this Act, as those provisions are expressed to have effect in relation to offences to which the extended time limit for prosecutions is to apply under sections 24, 25 and 26 above; but where proceedings for an offence under section 4A of the Commonwealth Immigrants Act 1962 would have been out of time but for this subsection, section 4A(4) (under which, in certain cases, a person not producing a passport duly stamped by an immigration officer is presumed for purposes of that section to have landed in contravention of it, unless the contrary is proved) shall not apply . . .'

I can see nothing retrospective in s 34(1). I use retrospective in the sense of authorising people being punished for what they did before the Act came into force. But there is nothing to prevent Parliament from authorising discrimination in the future between various classes of people and one ground of discrimination could be that if certain people have done a certain thing in the past or had a certain ancestry they shall be treated differently in future from those who have not done that thing or had a different ancestry. Whether that is good policy is a matter of opinion. But in my opinion that is what Parliament has done by this Act.

Section 34(1)(*a*) makes the 1971 Act apply to all 'entrants' and 'entrant' is defined in s 33 as 'a person entering or seeking to enter the United Kingdom'. His entry need not have been unlawful and it may have taken place a long time ago. Some entrants are given a right of abode here. Some are given indefinite leave to enter and remain here. The position of others is more precarious. I cannot see how s 34(1)(*a*) can be construed as having any reference to what any entrant may have done in this country before the Act came into force. All that it does is to subject to the provisions of the Act for the future anyone who entered in the past.

Section 34(1)(*b*) refers to 'the former immigration laws' which include the Acts of 1962 and 1968. It applies to anything 'done under or for the purposes of' those laws. So it does not apply to anything done contrary to, or to any offence against, those laws. And it certainly does not support the view that an act done before the 1971 Act came into force can be treated as an offence against that Act.

Section 35(3) requires more explanation. Under former immigration laws there was a time limit for prosecution of six months. Section 28 applied to certain offences against the 1971 Act a time limit of three years. Section 35(3) applies the new time limit to old offences against s 4A of the 1962 Act where, but only where, the provisions of s 35(3) are satisfied. Those provisions are complicated but the general effect appears to me to be that if prosecution for an old offence had become time-barred before the passing of the 1971 Act the old offence was not revived. So as the Act was passed on 28th October 1971 offences committed before 28th April 1971 remained time-barred. I do not think that s 35(3) can be said to have retrospective effect or that it can lend any support to the validity of the present prosecution. We are not concerned with any question whether in the circumstance of this case any charges could have been made of offences against former immigration laws.

This is a very clear case. I do not think it necessary to examine the details of the counts in this indictment.

I would dismiss the appeal. Costs are not usually awarded in cases of this kind but in view of the circumstances I would award to the respondent his costs in the House.

a

LORD MORRIS OF BORTH-Y-GEST. My Lords, I have had the advantage of reading the speech prepared by my noble and learned friend, Lord Reid. I am in agreement with it and accordingly would dismiss the appeal.

VISCOUNT DILHORNE. My Lords, I have read the speech of my noble and learned friend, Lord Reid. I agree with it and with his conclusion that the appeal should **b** be dismissed and the respondent awarded his costs in this House.

LORD SIMON OF GLAISDALE. My Lords, I have had the advantage of reading in draft the speech prepared by my noble and learned friend, Lord Reid. I agree with it, and I would therefore dismiss the appeal.

c **LORD SALMON.** My Lords, I, too, agree with my noble and learned friend, Lord Reid, and for the reasons he gives I would dismiss the appeal.

Appeal dismissed.

Solicitors: *Collyer-Bristow & Co*, agents for *Hetts, Stubbs & Kemp*, Scunthorpe (for the **d** appellant); *Joynson-Hicks & Co*, agents for *R A C Symes & Co*, Scunthorpe (for the respondent).

Christine Ivamy   Barrister.

e
Pollway Ltd and another v Abdullah

COURT OF APPEAL, CIVIL DIVISION
MEGAW, BUCKLEY AND ROSKILL LJJ
15th, 16th JANUARY, 1st FEBRUARY 1974

f *Bill of exchange – Cheque – Consideration – Auctioneer – Sale of property by auction – Deposit – Payment of deposit by purchaser – Payment by cheque drawn by purchaser in favour of auctioneer – Auctioneer waiving requirement for payment in cash – Auctioneer acting as agent for vendor – Cheque subsequently stopped by purchaser – Vendor accepting purchaser's repudiation and rescinding contract of sale – Right of auctioneer to sue purchaser on cheque – Consideration for cheque.*

g The vendors employed auctioneers to sell certain property. The auctioneers advertised that the property would be sold by auction and that it would be a condition of the sale that the purchaser would pay a deposit of 10 per cent of the purchase price to the auctioneers as agents for the vendors. At the auction the defendant made a successful bid of £5,550 for the property. A memorandum of sale was signed by the defendant as purchaser and by the auctioneers as agents for the vendors. **h** The defendant paid the deposit of £555 by a cheque drawn by himself in favour of the auctioneers. Subsequently, without any justifiable reason, he stopped the cheque and it was dishonoured on presentation. The vendors treated the defendant's conduct as repudiation of the contract between them and resold the property. The vendors and the auctioneers brought an action on the cheque against the defendant to recover the £555. The trial judge dismissed the action on the grounds that neither **j** the vendors nor the auctioneers were entitled to recover on the cheque as there had been a total failure of consideration once the vendors had accepted the defendant's conduct as repudiation of the contract of sale. The auctioneers appealed.

Held – The defendant was under an obligation to the auctioneers to honour the cheque by virtue of the contract between the defendant as the drawer of the cheque

and the auctioneers as the named payees. The obligation of the vendors to complete
the sale of the property could not properly be regarded as the consideration for the
cheque since that consideration did not move from the promisee, i e the auctioneers.
The consideration for the cheque was the warranty by the auctioneers that they had
authority to sign the memorandum on the vendors' behalf and to receive the cheque
payable to themselves as the named payees in diminution of the defendant's obligation
to pay the full amount of the purchase price to the vendors. Alternatively the consideration was the auctioneers' acceptance of the cheque in place of legal tender by
means of which the defendant was bound to discharge his obligation to pay the
deposit. As the consideration given by the auctioneers had never failed, they were,
as holders, entitled to sue on the cheque and the appeal would therefore be allowed
(see p 384 b to d and p 385 a to c and f g, post).

Per Curiam. Even if the consideration for the cheque was the vendors' obligation
to complete the sale, that consideration had not failed at the time when the breach
of contract by the defendant occurred and the subsequent rescission of the contract
of sale by the vendors could not operate to divest the auctioneers of their cause of
action (see p 384 f to h and p 385 f and g, post).

Notes
For consideration for bills of exchange etc, see 4 Halsbury's Laws (4th Edn) 164,
165, paras 379-382; for the rights of holders of such instruments, see ibid 169-171,
paras 388-391, and for cases on the subject, see 6 Digest (Repl) 280, 281, 2049-2059.

Case referred to in judgment
Diamond v Graham [1968] 2 All ER 909, [1968] 1 WLR 1061, CA, Digest (Cont Vol C)
53, 922a.

Cases also cited
Astley v Johnson (1860) 5 H & N 137, 157 ER 1131.
Fielding and Platt Ltd v Najjar [1969] 2 All ER 150, [1969] 1 WLR 357, CA.
Jackson v Warwick (1797) 7 Term Rep 121, 101 ER 888.
Lamont (James) & Co Ltd v Hyland Ltd [1950] 1 All ER 341, [1950] 1 KB 585, CA.
Solly v Hinde (1834) 2 Cr & M 516, 149 ER 865.
Wells v Hopkins (1839) 5 M & W 7, 151 ER 3.

Appeals
The plaintiffs, (1) Pollway Ltd and (2) May & Philpot (a firm), appealed against the
decision of his Honour Judge Stockdale, sitting at Westminister County Court on
22nd June 1973, whereby he gave judgment in favour of the defendant, Mohammed
Abdullah, holding that the plaintiffs had no right to sue on a cheque given by the
defendant to the second plaintiffs, as agents for the first plaintiffs, in payment of
a deposit of 10 per cent of the purchase price for certain property sold to the defendant
at an auction. The facts are set out in the judgment of Roskill LJ.

F Reynold for the plaintiffs.
F J C Goudie for the defendant.

                                                            Cur adv vult

1st February. **ROSKILL LJ** read the first judgment at the invitation of Megaw LJ.
The first named plaintiffs (whom I shall call 'the vendors') were the reversioners of
certain property in Purley, Surrey, of certain ground rents and rack rents relating to
which they wished to dispose. For this purpose they employed the second plaintiffs
(whom I shall call 'the auctioneers'). The auctioneers duly advertised the sale to
take place by auction on 25th April 1972 unless the property had previously been
sold privately which it was not. The conditions of sale were also advertised. It is
necessary only to refer to special condition 3:

a   'A deposit of 10 per cent. of the purchase price shall be paid on the making of this contract to [the auctioneers] as agents for the vendor.'

The auction took place on 25th April 1972. The defendant bid £5,550 for the property which was duly knocked down to him by the auctioneers. Thereupon he became liable to pay the 10 per cent deposit in accordance with condition 3. It is to be observed that, strictly speaking, he could only discharge this obligation

b   by paying cash, a cheque not being legal tender. Immediately following the auction a memorandum was duly signed by the defendant himself as purchaser and by the auctioneers as agents for the vendors who were named. That memorandum was dated 25th April 1972. By it the defendant acknowledged his purchase at the stated price, subject to the stated condition of sale, and that he had paid a deposit of £555 to the auctioneers in part payment of the purchase price. The deposit was in fact

c   paid by cheque drawn by the defendant in favour of the auctioneers as the named payees. It is not disputed that the auctioneers thereupon became the holders of that cheque as defined in s 2 of the Bills of Exchange Act 1882. It is also not disputed that the vendors were never the holders of that cheque.

Subsequently, for reasons which were admitted both at the trial and before this court to be without foundation and wholly unjustifiable, the defendant stopped

d   the cheque and it was dishonoured on presentation. The defendant was subsequently given time to comply with his obligations. He refused so to do. The vendors, as they were entitled to do, thereupon treated the defendant's conduct as a repudiation of the contract. They resold the property by subsequent auction, and we were told that the resale price was only £50 less than the price which the defendant agreed, but failed, to pay. The vendors' right to rescind and to claim damages was not

e   disputed. Both they and the auctioneers sued the defendant on the dishonoured cheque.

In a careful judgment, given on 22nd June 1973, his Honour Judge Stockdale, sitting at Westminister County Court, gave judgment for the defendant against both plaintiffs, holding that neither could recover on the cheque. His main reason

f   for so holding can be shortly stated. The consideration for the cheque was the vendors' undertaking to complete the sale. Once the vendors accepted the defendant's conduct as repudiation they were discharged from that obligation. There was then a total failure of consideration. Therefore the consideration for the cheque wholly failed, and the defendant ceased to be liable on it having properly discharged the burden resting on him to prove total failure of consideration. I will say at once that I think the learned judge was right in dismissing the vendors' claim on the cheque.

g   Indeed, that part of the judgment was not seriously challenged before us. There is a very short reason why the vendors cannot recover. They were never the holders of the cheque and cannot sue on it. I say no more of their claim.

The crucial question is whether the auctioneers can recover, contrary to the learned judge's conclusion. If they cannot, his decision, if upheld in this court, is

h   of great importance to auctioneers and others acting as agents for principals who may in the ordinary course of their business as agents accept cheques drawn in their favour by third parties. Indeed, as was pointed out during the argument, if the learned judge's view be right, no auctioneers can safely accept payment of a deposit from a purchaser to whom property is knocked down at an auction otherwise than in cash or by bankers' draft. This of course does not of itself mean that the

j   learned judge's view is wrong, but a conclusion which has so startlingly inconvenient a commercial result requires to have its foundation in point of law closely analysed before it can be accepted as correct.

It is, I think, necessary carefully to analyse the several contracts involved between the three parties concerned, the vendors, the auctioneers and the defendant. There are at least three. First, there is the contract between the vendors and the auctioneers under which the vendors employ the auctioneers to sell the property on the vendors' behalf. Secondly, there is the contract between the vendors, acting by the auctioneers, on the one hand, and the defendant, as purchaser, on the other, for the sale and purchase of the property. This is, in the first instance, an oral contract created when the property is knocked down to the defendant on acceptance by the auctioneers of his bid. But, by reason of s 40 of the Law of Property Act 1925, that oral contract is not enforceable unless and until the memorandum to which I have already referred is signed. When this is done (as it was done), then that contract between the vendor and the defendant becomes enforceable. Thirdly, there is (as I think) the contract created between the defendant as the drawer of the cheque sued on and the auctioneers as the named payees of that cheque whereunder the defendant agreed that that cheque would be duly met on presentation by the auctioneers or any person properly deriving title to the cheque from the auctioneers. It is true that the auctioneers, by reason of condition 3, received that deposit as agents for the vendors and are accountable to them for its proceeds. That accounting is a matter between the vendors and the auctioneers. The defendant is not concerned with the accounting. The auctioneers have warranted to him that they are authorised to accept the deposit as agents for the vendors and to give a good discharge to the defendant for his obligation to pay it. But that in no way divests the auctioneers of their rights as named payees, and, therefore, as holders of the cheque, as against the defendant.

I have ventured to emphasise this analysis of the contractual position because it is only on such analysis that what I consider to be true position regarding consideration for the cheque emerges.

The case appears to have been argued before the learned judge on the footing that the consideration for the cheque was the vendors' obligation to complete the sale. I will assume for the moment that this is correct. On this assumption, the contract of sale (the second of the three contracts already mentioned) still subsisted when the cheque was stopped. The vendors then still remained obliged to complete. True, the vendors became entitled to rescind immediately the cheque was stopped. But they did not immediately exercise that right. So long as they refrained from so doing their obligation to perform the sale contract remained. The stopping of the cheque immediately gave rise to a cause of action under the contract between the defendant and the auctioneers, the third of the three contracts already mentioned, a contract totally distinct from the second. At that time the consideration for the second contract had not failed, and it follows that if the consideration for the second contract were also the consideration for the third contract, equally, that consideration also had not then failed. Even if subsequently, on the vendors rescinding the second contract, the consideration for the second and third contracts then failed, the defendant was already liable to the auctioneers under the third contract by reason of his having stopped the cheque. None of the authorities to which we were referred support the conclusion reached by the learned judge, and I am unable to follow on what principle of law the vendors' subsequent rescission of the second contract can operate to divest the auctioneers of their already accrued cause of action under the third contract on the cheque, on which they alone could sue and of which they alone were at all material times the holders and the vendors were not.

Even if, therefore, that consideration did ultimately totally fail, and even if (which I very much doubt) the defendant can rely on such a total failure when brought about by his own wrongful act in stopping the cheque, I am quite unable to see how it affords a defence to the present case. I would, therefore, respectfully differ from the learned judge's conclusion on the premises on which the case was argued before him.

I must, however, confess to considerable doubt whether this was the consideration for the cheque. Even if one treats the signature of the memorandum (by which the vendors for the first time became bound to sell) and the giving to and the receipt by the auctioneers of the cheque as substantially concurrent, the resultant obligation of the vendors was consideration which did not move from the promisee—the payee of the cheque—that is to say, the auctioneers, and would not therefore support a simple contract between the auctioneers and the defendant: see s 27(1) of the Bills of Exchange Act 1882. On the other hand, at the moment when the cheque was given and received by the auctioneers they warranted to the defendant their authority to sign the memorandum on the vendors' behalf and to receive the cheque payable to themselves as named payees in diminution of the defendant's obligation to pay the full amount of the purchase price to the vendors. If this were the true consideration for the cheque (as I think it was) that consideration never failed and the suggested defence would fail in limine.

Another possibility (as was suggested by Buckley LJ during the argument) is that the true consideration was the auctioneers' acceptance of the cheque in place of legal tender by means of which, strictly speaking, the defendant was bound to discharge his obligation to pay the deposit.

Whatever the true view of the consideration may be, on no possible view did that consideration totally fail. For my part, I am not prepared to accept that in a case such as the present an agent who receives a cheque made payable to himself in the course of a transaction effected on behalf of his principal obtains no enforceable right against the drawer of that cheque if he stops payment without just cause, or that if that cheque were endorsed by the agent to his principal (as might well happen in the ordinary course of business), the principal equally in such circumstances obtains no right because of supposed lack of value.

The conclusion at which I have arrived makes it unnecessary to consider the decision of this court in *Diamond v Graham*[1], to which counsel most helpfully drew our attention after the conclusion of the argument. I must, however, confess to some doubts whether s 27(2) of the Bills of Exchange Act 1882 has any application to the present case, and had I wished to found this judgment on that decision I would have required to have further argument on certain questions which might arise under that subsection, and which do not (so far as appears from that report) seem to have been argued in that case, and were not argued on the present appeal.

I would allow this appeal and order judgment for the auctioneers to be entered for £555 with interest as claimed. I would dismiss the vendors' appeal without costs.

BUCKLEY LJ. I agree with the judgment that has just been delivered, and I hope that I shall not be regarded as guilty of any disrespect to the learned judge if I add nothing of my own.

MEGAW LJ. I agree fully with the judgment delivered by Roskill LJ. Out of respect for the learned judge, I would stress that he was called on to deal with a number of issues on which his conclusions of fact and law have not been challenged. Moreover, as to one issue on which his decision has been challenged, and successfully challenged, he seems to have been invited by both sides to deal with the issue on the assumption that the consideration, or value, for the cheque was something which in the view of each member of this court was not properly so to be regarded. The learned judge is not to be criticised for dealing with the case on that assumption; though, even if the erroneous hypothesis had been correct, I agree with Roskill LJ that it would not, in law, have provided a defence to the action by the auctioneers on the cheque.

Appeal of second plaintiffs allowed; judgment entered for second plaintiffs for £550. Appeal of first plaintiffs dismissed.

Solicitors: *Bailey & Peltz* (for the plaintiffs); *Blackett Gill & Langhams* (for the defendant).

A S Virdi Esq Barrister.

---

1 [1968] 2 All ER 909, [1968] 1 WLR 1061

Re Nicholson (deceased)
Nicholson v Perks

CHANCERY DIVISION
PENNYCUICK V-C
17th, 18th, 19th JULY 1973

Husband and wife – Property – Matrimonial home – Husband sole owner at law – Beneficial interests – Common intention of parties at date of acquisition – Wife making contribution to purchase price – Husband undertaking to pay mortgage instalments – Wife undertaking to pay off mortgage out of anticipated legacy – Wife's undertaking unenforceable – Wife paying off mortgage out of legacy five years later – Whether wife entitled to share of beneficial interest in home.

Husband and wife – Property – Improvement – Contribution by spouse in money or money's worth to improvement of property – Spouse acquiring enlarged share of beneficial interest – Valuation of enlarged share – Cost of improvement to be added to value of property and of spouse's share at date of improvement – Matrimonial Proceedings and Property Act 1970, s 37.

In April 1938 the plaintiff and her husband bought a house for £900. The house was conveyed into the sole name of the husband. The husband contributed £15 and the plaintiff £75 to the purchase money. The balance was raised on an instalment mortgage, repayable over a period of 18 years. At the date of the purchase the plaintiff expected to receive a substantial legacy from a relative. The understanding was that the husband would pay the instalments but that the plaintiff, on the death of the relative, would pay off the mortgage debt out of the legacy. The husband paid the mortgage instalments from May 1938 to July 1943. In May 1943 the plaintiff's relative died, leaving her residuary estate to the plaintiff. At the plaintiff's request a sufficient sum was paid out of the estate to redeem the mortgage. In 1966, when the market value of the house was some £6,000, the plaintiff paid £189 for the installation of gas central heating in the house. In 1969 the husband made a will in which he devised the house on trust to the plaintiff for life with remainder to the defendant absolutely. The husband died in July 1971. The plaintiff took out a summons for a declaration that immediately before the husband's death she was beneficially entitled to an undivided share in the proceeds of sale of the house.

Held – (i) The plaintiff could only establish her claim on an implication of a resulting trust based on the common intention of the parties at the date when the house was acquired. Just as an undertaking, though unenforceable, to pay mortgage instalments was a factor to be taken into account in determining the common intention of the parties, so also was an unenforceable undertaking to pay off the capital of the mortgage, whatever the source might be from which the spouse concerned intended to pay off the mortgage. Taking all the circumstances into account, i e the original contributions to the purchase price and the arrangement that the husband would pay the mortgage instalments and the plaintiff would pay off the mortgage when she received the legacy, the only legitimate inference was that it was their common intention that the beneficial interest in the property should belong to them in equal shares (see p 390 a and b and p 391 c to f, post).

(ii) The payment by the plaintiff for the installation of central heating represented a contribution of a substantial nature, within s 37[a] of the Matrimonial Proceedings and Property Act 1970, to the improvement of the property and accordingly when it

---

a Section 37 is set out at p 392 b and c, post

was installed the plaintiff acquired an enlarged share of the beneficial interest. Taking the value of the house as £6,000 at the date of installation, the effect of the installation was to increase the value of the house to £6,150 and the value of the plaintiff's share from £3,000 to £3,150, i e from a half share to a 21/41sts share (see p 392 d to g, post).

(iii) Accordingly a declaration should be made that the plaintiff was beneficially entitled to a share in the proceeds of sale, that share amounting to 21/41sts of the proceeds (see p 393 c, post).

Notes

For the determination of property rights between husband and wife, see 19 Halsbury's Laws (3rd Edn) 900, 901, para 1492, and for cases on the subject, see 27(1) Digest (Reissue) 304-315, 2267-2330.

For expenditure on improvements to property, see 19 Halsbury's Laws (3rd Edn) 840, para 1370.

For the Matrimonial Proceedings and Property Act 1970, s 37, see 40 Halsbury's Statutes (3rd Edn) 833.

Cases referred to in judgment

Cowcher v Cowcher [1972] 1 All ER 943, [1972] 1 WLR 425.
Gissing v Gissing [1970] 2 All ER 780, [1971] AC 886, [1970] 3 WLR 255, 21 P &CR 702, HL, 27(1) Digest (Reissue) 311, 2303.
Pettitt v Pettitt [1969] 2 All ER 385, [1970] AC 777, [1969] 2 WLR 966, 20 P & CR 991, HL, 27(1) Digest (Reissue) 102, 707.

Cases also cited

Davis v Vale [1971] 2 All ER 1021, [1971] 1 WLR 1022, CA.
Jones, Re, Farrington v Forrester [1893] 2 Ch 461.
Kowalczuk v Kowalczuk [1973] 2 All ER 1042, [1973] 1 WLR 930, CA.

Originating summons

By his will dated 4th July 1969, Lewis Herbert Nicholson devised his house, 29 Carding-ton Road, Bedford, to trustees in trust to permit the plaintiff, Elsie Ann Nicholson, his wife, to reside there during her life and subject thereto on trust for sale with power to postpone sale and to hold the rents and profits and all capital moneys and investments arising from any sale and the income thereof for the use and benefit of the plaintiff during her life and after her death on trust to convey and transfer the house or money and investments to the defendant, Phillis Claire Perks, absolutely. Mr Nicholson died on 1st July 1971 and letters of administration with the will annexed were granted to the plaintiff and the defendant on 29th December 1972. The plaintiff commenced proceedings under the Inheritance (Family Provision) Act 1938 which were stood over pending the hearing of a summons issued by the plaintiff on 15th January 1973 in which she sought the following relief: (i) a declaration that immediately before the death of Mr Nicholson she was beneficially entitled to an undivided share in the proceeds of sale of the house; (ii) that it might be declared whether the undivided share amounted to (a) eight-ninths, or (b) one-half, or (c) some other fraction of the proceeds of sale; (iii) further or other relief. The facts are set out in the judgment.

Timothy Lloyd for the plaintiff.
D Gidley Scott for the defendant.

PENNYCUICK V-C. This action, commenced by originating summons, relates to the estate of Lewis Herbert Nicholson and concerns the proceeds of sale of a property known as 29 Cardington Road, Bedford. The plaintiff is Mrs Elsie Ann Nicholson, who is the widow of Lewis Nicholson. The defendant, Miss Phillis Claire Perks, is the reversionary legatee under his will, the plaintiff being given a life interest. The issue in the action turns on the beneficial ownership of this property, 29 Cardington Road. The property was purchased on 11th April 1938 at a price of £900, and was conveyed into the sole name of Lewis Nicholson. It is common ground between counsel that the cash contribution made by Lewis Nicholson and the plaintiff towards the purchase price of the property should be regarded as £75 by the plaintiff and £15 by Lewis Nicholson. The balance of the purchase price was raised on an instalment mortgage in the sole name of Lewis Nicholson, the amount raised on mortgage being £860. That sum, together with the two sums of £75 and £15 which I have mentioned, makes £950. That represents the purchase price of £900, with £25 costs and £25 paid to a builder. The mortgage provided for repayment by monthly sums of £5 18s 3d over a period of 18 years.

I must now go, so to speak, sideways and backwards in order to mention certain facts concerning the family of Lewis Nicholson and the plaintiff. The latter had previously been married to Frederick Nicholson who was a cousin of Lewis Nicholson and who had died in 1912. Frederick Nicholson's mother was Mrs Esther Zillah Nicholson. Mrs Esther Nicholson had the plaintiff to live with her for some time, together with Arthur, who was an older brother of Lewis Nicholson, and also Lewis Nicholson himself. Arthur Nicholson died on 10th September 1938, having by a will dated 8th March 1937, appointed Mrs Esther Nicholson as his executrix and residuary legatee. His gross estate was £4,387. Esther Nicholson made a will dated 6th October 1938, whereby she gave her residuary estate to the plaintiff. I will refer later on to a codicil which she subsequently made.

It will be seen from those facts that at the date of the purchase, namely, 11th April 1938, Arthur Nicholson was still alive; but he had made a will the previous year giving everything to Mrs Esther Nicholson. The latter, in turn, made her will on 6th October 1938, shortly after the death of Arthur Nicholson.

To return to the property itself, the monthly instalments under the mortgage were paid from May 1938 to July 1943. The principal content of those payments was £162. It appears from the evidence that most of the payments were made by Lewis Nicholson himself, but on some occasions when he was short of money or the like the plaintiff paid the instalment out of her own money. In case the point is material, the proportion paid by the plaintiff is certainly something less than one-half, and I would put it at one-third. But that is largely guesswork, and the view which I take of the case does not depend on that matter.

I now return to Mrs Esther Nicholson. I have already mentioned that by her will dated 6th October 1938 she gave her residuary estate to the plaintiff. On 22nd November 1942 she made a codicil to her will in rather unusual terms. It looks as if the codicil, in holograph form, was written out by a doctor who had witnessed the will. The codicil, so far as material, runs as follows:

> 'I Esther Zillah Nicholson residing at One hundred and twenty eight Elstow Road, Bedford do hereby make the following Codicil to my Last Will and Testament dated 6th October 1938. I leave and bequeath to my nephew Lewis Herbert Nicholson residing at Twenty Nine Cardington Road Bedford my house property known as One hundred and twenty eight Elstow Road Bedford as his absolute property together with all furniture, bed and table linen and other contents of the said house and I also wish the mortgage on Twenty nine Cardington Road, if any, to be paid off out of my Estate if same is sufficient for that purpose and except as altered by this Codicil I confirm my said Last Will and Testament dated 6th October 1938.'

An obvious question of construction arises on that document to which I will return later. Mrs Esther Nicholson died shortly afterwards, on 11th May 1943.

Then, in August 1943, at the request of the plaintiff, the sum of £697 15s 9d was paid out of the estate of Mrs Esther Nicholson in redemption of the mortgage. The plaintiff

a
also claims to have made a number of payments between 1944 and 1970 for repairs and decorations to the house. She further claims to have made four specific payments, described as improvements, and those were as follows: on 25th May 1962 Eastern Gas Board £28 5s 0d (there was some little doubt on the evidence, but that appears to have been for a gas cooker); on 19th June 1963 a new gas fire, £22 17s 10d; on 19th November 1966 gas part central heating, £189; and on 7th December 1968 a new gas fire, £17 9s 6d.

b
In 1953 Lewis Nicholson and the plaintiff made mutual wills. However, on 4th July 1969 Lewis Nicholson made a new will under which he devised the house, 29 Cardington Road, on trust to permit his wife to reside there during her life—

c
'and subject thereto Upon trust for sale ... then Upon trust to convey and transfer the said house or money and investments to Phillis Claire Perks of 27 Goldington Road in the Borough of Bedford absolutely.'

She is the present defendant. Then there is a residuary gift to the plaintiff which did not have any operation because the net estate of Lewis Nicholson after payment of debts, including an overdraft to the bank, was represented entirely by the house.

d
Lewis Nicholson died on 1st July 1971. Lloyds Bank Ltd, which had been named as executor, renounced probate and ultimately letters of administration with the will annexed were granted to the plaintiff and the defendant. The plaintiff has started proceedings under the Inheritance (Family Provision) Act 1938, but they have been stood over pending the termination of the present action. The plaintiff did not claim a share in the house by virtue of contributions to it until 1972.

e
The present summons was issued on 15th January 1973. On the summons affidavit evidence was given by the plaintiff on the one hand, and by the defendant on the other hand. I have already sufficiently summarised the affidavit evidence and I need not refer again to the affidavits. The parties were both called to give oral evidence, first, by way of supplementing their affidavit evidence, and then by way of cross-examination. The plaintiff is 85 years old, but she is an altogether clear-minded

f
lady, and I found her a convincing witness. I will quote a few passages from her evidence. She said: 'I knew I would get the money from my mother-in-law and could then pay the mortgage off. She was there referring to the period in 1938 when the house was purchased. She referred to Mrs Esther Nicholson as her mother-in-law because that had been the relationship when she was married to her first husband. Then she said in cross-examination: 'My mother-in-law told me she was going to leave me everything she had.' Again she is referring back to the period in

g
1938. Then she said:

'Concerning the mortgage [again going back to 1938] I talked about buying the house on mortgage with my husband. My husband was supposed to pay the mortgage. He would give me the cash and I took the money to the building society. That was the arrangement when we bought the house.'

h
Then later on she said: 'I knew my mother-in-law had more than enough to pay off the mortgage. I always told my husband that when I got the money I would pay off the mortgage.' Then she said: 'I thought the house belonged to both of us.' She said 'There were no papers. When the house was bought we were not thinking about shares. We wanted the house for both of us—our house'. Finally, she said: 'When

j
I paid the builder there was no question of [my husband] paying it back. It was just towards the house.' I accept her evidence. The defendant, in the nature of things, had very little to contribute on the events of 1938.

What then is the proper conclusion on those facts. I was rightly, and rather shortly, referred to a series of well-known cases of properties acquired in the name of one party where another party, generally though not necessarily a spouse, claimed an

interest in the property, including, in particular, *Pettitt v Pettitt*[1] and *Gissing v Gissing*[2].
It is not, I think, in dispute between counsel that in circumstances such as the present
the party in whose name the property is not—that is to say, the plaintiff here—
must establish her claim, if she is to establish it at all, on an implication of a resulting
trust based on the common intention of the parties at the date of the acquisition of the
property. For this purpose, 'common intention' means, as I understand it, an intention
in some broad sense—may be a very broad sense—to provide the purchase price,
directly or indirectly, either equally or in certain proportions. I was referred on this
point to the judgment of Bagnall J in *Cowcher v Cowcher*[3], and in particular to a passage
in which he deals with what he calls 'money consensus' as defining the beneficial
interests under a resulting trust. I will not read that passage, but I respectfully agree
with the judge's reasoning. The common intention must be inferred from all the
circumstances, including what was actually done before and at the time of the
purchase. There is no doubt that in this connection great weight must be attached
to an undertaking, albeit not legally enforceable, of one party to make himself or
herself responsible for the amount owing under a mortgage where the house is
bought in part on mortgage and, in particular, though not universally, on an instalment mortgage: see, for example, per Viscount Dilhorne in *Gissing v Gissing*[4]:

> '. . . in determining whether or not there was such common intention, regard
> can of course be had to the conduct of the parties. If the wife provided part of
> the purchase price of the house, either initially or subsequently by paying or
> sharing in the mortgage payments, the inference may well arise that it was the
> common intention that she should have an interest in the house.'

And per Lord Diplock[5]:

> 'The conduct of the spouses in relation to the payment of the mortgage
> instalments may be no less relevant to their common intention as to the beneficial
> interests in a matrimonial home acquired in this way than their conduct in
> relation to the payment of the cash deposit.'

It is frequently impossible to quantify in money terms the amount of an unenforceable undertaking of this kind to pay mortgage instalments or the principal
under a mortgage. There is, however, no doubt that that is a factor which the court
must take into account in determining what was the common intention; and,
having ascertained that common intention, one should determine the trust on which
the property is to be regarded as held. It will be observed that the law as laid down
in the recent series of cases, although based on the old principle of resulting trusts,
has gone a considerable way beyond the original narrow framework of resulting
trusts. I am not, I think, concerned today to trace out any further, even if I were able
to do so, the precise path leading from common intention to resulting trust.

To return to the present case, the position is that the plaintiff made an original
contribution of £75 and Lewis Nicholson made an original contribution of £15.
So far there is no difficulty in quantification. Then, it is clear, I think, that Lewis
Nicholson undertook the obligation to pay the mortgage instalments vis-à-vis the
building society which advanced the money; and that appeared also to be the arrangement as between Lewis Nicholson and the plaintiff. As she says, her husband was
supposed to pay the mortgage: 'That was the arrangement when we bought the
house.' If there were no more to it than that, there would still be no great difficulty
in quantification, and it would appear that the share of Lewis Nicholson would be

---

1   [1969] 2 All ER 385, [1970] AC 777
2   [1970] 2 All ER 780, [1971] AC 886
3   [1972] 1 All ER 943 at 954, [1972] 1 WLR 425 at 436
4   [1970] 2 All ER at 786, [1971] AC at 900
5   [1970] 2 All ER at 791, [1971] AC at 906

a   much greater than the share of the plaintiff. Then, however, comes this circumstance
of critical importance in the present case; namely, that the plaintiff in 1938 was
expecting to receive the estate of Mrs Esther Nicholson which would be sufficient
to pay off the principal of the mortgage, and that she told her husband that when
she got the money she would pay off the mortgage. It seems to me that that is a factor
which must clearly be taken into account in assessing the common intention of the
parties. On the other hand, that factor is totally incapable of precise quantification.

b   Apart from the fact that Mrs Esther Nicholson might change her mind and not give
anything at all to the plaintiff there could be no certainty as to how long Mrs Esther
Nicholson would live.

Taking all the circumstances into account—that is, the original contribution, and
the arrangement that Lewis Nicholson would be responsible for the mortgage
instalments, but that the plaintiff when she got the money from Mrs Esther Nicholson

c   would pay off the mortgage—I have come to the conclusion that the only legitimate
inference is that their common intention was that the beneficial interest in this
property should belong to them in equal shares. I so hold.

Counsel for the defendant made the point that in 1938 the plaintiff possessed as
regards Mrs Esther Nicholson a mere expectation which is not an item of property

d   at all. It is, I think, clear enough that on the strict rule of resulting trust a mere
promise to pay off the mortgage when and if she got Mrs Esther Nicholson's estate
could not be regarded as a contribution to the purchase of the property. On the
other hand, on the principles which have been established in the present context,
there is no doubt that an undertaking, though unenforceable, to pay mortgage
instalments is a factor that must be taken into account in arriving at common intention, and I can see no reason why such a factor should be any less to be taken into

e   account where the undertaking is to pay off the capital of the mortgage and the
source from which the capital is to be paid off is some expected future legacy. For
the purposes of this case I think it quite immaterial what is the source from which
the spouse concerned intended to pay off the mortgage: for example, whether it is
future earnings or an expected legacy.

f   I come now to Mrs Esther Nicholson's will and codicil. On the view which I have
taken, these are only of significance insofar as they bear out the plaintiff's own
account of the understanding between herself and her husband in 1938. It is significant
in that respect that, whatever the effect of the codicil, Mrs Esther Nicholson did
indeed in the most express terms leave her money to be applied in the discharge of
the mortgage. If I had reached a different conclusion as to the plaintiff taking from
the start a beneficial interest in this property, then the terms of Mrs Esther Nicholson's

g   codicil would be of great significance. The position then would be that the property
belonged to Lewis Nicholson. I disregard for this purpose the small cash contribution made by the plaintiff. On the other hand, if the plaintiff herself provided
the amount paid to redeem the mortgage, then she would have a charge by way of
subrogation on the property. The question would then arise whether on this rather

h   odd document Mrs Esther Nicholson gave her whole residuary estate to the plaintiff
with a mere request to apply her estate pro tanto in the payment of the mortgage,
or whether it was a direct gift to Mr and Mrs Nicholson according to their respective
interests in the property for the purpose of discharging the mortgage on the property.
I regard that as an extremely moot point, and I do not think it is necessary to express
a view on it. Clearly if, as I have held, the plaintiff's interest should be regarded as a
beneficial share in the property by virtue of her undertaking to pay off the mortgage,

j   then the fact that she did in fact pay off the mortgage would be of no significance
in the quantification of her share: the payment could not increase her share.

I turn now to the other point which has been raised on this summons which is of
considerable interest, though on the facts of this case not of any outstanding practical
importance. It will be remembered that the plaintiff claims to have made four specified improvements to this property and I am satisfied from her evidence that she did

indeed pay the sums mentioned for the particular purposes mentioned; that is to say, the acquisition of a gas cooker, a gas fire, part installation of central heating and another gas fire. Section 37 of the Matrimonial Proceedings Property Act 1970 contains this entirely novel provision:

'It is hereby declared that where a husband or wife contributes in money or money's worth to the improvement of real or personal property in which or in the proceeds of sale of which either or both of them has or have a beneficial interest, the husband or wife so contributing shall, if the contribution is of a substantial nature and subject to any agreement between them to the contrary express or implied, be treated as having then acquired by virtue of his or her contribution a share or an enlarged share, as the case may be, in that beneficial interest of such an extent as may have been then agreed or, in default of such agreement, as may seem in all the circumstances just to any court before which the question of the existence or extent of the beneficial interest of the husband or wife arises (whether in proceedings between them or in any other proceedings).'

In the present case I have no doubt that the installation of central heating in November 1966 did constitute an improvement to this house which was paid for by the plaintiff, and that that payment represents a contribution of a substantial nature within the meaning of the section. The result of that is that I must treat her as having then—that is, at the date when the central heating was installed—acquired an enlarged share in her beneficial interest. It seems to me that, in principle, the proper way in which to work out that provision is to ascertain the value of the property at the date immediately before the making of the improvement, and then to ascertain what addition to the value of the property was due to that improvement. One should then treat the share of the party who makes the improvement as enlarged by a proportionate amount corresponding to the increase in value represented by the improvement. That can best be illustrated by taking simple figures. If the property before the improvement is worth £6,000 and the parties are entitled to it in equal shares, that is to say, £3,000 each, and if the improvement increases the value of the property by £1,000 then the respective shares instead of being three-sixths and three-sixths will become four-sevenths and three-sevenths. In the present case it is agreed between counsel that the increased value of the property in 1966, and indeed at the time when all these improvements, or so-called improvements, were made, was £6,000, and further, that the increase in the value of the property due to the installation of the central heating should be taken at £150. Taking those figures, the result is that instead of the shares being £3,000 in a property worth £6,000, the shares become £3,150 and £3,000 in a property worth £6,150. Counsel have worked out the proportions, and I am satisfied that the proportionate interests become 21/41sts to the plaintiff and 20/41sts to Lewis Nicholson.

I must say a word or two about the other three items claimed as improvements. On the face of it, one should, I think, read s 37 as applicable severally to each given improvement, and that would plainly be the position where one had, for instance, two improvements of a large amount separated by an interval of time. But a difficulty does arise in the case where one or other party carries out a series of relatively small improvements. It cannot, I think, be the position that the section requires that on each of what may be 20 occasions within a period of two years the shares of the parties have to be readjusted. It may well be that in such a case at least a legitimate course in deciding what is just, as the section requires one to do, is to look with hindsight at the series of repairs and treat them as, so to speak, a single improvement, and take some date at which that improvement should be taken as having been made. The whole subject seems to me to give rise to considerable difficulty, and it is not necessary for me on the facts of the present case to reach any decided view on it. I say it is not necessary on the facts of the present case because here one has three isolated items of a relatively small amount. The first is the gas cooker in 1962, which one must *a* assume (though there is no evidence about it) was installed in substitution for some existing cooker, in which case it may well be that it was not an improvement at all. I assume that the two gas fires could validly be treated as improvements. But, looking at the dates, I find it impossible in any way to lump them together with the central heating and treat them as, so to speak, a single improvement made at some date or other. The first gas fire was installed over three years before the central heating. Even *b* if it was an improvement the contribution of £22 17s 10d can hardly be treated by itself as of a substantial nature. Then, clearly, I think there must be an adjustment of shares in November 1966, when the one major improvement, the central heating, was made. But I cannot think that the new gas fire installed in December 1968, if it was an improvement, can in some way be lumped with the installation of the central heating, or that in itself the payment for it could be said to be a contribution of a substantial *c* nature. I do not think, therefore, that any adjustment of shares falls to be made in respect of the alleged improvements other than the central heating.

I conclude that I ought to make a declaration that immediately before the death of Lewis Nicholson the plaintiff was beneficially entitled to a share of the proceeds of sale of the property, 29 Cardington Road, that share amounting to 21/41sts of the proceeds of sale.

d *Declaration accordingly.*

Solicitors: *Mellows*, Bedford (for the plaintiff); *Hawkins & Co*, Hitchin (for the defendant).

Susan Corbett Barrister.

e
Lees v Arthur Greaves (Lees) Ltd

COURT OF APPEAL, CIVIL DIVISION
LORD DENNING MR, STAMP AND SCARMAN LJJ
2nd NOVEMBER 1973

f *Industrial relations – Unfair dismissal – Dismissal – Meaning – Notice to terminate contract of employment – Agreement to terminate employment during period of notice negativing dismissal – Evidence of termination by mutual consent – Need to prove employee had full knowledge of implications of agreement – Employers bringing pressure on employee to stop working for them before expiry of notice – Employee submitting to pressure – Whether employment terminated by agreement – Whether employee dismissed – Industrial Relations* *g* *Act 1971, s 23.*

The appellant had been employed by the employers for 18 years. His contract of employment provided for termination by six months notice by either party. In 1971 the employers gave the appellant notice terminating his employment on 31st March 1972 'unless otherwise agreed in the meantime'. During the period of notice the employers sought to persuade the appellant to leave before the expiry *h* of the notice. At an interview with the employers on 28th January 1972, the appellant was prevailed on to finish work with them on that date. He accepted two months full gross pay instead of working the remaining two months; he was given his insurance cards and other documents and left on the same day. The relevant provisions of the Industrial Relations Act 1971 came into force on 28th February 1972. The appellant applied for compensation under the 1971 Act on the ground that he had *j* been unfairly dismissed, contending that, under s 23(2) and (5)*ᵃ* of the 1971 Act, his dismissal had taken effect on the date when his notice expired, i e 31st March 1972. The Industrial Court affirmed a decision of an industrial tribunal dismissing the complaint, holding that the appellant had not been 'dismissed' since his employment had been terminated by mutual consent under the agreement of 28th January;

---
a Section 23, so far as material, is set out at p 395 *a* to *c*, post

alternatively that, if he had been dismissed, the dismissal had taken effect on 28th January and accordingly the provisions of the 1971 Act had no application. On appeal,

Held (Stamp LJ dissenting)—The appeal would be allowed for the following reasons—

(i) In order to prove the termination of a contract of employment by mutual consent during a period of notice it was necessary to show that the employee had agreed with full knowledge of the implications. It was impossible to infer from the primary facts that there had been a consensual termination of the appellant's contract on 28th January. The appellant had only stopped work because the employers insisted on it (see p 396 g and j, p 397 a and p 399 e to g, post); dictum of Sir John Donaldson P in *McAlwane v Boughton Estates Ltd* [1973] 2 All ER at 302 approved.

(ii) The proper inference was not that the appellant had been summarily dismissed on 28th January but that he was not required to work during the remainder of the period of his notice. It followed that his employment had terminated at the end of the period of notice, i e on 31st March, and the appellant was entitled to pursue his claim under the 1971 Act (see p 397 b and e and p 400 a and c to e, post).

Decision of the National Industrial Relations Court [1973] 2 All ER 21 reversed.

Notes

For the meaning of dismissal under the Industrial Relations Act 1971, see Supplement to 38 Halsbury's Laws (3rd Edn) 677B, 19.

For the Industrial Relations Act 1971, s 23, see 41 Halsbury's Statutes (3rd Edn) 2088.

Cases referred to in judgments

Brindle v H W Smith (Cabinets) Ltd [1973] 1 All ER 230, [1972] 1 WLR 1653, [1973] ICR 12, CA.

McAlwane v Boughton Estates Ltd [1973] 2 All ER 299, [1973] ICR 470, NIRC.

Marriott v Oxford and District Co-operative Society Ltd [1969] 3 All ER 1126, [1970] 1 QB 186, [1969] 3 WLR 984, CA, Digest (Cont Vol C) 689, 816Adc.

Appeal

The appellant, John R Lees, was employed by the respondents, Arthur Greaves (Lees) Ltd ('the employers'), under a contract of service which provided that it might be terminated by either party giving six months notice. On 1st October 1971 the appellant was orally given six months notice by the employers. The notice was confirmed by a letter from the employers dated 7th October which concluded: 'At the expiration of notice, March 31st 1972, your employment will be terminated unless otherwise agreed in the meantime.' The appellant continued to work for the employers until 28th January 1972 when, following an interview with the employers, he finished working for them. The appellant applied to an industrial tribunal for compensation for unfair dismissal under the Industrial Relations Act 1971, the relevant provisions of which came into force on 28th February 1972. On 19th July 1972 a tribunal sitting at Manchester dismissed the application holding that 'the effective date of the termination of the [appellant's] contract of service had been 28th January 1972', i e before the coming into force of the 1971 Act. On 14th December 1972 the National Industrial Relations Court[1] (Sir Samuel Cooke, Mr R Boyfield and Professor T L Johnston) dismissed an appeal by the appellant holding that he had not been 'dismissed', within s 23 of the 1971 Act since on 28th January 1972 he and the employers had agreed that his contract of service should be terminated forthwith and it had been so terminated; alternatively that, if the appellant had been dismissed, the contract had been terminated, and the dismissal had taken effect, on 28th January 1972. The appellant appealed.

Laurence Oates for the appellant.
Michael Howard for the employers.

---

1 [1973] 2 All ER 21

LORD DENNING MR. Under the Industrial Relations Act 1971 a man who is unfairly dismissed is entitled to compensation. The word 'dismissed' is defined in s 23(2). It says:

'... an employee shall be taken to be dismissed by his employer if, but only if, —(a) the contract under which he is employed by the employer is terminated by the employer, whether it is so terminated by notice or without notice ...'

Subsection (5) says:

'In this Act "the effective date of termination"—(a) in relation to an employee whose contract of employment is terminated by notice, whether given by his employer or by the employee, means the date on which that notice expires; (b) in relation to an employee whose contract of employment is terminated without notice, means the date on which the termination takes effect ...'

Those provisions of the Act came into force on 28th February 1972. It has been held in this court that a straddling notice is good—by which I mean a notice which is given before the Act came into force to expire after it came into force. That was decided in *Brindle v H W Smith (Cabinets) Ltd*[1]. So, as I go through the facts, remember that the critical date was 28th February 1972. If the effective date of termination was after 28th February 1972, he is entitled to compensation for unfair dismissal; but if the effective date of termination was before 28th February, he is not entitled to compensation.

Mr Lees, the appellant, has been 18 years with his employers. He had worked his way up from the bottom to the top. He had become works manager. On 31st October 1970 the terms of his employment were put into writing. He was to get £1,800 a year and there was this provision for termination: 'Notice of termination to be six months by either party.'

In 1971 the employers determined to have another works manager. They wrote to Mr Lees on 7th October 1971, this letter:

'Confirming the verbal notice given to you on Friday last, the 1st October, you are hereby given the requisite notice of 6 months under the terms of your agreement to terminate your employment as Works Manager. During the period of notice you will be responsible to the Works Manager who will be appointed to fill the position you now vacate, solely for the sales and production of General Sheet Metal Work, on your present terms and conditions. At the expiration of notice, March 31st, 1972, your employment will be terminated unless otherwise agreed in the meantime.'

By that letter Mr Lees's employment was terminated by notice which was to expire on 31st March 1972. If the matter stopped there, it would be a straddling notice. The effective date of termination would be 31st March 1972. He would be entitled beyond doubt to compensation for unfair dismissal.

But it is said that the notice never took effect. It is said that on 28th January 1972 the employment was terminated by agreement. So it was terminated before 28th February 1972, and Mr Lees is not entitled to any compensation at all.

The only evidence on this point was given by Mr Lees himself. He said:

'I was pressurised into leaving ... I was asked if I had got another job. I said I had notice to work [meaning 'I had to work out my notice']. After further meeting it was said I should leave on Friday, 28th January 1972. I said I should get compensation. He [i e the director] said he would go into it. I left on Friday, 28th January 1972. I was given for next two month—full wages for two months.'

In cross-examination he said:

1   [1973] 1 All ER 230, [1972] 1 WLR 1653

'I left on 28th January 1972 as being entitled to do so, I received two months
pay and cards and P45 on that day.'

The employers did not give any evidence, but submitted that on Mr Lees's own
evidence the effective date of termination was 28th January 1972, before the Act
came into effect; and so he had no claim to compensation. The tribunal made
this finding of primary facts:

'... that on 28th January 1972 [Mr Lees] was prevailed on to finish, and in
fact did finish, on that date, accepting two months full gross pay in lieu of working
the said two months; on that date he received in addition his insurance cards,
holiday pay entitlements, and his P45 tax form. [Mr Lees] signed on at the
employment exchange some time after 31st March 1972, and obtained new
employment in May 1972.'

The tribunal drew this conclusion from those primary facts:

'... the effective date of the termination of [Mr Lees's] contract of service had
been 28th January 1972 when he received all his monetary entitlements, his
insurance cards and P45 tax form, after which date there was no longer in
existence any contract between him and the [employers] and thenceforward
[Mr Lees] was entitled to offer his services to any other employer.'

So they rejected his application as his dismissal was before the Act came into force.
The Industrial Court[1] affirmed that decision. Mr Lees appeals to this court. He
says that on the primary facts the proper inference was that the effective date of
the termination was 31st March 1972.

We have held that in such cases as this the primary facts are for the tribunal;
and that the proper inference from them is a question of law which can be reconsidered
by this court. It was so held in *Marriott v Oxford and District Co-operative Society Ltd*[2],
and it has been applied repeatedly. In this case, what is the proper inference from
the primary facts found by the tribunal?

I start with this. By the letter of 7th October 1971 the contract of employment
of Mr Lees was terminated by notice. Applying s 23(5), the effective date of the
termination was the date on which that notice expired. That was 31st March 1972.
Next I ask: what was the effect of the happenings on 28th January 1972? It is suggested
that the parties came to an agreement whereby his contract of employment was
terminated on that day by agreement. I do not think that is a correct inference.
I find myself in full agreement with what was said by Sir John Donaldson P in
McAlwane v Boughton Estates Ltd[3]:

'We would further suggest that it would be a very rare case indeed in which
it could properly be found that the employer and the employee had got together
and, notwithstanding that there was a current notice of termination of the employment, agreed mutually to terminate the contract, particularly when one
realises the financial consequences to the employee involved in such an
agreement.'

Applying those observations here, it seems to me it would be quite wrong to find
there has been a consensual termination of this contract on 28th January 1972. It
is plain that Mr Lees did not want to stop work. He would have preferred to work
out his notice until 31st March. He only stopped work because the employers insisted
on it. He submitted to their insistence. But he did not agree to it. I decline to infer
any agreement by him when it would mean that he would be deprived of any
compensation at all.

1   [1973] 2 All ER 21
2   [1969] 3 All ER 1126 at 1128, [1970] 1 QB 186 at 192
3   [1973] 2 All ER 299 at 302

a   This point is of general importance because it may arise, not only in 'straddling notices', but also in notices given after the Act came into force. If the employment is terminated by agreement, then he gets no compensation. So the tribunal and the court should not find an agreement unless it is proved that he really did agree with full knowledge of the implications which it held for him.

   On the facts of this case, if there was no agreement by him, there are only two alternatives: either (1) he was dismissed out of hand summarily on 28th January
b 1972 by his employer, or, alternatively (2) he was still employed but not required to work after 28th January, but was paid his pay for the rest of his employment. As to the first alternative, no one suggests that he was dismissed without notice. So the second alternative holds. He was still employed but not required to work for the remaining period from 28th January to 31st March. So the effective date of termination of the employment remained as 31st March 1972, the date given in the
c written notice.

   The only point which has made me hesitate is the fact that his cards were only stamped up to 28th January 1972 and he took them away without comment. Although that is a point against him, I do not think it is sufficient grounds from which to infer a contractual termination of the whole contract. It is true that the cards ought to have been stamped up until 31st March 1972 and that he ought to have paid tax;
d but that still is not sufficient ground from which to infer a consensual termination. In some cases it might be evidence of a termination without notice, but not in this case.

   I cannot help thinking that if the tribunal had had the benefit of *McAlwane v Boughton Estates Ltd*[1], they would have decided differently. So would the Industrial Court. At all events, in my judgment on the primary facts the true inference in
e this case is that the effective date of termination was 31st March 1972. Mr Lees therefore comes within the 1971 Act. He is entitled to claim compensation for unfair dismissal. The preliminary objection fails. I would allow the appeal accordingly.

STAMP LJ. Immediately prior to 28th January 1972 the appellant was employed under a contract of employment which, by the effect of a notice given in October 1971,
f was due to terminate on 31st March 1972. The tribunal found that on 28th January 1972 the appellant was prevailed on to finish, and in fact did finish, on that day, that he accepted 'two months full *gross* pay in lieu of working the said two months'. They went on to say: '. . . on that date he received in addition his insurance cards, holiday pay entitlements, and his P45 tax form.' We are left to conclude that he stopped working on that day and his employers did not require him to do so thereafter.
g Now, on those facts it seems to me that on 28th January 1972 the contract of employment terminated. I cannot escape from that conclusion. It might have terminated —as I think the tribunal held, because they held it terminated 'legally'—by the effect of a mutual agreement; accord and satisfaction. I share the view that such an agreement was in the circumstances unlikely; but I think the tribunal probably did so find. But if the contract did not terminate by the effect of a mutual agreement,
h I cannot escape the conclusion that it terminated unilaterally by the effect of the employers dispensing forthwith with the applicant's services; in other words, they dismissed him forthwith. With all respect to Lord Denning MR I think there were facts in the appellant's own evidence which might have entitled the tribunal so to find. What the appellant said was:

j   'I was pressurised into leaving. 25th January 1972 I was asked if I had got another job. I said I had notice to work. After further meeting it was said I should leave on Friday, 28th January 1972. I said I should get compensation. He said he would go into it. I left on Friday, 28th January 1972.'

I think the tribunal might have found on those facts that the appellant was summarily dismissed on that date. But whether that be the correct view, it seems to me inescapable

1   [1973] 2 All ER 299

that the employment terminated on that day either by agreement or unilaterally; for as the result of what was said and done on that day, neither party thereafter had any right against or obligation to the other under the contract of employment.

With all respect to those who think otherwise, I cannot think that the notice which was given at the beginning of October 1971 affects the matter in the slightest degree. The only effect of that notice was to put a term to the appellant's employment; instead of him being employed for an unspecified period, a term was put to his employment and it remained a term of his employment that it would come to an end on 31st March 1972 unless otherwise agreed in the meantime. That in my view does not in the least prevent the contract of employment being brought to an end at an earlier date either, as I have said, by mutual consent or by summary dismissal. I see no reason for disagreeing with the tribunal's conclusion and I would dismiss the appeal.

SCARMAN LJ. I agree with Lord Denning MR that this appeal should be allowed. I think it is a pity that no evidence was called before the industrial tribunal by the employers. Nevertheless no evidence was called and the industrial tribunal had to do its best to draw the proper inferences from the evidence that was given. An industrial tribunal's findings of fact are final and an appeal to the Industrial Court and thereafter to this court must be confined to a question or questions of law. Nevertheless, whereas the primary facts found by the tribunal cannot be challenged either in the Industrial Court or in this court, it is proper both for the Industrial Court and thereafter for this court to test the inferences that the tribunal has drawn from those facts. The inferences, though of course they are concerned, as are all questions of law, with facts, are in truth a matter of law; and this has been clearly stated by Lord Denning MR in *Marriott v Oxford and District Co-operative Society Ltd*[1]. The passage I rely on is one sentence of Lord Denning MR where he says that the proper inference from facts found is a question of law with which this court can and should interfere. I think therefore it is important to see what were the primary facts. The history of the matter has been rehearsed by Lord Denning MR; I shall content myself with selecting what appear to me to be the critically important primary facts. The first in order of time was the notice given orally in October 1971 and confirmed by a letter written in that month.. It is convenient to take the notice then given as quoted in the letter of 7th October. That was a letter giving the requisite notice of six months to Mr Lees under the terms of his service agreement. It ends with these words: 'At the expiration of notice, March 31st 1972, your employment will be terminated unless otherwise agreed in the meantime'. So long as that notice governed the relationship between the appellant, Mr Lees, and his employers, so long was the effective date of termination of Mr Lees's employment 31st March 1972. That was a date after the coming into force of the Industrial Relations Act 1971, and therefore Mr Lees, if dismissed on that date, was entitled to present a claim for compensation for unfair dismissal. But there are other primary facts besides the giving of that notice. These primary facts were deposed to by Mr Lees, and, of course, by Mr Lees alone before the tribunal. The evidence has been quoted both by Lord Denning MR and by Stamp LJ, and I will not quote it again; but it is clear that Mr Lees in his evidence was speaking of the existence of some agreement between himself and his employers. He began his evidence on this point with the words: 'I finished on 28th January 1972.' That is the date which the employers say was the effective date of the termination of his service; and, being before the coming into force of the 1971 Act, would put Mr Lees out of court in his claim for compensation. Then Mr Lees went on: 'I was pressurised into leaving.' Had he been summarily dismissed on that day, that is not what he would have said. He would have said he had been told to go; but he said he was pressurised into leaving. And it is clear that the tribunal, viewing his evidence as a whole and

1   [1969] 3 All ER at 1128, [1970] 1 QB at 192

certainly taking into account that answer, came to the conclusion that there was an agreement as to his leaving on that day. When one turns to their reasons, one then begins to see the inferences that they draw as to the nature of that agreement. In para 1(iii) of their reasons they say that on—

'28th January 1972 [Mr Lees] was prevailed on to finish, and in fact did finish on that date, accepting two months full gross pay in lieu of working the said two months; on that date he received in addition [and these are also primary facts found by the tribunal] his insurance cards, holiday pay entitlements, and his P45 tax form.'

Counsel, who argued this case with great skill on behalf of the employers, did accept that the appropriate word to introduce as the object of the verb 'finish' in the passage I have quoted is 'working'. So there is a finding that he finished working on that day; and note that the tribunal has translated 'pressurised', which was Mr Lee's word, into being 'prevailed upon'—not, of course, language consistent with summary dismissal, but language consistent with reluctant agreement. Mr Lees was prevailed on to leave; that is to say, he agreed to go, but only after he had been prevailed on to do so. It will be observed that the facts I have just quoted, the primary facts, do not go so far as to contain a statement whether this was an agreement to end there and then the contract of employment or whether it was an agreement to advance the date of notice, or whether it was an agreement to finish working, while leaving untouched the expiry of his notice at the end of March. When one turns to para 2 of the reasons, one finds the tribunal proceeding on the basis that there was agreement on 28th January and drawing now the inference—and, of course, they had at some time to draw this inference or some other inference from the primary facts—that the contract of service was terminated on that date. I find it impossible to understand how from the evidence of Mr Lees as noted by the chairman of the tribunal one could jump to the conclusion that Mr Lees was speaking of an agreement which was a consensual discharge that day of his contract of employment. Of course, he might have been; but it is quite impossible to say that he certainly was; and this was a matter which had to be considered in the light of all the circumstances and an inference drawn. Had it been possible—and, of course, it was not—for the tribunal to have had their attention directed to the observations of Sir John Donaldson P in *McAlwane v Boughton Estates Ltd*[1] (I refer to the last paragraph of Sir John Donaldson P's judgment) it is extremely unlikely that they would have drawn this inference. Was the inference which they drew the proper inference from the facts deposed to by Mr Lees? I have come to the conclusion that it was not. There were, of course, indications to support the view of the tribunal, namely, that he was handed his cards, he was handed his tax form and he was paid the money due to him in lieu of notice gross—i e without deduction of tax. On the other hand, is it really conceivable that Mr Lees was then abandoning the notice provision that he had obtained in October and which was set out in the letter of 7th October? The tribunal did not really address themselves to this difficulty. As I say, they did not have the benefit of evidence from the employers. They had only the evidence to which I have alluded; and when one studies in detail the actual wording of their reasons and the language with which they chose to clothe or describe the agreement, they stop short of saying exactly what it was that was agreed. I think it would be doing an injustice to the tribunal's findings to infer that the tribunal thought Mr Lees was summarily dismissed. That would be an inference inconsistent with the clear finding of the tribunal that in fact he went, that is to say, he ceased working, pursuant to an agreement. The only question, therefore, is, what was the nature of the agreement? Was it an agreement that effectually ended his contract at that date, as the tribunal appears to have thought; or was it an agreement to go away and not work out his notice and to take his pay for the period during which he did not do any work? I have given my views for saying that I cannot believe it correct to draw the inference that it was the first of those cases. It cannot, for the reasons that I have given, be a case of summary dismissal; and therefore, of course, the only inference left is that it was pursuant to an agreement that he would no longer come to work there, but he would have his pay for the unexpired portion of his notice. Had the tribunal had the benefit that we have had of a full consideration of the 1971 Act, of the rights and duties of the parties arising under the October notice, and had they really considered the circumstances in January in the light of all these considerations, they could not have drawn the inference that they did. The inference which I draw from the evidence and which in my view it is correct for this court to draw is that on 28th January Mr Lees left his place of work on the understanding that he need not come back, and that he was paid his wages for the unexpired portion of his notice. This would be a very natural agreement to reach, bearing in mind that he was having to work under the man who had been appointed in his place; and one can see that there may have been many good reasons why, without prejudice to Mr Lees's rights under the notice given him, he should be prevailed on to finish working; and that, I think (in the words of the tribunal) is exactly what he was prevailed on to do; and I see no grounds for inferring that he was prevailed on to do any more.

For those reasons I think that the tribunal did err in law in inferring the character of the agreement as being one which meant that on that day Mr Lees's employment was effectually terminated. I think there was agreement, but I think it came only to not working out his notice. For these reasons I agree with Lord Denning MR.

Appeal allowed. Leave to appeal to the House of Lords refused.

Solicitors: *Seifert, Sedley & Co*, agents for *Casson & Co*, Salford (for the appellant); *Barlow, Lyde & Gilbert* (for the employers).

L J Kovats Esq Barrister.

Practice Direction

FAMILY DIVISION

Injunction – Interlocutory – Undertaking as to damages – Matrimonial and children's matters concerning personal conduct – High Court – County court – Undertaking not to be incorporated in order except in certain circumstances.

The form of interim injunction in a county court case (Form 79[1]) includes a reference to an undertaking by the applicant, by his counsel or solicitor, in respect of damages sustained by the respondent. While such undertakings may be required when an interlocutory injunction is granted in an action under the general jurisdiction of the county courts, they are unnecessary and inappropriate in High Court and county court matrimonial and children's matters concerning personal conduct. An undertaking as to damages will not be incorporated in an order for an injunction unless it is specifically required by the court and has been expressly given. This is likely to occur only when the injunction concerns property matters, and then only when the claim is to protect rights (as in applications under s 17 of the Married Women's Property Act 1882) rather than to invoke discretionary powers (such as applications for transfer of property).

Issued by the President of the Family Division with the concurrence of the Lord Chancellor.

R L BAYNE-POWELL

26th April 1974   Registrar

1   See County Court Practice 1973, p 699, Rayden on Divorce (11th Edn, 1971), p 2736

Butler and another v Broadhead and others

CHANCERY DIVISION
TEMPLEMAN J
14th, 15th NOVEMBER 1973

Company – Winding-up – Distribution of assets – Exclusion of creditor from benefit of distribution – Unjust enrichment – Liability of contributories to creditor – Sums overpaid to contributories at expense of creditor – Sums overpaid by mistake of fact – Creditor having failed to prove debt after notice by liquidator – Creditor having claim against company for breach of contract – Creditor ignorant of breach at date of notice and of distribution – Distribution of company's surplus assets to contributories – Company wound up – Whether creditor entitled in equity to claim against contributories for sums overpaid – Companies Act 1948, s 264 – Companies (Winding-up) Rules 1949 (SI 1949 No 330), r 106(1).

In 1960 a company, which had three shareholders, conveyed a plot of land to D in fee simple. In 1962 the company resolved to be wound up voluntarily and a liquidator was appointed. The three shareholders were the only contributories. In January 1964 the liquidator, in the company's name, by mistake conveyed the same plot of land to the plaintiffs. The liquidator, having paid the debts of the company, distributed all the surplus assets among the contributories and the company was dissolved in or about August 1964. In 1971 the plaintiffs discovered for the first time that the land had been conveyed twice over and that, at the date of the 1964 conveyance, the company had no title. The plaintiffs, having been dispossessed by D, and being unable to sue the company for damages for breach of the beneficial owner covenants, brought an action against two of the contributories and the personal representatives of the third who had died. By their statement of claim they alleged that, by a mistake of fact, the liquidator had failed to make any provision for the liability of the company to pay damages, estimated at £8,500, for breach of covenant, that he had therefore overpaid the contributories who had thereby been unjustly enriched at the expense of the plaintiffs, and that the plaintiffs were entitled to recover the overpayment. It was also pleaded that the company and each of the directors and contributories knew, or alternatively were to be treated as having known, that the land was conveyed to D by conveyance of 1960, but there was no suggestion of fraud or wrong dealing. On an application by the defendants to strike out the statement of claim as disclosing no cause of action, the plaintiffs contended that, since the company as the original debtor had been dissolved and the liquidator was innocent of any wrong dealing, they were entitled to proceed against the defendants on the ground that in equity the defendants were bound to refund to the plaintiffs the moneys which the liquidator had held on their behalf as creditors but had mistakenly paid to the defendants.

Held – The plaintiffs' claim was barred by s 264[a] of the Companies Act 1948 and r 106(1)[b] of the Companies (Winding-up) Rules 1949, since the plaintiffs had failed to prove their debt after notice by the liquidator. The word 'distribution' in r 106(1) included a distribution to contributories as well as to creditors. Accordingly, once the property of the company had been applied in satisfaction of debts proved after notice and thereafter distributed among the contributories, the plaintiffs were excluded by r 106(1) from the benefit of the distribution. Rule 106(1) therefore precluded the operation of any equitable principle whereby the defendants held the moneys received on trust for the plaintiffs. It followed that the statement of

---

a   Section 264 is set out at p 408 *b*, post
b   Rule 106(1) is set out at p 408 *c*, post

claim disclosed no cause of action and should be struck out (see p 408 *d e f* and *j* to
p 409 *a* to *c e g* and *j* to p 410 *a*, post).

Dictum of Roxburgh J in *Re House Property and Investment Co Ltd* [1953] 2 All ER
at 1534 applied.

Dictum of Lord Hanworth MR in *Re Aidall Ltd* [1932] All ER Rep at 303 explained.

Ministry of Health v Simpson [1950] 2 All ER 1137 distinguished.

Notes

For refund in favour of creditors, see 16 Halsbury's Laws (3rd Edn) 334-337, paras
646-656, and for cases on the subject, see 23 Digest (Repl) 441-443, 5104-5125.

For the effect of failure to prove debts in time in the winding-up of a company,
see 7 Halsbury's Laws (4th Edn) 723, para 1258, and for cases on the subject, see
10 Digest (Repl) 982, 6758-6760.

For the Companies Act 1948, s 264, see 5 Halsbury's Statutes (3rd Edn) 317.

For the Companies (Winding-up) Rules 1949, r 106, see 4 Halsbury's Statutory
Instruments (2nd Reissue) 163.

Cases referred to in judgment

Aidall Ltd, Re [1933] Ch 323, [1932] All ER Rep 296, 102 LJCh 150, 148 LT 233, 18 Tax
Cas 617, CA, 10 Digest (Repl) 954, 6565.

Anonymous (1683) 1 Vern 162, 23 ER 388, 23 Digest (Repl) 441, 5108.

Diplock's Case. See *Ministry of Health v Simpson.*

Greig v Somerville (1830) 1 Russ & M 338, 39 ER 131, 23 Digest (Repl) 441, 5113.

House Property and Investment Co Ltd, Re [1953] 2 All ER 1525, [1954] Ch 576, 10 Digest
(Repl) 1061, 7369.

Knowles v Scott [1891] 1 Ch 717, 60 LJCh 284, 64 LT 135, 10 Digest (Repl) 1047, 7257.

Ministry of Health v Simpson [1950] 2 All ER 1137, [1951] AC 251, HL, 47 Digest (Repl)
533, 4825.

Newman v Barton (1690) 2 Vern 205, 23 ER 733, 23 Digest (Repl) 437, 5065.

Thomas v Griffith (1860) 2 Giff 504, 66 ER 211; *on appeal* (1860) 2 De GF & J 555, 30
LJCh 465, 3 LT 761, 7 Jur NS 293, 45 ER 736, 24 Digest (Repl) 854, 8502.

Cases also cited

Armstrong Whitworth Securities Co Ltd, Re [1947] 2 All ER 479, [1947] Ch 673.

Kit Hill Tunnel, Re, ex parte Williams (1881) 16 Ch D 590.

Procedure summonses

By a writ issued on 28th February 1973, the plaintiffs, Russell Albert Butler and
Gordon George Butler, brought an action against the defendants, (1) Constance
Annie Broadhead, (2) John Macdonald Broadhead, (3) Elizabeth Rusby, (4) Patricia
Lesley Hickling, and (5) National Westminister Bank Ltd. By their amended state-
ment of claim the plaintiffs alleged that in the winding-up of a company called Arno
Estates Ltd they had been dispossessed of a sum of £8,500 or thereabouts in that the
company was liable to pay that sum to the plaintiffs as damages for breach of covenant
but by mistake of fact the liquidator had paid that sum to the contributories: (1)
Frank Arthur Broadhead, deceased, (2) the first defendant and (3) the fifth defendant;
that by reason of that mistake of fact the contributories had been overpaid by not
less than £8,500 or thereabouts, and that, by reason of that overpayment the contributories had been unjustly enriched at the expense of the plaintiffs. The plaintiffs
claimed against the first four defendants, as the personal representatives of Frank
Arthur Broadhead, deceased, against the first defendant personally, and against the
fifth defendant, an order for payment to the plaintiffs of all sums overpaid to the
contributories in the winding-up of the company. By a summons dated 19th April
1973, the fifth defendant, and by a summons dated 29th June 1973, the first four
defendants, sought orders that the statement of claim be struck out as disclosing

no reasonable cause of action. Both summonses were heard together. The facts are set out in the judgment.

P A Goodall for the first to fourth defendants.
William Goodhart for the fifth defendant.
Leolin Price QC and *Hubert Picarda* for the plaintiffs.

TEMPLEMAN J. In this action the plaintiffs introduce the ghost of Caleb Diplock[1] into the Companies Court. The defendants seek to exorcise that apparition by striking out the statement of claim on the grounds that it discloses no cause of action. RSC Ord 18, r 19, authorises the court to strike out a statement of claim which discloses no reasonable cause of action, but only in the circumstances described in the White Book[2] under the heading 'Exercise of Powers under this Rule', namely—

> 'in plain and obvious cases . . . when it can be clearly seen that a claim . . . is . . . "obviously unsustainable" . . . [The] rule "ought not to be applied to an action involving serious investigations of ancient law and questions of general importance".'

For the purposes of this application, the facts are to be assumed to be as follows. By a conveyance dated 30th August 1960 the company, Arno Estates Ltd, conveyed to a Mr Day in fee simple a plot of land in Nottingham. On 31st October 1962 the company resolved to be wound up voluntarily and a liquidator was appointed. The only shareholders in 1960 and the only contributories in 1962 were three in number, the first defendant, Mrs Broadhead, her husband, Mr Broadhead, and the fifth defendant, National Westminister Bank Ltd. On 16th January 1964 the company acting by the liquidator conveyed as beneficial owner the same plot of land in Nottingham to the plaintiffs in fee simple. This conveyance was an innocent mistake. In 1964 the liquidator paid the debts of the company, distributed all the surplus assets of the company, and thereupon the company was dissolved. Mr Broadhead died and the first four defendants are his personal representatives. In 1971 it was discovered for the first time by the plaintiffs and the defendants that the land in Nottingham had been conveyed twice over and that at the date of the 1964 conveyance the company had no title. The plaintiffs were dispossessed by Mr Day and the company was, or if in existence would have been, in breach of the beneficial owner covenants.

The plaintiffs are in a dilemma. They cannot sue the company because it no longer exists; they say they cannot sue the liquidator with any hope of success.

By their statement of claim the plaintiffs sue the defendants for £8,500 but will not seek to make any contributory liable for more than the contributory received from the liquidator. I think this claim may be too wide on any footing, but that would not make the statement of claim demurrable. The plaintiffs plead that by a mistake of fact the liquidator failed to make any provision for the liability of the company to pay damages now estimated at £8,500 for breach of the beneficial owner covenants; he overpaid the contributories who were thereby unjustly enriched at the expense of the plaintiffs, who are entitled to recover the overpayment. It is also pleaded that the company and each of the directors, including Mr and Mrs Broadhead, and the contributories, knew or must be treated as having known that the land was conveyed to Mr Day by the conveyance dated 30th August 1960. It is not alleged and was not suggested that there was any fraud or wrong dealing. This application was argued on the footing that the conveyance to the plaintiffs was

---

1 *Ministry of Health v Simpson (Diplock's Case)* [1950] 2 All ER 1137, [1951] AC 251
2 The Supreme Court Practice 1973, vol 1, pp 300, 301

in good faith, whoever was concerned in 1960 with the conveyance to Mr Day having gone or forgotten by 1964.

The first four defendants apply to strike out; the fifth defendant has a separate summons to strike out. The plaintiffs oppose both summonses.

Counsel for the plaintiffs said there was a law of restitution and a law of subrogation. He referred to Goff and Jones on The Law of Restitution[1], dealing with subrogation. He submitted that the plaintiffs were subrogated to the rights of the company under s 259 of the Companies Act 1948. That section empowers the court at any time after making a winding-up order to require any contributory to pay in manner directed by the order, any money due from him or from the estate of the person whom he represents to the company. By s 307 an order under s 259 can be made on a voluntary winding-up. It seems to me that the effect of s 259 died with the company when it was dissolved.

Counsel for the plaintiffs then relied, and placed his main argument, on equitable grounds culminating in the principle established by *Ministry of Health v Simpson* (the *Diplock* case)[2].

The first case to which counsel referred in support of his main argument was an anonymous case[3]. That runs as follows:

> 'A. being indebted unto B. makes C. his executor. C. wastes the estate and dies, and makes D. his executor, and by his will devises several legacies. D. pays the legacies. B. exhibits a bill against D. the executor of C. for his debt due from the first testator, and against the legatees in the will of C. to compel them to refund their legacies, there not being now sufficient assets of the first testator. Decreed that the legatees should refund.'

As between legatees and creditors the legatees must refund.

Counsel then pointed to s 302 of the Companies Act 1948, which provides:

> '. . . the property of a company shall, on its winding up, be applied in satisfaction of its liabilities pari passu, and, subject to such application, shall, unless the articles otherwise provide, be distributed among the members according to their rights and interests in the company.'

Counsel said that the plaintiffs as creditors of the company are in exactly the same position as the creditors in the 1683 case[3]; the contributories are in exactly the same position as the legatees. Therefore, the contributories should refund and only take what is left after the plaintiffs have been satisfied. There is force in the analogy, to which I shall return.

The second case to which counsel referred was *Newman v Barton*[4] in which it was said[5]:

> 'A creditor shall follow the assets in equity, into whosesoever hands they come. But where the executor had voluntarily paid the full legacy, and afterwards assets proved deficient to pay the other legacies, they conceived neither the executor nor any of the other legatees should compel him to refund . . . but if the payment had not been voluntary, but he had recovered his legacy by decree, there he should have refunded.'

---

1   (1966), pp 375-377
2   [1950] 2 All ER 1137, [1951] AC 251
3   (1683) 1 Vern 162
4   (1690) 2 Vern 205
5   (1690) 2 Vern at 205

A creditor, said counsel, whatever the rights between the executor and the beneficiaries, can follow the assets in equity. And so he can, with some qualifications,
in the administration of estates.

The third case was *Greig v Somerville*[1]:

> 'In a suit instituted in 1814, to administer the personal estate of an intestate
> who died in 1807, the Master reported that no debts had been proved; and by
> the decree on further directions, in 1817, the whole of the residue was apportioned
> and distributed; but as the Plaintiff was then an infant his share, amounting
> to 4-9ths of the fund, was retained and carried to his separate account. In 1825
> . . . a creditor of the intestate, petitioned for leave to prove his debt against the
> sum remaining in Court.'

It was held that the creditor, if he could establish a debt due from the intestate,
could, unless the personal representatives of the intestate could establish a defence,
take four-ninths of his debt out of the moneys in court. That was a case where there
had been full distribution save for a part which was retained because a beneficiary
not being of full age could not give a good receipt. Relief was obtained by the creditor,
after the infant had come of age, but limited to the deduction which the beneficiary
would have suffered if the debt had been provided out of the whole estate. Counsel
for the plaintiffs said that in the present case the position is the same. A creditor
did not prove before the company was dissolved because, until long after the company
was dissolved, the creditor had no reason to suspect that there was anything to prove
for. The creditor can now come against the contributories with more justification
than the creditor who appeared tardily in *Greig v Somerville*[1].

In the fourth case, *Thomas v Griffith*[2], in an administration suit, the chief clerk
disallowed debts alleged to have accrued due after the testator's death and distributed
the assets. The creditor, without moving to vary the chief clerk's certificate, was
allowed to sue the legatees for an account and for repayment of moneys paid to the
legatees. The decision turned mainly on whether the certificate was res judicata and it
was held that it was not, but Stuart VC said[3]:

> 'There is, however, this difficulty in the case. This is a bill, not against the
> executors, but against the legatees, who have been paid under the administration
> decree; the proper persons to resist the claim are the executors, and they are not
> before the Court; and the executors, it is said after the decree, might have des-
> troyed the documents. It is to be observed that the executors are exonerated by
> the decree; they are not before the Court, but the mere claim of the Plaintiff
> must have shewn the executors that the matters of the estate were not finally
> settled; but, however that may be, the Defendants are mere beneficiaries, and
> cannot hold the assets against creditors. Unquestionably it is objectionable to
> have an account taken in a suit in the absence of the legal personal representative,
> but it seems in this case unavoidable.'

Counsel for the plaintiffs said therefore it does not matter in the present case that the
original debtor was the company, or that the plaintiffs could originally look to the
liquidator. The company being dissolved and the liquidator being innocent, the
plaintiffs may proceed against the contributories without being faced with the riposte
that they ought to have sued someone else.

All these cases are a preliminary to *Ministry of Health v Simpson*[4]. That involved a
mistake of law, but the principle cannot be different in relation to a mistake of fact.
Caleb Diplock having by his will left his residue worth over £250,000 to be applied by

---

1   (1830) 1 Russ & M 338
2   (1860) 2 Giff 504
3   2 Giff at 508
4   [1950] 2 All ER 1137, [1951] AC 251

his executors for such charitable or benevolent objects as his executors might select, died in the mistaken belief that he had avoided intestacy. The estate was distributed to institutions selected by the executors and in due course the next-of-kin obtained a declaration that they were entitled to the estate. They then brought proceedings to recover from the institutions. Lord Simonds said[1]:

'Acting under a mistake the personal representatives of a testator whose residuary disposition is invalid distribute his residuary estate on the footing that it is valid. Have the next of kin a direct claim in equity against the persons to whom it has been wrongfully distributed? I think that the authorities clearly establish that, subject to certain qualifications which I shall state, they have such a claim. I think it is important in the discussion of this question to remember that the particular branch of the jurisdiction of the Court of Chancery with which we are concerned relates to the administration of assets of a deceased person. While in the development of this jurisdiction certain principles were established which were common to it and to the comparable jurisdiction in the execution of trusts, I do not find in history or in logic any justification for an argument which denies the possibility of an equitable right in the administration of assets because, as it is alleged, no comparable right existed in the execution of trusts.'

Counsel for the fifth defendant submitted that *Diplock's* case[2] applied only to the administration of estates and did not necessarily apply to trusts and a fortiori did not apply to the distribution of the assets of a company under the umbrella of the Companies Act 1948. Counsel for the plaintiffs pointed out that Lord Simonds, in *Diplock's* case[3], said that the equitable remedy available to unpaid creditors, legatees and next-of-kin in the administration of estates was—

'devised by the Court of Chancery . . . to avoid the evil of allowing one man to retain money legally payable to another and was applicable wherever it could appropriately be applied.'

So far the remedy only appears to have been allowed against a person who has received moneys held in trust for another. I have to consider whether such a trust is created by the Companies Act 1948 and if so what the terms of that trust are.

In *Diplock's* case[1] the claim of the next-of-kin was subject to one qualification. Lord Simonds said[4]:

'. . . it was clearly established that the right of an underpaid legatee to claim directly against the overpaid legatee is subject to this qualification, that he must first exhaust his remedy against the executor who has made the wrongful payment.'

Counsel for the plaintiffs submitted that this qualification, if it applied to the plaintiffs in the present circumstances at all, did not affect them because the company was dissolved before the plaintiffs were put on guard as regards their rights. So far as the liquidator is concerned, counsel for the plaintiffs told me that the statement of claim was drafted on the footing that the plaintiffs had no right against the liquidator which would avail the plaintiffs because they apprehended that he had done nothing wrong, everybody being in a state of ignorance about the two conveyances. So, said counsel, the way is in any event clear for the plaintiffs to sue the defendants.

I turn to see what the Companies Act 1948 has to say about the matter. Section 302, as I have mentioned, directs the property of the company to be applied in satisfaction

---

1 [1950] 2 All ER at 1140, [1951] AC at 265, 266
2 [1950] 2 All ER 1137, [1951] AC 251
3 [1950] 2 All ER at 1142, [1951] AC at 268
4 [1950] 2 All ER at 1142, [1951] AC at 267

of its liabilities pari passu, and subject to such application to be distributed between the contributories. Both counsel for the defendants contended that s 302 does not create a trust analagous to the trust considered in *Diplock's* case[1]. They relied on *Knowles v Scott*[2]. The headnote reads:

> 'A liquidator is not strictly speaking a trustee either for the creditors or the contributories of a company in liquidation, his position being that of agent of the company. Therefore, in the absence of fraud, *mala fides*, or personal misconduct, an action for damages will not lie against a liquidator at the suit either of a creditor or contributory for delay in paying the creditor's debt, or in handing over to the contributory his proportion of the surplus assets of the company.'

Of course, the position of a liquidator is not the same as the position of a trustee, but the duty cast on him by s 302 is very much the same duty as that cast on an executor; it is the duty of applying the assets in paying the creditors, then distributing the surplus among the beneficiaries or contributories. So, although for present purposes I need not decide the point, if s 302 stood alone I should have been inclined to think that there was a sufficient analogy between the position of an executor and a liquidator to enable equity to intervene in favour of unpaid creditors against overpaid contributories.

But the matter does not end with s 302 because the Companies Act 1948 makes express provisions governing the rights and liabilities of creditors and contributories. Section 259(1) provides:

> 'The court may, at any time after making a winding-up order, make an order on any contributory for the time being on the list of contributories to pay, in manner directed by the order, any money due from him or from the estate of the person whom he represents to the company, exclusive of any money payable by him or the estate by virtue of any call in pursuance of this Act.'

This provision was considered in *Re Aidall Ltd*[4]. A contributory holding 994 out of 1,000 issued shares was assessed to tax on a share of the company's profits made before winding up. The contributory refused to pay. The liquidator paid him a sum in excess of the tax. The Revenue applied under s 165 of the Companies (Consolidation) Act 1908, which was in the same terms as s 259 of the 1948 Act, for an order that the contributory refund to the company or liquidator the amount of the tax claimed and that the tax which, under the relevant surtax legislation, had been assessed on the company, might be paid out of the money so refunded. It was held that the contributory having received moneys from the liquidator on a distribution of surplus assets of the company in liquidation, with notice that the liquidator had not provided for a debt due from the company, ought to be ordered to pay the amount of the debt to the credit of the liquidator. Counsel for the plaintiffs relied on the judgment of Lord Hanworth MR[5]:

> 'The money is now asked for by way of return from the person who has been overpaid. He has received too much from the company, and he must repay some portion of that money, which never ought to have been handed over to him and which is needed for the purpose of paying the debts of the company.'

Counsel for the plaintiffs suggested that Lord Hanworth MR was applying a general principle: but, in my judgment, he was applying power vested in the court by s 165. So long as the company is in existence there is a method, now s 259, of putting right a mistake. There is no need or room for equity.

---

1   [1950] 2 All ER 1137, [1951] AC 251
2   [1891] 1 Ch 717
3   [1933] Ch 323, [1932] All ER Rep 296
4   [1933] Ch at 334, [1932] All ER Rep at 303

Then the Companies Act 1948 makes express provision for the proving of debts and for what is to happen if debts are not proved. Section 264 dealing with compulsory winding-up says:

'The court may fix a time or times within which creditors are to prove their debts or claims or to be excluded from the benefit of any distribution made before those debts are proved.'

Similarly, r 106(1) of the Companies (Winding-Up) Rules 1949[1], made under s 273(e) of the 1948 Act and applicable in the present case, provides:

'Subject to the provisions of the Act, and unless otherwise ordered by the Court, the Liquidator, in any winding-up may from time to time fix a certain day, which shall be not less than fourteen days from the date of the notice, on or before which the creditors of the Company are to prove their debts or claims, and to establish any title they may have to priority under section 319 of the Act, or to be excluded from the benefit of any distribution made before such debts are proved, or as the case may be from objecting to such distribution.'

So there is one very great difference between the law applicable to a company in liquidation and that applicable to the administration of an estate. The legislature has provided that a creditor who does not prove after notice is to be excluded from the benefit of a distribution. The provision enures for the benefit of the liquidator who makes the distribution and also for the benefit of those who receive the distribution. Counsel for the plaintiffs submitted that distribution in r 106 is confined to a distribution to creditors and does not comprehend a distribution to contributories. Fortified by the observations of Roxburgh J in *Re House Property and Investment Co Ltd*[2] I conclude that distribution in r 106 includes a distribution to contributories. That is supported by s 265 which provides:

'The court shall adjust the rights of the contributories among themselves and distribute any surplus among the persons entitled thereto.'

It appears that 'distribution' is an apt and proper word to govern a payment either to creditors or to contributories.

In the present case, if the liquidator did not advertise for claims, then he was in dereliction of duty and an action against the present defendants might only lie if proceedings had been brought against the liquidator and recovery had proved impossible from him. I say 'might' because both the plaintiffs and the defendants wish to be in a position to argue this. If advertisement was made, the plaintiffs, not knowing their unfortunate position, did not prove. They had a claim for which they could have proved, because s 316 provides:

'In every winding up . . . all debts payable on a contingency, and all claims against the company, present or future, certain or contingent, ascertained or sounding only in damages, shall be admissible to proof against the company, a just estimate being made, so far as possible, of the value of such debts or claims as may be subject to any contingency or sound only in damages, or for some other reason do not bear a certain value.'

The plaintiffs had the benefit of the beneficial owner covenants contained in their conveyance. There was a breach of covenant either by 1964 or in 1971 when the

---

1 SI 1949 No 330
2 [1953] 2 All ER 1525 at 1534, [1954] Ch 576 at 593

plaintiffs were dispossessed of the property they thought they had acquired. The claim of the plaintiffs to the enforcement of that covenant or to damages was a claim which could have been put forward when advertisement was made for claims against the company. Similarly, when a lessee company goes into liquidation its landlord has a claim and the landlord can ask for a sum to be set aside or prove for the value of the covenant: see *Re House Property and Investment Co Ltd*.[1]. Therefore, if the plaintiffs had a claim and if the liquidator advertised under r 106, then the plaintiffs were excluded from the benefit of any distribution made before they proved. It would be a contradiction of r 106 for equity to intervene and to require, notwithstanding that the plaintiffs were excluded from the benefit of the distribution, that the defendants hold that benefit, namely, the money received on trust for the plaintiffs.

Counsel for the plaintiffs felt the difficulty of claiming a carte blanche application of the principle found in *Diplock's* case[2] in the light of r 106 and attempted to narrow his claim. He said that the claim of a creditor against a contributory, where the creditor no longer has a remedy under the Companies Act 1948, can only be enforced if the loss of any remedy under the Companies Act did not arise from any failure or neglect of the creditor. This brings us back to r 106 if the creditor has failed or neglected to put in a proof after advertisement. But I think counsel for the plaintiffs intended to limit the claim of the creditor against a contributory to a claim which only existed in theory at the date of the advertisement and became serious after the dissolution of the company.

In the present case, for example, junior counsel for the plaintiffs said that in the normal course of events no purchaser would dream of putting in a proof just because he had a beneficial owner covenant from a vendor company. But it seems to me that the principle of *Diplock's* case[2] must apply in toto or not at all and that there cannot be some halfway house. If the creditor, whether it is his fault or not, does not put in a claim, then he is barred under r 106 and that is an end of the matter.

A company is a creature of statute and the rights of creditors and contributories are regulated by that statute, and the legislature, for good reason or bad, excludes from the benefit of a distribution a creditor who does not put in a proof. There may be practical reasons for this. In the case of a company there may be hundreds or thousands of contributories and it may be desirable to achieve certainty. A company cannot go into liquidation without the public becoming aware of the fact. A liquidator cannot be appointed without publishing the fact; he must advertise for claims and his accounts must be passed and his final accounts noted in the Companies Register.

The conclusion I have reached is that there can be no room for the operation of the principle of *Ministry of Health v Simpson*[2] in respect of a claim for which a proof could have been entered and for which there has been advertisement, not complied with, thus excluding the claim and the creditor from the distribution under r 106.

I say nothing as to what might be the position if there has been no advertisement, because in that case the plaintiffs wish to consider whether they have some remedy against the liquidator or against the defendants. I considered standing over this application until it had been established whether the liquidator advertised. But that would mean an entirely different pleading. If this statement of claim is struck out, the plaintiffs will not be debarred from asserting any remedies they think they have in the event of its turning out that the liquidator did not advertise. In the result, I think the present application falls within RSC Ord 18, r 19. Junior counsel for the plaintiffs urged that this is a difficult matter involving questions of law and general principle; but it raises a short point on the construction and effect of the Companies Act 1948 in the light of the decision in *Diplock's* case[2]. I have formed the view that

---

1 [1953] 2 All ER 1525, [1954] Ch 576
2 [1950] 2 All ER 1137, [1951] AC 251

r 106 leaves no room for equitable principles and I therefore strike out the statement
of claim.

Order accordingly.

Solicitors: *Field, Fisher & Martineau*, agents for *Browne, Jacobson & Roose*, Nottingham
(for the first to fourth defendants); *Church, Adams, Tatham & Co*, agents for *Dickinson,
Manser & Co*, Poole (for the fifth defendant); *Hewitt, Woollacott & Chown*, agents
for *Eking, Manning, Morris & Foster*, Nottingham (for the plaintiffs).

Jacqueline Metcalfe Barrister.

Trustees of Manchester Unity Life Insurance
Collecting Society v Sadler

CHANCERY DIVISION
WALTON J
28th MARCH 1974

*Mortgage – Possession of mortgaged property – Jurisdiction – High Court – Action by
mortgagee – Action for foreclosure or sale – County court having exclusive jurisdiction to
hear and determine action in which claim for possession made unless action is an action for
foreclosure or sale – Mortgagee in reality seeking payment or possession – Claim for foreclosure
or sale added as colourable device – Whether 'an action for foreclosure or sale' – Whether
High Court having jurisdiction to hear and determine it – Administration of Justice Act 1970,
ss 37, 38.*

The plaintiffs were the mortgagees of a dwelling-house which the defendant had
mortgaged to them by way of legal charge to secure the sum of £5,000. The defendant fell into arrears with payments under the mortgage and the plaintiffs brought
an action against him by summons in the High Court, claiming (i) payment, (ii)
possession, (iii) foreclosure or sale, (iv) further or other relief, and (v) costs. The
plaintiffs were not in fact interested in seeking foreclosure or sale. They contended,
however, that, although ss 37(1)[a] and 38(1)[b] of the Administration of Justice Act 1970
gave the county court exclusive jurisdiction to entertain an action by a mortgagee
in which he claimed 'payment or possession', their action was 'an action for foreclosure
or sale' within ss 37(2) and 38(2) of the 1970 Act and the High Court therefore had
jurisdiction to hear and determine it.

Held – The words 'an action for foreclosure or sale' in ss 37(2) and 38(2) meant an
action in which the mortgagee really was seeking foreclosure or sale and not an action
in which his real claim was for payment or possession and the claim for foreclosure
or sale had merely been added as a colourable device. Accordingly, since the mortgagee
was in reality seeking payment or possession, the action was not an 'action for foreclosure or sale' and accordingly the High Court had no jurisdiction to entertain it
(see p 413 b c and f, post).

Notes

For jurisdiction of the courts in actions for the recovery of possession by mortgagees,

---

a Section 37 is set out at p 411 j to p 412 a, post
b Section 38 is set out at p 412 b to d, post

a see 27 Halsbury's Laws (3rd Edn) 351, 352, paras 658, 659, and for cases on the subject, see 13 Digest (Repl) 395, 396, 240-243.
   For the Administration of Justice Act 1970, ss 37, 38, see 40 Halsbury's Statutes (3rd Edn) 1060, 1061.

Case referred to in judgment

b R v Judge Dutton Briant, ex parte Abbey National Building Society [1957] 2 All ER 625, [1957] 2 QB 497, [1957] 3 WLR 249, DC, Digest (Cont Vol A) 318, 165a.

Adjourned summons

   This was an application by originating summons dated 31st October 1973 by the plaintiffs, Ronald Henry Day, Ronald Arthur Perry and Rowland Arthur Vernon Bowler, the trustees of the Manchester Unity Life Insurance Collecting Society, in
c which they claimed against the defendant, William Ewart Sadler, (1) payment of all moneys due to the plaintiffs under a covenant in a legal charge made on 22nd May 1973 between the defendant of the one part and the plaintiffs of the other part whereby the defendant had charged to the plaintiffs a dwelling-house, 20 Adastral Close, Newmarket, in the county of Suffolk, to secure the sum of £5,000, 'and such
d costs as would be payable if this claim were the only relief granted', (2) an order that the legal charge be enforced by foreclosure or sale, (3) delivery by the defendant to the plaintiffs of possession of the charged property, (4) further or other relief and (5) costs. The facts are set out in the judgment.

   Peter Cowell for the plaintiffs.
e The defendant appeared in person.

   WALTON J. The facts here are of the simplest. The defendant, Mr Sadler, mortgaged the property, 20 Adastral Close, Newmarket, Suffolk, to the plaintiffs to secure the sum of £5,000 by a legal charge dated 22nd May 1973. This sum was repayable, together with interest, over a period of time by monthly instalments of
f £42·50 (or, if paid promptly, £40·75). He fell in serious arrears with his repayments, and on 31st October 1973 the plaintiffs issued the originating summons which is now before me claiming (1) payment, (2) possession, (3) foreclosure or sale, (4) further or other relief, (5) costs.
   This summons was issued in the Manchester District Registry of the High Court, and the first point which is raised is, has the High Court any jurisdiction to hear it?
g This depends on the true construction of three sections in the Administration of Justice Act 1970, namely ss 36(1), 37 and 38, which provide as follows:

       '36.—(1) Where the mortgagee under a mortgage of land which consists of or includes a dwelling-house brings an action in which he claims possession of the mortgaged property, not being an action for foreclosure in which a claim for possession of the mortgaged property is also made, the court may exercise any
h   of the powers conferred on it by subsection (2) below if it appears to the court that in the event of its exercising the power the mortgagor is likely to be able within a reasonable period to pay any sums due under the mortgage or to remedy a default consisting of a breach of any other obligation arising under or by virtue of the mortgage . . .
       '37.—(1) Where a mortgage of land consists of or includes a dwelling-house
j   and no part of the land is situated in Greater London, then, subject to subsection (2) below, if a county court has jurisdiction by virtue of section 48 of the County Courts Act 1959 or section 38 of this Act to hear and determine an action in which the mortgagee under that mortgage claims possession of the mortgaged property, no court other than a county court shall have jurisdiction to hear and determine that action.

'(2) This section shall not apply to an action for foreclosure or sale in which *a* a claim for possession of the mortgaged property is also made.

'(3) Nothing in this section shall be taken as affecting the jurisdiction of any court to hear and determine an action which is pending in that court at the date on which this section comes into force.

'38.—(1) If an action in which the mortgagee under a mortgage of land claims possession of the mortgaged property would, by virtue of section 48 of the *b* County Courts Act 1959, be within the jurisdiction of a county court had that claim been the only claim made in the action, a county court shall have jurisdiction to hear and determine the action notwithstanding that a claim for payment by the mortgagor of the amount owing in respect of the mortgage is also made in the action and that by reason of the amount claimed the last-mentioned claim is not within the jurisdiction of a county court.

'(2) Nothing in subsection (1) above shall be taken as empowering a county *c* court to hear and determine an action for foreclosure or sale which is not within the jurisdiction of a county court.

'(3) Without prejudice to section 102(3)(c) of the County Courts Act 1959 (which enables county court rules to authorise the registrar to hear and determine certain proceedings and actions), the registrar of a county court may hear and determine any action in which the mortgagee under a mortgage of land *d* claims possession of the mortgaged land, being an action which is within the jurisdiction of a county court.'

The scheme of this legislation is quite plain. In the case of all houses whose rateable value is less than £1,000 (see the Administration of Justice Act 1973, s 6 and Sch 2), claims for possession by a mortgagee are, in general, within the exclusive jurisdiction *e* of the county court. There are, I think, two obvious reasons for such an enactment. First, proceedings would have to be commenced in the county court for the district in which the mortgagor resides, which would therefore entail much less expense on his part in resisting the claim. Secondly, as admirably expressed by Lord Goddard CJ in *R v Judge Dutton Briant*[1], it would be very unfortunate if persons of modest means who are the principal borrowers were made liable for costs on the High *f* Court scale.

The reason for the exception of actions for foreclosure or sale is also easily understood. These actions require techniques of the taking of accounts and so forth which are readily available in the chambers of the Chancery Division, and each by its very nature provides for a very considerable period of delay before possession is obtained, which thus ensures full protection for the mortgagor. *g*

That being the position, the short point for decision is, is a mortgagee whose real claim throughout is 'payment or possession' entitled nevertheless to commence his proceedings in the High Court if he adds to those claims a claim for a remedy he does not in fact want and has no intention of in fact seeking, namely a claim for foreclosure or sale? The argument is that if he does this, he will have brought the situation within the precise wording of s 37(2) of the 1970 Act, and the county *h* court will no longer have the exclusive jurisdiction conferred by s 37(1), or for similar reasons the jurisdiction conferred by s 38(1). Of course Parliament may have so provided, either with intent or, as it were, per incuriam; but it would indeed be an astonishing result that, merely by using a meaningless incantation, the whole purpose of the relevant section could be completely frustrated. This is precisely the kind of mumbo jumbo which has, on occasion in the past, brought the law into disrepute. *j*

In the present case I think there is no real doubt as to what s 37(2) means. Counsel for the plaintiffs—who, if he will allow me to say so, took every point that could be taken in favour of the jurisdiction with force and clarity—foresaw that the words

---

1   [1957] 2 All ER 625 at 629, [1957] 2 QB 497 at 507, 508

a 'action *for* foreclosure' might be his downfall, and argued cogently that there was no such thing: that there was only an action *claiming* foreclosure. And he pointed to the language of s 36(1): 'action . . . in which [the mortgagee] claims possession', s 37(1): 'action in which the mortgagee . . . claims possession', and s 38(1): 'action in which the mortgagee . . . claims possession', as indicating the true analysis of the situation. Therefore, he argued, what is meant by an action *for* foreclosure in ss 37(2) *b* and 38(2) is an action *claiming* foreclosure, as is indeed one of the possible claims indicated in RSC Ord 88, r 1.

I draw entirely the opposite conclusion from the change of the statutory language from that drawn by counsel for the plaintiffs. The change of language involves, in my opinion, a change of intent. By 'an action for foreclosure' there is intended, in my opinion, to be indicated an action in which the plaintiff really is seeking foreclosure, and not an action in which he has never had any intention of seeking it, *c* but where it has been added as a mere colourable claim. In other words, in order to determine whether an action is 'for' anything one must ask the question: what is the plaintiff really seeking? and it is not sufficient to say: it is one of the claims made. If that is what the ambit of ss 37(2) and 38(2) was intended to be, they would simply say 'an action claiming' foreclosure.

d While the question does not strictly arise in the present case, where the plaintiffs have never sought to pretend that the claim for foreclosure was a relief in which they were at any time interested, I can, of course, envisage a situation where, when the originating summons is issued, the plaintiffs are genuinely seeking foreclosure, or at any rate really consider that this is a remedy they may genuinely wish to seek, and it may then happen that circumstances change their minds. I see no difficulty *e* in such a case; the plaintiffs will inform the master that the action is no longer one *for* foreclosure, and he will give them leave to amend the summons accordingly, and the proceedings will contemporaneously be transferred to the appropriate county court. This was the procedure which had been suggested to the plaintiffs by the district registrar in the present case, but one which they were ultimately not minded to accept.

f In the event, it appears to me that these proceedings, which are an action in which possession is claimed and are not an action for foreclosure, have been commenced in a court which has no jurisdiction to hear them, and I can only accordingly dismiss them with costs.

Summons dismissed.

g Solicitors: *Laytons*, agents for *John Gorna & Co*, Manchester (for the plaintiffs).

Jacqueline Metcalfe Barrister.

Hunter v Mann

QUEEN'S BENCH DIVISION
LORD WIDGERY CJ, BOREHAM AND MAY JJ
8th FEBRUARY 1974

Road traffic – Offence – Information – Duty to give information – Duty of any person to give information which it is in his power to give and may lead to identification of driver – Doctor – Information obtained by doctor in professional capacity – Whether 'any . . . person' to be construed restrictively so as not to include doctor under professional duty of confidence – Whether 'in [doctor's] power' to disclose information – Road Traffic Act 1972, s 168(2)(b).

An accident took place involving a motor vehicle. The driver of the vehicle and the passengers hurried away from the scene of the accident. On the same day the appellant, a doctor, treated a man and a girl in his surgery. The girl told him that she had been involved in a motor accident. The doctor advised them to see the police, but he did not seek their consent to disclose their identity to the police. Some days later a police officer requested the appellant to disclose the names and addresses of the man and the girl. The appellant refused on the ground that the information was confidential, having been obtained by him solely by reason of the relationship of doctor and patient. Subsequently the police officer served on the appellant a written notice requesting the information. The notice stated that the driver whose identification was sought was alleged to be guilty of dangerous driving. The appellant again, and for the same reason, declined to give the information. The appellant bona fide believed that it was not within his power to divulge the information and that such a disclosure would have been a breach of his professional code of ethics. The appellant was charged with failing to comply with a requirement under s 168(2)(b)[a] of the Road Traffic Act 1972 to give information which it was in his power to give and which might have led to the identification of the driver of the vehicle who was alleged to be guilty of dangerous driving, contrary to s 168(3)[b] of the 1972 Act. The appellant was convicted and appealed on the ground that in view of the professional duty of confidence which a doctor owed to his patient, the words 'any other person' in s 168(2)(b) did not extend to a doctor who had obtained confidential information in his professional capacity and that furthermore, in consequence of that duty, the information was such that it was not, within s 168(2)(b), 'in his power' to disclose it.

Held – Although a doctor was under a duty to his patient not to disclose voluntarily, without the consent of his patient, information which the doctor had gained in his professional capacity unless compelled by law to do so, it did not follow that the words 'any other person' in s 168(2) were to be construed in any restricted sense; they were wide enough to include a doctor who had obtained information in his professional capacity. Accordingly the appellant was guilty of the offence charged for, in the circumstances, it was in his power to give the information requested by the police officer. The appeal would therefore be dismissed (see p 419 *a b d e h* and *j*, post).

Notes
For the duty to give information as to the identity of a driver, see 33 Halsbury's Laws (3rd Edn) 649, para 1095.

Section 168(2), so far as material, is set out at p 417 *e*, post
Section 168(3), so far as material, is set out at p 417 *f*, post

a   For privilege in respect of communications to medical advisers, see 10 Halsbury's
Laws (3rd Edn) 479, 480, para 877, and for cases on the subject, see 22 Digest (Reissue)
457, 4566-4572.
    For the Road Traffic Act 1972, s 168, see 42 Halsbury's Statutes (3rd Edn) 1811.

Case referred to in judgment

b   *Parry-Jones v The Law Society* [1968] 1 All ER 177, [1969] 1 Ch 1, [1968] 2 WLR 397, CA,
Digest (Cont Vol C) 897, 830a.

Case also cited

Attorney-General v Mullholland, Attorney-General v Foster [1963] 1 All ER 767, [1963]
2 QB 477, CA.

c   **Case stated**

This was an appeal by way of a case stated by justices for the county of East Sussex
acting in and for the petty sessional division of East Grinstead in respect of their
adjudication as a magistrates' court sitting at East Grinstead on 25th June 1973.
    On 30th April 1973 an information was preferred by the respondent, Derrick Mann,
d   a chief inspector of police, against the appellant, John David William Hunter, that
he between 6th March 1973 and 21st March 1973 at East Grinstead in the county of
Sussex failed, contrary to s 168(3) of the Road Traffic Act 1972, to comply with a
requirement under s 168(2)(b) of that Act to give information which it was in his power
to give which might have led to the identification of the driver of a stolen motor
vehicle, index number BUF 769C, who was alleged to be guilty of the offence of
e   driving the motor vehicle in a manner dangerous to the public, contrary to s 2 of the
Road Traffic Act 1972, on 3rd January 1973.
    The justices found the following facts. (a) On 27th December 1972 one Pamela
Jean Werham discovered that her motor vehicle, BUF 769C, was missing from a
multi-storey car park opposite East Croydon railway station where it had been parked
five days earlier. (b) On 3rd January 1973 there was an accident involving the motor
f   vehicle, BUF 769C, whereby damage was caused to another vehicle. (c) The driver
and passengers of the motor vehicle, BUF 769C, hurried away from the scene of the
accident. (d) On that same day the appellant, a registered medical practitioner,
treated a man in evening surgery. (e) Later that same night, at the request of the
same man, the appellant treated a girl who told him she had been involved in a
motor car accident. (f) Although the appellant advised the man and the girl to visit
g   the police, he did not however seek their consent to disclose their identity to the
police. (g) On 22nd January 1973 Police Sergeant Davies personally requested the
appellant under s 168(2)(b) of the Road Traffic Act 1972 to divulge the name and/or
address of the man and the girl or alternatively to give him such information which
could lead to the police discovering those names and/or addresses. (h) The appellant
declined to divulge the information requested of him as he considered such infor-
h   mation was confidential, it having been obtained solely through his relationship of
doctor and patient, and he so informed the police officer at the relevant time. (i) On
7th March 1973 Police Sergeant Davies served on the appellant a written application
for information which might have led to the identification of the driver who was
therein alleged to be guilty of dangerous driving. (j) A letter dated 20th March 1973
was received from the appellant in which he declined to supply any information on
j   the grounds that it would be a breach of professional conduct. (k) The appellant
at the relevant time bona fide believed (i) that it was not in his power to divulge the
information, and (ii) that it would have been a breach of the professional code of
ethics. (l) The British Medical Association in its members' handbook for practitioners,
laid down a code of conduct for members and included the principle that a doctor
should refrain from disclosing voluntarily to a third party information which he had
learned directly or indirectly in his professional relationship with a patient subject

to exceptions, including the following: (i) the patient gave his consent, (ii) the information was required by law.

It was contended by the appellant that such information as he was requested to divulge was not within his power to give, within the meaning of s 168(3) of the 1972 Act, since he was precluded from giving it by the professional ethics of medical confidentiality.

It was contended by the respondent that such information as the appellant was requested to divulge was within his power to give as being within his knowledge.

The justices were referred to Archbold's Criminal Pleading, Evidence and Practice[1] in which authorities were cited for the view that there was no privilege entitling a medical practitioner to refuse to give in evidence statements made to him by a patient however confidential they might be.

The justices were of the opinion that that information was within the appellant's knowledge, was required by law, and was within his power to divulge and accordingly they found him guilty. They fined him £5.

The question for the opinion of the High Court was whether a medical practitioner who failed to comply with a requirement under s 168(2)(b) of the 1972 Act for information brought to his knowledge in the course of his professional relationship with a patient was guilty of an offence under s 168(3) of the 1972 Act.

Thomas Bingham QC and *Andrew Brooks* for the appellant.
Richard Carr for the respondent.

BOREHAM J delivered the first judgment at the invitation of Lord Widgery CJ. This is an appeal by way of case stated from a decision of justices acting for the county of East Sussex and sitting at East Grinstead on 25th June 1973.

On that date the appellant, who is a registered medical practitioner, appeared before them charged with an offence under s 168 of the Road Traffic Act 1972, namely, that he had failed to comply with a requirement under that section to give information which it was in his power to give and which might have led to the identification of the driver of a stolen motor vehicle who (that is the driver) was alleged to be guilty of dangerous driving.

The facts as they are found by the justices are, shortly, these. On 3rd January 1973 there was an accident involving the motor vehicle, BUF 769C, in which damage was caused to another vehicle and which led to the allegation that the driver of BUF 769C was guilty of dangerous driving. After the accident the driver and the passenger of the motor vehicle, BUF 769C, hurried away from the scene of the accident and no one was able to identify them. Nor was the owner, or, as it is now put, the keeper, of that vehicle able to assist in identification, for the vehicle had been taken without her consent or authority some time between 22nd and 27th December 1972.

On the same day as the accident, 3rd January, the appellant, in his capacity as a registered medical practitioner, treated a man at his evening surgery, and on the same evening he had, at the request of that man, treated a girl, who told him that she had been involved in a motor car accident. It is right that it should be emphasised —for it indicates, if indication is needed, that the appellant's attitude to this matter was an entirely responsible one—that he advised that man and that girl to visit the police; advice which clearly was not taken. But he did not seek to obtain their consent to disclose their identities to the police. Thus, when, on 22nd January, Police Sergeant Davies requested the appellant under s 168 to divulge the name and/or address of the man and the girl, or alternatively to give him other information

---

1   38th Edn (1973), p 633, para 1306

which could lead to their identification, he declined. He declined on the ground that he considered such information to be confidential because it had been obtained solely through the relationship of doctor and patient. He told the police officer his reason at the time. On 7th March there was served on him a written application for the sort of information that I have outlined. It was stated in that application that the driver whose identification was sought was alleged to be guilty of dangerous driving. By letter of 20th March the appellant again, and for the same reason, declined to give that information.

The justices find that the appellant bona fide believed (a) that it was not within his power to divulge the information required by the police and (b) that such disclosure would have been a breach of his professional code of ethics. The justices had before them, and they quote from it, the British Medical Association's handbook for the guidance of practitioners, which lays down a code of conduct for members of the medical profession. It includes this principle, that a doctor should refrain from disclosing voluntarily to a third party information which he has learned directly or indirectly in his professional relationship with a patient, subject to these, amongst other, exceptions: (1) the patient gives his consent to that disclosure; (2) the information is required by law. It may be a matter of some interest, if not of significance, to observe that the British Medical Association's code specifically refers to voluntary disclosure.

It would be useful to turn briefly to the provisions of s 168 of the 1972 Act. Subsection (1) I need not dwell on, for it is conceded that the section applies in this case because the unidentified driver was alleged to be guilty of dangerous driving. Section 168(2) provides:

> 'Where the driver of a vehicle is alleged to be guilty of an offence to which this section applies [para (*a*) deals with the person keeping a vehicle] (*b*) any other person shall if required as aforesaid give any information which it is in his power to give and may lead to the identification of the driver . . .'

'Any information aforesaid' refers to such information as to the identification of the driver as he may be required to give by or on behalf of the chief officer of police. Section 168(3) provides: '. . . a person who fails to comply with the requirement of subsection (2)(*b*) . . . shall be guilty of an offence.' It was that offence with which this appellant was charged and of which he was found guilty by the justices. As I understand it, it is not disputed that the appellant had in his possession information which might have led to the identification of the driver.

The contentions of counsel for the appellant are directed towards a construction of s 168. His first contention is this. He says that the appellant does not fall within the limits of the expression in sub-s (2)(*b*) 'any other person'. He says, and this is the basis of his submission on this aspect of the case, that it would not be right in the circumstances to give an unrestricted meaning to those words so as to include everyone except the driver or the keeper of the vehicle. He says that it would be wrong to give those words so unrestricted a meaning as to cause a doctor, or, as I understand it, any other professional man who stands in relation to his clients or patients in a position similar to a doctor, to act in breach of the duty of confidentiality on which a doctor's patient is entitled to rely.

He puts forward in support of that contention three propositions. He says first of all, and in effect this is a concession, that there is no absolute privilege in judicial proceedings for a doctor in respect of the disclosure of confidential information which was obtained by him in the course of his professional relationship with his patient. For my part at any rate I need no authority for that proposition; I accept it. The second proposition is this: that in common with other professional men, for instance a priest and there are of course others, the doctor is under a duty not to disclose, without the consent of his patient, information which he, the doctor, has gained in his professional capacity, save, says counsel for the appellant, in very exceptional circumstances. He quoted the example of the murderer still manic, who would be a menace to society. But, says counsel, save in such exceptional circumstances, the general rule applies. He adds that the law will enforce that duty.

I would accept that proposition if before the word 'disclosing' there were to be added the adverb 'voluntarily', as in the British Medical Association's handbook. I accept too counsel's cited authority for the proposition that the duty not to disclose information is enforceable at the behest of the patient in an action of contract or for breach of duty. But for my part at any rate I do not consider that that proposition covers the position where the doctor is compelled by law to disclose. In my judgment counsel for the appellant's second proposition relates only to voluntary disclosure. The third proposition is that protection is given to professional confidences to the extent that those who are bound by them are not ordinarily required to breach them and will only be compelled to do so by the order of a judge. Again counsel for the appellant has quoted authorities. I hope it will not indicate any lack of respect for him or for the authorities that he quoted if I do not cite them at this stage.

I would prefer to put the proposition in another way. I accept that the doctor, in accordance with the first proposition, has no right to refuse to disclose confidential information in the course of judicial or quasi-judicial proceedings; but I also accept that the judge in certain circumstances, and in the exercise of his, the judge's, judicial discretion, may refuse to compel him to do so. Further than this, in my judgment, the authorities which have been cited to us do not go. Moreover each one of those authorities was concerned with legal proceedings. In the present case it is important to bear in mind the distinction between privilege which is to be claimed in legal proceedings and a contractual duty not to disclose; that distinction is marked by a passage in the judgment of Diplock LJ in *Parry-Jones v The Law Society*[1]:

'So far as the plaintiff's point as to privilege is concerned, privilege is irrelevant when one is not concerned with judicial or quasi-judicial proceedings because, strictly speaking, privilege refers to a right to withhold from a court, or a tribunal exercising judicial functions, material which would otherwise be admissible in evidence. What we are concerned with here is the contractual duty of confidence, generally implied though sometimes expressed, between a solicitor and client. Such a duty exists not only between solicitor and client, but, for example, between banker and customer, doctor and patient, and accountant and client. Such a duty of confidence is subject to, and overridden by, the duty of any party to that contract to comply with the law of the land. If it is the duty of such a party to a contract, whether at common law or under statute, to disclose in defined circumstances confidential information, then he must do so, and any express contract to the contrary would be illegal and void.'

With those words in mind I proceed to the conclusion drawn by counsel for the appellant from his contentions. He says that when one comes to construe the statute one should approach it thus; that Parliament must not be taken to have overridden or to have attempted to override the duty of confidence to which reference has been made, except by clear language or necessary implication. He says, and this is the burden of his whole contention, that 'any other person' in s 168 must be read in a restricted way so that that duty is not breached. He quotes from Maxwell on the Interpretation of Statutes[2]. I shall not repeat the reference.

It seems to me that my first duty is to look at the section and give the words their ordinary natural meaning, and in the absence of equivocation or ambiguity to give effect to such meaning, unless of course there is something in the context of the

1 [1968] 1 All ER 171 at 180, [1969] 1 Ch 1 at 9
2 12th Edn (1969), p 116

section or of the Act itself which suggests that a special or restricted meaning should be given.

For my part I cannot find any ground for saying that a restricted meaning should be given. I find the words clear and unequivocal. I accept, as counsel for the appellant has suggested, that one should assume that Parliament has passed this Act, and this section in particular, with the existing law in mind. Accepting that, then it seems to me that Parliament must have been conscious of the use of very wide words here and, if it had been intended to create exceptions, it would have been easy enough to do so. It has not been done. Moreover I ask myself the question: if there is to be a restriction how far is it to go? Where is it to stop? I find it impossible to provide an answer to that question. In these circumstances I am driven to the conclusion that a doctor acting within his professional capacity, and carrying out his professional duties and responsibilities, is within the words 'any other person' in s 168(2)(b).

The next limb of counsel for the appellant's argument was directed to the words 'in his power' in the expression 'information which it is in his power to give'. He contends that power must include a legal right, that there is no legal right or power to disclose so far as a doctor is concerned and, therefore, that he is not caught by those words.

I am not going to attempt to define 'power'. It seems to me a word of fairly common understanding and reading it in its ordinary way I have no difficulty in coming to the conclusion that a doctor in the circumstances in which the appellant found himself had the power. It may be that but for the section in the Act he would not have exercised that power because of his duty to his patient, but that seems to me to beg the question, for that would have been in accordance with his duty not to make voluntary disclosure. Once it is decided that the appellant is a person to whom the statutory duty imposed by s 168 applies, then I have no doubt that he had the power. I think it would be no injustice to counsel for the appellant to say that this was the least strenuously argued of his points and I find it a point without substance.

In my view it is important when one is considering this section to have in mind that on many occasions serious accidents are caused by people who take away, without consent, other people's motor cars and who have no hesitation in leaving the scene as quickly as they possibly can so as to avoid detection. I therefore find it a comfort to think that the section gives the police a wide power for the purpose of detecting people who may cause damage to others.

May I say, before leaving this case, that I appreciate the concern of a responsible medical practitioner who feels that he is faced with a conflict of duty. That the appellant in this case was conscious of a conflict and realised his duty both to society and to his patient is clear from the finding of the justices, but he may find comfort, although the decision goes against him, from the following. First that he has only to disclose information which may lead to identification and not other confidential matters; secondly that the result, in my judgment, is entirely consistent with the rules that the British Medical Association have laid down and from which I have quoted in the course of this judgment.

In the result I have come to the conclusion that the justices were correct and that this appeal, therefore must be dismissed.

MAY J. I agree.

LORD WIDGERY CJ. I agree also. With all deference to counsel for the appellant's argument, I felt that he was claiming a degree of medical confidence wider than that which his authorities would support. I would compliment the authors of the British Medical Association handbook to which reference has already been made, for a brief and, I think, effective statement of the position. I repeat it:

'A doctor should refrain from disclosing voluntarily to a third party information which he has learnt professionally or indirectly in his professional relationship with a patient, subject to exceptions, including the following . . . (2) the
information is required by law.'

I would add one other point, namely, that if a doctor, giving evidence in court,
is asked a question which he finds embarrassing because it involves him talking about
things which he would normally regard as confidential, he can seek the protection
of the judge and ask the judge if it is necessary for him to answer. The judge, by
virtue of the overriding discretion to control his court which all English judges have,
can, if he thinks fit, tell the doctor that he need not answer the question. Whether
or not the judge would take that line, of course, depends largely on the importance
of the potential answer to the issues being tried. I too would dismiss the appeal.

*Appeal dismissed. The court certified under s 1(2) of the Administration of Justice Act 1960
that a point of law of general public importance was involved, viz, 'whether a medical
practitioner who failed to comply with a requirement under s 168(2)(b) of the Road Traffic
Act 1972 for information brought to his knowledge in the course of his professional relationship
with a patient was guilty of an offence under s 168(3) of the 1972 Act', but refused leave to
appeal to the House of Lords.*

Solicitors: *Hempsons* (for the appellant); *T Lavelle*, Lewes (for the respondent).

N P Metcalfe Esq   Barrister.

George Hensher Ltd v Restawile Upholstery (Lancs) Ltd

HOUSE OF LORDS
LORD REID, LORD MORRIS OF BORTH-Y-GEST, VISCOUNT DILHORNE, LORD SIMON OF GLAISDALE
AND LORD KILBRANDON
18th, 19th, 20th, 21st FEBRUARY, 1st MAY 1974

*Copyright – Artistic work – Work of artistic craftsmanship – Meaning of artistic – Plaintiffs
manufacturing suites of chairs and settees – Plaintiffs producing prototype for new type of
suite – Prototype consisting of frame nailed together and upholstered – Prototype used as
model and then destroyed when suites in production – Defendants selling copies of plaintiffs'
new suite under another name – Plaintiffs alleging defendants infringing their copyright in
prototype – Whether prototype qualifying as 'work of artistic craftsmanship' – Copyright Act
1956, s 3(1)(c).*

The plaintiff company manufactured upholstered furniture and in particular three
piece drawing room suites. One such suite, which was sold under the name 'Denver',
had a distinctive boat shape and was supported on spindle shaped legs. When the
sales of that suite began to decline, the managing director of the plaintiff company
and two of the plaintiffs' craftsmen collaborated to produce an improved design.
They stripped down the Denver to its frame, removed the legs and replaced the
legs by a sloped wooden plinth with casters on the corners and covered with a strip
of wood trim. The frame was nailed up and re-upholstered. The resulting article
was the prototype for a new suite that was to be known as 'the Bronx'. The prototype
was too flimsy to be used as a seat but it served as the model for the Bronx chairs
etc, which were copied from it and sold. Once the Bronx suite was in production,

the prototype was destroyed. The defendants, who also manufactured three piece suites, copied the Bronx suite and marketed the copies under the name 'Amazon'. The plaintiffs brought an action against the defendants for infringement of copyright in the prototype of the Bronx, which they contended was a 'work of artistic craftsmanship' within the meaning of s 3(1)(c)^a of the Copyright Act 1956. The defendants admitted that the prototype was a 'work of craftsmanship' but denied that it was of 'artistic' craftsmanship. At the trial, the principal buyer for a large retailing company gave evidence that the Bronx had 'eye appeal' and was, from the selling point of view, 'a winner'; she said it was a 'wonderful suite' although 'horrible', 'vulgar' and 'brash'. An experienced design consultant, who was also called as a witness, described the Bronx as 'typical of the middle of the road commercial type of production furniture'. He considered its design to be mediocre, although he could see that it had great appeal; he too thought it was slightly vulgar but that it was a good commercial design, having 'novelty . . . quite distinct individuality'.

Held – (i) The word 'artistic' in s 3(1)(c) of the 1956 Act had to be read in the context of the whole phrase 'works of artistic craftsmanship' and given its ordinary and natural meaning; no formula or test could be evolved to determine whether a work was one of artistic craftsmanship, for it was a matter of evidence in each case; it was the function of the court to decide on the evidence whether the work came within s 3(1)(c); in evaluating that evidence particular attention should be given to the evidence of experts, i e (per Lord Simon of Glaisdale) acknowledged artist-craftsmen or those concerned with the training of artist-craftsmen, and (per Lord Simon of Glaisdale and Lord Kilbrandon) to the conscious intention of the craftsman who produced the work (see p 423 f and g, p 426 b to d e h and j, p 430 g and h p 431 a, p 434 e, p 437 a b d and f and p 439 a b d f g and h, post).

(ii) The plaintiffs' prototype was not protected by copyright for the evidence merely established that it had originality in points of design aimed at appealing to the eye as commercial selling points and that was not sufficient to make it a work of 'artistic' craftsmanship within the meaning of s 3(1)(c) (see p 424 f and g, p 426 j to p 427 a and d, p 428 h, p 431 d and e, p 437 g and p 439 h, post).

Quaere. Whether so transient and incomplete a fabrication as the prototype could be described as a 'work of craftsmanship' (see p 423 a and b, p 425 h and j and p 428 e and f, post).

Decision of the Court of Appeal, Civil Division [1973] 3 All ER 414 affirmed on different grounds.

Notes

For copyright in artistic works, see 8 Halsbury's Laws (3rd Edn) 378-381, paras 695, 696, and for cases on the subject, see 13 Digest (Repl) 65, 66, 117-127.

For the Copyright Act 1956, s 3, see 7 Halsbury's Statutes (3rd Edn) 135.

Cases referred to in opinions

Blake v Warren (1931) [1928-35] MacG Cop Cas 268.
Britain v Hanks Brothers & Co (1902) 86 LT 764, 18 TLR 525, 13 Digest (Repl) 68, *136*.
Brutus v Cozens [1972] 2 All ER 1297, [1973] AC 854, [1972] 3 WLR 521, 56 Cr App Rep 799, [1972] Crim LR 56, HL.
Cuisenaire v Reed [1963] VR 719.
Cuisenaire v South West Imports Ltd [1968] 1 Ex CR 493, 37 Fox Pat C 93, 54 CPR 1; *affd* [1969] SCR 208, Digest (Cont Vol C) 171, **53a*.
Ealing (London Borough) v Race Relations Board [1972] 1 All ER 105, [1972] AC 342, [1972] 2 WLR 71, 70 LGR 219, HL.

---

a   Section 3(1) is set out at p 422 *g*, post

Hay and Hay Construction Co Ltd v Sloan (1957) 16 Fox Pat C 185.
Walter v Lane [1900] AC 539, 69 LJCh 699, 85 LT 289, HL, 13 Digest (Repl) 78, 221.

Appeal
This was an appeal by George Hensher Ltd against an order of the Court of Appeal[1]
(Russell, Stamp and James LJJ) dated 4th July 1973, allowing an appeal by the respondents, Restawile Upholstery (Lancs) Ltd, setting aside an order of Graham J[2], dated
31st October 1972, and dismissing an action brought by the appellants in respect
of, inter alia, alleged infringement of copyright by the respondents in the appellants'
prototype upholstered drawing room suites (each suite comprising two chairs and
a settee) and the chairs and settees. The suites were known respectively as the
Bronx, Continental, Manhattan and Atlantic suites. The facts are set out in the
opinion of Viscount Dilhorne.

R J Parker QC, *A Kynric Lewis* and *Hugh Laddie* for the appellants.
J N B Penny QC and *W Bruce Spalding* for the respondents.

Their Lordships took time for consideration.

1st May. The following opinions were delivered.

LORD REID. My Lords, the appellants manufacture upholstered chairs and
settees. Sales of their old types were falling off and they proposed to design a completely new type. After much consideration they evolved a prototype or 'mock-up'.
This consisted of a light frame with upholstery nailed on so as to look like a chair.
It was too flimsy to be used as a chair but served as a model for chairs which were
copied from it and sold. Once the new type was in production the prototype was
destroyed.
  This new type proved to be popular and sold well. Several other manufacturers
copied the appellants' products. The appellants thought that this was an infringement
of their rights and they took action. Only the respondents maintained that they
were not infringing the appellants' rights.
  The appellants did not register any design under the Registered Designs Act 1949.
They maintain that the respondents have infringed their copyright. Section 3(2) of
the Copyright Act 1956 provides that copyright shall subsist in every original artistic
work, and s 3(1) provides:

   'In this Act "artistic work" means a work of any of the following descriptions,
   that is to say,—(a) the following, irrespective of artistic quality, namely paintings,
   sculptures, drawings, engravings and photographs; (b) works of architecture,
   being either buildings or models for buildings; (c) works of artistic craftsmanship,
   not falling within either of the preceding paragraphs.'

The appellants maintain that the prototype of their furniture was a 'work of artistic
craftsmanship' within the meaning of s 3(1)(c). The respondents admit that the
prototype was a work of craftsmanship but deny that it was of 'artistic craftsmanship'.
  It is common ground that we must consider the prototype and not the furniture
put on the market by the appellants. Apparently this is because the articles put
on the market were not works of craftsmanship. But if there was copyright in the
prototype then the furniture put on the market by the appellants was copied from
it, and the respondents' products were copied from the furniture which the appellants
put on the market. The respondents do not deny that this would be infringement
of that copyright.

1 [1973] 3 All ER 414, [1973] 3 WLR 453
2 [1973] 1 All ER 160, [1973] 1 WLR 144

The respondents have not taken the point that such a prototype however artistic could not be a 'work of artistic craftsmanship', and the point was not argued. But I feel bound to say that I have great doubt about this matter. A work of craftsmanship suggests to me a durable, useful, handmade object and a work of artistic craftsmanship suggests something, whether of practical utility or not, which its owner values because of its artistic character. It appears to me to be difficult to bring within the terms or the intention of the statute an object which, however artistic it might appear to be, is only intended to be used as a step in a commercial operation and has no value in itself. I express no concluded opinion on this matter, on which the decision of this case can be of no authority. This case must I think be decided on the assumption that a real chair similar to those put on the market had been made by craftsmanship.

Section 3(1) is difficult to understand unless one takes account of its origin. The Copyright Act 1911 covered artistic works. Section 35 contains a definition: ' "Artistic work" includes works of painting, drawing, sculpture and artistic craftsmanship, and architectural works of art and engravings and photographs'. 'Architectural work of art' is defined as meaning any building or structure having an artistic character or design. This brought in artistic craftsmanship and buildings for the first time. It would seem that paintings, drawings, sculpture, engravings and photographs were protected whether they had any artistic character or not, but works of craftsmanship had to be of 'artistic' craftsmanship and buildings must have an 'artistic' character or design. There is no further explanation of what is meant by 'artistic'.

The 1956 Act in s 3(1)(a) makes explicit that the works to which it refers need have no artistic quality. Section 3(1)(b) removes the need for any artistic character or design in buildings. But s 3(1)(c) preserves the limitation that there must be 'artistic' craftsmanship.

The word 'artistic' is not an easy word to construe or apply not only because it may have different shades of meaning but also because different people have different views about what is artistic. One may have a word which substantially everyone understands in much the same way. Recently we had to consider such a word— 'insulting' (Brutus v Cozens[1]). Then the matter can and, indeed, must be left to the judge or jury for further explanation will confuse rather than clarify.

But here two questions must be determined. What precisely is the meaning of 'artistic' in this context and who is to judge of its application to the article in question? There is a trend of authority with which I agree that a court ought not to be called on to make an aesthetic judgment. Judges have to be experts in the use of the English language but they are not experts in art or aesthetics. In such a matter my opinion is of no more value than that of anyone else. But I can and must say what in my view is the meaning of the word 'artistic'.

I think we must avoid philosophic or metaphysical argument about the nature of beauty, not only because there does not seem to be any consensus about this but also because those who are ignorant of philosophy are entitled to have opinions about what is artistic. I think that by common usage it is proper for a person to say that in his opinion a thing has an artistic character if he gets pleasure or satisfaction or it may be uplift from contemplating it. No doubt it is necessary to beware of those who get pleasure from looking at something which has cost them a great deal of money. But if unsophisticated people get pleasure from seeing something which they admire I do not see why we must say that it is not artistic because those who profess to be art experts think differently. After all there are great differences of opinion among those who can properly be called experts.

It is I think of importance that the maker or designer of a thing should have intended that it should have an artistic appeal but I would not regard that as either

---

1   [1972] 2 All ER 1297, [1973] AC 854

necessary or conclusive. If any substantial section of the public genuinely admires and values a thing for its appearance and gets pleasure or satisfaction, whether emotional or intellectual, from looking at it, I would accept that it is artistic although many others may think it meaningless or common or vulgar.

I think that it may be misleading to equate artistic craftsmanship with a work of art. 'Work of art' is generally associated more with the fine arts than with craftsmanship and may be setting too high a standard. During the last century there was a movement to bring art to the people. I doubt whether the craftsmen who set out with that intention would have regarded all their products as works of art, but they were certainly works of artistic craftsmanship whether or not they were useful as well as having an artistic appeal.

I am quite unable to agree with the view of the Court of Appeal that[1]—

'there must at least be expected in an object or work that its utilitarian or functional appeal should not be the primary inducement to its acquisition or retention.'

The whole conception of artistic craftsmanship appears to me to be to produce things which are both useful and artistic in the belief that being artistic does not make them any less useful. A person who only wants, or has only room for, one of a particular kind of household object may be willing to pay more to get one which he regards as artistic; if a work of craftsmanship it is nonetheless of artistic craftsmanship because his primary purpose is to get something useful.

But on the other hand I cannot accept the appellants' submission or the view of Graham J[2]. Many people—probably too many—buy things on eye appeal or because they are of a new or original design. But they would not claim that therefore they thought that their purchase had artistic merit. They might say that they were not interested in art, or that they would like to have bought an artistic object but that there was none to be had, at least at a price they could pay. It is notorious that manufacturers go to great expense in providing packaging which will catch the eye of customers. But the customer does not regard the packaging as artistic—he throws it away.

In the present case I find no evidence at all that anyone regarded the appellants' furniture as artistic. The appellants' object was to produce something which would sell. It was, as one witness said, 'a winner' and they succeeded in their object. No doubt many customers bought the furniture because they thought it looked nice as well as being comfortable. But looking nice appears to me to fall considerably short of having artistic appeal. I can find no evidence that anyone felt or thought that the furniture was artistic in the sense which I have tried to explain. I am therefore of opinion that this appeal should be dismissed.

LORD MORRIS OF BORTH-Y-GEST. My Lords, by the time that this case reached this House there remained only one issue calling for consideration. Effectively, it raised the question whether a particular 'work' was a 'work of artistic craftsmanship' within the meaning of those words as they are contained in s 3(1) of the Copyright Act 1956. The 'work' was the prototype (or prototypes) for what became known as the Bronx suite. It consisted of what has been referred to as a 'knock-up' or 'mock-up', which was a sort of model for and which incorporated the features which would be seen in the new suites (consisting of sofas and chairs) which the appellants were going to produce. In succession to the suites which the appellants had previously

---

1 [1973] 3 All ER at 420, [1973] 3 WLR at 460
2 [1973] 1 All ER 160, [1973] 1 WLR 144

produced (including what was called the Denver suite) the new suites (the Bronx suite and variant suites with other names) would have the new features (prominent among which was the wooden plinth) devised by the appellants and put together in the 'knock-up'.

The nailed-up knock-up has long since ceased to exist. There must have come a time when it became scrap and was treated as scrap. We have read in the evidence descriptions of it. No photographs of it were taken. As a prototype it would portray the features which those setting out to manufature would have to reproduce. It was fully upholstered. But it was not a model in the sense that it was in all respects exactly like the things that were to be manufactured and produced. For example, though a chair or sofa is something to sit on the prototype or model or knock-up was not put together so as to be capable of bearing weight and would probably have disintegrated had anyone sat on it.

If the prototype (or prototypes) came within the words 'works of artistic crafts-manship' it is accepted that the appellants would be the owners of the copyright that would subsist in them. If there was such copyright it is not now in contest that the respondents infringed such copyright. Though the respondents did not actually see the prototype they unquestionably copied the Bronx suite which was derived from and which reproduced the prototype. Accordingly they reproduced the appellants' 'work' in a material form (see s 3(5)). They were not entitled to do so if it was a work of artistic craftsmanship. So the limited enquiry now remaining is whether it was. In deciding this question it is immaterial whether or not the appellants could have obtained advantage by taking action under the provisions of the Registered Designs Act 1949.

The Copyright Act 1911 (an amending and consolidating Act) laid down the conditions under which copyright would subsist in every original literary, drama-tic, musical and artistic work. By the interpretation section (s 35) it was pro-vided that unless the context otherwise required 'artistic work' included works of painting, drawing, sculpture and artistic craftsmanship, and architectural works of art and engravings and photographs. So the phrase 'work of artistic craftsmanship' is derived from the 1911 Act. In that Act the phrase 'architectural work of art' was further defined as meaning any building or structure 'having an artistic character or design, in respect of such character or design, or any model for such building or structure' with the proviso that the protection was to 'be confined to the artistic character and design' and was not to extend to 'processes or methods of construction'.

The arrangement of the words in the Copyright Act 1956 was to some extent varied. By s 3 of the Act it is provided that (subject to certain provisions) copyright subsists in every original 'artistic work' which is unpublished and of which the author in the terms of the section was a qualified person. There are the three descriptions of works which are artistic works. In the first are paintings, sculptures, drawings, engravings and photographs. All those are included 'irrespective of artistic quality'. In the second are works of architecture being either buildings or models of buildings. Then in the third are works not falling within the first two descriptions which are 'works of artistic craftsmanship'.

It must be manifest that to qualify as a work of artistic craftsmanship a work must at least be a work of craftsmanship: but it must not only be that: it must have the added character of being artistic. In the present case we were obliged to accept, because the point had been conceded, that the 'knock-up' qualified to be regarded as a work of craftsmanship. I would reserve for future consideration the question whether so transient and incomplete a fabrication as the described 'knock-up' did really come within what Parliament had in contemplation as a work of craftsmanship.

But if, by reason of admission and concession, we must regard the knock-up as having been a work of craftsmanship, did it fall within the more restricted description of having been a work of artistic craftsmanship? To the feature of its having been a work of craftsmanship was there added the feature of its having had an artistic character? Two questions arise. First, what does the word artistic denote? Secondly, how does a court reach a decision whether the character of being artistic was possessed?

As to the first of these I consider that in its place in the phrase 'work of artistic craftsmanship' the word 'artistic' will be well understood. As a word it can stand on and by its own strength. It needs no interpretation. That is not to say that there will not be differences of opinion whether some particular work of craftsmanship does or does not measure up to the standard which must be reached before the use of the word 'artistic' is warranted. But that is only because in this field personal judgment has to be formed: there are no absolute standards: there can be no scientific precision in measurement. Nor can there be unanimity in conclusion though a general consensus of opinion among those whose views command respect will surely be firm ground on which judgment in a court of law can be based.

If by reference to a dictionary it is thought that one sense in which the word 'artist' is understood is that of denoting 'one who cultivates one of the fine arts which please by perfection of execution' then there are conveyed some of the conceptions which the word 'artistic' suggests. But I would not seek to formulate any kind of judicial definition of a word which needs no such aid. If it is asked whether works which possess distinctive features of design and skill in workmanship or works which possess distinctive characteristics of shape, form and finish all qualify to be called artistic I would say that the word 'artistic' calls for something additional and different. If it is asked whether there is artistry if there is an appeal to the eye I would say that something more is needed. In any event, and apart from this, such questions would tend to suggest or to impose a clamp of rigidity and restriction in definition where none is needed.

In deciding whether a work is one of artistic craftsmanship I consider that the work must be viewed and judged in a detached and objective way. The aim and purpose of its author may provide a pointer but the thing produced must itself be assessed without giving decisive weight to the author's scheme of things. Artistry may owe something to an inspiration not possessed by the most deft craftsman. But an effort to produce what is artistic may, if forced or conscious, for that very reason fail. Nor should undue emphasis be given to the priorities in the mind of a possible acquirer. A positive need to purchase an object or thing in order to put it to practical use may be the primary reason for its acquisition but this may be reinforced by a full appreciation of its artistic merits if they are possessed.

So I would say that the object under consideration must be judged as a thing in itself. Does it have the character or virtue of being artistic? In deciding as to this some persons may take something from their ideas as to what constitutes beauty or as to what satisfies their notions of taste or as to what yields pleasure or as to what makes an aesthetic appeal. If, however, there is a resort to these or other words which may themselves have their own satellites of meanings there must follow a return to the word 'artistic' which is apt without exposition to contain and convey its own meaning.

As to the second question, I consider that as in all situations where a decision is required on a question of fact the court must pay heed to the evidence that is adduced. Though it is a matter of individual opinion whether a work is or is not artistic there are many people who have special capabilities and qualifications for forming an opinion and whose testimony will command respect. In practice a court will not have difficulty in weighing their evidence and in deciding whether it clearly points to some conclusion. In cases where the court is able to see the work which is in question that will not warrant a decision on the basis of a spot opinion formed by the court itself but it will be a valuable aid to an appreciation of the evidence.

In the present case the evidence fell short of establishing that the knock-up qualified to be characterised as a work of artistic craftsmanship. That a buyer for a retailing company approved of a design and shape and considered that the product would be a 'winner' only established that it would be likely to attract purchasers. Purchasers might be induced to buy for a variety of reasons which would not include the attraction of possessing a work of artistic craftsmanship. That buyer, who was a witness, expressed herself very clearly. Being asked about one suite which was a variant of the Bronx she said that young people would purchase it because in their case it had an 'eye appeal' and because the wide-arms of the suite were an added attraction: it was a 'wonderful suite' though it was 'horrible' and though it was 'vulgar' and though it was 'brash'. One witness (Mr Carter) had great knowledge and experience in regard to the designs of and the designing of furniture but his evidence did not support a claim that there was artistic character. He was asked about the design of the Bronx suite. In particular he was asked whether 'aesthetically speaking' he considered the design to be good. His revealing reply was, 'Personally I do not, no. I think it is mediocre, in my opinion, although I can see it has great appeal. I think it is slightly vulgar but it is obviously quite a good commercial design'. Though he considered that there was a 'distinctive shape' his nearest approach towards asserting an artistic character was when he said that there was a design concept in visual terms which provided artistic originality or lent artistic merit by possessing a strong individual character. The high water mark of his testimony is set out in the passage recited in the judgment of the Court of Appeal[1]. It was not high enough, in my view, to establish that the prototype (or prototypes) qualified to be described as a work of artistic craftsmanship within the meaning of s 3(1) of the 1956 Act.

I would dismiss the appeal.

VISCOUNT DILHORNE. My Lords, the appellants and the respondents are manufacturers of furniture. Among the types of suites of sofas and armchairs the appellants made was a suite to which they gave the name 'Denver'. They were described as 'boat-shaped' and stood on legs of a somewhat flimsy appearance. As sales of the 'Denver' suites were falling, Mr Hensher, their managing director, with Mr Sutton, their works director, and Mr Batchelor, their upholstery manager, decided to try to make the 'Denver' suite more saleable by making alterations to it. The 'Denver' suites, when altered, were called 'Bronx'.

Mr Batchelor in evidence described the process they followed thus: 'We started from the Denver chair, putting a temporary plinth on the Denver chair; then we had a prototype of the Bronx.' The legs of the Denver chairs were taken off and replaced by what may be called the four sides of a box, with castors being fixed on the bottom edges of the sides. Strips of a substance called 'afrormosia' were fixed horizontally along the sides of the box. This made what has been called a plinth. It had also two wings which extended upwards under the arms of the chair. The result was that the armchairs and settees so altered appeared to be standing on a solid base.

Suites of the Denver type on this plinth, now called the Bronx, were mass produced, and the appellants also mass produced variants of the Bronx. Their important feature was the presence of the plinth. Mr Sutton in evidence said that in a sense there was no other important difference between the Bronx and the Denver suites; the only other differences to which he drew attention being that the arms of the Bronx were made thicker at the top than those of the Denver and that a 'button back' was put on the Bronx.

The respondents at the hearing in this House did not contest that they had copied the Bronx suites as put on the market, that is to say, that they had copied the seats, arms, backs and shape of the Denver suite and the plinths on which the Denver suites were put.

---

1   [1973] 3 All ER at 417, 418, [1973] 3 WLR at 456, 457

When the Bronx suites were mass produced, the prototype from which they were made was destroyed. As the Bronx suites were copies of the prototype, the suites the respondents made were copies of that. The prototype appears to have consisted of a nailed up frame which was upholstered, resting on the plinth. The appellants contended that copyright attached to the prototype and that the respondents had infringed it by marketing their suites. The first question for consideration appears to me to be if copyright subsists in the prototype, does it subsist in the whole of it or in part of it, and if so, in which part.

Section 3(2) of the Copyright Act 1956 states that 'Copyright shall subsist ... in every original artistic work which is unpublished ...' and s 3(3) that it shall, if certain conditions are satisfied, subsist in an original artistic work which has been published.

The original part of the prototype was the plinth on which the Denver design was placed. It was no doubt for this reason that counsel for appellants conceded, in the course of the argument, that there was no breach of copyright in the prototype by copying the boat-shape, seat, arms and back. If copyright subsisted in the Denver suite, there might have been an infringement by the respondents of that copyright, but not of that in the Bronx. So if there was infringement of the appellants' copyright in the prototype, it consisted in the copying of the plinth and putting it under what was otherwise in all material respects a Denver type.

To succeed in this appeal the appellants must establish that that constituted an artistic work. 'Artistic work' is defined by s 3(1) of the Copyright Act 1956 as meaning:

'a work of any of the following descriptions, that is to say,—(a) the following, irrespective of artistic quality, namely, paintings, scuptures, drawings, engravings and photographs; (b) works of architecture, being either buildings or models for buildings; (c) works of artistic craftsmanship, not falling within either of the preceding paragraphs.'

The appellants contend that the destroyed prototype was a work of artistic craftsmanship. It has not to be considered in this appeal whether such a work must be a finished and complete work intended to be kept in existence and whether a prototype of the character of that in this case can properly be so described as a work of craftsmanship; for the respondents conceded in this House, perhaps rather surprisingly, that the prototype was a work of craftsmanship, apparently on the ground that those making it were craftsmen; but not everything produced by craftsmen is to be described as a work of craftsmanship. A work of craftsmanship is, in my opinion, something made by hand and not something mass produced.

This concession having been made, the only question for determination now is whether the 'original' part of the prototype was a work of artistic craftsmanship. Graham J came to the conclusion that the appellants' claim succeeded. In his view, the Bronx chairs and settees were works of artistic craftsmanship in that they had distinctive characteristics of shape, form and finish. He said[1]:

'They exhibit features of design and skill in workmanship which the words of definition "artistic craftsmanship" on their proper construction in their context connote.'

In view of the concession made, the question is not whether the Bronx chairs and settees in their entirety were such works, but whether the original part of them is to be so described, namely, the plinth on which the Denver chairs and settees were placed. It may be that before Graham J that concession was not made. However this may be, I do not think that the presence of distinctive features of shape, form and finish suffices to make a work artistic.

Russell LJ[2], delivering the judgment of the Court of Appeal, said that it seemed to that court that Graham J had come to the conclusion that in the field of furniture

---

1   [1973] 1 All ER at 164, [1973] 1 WLR at 152
2   [1973] 3 All ER at 418, [1973] 3 WLR at 458

all that is needed to qualify as a work of artistic craftsmanship is a sufficient originality of design to qualify as a design under the Registered Designs Act 1949. That court thought that this was not right in law. I agree. The Court of Appeal reversed Graham J, and it is from their decision that the appellants now appeal.

'Design' for the purposes of the Registered Designs Act 1949 is defined in s 1(3) as meaning:

> 'features of shape, configuration, pattern or ornament applied to an article by any industrial process or means, being features which in the finished article appeal to and are judged solely by the eye, but does not include a method or principle of construction or features of shape or configuration which are dictated solely by the function which the article to be made in that shape or configuration has to perform.'

If the appellants had registered the design they applied to the Denver chair in the course of its mass production, a design intended to have appeal to the eye and so to be more saleable—and sales of the Bronx were very satisfactory—they would have had the copyright in the registered design, that is to say—

> 'the exclusive right in the United Kingdom and the Isle of Man to make or import for sale or for use for the purposes of any trade or business, or to sell, hire or offer for sale or hire, any article in respect of which the design is registered, being an article to which the registered design or a design not substantially different from the registered design has been applied . . .' (Section 7(1) of the 1949 Act.)

The Copyright Act 1911 recognises that a design registrable under the Patents and Designs Act 1907 may be an artistic work (see s 22) and the Copyright Act 1956 recognised similarly that a design registered under the Registered Designs Act 1949 might be an artistic work (s 10), but it does not follow that all designs registrable under those Acts are artistic works within the meaning of the Copyright Acts.

The definition of 'artistic work' in the Copyright Act 1911 (s 35) also included 'works of artistic craftsmanship'. Parliament, when that phrase was used in the 1956 Act, must have intended it to have the same meaning as in the 1911 Act. The definition of 'artistic work' in the 1911 Act is in some respects different from that in the 1956 Act. The 1911 Act definition included all the things mentioned in s 3(1) of the 1956 Act (supra) except the words, 'irrespective of artistic quality'. The 1911 Act definition included architectural works of art which were in turn defined as meaning buildings or structures 'having an artistic character or design' or any model for such buildings or structures, but the protection given by the Act only extended to the artistic character or design. In relation to works of architecture the 1956 Act made no reference to artistic character or design.

Neither Act contains any express indication of the meaning to be given to 'works of artistic craftsmanship' but the wording of s 3(1)(c) of the 1956 Act recognises that some works covered by paras (a) and (b) of that subsection would be works of artistic craftsmanship, though some works which came within those paragraphs might not, were it not for the definition of 'artistic work', be so regarded. The definition of those words in the 1911 Act places greater emphasis on artistic character.

Apart from the slight indication of its meaning to be derived from its conjunction with the other parts of the definition of 'artistic work' in these Acts, I can see nothing in the other parts of those Acts which throws any light on the meaning to be given to the phrase 'works of artistic craftsmanship'.

How, then, is the phrase to be interpreted? An 'artistic work' is no more and no less than a work of art. Every work of art is an artistic work and vice versa. How does one distinguish between what is a work of art and what is not? Various tests have been suggested. In the Court of Appeal, Russell LJ said[1]:

---

1   [1973] 3 All ER at 418, 419, [1973] 3 WLR at 458

'In our judgment, if it can be said of a work of craftsmanship that it is an object which would be expected to be acquired or retained rather for its functional utility than for any appeal to aesthetic taste, it is not within the scope of the phrase "other works of artistic craftsmanship". Mere originality in points of design aimed at appealing to the eye as commercial selling points will not in our judgment suffice.'

And later he said[1]:

'... in order to qualify as a work of artistic craftsmanship, there must at least be expected in an object or work that its utilitarian or functional appeal should not be the primary inducement to its acquisition or retention.'

The Court of Appeal[1] agreed with Noël J's rejection in *Cuisenaire v South West Imports Ltd*[2] of the idea that, because a work or object was partly functional or utilitarian, it could not be an artistic work.

While I agree with the rejection of that idea and I agree that mere originality in design does not make a thing an artistic work of art, I do not think that whether or not a work is to be regarded as artistic depends on whether or not the primary inducement for its acquisition or retention is its functional character. To determine the primary purpose of possession of an article seems to me a very difficult and uncertain test for any court to apply: and I do not think that the words 'works of artistic craftsmanship' are to be interpreted as involving the application of any such test. A work which is one of artistic craftsmanship does not, I think, lose that character on account of its functional qualities.

Counsel for the appellants submitted that any work which is visible and which is made to have and has eye appeal is an artistic work and that a good design intended to appeal must also be an artistic design. He said that the work must be visible in order to exclude internal works such as a piece of machinery which is covered up. I do not think it possible to accede to this submission for I do not think it is right to say that every work which has eye appeal is necessarily a work of art, though some may be. This submission would appear to accord in all material respects with that of Graham J[3] which was, in my opinion, rightly rejected by the Court of Appeal[4]. If right, it would mean that every design registrable under the Registered Designs Act 1949 is a work of art or, if one prefers the expression, an artistic work.

Counsel for the respondents put forward two alternative tests. I do not think that I need discuss them for, in my opinion, the proper interpretation of the words of the statute does not involve the formulation of any test or the application of any particular formula. Indeed, to lay down any such test or formula is to add to what is contained in the Act and I can see no justification for doing so.

The phrase 'works of artistic craftsmanship' is made up of words in ordinary use in the English language. Unless the context otherwise requires, they must be given their ordinary and natural meaning. I can find nothing in the context to require that they should be given a different meaning from that.

So, in my view, it is simply a question of fact whether a work is one of artistic craftsmanship. Questions of fact are often difficult to decide but juries have to decide them. In many cases it will be easy to decide whether a work is or is not such a work, but there may be many borderline cases and I do not think that a clear line can be drawn between works which are and those which are not artistic. Nor, if the Court of Appeal's test is accepted, is a clear line laid down.

I am conscious, as was the Court of Appeal, of the need to avoid judicial assessment of artistic merits or quality, but I do not think that any such assessment is involved in deciding whether a work is an artistic work.

1 [1973] 3 All ER at 420, [1973] 3 WLR at 460
2 [1968] 1 Ex CR 493 at 513, 514
3 [1973] 1 All ER 160, [1973] 1 WLR 144
4 [1973] 3 All ER 414, [1973] 3 WLR 453

This question of fact in relation to copyright is decided not by a jury but by a judge sitting alone. Evidence may be called with regard to it. Expert witnesses may testify. At the end of the day, it will be for the judge to decide whether it is established that the work is one of artistic craftsmanship. If that is not established, the claim to copyright on that ground will fail. I do not think that it suffices to show that some section of the public considers the work to be artistic, though that fact will be one for the judge to take into account, for the decision has to be made by the judge and cannot be delegated.

In this case there was no evidence before Graham J that the prototype as a whole or that part of it which has been called a plinth was a work of an artistic character. Mrs Watney, who had been the principal buyer of the Times Furnishing Co, thought that the Bronx type was a 'winner' from the selling point of view. She regarded it as 'very flashy' and said 'It was horrible really'. She did not describe it as artistic; nor did Mr Carter, a design consultant. He said that the Bronx type was not, in his opinion, aesthetically speaking, a good design. He thought it slightly vulgar, but that it was obviously a good commercial design. While both these witnesses gave their opinions of the merits of the Bronx, neither of them said that the Bronx had an artistic character or was an artistic work of art.

In these circumstances, I do not think that the appellants established that either the prototype as a whole or that part of it which was original, namely, the plinth, was a work of artistic craftsmanship. I do not regard this as a borderline case but one which, in my view, fell clearly on the wrong side of the line from the appellants' point of view. No witness described, and I think it would have been surprising if a witness had, the Bronx chairs and settees as works of art.

I would therefore dismiss this appeal.

LORD SIMON OF GLAISDALE. My Lords, the appellants ('Henshers') and the respondents ('Restawile') are both manufacturers of upholstered furniture, including (and alone relevant to this appeal) mass-produced three-piece drawing-room suites consisting of two chairs and a settee. Henshers had from about 1963 or 1964 sold a suite called the Denver (with a variant). This had a distinctive 'boat-shape', which is more closely described in the judgment of the Court of Appeal[1], and it was supported on spindle-shaped legs. It had sold well until 1966, when sales started to fall off. Three employees of Henshers then set together to produce an improved design. They were Mr Hensher (the managing director), Mr Sutton (the works director) and Mr Batchelor (the prototype-maker)—the last two at least being admittedly craftsmen. Mr Hensher described their objective as follows:

'I decided that we would endeavour to make the Denver more attractive by bringing it down to the ground, and, at the same time, in doing so, incorporate various selling points.'

They stripped down the Denver to its frame, removed the legs, replaced the legs by a sloped wooden plinth all round with casters on the corners and covered with a strip of wood trim (afrormosia). The frame was nailed up (whereas the commercial product would be screwed and glued together), and re-upholstered. This was the prototype of the suite called the Bronx. The arms of the Denver were already wider than usual, providing at call extra seating (a significant selling point); but there were slight adjustments made to the height of the chair and the slope of the back. The main difference, however, between the Denver and the Bronx was the plinth replacing the legs, which gave the boat-shaped upper part a floating effect. As I read the evidence, it was a commercially bold and original design, though not calculated to appeal to fastidious taste. It was put into mass production as the Bronx (with variants bearing different names). They were a considerable commercial

1   [1973] 3 All ER at 416, [1973] 3 WLR at 455

success; so much so that other manufacturers, including Restawile, produced models bearing a marked similarity. Henshers started proceedings against such competitors. A number of issues arose which are no longer live. In particular, Restawile now admit that they copied the Bronx and that the prototype as a product of craftsmen was a work of 'craftsmanship' (though this, insofar as it involves the meaning of a word in a statutory phrase, might well be questionable). The sole issue before your Lordships is whether the prototype (which is no longer extant) was 'a work of artistic craftsmanship' within the meaning of s 3(1)(c) of the Copyright Act 1956. Graham J[1] decided this issue in favour of Henshers, but he was reversed by the Court of Appeal[2]. Henshers now appeal to your Lordships.

In *London Borough of Ealing v Race Relations Board*[3] I suggested to your Lordships that, in setting about the ascertainment of the meaning of a phrase in a statute, it was often useful to survey the social and legal backgrounds against which Parliament was legislating. Section 3 of the 1956 Act gives copyright in original artistic works, 'artistic work' being defined in sub-s (1) as meaning:

> 'a work of any of the following descriptions, that is to say,—(a) the following, irrespective of artistic quality, namely paintings, sculptures, drawings, engravings and photographs; (b) works of architecture, being either buildings or models for buildings; (c) works of artistic craftsmanship, not falling within either of the preceding paragraphs.'

The phrase 'work of artistic craftsmanship' was previously used—for the first time—in the Copyright Act 1911. Section 1 of that Act gave copyright protection, inter alia, to every original artistic work. By s 35 'artistic work' included: 'works of painting, drawing, sculpture and artistic craftsmanship, and architectural works of art and engravings and photographs'; and 'architectural work of art' meant—

> 'any building or structure having an artistic character or design, in respect of such character or design . . . provided that the protection afforded by this Act shall be confined to the artistic character and design . . .'

But, though the context of the phrase 'work of artistic craftsmanship' was different in 1911, there is nothing to suggest (nor has it been suggested in this appeal) that its meaning was any different in the two Acts. So it is the social and legal backgrounds to the 1911 Act which require investigation. When this is undertaken it will be found that they chime together remarkably, leaving no doubt as to what sort of work it was that Parliament was extending copyright protection in 1911.

The statutory background is that copyright in works of the description set out in s 3(1)(a) of the 1956 Act (paintings, sculptures, drawings, engravings and photographs) had been given protection by the Sculpture Copyright Act 1814 and the Fine Arts Copyright Act 1862 (replacing earlier statutes which protected engravings only), and copyright in works of the description set out in s 3(1)(b) of the 1956 Act (works of architecture, as distinct from architectural drawings, already protected by the 1862 Act) had been given protection for the first time by the 1911 Act, to the extent of their artistic character and design. The only other statutory provisions which require notice are in Part II of the Patents and Designs Act 1907, which gave protection to industrial designs. Part of the argument before your Lordships consisted of a close comparison of the terminology of these provisions of the 1907 Act (and their subsequent amendments and re-enactments up to the Design Copyright Act 1968) with that of the Copyright Acts 1911 and 1956. This terminological comparison did not finally yield any clinching result. But the fact that the 1911 Act supervened on,

1   [1973] 1 All ER 160, [1973] 1 WLR 144
2   [1973] 3 All ER 414, [1973] 3 WLR 453
3   [1972] 1 All ER 105 at 114, [1972] AC 342 at 361

without replacing, the 1907 Act suggests that, even though s 22 of the 1911 Act (cf s 10 of the 1956 Act, afterwards amended) recognised that a design registered under the 1907 Act might be an artistic work, the 1911 Act was not primarily concerned to protect works intended to lead to industrial (i e mass) production (see Copinger and Skone James on Copyright[1]). So the sole relevance of the legislation dealing with registered designs is to make it unnecessary, in order to give full and adequate protection, to read 'works of artistic craftsmanship' in an artificially extended sense. The words can bear their natural and ordinary meaning. The design of the Bronx might admittedly have been registred as an industrial design.

The significant feature of this part of the law before 1911 was that the artistic works given copyright protection were works of fine art. This accorded with the almost universal concept current in 1862: a work of art was a product of the fine arts and primarily an easel painting. But almost from the moment of the Fine Arts Copyright Act 1862, there was a reaction, which came to be known as the Arts and Crafts movement. In 1862 itself William Morris founded 'The Firm', producing a wide variety of work of decorative and applied art. In 1864 he produced his first wallpaper, hand-printed from wood blocks. In the 1880s at least five societies were founded to promote the guild ideal propagated by Ruskin and Morris. In 1888 the Arts and Crafts Exhibition Society began its work. In 1890 Morris set up the Kelmscott Press, to be followed by a number of other private presses within the decade. In 1893 came the Arts and Crafts Essays (of which eight were concerned with the design and decoration of furniture). In 1896 the Central School of Arts and Crafts was founded, with Lethaby and Frampton as joint principals. The tenth edition of the Encyclopaedia Brittannica[2] contained, for the first time, an article on 'Arts and Crafts' —by Walter Crane. In 1905 Cobden-Sanderson published The Arts and Crafts Movement. In 1908 the Central School moved to its present purpose-built premises in Southampton Row. These are no more than a handful of key events; but they put beyond doubt what it was that prompted Parliament in 1911 to give copyright protection to 'works of artistic craftsmanship'—namely, the Arts and Crafts movement with its emphasis on the applied or decorative arts.

For the essence of the Arts and Crafts ideology was that 'art' did not mean merely, or even primarily, the fine arts. Art was a way of life, standing in contrast to the prevailing life of industrialism and commercialism, which was seen as a threat to mankind's spiritual and physical well-being. 'On every hand', Carlyle had written, 'the living artisan is driven from his workshop, to make room for a speedier inanimate one'. So the handicraftsman must be restored to his creative role in society. Moreover, his creation, wherever appropriate, should be a work of art—creation par excellence; and the artist must in turn be a craftsman. The aim of Mackmurdo's Century Guild (1882) was, on the one hand, to render all branches of art no longer 'the sphere of the tradesman'; on the other, to 'restore building, decoration, glass-painting, pottery, wood-carving and metal to their proper place beside painting and sculpture'. The aesthetic of the movement was concerned with fitness and propriety, in contradistinction to irrelevant ornament (what Lethaby called 'sham artistic twaddle'). Functional efficiency and respect for the worked material would impose its own appropriate form, showing, to quote Lethaby again, that it was 'made for a human being by a human being'.

But although, in my view, there can be no doubt that, when Parliament, in 1911, gave copyright protection to 'works of artistic craftsmanship', it was extending to works of applied art the protection formerly restricted to works of the fine arts, and was doing so under the influence of the Arts and Crafts movement, and although the aesthetic of the Arts and Crafts movement was a handicraft aesthetic, Parliament used the words 'artistic craftsmanship', not 'artistic handicraft'. It seems likely that

---

1   11th Edn (1971), p 83, para 180
2   (1902-1903)

this was done advisedly: I have already indicated that s 22 of the 1911 Act envisaged that an industrial design might be an artistic work. Moreover, however ideologically opposed to current industrial and commercial society, at least some of the leaders of the Arts and Crafts movement recognised that they would have to come to terms with the machine. As early as 1859 Philip Webb designed table glassware for J Powell & Sons of Whitefriars. During the 1880s even Morris acknowledged that the machine could be useful in extinguishing 'all irksome and unintelligent labour, leaving us free to raise the standard of skill of hand and energy of mind of our workmen'. The private presses may have used hand-made paper and designed their own type-faces, but they printed on machines. Ashbee, who went to the United States in 1900 'to tilt at the great industrial windmill', by 1911, under the influence of Frank Lloyd Wright (who had lectured on 'The Art and Craft of the Machine'), could no longer deny to the unpretentious machine-made object an aesthetic value; and after the failure of his Guild and School of Handicraft he himself turned to industrial design. Much of Benson's metal-work was produced by machinery on a commercial scale. The Central School of Arts and Crafts, though foremost a school of handi-crafts, had as a declared aim to encourage 'the industrial application of decorative design'. So, although 'works of artistic craftsmanship' cannot be adequately con-strued without bearing in mind the aims and achievements of the Arts and Crafts movement, 'craftsmanship' in the statutory phrase cannot be limited to handicraft; nor is the word 'artistic' incompatible with machine production (see *Britain v Hanks Brothers and Co*[1]).

The concession that the prototype of the Bronx was a work of craftsmanship has tended to distort the argument by concentrating exclusively on the meaning of the word 'artistic' in the statutory phrase. But 'works of artistic craftsmanship' is a composite phrase which must be construed as a whole. There is nothing to suggest that any of the words is used in other than one of its ordinary senses. A work of craftsmanship, even though it cannot be confined to handicraft, at least presupposes special training, skill and knowledge for its production: see *Cuisenaire v Reed*[2] and *Cuisenaire v South West Imports Ltd*[3]. 'Craftsmanship', particularly when considered in its historical context, implies a manifestation of pride in sound workmanship—a rejection of the shoddy, the meretricious, the facile. But the craftsmanship—not the work itself—must, in addition, be artistic. Before turning to the various criteria which have been propounded it may be helpful to consider some examples. A cobbler is a craftsman, and those in the Arts and Crafts movement would have valued his vocation as such. But neither they, nor anyone else using the words in their common acceptation, would describe his craftsmanship as artistic, or his products as 'works of artistic craftsmanship'. A dental mechanic is a similar example; so is a pattern-maker, a boiler-maker, a plumber, a wheelwright, a thatcher. At the other extreme is the maker of hand-painted tiles. He too is a craftsman; but his craftsmanship would properly be described as artistic and his products as 'works of artistic crafts-manship'. In between lie a host of crafts some of whose practitioners can claim artistic craftsmanship, some not—or whose practitioners sometimes exercise artistic craftsmanship, sometimes not. In the former class, for example, are glaziers. The ordinary glazier is a craftsman, but he could not properly claim that his crafts-manship is artistic in the common acceptation. But the maker of stained glass windows could properly make such a claim; and indeed, the revival of stained glass work was one of the high achievements of the Arts and Crafts movement. In the latter class is the blacksmith—a craftsman in all his business, and exercising artistic craftsmanship perhaps in making wrought iron gates, but certainly not in shoeing a horse or repairing a ploughshare. In these intermediate—or rather, straddling—

---

1   (1902) 86 LT 764
2   [1963] VR 719
3   [1968] 1 Ex CR 493 at 514

classes come, too, the woodworkers, ranging from carpenters to cabinet-makers: some of their work would be generally accepted as artistic craftsmanship, most not. Similarly, printers, bookbinders, cutlers, needleworkers, weavers—and many others. In this straddling class also fall, in my judgment, the makers of furniture. Some of their products would be, I think, almost universally accepted as 'works of artistic craftsmanship'; but it would be a misuse of language to describe the bulk of their products as such. Where and how is the line to be drawn?

I think that the key passage of Graham J's judgment is the following[1]:

> 'My conclusion on this part of the case is therefore that these chairs and settees are "works of artistic craftsmanship" in that they have, whether one admires them or not, distinctive characteristics of shape, form and finish, which were conceived and executed by Mr Hensher and those working with him so as to result in articles which are much more than purely utilitarian. They exhibit in my judgment distinctive features of design and skill in workmanship which the words of definition "artistic craftsmanship" on their proper construction in their context connote.'

Though this approach receives some support from *Blake v Warren*[2], a decision of an official referee on the 'artistic character' of an 'architectural work of art' under the 1911 Act, I respectfully agree with the comment of the Court of Appeal[3]:

> 'It seems to us that the judge has in effect come to the conclusion that in the field of furniture all that is needed to qualify as a work of artistic craftsmanship is a sufficient originality of design to qualify as a design under the Registered Designs Act 1949. Is this right in law? We do not think so. It seems to us to give no sufficient effect to the word "artistic" in the definition in the 1956 Act. The phrase is not "a work of craftsmanship of original design" . . . Mere originality in points of design aimed at appealing to the eye as commercial selling points will not in our judgment suffice.'

Although there is, as I have pointed out, an area of overlap between the Copyright Acts and the Registered Designs Acts, the two classes of statute do not give co-terminous protection as regards subject-matter: if that had been the intention, interpretative cross-reference would have been the appropriate drafting technique. Moreover, although true originality (in the way of a new sensibility or ideology or world view or technique) may be relevant aesthetically, mere novelty can hardly be so. A gimmick is almost the negation of a work of art. Its appeal, as Russell LJ implied, is likely to be directed at satisfying other demands in the purchaser than the contemplation of beauty—desire for change, for modishness, for prestige , for example.

On the other hand, I cannot agree with the alternative criterion proposed by the Court of Appeal[4] that:

> '. . . in order to qualify as a work of artistic craftsmanship, there must at least be expected in an object or work that its utilitarian or functional appeal should not be the primary inducement to its acquisition or retention.'

Restawile's counsel did not attempt to support this test before your Lordships. It is, I fear, unworkable. One person may buy a chair because it is comfortable, another because it is beautiful, a third because it exactly fits the room, a fourth because it is the right price. Even without the third and fourth classes, which do not fit in the Court of Appeal's categorisation, it would be impracticable to decide on the artistic quality of the craftsmanship by a show of hands or a card vote. And in one purchaser

---

1 [1973] 1 All ER at 164, [1973] 1 WLR at 152
2 (1931) [1928-35] MacG Cop Cas 268
3 [1973] 3 All ER at 418, 419, [1973] 3 WLR at 458
4 [1973] 3 All ER at 420, [1973] 3 WLR at 460

alone the motives may be so mixed that it is impossible to say what is the primary inducement to acquisition or retention. Even more important, the whole antithesis between utility and beauty, between function and art, is a false one—especially in the context of the Arts and Crafts movement. 'I never begin to be satisfied', said Philip Webb, one of the founders, 'until my work looks commonplace'. Lethaby's object, declared towards the end, was 'to create an efficiency style'. Artistic form should, they all held, be an emanation of regard for materials on the one hand and for function on the other.

Hensher's counsel put forward an argument as follows. An object is artistic if it appeals to the eye of the beholder, giving him visual pleasure. The Bronx proved to be more appealing than the Denver. But, so far as utility or function was concerned, there was virtually nothing to choose between the two models. The greater appeal of the Bronx must, therefore, have been its 'eye-appeal'—that it gave significantly greater visual pleasure. The prototype Bronx was admittedly a work of craftsmanship. It inevitably follows, it was argued, that it was a work of artistic craftsmanship.

With all respect, and admitting its ingenuity, there seems to me to be much that is unacceptable in this argument. First, it is based on a hedonistic aesthetic theory (the essence of art is that it gives pleasure) which, although it has had distinguished proponents, has also been strongly disputed. Secondly, it then proceeds to stand the theory on its head—the essence of art is that it gives (visual) pleasure, therefore what gives visual pleasure is artistic. This is not only illogical, but manifestly untrue —a pretty girl or a landscape give visual pleasure without being artistic. Thirdly, this argument too is based on a contradistinction between art and function which is unsound, and particularly unsound in the instant context. Fourthly, the argument proceeds on the basis that the Bronx must have been bought in preference to the Denver for its greater utility or for its great visual appeal—and, since it was not the former, it must have been the latter. But there were many other reasons why the Bronx might have been bought—because the Joneses next door had just acquired such a suite, for example, or because no one in the neighbourhood had such a novelty, or because it struck the purchaser as being in the 'trend' of fashion (that word was actually used in evidence to explain the common appeal of these suites), or because it seemed to be the best general value for money of the available goods, or, no doubt, for a large variety of other reasons which have nothing to do with either function or eye-appeal.

Restawile's counsel, on the other hand, propounded two alternative criteria, both reflecting another theory of aesthetics—the idealistic. The first was: an article of craftsmanship is artistic if it can be seen from the article itself or from other evidence that the author is using a utilitarian article as a vehicle to carry an expression of his idea of beauty. Counsel defined neither 'idea' nor 'beauty'—widely, since philosophers have been at odds over these concepts for millennia. But without some explanation the proffered criterion is virtually tautological; since art, both in the discipline of aesthetics and in popular usage, is generally understood to be the expression or impression of beauty.

Counsel's second criterion was a variant on the first: craftsmanship is artistic if the craftsman is using a utilitarian article to give expression to an idea unassociated with the utilitarian purpose. This avoids the tautology implicit in the use of the word 'beauty', but at the cost of greater vagueness. Disregarding the metaphysical implications of the use of the word 'idea' in this context, this criterion would extend to the expression of ideas which would seem to be irrelevant to art—for example, novelty and gimmickry (which I have already referred to), or modishness, or obscenity, or racial prejudice. The example given by counsel was an 'archetypal' fork (a work of craftsmanship) with an ornament on the handle (making it a work of artistic craftsmanship). But, as I have ventured to point out, this whole contradistinction between art and utility, between function and ornament, is entirely alien to the concepts which lie behind s 3(1)(c) of the 1956 Act. An 'archetypal' spoon (assuming such a metaphysical concept can materialise) may itself be a work of artistic craftsmanship; an apostle spoon is neither more nor less likely to be so.

It is, my Lords, I confess, easier to question the criteria put forward by others than to propound one's own. The attempt must nevertheless be made. I start by re-emphasising that the statutory phrase is not 'artistic work of craftsmanship', but 'work of artistic craftsmanship'; and that this distinction accords with the social situation in which Parliament was providing a remedy. It is therefore misleading to ask, first, is this a work produced by a craftsman, and secondly, is it a work of art? It is more pertinent to ask, is this the work of one who was in this respect an artist-craftsman? It follows that the artistic merit of the work is irrelevant. (It is, no doubt, because s 3(1)(c) of the 1956 Act is concerned with works of artistic craftsmanship, and not with artistic works of craftsmanship, that it was unnecessary to repeat the words that appear in s 3(1)(a), 'irrespective of artistic quality', which, as comparison with the words 'artistic character' in the 1911 Act demonstrates, refer to artistic merit.) Not only is artistic merit irrelevant as a matter of statutory construction, evaluation of artistic merit is not a task for which judges have any training or general aptitude. Words are the tools and subject-matter of lawyers; but even in matters of literary copyright the court will not concern itself with literary merit: *Walter v Lane*[1]. Since the tribunal will not attempt a personal aesthetic judgment (Stewart J in *Hay v Sloan*[2]) it follows again, that whether the subject-matter is or is not a work of artistic craftsmanship is a matter of evidence; and the most cogent evidence is likely to be either from those who are themselves acknowledged artist-craftsmen or from those who are concerned with the training of artist-craftsmen—in other words, expert evidence. In evaluating the evidence, the court will endeavour not to be tied to a particular metaphysics of art, partly because courts are not naturally fitted to weigh such matters, partly because Parliament can hardly have intended that the construction of its statutory phrase should turn on some recondite theory of aesthetics—though the court must, of course, in its task of statutory interpretation, take cognisance of the social-aesthetic situation which lies behind the enactment, nor can counsel be prevented from probing the reasons why a witness considers the subject-matter to be or not to be a work of artistic craftsmanship. It is probably enough that common experience tells us that artists have vocationally an aim and impact which differ from those of the ordinary run of humankind. Given the craftsmanship, it is the presence of such aim and impact—what Stewart J[2] called 'the intent of the creator and its result'—which will determine that the work is one of artistic craftsmanship.

Against this construction of the statutory phrase, the result of the instant appeal cannot be in doubt: there was no, or certainly no adequate, evidence that the prototype of the Bronx chair was a work of artistic craftsmanship. A Mrs Watney, who had been the principal furniture buyer of the Times Furnishing Co, gave evidence for Henshers: some passages were quoted in the judgment of the Court of Appeal[3]. It is sufficient here to say that she nowhere stated that in her opinion any of the suites in question (or the prototype) was a work of artistic craftsmanship. Though she used the word 'eye-appeal', it was in the context of commercial potentially, selling-points. Of the Bronx she said, 'the shape . . . was new. It was very flashy. It was horrible really'. Of the Denver, in respect of its common features with the Bronx, she spoke of the 'trend that was coming in'. She used the word 'winner'—appropriate enough in its commercial context, but hardly apt for anything more.

Mr Carter, a design consultant specialising in furniture, also gave evidence for Henshers. He did use the word 'artistic'; but it was put into his mouth under the

---

1   [1900] AC 539
2   (1957) 16 Fox Pat C 185 at 190
3   [1973] 3 All ER at 416, 417, [1973] 3 WLR at 455, 456

misapprehension that he had already used it. Again, the key passages are set out in the judgment of the Court of Appeal[1]. Mr Carter agreed with Henshers' counsel that it was the intention of the designer to produce an article which appealed to the eye of the beholder; I have already ventured to indicate why this is an inadequate criterion of art or the artistic. He described the Bronx as 'typical of the middle of the road commercial type of production furniture'. He considered its design to be mediocre, although he could see that it had great appeal—slightly vulgar, though obviously quite a good commercial design, having 'novelty . . . quite distinct individuality'.

All this is very far from establishing the Bronx or its prototype as a work of artistic craftsmanship. I respectfully agree with the Court of Appeal[2] that at the most it established originality in points of design aimed at appealing to the eye as commercial selling points. I also agree that this does not suffice. If it were permissible to express a personal view, I would agree with the Court of Appeal[2] that Henshers' suites are perfectly ordinary pieces of furniture. It would be an entire misuse of language to describe them or their prototypes as works of artistic craftsmanship.

I would therefore dismiss the appeal.

LORD KILBRANDON. My Lords, there seems to be no dispute on the facts of this appeal—although there is room for some perplexity arising from admissions given during the course of the argument—and I can make a brief summary based for the most part on the case for the appellants. The appellants decided to make some modifications to their 'Denver' chair, the sales of which were falling off. So the managing director and two of the craftsmen on their staff—

'produced by a process of trial and error over a period of some six weeks ending in October 1966 and without any design drawings the "Bronx" prototype chair . . . The principal difference between the "Bronx" and its predecessor the "Denver" lay in the fact that whereas the "Denver" stood on four legs the "Bronx" had and was intended to have a more attractive lighter floating appearance imparted to it by the substitution, for the four legs which supported the "Denver", of a wooden plinth.'

The prototype was a mock-up, nailed together and then upholstered. It was not a chair, in the sense that it could not be sat on because it would not bear such a weight. It was destroyed after it had served its purpose, and no intelligible visual records of it were preserved. The 'Bronx' was very successful commercially when it was put on the market. The respondents copied the 'Bronx' chair and put the copies on the market under the name 'Amazon'.

The appellants originally claimed copyright in artistic works being the 'Bronx' and related suites and the several individual chairs and settees therein comprised. By amendment they claimed copyright 'in the several original prototypes for the foregoing', and this is now the extent of the claim as maintained. The basis of the claim is that the prototypes (of which the 'Bronx' chair is taken as a specimen) are artistic works within the meaning of s 3 of the Copyright Act 1956, being works of artistic craftsmanship. The respondents concede that the prototype is (or was) a work of craftsmanship, but dispute the applicability to it of the adjective 'artistic', and that is the extent of the present controversy. I express no opinion whether that concession was or was not properly made.

In my opinion, the first essential of a work of art (which I think an artistic work must be) if it is to be distinguished from a work of craftsmanship—a distinction on which Parliament insists—is that it shall have to come into existence as the product of an author who is consciously concerned to produce a work of art. The work either is or is

---

1 [1973] 3 All ER at 417, 418, [1973] 3 WLR at 456, 457
2 [1973] 3 All ER at 419, [1973] 3 WLR at 458

not a work of art before anyone except the author has seen it; it does not depend for its artistic character on the criticism, whether favourable or unfavourable, of other people who may make value judgments about it. It must be possible to deduce the conscious purpose of artistic creation from the work itself or from the circumstances of its creation, but this act arises only when the question whether it is a work of art becomes one for discussion or decision by others than the author. Merit is another matter altogether. It has been said that the courts will be reluctant to make aesthetic appreciations, and that is right, not because so to do is for a judge difficult or unseemly, but because it is a decision which, in this context, is not required. I do not think it is possible to add, as it were, some artistic character to an object, and by so doing to justify a conclusion that the object is not only a work of craftsmanship but artistic to boot. To do so is almost certainly to make an aesthetic value judgment. An example was given in the course of the argument—the five-barred gate made by a craftsman, blacksmith or carpenter. It was suggested that a gate might be regarded as an artistic work if its proportions were right. But what does 'right' mean? It only means 'I like them', unless it means no more than that that gate will be effective for controlling stock, which is the requirement demanded of the 'mere' craftsman. The conscious intention of the craftsman will be the primary test of whether his product is artistic or not; the fact that many of us like looking at a piece of honest work, especially in the traditional trades, is not enough to make it a work of art.

Whether a given object is a work of artistic craftsmanship can be posed as a question of fact. but only after the meaning of the word 'artistic' has been determined; what that meaning is, is a question of law, since it involves a decision of what Parliament meant by the word Parliament used. I do not believe that it is possible, as matter of law or of exegesis, to arrive at a comprehensive definitive interpretation of such a familiar English word, so as to be armed with a test which will enable one, by the application of it, at a glance, to exclude all that does not properly fall within the scope of the simple word itself. It is, indeed, seldom that a simple word can, by translation into some easier or more difficult phrase, be rendered the more capable of furnishing such a test. But it is quite plain, in my opinion, that you cannot get on without exercising, in any case in which this kind of dispute arises, the judicial function of holding whether the facts bring the object within the meaning of the statutory definition. You will get no assistance, until you have exercised that judicial function, by asking the opinion of an expert; if he says, 'I regard that object as artistic', the next question which must be asked in order to make his last answer intelligible is, 'What do you mean by artistic?' That question is incompetent, because the answer would be irrelevant. Since the word is a word of common speech, it requires, and permits of, no interpretation by experts. It is for the judge to determine whether the object falls within the scope of the common meaning of the word.

The evidence given in the present case is instructive in this connection. Quite properly, no witness was specifically asked whether the prototype—and so the chair—was artistic, but certain epithets of an uncomplimentary character were attached to it by some of the witnesses: 'vulgar', 'brash', and 'horrible' were examples. Such words on the issue of artistic or no, are colourless. They neither claim nor deny—artistic character, though they might go to an assessment of artistic merit, were that in question. The story of the birth of the Bronx prototype tells of other than artistic aims and achievements on the part of the craftsmen. The objective, as I have already said, was the retrieval of commercial success in the furniture line. That objective was attained, and the epithets bestowed by the witnesses on the product are again instructive: 'a winner', 'great appeal', 'a good commercial design', and so on. It is not that these encomia are fundamentally inappropriate to a work of artistic craftsmanship as reflecting on its artistic mertis; they are not. The point is that they throw a clear light on the process which was taking place in that factory as those craftsmen worked on their job. No one thought he was assisting at the delivery of a work of art. If in the course of the labour Mr Batchelor had been able to say—'There, I have made a work of art' it would have been quite probable that the sales manager would have retorted, 'So you have. It is beautiful. But since no one would buy it, you must scrap it and try again'. During all the hours and weeks of hard work which the witnesses describe there was no suggestion that there was present to their mind any desire to produce a thing of beauty which would have an artistic justification for its own existence. The objective was the equally honourable but fundamentally different one of producing a commercially successful chair, whether its creators thought that it had intrinsic beauty or that it had not.

In the result I have failed, perhaps inevitably, to find a substitute formula which will replace the word 'artistic', and be one which will serve to qualify as artistic or non-artistic any given piece of craftsmanship. I do not think it is necessary to do so. I would put it in this way, that in my opinion the common meaning of the word 'artistic' does not permit that word to be used as a description of the craftsmanship involved in the production of the prototype 'Bronx' chair, having regard to all the evidence of the circumstances surrounding its manufacture, and I have endeavoured to show the reason why that should be so. I have found no assistance in the terms of the 1911 Act or of the other parts of the 1956 Act. Nor could I draw any conclusions from the Registered Designs Act 1949; there is a considerable area of overlap between that Act and the 1956 Act. No explanation was offered, nor was it required, of why the appellants had not registered their goods under the 1949 Act, as it seems they could have done. It may be that the relative functions and ambits of the two Acts would merit the scrutiny of the legislature. Certainly it is to be hoped that the question which the circumstances of this appeal poses will not often arise. Your Lordships' House has been offered 'definitions' of the word 'artistic' framed by each of Graham J[1] the Court of Appeal[2], counsel for the appellants together with two by counsel for the respondents, and has rejected them all. In addition, I rather gather that there is no definition framed by a member of the appellate committee which is altogether acceptable to any other member; this means that each of their Lordships has rejected, or at least refrained from adopting, nine solutions of the problem. It may be that Copinger[3] is right when he says:

'Copyright law is, in essence, concerned with the negative right of preventing the copying of physical material existing in the field of literature and the arts. Its object is to protect the writer and the artist from the unlawful reproduction of his material.'

Since ample protection is provided aliunde for those preparing designs for commercial reproduction, it would not be doing any injustice were it made clear that the Copyright Act is not concerned to protect, eg, the Bronx prototype.

I would dismiss the appeal.

Appeal dismissed.

Solicitors: *Simmonds, Church, Rackham* (for the appellants); *Simpson, Silvertown & Co* (for the respondents).

Christine Ivamy Barrister.

1 [1973] 1 All ER 160, [1973] 1 WLR 144
2 [1973] 3 All ER 414, [1973] 3 WLR 453
3 Copinger and Skone James on Copyright (11th Edn, 1971), p 3, para 1

Harper and others v National Coal Board

COURT OF APPEAL, CIVIL DIVISION
LORD DENNING MR AND STEPHENSON LJ
20th DECEMBER 1973

Limitation of action – Extension of time limit – Material fact outside knowledge of plaintiff – Knowledge of facts on which action founded – Lack of knowledge that facts founding worthwhile cause of action – Reasonable steps taken by plaintiff to ascertain whether a cause of action – Whether time beginning to run when plaintiff acquiring knowledge of relevant facts or when discovering that he has worthwhile cause of action – Limitation Act 1963, s 1(3) (as amended by the Law Reform (Miscellaneous Provisions) Act 1971, s 1(1)).

Judgment – Judicial decision as authority – Ratio decidendi – House of Lords – Majority decision of House of Lords – No discernible ratio decidendi common to majority speeches – Reasoning of House of Lords not binding – Court of Appeal free to adopt reasoning which appears to it to be correct – Court of Appeal bound to adopt reasoning which supports House of Lords decision.

The proposed plaintiff was a coal-miner who had worked underground for 34 years. He was at all material times a member of a trade union. In February 1968 he was certified as suffering from pneumoconiosis. He did not then realise that he could make a claim against his employers for damages and, when he sought their advice, his union did not suggest to him that he could. He thought that his only remedy was to claim disablement benefit. As a result of a case published in the newspapers in 1971 the plaintiff again sought the advice of his union. In August 1971 he discovered for the first time, when he saw the union's solicitors, that he had a worthwhile cause of action against the employers; they advised him that he should seek leave under the Limitation Act 1963 to bring proceedings. In September 1973 he applied for leave pursuant to s 1(1)[a] of the 1963 Act. The judge refused to grant leave, taking the view that the plaintiff had failed to fulfil the requirements of s 1(3)[b] of the 1963 Act, in that he had knowledge of all the material facts on which his action was based in 1968, i e more than three years before the action was brought. The judge based his decision on the speeches in the House of Lords in *Central Asbestos Co Ltd v Dodd*[c]. In that case the House of Lords, by a majority of three to two, affirmed a majority decision of the Court of Appeal[d], which had held, following its own earlier decisions, that time did not begin to run against the plaintiff under s 1(3) until he discovered that he had a worthwhile cause of action. The majority of the House of Lords were, however, divided in their reasoning; two took the same view of the law as that taken by the majority of the Court of Appeal, while the third took another view of the law which in substance accorded with that of the

---

a Section 1(1) provides: 'Section 2(1) of the Limitation Act 1939 (which, in the case of certain actions, imposes a time-limit of three years for bringing the action) shall not afford any defence to an action to which this section applies, in so far as the action relates to any cause of action in respect of which—(a) the court has, whether before or after the commencement of the action, granted leave for the purposes of this section, and (b) the requirements of subsection (3) of this section are fulfilled.'

b Section 1(3), as amended, provides: 'The requirements of this subsection are fulfilled in relation to a cause of action if it is proved that the material facts relating to that cause of action were or included facts of a decisive character which were at all times outside the knowledge (actual or constructive) of the plaintiff until a date which was not earlier than three years before the date on which the action was brought.'

c [1971] 2 All ER 1135

d [1971] 3 All ER 204

minority of the House, i e that time began to run under s 1(3) as soon as the plaintiff knew of the facts on which his action was based. The plaintiff appealed against the refusal to grant him leave.

Held – The appeal should be allowed for the following reasons—

(i) Since there was no discernible ratio decidendi common to the majority in the speeches in the House of Lords in *Dodd's* case[e], the Court of Appeal was not bound by the reasoning in those speeches and was free to adopt any reasoning which appeared to the court to be correct provided that it supported the actual decision of the House. In those circumstances the court should adopt the reasoning of the Court of Appeal in *Dodd's* case[f], and in the earlier cases in the Court of Appeal decided before the House of Lords' decision; those cases had not been overruled by the House of Lords and were therefore binding on the court (see p 446 *b* to *d* and *g* to *h* and p 447 *f* to *h*, post); dicta of Viscount Dunedin in *Great Western Railway Co v Mostyn (Owners)* [1927] All ER Rep at 121 and of Viscount Simonds in *Scruttons Ltd v Midland Silicones Ltd* [1962] 1 All ER at 7 applied.

(ii) Accordingly time did not begin to run against the plaintiff for the purposes of s 1(3) until August 1971, for prior to that date he had done all that was reasonable by consulting his union to find out if he had a claim against the employers and he was not at fault in failing to discover before then that he had a worthwhile cause of action; accordingly it was a proper case for the court to give leave to bring an action (see p 447 *b* and *f* to *h*, post).

Pickles v National Coal Board [1968] 2 All ER 598; *Skingsley v Cape Asbestos Co Ltd* [1968] 2 Lloyd's Rep 210; *Newton v Cammell Laird & Co (Shipbuilders and Engineers Ltd)* [1969] 1 All ER 708, *Drinkwater v Joseph Lucas (Electrical) Ltd* [1970] 3 All ER 769, *Smith v Central Asbestos Co Ltd* [1971] 3 All ER 204 and *Knipe v British Railways Board* [1972] 1 All ER 673 followed.

Central Asbestos Co Ltd v Dodd [1972] 2 All ER 1135 considered.

Notes

For extension of the limitation period in personal injury actions, see Supplement to 24 Halsbury's Laws (3rd Edn) para 381, and for cases on the subject, see Digest (Cont Vol B) 500-502, 1933a-2022Aa, and Digest (Cont Vol C) 641-644, 1933b-2022Ad.

For the binding force of the ratio decidendi for a decision, see 22 Halsbury's Laws (3rd Edn) 796, 797, para 1682, and for cases on the subject, see 30 Digest (Reissue) 253-256, 599-623.

For the Limitation Act 1963, s 1, see 19 Halsbury's Statutes (3rd Edn) 103.

For the Law Reform (Miscellaneous Provisions) Act 1971, s 1, see 41 Halsbury's Statutes (3rd Edn) 846.

Cases referred to in judgments

Cartledge (Widow and Administratrix of the Estate of Fred Hector Cartledge (deceased)) v E Jopling & Sons Ltd [1963] 1 All ER 341, [1963] AC 758, [1963] 2 WLR 210, [1963] 1 Lloyd's Rep 1, HL; *affg* [1961] 3 All ER 482, [1962] 1 QB 189, [1961] 3 WLR 838, [1961] 2 Lloyd's Rep 61, CA, 32 Digest (Repl) 401, 259.

Central Asbestos Co Ltd v Dodd [1972] 2 All ER 1135, [1973] AC 518, [1972] 3 WLR 333, [1972] 2 Lloyd's Rep 413, HL; *affg* sub nom *Smith v Central Asbestos Co Ltd* [1971] 3 All ER 204, [1972] 1 QB 244, [1971] 3 WLR 206, [1971] 2 Lloyd's Rep 151, CA.

Drinkwater v Joseph Lucas (Electrical) Ltd [1970] 3 All ER 769, CA, Digest (Cont Vol C) 644, 2022Ad.

Great Western Railway Co v Mostyn (Owners), The Mostyn [1928] AC 57, [1927] All ER Rep 113, 97 LJP 8, 138 LT 403, 92 JP 18, HL; *rvsg* [1927] P 25, 96 LJP 1, 135 LT 693, CA, 30 Digest (Reissue) 254, 609.

---

e [1972] 2 All ER 1135
f [1971] 3 All ER 204

a *Howell v West Midland Passenger Transport Executive* [1973] 1 Lloyd's Rep 199, CA.
Knipe v British Railways Board [1972] 1 All ER 673, [1972] 1 QB 361, [1972] 2 WLR 127, [1972] 1 Lloyd's Rep 122, CA.
Newton v Cammell Laird & Co (Shipbuilders and Engineers) Ltd [1969] 1 All ER 708, [1969] 1 WLR 415, [1969] 1 Lloyd's Rep 224, CA, Digest (Cont Vol C) 644, 2022Ac.
Pickles v National Coal Board [1968] 2 All ER 598, [1968] 1 WLR 997, CA, Digest (Cont
b   Vol C) 641, 1933c.
Scruttons Ltd v Midland Silicones Ltd [1962] 1 All ER 1, [1962] AC 446, [1962] 2 WLR 186, sub nom *Midland Silicones Ltd v Scruttons Ltd* [1961] 2 Lloyd's Rep 365, HL; *affg* [1960] 2 All ER 737, [1961] 1 QB 106, [1960] 3 WLR 372, [1960] 1 Lloyd's Rep 521, CA; *affg* [1959] 2 All ER 289, [1959] 2 QB 171, [1959] 2 WLR 761, [1959] 1 Lloyd's Rep 289, Digest (Cont Vol A) 271, 261a.
c *Skingsley v Cape Asbestos Co Ltd* [1968] 2 Lloyd's Rep 201, CA.
Walsh v Curry [1955] NI 112, 45 Digest (Repl) 294, *57.

Cases also cited

East London Railway Joint Committee v Greenwich Union Assessment Committee [1913] 1 KB 612, CA.
d *Quinn v Leathem* [1901] AC 495, [1900-03] All ER Rep 1, HL.
Usher's Wiltshire Brewery v Bruce [1915] AC 433, HL.

Interlocutory appeals

e These were ex parte appeals by the proposed plaintiffs, Wilfred Arthur Harper, Jack Ward, Wlodzimerz Komorowski, Jack Brownlow and James Albert Pearson, pursuant to leave of Thesiger J, against the order of Thesiger J, made on 9th November 1973, refusing them leave pursuant to the Limitation Act 1963, as amended, to bring an intended action for damages for personal injury, namely, pneumoconiosis, caused by breach of statutory duty and/or negligence on the part of the proposed defendants, the National Coal Board.   The grounds of the appeal were, inter alia, (1) that the judge had misdirected himself in failing to give any or adequate weight
f to the proposition that time did not run under s 1(3) of the 1963 Act until a proposed plaintiff not only had knowledge of the disease from which he was suffering but also had knowledge that the disease was attributable to fault on the part of the proposed defendants, and (2) that the judge had misdirected himself in holding that time ran against the proposed plaintiffs from the date when they first knew that they were in fact suffering from pneumoconiosis.   The facts are set out in the judgment of Lord
g Denning MR.

Charles McCullough QC and *I McClaren* for the proposed plaintiffs.

LORD DENNING MR.   In the years before 1963 miners were often found to be suffering from pneumoconiosis. This was due to the inhaling of dust. They
h had to give up work. They received disablement benefits. None of them thought they had any cause of action in the courts against the Coal Board. Some years later it appeared that the Coal Board might have been guilty of negligence or breach of statutory duty. But then it was far too late for the men to make a claim. They were barred by the Statute of Limitations[1]. It was so held by the House of Lords in *Cartledge v E Jopling & Sons Ltd*[2]. The Limitation Act 1963 was passed to remedy that
j injustice. It provided[3], in effect, that if a man brought an action within 12 months of getting to know (actually or constructively) that he had a worthwhile cause of action, then his action would not be barred. He had to bring his action within

---

1   The Limitation Act 1939, s 2(1)(a)
2   [1963] 1 All ER 341, [1963] AC 755
3   Section 1(1), (2) and (3)

12 months of getting to know. The 12 months has been extended recently by the Law Reform (Miscellaneous Provisions) Act 1971[1] to three years; but the principles remain just the same as before.

We have before us applications on behalf of five coal-miners. They have applied ex parte for leave to bring an action so as to get the benefit of the Limitation Act 1963. In order to get leave under s 2(2) of the Act, the man has to show (a) a prima facie case that he would have a cause of action for negligence or breach of duty, and also (b) satisfy the requirement that he did not know that he had a worthwhile cause of action until within the last three years. The five cases are much alike. I will take as typical Mr Brownlow's case. He had worked underground for 34 years. On 7th February 1968 he was certified as suffering from pneumoconiosis. He said:

'... I was not aware [that I was suffering from it] until on or about that date ... At all material times I was a member of the National Union of Mineworkers. However I was not aware that my contracting pneumoconiosis gave me any potential cause of action against the Defendants and I thought that my only remedy was to claim for Industrial Disablement Benefit and this so far as I was at that time aware was all that other miners, suffering from pneumoconiosis, were claiming ... I told the branch secretary of the National Union of Mineworkers of this at the time. I did not think that there was any question of suing for damages for pneumoconiosis as I had never heard of anyone doing this. The branch secretary did not suggest that I could. Like any other trade union member I relied upon him to tell me of my rights ... it was not until June 1971 that I heard of the result in the case of *Pickles v National Coal Board*[2] where I verily believe that the Plaintiff recovered damages against the Defendants for pneumoconiosis. Thereafter I sought advice concerning the likelihood of my having a similar cause of action. I was referred to the Union Solicitors whom I saw on the 20th day of August 1971 and who then advised me that I should seek leave to bring the intended action and this was the first time that I knew or realised that I had a worthwhile action against the Defendants.'

So Mr Brownlow says he did not get to know until 20th August 1971. He made his application for leave in September 1973. That is within three years of getting to know. Mr Brownlow mentions *Pickles v National Coal Board*[2]. In 1968 this court gave leave to Pickles to bring an action against the National Coal Board. No doubt Pickles brought his action. It was not settled until 1971 when he received compensation. The result was published in the middle of 1971 in some newspapers. That is how these five men got to know that they might have a claim.

The application of these five men for leave was made to Thesiger J when he was on circuit at Nottingham. He dealt with them on the affidavits without any oral arguments. He refused to grant leave to any of them. He made a note that he did so because of—

'the speeches in the House of Lords in *Central Asbestos Co Ltd v Dodd*[3] which case I decided at first instance on 8th July 1970. The speech of Lord Pearson indicates that he decided the case in favour of the Respondents on the facts, but agreed with Lord Simon of Glaisdale and Lord Salmon on the law.'

The root issue is on this point of law: what is the knowledge which bars a man from getting leave? is it his knowledge of the facts or his knowledge of the law? According to one point of view, time begins to run against a man as soon as he acquires knowledge of all the material facts, even though he does not know the law and does not

---

1 Section 1(1)
2 [1968] 2 All ER 598, [1968] 1 WLR 997
3 [1972] 2 All ER 1135, [1973] AC 518

a   know that he has a worthwhile cause of action. According to the other point of view, time does not begin to run against him until he acquires knowledge not only of the material facts but also that he has a worthwhile cause of action.

Prior to the decision of the House of Lords[1], this court held in a series of cases that time did not run against a man until he knew that he had a worthwhile cause of action. Those were such cases as: *Pickles v National Coal Board*[2], *Skingsley v Cape Asbestos Co Ltd*[3], *Newton v Cammell Laird & Co*[4], *Drinkwater v Joseph Lucas Ltd*[5], *Smith v Central Asbestos Ltd*[6] and *Knipe v British Railways Board*[7]. None of those cases were overruled by the House of Lords in *Central Asbestos Co Ltd v Dodd*[1]. But the speeches in the House give rise to much uncertainty as to the correct legal position.

b

Dodd suffered from asbestosis due to his work. He knew it when he had to give up work in 1965 because of it. But he did not know that he had any cause of action for damages until about 1967. He then learned that a fellow workman was suing the employers for damages. He went to a solicitor and was told that he (Dodd) might have a cause of action. He got leave in October 1967, within 12 months of getting to know that he had a cause of action, but more than 12 months of getting to know the facts. This court[8] held that he was within time. The House of Lords[1] affirmed the decision, but only by a majority of three to two. The speeches show a perplexing difference of view. Two of the majority accepted the view of the Court of Appeal that time did not run against a man until he knew that he had a worthwhile cause of action. These were Lord Reid and Lord Morris of Borth-y-Gest. Their view was well expressed by Lord Morris of Borth-y-Gest[9].

c

d

e

> 'A typical case will be that of someone who knows or comes to know that he has suffered injuries in such a form as pneumoconiosis or asbestosis and who knows or comes to know that he has suffered those injuries while at work and because of the nature of his work but has no idea that he can in any way blame his employer or sue his employer. He would say: "I did not know that I could put my injuries down to his negligence or breach of duty; I did not know that I could ascribe them or attribute them to his negligence. I did not know I could sue him." In my view, by enacting the sections now under consideration Parliament decided that such a plaintiff who has proved his case should not be debarred from recovery provided always that his ignorance was excusable.'

f

So those two held that Dodd was all right. His claim was not barred.

The two in the minority disagreed. They took the view that time ran against a man as soon as he knew all the material facts, even though he did not know that he had a worthwhile cause of action. These were Lord Simon of Glaisdale and Lord Salmon. Their view was well expressed by Lord Salmon[10]:

g

> '... the purpose of the legislature was to protect persons against their lack of knowledge of facts which they could not reasonably have ascertained. No doubt as a matter of policy the legislature might have protected ignorance of the law as well as ignorance of fact, but it did not do so.'

h

So those two would have held that Dodd failed. His claim was barred.

---

1   [1972] 2 All ER 1135, [1973] AC 518
2   [1968] 2 All ER 598, [1968] 1 WLR 997
3   [1968] 2 Lloyd's Rep 201
4   [1969] 1 All ER 708, [1969] 1 WLR 415
j 5   [1970] 3 All ER 769
6   [1971] 3 All ER 204, [1972] 1 QB 244, CA (*affd* sub nom *Central Asbestos Co Ltd v Dodd* [1972] 2 All ER 1135, [1973] AC 518)
7   [1972] 1 All ER 673, [1972] 1 QB 361
8   [1971] 3 All ER 204, [1972] 1 QB 244
9   [1972] 2 All ER at 1146, 1147, [1973] AC at 539
10 [1972] 2 All ER at 1161, [1973] AC at 556

Lord Pearson was the odd man out. He held that time did not run against Dodd until April 1967 because[1]—

'he did not appreciate that the appellants were at fault and that his injuries were attributable to their fault.'

On that ground he agreed with Lord Reid and Lord Morris of Borth-y-Gest that Dodd succeeded. His claim was not barred. But he went on to say[1] that he agreed, in substance at any rate, with the opinion of Lord Simon of Glaisdale and Lord Salmon as to the proper construction of the statute.

How then do we stand on the law? We have listened to a most helpful discussion by counsel for the proposed plaintiffs on the doctrine of precedent. One thing is clear. We can only accept a line of reasoning which supports the actual decision of the House of Lords. By no possibility can we accept any reasoning which would show the decision itself to be wrong. The second proposition is that, if we can discover the reasoning on which the majority based their decision, then we should accept that as binding on us. The third proposition is that, if we can discover the reasoning on which the minority base their decision, we should reject it. It must be wrong because it led them to the wrong result. The fourth proposition is that if we cannot discover the reasoning on which the majority based their decision we are not bound by it. We are free to adopt any reasoning which appears to us to be correct, so long as it supports the actual decision of the House.

In support of those propositions, I would refer to the speeches of Viscount Dunedin in *Great Western Railway Co v Mostyn (Owners)*[2], and of Lord MacDermott CJ in *Walsh v Curry*[3], and Viscount Simonds in *Scruttons Ltd v Midland Silicones Ltd*[4].

Applying the propositions to the decision in *Central Asbestos Co Ltd v Dodd*[5] the position stands thus. (1) The actual decision of the House in favour of Dodd must be accepted as correct. We cannot accept any line of reasoning which would show it to be wrong. We cannot therefore accept the reasoning of a minority of two—Lord Simon of Glaisdale and Lord Salmon—on the law. It must be wrong because it led them to the wrong result. (2) We ought to accept the reasoning of the three in the majority *if* we can discover it. But it is not discoverable. The three were divided. Lord Reid and Lord Morris of Borth-y-Gest took one view of the law. Lord Pearson took another. We cannot say that Lord Reid and Lord Morris of Borth-y-Gest were correct, because we know that their reasoning on the law was in conflict with the reasoning of the other three. We cannot say that Lord Pearson was correct because we know that the reasoning which he accepted on the law led the other two (Lord Simon of Glaisdale and Lord Salmon) to a wrong conclusion. So we cannot say that any of the three in the majority was correct. (3) The result is that there is no discernible ratio among the majority of the House of Lords. In these circumstances I think we are at liberty to adopt the reasoning which appears to us to be correct.

In my opinion we should adopt the reasoning which was accepted in this court in the long line of cases before the decision of the House of Lords. None of these was overruled. They may therefore be said to be binding on us. But in any case we should follow their reasoning, especially as it was accepted by two of their Lordships who were in the majority and was expressed convincingly by Lord Morris of Borth-y-Gest in the passage I have quoted.

I would add that in the recent case of *Howell v West Midland Passenger Transport Executive*[6] we expressed the same view where I tried to summarise the position in these words:

---

1 [1972] 2 All ER at 1152, [1973] AC at 546
2 [1928] AC 57, at 73, 74, [1927] All ER Rep 113 at 121
3 [1955] NI 112 at 124
4 [1962] 1 All ER 1 at 7, [1962] AC 446 at 468, 469
5 [1972] 2 All ER 1135, [1973] AC 518
6 [1973] 1 Lloyd's Rep 199 at 201, citing the statement made by Lord Denning MR in *Smith v Central Asbestos Ltd* [1971] 3 All ER at 210, [1972] 1 QB at 258

a   'A man is taken to have constructive knowledge as soon as he could reasonably
     be expected to put the facts before a legal adviser and be advised that he had a
     worthwhile cause of action. From that moment time runs against him. But
     if he is put off by some circumstance which affords him a reasonable excuse—
     so that he could not reasonably be expected to go to a legal adviser—then his
     time will be extended till his misapprehension is removed . . .'

b   On the facts the present case is stronger than Dodd's case[1]. Dodd knew that the
     Asbestos Co had been found guilty of criminal offences and had been fined. So
     (pace Lord Pearson) he must have appreciated that the employers were at fault.
     In the present case the Coal Board have not been prosecuted or fined. The men
     did all that was reasonable to find out if they had a claim. They went to their trade
     union and were told they had no claim. The men were not at fault in the least in
c   not getting to know any earlier about the possibility of suing the Coal Board. In
     my judgment this is a proper case for us to give leave.
         I know that in giving leave we are acting on ex parte statements of the men. The
     defendants have not been heard. There are safeguards available to them. They
     will be able to canvass the matter on a hearing inter partes, either on a preliminary
     issue or on a full trial, at a later date. By granting leave, however, we do help
d   the men to this extent. They are not to be barred for ever. I think we should take
     a different view from Thesiger J; we should grant leave for the purposes of the 1963
     Act in each one of these five cases.

         STEPHENSON LJ. I agree. I cannot find any discernible ratio decidendi common
     to the majority of the House of Lords in deciding Dodd's case[1]. Their Lordships
e   were divided three to two in the decision to affirm the judgment of the Court of
     Appeal; but in the reasons for their decision they appeared to be divided two to two,
     Lord Pearson taking a third view which perhaps came closer to the view of the
     minority. In those circumstances I do not think that we can treat the reasoning of
     the majority of the majority—Lord Reid and Lord Morris of Borth-y-Gest—as the
     ratio decidendi of the House. It is the ratio given by only two out of five. Still less can
f   we treat the 'ratio dissentiendi' appearing from the speeches of the minority—Lord
     Simon of Glaisdale and Lord Salmon—as binding if added to Lord Pearson's. That
     seems to have been the view of Thesiger J; but having had the advantage denied to
     him of counsel's argument, I respectfully disagree with him. We are therefore bound
     by the decision of the House of Lords affirming the decision of this court, but not by
     the reasoning in the speeches of their Lordships. That, in my judgment, sends us back
g   to the decision of this court[2] and the ratio of its decision. If there is in the Court of
     Appeal a discernible reason for their decision common to the majority, it stands and
     binds us. I think that there is. I agree that we should take the same view of the
     1963 Act as was taken by the Court of Appeal in Dodd's case[1], confirmed as it is most
     persuasively by the approval of Lord Reid and Lord Morris of Borth-y-Gest in the
     House of Lords[1]. Applying that construction of the Act to the circumstances of this
h   case, I agree with Lord Denning MR that they are stronger on the facts, as we have
     them on affidavit only, than those which enabled Dodd to bring himself, not without
     difficulty, within the Act. I therefore concur in allowing this appeal and giving the
     appellants leave.

     Appeal allowed; leave given to bring an action.

j   Solicitors: *Sharpe, Pritchard & Co*, agents for *Bertram Mather & Co*, Chesterfield (for
     the appellants).

                                                        Wendy Shockett Barrister.

     1 [1972] 2 All ER 1135, [1973] AC 518
     2 [1971] 3 All ER 204, [1972] 1 QB 244

Erinford Properties Ltd v Cheshire County Council   *a*

CHANCERY DIVISION
MEGARRY J
12th, 13th, 14th, 15th, 18th MARCH 1974   *b*

Injunction – Jurisdiction– Injunction pending appeal – Motion for interlocutory injunction – Dismissal of motion by judge – Jurisdiction of judge to grant applicant injunction pending appeal against dismissal of motion.

Where a judge dismisses an interlocutory motion for an injunction he has jurisdiction to grant the unsuccessful applicant an injunction pending an appeal against the dismissal; it is not necessary for the applicant to apply to the Court of Appeal (see p 453 *a b* and *d*, post).   *c*

There is no inconsistency in granting such an injunction after dismissing the motion, for the purpose of the order is to prevent the Court of Appeal's decision from being rendered nugatory should that court reverse the judge's decision (see p 454 *a b d e* and *f*, post).   *d*

Polini v Gray (1879) 12 Ch D 438, *Wilson v Church (No 2)* (1879) 12 Ch D 454 and *Orion Property Trust Ltd v Du Cane Court Ltd* [1962] 3 All ER 466 applied.

Dictum of Jessel MR in *Wilson v Church* (1879) 11 Ch D at 578 explained.

Dicta of Jessel MR and Cotton LJ in *Otto v Lindford* (1881) 18 Ch D at 394, 395 not followed.   *e*

Notes

For effect of pending appeal on injunction, see 21 Halsbury's Laws (3rd Edn) 357, para 746, and for cases on the subject, see 28(2) Digest (Reissue) 986, 987, 206-209.

For appeals against orders made on an interlocutory motion for an injunction, see 21 Halsbury's Laws (3rd Edn) 426, para 896.   *f*

Cases referred to in judgment

Cropper v Smith (1883) 24 Ch D 305, 53 LJCh 170, 49 LT 548, CA, 21 Digest (Repl) 533, 312.

Harrison's Share under a Settlement, Re, Harrison v Harrison, Re Ropner's Settlement Trusts, Ropner v Ropner [1955] 1 All ER 185, [1955] Ch 260, [1955] 2 WLR 256, CA, 51 Digest (Repl) 870, 4206.   *g*

Lawrence's Will Trusts, Re, Public Trustee v Lawrence [1971] 3 All ER 433, [1972] Ch 418, [1971] 3 WLR 188.

Orion Property Trust Ltd v Du Cane Court Ltd, General London and Urban Properties Ltd v Du Cane Court Ltd [1962] 3 All ER 466, [1962] 1 WLR 1085, 28(2) Digest (Reissue) 987, 209.

Otto v Lindford (1881) 18 Ch D 394, 51 LJCh 102, CA, 21 Digest (Repl) 533, 311.   *h*

Pickwick International Inc (GB) Ltd v Multiple Sound Distributors Ltd [1972] 3 All ER 384, [1972] 1 WLR 1213, [1972] RPC 786.

Polini v Gray, Sturla v Freccia (1879) 12 Ch D 438, 41 LT 173, CA, 28(2) Digest (Reissue) 986, 208.

Wilson v Church (1879) 11 Ch D 576, 48 LJCh 690, CA, 28(2) Digest (Reissue) 986, 207.

Wilson v Church (No 2) (1879) 12 Ch D 454, 41 LT 296, CA, 21 Digest (Repl) 535, 354.   *j*

Motion

This was an ex parte motion by the defendants, Cheshire County Council ('the county council'), to discharge an injunction granted ex parte by Megarry J to the plaintiffs, Erinford Properties Ltd, pending an appeal by the plaintiffs against the order of

Megarry J made on 14th March 1974 dismissing a motion by the plaintiffs for an interlocutory injunction against the county council. The plaintiffs appeared in opposition to the ex parte motion. The facts are set out in the judgment.

J A R Finlay QC and Lesley Appleby for the county council.
George Newsom QC and R M K Gray for the plaintiffs.

MEGARRY J. In this case the plaintiffs moved for an interlocutory injunction to restrain the defendant county council from considering the plaintiffs' planning applications otherwise than concurrently with a different planning application for adjoining land made by joint applicants who were not parties to the action; and for the reasons that I have given I dismissed that motion. Counsel for the plaintiffs thereupon moved ex parte for an injunction in the same terms pending an appeal by the plaintiffs. The county council had previously been bound by an undertaking in similar terms, but this came to an end with the dismissal of the motion, and counsel for the county council had no instructions to renew it or offer any other undertaking. He volunteered, however, that the next meeting of the appropriate body of the county council would not be until 28th March, and in the end counsel for the plaintiffs was content to seek an ex parte injunction only over 20th March, which he said would allow time for him to give notice of appeal and to serve notice of motion to extend the injunction. Ultimately I held that I should grant the injunction in this modified form. Counsel for the county council thereupon acted on an intimation that he had already made and moved ex parte to discharge or modify the injunction, primarily on the ground that I had no jurisdiction to grant it, and that only the Court of Appeal could do so. After a brief discussion, I adjourned this motion to the next day so that the authorities could be consulted; and as a result I have heard substantial argument on the point. Although the county council's motion was ex parte, I indicated that I would hear what could be said on behalf of the plaintiffs; and in the end I had the advantage of an argument by junior counsel for the plaintiffs, so that the motion of counsel for the county council became what in *Pickwick International Inc (GB) Ltd v Multiple Sound Distributors Ltd*[1] was described as an opposed ex parte motion.

After some discussion counsel for the county council accepted that there was plainly still a subsisting action and that I had not become wholly functus officio, at all events so long as my order remained unperfected. He also accepted that if on the main motion I had granted an injunction it would still have been open to me to suspend it or otherwise modify its effect pending an appeal. But he said that when I had held (as I did) that the plaintiffs were not entitled to an injunction, I had no jurisdiction, or alternatively it would be quite wrong, to sit on appeal from myself, as it were, and hold that an injunction should be granted to preserve the status quo pending an appeal: the grant of such an injunction would be wholly inconsistent with my decision on the main motion that no injunction should be granted. By refusing an injunction on motion a judge showed that it was not right to preserve the status quo pending trial or at all, and so showed that it was not right to preserve the status quo pending appeal. He was functus officio quoad granting an injunction in that case. The settled practice, counsel asserted (without citing authority), was that if the motion for an injunction failed and the unsuccessful party sought an injunction pending an appeal against the refusal, he should make no application to the judge but should at once take himself to the Court of Appeal and there seek his injunction pending the appeal. Counsel emphasised that apart from the plaintiffs' expression of a probable intention to appeal, nothing new had happened since the refusal of the injunction which would make it proper to grant now, even in a temporary form, what had been refused then.

---

1   [1972] 3 All ER 384, [1972] 1 WLR 1213

Counsel for the plaintiffs, on the other hand, dwelt on the merits of speed and convenience. The judge already knew all the facts of the case and so the point could be argued and decided with relative speed and convenience at the conclusion the main motion, whereas an application to the Court of Appeal involved seeking to disturb the existing business of that court at short notice in what sometimes would be circumstances of great urgency, and putting that court sufficiently in possession of the facts and law involved to enable a decision to be given on the ex parte application. Counsel for the plaintiffs contended that the essence of the matter was the power of the court to preserve the subject-matter of the dispute pending the determination of the appeal, and that in the present case, once the county council had decided the rival joint planning application, the subject-matter of the alleged agreement by the county council (namely, that the plaintiffs' planning applications would not be decided otherwise than concurrently with the joint planning application) would be destroyed, leaving the plaintiffs to a complex and unsatisfactory claim in damages.

The most recent case put before me was *Orion Property Trust Ltd v Du Cane Court Ltd*[1]. In this Pennycuick J said[2] that he found considerable difficulty in reconciling entirely what was said in the four cases which had been cited to him. All were decisions of the Court of Appeal, and 'it may be that only the Court of Appeal itself can give an authoritative statement as to the principle to be applied in these cases'. In view of the judge's ample discussion of the cases, I do not propose to say more about them than seems necessary, merely adding my respectful concurrence with his comments. The four cases were all, I may say, cases of final and not interlocutory orders. Broadly, the conflict may be said to centre round dicta in two very short judgments by Jessel MR in the Court of Appeal in *Wilson v Church*[3] and *Otto v Lindford*[4], on the one hand, and on the other hand the more substantial judgments in the Court of Appeal in *Wilson v Church (No 2)*[5] and *Polini v Gray*[6]. At least at first sight the dicta support the view that a judge who has dismissed an action has no jurisdiction to grant an injunction restraining the successful defendants from parting with the subject-matter of the action pending an appeal. The decisions, on the other hand, support the opposite principle. In the words of Pennycuick J in the *Orion* case[2], the effect of the principle is that 'the court of first instance has jurisdiction to make an order preserving the subject-matter of the action in the appeal, even though the action has wholly failed'. Such a principle plainly seems to be consonant with the undoubted jurisdiction of a judge who has made an order to grant a stay of execution of that order pending an appeal, a jurisdiction which is the subject of Rules of Court.

I think I should say something about the two cases which appear to be opposed to the principle. In *Wilson v Church*[3] there had been a claim against trustees for moneys in their hands. Fry J dismissed it, and the plaintiffs thereupon entered an appeal and, without applying to the judge, moved the Court of Appeal for an injunction to restrain the defendants from parting with the trust funds pending the appeal. The Court of Appeal held that it had jurisdiction and granted the injunction. Jessel MR is reported as delivering a two-sentence judgment with which Brett and Cotton LJJ simply concurred. The first sentence runs[7]:

'The action having been absolutely dismissed by Mr. Justice *Fry*, he had no jurisdiction to stay the proceedings pending the appeal, and this application for an injunction was properly made to the Court of Appeal.'

1   [1962] 3 All ER 466, [1962] 1 WLR 1085
2   [1962] 3 All ER at 471, [1962] 1 WLR at 1090
3   (1879) 11 Ch D 576
4   (1881) 18 Ch D 394
5   (1879) 12 Ch D 454
6   (1879) 12 Ch D 438
7   11 Ch D at 578

Before me, counsel for the county council naturally relied on these words as showing that I had had no jurisdiction to grant the injunction that counsel for the plaintiffs had obtained.   That, indeed, seems to be the view of the editors of the Supreme Court Practice 1973[1], where the case is cited as authority for the proposition that—

> 'Where an action has been dismissed in the Court below, that Court has no jurisdiction, e.g., to restrain a defendant from parting with a trust fund pending an appeal: the application for that injunction must be made to the Court of Appeal.'

This repeats words in the Annual Practice 1962[2] to which Pennycuick J referred in the *Orion* case[3].

I do not think that this is right.   In *Wilson v Church*[4] it had been argued that the application for an injunction was in substance an application to stay proceedings pending an appeal, so that just as under what was then RSC Ord 58, rr 16 and 17, and is now RSC Ord 59, rr 13 and 14, any application for a stay ought to be made in the first instance to the trial judge, so the application for the injunction ought to have been made initially to Fry J.   The answer to this was that no question of staying proceedings could arise, for the action had been dismissed and so there was nothing to stay.   The rule requiring an application for a stay to be made in the first instance to the trial judge accordingly had no application, and the Court of Appeal could properly grant the injunction.   In other words, I think Jessel MR was directing himself not to what jurisdiction remained in a judge once he had given judgment, but to the nature of the particular application being made to the court.

The point seems to be made somewhat clearer by the report of the same case in the Law Journal Reports[5].   That reports the argument of counsel that the application was to stay proceedings pending appeal and ought to have been made to the court below, whereat Jessel MR said[6]:

> 'No one can say that this is an application to stay proceedings in the action. The action was dismissed. This is an original motion.'

Counsel then argued that the case was not one for an injunction: and counsel on the other side were not called on.   The judgment of Jessel MR is then reported without the first sentence that appears in the Law Reports and that I have quoted, simply granting the injunction and advancing the hearing of the appeal.   It looks as if an interlocutory observation which stopped counsel from pursuing a fallacious argument has in the Law Reports version[4] been transformed into part of the judgment;   and the Law Journal version[5] seems to me to be the more probable.

That, however, does not take into account the other case, *Otto v Lindford*[7].   What had happened there was that Bacon V-C had dismissed an action with costs.   The defendant appealed, and applied to the Court of Appeal for leave to serve short notice of motion to restrain the plaintiff from enforcing the order for costs pending the appeal.   When asked if he had applied to Bacon V-C, counsel replied that he had not done so because *Wilson v Church*[4] had held that if an action had been dismissed the court below had no jurisdiction to stay proceedings, and the application must be made to the Court of Appeal.   The Court of Appeal held that where the application was to stay any proceedings under the order made by the court below (in that case

---

1   Volume 1, p 856
2   Page 1693
3   [1962] 3 All ER at 470, [1962] 1 WLR at 1089
4   (1879) 11 Ch D 576
5   48 LJCh 690
6   48 LJCh at 690
7   (1881) 18 Ch D 394

the order for costs) the application should be made initially to the trial judge. However, Jessel MR began his short judgment with these words[1], referring to *Wilson v Church*[2]:

'That was a case of an entirely different description. The plaintiffs there were asking for an injunction to restrain the trustees from parting with the trust funds pending the appeal. That was not an application to stay proceedings under the order appealed from, for that order did not give any directions for dealing with the funds, and the Court below having dismissed the action, had no jurisdiction to grant such an injunction.'

These latter words, of course, plainly provide some support for the view that *Wilson v Church*[2] was concerned with the jurisdiction remaining in a judge who had dismissed an action. Furthermore, Cotton LJ said[3]:

'I also was a party to the decision in *Wilson* v. *Church*[2], and I agree with the view taken of it by the Master of the Rolls.'

On this, there are two things that I should say with the greatest respect. First, it is easy to see how a court which has had cited to it the words relating to juridiction which appear in the Law Reports version of *Wilson v Church*[2] might easily, when dealing briefly with a short application where the point for decision was quite different, refer to that case in the same kind of language: *Wilson v Church*[2] came into the matter no more than being a case of an entirely different description which required to be distinguished. The words in question in the Law Reports version of *Wilson v Church*[4] are, of course, 'no jurisdiction to stay the proceedings pending the appeal', and these are not the same as 'no jurisdiction to grant such an injunction' that appear in *Otto v Lindford*[5]. Second, *Otto v Lindford*[6] and another decision of Jessel MR were subsequently explained and in some degree disapproved by the Court of Appeal in *Cropper v Smith*[7]. This dealt with the rules that applications to stay proceedings must be made in the first instance to the trial judge. Jessel MR had expressed the view that if the trial judge refused a stay, the application to the Court of Appeal must necessarily be a motion by way of appeal, and the Court of Appeal and the court below could not have co-ordinate jurisdiction. Brett MR and Cotton and Bowen LJJ all held that this was not accurate, and that there was concurrent jurisdiction in the court below and in the Court of Appeal. Brett MR read[8] the whole of the judgment of Jessel MR in *Otto v Lindford*[6] and then said: 'That is nothing more than rule 17', that is, the then RSC Ord 58, r 17, requiring any application for a stay to be made to the trial judge in the first place; and Cotton LJ[9] expressed himself similarly. (Oddly enough, Bowen LJ[10] compared the Law Reports and Law Journal Reports versions of an earlier decision[11] in demonstrating that Jessel MR had misunderstood the effect of that earlier case.) I do not, of course, say that considerations such as these dispose of the phrase 'had no jurisdiction to grant such an injunction' in *Otto v Lindford*[5], but they cannot add to the weight of a phrase which was admittedly not of the ratio.

---

1 (1881) 18 Ch D at 394, 395
2 (1879) 11 Ch D 576
3 18 Ch D at 395
4 11 Ch D at 578
5 18 Ch D at 395
6 18 Ch D 394
7 (1883) 24 Ch D 305
8 24 Ch D at 311
9 24 Ch D at 314
10 24 Ch D at 316
11 *Cooper v Cooper* (1876) 2 Ch D 492, 45 LJCh 667

As against that phrase, there are the substantial judgments in *Polini v Gray*[1] and *Wilson v Church*[2] which Pennycuick J discussed and relied on in the *Orion* case[3] (and I shall not repeat), and also the actual decision in the *Orion* case[3] itself. All of these point to a judge not being stripped of his jurisdiction as soon as he dismisses the proceedings before him. It is true that the motion before me is merely an interlocutory one, whereas the authorities discussed in the *Orion* case[3], and the *Orion* case[3] itself, were all concerned with trials, or, in some cases, pending appeals from the Court of Appeal to the House of Lords. However, these considerations seem to me to make the case before me a fortiori. It is less difficult to contend that a trial judge is functus officio if he has dismissed an action than if he has merely dismissed a motion in an action that is still very much alive. Furthermore, it may be technically less difficult to contend that the Court of Appeal is functus officio when it has dismissed an appeal and the loser wishes to appeal to the House of Lords than to contend that a trial judge is functus officio when he has dismissed an action and the loser wishes to appeal to the Court of Appeal: for in the latter case, as contrasted with the former, the proceedings are still within the same court, the Supreme Court. Again, in the case before me no order dismissing the motion has yet been perfected, and until it has been it is open to this court to modify or even revoke the decision, as may be considered proper: see *Re Harrison's Share under a Settlement*[4]. Yet again, an application for an injunction to restrain a successful defendant from acting on his success seems to constitute an original motion, and I do not see what there is to exclude the jurisdiction of the court to hear and decide such motions in this one limited class of case. It seems to me that on principle and on authority, despite the words of Jessel MR that I have quoted, I had jurisdiction to grant the injunction that I granted.

I turn to the other way that counsel for the county council put his case, that of inconsistency: and as I indicated to him during the argument, that, rather than jurisdiction, seemed to me to be his real case. Having held that it would be wrong to grant the plaintiffs an injunction, how can a judge, consistently with his judgment, hold that it is right to grant them a similar though more limited injunction? Counsel for the county council did not challenge the decision in *Orion*[5], but he distinguished it: the complicated facts of that case, I may say, are more fully set out in the report in the All England Law Reports. In that case, said counsel, the decision by the trial judge had been as to the ownership of certain shares, and the injunction granted pending appeal was merely to restrain the successful defendants from acting on their success pending the appeal. That was not a case in which an injunction had been sought in the action and refused, and the judge had then granted an injunction pending an appeal. Furthermore, in that case subsequent events had occurred (the defendant company had issued some new shares), whereas here there was no new event: the intimation of a probable intention to appeal was not such an event.

I do not think that these contentions are sound. Counsel for the county council disclaimed any contention that injunctions stood in a category by themselves, and said that if, for example, the plaintiff failed in a claim to have a receiver appointed, the judge could not appoint a receiver pending an appeal, and only the Court of Appeal could. The argument seemed in the end to come to the alleged inconsistency between granting, pending appeal, the selfsame relief that had been refused at the trial or on motion. On this argument, such a case should, it seems, be treated quite differently from the case of an inconsistency between a declaration or decision that A owns certain property and an injunction fettering A's rights of ownership pending appeal,

1 (1879) 12 Ch D 438
2 (1879) 11 Ch D 576
3 [1962] 3 All ER 466, [1962] 1 WLR **1805**
4 [1955] 1 All ER 185, [1955] Ch 270
5 [1962] 3 All ER 466, [1962] 1 WLR **1085**

as by enjoining him from making any distribution of the property pending the appeal; the latter form of inconsistency was no bar to the judge granting the injunction.

I can see no real inconsistency in any of these cases. The questions that have to be decided on the two occasions are quite different. Putting it shortly, on a motion the question is whether the applicant has made out a sufficient case to have the respondent restrained pending the trial. On the trial, the question is whether the plaintiff has sufficiently proved his case. On the other hand, where the application is for an injunction pending an appeal, the question is whether the judgment that has been given is one on which the successful party ought to be free to act despite the pendency of an appeal. One of the important factors in making such a decision, of course, is the possibility that the judgment may be reversed or varied. Judges must decide cases even if they are hesitant in their conclusions; and at the other extreme a judge may be very clear in his conclusions and yet on appeal be held to be wrong. No human being is infallible, and for none are there more public and authoritative explanations of their errors than for judges. A judge who feels no doubt in dismissing a claim to an interlocutory injunction may, perfectly consistently with his decision, recognise that his decision might be reversed, and that the comparative effects of granting or refusing an injunction pending an appeal are such that it would be right to preserve the status quo pending the appeal. I cannot see that a decision that no injunction should be granted pending the trial is inconsistent, either logically or otherwise, with holding that an injunction should be granted pending an appeal against the decision not to grant the injunction, or that by refusing an injunction pending the trial the judge becomes functus officio quoad granting any injunction at all.

There may, of course, be many cases where it would be wrong to grant an injunction pending appeal, as where any appeal would be frivolous, or to grant the injunction would inflict greater hardship than it would avoid, and so on. But subject to that, the principle is to be found in the leading judgment of Cotton LJ in *Wilson v Church (No 2)*[1], where, speaking of an appeal from the Court of Appeal to the House of Lords, he said, 'when a party is appealing, exercising his undoubted right of appeal, this Court ought to see that the appeal, if successful, is not nugatory'. That was the principle which Pennycuick J applied in the *Orion* case[2]; and although the cases had not then been cited to me, it was on that principle, and not because I felt any real doubts about my judgment on the motion, that I granted counsel for the plaintiffs the limited injunction pending appeal that he sought. This is not a case in which damages seem to me to be a suitable alternative.

I accept, of course, that convenience is not everything, but I think that considerable weight should be given to the consideration that any application for a stay of execution must be made initially to the trial judge. He, of course, knows all about the case and can deal promptly with the application. The Court of Appeal will not be troubled with it unless one of the parties is dissatisfied with the decision of the judge, in which case the Court of Appeal will at least have whatever assistance is provided by knowing how the judge dealt with the application. Although the type of injunction that I have granted is not a stay of execution, it achieves for the application or action which fails the same sort of result as a stay of execution achieves for the application or action which succeeds. In each case the successful party is prevented from reaping the fruits of his success until the Court of Appeal has been able to decide the appeal. Except where there is good reason to the contrary (and I can see none in this case), I would apply the convenience of the procedure for the one to the other. Accordingly, for these reasons the county council's motion to discharge the injunction fails and the ex parte injunction stands. I decide nothing on whether it ought to be

---

1 (1879) 12 Ch D at 458
2 [1962] 3 All ER 466, [1962] 1 WLR 1085

extended: that I leave for argument and any evidence that may be adduced if an extension is sought.

I should add this. Neither the Law Journal report of *Wilson v Church*[1] nor *Cropper v Smith*[2] was cited during argument, and I therefore considered whether before giving judgment I ought to restore the case for further argument on those authorities. However, they merely seemed to confirm to some extent the view that I had already formed without their aid, and so in accordance with *Re Lawrence's Will Trusts*[3] I have not sought further argument. However, if it is desired to make any submissions on this point I will of course hear them.

Motion to discharge injunction dismissed.

Solicitors: *Sharpe, Pritchard & Co* (for the county council); *Hancock & Willis*, agent for *Ellis Moxon*, Crewe (for the plaintiffs).

R W Farrin Esq Barrister.

Reiterbund v Reiterbund

FAMILY DIVISION   Affirmed CA [1975] 1 All ER 280

FINER J

16th JANUARY, 18th FEBRUARY 1974

Divorce – Separation – Five year separation – Decree nisi – Refusal – Grave financial or other hardship – Loss of chance of acquiring benefit – Pension rights – Widow's pension – Loss of chance constituting hardship – Onus of proving hardship grave – Onus on wife of proving that discrepancy between amount of widow's pension and amount of alternative benefits sufficiently large to constitute grave hardship – Matrimonial Causes Act 1973, s 5(3).

Divorce – Separation – Five year separation – Decree nisi – Refusal – Grave financial or other hardship – Social security benefits – Relevance – Loss of chance of widow's pension – Right to social security benefits of similar amount to pension – Duty of husband to maintain wife irrelevant in situation where husband assumed to be dead – Entitlement to social security benefits to be taken into account – Matrimonial Causes Act 1973, s 5.

The parties married in 1942 and had two children born in 1943 and 1950. In 1956 the parties separated and never lived together again. The husband suffered from chronic bronchitis and was a registered disabled person. He was unable to work and received £12·60 a fortnight from the Ministry of Social Security. He lived with his sister, contributing to the household expenses. The wife had for some time required psychiatric treatment and therefore could only do some form of sheltered work. She earned £1 a week working in a day-centre and was in receipt of supplementary benefits at the rate of £7·75 a week. Out of that sum she paid £4·55 to a private charity which looked after her. It was unlikely that she would ever be able to earn her own living. The husband was 54 years of age and the wife 52. The husband petitioned for divorce relying on the fact that the parties had lived apart for a period of five years as provided in s 1(2)

---

1   (1879) 48 LJCh 690
2   (1883) 53 LJCh 170
3   [1971] 3 All ER 433 at 447, 448, [1972] Ch 418 at 436, 437

(e) of the Matrimonial Causes Act 1973. The wife, relying on s 5[a] of the 1973 Act, opposed the petition on the ground that she would suffer grave financial hardship, in that she stood to lose her pension rights as a married woman if a decree were granted, and that in all the circumstances it would be wrong to dissolve the marriage. Although it was possible to infer from the fact that the husband had an invalidity benefit that he had satisfied one condition for a retirement pension, there was no other evidence before the court of the parties' respective rights under the national insurance legislation. In particular there was no evidence of the wife's national insurance record, or whether she would be able to pay, or be excused from payment, of contributions as from the date of a divorce, and no means of determining whether, so far as her retirement benefit was concerned, she would or was likely to be better or worse off if she were divorced or remained married to the husband. The evidence showed however that the wife was and would remain at least as well off receiving supplementary benefits as with a widow's or retirement pension. The wife contended that her receipt of supplementary benefits should be excluded from consideration in determining whether a decree would result in grave financial hardship.

Held – (i) If the marriage were dissolved the wife would lose some chance, whether large or small, of obtaining a widow's benefit and therefore it followed that dissolution would cause some hardship within s 5(3) of the 1973 Act which did not define the odds to be established for the chance, to which the subsection referred, eventuating. The size of the odds and the question whether there would or might be compensations, if the chance were lost, were vital matters in considering whether the hardship constituted by the loss of the chance was grave. The evaluation of that hardship required the wife, on whom the burden of proof lay, to take the necessary steps to place the relevant information before the court. In the circumstances the wife had failed to prove that the hardship which she would suffer was a grave one (see p 460 f to h and p 462 a, post).

(ii) Although the fact that social security benefits were available to a wife was not a reason for her husband refusing to carry out, or being excused from carrying out, his obligation to maintain her, that principle could not be applied to the situation where the husband was assumed to have died and could no longer be required to maintain his wife. In those circumstances the state provided an unsupported widow with a benefit as it did to anyone whose means fell below subsistence level. Accordingly in assessing the gravity of the wife's hardship social security benefits were to be taken into account and therefore the wife had failed to prove grave financial hardship since she would be as well off with supplementary benefits as with a widow's or retirement pension (see p 463 a to d and g, post); dictum of Sir George Baker P in *Dorrell v Dorrell* [1972] 3 All ER at 348 not followed.

Per Finer J. In considering, under s 5 of the 1973 Act, whether it would in all the circumstances be wrong to dissolve the marriage, the court must exclude from consideration that the petition may have been brought under s 1(2)(e) by a 'guilty' husband against a non-consenting wife (see p 464 d, post).

---

a Section 5, so far as material, provides:
'(1) The respondent to a petition for divorce in which the petitioner alleges five years' separation may oppose the grant of a decree on the ground that the dissolution of the marriage will result in grave financial or other hardship to him and that it would in all the circumstances be wrong to dissolve the marriage.
'(2) Where the grant of a decree is opposed by virtue of this section, then . . . the court shall consider all the circumstances . . . and if of opinion that the dissolution of the marriage will result in grave financial or other hardship to the respondent and that it would in all the circumstances be wrong to dissolve the marriage it shall dismiss the petition.
'(3) For the purposes of this section hardship shall include the loss of the chance of acquiring any benefit which the respondent might acquire if the marriage were not dissolved.'

Notes
For the refusal of a decree on the ground of hardship, see Supplement to 12 Halsbury's Laws (3rd Edn) para 437A, 6, and for cases on the subject, see 27(1) Digest (Reissue) 361, 362, 2638-2644.
  For the Matrimonial Causes Act 1973, ss 1, 5, see 43 Halsbury's Statutes (3rd Edn) 541, 548.

Cases referred to in judgment
Brickell v Brickell [1973] 3 All ER 508, [1973] 3 WLR 602, CA.
Dorrell v Dorrell [1972] 3 All ER 343, [1972] 1 WLR 1087.

Cases also cited
Banik v Banik [1973] 3 All ER 45, [1973] 1 WLR 860, CA.
Julian v Julian (1972) 116 Sol Jo 763.
Lee v Lee (1973) 117 Sol Jo 616.
Mathias v Mathias [1972] 3 All ER 1, [1972] Fam 287, [1972] 3 WLR 201, CA.
Parker v Parker [1972] 1 All ER 410, [1972] Fam 116, [1972] 2 WLR 21.

Petition
By a petition presented on 18th February 1971 the husband prayed for the dissolution of his marriage to the wife on the ground that it had irretrievably broken down, relying on the fact that the parties had lived apart for a continuous period of five years immediately preceding the presentation of the petition. By para (1) of the prayer in her answer, the wife opposed the decree on the ground that the dissolution of her marriage would cause her grave financial or other hardship and that it would, in all the circumstances, be wrong to dissolve the marriage. The facts are set out in the judgment.

Mordecai Levene for the husband.
John Samuels for the wife.

Cur adv vult

18th February. **FINER J** read the following judgment. By his petition filed on 18th February 1971 the husband seeks the dissolution of his marriage to his wife, alleging that the marriage has broken down irretrievably, and relying solely for proof of such breakdown on s 2(1)(e) of the Divorce Reform Act 1969, namely, that the parties had lived apart for a continuous period of at least five years immediately preceding the presentation of the petition. Under Sch 1, para 2, to the Matrimonial Causes Act 1973 the suit is deemed to proceed under the corresponding provision of that Act, which is s 1(2)(e). The wife resists the petition by relying on s 5 of the 1973 Act, claiming that the dissolution of the marriage would result in grave financial hardship to her, and that it would be wrong in all the circumstances to dissolve the marriage. The answer relied also on the other limb of s 5 by pleading a hardship other than a financial one, to the effect that the prospect of divorce was anathema to the wife on both religious and moral grounds. However, this plea was expressly abandoned at the outset of the hearing, so that the hardship relied on is now financial hardship only.
  The marriage took place on 18th January 1942 when the husband was 22 and the wife 20 years of age. It was a first marriage for both of them. There are two children of the marriage, a girl born in 1943 and a boy in 1950, and both therefore adult. The parties separated in 1956, that is to say, some 15 years before the commencement of these proceedings, and have not lived together since. On 17th August 1956, on the wife's complaint, the North London stipendiary magistrate found that the husband had deserted her, gave her custody of the two children, and ordered the husband to pay her £5 a week for her own maintenance and 15s a week for the maintenance of each of the two children. In 1958 the husband brought divorce proceedings based on alleged cruelty, but they were dismissed after a contested hearing on 15th October 1959.

The evidence before me was distinctly on the exiguous side. The wife was not called, and the cross-examination of the husband, who is currently in receipt of invalidity benefit at the rate of £8·25 a week, was largely, and with only indifferent success, concerned to establish that he had other financial resources. There was also an agreed bundle of correspondence from which some information could be extracted regarding the circumstances of the parties.

The husband has not for many years paid any of the maintenance he was ordered to pay in 1956. The wife says that he stopped paying in 1959, and was dilatory in his payments before then. The husband says that he stopped paying because he was unemployed. He told me that he had been out of work for three years, and that he was a chronic bronchial case. The wife lives on supplementary benefits at the rate, as at 2nd November 1973, of £7·75 weekly. A letter from her solicitors dated 23rd August 1972 states that out of the then payment of £6 a week for supplementary benefit she paid £4·55 a week for her keep to a charitable institution that was looking after her, and was earning up to £1 a week for working during the day for a day-centre. She had no savings or capital, and her clothing was largely provided by the charity. The answer filed in June 1971 alleges that the wife has for some time required psychiatric treatment as an in-patient in a mental hospital and, although now employed at a day-centre, is unable to seek other than a sheltered form of employment from which she could not earn enough for her keep if not assisted by private charity. All this leaves her precise current circumstances rather obscure, but I am satisfied (and it has never been contested by the husband, who, indeed, himself asserts that his wife was mentally disturbed when he left her) that the wife is, and will in the future, remain incapable of earning her own living, and will have to continue to rely on external sources of support. She is now 52 years of age.

The husband is now 54 years of age. In his earlier petition he described himself as a tailor's machinist, and I gather that this remained his trade. In an affidavit sworn 15th December 1971 he asserts that chronic bronchitis prevented him for the previous two years from working as a tailor's machinist or otherwise; and that because of this condition he was on 3rd November 1970 issued with a certificate of registration under the Disabled Persons (Employment) Acts 1944 and 1958, the certificate expiring on 2nd November 1975.

This was neither challenged nor further explained at the trial. Reference to the Acts, however, shows that their purpose is to rehabilitate and train disabled persons and to enable them to secure employment or work on their own account. Employers having more than a certain number of employees have an obligation to employ a quota of registered disabled persons. A disabled person is defined as one who—

'on account of ... disease ... is substantially handicapped in obtaining or keeping employment, or in undertaking work on his own account, of a kind which apart from that ... disease ... would be suited to his age, experience and qualifications.'

The husband produced an invalidity benefit order book issued on 19th October 1973 and valid for three months. Each of the weekly orders in the book is for the amount of £8·25. Again, there was no investigation at trial into the precise nature of the terms of eligibility for this benefit. These are, in fact, that the beneficiary should, in respect of a period of interruption of employment, have been entitled to sickness benefit for 168 days and should also have paid not less than 156 national insurance contributions as an employed or self-employed person: see the National Insurance Act 1971, s 3. The current rates of benefit which became operative as from October 1973 are £7·75 a week for the invalidity pension, plus £0·50 invalidity allowance for a man aged at least 45 but under 60 at the onset of the incapacity. Hence the £8·25 payable to the husband. Thus, the invalidity benefit is consistent with the husband's case that he has not worked for a long time, but it also shows that he must have at least 156 stamps on his national insurance record.

In his affidavit of 15th December 1971, to which I have already referred, the husband said that he was then in receipt as his sole income of £12·60 a fortnight from the Ministry of Social Security. I do not know whether this is a reference to invalidity benefit or supplementary benefit.

The husband lives with his sister, apparently rent-free, although he contributes towards the costs of the household. He drives a Ford car—in evidence he said it was an Escort, although I observe that reference is made by his solicitors in the correspondence to a 1966 Cortina. There was some obscurity about the ownership of this car, it being said at different times both that the owner is the husband and that, although the car is registered in his name, it belongs to a lady friend of his, a widow, whom—and, again, it was all left vague—he may be intending to marry. The husband was also cross-examined about money that he made on the side in acting as master of ceremonies, commenting on boxing matches, and singing at a club at the weekends. I find that he does make a few pounds from time to time in activities of this kind, but certainly no substantial income. For the purposes of legal aid in these proceedings, his disposable income was assessed at £211, his disposable capital as nil, and his contribution as nil.

It is to be observed, further, that although he has not been paying under the magistrate's maintenance order, he has not been pursued to pay, either by the wife or by the Supplementary Benefits Commission. Since the latter are paying the wife supplementary benefit, they would have an interest in causing her to proceed for the maintenance against the husband (which would, under what is known as the 'diversion procedure', then be paid direct to the commission by the court collecting officer up to the amount of the supplementary benefit paid out). Alternatively, they could proceed themselves against the husband by way of complaint to a magistrates' court under s 23 of the Ministry of Social Security Act 1966. Since neither of these events have happened, one may perhaps infer that the commission have taken the view that the husband is too poor to be worth pursuing.

On the whole of the evidence, including the agreed documents, I find that the husband is himself a poor man, dependent for the most part on support from state benefits, and not very likely to be able to break out of that situation in the future.

I have now recited all the material facts, either as they emerged in or may be inferred from the evidence. The five years of continuous living apart is established, and none of the other 'facts' under s 1(2) of the 1973 Act is relevant. Apart from s 5, I would grant a decree on the petition. The question then becomes: has the wife established her defence under that section?

For that purpose, her assertion, as pleaded, is that:

> 'If a decree of dissolution is granted to the [husband] the [wife] will lose her pension rights as a married woman, and, in the future, as a widow under the prevailing regulations of the Department of Health and Social Security.'

The argument is that the loss of these rights will amount to a grave financial hardship, and that in these, and all other circumstances of the case—including, at this point, the husband's desertion of the wife, his failure to pay maintenance, and the unsatisfactory disclosure regarding his present financial means—it would be wrong to dissolve the marriage.

A plea of this kind must surely involve the wife in establishing from the outset, with such reasonable precision as is possible, the nature and extent of the rights which it is claimed will be, or are likely to be, lost to her, so as to demonstrate the hardship to the satisfaction of the court. The wife's solicitor did make an attempt to extract figures for a number of different contingencies from the department, but with not very illuminating results. I am left, therefore, to make a few observations of my own on the rights in question.

The reference in the answer to 'loss [of] . . . pension rights as a married woman'
must, I think, refer to loss of retirement pension. But a married woman may
qualify for a retirement pension in one of two ways. She can opt to pay her own
contributions. If she does so, she can qualify for a flat-rate pension at the age of 60
of a maximum amount (at current rates) of £7·75 a week. She must, to qualify for
any pension, have paid at least 156 contributions. Then, to gain the full pension of
£7·75, she must also have a yearly average of 50 payments made or credited over a
period of 44 years; the rate of the pension decreasing as this yearly average reduces.
Alternatively, a married woman may rely on her husband's contributions and qualify
for a full retirement pension of her own of (at current rates) £4·75 a week if her
husband has made sufficient contributions to qualify for his full retirement pension,
or for a lesser amount, in proportion to whatever his entitlement may be. A divorced
woman can, if it suits her, take the benefit of her former husband's contributions;
that is to say, she must pay her own contributions as a single woman from the date
of the divorce, and when she reaches 60 can add those contributions to the contributions made by her former husband down to the date of the divorce, and become
eligible for a retirement pension up to £7·75 a week.

I shall not cite the statutory provisions relevant to this short explanation of retirement benefits, none of which were discussed in argument, since it is intended only to
demonstrate the point that I have nothing like sufficient information to enable me
to determine what the wife's situation is likely to be at the age of 60 if she is now
divorced as compared with that situation if she remains married. I do know, only
by inference from the fact that the husband has an invalidity benefit, that he has
satisfied one condition for a retirement pension, namely, payment of 156 contributions. Nothing else is clear. I have no evidence at all concerning the wife's national
insurance record until now; no evidence on whether she will be able to pay contributions as from the date of a divorce; or be excused payment as being in receipt of a
small income (the current exemption is for incomes under £520 a year); or be
credited with payments, as is in certain circumstances possible; and, indeed, no means
beyond a speculation of determining whether, so far as her retirement benefit is
concerned, she will, or is likely to be better, worse or just as well off if she is divorced
now or remains married to the husband.

Similarly, the wife's situation regarding widow's benefits depends on a number of
variables on which I was given very little information. I appreciate, of course, that
s 5(3) of the 1973 Act provides that 'hardship' includes the loss of the chance of acquiring any benefit which the respondent might acquire if the marriage were not dissolved. But the evaluation of the hardship considered as a loss of a chance, and in
particular the determination of whether the hardship is 'grave', in my view requires
the wife, on whom lies the burden of proof, to take those steps which are open to
her to place the available relevant information before the court.

It is beyond doubt that if the marriage is dissolved, the wife must lose some chance,
whether it is a large or a small one, of acquiring the widow's benefit. It follows that
dissolution must cause hardship within the meaning of s 5(3), which does not define
the odds to be established for the chance eventuating to which the subsection refers.
I suppose that anything more than a de minimis chance is sufficient. But the size
of the odds, and the question whether there will or may be compensations if the
chance is lost, are vital matters for consideration when it comes to the question
whether the hardship constituted by the loss of the chance is a grave hardship.

In the present case, it seems not merely possible, but quite likely that a divorce
will deprive the wife of a widow's pension that she would otherwise have received in
due course. I have no evidence of her state of physical, as distinct from mental
health, but I do know that the husband is not in the best of health. There is not
much between them in age, but it is not unreasonable to suppose that she will survive
him, and one sees little prospect for her marrying again.

On the other hand, I have no material from which to determine the amount of the widow's pension she risks losing. The full standard of widow's pension is at present £7·75 a week for widows of 50 or over. I exclude the widow's allowance from consideration. The standard rate of the allowance is £10·85 a week, and it is payable for the first 26 weeks after the husband's death. This is a very useful benefit, but it is by way of temporary provision only, and I cannot think that it was intended to make the grant or refusal of a divorce dependent on a benefit of this kind. However, the rate of entitlement to widow's pension, as distinct from an allowance, up to the full amount of £7·75 a week depends on the yearly average of contributions paid by or credited to the husband, and in the present case I have no information on that subject at all.

As far as I can see from the limited extent to which I have gone into the pension provisions, it is quite possible for a widow to be better off on a retirement pension than on a widow's pension; and although she can have the better of the two, she cannot have both. If, therefore, the wife were over 60 years of age when the husband dies (a circumstance which can be regarded as very likely) and thus eligible for a retirement pension, the loss of the widow's pension, had she meantime been divorced, might be of no account. Whether this would be so or not depends on a large number of factors on which I do not intend further to elaborate; nor shall I give chapter and verse from the National Insurance Acts and the various regulations made thereunder in support of these various propositions. The point I am concerned to demonstrate is that I am given virtually none of the basic information which is needed to evaluate the chances and their consequences.

I would not like to give the impression of being willing unduly to complicate matters. But I have to determine whether the wife is likely to suffer a grave financial hardship. Comparatively small amounts are involved, but this underlines, rather than diminishes, the need for as much accuracy as possible, since the loss of a pound or two in an income of £8 or £10 is far more likely to produce grave hardship than the loss of the same proportion of a higher total. Two general points of practical application seem to me to emerge.

First, in the Family Division at any rate, we should recognise that much of the law of national insurance and supplementary benefits is of the greatest possible importance in the daily work of the Division. None of us can afford, in this respect, to make the always suspect separation between lawyer's law that we have to know, and the other law which we have to look up when necessary. The law of pensions and supplementary benefits requires as much expertise and demands as much study from practitioners as any other branch of the family law, of which it is, essentially, a part.

Secondly, it seems to me that when questions of the kind that I am considering arise in proceedings, the proper and convenient course is for the parties to obtain as much relevant information as possible from the records kept by the Department of Health and Social Security, and then, so far as possible, to agree the information thus obtained. It would also be desirable for the parties to agree what the consequences might be, in terms of pension and benefit entitlement, of the contingencies which seem to be the most relevant ones to consider. Procedures of this kind are common form for the purpose of assisting the court to fix damages, and it seems to me that it would be most helpful if they were adopted in the field I now have under consideration.

My first conclusion may, on the basis of the preceding discussion, be thus stated. If I grant the husband a decree and he dies within the next eight years or so, before the wife is 60 years of age, she will have lost a widow's pension before becoming eligible for a retirement pension. She will continue over these eight years to be eligible for supplementary benefit, but I am at this stage excluding that factor from consideration. If he dies after she reaches the age of 60, she will have lost a widow's pension, but will be entitled to a retirement pension. I have no information sufficient to enable me to determine the amount of either pension, or whether one, and if so which, would be larger than the other (although I suspect that they might be equal), principally because I do not know enough about the insurance records of the parties. A divorce will therefore cause a hardship to the wife within the meaning of s 5(3) of the 1973 Act, but I do not consider that she has sufficiently proved that the hardship is a grave one.

If I am wrong in this conclusion, it becomes necessary to consider another feature of the case. The wife has been for many years almost exclusively dependent on supplementary benefits. As has already appeared, she now receives supplementary benefit at the rate of £7·75 a week. This happens to coincide with the maximum current rates for both widow's benefit and retirement benefit. I do not know how the wife's supplementary benefit at £7·75 a week has been calculated. The ordinary scale rate of supplementary benefit for a single householder is now £7·15 a week and for a single non-householder £5·70 a week; but a person such as the wife is probably in receipt of the long-term addition. Further, the Supplementary Benefits Commission will also pay her rent. It is reasonable to suppose that the comparative rates of the various benefits and pensions to which I have referred will continue in the future to march in step as they are reviewed periodically under the arrangements which exist for that purpose. I am satisfied that in terms of the amounts receivable, bearing in particular in mind that rent is paid with supplementary benefit, the wife is and would remain at least as well off under supplementary benefits as with a widow's or a retirement pension.

Counsel for the wife says that I cannot take supplementary benefits into account at all in deciding whether a decree will result in grave financial hardship. In support of this proposition he relies on *Dorrell v Dorrell*[1]. The facts as found, so far as they are material, were, in that case, that if a decree were granted to the wife, who was then over 60, she would have a retirement pension of £6 a week; if, instead, she became a widow, she would have a widow's pension of the same amount. As a widow, however, she would become entitled also to a further pension from a local authority of £2 a week, thus bringing up her income to £8. The wife was on supplementary benefit with an entitlement of £8·25 a week. The argument advanced on behalf of the husband was that the loss of the chance of the £2 local authority pension that would follow from a decree being granted was no grave financial hardship, because the wife would make good the deficiency from supplementary benefits; that is to say, if she received only £6 a week either as a retirement pensioner or as a widow, she would still be entitled to another £2·25 a week from the Supplementary Benefits Commission.

In rejecting this argument Sir George Baker P observed[2]:

'This is a novel argument but I am not disposed to accept it for I do not think it can be right. I think you have to look at the position of this lady, quite apart from social security. That is my understanding of the law which has been applied in these courts for many years in relation to magistrates' orders. The fact that social security is available to a wife is not a reason for a man refusing to carry out, or being excused from carrying out, his obligation to maintain his wife. The fact that such maintenance as he can pay will go to repay in whole or in part the social security paid to the wife, is not a reason for reducing the sum which the husband ought to pay. The argument so well and clearly put by counsel for the husband founders on the same rock; in my judgment it is wrong and this lady will suffer grave financial hardship. (For the purposes of s 4 [of the Divorce Reform Act 1969] hardship includes the loss of the chance of acquiring any benefit which the respondent might acquire if the marriage were not dissolved; that provision in s 4(3) clearly covers this pension.)'

---

1   [1972] 3 All ER 343, [1972] 1 WLR 1087
2   [1972] 3 All ER at 348, [1972] 1 WLR at 1093

Dorrell v Dorrell[1] was considered in *Brickell v Brickell*[2] but on another point. With natural hesitation and reluctance I find myself unable to agree with the proposition of Sir George Baker P to which I have just made reference. The general rule against mitigating one spouse's liability to maintain by reference to the other's entitlement to supplementary benefit is, of course, established in a number of cases which are too well known to need citation. They will be found set out in Rayden on Divorce[3]. I cannot for myself see, however, how it applies to the situation where, hypothetically, the husband is dead, and one is considering the financial situation of his widow. The basis of the rule is that a husband who ought to pay maintenance and can afford to do so should not be allowed to pass on his responsibility to the state. That would hold good whether the court grants a decree or not. But I do not understand how it can apply to the situation where the husband is assumed to have died, and can no longer be required to maintain his wife. No question then arises of the husband shuffling off his liability on the public. The widow is both unsupported and unable to look to a husband for support. In such circumstances, the state provides her, as it does everyone else whose means fall below the level set for subsistence, with a benefit. I see no reason at all why this benefit should not be taken into account when considering the financial circumstances of a widow, as of a spinster or a bachelor or anyone else.

When I put this point to counsel in argument, he was inclined to concede that it might have some logical merit, but changed the grounds of the objection. It was, he said, broad policy, rather than the facts in any particular case, which required the court to pay no attention to supplementary benefits. Many people were reluctant to apply for supplementary benefits. They were in the nature of a hardship benefit, and in a different category from national insurance benefits.

I reject this argument completely. It seeks to revive the stigma of the poor law which it has been a prime object in the field of social welfare since the National Assistance Act 1948 to root out and destroy. For $3\frac{1}{2}$ centuries from the Poor Relief Act 1601[4] it was an avowed purpose of the English poor law to stigmatise its recipients. Section 1 of the 1948 Act enacted: 'The existing poor law shall cease to have effect . . .' National assistance, and its successor, supplementary benefits, were designed to close this chapter in English social history. The whole emphasis of the present law and its administration is to insist that supplementary benefits are the subject of rights and entitlement, and that no shame attaches to the receipt of them. I recognise, of course, that it takes more than a few years to eradicate an attitude bred over the centuries, and that it is true that there are many who still regard it as a reflection on a man or woman to be in need of supplementary benefit. However, in my opinion a court responsive to the policy of the law has a duty to discourage rather than foster this attitude.

Accordingly, in the circumstances of the present case, I hold as a second ground for the conclusion that the wife has not proved grave financial hardship that she will be as well off with supplementary benefits as with widow's or retirement pension, or that, at any rate, no such difference has been established between the alternatives as inclines me to think that any financial hardship would be grave.

I would add that it is financial hardship that must be demonstrated to be grave. If stigma were relevant at all, it would only be in connection with the second limb of the statutory defence, which requires me to consider whether it would in all the circumstances be wrong to dissolve the marriage. I do not arrive at the second limb until I am satisfied that grave financial hardship has been established.

I would add, further, that there might well be circumstances in which a substantial financial difference could be established between the position of a woman in receipt

---

1   [1972] 3 All ER 343, [1972] 1 WLR 1087
2   [1973] 2 All ER 508, [1973] 3 WLR 602
3   11th Edn (1971), pp 724, 1134, 1135, 1169
4   43 Eliz 1 c 2

of widow's benefit or retirement benefit, and her position on supplementary benefits. No deduction is made from a widow's benefit for any of her earnings; and, at present rates, a retirement pensioner may earn up to £9·59 a week without suffering any deduction. The earnings disregard in supplementary benefits is only £2 a week. In the present case, however, the wife has never, on the evidence, earned enough to use up her supplementary benefits disregard, and I cannot discern any prospect of her doing so in the future. This, moreover, does not take into account the possibility of a future increase in the supplementary benefits disregard for earnings, which has remained unchanged for a very long time.

Finally, I would add a word on the second limb of the defence. It seems to me that the word 'wrong' must there be construed to mean 'unjust'. However, in determining whether in all the circumstances it would be wrong, or unjust, to dissolve the marriage, it seems to me that the court must be careful to avoid subverting the policy which led to the inclusion of s 1(2)(e) as one of the facts establishing irretrievable breakdown by, so to speak, treating the para (e) 'fact' as of a lower order than the other four. Irretrievable breakdown is now the sole ground for divorce, and it may be established through any one of the matters set out in s 1(2), all of which carry equal weight in expressing the object of the legislation. It seems to me, therefore, that in considering the s 5 defence, the court has to exclude from its consideration that a petition based on five years separation is brought by a 'guilty' husband (in the phraseology of the old law) against a non-consenting wife, for this would be tantamount to striking s 1(2)(e) out of the Act altogether. (I might parenthetically point out that the Civil Judicial Statistics for 1972 [Table 10] show that of the 19,270 petitions for dissolution filed that year based on five years separation, 10,003 were by husbands and 9,267 by wives; so that the fear, to which s 5 was largely a response, that the five years separation rule constituted, as it was said, a Casanova's charter, might with roughly equal ineptitude have been expressed by a reference to Messalina.) In the course of the argument I was referred to the bulk of the authorities so far decided on the construction and application of the s 5 defence; I do not find any of them inconsistent with the view I have just expressed. The parties in this case are not young, but even if there were no prospect at all of the husband marrying again (and, as I said previously, there is at least a hint that he may) I do not consider that it would be wrong to dissolve this marriage. On the contrary, I think it is a case which is well within the policy embodied in the new law which aims, in all other than exceptional circumstances, to crush the empty shells of dead marriages.

I therefore pronounce a decree nisi on the prayer of the petition and reject para (1) of the prayer of the answer. The wife's claim for financial provision will be adjourned, if it is to be pursued, to chambers. I declare that for the purposes of s 41 of the 1973 Act there are no children of the family to whom that section applies.

Decree nisi.

Solicitors: *Herbert Oppenheimer, Nathan & Vandyk* (for the husband); *Stanley Sovin* (for the wife).

R C T Habesch Esq Barrister.

Grant and another v Southwestern and County Properties Ltd and another

Applied in SENIOR v HOLDSWORTH
[1975] 2 All ER 1009

CHANCERY DIVISION
WALTON J
30th JANUARY, 21st FEBRUARY 1974

Discovery – Production of documents – Document – Meaning – Tape recording – Tape recording of conversation between parties – Whether tape recording a 'document' – RSC Ord 24, r 10(1).

Discovery – Production of documents – Inspection of documents to which reference made in pleadings or affidavits – Reference to document – Record of conversation – Tape recording – Allegation in pleading that conversation between parties 'was being recorded' – Whether tape recording a document to which 'reference is made' in pleading – RSC Ord 24, r 10.

Discovery – Production of documents – Privilege – Legal professional privilege – Document brought into existence when litigation contemplated – Document for purpose of litigation – Document prepared by plaintiff for purpose of instructing solicitor and obtaining advice – Tape recording by plaintiff of conversation with defendant – Whether tape recording a document prepared by plaintiff for solicitor.

The plaintiffs brought an action against the defendants claiming (i) a declaration that they and the first defendants had become partners in a venture to acquire and develop certain properties, and (ii) dissolution of the partnership. Paragraph 6 of the statement of claim alleged that the second defendant had conspired with the first defendants and others unknown to defraud the plaintiffs by procuring the first defendants to purchase certain properties for their own sole use and benefit, and depriving the plaintiffs of their share of the profits. The particulars given of that allegation included the following: '. . . the 2nd Defendant orally represented, at first that he had intended to tell the Plaintiffs of the said purchases by the 1st Defendants or their subsidiaries or associates and would, in due course, ensure that the Plaintiffs participated in the proposed development; but shortly thereafter, when he appreciated that the conversation was being recorded, sought to maintain that the venture upon which the 1st Defendants were then engaged . . . was other than that upon which the Plaintiffs and 1st Defendants had agreed to engage together.' The defendants served notice on the plaintiffs under RSC Ord 24, r 10(1)[a], requiring the plaintiffs to produce for inspection the tape recording of the conversation referred to in the particulars and, when the plaintiffs objected, the defendants applied for an order that the plaintiffs should deliver up the tape recording for inspection. The plaintiffs contended, inter alia, that the tape recording was not a 'document', within RSC Ord 24, r 10(1), and, alternatively, that, since the recording had been made by the second plaintiff because he contemplated that litigation between the parties might ensue and in order that he might better instruct his solicitors and seek advice on the matter, it was therefore privileged from production as material brought into existence in contemplation of, and for the purposes of, litigation.

Held – (i) A tape recording was a document if what was recorded was information or evidence and a tape recording of a conversation could properly be described as documentary evidence of the conversation. The interposition of necessity of an

_____
a Rule 10(1) is set out at p 467 *j*, post

R

instrument for decyphering the information made no difference in principle. Furthermore, although the tape recording provided no information to the eye, it was nonetheless a document that could be produced for inspection, within RSC Ord 24, r 10(1), since the word 'inspection' was not limited to ocular inspection but included scrutiny or examination by any of the senses (see p 474 h to p 475 d and h to p 476 b, post); *Da Mata v Menfred Properties (Pty) Ltd* 1969 (3) SA 332, and *Cassidy v Engwirda Construction Co* [1967] QWN 16 followed; *Re Alderton and Barry's Application* (1941) 59 RPC 56, *Lyell v Kennedy (No 3)* (1884) 27 Ch D 1, *R v Daye* [1908] 2 KB 333, *Hayes v Brown* [1920] 1 KB 250 and *Hill v R* [1945] 1 All ER 414 applied; *Beneficial Finance Corpn Co Ltd v Conway* [1970] VR 321 not followed.

(2) The claim to privilege could not be sustained since it did not appear in any relevant sense that the tape had been prepared by the plaintiffs for their solicitors. It was a recording of (a) communications made by the plaintiffs as they were being made to the other side and (b) communications made by the other side, which were not in any way being made for the benefit of the plaintiffs' solicitors (see p 477 b, post).

(3) The application would, however, be refused since the tape was not a document to which 'reference [was] made' in the plaintiffs' particulars, within the meaning of RSC Ord 24, r 10(1); the particulars referred to the act of recording, not the recording itself, and it was quite impossible to be certain from the particulars what was the form of the record which was being made (see p 477 g, post).

Notes

For discovery and inspection of documents, see 12 Halsbury's Laws (3rd Edn) 26-39, paras 35-55.

For privilege of documents prepared with a view to litigation, see ibid 44-46, paras 62, 63, and for cases on the subject, see 18 Digest (Repl) 103-105, 879-896.

Cases referred to in judgment

Alderton and Barry's Application, Re (1941) 59 RPC 56, 36 Digest (Repl) 657, *131*.

Averill v Sunday Pictorial Newspapers (1920) *Ltd* [1959] The Times, 22nd April.

Beneficial Finance Corpn Co Ltd v Conway [1970] VR 321, Digest (Cont Vol C) 298, **33a*.

Carew v Carew [1891] P 360, 61 LJP 24, 65 LT 167, 18 Digest (Repl) 65, *512*.

Cassidy v Engwirda Construction Co [1967] QWN 16.

Da Mata v Menfred Properties (Pty) Ltd 1969 (3) SA 332.

Flight v Robinson (1844) 8 Beav 22, 13 LJCh 425, 50 ER 9; *subsequent proceedings* sub nom *Robinson v Wall* (1847) 10 Beav 73, 18 Digest (Repl) 95, *789*.

Glyn v Western Feature Film Co [1916] 1 Ch 261, 85 LJCh 261, 114 LT 354, 51 Digest (Repl) 899, *4502*.

Hayes v Brown [1920] 1 KB 250, [1918-19] All ER Rep 1159, 89 LJKB 63, 122 LT 313, DC, 13 Digest (Repl) 432, *575*.

Hill v R [1945] 1 All ER 414, [1945] KB 329, 114 LJKB 438, 172 LT 255, 17 Digest (Repl) 482, *289*.

Lyell v Kennedy (No 3) (1884) 27 Ch D 1, [1881-85] All ER Rep 814, 53 LJCh 937, 50 LT 730, CA, 18 Digest (Repl) 52, *399*.

R v Daye [1908] 2 KB 333, 77 LJKB 659, 99 LT 165, 72 JP 269, 21 Cox CC 659, DC, 22 Digest (Reissue) 474, *4769*.

R v Robson, R v Harris [1972] 2 All ER 699, [1972] 1 WLR 651, 56 Cr App Rep 450, [1972] Crim LR 316.

Cases also cited

Baker v London and South Western Railway Co (1867) LR 3 QB 91.

R v Maqsud Ali, R v Ashiq Hussain [1965] 2 All ER 464, [1966] 1 QB 688, CCA.

Saxton (deceased), Re, Johnson v Saxton [1962] 2 All ER 618, [1962] 1 WLR 859.

Procedure summons

By a summons dated 29th November 1973 (1) Southwestern and County Properties Ltd and (2) Richard M Cyzer, the defendants to an action by Roger Lloyd Jamie Grant and Stuart Glyn, applied for an order that the plaintiffs deliver up for inspection the tape recording of the conversation between the plaintiffs and the second defendant dated 13th June 1973 referred to in para 6(4) of the plaintiffs' statement of claim and grant to the defendants and both of them facilities to take a transcript thereof. The facts are set out in the judgment.

Gerald Levy for the defendants.
Christopher Hordern for the plaintiffs.

Cur adv vult

21st February.   **WALTON J** read the following judgment. This is an action which, basically, claims a declaration that the plaintiffs and the first defendant became partners in a venture to acquire and develop certain properties, and dissolution of that partnership, with consequential relief. Damages are claimed against the second defendant, including exemplary damages, and an injunction restraining disposal of all the partnership properties as against both defendants.

One of the allegations in the statement of claim (para 6) is that the second defendant conspired with the first defendants and with others unknown to defraud the plaintiffs by procuring the first defendants to purchase certain properties for their own sole use and benefit, with the intention of developing the same for their own sole benefit, and depriving the plaintiffs of their share of the profits therefrom. Among the particulars which are given of that allegation is the following, para (4):

'On or about the 13th June 1973 the 2nd Defendant orally represented, at first that he had intended to tell the Plaintiffs of the said purchases by the 1st Defendants or their subsidiaries or associates and would, in due course, ensure that the Plaintiffs participated in the proposed development; but shortly thereafter, when he appreciated that the conversation was being recorded, sought to maintain that the venture upon which the 1st Defendants were then engaged at South Road was other than that upon which the Plaintiffs and 1st Defendants had agreed to engage together.'

It is out of these particulars that the present summons which is now before me arises; for the defendants on 20th November 1973 served a notice on the plaintiffs in the following terms:

'Take notice that the Defendants require you to produce for their inspection the following Document referred to in your pleading, namely: "The tape recording of the conversation between the Plaintiffs and Mr Richard Cyzer, the second Defendant dated 13th June 1973 referred to in paragraph 6 (iv) of the Statement of Claim' [which I have just read].

Though not expressly so stated therein, such notice was of course given under the provisions of RSC Ord 24, r 10(1), which provides as follows:

'Any party to a cause or matter shall be entitled at any time to serve a notice on any other party in whose pleadings or affidavits reference is made to any document requiring him to produce that document for the inspection of the party giving the notice and to permit him to take copies thereof.'

Rule 10(2) provides as follows:

'The party on whom a notice is served under paragraph (1) must, within 4 days after service of the notice, serve on the party giving the notice a notice stating a time within 7 days after the service thereof at which the documents, or such

of them as he does not object to produce, may be inspected at a place specified
in the notice, and stating which (if any) of the documents he objects to produce
and on what grounds.'

On 23rd November 1973 the plaintiffs served a notice under that sub-rule on the
defendants in the following terms:

'TAKE NOTICE that the plaintiffs object to the production of any such material
as is referred to in the defendants' notice herein dated 20th November 1973 for
the following reasons:—1. No such material is referred to in the statement of
claim herein as alleged in the said notice or at all 2. Any such material is in
any event not a discoverable document 3. Further or in the alternative any such
material was brought into existence in contemplation of or for the purposes of
litigation and is thereby privileged from production.'

Consequent on such refusal, the defendants took out a summons on 29th November
1973 in the following terms, omitting the formal parts:

'. . . an application on the part of the First and Second Defendants for an Order
that the Plaintiffs do deliver up for inspection the tape recording of the conversation between the Plaintiffs and Mr. Richard Cyzer, the Second Defendant, dated
the 13th day of June, 1973 referred to in paragraph [6(4)] of the Statement of
Claim served herein and do grant the Defendants and both of them facilities
to take a transcript thereof AND for an order that the Defendants' time for filing
their respective Defences be extended until 21 days after production of the said
tape and the granting of such facilities.'

This summons came before the master on 21st December 1973, when he intimated
that in his view there ought to be no discovery before a defence had been served, and
the defendants' time for delivery of defences was extended until 28th January 1974.
In fact, within this time the defendants have delivered a defence, so that, strictly
speaking, the whole purpose of the summons has been frustrated. However, in the
meantime the master, as requested, adjourned the summons to the judge, and the
matter has come before me in this way. Both counsel for the defendants and counsel
for the plaintiffs has asked me to decide what are really the three crucial issues in
dispute between the parties, namely: (i) on the assumption that the method of
recording referred to in the relevant particulars to which I have referred above is by
means of a tape (which is certainly not therein so stated, but which counsel for the
plaintiffs informed me was in fact the case), is that tape a 'document' within the
meaning of RSC Ord 24 at all? (ii) Secondly, if it is, is it, in the circumstances under
which it was made, privileged from production? (iii) If the answer to both the
foregoing questions is in the negative, so that the tape is not a discoverable document
but equally there is no privilege attaching to it, can the defendants in effect secure
its discovery by utilising the machinery of RSC Ord 29, r 2(1)? Rule 2(1) is in the
following terms:

'On the application of any party to a cause or matter the Court may make an
order for the detention, custody or preservation of any property which is the
subject-matter of the cause or matter, or as to which any question may arise
therein, or for the inspection of any such property in the possession of a party
to the cause or matter.'

Of course, there also remains in dispute between the parties the question whether,
in any event, the tape can be said to be 'referred to' in the particulars in question but,
since the parties require in any event a decision on the questions of 'document or no
document' and 'privilege or no privilege', which questions are bound to arise in connection with the ordinary automatic discovery of documents, this last question goes
only towards the ultimate question of costs.

The first question which arises is therefore: is a tape recording a document? For, if it is not a 'document', none of the provisions of RSC Ord 24 will apply thereto at all, and a fortiori the provisions of r 10 will not apply.

There is no definition of the word 'document' in the Rules of the Supreme Court (see RSC Ord 1, r 4(1)). It is interesting to observe that there is a definition in extremely wide terms in the Iron and Steel Act 1967, Sch 2, as 'any device by means of which information is recorded or stored'. There is also a definition in s 10(1) of the Civil Evidence Act 1968, again in exceedingly wide terms, which expressly includes tapes. These definitions, however, are of little assistance in themselves.

There are a number of cases in which the meaning of the word 'document' has been discussed in varying circumstances. Before briefly referring to such cases, it will, I think, be convenient to bear in mind that the derivation of the word is from the Latin 'documentum': it is something which instructs, or provides information. Indeed, according to Bullokar's English Expositer, 1621, it meant a lesson. The Shorter Oxford English Dictionary has as the fourth meaning for the word the following: 'Something written, inscribed, etc., which furnishes evidence or information upon any subject, as a manuscript, title deed, coin, etc.', and it produces as the relevant quotation: 'These frescoes . . . have become invaluable as documents', the writer being Mrs Anna Brownell Jameson who lived from 1794 to 1860.

I think that all the authorities to which I am about to refer have consistently stressed the furnishing of information—impliedly other than as the document itself—as being one of the main functions of a document. Indeed, in *Re Alderton and Barry's Application*[1] Morton J expressly doubted whether blank workmen's time sheets could be classified as documents within s 11(1)(*b*) of the Patent and Design Acts 1907-1939 expressly because in their original state they conveyed no information of any kind to anybody. He said[2]:

'In order to establish that the present case comes within Section 11(1)(*b*), the opponents have to satisfy me upon three points: (*a*) that the cards upon which they rely are "documents" within the meaning of the subsection [and then (b) and (c) which are not material for the present purposes]. As to (*a*), I incline to the view that Mr. *Wale* was right in holding that the cards in question are documents, but feel considerable doubt on the point, having regard to the observations quoted above, as the cards may equally well be described as "examples or models of the invention itself". Further, it is true to say that they convey no information at all until they have been put into a time-recording machine and have had records of time stamped upon them. In various dictionary definitions the conveying of information is treated as being an essential feature of a document. For instance, in the Shorter Oxford Dictionary, I find the definition: "Something written, inscribed, etc., which furnishes evidence or information upon any subject, as a manuscript, title-deed, coin, etc." In *Webster's* New International Dictionary (1911) the definition is: "An original or official paper relied upon as the basis, proof, or support of anything else; in its most extended sense, including any writing, book, or other instrument conveying information . . ." This feature is wholly lacking on the cards in question.'

The debate here in question has raged, I think, in a very narrow field. It really is whether the kind of material alleged to be a document is confined to material which makes an appeal to the eye, as distinct from material which makes an appeal to the ear, or, I may add, which makes an appeal to the nose or indeed any other sense.

That one is not confined to written, printed, or inscribed materials is, I think, quite clear. It was accepted without question by a very strong court (Cotton, Bowen and

---

1 (1941) 59 RPC 56
2 (1941) 59 RPC at 60

Fry LJJ) in *Lyell v Kennedy* (*No 3*)[1], as reported in the Law Times Reports[2], that
photographs of tombstones and houses were 'documents' for the purposes of discovery, and I do not think that this has ever since been questioned. From this it
must, of course, follow that a moving cinematograph film is also a document. There
is some suggestion in Phipson on Evidence[3] that a cinematograph film is not a document provable by production under the rule enunciated at the commencement of the
relevant paragraph. For that *Glyn v Western Feature Film Co*[4], presumably as reported
in the Law Journal Reports[5], is cited;   but in my judgment there is nothing therein
which is of any assistance in the present case.

I think that the well-established acceptance of photographs as documents had
eluded Darling J when he gave his often quoted definition of a document in *R v Daye*[6],
where he said:

> 'On behalf of the bank it has been contended that the sealed envelope and what
> is inside it does not come within the term "document." I think that it is per-
> fectly plain that the sealed envelope itself might be a document. Nothing but
> the sealed envelope might be required. But I should myself say that any written
> thing capable of being evidence is properly described as a document and that it
> is immaterial on what the writing may be inscribed. It might be inscribed on
> paper, as is the common case now; but the common case once was that it was not
> on paper, but on parchment; and long before that it was on stone, marble, or
> clay, and it might be, and often was, on metal. So I should desire to guard
> myself against being supposed to assent to the argument that a thing is not a
> document unless it be a paper writing. I should say it is a document no matter
> upon what material it be, provided it is writing or printing and capable of being
> evidence.'

In any event, the point of that case was that the document there in question could
not be withheld from the court merely by being placed in an envelope which could
be argued not, by itself, to be a document. In *Hayes v Brown*[7] the actual decision was
that a plan made purely for the purposes of illustration was not a document which
required to be included in a notice to admit documents served in the county court.
The Divisional Court, however, recognised that there were many plans which were
documents in the nature of evidence, and to which the notice to admit would
therefore clearly apply. Lush J said[8]:

> 'It is contended that the plan was a "document" within the meaning of that
> rule, and that as no notice was given to admit it the costs of proving it could not
> be allowed. In my opinion that contention is not sound. Order xviii., r. 6,
> only applies to documents which a party "desires to give in evidence," and a
> plan like this which is intended, not as evidence of any facts, but merely to
> illustrate the party's case, is not such a document . . . I do not say that no plan
> can be a document within Order xviii., r. 6. There are many plans which are
> documents in the nature of evidence. But the question is whether this
> particular plan which was prepared only for the purpose of illustrating the
> plaintiff's case is such a document. I think it is not.'

---

1   (1884) 27 Ch D 1, [1881-85] All ER Rep 814
2   50 LT 730
3   11th Edn (1970), p 738, para 1681
4   [1916] 1 Ch 261
5   85 LJCh 261
6   [1908] 2 KB 333 at 340
7   [1920] 1 KB 250, [1918-19] All ER Rep 1159
8   [1920] 1 KB at 252, [1918-19] All ER Rep at 1160, 1161

Sankey J said[1]:

'I agree.   The question is not whether all plans are documents within Order
xviii., r. 6, but whether this particular plan was so.   I think it was not, but came
within Order liii., r. 44.   It was not an evidential document but was only
illustrative.'

In *Hill v R*[2], which was a case under the War Damage Act 1943, Humphreys J
said[3]:

'Although the construction of an Act of Parliament must always be a question
of law, I agree with Mr. Pritt that where the construction involves the right meaning to be given to a word in such common use in business as the word "document"—a word of which every-one thinks he knows the meaning—the court
should endeavour to give to it a meaning with which the ordinary educated
business man would agree.   Whether I regard the derivation of the word "document" from Latin, or the decisions of the courts on the meaning of the word, I
find that a document must be something which teaches you and from which you
can learn something, i.e., it must be something which affords information.   In
the dictionaries the word is repeatedly defined as something which is "evidence,"
not in the sense that it is something admissible in a court of law, but as being
something which makes evident that which otherwise would not be evident.
To constitute a document, the form which it takes seems to me to be immaterial; it may be anything on which the information is written or inscribed—
paper, parchment, stone or metal.   In Stroud's Judicial Dictionary[4] the first
words which I find on the meaning of "document" are: "a ledger, including a
partnership ledger, is a document within r. 191, Divorce Court Rules," and the
reference is to *Carew* v. *Carew*[5].   That case is not an authority for that proposition, but it was assumed by the parties that the ledger in that case was a "document" within the meaning of r. 191: "If he (the registrar) thinks fit he shall be at
liberty to require the attendance of the husband, for the purpose of being examined or cross-examined, and to take the oral evidence of witnesses, and to require
the production of any document . . ."   The petitioner, a wife, made an application for alimony pendente lite.   The registrar issued a subpoena duces tecum
directing the respondent, the husband, and his partner, to produce their books.
They produced a ledger relating to the last year's business, but refused to allow
it to be inspected.   The registrar made an order granting inspection of the
ledger, but the respondent and his partner failed to comply with the order and
the petitioner moved for their attachment.   But counsel, it seems, did not think
it even arguable that the word "document" in the rule did not include the
ledger.'

Then he refers to *R v Daye*[6] which I have already referred to.   After quoting a
passage from Darling J, he goes on[7]:

'The following words might have been added to this passage, as I have indicated:
"in that it furnishes information."   That decision was dealing with the terms of a
different statute, but I agree with the decision and with the judgment of Darling
J.   Morton J., in *In the Matter of an Application for a Patent by Alderton and Barry*[8]

---

1   [1920] 1 KB at 252, [1918-19] All ER Rep at 1161
2   [1945] 1 All ER 414, [1945] KB 329
3   [1945] KB at 332, 333, cf [1945] 1 All ER at 417
4   2nd Edn (1903)
5   [1891] P 360
6   [1908] 2 KB at 340
7   [1945] KB at 334, cf [1945] 1 All ER at 419
8   (1941) 59 RPC 56

expressed doubt whether cards which by means of a machine would give informa- *a*
tion as to the time a workman clocked in or out, before they had been so used,
were documents within the meaning of [the statute in question] since they did
not convey any information to any-one at that time. The same point might be
taken about an apparently blank piece of paper, that it is not a document, but
once secret writing has been developed on it then it might properly be described
as a document.'   *b*

I think it is fair to say that all these cases, in different ways, stress that the essential
feature of a document is the information thereby conveyed: they all hark back to the
Latin origin and meaning of the word. Although there are, of course, expressions
in them which, if taken literally, might be considered to exclude tapes from the ambit
of documents, I conclude that the tenor of such cases is strongly in favour of the
admission of the tapes to the category of documents. The matter is, however, not *c*
wholly untouched by direct authority.

In *Averill v Sunday Pictorial Newspapers (1920) Ltd*[1] the debate appears to have
proceeded throughout on the basis that tape recordings were documents. It is
fair to say that the matter was not argued; but the judge was that particularly
acute master of Chancery procedure, Danckwerts J. Certainly, a conclusion that
the tape was not a document would have produced an even shorter end to the appli- *d*
cation before him. The judge himself certainly directly speaks of a tape as a document. Although the status of the tape was a matter of tacit assumption before
Danckwerts J, it was a matter of argument in the South African case of *Da Mata v
Menfred Properties (Pty) Ltd*[2]. In that case Theron J, after argument, but unfortunately without the delivery of a reasoned judgment, clearly decided that tapes
were documents for the purposes of discovery. The same conclusion was reached *e*
in a different jurisdiction in Queensland by Hoare J in *Cassidy v Engwirda Construction Co*[3]. I think it is fair to say that he relied really on two matters; first, what I
may venture to call the instructional aspect, and, secondly, his view that[4]—

'Nothing is more likely to destroy the effectiveness of the law and our legal
system than a timid, restrictive, interpretation of procedural provisions.' *f*

I would for myself agree with this last sentiment, but subject to the proviso that one
is not, under cover of 'interpretation', laying down the law not as it is but as it ought
to be, which is, of course, the classic temptation.

So far the decisions whether tapes were documents were unanimously in favour
of their being so; but three years later there came a very powerful judgment in a
contrary sense, namely, the judgment of McInerney J in *Beneficial Finance Corpn* *g*
Co Ltd v Conway[5]. I think it is desirable that I should read a considerable portion
of this judgment. The learned judge said[6]:

'A "document" is defined in the *Oxford English Dictionary* as "Something
written or inscribed which furnishes evidence or information upon any subject-
matter, as a manuscript, title-deed or coin" etc., and in *Osborne's Concise Law* *h*
Dictionary, 4th ed., p. 121, it is defined as "Something on which things are written,
printed or inscribed and which gives information any written thing capable of
being evidence". In *Phipson on Evidence*, 10th ed., para 1681, there is a discussion of what are documents within the meaning of the rule of evidence that
the contents of public and judicial documents are provable either by primary

1 [1959] The Times, 22nd April
2 1969 (3) SA 332
3 [1967] QWN 16
4 [1967] QWN 16 at 31
5 [1970] VR 321
6 [1970] VR at 322

or more usually by secondary evidence. The contents of private documents must be proved by primary evidence except in the cases specifically mentioned as exceptions in a subsequent part of the book.'

Then the learned judge quoted the passage from *R v Daye*[1] which I have already referred to and continued[2]:

'In the passage in para 1681 of *Phipson*, to which I referred earlier, cases are collected in which it has been held that the term "document" included, or was applicable to, Exchequer tallies, wooden scores used by milkmen and bakers, inscriptions on walls, coffin plates and rings. But, on the other hand, labels on decanters or parcels have been held not to be documents but merely objects to be identified and there are authorities also in which inscriptions on flags and placards exhibited to public view were held to be of a character rather than of writing and so not to be subject to the rules relating to documents. The word "document" is, etymologically derived from the Latin word "documentum", that which teaches, a lesson, an example for instruction or warning. The common feature of documents, as the term is popularly understood, I think, is that the writing or printing or inscription of is something capable of being discerned by the eye, with or without the aid of optical instruments. The communication of the information onto the document is usually achieved through the organ of touch, and the apprehension of the information contained in the document is achieved usually by the organ of sight, or, sometimes, as in the case of a document in Braille, by the organ of touch. In a magnetic tape record the process of recording is one whereby, as I understand it, electrical soundwaves, or vibrations, are caught by a microphone, which converts the sound energy into electrical energy, which varies according to the nature and intensity of the soundwaves, and the electrical energy into which the sound energy has been so converted, is in turn converted by a magnetic coil in the magnetic head of the tape recorder, into magnetic energy which is then recorded on iron oxide particles or other particles of that nature, on the plastic tape. To that extent the characteristic soundwaves originally spoken into the microphone are recorded onto the tape, the iron oxide or other particles being magnetized in a manner which corresponds substantially with the pattern of the soundwaves. When the tape is rewound and played it passes a magnetic head which scans the magnetic pattern of the iron oxide particles on the tape, converting the magnetic energy back to electrical energy, which in turn is conveyed to the speaker or earphones, in which it is converted back to sound energy or sound waves, capable of being heard. So far as I am aware, at no stage is it possible to read the magnetic tape itself. The communication of the information on to the tape is through the organ of speech, and the apprehension of that information from the tape is through the organ of hearing. If this be the process of tape recording, as I understand it is, then, in my view, although the tape recording conveys information and serves a function corresponding to that of a document, as was said by Darling, J., in *Daye's Case*[1], to which reference has already been made, and Humphreys, J., in *Hill* v. *R.*[3], it does not necessarily follow that a tape recording is a document. It may be that it partakes more of the character of the unprocessed time machine cards which were considered by Morton, J., in [*Re Alderton and Barry's Application*[4]]. In that case, Morton, J., held that unprocessed time machine cards were not documents because they conveyed no information to anybody. In the present case the tape recording would convey, as I understand it, no information to

1   [1908] 2 KB at 340
2   [1970] VR at 323, 324
3   [1945] 1 KB at 334, [1945] 1 All ER at 419
4   (1941) 59 RPC 56

anyone on a mere visual inspection of the tape recording. I have, however, been pressed with the decision of Hoare, J., of the Supreme Court of Queensland in *Cassidy* v. *Engwirda Construction Co*[1]. In that case Hoare, J., held that a tape recording was a document within the meaning of the rules as to discovery and he made an immediate order for discovery of the text of the tape recording. He said he could see no reason in principle why the recording in some permanent or semi-permanent manner of the human voice or other sounds which are relevant to the issues to be determined, provided that it furnishes information, could not be a document. He owned, however, to some difficulty as to whether the existing Rules of the Supreme Court were adequate to cover the procedure whereby inspection and copies of such a tape recording could be obtained. I own to every sympathy with the view which was adopted by Hoare, J., and I do not think that procedural rules ought to be restrictively construed. Nevertheless, they are rules under which parties regulate their conduct of litigation and if according to the accepted interpretation of the terms used therein parties have regulated their behaviour, it is not always the most useful service which a court can render to the promotion of justice to give rules an interpretation beyond that which they can fairly bear. In my view, Hoare, J's decision goes further than I, sitting as a single judge, am prepared to go. The present case, I think, does point out the need for an amendment of the existing Rules of Supreme Court to make provision for what has become a practice, and will no doubt in the future become an increasingly prevalent practice, namely, the practice of making tape recordings of conversations and using the tape recordings afterwards as evidence. But the difficulties to which Hoare, J., adverted in *Cassidy's Case*[1] as to how the process of inspection and taking copies, obtaining copies of the contents, or a transcript of a tape recording plainly would require to be the matter of some careful consideration by the framers of any new rules designed to make provision for this class of case.'

So there the learned judge came to the conclusion that the tape recordings were not documents.

This is a very persuasive judgment, but I think there are two criticisms to be made of it. First, he misquotes—and the misquotation is a subtle and devastating one—from the Oxford English Dictionary. The words he uses are, 'Something written or inscribed which furnishes evidence or information upon any subject-matter, as a manuscript, title-deed or coin', i e omitting the important word 'etc', and indeed shifting it and so giving it a different interpretation, whereas what it actually says is as I have indicated above. The point is that the given example of 'frescoes' quite clearly would not fall within his amended definition which suggests a genus for 'manuscript, title deed and coin' that the dictionary clearly does not intend. The second is that he appears to equate the tapes with the workmen's time sheets in Morton J's case[2]. This really will not do. The point of this latter case was that what was alleged to be a document contained no information; there can be no doubt but that the tapes do contain information. The two are poles apart.

I therefore think that the real virtue of this judgment of McInerney J lies simply in the distinction which it draws between information which appeals to the eye, and information which appeals to the ear, which was, indeed, as I have already noted, precisely the distinction which counsel for the plaintiffs drew in argument. It is, I think, quite clear that the mere interposition of necessity of an instrument for decyphering the information cannot make any difference in principle. A litigant who keeps all his documents in microdot form could not avoid discovery because in order to read the information extremely powerful microscopes or other sophisticated

---

1   [1967] QWN 16
2   *Re Alderton and Barry's Application* (1941) 59 RPC 56

instruments would be required. Nor again, if he kept them by means of microfilm which could not be read without the aid of a projector.

Does such a difference exist? In my view it does not. It appears to me that written or printed words are, after all, only encapsulated sound—and in a sense badly encapsulated sound, in that they often do not, when they purport to be a record of direct speech, embody the tone of voice, the inflexions, the subtleties of phrasing and pauses, which form the warp and woof of real-life conversation. If two parties to litigation have a record of a vital conversation, one in the form of a shorthand note, and the other in the form of a tape recording, I think that both would be justified, under normal English usage, in saying that they held 'documentary proof' of the conversation. If there was in existence a tape recording of Queen Elizabeth I's speech to her troops at Tilbury would not all the world say that that was a priceless historical document?

It is, I think, noteworthy that instructional films have for many years now been called 'documentary films'. This strengthens my belief that in ordinary current English usage a document is primarily something that instructs and is by no means to be confined to 'books, clothed in black and red, of Aristotle and his philosophie' which the Clerk of Oxenford had in days gone by, or things ejusdem generis therewith. A film is a documentary film, notwithstanding that the sound is, of course, incorporated in the print. I do not think that popular speech makes any distinction between the visual and oral parts of what is all one subject-matter.

Though only of persuasive authority, I observe that in the recent case of *R v Robson*[1] Shaw J records, without adverse comment, the submissions which had been made by the very experienced counsel before him concerning the admissibility of tapes in a criminal trial:

> 'It was not contended that the tape recordings were, as such, inadmissible evidence of what was recorded on them. The objections taken were put under the following heads: first, it was said that the recordings, being in the nature of documentary evidence, must be excluded unless either (a) they were shown to be originals, or (b) the absence of the originals was satisfactorily explained and it was shown that the recordings it was sought to be put in evidence were true copies of those originals. This objection was, of course, founded on the strict rule requiring that the best evidence must be tendered or its absence accounted for before secondary evidence can be received. The application of the rule in a trial by jury can give rise to difficulties in delimiting the function of the judge in deciding admissibility while at the same time avoiding any unnecessary or unwarranted incursion into matters which go to cogency and weight which are for the jury to consider and to decide.'

In the upshot I conclude that a tape recording, provided of course that what is recorded is indeed information—relevant sounds of some description—is a document. Counsel for the plaintiffs' argument did not, however, stop there, because he argued that the heading to RSC Ord 24 of 'Discovery and Inspection of Documents' implied that its provisions extended only to such documents as could usefully be 'inspected', and that once again this led one back to something which provided information to the eye.

Here again the help of the Oxford English Dictionary is invaluable. The Shorter Oxford English Dictionary defines 'Inspection' as follows:

> 'The action of inspecting or looking narrowly into; careful scrutiny or survey; close examination.'

From this it is, I think, quite clear that inspection is not confined to mere ocular inspection. Clearly, for example, inspectors appointed under the Companies Act

---

1 [1972] 2 All ER 699 at 700, [1972] 1 WLR 651 at 653

1948, s 164, are not there merely to glare about them; they will use every sense which
they possess to enable them officially to examine the past proceedings of the company
in question, proceedings which can no longer feasibly be discerned by the eye.

I therefore conclude that there is nothing in the heading to the RSC Ord 24, or
indeed in any of the specific rules of that order which, given that a tape is a document,
renders the provisions of that order inapplicable thereto.

I am, of course, not insensible of the dangers and difficulties which occurred to
Hoare J[1] in relation to inspection of a tape, and certain events in yet another jurisdiction have alerted the whole world to the possibility of tampering with tape recordings.   But it seems to me that the simplest and most foolproof method of 'inspection'
in these cases is for the party giving discovery to play the tape to the party to whom
discovery is being given, and for that party to make his own recording as it is played.

Accordingly, I answer the first question in favour of the defendants.   I am glad
to be able to reach this conclusion, because otherwise the general purposes of discovery might, purely accidentally, by reason of the crystallisation of the rules relating
to discovery in the Rules of the Supreme Court, have been frustrated.   Discovery
was an invention of the courts of equity, and there can be no doubt at all but that the
general rule is accurately set forth in *Flight v Robinson*[2] as follows:

'The general rule is, that a Defendant is bound to discover all the facts within
his knowledge, and to produce all documents in his possession, which are material
to the case of the Plaintiff.   However disagreeable it may be to make the disclosure—however contrary to his personal interests—however fatal to his claims,
he is compelled to set forth, on oath, all he knows, believes, or thinks in relation
to the matters in question.'

Discovery is full, and not partial, discovery.

I would only finally add on this topic that it was, of course, accepted by both counsel
that visual reading of the tape here in question was impossible, and there was certainly no evidence that it could be so read before me.   I need say no more than that,
if that matter ever became a live issue in any subsequent case, the party desiring
inspection would be well advised to investigate the present state of the art.

I now turn to the second point, the claim for privilege.   This is made in an affidavit
of Nicholas Norton Jeremy Smith, a partner in the firm of Oswald Hickson, Collier &
Co, the solicitors for the plaintiffs, in the following terms:

'1.   I have the joint conduct of this action on behalf of the Plaintiffs.
'2.   The Plaintiffs first consulted my firm and sought advice in this matter
on the 12th June, 1973, the day before the telephone conversation in question
took place.   I am informed by the second Plaintiff and verily believe that any
record which he made of the said conversation was made because he contemplated that litigation between the parties would or might ensue and in order to
be able the better to instruct my firm and seek advice upon the matter.
'3.   The Plaintiffs claim that any such record is privileged from production
on the grounds that it was brought into existence when litigation was contemplated and with a view to giving instructions to and obtaining advice from legal
professional advisers.'

It is, of course, well established that a communication from the other side in litigation
cannot be privileged, and it is obvious common sense that a communication to the
other side in litigation cannot be privileged.   Is the tape in the present case anything
more than a summation of such unprivileged communications?   Counsel for the
plaintiffs accepts, of course, the principles I have set out above, but says, and correctly
says, that a document prepared for the use of one's own solicitor is, or at any rate

1 [1967] QWN 16
2 (1844) 8 Beav 22

is capable of being, privileged, even although it may take the form of a summary of one's recollection of conversations with the other party to the litigation. So here, he says, this was merely a more accurate note, made at the time for the benefit of the plaintiffs' solicitors and is, therefore, privileged.

I regret that I cannot accept this submission. It does not appear to me that, in any relevant sense, the tape was prepared by the plaintiffs for their solicitor. It was a recording of two things: (a) communications made by the plaintiffs as they were being made to the other side and (b) communications made by the other side, which were not in any way being made for the benefit of the plaintiffs' solicitors. The fact that when made the tape might be useful to the plaintiffs is, of course, neither here nor there. I, therefore, reject any claim to the privilege under this head completely.

I am glad to reach this conclusion from a practical point of view. As the tape is being recorded, it cannot be predicted how it will turn out, i e whether it will be useful to the person making the recording in subsequent litigation which is even at that stage assumed to be contemplated, or not. It would be the height of absurdity if, having taken the tape and it proving to be wholly in the other side's favour, that privilege could then be claimed for it.

Although in the event the question does not, in my opinion, arise, I must now deal with counsel for the defendants' alternative submission to the effect that, even if the tape was not a document disclosable under RSC Ord 24, r 10(1), it was 'property' which fell within RSC Ord 29, r 2(1). He said that the conditions of that rule were satisfied, because there did indeed arise with respect to the tape a very simple question: what is on it? I regret that I am wholly unable to accept this submission. The tape is evidence merely—or to be absolutely precise, it is on this hypothesis something other than a document which will supply evidence as to what happened in the course of the vital telephone conversation. But the strength, or even the existence, of the evidence in relation to a particular question which does arise in the trial is not itself a matter as to which any question arises. Any questions as to this are at one remove from the questions in the action. Had this matter fallen for decision, therefore, I would have been against counsel for the defendants' submission on this point.

Finally, there remains the question: is the tape a document to which, on a fair reading of the relevant particulars, reference is made within the meaning of RSC Ord 24, r 10(1)? In my opinion, the answer is clearly in the negative. What is mentioned in those particulars is the act of recording, not the recording itself. Indeed, so clear is this that it is quite impossible to be certain from the relevant particulars what the form of the record which was being made was. There is a reference to the act of recording; there is, in my judgment, no relevant reference to the record being made.

In the result, although I find that the summons actually issued by the defendants was misconceived, on the matters which the parties wished to have decided, because they are bound to arise, the defendants have succeeded, although not on all of the limbs of their argument. In the circumstances, I must invite submissions as to the proper order which I should make in relation to costs.

No order on summons save that plaintiffs pay half defendants' costs.

Solicitors: *Nabarro, Nathanson & Co* (for the defendants); *Oswald Hickson, Collier & Co* (for the plaintiffs).

Jacqueline Metcalfe Barrister.

Probatina Shipping Co Ltd v Sun Insurance Office Ltd

QUEEN'S BENCH DIVISION
KERR J
31st JULY, 2nd OCTOBER 1973

COURT OF APPEAL, CIVIL DIVISION
LORD DENNING MR, BUCKLEY AND ROSKILL LJJ
19th, 20th FEBRUARY, 15th MARCH 1974

Discovery – Marine insurance actions – Order for ship's papers – Order before delivery of defence – Scuttling cases – When order should be made – Factors to be considered by judge – Factors to be considered in deciding whether to order stay pending compliance with order for ship's papers – RSC Ord 72, r 10(1)(2).

The plaintiffs were the owners of a vessel which ran on to rocks and became a total loss. They brought an action against the underwriters claiming under a policy of marine insurance for the total loss of the vessel by perils of the sea. Points of claim and some further particulars of the claim were delivered but before delivery of the defence the defendants, pursuant to RSC Ord 72, r 10[a], applied for an order for ship's papers in Form 94[b] in Appendix A to the Rules of the Supreme Court, and that meanwhile all further proceedings in the action should be stayed. At the hearing of the application counsel for the defendants told the judge that it was intended to plead in the defence that the vessel had been scuttled and he gave some indication of the reasons for the plea. The plaintiffs had already disclosed to the defendants certain documents but those were sketchy and, in content and substance, considerably less than the documents which might be expected to be disclosed in an affidavit of ship's papers. In the exercise of his discretion under RSC Ord 72, r 10, the judge (i) refused to make an order for ship's papers or, for the time being, any other order for discovery but invited the parties to agree what further documents should be disclosed by the plaintiffs, indicating that, if the parties failed to agree, the matter should be brought back to the court to consider what further order should be made; (ii) refused to stay the action. Subsequently he ordered the defendants to serve points of defence within three weeks of the availability of the transcript of his judgment. The defendants appealed.

Held – (i) An order for ships' papers before delivery of defence should not be made automatically in cases where scuttling was alleged (see p 494 h, p 495 e and p 500 b, post).

(ii) Such an order however might be properly made (either in the terms of Form 94 or in such other form as the judge thought fit) where the assured went ahead with his action without voluntarily producing all the relevant documents and all other documents that the insurers reasonably asked to see (see p 494 g, p 495 e, p 499 j, p 500 c and p 501 d, post).

(iii) In making an application for ship's papers counsel for the insurers need not disclose the grounds for the allegation of scuttling but should put before the judge such reasons for making the order as he could properly give without embarrassing his clients' case which (per Buckley LJ) might include indicating the basis of the allegation of scuttling (see p 494 h and j, p 496 c and d and p 501 h and j, post).

(iv) If an order for ship's papers were made, the action should not necessarily be stayed until the assured had complied with it even though the insurers were required

---

Rule 10, so far as material, is set out at p 480 b and c, post
Form 94 is set out at p 486 j to p 487 d, post

to give the best particulars they could of the allegation of scuttling. If a stay were refused the insurers would have to deliver their defence giving the best particulars of the allegation they could then give, unless (per Roskill LJ) it would be unjust to require them to do so before they had obtained discovery of further documents, for on discovery leave could be given to supplement or amend the particulars (see p 495 *c*, p 496 *e*, p 500 *c* and p 501 *b*, post).

(v) In the circumstances the judge had properly exercised his discretion under RSC Ord 72, r 10; accordingly the appeal would be dismissed (see p 495 *d*, p 497 *c* and p 502 *e* and *j*, post).

Notes

For discovery of ship's papers, see 22 Halsbury's Laws (3rd Edn) 173-175, paras 331-334, and for cases on the subject, see 18 Digest (Repl) 60-62, 462-491.

Cases referred to in judgments

Astrovlanis Compania Naviera SA v Linard [1972] 2 All ER 647, [1972] 2 QB 611, [1972] 2 WLR 1414, [1972] 1 Lloyd's Rep 331, CA *subsequent proceedings* [1972] 2 Lloyd's Rep 187.

China Transpacific Steamship Co v Commercial Union Assurance Co (1881) 8 QBD 142, LJQB 132, 45 LT 647, CA, 18 Digest (Repl) 62, 483.

China Traders' Insurance Co Ltd v Royal Exchange Assurance Corpn [1898] 2 QB 187, 67 LJQB 736, 78 LT 783, 8 Asp MLC 409, 3 Com Cas 189, CA, 18 Digest (Repl) 60, 467.

Dias, The, Palamisto General Enterprises SA v Ocean Marine Insurance Co Ltd [1972] 2 All ER 1112, [1972] 2 QB 625, [1972] 2 WLR 1425, [1972] 2 Lloyd's Rep 60, CA.

Disney v Longbourne (1876) 2 Ch D 704, 45 LJCh 532, 35 LT 301, 18 Digest (Repl) 167, 1451.

Goldschmidt v Marryat (1809) 1 Camp 559, 170 ER 1057, 18 Digest (Repl) 61, 476.

Keevil and Keevil Ltd v Boag [1940] 3 All ER 346, 163 LT 238, 57 Lloyd's Rep 263, 19 Asp MLC 387, CA, 18 Digest (Repl) 61, 475.

Leon v Casey [1932] 2 KB 576, [1932] All ER Rep 484, 101 LJKB 578, 147 LT 165, 37 Com Cas 330, 18 Asp MLC 300, CA, 18 Digest (Repl) 61, 472.

Mania Maritime and Commercial Co v Sun Insurance Office Ltd (4th May 1973) unreported.

Tropaioforos, The, Compania Naviera Santi SA v Indemnity Marine Assurance Co Ltd [1960] 2 Lloyd's Rep 469, 29 Digest (Repl) 228, 1710.

West of England Bank v Canton Insurance Co (1877) 2 Ex D 472, 18 Digest (Repl) 60, 462.

Application

By a writ issued on 5th April 1973 the plaintiffs, Probatina Shipping Co Ltd, claimed against the defendants, Sun Insurance Office Ltd, as representative underwriters, £1,640·29, due under a policy of marine insurance, being the defendants' proportion of the insured value of the plaintiffs' vessel, the Sageorge, which was a total loss as a result of stranding off Crete on 29th April 1972, together with interest thereon, pursuant to the Law Reform (Miscellaneous) Provisions Act 1934. The plaintiffs delivered points of claim and at the defendants' request gave certain further and better particulars of their claim. By a summons, dated 25th July 1973, the defendants applied (i) for an order for ship's papers in the terms prescribed in Form 94 of Appendix A to the Rules of the Supreme Court, pursuant to RSC Ord 72, r 10, and (ii) for an order that pending compliance therewith all further proceedings should be stayed. The summons was heard in chambers and adjourned to open court for judgment. The facts are set out in the judgment.

Kenneth Rokison for the defendants.
R A MacCrindle QC and *Nicholas Phillips* for the plaintiffs.

Cur adv vult

2nd October.   **KERR J** read the following judgment. This is the defendants' application for what is commonly known as an order for 'ship's papers' to be collected and disclosed by the plaintiffs pursuant to RSC Ord 72, r 10(1). The form of order asked for is that set out in Form 94 of Appendix A to the rules. The defendants also ask for a stay of the action under r 10(2) of this order pending compliance with the order for ship's papers. I should set out the relevant parts of Ord 72, r 10:

> 'Production of certain documents in marine insurance actions. (1) Where in an action in the commercial list relating to a marine insurance policy an application for an order under Order 24, rule 3 [that is an order for discovery], is made by the insurer, then, without prejudice to its powers under that rule, the Court, if satisfied that the circumstances of the case are such that it is necessary or expedient to do so, may make an order either in Form No. 94 in Appendix A or in such other form as it thinks fit, for the production of such documents as are therein specified or described. (2) An order under this Rule may be made on such terms, if any, as to staying proceedings in the action or otherwise as the Court thinks fit. . .'

The action is a claim by the plaintiffs under a policy of marine insurance issued by the defendants in respect of the loss of the plaintiffs' vessel Sageorge. It is what is commonly known as a scuttling case in that the defendants have stated through their counsel on this application that they not only propose to deny liability under the policy and to put the plaintiffs to proof that the vessel was lost by insured perils, but that they also propose to plead, in the time-honoured phrase, that she was wilfully cast away with the connivance of the plaintiffs. The defendants' counsel has put before the court some indication of the reasons why he is satisfied that this is a proper plea in the circumstances of this case, and I shall have to revert to this hereafter.

I adjourned this summons into open court for judgment for two reasons. First, it became clear in the course of the argument that the case is being treated by the plaintiffs as raising an issue of principle, viz whether it is or should be the practice of the Commercial Court to make orders for ship's papers in scuttling cases, as I have described them, as a matter of course, whether with or without a stay, or whether even in scuttling cases the court should only do so if and when satisfied 'that the circumstances of the case are such that it is necessary or expedient to do so' within the wording of the rule. The second reason is that since the decision of the Court of Appeal in *Keevil and Keevil Ltd v Boag*[1] there has been no reported decision on any application for an order for ship's papers, although there have been many such applications before different commercial judges. For over 30 years there has therefore been no official record of the practice of this court on such applications. Evidence of the practice primarily exists in the experience of the counsel and solicitors who have dealt with such applications over the years. In addition it so happens that the solicitors acting for the defendants in this case have also acted for the insurers in all, or nearly all, scuttling cases for many years, if not decades, and that the solicitors acting for the plaintiffs in this case have also on many occasions represented the plaintiffs in such cases. Over a number of years the defendants' solicitors have kept notes of the submissions of counsel and of the remarks of commercial judges on applications for ship's papers in chambers, and it has thereby increasingly become the practice, as it were by a series of private mini-law reports, to refer to the events in earlier applications for ship's papers and to put these notes before the judge in question in order to assist him to see what the practice has been or is said to have been. This happened a good deal within my own experience at the Bar, and the present case is the second occasion on which I have been asked to make an order for ship's papers partly on the basis of notes or statements by counsel as to what happened on similar applications in the past. This practice is useful so far as it goes, but there obviously comes a time when it ceases to be either convenient or desirable. In my view this time has now

1 [1940] 3 All ER 346

_a_ come, particularly since the present case also seeks to raise the issue of principle which I have already mentioned.

In order to put the whole position in perspective it is necessary shortly to summarise the history of the order for ship's papers. Broadly speaking, an order for ship's papers goes beyond the ordinary order for discovery by requiring plaintiffs not only to disclose documents which are or have been within their possession or power, but

_b_ also to use their best endeavours to obtain from any source documents, or classes of documents, in the possession or power of other persons. It can therefore involve very far-reaching enquiries, expense and delays.

Before 1936 the order did not rest on any rule of the Supreme Court, but it had been the settled practice of the common law courts for well over 100 years to grant such orders as of right to defendants to claims under marine policies irrespective of whether

_c_ allegations of scuttling or other fraud were to be raised or not. A full account of the historical development of the order is to be found in the judgment of Scrutton LJ in _Leon v Casey_[1]. The historical explanation of the fact that this order was only made on claims under marine policies is simply that it originated at a time when the only prevalent type of insurance was marine insurance. The original reason for the order was that the defending insurers would, or would normally, not have any means

_d_ of knowledge of the circumstances of the loss or any means to assess the bona fides of the claim. However, with the proliferation of different types of insurance and the vast changes in means of communication and opportunities for investigation by insurers, both of these raisons d'être no longer have the same validity. An almost equally strong case for orders of this kind could in principle now be made in relation to insurance in some other fields. But there has been no pressure from in-

_e_ surers to enlarge the field beyond that of marine insurance in which such orders are made, with the result that the present rule still only applies to claims under marine policies. On the other hand, changes in means of communication and investigation, even within the field of marine insurance, ultimately led to a change in the practice of granting the order as of right. The inequity of the prior practice was vividly described by Greer LJ in _Leon v Casey_[2], and it is worthwhile setting out the passage in full because

_f_ it is still capable of affecting cases under the present practice. He said:

'I have come with regret to the conclusion that the authorities oblige me to hold that we cannot interfere with the order of MacKinnon J. Before dealing with the facts of this case and the law relating to them, I should like to make two general observations. The first is that no more unpleasant duty has to be per-formed by a judge than that of giving, in accordance with binding authority,

_g_ a decision which upon the facts before him he considers both unreasonable and unjust. That is the task which I have before me in this particular case.'

Having dealt with the facts he then went on to say this:

'The other general observation is this, that custom and habit tend to blind the

_h_ vision. At a time when the criminal law of this country was in a state to disgrace a half-civilized country, judges of high authority and writers of text-books had been brought up to regard it as the "perfection of reason"; and I cannot help thinking that those members of the profession, who both at the Bar and on the Bench have been largely engaged in matters of marine insurance, have come to believe that the rules which have hitherto been applied in marine insurance are those which ought to be applied, and that the law as it stands is incapable of improve-ment. I take a very different view. In my opinion the order for ship's papers was invented at a time when it was necessary in order to do justice to the case of the insurer; it has now become an unfair and unjust weapon in the

---

1   [1932] 2 KB 576, [1932] All ER Rep 484
2   [1932] 2 KB at 587-589, [1932] All ER Rep at 490-491

hands of the insurer. I have known of case after case in the Commercial List
where defendants, who had no real defence, have been enabled by means
of this instrument of oppression to keep plaintiffs out of their insurance money
for long periods of time; and I regret that the Court has not felt itself justified
in holding a tighter hand upon this practice than it has done. But it has ultimately
been decided that if in a case of marine insurance there is a single document
which has not been accounted for by the plaintiff, the defendant can hold up
the case until the plaintiff searches the world over for that document, which is
often just as obtainable by the insurers as it is by the assured. It would be possible
under the powers of the Court to confer on the judge hearing the summons for
directions greater control over the practice of ordering discovery of ship's papers,
so that he might exercise his discretion according as the practice is being used for
the necessary purposes of justice or is being abused as a means of oppression in
the hands of the insurance company or Lloyd's underwriter. I doubt whether
this can be done under the existing Rules of Court, but, if it could be done, I
should think the change would be a welcome one to all who desire that justice
shall be done and that there shall be a speedy end to litigation.'

The consequence, probably of this judgment, was the introduction in 1936 of the
predecessor of the present RSC Ord 72, r 10. The change made was to give a discretion to the court whether or not to order the production of ship's papers and,
if so, whether or not to impose a stay meanwhile. Its wording is conveniently set out
in the judgment of Goddard LJ in *Keevil and Keevil Ltd v Boag*[1]. I need not set it out
here. In substance it only differed from the present Ord 72, r 10, in that the court
could then only make the order in the terms of what is now Form 94 of Appendix A,
whereas the present rule enables it to do so in such other form as it may think fit.
This is a further valuable development, because in my experience it is generally
accepted, and indeed obvious from the wording of this form, as mentioned below,
that parts of it are archaic and other parts too wide, or perhaps in some cases too
narrow, to be sensible or efficaceous.

The importance of *Keevil and Keevil Ltd v Boag*[1] is that it is the only reported case
which considered the newly introduced discretion to refuse the order. Singleton J
had refused to make the order on a summons for directions but had added 'Liberty
to apply for affidavit of ship's papers hereafter if so advised'. This was upheld by the
Court of Appeal as a proper exercise of his discretion in the circumstances of that case,
and the court for the same reason also refused to order discovery before pleadings.
But the important point about *Keevil and Keevil Ltd v Boag*[1] is that it was not a scuttling
case; it was a claim under a marine warehouse-to-warehouse policy in which the
intended defence was a plea of inherent vice of the goods insured. The effect of this
decision on the practice relating to orders for ship's papers was however that applications for such orders appear thereafter to have been limited to scuttling cases;
at any rate I have never heard of any case since then other than a scuttling case,
whether only relating to ship or to both ship and cargo, in which such an order has
been asked for, let alone made.

In effect, therefore, applications for orders for ship's papers have since the last
war been limited to scuttling cases. On the other hand, neither the experienced solicitors and counsel in the present case, nor I, know of any scuttling case in which such
an order has ever been refused. To the extent that such applications have always
ultimately been successful in scuttling cases it can therefore be claimed, as the defendants claim here, that a settled practice has crystallised. But it is also within my
own experience, and evident from the notes relating to earlier applications which
were put before me, that there have been many instances in which applications for
ship's papers in scuttling cases have been strongly resisted, though ultimately always

1 [1940] 3 All ER 346

unsuccessfully. To give some idea of the extent of the practice, if it can be called a practice, I would say that on the average something of the order of two to five applications for ship's papers have come before the Commercial Court annually over the last 15 years or so, but that with the exception of two of them, *The Tropaioforos*[1] and *Astrovlanis Compania Naviera SA v Linard*[2], no scuttling cases have ultimately been fought. Such cases have therefore either been abandoned or, no doubt in the vast majority of cases, settled. But I have no doubt that in many, if not all, of the settled cases the existence of the order for ship's papers played a part in the settlement and that many, if not most, such cases were in fact settled before the order was fully complied with.

The reason for this lies in the expense and delay which the order necessarily entails. I have been informed that in the experience of the solicitors for the plaintiffs in the present case compliance with such an order has involved costs as high as £30,000 and that it has taken as long as two to three years to obtain all the documents which can be claimed by the defendant insurers to fall within the scope of the order. They also say that from their experience as little as about 20 per cent of copies of the obtained documents may then ultimately be bespoken for use at the hearing after inspection by the defendants. No doubt these are extreme figures and it would be dangerous to generalise from them, though I have no reason to doubt them. But there is equally no doubt that if and insofar as the court retains a discretion, even in scuttling cases, it is right to take account of the facts that compliance with the order undoubtedly involves plaintiffs in considerable expense and that if the order is accompanied by a stay it substantially postpones any possibility of getting the action to trial for a very long time.

In the most recent application for ship's papers, *Mania Maritime and Commercial Co v Sun Insurance Office Ltd*[3], which came before me in May 1973, the application for a stay was not resisted after I had indicated that I was going to grant the order, because on the facts of that case it was accepted that it made little difference whether the inevitable delay entailed by compliance with the order occurred before or after the insurers were required to serve their points of defence. On reflection I think that this may be an over-simplification. In the present case a stay is strongly opposed even if an order for ship's papers is granted, and I must therefore revert to this point hereafter.

Another aspect of the practical effect of the order for ship's papers is that I have not heard of a case in which the insurers have, at any rate in recent times, derived any really important benefit from the documents collected and disclosed as the result of the order. On past applications by defendants it has again and again been pointed out by counsel for the plaintiffs, and often also by judges of this court, that if a ship-owner plans to scuttle his ship and does so, there are unlikely to be documents showing or suggesting that this may have happened. Or, if there are any such documents in existence, they are in any event unlikely to be disclosed by him. Although the solicitors for the insurers in the present case have represented insurers in virtually every scuttling case which has come before this court for many years, their counsel only referred to one instance in which the disclosed documents gave some indirect assistance to underwriters by corroborating the reliability on other points of a witness whom the insurers called to testify about a conversation which he overheard between members of the crew and which supported the inference that the ship had in fact been scuttled. But I do not think that the potential uselessness of the order in practice is a weighty argument, because one never knows what may turn up in documents and lead to the exploration of further aspects or the drawing of inferences which may support the allegation of scuttling. Nevertheless I am bound to say that I do not

---

1   [1960] 2 Lloyd's Rep 469
2   [1972] 2 Lloyd's Rep 187
3   (4th May 1973) unreported

think that anybody experienced in this work would have any doubt that the real value of an order for ship's papers to the defendant insurers is nowadays infinitely greater as a means of obtaining a settlement of the claim than as a means of discovering the truth about the claim.

I must next mention a further important recent development in relation to scuttling cases generally, which is of some relevance to orders for ship's papers in such cases. This is the fact that it is now incumbent on insurers who raise a plea of scuttling to particularise this allegation in the same way as any other plea of fraud. This was the view of the majority of the Court of Appeal in *Astrovlanis Compania Naveria SA v Linard*[1], but it was there obiter because the particulars were refused due to the imminence of the trial. The point was however decided by a differently constituted Court of Appeal, though again only by a majority, in *The Dias*[2]. There are two reasons why these cases are relevant in the present context. First, since the insurers are now obliged to give particulars of the facts relied on in support of the plea of scuttling, and are therefore at any rate to some extent restricted in relation to the material which they can introduce at the trial in support of this plea (though it is undesirable to consider here how this will work out in particular cases), they can now justifiably contend that an application for ship's papers to some extent rests on an even stronger basis than under the former practice when no particulars of scuttling had to be given. Secondly, there are passages in the judgments of Edmund Davies and Stephenson LJJ in the first of these cases which, although strictly obiter and without the court having had the benefit of argument on the present aspects, go some way to support the defendants' contention on the present application. Edmund Davies LJ said[3]:

'In marine insurance cases such as the present the defendant already has the almost (if not wholly) unique advantage of not being obliged to plead until after discovery, and that has been completed in the present case. If the ship's documents thereby obtained are his only source of information and they afford no substantiation of complicity in scuttling, such a grave allegation should not have been advanced.'

However, in parenthesis I would respectfully venture to doubt the reality of an expectation that the documents disclosed on an order for ship's papers are in practice likely materially to influence the knowledge or suspicions of underwriters whether or not the ship was in fact scuttled. I think that their knowledge and suspicions will be much the same after compliance with the order as they have been before. Stephenson LJ said[4]:

'But those who do put forward this defence [i e of scuttling] already have at least one advantage over most litigants which is within the rules of the Supreme Court: they are generally, if not always, given exceptionally full discovery by an order for ship's papers under RSC Ord 72, r 10, and, like this defendant, they will probably not be asked for particulars until after discovery, whereas defendants usually have to give them before discovery.'

In dealing with the present application I therefore bear in mind this twofold relevance of these recent decisions.

Before turning to the circumstances of the present case I must deal with what the plaintiffs have referred to as an issue of principle. Since RSC Ord 72, r 10, expressly empowers the court to exercise its discretion in at least three respects, viz whether or not to make an order for ship's papers and, if so, in what form, and whether or not

---

1 [1972] 2 All ER 647, [1972] 2 QB 611
2 [1972] 2 All ER 1112, [1972] 2 QB 625
3 [1972] 2 All ER at 655, [1972] 2 QB at 621
4 [1972] 2 All ER at 657, [1972] 2 QB at 624

accompanied by a stay, there is in my judgment no short or general answer as to what should happen in individual cases. It may, however, be helpful if I summarise my views on these three important aspects insofar as it is possible to do so in general terms, and this is also necessary as a basis for my decision in the present case.

First, generally speaking I think that it is at least prima facie 'expedient' within the wording of the rule to make some order in the nature of an order for ship's papers in cases in which the court is satisfied that a plea of scuttling is going to be made and that there is prima facie justification for such a plea. This is putting it at its lowest from the point of view of the insurers, but if it were otherwise, then the existence of the power to make such an order in claims under marine policies would have no, or virtually no, remaining purpose. This conclusion is also in accordance with the practice of this court because, as already mentioned, an order for ship's papers has in fact never been refused in such circumstances. Further, the prima facie entitlement of insurers to an order in such circumstances is in my view somewhat strengthened by the recent change in the practice whereby they must now give particulars of the facts relied on in support of their allegation that the ship was scuttled. On the other hand, the insurers' prima facie entitlement in such cases to an order which goes beyond the ambit of normal discovery does not, in my view, absolve the court from considering in each case what order in the words of the rule is 'necessary or expedient' in the particular circumstances. I agree that it would be wrong, to use the phrase of counsel for the plaintiffs, that there should be some kind of automatic Pavlovian reaction by the court invariably to make the order simply on being informed by counsel, usually in tones of suitable gravity, that the insurers intend to plead that the vessel was wilfully cast away with the privity of her owners and that in counsel's view this is a proper plea on the information before him. In this connection there is, in my experience, no settled practice about the extent to which the court requires to be satisfied about the propriety of a plea of scuttling and the consequential prima facie entitlement of the insurers to an order in the nature of an order for ship's papers. Whereas judges have in some cases made the order on the basis of the simple ipse dixit of counsel that a plea of scuttling is going to be raised, in other cases within my own experience judges of this court have shown a disinclination to make the order unless they were given at any rate some indication of the reasons why the insurers were proposing to put forward a positive case of scuttling. In my view this is the correct approach in principle, because the court cannot otherwise decide what is necessary or expedient in the interests of justice in the particular case. Of course it would be wrong to compel underwriters to disclose in any detail evidence or suspicions which they may have and hope to justify at the trial. But there is no need to go so far as this by pressing for any detailed disclosures. Further, the consequence of the recent decisions in the Court of Appeal is that a plea of scuttling now in any event requires a degree of particularisation of the facts relied on in support of it. Although counsel appearing for insurers have in my experience always been careful to assert and to seek to retain an alleged right of insurers to obtain an order for ship's papers merely on the basis that it is intended to plead scuttling, without giving any justification for the propriety of the plea other than counsel's statement that the plea will be made, in practice they have then usually, if not always, gone further and provided the court with some general indications of the grounds justifying the plea in the particular case. I know of no case in which this has caused any embarrassment to the insurers, and the present case, as mentioned below, is no exception. The obligation to particularise the plea must now reduce the possibility of embarrassment still further. I therefore consider that counsel for the insurers should always give some sufficient indication to the court of the justifiability of the plea before any question of a prima facie entitlement to an order for ship's papers can arise. Otherwise the court is in the dark as to what may be necessary or expedient in the particular case and one is merely left with what counsel for the plaintiffs described as a Pavlovian reaction by the court. This is the first general aspect.

Secondly, I consider that there is not, nor ever should be, any settled practice whether or not an order for ship's papers is to be accompanied by a stay of the action meanwhile. Indeed, in many, if not in most, cases, it may be much more sensible to refuse a stay. As already mentioned, the application for ship's papers in scuttling cases now ex hypothesi rests on the basis that the insurers are already in a position to put forward a plea of scuttling with some degree of particularisation. Further, the insurers' own means of investigation are nowadays in practice likely to be much more efficacious to enable them to contest the plaintiffs' account of the casualty and to put forward a positive case of scuttling than any additional assistance which they may possibly derive from the documents disclosed as the result of the order. If such disclosure should throw up further facts relied on in support of the allegation of scuttling the court would no doubt always give leave to amend the particulars of this plea. The advantage of refusing a stay is that the action does not come to a halt for what may be a period of well over a year while the plaintiffs set about collecting the various documents which are required. As experience shows, in the rare cases in which scuttling cases are actually fought, the trial is likely to occupy many weeks. Witnesses have to be brought from all over the world and it may be necessary to all concerned for a date to be fixed for as much as a year in advance. But if a stay is imposed then one of its effects is that a date cannot be fixed until the stay is lifted after every document of potential relevance has been collected and considered. It is generally much more profitable, after the main issues have been crystallised in the pleadings, to use this waiting period in the preparation for the trial and the collection and consideration of the remaining documents to be obtained and disclosed by the plaintiffs, and for both parties to work towards a definite date during this period. The inevitable intervening delay also gives ample opportunity to the insurers to consider any further amendment to their pleadings or, in extreme cases, to apply for an adjournment if the plaintiffs are dilatory in complying with the order. As one knows, in practice it is virtually inevitable for the final preparations for the trial only to be made at a late stage, because solicitors, counsel and expert witnesses are too busy with other matters to deal with pending cases a long time ahead. It is therefore in my view a complete unreality to contend that the documentation should be virtually ready for trial before the stay is lifted and a date for the trial can be applied for, which, in the nature of things, cannot be until many months ahead. The practical effect of a stay is therefore in most cases to delay an eventual trial to such an extent that the plaintiffs prefer to settle rather than to wait more or less indefinitely, and that an order for ship's papers accordingly provides the insurers with an unwarranted bargaining factor. In these circumstances it is not surprising that, as I am informed, both in *Astrovlanis Compania Naviera SA v Linard*[1] and *The Dias*[2] there was an order for ship's papers but without any stay. I cannot now recall the timetable of events prior to the application for ship's papers in *Mania Maritime and Commercial Co v Sun Insurance Office Ltd*[3], but I might well have refused a stay if the order of a stay had been opposed and the point fully argued.

The third general aspect relates to the form of the order, as to which the court now also has a discretion. For this purpose it is necessary to set out the wording of Form 94, though I have never yet heard it read, nor analysed in detail, on any application for ship's papers except in order to show its general deficiencies. It would appear that its wording dates from the last century and it reads as follows:

'It is ordered that the plaintiff and all other persons interested in this action, and in the insurance the subject of this action, do produce and show to the defendant, his solicitors or agents on oath [*or* by oath of their proper officer]

---

1   [1972] 2 All ER 647, [1972] 2 QB 611
2   [1972] 2 All ER 1112, [1972] 2 QB 625
3   (4th May 1973) unreported

all insurance slips, policies, letters of instruction or other orders for effecting
such slips or policies, or relating to the insurance or the subject-matter of the
insurance on the ship   , or the cargo on board thereof, or the freight thereby,
and also all documents relating to the sailing or alleged loss of the ship, cargo
or freight, and all correspondence with any person relating in any manner to
the effecting of the insurance on the said ship, cargo or freight, on the voyage
insured by the policy sued on in this action, or any other policy whatsoever
effected on the said ship, or the cargo on board thereof, or the freight thereby
on the same voyage.   Also all correspondence between the captain or agent of
the ship and any other person with the owner or any person before the commencement of or during the voyage on which the alleged loss happened.   Also all
books and documents, whatever their nature and whether originals, duplicates
or copies, which in any way relate or refer to any matter in question in this action
and which are now in the custody, possession or power of the plaintiff or any
other person on his behalf, his or their, or any of their brokers, solicitors or
agents, with liberty for the defendant, his solicitors or agents to inspect and take
copies of, or extracts from, any of those books or documents.   And that in the
like manner the plaintiff and every other person interested as aforesaid do account
for all other books and documents relating or referring to any matter in question
in this action which were once but are not now in his custody, possession and
power.'

It will be seen that it contains four sentences. The first sentence deals broadly
with all documents in any way relating to the insurance of the ship, cargo or freight
and to documents relating to the sailing and loss of the vessel.   Most of the insurance
documents are nowadays in any event readily available to underwriters. I have
never yet heard of a case in which the collection and disclosure of every document
referred to in the first sentence has resulted in any benefit to the insurers affecting
the merits of the claim or of the allegation of scuttling.   This is not to say that the
insurers should not be entitled to call for any document or class of document which
falls within this sentence if this is necessary or expedient in the particular case.   In
some cases, for instance, there may be a suspicion that the owners of the ship are in
some way associated with the owners of the cargo and that both may have been
fraudulently destroyed, but even in such cases the painstaking assembly of what may
be hundreds of formal or colourless documents has never to my knowledge been
claimed to serve any useful purpose.   The important facts relating to the insurance
of the ship and cargo are always known to underwriters at an early stage and usually
mentioned on their application for ship's papers, viz whether or to what extent
there is over-insurance in comparison with the market value of the ship, which is
common, and when the insurance was effected in relation to the date of the loss.

Turning to the second sentence, which requires the production of all correspondence between the captain or ship's agent before and during the voyage, this is
wholly unlimited in its terms and obviously far too wide to make sense. It does
make sense, however, if it is limited to correspondence relating to the ship and
cargo and to the voyage on which the loss occurred and perhaps previous similar
voyages.   The latter point may well be relevant in the present case for the reasons
mentioned below.

As regards the third and fourth sentences, it is to be noted that they in fact go
little further than the ordinary order for discovery. They apply to documents
'which in any way relate or refer to any matter in question in this action', but unlike
the documents referred to in the first and second sentences, in relation to which there
is no limitation as regards the persons in whose power or possession they may be,
the documents referred to in the third and fourth sentences are limited to documents
in the possession or power of the plaintiffs and, in effect, any agent or sub-agent of
the plaintiffs or which had previously been in the power or possession of such persons.

However, apart from the wording of Form 94 there may well be classes of documents, as mentioned below, which fall within none of the four sentences but in relation to which an order for disclosure should in a particular case be made in favour of the insurers. The mere making of the order in the terms of Form 94 in every scuttling case is therefore in many cases no more than an unthinking exercise. Having regard to the clumsy and unsatisfactory form of the order, it is very important to note, in particular in connection with cases like the present which is in many ways typical, that what in fact usually happens when an order for ship's papers has been made and the action is not thereupon settled or, partially as a result of the order, gradually drifts towards a settlement, is that after the initial wave of documents has been collected and disclosed, either voluntarily or as the result of the order, the solicitors acting for the insurers ask for specific classes of documents in which they are interested because of the particular circumstances of the case. I am assuming that there will not be an intermediate stage during which there is insistence on the collection and disclosure of documents referred to in the disclosed documents, and so on, without any real consideration of their potential value, though the form of the order in fact gives considerable latitude for spinning out this process, as pointed out by Greer LJ[1] 40 years ago. The documents required by the defendants' solicitors will in practice fall within their interpretation of the words 'which in any way relate or refer to any matter in question in this action' governing the third and fourth sentences. Most of such classes of documents will be within the ambit of these sentences, but others may lie outside. For instance, crew lists and survey reports relating to the vessel and cargo will be within them, but the bank statements of individuals who may have a financial interest in the companies owning the ship or cargo, or their past record in maritime ventures, would not be within them. These may however be of considerable importance, and to that extent the wording of the order may in fact be too narrow. But in practice the wording of the order makes little difference to the course of events, because in my experience the subsequent process of requests for classes of documents by the solicitors acting for the insurers and the reaction of the solicitors acting for the plaintiffs, whose clients will be anxious to show or to appear to show that they have nothing to hide, normally takes place without either side concerning itself to any extent with the wording of the order, but much more with the sanction of a further application to the court for specific documents or classes of documents which the insurers' solicitors may claim to be material. This is what happens in practice, and in view of the wording of Form 94 there is really no other way in which the disclosure of ship's papers in a scuttling action can sensibly work in practice. The relative uselessness of the general wording of Form 94 is also illustrated by the fact that in many applications for ship's papers counsel for the insurers readily agree that if an order is made it may be more helpful, instead of making it in the terms of Form 94, for the parties to try to agree on a form of order containing classes of documents which are really relevant to the particular facts of the case. This was offered by counsel for the defendants in the present case, and it was also agreed to by both counsel when I recently made an order for ship's papers in *Mania Maritime and Commercial Co v Sun Insurance Office Ltd*[2]. In my view this form of procedure is far more efficacious than merely to make an order in the terms of Form 94, because it requires the parties to co-operate, under the sanction of an application to the court, to assemble documents which may be of some direct relevance to the particular case and thereby to focus on the real issues in the action. It avoids the worst feature of a bare order for ship's papers of erecting something like a barrier in front of the plaintiffs' claim which stifles any meaningful progress in the action for a period of months, if not years.

These general considerations in my view apply in particular to cases such as the

---

1 See *Leon v Casey* [1932] 2 KB at 588, 589, [1932] All ER Rep at 490, 491
2 (4th May 1973) unreported

present, which is by no means an unusual case, because of the amount of documentation which may already have been disclosed to the insurers' solicitors, either
voluntarily or at their request, because of the information which these solicitors
may already possess as the result of independent enquiries, and because of the delay
which may already have occurred. But, notwithstanding all this, such a case may still
be one in which the insurers should be entitled to the protection of being able to
require the production of documents and classes of documents which go beyond the
ambit of ordinary discovery and beyond what has already been disclosed.

In the light of these general considerations I must now turn to the circumstances
of the present case. As put before me by counsel they are shortly as follows. The
Sageorge was built in 1953 and acquired by the plaintiffs, her present owners, in 1970.
She is registered in Cyprus. From October 1971 she operated under a time charter
for six months. The charterers had the right to extend this period by a further
six months and did so. The casualty occurred on 29th April 1972 while she was on
a voyage from Ashdod in Israel to Genoa, Italy. Her insured value was £75,000.
It will therefore be seen that by present day standards this is by no means a very
large case in terms of money, but if the plaintiffs are entitled to the insured value
there may be considerable hardship in keeping them out of their money for a lengthy
and more or less indefinite time. She stranded on a small rocky island near the
south-east corner of Crete. She apparently became a total loss, but her wreck has
survived and has at different times been examined by surveyors on behalf of both
parties. The circumstances of the casualty were investigated on behalf of the plaintiffs and detailed statements were taken from the crew. Although there was of
course no obligation to do so, and the statements would by now no doubt have
become privileged documents, the crew's statements were then voluntarily disclosed
to the insurers through the plaintiffs' brokers. By August 1972 Messrs Ince had
been instructed to act for the insurers and had seen the crew's statements. They
asked for all relevant documents and for a chart referred to in the master's statement.
I understand that all immediately available and apparently relevant documents
were then disclosed, together with this chart. In September Messrs Holman, Fenwick and Willan, the solicitors acting for the plaintiffs, then offered to meet Messrs
Ince to discuss what further documents or information the insurers might require.
This was declined as it was felt that a meeting would not greatly assist at that stage.
In October the plaintiffs' solicitors then wrote to the effect that without knowing
what further information or documents were required by underwriters they did not
know for what further material they should ask the plaintiffs. Messrs Ince replied
to the effect that they were still making enquiries and that a meeting would therefore
not be helpful, but they asked for any further statements from the crew, copies of
the charts on board, a copy of the report of a survey carried out at the port of loading,
and a list of the crew. These requests were complied with to the extent to which
the documents then existed or were readily available; in particular certain further
statements and the crew list were sent. Messrs Ince were then asked for underwriters' decision. In November further statements were sent which had meanwhile
been taken and also notes of the master's previous experience. In late November
or early December Messrs Ince then asked for a number of prior survey reports and
for a copy of the charterparty. These were sent in early January 1973 and the position
about a mortgage on the ship was also explained. There was, as I understand, a
mortgage of £30,000, but I can see no immediate relevance in this. The plaintiffs'
solicitors again offered to discuss the position and pointed out that eight months had
by now elapsed since the casualty. Messrs Ince then asked for details relating to the
engagement of a new radio operator and also for certain information relating to the
profitability of the vessel and her previous charterparties. The information relating to
the radio operator was supplied and it was also stated, but without giving details,
that the charterparty had been reasonably profitable to date. In February 1973
Messrs Ince then insisted that this general statement should be particularised, and in

March they were supplied with a detailed breakdown showing the daily profit made
by the vessel under the charter. The plaintiffs' solicitors then pointed out that nine
months had by now passed and threatened the issue of a writ. Messrs Ince replied
that they needed still further time to consider the position. The plaintiffs' solicitors
were then instructed to issue a writ and the name of a representative underwriter
was put forward for this purpose. The writ in this action was issued on 5th April
1973 and the points of claim were served on 19th April, a little under a year since the
casualty. On 21st May Messrs Ince were asked to serve points of defence. On
29th May Messrs Ince asked for certain further and better particulars before defence.
The defendants' entitlement to further and better particulars before defence was
a matter which was also argued before me and it was agreed, without the necessity
for an order, that certain further and better particulars should be given. I need
not discuss these here, because although I think that the defendants were entitled
to some of them, they do not affect the issue concerning ship's papers, and no one
suggested they did,

Nothing then happened until 25th July when the present summons for an order for
ship's papers was issued by the defendants a few days before the Long Vacation. With
some difficulty a hearing was arranged for the last day of the legal year. It is clear
that this summons could have been taken out at any time after the issue of the writ
on 5th April. There had been no prior indication that an order for ship's papers
was going to be asked for; nor any suggestion of scuttling. On the application for
ship's papers the defendants stated for the first time through counsel that a plea of
scuttling was going to be made. In support of the application he gave certain reasons
why the defendants had decided to take this course. I think that he was quite right
to do so and that nothing he said caused any embarrassment to the defendants or
revealed anything to the plaintiffs which they did not already know or suppose as
being within the knowledge or belief of the insurers. Most of what he said would in
any event have to be pleaded by the defendants by way of particulars under the new
practice. In order to explain my conclusion on the present application it is necessary
that I should briefly refer to what he said. This cannot prejudice anyone, since it
will in any event be reflected in the pleadings or emerge at an early stage of the trial.

The facts which counsel for the defendants summarised were partly based on the
documents which had already been disclosed, in particular the substantial number of
statements of witnesses, and partly on the insurers' own investigations. He mentioned the following facts or contentions. The stranding occurred at a position
well north of what one would have expected the vessel's ordinary course to be and
while she was navigating through a narrow channel between Crete and the rocky
islet on which she stranded. There was no apparent reason for taking this northerly
course, but the master evidently claimed in his statement that this had been his
invariable practice on similar previous voyages. The defendants are in my view
clearly entitled to any documentary evidence which may exist and which either
supports or militates against this assertion. The plaintiffs' case is that the vessel
encountered squally weather conditions in this narrow channel, but the defendants
contend that this is not consistent with the meteorological information which they
have obtained independently. Next, the crew's statements which were disclosed
evidently claimed that the vessel had then been swept on to the rocks by three huge
waves. On the advice which the defendants have obtained from their experts
this is considered by them to be most unlikely, and they also contend that queries
and inconsistencies relating to the vessel's contemporary heading and engine
movements are apparent from the crew's statements. It is therefore clear that the
defendants and their advisers already have a great deal of information about the
circumstances or alleged circumstances of the casualty. The logs were lost by the
master when the crew got away from the ship.

Counsel for the defendants then turned to the other aspect of every scuttling case,
viz the question of the owners' privity. He said that the persons who were in reality

a
the owners, i e the moving spirits of the owning company, as well as the master, had a prior record of losses which was said to be material to the present claim. I must pause here for a moment to consider this contention in relation to an order for ship's papers. This information has presumably come to the underwriters either by way of general knowledge in the market or as the result of their own investigations. Since losses of ships usually result in some form of public enquiry it is often possible for marine underwriters and their advisers to obtain the reports and other documents

b
relating to such enquiries. On the other hand, further documents relating to these matters may also be or have been in the power or possession of the owners and the master or their agents. Whether or not they would fall within the ambit of Form 94 as it stands is doubtful. But, depending on the circumstances and their comparability with the present loss, it may well be right that the underwriters should have disclosure of some or all of such documents. However, whether or not they are so

c
entitled is not resolved by simply making an order in the terms of Form 94. This merely invites argument between the solicitors and the likelihood of the court being called on to make or refuse some further specific application at a later stage. There is therefore no point in postponing this process indefinitely. The right course is to exhort the parties to try to agree now as to what further documents or classes of documents are disclosable under this head, and, if they cannot agree, to come back to

d
the court as quickly as possible.

Finally counsel for the defendants mentioned that underwriters 'had a witness'. His identity and what he might be able to say in relation to the plea of scuttling were rightly not mentioned, though it was also clear that the existence or alleged existence of the witness was already known to the plaintiffs and their advisers. This again is not an unusual situation, but I need not say any more about it since it does

e
not add anything to the present position.

This then is the picture on the present summons. To return to Ord 72, r 10, the question for the court is now to decide what, in the interests of justice, it is necessary or expedient to do in these circumstances on the defendants' application for an order for ship's papers in the terms of Form 94 and for a stay meanwhile.

f
It seems to me, first, that this is properly to be described as a scuttling case, in the limited sense, of course, that I am satisfied on the general information put before the court that a plea of scuttling is justifiable. I am therefore also satisfied, for the reasons already given, that it is prima facie expedient and in accordance with the practice of the court that the insurers should be entitled to a wider range of discovery than the ordinary discovery afforded by the rules. On the other hand, having regard to the large amount of documentary material already disclosed, in particular

g
the statements of witnesses, and the large amount of information already available to the defendants from their own investigations, and also having regard to the long delay which has already occurred and the lateness of this application, I consider that it would be quite wrong at this stage merely to make an order for ship's papers in the terms of Form 94. This would merely be what I have already referred to as an

h
unthinking exercise. It would give to the defendants a formal order which would have great bargaining value in any negotiations for a settlement, but the contents and effect of the order would have little or no relevance to the necessity or expediency of the circumstances as required by the rule. It would also be wrong to order a stay, since the defendants already have ample material to plead their points of defence with adequate particulars. In this situation counsel for the plaintiffs submitted that

j
I should do no more than take the same course as that taken by Singleton J and approved by the Court of Appeal in *Keevil and Keevil Ltd v Boag*[1], viz to make no order but to give liberty to the defendants to apply for an affidavit of ship's papers hereafter if so advised. But that course was taken at a time when the predecessor to the present rule gave no discretion to the court except to make an order, if at all,

1 [1940] 3 All ER 346

in the terms of Form 94. The present rule gives a wider discretion and enables the
court in effect to consider and decide what documents or classes of documents should
be disclosed insofar as the parties may be at issue about this. In my view this is the
right line on which to proceed. The defendants' solicitors should as soon as possible
request the production of such further documents or classes of documents as they
consider to be material. The plaintiffs' solicitors should then consider such request
with equal expedition. In effect, the parties should therefore in the first instance try
to agree what should be the contents of an order for the balance of the ship's papers
at this stage. If and to the extent to which they cannot agree the matter should come
back to the court for decision. All the documents disclosed, whether in the past
or hereafter as the result of agreement or further order, should then be verified by
the plaintiffs on affidavit. There should be no stay meanwhile, and the defendants
should serve their points of defence within a time on which I will hear counsel. This
will also enable the plaintiffs' advisers to obtain further statements from their witnesses on the basis of the allegations put forward in the points of defence without the
lengthy delay which would otherwise elapse before these are put on paper. It
should then be open to either party to apply for a date for the trial. The trial has
every prospect of being lengthy, with witnesses having to be assembled from abroad.
A date should therefore be fixed well in advance. The kind of time-table which I
have in mind as appearing reasonable at the present stage is that any dispute about
the disclosure of documents should be resolved during the present term and that
a date for trial should then be obtained either for the autumn of next year or early
in 1975. The production and disclosure of the remaining documents should then
take place during this waiting period, and if necessary further applications can be
made to the court if difficulties arise. In this way the action can come to trial within
a reasonable time instead of being dragged out more or less indefinitely. Having
indicated in general terms the course which the action should, in my view, now take,
the formal result of my judgment is accordingly that I make no order on the
defendants' application save that they have liberty to apply.

No order but defendants to have liberty to apply. Leave to appeal if desired.

12th October. Kerr J ordered (i) that time for notice of appeal be extended for three
weeks from the date when the transcript of his judgment was available and (ii) that
time for service of points of defence be extended for the same period of three weeks
but if notice of appeal was served within three weeks of the availability of the transcript of his judgment (and on the defendants undertaking to prosecute the appeal
with due speed) time for service of points of defence be extended to three weeks
from determination of the appeal.

Solicitors: *Ince & Co* (for the defendants); *Holman, Fenwick & Willan* (for the plaintiffs).

E H Hunter Esq Barrister.

Interlocutory appeal

The defendants appealed from (i) so much of the judgment of Kerr J[1] given on 2nd
October 1973 as adjudged that the defendants were not entitled to an immediate order
for ship's papers and a stay of proceedings pending the plaintiffs' compliance with the
order, and (ii) so much of the order of Kerr J made on 12th October 1973 as ordered
that the defendants serve points of defence within three weeks of the availability of
the transcript of judgment.

Michael Mustill QC and *Kenneth Rokison* for the defendants.
R A MacCrindle QC and *Nicholas Phillips* for the plaintiffs.

---

1 See p 479, ante

Cur adv vult

a 15th March. The following judgments were read.

LORD DENNING MR. On 29th April 1972 the vessel Sageorge ran on to the rocks of a small island near Crete. She became a total loss, but the wreck is still there. She was insured for £75,000. Her owners claim against the underwriters for the loss. The underwriters have not paid. They say that the vessel was scuttled.

b On 5th April 1973 the owners issued a writ. They delivered points of claim for loss by perils of the sea, and gave some particulars as asked. The underwriters have not yet delivered their points of defence. They ask for an order for ship's papers in the form appended to RSC Ord 72, r 10; and that, meanwhile, all further proceedings be stayed. The underwriters recognise that, in due course, when they deliver their points of defence, then, if they allege therein that the vessel was scuttled or words

c to that effect, they will be bound to give the best particulars they can of that allegation. That was settled in *Astrovlanis Compania Naviera SA v Linard*[1] and *The Dias*[2]. But, before delivering the defence, the underwriters seek discovery of 'ship's papers'.

In all ordinary actions a defendant is not allowed discovery before delivering his defence. He must first put in his defence and then apply afterwards for discovery.

d It was so held by Jessel MR shortly after the enactment of the Judicature Acts: see *Disney v Longbourne*[3]. The usual form of pleading is that the defendant cannot give particulars—or further particulars—until after discovery. But for many years marine insurance has been an exception. It arose in the days of sailing ships, when an action was brought on a policy in the courts of King's Bench or Common Pleas (which sat in Westminster Hall), and the attorneys for the underwriters used to hurry down to the bottom end of the hall and up the stairs to the Court

e of Exchequer. That court had jurisdiction in equity. There the attorneys used to apply for and obtain an order for discovery of ship's papers; and, furthermore, an order for a stay of the proceedings in the King's Bench or Common Pleas until such discovery was given. That caused a great deal of delay, expense and litigation. In order to obviate this, the judges of the King's Bench and Common Pleas from about 1800 took it on themselves to make an order for ship's papers and a stay

f meanwhile. That appears from the report of *Goldschmidt v Marryat*[4]. The practice thus established was continued after the Judicature Acts: see *West of England Bank v Canton Insurance Co*[5]. In 1881 Brett LJ[6] gave this justification for it:

> 'The underwriters have no means of knowing how a loss was caused; it occurs abroad and when the ship is entirely under the control of the assured. In
g > addition to this the contract of insurance is made, in peculiar terms, on behalf of the assured himself and all persons interested, and who these persons are, especially at the time of the loss, is entirely unknown to the underwriters.'

In 1898 the practice was extended so as to enable a re-insurer to get an order for ship's papers: see *China Traders' Insurance Co v Royal Exchange Assurance Corpn*[7]. In 1932

h it was held to apply to marine policies with land risks; so that, when an insurance contained a warehouse-to-warehouse clause—and the loss occurred on land—an order for ship's papers was made: see *Leon v Casey*[8]. It was in that case that Greer LJ made severe criticism of the practice. He said[9]:

---

1   [1972] 2 All ER 647, [1972] 2 QB 611
2   [1972] 2 All ER 1112, [1972] 2 QB 625
j 3   (1876) 2 Ch D 704
4   (1809) 1 Camp 559
5   (1877) 2 Ex D 472
6   See *China Transpacific Steamship Co v Commercial Union Assurance Co* (1881) 8 QBD 142 at 145
7   [1898] 2 QB 187
8   [1932] 2 KB 576, [1932] All ER Rep 484
9   [1932] 2 KB at 588, [1932] All ER Rep at 490

'. . . the order for ship's papers was invented at a time when it was necessary   *a*
in order to do justice to the case of the insurer; it has now become an unfair and
unjust weapon in the hands of the insurer.'

His criticisms had effect. In 1936 the Rules of Court were amended (by Ord 31,
r 12A) so as to enable a judge to refuse an order for ship's papers unless he was satisfied
that it was 'necessary or expedient' and also giving him a complete discretion as to
whether he should order a stay, or not.   *b*

Soon after that amendment, there was *Keevil and Keevil Ltd v Boag*[1]. A consignment of eggs was damaged by excess of damp in the ship's hold. An order for
ship's papers was refused. Goddard LJ said[2] it showed 'how fortunate it is that
the rule has been altered'. Since that time it has been very rare for an order
for ship's papers to be made save when the underwriters say that they are going to
allege that the vessel was scuttled. In such a case we are told that an order for   *c*
'ship's papers' is still made and a stay meanwhile. There is no scuttling case in which
it has been refused.

The time has now come for the practice to be revised, even in scuttling cases. It
should be brought up to date. It arose in the days of sailing ships when underwriters
in Lloyd's Coffee House were completely in the dark as to the loss of the vessel.
It is not appropriate in the present day when underwriters at Lloyd's get information   *d*
as soon as anyone of a loss, and of the circumstances in which it occurred. The order
itself is in a form which is appended to the Rules of Court. But this form is so long,
so full of repetitive detail, and so obscure that it must have been drafted by a con-
veyancer in the days when payment was so much a folio. The only people who
know how it works are the few firms of solicitors in the City of London who handle
these cases. The claimant has to produce not only his own documents but also those   *e*
of many other people, all over the face of the globe, or else show that he has made
reasonable endeavours to find them, and has failed. The cost of it all may run into
thousands of pounds. The time taken may be months and months. It may be
that in the haystack of paper, the defendants may find a needle which will enable
them to draw blood. But, this is a very remote chance. It is not sufficient to justify
the burden which this order puts on the plaintiff. He may find it so onerous that he   *f*
will settle at any price rather than be harassed further. I do not say that it has
happened. But it is open to abuse. So it must be remedied.

The singular feature about an order for ship's papers is that it is an order on the
plaintiff to give discovery of documents before the defendant delivers his defence.
This feature should be retained. In scuttling cases it may still serve a useful purpose.
When a shipowner claims on a policy for loss by perils of the sea, he will be anxious   *g*
that the underwriters should admit his claim as soon as may be. He will, therefore,
or at any rate should, produce all papers that are relevant to his claim; and, in
addition, all other papers that the underwriters reasonably ask to see. If he does not
do so, but instead goes ahead with his action, it will be open to the defendants to apply
for an order for ship's papers before defence. But the order should not be made
automatically. The judge should see whether or not it is a proper case for it. For   *h*
this purpose counsel should put before the judge the reasons for it. Counsel will
not, of course, disclose any material which would be privileged or which it would be
inadvisable to mention. But he should give such reasons as he can properly disclose
without embarrassment or giving away too much of his client's case. That is what
Kerr J suggested[3], and I agree with it. If the reasons are such as to warrant an order
for discovery before defence, the judge will make it.   *j*

If the order is made, it may be made in the form appended to RSC Ord 72, r 10. But
I venture to suggest that it might be shortened so as to require the plaintiff to disclose

1   [1940] 3 All ER 346
2   [1940] 3 All ER at 348
3   Page 485, ante

a   all documents relating to the insurance of the ship and cargo, and to the adventure on which she was engaged, which are or have been in the possession or power of the plaintiff and any persons interested in such insurance and adventure. In order to comply with this order, the plaintiff must apply to the persons interested and get the documents, if he can, or else show that he is unable to get them. If the defendants are not satisfied with the documents disclosed, they can make a request for specific documents; and if it is refused, apply to the judge.

b   So much for the order for ship's papers. But should the plaintiff's action be stayed until he complies with the order? Under the old practice before 1936 the action was automatically stayed until the order was complied with. Under the rules now, it is in the discretion of the judge whether to order a stay, or not. In exercising this discretion, it is important that the action should not be unduly delayed pending the discovery. After all, if the defendants have sufficient reason for alleging scuttling,

c   they should have sufficient material to plead it in their defence, and to give particulars of it. Accordingly, as Kerr J said[1]: '... in many, if not in most, cases, it may be much more sensible to refuse a stay.' The defendants should deliver their defence, giving the best particulars they can at that stage: and then give further particulars after the discovery has been had, or, if need be, amending the defence after discovery. But, on the other hand, there may be some cases where the plaintiff has been so unco-

d   operative and so unforthcoming that the judge may feel it proper to stay the action until he does give the discovery that is asked.

I would, therefore, endorse the principles stated by the judge; and I agree with his application of them in the present case. I would dismiss the appeal.

e   **BUCKLEY LJ** (read by Roskill LJ). I agree. It is with great diffidence that I offer any observations of my own, for my experience of marine insurance litigation is negligible compared to that of Lord Denning MR and with that of Roskill LJ, both of whose judgments I have had the advantage of reading.

An order for ship's papers is an order for discovery which is exceptional in at least two respects: first, it is not confined to documents which are or have been in the

f   possession or control of the plaintiff, but extends or, as we were told, is treated by practitioners as extending to almost any document capable of throwing the smallest light on the possible fate of the ship, the production of which the plaintiff might be able to procure in whosever possession or control the document may be; and secondly, it is customarily made before delivery of defence. The genesis of this type of order was clearly the difficulty under which defendant insurers were in days

g   when means of communication were very limited and it was consequently very hard for them to obtain reliable information about the relevant facts. Nowadays circumstances are very different. The telephone and the aeroplane have to a great extent contracted distances and abbreviated time. In these days the need for such discovery as is procured by means of an order for ship's papers seems to me to be much less than in the past. But there may well still be cases in which the order will serve a

h   useful purpose, and it should not be forgotten that in scuttling cases the physical evidence may be at the bottom of the sea and therefore inaccessible.

In my judgment it is the duty of a judge, who is asked to make an order for ship's papers, to weigh the advantages which may result in the search for truth against the disadvantages of delay and expense involved in discovery of this kind. That delay and expense may be very substantial. If the judge considers that the advantages

j   outweigh the disadvantages, he will make an order for ship's papers; but otherwise, in my opinion, he should not, notwithstanding that the defendants indicate that they intend to plead scuttling. It goes without saying that the judge should not make such an order if he has reason to suppose that it is being sought as a means of extorting a settlement.

1 Page 486, ante

Whether on an application for ship's papers counsel should disclose to the court
the grounds on which a plea of scuttling is proposed to be put forward must, in
my opinion, be a question for counsel to decide. The circumstances of the case may
be such that the judge is unlikely to make an order for ship's papers without some
indication of the kind of suspicions entertained by the defendants. In such a case
counsel may consider it desirable to tell the court the nature of his client's suspicions.
If he chooses to disclose any evidence that may be known to his clients, that is a matter
for him. If by the words[1] 'counsel for the insurers should always give some sufficient
indication to the court of the justifiability of the plea before any question of a prima
facie entitlement to an order for ship's papers can arise' the learned judge meant
something more than this, I venture to think that he went too far. It cannot, I think,
be right to require counsel to disclose his client's case at an interlocutory stage in the
action and more particularly before pleadings are closed, but counsel may very
possibly feel able to indicate the nature of the defendants' belief or suspicions without
making any undesirable disclosure and he may think that to do so will assist him in
his application for an order for ship's papers. The court should not, I think, readily
suppose that an experienced and responsible counsel would associate himself with an
allegation of scuttling—a grave charge of fraud—without sufficient reason; but some
indication of the basis of the allegation may well be necessary for deciding what kind
of discovery of documents would fit the case.

Whether, where an order for ship's papers is made, it should be accompanied by a
stay until the order has been complied with, is a matter which must rest in the
discretion of the judge and depends on the particular facts of the case. RSC Ord 72,
r 10(2), so provides. The circumstances that the defendants may be called on to give
particulars of their plea of scuttling does not, in my opinion, necessarily mean that
they should not be required to plead before an order for ship's papers had been fully
complied with. Particulars can be given or amended at any stage in the proceedings
before or even at the trial, if the circumstances justify this course.

To one who is unaccustomed to marine insurance litigation the form of order for
ship's papers which is to be found in Form 94 in Appendix A to the Rules of the
Supreme Court appears a strange document. We were told that when an order is
made in this form practitioners pay little attention to its actual terms but know what
practical effect the order is intended to have. This seems to me to be a regrettable
state of affairs. An order of the court should be framed in language which is intelligible and which expresses the intention of the court. It should be possible to say
whether it has been obeyed in accordance with its spirit by reading its language. I
think that Form 94 merits revision. The learned judge in the course of his very
careful judgment said[2]:

'The relative uselessness of the general wording of Form 94 is also illustrated
by the fact that in many applications for ship's papers counsel for the insurers
readily agree that if an order is made it may be more helpful, instead of making
it in the terms of form 94, for the parties to try to agree on a form of order containing classes of documents which are really relevant to the particular facts of
the case.'

This sounds to me, if I may say so, to be eminently sensible. Later in his judgment
after referring to the course taken in *Keevil and Keevil Ltd v Boag*[3], the learned judge
pointed out that at the time of that decision the predecessor of the present rule gave
no discretion to the court except to make an order, if at all, in the terms of Form 94.
He went on[4]:

'The present rule gives a wider discretion and enables the court in effect to

1 Page 485, ante
2 Page 488, ante
3 [1940] 3 All ER 346
4 Page 492, ante

consider and decide what documents or classes of documents should be disclosed insofar as the parties may be at issue about this. In my view this is the right line on which to proceed. The defendants' solicitors should as soon as possible request the production of such further documents or classes of documents as they consider to be material. The plaintiffs' solicitors should then consider such request with equal expedition. In effect, the parties should therefore in the first instance try to agree what should be the contents of an order for the balance of ship's papers at this stage. If and to the extent to which they cannot agree the matter should come back to the court for decision. All the documents disclosed, whether in the past or hereafter as the result of agreement or further order, should then be verified by the plaintiffs on affidavit. There should be no stay meanwhile and the defendants should serve their points of defence within a time on which I will hear counsel.'

In my judgment, that was a very sensible and practical way in which to deal with the present case. I would consequently dismiss this appeal.

ROSKILL LJ. This is an appeal by the defendant underwriters against the refusal of Kerr J[1] on 2nd October 1973 to grant an application made by the underwriters for an affidavit of ship's papers in the terms prescribed in Form 94 of Appendix A, pursuant to RSC Ord 72, r 10. The learned judge gave leave to appeal against his refusal in order that the matters to which this appeal gives rise may be ventilated in this court. The plaintiffs are a Cyprus-registered company who were at the material time the owners of a small ship named Sageorge. That vessel stranded off the south-east corner of Crete on 29th April 1972. The plaintiffs claim a total loss under a policy of insurance on her hull underwritten by (amongst other underwriters) the defendants. The defendants by their counsel have informed the learned judge that they intend to allege that the vessel was wilfully cast away, that is to say 'scuttled'. Points of claim have been delivered by the plaintiffs. Points of defence alleging scuttling have not yet been delivered by the defendants.

This appeal represents yet another step in what might be described as the saecular struggle between shipowners' defence clubs and hull and cargo underwriters regarding the practice and procedure to be adopted in the Commercial Court in interlocutory proceedings in cases of alleged scuttling. The former recently obtained a victory over the latter in two successive appeals to this court, regarding the giving of particulars of an allegation of scuttling by underwriters: see *Astrovlanis Compania Naviera SA v Linard*[2] and *The Dias*[3]. In each of those cases this court by a majority ordered underwriters to give particulars of the allegations of scuttling there made in the points of defence.

Early in his admirably clear and helpful judgment in the present case Kerr J[4] drew attention to a passage in the judgment of Greer LJ in *Leon v Casey*[5] in which the learned Lord Justice strongly criticised the then state of the law which entitled underwriters when sued by their assured on a policy of marine insurance to obtain as of right an affidavit of ship's papers. Greer LJ said[6]:

'... I cannot help thinking that those members of the profession, who both at the Bar and on the Bench have been largely engaged in matters of marine insurance, have come to believe that the rules which have hitherto been applied in marine insurance are those which ought to be applied, and that the law as it

1 Page 479, ante
2 [1972] 2 All ER 647, [1972] 2 QB 611
3 [1972] 2 All ER 1112, [1972] 2 QB 625
4 Page 481, ante
5 [1932] 2 KB 576 at 587-589, [1932] All ER Rep 484 at 490, 491
6 [1932] 2 KB at 588, 589, [1932] All ER Rep at 490

stands is incapable of improvement. I take a very different view. In my opinion the order for ship's papers was invented at a time when it was necessary in order to do justice to the case of the insurer; it has now become an unfair and unjust weapon in the hands of the insurer. I have known of case after case in the Commercial List where defendants, who had no real defence, have been enabled by means of this instrument of oppression to keep plaintiffs out of their insurance money for long periods of time; and I regret that the Court has not felt itself justified in holding a tighter hand upon this practice than it has done.'

Those strong words of the learned Lord Justice did not fall on deaf ears. In 1936 the Rules of the Supreme Court were altered. By a new RSC Ord 31, r 12A, a discretion was given to the commercial judge whether he would order an affidavit of ship's papers or not. As counsel for the plaintiffs pointed out, hitherto there had been no relevant rule of the Supreme Court. The matter was treated as one of substantive law and practice dating back to at least the latter part of the 18th century. The only other case which has come to this court regarding affidavits of ship's papers since *Leon v Casey*[1] is *Keevil and Keevil Ltd v Boag*[2].

I hope I have at all times borne Greer LJ's warning well in mind particularly as Kerr J went on to criticise the more modern practice whereunder, according to him, some judges now or formerly in charge of the commercial list are alleged almost automatically to have exercised the discretion now accorded to them under RSC Ord 72, r 10, and previously accorded by its predecessor, in favour of ordering such an affidavit merely on being told by counsel for underwriters that it was intended to plead scuttling by way of defence to a claim for total loss on a hull or cargo policy of marine insurance. If it be the fact that some judges have shown what in the court below counsel for the plaintiffs is reported[3] as having called 'some kind of automatic Pavlovian reaction' to such a statement by counsel, the criticism of Kerr J is well justified, for the exercise of a judicial discretion must never be automatic; still less must it ever be allowed to be Pavlovian. Counsel for the plaintiffs before this court reinforced this criticism by urging that the attitude of the courts in recent years in relation to questions of ship's papers was still largely influenced by the practice of former times, and ignored the fact that the modern RSC Ord 72, r 10, and its predecessors conferred a wide discretion on the court, the existence of which had in practice been ignored. He claimed that the judgment of Kerr J represented what he called a milestone in the march of progress from the rigidity of former times.

Kerr J not only refused to order an affidavit of ship's papers but he also refused, for the time being, to make any other order for discovery as RSC Ord 72, r 10, empowered him to do. He also refused to stay the action. He invited the parties through their respective experienced solicitors to reach agreement on what further documents beyond those already vouchsafed by the plaintiffs should be disclosed. But whilst refusing the order, he made it plain in an observation[4] at the end of his judgment, that in his view the defendants were entitled to the same protection as an order for ship's papers of some kind would give. He also made it plain that if his suggested proposal for agreement did not bear fruit, the parties should return to him and he would then consider what further order to make.

The real problem in the present appeal seems to me to arise from the learned judge's refusal to order a stay of the action pending agreement between the two parties what discovery should now be given, or, failing such agreement pending compliance with any order for ship's papers or other discovery which, in furtherance of what I have just said, the learned judge might ultimately make. Before the two recent cases to which I have just referred, which decided that underwriters must

1   [1932] 2 KB 576, [1932] All ER Rep 484
2   [1940] 3 All ER 346
3   Page 485, ante
4   Page 491, ante

—at any rate in most cases—give particulars of a plea of alleged scuttling, it was by no means unknown for the commercial judge, whilst ordering an affidavit of ship's papers to be made by a plaintiff, to refuse a stay of the action, so that the points of defence with a plea of scuttling in the old form were delivered before the plaintiff had complied with the order for ship's papers. Since no particulars of scuttling had then to be given, underwriters were rarely worse off since within that plea of scuttling in the old form they could later make use in cross-examination at the trial of any information derived from the documents disclosed after the points of defence had been filed.

But since the change in the practice regarding particulars, it is said that if underwriters have to give particulars of scuttling—at any rate to the extent suggested by Buckley LJ in *The Dias*[1]—it is wrong that they should be made to plead scuttling with appropriate particulars until an affidavit of ship's papers has been ordered and delivered or at least until an order for more limited discovery has been made and complied with. Otherwise it is said something may emerge from the documents ultimately disclosed which will necessitate amendments and reamendments to the first version of the points of defence.

It should be observed, as Buckley LJ pointed out during the argument, that in any other type of case where a defendant charges fraud against a plaintiff, the defendant is nearly always at a disadvantage until he sees the plaintiff's documents. Yet the mere existence of a plea of fraud has not hitherto been regarded in the ordinary Queen's Bench action as sufficient justification for ordering discovery before defence. Moreover in an action on a non-marine policy of insurance where the defence is fraud, it is unusual though not impossible for the defendant underwriter to obtain discovery before defence. To this extent the marine underwriter has for some 200 years been in a privileged position. The reason for this is largely historic as counsel for the plaintiffs pointed out and many of the reasons which originally justified the privilege have disappeared with the passage of time. Rapid communication with distant scenes of strange and apparently inexplicable marine casualties were, until comparatively recently, difficult if not impossible. Now it is an everyday occurrence. At least as useful and perhaps far more useful information regarding a possibly suspicious loss can be quickly obtained by the swift despatch of a highly skilled solicitor specialising in this work to the other side of the world than by waiting for some months or even years for a supposed cornucopia of documents to be derived from an affidavit of ship's papers sworn and delivered at some much later date.

Nonetheless I have some sympathy with the attitude of underwriters in these cases without I hope being guilty of the mental attitude complained of by Greer LJ in the passage quoted or any of the offences which counsel for the plaintiffs attributed to the commercial judges of more recent times. Ships are from time to time scuttled. So are cargoes. There are plenty of examples of scuttled ships found recorded in the reports between about 1920 and 1970. Where suspicious losses arise, it is not easy for underwriters to probe or ascertain the truth. Their enquiries may sometimes run up against the blank wall of the dishonest who hope by silence to avoid detection. In such a case, especially where the facts are all within the knowledge of the assured, his servants or agents, the requirement of the affidavit of ship's papers may be an invaluable weapon to help seek out the truth. In such a case I think the commercial judge should not hesitate to exercise his discretion to order such an affidavit and to order it before defence if he thinks it is right to do so and to back his order by a stay if he thinks that right as well. After all, whatever may be said against affidavits of ship's papers, the provisions which now appear in RSC Ord 72, r 10, have survived the changes of 1964 and the futher changes of 1971. Those provisions cannot be ignored. So long as those provisions exist, underwriters are entitled to invite the court to make use of them to underwriters' advantage in a suitable case and a court has a far reaching

---

1   [1972] 2 All ER at 1125, [1972] 2 QB at 645

discretion whether or not in a particular case to order an affidavit of ship's papers o
whether to order more limited discovery, and whether to do either before defenc
and whether to back any such order by a stay.

Cases of alleged scuttling vary infinitely. There are ships which disappear with o
without sufficient explanation. There are ships which strand with or without suffici
cient explanation. Ships sometimes suffer mysterious explosions or are the victims o
unexplained fires. I do not think it possible to lay down hard and fast rules how th
judicial discretion should be exercised in these cases. For my part I would, as I hav
already said, accept that there should never be an automatic order for ship's paper
merely because scuttling is alleged. Nor should there be an automatic stay even wher
a judge makes an order for an affidavit of ship's papers or makes a more limited orde
for discovery whether before defence or not. In this respect I find myself in entir
agreement with Kerr J[1]. Where a ship sinks or is burned out there may (I stress th
word 'may') be a stronger case for an order for an affidavit of ship's papers than wher
she strands and physical investigation of the wreck remains practicable. Much wil
depend on what documents an assured has already voluntarily vouchsafed to under
writers before or immediately after the issue of the writ in the action.

Clearly an affidavit of ship's papers must never be allowed to become a weapo
of oppression nor used to attempt to force a settlement on an impoverished plaintif
shipowner. The learned judge suggests that both these are still possibilities even to
day. If that be right it is regrettable and should never be tolerated by the commercia
judge. I must confess, however, that my own experience (for what it is worth and it i
far less recent than Kerr J's) does not in this respect accord with his. Nor would
accept that underwriters do not derive benefit from documents disclosed as a resul
of the order for an affidavit of ship's papers. Surprising details often emerge on th
disclosure of documents which become a valuable weapon in the armoury of counse
cross-examining the plaintiffs' witnesses on behalf of underwriters at the trial. No
are the figures given[2] by the learned judge in his judgment in line with those vouch
safed to us by counsel for the defendants. He informed us on instructions that in th
last 15 years Lloyd's claims department had handled 5,738 total loss cases. Of these
only 100 had been referred to solicitors. Of those 100, orders for an affidavit of ship'
papers had only been made in 17 cases. Of those 17 cases we were told two went fo
trial. Underwriters won each. One was struck out, two were abandoned, six wer
settled and six were still pending. If this information was accurate the learned judge'
estimate—no doubt based on his own recollection—that over the last 15 years some
thing of the order of two to five applications for ship's papers had come before th
commercial judge annually is not, with great respect to him, correct. Further it i
perhaps worth recording that there have been cases other than scuttling cases, sinc
the last war, in which affidavits of ship's papers have been ordered, as for exampl
where a defence of non-disclosure has been raised. But these criticisms, though validl
made by counsel for the defendants, are of the detail of the learned judge's judgment
They are not criticisms of the substance of that judgment.

The real question is how the judge's discretion should be exercised in principle an
whether Kerr J exercised his discretion properly in the present case. It seems to me
as I have already said, that he intended to give the defendants the practical benefit o
an order for ship's papers, but in the first instance by means of a suggested agreemen
to be reached between the solicitors involved with the sanction of an order in th
background, all this to be done without a stay. The learned judge recorded[3] what ha
passed to date between the solicitors for the parties regarding discovery of documents
He laid some stress on the extent of the documents which had already been mad
available to underwriters' solicitors. It does not appear from the judgment whethe

---

1 Page 486, ante
2 Page 483, ante
3 Pages 489, 490, ante

CA   Probatina Shipping v Sun Insurance (Roskill LJ)   501

or not the learned judge actually saw copies of these documents to which he refers. I would opine he did not. But in the course of his reply, counsel for the defendants showed us copies of those documents. I feel bound to say that they are extremely sketchy and in content and substance considerably less than one would expect to be disclosed in an affidavit of ship's papers even by the owners of a comparatively small and not particularly valuable ship.

The question therefore arises whether it is unjust to require underwriters to plead with the best particulars which they can give before they obtain further documents? If I thought that it was unjust or if I thought that it was impossible for anything but the sketchiest defence to be pleaded without more documents, I would not hesitate to order an affidavit of ship's papers and to back that order with a stay if necessary. But somewhat sketchy as the documents previously disclosed are, I do not think that the present is such a case. Leave to supplement the particulars or to amend them should always readily be given where the information sought to be pleaded has only subsequently come to light.

I think a crucial question—not necessarily the only question—which the commercial judge should ask himself is not (with all respect to Kerr J) whether there is a prima facie case for pleading scuttling but whether when the application for ship's papers is made, the plaintiffs have already voluntarily given sufficient disclosure of documents whether before or after action brought. If they have I see no reason why in such cases the points of defence should not be delivered with the best particulars then available. But if the plaintiffs have not, then I think a judge can and should order further discovery either in Form 94 or in such other form as he thinks fit, as for example by ordering discovery of specific classes of documents with or without stay. If therefore a plaintiff wants to avoid the risk of an order for ship's papers and the attendant delay and expense, he will be wise in most cases (especially if he is completely innocent) to disclose everything as early as possible and perhaps even more than he is strictly obliged to disclose even under an affidavit of ship's papers.

Where I most respectfully but emphatically part company with the learned judge is when in his judgment he said[1]:

'I therefore consider that counsel for the insurers should always give some sufficient indication to the court of the justifiability of the plea before any question of a prima facie entitlement to an order for ship's papers can arise. Otherwise the court is in the dark as to what may be necessary or expedient in the particular case ...'

At the end of his judgment he said[2]:

'... I am satisfied on the general information put before the court that a plea of scuttling is justifiable. I am therefore also satisfied, for the reasons already given, that it is prima facie expedient in accordance with the practice of the court that the insurers should be entitled to a wider range of discovery than the ordinary discovery afforded by the rules.'

I cannot, with great respect, think that it can be right for counsel for underwriters to be obliged as distinct from volunteering to tell the court what his view is about the strength (for that is what it amounts to) of the intended plea of scuttling. For him to be required to do so comes near to infringing the fundamental rules of privilege. Counsel may in the course of his application choose to tell the commercial judge what the factual foundation for the plea of scuttling is in order to make his application for ship's papers or for discovery more attractive to the learned judge; but that must be a matter for him without becoming in any way obligatory for him to do so.

---

1   Page 485, ante
2   Page 491, ante

For the commercial judge to use the language I have quoted above from the judgment[1], is, with respect, susceptible of giving a plaintiff shipowner, were he to be sitting in the back of the court during the hearing of the summons, the impression that the judge was not only prejudging the crucial issue but was prejudging it against him. After all, scuttling is a criminal offence and to say that there is a prima facie case for pleading scuttling means, if stated in terms of the criminal law, that if the plaintiff had been appropriately charged, the evidence justified committal for trial. I cannot think that that is right nor did counsel for the plaintiffs seek to support that part of the learned judge's judgment. For my part, I was unaware that the practice of requiring this information from counsel for underwriters had grown up. If it has, it is, so far as I am aware, recent and I venture to think it ought not to be continued. It is unfair to a plaintiff and it puts counsel for underwriters into a difficult if not impossible position where underwriters have some genuine grounds for suspicion which at the time of the summons seem likely to fall short of ultimate proof but which may well later be reinforced by some documents still to be disclosed by the plaintiff.

The only matter which has given me cause for hesitation in this case is the sketchiness of the documents hitherto disclosed by the plaintiffs. These, as I have already said, fall far short of what could reasonably be required of a plaintiff under an affidavit of ship's papers. It is therefore incumbent on the plaintiffs, if the learned judge's present order is to stand, rapidly to comply with any reasonable request made by the solicitors for underwriters for documents or classes of documents to be furnished as soon as possible. On the whole, I think the learned judge on the facts of this case was entitled to exercise his discretion as he did and I for my part would not wish to interfere with that discretion. But if the agreement suggested by the learned judge is not readily and satisfactorily forthcoming, the learned judge will no doubt not hesitate to make an order for ship's papers or other discovery in such terms as he thinks fit and to back that order with a stay at some later stage of the proceedings. The defendants are entitled to the fullest discovery. It is the duty of the court to see that they should have it. But I see no reason why, again on the facts of this case, they should not deliver their pleading in the near future. Counsel for the defendants made plain to the learned judge what the basic facts were which led the underwriters to allege scuttling. Those can without difficulty be sufficiently incorporated at this stage into particulars of scuttling.

Many harsh things have been said during the hearing of this appeal about Form 94. It has come under attack both from counsel for the defendants and from counsel for the plaintiffs. That the form is archaic cannot be doubted. That it requires a plaintiff to disclose more than he would be required to disclose under an ordinary order for discovery equally cannot be doubted. Curiously enough, it also makes less wide provision for discovery than is sometimes given by plaintiffs in pursuance of an order for an affidavit of ship's papers. I feel bound to say that I think most of the criticisms are justified. But when RSC Ord 72, r 10, was introduced in 1964, Form 94 was deliberately retained in its present form, though the form seems to have been altered from time to time during the last 40 or 50 years. If the form is thought to be defective by those engaged in marine insurance cases, I do not doubt that the rules committee of the Supreme Court would be willing to consider its revision if asked so to do. If in a particular case a judge is of the opinion that Form 94 is unsatisfactory, RSC Ord 72, r 10, empowers him to make such other order as he thinks right and in appropriate cases he can either order ordinary discovery or discovery of specific classes of documents.

For these reasons I think Kerr J exercised his discretion correctly and I would not interfere with that exercise. I would therefore dismiss the appeal.

Appeal dismissed.

Solicitors: *Ince & Co* (for the defendants); *Holman, Fenwick & Willan* (for the plaintiffs).

Wendy Shockett   Barrister.

---

1   Page 485, ante

George Ballantine & Son Ltd and others
v F E R Dixon & Son Ltd and others

CHANCERY DIVISION
WALTON J
21st MARCH 1974

Discovery – Production of documents – Similar transactions – Relevance – Discovery directed solely to credit – Passing-off action – Allegation in statement of claim that defendant supplied Scotch whisky to importers in specified countries for admixture with local spirits – Admixture passed off in those countries as genuine Scotch whisky – Application by plaintiffs for discovery of other documents alleged to relate to similar transactions in other countries and in connection with other spirits – Evidence of defendants' knowledge of and complicity in activities of foreign importers – Whether discovery should be ordered.

The plaintiffs, well-known blenders and exporters of Scotch whisky, brought an action against the defendants alleging that they were passing off goods by supplying Scotch whisky, together with bottles, cartons, closures, labels and other similar incidents, to importers in Greece, Spain, Guatemala, Lebanon and Cyprus, who then diluted the original genuine Scotch whisky with locally produced spirits and sold the resultant admixture under such a get-up as to lead the general public in those countries to imagine that it was genuine Scotch whisky. The defence was that the defendants were simply suppliers of Scotch whisky; that they had no direct control over the importers in the countries concerned to whom they sold the whisky; that they had always traded honestly and at all times used their best endeavours to prevent their customers from using any trade mark, brand name, advertisement or get-up which could be misleading. In their statement of claim, the plaintiffs complained of 13 get-ups in the five countries named. In an affidavit sworn on behalf of the plaintiffs it was stated that they believed that the defendants were 'involved in the admixture trade ... in other countries of the world, and also, in the 5 countries in question, under other get-ups; and also in respect of spirits other than Scotch Whisky'. Alleging that the defendants' case was that they had at all times traded honestly, the affidavit stated that the plaintiffs believed that the documents in the defendants' possession relating to that trading and, in particular, relating to the adoption of the get-ups in question, and the steps which the defendants had taken to see that the admixed end-product was not being used improperly, were material to the issues in the case, on the ground that the intentions and conduct, honourable or otherwise, of the defendants in relation to all their other business was relevant to the intentions and honesty of the conduct of their business in relation to the five countries of which complaint was specifically made. Accordingly the plaintiffs applied to the court for discovery of those documents.

Held – The application should be dismissed since it was directed exclusively to credit in that it was simply and solely directed towards putting the plaintiffs in a position to assert that, since the defendants had been guilty of dishonest trading in one country, they were the sort of people who would trade dishonestly in the five countries in question. Even if the conclusion that, as a matter of strict law, the proposed discovery ought not to be allowed was wrong, it should not, as a matter of discretion, be allowed since it was not necessary either for disposing fairly of the action or for saving costs but would, on the contrary, be oppressive and entail additional costs (see p 509 g to j, post).

Kennedy v Dodson [1895] 1 Ch 334 applied.

Notes

For the circumstances in which discovery will be granted, see 12 Halsbury's Laws
(3rd Edn) 2-8, paras 1-8, and for cases on the subject, see 18 Digest (Repl) 9-19, 48-133.

Cases referred to in judgment

Compagnie Financière et Commerciale du Pacifique v Peruvian Guano Co (1882) 11 QBD
55, 52 LJQB 181, 48 LT 22, CA, 18 Digest (Repl) 42, *334.*
Kennedy v Dodson [1895] 1 Ch 334, 64 LJCh 257, 72 LT 172, CA, 18 Digest (Repl) 176,
1516.

Procedure summons

This was an application by the plaintiffs, George Ballantine & Son Ltd, John Dewar
& Sons Ltd and John Walker & Sons Ltd, for discovery of certain documents in a
passing-off action brought by the plaintiffs against the defendants, F E R Dixon &
Son Ltd, The House of Dixon Ltd and Sornbeg Blending Co Ltd. The facts are set
out in the judgment.

Donald Nicholls for the plaintiffs.
Julian Jeffs for the defendants.

WALTON J.   This is an application by the plaintiffs for further discovery from
the defendants, and raises yet once again the always troublesome and difficult
question of the extent to which discovery ought properly to be made by a party of
what may conveniently be termed parallel transactions.

The action is an unusual one. It is one for passing off, the goods being passed off
being Scotch whisky (in the goodwill of which description the plaintiffs, who are
well-known blenders and exporters thereof, have a share), and the method of passing
off being by the supply of genuine Scotch whisky, together with bottles, cartons,
closures, labels and other similar incidents, to importers in Greece, Spain, Guatemala,
Lebanon and Cyprus, who then dilute the original genuine Scotch whisky (whose
technical description is of no present moment) with locally produced spirits and sell
the resultant admixture under such a get-up as to lead the general public in those
countries to imagine that the admixture is genuine Scotch whisky.

The statement of claim accordingly pleads, in paras (4), (5) and (6) thereof, as
follows:

'(4) The trade marks and brand names, the wording and devices on the labels
cartons caps capsules or other closures, and the advertising used in relation to
the mixtures referred to in Paragraph 3 are calculated and (furthermore)
intended to lead purchasers to believe that the contents of the respective bottles
are Scotch Whisky whereas in fact they are not Scotch Whisky but a mixture of
Scotch Whisky and spirit distilled locally from divers local materials. By
reason of the premises purchasers in Greece, Spain, Guatemala, Lebanon and
Cyprus of the mixtures sold under the above-mentioned names would be
deceived into thinking that the product was Scotch Whisky.

'(5) The Defendants or one or other of them have with the fraudulent intention
mentioned in paragraph (4):—(i) Licensed or permitted the use of the trade
marks, brand names and labels referred to in Paragraph 3 in relation to the
said mixtures; and/or (ii) Supplied the bottles, labels, cartons, caps, capsules
or other closures referred to in Paragraph 3 knowing that they would be
used in relation to the said mixtures and that such mixtures would be offered
for sale and sold under the trade marks, brand names, labels, cartons, caps,
capsules or other closures and advertising referred to in Paragraphs 3 and 4;
and/or (iii) Supplied Scotch Whisky knowing that it would be used in the manufacture of the said mixtures and that such mixtures would be offered for sale

and sold under the trade marks, brand names, labels, cartons, caps, capsules or other closures and advertising referred to in Paragraphs 3 and 4.

'(6) The said acts of the Defendants and each of them are calculated and (furthermore) intended by each Defendant to lead purchasers in Greece, Spain, Guatemala, Lebanon and Cyprus to believe that the respective mixtures mentioned in Paragraph 3 are Scotch Whisky and to lead to the passing off as and for Scotch Whisky of products consisting of or including spirits not obtained by distillation in Scotland from a mash of cereal grain saccharified by the diastase of malt.'

The defence to the action, put shortly, is that the defendants are simply suppliers of Scotch whisky; that they have no direct control over the importers in the countries concerned to whom they sell the whisky; they themselves have always traded honestly, and have at all times used their best endeavours to prevent their customers from using any trade mark, brand name, advertisement or get-up which could be misleading.

The defendants' business is not, however, confined to the five countries already named, nor is it confined to dealing in whisky. They also deal in gin (and, I gather, other spirits) which is also locally admixed in the same kind of manner as the Scotch which they supply, and I was indeed informed that their trade is known as 'the admixture trade'.

Basing himself on this, counsel for the plaintiffs first of all requested disclosure of the defendants' trading in gin; and I gather that, although counsel for the defendants considered such documents wholly irrelevant to any matter in issue in the action, since they were very few in number, sensibly and commendably advised that they should be disclosed rather than have the matter argued out. But he objects strongly to producing the other documents sought, the nature of which appears from the mandatory affidavit in support of the application sworn by a partner in the plaintiffs' solicitors on 21st February 1974, which I can conveniently take up at para 4:

'As appears from the Statement of Claim herein the form in which the passing off complained of takes place is not so crude or blatant as a simple description of the admixture as "Scotch Whisky". In this case the method employed is more subtle and sophisticated, in that in many if not all instances the actual wording of the label on the admixture is, when read carefully and literally, true. But it is the Plaintiffs' case that when the get-up as a whole is considered, and the circumstances in which the spirits will often be offered for sale are borne in mind, and taking into account the fact that the labels include prominent references to Scotland and are worded wholly or predominently in the English language although they are intended for use in non-English-speaking countries such as Guatemala and Greece, the conclusion of fact to be reached is that such get-up is calculated to deceive as mentioned above. Moreover—and this is an important part of the Plaintiffs' case—this form of get-up has not been adopted by the Defendants in the ordinary course of trading, with no intention or awareness of the ultimate purchasers of the admixtures being misled: on the contrary this form has been deliberately adopted with the intention that local purchasers may think that the product which they are purchasing is Scotch Whisky; the intention is that, if possible, local purchasers should be misled into so thinking; and to this end the Defendants are in their choice of get-up sailing as close to the wind as they dare.

'5. The fact that throughout parts of the world the sale of Scotch Whisky admixed with local spirits is sold and sought to be passed off as Scotch Whisky is something which is well known throughout the trade. By their choice of get-up the Defendants are, with their eyes wide open, deliberately placing on the local markets a product which is nothing less than an instrument of deception

—a product in a get-up which is inherently likely to be used for improper trading purposes.

6. I am advised by counsel that in this action proof of the Defendants' intention in and about its trading in the admixture field as a whole is of importance. It is in this connection that further discovery is being sought.

'7. In the Statement of Claim complaint is made in respect of 13 get-ups in a total of 5 countries: Greece, Spain, Guatemala, Lebanon, and Cyprus. The Plaintiffs believe, and so far as I am aware this is not denied, that the Defendants are involved in the admixture trade (as shortly described above) in other countries of the world, and also, in the 5 countries in question, under other get-ups; and also in respect of spirits other than Scotch Whisky.

'8. The Defendants' case is that at all times they have traded honestly and with no proper intention. On this issue the Plaintiffs believe that the documents in the Defendants' possession relating to their trading mentioned in paragraph 7 (and in particular relating to the adoption of the get-ups in question, and the steps which the Defendants have taken to see that the admixed end-product is not being used improperly) are most material to the issues in the present case. If such documents show a readiness by the Defendants to trade improperly in relation to admixtures in (say) Ecuador, then such evidence is of the utmost importance when evaluating what was the Defendants' state of mind when trading in the admixtures complained of in Guatemala.'

Counsel for the plaintiffs' point is that the intentions and honourable, or otherwise, conduct of the defendants in relation to all their other business must be relevant to the intentions and honesty, or otherwise, of their conduct of their businesses in relation to the five countries of which complaint is specifically made in the action. He admits that before being discoverable there must be something in the nature, or alternatively, the contents, of the documents which makes them relevant to the issues in the action; he submits that of their own nature the documents of which he seeks discovery must be relevant, or, if that is not so, then their contents must be relevant, either to condemn the defendants' whole trading methods, or to exonerate them.

Counsel for the defendants, on the other hand, argues that the documents of which discovery is sought do not go to any issues in the action, which relates to the defendants' business with the five named countries and that alone. Moreover, he says that the discovery now sought would be oppressive, and that since discovery is a matter of discretion rather than right, it would not be a proper exercise of my discretion to grant it in the form now sought. His factual basis for that allegation is set out in an affidavit of the managing director of the three defendant companies, Group-Captain F E R Dixon, sworn on 18th March 1974 of which the last two paragraphs read as follows:

'8. The Plaintiff companies are three of the largest whisky distillers and blenders. They do business throughout the world and I verily believe they have agents everywhere where my companies do business. The Statement of Claim herein gives a good indication of the extent of their enquiries and how closely they have been watching the business activities of my Companies. My own case is that I have never done anything illegal or of which I need be ashamed in the countries which they have referred to or anywhere else. If my Companies' activities had been objectionable to them anywhere I have no doubt they would have detected them right away.

'9. I verily believe that the discovery they are now seeking is just in the hope of finding another stick to beat me with. If this case lasts the weeks that I am already advised that it will, the financial burden to my Companies could well be disastrous. The Plaintiffs have already pleaded enough matters to enable them thoroughly to investigate my Companies' manner of trading. I am

a advised that the discovery that they now seek will entail my producing practically every trading file in my Companies' possession; that it would take a very
   long time; that it will completely disrupt our business activities; that it would
   cost a great deal in legal fees that we can ill afford and that it would delay the
   trial.'

b Counsel for the plaintiffs in reply did not accept the difficulties which would face the
   three defendant companies if an order as he sought was made, but I do not think that
   on a matter of this nature I could go behind the oath of the deponent, at any rate
   without sufficient material on which to do so, and here there is no material at all
   beyond counsel's attractive, but purely forensic, assertions.
       What, then, ought to be done? The leading case on discovery in relation to similar
   transactions is of course *Kennedy v Dodson*[1]. This was a case relating to interroga-
c tories, but the delivery of interrogatories is merely one branch of discovery, and
   indeed this so appears from the case itself. The headnote reads:

       'An action was brought for a declaration that a piece of land which had been
       purchased by the Defendant and C. in 1873 was purchased by them as co-partners,
       and for accounts of the partnership and consequential relief. The Defendant
d   denied the partnership. The Plaintiff exhibited interrogatories to the Defendant
       asking for particulars of purchases of land by the Defendant and C. previous
       and subsequent to 1873, in order to prove that they had been co-partners in
       various other purchases similar to that of 1873:—*Held* (reversing the decision of
       the Vice-Chancellor of the County Palatine of *Lancaster*), that the interrogatories
       were irrelevant to the issue in the action and oppressive, and that they ought
e   not to be allowed.'

   I will now read first a passage from Lord Herschell LC's judgment[2]:

       'In my opinion, these interrogatories are not such that the answers to them
       would be relevant to the issue. Suppose the Defendant says, "I did enter into
       such and such transactions at such and such dates on such and such terms,"
f   would that be relevant to the issue, what were the terms on which this property
       was purchased? Could the truth of his statement be tried in this action? Could
       the Plaintiff say, "I will shew you that *Carswell* and the Defendant purchased
       twenty properties on certain terms before 1873, and that they purchased ten
       properties on the same terms afterwards"? Would the Judge be bound to try
       the question on what terms all these properties were purchased for the purpose
g   of determining the terms upon which the property involved in this action was
       purchased? No doubt there are cases in which evidence of what happened in
       one transaction may be relevant to the question what happened in another. I
       do not dispute that general proposition. In the present case the suggestion is this,
       that if it can be proved that in a number of prior transactions *Carswell* and the
       Defendant had been purchasing land on partnership terms, that would render it
h   probable that such was the nature of this transaction also. But that is not rele-
       vant evidence. Cases of this description are not determined upon probabilities,
       but upon evidence of what happened upon the particular occasion. It is said
       that many of these questions might be put to the Defendant in cross-examination;
       but that would not be for the purpose of proving what the particular transaction
       had been, except only to the extent of shewing that the Defendant's evidence
j   as to this particular transaction was not to be credited because of the admissions
       made by him with regard to the other transactions. But because those questions
       might be put to the Defendant in cross-examination, it by no means follows that

─────────────────────────────
1 [1895] 1 Ch 334
2 [1895] 1 Ch at 338

evidence as to such transactions would be relevant evidence to be given in chief
by the Plaintiff.   I entertain a strong opinion that interrogatories of this descrip-   *a*
tion, unless strictly relevant to the question at issue in the action, ought to be
rigorously excluded.   They cause a great amount of hardship and oppression.
They cast upon the Defendant, merely because a writ has been served upon
him, the burden of an intolerable amount of trouble and annoyance, and if he
refuses to answer he may be sent to prison.   Here the Defendant is asked to give   *b*
a list of all the properties prior to 1873 in which he and the bankrupt were jointly
interested, and to state the terms and conditions on which such properties were
purchased.   In order to answer that question he must rake up all these transactions—it may be for a period of twenty years before 1873.   It is said that he may
have diaries relating to these transactions.   So much the worse for him.   He
will be a lucky man if he has destroyed them.   Nothing shews better than this
the wisdom of destroying books and papers relating to transactions which are   *c*
done with.   In my opinion, there has sometimes been great laxity in times past
in allowing interrogatories.   It is that system which has made the very name of
law stink in the nostrils of many sensible men of business.   They say they would
rather pay a claim for which they are not legally responsible than take the trouble
necessary to answer interrogatories of this description, which cause a vast amount
of trouble and difficulty, unless they are clearly relevant to the issue.'   *d*

Lindley LJ said[1]:

'I am of the same opinion.   Under ordinary circumstances we should not think
of interfering with the decision of the Judge in the Court below in a matter which
is very much a matter of discretion.   But I cannot help thinking that these interro-   *e*
gatories are vexatious and oppressive to such an extent that the Defendant ought
not to be compelled to answer them.   They are opposed to the fundamental
principles of discovery which are stated in Sir J. Wigram's treatise on Discovery[2].
The second proposition stated is as as follows[3]: "It is the right, as a general rule,
of a plaintiff in equity to exact from the defendant a discovery upon oath as to
all matters of fact which, being well pleaded in the bill, are material to the   *f*
plaintiff's case about to come on for trial, and which the defendant does not by
his form of pleading admit."   That renders it necessary to say a few words as to
what are "matters of fact which being well pleaded in the bill are material
to the plaintiff's case."   What ought a properly drawn bill to contain?   It ought
to contain a statement of those facts, and those facts only, which, if proved, will
entitle the plaintiff to relief.   It ought not to contain the evidence of those facts.   *g*
Of course, it is in some cases difficult to draw the line between those facts which
are properly contained in the bill and those which are not; but in case of doubt
it has always been the practice of the Court to find out whether the facts as to
which information is required are so material as to render discovery reasonable.
Sir J. Wigram says this[4]: " In determining whether *particular* discovery is material
or not, the Court will exercise a discretion in refusing to enforce it, where it is   *h*
remote in its bearings upon the real point in issue, and would be an oppressive
inquisition."   The facts properly stated in this statement of claim are that
Carswell and the Defendant bought a certain property in *Manchester*, and the
Plaintiff alleges that that property is partnership property, and relief is sought
on that footing.   The Plaintiff is entitled to discovery with reference to those
allegations;   but he wants information as to a number of other transactions   *j*

1   [1895] 1 Ch at 340, 341
2   The Law of Discovery (2nd Edn, 1840)
3   Ibid, p 15
4   Ibid, p 165

a which took place between *Carswell* and the Defendant in order to raise a probability that this was a partnership transaction. To ask the Defendant to take the trouble to go through his books and papers for so many years is vexatious and oppressive. The vexation and oppression can only be estimated by persons who have to answer interrogatories of this kind. I doubt whether this information would be admissible in evidence; but suppose it would, it does not follow that
b the Plaintiff would be entitled to discovery of it. Examining witnesses at a trial and obtaining discovery before the trial are two totally different matters. If the decision of the Vice-Chancellor were anywhere near the line, I should be slow to differ from him in a matter which is largely a matter of discretion; but, in my opinion, to compel the Defendant to answer these interrogatories would be most oppressive. I think the appeal should be allowed.'

c A L Smith LJ said[1]:

'Then the Plaintiff administers interrogatories to the Defendant. What does he ask him? Does he ask him a single question relevant to that issue? Does he ask him whether he entered into partnership with *Carswell* as regards that piece of land? He does nothing of the kind. What he does ask him is this: "Prior
d to 1873, and subsequently to 1873, did you have any dealings with *Carswell* as regards land?" He may have had twenty dealings with *Carswell* with regard to other properties; the issue is what was the dealing with regard to this property. I agree that if the Defendant were in the witness-box and denied that he ever was in partnership with *Carswell*, it would be relevant to the question whether he was telling the truth to ask him whether he did not have dealings with regard to
e properties A, B, and C, and whether he was not in partnership with *Carswell* in respect of each of those properties. But that is pure cross-examination and not the subject-matter for interrogatories. In my opinion, these interrogatories ought not be admitted, and the appeal ought to be allowed.'

From that case I think one extracts the two principles: (i) that discovery which relates
f solely to credit is not allowed; and (ii) that discovery is confined to matters which are in question in the action.

Of course, I entirely accept in relation to (ii) what was said by Brett LJ in *Compagnie Financière du Pacifique v Peruvian Guano Co*[2] as to this extending to any document containing information which might—not which must—enable the party requiring the discovery either to advance his own case or to damage the case of his adversary.

It appears to me, however, that if the present application for discovery is not a pure
g fishing expedition—as was asserted by counsel for the defendants but denied by counsel for the plaintiffs—then it is really one which is directed exclusively to credit, since it is simply and solely directed towards putting the plaintiffs in a position to say: 'You did a wicked act in Ecuador (or wherever), ergo you are a person who would do a dirty deed in the five countries with which the action is specifically concerned.' In other words, give a dog a bad name and hang him.

h I therefore conclude that I ought not to accede to the present application. If, however, I am wrong in my conclusion that as a matter of strict law this proposed discovery ought not to be allowed, then certainly as a matter of discretion I am wholly in favour of disallowing it. I see nothing to displace Group-Captain Dixon's oath as to the difficulties which the giving of such discovery would cause to his firm, even if the actual trial of the action were not thereby held up. I am quite clearly of the
j opinion that the discovery sought is not necessary, even if relevant, which as I have said I do not think it is, either for disposing fairly of the action or for saving costs. On the contrary, it will be oppressive and will entail additional costs.

---

1 [1895] 1 Ch at 341, 342
2 (1882) 11 QBD 55 at 63

Whilst it forms no part of my grounds for deciding against the plaintiffs in this
application, I cannot bring myself to believe, as a practical matter, that if there was
anything relevant in the state of Denmark, or elsewhere, the plaintiffs would not
perfectly well know all about it, as suggested by Group-Captain Dixon in para 8 of
his affidavit. Indeed, I do not know where, if the kind of discovery now sought is to
be allowed, it ought to stop. Presumably the plaintiffs have investigated the activities
of the defendants in countries other than the five they have chosen; have they disclosed their files giving the defendants a clean bill of health in those countries?
Obviously—and rightly—not. But if general credit were to be one of the real issues in
the action—which it is not—I certainly do not know where the line could ever be
drawn. The application is dismissed.

Application dismissed. Leave to appeal.

Solicitors; *Ince & Co* (for the plaintiffs); *Norton Rose Botterell & Roche* (for the
defendants).

Jacqueline Metcalfe Barrister.

New Windsor Corporation v Mellor and others

CHANCERY DIVISION
FOSTER J
19th, 20th, 21st, 22nd FEBRUARY, 20th MARCH 1974

*Commons – Registration – Town or village green – Land on which inhabitants of any locality
have customary right – Right to indulge in lawful sports and pastimes – Custom – Use of
land since time immemorial – Evidence of long usage – Usage as of right – Evidence that right
confined to inhabitants of locality – Land in town centre – Indirect evidence that land used as
of right by local inhabitants for sports and pastimes between 1651 and 1875 – Inference of
customary right since time immemorial – Commons Registration Act 1965, ss 1(1), 22(1).*

The respondent caused certain land in the centre of the borough of New Windsor
to be registered in the register of town or village greens maintained by the registration
authority under s 3 of the Commons Registration Act 1965, claiming that the inhabitants of the borough had by custom acquired a right to indulge in lawful sports
and pastimes on it. The borough objected to the registration and an inquiry was
held by the Chief Commons Commissioner. The evidence before the Commissioner
showed that in 1651 a lease of the land had been granted by the borough for 40 years,
the lease containing a covenant by the lessee that it should be lawful for the 'Mayor
Bailiffs and Burgesses and . . . all and every other person and persons to have access'
to the land 'as well as to exercise and use shooting or any other lawful pastime for
their recreation at all convenient times'. The lessee also covenanted to set up a
pair of butts 'for the inhabitants of the . . . town to shoot at' and to repair and maintain them, and not to do anything which might be 'hurtful to the shooting or any
other pastime then to be exercised for recreation of the people'. Further leases
of the land for 40 year terms, containing similar covenants, were granted in 1704 and
1749. In 1819 the corporation granted a three year lease, the lease being made subject
to the right 'of the Native Bachelors of Windsor of exercising all lawful sports games
and pastimes' over the land, and, in 1822, a similar lease 'subject to the rights and
privileges of the Bachelors of Windsor who are entitled to use the [land] for all lawful
recreations and amusements'. After the Inclosure Act 1813 the borough held the
land by virtue of their statutory title under that Act. Following an inclosure award in

1819, they held it free from any rights of common of pasture or turbary, but still subject to any rights to use it for lawful sports and pastimes to which it was formerly subject. The land was used annually for 'revels' until the 1840s. There were also in evidence extracts from newspaper reports and reports of meetings, a newspaper extract of October 1875 recording that the land had been used for sports by a large number of people and that the mayor had vetoed the holding of the sports, on wrong advice given to him by the town clerk on the legal effect of the inclosure award. From 1875 onwards the borough refused to recognise that the inhabitants had any right to use the land for recreation and accordingly it was no longer used for that purpose. At the time of the respondent's registration the land had for some years been used partly as a school sports ground and partly as a car park. It was listed in the development plan for the borough as the site for a multi-storey car park. On the evidence the Commissioner confirmed the registration, holding that a customary right to indulge in lawful sports and pastimes on the land had been acquired by the inhabitants of the locality from time immemorial and that the land was therefore a 'town or village green' within ss 1(1)^a and 22(1)^b of the 1965 Act. The borough appealed, contending, inter alia, (i) that the evidence did not support the conclusion of long usage since there was no direct evidence of any user and the Commissioner had found that there had been no such user since 1875, and (ii) that the user was incapable of existing as a custom since, from the terms of the covenants in the 1651 lease, the user was not confined to the inhabitants of the borough , i e the 'Burgesses', but extended to 'all and every other person', i e persons residing outside the borough.

Held – The appeal would be dismissed for the following reasons—

(i) In order to reverse the Commissioner's conclusion that there had been long usage of the land by the local inhabitants for lawful pastimes, it had to be shown that the commissioner had not only been wrong in the inferences of fact which he had drawn but that no person properly instructed in the law and acting judicially could have reached that conclusion. There was, however, ample evidence on which the Commissioner could come to the conclusion that long usage had been established and that the user had been as of right (see p 518 *d* and *e*, post); dictum of Lord Radcliffe in *Edwards (Inspector of Taxes) v Bairstow* [1955] 3 All ER at 57 applied.

(ii) The right claimed was one which was capable of existing as a custom since it was one which was confined to the inhabitants of a particular locality, i e the borough. The expression 'Mayor Bailiffs and Burgesses' in the 1651 lease referred to the body corporate and, although the words 'all and every other person' and 'the people' in the lease were words of potentially wide import, they had to be read in their context; the covenant to set up a pair of butts 'for the inhabitants of the said town to shoot at', showed that the words were to be confined to people living in the borough (see p 518 *f* and *g* and p 519 *b*, post).

(iii) Once it had been established that there had been long usage of the land for lawful sports and pastimes, that such usage had been as of right and that it was capable of subsisting as a custom, the court would be astute to find the origin from time immemorial and the Commissioner had been right to do so (see p 519 *f*, post).

Notes
For the meaning of 'town or village green', see 6 Halsbury's Laws (4th Edn) 187, para 525.

For the presumption of the immemorial existence of a custom, and for proof of custom, see 11 Halsbury's Laws (3rd Edn) 160-162, 171, 172, paras 300, 301, 319, 320, and for cases on the subject, see 17 Digest (Repl) 8-12, 18, 19, 51-99, 202-220.

---

a   Section 1(1), so far as material, is set out at p 513 *e*, post
b   Section 22(1), so far as material, is set out at p 513 *h*, post

For the Commons Registration Act 1965, ss 1, 3, 22, see 3 Halsbury's Statutes (3rd
Edn) 920, 921, 933.

Cases referred to in judgment
Cocksedge v Fanshaw (1779) 1 Doug KB 119, 99 ER 80, 17 Digest (Repl) 7, 43.
Edwards (Inspector of Taxes) v Bairstow [1955] 3 All ER 48, [1956] AC 14, [1955] 3 WLR
    410, 34 ATC 198, 48 R & IT 534, HL, 28(1) Digest (Reissue) 567, 2089.
Forbes v Ecclesiastical Comrs for England (1872) LR 15 Eq 51, 42 LJCh 97, 27 LT 511,
    36 Digest (Repl) 351, 5.
Hammerton v Honey (1876) 24 WR 603, 17 Digest (Repl) 4, 9.
Johnson v Barnes (1872) LR 7 CP 592, 41 LJCP 250, 27 LT 152; *affd* (1873) LR 8 CP 527,
    19 Digest (Repl) 58, 316.
Malcomson v O'Dea (1863) 10 HL Cas 593, 9 LT 93, 11 ER 1155, 9 Jur NS 1135, 27 JP 820,
    HL, 25 Digest (Repl) 17, 156.
Mercer v Denne [1904] 2 Ch 534, 74 LJCh 71, 91 LT 513; *affd* [1905] 2 Ch 538, [1904-7]
    All ER Rep 71, 74 LJCh 723, 93 LT 412, CA, 17 Digest (Repl) 4, 11.
Scales v Key (1840) 11 Ad & El 819, 113 ER 625, 17 Digest (Repl) 16, 177.
Simpson v Wells (1872) LR 7 QB 214, 41 LJMC 105, 26 LT 163, 36 JP 774, 17 Digest
    (Repl) 8, 54.
Spicer v Warbey [1953] 1 All ER 284, [1953] 1 WLR 334, DC, 33 Digest (Repl.) 323,
    1473.
Wyld v Silver [1962] 3 All ER 309, [1963] Ch 243, [1963] 1 QB 169, [1962] 3 WLR 841,
    CA, Digest (Cont Vol A) 1123, 11a.

Cases also cited
Atwood v Chichester (1878) 3 QB 722, CA.
Beckett (Alfred F) Ltd v Lyons [1967] 1 All ER 833, [1967] Ch 449, CA.
*British Launderers' Research Association v Central Middlesex Assessment Committee and
    Hendon Rating Authority* [1949] 1 All ER 21, [1949] 1 KB 462, CA.
Carr v Lambert (1866) LR 1 Ex 168.
Fitch v Rawling (1795) 2 Hy Bl 394, [1775-1802] All ER Rep 571.
Goodman v Mayor of Saltash (1882) 7 App Cas 633, [1881-5] All ER Rep 1076, HL.
Warrick v Queen's College, Oxford (1870) LR 10 Eq 105.

Case stated
The respondent, Doris Evelyn Mellor, caused land in the centre of the Royal Borough
of New Windsor known as 'Bachelors' Acre' to be registered at entry no 1 in the land
section of the register unit no VG 21 in the Register of Town or Village Greens maintained by the Berkshire County Council under s 3 of the Commons Registration Act
1965. New Windsor Corporation ('the borough') objected to the registration.
On 6th November 1972 G D Squibb Esq QC, Chief Commons Commissioner, after an
inquiry held on 10th and 11th October 1972, confirmed the registration. At the
request of the borough the commissioner stated a case for the decision of the High
Court pursuant to s 18(1) of the 1965 Act. By an originating motion dated 12th July
1973 the borough sought the determination of the question of law set out in the case
stated by the commissioner, and set out its grounds of appeal as follows: (i) the commissioner had erred in law in drawing the following conclusions from the evidence
to which he had referred in his decision, namely, (1) that Bachelors' Acre had been
used for archery and other lawful pastimes from time immemorial; (2) that those
indulging in sports and pastimes on Bachelors' Acre did so as a matter of right as
against the borough rather than by permission of the borough; (3) that the rights to
indulge in sports and pastimes on Bachelors' Acre were confined to the inhabitants
of any particular locality; (ii) the commissioner had failed to give sufficient weight
to his finding that there had since 1875 been no user of the land for recreation; and

(iii) the commissioner had erred in law in holding that a customary right of the kind in question could not as a matter of law be abandoned.   The third ground was not proceeded with at the hearing but counsel for the borough reserved the point for argument in a higher court.   The facts are set out in the judgment.

Patrick Freeman QC and *Konrad Schiemann* for the borough.
Oliver Lodge for the respondent.

Cur adv vult

20th March.   **FOSTER J** read the following judgment.   This is an appeal, by way of case stated, by the mayor, aldermen and burgesses of the Royal Borough of New Windsor (which I will call 'the borough') from a decision of the Chief Commons Commissioner (whom I will call 'the Commissioner') in which he confirmed the registration as a common of land known as Bachelors' Acre in the centre of New Windsor. The respondent is Miss D E Mellor, who is a member of the Windsor and Eton Society, and who caused Bachelors' Acre to be registered as a common under the Commons Registration Act 1965.

Statutory provisions
By s 1(1) of the 1965 Act it is provided:

> 'There shall be registered, in accordance with the provisions of this Act and subject to the exceptions mentioned therein,—(a) land in England or Wales which is common land or a town or village green . . .'

Section 4 provides for provisional registration and for an application for the registration of any land as a town or village green to be made by any person.   Section 5 provides for notification and objections to registration, and s 6 provides that a commons commissioner should inquire into any disputed claims and either confirm the registration with or without modification or refuse to confirm it.   Section 17 provides for the appointment by the Lord Chancellor of commons commissioners, one of whom shall be the Chief Commons Commissioner.   Section 18(1) is in these terms:

> 'Any person aggrieved by the decision of a Commons Commissioner as being erroneous in point of law may, within such time as may be limited by rules of court, require the Commissioner to state a case for the decision of the High Court.'

In s 22(1) the words 'town or village green' are defined as meaning—

> 'land which has been allotted by or under any Act for the exercise or recreation of the inhabitants of any locality or on which the inhabitants of any locality have a customary right to indulge in lawful sports and pastimes or on which the inhabitants of any locality have indulged in such sports and pastimes as of right for not less than twenty years.'

RSC Ord 93, r 16, provides that proceedings under s 18 of the 1965 Act shall be heard and determined by a single judge of the Chancery Division and that an aggrieved person must require the commons commissioner to state a case for the opinion of the High Court within six weeks from the date on which notice of the decision was sent to the aggrieved person.   At present, the Chief Commons Commissioner is Mr G D Squibb QC, and he held a hearing on 10th and 11th October 1972 and gave his decision on 6th November 1972.   The borough as an aggrieved person asked for a stated case and this is dated 26th June 1973.

Application to vary case stated

At the hearing before me, counsel for the respondent applied to have the case stated varied by this court. Under RSC Ord 56, r 11, it is provided:

'The Court hearing a case stated by a Minister, tribunal, arbitrator or other person may amend the case or order it to be returned to that person for amendment, and may draw inferences of fact from the facts stated in the case.'

Lord Goddard CJ in a practice note[1] said this in regard to a case stated by justices:

'As the Case has been in the hands of the respondent's advisers all these months [in fact 3½ months], we cannot now send it back to the justices for amendment merely on a statement on behalf of the respondent that certain facts have been omitted. It was the respondent's duty to act promptly in the matter ...'

Counsel in this case said that in fact the borough knew of the application late in December 1973 or early in January 1974 (a delay of nearly six months). He did not ask that the case should be remitted to the Commissioner but asked that I should myself allow an amendment, and if I was not disposed to allow an amendment, he would withdraw his application as the respondent could not financially afford to pay the costs of the adjournment and of the remission back. I was told that at the hearing before the Commissioner the respondent gave evidence and was cross-examined, as was also the town clerk of the borough. In addition, the Commissioner received proofs from four witnesses who were present but who were not cross-examined, and two affidavits were read which were sworn by deponents who were not present, but no application was made to cross-examine them. It was said that those proofs and affidavits did not justify the Commissioner's conclusion that since 1875—

'the [borough] has continued to refuse to recognise any right to use the land for recreation by the inhabitants of the town and it has not been so used.'

The application was that I should allow the four proofs and two affidavits to be annexed to the case before me, and that application was strenuously opposed by counsel for the borough. I was not prepared to allow these documents to be added as the result would be that there would be no record before this court of the evidence given by the respondent and the town clerk (and apparently there was no note taken of the cross-examination, though the proofs of those two witnesses were available). I was, however, prepared to remit it to the Commissioner for amendment, but in view of the fact that the borough would then ask for the costs of the adjournment, the application was withdrawn.

The main question

This can be stated as follows. Is Bachelors' Acre land on which the inhabitants of New Windsor have a customary right to indulge in lawful sports or pastimes and therefore a town or village green within the meaning of the Act? The grounds of the borough's appeal are set out in the originating motion as follows:

'1. The learned Chief Commons Commissioner erred in law in drawing the following conclusions from the evidence to which he refers in his decision, namely (1) That Bachelors' Acre has been used for archery and other lawful pastimes from time immemorial; (2) That those indulging in sports and pastimes on Bachelors' Acre did so as a matter of right as against the [borough] rather than by permission of the [borough]; (3) That any rights to indulge in sports and pastimes on Bachelors' Acre were confined to the inhabitants of any locality.

---

1   *Spicer v Warbey* [1953] 1 All ER 284 at 285, [1953] 1 WLR 334 at 335

'2. The learned Chief Commons Commissioner failed to give sufficient weight to his finding that there had since 1875 been no user of the land for recreation.

'3. The learned Chief Commons Commissioner erred in law in holding that a customary right of the kind in question could not as a matter of law be abandoned.'

In regard to the third ground it was admitted on behalf of the borough that the point is concluded against it by several cases, the most recent one being in the Court of Appeal, *Wyld v Silver*[1], which, inter alia, decided that once a custom has been established it cannot be waived or abandoned (see Lord Denning MR[2]). Counsel for the borough reserved the point for argument in a higher court.

Bachelors' Acre

Despite its name, this land consists of more that two acres in the centre of New Windsor. It is now used partly as a sports ground for a school and partly as a car park. It is listed on the development plan for New Windsor for building a multi-storeyed car park.

The claim

The claim made by the respondent is that the inhabitants of the borough have by custom acquired a right to indulge in lawful sports and pastimes on Bachelors' Acre. The onus of proving such a custom must, I think, rest on the respondent and the Commissioner has found that she discharged that onus and has proved to his satisfaction that such a custom has been acquired by such inhabitants from time immemorial. For the borough, it is submitted that the evidence before the Commissioner was not sufficient in law for him to draw the conclusions which he did. Both parties agreed that the court must be satisfied on the evidence: (1) that there has been long usage; (2) that the claim has been made as of right; (3) that the right claimed is capable of existing as a custom; and (4) if the first three points are proved satisfactorily, the court will be astute to infer an origin from time immemorial and thus create a custom at common law.

(1) *Long usage*

The first document before the Commissioner was one called a full transcript from the register of leases kept in the Windsor Corporation's Book of Leases. The first entry was a lease by the corporation to Richard Hale of Bachelors' Acre, commencing on Lady Day 1651 and expiring on Lady Day 1691. But in the parcels the land is described as—

'all that parcell of land and pasture ground with the Appurtenances called Bachelors' Acre where the Butts were usually sett and made situate in New Windsor.'

The lessee covenanted as follows:

'... that it shall and may be lawful to and for the Mayor Bailiffs and Burgesses and to all and every other person and persons to have access recess ingress egress and regress unto and from the said ground as well to exercise and use shooting or any other lawful pastime for their recreation at all convenient times during the said terms without let or disturbance. And that he his executors administrators or assignees shall and will within one year ensuing the date hereof make and set up in and upon the said parcel of ground one sufficient pair of Butts for the inhabitants of the said town to shoot at and the said two Butts being so made

1   [1962] 3 All ER 309, [1963] Ch 243
2   [1962] 3 All ER at 313, [1963] Ch at 255

and sett shall at his and their proper cost and charges repair amend maintain and keep sufficiently during the said term. And not to dig or mine in the same ground or do any other act or thing which shall or may be hurtful to the shooting or any other pastime there to be exercised for recreation of the people and to level the pits in the said ground.'

A further lease was granted to one Anthony Moysey from Lady Day 1704 for 40 years, expiring on Lady Day 1744. It contained a similar covenant. There is a gap between 1744 and 1749, but at Michaelmas 1749 the borough granted a lease to one William Tyrrell for a period of 40 years, expiring at Michaelmas 1789, and again it was granted subject to the use of the ground for any lawful pastime for the recreation of the people. There is another gap from 1789 until 1819 when a lease of Bachelors' Acre was granted by the borough to William Perryman for three years, expiring on 24th June 1822, again subject to the use of the ground for lawful pastimes, but this time, for the first time, the right is described as that 'of the Native Bachelors of Windsor of exercising all lawful sports games and pastimes' over Bachelors' Acre. This is confirmed by minutes of the council dated 11th May 1819, an advertisement from the Windsor and Eton Express dated 16th May and 23rd May 1819 and minutes of the council dated 22nd June 1819 confirming the decision to let to Mr Perryman. On 31st August 1822 Bachelors' Acre was again advertised for letting subject to 'the rights and privileges of the Bachelors of Windsor who are entitled to use the [land] for all lawful recreations and amusements'. It was let to George Cooper for three years on the terms of the advertisement.

Meanwhile, on 21st July 1813, there was passed an Inclosure Act[1] in regard to certain parts of Windsor Forest and for enclosing the open commonable lands within the said forest. It seems that Bachelors' Acre came within s 50 of that Act. This Act seems to have given birth to what has been called a pressure group, namely, the Bachelors of Windsor, who actively campaigned to retain the right to carry on lawful sports and pastimes on Bachelors' Acre. In evidence, there was a booklet published by Knight and Son dated 1817 and it is entitled 'Proceedings of the Committees of Bachelors of New Windsor'. It records the proceedings of Bachelors from 1809 and the relevant extracts from that book are numerous. On p 6 it is said:

'Many venerable inhabitants of Windsor and the neighbourhood now relate with much pleasure the actions of their youthful days, when as Bachelors they asserted their right, and successfully resisted every attempt to deprive them of it...'

When one comes to the proceedings of the committee, there is constant reference to 'the Bachelors and Inhabitants of Windsor'. Representations were made to the Commissioner, and at p 39 it is said:

'... the Chairman informed him the Bachelors wished nothing more than their just right of playing over every part of the Bachelors' Acre, as stated in their Claim.'

On p 40 there is a statement dated 23rd January 1815:

'In support of the Claim of the Bachelors, a number of the oldest inhabitants of Windsor and the neighbourhood were examined by Mr. Richards, and their evidence fully proved the right of playing in and over every part of the Bachelors' Acre, to have been enjoyed by the Bachelors from the earliest period of their recollection (in some instances near 80 years) to the present time; and that they had at all times asserted the same, and removed every obstruction to their pastime therein.'

---

1 53 Geo 3 c 158

The Commissioner, under the Inclosure Act 1813, informed the members of the committee that he would not interfere in his award with Bachelors' Acre. However, the Commissioner, in his New Windsor Inclosure Award 1819 did make an award in regard to Bachelors' Acre. He awarded part of Bachelors' Acre one way and another part another way, but it is agreed that the effect of the award was that although the rights of pasture and turbary were abolished, it did not in law affect a customary right for the inhabitants to indulge in lawful pastimes if such a custom was proved (see *Forbes v Ecclesiastical Commissioners*[1]). In the record it was further stated in an appendix dated 25th October 1817 that the Bachelors of Windsor celebrated the birthday of the Prince Regent on 12th August by a revel in their acre, at which valuable prizes were given for the usual rural sports; and that it was proposed to continue the revel annually. At p 5 of his decision, the Commissioner found as a fact, 'It was used annually for "revels" until the 1840s.' In Wharton's Law Lexicon[2] 'Revels' are defined as 'sports of dancing, masking, etc.'

To complete the history, there was an excerpt from the Windsor and Eton Express dated 19th June 1847 containing a report of what was called, 'The Battle of Bachelors' Acre'. The report starts with the words:

'This celebrated spot at Windsor, appropriated from time immemorial to the lawful sports and recreation of the people, was on Monday, Tuesday and Wednesday, the scene of a remarkable commotion.'

Apparently the Commissioners of Pavement tried to sink a well to erect a pump on Bachelors' Acre, which was successfully arrested.

In the issue of Saturday, 3rd July 1847, the Windsor and Eton Express reports:

'For his own part he [the Mayor] had no inclination to abridge the rights of the people in Bachelors' Acre. Although not a bachelor himself he had exerted himself in favour of them previous to Bachelors' Acre putting on its present decent appearance; but he was anxious to guard the rights of the Corporation as well as of the bachelors. Certainly they had an immemorial right to recreation there ...'

It was then reported that the mayor was requested to arrange with the Commissioners of Pavement for a proper site in the Acre 'so as not to interfere with the enjoyment of the same by the inhabitants ...'

The last extract is again from the Windsor and Eton Express dated 2nd October 1875. This recorded that Bachelors' Acre had been used for sports by a large number of people, that the mayor had vetoed the holding of the sports (on the wrong advice given to him by the town clerk on the legal effect of the inclosure award). Mr Alderman Cantrell is reported as saying that—

'He hoped that there would not be now or at any future time a majority in the Council who would deprive the youths of the town of the only spot where there could be any recreation.'

Since 1875, and on wrong advice, the right of the inhabitants has been disputed by the borough, and on the evidence as it now stands there has been no further use of the ground since 1875 by the inhabitants.

On this evidence, the Commissioner came to the conclusion that there had been long usage of Bachelors' Acre by the inhabitants for lawful pastimes. It was strongly argued for the borough that the evidence did not support such a conclusion. In particular, it was pointed out that there was no direct evidence of any user at all, that there was a finding that it had not been so used since 1875 and such a long period of non-user raises a strong presumption that there never was such a custom

---

1   (1872) LR 15 Eq 51
2   14th Edn (1938)

(*Hammerton v Honey*[1]). And in any event there was no evidence who the bachelors were.

Finally, it was submitted that the evidential value of newspaper reports and of reports of meetings is small if not negligible. In regard to the long period of non-user, if a custom is once established it cannot be abandoned or be extinguished except by an Act of Parliament (*Hammerton v Honey*[1] and *Wyld v Silver*[2]). In *Scales v Key*[3] there had been no user since 1689, but the custom was upheld. It is true that not a great deal of weight can be placed on newspaper reports, but they carry some weight, for in *Wyld v Silver*[4] Harman LJ quotes from the same paper.

It must, however, be remembered that this is an appeal by way of case stated, and an appeal only lies on a question of law. To use the well-known words of Lord Radcliffe in *Edwards v Bairstow*[5]:

'But, without any such misconception appearing ex facie, it may be that the facts found are such that no person acting judicially and properly instructed as to the relevant law could have come to the determination under appeal. In those circumstances, too, the court must intervene.'

In order to succeed, the borough must show that the Commissioner was not only wrong in the inferences of fact which he drew, but that no person acting judicially and properly instructed could have reached such a conclusion. There was, in my judgment, ample evidence on which the Commissioner could come to the conclusion that there had been long usage, and I, for my part, on that evidence would have come to the same conclusion.

(2) *That the claim had been made as of right*

The Commissioner came to the conclusion that the user has been as of right, in view of the leases granted, subject to the right and to the events in 1819 and 1822, to which I have referred. In my judgment, his conclusion was right.

(3) *That the right claimed is capable of existing as a custom*

It is well established that to create a custom the user must have been, by the inhabitants of an area, defined by reference to the limits of some recognised division of land such as a town (see Coke on Littleton[6], and *Mercer v Denne*[7]). This raises a question of construction of the words used in the lease of 1651. The Commissioner held that the words 'all and every other person or persons' and the words 'the people' must be read in their context and the covenant to set up a pair of butts 'for the inhabitants of the said town' to shoot at shows that those wide expressions should be limited to the inhabitants of the town. He therefore concluded that the custom was confined to the inhabitants of a particular locality.

Counsel for the borough submitted that the word 'burgesses' included all the inhabitants of the town, so that the expression 'all and every other person' must refer to persons residing outside the town, and reliance was placed on the definition of 'burgesses' in Wharton's Law Lexicon[8]: 'Generally the inhabitants of a borough or walled town'. In Stroud's Judicial Dictionary[9], 'Burgesses' is defined as referring to men of trade. Earlier in the lease there are found the words 'Mayor Bailiffs

---

1   (1876) 24 WR 603
2   [1962] 3 All ER 309, [1963] Ch 243
3   (1840) 11 Ad & El 819
4   [1962] 3 All ER at 316, [1963] Ch at 261
5   [1955] 3 All ER 48 at 57, [1956] AC 14 at 36
6   Page 110b
7   [1905] 2 Ch 538, [1904-7] All ER Rep 71
8   14th Edn (1938)
9   4th Edn (1971), vol 1, p 346

a Burgesses and their Successors', showing that the words 'Mayor Bailiffs and Burgesses' refer to the body corporate rather than to every person living in the town. It might well be ultra vires for the corporate body to provide benefits for persons not living within its boundaries, and it may be, but this is pure surmise, since there is only an extract from the lease, that after the words 'all and every other person or persons' there may have followed some words such as 'being inhabitants of the town', which occur later. I have, however, come to the conclusion that the Commissioner was *b* correct in confining the expressions used to the inhabitants of the town.

(4) *Does the custom arise from time immemorial?*

Counsel for the respondent submitted that once the first three points were established the court should be astute to find that the origin of the custom was from time immemorial, and he relied for his submission on three cases: *Cocksedge v Fanshaw*[1], *c* *Malcomson v O'Dea*[2] and *Johnson v Barnes*[3]. Counsel for the borough referred me to a statute of Henry VIII[4] which was not cited to the Commissioner, to show that the origin of the usage stemmed from that statute and not from time immemorial. If it could be shown that the right to use Bachelors' Acre stems from a statute passed after 1189, then the claim of a custom would be defeated (see *Simpson v Wells*[5]).

Section 4 of that statute is in these terms:

d '...(4) and also that Butts be made on this Side the Feast of St. *Michael* the Archangel next coming, in every City, Town and Place, by the Inhabitants of every such City, Town and Place, according to the Law of ancient Time used; (5) and that the Inhabitants and Dwellers in every of them be compelled to make and continue such Butts, upon Pain to forfeit for every three Months so lacking, xx.s. *e* (6) and that the said Inhabitants shall exercise themselves with Long-Bows in shooting at the same, and elsewhere, in holy Days and other Times convenient.'

But from the terms of s 4(4) the words 'according to the Law of ancient Time used' show that the making of butts was not started by virtue of that Act. The provisions do not negative the right having existed from time immemorial.

The court should therefore be astute to find the origin from time immemorial *f* and, in my judgment, the Commissioner was right to do so. For these reasons, in my judgment the appeal fails and I propose to dismiss it.

Appeal dismissed.

Solicitors: *Marris & Shepherd*, agents for *Town Clerk*, New Windsor (for the borough); *Gamlens*, agents for *Lovegrove & Durant*, Windsor (for the respondent).

g
                                       Jacqueline Metcalfe Barrister.

---

1 (1779) 1 Doug KB 119
2 (1863) 10 HL Cas 593
3 (1872) LR 7 CP 592
h 4 33 Hen 8 c 9
5 (1872) LR 7 QB 214

a

Buswell v Inland Revenue Commissioners

COURT OF APPEAL, CIVIL DIVISION
RUSSELL, STAMP AND ORR LJJ
15th, 18th, 19th, 20th FEBRUARY, 27th MARCH 1974

b

*Income tax – Domicile – Income arising from overseas securities and possessions – Taxpayer
not domiciled in United Kingdom – Assessment on a remittance basis – Change of domicile –
Acquisition of English domicile of choice – Onus of proof – Taxpayer having South African
domicile of origin – Taxpayer coming to United Kingdom and obtaining employment – Statement by taxpayer in answer to Revenue questionnaire that he intended to remain permanently* c
*in United Kingdom – Whether sufficient to establish taxpayer's acquisition of English domicile
of choice – Income Tax Act 1952, s 132(2)(a).*

The taxpayer's father, who was English, went to South Africa as a young man and
acquired a South African domicile of choice. The taxpayer was born in Johannesburg
in August 1921 and had a domicile of origin in South Africa. In 1928 his parents brought d
him to England to be educated there in compliance with the provisions of a trust
established by his grandfather's will. The taxpayer's father intended to return to
South Africa when the taxpayer's education was completed but, in the event, because
of the outbreak of war and subsequent ill-health, that proved impracticable. In
July 1941 the taxpayer was called up for military service and, having obtained a
commission in the Indian Army, went to India in December 1941. On demobilisation e
in 1945, he obtained two successive civilian employments in India, the second of
them with a firm of importers who had connections with a firm in Johannesburg.
In 1949 he spent a three month holiday in England and on the Continent. In July
1952 he returned to England mainly because of his father's ill-health. After his
arrival he obtained employment with an English company but after six months f
left them and went to work with British Olivetti in whose employment he remained
for ten years. The taxpayer's reason for joining the latter company was its international character and the hope that an opportunity might arise of his being posted
abroad. In November 1952 the taxpayer received a questionnaire from the Inland
Revenue, which included the following questions: 'Do you propose to remain
permanently in the United Kingdom? . . . If not, how long do you expect to remain
in this country?' It was not the purpose of that form to ascertain the taxpayer's g
domicile but to ascertain his entitlement to certain income tax allowances which
depended on residence in the United Kingdom. The taxpayer answered 'Yes' to the
first question, and put a dash against the second question. In 1955 the taxpayer
obtained a South African passport. In 1958 and subsequently the taxpayer expressed
to relatives his intention of returning to South Africa. The taxpayer's father died
in 1959. In 1961 the taxpayer married. His wife was in receipt of a substantial income h
from overseas sources. After South Africa left the Commonwealth in 1961 the
taxpayer elected to acquire South African nationality and subsequently he took
steps to register his two children as South African citizens. In 1963 the taxpayer
gave up his employment with British Olivetti. In 1968 the taxpayer and his wife
visited South Africa and bought a farm there on which they spent substantial sums
of money. Thereafter they regularly visited South Africa for some three months j
each year to supervise the harvesting and marketing of farm produce. They intended
to settle permanently in South Africa in 1976. The taxpayer was assessed to tax
on the full amount of his income arising from overseas possessions and securities
for the years 1961-62 to 1967-68. The taxpayer appealed against those assessments,
contending that during the relevant years he was 'not domiciled in the United

Kingdom' and therefore, under s 132(2)(*a*)(3)[a] of the Income Tax Act 1952, tax was chargeable on that income only on a remittance basis. The Special Commissioners affirmed the assessments holding that the contemporary evidence, in particular the taxpayer's answers to the Revenue questionnaire, established that, after he had come to England, he had acquired an English domicile of choice by November 1952. On appeal Pennycuick V-C[b] affirmed the decision holding that, on the facts, it was reasonable for the commissioners to have come to that conclusion. The taxpayer appealed.

Held – Apart from the answers given by the taxpayer to the questionnaire, there was no sufficient evidence on which the commissioners could reasonably have held that, in November 1952, less than five months after his arrival in England, the taxpayer had acquired a domicile of choice in place of his domicile of origin. In concluding that the taxpayer had acquired a domicile of choice in England the commissioners had attributed to the taxpayer's answers on the questionnaire a weight which, in all the circumstances, they could not reasonably bear. The commissioners had ignored the fact that, to a person who was not a lawyer, the meaning of the words 'propose to remain permanently' was by no means necessarily clear, and that, because of the way in which the questions had been put, a person who was uncertain of his future intentions might well have answered them in the manner in which the taxpayer had done. In consequence the taxpayer's answer to the first question was not a reliable pointer to his domiciliary intention and in attributing a decisive importance to the answer the commissioners had acted on a view of the facts which could not reasonably be entertained. The appeal would therefore be allowed (see p 527 *c d* and *g* to p 528 *d* and *j* to p 529 *b* and *d* and p 530 *b*, post).

Dicta of Lord Atkin in *Wahl v Attorney-General* [1932] All ER Rep at 926, and of Scarman J in *Re Fuld (decd) (No 3)* [1968] P at 684, 685, 686 applied.

Dictum of Scarman J in *Re Fuld (decd) (No 3)* [1968] P at 685 explained.

Per Stamp LJ. Even if, when he answered the questionnaire, the taxpayer did propose to remain permanently in the United Kingdom, it did not follow that he had the settled intention to remain which had to be shown in order to establish the abandonment of a domicile of origin by the acquisition of a domicile of choice (see p 529 *e*, post).

Notes

For change of domicile, see 7 Halsbury's Laws (3rd Edn) 18-23, paras 33-43, and for cases on the subject, see 11 Digest (Repl) 331-333, 54-68.

For the Income Tax Act 1952, s 132, see 31 Halsbury's Statutes (2nd Edn) 128.

For 1970-71 and subsequent years of assessment, s 132 of the 1952 Act has been replaced by s 122 of the Income and Corporation Taxes Act 1970.

Cases referred to in judgments

Bell v Kennedy (1868) LR 1 Sc & Div 307, HL, 11 Digest (Repl) 329, 39.

---

a   Section 132, so far as material, provides:

'(1) Subject to the provisions of this and the two next following sections, tax chargeable under Case IV or Case V of Schedule D shall be computed on the full amount of the income arising in the year preceding the year of assessment, whether the income has been or will be received in the United Kingdom or not ...'

'(2) Subsection (1) of this section shall not apply—(*a*) to any person who satisfies the Commissioners of Inland Revenue that he is not domiciled in the United Kingdom ...'

'(3) In the cases mentioned in subsection (2) of this section, the tax shall ... be computed [on a remittance basis] ...'

b   [1973] STC 267

Edwards (Inspector of Taxes) v Bairstow [1955] 3 All ER 48, [1956] AC 14, 36 Tax Cas
  207, [1955] 3 WLR 410, 34 ATC 198, [1955] TR 209, 48 R & IT 534, HL, 28(1) Digest
  (Reissue) 566, 2089.
Fuld (decd) (No 3), Re, Hartley v Fuld [1968] P 675, [1966] 2 WLR 717.
Wahl v Attorney-General [1932] All ER Rep 922, 147 LT 382, HL, 11 Digest (Repl)
  345, 145.
Winans v Attorney-General [1904] AC 287, [1904-7] All ER Rep 410, 73 LJKB 613, 90
  LT 721, HL, 11 Digest (Repl) 329, 41.

Cases also cited

Steiner v Inland Revenue Comrs [1973] STC 547, CA.
Udny v Udny (1869) LR 1 Sc & Div 441, HL.

Appeal

The taxpayer, Leslie Charles Croft Buswell, appealed against an order of Pennycuick
V-C[1] made on 23rd March 1973 whereby, on a case stated by the Commissioners
for the Special Purposes of the Income Tax Acts, he dismissed the appeal by the
taxpayer against the decision of the commissioners rejecting the taxpayer's claim
that for the years 1961-62 to 1967-68 inclusive he was not domiciled in the United
Kingdom and so was entitled under s 132(2)(a)(3) of the Income Tax Act 1952 to have
his liability to tax for those years in respect of income from foreign possessions and
securities computed in accordance with s 132(3). The facts are set out in the judgment
of Orr LJ.

C N Beattie QC and *M E P Jump* for the taxpayer.
Martin Nourse QC, *Patrick Medd QC* and *Harry Woolf* for the Crown.

27th March. The following judgments were read.

Cur adv vult

ORR LJ read the first judgment at the invitation of Russell LJ. This is a taxpayer's appeal against a judgment of Pennycuick V-C[1] dated 23rd March 1973
whereby he affirmed a determination of the Special Commissioners in favour of
the Crown.

  The question arising in the appeal is as to the taxpayer's domicile for the income
tax years 1961-62 to 1967-68, and the relevant statutory provisions are contained in
s 132 of the Income Tax Act 1952, which, so far as material, provides that a taxpayer
shall be chargeable on the full amount of his income (which includes for the present
purposes his wife's income) arising in the year preceding the year of assessment,
whether or not it has been received in the United Kingdom, unless he satisfies the
Inland Revenue Commissioners that he was not in the relevant period 'domiciled
in the United Kingdom', in which event he is taxable only on what is commonly
called a remittance basis, that is to say on 'the full amount . . . of the sums received
in the United Kingdom' during the year in question. The taxpayer in the present
case made a claim that in the years 1961-68 he was not domiciled in the United Kingdom and was therefore entitled to be taxed on a remittance basis, but the Inland
Revenue Commissioners rejected that claim and he appealed against that rejection
to the Special Commissioners whose determination was that on the evidence he was
during the period in question domiciled in the United Kingdom.

  The taxpayer was born in Johannesburg on 3rd August 1921; his father, who had
an English domicile of origin and was originally a British national, having gone as
a young man to live in the Transvaal and having married in South Africa, as his
second wife, the taxpayer's mother who had been born in South Africa of English

a parents. The taxpayer lived in Johannesburg with his parents until 1928, when, because of the insistence of the trustees of the taxpayer's grandfather's will (under which the taxpayer's father was a beneficiary) that the taxpayer should be educated here, they came to England where the taxpayer attended a boarding school until December 1939, while his parents found temporary accommodation in different places. There was evidence that the father came to England reluctantly but the

b mother willingly, since she wished the boy to be educated here and also wished to get her husband away from Johannesburg.

On leaving school, the taxpayer was employed temporarily as a teacher until he was called up for military service in July 1941. During this period, in 1940, his parents moved to a rented house in Stoke Mandeville, where they continued to live until the father died in 1959, and in which the mother is still living, the trustees of the

c grandfather's will (who had previously bought the house) having conveyed it to her after her husband's death. In December 1941 the taxpayer went to India, where he had obtained a commission in the Indian Army, but he later transferred to the Indian Navy in which he served until demobilised in late 1945. Thereafter, he obtained two successive civilian employments in India, the second of them with a firm of importers who had connections with a firm in Johannesburg. During this period,

d in 1949, he had spent a three month holiday in England and on the Continent, and in July 1952 he finally left India and came here. The Special Commissioners were satisfied that he liked India and, but for Indian independence, might well have settled there, but it was not suggested that he had at any time acquired an Indian domicile of choice.

There was evidence before the commissioners, which they accepted, that during

e the pre-war years the father, who never engaged in any work in England save for a brief period in 1935-36, often said that if it were not for his son he would not be here and often spoke of his intending to go back to South Africa. The commissioners also accepted that during the war the taxpayer's parents had not considered it practicable to return to South Africa and after the war had continued to live at Stoke Mandeville partly for financial reasons and partly because, so long as the taxpayer

f remained in India, they wished to wait and see what he would eventually decide to do; and they found that it was not until some years before 1958 that the father abandoned any realistic hopes of returning to South Africa.

At this point in the narrative of events it is convenient to refer to the three issues which arose before the commissioners. The first of these was whether at the time of the taxpayer's birth his father retained his English domicile of origin, or had acquired a South African domicile of origin. The second question was whether,

g before the taxpayer attained his majority, his father had reverted to his English domicile of origin with the result that the taxpayer would also have acquired a domicile here. The third question was whether, if the taxpayer on the date of his attaining his majority had a South African domicile of origin, he subsequently, between that date and the tax years in question, acquired a domicile of choice in England.

h On the material which I have so far reviewed, the commissioners decided the first two of these questions in favour of the taxpayer. They held that his father had before the taxpayer's birth acquired a South African domicile of choice and had not during the taxpayer's minority reverted to his English domicile of origin, with the result that the taxpayer had on obtaining his majority a South African domicile, and these conclusions were not challenged by the Crown on the appeal to Pennycuick

j V-C[1]. But the commissioners went on to decide the third issue, as to the taxpayer's acquisition, after attaining his majority but before 1961, of an English domicile of choice, in favour of the Crown, and to the evidence on that issue, which was the only issue before Pennycuick V-C, I now turn.

1 [1973] STC 267

The taxpayer, as I have said, left India in 1952 and came to England, and in deciding   *a*
to do so the commissioners found that he had in mind mainly his father's poor
state of health and also that a girl he had met in India had returned here. After his
arrival in England he obtained, in November 1952, employment with George Newnes,
the publishers, but after six months left them and went to work for British Olivetti,
in whose employment he remained for ten years. The commissioners found that
one of his reasons for joining this company was its international character and the   *b*
hope that an opportunity might arise of his being posted abroad.

On 11th November 1952 the taxpayer answered in writing an Inland Revenue
questionnaire (Form P 86) which he had almost certainly received as a result of
accepting employment with George Newnes, since they would wish to know what
tax coding should be applied to his remuneration. In answer to the first two questions
on this form, he correctly stated that he was a British subject and had arrived in the   *c*
United Kingdom on 8th July 1952. To the third question, which enquired when and
by whom he had been employed prior to his arrival and for how long, he replied,
'Bombay, India. Messrs. J. Stevenson & Co. Bombay 10 1945-1952', and this answer
was not entirely accurate since he had during part of that period been in other
employment. To question 5(a), 'Do you propose to remain permanently in the
United Kingdom?', he replied, 'Yes', and against question 5(b), 'If not, how long   *d*
do you expect to remain in this country?' he put a dash.

Because in the event the commissioners clearly attached very great importance
to his answer to question 5(a) on this form, it is necessary to refer both to the object
of the form and to the taxpayer's evidence before the commissioners as to the circumstances in which he filled it in. Counsel for the Crown has made it clear that it is
no part of the purpose of this form to ascertain domicile, that being an issue which   *e*
the Revenue leave to the taxpayer to raise if he so desires, and in fact at the time
when these answers were given, the taxpayer's domicile was irrelevant to his taxation
since he had no income from abroad. It was, however, one of the objects of the form
to ascertain whether the signatory was entitled to personal allowances for the purposes
of United Kingdom income tax, the entitlement to which depends on residence
here; and as to that matter it is clear that the taxpayer was at the time not only   *f*
resident but ordinarily resident here.

The taxpayer's evidence was that the form bore his signature but that he did not
remember completing it. He thought, however, that his attitude would have been
that the answers should be true in essence but preferably short and simple. He had
not appreciated the need for complete accuracy, as he claimed was indicated by
his answer to question 3, and he thought that any other answer than he had given to   *g*
question 5(a) would have had to be followed by an explanation about his father's
health, and that as he was expecting to stay in the United Kingdom indefinitely,
perhaps for four years or so, he could properly say that he proposed to remain here
permanently.

After his return to England the taxpayer for some years spent part of his time
with his parents and the rest of it in rented accommodation in London. He had   *h*
on his return from India an Indian passport in which he was described as a British
subject born in South Africa. In July 1955 he went to South Africa House and, on
being informed that since he had been born in South Africa it was open to him to
apply for a South African passport, he did so and obtained one. In 1958 a Miss Denise
Bywater (now Mrs Milroy), the daughter of a first cousin of his living in South Africa,
visited England for some months and her evidence was that he mentioned several   *j*
times to her an intention of going back to South Africa but said that he could not
do so for the time being partly because his mother was unwell and did not want
to return there, and partly because he could not afford to establish himself in business
there. During the same period, in October 1958, he wrote to Denise's mother a letter
which contained the following passage:

'I am quite sure that one day I will come back to South Africa. I have been *a* back in England some seven years now—and I can never get used to this god-forsaken climate. In fact but for my parents I would never have stopped this long.'

In March 1960, the year following his father's death, the taxpayer bought a property in Osten Mews, London, as a residence for himself, but shortly afterwards he met his present wife, whose father is Lord Fisher of Kilverston and her mother an American,
b and who receives a substantial income from overseas sources, and they married on 21st July 1961. His wife owns a London house in which they began their married life, and the Osten Mews property was sold. In 1962 they bought a house at Burgess Hill at a cost of some £10,000 and spent a further £30,000 on rebuilding it, and since then have normally lived there or in the wife's London house.

In 1963 the taxpayer gave up his employment with British Olivetti. Thereafter,
c he had for a time interests in certain businesses, but for the most part devoted himself to the garden at Burgess Hill and regularly visited his mother. He and his wife have two children, a son born in 1965, who at the time of the hearing had begun to go to school in this country, and a daughter born in 1968. After South Africa left the Commonwealth in 1961 the taxpayer elected to acquire South African nationality and he has since taken the appropriate steps to have the children also registered as
d South African citizens.

In July 1967 the taxpayer answered in writing a number of questions by the inspector of taxes, stating that he considered himself domiciled in South Africa because that was his domicile of origin which he claimed never to have abandoned; that he had no business connections but many family connections with that country; and that his future intentions were indefinite since he had made no long-range
e plans.

In January 1968 the taxpayer and his wife paid a two month visit to South Africa, this being the first visit (apart from a wartime transit stop) which he had paid to that country since leaving it in 1928. The objects of the visit were to introduce his wife to South Africa and to look for a suitable property in which they could settle down, and they in fact arranged during the visit to buy a property, Seaton Farm,
f Stellenbosch, Cape Province, for £40,000, and on rebuilding and improving it have since spent a further £80,000. Since then they have regularly visited South Africa for some three months in each year, going early in the year so that the taxpayer can supervise the harvesting and the marketing of the farm produce.

The evidence of the taxpayer and his wife, which the commissioners accepted, was that they had before their marriage discussed where they would subsequently
g live, and neither of them wished to live in England. The taxpayer at that time had in mind going back some time to South Africa and his wife welcomed this idea, but they had obligations towards the taxpayer's mother, who did not wish to leave England. They had hoped that she would make her home with them at Burgess Hill, but she has been unwilling to do so. As to the children, they considered it desirable that both should complete their education in England, but their intention
h at the time of the hearing was to settle in South Africa in 1976 with a view to the children travelling to and fro for holidays during the remaining years of their education.

Apart from his own and his wife's evidence, the taxpayer's case was supported by affidavit evidence, which the commissioners accepted, that on many occasions after his marriage he had told South African relations of his intention to return there event-
j ually, and he had mentioned this also to Mr Simpson, the architect employed in relation to the rebuilding at Burgess Hill. The commissioners, however, while they did not doubt the taxpayer's honesty, were entitled, as respects declarations made by him in this period, to bear in mind that after his marriage it was very much in his interest to have retained a South African domicile.

On the material I have summarised the commissioners, in relation to the issue as to the acquisition by the taxpayer of a domicile of choice in England, took the view

that they had to consider very carefully the position in 1952 when he returned
to England from India. They referred to the background of the taxpayer, his circum-   *a*
stances (including his age at 31 which they apparently considered a suitable age for
settling down), and his accepting employment in this country, and formed the view
that at that time his acquiring a domicile of choice here was by no means an unlikely
event.

They then considered his written answers to the questions put to him on form P 86   *b*
in November of that year and his explanation of those answers which they accepted
as entirely honest, but rightly considered that they could not accept as accurate
evidence of what had been in his mind at the time, since he did not remember
filling in the form. They concluded that there was no adequate reason to read the
questions or the answers as meaning anything other than they appeared to mean,
giving the words used their ordinary meaning; and on the evidence came to the   *c*
conclusion that, apart from consideration of subsequent events, the Crown had
discharged the onus of showing that the taxpayer acquired in 1952 a domicile of
choice in England. They then proceeded, however, to consider whether subsequent
happenings might lead them to think that this conclusion would be wrong and in
so doing accepted that, if the taxpayer had had to answer the questionnaire in 1955
or later, he might well have answered it differently, but in the end they found that   *d*
the subsequent happenings did not justify their arriving at a different conclusion
from that which they had reached on the circumstances existing in 1952, and they
accordingly dismissed the appeal.

On the taxpayer's appeal against this determination, Pennycuick V-C found it
impossible to hold that the commissioners had, in the words of Viscount Simonds
in *Edwards (Inspector of Taxes) v Bairstow*[1], acted 'on a view of the facts which could   *e*
not reasonably be entertained', and he therefore dismissed the appeal. In the course
of his judgment, he referred to two questions of law, the first as to the nature of the
intention which must be proved in order to establish the acquisition of a domicile
of choice in place of a domicile of origin, and the second as to the standard of proof
which has to be satisfied for that purpose, and as to both these questions cited passages
from the judgment of Scarman J in *Re Fuld (No 3)*[2].   *f*

As to the intention to be proved Scarman J, after referring to the 'strongly adhesive
quality' of the domicile of origin, and to the leading authorities, said[3]:

> '... a domicile of choice is acquired only if it be affirmatively shown that the
> propositus is resident within a territory ... with the intention, formed indepen-
> dently of external pressures, of residing there indefinitely. If a man intends to
> return to the land of his birth upon a clearly foreseen and reasonably anticipated   *g*
> contingency, e.g., the end of his job, the intention required by law is lacking;
> but if he has in mind only a vague possibility, such as making a fortune (a modern
> example might be winning a football pool), or some sentiment about dying
> in the land of his fathers, such a state of mind is consistent with the intention
> required by law. But no clear line can be drawn; the ultimate decision in each
> case is one of fact ...'   *h*

As to the second question Scarman J, after rejecting the application in this context
of the criminal standard of proof beyond reasonable doubt, said[4]:

> 'Two things are clear—first, that unless the judicial conscience is satisfied by
> evidence of change, the domicile of origin persists: and secondly, that the acquisi-
> tion of a domicile of choice is a serious matter not to be lightly inferred from   *j*
> slight indications or casual words.'

1   [1955] 3 All ER 48 at 53, [1956] AC 14 at 29, 36 Tax Cas 207 at 224
2   [1968] P 675
3   [1968] P at 684, 685
4   [1968] P at 686

a On this appeal the accuracy of these statements has not been in dispute and it
was not contended that Scarman J was wrong in rejecting in this context the criminal
standard of proof. I too accept the statements as accurate and would only add that
in referring to the judicial conscience I am satisfied that Scarman J was not recognising
the existence of some general standard of proof intermediate between the criminal
and civil standards but was merely emphasising that in the application of the civil
standard the degree of proof required will vary with the subject-matter of the case.
b Hereunder, reference may be made to the description of the domicile of origin as
strongly adhesive.

In these circumstances, there being no issue as to the principle of law applicable,
counsel for the taxpayer has in this court based his arguments solely on the proposition
that in arriving at their determination the commissioners acted, in the words of
Viscount Simonds[1] already quoted, 'on a view of the facts which could not reason-
c ably be entertained'. He argued first that, apart from the answers given by the
taxpayer on the form P86, there was no sufficient evidence on which the commissioners could reasonably have held that in November 1952, less than five months
after his arrival in this country in the circumstances to which I have referred, he
acquired a domicile of choice here in place of his domicile of origin, and secondly
that in arriving at their determination they attributed an unreasonable weight to
d those answers.

In my judgment, the first of these arguments is well-founded. There were indeed
matters which might have led the taxpayer to acquire in 1952 an English domicile;
these including his English background on his father's side until the father emigrated
to South Africa and on his mother's side until her parents settled there; the fact
that his formative years from the age of seven to 20, when he left for India, were
e spent in England; that his departure from England in 1941 was due to the war;
and that it was to England and not to South Africa that he returned in 1952, although
this last fact may call for no further explanation than that his parents were here and
his father in poor health.

On the other side were his birth and childhood in South Africa; his having chosen
f to enter in India an employment with a South African connection; and his father's
hopes of returning to that country. Moreover, if regard is had to later events, his
joining British Olivetti with a view to a possible foreign posting, although it did
not necessarily point to South Africa, certainly gave no support at that time to an
inference of intention to acquire an English domicile; and his acquiring in 1955 a
South African rather than an English passport and his declaration to Denise and,
by letter, to his mother, pointed towards South Africa.

g Weighing these factors, the commissioners were entitled to conclude that it was
possible, and may even have been quite likely, that he might in 1952 acquire an
English domicile of choice, but if the answers on the form P86 are disregarded, the
only evidence of his having actually done so would be his acceptance of an employment with George Newnes which in the event lasted only for six months. This fact
was, in my judgment, plainly insufficient evidence for that purpose, and it is clear
h that the commissioners also thought so and that without the answers on the form
P86 they would not have found an English domicile.

The crucial question in the appeal is therefore whether the commissioners, in
coming to their conclusion, attributed to the answers on form P86 a weight which
in all the circumstances they could not reasonably bear. For this purpose it is neces-
j sary to consider both the terms of the questions asked on the form and the circumstances in which it may reasonably be supposed that the taxpayer answered them.
As I have already said, the form was not intended by the Revenue to ascertain
domicile and it nowhere used that word. It does enquire in question 5(a) whether
the addressee proposes to remain permanently in the United Kingdom, and to a

---

1   [1955] 3 All ER at 53, [1956] AC at 29, 36 Tax Cas at 224

lawyer an intention to remain permanently in a country is the test of domicile, but the meaning of 'propose to remain permanently' is by no means necessarily clear to a layman, and on the form this question is immediately followed by the further question 5(b), 'If not, how long do you expect to remain in this country?', which might well convey to the addressee that unless he is able to put against that question a date or an approximate date of proposed departure from this country, the answer to the preceding question must be, Yes. A person uncertain of his intentions as to the future, faced with these (in terms) mutually exclusive questions, would, I think, be very likely to consider that he was not expected to say 'I do not know' in answer to the second question, an answer which would have to be given if he said, No, to the first.

It was suggested for the Crown that the logical difficulty, arising from the introductory words 'If not' in question 5(b), might be overcome by bracketing the two questions and giving a single answer, but persons filling in public forms may hesitate to bracket questions, and I do not find this solution at all satisfactory. It is clear that the commissioners attached very great importance to the taxpayer's answer to question 5(a) and also that they did so because they ignored the factors that I have mentioned and those stated (by way of supposition rather than evidence) by the taxpayer, which factors in my judgment make the answer quite unreliable in the present case as a pointer to domiciliary intention.

I have borne in mind, in reaching this conclusion, that the commissioners enjoyed the advantage, which this court has not had, of seeing and hearing the taxpayer, and for this reason I would have hesitated long before criticising the determination but for the facts that they found him to be an honest witness and that they were not concerned with evidence as to what he had thought but with argument as to what he might have thought.

We were referred in the course of argument to the speeches of the majority of the House of Lords in *Wahl v Attorney-General*[1], in which the deceased, whose domicile at the time of his death was in issue for estate duty purposes, had many years before his death applied for and obtained naturalisation as a British subject, and had in his memorial for that purpose, which he deposed by a statutory declaration to be true, stated that he intended to continue to reside permanently within the United Kingdom. The House (Lord Macmillan dissenting) held, reversing a decision of this court, which had upheld a judgment of Rowlatt J, that notwithstanding this statement the deceased at his death retained a German domicile, and Lord Atkin said[2]:

'I am far from saying that an application for naturalisation is not a matter to be carefully considered as part of the evidence in a case of domicil, but it must be regarded as one of the totality of facts, and it cannot assume the dominant importance attached to it in the judgment of the trial judge.'

In my judgment, the concluding words of this passage are applicable with even greater force to the commissioners' determination in the present case since in that case, as in this, a decisive importance was clearly attributed to the statement in question, but in that case, unlike this, the statement was deposed by statutory declaration to be true, which gave it an added solemnity. I am far from thinking that the facts of *Wahl's* case[1] were at all close to those with which we are now concerned, but I find in Lord Atkin's statement additional support for the view I would have taken without reference to *Wahl's* case[1], that in attributing a decisive importance to the taxpayer's answers on the form P86, given at the time when he had been back in this country for less than five months after an absence of ten years, and against the background to which I have referred, the commissioners acted 'on a view of the facts which could not reasonably be entertained'[3].

1 [1932] All ER Rep 922
2 [1932] All ER Rep at 926
3 See *Edwards (Inspector of Taxes) v Bairstow* [1955] 3 All ER at 53, [1956] AC at 29, 36 Tax Cas at 224, per Viscount Simonds

I have reached this conclusion with great respect for the view taken by two experienced commissioners and for the judgment of Pennycuick V-C, who dismissed the appeal; but, in my judgment, the evidence in the case was not sufficient to justify an inference that in 1952 the taxpayer acquired a domicile of choice in place of his domicile of origin, and for these reasons I would allow the appeal.

RUSSELL LJ. I agree with the judgment that has just been delivered. In the course of argument, our attention was drawn to a slip in the judgment of Scarman J as reported in *Re Fuld (decd) (No 3)*[1], and I take this occasion to correct it. It is there stated that if a man—

> 'has acquired but *abandoned* a domicile of choice *either* because he no longer resides in the territory *or* because he no longer intends to reside there indefinitely, the domicile of origin revives . . .'

This is not a correct statement of the law. Neither of those two facts per se amounts to abandonment of the domicile of choice. I make this correction with the approval of Scarman LJ, with whom I have discussed it.

STAMP LJ (read by Russell LJ). I agree with the judgment of Orr LJ. I am, however, prepared to assume that the taxpayer did in truth, at the moment of time when he signed the form P86, '*propose* to remain permanently in the United Kingdom'. It does not, however, follow that he had then that settled intention so to remain which is to be shown in order to show the abandonment of a domicile of origin by the establishment of a domicile of choice. He had been over ten years in India, and accepting that in the circumstances in which he found himself he might have been expected in due course to settle in England, I cannot accept that it was at all probable that a young man of 31 would after just over four months in this country have firmly made up his mind, or determined, to do so. Having obtained employment with George Newnes & Co, he probably did, as he said in answer to the question, then propose to remain here permanently; but it does not in the least follow that, asked the same question a week earlier, or a month after he had entered that employment, he would have answered it in the same sense or been of the same mind. If today I 'propose' to spend my next summer holiday in such and such a place, it does not in the least follow that next week I will not change my mind.

The question asked in the form P86 would have been more apt for the purpose of obtaining an answer relevant to domicile if it had been in the form: 'Are you sure that you have quite made up your mind to live permanently in England and not elsewhere?' But even had that been the question, I would have thought the affirmative answer given at that moment of time would have been a fragile foundation for the commissioners' finding.

The problem of determining the strength of the evidence required to prove the establishment of a new domicile in another country displacing the domicile of origin perhaps almost disappears if it be remembered that what is required, so far as the animus is concerned, is proof, to quote the words of Lord Westbury in *Bell v Kennedy*[2], of a 'settled fixed intention of being permanently resident' in that country: see also the speeches of Lord Chelmsford[3] and Lord Cairns LC[4], both of whom used the expression 'fixed intention'. It is to be noted in this connection that Scarman J in *Re Fuld (decd)*

---

1 [1968] P 675 at 685
2 (1868) LR 1 Sc & Div 307 at 321
3 (1868) LR 1 Sc & Div at 319
4 (1868) LR 1 Sc & Div at 318

(*No 3*)[1] referred to *Bell v Kennedy*[2] and to *Winans v Attorney-General*[3] (where Lord Macnaghten insists on the necessity of 'a fixed and settled purpose') as illustrative of 'the adhesive character' of a domicile of origin.

It may be, and I express no concluded opinion because the question was only touched on in the course of the arguments, that so far as the standard of proof of the animus manendi is concerned it is enough that it should be shown clearly that the propositus had a fixed and settled intention to live permanently in the chosen country. However that may be, that fixed intention is not to be deduced from a single statement in a form P86.

Appeal allowed.   Leave to appeal to the House of Lords refused.

Solicitors: *Riders* (for the taxpayer); *Solicitor of Inland Revenue.*

Rengan Krishnan Esq Barrister.

Re Mallinson Consolidated Trusts
Mallinson and others v Gooley and others

CHANCERY DIVISION
TEMPLEMAN J
14th MARCH, 3rd APRIL 1974

Settlement – Contingent interest – Contingent interest distinguished from vested interest liable to be divested – Interest subject to condition precedent or subsequent – Gift over on failure of condition – Appointment – Appointed funds to be held on trust for beneficiary 'if she shall attain the age of 21-years and subject as aforesaid' for two other persons – Whether beneficiary having vested interest liable to be divested.

By an appointment made in September 1963, pursuant to a power in a settlement to appoint in favour of the settlor's issue, the trust fund was appointed on trust for the settlor's daughter 'if she shall attain the age of 21-years and subject as aforesaid upon trust for such of [the settlor's two other children] as shall attain the age of 30 years and if both in equal shares'.   Clause 3 of the appointment directed that s 31 of the Trustee Act 1925 should apply.   The appointment was revocable.   Subject to the appointment, the trust fund was held on the powers and subject to the trusts of the settlement, which included a power to apply income for the benefit of the settlor's issue, and a trust for such of his children who should be living on a defined perpetuity date and should attain the age of 21 years.   The daughter, who was born in September 1947, married in July 1965.   The appointment was revoked in September 1966, and the daughter attained the age of 21 in September 1968.   On a summons by the trustees of the settlement to determine the destination of the income of the property subject to the trusts accruing between October 1963 and September 1966, the daughter contended that, since the appointment and the settlement provided for remainders taking effect if her interest failed or was revoked, she had a vested interest liable to be divested and was accordingly entitled to the accumulations.

Held – For an interest to subsist as a vested interest liable to be divested rather than as a contingent interest, there had to be an express gift over which spelt out the

---

1 [1968] P 675 at 684
2 (1868) LR 1 Sc & Div 307
3 [1904] AC 287, [1904-7] All ER Rep 410

conditions on which the gift over would take place, and those conditions had to include the counterparts, though not necessarily identical counterparts, of the conditions applicable to the prior gift; under the appointment there was no such gift over after the gift to the daughter; her interest was therefore a contingent one and accordingly the income accumulated during her minority was added to capital, to which she was not entitled in view of the revocation of the appointment (see p 532 *c* and p 534 *d* to *h*, post).

Phipps v Ackers (1842) 9 Cl & Fin 583 explained.

Notes

For the rule in *Phipps v Ackers*, see 39 Halsbury's Laws (3rd Edn) 1124, 1125, para 1660; for contingent gifts over, see ibid 1127, 1128, para 1664; and for cases on the subject, see 49 Digest (Repl) 974-979, 9154-9187.

For the Trustee Act 1925, s 31, see 38 Halsbury's Statutes (3rd Edn) 137.

Cases referred to in judgment

Heath, Re, Public Trustee v Heath [1936] Ch 259, [1935] All ER Rep 677, 105 LJCh 29, 154 LT 536, 49 Digest (Repl) 1037, 9711.

Penton's Settlements, Re, Humphreys v Birch-Reynardson [1968] 1 All ER 36, [1968] 1 WLR 248, Digest (Cont Vol C) 874, 2715*a*.

Phipps v Ackers (1842) 9 Cl & Fin 583, [1558-1774] All ER Rep 381, 4 Man & G 1107, 8 ER 539, HL, 49 Digest (Repl) 975, 9163.

Cases also cited

Blackwell, Re, Blackwell v Blackwell [1925] Ch 312; *affd* [1926] Ch 223, [1925] All ER Rep 498, CA.

Finch v Lane (1870) LR 10 Eq 501.

Kilpatrick's Policies Trusts, Re, Kilpatrick v Inland Revenue Comrs [1966] 2 All ER 149, [1966] Ch 730, CA.

McGredy and McGredy's Trustees v Inland Revenue Comrs (1951) 32 Tax Cas 338.

Sharp's Settlement Trusts, Re, Ibbotson v Bliss [1972] 3 All ER 151, [1973] Ch 331.

Turner's Will Trusts, Re, District Bank Ltd v Turner [1936] 3 All ER 1435, [1937] Ch 15, CA.

Whitter v Bremridge (1866) LR 2 Eq 736.

Adjourned summons

By an originating summons dated 30th April 1973, the plaintiffs, Sir William Paul Mallinson, Raymond Evans Bussell and Denis John Parr, the trustees of the Mallinson Consolidated Trusts, sought the determination by the court of the question whether, on the true construction of (a) two deeds of revocation and appointment dated 27th September 1963 and 23rd September 1966 made by the plaintiffs, and (b) s 31 of the Trustee Act 1925, the income of the property subject to the trusts of the deeds accruing between 7th October 1963 and 23rd September 1966 (and the investments representing the accumulations thereof) were in the events which had happened held (a) in trust for the first defendant, Hilary Eila Gooley, absolutely, or (b) on the trusts affecting the property subject to the deed of revocation and appointment dated 23rd September 1966, or (c) on some other, and if so what, trusts. The second to seventh defendants were Hannah Scrase, James Ivan Scrase, Paul Achilles St Clair Barrow, William James Mallinson, Kate Sophia Mallinson and Tristan Patrick Gooley, representing persons interested in the capital or income of the property subject to the deed of revocation and appointment dated 23rd September 1966. The facts are set out in the judgment.

Richard Scott for the plaintiffs.
Philip Rossdale for the first defendant.
Robert Walker for the second to seventh defendants.

Cur adv vult

3rd April. **TEMPLEMAN J** read the following judgment. This summons concerns the rule in *Phipps v Ackers*[1] and the distinction between a contingent interest and a vested interest liable to be divested. The rule was respectably ancient even in 1842; its secrets lurk in the chain Bibles of Chancery practitioners. The rule, which has outlived its usefulness, usually applies as a result of poor and verbose drafting which defeats the inclination of the testator or settlor; it sometimes favours the Revenue and sometimes affords relief to the taxpayer. Unless and until the rule is swept away by the Law Commission this case will serve as a useful illustration of the simple method of avoiding the rule.

The question in this case is whether there was appointed to the first defendant, Mrs Gooley, a contingent interest or a vested interest liable to be divested. The answer to this abstruse question involves practical consequences; if the interest of Mrs Gooley was contingent, then the income accumulated under the appointment during her minority became capital which in view of the subsequent revocation of the appointment does not belong to her. If the interest of Mrs Gooley was a vested interest liable to be divested then the accumulated income belongs to her; the Revenue, as they have intimated, will be entitled to consequential surtax and capital gains tax. A decision must therefore be reached and counsel for Mrs Gooley submitted strenuously and comprehensively that her interest was vested liable to be divested.

The appointment was made pursuant to a power in a settlement to appoint in favour of the issue of Sir Paul Mallinson. The trust fund was appointed on trust for Mrs Gooley, then Hilary Eila Mallinson—

'if she shall attain the age of 21-years and subject as aforesaid upon trust for such of the said ANGELA MARY MALLINSON and WILLIAM JOHN MALLINSON as shall attain the age of 30 years and if both in equal shares'.

The appointment contained a power of revocation and new appointment. Subject to the appointment, the trust fund was held with the powers and subject to the trusts of the settlement, namely the power exercised by the appointment, a power to apply income for the benefit of the issue of Sir Paul Mallinson and a trust for the children of Sir Paul who shall be living on a defined perpetuity date and shall attain the age of 21 years.

The appointment was dated 27th September 1963. Mrs Gooley married on 3rd July 1965. The appointment was revoked on 23rd September 1966. Mrs Gooley attained 21 on 9th September 1968.

Clause 3 of the appointment directed that:

'THE provisions of Section 31 of the Trustee Act 1925 as made applicable to the Settlement shall apply to the income of the interests hereby created pending the vesting thereof.'

The settlement applied s 31 as if the trustees had an absolute discretion to determine whether and if so how much income they would apply for the benefit of an infant.

Section 31 of the Trustee Act 1925 provides that where any property is held by trustees in trust for any person for any interest whatsoever, whether vested or contingent, the trustees during the infancy of any such person, if his interest so long continues, may apply the whole or part of the income for the benefit of that infant and shall accumulate any residue. If any such person—

'attains the age of twenty-one years, or marries under that age, and his interest in such income during his infancy or until his marriage is a vested interest ... the trustees shall hold the accumulations in trust for such person absolutely ...'

---

1 (1842) 9 Cl & Fin 583, [1558-1774] All ER Rep 381

If Mrs Gooley had a vested interest liable to be divested she thus became entitled to the accumulations. If she only had a contingent interest the accumulated income became capital under further provisions of s 31.

Counsel admits that an interest for Mrs Gooley 'if she shall attain the age of 21 years', if it stood alone, would be a contingent interest. But, he says, because the appointment and the settlement in fact provided remainders taking effect if the interest of Mrs Gooley failed or if the appointment were revoked, the rule in *Phipps v Ackers*[1] converted the contingent interest into a vested interest liable to be divested. The rule has been so extended, it is argued, that there are only two methods of creating a contingent interest, first by expressly directing that the interest shall be contingent and secondly by creating one interest only, namely a contingent interest with no remainders so that on failure of the contingency there is a resulting trust. It is common ground that the reason for the rule is to be found in a medieval horror of a vacuum, so that equity leans in favour of early vesting but I shall be reluctant to conclude that equity has leaned so far as to fall flat on her face. It is necessary to consider not the reason for the rule but what it is that brings the rule into play and converts what would otherwise be a contingent interest into a vested interest liable to be divested.

In *Phipps v Ackers*[1] a devise to the testator's godson 'when and as soon as he . . . shall attain his age of 21 years' was followed by a direction that 'in case my said godson . . . shall depart this life before he attains the said age of 21 years without . . . issue', the property shall fall into residue. The judges advised[2]—

> 'that the subsequent gift over in the event of the devisee dying under 21, sufficiently shows the meaning of the testator to have been that the first devisee should take whatever interest the party claiming under the devise over is not entitled to, which of course gives him the immediate interest, subject only to the chance of its being devested on a future contingency.'

In *Re Heath*[3] the testator gave his granddaughter £5,000—

> 'if she shall be living at the date of the death of the survivor of myself and my wife and shall attain the age of 21 years or marry under that age. In case [she] shall predecease me or shall survive me, but shall not attain the age of 21 years or marry under that age [there was a gift to a second donee].'

Farwell J[4] quoted the then current edition of Hawkins on Wills[5] stating the rule in *Phipps v Ackers*[1] in this way:

> 'If real estate be devised to A., "if" or "when" he shall attain a given age, with a limitation over in the event of his dying under that age, the attainment of the given age is held to be a condition subsequent and not precedent, and A. takes an immediate vested estate, subject to being divested upon his death under the specified age.'

Farwell J applied the rule to a will of personalty and said[6] 'the whole basis of the decision in *Phipps v. Ackers*[1] rests upon the fact that there is a gift over'.

In *Re Penton's Settlements*[7] Ungoed-Thomas J referred to the rule in *Phipps v Ackers*[1] as extended in later cases—

---

1   (1842) 9 Cl & Fin 583, [1558-1774] 1 All ER Rep 381
2   9 Cl & Fin at 592, [1558-1774] All ER Rep at 384
3   [1936] Ch 259, [1935] All ER Rep 677
4   [1936] Ch at 262, [1935] All ER Rep at 678
5   3rd Edn (1925), p 286
6   [1936] Ch at 265, [1935] All ER Rep at 680
7   [1968] 1 All ER 36 at 42, [1968] 1 WLR 248 at 255

'that if there is a gift to individuals or to a class if or when they attain a specified age or survive a specified time or person and there is a gift over on failure to attain that age or so survive or on such occurrence and some further occurrence such as that they leave children, the interests of such individuals or class are not contingent on attaining that age or so surviving, but are vested subject to being divested if they die under that age or do not so survive.'

Later the learned judge said[1] that the rule is founded on a principle of law—

'based on intention ascertained as a matter of construction. Further—and this is crucial—an examination of cases clearly reveals that that intention is ascertained, not by reference to the non-disposal of income which would arise before the contingency occurred if the gift were treated as contingent, but by reference to the gift over being dependent upon that contingency not occurring. The contingency applicable to the prior gift and the gift over are the counterparts of each other, hinging on the same event. When read together, as they should be, as a matter of construction, they indicate an intention that the prior donee should take, subject only to the subsequent contingency of the gift over being satisfied.'

As a result of these authorities I accept the submission lucidly advanced by counsel on behalf of the beneficiaries interested in capital, that for the rule in *Phipps v Ackers*[2] to apply there must be an express gift over which spells out the conditions on which the gift over will take place and includes amongst those conditions the counterparts, though not necessarily identical counterparts, of the conditions applicable to the prior gift. Faced with a prior gift which creates a condition precedent followed by a gift over which creates a condition subsequent in relation to the same events, the court being in favour of early vesting resolves the dilemma by accepting the condition subsequent which achieves early vesting. The terms of the gift over alter the construction of the prior gift and convert what would otherwise be a contingent interest into a vested interest liable to be divested. In the absence of a gift over there is nothing to alter the construction of the prior gift and to convert the contingent interest.

In the present case there is no gift over necessary to satisfy the rule in *Phipps v Ackers*[2]. After the gift to Mrs Gooley the appointment contains remainders in favour of two named beneficiaries 'subject as foresaid' that is to say, subject to the limitations (in the present case contingent limitations) which have gone before in favour of Mrs Gooley so far as they are effective. The appointment does not create the dilemma of a prior gift subject to a condition precedent followed by a gift over in terms which suggest a condition subsequent enabling the court to solve the dilemma in favour of early vesting by construing the prior gift as being vested liable to be divested.

In the result there is nothing in the appointment which tempts or compels me to treat the interest of Mrs Gooley 'if she shall attain the age of 21 years' as being anything other than the contingent interest it appears to be.

Declaration accordingly.

Solicitors: *Bird & Bird* (for the plaintiffs and second to seventh defendants); *William Heath & Co* (for the first defendant).

Jacqueline Metcalfe   Barrister.

---

1   [1968] 1 All ER at 43, [1968] 1 WLR at 256
2   (1842) 9 Cl & Fin 583, [1558-1774] All ER Rep 381

Re Wyvern Developments Ltd

CHANCERY DIVISION

TEMPLEMAN J

16th, 17th NOVEMBER 1972

Company – Winding-up – Liquidator – Powers – Sale of land – Power to concur in and execute conveyance of land on behalf of company – Consideration for promise of liquidator to join in conveyance – Equitable estoppel – Company having beneficial interest in land under contract of sale – Vendor having lien on land for unpaid purchase money – Vendor proposing to enter into contract for sale of land to third party – Liquidator agreeing to join in conveyance on behalf of company – Vendor refraining from applying to court to enforce lien – Vendor entering into agreement with third party to sell land – Whether liquidator bound to execute conveyance to third party.

In 1966 G Ltd agreed to sell certain land to W Ltd. Subsequently G Ltd obtained an order for specific performance of the agreement against W Ltd. The land remained vested in G Ltd on trust for W Ltd, subject to an unpaid vendor's lien in favour of G Ltd for £20,598. In 1969 W Ltd was compulsorily wound-up, and the Official Receiver became the liquidator. In July 1970 G Ltd instructed a firm of estate agents to find a purchaser for the land. Various offers, in the region of £15,000–£18,000, were received but were later withdrawn. The applicant, who had owned 98 out of the 100 shares in W Ltd when it went into liquidation, instructed another firm of estate agents, who, in December 1970, valued the land at £38,000. G Ltd's estate agents considered that that figure was frivolous. In June 1971 a building contractor ('the purchaser') made a firm offer of £16,000 for the land, subject to contract. G Ltd's solicitors wrote to the Official Receiver's solicitors stating that G Ltd were prepared to accept that offer subject to contract, and asking whether they would confirm that W Ltd, acting by the Official Receiver as liquidator, would be prepared to join in the conveyance of the land to the purchaser in order to save the costs of an application to the court by G Ltd to enforce its lien. The Official Receiver agreed on condition, inter alia, that the conveyance to the purchaser was approved on his behalf before it was executed by W Ltd. In December 1971 G Ltd's solicitors sent the Official Receiver's solicitors the draft contract and a copy of the proposed conveyance. They were returned, slightly amended, with a letter from the Official Receiver's solicitors asking for confirmation from G Ltd's estate agents that £16,000 continued to represent a fair price for the land. That confirmation was given, and contracts were exchanged on 22nd March 1972. G Ltd agreed to sell the land to the purchaser for £16,000 and completion was to take place on 20th April. Clause 6(b) of the contract stated that W Ltd had confirmed to G Ltd that it would join in the conveyance of the land to the purchaser for the purpose of (i) authorising and acknowledging the payment of the purchase price of £16,000 to G Ltd and (ii) conveying and confirming unto the purchaser its interest in the property and that the contract was conditional on W Ltd joining in the conveyance. Clause 6(c) provided that a rider would be incorporated into the conveyance to the effect that, as there was no vesting of W Ltd's assets in the liquidator, W Ltd would convey and confirm unto the purchaser its interest in the property and the Official Receiver would not be a party to the conveyance. On 10th April the draft conveyance was sent to the Official Receiver's solicitors for execution by W Ltd. It was in the form approved by the Official Receiver and the operative part provided that, in consideration of £16,000 paid by the purchaser to G Ltd, G Ltd as beneficial owner conveyed and W Ltd conveyed and confirmed unto the purchaser the land. The applicant applied for an order under s 246(5)[a] of the Companies Act 1948 that the decision of the Official Receiver to concur in and execute the conveyance on behalf of W Ltd be reversed or modified. She contended (i) that the sale for £16,000 on 22nd March 1972 was a sale at an undervalue, and (ii), alternatively, that even if the contract did not constitute a sale at an undervalue, the Official Receiver was not bound to execute the conveyance to the purchaser on behalf of W Ltd since there was no consideration to support his promise to concur in the sale. Evidence was submitted on the applicant's behalf that another purchaser was ready, willing and able to purchase the land for £35,000.

Held – The court would make no order on the summons for the following reasons—

(i) There had not been a sale at an undervalue. On the evidence G Ltd, W Ltd and the Official Receiver were entitled to enter into a binding contract on 22nd March to sell the land to the purchaser for £16,000 (see p 540 j, post).

(ii) The Official Receiver was contractually bound to execute the conveyance because (a) there was a tripartite contract formed by the correspondence between G Ltd's solicitors and the Official Receiver's solicitors and by the contract executed by G Ltd and the purchaser; G Ltd had entered into that contract pursuant to the authority granted by W Ltd, and it was immaterial that W Ltd had not received any part of the purchase price, since it was sufficient that the consideration, i e the promise of G Ltd to convey the land and that of the purchaser to pay the price, had moved from the promisees, G Ltd and the purchaser (see p 541 f and g, post); (b) in any event the Official Receiver had received consideration for agreeing to execute the conveyance on behalf of W Ltd, i e the implied promise by G Ltd that, instead of enforcing its lien by application to the court, it would contract to sell its legal estate plus its right of lien (see p 541 h and p 542 b d and e, post).

(iii) Furthermore, the Official Receiver, by giving his approval to cl 6(b) of the contract, would be estopped from denying that he was bound to execute the conveyance on behalf of W Ltd, since he had made a promise knowing and intending that G Ltd and the purchaser would irretrievably alter their relationship by entering into a contract that bound them both (see p 542 e and p 543 c, post); *Central London Property Trust Ltd v High Trees House Ltd* (1946) [1956] 1 All ER 256 applied.

(iv) In any event, the Official Receiver was bound by the high standard of conduct imposed on him by virtue of his office to comply with the promise that he had given for if he did not there would be an enrichment of the assets of the insolvent company, W Ltd, at the expense of the purchaser (see p 543 f and h to p 544 a, post); *Ex parte James* (1874) LR 9 Ch App 609 applied.

Notes

For control of the court over a liquidator, see 7 Halsbury's Laws (4th Edn) 650, para 1114; and for cases on the position of a liquidator, see 10 Digest (Repl) 915-917, 6250-6263.

For promissory estoppel, see 15 Halsbury's Laws (3rd Edn) 175-176, para 344, and for cases on the subject, see 21 Digest (Repl) 376, 377, 392, 393, 1133-1135, 1220, 1221.

For the Companies Act 1948, s 246, see 5 Halsbury's Statutes (3rd Edn) 307.

Cases referred to in judgment

Buttle v Saunders [1950] 2 All ER 193, 47 Digest (Repl) 415, 3711.

Central London Property Trust Ltd v High Trees House Ltd (1946) [1956] 1 All ER 256, [1947] KB 130, [1947] LJR 77, 175 LT 332, 21 Digest (Repl) 376, 1133.

Combe v Combe [1951] 1 All ER 767, [1951] 2 KB 215, CA, Digest (Cont Vol A) 280, 1366a.

---

a   Section 246(5) provides: 'If any person is aggrieved by any act or decision of the liquidator, that person may apply to the Court, and the Court may confirm, reverse or modify the act or decision complained of, and make such order in the premises as it thinks just.'

Debtor (No 400 of 1940), Re A, Ex parte The debtor v Dodwell (The trustee) [1949] 1 All ER 510, [1949] Ch 236, [1949] LJR 907, 4 Digest (Repl) 260, 2354.

Government of India, Ministry of Finance (Revenue Division) v Taylor [1955] 1 All ER 292, [1955] A C 491, [1955] 2 WLR 303, 48 R & IT 98, sub nom *Re Delhi Electric Supply & Traction Co Ltd* 34 ATC 10, HL, Digest (Cont Vol A) 217, 7b.

James, Ex parte, Re Condon (1874) LR 9 Ch App 609, [1874-80] All ER Rep 388, 43 LJ Bcy 107, 30 LT 773, 4 Digest (Repl) 226, 2031.

Miles v New Zealand Alford Estate Co (1886) 32 Ch D 266, 55 LJCh 801, 54 LT 582, CA, 9 Digest (Repl) 355, 2276.

Robertson v Minister of Pensions [1948] 2 All ER 767, [1949] 1 KB 227, [1949] LJR 323, 21 Digest (Repl) 399, 1259.

Case also cited

General Share & Trust Co v Wetley Brick and Pottery Co (1882) 20 Ch D 260, CA.

Summons

This was an application, by a summons dated 23rd May 1972, by Norah Margaret Wells, a contributory of Wyvern Developments Ltd ('Wyvern'), which had been compulsorily wound-up by an order of the court dated 6th October 1969. The applicant sought an order under s 246(5) of the Companies Act 1948 that the decision of the Official Receiver, as liquidator, to concur in and execute on behalf of Wyvern a conveyance intended to be made by Gresham Trust Ltd of freehold land at Lincombe Drive, Torquay, might be reversed or modified or that such other order might be made relating thereto as the court thought just. The facts are set out in the judgment.

Muir Hunter QC and *J H Weeks* for the applicant.
C A Settle QC and *Eben Hamilton* for the Official Receiver.

TEMPLEMAN J. This is an application by a Mrs Wells, who held 98 out of 100 shares in Wyvern Developments Ltd ('Wyvern') when it went into liquidation. She seeks an order under s 246(5) of the Companies Act 1948 that the decision of the Official Receiver to concur in and execute on behalf of Wyvern a conveyance intended to be made by Gresham Trust Ltd ('Gresham') of freehold land adjoining Danby Lodge, Lincombe Drive, Torquay, may be reversed or modified or that such other order may be made relating thereto as the court thinks just. What the applicant is asking for is an order directing the Official Receiver, the liquidator of Wyvern, not to execute that conveyance on behalf of Wyvern.

On 27th April 1966 Wyvern conveyed the land in question and other land to Gresham for £33,500, and by a contract of the same date Gresham agreed to sell the land back to Wyvern for £33,835. Subsequently, with the consent of Wyvern, part of the land comprised in the 1966 contract was sold to a third party for £13,500. On 24th April 1968 Gresham obtained an order for specific performance of the 1966 agreement, so far as it was still uncompleted, against Wyvern. The land remained vested in the vendor Gresham on trust for the purchaser Wyvern, subject to an unpaid vendor's lien in favour of Gresham for a sum which is now £20,598. On 6th October 1969 this court ordered Wyvern to be wound up, and the Official Receiver became liquidator. The creditors of Wyvern consists of the Inland Revenue Commissioners, creditors for £600, and Gresham, creditors for £20,598, secured by a lien on the land.

In June 1970 Gresham instructed Messrs Nicolles, auctioneers and estate agents in Torquay, to find a purchaser for the land. The land was widely advertised for sale and most of the local builders were advised that the site was available. A fair number of builders expressed an interest, but after investigation decided that the development of the site was not an economic proposition. Twenty or thirty people were interested, including such well-known builders as John Mowlem & Co Ltd and George Wimpey & Co Ltd. In September 1970 Mowlem offered £15,000, but then withdrew. In December 1970 Messrs Lyndon James & Co, another firm of estate agents in Torquay, instructed by the applicant or her husband, valued the land at £38,000. Messrs Nicolles considered this valuation and advised that the figure of £38,000 was quite frivolous. In January 1971 an offer of £18,000 was received from South West Investments Ltd, but the offer was withdrawn in May 1971. On 2nd June 1971 Messrs Nicolles wrote to Gresham's solicitors, Messrs Coward Chance & Co. The letter was headed in the matter of the land in question, and said:

'Further to the instructions contained in your letter of the 6th instant, we have continued to offer for sale the above mentioned land. We have introduced this site to Mr. F. Winter, a well known local building contractor, who has today submitted a firm offer of £16,000 for the land, subject to contract. We appreciate this figure is less than that at which Messrs. Draycotts intended to purchase but we refer you to our letter of 15th May last year in which we quoted a figure of £15,000 as fairly representing todays value of this site. Mr. Winter is well known to this firm and he has recently completed a successful development of approximately the size of Danby Lodge. We have every confidence therefore that the offer made by this builder is firm.'

On 8th June 1971 Gresham's solicitors wrote to the Official Receiver's solicitors, Messrs Stafford Clark & Co, reported the offer of £16,000 from Mr Winter and said that Gresham were prepared to accept the offer subject to contract. Then follows this important passage:

'In order to save the costs of an application to the Court by our clients to enforce their lien, we shall be glad if you would please confirm that Wyvern Developments Limited, acting by the Official Receiver as Liquidator, would be prepared to join in the conveyance of the land to Mr. Winter.'

The Official Receiver's solicitors, in a letter dated 21st June 1971, replied that the Official Receiver was—

'prepared to assist in this matter as indicated in the Conveyance of the land in question to Mr. Winter subject to the same conditions as before namely with regard to his costs being met and also with regard to the form of Conveyance being approved on his behalf before it is executed by the Company.'

It is the usual practice for the Official Receiver not to insist on a person who holds a lien or a mortgage applying to the court to order a sale. If the Official Receiver is satisfied with the sale, he joins in and assists. The letter from the Official Receiver's solicitors was acknowledged on 22nd June 1971 by Gresham's solicitors, who said they were glad to hear that the Official Receiver was prepared to assist and they enclosed a copy of the draft agreement submitted to Mr Winter. There was then an interval until December 1971, occupied by some difficulties over restrictive covenants and the removal of some form of charge. By 28th December 1971 Gresham's solicitors sent to the Official Receiver's solicitors the draft contract and a copy of the proposed conveyance. That draft contract and that draft conveyance were returned by the Official Receiver's solicitors, slightly amended, with a letter dated 30th December 1971, and apart from giving reasons for the amendment—which I need not trouble to read—the letter contained this paragraph:

'It is now some 6 months since you indicated that the offer from Mr. Winter had been received. We understand that investigations have had to be made by the proposed purchaser but in view of the length of time that has elapsed we feel that the Official Receiver should have on his file an up to date recommendation from Messrs. Nicolles that the sum of £16,000 represents a fair figure

a   at which the proposed sale may proceed at this stage. Will you kindly obtain
      such a letter for us addressed to the Official Receiver and Liquidator.'

      In response to this, Messrs Nicolles wrote directly to the Official Receiver, care
      of his solicitor, saying,

b   'Whilst we appreciate a period of six months has elapsed from the time a
      price was agreed for the purchase of this land, we are satisfied that a figure of
      £16,000 continues to represent a fair price for the land and we recommend
      a sale at this figure. Property and land prices are, of course, increasing consider-
      ably. However, the high costs likely to be involved in developing this particular
      site with its extremely difficult contours will certainly offset any advantages in
      increased property values.'

c   The next material thing that happened was the exchange of contracts dated 22nd
      March 1972. Gresham agreed to sell the land to Frederick Winter Ltd for £16,000,
      completion to take place on 20th April 1972. That was the price which Messrs
      Nicolles had recommended. The contract contained cl 6(a):

d   'By an Agreement dated the 27th April 1966 and made between the Vendor
      [Gresham] of the first part the Company [Wyvern] of the second part and
      Leonard William Wells of the third part the Company [Wyvern] agreed to
      purchase (inter alia) the property but no conveyance has hitherto been taken
      by [Wyvern] of the property. [That was perfectly accurate]
      '(b) the Company has confirmed to the Vendor [i e, Wyvern has confirmed
      to Gresham] that it will join in the Conveyance of the property to the Purchaser
e   for the purposes of (i) authorizing and acknowledging the payment of the said
      purchase price of £16,000·00 to the Vendor and (ii) conveying and confirming
      unto the Purchaser its interest in the property and this contract shall be
      conditional upon the Company [Wyvern] so joining in the said conveyance.'

      That is perfectly accurate; the Official Receiver, acting on behalf of Wyvern, had
f   confirmed to Gresham that Wyvern would act in the manner set out in (b).
      Then (c) goes on:

      'The recitals and other provisions set out in the Rider hereto shall be incor-
      porated in such Conveyance and the said conveying and confirming by the Com-
      pany shall be effected in accordance with such recitals and provisions.'

      The rider provides:
g
      'As there is no vesting of [Wyvern's] assets in the Liquidator [Wyvern] (which
      will be described as "In Liquidation") will convey and confirm unto the Purchaser
      its interest in the property. The Official Receiver and Liquidator will not be a
      party to the Conveyance.'

h   That is the usual method. Then there are certain recitals to be incorporated in the
      conveyance relating to the winding-up order and the appointment of the Official
      Receiver and liquidator. Then the rider continues:

      'THE Recital of the agreement to join in the Conveyance will be by [Wyvern]
      and not by the Official Receiver. [Wyvern] being a Company in liquidation
      will give no covenants for Title . . .'

j   Finally, 'THE Company's seal [Wyvern's] when affixed to the Conveyance will be
      witnessed as affixed by the Official Receiver and Liquidator'.
      On 10th April 1972 a draft conveyance was sent to the Official Receiver's solicitors
      for execution by Wyvern. That conveyance was in the form approved by the Official
      Receiver and contained recitals in accordance with the contract. In particular, recital
      (6) says that the vendor (Gresham)—

'with the agreement of the Company [Wyvern] has agreed with the Purchaser   *a*
for the sale to it of the said property for the said estate at the price of Sixteen
Thousand Pounds and [Wyvern] has agreed that the whole of the said purchase
price shall be paid to [Gresham] and that [Wyvern] shall join herein in the
manner hereinafter appearing.'

The whole purchase price must be paid to Gresham, because £16,000 will not be
sufficient to discharge the claim and lien of Gresham, which amount to over £20,000.   *b*
The operative part provides this: in consideration of £16,000 paid by Winter to
Gresham (the receipt and payment whereof Gresham and Wyvern acknowledge)
Gresham as beneficial owner conveys and Wyvern conveys and confirms unto the
purchaser the land described in the conveyance.

In a letter dated 27th April 1972 Messrs Lyndon James & Co, who had previously
valued the land at £38,000, writing to solicitors then instructed by the applicant or   *c*
her husband, said this:

'Acting upon the instructions of out mutual Client, Mr. L. Wells, we have
to-day agreed to sell the above Land [that is the land with which I am concerned]
to our Applicants, Messrs. Morris and Jacombs Ltd ... for the sum of £36,000
... subject to contract.'
                                                           d

In a letter dated 2nd May 1972 Messrs Lyndon James & Co wrote again to the solicitors
acting for the applicant or her husband reporting that—

'On the direct instructions of our mutual Client, Mr. Leonard Wells, to-day
we have agreed on his behalf to sell the above site to Mr. Edward Goldstein
... at the sum of £40,000 ... subject to contract.'
                                                           e

Nothing appears to have resulted from these letters. Neither Morris and Jacombs Ltd
nor Mr Goldstein has taken any part in the present proceedings. Nor has Mr Wells.
This summons was issued on 23rd May 1972 and the persons who seem to be
interested in purchasing the land are two, namely the Winter company relying on
the contract dated 22nd March 1972, and Mrs Goldstein, who has sworn, in an
affidavit, that she is ready, willing and able to purchase the land in question for   *f*
£35,000. The Official Receiver does not accept that Mrs Goldstein's offer is genuine,
nor that the land can be now sold for more than £16,000, but these are problems
which I need not resolve and which I would have found impossible to resolve in the
absence of further evidence and cross-examination. I must consider the position, as
at 22nd March 1972 when contracts with the Winter company were exchanged.

Counsel for the applicant submitted, in the first place, that the sale for £16,000   *g*
on 22nd March 1972 was a sale at an undervalue. I am not satisfied that more than
£16,000 could have been obtained on 22nd March 1972. I am quite satisfied that
Gresham and the Official Receiver reasonably thought that £16,000 was a fair price.
That was the advice given by Messrs Nicolles. There is no evidence that Winter
thought they were buying at an undervalue. True, Messrs Lyndon James & Co
had valued the land at £38,000, but they had been trying to sell the property for   *h*
some years without success until they produced too late, at the end of April 1972,
an alleged purchaser subject to contract. Land is worth what purchasers will pay.
Before 22nd March 1972, despite the advertising and efforts of Messrs Nicolles and
Messrs Lyndon James & Co, no purchaser appears to have offered more than £18,000,
and that offer was withdrawn. I conclude, on the evidence, that Gresham, Wyvern
and the Official Receiver were entitled to enter into a binding contract on 22nd   *j*
March 1972 to sell the land to Winter for £16,000.

Counsel's alternative submission, made on behalf of the applicant, was that even
if the contract dated 22nd March 1972 did not constitute a sale at undervalue, nevertheless the Official Receiver is not bound to execute the conveyance to Winter on
behalf of Wyvern and the Official Receiver should be directed not to execute the

a conveyance because a price of £35,000 can now be obtained. That proposition I gladly reject. By the letters dated 21st June 1971 and 30th December 1971 and by the approval of the terms of the contract and the conveyance, the Official Receiver made a clear and express promise to Gresham that Wyvern would execute the conveyance. Gresham could not have been advised to enter into that contract without such a promise. The promise was conveyed to Winter and when they agreed to buy,

b and paid their deposit, no doubt they arranged their affairs on the assumption that people would do what they promised, and they believed that the Official Receiver would fulfil his promise. The Official Receiver is anxious to perform his promise. The promise was given and accepted in good faith and it was a promise the Official Receiver was entitled to make, provided that I am satisfied, as I am, that the sale was bona fide and at a price which did not appear to be at undervalue. Breach of that promise will involve Gresham in expense, delay and possibly damages. Breach of

c that promise will involve Winter in delay, expense and possibly litigation and damages. How can it be right for the court to direct the Official Receiver to break his promise in these circumstances? Counsel for the applicant submitted that the Official Receiver is not contractually bound and cannot be allowed to fulfil his promise, unless he can be made liable in damages for breach. The argument was that the Official Receiver is not contractually bound because he received no consideration

d for his promise to concur in the conveyance. This stems from the fact that the sale is for £16,000 and the lien is for £20,000 and it follows that there is going to be no surplus payable to Wyvern. In brief, Wyvern will not receive a penny for the sale.

    Now the sale to Winter could have been carried through by a contract whereby Gresham, as the legal owner and entitled to a lien, and Wyvern, as equitable owner of the land subject to the lien, agreed to join in the conveyance of the land to Winter

e for £16,000 to be paid to Gresham. In other words, the Official Receiver and Wyvern could have been made parties to the contract which in fact was made between Gresham and Winter. This tripartite contract would, in my judgment, have bound Gresham, Winter and Wyvern. The consideration for Wyvern entering into a commitment under that contract would have been the promise of Gresham to convey the legal estate to Winter and the promise of Winter to pay the purchase price to

f Gresham, albeit that no money would be received by Wyvern. By the correspondence to which I have referred, Wyvern authorised Gresham to enter into a contract reciting that Wyvern had agreed to join in a conveyance of the land for £16,000. In my judgment, there was in fact a tripartite contract formed by the correspondence and by the contract which was executed by Gresham and Winter. The contract which Gresham entered into pursuant to the authority granted by Wyvern is just

g as much binding on Wyvern as it is on Gresham. On well-established principles it is not necessary for Wyvern to receive any part of the purchase price or any other consideration provided that consideration moves from the promisees, Gresham and Winter.

    In the alternative, counsel for the Official Receiver, submitted—and I accept— that there *was* consideration received by the Official Receiver for agreeing to execute

h the conveyance on behalf of Wyvern. Counsel drew my attention to the duties of the Official Receiver and to the warning given in Palmer's Companies Precedents[1], which says:

    'Nor should the liquidator, where there is no substantial dispute, insist on resisting well-founded claims, and compel litigation which is not really necessary.'

j The Official Receiver, says counsel, was carrying out his duty not to be over-litigious when he agreed to join in the conveyance. If he had not done so and had forced Gresham to apply to the court to enforce their lien, then even if the Official Receiver did not appear and incurred no costs, it is admitted that Gresham would, or might, have been able to obtain an order adding their costs to their security. Any balance

---

1 17th Edn (1960), Part II, p 178

due to them from Wyvern not satisfied by the sale to Winter, including the extra costs caused by the application to the court, could have been proved as unsecured debts owed by Wyvern to Gresham in competition with any other creditors. Counsel for the applicant says there were no other creditors and that, in any event, there was no other property out of which the debts could have been satisfied. That would not be known for certain unless and until the liquidation of Wyvern ended in its dissolution. In my judgment, the implied promise of Gresham not to apply to the court to enforce their lien was consideration for the promise of the Official Receiver to execute the conveyance, thus making an application to the court unnecessary.

Counsel for the applicant cited *Miles v New Zealand Alford Estate Co*[1]. That was a case where four members—the judge below and three members of the Court of Appeal—were nicely split, two and two. It was decided that there was no consideration in that case for a guarantee given by a shareholder and director that a dividend would be paid. Counsel relied on certain passages[2] to show that there could be no consideration in the present case unless Gresham bound themselves not to apply to the court. Gresham entered into the contract relying on the promise made by the Official Receiver and once they entered into that contract then, of course, they were barred from going to the court to enforce their lien; they had committed themselves and could do nothing but carry out that contract. Accordingly, in my judgment, the consideration for the promise of the Official Receiver was the promise by Gresham that instead of enforcing their lien by application to the court they would contract to sell their legal estate plus their right of lien; and in consideration of Gresham's promise, the Official Receiver agreed to concur by conveying the equitable interest of Wyvern, thus completing the title of Winter. That is sufficient to dispose of this application, because, in my judgment, the Official Receiver is contractually bound to do that which he promised to do and is anxious to do.

I should, however, mention the alternative submissions which were made. In the first place, counsel for the Official Receiver says that the approval by the Official Receiver of cl 6(b) of the contract created an estoppel and he prays in aid the principle of promissory estoppel exemplified in *Central London Property Trust Ltd v High Trees House Ltd*[3]. The well-known passage in the headnote reads[4]:

'... where parties enter into an arrangement which is intended to create legal relations between them and in pursuance of such arrangement one party makes a promise to the other which he knows will be acted on and which is in fact acted on by the promisee, the court will treat the promise as binding on the promisor to the extent that it will not allow him to act inconsistently with it even although the promise may not be supported by consideration in the strict sense and the effect of the arrangement made is to vary the terms of a contract under seal by one of less value.'

Counsel for the applicant, citing Snell's Principles of Equity[5] and *Combe v Combe*[6] said promissory estoppel only applies as a form of defence. The headnote in *Combe v Combe* reads[7]:

'The principle stated in *Central London Property Trust Ld. v. High Trees House Ld.*[3] and *Robertson v. Minister of Pensions*[8], is that, where one party has, by his words or conduct, made to the other a promise or assurance which was intended to

1   (1886) 32 Ch D 266
2   32 Ch D at 284, 285
3   (1946) [1956] 1 All ER 256, [1947] KB 130
4   [1947] KB at 130
5   26th Edn (1966), p 627
6   [1951] 1 All ER 767, [1951] 2 KB 215
7   [1951] 2 KB at 215
8   [1948] 2 All ER 767, [1949] 1 KB 227

affect the legal relations between them and to be acted on accordingly, then, once the other party has taken him at his word and acted on it, the party who gave the promise or assurance cannot afterwards be allowed to revert to the previous legal relationship as if no such promise or assurance had been made by him, but he must accept their legal relations subject to the qualification which he himself has so introduced, even though it is not supported in point of law by any consideration, but only by his word. But this principle does not create any new cause of action where none existed before; so that, where a promise is made which is not supported by any consideration, the promisee cannot bring an action.'

In my judgment, the situation is different and estoppel applies where the promisor knows and intends that the promisee will irretrievably alter his position in reliance on the promise. The Official Receiver put into circulation a promise, on the strength of which both Gresham and Winter altered their legal relationships. They did so by entering into a contract which bound them both. Once that was done, the Official Receiver was estopped from denying that he was entitled and bound to perform his promise. I accept counsel for the Official Receiver's submission.

As a further alternative, counsel for the Official Receiver relied on the principle of *Ex Parte James*[1]. In Williams on Bankruptcy[2], a work with which counsel for the applicant is familiar, I find[2] under the heading '*Rule in Ex p. James*', the passage:

'Generally, the trustee will be ordered, as an officer of the court, to do the fullest equity, and in certain cases, an even higher standard of conduct is imposed on him. It is not easy to define the exact bounds of a principle based upon the control exercised by the court over its officer, which, since it operates in a field not covered by the established rules of law and equity, is incapable of reduction to an exact formula, and must in its application be governed in part by ethical considerations.'

Counsel for the Official Receiver says, even if there is no contract and no estoppel, a high standard of conduct and ethical considerations require the Official Receiver to comply with his promise. Various examples of the application of the rule are given in Williams on Bankruptcy and they are all cases where there was a refund of money paid under a mistake of law. Counsel for the applicant cited and relied on the judgment of Lord Keith of Avonholm in *Government of India v Taylor*[3], where Lord Keith, dealing with the rule in *Ex parte James*[1], said:

'The rule, however, which is at best exercised as a discretionary power by the court, appears to have been exercised only in cases where there has been some form of enrichment of the assets of a bankrupt or insolvent company at the expense of the person seeking recoupment. No case has been brought to our notice of the application of the rule where there has been no enrichment of one party with corresponding loss to the other.'

It is quite true that Gresham and Winter are not seeking recoupment, but there undoubtedly would be enrichment of the assets of the insolvent company Wyvern at the expense of Winter if, by dint of a refusal by the Official Receiver to perform his promise, supported by an order made by me, Winter lost a contract under which it is to buy land for £16,000, when the present value of the land, if Mrs Goldstein is a genuine purchaser, is £35,000. In my judgment, these are extreme circumstances and I see no reason why *Ex parte James*[1] should not apply or be extended if necessary

1   (1874) LR 9 Ch App 609
2   18th Edn (1968), p 275
3   [1955] 1 All ER at 300, [1955] AC at 513

to allow the Official Receiver to comply with an express promise made by him in the circumstances in which he was placed.

Finally, counsel for the Official Receiver prayed in aid general equitable principles. He said that it is not right that I should make any order in the present case and that I have a discretion. I was referred again to Williams on Bankruptcy[1], setting forth s 80 of the Bankruptcy Act 1914, corresponding to s 246(5) of the Companies Act 1948 with which I am dealing. These sections enable a person aggrieved by any act or decision of a trustee in bankruptcy or liquidation to apply to the court which 'may confirm, reverse or modify the act or decision complained of, and make such order in the premises as it thinks just'. The note to s 80 says it was introduced in 1883 in part to remedy the injustice created by the disability of the bankrupt to sue even where he had been gravely wronged. This does not assist counsel for the applicant because, in my judgment, it cannot be said that Wyvern and the applicant have been gravely wronged.

In *Re A Debtor*[2] Harman J took the view that s 80 of the Bankruptcy Act 1914 did not—

> 'justify interference in the day to day administration of the estate, nor can [it] entitle the bankrupt to question the exercise by the trustee in good faith of his discretion, nor to hold him accountable for an error of judgment.'

This also does not assist counsel. But counsel for the applicant was on stronger ground when he referred to the analogous case of a trustee in *Buttle v Saunders*[3]. The headnote reads:

> 'When negotiations for the sale of property, which was held by trustees on the statutory trusts for sale, were in an advanced stage, the trustees received a higher offer from one of the beneficiaries, but they considered themselves bound by commercial morality to complete with the original purchaser, and, therefore, they refused the higher offer.'

It was held that the trustees had an overriding duty to obtain the best price for their beneficiaries.

In my judgment, the same must be said about the Official Receiver. He has no general discretion to sell for £16,000. Unless he is bound contractually or bound by estoppel or entitled to execute the conveyance on the principle of the rule in *Ex parte James*[4], then that is the end of the matter. He must do his best by his creditors and contributories. He is in a fiduciary capacity and cannot make moral gestures, nor can the court authorise him to do so.

For the reasons which I have given, I have come to the conclusion that the Official Receiver is bound by contract or alternatively by estoppel or alternatively can rely on the rule in *Ex parte James*[4] to fulfil the promise which he made to Gresham and Winter. I do not therefore propose to make any order on the summons.

No order on summons.

Solicitors: *Bridges, Sawtell & A J Adams* (for the applicant); *Stafford Clark & Co* (for the Official Receiver).

Jacqueline Metcalfe Barrister.

---

1 18th Edn (1968), pp 474, 475
2 [1949] 1 All ER 510 at 512, [1949] Ch 236 at 241
3 [1950] 2 All ER 193
4 LR 9 Ch App 609

Simpson (Inspector of Taxes) v John Reynolds & Co (Insurances) Ltd

CHANCERY DIVISION   Affirmed CA [1975] 2 All ER 88
PENNYCUICK V-C
19th, 20th, 21st MARCH 1974

Income tax – Profits of trade, profession or vocation – Trade – Profits arising or accruing from trade – Voluntary payment – Client terminating trading connection with taxpayer – Client making voluntary payment to taxpayer in recognition of past services – Services provided by way of trade – Whether payment chargeable to tax as a trading receipt – Income Tax Act 1952, ss 122, 123 (Sch D, Case I).

The taxpayer company, which carried on business as insurance brokers, had for many years acted as adviser to C Ltd on all its insurance matters including pension schemes. In 1965 ICI Ltd acquired a large shareholding in C Ltd and required the latter to place all its insurances with another insurance company. Thereupon C Ltd informed the taxpayer company that its services would no longer be required. In or about September 1965 C Ltd wrote to the taxpayer company volunteering to pay the latter £1,000 per annum for a period of five years commencing in March 1966. The letter stated that the payment was in recognition of the taxpayer company's past services as insurance brokers and was calculated on the basis that in the past the annual earnings of the taxpayer company by way of commission in respect of C Ltd's business had been in the order of £2,000. The taxpayer company was assessed to corporation tax for the accounting period ended 31st March 1970, on the basis that the annual instalment of £1,000 received by the taxpayer company from C Ltd was a trading receipt liable to tax under ss 122[a], 123(1)[b] (Sch D, Case I), of the Income Tax Act 1952. On appeal the commissioners held that the payment from C Ltd was not chargeable to tax and discharged the assessment. The Crown appealed.

Held – Where a customer chose to make a voluntary payment to a trader on the cessation of their trading connection, that payment, on proper principles of commercial accounting, could not be treated as a receipt in ascertaining the profits arising from the trade, since it was not received in return for activities carried on by the trader in his trade, but was simply a windfall in the nature of a gift. Accordingly, since the payment by C Ltd to the taxpayer company was a purely voluntary payment, being in recognition of its past services, it was not taxable as trading income in the hands of the taxpayer company and the appeal would be dismissed (see p 558 *g* and p 559 *g* and *h*, post).

Chibbett v Joseph Robinson & Sons [1924] All ER Rep 684, and *Walker (Inspector of Taxes) v Carnaby, Harrower, Barham & Pykett* [1970] 1 All ER 502 applied.

Inland Revenue Comrs v Fleming & Co (Machinery) Ltd 1952 SC 120 distinguished.

Dictum of Vaisey J in *Temperley (Inspector of Taxes) v Smith* [1956] 3 All ER at 95 doubted.

Notes
For trade receipts, see 20 Halsbury's Laws (3rd Edn) 149-158, paras 262-276, and for cases on the subject, see 28(1) Digest (Reissue) 23-57, 85-226.

For the Income Tax Act 1952, ss 122, 123, see 31 Halsbury's Statutes (2nd Edn) 112, 116.

---

a Section 122, so far as material, is set out at p 547 *e* and *f*, post
b Section 123(1), so far as material, is set out at p 547 *g*, post

For the year 1970-71 and subsequent years of assessment, ss 122, 123 of the 1952 Act have been replaced by the Income and Corporation Taxes Act 1970, ss 108, 109.

Cases referred to in judgment

Australia (Commonwealth) Comr of Taxation v Squatting Investment Co Ltd [1954] 1 All ER 349, [1954] AC 182, [1954] 2 WLR 186, 33 ATC 38, [1954] TR 37, PC, 28(1) Digest (Reissue) 58, *57.

Blackburn v Close Brothers Ltd, Inland Revenue Comrs v Close Bros Ltd (1960) 39 Tax Cas 164, 39 ATC 274, [1960] TR 161, 53 R & IT 430, 28(1) Digest (Reissue) 48, 200.

Bush, Beach & Gent Ltd v Road [1939] 3 All ER 302, [1939] 2 KB 524, 22 Tax Cas 519, 108 LJKB 801, 161 LT 117, 28(1) Digest (Reissue) 32, 125.

Chibbett (Inspector of Taxes) v Joseph Robinson and Sons, Inland Revenue Comrs v Joseph Robinson and Sons (1924) 9 Tax Cas 48, sub nom *Chibbett v Joseph Robinson & Sons* [1924] All ER Rep 684, 132 LT 26, 28(1) Digest (Reissue) 32, 124.

Cowan v Seymour (Surveyor of Taxes) [1920] 1 KB 500, 7 Tax Cas 372, 89 LJKB 459, 122 LT 465, CA, 28(1) Digest (Reissue) 323, 1148.

Ellis (Inspector of Taxes) v Lucas [1966] 2 All ER 935, [1967] Ch 858, 43 Tax Cas 276, [1966] 3 WLR 382, 45 ATC 90, [1966] TR 87, 28(1) Digest (Reissue) 242, 750.

Hochstrasser (Inspector of Taxes) v Mayes [1959] 3 All ER 817, [1960] AC 376, 38 Tax Cas 673, [1960] 2 WLR 63, 38 ATC 360, [1959] TR 355, 53 R & IT 12, HL; affg [1958] 3 All ER 285, [1959] Ch 22, [1958] 3 WLR 215, 37 ATC 205, [1958] TR 237, 51 R & IT 767, CA; affg [1958] 1 All ER 369, [1958] 2 WLR 982, 36 ATC 356, [1957] TR 365, 51 R & IT 321, 28(1) Digest (Reissue) 326, 1164.

Holden (Isaac) & Sons Ltd v Inland Revenue Comrs (1924) 12 Tax Cas 768, 28(1) Digest (Reissue) 593, 2201.

Hunter (Inspector of Taxes) v Dewhurst (1932) 16 Tax Cas 605, [1932] All ER Rep 753, 146 LT 510, HL, 28(1) Digest (Reissue) 328, 1175.

Inland Revenue Comrs v Fleming & Co (Machinery) Ltd 1952 SC 120, 33 Tax Cas 57, 30 ATC 418, [1951] TR 415, 45 R & IT 541, 28(1) Digest (Reissue) 77, *237.

Kelsall Parsons & Co v Inland Revenue Comrs 1938 SC 238, 21 Tax Cas 608, 28(1) Digest (Reissue) 202, *661.

Odeon Associated Theatres Ltd v Jones (Inspector of Taxes) [1972] 1 All ER 681, [1973] Ch 288, 48 Tax Cas 257, [1972] 2 WLR 331, [1971] TR 373, CA.

Temperley (Inspector of Taxes) v Smith [1956] 3 All ER 92, 37 Tax Cas 18, [1956] 1 WLR 931, 35 ATC 291, [1956] TR 275, 49 R & IT 650, 28(1) Digest (Reissue) 246, 770.

Walker (Inspector of Taxes) v Carnaby, Harrower, Barham & Pykett [1970] 1 All ER 502, 46 Tax Cas 561, [1970] 1 WLR 276, 48 ATC 439, [1969] TR 435, 28(1) Digest (Reissue) 49, 201.

Cases also cited

Anglo-French Exploration Co Ltd v Clayson (Inspector of Taxes) [1956] 1 All ER 762, [1956] 1 WLR 325, 36 Tax Cas 545, CA.

Bridges (Inspector of Taxes) v Hewitt, Bridges (Inspector of Taxes) v Bearsley [1957] 2 All ER 281, [1957] 1 WLR 674, 37 Tax Cas 289, CA.

Herbert v McQuade [1902] 2 KB 631, 4 Tax Cas 489, CA.

Moorhouse (Inspector of Taxes) v Dooland [1955] 1 All ER 93, [1955] 1 Ch 284, 36 Tax Cas 1, CA.

Mudd v Collins (Inspector of Taxes) (1925) 9 Tax Cas 297.

Pritchard (Inspector of Taxes) v Arundale [1971] 3 All ER 1011, [1972] Ch 229, 47 Tax Cas 680.

Severne (Inspector of Taxes) v Dadswell, Inland Revenue Comrs v Dadswell [1954] 3 All ER 243, [1954] 1 WLR 1204, 35 Tax Cas 649.

Case stated

At a meeting of the Commissioners for the Special Purposes of the Income Tax Acts held at Manchester on 10th May 1972, John Reynolds & Co (Insurances) Ltd ('the company') appealed against an assessment to corporation tax made on it under Sch D, Case I, in respect of a sum of £1,000, being an annual instalment of a sum of £5,000 receivable from a former client of the company.   The commissioners allowed the appeal and discharged the assessment.   Immediately after the determination of the appeal the Crown declared its dissatisfaction therewith as being erroneous in point of law and in due course required the commissioners to state a case for the opinion of the High Court pursuant to the Taxes Management Act 1970, s 56.   The case stated, so far as material, is set out in the judgment.

Peter Rees QC and *Harry Woolf* for the Crown.
Michael Nolan QC and *James Holroyd Pearce* for the company.

PENNYCUICK V-C.   I have before me an appeal by the Crown against a decision of the Special Commissioners whereby they allowed an appeal by the present respondent, John Reynolds and Co (Insurances) Ltd (to which I shall refer as 'the company'), against an assessment to corporation tax in respect of the accounting period 1969-70.   Very summarily, the company carries on the trade of insurance brokers, and is chargeable under Case I of Sch D on its profits from that trade.   In 1965 one of its clients withdrew its connection and decided to make to the company a voluntary payment of £5,000 by five yearly instalments of £1,000 in recognition of the company's past services.   This sum was duly paid by the five specified instalments, and the question is whether the instalment received in the relevant year should be treated as a receipt of the company's trade.

Before reading the case stated I should refer to the relevant charging provisions under the Income Tax Act 1952.   Section 122 provides:

'The Schedule referred to in this Act as Schedule D is as follows—Schedule D 1. Tax under this Schedule shall be charged in respect of—(a) the annual profits or gains arising or accruing ... (ii) to any person residing in the United Kingdom from any trade, profession, or vocation, whether carried on in the United Kingdom or elsewhere ...'

Then, s 123(1):

'Tax under Schedule D shall be charged under the following Cases respectively, that is to say—Case I—tax in respect of any trade carried on in the United Kingdom or elsewhere ...'

Nothing here turns on the specific provisions of the Act relating to Case I.   Those provisions are made applicable to corporation tax and I need not take up time reading the statutory provisions which produce that result.   It is well established that for the purpose of Case I of Sch D the profits of a trade must be ascertained in accordance with the principles of commercial accounting.   For a recent statement of this principle, see *Odeon Associated Theatres Ltd v Jones*[1].

I will now read the material parts of the case stated.   Paragraphs 1 to 4 set out various formal matters, including the evidence called and the documents proved or admitted before the Special Commissioners.   No question of primary fact is involved on this appeal.   Then, para 5:

'As a result of the evidence both oral and documentary adduced before us we find the following facts proved or admitted: (a) In or about 1912 one Alfred Evans (hereinafter called "Mr Evans") started a business of insurance brokers (hereinafter called "the business") under the name John Reynolds & Co.   In 1918 Mr Shaw entered into partnership with Mr Evans and the business was

---

1   [1972] 1 All ER 681, [1973] Ch 288, 48 Tax Cas 257

continued by the partnership. In 1945 the Company was incorporated and took
over the business, Mr Evans and Mr Shaw becoming the controlling shareholders and directors. In 1950 Mr Evans died and the bulk of his shareholding
was acquired by Mr Shaw and members of the latter's family. [I interpose
the observation that Mr Shaw was the only witness heard before the Special
Commissioners.]

'(b) The Company's income was derived from commissions received from
insurance companies.

'(c) Insurance brokerage is a competitive business and generally brokers have
to seek out their business, although occasionally they are approached by a client.
Insurance companies want business and the Company as brokers obtain it for
them although as broker the Company always acted as agent of the insured
client. The Company's method was to make its own survey of an insurable
property and to prepare a report showing advantageous insurance quotations.
That method enabled the company to keep the prospective client and to advise
him the price at which the risk should be placed. After acceptance by the
client the Company's report was sent to the insurer selected on behalf of the
client, together with an estimate of the premium involved. The selection of
the insurer depended on the Company's knowledge of the particular type of
risk favoured by the insurer. Such knowledge was gained by experience and
contact. When the risk was large, it was necessary to schedule or spread the
insurance over a number of insurers of good standing who accepted that kind
of risk. Sometimes the Company had to correct or amend its estimate of premium
at the insistence of the insurers, but it had to stand by the quotation which it
had given to its client.

'(d) The Company received the amount of the estimated premium from its
client and placed the insurance. When the policy was issued, the Company
passed over to the insurer the amount of the policy premium, less a brokerage
commission, which ranged between 10% and 15% of that amount. The amount
of commission was a matter of agreement between the Company and the
insurers, and was a matter in which the client had no say. If the estimated premium exceeded the policy premium, the saving was not retained by the Company,
but was returned to the client. On the other hand, if the policy premium
exceeded the estimate, the Company did not charge the client the extra amount.

'(e) The Company had built up a large clientele, the composition of which
changed from time to time. There was not a lot of change each year but over
the years there was considerable change. For example, in the year before the
one under appeal, the Company had lost two or three clients and had acquired
six new ones. The Company had at least one client for whom it or its predecessor
had acted since 1925. Many of the Company's clients had been in the textile
trade, and to that extent the Company's business was a specialised one.

'(f) One of the oldest clients of the Company had been Carrington & Dewhurst
Limited (hereinafter called "Carrington Dewhurst"), which had been very successful in the textile trade. For forty years Mr Shaw had been their adviser on all insurance matters, including pension schemes, and had developed a close business
relationship with their managing director, a Mr Sager. In 1965 Imperial Chemical
Industries Ltd acquired a large shareholding in Carrington Dewhurst, whose
name was subsequently changed to Carrington Viyella Ltd, (hereinafter called
"Carrington Viyella") and required the latter thereafter to place all its insurances
with the Royal Insurance Group. Mr Sager accordingly informed Mr Shaw that
the services of the Company would probably be no longer needed.

'(g) In or about September 1965 Mr Shaw was asked to wait on the Board of
Carrington Dewhurst. He went to see the directors expecting no more than a
friendly parting, but was greatly surprised to be told by the then Chairman,
Charles Riding (hereinafter called "Mr Riding") that the Board had decided

to make "him" a gift of £5,000. By "him", Mr Shaw assumed that the Company was meant. He had never received a gift on the cessation of a business association, for himself or for the Company. He had not expected Carrington Dewhurst to give him or the Company anything and did not consider that there was any obligation on the part of Carrington Dewhurst to do so. Subsequently on 21 September 1965 the Secretary of Carrington Dewhurst wrote to Mr Shaw in the following terms: "Dear Mr Shaw, The writer has been away on holiday for a fortnight and has not had an opportunity of writing to you since our last discussion at Eccleston. We think it is right that we should confirm the financial arrangement which [Carrington Dewhurst] have volunteered to make with you in recognition of the long period during which you have acted as broker and adviser on all insurance matters to Carrington and Dewhurst Limited. The basis of our proposal is that we have estimated your commission earned in the past to be approximately £2,000 p.a. and on that basis we are willing to pay one half of this estimated figure each year for a period of five years. In other words we are placing an upper limit of £1,000 p.a. for a five year period on our voluntary offer which we think you will agree is a very fair arrangement. We would propose to pay the annual amount of £1,000 to your firm in March of each year, commencing March 1966 and terminating in March 1970. Yours sincerely," In arriving at the estimate contained in the penultimate paragraph of the above letter Carrington Dewhurst would have known the amount of premiums which they had paid to the Company, but they would not have known the percentage earned by the Company as commission. Moreover, that estimate had no reference to pension scheme business handled by the [company].

'(h) The first £1,000 was paid by Carrington Dewhurst to the Company in 1966. The fourth payment of £1,000 was recorded in the Company's Corporation Tax Computation for the year ended 31 March 1970 as a deduction from "Profit per accounts" under the heading "Gift from Carrington Dewhurst", and was included as a gross trading receipt in the amount of £51,334 shown in the Company's Trading Account for the same period under the heading "Insurance Commissions", payments in previous years having been similarly dealt with.

'(i) Having accepted the verbal offer of the gift Mr Shaw did not at the time attach much importance to the precise wording of the said letter dated 21 September 1965 and gave no thought to the tax position. In 1970, however, his attention was drawn to the decision in *Walker* v. *Carnaby Harrower, Barham & Pykett*[1]. As a result, he wrote on 18 December 1970 to Mr Riding (who had then ceased to be Chairman of Carrington Viyella) in the following terms . . .'

There follows a correspondence between Mr Shaw and Mr Riding, culminating in a letter dated 18th January 1971 from Mr Riding to Mr Shaw's accountants on the lines of a draft supplied by Mr Shaw. I do not think any useful purpose would be served in reading those letters. They plainly represent a perfectly bona fide attempt by Mr Shaw to have the terms on which Carrington Dewhurst promised to pay the sum clarified and set out in terms which would bring his case as near as might be within the decision of *Walker v Carnaby, Harrower, Barham & Pykett*[1]. However, in considering the terms on which that promise was in fact made, one must go back to the terms of the original letter written on 21st Spetember 1965. The case stated continued:

'(k) After the loss of the Carrington Dewhurst business, none of the Company's staff had become redundant, but the Company's premium turnover had dropped by (very roughly) £30,000 for a year or so as against an annual premium turnover of about £500,000.'

---

1   [1970] 1 All ER 502, [1970] 1 WLR 276, 46 Tax Cas 561

Paragraph 6:

'It was contended on behalf of the Company: (a) That the circumstances of this appeal were similar to those in the *Carnaby Harrower* Case[1]. (b) That broker-age commission was not an "asset" in the ordinary meaning of that word, as it was terminable at any time without notice, and was not saleable. (c) That the £5,000 received by the Company was not assessable, although it had been included (in instalments of £1,000) in the Company's accounts for the earlier years, until the decision in the *Carnaby Harrower* Case[1] had become known. (d) That the appeal should be upheld.'

Paragraph 7:

'It was contended on behalf of the [Crown]: (a) That the facts of the *Carnaby Harrower* Case[1] were distinguishable from those in the present appeal. (b) Alternatively, that the decision in the said Case was per incuriam, because other cases in which it had been held that gifts were chargeable to tax under Schedule D of the Income Tax Act 1952 were not cited to the Court. (c) That the said £1,000 was properly assessable to Corporation Tax. (d) That the appeal should be dismissed.'

Paragraph 8: 'The following cases were cited by the parties', and then there are a number of cases[2] set out, some but not all of which were cited before me. Paragraph 9:

'We the Commissioners who heard the appeal gave our decision orally as follows: Having referred to the evidence both oral and documentary, the arguments addressed to us and the cases cited, we were not disposed to regard the decision in the *Carnaby Harrower* Case[1] as per incuriam. That decision, it seemed to us, covered broadly the situation in the present appeal. The fact that the payment in question had been unsolicited was not in itself decisive, but it had been made by the donor in respect of a long period of close business relationship, unlike payments in the cited cases relied on by the Solicitor for the Crown—in those cases payments had been made for loss of payments which might otherwise have been expected from the donor. In the present appeal, if the payment related to anything, it appeared to relate to payments which might otherwise have been expected from third parties, namely insurance companies. We held that the appeal succeeded in principle for the accounting period to 31 March 1970 in respect of the payment of £1,000, and we left figures to be agreed between the parties.'

Paragraph 10:

'Figures were agreed between the parties on 5 July 1972 and on 26 July 1972 we reduced the assessment to £22,631.'

Paragraph 11 contains the expression of dissatisfaction. Paragraph 12:

1   [1970] 1 All ER 502, [1970] 1 WLR 276, 46 Tax Cas 561

2   *Herbert v McQuade* [1902] 2 KB 631, 4 Tax Cas 489, CA; *Inland Revenue Comrs v Brander & Cruickshank* [1971] 1 All ER 36, [1971] 1 WLR 212, 46 Tax Cas 574, HL; *Inland Revenue Comrs v Fleming & Co (Machinery) Ltd* 1952 SC 120, 33 Tax Cas 57; *Mills (John) Productions Ltd (in liquidation) v Mathias (Inspector of Taxes)* (1967) 44 Tax Cas 441; *Moorhouse (Inspector of Taxes) v Dorland* [1955] 1 All ER 93, [1955] 1 Ch 284, 36 Tax Cas 1, CA; *Mudd v Collins (Inspector of Taxes)* (1925) 9 Tax Cas 297; *Severne (Inspector of Taxes) v Dadswell, Inland Revenue Comrs v Dadswell* [1954] 3 All ER 243, [1954] 1 WLR 1204, 35 Tax Cas 649; *Temperley (Inspector of Taxes) v Smith* [1956] 3 All ER 92, [1956] 1 WLR 931, 37 Tax Cas 18; *Walker (Inspector of Taxes) v Carnaby, Harrower, Barham & Pykett* [1970] 1 All ER 502, 1970 1 WLR 276, 46 Tax Cas 561; *Wing v O'Connell* [1927] IR 84; *Young v Bristol Aeroplane Co* [1944] 2 All ER 293, [1944] KB 718, CA; *affd* [1946] 1 All ER 98, [1946] AC 163, HL

a

'The question of law for the opinion of the Court is whether our decision was erroneous in point of law.'

Notice of an additional contention was given on behalf of the Crown; namely, that the *Carnaby, Harrower* case[1]—

b

'was wrongly decided and that the payments to the [company] were made as compensation for the cancellation of its contract with Carrington and Dewhurst and therefore the sums in question were trading receipts of an income nature which should be brought into account in computing the profits and gains of the [company's] trade, for the purpose of assessment to Corporation Tax.'

I will refer in a few moments to the *Carnaby, Harrower* case[1], which was a decision of my own. Before doing so I will refer to three previous cases relating to payments

c made by way of consolation or compensation for the loss of a trading connection, the receipts of which whilst the connection lasted had fallen to be included as receipts in ascertaining the profits of the trade. I should mention that in the *Carnaby, Harrower* case[1] the taxpayers were not legally represented, and whilst I received every assistance from counsel for the Crown I did not have the advantage of a full citation of the relevant authorities.

d   The first and to my mind the most important case for the present purpose is *Chibbett (Inspector of Taxes) v Joseph Robinson and Sons*[2]. The headnote runs as follows[3]:

'*Income Tax, Schedule D – Excess Profits Duty – Ship-managers – Profits of trade – Compensation for loss of employment.* The Respondents, a firm of ship-managers, were employed in that capacity by a certain steamship Company, their remunera-tion consisting in part of a percentage of the Company's annual net profits,

e including interest on its investments, which were considerable. The Company went into voluntary liquidation in 1918, and in general meeting authorised the liquidator to distribute some £800,000 worth of its investments among the shareholders, and to transfer £50,000 of 5 per cent. National War Bonds to the Respondents "as compensation for loss of office," the Articles of Association having been specifically amended to enable this to be done. The said Bonds

f were duly transferred to the Respondents in October, 1918. Subsequently, in pursuance of arrangements already made, the undertaking of the old Company, including two ships and its remaining assets, was transferred to a new Company of the same name consisting of the same shareholders. The Articles of Associa-tion of the new Company provided that its first managers should be the Res-pondent firm, though there had been no bargain to that effect, and that their

g remuneration should be on similar lines to that formerly received by them from the old Company. In computing the Respondent firm's liability to Income Tax and Excess Profits Duty, the said sum of £50,000 was treated as part of the profits arising from their business as ship-managers, but, on appeal to the General Commissioners, they contended (inter alia) that the sum in question was a voluntary payment made to them as compensation for the loss of the profits of

h their employment under the old Company which had terminated, and that it was not chargeable to Income Tax or Excess Profits Duty. The General Commissioners decided that it was not a profit liable to Income Tax or Excess Profits Duty. *Held*, that, on the findings of the Commissioners as to the nature of the payment, which there was evidence to support, the said sum of £50,000 was not a profit liable to Income Tax or Excess Profits Duty.'

j   It will be seen from that headnote and from the case stated[4] that the respondents were assessed in respect of their remuneration from the Stag Line under Case I of

1   [1970] 1 All ER 502, [1970] 1 WLR 276, 46 Tax Cas 561
2   (1924) 9 Tax Cas 48, [1924] All ER Rep 684
3   9 Tax Cas at 48, 49
4   9 Tax Cas at 55

Sch D, that remuneration being brought in as a receipt of the trade. One should *a*
observe that that was the only available head of charge for the years of assessment
involved, since remuneration from private offices and employments was not transferred from Case I of Sch D to Sch E until 1922. The fact remains that this is a decision
under Case I of Sch D, the question being whether this item should or should not have
been brought into account as a receipt of the trade of the managers. I turn now to the
judgment of Rowlatt J[1]:
b

> 'This case, like all cases of a similar nature, is very troublesome; because all
> these cases turn upon nice questions of fact, and at least I find very great difficulty
> in apprehending any permanent and clear line of division between the cases
> which are within and the cases which are without the scope of the Income Tax
> Acts. I think everybody is agreed, and has been agreed for a long time, that in
> cases of this kind the circumstances that the payment in question is a voluntary   *c*
> one does not matter. As Sir Richard Henn Collins said, you must not look at
> the point of view of the person who pays and see whether he is compellable to
> pay or not; you have to look at the point of view of the person who receives, to
> see whether he receives it in respect of his services, if it is a question of an office,
> and in respect of his trade, if it is a question of trade, and so on. You have to
> look at his point of view to see whether he receives it in respect of those con-   *d*
> siderations. That is perfectly true. But when you look at that question from
> what is described as the point of view of the recipient, that sends you back again,
> looking, for that purpose, to the point of view of the payer: not from the point
> of view of compellability or liability, but from the point of view of a person
> inquiring what is this payment for; and you have to see whether the maker of   *e*
> the payment makes it for the services and the receiver receives it for the
> services.'

Then, after a discussion of *Cowan v Seymour*[2], the learned judge goes on as follows.
I should mention that this statement[3], and in particular one sentence, could not I
think stand with certain other authorities without some qualification: that has been
pointed out in two subsequent cases[4]. What the learned judge said was this: *f*

> 'In this case we have the position that it is possible to make this payment as a
> compensation for loss of office, and it is so expressed in the resolution, and there
> is certainly no finding by the Commissioners that that resolution does not repre-
> sent the facts, namely, that it is fallacious to say that the company gave and the
> firm received this sum as compensation for the loss of profits of their employ-   *g*
> ment which was terminated. If it was a payment in respect of the termination
> of their employment I do not think that is taxable. I do not think that is taxable
> as a profit. It seems to me that a payment to make up for the cessation for
> the future of annual taxable profits is not itself an annual profit at all.'

Then he goes on a little later[5]:   *h*

> 'But the real crux of this case is this. It has been argued by the Attorney-
> General that, in spite of what must be taken to be the view of the Commissioners
> upon the point, this is not compensation for loss of office. The way he puts it
> is this. Here was a firm carrying on this business and acting for this company,

j

1   (1924) 9 Tax Cas at 60, [1924] All ER Rep at 690
2   [1920] 1 KB 500, 7 Tax Cas 372
3   9 Tax Cas at 61, [1924] All ER Rep at 691
4   See *Hunter v Dewhurst* (1932) 16 Tax Cas 605, [1932] All ER Rep 753; *Bush, Beach & Gent
    Ltd v Road* [1939] 3 All ER 302, [1939] 2 KB 524, 22 Tax Cas 519
5   9 Tax Cas at 61, 62, [1924] All ER Rep at 691, 692

this line of steamers. They were acting for them and continued to act for them, but in the middle of the time there came a reconstruction, and there was in the course of reconstruction this valuable windfall which fell to the company—and fell to the company because of their position of managers to this line of steamers. Therefore he says it is not to be looked upon as compensation for loss of office or employment; it has nothing to do with it; it was just simply a windfall in the course of the history of this firm. That is attractive at first sight, but I do not think it will do. In this case there was a difference. There were large investments which contributed to the income of the company, upon which these gentlemen got their percentage as part of their remuneration. So I understand. Therefore it was wholly illusory; they were losing something; the company which they had served was being wound up. There was a great surplus of assets. The company as then constituted certainly came to an end, and when it came to an end they gave this solatium to this firm out of their abundant prosperity, once for all, not because of anything they were doing, but really very much, I think, as the Master of the Rolls put it, as a testimonial for what they had done in the past in their office which had now terminated.

'Of course it is true that it is a trade receipt in this sense, that if these people had not been managers they never would have got it. It was not a gift to them as individuals or anything of that sort; it was because they were people of this kind. A question has been raised as to how it ought to be dealt with in the partnership accounts, and so on, but I do not think that really affects it. If it had been one man instead of a firm it would have been just the same, in which case there would have been no partnership accounts at all, and the question would have been, what is the position when his office comes to an end and reconstitution is taking place by which he will lose something, and, after all, the old arrangement has come to an end and he gets this lump sum given him as compensation for loss of office, if you like to put it that way, or if you like to put it as a testimonial because of the work he had done in the past, work which was now at an end. If it is that, which I think the Commissioners have found it is, and I think there was sufficient evidence for them to find it, I think the tax is not exigible, and therefore, this appeal must be dismissed and the decision of the Commissioners affirmed.'

As I indicated earlier, the statement[1]:

'If it was a payment in respect of the termination of their employment I do not think that is taxable. I do not think that is taxable as a profit. It seems to me that a payment to make up for the cessation for the future of annual taxable profits is not itself an annual profit at all'

must now be regarded as too wide: see on this point *Hunter v Dewhurst*[2], in the House of Lords per Lord Macmillan in his dissenting judgment. He said[3]:

'And as to *Chibbett's* case[4] [which had been commented on in argument adversely by counsel for the Crown], there a firm of ship managers who had been employed by a steamship company lost the benefit of this employment in consequence of the company going into liquidation and received by way of compensation a sum of money out of the surplus assets of the company. The terms on which the ship managers had been employed gave them no right whatever to this sum and their services had already received full remuneration. It was in the course of his judgment holding the payment to the ship managers

---

1   (1924) 9 Tax Cas at 61, [1924] All ER Rep at 691
2   (1932) 16 Tax Cas 605, [1932] All ER Rep 753
3   16 Tax Cas at 653, [1932] All ER Rep at 766
4   (1924) 9 Tax Cas 48, [1924] All ER Rep 684

not to be a taxable profit of their employment that Mr. Justice Rowlatt used the words which I have quoted above and which he himself quoted in his judgment in the present case. I am disposed to regard them as too widely expressed, for remuneration for services may take, in part, the form of a payment at the end of the employment, and a payment does not necessarily cease to be remuneration for services because it is payable when the services come to an end. Here, however, the circumstances, as I have pointed out, are quite different from those in *Chibbett's* case[1].'

So, Lord Macmillan points out that Rowlatt J's statement is too widely expressed. In particular, I think, it is not correct in its application to the case where, on determination of an employment, the individual concerned receives a payment as compensation for future profit to which he would have been entitled under the terms of his employment. Nonetheless, there is nothing in Lord Macmillan's comments which indicates that Rowlatt J's judgment in *Chibbett v Joseph Robinson and Sons*[1] was wrong. On the contrary, he says[2]: 'Here, however, the circumstances, as I have pointed out, are quite different from those in *Chibbett's* case[1].' All he says is that the statement is too widely expressed. I see no reason to think that that statement has been said to be incorrect or has been judicially doubted insofar as the statement relates to a purely voluntary payment made at the end of an employment. I have referred to an employment: the same applies, mutatis mutandis, I think, to the case of a payment to a trader made on the determination of some trade connection. I should perhaps mention at this stage that in *Bush, Beach and Gent Ltd v Road*[3] Lawrence J similarly commented that Rowlatt J's statement[4] was too wide.

Before leaving that case, my conclusion on it is that it is a valid and binding authority with only this qualification, that the statement[4] quoted above is too wide, and I think it is still applicable and appropriate to payments which are purely voluntary payments made at the end of an employment or trade connection. Perhaps I should mention at this stage that payments on retirement from offices are now chargeable with tax: see the Finance Act 1960, s 37. It is not suggested that this section has any application to voluntary payments received by a trader and chargeable under Case I of Sch D.

The next case to which I was referred dealing with payments to a trader on the termination of some trading connection is *Inland Revenue Comrs v Fleming & Co (Machinery) Ltd*[5] in the Court of Session. The headnote runs as follows[6]:

'The Company carried on business as manufacturers' agents and general merchants. Since before 1903 the Company and its predecessors had been sole selling agents in Scotland for certain products of a manufacturer but in 1948 at the instance of the manufacturer the agency was terminated by an agreement under which the Company received inter alia a payment as compensation for the loss of the agency. On appeal before the General Commissioners it was contended for the Company that the compensation was a capital receipt and the Commissioners allowed the appeal. *Held,* that the compensation was a trading receipt.'

I was much pressed with the judgment of Lord Keith in which he said[7]:

'I agree that the sum of £5320 must be treated as an income payment. The question is a narrow one. The payment is expressed to be compensation for the

1   (1924) 9 Tax Cas 48, [1924] All ER Rep 684
2   (1932) 16 Tax Cas at 653, [1932] All ER Rep at 766
3   [1939] 3 All ER 302 at 305, [1939] 2 KB 524 at 533, 22 Tax Cas 519 at 524
4   (1924) 9 Tax Cas at 61, [1924] All ER Rep at 691
5   1952 SC 120, 33 Tax Cas 57
6   (1951) 33 Tax Cas at 57
7   1952 SC at 130, 33 Tax Cas at 64, 65

loss of the agency.   This might be thought to suggest compensation for the loss
of a profit-earning asset and therefore make the payment a capital receipt.
But such an expression leaves the whole question, I think, open.   In *Kelsall Parsons & Co. v. Inland Revenue*[1] the words used were "compensation for termination" of an agency agreement; yet the payment was held to be an income
payment.   I am influenced in reaching my decision by the following considerations [He then sets out a number of specific considerations, and concludes:]
I think accordingly that the sum of £5320 must be regarded as compensation
for loss of profits and not for loss of a profit-earning asset.'

That case, I think, takes one no further in the present case.   The payment was
made pursuant to a contract for valuable consideration under which an agency and
a restrictive covenant were terminated and a sum was paid for the assignment of
certain leases, a particular part of the consideration being allocated to each of those
three items.   It appears that the sum allocated to the loss of the agency may have
been rather high bearing in mind the terms of the agency.   Apparently the letter
appointing the company as agent did not specify the period of appointment and made
no provision for compensation on cessation of the agency.   Nonetheless, the company
had certain contractual rights against the manufacturer which made the payments,
and those rights were compromised for valuable consideration under the terms of
the agreement.   That being the position, the question before the Court of Session
was simply whether this should be treated as a capital receipt, as representing compensation for the loss of a profit-earning capital asset, or whether it should be treated
as a revenue receipt; and it was held on the particular facts that the latter was the
proper view.   The court was not at all concerned with the question of a purely
voluntary payment.

The only other case cited to me in this connection was that of *Temperley v Smith*[2],
where the headnote runs as follows[3]:

'Income Tax Schedule D – Assignment to member of hospital's honorary medical
staff of endowment assurance policy – Whether surrender value assessable.   The Board
of Management of a voluntary hospital had taken out endowment assurance
policies on the lives of members of its honorary medical staff, of whom the
Respondent was one, under a scheme which provided that in the event of the
hospital ceasing to be a voluntary hospital the policies would become the sole
property of the members of the scheme.   The National Health Service Act,
1946, was passed in November 1946, and the National Health Service came into
operation in July, 1948.   Under an agreement made in February 1947, the Respondent was granted a new contract of service from 1st January, 1947, similar
contracts being offered to the other members of the medical staff.   No premiums
were paid by the Board of Management after 31st December, 1946, and in
pursuance of resolutions dated 4th November, 1947, and 27th January, 1948,
the policy was in May, 1948, formally assigned to the Respondent, who had
paid the premiums falling due on and after 1st January, 1947.   On appeal before
the General Commissioners against alternative additional assessments under
Case II of Schedule D for the years 1947-48 and 1948-49 in respect of the surrender
value of the policy, the Respondent contended that the policy was not a receipt
of his profession.   The Commissioners upheld the Respondent's contention.
Held, that the surrender value of the policy was a receipt of the Respondent's
profession and was liable to tax.'

The facts in that case are not very relevant to those in the present case, but I was
referred to two paragraphs in the judgment of Vaisey J.   He said[4]:

1   1938 SC 238, 21 Tax Cas 608
2   [1956] 3 All ER 92, [1956] 1 WLR 931, 37 Tax Cas 18
3   (1956) 37 Tax Cas at 18
4   [1956] 3 All ER at 95, [1956] 1 WLR at 934, 37 Tax Cas at 23

'The assessment in this case is under Sch. D, and the sum in question is alleged to be part of the annual profits or gains accruing to the taxpayer from his profession of a medical practitioner. Many of the authorities relate to assessments under Sch. E, but in my judgment the authorities under both Schedules all rest on the same general principles.'

He continued[1]:

'The crucial test, in my judgment, is the character in which the recipient of a benefit takes it, and if it came to him in virtue of his office or in virtue of his profession or vocation and otherwise than as a mere present, I think that it is liable to tax. I cannot accept the view that the taxpayer's services at the hospital were not within the scope of his profession, and in the circumstances of the case my decision here must be for the Crown . . .'

With great respect to Vaisey J, his statement[2] that 'the authorities under both Schedules all rest on the same general principles', and the application of Sch E principles to Case I of Sch D, seem to me to require some qualification. I will not elaborate the distinction between, on the one hand, Sch D, Case I, and, on the other hand, Sch E beyond pointing out something which is of considerable importance in the present case; namely, that in the case of a trade, unlike that of an office or employment, a particular connection may terminate leaving the trade continuing. The position of a trade in this respect is more favourable to the Crown than that of an office or employment, and indeed counsel for the Crown relied to a great extent on this circumstance.

I come now to *Walker v Carnaby, Harrower, Barham & Pykett*[3]. The headnote, so far as material, reads as follows[4]:

'The Respondents, a firm of accountants, had for many years acted as auditors to six associated companies. As a result of the reorganisation of the group's accounting system, they were asked, after completing the 1962 audit, not to seek reappointment for 1963. They complied, and their charges of £2,567 for the 1962 audits were duly paid. Later they were given an unsolicited ex gratia payment of £2,567 "as solatium for the loss of the office of auditors". That sum was not a gift to any individual partner.'

The next paragraph of the headnote is addressed to two cases; namely, *Blackburn v Close Brothers Ltd*[5] and *Ellis v Lucas*[6], which played a large part in the argument in *Walker v Carnaby, Harrower, Barham & Pykett*[3] but with which I do not have to deal in the present case. Then[4]:

'*Held*, that but for being voluntary the payment would have fallen to be taken into account as part of the profits of the profession, but that ordinary commercial principles did not require the bringing into account of a voluntary payment made, not as consideration for past services, but as a recognition of past services or by way of consolation for the termination of a contract.'

In my judgment, after setting out the case stated, I said[7]:

'It will be seen that the taxpayers for many years held the office of auditors under the six companies. That is an office to which auditors are appointed

---

1 [1956] 3 All ER at 96, [1956] 1 WLR at 935, 936, 37 Tax Cas at 24
2 [1956] 3 All ER at 95, [1956] 1 WLR at 934, 37 Tax Cas at 23
3 [1970] 1 All ER 502, [1970] 1 WLR 276, 46 Tax Cas 561
4 (1969) 46 Tax Cas at 561
5 (1960) 39 Tax Cas 164
6 [1966] 2 All ER 935, [1967] Ch 858, 43 Tax Cas 276
7 [1970] 1 All ER at 505, [1970] 1 WLR at 280, 46 Tax Cas at 566

annually under the Companies Acts.   There was no contract between the taxpayers and the various companies, nor had the taxpayers any contractual or
other legal right to receive compensation under the termination of that office.
It was accepted by the taxpayers that their appointment as auditors was made
in the course of the taxpayers' business as accountants, that the payments
received might be considered as compensation for the loss of an audit, and that
the payment was made to the firm as a whole.   It was not by way of a personal
gift to any one or more of the members of the firm.   The Special Commissioners
reached their conclusion in favour of the taxpayers on two distinct grounds:
first, that the payment was an ex gratia payment and unsolicited; and, secondly,
on the ground, as expressed, that the facts were quite different from those in
Blackburn v Close Bros Ltd.[1]'

The next part of the judgment is devoted to a review, at considerable length, of
Blackburn v Close Brothers Ltd[1] and *Ellis v Lucas*[2], and none of that is material now.
Then[3]:

'I turn now to the other point which is the first point made by the Special
Commissioners, namely, that the payment here was an ex gratia payment.
There is, as is well known, a great volume of authority on voluntary payments
made to the holder of an office.   There is no doubt that in many circumstances
a payment, although voluntary, may yet when looked at from the point of
view of the recipient be regarded as a payment arising from that office.   There
is curiously little authority on voluntary payments made to someone who is
carrying on a trade or profession, chargeable under Case I or Case II of Schedule
D.   It may be that traders do not frequently receive voluntary payments from
their clients or customers or from former clients or former customers.   The
test must be whether a voluntary payment made to someone carrying on a
trade or profession is properly to be regarded as a receipt to be taken into account
in computing the profit of that trade or business.   To avoid misunderstanding,
the position is quite different from that in respect of voluntary payments of a
pure income character.'

I then went on to consider *Australia (Commonwealth) Comr of Taxation v Squatting
Investment Co Ltd*[4] with which I had been pressed.   I will refer to that much more
shortly in a few moments.   Then[5]:

'In the present case the commissioners have concluded that the fact that the
payment was ex gratia and unsolicited is a ground for holding that it ought not
to be brought into account.   I do not think I ought, having regard to the way in
which the decision of the commissioners is framed, to regard that as the kind of
finding of secondary fact to which the court should pay very great importance.
I ought, I think, to reach my own conclusion on this point, but my conclusion—
I say at once—is the same as that of the commissioners.   When one looks at
the particular facts of this case one finds that the taxpayers were carrying on the
business of chartered accountants, which consists in rendering services of a certain
professional character in return for reward.   They rendered those services to
these six companies over a number of years and duly received their reward for
so doing.   At the end of their final term of office they had no legal claim of any
description to receive any further payment from the companies.   The companies then proceeded to make a wholly voluntary payment to the taxpayers.

---

1   (1960) 39 Tax Cas 164
2   [1966] 2 All ER 935, [1967] Ch 858, 43 Tax Cas 276
3   [1970] 1 All ER at 509, [1970] 1 WLR at 285, 46 Tax Cas at 570, 571
4   [1954] 1 All ER 349, [1954] AC 182
5   [1970] 1 All ER at 511, 512, [1970] 1 WLR at 287, 288, 46 Tax Cas at 572, 573

It is, I think, irrelevant that the companies elected to make that payment in an amount identical to a penny with the fees paid to the firm during their last year of office. It seems to me that a gift of that kind made by a former client cannot reasonably be treated as a receipt of a business which consists in rendering professional services. The subject-matter of the assessments under Cases I and II is the full amount of the profits or gains of the trade or profession. Those profits have to be computed, it is well established, on ordinary commercial principles. It does not seem to me that ordinary commercial principles require the bringing into account of this sort of voluntary payment, not made as the consideration for any services rendered by the firm, but by way of recognition of past services or by way of consolation for the termination of a contract. It is difficult to amplify the point any further. I fully appreciate that the taxpayers would not have received this payment if they had not previously rendered professional services to the companies. Again, I fully appreciate that the payment was made to them as a firm and not because the companies had a particular affection for any member of the firm personally. As I have said, counsel for the Crown, who is of course familiar with all the cases, has been unable to cite any authority one way or the other which is directly in point. I must, I think, decide this point on general principles, and I do not think that there is anything in the charging words of Sch D Cases I and II which make it necessary to take a wider view as regards voluntary receipts. I need hardly say that the facts of the present case are sharply distinguishable from those in *Australia (Commonwealth) Comr of Taxation v Squatting Investment Co Ltd*[1] in which the payment was in effect by way of an additional payment in respect of the purchase price for goods sold.'

The Crown intends to contend in a higher court that that decision was wrong. To avoid misunderstanding, I think that when the words 'per incuriam' are used in the contention before the commissioners they mean only that that decision was given without my having had cited to me all the authorities which might have affected the conclusion. I am not myself persuaded that this decision was wrong. On the contrary, I think that it is directly in line with the decision in *Chibbett v Joseph Robinson and Sons*[2], although that decision was not in fact cited; and, further, that it is in accordance with proper principles. I do not see on what principle of commercial accounting, if a customer chooses to make a voluntary payment to a trader on the cessation of their trading connection, that payment should be treated as a receipt in ascertaining the profits arising from the trade. It is not received in return for activities carried on by the trader in his trade—e g the provision of goods or services—but is simply a windfall in the nature of a gift. In other words, it is a by-product of the trade rather than an operation in the carrying on of the trade.

Counsel for the Crown referred me to, and placed some reliance on, the line of cases which includes *Australia (Commonwealth) Comr of Taxation v Squatting Investment Co Ltd*[1], to which I have already referred, and also the earlier English case of *Isaac Holden & Sons Ltd v Inland Revenue Comrs*[3], in which a payment was made to a trader in respect of goods which had been purchased from him under wartime conditions some time previously and in respect of which the full contractual purchase price had been paid. The additional sum was voluntary in the sense that payment could not have been enforced, but the additional sum yet represented in substance an addition to the price of the goods sold. In those circumstances, the additional payment was held to be what it certainly was in substance, namely, an additional part of the price of the goods sold, and not a mere gift. Those cases are wholly distinguishable from

1   [1954] 1 All ER 349, [1954] AC 182
2   (1924) 9 Tax Cas 48, [1924] All ER Rep 684
3   (1924) 12 Tax Cas 768

cases such as the present, where the payment is not on any view an additional price for services already rendered but simply a recognition of past services or consolation for the determination of the connection in the future.

I was also referred to a line of cases relating to payments received by the holder of an office or employment and chargeable, if at all, under Sch E. No assistance is to be derived from cases on receipts while the office continues; the liability for tax on such receipts turns on entirely different considerations from those at issue here. No Sch E case has been cited to me in which it has been held that a voluntary payment made to the holder of an office on the termination of that office merely by way of gift or consolation, or the like, and for no other reason, has been held to be chargeable as a profit from the office. On the contrary, as I understand it, until the law was altered in 1960 such payments did not fall to be brought into charge under Sch E. One must of course distinguish cases in which a payment has been made by way of compensation for premature determination of a contract, and the like.

I do not think it would be useful to go any further into these Sch E cases. However, it may be worthwhile to cite a single paragraph from the speech of Viscount Simonds in *Hochstrasser v Mayes*[1]:

'UPJOHN, J., before whom the matter first came, after a review of the relevant case law, expressed himself thus in a passage which appears to me to sum up the law in a manner which cannot be improved on. He said[2]: "In my judgment the authorities show this, that it is a question to be answered in the light of the particular facts of every case whether or not a particular payment is or is not a profit arising from the employment. Disregarding entirely contracts for full consideration in money or money's worth and personal presents, in my judgment not every payment made to an employee is necessarily made to him as a profit arising from his employment. Indeed, in my judgment, the authorities show that to be a profit arising from the employment, the payment must be made in reference to the service the employee renders by virtue of his office, and it must be something in the nature of a reward for services past, present and future." In this passage the single word "past" may be open to question, but apart from that it appears to me to be entirely accurate.'

To return to the present case, the promise to pay £5,000 and the subsequent payment of £1,000 in each year represented a purely voluntary disposition on the part of Carrington Dewhurst; in other words, each payment represented a gift to the company, the motive for the gift being, as is stated in the letter of 21st September 1965, 'recognition of the long period during which you have acted as broker and adviser on all insurance matters to Carrington and Dewhurst Limited'. No evidence has been produced on either side as to the principles of commercial accounting. In the absence of such evidence—and, indeed, the court must in any event have the last word on the question—it seems to me that this payment is not a receipt which on the proper principles of commercial accounting should be brought into account in calculating the profit of the trade, which consists in rendering services for reward. I need not repeat what I said in the *Carnaby, Harrower* case[3], but what I said there is to my mind immensely fortified by what was said by Rowlatt J in *Chibbett v Joseph Robinson and Sons*[4].

Counsel for the Crown relied on a number of miscellaneous circumstances; namely, (1) that the recipient of the payment is a limited company, (2) that the payment was quantified by reference to commission earned in past years, (3) that the payment was by five yearly instalments and (4) that the taxpayer company in fact brought the

---

1 [1959] 3 All ER 817 at 821, [1960] AC 376 at 387, 388, 38 Tax Cas 673 at 705
2 [1958] 1 All ER 369 at 374, [1959] Ch 22 at 33, 38 Tax Cas at 685
3 [1970] 1 All ER 502, [1970] 1 WLR 276, 46 Tax Cas 561
4 (1924) 9 Tax Cas 48, [1924] All ER Rep 684

instalment into account as a trading receipt before seeing the green light of the decision in the *Carnaby, Harrower* case[1]. These circumstances might all be highly relevant on a consideration of whether the transaction was really a voluntary payment at all, but once it is conceded that the payment is indeed a voluntary payment and nothing else, these circumstances seem to me to have no significance.   There is no reason in principle why a gift could not be made to a limited company.   It may be an unusual transaction, but not at all an unknown one in the case of what one may call a one-man company.   Again, the quantification of the payment and the circumstance that it is payable by instalments cannot affect its quality as a voluntary payment; and, finally, I think it is irrelevant that this company made a mistake as to the nature of this payment during the first years under review.   It seems to me that unless one is constrained to hold that a gift by a customer to a trader as such— i e there being no other relevant connection between them—must ipso facto be treated as a receipt of the trade, then there is no reason why this receipt should be so treated.   The commissioners have held that this payment is not such a receipt, and I agree with their decision.   I put it like that because I think this is ultimately a question of law rather than of fact.

I have not overlooked the fact that during the currency of its agency the company received its commission not from Carrington Dewhurst but from the insurance company.   This circumstance certainly emphasises the nature of the transaction as a pure gift.   However, counsel for the company has not (rightly, I think) laid too much stress on this circumstance, which cannot be in any way conclusive.   If a mere gift to a trader by a customer is taxable, I see no reason why a gift to a broker by one of two parties whom the broker brings together should be any less taxable by reason of the fact that the broker receives his commission from the other party.

For the reasons I have given, I think the appeal must be dismissed.

Appeal dismissed.

Solicitors: *Solicitor of Inland Revenue; Taylor, Hindle & Rhodes,* Manchester (for the company).

Rengan Krishnan Esq Barrister.

---

1   [1970] 1 All ER 502, [1970] 1 WLR 276, 46 Tax Cas 561

R v John (Graham)

COURT OF APPEAL, CRIMINAL DIVISION
ROSKILL, JAMES LJJ AND CAULFIELD J
15th MARCH 1974

Road traffic – Driving with blood-alcohol proportion above prescribed limit – Evidence – Failure to supply specimen – Reasonable excuse – What amounts to reasonable excuse – Religious belief – Belief precluding motorist from supplying specimen of blood – Whether belief capable in law of amounting to reasonable excuse – Road Safety Act 1967, s 3(3).

The appellant was charged with failing, without reasonable excuse, to supply a specimen of blood for a laboratory test, contrary to s 3(3)[a] of the Road Safety Act 1967. The appellant genuinely and sincerely held the belief that he was possessed of certain faith healing powers derived from the presence in his blood of divinely given gifts. He contended that those beliefs precluded him from supplying a specimen of blood and that in consequence he had a 'reasonable excuse' for refusing to do so. The trial judge ruled that the appellant's beliefs could not in law amount to a 'reasonable excuse' within s 3(3), and thus there was no defence to the charge. The appellant was convicted. On appeal,

Held – For an excuse to be capable of being a 'reasonable excuse' within s 3(3), it had to be one which related to the physical or mental capacity of the person concerned to supply a specimen; a person's religious beliefs, however sincerely held, could not in law amount to a reasonable excuse for failing to supply a specimen. Accordingly the appeal would be dismissed (see p 565 h to p 566 a, post).

Dictum of Lawton LJ in *R v Lennard* [1973] 2 All ER at 834 applied.

Notes

For failure to provide a specimen of blood or urine for a laboratory test without reasonable excuse, see Supplement to 33 Halsbury's Laws (3rd Edn) para 1061A, 8.

For the Road Safety Act 1967, s 3, see 28 Halsbury's Statutes (3rd Edn) 465.

As from 1st July 1972 s 3 of the 1967 Act has been replaced by the Road Traffic Act 1972, s 9.

Cases referred to in judgment

Hunter v Mann p 414, ante, [1974] 2 WLR 742, DC.
Law v Stephens [1971] RTR 358, DC.
R v Lennard [1973] 2 All ER 831, [1973] 1 WLR 483, 57 Cr App Rep 542, [1973] RTR 252, CA.
R v Najran [1973] RTR 451, CA.
R v Reid (Philip) [1973] 3 All ER 1020, [1973] 1 WLR 1283, 57 Cr App Rep 807, [1973] RTR 536, CA.

Cases also cited

Rowland v Thorpe [1970] 3 All ER 195, DC.
Scobell v Graham [1970] RTR 358, DC.

Appeal

This was an appeal by Graham John against his conviction on 23rd January 1973 in the Crown Court at Middlesex before his Honour Judge Edie and a jury of failing, without reasonable excuse, to provide a specimen for a laboratory test, contrary to s 3(3) of the Road Safety Act 1967. He was disqualified from holding a driving

---

a   Section 3(3), so far as material, is set out at p 562 f, post

licence for 12 months, fined £40, and ordered to pay £20 towards the costs of prosecution. The facts are set out in the judgment of the court.

P Coni for the appellant.
Donald Farquharson QC and *R J Prendergast* for the Crown.

ROSKILL LJ delivered the following judgment of the court. This appeal brought by leave of the full court, granted on 8th October 1973, raises a point of general importance in connection with what is popularly called breathalyser law. The court is grateful to counsel for the appellant and the Crown for the clear way in which they have placed the rival contentions before it. In a sentence the point is this: where a man is required by law, after all due formalities have been complied with, to supply a sample in accordance with the provisions of the Road Traffic Act 1972, is it a reasonable excuse for him to say to the police officer: 'My personal religious belief or faith or tenet does not allow me to comply with that request, albeit it is one which you properly make to me in accordance with your duty under the statute?' It was to enable that point to be argued that the full court gave leave.

The facts fall within a very narrow compass. On the night of 2nd May 1972—why this case has taken so long to come on is not the fault of the court—the appellant drove on a restricted road at a speed exceeding 30 m p h. He was stopped. His breath smelt of drink. A breathalyser test taken at 9.40 p m was positive. It is not disputed that he was then properly arrested. He was taken to the local police station. He was breathalysed a second time at 10.01 p m. That second breath test proved positive. He was asked for a sample of blood. He refused for the reason I have already indicated. The statutory procedure laid down in s 9 of the 1972 Act was then gone through. A first sample of urine was taken and thrown away, as the statute requires. He was unable, and the reason was genuine, to supply a second. He was asked for a second sample of blood. Again he refused. Accordingly he was charged with an offence against s 3(3) of the Road Safety Act 1967 (now s 9(3) of the 1972 Act), which provides:

> 'A person who, without reasonable excuse, fails to provide a specimen for a laboratory test in pursuance of a requirement imposed under this section shall be guilty of an offence . . .'

The sole question is whether or not the appellant had reasonable excuse. Counsel on his behalf says that he had. His personal belief can be shortly and simply stated. No one has doubted its sincerity or his sincerity. He is apparently a follower of, and a believer, in the doctrines enunciated in the last century by Mesmer. He believes that he is possessed of certain faith healing powers derived from the presence in his blood of divinely given gifts. It is not for this court to presume to comment on those beliefs. They are, it is accepted on all sides, genuinely and sincerely held. It was for that reason that he said, and there is no doubt that he believed, that his beliefs precluded him from complying with what would otherwise have been his obligation. Is that a reasonable excuse? It is said that it is. When the matter came before the trial judge, he heard the evidence of the appellant. After hearing arguments advanced by counsel on both sides, he ruled as a matter of law—and he did not have the benefit, if benefit it be, of the citation of authorities which we have had—that those beliefs were incapable of affording the appellant a reasonable excuse. Accordingly, and perfectly properly in accordance with his view of the law, he directed the jury that there was no defence and the jury, under his direction, returned a verdict of guilty. The appellant, a man of otherwise impeccable antecedents, was thereupon fined £40, disqualified from driving for 12 months and ordered to pay £20 towards the costs of the prosecution.

We have been referred to a number of authorities in this field. I do not propose to go through all of them. In *Law v Stephens*[1], the Divisional Court stated categorically

1 [1971] RTR 358

a   when considering what was capable of being a reasonable excuse, that that question
     was in the first instance a question of law. Lord Parker CJ said[1]:

> 'In that connection I think it is only right to say that it is a question of law in
> the first instance whether something put forward is capable of being a reason-
> able excuse; if it is capable of being one, then it becomes a matter of fact and
> degree as to whether or not it amounts to a reasonable excuse, and the burden
b   > of course then is on the prosecution to negative it.'

     Counsel for the appellant in this court has not challenged that statement. This
     court therefore proceeds on the basis, accepted on both sides, that the first question
     it has to ask is whether or not a particular excuse is capable in law of being a reason-
     able excuse. If the present facts are capable in law of being a reasonable excuse, then
     the judge's ruling and direction to the jury were wrong, and this conviction must
c   be quashed. But if those facts are incapable in law of being a reasonable excuse, it
     was of course the judge's duty to rule as he did, and his ruling was plainly right.
     Since that decision of the Divisional Court[2], there have been three decisions of
     this court to which it is necessary to refer. This court on each occasion included
     Lawton and Scarman LJJ. The first is R v Lennard[3]. Lawton LJ read the reserved
d   judgment of the court. It is not necessary to relate the facts. In it he said[4]:

> 'The problem whether an excuse such as that put forward by this appellant is
> capable of being a reasonable one necessitated the court construing s 3(3) [of the
> 1967 Act] in its context and considering a number of authorities.'

     Lawton LJ then went on to deal with the various statutory provisions, and continued:

e   > 'In our judgment no excuse can be adjudged a reasonable one unless the person
> from whom the specimen is required is physically or mentally unable to provide
> it or the provision of the specimen would entail a substantial risk to his health.'

     Counsel for the appellant realistically accepted that if those final words used by
     Lawton LJ were to be followed without qualification, they presented difficulties
f   for him in this appeal.
     Immediately after R v Lennard[3], this court, in fact on the very next day, again
     had to consider the same point in R v Najran[5]. There the recorder at Birmingham
     Crown Court had expressed the view that the excuse put forward was incapable
     of being a reasonable excuse. But notwithstanding that that was his view, he left
     the matter to the jury. Accordingly the point that had arisen in R v Lennard[3] and
     arises in this case was not the subject of direct decision in R v Najran[5]. Scarman LJ,
g   in giving judgment in R v Najran[6], said:

> 'Whether or not the recorder was right in law in assuming that a refusal to
> give a blood specimen on religious grounds was capable of constituting a reason-
> able excuse, again is neither here nor there for the purposes of this application.
> Favourably to the applicant, the recorder left that issue, as he also left the issue
h   > of the warning, to the jury to be considered and indicated, as was indeed the
> fact, that there was a conflict of evidence about those matters between the police
> and the applicant and that conflict of evidence, according to the well-known
> principles of proof in these courts, had to be dealt with and determined by the
> jury.'

     Later he said[7]:

j   1   [1971] RTR at 361
     2   [1971] RTR 358
     3   [1973] 2 All ER 831, [1973] 1 WLR 483
     4   [1973] 2 All ER at 834, [1973] 1 WLR at 486
     5   [1973] RTR 451
     6   [1973] RTR at 455
     7   [1973] RTR at 456

'During the evidence it is alleged that the recorder expressed the view in the presence of the jury on more than one occasion that the religious beliefs of the applicant on the giving of a blood sample were irrelevant. In the light of this court's decision in *R v Lennard*[1] the recorder may well have been right in taking that view, but whether he was wrong or right he had put it fairly to the jury, sought their verdict and obtained it.'

There was nothing in that judgment to cast any doubt on what was stated in *R v Lennard*[1].

I come to the third authority, *R v Reid*[2]. The same two Lords Justices, together with Ackner J, constituted the court. The judgment was delivered by Scarman LJ who said[3]:

'I come now to the second point taken by counsel that the appellant, when he failed to provide a specimen, had a reasonable excuse for that failure. The learned judge did not leave the issue of reasonable excuse to the jury.'

Pausing there for a moment; the judge there concerned, Judge Stock, acted as Judge Edie did in the present case. Scarman LJ continued:

'He felt, as a matter of law, that, on the facts disclosed by the prosecution case, there could be no reasonable excuse. Subsequent to his summing-up, this court has had to consider the meaning of "reasonable excuse" in the context of s 3(3) of the 1967 Act, and has reached a decision that abundantly justifies the approach of the learned judge to the question in this summing-up. I refer to *R v Lennard*[1]. I make only this observation. We are, of course, bound by that decision, but, even if at any time hereafter it should be considered that this court was too restrictive in its interpretation of the words "reasonable excuse", it is abundantly plain in my view that on the facts of the present case there can be no reasonable excuse.'

So there this court was suggesting that perhaps the language used in *R v Lennard*[1] might be a little too restrictive, and might be thereafter interpreted as exhaustive, when that had not been the intention of the court.

It is against that background of authority that we turn to consider the crucial question. It is right to say, of course, that any state of affairs which involves persons committing criminal offences because of beliefs sincerely held by them, is, to put it at its lowest, highly distasteful for any court. Ever since the early or middle part of the 18th century, the courts of this country have prided themselves on the liberality of their approach to matters of conscience. That attitude has continued for the last 200 years at least. Accordingly, any argument such as that to which this court has listened on behalf of the appellant is entitled to and must receive respect. For a man to be punished for an offence which is committed by reason only of his adherence to his own religion or belief can only be justified if the court is satisfied that the clear intention of the statute creating the offence was in the interests of the community as a whole to override the privileges otherwise attaching to freedom of conscience and belief, which it must always be the duty of the courts to protect and defend. There are examples mentioned in argument where this has happened. One is the National Service Acts before, during and after the 1939-45 war. Persons holding sincere objection to military service were nonetheless compelled to serve in one or other of various spheres of activity subject to due safeguards. Another is the recent case[4] in the Divisional Court where a doctor, whose professional etiquette precluded him from giving certain information which the statute required him to give,

1　[1973] 2 All ER 831, [1973] 1 WLR 483
2　[1973] 3 All ER 1020, [1973] 1 WLR 1283
3　[1973] 3 All ER at 1025, [1973] 1 WLR at 1289
4　*Hunter v Mann* p 414, ante, [1974] 2 WLR 742

a was prosecuted and fined. Other examples can be found in the law of evidence. There is no privilege attaching to the confessional. There is no privilege attaching to communications between doctor and patient. In these matters Parliament and the courts have found it necessary, in the interests of the community as a whole, to override the personal right of the individual to maintain his own belief. The position is by no means uncommon.

b It is against that background that one turns to consider the position under the road traffic legislation. Anyone recollecting the introduction of these provisions in 1967 will recall that they were bitterly opposed, on the ground that they restricted individual liberty. They rendered persons liable to arrest on the road if a breath test proved to be positive. That was an infringment of personal liberty, albeit only for a limited period, by enabling the alleged offender to be taken to a police station. Nonetheless Parliament found it necessary, because of the difficulty of

c enforcing the former law in relation to driving when ability to drive was allegedly impaired through drink or drug, to introduce the code which first found its place on the statute book in 1967. It was in many respects a drastic code which infringed the personal liberty of individuals. But Parliament found it necessary to introduce that code in the interests of the public as a whole, to prevent the public as a whole being victimised by those who were persistently driving after consuming an excessive

d quantity of alcohol but who all too often were not brought to justice because of the difficulty of bringing home a charge in the courts. The very introduction of the limit of 80 milligrammes was itself an infringement of individual rights.

It is therefore against the background of a statute which by its very terms does restrict individual rights that one has to construe the crucial words that are now in s 9(3) of the 1972 Act, 'without reasonable excuse'. It is suggested that any excuse

e will do, if based on belief sincerely held. But that, with great respect to the skill with which the argument has been advanced, involves making the person seeking to set up that excuse as reasonable the judge in his own cause. He becomes entitled to say, 'Because I believe a certain thing, that belief of my own, personal to myself, affords me a reasonable excuse for not complying with what other people would

f have to comply. In other words the person concerned is really seeking to say not 'I cannot', but 'I ought not'.

In the view of this court, that is not well founded. As I said a few moments ago, the 1972 Act provides rules for the safety of the public. It provides rules to protect the public from certain classes of users of the road. The securing of that protection involves restriction on the liberty of individuals.

g It is against that background that one returns to consider the language used in R v Lennard[1]. It may be—and we say this with the utmost respect to the Lords Justices concerned—that the language used, if construed too strictly, might involve an over-rigid approach to the language of s 3(3) of the 1967 Act. Certainly, in the view of this court and in the light of what was said by Scarman LJ in R v Reid[2], the court did not intend to lay down something rigid and exhaustive. In truth what

h the court was there saying was that for an excuse to be capable of being a reasonable excuse, it must be an excuse which is related to the capacity of the person concerned to supply a sample, be it of urine or be it of blood. It is not related to his belief whether or not he ought, because of his personal faith or belief, to be required to supply a sample of urine or blood. There is, in the view of this court, this very marked difference between the two positions. One depends on whether or not, for example,

j he is in a mental or physical condition which enables him physically to give the sample. It may be in some cases that he will not be in that condition. Such facts, if proved, may at least be capable of affording a reasonable excuse for not giving the sample. But it is not enough for someone to come along and say, 'True, others

1   [1973] 2 All ER 831, [1973] 1 WLR 483
2   [1973] 3 All ER at 1025, [1973] 1 WLR at 1289

are obliged to comply with the law, but my personal faith or belief frees me from *a* the obligation which rests on others'.

That, with all respect to the appellant and to the sincerity of his beliefs, is what he is seeking to say in this court. This court must reject that argument. This conclusion does involve to some extent a restriction on the liberty of the individual, but it is a consequence that flows from what Parliament found necessary when these provisions were first introduced in 1967 for the benefit of the public as a whole. *b*

I have dealt with this matter, I am afraid, at some length because it is a point of general importance. In the view of this court this appeal must fail and must be dismissed.

Appeal dismissed.

c

Solicitors: *Registrar of Criminal Appeals* (for the appellant); *Solicitor, Metropolitan Police.*

Lea Josse Barrister.

d

Practice Direction

CHANCERY DIVISION

e

Originating summons – Summons to which appearance not required – Procedure – Insertion of particulars of hearing by master – RSC Appendix A, Form 10.

1. It has come to notice that when an originating summons for the grant of a new business tenancy under Part II of the Landlord and Tenant Act 1954 is issued in Form 10 of Appendix A to the Rules of the Supreme Court the solicitors issuing the *f* summons sometimes do not take an appointment for hearing but leave the details blank. This has the effect of adjourning the proceedings indefinitely, unless it can be said that they are ineffective or never properly commenced or that service with the hearing date left blank is insufficient service.

2. Form 10 is designed to ensure that the matter reaches the master at an early date. This is also the reason for the requirement that an originating summons for *g* a new business tenancy must be served within one month. Unless the summons comes on for hearing quickly the court cannot ensure that service has been effected and there may be an unjustifiable extension of security of tenure.

3. In future the Central Office will not seal an originating summons in Form 10 in any Chancery proceedings (whether they are under the Landlord and Tenant Act 1954 or not) until the particulars of the hearing by the master have been inserted. *h* Those issuing such a summons must first obtain from the Central Office a provisional allocation to a group; the form of summons must then be produced to the appropriate master's summons clerk, who will insert particulars of the hearing; the summons must then be taken back to the Central Office for sealing and finally produced to the master's summons clerk, who will note that it has in fact been issued.

By the direction of the Vice-Chancellor and with the concurrence of the Senior *j* Master.

R E BALL
15th May 1974　　　　　　　　　　　　　　　　　　　　　　　Chief Master

Starside Properties Ltd v Mustapha

COURT OF APPEAL, CIVIL DIVISION
EDMUND DAVIES, CAIRNS AND LAWTON LJJ
20th, 21st FEBRUARY 1974

Equity – Forfeiture – Relief – Jurisdiction of court – Jurisdiction to vary previous order granting relief – Relief by way of extension of time for payment – Sale of land – Purchase price payable by instalments – Provision for rescission of contract and forfeiture of sums paid on failure of purchaser to pay instalments in due time – Purchaser failing to pay instalment – Action by vendor for possession – Order granting purchaser extension of time for payment – Application by purchaser for further extension of time – Whether court having jurisdiction to grant further extension – Whether jurisdiction limited to cases of forfeiture for non-payment of rent.

By an agreement dated 9th November 1970 the plaintiffs agreed to sell to the defendant the freehold of a dwelling-house for £5,950. The agreement allowed the defendant on payment of an initial deposit of £350 to enter into occupation as a licensee pending completion of the sale in accordance with the terms of the agreement. By those terms the defendant undertook to pay ten per cent per annum interest on the balance of the purchase price, which amounted to £46 13s 4d a month, and a further sum of £15 13s 4d a month off the purchase price and towards what was described as the total deposit of £1,250. Within one month of paying that latter sum the defendant was entitled to call for a conveyance. Provision was made for the balance of the purchase price to be left outstanding on the security of a mortgage of the property. Clause 7 of the agreement provided that if the defendant was in arrears with payments of interest and/or deposit for a period exceeding 14 days the plaintiffs would be entitled to rescind the contract and forfeit all sums paid by the defendant by way of deposit and the defendant would forthwith vacate the property. For a time the defendant paid the instalments but on 9th May and 9th June 1971 she failed to do so. On 12th June the plaintiffs' solicitors wrote determining the whole arrangement under the provisions of cl 7 and they asked the defendant to vacate the property within 14 days. The defendant failed to comply with that request and, on 17th September, the plaintiffs commenced proceedings in the county court claiming possession and a declaration that the defendant was a licensee of the plaintiffs in the premises and that the plaintiffs were entitled to forfeit all sums already paid to them by the defendant. The defendant counterclaimed for relief from forfeiture. On 1st February 1973 the judge found that cl 7 was a penalty clause and, while granting a declaration that the defendant was a licensee, postponed the order for possession for three months until 30th April 1973 to enable the defendant to raise the money to acquire the property from the plaintiffs at the original contract price. The defendant was unable to raise the money in time and on 27th April she applied for a further extension of time on the ground that she had contracted to sell the property at a figure which would bring her in a profit of £3,000 to £4,000 and that completion was fixed for 12th July. On 26th June the judge dismissed her application on the ground that he had no jurisdiction to vary the order of 1st February, since only in cases where relief from forfeiture for non-payment of rent was sought did the court have jurisdiction to vary the terms of its earlier order granting relief. The defendant appealed.

Held – The court had jurisdiction to grant relief against forfeiture when the provision for forfeiture was penal in character. Relief would be granted in such circumstances as justice required and on such terms as were equitable in those circumstances. Where it later appeared that relief granted by way of an extension of time ought to

be extended, and that in fairness to the other party it could be done, the court
had jurisdiction to grant a further extension. No distinction could be drawn between
cases of relief for non-payment of rent and other cases where relief against forfeiture
was sought. It followed that the judge had jurisdiction to grant the relief asked for
by the defendant. The appeal would therefore be allowed and the case remitted to
him to consider the defendant's application on its merits (see p 574 *c d* and *f*, p 575
b d e and *h* and p 576 *b* and *c*, post).

Chandless-Chandless v Nicholson [1942] 2 All ER 315 applied.
Dictum of Romer LJ in *Stockloser v Johnson* [1954] 1 All ER at 643 explained.

Notes

For equitable relief against penalties and forfeitures, see 14 Halsbury's Laws (3rd Edn)
620-623, paras 1147-1153, and for cases on the subject, see 20 Digest (Repl) 548-550,
2560-2579.

Cases referred to in judgments

Barton, Thompson & Co Ltd v Stapling Machines Co [1966] 2 All ER 222, [1966] Ch 499,
   [1966] 2 WLR 1429, 31(2) Digest (Reissue) 819, 6815.
Campbell Discount Co Ltd v Bridge [1961] 2 All ER 97, [1961] 1 QB 445, [1962] 2 WLR 596,
   CA; *rvsd sub nom Bridge v Campbell Discount Co Ltd* [1962] 1 All ER 385, [1962]
   AC 600, [1962] 2 WLR 439, HL, Digest (Cont Vol A) 648, 39a.
Chandless-Chandless v Nicholson [1942] 2 All ER 315, [1942] 2 KB 321, 112 LJKB 19,
   167 LT 198, CA, 31(2) Digest (Reissue) 818, 6810.
Dagenham (Thames) Dock Co, Re, ex parte Hulse (1873) 8 Ch App 1022, 43 LJCh 261,
   38 JP 180, LJJ, 20 Digest (Repl) 544, 2535.
Dixon, Re, Heynes v Dixon [1900] 2 Ch 561, 69 LJCh 609, 83 LT 129, CA, 7 Digest (Repl)
   221, 579.
Galbraith v Mitchenall Estates Ltd [1964] 2 All ER 653, [1965] 2 QB 473, [1964] 3 WLR 454,
   Digest (Cont Vol B) 242, 2579a.
Kilmer v British Columbia Orchard Lands Ltd [1913] AC 319, 82 LJPC 77, 108 LT 306,
   PC, 20 Digest (Repl) 544, 2536.
Maynard v Moseley (1676) 3 Swan 651, 36 ER 1009, sub nom *Maynard's Case* Freem Ch 1,
   LC, 40 Digest (Repl) 382, 3060.
Mussen v Van Diemen's Land Co [1938] 1 All ER 210, [1938] Ch 253, 107 LJCh 136, 158
   LT 40, 20 Digest (Repl) 545, 2538.
Steedman v Drinkle [1916] 1 AC 275, [1914-15] All ER Rep 298, 85 LJPC 79, 114 LT 248,
   PC, 20 Digest (Repl) 544, 2537.
Stockloser v Johnson [1954] 1 All ER 630, [1954] 1 QB 476, [1954] 2 WLR 439, CA, 20
   Digest (Repl) 548, 2565.

Case also cited

McPhail v persons, names unknown, Bristol Corpn v Ross [1973] 3 All ER 393, [1973] Ch 447,
   CA.

Interlocutory appeal

This was an appeal by the defendant, Ayfer Mustapha, against an order of his Honour
Judge Fife at the Bromley County Court on 26th June 1973 in proceedings by the
plaintiffs, Starside Properties Ltd, for, inter alia, possession of premises known as
68 Knighton Park Road, London, SE26. The facts are set out in the judgment of
Edmund Davies LJ.

Roger Ellis for the defendant.
Isaac Jacob for the plaintiffs.

EDMUND DAVIES LJ. This is a defendant's appeal from the order of his Honour
Judge Fife sitting at the Bromley County Court on 26th June 1973. On 1st February
1973 the same learned judge made an order (1) declaring that the defendant was a

a licensee of the plaintiffs in relation to 68 Knighton Park Road, SE26, (2) adjudging that the plaintiffs were entitled to recover possession of those premises, and (3) ordering that the defendant give possession to the plaintiffs on 30th April 1973. Three days before the last-mentioned date, that is to say on 27th April, the defendant applied for an order extending the time for delivery of possession for a period of eight weeks from 30th April on grounds to which I shall refer later. The eight weeks

b period sought expired on 25th June, and it was on the next day that the application was heard. The defendant then asked that her time be extended to 13th July on the ground that she had already contracted to sell the premises at a figure which would have brought her in a profit of between £3,000 and £4,000, and that completion was fixed for 12th July. But her application was dismissed, the learned judge holding ('with a certain amount of reluctance', as he put it) that he had no jurisdiction to entertain it. It is against this second order that the defendant now appeals.

c   The material facts are not in dispute. In November 1970 the plaintiffs agreed to sell the freehold of 68 Knighton Park Road to the defendant for £5,950. The plaintiffs' letter of 9th November 1970 confirmed the terms of this agreement. It required the defendant to pay an initial deposit of £350 (which she did), and thereupon she entered into occupation as a licensee pending completion of the sale on the conditions

d therein set out. Thereby the defendant undertook to pay ten per cent interest per annum on the purchase price of £5,950, less the initial deposit of £350, which amounted to £46 13s 4d a month, and also to pay a further £16 13s 4d monthly off the purchase price and towards what was described as the total deposit of £1,250. The later parts of the letter must be quoted verbatim. Paragraph 4 was in these terms:

e   'On or before one month after you have paid a total deposit of £1250. off the purchase price (being the aggregate of the said initial deposit of £350. and the instalments referred to ... above) we will complete the sale and you will complete the purchase of the property and thereupon pay us the balance of the purchase price of £4700. Nothing in this Agreement contained shall prevent you from paying us the balance of the said deposit at any time whereupon completion shall take place in accordance with this paragraph.'

f Paragraph 5 provided:

        'On receiving a request from you in writing we undertake to leave the said balance of the price outstanding on the security of a first mortgage of the property for ten years carrying interest at the flat and non-reducing rate of 10% per annum repayable by monthly instalments of £78. 6. 8. each, the first such payment to be

g made one month after completion.'

Then para 7 provided:

        'If you are in arrear with your payments of interest and/or deposit for a period exceeding fourteen days we shall have the right to rescind the contract and for-feit all sums paid by you by way of deposit and you will forthwith vacate

h the property.'

    The defendant went into possession of the premises. For a time she duly paid the agreed instalments. But thereafter she fell into arrears, failing to pay the instalments due on 9th May and 9th June 1971. On 12th June the plaintiffs' solicitors wrote to her in these terms:

j   'Under clause 7 of the contract our clients have the right to rescind the contract and to forfeit all sums paid by you by way of deposit if you are in arrears with your payments of interest and/or deposit for a period exceeding 14 days. You are more than 14 days in arrears with your deposit and interest and we therefore hereby give you notice rescinding the said contract pursuant to clause 7 thereof. The contract also provides that on rescindation of the contract you will forthwith vacate the property. We hereby terminate the licence conferred upon you ª by clause 3 of the said contract and require you to vacate this property within 14 days of today's date.'

The letter went on to indicate that in the event of non-compliance with that demand proceedings would be instituted.

Well, the defendant did not comply, and on 17th September the plaintiffs instituted county court proceedings claiming therein: ᵇ

'1. The declaration that the Defendant was a licensee of the Plaintiffs in the said premises. 2. Possession of the said premises. 3. The declaration that the Plaintiffs are entitled to forfeit and retain: (a) The initial deposit of £350, (b) The payments of £63·33 per month received on and since the 9th day of December 1970.' ᶜ

Various pleas were raised in the defence, but (with one exception) all were held invalid by the learned judge when he dealt with the proceedings on 1st February 1973 and against his judgment neither party appealed. The one plea which he upheld (and rightly, in my judgment) was that cl 7 of the agreement of sale imposed a penalty on the defendant. The judge said: ᵈ

'. . . one only has to consider the case where the defendant goes on paying regularly right up to a state where she has nearly accumulated a deposit of £1,250 and then defaults. If she loses all her payments to date it cannot be argued that this provision is not a penalty. It cannot be a penalty one year and not the next and therefore I am in no doubt that this is a penal provision.'

The defendant having counterclaimed relief from forfeiture, the learned judge went ᵉ on to say that he considered it a proper case to exercise his discretion so as to relieve her from that penal provision. Accordingly, while making the declaration sought by the plaintiffs that the defendant was in occupation as a licensee, he said:

'. . . in the circumstances I am going to postpone the order for possession that I am going to make for three months in order to enable the defendant to raise ᶠ the money to acquire this property from the [plaintiffs] at the original contract price.'

The court's order was that the defendant surrender possession on 30th April, but, pursuant to the terms of cl 4 of the contract, she negotiated to raise sufficient money to buy off the plaintiffs, or, failing that, to find someone prepared to buy the property from her on terms profitable to her. But as time was running out, on 27th April ᵍ she made the application already referred to. On 26th June it was dismissed, it being ordered that execution of the possession order be stayed pending appeal. The two questions raised before the learned judge were (1) whether he had jurisdiction to extend the time granted to the defendant by his order of 1st February; and (2), if he had, whether he ought to. He answered question (1) in the negative, and found it unnecessary to deal with question (2). He expressed his conclusion from the ʰ cases cited in this way:

'. . . I have no jurisdiction in the ordinary case to vary an order drawn up . . . I do not consider that the cases cited go beyond . . . forfeiture for non-payment of rent';

and, since this was not such a case, he added: ʲ

'Thus I do not accept that the cases cited provide any authority for my having jurisdiction to vary the order made on 1st February.'

The attack on that finding by counsel for the defendant was by way of the following submissions: (1) the order of 1st February was made pursuant to the court's power to grant equitable relief against forfeiture; (2) the defendant's claim for relief was analogous to a claim for relief against forfeiture for non-payment of rent; (3) accordingly, the court had jurisdiction on 26th June to grant the further relief sought, notwithstanding that it involved a variation of the February order.

On the other hand, in seeking to uphold the learned judge's order, counsel for the plaintiffs has submitted: (1) that equity will not interfere with the bargain made between parties merely because it turned out to be improvident for one of them; (2) that equity will give 'a limited and conditional relief' to purchasers who default in payment on the footing that a clause whereby instalment payments already made are forfeited is in the nature of a penalty, *provided* that the defaulting party has obtained no profit from the agreement over and above the right to complete the contract on payment of the agreed instalments; (3) that in such circumstances a defaulter will be given a further chance and a further time to pay the money due only if he is able and willing to do so when he seeks that chance, the only exception to this condition being where relief against forfeiture for non-payment of rent is sought; (4) that, with one possible exception, the reported decisions do not show that any further relief from forfeiture will be granted 'if [the defaulter] failed . . . to take advantage of the limited relief which was extended to him'. The quoted words are those of Romer LJ in *Stockloser v Johnson*[1] which must later be referred to.

Was the learned judge right in holding that only in cases where relief from forfeiture for non-payment of rent is sought does the court have jurisdiction to vary the terms of its earlier order granting relief? If he was, what is the legal or equitable basis for so restricting the court's power? That the contract between the parties imposed a penalty is unchallenged, and that the nature or dimensions of the penalty were such as to satisfy the court that justice required that relief therefrom should be granted was demonstrated by the original order from which the plaintiffs did not appeal. Then is there some unique quality about the penalty of forfeiture for non-payment of rent putting such cases into a category of their own which confers on the court wider powers in reversing its orders than it possesses in any other case where equitable relief against forfeiture has been granted on terms? If so, what is this unique quality and why should it attract to itself special treatment? In order to answer these questions, I proceed to consider the relevant decisions, first pointing out in fairness to the learned judge that more have been cited to us than are referred to in his judgment.

It is clear on the authorities that the power of the court to grant relief against forfeiture resulting from breach of a penal clause is *not* restricted to cases of forfeiture for non-payment of rent. Snell[2] summarises the law in this way:

> 'The principle is that in appropriate and limited cases courts of equity will grant relief against forfeiture for breach of covenant or condition where the primary object of the bargain is to secure a stated result and the provision for forfeiture is added as security for the production of that result. In determining whether a case is appropriate for relief, the court considers the conduct of the applicant for relief (and in particular whether his default was wilful), how grave the breaches were, and what disparity there is between the value of the property forfeited and the damage caused by the breach. In general, equity granted relief only where the forfeiture in substance was merely security for payment of a monetary sum; but the jurisdiction is not confined to such cases, and it applies, e.g., to a right of entry reserved on an assignment of leasehold premises in respect of the assignee's breaches of positive and restrictive covenants designed to protect the assignor's adjoining premises.'

---

1   [1954] 1 All ER 630 at 642, [1954] 1 QB 476 at 498
2   Principles of Equity (27th Edn, 1973), pp 537, 538

Amongst the cases cited to us were *Re Dagenham (Thames) Dock Co*[1], where relief against forfeiture was granted in relation to a contract to purchase land, and this was followed by the Privy Council in *Kilmer v British Columbia Orchard Lands Ltd*[2].

Chandless-Chandless v Nicholson[3] related, as his Honour Judge Fife stressed, to relief from forfeiture for non-payment of rent, this court holding that where such relief was granted on terms to be performed within a specified time, it has jurisdiction to extend that time if the circumstances are such as to make an extension just and equitable. Its importance lies in the fact that the Court of Appeal appeared to entertain no doubt that there was power to extend the period of indulgence granted by an earlier order. Furthermore, I do not read the judgment of Lord Greene MR as indicating that he considered that there was any unique quality in that class of case. He said[4]:

'The court in exercising its jurisdiction to grant relief in cases of non-payment of rent is, of course, proceeding upon the old principles of the Court of Equity. The Court of Equity always regarded the condition of re-entry as being merely security for payment of the rent, and, provided the landlord could get his rent, relief was given . . . if an order of this kind in which relief is granted on terms to be observed within a limited time is to be treated as one which the court has no jurisdiction to modify in point of time if circumstances justify it, then the order becomes as vicious as the original forfeiture clause itself.'

In *Barton, Thompson & Co Ltd v Stapling Machines Co*[5] Pennycuick J was dealing with a hiring agreement whereby the defendants leased to the plaintiffs for 25 years certain machines, the agreement providing for rental and other payments. In case of breach of any term of the agreement the defendants were entitled to serve a notice requiring the plaintiffs to remedy the breach within 30 days and in default to terminate the agreement. The plaintiffs failed to make due payments and did not comply with a notice requiring payment within 30 days, and the defendants then sent a notice of immediate termination. That same day, the plaintiffs took out an originating summons seeking relief from forfeiture. In proceedings to strike out the summons, counsel for the defendants submitted that there is no principle of English law providing for relief from forfeiture in the case of bailment of chattels, except where a party seeking forfeiture has acted unconscionably, and that no such relief could be granted in commercial contracts. Counsel for the plaintiffs, on the other hand, contended that the basic principle on which relief against forfeiture is afforded is applicable to subject-matter other than land.

Having cited the observations of Rigby LJ in *Re Dixon, Heynes v Dixon*[6], and those of Lord Greene MR in *Chandless-Chandless v Nicholson*[4] to which I have just referred, Pennycuick J concluded[7]:

'I am not prepared to hold that it is plain and obvious as a matter of law that in the absence of unconscionable behaviour the court has in no circumstances power to relieve against forfeiture under any conceivable lease of a chattel.'

He added:

'The precise length of time is a matter of discretion and the time may be extended on subsequent application, but the imposition of the condition is not a matter of discretion . . .'

---

1   (1873) 8 Ch App 1022
2   [1913] AC 319
3   [1942] 2 All ER 315, [1942] 2 KB 321
4   [1942] 2 All ER at 317, [1942] 2 KB at 323
5   [1966] 2 All ER 222, [1966] Ch 499
6   [1900] 2 Ch 561 at 576
7   [1966] 2 All ER at 225, [1966] Ch at 509, 510

He then went on to consider what he regarded as the conditions before relief can
be granted to an applicant. I am, of course, alive to the fact that the learned judge
was there finally committing himself to no view and merely declined to strike out
the summons, but I respectfully attach importance to the fact that so experienced a
judge (who is now Vice-Chancellor of the Chancery Division) was not prepared to
regard as irrefutable the submission of defence counsel.

I turn finally to consider *Stockloser v Johnson*[1], where Romer LJ gave a judgment on
which counsel for the plaintiffs places great weight. It concerned a contract to buy
plant and machinery, payment to be made by instalments. It provided that if the
purchaser defaulted for more than 28 days in paying any instalment the vendor
should be entitled to rescind the contract, forfeit the instalments already paid and
retake possession of the plant and machinery. These events having occurred, the
purchaser (who was unable or unwilling to complete the contract) claimed the return
of the paid instalments on the ground that the effect of the forfeiture clause was
penal and unconscionable and that in equity he was entitled to relief. All three
members of the court were united in refusing the purchaser the relief he sought,
but whereas Somervell and Denning LJJ held that the court had jurisdiction to relieve
against forfeiture of instalments after rescission if in the circumstances of the case it
would be unconscionable for the vendor to retain them, Romer LJ held that the court
had *no* such jurisdiction in the absence of unconscionable conduct by the vendor.

The passage in Romer LJ's judgment particularly relied on by counsel for the
plaintiffs as supporting the view adopted by the learned trial judge in the present
case (though *Stockloser v Johnson*[1] was apparently not cited to him) is in these terms[2]:

'... it appears to me that the cases establish that, if a purchaser defaults
in punctual payment of instalments of purchase money, the court will, in a proper
case, relieve the purchaser from his contractual liability to forfeit instalments
(apart from the deposit) already paid to the extent of giving him a further chance
and further time to pay the money which is in arrear if he is able and willing to
do so. But the cases do not, in my judgment, show that the court will relieve
such a purchaser to any further extent than this.'

Counsel for the plaintiffs stresses the final words of this passage and construes them
as indicating that, once the court has given a defaulter 'a further chance and a further
time to pay' it cannot thereafter grant yet another chance and more time. I have to
say that I disagree. The 'further extent' of which Romer LJ was speaking in his final
words does not, in my judgment, relate to the court's power (or, rather, its lack of
power) to grant further time, but rather to the granting of relief which was 'further'
in the sense of being over and above and different from an extension of time, and the
treatment of *Steedman v Drinkle*[3], which immediately follows the above quotation
from Romer LJ's judgment, appears to demonstrate that this is so. The difference
between Romer LJ and the other members of the court was simply that the latter
took the view that, as Somervell LJ put it[4]:

'... the cases do not establish (i) that relief could never be given unless the
plaintiff could show that he is financially in a position to complete and would
be willing to do so if the defendant were himself prepared to waive the breach
and complete the contract, or (ii) that after rescission no relief can be given unless
there is fraud or sharp practice.'

Denning LJ was of the same view, whereas Romer LJ, citing[5] an observation of

1 [1954] 1 All ER 630, [1954] 1 QB 476
2 [1954] 1 All ER at 643, [1954] 1 QB at 499
3 [1916] 1 AC 275, [1914-15] All ER Rep 298
4 [1954] 1 All ER at 636, [1954] 1 QB at 487, 488
5 [1954] 1 All ER at 640, [1954] 1 QB at 495

Lord Nottingham[1] that 'Chancery mends no man's bargain', and reviewing *Kilmer's* case[2] and the *Dagenham Dock* case[3], concluded[4] that all the courts had there done was to intervene 'by giving a purchaser, who, ... desired a further chance of completing his purchase, an opportunity of doing so'. He added:

> 'So far as I can see, in neither of these cases did the court declare, or even intimate, that the purchaser should be relieved from the forfeiture if he failed, through want of funds, to take advantage of the limited relief which was extended to him—although, admittedly, there was little reason to deal with this point in *Kilmer's* case[2], as the purchaser had brought the whole of the unpaid purchase money and interest into court.'

Such was the 'further extent' that Romer LJ was adverting to, as I think, in the later passage of his judgment on which counsel for the plaintiffs so strongly relies.

The conclusion I have come to in the light of the cases to which our attention has been directed is that, certainly in relation to the jurisdiction of the court to vary an order granting an extension of time by granting a further extension, no distinction is to be drawn between cases of relief against forfeiture for non-payment of rent and other cases where relief against forfeiture is sought. The common feature in all these cases is that a penal provision is involved and the court grants relief against the forfeiture which would otherwise follow therefrom in such circumstances as justice requires, and it does so on such terms as are equitable in these circumstances. If it should later appear that the relief by way of extension of time first granted ought to be extended, and that in fairness to the other party this can be done, I see no difficulty in holding that the court has the jurisdiction to do that which the justice of the case is seen to require. Naturally enough, the court will scrutinise with particular care an application for further relief and will be more reluctant to grant it than in the case of a first application; but that goes to the likelihood of the later application succeeding and not to the court's jurisdiction to entertain it. No case cited to us supports counsel for the plaintiffs' submission—certainly not *Stockloser v Johnson*[5], nor the later cases to which we were referred, such as *Galbraith v Mitchenall Estates Ltd*[6] and *Campbell Discount Co Ltd v Bridge*[7]—and *Chandless-Chandless v Nicholson*[8] affords support to the contrary submission advanced by counsel for the defendant. I am therefore of the view that the learned county court judge was in error in arriving at his reluctant conclusion as to jurisdiction.

The notice of appeal gives as its second ground: 'That the learned Judge ought in the exercise of his discretion to have granted the application of the April 27th 1973'. But, as I have already observed, he came to no conclusion on this point, and I do not consider that we should approach this appeal as though he had exercised his discretion adversely to the defendant. It is true that the Court of Appeal in *Chandless-Chandless v Nicholson*[8] did proceed to exercise its own discretion, but the facts there were less complicated than those of the present case. The conflicting views expressed in *Stockloser v Johnson*[6] are here pertinent, and there are other relevant authorities (including, in particular, the *Barton, Thompson & Co* case[9]—and I have here in mind the already-quoted observations of Pennycuick J[10]) which would need to be considered. I confess that I have formed a purely tentative view on the matter,

---

1   See *Maynard v Moseley* (1676) 3 Swan 651 at 655
2   [1913] AC 319
3   (1873) 8 Ch App 1022
4   [1954] 1 All ER at 642, [1954] 1 QB at 498
5   [1954] 1 All ER 630, [1954] 1 QB 476
6   [1964] 2 All ER 653, [1965] 2 QB 473
7   [1961] 2 All ER 97, [1961] 1 QB 445; *on appeal* [1962] 1 All ER 385, [1962] AC 600
8   [1942] 2 All ER 315, [1942] 2 KB 321
9   [1966] 2 All ER 222, [1966] Ch 499
10   [1966] 2 All ER at 225, [1966] Ch at 509, 510

a but I have no intention of disclosing its nature. All I would say is that when he comes to consider how he should exercise that discretion which, as I have held, he possesses, his Honour Judge Fife will bear in mind that this is *not* a case where the purchaser is counterclaiming to recover instalments already paid, and is therefore to be distinguished from *Mussen v Van Diemen's Land Co*[1] and other cases cited in Snell's Equity[2].

b For the reasons I have sought to give, I would allow the appeal and direct that the matter be remitted to his Honour Judge Fife so that he may consider the defendant's application on its merits.

CAIRNS LJ. I agree that this appeal should be allowed, and because we are differing from the learned county court judge, and out of respect for the helpful argument addressed to the court by counsel for the plaintiffs, I will briefly express my reasons
c in my own words. It appears to me that *Chandless-Chandless v Nicholson*[3] is conclusive authority that the learned judge had jurisdiction to extend the time unless that case can be distinguished on one of two grounds submitted by counsel for the plaintiffs: first, that the ruling in that case is confined to relief from forfeiture for non-payment of rent under a lease of land; secondly, that the defendant was not in this case able to pay the outstanding debt on the day when the application for
d extension of time was before the court.

As to the first of those points, it appears to me that there is no reason in principle why the ruling in *Chandless-Chandless v Nicholson*[3] should be confined to cases of non-payment of rent. There is nothing in the language of Lord Greene MR to limit it in that way. Counsel for the plaintiffs points to the words[4] 'an order of this kind'. But the 'kind' to which Lord Greene MR is referring is indicated by the words which
e follow, 'which gives relief on terms to be observed within a limited time'. Pennycuick J certainly did not consider that the doctrine should be restricted in the way now argued for when he was deciding *Barton, Thompson & Co Ltd v Stapling Machines Co*[5], and in my judgment the rule is not so restricted.

As to the second point, I do not consider that the expression 'able, ready and willing to perform' means 'able to perform on that very day'. The condition of
f being 'able, ready and willing to perform' is applicable not only when an extension of time is asked for, but also when the original application for relief is made. It is to be noted that in the *Chandless* case[3] itself the original order for relief was on condition that payment of arrears was made within three months, and I believe it to be common for time to pay to be given, which would never be appropriate if it were a condition of relief that the applicant for relief should be able to pay immediately. In *Barton,*
g *Thompson & Co Ltd v Stapling Machines Co*[5] the applicants failed because their evidence gave no indication that they would ever be able to pay.

I agree that there is nothing in the judgment of Romer LJ in *Stockloser v Johnson*[6]— even assuming that judgment to be preferable to the views of the majority of the court there—which supports the proposition that an extension of time cannot be given in a case where relief from forfeiture can be given at all. I am therefore of
h opinion that the jurisdiction to extend the time is established by *Chandless-Chandless v Nicholson*[3], and accordingly I agree that this appeal should be allowed.

LAWTON LJ. I, too, agree that this appeal should be allowed and that the case should be remitted to the learned county court judge for him to exercise the discretion which this court in this appeal had adjudged that he has. I have reached that
j

---

1 [1938] 1 All ER 210, [1938] Ch 253
2 27th Edn (1973), p 537, footnote 23
3 [1942] 2 All ER 315, [1942] 2 KB 321
4 [1942] 2 All ER at 317, [1942] 2 KB at 323
5 [1966] 2 All ER 222 [1966] Ch 499
6 [1954] 1 All ER 630, [1954] 1 QB 476

conclusion by the application of what I believe to be precise and well-established equit- *a*
able principles. At the trial the defendant asked for, and obtained, equitable relief
against what the learned judge had found to be a penalty clause. In this court the
plaintiffs have not submitted that he had no jurisdiction to give that relief. No doubt
they made the concession they did because the authorities clearly establish that
those who are enmeshed in a penalty clause are entitled to come to the court for
limited equitable relief: see *Re Dagenham (Thames) Dock Co, ex parte Hulse*[1] and *b*
Kilmer v British Columbia Orchard Lands Ltd[2].

The plaintiffs' case was that once equitable relief had been given it could never be
given again. In my judgment, this submission is contrary to precise and well-established equitable principles. Once the existence of an equity is established, the court
clearly has jurisdiction to give such equitable relief as may be necessary to protect it.
What is necessary will depend on the evidence in each case; and events may occur *c*
which may make necessary that which was not foreseen to be necessary at the beginning. In most cases the applicant for further equitable relief may have difficulty in
establishing entitlement. But, as was pointed out in argument, cases can be envisaged
where there would be manifest injustice if further equitable relief was not granted.

In exercising its jurisdiction to protect a clearly-defined equity, the court is not
making its decision by what it considers to be the length of the Chancellor's foot, nor *d*
by taking on the role of a fussing judicial nanny seeking to protect the improvident
from their folly in entering into disadvantageous contracts. What it is doing is
protecting that which the law recognises to exist, namely, an equity. This is what
Harman LJ pointed out in *Campbell Discount Co Ltd v Bridge*[3] was the duty of the
court to do. It seems to me, therefore, that the learned county court judge failed
to recognise that what he was being asked to do was to protect an equity which he *e*
had found to exist.

Appeal allowed.

Solicitors: *Armstrong & Co* (for the defendant); *Cowan, Lipson & Rumney* (for the
plaintiffs).

Mary Rose Plummer Barrister. *f*

---

1   (1873) 8 Ch App 1022
2   [1913] AC 319
3   [1961] 2 All ER 97, [1961] 1 QB 445

Number 20 Cannon Street Ltd v Singer & Friedlander Ltd

CHANCERY DIVISION
MEGARRY J
6th, 7th, 8th, 13th FEBRUARY 1974

Landlord and tenant – Rent – Limitation – Prohibition on increase in rate of rent – Business premises – Counter-inflation legislation – Rent not payable at rate exceeding standard rate – Standard rate – Rate at which rent was payable in respect of premises on specified date – Different tenancies of separate parts of premises subsisting on specified date – Subsequent lease of premises – Single tenancy of whole premises – Whether 'standard rate' for premises as a whole – Counter-Inflation (Business Rents) Order 1972 (SI 1972 No 1850), paras 2(2), 4 – Counter-Inflation (Business Rents) Order 1973 (SI 1973 No 741), arts 3, 4, 5.

Statute – Construction – Generalia specialibus non derogant – Statute containing two prohibitions – Wide and limited prohibitions – Limited prohibition subject to exception – Limited prohibition wholly within wide prohibition – Whether wide prohibition to be treated as applying to cases within limited prohibition.

Statute – Construction – Number – Words in singular to include words in plural – Selective reading of words in plural – Whether permissible – Interpretation Act 1889, s 1(1)(b).

Three floors of a building were separately let on business tenancies at rents which totalled £39,150 a year. On 5th November 1972 those tenancies were still in existence but by then they had become vested in a single tenant. That tenant vacated the premises on 4th December 1972. On 22nd January 1973 the defendants ('the tenants') went into occupation of the three floors ('the demised premises') on the terms of an unexecuted lease granting them a single tenancy of the whole premises. The lease provided for a rent of £191,650 a year payable in advance on the usual quarter days. The first full quarter's payment of rent therefore fell due on 25th March 1973. Meanwhile, on 1st December 1972, the Counter-Inflation (Business Rents) Order 1972 had come into force and remained in force for a period which expired at midnight on 28th April 1973. That order was replaced by the Counter-Inflation (Business Rents) Order 1973, which came into force on 29th April 1973. The general purpose of those orders was to restrict the rent payable under tenancies of business premises to the rate at which rent was payable in respect of those premises on 5th November 1972. The lease of the demised premises was eventually executed on 6th February 1974. Meanwhile the tenants, relying on para 4[a] of the 1972 order in respect of the period from 22nd January to 28th April 1973 and on art 5[b] of the 1973 order for the period commencing on 29th April 1973, refused to pay rent for the demised premises in excess of a rate of £39,150 a year, contending that that figure was the 'standard rate' for the demised premises under para 2(2)[c] of the 1972 order and art 4[d] of the 1973 order and that para 4 and art 5 of the respective orders prohibited the payment of rent in excess of that rate.

Held – (i) Paragraph 4 of the 1972 order prohibited the payment of rent to the landlords at a rate exceeding £39,150 since the business tenancy of each of the three floors had come to an end after 6th November 1972, 'the premises' (i e each of those floors)

---

a Paragraph 4 is set out at p 582 *f*, post
b Article 5 is set out at p 590 *g*, post
c Paragraph 2(2), so far as material, is set out at p 581 *j*, post
d Article 4, so far as material, is set out at p 590 *d* to *f*, post

had been relet, and each floor had a 'standard rate' within para 2(2) of the 1972 order, i e the rent payable under the tenancy of that floor subsisting on 5th November 1972. It followed that the payment of rent in excess of the aggregate of the standard rates for the three floors would contravene para 4 since that rent would necessarily exceed for at least one floor the standard rate for that floor; alternatively the words 'tenancy', 'premises' and 'standard rate' in para 4 were to be construed as including the plural and para 4 was therefore to be construed as prohibiting payment of rent for the demised premises at a rate in excess of the aggregate of the standard rates for the three floors (see p 585 f to p 586 a and h, p 587 a c to e and h and p 588 j to p 589 a and f to h, post).

(ii) Article 5 of the 1973 order did not however prohibit the payment of rent at a rate exceeding £39,150, and accordingly under the 1973 order the full amount of the rent reserved under the tenancy was payable to the landlords. Article 5 only applied where there was a standard rate for the premises as a whole since it referred in terms to 'those premises', i e the identical premises in relation to which there was a 'standard rate', and the express provisions in art 4(2) for aggregating standard rates excluded any implied process of aggregation such as that which could be implied into para 4 of the 1972 order. Furthermore art 4(2) only applied to premises comprised in a 'tenancy granted after the coming into force' of the 1973 order, i e 29th April 1973; it did not therefore apply to the new tenancy granted by the landlords, for that tenancy had been 'granted' when the tenants went into occupation, i e on 22nd January 1973, and not when the lease was eventually executed on 6th February 1974. In any event, under art 3(1)[e] of the 1973 order, nothing in that order applied to the new tenancy since the tenancy was 'new lettings' within art 3(2), in that it had been granted after 5th November 1972 and consisted of premises 'in relation to which there is not a standard rate' (see p 590 j to p 591 h and p 592 e to h, post).

(iii) Although the quarter's rent payable in advance on 25th March 1973 fell due during the period when the rent was restricted under the provisions of the 1972 order, it did not follow that the whole of that quarter's rent was to be restricted to the rate of £39,150 a year, i e a sum of £9,787·50, for the mechanics of payment were irrelevant; what was decisive was the period during which the statutory restriction ran. Accordingly the tenants were liable for rent in respect of that quarter at the rate of £9,787·50 until the end of 28th April 1973 and thereafter at the rate of £47,912·50 for the rest of the quarter (see p 593 j to p 594 b, post).

(iv) It followed that the tenants were liable to pay rent at the restricted rate (i e £39,150 a year) for the period of 22nd January 1973 to 28th April 1973 and at the full rate reserved under the tenancy agreement thereafter, and the amount of rent payable on 25th March 1973 was to be apportioned and calculated accordingly (see p 594 c and d, post).

Per Megarry J. (i) If an enactment contains two similar prohibitions, one wide and the other applying only to a limited class of case wholly within the wide prohibition, the wide prohibition is to be treated as not applying to cases within the limited prohibition, especially if the limited prohibition is made subject to some exception and the wide prohibition is not (see p 583 c to e, post).

(ii) The provision in s 1(1)(b) of the Interpretation Act 1889 that words in the singular include the plural authorises a process of selective pluralising (see p 587 j to p 588 c, post).

(iii) Statutory definitions explain the meaning of the words defined, but for grammatical purposes they are not to be treated as being substituted for the words defined (see p 586 f and g, post).

Notes

For the limitation of general provisions in the construction of statutes, see 36 Halsbury's Laws (3rd Edn) 396-398, paras 596-600.

---

e Article 3 is set out at p 590 h and j, post

a For the rule that words in the singular include the plural, see 36 Halsbury's Laws (3rd Edn) 386, 387, para 575, and for cases on the subject, see 44 Digest (Repl) 268, 945-947.

For statutory restrictions on amount of rent, see 23 Halsbury's Laws (3rd Edn) 540, para 1198.

For the Interpretation Act 1889, s 1, see 32 Halsbury's Statutes (3rd Edn) 435.

b **Cases referred to in judgment**

Gluchowska v Tottenham Borough Council [1954] 1 All ER 408, [1954] 1 QB 438, [1954] 2 WLR 302, DC, 31(2) Digest (Reissue) 1132, 8759.

Luke v Inland Revenue Comrs [1963] 1 All ER 655, [1963] AC 557, [1963] 2 WLR 559, HL, 28(1) Digest (Reissue) 332, 1200.

Vaughan v Shaw [1945] 2 All ER 52, [1945] KB 400, 114 LJKB 350, 173 LT 6, CA, 31(2)
c Digest (Reissue) 1041, 8229.

Veale v Cabezas [1921] WN 311, DC, 31(2) Digest (Reissue) 1040, 8219.

Action

By a writ issued on 5th July 1973 the plaintiffs, Number 20 Cannon Street Ltd ('the landlords'), brought an action against the defendants, Singer & Friedlander Ltd ('the tenants'), claiming £128,369·29 as arrears of rent due under an agreement for
d a lease for a term commencing on 22nd January 1973 and expiring on 21st June 1982 of the third, fourth and fifth floors of a building known as 20 Cannon Street, London, EC4, at the yearly rent of £191,650 by equal quarterly payments in advance on the usual quarter days. By their defence the tenants contended that no rent was payable in respect of the demised premises in excess of the standard rate ascertained under the provisions of the Counter-Inflation (Business Rents) Order 1972[1] and the
e Counter-Inflation (Business Rents) Order 1973[2] and that they were willing to pay such rent as might be lawfully payable. The tenants contended that the standard rate was £39,150 per annum. By their counterclaim they sought the determination of the court as to the amount of the rent which was payable by them by virtue of the provisions of the 1972 and 1973 orders. By an amended statement of claim the
f landlords also sought the determination of similar questions arising on the construction of those orders. The facts are set out in the judgment.

P R Oliver QC and *Alan Fletcher* for the landlords.
Ronald Bernstein QC and *Christopher Priday* for the tenants.

Cur adv vult

g 13th February. **MEGARRY J** read the following judgment. This is a landlord and tenant case concerning the rent payable by business tenants under the counter-inflation legislation. In broad terms the question is whether the yearly rent that the tenants must pay is a little over £39,000 or rather over £190,000; and this depends on the construction of two statutory instruments of general importance which do not seem to have been the subject of any relevant reported decision. The premises with which I am
h concerned (which I shall call 'the demised premises') consist of the top three floors of 20 Cannon Street, London, EC4, an office building with six floors. There are certain ancillary rights relating to parking places in the basement on which nothing turns, and I shall ignore these. There is also a hierarchy of leases, and there have been a number of transactions relating to the demised premises and other floors in the same building; but again nothing turns on these, and I shall similarly ignore them. The case has been argued, and I shall decide it, as a simple case of a letting of the
j demised premises by the plaintiffs, whom I shall call 'the landlords', to the defendants, whom I shall call 'the tenants'. The tenancy began on 22nd January 1973, when the tenants went into occupation of the demised premises as business tenants on the terms of an unexecuted lease which provided for a rent of £191,650 a year,

1 SI 1972 No 1850
2 SI 1973 No 741

payable quarterly in advance. Matters continued on that footing until 6th February *a*
1974, when, as the parties now agree, the lease is to be treated as having been finally
executed, with insignificant variations. I may say that during the three days of the
hearing before me a good deal happened by way both of the occurrence of new
facts and the advancing and withdrawal of a number of arguments and contentions,
and that when counsel had justifiably concluded at the end of Day 2 that the arguments
were at an end, most of Day 3 was consumed in further argument to assist me in *b*
difficulties in construing the relevant legislation that had occurred to me during
the adjournment. However, I do not think that I need discuss these matters, and so
I shall proceed to the net result, and attempt to construe the difficult legislation
which confronts me. Counsel, I may say, were unable to put before me any authorities which provided any real assistance on the principles of statutory construction
which gave rise to difficulty.

c

The legislation in question consists of two statutory instruments, the Counter-
Inflation (Business Rents) Order 1972[1] and the Counter-Inflation (Business Rents)
Order 1973[2]: I shall refer to them as 'the 1972 order' and 'the 1973 order' respectively.
The 1972 order was made under the Counter-Inflation (Temporary Provisions) Act
1972, s 2(4), which as set out in Halsbury's Statutes[3] has, I regret to say, been the
victim of a homoeoteleuton; the 1973 order was made under the Counter-Inflation *d*
Act 1973, s 11. The 1972 order was in force from 1st December 1972 until 28th
April 1973, both dates inclusive. As will appear, this order took 5th November 1972
as the date at which certain matters were to be determined, this being the date, I
was told, on which it was announced that the legislation was to be enacted. Under
this order I have to determine the tenants' liability for rent during what I may call
'the first period', from the creation of the tenancy on 22nd January 1973 until the *e*
expiration of the order at the end of 28th April 1973. During this period, two gales
of rent fell due, the first, of £32,544·25 for the broken quarter, on 22nd January, and
the second, for a full quarter's rent of £47,912·50, on 25th March. The second period
began on 29th April 1973, when the 1973 order came into force, and this period is still
running. The writ was issued on 5th July 1973, and by the statement of claim
endorsed on it, the landlords claimed the two gales of rent that I have mentioned, *f*
and also the sum of £47,912·50 as being the quarter's rent due on 24th June 1973.
The landlords' claim is thus a simple money claim for these three sums, totalling
£128,369·25.

The tenants admit that they have paid no rent. They say that they have always
been prepared to pay such rent as is lawfully due, but they contend that by reason
of the two orders the landlords are not entitled to the whole of the sum claimed.
The tenants counterclaim for a determination by the court as to the amount of rent *g*
which is payable by them by virtue of the orders. Each of the orders, I may say,
contains provisions which confer jurisdiction on the court to make such a determination: see the 1972 order, para 8, and the 1973 order, art 13. The principal questions
are thus what rent is payable by the tenants to the landlords for each of the two
periods. There are also two further questions that may arise. The first is whether *h*
any difference is made by the lease having been executed on 6th February 1974; for
this was after the date when the 1973 order came into force, whereas the tenancy
began before that date, when the tenants went into occupation on 22nd January 1973.
The second question is one of apportionment. If the 1972 order restricts the tenants'
liability for rent but the 1973 order does not, it is disputed whether the tenants'
liability in respect of the quarter's rent due on 25th March 1973 is restricted only in *j*
respect of the remainder of the first period (namely, until 28th April 1973), or whether

---

1 SI 1972 No 1850
2 SI 1973 No 741
3 3rd Edn, vol 42, p 2238

it is restricted in respect of the whole of the quarter. In other words, as the quarter's rent fell due on 25th March 1973 and this was during the first period, are the tenants liable only at the restricted rate in respect of the entire quarter's rent, or are they liable at the restricted rate in respect of the first month or so and then at the full contractual rate in respect of the rest of the quarter?

Before I turn to the orders, I must state certain further facts. In 1961 each of the three floors of the demised premises had been separately let on business tenancies to separate tenants, the third floor at £13,050 per annum, the fourth at £13,200 and the fifth at £12,900. On 5th November 1972 an important date for the purposes of both orders, these tenancies were still in existence, though by then they had become vested in a single tenant. The tenant vacated the premises on 4th December 1972, and this made it possible for the landlords to grant to the tenants, on 22nd January 1973, the tenancy with which I am concerned. The essential sequence of events is thus that on 5th November 1972 the three floors which together make up the demised premises were separately let at rents which totalled £39,150 a year, that the 1972 order came into force on 1st December 1972, and that the tenants' tenancy of the demised premises as a whole at a rent of £191,650 a year commenced on 22nd January 1973 during the first period. Put in the shortest possible form, the basic question is whether the 1972 order prevents rent at a rate greater than £39,150 out of the £191,650 annual rent reserved under the tenancy from being payable during the first period, or whether the 1972 order imposes no such restriction, and leaves the tenant liable for the whole of the rent reserved by the tenancy. Counsel for the tenants contended for rent at the rate of £39,150 a year, while counsel for the landlords contended for rent at the rate of £191,650 a year.

With that, I must turn to the 1972 order. Paragraph 2(1) provides:

'The Interpretation Act 1889 shall apply for the interpretation of this Order as it applies for the interpretation of an Act of Parliament.'

This provision assumed considerable importance in the argument of counsel for the tenants, who relied on s 1(1)(b) of the 1889 Act, whereby in the absence of a contrary intention 'words in the singular shall include the plural'. I shall discuss the application of this in due course. Paragraph 2(2) of the 1972 order then sets out certain definitions which apply 'unless the context otherwise requires'. The term—

' "business tenancy" means any tenancy where the property comprised in the tenancy is or includes premises which are occupied by the tenant and are so occupied for the purposes of a business carried on by him or for those and other purposes but does not include a tenancy of or a right to occupy land used for agriculture.'

'Business' is defined in wide terms made familiar by the Landlord and Tenant Act 1954, s 23(2), but I need not set these out as it was common ground that all the tenancies with which I am concerned were business tenancies. Then there is 'rent':

' "rent" means the rent payable under a business tenancy, and includes the amount of any premium rateably apportioned over the period of the tenancy, but excludes any sums payable by the tenant in respect of rates, services, repairs, maintenance or insurance'.

Next there is 'standard rate' which—

'in relation to any premises means—(i) where a business tenancy was subsisting on 5th November 1972 the rate at which rent was payable (whether or not then determined as to amount) under that tenancy at that date; (ii) where there was no business tenancy subsisting on 5th November 1972 but a business tenancy had subsisted in respect of the premises on or after 5th November 1971, the rate at which rent was payable at the date upon which such tenancy or, where there were successive tenancies, the last such tenancy came to an end'.

I pause there. The 'standard rate', broadly speaking, is the rate of rent which is not to be exceeded. For the purpose of ascertaining the standard rate in relation to any premises, the year and a day ending at midnight on 5th November 1972 is to be taken. If on 5th November 1972 a business tenancy subsisted, the rent then payable under that tenancy determines the standard rate; otherwise the standard rate is determined by the rent payable at the end of the last business tenancy subsisting during the preceding year. Plainly there are many premises for which there will be no standard rate under this provision. If during the whole of the year and a day the premises were owner-occupied, or vacant, or occupied under a tenancy that was not a business tenancy, there would be no standard rate for those premises; and tenancies of premises which lacked a standard rate escaped any restriction under the order, since the prohibitions of the order are framed in terms of standard rates: no standard rate, no control.

Of the other provisions of the 1972 order, I may mention briefly the definition of 'the standstill period' in para 2(2). This means the period during which s 2 of the 1972 Act remains in force after the order came into operation; and as events turned out, this period was from 1st December 1972 to the end of 28th April 1973. By para 8, any person who 'requires or accepts' any payment in contravention of the order is liable to certain penalties on conviction. Counsel for the landlords placed some weight on this provision as an aid to construction, emphasising that in case of doubt the order should be construed so as to restrict the ambit of penal consequences.

I can now turn to the two paragraphs which were at the centre of the argument, paras 3 and 4. They read as follows:

'3. Rent shall not be payable in respect of the standstill period at a rate exceeding the standard rate and, where the terms of any tenancy provide for an increase of rent on or after 6th November 1972, the amount of that increase shall not be payable in respect of the standstill period.

'4. Where a business tenancy comes to an end on or after 6th November 1972 and the premises are re-let (whether to the previous tenant or not) the rate at which rent is payable in respect of the standstill period shall not exceed the standard rate, except to the extent that any such excess is properly attributable to a variation in the terms of the tenancy.'

Now in the case before me a business tenancy of each of the three floors came to an end after 5th November 1972, and each of the three floors was then relet by being included in the letting of the demised premises. It is therefore at least arguable that the case falls within para 4, as well as falling within para 3, and so the question arises of the relationship between these two paragraphs, and which of them applies to the present case, or whether both do. Each paragraph contains two limbs, and in each the first limb is prohibitory. The first limb of para 3 runs, 'Rent shall not be payable in respect of the standstill period at a rate exceeding the standard rate'. The second limb then adds a further explicit prohibition in respect of increases of rent payable under the terms of a tenancy. The first limb of para 4 similarly prohibits payments which exceed the standard rate, but it does this only in a limited class of case, namely, where a business tenancy came to an end after 5th November 1972 and the premises were relet. The second limb of para 4, beginning with the word 'except', makes an exception from the prohibition of the first limb of para 4 where the excess in the rent is 'properly attributable to a variation in the terms of the tenancy'.

The role of para 4 gave rise to considerable discussion. Nobody was able to suggest anything that the first limb prohibited which the first limb of para 3 had not already prohibited. Each of the prohibitions was in the same form of providing that rent in respect of the standstill period should not be payable at a rate exceeding the standard rate, and all that the first limb of para 4 did was to take the same prohibition as the first limb of para 3 imposed quite generally and impose it on a limited class of case, namely, where a business tenancy ended after 5th November 1972 and the premises were relet. To this extent, para 4 seemed merely a partial repetition. Further, the limited exception in the second limb is in terms merely an exception from the first limb of para 4, and does nothing to exclude the wider prohibition of para 3. However, to read the two paragraphs literally in this way would produce an absurd result: an excess attributable to variations in the terms of a tenancy would escape the prohibition of para 4 only to be caught by the prohibition of para 3, and so the whole of para 4 would be nugatory, the first limb as being a partial repetition, and the second limb as saving nothing from the prohibitions of the order. Accordingly, I think that para 4 must be read as excluding para 3 to the extent of the overlap. In other words, it is para 3 that imposes the general prohibition, but in the limited class of case covered by para 4, it is para 4 and not para 3 that imposes the operative prohibitions, thus carrying with it the exception. In this way effect is given to the whole of both paragraphs. Such an approach bears at least some relationship to the familiar maxim generalia specialibus non derogant. Put formally, it seems to me that the proper principle to apply if an enactment contains two similar prohibitions, one wide and the other applying only to a limited class of case wholly within the wide prohibition, is to treat the wide prohibition as not applying to cases within the limited prohibition, especially if the limited prohibition is made subject to some exception and the wide prohibition is not. Accordingly, in my judgment if the present case falls within para 4, it is para 4 alone that applies: if it does not, then the question is whether para 3 applies. Counsel for the landlords ultimately came to accept that it would not suffice him to show that para 4 did not apply unless he could also show that he was not caught by para 3. He had to plot a course which escaped both Scylla and Charybdis.

I pause merely to remark one curiosity of para 4. If premises were relet in, say, January 1973, and previously a business tenancy of the same premises had come to an end, the operation of para 4 depended entirely on whether that business tenancy ended after 5th November 1972, or before 6th November 1972. If it ended on, say, 7th November, para 4 applied, and so under the exception the excess over the standard rate could lawfully be charged if it was properly attributable to a variation in the terms of the tenancy. But if the business tenancy had ended on, say, 4th November 1972, the case was outside para 4, and so neither the prohibition of para 4 nor its exception for a proper excess applied. Instead, the case fell within para 3, which provided no exception. Nobody could suggest why what could be done on granting the new tenancy in January 1973 should depend on this; but whatever the reason, it illustrates the limited scope of para 4.

I must now turn to construing paras 3 and 4 in relation to the facts of this case. Counsel for the landlords' basic contention was that neither paragraph applied unless there was complete identity between the premises which yielded the standard rate and the premises comprised in the tenancy in question. The 1972 order contained no provision for apportioning the standard rate of premises in order to ascertain the standard rate for a mere part of the premises, and it also contained no provision for adding together the standard rates of each separate part of the premises in order to ascertain the standard rate of the whole. These cases escaped any restriction by the 1972 order. If a standard rate of £50,000 had been established for a five-storey building which had been let as a whole, then under the 1972 order the building as a whole could not be relet for more than £50,000, but the landlord was free to let each floor for, say, £100,000, or, indeed, the entire building minus enough of it to escape the label of de minimis for £500,000. Correspondingly, if instead each floor of the building had a standard rate of £10,000, but the building had never been let as a whole, the entire building, or, indeed, any combination of floors or parts of floors which did not exactly coincide with one single floor, could be let at whatever rent the landlord could get. Nothing save a complete identity of premises subjected what was let to the standard rate.

Of course, statutes do sometimes miscarry ; and statutory instruments drafted to carry out what is plainly emergency legislation are perhaps particularly liable to miscarriage. Nevertheless, in a statutory instrument made under an Act with the long title 'An Act to authorise measures to counter inflation', one would not readily put on the words used a construction which makes the countering of inflation so capricious and easily escapable. I bear in mind that of one provision in a Finance Act, Lord Reid once said[1]:

> 'To apply the words literally is to defeat the obvious intention of the legislation and to produce a wholly unreasonable result. To achieve the obvious intention and produce a reasonable result we must do some violence to the words.'

Counsel for the landlords delicately refrained from suggesting that the degree of violence that a puisne could properly do was less than that open to the House of Lords; but the thought is not absent from my mind. In any case, the first task is to try to put a fair meaning on the words used, in their proper context, before admitting any thoughts of violence. In doing that, I feel no doubt that in any case of uncertainty, sense may be preferred to nonsense, and efficacy to impotence.

Counsel for the tenants put his contentions under two main heads. First, he argued that by a judicious application of s 1(1)(b) of the Interpretation Act 1889, the appropriate words in paras 3 and 4 could be read in the plural in such a way as to produce the result that the rent of the whole must not exceed the aggregate of the standard rates of the parts. I shall call this approach the 'aggregate standard rate construction'. Counsel for the landlords' reply was that this was a difficult task, especially if one first applied para 2 of the order and read into paras 3 and 4 the full meaning of 'business tenancy', 'rent' and 'standard rate'. Furthermore, even if this could be done, there was nothing in the result to authorise the process of adding together the standard rates of the parts: to read 'standard rate' as 'standard rates' was one thing, to read 'standard rate' as 'the aggregate of standard rates' was another, and there was nothing in the Interpretation Act 1889 or anywhere else to authorise such a process.

The second and perhaps simpler way that counsel for the tenants put his contention was that the three floors, each with its standard rate, should be looked at separately, and then the rent payable for the demised premises as a whole should be considered. If the rent for the whole exceeded the aggregate of the standard rates of the parts, that showed that the rent payable in respect of at least one of the floors, if not all of them, exceeded the standard rate for that floor. True, none of the separate floors was presently let as a separate entity at its own rent, but each was nevertheless let as part of the whole, and it is ancient law that rent under a tenancy issues out of every part of what is demised. I shall call this approach the 'individual standard rate construction'. To this, counsel for the landlords objected that the 1972 order was a penal statute, and as it could not be said with reasonable certainty what excess was attributable to each floor, there was not the certainty that there ought to be in a penal statute if this construction was adopted. I should add that in opposition to each of counsel for the tenants' contentions counsel for the landlords laid great stress on the presence in paras 3 and 4 (either actual or by means of the definitions in para 2) of words which indicated that the paragraphs applied only where there was identity of premises between the premises comprised in the tenancy which established the standard rate and those which were in dispute. For this purpose, para 4, with its explicit reference to 'the premises', was on the face of it more helpful than para 3, which was innocent of any such reference.

I shall first consider counsel for the tenants' second submission, that based on the individual standard rate construction. Looking at each floor separately, it is undisputed that the opening words of para 4 are satisfied: 'Where a business tenancy comes to an end on or after 6th November 1972 . . .' In that phrase, 'business tenancy',

---

1 See *Luke v Inland Revenue Comrs* [1963] 1 All ER 655 at 664, [1963] AC 557 at 577

a by virtue of the definition in para 2, 'means any tenancy where the property comprised in the tenancy is or includes premises which are occupied by the tenant' for business purposes. The next words in para 4 are 'and the premises are re-let'. I do not think that counsel for the landlords seriously denied that each floor was relet: but he stressed heavily that it could not be said that each floor was relet as an entity under a separate business tenancy. In this connection he referred me to a number of auth-

b orities relating to standard rent under the Rent Acts, including *Veale v Cabezas*[1] and *Vaughan v Shaw*[2], as showing that the standard rent of premises under those Acts would not be ascertained by adding together the standard rents established for the constituent parts of those premises. These cases, of course, were also (and mainly) relied on for the general proposition that no process of aggregating standard rates was authorised by the order. It was pleasant to revisit old friends such as these, but

c I think that counsel for the tenants' contention that they had no application is inescapable. One of the fundamentals of the Rent Acts is that they are dealing with 'a house or a part of a house let as a separate dwelling'. If in the 1972 order there had been any corresponding concept, confining its operation to cases where premises are let or relet 'as a separate entity' or the like, then there would have been some force in the parallel: but the order contains no such requirement.

d However, counsel for the landlords had another way of putting his argument. The words 'the premises', he said, almost of necessity refer back to the opening phrase 'Where a business tenancy comes to an end'; and the definition of 'business tenancy' in para 2(2) states that the phrase 'means any tenancy where the property comprised in the tenancy is or includes premises which . . .', and so on. Therefore, he said, 'the premises' must mean the property comprised in the business tenancy that has come to an end (here, the individual floor), and could not mean that property

e together with other property (namely, the other two floors). I can see the force of this, but I cannot see how it helps counsel for the landlords. Assume that the words 'the premises' mean 'the self-same premises which were the subject of the business tenancy that has come to an end', and it still can properly be said that these premises have been relet; true, they have not been relet as a separate entity, but still they have

f been relet, and the order contains no requirement that they should have been relet as a separate entity. In my judgment the words 'and the premises are re-let' are satisfied by the premises being relet as part of a larger unit. If one looked at an individual floor immediately after the tenancy of the demised premises had been granted, I do not see how it could be said that that floor was not 'let', or had not been 're-let'.

With these requirements satisfied, para 4 then provides that 'the rate at which rent is payable in respect of the standstill period shall not exceed the standard rate'.

g By para 2(2) ' "rent" means the rent payable under a business tenancy', and so on: and it is plain that the rent for the demised premises is payable under a business tenancy. Accordingly, apart from the exception at the end of para 4 relating to variations in the terms of the tenancy, para 4 is capable of applying to the case before me. I shall consider that exception shortly; but first I must discuss counsel for

h the landlords' submission that even if the requirements of para 4 are satisfied, the order cannot operate properly in a case such as this, in that this legislation is penal, and it cannot be said with the requisite certainty that more than the standard rate of rent is payable in respect of each floor.

I pause to mention certain facts again. In round figures, each of the three floors has a standard rate of £13,000, and the rent for the demised premises, comprising the three floors, is £190,000. The act of letting the demised premises was a single act.

j Yet it is said that there is or may be some uncertainty about whether the three standard rates for the three floors has been exceeded by such a letting. What that uncertainty is I was never really able to discover. Thus if it be said that the fraction

---

1   [1921] WN 311
2   [1945] 2 All ER 52, [1945] KB 400

of the rent properly attributable to two of the three floors is no more than the
standard rate of £13,000 each, that seems to me to lead to the inescapable conclusion
that £164,000 is attributable to the remaining floor with its standard rate of £13,000.
However the rent is attributed, the order must be contravened if a rent of £190,000
is demanded.

If one of the floors had had no standard rate, then of course the position might
have been very different. If two floors have a standard rate of £13,000 each and the
third has none, then a letting of the three together for £40,000 or £50,000 might
well fall outside para 4; for it could indeed be contended that the floor without a
standard rate carried the excess, so that it could not be shown that the other two
floors had been let for more than their standard rates of £13,000 each. Even then,
in a case like this, it might be contended that when the whole had been let for
£190,000, it was impossible to believe that £164,000 was attributable to the floor
with no standard rate. However, such a case is not before me for decision, and I
do no more than indicate possible contentions which may fall to be argued hereafter.
It may be that if any part of the property demised is free from a standard rate, the
order does not apply at all, any more than it applies to a letting of premises wholly
devoid of any standard rate.

I turn, then, to the concluding words of para 4, 'except to the extent that any such
excess is properly attributable to a variation in the terms of the tenancy'. Counsel
for the landlords emphasised the words 'the tenancy', and contended that this helped
to demonstrate that there must be identity between the premises comprised in the
tenancy that has come to an end and the tenancy created by the reletting: only if
you could compare the terms of the two tenancies of identical premises could you
assess what variation there has been in the terms of 'the tenancy'. I can see some
force in this, but I do not think that it really affects the construction of the paragraph
in the way that counsel for the landlords would have it. The words 'the tenancy'
must, I think, refer back to the only other express mention of a tenancy in the
paragraph, in the phrase: 'Where a business tenancy comes to an end . . .' True, the
expressions 'standard rate' and 'rent' are nearer antecedents, and the definitions of
them in para 2(2) each have more than one reference to 'tenancy' in them; but I do
not think that statutory definitions require you bodily to substitute the definitions
for the words defined so as to enable you as a matter of grammar to treat words
in the definitions as being antecedents of words actually appearing later in the statutory provision. The definitions explain what the expressions mean in the statutory
provision, but they remain outside that provision and for grammatical purposes
leave unchanged in the provision the actual words that are there, even though they
have become freighted with their statutory meanings. At all events, with no
authority to assist me on the point, that is what appears to me to be the principle.

Accordingly, the words 'the tenancy' mean the 'business tenancy' which has come
to an end on or after 6th November 1972, that is, the business tenancy of each of the
three floors. What have to be compared with the terms of that tenancy, for each
floor, are the terms of the new tenancy of the three floors as a whole which comprise
the demised premises. Counsel for the landlords accepted and asserted that 'terms'
did not include the extent of the property demised, but related to the covenants
and other contractual provisions of the tenancy. In some cases there obviously may
be room for argument, but I cannot see anything impossible in the process of taking
each floor separately, contrasting the terms of the tenancy of that floor which came
to an end after 5th November 1972 with the terms of the new tenancy of the three
floors together, and then seeing whether the excess of the rent of the whole over the
total of the three standard rates could properly be attributed to the variations. If,
for example, there were changes in the repairing obligations, with the obligations
becoming more burdensome on the tenant for one floor and less burdensome for
the other two floors, I cannot believe that it would be beyond the skill of valuers to
quantify this difference, with the usual allowances for differences of opinion. In

any case, the paragraph is admittedly assumed to work where there is identity between the premises which are let under each tenancy.

In the result, it seems to me that counsel for the tenants is right in his argument under this head, and that para 4 applies to this case so as to limit the rent payable to the rate of £39,150 a year. If para 4 did not apply, then I can see no ground why para 3 should not produce the same result. Its operative words are simpler, and there is no express reference to 'premises' to help counsel for the landlords. Paragraph 3 runs: 'Rent shall not be payable in respect of the standstill period at a rate exceeding the standard rate . . .'; and it then goes on to deal with tenancies containing a term providing for an increase of rent. Even after the definitions of 'rent' and 'standard rate' in para 2(2) have been applied, para 3 seems to me to be apt for this case. If para 3 is expanded by reading into it the relevant parts of the definition it runs 'Rent payable under a business tenancy shall not be payable in respect of the standstill period at a rate exceeding the standard rate': and the words 'standard rate' import the complex definition which relates to 'a business tenancy' existing on 5th November 1972 or in the previous year. In other words, rent which is payable under the present business tenancy of the whole must not be paid at a rate exceeding the standard rate: each floor has its standard rate: and if for any floor it can be said that the rent which is payable under the present business tenancy exceeds for that floor the standard rate for the floor, or if for all three floors together it can be said that the rent which is payable under the present business tenancy exceeds for all three floors together the standard rates for those three floors, then the prohibition is contravened. Expressed in the latter form, the singular is to be read as including the plural: but under the Interpretation Act 1889 there is no difficulty in doing this.

I turn to the other way in which counsel for the tenants put his case, based on the aggregate standard rate construction. This depends on a liberal application of the Interpretation Act 1889 in substituting the plural for the singular where this is appropriate. Here, as I have indicated, the process is not to show that the individual standard rates of each floor are exceeded, but to show that the demised premises as a whole have a composite standard rate which is exceeded by the rent for the demised premises. In many cases, if not most, this approach doubtless produces the same result as the individual standard rate construction: but there are differences. Thus if two floors each have a standard rate but the third does not, and the entirety is then let, under the individual standard rate construction the rent of the entirety may be so great as to leave little or no doubt that the two standard rates have each been exceeded (a matter on which, as I have indicated, I decide nothing), whereas under the aggregate standard rate construction the order, being incapable of producing any aggregate standard rate for the entirety, seems impossible of application.

Under the aggregate standard rate construction, counsel for the tenants would read para 4, in its application to the present case, as being 'Where business tenancies come to an end on or after 6th November 1972 and the premises are re-let . . . the rate at which rent is payable in respect of the standstill period shall not exceed the standard rates . . .' In that reading of para 4, the word 'premises' is to be read as being plural, and as referring to two or more different entities. 'Premises' is an awkward word, for grammatically it is plural even when it refers only to one entity; and counsel for the tenants said that if instead para 4 had used the word 'hereditament', then in his reading of the paragraph as applying to the present case he would read it as 'hereditaments'.

On this a number of points arose. First, counsel for the landlords emphasised that although under the Interpretation Act 1889, s 1(1)(b), 'words in the singular . . . include the plural', this was only 'unless the contrary intention appears'; and he said that here there was a contrary intention. However, I do not think that he ever made good this submission. Second, it will be observed that counsel for the tenants' reading left some words in the singular (notably 'rate' and 'rent') and turned many others into the plural. There was some discussion of this process of eclectic pluralising but in the end it was not seriously contended that under the Interpretation Act 1889 this process was illegitimate. I think that this must be so, though I was referred to no authority on the point: indeed, authorities on this part of the Interpretation Act 1889 seem meagre. I do not see why this provision should not be applied distributively. Further, to 'include' the plural does not mean that the word must discard its singularity: the Act adds to the meaning of the word, rather than changing it. It would indeed be remarkable if, for example, a statute worded in terms of 'landlord' and 'tenant' applied to every case where there was a landlord and a tenant in the singular or landlords and tenants in the plural, but not to cases where there were plural landlords and a singular tenant, or vice versa. In my judgment, subject always to the context, the Interpretation Act 1889 authorises a process of selective pluralising or, for that matter, singularising.

Third, as I have indicated, counsel for the landlords' primary answer to counsel for the tenants' reading of para 4 was that it ignored the definitions of 'business tenancy', 'rent' and 'standard rate' to be found in para 2(2) of the order, and that when these definitions were read in, counsel for the tenants' method of construction would not work. I do not think this is so. As I have already indicated for another purpose, I cannot see that para 2(2) requires the definitions to be substituted for the words in para 4 that are defined. Thus in para 4 the phrase 'business tenancy' must be read and understood with the meaning ascribed to it by para 2(2), but if it is read as including the plural 'business tenancies' I do not see why each of those tenancies should not also be understood as bearing the meaning to be found in para 2(2). If I am wrong and the definition of 'business tenancy' in para 2(2) is required to be transposed bodily into para 4, I cannot see why, when it has arrived there, its constituent parts should not be read with the requisite plurality. At all events, in his expanded version of para 4 counsel for the landlords failed to demonstrate to me any impossibility or impracticability in such a reading.

Fourth, counsel for the landlords took as an example of the frailties in counsel for the tenants' approach the case of a two-storey building in which the business tenancy of the ground floor ended on 1st November 1972, and that of the first floor ended on 7th November 1972, whereupon the entire building was relet on 10th November 1972 on a new business tenancy of the whole. In such a case, the standard rate for the ground floor would be ascertained not under para 2(2)(i) (for no business tenancy was subsisting on 5th November) but under para 2(2)(ii), by reference to the rent on 1st November, whereas the standard rate for the first floor would be ascertained under para 2(2)(i) as being the rent on 5th November. Neither rent could therefore, he said, provide a standard rate for the whole. Furthermore, where a business tenancy ended before 6th November (as with the tenancy of the ground floor) no excess could be permitted under para 4 by reason of a variation in the terms of the tenancy.

I do not find these contentions persuasive. As regards the latter, I have already commented on the curiosity of an excess by reason of a variation in the terms of the tenancy being permitted if the previous tenancy ended after 5th November but not if it ended before 6th November; and with this curiosity existing in the case where the premises under the old tenancy and the new are identical, I cannot see how its operation in the case where this identity is lacking demonstrates that counsel for the tenants is wrong. As regards counsel for the landlords' example of the standard rates being ascertained by reference to different dates, one being 1st November and the other 5th November, and the impossibility of applying para 4 to such a case, counsel for the tenants saw no difficulty; nor do I. He never contended that the standard rate for the whole would be established by taking the standard rate for a mere part. His contention was that if every part had its own standard rate, the rent for the whole must not exceed the aggregate of the standard rates of the parts; and for this purpose it does not matter that those standard rates have been ascertained by reference to different dates. Furthermore, the only effect of showing that such a

case does not fall within para 4 is to leave it to fall within para 3, where these difficulties do not arise.   When all is considered, I reach the conclusion that the aggregate
standard rent construction is sound.

Before I leave this branch of the case, I must say something about the decision of a
Queen's Bench Divisional Court in *Gluchowska v Tottenham Borough Council*[1], on which
counsel for the landlords placed some weight.   This was a case on the Furnished
Houses (Rent Control) Act 1946, s 4(1) of which provided that where the rent 'payable
for any premises' was entered in the register under the Act, it was not lawful thereafter to require or receive on account of rent 'for those premises' payment of any sum
in excess of the rent so entered.   The rent of an entity consisting of three rooms and
a kitchen was registered, and afterwards a part of that entity was let at a rent higher
than the rent registered for the whole.   The landlord was convicted of contraventions
of the Act, but Parker and Byrne JJ, over the dissent of Lord Goddard CJ, quashed
the conviction.   The majority held that the language of s 4(1) required the 'any
premises' and 'those premises' to be identical, and that the tenant's remedy for the
apparent absurdity of the landlord being able to charge more for the part than he
could for the whole was for the tenant to apply forthwith for the determination and
registration of the proper rent for that part.

That case differs from this case in a number of respects.   The statutory language
is quite different, and of course the question there was one of a rent for the whole
being applied on the letting of a part, whereas here I am concerned with rents for the
parts being applied on a letting of the whole.   Furthermore, there was the remedy
that was open to the tenant in that case but is not in this.   There is also, if I may say
so, considerable force in Lord Goddard CJ's dissent, based as it was on the greater
including the less, and the fact that even if the tenant obtained the registration of a
proper rent for the part, that would do nothing to give him back excessive payments
that he had already made.   Giving full weight to the views of the majority, I can
only say that I can see nothing in them to compel or even persuade me to a conclusion on the significantly different language of the 1972 order which does not
accord with the conclusion that I would reach without their aid.

On the footing that the individual standard rate construction and the aggregate
standard rate construction are both sound, questions may arise as to which of the two
is the true construction, or whether both are right, and, if so, what is the effect of
two different constructions of a particular provision both being right.   I do not
think that I have to resolve these puzzles.   There has been no suggestion that on
the facts of this case the two constructions produce different results, and so each
provides an alternative ground for reaching the conclusion that I think is right.   One
day it may be necessary to decide these matters; and I am content, and, indeed,
happy to leave them for whatever court encounters them.   However, for the assistance of those who may be concerned with other cases in the meantime I may indicate
that if it were necessary for me to choose, I think that as at present advised I should
rest my decision on the individual standard rate construction.

I can now at last turn to the 1973 order and its effect in relation to the second period,
the period after 28th April 1973.   Counsel for the landlords' submission was that this
order did not apply to the present case and so there was no restriction on the contractual rent.   After counsel for the tenants had heard the submission of counsel
for the landlords and had had the opportunities for consideration afforded by the
overnight adjournment, he said that he was unable to sustain any argument to the
contrary.   However, I do not think that I ought simply to enter judgment for the
landlords for the rent claimed, saying no more, especially in view of the tenants'
counterclaim for a determination 'as to the amount of the rent which is payable' by
the tenants 'by virtue of the provisions' of the orders of 1972 and 1973.   But I can
consider the matter with a brevity which, unfortunately, is only relative.

---

1   [1954] 1 All ER 408, [1954] 1 QB 438

The 1973 order is about twice as long as the 1972 order, and contains many changes and additions, as well as many similarities. Most of the definitions in art 2(2) of the 1973 order are much the same as those in the 1972 order. The definition of 'business' is identical. The definition of 'business tenancy' is the same, apart from building leases being made an additional exception, and the word 'purposes' in the phrase 'for the purposes of a business carried on by him' being cast into the singular. This seems to be a mere slip, for the subsequent words 'for those and other purposes' remain in the plural. The definition of 'rent' loses the words 'means the rent payable under a business tenancy, and', but otherwise is unchanged.' Standard rate' is dealt with quite differently, art 2(2) merely providing that the expression has the meaning assigned to it in art 4. Article 4 is divided into three paragraphs. Paragraph (1) is identical with the twofold definition of 'standard rate' in the 1972 order, save that it is expressed to be subject to certain other provisions of the order, and it concludes by saying that in each case there is to be the addition 'of any increase in that rate as a result of an increase of rent permitted by the provisions of the 1972 Order, where those provisions applied'. Paragraphs (2) and (3) are completely new. They run as follows:

'(2) Where in relation to the premises comprised in a business tenancy granted after the coming into force of this order a standard rate is not ascertainable by the application of paragraph (1) of this article and the premises—(a) form part of larger premises in relation to which there is a standard rate, the standard rate in relation to the premises comprised in the business tenancy shall be a just part of the standard rate in relation to the larger premises; (b) consist of two or more premises in relation to each of which there is a standard rate (and those premises together make up the whole of the premises comprised in the business tenancy), the standard rate in relation to the premises comprised in the business tenancy shall be a just amount based on the aggregate of the standard rates in relation to the constituent premises.

'(3) The just part and the just amount referred to in paragraph (2) of this article shall be such amount as may be agreed in writing between the landlord and the tenant or determined by the court under article 13.'

There are two other provisions of the 1973 order that I must set out. First, the substantive restriction of rent is now effected by a single article, art 5, in place of the two paragraphs of the 1972 order, paras 3 and 4, that I have discussed. Article 5 of the 1973 order is as follows:

'Subject to the provisions of this order, where in relation to any premises there is a standard rate, rent under a business tenancy (whether granted before or after the coming into force of this order) of those premises shall not be payable in respect of any part of the time during which this order is in force at a rate exceeding the standard rate.'

Second, there is art 3:

'(1) Nothing in this order shall apply to—(a) any rent increase in respect of a business tenancy or superior tenancy taking place before 29th April 1973, or (b) any new lettings.

'(2) "New lettings" means, for the purposes of this article, any business tenancy which is granted after 5th November 1972 where the property comprised in the tenancy consists of or includes premises in relation to which there is not a standard rate and any superior tenancy granted after that date.'

I begin with art 5. The reference which it makes to 'any premises' and 'those premises' plainly makes it difficult to put on the article either the aggregate standard rate construction or the individual standard rate construction. On a simple reading of the article the rent which is restricted is the rent under a business tenancy of the very premises for which there is a standard rate, so that on this wording, which is significantly different from the corresponding language of the 1972 order, counsel for the landlords' argument that there must be identity between the premises which established the standard rate and the premises which are let is greatly strengthened. Furthermore, and in my judgment decisively, there are the provisions for ascertaining the standard rate by the processes of apportionment and aggregation which are set out in art 4(2).   Even if the process of aggregation there prescribed had been one of simple addition, its presence would have been a powerful argument against reading into art 5 any implied process of aggregation: expressum facit cessare tacitum.   In fact, of course, the prescribed process is one of ascertaining 'a just amount based on the aggregate of the standard rates', so that the process is one not of simple addition but of simple addition tempered with justice.   I do not see how it could be possible to find an implied process of simple addition in art 5 which could co-exist with the express process of justice based on aggregation set out in art 4(2).

That is not all.   Article 4(2) is in terms confined to 'a business tenancy granted after the coming into force of this order'; and this coming into force occurred on 29th April 1973. If the language of art 5 were otherwise capable of yielding an implied process of simple addition of standard rates, I do not see how that implication could survive the impact of art 4(2), with its provision of a different process for tenancies granted after the order came into force.   The self-same words in art 5 would have to be read as bearing different meanings, depending on whether the business tenancy in question was granted after the 1973 order came into force or before: if before, the words of art 5 would carry an implied process of aggregation different from that of art 4(2); if after, those words would carry no implication of any process of aggregation. In my judgment, under the 1973 order, the only process of aggregation of standard rates that is authorised or required is that laid down by art 4(2).

That seems to me to be decisive of this part of the case. The tenancy with which I am concerned was granted before the 1973 order came into force: by the express words of art 4(2) the process of aggregation tempered with justice that it lays down is limited to the case of a business tenancy granted after the order came into force: therefore that process does not apply to the tenancy with which I am concerned. The premises comprised in that tenancy therefore have no standard rate, and so the prohibition in art 5 can do nothing.

That by itself would be enough: but there is more. By art 3(1) nothing in the order applies to 'new lettings'. By art 3(2) 'new lettings' means 'any business tenancy which is granted after 5th November 1972' which satisfies a further requirement. (In a case which has abounded with singulars and plurals, I pause only to wonder why 'new lettings', in the plural, should have been made to mean a particular type of business tenancy, in the singular.) The further requirement is that the property comprised in the tenancy 'consists of or includes premises in relation to which there is not a standard rate'. This is a provision of remarkable width. For tenancies granted after 5th November 1972 the operation of the order is excluded in any case where there is no standard rate for the premises as a whole or else there is no standard rate for any premises which are included in the premises as a whole. Let any of the constituent premises which go to make up the whole lack a standard rate, and the whole is outside the order. Thus if on 5th November 1972 three floors were then let as one unit, and after that date a new tenancy of the same unit is granted, that unit plainly has a standard rate. But the order will not apply at all if there is not a standard rate for, say, one of those floors. If the new tenancy of the whole was granted after 28th April 1973 (but not otherwise), the standard rate for any floor can be ascertained under arts 4(2) and (3) by determining the 'just part' of the standard rate of the whole by agreement in writing or by a decision of the court. It may be that the assumption of art 3(2) is that all premises included in a letting of a larger unit necessarily have their standard rates by potential apportionment, even before the 'just part' has been duly ascertained. If this is not so, then art 3 would be so extensive in its operation as to make the whole almost nugatory.

However that may be, if, as in the present case, the new tenancy was granted before 29th April 1973, art 4(2) can do nothing. The case before me is in some respects the converse of the example that I have been discussing, in that it is a case not of there being a standard rate for the whole and none for the parts, but one of there being standard rates for the parts and none for the whole. In the inelegant language of art 3, the tenancy before me is thus 'new lettings' and so is outside the order. The case is one in which the order does not apply to the tenancy, and even if it did it would do nothing because it yields no standard rate for the demised premises.

The conclusion that the rent is restricted by the 1972 order but not by the 1973 order is somewhat surprising. It is not easy to see the legislative purpose that lies behind such a result; but the differences in the drafting of the two orders seem to me to lead inescapably to this conclusion. I may add that although something was said on the point, it was not seriously contended that the presence in the 1973 order of the express provisions for the apportionment and aggregation of standard rates that I have discussed does anything to affect the construction of the 1972 order, for example, by indicating that the absence of any such provisions from the 1972 order must lead to the conclusion that without them the order could not be read as authorising any such process. The 1972 order bore a meaning as soon as it was made, and I do not think that this meaning has been altered by another order made over four months later for a similar purpose containing provisions absent from the earlier order. Provisions may, of course, be inserted ex abundanti cautela or for the avoidance of doubt; and even though a later Act of Parliament may sometimes be used to assist in the construction of an earlier Act, I doubt very much whether a later statutory instrument made under a later Act can provide much legitimate assistance in construing an earlier statutory instrument made under an earlier Act.

That brings me to the first of the two subsidiary questions which I mentioned at the outset. Does the execution of the lease on 6th February 1974 make any difference to the operation of the 1973 order? The point, of course, is that arts 3 and 4(2) prevent the 1973 order from applying if the operative transaction is the commencement of the tenancy on 22nd January 1973, before the 1973 order came into operation, but not if the operative transaction is the grant of the lease on 6th February 1974, after that order had come into operation.

I think the answer is plainly No; and in the end counsel for the tenants, whose point it was, found himself unable to press it. The orders are expressed in terms of 'tenancy', and I can see no reason why any tenancy should not suffice, whether legal or equitable. If a tenant is in possession under an enforceable agreement for a lease, he is a tenant holding under a tenancy, and I cannot see how for the purposes of the orders the subsequent clothing of his interest with the legal estate by the formal grant of a formal lease can make any difference to his having had a tenancy ab initio. In this case I am concerned with 'a business tenancy granted' before the 1973 order came into force, and in my judgment the subsequent granting of the lease made no difference.

Finally, I turn to the second of the two subsidiary points, that of the landords' claim that the quarter's rent payable in advance on 25th March 1973 should be apportioned as between the restricted rate and the unrestricted. On 25th March 1973, while the 1972 order was still in force, the tenants became liable for a quarter's rent in advance. By virtue of the 1972 order, rent was not payable at a rate exceeding the standard rate of £39,150 a year, so that on that footing a quarter's rent would be £9,787·50. However, at midnight on 28th April 1973, when little more than one-third of the quarter had run, the 1972 order expired, and, as I have held, the 1973 order did not apply to the tenancy. In those circumstances, are the tenants liable for rent at the restricted rate of £9,787·50 for the first part of the quarter and at the contractual rate of £47,912·50 in respect of the remainder of the quarter, or will their liability for the entire quarter be discharged by paying £9,787·50?

It has not been contended that by reason of the quarter's rent remaining wholly unpaid the tenants are in any position different from that in which they would have been had they paid or tendered £9,787·50 on 25th March 1973. It was also common ground that the Apportionment Act 1870 had no application. Counsel for the landlords emphasised that paras 3 and 4 of the 1972 order were expressed in terms of the 'rate' at which rent was payable, and also that the paragraphs were expressed to operate 'in respect of' rather than 'during' the standstill period. Each of these expressions, he contended, showed that the order was intended to operate de die in diem rather than govern the payment of individual sums on particular dates. He also relied on para 10 of the order, which runs:

'Subject to the provisions of this Order relating to rent payable in respect of the standstill period, nothing in this Order shall render unlawful or invalid any agreement, determination or notice relating to rent.'

Counsel for the tenants, on the other hand, emphasised the act of payment. He contended that the obligation of the tenants was to pay a particular sum at a particular time, and that if the tenant discharged his obligation by paying what under the law in force at that time was the proper sum, no further liability could arise from a subsequent change in the law.

This, like other points under the order, is far from easy. The order operates by making rent not 'payable in respect of the standstill period'. This wording is curious. Rent in advance may well be said to be payable 'in respect of' the tenancy and 'in respect of' the quarter or other period of the tenancy in question, but it is not in any purposive sense of the words payable 'in respect of' the standstill period: that period merely happens to be running at the time when the rent is payable 'in respect of' the period under the reddendum, here the quarter beginning on 25th March 1973. Accordingly, unless the order is to be singularly ineffective, the phrase 'in respect of the standstill period' must be given some other meaning. I do not feel much difficulty about doing this, as 'in respect of' is a flexible phrase which I think can be satisfied by any of a wide range of connections or relationships between the two matters in question.

Some indication of the true construction of paras 3 and 4 on this point seems to be given by the definition of 'standard rate' in para 2(2). In each limb of this the phrase 'the rate at which rent was payable' is used in relation to a fixed date which only by chance will be a gale day, in one case 5th November 1972, and in the other case the date before that on which the tenancy came to an end. The word 'payable' is thus of necessity directed not to the obligation to perform the act of payment but to the continuing liability for rent at that rate. Paragraphs 3 and 4 should be construed in the same way. For the first month or so of the quarter, the contractual liability for rent at the higher rate was negatived by the order for all rent in excess of the standard rate; for the rest of the quarter the contractual liability remained unimpaired. The scheme of the order necessarily means that not until the expiry of any rental period can it be known whether the contractual liability for rent has been curtailed for the entire period or only for some initial part of the period. Counsel for the landlords' contentions based on the expressions 'the rate' and 'in respect of' seem to me to have much force. If the rent had been made payable in arrear instead of in advance, it is difficult to see how counsel for the tenants could have sustained any real argument on the point; and with the objects of the legislation in mind, it is difficult to see why rent in respect of a period during which no restriction is in force should nevertheless be restricted if the rent is payable in advance but not if it is payable in arrear.

Looking at the matter as a whole, it seems to me that the legislation is best effectuated by holding that the mechanics of payment are irrelevant, so that it does not matter whether the rent is payable in advance or in arrear, or whether it is paid punctually or late, and that what is decisive is the period during which the statutory restriction runs; and I think that the statutory language supports this view. I accept that on this view there is some difficulty in pointing to the moment of time when the balance of rent for the period after the standstill period has ended must be paid,

Y

but this does not seem to me to offset the effect of the statutory language. The moment of time, I think, cannot be later than the end of the rental period in question, here the end of the second quarter of 1973, and no question on this has arisen in this case. Accordingly in my judgment the tenants are liable for rent in respect of that quarter at the rate of £9,787·50 until the end of 28th April 1973 and thereafter at the rate of £47,912·50 for the rest of the quarter.

I need hardly say that I am not alone in regretting the length of this judgment: but the orders present formidable difficulties of construction and application, and they are, of course, drastic and far-reaching in their operation. Mapping untrodden territory is necessarily more laborious than plotting a course from maps made by others. For the reasons that I have given I hold that the landlords are entitled to part but not all of the £128,369·25 that they claim. Of the first sum, due on 22nd January 1973, for the period from then until 25th March 1973, they are entitled not to the whole of the £32,544·25 claimed, which is calculated at the rate of £191,650 a year, but only to such part of it for the same period as is appropriate to rent at the rate of £39,150 a year. Of the second sum, one of £47,912·50 claimed as being due on 25th March 1973, they are entitled to such part of it as corresponds to a sum calculated at the rate of £39,150 a year for the period from 25th March 1973 to the end of 28th April 1973, together with a further sum for the remainder of the quarter calculated at the rate of £191,650 a year. They are also entitled to the whole of the third sum, £47,912·50, for the quarter beginning on 24th June 1973. I shall leave to counsel or those instructing them the pleasure of working out these figures: no doubt they will be able to agree them. I will accordingly order judgment to be entered for the landlords for the sum so agreed, or, in default, as may be determined by me on the case being mentioned to me for that purpose.

That disposes of the claim. The counterclaim seeks—

'a determination by the Court as to the amount of the rent which is payable by the [tenants] ... by virtue of the provisions of the said Orders.'

In respect of the first period, while the 1972 order was in force, the amount of rent payable by the tenants consists of the whole of the first and second sums for that period as determined in accordance with the order on the claim that I have just made. Apart from that, my jurisdiction to make the order sought is not very clear. Article 13(1)(a)(ii) of the 1973 order confers jurisdiction on the court on an application by the landlord or tenant of premises—

'to determine any question arising under this order ... as to the amount of rent which is payable under any tenancy of those premises by virtue of this order ...';

and doubtless the prayer in the counterclaim followed the language of this provision. As I have decided that the 1973 order does not apply to the tenancy, and that even if it did it would not restrict the rent, it is difficult to see what rent is payable under the tenancy 'by virtue of this order': the rent is payable by virtue of the terms of the tenancy, and the order has nothing to do with it, any more than it would have if the tenancy were outside the order because it fell within the express exclusion of a building lease or agricultural tenancy. It may be that a determination that the order does not apply to the tenancy could be made under art 13(1)(a)(i), subject, of course, to art 13(3); but I shall leave the question of what further order, if any, I can properly make on the counterclaim until after I have heard counsel on the point.

Determination (i) that by virtue of 1972 order rent payable in respect of period from 22nd January 1973 to 28th April 1973 at the rate of £39,150 a year; (ii) that provisions of 1973 order do not apply to tenancy.

Solicitors: *Allen & Overy* (for the landlords); *Clifford-Turner & Co* (for the tenants).

R W Farrin Esq Barrister.

Way v Underdown (Inspector of Taxes) (No 2)

CHANCERY DIVISION
PENNYCUICK V-C
25th MARCH 1974

Income tax – Persons chargeable – Profits and interest of money – Person entitled to income chargeable – Commissions on insurance premiums – Taxpayer agent for insurers – Taxpayer entitled to deduct amount of commission from premium paid by insured – Taxpayer reimbursing insured amount of commission – Insured limited company – Taxpayer director of company – Cheque for premium less commission drawn on behalf of company and paid direct to insurers – Agent not receiving commission – Whether agent 'entitled' to commission – Income Tax Act 1952, s 148.

At all material times the taxpayer was an agent of an insurance company, N Ltd. N Ltd paid its agents commission in respect of insurance policies effected by them on behalf of N Ltd. The normal practice was for the insured to pay the full amount of the premium to the agent who had effected the policy. The agent then deducted his commission from that sum and paid the balance to N Ltd. The taxpayer effected policies of insurance with N Ltd on behalf of M and on behalf of J Ltd, of which he was a director. Under a 'friendly agreement' between the taxpayer and M, the taxpayer handed over to M all the commissions that he had retained against N Ltd. In respect of policies taken out on behalf of J Ltd, the premiums less commission were paid direct to N Ltd by cheques drawn on J Ltd. The taxpayer himself never received any commission in respect of those policies. The taxpayer was assessed to tax under Sch D on the commissions in respect of the policies effected on behalf of M and J Ltd by virtue of s 148ᵃ of the Income Tax Act 1952 on the ground that he had 'received' or was 'entitled' to those commissions.

Held – (1) Since there was no contractual obligation on the part of the taxpayer to pay over to M the commissions on M's policies, it followed that the taxpayer was 'entitled' to the commissions. Even if he was under a contractual obligation to M, the taxpayer was liable to tax in respect of the commissions since they were income which he had in fact 'received', within s 148 (see p 600 *e* to *h*, post).

(2) Since the taxpayer had only acted as a channel through which cheques of J Ltd for the premiums less commission passed directly to N Ltd, it was impossible to say that the taxpayer had 'received' commissions from J Ltd or N Ltd; nor was it possible to say he was ever 'entitled' to the commissions, for the course of dealing was for the premium to be paid direct to N Ltd less an amount equal to the commission to which he would have been entitled in the ordinary course; in those circumstances he had not become entitled to the commissions and disposed of them, but had foregone them. Accordingly, the taxpayer was not liable to tax on the commissions in respect of the policies taken out on behalf of J Ltd (see p 601 *a* to *f*, post).

Notes

For the persons chargeable to tax under Sch D, see 20 Halsbury's Laws (3rd Edn) 101, 102, para 182.

For the Income Tax Act 1952, s 148, see 31 Halsbury's Statutes (2nd Edn) 145.

For 1970-71 and subsequent years of assessment s 148 of the 1952 Act has been replaced by s 114(1) of the Income and Corporation Taxes Act 1970.

---

a Section 148 is set out at p 600 *c*, post

Cases referred to in judgment

Pierson v Belcher (1959) 38 Tax Cas 387, 38 ATC 258, [1959] TR 165, 52 R & IT 375, 28(1) Digest (Reissue) 562, 2059.

Regal (Hastings) Ltd v Gulliver [1942] 1 All ER 378, [1967] 2 AC 134, HL, 9 Digest (Repl) 523, 3447.

Royal Choral Society v Inland Revenue Comrs [1943] 2 All ER 101, 25 Tax Cas 263, 112 LJKB 648, 169 LT 100, CA, 28(1) Digest (Reissue) 478, 1726.

Cases also cited

Brocklesby v Merricks (Inspector of Taxes) (1934) 18 Tax Cas 576, CA.

Cole v Inland Revenue Comrs (1933) 18 Tax Cas 387, CA.

Perkins' Executor v Inland Revenue Comrs (1928) 13 Tax Cas 851.

Ransom (Inspector of Taxes) v Higgs [1973] 2 All ER 657, [1973] 1 WLR 1180, [1973] STC 330, CA.

Case stated

At a meeting of the Commissioners for the General Purposes of Income Tax Acts for the Cheltenham division in the county of Gloucester held on 27th July 1966, the taxpayer, William Morris Way, appealed against, inter alia, assessments to income tax made on him under Sch D, Case VI, in respect of insurance commissions for the years 1959-60 to 1964-65. The commissioners dismissed the appeal on 21st February 1967. Immediately after the determination of the appeal, the taxpayer expressed his dissatisfaction therewith and asked for a case to be stated for the opinion of the High Court pursuant to s 64 of the Income Tax Act 1952. The case stated, so far as material, is set out in the judgment.

Marcus Jones for the taxpayer.
Patrick Medd QC and *D K Rattee* for the Crown.

PENNYCUICK V-C. I have before me an appeal by way of case stated from certain assessments to income tax made under Case VI of Sch D. The assessments appealed against are in a series of very small sums, the years of assessment being 1959-60 to 1964-65 inclusive. The appeal is from a decision of the General Commissioners for the Cheltenham Division given as long ago as 1967. I have been told very broadly the reason for the delay. It will be sufficient to say that responsibility for the delay cannot be attributed to either of the parties to this appeal, and I do not propose to go into it any further. It is sufficient to say that I now have this appeal by way of case stated before me. The case stated was ultimately signed on 13th February 1973, which was itself about six years after the date of the decision. Perhaps not unnaturally, by that time the detail had slipped from the memory of those who drew the case stated, and I am bound to say that it is an unsatisfactory document. If the case stated had been drawn within a reasonable time after the decision, this difficulty would have been avoided.

Summarily, the taxpayer acted in certain family matters during the years under assessment as agent for the Norwich Union Insurance Co. He effected policies on behalf of a Mr Marshall and, as I understand it, considerably more importantly, on behalf of a company known as John Walker (Cheltenham) Ltd, of which he was a director. The assessments were on certain sums paid, or claimed by the inspector of taxes to have been paid, by way of commission on the effecting of those policies.

I will read the case stated without comment in the first place.

'1. At a meeting of the said Commissioners held on the 27th July, 1966 at ... Cheltenham William Morris Way (hereinafter called "the [taxpayer]") appealed against, inter alia, the following assessments to Income Tax made upon him under Case VI of Schedule D: [Then, for the years 1959-60 to 1964-65, on 'Insurance and other Commissions', there is an estimated figure of £200 for each year.]

'2.   The question for our decision was whether or not the [taxpayer] had beneficial title to the said commissions, allegedly allowed to him by the Norwich Union Insurance Company. The hearing was adjourned in view of the paucity of information and precepts issued by the Commissioners. It was resumed at ...Cheltenham on the 8th February 1967 when the [taxpayer] had given no information in reply to the precepts. We decided to hear the Appeal and that Hearing also concerned Schedule "E" Tax against the same [taxpayer]. The Hearing was adjourned to 13th February 1967 at the same venue and a reserved written decision was communicated to the parties at a Meeting of the Commissioners held on the 21st February 1967 ... The Case here stated relates solely to Schedule "D" Tax and we have stated a separate Case in respect of Schedule "E" Tax.   [I interpose to say that the taxpayer's appeal against the Sch E assessments has been abandoned.]

'3.   Evidence was given before us by the [taxpayer], Mr. Marshall, Mr. Jenkins, an employee of the Norwich Union Insurance Company Limited and Mr. Guest, a Senior Inspector of Taxes.

'4.   The following facts were proved or admitted: (i) At all relevant dates the [taxpayer] was an agent of the Norwich Union Insurance Company Limited and a director of John Walker (Cheltenham) Ltd, Fruit Merchants (ii) The [taxpayer] had received payments from a Mr. Marshall in respect of certain policies effected with the Norwich Union insurance Company (iii) The [taxpayer] was also entitled to commissions in respect of certain policies of insurance on John Walker (Cheltenham) Ltd (iv) The amount of commission payable to the [taxpayer] by the Insurance Company in respect of the relevant premiums, namely in respect of Mr. Marshall's policies and policies on John Walker (Cheltenham) Ltd was as follows: 1959/60 £70; 1960/61 £120; 1961/62 £57; 1962/63 NIL; 1963/64 £109; 1964/65 £65.

'5.   Evidence was given by Mr. Marshall that: (i) He had taken out Policies of Assurance through the agency of the [taxpayer] with the Insurance Company and that it had been a mutual arrangement between them that the [taxpayer] would allow him the amount of the [taxpayer's] commission. (ii) the premium payments had been made gross to the [taxpayer] and that he had subsequently received back from the [taxpayer] cash to the value of the [taxpayer's] commission. He had neither told his Accountant he was getting the cash nor disclosed it in his own Income Tax returns. There were no receipts for the cash as it was only a friendly agreement.

'6.   Evidence was given by Mr. Jenkins that: (i) He was [an] employee of the Norwich Union Insurance Company working in its Fire Department (ii) It was his practice to collect premiums from [the taxpayer]. As far as he could remember they were received net after deduction of commission. (iii) The Life Assurance business was dealt with by a separate Company in the same group but the procedure as to commissions was identical. He personally had nothing to do with the Life business. (iv) The premiums were received by cheque, but he could not say whether it was a cheque drawn on the [taxpayer's] own account or not. (v) The Agent issued a receipt for the whole amount to the Policy Holder but accounted to the Insurance Company after deducting his own commission. No receipt was issued since the coming into force of the Cheques Act [1957], but the cheque was acknowledged by the Company. (vi) The Policy holder was taken as paying the gross premium and the Agent as having received the commission. The Company made a return of such commissions to the Revenue every five years. J. Walker (Cheltenham) Limited was not an agent of the Norwich Union Insurance Company Ltd.

'7. Evidence was given by the [taxpayer] that: (i) He had an insurance agency with the Norwich Union Insurance Company only in respect of business for his Companies and his family (ii) The relevant premiums were paid by cheque drawn on J. Walker (Cheltenham) Ltd, less commission. He did not act as agent for his own personal insurances, though these were effected with the same company. In effect tax had been borne on the commissions as they had been included in the Cheltenham Company's return. So far as he could remember he had never received any commission.

'8. The following authorities were cited to us: *Pierson v. Belcher*[1]; *Regal (Hastings) v. Gulliver*[2].

'9. It was contended on behalf of the [taxpayer] (i) that the Revenue had made no discovery (ii) that J. Walker (Cheltenham) Ltd was entitled to the commissions in respect of the Company because of the fiduciary relationship existing between the [taxpayer] and the Company (iii) the Commission in respect of the Company had never been received by the [taxpayer]: the commissions being credited against the premiums payable by J. Walker (Cheltenham) Ltd and were reflected in its taxable profits and net payments being made to the Insurance Company concerned (iv) that the commission in respect of Mr Marshall's premiums had been repaid to Mr. Marshall and that it belonged to Mr. Marshall not the [taxpayer] (v) that he stood in a fiduciary capacity to Mr. W. C. Marshall (vi) that no records were available because of a fire in the office of the Accountants for John Walker (Cheltenham) Ltd. This point was not brought forward when we heard the [taxpayer] as to precepts. No evidence given before us enabled us to find as a fact that there was such a fire. The [taxpayer] refused to call the Accountants to testify as to the fire and we were accordingly unable to take this point into account in out findings (vii) that the [taxpayer] was not liable to Tax on the Commission and that the appeal be allowed.

'10. It was contended by [the Crown]: (i) that the evidence was that the [taxpayer] was credited with the commissions and the Insurance Company charged the tariff rate. (ii) that whether or not the [taxpayer] was in a fiduciary capacity was irrelevant. (iii) that the [taxpayer] had failed to show that the assessments were excessive or incorrect. (iv) that the [taxpayer] was accordingly assessable under Schedule D in respect of the commissions. (v) that the appeal be dismissed.

'11. We, the Commissioners, who heard the appeal gave our decision in writing on 21st February, 1967 as follows: "As to Schedule 'D' Tax the Commissioners heard evidence that these were on Insurance Premiums received by the [taxpayer] and the amount of those premiums is common ground. It was submitted to them that the [taxpayer] allowed his own commission on certain Insurances to the Insured and heard the evidence of the [taxpayer] and the Insured, Mr. William Cyril Marshall. On that evidence they are satisfied that there was a receipt of the commission by the [taxpayer] who subsequently repaid the money in cash to Mr. Marshall. The [taxpayer] accordingly is liable to Schedule 'D' Tax on such commission. The Commissioners therefore reduce the assessments and determine them in the agreed amounts as follows: [There follow amounts corresponding exactly to those which I have read in para 4 (iv).] We add to that decision that we found as fact that there was a discovery. [I mention in parenthesis that that point has not been pursued.]"

'12. Immediately after our decision the [taxpayer] expressed dissatisfaction therewith and asked for a case to be stated under Section 64 of the Income Tax Act 1952.

---

1   (1959) 38 Tax Cas 387
2   [1942] 1 All ER 378, [1967] 2 AC 134

'13. The point of law for the opinion of the High Court is whether on the facts found by us, there was evidence on which we could properly arrive at our decision and whether our decision was correct in law: specifically whether the [taxpayer] had beneficial title to the commissions receivable by him during the material years of assessment.'

Notice of an additional contention was given on behalf of the Crown; namely—

'that the [taxpayer] was properly assessed to tax in respect of the commissions relating to the policies of insurance effected for John Walker (Cheltenham) Ltd. because he was the person "entitled" to those commissions, and, therefore, the tax was properly charged on him in accordance with the provisions of Section 148, Income Tax Act, 1952.'

The case stated is rather an unhappy document. Not unnaturally, after six years the memory of the commissioners would not be very clear. Moreover, in paras 5, 6 and 7 they set out evidence given by Mr Marshall, Mr Jenkins and the [taxpayer] respectively without saying whether or not they accepted that evidence and, if they did not accept it, to what extent they did not accept it. Then, in their decision, they deal with the insurances on behalf of Mr Marshall but omit altogether to mention the insurances on behalf of John Walker (Cheltenham) Ltd.

It would not be profitable to enter into a detailed analysis of the case stated. However, I will mention that I was referred to the judgment of Lord Greene MR in *Royal Choral Society v Inland Revenue Comrs*[1] in which Lord Greene MR, in a well-known passage, said:

'The next matter relates to the evidence given before them by Sir George Dyson. In dealing with that evidence, they have adopted a form which I have always thought, and on occasions have said, is not a desirable form to use in these cases. They say: "Sir George Dyson gave evidence before us and stated (*inter alia*)"; and then they set out what his evidence was. To my mind it is quite impossible to interpret that as meaning that, although Sir George Dyson said that, they did not believe him. The only significance and interpretation that can be given to that paragraph is that they accepted that evidence as evidence of fact; otherwise the paragraph is meaningless, if not misleading.'

Counsel for the Crown very fairly and properly accepted that except where the commissioners themselves qualify their summary of the evidence I should treat the evidence as being accepted. The important qualification is the matter referred to in para 9(vi) of the case; namely, the alleged fire in the offices of the accountants of John Walker (Cheltenham) Ltd. However, I need not pursue that because the commissioners themselves refused to take that point into account in their findings; in other words, they did not accept that evidence.

It seems to me that quite different considerations apply to the commission in respect of Mr Marshall's insurances on the one hand and the commission in respect of John Walker (Cheltenham) Ltd's insurances on the other hand. I will do my best to state how, on the facts as found in the case stated, the legal position seems to me to stand in respect of Mr Marshall's insurances and John Walker (Cheltenham) Ltd's insurances respectively. It will be convenient to mention first, by way of preface, what I think is the normal procedure where an insurance agent is employed by an insurance company to obtain business on commission and that agent finds clients willing to take out insurance policies with the insurance company. There is, of course, no finding of fact on this, but I do not think this general statement will be in dispute. What happens is that the agent finds a client and, the terms of the policy having been negotiated, the

---

1 [1943] 2 All ER 101 at 103, 25 Tax Cas 263 at 271

client pays the premium— that is, the whole premium—to the agent. The agent then
pays over the equivalent of the premium to the insurer subject, however, to a deduction from the amount of the premium of the amount of his own commission. The
agent does not normally receive any commission from the client, although I suppose
that, in a sense, he is the agent of the client in negotiating the policy. In the normal
case there is no doubt that the agent is entitled to commission and that he in fact
receives commission from the insurer.

The significance of those words, 'receive' and 'entitled', is to be found in s 148 of
the Income Tax Act 1952, which is among the 'Miscellaneous Provisions as to Schedule
D' and contains this provision:

> 'Persons chargeable. 148. Tax under Schedule D shall be charged on and paid
> by the persons receiving or entitled to the income in respect of which tax under
> that Schedule is in this Act directed to be charged.'

I come now more particularly to the facts of Mr Marshall's insurances. In this
case it appears that what I have described as the ordinary procedure was followed;
that is to say, when the terms of the policy had been arranged, Mr Marshall paid the
amount of the premium in full to the taxpayer and the taxpayer then paid to the
Norwich Union a sum equivalent to the amount of the premium less the amount of
his own commission. That amount he retained as against the Norwich Union, but
instead of keeping it for his own benefit he handed it over to Mr Marshall. If there
had been a binding arrangement between Mr Marshall and the taxpayer that the
transaction should take that course, certainly the taxpayer would have been under
at least a contractual obligation to Mr Marshall to pay over to him the equivalent
of the commission. It may be that he would have been in a fiduciary capacity,
although I am not clear, on the facts, what would have been the subject-matter of
the trust. However, on Mr Marshall's own evidence that was not the position.
What Mr Marshall said was: 'There were no receipts for the cash as it was only a
friendly agreement.' Those words 'as it was only a friendly agreement', seem to
me to be incompatible with the existence of a legally binding obligation, and I think
I must proceed here on the footing that the evidence given by Mr Marshall and
accepted by the commissioners did not establish any legal obligation on the part of
the taxpayer to pay over the amount of his commission to Mr Marshall. Counsel
for the taxpayer contended with force that the words 'as it was only a friendly agreement' form part of the same sentence as the words 'There were no receipts for the
cash' and should be discounted as being no more than an explanation as to why there
were no written receipts. I think, however, that that gives insufficient force to those
words, 'as it was only a friendly agreement', and I am not inclined to treat this as
being a contractually binding obligation. I would add that, in any event, I am not
at all clear why, if indeed the taxpayer received his commission from the Norwich
Union and then proceeded to pay it over to Mr Marshall under a binding obligation,
this transaction should not come within s 148 on the ground that this was income
which the taxpayer had received. On that basis, no doubt, he would have been
entitled to some form of recoupment from Mr Marshall; but that is neither here
nor there.

The position as regards John Walker (Cheltenham) Ltd's policies seems to me to
be entirely different. The evidence with regard to those policies was: 'The relevant
premiums were paid by cheque drawn on John Walker (Cheltenham) Limited, less
commission'. That is to say, by arrangement between himself and the company
(of which, it will be remembered, he was a director) the taxpayer arranged the
policies with the Norwich Union but then, instead of following what would have
been the normal procedure—that is, of receiving the total amount of the premiums
himself from John Walker (Cheltenham) Ltd and then paying over the amount of
the premiums less his commission to the Norwich Union—he adopted quite a

different procedure; that is, he acted merely as a channel through which John Walker (Cheltenham) Ltd's own cheques passed directly to the Norwich Union, the amount of the cheques being for the premium less commission.

That being the transaction, it seems to me impossible to say that the taxpayer in any sense received this commission. The simple fact is that he did not receive it: he received nothing, either from John Walker (Cheltenham) Ltd or from the Norwich Union. Nothing ever went into his own pocket. Nor is it possible, it seems to me, to say that he was ever entitled to this commission.

Looking at the matter as between himself and the Norwich Union, in the ordinary course he would have been entitled to receive a commission from the Norwich Union by way of hold-back or deduction of the commission from the premium which he had received from John Walker (Cheltenham) Ltd. That was the method, and the only method, by which, as between himself and the Norwich Union, he was entitled to receive a commission. In this particular case, however, the course of dealing was for the premium to be paid direct to the Norwich Union less an amount equal to the commission to which he would have been entitled in the ordinary course, thus preventing the asset to which he would have had recourse for payment of his commission from coming into existence at all. On these facts the proper view, I think, is not that he became entitled to commission and disposed of it but that he forewent it.

Looking at the matter as between himself and John Walker (Cheltenham) Ltd, there is, I think, no conceivable ground on which he could have claimed to be entitled to commission against John Walker (Cheltenham) Ltd. It would not be John Walker (Cheltenham) Ltd to which he would look for commission in the ordinary course; and in the particular circumstances, so far from being entitled to look to John Walker (Cheltenham) Ltd for commission, his course of dealing with it was totally inconsistent with such being the case.

It seems to me that one could only treat the taxpayer here as either having received or having been entitled to commission by setting up some entirely imaginary framework under which the Norwich Union must be treated as having paid him commission in a way quite different from that in which commission was in fact, according to the practice between them, paid and he in turn must be treated as having paid that commission to John Walker (Cheltenham) Ltd. I do not think there is any ground on which one would be justified in setting up that imaginary framework.

I conclude, then, that as regards the commission on John Walker (Cheltenham) Ltd's policies this appeal must succeed, and that will involve a scaling down of the amount of commission to be brought into charge for each of the years by excluding the amounts of commission notionally received in respect of John Walker (Cheltenham) Ltd's policies and confining the commission to the amount actually received in respect of Mr Marshall's policies.

Appeal allowed in part. Case to be remitted to commissioners for determination of amount to be assessed in default of agreement.

Solicitors: *Pritchard, Englefield & Tobin; Solicitor of Inland Revenue.*

Rengan Krishnan Esq Barrister.

George Wimpey & Co Ltd v Inland Revenue Commissioners

CHANCERY DIVISION　　　　　　　Affirmed CA [1975] 2 All ER 45
BRIGHTMAN J
14th, 15th MARCH, 5th APRIL 1974

Stamp duty – Conveyance on sale – Instrument whereby property or interest in property on sale thereof vested in purchaser – Option to purchase land – Agreement in writing whereby for a consideration option granted to purchase land – Whether option 'property' or an 'interest in property' – Whether agreement 'conveyance on sale' – Stamp Act 1891, s 54.

M was the beneficial owner of certain land. By an agreement dated 12th June 1972 M granted the taxpayer company an option to purchase the land for a consideration in the sum of £15,000. The Inland Revenue Commissioners held that the agreement attracted ad valorem stamp duty on the amount of the consideration paid for the option under s 1 of, and Sch 1[a] to, the Stamp Act 1891 as an instrument of conveyance on sale. The taxpayer company appealed.

Held – An option to purchase land was 'property' or an 'interest in property' within s 54(1)[b] of the 1891 Act; accordingly an instrument which created an option to purchase land was an instrument whereby property or an interest in property, on the sale thereof, was vested in the purchaser within s 54(1). It followed that the agreement granting an option to the taxpayer company to purchase land was a 'conveyance on sale' and was liable to ad valorem duty. The appeal would therefore be dismissed (see p 608 *a* and p 610 *e* and *f*, post).

London and South Western Railway Co v Gomm (1881) 20 Ch D 562 and *Re Button's Lease* [1963] 3 All ER 708 applied.

Muller & Co's Margarine Ltd v Inland Revenue Comrs [1900] 1 QB 310 explained.

Notes

For the meaning of conveyance on sale, see 33 Halsbury's Laws (3rd Edn) 307, 308, para 538, and for cases on the subject, see 39 Digest (Repl) 321-323, 654-673.

For the Stamp Act 1891, ss 1, 54, Sch 1, see 32 Halsbury's Statutes (3rd Edn) 136, 148, 170.

Cases referred to in judgment

Button's Lease, Re, Inman v Button [1963] 3 All ER 708, [1964] Ch 263, [1963] 3 WLR 903, 31(1) Digest (Reissue) 162, 1415.

Cory (Wm) & Son Ltd v Inland Revenue Comrs [1965] 1 All ER 917, [1966] AC 1088, [1964] 2 WLR 924, 44 ATC 61, [1965] TR 77, [1965] 1 Lloyd's Rep 313, HL, Digest (Cont Vol B) 99, 2718a.

Danubian Sugar Factories Ltd v Inland Revenue Comrs [1901] 1 KB 245, 70 LJQB 211, 84 LT 101, 65 JP 212, CA, 39 Digest (Repl) 323, 673.

Griffith v Pelton [1957] 3 All ER 75, [1958] Ch 205, [1957] 3 WLR 522, CA, 31(1) Digest (Reissue) 168, 1447.

Inland Revenue Comrs v Muller & Co's Margarine Ltd [1901] AC 217, [1900-3] All ER Rep 413, 70 LJKB 677, 84 LT 729, HL; *affg sub nom Muller & Co's Margarine Ltd v Inland Revenue Comrs* [1900] 1 QB 310, 69 LJQB 291, 81 LT 667, CA, 39 Digest (Repl) 321, 660.

---

a　Schedule 1, so far as material, is set out at p 605 *c*, post
b　Section 54 is set out at p 605 *d*, post

Limmer Asphalte Paving Co Ltd v Inland Revenue Comrs (1872) LR 7 Exch 211, 41 LJ Ex 106, 26 LT 633, 39 Digest (Repl) 301, 470.

London and South Western Railway Co v Gomm (1881) 20 Ch D 562, 51 LJ Ch 530, 46 LT 449, CA, 37 Digest (Repl) 81, 203.

Mersey Docks and Harbour Board v Inland Revenue Comrs [1897] 1 QB 786, 66 LJQB 480, 76 LT 596, DC; affd [1897] 2 QB 316, 66 LJQB 697, 77 LT 120, CA, 39 Digest (Repl) 331, 712.

Muller & Co's Margarine Ltd v Inland Revenue Comrs. See *Inland Revenue Comrs v Muller & Co's Margarine Ltd,* supra.

Stromdale and Ball Ltd v Burden [1952] 1 All ER 59, [1952] Ch 223, 31(1) Digest (Reissue) 168, 1446.

Wright v Dean [1948] 2 All ER 415, [1948] Ch 686, [1948] LJR 1571, 31(1) Digest (Reissue) 168, 1449.

Cases also cited

Chesterfield Brewery Co v Inland Revenue Comrs [1899] 2 QB 7.

English, Scottish and Australian Bank Ltd v Inland Revenue Comrs [1932] AC 238, [1931] All ER Rep 212, HL.

Faber (Oscar) v Inland Revenue Comrs [1936] 1 All ER 617.

Great Northern Railway Co v Inland Revenue Comrs [1901] 1 KB 416, CA.

Inland Revenue Comrs v G Angus & Co, Inland Revenue Comrs v J Lewis and Sons (1889) 23 QBD 579.

Littlewoods Mail Order Stores Ltd v Inland Revenue Comrs [1961] 3 All ER 258, [1961] Ch 597, CA; affd sub nom *Inland Revenue Comrs v Littlewoods Mail Order Stores Ltd* [1962] 2 All ER 279, [1963] AC 135, HL.

Mountford v Scott [1974] 1 All ER 248, [1973] 3 WLR 884.

Oughtred v Inland Revenue Comrs [1959] 3 All ER 623, [1960] AC 206, 38 ATC 317, HL.

Potter v Inland Revenue Comrs (1854) 10 Exch 147.

Smelting Co of Australia Ltd v Inland Revenue Comrs [1897] 1 QB 175, CA.

United Dominions Trust (Commercial) Ltd v Eagle Aircraft Services Ltd, United Dominions Trust (Commercial) Ltd v Eagle Aviation Ltd [1968] 1 All ER 104, [1968] 1 WLR 74, CA.

West London Syndicate Ltd, The v Inland Revenue Comrs [1898] 1 QB 226.

Case stated

An agreement dated 12th June 1972 was made between Jeffrey Morgan of the one part and George Wimpey & Co Ltd ('Wimpeys') of the other part, whereby, in consideration of the sum of £15,000, Mr Morgan, as the beneficial owner of certain land at Sully in the county of Glamorgan, granted to Wimpeys an option to purchase that land. The agreement was presented for adjudication under s 12 of the Stamp Act 1891. On 22nd July 1973 the commissioners held that the agreement was chargeable to stamp duty under s 60 of the 1891 Act as an instrument securing a right not before in existence on a sale thereof. For the purpose of appealing against the assessment under s 13 of the 1891 Act Wimpeys required the commissioners to state a case for the opinion of the High Court. On 30th August the commissioners gave notice that at the hearing of the appeal they would contend in the alternative that the agreement was liable to duty under s 54 of the 1891 Act as an instrument whereby an estate or interest in property, on the sale thereof, was transferred to, or vested in, a purchaser. On 10th December the commissioners signed the case stated. Paragraphs 1 and 2 of the case described the agreement and recited that it had been presented for adjudication. Paragraphs 3-7 were in the following terms:

'3. The Commissioners were of the opinion that the Agreement was an instrument securing a right not before in existence upon a sale thereof, within Section 60 of the Stamp Act 1891, and is therefore to be charged with the same duty as an actual grant or conveyance and is for the purpose of that Act to be deemed an instrument of conveyance on sale.

'4. The Commissioners accordingly assessed the duty under the provisions of
the said Section 60 by reference to Section 1 of the Stamp Act 1891 and the head
of charge "Conveyance or transfer on Sale" in the First Schedule to that Act as
follows:

Ad valorem Conveyance on Sale duty at the rate of 50p for every £50
on the amount or value of the consideration for the option, namely,
£15,000   £150

'5. [Wimpeys] contended that the Agreement did not constitute a transaction
of sale and did not, in any event, require to be completed by grant or
conveyance.

'6. [Wimpeys] being dissatisfied with the assessment made and having paid
the duty in accordance therewith appealed against the said assessment to the
High Court and for that purpose required the Commissioners to state and sign
a Case setting out the questions on which their opinion was required and the
assessment made by them and the Commissioners do sign this Case accordingly.

'7. The questions for the opinion of the Court are—(i) whether the Agreement
is liable to duty as assessed by the Commissioners; (ii) if not, to what duty (if
any) it is liable.'

Peter Rees QC and *A L Potez* for Wimpeys.
Christopher Slade QC and *Peter Gibson* for the commissioners.

Cur adv vult

5th April.   **BRIGHTMAN J** read the following judgment.   The question in this
case is whether an instrument creating an option to purchase attracts ad valorem
stamp duty on the amount of the consideration paid for the option.   I have been told
by counsel that there is no reported decision directly in point and that there is no
settled Revenue practice.

Mr Morgan is the owner of 30 acres of potential building land in Glamorgan.   On
12th June 1972 he entered into a written agreement with George Wimpey & Co Ltd,
which I shall call 'Wimpeys'.   In the agreement, Mr Morgan is called 'the intending
Vendor' and Wimpeys are called 'the intending Purchaser'.   Clause 1 of the agreement
reads as follows:

'IN consideration of the sum of [£15,000] paid by the intending Purchaser to
the intending Vendor (the receipt whereof the intending Vendor hereby acknowledges) the intending Purchaser shall have the option of purchasing the
property for an estate in fee simple in possession subject as hereinafter mentioned
but otherwise free from encumbrances on the terms and conditions set forth in
the Second Schedule hereto'.

The option is expressed to be for a period of five years, and is to be exercisable within
15 days after outline planning permission has been obtained.   The purchase price
for the property is to be at the rate of £10,000 an acre if the option is exercised during
the first three years, and £12,000 an acre if exercised during the last two years.

Clause 5, which is the only other clause of the agreement to which I need refer,
reads as follows:

'UPON the exercise of the said option the intending Purchaser shall pay to the
intending Vendor's Solicitors as Stakeholders by way of deposit the sum which
shall represent ten per cent of the balance purchase price payable as shall be
determined with reference to the preceding Clause hereof after taking into
account the consideration of [£15,000] already paid to the intending Vendor on
the execution thereof which in the event of the option being exercised shall be
deemed to form part of the purchase price payable'.

a The agreement was presented for adjudication under s 12 of the Stamp Act 1891. The commissioners were of the opinion that the agreement was chargeable with duty at £150, being ad valorem conveyance on sale duty at the rate of 1 per cent. Wimpeys were dissatisfied with the assessment, and required the commissioners to state and sign a case accordingly. The commissioners originally took the view that liability to ad valorem duty arose under s 60 of the 1891 Act. The case stated is drawn on that basis. The commissioners later informed Wimpeys that duty would be

b claimed in the alternative under s 54. It has not been argued before me that the commissioners are disentitled to shift their ground. Indeed, s 13(3) requires the court, if the instrument in question is in the opinion of the court chargeable with any duty, to assess the duty with which it is chargeable.

Schedule 1 to the 1891 Act sets out the heads of charge under which instruments become chargeable to stamp duties under s 1. One head of charge is, 'Conveyance or

c Transfer on sale—Of any property . . .' Underneath this heading in the schedule are inserted the words 'And see sections 54, 55, 56, 57, 58, 59, 60 and 61'. The sections to which it is relevant to look for present purposes are ss 54, 59(1) and 60. Section 54 enacts:

d   'For the purposes of this Act the expression "conveyance on sale" includes every instrument, and every decree or order of any court or of any commissioners, whereby any property, or any estate or interest in any property, upon the sale thereof is transferred to or vested in a purchaser, or any other person on his behalf or by his direction.'

Section 59(1) imposes duty on instruments which are not in the strict sense instruments of transfer or vesting, but mere contracts. There are two limbs to the sub-

e section. The first limb, as amended by the Revenue Act 1909, is, shortly stated, 'Any contract or agreement . . . for the sale of any equitable estate or interest in any property whatsoever . . .' The second limb is, 'any contract or agreement . . . for the sale of any estate or interest in any property except lands . . . or property locally situate out of the United Kingdom' etc. Before amendment, this

f subsection did not apply to a contract or agreement made abroad. Under each limb of the subsection the contract or agreement is to be charged with the same ad valorem duty, 'as if it were an actual conveyance on sale of the estate, interest, or property contracted or agreed to be sold.'

Section 60 is in the following terms:

g   'Where upon the sale of any annuity or other right not before in existence such annuity or other right is not created by actual grant or conveyance, but is only secured by bond, warrant of attorney, covenant, contract, or otherwise, the bond or other instrument, or some one of such instruments, if there be more than one, is to be charged with the same duty as an actual grant or conveyance, and is for the purposes of this Act to be deemed an instrument of conveyance on sale.'

h Although the commissioners relied on s 60 in the first instance, s 54 was the mainstay of the commissioners' argument before me, and I propose to deal with that section first. If a charge to duty does arise under s 54, it will be unnecessary to devote further consideration to s 60. No duty can arise in the present case under s 59 because an option to purchase land is not a contract for the sale of an equitable estate or

j interest in the land, nor indeed a contract for sale at all: *Wm Cory & Son Ltd v Inland Revenue Comrs*[1].

The requisites of s 54 are these. First, there must be an instrument or a decree or order of any court or of any commissioners. Secondly, the instrument, decree or

---

1 [1963] 3 All ER 708, [1964] Ch 263

order must be one which affects property or any estate or interest in any property.
Thirdly, there must be a sale of that property or estate or interest. Fourthly, it must
be on that sale that the property, estate or interest is transferred to or vested in a
purchaser or other person on his behalf or by his direction.

There is no dispute that the 1972 agreement is an instrument, and that therefore
the first requisite is satisfied. Wimpeys deny, however, that the instrument is one
whereby any property or estate or interest in any property, on the sale thereof, is
transferred to or vested in a purchaser or another. On this aspect of the case counsel
for Wimpeys submitted that the agreement is not in form or substance a sale. It is,
he said, a prelude to a possible sale, and not the sale itself. An option to purchase is
no more than an offer which, by virtue of the existence of consideration or a seal
or perhaps some other binding factor, is incapable of revocation at the will of the
offeror. It has been held, he submitted, that a contract for sale of an option to purchase property is not a contract for the sale of an equitable estate or interest in
property within s 59(1): see *Muller & Co's Margarine Limited v Inland Revenue Comrs*[1],
a case to which I shall have to return later. It must follow, submitted counsel, that
an instrument conferring an option is not an instrument whereby any property, or
any estate or interest in any property, is transferred to or vested in a purchaser within
the meaning of s 54.

I deal with one preliminary point about which there can, I think, be no dispute.
Although s 54 speaks of an instrument whereby property or an estate or interest in
property is transferred to or vested in a purchaser, the section applies as much to
an instrument which creates an interest in property de novo as to an instrument
which transfers an estate or interest previously created. This proposition was submitted to and clearly accepted by the Court of Exchequer in *Limmer Asphalte Paving Co
Ltd v Inland Revenue Comrs*[2] under s 70 of the Stamp Act 1870, which was the precursor
of s 54 of the 1891 Act. In *Mersey Docks and Harbour Board v Inland Revenue Comrs*[3] a
Divisional Court of the Queen's Bench Division considered that the grant de novo
of an annuity by the Mersey Docks and Harbour Board on the security of its rates
came within s 54 as well as s 60 of the Act. The brief judgments in the Court of
Appeal[4] do not specifically mention s 54, but there is no reason to suppose that they
disagreed with that view.

Counsel for the commissioners submitted that an option is property within the
meaning of s 54, and that the 1972 agreement vested that property in Wimpeys on
the sale thereof. Accordingly, it is said, the 1972 agreement is a conveyance on sale
within the meaning of s 54 and is liable to ad valorem duty on the £15,000 consideration money payable on the creation of that property. The crucial question, therefore,
is whether the option in the present case is property or an interest in property within
the meaning of s 54. If it is, I do not see that there is room for disputing that such
property or interest was created by the 1972 agreement and thereby vested in
Wimpeys, and that the option so acquired by Wimpeys was granted to them in
consideration of the sum of £15,000 and therefore sold to Wimpeys at that figure.

Leaving on one side for a moment the *Muller* case[1], there is a long line of authority
which establishes that an option to purchase land creates a contingent interest in
land. The starting point is *London and South Western Railway Co v Gomm*[5]. In that
case the railway company conveyed a piece of land near one of their stations to
Powell for £100. In the conveyance Powell covenanted for himself and his assigns
that if the company needed the land for its railway he would reconvey it for the same

---

1   [1900] 1 QB 310; *affd* [1901] AC 217, [1900-3] All ER Rep 413
2   (1872) LR 7 Exch 211
3   [1897] 1 QB 786
4   [1897] 2 QB 316
5   (1881) 20 Ch D 562

a sum. Powell sold to the defendant. In 1880 the company gave notice to the defendant to repurchase, and ultimately sued for specific performance. Among a number of defences it was argued, in effect, that if Powell's covenant did not create an interest in land it must be personal to Powell and could not bind the defendant. If, on the other hand, it did create an interest in land it was void for perpetuity. The latter argument prevailed. Jessel MR said[1]:

b   'The right to call for a conveyance of the land is an equitable interest or equit-able estate. In the ordinary case of a contract for purchase there is no doubt about this, and an option for repurchase is not different in its nature. A person exercising the option has to do two things, he has to give notice of his intention to purchase, and to pay the purchase-money; but as far as the man who is liable to convey is concerned, his estate or interest is taken away from him without

c   his consent, and the right to take it away being vested in another, the covenant giving the option must give that other an interest in the land. It appears to me therefore that this covenant plainly gives the company an interest in the land . . .'

Sir James Hannen and Lindley LJ agreed. There are similar statements in later cases:
d see *Wright v Dean*[2] where Wynn-Parry J said: 'The option confers [on its exercise] a right to call for a conveyance of the freehold, and, therefore, it creates an interest in land.' In *Griffith v Pelton*[3] Jenkins LJ, delivering the judgment of the court, said: ' . . . the option creates in favour of the grantee of the option a contingent interest in the land.'

In *Re Button's Lease*[4] the question arose whether an option in a lease to purchase
e the freehold was exercisable by the assignee of the original tenant. After referring to certain cases, Plowman J said[5]:

    ' . . . I accept those cases as establishing that an option to purchase does not of itself constitute a contract; but to my mind the relevant consideration is not whether an option to purchase constitutes a contract but whether it operates to create property—I use the word "property" in the widest sense—which in

f   principle is capable of assignment. To my mind there is no doubt that it does. *Griffith v. Pelton*[6] itself is a decision on that point, but there are many others. I notice that in *Stromdale & Ball, Ltd. v. Burden*[7], to which counsel for the defen-dant referred me in the course of his argument, DANCKWERTS, J., said[8]: "In the present case, for the purposes of s. 56(1) [i.e. s. 56(1) of the Law of Property Act, 1925] the 'land' is No. 40, Romford Road, and an option to purchase a lease-

g   hold interest in that land seems to me to create an interest in it and to be an agreement respecting it, and so to be within the precise words of the sub-section."'

Plowman J added[9]:

    'Apart from authority, one would have thought that prima facie the piece of
h   property created by an option to purchase was, like any other piece of property, assignable. It is inherent in the nature of a piece of property that the owner of it should be able to dispose of it.'

---

1 (1881) 20 Ch D at 581
2 [1948] 2 All ER 415 at 417, [1948] Ch 686 at 693
j 3 [1957] 3 All ER 75 at 83, [1958] Ch 205 at 225
4 [1963] 3 All ER 708, [1964] Ch 263
5 [1963] 3 All ER at 713, [1964] Ch at 271
6 [1957] 3 All ER 75, [1958] Ch 205
7 [1952] 1 All ER 59, [1952] Ch 223
8 [1952] 1 All ER at 65, [1952] Ch at 234
9 [1963] 3 All ER at 713, 714, [1964] Ch at 272

And later he said[1]:

'If I am right so far in thinking that an option is assignable unless there is some context to the contrary, the next question is whether there is anything in the lease which is before me to negative the right of the owner of this piece of property to dispose of it as he wishes.'

In the result, to deny an option to purchase land the status of 'property' or, if preferred, 'an interest in property' would seem to me to run counter to the clear current of authority. I must however deal with the *Muller* case[2], which appears to stand on its own. The essential facts are these. Muller manufactured margarine in a town in Germany. Newman, as trustee for Wigley, acquired from Muller an option to purchase the business for £80,000. Newman, as such trustee, sold his option to the General Purposes Syndicate (No 2) Ltd for £9,500. An agreement was then made in the year 1897 between Muller of the first part, Newman of the second part, Wigley of the third part, the syndicate of the fourth part and Muller & Co's Margarine Ltd of the fifth part. By that agreement Muller, by the direction of Newman, Wigley and the syndicate, agreed to sell and the Margarine Co agreed to purchase six items: first, the goodwill; secondly, certain land in Germany; thirdly, certain patents; fourthly, equipment; fifthly, pending contracts; and, sixthly, trade documents. The total consideration was £122,500, whereof £80,000 was to be paid to Muller, being the sum due on the exercise of his option, and £42,500 to the syndicate, thus yielding a profit to the syndicate of £33,000. The issue arose only in respect of the property first and fifthly described; that is to say, the goodwill and the pending contracts. The apportioned price for these items was £77,418. Ad valorem stamp duty was assessed on that amount at the then rate of 10s per cent. Duty was claimed on the agreement under s 59(1). The Divisional Court upheld the assessment, but their decision was reversed on appeal[3].

It was argued before the Court of Appeal[3] on behalf of the taxpayer that the agreement was not made in England—an argument available before the 1909 amendment which has no relevance to the present case. That submission failed. It was then argued for the taxpayer that the contract was not for the sale of an equitable interest in property; Muller had agreed to sell only the legal interest; the syndicate (I quote from the argument)[4]—

'did not sell any interest in property at all, whether equitable or otherwise. All that the intermediaries had to sell was an option. What they had acquired from the vendor Muller was nothing more than a right to dictate to him to whom he should sell.'

After submitting that the contract was made in England, it was argued for the Crown that the contract was for the sale of an equitable interest; the syndicate, it was submitted, were the real owners in equity of the whole business and they were the real vendors. Alternatively, there was a sale of an equitable interest to the extent of the £42,500 which the syndicate received as their share.

The first judgment was delivered by A L Smith LJ. Having decided that the agreement was made in England, he continued as follows[5]:

'The next question is, whether it was an agreement for the sale of an "equitable estate or interest" in property. On that point Mr. Danckwerts' contention [Mr Danckwerts was for the Crown] was that the syndicate were the vendors,

1 [1963] 3 All ER at 714, [1964] Ch at 273
2 [1901] AC 217, [1900-3] All ER Rep 413, HL; *affg* [1900] 1 QB 310, CA
3 [1900] 1 QB 310
4 [1900] 1 QB at 314
5 [1900] 1 QB at 318

and that the only interest in the property that they had to sell was an equitable one. I have already intimated, when dealing with the first question (although it was unnecessary for me then to decide the point), that in my opinion the real vendor was Muller, and not the syndicate. It seems to me perfectly plain from the recitals in this agreement that what the intermediate parties had acquired from the vendor was not any estate or interest in the property at all, but a mere option or right to purchase, and it was only that option or right to purchase which they transferred. The Crown's contention on this point, therefore, fails.'

He finally concluded that the goodwill etc were property situate out of England, with the result that no ad valorem duty was payable. Collins and Vaughan Williams LJJ concurred. In the course of his judgment, Collins LJ said[1]:

'Mr. Danckwerts contended that even if (contrary to his contention) Muller was to be regarded as the vendor of the whole of the legal interest to the company, still, as he did not get the whole of the purchase-money, the rights which the syndicate parted with as the consideration for the balance of the purchase-money must have been an agreement for the sale of an equitable interest to the extent of 42,000l. But with that contention I cannot agree. I do not think that an option to purchase at a particular price can be properly described as an equitable estate or interest in property.'

Vaughan Williams LJ did not deal with this particular aspect of the case. The matter ultimately went to the House of Lords[2], where the appeal was dismissed without comment on the particular passages I have quoted.

At first sight the observations of the Court of Appeal in the *Muller* case[3] might seem to be a formidable authority in favour of the contention of Wimpeys that an option to purchase land is not an interest in land, and that the creation of an option for value is outside s 54. But on closer analysis I do not think that that is the correct conclusion to be drawn. The only point argued in the *Muller* case[3] on this particular aspect was whether the agreement was a contract for the sale of an equitable interest in property within s 59(1). The case was considered and analysed by Collins LJ in the later case of *Danubian Sugar Factories Ltd v Inland Revenue Comr*[4], where he said:

'Two matters only were made the subject of discussion before, and considered by this Court in that case, namely, the matters mentioned in clause 1 and in clause 5 of the agreement; that is to say, the goodwill of the business, and the pending contracts, engagements, and orders in connection with the business. With reference to those we all thought that the sale was by Muller, though the intermediaries were made parties to the agreement, and that the sale was of the goodwill of the business, and not of an option to purchase it. As I have said, one of the intermediaries had acquired the option of purchasing the business, but the subject-matter which, by the terms of the agreement, the vendor, by the direction of the parties of the second and third part, and the parties of the fourth part agreed to sell, and the company to purchase, was the goodwill of the business. Whatever right the parties joining in the sale may have had, what they agreed to sell was the goodwill. There was no sale of an option to purchase. The question was raised whether the parties of the fourth part—i.e., the syndicate, who purported to join in selling, had what amounted to an equitable estate or interest, so as to let in the operation of the section. It is with reference to what was said on that subject that the judges in the Court below [i e the

1 [1900] 1 QB at 319, 320
2 [1901] AC 217, [1900-3] All ER Rep 413
3 [1900] 1 QB 310
4 [1901] 1 KB 245 at 251-253

Divisional Court which heard the *Danubian* case] seem to have fallen into a misconception. What the Court [i e the Court of Appeal in the *Muller* case[1]] was there considering was whether there was a sale of an equitable estate or interest. We came to the conclusion that, assuming the syndicate to be vendors of an option, what they sold being only an option to purchase property at a particular price, there was not a sale of an equitable estate or interest. That was all that we had to decide in that case. We did not decide that there was a sale of an option, but that, even if there were, it was not a sale of an equitable estate or interest within the section. This did not involve any decision of the question whether a sale of a person's interest under an option would not be a sale of "property." Having decided that there was no sale of an equitable estate or interest, we proceeded to consider the main question, namely, whether the sale of the goodwill of the business, and of the contracts incident thereto, though prima facie a sale of property, was taken out of the provisions of the first part of the section by reason of its being within the exception in respect of "property locally situate out of the United Kingdom." With regard to that question we thought that, though the goodwill of the business, and the contracts incident thereto, were clearly property, they came within the exception; because, as property annexed to the factory which was locally situated out of the United Kingdom, the goodwill itself and its incidents were locally situate out of the United Kingdom. So that really our decision involved the view that the goodwill and the contracts incidental thereto were property within the section, and that the agreement for sale of them would have been liable to the duty but for the fact that we came to the conclusion that they were within the exception.'

In the light of that explanation of the *Muller* case[1], and having regard also to the fact that *London and South Western Railway Co v Gomm*[2] was not mentioned either in the *Muller* case[1] or in the *Danubian* case[3], I think that I am bound to treat an instrument which, in consideration of money, creates an option to purchase land as an instrument whereby property, or an interest in property, on the sale thereof is vested in a purchaser. I accordingly hold that the 1972 agreement is liable to ad valorem duty under s 54. It is not necessary for me to consider the possible alternative liability under s 60.

Appeal dismissed Agreement liable to duty as assessed by commissioners.

Solicitors: *P J Ward* (for the taxpayer company); *Solicitor of Inland Revenue.*

Rengan Krishnan Esq Barrister.

---

1 [1900] 1 QB 310; affd [1901] AC 217, [1900-3] All ER Rep 413
2 (1881) 20 Ch D 562
3 [1901] 1 KB 245

Black-Clawson International Ltd v Papierwerke Waldhof-Aschaffenburg AG

COURT OF APPEAL, CIVIL DIVISION   Reversed HL [1975] 1 All ER 810
LORD DENNING MR, MEGAW AND SCARMAN LJJ
27th, 28th, 29th FEBRUARY, 19th MARCH 1974

Conflict of laws – Foreign judgment – Conclusiveness in English proceedings – Recognition of judgment as conclusive between the parties in proceedings founded on same cause of action – Reliance on judgment by way of defence – Foreign judgment dismissing action by plaintiff – Judgment based on limitation period and not on merits of claim – Plaintiff bringing proceedings in English courts founded on same cause of action – Whether defendant entitled to rely on foreign judgment by way of defence – Whether judgment to be recognised as conclusive between parties – Foreign Judgments (Reciprocal Enforcement) Act 1933, s 8(1).

In 1961 an English company entered into a contract to sell to a German company certain machines to be installed in the latter's factory in West Germany. It was agreed that the price should be paid by 20 bills of exchange drawn by the English company and accepted by the German company, and payable by a bank in London between 1963 and 1967. On 24th August 1972 the English company commenced proceedings against the German company, which had no assets or place of business in England, in the Provincial Court of Munich, claiming the amount due on two of the bills of exchange which had fallen due on 1st September 1966 but had been dishonoured. Realising however that the action might be barred under the German three year limitation period, the English company, on 29th August, obtained leave to issue a writ in the High Court claiming against the German company the amount due on the same two bills, and to serve notice of the writ out of the jurisdiction. In November 1972 the Munich court dismissed the English company's claim on the ground that it was time-barred. In August 1973 the English company served notice of their writ. On an application by the German company to set aside the English proceedings on the ground that, under s 8(1)[a] of the Foreign Judgments (Reciprocal Enforcement) Act 1933, the judgment of the Munich court was to be recognised as conclusive between the parties in the English proceedings, the English company contended (i) that s 8(1) applied only to foreign judgments in favour of a plaintiff and not to judgments which merely dismissed a plaintiff's claim, and (ii) that, alternatively, the Munich judgment was not to be recognised as conclusive under s 8(1), since it was not a judgment on the merits of their claim.

Held – On the true construction of s 8(1) of the 1933 Act a foreign judgment was conclusive in English proceedings founded on the same cause of action irrespective of the reasons on which the judgment was based. Furthermore, since s 8(1) provided that the foreign judgment might be 'relied on by way of defence', it was open to a defendant to rely on a foreign judgment dismissing the plaintiff's claim as conclusive in proceedings brought by the plaintiff in the English courts. It followed that, since the English company's claim was based on the same cause of action, i e the dishonoured bills, as the proceedings in the Munich court, the judgment of that court was to be recognised as conclusive and the German company had an unanswerable defence in law to the action. Accordingly the leave to serve the writ out of the

---

a Section 8(1) provides: 'Subject to the provisions of this section, a judgment to which Part I of this Act applies or would have applied if a sum of money had been payable thereunder, whether it can be registered or not, and whether, if it can be registered, it is registered or not, shall be recognised in any court in the United Kingdom as conclusive between the parties thereto in all proceedings founded on the same cause of action and may be relied on by way of defence or counterclaim in any such proceedings.'

jurisdiction should be set aside (see p 615 c and h, p 616 b to d, p 618 c to e and j to
p 619 d and p 623 f and j to p 624 a e and g, post).
  Harris v Quine (1869) LR 4 QB 653 distinguished.

Notes
For the conclusiveness of foreign judgments in English proceedings, see 7 Halsbury's
Laws (3rd Edn) 165, 166, para 296, and 15 ibid 214, para 401.
  For s 8 of the Foreign Judgments (Reciprocal Enforcement) Act 1933, see 6 Halsbury's
Statutes (3rd Edn) 372.

Cases referred to in judgments
Barclays Bank v Aschoffenburger Zellstoffwerke AG [1967] 1 Lloyd's Rep 387, CA.
Carl-Zeiss-Stiftung v Rayner and Keeler Ltd (No 2) [1966] 2 All ER 536, [1967] 1 AC 853,
  [1966] 3 WLR 125, HL; *rvsg* [1965] 1 All ER 300, [1965] Ch 525, [1965] 2 WLR 277,
  Digest (Cont Vol B) 249, 278b.
Fidelitas Shipping Co Ltd v V/O Exportchleb [1965] 2 All ER 4, [1966] 1 QB 630, [1965]
  2 WLR 1059, [1965] 1 Lloyd's Rep 223, CA, Digest (Cont Vol B) 248, 278a.
Harris v Quine (1869) LR 4 QB 653, 10 B & S 644, 38 LJQB 331, 20 LT 947, 17 WR 967,
  11 Digest (Repl) 554, 1601.
Huber v Steiner (1835) 2 Bing NC 202, 1 Hodg 206, 2 Scott 304, 132 ER 80, 6 Digest
  (Repl) 409, 2902.
Thoday v Thoday [1964] 1 All ER 341, [1964] P 181, [1964] 2 WLR 371, CA, Digest
  (Cont Vol B) 365, 4179a.
Tyne Improvement Comrs v Armement Anversois SA, The Brabo [1949] 1 All ER 294,
  [1949] AC 326, 82 Lloyd LR 251, [1949] LJR 435, HL; *affg* [1947] 2 All ER 363, [1948]
  P 33, 80 Lloyd LR 570, CA, 50 Digest (Repl) 364, 842.

Interlocutory appeal
By an order dated 29th August 1972 Master Elton gave the plaintiffs, Black-Clawson
International Ltd, leave to issue a writ against the defendants, Papierwerke Waldhof-
Aschaffenburg AG, and to serve notice of the writ on them at 8201 Raubling,
Redenfelden, or elsewhere in West Germany. Notice of the writ was served on the
defendants on 14th August 1973. By a summons dated 3rd September 1973 the
defendants applied for an order that Master Elton's order, the writ issued pursuant
to the order, the service of notice of the writ and all subsequent proceedings be set
aside. On 6th December Master Bickford-Smith in chambers ordered that the
defendants' application be dismissed and on 15th February 1974 Talbot J in chambers
dismissed an appeal by the defendants against that order. The defendants applied
to the Court of Appeal for leave to appeal against the order of Talbot J. The Court
of Appeal, having granted leave to appeal, immediately proceeded to hear the appeal.
The facts are set out in the judgment of Lord Denning MR.

Anthony Lincoln QC and *Stanley Brodie* for the defendants.
Conrad Dehn QC and *Peter Scott* for the plaintiffs.

                                                                    Cur adv vult
  19th March. The following judgments were read.

LORD DENNING MR. We are here concerned with a new point about the
recognition of foreign judgments. An English company brought an action against
a German company in the German courts, but that action failed. It was dismissed
by the German court. The English company now seek to bring another action for
the same cause in England. The question is whether it can do so. The German
company invoke the maxim which prevails in both systems of law: nemo debet
bis vexari pro eadem causa.
  The English company are Black-Clawson International Ltd. They are an English
subsidiary of an American parent company. The German company are Papierwerke
Waldhof-Aschaffenburg AG or their predecessor. In 1961 the English company agreed

to supply the German company with machines for a paper factory in Germany. In order to pay the price, the German company accepted 20 bills of exchange, each for £48,406 payable at Barclays Bank, London. They were clearly English bills governed by English Law. The 20 bills were so drawn that two bills matured every half year over five years. The English company supplied the machinery. The German company paid a number of the bills as they fell due. But the German company then complained that the machinery was defective and that there were delays in deliveries. They stopped payment of the bills. In 1965 the dispute was referred to arbitration in Zurich. Unfortunately that arbitration has taken an interminable time. It is not yet concluded in 1974, and may not be concluded for some years yet. Now the English company seek payment of the bills. They sue on two bills which fell due as long ago as 1st September 1966. At once, therefore, the question arises whether they are barred by lapse of time. And here is the crux of the case. In England, an action on a bill of exchange can be brought within six years of the time when it fell due. But in Germany it must be brought within three years. Furthermore, in England the law of limitation has been held to affect the *procedure* by which a claim is enforced, and not the *substance* of the obligation itself; and accordingly the time limit is that presented by lex fori: see *Huber v Steiner*[1]; whereas in Germany and most continental countries the law of limitation is held to go to the substance of the obligation, and accordingly the time limit is that prescribed by the proper law of the contract: see Cheshire's Private International Law[2].

After that introduction, I turn to the particular facts. On 1st September 1966 two bills of exchange accepted by the German company fell due for payment to the English company at Barclays Bank, London. Each was for £48,406. They were duly presented for payment, but they were dishonoured and thereupon were duly protested for non-payment. On 24th August 1972 the English company issued proceedings in Germany against the German company. They issued those proceedings in the Provincial Court of Munich, claiming £96,812 (the amount of the two bills) plus interest and costs. The German company resided in Germany and had their assets there. They did not reside in England. They had no assets here. They would probably not submit to jurisdiction of the English courts. So, naturally enough, the English company sought to get judgment in Germany. The English company realised, however, that those proceedings might be barred by the three-year limitation prevailing in Germany. In order to protect themselves, they took parallel proceedings in England. On 29th August 1972 (just within the six years) the English company applied for leave to issue a writ in the High Court in London, claiming against the German company, on the same two bills, £96,812 plus interest and costs. On the same day, 29th August 1972, the English company were granted leave to issue the writ and to serve notice of the writ out of the jurisdiction on the German company. On the same day, 29th August 1972, the English company issued the writ, but they did not at that time give notice of it to the German company. They had one year in which to do it. They took advantage of that year to do nothing in the English proceedings. But meanwhile they took active steps in the German proceedings so as to get judgment there, if they could.

On 30th November 1972 the Provincial Court of Munich gave their decision. They dismissed the claim of the English company on the bills. They did so on the ground that it was barred by the three-year limitation which prevailed in German law. We have before us the grounds of the decision translated into English. I am not at all confident that I have understood it rightly, but the reasoning would appear to be as follows. The bills were payable in London and the substantive obligations under them were to be determined according to English law. Now English law says that a period of limitation for bills is not part of the substantive law, but is only procedure.

---

1 (1835) 2 Bing NC 202
2 8th Edn (1970), p 665

It does not take away the right to payment, but only bars the remedy. Being a matter of procedure, it is governed by the lex fori. The German courts applied that English law. They held that the remedy in Germany was subject to the German period of limitation, which is three years. Accordingly, the Provincial Court of Munich dismissed the claim. The English company have appealed from that decision to the Bavarian Supreme Court. The English company argue that, according to German law, a period of limitation belongs to the substantive law and not to procedure. The German court should, therefore, apply the English law, including the six years limitation. We do not know the result of the appeal, but it is expected shortly.

Now I return to the English proceedings. As I said, the English company issued the writ in England on 29th August 1972. They had a year in which to serve notice of it on the German company. When the year was nearly up, on 24th August 1973, they did serve notice of it on the German company. The German company did not enter an appearance. They applied to set aside the English proceedings. They did so on the ground that the English company had already sued the German company in Germany on these very two bills, and that action had been dismissed. So the English company should not be allowed to sue on the bills in England. The master and the judge refused to set the English proceedings aside. They did so on the authority of *Harris v Quine*[1], which appeared to be directly in point.

Before us, however, the German company took a new point. They said that England and Germany entered into a convention on 14th July 1960 which provided for the reciprocal enforcement of judgments, and that, by reason of the Foreign Judgments (Reciprocal Enforcement) Act 1933, the judgment of the Munich court is conclusive of the cause of action on the bills. The material provisions are contained in s 8 of the 1933 Act. Section 8(1) deals with 'cause of action estoppel'. Under our English law, if one party brings an action against another for a particular cause and judgment is given on it—whether for him or against him—there is a strict rule of law that he cannot bring another action against the same party for the same cause: see *Thoday v Thoday*[2] and *Fidelitas Shipping Co v V/O Exportchleb*[3]. The effect of s 8(1), as I see it, is to make a judgment of a German court likewise binding on an English court in respect of the same cause of action. Take a judgment given by a superior court in Germany, which is final and conclusive in Germany as between the parties thereto. There may, or may not, be an appeal pending in Germany to a higher court there: see s 1(2)(3) of the 1933 Act. Nevertheless, it is a judgment which comes within the provisions of s 8(1), which says that the judgment—

> 'shall be recognised in any court in the United Kingdom as conclusive between the parties thereto in all proceedings founded on the same cause of action and may be relied on by way of defence or counterclaim in any such proceedings.'

Counsel for the English company submitted that that provision applies only to a judgment in favour of a plaintiff, and not to a judgment in favour of a defendant. This submission was effectively answered by counsel for the German company. He drew attention to the words: 'may be relied on by way of defence'. Those words are appropriate to meet this very case where the plaintiff has brought proceedings in this country founded on the same cause of action; the defendant may rely on the judgment as conclusive 'by way of defence'. I see no content for those words except to avail a defendant.

Counsel for the English company next submitted that s 8(1), in saying that the judgment was to be recognised as 'conclusive between the parties thereto' meant only that it was to be conclusive as to the matters adjudicated on, and not as to other matters. This submission, too, was effectively answered by counsel for the German

1   (1869) LR 4 QB 653
2   [1964] 1 All ER 341 at 352, [1964] P 181 at 197, per Diplock LJ
3   [1965] 2 All ER 4, [1966] 1 QB 630

company. He drew attention to the difference between s 8(1) and s 8(3). Section 8(1) says that the judgment is 'conclusive between the parties'. Section 8(3) says that it is 'conclusive of any matter of law or fact decided therein'. This difference is because the two subsections are dealing with different subjects. Section 8(1) deals with 'cause of action' estoppel. Section 8(3) deals with 'issue estoppel'. Under our English law, once an issue has been raised and distinctly determined between the parties there is a general rule that neither party can be allowed to fight that issue all over again: see the dictum of Lord Wilberforce in *Carl-Zeiss-Stiftung v Rayner and Keeler (No 2)*[1]. Section 8(3) preserves that rule in respect of issues raised and decided. It limits 'conclusive' to matters decided, whereas s 8(1) does not so limit it.

In my opinion, therefore, s 8(1) is to be given its natural meaning. The judgment of the Munich court is to be recognised by the English court 'as conclusive between the parties thereto in all proceedings founded on the same cause of action and may be relied on' by the German company by way of defence in the English proceedings. Now, the English action is undoubtedly founded on the same cause of action. It is brought on the self-same bills. The judgment of the German court is 'conclusive'. This means, I think, that the ultimate ruling is binding on the English courts. Test it by two examples.

(1) A bill of exchange in favour of the English company is accepted by the German company payable in Munich in 1966. It would clearly be governed by German law. Suppose the English company brought proceedings in Munich against the German company. The claim would be dismissed by the Munich court on the ground that it was barred by the three years limitation prevailing in German law. Suppose that afterwards, in 1971, the English company brought proceedings in the English court for the same amount on the same bill. The claim would be within the six years allowed by English law. But it would be quite wrong for the English court to give the go-by to the decision of the German court in what was, after all, a German transaction: see Cheshire[2]. The English court would dismiss the action in England because of s 8(1) of the 1933 Act. It would be bound to recognise the judgment of the German court as 'conclusive'.

(2) A bill of exchange in favour of the English company is accepted by the German company payable in London in 1966. It would clearly be governed by English law. Suppose that the English company in 1970 brought proceedings in London against the German company. Those proceedings are within the six years allowed by English law. So the English company get judgment for the amount of the bill. The German company, however, do not pay. Under the reciprocity provisions, the English company can at once go to Germany and register the judgment there and enforce payment, even though the claim would have been barred in Germany because of the three years limitation.

Those two examples satisfy me that, once a party brings proceedings against another in Germany and proceeds to judgment—whether for or against him—then that judgment is conclusive between them. If the plaintiff wins and gets a money judgment, he can register it in England and enforce payment. If the plaintiff fails and his claim is dismissed, then the defendant can set it up as a defence to any proceedings in England for the same cause. This is, I think, the result of the 1933 Act. It might have been different at common law, that is if *Harris v Quine*[3] was rightly decided. But we are here concerned, not with the common law, but with the effect, of the 1933 Act.

In the present case I have no doubt that the English company were well advised to bring proceedings against the German company in Munich, because the German company are in Germany, their assets are there, and, if the English company are to

---

1   [1966] 2 All ER 536 at 584, 585, [1967] 1 AC 853 at 964-967
2   Private International Law (8th Edn, 1970), p 666
3   (1869) LR 4 QB 653

recover any money, it is in Germany that they are most likely to do so. If the English
company should get leave to sue the German company in England, it is pretty plain
that the German company will not submit to the jurisdiction of the English courts
—so that a judgment in England will not do them much good, as it will not be
recognised in Germany or be registered there. In any case, however, I think that, once
judgment was given in the Munich court, that judgment must be recognised
as conclusive by the English courts. If the judgment had been in favour of the English
company for money to be paid by the German company, the English company could
at once have registered that judgment in England and enforced it if there were any
assets here. The German company could not have gainsaid that judgment in the least.
It would have been conclusive. Now that the judgment was in favour of the German
company, dismissing the claim, that judgment is also conclusive. The English
company cannot go behind it and sue in the English courts. By going to Germany
and seeking judgment there, the English company have burnt their boats. They
have committed the case to the judgment of the German courts and must abide
by it. They cannot now resort to the English courts.

This being a point of law—none of the facts being in dispute—I think we must
take the responsibility of deciding it: see *Tyne Improvement Comrs v Armement
Anversois*[1]. Seeing that we decide it against the English company, I think we should
refuse leave to serve the writ out of the jurisdiction. Apart from this point, however,
I doubt whether it would be a case for leave. There is no doubt that the most effective
remedy would be a judgment given by the German courts, because the German
company are there and their assets there. The German courts may, on appeal, give
that remedy. But, even if they do not, the English company would be able, I should
think, to recover in the arbitration any amount which may justly be due to them
for the price of the goods with interest. So, as a matter of discretion, leave might be
refused. I put my decision, however, on the ground that the German judgment
is conclusive. I would therefore allow the appeal.

MEGAW LJ. I agree that the appeal should be allowed. On the arguments
presented before Master Bickford-Smith and Talbot J, their decisions were in my
opinion right, including their exercises of the discretion under RSC Ord 11, r 1. But
in this court for the first time a submission has been made founded on s 8 of the
Foreign Judgments (Reciprocal Enforcement) Act 1933.

That Act has become relevant in respect of judgments of superior courts of the
Federal Republic of Germany by virtue of the Reciprocal Enforcement of Foreign
Judgments (Germany) Order 1961[2]. By para 1 of that order it is provided that
Part I of the 1933 Act shall extend to the Federal Republic of Germany. Section 8
of the Act is not included in Part I of the Act. It is the first section in Part II. But it
has not been argued before us, and in my opinion it could not successfully be argued,
that s 8 of the Act does not have effect in respect of a German judgment to which
Part I of the Act is made applicable by virtue of the order. The wording of s 8 makes
it plain that, whatever the effect of the section may be, that effect is given to any
judgment which, by virtue of the order, is 'a judgment to which Part I of this Act
applies . . .'

The relevant judgment is a judgment of the Landgericht München I, the Munich
Provincial Court, published on 30th November 1972. By that judgment the claim
of Black-Clawson International Ltd, the potential plaintiffs in the intended English
action, was dismissed. The potential defendants in the English action, Papierwerke
Waldhof-Aschaffenburg AG, in this appeal are seeking to set aside the order by which
leave was granted to the potential plaintiffs to serve notice of the writ in the intended
English action out of the jurisdiction.

---

1   [1949] 1 All ER 294 at 298, [1949] AC 326 at 338, per Lord Porter
2   SI 1961 No 1199

The intended action in the English courts involves a claim by the plaintiffs (for simplicity I shall omit the word 'potential' hereafter in respect of both the potential plaintiffs and the potential defendants) on two bills of exchange, governed by English law, which were accepted by the defendants and subsequently dishonoured. The action in the Munich Provincial Court was brought by the plaintiffs against the defendants on the same two bills of exchange. It was dismissed because of German law as to limitation or 'prescription'. The German period in respect of actions on bills of exchange is three years, whereas the English period is six years. The Munich court accepted that the proper law of the contract of these bills of exchange was English law, but it held that, applying English law, including therein English rules of private international law, the German period was applicable. As the German action had been started by the plaintiffs outside the three year period, though within the six year period, the action therefore failed. The decision of the Munich court is now subject to appeal by the plaintiffs to a higher court in Germany.

There is no doubt that the Munich judgment would be a judgment to which Part I of the 1933 Act, as made operative by the 1961 order, would apply, if it had been a judgment under which a sum of money was payable. It possesses all the other necessary characteristics stipulated by s 1 of the 1933 Act read along with the definition of 'judgment' in s 11. The Munich court is a relevant superior court as defined in the 1961 order. The judgment is 'final and conclusive' within the meaning of those words in s 1 of the 1933 Act. The fact that it is subject to appeal does not, because of s 1(3), alter its character of 'final and conclusive'.

It is, however, not a judgment under which a sum of money is payable. It is a judgment in which the claim by the plaintiffs was dismissed. It was conceded, rightly, before us on behalf of the defendants that the fact that the order of the Munich court makes provision as to liability of the plaintiffs for costs does not make it a 'judgment under which a sum of money is payable'. For that reason it is not a judgment on which Part I of the Act has any direct operation. Part I deals with the registration of foreign judgments, providing a simple and expeditious means of enforcing them, in proper cases, in England. This judgment could not be registered under Part I. But that does not, according to the defendants' argument asserting the relevance of the 1933 Act in the present proceedings (being the argument which was presented for the first time in this appeal), prevent s 8 of the 1933 Act from being applicable. For s 8 relates to 'a judgment to which Part I of this Act applies or *would have applied if a sum of money had been payable thereunder*'. The judgment of the Munich court, the defendants say, is such a judgment. Though Part I of the Act, providing for the registration of foreign judgments, does not apply to judgments in favour of a defendant whereby a claim is dismissed, s 8, by its clear and express words, removes the limitation which exists in Part I of the Act and brings within the scope of the section any judgment which fulfils the other requirements of s 1, even though it is not a judgment under which a sum of money is payable. It thus operates on a judgment such as this Munich judgment, the effect of which is to dismiss a claim.

The plaintiffs, in their first answer to that contention, submit that the extension which s 8 gives, in respect of the kinds of judgment to which it applies, is limited to foreign judgments in favour of a plaintiff where the judgment is not for a sum of money, but is, for example, a judgment ordering the return of a chattel. The 1933 Act in general, and s 8 in particular, say the plaintiffs, do not apply to judgments in favour of a defendant, other, of course, than a judgment on a counterclaim. They do not apply where the foreign judgment involves the dismissal of a plaintiff's claim, Insofar as the English courts may give effect to any such foreign judgment—a judgment dismissing a plaintiff's claim—their power to do so arises solely on the common law of England, and not in any shape or form on the 1933 Act. The common law applies the principle set out in *Harris v Quine*[1]. A judgment of a foreign court (in

---

1 (1869) LR 4 QB 653

that case a Manx court), whereby a plaintiff's claim had been defeated by reason
of the application of a period of limitation applicable in the foreign jurisdiction,
was held not to prevent the plaintiff from suing on the same cause of action in the
English courts where, because of a longer period of limitation, he could not be met
with that defence. In the present case, therefore, the foreign court's dismissal of
the plaintiffs' claim because of the application of the German period of limitation
would not affect or prejudice, or provide a defence to, the contemplated English
action.

It would be strange if the 1933 Act, while dealing with foreign judgments in favour
of a plaintiff, omitted to deal with foreign judgments in favour of a defendant. It
is, of course, clear why the provisions as to registration are confined to money judgments in favour of a plaintiff, and why, therefore, Part I of the Act is so confined.
But s 8, on any view, extends the provisions of Part I, both as to the nature or class
of judgments included and as to the effect to be given to them by English courts.
That judgments in favour of a defendant, dismissing the plaintiff's claim, are included
in s 8 is, I think, clear beyond doubt from the concluding words of s 8(1). It is there
provided that foreign judgments coming within the subsection 'may be relied on
by way of defence' in all proceedings in the English courts founded on the same
cause of action; that is, the same cause of action as the cause of action in respect of
which the foreign judgment was given. I am unable to see what the intention,
purpose or effect of these words 'may be relied on by way of defence' could be,
unless the judgments which are relevant for purposes of the subsection include
judgments which merely dismiss a plaintiff's claim. Thus the first answer offered
by the plaintiffs to the defendants' reliance on s 8 of the 1933 Act cannot prevail.
As a matter of construction, in my opinion, it is wrong.

The plaintiffs' second, and alternative, answer to the defendants' submission on
s 8 is that, even if that section on its true construction includes foreign judgments
dismissing a plaintiff's claim, nevertheless the word 'conclusive' in the section should
be narrowly construed. That is, in the phrase in s 8(1):

'... shall be recognised ... as conclusive between the parties thereto in all
proceedings founded on the same cause of action ...'

The conclusiveness of the judgment, as regards the cause of action as a whole, arises
only where the foreign court has decided the action, as it is put, 'on the merits'.
If the foreign court has decided the action, as here, on some point, procedural or
otherwise, such that the decision is not properly to be described as 'on the merits',
then s 8 makes that foreign judgment conclusive only in respect of the point on
which the decision rested. There is, it is suggested, an issue estoppel only, not a cause
of action estoppel. So, in this case, the Munich court's decision was not 'on the merits'.
It was giving effect to the German rule of limitation. The decision on that issue,
however 'conclusive' it may be, is irrelevant in the intended English action, which
is not concerned with the German period of limitation.

The phrase 'on the merits' is taken from the judgment of Cockburn CJ in *Harris
v Quine*[1]:

'... there is no judgment of the Manx Court barring the present action, as
there was no plea going to the merits ...'

I fear that I have been unable to understand what is meant by 'on the merits' in this
context. I do not see any proper basis for reading any such words, whether or not
they are capable of any reasonably precise definition, into the words which have
been used by the legislature in s 8(1) of the 1933 Act. Where s 8 is applicable, *Harris
v Quine*[1] has ceased to be applicable. Section 8(1) gives rise to a cause of action

---

1   (1869) LR 4 QB 653 at 657

estoppel in a case such as the present. I agree in their entirety with the reasons given by Scarman LJ.

The result is that if the plaintiffs were allowed to maintain the service out of the jurisdiction, and the intended action were thus to be allowed to proceed, the defendants would have an unanswerable defence to this claim on the two bills of exchange. That defence is that the plaintiffs brought their action in the Munich court—the selfsame cause of action; judgment has been given in the Munich court dismissing that action; that judgment has to be recognised by the English courts as being conclusive between the parties in all proceedings founded on the same cause of action; it may be relied on by way of defence in those proceedings; and, being relied on, it is conclusive. It is conclusive against the plaintiffs' claim on this cause of action.

That being so, the principles applicable to the granting of leave under RSC Ord 11, r 1, as interpreted or confirmed by the decision of the House of Lords in *Tyne Improvement Comrs v Armement Anversois*[1], require that leave to serve notice of the writ out of the jurisdiction should not be granted; or, having been granted, should be set aside. I too would allow the appeal but, I say again, only because of a submission made to us which was not made, nor hinted at, in the courts below.

SCARMAN LJ. The defendants, whom I shall call 'Papierwerke', manufacture paper products in Western Germany. They own a number of mills, including one at Stockstadt. They have neither a place of business nor any assets in England. The plaintiffs, whom I shall call 'Black-Clawson', are an English company which carry on business in England and are a subsidiary of an American corporation. They manufacture paper-making machinery.

By a contract in writing dated 29th December 1961, Black-Clawson agreed to supply a company, whose rights and liabilities have now passed to Papierwerke, with machinery to be delivered to Stockstadt. The purchase price was well over £1,000,000, 80 per cent of which, it was agreed, would be paid by the purchaser's acceptance of a series of 20 bills of exchange, each with a face value of £48,406, payable in London. The bills were duly drawn by Black-Clawson and accepted by Papierwerke for payment in London. They were English bills and the series were due to mature between 31st August 1963 and 28th February 1968, four bills a year, two on 28th February and two on 31st August of each year.

Disputes arose in the performance of the contract. Papierwerke complained of delays in delivery and of defects in the machinery; they alleged, and continue to allege, that Black-Clawson's breaches of contract have involved them in loss (including loss of profits) and expense totalling some £5,000,000—more than three times as much as the price of the goods delivered.

The contract contained a remarkable arbitration clause providing for arbitration in Zurich, English law to be applied if the reference be by Papierwerke, but German if the reference be by Black-Clawson. Papierwerke referred the dispute to arbitration on 2nd July 1965. From that day to this the arbitration has wound its slow and complex way, but no result has yet been achieved. We were told that there was a meeting of the arbitrators taking place in Zurich at the same time as we were hearing this appeal, but no one expects an early decision in the arbitration. In an affidavit Black-Clawson's solicitor permitted himself a description of the arbitration as 'proceeding with seemingly interminable delays'—moderate language, I think.

One of the consequences of the dispute and its reference to arbitration was that Papierwerke gave thought to their position as acceptors of the London bills, the history of which I now relate. Drawn and accepted for payment in London, they were discounted by Black-Clawson with Barclays Bank, who paid to Black-Clawson approximately 74 per cent of their value, but the bank required and obtained the Export Credit Guarantee Department's guarantee before they discounted them. Bills

---

1   [1949] 1 All ER 294, [1949] AC 326

1, 2, 3, 4, 7 and 8, maturing on dates between 31st August 1963 and 28th February 1965, were met by Papierwerke, but in 1965 Papierwerke, concerned to avoid any further payments pursuant to a contract which they now saw as ruinous, failed to honour any further bills in the series, a default which has led to legal proceedings in England and Germany. Bills 11 and 12 were among those dishonoured. Barclays Bank, as holders, sued Papierwerke and, after being taken to the House of Lords[1] were ultimately successful, to the extent, at least, of their 74 per cent interest in the bills.

Bills 13 and 14 matured on 31st August 1966. They were presented for payment on 1st September 1966 and dishonoured. Having burnt their fingers on the bills, the bank pressed the Export Credit Guarantee Department to honour their guarantee, and the department in its turn reminded Black-Clawson of their obligation to indemnify. So it was that in August 1972 Black-Clawson bought back (from the Export Credit Guarantee Department who had bought them from the bank) the outstanding bills, thereby becoming holders for value. When they did so, Black-Clawson were alive to the fact that time was running out on bills 13 and 14. To make sure, if they could, that they were not statute-barred, Black-Clawson began legal proceedings against Papierwerke in Germany and England. The German suit, begun on 24th August 1972, was dismissed by a judgment of the Munich Landgericht published on 30th November 1972. The judgment is now under appeal and a further appeal lies to the Supreme Court at the instance of the party who fails in the appellate court where the suit now is.

The English proceedings were begun by Black-Clawson on 29th August 1972 by an ex parte application to a master of the Queen's Bench Division for leave to issue the writ and serve notice of it outside the jurisdiction. The order sought was made and Papierwerke were given 21 days after service within which to enter an appearance. The writ was issued on the same day—a few days before the expiry of the English limitation period of six years from date of dishonour. Notice of the writ was not, however, served on Papierwerke until mid-August 1973, 11½ months after its issue. On receipt of the notice, Papierwerke chose not to enter an appearance but to apply to set aside the writ. Their application was dismissed first by the master and then by the judge in chambers, who refused them leave to appeal. Papierwerke now seek from this court leave to appeal and, if leave be given, to prosecute their appeal. Accordingly, we have heard full argument on the merits of the appeal as well as on the application. We have been told that the bills subsequent in series to nos 13 and 14 are the subject of legal proceedings, the course of which may to some extent be determined by the result of the litigation with which we are now concerned.

The application for leave to issue the writ was made by Black-Clawson pursuant to RSC Ord 11, r 1(1)(g). The action is in respect of a breach committed within the jurisdiction of a contract made within the jurisdiction, namely the dishonour in London of two English bills of exchange. Leave can, therefore, be granted if it should be made sufficiently to appear to the court that the case is a proper one for service out of the jurisdiction (RSC Ord 11, r 4(2)). Papierwerke's case before the master and the judge was that it had not been made so to appear; they argued that to grant leave was a wrong exercise of the court's discretion, urging in support of their case the existence of the German judgment, the currency of the Swiss arbitration and the 'inconvenience and annoyance', as one of the decided cases calls it, of their being brought here to contest their rights, though their business, the dispute, and proceedings to determine it, are all outside the jurisdiction. In addition to their general case against the exercise of the discretion, they took a specific point. They submitted that the English action was bound to fail, the German judgment (which, subject only to appeal, is a final and conclusive judgment) constituting an estoppel per rem judicatam.

---

1 See *Barclays Bank v Aschaffenburger Zellstoffwerke AG* [1967] 1 Lloyd's Rep 387

The German judgment was a dismissal of Black-Clawson's suit. The ground of decision was that the suit was out of time, three years being the period of limitation by German law. Limitation (or prescription) is in Germany a matter of substantive not procedural law; nevertheless, it operates not to extinguish the right but to bar the remedy. The court found the proper law of the bills to be English, but commented: 'English Law refers the matter of prescription to the lex fori. Thus in the present case it refers back to German Law.' Accepting the renvoi, it applied the German period of limitation, and dismissed the suit.

The judge in chambers accepted this analysis of the German judgment and held that it was not 'res judicata'; for it contained no adjudication 'on the merits' of the dispute but only barred a remedy in Germany; he based himself on *Harris v Quine*[1]. He was also unimpressed by Papierwerke's general case, recalling that the bills were for payment in London and were supposed to be the equivalent of cash, but, if Papierwerke were right, were worth no more than part of a counterclaim for the price in the unterminated and seemingly interminable arbitration in Zurich. If the judge was correct in law in holding that the German judgment was not 'res judicata', I do not think that his exercise of discretion can be successfully challenged in this court. But counsel for Papierwerke has addressed to us an argument, based on s 8(1) of the Foreign Judgments (Reciprocal Enforcement) Act 1933, which was not addressed to the judge. If correct, it is of such importance that it may not be disregarded, belated though its appearance is. Fortunately, his point has been fully argued before us, and we have had the benefit of a sustained and vigorous argument from counsel for Black-Clawson.

Put shortly, counsel for Papierwerke's submission is this. The Munich judgment is a final and conclusive judgment of a superior court of the Federal Republic of Germany, a country with whom Her Majesty has concluded a convention under s 1 of the 1933 Act. Section 8(1) provides that such a judgment shall be recognised in the courts of the United Kingdom as—

'conclusive between the parties thereto in all proceedings founded on the same cause of action and may be relied on by way of defence or counterclaim in any such proceedings.'

The English action is founded on the same cause of action. If, therefore, Papierwerke should rely on the German judgment as a defence in the English action, Black-Clawson are bound to fail. Papierwerke should not be put to the inconvenience, annoyance and expense of being brought to England to contest an action that has no chance of success. Accordingly, it was an improper exercise of the discretion to grant leave to issue the writ.

If the point be a good one, *Harris v Quine*[1], a decision which has stood for over 100 years and is treated by the textbook writers as authoritative, has no application to a foreign judgment which is entitled to recognition under s 8(1) of the 1933 Act. Indeed counsel for Papierwerke does not shrink from submitting that the Act, once it is made applicable to the judgments of the superior courts of another country by Order in Council, is a code of reciprocity displacing the common law as to the enforcement and recognition of those judgments (except where expressly saved as in s 8(3)).

The English common law has traditionally favoured the recognition and enforcement in England of the judgments of foreign courts of competent jurisdiction. Enforcement was, and is, by action; the defendant cannot be heard to challenge the judgment save on certain specific and well-known grounds. A plaintiff can apply for a summary judgment, and, unless the defendant can show cause, will obtain it; for a concise description of the common law, see Dicey[2]. But a foreign

1 (1869) LR 4 QB 653
2 Dicey and Morris, *Conflict of Laws* (9th Edn, 1973), p 988

judgment, as well as being a weapon of offence in the hands of a plaintiff, is also recognised by the common law as a weapon of defence available to a defendant. As with enforcement, so also its recognition as a defence is open to challenge only if one of a narrow range of specific causes can be established; in the absence of a successful challenge, it is a good defence.

Harris v Quine[1] was a case in which a defendant sought to rely on a foreign judgment. The plaintiff sued in England for money due on a work and labour contract (he was an attorney who had conducted legal business in the Isle of Man on behalf of the defendant); he was met with the defence that in proceedings he had instituted in the Isle of Man the Manx court had dismissed his claim. The English court examined the Manx judgment and observed that the plaintiff had failed because, by the Manx statute of limitations, his action was out of time and his remedy was, accordingly, barred. The court held that the Manx court had not adjudicated on the merits of the plaintiff's claim, i e on his right or cause of action, but had merely barred his remedy Cockburn CJ accepted that the Manx statute of limitations was a matter of procedure and did not apply to the substance of the contract, and then said[2]:

> '... there is no judgment of the Manx Court barring the present action, as there was no plea going to the merits ... and the issue which the Manx Court decided in favour of the defendant is not the same issue as is raised in the present action.'

The Manx judgment, therefore, was no defence to the claim, since it had not adjudicated on the 'res' in issue, that is to say whether or not the plaintiff had a right to the money he was claiming.

That *Harris v Quine*[1] was a correct decision has never been doubted. It was consistent with previous case law and, in my opinion, fairly reflects the principle of the common law. The learned judge was right to treat it as an accurate statement of the common law. Counsel for Papierwerke can succeed only if he can show that, so far as German superior court judgments are concerned, the common law has been displaced by statutory provision.

Over the last 100 years or so Parliament has intervened not to destroy but to strengthen the law favouring the enforcement and recognition of foreign judgments. The Judgments Extension Act 1868, which continues in force in England, Scotland and Northern Ireland, dispenses with the necessity of an action to enforce in one United Kingdom law district a judgment obtained in another. Such judgments may be registered, whereupon they acquire the force of a local judgment and are beyond challenge. In 1920 the Administration of Justice Act extended registration to the superior courts of those Commonwealth countries which were prepared to offer the like facilities to United Kingdom judgments, but it stopped short of treating Commonwealth judgments as though they were local judgments. Registration was not of right, but discretionary; and the statute retained the common law challenges to the enforcement of a foreign judgment. In 1933 the Foreign Judgments (Reciprocal Enforcement) Act—the Act on which counsel for Papierwerke relies—was passed, going substantially further than the 1920 Act. The policy of the 1933 Act is that foreign judgments to which it is made applicable shall, subject to certain challenges, which are, indeed, taken from the common law, be treated as though they were judgments given by an English court. Money judgments may be registered and, after registration, executed as if they were British judgments. Other judgments, if they meet the requirements of s 8(1), shall be recognised by the United Kingdom courts as conclusive; this statutory recognition does not displace but is additional to the common law of recognition: see s 8(3) of the 1933 Act.

1 (1869) LR 4 QB 653
2 LR 4 QB at 657

a   So far as concerns enforcement, the common law is displaced, although the statute accepts its principles. In one important respect, the common law is abrogated; a foreign judgment which may be registered cannot be enforced by action: see s 6 of the 1933 Act. Recognition is dealt with in s 8—the first section in Part II of the Act Textbook writers have been puzzled by s 8(1). For instance, the learned editor of Dicey[1] describes it as 'a tortuously drafted provision'. But there is no puzzle if it is seen in context and construed as part of a statute adding to, and going further than,

b   the common law. I have no doubt that this is the context of the subsection. If on such a construction it is seen to modify or abrogate a common law rule, so be it. The Act is no mere restatement in statutory form of the common law but, to the extent that its language indicates, new law.

Accordingly, I think it wrong to torture the language of s 8(1) or read into it words which are not there solely so as to make its effect consistent with the common law.

c   If the subsection does within the limited range of its application displace *Harris v Quine*[2], it does so by increasing, not diminishing, the efficacy of the foreign judgment, which, to qualify for recognition under the subsection, has to be one to which the Act applies; and this, in my judgment, is wholly consistent with the policy and intent of the Act.

When one turns to s 8(1), three questions have to be answered: (1) To what judg-

d   ments does it apply? (2) Of what is a foreign judgment to which the subsection applies conclusive? (3) What is the meaning of the phrase 'founded on the same cause of action'? On the first question, counsel for Black-Clawson submits that s 8(1)—and, indeed, the whole Act—applies only to judgments in favour of a plaintiff or claimant. Judgments for defendants are left to the common law. The Act, he says, is primarily, concerned with enforcement; only incidentally with recognition,

e   and then only with the recognition of a plaintiff's judgment, which, because it has been satisfied or affords a remedy (e g delivery up of a chattel) other than an order for the payment of money, cannot be registered, though otherwise qualifying for registration. The difficulty of this approach is that the subsection appears to be dealing in terms with the use a defendant can make of a foreign judgment. It con-

f   templates proceedings in the United Kingdom founded on the same cause of action as was the foreign judgment, and it provides that a party in the United Kingdom proceedings may rely on it as a defence 'in such proceedings'. It is not possible, in my opinion, to exclude from the scope of s 8(1) a judgment in favour of a defendant dismissing the plaintiff's claim.

On the second question, counsel submits that 'conclusive' means 'conclusive of the matter adjudicated on'. He would introduce into s 8(1) of the 1933 Act words

g   which are not there, and he says the justification for so doing is that it brings the subsection into line with the common law as declared in *Harris v Quine*[2] I think this is his best point. It would produce a sensible result without displacing the common law rule. But there is objection, which I find overwhelming. Had the legislature intended to define more narrowly the subject-matter of 'conclusiveness', it could have done so, and did so in another context: see s 8(3). If these words were intended

h   to be implied, what useful purpose was to be served by the words 'founded on the same cause of action'?

More fundamentally, if these words are to be read into s 8(1), why was the subsection enacted? On this construction it would add nothing to the common law, which for situations outside the scope of the Act is expressly preserved by s 8(3). The subsection is difficult only if one assumes it has to be consistent with the common

j   law. Once it is accepted that it may be an innovation, displacing within its limited range the common law, its interpretation is no problem. It means what it says. Accordingly, I read s 8(1) as declaring that foreign judgments to which it applies are

1   9th Edn (1973), p 1021
2   (1869) LR 4 QB 653

conclusive in all United Kingdom proceedings founded on the same cause of action.
Such judgments are in like case with English, Scottish and Northern Ireland judg- *a*
ments, binding on the parties irrespective of their reasons provided that the subsequent proceedings are themselves founded on the same cause of action: see *Fidelitas
Shipping Co Ltd v V/O Exportchleb*[1].

If this be right, the third question is critical. What is the meaning of the phrase
'founded on the same cause of action'? It must be a reference to the right the plaintiff
seeks to establish. There can be no doubt that Black-Clawson seek to establish in *b*
the English proceedings the same cause of action as in the German proceedings;
their action is founded on the cause of action on which they failed to get judgment
in Germany. 'Conclusive' means, on this view of the subsection, simply 'that's that',
and equates the foreign judgment with an earlier British judgment between the
same parties.

At first sight, s 8(1) of the 1933 Act, on this view of its meaning, may appear to *c*
work injustice. But I do not think so. A plaintiff, in a case such as the present, has
his choice of tribunal. If he elects to proceed in the German court, the law requires
him to accept its decision as decisive on his claim. The policy of the law, being to
treat the judgment as though it were a British judgment final and conclusive between
the parties, discourages multiplicity of action. It is not surprising, therefore, that s 8(1)
should make impossible a successful United Kingdom action founded on the same *d*
cause of action as was litigated unsuccessfully in Germany, even though the German
judgment barred the remedy without extinguishing the right.

For these reasons I have reached the conclusion that Papierwerke have only to
rely on the German judgment to defeat Black-Clawson's action in England. The
conclusion derives from the 1933 Act, to which no attention was paid by the parties
or the court until counsel for Papierwerke opened the appeal in this court. Counsel *e*
for Black-Clawson has submitted that it would be wrong to set aside the writ, even
if counsel for Papierwerke's argument be accepted; the defence based on the statute
should be pleaded and argued at the trial. But the point has been fully argued.
No facts other than those already known and undisputed need to be established,
and this court, rightly or wrongly, has reached the unanimous conclusion that the
German judgment bars the English action. That being the case, the court is, I think, *f*
obliged to act now on its view of the law: see *Tyne Improvement Comrs v Armement
Anversois*[2]. Any other course would impose on the foreign defendant the inconvenience, annoyance and expense of being brought here to contest an action which
in our view is, as a matter of law, not sustainable.

I agree with Lord Denning MR and Megaw LJ. I would allow the appeal and
refuse leave to issue the writ. *g*

Appeal allowed. Leave to appeal to the House of Lords.

Solicitors: *Herbert Smith & Co* (for the defendants); *Slaughter & May* (for the
plaintiffs).

L J Kovats Esq Barrister. *h*

---

1   [1965] 2 All ER 4 at 8, [1966] 1 QB 630 at 640, per Lord Denning MR
2   [1949] 1 All ER 294, [1949] AC 326

Northern Counties Securities Ltd v Jackson & Steeple Ltd

CHANCERY DIVISION
WALTON J
22nd, 28th MARCH 1974

Company – Director – Duty – Extent of duty – Duty in respect of court order – Order for specific performance of agreement to allot and issue shares – Undertaking by company to use best endeavours to obtain quotation for and permission to deal in shares and issue same to plaintiffs – Stock exchange requiring that issue be subject to consent of 'company in general meeting' – Extraordinary general meeting summoned – Circular accompanying notice of meeting stating that no recommendation was being made by directors – Circular in effect inviting rejection of resolution to issue shares – Whether directors bound to recommend members to vote in favour of resolution – Whether directors in capacity of shareholders bound to vote in favour of resolution.

Contempt of court – Company – Shareholders – Order for specific performance of shares agreement – Company undertaking to use best endeavours to obtain quotation for and permission to deal in shares and issue same – Stock exchange requiring that issue be subject to consent of 'company in general meeting' – Whether shareholders would be in contempt of court if voting against resolution to issue shares.

An agreement made between the plaintiffs and the defendants ('the company') provided, inter alia, that, on the completion of a certain option, the plaintiffs should deliver to the company a duly executed transfer or transfers of certain shares in favour of the company or their nominee, and the company should issue to the plaintiffs certain shares ranking pari passu with the company's other shares and 'with permission to deal in and quotation for such shares' on the London Stock Exchange. The plaintiffs fulfilled their part of the agreement but the company did not issue the shares to them. The plaintiffs brought an action for specific performance of that portion of the agreement and applied for summary judgment under RSC Ord 86. In December 1972 it was ordered (i) that the agreement be specifically performed; (ii) that an enquiry be taken as to the shares and an account taken of the dividends that would have been payable to the plaintiffs if the shares had been allotted to plaintiffs on 3rd June 1969; (iii) that the company, undertaking 'forthwith at their expense to apply for and to use their best endeavours to obtain quotation for and permission to deal on the London Stock Exchange' in the shares concerned, allot and issue the shares to the plaintiffs within 28 days of such quotation being obtained. The company further undertook not until after the allotment and issue of the shares to the plaintiffs, without the plaintiffs' prior written consent, to increase the authorised share capital of the company or do any other thing requiring the authority of the members of the company in general meeting. In November 1973 the company discovered that the stock exchange required that the issue of the shares be subject to the consent of 'the company in general meeting', and that a class 1 circular to shareholders including an accountants' report would have to be issued. No such meeting of the company having been summoned by the directors by 19th March 1974, the plaintiffs applied, inter alia, for (1) an order that the company and the directors should despatch to all members a notice convening an extraordinary general meeting of the company to approve a resolution for the issue and allotment to the plaintiffs of the shares; (2) an order that the notice should include, or be accompanied by, a circular including all relevant information calculated to induce the members of the company to vote in favour of the resolution; (3) an order that the notice should include, or be accompanied by, a circular including a recommendation by the directors to the members to vote in favour of the resolution; and (4) an order restraining the directors from voting against it. On the same day (i e 19th March) the company gave its shareholders notice of an extraordinary general meeting to be held on 5th April when the following resolutions would be proposed: (i) that the capital of the company be increased by the creation of 370,000 ordinary shares, ranking pari passu as to dividend with the ordinary shares of the company; (ii) that the directors be authorised to issue those shares fully paid to the plaintiffs and that the shares should, when issued, carry dividend at the rates declared from 3rd June 1969. The notice was accompanied by a circular which stated, inter alia, that the company had taken the opinion of leading counsel as to the rights and obligations of the board, the company, and its shareholders as a result of the court order and that in accordance with that advice the shareholders were free to vote in whatever way they wished. In view of that the board were making no recommendation to the shareholders but leaving the decision on how to vote to the individual judgment of the shareholders. The circular pointed out that if the resolution were passed the company would have to pay £300,873 for the asset it had acquired from the plaintiffs, but, if it were not, the cost would not be much over £183,873. A summary of the advice of leading counsel was set out in an appendix to the circular. It stated, inter alia, (i) that the undertaking and court order did not bind the shareholders, so there could be no penalty on them if they did not approve the issue of the shares to the plaintiffs, and (2) that if the quotation for and permission to deal in the shares were not obtained, the order for the allotment of the shares could not take effect. It was admitted that the company had sufficient unissued shares to enable them to make the required issue without increasing the company's capital.

Held – (1) The meeting convened for 5th April 1974 should not be allowed to proceed, and the first three orders sought by the plaintiffs should be made, for the following reasons—

(i) the circular could not stand in the form in which it had been issued; in order to comply with the company's undertaking to the court to use its best endeavours to see that the shareholders passed a resolution for the issue of the shares to the plaintiffs, it had to be phrased in positive terms, inviting a favourable response (see p 636 e, post);

(ii) in any event, the first resolution was, in the absence of the plaintiffs' written consent, a breach of the undertaking given by the company in December 1972; and the second resolution was misconceived in that (a) in the circumstances the proposed backdating would involve a form of double payment, and (b) once a company's accounts for any year had been duly passed, they could not be retrospectively reopened in the manner proposed (see p 632 a to d, post).

(2) No order would however be made restraining the directors from voting against the resolution for they were only bound in their capacity as directors to cause the company to comply with the undertaking given to the court (i e by convening the requisite meeting and placing a positive circular before the members); once they had fulfilled that obligation they were entitled as individual shareholders to enjoy the same unfettered and unrestricted right of voting at general meetings of the members of the company as they would have had if they were not directors (see p 637 c e to g and j to p 638 a, post).

Per Walton J. (i) While the defeat of the resolution would prevent the shares from receiving a quotation, it would not prevent their allotment and issue to the plaintiffs for there was nothing conditional about the obligation undertaken by the company under the agreement and the court order did not make that absolute obligation a conditional one (see p 630 b and p 634 b and c, post).

(ii) For a shareholder to vote against a resolution to issue the shares to the plaintiffs would not be a contempt of court for decisions taken by a 'company in general *a* meeting' and the resolutions passed thereat are decisions taken by, and resolutions passed by, the members of the company and not the company itself. When a shareholder casts his vote in general meeting he is not casting it as an agent of the company (see p 634 *j* to p 635 *a d* to *g* and p 636 *a*, post).

Notes

b For powers and duties of directors, see 7 Halsbury's Laws (4th Edn) 265-296, paras 496-510, and for cases on the subject, see 10 Digest (Repl) 1241-1242, 8730-8737.

For contempt of court by strangers to the action, see 8 Halsbury's Laws (3rd Edn) 21, para 39, and for cases on the subject, see 16 Digest (Repl) 45, 397-409.

Cases referred to in judgment

c *Bower v Bantam Investments Ltd* [1972] 3 All ER 349, [1972] 1 WLR 1120.

Ford-Hunt v Raghbir Singh [1973] 2 All ER 700, [1973] 1 WLR 738.

Lennard's Carrying Co Ltd v Asiatic Petroleum Co Ltd [1915] AC 705, [1914-15] All ER Rep 280, 84 LJKB 1281, 113 LT 195, 13 Asp MLC 81, 20 Com Cas 283, HL, 41 Digest (Repl) 295, 1073.

Monkland v Jack Barclay Ltd [1951] 1 All ER 714, [1951] 2 KB 252, CA, 39 Digest (Repl)
d 676, 1730.

Sheffield District Railway Co v Great Central Railway Co (1911) 27 TLR 451, 14 Ry & Can Tr Cas 299, 38 Digest (Repl) 377, 482.

Case also cited

Thorne Rural District Council v Bunting (No 2) [1972] 3 All ER 1084, CA.

e ### Motion

By a writ issued on 30th March 1972, the plaintiffs, Northern Counties Securities Ltd, brought an action against the defendants, Jackson & Steeple Ltd ('the company') claiming (1) specific performance of an agreement in writing dated 23rd December 1968 for the allotment and issue by the company to the plaintiffs of 370,000 shares of 2s each
f in the company or of such other number of such shares as represented not less than 37/202 of the equity share capital of the company at the date of allotment and issue; (2) an account of the dividends that would have been payable to the plaintiffs in respect of the shares if they had been duly allotted and issued to the plaintiffs in accordance with the agreement and payment of the sum found due; (3) damages in addition to or in lieu of specific performance; and (4) further or other relief. They applied for summary judgment under RSC Ord 86 and, on 8th December 1972,
g Brightman J ordered (i) that the agreement be specifically performed; (ii) that an account and enquiry be taken; and (iii) that the company, undertaking by their counsel forthwith at their expense to apply for and use their best endeavours to obtain quotation for and permission to deal on the London Stock Exchange in the shares, allot and issue to the plaintiffs the correct number of shares within 28 days of such
h quotation being obtained. By notice of motion, dated 19th March 1974, the plaintiffs sought the following relief: (1) An order that the company and William John Beggs, John Hitchon Cudworth, John Roy Finch, Joseph Menagie and Harold Hinde ('the directors') and each of them as directors of the company should procure that the company as soon as might be practicable despatch to all the members of the company a notice accompanied by such documents as the stock exchange might require
j convening an extraordinary general meeting of the company for the purpose of approving a resolution for the issue and allotment to the plaintiffs of the shares. (2) An order that the company and the individual directors and each of them as directors of the company should procure that the notice should include or alternatively be accompanied by a circular including all relevant information calculated to induce the members of the company to vote in favour of the resolution, and in particular the following information: (i) that the company were under a subsisting contractual

obligation to the plaintiffs to issue the new shares with permission to deal and a quotation for such shares on the stock exchange being granted, and that the company had given an undertaking to the court to use their best endeavours to obtain such quotation and permission to deal; (ii) that the stock exchange had made it a condition of quotation and permission to deal that the issue of the shares should be approved by the company in general meeting; (iii) that it was a contempt of court for any person knowingly to take any steps which would prevent the company from fulfilling their undertaking to the court; (iv) that the defeat of the resolution would amount to a contempt of court on the part of the company which could result in the payment of a substantial fine by the company or in the sequestration of the assets of the company; (v) that while the defeat of the resolution would prevent the new shares from receiving a quotation, it would not prevent their issue, to which the plaintiffs remained contractually entitled; (vi) that accordingly the only effect of defeating the resolution would be to expose the company to proceedings for contempt of court; to deprive the plaintiffs of a quotation for the shares which the company would still be bound to issue to them if they elected to take them without a quotation; and whether or not the plaintiffs so elect, to expose the company to heavy damages; (vii) and that the company had undertaken to the court not until after the allotment and issue of the shares to the plaintiffs without the prior written consent of the plaintiffs to increase the authorised share capital of the company or do any other thing requiring the authority of the members of the company in general meeting, which included the payment of dividends, appointment of directors, etc. (3) (i) An order that the company and the individual directors and each of them as directors of the company should procure that the notice should include or alternatively be accompanied by a circular including a recommendation by the directors of the company to the members to vote in favour of the resolution; (ii) alternatively, an order that the company and the individual directors and each of them as directors of the company should procure that there should be included in the notice or circular no recommendation by the directors of the company to the members to vote against the resolution. (4) An order restraining the individual directors and each of them from voting against the resolution. (5) An order restraining the company until after the allotment and issue of the shares to the plaintiffs or further order without the prior written consent of the plaintiffs from (i) increasing the authorised share capital of the company (ii) doing any other thing (including but without prejudice to the generality of the foregoing appointing directors, declaring final dividends, or approving accounts) requiring the authority of the members of the company in general meeting or (iii) disposing of the assets of the company otherwise than in the ordinary course of business. The facts are set out in the judgment.

Leolin Price QC and *Peter Millett QC* for the plaintiffs.
Ian McCulloch for the company.
Ralph Instone for the directors.

Cur adv vult

28th March. **WALTON J** read the following judgment. By an agreement dated 23rd December 1968, and made between the plaintiffs of the one part and the defendants ('the company') of the other part, a particular option was granted, and as part thereof it was provided, inter alia, by cl 5 of the agreement as follows:

'On completion of either option [the plaintiffs] shall deliver to [the company] a duly executed Transfer or Transfers in favour of [the company] or [their] Nominee [of certain shares] . . . and [the company] shall issue to [the plaintiffs] the shares required (ranking pari passu in all respects with the other shares of [the company] and with permission to deal in and quotation for such shares being granted either absolutely or subject to allotment) and shall pay to [the plaintiffs] any balance of the said price that may be due.'

The option was not in fact exercised, but the parties by their conduct treated it as exercised. The company did not, however, issue the shares which it should have done, to the plaintiffs and the present action had to be commenced for specific performance of that portion of the agreement between the parties (the plaintiffs having fulfilled their part) by writ dated 30th March 1972. By summons dated 30th March 1972 the plaintiffs applied in the action for summary judgment under RSC Ord 86, and on 8th December 1972 Brightman J made an order accordingly.

It is, I think, important to consider the form of that order carefully. The first operative part of the order is as follows:

'THIS COURT DOTH DECLARE that the Agreement in the Writ of Summons mentioned and constituted by (i) an option agreement dated 23rd December 1968 and (ii) the conduct of the parties in treating the said option as duly exercised ought to be specifically performed and carried into execution AND DOTH ORDER AND ADJUDGE the same accordingly',

and the remainder of the order is geared to that declaration and order. It proceeds:

'And the plaintiffs by their Counsel reserving any claim against the [company] to the further performance of the said Agreement AND THE [company] by their Counsel reserving any claim to damages which they might wish to make against the plaintiffs IT IS ORDERED that the following Account and Inquiry be taken and made that is to say 1. An Inquiry what number of shares of 2/- each in the [company] represented 37/202 of the equity share capital of the Defendants on 3rd June 1969 and 2. An account of the dividends that would have been payable to the Plaintiffs in respect of the said shares and the shares from time to time representing the same if the number of shares of 2/- each in the [company] found upon taking the said Inquiry Number 1 had been allotted and issued to the Plaintiffs on 3rd June 1969 AND the [company] by their Counsel undertaking forthwith at their expense to apply for and to use their best endeavours to obtain quotation for and permission to deal in the London Stock Exchange in the shares hereinafter mentioned IT IS ORDERED that the [company] do within twenty-eight days of such quotation being obtained allot and issue to the plaintiffs [the correct number of shares].'

I do not think that I need read any more of that order; but the whole of the remainder of the order is, as I have said, geared to the original declaration and order. Hence, when the order provides that—

'the [company] by their Counsel undertaking forthwith at their expense to apply for and to use their best endeavours to obtain quotation for and permission to deal on the London Stock Exchange in the shares hereinafter mentioned',

if for any reason no quotation for such shares can in fact be obtained, there can be no question of the company having found an escape route from its obligations. Under the liberty to apply which is reserved in the order, the plaintiffs would then be entitled to apply for whatever, in the changed circumstances, was the correct order for the court to make having regard to the overriding determination that the contract should be specifically enforced. That there is clear jurisdiction in the court to make a supplemental order of this nature on the proof of a changed state of affairs since the order for specific performance was made appears quite clearly from a recent decision of Brightman J, reviewing the earlier authorities, in *Ford-Hunt v Raghbir Singh*[1]. Moreover, although I do not think that this reservation is in any way essential to the plaintiffs' right to claim damages or an alternative order for transfer of what the company can in any event issue to them, namely, the shares without the benefit of a

---

1   [1973] 2 All ER 700, [1973] 1 WLR 738

stock exchange quotation, together with damages for the difference of the subject-   *a*
matter transferred (that is the difference in the value between the shares with and
without such a quotation), nevertheless it is to be observed that the order expressly
states (and thereby sanctions the fact) that the plaintiffs by their counsel reserved any
claim against the company to the further performance of the agreement.

At the risk of repetition, but for a reason which will become apparent later, there is
nothing conditional about the obligation undertaken by the company under cl 5 of   *b*
the agreement of 23rd December 1968; and the order of 8th December 1972 was never
intended to and never in fact did turn any obligation of the company thereunder into
a conditional obligation. It was directed to ensuring the discharge of the company's
obligations, not towards turning absolute obligations into conditional ones.

All this is, of course, quite elementary; and but for subsequent events I should not
have taken up time delving into it. Although there was a great deal of correspondence   *c*
between the parties, nothing effective had been done by the company to issue the
shares it was obliged to issue prior to 19th March 1974. It had, however, been
discovered in the meantime (although I do not think that this would have come as a
surprise to anybody versed in stock exchange practice) that the stock exchange
required that the issue of the shares should be made subject to the consent of the
company in general meeting, and that a class 1 circular to shareholders including an   *d*
accountants' report would have to be issued. This requirement was known by early
November 1973 and the company was required by the order of 8th December 1972
forthwith to use its best endeavours to obtain the quotation and permission to deal.
Yet no such meeting of the company as was requisite had been summoned by the
directors by 19th March 1974.

On that day the plaintiffs issued their notice of motion, which is presently before me,   *e*
addressing it not only to the defendant company but also to the individual directors
thereof. It claimed the following relief:

'1. An Order that the Defendants ("the Company") do and that the individual
Respondents and each of them as Directors of the Company do procure that the
Company do as soon as may be practicable despatch to all members of the Com-   *f*
pany a notice accompanied by such documents as the Stock Exchange may require
convening an Extraordinary General Meeting of the Company for the purpose of
approving a resolution for the issue and allotment to the Plaintiffs of the shares
referred to in the Order herein dated the 8th December 1972.

'2. An Order that the Company and the individual Respondents and each of
them as Directors of the Company do procure that the said notice shall include or
alternatively be accompanied by a circular including all relevant information   *g*
calculated to induce the members of the Company to vote in favour of the said
resolution, and in particular the following information:—(i) that the Company
are under a subsisting contractual obligation to the Plaintiffs to issue the new
shares with permission to deal and a quotation for such shares on the Stock
Exchange being granted, and that the Company have given an undertaking to the   *h*
Court to use their best endeavours to obtain such quotation and permission to
deal; (ii) that the Stock Exchange has made it a condition of quotation and permission to deal that the issue of the shares shall be approved by the Company in
general meeting; (iii) that it is a contempt of Court for any person knowingly to
take any steps which will prevent the Company from fulfilling their undertaking
to the Court; (iv) that the defeat of the resolution will amount to a contempt of   *i*
court on the part of the Company, which could result in the payment of a substantial fine by the Company or in the sequestration of the assets of the Company;
(v) that while the defeat of the resolution will prevent the new shares from receiving a quotation, it will not prevent their issue, to which the Plaintiffs remain
contractually entitled; (vi) that accordingly the only effect of defeating the resolution will be to expose the Company to proceedings for contempt of Court; to

a deprive the Plaintiffs of a quotation for the shares, which the Company will still be bound to issue to them if they elect to take them without a quotation; and, whether or not the Plaintiffs so elect, to expose the Company to heavy damages; (vii) and that the Company have undertaken to the Court not until after the allotment and issue of the shares to the Plaintiffs without the prior written consent of the Plaintiffs to increase the authorised share capital of the Company

b or do any other thing requiring the authority of the members of the Company in general meeting, which includes the payment of dividends, appointment of directors, etc.

'3. (1) An Order that the Company and the individual Respondents and each of them as Directors of the Company do procure that the said notice shall include or alternatively be accompanied by a circular including a recommendation by the Directors of the Company to the members to vote in favour of the resolution.

c (2) Alternatively an Order that the Company and the individual Respondents and each of them as Directors of the Company do procure that there shall be included in the said notice or circular no recommendation by the Directors of the Company to the members to vote against the resolution.

'4. An Order restraining the individual Respondents and each of them from voting against the resolution.

d '5. An Order restraining the Company until after the allotment and issue of the said shares to the Plaintiffs or further Order without the prior written consent of the Plaintiffs from (i) increasing the authorised share capital of the Company (ii) doing any other thing (including but without prejudice to the generality of the foregoing appointing directors, declaring final dividends, or approving accounts) requiring the authority of the members of the Company in general meeting or

e (iii) disposing of the assets of the Company otherwise than in the ordinary course of business.'

As regards that last requirement, in the order of 8th December 1972 the defendants had by their counsel given an undertaking—

f '(i) not until after the allotment and issue of shares to the Plaintiffs as aforesaid or further order without the prior written consent of the Plaintiffs to increase the authorised share capital of the Defendants or do any other thing requiring the authority of the Members of the Defendant Company in general meeting and (ii) to prosecute any Appeal from this Order [in fact no appeal was made] with all due diligence.'

g Counsel for the company specifically called my attention to the fact that the notice of motion does not claim any relief in relation to the question of costs. This is true; but it does not, in my judgment, in any way diminish my jurisdiction to award them if I think it right. At the highest, all that would be required would be a simple amendment of the notice of motion, for which I would unhesitatingly give leave. The motion was issued for 22nd March; and in the meantime, namely on the same 19th March, the

h company duly gave its shareholders notice of an extraordinary general meeting for 5th April 1974 accompanied by a circular.

The resolutions which it is stated were intended to be proposed at the meeting were as follows:

i '*First Resolution*: "THAT the capital of the Company be increased by the creation of 370,000 ordinary shares of 10p each ranking pari passu as to dividend with the present Ordinary Shares of the Company" *Second Resolution*: "THAT the Directors be authorised to issue the said Ordinary Shares as fully paid up to [the plaintiffs] and THAT the said shares when issued do carry dividend at rate declared by the Company from and since 3rd June 1969 and that the proper officer of the Company be authorised to pay such dividend upon the issue of the said shares to the persons who are to be registered as the holders thereof".'

They appear to be wholly misconceived. It is admitted that the company has in fact *a*
amply sufficient unissued shares to enable those which it will or may have to issue to
the plaintiffs to be issued without any increase in the capital being required. Moreover,
the suggestion that the dividend payable on the shares should be backdated to 3rd
June 1969 appears to me to be also wholly misconceived, really on two grounds:
first, that the order in fact expressly made provision for the amount of the dividends
which would have been paid on the shares if they had been issued on 3rd June 1969 to *b*
be calculated and for the payment of the sum so found due to be paid by the defendants to the plaintiffs, so that the proposed backdating would have involved a form of
double payment. Secondly, I do not think that it is possible, at any rate under most
usual forms of articles, for this kind of backdating of the right to dividends to take
place. Whilst there can be no possible objection to backdating within the current
financial year in which the shares are actually issued, once the accounts of the *c*
company for any one year have been duly passed I do not see how they can be
retrospectively reopened in this manner.

There is, of course, the further and overriding point that any increase in the capital of
the defendant company without the prior written consent of the plaintiffs would be
a breach of the undertaking by the defendant company contained in the order of 8th
December 1972. It is therefore at once apparent that this meeting could not, on the *d*
foregoing grounds alone, be allowed to proceed.

It will be recalled that a further part of the order of 8th December 1972 was that
the company had undertaken by its counsel to use its best endeavours to obtain the
quotation for and permission to deal on the London Stock Exchange for these shares.
The words 'use their best endeavours' are, perhaps, not the most certain of all phrases;
see the criticisms of Goff J in *Bower v Bantam Investments Ltd*[1]; but note also that it did *e*
not appear to cause the Court of Appeal any problems in *Monkland v Jack Barclay Ltd*[2]
any more than it had caused any difficulty to the Railway and Canal Commission in
Sheffield District Railway Co v Great Central Railway Co[3], where it was pointed out[4] that
the words mean what they say; they do not mean 'second-best endeavours'.

Certainly in their context in the order of 8th December 1972 I do not think the words
cause any real difficulty. The company has to use its best endeavours to see that the *f*
shareholders pass the resolution for the issue of the shares to the plaintiffs.

How does it propose to discharge that obligation, as indicated in the circular to
which I have referred? Inter alia, it reads as follows:

> 'The Board, on behalf of your Company, have taken the opinion of [a leading
> counsel] (who did not act and was not concerned in either of the litigation matters
> hereinbefore mentioned on behalf of your Company or any other party thereto), *g*
> as to the rights and obligations of the Board, your Company and its shareholders
> as a result of the Court Order set out in Appendix 1. His conclusions are set out in
> one paragraph which is contained in Appendix 4 to this circular.'

Then later it says:

> 'Shareholders should seek advice as to their position from their Solicitor, *h*
> Accountant or Bank Manager, if they are in doubt as to how to cast their votes.
> In accordance with the advice which has been given by Counsel, Shareholders are
> entitled to vote in whatever way they wish. In view of this the Board is making no
> recommendation to them but is leaving the decision on how to vote to the judg-
> ment of individual members. Whatever the outcome it will have no effect on
> your Company's quotation for its existing shares. At the time the acquisition in *i*

---

1   [1972] 3 All ER at 355, [1972] 1 WLR at 1126
2   [1951] 1 All ER 714, [1951] 2 KB 252
3   (1911) 27 TLR 451
4   27 TLR at 452

a

Logan was negotiated between your Company and [the plaintiff company] in December 1968 I was Chairman of [the plaintiff company] as well as being Chairman of your company. When the dispute arose between your company and [the plaintiff company] I chose to resign my position with [the plaintiff company], which took effect from the 6th April, 1972. It has been suggested by your Company's Brokers that it would be invidious for me to vote. Accordingly I have considered this and for this reason alone I shall abstain from voting.'

b

The following passage I am about to read is contained in appendix 3 entitled: 'General Information'. Item 14 is:

'*The cost of Investment by [the company] in Logan*
(a) If the Resolutions to be put before the Company in General Meeting are passed the cost to your Company of the acquisition will be £276,373 consisting of:

c

		£
(i)	Cash consideration	150,000
(ii)	Consideration attributable to the 370,000 Ordinary Shares previously referred to	92,500
(iii)	Acquisition costs	33,873

d

Subject to further legal fees to be ascertained
(b) In addition if the Resolutions are passed a sum of £54,500 will be payable to [the plaintiff company] in respect of arrears of dividend calculated from the 3rd June 1969 up to and including the interim dividend for the year ended 28th December 1973.
(c) If the Resolutions are rejected the cost to your Company will be £183,873 and further legal fees, as yet unascertained on the basis of the advice of Leading Counsel.'

e

Then a summary of the advice of leading counsel was given as follows:

'(1) The undertaking to and Order of the Court in the action between [the plaintiffs] and [the company] do not bind the shareholders of the company in their capacity of shareholders. (2) There is no compulsion on the shareholders of the Company to approve the proposed issue of shares to [the plaintiffs]. If they do not approve there can be no penalty upon them. (3) The Directors, Officers and other agents of the Company must, in those capacities, take normal proper steps to seek quotation for and permission to deal in the shares: but this does not in any way affect their position as shareholders: in that capacity they are entitled to decline to approve the issue, even if that has the effect of preventing the Company from obtaining quotation and permission to deal. (4) If quotation for and permission to deal in the shares are not obtained, the Order for the allotment and issue of the shares never takes effect. In these circumstances [the plaintiffs] could not get the shares, even if they were willing to take the share without quotation; nor can they get anything else in compensation.'

f

g

h

In view of the fact that at least two of the passages which I have just read either are, or are based directly on, the opinion of leading counsel referred to, it is perhaps difficult to come to the conclusion that the company, activated by its directors, was intending deliberately to place itself in contempt of court by cold-bloodedly breaking the terms of its undertaking to the court. But there can hardly be any question but that to tell shareholders 'If you pass the resolutions, the company will have to pay £330,873 for the asset it has acquired from the plaintiffs, whereas if you do not pass them the cost will be something not much over £183,873' is to invite the shareholders to reject the resolution. Not even—as might have been expected, even if the advice of leading counsel was accepted wholly—words along the lines 'But as honourable men running an honourable company we ought to stick to our bargain even although we might, through a legal technicality, be able to save ourselves £140,000' are there.

j

As I say, I feel able to exonerate the directors from the charge of deliberately flouting
the order of the court, although I can well understand that others, including the
plaintiffs, may not take such a charitable view of their actions. But that the circular
cannot be allowed to stand is, in my view, beyond all possible argument. It is founded
on a wholly false premise. I cannot for one moment accept the concluding paragraph
of the extract from counsel's opinion which I have read. He has overlooked altogether
that the order, into which he correctly states the rights of the plaintiffs have been
transmuted, is one for the execution of the contract between the parties, and that if
this cannot take place exactly as ordered, obviously a supplemental order must be
made along the lines I have previously indicated. Counsel's conclusions lack, not
only sound legal conclusions, but also elementary notions of right. Counsel for
the directors, with studied meiosis, called the conclusions 'somewhat surprising'.
For my part, I am sorry that such a conclusion should ever have gone out under the
imprimatur of Lincoln's Inn.

But this is by no means the end of the matter; it is one thing to condemn the
circular as actually sent out, quite another to decide what must go into it. I therefore
turn to para 2 of the plaintiffs' notice of motion. I do not think that any question
arises as to (i) and (ii), these being simply highly relevant matters of fact; (iii) was
eventually abandoned by counsel for the plaintiffs; and, rather more reluctantly, he
finally abandoned (iv) as being necessarily involved with the abandonment of (iii).
Involved in this abandonment, however, was a consideration of the precise scope and
effect of the well-worn company law phrase 'the company in general meeting' in
relation to which, out of deference to the extremely persuasive arguments of both
counsel for the plaintiffs and counsel for the directors, I think it right to say a few
words.

Counsel for the plaintiffs argued that, in effect, there are two separate sets of persons in whom authority to activate the company itself resides. Quoting the well-
known passages from Lord Haldane in *Lennard's Carrying Co Ltd v Asiatic Petroleum
Co Ltd*[1] he submitted that the company as such was only a juristic figment of the
imagination, lacking both a body to be kicked and a soul to be damned. From this it
followed that there must be some one or more human persons who did, as a matter of
fact, act on behalf of the company, and whose acts therefore must, for all practical
purposes, be the acts of the company itself. The first of such bodies was clearly the
body of directors, to whom under most forms of articles (see art 80 of Table A, or
art 86 of the defendant company's articles which is in similar form) the management
of the business of the company is expressly delegated. Therefore, their acts are the
company's acts; and if they do not, in the present instance, cause the company to
comply with the undertakings given by it to the court, they are themselves liable for
contempt of court. And this, he says, is well recognised: see RSC Ord 45, r 5(1),
whereunder disobedience by a corporation to an injunction may result directly in the
issue of a writ of sequestration against any director thereof. It is of course clear that
for this purpose there is no distinction between an undertaking and an injunction (see
the Supreme Court Practice 1973[2]).

This is, indeed, all well-established law, with which counsel for the directors did not
quarrel and indeed I think his first proposition asserted. But, continues counsel for the
plaintiffs, this is only half of the story. There are some matters in relation to which the
directors are not competent to act on behalf of the company, the relevant authority
being 'the company in general meeting', that is to say, a meeting of the members.
Thus in respect of all matters within the competence—at any rate those within the
exclusive competence—of a meeting of the members, the acts of the members are the
acts of the company, in precisely the same way as the acts of the directors are the acts
of the company. Ergo, for any shareholder to vote against a resolution to issue the

1　[1915] AC 705, [1914-15] All ER Rep 280
2　Volume 1, p 685, para 45/5/3

shares here in question to the plaintiffs would be a contempt of court, as it would be a step taken by him knowingly which would prevent the company from fulfilling its undertaking to the court. Counsel for the plaintiffs admitted that he could find no authority which directly assisted his argument, but equally confidently asserted that there was no authority which precluded it.

Counsel for the directors indicted the argument of counsel for the plaintiffs as being based on a nominalistic fallacy. His precise proposition was formulated as follows:

'Whilst directors have special responsibilities as executive agents of the company to ensure that the company does not commit a contempt of court, a shareholder when the position has been put before them generally who chooses to vote against such approval will not himself be in contempt of court'.

Putting this into less formal language, what counsel for the directors submitted was that although it is perfectly true that the act of the members in passing certain special types of resolutions binds the company, their acts are not the acts of the company. There would, he submitted, be no real doubt about this were it not for the use of the curious expression 'the company in general meeting'—which, in a sense, drags in the name of the company unnecessarily. What that phrase really means, he submitted, is 'the members (or corporators) of the company assembled in a general meeting', and that if the phrase is written out in full in this manner it becomes quite clear that the decisions taken at such a meeting, and the resolutions passed thereat, are decisions taken by, and resolutions passed by, the members of the company, and not the company itself. They are therefore in the position of strangers to the order and not in contempt by their act in voting as they please, whatever its effect may be.

In my judgment, these submissions of counsel for the directors are correct. I think that in a nutshell the distinction is this. When a director votes as a director for or against any particular resolution in a directors' meeting, he is voting as a person under a fiduciary duty to the company for the proposition that the company should take a certain course of action. When a shareholder is voting for or against a particular resolution he is voting as a person owing no fiduciary duty to the company who is exercising his own right of property to vote as he thinks fit. The fact that the result of the voting at the meeting (or a subsequent poll) will bind the company cannot affect the position that in voting he is voting simply as an exercise of his own property rights.

Perhaps another (and simpler) way of putting the matter is that a director is an agent, who casts his vote to decide in what manner his principal shall act through the collective agency of the board of directors; a shareholder who casts his vote in general meeting is not casting it as an agent of the company in any shape or form. His act, therefore, in voting as he pleases cannot in any way be regarded as an act of the company.

Counsel for the directors was, in his second proposition, which was as follows:

'Where it is necessary for the proper performance of a contract that something should first be approved by a third party who is not under the control of a party to the contract, the withholding of such approval with the result that the contract cannot be performed does not create a breach of contract',

enunciating a proposition which he intended to relate to the shareholders in the company. His 'third party' is intended to be the shareholders, and they are not (in his words) 'under the control' of the company. I would accept this as far as it goes, but although an acceptable proposition in the abstract, it does not, of course, have any relevance to the present case, where the contract is not in any way conditional, and the order of the court is directed merely to ensuring that, if at all possible, the company performs it to the letter rather than performs it partly with compensation, or not at all with damages.

It is, I think, equally clear that the shareholders are not abetting the company to commit a contempt of court; the company is, indeed, by convening the requisite meeting and putting a positive circular before the members duly complying with the obligations which rest on it. It will have done its best, and the rest is in the lap of the gods in the shape of the individual decisions of the members.

It would, of course, be otherwise if one could envisage any circumstances in which an order was made by the courts on a company to do something, for example to increase its capital (as distinct from using its best endeavours to increase its capital), which must of necessity involve the shareholders voting in a particular manner. But I at any rate cannot envisage any ordinary situation (as distinct from, for example, a situation where all the shareholders were before the court and bound by the order) where such an order would ever be made.

It is for these reasons that I cannot accept paras 2(iii) and 2(iv) of the notice of motion. Passing from these topics for a moment, it also follows from what I have said earlier that I accept para 2(v) of the notice of motion. I cannot wholly accept para 2(vi); I think the words 'to expose the Company to proceedings for contempt of Court' are inaccurate, and I have no means of knowing at present whether the damages payable to the plaintiffs in the event they should elect to take the shares without a stock exchange quotation would be 'heavy'. In any event, I think the damages position ought to be explained fully in the circular. Paragraph 2 (vii) is again factual and should go in, slightly expanded to refer to what the terms of the current undertaking of the company will actually be.

Having dealt so far with what the plaintiffs seek to have included in the circular, it appears to me that in a sense the most important matter has not been dealt with; that is to say, it must be a circular which, in order to comply with the company's undertaking to the court, must be one inviting a favourable response. The question which it poses must be one which Latinists would preface with the word 'nonne' and not with the word 'num'. In other words, I accede to para 3(1) of the notice of motion; I do not consider that the circular should be left neutral.

This only leaves for consideration the question in what manner the circular should, as a practical matter, be drafted. For even granted that the lines of the circular are fixed, there is clearly room for a considerable amount of light and shade therein. I think that, strictly, having regard to the issue of the present clearly offending circular, the correct course would be to refer the settlement of the circular to the master. This, however, would, I think, be a remedy which neither plaintiffs nor defendants would welcome; and, having regard to the attitudes which counsel for the company and counsel for the directors have taken up before me, I am hopeful that it will be sufficient if I order that the circular which is to go out is to be as agreed between the plaintiffs and the defendants in accordance with the foregoing principles, and only in default of agreement is to be so settled.

I now come to para 4 of the notice of motion, which seeks an order restraining the individual respondents and each of them from voting against the resolution. Counsel for the plaintiffs says that, as the executive agents of the company, they are bound to recommend to its shareholders that they vote in favour of the resolution to issue the shares, and hence, at the least, they cannot themselves vote against it, for they would thereby be assisting the company to do that which it is their duty to secure does not happen. If as executive officers of the company they are bound to procure a certain result, if at all possible, how can they, as individuals, seek to frustrate that result?

I regret, however, that I am unable to accede to counsel's arguments in this respect. I much regret it, because I cannot see how, in common honesty, directors who have committed a company to a particular course of action can themselves seek by their own acts as individuals to frustrate it, more especially when they will thereby be rendering the company liable to pay damages, and possibly very heavy damages indeed. But even if that were not the case, the point on commercial honesty would remain.

However, I do not see where this is meant to lead me. Suppose, for example, that a minority of the board had been throughout strenuously opposed to the company entering into this contract, are they nevertheless as individuals to lose control of their right to vote adversely thereto? Suppose that, before the question of implementation arose, there had been a complete change in the character of the composition of the board, and the existing board were all bitterly hostile to their predecessors' actions? True it is that they would still be bound to procure the company to honour its undertakings, but it is far from clear to me on what principle they would be obliged, at the least, to have their own votes as members sterilised. Suppose that the members of the present board resigned on the eve of this meeting; would they then be entitled to vote as ordinary members, or not? These examples show, I think, that counsel's proposition is far from self-evident. I think it is wrong. I think that a director who has fulfilled his duty as a director of a company by causing it to comply with an undertaking binding on it is nevertheless free, as an individual shareholder, to enjoy the same unfettered and unrestricted right of voting at general meetings of the members of the company as he would have if he were not also a director.

The propositions of counsel for the directors bearing on this point were as follows:

> '4. Where a court makes an order directing a party to an action to observe or do some act, this does not impose an obligation on someone who is not a party to the action to do anything. 5 (a) Directors of the defendant company who are not parties to the action but have either legally or by commercial custom a duty to advise shareholders as to their interests in approving or otherwise an acquisition are free to advise them as they the directors *bona fide* think fit. (b) All the shareholders, directors or not, are free to vote at relevant meetings as they think fit.'

I would accept counsel's proposition 4 as a purely general statement of law, but if applied to the directors of the company subject to such an order of the court it is misleading. The directors, although not in express terms parties to the action, do come under an obligation to procure that the company acts in conformity with the order of the court, for the simple reason that if they did not there would never be any effective remedy of this nature against a company. The provisions of RSC Ord 45, r 5(1), stand as an awful warning that this proposition cannot be pushed to the lengths to which counsel would perforce push it. It follows inevitably that his propositions 5(a)—both (a) and (b) being stated by him to follow from 4—is again too wide if it is intended to link up with proposition 4. I have no doubt that where a conditional contract is entered into—conditional, for example, on the shareholders approving an increase in the capital of the company—there is, in general, no duty on the company to procure the fulfilment of the condition, and in those circumstances proposition 5(a) would be correct. But I think a great deal must depend on the precise condition, and the precise construction of the contract into which the company has entered. In any event, of course, this proposition is not geared to the facts of this case, where the question never has been whether the company shall make the acquisition (it has already done so) but whether it will fairly and squarely discharge the obligation which lies on it to satisfy the purchase consideration, or whether it will, in lieu, pay damages.

However, as I have already stated, I agree with proposition 5(b) though not as a deduction from proposition 4. I would under this head finally call attention to s 138 of the Companies Act 1948 under which it will be noted that on a poll a member may cast his votes both for and against any particular resolution. This provision was, as is well known, introduced to meet the difficulties of large trust corporations which might hold shares in a company on behalf of two or three more trusts, whose respective interests might well require different exercises of its votes. This recognition of the fact that a shareholder in a company may have more than one capacity, and that in each capacity he is entitled to act as necessitated by such capacity, appears to me to be fully consistent with my view that in relation to the matters here in question, a director who is, as a director, bound to take one course, may as an individual shareholder take quite another.

As regards para 5 of the notice of motion, counsel for the company exercising, if I may say so, his usual admirable discretion, offered, as soon as the matter was raised, to give the undertaking thereby sought. This renders it wholly unnecessary for me to say anything about the circumstances giving rise to the claim for this extended relief.

In the upshot, the final outcome is as follows. First, I accepted counsel for the company's undertakings in the terms of para 5 of the notice of motion on the hearing on Friday, 22nd March 1974. Second, I then ordered that the meeting convened for 5th April should not take place, or, if it took place, should merely be adjourned sine die without proceeding to any business. The parties agreed that the best method of effecting this would be by means of a suitable press announcement together with a circular letter to the members of the company informing them that the meeting would not proceed to business and that they should ignore the present circular, or words to the like effect. I understand that a suitable announcement and letter was agreed between all parties. Thirdly, I make an order in terms of para 1 of the notice of motion, and order that the notice convening the meeting is to be accompanied by a circular, both to be in terms approved by the plaintiffs, or, in default of such approval, to be settled by the master in conformity with the directions contained in this judgment. Fourthly, I make no order under para 4 of the notice of motion.

As regards costs, counsel for the directors wisely conceded that the motion could not be described as premature; he was, however, vitally concerned chiefly with those parts of the motion of counsel for the plaintiffs which I have held to have failed. I therefore think that the proper order so far as the directors are concerned is to say that there is to be no order with regard to costs either way.

So far as the company is concerned, in my view the motion, although seeking in some respects rather more by way of relief than that to which I have held the plaintiffs entitled, was fully justified, and I think the company must accordingly pay to the plaintiffs the costs thereof. I am minded to make an order for the immediate taxation and payment of such costs, not in any sense as a mark of the court's displeasure but merely because, having regard to the absolutely correct attitude exhibited by the defendant company through their present representative at the hearing, I would be very loth to think that there will now be any other event in this most unfortunate action.

Order accordingly.

Solicitors: *Herbert Smith & Co* (for the plaintiffs); *Bull & Bull*, agents for *Elliott & Buckley*, Manchester (for the company and the directors).

Jacqueline Metcalfe   Barrister.

Applied in R v Wehner [1977]
3 All ER 553

R v Tucker

COURT OF APPEAL, CRIMINAL DIVISION
ROSKILL, JAMES LJJ AND CAULFIELD J
14th MARCH 1974

Distinguished in R v Marquis
[1974] 2 All ER 1216

Criminal law – Appeal – Sentence – Probation order – Right of appeal against order – Whether offender against whom order made having right of appeal – Criminal Justice Act 1948, s 12(1).

There is no right of appeal against a probation order made by the Crown Court since, under s 12(1)[a] of the Criminal Justice Act 1948, a conviction of an offence for which an order is made placing the offender on probation is deemed not to be a conviction for the purposes of an appeal and, if there has been no conviction, there is no right of appeal against sentence (see p 640 *b* and p 641 *a* and *d*, post).

Notes
For the effects of probation, see 10 Halsbury's Laws (3rd Edn) 507, 508, para 922.

For the Criminal Justice Act 1948, s 12, see 8 Halsbury's Statutes (3rd Edn) 352.

Cases referred to in judgment
R v Colbourn (31st May 1967) unreported, CA.
R v Thayne [1969] 3 All ER 652, [1970] 1 QB 141, [1969] 3 WLR 480, 53 Cr App Rep 582, CA, Digest (Cont Vol C) 240, 6836c.

Appeal
On 25th October 1973 in the Crown Court at Croydon before Judge Grieves QC and a jury the appellant, Richard Tucker, was convicted of driving a motor vehicle when unfit to drive through drink or drugs, contrary to s 5(1) of the Road Traffic Act 1972. He was disqualified for 12 months and remanded on bail for a social enquiry report and, if need be, for a medical report. On 16th November 1973 he was made the subject of a probation order under s 4 of the Criminal Justice Act 1948 with a condition of residence at Tooting Bec Hospital. He was given leave to appeal against sentence by the single judge. The facts are set out in the judgment of the court.

I G Bing for the appellant.
I R Stanbrook for the Crown.

ROSKILL LJ delivered the following judgment of the court. The appellant, Richard Tucker, was given leave to appeal by Bristow J against a probation order made at Croydon Crown Court by Judge Grieves on 16th November 1973. It was not what one might call an ordinary probation order. It was a probation order subject to s 4 of the Criminal Justice Act 1948, and had attached to it a condition of residence at Tooting Bec Hospital. The order was made by the trial judge after considerable enquiry into the appellant's condition, and with the benefit of the best medical advice which could be made available to him.

The offence in question was driving a motor vehicle when unfit to drive through drugs. Of that offence the appellant had been convicted on 25th October 1973 before the trial judge and a jury. The judge ordered him to be disqualified for 12 months.

When the single judge gave leave to appeal, he did not, naturally enough, have drawn to his attention the statutory provisions which give rise to the question we have to decide, namely whether there is in these circumstances a right of appeal

---

a Section 12(1) is set out at p 640*j*, post

to this court against a probation order made by a Crown Court. Curiously enough, neither in the days of assizes and quarter sessions, nor since 1972, when the Crown Court came into existence, has this point arisen for decision in this court. Therefore, with the help we have had from counsel for the appellant and counsel for the Crown, we have gone into the matter with some care. We have reached the conclusion, and I will say it now, that there is no such right of appeal to this court. In order to explain why we have reached that conclusion, it is necessary to look in detail at a number of statutory provisions.

The starting point must be the statute which creates this court. The jurisdiction of this court is solely statutory—that is elementary and well known. The relevant section is s 9 of the Criminal Appeal Act 1968, which provides:

'A person who has been convicted of an offence on indictment may appeal to the Court of Appeal against any sentence (not being a sentence fixed by law) passed on him for the offence, whether passed on his conviction or in subsequent proceedings.'

That provision gives rise at once to two separate questions: first, has the appellant been convicted, and secondly, has he been sentenced. I will take the second first. 'Sentence' is defined in s 50 of the 1968 Act. Section 50(1) provides thus:

'In this Act, "sentence", in relation to an offence, includes any order made by a court when dealing with an offender (including a hospital order under Part V of the Mental Health Act 1959, with or without an order restricting discharge) . . .'

It is therefore plain, in the view of this court, that the word 'sentence' in s 9, when read with s 50, is not limited to meaning fine or imprisonment or other sentence of that kind, but includes an order, such as the order which was made in the present case.

It is quite true, as counsel for the appellant helpfully reminded us, that when one looks back at s 3(1) of the Criminal Justice Act 1948, one finds:

'Where a court by or before which a person is convicted of an offence (not being an offence the sentence for which is fixed by law) is of opinion that having regard to the circumstances, including the nature of the offence and the character of the offender, it is expedient to do so, the court may, instead of sentencing him, make a probation order, that is to say, an order requiring him to be under the supervision of a probation officer for a period to be specified in the order of not less than one year nor more than three years.'

At first sight it does seem a little curious that one should treat a probation order as a sentence for the purpose of ss 9 and 50 of the Criminal Appeal Act 1968 when the very statute which empowers the making of such an order says that it is an order made instead of a sentence. Nonetheless, we are satisfied, having heard counsel, that an order such as that from which the appellant seeks to appeal, is a sentence for the purpose of s 9 of the Criminal Appeal Act 1968.

That enables me to turn to what is the more difficult question, namely whether the appellant has been 'convicted'. Of course the jury in this case returned a verdict of guilty, and that in ordinary language is a conviction. But the matter does not end there, because s 12(1) of the Criminal Justice Act 1948 provides:

'Subject as hereinafter provided, a conviction of an offence for which an order is made under this Part of this Act placing the offender on probation or discharging him absolutely or conditionally shall be deemed not to be a conviction for any purpose other than the purposes of the proceedings in which the order is made and of any subsequent proceedings which may be taken against offender under the foregoing provisions of this Act.'

It has not been suggested that an appeal to this court is part of the proceedings in which the order is made. It seems to this court clear that the effect of that subsection is to ensure that a person who, though 'convicted' in the ordinary sense of that word, is thereafter made subject to a probation order, should not have that conviction counted against him for any subsequent purpose save for those few to which our attention has been drawn, such as the Civil Evidence Act 1968, s 11(5), where an exception is made to the provisions of s 12(1) of the 1948 Act.

In the view of this court, s 12(3)(a) of the 1948 Act, to which counsel for the appellant also referred, supports this conclusion, because it provides:

'The foregoing provisions of this section shall not affect—(a) any right of any such offender as aforesaid to appeal against his conviction, or to rely thereon in bar of any subsequent proceedings for the same offence . . .'

In other words although by virtue of s 12(1) once an offender is placed on probation, his conviction does not for any other purpose count as a conviction, nonetheless it still will be treated as a conviction to enable him to appeal to this court against the verdict of the jury and subsequently to plead autrefois acquit or convict. In those circumstances we have been driven to the conclusion that the appellant has not been 'convicted' in any relevant sense of that word, and unless he has been convicted, he has no right of appeal against sentence.

I said earlier that this question had not previously come before this court. The researches of the learned registrar's staff have brought to light a decision of this court on 31st May 1967, R v Colbourn[1]. The court consisted of Lord Parker CJ, Sachs LJ and Waller J. Colbourn had pleaded guilty to child detention at Hampshire Quarter Sessions in December 1966. A probation order was made with a condition of residence. Colbourn sought to complain of that condition of that order, and this court did in fact deal with the application on its merits. For that purpose it assumed that it had jurisdiction and Sachs LJ, after pointing out that it was always open to the court which made the probation order to revise or alter the conditions of that order, said:

'Suffice it to say that so far as this court is concerned, this is not an application which, even if it had jurisdiction, which it assumes for the purpose of this judgment that it has got, it could accede to . . .'

At first sight, of course, as Lord Parker CJ pointed out in R v Thayne[2], it may seem odd that there can be any sentence or order of a Crown Court which should not be the subject of appeal to this court. In Thayne's case[2] the sentence against which no appeal lay arose from estreating bail. But in the present case the position is different. The Criminal Justice Act 1948 in Sch 1 creates a complete—and one might call it self-contained—code for dealing with probation orders. Paragraph 1 of Sch 1 reads:

'The court by which a probation order was made may, upon application made by the probation officer or by the probationer, discharge the order.'

Paragraph 2(1) reads:

'If the supervising court is satisfied that a probationer proposes to change, or has changed his residence from the petty sessional division named in the probation order to another petty sessional division, the court may, and if application in that behalf is made by the probation officer, shall, by order amend the probation order . . .'

He has to go back to that court or invite the probation officer to go back and the matter can be then dealt with.

---

1   Unreported
2   [1969] 3 All ER 652, [1970] 1 QB 141

There is another reason why it is not surprising that there should not be a right of appeal. Section 3(5) of the Criminal Justice Act 1948, after providing that the court should explain the practical effect of a probation order in ordinary language, continues:

> '... and if the offender is not less than fourteen years of age the court shall not make the order unless he expresses his willingness to comply with the requirements thereof.'

In other words the court cannot, in the case of someone over 14, make a probation order without express consent given in open court by the offender. In those circumstances, it would be wrong if there were a right of appeal to this court against an order to the making of which the offender is required to consent and has publicly consented when its effect in accordance with s 3(5) has been fully explained to him.

In those circumstances this court, notwithstanding that the single judge gave leave to appeal, is of the opinion that he had no jurisdiction to do so, and that this court has no jurisdiction to entertain the appeal.

The matter cannot unfortunately be left there. There are before us reports from doctors and also the probation service. The most relevant for present purposes is the report, dated 12th March 1974, to the liaison probation officer of this court, Mr Dashwood, from the probation officer concerned. I will not read it. That officer makes it plain that the appellant has taken the law into his own hands and has walked out of the hospital where he is required to reside. Indeed we are told by counsel he is in court today. In those circumstances there is certainly a strong prima facie case for saying that he is in breach of the probation order.

This court must, in those circumstances, direct that the attention of the probation officer should formally be drawn to this fact—no doubt he is well aware of it. The appellant should be brought back promptly before Judge Grieves or other appropriate judge of the Crown Court for any breach (if proved) to be dealt with. That does not preclude an application being made to vary the order. That is entirely a matter for the court in the light of up-to-date medical reports. This court is expressing no view on the propriety of the original order, whether it should be continued or whether it should now be varied, so far as the condition of residence is concerned. That must be a matter for the learned circuit judge in the light of the best help he can get. This court is not prepared, where persons have assented to the making of probation orders, including s 4 orders with conditions of residence, to tolerate probationers taking the law into their own hands, as it seems the appellant may have done, because they think the hospital cannot do them any good, and just walking out of the hospital. That defeats the whole purpose of the order. The sooner the appellant realises that the better.

In these circumstances we must refuse to entertain this appeal.

Order accordingly.

Solicitors: *Montague, Gardner & Howard*, Mitcham (for the appellant); *Solicitor, Metropolitan Police*.

N P Metcalfe Esq Barrister.

R v London Borough of Hillingdon, ex parte Royco Homes Ltd

QUEEN'S BENCH DIVISION
LORD WIDGERY CJ, MELFORD STEVENSON AND BRIDGE JJ
7th, 8th, 11th MARCH 1974

Certiorari – Jurisdiction – Bodies amenable to jurisdiction – Bodies having legal authority to determine rights of subjects – Whether necessary that body should have the duty to act judicially.

Certiorari – Jurisdiction – Planning authority – Decision of authority – Permission for development – Grant of permission subject to conditions – Permission granted to applicant subject to conditions – Applicant alleging conditions ultra vires – Applicant seeking order of certiorari – Whether remedy of certiorari available.

Town and country planning – Development – Permission for development – Condition – Reasonableness – Ultra vires – Severability – Permission granted to private developer – Permission subject to conditions – Conditions requiring developer to make dwellings suitable for local authority tenants – Conditions requiring dwellings to be occupied by local authority tenants – Whether conditions ultra vires – Whether conditions severable.

A local planning authority granted the applicants planning permission, under s 29(1)[a] of the Town and Country Planning Act 1971, to erect seven blocks of three-storey flats, subject to the following conditions: (1) that the dwellings were designed so as to provide space and heating to the standards required for local authority housing; (2) that the dwellings were constructed at a cost per dwelling not exceeding the relevant housing cost yardstick (i e the yardstick appropriate to local authorities who sought to obtain government subsidies for the houses which they erected); (3) that the dwellings should first be occupied by persons who were on the local authority's housing waiting list; and (4) that the dwellings should, for a period of ten years from the date of first occupation, be occupied as the residence of a person who occupied by virtue of a tenure which could not be excluded from the protection of the Rent Act 1968 by any provision of s 2 of that Act. The applicants moved for, inter alia, an order of certiorari to bring up and quash the grant of the planning permission on the grounds that the four conditions attached to it were ultra vires the planning authority.

Held – The applicants were entitled to an order of certiorari for the following reasons—
    (i) Certiorari would lie in appropriate cases to control the exercise by a local planning authority of its jurisdiction under the planning Acts, i e in clear cases where the issue was a matter of law and the matter of law appeared on the face of the record. It was immaterial that the planning authority was not a body which had the duty to act judicially, for certiorari would issue to any body which had jurisdiction to determine the rights of subjects whether or not it was required to act judicially (see p 648 e and f, p 649 b and p 652 b and c, post); *R v Hendon Rural District Council, ex parte Chorley* [1933] All ER Rep 20 and dictum of Lord Reid in *Ridge v Baldwin* [1963] 2 All ER at 77 applied.
    (ii) Although s 29(1) gave the planning authority very wide powers to impose such conditions as they thought fit, conditions 3 and 4 were so unreasonable as to go beyond anything that Parliament could have intended, or that any reasonable authority could properly have imposed, since they, in effect, required the applicants

---

a   Section 29(1), so far as material, is set out at p 649 *d* and *e*, post

to assume at their own expense a significant part of the duty of a local authority as *a* housing authority. Accordingly those conditions were ultra vires (see p 651 *e* to *g* and p 652 *b d* and *f*, post).

(iii) Although conditions 1 and 2 were not themselves clearly ultra vires, they could not be severed from conditions 3 and 4 because they were all designed for a single purpose (see p 651 *g* and *h* and p 652 *b* and *c*, post).

(iv) The four conditions were fundamental to the whole planning permission, which *b* was accordingly void (see p 651 *j* and p 652 *b* and *d*, post).

Dictum of Lord Denning in *Pyx Granite Co Ltd v Ministry of Housing and Local Government* [1958] 1 All ER at 633 and *Hall & Co Ltd v Shoreham-by-Sea Urban District Council* [1964] 1 All ER 1 applied.

Notes
For certiorari, see 1 Halsbury's Laws (4th Edn) 150-160, paras 147-167, and for cases *c* on jurisdiction to grant certiorari, see 16 Digest (Repl) 471-485, *2905-3038*.

For conditions attaching to planning permission, see 37 Halsbury's Laws (3rd Edn) 304-307, para 414, and for cases on the subject, see 45 Digest (Repl) 340-343, *56-64*.

For the Rent Act 1968, s 2, see 18 Halsbury's Statutes (3rd Edn) 784.

For the Town and Country Planning Act 1971, s 29, see 41 Halsbury's Statutes (3rd Edn) 1619. *d*

Cases referred to in judgment
Associated Provincial Picture Houses Ltd v Wednesbury Corpn [1947] 2 All ER 680, [1948] 1 KB 223, [1948] LJR 190, 177 LT 641, 112 JP 55, 45 LGR 635, CA, 45 Digest (Repl) 215, *189.*

Hall & Co Ltd v Shoreham-by-Sea Urban District Council [1964] 1 All ER 1, [1964] 1 WLR *e* 240, 128 JP 120, 62 LGR 206, 15 P & CR 119, CA, 45 Digest (Repl) 342, *61.*

Mixnam's Properties Ltd v Chertsey Urban District Council [1963] 2 All ER 787, [1964] 1 QB 214, [1963] 3 WLR 38, 127 JP 446, 61 LGR 489, CA; *affd* [1964] 2 All ER 627, [1965] AC 735, [1964] 2 WLR 1210, 128 JP 405, 62 LGR 528, HL, 45 Digest (Repl) 359, *126.*

Pyx Granite Co Ltd v Ministry of Housing and Local Government [1958] 1 All ER 625, *f* [1958] 1 QB 554, [1958] 2 WLR 371, 122 JP 182, 56 LGR 171, CA; *rvsd* [1959] 3 All ER 1, [1960] AC 260, [1959] 3 WLR 346, 123 JP 429, 58 LGR 1, 10 P & CR 319, HL, 45 Digest (Repl) 336, *37.*

R v Electricity Comrs, ex parte London Electricity Joint Committee Co (1920) Ltd [1924] 1 KB 171, [1923] All ER Rep 150, 93 LJKB 390, 130 LT 164, 88 JP 13, 21 LGR 719, CA, 16 Digest (Repl) 433, *2381.* *g*

R v Hendon Rural District Council, ex parte Chorley [1933] 2 KB 696, [1933] All ER Rep 20, 102 LJKB 658, 149 LT 535, 97 JP 210, 31 LGR 332, DC, 45 Digest (Repl) 336, *36.*

Ridge v Baldwin [1963] 2 All ER 66, [1964] AC 40, [1963] 2 WLR 935, 127 JP 295, 61 LGR 369, HL, 37 Digest (Repl) 195, *32.*

Cases also cited
h
Fawcett Properties Ltd v Buckingham County Council [1960] 3 All ER 503, [1961] AC 636, HL.

Pilling v Abergele Urban District Council [1950] 1 All ER 76, [1950] 1 KB 636, DC.

R v Bradford-on-Avon Urban District Council, ex parte Boulton [1964] 2 All ER 492, [1964] 1 WLR 1136, DC. *j*

Motion for certiorari and mandamus
This was an application by way of motion on behalf of Royco Homes Ltd for (1) an order of certiorari to bring up and quash a purported grant of planning permission by the respondents, the London Borough of Hillingdon ('the planning authority'), dated 12th December 1973, permitting the development of a parcel of land known

as Buntings, Swakeleys Road, in the London Borough of Hillingdon, for residential development; (2) an order of mandamus directed to the planning authority requiring them to reconsider the planning application on which the planning permission was based and to decide it afresh according to law.   The facts are set out in the judgment of Lord Widgery CJ.

John Drinkwater QC, B A Payton and *B Sawbridge* for the applicants.
Michael Chavasse QC and *Michael Rich* for the planning authority.

LORD WIDGERY CJ. In these proceedings counsel moves on behalf of Royco Homes Ltd for an order of certiorari to bring up into this court with a view to its being quashed a purported grant of planning permission by the London Borough of Hillingdon dated 12th December 1973 and permitting the development of a parcel of land in the borough of Hillingdon known as 'Buntings', Swakeleys Road, for residential development.   The permission was subject to certain conditions to which I will refer in a great deal more detail later on.   If counsel for the applicants succeeds in obtaining an order for certiorari and the quashing of the planning permission in question, he then moves for an order of mandamus to require the planning authority, the London Borough of Hillingdon, to reconsider the planning application on which the planning permission is based and to decide it afresh according to law.

The whole matter, as I have said, arises out of the future of a small parcel of land at Hillingdon by the name of Buntings.   It is land which on any view of the matter is appropriate for development and appropriate for development by the building of residential homes.   The issue between the parties is whether this land should be developed by the planning authority, the borough council, under its duties as a housing authority for the provision of homes for those for whom the housing authority is responsible, or in the alternative whether it should be developed for residential purposes by its present owners, who are the applicants in this case.

The matter began on 18th May 1973 when the applicants made an application for permission to develop the land for residential purposes.   This application was refused by the borough in its capacity as planning authority, and the reason for the refusal which was given was in these terms: 'The site is required by the Local Authority for municipal housing purposes.'   That refusal was given on 31st August 1973.   The planning authority, having refused permission in the terms to which I have referred, went on to set out in a great deal of detail the conditions under which the development of this site would have been permitted but for the overriding difficulty of its being required by the local authority for municipal housing purposes.   Under the cross-heading of 'Informative' the planning authority go on to say: 'You are advised that if this site had not been required for municipal housing purposes then outline permission would have been given subject to the following conditions', and then a whole number of conditions are attached.

Just exactly what happened following the refusal to which I have referred is not important and the court has not been burdened with the detail of it.   It seems clear and I think counsel for the planning authority told us this, that the authority had some doubts as to the propriety of the reason which was given for refusing permission, and the upshot of it all was that the applicants made a further application for planning permission on 2nd October 1973.   This was again an outline application and some pains seem to have been taken to ensure that the conditions which had been antici-pated by the informative section of the earlier refusal were complied with.   The effect, therefore, was to narrow the question of whether the grant of planning per-mission should be made to the simple issue of whether it was appropriate for the local authority or for the private developer to have the privilege and duty of developing it.

Following on that second application the planning authority made a further

determination and in this case it was a determination to grant permission. The form
of the permission, which is dated 12th December 1973, is to—

'GRANT permission for . . . Erection of 7 blocks of 3 storey flats to provide 36
two bedroom flats with garaging and parking and estate road at The Buntings . . .'

The permission is made subject to conditions, many of which are not controversial
and raise no sort of issue before us, but within the ambit of the conditions are four
which constitute the basis of counsel for the applicants' submission that this grant
of permission is a nullity.

Condition 2:

'The dwellings hereby approved shall be so designed as to provide space and
heating standards at least to the standards (a) defined in Appendix I to Circular
36/67 dated 25th April, 1962 issued by the then Ministry of Housing and Local
Government, and (b) which shall have been designated as mandatory requirements for local authority housing schemes qualifying for Government subsidy
or loan sanction, and the detailed drawings required by condition No. 6 shall
show compliance with such standards.'

What that comes to is that the planning authority are insisting as a condition of the
planning permission that the dwellings shall be designed so as to provide space and
heating to the standards required for local authority housing. For myself I would
not have thought this condition on its face was a departure from the functions and
powers of the planning authority to which reference must later be made, but counsel
for the applicants, apart from other arguments designed to show that this permission
is invalid, says that it is outside the powers of a planning authority to lay down conditions as to the internal design of houses or flats the erection of which it authorises.
He says, as is the fact, that once a house has been built in accordance with planning
permission, its internal arrangements can be varied to any degree without further
planning permission. He, therefore, contends that it would be wholly illogical if
a planning authority when granting planning permission tried to dictate the internal
arrangements in the detail which this condition contemplates. For my part I do not
find it necessary to reach a conclusion on that argument of counsel for the applicants
and I deliberately do not attempt to pursue the matter further on that particular
point.

Condition 3:

'The dwellings hereby approved shall be constructed at a cost per dwelling
which shall not exceed the relevant housing cost yardstick (as defined by
Circular 36/67) . . .'

The condition goes on to further detail but the essence of it is contained in the
sentence which I have read. The effect of it, if it is valid, is that the houses to be
erected pursuant to this planning permission must be erected to a maximum cost
equivalent to that to which local authorities are subject if they seek to obtain normal
housing subsidies for development which they have carried out. This is a condition
then the effect of which is to restrict the maximum cost per dwelling and in fact the
yardstick chosen is the yardstick appropriate to the local authorities who seek, as
they naturally would, to obtain the appropriate government subsidies for the houses
which they erect.

Condition 4:

'The dwellings hereby approved shall be first occupied by persons (together
with their families and/or dependents) who on the qualifying date shall have been
recorded on the Housing Waiting List of the Hillingdon London Borough Council
(as distinct from the Council's statutory register of applications for accommodation) for a period of not less than 12 months immediately preceding the qualifying date. The qualifying date for any person shall be any date within the period

of 6 months before the commencement of his occupation of one of the dwellings hereby approved.'

Again cutting through the detail of the language, this is a requirement that if the houses are erected pursuant to the permission obtained by the applicants, the occupiers of those houses shall not be occupiers chosen by the developers themselves but shall be persons who are on the local authority's housing waiting list in the terms of the condition which I have read. That is on any view an extremely serious restriction on the character of the occupier who is to go into these houses if they are built pursuant to this permission.

Finally, condition 5:

'The dwellings hereby approved shall for a period of 10 years from the date of first occupation be occupied as the residence of a person who occupies by virtue of a tenure which would not be excluded from the protection of the Rent Act 1968 by any provision of Section 2 of that Act.'

Again the provision with regard to the security of tenure to be enjoyed by the respective tenants is there restricted when compared with the freedom which a developer would normally have in choosing not only the tenants who occupy his property but the terms on which they should so occupy it.

The case for the applicants before us today is that those four conditions are as a matter of law ultra vires as being in excess of the power to impose conditions enjoyed by a planning authority when granting a planning permission. Counsel for the applicants further submits that those conditions being void on that account, they are fundamental to the grant of planning permission, and if they are to be held to be null and void, the whole planning permission must fall with them, hence his application for certiorari.

This case involves a number of important and interesting points. The first one to be considered, strangely enough for the first time since the passing of the Town and Country Planning Act 1947, is whether certiorari will go at all to control the exercise by a planning authority of its jurisdiction under the planning Acts. In other words, the first question which we have to face squarely for the first time is whether the procedure of the prerogative orders goes to a planning authority exercising its jurisdiction under the Acts. There is, as I have said, no authority on this point on the modern town planning legislation, but there is a case on the earlier Acts which really stands alone as the only authority for the assistance of this court. It is *R v Hendon Rural District Council*[1]. The facts I take from the headnote[2]:

'A certiorari will lie to bring up a decision of a local authority to permit development pending the final approval by the Minister of Health of a town-planning scheme ... Resolutions had been passed by a rural district council for the preparation of a town-planning scheme, and the scheme was awaiting the approval of the Minister of Health, who had made, under s. 4 of the Town Planning Act, 1925, an Interim Development Order, under which persons could apply to the council for permission to build, pending the approval of the scheme by the Minister. This permission, if granted, would safeguard the applicants' right to compensation under s. 10 of the Town Planning Act, 1925, in the event of their property being injuriously affected by the making of the town-planning scheme. An application was made to the council for permission to develop certain premises in the area covered by the proposed town-planning scheme. Objections were invited and considered by the council, who unanimously decided to permit the proposed development, pending the final approval by the Minister of Health of the town-planning scheme:—*Held*, that as the decision of the council to permit the development in question conferred a legal

---

1   [1933] 2 KB 696, [1933] All ER Rep 20
2   [1933] 2 KB at 696

right to compensation in certain events and affected the rights of subjects, it *a* was sufficiently near a judicial decision to be the subject of a writ of certiorari.'

In the course of the judgments in this court in the *Hendon* case[1] reference was made to a frequently quoted observation of Atkin LJ in *R v Electricity Comrs*[2]. What Atkin LJ said was[3]:

'Wherever any body of persons having legal authority to determine questions *b* affecting the rights of subjects, and having the duty to act judicially, act in excess of their legal authority they are subject to the controlling jurisdiction of the King's Bench Division . . .'

In view of that clear dictum from Atkin LJ it is surprising that so little use has been made of the prerogative orders in this particular field, and I think that counsel for the planning authority may have put his finger on the explanation when he referred *c* to the fact that Atkin LJ's dictum required not only that the body to whom certiorari was to go had legal authority to determine questions affecting the rights of subjects, but also required that that body should have the duty to act judicially, a phrase which is rather less clear and indeed very difficult of definition. Accordingly it may be that previous efforts to use certiorari in this field have been deterred by Atkin LJ's reference to it being necessary for the body affected to have the duty to act *d* judicially. If that is so, that reason for reticence on the part of applicants was, I think, put an end to in the House of Lords in *Ridge v Baldwin*[4]. It is a case the facts of which are very far from the present and indeed have nothing to do with planning at all. But in the course of his speech Lord Reid made reference[5] to that oft-quoted dictum of Atkin LJ and pointed out that the additional requirement of the body being under a duty to act judicially was not supported by authority. Accordingly *e* it seems to me now that that obstacle, if obstacle it were, has been cleared away and I can see no reason for this court holding otherwise than that there is power in appropriate cases for the use of the prerogative orders to control the activity of a local planning authority. To put it the other way round, I see no general legal inhibition on the use of such orders, although no doubt they must be exercised only *f* in the clearest cases and with a good deal of care on the part of the court.

In particular, it has always been a principle that certiorari will go only where there is no other equally effective and convenient remedy. In the planning field there are very often, if not in an almost overwhelming number of cases, equally effective and convenient remedies. As is well known, there is now under the Town and Country Planning Act 1971 a comprehensive system of appeals from decisions of local planning authorities. In the instant case the applicants could, had they wished, have gone to *g* the Secretary of State for the Environment in the form of a statutory appeal under the Act instead of coming to this court. There would, if they had taken that course, have been open to them a further appeal to this court on a point of law following on the decision of the Secretary of State.

It seems to me that in a very large number of instances it will be found that the statutory system of appeals is more effective and more convenient than an application *h* for certiorari, and the principal reason why it may prove itself to be more convenient and more effective is that an appeal to the Secretary of State on all issues arising between the parties can be disposed of at one hearing. Whether the issue between them is a matter of law or fact, or policy or opinion, or a combination of some or all of those, one hearing before the Minister has jurisdiction to deal with them all, whereas of *j*

1 [1933] 2 KB 696, [1933] All ER Rep 20
2 [1924] 1 KB 171 at 205, [1923] All ER Rep 150 at 161
3 [1924] 1 KB at 205, [1923] All ER Rep at 161
4 [1963] 2 All ER 66, [1964] AC 40
5 [1963] 2 All ER at 77-79, [1964] AC at 74-76

a course an application for certiorari is limited to cases where the issue is a matter of law and then only when it is a matter of law appearing on the face of the order.

Furthermore of course there are in some instances reasons for saying that an action for a declaration is more appropriate and more convenient than an order of certiorari, and in cases where such an argument can be used certiorari should not in my opinion go because to allow it to go would be contrary to the necessary restrictions on its use.   But an application for certiorari has this advantage that it is speedier
b and cheaper than the other methods, and in a proper case, therefore, it may well be right to allow it to be used in preference to them.   But I would define a proper case as being a case where the decision in question is liable to be upset as a matter of law because on its face it is clearly made without jurisdiction or made in consequence of an error of law.

c Given those facts I can well see that it may be more efficient, cheaper and quicker to proceed by certiorari, and in those cases when they arise it seems to me proper that remedy should be available.

Thus one comes to consider the four conditions complained of in the present case. That the planning authority has wide power to impose conditions has been a common feature of this legislation ever since 1947, or indeed it may be before that.   The
d power is presently contained in s 29(1) of the 1971 Act which provides:

'Subject to the provisions of sections 26 to 28 of this Act, and to the following provisions of this Act, where an application is made to a local planning authority for planning permission, that authority, in dealing with the application, shall have regard to the provisions of the development plan, so far as material to the application, and to any other material considerations, and—(a) subject to
e sections 41, 42, 70 and 77 to 80 of this Act, may grant planning permission, either unconditionally or subject to such conditions as they think fit . . .'

Those wide words 'subject to such conditions as they think fit' confer authority for a wide range of conditions to be attached to planning permissions.   However those words are clearly too wide to be given their literal meaning and a number of
f years ago they were restricted by a dictum of Lord Denning, which is constantly quoted in these matters.   The dictum appears in the decision of the Court of Appeal in *Pyx Granite Co Ltd v Ministry of Housing and Local Government*[1], where Lord Denning said this:

'The principles to be applied are not, I think, in doubt.   Although the planning authorities are given very wide powers to impose "such conditions as they think
g fit", nevertheless the law says that those conditions, to be valid, must fairly and reasonably relate to the permitted development.   The planning authority are not at liberty to use their powers for an ulterior object, however desirable that object may seem to them to be in the public interest.'

There, of course, is counsel for the applicants' case in a sentence.   He says that these
h four conditions were imposed to suit an ulterior purpose, a purpose ulterior to the duty of the borough council as planning authority.   He says their purpose was to ensure that if a private developer was allowed to develop this land, he should have to use it in such a way as to relieve the local authority of a significant part of its burden as housing authority to provide houses for the homeless, and whether it is put as being a condition which is unreasonable or one not related to the development, or
j for an ulterior purpose, the argument for the applicants is that, however you look at it, these conditions are ultra vires and that they bring the whole planning permission down.

Of the cases which followed *Pyx Granite*[2] the one which is nearest to the present is

---

1   [1958] 1 All ER 625 at 633, [1958] 1 QB 554 at 572
2   [1958] 1 All ER 625, [1958] 1 QB 554

Hall & Co Ltd v Shoreham-by-Sea Urban District Council[1].   The facts of this case are a
little complex, but the essential features of it were these. The plaintiffs wanted to
develop some industrial land which fronted on a very heavily used highway. The
planning authority were concerned at the prospect of this development taking place
with its possible addition to the traffic using this already very congested road. In
granting permission for the development they made it a condition that the developers
should set aside from land in their own ownership a strip of land on the frontage
which was to be used for what is described as 'an ancillary roadway'. That by itself
might not have been objectionable if the ancillary roadway had simply been a service
road for the use of traffic coming to the site in question, but the terms on which the
council required this ancillary road to be used were such as almost to make it equivalent to a public highway. Thus complaint was made that the conditions requiring
the construction of the ancillary road were ultra vires on a great many grounds,
including the ground that they were for the ulterior purpose of requiring the developer to take on a part of the local authority's duty as highway authority. The view
of the Court of Appeal is well summarised in the headnote in these terms[2]:

> '... (2) That although the object sought to be attained by the [planning
> authority] was a perfectly reasonable one, the terms of the conditions, requiring
> the plaintiffs to construct an ancillary road at their own expense for the use of
> persons proceeding to and from adjoining properties and amounting to a re-
> quirement that the plaintiffs should in effect dedicate the road to the public
> without any right to compensation, there being a more regular course available
> under the Highways Act, 1959, were so unreasonable that they were ultra vires.'

Before I leave the headnote I mention, because it is relevant in a moment, a further
conclusion in *Hall's* case[1], namely[2]:   '(3) That the ultra vires conditions were
fundamental to the whole planning permission which was, accordingly, void.'
     The position is well set out in the judgment of Willmer LJ. An issue had been
raised in *Hall's* case[1] that the conditions were void for uncertainty, but that submission was rejected and is of no interest to us today. Willmer LJ then came down
to the issues which are of vital importance today. He said[3]:

> 'It is contended that the effect of these conditions is to require the plaintiffs
> not only to build the ancillary road on their own land, but to give right of passage
> over it to other persons to an extent that will virtually amount to dedicating it to
> the public, and all this without acquiring any right to recover any compensation
> whatsoever. This is said to amount to a violation of the plaintiffs' fundamental
> rights of ownership which goes far beyond anything authorised by the statute.
> In the course of the argument for the plaintiffs we were referred to the recent
> decision of this court in *Mixnam's Properties Ltd. v. Chertsey Urban District Council*[4].
> [He explained how that case arose and he went on:] The members of the court
> differed as to whether the particular conditions sought to be imposed were
> ultra vires; but all of us, I think, were agreed as to the principles to be followed.
> I can summarise the effect of what we said under three heads as follows: (i) The
> conditions must not be such as to effect a fundamental alteration in the general
> law relating to the rights of persons on whom they are imposed unless the power
> to effect such an alteration is expressed in the clearest possible terms. (ii) The
> conditions imposed must fairly and reasonably relate to the permitted develop-
> ment. (iii) The conditions imposed must not be so unreasonable that it can be
> said that Parliament clearly cannot have intended that they should be imposed.
> It has been contended on behalf of the plaintiffs that the conditions sought to be
> imposed in the present case violate all three of these principles.'

---

1   [1964] 1 All ER 1, [1964] 1 WLR 240
2   [1964] 1 WLR at 241
3   [1964] 1 All ER at 7, [1964] 1 WLR at 247
4   [1963] 2 All ER 787, [1964] 1 QB 214

Then in a later passage[1] he went on to deal with the issues then before the court:

'It appears to me that the object sought to be attained by the [planning authority] in the present case is a perfectly reasonable one. I agree with the view of the learned judge that to require the construction of an ancillary road and to limit the points at which traffic may enter or leave the main road, is "consistent with good traffic engineering". It is said, however, that the terms of the conditions actually imposed, particularly the requirement that the plaintiffs should give right of passsage to and from the ancillary roads to be constructed on the adjoining land, are so unreasonable as to go beyond anything that Parliament can have intended or that any reasonable authority could properly have imposed.'

Then he went on to deal with the effect of the conditions then before the court, and he justified the conclusion that the conditions were ultra vires in that case on the basis that they were so unreasonable that no reasonable authority, properly directing itself, could have imposed them. He reached that conclusion[2] having referred to *Associated Provincial Picture Houses Ltd v Wednesbury Corpn*[3] and the classic judgment of Lord Greene MR in that case.

I find *Hall's* case[4] helpfully similar to the situation which is before us. In *Hall's* case[4] the local authority, with the best of motives, wanted in effect a new extension to the public highway and thought it right to require the developer to provide it at his own expense as a condition of getting planning permission. That was rejected in the Court of Appeal because it was a fundamental departure from the rights of ownership and it was so unreasonable that no planning authority, appreciating its duty and properly applying itself to the facts, could have reached it. I think exactly the same can be said of the conditions in issue in this case.

Taking nos 4 and 5 first of all, they undoubtedly in my judgment are the equivalent of requiring the private developer to take on at his own expense a significant part of the duty of the local authority as housing authority. However well intentioned and however sensible such a desire on the part of the planning authority may have been, it seems to me that it is unreasonable in the sense in which Willmer LJ was using the word in *Hall's* case[4]. I, therefore, have no doubt for myself that conditions 4 and 5 are clearly ultra vires, but I have for some time thought that conditions 2 and 3 might be saved. Conditions 2 and 3, however strange and perhaps oppressive, do not by themselves appear to me to have a clear badge of ultra vires on them, although I would expect the Secretary of State on an appeal to him to have something to say about them. By themselves, however, I doubt whether they would have justified the allegation that they were clearly in excess of jurisdiction and clearly ultra vires. But I am persuaded in the end that one must not sever conditions 2 and 3 from conditions 4 and 5 because they are all designed to the single purpose. Conditions 2 and 3 are designed to see that the houses physically should be suitable for local authority tenants and conditions 4 and 5 are designed to see that in fact they should be occupied by the local authority tenants. I think the four being different facets of the single purpose stand or fall together and with that approach they must unquestionably fall in my opinion.

On the authority of *Hall's* case[4], the conditions being fundamental to the planning permission, I think they bring the planning permission down with them and that means that the applicants are entitled to the order of certiorari which they seek.

What happens after that is a matter which I do not think this court can finally deal with today. In my view the position following the order that certiorari should

---

1   [1964] 1 All ER at 8, [1964] 1 WLR at 249
2   [1964] 1 All ER at 8, [1964] 1 WLR at 248
3   [1947] 2 All ER 680 at 685, [1948] 1 KB 223 at 233
4   [1964] 1 All ER 1, [1964] 1 WLR 240

go is that the planning authority will now be required to reconsider the second
application for planning permission and reach a conclusion on it according to law.
I have little doubt that the local authority will do what is required of it under those
circumstances and, therefore, at the moment it would be, I think, wholly premature
for this court to consider an order of mandamus. I would for myself say that certiorari should go but that the application for mandamus should be adjourned sine die
with liberty to apply in case it proves necessary hereafter to achieve the proper
solution to this problem.

MELFORD STEVENSON J. I agree.

BRIDGE J. I also agree, and add a word only because this is the first time since the
passing of the Town and Country Planning Act 1947 that this court has made an order
of certiorari to quash a grant of planning permission. Clearly that is a strong step
and one which, in agreement with Lord Widgery CJ, I think should only be taken in
a clear case. This is, in my judgment, as clear a case as one could expect to find of
conditions being imposed which are ultra vires because the local authority are seeking
to impose on the citizen the performance of a duty which statute puts on them.

Everything possible is sought to be achieved by the four conditions in question,
which again in agreement with Lord Widgery CJ, I think one has to look at together,
to make the development which the applicant is permitted to carry out perform the
functions of a municipal housing estate. It is to conform to the physical standards
of a municipal housing estate and be built within the cost limits applicable to a
municipal housing estate. Finally it is to perform the function of municipal housing
by housing those who are on the local authority's housing waiting list and giving them
comparable security of tenure.

It is difficult to see how any authority could go further towards unburdening themselves and placing on the shoulders of the applicant the duty to provide housing
accommodation which Parliament has said in Part V of the Housing Act 1957 shall be
performed by the local authority in the various ways in which it can be performed
under that part of that Act, all of them requiring acquisition of the land by the local
authority.

Certiorari granted. Application for mandamus adjourned.

Solicitors: *Harold Benjamin & Collins*, South Harrow (for the applicants); *S H Stansfield*,
Hayes, Middlesex (for the planning authority).

N P Metcalfe Esq Barrister.

a

Bentley-Stevens v Jones and others

CHANCERY DIVISION
PLOWMAN J
15th, 18th MARCH 1974

b *Company — Director — Removal — Resolution to remove director — Interlocutory injunction to restrain company acting on resolution — Quasi-partnership — Irregularity in convening meeting — Irregularity capable of being cured by going through proper processes — Whether director entitled to interlocutory injunction.*

The defendant company was a wholly-owned subsidiary of another company, H
c Ltd, of which the plaintiff and the first and second defendants, J and H, were the three directors. They were also three of the four directors of the defendant company. J and H held between them 58 per cent of the issued share capital of H Ltd. They wished to remove the plaintiff from the board of the defendant company, under s 184 of the Companies Act 1948, and on 27th January 1974 J sent the plaintiff a letter notifying him of a board meeting of H Ltd to be held the next morning at which it was to be
d resolved that H Ltd should convene an extraordinary general meeting of the defendant company for the purpose of removing the plaintiff from the board. The plaintiff did not receive the letter until after (i) J and H had met and passed the resolution, (ii) H Ltd had requisitioned the extraordinary general meeting and (iii) J, as a director of the defendant company, had called an extraordinary general meeting of that company for 26th February. The notice convening that meeting purported to be given by order of
e the board but no board meeting of the company was held. The extraordinary general meeting was held on 26th February and the votes of H Ltd were cast in favour of removing the plaintiff from the board. The plaintiff brought an action against the defendants and applied for an interlocutory injunction restraining them from acting on the resolution of 26th February.

f **Held** — The plaintiff was not entitled to an interlocutory injunction for the following reasons—
  (i) The court would not grant an interlocutory injunction in respect of irregularities which could be cured by going through the proper processes. If, for example, the proceedings that followed the board meeting of 28th January were invalid because proper notice had not been given, the invalidity could be cured by the giving of a
g valid notice (see p 655 *f* to *h*, post); dictum of Lindley LJ in *Browne v La Trinidad* (1887) 37 Ch D at 17 applied.
  (ii) Assuming that the plaintiff was a quasi-partner he could still be expelled; the defendant company had a statutory right to remove him from its board and his only remedy was to apply for a winding-up order on the ground that it was just and equitable for the court to make such an order (see p 655 *f* and *j*, post); *Ebrahimi v Westbourne*
h *Galleries Ltd* [1972] 2 All ER 492 explained.

Notes

For convening of meetings of a company, see 7 Halsbury's Laws (4th Edn) 330-334, paras 560-566; and for cases on the validation and waiver of irregular notice, see 9 Digest (Repl) 604, 4000-4004.
j For the Companies Act 1948, s 184, see 5 Halsbury's Statutes (3rd Edn) 255.

Cases referred to in judgment

Browne v La Trinidad (1887) 37 Ch D 1, 57 LJCh 292, 58 LT 137, CA, 9 Digest (Repl) 604, 4003.
Ebrahimi v Westbourne Galleries Ltd [1972] 2 All ER 492, [1973] AC 360, [1972] 2 WLR 1289, HL.

Case also cited
Bainbridge v Smith (1889) 41 Ch D 462, CA.

Motion
By notice of motion dated 26th February 1974 Charles Edward Bentley-Stevens, the plaintiff in an action commenced by writ issued on 26th February 1974 against the defendants, (1) D Gareth Jones, (2) Gerald S J Hyam and (3) Sloane Nursing Home Ltd, sought an order restraining the defendants and each of them until the trial of the action or further order from acting on the resolution purported to have been passed by the defendant company at a purported extraordinary general meeting thereof held at 9.30 am on 26th February 1974 removing the plaintiff as a director of the defendant company. The facts are set out in the judgment.

Allan Heyman QC and *M K I Kennedy* for the plaintiff.
Ralph Instone for the defendants.

PLOWMAN J. The notice of motion which is before me asks for an order on behalf of the plaintiff—

'restraining the Defendants and each of them until the trial of the action or further order from acting upon the resolution purported to have been passed by the Defendant Company at a purported Extraordinary General Meeting thereof held at 9.30 a.m. on the 26th February 1974 removing the Plaintiff as a Director of the Defendant Company.'

The facts giving rise to this motion are as follows. The defendant company, Sloane Nursing Homes Ltd, is a wholly owned subsidiary of a company called J & B S Holdings Ltd, which I will call 'Holdings'. The plaintiff and the first defendant, Mr Gareth Jones, each hold 42 per cent of the issued share capital of Holdings, and the second defendant, Mr Gerald Hyam, holds the remaining 16 per cent. The plaintiff and the first and second defendants are the three directors of Holdings and they are three of the four directors of the defendant company, the fourth director of the defendant company being the matron of the defendant company's nursing hime.

In the latter part of last year differences arose between the plaintiff and the first two defendants, the nature of which is not, I think, important for the purposes of this motion, but those differences led to this, that on Sunday, 27th January 1974, the first defendant wrote a letter to the plaintiff, part of which I will read. He said:

'... Gerald [that is, the second defendant] and I have, as majority shareholders of J. & B.S. Holdings Ltd. no alternative but to procure J. & B.S. Holdings Ltd. to seek the convening of an E.G.M. of Sloane Nursing Homes Ltd. for purposes of removing you from its board of directors.'

Later on in the letter he said:

'Please take notice of a meeting of the directors of J. & B.S. Holdings Ltd. on Monday 27th [that should be 28th] January 1974 at 09.30 hours at the Sloane Nursing Home, 129/133 Albemarle Road, Beckenham, Kent, for the purpose of resolving the necessary action to give effect to the above.'

The plaintiff happened to be away from home for the weekend and he did not receive that letter until 9 o'clock on the Monday evening when he got back. Nor did he receive a telephone call which the first defendant made to him, or tried to make to him, on the Sunday because there was nobody there to answer the telephone. By Monday evening when the plaintiff received the letter a number of things had happened. In the first place the board meeting of Holdings took place at 9.30 in the a morning and a resolution was passed, which is set out in para 16 of Mr Gareth Jones's affidavit as follows:

> 'The Board meeting of Holdings attended by Mr. Hyam and myself was held at 9.30 a.m. on Monday, 28th January 1974 and we resolved "that Mr. D. G. Jones (i.e. myself) be and is hereby authorised to give special notice on behalf of the Company to (Sloane) for the purpose of removing (the Plaintiff) from the Board
b of that Company under Section 184 of the Companies Act 1948 and to vote on behalf of Company at the EGM convened for such purpose".'

Secondly, Holdings had requisitioned an extraordinary general meeting of the defendant company for that purpose; and thirdly, as a director of the defendant company the first defendant had called an extraordinary general meeting of that company
c for 26th February. The notice convening that meeting was expressed to be given by order of the board, but in fact no board meeting of the defendant company was held. The first and second defendants had acted on their own initiative without notice to the plaintiff and without notice, I infer from the evidence, to the matron. In due course that extraordinary general meeting was held and the votes of Holdings were cast in favour of the resolution removing the plaintiff as a director of the defendant company.
d Those in outline are the facts.

The plaintiff's case is first of all that proper notice of the board meeting of Holdings on Monday, 28th January 1974, was not given, with the consequence that the proceedings of that meeting, and everything that flowed from them, were invalid. Secondly, it was submitted on behalf of the plaintiff that even if sufficient notice of the meeting was given, a board meeting of the defendant company was necessary before
e an extraordinary general meeting of that company could be validly convened, and no such meeting was ever held, with the consequence that the extraordinary general meeting was not properly convened and its proceedings were therefore a nullity. Alternatively, counsel for the plaintiff submitted that this is what is popularly known as a 'quasi-partnership' case and that on the principles enunciated by the House of Lords in *Ebrahimi v Westbourne Galleries Ltd*[1], the court should restrain the first and
f second defendants, as two of the three partners in the quasi-partnership, from expelling the third partner, namely, the plaintiff.

I will deal with the first and second submissions together. In my judgment, even assuming that the plaintiff's complaint of irregularities is correct, this is not a case in which an interlocutory injunction ought to be granted. I say that for the reason that the irregularities can all be cured by going through the proper processes and the ultimate result would inevitably be the same. In *Browne v La Trinidad*[2] Lindley LJ
g said:

> 'I think it is most important that the Court should hold fast to the rule upon which it has always acted, not to interfere for the purpose of forcing companies to conduct their business according to the strictest rules, where the irregularity complained of can be set right at any moment.'
h
It seems to me that the motion which is before me falls within the principle stated by Lindley LJ.

However, that still leaves the *Westbourne Galleries*[1] point. But in my judgment there is nothing in that case which suggests that the plaintiff is entitled to an injunction to interfere with the defendant company's statutory right to remove the plaintiff
j from its board. What it does decide is that if the plaintiff is removed under a power valid in law then he may, in appropriate circumstances, be entitled to a winding-up order on the just and equitable ground.

---

1 [1972] 2 All ER 492, [1973] AC 360
2 (1887) 37 Ch D 1 at 17

For those reasons the plaintiff is not, in my judgment, entitled to the relief which he
seeks on this motion, and I must dismiss it.

Motion dismissed.

Solicitors: *A Kramer & Co* (for the plaintiff); *Norton, Rose, Botterell & Roche* (for the
defendants).

Jacqueline Metcalfe Barrister.

Riverlate Properties Ltd v Paul

COURT OF APPEAL, CIVIL DIVISION
RUSSELL, STAMP AND LAWTON LJJ
18th, 19th, 20th MARCH, 8th APRIL 1974

*Mistake – Rescission – Unilateral mistake – Lease – Mistake of lessor in drafting lease –
Lessee unaware of mistake – Mistake not attributable to anything said or done by lessee –
Claim by lessor for rescission subject to rectification at lessee's option – Whether mere
unilateral mistake ground for rescission.*

The lessor, a limited company, was the owner of a building, the ground and basement floors of which were subject to a lease for use as a shop. The lessor wished
to dispose of the first and second floors, a self-contained maisonette, on a 99 year lease
at a price of £6,500 with a ground rent exclusive of rates of £25 per annum. The
lessee instructed her solicitor to make an offer for the premises and to carry through
the acquisition. It was the lessee's understanding that she was not to be responsible
for any part of the expense of exterior and structural repairs to the building. Solicitors
for the lessor submitted a draft contract to which was annexed a draft of the proposed
lease. Ultimately the contracts were exchanged and the lease and counterpart
executed. By cl 5(iii) of the lease the lessee covenanted to contribute and pay half
of the reasonable costs, expenses, outgoings and matters for which the lessor was
responsible by virtue of the provisions of cl 6(b), (c) and (d) of the lease, i e (b) insurance of the building, (c) decoration of the exterior of the building and (d) water
rates.   Under cl 6(a) the lessor was responsible for the exterior and structural repairs
of the building. The effect of the lease as executed was that it threw the entire
responsibility for those repairs on the lessor. It was, however, the lessor's intention
that the lessee should contribute to the cost of exterior and structural repairs, but
neither the lessee nor her solicitor appreciated that that was the case. It was not
the lessee's solicitor's intention that the lessee should be liable for such a contribution
and, on examining the draft lease, he did not appreciate that the reference in cl 5(iii)
to cl 6(b) (c) and (d) was an error in drafting and that the reference should have
been to cl 6(a), (b) and (c). In September 1971 the lessor commenced an action in
which it claimed, inter alia, that there had been a unilateral mistake on its part of
such a character as to entitle the lessor to rescission or annulment of the lease subject
to the lessee being put to her election whether or not to retain the lease subject to
rectification by the substitution in cl 5(iii) of a reference to cl 6(a), (b) and (c).

Held – Mere unilateral mistake in a lease was not a ground for rescission. Since
the lessee had neither directly nor through her solicitors known of the lessor's
mistake and since the mistake was in no way attributable to anything said or done
by her, the lessor was not entitled to rescission of the lease, either with or without
the option to the lessee to accept rectification to cure the mistake (see p 661 *d* to *f*
and p 665 *d* to *e*, post).

Dictum of Farwell J in *May v Platt* [1900] 1 Ch at 623 approved.
Garrard v Frankel (1862) 30 Beav 445 distinguished.
Harris v Pepperell (1867) LR 5 Eq 1 and dictum of Bacon V-C in *Paget v Marshall* [1881-85] All ER Rep 290 disapproved.

Notes
For rescission after conveyance in cases of mistake, see 26 Halsbury's Laws (3rd Edn) 912, 913, para 1695, and for cases on the subject, see 35 Digest (Repl) 130, 131, *255-259*.

Cases referred to in judgment
Blay v Pollard and Morris [1930] 1 KB 628, [1930] All ER Rep 609, 99 LJKB 421, 143 LT 92, CA, 35 Digest (Repl) 123, *212*.
Bloomer v Spittle (1872) LR 13 Eq 427, 41 LJCh 369, 26 LT 272, 35 Digest (Repl) 119, *173*.
Devald and Devald v Zigeuner and Zigeuner (1958) 16 DLR (2d) 285, [1958] OWN 381, 35 Digest (Repl) 133, *95*.
Garrard v Frankel (1862) 30 Beav 445, 31 LJCh 604, 26 JP 727, 8 Jur NS 985, 54 ER 961, 35 Digest (Repl) 138, *311*.
Harris v Pepperell (1867) LR 5 Eq 1, 17 LT 191, 32 JP 132, 35 Digest (Repl) 118, *172*.
May v Platt [1900] 1 Ch 616, 69 LJCh 357, 83 LT 123, 35 Digest (Repl) 108, *91*.
Paget v Marshall (1884) 28 Ch D 255, [1881-85] All ER Rep 290, 54 LJCh 575, 51 LT 351, 35 Digest (Repl) 136, *300*.
Redbridge (London Borough) v Robinson Rentals Ltd (1969) 211 Estates Gazette 1125.
Roberts (A) & Co Ltd v Leicestershire County Council [1961] 2 All ER 545, [1961] Ch 555, [1961] 2 WLR 1000, 59 LGR 349, 35 Digest (Repl) 138, *316*.
Solle v Butcher [1949] 2 All ER 1107, [1950] 1 KB 671, CA, 31(2) Digest (Reissue) 1042, *8232*.

Case also cited
Joscelyne v Nissen [1970] 1 All ER 1213, [1970] 2 QB 86, CA.

Appeal
By a writ issued on 2nd September 1971, and subsequently amended and reamended, the plaintiff, Riverlate Properties Ltd, brought an action against the defendant, Laura Caroline Paul, in which it alleged that, by a lease dated 28th July 1969, the plaintiff had demised to the defendant for the term of 99 years from 25th March 1969 a maisonette on the first and second floors of freehold property known as 22 Blenheim Terrace, London, NW8; that the demise had been made pursuant to a contract dated 20th May 1969, and made between the plaintiff and the defendant, which incorporated the draft of a lease containing substantially the same terms and in substantially the same form as the lease dated 28th July 1969. The plaintiff claimed (i) an order that the draft lease and the lease be rectified by substituting in cl 5 (iii) thereof the words: 'Clause 6 paragraphs (a) (b) and (c)', for the words: 'Clause 6 paragraphs (b) (c) and (d)'; (ii) alternatively, rescission of the contract and the lease unless the defendant elected to have them rectified in the manner set out above. On 23rd March 1973 Templeman J dismissed the plaintiff's action and the plaintiff appealed. The facts are set out in the judgment of the court.

H E Francis QC and *Robert Wakefield* for the plaintiff.
Michael Eastham QC and *Peter Slot* for the defendant.

Cur adv vult

8th April. **RUSSELL LJ** read the following judgment of the court. 22 Blenheim Terrace, St John's Wood, is at the end of a terrace. In 1969 the ground and basement floors were subject to a lease for use as a shop. The first and second floors were a self-contained maisonette with a separate outside front door and staircase from ground level. The plaintiff company—a £100 property dealing company part of a group—wished to dispose of the maisonette on a 99 year lease at a price of £6,500 with a ground rent exclusive of rates of £25 per annum and put it in the hands of agents. The defendant, Mrs Paul, a recent widow not in very good health, was attracted by it. She saw the property and the estate agents and went to solicitors in which the relevant partner was a Mr Mills, to act for her in making an offer and carrying through the acquisition of the property. Solicitors for the plaintiff submitted a draft contract to which was annexed a draft of the proposed 99 year lease. Ultimately the contracts were exchanged and the lease and counterpart executed. A friend of the defendant's son was a surveyor: he looked at the property and found defects that he thought should be remedied before completion by the lessor, and the contract provided for this. The accepted price or premium was £6,250.

The lease as executed provides that the lessor shall be responsible for exterior and structural repairs of the building, no 22, and contains no provision for any part of the cost falling on the lessee. This action seeks rectification of the lease so as to make the lessee obliged to reimburse to the lessor one-half of the cost of such repairs. The alleged error in the form of the lease, which was executed in July 1969, was first asserted by the plaintiff in 1971. The plaintiff claims that the lease was executed in a form which does not throw on the defendant any obligation to bear part of the cost of exterior and structural repairs by a mistake common to both parties; alternatively, on the ground that the plaintiff made the mistake and the defendant knew that the plaintiff was making it, which equally it is said entitles the plaintiff to rectification. In the further alternative the plaintiff contends that the case is one in which, albeit there was only unilateral mistake not known to or contributed to by the defendant, the defendant should be put to her election whether to submit to rescission of the lease or to rectification such as to cure the plaintiff's mistake.

First we turn to the contents of the lease as executed, which in particular are relied on by the plaintiff as showing that at least something has gone wrong. Clause 3 contained lessee's covenants to pay rent, rates and taxes charged on the maisonette and to pay the proper proportion of such outgoings as were attributable to the maisonette so far as they were charged on the building as a whole. The building was the whole of no 22. Clause 3 also required the lessee to deal with interior maintenance and decoration of the interior of the maisonette, and other usual tenant's covenants. Clause 4 provided that it was for the lessor to decide the appropriate proportion of rates and taxes etc attributable to the maisonette subject, in the event of a dispute, to decision of an independent surveyor: this is relevant to a later reference to water rate. We come then to cl 5(iii) whereby the lessee covenants to contribute and pay one-half of the reasonable costs, expenses, outgoings and matters for which the lessor is responsible by virtue of the provisions of cl 6(b), (c) and (d) thereof. Herein is the nub of the dispute. Clause 6 imposes obligations on the lessor. Clause 6(a) relates to exterior and structural repairs. Clause 6(b) was a covenant by the lessor to insure the building—the building being, of course, the whole of no 22. Clause 6(c) required the lessor to decorate the exterior of the building. Clause 6(d) required the lessor to pay the water rates on the building.

It would obviously make good sense if you combine cl 5(iii) with cl 6(a), (b) and (c). If you combine cl 5(iii), as required by it, with cl 6(b), (c) and (d), it throws on the lessor the entire financial liability for exterior and structural repairs, without putting on the lessee an obligation to contribute a suitable proportion of such expenditure by the lessor. Moreover, by putting on the lessee one-half of the water rate on the whole building, it would appear to conflict with the obligation under cl 4 for the lessee to bear an appropriate proportion of, inter alia, water rate, whether it be half or not.

There is this further to be considered. Clause 6 (f) and (g) require the lessor to keep accounts of his expenditure under cl 6(a), (b) and (c) and from time to time (half-yearly) that an audit should certify the total expenditure under these three heads. Here it is said is a system which must be designed to produce *a sum* of expenditure by the lessor to which can be applied the obligation of the lessee under cl 5(iii) to contribute half.

In short, it is said, every provision works well and intelligibly if you substitute in cl 5(iii) the reference to cl 6(a), (b) and (c) for cl 6(b), (c) and (d): and that if you do not do this, you find a situation, at the very least unusual, in which (i) at this ground rent of £25 the lessor is for 99 years wholly liable for exterior and structural repairs relevant to the maisonette, (ii) while at the same time the lessee is liable to contribute an appropriate proportion to the cost of external decoration such as painting of ironwork and outer parts of window-sills, (iii) there is an apparent conflict as to water rate between liability on the lessee of a proper proportion of the water rate on the whole of the building and a liability for half that whole under cl 6(d) regardless of relative consumption of water on relative rateable values, and (iv) the accounts to be kept and the *total* expenditure to be certified are to include an element (cl 6(a) exterior and structural repairs) which are no concern of the lessee, for whose benefit it is to be assumed that the auditor's certificate is to be prepared.

Under all these heads there is good ground for thinking that something has gone wrong. But these heads are not sufficient by themselves to justify *construction* of the lease in the sense suggested by the lessor—which indeed is not suggested as possible.

The defendant herself gave evidence which was accepted by the judge and is not challenged. Her memory of 1969 was, not surprisingly, vague, but she was clear that it was always her understanding that the lessor was to be responsible for exterior and structural repairs of the building and that she was not to be liable for any part of that expense. For the plaintiff it was accepted that if her state of mind was the only relevant one for the purpose of founding a claim to rectification on either common mistake or on unilateral mistake by one party known to the other party, the latter lying low and saying nothing (like a combination of Brer Fox and the Tar Baby in Uncle Remus), it did not suffice. What was contended was that the proper conclusion from events and from the evidence of Mr Mills was that he, the agent of the defendant, either intended the lease to put on the defendant an obligation to pay half the lessor's expenses from time to time on exterior and structural repairs, or that he appreciated that the form of lease prepared by the plaintiff failed by a mistake of the plaintiff or its advisers to achieve that result because cl 5(iii) referred to cl 6(b), (c) and (d) instead of cl 6(a), (b) and (c). He could not, it was said, have failed to appreciate this. There is one point to be particularly mentioned in this connection. An amendment was introduced into cl 4 of the draft of the lease by Mr Mills (and accepted by the plaintiff's solicitor) by way of a reference subjecting it to cl 6(d). It is plain from this that Mr Mills recognised that, so far as water rate might be charged on the whole building, cl 6(d) in conjunction with cl 5(iii) put liability for half on the lessee, while cl 4 put on her liability for a 'proper proportion': hence the amendment to make cll 6(d) and 5(iii) govern the situation. But this certainly shows that Mr Mills did not think that cl 5(iii) erred in referring to cl 6(d). Another point is this. It is, we think, reasonably plain that the draft lease prepared by Mr Butcher, the plaintiff's solicitor, was based on an earlier lease of the maisonette at no 20, next door, to one Webb, for which Mr Butcher was also responsible. That was also for 99 years at a £25 ground rent for a premium payment of an amount unknown, and equally referred to cl 6(b), (c) and (d), and not (a), (b) and (c). The point here is that in that case also the solicitor for the *lessee* seems not to have assumed a mistake on the lessor's side: unless, of course, he was somewhat dishonestly emulating the Uncle Remus combination.

The summary of Mr Mills's evidence is this: and it must be remembered that he was trying to reconstruct his thoughts in the face of a minute examination of the implications of various parts of the lease when the question had been first raised two years after the relevant events. His recollection which he constantly reiterated was that he had been instructed that the plaintiff was to be responsible for all exterior and structural repairs to the building and that no part of this burden was to fall on the defendant, his client: that he had thought this unusual in a lease of this kind: but that when the lessor itself produced a draft lease which coincided with his instructions, he took it that it was so intended. He said that without such instructions he would have queried to the plaintiff whether there was not a mistake in the draft lease, but that the combination of his instructions and the form of the draft lease coming from the plaintiff made query out of place. The plaintiff challenged forcefully the evidence that Mr Mills had ever had such instructions: the defendant, it was said, did not testify to such instructions, but of course her recollections were very vague. It was said that whatever view the judge may have had about Mr Mills as a witness by observing his demeanor (which was favourable), the judge did not make an express finding on his evidence as to his instructions, and that unless there were such instructions Mr Mills had condemned his attitude out of his own mouth as a person who without them would have queried the form of draft lease as perhaps or certainly containing an error from the plaintiff's viewpoint. We think it is correct that the judge made no precise finding in his judgment on the evidence of instructions from the defendant. On the other hand, it is quite plain that the judge, after hearing his evidence and his reactions to what was a very thorough, searching and able cross-examination by counsel for the plaintiff, was not prepared to conclude that Mr Mills either (a) intended that the lease should put on the lessee a contribution to the lessor's expenditure on exterior and structural repairs or (b) appreciated that the lessor's solicitors had made a mistake in this regard in drafting the lease. In those circumstances it seems to us impossible to differ from the judge on these points. In this connection it is important to remember that the acceptable and accepted evidence of the defendant is that she always understood that she was to bear no part of the expense of exterior and structural repairs to the building. If this was her view, it would be surprising if it was not communicated to Mr Mills, and it would be easy to understand that it would colour his approach to a draft lease from the other side which coincided with that view. By this we mean that the absence of evidence of an agreement by the defendant with the plaintiff through, for example, its estate agents does not show that Mr Mills either intended a liability on the defendant to contribute to the cost of exterior and structural repairs (that is to say, a common mistake requiring convincing proof) or a knowledge by Mr Mills that the plaintiff's advisers were making a damaging mistake in putting forward the lease in the particular form, a form of dishonesty or sharp practice which might well require proof beyond reasonable doubt, or, as we believe it is now phrased in criminal law, require the tribunal of fact to be 'sure'.

For these reasons, it appears to us that there is no justification, assuming a mistake on the side of the plaintiff, for rectification either on the ground of a common mistake, or on the ground of knowledge on the defendant's side at the time of the execution of the contract or the lease that the plaintiff in putting forward the lease in its particular form was making a mistake. It may be that the original conception of reformation of an instrument by rectification was based solely on common mistake: but certainly in these days rectification may be based on such knowledge on the part of the defendant: see, for example, *A Roberts & Co Ltd v Leicestershire County Council*[1]. Whether there was in any particular case knowledge of the intention and mistake of the other party must be a question of fact to be decided on the evidence. Basically it appears to us that it must be such as to involve the defendant in a degree of sharp practice.

Thus far we have proceeded on an assumption that the evidence reveals, as the judge held, a mistake on the part of the plaintiff. It was contended before us for the defendant that the judge was wrong in so holding, the prime contention being that Mr Butcher never said in terms that he intended to put forward a lease in a form which

---

1   [1961] 2 All ER 545, [1961] Ch 555

brought the lessor's expenditure on external repairs under cl 6 (a) within the ambit of the lessee's liability under cl 5(iii) to contribute half of the expenditure. But basically the question is whether from the evidence as a whole and all the facts it is convincingly shown that the document was not in accordance with the lessor's intentions: and, without discourtesy to the arguments adduced, we think we may content ourselves with saying that in our view the judge was right on this point.

Finally, the proposition is put forward for the plaintiff that there was unilateral mistake by the plaintiff of a character which entitles the plaintiff to rescission or annulment of the lease, subject only to this, that the defendant can escape rescission or annulment by agreeing to retain the lease subject to variation in the manner suggested as appropriate to correct the plaintiff's unilateral mistake—here, for example, by variation substituting in cl 5(iii) reference to cl 6(a), (b) and (c) for 6(b), (c) and (d). It is to be observed that this contention does not depend in any way on the knowledge or state of mind of the other party at the time of the transaction in question. It is further to be observed that we are not concerned with a case in which a party is seeking an equitable remedy under a contract such as specific performance, where in an appropriate case the court may refuse specific performance if the defendant has made a unilateral mistake. Here the lessee seeks no equitable remedy: she is in possession under a lease.

Is the plaintiff entitled to rescission of the lease on the mere ground that it made a serious mistake in the drafting of the lease which it put forward and subsequently executed, when (a) the defendant did not share the mistake, (b) the defendant did not know that the document did not give effect to the plaintiff's intention, and (c) the mistake of the plaintiff was in no way attributable to anything said or done by the defendant? What is there in principle, or in authority binding on this court, which requires a person who has acquired a leasehold interest on terms on which he intended to obtain it, and who thought when he obtained it that the lessor intended him to obtain it on those terms, either to lose the leasehold interest, or, if he wish to keep it, to submit to keep it only on the terms which the lessor meant to impose but did not? In point of principle, we cannot find that this should be so. If reference be made to principles of equity, it operates on conscience. If conscience is clear at the time of the transaction, why should equity disrupt the transaction? If a man may be said to have been fortunate in obtaining a property at a bargain price, or on terms that make it a good bargain, because the other party unknown to him has made a miscalculation or other mistake, some high-minded men might consider it appropriate that he should agree to a fresh bargain to cure the miscalculation or mistake, abandoning his good fortune. But if equity were to enforce the views of those high-minded men, we have no doubt that it would run counter to the attitudes of much the greater part of ordinary mankind (not least the world of commerce), and would be venturing on the field of moral philosophy in which it would soon be in difficulties.

What then of authority? There are a number of authorities at first instance, of some antiquity, to which our attention was drawn, which it was said decided that in cases of mere unilateral mistake rescission could be ordered, but with the opportunity being given to the defendant to retain the benefit of the transaction if he consent to a variation (that is to say, rectification) which will mend the plaintiff's mistake. The first was *Garrard v Frankel*[1] (Lord Romilly MR). There the parties, after correspondence and conversation in which the plaintiff (proposed lessor) had made it clear to the defendant (proposed lessee) that the rent could not be less than £240 per annum, finally agreed in August orally on a rent of £230 plus a premium of £125. On 20th August the parties signed an agreement, in the fold of the draft of the lease to the previous tenant, for the grant of a lease for 21 years from Michaelmas '*at the rent of £230 clear of all taxes, and in all respects on the terms of the within lease*': provision was also made for the premium. By a slip the lessor subsequently inserted £130 as the rental figure

---

1   (1862) 30 Beav 445

in the draft and it was so engrossed and executed. The lessee refused to pay except at
the rate of £130. The lessor sued for rectification by substituting £230 for £130; or
alternatively for delivery up and cancellation of the lease (that is to say, rescission), at
the same time offering a new lease on the same terms at £230 rent. Lord Romilly MR
stated that, for rectification, ordinarily common mistake was required: but continued
by saying that the court 'would interfere' in cases of mistake where one party being at
the time cognisant of the fact of the error seeks to take advantage of it. He then
(quite incomprehensibly to us) declined to find that the lessee intended the lease to be
at £230 per annum, basing himself on the proposition that the draft of the previous
lease with the agreement written within the fold was as one document self-contradictory. He seems to have assumed that the draft lease contained a figure for rent of £130:
but if the draft lease contained any figure for rent at all, it would have been the previous
lessee's rent of £230: and in fact it appears from the report that if the document contained the figure of £130, it was inserted by the lessor *after* the agreement had been
written and signed within the fold. In any event, if there was a difference between the
rent in the agreement and in the draft lease, it seems to us to be a wholly perverse
construction of the written agreement to say that the phrase 'and in all respects on
the terms of the within lease' meant anything except in all respects *other than* the rental
figure. Lord Romilly MR[1] then found himself 'disposed to believe' that the lessee
'when she signed' the agreement, knew that the within lease contained the figure of
£130 (which it then did not) and knew that the agreement said £230. He then doubted
whether he could compel the lessee to be bound by a lease—

   'inconsistent with a portion of the agreement which she signed, and which,
   in one view which might be taken of it, might govern the other portion.'

He then said[1]:

   'I am quite clear that I cannot compel the Plaintiff [lessor] to be bound by
   the terms of lease as it stands, or permit the Defendant [lessee] to derive any
   advantage from this mistake, and, in that respect, the Plaintiff is ... entitled to
   relief.'

He then dealt with the situation by in effect saying that unless the defendant chose
to agree to retain the lease rectified by the insertion of £230 as the rent, he would
set aside the lease and order her to pay for use and occupation at the rate of £230
per annum (the previous tenant's rent). He would not allow her any expenses of
having established herself there, his reason for this being that[2]—

   'the evidence ... convinces me ... that she must, at the time when she executed
   the lease, be taken to have been cognizant of the mistake which had been
   committed by the Plaintiff.'

There it is, plainly stated, a fact which now would be taken as entitling the plaintiff
to rectification. We are unable to explain this case except on the basis that such
knowledge was not then considered to be a ground for rectification but rather for
rescission, to which alone Lord Romilly MR considered the plaintiff to be entitled; but
that he was prepared to give the defendant a chance of accepting rectification, which
had of course been offered by the plaintiff. At any rate, this case is not authority
for the proposition that a plaintiff is entitled to rescission of a lease on the ground
of mere unilateral mistake: and if it so decided it was, in our judgment, wrong.
   The next case was *Harris v Pepperell*[3] (also Lord Romilly MR), where a conveyance
by reference to a plan thereon embraced a piece of land which the plaintiff vendor

---

1   (1862) 30 Beav at 457
2   30 Beav at 458
3   (1867) LR 5 Eq 1

did not intend to convey. The plaintiff sought rectification to exclude that piece from the plan. As we understand the report of the case, the defendant sent a plan which he proposed to incorporate in the conveyance; the plaintiff said that it was wrong and sent a correct plan; later, at the request of the defendant, the plaintiff returned the defendant's erroneous plan; when the engrossment of the conveyance was submitted by the defendant, it incorporated the defendant's erroneous plan and not the plan sent by the plaintiff; this the plaintiff did not notice and executed the conveyance. Lord Romilly MR appears to have considered that there was not a mistake common to both parties. He said[1]:

> 'In the present case it is clear that the Court can put the parties in the same position as before the conveyance was executed, for if I hold that there has been a mistake, and that the deed ought to have been rectified, then I can give the Defendant the option of having the whole contract annulled, or else of taking it in the form which the Plaintiff intended. It is, therefore, a case where the Court can grant relief, and I am of opinion that the mistake was clearly proved.'

When discussing costs, he said that in a case when the defendant has been aware of the mistake from the beginning and refused to rectify it, then the costs must be given against him; he was not referring to that particular case, but this again reflects the view that knowledge by the defendant that the plaintiff was making a mistake would not entitle the plaintiff to rectification, but only to rescission. In the end he declared that the plaintiff did not intend to convey the additional piece of land[1] 'and is entitled to have the conveyance rectified accordingly, with an option to the Defendant to annul the contract'. This case we find very puzzling. In the end the order was substantially the same as in *Garrard v Frankel*[2], though put the other way round; that is to say, that the plaintiff would be entitled to rescission of the conveyance unless the defendant agreed to rectification. It may be that the decision could be supported on the ground that the plaintiff's mistake was in some sort procured by the defendant embodying in the engrossment a plan which the plaintiff had told him was wrong without the defendant saying that he was not putting forward the plan which obviously the plaintiff would have expected him to. But, however that may be, if the basis of the decision was that a mere unilateral mistake on the part of the plaintiff would entitle him to either rectification or rescission, it was in our judgment wrongly decided.

Next was *Bloomer v Spittle*[3], also Lord Romilly MR. This does not really assist. It was a case of common mistake resulting in the exception of minerals from a conveyance. But, since a considerable time had elapsed and the vendor had died, Lord Romilly MR was not prepared absolutely to order rectification at the suit of the purchaser plaintiff, but gave the vendor's personal representatives the option of submitting to rectification or the whole transaction being set aside.

Next came *Paget v Marshall*[4] (Bacon V-C). There the plaintiff lessor had included by mistake in the lease of a number of adjoining buildings the first floor of one. The statement of claim asserted the plaintiff's mistake and that the defendant lessee knowingly took advantage of the error. The plaintiff claimed a declaration that the lease ought not to have comprised the particular first floor, and that the defendant be ordered to elect between annulment of the lease and its rectification accordingly, and that if the defendant refuse to consent to rectification, the lease be rescinded. Here again is reflected the attitude that the defendant's knowledge of the plaintiff's mistake at the time would entitle the plaintiff to rescission but not to rectification. The defence alleged no mistake at all, or, if any, that it was the plaintiff's only and not common. Bacon V-C said this in general terms[5]:

---

1   (1867) LR 5 Eq at 5
2   (1862) 30 Beav 445
3   (1872) LR 13 Eq 427
4   (1884) 28 Ch D 255, [1881-85] All ER Rep 290
5   28 Ch D at 263, [1881-85] All ER Rep at 292

'But the law I take to be as stated this morning by Mr. *Hemming*. If it is a case
of common mistake—a common mistake as to one stipulation out of many
provisions contained in a settlement or any other deed, that upon proper evidence
may be rectified—the Court has the power to rectify, and that power is very
often exercised. The other class of cases is one of what is called unilateral mistake,
and there, if the Court is satisfied that the true intention of one of the parties
was to do one thing, and he by mistake has signed an agreement to do another,
that agreement will not be enforced against him, but the parties will be restored
to their original position, and the agreement will be treated as if it had never
been entered into. That I take the clear conclusion to be drawn from the
authorities.'

However, it is, it appears to us, clear from the judgment[1] that Bacon V-C, while
thinking that it was very nearly a case of common mistake, certainly concluded that
the defendant at the time knew that the plaintiff had included the relevant first
floor by mistake. Consequently, he took the view that the plaintiff was entitled to
rescission, but gave the defendant the opportunity (which he took) of submitting to
rectification. The decision appears to be correct on the basis of what was claimed
by the plaintiff. But if the passage quoted[2] is to be taken as laying down that a
mere unilateral mistake entitles the plaintiff to rescission, it is in our judgment
wrong in law.

In *May v Platt*[3] Farwell J said (obiter):

'In my judgment, in order to get rescission after conveyance, the allegations
would have had to be very different. I have always understood the law to be
that in order to obtain rectification there must be a mistake common to both
parties, and if the mistake is only unilateral, there must be fraud or misrepresentation amounting to fraud.'

He said of the three cases, *Harris v Pepperell*[4], *Garrard v Frankel*[5] and *Paget v Marshall*[6],
that they could only be justified as treating the defendants' conduct as equivalent
to fraud, and continued[7]: 'Rescission after conveyance of land can only be obtained
on the ground of unfair dealing'. On these dicta see also *Blay v Pollard and Morris*[8],
per Scrutton LJ.

Solle v Butcher[9] (in this court) was a case of common mistake: the order made was
analogous to those made in *Garrard v Frankel*[5] and *Paget v Marshall*[6], in that the
defendant was given an option, those cases being referred to by Denning LJ[10] in that
respect. But the details of those cases and their rationes decidendi did not fall for
consideration, and insofar as they may be said to support the view that rescission
may be grounded on mere unilateral mistake they are not to be regarded as having
been approved.

Our attention was drawn to a case in the High Court of Ontario, *Devald and Devald
v Zigeuner and Zigeuner*[11] (McRuer CJ). That was a case in which a building was
included in a conveyance by a mistake on the part of the vendor. On the assumption

1   (1884) 28 Ch D at 265, 266, [1881-85] All ER Rep at 293, 294
2   28 Ch D at 263, [1881-85] All ER Rep at 292
3   [1900] 1 Ch 616 at 623
4   (1867) LR 5 Eq 1
5   (1862) 30 Beav 445
6   (1884) 28 Ch D 255, [1881-85] All ER Rep 290
7   [1900] 1 Ch at 623
8   [1930] 1 KB 628 at 633, [1930] All ER Rep 609 at 612
9   [1949] 2 All ER 1107, [1950] 1 KB 671
10 [1949] 2 All ER at 1122, [1950] 1 KB at 696
11 (1958) 16 DLR (2d) 285

a that there was no common mistake, rescission was ordered, but with an option to the defendant to submit to rectification.   McRuer CJ[1] made it clear that in his view rectification could only be ordered if common mistake was shown.   As we read the report, it must have been the situation that the defendant knew at the time of the conveyance that the building was included by a mistake on the part of the plaintiff, as indeed is suggested in the headnote[2].   On that basis, the decision allowing

b rescission with an option in the defendant to accept rectification is supportable, though on that basis, as we have indicated, the courts here would order rectification.   The learned Chief Justice referred[3] to the dicta of Farwell J in *May v Platt*[4], but remarked that notwithstanding those dicta *Garrard v Frankel*[5] and *Paget v Marshall*[6] had been approved in *Solle v Butcher*[7].   We have already explained that that approval was only in a limited sense.   Here also, if the ratio in *Devald and Devald v Zigeuner and*

c *Zigeuner*[8] were that mere unilateral mistake in conveyance entitles the plaintiff to rescission, it would in our judgment be (according to English law) wrong.   There is then the decision of Stamp J in *London Borough of Redbridge v Robinson Rentals Ltd*[9].   In that case it was clearly held that mere unilateral mistake on the part of the plaintiff, unknown to the defendant, was no ground for rescission of the lease in question, and consequently there was no jurisdiction to make an order for rescission with an

d option to the defendant to accept rectification.   This is, in our view, correct.

It follows from this review of the authorities cited to us that there is no authority binding on this court which requires us to arrive at a conclusion for which, as we have indicated, there is no justification in principle.

Consequently, since the defendant neither directly nor through her solicitor, Mr Mills, knew of the plaintiff's mistake, and was not guilty of anything approaching

e sharp practice in relation thereto, it is a case of mere unilateral mistake which cannot entitle the plaintiff to rescission of the lease either with or without the option to the defendant to accept rectification to cure the plaintiff's mistake.

We accordingly dismiss the appeal.

Appeal dismissed.   Leave to appeal to the House of Lords refused.

f Solicitors: *Charles Caplin & Co* (for the plaintiff); *Dibsdall & Mills* (for the defendant).

Mary Rose Plummer Barrister.

---

g
1   (1958) 16 DLR (2d) at 290
2   16 DLR (2d) at 285
3   16 DLR at 292, 293
4   [1900] 1 Ch at 623
5   (1862) 30 Beav 445
6   (1884) 28 Ch D 255, [1881-85] All ER Rep 290
7   [1949] 2 All ER at 1122, [1950] 1 KB at 696
8   (1958) 16 DLR (2d) 285
9   (1969) 211 Estates Gazette 1125

R v Oddy

COURT OF APPEAL, CRIMINAL DIVISION
LAWTON LJ, MAIS AND PHILLIPS JJ
14th MARCH 1974

Criminal law – Compensation – Compensation order – Principle to be applied when making order – Means and prospect of rehabilitation – Relevance – No order to be made where liable to be self-defeating – Circumstances in which order liable to be self-defeating – Offender unlikely to have sufficient means to comply with order – Temptation to resort to crime in order to make necessary payment – Criminal Justice Act 1972, s 1(1)(4).

Criminal law – Compensation – Compensation order – Form of order – Criminal Justice Act 1972, s 1(1).

The appellant opened four banking accounts and thereafter proceeded to obtain goods and money, totalling £3,704, on dud cheques. On arrest he was found to have in his possession £1,200 worth of goods that he had obtained dishonestly. He was charged with, and pleaded guilty to, four offences of obtaining property by deception and two offences of knowingly making a false statement to procure a passport. He asked for 28 other offences to be taken into consideration. He was sentenced to 3½ years imprisonment and, in addition, was ordered to pay, under s 1(1)[a] of the Criminal Justice Act 1972, compensation in the sum of £2,000. The appellant had £300 and he was ordered to pay £200 to one named firm and £50 to each of two other firms. The total sum of £2,000 was to be paid within two years of the appellant being released from prison. The appellant was 27 years of age. He appealed against the compensation order.

Held – The appeal would be allowed and the compensation order discharged for the following reasons—
(i) The court's jurisdiction under s 1 of the 1972 Act to make compensation orders had to be applied in a realistic way, and account had to be taken, under s 1(4), of the means of the accused, and of the prospects of rehabilitation. No order should be made where it might result in the accused committing further offences in order to discharge his obligations. The compensation order imposed on the appellant was inappropriate since it was unlikely that on his release from prison he would be able to obtain employment that would enable him to earn sufficient money to comply with the order and as a result he would be tempted to think up new and dishonest ways of obtaining money quickly (see p 670 j to p 671 a c and f, post).
(ii) The order was defective in form for (a) s 1(1) required the compensation order to relate to a specific offence (i e either an offence in the indictment or an offence taken into consideration) and to personal injury, loss or damage suffered by a particular person as a result of that offence, and the global sum of £2,000 was not related to any specific offence or to any specific loser; and (b) it was not known whether the £1,200 worth of property recovered related to any of the counts in the indictment or to the offences taken into consideration (see p 669 j to p 670 a and p 671 g and h, post).
(iii) The part of the order that related to the £300 could not stand because the existence of £1,200 worth of property recovered made it impossible to determine to which counts in the indictment and to which offences taken into consideration it could be allocated (see p 671 j to p 672 a and c, post).

_____

[a] Section 1, so far as material, is set out at p 669 h to p 670 b, post

Notes

For compensation orders, see Supplement to 10 Halsbury's Laws (3rd Edn) para 1020B.
For the Criminal Justice Act 1972, s 1, see 42 Halsbury's Statutes (3rd Edn) 102.

Cases referred to in judgment

R v Bradburn (1973) 57 Cr App Rep 948, CA.
R v Daly [1974] 1 All ER 290, [1974] 1 WLR 133, CA.
R v Ironfield [1971] 1 All ER 202, [1971] 1 WLR 90, 135 JP 156, 55 Cr App Rep 91, CA.
R v Lovett (1870) 23 LT 95, 11 Cox CC 602, 14 Digest (Repl) 685, 7021.
R v McIntosh [1973] Crim LR 378, CA.

Appeal

On 26th November 1973 in the Crown Court at Southampton the appellant, Julian
Farrar Oddy, pleaded guilty to four counts (1 to 4) of obtaining property, belonging
to Comet Radiovision Services Ltd, by deception, and to two counts (4 and 6) of
knowingly making a false statement to procure a passport. After asking for 28 other
offences to be taken into consideration he was sentenced by his Honour Judge
McCreery QC to concurrent terms of 30 months imprisonment on counts 1-4 inclusive
and to 12 months imprisonment on counts 5 and 6 concurrent with each other but
consecutive to the sentences imposed on counts 1-4, making a total of 3½ years imprisonment in all. In addition he was ordered to pay compensation of £4,640, £300 of
which was to be paid within seven days. On 29th November 1973 the judge directed
that the £300 be paid to three named losers and varied the amount of compensation
to £2,000 payable within two years of the appellant's release from prison. The
appellant appealed by leave of the single judge against both his sentence of imprisonment and the order for compensation. The facts are set out in the judgment of the
court.

Adrian Whitfield for the appellant.
The Crown did not appear and were not represented.

LAWTON LJ delivered the following judgment of the court. On 26th November
1973 at Southampton Crown Court the appellant pleaded guilty to four offences of
obtaining property by deception (counts 1-4) and to two offences of knowingly
making a false statement to procure a passport (counts 5 and 6). He was sentenced
by his Honour Judge McCreery to concurrent terms of 30 months imprisonment
on each of counts 1 to 4 inclusive, and to 12 months imprisonment on counts 5 and 6
concurrent with each other but consecutive to the sentences imposed on counts
1 to 4. That means there was a sentence of 3½ years imprisonment in all. Twenty-
eight other offences were taken into consideration. In addition he was ordered to
pay compensation in the sum of £4,640, £300 of which was to be paid within seven
days.

Someone seems to have called the trial judge's attention to a defect in that order
for compensation. The result was that on 29th November 1973 the case was relisted
and on that occasion, after some argument, the learned judge decided to alter the
order for compensation. He did it in this way, and I quote from the transcript:

'When this case was before me on 26th November I ordered the accused to
pay a sum of money by way of compensation and directed that £300 of that
sum should be payable within seven days. The total amount I ordered him to
pay was £4,640. So far as the £300 is concerned, I now direct that £200 of that
should be paid to Comet Radiovision Services Ltd, £50 to Marks and Spencers
Ltd and £50 to St Georges Audio. So far as the total amount of compensation
payable is concerned, I have reconsidered the matter and have decided that I

will substitute for the figure of £4,640 the figure of £2,000. I direct that that *a* sum shall be payable within two years of the accused being released from the prison sentence which I imposed on him on Monday.'

The appellant now appeals by leave of the single judge against both his sentence of imprisonment and the order for compensation.

The facts out of which the appeal arises can be stated shortly. In 1973 the appellant, who is now 27 years of age and a man of considerable intelligence, set out deliberately *b* on a course of fraudulent conduct. He opened four banking accounts, thereby obtaining cheque books. He then proceeded over a wide area of this country to obtain goods and money on dud cheques. The amount of property and money which he obtained in this way totalled £5,800, of which £3,704 related to offences taken into consideration.

On arrest he was found to be in possession of goods, dishonestly obtained, to a *c* total value of £1,200. One of the problems which has arisen in this case with regard to the order of compensation arises from the fact that property of that value was recovered. The trial judge does not seem to have had any information as to which specific counts in the indictment or to which specific offences amongst those taken into consideration were referable to the property recovered.

In the course of carrying out this series of frauds, the appellant had to produce *d* identifying documents and he showed a considerable amount of cunning in doing so. Amongst the documents that he produced was a passport which he had obtained by making false statements. The trial judge, as I have already recounted, made the sentences for the offences relating to the obtaining of that passport consecutive, and it was argued before us by counsel that the judge should not have done so as the use of a false passport was part of the fraud. What has got to be remembered is *e* this; the use of a passport obtained improperly was undoubtedly one of the ways he used to convince tradesmen to part with goods, but that passport had been obtained by a separate course of criminal conduct. In those circumstances this court can see no reason why the sentences in respect of the passport should not have been ordered to run consecutively to the sentences in respect of the fraud.

From these facts it must be obvious that this was a serious offence and one which *f* called for a sentence of immediate imprisonment, and imprisonment for a longish period. As I have already said, this young man is of high intelligence. He has had every advantage in life. The only excuse which he put forward at the trial for starting on this series of crimes was that he was suffering from considerable emotional distress because of marital problems. That may be so, but it provides no excuse whatsoever for his criminal conduct. I should say at once that this court can see *g* no reason at all for interfering with the sentences totalling 3½ years imprisonment and in relation to those sentences the appeal is dismissed.

Different considerations, however, arise with regard to the order for compensation. This court has had the benefit of a very clear and well-researched argument by counsel and we are grateful to him for the care which he has taken. It is important for this court to remember that the law relating to the making of orders of compen- *h* sation by the criminal courts was substantially altered by the Criminal Justice Act 1972. It is necessary, however, for the purposes of considering the problem which arises in this case to go back to the Forfeiture Act 1870, which is the foundation of the modern law relating to compensation orders. Shortly after that Act was passed, in *R v Lovett*[1] it was submitted to the court that a compensation order under the Forfeiture Act 1870 might be considered as an alternative to a sentence. The trial *j* judge, who was Mr Sergeant Cox, firmly rejected that submission. He referred to the Act and he said[2]:

---

1   (1869) 11 Cox CC 602
2   11 Cox CC at 603

'This [i e s 4 of the 1870 Act] was manifestly designed to be in the nature of a remedy for the wrong done to the individual, and to be in addition to, and not as a substitute for, the punishment due to the crime.'

That was the approach of the courts from 1870 up to 1972, and as recently as 1971 in *R v Ironfield*[1] this court laid down the principles which were applicable for the making of compensation orders under the Forfeiture Act 1870. The court was presided over by Lord Parker CJ and he delivered the judgment. One part of the judgment is relevant to the problem, which we have had to consider in this case. It is as follows[2]:

'Counsel for the appellant has argued in connection with this compensation order that it would be wrong in principle to allow it to stand in the case of a convicted person who has no means, and who on his eventual release from prison will require such money as he can earn to rehabilitate himself, and that it would be wrong to make a compensation order in a case of a convicted person subjected to a considerable period of imprisonment who has no means. He points by analogy to rulings of this court in that connection relating to fines or costs. This court is quite satisfied that a completely different principle applies in the case of compensation. If a man takes someone else's property or goods, he is liable in law to make restitution, or pay compensation even if no compensation order is made by the court before which he is convicted. A victim who wishes to assert his rights need not be put to the additional trouble and expense of independent proceedings, and certainly cannot be required to forego his rights in order to facilitate the rehabilitation of the man who has despoiled him. In contrast, liability to pay a fine or costs can only arise from an order of the court and, in the case of a fine, is entirely punitive.'

It follows that if the principles laid down in *R v Ironfield*[1] are applicable to this case, then it was appropriate for the trial judge, if he was so minded, to make an order of compensation for a substantial sum. The problem for us has been whether those principles are still applicable under the Criminal Justice Act 1972. During the passage of that Act through Parliament there was a good deal of discussion about the value of compensation orders as one of the instruments of the courts in dealing with crime and criminals, and no doubt because of the public interest in the use of compensation orders there were a number of provisions in the Act to extend the jurisdiction of the courts to make compensation orders. It is necessary to look in some detail at those provisions.

The first provision and the most important is in s 1(1), which is as follows:

'Subject to the provisions of this Part of this Act, a court by or before which a person is convicted of an offence, in addition to dealing with him in any other way, may, on application or otherwise, make an order (in this Act referred to as "a compensation order") requiring him to pay compensation for any personal injury, loss or damage resulting from that offence or any other offence which is taken into consideration by the court in determining sentence.'

It is important to bear in mind that what the Act empowers the court to do is to make an order requiring the accused to pay compensation for any personal injury, loss or damage resulting *from that offence or any other offence*. It seems to us that it is clear from the wording of the Act that any order for compensation must be related to a specific offence whether that offence be in the indictment or it be an offence taken into consideration. There must, of course, also be a person who has suffered

---

1   [1971] 1 All ER 202, [1971] 1 WLR 90
2   [1971] 1 All ER at 202, 203, [1971] 1 WLR at 91

personal injury, loss or damage, so a court when making a compensation order must pay regard not only to the offence but to the victim of a specific offence.

In the same section, by sub-s (4), Parliament provided as follows:

'In determining whether to make a compensation order against any person, and in determining the amount to be paid by any person under such an order, the court shall have regard to his means so far as they appear or are known to the court.'

Section 1(4) introduces an entirely new factor into the discretion of the court. Why was that factor introduced? Having regard to the general policy of the 1972 Act, which was an Act to make further provisions with regard to the administration of criminal justice, it seems to us that that section must be construed as extending the powers of the court and of the objectives for which compensation orders are made, because, if the sole object of making compensation orders is, as it was under the 1870 Act, to give the equivalent of a quick and easy civil remedy, then the means of the accused would be irrelevant. The means of the accused are relevant for a number of reasons. The courts have got to be realistic. It is no good courts making compensation orders which can never be discharged by an accused person, and equally it is no good making compensation orders which, to use counsel's phrase, are likely to be counter-productive in the sense that they may result in the accused committing further offences to discharge an order.

Those of us who have had longish experience of the administration of criminal justice have met time and time again cases in which crimes have been committed in order to get the money with which to pay fines and similarly it seems to us there is a danger, if the courts are not realistic, that those who are ordered to pay compensation in sums which are far outside their reasonable expectations of ever being able to pay may be tempted to commit more crimes in order to discharge their obligations. Since the passing of the 1972 Act there have been a number of cases in which the court has had to consider the effect of that Act and the indications are that the courts have taken a much more liberal view of their jurisdiction than they ever did or could do before 1972.

In *R v McIntosh*[1], which is very shortly reported in the Criminal Law Review, this court presided over by Cairns LJ decided that the making of a compensation order was discretionary, and since the coming into force of s 1 of the Criminal Justice Act 1972 regard must be paid to the means of the defendant. In that case the court decided on the evidence that the accused had no means and might be unable to find work on release: the order for compensation was quashed. A comment was made on that case by the editors of the Criminal Law Review which is worth mentioning; it was in these terms[2]:

'Prior to the enactment of the Criminal Justice Act 1972 the court held in *Ironfield*[3] that in making an order for compensation under the Forfeiture Act 1870 a sentencer was not bound by the principle governing fines and orders for payment of prosecution costs that in imposing a financial penalty regard should be paid to the means of the defendant. The effect of section 1 of the 1972 Act is to assimilate compensation orders, which may now be made on a wider basis than previously, to fines in this respect.'

The court is not prepared to go as far as the editors went in their comment. What it is prepared to say is that the courts must apply their jurisdiction to make compensation orders in a common sense, realistic way, and that one of the factors to be taken

---

1 [1973] Crim LR 378
2 [1973] Crim LR at 378
3 [1971] 1 All ER 202, [1971] 1 WLR 90

a into consideration is the danger which I have already referred to of a compensation order becoming counter-productive.
  We find support for that proposition in a decision of this court in *R v Bradburn*[1].
The court was presided over by Lord Widgery CJ and had to consider whether a
compensation order had been made in accordance with the proper principle. In the
course of his judgment Lord Widgery CJ pointed out that the fact a man had got
b no means did not necessarily mean that he should not pay compensation. He said[2]:

  'There are good moral reasons for making compensation orders which will in
  a measure hurt the defendant's pocket and act to remind him of what he has
  done. But the Court must try to steer a common sense path through these
  various considerations and come up with a solution which satisfies them.'

c In that case Lord Widgery CJ does not seems to have had his attention drawn, as
far as we can see, to this problem of the rehabilitation of a man when he comes out
of prison subject to a compensation order; but we are of the opinion looking at his
judgment that he was inviting courts to keep in mind all the common sense factors
and the factor of rehabilitation is, in our judgment, one.
  When those principles are applied to the facts of this case, what is the result?
d I will deal with the application in its broadest aspect before I deal with the detail.
It was pointed out to us by counsel, who has done the arithmetic, that if the
appellant gains all his remission and he starts paying off the compensation as soon
as he comes out of prison and it is paid regularly, he will not have discharged his
liabilities under the order until March 1978. By that time he will be in his early
30's and weekly payments will have been at the rate of £16·34. What sort of job
e is the appellant going to get when he comes out of prison with a sentence of 3½ years
behind him for fraud which will enable him to make payments of that kind? The
answer is, it is most unlikely he is ever going to have a job of that calibre for very
many years indeed. But it is clear from the facts of this case that he is a man who can
use his high degree of intelligence for criminal purposes and it seems to this court
very likely that if he left prison with that kind of order for compensation over his
f head in a very short time he would be using his intelligence to think up new ways
of getting money quickly and almost certainly dishonestly. If there ever was a case
where an order for compensation was likely to be counter-productive this is it. On
that ground alone we would discharge the order for compensation, but there are
other reasons for discharging it.
  Counsel has pointed out to us that the global sum of £2,000 was not related to
g any specific offence or to any specific loser. This is a grave defect in the order; and
it is not merely on legalistic grounds, because if any loser does seek to proceed by
way of civil action how is he to know what he is going to get out of the compensation
order? The defect is made more grave in this case by the fact that £1,200 worth of
property has been recovered. To what counts in the indictment and amongst the
offences taken into consideration does that property relate? For example, the first
h count in the indictment relates to a firm called Comet Radiovision Services Ltd.
The amount involved in that count was just over £700. Does the £1,200 worth
of property relate to that count? How much of it relates to that count, if any of it
does? These are practical problems and it seems to this court that in form the order
was defective.
  At the hearing the appellant through his counsel said that he was in possession of
j £300 and was anxious that it should be used to compensate the losers. The judge,
bearing that in mind, gave a direction as to how it was to be split up. We have sought
in this court to be realistic and to ask ourselves to what counts in the indictment and
amongst the offences taken into consideration could this £300 be allotted? The

---

1 (1973) 57 Cr App Rep 948
2 57 Cr App Rep at 952

existence of £1,200 worth of property recovered makes the task of allocation impossible. We would like to call attention to what was said by this court in R v Daly[1].
The facts of that case are not important. The court was considering whether a compensation order was realistic, but in the course of his judgment Lord Widgery CJ said[2]:

> 'It must be remembered by courts making compensation orders that the civil
> remedy for the damage still exists. The machinery of the compensation order is
> a quick and simple way for dealing with the claim in simple cases, and in particular
> it should not be used where recompense involves a weekly payment over such
> a long period as the present.'

We endorse that and adopt it. This is not the sort of case which could possibly be
described as simple for this purpose and the facts which I have already recounted
indicate the difficulties of allotting particular sums to particular counts and particular
persons.

With considerable regret we have come to the conclusion that we cannot support
even that part of the trial judge's order which ordered the sum of £300 to be paid
out by way of compensation. The appellant informed the court, through his counsel,
that he still had the money and he might find it in his own interest to give instructions
to his lawyers to pay it over without an order of the court. Under the Criminal
Justice Act 1967 his case will come up for consideration for parole in due course and
his behaviour in respect of compensation might be a factor which the parole board
would take into consideration.

We quash the order for compensation.

Appeal allowed in part. Compensation order quashed.

Solicitor: *Registrar of Criminal Appeals* (for the appellant).

J K Anklesaria Esq Barrister.

Barclay v Prospect Mortgages Ltd

CHANCERY DIVISION
GOULDING J
7th, 8th, 11th FEBRUARY 1974

*Moneylender – Security – Enforcement – Security given by the borrower or by his agent –
Security given by third party – Memorandum insufficient – Security given by borrower not
enforceable – Security given by third party – Whether 'security given by the borrower' –
Whether enforceable – Moneylenders Act 1927, s 6(1).*

*Moneylender – Security – Enforcement – Security not enforceable – Meaning of 'enforceable'
– Mode of enforcement – Deposit of assets by surety with lender as security for loan – Memorandum of loan insufficient – Whether security enforceable by means other than legal proceedings – Whether surety entitled to order for delivery up of assets – Moneylenders Act
1927, s 6(1).*

A company wished to borrow £12,000 from the defendants, who were registered
moneylenders. In connection with the loan two documents were drawn up and
executed. The first was described as a 'Note or Memorandum' of the contract of
loan. It set out the amount of the principal sum and the method of calculating
interest and repayment. It stated that the loan was to be made on the security of a
charge on certain securities listed in a schedule forming part of the memorandum.

---

1 [1974] 1 All ER 290, [1974] 1 WLR 133
2 [1974] 1 All ER at 291, [1974] 1 WLR at 134

a The memorandum concluded by stating that it had been signed by two directors for and on behalf of the company both before the loan had been made or the security taken and subsequently in acknowledgment that since the first signature the sum of £12,000, together with a true copy of the memorandum, had been received by the company. The memorandum did not, however, specify the date on which the loan was to be made and did not therefore comply with s 6(2)[a] of the Moneylenders Act 1927. The second document was described as a deed of mortgage and agreement

b ('the deed'). It was made between the company, the defendants and the plaintiff. The deed recited that the defendants had agreed to advance £12,000 to the company and that the plaintiff had 'transferred into the name' of the defendants the securities listed in the schedule to the deed together with blank transfers thereof signed by the plaintiff. The deed provided for the repayment of the principal sum and interest by the borrower in specified monthly instalments and gave the defendants a power

c of sale over the securities which was exercisable 'at any time after the principal sum ... hereby secured shall have become payable...' The plaintiff did not in fact transfer the securities into the name of the defendants but deposited with them the certificates of title to the securities and the blank transfers. On a summons by the plaintiff for a declaration that the deed was unenforceable against her and for an order for the cancellation and delivery up of the deed and blank transfers and delivery

d up of the certificates of title, the defendants contended (i) that, although the memorandum failed to comply with s 6 of the 1927 Act, it did not follow that the security was unenforceable under s 6(1) since the security had not been 'given by the borrower' or his agent, but by the plaintiff, and (ii) that, even if the security were unenforceable under s 6, it was not therefore void and there was nothing in the 1927 Act to prevent the defendants, by their own actions and without the court's assistance,

e from operating the security so as to recover their money.

Held – (i) Where a borrower offered the deposit of a third party's investments or other assets as security for a loan those assets were a 'security given by the borrower' within s 6(1) of the 1927 Act. Since any security, given by a borrower was unenforceable under s 6(1) where the formalities required by s 6 had not been complied

f with, the plaintiff was entitled to a declaration that the deed was unenforceable against her (see p 680 *b* to *e*, post); *Temperance Loan Fund Ltd v Rose* [1932] All ER Rep 690 and *Central Advance and Discount Corporation Ltd v Marshall* [1939] 3 All ER 695 applied.

(ii) Furthermore, the word 'enforceable' in s 6 (1) was not limited to any particular mode of enforcement, e g by legal proceedings, but included the performance of

g such acts as the exercise of a power of sale over a deposited security in assertion of the right to repayment. Accordingly the plaintiff was entitled to an order for the delivery up of the certificates and the blank transfers but, since the judgment did not as a matter of law benefit the company, she was not entitled to the cancellation and delivery up of the deed (see p 682 *a* to *e* and *h*, post); *Kasumu v Baba-Egbe* [1956]

h 3 All ER 266 applied.

Notes
For the form of a note or memorandum of a moneylender's contract, see 27 Halsbury's Laws (3rd Edn) 32, para 50, and for cases on the subject, see 35 Digest (Repl) 241-247, 401-447.
For the Moneylenders Act 1927, s 6, see 22 Halsbury's Statutes (3rd Edn) 709.

j **Cases referred to in judgment**
Central Advance and Discount Corporation Ltd v Marshall [1939] 3 All ER 695, [1939] 2 KB 781, 109 LJKB 58, 162 LT 237, CA, 35 Digest (Repl) 246, 446.
Congresbury Motors Ltd v Anglo-Belge Finance Co Ltd [1970] 3 All ER 385, [1971] Ch 81, [1970] 3 WLR 683, CA, Digest (Cont Vol C) 711, 429a.

a Section 6 is set out at p 647 *h* to p 675 *b*, post

Conley, Re, Ex parte The Trustee v Barclays Bank Ltd [1938] 2 All ER 127, 107 LJCh 257, 158 LT 323, CA, 5 Digest (Repl) 921, 7592.

Eldridge and Morris v Taylor [1931] 2 KB 416, [1931] All ER Rep 542, 100 LJKB 689, 145 LT 499, CA, 35 Digest (Repl) 245, 438.

Kasumu v Baba-Egbe [1956] 3 All ER 266, [1956] AC 539, [1956] 3 WLR 575, PC, 35 Digest (Repl) 243, *232.

Reading Trust Ltd v Spero [1930] 1 KB 492, [1929] All ER Rep 405, 99 LJKB 186, 142 LT 361, CA, 35 Digest (Repl) 245, 437.

Temperance Loan Fund Ltd v Rose [1932] 2 KB 522, [1932] All ER Rep 690, 101 LJKB 609, 147 LT 330, CA, 35 Digest (Repl) 241, 412.

Cases also cited

Askinex Ltd v Green [1967] 1 All ER 65, [1969] 1 QB 272, CA.
Chapman v Michaelson [1909] 1 Ch 238, CA.
Cohen v J Lester Ltd [1938] 4 All ER 188, [1939] 1 KB 504.
Dunn Trust Ltd v Feetham [1936] 1 KB 22, [1935] All ER Rep 280, CA.
Edgware Trust Ltd v Lawrence [1961] 3 All ER 141, [1961] 1 WLR 1354.
Gaskell Ltd v Askwith (1929) 45 TLR 566, CA.
Leroux v Brown (1852) 12 CB 801, 138 ER 1119.
Lodge v National Union Investment Co Ltd [1907] 1 Ch 300, [1904-7] All ER Rep 333.
Lyle (B S) Ltd v Chappell [1932] 1 KB 691, [1931] All ER Rep 446, CA.
National Assistance Board v Wilkinson [1952] 2 All ER 255, [1952] 2 QB 648.
Pulbrook v Lawes (1876) 1 QBD 284.

Adjourned summons

By an originating summons dated 15th June 1973, as amended, the plaintiff, Angela Mary Barclay, the owner of certain stock and share certificates and blank transfers which had been deposited with the defendants, Prospect Mortgages Ltd, registered moneylenders, as security for a loan of £12,000 made by the defendants to Seaswept Estates Ltd ('the borrower'), claimed against the defendants: (i) a declaration that a deed of mortgage and agreement ('the deed') dated 6th September 1973 and made between the plaintiff, the defendants and the borrower was unenforceable against the plaintiff; (ii) an order for the cancellation and delivery up of the deed and the blank transfers referred to therein and for the delivery up of the certificates relating to the stocks and shares set out in the schedule to the deed. The facts are set out in the judgment.

D Gidley Scott for the plaintiff.
Gerald Owen QC and *R A Payne* for the defendants.

GOULDING J. This originating summons relates to a question under s 6 of the Moneylenders Act 1927, and I can conveniently begin my judgment by reading that section. It is in two subsections and provides:

'(1) No contract for the repayment by a borrower of money lent to him or to any agent on his behalf by a moneylender after the commencement of this Act or for the payment by him of interest on money so lent and no security given by the borrower or by any such agent as aforesaid in respect of any such contract shall be enforceable, unless a note or memorandum in writing of the contract be made and signed personally by the borrower, and unless a copy thereof be delivered or sent to the borrower within seven days of the making of the contract; and no such contract or security shall be enforceable if it is proved that the note or memorandum aforesaid was not signed by the borrower before the money was lent or before the security was given as the case may be.

a
'(2) The note or memorandum aforesaid shall contain all the terms of the co-tract, and in particular shall show the date on which the loan is made, the amount of the principal of the loan, and, either the interest charged on the loan expressed in terms of a rate per cent. per annum, or the rate per cent. per annum represented by the interest charged as calculated in accordance with the provisions of the First Schedule to this Act.'

b
The facts in the present case are not in dispute between the parties. The borrower, a company named Seaswept Estates Ltd, desired to borrow money from the defendants, Prospect Mortgages Ltd, who were registered moneylenders. In connection with that loan, two documents were drawn up and executed which have given rise to the questions in the present litigation. The two documents are, in quantity, brief and, in quality, ill drawn. I will read them both before I go further.

c
One of them in its present condition bears the date 6th September 1972, and reads:

'NOTE OR MEMORANDUM of Contract for a loan to be made by Prospect Mortgages of 378 Ilford Lane, Ilford, Essex, to me
'1.   The Principal sum shall be £12,000·00p.
'2.   The Interest shall be calculated on the principal sum at the rate of £12·00p

d
per centum per calendar month which represents interest at £23·6064% per annum as calculated in accordance with the 1st Schedule of the Moneylenders Act of 1927.
'3.   The said loan is to be repaid by 60 consecutive monthly payments of £320·00p.
'4.   The said loan shall be made on the 6th day of September 1972 upon the

e
security of a charge on a Schedule of Shares hereto, and forms part of this Memorandum.
'SIGNED by me before the loan was made or the security taken.'

Then follow the signatures of two persons, followed by the description 'Directors for and on behalf of [the borrower]'. Below that comes another paragraph, which reads:

f
'I hereby acknowledge that since the signature by me of the above Memorandum I have received the sum of £12,000·00p., together with true copy of this Memorandum.'

That paragraph bears the same two signatures and the same description of the signatories' office as directors of the borrower, and their signature is witnessed by a

g
Mr Bellis, a solicitor.
The other document is expressed to be made between three parties, and it begins as follows:

h
'This MORTGAGE and AGREEMENT is made the Sixth day of September one thousand nine hundred and seventy two BETWEEN [the defendants], whose Registered Office is situate at 378 Ilford Lane Ilford in the London borough of Redbridge (hereinafter called "the lender") of the first part; [the plaintiff] of 134 Somerset Road London S.W.19 (hereinafter called "the owner of the shares") of the second part and [the borrower] whose Registered Office is situate at 134 Somerset Road aforesaid (hereinafter called "the Borrower") of the third part.'

j
There follow two recitals, of which the first appears clear and the second appears extremely obscure:

'WHEREAS:—
'1.   The Lender has agreed to advance to the Borrower the sum of TWELVE THOUSAND POUNDS (£12,000·00) upon having the repayment thereof with interest secured in a manner hereinafter appearing . . .

'2. The Owner of the shares has transferred into the name of the Lender ALL THOSE stocks, shares and securities particulars of which are contained in the Schedule hereto TOGETHER WITH transfers thereof in blank duly signed by the Owner of the shares . . .'

It has been common ground before me that what actually happened was not that the stocks and shares were transferred by the plaintiff into the name of the defendants, but that stock and share certificates with blank transfers were handed over to the defendants. The operative part of this deed is in these terms:

'1. IN consideration of the sum of TWELVE THOUSAND POUNDS (£12,000·00) this day paid by the Lender to the Borrower (the receipt whereof the Borrower hereby acknowledges) the Borrower hereby agrees that he will on the Sixth day of October next pay to the Lender the sum of TWELVE THOUSAND POUNDS £12,000·00) with interest thereon from the date hereof at the rate of £23·6064 per cent per annum and that after the said Sixth day of October One thousand nine hundred and seventy two he will pay to the Lender by equal monthly payments, commencing on the Sixth day of October next the sum of THREE HUNDRED AND TWENTY POUNDS (£320·00) representing a combined payment of principal and interest, and will continue these payments for five years from the date hereof making sixty monthly payments of THREE HUNDRED AND TWENTY POUNDS (£320·00) as aforesaid until the total sum of NINETEEN THOUSAND TWO HUNDRED POUNDS (£19,200·00) being the total of the principal and interest, has been repaid . . .

'2. PROVIDED THAT if the Borrower shall on the Sixth day of October next pay to the Lender the sum of TWELVE THOUSAND POUNDS (£12,000·00) with interest thereon as from the date hereof at the rate hereinbefore provided the Lender will thereafter at the request and cost of the Borrower re-transfer and re-deliver the Certificates and Transfers deposited by the Owner of the shares to the Owner of the shares or as she shall direct . . .

'3. THE OWNER of the shares hereby irrevocably APPOINTS the Lender and its duly appointed agent or its attorney [I interject to say that the case has been argued on the footing that the words "or its attorney" ought to be "as her attorney"] to insert the name or names of the Lender or its assigns or any alteration or addition as regards the particulars of the shares affected thereby in the aforesaid Transfers or any of them and to re-deliver the same after any alteration or addition has been made thereto . . .

'4. PROVIDED FURTHER that:—(i) So long as the borrower shall duly pay the combined payments of capital and interest on the due dates the dividends upon the property for the time being SUBJECT to this security shall belong and be paid to the Owner of the shares . . . (ii) The Statutory Power of Sale shall be exercisable at any time after the principal sum of TWELVE THOUSAND POUNDS (£12,000·00) hereby secured shall have become payable, and Section 103 of the Law of Property Act 1925 shall not apply to this security.'

I need not read the final clause (cl 5) which defines the terms 'the borrower', 'the owner of the shares' and 'the lender' to include persons deriving title under the respective parties. Nor need I read the schedule which contains a list of marketable shares and stock. The deed was executed under the seal of the defendants and of the borrower. The plaintiff also executed the document under seal.

In case the matter goes further, I should mention one other fact that does not fully appear from the affidavit evidence. At some stage—and this, I think, does appear from an affidavit—a photographic copy of a completed draft of the deed was attached by a staple to the note or memorandum, which was the first document that I read. It has not been shown exactly when that happened, but the two documents, the note or memorandum and the photographic copy of the completed draft mortgage, were detached one from the other by counsel in this court, hence they are not attached at the present moment.

The borrower is not a party to the present proceedings and has not appeared before me. The proceedings are brought by originating summons. The plaintiff was, I was informed, the wife of one of the directors of the borrower. She contends that the note or memorandum which I have read is not in accordance with s 6 of the 1927 Act, and therefore she claims a declaration that the deed is unenforceable against her. She also claims certain consequential relief which I shall come to at a later point in my judgment.

So the first question which arises on the accepted facts is whether the memorandum does or does not comply with the requirements of s 6. Counsel for the plaintiff made four criticisms of the memorandum, any one of which, he submitted, was enough to show that it was insufficient to satisfy the statutory requirements.

The first criticism depended on the true construction of the deed of mortgage and agreement. Counsel submits that, reading cl 1 of the deed, it is provided that by way of repaying the loan of £12,000 with interest, the borrower was obliged to pay at the end of one month the sum of £12,000 with interest at the stipulated rate of a little over 23½ per cent per annum, and thereafter to make 60 monthly payments of £320 each, making, if my arithmetic is correct, an aggregate of £31,436·06p. Counsel for the defendants, on the other hand, say that the true interpretation of the deed, reading it as a whole, is that principal and interest will be fully repaid, and were only intended to be repaid, by 60 monthly instalments of £320 each, making £19,200 in all. If counsel for the plaintiff's reading of the deed is correct, then, of course, the financial statements in the memorandum are hopelessly incorrect, and it fails to comply with the 1927 Act.

The second point which counsel took was that even on the defendants' view of the deed, para 2 of the memorandum is wrong, and is in itself inconsistent because it stipulated for interest at 12 per cent per mensem, stating that it represents interest calculated under the statutory schedule at 23.6064 per cent per annum. The answer made to that is that the words 'per calendar month' are an obvious slip for 'per annum', and that reading the memorandum as a whole there is no real doubt it correctly states interest.

The third attack made on the memorandum was that it omits to state the date at which the first of the 60 monthly payments of £320 would become due. The answer to that was that the detail is one that could be inferred from the other provisions as being a date one month after the loan was made, or alternatively that any omission was cured because the fourth paragraph of the memorandum incorporates by reference the provisions of the deed. That argument as to incorporation was also relied on as a further answer to the first two points.

The fourth point made by counsel for the plaintiff was that when the memorandum was executed the date in para 4 stating when the loan should be made was blank. It is common ground that the date was blank because it was not known when the memorandum was signed that the transaction could necessarily be completed on the same day.

In the course of argument, I raised a possible fifth point on the memorandum by remarking that the name of the defendants is given as Prospect Mortgages, whereas the true name, and also the registered name under the Moneylenders Acts, of the defendants was, of course, Prospect Mortgages Ltd.

Those various criticisms raise a number of questions of construction and law, some of which are touched by reported dicta, if not by decisions, in the Court of Appeal. In this branch of the law it would, I think, be wrong for me to muddy the waters by making observations on points that are not needed for my decision.

Now, it appears to me that there is one of the points which have been raised which is quite unanswerable. I therefore propose to confine myself to that and not to

touch the other four. Section 6(1) of the 1927 Act, it will be remembered, says that
no contract and no security of the kinds there referred to shall be enforceable unless
the memorandum is made and a copy delivered as required, and it continues by
saying that—

> 'no such contract or security shall be enforceable if it is proved that the note
> or memorandum ... was not signed by the borrower before the money was
> lent or before the security was given as the case may be.'

Then s 6(2) requires, among other things, that the 'Note or memorandum ...
shall show the date on which the loan is made ...'. Therefore, the note or
memorandum, to be effective, must be signed before the money is lent and must
show the date on which it is to be lent. Signing a note or memorandum with a
blank for the date on which the loan shall be made is, in my judgment, clearly no
sufficient compliance with s 6 of the 1927 Act.

I express no view on the argument that the terms of the deed are incorporated by reference in the memorandum. Even if they are, the argument
cannot avail the defendants on this particular point, because at the date when the
note was signed any draft or engrossment of the deed was still, so far as the date was
concerned, in blank. Thus the plaintiff succeeds on her first contention that there
is no sufficient memorandum to comply with s 6 of the 1927 Act.

Then the plaintiff takes a further step. She says that if the memorandum is defective, s 6 provides that the security provided by the deed is unenforceable. The
answer made to that contention, as put forward by counsel in argument, was twofold, though it appears to me on reflection that one of the alternative answers really
belongs to a different and later branch of the matter.

The two answers made were these. First of all, it was said that the provisions of
s 6 only render unenforceable a security given by the borrower or by an agent on his
behalf. Here it is contended the security was not given by the borrower, and the
plaintiff was no agent of the borrower; therefore the security, it is said, is not one
struck at by the 1927 Act. The answer made by counsel for the plaintiff is that the
courts have interpreted s 6 in such a way that where a borrower, to obtain a loan,
offers the security, personal or real, of a third party, that is a security given by the
borrower within the meaning of the section. That argument I shall have to examine
in a moment. The other answer made on this point was that the security would not
be affected by the section unlesss the obligation of the borrower became not merely
unenforceable but discharged. That, I think, is out of place in this context. Section 6
says in plain terms that unless the formalities required are complied with, no contract
by a borrower for repayment shall be enforceable, and no security given by a borrower or his agent shall be enforceable. Therefore, if the contract containing the
obligation of a borrower becomes unenforceable, a security within the section also
becomes unenforceable. It may be that the consequences of being unenforceable
differ according to whether the obligation of a borrower has merely become unenforceable or has been actually discharged, but that is not the point on this particular
contention.

This branch of the matter is not free from authority. I have been referred in
particular to *Eldridge and Morris v Taylor*[1], *Temperance Loan Fund Ltd v Rose*[2], and
Central Advance and Discount Corporation Ltd v Marshall[3], all of which were decisions
of the Court of Appeal. I propose to read certain short passages from the judgments
in *Temperance Loan Fund Ltd v Rose*[2] to show how the Lords Justices there looked at
s 6 of the 1927 Act. The case was one in which a borrower and another party who
joined as surety had entered into a joint and several promise to pay the lender, and it

---

1 [1931] 2 KB 416, [1931] All ER Rep 542
2 [1932] 2 KB 522, [1932] All ER Rep 690
3 [1939] 3 All ER 695, [1939] 2 KB 781

was a case in which s 6 of the 1927 Act had not been complied with. Those same features were present in the earliest of the three cases, *Eldridge and Morris v Taylor*[1]. In *Temperance Loan Fund Ltd v Rose*, Scrutton LJ, who delivered the first judgment, said[2]:

'[It was contended] on behalf of the money-lenders that even if, as against [the borrower], the memorandum is bad, it is good as against the surety, because several cases connected especially with companies have decided that there may be a surety guaranteeing the debt of a company which the company is not liable to pay. A sum may be borrowed by a company, and the lender says: "I must have someone to guarantee the debt", and thereupon the guarantor guarantees that the company will pay. It has been held that in such a case, if the borrowing was ultra vires the company, the principal is not liable, but the surety is liable. The same point has been decided in the case of a father guaranteeing the debt of his infant son, where it has been sought to make the father liable. Those cases, however, do not affect the question under s. 6 of the Moneylenders Act, 1927. I am relieved from considering these authorities, because this action is upon a promissory note; that note is a security given by a borrower to money-lenders; that security includes a promise by a third party that he will pay, and the Act says that that security shall be unenforceable unless a memorandum complying with the statute has been signed. That is a sufficient answer to the point made by the money-lenders. Consequently the appellant is discharged and the appeal must be allowed.'

Greer LJ said[3]:

'If the second contention urged by Mr. Croom-Johnson—namely, that the Act makes the contract unenforceable only as against the borrower, were sound, the effect would be that the statute would give a defence to the borrower who has no merits and who has had the money, but refuses a similar defence to a person who signs merely as guarantor and who has not had the money. I decline to construe the section in that way. The section is not confined in its operation to a contract for the repayment of money lent. It says that any security given shall be unenforceable unless certain conditions are complied with. Sect. 6 clearly applies to a promissory note, bill of exchange, or any other security given by a third party and received by the money-lenders as security for the payment of the money lent. Even if I had any doubt about the meaning of s. 6, I should hold myself bound by the decisions of this Court in *Eldridge & Morris v. Taylor*[1] [and two other cases].'

Slesser LJ finally, after remarking that in the case before the Court of Appeal the obligation was joint and several, went on to give an alternative ground for his decision as follows[4]:

'Moreover a security "given by the borrower" may take the form of a guarantee given by a third party; it is a security given to the money-lender in order that he may lend money to the borrower. This point was not directly taken in *Eldridge & Morris v. Taylor*[1], but be that as it may, I have come to the conclusion that on the proper interpretation of s. 6 it is not necessary to consider the cases which decided that where a company acts ultra vires in incurring a debt the surety who guaranteed the debt may be liable although the company may not be liable. Here it is sufficient to say that s. 6 specifically provides that "no

---

1 [1931] 2 KB 416, [1931] All ER Rep 542
2 [1932] 2 KB at 529, cf [1932] All ER Rep at 693
3 [1932] 2 KB at 531, cf [1932] All ER Rep at 694
4 [1932] 2 KB at 533, 534, cf [1932] All ER Rep at 695

security given by the borrower ... shall be enforceable" unless certain conditions are fulfilled, and a security is given by the borrower when he produces the guarantee of a surety.'

The third of the cases that I mentioned, *Central Advance and Discount Corporation Ltd v Marshall*[1], was again one where a personal guarantee had been given by a third party, but it differed from the two earlier cases in that the guarantee was not given by way of joint and several promise, but appeared in a separate document executed by the guarantors. The result, however, was the same, that the guarantee was not enforceable because s 6 of the 1927 Act had not been complied with.

Those cases show that where a surety gives a personal guarantee to secure a borrower's debt, that guarantee is a security given by the borrower within the meaning of s 6, and therefore becomes unenforceable if the borrower's own contract to repay becomes unenforceable. Is there any reason why s 6 should not similarly affect the case where, instead of offering the personal security of a surety's promise, a borrower offers the deposit of a third party's investments or other assets? I can see no reason in principle why the liability of deposited securities should be preserved if the personal liability of a surety who gives a promise is not preserved. The similarity of the two situations is emphasised in a decision of the Court of Appeal, on a different subject, *Re Conley*[2]. Moreover, the case is covered, to my mind, by the reasoning of Greer and Slesser LJJ in *Temperance Loan Fund Ltd v Rose*[3].

Accordingly, I conclude on this point that the plaintiff has not only shown that the note or memorandum was insufficient to satisfy the section, but is also entitled to the declaration that she seeks that the deed of mortgage and agreement constituting the defendants' security is unenforceable against her.

Now I come to the last point in the case. By her originating summons the plaintiff not only claims the declaration to which I have just referred, but she also claims an order for the cancellation and delivery up of the deed and of the blank transfers referred to therein, and the delivery up of her stock and share certificates.

The defendants resist that relief and submit that although the security may be made unenforceable by the 1927 Act, it does not thereupon become void. There is merely, say the defendants, a situation in which the court will not lend its aid to a lender to enforce a security, but if the lender, by his own actions, without the assistance of the court, can operate the security so as to recover his money, there is nothing in the 1927 Act to prevent him.

Questions of this sort have been before the courts previously, and the most recent directly relevant authority is *Kasumu v Baba-Egbe*[4] in which the judgment of the West African Court of Appeal was affirmed by the Privy Council. That decision related to a Nigerian ordinance concerning moneylenders, but the English cases were reviewed and commented on. There the transaction of loan had become unenforceable for failure to comply with the requirements of the ordinance as to the recording of the transaction. The borrower himself, if I understand the facts correctly, had provided a mortgage of leasehold property by way of security, and it was contended that, although the loan transaction might have become unenforceable, the court ought not, as it had done, to make an order in favour of the borrower for possession of the mortgaged property, cancellation of the mortgage, and delivery up of the title deeds, unless he were required as a condition of that relief to repay the outstanding balance of the loan. The Judicial Committee, consisting of Lord Radcliffe, Lord Cohen and Lord Somervell of Harrow, decided, after a review of the facts and the authorities, that the West African Court of Appeal had been quite correct, and that if a court were to impose terms of repayment as a condition of setting the security aside, it would be expressing a policy of its own in regard to such transactions in conflict with the policy,

1   [1939] 3 All ER 695, [1939] 2 KB 781
2   [1938] 2 All ER 127 at 131
3   [1932] 2 KB at 531, 533, 534 cf [1932] All ER Rep at 694, 695
4   [1956] 3 All ER 266, [1956] AC 539

a   in Lord Radcliffe's words[1], 'of the Acts themselves', and I think he meant of the
ordinance which forms the comparable legislation in Nigeria.

Once the first and second contentions of the plaintiff have succeeded, it appears to
me that I ought to follow *Kasumu v Baba-Egbe*[2], although that case is not technically
binding on me, unless some valid distinction or irresistible attack can be made in
relation to it.

b   It has been submitted on behalf of the defendants that there are three grounds on
which I ought not to follow *Kasumu v Baba-Egbe*[2]. First of all, the terms of the legislation in contest there were different from those of the Moneylenders Act 1927. That
is perfectly true. The Nigerian ordinance does not say that no contract or security
shall be enforceable unless the statutory requirements are complied with. What it
says is that:

c   'Any moneylender who fails to comply with any of the requirements . . . shall
        not be entitled to enforce any claim in respect of any transaction in relation to
        which the default shall have been made.'

Further, the ordinance adds a penal sanction in the form of a fine, thus making a transaction which does not comply with the ordinance illegal as well as unenforceable.
Those are valid distinctions between the two pieces of legislation, but I do not think it
d   would be right for me to hold that they are critical for present purposes, because the
Judicial Committee do not appear to have attached any importance to them. They
remarked on the general analogy between the British and the Nigerian legislation and
examined the English authorities, as I have said, without apparently relying on any
vital difference between the law of the two countries. I think, therefore, that I ought
not to distinguish *Kasumu v Baba-Egbe*[2] on that ground.

e   Secondly, it was submitted that I ought to be persuaded that *Kasumu v Baba-Egbe*[2]
was wrongly decided, even though by a tribunal of such high authority as the Judicial
Committee, and to decline to follow it since it is not a decision strictly binding on the
High Court. The main ground for that contention was that the judgment in *Kasumu's*
case is out of line with decisions on the Statute of Frauds 1677 and enactments derived
from it such as s 4 of the Sale of Goods Act 1893, now repealed, or s 40 of the Law of
f   Property Act 1925, and with decisions on the Limitation Acts. Under the Statute of
Frauds and the Limitation Acts, lawyers are familiar with unenforceable contracts
which, while they will not in general be enforced by the courts, are still for many legal
purposes of effect as agreements between the parties. It was said that the result in
Kasumu v Baba-Egbe[2] would have been different had the attention of the Lords of the
Privy Council been drawn to decisions on the Statute of Frauds and the other enact-
g   ments I have mentioned in relation to the words 'entitled to enforce' in the Nigerian
ordinance. I was reminded that in *Reading Trust v Spero*[3] Greer LJ said:

        'The words of s. 6 are that without such a note no contract of loan shall be
        enforceable. They are analogous to the words of the Statute of Frauds, and the
        Sale of Goods Act 1893.'

h   Greer LJ was there drawing the analogy for the purpose of seeing whether a document
could be incorporated by reference in a note or memorandum under s 6. Reference
was also made to what was said by Scrutton LJ in *Eldridge and Morris v Taylor*[4], to which
I have already referred, though there is there no express mention of other statutes. I
am not convinced by that argument. The Statute of Frauds, the Sale of Goods Act 1893,
the Law of property Act 1925, the Limitation Acts, all use different language: 'No
j   action shall be brought'; 'A contract . . . shall not be enforceable by action'; 'No action
may be brought'; 'The following actions shall not be brought after the expiration of

1   [1956] 3 All ER at 272, [1956] AC at 552
2   [1956] 3 All ER 266, [1956] AC 539
3   [1930] 1 KB 492 at 507, cf [1929] All ER Rep 405 at 411
4   [1931] 2 KB at 420, [1931] All ER Rep at 544

six years', and so on; such language expressly refers in every case to judicial proceedings. Here, on the contrary, Parliament seems to have been careful to put in the word 'enforceable' without any limitation to a particular mode of enforcement. Secondly, not only is the language different, but the purpose and character of the legislation are different. The Statute of Frauds requiring a memorandum signed by the party to be charged operated indifferently, whichever party was the potential defendant. That, and the Limitation Acts too, were concerned to avoid litigation in circumstances where evidence was likely to be unsatisfactory as between subjects of the realm in general. Moneylenders' legislation, on the other hand, is expressly aiming at the protection of one class of persons against another, and the construction of any particular term in the legislation such as 'enforceable' should be considered with that purpose in mind. As Lord Radcliffe said, delivering the advice of the Judicial Committee in *Kasumu v Baba-Egbe*[1]:

'... their Lordships are satisfied that the words of deprivation "not be entitled to enforce any claim in respect of any transaction" are very widely drawn, and that they should not be confined to the assertion of rights by means of, or in the course of, legal proceedings. Thus, the performance of such acts in the law as the exercise of a right of sale over property mortgaged or charged, or the retention or taking possession of such property in assertion of the claim to repayment, is also precluded.'

The reasoning lying behind that statement seems to me equally applicable to the English Act.

The third and last ground on which I was urged to distinguish *Kasumu v Baba-Egbe*[2] is that there the borrower who had provided security had claimed to have the security set aside and his premises and deeds returned, and the lender claimed that as a condition of such relief the borrower should be required to repay the money still owing. In the present case, say counsel for the defendants, the lender is not asking that any condition should be imposed; the lender simply asks that no relief should be given by way of setting the security aside. 'We are perfectly content', say counsel for the defendants, 'that the securities should be left in our hands. We do not ask that some condition should be imposed as a term of recovering them.' I am quite unable to see how that greater rigidity of attitude on the part of the defendants can improve their position.

Reference was also made to a recent case of *Congresbury Motors Ltd v Anglo-Belge Finance Co*[3]. That was a case where a transaction of loan was rendered unenforceable by the 1927 Act and a security given in the form of a mortgage was cancelled as a result. The courts held that the lender was able indirectly to secure his right to repayment by subrogation to the lien of the vendor of property that the lender had paid for as part of the transaction. That decision, turning as it did on the special doctrine of subrogation, cannot in my view assist the defendants on the quite different facts of the present case.

Accordingly, in my judgment the plaintiff is entitled not only to a declaration that the deed is unenforceable against her, but also to an order for delivery up of the stock and share certificates and of the blank transfers referred to in the deed. It is not so clear to me that she is entitled, as she asks, to cancellation and delivery up of the deed itself, since my judgment does not, as a matter of law, redound to the benefit of the borrower. Therefore I limit my order under para 2 of the originating summons to delivery up of the certificates and blank transfers.

Order accordingly.

Solicitors: *Monier-Williams & Keeling* (for the plaintiff); *Edward Oliver & Bellis*, Ilford (for the defendants).

Evelyn Budd Barrister.

---

1 [1956] 3 All ER at 268, [1956] AC at 546
2 [1956] 3 All ER 266, [1956] AC 539
3 [1970] 3 All ER 385, [1971] Ch 81

Re Bryant Investment Co Ltd

CHANCERY DIVISION
PLOWMAN J
29th, 30th APRIL 1974

Company – Winding-up – Compulsory winding-up – Creditor's petition – Inability to pay debts – Statutory demand – Neglect by company to comply with demand by creditor for payment of debt – Debt not payable at date of demand – Dispute whether debt payable at date of demand – Whether company should be deemed unable to pay its debts – Companies Act 1948, ss 222(e), 223(a).

A company was formed as a property investment company. It had three shareholders, E, B and D, who were also the directors. The plan was that D, who was a surveyor, would find suitable properties for the company to acquire and E and B would provide the necessary finance through a company ('Metals') which they owned or controlled. The company acquired a number of properties, the acquisitions being financed by Metals to the extent of £92,386. Subsequently E and B, who between them owned a majority of the shares in the company, secured the removal of D from the board under s 184 of the Companies Act 1948. Metals made a formal demand on the company for the repayment of the £92,386. The company did not comply with the demand and Metals petitioned for the winding-up of the company under s 222 (e)^a of the 1948 Act on the ground that, under s 223(a)^b, it should be deemed unable to pay its debts since it had neglected to comply with the demand to repay the debt of £92,386. The petition was opposed by D who alleged that the agreement between the parties was that properties acquired by the company would only be sold when it appeared financially expedient to do so and that Metals would not be entitled to repayment of money lent on demand but only when the money became available on the sale of the company's properties.

Held – Section 223(a) of the 1948 Act was confined to the case of a debt which was payable; it had no application where the debt was not yet due. Accordingly, since the question whether the sum owed to Metals was due was in dispute, a winding-up order on the basis that there had been neglect to comply with the statutory demand would be refused (see p 685 b and c, post).

Notes

For a company's inability to pay debts, see 7 Halsbury's Laws (4th Edn) 593, para 999, and for cases on the subject, see 10 Digest (Repl) 853-855, 5620-5637.

For the Companies Act 1948, ss 184, 222, 223, see 5 Halsbury's Statutes (3rd Edn) 255, 289, 292.

Case cited
Re Stockton Malleable Iron Co (1875) 2 Ch D 101.

Petition
This was a petition by E & B Metals Ltd ('Metals') in which they sought an order that Bryant Investment Co Ltd ('the company') be wound up by the court under the provisions of the Companies Act 1948. The petition alleged that the company was indebted to Metals in the sum of £92,386, that, by a letter dated 18th January 1974 and delivered by hand to the company, Metals had demanded payment of that sum,

---

a Section 222, so far as material, is set out at p 684 j, post
b Section 223, so far as material, is set out at p 685 a and b, post

and that, for a period of over three weeks, the company had neglected to comply *a*
with that demand. The petition further alleged that the company was insolvent and
unable to pay its debts and that, in the circumstances, it was just and equitable that it
should be wound up. The petition was supported by Bernard Seymour Ellis and
Gerald Bean, two of the three contributories of the company, and opposed by
Joseph Harold Dobinson, the third contributory. The company did not oppose the
petition. The facts are set out in the judgment.   *b*

Dennis Levy for the petitioners.
G R A Argles for Mr Dobinson.

PLOWMAN J. This is a winding-up petition based on a statutory demand for
£92,386 odd in respect of money lent. It is supported by two of the three contribu- *c*
tories, namely Mr Ellis and Mr Bean, and opposed by the third contributory, Mr
Dobinson. The company itself does not oppose the petition, and I will say more
about that in a moment.

Mr Dobinson owns or controls 40 out of the 100 issued £1 shares of the company,
and Mr Ellis and Mr Bean each hold 30. The company was incorporated on 17th
May 1971 as a property investment company. It was formed pursuant to what *d*
I may call a quasi-partnership arrangement between the three shareholders. The
plan was that Mr Dobinson, who is a surveyor by profession, should find the properties for the company to acquire and that Mr Ellis and Mr Bean would put up
the finance through a company which they own or control called E & B Metals
Ltd. E & B Metals Ltd are the present petitioners. Since its incorporation, the company
has acquired 14 properties, and their acquisition has been financed by the petitioners *e*
to the extent of the £92,386 which I have mentioned.

Originally, all three contributories were directors, but on 18th February 1974 Mr
Dobinson was removed from the board, pursuant to s 184 of the Companies Act
1948. The curious and unusual position therefore arises that the petitioners, who
are controlled by Mr Ellis and Mr Bean, are seeking to wind up the company which
they also control, with the result that the company does not oppose the petition *f*
to wind it up. Mr Dobinson does oppose the petition on the ground that the debt
on which the petition is based is not at present due, and I think that in the circumstances Mr Dobinson's views are entitled to more weight than would usually be
the case on a creditor's petition. Mr Dobinson says this in para 7 of the affidavit
which he has sworn:

                                                                          g
'It was at all times agreed that properties purchased by the Company would
be purchased as a long term investment and that they should only be sold
when it appeared financially expedient on the part of the Company as a whole
to do so. It was therefore agreed that the Petitioner would not be entitled to
any repayment of the money lent as aforesaid until such money became available
on the sale of the Company's properties. It was at no time agreed that such *h*
moneys should be repayable on demand.'

The submissions made on his behalf are twofold. In the first place it is submitted
that it was not competent for the petitioners to make a statutory demand because
there was no present debt. That submission is based on the construction of s 223
of the Companies Act 1948. Before I refer to that section, I should just notice that *j*
s 222 provides:

'A company may be wound up by the court if—[inter alia] (e) the company
is unable to pay its debts . . .'

Section 223 provides:

a
'A company shall be deemed to be unable to pay its debts—(a) if a creditor, by assignment or otherwise, to whom the company is indebted in a sum exceeding fifty pounds then due has served on the company, by leaving it at the registered office of the company, a demand under his hand requiring the company to pay the sum so due and the company has for three weeks thereafter neglected to pay the sum or to secure or compound for it to the reasonable satisfaction of the creditor...'

b
In my judgment, that paragraph is only consistent with the view that it is confined to the case of a debt presently payable. The words, 'is indebted' and 'then due', followed by a reference to payment of the sum 'so due', are not, in my judgment, appropriate to a debt which is not yet due. The petitioners say that the debt is due, and, as I have already said, the company does not challenge that assertion. But on
c
the evidence, the matter is clearly disputed, and in those circumstances, I am not prepared to make a winding-up order on the basis of the statutory demand.

The petitioners then say that the company is insolvent. The relevant statutory provision there is para (d) of s 223 which provides:

d
'A company shall be deemed to be unable to pay its debts—... (d) if it is proved to the satisfaction of the court that the company is unable to pay its debts, and, in determining whether a company is unable to pay its debts, the court shall take into account the contingent and prospective liabilities of the company.'

I am not satisfied, on the evidence, that the company is unable to pay its debts. Mr Dobinson who, as I have already said, is a surveyor, estimates that the total
e
liabilities of the company are about £300,000, while the current market value of its properties is between £438,000 and £663,000. He says these figures assume that sales would take place otherwise than in a liquidation. The only challenge to the company's solvency is in the affidavit of Mr Ellis, sworn in reply to Mr Dobinson's affidavit, where he says this in paras 5 and 6:

f
'We [that is to say Mr Bean and himself] had instructed our Solicitors, Messrs Howard Kennedy & Rossi, to petition this Honourable Court for a winding up of the Company on the "quasi partnership" grounds, but we received advice that unless we were able to swear in an Affidavit that the Company was solvent, it might not be proper for us to bring such a petition. On the valuation advice we received neither Mr Bean not I were able to swear that on a liquidation the
g
Company would be solvent.'

I pause there to say that there is no evidence at all as to what that valuation advice was nor whose advice it was. The affidavit goes on:

'We therefore did not commence proceedings on the quasi partnership basis.
h
However, it was clearly unsatisfactory to us as directors of [the petitioners] that large sums of [the petitioners'] money should be tied up in the Company's investments. We therefore called in the sums due. The Company had and has no liquid funds to pay the debt, therefore as directors of the Company we did and do not oppose this Petition.'

j
There is no evidence at all that I can see that the company cannot meet its current liabilities as they fall due, and of course, in saying that, I am ignoring the money advanced by the petitioners. On that evidence, as I have said, I am not satisfied that it has been proved that the company is unable to pay its debts, and on those grounds I would prima facie propose to dismiss the petition. But counsel for the petitioners has asked that if I am not prepared to make a winding-up order I should give leave for Mr Ellis and Mr Bean to be substituted as petitioners; for the petition to be

amended to proceed on the just and equitable basis, and I have not yet heard what, if anything, is said in opposition to that.

Leave to amend by substituting Mr Ellis and Mr Bean as petitioners; petition stood over for 14 days.

Solicitors: *Howard, Kennedy & Rossi* (for the petitioners); *Collyer-Bristow & Co*, agents for *Walter Wilson, Dalton & Co*, Harrow (for Mr Dobinson).

Jacqueline Metcalfe Barrister.

The Golden Trader

Danemar Scheepvaart Maatschappij BV v Owners of the motor vessel Golden Trader

QUEEN'S BENCH DIVISION (ADMIRALTY COURT)

BRANDON J

4th, 5th, 28th FEBRUARY 1974

Admiralty – Jurisdiction – Action in rem – Arrest of ship – Stay of proceedings – Arbitration agreement – Protocol agreement – Court bound to grant stay – Whether court bound to order release of ship from arrest – Arbitration Act 1950, ss 4(2), 28, Sch 1.

The charterers, a company registered and carrying on business in the Netherlands, chartered a ship from the owners, a company registered and carrying on business in Eire. Under the charterparty the owners undertook certain obligations with regard to the seaworthiness of the ship on delivery and the maintenance of seaworthiness during service. The charterparty contained a clause providing that disputes arising under the charter were to be referred to arbitration. The charterers began an action in rem against the ship alleging breaches of the charterparty arising out of the owners' failure to maintain the ship. The writ was served and the ship arrested in the port of Milford Haven where she was undergoing repairs. On an application by the owners for an order that all further proceedings in the action be stayed, it was established that the court had jurisdiction to entertain the action and to arrest the ship under ss 1(1)(h) and 3(4) of the Administration of Justice Act 1956 and that the case was one to which the Protocol on Arbitration Clauses, set out in Sch 1 to the Arbitration Act 1950, applied and therefore the court was bound to grant a stay of proceedings under s 4(2)[a] of the 1950 Act. The charterers contended, however, that the court should refuse to make an order releasing the ship from arrest so that the security could be maintained

---

a Section 4(2), so far as material, provides: '. . . if any party to a submission to arbitration made in pursuance of an agreement to which the protocol set out in the First Schedule to this Act applies, or any person claiming through or under him, commences any legal proceedings in any court against any other party to the submission, or any person claiming through or under him, in respect of any matter agreed to be referred, any party to those legal proceedings may at any time after appearance, and before delivering any pleadings or taking any other steps in the proceedings, apply to that court to stay the proceedings, and that court or a judge thereof, unless satisfied that the agreement or arbitration has become inoperative or cannot proceed or that there is not in fact any dispute between the parties with regard to the matter agreed to be referred, shall make an order staying the proceedings.'

a to satisfy any award that might be made in the arbitration proceedings, or, alternatively, to satisfy the judgment which the charterers might obtain in the action should the stay be removed in the event of the arbitration agreement or proceedings becoming inoperative or incapable of proceeding.

Held — The owners were entitled to an unconditional order for the release of the ship for the following reasons—

b (i) The possibility of the court removing the stay, in the event of the arbitration agreement or arbitration proceedings becoming inoperative or incapable of proceeding, or of the defendants failing to pay under the award, was so remote that it would not be right to maintain the arrest solely to cater for it (see p 695 *c* to *e*, post).

(ii) Where an order was made staying further proceedings in an action in rem, the court had no jurisdiction to order the retention of an arrested ship as security to
c satisfy an award in arbitration proceedings or a judgment of a foreign court (see p 690 *j*, p 694 *c* and *d*, p 695 *f* and p 696 *c*, post); *The Cap Bon* [1967] 1 Lloyd's Rep 543 followed.

(iii) In protocol arbitration cases the grant of a stay under s 4(2) of the 1950 Act was mandatory and accordingly, under s 28^b of the 1950 Act, the court had no power to make the provision of alternative security a term of the order staying the action.
d Furthermore since the court could only retain the security to satisfy a judgment or compromise in the action itself, it followed that, where the court stayed the action, with the result that, in all probability, there would be no judgment or compromise in the action, the court was bound to release the security. Accordingly where the court was bound to grant a stay it was also bound to grant a release since a release was a necessary consequence of a stay (see p 696 *c* to *e*, post).
e

Notes

For jurisdiction of High Court in Admiralty cases, see 1 Halsbury's Laws (4th Edn) 212, 213, para 307.

For jurisdiction to stay court proceedings in arbitration cases, see 2 Halsbury's Laws (4th Edn) 285-287, paras 555-557, and for cases on the subject, see 2 Digest (Repl) 480,
f 481, 369, 482-485, 377-395.

For the Arbitration Act 1950, ss 4, 28, Sch 1, see 2 Halsbury's Statutes (3rd Edn) 437, 457, 466.

For the Administration of Justice Act 1956, ss 1, 3, see 1 Halsbury's Statutes (3rd Edn) 21, 26.

g **Cases referred to in judgment**
Athenee (Owners of cargo Ex) v Athenee (1922) 11 Lloyd LR 6, CA.
Atlantic Star, The, The owners of the Atlantic Star v The owners of the Bona Spes [1973] 2 All ER 175, [1973] 2 WLR 795, HL; *rvsg* [1972] 3 All ER 705, [1973] QB 364, [1972] 3 WLR 746, [1972] 2 Lloyd's Rep 446, CA; *affg* [1972] 1 Lloyd's Rep 534.
Banco, The, Owners of the motor vessel Monte Ulia v Owners of the ship Banco and others
h [1971] 1 All ER 524, [1971] P 137, [1971] 2 WLR 335, [1971] 1 Lloyd's Rep 49, CA.
Bremer Oeltransport GmbH v Drewry [1933] 1 KB 753, [1933] All ER Rep 851, 102 LJKB 360, 148 LT 540, CA, 2 Digest (Repl) 700, 2128.
Cap Bon, The [1967] 1 Lloyd's Rep 543.
Cooper v Williams [1963] 2 All ER 282, [1963] 2 QB 567, [1963] 2 WLR 913, CA, Digest (Cont Vol A) 1211, 1208c.
j *Eleftheria, The, Owners of Cargo lately laden on board ship or vessel Eleftheria v Owners of ship or vessel Eleftheria* [1969] 2 All ER 641, [1970] P 94, [1969] 2 WLR 1073, [1969] 1 Lloyd's Rep 237, Digest (Cont Vol C) 156, 1511b.

---

b Section 28 provides: 'Any order made under this Part of this Act may be made on such terms as to costs or otherwise as the authority making the order thinks just: Provided that this section shall not apply to any order made under subsection (2) of section four of this Act.'

Fehmarn, The [1958] 1 All ER 333, [1958] 1 WLR 159, [1957] 2 Lloyd's Rep 551, CA;
    affg [1957] 2 All ER 707, [1957] 1 WLR 815, [1957] 1 Lloyd's Rep 511, 1 Digest (Repl) *a*
    175, 606.
Foresta Romana SA v Georges Mabro (Owners) (1940) 66 Lloyd LR 139.

Cases also cited
Beldis, The [1936] P 51, [1935] All ER Rep 760, CA.
Brazendale & Co Ltd v St Freres SA [1970] 2 Lloyd's Rep 34.   *b*
Bustros v Lenders (1871) LR 6 CP 259.

Motion
This was a motion by the defendants, Commercial Ferries Ltd, the owners of the
motor vessel Golden Trader, for an order that all further proceedings in the action
between themselves and the plaintiffs, Danemar Scheepvaart Maatschappij BV, the   *c*
charterers of the vessel, be stayed pursuant to s 4(2) of the Arbitration Act 1950, the
plaintiffs and defendants having by an agreement dated 14th May 1973 agreed to refer
to arbitration the matters in respect of which the action was commenced, and for an
order that the warrant of arrest be set aside.   The facts are set out in the judgment.

Michael Dean for the defendants.   *d*
Jonathan Gilman for the plaintiffs.

5th February.   At the conclusion of argument Brandon J ordered that all further
proceedings in the action be stayed and that the vessel be released from arrest. His
Lordship stated that his reasons for making the order would be given at a later date.
                                                                                          e

28th February.   **BRANDON J** read the following judgment.   The question which
arises in this case is whether, where a ship has been arrested in an action in rem, and
the defendants subsequently obtain an order for a stay under s 4(2) of the Arbitration
Act 1950, they are also entitled to a further order releasing the ship from arrest. On
5th February 1974 I decided that they were so entitled and made an order accordingly. *f*
I thought it desirable, however, since the question raised is one of considerable general
importance in the field of maritime contracts, to reserve the reasons for my decision,
which I now give.
    The facts giving rise to the question are these.   The plaintiffs in the action are Dane-
mar Scheepsvaart Maatschappij BV, a company registered and carrying on business in
the Netherlands, and the defendants are Commercial Ferries Ltd, a company regis- *g*
tered and carrying on business in Eire.   By a charterparty made in Rotterdam and
dated 11th May 1973, the plaintiffs time-chartered from the defendants their motor
vessel Golden Trader, which I shall call 'the ship'.   By cll 1 and 26 of the charterparty
the hire was to be for three months, with an option to the plaintiffs to extend it for
three further periods of three months each.   By cll 13 and 44 the defendants undertook
certain obligations with regard to the seaworthiness of the ship on delivery and the *h*
maintenance of such seaworthiness during service.
    Clause 23 of the charterparty further provided:

    'Any dispute arising under the Charter to be referred to arbitration in London
    (or such other place as may be agreed) one Arbitrator to be nominated by the
    Owners and the other by the Charterers, and in case the Arbitrators shall not *j*
    agree then to the decision of an Umpire to be appointed by them, the award of
    the Arbitrators or the Umpire to be final and binding upon both parties.'

On 21st January 1974 the plaintiffs began an action in rem against the ship, and on
the same day caused the writ to be served and the vessel to be arrested in the port of
Milford Haven where she was being repaired.   The plaintiffs' claim, as endorsed on the

writ, was for breach or breaches of the charterparty arising out of the defendants' failure to maintain the vessel in a thoroughly efficient state, alternatively an indemnity under the charterparty for loss and/or damage sustained as a result of such failure.

On 30th January 1974 the defendants entered an appearance in the action by solicitors, and by notice of motion of the same date applied for an order that all further proceedings in the action be stayed pursuant to s 4(2) of the Arbitration Act 1950, and that the warrant of arrest be set aside.

The motion came on for hearing before me on 4th and 5th February 1974, when an affidavit in support of it by Mr Hall, an assistant solicitor with Messrs Clyde & Co, the defendants' solicitors, and three exhibits to it, were read. This evidence proved the facts to which I have already referred, and further established that both the Netherlands and Eire are signatories to the Protocol on Arbitration Clauses, Geneva, 24th September 1923, set out in Sch 1 to the Arbitration Act 1950.

The following matters were agreed between the parties. First, that the court had jurisdiction to entertain the action, and to arrest the ship in it, under ss 1(1)(h) and 3(4) of the Administration of Justice Act 1956. Second, that the case came within s 4(2) of the 1950 Act, as a protocol case, and that the court was therefore bound to make an order staying the proceedings. Third, that s 28 of the 1950 Act prevented the court from attaching any term of any kind to the order for stay. There was, however, a dispute as to whether the arrest of the ship should continue or be brought to an end. For the defendants it was contended that the court, having made an order staying the action, should forthwith make a further order releasing the ship from arrest in it. For the plaintiffs it was contended that the arrest should continue, at any rate for the time being.

So far as procedure is concerned, I think that, if the arrest is to be brought to an end, the right way to achieve that result is not to make an order setting aside the warrant of arrest, as asked for in the defendants' notice of motion, but to make an order for the release of the ship under RSC Ord 75, r 13(4). This is because the arrest was, as has been conceded by the defendants, lawfully made, and there can therefore be no justification for setting it aside, though there may be good reason, since the action is to be stayed, for ending it by release. This view as to the right form of order to be made is supported by *Foresta Romana SA v Georges Mabro (Owners)*[1], a case which I shall be discussing later.

While the question for decision in this case arises on a stay granted under s 4(2) of the 1950 Act, it is part of a larger problem which arises whenever an action in rem, in which the property proceeded against has been arrested or bail or other security has been given to prevent or to obtain release from arrest, is subsequently stayed on the ground that the dispute ought properly to be decided by another tribunal. The problem is what order should be made with regard to the security so obtained.

There are four categories of cases in which that problem can arise. First, cases where the parties have agreed to refer the dispute to arbitration and s 4(1) of the 1950 Act applies. Second, cases where the parties have agreed to refer the dispute to arbitration and s 4(2) of the 1950 Act applies. Third, cases where the parties have agreed to submit the dispute to the jurisdiction of a foreign court. Fourth, cases where, because a foreign court is much the more appropriate forum, the bringing or continuation of an action in England is vexatious or oppressive. I shall refer to these four categories of cases as 'non-protocol arbitration cases', 'protocol arbitration cases', 'foreign jurisdiction clause cases', and 'vexation cases' respectively. I shall also refer to the arrested property, or to the bail or other security given to prevent or to obtain release from arrest, simply as 'the security'.

There are, as it seems to me, in principle, three ways in which the problem to which I have referred, namely what to do with regard to the security when a stay is granted

---

1   (1940) 66 Lloyd LR 139

in such cases, can be dealt with. First, the security can be retained to satisfy any judgment or award of the other tribunal. Second, the security can be released, but only on condition that the defendant provides other equivalent security outside the court to satisfy the judgment or award of the other tribunal. Third, the security can be released unconditionally. I shall refer to the first and second of these ways of dealing with the problem as the 'retention method' and 'the alternative security method' respectively.

There are various arguments of policy and convenience which can be advanced both for and against each of these methods. It seems to me clear, however, that the International Convention for the Arrest of Sea-going Ships 1952[1], to which the United Kingdom is a party, contemplates that the retention method will be used.

The relevant provisions of the convention are contained in art 7. Article 7(1) provides that the court which has arrested a ship in respect of a maritime claim (see arts 1 and 3) shall have jurisdiction to decide the merits of the dispute if the domestic law of that court gives it such jurisdiction and anyhow in six specified cases. Article 7(2) states that, where the court of arrest has no jurisdiction to decide the merits, bail or other security given to procure the release of the ship shall specifically provide that it is given to satisfy the judgment of any court which does have such jurisdiction. It further provides that the court of arrest may fix the time within which the plaintiff shall bring an action before a court having such jurisdiction. Article 7(3) provides that, where the parties have agreed to submit the dispute to the jurisdiction of another court or to arbitration, the court of arrest may fix the time within which the plaintiff shall bring proceedings in that court or in an arbitration. Article 7(4) provides that, if in any case where time for bringing the proceedings has been fixed under art 7(2) or (3), the plaintiff does not bring proceedings within that time, the defendant may apply to the court of arrest for release of the security.

It is, in my view, necessarily to be implied from these provisions that, where the court of arrest has no jurisdiction on the merits, or where the parties have agreed to submit the dispute to a foreign court or to arbitration, then, provided that the plaintiff brings proceedings in a court which has jurisdiction on the merits, or in the agreed foreign court or before the agreed arbitration tribunal, within a time allowed by the court of arrest, the security will not be released, but will remain in the court of arrest to satisfy any judgment in the other court or any award in the arbitration.

The domestic law of this country intended to give effect to the 1952 arrest convention is the Administration of Justice Act 1956 (see *The Banco*[2]). By that Act the High Court in England was given jurisdiction on the merits in respect of every claim which is a maritime claim under the convention (see art 1 of the convention and s 1(1) of the 1956 Act). The result of that is that there cannot at present be any case in which, where a ship has been arrested in the Admiralty Court in respect of a maritime claim, that court will not also have jurisdiction on the merits, and it follows that there can never at present be a case where it would be appropriate to use the procedure contemplated by art 7(2), even if such procedure were available. Whether that will still be the situation when and if effect is given by domestic legislation to the European Judgment Convention 1968 remains to be seen.

There is, however, nothing in the 1956 Act, or the general law of England, to prevent parties from agreeing to submit the disputed maritime claim to the jurisdiction of a foreign court or to arbitration. It follows that there can readily be cases, of which the present one is an example, in which the use of the procedure contemplated by art 7(3) and (4) would be appropriate, if it were available. The question, however, is whether under English law as it has developed until now, that procedure is available for use in such cases. In order to answer that question it is necessary to examine the authorities which I shall now do.

---

1 Cmd 8954
2 [1971] 1 All ER 524, [1971] P 137

In *The Athenee*[1] there was a claim for damage to goods carried from Alexandria to Hull in a French ship under a bill of lading which contained a clause providing for all disputes under it to be brought before the Commercial Court of Marseilles. The cargo owners brought an action in rem against the shipowners in the Admiralty Court in respect of the claim and the defendants applied for a stay. It was, therefore, a foreign jurisdiction clause case. Sir Henry Duke P refused a stay and an appeal from his decision to the Court of Appeal was dismissed. It does not appear from the report of the case whether the ship had been arrested or not. I have, however, had the record searched, and it shows that the ship had been arrested before the application to Sir Henry Duke P and was released, presumably on security being given, between the time of his decision and the hearing of the appeal. In his judgment supporting the refusal of a stay, Atkin LJ said[2]:

> 'The question arises in respect of a clause to refer to a foreign tribunal as to a clause to refer to a domestic tribunal, whether there are proper reasons for not enforcing it. To my mind there were ample reasons for the learned President not enforcing it in this case. I think the balance of convenience and the substantial advantage which the plaintiffs have by suing in this country (and which they lose by not being able to proceed *in rem* against this ship), and many other advantages such as in respect of proof of loss . . . all those grounds seem to me to afford ample reason for the learned President coming to the conclusion that . . . the clause in the contract should not be given effect to.'

Atkin LJ is there saying that there were various reasons to justify the refusal of a stay, and one such reason was that, if a stay were granted, the plaintiffs would lose the substantial advantage of being able to proceed in rem against the ship. It seems to me to be implicit in this reasoning that Atkin LJ thought that there was no procedure by which the plaintiffs could obtain security for their claim by arresting the ship, and then, on a stay of the action being granted, retain that security to satisfy the judgment of the agreed foreign court. I say that because, if he had thought that such a procedure was available, it is likely that he would have referred to it.

In *Foresta Romana SA v Georges Mabro (Owners)*[3] there was a claim for breach of a charterparty relating to an Egyptian ship. The charterparty contained a London arbitration clause. The charterers began an action in rem against the shipowners in the Admiralty Court in respect of the claim and arrested the ship. The shipowners applied to the Admiralty registrar for the action to be stayed under s 4 of the Arbitration Act 1889 and for the ship to be released from arrest. It was, therefore, a non-protocol arbitration case. The registrar allowed the application and his decision was upheld on appeal by Langton J. No point was raised for the plaintiffs that, if the action were stayed, the arrest should nevertheless continue, and there is therefore, nothing in the report of the case relating to that point. The fact that it was not raised, however, appears of itself to indicate that it was not at that time thought that such a result could be achieved.

The approach adopted in *The Athenee*[1] was followed in *The Fehmarn*[4], another foreign jurisdiction clause case. In that case there was a claim for damage to goods carried from Ventspils in the USSR to London in a German ship under a bill of lading which contained a clause providing for all disputes under it to be judged in the USSR. The cargo owners brought an action in rem against the shipowners in the Admiralty Court in respect of the claim, but did not at that stage arrest the ship. The shipowners applied for a stay of the action. Willmer J[5] refused the stay and his decision was

1 (1922) 11 Lloyd LR 6
2 11 Lloyd LR at 7
3 (1940) 66 Lloyd LR 139
4 [1958] 1 All ER 333, [1958] 1 WLR 159; *affg* [1957] 2 All ER 707, [1957] 1 WLR 815
5 [1957] 2 All ER 707, [1957] 1 WLR 815

upheld by the Court of Appeal[1].   One of the matters taken into account by Willmer J
in exercising his discretion was the security which the plaintiffs might expect to obtain
by a subsequent arrest of the ship. As to this he said[2]:

> 'It is, however, the fact that, if I were to stay these proceedings which have
> already been launched, I might be depriving the plaintiffs of any remedy at all.
> It is not as though the defendant's ship was a Russian ship belonging to an organi-
> sation domiciled in Russia. There seems to be no possible guarantee that, if I
> ordered these proceedings to be stayed so as to enable the plaintiffs to start
> alternative proceedings in Russia, any judgment obtained would necessarily be
> of any value to them at all.'

Here again it seems to be implicit in the reasoning of Willmer J that he thought
that there was no procedure by which the plaintiffs could obtain security for their
claim by arresting the ship, and then, on a stay of the action being granted, retain
the security to satisfy the judgment of the agreed foreign court.

The next case for consideration is *The Cap Bon*[3], a decision of my own which bears
directly on the matter under discussion. In that case there was a claim by charterers
against the owners of a French ship arising out of a charterparty which contained a
London arbitration clause. The charterers began an action in rem against the shipowners in the Admiralty Court in respect of the claim and arrested the ship. The
defendants appeared and gave bail to obtain the release of the ship from arrest. The
bail bond purported to secure payment not only of any judgment in the action but
also of any award in any arbitration proceedings. Subsequently the charterers
began arbitration proceedings against the shipowners, who raised a counterclaim in
them. The charterers did not serve any statement of claim in the action, and the
shipowners therefore applied by summons to the Liverpool district registrar for an
order that, unless a statement of claim were served by a specified date, the action
should be dismissed. The district registrar declined to make the order asked for, and
made instead an order that the summons should stand adjourned while arbitration
proceedings were continued with due diligence. The shipowners appealed against that
order and I allowed the appeal, setting aside the order of the district registrar and
substituting for it an order that, unless the charterers served a statement of claim
within 21 days, the action should stand dismissed, and the bail bond, as a bail bond
in the action, should be cancelled. The principal ground on which I decided the appeal
appears from the following passages in my judgment. I said[4]:

> 'The plaintiffs' case on the appeal, as I understood it, was this. They wish to
> have what I hope I have not unfairly described as the best of both worlds; they
> desire to keep the action alive while not proceeding with it for the sole purpose of
> keeping the security which they have obtained, but they wish to have their claim
> determined by arbitration in accordance with the arbitration clause in the
> charterparty. For those reasons they seek to support the order made by the
> District Registrar which keeps the action alive while relieving them of their duty
> to prosecute it. In my view the plaintiffs' approach to this matter is based on a
> misconception. In my view, when an action *in rem* is brought the security thereby
> obtained is security in respect of any judgment which may be given by the Court
> after hearing and determining the claim. The security so obtained also covers the
> payment of any sum which may become due under an agreement whereby the
> action is settled. But the security so obtained is not in my view available for the
> purpose of ensuring payment of the judgment of some other Court or for the
> purpose of ensuring payment of the award of an arbitration tribunal. It seems to

1   [1958] 1 All ER 333, [1958] 1 WLR 159
2   [1957] 2 All ER at 711, [1957] 1 WLR at 821
3   [1967] 1 Lloyd's Rep 543
4   [1967] 1 Lloyd's Rep at 546, 547

a   me that this is a necessary inference from the terms of the Administration of
     Justice Act, 1956, which gives the Court power to entertain proceedings *in rem*.'

I then referred to the provisions of ss 1(1) and 3(4) of the 1956 Act and continued[1]:

b
     'It is to be inferred from that that the object of the process *in rem* is to provide
     security for a plaintiff in respect of any judgment which he may obtain as a result
     of the hearing and determination of a claim. That is the purpose of the proceeding
     in rem and, subject to the point I made, that it covers also payment of a sum due
     under a settlement in an action, it is the sole purpose of such process. It seems to
     me that in the present case the plaintiffs have sought to invoke the Admiralty
     jurisdiction of the Court *in rem* for a wholly different purpose, or at any rate seek
     now to maintain that process for a wholly different purpose. That different pur-
c   pose is not security for the payment of a judgment of the Court or security for the
     payment of a sum due under the settlement of an action in the Court, but security
     for the payment of an award in an arbitration conducted pursuant to cl 33 of the
     charter-party. In my view the Admiralty Court has no jurisdiction to arrest ships
     or to keep ships under arrest for that purpose; it only has jurisdiction to arrest
     ships and keep ships under arrest for the purpose of providing security for a
d   judgment of the Court. Bail in an Admiralty action *in rem* represents the *res*,
     and it follows, in my view, that the Admiralty Court has no jurisdiction to require
     bail as a condition of release, or to maintain that bail, for the collateral purpose to
     which I have referred.'

Finally I said[2]:

e
     'On the view I take of the effect of what the plaintiffs have done, or, rather, the
     non-effect, it seems to me that the whole of the plaintiffs' scheme falls to the
     ground. There would be no advantage to the plaintiffs, if they mean to arbitrate
     their claim, in keeping the action alive. No benefit would accrue to them in that,
     even if the action were kept alive, they would not be able to enforce any award in
     the arbitration against the bail given.'

f
     I shall refer finally to two still more recent cases, which illustrate the use of the
alternative security method of dealing with the problem. These are *The Eleftheria*[3],
which was another foreign jurisdiction clause case, and *The Atlantic Star*[4], which was a
vexation case. In *The Eleftheria*[3] there was a claim by English cargo owners against
the owners of a Greek ship for damage to goods carried under a bill of lading which
provided in effect that all disputes under it should be decided in Greece and according
g   to Greek law. The cargo owners began an action in rem against the shipowners in the
Admiralty Court and arrested the ship. The shipowners obtained her release by
providing security and applied for a stay of the action. They offered to accept, as a
condition of the stay, that the security already given, or other equivalent security,
should be available to satisfy any judgment of a Greek court. I allowed the applica-
h   tion and granted a stay, subject to appropriate terms about security in accordance
with the shipowners' offer.
     In *The Atlantic Star*[4] there had been a collision in fog in the port of Antwerp between
a Dutch ship under way and two moored barges, one Dutch and the other Belgian.
There was a preliminary enquiry, at the request of the two barge owners, by a surveyor of the Commercial Court of Antwerp, and later various actions arising out of the
j   collision, including an action by the Belgian barge owners, were brought against the
Dutch shipowners in that court. The Dutch barge owner, however, being dissatisfied

1 [1967] 1 Lloyd's Rep at 547
2 [1967] 1 Lloyd's Rep at 548
3 [1969] 2 All ER 641, [1970] P 94
4 [1973] 2 All ER 175, [1973] 2 WLR 795

with the surveyor's report, which tended to exonerate the Dutch ship, began an action   a
in rem against the Dutch shipowners in the Admiralty Court here, and the latter provided security to avoid arrest. They then applied for a stay of the action on the ground
that the Commercial Court of Antwerp was much the more appropriate forum and
that to proceed in England was vexatious and oppressive. They offered to provide
equivalent security to satisfy any judgment of the Commercial Court of Antwerp. I
refused a stay and my decision[1] was affirmed by the Court of Appeal[2]. There was a   b
further appeal to the House of Lords[3] which by a majority reversed the decision
below and granted a stay. In considering whether a stay should be granted or not the
members of the appellate committee who formed the majority all treated as a relevant matter the fact that the defendants were willing to provide alternative security to
satisfy any judgment of the Belgian court, and it is clear that the stay was granted on
that basis. See per Lord Reid[4], Lord Wilberforce[5] and Lord Kilbrandon[6].
    I think that the effect of these authorities can be summarised in this way. The first   c
three cases, *The Anthenee*[7], *Foresta Romana SA v Georges Mabro (Owners)*[8] and *The
Fehmarn*[9], while not deciding that the retention method is not available in English
law, nevertheless suggest strongly that it is not. The fourth case, *The Cap Bon*[10],
decides expressly that this method is not available. The last two cases, *The Eleftheria*[11]
and *The Atlantic Star*[3], show that, where a stay is discretionary, as it is in all cases
under consideration except protocol arbitration cases, the alternative security method   d
may, if the court thinks fit, properly be used.
    I turn now to the arguments in the present case. Counsel for the defendants ad-
vanced two propositions. The first proposition was that the court had no power, in
any case where a stay of an action in rem was granted, either under s 4(1) or (2) of the
1950 Act, to retain the security to satisfy any award in the arbitration. For this he
relied on *The Cap Bon*[10] and the three earlier cases discussed above. The second propo-   e
sition was that, where a stay was granted under s 4(2) of the 1950 Act (that is to say in a
protocol arbitration case), s 28 expressly forbade the court to attach any term to the
stay, so that the court, on granting a stay had no alternative but to release the security
unconditionally.
    Although it was open to counsel for the plaintiffs to contend that *The Cap Bon*[10]   f
was wrongly decided and should not be followed, he did not do so. Faced with that
decision, and accepting it as correct, he was obliged to put his case for keeping the ship
under arrest, despite the grant of a stay, on other grounds.
    The first ground on which he relied was that the stay was not final and that the
security should be maintained in case it were later removed. In this connection he said
that a stay of an action was not the same as a dismissal or discontinuance, in that a stay
could later, if circumstances justified it, be removed and the action allowed to proceed: g
Cooper v Williams[12]. This could happen if the circumstances contemplated in s 4(2) of
the 1950 Act, as justifying the refusal of a stay in the first place, namely the arbitration
agreement or an arbitration begun pursuant to it becoming inoperative or incapable of
proceeding, were to supervene at any time in the future after a stay had been granted.
It might also happen, so the argument went, if, after an arbitration had taken place   h

1   [1972] 1 Lloyd's Rep 534
2   [1972] 3 All ER 705, [1973] QB 364
3   [1973] 2 All ER 175, [1973] 2 WLR 795
4   [1973] 2 All ER at 182, [1973] 2 WLR at 801
5   [1973] 2 All ER at 195, 196, [1973] 2 WLR at 815, 816
6   [1972] 2 All ER at 202, 203, [1973] 2 WLR at 823
7   (1922) 11 Lloyd LR 6
8   (1940) 66 Lloyd LR 139
9   [1958] 1 All ER 333, [1958] 1 WLR 159
10   [1967] 1 Lloyd's Rep 543
11   [1969] 2 All ER 641, [1970] P 94
12   [1963] 2 All ER 282, [1963] 2 QB 567

and an award had been made, the defendants failed to pay under it. In the event of the stay being lifted in this way, the plaintiffs would be able to go on with the action and obtain a judgment in it, and the security should therefore be maintained as a means of satisfying such a judgment.

The second ground put forward for the plaintiffs was based on s 12(6)(f) of the 1950 Act. It was said that, once the plaintiffs had commenced an arbitration, they would be able to apply to the court under s 12(6)(f) for an order securing the amount in dispute in the reference, and that, on such application, the court would have power to order the arrest of the ship in order to provide such security. In these circumstances it was right to maintain the existing arrest until the plaintiffs had had an opportunity of making such an application and the court had adjudicated one way or the other on it.

As regards the first argument, I accept that, if the arbitration agreement, or an arbitration begun pursuant to it, should hereafter become inoperative or incapable of proceeding, there might well be grounds for the court making an order removing the stay and allowing the action to proceed. There was, however, no evidence of any kind to show that this was liable to happen in this case, and, in the absence of such evidence, I consider that the possibility can fairly be regarded as remote. Since it is remote, I do not think that it would be right to maintain the arrest solely to cater for it.

As regards the possibility of the defendants not paying under an award, I do not think that, if this occurred, it would necessarily justify removal of the stay. Rather do I think that, in that event, the plaintiffs should, in most cases at any rate, be left with the two remedies available to them, first of enforcing the award as a judgment under s 26 of the 1950 Act, and, secondly, of suing for breach of the agreement to arbitrate (see *Bremer Oeltransport GmbH v Drewry*[1]). Apart from this, there was no evidence to suggest that the defendants, if an award was made against them, would not pay under it.

As regards the second argument based on s 12(6)(f) of the 1950 Act, I think that this is founded on a misconception about the meaning of that provision. It seems to me that the power of the court there referred to is the power given by certain rules of court, such as RSC Ord 29, rr 2(3) and 6. I certainly do not think that the power referred to has anything whatever to do with the arrest of a ship by the court in an Admiralty action in rem or otherwise. Accordingly, while there are other difficulties about this second argument for the plaintiffs, I would reject it on that ground alone.

I have earlier expressed my view that the authorities are against retention of the security in order to satisfy an arbitration award, and I have now rejected the two other grounds for such retention put forward on behalf of the plaintiffs. It follows that I am satisfied that the court must release the ship. There remains, however, the question whether the release should be conditional, that is to say subject to alternative security being provided to satisfy any award in the arbitration, or unconditional.

As a matter of procedure only, there are two possible ways in which the court can give effect to the alternative security method. The first way is by making the provision of alternative security a term of the order for stay. The second way is by making it a term of the order for release. As I have shown earlier, the authorities support the use by the court of the first way, if it thinks fit, in cases where the grant of a stay is discretionary, that is to say in non-protocol arbitration cases, foreign jurisdiction clause cases and vexation cases. That way, however, is clearly not available in protocol arbitration cases, where the grant of a stay is mandatory and s 28 of the 1950 Act forbids the attachment of any term to the order for such stay. The question then is whether the court can properly, if it thinks fit, use the second way, namely attaching the term not to the order for a stay but to the order for release.

I believe that I am right in saying that counsel for the plaintiffs did not, until I suggested the possibility at any rate, invite me to proceed in this way. Perhaps he was wise not to do so. The point arises, however, and I think that I should deal with it.

---

1   [1933] 1 KB 753, [1933] All ER Rep 851

In theory I do not see why, if it is appropriate to use the alternative security method in non-protocol arbitration cases, foreign jurisdiction clause cases and vexation cases, where the grant of a stay is discretionary, it should not also be appropriate to use it in protocol arbitration cases, where the grant of a stay is mandatory, even if the procedure employed for the purpose has to be slightly different. On further examination of the point, however, I think that protocol arbitration cases must, in this respect, be treated differently.

Counsel for the defendants argued that to attach a term for the provision of alternative security to the order for release, while not offending against the letter of s 28 of the 1950 Act, would offend against its spirit. While this may be the right way to put the matter, I should prefer to put it differently as follows.

The starting point, if The Cap Bon[1] is right, is that the court can only retain the security to satisfy a judgment or a compromise in the action itself. It follows that, if the court stays the action, so that there will, in all probability at least, be no judgment or compromise in the action to be satisfied, it must then release the security. Putting it shortly, if there is a stay, there must, as a necessary consequence, be a release. In cases where the grant of a stay is discretionary, the court can refuse a stay unless alternative security is provided. The defendant then has to choose between having a stay subject to a term for the provision of such security and not having a stay at all. If he chooses the former, then, subject to his complying with the term, he gets both a stay and release; if he chooses the latter, he gets neither. By contrast, in protocol arbitration cases, where the grant of a stay is mandatory, the court cannot refuse a stay unless alternative security is granted. It is bound to grant a stay in any event, and, since release is a necessary consequence of a stay, it is bound also to grant a release.

For the reasons which I have given I formed the view, at the conclusion of the argument on the motion, that the defendants were entitled not only to an unconditional order for a stay, but also to an unconditional order for the release of the ship, and I made both orders accordingly.

I would add this. If I am right in the views which I have expressed, first that paras (2), (3) and (4) of art 7 of the 1952 arrest convention, to which the United Kingdom is a party, contemplate the use of the retention method in all cases where a dispute in respect of a maritime claim should properly be referred to another tribunal, and secondly that English law, as contained in the 1956 Act, does not at present give effect to what is contemplated by those paragraphs, then there is a situation which cannot be regarded as satisfactory and which it would be desirable for Parliament to remedy, anyhow in relation to persons belonging to states which have ratified the convention. In order to effect such remedy it would be necessary to give the court the power to retain the security obtained through arrest not only in cases where the grant of a stay is discretionary but also in cases where it is mandatory. It is right to point out, however, in relation to the present case, that neither of the states to which the parties belong has ratified the convention, so that there is no reason why its provisions should, as a matter of international treaty obligation, govern the relationship between them.

Order that action be stayed and vessel released from arrest.

Solicitors: *Clyde & Co* (for the defendants), *Holman, Fenwick & Willan* (for the plaintiffs).

N P Metcalfe Esq Barrister.

---

1   [1967] 1 Lloyd's Rep 543

Kavanagh v Chief Constable of Devon and Cornwall

COURT OF APPEAL, CIVIL DIVISION
LORD DENNING MR, STAMP AND ROSKILL LJJ
27th MARCH 1974

Firearms – Appeal – Decision of police authority – Refusal of certificate – Refusal of registration as firearms dealer – Appeal to Crown Court – Hearing of appeal – Evidence – Hearsay – Court not bound by rules of evidence.

When hearing an appeal under s 44 of the Firearms Act 1968 against the refusal of a chief officer of police to grant a firearm or shotgun certificate or to register a person as a firearms dealer, the Crown Court is not bound by the rules of evidence applicable in civil or criminal proceedings but is entitled to take into consideration all the matters, including hearsay evidence, which were before the chief officer of police in coming to his decision (see p 698 *h* to p 699 *c*, post).

Decision of the Divisional Court of the Queen's Bench Division [1973] 3 All ER 657 affirmed.

Notes

For the admissibility of evidence in courts and other tribunals, see 15 Halsbury's Laws (3rd Edn) 260-262, paras 474, 475.

For appeals against the refusal of firearms certificates, see 30 Halsbury's Laws (3rd Edn) 139, paras 223, and for a case on the subject, see 15 Digest (Repl) 804, 7648.

For the Firearms Act 1968, s 44, see 8 Halsbury's Statutes (3rd Edn) 756.

Case referred to in judgment

Miller (T A) Ltd v Minister of Housing and Local Government [1968] 2 All ER 633, [1968] 1 WLR 992, 66 LGR 539, CA, Digest (Cont Vol C) 958, 4a.

Appeal

This was an appeal by James Kevin Patrick Kavanagh against the decision of the Divisional Court of the Queen's Bench Division[1] (Lord Widgery CJ, Cusack and Mars-Jones JJ) dismissing his appeal by way of a case stated by the Crown Court (appeals) (chairman his Honour Judge Willcock QC) sitting at Bodmin against a decision of the court on a question which arose during the hearing of an appeal by the appellant against the refusal of the respondent, the chief constable of Devon and Cornwall, to grant him certificates under ss 26, 33 and 34 of the Firearms Act 1968. The facts are set out in the judgment of Lord Denning MR.

John Reide for the appellant.
Neil Butterfield for the respondent.

LORD DENNING MR. Mr Kavanagh wants to have a gun, perhaps many guns. To do so, he has to get the permission of the chief officer of police for his area. He applied for a shot gun certificate under s 26 of the Firearms Act 1968. He applied for registration as a firearms dealer under ss 33 and 34 of that Act. His application was considered by the chief constable of Devon and Cornwall. The chief constable had before him a good deal of information about Mr Kavanagh. In particular he had reports in writing from people in Gloucestershire and Ireland. These, we may assume, were not much help to Mr Kavanagh. At any rate the chief constable refused Mr Kavanagh's application.

---

1   [1973] 3 All ER 657, [1973] 3 WLR 415

Under s 44 of the 1968 Act Mr Kavanagh was entitled to appeal to quarter sessions.   *a*
That jurisdiction is now vested in the Crown Court under s 8 of the Courts Act 1971.
Mr Kavanagh duly appealed to the Crown Court. His appeal was heard at Bodmin.
The case proceeded for a day and a half. Witnesses were called. They were
examined and cross-examined according to the rules normally applied in a criminal
case. After they had all given evidence, in the course of speeches of counsel, the
circuit judge, who was presiding, asked these questions: What are the rules as to
admissibility of evidence in this case? Are they the rules as to admissibility of   *b*
evidence which apply in criminal cases or those which apply in civil cases? Ought
not the court to have before it the matters which influenced the chief constable even
though they were hearsay?

After hearing argument, the court held:

> 'We were of the opinion that we were entitled to hear of all the matters which   *c*
> had influenced the chief constable in reaching his decision with regard to the
> appellant, whether the matters were hearsay evidence, were not strictly proved,
> or were otherwise inadmissible by the rules of evidence applied in ordinary
> Courts of law.'

Seeing that the point was of some importance, application was made for a case to   *d*
be stated for the opinion of the High Court. The Crown Court stated this question:

> 'In an appeal of this nature, is the Court to be governed by the rules of evidence
> normally applied in the criminal and/or civil Courts, or is it entitled to hear or
> see all such matter as was originally before the Executive Officer who made
> the decision which is now the subject of appeal?'

  e

The Divisional Court held[1] that it was entitled to hear and see all such matter as was
before the executive officer. Now there is an appeal by leave to this court.

It seems to me that the Crown Court is in the same position as the court of quarter
sessions. The Crown Court is to try cases according to the same rules as the court
of quarter sessions used to do. The court of quarter sessions, when trying criminal
cases, applied the rules of evidence applicable to criminal cases. But from time   *f*
immemorial the court of quarter sessions exercised administrative jurisdiction.
When so doing, the justices never held themselves bound by the strict rules of
evidence. They acted on any material that appeared to be useful in coming to a
decision, including their own knowledge. No doubt they admitted hearsay, though
there is nothing to be found in the books about it. To bring the procedure up to
modern requirements, I think they should act on the same lines as any administrative   *g*
body which is charged with an enquiry. They may receive any material which is
logically probative even though it is not evidence in a court of law. Hearsay can be
permitted where it can fairly be regarded as reliable. No doubt they must act
fairly. They should give the party concerned an opportunity of correcting or contradicting what is put against him. But it does not mean that he has to be given a chance
to cross-examine. It is enough if they hear what he has to say. This was all made   *h*
clear by the decision of this court in *T A Miller Ltd v Minister of Housing and Local
Government*[2]. In an appeal under the Firearms Act 1968, it seems to me essential
that the Crown Court should have before it all the material which was before the chief
officer of police. After all, the chief officer is the person to give the decision in the first
instance. Under s 27 it is he who is to be 'satisfied'. Under s 34 he may refuse if he is
'satisfied' of what is said there. It is plain that he can take into account any information
that he thinks fit. He need not hold any hearing. He can decide on paper. If he refuses   *j*
and the applicant appeals to the Crown Court, then the Crown Court must see whether
or not the chief officer was right in refusing. For that purpose the Crown Court

---

1   [1973] 3 All ER 657, [1973] 3 WLR 415
2   [1968] 2 All ER 633, [1968] 1 WLR 992

ought to know the material that was before him and what were the reasons which operated on his mind. It can also consider any other material which may be placed before it. In the end it must come to its own decision whether a firearm certificate should be granted or refused, or whether a person should be registered as a firearms dealer. It will then dismiss or allow the appeal accordingly.

I think the answer which was given by the Crown Court and afterwards by the Divisional Court was correct. I would dismiss the appeal.

STAMP LJ. I agree and because I find the judgments in the court below wholly convincing, I would dismiss this appeal.

ROSKILL LJ. I also entirely agree and would adopt as my own the judgment in the Divisional Court given by Cusack J. He observed[1] that he did not think it useful to consider whether the proceedings on the appeal were civil or criminal. I entirely agree. The question is not whether the proceedings are civil or criminal, but whether the Crown Court when hearing an appeal under the Firearms Act 1968 is bound by the ordinary rules of evidence, and in particular the rule which exists in criminal courts as to inadmissibility of hearsay evidence. It has been said by counsel for the appellant—almost as a matter of complaint—that there is no authority on this point in relation to appeals under the Firearms Act 1968. I venture to think that the reason why there is no authority is that until the present case nobody has been brave enough to put forward the submissions to which we had the benefit of listening today. The relevant jurisdiction of the Crown Court under the statute derives from what was until 1971 part of the old administrative jurisdiction of quarter sessions. As Lord Denning MR has pointed out, from medieval times until 1971 a court of county quarter sessions had wide jurisdiction only a part of which involved the trial of criminal cases. The administrative jurisdiction included the hearing of appeals of this kind and the fulfilment of many different duties which had descended from earlier times. Before county councils existed quarter sessions were the main administrative body for a county. When in the last century county councils were created, they were given certain administrative duties. But the courts of quarter sesssions retained other administrative duties which have since been added to. When problems of controlling the possession of firearms arose and the right and obligation to grant or to refuse to grant firearms and other related certificates were given to senior police officers, it was natural in the circumstances that any appeal from their decisions should be to quarter sessions. Lord Denning MR has pointed out that when one looks at the relevant sections of the Firearms Act 1968 one finds references to the need for the officers concerned to be 'satisfied' of certain matters. That seems to me the key to the present case. In reaching a decision whether or not he is 'satisfied', he is entitled and indeed obliged to take into account all relevant matters, whether or not any reports and information given to him would be strictly admissible in a court of law. The statutory right of appeal originally lay to quarter sessions. Now it lies to the Crown Court. It would be strange indeed if the appeal which formerly lay to quarter sessions and now lies to the Crown Court had to be dealt with on a wholly different evidential basis from that on which the senior police officers concerned had to deal with the original application. For my part I think the reasons given by the Divisional Court are unanswerable, and, like Lord Denning MR and Stamp LJ, would dismiss the appeal.

Appeal dismissed.

Solicitors: *Philip Kossoff, Sheratte & Co* (for the appellant); *Frank & Caffin*, Truro (for the respondent).

L J Kovats Esq   Barrister.

---

1   [1973] 3 All ER at 660, [1973] 3 WLR at 419

Keppel Bus Co Ltd v Sa'ad bin Ahmad

PRIVY COUNCIL
LORD CROSS OF CHELSEA, LORD KILBRANDON AND SIR HARRY GIBBS
1st APRIL, 20th MAY 1974

Vicarious liability – Master and servant – Act of servant in course of employment – Authority of servant – Scope of authority – Implied authority – Bus conductor employed by defendants – Implied authority of conductor to keep order among passengers – Conductor assaulting passenger – No evidence of disorder or of emergency situation requiring forcible action – Whether conductor acting within scope of implied authority – Whether defendants vicariously liable for conductor's act.

The appellants were a bus company. The respondent was a passenger on one of their buses. In the course of the journey the conductor, who was employed by the appellants, was rude to an elderly lady who wished to get off the bus. The respondent remonstrated with the conductor. An altercation broke out between them but the other passengers prevented them from coming to blows. Thereafter the bus stopped, the lady got off and other passengers got on. The conductor began collecting fares. As he did so he abused the respondent in insulting terms. The respondent stood up and asked the conductor not to use abusive language; he then sat down. After he had done so the conductor struck him in the eye with his ticket-punch, breaking the respondent's glasses and causing the loss of the sight of his eye. In an action by the respondent in the High Court of Singapore against the appellants and the conductor, the trial judge found that, when he hit the respondent, the conductor was acting in the course of his duties in that he was 'maintaining order amongst the passengers. He was in effect telling the [respondent] by his act not to interfere with him in the due performance of his duties.' The judge therefore held that the appellants were vicariously liable for the conductor's act and his decision was affirmed by the Court of Appeal. On appeal,

Held – Although the question whether on the facts the act done, albeit unauthorised and unlawful, had been done in the course of the employment, was itself a question of fact, a jury would only be entitled to find that an act had been done in the course of employment if facts had been proved which established the extent of the master's delegated authority, express or implied, and that the servant's act was done under that authority, as part of his duty to his master. On the assumption that the keeping of order among the passengers was part of the duties of a conductor, there was no evidence of any disorder among the passengers or other circumstances from which it could be inferred that there was an emergency situation calling for forcible action, justifiable on any express or implied authority with which the appellants could be said on the evidence to have clothed the conductor. Accordingly the appeal would be allowed (see p 702 *e* and *f* and p 703 *c e f* and *g*, post).

Dicta of Sir Montague Smith in *Bank of New South Wales v Owston* (1879) 4 App Cas at 290 and of Lord Atkinson in *Riddell v Glasgow Corpn* 1911 SC (HL) at 36, 37 applied.

Notes

For the liability of a master for the tortious acts of his servant, see 25 Halsbury's Laws (3rd Edn) 535-544, paras 1021-1032, and for cases on the subject, see 34 Digest (Repl) 157-165, 1093-1140.

Cases referred to in opinion

Baker v Snell [1908] 2 KB 352, 77 LJKB 726; *affd* [1908] 2 KB 825, [1908-10] All ER Rep 398, 77 LJKB 1090, 99 LT 753, 21 Cox CC 716, CA, 34 Digest (Repl) 164, *1136*.

Bank of New South Wales v Owston (1879) 4 App Cas 270, 48 LJPC 25, 40 LT 500, 43 JP 476, 14 Cox CC 267, PC, 1 Digest (Repl) 382, *488*.

Canadian Pacific Railway Co v Lockhart [1942] 2 All ER 464, [1942] AC 591, 111 LJPC 113, 167 LT 231, PC, 34 Digest (Repl) 172, *1217*.

Daniels v Whetstone Entertainments Ltd [1962] 2 Lloyd's Rep 1, CA, Digest (Cont Vol A) 1131, *1331a*.

Deaton's Pty Ltd v Flew (1949) 79 CLR 370, 23 ALJ 522, 50 SRNSW 50, 34 Digest (Repl) 186, **737*.

Pettersson v Royal Oak Hotel [1948] NZLR 136, 34 Digest (Repl) 188, **756*.

Poland v John Parr & Sons [1927] 1 KB 236, [1926] All ER Rep 177, 97 LJKB 152, 136 LT 271, CA, 34 Digest (Repl) 146, *1002*.

Riddell v Glasgow Corpn 1911 SC (HL) 35.

Warren v Henlys Ltd [1948] 2 All ER 935, 34 Digest (Repl) 188, *1323*.

Appeal

By a writ issued on 18th December 1968 in the High Court of Singapore the respondent, Sa'ad bin Ahmad, brought an action against (1) the appellants, Keppel Bus Co Ltd, and (2) Chiu Eng Kiam, claiming damages for personal injuries and consequent loss and expense caused by the assault and battery of the respondent by the second defendant, the servant or agent of the appellants. On 5th April 1971 Kulasekaram J gave judgment for the respondent awarding him $20,000 by way of general damages and $290 by way of special damages against the appellants and the second defendant. The second defendant did not appeal against the order. On 31st July 1972 the Court of Appeal in Singapore (Wee Chong Jin CJ, Chua and Tan Ah Tah JJ) dismissed an appeal by the appellants. On 20th November the court gave the appellants leave to appeal to the Privy Council. The facts are set out in the opinion of the Board.

J G Le Quesne QC, Kenneth Hilbourne (of the Singapore Bar) and *Stuart MacKinnon* for the appellants.

T O Kellock QC and *Ian Ballieu* for the respondent.

LORD KILBRANDON. The respondent (plaintiff) was a passenger in a bus belonging to the appellants (first defendants). They employed as conductor of the bus the second defendant, who was a party neither to the proceedings before the Court of Appeal in Singapore nor to the present appeal. In the course of his journey the respondent was assaulted by the conductor. He brought an action claiming damages against both the conductor and also the appellants, as vicariously liable for the wrong committed by their servant. Kulasekaram J, before whom the case was tried, decided for the respondent against both defendants, and assessed the damages at $20,290. The Court of Appeal dismissed the appeal of the first defendants, and gave leave to appeal to the Board.

The facts, as they were found by the learned judge, may be stated as follows. At one point on the journey, an elderly Malay lady indicated that she wanted to get off the bus. The conductor ordered her 'in a loud and rude manner' to go and wait near the exit. The respondent took exception to this instruction and the manner in which it was given; he remonstrated that it was not safe for the lady to stand by the exit, which was also the entrance. An altercation broke out between him and the conductor, in the course of which each tried to hit the other. The passengers intervened and separated them. The bus stopped, the lady got off, and some passengers got on. The conductor began collecting fares. As he did so he abused the respondent in Chinese, using a very rude expression, of which an English translation has not been furnished. The respondent stood up and asked the conductor not to use abusive language; he then sat down. After he had sat down the conductor struck him in the eye with the ticket-punch, breaking his glasses, and causing the loss of the sight of the eye. The learned judge specifically rejected the conductor's version that the ticket-punch accidentally struck the glasses. The learned judge's account of these facts was accepted by the Court of Appeal; there are therefore concurrent findings of these facts, which, in accordance with their usual practice, their Lordships would not review.

The question in the case is whether the conductor did what he did 'in the course of his employment'. The course of the employment is not limited to the obligations which lie on an employee in virtue of his contract of service. It extends to acts done on the implied authority of the master. In *Poland v John Parr & Sons*[1] a carter, who had handed over his wagon and was going home to his dinner, struck a boy whom he suspected, wrongly but on reasonable grounds, of stealing his master's property. The master was held liable for the consequences, since a servant has implied authority, at least in an emergency, to protect his master's property.

> 'Maybe his action was mistaken and maybe the force he used was excessive; he might have pushed the boy instead of striking him. But that was merely acting in excess of what was necessary in doing an act which he was authorized to do. The excess was not sufficient to take the act out of the class of authorized acts . . . (per Scrutton LJ[2]).'

There is no dispute about the law. The Court of Appeal relied on the well-known passage from Salmond on Torts[3] which was approved in *Canadian Pacific Railway Co v Lockhart*[4]; it is not necessary to repeat it.

The Court of Appeal rightly point out that the question in every case is whether on the facts the act done, albeit unauthorised and unlawful, is done in the course of the employment; that question is itself a question of fact. In *Baker v Snell*,[5] Channell J, after saying that the defendant's liability would depend on whether his servant's wrongful act was done in the course of his employment, went on, 'the question is one of fact which ought to have been left to the jury'. A jury, however, would be entitled to find that the act was done in the course of the employment only if there were facts proved which established the extent of the master's delegated authority, express or implied, and that the servant's act was done under that authority, as part of his duty to his employer. In *Riddell v Glasgow Corpn*[6] it was alleged that a rate-collector had defamed the appellant by charging her with forging a receipt, and that the corporation, his employers, were vicariously liable. The question was whether the pleadings disclosed a relevant case. Lord Atkinson observed[7]:

> '. . . there is nothing, in my opinion, on the face of the pleadings to show expressly or by implication that Gilmour was clothed with authority to express on behalf of the Corporation to ratepayers any opinion he might form on the genuineness of any receipts which might be produced to him for payment of rates . . . it was not shown by the pursuer's pleadings, as I think it should be, that the expression of such an opinion was within the scope of Gilmour's employment; from which it follows, on the authorities, that the Corporation are not responsible for a slander uttered by him in the expression of that opinion.'

It is necessary, accordingly, in the present appeal to examine the grounds on which the learned judge held that, on the facts, this assault was committed in the course of carrying out, by a wrong mode, work which the conductor was expressly or impliedly authorised and therefore employed to do, and to see whether there is

---

1　[1927] 1 KB 236, [1926] All ER Rep 177
2　[1927] 1 KB at 244, [1926] All ER Rep at 180
3　9th Edn (1936), p 95; see now 16th Edn (1973), p 474
4　[1942] 2 All ER 464 at 467 [1942] AC 591 at 599
5　[1908] 2 KB 352 at 355; *affd* [1908] 2 KB 825, CA
6　1911 SC (HL) 35
7　1911 SC (HL) at 36, 37

any evidence to support them. If there be no evidence, it is a matter of law that his conclusions could not stand. The passage in which those grounds are stated is as follows:

'I find that the conductor when he hit the [respondent] was acting in the course of his duties. He was then maintaining order amongst the passengers in the bus. He was in effect telling the [respondent] by his act not to interfere with him in his due performance of his duties. He may have acted in a very high handed manner but nonetheless I am of the opinion that he was acting in the due performance of his duties then.'

On the facts as found by the learned judge, and after examining, with the assistance of learned counsel, the testimony of those witnesses whom the judge accepted as credible, their Lordships are unable to find any evidence which, if it had been under the consideration of a jury, could have supported a verdict for the respondent. It may be accepted that the keeping of order among the passengers is part of the duties of a conductor. But there was no evidence of disorder among the passengers at the time of the assault. The only sign of disorder was that the conductor had gratuitously insulted the respondent, and the respondent had asked him in an orderly manner not to do it again. Their Lordships do not consider the question whether the events of that morning are to be regarded as one incident, or as two incidents separated by a gap, to be of much importance. Certainly the end result can be related back to the treatment of the Malay lady; on the other hand she had by now left the bus, normalcy had been restored, except, apparently, for some simmering resentment in the conductor which caused him to misbehave himself. But to describe what he did in these circumstances as an act of quelling disorder seems to their Lordships to be impossible on the evidence; on the story as a whole, if any one was keeping order in the bus it was the passengers. The evidence falls far short of establishing an implied authority to take violent action where none was called for. In *Bank of New South Wales v Owston*[1], where the question was whether a bank manager was within his authority in bringing a criminal charge, Sir Montague Smith observed in relation to evidence that such an action might be taken in an emergency:

'An authority to be exercised only in cases of emergency, and derived from the exigency of the occasion, is evidently a limited one, and before it can arise a state of facts must exist which shews that such exigency is present, or from which it might reasonably be supposed to be present.'

Their Lordships are of opinion that no facts have been proved from which it could be properly inferred that there was present in that bus an emergency situation, calling for forcible action, justifiable on any express or implied authority, with which the appellants could be said on the evidence to have clothed the conductor.

A similar criticism can be levelled at the second ground on which the learned judge found that the conductor was acting under authority. There is no evidence that the respondent was interfering with the conductor in his due performance of his duty. His interference, if so it could be described, was a protest against the conductor's insulting language. Insults to passengers are not part of the due performance of a conductor's duty, as the learned judge seems to recognise in the paragraph of his judgment which follows.

The function of a bus conductor, from which could be deduced the scope of the authority committed to him, was attractively put by counsel for the respondent as 'managing the bus'; it was said that what he did arose out of that power and duty of management. But this concept, it seems, if pushed to its extreme, could serve to bring anything which the conductor did during his employment within the class of things done in the course of it. There must be room for some distinction between

---

1   (1879) 4 App Cas 270 at 290

the acts of a manager, however foreign to his authority, and acts of management, properly so called. Probably this way of putting the case is fundamentally no different from that which the learned trial judge adopted and their Lordships reject, because there is no evidence of circumstances which would suggest that what the manager actually did was, although wrongful, within the scope of his authority, express or implied, and thus an act of management.

Although each case on this branch of the law must stand on its own facts, it was natural and proper that their Lordships should have been referred to other cases by way of analogy. There is no difficulty about *Daniels v Whetstone Entertainments Ltd*[1]; in that case an assault was committed by a servant in circumstances which showed not a possibly excessive exercise of implied authority but, as Davies LJ pointed out[2], a contumacious repudiation of a direct order. In *Warren v Henlys Ltd*[3] the master's business with the plaintiff, which had been transacted by the servant, was long over when the servant assaulted the plaintiff. As regards the two public-house cases cited, *Deatons Pty Ltd v Flew*[4] and *Petterson v Royal Oak Hotel*[5], their Lordships have some difficulty in reconciling them, except on the possible ground that while in both the servant was retaliating for a personal affront, in the latter, though not the former, he was also encouraging the undesirable he assaulted to leave the premises. If either of those cases assist, by analogy, the present, it would seem that more assistance might be obtained from the former.

A question which does not appear to have been argued below is whether, supposing that implied authority had been proved, there was not here that excessive violence which Scrutton LJ[6] held might pass beyond the description of an unauthorised mode of doing an impliedly authorised act. Their Lordships do not find it necessary to consider the point. They conclude that there was no evidence which would justify the ascription of the act of the conductor to any authority, express or implied, vested in him by his employers; there is, accordingly, no legal ground for holding that the facts of this case justify a departure from the ordinary rule of culpa tenet suos auctores.

Their Lordships will therefore allow the appeal, set aside the order of the Court of Appeal and also set aside the judgment of the trial judge insofar as it was a judgment against the appellants. The respondent must pay the costs of the appellants before the trial judge, in the Court of Appeal and before their Lordships.

Appeal allowed.

Solicitors: *Coward Chance* (for the appellants); *Le Brasseur & Oakley* (for the respondent).

Christine Ivamy Barrister.

1   [1962] 2 Lloyd's Rep 1
2   [1962] 2 Lloyd's Rep at 9
3   [1948] 2 All ER 935
4   (1949) 79 CLR 370
5   [1948] NZLR 136
6   [1927] 1 KB at 244, [1926] All ER Rep at 180

The Esso Malaysia
Cox v Owners of the Esso Malaysia

QUEEN'S BENCH DIVISION (ADMIRALTY COURT)

BRANDON J

25th, 26th, 27th FEBRUARY, 18th MARCH 1974

Fatal accident – Action – Competency – Alien – Action by alien against another alien – Collision between foreign vessels on high seas – Death of foreign seaman on board vessel in consequence of collision – Collision caused or contributed to by negligence of other vessel – Action by personal representatives of deceased against owners of other vessel – Whether personal representatives entitled to recover damages on behalf of deceased's dependants from foreign owners – Fatal Accidents Act 1846, ss 1, 2.

Where a collision takes place between two foreign vessels on the high seas, outside the territorial jurisdiction of the United Kingdom, and a foreign seaman on board one of the vessels loses his life in consequence of the collision, the personal representatives of the deceased may recover damages for the benefit of the deceased's dependants from the owners of the other vessel, under ss 1^a and 2^b of the Fatal Accidents Act 1846, if the collision was caused or contributed to by the negligence of the other vessel (see p 707 *c* and p 711 *b* and *g*, post).

Davidsson v Hill [1900–3] All ER Rep 997 applied.

Notes

For claims for negligence under the Fatal Accidents Acts, see 28 Halsbury's Laws (3rd Edn) 35-38, paras 31, 32, and for cases on the subject, see 36 Digest (Repl) 208, 209, 1091-1105.

For personal injuries and death in Admiralty actions in rem, see 35 Halsbury's Laws (3rd Edn) 717, 718, para 1086, and for cases on the subject, see 1 Digest (Repl) 169, 170, 552-558.

For local limits of operation and persons to whom statutes apply, see 36 Halsbury's Laws (3rd Edn) 429, 430, para 650, and for cases on the subject, see 44 Digest (Repl) 277-278, 1051-1081.

For the Fatal Accidents Act 1846, ss 1, 2, see 23 Halsbury's Statutes (3rd Edn) 780, 781.

Cases referred to in judgment

Adam v The British and Foreign Steamship Co Ltd [1898] 2 QB 430, 67 LJQB 844, sub nom *Adam v British and Foreign SS Co Ltd, Stevart v Same, Michiels v Same, Yseboot v Same* 79 LT 31, 8 Asp MLC 420, 44 Digest (Repl) 277, *1060.*

Admiralty Commissioners v Steamship Amerika (Owners), The Amerika [1917] AC 38, [1916-17] All ER Rep 177, 86 LJP 58, sub nom *The Amerika* 116 LT 34, 13 Asp MLC 558, HL; *affg* [1914] P 167, CA, 36 Digest (Repl) 207, *1084.*

Aizkarai Mendi, The [1938] 3 All ER 483, [1938] P 263, 107 LJP 141, 159 LT 490, 61 Lloyd LR 274, 19 Asp MLC 228, 36 Digest (Repl) 230, *1221.*

Arum, The [1921] P 12, 90 LJP 166, 42 Digest (Repl) 929, *7205.*

Chartered Mercantile Bank of India, London and China v Netherlands India Steam Navigation Co (1883) 10 QBD 521, 52 LJQB 220, 48 LT 546, 47 JP 260, 5 Asp MLC 65, CA, 1 Digest (Repl) 119, *54.*

---

a   Section 1 is set out at p 708 *d*, post

b   Section 2 is set out at p 708 *e* and *f*, post

Cooke v Charles A Voegler Co [1901] AC 102, [1900-3] All ER Rep 660, 70 LJQB 181, *a*
　　84 LT 70, HL; *affg* sub nom *Re A B & Co* [1900] 1 QB 541, 69 LJQB 375, 82 LT 169,
　　CA, 44 Digest (Repl) 277 *1061*.
Cope v Doherty (1858) 2 De G & J 614, 27 LJCh 600, 31 LTOS 307, 44 ER 1127, 44 Digest
　　(Repl) 224, *411*.
Davidsson v Hill [1901] 2 KB 606, [1900-3] All ER Rep 997, 70 LJKB 788, 85 LT 118,
　　9 Asp MLC 223, DC, 2 Digest (Repl) 172, *25*. *b*
Draper (CEB) & Son Ltd v Edward Turner & Son Ltd [1964] 3 All ER 148, [1965] 1 QB
　　424, [1964] 3 WLR 783, [1964] 2 Lloyd's Rep 91, CA, 44 Digest (Repl) 277, *1054*.
Explorer, The (1870) LR 3 A & E 289, 40 LJ Adm 41, 23 LT 604, 3 Mar LC 507, 1 Digest
　　(Repl) 169, *554*.
Fabiola, The (1965) unreported.
Franconia, The (1877) 2 PD 163, 46 LJP 33, 36 LT 640, 3 Asp MLC 435, CA, 1 Digest *c*
　　(Repl) 169, *556*.
Guldfaxe, The (1868) LR 2 A & E 325, 38 LJ Adm 12, 19 LT 748, 3 Mar LC 201, 1 Digest
　　(Repl) 169, *553*.
Jefferys v Boosey (1854) 4 HL Cas 815, 24 LJ Ex 81, 23 LTOS 275, HL, 44 Digest (Repl)
　　277, *1057*.
Rosberg, The (1963) unreported. *d*
Saxonia, The, and The Eclipse (1862) Lush 410, 31 LJP M & A 201, 6 LT 6, 1 Mar LC 192,
　　167 ER 179, sub nom *Hamburgh American Steam Navigation Co v North of Scotland
　　Banking Co, The Eclipse, The Saxonia* 15 Moo PCC 262, PC, 42 Digest (Repl) 615,
　　3717.
Seward v Vera Cruz (Owner), The Vera Cruz (1884) 10 App Cas 59, [1881-85] All ER Rep
　　216, 54 LJP 9, 52 LT 474, 49 JP 324, 5 Asp MLC 386, HL, 1 Digest (Repl) 169, *557*. *e*
Smith v Brown (1871) LR 6 QB 729, 40 LJQB 214, 24 LT 808, 36 JP 264, 1 Asp MLC
　　56, 1 Digest (Repl) 169, *555*.
Tomalin v S Pearson & Son Ltd, [1909] 2 KB 61, 78 LJKB 863, 100 LT 685, CA, 34 Digest
　　(Repl) 355, *2702*.
Yorke v British & Continental SS Co Ltd (1945) 78 Lloyd LR 181, CA, Digest (Cont Vol
　　B) 298, *110a*. *f*
Zollverein, The (1856) Sw 96, 27 LTOS 160, 166 ER 1038, 42 Digest (Repl) 614, *3704*.

Case also cited
Bernina, The, Mills v Armstrong (1888) 13 App Cas 1, [1886-90] All ER Rep 823, HL.
Gaetano and Maria, The (1882) 7 PD 137.
Johann Friederich, The (1839) 1 Wm Rob 36, 166 ER 487. *g*
Tojo Maru, The [1971] 1 All ER 1110, [1972] AC 242, HL.

Preliminary point of law
The plaintiff, William Edward Cox, the surviving administrator of the estates of
Ernests Ekabovich Ekabsons and others (the master and entire crew of the SRT 4553
Pavilosta of the Port of Liepaia, Latvia), brought an action against the owners of *h*
the vessel Esso Malaysia, who were at the material time the owners of the vessel
Esso Honduras. The plaintiff claimed damages under the Fatal Accidents Acts 1846
to 1959 and the Law Reform (Miscellaneous Provisions) Act 1934 and for the loss
of effects and generally, arising out of and occasioned by a collision between the
SRT 4553 Pavilosta and the defendant vessel Esso Honduras off the coast of Oregon
Inlet, North Carolina, on or about 13th March 1969, as a result of which the estates *j*
and dependants of the deceased master and crew of the SRT 4553 Pavilosta suffered loss
and damage due to the negligence of the defendants or their agents. By their defence,
served on 23rd March 1973, the defendants denied that they were under any liability
to the plaintiff on the ground that the Fatal Accidents Acts 1846 to 1959 could have
no application to the loss of life of foreign seamen resulting from the collision so
that no claim could be made on behalf of the dependants of the deceased seamen

a under those Acts. By order of Brandon J, dated 11th June, the question whether the Fatal Accidents Acts 1846 to 1959 imposed on the defendants a liability in damages in respect of the deaths of the deceased seamen was ordered to be tried as a preliminary issue. The facts are set out in the judgment.

Michael Thomas QC and *Simon Gault* for the plaintiff.

b *Nicholas Phillips* for the defendants.

Cur adv vult

18th March. **BRANDON J** read the following judgment. The court has before it a preliminary question of law in an action for damages for loss of life brought in rem

c against a sister-ship. The question is whether, where two foreign ships collide on the high seas in international waters by the fault of both, and foreign seamen on board one ship lose their lives in consequence of the collision, the personal representatives of those seamen can recover damages from the owners of the other ship under the Fatal Accidents Acts 1846 to 1959. This question was raised by the defendants in their defence and was ordered to be tried as a preliminary issue on 11th June 1973. Certain

d other preliminary issues were also ordered to be tried at the same time, but agreement has since been reached on these, so that the court is no longer concerned with them.

The nature of the action, and the facts out of which it arises, appear from the agreed statement of facts. This reads:

e '1. At about 0500 hours on the 13th March, 1969, a collision occurred on the high seas outside territorial waters, off the East coast of the United States of America between the Defendant Motor Tanker "Esso Honduras" and the Trawler S.R.T. 4553 known as "Pavilosta". S.R.T. 4553 was so severely damaged as a result of this collision that she sank immediately and was totally lost. All 24 members of the crew of S.R.T. 4553 were killed.

f '2. The "Esso Honduras" was registered in Panama; her owners were Esso Transport Company Incorporated, a company incorporated and resident in the Republic of Panama; the nationality of her crew was principally Spanish.

'3. The S.R.T. 4553 was registered in Liepaia in the Republic of Latvia, a republic of the Union of Soviet Socialist Republics; her owners were the fishing Kolkhoz "Bolshevik" resident in Liepaia; the domicile and residence of the crew was Liepaia and many of the dependants of the crew are also resident and domiciled

g in Liepaia, although some dependants are resident and domiciled in other parts of the Union of Soviet Socialist Republics. The nationality of both crew and dependants is Russian.

'4. The collision and the consequent deaths of the crew of S.R.T. 4553 were caused in part by the negligence of the servants or agents of the defendants aboard "Esso Honduras". The parties have agreed that the degree of fault

h causing the collision should be apportioned 85 per cent to "Esso Honduras" and 15 per cent to S.R.T. 4553.

'5. The Plaintiff is the surviving administrator of the estates of all 24 members of the crew of S.R.T. 4553. He brings this action for the benefit of the estates of the deceased persons under the Law Reform (Miscellaneous Provisions) Act 1934, and makes a further claim on behalf of the dependants of the deceased

j persons under the Fatal Accidents Acts 1846 to 1959.

'6. The parties agreed that this action should be tried by the English Courts. By an undertaking dated the 26th August 1969 the Esso Petroleum Company Limited on behalf of the Defendants agreed to pay on demand such sums as may be adjudged by the English High Court of Justice or agreed to be recoverable from the Defendants in respect of, inter alia, the Plaintiff's claim, interest and

costs up to the amount of the statutory limit of liability of the Defendants
calculated in accordance with the English Merchant Shipping Acts.'

Certain matters may be got out of the way first. It is not in dispute that, if the plaintiff
has a good cause of action under the Fatal Accidents Acts 1846 to 1959, the Admiralty
Court has jurisdiction to hear and determine the claim in an action in rem against
a sister-ship under ss 1(1)(f) and 3(4) of the Administration of Justice Act 1956. There
is, therefore, no particular significance in the fact that the claim has been made in
the Admiralty Court, or that the action is one in rem against a sister-ship. The same
question of law about the existence of the cause of action relied on would arise if
the claim had been made in an ordinary action in the Queen's Bench Division,
assuming that service on the defendants of the writ in such an action could have
been effected by agreement or otherwise. The question is further unaffected by the
circumstance that both ships were to blame for the collision; it would arise in the
same way if the Esso Honduras had been alone to blame.

Before the passing of the Fatal Accidents Act 1846 English law gave no right of
action against a person who wrongfully caused the death of another person. This
deficiency was remedied by the 1846 Act which, as later amended, provides:

> '1. Whensoever the death of a person shall be caused by wrongful act, neglect,
> or default, and the act, neglect or default is such as would (if death had not ensued)
> have entitled the party injured to maintain an action and recover damages
> in respect thereof, then and in every such case the person who would have been
> liable if death had not ensued shall be liable to an action for damages, notwith-
> standing the death of the person injured.
>
> '2. Every such action shall be for the benefit of the wife, husband, parent, and
> child of the person whose death shall have been so caused, and shall be brought
> by and in the name of the executor or administrator of the person deceased;
> and in every such action the jury may give such damages as they may think
> proportioned to the injury resulting from such death to the parties respectively
> for whom and for whose benefit such action shall be brought; and the amount
> so recovered, after deducting the costs not recovered from the defendant, shall
> be divided amongst the before-mentioned parties in such share as the jury by
> by their verdict shall find and direct . . .
>
> '6. Nothing herein contained shall apply to Scotland.'

The reason for s 6 is that Scottish law already provided a remedy: see *Admiralty
Commissioners v Steamship Amerika*[1], per Lord Sumner.

For the plaintiff two propositions were put forward. The first proposition was that,
if the deceased seamen had only been injured instead of being killed, they would
themselves have been entitled to maintain an action against the defendants in negligence, and to recover damages in respect of their injuries, in an English court, even
though (a) they were foreigners serving at the material time on board a foreign ship,
(b) the Esso Honduras was a foreign ship owned by the defendants who were foreigners
and manned by the defendants' servants who were also foreigners, and (c) the collision took place on the high seas in international waters. The second proposition
was that in these circumstances, ss 1 and 2 of the 1846 Act as set out above made the
defendants liable to an action for damages at the suit of the plaintiff for the benefit
of the families of the seamen, even though the latter had been killed.

In support of the first proposition counsel for the plaintiff relied on the judgment
of Brett LJ in *Chartered Mercantile Bank of India v Netherlands India Steam Navigation Co*[2].
In support of the second proposition he relied on the express terms of ss 1 and 2,
which he said should not be construed as impliedly subject to any limitation in their

---

1   [1917] AC 38 at 51, 52, [1916-17] All ER Rep 177 at 185
2   (1883) 10 QBD 521 at 537

scope, by reference either to the place of the wrong or death, or to the nationality, domicile, or place of residence of the persons concerned.

Although the first proposition might at first sight appear surprising, counsel for the defendants recognised that it was well established by authority and practice, and did not seek to dispute its correctness. He did, however, dispute the second proposition, arguing that the provisions of the 1846 Act relied on, whatever effect they might have either extra-territorially or in relation to foreigners or both, did not, on their true construction, confer a right of action on a foreigner against a foreigner in respect of a death occurring on the high seas outside the territorial waters of the United Kingdom. Although I was referred by counsel to numerous cases in the course of the argument, there is, so far as I know, no reported case in which the precise point now before me has been raised for decision.

Among the authorities cited to me was a group of cases decided between 1868 and 1884, which related to claims for loss of life caused by collisions on the high seas brought in the High Court of Admiralty, or its successor in title under the Supreme Court of Judicature Act 1873. These cases were: *The Guldfaxe*[1]; *The Explorer*[2]; *Smith v Brown*[3]; *The Franconia*[4]; and *The Vera Cruz*[5]. In none of these cases were both the colliding ships foreign, but in three of them, namely *The Guldfaxe*[1], *The Franconia*[4] and *The Vera Cruz*[5], the ship proceeded against, and therefore the defendants, were foreign, and in the first two of these, though not the third, the collisions took place outside territorial waters. In all these cases, including the three just mentioned, the only point decided was whether s 7 of the Admiralty Court Act 1861 gave the High Court of Admiralty, or its successor the Probate, Divorce and Admiralty Division of the High Court, jurisdiction over a claim for loss of life. After a series of conflicting decisions on that point it was finally decided by the House of Lords in *The Vera Cruz*[5] that it did not. The effect of this last decision was later reversed by the legislature in s 5 of the Maritime Conventions Act 1911, and that provision was subsequently repealed and re-enacted with modifications, first in ss 22(1)(*a*)(iv) and (2) and s 33(2) of the Supreme Court of Judicature (Consolidation) Act 1925 and later in the provisions of the Administration of Justice Act 1956, to which I referred earlier.

Because the only point decided in those cases was that relating to jurisdiction, I do not consider that they afford any real assistance in resolving the question of the extent to which ss 1 and 2 of the 1846 Act apply for or against foreigners, or in respect of wrongs or deaths occurring on the high seas outside the territorial waters of Great Britain. It is right to observe, however, that in both *The Guldfaxe*[1] and *The Franconia*[4] it seems to have been assumed that, subject to the question of Admiralty jurisdiction, the Act gave a cause of action against a foreigner in respect of the death of a British seaman on the high seas outside territorial waters. Further Lord Blackburn, in his speech in *The Vera Cruz*[5], where the collision was in fact within the territorial waters of Great Britain, appears, on the hypothesis that it had occured outside such waters, to have been willing to make the same assumption.

I was referred next to two cases in the Queen's Bench Division in which the question of the application of the 1846 Act, as against the owners of a British ship, in respect of the death of a foreigner in consequence of a collision on the high seas outside territorial waters, was expressly raised for decision. In the first case, *Adam v The British and Foreign Steamship Co Ltd*[6], there had been a collision between a Belgian ship and a British ship on the high seas outside territorial waters, in consequence of which the Belgian ship sank and several members of her crew, who were

1   (1868) LR 2 A & E 325
2   (1870) LR 3 A & E 289
3   (1871) LR 6 QB 729
4   (1877) 2 PD 163
5   (1884) 10 App Cas 59, [1881-85] All ER Rep 216
    [1898] 2 QB 430

Belgian subjects, were drowned. The mother of one of the deceased crew sued the   *a*
owners of the British ship for damages under the Fatal Accidents Acts. It was held
by Darling J that those Acts did not apply for the benefit of aliens abroad, and that the
plaintiff therefore had no cause of action. He based himself on the principle, for which
he cited a number of authorities, that an Act of Parliament does not apply to aliens,
at least if they are not resident in this country, unless it refers expressly to them. In
the second case, *Davidsson v Hill*[1], there had been a collision between a Norwegian   *b*
ship and a British ship on the high seas outside territorial waters, in consequence of
which the Norwegian ship sank and a member of her crew was drowned. The
action was brought by the widow of the deceased man against the owners of the
British ship for damages under the Fatal Accidents Acts. It was held by Kennedy
and Phillimore JJ, sitting as a Divisional Court, that the Acts applied for the benefit
of the personal representatives of a deceased foreigner, anyhow as against an English   *c*
wrongdoer, and that the plaintiff accordingly had a good cause of action. The court
expressly disagreed with the decision of Darling J in *Adam v The British and Foreign
Steamship Co Ltd*[2] referred to above. Kennedy J further expressed obiter his provisional opinion that the result would have been the same if the defendants had
been foreigners, and, although Phillimore J did not refer to the matter specifically
in his judgment, he began by stating generally his agreement with the judgment of   *d*
Kennedy J, and I think it can therefore be inferred that he agreed with him on this
point also.

    Kennedy J, after referring to various cases cited in support of the principle that
statutes do not apply to aliens not resident within the jurisdiction, unless they
expressly so provide, said[3]:

> 'It seems to me that the Fatal Accidents Acts which are under our consideration   *e*
> in the present case embody legislation which is of a very different character.
> The basis of the claim to which they give statutory authority is negligence causing
> injury, and that is a wrong which I believe the law of every civilised country
> treats as an actionable wrong. They create, no doubt, a new cause of action
> (see per Lord Selborne in *Seward* v. *Vera Cruz*[4]), for previously the relatives of
> the deceased could not in England sue the wrong-doer. The measure of damages   *f*
> is not the same as in an action by the injured man, as the death is an essential
> constituent of the right of action. None the less, as I venture to think, is it true to
> say that in substance the purpose and effect of the legislation is to extend the
> area of reparation for a wrong which civilised nations treat as an actionable
> wrong ... It appears to me, under all the circumstances and looking at the
> subject-matter, more reasonable to hold that Parliament did intend to confer   *g*
> the benefit of this legislation upon foreigners as well as upon subjects, and
> certainly that as against an English wrong-doer the foreigner has a right to
> maintain his action under the statutes in question. It is not necessary to decide
> whether—assuming, of course, that no technical difficulty arises as to the service
> of proceedings—the action could be maintained in the English Courts, the
> death occuring through negligence in a collision upon the high seas, where   *h*
> both parties were foreigners, or where the wrong-doers were foreigners and
> the sufferers English. My present opinion is that an action could be maintained,
> but I desire to be understood as not expressing, as it is not necessary to express,
> a decided opinion upon this point. Here the plaintiff seeks to enforce her claim
> against an English subject, and I cannot see why she should not do so. If she
> has not the right we should have the anomaly, as it seems to me, that if a foreigner   *j*
> and an Englishman serving on the same ship were both drowned on the high

1   [1901] 2 KB 606, [1900-3] All ER Rep 997
2   [1898] 2 QB 430
3   [1901] 2 KB at 613-615, [1900-3] All ER Rep at 1001, 1002
4   (1884) 10 App Cas 59, [1881-85] All ER Rep 216

seas by the same collision negligently caused by an English vessel, the widow of the one could, and the widow of the other could not, obtain by suing the owners of the ship in fault in personam that reparation which our Legislature in these statutes has declared to be a just reparation.'

During the period of over 70 years since *Davidsson v Hill*[1] was decided it has, I think, been generally assumed that the Fatal Accidents Acts gave a cause of action against a foreign shipowner in respect of the death of a foreigner caused by a collision on the high seas outside United Kingdom territorial waters, and it is my belief that a significant number of Admiralty actions have been brought on that basis without the validity of such cause of action being challenged. An example of such an action is to be found in *The Aizkarai Mendi*[2] (where the collision was between a Spanish ship and a French ship in the North Sea). Enquiries in the Admiralty registry show that two actions raising similar claims were brought in recent years, both of which were settled. These were *The Fabiola*[3] (where the collision was between a Spanish ship and a French ship in the Atlantic), and *The Rosberg*[4] (where the collision was between a French ship and a Danish ship in the Kattegat).

Counsel for the defendants, in seeking to support the opposite view, referred me to numerous cases in which it was held that statutes of various kinds did not apply extra-territorially, or to the advantage or disadvantage of foreigners, or both. These cases included: *Jefferys v Boosey*[5], *The Zollverein*[6], *Cope v Doherty*[7], *The Saxonia and The Eclipse*[8], *Cooke v Charles A Voegler Company*[9], *Tomalin v S Pearson & Son Ltd*[10], *The Arum*[11], *Yorke v British and Continental Steamship Co Ltd*[12] and *Draper v Turner*[13]. The first three of these cases were considered and referred to, along with other cases on the same lines, in *Davidsson v Hill*[1]. I do not think it would serve any useful purpose for me to examine these cases individually, for I share the view expressed by Kennedy J in *Davidsson v Hill*[1] that the Fatal Accidents Acts embody legislation of a different character from that which has been the subject-matter of the decisions relied on.

The nature of the difference is, in my opinion, well stated in Dicey and Morris, Conflict of Laws[14] as being between statutes which, on the one hand, create new rules of conduct, and those which, on the other hand, remove exceptions to common law liabilities, or attach new liabilities to the violation of existing rules of conduct. The 1846 Act falls into the second part of the second category, being a statute which attached new liabilities to the violation of existing rules of conduct.

The actual decision in *Davidsson v Hill*[1], being that of a Divisional Court, is binding on me. The further expressions of opinion in the case do not bind me, but they are of considerable persuasive authority, which is to my mind immensely strengthened by the fact that their correctness appears to have gone unchallenged for over 70 years. I agree with them and have no doubt that I should follow them.

Counsel for the defendants, in the course of his able and interesting argument, invited me to consider the applicability of the 1846 Act to deaths occurring abroad

 1   [1901] 2 KB 606, [1900-3] All ER Rep 997
 2   [1938] 3 All ER 483, [1938] P 263
 3   (1965) unreported
 4   (1963) unreported
 5   (1854) 4 HL Cas 815
 6   (1856) Sw 96
 7   (1858) 2 De G & J 614
 8   (1862) Lush 410
 9   [1901] AC 102, [1900-3] All ER Rep 660
10   [1909] 2 KB 61
11   [1921] P 12
12   (1945) 78 Lloyd LR 181
13   [1964] 3 All ER 148, [1965] 1 QB 424
14   9th Edn (1973), p 952

or in foreign territorial waters, and referred me to a number of authorities, including
Commonwealth cases, bearing on such questions. The present case, however, does
not require the court to go into these further problems, and I do not therefore
propose to express any view on them.

For the reasons which I have given I hold that the Fatal Accidents Acts 1846 to
1959 apply to the present case, and that the plaintiff has a good cause of action against
the defendants for damages under them. There will be a declaration accordingly.

Order accordingly.

Solicitors: *Clyde & Co* (for the plaintiff); *Ince & Co* (for the defendants).

N P Metcalfe Esq Barrister.

Hellyer and another v Sheriff of Yorkshire and another

COURT OF APPEAL, CIVIL DIVISION
RUSSELL, BUCKLEY AND LAWTON LJJ
25th, 26th, 27th MARCH 1974

*Execution – Company – Winding-up – Creditors' rights – Duties of sheriff – Notice served
on sheriff – Notice relating to proposed winding-up of company – Service on sheriff's officer
and not on sheriff or under-sheriff – Effect – Writ of fi fa issued and sent to under-sheriff –
Warrant issued to sheriff's officer – Sums received by officer in execution of warrant – Notice
served on sheriff's officer of meeting of company at which winding-up resolution to be
proposed – Whether service of notice on sheriff's officer constituting service on sheriff –
Whether notice effective – Companies Act 1948, s 326(2) – Companies (Winding-up) Rules
1949 (SI 1949 No 330), r 43.*

*Costs – Appeal to Court of Appeal – Leave – Requirement of leave – Order of High Court or
judge thereof – Order as to costs only – Costs in discretion of judge – Leave of judge making
order – Joint defendants – Point of law decided against defendants – Substantive order against
one defendant – Order for costs against both defendants – Appeal by second defendant –
Central point of law wrongly decided by judge – No material on which to exercise discretion
that defendants should pay costs – No leave required by second defendant to appeal against
order as to costs – Supreme Court of Judicature (Consolidation) Act 1925, s 31(1)(h).*

On 11th November 1968 a judgment creditor obtained judgment in the High Court
against a limited company for a sum of £580. A writ of fieri facias was issued on the
same day and, on the following day, the under-sheriff issued a warrant to the sheriff's
officer. The officer took possession of goods belonging to the company and, on 7th
and 14th December, he received sums totalling £630 which were paid to avoid a sale
of the goods. On 21st December, i e within the 14 day period provided for in s 326(2)[a]
of the Companies Act 1948, the sheriff's officer received notice of a meeting of the
company at which a resolution was to be proposed for the voluntary winding-up of
the company. The notice was not, however, sent to the under-sheriff; the sheriff's
officer, assuming that, in accordance with the usual practice, the under-sheriff had

---

a Section 326(2), so far as material, is set out at p 715 d and e, post *a* received it, did not inform him of the notice until some time in January 1969. Subsequently the sheriff's officer released the sum of £580 to the judgment creditor. On a motion by the liquidators of the company, to which the sheriff and the judgment creditors were the respondents, the judge held that the notice of the meeting served by the liquidators on the sheriff's officer constituted an effective service of notice on the sheriff for the purpose of r 43[b] of the Companies (Winding-up) Rules 1949 and

b accordingly ordered the judgment creditor to pay the sum of £580 to the liquidators. He further ordered the sheriff and the judgment creditor to pay the liquidators' costs jointly and severally. The sheriff appealed against that order. At the hearing of the appeal it was contended, inter alia, that, by virtue of s 31(1)(h)[c] of the Supreme Court of Judicature (Consolidation) Act 1925, the court had no jurisdiction to hear the appeal, since the appeal was against an order as to costs only, and the leave of the

c judge below had been neither given nor sought.

Held – The court had jurisdiction to hear the appeal, and the appeal would be allowed, for the following reasons—

(i) It was not implicit in the duties of a sheriff's officer, by reason of the warrant issued to him, that he should inform the sheriff, or under-sheriff, of the receipt by

d him of a notice served under r 43 of the 1949 rules. Accordingly receipt of the notice by him could not be regarded as notice to the sheriff or the under-sheriff. It followed that, since the sheriff had not received a proper notice within the 14 day period under r 43, he was entitled, and obliged, to pay over the money to the judgment creditor (see p 717 *e f* and *h*, p 718 *a* and *j* and p 719 *a*, post); *Re Holland, Ex parte Warren* (1885) 15 QBD 48 and *Bellyse v M'Ginn* [1891] 2 QB 227 applied.

e (ii) Since the judge had gone wrong on the central point of law in the case there was no relevant material on which he could properly have exercised his discretion as to costs by ordering the sheriff to pay the unsuccessful liquidators' costs of the summons. In those circumstances leave to appeal was not required under s 31(1)(h) of the 1925 Act (see p 718 *f g* and *j* and p 719 *a* post).

f **Notes**
For the sheriff's duties when a company's goods are taken in execution, see 7 Halsbury's Laws (4th Edn) 767, para 1356, and for cases on the subject, see 10 Digest (Repl) 1016-1019, 6990-7013.

For the right of appeal against an order as to costs only, see 30 Halsbury's Laws (3rd Edn) 423, para 798, and for cases on the subject, see 51 Digest (Repl) 984-986,

g 5237-5257.

For the Supreme Court of Judicature (Consolidation) Act 1925, s 31, see 7 Halsbury's Statutes (3rd Edn) 590.

For the Companies Act 1948, s 326, see 5 Halsbury's Statutes (3rd Edn) 355.

For the Companies (Winding-up) Rules 1949, r 43, see 4 Halsbury's Statutory Instruments (2nd Reissue) 147.

h

Cases referred to in judgment
Bellyse v M'Ginn [1891] 2 QB 227, 65 LT 318, DC, 5 Digest (Repl) 885, 7369.
Engineering Industry Training Board v Samuel Talbot (Engineers) Ltd [1969] 1 All ER 480, [1969] 2 QB 270, [1969] 2 WLR 464, CA, Digest (Cont Vol C) 120, 7013b.
Holland, Re, Ex parte Warren (1885) 15 QBD 48, 54 LJQB 320, 53 LT 68, 2 Morr 142, CA,
j 5 Digest (Repl) 987, 7956.

---

b Rule 43, so far as material, is set out at p 715 *c*, post
c Section 31(1), so far as material, provides: 'No appeal shall lie ... (h) without the leave of the court or judge making the order, from an order of the High Court or any judge thereof ... as to costs only which by law are left to the discretion of the court ...'

Case also cited

Wheeler v Somerfield [1966] 2 All ER 305, [1966] 2 QB 94, CA.

Appeal

On 30th October 1969 Union Rubber Works Ltd ('the judgment creditor') issued a writ in the Queen's Bench Division against E H Clay Ltd ('the company') claiming the sum of £561 9s 6d, the balance of the price of goods sold and delivered. No appearance was entered to the writ and, on 11th November 1968, the judgment creditor obtained judgment in default of appearance in the Leeds District Registry for the whole of the sum claimed and £15 11s 6d costs. On the same day the judgment creditor obtained the issue of a writ of fieri facias and despatched the writ to the under-sheriff of Yorkshire. By letter dated 12th November the under-sheriff gave notice that he had issued a warrant to Mr R B Holroyd, the sheriff's officer in Dewsbury. The assistant sheriff's officer, Mr J M Holroyd, took possession of goods belonging to the company and, on 7th December and 14th December, received sums totalling £580 10s which were paid to avoid a sale of the goods. On 19th December the sheriff's officer wrote to the judgment creditor's solicitors informing them that he had received the sum of £580 10s and that that sum would be forwarded to them on 28th December 'if no bankruptcy intervenes'. On 21st December the sheriff's officer received a notice dated 19th December convening a meeting of the company, to be held on 8th January 1969, at which a resolution would be proposed for the winding-up of the company. The sheriff's officer did not send the notice to the under-sheriff at York since the usual practice was for such notices to be sent direct to the under-sheriff. The sheriff's officer assumed that that had been done and that a copy of the notice had been sent to the under-sheriff for his information. The extraordinary general meeting of the company was held on 8th January 1969 and a resolution was duly passed that the company be wound up. On 9th January the judgment creditor's solicitors wrote to the sheriff's officer asking for the release of the moneys held by him. On 18th January the sheriff's officer wrote to the under-sheriff raising certain queries concerning the notice of the meeting and asking whether the under-sheriff had received a copy of the notice. The under-sheriff replied on the following day stating that the form of notice was 'not sufficient to prevent your parting with the proceeds of sale or money received' and further that 'no Notice was received at the office, where they must be served in the first instance'. On 23rd January the sheriff's officer wrote to the judgment creditor's solicitors enclosing a cheque for £580 10s 'being full settlement of debt and costs'. On 26th March the solicitor acting for the liquidator of the company wrote to the judgment creditor's solicitors stating that 'the proceeds of the execution should have been paid to the liquidator under Section 326(2) of the Companies Act 1948' and demanding the payment of the sum of £580 10s.

By an originating motion dated 1st September 1972 Robert Wheaton Hellyer and Barrie Price, the joint liquidators of the company, applied, inter alia, for (i) a declaration that they were entitled, under s 326(2) of the 1948 Act, to recover from the first respondent, the sheriff of Yorkshire, alternatively from the second respondent, the judgment creditor, the sum of £580·50; (ii) an order for the payment by the sheriff, alternatively the judgment creditor, to the joint liquidators of that sum with interest, and (iii) an order that the respondents, or one or other or both of them, pay the costs of or incidental to the motion. On 14th May 1973 in the Companies Court, sitting at Leeds, Blackett-Ord V-C held that the notice of 19th December 1968 convening a meeting of the company had been effectively served on the sheriff under r 43 of the Companies (Winding-up) Rules 1949[1], and that it was therefore a valid notice under s 326(2) of the 1948 Act. Accordingly he declared that the liquidators were entitled to recover the sum of £580·50 from the judgment creditor. He further

---

1   SI 1949 No 330

ordered that the judgment creditor pay that sum to the liquidators with interest at five per cent from 26th March 1969 until the date of payment, that the respondents pay the liquidators' costs jointly and severally, and that there be no order for costs between the respondents. The sheriff appealed against the order.

Brian Parker for the sheriff.
Eben Hamilton for the liquidators.

RUSSELL LJ. The point in this appeal is a short one. A company called Union Rubber Works Ltd on 11th November 1968 obtained a judgment in the High Court in default of appearance against E H Clay & Co Ltd, the company with which we are concerned, for a sum of some £580, and a writ of fieri facias was issued on the same day. The under-sheriffs for Yorkshire, on 12th November, issued the relevant warrant to the sheriff's officer at Dewsbury, a Mr R B Holroyd. The sheriff's officer, either personally or through an assistant (who was I think his son), took possession of some goods the property of the company; and on 7th and 14th December, respectively, he received sums totalling about £630 which were paid to avoid sale of the goods that were seized.

Now under s 326(2) of the Companies Act 1948 it is provided:

'... the sheriff shall deduct the costs of the execution from the proceeds of the sale or the money paid and retain the balance for fourteen days, and if within that time notice is served on him ... of a meeting having been called at which there is to be proposed a resolution for the voluntary winding up of the company and an order is made or a resolution is passed, as the case may be, for the winding-up of the company, the sheriff shall pay the balance to the liquidator who shall be entitled to retain it as against the execution creditor.'

There is involved in that, that if an appropriate notice is not given in the appropriate manner within the 14 days, the sheriff is entitled and indeed obliged to pay over to the judgment creditor—in this case Union Rubber—the amount of the judgment debt; and this in fact was done.

Returning to s 326, sub-s (4) provides that in that section 'the expression "sheriff" includes any officer charged with the execution of a writ or other process'. I pause there to say that it has been made plain on authority (and it appears also from the relevant winding-up rule) that 'any officer charged with the execution of a writ or other process' is intended to cover persons who are in the equivalent situation, so far as execution is concerned, of the sheriff in respect of courts other than the High Court.

I turn to r 43 of the Companies (Winding-up) Rules 1949, which says:

'For the purposes of section 326 of the [Companies Act 1948] a notice that ... a meeting has been called at which there is to be proposed a resolution for the voluntary winding-up of the company ... shall be in writing and shall be addressed, where the execution is in respect of a judgment of the High Court, to the Sheriff, and in any other case, to the officer charged with the execution, and may be served by being delivered by hand or by registered post, in the case of a notice to a Sheriff, at the office of the Under-Sheriff, and in any other case, at the office of the officer charged with the execution ...'

Now in this case a notice that a relevant meeting had been called was sent to the office of the sheriff's officer, Mr Holroyd, at Dewsbury, and was not sent to the under-sheriff's office at York. The learned vice-chancellor decided that the word 'sheriff' in rule 43 includes officers of the sheriff who are his agents for the purpose of carrying out the duties which he deputes to them and that those include, in a case of this kind, the receipt of such a notice as this. The question is whether the vice-chancellor was right in that conclusion.

I observe at once that, whereas the under-sheriff or under-sheriffs are generally *a* in the position under which they are required to act as (so to speak) pro sheriffs, in the case of a sheriff's officer he acts, and acts only, on the basis of individual warrants to carry out execution, such as the warrant which was issued by the under-sheriff to Mr Holroyd in the present case. The sheriff's officer is, so to speak, a piece-worker.

Now the matter of this kind of notice and on whom it shall be served has been considered in other cases, the first of which, to which our attention was drawn, was *Re b Holland, Ex parte Warren*[1], which was a case in this court. The details of that case are not of importance. One Hillyer was in the process of carrying out the execution of a writ of fieri facias on behalf of the sheriffs of London, he being in the situation of a sheriff's officer. There was also a judgment in the Mayor's Court of London, the appropriate writ had been issued for execution on that judgment, and in the case of that court if one was to enforce a judgment by execution, the appropriate officer charged *c* with the execution was not the sheriff, but the serjeant-at-mace of the Mayor's Court of London. As was the convenient practice, when the serjeant-at-mace proceeded to seek to enforce that judgment, and found Hillyer as the sheriff's officer in possession, he entrusted him with the execution of the Mayor's Court warrant for that particular judgment. What happened was that the relevant notice (in fact in that case) of a bankruptcy petition—there being parallel provisions in the bankruptcy *d* code to those found now in s 346 of the 1948 Act—was given to Hillyer, the sheriff's officer. It is perfectly true to say that in that case it was held that notice to Hillyer could not be relevant to the situation as to the moneys levied by Hillyer and paid over to the serjeant-at-mace, because the notice that Hillyer received was in fact after he had paid over the moneys to the serjeant-at-mace at a time when he could not in any event have been any longer acting in any manner as agent for the serjeant- *e* at-mace. I do not pause to quote in detail, but it is quite plain from the judgment of Brett MR and also from the judgment of Baggallay LJ (Bowen LJ expressing himself briefly to be of the same opinion) that they were of the opinion that in any event service of such a notice on somebody who was only in the position of sheriff's officer would not be a due service of the notice on the sheriff or the equivalent in the Lord Mayor's Court, namely, the serjeant-at-mace. It was not an actual decision to that *f* effect, but it was very strongly expressed in that regard, particularly by Brett MR.

Some years later a similar question came before the Divisional Court in *Bellyse v M'Ginn*[2]. I will not rehearse the detail. In that case one Ambler was quite plainly in the same position as was Mr Holroyd in the present case, namely, he was a sheriff's officer. Mathew J, relying on what had been said in *Warren*[1], plainly came to the conclusion that the employment of Ambler as sheriff's officer was not such as would make him charged with the duty of receiving a notice such as we are now concerned *g* with. Vaughan Williams J said[3] in terms of Ambler: '... nor do I think that his employment was such as to render him the agent of the sheriff for the purpose of receiving [the] notice.'

Now, those views expressed and reported have not, so far as I am aware, been challenged. It has not been suggested that they do not represent the law insofar as *h* they say that a sheriff's officer (as distinct, of course, from an under-sheriff) is a person on whom the notice which we now have under discussion may be served.

In 1969 *Engineering Industry Training Board v Samuel Talbot Ltd*[4] was decided in this court, to which I was a party. So far as the report goes, it would appear that the only notice was one given to the sheriff's officer. The whole debate was whether the notice in its form was a sufficient indication of the proposed relevant meeting, and it was not suggested that there was any defect in the notice by reason of it having been *j*

---

1 (1885) 15 QBD 48
2 [1891] 2 QB 227
3 [1891] 2 QB at 230
4 [1969] 1 All ER 480, [1969] 2 QB 270

a given to the sheriff's officer and not to the sheriff, or, rather, to the under-sheriff. It is my plain recollection that the point was never for consideration by the court. If—and I say 'if' because one does not know—there was no notice in that case other than the notice given to the sheriff's officer, then it would appear, if the decision of the vice-chancellor in this case below is erroneous, that a point there was missed. But I do not think that really we can get any guidance from that case. First, we do *b* not know for certain that there had not also been a notice given to the under-sheriff's office, and we do know for certain that the point was never canvassed at all. It cannot therefore be regarded as in any way an indication of authority in favour of the decision by the vice-chancellor in this case below. Indeed, he himself readily accepted that it was not, and considered the point was open to him.

Now I would be very loth to take a view of this which runs counter to the view which, as far as I can judge, has been taken for many years in the textbooks, following *c* the expressions of judicial opinion to which I have referred. I would be very loth to reverse it, and would only do so if I thought it was necessary, because I apprehend it may well be that rights have been determined one way or another on the basis of what was understood to be the law. But, in my view, the vice-chancellor came to his conclusion simply by (if I may say so) so saying. Here, says the vice-chancellor, is a man who is the agent of the sheriff for the purposes that are indicated, and he then *d* immediately says that he would construe the word 'sheriff' as—

> 'including the officers of the sheriff who are his agents for the purpose of carrying out the duties which he deputes to them, including in my judgment the receipt of a notice in a case of this kind . . .'

e There is no ground in the evidence at all for saying that the sheriff, or the under-sheriff on his behalf, had deputed to the sheriff's officer the duty of receiving a notice of this kind. There is no ground in the evidence for that at all. I do not see why, having regard to the language of the section and the rule, it should be thought that it was implicit in the duties which are imposed on the sheriff's officer by reason of the warrant issued to him, which I have described as 'piece-work', to inform the *f* sheriffs or the under-sheriffs of the receipt by him of a notice, so that the receipt by him of the notice is to be regarded as notice to the sheriffs or the under-sheriffs, which it is not.

We had our attention drawn by counsel for the liquidators in particular to a passage in Halsbury's Laws of England[1], which is headed 'Knowledge imputed to sheriff':

> 'The knowledge of a sheriff's officer of any fact or circumstance connected *g* with his employment which it is his duty to communicate to the sheriff or under-sheriff operates as notice thereof to the sheriff.'

As I remarked to counsel when he drew our attention to that as being a passage in his favour, if it had simply said that the knowledge of a sheriff's officer of any fact or circumstance connected with his employment operates as notice thereof to the *h* sheriff, it would be very good ammunition for his argument. But to cite it in support of the vice-chancellor's decision seems to me, with respect, to beg the question whether it is the duty of the sheriff's officer to communicate to the sheriff or under-sheriff the receipt by him of a notice such as this. I do not think it is. Mr Holroyd did not think it was, and I think he was right, because Mr Holroyd, on receiving this notice at the sheriff's office, for his part assumed that it was simply a copy of a notice *j* which had already been sent to the under-sheriff's office by those connected with the company, sent also to him for information. That indeed would be a very sensible thing to do and I am sure is quite common in practice, that you not only give notice to the under-sheriff but you also give a copy of the notice to, or inform, the sheriff's officer who is directly responsible for the execution at the same time.

---

1   3rd Edn, vol 34, p 699, para 1242

Accordingly, in my view, this notice was not properly given, and the sheriff was entitled and indeed obliged, not having received a proper notice within the 14 day period, to pay over the money to the judgment creditor.

Now a preliminary point in this appeal was taken against it, namely, that it is an appeal by the sheriff as to costs only, and therefore does not lie at all to this court without the leave of the judge below, because of the language of s 31(1)(h) of the Supreme Court of Judicature (Consolidation) Act 1925, and that leave was neither given nor sought. It was argued on the part of the sheriff that the leave was in effect given, because, at the request of counsel for the sheriff below, some stay was ordered pending the appeal, and the only order that had been made against the sheriff, since the money had been ordered to be paid to the liquidators by the judgment creditor and not by the sheriff, was that the sheriff be jointly and severally liable for the liquidators' costs. So it is said: here is an application by the sheriff's counsel for a stay pending an appeal, and a stay granted, and that must be the equivalent of giving the sheriff leave to appeal on the question of costs only.

I do not myself think that that argument is correct. I think it is more likely either that everyone assumed that the judgment creditor would also appeal, or that they overlooked the question of leave being either necessary or desirable if the sheriff alone were to appeal on costs. I am bound to say that if leave had been sought on the basis that the fundamental decision on which the order as to costs depended was to be challenged on appeal by the sheriff, I have no doubt that the vice-chancellor would have given leave.

It was canvassed whether the question could be dealt with, or the issue could be dodged, if that is another way of putting it, by an adjournment to enable the vice-chancellor to be approached and asked for leave. It was alternatively canvassed whether any defect could be cured by joining the judgment creditor out of time in the present appeal, a step which apparently, if suitably indemnified, he was prepared to take. But, in the end, we formed the view, which we announced at the outset, that neither of these courses was necessary.

It is not essential to an ability to appeal against an order as to costs only that there should be leave when those costs are in the discretion of the judge. I refer in this connection to the notes in the Supreme Court Practice 1973[1]. In the present case, if it should be held, as I would hold, that the learned judge was wrong on the central point of law in the case, it is in my view quite clear that there was no relevant material on which he could properly have exercised his discretion as to costs by ordering the sheriff to pay the unsuccessful liquidators' costs of the originating motion; and in those circumstances, in my view, leave to appeal was not required. The particular order for costs would have been made without (in law) any material on which it could be justified as an exercise of the judicial discretion over costs. For those reasons, we decided that this was a case in which the appeal lies without the leave of the judge below.

Accordingly, I for my part would admit the appeal and allow it, set aside that part of the judgment as orders the sheriff to pay any part of the liquidators' costs, and I apprehend in lieu order the liquidators to pay the sheriff's costs of the motion and of this appeal, subject to discussion.

BUCKLEY LJ. I entirely agree with the judgment Russell LJ has delivered both on the substantive matter in the appeal and on the point about the jurisdiction of this court to hear this appeal without the leave of the learned vice-chancellor; and, although we are differing from the vice-chancellor, I do not wish to add anything of my own.

---

1   Volume 1, p 884, paras 62/2/25, 62/2/26

LAWTON LJ. I too agree on both points.

Appeal allowed. Order of Blackett-Ord V-C discharged so far as it ordered the sheriff to be jointly and severally liable for the liquidators' costs; order that the liquidators pay the sheriff's costs in the court below and of the appeal.

Solicitors: *Grobel, Willey, Hargrave & Co*, agents for *Willey Hargrave & Co*, Leeds (for the sheriff); *Saffman & Co*, Leeds (for the liquidators).

A S Virdi Esq Barrister.

R v Bristol Coroner, ex parte Kerr

QUEEN'S BENCH DIVISION
LORD WIDGERY CJ, WALLER AND PHILLIPS JJ
8th, 9th APRIL 1974

Coroner – Inquest – Custody of body – Adjournment of inquest sine die – Criminal proceedings pending – Coroner's right to detain body until completion of inquest – Power to order release of body before completion of inquest – Coroners (Amendment) Act 1926, s 14(2).

The deceased, a 20 year old Rhodesian, died a violent death from multiple stab wounds. Two days later a man was charged with his murder and remanded in custody. On the same day the coroner started an inquest on the body and heard the evidence of a pathologist as to the physical cause of death. In view of the prospective criminal proceedings the coroner then adjourned the inquest sine die under s 20(1)[a] of the Coroners (Amendment) Act 1926. Subsequently the deceased's parents, wishing to take his body back to Rhodesia for burial, applied to the coroner to release it. The coroner refused, taking the view that he should not do so until he was satisfied that further examination of the body would not be required in connection with the murder case. At that time the prosecution had indicated that they were willing for the body to be released so long as the defence agreed. The solicitors for the accused had stated that they could not immediately say that a further examination would not be required but hoped to reach a conclusion as soon as possible. The deceased's father applied for an order of certiorari to quash the coroner's refusal on the ground that he had no right to the custody of the body once the post mortem examination had been completed; alternatively that, if the coroner had a discretion under s 14(2)[b] of the 1926 Act to retain the body, he had wrongly exercised it because the refusal was related not to the coroner requiring the body any longer but to the requirement of the defence advisers in the criminal proceedings, and the latter was a requirement to which the coroner could not in law have regard.

Held – It was the right and duty of a coroner to take possession of the body of anyone who had been killed violently and to retain possession until the completion of the inquest. Accordingly the coroner's authority over the physical control of the body arose as soon as he decided to hold an inquest and lasted until the inquest itself had been determined. It followed that the coroner had the right to retain the deceased's body at the relevant time. Furthermore, the desire of the defence advisers in the murder trial to have access to the body was highly relevant to the exercise of the coroner's discretion under s 14(2) of the 1926 Act, and it was therefore impossible to

---

a   Section 20(1) is set out at p 721 *b*, post
b   Section 14(2) is set out at p 721 *d*, post

say that the coroner had exercised his discretion wrongly at the time of his refusal or
that he had acted in excess of his jurisdiction.   Accordingly the application would be
refused (see p 722 *j* to p 723 *a* and *e* to *j*, post).

Notes
For adjournment of inquest when charge of murder is made, see 8 Halsbury's Laws
(3rd Edn) 511, 512, paras 964, 965, and for cases on the subject, see 13 Digest (Repl)
158, 159, *190-196*.
    For the Coroners (Amendment) Act 1926, ss 14, 20, see 7 Halsbury's Statutes (3rd
Edn) 271, 273.

Case cited
R v Ferrand (1819) 3 B & Ald 260.

Motions for certiorari, prohibition and mandamus
This was an application by way of motion by Wellesley Kerr, of Salisbury, Rhodesia,
as administrator of the estate of Simon Wellesley Kerr, deceased, who died on 16th
March 1974 at Bishopston, Bristol, for an order of certiorari to bring up and quash
an order or instruction issued by HM Coroner for the city and county of Bristol on
or about 28th March 1974 to his servants or agents and/or to employees of the corporation of Bristol at the Bristol city mortuary whereby those employees were ordered
to detain the body of the deceased and not to permit the body to be removed from
the Bristol city mortuary or on behalf of the applicant.   The applicant also applied
for an order prohibiting the coroner from ordering the removal of the body from the
Bristol city mortuary or other place, and an order of mandamus directing the coroner
to deliver up the body to the applicant.   The grounds of the application were (1) that
the coroner had acted without jurisdiction in issuing the order or instruction in that
(a) the coroner had no legal power to detain the body or prevent the applicant from
taking possession of it; alternatively, (b) if the coroner had such power, he had no
reasonable ground for exercising it in the circumstances of the case; and (2) that the
coroner had wrongly refused to deliver the body, or to order that it be delivered up
into the possession of the applicant's servants or agents who were lawfully entitled
to possession of the body, when required to do so.   The facts are set out in
the judgment of Lord Widgery CJ.

David Fletcher for the applicant.
L Herrick Collins for the coroner.

LORD WIDGERY CJ.   In these proceedings counsel moves on behalf of one
Wellesley Kerr for an order of certiorari to remove into this court with a view to its
being quashed an order or instruction issued by Her Majesty's Coroner for the city
and county of Bristol on 28th March 1974 to his servants or agents and/or to employees
of the corporation of Bristol at the Bristol city mortuary whereby the said employees
were ordered to detain the body of Simon Wellesley Kerr deceased and not to permit
the said body to be removed from the Bristol city mortuary or on behalf of the
applicant.
    There is a further application for an order of prohibition prohibiting any similar
orders being made by the coroner in future if the initial order is duly quashed under
the application for certiorari.
    This is a very sad case, as so many cases arising under this branch of the law tend to
be.   Simon Kerr came to this country from Rhodesia to join the Gloucestershire
Cricket Club, and after unhappily a very short time in this country he died a violent
death on the night of 16th March 1974, that is to say about three or four weeks ago;
the cause of death was multiple stab wounds.   The police made an arrest quite
promptly, and on 18th March, two days after the death, a man was charged before

a the Bristol magistrates with the murder of Simon Kerr and he was remanded in custody on that date.

On the same date, 18th March, Her Majesty's Coroner for Bristol started an inquest on the body of Simon Kerr; he heard the evidence of a pathologist as to the physical cause of death, and he then adjourned the inquest sine die. In doing that the coroner acted on the best authority, because it is provided by s 20(1) of the Coroners *b* (Amendment) Act 1926:

'If on an inquest touching a death the coroner is informed before the jury have given their verdict that some person has been charged before examining justices with the murder, manslaughter or infanticide of the deceased, he shall, in the absence of reason to the contrary, adjourn the inquest until after the conclusion of the criminal proceedings and may if he thinks fit discharge the jury.'

c And that is exactly what the coroner did in the circumstances, as was entirely proper. At one time an adjournment of the inquest may have necessarily postponed the date on which the body could be disposed of, but that is no longer so today, because under s 14(2) of the same Act it is provided:

d 'Subject to the provisions of any rules made under this Act an order of a coroner authorising the burial of a body upon which he has decided to hold an inquest may be issued at any time after he has viewed the body.'

So there is a clear discretionary power for the coroner to give authority for the burial of the body at any time after he had viewed it, and it was therefore within the coroner's undoubted discretion to make such burial order from the date on which the inquest *e* was begun and adjourned.

What happened thereafter was that the applicant and his wife, the parents of Simon Kerr, wishing to take his body back to Rhodesia for burial, made application to the coroner for the release of the body, or his authority for the body to be taken to Rhodesia, and they were met with a refusal.

f The form of the documents dealing with the request for delivery up of the body was this. We have before us first of all a notice dated 22nd March 1974 whereby the applicant, in pursuance of s 4 of the Births and Deaths Registration Act 1926 gave notice to the coroner that he intended to remove the body out of England and Wales. The reason why that notice was given was because, as I have already said, the intention was to remove the body to Rhodesia, and a notice of that kind to the coroner is an essential prerequisite for such removal, whatever the circumstances in which the *g* death occurred.

The coroner by a formal notice dated 25th March acknowledged receipt of that notice, but said:

'My inquest stands adjourned sine die, and until the inquest is concluded I cannot give any order consenting to the removal of the body out of England *h* which now lies within my jurisdiction.'

Disappointed, as the parents obviously were, at that reaction from the coroner, the applicant made a formal request at the mortuary for the delivery up of the body on 28th March, and he was formally refused custody of the body by a police officer acting as the coroner's officer at that place.

j It is quite clear from the evidence subsequently put before this court that the coroner's attitude was simply this. He took the view that he should not release the body from his direct custody and control until he was satisfied that further examination of the body would not be required in connection with the murder case. The prosecution had already indicated that so far as they were concerned they did not require any further examination, and were willing that the body be released, as long as the defence agreed. The attitude of the solicitors for the defence in the

murder case was that they could not immediately say that they would not require   a
further examination of the body, saying they would reach a conclusion as early as
possible.   The coroner's affidavit, carrying as it does considerable overtones of
sympathy with the applicant, was to the effect that he was prepared to consider
releasing the body as soon as he got a clearance from the solicitors acting for the
defence; that was going to take days at any rate, and in his view he should not
release the body until he was satisfied on that score.   So the applicant comes to this   b
court asking for an order of certiorari to set aside the coroner's refusal to release the
body.

Counsel for the applicant puts his argument on two main planks.   He challenges
first of all the right of the coroner to custody of the body at all once the post mortem
has been completed; alternatively he says that if the coroner had a discretion to
retain the body, it was a discretion which was wrongly exercised because a refusal   c
was not related to the coroner requiring the body any longer, but related to a requirement of that kind from the defence advisers in the murder case, a requirement
which counsel says the coroner could not in law have regard to.   The point is thus
a short one and not as fully illustrated by authority as one might at first sight expect.

Counsel for the applicant approaches the matter in this way.   He says that if
you look through the modern statutes dealing with coroners, there is a remarkable   d
omission in that at no point is there a section which says the coroner may retain
control over the body until a given date.   On the other hand, says counsel for the
applicant, in s 24(1) of the Coroners (Amendment) Act 1926 one finds express provision
to this effect:

> 'Where by the direction or at the request of a coroner a post-mortem examina-
> tion of a body is to be made, the coroner may, subject as hereinafter provided,   e
> order the removal of the body to any place which may be provided for the
> purpose either within his jurisdiction or within any adjoining area in which
> another coroner has jurisdiction ...'

It is remarkable, says counsel, that Parliament thought it necessary to give the
coroner direct authority to move the body to a convenient place for a post mortem
if the coroner had a general and overriding authority to move the body anywhere   f
else.   Counsel for the applicant recognised, I think, there would be difficulty in
burying the body in this country even if he obtained custody of it because by s 1 of
the Births and Deaths Registration Act 1926 the coroner's authority, or a certificate
of a registrar, is necessary for the disposal of the body whoever has its physical custody.

However, the applicant is obviously of opinion if he can obtain possession of the
body, his intention being to go to Rhodesia with the body, the absence of a coroner's   g
certificate will not stand in his way.   I express no view on that; that is not a point
we have to decide.

The point is whether the coroner has general overriding custody and control of the
body prior to the termination of the inquest.   Counsel's submission on behalf of
the coroner is that at common law the coroner possessed that right and retains   h
it today.   In the submission of the coroner the law in regard to coroners is still largely
governed by the common law, the modern statutes merely having made adjustments and amendments to the common law.   Counsel submits that it has always
been the right and duty of the coroner to take possession of the body of anyone who
has been killed violently, and at common law to retain possession until the completion of the inquest.   It is now recognised that s 14(2) of the Coroners (Amendment)
Act 1926 made earlier release possible as a matter of discretion.

According to counsel for the coroner the right to retain the body arises at common
law as soon as the report reaches the coroner that a person has been killed or has
died violently, and remains until the conclusion of the inquest.

I am left in no doubt at the end of the argument that counsel for the coroner is
right.   The reason why there is so little authority on the point no doubt is because

the coroner's office is a very ancient one, and many of the principles on which his rights are based are principles of common law which have never been challenged in recent years. But we have been referred to one or two indications that counsel for the coroner is right, and more particularly in The King's Coroner[1] by Mr R Henslowe Wellington. This fascinating book takes one in detail through all the duties of a coroner, and what he should do and what he should say and what documents he should prepare from time to time. One gets to 'The Burial Order' where the learned author says this[2]:

> 'When all this is done the Coroner should fill in and sign the burial order, and hand it to the relative, friend, or legal representative of the deceased having charge of or being responsible for the burial, instead of delivering it to the person who buries or performs any funeral or religious service for the burial of the body of the deceased, as was enacted by the Registration of Births and Deaths Act, 1874 . . . If the inquest has been upon one who is unidentified, the Coroner will give the order to his officer, who must deliver it to the overseers of the parish, or relieving officer when acting on their behalf, in which the body is lying, and whose duty it is to attend to the interment, the Coroner having no power to spend money in regard to any burial. The burial order may be given at the termination of the first sitting in the event of an adjournment, or after view of the body, and before registry of the death . . . Having once given the order for burial, the jurisdiction of the Coroner over the body itself now ceases, as, in the same manner, when once he issues his warrant to summon a jury his jurisdiction commences, and any interference with the body which would hinder or prevent the Coroner from holding an inquest upon it when an inquest ought to be held is an indictable offence at common law . . .'

That clearly supports the view that the coroner's authority over the physical control of the body arises as soon as he decides to hold an inquest, and lasts at common law until the inquest itself is determined. I am in no doubt that counsel for the coroner is right in his principal submission, namely that the coroner had the right to retain control of the body at the relevant times in this case.

The alternative argument put forward by counsel for the applicant is that even if that right existed, there was a discretion under s 14(2) of the 1926 Act to release the body, and the discretion was wrongly exercised because it was exercised in consequence of an irrelevant fact, that is to say the desire of the defence solicitors in the murder case to have access to it. All I find it necessary to say is that far from an irrelevant fact, it is a highly relevant fact, and although one hopes in all these cases the utmost expedition takes place in the release of the body, nevertheless it is impossible to say that the coroner's refusal at the time when it was given was an excess of jurisdiction or disclosed any error of law, and I would refuse the application.

WALLER J. I agree.

PHILLIPS J. I agree also.

Certiorari refused.

Solicitors: *Vizards*, agents for *Dolmans*, Bristol (for the applicant); *Lawrence & Co*, Bristol (for the coroner).

N P Metcalfe Esq Barrister.

---

1 (1906), vol 2, p 83
2 Volume 2, pp 82, 83

R v National Insurance Commissioner,
ex parte Viscusi

COURT OF APPEAL, CIVIL DIVISION
LORD DENNING MR, BUCKLEY AND ROSKILL LJJ
15th, 18th, 19th FEBRUARY 1974

Industrial injury – Medical appeal tribunal – Jurisdiction – Claim for disablement benefit – Scope of jurisdiction – Previous finding by statutory authority (another medical appeal tribunal) on claim for benefit that injured workman suffered serious disablement as result of accident – Decision of statutory authority on claim 'final' – Statutory authority making provisional assessment for specified period – Medical appeal tribunal discharging assessment made in respect of subsequent period – Whether medical appeal tribunal bound to accept finding of earlier tribunal – National Insurance (Industrial Injuries) Act 1965, s 50(1).

Industrial injury – Disablement benefit – Claim – Nature of proceedings – Medical appeal tribunal – Onus of proof – Discharge of assessment – Assessment made by medical board – Appeal tribunal suspicious that claimant malingering – Report of consultant before tribunal – Report suggesting claimant malingering – Whether tribunal bound to make positive finding of malingering before discharging assessment.

Natural justice – Medical appeal tribunal – Duty to make due enquiry – Extent of duty.

Industrial injury – Determination of claims – Powers of Minister or insurance tribunal – Power to refer to medical practitioner for examination and report – Medical appeal tribunal requesting opinion of consultant – Medical officer from Ministry transmitting papers etc to consultant – Whether essential reference made by tribunal – National Insurance (Industrial Injuries) (Determination of Claims and Questions) (No 2) Regulations 1967 (SI 1967 No 1571), reg 19(2).

Industrial injury – Medical appeal tribunal – Record and notice of decision – Contents – Statement of reasons and findings on all questions of fact – Detail required – National Insurance (Industrial Injuries) (Determination of Claims and Questions) (No 2) Regulations 1967 (SI 1967 No 1571), reg 12(1).

In July 1965 the applicant trod on a nail at work and twisted his right knee. He was paid injury benefit, and then claimed disablement benefit pursuant to the National Insurance (Industrial Injuries) Acts 1946 to 1964. In January 1966 he came before a medical board, which found that his walking was impaired and made a provisional assessment of 50 per cent disablement in respect of the knee for a period of six months. That provisional assessment was subsequently affirmed by a medical appeal tribunal, which extended the period of its duration to September 1966. In September 1966 a second medical board found that the applicant's right leg was swollen but did not continue the award for it considered that the swelling had been artificially induced and that the applicant was malingering. In January 1967 the applicant appealed to a medical appeal tribunal ('the second tribunal'), which allowed the appeal holding that the right leg condition was a serious disablement and had arisen from the accident. They made a further provisional assessment of 50 per cent and extended its duration to 25th June. In June the applicant came before a reassessment medical board, which made a final life assessment of 50 per cent in respect of the right knee. The Ministry referred that decision to another medical appeal tribunal ('the third tribunal'). The third tribunal stated that before adjudicating they wished to have an opinion from a consultant, whom they named, as to the cause of the swelling and its relevance to the industrial accident in July 1965. Pursuant to that request the medical officer of the Ministry sent the consultant a history of the applicant's case and the findings of fact of the three medical boards. He did not give the consultant the decisions or remarks of the three medical boards or any part of the records of the three medical appeal tribunals. The consultant examined the applicant and reported that he could not explain the swelling of the right leg; he said that in the circumstances 'there must be a strong suspicion of lymphoedema artefacta', i e that the swelling had been artificially induced by the applicant. He suggested that a lymphangiography might confirm his view. No lymphangiography was taken. A copy of the consultant's report was sent to the applicant's representatives, together with the papers that had been submitted to the consultant. They did not make any adverse comment on the way in which the matter had been submitted to the consultant or ask for a further examination by lymphangiography. They and the applicant attended the hearing. The tribunal decided that the applicant was no longer entitled to benefit. They said 'After examination, we accept the report of [the consultant] and agree with his findings and opinions. Whatever may have been the [applicant's] condition up to 25-6-67, the condition of his right lower limb thereafter is not attributable to the relevant accident. The assessment must be discharged.' The applicant appealed unsuccessfully against that decision to the Commissioner of Insurance. He then applied for an order of certiorari to bring up and quash the decision of the commissioner, contending (i) that the third tribunal could not reverse the decision of the second tribunal because they were bound, by s 50(1)[a] of the National Insurance (Industrial Injuries) Act 1965, to treat the decision of the second tribunal as 'final'; (ii) that the desire expressed by the third tribunal to have the opinion of the consultant was a reference to a medical practitioner for examination and report under reg 19(2)[b] of the National Insurance (Industrial Injuries) (Determination of Claims and Questions) (No 2) Regulations 1967 and accordingly ought to have been referred by the tribunal itself and not by a medical officer of the Ministry; (iii) that the tribunal's decision was contrary to the rules of natural justice in that (a) they made their decision without 'due enquiry', for they had not followed up the consultant's suggestion for a further investigation by way of lymphangiography, and (b) they could not find against the applicant merely on a suspicion that his disablement was caused by an artefact; there had to be a positive finding of fraud or malingering; (iv) that it was a breach of the rules of natural justice for the Ministry to send only the clinical findings to the consultant in relation to the applicant and to omit the decisions of the three medical appeal tribunals; and (v) that the tribunal had failed to comply with the requirements of reg 12(1)[c] of the 1967 regulations by not stating all their findings of fact which had led them to depart from the views of the earlier tribunals.

Held – The application for certiorari would be refused for the following reasons—
    (i) The decision of the second tribunal was 'final' only in respect of the specified period for which its provisional assessment was made; it was not binding in respect of subsequent periods. Accordingly the third tribunal were entitled, in relation to the period with which they were concerned, to reconsider the matter de novo and to discharge the assessment (see p 729 h, p 730 b, p 732 a and p 734 f, post); *R v Industrial Injuries Commissioner, ex parte Howarth* (1968) 4 KIR 621 applied; *Jones v Secretary of State for Social Services* [1972] 1 All ER 145 distinguished.

---

a   Section 50(1) is set out at p 729 g, post
b   Regulation 19(2), so far as material, provides: '... the Minister or an insurance tribunal, as the case may be, may refer to a medical practitioner for examination and report any question arising for his or their determination.'
c   Regulation 12(1), so far as material, provides: 'A medical appeal tribunal shall in each case record their decision in writing in such form as may from time to time be approved by the Minister, and shall include in such record ... a statement of the reasons for their decision, including their findings on all questions of fact material to the decision.'

(ii) The request to the consultant was not a reference under reg 19(2), since that regulation did not prevent a tribunal from asking a Minister to obtain a report. A tribunal was entitled to obtain a report by that means and to use it, provided that the tribunal gave the person whom it concerned an opportunity of seeing the report and dealing with it. In any event, even if the request etc was a reference under reg 19(2) the applicant had not been prejudiced in any way (see p 731 *f* to *h*, p 733 *b* and *f*, p 735 *f* and p 736 *g*, post).

(iii) The third tribunal had not been guilty of any 'want of due enquiry'; its duty was to act fairly and to make all reasonable enquiries in order to enable them to reach a conclusion. They were not bound to explore every possibility. They were the masters of their own procedure and on the evidence there were no grounds for saying that they had acted unfairly by acting on the consultant's report and not requiring a confirmatory examination (see p 731 *b* to *d*, p 732 *d* to *g* and p 735 *h* to p 736 *a*, post).

(iv) Proceedings on an application for insurance benefits were not adversary proceedings but were investigatory; and in such proceedings it was not necessary for the tribunal positively to find fraud or malingering; if there were any circumstances which appeared to throw suspicion on a claim it was the tribunal's duty to investigate them. If the tribunal then concluded that there was a grave doubt whether the loss of faculty was the result of the injury, they could discharge the assessment (see p 729 *d*, p 730 *e* to *h*, p 732 *c* and *d* and p 736 *f*, post).

(v) The consultant was being asked to give an independent diagnosis and there was nothing unfair in not sending him the decisions of the three medical appeal tribunals, especially (per Lord Denning MR) as the applicant's representatives had made no complaint to the third tribunal about it (see p 731 *d* and *e*, p 733 *d* and *e* and p 735 *e* and *g*, post).

(vi) The third tribunal had complied with the requirements of reg 12(1); it was sufficient for the purposes of that regulation for them to state that they accepted the consultant's report and agreed with his finding and opinion (see p 730 *h* to p 731 *a*, p 733 *f* and *g* and p 736 *d* and *e*, post).

Notes

For disablement benefit, see 27 Halsbury's Laws (3rd Edn) 824, 825, paras 1451, 1452, and for the determination of industrial injury claims and questions, see ibid 853-866, paras 1495-1513.

For the National Insurance (Industrial Injuries) Act 1965, s 50, see 23 Halsbury's Staututes (3rd Edn) 534.

For the National Insurance (Industrial Injuries) (Determination of Claims and Questions) (No 2) Regulations 1967, regs 12, 19, see 15 Halsbury's Statutory Instruments (3rd Reissue) 394, 398.

Cases referred to in judgments

Hudson v Secretary of State for Social Services. See *Jones v Secretary of State for Social Services, Hudson v Secretary of State for Social Services*, infra.

Jones v Secretary of State for Social Services, Hudson v Secretary of State for Social Services [1972] 1 All ER 145, [1972] AC 944, [1972] 2 WLR 210, HL; *rvsg* sub nom *R v National Insurance Comr, ex parte Hudson and Jones* [1970] 1 All ER 97, [1970] 1 QB 477, [1970] 2 WLR 182, CA; *affg* sub nom *R v National Insurance Commissioner, ex parte Hudson* [1969] 2 All ER 631, [1969] 2 WLR 639, DC.

Minister of Social Security v Amalgamated Engineering Union [1967] 1 All ER 210, [1967] 1 AC 725, [1967] 2 WLR 516, HL; *affg* sub nom *R v Deputy Industrial Injuries Commissioner, ex parte Amalgamated Engineering Union, Re Dowling* [1966] 1 All ER 705, [1967] 1 QB 202, [1966] 2 WLR 1301, CA, Digest (Cont Vol C) 704, 4585a.

R v Industrial Injuries Comr (Deputy), ex parte Howarth (1968) 4 KIR 621, 112 Sol Jo 542, CA, Digest (Cont Vol C) 704, 4587b.

a   *R v Medical Appeal Tribunal (North Midland Region), ex parte Hubble* [1959] 3 All ER 40,
    [1959] 2 QB 408, [1959] 3 WLR 456, CA; *affg* [1958] 2 All ER 374, [1958] 2 QB 228,
    [1958] 3 WLR 24, DC, 34 Digest (Repl) 665, 4585.

Appeal

b   This was an appeal by Georgio Viscusi ('the applicant') against the order of the
    Divisional Court of the Queen's Bench Division (Lord Widgery CJ, Melford Stevenson
    and Brabin JJ) dated 14th November 1972, dismissing his application for an order
    of certiorari to bring up and quash the decision, dated 12th February 1969, of J S
    Watson Esq QC, a national insurance commissioner, affirming the decision of a
    medical appeal tribunal at London, dated 30th November 1967, to discharge the
    assessment made by a medical board at Guildford on 6th June 1967 in respect of the
c   applicant's claim for disablement benefit, pursuant to the National Insurance
    (Industrial Injuries) Acts 1946 to 1964, for the loss of faculty resulting from an accident
    on 28th July 1965. The facts are set out in the judgment of Lord Denning MR.

    David Turner-Samuels QC and *Alexander Irvine* for the applicant.
    Gordon Slynn for the commissioner and the Secretary of State for Health and Social
d   Security.

LORD DENNING MR.   This case raises several questions of interest to those who
administer industrial insurance.

    The applicant, Mr Viscusi, came to this country from Italy. He cannot read or
write. He cannot speak English. He worked in the woodlands near Haslemere,
e   Surrey. In July 1965, when he was 55, he trod on a nail and twisted his knee. In
October 1965 it was operated on at the Haslemere Hospital. He was paid injury
benefit and afterwards disablement benefit. The question is: for how long is he
entitled to benefit? The insurance history has three chapters.

f   *The first chapter*
    On 27th January 1966 Mr Viscusi had the *first* medical board. It was found that
his walking was impaired. The board made a provisional assessment of 50 per cent
to continue for six months. The Ministry thought this was an over-assessment.
They referred it to the *first* medical appeal tribunal. On 3rd March 1966 that tribunal
affirmed the 50 per cent as reasonable. It extended the period to 25th September
1966. Meanwhile on 14th July 1966 he was examined by a consultant at the Haslemere
g   Hospital, who reported that he was fit for work and added:

> 'His imagined disability is the result of injury that was cured by operation
> 20/10/65 when it was found there was no ligament damage. This seems to be
> a psychological problem.'

h   *The second chapter*
    On 12th September 1966 there was the *second* medical board. They found that his
right leg was swollen. They found that he was handicapped 'not at all', and added
this remark:

> 'The Board is of the opinion, having studied the hospital report and examined
j   the case carefully, that the swelling of the right leg and the physically abnormal
> findings are an artefact and that [Mr Viscusi] is malingering.'

(I may say that the word 'artefact' means that it was caused by himself.) So that
board did not continue the award. He appealed to the *second* medical appeal tribunal.
Prior to the hearing he went to the Italian Hospital in Queen Square, London, and
was kept there a week. The surgeon there reported that the 'man has reached a

permanent state in the condition of his right knee which can be classified as traumatic elephantiasis'. With that report, the case went to the *second* medical appeal tribunal. They allowed his appeal. They found:

> 'His right leg is swollen and tense from the upper thigh to foot, as a result, in our opinion, of a deep femoral vein thrombosis ... The right leg condition is a serious disablement and in our opinion has arisen from the accident.'

They made a provisional assessment of 50 per cent and extended it to 25th June 1967.

The third chapter

On 6th June 1967 he had the *third* medical board. The board found that his walking was impaired and made a final assessment of 50 per cent *for life*. The Ministry referred that to the *third* medical appeal tribunal. On 23rd August 1967 the appeal tribunal said that they desired to have a further opinion:

> 'Before adjudicating we desire to have an opinion from Mr Noel Thompson of the Middlesex Hospital as to the cause of the swelling and its relevance to the industrial accident of 28/7/65.'

In pursuance of that request the medical officer of the Ministry prepared a history of the case and appended to it the *findings* of fact of the three medical boards, but not their decisions or remarks. He did not append any part of the records of the three medical appeal tribunals.

On receiving those papers, Mr Noel Thompson himself examined Mr Viscusi. He studied the papers and gave his report on 4th October 1967. It is of particular significance in the case. Mr Thompson described the man's condition on examination and gave the measurement of the leg. It showed swelling of the right leg. Mr Thompson said:

> 'I cannot explain these findings: there must be a strong suspicion of lymphoedema artefacta, for the following reasons ...'

Putting that into English, it means a swelling artificially induced by himself. Mr Thompson then gave his reasons in medical terms, including this, that the swelling was in mid-thigh well above the knee, and at that level it was—

> 'suspect as [being] the level at which a self applied tourniquet bandage might be applied. The latter by applying compression, together with disuse-atrophy might explain the wasting in the upper thigh. I agree with the late Prof Ian Aird that oedema of the sole of the foot in an ambulant patient is strongly indicative of a self-inflicted cause.'

Mr Thompson suggested that a further investigation might confirm his view: 'Lymphangiography would confirm these conclusions.' 'Lymphangiography', as we were told, means the injecting a fluid into the vein and seeing the result rather like an X-ray does. Although Mr Thompson suggested lymphangiography, it was not held.

The Ministry sent a copy of Mr Thompson's report to the representatives of Mr Viscusi together with the papers submitted to Mr Thompson. Mr Viscusi's representatives had every opportunity of considering them. They did not make any adverse comment on the way in which the matter was submitted to Mr Thompson. They did not ask for a further examination by lymphangiography. They attended at the hearing of the third medical appeal tribunal. They argued that Mr Viscusi was a genuine case and that he would not have enough medical knowledge to fake

these symptoms. After hearing these submissions, the third medical appeal tribunal
on 30th November 1967 decided that he should no longer be entitled to benefit.
They said:

> 'After examination, we accept the report of Mr Noel Thompson and agree
> with his findings and opinion. Whatever may have been [Mr Viscusi's] condition
> up to 25-6-67, the condition of his right lower limb thereafter is not attributable
> to the relevant accident. The assessment must be discharged.'

So the *third* medical appeal tribunal discharged the assessment altogether on the
ground that he was malingering. He had tied a bandage himself round his leg and
caused the swelling himself.

From that decision Mr Viscusi appealed to the Commissioner of Insurance. That
appeal is only on points of law. On behalf of Mr Viscusi it was said that natural
justice had not been observed; that there should have been further investigation,
and so forth. On 12th February 1969 the commissioner, Mr J S Watson, gave a
reasoned opinion in which he dismissed the appeal. Thereupon an application was
made to the Divisional Court of the Queen's Bench Division for certiorari. It was
refused. Now there is an appeal to this court.

At the outset I would like to say a word about the proceedings on an application
for insurance benefit. The proceedings are not to be regarded as if they were a
law suit between opposing parties. The injured person is not a plaintiff under a
legal burden of proof. They are more in the nature of an enquiry before an investigating body charged with the task of finding out what happened and what are the
consequences. The man tells about the accident and his injury. He describes his
disablement. The Ministry are not there to oppose him. They are simply there to
help the tribunal to come to a correct decision. It is very proper for the Ministry
to make investigations, to get medical reports and to put them before the tribunal.
They do it not as trying to defeat the man's claim, but simply to see whether his
case is a true one or not.

I turn now to the several points which have been raised. The first point was as
to 'finality'. It was argued for Mr Viscusi that the second medical appeal tribunal
had considered the charge of malingering and rejected it. It was contended that that
decision was 'final' on the point.

Section 50(1) of the National Insurance (Industrial Injuries) Act 1965 says:

> 'Except as provided by this Part of this Act, any decision of a claim or question
> in accordance with this Part of this Act shall be final.'

The question of finality has been considered in *Minister of Social Security v Amalgamated
Engineering Union*[1] in the House of Lords; and more recently in *Jones v Secretary of
State for Social Services*[2]. Those cases concerned the decisions of the statutory authori-
ties. In the present case we are concerned with the decision of the medical authorities.
It appears to me that a 'provisional assessment' is, as the very word says, provisional.
It is not final. It only applies for the period for which assessment is made. It is not
binding on a future tribunal in regard to subsequent periods. In *R v Industrial Injuries
Commissioners, ex parte Howarth*[3], we considered this point. We said:

> 'But they were only final in respect of the periods stated in them. Each of those
> boards made provisional assessments in respect of specified periods. They were
> final for those periods only. They were not final for any subsequent periods.'

I would adhere to what we said then. These provisional assessments are not binding
on the *subsequent* periods.

---

1   [1967] 1 All ER 210, [1967] 1 AC 725
2   [1972] 1 All ER 145, [1972] AC 944
3   (1968) 4 KIR 621 at 625

It would be different if it was sought to reverse the assessments for the selfsame period—to reverse the assessment which had already been made. It would then be a question for review under s 40 of the 1965 Act. A review could be had if there were fresh evidence. That section should be interpreted liberally. That appears from *R v Medical Appeal Tribunal (North Midland Region), ex parte Hubble*[1], which was applied by Sir Robert Micklethwait, Chief Commissioner, in decision no R(1) 17/66. Fresh evidence includes evidence which the claimant could not reasonably have been expected in the circumstances to produce at the last hearing.

The result is this. If it is sought to reverse a previous assessment for a previous period, then it must be done by way of review. But when it is simply a new fresh period to be considered, there is no finality about the previous decision. It is open to the subsequent tribunal to discharge the assessment altogether, even though it means contradicting the finding of a previous tribunal in regard to the previous period.

Now about the onus of proof. This was discussed in this court in *R v National Insurance Commissioner, ex parte Hudson and Jones*[2]; and received the approval of Lord Simon of Glaisdale in *Jones v Secretary of State for Social Services, Hudson v Secretary of State for Social Services*[3]. Once a man has lost a faculty—say the loss of a finger—he is presumed to suffer all the disabilities which a normal man would suffer from that loss of faculty. See Sch 4 to the 1965 Act. But if he alleges that he is disabled to a greater extent than a normal man would be, the burden is on him to show it. But that does not touch the question we have here. This case appears to me to rest in this way. The man makes a prima facie case by showing circumstances which point to the loss of faculty—in this case the swollen leg—being the result of the injury. If it appears to the tribunal that there are circumstances which throw suspicion on his claim—so that the tribunal are not satisfied that the claim is genuine—then they should investigate it. The tribunal must balance the pros and cons. They must regard the probabilities. If in the end the tribunal are left in grave doubt whether the loss of faculty was the result of the injury—such that the balance is against the man—then they can discharge the assessment. It is not necessary for them positively to find fraud. It is not necessary for them positively to find malingering. If the suspicion is such as to throw serious doubt on the man's claim as he puts it forward— so that on balance it is against him—they can say at the end of the case: 'We do not think that his claim is well founded'.

Applying it to this case, it seems to me that the third medical appeal tribunal here were entitled to say, looking at Mr Noel Thompson's report and with their own investigations, there was such grave doubt about his claim that they could not accept it. As they said:

'Whatever may have been [Mr Viscusi's] condition up to 25th June 1967, the condition of the right lower limb thereafter is not attributable to the relevant accident.'

That seems to me sufficient without their positively finding fraud or malingering.

The next question is as to the findings of the tribunal. Regulation 12(1) of the National Insurance (Industrial Injuries) (Determination of Claims and Questions) (No 2) Regulations 1967[4] says that the tribunal's decision must include a statement of the reasons for their decision, including their findings on all questions of fact material to the decision. It was said that they had not stated their findings sufficiently in the paragraph I have read. In particular, that they had not said whether they had found fraud—malingering—or not. This is covered by what I have just said about

---

1 [1958] 2 All ER 374, [1958] 2 QB 228
2 [1970] 1 All ER 97, [1970] 1 QB 477
3 [1972] 1 All ER at 198, [1972] AC at 1025
4 SI 1967 No 1571

a the burden of proof. It was not necessary for them to find positively that there was malingering. It was sufficient for them to say they accepted the report of Mr Noel Thompson and agreed with his finding and opinion.

Next, it was said by counsel for Mr Viscusi that the tribunal did not conform to the rules of natural justice. He said that in an enquiry of this kind—and he quoted some cases on coroners—there ought to be 'due enquiry' into the matter. The *b* tribunal, he said, had not made due enquiry because they had not required a lymphangiography. I agree that the tribunal should make due enquiry, but I do not think this means that they must follow up every suggestion and explore every avenue. They must do what is fair but need not go further. The opinion of Mr Thompson threw grave doubt on Mr Viscusi's claim. He thought that there was a strong suspicion of malingering. That was quite good enough for a tribunal to act on. *c* On reading Mr Noel Thompson's report and on their own examination, they could say: 'There is no need for us to go further into the matter and have any further examination'. Especially, I may say, when the representatives of Mr Viscusi did not suggest a lymphangiography or did not even ask for it. It seems to me that the tribunal were quite entitled to decide on the material that was before them, without requiring this confirmatory examination.

d Then it was suggested that the Ministry did not put before Mr Thompson all the relevant material. In particular, they did not put before him the decision of the second medical appeal tribunal which rejected the charge of malingering. They only put before him the clinical findings and history. I see nothing unfair in that. It seems to me that, from a medical point of view, it is the clinical findings and history that Mr Thompson would wish to know. It was not necessary to give him the decision of the three medical appeal tribunals. Again, on this point the representatives *e* of Mr Viscusi did not complain of it. They did not submit to the tribunal that there was anything wrong about it. In those circumstances it cannot be suggested that there was anything unfair.

The last matter is reg 19(2) of the 1967 regulations. It says that the Minister 'may refer to a medical practitioner for examination and report any question arising for his *f* or their determination'. It was said that the request to Mr Thompson ought to be regarded as a reference under reg 19(2), that it ought to have been referred by the medical appeal tribunal themselves and not dealt with by the medical officer of the Ministry. I do not think this complaint is well founded. This was not a reference under reg 19(2). It was a consultant's report obtained to assist the tribunal. The tribunal are entitled to obtain reports and information to assist them. They might, for instance, require information from an employer. There is nothing wrong in this, so long as *g* they give the man or his representatives an opportunity of seeing the report and of dealing with it. We are told that, in the past, in some thousands of cases, the Minister has obtained a consultant's report for the assistance of boards and tribunals. I see nothing wrong in this at all. It is not necessary to go through the requirements of reg 19(2). That is one step available to the tribunal. It does not exclude the other step of asking the Minister to obtain a consultant's report.
h I hope I have gone through all the points in the case now. It seems to me that none of them are well taken. There was no error in point of law in the third medical appeal tribunal or in the commissioner or in the Divisional Court.

I would dismiss the appeal.

j **BUCKLEY LJ.** I agree that this appeal should be dismissed. In view of the very full way in which Lord Denning MR has dealt with the case, I think I can express what I wish to say in I hope a very few sentences.

The first point is the point of finality which arises under s 50(1) of the 1965 Act. On first impression I think the argument presented to us by counsel for the applicant has an attractive quality both as an exercise in construction of the subsection

and as tending to produce certainty in the administration of the scheme of the Act.
But I do not think that that question is open to us. It has been decided in *R v Industrial*
Injuries Comr, ex parte Howarth[1], to which Lord Denning MR has already referred;
and I am not at all sure on consideration that the contrary view would really be
advantageous to claimants to benefits under the Act. If a provisional decision by
the first medical board before which a case happened to come were capable of being
binding on tribunals before which the case might subsequently come under the Act,
it might well become more difficult to obtain and to hold a favourable first provisional
decision, and appeals at that stage might be multiplied. I would only add that in
my view nothing in the decision in *Jones v Secretary of State for Social Services*[2] affects
the decision in the *Howarth* case[1].

As regards the burden of proof, as Lord Denning MR has pointed out, these are
not adversary proceedings; they are inquisitorial proceedings; and in such proceedings questions of burden of proof do not arise in the same way in which they
would in proceedings between parties in a law suit. It is for the medical board or the
medical appeal tribunal, as the case may be, to investigate the case inquisitorially
and to decide whether the claimant is entitled to benefit under the Act. But, of
course, the fact remains that the medical board or the medical appeal tribunal,
as the case may be, must be satisfied that the claimant is entitled to benefit; and
so, in a sense, and subject to such statutory assumptions as are prescribed by the
Act itself, it does rest with the claimant in the end to make out his claim. The tribunal
have in my view a duty to make all reasonably necessary enquiries in order to enable
their to reach a conclusion; but they are not, I think, bound to do more than what it
considers to be reasonable. Where there is any doubt whether a claimant is or is not
entitled to benefit, the claimant can himself advance his own case by bringing evidence
before the board or tribunal, or by drawing their attention to such matters as he
thinks will assist him; and the tribunal must themselves consider whether there is
any further information or further expert assistance that is likely to enable them to
reach a proper conclusion. But it is, in my judgment, for the tribunal to decide
whether any further investigation is likely to serve a useful purpose; and in the
present case it was for the third medical appeal tribunal to decide, in the light of
Mr Thompson's report, whether a lymphangiographical exploration or investigation
would be useful. It was not suggested on behalf of the applicant that such an investigation should be made. That was not urged on his behalf; and the medical appeal
tribunal, who in this respect are perfectly entitled to use their own expertise, evidently
thought that it would not assist or throw any light on Mr Thompson's report, and
they reached the conclusion which they did, which can perhaps be framed in either
of two ways: either that they were not satisfied that the applicant had established
that any disability from which he was suffering was causally connected with the
accident in respect of which he was making his claim; or, alternatively, that on the
balance of probability they came to the conclusion that there was not such a causal
connection; and that was a conclusion to which in my judgment in the circumstances
of the case they were fully entitled to come.

Thirdly, I will say a word about the natural justice point. Again I emphasise that
these are not proceedings in an action. It is an inquisitorial proceeding, and I fully
agree with what Lord Denning MR has said, that in such proceedings it is the duty
of the board or tribunal to act with fairness; but the considerations which more
normally arise in connection with points taken under natural justice do not directly
arise, I think. It was said that as the charge against the applicant, or the accusation
levelled at him, was that he was a malingerer, that is to say that he was fraudulently
seeking to deceive the tribunal as to the state of his injury or disability, that that
should have been put forward with particularity in order that he might know

---

1   (1968) 4 KIR 621
2   [1972] 1 All ER 145, [1972] AC 944

a precisely what case he had got to meet. Well, Mr Thompson's report was in the hands of the applicant or his advisers on, I think it was said, 13th October, some weeks before the adjourned hearing of the third medical appeal tribunal at which that report was considered, and at that adjourned hearing the question of whether or not he was a malingerer was raised and fully debated. The fact that it was a point taken at that hearing appears from the written report that we have amongst the papers. It cannot, in my judgment, be suggested with any justification that the appli-

b cant or his advisers were taken by surprise in that respect or that they did not know the nature of the suggestions that were being made in that respect. It does not seem to me that the applicant was in any way prejudiced by the fact that the circumstances of the case were transmitted to Mr Thompson for his opinion not by an officer of the medical appeal tribunal, but by a medical officer of the Ministry. The matter was fairly put before Mr Thompson with a full case history, all the medical facts;

c but it was placed before him without intimation of the opinions that had been formed by members of the boards or appeal tribunals in the earlier stages of the case, and, in particular, the views rather than the findings expressed by the various boards and tribunals which have considered the case. As I understand the position, the reason for seeking a report from Mr Thompson was that the tribunal were anxious to have a fresh and uninfluenced opinion on the case. It has been urged by counsel

d for the applicant that among the facts of the case which ought to have been put before Mr Thompson was the fact that certain doctors had taken certain views one way or the other on the malingering aspect. Of course, the views expressed by doctors are in a sense facts; but they are also matters of opinion. It is a fact that the doctor expressed an opinion; but in my judgment it was perfectly fair not to place those views before the expert when the expert was asked to give his expert opinion

e on the case, and in this connection I may say that it seems to me really to be irrelevant whether this was a reference under reg 19(2) of the National Insurance (Industrial Injuries) (Determination of Claims and Questions) (No 2) Regulations 1967[1]. For, even if it were—and I am inclined to the view that it was not—I do not think that the applicant was in any way prejudiced by the course that was taken.

f One final point with which I should perhaps deal is that it was submitted that there had been a failure to comply with the full requirements of reg 12 of these regulations which requires a medical appeal tribunal to record their decision in writing and to include therein findings on any questions of fact material to the decision. A complaint was made as to the form in which the third medical appeal tribunal dealt with the matter, because, it was said, they departed from the views expressed by the earlier medical appeal tribunals which accepted that the applicant's disability was genuinely

g a result of the accident he had suffered, and yet there are no findings of facts to show what circumstances were relied on for that change of view. But this argument in my judgment really proceeds on a misconception of the effect of the findings of the earlier tribunals. That is the finality point with which I dealt at the beginning of this judgment. I think this part of the argument really proceeds on a misapprehen-

h sion as to the effect of s 50(1) of the 1965 Act. It was not incumbent, in my view, on the third medical appeal tribunal to explain why they were differing from the findings of the earlier tribunals for the reason that those earlier findings were final only in relation to the period with which those bodies were dealing at the time. On the construction of the decision of the third medical appeal tribunal, as I say, I understand them to be saying that they have arrived at their conclusion either on the basis that they had grave suspicion as a result of which they were not satisfied that the

j applicant had made out his case, or that on the balance of probability there was no connection between the disability from which the applicant was then suffering and the accident of which he was the victim.

For these reasons and those given by Lord Denning MR, I agree that this appeal fails.

1 SI 1967 No 1571

ROSKILL LJ. I agree that this appeal fails. I think the Divisional Court was *a* manifestly right in refusing the order of certiorari sought on behalf of the applicant. The regrettable delay in this case cannot affect the result. But it is to be observed that the decision of the commissioner, Mr J S Watson QC, which it was sought to quash was given as long ago as 12th February 1969, while the decision of the medical appeal tribunal (which is the real target of the applicant's attack) was given as long ago as 30th November 1967, over six years ago. Since, however, the argument on *b* the appeal was far reaching, I would add a few observations on certain points to those which have been made by Lord Denning MR and Buckley LJ.

First, the question of finality. Founding his argument on the language of s 50(1) of the 1965 Act, counsel for the applicant strongly contended that the medical appeal tribunal (which, to avoid confusion, I will call 'the third medical appeal tribunal' had no right to conclude the crucial question of fact in this case adversely to the *c* applicant. That issue was whether the condition of the applicant's right lower limb was attributable to the accident which admittedly took place on 23rd July 1965 when apparently he trod on a nail at work and twisted his right knee. It was argued that the decision of the second medical appeal tribunal dated 18th January 1967 that 'the right leg condition is a serious disablement and in our opinion has arisen from the accident', was final in the strict sense of that word, save only that it might *d* be reviewed under s 40 of the 1965 Act if subsequently discovered evidence justified an application for review. Section 50(1) of the Act reads thus:

'Except as provided by this Part of this Act, any decision of a claim or question in accordance with this Part of this Act shall be final.'

The argument advanced by counsel for the applicant is that that simple language *e* means what it says. Such an argument readily appeals to any court. But the answer is not as simple, for the very simplicity of the language at once invites the question: in respect of what period is the decision in question to be final? The answer to that question to my mind is concluded in this court by authority—namely, the decision referred to by Lord Denning MR, *R v Industrial Injuries Commissioner, ex parte Howarth*[1]. Lord Denning MR has already read the relevant passages. Suffice it to say *f* that I respectfully agree with that decision, which is in no way invalidated by the subsequent decision of the House of Lords in *Jones v Secretary of State for Social Services*[2]. The decisions of the relevant tribunals in *Howarth*[3], like the earlier decisions of the first and second medical appeal tribunals concerned in the present case, are final only in relation to the period stated in them. None is final for all time. That decision, as I have already said, binds this court unless it can be shown to be incon- *g* sistent with some later decision of the House of Lords and therefore wrong. Counsel for the applicant understandably shrank from going so far as to say that the decision in *Howarth*[3] was wrong, but limited his contention to saying it had been 'refined' (the word was his) by the decision in *Jones's* case[2]. If, as counsel for the applicant argued, the earlier decision was on what he called a 'gateway' question, then it was final. By that expression, which he borrowed from some of the speeches in *Jones's* *h* case[2], he meant a question the answer to which enabled an applicant to proceed with the next stage of his argument in support of his claim for benefit. But with respect, I do not think this argument is well founded. *Howarth*[3] is not referred to in the report of *Jones*[2], though counsel for the commissioner told us it had been casually referred to during the argument before their Lordships' House. I can see nothing in the speeches in *Jones*[2] which requires reconsideration of the decision of this court in *i* *Howarth*[3]. Accordingly, the third medical appeal tribunal was fully entitled in relation to the period with which they were concerned to reconsider the matter de novo.

1 (1968) 4 KIR 621 at 624, 625
2 [1972] 1 All ER 145, [1972] AC 944
3 4 KIR 621

a There was some discussion on the scope of s 40(1) of the 1965 Act regarding reviews of previous decisions of medical boards or medical appeal tribunals on any of the grounds provided for in that subsection. Since this question does not arise directly for decision in this present appeal, I would only make these comments on one submission made by counsel for the commissioner. The subsection was considered by the Divisional Court[1] and by this court[2] in *R v Medical Appeal Tribunal, ex parte Hubble*. The Divisional Court took a somewhat narrow view of the powers accorded

b by that section: see the judgment of Diplock J[3]. But the Court of Appeal[2] in the judgments of Morris and Ormerod LJJ took a wider view though. Even on that wider view the appellant's claim failed. We were also referred to a decision (No R(1) 17(66)) of Sir Robert Micklethwait QC, the Chief Commissioner, in which the relevant authorities were considered. For my part, if I may respectfully say so, like Lord Denning MR, I see nothing susceptible of criticism in the learned commissioner's

c analysis of the legal position, which in my judgment is entirely correct. I only mention this matter because of the concluding paragraphs in the speech of Viscount Dilhorne[4] in *Jones's* case. From what counsel for the commissioner told us, the matter was not argued before the House of Lords and the authorities to which I have referred were not drawn to their Lordships' attention. As I understood counsel for the commissioner, the department have most properly, if I may say so, in the light of the

d 1966 decision of Sir Robert Micklethwait, adopted a wider and more benevolent construction of s 40 of the 1965 Act than the decision of the Divisional Court in *Hubble's* case[1] would suggest. This no doubt explains the absence of judicial decision on its scope since 1959.

So far as counsel for the applicant's other arguments are concerned, I can see no foundation for his complaint that the department did not, as is now clear, send the

e conclusions of the previous medical appeal tribunals to Mr Noel Thompson on 14th September 1971 to accompany the other documents then sent. Nor can I see any reason why the papers sent to Mr Noel Thompson should not have been sent by the department rather than by the secretariat of the tribunal. It is an example, as Lord Denning MR has pointed out, of a government department, in fulfilment

f of its general duty to see that all relevant factual material is placed before the medical appeal tribunal or any specialist whom the medical appeal tribunal may wish to consult, fulfilling that duty. Previous conclusions of other tribunals, though doubtless of value, were not primary or clinical facts of which it was necessary to make Mr Noel Thompson aware. They were conclusions or inferences of fact drawn by the distinguished doctors concerned from primary or clinical facts previously submitted to them. What was wanted from Mr Noel Thompson was an independent diagnosis

g founded on his own examination of the applicant and on his own assessment of those primary or clinical facts submitted to him—properly, as I think—uninfluenced by the prior conclusions of others.

Then it was argued that the third medical appeal tribunal was at fault in not following up Mr Thompson's suggestion of a further investigation by way of lymphangiography. This seems to me to be entirely a matter for that tribunal. They saw

h the applicant. They saw Mr Thompson's report and conclusions. They had the previous reports and the previous conclusions. I am afraid I cannot see why the third medical appeal tribunal was in any way guilty of what counsel for the applicant described as 'want of due enquiry' merely because they failed to follow up Mr Noel Thompson's suggestion. They were the masters of their own procedure; they were entitled to use their own expertise and it is not for the court to dictate to them how

j they use their expertise or how they should conduct their proceedings within the

1 [1958] 2 All ER 374, [1958] 2 QB 228
2 [1959] 3 All ER 40, [1959] 2 QB 408
3 [1958] 2 All ER at 382, [1958] 2 QB at 242, 243
4 [1972] 1 All ER at 171, [1972] AC at 993, 994

limits of fairness. This is not, as Lord Denning MR has pointed out, a law suit con- *a*
ducted between parties. It is an enquiry to determine whether or not a particular
applicant is entitled to certain statutory benefits to which he becomes entitled if
it is found that certain conditions are fulfilled. It is important to observe in this
connection that the representative of the applicant was aware before the resumed
hearing of the third medical appeal tribunal of what had been sent to Mr Noel
Thompson and that the third medical appeal tribunal did not propose to have the *b*
further investigation carried out which Mr Thompson suggested.

As regards counsel for the applicant's point on reg 12[1], that regulation reads:

> 'A medical appeal tribunal shall in each case record their decision in writing
> in such form as may from time to time be approved by the Minister, and shall
> include in such record, which shall be signed by all the members of the tribunal,
> a statement of the reasons for their decision, including their findings on all *c*
> questions of fact material to the decision.'

Counsel for the applicant argued that they had not complied with that statutory
requirement because they had not set out in detail or indeed at all why they had
concluded that the applicant had made a fraudulent claim to benefit, and indeed
had not set out their reasons for disagreeing with the conclusions of the second *d*
medical appeal tribunal. In my judgment there was no reason why the third medical
appeal tribunal should set out the contents of Mr Noel Thompson's report in detail.
Nor was there any reason why they should set out in further detail beyond what
they did what the reasons for their conclusions were. It was enough for them to
conclude, as they did conclude, that the disability relied on was not attributable to
the accident. They need not go further than that. For the reasons which they *e*
sufficiently set out, they accepted Mr Noel Thompson's clinical findings and his
conclusion that 'there must be a strong suspicion of lymphoedema artefacta'. Founding themselves on that and on their own examination, they reached their conclusion
and I see no reason why they should have spelt out further their reasons for rejecting
the claim.

So far as onus of proof is concerned, I agree with what has fallen from Lord Denning *f*
MR and in particular with what was said by Lord Parker CJ in the Divisional Court
in *Hudson*[2] and by Lord Denning MR[3]. Nothing said in the House of Lords casts
any doubt on what was then said.

Like Buckley LJ, I do not think this was a case of a reference under reg 19. But
I do not think it matters whether or not it was.

For these reasons, in addition to those Lord Denning MR and Buckley LJ have *g*
given, the application for an order of certiorari was rightly refused and the appeal
should be dismissed.

Appeal dismissed.

Solicitors: *W H Thompson* (for the applicant); *Solicitor, Department of Health and* *h*
Social Security.

L J Kovats Esq Barrister.

---

1   SI 1967 No 1571
2   [1969] 2 All ER 631 at 635, [1970] 1 QB 477 at 484
3   [1970] 1 All ER 97 at 102, [1970] 1 QB at 500

a
Robinson v The Post Office and another

COURT OF APPEAL, CIVIL DIVISION
DAVIES, BUCKLEY AND ORR LJJ
2nd, 3rd, 5th, 6th, 9th, 10th JULY, 25th OCTOBER 1973

b

Damages – Remoteness of damage – Negligence – Foreseeability – Type but not extent of injury foreseeable – Physical condition of plaintiff such as to aggravate extent of injury – Treatment of injury – Necessity for medical treatment foreseeable – Plaintiff allergic to treatment administered by doctor – Doctor not negligent – Treatment not novus actus interveniens – Plaintiff suffering extensive injury in consequence of treatment – Whether defendant liable c *for full extent of injury.*

On 15th February 1968 the plaintiff, a technician employed by the Post Office, slipped as he was descending a ladder from one of the Post Office's tower wagons. The slipping was caused by oil on the ladder due to leakage of a pump. The plaintiff sustained a wound to his left shin. Some eight hours later he visited his doctor d and was given an injection of anti-tetanus serum ('ATS'). The plaintiff had, to the doctor's knowledge, been given a dose of ATS following an accident in 1955. Where a patient had had a previous dose of ATS it was essential, because of the risk of reaction, to give a test dose before administering a full dose. The recognised test procedure in 1968 entailed waiting half an hour after injecting a small quantity of ATS to see whether the patient showed any reaction. The doctor did not follow e that procedure but followed one of his own, waiting only a minute for a reaction before administering the balance of the full dose. The plaintiff did not suffer any reaction until 24th February when he began to show signs of a reaction. On 26th February he was admitted to hospital suffering from encephalitis. It was known that encephalitis was a possible, though rare, consequence of the administration of ATS. The plaintiff suffered brain damage in consequence of the encephalitis. f He brought an action for damages against the Post Office and the doctor. The trial judge found that the Post Office were negligent in allowing the oil to leak on to the ladder and that the doctor was not negligent in deciding to administer ATS. The judge absolved the doctor from liability holding that, although he had been negligent in failing to administer a test dose, 'a proper test dose would have made no difference' since it would not have produced a reaction within half an hour. Accordingly he g held the Post Office wholly liable for the plaintiff's injury. The Post Office appealed, contending, inter alia, that an essential link between the negligent act and the plaintiff's injury was missing in that it could not have been foreseen that administration of a form of an anti-tetanus prophylaxis would itself give rise to serious illness.

Held – The appeal would be dismissed for the following reasons—

h   (i) In the light of the plaintiff's subsequent history it was most unlikely that, if the proper test dose procedure had been followed, the plaintiff would have shown a reaction within the period of half an hour before the administration of the full dose. The negligence of the doctor in failing to administer a proper test dose did not therefore cause or materially contribute to the plaintiff's injury (see p 746 *b* to *d* and p 747 *a* and *b*, post); *Bonnington Castings Ltd v Wardlaw* [1956] 1 All ER 615 j applied.

(ii) The administration of ATS by the doctor was not a novus actus interveniens since (a) he had not been negligent or inefficient in deciding to administer ATS, and (b) his failure to administer a proper test dose had had no causative effect (see p 747 *h* to p 748 *a* and *d*, post).

(iii) Since it was foreseeable that, if oil were negligently allowed to escape on to a ladder, a workman would be likely to slip and sustain the type of wound in question

and that such an injury might well require medical treatment, it followed that the
Post Office were liable for the encephalitis suffered by the plaintiff in consequence
of that injury. The Post Office were bound to take the plaintiff as they found him,
i e with an allergy to a second dose of ATS, and if it was foreseeable that as a result
of their wrongful act he might require medical treatment, they were, in the absence
of a novus actus interveniens, liable for the consequences of the treatment applied
even though they could not have reasonably foreseen those consequences or that
they could be serious (see p 750 *a* and *c* to *e*, post); *Smith v Leech Brain & Co Ltd* [1961]
3 All ER 1159 and *Winteringham v Rae* (1966) 55 DLR (2d) 108 applied; *Tremain v Pike*
[1969] 3 All ER 1303 distinguished.

Notes

For the remoteness of damage in general, see 11 Halsbury's Laws (3rd Edn) 268-274,
paras 445-452, and for cases on the subject, see 17 Digest (Repl) 114, 115, 268-276.

Cases referred to in judgment

Barnett v Chelsea and Kensington Hospital Management Committee [1968] 1 All ER 1068,
  [1969] 1 QB 428, [1968] 2 WLR 422, Digest (Cont Vol C) 666, 112*a*.
Bloor v Liverpool Derricking and Carrying Co Ltd [1936] 3 All ER 399, CA, 36 Digest
  (Repl) 43, 233.
Bolam v Friern Hospital Management Committee [1957] 2 All ER 118, [1957] 1 WLR 582,
  33 Digest (Repl) 527, 81.
Bonnington Castings Ltd v Wardlaw [1956] 1 All ER 615, [1956] AC 613, [1956] 2 WLR
  707, 54 LGR 153, HL, 34 Digest (Repl) 268, 1899.
Bradford v Robinson Rentals Ltd [1967] 1 All ER 267, [1967] 1 WLR 337, Digest (Cont
  Vol C) 729, 89*c*.
Cummings (or McWilliams) v Sir William Arrol & Co Ltd [1962] 1 All ER 623, [1962]
  1 WLR 295, 1962 SC 70, 1962 SLT 121, HL, Digest (Cont Vol A) 592, 277*c*.
Hogan v Bentinck West Hartley Collieries (Owners) Ltd [1949] 1 All ER 588, [1949] LJR 865,
  41 BWCC 185, HL, 34 Digest (Repl) 568, 3887.
Hughes v Lord Advocate [1963] 1 All ER 705, [1963] AC 837, [1963] 2 WLR 779, 1963
  SC 31, 1963 SLT 150, HL, Digest (Cont Vol A) 1143, 89*a*.
McGhee v National Coal Board [1972] 3 All ER 1008, [1973] 1 WLR 1, 13 KIR 471, HL.
Oman v McIntyre 1962 SLT 168.
Overseas Tankship (UK) Ltd v Morts Dock & Engineering Co Ltd [1961] 1 All ER 404,
  [1961] AC 388, [1961] 2 WLR 126, [1961] 1 Lloyd's Rep 1, [1961] ALR 569, PC,
  Digest (Cont Vol A) 1148, 185*a*.
Polemis and Furness, Withy & Co Ltd, Re [1921] 3 KB 560, [1921] All ER Rep 40, sub
  nom *Polemis v Furness, Withy & Co Ltd* 90 LJKB 1353, 126 LT 154, 15 Asp MLC 398,
  27 Com Cas 25, CA, 17 Digest (Repl) 114, 269.
Rothwell v Caverswall Stone Co Ltd [1944] 2 All ER 350, 113 LJKB 520, 171 LT 289, 37
  BWCC 72, CA, 34 Digest (Repl) 568, 3885.
Smith v Leech Brain & Co Ltd [1961] 3 All ER 1159, [1962] 2 QB 405, [1962] 2 WLR 148,
  Digest (Cont Vol A) 464, 155*a*.
Tremain v Pike [1969] 3 All ER 1303, [1969] 1 WLR 1556, 67 LGR 703, Digest (Cont Vol C)
  698, 1790*j*.
Wagon Mound, The. See *Overseas Tankship (UK) Ltd v Morts & Engineering Co Ltd*,
  supra.
Warren v Scruttons Ltd [1962] 1 Lloyd's Rep 497.
Wigley v British Vinegars Ltd [1962] 3 All ER 161, [1964] AC 307, [1962] 3 WLR 731,
  61 LGR 1, HL, Digest (Cont Vol A) 592, 277*a*.
Winteringham v Rae (1966) 55 DLR (2d) 108, [1966] 1 OR 727, Digest (Cont Vol B) 23,
  605c.

Cases also cited

Burke (James) v John Paul & Co [1967] IR 277.

Davies v Liverpool Corpn [1949] 2 All ER 175, CA.

Doughty v Turner Manufacturing Co Ltd [1964] 1 All ER 98, [1964] 1 QB 518, CA.

Heron II, The, Koufos v C Czarnikow Ltd [1967] 3 All ER 686, [1969] 1 AC 350, HL.

Home Office v Dorset Yacht Co Ltd [1970] 2 All ER 294, [1970] AC 1004, HL.

Lord v Pacific Steam Navigation Co Ltd, The Oropesa [1943] 1 All ER 211, [1943] P 32, CA.

McKew v Holland & Hannen & Cubitts (Scotland) Ltd [1969] 3 All ER 1621, HL.

Roe v Ministry of Health, Woolley v Ministry of Health [1954] 2 All ER 131, [1954] 2 QB 66, CA.

Vacwell Engineering Co Ltd v BDH Chemicals Ltd (Formerly British Drug Houses Ltd) [1969] 3 All ER 1681, [1971] 1 QB 88; *rvsd* [1970] 3 All ER 553, CA.

Wagon Mound (No 2), The, Overseas Tankship (UK) Ltd v The Miller Steamship Co Pty Ltd [1966] 2 All ER 709, [1967] 1 AC 617, PC.

West v Hughes of Beaconsfield [1971] RTR 298.

Wieland v Cyril Lord Carpets Ltd [1969] 3 All ER 1006.

Appeal and cross-appeal

At all material times the plaintiff, Keith Robinson, was employed by the first defendants, the Post Office, as a jointer. On 15th February 1968, in the course of his employment, he was working on a tower wagon owned by the Post Office when he slipped as he was descending the ladder from the tower wagon and suffered laceration to his left leg. Subsequently he visited his doctor, the second defendant, Malcolm MacEwan ('Dr MacEwan'), who gave him an injection of anti-tetanus serum. In consequence of the injection the plaintiff contracted encephalitis. By a writ issued on 12th March 1970 the plaintiff brought an action against the Post Office claiming damages for personal injuries and loss sustained in consequence of the accident. On 30th December 1970 Dr MacEwan was joined as a defendant to the action. On 21st December 1972, at the trial of the action, Ashworth J dismissed the claim against Dr MacEwan, entered judgment for the plaintiff against the Post Office and awarded him damages of £20,157·77 with interest and costs. The Post Office appealed and the plaintiff cross-appealed against so much of the judgment as ordered that judgment be entered for Dr MacEwan against the plaintiff. The facts are set out in the judgment of the court.

John Newey QC and *Robin Auld* for the Post Office.

John Griffiths QC and *Peter Lewis* for the plaintiff.

John Spokes QC for Dr MacEwan.

Cur adv vult

25th October. **ORR LJ** read the following judgment of the court. This is an appeal by the Post Office against a judgment of Ashworth J, given on 21st December 1972, by which he held the Post Office, who were the first defendants in an action for damages for personal injuries, liable to the plaintiff in damages of £20,157·77 and interest, and also ordered them to pay to the second defendant, Dr MacEwan, his costs of defending the action.

The plaintiff in the action, Mr Robinson, had been in the service of the Post Office since 1955 and was, at the time of the accident complained of, 34 years of age and employed by the Post Office as a technician, class 1. The circumstances of the accident, which took place between 10.00 and 10.30 a m on 15th February 1968, were that he slipped when descending the ladder of one of the Post Office's tower wagons and sustained a wound some three inches long on his left shin. It was not in dispute that the cause of his slipping was the presence of oil on the ladder due to leakage of a pump and that the Post Office were liable for such modest damages as would have been attributable to the plaintiff's wound had nothing further supervened, but unfortunately, as a result of the medical treatment given to the plaintiff, very grave consequences supervened, and the contest in the action was as to the Post Office's liability for these consequences.

The plaintiff after his fall was able to carry on working until knocking-off time at 5.30 p m, after which he went to his general practitioner, Dr MacEwan, who saw him just after 6.00 p m and, after examining the wound, ascertaining its circumstances and that it had been caused some 7½ to eight hours before, and enquiring what anti-tetanus injections the plaintiff had previously had, sent him to a chemist for anti-tetanus serum (hereinafter in this judgment referred to as 'ATS') and on his return gave him an injection of the serum. The plaintiff's own evidence was that from then until 24th February he felt perfectly well, was playing with his children, and was only absent from work because of the wound. His mother, however, gave evidence of his suffering, at the earliest three days after the injection, from an irritation which is referred to in the paragraph entitled 'History' in a report dated 23rd April 1968 by the medical registrar at the Ipswich Hospital and was taken by him to have been giant urticaria. On 24th February, nine days after the injection, the plaintiff showed signs of reaction which were not at first thought to be serious but on the following day he became delirious and on 26th February he was admitted to hospital and was on admission unable to speak. It was not in dispute at the trial that the plaintiff had at this time, as a result of the injection, contracted encephalitis, which is a possible, though a rare, consequence of the administration of ATS; and that the brain damage so sustained has been followed by very severe consequences. The plaintiff appeared at first to make a very good recovery but the improvement was short-lived. He had in early 1969, as a direct result of the brain damage, two attacks of an epileptic character and although there have been no further such attacks there is a risk of their recurrence. He is, as the judge found, a very different man from what he would have been if the accident had not befallen him.

In the action the plaintiff originally sued only the Post Office but, they having in their defence made allegations of negligence on the part of Dr MacEwan, he was, by amendment of the writ and statement of claim, joined as a co-defendant; the allegations made against him in the amended statement of claim being identical with those set out in the Post Office's defence.

At the trial the main issues which arose were, first, whether Dr MacEwan had, in all the circumstances, been negligent in injecting ATS; secondly, whether he had been negligent in injecting a full dose of ATS without administering a proper test injection beforehand; thirdly, whether, if he had been negligent in the second of these respects, such negligence caused or materially contributed to the encephalitis; and fourthly, whether, if Dr MacEwan was not liable in negligence to the plaintiff (it being admitted that, if he was, the chain of causation between the Post Office's breach of duty and the encephalitis would be broken), the Post Office were entitled in law to be held not liable for the damage attributable to the encephalitis on the ground that that illness was not foreseeable in the circumstances or was otherwise too remote a consequence of their admitted negligence.

As to the first and second of these issues, the judge held that it had not in the circumstances been negligent of Dr MacEwan to administer ATS but that he had been negligent in failing to administer a proper test dose. He went on, however, to find as a fact that if a proper test dose had been administered the plaintiff would not have shown any reaction to it and therefore the failure to administer a proper test dose had not caused or materially contributed to the encephalitis; and as to the fourth issue he held that the Post Office were liable in law for the encephalitis as well as for the wound. He also made certain findings of fact, to which reference will be made later in this judgment, as to the plaintiff's medical history of anti-tetanus injections, and, with reference to complaints made in the Post Office's defence and the amended statement of claim as to the insufficiency of the wound toilet applied by Dr MacEwan and as to his failure to administer an antibiotic, refused to find that the doctor had been negligent in either of these respects. These last conclusions have not been challenged in this appeal, nor has Dr MacEwan in this appeal sought to challenge the judge's finding that he was negligent in failing to administer a proper test dose.

In the result the three issues in the appeal are whether the judge was right in holding (1) that it was not negligent of Dr MacEwan to administer ATS, (2) that the failure to administer a proper test dose did not cause or materially contribute to the encephalitis, and (3) that the Post Office were liable for the damages attributable to that illness.

Before turning to the first of these issues it should be mentioned that counsel for the Post Office criticised the judge for considering separately the question whether Dr MacEwan was wrong to administer ATS at all and whether he was negligent in administering it without a proper test dose, but these are in fact distinct questions and we see no reason to suppose that in considering either question the judge overlooked any relevant evidence in relation to the other.

By way of introduction to the first issue it is necessary to refer to certain general evidence, given at the trial and not in dispute, as to the history of anti-tetanus precautions and also to the more important of a very large number of published or circulated papers on the subject which would have been available to a general practitioner before the date of the accident.

ATS first came into use about the beginning of this century. It may take the form of horse serum or human or bovine serum but it has always, for practical purposes, denoted horse serum since stocks of human or bovine serum are restricted to a very few centres in the country, and, while it was common ground at the trial that certain risks associated with horse serum and referred to in the medical literature are far less serious in the case of human or bovine serum, it was also common ground that Dr MacEwan could not, in the circumstances of this case, have obtained either human or bovine serum in sufficient time for it to have any effect. The abbreviation 'ATS' is therefore used throughout this judgment to denote ATS in the form of horse serum.

ATS was widely used in the 1914-18 war but it was found that a considerable number of those injected with it developed symptoms afterwards and some died. This led to research with the object of finding an alternative for it and an alternative was found in anti-tetanus toxoid of which an improved form became available in 1963 but it will be convenient to refer alike to the toxoid injected before and after that date as APT (alum-precipitated toxoid). During the 1939-45 war APT was administered both to the British and American forces, whereas for civilians ATS continued to be used. For a short period from about 1945-48 the British Army stopped using APT but thereafter reverted to it. An essential difference between APT and ATS is that the former, administered in three doses, provides future immunity from tetanus for a period of years as to the duration of which different views have been held at different times, and within limits of time its efficacy can be restored by a single booster dose, but it is not, whereas ATS may be, efficacious to prevent the onset of tetanus in a wound in which, before the injection is made, there has been time for tetanus toxin to develop.

After the second world war APT was increasingly used and from the 1940s onwards increasing doubts were felt as to the desirability of using ATS, and those doubts are reflected in the medical literature on the subject, a very large volume of which was before the learned judge. It is, for the present purposes, necessary to refer to only five of these documents. [His Lordship then considered the documents and continued:] The medical literature represented by these documents reveals that for a period of years before 1968 there had been a growing tendency to discontinue the use of ATS in favour of APT and antibiotics but reveals also that there were two schools of thought on this subject, the first, represented by Mr W J W Sharrard[1], that ATS should be given only in very exceptional circumstances, and

---

1 Senior consultant at the Accident and Orthopaedic Department of the Sheffield Royal Infirmary and a witness at the trial on behalf of the Post Office

the other, represented by Dr J W Granville-Smith[1], that the administration of ATS remained the wiser course in the case of a non-immunised patient with a contaminated wound over six hours old, but with the qualification that it should, if it were at all reasonable to do so, be withheld from a patient who had had ATS before. It was, however, common ground between the two schools that if a patient had had a previous dose of ATS there were two serious drawbacks of administering another, the first that its prophylactic value would be greatly diminished by the speed of its elimination, and the second that it would involve much greater risks of reactions, and these would include, as well as local skin irritation, the risks, admitted to be rare, of the patient dying from anaphylactic shock or contracting encephalitis. In these circumstances the evidence as to the plaintiff's previous medical history, and the judge's findings on it, are of great importance in the case. The plaintiff had in 1940, at the age of seven, sustained injury by a nail going through his right hand, for which he was admitted to hospital, but no records were available to show what treatment he had received. Since at that time ATS was widely used as a prophylactic against tetanus the judge thought it quite likely that it would have been administered but was not satisfied on a balance of probabilities that it had been, and this finding has not been challenged in the appeal. Between 1952 or 1953 and 1955 the plaintiff had served in the Royal Corps of Signals. His pay-book (from which the relevant pages had been removed) did not reveal any injection but the judge drew the inference that he would have been injected with APT, which was, during that period, being used in the Forces. In September 1955, some months after joining the Post Office, the plaintiff suffered an accident for which Dr MacEwan sent him to hospital, and a letter, dated 9th November 1955, from the consultant orthopaedic surgeon in charge of his case to Dr MacEwan reveals that he was at this time given 1,500 units of ATS. Dr MacEwan's evidence at the trial was that he did not have this letter (which was in the surgery of his son, a partner in the practice) when the plaintiff consulted him on 15th February 1968, but made the assumption that the plaintiff would, when in hospital, have had an injection of ATS.

In August 1965 the plaintiff sustained, in climbing out of a manhole, an injury to his left shin, for which he consulted Dr MacEwan, and his evidence, which the judge accepted, was that the doctor on that occasion gave him an injection. There was no entry on his card in relation to this visit and Dr MacEwan could not recall it but his evidence was that if he had injected ATS he would have recorded it. The judge considered it possible that on this occasion the doctor administered penicillin, which would have been available at the surgery whereas ATS would have involved, as in 1968, a visit by the plaintiff to a chemist, and, in the absence of any evidence by the plaintiff as to such a visit in 1965, came to the conclusion that penicillin and not ATS had been administered, and this conclusion also has not been challenged in the appeal. Accordingly the relevant circumstances in the plaintiff's medical history must be taken to be that he had had a dose of APT prior to February 1955, and a dose of ATS in the autumn of the same year.

From this background of medical literature and of the plaintiff's medical history we now turn to Dr MacEwan's own evidence as to the considerations which led him to inject ATS, and to the evidence of other medical witnesses as to the propriety of his doing so. Dr MacEwan qualified in 1924 and, apart from very distinguished active service in the second world war, has been in general practice in Ipswich since 1927. He gave evidence that when he started in practice there he was warned by the medical officer of health for Ipswich that the whole of the Suffolk-Norfolk borders were tetanus-prone country and that as a casualty officer he should be particularly careful in that regard. He had in his practice encountered three or four cases of tetanus, two involving agricultural labourers, one of whom had sustained no more than a slight

---

1 Consultant deputy myologist in a public health laboratory at Colindale and a witness at the trial on behalf of Dr MacEwan

graze from a kick by a cow, and he took the view that Post Office workers were subject to a tetanus risk because their work took them on the land and they could carry tetanus infection on their footwear. He had read much material about tetanus precautions in the medical journals which had revealed conflicting views. His own approach had been that in deciding whether or not to inject ATS the major considerations were (1) the age of the wound, (2) the length of the period since the patient had been actively immunised, and (3) whether the patient had had ATS before. In the case of a patient who had had no active immunisation in the past ten years his practice would be to administer ATS if he thought there was any risk at all of tetanus being present and developing toxin. If there was no such risk he would start active immunisation in the form of APT.

On 15th February 1968 the plaintiff had come to his surgery about 6 p m and had told him that the injury had been sustained by his slipping on the ladder of a tower wagon about 10 a m, which would make it about eight hours old. The injury itself could be described as an abrasion or graze 2½ to three inches long, surrounded by some devitalised tissue but not particularly dirty. He formed the view that tetanus infection could have been deposited on the ladder from the footwear of Post Office employees and that in eight hours there had been ample time for tetanus toxin to develop in the wound, which he described as superficial but of great significance. The judge, after referring to evidence of the plaintiff that the wound went down to the bone and that he had attempted to clean it before going to the surgery, concluded, and in our view justifiably, that it was by no means trivial.

Dr MacEwan's evidence was that, having examined the wound and obtained information as to when and how it was caused, he then asked the plaintiff when he had had his last tetanus injection and the plaintiff replied that this had been in 1955 but that he did not remember where he was given it. The doctor assumed (what he later confirmed from the surgeon's letter) that the plaintiff would have had ATS at the hospital in the autumn of that year, and, since he knew of the plaintiff's military service, also assumed that he would have had APT, probably soon after the commencement of that service. In these circumstances he took the view that, since the plaintiff's only active immunisation had been more than ten years before, he must be regarded as non-immunised. The plaintiff's evidence as to this part of the case was that when asked about his last injection he had replied 'three or four years ago', but it was not in dispute that Dr MacEwan had, either on 15th February 1968 or on the following day, entered on the plaintiff's medical card that his last previous injection had been in 1955, and the judge accepted the doctor's evidence that this was what he was told by the plaintiff.

Dr MacEwan's evidence as to what followed was that, having examined the wound and obtained the foregoing information, he decided to inject ATS, sent the plaintiff to a chemist to get it, and on his return proceeded to administer it in a manner to which reference will be made later in this judgment. He did not excise the devitalised tissues round the wound and left the wound itself uncovered in order to allow light to get at it, and he did not administer any antibiotic systemically but sprayed the wound with an antibiotic called Terra-Cortril. He did not administer APT. He gave as his reason for not excising the tissue that very extensive excision would have been necessary, which he did not consider it good surgery to perform, and that it would have involved sending the plaintiff to hospital, and, as his reason for not giving an antibiotic systemically, that it would have had no effect against toxin which could already have developed in the wound. The judge was not satisfied with these explanations but was not prepared to find that the doctor had been negligent in either of these respects, and these conclusions have not been challenged in the appeal.

As regards the administration of ATS Dr MacEwan admitted that he had been influenced by the consideration that if he did not take this precaution and the plaintiff died of tetanus he might have to face a law suit, but he claimed to have weighed in

his mind the conflicting considerations which arose, and in essence the justification a
which he offered for the course taken was that the circumstances in which the wound
had been caused involved a risk of tetanus infection; that the patient fell to be treated
as non-immune; that sufficient time had elapsed for tetanus toxin to develop in the
wound; and that, if it had developed, ATS was the only means of preventing tetanus.

On the question whether in the circumstances Dr MacEwan was justified in administering ATS, views were expressed by a number of medical witnesses. Dr Thompson, b
consultant bacteriologist at the Middlesex Hospital and called for the plaintiff, took
the view that it was properly administered, having regard in particular to the time
that had elapsed since the wound was sustained, and he thought that the critical
period in that respect would be five hours. He considered that in all the circumstances there was a strong indication for ATS whether or not some practitioners
might not have given it. c

Mr Sharrard, called for the Post Office, gave evidence that he would not ordinarily
have expected a general practitioner to give ATS in the circumstances and would
have expected that if he did so he would take very careful precautions having regard
to the circumstance that the plaintiff had had a previous injection of ATS. He agreed,
however, that an antibiotic could not have been effective if toxin had already
formed in the wound before its administration, and he said that he would not d
criticise a general practitioner for thinking in 1968 that a patient was non-immunised
after the expiry of ten years from his last inoculation. He also accepted that any
general practitioner would be justified in thinking that in the circumstances of this
case he must take some measures to combat the possibility of tetanus infection.

Dr Taylor, chief medical officer to the Post Office and called on their behalf, gave
evidence that he would not have administered ATS in the circumstances but that he e
was in this respect expressing a personal view and was not saying that no practitioner
could take the view that ATS should be administered, and he too accepted that it
would in the circumstances have been wrong to ignore any tetanus precautions at all.
As an example of the kind of wound for which he himself would have given ATS to a
non-immune patient who had had ATS before, he instanced one that had been
sustained 'literally in manure'. f

Dr Granville Smith, called for Dr MacEwan, gave evidence that on balance he would
have been inclined to give ATS in the circumstances of this case because of the dangers
of toxin having developed in the wound in the period since it was sustained. He
thought that he would have taken this course notwithstanding the plaintiff's having
had ATS on one previous occasion but he would not have given it if the plaintiff
had had ATS twice before.

Finally there was evidence from two medical witnesses neither of whom claimed g
to have made any specialised study of anti-tetanus precautions. Dr Hughes, called for
the plaintiff and who had attended him for the encephalitis, took the view that ATS
had been reasonably administered, and Dr Williams, a general practitioner in Northampton, considered that in the circumstances there was a strong indication for its
administration.

As to this issue the learned judge, on the evidence which we have summarised, h
came to the conclusion that Dr MacEwan had not been negligent in deciding to inject
ATS. On this appeal it has been attractively argued by counsel for the Post Office
that this conclusion was wrong. He accepted that there was in the circumstances
of the case some degree of risk of the ladder being infected by tetanus from the
footwear of Post Office employees but claimed that the risk of the wound having
been infected was slight and that the case was far removed from the instance given j
by Dr Taylor of an injury caused 'literally in manure'. In our judgment, however,
the judge's conclusion on this issue was fully justified on the evidence and we agree
with it.

The judge, rightly in our view, accepted that in deciding whether Dr MacEwan had
been negligent the test to be applied was that contained in the following well-known

passage from the judgment of McNair J in *Bolam v Friern Hospital Management Committee*[1]:

> 'I myself would prefer to put it this way: A doctor is not guilty of negligence if he has acted in accordance with a practice accepted as proper by a responsible body of medical men skilled in that particular art... Putting it the other way round, a man is not negligent, if he is acting in accordance with such a practice, merely because there is a body of opinion that takes a contrary view. At the same time, that does not mean that a medical man can obstinately and pig-headedly carry on with some old technique if it has been proved to be contrary to what is really substantially the whole of informed medical opinion.'

Applying this test to the medical literature to which reference has been made it is clear, in our judgment, that Dr MacEwan was not bound in the exercise of due care to adopt the Sharrard in preference to the Smith school of thought. So far as the oral evidence was concerned, two witnesses with specialist knowledge in this field, Dr Granville Smith and Dr Thompson, approved of the course taken, and Dr Taylor, while he would not himself have given ATS, made it clear that he was expressing a personal opinion, and both he and Mr Sharrard accepted that the case was one in which it would have been wrong to ignore any anti-tetanus precautions at all. Dr MacEwan, as already stated, himself accepted that in coming to his decision there had been present in his mind the possibility that he might be criticised, and perhaps sued, if he did not administer ATS and the patient then died of tetanus, but it is, in our view, asking too much of human nature that he should have excluded such a consideration entirely from his mind, and his evidence, which the judge clearly accepted, was that he considered the hazards both of giving and of withholding ATS. The judge obtained the impression that Dr MacEwan was 'so to speak, wedded to ATS', and it is, we think, clear that the doctor's approach to the problem was that, if there was a real risk of tetanus having developed in a wound, ATS should be given. The decision which he had to take, and to take as a matter of urgency, was a difficult one, and if in arriving at it he had put rather too much weight in the balance on one side we should have hesitated before finding him negligent but, like the judge, we see no reason to conclude that he came, in all the circumstances, to a wrong decision. It was, in our judgment, a very relevant consideration that, although the risks of tetanus having developed in the wound did not amount to any high probability, they could not be dismissed as unreal, and the consequence, if they had materialised, would be likely to be fatal unless ATS were administered.

We turn now to the second issue in the appeal. The clear effect both of the literature and of the oral evidence before the judge at the trial was that in the case of a patient who had already had an injection of ATS it was essential (and was probably in all cases desirable) that before injection of a full dose of 1,500 units of ATS a test dose should be administered with a view to ascertaining whether there was any reaction from the patient, and the procedure for this purpose, which the judge found was well recognised in 1968, was to inject just below the skin a test dose of 100 or 200 units and then, before administering the balance of the full dose, to wait for half an hour in order to see whether the patient showed any reaction, in which event it would be unwise to administer the rest of the dose. Mr Sharrard's own practice had been to adopt a more elaborate procedure involving consecutive tests for skin reaction and reaction from the deep tissues, but Dr Thompson gave evidence that it was not usual in 1968 to apply more than one test. On the basis, however, which the judge accepted, of the single test, it was clear from the evidence of Dr MacEwan that he had not followed the recognised procedure but had used a procedure of his own, which was to inject a test dose of 300 units just below the skin, wait for half a minute or a minute with the

---

1   [1957] 2 All ER 118 at 122, [1957] 1 WLR 582 at 587

needle in, and then in the absence of any reaction push in the needle deeper and administer the rest of the full dose. The reason he gave for adopting this procedure was that in his view a reaction by way of anaphylactic shock would manifest itself within the period of delay which he allowed, and in the absence of such a reaction he considered it safe to proceed. The evidence, however, of Dr Thompson was that such a brief delay was almost valueless and of Dr Granville Smith that it was not of great value, and the judge found that Dr MacEwan, in directing his test solely to anaphylactic shock, had left out of account other forms of reaction of which he must have been aware, and to which the judge (apparently rejecting in this respect certain evidence given by Dr Smith) found that the established test procedure was directed, including local skin reaction and encephalitis. On this basis, and rejecting as unconvincing a claim by Dr MacEwan that it was not possible to keep patients in a busy surgery for half an hour, the judge found that the doctor had been negligent in respect of his test dose procedure but, having made this finding, went on to hold, in the light of the plaintiff's subsequent history, that if the proper test dose procedure had been followed by waiting half an hour before administering the full dose there would most probably in that time have been no reaction from the plaintiff and the full dose would then have been properly administered; and that on this basis the doctor's negligence as to the test procedure did not cause or materially contribute to the plaintiff's injury. The validity of these conclusions, which forms the second issue in the appeal, involves questions of both fact and of law, of which it will be convenient to deal first with the questions of fact.

The medical evidence on this issue, which was very brief and in some respects not entirely satisfactory, may be summarised as follows. Dr Thompson gave evidence that there could after administration of ATS be a subsequent general reaction of which a test dose properly administered had given no indication. In answer to the question whether, in the light of the plaintiff's subsequent history, a test dose properly administered would have had no effect, he replied 'I do not think one can categorically say that'. There follows a passage in the transcript which does not make sense and we accept (on the basis of a note made at the time by leading counsel for the Post Office) that he may have said in answer to a further question that if the test dose had been properly administered there might or might not have been a reaction.

Mr Sharrard accepted that, in an article 'Tetanus Prophylaxis', published in April 1965, he had referred to 'the liability to delayed reactions even where all precautions, including a test dose, have been taken', and that delayed reactions could arise in such circumstances, but later in his evidence claimed that, if a patient was so sensitive that he was liable to develop encephalitis or to be killed by the effects of the algae, the single test dose procedure would be quite enough to show it. Dr Granville Smith, when referred to this last answer of Mr Sharrard, replied 'I do not think this is true'.

The judge on this evidence found as a fact that, important as the test procedure was, it was not by any means a certain safeguard against reaction in that, even if the proper test dose procedure were observed and no sign of reaction appeared in half an hour, a patient could still react after a full dose was administered, and in such circumstances he considered that, provided the doctor had not been negligent in deciding to inject ATS at all, what followed would be the patient's misfortune and not the doctor's fault, and he went on to find that in the light of the plaintiff's subsequent history it was 'as near certain as anything can be on an issue of this sort that a proper test dose would have made no difference'. In reaching these conclusions he made no reference to the medical evidence but we have no doubt that he had it in mind and in our judgment he was fully entitled, if he thought fit, to prefer the view expressed on this question by Dr Smith to that of Mr Sharrard, and in addition to conclude that Dr Thompson, having regard to his first answer quoted above, had fallen short of saying that a proper test dose procedure would have been *a* as likely as not to produce a reaction. But in any event this matter, in our view, was largely one of common sense and as a matter of common sense we entirely agree with the judge's conclusion that a reaction which did not, after administration of even the full dose, arise on the plaintiff's way home or in his home until at earliest three days after the injection, was most unlikely to have manifested itself during the period of half an hour for which, if the test had been properly administered, he

b would have had to wait in the doctor's surgery before a decision was taken to administer the full dose.

The remaining question on this part of the appeal is whether the judge, having made these findings of fact which we hold to have been fully justified, was right in law in holding that Dr MacEwan was not liable in damages to the plaintiff in respect of his negligence in the administration of the test dose, and we have come without

c any difficulty to the conclusion that he was right in so holding. Counsel for the Post Office, rightly in our judgment, accepted that the question which, on the authority of *Bonnington Castings Ltd v Wardlaw*[1], the judge had to ask himself for this purpose was whether the doctor's negligence in this respect had caused or materially contributed to the plaintiff's injury, and plainly on the judge's findings it had not. Recent applications of this principle are to be found in *Cummings (or McWilliams) v*

d *Sir William Arrol & Co Ltd*[2] and *Wigley v British Vinegars Ltd*[3], where employers were found to have been in breach of duty in failing to supply safety belts to, in the first case, a steel erector and, in the second, a window cleaner, but it was found in each case that the employee would not have worn the belt if it had been provided, and that on this basis the employers were not liable. A further example, closer to the present facts, of the application of the same principle is *Barnett v Chelsea and Kensington*

e *Hospital Management Committee*[4], where it was held by Nield J that, although a hospital casualty officer had been negligent in failing to see and examine a man, and in failing to admit him to the wards for treatment, the claim failed because, on the evidence, the man would have died of poisoning even if he had been admitted and treated with all due care. The same principle is, in our judgment, equally applicable to the present facts, and the decision of the House of Lords in *McGhee v National Coal Board*[5]

f (the first published report of which became available on the last day of hearing of the present case and was brought to the judge's attention) is, in our judgment, no authority to the contrary.

We would add, before leaving this issue, that it was accepted for the respondents that on them rested the onus of establishing on a balance of probabilities that the negligence of Dr MacEwan in respect of the test dose did not cause or materially contribute to the injury, but in view of the terms of the judge's findings nothing

g turns on the question of onus.

There remains the final issue in the appeal, namely, whether the Post Office are entitled to be absolved from liability for the plaintiff's encephalitis on the ground that they could not reasonably have foreseen that illness as a consequence of their admitted negligence, or that it was otherwise in law too remote a consequence of

h that negligence.

With the second of these questions, which involves the concept of novus actus interveniens, we can deal very shortly having regard to the judge's findings of fact which we have upheld, and it will be convenient to deal with it first. The judge having found that Dr MacEwan was not negligent in deciding to administer ATS, and that, although he was negligent in failing to administer a proper test dose, such

j negligence had no causative effect, it is, in our judgment, impossible for the Post

1 [1956] 1 All ER 615, [1956] AC 613
2 [1962] 1 All ER 623, [1962] 1 WLR 295
3 [1962] 3 All ER 161, [1964] AC 307
4 [1968] 1 All ER 1068, [1969] 1 QB 428
5 [1972] 3 All ER 1008, [1973] 1 WLR 1

Office to rely on any negligence of the doctor as a novus actus interveniens. It was, *a* however, argued by counsel for the Post Office that conduct of the doctor's falling short of negligence could amount to a novus actus. He relied in this respect on Lord Simonds's approval in *Hogan v Bentinck West Hartley Collieries (Owners) Ltd*[1] (a case involving the words 'where . . . incapacity for work results from the injury' in s 9(1) of the Workmen's Compensation Act 1925) of a passage in which du Parcq LJ, in his judgment in *Rothwell v Caverswall Stone Co Ltd*[2], had referred in the same context *b* to 'negligent or inefficient treatment by a doctor' as capable of amounting to a novus actus. We are by no means satisfied, having regard to subsequent references which he made[3] to 'the later negligent act of a doctor' and the 'negligence of a surgeon', that in approving this passage Lord Simonds was intending to convey that treatment by a doctor falling short of want of reasonable care could amount to a novus actus; and it is to be noted that Lord Reid[4], in his dissenting speech in *c* the same case (quoted in the judgment under appeal), considered that the dividing line in this respect was between 'that degree of lack of skill or care which may make the doctor liable in damages and that which will not'. But it is unnecessary to pursue this question further for even if, which we doubt, the law is as counsel for the Post Office claimed, the short answer to his argument is that there was in the present case no finding by the judge, or indication that he thought, that Dr MacEwan had *d* been inefficient in deciding to inject ATS, nor, in our view, would the judge have been justified in making such a finding.

Counsel for the Post Office's main argument, however, was that the onset of encephalitis was not reasonably foreseeable and that on the basis of the decision of the Privy Council in *Overseas Tankship (UK) Ltd v Morts Dock & Engineering Co (The Wagon Mound)*[5] the Post Office should not be held liable for that consequence *e* of the injury. In answer to this argument the respondent plaintiff relied on the judgment of Lord Parker CJ in *Smith v Leech Brain & Co Ltd*[6]. In that case an employee already suffering from premalignant changes had, as a result of his employers' negligence, sustained a burn which the judge found to have been the promoting agent in the development of cancer from which the employee died, and in a fatal accident claim by his widow it was argued for the defendant employers that the *f* development of cancer was unforeseeable and that on the basis of *The Wagon Mound*[5] decision the claim should be dismissed. Lord Parker CJ, however, rejected this argument in the following passages from his judgment[7] which are quoted in the judgment now under appeal:

'For my part, I am quite satisfied that the Judicial Committee in *The Wagon Mound*[5] did not have what I may call, loosely, the "thin-skull" cases in mind. *g* It has always been the law of this country that a tortfeasor takes his victim as he finds him ... The test is not whether these defendants could reasonably have foreseen that a burn would cause cancer and that Mr. Smith would die. The question is whether these defendants could reasonably foresee the type of injury which he suffered, namely, the burn. What, in the particular case, is the amount of damage which he suffers as a result of that burn, depends on the *h* characteristics and constitution of the victim.'

It is to be noted, as pointed out in the judgment under appeal, that the last of these passages is supported by very similar language used by Lord Reid in the later case

1 [1949] 1 All ER 588 at 592
2 [1944] 2 All ER 350 at 365
3 [1949] 1 All ER at 593, 594
4 [1949] 1 All ER at 607
5 [1961] 1 All ER 404, [1961] AC 388
6 [1961] 3 All ER 1159, [1962] 2 QB 405
7 [1961] 3 All ER 1159 at 1161, 1162, [1962] AC 388 at 414, 415

_a of *Hughes v Lord Advocate*[1]. We have been referred on this issue to a large number of cases, most of them decided at first instance, and in refraining from referring to them all we intend no disrespect to the very helpful arguments addressed to us on both sides.

The decision which in our view is closest on its facts to the present case is that of Parker J in the Ontario High Court in 1966 in *Winteringham v Rae*[2]. There the
_b plaintiff, who had been bitten by the defendant's dog, was given ATS by a doctor in a normal and approved manner but toxic reaction set in, leading to serum neuritis, with the result that the plaintiff sustained permanent partial paralysis. The judge was not, apparently, referred to the *Leech Brain* case[3] but, in agreement with the conclusion reached by Lord Parker CJ in that case, held the defendant liable for the serum neuritis resulting from the treatment on the basis that a wrongdoer is liable
_c for any increased injury to his victim which is due to the latter's abnormal physical susceptibility, and that this principle had been accepted in English law long before the decision in *Re Polemis*[4], which the Privy Council in *The Wagon Mound*[5] considered to be wrong in law.

Among the relevant United Kingdom decisions is that of this court in *Bloor v Liverpool Derricking and Carrying Co Ltd*[6], where a derricker who had suffered a minor
_d injury by falling in the hold of a barge later collapsed and died, by reason of a pre-existing heart condition, when an anaesthetic was administered to him in hospital, and it was held that this employers were liable for his death. This case, however, was argued on novus actus interveniens and we bear in mind that it was decided before *The Wagon Mound*[5] and under the dominance of the earlier decision in *Re Polemis*[4]. Among the relevant cases since *The Wagon Mound*[5] are, however, the Scottish fatal
_e accident claim in *Oman v McIntyre*[7], where a fat embolism resulted from leg fractures sustained by an employee, with the consequence that he died from broncho-pneumonia, and Lord Milligan found in the judgment of Lord Parker CJ in the *Leech Brain* case[3] reinforcement of his own view that it was not necessary for the defendants to have foreseen the precise type of physical injury which resulted; and in the English decisions of Paull J in *Warren v Scruttons Ltd*[8] (fractured finger tip giving rise to ocular
_f deterioration) and of Rees J in *Bradford v Robinson Rentals Ltd*[9] (frost-bite suffered by a mobile service engineer sent on a long journey in severe winter conditions in a van inadequately equipped for that purpose). In contrast to these decisions is that of Payne J in *Tremain v Pike*[10], where a herdsman employed by the defendants contracted Weil's disease, which is communicated by contact with rats' urine. The incidence of that disease is very rare among humans and there was no evidence that the farming
_g community knew or should have known of its existence or that any disease could be contracted by merely handling matter contaminated by rats. On these facts Payne J dismissed the claim, holding that there had been no breach of duty by the defendants in failing to take further precautions but that, even if there had been, the damage suffered would be too remote to be recoverable, and he distinguished the *Leech Brain*[3] and *Bradford*[9] cases on the basis that both the burn and the extreme
_h cold were foreseeable and it was only the degree of injury and the development of the sequelae which were not foreseeable, whereas in the case with which he was concerned the initial risk of infection was not foreseeable.

1 [1963] 1 All ER 705 at 706, 707, [1963] AC 837 at 845
2 (1966) 55 DLR (2d) 108
3 [1961] 3 All ER 1159, [1962] 2 QB 405
_j 4 [1921] 3 KB 560, [1921] All ER Rep 40
5 [1961] 1 All ER 404, [1961] AC 388
6 [1936] 3 All ER 399
7 1962 SLT 168
8 [1962] 1 Lloyd's Rep 497
9 [1967] 1 All ER 267, [1967] 1 WLR 337
10 [1969] 3 All ER 1303, [1969] 1 WLR 1556

In the present case the judge held that it was plainly foreseeable (1) that if oil *a*
was negligently allowed to escape on to a ladder a workman was likely to slip and
sustain the type of wound in question; and (2) that such injury might well require
medical treatment; and on this basis alone he was prepared to hold the defendants
liable for encephalitis, but he held in addition that, having regard to the nature of
the plaintiff's work and the area in which he was working, it was also foreseeable
that some form of anti-tetanus prophylactic would be deemed necessary. In the *b*
result he concluded that every relevant matter was foreseeable except the terrible
extent of the injury which was due to the plaintiff's allergy to a second dose of ATS,
in which respect the Post Office must take their victim as they found him.

On this appeal counsel for the Post Office did not challenge the correctness of
Lord Parker CJ's reasoning and conclusion in the *Leech Brain* case[1] and accepted that
some at least of the subsequent decisions fell within the same principle, but he claimed
that an essential link which was missing in the present case was that it was not fore- *c*
seeable that administration of a form of anti-tetanus prophylaxis would itself give
rise to a rare serious illness. In our judgment, however, there was no missing link
and the case is governed by the principle that the Post Office had to take their victim
as they found him, in this case with an allergy to a second dose of ATS. On this basis
the judge, in our view, was right in concluding that the first two of his findings, above *d*
referred to, were sufficient to impose liability on the Post Office, and a fortiori was
right in coming to the same conclusion on his additional third finding which we
consider to have been fully justified on the evidence. In our judgment the principle
that a defendant must take the plaintiff as he finds him involves that if a wrongdoer
ought reasonably to foresee that as a result of his wrongful act the victim may require
medical treatment he is, subject to the principle of novus actus interveniens, liable
for the consequences of the treatment applied although he could not reasonably *e*
foresee those consequences or that they could be serious.

For these reasons this appeal fails and must be dismissed.

Appeal and cross-appeal dismissed. Leave to appeal to the House of Lords granted.
f
Solicitors: *Post Office Solicitor; Shaen, Roscoe & Bracewell* (for the plaintiff); *Le Brasseur,
& Oakley* (for Dr MacEwan).

Mary Rose Plummer Barrister.

---

1   [1961] 3 All ER 1159, [1962] 2 QB 405   *g*

Pilgram v Dean

QUEEN'S BENCH DIVISION
LORD WIDGERY CJ, MACKENNA AND MAY JJ
22nd JANUARY 1974

Road traffic – Licence – Excise licence – Exhibition of licence on vehicle – Offence – Failure to exhibit licence – Defendant not in possession of licence – Defendant convicted of not having licence in force for vehicle – Whether fact that defendant has no licence defence to charge of failing to exhibit it – Vehicles (Excise) Act 1971, ss 8(1), 12(4).

A person who uses a vehicle on a public road without having an excise licence for that vehicle may be convicted both of using a vehicle for which a licence is not in force, contrary to s 8(1)*a* of the Vehicles (Excise) Act 1971, and of using a vehicle without a licence being fixed to and exhibited on that vehicle in the prescribed manner, contrary to s 12(4)*b* of the 1971 Act. It is no defence to a charge under s 12(4) that the defendant has no licence to exhibit (see p 753 *h* to p 754 *a*, post).

Notes

For the exhibition of motor vehicle licences, see 33 Halsbury's Laws (3rd Edn) 439, 440, para 742.

For the penalty for keeping or using a vehicle for which a licence is not in force, see ibid, 449, para 762.

For the Vehicles (Excise) Act 1971, ss 8, 12, see 41 Halsbury's Statutes (3rd Edn) 433, 440.

Case stated

On 6th April 1973 the appellant, Peter Pilgram, laid informations against the respondent, John Patrick Dean, alleging (i) that on 24th November 1972 at Thetford in the county of Norfolk he had used on a certain public road a motor vehicle for which a licence under the Vehicles (Excise) Act 1971 was not in force, and (ii) that at the same time and place he had used the same vehicle—

'when the licence issued under the Vehicles (Excise) Act, 1971 was not fixed to and exhibited on the said vehicle in the prescribed manner, contrary to Regulation 16 of the Road Vehicles (Registration and Licensing) Regulations, 1971[1].'

The informations were heard on 17th May 1973 by justices for the county of Norfolk acting in and for the petty sessional division of Thetford and Grimshoe sitting as a magistrates' court at Thetford. The justices convicted the respondent of using the vehicle without a licence but, being of the opinion that 'the offences of using a vehicle without an excise licence, and of failing to exhibit a current excise licence were alternative to one another', they dismissed the charge of failing to exhibit the licence. The appellant, being dissatisfied with the determination of the justices, applied for a case to be stated for the opinion of the High Court.

John Marriage QC and *T Cassel* for the appellant.
The respondent did not appear and was not represented.

LORD WIDGERY CJ. This is an appeal by case stated by the justices for the county of Norfolk sitting as a magistrates' court at Thetford on 17th May 1973.

---

a Section 8(1), so far as material, it is set out at p 752 *g*, post
b Section 12(4) is set out at p 753 *j*, post
1 SI 1971 No 450

On that day there were before them two informations laid by the appellant against the respondent. One alleged that the respondent on 24th November 1972 had used a motor car on a public road when no licence issued under the Vehicles (Excise) Act 1971 was in force for the vehicle. The other alleged that he used the same vehicle at the same time and place when the licence issued under the Vehicles (Excise) Act 1971 was not affixed to and exhibited on the vehicle in the prescribed manner, contrary to reg 16 of the Road Vehicles (Registration and Licensing) Regulations 1971.

When these two charges came before the justices they dealt first with the charge under s 8 of the Vehicles (Excise) Act 1971, namely, the keeping of this motor car on the road without there being a licence in force. They convicted of the charge and imposed a penalty the details of which are not before us. They then turned to consider the second charge, which, as I have already said, related to the use of the same vehicle on the same road at the same time but where the offence was laid under s 12(4) of the Vehicles (Excise) Act 1971 and where, therefore, the substance of the offence was a failure to exhibit the excise licence in force in respect of the motor car.

The justices, having convicted on the first charge of using the vehicle when no licence was in force, were at once somewhat hesitant whether they should impose a further penalty in respect of using the vehicle when the licence was not exhibited.

If I may say so with deference to the justices, it is understandable enough that it should strike them as a little odd that this man was being prosecuted for a second offence, namely, failure to exhibit the licence, when he had not got a licence to exhibit and had already been made subject to a penalty by the same court on the same day in respect of that offence. In the end the justices took the view that the two charges in this case were alternative and that therefore there was a defence to the second charge. They acquitted on the second charge and the matter comes before us at the instance of the prosecutor.

As counsel for the appellant vividly said when opening the case:

'This case raises the question: is it an answer to a charge of failing to exhibit an excise licence to say, "I have no licence to exhibit"?'

Put rather more formally, the question is: are these offences cumulative in the sense that both can be committed at the same time, or are they alternative?

Turning to the 1971 Act, s 8(1) provides:

'If any person uses or keeps on a public road any mechanically propelled vehicle for which a licence is not in force, not being a vehicle exempted from duty under this Act by virtue of any enactment (including any provision of this Act), he shall be liable to the greater of the following penalties, namely [and then certain excise penalties are specified].'

I pause to emphasise the fact that breach of s 8 does not result in a fine in the conventional sense, but it results in the imposition of an excise penalty.

When one turns to s 12, which deals with a failure to exhibit a licence, sub-ss (1), (2) and (3) contain provisions in regard to the obtaining of licences and their issue, and sub-s (4) creates the obligation to display an excise licence. Section 12(4) provides:

'Subject to the provisions of regulations under this Act, and without prejudice to section 8 thereof, any person who uses or keeps on a public road any mechanically propelled vehicle on which duty under this Act is chargeable without there being fixed to and exhibited on that vehicle in the prescribed manner a licence for, or in respect of the use of, that vehicle issued under this Act and for the time being in force, shall be liable on summary conviction to a fine not exceeding £20.'

a Pausing there, it would seem to me at first sight that it is possible for a person simultaneously to commit both these offences, and the indication of that which I find in the language of the Act is that s 12(4) specifically provides that the penalty thereupon imposed is to be imposed without prejudice to s 8, the section which had created the obligation to take out an excise licence.

b The justices may have been somewhat influenced by the reference in s 12(4) to regulations to be made under the Act. The regulation in question is reg 16 of the Road Vehicles (Registration and Licensing) Regulations 1971. Regulation 16(1) reads:

'Every licence issued under the Act and in force for a mechanically propelled vehicle, excepting a tramcar, shall be fixed to and exhibited on the vehicle in accordance with the provisions of this Regulation at all times while the vehicle is being used or kept on a public road . . .'

c If one just looks at those provisions of the regulation, it does look as though they are concerned only with the case of a man who has a licence and who has therefore to exhibit it because he has it. However, as was pointed out in argument, the offence of failing to exhibit a licence is not created by reg 16, which is concerned with the manner of exhibition only, and accordingly it seems to me that nothing in the terms d of reg 16(1) should be treated as counter-balancing the language of s 12(4) of the 1971 Act to which I have already referred, where it is precisely stated that the operation of that section shall be without prejudice to s 8.

But finally, if the matter is to be put beyond doubt, it is, I think, resolved by counsel for the appellant's last argument in which he draws our attention to the fact that in each of the three pieces of legislation to which I have referred, namely, ss 8 and 12 e of the 1971 Act, and reg 16 of the 1971 regulations, there is a special defence or escape clause to protect people at a time when one licence is expiring and another has to be obtained against the possibility that a driver may inevitably for a time during that operation fail to exhibit a licence on his car as required.

Section 8 contains an exemption the details of which need not be referred to, which is designed to cover a man who, for the time being, has not got a licence because f there has been delay in issue of the new one. Section 12(5) contains a similar escape clause in respect of a driver who fails to exhibit his licence for similar reasons.

Counsel for the appellant says, and I think with great force, that it would be totally unnecessary to have made this special defence available under s 12(4) if there were built into the legislation a simple defence to the effect that if you have not got a licence there is no obligation to exhibit one.

g If that had been the case, and if that defence had been available, it would have been unnecessary in my judgment to put in special defences under s 12(4), or again a somewhat similar provision in reg 16(1) of the 1971 regulations. The fact that the draftsman thought it necessary to include those special defences shows conclusively, I think, that the draftsman did not consider that it was an answer to a charge of failing to exhibit simply to say, 'I have not got a licence to exhibit'.

h For those reasons, although I have every sympathy with the justices, I think they misdirected themselves. I think there is no obstacle in law to the respondent being charged with both these offences in respect of one single incident, and I would send the case back to the justices with a direction that they should either complete the hearing or, if the hearing was already completed, that they should convict.

j **MACKENNA J.** I agree that an excise penalty can be imposed under s 8 as well as a fine under s 12 of the 1971 Act. The two provisions are not alternative. If in the exercise of their discretion the justices decide that only a small or nominal fine is called for in the present case, I do not think that anyone could say that their decision was unreasonable. I agree that the appeal should be allowed.

MAY J. I agree with both judgments which have been delivered and that the appeal
should be allowed.

Appeal allowed.

Solicitors: *Sharpe, Pritchard & Co*, agents for *J V Bates*, Norwich (for the appellant).

Jacqueline Charles Barrister.

Gian Singh & Co Ltd v Banque de l'Indochine

PRIVY COUNCIL

LORD WILBERFORCE, LORD DIPLOCK, LORD CROSS OF CHELSEA, LORD KILBRANDON AND SIR
HARRY GIBBS

18th, 19th MARCH, 6th MAY 1974

*Bank – Documentary credit – Irrevocable credit – Duty of bank to ensure requirements of
credit complied with – Special requirements of letter of credit – Credit opened on application
of company – Payment to be made to beneficiary against presentation of sight draft drawn
on company – Special condition – Draft to be accompanied by certificate signed by person named
holder of specified passport – Certificate and passport presented to bank – Signatory described
on certificate as managing director of company – Signature in representative rather than
personal capacity – Payment made by bank – Signature on certificate forgery – Whether
certificate appearing on its face to conform with requirements of letter of credit – Whether
issuing bank entitled to rely on certificate.*

The appellant company, Gian Singh & Co Ltd, carried on business in Singapore
and its managing director was Balwant Singh. On the company's instructions, the
respondent bank ('the issuing bank') opened an irrevocable documentary credit for
US $45,000 in favour of T ('the beneficiary') for the purchase of a fishing vessel built
in Taiwan. Payment under the credit was to be made against presentation of a sight
draft, drawn on the company and accompanied by, inter alia, 'a Certificate signed
by Balwant Singh holder of Malaysian Passport E-13276 . . . certifying that the
vessel has been built according to specifications and is in fit and proper condition
to sail'. Subsequently C handed to the beneficiary a certificate on the company's
letter heading. The certificate referred to the letter of credit and certified that 'I,
Balwant Singh' had inspected the vessel and that it was built according to specifications etc. It concluded with the words 'Yours faithfully, I, Balwant Singh, Passport
No. E-13276 issued at 11th Nov. 1964, GIAN SINGH & CO. LIMITED, Sd. Balwant Singh,
DIRECTOR'. The words 'GIAN SINGH & CO LIMITED' and 'DIRECTOR' were rubber
stamped. With the certificate C produced a Malaysian passport E-13276 in the name of Balwant
Singh and purporting to bear his signature. The passport and the signature were in
fact both forgeries. The certificate and passport were presented to a bank in Taipeh
('the notifying bank'), an agent of the issuing bank. The notifying bank checked
the signature on the certificate with the signature on the passport and found that they
appeared to correspond. The US $45,000 was thereupon paid to the beneficiary by
the notifying bank. The company brought an action in the High Court of Singapore
against the issuing bank in which it claimed that it had been wrongly debited with
the sum paid to the beneficiary by the notifying bank, contending, inter alia, that the
certificate did not conform with the terms of the credit since (a) the signature of
Balwant Singh was a forgery, and (b) the certificate did not, in any event, purport
to be signed by Balwant Singh personally but by the company. The trial judge

dismissed the company's claim and, on appeal, his decision was affirmed by the Court of Appeal of Singapore. On appeal,

Held – The fact that the signature was a forgery did not prevent the issuing bank from debiting the company with the sum paid by the notifying bank to the beneficiary if it had taken reasonable care to ascertain that the certificate appeared, on its face, to conform with the requirements of the documentary credit. In the circumstances the notifying bank had taken reasonable care to examine the documents and the certificate presented to it did appear to be a certificate signed by 'Balwant Singh holder of Malaysian passport E-13276' for (i) on its true construction it was clear that it was signed by 'Balwant Singh' in a personal capacity and that the rubber-stamped words were merely words of description, and (ii) in any event, the credit merely required that the certificate should bear the actual holograph signature of Balwant Singh; it did not require it to be a certificate of Balwant Singh. Accordingly the appeal would be dismissed (see p 757 *j* to p 758 *d* and p 759 *a* and *h* to p 760 *b*, post).

Equitable Trust Company of New York v Dawson Partners Ltd (1927) 27 Lloyd LR 49 applied.

Notes

For letters of credit, see 3 Halsbury's Laws (4th Edn) 99-106, paras 131-141, and for cases on the subject, see 3 Digest (Repl) 282-285, 846-858.

For the principles on which the Court of Appeal acts on hearing appeals, see 30 Halsbury's Laws (3rd Edn) 470, 471, para 886, and for cases on the subject, see 51 Digest (Repl) 814-817, 3707-3726.

Case referred to in opinion

Equitable Trust Co of New York v Dawson Partners Ltd (1927) 27 Lloyd LR 49, HL.

Appeal

This was an appeal by Gian Singh & Co Ltd against an order of the Court of Appeal of Singapore (Wee Chong Jin CJ and Tan Ah Tah J, Choor Singh J dissenting), dated 1st March 1972, dismissing an appeal by the appellant against the judgment of Chua J, dated 22nd March 1971, dismissing the appellant's claim for a declaration that the respondent, Banque de L'Indochine, had wrongfully debited the appellant's account with the respondent with the sum of $139,496·43 and that the respondent owed that sum together with interest at 8½ per cent per annum from 16th July 1968 to the appellant. The facts are set out in the opinion of the Board.

R J Parker QC and *Gordon Pollock* for the appellant.
Michael Mustill QC and *A P Goodwin* (of the Singapore Bar) for the respondent.

LORD DIPLOCK. The question in this appeal from the Court of Appeal in Singapore is whether the respondent ('the issuing bank') was entitled to debit the appellant ('the customer') with the sum of $139,496·43 paid by the Bank of Taiwan ('the notifying bank') to Messrs Thai Lung Ship Machine Manufactory ('the beneficiary') under an irrevocable documentary credit opened by the issuing bank on the instructions of the customer. The credit was expressed to be subject to the Uniform Customs and Practice for Documentary Credits (1962 Revision).

The customer is a company carrying on business in Singapore. Its managing director was Balwant Singh. The credit was opened on the application of the customer to finance the purchase by a third party, at a price of US $45,000, of a fishing vessel built in Taiwan. Payment under the documentary credit was to be made against presentation of a draft at sight, drawn on the customer and accompanied by signed commercial invoices in duplicate, and a certificate of origin, together with a document referred to under the heading 'Special Instructions' on the back of the application for the credit. This reads as follows:

'A specific condition of this L/C is that a Certificate signed by Balwant Singh holder of Malaysian Passport E-13276 ... certifying that the vessel has been built according to specifications and is in fit and proper condition to sail. In the absence of such a certificate, the L/C is not to be allowed "NEGOTIATION".'

In June 1968 documents were presented to the notifying bank in Taipeh under the credit and payment of a sight draft for US $45,000 made to the beneficiary. The only question which arises is whether the issuing bank were entitled to accept as conforming with the requirements of the letter of credit the certificate purporting to be signed by Balwant Singh which was presented. It was on paper bearing the letterhead of the customer and in the following terms:

'CERTIFICATE

'Reference to the Letter of Credit No. 2693, U.S. Dollars Forty-Five Thousand, issued by the Bank of BANQUE DE L'INDOCHINE Singapore, covering shipment of one Fishing Boat "M/V WEI CHING No. 6" Gross tonnage 80 Tons, Main Engine 5 Cylinders Diesel Engine, Horsepower 220, Built in wood. I, Balwant Singh, Holding the Malaysian Passport No. E-13276, certify that, the Fishing Boat had been inspected and built according to the specification and in the fit and proper conditions to sail. I, agreed Messrs. Thai Lung Ship Machine Manufactory, No. 51 3rd Chung Cheng Road, Keelung, Taiwan, to Negotiate the Letter of Credit No. 2693 without any objection.

Yours faithfully,
I, Balwant Singh,
Passport No. E-13276
issued at 11th Nov. 1964
GIAN SINGH & CO. LIMITED,
Sd.   Balwant Singh
DIRECTOR.'

The customer brought an action against the issuing bank in which it claimed that it had been wrongly debited with the equivalent in Singapore currency of the US $45,000 paid to the beneficiary by the notifying bank. It contended: (1) that the signature 'Balwant Singh' on the certificate was a forgery, and (2) that whether or not the signature was a forgery, the certificate did not conform with the terms of the documentary credit.

The issue of forgery

It is not disputed that when the certificate was presented to the notifying bank there was also shown to that bank a Malaysian Passport E-13276 in the name of Balwant Singh and purporting to bear his signature. Nor is it disputed that the notifying bank checked the signature on the certificate with the signature on the passport and found them to correspond. The passport, together with the certificate, had been produced by a Mr Chew, who himself held a Singapore passport no 16746. Mr Chew was subsequently identified as a man with an unsatisfactory record who was no longer in Singapore.

At the trial in the High Court before Chua J, Balwant Singh gave evidence that he had not signed the certificate and that what purported to be his signature was a forgery. His own passport was produced. Its authenticity was not in doubt. It showed that he had not left Singapore at any time after 26th April 1967. More important, it bore the date of issue, 18th September 1964, whereas on the certificate the date of issue of passport no E-13276 is stated by the signatory to be 11th November 1964. The evidence of the Assistant Controller of Immigration was that 'it is not possible for another passport issued on another day to bear the same number'. The inference is therefore that the passport no E-13276 handed to the beneficiary by Mr Chew was itself a forgery.

Chua J, however, found Balwant Singh to be an unsatisfactory witness. On a number of matters his evidence conflicted with that of the manager of the issuing bank, and where this was so the judge preferred the evidence of the latter. He also disbelieved Balwant Singh's story that he had not signed the certificate, though here there was no direct evidence to the contrary. His reasons for rejecting this part of Balwant Singh's evidence were: (1) that no hand-writing expert had been called to say that the signature on the certificate was a forgery; (2) that the certificate was on the customer's letterhead and Balwant Singh was not able to explain how this came about; and (3) that he, the judge, himself thought the signature on the certificate was 'much like' Balwant Singh's signature on his genuine passport and on the application for the documentary credit.

The Court of Appeal (Wee Chong Jin CJ, Tan Ah Tah and Choor Singh JJ) unanimously reversed the finding of fact of Chua J that the signature on the certificate was not a forgery. It has been contended before their Lordships that the judge's finding depended on his assessment of the credibility of Balwant Singh and that an appellate court was not entitled to reverse this finding. Their Lordships agree that an appellate court is seldom justified in holding that the trial judge was wrong in disbelieving evidence given by a witness whom he had an opportunity of hearing and observing in the witness box—an advantage which the appellate court does not share. But, in the instant case, the only direct evidence whether the signature on the certificate was genuine or not was that of Balwant Singh. There was no evidence which conflicted with it except the judge's own impression that the signature on the certificate was much like a specimen of Balwant Singh's signature which was admittedly genuine. This, however, is a common feature of successful forgeries, and it is notoriously dangerous for judges, in the absence of expert evidence, to rely on their own impression whether two signatures are by the same hand. Nevertheless if there had been no circumstantial evidence to support the bare denial by Balwant Singh that he had signed the certificate, it might well have been improper for the Court of Appeal to reverse the judge's finding. In their Lordships' view, however, there was powerful circumstantial evidence corroborating the direct evidence of Balwant Singh which it is clear the judge had overlooked in making up his mind as to the credibility of Balwant Singh's evidence on the issue of forgery. Although the judge accepted that the entries on Balwant Singh's passport, which was produced in court, proved that he himself could not have gone to Taiwan to present the documents, this of itself was not inconsistent with his having provided Mr Chew with that passport as well as with the certificate. What the judge failed to appreciate was the significance of the date, 11th November 1964, stated on the certificate as being the date of issue of the passport which Mr Chew had handed to the notifying bank and which contained the purported signature of Balwant Singh that the notifying bank had found to correspond with the signature on the certificate. As their Lordships have already pointed out, the divergence between that date and the date of issue of Balwant Singh's genuine passport gives rise to the inference that the passport handed to the notifying bank, and the signature of Balwant Singh on it, was a forgery.

This, together with the evidence as to Mr Chew's movements, in their Lordships' view provides strong corroboration of Balwant Singh's oral evidence that his purported signature on the certificate was also forged. Chua J's failure to appreciate this vitiates his finding that Balwant Singh was lying when he denied that he had signed the certificate and justified the Court of Appeal in reversing it.

The issue of conformity

The fact that a document presented by the beneficiary under a documentary credit, which otherwise conforms to the requirements of the credit, is in fact a forgery does not, of itself, prevent the issuing bank from recovering from its customer moneys paid under the credit. The duty of the issuing bank, which it may perform either by itself, or by its agent, the notifying bank, is to examine documents with

reasonable care to ascertain that they appear on their face to be in accordance with
the terms and conditions of the credit. The express provision to this effect in art
7[1] of the Uniform Customs and Practice for Documentary Credits does no more
than restate the duty of the bank at common law. In business transactions financed
by documentary credits banks must be able to act promptly on presentation of the
documents. In the ordinary case visual inspection of the actual documents presented
is all that is called for. The bank is under no duty to take any further steps to investigate the genuineness of a signature which, on the face of it, purports to be the
signature of the person named or described in the letter of credit.

The instant case differs from the ordinary case in that there was a special requirement that the signature on the certificate should be that of a person called Balwant
Singh, and that that person should also be the holder of Malaysian passport no
E-13276. This requirement imposed on the bank the additional duty to take reasonable care to see that the signature on the certificate appeared to correspond with
the signature on an additional document presented by the beneficiary which, on
the face of it, appeared to be a Malaysian passport number E-13276 issued in the name
of Balwant Singh. The evidence is that that is what the notifying bank had done
when the certificate was presented. The onus of proving lack of reasonable care in
failing to detect the forgery of the certificate lies on the customer. In their Lordships'
view, in agreement with all the members of the Court of Appeal, the customer
did not succeed in making out any case of negligence against the issuing bank or
the notifying bank which acted as its agent, in failing to detect the forgery.

Before the trial judge and in the Court of Appeal, the customer sought to infer
absence of reasonable care from the fact that the purported signature of Balwant
Singh on the certificate appeared between the rubber-stamped words 'Gian Singh
& Co Limited' above it and 'Director' below it. This, they submitted, ought to have
roused the suspicions of the notifying bank as to the genuineness of the signature,
and to have caused that bank to refer back to the issuing bank and the issuing bank
to refer back to the customer before making any payment under the credit. If this
had been done, the fraud would have been detected and no payment made.

In their Lordships' view the presence of the rubber-stamped words above and below
the holograph signature 'Balwant Singh' would give no ground for suspicion unless
they had the consequence of making the certificate one that did not conform with
the requirements of the credit. But if it did not conform, the customer does not need
to rely on any negligence by the issuing or notifying bank in failing to detect the
forgery; for, independently of negligence, the issuing bank would be in breach of
its contract with the customer if it paid the beneficiary on presentation of that
document.

So this appeal ultimately turns on the only question on which there was a difference
of opinion in the Court of Appeal, viz, whether the certificate, on the face of it,
conformed with the requirements of the documentary credit.

The law to be applied in answering this question is clear and simple. It was stated
succinctly by Viscount Sumner in *Equitable Trust Company of New York v Dawson
Partners Ltd*[2] in the following passage from his speech:

'It is both common ground and common sense that in such a transaction the
accepting bank can only claim indemnity if the conditions on which it is authorised
to accept are in the matter of the accompanying documents strictly observed.
There is no room for documents which are almost the same, or which will do
just as well. Business could not proceed securely on any other lines. The bank's
branch abroad, which knows nothing officially of the details of the transaction

---

1   Article 7 provides: 'Banks must examine all documents with reasonable care to ascertain
    that they appear on their face to be in accordance with the terms and conditions of the
    credit.'
2   (1927) 27 Lloyd LR 49 at 52

a   thus financed, cannot take upon itself to decide what will do well enough and what will not. If it does as it is told, it is safe; if it declines to do anything else, it is safe; if it departs from the conditions laid down, it acts as its own risk.'

This oft-cited passage has never been questioned or improved on. The later cases, many of which are cited in the dissenting judgment of Choor Singh J in the Court of Appeal, are but examples of the application of this principle by individual judges
b   to the particular terms of the letter of credit and documents with which the particular case was concerned. Their Lordships do not find it necessary to refer to them in detail, nor to express any view whether on their particular facts each one of them was rightly decided.

So the question on which this appeal turns can be stated thus: did the certificate presented to the notifying bank appear on its face to be 'a certificate signed by Balwant
c   Singh, holder of Malaysian passport E-13276, certifying that the vessel has been built according to specifications and is in fit and proper condition to sail'?

This can be sub-divided into three questions. First, apart from the signature was it a certificate in the terms called for? Second, did it appear on its face to be a certificate signed by Balwant Singh? Third, did it appear on the face of the certificate and the passport presented with it that the signatory was the holder of Malaysian passport
d   E-13276?

On the first question the customer took no point before the trial judge or before the Court of Appeal. Reliance was placed on the form of the signature alone. Before their Lordships leave was sought to rely also on minor variances between the wording of the description in the credit of the certificate required and the wording of the certificate actually presented; such as the insertion in the latter of the words 'Built in wood'
e   as descriptive of the vessel, and the use of the singular 'the specification' instead of the plural 'specifications' which appears in the credit itself. In their Lordships' opinion it is too late for the customer to take these new points for the first time now. The relevance of minor variations such as these depends on whether they are sufficiently material to disentitle the issuing bank from saying that in accepting the certificate it did as it was told. Their Lordships would not think it proper to decide issues of
f   this kind without having the benefit of the opinion of the local courts on the significance, if any, which would be attached by those who transact business in Singapore to particular minor variations in the precise words used in their transactions.

The third question their Lordships have already disposed of in dealing with the allegation of negligence in failing to detect the forgery. It is the second that is the crucial question: did the certificate appear on its face to be a certificate signed by
g   Balwant Singh?

The customer's contention can be stated in a sentence. The signature was not that of Balwant Singh but of the customer on whose behalf Balwant Singh wrote his name on the document in a representative capacity only.

Where a natural person's holograph signature to a document which creates contractual rights is associated with a reference to his being a director or manager of
h   a corporate person, it may sometimes be a difficult matter to determine whether he is signing it in a personal capacity and the reference is merely descriptive of him or whether he is signing in a representative capacity only, and not in a personal capacity at all. In their Lordships' view there is no such difficulty in the instant case. Not only is the body of the certificate couched in the first person singular, 'I, Balwant Singh', but even more significant, at the end of the certificate, after the words 'Yours
j   faithfully' and thus as much part of the signature itself as the rubber-stamped words 'Gian Singh & Co Limited' and 'Director', are the typewritten words, 'I, Balwant Singh, Passport No. E-13276 issued at 11th Nov. 1964'. This, in their Lordships' view, puts it beyond doubt that the rubber-stamped words are to be understood as words of description only.

Even apart from this, however, their Lordships agree with the majority of the Court of Appeal that the only requirement of the documentary credit is that the

certificate should bear the actual holograph signature of Balwant Singh. It does not
require that the certificate shall be the certificate *of* Balwant Singh, but merely
that whoever else the certifying party might be, the certificate should be *signed* by
him. It was. So the literal requirement of the credit was complied with. There was
no reason discernible on a mere reading of the terms of the credit for construing
the requirement that the certificate should be signed by Balwant Singh otherwise
than literally. The notifying bank did as it was told; so the issuing bank is safe. The
appeal must be dismissed with costs.

Appeal dismissed.

Solicitors: *Linklaters & Paines* (for the appellant); *Parker, Garrett & Co* (for the
respondent).

Christine Ivamy Barrister.

Nottingham Corporation v Newton
Nottingham Friendship Housing Association
Ltd v Newton

Approved in SALFORD CC v McNALLY
[1975] 2 All ER 860

QUEEN'S BENCH DIVISION
LORD WIDGERY CJ, ASHWORTH AND PHILLIPS JJ
5th APRIL 1974

*Nuisance – Statutory nuisance – Nuisance order – Duty of justices – Justices bound to make
order on finding that nuisance exists – Discretion as to implementation of order – Power
to delay operation of order – Duty of justices to take into account surrounding circumstances –
House constituting nuisance subject to unconfirmed compulsory purchase order under slum
clearance programme – Power of justices to delay operation of order in view of prospective
demolition of house – Public Health Act 1936, s 94(2).*

The tenant of a house made a complaint before justices under s 99[a] of the Public
Health Act 1936 alleging that the house was in such a state as to constitute a statutory
nuisance within s 92[b] of the 1936 Act and that the local authority and the landlords
had made default in complying with a notice by the tenant requiring them to abate
the nuisance. The complaint was heard by the justices on 18th July 1973. The
justices found that the premises were in a state of disrepair and in consequence were
a statutory nuisance. They also found that the local authority, as part of an extensive
slum clearance programme, had declared a clearance area and made a compulsory
purchase order under Part III of the Housing Act 1957. That order included the
tenant's house which had been represented by the medical officer of health as unfit
for human habitation and incapable of being made fit. The justices found that the
Secretary of State for the Environment had directed a public inquiry to be held in
November 1973 and that it was probable that confirmation of the order would follow
in February or March 1974. The local authority and the landlords opposed the
making of a nuisance order on the ground that the justices had a discretion under
s 94(2)[c] of the 1936 Act to refuse to make an order and that, in view of the imminent
demolition of the tenant's house under the slum clearance programme, no order
should be made. The justices however held that the terms of s 94(2) were mandatory

---

a Section 99 is set out at p 764 e, post
b Section 92, so far as material, is set out at p 763 d, post
c Section 94(2), so far as material, is set out at p 764 b to d, post

and accordingly made an order against the local authority and the landlords.   On appeal,

Held – Once the justices were satisfied that the house constituted a statutory nuisance, they were bound to make a nuisance order under s 94(2) of the 1936 Act but, within the framework of s 94, they had a considerable tolerance as to the precise terms which the order should take.   In particular the section gave the justices a discretion in regard to the time within which the work had to be done.   In deciding what the terms of the order should be, it was the duty of the justices to look at the whole circumstances of the case and try to make an order which was in its terms sensible and just having regard to the entire prevailing situation.   Accordingly, the justices ought to have considered the current proceedings under the 1957 Act and the imminence of demolition, in which case they might, having regard to those factors, have provided for the nuisance to be abated by March 1974 so that, if demolition proceedings had taken effect meanwhile, the danger of money being spent on the house abortively would be avoided.   Accordingly, the appeal would be allowed and the case sent back to the justices for reconsideration (see p 765 d h and j and p 766 b to e, post).

Notes

For statutory nuisances outside London, see 31 Halsbury's Laws (3rd Edn) 367-369, para 546, and for cases on the subject, see 36 Digest (Repl) 272, 273, 241-254.

For power of abatement of statutory nuisances, see 31 Halsbury's Laws (3rd Edn) 363, 364, para 540.

For the Public Health Act 1936, ss 92, 94, 99, see 26 Halsbury's Statutes (3rd Edn) 270, 272, 275.

Cases cited

R v Bristol Corpn, ex parte Hendy [1974] 1 All ER 1047, [1974] 1 WLR 498, CA.
R v Epsom and Ewell Corpn, ex parte R B Property Investments (Eastern) Ltd [1964] 2 All ER 832, [1964] 1 WLR 1060, DC.
Salisbury Corporation v Roles [1948] WN 412, DC.

Cases stated

Nottingham Corporation v Newton

This was an appeal by way of case stated by justices for the city of Nottingham in respect of their adjudication as a magistrates' court sitting at Nottingham on 18th July 1973.

1.   On 13th June 1973 a complaint was preferred by the respondent, Ivy Newton, that she was a person aggrieved as stated in s 99 of the Public Health Act 1936 and that on 2nd April 1973 a statutory nuisance existed and continued to exist at 55 Hawthorn Street Meadows in the city of Nottingham and that the Nottingham Friendship Housing Association Ltd ('the association'), being the owners of the property on which the nuisance arose, and the appellants, Nottingham Corporation ('the corporation'), being the local authority in whose area the property was, had each received a letter dated 24th April 1973 requiring them to abate the statutory nuisance by carrying out the works specified in a specification attached to the letters and that the association had made default in failing to abate the nuisance; and that the corporation had made default in failing to ensure the abatement of the nuisance.

2.   The justices found the following facts.   (a) At all material times the respondent was the occupier of the premises known as 55 Hawthorn Street Meadows in the city of Nottingham and the association were the owners thereof for the purposes of the Public Health Act 1936.   (b) The corporation were the public health authority for the city of Nottingham.   (c) On 2nd April 1973 the premises were in disrepair and by reason of such disrepair the premises were in such a state as to be a statutory nuisance under s 92(1)(a) of the 1936 Act.   (d) On 8th June 1973 the corporation served on the

association an abatement notice requiring the following works to be done: make good the dropped portion of the rear main roof eavesgutter and leave in a sound and watertight condition; suitably cover up the fireplace opening to the first floor front right room; suitably cloak the gap at the top of the upper sash of the first floor front right room window so as to reduce the draught at that point when the sash was closed; secure the loose parting bead to the rear upper landing window; make good the hole in the plaster to the ceiling of the scullery; make safe and secure the loose entrance step into the bathroom. (e) The association carried out the works in accordance with the abatement notice. (f) Save as aforesaid, the corporation had not since 2nd April 1973 served on the association any abatement notice nor had the association carried out any works to remedy the defects set out in the schedule, and the premises continued to be a statutory nuisance. (g) On 2nd April the corporation, as part of their very extensive slum clearance programme, declared a number of clearance areas and made the Nottingham (Meadows No 3) Clearance Compulsory Purchase Order under Part III of the Housing Act 1957. The order applied to 1,674 homes and, of those, 1,450, including 55 Hawthorn Street, had been represented by the medical officer of health as unfit for human habitation and incapable of being made fit at reasonable expense. (h) The condition of 55 Hawthorn Street was no worse than that of many other houses to which the order applied. (i) The Secretary of State for the Environment directed that a public inquiry into the order should be held on 13th November 1973 and it was probable that he would confirm the order in February or March 1974; on confirmation of the order the corporation would begin demolishing the houses to which the order applied.

3. The corporation and the association contended that on a true construction of Part III of the Public Health Act 1936, and in particular ss 93 and 94 thereof, a public health authority had a discretion whether to cause a statutory nuisance to be abated by summary procedure under that Act or by some other procedure and that the justices had a similar discretion in proceedings brought under s 99 of the 1936 Act and that by reason of the facts set out in para 2 (g), (h) and (i) above the justices should exercise their discretion and not make a nuisance order against the association.

4. The respondent contended that the provisions of s 93 of the 1936 Act were mandatory and that, having found the facts set out in para 2(a), (b), (c), (d), (e) and (f) above, the justices were legally bound to make a nuisance order against the association.

[Paragraph 5 noted the cases to which the justices were referred.]

6. The justices were of the opinion that, having found the facts set out in para 2(a), (b), (c), (d), (e) and (f) above, they were legally bound to make a nuisance order against the association and had no discretion to take into account the other facts set out in para 2, and accordingly they made an order against the association requiring them to carry out by 30th September 1973 such of the work in the specification as should be sufficient to abate the statutory nuisance. Furthermore, in the exercise of their discretion under s 99 of the 1936 Act, they ordered that the corporation abate the nuisance by carrying out such of the work as remained by that date to be completed.

Nottingham Friendship Housing Association Ltd v Newton

The case stated was in similar terms to that stated in *Nottingham Corporation v Newton* above.

Alan Fletcher for the corporation.
D J R Wilcox for the association.
James Harper for the respondent.

LORD WIDGERY CJ. These are two appeals by case stated by justices for the city of Nottingham in respect of their adjudication as a magistrates' court at Nottingham on 18th July 1973. The two appeals arise out of identical facts and raise the *a* identical point, therefore it is sufficient for present purposes if I deal with the first one, which is Nottingham Corporation against the respondent, Mrs Ivy Newton.

The appeals arise out of the fact that within the city of Nottingham at 55 Hawthorn Street there is a house occupied by the respondent as the tenant. Of that house the Nottingham Friendship Housing Association Ltd ('the association') are the owners, and the corporation are of course the local authority for the area in which the house
b is situated. At the relevant time, which means about the middle of 1973, the house was out of repair to such a state as to be prejudicial to health. When that situation arises there are a number of ways in which it can be corrected. Of the ways in which a defective house can be rendered in proper repair for occupation, the two outstanding ones relevant to the present appeals are first the power of the local authority or other aggrieved persons to instigate summary proceedings under the terms of the
c Public Health Act 1936, and secondly the power that the housing authority possess under the Housing Act 1957, which is in the main directed to the house being made fit at the expense of the owner or being demolished either alone or as part of a substantial area of redevelopment.

The course that was adopted in this case was the Public Health Act 1936. Section 92 has the cross-heading 'Statutory nuisances'. Subsection (1) provides:

d 'Without prejudice to the exercise by a local authority of any other powers vested in them by or under this Act, the following matters may, subject to the provisions of this Part of this Act, be dealt with summarily, and are in this Part of this Act referred to as "statutory nuisances", that is to say:—(a) any premises in such a state as to be prejudicial to health or a nuisance...'

e So this house was a statutory nuisance within the definition in s 92.

Section 93 provides:

'Where a local authority are satisfied of the existence of a statutory nuisance, they shall serve a notice (hereinafter in this Act referred to as "an abatement notice") on the person by whose act, default or sufferance the nuisance arises or continues, or, if that person cannot be found, on the owner or occupier of the
f premises on which the nuisance arises, requiring him to abate the nuisance...'

So, taking the literal text of the Act, as soon as the local authority are satisfied that this house is in such a state as to be prejudicial to health, it would appear that they are bound to serve a notice initiating proceedings under the Act. In fact it is quite clear to me and not disputed by counsel for the respondent that the fact that the imperative word 'shall' is used in that context does not mean that the local authority
g are bound to choose this method of dealing with the statutory nuisance in preference to any others which may be open to them. In particular I am satisfied that if in a particular case the local authority can, of the two Acts of Parliament in question, legally take either, namely summary proceedings under the Public Health Act 1936 or alternatively proceedings under the Housing Act 1957, the local authority have a choice in the matter and is not compelled to take proceedings under the 1936 Act.
h To that extent the word 'shall' is not as mandatory as it appears.

Section 94(1) provides:

'If the person on whom an abatement notice has been served makes default in complying with any of the requirements of the notice, or if the nuisance, although abated since the service of the notice, is, in the opinion of the local
j authority, likely to recur on the same premises, the authority shall cause a complaint to be made to a justice of the peace, and the justice shall thereupon issue a summons requiring the person on whom the notice was served to appear before a court of summary jurisdiction.'

In my view the use of the word 'shall' there in regard to the authority again leaves open to the authority the alternative courses under different statutes which may be

available to it; but if the authority causes complaint to be made to a justice of the   *a*
peace, the justice of the peace in my view is bound to issue a summons. The word
'shall' as applied to him has its normal imperative meaning, because no alternative
meaning is appropriate or appears from the language of the section.

Section 94(2) provides:

'If on the hearing of the complaint it is proved that the alleged nuisance exists,
or that although abated it is likely to recur on the same premises, then, subject   *b*
to the provisions of subsections (4) and (5) of this section the court shall make an
order (hereafter in this Act referred to as "a nuisance order") for either, or both,
of the following purposes—(*a*) requiring the defendant to comply with all or
any of the requirements of the abatement notice, or otherwise to abate the
nuisance, within a time specified in the order, and to execute any works necessary
for that purpose; (*b*) prohibiting a recurrence of the nuisance, and requiring   *c*
the defendant, within a time specified in the order, to execute any works necessary
to prevent a recurrence ... Where a nuisance proved to exist is such as to render
a building, in the opinion of the court, unfit for human habitation, the nuisance
order may prohibit the use of the building for that purpose until a court of
summary jurisdiction, being satisfied that it has been rendered fit for human
habitation, withdraws the prohibition.'   *d*

Lastly at this stage I refer to s 99 of the Act, which gives authority for an aggrieved
person other than the local authority to initiate proceedings. Section 99 provides:

'Complaint of the existence of a statutory nuisance under this Act may be
made to a justice of the peace by any person aggrieved by the nuisance, and
thereupon the like proceedings shall be had, with the like incidents and   *e*
consequences as to the making of orders, penalties for disobedience of orders
and otherwise, as in the case of a complaint by the local authority, but any order
made in such proceedings may, if the court after giving the local authority an
opportunity of being heard thinks fit, direct the authority to abate the nuisance.'

What happened in this case was that the house in question being in such a condition   *f*
as to be prejudicial to health and no action having been taken by the corporation,
the respondent wrote to the corporation and to her landlord, the association, requiring
them to abate the statutory nuisance constituted by the fact that these premises
were in a state prejudicial to health.

The association did nothing in consequence of that notice directly, but on 8th June
1973 the corporation served on the association an abatement notice under the 1936
Act, requiring them to do a limited amount of work, less than the totality of the   *g*
schedule which was relied on by the respondent in claiming that the premises were
in a state prejudicial to health. The association did that limited amount of work
which the corporation required them to do, but did no more, and in due course the
matter came before the justices consequent on a complaint made by the respondent.

On 18th July, when the matter was before the court, the justices found that at all   *h*
material times the respondent was the occupier of the premises and that the association were the owners. Further they found that the corporation were the public
health authority for the city of Nottingham. They found as a fact that on 2nd April
1973 the premises were in disrepair, and the particulars of disrepair are comprised
in the longer of the two schedules to which I earlier referred, namely the description
of the totality of the work necessary to put them in a state of repair, and the justices
found that in the state in which they were, the premises were a statutory nuisance   *j*
under s 92(1).

The corporation resisted the making of a nuisance order by the justices on that
material for this single and understandable reason. The corporation were already
involved in substantial redevelopment of the city of Nottingham and they had plans
well advanced for demolishing the houses in the area in which the respondent's

a house was, and they took the view, which is sensible enough in all conscience, that there was no point in spending a great deal of money on this house if it was going to be demolished with the rest of the street in a short time. The justices found that on 2nd April the corporation, as part of a very extensive slum clearance programme, had declared a clearance area and made a compulsory purchase order in respect of the area in which the respondent's house stood. The order applied to no less than

b 1,674 homes, and, of those, 1,450, including the respondent's house, had been represented by the medical officer of health as unfit for human habitation and incapable of being made fit at a reasonable expense. They found 55 Hawthorn Street was no worse and probably no better than other houses in the clearance area, that the Secretary of State for the Environment had directed a public inquiry to be held in November 1973, three or four months after the justices' hearing and that it was

c probable that the result of the inquiry, and probably confirmation of the orders, would follow in February or March 1974.

Before the justices the corporation and the association took what seems to me, I must say, to be a very bold line of argument, that the justices had a discretion to make no order at all on the respondent's complaint, and that the justification for their making no order would be the imminent demolition of the premises pursuant

d to the plans made by the local authority to which I have already referred.

The justices would not accept that contention; they looked at s 94, saw that the section provided that the justices shall make an order, and they took the word 'shall' to have its ordinary meaning, and I think they were right. I think the word is imperative in the sense that there is no general discretion in s 94 for the justices to say, although the basic facts have been proved to establish a statutory nuisance, we will make no order at all; I think they are required to make an order.

e The justices having rejected the main argument for the corporation then imposed restrictions on themselves which I think were unjustified, because when one comes to para 6 of the case and sees what the justices' opinion was, it was to this effect:

'We were of the opinion that, having found the facts as set out in para. 2 (a) (b) (c) (d) (e) and (f) above we were legally bound to make a nuisance order against

f the Association [I pause to say the facts referred to in para. 2 (a), (b), (c), (d), (e) and (f) are the facts I have already read up to but excluding the findings in regard to the Housing Act 1957 proceedings; the justices went on to say:] and had no discretion to take into account the other facts set out in para. 2, [in other words they are as I see it directing themselves that in deciding what order to make, they should disregard the Housing Act proceedings and the imminence of

g demolition altogether; they go on: and we accordingly made an order against the Association requiring them to carry out by 30 September 1973 such of the work in the said specification as should be sufficient to abate the statutory nuisance. And, in the exercise of our discretion under s. 99 of the said Act, we further ordered that the [corporation] abate the said nuisance by carrying out such of the said work as remained by that date to be completed.'

h In my view the position of the justices as a matter of law was this: once they were satisfied that the house constituted a statutory nuisance they were bound to make a nuisance order under s 94 but they have within the framework of the section a considerable tolerance as regards the precise terms which the nuisance order shall take.

i It must be directed, of course, to the abatement of the nuisance, that is the purpose of the order, but the section makes it clear that the justices have a discretion whether to require the owner to do the whole of that work which was referred to in the abatement notice as opposed to only part of it. Further the section expressly gives a discretion in regard to the time within which the work has to be done, and in my judgment would certainly enable the justices to divide the work into phases or programmes requiring some to be done quickly and others to be done at a later time.

If there is real danger to the health of the occupier of the house, the justices of
course, within the terms of s 94, can impose a prohibition on the house being lived in
until the work is done, a prohibition which might have been unpopular with the
respondent, but nevertheless it was urged by her counsel as one of the factors which
might be taken into account.

In deciding within that wide ambit of detailed discretion just what the terms of
the nuisance order should be, I have no doubt it is the duty of the justices, as common
sense dictates, to look at the whole circumstances of the case and to try and make an
order which is in its terms sensible and just having regard to the entire prevailing
situation. They were wrong in my judgment in closing their eyes to the Housing
Act proceedings and the imminence of demolition, and had they had regard to those
factors as well as all the other relevant factors, it may be that they would have provided for the nuisance to be abated by perhaps March 1974 so that if the demolition
proceedings had taken effect meanwhile, the danger of money being spent on the
house abortively in view of the subsequent demolition would be avoided.

I think the justices were very nearly right in this case, but I conclude that they were
wrong in restricting the factors to which they had regard, and I think this appeal
should be allowed to the extent that the case should be sent back to the justices asking
them to reconsider their decision in the light of the discretion within the precise terms
of s 94(2), and in the light of all the prevailing circumstances, and endeavour to come
to what seems to them to be a sensible and just conclusion.

ASHWORTH J. I agree.

PHILLIPS J. I also agree.

Appeal allowed. Case remitted.

Solicitors: *Sharpe, Pritchard & Co* (for the corporation); *Hunt, Dickson & Willatt*,
Nottingham (for the association); *H E G Hodge*, Child Poverty Group (for the
respondent).

N P Metcalfe Esq Barrister.

Livingstone-Stallard v Livingstone-Stallard

FAMILY DIVISION
DUNN J
18th, 19th MARCH 1974

*Divorce – Behaviour of respondent – Behaviour such that petitioner cannot reasonably be
expected to live with respondent – Reasonableness – Test to be applied – Conduct amounting
to constructive desertion – Gravity of conduct such as to justify dissolution – Relevance as
criteria – Issue to be determined as question of fact taking into account characters and
personalities of parties – Matrimonial Causes Act 1973, s 1(2)(b).*

In construing s 1(2)(b)[a] of the Matrimonial Causes Act 1973 it is not appropriate to
import notions of constructive desertion or to analyse the degree of gravity of
conduct which would be sufficient to justify dissolution of the marriage. The proper

---

a   Section 1(2), so far as material, provides: 'The court hearing a petition for divorce shall not
    hold the marriage to have broken down irretrievably unless the petitioner satisfies the
    court of one or more of the following facts, that is to say . . . (b) that the respondent has
    behaved in such a way that the petitioner cannot reasonably be expected to live with the
    respondent . . .'

a   approach is to determine as a question of fact whether the respondent has behaved in such a way that the particular petitioner before the court cannot reasonably be expected to live with him, taking into account the whole of the circumstances including the characters and personalities of the parties (see p 770 *g* and *h* and p 771 *b* and *c*, post).

    Dictum of Ormrod J in *Pheasant v Pheasant* [1972] 1 All ER at 591 doubted.

b   **Notes**
For proof that the respondent has behaved in such a way that the petitioner cannot reasonably be expected to live with the respondent, see Supplement to 12 Halsbury's Laws (3rd Edn) para 437A, 3, and for cases on the subject, see 27(1) Digest (Reissue) 358, 359, 2630-2633.

c   **Cases referred to in judgment**
Ash v Ash [1972] 1 All ER 582, [1972] Fam 135, [1972] 2 WLR 347, 27(1) Digest (Reissue) 358, 2630.
Katz v Katz [1972] 3 All ER 219, [1972] 1 WLR 955.
Pheasant v Pheasant [1972] 1 All ER 587, [1972] Fam 202, [1972] 2 WLR 353, 27(1) Digest (Reissue) 358, 2631.

d   **Petition**
By a petition dated 29th January 1973 the wife, Brenda Vera Livingstone-Stallard, sought the dissolution of her marriage alleging that the husband, Herbert James Livingstone-Stallard, had behaved in such a way that she could not reasonably be expected to live with him. The husband by his answer denied that the marriage

e had broken down or that he had behaved in the manner alleged in the petition. The facts are set out in the judgment.

    Michael Beckman for the wife.
    E V Paynter Reece for the husband.

f

    DUNN J. In this suit the wife seeks a dissolution of her marriage on the ground of irretrievable breakdown under s 1(2)(*b*) of the Matrimonial Causes Act 1973. The husband by his answer denies that the marriage has broken down irretrievably and he denies that he has behaved in the manner alleged by the wife in her petition.

    The parties were married on 5th December 1969, the husband being then 56 and

g the wife 24 years of age. He had been married before in 1942 to a lady some 15 years his junior. There was one son of that marriage who was born in 1944 and the marriage ended in divorce in the middle of the 1960s, the first wife having obtained a decree nisi in a defended suit on the ground of cruelty.

    Shortly after the war the husband started an insurance broking business at Westcliff-on-Sea, and his son, in due course, followed him into the business. He has

h quite recently retired from the business and is living in the former matrimonial home at 8 Branscombe Gardens, Thorpe Bay.

    The parties met some years before they were married. The wife's father is a clerk employed by the Customs and Excise. She herself was employed by that department before her marriage, although for a short time she was employed part-time in the husband's office. They became engaged in about 1968. The

j engagement was a stormy one and was broken off twice. The husband, not surprisingly, had doubts about the difference in age. The wife frankly told me that she herself had doubts about his temper and dominant character, but in the end she came to the conclusion that once they were married, things would improve and their marriage could be a success; in due course they were married. The marriage was neither easy nor long-lived, because within two months of the marriage the wife had left and gone back to her parents. The parties remained apart until November 1970 when the husband joined the wife at a flat at Cotswell Road, Westcliff-on-Sea, which she had bought jointly with her mother from the proceeds of a gift which had been made her by a cousin.

They lived together there for some two years during which the one child of the family, Jason, was conceived and born. In August 1972 there was bought in their joint names a house at 8 Branscombe Gardens, Thorpe Bay, which was conveyed to them jointly as tenants in common, on terms that on any sale of the house the wife should receive a payment of £5,000 and the balance should be split equally between them. That is set out in the conveyance; the reason for it I was told is that the wife provided £5,000 for the purchase, the balance being found from a bank loan and moneys put up by the husband. It is right to say that the husband disputes the validity of that division of the property as set out in the deed, saying that he never intended the deed to be drawn up in that way.

The wife moved from the flat to 8 Branscombe Gardens in October 1972, and a month later she left, taking the child back to her parents. In January 1973 she filed her petition seeking the dissolution of marriage. As the house partly belonged to her, she was naturally reluctant to leave it. She moved back with the child in June 1973, though living quite separate from her husband. This arrangement did not work, so the child went back to the wife's parents, and since then the wife has been living partly at the former matrimonial home—at any rate sleeping the night there—and partly at her parents' house.

Her case is that her husband was, as she put it, a critical and non-loving man who treated her from the very first, not as a wife but as a rather stupid child. She said that even on their honeymoon, when they spent a week at the Cumberland Hotel, her husband was abusive to her. It is quite plain from the evidence of the husband that even at that stage there were difficulties between them. The wife had referred to her holiday with a female cousin the previous summer. The husband objected to this and I accept the wife's evidence that the result was to make him rude, boorish and critical of her during the honeymoon.

They first went to live at 69 Cavendish Gardens, Westcliff-on-Sea. The wife complained that from the time that they started married life together he criticised her behaviour, her friends, her way of life, her cooking and he even criticised her dancing. 'They were all petty little things' she said 'but my life was not my own. I dreaded hearing his latch-key in the door'. The husband agreed that he did criticise her, but he said that he was quite justified in so doing, because she was what he called a very constructive person. I had some difficulty in understanding what he meant by that or how it could be said to justify his criticism. But it appeared at the end, after he had been cross-examined, that he formed the opinion that she was worthy of criticism, because she was a person who potentially did things well and by his criticism would be able to do things even better.

An indication of his attitude towards his wife was, that in the witness box, he referred to her variously as 'the girl', 'the lady' and 'Brenda Foster' which was her maiden name—but not as 'my wife' or 'Brenda'. I accept her complaint that right from the very start he did criticise her over these petty things in the way she described them.

On one occasion, she said, in the course of an argument, he spat at her. He denies this and I do not accept his denial. I found his evidence evasive on this issue. She also told me that when he was angry he called her names and she described them. In the witness box he spoke in a quiet carefully modulated voice; I do not believe that it was his real voice, particularly when he was angry. This was a man who was capable of controlled anger and I accept her evidence that he called her names when he was angry. The only name he would admit to having called her was a bastard. No doubt he called her that and many other names as well.

She also told me that on one occasion he tried to kick her out of bed. His explanation was that he was a restless sleeper and that he jumped and jerked about in his sleep. He denied that he ever kicked his wife intentionally. I do not accept that explanation and I do not believe that the wife made that up. I am satisfied that on that occasion he did try to knock her out of bed, as she said, because he was bad-tempered.

Another incident, small in itself, related to the washing of the wife's underclothes. She said that he complained because she left her washing soaking in the sink overnight, and said that it was indicative of the way she was brought up. This particularly annoyed her because the husband did exactly the same thing himself. He denied either washing his underclothes and leaving them in the sink or of criticising her about it. I am satisfied that the evidence of the wife had a ring of truth about it. I thought that the husband was a man who was very set in his ways and had a good conceit of himself. He was inclined to look down on his wife, her background and upbringing. I accept that on that occasion he criticised her in that way and added the twist that it was indicative of how she had been brought up.

The wife also complained about another incident which was, perhaps, the most illuminating incident so far as the husband's character was concerned. They had had some photographs taken at their wedding, and not very long afterwards the photographer came round with the wedding album. The husband was out and the wife, exercising what one would imagine was normal courtesy and hospitality, offered the photographer a glass of sherry which he accepted and she had a glass of sherry too to keep him company. When the husband came home he went to his cocktail cabinet, took out the sherry bottle and said: 'You have drunk half a bottle of sherry. Don't you ever go to my cocktail cabinet again'. He asked her who she had been drinking with, and she told him what had happened. He forbade her to 'give refreshment to tradespeople again'. He was naturally cross-examined about his attitude and it appeared to be that if his wife took a glass of sherry with a tradesman —and he apparently classed the photographer as a tradesman—then the glass of sherry might, as he put it, impair her faculties, so that the tradesman might make some kind of indecent approach to her, and that was the justification of his conduct on that occasion. To my mind it is typical of the man.

Not very long after that the wife left. She left as the result of one of the few scenes of violence which took place during the marriage. I have no doubt that the wife was right when she said the husband came back in bad temper, and although there is a dispute between the two of them as to the details of what happened, there is no doubt whatever that the husband took hold of the wife, bundled her out of the house on a cold February evening and locked the door so that she could not get back in again. She was exceedingly upset, and being a young woman of spirit she broke a pane of glass to try and get in again. The husband, in order to prevent her getting in, got a bowl of water and threw it through the broken glass. She said it soaked her and I accept that it did. It may very well be, as the husband says, that she also threw some water through the window, but he was, after all, in possession of the house and she was being excluded from it. She went across to her mother's, which was very close, and stayed there. A few days later she went to her doctor, who found that she had bruise marks on her arms and legs and that her injuries were consistent with her having been violently assaulted. He said that she was in a very nervous state for about six weeks and required sedation.

She bought the flat, 66 Cotswell Road, and moved there. I accept that the husband was continually attempting to annoy her by going to the flat, trying to get in, following her in his car and things of that kind. But in the late summer of 1970 she agreed to a reconciliation and the husband moved into the flat. One of the criticisms which is made by counsel for the husband of the wife's case is that there is no specific incident either pleaded or referred to in evidence during the two years that they lived there together. The husband's case was that those two years were perfectly happy. The wife agreed that they were happy at times, but she said:

'He did not really want me, he only wanted to annoy me. He was always packing his bags and threatening to go away, he was always nasty, he was unkind, he belittled me in front of people and refused to meet my friends, he belittled my opinions.'

He said to her on more than one occasion: 'In order for them to be happy, wives have to be subservient to their husbands'.

I accept the wife's evidence as being completely consistent with the husband's character and attitude as I saw it in the witness box. I accept the submission of counsel for the wife that in a case which depends on a course of conduct and on the character of the other spouse rather than on a series of dramatic incidents, perhaps of violence, the effect of the conduct may be nonetheless serious in the long run even though it is not practical to specify particular incidents as having impinged on the memory of the wife as incidents in their own right.

In October 1972 the wife moved with Jason, who, by that time, was nearly a year old, to join the husband at 8 Branscombe Gardens. She said they did not get on there; he vented his anger with other people on her, blaming her for the mistakes which the decorators had made, that his temper was very easily roused, that he slammed the doors, pushed her about and adopted a generally menacing attitude towards her. I accept that evidence of hers.

The marriage ended for practical purposes on 13th November 1972. On that day the husband was late for his evening meal. According to the wife he was very offhand when he arrived. He sat down and simply picked up a newspaper and started to read it, and she, in exasperation, took it away from him and he said 'I will kill you' and that developed into an argument. She said he was in a terrible rage by the end of the evening. She could not take any more and she took the child to her parents and followed herself in January when her petition was filed.

The husband said at the end of his evidence that he was anxious for a reconciliation and although his wife was constructive, honest and reliable, she had some of his own failings; unhindered, they could make a success of their marriage as he loved her very dearly. If by the word 'unhindered' the husband intended to convey the impression that the wife's mother had a hand in the breakdown of this marriage, I reject that suggestion. I saw the wife's mother in the witness box. She impressed me as being an objective and sensible person. There was put to her in cross-examination a letter which she wrote to her future son-in-law on 18th March 1969, which showed that even at that time there had been some quarrel between the parties. The wife's mother was, in effect, taking the husband's side and apologising for her daughter's behaviour, saying that she had an arbitrary streak in her.

I am quite satisfied that this marriage has broken down irretrievably. The wife told me that in no circumstances would she continue to live with her husband, partly because he is so irresponsible with Jason and takes so little interest in him. I cannot, of course, dissolve this marriage unless I am satisfied that the husband has behaved in such a way that the wife cannot reasonably be expected to live with him. That question is, to my mind, a question of fact, and one approach to it is to assume the case was being tried by a judge and jury and first to consider what the proper direction to the jury would be, and then to put oneself in the position of a properly-directed jury in deciding the question of fact.

Counsel for the husband has referred me to the cases—all of which have been so far decided at first instance—of *Ash v Ash*[1], *Pheasant v Pheasant*[2] and *Katz v Katz*[3], and has submitted that incompatibility of temperament is not enough to entitle a petitioner to relief. The behaviour must be of sufficient gravity so that the court can say that it would, under the old law, have granted a decree of divorce on the ground of constructive desertion. He also submitted that the best approach is to

1 [1972] 1 All ER 582, [1972] Fam 135
2 [1972] 1 All ER 587, [1972] Fam 202
3 [1972] 3 All ER 219, [1972] 1 WLR 955

apply the test which was applied in the constructive desertion cases, bearing in mind that the parties are married and that the conduct must be sufficiently grave to justify a dissolution of the marriage; weighing the gravity of the conduct against the marriage bond or, as he put it, against the desirability of maintaining the sanctity of marriage. I have, in the past, followed the reasoning of Ormrod J in *Pheasant v Pheasant*[1], but, on reflection and with respect to that learned judge, I am not sure how helpful it is to import notions of constructive desertion into the construction of this statute. Nor, speaking for myself, do I think it helpful to analyse the degree of gravity of conduct which is required to entitle a petitioner to relief under s 1(2)(*b*) of the 1973 Act. The Act, as Lord Denning MR has emphasised in another context, is a reforming statute and the language of the subsection is very simple and quite easy for a layman to understand. Coming back to my analogy of a direction to a jury, I ask myself the question; would any right-thinking person come to the conclusion that this husband has behaved in such a way that this wife cannot reasonably be expected to live with him, taking into account the whole of the circumstances and the characters and personalities of the parties? It is on that basis that I approach the evidence in this case.

The wife was young enough to be the husband's daughter and plainly considerable adjustment was required on both sides. Counsel for the husband submitted that she had known him a long time and that she knew exactly the kind of man that she was marrying and the complaints which she made are trivial. She cannot bring herself within the subsection, simply because the character of her husband does not suit her. He further submitted that the reality of this case was that this young woman had simply got fed up and walked out, and walked out pretty soon too. I accept that she was a strong-minded young woman but I am satisfied that she was anxious for the marriage to last. She wished it to continue and wished to have children, bring them up, have her own home and did her best so far as she was able to adjust to her husband's character. He was said, by his counsel, to be meticulous. I agree with counsel for the wife that more suitable adjectives would be self-opinionated, didactic and critical and I accept that the husband's approach was to educate her to conform entirely to his standards.

In my judgment, he patronised her continually and submitted her, as I have found, to continual petty criticisms. His general attitude is well exemplified by the incident of the sherry and the photographer, whom he called 'the tradesman'. I accept that many of the incidents were, or might appear to be, trivial in themselves and that there is a paucity of specific incidents between September 1970 and November 1972. But taking the facts as I have found them in the round in relation to the husband's character, in my judgment they amount to a situation in which this young wife was subjected to a constant atmosphere of criticism, disapproval and boorish behaviour on the part of her husband. Applying the test which I have just formulated, I think that any right-thinking person would come to the conclusion that this man had behaved in such a way that this woman could not reasonably be expected to live with him. There will accordingly be a decree nisi under s 1(2)(*b*) of the Matrimonial Causes Act 1973.

Decree nisi.

Solicitors: *Mervyn Beecham & Bodiam*, Southend-on-Sea (for the wife); *Elman, Flint, Jefferies & Co*, Southend-on-Sea (for the husband).

R C T Habesch Esq Barrister.

---

1 [1972] 1 All ER at 591, [1972] Fam at 208

Paterson v Chadwick
Paterson v Northampton and District
Hospital Management Committee

QUEEN'S BENCH DIVISION

BOREHAM J

28th JANUARY, 22nd FEBRUARY 1974

Distinguished in ACKBAR v GREEN
[1975] 2 All ER 65

Discovery – Production of documents – Parties – Order for discovery against person not a party to proceedings – Claim in respect of personal injuries or death – Meaning of 'in respect of' – Claim for personal injuries against hospital – Plaintiff's solicitors allowing claim to become statute-barred – Action against solicitors for breach of duty – Documents relating to injury in possession of hospital – Application for order for discovery against hospital – Whether claim against solicitors claim 'in respect of' personal injuries – Administration of Justice Act 1970, s 32(1).

In February 1969 the plaintiff visited a hospital, under the management and control of the appellants, for dental treatment. In the course of that treatment she was given an anaesthetic by injection. Subsequently she alleged that the injection had been given negligently and that in consequence she had sustained personal injuries. Some months later she consulted solicitors and instructed them to act for her in a claim for damages against the appellants. The solicitors took certain steps in the matter but no proceedings were commenced by February 1972 when the plaintiff's claim against the appellants became barred by effluxion of time. In February 1973 the plaintiff issued a writ against the solicitors claiming damages for breach of contract or duty in allowing her claim to become statute-barred. For the purpose of that action the plaintiff's advisers considered it necessary to obtain from the appellants discovery of the medical records and other documents relating to her injury. Accordingly the plaintiff applied under s 32(1)[a] of the Administration of Justice Act 1970 for an order for discovery of those documents on the ground that they were relevant to an issue arising in her claim against the solicitors. The master made the order sought. On appeal, the appellants contended that the plaintiff was not entitled to the order since the proceedings against the solicitors were not, within s 32(1), proceedings in which a claim was being made 'in respect of personal injuries'.

Held – The words 'in respect of' in s 32(1) were words of the widest import signifying some connection or relation between the two subject-matters referred to. Since the nature and extent of the plaintiff's personal injuries formed an essential ingredient in the proof of her claim against the solicitors, there was a clear connection or relation between the claim and the personal injuries. It followed therefore that the plaintiff was a party to proceedings in which a claim was being made 'in respect of personal injuries' and accordingly the appeal would be dismissed (see p 775 c to h, post).

Dictum of Mann CJ in *Trustees, Executors & Agency Co Ltd v Reilly* [1941] VLR at 111 applied.

Notes

For discovery against persons not parties to proceedings in personal injuries claims, see Supplement to 12 Halsbury's Laws (3rd Edn) para 10A.

For the Administration of Justice Act 1970, s 32, see 40 Halsbury's Statutes (3rd Edn) 1102.

---

a   Section 32(1), so far as material, is set out at p 774 a and b, post

Case referred to in judgment
Trustees, Executors & Agency Co Ltd v Reilly [1941] VLR 110, 47 ALR 105, 2 Digest (Repl)
155, *690.

Interlocutory appeal
This was an appeal by Northampton and District Hospital Management Committee
against an order of Master Jacob made on 15th October 1973 whereby he ordered
discovery of certain documents on the application of the respondent, Sarah Paterson
('the plaintiff'), the plaintiff in an action against Francis Claude Basil Chadwick. The
appeal was heard in chambers but judgment was delivered in open court. The facts
are set out in the judgment.

Colin Colston for the appellants.
Alan Cooper for the plaintiff.

Cur adv vult

22nd February. **BOREHAM J.** read the following judgment. This is an appeal
by the Northampton and District Hospital Management Committee (whom I shall
refer to as the 'appellants' from a decision of Master Jacob given on 15th October
1973, whereby he ordered the discovery of various medical case notes and other
medical documents. This appeal was heard in chambers by me and has been
adjourned into open court for judgment at the request of both parties.

It would, in the circumstances, be inappropriate to deal with the facts in any
greater detail than is necessary for an understanding of the issues which arise on
this appeal. The short facts are these. On 14th February 1969 Mrs Paterson (whom,
for convenience, I will refer to as 'the plaintiff') attended the Northampton Hospital,
a hospital which is under the management and control of the appellants, for dental
treatment. For the purpose of that treatment, or in the course of it—it matters not
which—she was given an anaesthetic by injection and she alleges that that injection
was negligently given by a servant or agent of the appellants, with the result, as
she further alleges, that she has sustained a serious and permanent disability of her
left hand.

Some time after that event, she says in July 1969—I think her solicitors, or her
then solicitors, put the date at somewhere about May 1970, but for the present
purpose the difference is immaterial—she consulted solicitors, Messrs Douglas and
Douglas, and instructed them to act for her in connection with a claim for damages
for personal injuries against the appellants. It is sufficient to say that it appears that
the solicitors made certain enquiries, and obtained medical opinions, but in fact no
proceedings were commenced. In the result, the plaintiff's claim against the
appellants was barred by effluxion of time in February 1972.

Thereafter, the plaintiff consulted other solicitors and on 22nd February 1973
a writ was issued against her former solicitors claiming damages for their breach
of contract or breach of duty. It is unnecessary to pursue the steps that have been taken
so far in those proceedings in any detail. It is sufficient to say that by April 1973
the plaintiff's statement of claim and the defence in the action had been served.

It was then considered necessary for the plaintiff's present advisers to obtain from
the appellants discovery of the medical records and other documents relating to the
plaintiff's injury. On 5th July 1973 the plaintiff applied by summons, pursuant to
RSC Ord 24, r 7A, for an order for discovery by the appellants of various documents
on the ground that they are documents material to the issues raised in the proceedings between the plaintiff and her former solicitors. Happily there is no need
to particularise those documents because the appellants have very fairly conceded
that, if the plaintiff is otherwise entitled to discovery, then these are all material
documents. As I have already indicated on 15th October 1973 Master Jacob made
the order for discovery and it is from his order that the appellants now appeal.

The procedure is new and the enabling provisions are to be found in Part III, and in particular in s 32(1), of the Administration of Justice Act 1970. Part of that sub-section reads thus:

'On the application, in accordance with rules of court, of a party to any proceedings in which a claim in respect of personal injuries to a person or in respect of a person's death is made, the High Court shall, in such circumstances as may be specified in the rules, have power to order a person who is not a party to the proceedings and who appears to the court to be likely to have or to have had in his possession, custody or power any documents which are relevant to an issue arising out of that claim [to disclose and produce those documents].'

It is not disputed, as I have understood it, that the application has been made in accordance with the rules of court. What is said by the appellants is that the plaintiff is not a party to any proceedings in which a claim in respect of personal injuries is made. This harks back to the precise wording of s 32(1). The argument proceeds thus. Her claim, it is said, against her erstwhile solicitors is a claim in respect of a lost cause of action, or in respect of a lost chance. It is not a claim in respect of personal injuries. The effect of this argument, as I understand it, would be to limit the claim referred to in s 32(1) to a claim against the person or persons who caused the injuries, or against those vicariously liable for those injuries. In support of that contention, the appellants rely first on the Report of the Committee on Personal Injuries Litigation[1], and particularly on that part of the report which deals (and I use the expression compendiously) with medical evidence and medical reports. It is unnecessary, in my judgment, for me to go in detail into the various parts of the report which were quoted to me, because I gain no assistance for present purposes from such passages. It may well be, as the appellants have argued, that the Winn Committee had uppermost in their minds what are usually called, or what usually fall under the heading of, claims for damages for personal injuries in the restricted sense contended for by counsel for the appellants, but I do not find it possible to allow anything in that report to restrict the meaning of the statutory provisions which I have to interpret.

Next it is contended that s 32(1) of the 1970 Act is a section which is not of general application, and that the words 'proceedings in which a claim in respect of personal injuries is made' are words of limitation. Counsel for the appellants has compared those words with, for instance, the provisions of the Limitation Act 1963, s 1(2). He contends that the words in s 1(2) of the 1963 Act would be wide enough to include the plaintiff's present proceedings against her solicitors. I think it unnecessary to read that subsection. He goes on to contend that the words of s 1(2) of the 1963 Act, or similar words, would have been adopted in s 32(1) of the 1970 Act if the wide meaning which Master Jacob accepted had been intended by the legislature.

With respect to counsel's argument, I for my part obtain no assistance from a comparison of s 32(1) of the 1970 Act and s 1(2) of the 1963 Act. The 1963 Act as in the case of all Acts of that kind, is of necessity dealing with causes of action, and s 1(2) first refers to the various causes of action and then goes on to limit by description the types of claim which that subsection is intended to cover. Section 32(1) of the 1970 Act, on the other hand, makes no mention of, and is not concerned with, causes of action. It refers to claims, on whatever causes of action those claims may be founded. In my view, the difference in the language between those two subsections is accounted for by this difference in emphasis, and I find it impossible, in present circumstances, to give any greater significance to that comparison.

Counsel has also referred me to a number of decisions in which the words 'in respect of' have been considered by the courts of this country and the courts of Australia. They were referred to by counsel for the appellants in order to distinguish *a* them. I think it sufficient that I say, without going into any detailed analysis of those cases (and I say it with deference both to the authorities and to counsel's submission), that I do not find those decisions in the main of assistance. In each case to which reference was made the words were given their ordinary and unrestricted meaning. In each case the court was considering the words 'in respect of' in different contexts. For my part it is sufficient that I leave those cases there, save for one. That one is

b a decision of the Supreme Court of Victoria, in *Trustees, Executors & Agency Co Ltd v Reilly*[1], and it is the judgment of the Chief Justice, Mann CJ. I refer to it for this reason: that it is the one case in which reference was made and an explanation attempted—an explanation rather than a definition—of these words 'in respect of', again in the particular context in which Mann CJ found them. It is right that one should say this. This was a decision given under the Farmers Protection Act 1940, by s 5 of which

c farmers were protected from process or proceedings 'in respect of' a debt unless a notice had been served on the farmer in question. In the decision, Mann CJ was faced with the contention that the proceedings were ejectment proceedings; that they were not proceedings in respect of a debt, but in respect of failure to deliver up possession. In the course of giving his judgment[2], Mann CJ attempted this explanation of the words 'in respect of':

d 'The words "in respect of" are difficult of definition but they have the widest possible meaning of any expression intended to convey some connection or relation in between the two subject-matters to which the words refer.'

I think it unnecessary for me to go any further. For me those words of Mann CJ provide helpful guidance, at any rate as to the ordinary meaning of the words 'in

e respect of', and I accept that guidance.

In my view there is nothing in the arguments of counsel for the appellants which can induce me to take the view that anything except the ordinary and natural meaning of those words should be applied in construing this particular section of the 1970 Act. In my judgment the words 'in respect of' in s 32(1) convey some connection or relation between the plaintiff's claim and the personal injuries that she

f sustained, that is, a claim against her ex-solicitors.

If this is the correct approach, then there remains this question: is there in the proceedings brought by the plaintiff against her solicitors a connection or relation between her claim and her personal injuries? To answer that question it suffices, in my view, to say that the nature and the extent of her personal injuries form an essential ingredient in the proof of her claim. Unless she can prove such injuries, she will fail. In these circumstances, it seems to me, whatever her cause of action

g may be—and I accept, as counsel for the appellants contends, that it lies in contract —there is a clear and firm connection or relation between her claim and her personal injuries.

In my judgment, therefore, to quote the words of s 32(1) of the 1970 Act, she is a person who is a party to 'proceedings in which a claim in respect of personal injuries

h to a person' is made, and, as such, she is entitled to the order made by Master Jacob.

In the result, my judgment is that this appeal fails and must be dismissed.

Appeal dismissed. Leave to appeal to the Court of Appeal granted.

Solicitors: *Bower, Cotton & Bower*, agents for *Becke, Phipps*, Northampton (for the

j appellants); *Williams & Co*, Bedford (for the plaintiff).

E H Hunter Esq Barrister.

---

1 [1941] VLR 110
2 [1941] VLR at 111

Maris v Rotherham Corporation

NATIONAL INDUSTRIAL RELATIONS COURT
SIR HUGH GRIFFITHS, MR R BOYFIELD AND MR H ROBERTS
4th FEBRUARY, 11th, 28th MARCH 1974

Dictum of SIR HUGH GRIFFITHS at
779 disapproved in DEVIS & SONS v
ATKINS [1977] 3 All ER 40

*Industrial relations – Unfair industrial practice – Compensation – Assessment – Matters to
which complaint relates caused or contributed to by aggrieved party – Reduction of award
where just and equitable – Unfair dismissal – Matters to which complaint relates – Meaning
– Conduct of employee having caused dismissal – Conduct of employee not having contributed
to unfair character of dismissal – 'Matters to which complaint relates' not restricted to unfair
character of dismissal – All circumstances surrounding dismissal to be taken into account –
Whether employers entitled to reduction in award in consequence of employee's conduct –
Industrial Relations Act 1971, s 116(3).*

The employee who worked as a superintendent of a corporation cleansing department was convicted on a number of charges of dishonesty in connection with his
employment. The employee had been suspended on full pay by his employers
pending the criminal proceedings. Following his conviction the employers were
advised that if he was reinstated in his former employment his fellow workers
in the department would not object. The employee was reinstated accordingly.
In the event the employee's fellow workers took strong exception to the employee's
reinstatement. Faced with the prospect of industrial action the employers decided
to reverse their earlier decision and to dismiss the employee. On a complaint of
unfair dismissal by the employee, the industrial tribunal found that the reason
for the employee's dismissal was the threat to the employers of industrial action.
Since s 33(1) of the Industrial Relations Act 1971, however, precluded them from
taking account of that threat as a reason for dismissal, they were constrained to
hold that the employee had been unfairly dismissed, but in assessing compensation
they held that, since the employee's loss had stemmed wholly from his own breach
of duty, it would not be 'just and equitable in all the circumstances', within s 116(1)[a]
of the 1971 Act, to award him any compensation. The employee appealed, contending that the tribunal was not entitled to reduce his award under s 116(1) on
account of his own conduct and furthermore that the award could not be reduced
under s 116(3)[b] since he had in no way caused or contributed to the unfairness of his
dismissal which had been occasioned solely because of the industrial pressure brought
against the employers.

Held – The tribunal, having found that the dismissal was unfair, was not entitled
to make a reduction in the award of compensation under s 116(1) for that subsection
was concerned solely with the fair assessment of compensation on the assumption
that some award should be made. The tribunal was however entitled to take
into account under s 116(3) the extent to which 'the matters to which the complaint

---

a Section 116(1) provides: 'Where in any proceedings on a complaint under this Act the
   Industrial Court or an industrial tribunal makes an award of compensation to be paid by
   a party to the proceedings (in this section referred to as "the party in default") to another
   party (in this section referred to as "the aggrieved party"), the amount of the compensation
   shall, subject to the following provisions of this Part of this Act, be such amount as the
   Court or tribunal considers just and equitable in all the circumstances, having regard to
   the loss sustained by the aggrieved party in consequence of the matters to which the complaint relates, in so far as that loss was attributable to action taken by or on behalf of the
   party in default.'

b Section 116(3) is set out at p 780 j to p 781 a, post

relates' had been caused or contributed to by the employee's conduct, and to reduce its assessment accordingly.   The words 'the matters to which the complaint relates' in s 116(3) were not restricted to the conduct of the employers in dismissing the employee unfairly but brought into consideration all the circumstances surrounding his dismissal and required the tribunal to decide what, if any, part the employee's own conduct had played in contributing to his dismissal and what, if any, reduction should be made in consequence; for that purpose it was not necessary to show that the employee's conduct had contributed to the unfair character of his dismissal.   The tribunal was therefore entitled to treat the employee's conduct as extinguishing any right to compensation under s 116(3) and the appeal would be dismissed accordingly (see p 779 h, p 780 j and p 784 b and e to g, post).

Dictum of Sir John Donaldson P in *Earl v Slater & Wheeler (Airlyne) Ltd* [1973] 1 All ER at 151 disapproved.

Notes
For fair and unfair dismissal, see Supplement to 38 Halsbury's Laws (3rd Edn) para 677B, 20, and for the general principles as to assessment of compensation on a complaint to the Industrial Court or an industrial tribunal, see ibid para 677F, 20.

For the Industrial Relations Act 1971, ss 33, 116, see 41 Halsbury's Laws (3rd Edn) 2098, 2143.

Cases referred to in judgment
Earl v Slater & Wheeler (Airlyne) Ltd [1973] 1 All ER 145, [1973] 1 WLR 51, [1973] ICR 508, NIRC.
Morris v Gestetner Ltd [1973] 3 All ER 1168, [1973] 1 WLR 1378, [1973] ICR 587, NIRC.
Norton Tool Co Ltd v Tewson [1973] 1 All ER 183, [1973] 1 WLR 45, [1973] ICR 501, NIRC.
Scottish Co-operative Wholesale Society Ltd v Lloyd [1973] ICR 137, NIRC.
Springbank Sand and Gravel Co Ltd v Craig [1974] ICR 7, NIRC.
Street v Wrights Insulations Ltd (1973) 8 ITR 5, NIRC.
Winterhalter Gastronom Ltd v Webb [1973] ICR 245, NIRC.
York Trailer Co Ltd v Sparkes [1973] ICR 518, NIRC.

Cases also cited
Carling v National Union of General & Municipal Workers [1973] ICR 267, NIRC.
Clarkson International Tools Ltd v Short [1973] ICR 191, NIRC.
Donnelly v Feniger & Blackburn Ltd [1973] ICR 68, NIRC.
Goad v Amalgamated Union of Engineering Workers [1972] ICR 429, NIRC.
Monksfield v National Society of Operative Printers, Graphical & Media Personnel [1972] ICR 469, NIRC.
Morrish v Henlys (Folkestone) Ltd [1973] 2 All ER 137, NIRC.
Munif v Cole & Kirby Ltd [1973] ICR 486, NIRC.
St Anne's Board Mill Co Ltd v Brien [1973] ICR 444, NIRC.
Shipside (Ruthin) Ltd v Transport and General Workers Union [1973] 3 All ER 514, NIRC.
Vokes Ltd v Bear [1974] ICR 1, NIRC.
Wellman Alloys Ltd v Russell [1973] ICR 616, NIRC.

Appeal
This was an appeal by George Robert Maris against the decision of an industrial tribunal (chairman A J H Morrison Esq) sitting in Sheffield, dated 1st November 1973, that the appellant was not entitled to compensation for unfair dismissal from the respondents, Rotherham Corporation.   The facts are set out in the judgment of the court.

James Mitchell for the appellant.
Seddon Cripps for the corporation.

Cur adv vult

28th March. **SIR HUGH GRIFFITHS** read the following judgment of the court. The appellant appeals against the refusal of an industrial tribunal to award him compensation for unfair dismissal.

The appellant was employed by the respondent corporation as superintendent of the cleansing department at a salary in excess of £2,600 per annum. He was first employed in 1967 and for some years gave good service to the corporation but then he fell from grace. In February 1973 the corporation discovered that he had been rendering fraudulent claims for expenses. On 25th July 1973 he was prosecuted at Doncaster Crown Court where he pleaded guilty to eight cases of attempting to obtain property by deception and other offences of fraud and asked for a further 24 offences of a similar nature to be taken into consideration. He was fined and ordered to contribute to the prosecution's costs. The tribunal expressed their view of these offences in the following language:

'It is clear to the tribunal that in committing these offences he was in grave breach of his duty to the corporation and his offences involved dishonest misappropriation of ratepayers' money. He must also be held to have set a deplorable example to the other corporation employees.'

Since the offences first came to light in February the appellant had been suspended on full pay. On 15th August 1973 the corporation's highways committee considered the question of his future employment by the corporation. The highways committee were naturally anxious about the effect that his reinstatement might have on the men in the cleansing section. The committee were advised by the borough engineer, who had overall responsibility for the cleansing department, that the appellant would be readily accepted by the men. The committee accepted this advice and recommended that the appellant be reinstated on condition that he was removed from the list of persons authorised to use his car on corporation business and that he was asked to repay an amount to be determined in respect of the car claims estimated at something over £100. The appellant resumed his full duties on 17th August 1973.

The borough engineer had been wholly mistaken in the advice he gave to the highways committee. The men took grave exception to the reinstatement of the appellant and they passed a resolution in the following terms:

'We, the work force of the Rotherham Corporation Cleansing Department, deplore the reinstatement of [the appellant]. We would point out that [the appellant] was convicted of defrauding rate-payers. We understand that he has been suspended on full pay up to the time of his trial; he was fined £200 for the crime, therefore his punishment was nil. We further point out that a dangerous precedent is being set here insomuch that any workman found guilty of stealing Corporation property, etc. must, in all fairness, now continue to hold his job. We therefore urge the Highways Committee to reconsider their decision in regard to [the appellant]. We further urge that the rate-payers of Rotherham take note of our action and give us their support. We further request that the Highways Committee receive a delegation of shop stewards and branch secretaries in order to discuss the problem. At this time in the day we will accept Mr. D. Simpson's suggestion to carry on working under protest without prejudice to any action we may contemplate in the future.'

As the direct consequence of this resolution the highways committee met again on 20th August 1973 when they saw representatives of the men's unions and reconsidered their earlier decision. The highways committee feared that in the event of *a* reinstatement of the appellant they would be faced with either a strike or industrial action short of strike on the part of the employees in the department. They therefore determined to reverse the decision that they had taken three days earlier and on 21st August 1973 they informed the appellant that they had decided to terminate his employment as a cleansing superintendent. The appellant was offered alternative employment with the corporation as highways maintenance coordinator which

b involved a reduction of salary in the order of £500 a year. The appellant appealed against the decision through the corporation's domestic appeals procedure but his appeal was dismissed on 14th September 1973. On 19th September 1973 the appellant was given one month's notice to terminate his employment as cleansing superintendent which expired on 20th October 1973 and he then took up duties as highways maintenance co-ordinator on the following day.

c The tribunal came to the following conclusions: first, that the appellant was, in the course of his employment, in grave breach of duty; secondly, that if on the occasion of the first meeting of the highways committee on 15th August 1973 they had decided not to recommend reinstatement but had recommended dismissal no industrial tribunal would have come to the conclusion that that dismissal was in all the circumstances otherwise than fair. Thirdly, the tribunal were satisfied that

d the true reason for the appellant's dismissal was because the corporation were faced with a threat of industrial action on the part of the union members in the cleansing department if they continued to employ the appellant as superintendent of the cleansing department.

The tribunal were satisfied that this was pressure applied 'in the course of an industrial dispute' within the meaning of s 167 of the Industrial Relations Act 1971.

e They were satisfied that the men's threat of action was of the description included in s 33(2) of the 1971 Act and they therefore concluded that the provisions of s 33(1) of the 1971 Act precluded them from taking any account of that pressure when deciding whether or not the corporation had established a reason for the dismissal within the meaning of s 24(1) of the 1971 Act. The tribunal were therefore driven to the conclusion that the corporation having failed to establish a reason for the

f dismissal they must deem it to have been unfair. They expressed themselves as follows:

> 'It follows therefore that the tribunal must come to the conclusion, as it does, that the dismissal was unfair, even though we are unanimously satisfied that the [appellant] was the author of his own misfortune by reason of his offences.'

g In a later passage the tribunal said: 'We consider that all his loss stemmed directly from and was caused by his own breach of duty.'

Against these findings it comes as no surprise to this court that the tribunal refused to award compensation. We are quite satisfied that they were right to do so. Technically, however, we are satisfied that they arrived at this sensible conclusion by the wrong route.

h The tribunal relied on the provisions of s 116(1) of the 1971 Act as entitling them to award no compensation because they did not consider it was 'just and equitable in all the circumstances' to do so. This subsection, however, is not concerned with whether or not relief should be given; it is concerned solely with the fair assessment of compensation on the assumption that some award should be made. This construction of the section was adopted by this court in *Norton Tool Co Ltd v Tewson*[1] and consistently applied by the court since then.

j In *Morris v Gestetner Ltd*[2] Sir John Donaldson P, in giving guidance to tribunals on the general approach to the assessment of damages, said this of s 116(1):

---

1 [1973] 1 All ER 183, [1973] 1 WLR 45
2 [1973] 3 All ER 1168 at 1175, [1973] 1 WLR 1378 at 1385

'Assume also that, contrary to the fact, the wrongful action was taken volun- *a*
tarily and in no way as a result of pressure by the third party. On these assumptions, assess compensation in accordance with s 116(1). This involves the tribunal in asking itself the question: "On these assumptions, what sum would it
be just and equitable to award to the complainant in all the circumstances
(including those which are being assumed for the purposes of this stage of the
assessment) having regard to the loss sustained by the complainant in conse- *b*
quence of the matters to which the complaint relates, in so far as that loss was
attributable to action taken by or on behalf of the party in default?" We apolo-
gise for the complexity of the question, but it has necessarily to follow the wording of the statute. The answer provides a figure to which we will refer as "the
base figure".'

Unfair dismissal is one of a number of unfair industrial practices about which *c*
complaint may be made to a tribunal. In the case of complaints other than those
relating to dismissal s 106(2) and (3) of the 1971 Act provide as follows:

'(2) If on a complaint under this section, other than a complaint relating to
dismissal, the industrial tribunal finds that the grounds of the complaint (as
specified in paragraphs (*a*) to (*c*) of the preceding subsection) are well-founded, *d*
the tribunal may, if it considers that it would be just and equitable to do so,
grant to the complainant either or both of the remedies specified in the next
following subsection, as the tribunal considers appropriate.
'(3) The remedies which may be granted are—(*a*) an order determining the
rights of the complainant and of the employer in relation to the action specified
in the complaint; (*b*) an award of compensation, to be paid by the employer to *e*
the complainant, in respect of that action.'

The tribunal is charged by these subsections with the duty of deciding whether or
not it would be just and equitable to make an award of compensation. It is only
if it decides that it should make such an award that it then turns to s 116(1) of the 1971
Act for guidance as to the principles it should follow in assessing the award. Section *f*
116(1) does not require the tribunal to ask itself again the same question which it
has already decided under s 106(3), namely whether an award should be given or
not. Section 109 provides similar provision in respect of complaints under ss 107
and 108.

The position in respect of a claim relating to unfair dismissal is somewhat different.
Section 106(4) requires the tribunal first to consider whether or not it should recommend re-engagement. Then sub-s (5) provides: *g*

'Where on such a complaint the industrial tribunal finds that the grounds
of the complaint are well-founded, but—(*a*) the tribunal does not make such a
recommendation as is mentioned in subsection (4) of this section, or (*b*) the
tribunal makes such a recommendation, and (for whatever reason) the recommendation is not complied with, the tribunal shall make an award of com- *h*
pensation, to be paid by the employer to the complainant, in respect of the
dismissal.'

So the position is that if the tribunal finds that the dismissal is unfair it is required
to assess compensation.

For the reasons already given it is not entitled to refuse to make an award by *j*
virtue of the provisions of s 116, but it is required to take into account the provisions
of s 116(3), which provides:

'Where the Industrial Court or industrial tribunal finds that the matters to
which the complaint relates were to any extent caused or contributed to by any
action of the aggrieved party in connection with those matters (whether that

action constituted an unfair industrial practice on his part or not), the Court or tribunal shall reduce its assessment of his loss to such extent as, having regard to that finding, the Court or tribunal considers just and equitable.'

It is submitted on behalf of the appellant that this subsection can have no application to the facts of this case because the appellant in no way contributed to the unfairness of his dismissal. It is said that once the highways committee had decided to reinstate the appellant they had forgiven his past misconduct and had waived any right to rely on that as a ground for dismissing him. They dismissed him solely because of the industrial pressure placed on them for which the appellant was in no way directly responsible. So it is said that in this case the appellant is entitled to full compensation without any reduction by virtue of his own misconduct. If it is right to look solely at the 'unfair' feature of the dismissal there is force in this submission, although the result would appear to be an affront to common sense.

The first authority on which the appellant relies is *Earl v Slater & Wheeler (Airlyne) Ltd*[1]. In that case an estimating and planning engineer was taken ill and was absent from work. During his absence the employers discovered certain matters which indicated that his work was unsatisfactory. On his return to work he was handed a letter of dismissal informing him that he was being dismissed because his work was unsatisfactory and that a replacement had been appointed. He was given no opportunity to deal with the complaints made against him or to state his case before being dismissed. The court held that the dismissal was unfair because the employee had been given no opportunity to give an explanation of his unsatisfactory work. The court was, however, also satisfied that if he had been given the opportunity he would have been unable to put forward a satisfactory explanation and dismissal was inevitable. In dealing with compensation the court said[2]:

'This brings us to whether the employee is entitled to any compensation and, if so, how much. Compensation falls to be assessed in accordance with the general principles set out in s 116 of the 1971 Act.'

Then after setting out s 116(1) and (3) the judgment continues[2]:

' "The matters to which the complaint relates" is the conduct of the . . . employers in dismissing the appellant unfairly, contrary to his rights under s 22 of the 1971 Act. It was the appellant's own conduct or lack of capability which led to his dismissal, but he in no way caused or contributed to its unfair character which is the essence of his complaint. There are, therefore, no grounds for reducing the assessment of compensation under s 116(3). But what alone rendered the dismissal unfair was that the appellant was not given any opportunity to explain the various matters which had come to light during his absence. On the findings of the tribunal that he has in fact no valid explanation to offer, the unfairness of the dismissal, i e the failure to give him an opportunity of attempting to do so, appears to have caused him no loss. We do not think that there is any room in this field for the award of nominal compensation and in the light of the tribunal's finding that the appellant suffered "no conceivable injustice" they must, even if they had found unfair dismissal, have assessed the compensation at "nil".'

This decision was followed in *Winterhalter Gastronom Ltd v Webb*[3] where the court said:

'This approach to the valuation of compensation is open to a number of valid criticisms. In the first place, upon the tribunal's findings that the employee

1   [1973] 1 All ER 145, [1973] 1 WLR 51
2   [1973] 1 All ER at 151, [1973] 1 WLR at 58
3   [1973] ICR 245 at 250, 251

was dismissed not by reason of any misconduct but because he did not appear to be capable of doing the job properly, it is difficult to see how any deduction from the compensation falls to be made pursuant to section 116(3) of the Industrial Relations Act 1971 ... The complaint in this case referred not to dismissal but to unfair dismissal. Of course lack of capability caused the dismissal, but how did it cause or contribute to the unfairness of the dismissal, which is the essence of the complaint?: see *Earl* v. *Slater & Wheeler (Airlyne) Ltd*[1]. In the absence of any evidence that any conduct on the part of the employee contributed to the failure to give him a proper warning, there should have been no deduction, pursuant to section 116(3).'

In Scotland the court appears to have adopted a wider construction of the subsection. The first decision is *Street v Wrights Insulations Ltd*[2]. An employee had been summarily dismissed for leaving the site where he was working before the time he should have stopped work. The industrial tribunal decided that his dismissal was unfair but reduced the amount of compensation payable by four-fifths because they thought that the employee was largely to blame for his dismissal by leaving the site before time. Lord Thomson, in giving the judgment of the court, said[3]:

'The tribunal found that the appellant was aware that he should have remained on the site until 4.30 p.m. and upon the evidence which they heard they took the view that the appellant himself: "... was very largely to blame for his dismissal through his action in leaving the site before the time which he knew was the proper time for doing so."

'In our judgment the tribunal were entitled to take that view and, so taking it, to find that the matter to which the complaint relates, that is to say, his dismissal, was to some extent caused or contributed to by his own action, that is to say, in leaving before the time which he knew was the proper time for him to leave.'

This passage does not distinguish between the dismissal and the unfair nature of the dismissal although it might be said that in this case even if one took the narrower test of the unfair nature of the dismissal the man's conduct had directly contributed to it.

The next decision is *Scottish Co-operative Wholesale Society Ltd v Lloyd*[4]. In that case an area manager was dismissed by his employer, after 26 years employment, on the grounds of inefficiency. The court upheld the tribunal's finding of unfair dismissal, but they reduced the compensation applying the provisions of s 116(3). Lord Thomson said[5]:

'The tribunal stated with reference to [s 116(3)]: "We do not consider that the matters to which the [employee's] complaint relates were caused or contributed to by any action of the [employee]. No adjustment of an assessment of [his] loss is necessary under this subsection." We accept that the tribunal were entitled to find that in terms of section 24(6) of the Act of 1971 the employee's dismissal was unfair. But having considered with care the whole evidence in the case, including the correspondence and productions, we are driven to the conclusion his dismissal was at least to some extent caused or contributed to by his own actions. The tribunal having heard the witnesses plainly thought that there was a personal issue between the employee and the regional manager and on some points at least preferred the evidence of the employee. This we

---

1   [1973] 1 All ER 145, [1973] 1 WLR 51
2   (1973) 8 ITR 5
3   8 ITR at 6
4   [1973] ICR 137
5   [1973] ICR at 143, 144

accept. But there can in our opinion be no doubt that he failed to respond satisfactorily to the numerous letters of complaint addressed to him, he failed to obey the instructions given to him regarding stock reduction and he failed as regards sales to reach his own target far less that of the regional manager. We would add that in the matter of the offer of alternative employment the employers in our view did all that could reasonably be expected of them. In our opinion the employers' real fault lay in their failure to give the employee plain and specific warning that, if he showed himself in the result incapable of complying with their instructions as regards the running of the stores in his area and in reaching the target they desiderated, he would be dismissed. In our judgment in all the circumstances the employee can fairly be held as being in part responsible for his own dismissal and his contribution we assess at 30 per cent.'

Finally we were referred to *Springbank Sand and Gravel Co Ltd v Craig*[1]. The employee was the driver of a mechanical shovel which broke down through lack of lubrication. The employers blamed the driver and dismissed him. The tribunal were satisfied that the breakdown was due to the employee's negligence in failing to check the oil. Considering that the penalty was disproportionate to the offence, they held that the dismissal was unfair. The tribunal refused to reduce the award of compensation by virtue of the employee's conduct. Dealing with the employer's appeal from that part of their decision Lord Thomson said[2]:

'It may be that at some later date the decision of this court in *Scottish Co-operative Wholesale Society Ltd v. Lloyd*[3] and *Earl v. Slater & Wheeler (Airlyne) Ltd.*[4] will be found to be irreconcilable in their differing construction of the meaning and application of section 116(3) of the Act of 1971. We do not think we need to enter on to that somewhat delicate territory now. In our opinion the present case on its facts and in its presentation is radically different from *Earl v. Slater & Wheeler (Airlyne) Ltd*[4]. In *Earl*[4] the tribunal found the employee was not entitled to any compensation for unfair dismissal because of his conduct. The court reached the same conclusion "for reasons which differ slightly from those given by the tribunal". In the present case the tribunal, applying in their view the approach to section 116(3) followed in *Earl v. Slater & Wheeler (Airlyne) Ltd.*[4], have found the employee entitled to the same compensation as that to which he would have been entitled if his negligence had not led to his dismissal. They reached the result because "in our opinion he in no way caused or contributed to the unfair character of his dismissal which is the essence of his complaint." As we understand the employee's position "the unfair character of his dismissal", i.e. breach of proper and fair procedure as regards his dismissal, has never been and certainly when he appeared before us was not "the essence of his complaint". His complaint was and is that he was dismissed because there was a lack of oil in the differential of his loader and the responsibility for that according to him was not his. "I am innocent" was his reiterated protest. We agree with the tribunal that the method of dismissal was unfair and that the dismissal was unfair in terms of the Industrial Relations Act 1971, but in our opinion in circumstances like the present when the dismissal is held to have resulted from negligence on the employee's part it is for the tribunal to consider in terms of section 116(3) to what extent if any they consider a reduction in their assessment of compensation would be just and equitable.'

1   [1974] ICR 7
2   [1974] ICR at 11, 12
3   [1973] ICR 137
4   [1973] 1 All ER 145, [1973] 1 WLR 51

It has been previously recognised that the decisions of the court sitting in Scotland and that sitting in England have adopted a different construction and approach to s 116(3), but it has not as yet been necessary to decide between them (see *York Trailer Co Ltd v Sparkes*[1]). The time has now come, however, in this case when the court must decide which line of authority it will follow. Having had the advantage of full argument we are satisfied we should follow the Scottish decisions. 'The matters to which the complaint relates' in the subsection are words of wide import and bring into consideration all the circumstances surrounding the dismissal, requiring the tribunal to take a broad common sense view of the situation and to decide what, if any, part the applicant's own conduct played in contributing to his dismissal, and then in the light of that finding decide what, if any, reduction should be made in the assessment of his loss.

It appears that it was this broad approach to s 116(3) that was adopted in *Morris v Gestetner Ltd*[2]. After dealing with the assessment of damage under s 116(1) in a s 33 situation to which we have already referred the court then continued[3]:

'Assuming again that the wrongful action was taken voluntarily and in no way as a result of pressure, the tribunal should next ask itself the question: "To what extent (if any) is it just and equitable that the base figure should be reduced having regard to the extent (if any) to which we find that the matters to which the complaint relates (e g the unfair dismissal) were caused or contributed to by any action of the complainant in connection with those matters (whether that action constituted an unfair industrial practice on his part or not)?" The answer will either leave the base figure unchanged or reduce it or, in an exceptional case, extinguish it.'

This test directs one to ignore the technical reason why the dismissal is unfair, namely the industrial action, but to look rather at the realities of the situation to see to what extent, if any, the appellant has contributed to his own ultimate dismissal. Adopting the broad approach we have no doubt that the tribunal were right in concluding that the appellant brought this dismissal on himself by his own dishonesty and that it would not in the circumstances be just and equitable to make any award of compensation against his employers. The tribunal should, however, have reached this conclusion not by refusing to award compensation under s 116(1), but by regarding this as that exceptional case in which a consideration of the appellant's conduct under s 116(3) extinguished any right to compensation.

Appeal dismissed.

Solicitors: *J G Haley* (for the appellant); *Sharpe, Pritchard & Co*, agents for *D Buckley*, Solicitor, County Borough of Rotherham (for the corporation).

Gordon H Scott Esq Barrister.

---

1 [1973] ICR 518
2 [1973] 3 All ER 1168, [1973] 1 WLR 1378
3 [1973] 3 All ER at 1175, [1973] 1 WLR at 1185, 1186

Diment v N H Foot Ltd

CHANCERY DIVISION
PENNYCUICK V-C
4th, 5th, 6th FEBRUARY 1974

Easement – Right of way – Prescription – User by dominant owner – Knowledge of servient owner – Means of knowledge – Acts of diligent landowner – Agricultural land – Servient land subject to successive agricultural tenancies – Use of way across field by owner of neighbouring farm – Use of way with vehicles between six and ten times a year during period of tenancies – Gate between field and neighbouring farm – Occasional visits to farm by owner – Whether owner having means of knowledge of user.

Easement – Right of way – Prescription – User by dominant owner – Knowledge of servient owner – Burden of proof – Knowledge of servient owner's agent – Absent landowner employing agents to manage agricultural land – Use of way across field by owner of neighbouring farm – Whether presumption that agents had knowledge of user – Whether burden on person claiming right of way to prove agents had knowledge.

Bookham Farm had been in the possession of F or his father since 1920. At the north-west corner of Bookham Farm there was a narrow tongue or 'panhandle' of land which on its western side adjoined a field which formed part of the neighbouring Sanctions Farm. The field on its western side was bounded by a public road. In 1936 the plaintiff was registered as proprietor of Sanctions Farm. From 1936 until 1967 she let Sanctions Farm under four separate agricultural tenancies. During that time she was away from the area, though she occasionally visited Sanctions Farm to look over it. She employed a firm of chartered surveyors to act as her agents in making the tenancies and dealing with matters relating to the rents. There was no evidence as to the other activities carried on by the surveyors and, in particular, no evidence that they did anything on the land by way of inspection. At all material times there had been a gateway between the field and the 'panhandle' and after the commencement of the first tenancy of Sanctions Farm in 1936 the field had been used by F and his father on between six and ten occasions in each year as a means of access for farm vehicles to Bookham Farm from the public road. Due to the lie of the land the north-west tip of the 'panhandle' was inaccessible to vehicles except by that route. In 1967 the plaintiff returned to live at Sanctions Farm. She was told then by her last tenant that F was 'coming in tomorrow to keep the right of way [over the field] open'. That was the first time that the plaintiff had heard that a right of way was alleged to exist over the field. In February 1970 the plaintiff noticed the track marks of vehicles on the field. She telephoned F who said that he had a right of way over the field. The plaintiff said that he had none. In December 1970 F's tractor driver, acting on F's instructions, took six trailer loads of chalk across the field from the public road into the 'panhandle'. The plaintiff brought an action for an injunction to restrain F from entering or driving any vehicle on the field. After the commencement of the action F conveyed Bookham Farm to himself and his wife and transferred the farming business to a company who became the defendants to the action. The defendants contended that a right of way had been created by prescription on the grounds (i) that the plaintiff was to be treated as having had the means before 1967 of acquiring the knowledge that F and his father were using the field for access to Bookham Farm by reason of the existence of the gateway from the field into the 'panhandle', and (ii) that any actual or imputed knowledge by the firm of chartered surveyors that F and his father were using the field as a means of access to their own farm, was to be treated as the plaintiff's own knowledge.

Held – (i) The user of the way over the field was sufficient in extent and regularity to be capable of creating a right of way (see p 788 *e*, post).

(ii) Since the plaintiff had never heard before 1967 that F or his father had been using the field for access to their farm, the plaintiff had no actual knowledge of the user of the way over the field. Furthermore, since it was not certain that the plaintiff, in doing all the acts which a diligent landowner would have done, would have seen the gateway between the field and the 'panhandle', or that, even if she had, the mere sight of it would have set her on enquiry, it was not possible to impute to her knowledge of the user (see p 791 *b* and *d* to *f*, post).

(iii) Although the burden of proof was on an owner of land to rebut the presumption that he had knowledge of long user of a way over his land, where an owner employed an agent to act in connection with his property, the burden of establishing the agent's knowledge or means of knowledge rested on the party wishing to establish it and that burden had to be discharged by inference from all the surrounding circumstances. Since there was no evidence as to the precise activities carried on by the surveyors other than arranging the tenancies and dealing with rents, there was no ground for holding that the firm had knowledge or the means of knowledge of the user (see p 791 *h* and p 792 *b* to *e*, post); *Pugh v Savage* [1970] 2 All ER 353 distinguished.

(iv) Accordingly, before 1967, the plaintiff had no knowledge or means of knowledge, either by herself or through her agents, of the user of the way over the field. It followed that the defendants had failed to establish the existence of a right of way and the plaintiff was entitled to the injunction sought (see p 792 *f*, post).

Notes

For creation of rights of way by prescription, see 12 Halsbury's Laws (3rd Edn) 576, para 1250, and for cases on the subject, see 19 Digest (Repl) 112, 113, 684-696.

For knowledge of servient owner, see 12 Halsbury's Laws (3rd Edn) 547, 549, paras 1186, 1189, and for cases on the subject, see 19 Digest (Repl) 74, 75, 420-424.

Cases referred to in judgment

Dalton v Henry Angus & Co, The Comrs of Her Majesty's Works and Public Buildings v Henry Angus & Co (1881) 6 App Cas 740, [1881-85] All ER Rep 1, 50 LJQB 689, 44 LT 844, 46 JP 132, HL, 19 Digest (Repl) 6, 4.

Link v Wimble (1st February 1967) unreported.

Pugh v Savage [1970] 2 All ER 353, [1970] 2 QB 373, [1970] 2 WLR 634, 21 P & CR 242, CA, Digest (Cont Vol C) 303, 686a.

Union Lighterage Co v London Graving Dock Co [1902] 2 Ch 557, [1900-3] All ER Rep 234, 71 LJCh 791, 87 LT 381, CA, 19 Digest (Repl) 19, 68.

Cases also cited

Cross v Lewis (1824) 2 B & C 686.

Davies v Du Paver [1952] 2 All ER 991, [1953] 1 QB 184, CA.

Action

By writ issued on 21st December 1970, the plaintiff, Margaret Eileen Diment, the owner of Sanctions Farm, Buckland Newton, Dorset, brought an action against the defendant, N H Foot Ltd, a company engaged in farming Bookham Farm, Buckland Newton, Dorset, for: (i) an injunction to restrain the defendant by itself its agents or servants or howsoever otherwise from entering or driving any vehicle on any part of her land and yard marked on the ordnance survey sheet for Dorset as OS 415, and (ii) damages for wrongfully entering her land, ripping up the turf and making vehicle track marks thereon. The defendant counterclaimed for damages for alleged wrongful obstruction of the defendant's right of way across the land and for an injunction restraining the plaintiff, her servants or agents, from repetition or continuance of the acts of obstruction. The facts are set out in the judgment.

J A R Finlay QC for the plaintiff.
John Bradburn for the defendant.

PENNYCUICK V-C. This action and also the counterclaim are concerned with a right of way claimed by the defendant company—or perhaps, more accurately, certain individuals who are interested parties—over a field, being 415 on the ordnance survey map, at Buckland Newton in Dorset.

I will first state the facts as I find them. In truth there is very little issue of relevant primary fact which is in dispute. The defendant—I will use that word collectively to describe the defendant company and any personal interests of a Mr N H Foot and his wife in it—is the owner of a farm known as Bookham Farm. It is a large area and at the extreme north-west corner there is a narrow tongue of land, something like what is sometimes called 'a tongue' or 'a panhandle'. That land was adjoined on the west side by a farm known as Sanctions Farm. Sanctions Farm has now been sold (so far as material) sold except for one field in the corner—that is field 415—which contains something under nine acres. Field 415 adjoins what I have called 'the panhandle' of Bookham Farm. Bookham Farm has been in the possession of the defendant or members of the Foot family since about 1920. In that year Bookham Farm was acquired by the father of Mr N H Foot. He farmed Bookham Farm until his death and then in 1969 Mr N H Foot purchased Bookham Farm from his father's personal representatives. At some date in 1971, subsequent to the commencement of this action, Mr N H Foot conveyed Bookham Farm to himself and his wife, but he transferred the farming business carried on from Bookham Farm to the defendant company.

Sanctions Farm was likewise in the possession of one family for a very considerable time. The history begins somewhere in the 1860s with the plaintiff's great-grandfather. Sanctions Farm devolved successively on certain relations—details of whom are not relevant—and in 1933 the plaintiff's mother was registered as proprietor. Then on 20th August 1936 the plaintiff was registered as proprietor. I mention at this stage, out of chronological order, that at a much later date, namely in 1970, the plaintiff sold the bulk of Sanctions Farm but for some reason retained field 415.

To return to the plan, the 'panhandle' is a relatively narrow field which slopes down a hillside to its north-west corner where there is a drinking pool used for cattle. The slope at the end is extremely steep and would not be negotiable by a wheeled vehicle. For most of its length the 'panhandle' adjoins field 415. Field 415 itself is bounded on the west side by a public road known as Landscombe Lane. At all material times there has been a gateway between field 415 and the 'panhandle' at a point which is marked B on the plan. It is possible to go with a wheeled vehicle along the northern boundary of field 415 from a point A in Landscombe Lane to point B and then through that gate on to the 'panhandle'. That access to the 'panhandle' is useful to the occupiers of Bookham Farm because it is the only practical way of getting a wheeled vehicle on to the northern end of the 'panhandle' where the drinking pool is situated.

As I have said, the plaintiff was registered as the proprietor of Sanctions Farm, including field 415, on 20th August 1936. Her mother had recently died, her father married again and for various personal reasons she left home and was continuously away from the Dorset area from 1936 until 1967. During much of that time she was at a very considerable distance away—sometimes abroad. I should mention that her occupation is that of a physiotherapist. She never farmed Sanctions Farm herself. In 1936 she created a tenancy of Sanctions Farm in favour of one House. It appears from one document which is in evidence that that tenancy began on the March quarter day. Thenceforward Sanctions Farm was continuously in the occupation of tenants until Lady Day 1967. There was first Mr House from 1936 to 1938, then Mr Cable to 1943, then Mr McAllister to 1946 and then Mr Billen for a long period until 1967. These tenancies were in each case separate agricultural tenancies and not one continuous tenancy with successive tenants. There may have been an interval of days or weeks between the successive tenancies, but I think it is clear that nothing significant could turn on that. There is in fact no evidence that there were such intervals. In May 1967, when she was about to settle again in Dorset, the plaintiff made an abortive attempt to sell Sanctions Farm. She returned to live in Buckland Newton at the end of 1967. She has lived there ever since and, as I have said, in 1970 she sold the best part of Sanctions Farm, but she still retains field 415.

I turn now to the use which the defendant company or its individual predecessors have made of field 415. According to the evidence of Mr N H Foot, the earliest date within his recollection at which his father was using field 415 as a method of access to his own land was 1936. That, it will be remembered, was the selfsame year in which the plaintiff acquired Sanctions Farm and in which she made the first of the lettings which I have mentioned—there had been previous lettings. There is no evidence of any user of field 415 for access before 1936. There may have been such user, but there is no evidence of it. Since that date there has been a user and a continuous user of field 415. User has been limited to quite a few occasions in each year and particulars of this user were given in evidence both by Mr N H Foot himself and by Mr Mitchell, his tractor driver. The occasions of user were these. In the early summer there was a check on the fences around the 'panhandle', and where necessary fencing gear was taken to the 'panhandle'. In midsummer, perhaps about June, there was hedge trimming and cutting of thistles. Again, from time to time, the drinking pool was cleared out and whatever drainage work was necessary was done. It appears that field 415 was not used more than on perhaps six to ten occasions in each year. To get the point out of the way, I have no doubt that the user was sufficient in extent and regularity to be capable of creating a right of way. On the other hand, obviously it would only be apparent to anybody who happened to be there on one of those ten or so days in the year, apart from whatever traces were left on field 415 by vehicles passing across it.

I now mention the particular passage of vehicles which has given rise to the present action. Every six years it became necessary to carry chalk across to the 'panhandle'. In December 1970 Mr Mitchell was instructed to take a series of loads of chalk in a trailer attached to the tractor across field 415. He made in all six journeys in each direction, i e he crossed field 415 12 times. It was a wet day and getting wetter and he made deep indentations along the north side of field 415. It had been the practice of Mr Foot when one of his vehicles crossed field 415 and left traces to obliterate them the next day by running a tractor over the edge of the wheel marks, but unfortunately on this occasion in December it was a Friday, so nothing could be done until the next Monday. When Monday came and Mr Mitchell was instructed to go and erase the marks he found that the plaintiff had locked the gate from Landscombe Lane, so that he could not get into field 415.

The plaintiff first heard that Mr Foot was making use of field 415 as the result of a conversation with the last of the tenants in 1967. Just before Mr Billen left he told her that his neighbour, i e Mr Foot, was 'coming in tomorrow to keep the right of way open'. The plaintiff had never heard of any right of way before. The next occasion on which the use of field 415 was brought to her notice was on a date in February 1970 when she noticed track marks. She appreciated that it was probably Mr Foot or his employees who had made those marks, and she had a telephone conversation with Mr Foot. In that conversation she asked Mr Foot whether he was claiming a right of way and he said he had had one for 50 years and she said he had none. Mr Foot himself kept a contemporary record of the same telephone conversation. The substance of his record corresponded almost exactly with the plaintiff's recollection of it. That telephone conversation did not itself spark off any further proceedings on the part of the plaintiff. On the other hand, when she observed the deep track marks left in December 1970 then, as I have said, she locked the gate leading into field 415 from Landscombe Lane and almost immediately afterwards issued the writ in the present action.

a The writ takes the form of the statement of claim and I think it is possibly a home-made document. The plaintiff claims an injunction—

'to restrain the defendants, by themselves, their agents or servants or howso-ever otherwise from entering or driving any vehicle upon any part of her land and yard marked on the relevant Ordnance Survey sheet for Dorset as O.S. 415 . . .'

b
I should have mentioned that the yard is situated just to the north of the gate at point B. Then there is a claim for damages for wrongfully entering her land with a tractor and trailer, ripping up turf and making tracks—and particulars about that are given.

The defence alleges that:

c
'2. A right of way has been continuously exercised as of right for the passage of farm and agricultural vehicles by the occupiers for the time being of a tenement known as and situate at Bookham Farm, Buckland Newton, in the County of Dorset across a field Ordnance Survey Number 415 between the points marked A and B as delineated on the map annexed hereto. The said user by the said occupiers of the said tenement was for the benefit of the said tenement in giving access to and from a thoroughfare known as Landscombe Lane.

d
'3. The user referred to in paragraph [2] has continued since time immemorial, alternatively for a period of 40 or 20 years before this action, alternatively for a period of more than 20 years.

'4. By reason of the matters referred to above, the owners and occupiers of the said tenement are entitled to the said right by prescription at common law, alternatively under the Prescription Act, 1832, alternatively by virtue of the doctrine of Lost Modern Grant.'

e

Then there is a counterclaim in which the defendant company claims an injunction restraining the plaintiff from repetition or continuance of the action referred to under para 2 of the counterclaim, i e locking the gate at point A or any other acts preventing *f* the defendant from exercising the right of way and a declaration that the defendant as occupier for the time being is entitled to the said right of way. I mention at this point that I think, strictly speaking, the person entitled to that declaration would be the freehold owners of Bookham Farm rather than the defendant company which was carrying on farming business presumably under lease from the freehold owners. The freehold owners are now—though they were not at the date of issue *g* of the writ—Mr N H Foot and his wife. Nothing has been made of that point and I need say nothing more at all about it.

Then there is a defence to the counterclaim of which I read two paragraphs:

'2. A right of way has not been continuously exercised as of right for the passage of farm and agricultural vehicles by the said occupiers . . . of Bookham Farm . . .
h '3. If the defendants enjoyed access to and from Landscombe Lane through O.S. 415 such enjoyment has not been of right but has been a secret enjoyment without the knowledge of plaintiff or her predecessors in title owners of the freehold of O.S. 415 or alternatively without such knowledge save since 1967 or thereabouts and further or alternatively the plaintiff and such predecessors as aforesaid had no means of discovering the user alleged.'

j Then there is an allegation of occasional and intermittent user which has not been pursued at the hearing.

The action came on for hearing before me two days ago. The principal witnesses were the plaintiff on the one hand—indeed she called no other witness—and Mr N H Foot on the other hand—and he called one other witness, namely Mr Mitchell, his tractor driver. The plaintiff and Mr Foot, although strikingly different personalities, were each outstandingly clear and, to my mind, truthful witnesses. They gave their answers simply and without any attempt to cover up matters unfavourable to themselves. As I have said, in the event there is no real conflict of evidence between them on any significant matter of particular fact. I do not think therefore that it is necessary to weigh their evidence any further. I can, for all practical purposes, accept what each of them said and then I have to decide what are the proper inferences of fact and conclusions of law to be drawn from that evidence.

I would mention this point: no suggestion was made by counsel for the defendant company that if no right of way had been acquired by 1967, or had been inchoate before 1967, it would be possible to maintain that a right of way had been acquired during the short period between 1967 and 1970. If the defendant is to succeed at all under any of the heads under which a right of way can be acquired it has to go back to a starting point a long time before 1967, and let me say at once that I think 1936 would be quite far enough back so far as time is concerned.

I turn now to the law and I will read first the statement of principle made by Fry J in *Dalton v Henry Angus & Co*[1]. I should perhaps mention that this was not a decision of the court, but was advice given by a number of judges to the House of Lords under the procedure which was then sometimes adopted. Fry J's statement has been repeatedly confirmed since then and I think may be taken as an authoritative statement of the law. He says[2]:

'But leaving such technical questions aside, I prefer to observe that, in my opinion, the whole law of prescription and the whole law which governs the presumption or inference of a grant or covenant rest upon acquiescence. The Courts and the Judges have had recourse to various expedients for quieting the possession of persons in the exercise of rights which have not been resisted by the persons against whom they are exercised, but in all cases it appears to me that acquiescence and nothing else is the principle upon which these expedients rest. It becomes then of the highest importance to consider of what ingredients acquiescence consists. In many cases, as, for instance, in the case of that acquiescence which creates a right of way, it will be found to involve, 1st, the doing of some act by one man upon the land of another; 2ndly, the absence of right to do that act in the person doing it; 3rdly, the knowledge of the person affected by it that the act is done; 4thly, the power of the person affected by the act to prevent such act either by act on his part or by action in the Courts; and lastly, the abstinence by him from any such interference for such a length of time as renders it reasonable for the Courts to say that he shall not afterwards interfere to stop the act being done.'

So, the third requirement is knowledge of the person that the act is done and the fourth requirement is the power of that person to prevent such act. The requirement of knowledge has subsequently been expanded so as to include imputed knowledge. I will refer to *Union Lighterage Co v London Graving Dock Co*[3], where Romer LJ says this:

'... on principle, it appears to me that a prescriptive right to an easement over a man's land should only be acquired when the enjoyment has been open —that is to say, of such a character that an ordinary owner of the land, diligent in the protection of his interests, would have, or must be taken to have, a reasonable opportunity of becoming aware of that enjoyment.'

Then Romer LJ goes on to cite *Dalton v Henry Angus & Co*[1]. Stirling LJ says[4]: 'I think that *Dalton v. Angus*[1] establishes that there must be some knowledge or means of

1 (1881) 6 App Cas 740, [1881-85] All ER Rep 1
2 (1881) 6 App Cas at 773, 774, [1881-85] All ER Rep at 30
3 [1902] 2 Ch 557 at 570, 571, [1900-3] All ER Rep 234 at 240
4 [1902] 2 Ch at 574, [1900-3] All ER Rep at 242

knowledge on the part of the person against whom the right is claimed'. Vaughan
Williams LJ in his judgment dissented from the others, but expressed the same view
on means of knowledge. So in order that there may be the necessary acquiescence
the owner of the servient tenement must have knowledge or the means of knowledge
that the act is done—the act being here user of these lands for passage to create a
right of way. I will refer in a moment to the way in which the point was put—I
think rather differently—in a recent case in the Court of Appeal[1].

Coming to the facts of the present case, I have already held that the plaintiff
had never heard that the predecessors of the defendant had been using field 415
for access to their own land until Mr Billen told her something in 1967. I have
already made clear that I accept that evidence, so that she did not have actual
knowledge at any time before 1967. Were the circumstances such that if she had
followed up any clues she would have ascertained that the relevant acts were being
done? I have reached the clear conclusion that the plaintiff did not possess any such
means of knowledge.

Counsel for the defendant company contended that the plaintiff must be treated
as having such means of knowledge by reason of the existence of the gateway at
point B, when considered in connection with the lie of the land which made the
extreme north-west tip of the 'panhandle' virtually inaccessible to vehicles except
through that gate. I am not at all certain that the plaintiff, doing all the acts which
a diligent landowner could have done, would have even seen gate B when she made
her inspections of Sanctions Farm during this period from 1936 to 1967. During this
period the plaintiff came down to Buckland Newton perhaps once a year to look
over Sanctions Farm. Field 415 was an outlying part of a large farm and there is
no reason I can see why one should infer that the plaintiff, looking over the farm
as a whole, should have walked along the boundary of this outlying field. Even if
she had done so, I am not persuaded that the mere sight of a gate at point B leading
to the 'panhandle' would have put her on any further enquiry as to why that gate
was there. There can be all sorts of reasons why a gate stands between two pieces
of land which are not at present in common ownership and I should not have thought
that the mere sight of the gate would have put her on enquiry whether the gate was
in current use by the owner or occupier for the time being of Bookham Farm for the
purposes of access over field 415. I conclude that it is not possible to impute to the
plaintiff personally any means of knowledge.

Counsel for the defendant company put his contention of knowledge in one rather
different way. I mention now the case to which I alluded previously in this judgment,
namely, *Pugh v Savage*[2], in which Cross LJ said:

'When long user—here user for 36 years—of a way has been shown, I think
that the law should support it if it can, and that we ought to presume, in the
absence of any evidence to the contrary, that the owners of 457 in the period
1932 to 1940 knew of the user and that Mr Ralphs knew of it.'

There Cross LJ—and both Harman and Salmon LJJ agreed—was stating that there
is a presumption that the owner concerned knows of the relevant user of a way but,
as Cross LJ said, it is obvious that the presumption can be rebutted by evidence
that the owner did not have such knowledge. The effect of that statement is to
throw the burden of proof on the owner concerned, that is to say instead of the other
party having to establish affirmatively that he did have knowledge, the owner
must establish that he did not have knowledge.

Accepting that as a correct statement of the law, it is I think an enlargement of the
principle stated in *Dalton v Henry Angus & Co*[3]. The plaintiff herself did not have

---

1   *Pugh v Savage* [1970] 2 All ER 353, [1970] 2 QB 373
2   [1970] 2 All ER at 359, [1970] 2 QB at 384
3   (1881) 6 App Cas 740, [1881-85] All ER Rep 1

such knowledge and so, as far as she is concerned, she has rebutted the presumption. But what was said by counsel for the defendant company was this: that during these years the plaintiff employed a firm of chartered surveyors known as Henry Duke & Son of Dorchester to act for her in connection with Sanctions Farm including the making of agreements with the successive tenants in occupation of field 415. That is undoubtedly so. Then he said that any knowledge or imputed knowledge on the part of the plaintiff's agent must be treated for this purpose as her own knowledge as principal and went on to contend that this presumption applies as regards Henry Duke & Son, with the consequence that it could only be rebutted by showing that Henry Duke & Son did not in fact have knowledge of the user of the way, or means of such knowledge. I do not think the presumption can legitimately be carried so far where a landowner employs an agent in connection with his property. There cannot, I think, be a presumption, merely by reason of that relation and without reference to the particular circumstances, that the agent has knowledge or means of knowledge of any particular act on the land. That would be carrying this presumption altogether beyond anything that was said in *Pugh v Savage*[1] and would, I venture to think, lead to some very odd consequences. It seems to me that where one is concerned with an agent the role of establishing knowledge or means of knowledge must rest on the other party concerned who may discharge that burden by positive evidence or inference—the inference depending on all the particular circumstances. There is no evidence here as to the precise activities carried on by Henry Duke & Son apart from the fact that they were responsible for making the tenancies and dealing with matters of rents and so forth. There is no evidence as to what members or representatives of that firm did physically on Sanctions Farm or field 415 by way of inspection and I see no ground on which I would be entitled to hold that Henry Duke & Son had knowledge or means of knowledge of the user of this way by Mr Foot or the defendant company.

That is sufficient to decide this case because the defendant company has failed to establish that the plaintiff either had knowledge of the use of this way or the means of such knowledge and that is the third of Fry LJ's requirements.

Strictly speaking it is therefore unnecessary for me to go on and deal with the fourth requirement[2], namely, 'power ... to prevent such act either by act on his part or by action in the Courts'. I will limit myself to a very few observations on that point. The difficulty in the way of the defendant company here is that throughout the relevant period, 1936 to 1967, Sanctions Farm was in the occupation of a succession of tenants who alone could have brought proceedings in trespass. A useful general statement of the principle applicable here is contained in Gale on Easements[3], where it is said:

'... and even as to some positive easements, such as a right of way, it is doubtful whether the reversioner could maintain an action; and during the continuance of the tenancy he may be unable either to interrupt the enjoyment or to compel his tenant to do so. Unless, therefore, some positive act, as a notice, intimating his dissent, be sufficient to obviate the effect of the user giving a right, he would not be brought into the condition of a *valens agere*, without which the prescription ought not to run against him.'

The same point is taken up in one paragraph of Cross LJ's judgment in *Pugh v Savage*[4] where he says:

'That a distinction may be drawn between cases where the tenancy was in existence at the beginning of the period of user and cases where the tenancy came

1   [1970] 2 All ER 353, [1970] 2 QB 373
2   See (1881) 6 App Cas at 774, [1881-85] All ER Rep at 30
3   14th Edn (1972), p 181
4   [1970] 2 All ER at 359, [1970] 2 QB at 383, 384

a into existence in the course of the period of user, is surely only common sense. If a tenancy is in existence at the beginning of a period of user, it may well be unreasonable to imply a lost grant by the owner at the beginning of the user. He might not have been able to stop the user, even if he knew about it. If, on the other hand, one has a period of user against an owner or owners without any evidence that they did not know about it when they were in possession,

b and then afterwards the grant of a tenancy, though undoubtedly such a tenancy during the period of user is a matter to be considered, it would be quite wrong to hold that it is a fatal objection to presuming a grant, or to a claim under the Prescription Act 1832.'

It appears logically to follow that even if the plaintiff had been fully aware of the use of this way during these years 1936 to 1967, it might still have been impossible

c for the defendant company to satisfy the fourth of Fry J's requirements.

Counsel for the defendant company sought to escape that result by saying that two remedies would have been open to the plaintiff in such circumstances. Either she could have financed an action by her tenant or she could have called on the tenant to fence off the property under a term in his tenancy agreement. We have Mr Billen's tenancy agreement in evidence under which the tenant was bound to keep and leave in

d good tenantable repair and condition, inter alia, the fences on the demised property. I do not think it is necessary for me to express a concluded view on those remedies, but I must say I do not see how the plaintiff could have compelled her tenant to bring an action and I feel considerable doubt whether she could have required him to block this way under the tenancy agreement. However that may be it seems to me, having decided this case on the third requirement, that it is better I should not

e express a concluded view of the law under the fourth requirement which does present considerable difficulties.

I should refer to a judgment of my own in *Link v Wimble*[1], in which I dealt at some length with the third and fourth requirements. I do not want to take up time in quoting what I said then but, as at present advised, I see no reason to form a different view today.

f I do not think I need say anything about damages. Counsel for the plaintiff did not make any point on damages and the difficulty, apart from the fact that the damages would not be very substantial, is that by locking the gate into Landscombe Lane, the plaintiff prevented the defendant company from doing the remedial work which it would otherwise have done and which would have reduced the damage, according to the evidence of Mr Foot, to minimal proportions. For all practicable

g purposes the tracks could have been obliterated. I do not think therefore that this is a case where I ought to make any award of damages.

I must then make an injunction substantially in the terms of the statement of claim.

Injunction restraining the defendant from entering or driving across the land with any vehicle. Counterclaim dismissed.

h Solicitors: *Gregory, Rowcliffe & Co* (for the plaintiff); *Moon, Beever & Hewlett,* agents for *Andrews, Son & Huxtable,* Dorchester (for the defendant).

Evelyn Budd   Barrister.

j 1 (1st February 1967) unreported

Practice Note

COURT OF APPEAL, CRIMINAL DIVISION
LORD WIDGERY CJ, PARK AND FORBES JJ
4th JUNE 1974

Criminal law – Bail – Bail during trial – Discretion of judge.

Notes

For bail generally, see 10 Halsbury's Laws (3rd Edn) 373-376, paras 677-682, and for cases on the subject, see 14 Digest (Repl) 170-181, *1332-1480*.

LORD WIDGERY CJ gave the following practice direction, after consultation with the judges of the Queen's Bench Division and the Family Division, on the grant of bail in the course of a trial.

Once a trial has begun, the further grant of bail, whether during the short adjournment, or overnight, is in the discretion of the trial judge. It may be a proper exercise of this discretion to refuse bail during the short adjournment if the accused cannot otherwise be segregated from witnesses and jurors.

An accused who was on bail while on remand should not be refused overnight bail during the trial, unless in the opinion of the judge there are positive reasons to justify this refusal. Such reasons are likely to be: (1) that a point has been reached where there is a real danger that the accused will abscond, either because the case is going badly for him, or for any other reason; (2) that a there is a real danger that he may interfere with witnesses or jurors.

There is no universal rule of practice that bail shall not be renewed when the summing-up has begun. Each case must be decided in the light of its own circumstances, and having regard to the judge's assessment from time to time of the risks involved.

Once the jury has returned a verdict, a further renewal of bail should be regarded as exceptional.

N P Metcalfe Esq Barrister.

Stewart v Stewart

COURT OF APPEAL, CIVIL DIVISION
DAVIES, STAMP LJJ AND SIR SEYMOUR KARMINSKI
11th, 12th, 13th MARCH, 9th APRIL 1974

Legal aid – Costs – Unassisted person's costs out of legal aid fund – Costs incurred in proceedings in which apart from Act no order for costs would have been made – No order to be made in favour of unassisted party – Divorce proceedings – Petition by impecunious wife – Unsuccessful petition – Practice of divorce courts not to make order for costs against impecunious wife – Statutory discretion as to costs – Wife legally aided with nil contribution – Whether proceedings in which apart from Act order would have been made against wife – Whether court precluded from making order for payment to husband of costs out of legal aid fund – Supreme Court of Judicature (Consolidation) Act 1925, s 50 – Legal Aid Act 1964, s 1(4).

Legal aid – Costs – Unassisted person's costs out of legal aid fund – Just and equitable – Divorce proceedings – Unsuccessful petition by wife – Petition containing false and scandalous allegations – Wife legally aided – Decree awarded to husband on answer – Parties found equally to blame for breakdown of marriage in subsequent ancillary proceedings – Husband ordered to pay costs of ancillary proceedings – Whether just and equitable that husband should be awarded costs of divorce proceedings out of legal aid fund – Legal Aid Act 1964, s 1(2).

Legal aid – Costs – Unassisted person's costs out of legal aid fund – Severe financial hardship – Broad interpretation – Divorce proceedings – Financial hardship to husband – Husband enjoying substantial salary – Husband living in house too large for needs – Husband subject to heavy financial commitments – Legal Aid Act 1964, s 1(3)(b).

The wife petitioned for divorce under s 2(1)(b) of the Divorce Reform Act 1969 alleging that the husband had behaved in such a way that she could not reasonably be expected to live with him. Her petition was full of scandalous and offensive allegations against the husband. After a six day hearing the judge found that the allegations were false and dismissed the petition. He granted the husband a decree, on his answer, under s 2(1)(a) and (b) of the 1969 Act, having found that the wife had committed adultery with two men and that her behaviour, including the making of the false and scandalous allegations in her petition, had been such that the husband could not reasonably be expected to live with her. The wife was legally aided with a nil contribution, and costs of the suit were reserved. At the subsequent hearing of the wife's application for financial provision the same judge found that each party was equally to blame for the breakdown of the marriage; he ordered the husband to pay the wife a lump sum of £6,000 and interim maintenance and periodical payments of £1,820 a year. He ordered the husband to pay the costs of the ancillary proceedings. The husband applied under s 1[a] of the Legal Aid Act 1964 for payment of his costs of the divorce suit out of the legal aid fund. The Law Society opposed the husband's application. The husband's principal asset was the former matrimonial home, which was worth £50,000 but was subject to a mortgage of £21,000. In order to pay the wife the lump sum of £6,000 the husband had taken out a second mortgage on the property of £9,000. He had shares worth £3,180 and a sum of £1,500 on deposit with his solicitors against costs. His income was £8,000 a year out of which he had to pay £2,500 to a former wife and children, £1,820 to the wife under the judge's order and £3,600 in mortgage interest. His living expenses were £2,645 a year. His costs of the divorce suit were £5,330 and, together with the costs

a Section 1, so far as material, is set out at p 798 g, post

of the ancillary proceedings which he had been ordered to pay, his total liability for
costs was likely to amount to £9,000 or £10,000, less the £1,500 already paid to the *a*
solicitors. The judge, having referred to his finding in the financial proceedings
that each party had contributed equally to the breakdown of the marriage, concluded that the proper order for costs of the divorce proceedings would have been
for the husband to pay half the wife's costs, and that it would not be just and equitable
for the husband to obtain a full order against the Law Society when he would only
have obtained an order for one-half of the costs against the wife. The judge further *b*
found that the husband would not suffer severe financial hardship within s 1(3)(*b*)
of the 1964 Act even if he were ordered to pay the whole of his costs and that it would
not be 'just and equitable', within s 1(2) of the 1964 Act, to order that any of his costs
should be paid out of public funds, if only because he had increased his liability by
choosing to live in, and bear the expense of, a house which was, on the evidence,
plainly too large for his needs and means. Accordingly the judge refused the husband's *c*
application. On appeal by the husband, the Law Society contended that, apart
from the 1964 Act, the court would not have made an order for costs against an
impecunious wife and that accordingly s 1(4) of the 1964 Act precluded an order for
payment of the husband's costs out of public funds.

Held – The appeal should be allowed for the following reasons— *d*
    (i) In considering whether s 1(4) of the 1964 Act precluded an order for payment
of an unassisted husband's costs out of the legal aid fund, what had to be determined
was not whether an order would have been made for payment of his costs if the wife
had not been legally aided, but whether, if there had been no 1964 Act, no order
would have been made. In considering that question the court had to bear in mind,
that, although there was no general practice that, on the dismissal of a wife's petition, *e*
costs should follow the event, the judge's discretion as to costs under s 50 of the
Supreme Court of Judicature (Consolidation) Act 1925 was untrammelled by any
former practice that costs should not be awarded against an unsuccessful and impecunious wife. Taking into account the fact that, by bringing proceedings against
her husband unsuccessfully, the wife had thrown on to him a burden of costs which
as a successful litigant he ought not to have to bear and in particular that she had *f*
made allegations in her petition which no husband could have been expected to leave
unchallenged, the judge had been justified in coming to the conclusion that an
order ought to be made against her and that he was not, therefore, precluded by
s 1(4) from making an order under the 1964 Act (see p 799 *e* and *h*, p 801 *j* to p 802 *b*,
p 803 *b* to *d* and p 804 *j*, post); *Gooday v Gooday* [1968] 3 All ER 611 applied; *Nowotnik
v Nowotnik* [1965] 3 All ER 167 distinguished. *g*
    (ii) For the purpose of s 1(3)(*b*) of the 1964 Act the question was not whether the hus-
band ought not to have got himself in such a position that he would suffer severe
financial hardship unless the order was made, but whether he would in fact suffer
severe financial hardship. The husband's financial position was such that in default
of such an order he would suffer severe financial hardship and accordingly s 1(3)(*b*)
did not preclude the making of an order under the 1964 Act (see p 800 *e* and *j*, p 804 *e* *h*
and p 805 *b*, post); dicta of Lord Denning MR in *Nowotnik v Nowotnik* [1965] 3 All ER
at 172, and of Salmon LJ in *Hanning v Maitland (No 2)* [1970] 1 All ER at 819 applied.
    (iii) Having regard to the nature of the charges made against the husband in the wife's
petition and his successful defence of those charges, and the fact that in the financial
proceedings the judge had already taken into consideration the husband's share for
the breakdown of the marriage, it was just and equitable that the whole of the *j*
husband's party and party costs of the divorce proceedings should be paid out of the
legal aid fund (see p 801 *b*, p 803 *h* and *j* and p 805 *c*, post).

Notes
For the awarding of costs to an unassisted person out of the legal aid fund,
see Supplement to 30 Halsbury's Laws (3rd Edn) para 933A.

a   For the Supreme Court of Judicature (Consolidation) Act 1925, s 50, see 25 Halsbury's Statutes (3rd Edn) 721.

For the Legal Aid Act 1964, s 1, see 25 Halsbury's Statutes (3rd Edn) 789.

For the Divorce Reform Act 1969, s 2, see 40 Halsbury's Statutes (3rd Edn) 770.

As from 8th May 1974 s 1 of the 1964 Act has been replaced by s 13 of the Legal Aid Act 1974. As from 1st January 1974 s 2 of the 1969 Act has been replaced by s 1 of the Matrimonial Causes Act 1973.

b

Cases referred to in judgments

Daley v Diggers Ltd [1951] 1 All ER 116, [1951] 1 KB 661, DC, 50 Digest (Repl) 492, *1734.*

Gooday v Gooday [1968] 3 All ER 611, [1969] P 1, [1968] 3 WLR 750, CA, 27(2) Digest (Reissue) 750, *5919.*

c   *Hanning v Maitland (No 2)* [1970] 1 All ER 812, [1970] 1 QB 580, [1970] 2 WLR 151, CA, Digest (Cont Vol C) 1087, *1736a.*

Nowotnik v Nowotnik (Hyatt intervening) [1965] 3 All ER 167, [1967] P 83, [1965] 3 WLR 920 CA, 27(2) Digest (Reissue) 769, *6144.*

Povey v Povey [1970] 3 All ER 612, [1972] Fam 40, [1971] 2 WLR 381, DC, 27(2) Digest (Reissue) 770, *6146.*

d   *Saunders (Executrix of the estate of Rose Maud Gallie (deceased)) v Anglia Building Society (formerly Northampton Town and County Building Society) (No 2)* [1971] 1 All ER 243, [1971] AC 1039, [1971] 2 WLR 349, HL.

Saxton, Re, Johnson v Saxton [1962] 3 All ER 92, [1962] 1 WLR 968, CA, 51 Digest (Repl) 609, *2291.*

e   **Cases also cited**

Clifford v Walker [1972] 2 All ER 806, [1972] 1 WLR 724, CA.

Tiverton Estates Ltd v Wearwell Ltd [1974] 1 All ER 209, [1974] 2 WLR 176, CA.

Appeal

f   This was an appeal by the husband, Charles Henry Stewart, against an order of Hollings J dated 13th July 1973 whereby he refused the husband's application for payment out of the legal aid fund of all or part of his costs in defending divorce proceedings brought against him by his wife, Mary Felicity Stewart, under s 2(1)(*b*) of the Divorce Reform Act 1969. The Area Secretary to the Law Society No 13 (London East) Legal Aid Area opposed the husband's application. The facts are set out in the judgment of Davies LJ.

g

Bruce Campbell QC and *Robert Johnson* for the husband.
Leolin Price QC and *Duncan Matheson* for the Law Society.

Cur adv vult

h   9th April.   **DAVIES LJ** (read by Stamp LJ). This is an appeal by a respondent husband against an order of Hollings J dated 13th July 1973 whereby he refused an application made by the husband under s 1 of the Legal Aid Act 1964 (shortly to be replaced by s 13 of the Legal Aid Act 1974) for the payment to him out of the legal aid fund of his costs of a divorce suit brought against him by his wife. In that suit in the event the wife's petition had, after a six day hearing, been dismissed and the husband had obtained a decree on his answer. The wife had been legally aided with a nil contribution; the husband had been unassisted. In the present application and appeal the wife took no part; but the Law Society were represented by counsel to oppose the husband's application.

j

The parties were married in 1963. There was one child of the family, born on 21st August 1971, but as a result of a blood test it has been ascertained that the husband is not the father of that child.

The wife's petition alleging intolerable conduct was filed on 2nd February 1972. *a*
I think that counsel for the husband was right when he said that it was full of scandalous and offensive allegations.   There is no need to go into any detail about them
here.   In substance it was alleged (i) that the husband constantly sought to persuade
the wife to take lovers and become a prostitute and (ii) that he constantly forced her
to submit to abnormal and unpleasant sexual practices.   The judge found against
her on both allegations.   He found that there was no compulsion or persuasion *b*
to commit adultery; there was earlier in the marriage permission by the husband,
but the wife enjoyed it, and later adultery with at least two men of whom the husband was ignorant.   As to the unusual sexual practices, the judge found that the
wife consented.

In the event, on 7th February 1973, after, as I have said, a six day hearing, Hollings J
granted a decree to the husband on the ground both of adultery with two men and *c*
of intolerable conduct, including the making of the false and scandalous allegations
in her petition.   At that stage the question of costs was not dealt with.

On 16th April, on the wife's application for financial provision, the same judge
ordered that the husband should pay interim maintenance and periodical payments
at the rate of £1,820 per annum less tax and also a lump sum of £6,000 payable in
three months.   So far as the costs of that application were concerned, the question *d*
was left over until the hearing of the application against the legal aid fund.   The
judge eventually ordered the husband to pay those costs.   The judge's reason for
making that order was the fact that it had been contended on behalf of the husband
in the financial proceedings that, in the light of her conduct, the wife ought not to be
granted any financial provision at all, whereas the judge had found that each party
had contributed equally to the breakdown of the marriage and had made his award *e*
accordingly.

The provisions of the Legal Aid Act 1964 as to the circumstances in which the court
is empowered to order the payment to an unassisted party of his costs out of the
legal aid fund have been so fully discussed in a number of authorities which were
cited to us that it is unnecessary to recite them at length.   In substance it amounts
to this.   The proceedings must have been finally decided in favour of the unassisted *f*
party (s 1(1)).   It must be 'just and equitable' that provision for the costs should be
made out of public funds (s 1(2)).   So far as concerns costs in a court of first instance,
the proceedings must have been instituted by the assisted party (s 1(3)(a)), and the court
must be satisfied that the unassisted party will suffer severe financial hardship unless
the order is made (s 1(3)(b)).   And finally s 1(4) provides:

> 'An order under this section shall not be made by any court in respect of costs *g*
> incurred by the unassisted party in any proceedings in which, apart from this
> Act, no order would be made for the payment of his costs.'

In the judgment which he is about to read, Stamp LJ will discuss the statute and the
authorities.   I will therefore forbear to deal with them here.

The main controversy on the hearing of the application before the learned judge *h*
was on the points of 'just and equitable' and 'severe financial hardship'.   In this
court there was also a great deal of discussion of s 1(4) in the light of such decisions
as *Nowotnik v Nowotnik*[1], *Gooday v Gooday*[2] and *Hanning v Maitland (No 2)*[3].

It is convenient at this stage to set out in round figures the husband's financial
position.   So far as concerns capital, his principal asset is the former matrimonial
home, 'Pantiles', Leatherhead.   This was valued at £50,000, but was subject to a *j*
mortgage of £21,000, and there is now a second mortgage of £9,000, raised by the

1   [1965] 3 All ER 167, [1967] P 83
2   [1968] 3 All ER 611, [1969] P 1
3   [1970] 1 All ER 812, [1970] 1 QB 580

a   husband to cover the lump sum of £6,000 ordered to be paid by him to the wife. In addition he has shares of the value of £3,180. It must, of course, be realised that as of this moment some of those values may be lower. In addition he has a sum of £1,500 on deposit with his solicitors against costs. Turning now to income, he has a salary of £8,000. Under a court order he has to pay to a former wife and children £2,500, leaving £5,500. Under the order of Hollings J he has to pay to the

b   petitioner £1,820; then his mortgage interest amounts to £3,600, making a total of £5,420. These figures would show that he has very little left on which to live. He has exhibited a schedule purporting to show general living expenses amounting to £2,645. This, of course, may be on the high side, but it is obvious that on any view things must be very tight.

His position with regard to costs is most unhappy. His costs of the main suit are

c   estimated at £5,330. In addition he has to pay his own and the wife's costs of the ancillary proceedings. His total liability may amount to £9,000 to £10,000, less the £1,500 already paid to his solicitors. It is estimated that he may have to pay some £4,000 to £5,000 even if he obtained the order for which he applied to the judge.

I now turn to the decision of the judge as to costs and his reasons for refusing to make an order against the Law Society. Having referred to his finding in the financial

d   proceedings that both parties must take equal responsibility for the ultimate break-down of the marriage, he stated:

> 'Having regard to all these matters I am satisfied that the proper order for costs of the divorce proceedings would have been that the [wife] should pay half of the [husband's] costs.'

And after dealing with the costs of the financial procedings, he refers to himself as

e   having 'decided that an order would have been made, though only in respect of half the costs, against the [wife] ...'

This finding seems to me to be a finding that the condition prescribed in s 1(4) of the 1964 Act is satisfied, namely, that an order would have been made against the wife. And, with great respect to the judge, I do not think that he is right when he proceeds to say that it would not be just and equitable for the husband to obtain a

f   full order for costs against the Law Society when he would only have got one-half from the wife. For, in the first place, the Act does not so provide and, secondly, if the husband were to obtain an order against the Law Society the order would not necessarily be a full order; it might—though it might not—be confined to the one-half which the judge would have awarded against the wife.

There was, I thought, considerable force in counsel for the husband's argument

g   that, as the judge had in the financial proceedings taken into account the husband's joint responsibility for the breakdown of the marriage, it was wrong to take this fact again into account in assessing the wife's liability for costs and penalising the husband in that regard. Conduct in the marriage might well, it was said, be relevant on financial matters, but costs should depend on the conduct of the suit.

The finding of the judge that he would have made an order for costs against the

h   wife tends, in my judgment, to distinguish this case from *Nowotnik v Nowotnik*[1]. This court in that case gave a number of reasons for its decision, but it would seem that the fundamental reason was that the view was taken that, in accordance with accepted practice, an order for costs would not have been made against the wife (see per Lord Denning MR[2]). This view as to the accepted practice was stated not to be correct in the later case of *Gooday v Gooday*[3].

j   On the question of severe financial hardship, the judge summed up the husband's financial position in terms somewhat similar to those set out above and continued as follows:

1 [1965] 3 All ER 167, [1967] P 83
2 [1965] 3 All ER at 172, [1967] P at 101, 102
3 [1968] 3 All ER 611, [1969] P 1

'He has maintained the large mortgage payments notwithstanding his com- *a*
mitments to his first wife, which I found amount to some £2,500 gross per
annum, and his other expenses as set out in the other exhibit to his affidavit,
and I was told that, in order to raise the £6,000 lump sum I ordered, he proposes
not to sell Pantiles but to remortgage it in an even greater amount, and so
impose upon himself even greater mortgage payments while still incurring the
considerable expense of running Pantiles and also in the knowledge that he has *b*
to pay the [wife] for the next few years £1,820 per annum. I must, I realise,
bear in mind that the [husband] has now a liability to pay the [wife's] costs in
the chambers proceedings and that he will have to bear himself the difference
between his own party and party costs and solicitor and client costs, including
probably a large part of the enquiry agents' fees. Even so, in the circumstances
I have outlined, I consider it plain that to pay a sum of about £2,500 would in *c*
the circumstances be no hardship to him, let alone severe hardship. Indeed,
in my judgment, it would not be severe hardship for him to pay the whole of
his costs, even amounting to £5,000. In addition I consider it would not be just
and equitable that public funds should be ordered to pay any of his costs if only
because he has increased his liability by choosing to live in and bear the expenses
of a house which is, on the evidence, plainly too large for his needs and means *d*
and which is not, as I have found, necessary for his employment or business.
I therefore refuse the application.'

It seems to me that the learned judge in that passage adopted the wrong approach.
The question is not whether the husband ought not to have got himself in such a
position that he will suffer severe financial hardship unless the order is made but
whether he will in fact suffer severe financial hardship.   *e*
    Guidance in this matter may, I think, be derived from two observations in the
decided cases. In *Nowotnik v Nowotnik*[1] Lord Denning MR said this:

    'If, however, his finances are so nicely balanced that, in order to meet his costs,
    he has to restrict his activities considerably, or seriously deplete his capital, then
    we think he would suffer severe financial hardship.'   *f*

And in *Hanning v Maitland (No 2)*[2] Salmon LJ said:

    'I do not think that the words "just and equitable" and "severe financial
    hardship" are used in the Act as terms of art. Nor are they capable of precise
    definition. The words should be interpreted broadly to mean just what they
    say. To my mind for a man in the defendant's modest financial position to *g*
    have to pay out £325 costs in the circumstances of this case is obviously a severe
    financial hardship. If it is not then it is very difficult to imagine a case in which
    it would be. I do not believe that it is legitimate for any court to say that be-
    cause all his life he has lived frugally, there is no severe financial hardship in his
    having to pay £325 costs, any more than I think it would be legitimate for a
    court to say that no financial hardship is involved because a defendant has chosen *h*
    to spend his money liberally on drink or tobacco or indeed for any other purpose.'

In the light of those observations and of the figures of the husband's financial position
as set out above, I am, with respect, of the opinion that the judge's conclusion was
wrong. I have no doubt that in the circumstances it was just and equitable that an
order should be made in his favour and that in default of such an order he would
suffer severe financial hardship. The only doubt in my mind has been whether *j*
the proper order would be that he should receive half his costs, the amount which
the judge would have thought appropriate had he thought fit to make an order, or
whether, in view of the fact that the judge does appear to have taken his finding of

1 [1965] 3 All ER at 172, [1967] P at 103
2 [1970] 1 All ER at 819, [1970] 1 QB at 591

a   'equally to blame' into consideration both on the question of financial provision and
     also on the assessment of the wife's liability for costs, it would be more just and
     equitable to make an order against the Law Society for the payment of the whole of
     the husband's costs of the main suit.

         I have had some doubt on this point but on the whole, in the light of the nature
     of the charges made in the wife's petition and their falsity, as found by the judge, the
b   manner in which they were persisted in during such a protracted hearing, and the
     fact that in the financial proceedings the judge had already taken into consideration
     the husband's share of blame for the breakdown of the marriage, I have come to the
     conclusion that the proper order against the legal aid fund would be for the payment
     of the whole of the husband's party and party costs of the main suit.

c   **STAMP LJ.** The Legal Aid Act 1964 recognises, subject to important exceptions,
     that where a suit is unsuccessfully maintained out of public funds, the successful party,
     if unassisted by legal aid, may have his costs paid out of public funds. It provides
     by s 1(1):

         'Where a party receives legal aid in connection with any proceedings between
         him and a party not receiving legal aid (in this Act referred to as "the unassisted
d   party") and those proceedings are finally decided in favour of the unassisted
         party, the court by which the proceedings are so decided may, subject to the
         provisions of this section, make an order for the payment to the unassisted party
         out of the legal aid fund of the whole or any part of the costs incurred by him in
         those proceedings.'

e   The limitations are set out in sub-ss (2), (3) and (4) of s 1 of that Act as follows:

         '(2) An order may be made under this section in respect of any costs if (and only
         if) the court is satisfied that it is just and equitable in all the circumstances that
         provision for those costs should be made out of public funds; and before making
         such an order the court shall in every case (whether or not application is made in
         that behalf) consider what orders should be made for costs against the party
f   receiving legal aid and for determining his liability in respect of such costs.
         '(3) Without prejudice to subsection (2) above, no order shall be made under
         this section in respect of costs incurred in a court of first instance, whether by that
         court or by any appellate court, unless—(a) the proceedings in the court of first
         instance were instituted by the party receiving legal aid; and (b) the court is
         satisfied that the unassisted party will suffer severe financial hardship unless
g   the order is made.
         '(4) An order under this section shall not be made by any court in respect of
         costs incurred by the unassisted party in any proceedings in which, apart from
         this Act, no order would be made for the payment of his costs.'

     On behalf of the Law Society it is submitted, and I summarise the submissions in the
h   order in which they were made: first, that apart from the 1964 Act no order would
     have been made for the payment of the husband's costs of the petition and that
     accordingly sub-s (4) precludes an order for payment out of public funds; second,
     that the husband would not suffer severe financial hardship if the order sought was
     not made so that sub-s (3)(b) precludes such an order; and third, that in all the
     circumstances of this case it is not just and equitable that provision for the husband's
j   costs should be made out of public funds so that sub-s (2) precludes such an order.
     I will consider each of these submissions in the same order.
         With reference to the first submission it is, I think, convenient to emphasise at the
     outset, because I think some confusion has been introduced by making the contrary
     assumption, that on the plain meaning of s 1(4) what has to be determined is not
     whether an order would be made for payment of the husband's costs if the wife had
     not been legally aided but whether, if there had been no Legal Aid Act 1964, no

order would be made. An order for payment of costs of an unassisted party out of public funds under the 1964 Act is not to be made if the unassisted party would have obtained no order for payment of his costs apart from that Act. If the construction of s 1(4) in this regard was otherwise in doubt it is made clear by s 1(2), which provides that before making an order for payment out of public funds the court shall consider what order should be made for costs against the party receiving legal aid and for determining his liability in respect of such costs. If the court on that consideration concludes that no order should be made against the party receiving legal aid then, as I see it, s 1(4) comes into play, but not otherwise.

It is also, I think, convenient to add a further preliminary observation, namely, that by the effect of s 1(7)(b) of the Legal Aid and Advice Act 1949, the principles on which the court acts in exercising the discretion as to costs which is conferred by s 50(1) of the Supreme Court of Judicature (Consolidation) Act 1925 is not to be affected by the rights conferred on assisted persons by that Act: see *Daley v Diggers Ltd*[1] and *Re Saxton*[2]. So if he would otherwise have done so a judge should, if invited to do so, make an order for costs against an unsuccessful party notwithstanding that he is assisted by legal aid. Only his liability to pay the costs is (by the effect of s 2(2)(e) of the 1949 Act) limited.

Having made these preliminary observations I turn to consider counsel for the Law Society's submission that an order for costs ought not to be made against this unsuccessful petitioning wife. This submission is based, as I understand it, on the proposition laid down in this court in *Nowotnik v Nowotnik*[3] that it was not the practice of the Divorce Court to make awards for costs against an unsuccessful wife unless she had sufficient means of her own with which to pay her costs and also her husband's costs. Just three years later, in *Gooday v Gooday*[4] this court pointed out that the discretion as to costs is a statutory discretion conferred on the judges by s 50(1) of the 1925 Act, and the court refused to interfere with an order for costs made in the court below against an almost impecunious wife. Diplock LJ remarked in the course of his judgment that today, where the spouses in the case of many married couples are equally capable of earning their own living and equally likely to have a joint interest in property or to have property of their own, he could see no rational ground for saying that there should continue to be a settled practice without regard to the individual features of each case. Widgery LJ expressed a somewhat similar view but added that this was not to say that the old so-called practice would not be followed thereafter, because there would still be many cases in which a wife is entirely dependent on her husband and therefore is in the situation which gave rise to the practice. Willmer LJ, who had been a member of the court which decided the *Nowotnik*[3] appeal, agreed that the reason for the existence of the practice had largely disappeared.

Gooday v Gooday[4] was followed by the Matrimonial Proceedings and Property Act 1970. After that Act had been passed Sir Jocelyn Simon P in *Povey v Povey*[5] traced the practice of not awarding costs against an unsuccessful wife to the fact that by and large her property formerly vested in her husband and that in return the law imposed on the husband the duty to maintain his wife; a duty which, as he put it, was vindicated by recognising her right to pledge his credit for necessaries. Among such necessaries, remarked Sir Jocelyn Simon P, was the wife's assertion or defence of her rights under the matrimonial law. So it became the practice in matrimonial causes that even an unsuccessful litigant wife should (unless she had adequate independent means) ordinarily have her costs paid by her husband, at least up to such sum as he had been ordered to provide (as he frequently was) by way of security for her costs, or, at any rate, she should not be ordered to pay his.

1　[1951] 1 All ER 116, [1951] 1 KB 661
2　[1962] 3 All ER 92, [1962] 1 WLR 968
3　[1965] 3 All ER 167, [1967] P 83
4　[1968] 3 All ER 611, [1969] P 1
5　[1970] 3 All ER 612, [1972] Fam 40

At the moment when judgment was given in *Povey v Povey*[1] the Matrimonial Proceedings and Property Act 1970 had not come into force; but Sir Jocelyn Simon P pointed out that, by the effect of s 41 of that Act, which was to come into force on 1st August 1970, the wife's agency of necessity was abolished. Any special practice as to the wife's security for costs in matrimonial proceedings would in his view disappear with it.

Sir Jocelyn Simon P went on to indicate that it did not follow that that uniform practice should be replaced by a general practice that costs should follow the event, pointing out that this would often be inappropriate or unjust. This, is of course, always so, and the discretion conferred by s 50(1) of the 1925 Act must be exercised. But it does, I think, mean that a judge in exercising his discretion ought to have regard to the fact, if such it be, that the wife has brought proceedings against her husband unsuccessfully and has thrown a burden of costs on her husband which he as the successful litigant ought not to bear. And if, as in the instant case, the wife in her petition makes wicked and untrue charges against her husband which no husband could be expected to leave unchallenged, I entertain no doubt that an appropriate order for costs ought to be made against her.

I agree, therefore, with the conclusion of the judge in the court below that the judge's discretion under s 50(1) of the 1925 Act is untrammelled by any former practice and that he was right in his conclusion that he was not precluded from making an order under the Legal Aid Act 1964 by the effect of s 1(4) of that Act.

Having come to this conclusion, it is not necessary to consider whether, in view of the order of 16th April 1963, whereby the husband was ordered to pay the wife £1,820 per annum and a lump sum of £6,000, it would in any event have been right, in considering the appropriate order for costs of the wife's petition, to treat her as an impecunious wife. On behalf of the Law Society it was pointed out that on 7th February 1973, when the order was made rejecting the wife's prayer for the dissolution of the marriage, she was in truth impecunious. But it would in my judgment have been wrong for the judge to exercise his discretion as to the costs of the wife's petition on the footing that the wife was impecunious while there was pending an application which might, and in the event did, put substantial funds into her hands.

The judge in relation to the application under the Legal Aid Act 1964, with which we are concerned, expressed himself satisfied that the proper order for costs of the divorce proceedings would have been that the wife should pay half of the husband's costs. In coming to that conclusion the learned judge, after indicating that the case was one in which a wife with means would have been ordered to pay costs, remarked that the outcome of the divorce proceedings and the way in which they were initiated and conducted was not all that had to be considered. And, after he had gone on to emphasise that in the proceedings relating to financial provision he had not been able to absolve the husband of a considerable share of the blame and had concluded that both parties must take equal responsibility, the learned judge said that having regard to all those matters the wife should pay half the husband's costs.

In my judgment the learned judge, in deciding that because the husband must bear half the responsibility for the breakdown of the marriage he should have had an order for no more than half of his costs of the divorce proceedings, fell into error. In the first place it appears to me that the husband's responsibility for the breakdown of the marriage was reflected in the financial provision which he was ordered to make for his wife. Secondly, it had nothing at all to do with the conduct of the divorce proceedings and was not, in my judgment, a ground for reducing the amount of costs which otherwise ought to have been ordered to be paid to him in respect of his costs in successfully resisting over a period of days a petition which contained the most serious and unjustified allegations against him. In my judgment the appropriate order ought to have been that the wife should pay the whole of the husband's costs of the divorce proceedings. It is convenient to add at this point that the learned

1 [1970] 3 All ER 612, [1972] Fam 40

judge in the course of his judgment indicated that (acting pursuant to s 1(2) of the
1964 Act) he would have determined the wife's liability under any order for costs
against her either at nil or an amount insignificant for the purposes of the application
before him. We have not been invited to disagree with this assessment.

I turn to consider, which I can do very briefly, whether the husband will suffer severe
financial hardship unless the order sought by him is made. The judge answered that
question in the negative. He said that the house in which the husband lives, which was
his only substantial asset, was too large for him and an unnecessary extravagance. He
took its value at £50,000 less the mortgage on it amounting to £21,000, leaving an equity
of £29,000. If the husband sold the house he would, after paying the wife £6,000
payable under the financial provision order, have £23,000 left. With that he could, in
the view of the judge, buy a more appropriate smaller house, again on mortgage.
Well, we were told—and counsel on behalf of the Law Society did not really challenge
it—that his total bill to his solicitors (including the costs relating to the contest over
the financial provisions made for the wife) will be in the region of £9,000; to which,
of course, would have to be added the costs incidental to the sale and purchase, the
negotiating of a new mortgage, as well as the expense of moving into a new residence.
The husband's available income, after meeting the charges on it, is exiguous and, on
the figures given to us, not sufficient to provide him with food and clothing. Even
applying the strict test of 'severe financial hardship' laid down in *Nowotnik v Nowotnik*[1], and without resort to the more expansive interpretation of the phrase preferred
in *Hanning v Maitland (No 2)*[2], the husband's situation would in my judgment fall
within it. His financial position was, on the figures before the judge, worse than (I
quote a passage in the former case[3]) 'so nicely balanced that, in order to meet his
costs, he has to restrict his activities considerably, or seriously deplete his capital',
a situation which the Court of Appeal in that case would have regarded as 'severe
financial hardship'. He would have to do both. In this respect the more up-to-date
figures with which we have been supplied do not alter his situation.

Finally I have to consider the submission that it would not be just and equitable that
provision for the husband's costs should be made out of public funds. The submission
to that effect was based on the proposition accepted by the learned judge that because
the husband had a house which he could sell and out of the proceeds of which he could
pay the costs and buy another smaller house in which he could live at less expense, it
was not equitable that the costs should be paid out of public funds. In my judgment
this submission is not well founded. Although there may be cases in which the
assisted person's capacity to bear his costs falls to be taken into account, it would be
to fly in the face of *Saunders v Anglia Building Society (No 2)*[4] to hold that in the generality of cases it is not 'just and equitable' within the meaning of s 1(2) of the 1964 Act
that his costs should be paid out of public funds merely because he is able to pay them
himself. There the unassisted party, a building society, having, as Lord Pearson said[5],
very large resources, did obtain an order under s 1 of the 1964 Act. Here the husband
successfully contested serious and untrue charges made against him in proceedings
maintained at the public expense and, it not being suggested that he ought not to have
done so, it is in my judgment just and equitable that he should have the whole of his
party and party costs out of public funds.

I too would allow the appeal.

SIR SEYMOUR KARMINSKI. I have had the advantage of reading the judgments
of Davies and Stamp LJJ, and I agree with them. There is no doubt in my mind that

1   [1965] 3 All ER 167, [1967] P 83
2   [1970] 1 All ER 812, [1970] 1 QB 580
3   [1965] 3 All ER at 172, [1967] P at 103
4   [1971] 1 All ER 243, [1971] AC 1039
5   [1971] 1 All ER at 253, [1971] AC at 1054

a Hollings J was wrong in refusing to order that the husband's costs be paid out of public funds.

The wife brought serious charges against the husband, who contested those charges successfully. The husband was granted a decree against the wife on the grounds of her adultery with two men and of intolerable conduct on her part. The wife was given legal aid. She had no means and was not ordered to make any contribution towards

b her legal aid. The husband had no legal aid and had to contest a long hearing at his own expense, which may amount in all to about £10,000. He is not a rich man, though his salary is £8,000 a year. Out of this he has first to pay £2,500 to a former wife and her children. In the present case the husband has to pay the wife substantial maintenance and a further lump sum of £6,000. I entertain no doubt that the costs of the present litigation will be so heavy as to cause the husband severe financial hardship.

c Equally in my view the whole or part of such costs should be paid out of public funds. Having regard to the nature of the charges made against the husband by the wife, and to his successful defence against those charges, I am of the opinion that the whole of the taxed party and party costs incurred by the husband should be repaid to him out of public funds.

Appeal allowed. Law Society to pay husband's costs in Court of Appeal and below. Order
d *for payment out of legal aid fund of whole of husband's party and party costs of divorce suit down to date of decree nisi.*

Solicitors: *Herbert Smith & Co* (for the husband); *The Law Society.*

Mary Rose Plummer Barrister.

e

Practice Note

COURT OF APPEAL, CRIMINAL DIVISION
LORD WIDGERY CJ, PARK AND FORBES JJ
4th JUNE 1974

f *Legal aid – Criminal cases – Practice –Appeal – Legal aid order – Legal Aid Act 1974, s 30(7).*

Notes
For legal aid in Court of Appeal, Criminal Division, see 10 Halsbury's Laws (3rd Edn) 530, para 974.

For the Legal Aid Act 1974, s 30, see Halsbury's Statutes (3rd Edn) Current Statute
g Service, p 79.

LORD WIDGERY CJ delivered the following direction at the sitting of the court:
1. The attention of solicitors and counsel is directed to s 30(7) of the Legal Aid Act 1974 and to the pamphlet 'Preparation for proceedings in the Court of Appeal Criminal Division' which has been issued by the registrar today with the approval of the court.

h 2. Solicitors should bear in mind especially that any reasonable possibility of calling fresh evidence should be properly explored at the earliest possible moment and that a legal aid order as extended by s 30(7) will apply as described in the pamphlet.

3. When legal aid is granted for an oral hearing before the court the order will
j be restricted to 'counsel only' if it appears from the notice of appeal that counsel requires no instructions beyond those contained in the papers. If, however, there is good reason to assign a solicitor, e g if it appears that reports, witness statements or other new material are or may be required, the court will order 'full legal aid' (i e solicitor and counsel) either of its own motion or at the request of counsel assigned to the appellant.

N P Metcalfe Esq Barrister.

R v Howell

CROWN COURT AT SWANSEA
WIEN J
29th, 31st OCTOBER, 1st, 2nd, 5th NOVEMBER 1973

Criminal law – Manslaughter – Mens rea – Causing death by unlawful act – Intoxication – Self-induced intoxication – Accused incapable of forming intent to cause harm to victim – Whether defence to charge of manslaughter.

On 29th June 1973 the body of a woman was found partly concealed in the airshaft of an old mine. She had last been seen alive on 20th June in the company of the defendant who was subsequently charged with her murder. The defendant pleaded not guilty and raised the defence that at the material time he was so affected by alcohol and drugs that he was unable to form the necessary intent. During the trial the judge was invited by counsel for the defendant to direct the jury that if they found that the degree of intoxication was so great as to render the defendant incapable of having an intention to cause some harm to the victim they would be entitled to acquit the defendant of the alternative offence of manslaughter as well as of murder.

Held – Intoxication in relation to manslaughter stood on its own and it was not right to introduce into cases of intoxication those concepts of intention or realisation of harm that were necessary in other forms of manslaughter. Self-induced intoxication resulting from drink or drugs or both was no defence to manslaughter however great the degree of intoxication (see p 810 *b* and *c*, post).

Director of Public Prosecutions v Beard [1920] All ER Rep 21, *Bratty v Attorney-General for Northern Ireland* [1961] 3 All ER 523, *Attorney-General for Northern Ireland v Gallagher* [1961] 3 All ER 523 and *R v Lipman* [1969] 3 All ER 410 applied.

Gray v Barr [1971] 2 All ER 949 distinguished.

Notes

For the effect of drunkenness, see 10 Halsbury's Laws (3rd Edn) 713, para 1364, and for cases on the subject, see 14 Digest (Repl) 69-72, *315-332*.

Cases referred to in judgment

Attorney-General for Northern Ireland v Gallagher [1961] 3 All ER 299, [1963] AC 349, [1961] 3 WLR 619, 45 Cr App Rep 316, HL, Digest (Cont Vol A) 331, *259a*.

Bratty v Attorney-General for Northern Ireland [1961] 3 All ER 523, [1963] AC 386, [1961] 3 WLR 965, 45 Cr App Rep 1, HL, Digest (Cont Vol A) 332, *269a*.

Director of Public Prosecutions v Beard [1920] AC 479, [1920] All ER Rep 21, 89 LJKB 437, 122 LT 625, 84 JP 129, 26 Cox CC 573, 14 Cr App Rep 159, HL, 14 Digest (Repl) 71, *332*.

Gray v Barr (Prudential Assurance Co Ltd, third party) [1971] 2 All ER 949, [1971] 2 QB 554, [1971] 2 WLR 1334, [1971] 2 Lloyd's Rep 1, CA.

R v Church [1965] 2 All ER 72, [1966] 1 QB 59, [1965] 2 WLR 1220, 129 JP 366, 49 Cr App Rep 206, CCA, Digest (Cont Vol B) 197, *9203a*.

R v Lamb [1967] 2 All ER 1282, [1967] 2 QB 981, [1967] 3 WLR 888, 131 JP 456, 51 Cr App Rep 417, CA, Digest (Cont Vol C) 255, *9325a*.

R v Lipman [1969] 3 All ER 410, [1970] 1 QB 152, [1969] 3 WLR 819, 133 JP 712, 53 Cr App Rep 600, CA, Digest (Cont Vol C) 183, *322a*.

Ruling

On 29th June 1973 the body of Linda Thomas, a taxi driver, was found partly concealed in the airshaft of an old mine. She had last been seen alive on 20th June in

a   the company of the defendant, Trevor Thomas Henry Howell. On 29th October the defendant was arraigned in the Crown Court at Swansea before Wien J and pleaded not guilty to the murder of the deceased on 20th June. According to the defendant's evidence, he had been drinking on that day and had also taken drugs. He could only remember certain events, and could not recall all the circumstances leading up to the deceased's death. He could remember inflicting physical blows
b   on her but could not recall why he had acted in that way. He explained that at the material time he had no intention of harming her and had no control over his actions. Before the case for the defence had been concluded, counsel for the defendant invited his Lordship to rule whether self-induced intoxication through drink or drugs was a defence to manslaughter. After hearing argument his Lordship gave a considered judgment on the issue raised.

c   *Aubrey Myerson QC* and *Gerald Price* for the defendant.
Michael Evans QC and *Patrick Webster* for the Crown.

Cur adv vult

5th November. **WIEN J** read the following judgment. Counsel for the defendant
d   in this case invites me to direct the jury that if they find that the degree of intoxication by the defendant was so great as to render him incapable of having any intention to cause some harm to the dead girl then they would be entitled to acquit the defendant altogether.

It is a proposition that has some attraction because it has the merit of logic. Counsel for the defendant, who has cited many authorities most of which are, as he frankly
e   concedes, against the proposition that he puts forward, places reliance on, first of all, *Gray v Barr*[1]. He also relies on criticisms of *R v Lipman*[2] made by the learned editors of Smith and Hogan's Criminal Law[3].

The starting point of the question of intoxication in relation to manslaughter must be the leading case of *Director of Public Prosecutions v Beard*[4]. Before I consider that case I think it important to underline the fact that intoxication in relation to man-
f   slaughter stands on a separate footing entirely from any other form of manslaughter, for example manslaughter based on negligence. In *Beard's* case Lord Birkenhead LC said[5], after referring to some previous cases:

'... these decisions establish that where a specific intent is an essential element in the offence, evidence of a state of drunkenness rendering the accused incapable of forming such an intent should be taken into consideration in order to deter-
g   mine whether he had in fact formed the intent necessary to constitute the particular crime. If he was so drunk that he was incapable of forming the intent required he could not be convicted of a crime which was committed only if the intent was proved. This does not mean that the drunkenness in itself is an excuse for the crime but that the state of drunkenness may be incompatible with the actual crime charged and may therefore negative the commission of that crime. In a
h   charge of murder based upon intention to kill or to do grievous bodily harm, if the jury are satisfied that the accused was, by reason of his drunken condition, incapable of forming the intent to kill or to do grievous bodily harm, unlawful homicide with malice aforethought is not established and he cannot be convicted of murder. But nevertheless unlawful homicide has been committed by the accused, and consequently he is guilty of unlawful homicide without malice
j   aforethought, and that is manslaughter ...'

1   [1971] 2 All ER 949, [1971] 2 QB 554
2   [1969] 3 All ER 410, [1970] 1 QB 152
3   3rd Edn (1973), p 249
4   [1920] AC 479, [1920] All ER Rep 21
5   [1920] AC at 499, 500, [1920] All ER Rep at 27, 28

This reasoning may in the eyes of some persons be sound or unsound. Whether *a* the principle be truly expressed in this view or not the law is plain beyond all question that in cases falling short of insanity a condition of drunkenness at the time of committing an offence causing death can only, when it is available at all, have the effect of reducing the crime from murder to manslaughter. Hence the submission made on behalf of the Crown in this case that anything short of insanity—and counsel for the Crown qualified insanity by the word 'temporary'—does not provide a complete *b* defence and that submission of his is supported by the leading case of *Beard*[1]. Has the law changed since 1920? The Court of Appeal, Criminal Division, thought it had not. In *R v Lipman*[2] this very matter arose for consideration by the court. In that case the appellant was a United States citizen. He gave evidence of having gone with a girl to her room and there experienced what he described as an 'LSD trip'. He explained during the course of his evidence how he had the illusion of descending to the centre *c* of the earth and being attacked by snakes, which he fought. It was not seriously disputed that he had killed his victim in the course of this experience but he said that he had no knowledge of what he was doing and no intention of harming her. The jury apparently accepted that he lacked the specific intention either to kill his victim or to cause her really serious bodily harm and in the result they found him guilty of manslaughter. Widgery LJ in giving the judgment of the court referred *d* not only to *Beard's* case[1] but to several other cases in which the question of intoxication had arisen and for present purposes I wish to emphasise, in view of the case counsel for the defendant has referred to, namely *Gray v Barr*[3], that there were cases referred to by Widgery LJ, to which Lord Denning MR was a party, which dealt with the question of intoxication. One is *Bratty v Attorney-General for Northern Ireland*[4]. In that case Lord Denning said[5]: *e*

> 'Another thing to be observed is that it is not every involuntary act which leads to a complete acquittal. Take first an involuntary act which proceeds from a state of drunkenness. If the drunken man is so drunk that he does not know what he is doing, he has a defence to any charge, such as murder or wounding with intent, in which a specific intent is essential, but he is still liable to be convicted of manslaughter or unlawful wounding for which no specific intent is *f* necessary ...'

and Lord Denning referred to *Beard's* case[6] as authority for that proposition. Again, there was another case in which Lord Denning spoke about manslaughter in relation to drunkenness and that was *Attorney-General for Northern Ireland v Gallagher*[7], where he said: *g*

> 'If a man is charged with an offence in which a specific intention is essential (as in murder, though not in manslaughter), then evidence of drunkenness, which renders him incapable of forming that intent, is an answer ...'

There again he relied on *Beard's* case[8].

In the course of his judgment, in *Lipman's* case[9], Widgery LJ referred to s 8 of the *h* Criminal Justice Act 1967 and said:

> 'If the applicant's argument be sound, it follows that we have come a long way since [*Beard's* case[1]] and that events have moved very fast.'

1 [1920] AC 479, [1920] All ER Rep 21
2 [1969] 3 All ER 410, [1970] 1 QB 152
3 [1971] 2 All ER 949, [1971] 2 QB 554	*j*
4 [1961] 3 All ER 523, [1963] AC 386
5 [1961] 3 All ER at 533, [1962] AC at 410
6 [1920] AC at 494, 498, 504, [1920] All ER Rep at 25, 27, 30
7 [1961] 3 All ER 299 at 313, [1963] AC 349 at 381
8 [1920] AC at 501, 504, [1920] All ER Rep at 28, 30
9 [1969] 3 All ER at 415, [1970] 1 QB at 159

a   I interpose here to say that the argument on behalf of the applicant was that the jury should have been directed that it was necessary for the Crown to prove that the defendant intended to do acts likely to result in harm, or foresaw that harm would result from what he was doing. Widgery LJ went on[1]:

b   'In our judgment, there is a flaw in the applicant's argument; and the flaw lies in the assumption that *R. v. Church*[2] introduced a new element of intent or foreseeability into this type of manslaughter. All that the judgment in *R. v. Church*[2] says in terms is that whereas, formerly, a killing by any unlawful act amounted to manslaughter, this consequence does not now inexorably follow unless the unlawful act is one in which ordinary sober and responsible people would recognise the existence of risk.'

c   Finally Widgery LJ said[1]:

'We can dispose of the present application by reiterating that when the killing results from an unlawful act of the accused no specific intent has to be proved to convict of manslaughter, and self-induced intoxication is accordingly no defence. Since in the present case the acts complained of were obviously
d   likely to cause harm to the victim (and did, in fact, kill her) no acquittal was possible and the verdict of manslaughter, at the least, was inevitable.'

Counsel for the defendant relies principally on *Gray v Barr*[3] which was a case of a similar nature involving an incident where a person presented a loaded firearm at the victim, fired one shot deliberately into the ceiling and fired another shot, taking the consensus of the judgments of the various members of the court, accidentally.
e   That was a case that was not concerned in any way with intoxication. It was a case where an insurance company asserted that it was not liable to indemnify because there was, in fact, at least manslaughter and they were under no obligation at law to make any indemnity. During the course of his judgment, Lord Denning MR said[4]:

'There is no doubt, to my mind, that Mr Barr was guilty of manslaughter. I know that at the criminal trial he was acquitted altogether. But that was a
f   merciful verdict: and in this civil action we must, when called upon, give the true decision according to law.'

A little further on he said[5]:

'But I do not think it necessary to go into the matter at length. I would only say this: in manslaughter of every kind there must be a guilty mind. Without
g   it, the accused must be acquitted: see *R v Lamb*[6]. In the category of manslaughter relating to an unlawful act, the accused must do a dangerous act with the *intention* of frightening or harming someone, or with the *realisation* that it is likely to frighten or harm someone, and nevertheless he goes on and does it, regardless of the consequences.'

h   So far as any form of manslaughter is concerned that is unrelated to intoxication, I would respectfully agree and adopt what Lord Denning MR said in *Gray v Barr*[3] but he was not dealing with intoxication and one knows from what he has said in other cases, for example in *Bratty's* case[3], what his views were about intoxication. At no time, so far as researches show, has he sought to resile from what has been said in *Beard's* case[8] and what is said to have been the law for very many years indeed.

j   1   [1969] 3 All ER at 415, [1970] 1 QB at 159
2   [1965] 2 All ER 72, [1966] 1 QB 59
3   [1971] 2 All ER 949, [1971] 2 QB 554
4   [1971] 2 All ER at 956, [1971] 2 QB at 567, 568
5   [1971] 2 All ER at 956, [1971] 2 QB at 568
6   [1967] 2 All ER 1282, [1967] 2 QB 981
7   [1961] 3 All ER 523, [1963] AC 386
8   [1920] AC 479, [1920] All ER Rep 21

So one goes from there to the criticism that has been made of *Lipman's* case[1] (and
one supposes of *Beard's* case[2] since *Lipman's* case only followed *Beard's* case) by the
editors of Smith and Hogan[3]. Some criticism is made of that case and the editors
try their best to deal with the matter logically. I come to the view that it is quite
impossible to deal with this matter logically. Intoxication in relation to manslaughter
stands on its own and it is not right to introduce into cases of intoxication those
concepts of intention or realisation of harm that are necessary in other forms of
manslaughter. Accordingly I propose to direct the jury as follows in this case.

If they are satisfied that the defendant's acts caused the death of Linda Thomas, that
is he killed her and his acts were unlawful and dangerous, a self-induced intoxication
resulting from drink or drugs or both is no defence to manslaughter however great the
the degree of intoxication. If the defendant's acts were likely to cause harm to Linda
Thomas then an acquittal is impossible and at the very least there must be a verdict
of guilty of manslaughter. It follows that I reject the submission of counsel for the
defendant though it was put forward with great persuasion and considerable ability.
I am greatly assisted by counsel on both sides in this matter. I only add this, that I
have permitted argument at this stage although I am told that there is one more
witness to be called for the defence because that witness was not available yesterday
afternoon and there was time for this matter to be canvassed. It was canvassed
with the agreement of both counsel in the absence of the jury and my ruling has,
of course, been given in the absence of the jury.

Ruling accordingly. Subsequently, the jury found the defendant guilty of murder.

Solicitors: *R B Whittingham & Sons*, Bridgend (for the defendant); *Director of Public
Prosecutions.*

Gerald Price Esq Barrister.

---

1 [1969] 3 All ER 410, [1970] 1 QB 152
2 [1920] AC 479, [1920] All ER Rep 21
3 Criminal Law (3rd Edn, 1973), p 249

a

R v Noble

COURT OF APPEAL, CRIMINAL DIVISION
JAMES LJ, MOCATTA AND MICHAEL DAVIES JJ
7th, 10th MAY 1974

b

Criminal law – Evidence – Admissibility – Evidence of husband or wife – Husband or wife competent witness where one of them charged with offence with reference to the other or his property – Meaning of 'with reference to' – Wife writing husband's name and her own on loan agreement – Finance company believing signatures written by two different people – Finance company making loan on that assumption – Wife subsequently charged with forging
c *husband's signature on agreement – Prosecution seeking to call husband to give evidence that he had not authorised wife to sign on his behalf – Whether husband competent witness – Theft Act 1968, s 30(3).*

The accused wrote her name and that of her husband on (i) a form applying to a finance
d company for a loan of £120 and (ii) the subsequent loan agreement, under which the
accused received £120 from the finance company. The finance company thought that
the names on the application form were the signatures of two different people. They
would not have considered the application if they had known that it had been signed
by the accused alone. The accused was charged, under the Forgery Act 1913, with
forging her husband's signature on both documents. At the trial her defence was
that she had acted on the bona fide belief that she had her husband's authority to
e put his name to the documents. The prosecution, relying on s 30(3)[a] of the Theft
Act 1968, sought to call the husband to give evidence that that was not so. The
accused contended that he was not a competent witness under s 30(3) on the grounds
(i) that s 30(3) only applied to proceedings for offences under the 1968 Act, and (ii) that,
in any event, the offences with which she was charged were not offences
'with reference to' the husband or his property since they were not offences against
f him or his property.

Held – The husband's evidence was admissible under s 30(3) for (i) the words 'with
reference to' did not have the effect of limiting the subsection to offences against
the husband or his property or to offences under the 1968 Act, and (ii) the offences
with which the accused was charged were, within s 30(3), offences 'with reference to'
g the husband since the signatures, if they were authorised, would directly affect his
rights and obligations (see p 814 *f* to *j* and p 815 *a* and *b*, post).

Notes
For calling of spouse of defendant, under the Theft Act 1968, as witness for prosecution
h or defence, see Supplement to 10 Halsbury's Laws (3rd Edn) para 884.
For the Theft Act 1968, s 30, see 8 Halsbury's Statutes (3rd Edn) 801.

Case referred to in judgment
National Assistance Board v Wilkinson [1952] 2 All ER 255, [1952] 2 QB 648, 116 JP 428,
40 LGR 454, DC, 27(1) Digest (Reissue) 86, 661.

j
Cases also cited
Arthur v Bokenham (1708) 11 Mod Rep 148.
*Eastman Photographic Materials Co Ltd, The v The Comptroller General of Patents, Designs
and Trademarks* [1898] AC 571, HL.

---

a Section 30(3), so far as material, is set out at p 813 *g*, post

Haydon's Case (1584) 3 Co Rep 7a.   *a*
Holme v Guy (1877) 5 Ch D 901, CA.
Lincoln College's Case (1595) 3 Co Rep 53a.

Appeal
On 5th November in the Crown Court at Plymouth, before his Honour Judge
Goodall, the appellant, Irene Noble, was convicted by a majority verdict of 11 to one   *b*
on two charges of forgery under the Forgery Act 1913. She was sentenced to concurrent sentences of six months imprisonment suspended for 12 months on each
count and was ordered to pay £30·65 to the Mercantile Credit Co Ltd by way of
compensation. She appealed against her conviction by leave of the single judge
(May J). The facts are set out in the judgment of the court.

F L Coombs for the appellant.   *c*
M R Selfe for the Crown.

Cur adv vult

10th May.   **MOCATTA J** read the following judgment of the court. This is an
appeal against conviction by Mrs Irene Noble, who, after a trial at Plymouth Crown   *d*
Court was on 5th November 1973 convicted on two charges of forgery (counts 5 and
6), but acquitted on two other charges of forgery (counts 1 and 3) and two of obtaining
property by virtue of a forged instrument (counts 2 and 4). She was sentenced to
concurrent sentences of six months imprisonment suspended for 12 months on each
count. In the case of each count in the indictment the Crown's case against her was
that she had forged her husband's signature on the relevant document.
In order to establish the charges against the appellant, the prosecution wished to   *e*
call her husband to give evidence to the effect that he had not given her authority
to sign his name. After arraignment but before the jury were empanelled the trial
judge (his Honour Judge Goodall) heard lengthy submissions by counsel whether
the husband was a competent witness to give evidence for the prosecution by reason
of the provisions in s 30(3) of the Theft Act 1968. The learned judge ruled in favour   *f*
of the prosecution on this matter and the main and important question of law arising
on the appeal is whether his ruling was correct. Since this was a pure point of law,
the appellant did not need leave to appeal. The single judge, however, lest there
be any doubt on the matter, gave leave to appeal.
In the grounds of application for leave to appeal three other points in addition to
the issue of the competence of the husband as a witness for the Crown were taken,
each on the assumption that he was competent. It is convenient to dispose of these   *g*
at the outset.
The appellant admitted that she wrote her husband's name on each of the documents mentioned in the six counts, but her case was that she either had his authority
so to do or honestly believed that she had. The documents in question were all dated
in 1971 by which time relations between husband and wife, who had not lived as   *h*
man and wife since 1968, were distinctly strained. She continued to live with her
husband until the middle of June 1972 when in consequence of his alleged brutality
to her she took proceedings against him before the magistrates. Although she
succeeded in these and obtained an order against him, this was set aside and a fresh
hearing ordered by the Divisional Court on the basis that the husband had never
received the summons to appear before the magistrates. The matter is apparently   *j*
now proceeding by way of a petition for divorce.
Two of the subsidiary grounds advanced in support of the appeal have relation to
these matters. It was said on behalf of the appellant that the learned judge in his
summing-up failed to direct the jury sufficiently on the importance of the credibility
to be attached to the husband's evidence, the appellant's case being that he was
perjuring himself by way of revenge. The learned judge put the appellant's case on

a this clearly to the jury and the criticism is without foundation. Similarly there is nothing in the further point that the learned judge erred in excluding evidence by a doctor as to what had been said to him by the appellant in relation to how her multiple injuries had been caused.

Another ground, which at first sight was more plausible, was that the verdicts of the jury were inconsistent or perverse in that the appellant was acquitted on the first *b* four counts in respect of which, as in the case of counts 5 and 6 on which she was found guilty, her evidence was that she was authorised to sign her husband's name. The matter was, however, dealt with in the evidence and discussed with the jury at some length in the summing-up. In the case of the documents mentioned in the first four counts only what purported to be the husband's signature appeared. In the case of the two documents on which counts 5 and 6 were based there were signa-*c* tures of the appellant and what purported to be those of her husband. She was unable to explain why 'R. Noble', which she admitted she wrote, was written in a different colour ink from her own signature and was different from her ordinary handwriting in which she had written 'R. Noble' on the documents with which the first four counts were concerned. It is unnecessary to go into this matter in further detail since sufficient has been said to show that there was evidence justifying the *d* different verdicts reached by the jury.

We now pass to the main point in the case. In count 5 the appellant was charged with forgery of a document in that on or about 24th April 1971, with intent to defraud, she forged a certain document purporting to be an application to the Mercantile Credit Co Ltd for a loan and to be signed by herself and her husband, Robert Noble. The sixth count was in similar terms referring to the signature by herself and her *e* husband on or about 27th May 1971 of a loan agreement. As a result of this agree-ment the appellant received £120 which she required for the purchase of a washing machine. Evidence was given by a representative from the Mercantile Credit Co Ltd to the effect that he thought the signatures on the application form were those of two different people, that the company would not have considered the application had it been signed by the appellant alone and that the company's policy was not to *f* grant loans to persons who were not householders unless there was a guarantee by a householder or a guarantee card.

The main provision of s 30(3) of the Theft Act 1968 reads:

'Where a person is charged in proceedings not brought by that person's wife or husband with having committed any offence with reference to that person's wife or husband or to property belonging to the wife or husband, the wife or *g* husband shall be competent to give evidence at every stage of the proceedings, whether for the defence or for the prosecution, and whether the accused is charged solely or jointly with any other person . . .'

We omit the proviso dealing with compellability since counsel for the Crown made it clear at the outset both below and on the hearing of the appeal that he was not *h* arguing that the husband was a compellable witness.

Since it is clear that prior to the Theft Act 1968 the husband would not have been a competent witness in similar proceedings against his wife, stress was laid in the argu-ment advanced for the appellant on various well-known principles applicable to the construction of statutes. Of these it is sufficient to mention only two. The first is that the presumption is that the legislature does not intend to make a substantial *j* alteration in the law beyond what it expressly declares: see, for example, per Lord Goddard CJ in *National Assistance Board v Wilkinson*[1]. The second is that since the 1968 Act is a penal statute it should be interpreted in favour of the liberty of the subject.

---

1   [1952] 2 All ER 255 at 259, [1952] 2 QB 648 at 658, 659

Whilst nothing that is said in this judgment should be taken as in any way deroga- *a* ting from either of the two principles of construction mentioned, it is right in approaching the problem arising here as to the meaning of s 30(3) to bear in mind the far-reaching changes made in the law by the two preceding subsections of s 30. Thus at common law husbands and wives could not steal from one another, at least when living together, owing to the doctrine that in law they were one person. Certain limited inroads were made on this principle by the provisions of ss 12 and 16 of the *b* Married Women's Property Act 1882 and s 1 of the Married Women's Property Act 1884 as well as by the closely similar provisions of s 36 of the Larceny Act 1916, but although these enactments gave the parties to a marriage the right to bring criminal proceedings against each other for offences against one another's property, such proceedings might not be brought whilst the parties were living together, or even when they were living apart in respect of offences committed when they were *c* living together, unless at the time of the offence the offender was leaving or deserting or about to leave or desert the wronged party.

Section 30(1) of the 1968 Act provides that the Act shall apply in relation to the parties to a marriage and their property as it would apply as if they were not married, thus doing away with the common law doctrine. Section 30(2) gives a person the same right to bring proceedings against that person's wife or husband for any offence, *d* whether under the 1968 Act or otherwise, as if they were not married and further provides that a person bringing any such proceedings shall be competent to give evidence for the prosecution at every stage of the proceedings. The provisions of ss 12 and 16 of the Married Women's Property Act 1882 and of the 1884 Act as well as the Larceny Act 1916 were repealed. This subsection therefore goes substantially beyond the offences under the 1968 Act committed by one spouse against another. *e* It should perhaps also be noticed that in sub-s (2) as in sub-s (3) the 1968 Act in relation to the competence of a spouse as a witness in proceedings against another spouse departs from the specific enumeration of exceptions to the general rule adopted in s 4 of the Criminal Evidence Act 1898.

When one comes to the language of sub-s (3) itself the wide and somewhat vague phrase 'with reference to' is immediately noticeable in contrast to the use of the *f* word 'against' in sub-s (2) and also in the Married Women's Property Acts. Prima facie it would seem that the words 'with reference to' have been intentionally used in preference to 'against' in order to widen the category of criminal proceedings against a spouse in which the other spouse shall be competent to give evidence. Whether this be right or not, the words in fact used are ordinary non-technical English words carrying a wider meaning than the word 'against' had it appeared in this context in *g* their stead.

As against the argument for the Crown, it was sought to limit the construction to be placed on 'any offence with reference to that person's wife or husband' in two ways. The first was by reference to the long title to the Act to which it was argued that the ejusdem generis rule applied so as to limit the ambit of the words 'and for other purposes connected therewith'. We have been unable to derive any assistance from *h* this argument, since we cannot discern a relevant genus covering the preceding words in the long title. It was further argued that 'any offence' in sub-s (3) meant any offence under the 1968 Act and therefore did not include offences under the Forgery Act 1913. The words 'any offence' are very wide and since they are made applicable not only to property belonging to the husband or wife, we can find no justification for limiting their application to proceedings in respect of offences *j* under the 1968 Act.

It is no doubt possible, as is often the case when considering the application of a statutory provision or a legal principle, to think of sets of facts some of which would be clearly within and others clearly without the application of the provision or principle and further to imagine difficult borderline cases. We are not called on today to lay down some general criterion by which to determine in the infinite *a* variety of facts that may arise whether the wide phrase used in sub-s (3) would render the particular spouse concerned a competent witness. We have to determine, having decided that 'with reference to' bears a wider meaning than 'against', whether the offence with which the appellant was charged here of forging her husband's signature to an application for a loan and to a loan agreement were offences 'with reference to' her husband. The signatures if genuine or authorised would have directly affected the rights and obligations of the husband. In our judgment, like *b* that of the learned judge, the offences of forging her husband's signature were offences 'with reference to' the appellant's husband.

Appeal dismissed. Leave to appeal to the House of Lords refused but the court certified that the following question of law of general public importance was invloved, viz, 'Whether in s 30(3) of the Theft Act 1968 the words "with reference to that person's wife or husband or to property belonging to the wife or husband" limit the preceding words "any offence" to offences against the person or property of the wife or husband of the accused?'

Solicitors: *Registrar of Criminal Appeals* (for the appellant); *L D Lipson*, Plymouth (for the Crown).

d S Munasinghe Esq Barrister.

Kenilworth Industrial Sites Ltd v E C Little & Co Ltd

e
CHANCERY DIVISION
MEGARRY J   Affirmed CA [1975] 1 All ER 53
21st JANUARY 1974

Landlord and tenant – Rent – Review – Notice – Time limits – Failure to comply with time
f *limits – Effect – Clause providing machinery for determination of rent for specified period of term – No other provision in lease for rent during that period – Notice to operate clause to be given by landlord within specified time limits before termination of preceding period of term – Landlord failing to give notice within time limits – Notice given reasonable time before expiry of preceding period – Whether notice valid.*

g The landlord granted the lease of a factory to the tenant for a term of 21 years from 19th January 1968 at a rent of £2,980 per annum for the first five years and thereafter at a rent to be agreed in accordance with cl 5 of the lease. Clause 5 provided: 'NOT more than twelve months not less than six months before the expiration of the fifth tenth and fifteenth years of the term the Landlord shall serve upon the Tenant a notice to agree the rent of the said property for the ensuing five years . . .' The clause *h* provided for the determination of the new rent by arbitration in default of agreement and was subject to a proviso 'that any failure to give or receive such notice shall not render void the right of the Landlord hereunder to require the agreement or determination as aforesaid of a new rent'. The landlord failed to serve a notice before 18th July 1972, which was the date six months before the expiration of the first five years, but served a notice on 10th October 1972. The tenant contended that the *j* proviso to cl 5 of the lease was repugnant to the main body of the clause and therefore void and that the notice of 10th October was ineffective since the landlord had failed to comply with time limits stipulated by cl 5.

Held – Clause 5 provided machinery for the determination of the rent under the lease and imposed an obligation on the landlord to set that machinery in motion by giving notice; the clause was not one which conferred on the landlord an option

to require the review of an agreed rent. Accordingly the requirement of strict a
compliance with conditions precedent in the case of the privilege conferred by an
option did not apply to cl 5. Furthermore the proviso to cl 5 confirmed that the
obligation imposed on the landlord to comply with the time limits was not mandatory but merely directory, and failure to comply did not therefore render a
notice by the landlord void. Accordingly there was no necessary repugnancy between the proviso and cl 5. Since the notice had been given on 10th October, i e a b
reasonable time before the first five year period had expired, it operated as a valid
notice under cl 5 to agree the rent for the second five years (see p 818 b to h, post).
     Finch v Underwood (1876) 2 Ch D 310 and *Samuel Properties (Development) Ltd v Hayek*
[1972] 3 All ER 473 distinguished.

Notes
For agreements to review rents subject to a time limit for giving notice, see Supple- c
ment to 23 Halsbury's Laws (3rd Edn) para 1197, and for a case on the subject, see
31(1) Digest (Reissue) 481, 3952.

Cases referred to in judgment
Finch v Underwood (1876) 2 Ch D 310, 45 LJCh 522, 34 LT 779, CA, 31(1) Digest (Reissue)
   293, 2394. d
Forbes v Git [1922] 1 AC 256, 91 LJPC 97, 126 LT 616, PC, 17 Digest (Repl) 359, 1655.
Samuel Properties (Development) Ltd v Hayek [1972] 3 All ER 473, [1972] 1 WLR 1296,
   24 P & CR 233, CA, 31(1) Digest (Reissue) 481, 3952.

Summons
By an originating summons dated 22nd August 1973 the plaintiff, Kenilworth Industrial Sites Ltd ('the landlord'), sought: 1. a declaration that on the true construction e
of a lease dated 19th January 1968 and made between the landlord and the defendant,
E C Little & Co Ltd ('the tenant'), (a) the letter dated 10th October 1972 from the
landlord to the tenant operated as a valid notice to agree the rent for the second five
years of the term created by the lease for the purposes of cl 5 thereof; (b) alternatively, that the notice dated 9th February 1973 as varied by the terms of a letter f
dated 29th March 1973 operated as a valid notice for those purposes; 2. such further
or other declarations or relief as might seem to the court necessary or just. The
facts are set out in the judgment.

Edwin Prince for the landlord.
C P F Rimer for the tenant.
                                                                                      g

MEGARRY J. This originating summons raises a short point on a rent revision
clause in an ill-drafted lease of a factory. The lease was granted by the plaintiff
company (which I shall call 'the landlord') to the defendant company (which I shall
call 'the tenant') for a term of 21 years from 19th January 1968. In cl 1 the reddendum provides for a rent of £2,980 a year until 18th January 1973 (that is, for the first h
five years), '... and thereafter at a rent to be agreed as hereinafter mentioned in
clause 5 hereof...' The rent was made payable quarterly in advance on the usual
quarter days.
     I turn to cl 5. This reads as follows:

     'NOT more than twelve months nor less than six months before the expiration f
     of the fifth tenth and fifteenth years of the term the Landlord shall serve upon
     the Tenant a notice to agree the rent of the said property for the ensuing five years
     and thereupon the parties hereto shall agree a new rent as aforesaid and failing
     agreement such rent shall be determined by a single arbitrator to be appointed
     by the President of the Royal Institute of Chartered Surveyors whose decision
     shall be binding and final on the parties hereto PROVIDED always that such new

a
rent shall not be lower than the rent payable in respect of the premises for the last year of the term before such determination of the new rent AND PROVIDED always that any failure to give or receive such notice shall not render void the right of the Landlord hereunder to require the agreement or determination as aforesaid of a new rent.'

It may be observed that this appears to make no provision for the rent during the last year of the term.

b
What happened was that the landlord failed to serve any notice under cl 5 before 18th July 1972, which was the date six months before the expiration of the first five years of the said term. The landlord did, however, serve a notice on 10th October 1972. This notice was accordingly nearly three months late, though over three months before the second five years of the term began to run. The landlord also

c
served a second notice on 9th February 1973, and purported to vary it by a letter dated 29th March 1973; and reliance is placed on the second notice if the first is ineffective. The summons seeks in the alternative declarations that each notice operated as a valid notice to agree the rent for the second five years of the term. Counsel for the landlord primarily contends for the validity of the first notice. Counsel for the tenant contended that both notices were ineffective.

d
Counsel for the tenant's attack was, in effect, threefold. First, he contended that the second proviso to cl 5 was repugnant to the main body of the clause, and as it was the later of two inconsistent provisions contained in a deed it was therefore void; and Forbes v Git[1] was cited. Second, he said that in any event the words 'such notice' in the second proviso related only to the contents of the notice and not to the time within which the notice was to be given. Third, he said that just as the notice re-

e
quired to operate the rent review clause in Samuel Properties (Developments) Ltd v Hayek[2] was held to be ineffective because it was not served in due time, so the notice in the present case was ineffective; for in such clauses time limits are inflexible and mandatory. Counsel for the landlord, of course, sought to repel these attacks.

It seems to me that the courts are slow to conclude that two provisions in an instrument are so irreconcilable that one of them is void for repugnancy: only if

f
the conflict is necessary and inescapable will one be held void. So far as is reasonably possible the court should give effect to the whole of what the parties have agreed. In doing this, it is important to consider the language used, in its context, and the general purpose of the clause in question. In the Samuel case[2], the Court of Appeal was concerned with an underlease for 21 years in which the rent had been agreed for the entire term, though this was subject to an option for the landlords to increase the rent at the end of the seventh and fourteenth years. Both as a matter of wording and

g
as a matter of substance, that right of the landlords was an option, conditioned on serving a notice of a specified length. In the words of Russell LJ[3] (with whom Stamp LJ concurred), the language was that of a 'condition precedent in the context of what is described as an option'. It has long been settled that to exercise an option under a lease there must be strict compliance with the requirements of the option.

h
As was pointed out in Finch v Underwood[4], the right to exercise such an option is a privilege which requires due compliance with any conditions precedent. The present case seems to me to be very different. First, the lease reserves no rent beyond the first five years. The question is not one of the landlord having an option to displace an agreed rent for the later years of the term. If no new rent is ever ascertained, then as a matter of obligation under the terms of the lease, no rent at all is reserved for

j
the last 16 years of the term. Counsel for the tenant repudiated any idea that the tenant could remain rent-free after the first five years, and accepted and asserted that the tenant must pay rent at the rate initially reserved, namely, £2,980 a year. This,

1 [1922] 1 AC 256
2 [1972] 3 All ER 473, [1972] 1 WLR 1296
3 [1972] 3 All ER at 478, [1972] 1 WLR at 1301
4 (1876) 2 Ch D 310 at 314, 315

however, is not what the lease says, and counsel had to rely on a term to this effect
being implied in the lease. Such a term, however, would be entirely contrary to
the mechanism laid down by cl 5, and would have to be a term implied if, and only
if, the landlord failed to operate cl 5 according to its tenor. There seem to me to be
considerable difficulties in implying a conditional term of this kind.

Second, cl 5 is framed in terms not of option but of obligation: 'the Landlord
shall serve upon the tenant . . .', and so on. Clause 5 is a machinery clause designed
to fill the void left by the reddendum. I do not think that it is framed in a way
which supports counsel for the tenant's contention that the effect of the clause is as
if it had all been governed by the word 'If'. Furthermore, it does not seem to me
that there is any reason why the requirement of strict compliance with conditions
precedent in the case of the privilege conferred by an option clause should apply to
a clause imposing on the landlord an obligation to operate machinery intended to
fill a gap. If the landlord fails to comply with such a clause, he will no doubt be in
breach of his obligations under the lease; but belated compliance with obligations
is a commonplace as between landlord and tenant. No authority for applying to
a machinery provision the strict requirements for options has been put before me,
and in the absence of such authority I would not extend the principle of the option
cases in this way.

To these considerations one must add the terms of the second proviso to cl 5.
That seems to me to provide strong support for the view that I have indicated. If
the landlord is late in serving the notice, the landlord remains in breach of obligation,
but this is not to invalidate the landlord's right to require the new rent to be ascertained. So far as the ascertainment of a new rent is concerned, the time limits are
not mandatory but merely directory, with due observance an obligation of the lease
but not a condition precedent to the validity of the revision of rent. The proviso
refers to 'any failure to give . . . such notice' as not rendering the landlord's right void.
As a matter of construction, this seems to me to be wide enough to embrace both a
failure in the contents of a notice and a failure in the giving of a notice. In other
words, it covers both an inadequate notice given in time and an adequate notice
given late. No doubt, as counsel for the landlord accepted, the landlord could not
wait for several years after the first five years had run, and then demand what in
effect would be a retrospective increase of rent for the whole of the second five years:
but that is not what has happened. The landlord has in fact served a good notice.
Service was late, but nevertheless it was effected over three months before the first
five years had expired; and although the landlord was in breach of obligation in not
serving the notice sooner, by the second proviso to cl 5 the landlord's right to require
a new rent was not to be rendered void by the delay. (This delay, I may mention,
was said to have been one of the consequences of the death of the secretary to
the plaintiff company in December 1971.) I cannot see what there is to invalidate
a notice given, as this notice was, a reasonable time before the expiration of the first
five years. I do not have to decide what would have been the effect of a notice not
given a reasonable time before then.

I turn to repugnancy. On the construction that I have discussed, I can see no
necessary repugnancy between the second proviso to cl 5 and the body of the clause.
Reasonable effect can be given to each without straining the language, and so neither
is void. I do not say that no difficulties of construction remain, but I am only required to answer the questions put before me by the summons. Subject to anything
counsel may say, I would therefore make a declaration in the sense of question 1(a),
on which footing question 1(b) does not arise. Nothing arises under question 2,
and I shall deal separately with costs.

Declaration accordingly.

Solicitors: *White & Leonard*, agents for *J Arch & Co*, Coventry (for the landlord);
Martin & Nicholson, agents for *Pitt & Derbyshire*, Birmingham (for the tenant).

R W Farrin Esq Barrister.

Holden and another v Inland Revenue Commissioner

PRIVY COUNCIL

LORD WILBERFORCE, LORD DIPLOCK, LORD CROSS OF CHELSEA, LORD SALMON AND SIR ERIC SACHS

25th, 26th, 27th FEBRUARY, 6th MAY 1974

Privy Council – New Zealand – Income tax – Profits or gains derived from sale of property – Profits or gains – Meaning – Conversion of sterling funds into New Zealand currency – Purchase of United Kingdom securities with sterling funds and simultaneous sale of securities for New Zealand currency – Transactions yielding premium over amount of New Zealand currency receivable by converting sterling at official rate of exchange – Transactions of that kind in common use for purpose of converting sterling into New Zealand currency – Whether premium a profit derived from sale of United Kingdom securities – Land and Income Tax Act 1954 (New Zealand), s 88(1)(c).

The taxpayer, who was resident in New Zealand, became entitled to sterling funds in the United Kingdom. He wished to convert those assets into New Zealand currency available in New Zealand. There were two principal methods by which sterling funds in the United Kingdom could be converted into New Zealand currency: (i) by remitting the funds to New Zealand through the banking system at the official rate of exchange; (ii) by using the funds to purchase United Kingdom assets which could then be sold for New Zealand currency in New Zealand. The latter method, which was approved by the authorities, was the one in common use, for by adopting it the holder of sterling funds received a premium of between 12 and 13 per cent over the amount of New Zealand currency that he would receive for sterling at the official rate of exchange. There was therefore an alternative de facto exchange rate for sterling and the amount of the current premium could be ascertained by reference to market quotations. The taxpayer decided to adopt the second method and instructed his sharebroker to make the necessary arrangements. The broker arranged in New Zealand a price in New Zealand currency for selected United Kingdom securities on a particular day, and instructed his agent in London to buy those securities with the sterling funds and simultaneously to sell them for New Zealand currency. The Inland Revenue Commissioner assessed the taxpayer to income tax on the difference between the amount that the taxpayer had received in New Zealand currency from the sale of the securities and the value of the sterling funds in terms of New Zealand currency at the official rate of exchange, on the ground that it constituted 'profits or gains derived from the sale of personal property' within s 88(1)(c)[a] of the Land and Income Tax Act 1954. The taxpayer appealed.

Held – If one considered the substance of the transaction, all that the taxpayer had done was to exchange one currency for another. Because the method of conversion adopted by the taxpayer bought more New Zealand currency than would have been the case had he used the official rate of exchange it could not be said that the taxpayer had made a profit from the transaction for, in order to determine whether or not the taxpayer had made a profit, his sterling funds in London had to be valued at what they were worth in the market which the taxpayer had legitimately used rather than their worth at the official rate of exchange. Accordingly the appeal would be allowed (see p 824 g to j and p 825 b, post).

Notes

For the computation of 'profits or gains' for income tax purposes, see 20 Halsbury's Laws (3rd Edn) 139, 140, para 247, and for cases on the subject, see 28(1) Digest (Reissue) 120-127, 351-376.

---

a   Section 88(1), so far as material, is set out at p 820 j to p 821 a, post

Cases referred to in opinion

Eder v Internal Revenue Comr (1943) 138 F (2d) 27.

Inland Revenue Comr v Hunter [1970] NZLR 116, 28(1) Digest (Reissue) 129, *410.

Inland Revenue Comr v Walker [1963] NZLR 339, 28(1) Digest (Reissue) 104, *350.

Weil (Edmond) Inc v Internal Revenue Comr (1945) 150 F (2d) 950.

Appeals

Duncan Holden and Maurice Campbell Menneer ('the taxpayers') appealed against a decision of the Court of Appeal of New Zealand (Wild CJ and Richmond J, Turner P dissenting) dated 29th September 1972 dismissing an appeal by the taxpayers against a decision of Haslam J given in the Supreme Court of New Zealand on 7th March 1972 whereby he held that the respondent, the Commissioner of Inland Revenue ('the commissioner'), had not acted incorrectly in making certain assessments of liability for income tax on the taxpayers respectively. The cases of the two taxpayers were treated as raising identical questions and at all stages were heard together. The facts are set out in the opinion of the Board.

G P Barton and *R F Pethig* (both of the New Zealand Bar) for the taxpayers.

The Solicitor General (R C Savage QC) and *I L M Richardson* (of the New Zealand Bar) for the commissioner.

LORD WILBERFORCE. These appeals are from a judgment of the Court of Appeal of New Zealand which, by a majority, Turner P dissenting, dismissed an appeal from a judgment of the Supreme Court of New Zealand. The issue is identical with that previously raised in *Inland Revenue Comr v Hunter*[1]. In that case the Court of Appeal by a majority, Turner J dissenting, allowed an appeal from a judgment of McGregor J in the Supreme Court in favour of the taxpayer.

In each of the cases now under review the taxpayer, a resident in New Zealand, became entitled to sterling funds in the United Kingdom. He wished to convert these assets into New Zealand currency available in New Zealand, and instructed his sharebroker to make the necessary arrangements. The sharebroker arranged in New Zealand a price in New Zealand currency for selected United Kingdom securities on a particular day, and instructed his agent in London to buy these securities with the sterling funds and simultaneously to sell them for New Zealand currency. The result of these transactions was that the taxpayer received in New Zealand more New Zealand currency than he would have received if he had remitted his sterling funds to New Zealand for exchange into New Zealand currency through the banking system at the official rate of exchange. In fact, whereas for each £100 sterling at the official rate, he would have received approximately £NZ100 7s 6d, he obtained through the transactions in securities an amount which varied from £NZ105 to £NZ113. The commissioner, in each case, assessed the taxpayer to income tax on the difference between the two resulting amounts, and the question for decision is whether these assessments were correct in law.

The assessments were based on s 88(1)(c) of the Land and Income Tax Act 1954, which is as follows:

'Without in any way limiting the meaning of the term, the assessable income of any person shall for the purposes of this Act be deemed to include, save so far as express provision is made in this Act to the contrary—... (c) All profits or gains derived from the sale or other disposition of any real or personal property or any interest therein, if the business of the taxpayer comprises dealing in such property, or if the property was aquired for the purpose of selling or otherwise disposing of it, and all profits or gains derived from the carrying on or carrying

---

1   [1970] NZLR 116

a
out of any undertaking or scheme entered into or devised for the purpose of
making a profit.'

The commissioner relied on the second limb of para (c) so that he set out to show:
(1) that the amounts in question constituted a profit or gain derived from the sale
of personal property, (2) that the property was acquired for the purpose of sale. The
validity of each of these steps was contested by the taxpayers.

b
Their Lordships deal first with the second point, and do so briefly since they are in
agreement with the Court of Appeal, which on this point was unanimous in these
cases and in *Hunter's* case[1], that the commissioner's contention is correct. It is clear
that the relevant enquiry is for what purpose was the property acquired, and if
there was more than one purpose, what was the dominant purpose (see *Inland Revenue
Comr v Walker*[2]). In the present cases it is not relevant to enquire what was the
c
dominant purpose, since the only purpose for which the securities were bought was
that they should, immediately, be sold. The taxpayers argued that this purpose was
only incidental to the wider and more essential purpose, which each taxpayer set
out to achieve, namely, to remit funds from the United Kingdom to New Zealand
but that, in their Lordships' opinion, is irrelevant. There can be only one answer to
the question for what purpose the securities were bought, and the fact that the
d
purchase and sale were part of a wider objective cannot affect that answer. *Walker's*
case[2] on its facts and ratio decidendi is clearly distinguishable from the present.

Their Lordships turn to consider the first point, which raises a question of some
difficulty, and on which the Court of Appeal was divided in opinion. It is necessary
first to refer in more detail to the evidence. It is not disputed that, although the
commissioner set out his view of the facts in a case stated, it is open to the courts to
e
consider the actual evidence which was adduced before him. Moreover, although
for convenience some essential points were embodied in an agreed statement of facts
(set out in the judgment of Haslam J in the Supreme Court), each side reserved their
right to make 'limited submissions on the facts' and to raise 'such contentions as
might be open on the evidence'. There was, in fact, no essential difference between
the evidence of the various witnesses, and there is really no room for differences in
f
the interpretation to be placed on the critical passages in the testimony. It should
be mentioned that the evidence in the present case was in some respects fuller than
that in *Hunter's* case[1], and indeed was directed to fill some lacunae which that case
had revealed.

It is clear that, at all material times, there were three ways in which sterling funds
in the United Kingdom belonging to a New Zealand resident could be turned into
g
New Zealand currency. Each of these was legitimate, and was known to the
authorities.

1. The funds could be remitted to New Zealand through the banking system at
the official rate of exchange. This rate was fixed by the Minister of Finance in accordance with the Reserve Bank of New Zealand Act 1964 and the evidence was that,
prior to November 1967 when a devaluation took place, the £NZ was overvalued
h
in the sense that it could not have been maintained without a system of controls.
In 1965 and 1966 the official telegraphic transfer buying rate was £100 sterling=
£NZ100 7s 6d. There was no other legal means of effecting straight currency-to-
currency exchange, i e there was no separate 'commercial' or 'financial' rate. If
any black market rate existed, there was no evidence of it, and no argument was
based on the existence, if any, of such a rate. A counterpart of this was that
New Zealand residents were severely restricted in the purchase of sterling currency
in London. One of the witnesses—Mr J W Rowe—said indeed that if a New Zealand
resident wished to purchase sterling, he would have to operate the method referred

1   [1970] NZLR 116
2   [1963] NZLR 339

to in 3 below in reverse, i e to purchase United Kingdom securities at a premium and
to sell them for sterling, because that was the only way he had.

2. The fund could be sold to another New Zealand resident for New Zealand
currency provided that the sale was effected at the current official rate of exchange.

3. The funds could be used to purchase foreign assets which could then be sold for
New Zealand currency in New Zealand.

The evidence was that the third of these methods (in fact used by each of the
taxpayers and by the taxpayer in *Hunter's* case[1]) was most commonly adopted, in
the case of sterling funds, by the purchase of sterling securities. Considerable
amounts of such securities were purchased and sold. The working of these transactions and the manner in which a 'premium' was obtained is well explained by Mr J W
Rowe, an expert witness called by the taxpayers. He said:

'On the one hand there were many people in New Zealand anxious to purchase assets overseas in excess of those they might acquire with foreign currency
via the banking system because of the restrictive exchange controls then in
force, and such people were prepared to pay a significant margin in order to do
so. On the other hand there were people with assets in the United Kingdom,
Australia and elsewhere who wished to exchange these assets for New Zealand
currency and they were naturally not unwilling to do so at a rate more favourable
than that available via the banking system. The existence of such a de facto
exchange rate of course indicates that the volume of funds seeking to leave New
Zealand was greater than the reverse flow would have been at the official exchange rate (in the absence of exchange controls) and the difference at any one
time reflected the relative magnitude of the two flows.'

Evidence was also given that the great majority of purchases of sterling securities
were made for this purpose, i e as a means of remitting funds, rather than for
investment.

Elsewhere in his evidence Mr Rowe described these operations as producing a
'well-known alternative de facto but legal exchange rate', and as a 'legal double
(or multiple) exchange rate in respect of foreign property-to-local currency transactions'. The word 'multiple' was used because transactions of this kind took place
in Australian shares, and also in motor cars, producing separate, and possibly different,
'premia'. Moreover, even as regards sterling securities there might be slightly
different premia according to the stock selected: it was the task of the broker to
select the security best suited to the operation and to the demand in New Zealand.

The essence of this factual situation is, in their Lordships' opinion, undisputed.
Because the 'official rate' placed too high a value on New Zealand currency, and
because of the large demand by New Zealand residents for sterling currency, which
could not be satisfied by exchange through banking channels, there had developed,
and there was extensively used, the alternative method through the purchase and sale
of sterling securities, which both enabled New Zealand residents to obtain sterling
funds and also enabled New Zealand holders of sterling funds to obtain New Zealand
currency. Because of the working of supply and demand, the former class had to
pay and the latter class obtained the 'premium'. The amount of the current premium
could be ascertained by reference to market quotations; at the relevant time it was
about 12 to 13 per cent. All of this was legitimate, and was known to the authorities.
There was in evidence a letter of the Inland Revenue Department referring to the
'then ruling' premium on sterling in terms which show that buying and selling
of securities was both established and accepted practice. The bulletin of the Reserve
Bank of New Zealand in July 1966 contained this passage:

'... the proceeds from the sale of overseas securities, interest and dividends
on overseas securities, immigrants' funds and legacies could either be retained
overseas or transferred to New Zealand through a security transaction. The

---

1   [1970] NZLR 116

a   banking system was used to only a moderate extent for such transfers because of the premium to be obtained on the security market.'

It is not necessary to refer in greater detail to the evidence since the difficulty of this case does not lie in the facts, but in the legal consequences which ought to follow from them. The question is, whether, in relation to the transactions described above, the taxpayers derived any profits or gains from the sale of the purchased securities.

b   At first sight, it would appear that this could not be so. It is difficult to understand how a profit can be derived from the sale of property, made instantaneously after its purchase, when the property as such—viz the securities—neither rises nor falls in value. Particularly in the case of a quoted security, the presumption is that the purchaser paid for it precisely its value, and not something less than its value: no question of profit, or loss, could seem to arise. Moreover if one considers the

c   substance of the transaction, it can be said that all that the taxpayers were doing was to exchange one currency for another. Admittedly more New Zealand currency was obtained by using the particular method adopted than would have resulted from using the official rate—but merely to choose one of two available rates of exchange does not, it could be said, bring the section into play, or bring about a profit.

On the other hand the taxpayers, in choosing the method they did, adopted one

d   which involved the purchase and sale of securities: and since they did this, it is legitimate, even necessary, to examine the purchase and sale and see if a profit was made on the sale. A profit on a sale arises if the sale proceeds exceed the purchase price: the sale proceeds are known, viz the amount of New Zealand currency, including the 'premium' which the taxpayers obtained: the only question is as to the value of the purchase price.

e   The argument of the Solicitor-General as to this was simple. The purchasers, he contended, paid a price expressed in sterling: there is only one way in which to ascertain its value in New Zealand currency, and that is by converting it at the official rate. Thus: each £100 sterling was worth £NZ100 7s 6d, not more. Since, on the sale, the taxpayers received, for each £100 sterling, £112 to £NZ113, the difference represents the profit. This argument, which has an attractive clarity, in substance

f   was accepted by the majority in the Court of Appeal. It was forcibly put in the judgment of Richmond J in these words:

> 'However the vital question seems to me to be this. Can one properly to go one extra step and say that the *particular sterling funds owned by the* [*taxpayers*] were, as such, worth more than their value at the official rate? There is no
>
> g   doubt that they carried with them the potential of eventually realising a larger figure in New Zealand currency if they were utilised in the purchase of United Kingdom stock. There can also be no doubt that United Kingdom stock commanded a particular value to persons able to purchase it for New Zealand currency. As I see it however, the particular funds owned by the [taxpayers] (prior to their investment in United Kingdom stock) commanded no special
>
> h   value in themselves to any New Zealander anxious to acquire sterling. As such they were inaccesssible to such a person except at the official rate of exchange or in breach of the regulations.'

The opposite view was expressed by Turner P whose words repay quotation:

> j   'In this case it is necessary for the commissioner to show a *profit* or *gain* on the sale of the consols. What they realised in New Zealand currency is certain. What is not so certain is what the taxpayer gave for them, *measured in New Zealand currency*. We know, of course, what he gave for them *measured in English currency*. To say that the value of this English currency, measured in New Zealand currency, must be its value at the official rate, seems to me entirely to beg the question before us. I think that these English funds in England were

worth in New Zealand (as everything else is always worth) what they would
bring in the market. If there had been only one market—i e only one feasible *a*
way of realising them, viz the official channel, via the Reserve Bank—the question
would answer itself. But there were in my opinion two methods of realisation
—i e two markets—open to the taxpayer. Both were completely legitimate,
both were in fact open to the taxpayer, and both were being used daily by large
numbers of persons with the open approval of the authorities. These two *b*
methods were (a) the official method of remission through the Reserve Bank
and (b) the method followed by the taxpayer, and by many other taxpayers,
which furnished an *alternative* market for the funds. Where there are two markets
and the question is what is the value, the economists tell us that the question is
begged by selecting arbitrarily one of the available markets rather than the other.
In such case the value is the value in the market *actually used*, or, if neither is
yet used, the value in the higher of them.' *c*

In their Lordships' view, the opinion of Turner P is to be preferred. Looking at
the matter broadly, there can be no doubt that this corresponds more closely to the
reality of the transaction. The taxpayers were in truth making use of what had
come to be established as an alternative or parallel rate of exchange. This had
become so current, that the official method of transfer through the banking system *d*
was hardly used. The taxpayer or his adviser knew in advance what 'rate', under
the alternative method, in New Zealand was going to be obtained—there was in
fact a market rate—and all that the taxpayer had to do was to instruct his broker to
arrange remittance in this way and at this rate. That this corresponded to the
official view of the matter is shown by a passage from the bulletin of the Reserve Bank
of New Zealand for July 1966: *e*

'It should be remembered that all sales of sterling securities in the free market
in exchange for New Zealand currency represent the transfer of a New Zealander's
overseas assets into New Zealand currency, but without benefit to the official
reserves.'
f
But their Lordships accept, as the Solicitor-General contended, that, in a matter
in which taxation is involved, it is insufficient to look too broadly at the 'substantial
result' of what was done. Analysis must be made of the method actually chosen by
the taxpayer. If he has made use of a method which brings him within a taxing
provision, then the tax attaches. But this analysis does not, in their Lordships' opinion
lead to any different result. The essential fallacy of the commissioner's argument, in *g*
their Lordships' opinion, lies in valuing the sterling funds, which it was sought to
remit, at the official rate. The argument that they should be so valued may be
answered in the words of Turner P by saying that the funds must be valued for what
they were worth in the better market, in fact in the market which was used, and that,
on the evidence, there was a better market in a real sense. Another way of putting
it is to say that sterling funds in London had a premium value to a New Zealand *h*
resident. This in fact they had, otherwise the premium would not have existed, for
a New Zealand resident could only have obtained them by operating the taxpayers'
method in reverse—i e by purchasing United Kingdom securities with New Zealand
currency, at a premium, and then selling them for sterling. Funds available in
London must be treated as having, for a New Zealand resident, the same value as
he would have had to pay to obtain them. *j*
The point was clearly made by a banker witness—Mr G A Lau—in these words:

'As a result of the foregoing overseas assets held by a New Zealand resident
attained a new value at the time the government measures were first announced.
As indicated, this did not apply only to securities held by overseas residents but
also funds held in banks or on loan, as they were immediately convertible into

a   overseas securities which could be sold in New Zealand at the rate applicable
to such securities.'

This is really the point at which their Lordships respectfully differ from Richmond J. The funds owned by the taxpayers did, in truth, have a special, i e premium,
value to a New Zealand resident.   And so far from their being inaccessible except
at the official rate, they were inaccessible, in the sense that they could not have
b   been bought, at that rate.   They were only accessible if he paid the premium.   To
treat them, therefore, as having only their official rate value, is to disregard the fact
that they were freely available for external use, and for that reason, commanded a
premium value.   Thus they had the same value (disregarding brokerage, etc) as
the purchased securities.   No profit was made on the sale.

Their Lordships were referred to two United States cases, *Eder v Internal Revenue*
c   *Comr*[1] and *Edmond Weil Inc v Internal Revenue Comr*[2], both cited in Mann on The Legal
Aspect of Money[3], but these relate to different situations from those with which their
Lordships are concerned.

Their Lordships will humbly advise Her Majesty that the appeals be allowed.
Since there may be other contentions bearing on the cases which have not been
disposed of, the cases will be remitted to the Court of Appeal of New Zealand for
d   final disposal.

The commissioner must pay the costs of the taxpayers before the Board and in the
courts below.

Appeals allowed.

e   Solicitors: *Wray, Smith & Co* (for the taxpayers); *Allen & Overy* (for the commissioner).

Rengan Krishnan Esq Barrister.

---

1   (1943) 138 F (2d) 27
f   2   (1945) 150 F (2d) 950
3   3rd Edn (1971), p 475

Re Smith Kline & French Laboratories Ltd's applications

COURT OF APPEAL, CIVIL DIVISION
RUSSELL, BUCKLEY AND LAWTON LJJ
4th, 5th, 8th, 9th, 10th APRIL, 8th MAY 1974

Trade mark – Mark – Meaning – Representation or description of external appearance of goods – Colour scheme – Scheme a complete representation of goods as they appear to eye – Capsules containing drugs – Colour scheme for complete capsule – Scheme denoting origin of drug – Whether 'mark' must be something which can be described or represented separately from goods – Whether colour scheme applied to capsules a 'mark' – Trade Marks Act 1938, s 68(1).

The applicants applied for registration, in Part A of the register, of ten trade marks in respect of 'Pharmaceutical substances sold in capsules'. Each application was advertised before acceptance. On advertisement, the general specification was of 'Pharmaceutical substances sold in pellet form within capsules'. Application 849769 on advertisement contained the following more particular description which was typical of the ten: 'The trade mark consists of a dark grey colour applied to one half of the capsule at one end, the other half being colourless and transparent, and grey, red and white colour being each applied to a substantial number of pellets so that each pellet is of one colour only'. The opponents opposed the registrations on the ground, inter alia, that the colour scheme was not a 'mark' within s 68(1)[a] of the Trade Marks Act 1938, and was not therefore registrable as a trade mark.

Held – The ordinary meaning of 'mark' in relation to goods did not extend to something which amounted to an entire and complete description or representation of the external appearance of the goods in question. A mark, to be registered as a trade mark in respect of goods, had to be something which could be represented or described separately from the goods in relation to which it was to be used in the sense that it was not merely a description of the goods as they appeared to the eye. The capsule in each of the applications was recognisable by its whole appearance rather than by the fact that it bore an indicative mark. Accordingly none of the colour schemes was registrable (see p 835 *b* to *d*, p 837 *j* and p 838 *h* to p 839 *b* and *g*, post).

Re James's Trade-Mark (1886) 33 Ch D 392 applied.

Smith Kline and French Laboratories (Australia) Ltd v Registrar of Trade Marks [1972] RPC 519 approved.

Re F Reddaway & Co Ltd's Application [1914] 1 Ch 856 distinguished.

Decision of Graham J [1974] 1 All ER 529 reversed.

Notes

For the meanings of 'mark' and 'trade mark', see 38 Halsbury's Laws (3rd Edn) 513, para 852.

For the Trade Marks Act 1938, s 68, see 37 Halsbury's Statutes (3rd Edn) 936.

Cases referred to in judgments

Goodall (Charles) & Son Ltd v John Waddington Ltd (1924) 41 RPC 658, CA, 46 Digest (Repl) 66, 365.

Hoffmann-La Roche (F) & Co AG v DDSA Pharmaceuticals Ltd [1972] RPC 1, [1969] FSR 391, CA.

a Section 68(1), so far as material, is set out at p 828 *j*, post

a *James's Trade-Mark, Re, James v Soulby* (1886) 33 Ch D 392, sub nom *James & Sons v Parry & Co, Re James & Sons' Trade Mark*, 55 LJCh 915, 55 LT 415, 3 RPC 340, CA; rvsg (1885) 31 Ch D 340, DC, 46 Digest (Repl) 38, 190.

Parke Davis & Co v Controller of Patents, Designs and Trade Marks (13th December 1971), unreported, High Court of Ireland.

Reddaway (F) & Co Ltd's Application, Re [1914] 1 Ch 856, 83 LJCh 705, 31 RPC 147.

b *Roche Products Ltd v Berk Pharmaceuticals Ltd* [1973] RPC 473, [1973] FSR 345, CA.

Smith Kline and French Laboratories (Australia) Ltd v Registrar of Trade Marks [1972] RPC 519.

United States Playing Card Co's Application, Re [1908] 1 Ch 197, 77 LJCh 204, 98 LT 435, 46 Digest (Repl) 5, 2.

c **Cases also cited**

Banham (George) & Co Ltd v F Reddaway & Co Ltd [1927] AC 406, 44 RPC 27, HL; rvsg [1925] 42 RPC 397, CA.

Berlei (UK) Ltd v Bali Brassiere Co Inc [1969] 2 All ER 812, [1969] 1 WLR 1306, HL.

General Electric Co v The General Electric Co Ltd [1972] 2 All ER 507, [1973] RPC 297, HL.

d *Pentagon Trade Mark* [1964] RPC 138.

Pirie and Sons v Goodall and Sons (1891) 9 RPC 17, CA.

Registrar of Trade Marks v W & G Du Cros Ltd [1913] AC 624, 30 RPC 660, HL.

Samson Cordage Works' Application, Re (1927) 44 RPC 313.

Smith Kline and French Laboratories Ltd's Design Application [1974] RPC 253.

Williams (J B) Co v H Bronnley & Co Ltd, J B Williams Co v J H Williams (1909) 26 RPC 765, CA.

e *Winterbottom Book Cloth Co Ltd's Application, Re* (1925) 42 RPC 450.

Yorkshire Copper Works Ltd v Trade Marks Registrar [1954] 1 All ER 570, 71 RPC 150, HL.

Appeal

f On 29th May 1963 the applicants, Smith Kline & French Laboratories Ltd, applied for registration, in Part A of the register, of ten trade marks in respect of pharmaceutical substances sold in capsules. The Sterling-Winthrop Group Ltd opposed the applications. On 2nd November 1971 the Assistant Registrar of Trade Marks[1] (Mr R L Moorby) refused to register the marks. The applicants appealed and on 14th June 1973 Graham J[2], allowing the appeal, granted the applications but limited the registration to particular drugs. The opponents appealed. The facts are set out in *g* the judgment of Russell LJ.

G D Everington QC and *Anthony Rogers* for the opponents.
T A Blanco White QC and *Robin Jacob* for the applicants.

h   *Cur adv vult*

8th May. The following judgments were read.

RUSSELL LJ. This is an appeal by the opponents from a decision of Graham J[2] dated 14th June 1973, by which he (in effect) directed the Registrar of Trade Marks to accede to ten applications by the respondents to this appeal for registration of *j* ten trade marks. Each application was in connection with a particular get-up of a soluble capsule containing a drug in pellet form, which get-up was on the evidence distinctive of the applicants' goods. The get-up of the applicants' capsules consisted

---

1   [1972] RPC 247
2   [1974] 1 All ER 529, [1973] 1 WLR 1534

in one half being coloured (sometimes opaque and sometimes translucent), the other
half being colourless and transparent, the actual drug being in pellet form, and the
pellets being each coloured with one of two or more colours (including white), thus
giving a speckled or stippled effect to the uncoloured transparent half of the capsule.

It is convenient to take one application as typical of all, and I take no 849769 in
which the applicants marketed a drug called by it 'Eskornade', of which the chemical
make-up, or approved name, is diphenylpyraline hydrochloride, isopropamide
iodide and phenylpropanolamine hydrochloride. The application in its original
form in May 1963 consisted of a coloured photograph of the capsule and the legend:

> 'The trade mark consists of a capsule of which one half is coloured opaque
> dark grey, the other half colourless, containing pellets coloured grey/red/
> white.'

Registration was sought in respect of 'Pharmaceutical substances sold in capsules'.
Later it is to be assumed that the application was amended, for as advertised in the
Trade Marks Journal it was related to 'Pharmaceutical substances sold in pellet
form within capsules' and was thus described:

> 'The Trade Mark consists of a dark grey colour applied to one half of the cap-
> sule at one end, the other half being colourless and transparent, and grey, red
> and white colour being each applied to a substantial number of pellets so that
> each pellet is of one colour only. A specimen of the Mark may be seen at the
> Trade Marks Registry . . .'

In his decision the registrar (a) considered that there was here a mark capable of
being a trade mark, but (b) refused the application on the ground that it (the mark)
was not inherently adapted to distinguish goods of the proprietor of the mark from
other goods. On the originating motion by the applicants by way of appeal from
that decision, Graham J agreed with the registrar on point (a) but disagreed on
point (b) and allowed the appeal.

Two points may be conveniently here mentioned. It had been agreed below by
the opponents that s 11 of the Trade Marks Act 1938 prevented registration: but that
point was not really pursued in this court. Secondly, the judge by his order narrowed
in each case the application of the mark to goods, by adding to the general reference
to 'Pharmaceutical substances sold in pellet form within capsules' the approved
name or description of the particular drug sold in the particular colour combination.
This was the subject of the cross-appeal by the applicants. The learned judge
appreciated that this could have the effect of enabling a rival to use any of the marks,
providing that he put a different or somewhat different drug in the capsule, without
infringing the trade mark, but considered that the law of passing-off would sufficiently protect the applicants in such a case. The opponents in this court did not
resist the cross-appeal, should the appeal fail, and I think rightly. Granted all else
in favour of the applicants, I consider that the particular restriction was not justified.

Consequently, the issues are narrowed to two. First, whether there is here a
'mark' within the Trade Marks Act 1938. Second, if so, whether it is not only in
fact adapted to distinguish but also inherently so adapted.

The interpretation section, s 68(1), provides:

> '. . ."trade mark" means . . . a mark used or proposed to be used in relation
> to goods for the purpose of indicating, or so as to indicate, a connection in the
> course of trade between the goods and some person having the right . . . as
> proprietor . . . to use the mark . . .'

The section also provides:

> '. . ."mark" *includes* a device, brand, heading, label, ticket, name, signature,
> word, letter, numeral, or any combination thereof . . .'

a   Section 68(2) is in these terms:

'References in this Act to the use of a mark shall be construed as references to the use of a printed or other visual representation of the mark, and references therein to the use of a mark in relation to goods shall be construed as references to the use thereof upon, or in physical or other relation to, goods.'

b   Reference to colour in trade marks was first introduced in 1905[1], and is now to be found in s 16 of the 1938 Act as follows:

'A trade mark may be limited in whole or in part to one or more specified colours, and in any such case the fact that it is so limited shall be taken into consideration by any tribunal having to decide on the distinctive character of the trade mark. If and so far as a trade mark is registered without limitation
c   of colour, it shall be deemed to be registered for all colours.'

Section 9 of the 1938 Act deals with the distinctiveness requisite for registration in Part A of a trade mark. It must contain or consist of at least one of the following essential particulars: (a) the name of a company, etc, represented in a special or particular manner; (b) the signature of the applicant for registration or some predecessor
d   in his business; (c) an invented word or invented words; (d) a word or words having no direct reference to the character or quality of the goods, and not being according to its ordinary signification a geographical name or surname; '(e) any other distinctive mark . . .' It is under (e) that the applicants contend for registration. Section 9(2) provides:

e   '. . ."distinctive" means adapted, in relation to goods in respect of which a trade mark is . . . proposed to be registered, to distinguish goods with which the proprietor of the trade mark is . . . connected in the course of trade from goods in the case of which no such connection subsists . . .'

Section 9(3) is as follows:

f   'In determining whether a trade mark is adapted to distinguish as aforesaid the tribunal may have regard to the extent to which—(a) the trade mark is inherently adapted to distinguish as aforesaid; and (b) by reason of the use of the trade mark or of any other circumstances, the trade mark is in fact adapted to distinguish as aforesaid.'

It is under (a) that there is a difference of view between the registrar and the learned
g   judge.
On the first question in this appeal, which is I apprehend the question of the greater general importance, it is I think of the first importance to observe this fact: that in the case of no 849769 (and of course each other application) it is not possible to describe or represent that which is said to be the mark without describing or representing the whole exterior appearance of the goods in relation to which it is proposed
h   to be used. I believe that the one question is whether such is properly to be regarded as a 'mark'. In perhaps an over-simplified form, it was asked in the course of argument whether there was a distinction between a badge and an overall livery. Applying the question to a specific case in the books[2], where a blue/red/blue stripe throughout the length of Reddaway's fire hose was registrable as a trade mark, would the answer have been otherwise had the stripes been accustomed to be applied round the
i   whole circumference of the hose as distinctive of the applicant's goods and had the mark applied for been equally extensive?
At this point it should I think be noticed that the fact that we are concerned here

1   See the Trade Marks Act 1905, s 10
2   *Re F Reddaway & Co Ltd's Application* [1914] 1 Ch 856

with colours does not by itself answer the question.   Section 16 of the 1938 Act does
not provide that any colour or colour scheme is necessarily a mark, though in a given
case it may be only by the use of colour that a mark is discernible, as in *Reddaway's*
case[1], where there could not have been three stripes of the same neutral colour as
the rest of the fire hose: see contra the argument in *Reddaway's* case[2].   In the present
case what is relied on in, for example, no 849769, is described in argument as the
pattern, which is exhibited in fact by the capsule.

The definition of 'mark' in the statute is of course not confined to the items which
it is said to include, and we were invited to consider a number of dictionary definitions.
Chambers (1901) includes 'a visible sign'; 'that by which anything is known'; 'a
badge'.   Chambers (1952) includes 'a visible indication or sign'; 'a distinctive device';
'a brand'; 'a streak, smear or other local modification of appearance'.   Murray's
Oxford Dictionary has a main heading III, 'a sign, token, indication', and thereunder
numbered Arabic 10 'an appearance, action or event that indicates something: a
sign, token, symptom': and further numbered Arabic 11, 'a sign affixed or impressed
for distinction', and '(a) a device, stamp, seal, label, brand, inscription, written
character, or the like placed upon an article as an indication of ownership or origin'.

In *Re F Reddaway & Co Ltd's Application*[1], already referred to, the trade mark
proposed and registered consisted of a stripe of three lines blue/red/blue for use on
or in relation to hoses.   It was considered that the mark as shown on the application
form—which was simply a length of those stripes—was not adapted to distinguish;
but it would be so if made subject to a condition of limiting protection to use throughout the whole length of the hose.   The Comptroller-General appears[3] to have rejected the application on a more general ground, namely, that the definition of
'mark' did not appear to him—

'to cover the mere pattern or design of an article, or, as here, lines of a particular
colour woven in Hose.   The idea underlying the definition would appear to be
that a mark is some definite device or symbol affixed to goods and, not merely
the peculiar fabric, pattern, or construction which characterises the articles.'

On the appeal it was argued for the registrar that registration would be protecting
a get-up 'and that is not what the statute is intended to protect . . .'   Warrington J[4]
saw 'no reason why three lines of colour woven into a fabric should not be a mark'.
The mark was, as I have said, three lines of colour blue/red/blue; it was proposed to
be used on or in connection with hoses; the judge considered that the fact that the
mark was woven and to be woven into a fabric was nonetheless a user on the goods,
thus answering part of the objection of the Comptroller-General to it being regarded
as a trade mark.

Our attention was drawn to remarks of Sargant LJ in *Charles Goodall & Son Ltd v
John Waddington Ltd*[5].   He said[6]:

'A trade mark and a design are two quite different things, ordinarily speaking.
A design forms part of the goods themselves.   A trade mark is something which is
extra, which is added to the goods for the purpose of denoting the origin of the
goods, and, speaking generally of trade mark and design, the same thing is not a
trade mark and a design.'

1 [1914] 1 Ch 856
2 [1914] 1 Ch at 860
3 See 31 RPC 147 at 148
4 [1914] 1 Ch at 862
5 (1924) 41 RPC 658
6 41 RPC at 668

a   He then referred to a view of Swinfen Eady J that registration as a design and as a trade mark are not mutually exclusive: see *Re United States Playing Card Co's Application*[1]. These comments were obiter, and do not I think greatly assist to answer the question which I conceive arises in the present case.

Reliance was placed on a phrase in the judgment of Harman LJ in *F Hoffmann-La Roche v DDSA Pharmaceuticals Ltd*[2]—the green and black CDP capsule passing-off
b   case. He said[3]: '... in a get-up it is quite different: it is not a description, it is mark just as if here they had said "Roche's product" ...' This it was said was a natural and instinctive use of the word 'mark' as applicable to an overall get-up or livery. I do not derive assistance from this. The question what is or can be a 'mark' for trade mark purposes was not for consideration. I note also that Harman LJ[4] had quoted extensively from a judgment of Jenkins LJ[5] in which the latter would seem to use on seven occasions the phrase 'mark or get-up' as indicating different
c   things.

Re James's Trade-Mark[6] was relied on by the opponents. The question was whether a representation or drawing of a block of blacklead in domed shape was properly registered under the 1875 Act[7] as 'a distinctive device, mark ...' Pearson J[8] held that, if registrable at all, it must be as a 'distinctive device'; he ignored the word 'mark'. He held that it was not registrable, being 'nothing more than a representa-
d   tion of the article which is sold', and analogous to a merely descriptive word. In the Court of Appeal[9] it was successfully contended that it was a 'distinctive mark' to be used on or in connection with blacklead sold in any shape by the proprietor; it could not prevent others selling blacklead in a dome shape. Cotton LJ agreed with Pearson J that if it was merely an attempt to register a picture of the thing sold as a trade mark it would be bad, but indicated that this was not the case; the mark
e   was one which could be by the proprietor annexed to or connected with blacklead in any shape. Lindley LJ said[10]:

'A mark must be something distinct from the thing marked. The thing itself cannot be a mark of itself, but here we have got the thing and we have got a mark on the thing ...'

f   Lopes LJ[11] dealt with the contention that it could not be registered because it was a pictorial representation of the thing itself (which in general he would appear to accept) by saying that it could nevertheless be a distinctive mark *on* the article whatever the shape of the article.

This case appears to me to be authority for the proposition that you cannot register as a trade mark that which, at any rate so far as shape is concerned, is nothing but a
g   representation or description *of the article in question.* (It is to be observed that the dome shape had formerly been registered as a *design*.) It is not of course authority for a proposition that a mark must be something which is put on an article after the article is produced, and in *that* sense distinct; for clearly an article may be manufac- tured by a process which simultaneously incorporates the mark, as in the *Reddaway* case[12]. Now the shape is the whole external appearance of the article: and it is
h

1   [1908] 1 Ch 197
2   [1972] RPC 1
3   [1972] RPC at 21
4   [1972] RPC at 19
5   In *T Oertli AG v E J Bowman (London) Ltd* [1957] RPC 388 at 397; *affd* HL [1959] RPC 1
j   6   (1886) 33 Ch D 392
7   Trade Marks Registration Act 1875
8   (1885) 31 Ch D 340
9   (1886) 33 Ch D 392
10 33 Ch D at 395
11 33 Ch D at 396
12 [1914] 1 Ch 856

contended in the present case that what is sought to be registered under application
no 849769 is nothing but the whole external appearance of the article, albeit by
reference to colours and colour pattern deployed over a substantially standard
capsule shape. In the one case the shape was the overall get-up. In the present
case the colour pattern is the overall get-up. There is no question here of using a
painting or colour reproduction of the finished article as a mark on the goods or on
packaging of the goods; to see the 'mark' is to see the goods.

I take next the decision in the Irish case of *Parke Davis & Co v Controller of Patents,
Designs & Trade Marks*[1] in 1971. Under a substantially similar legislation a blue
colour band encircling the middle of capsules containing pharmaceutical substances
was held to be a mark. (I observe that Parke Davis have obtained registration in
Great Britain of coloured bands so applied.) This decision in no way helps to solve
the main question in this appeal.

Finally, there is the decision of Windeyer J on parallel applications for registration
by the present applicant in Australia: see *Smith Kline and French Laboratories (Australia)
Ltd v Registrar of Trade Marks*[2]. There, says the headnote, a trade mark must be
capable of being described and depicted as something apart from the goods in relation
to which it is to be used; a mere description of goods by shape, size or colour cannot
be a trade mark in respect of those goods. As in the present case, the applications
considered by the judge were not in their original form, but in the final form as
exemplified in the previously quoted advertisement from the Trade Marks Journal[3].
Windeyer J, in considering whether there was a relevant mark, was thus addressing
his mind to the same question that was before Graham J[4] and is now before us.
Windeyer J says this[5]:

'A trade mark is defined in the Act[6] as "a mark used or proposed to be used
in relation to goods" for the purposes stated. This definition assumes, it seems
to me, that the mark is something distinct from the goods in relation to which
it is used or to be used. It assumes that the goods can be conceived as something
apart from the mark and the mark is not of the essence of the goods. The goods
are assumed to have an existence independently of the mark. As Sargant L.J.
put it, in stating the difference between a design and a trade mark, "A trade mark
is something which is extra, which is added to the goods for the purpose of denoting the origin of the goods": *Charles Goodall & Son Ltd. v. John Waddington
Ltd*[7]. And Lord Lindley, then Lindley L.J., said *In re James's Trade-Mark*[8]:
"We must be careful to avoid confusion of ideas. A mark must be something
distinct from the thing marked. A thing cannot be a mark of itself...".'

I continue the quotation from Windeyer J[9]:

'This does not mean that today a trade mark must be a mark to be physically
applied to the goods. It may now be a mark to be used in other ways in relation
to goods. A thing can always be described and distinguished in appearance by
any visible characteristic which it has, its shape, colour or any mark which it
bears. But the test is not—Can the goods be described or depicted without
reference to their markings? As I see it, a mark for the purposes of the Act must

---

1   13th December 1971 (unreported)
2   [1972] RPC 519
3   See [1972] RPC 519 at 527
4   [1974] 1 All ER 529, [1973] 1 WLR 1534
5   [1972] RPC at 527, 528
6   Trade Marks Act 1955-1958 (Australia)
7   (1924) 41 RPC 658 at 668
8   (1886) 33 Ch D 392 at 395
9   [1972] RPC 519 at 528

be capable of being described and depicted as something apart from the goods to which it is to be applied, or in relation to which it is to be used. This view is supported by the provisions of s. 107 of the Act. It accords too with the various things included in the definition of "mark". That list is not expressed as exhaustive but it is certainly illustrative. I do not think that a mere description of goods simply by shape, size or colour can be a trade mark in respect of those goods.'

As I read that passage in the judgment, Windeyer J is concluding that the applications should fail because that which was merely a description or representation of the total get-up, the total external appearance, of the article could not properly be regarded or treated as a 'mark' used on the article in the trade mark context. We are therefore faced with the task of deciding on this point whether we prefer the views of Graham J[1] or of Windeyer J[2], which appear to me to be irreconcilable.

I turn to the reasons given by Graham J for his conclusion. He rehearses[3] that which he took to be a short statement of the argument for the opponents—

'that nothing could be a mark . . . unless it could be separately depicted or represented and separately applied to an existing article. Nothing, he said, could be a mark unless it could in effect be stamped or otherwise applied to the article in respect of which it was registered.'

The learned judge then referred to *Reddaway's* case[4] as being relied on by the applicants. If this passage suggests that the opponents' argument was based simply on the proposition that you must first have your article and then apply the mark to it, it is not the argument which I understood to have been put before this court. As I have said, it is plain that you can have a mark, such as the coloured stripes in Reddaway's hoses, which is used on or in connection with goods notwithstanding that it is formed as an integral part of the process of production of the goods by being, for example, woven into the goods. Perhaps the reference to the applicants' reliance on *Reddaway's* case[4] shows that the judge had a narrow understanding of the opponents' submissions. The learned judge then referred to the reference by Harman LJ to 'mark' in the green/black capsule case[5] which I have already mentioned; he also, I think with respect irrelevantly, referred to the decision in another passing-off case in this court, *Roche Products Ltd v Berk Pharmaceuticals Ltd*[6], in which there was no occasion to comment on or even notice Harman LJ's use of the word 'mark'. Graham J said[7]: 'If, as it normally is, get-up is something which can be registered as a trade mark . . .' Counsel were unable to cite any authority in support of that wide proposition; indeed there is no case, of which we were made aware, in which there has been registration as a trade mark of nothing but the total get-up—the total external appearance—of the goods in question. If of course the judge's phrase means no more than that a trade mark may be used on goods so as in that sense to form *part* of the-get up, I do not quarrel with it. The judge then concluded[8] that the upshot of all the cases referred to was 'to establish that a scheme of colouring applied to goods may be a "mark"': the cases were *Re James's Trade-Mark*[9], *Reddaway's* case[4], *Hoffmann-La Roche's* case[10], and *Roche Products Ltd v Berk Pharmaceuticals Ltd*[6]. Insofar as the

1 [1974] 1 All ER 529, [1973] 1 WLR 1534
2 [1972] RPC 519
3 [1974] 1 All ER at 533, [1973] 1 WLR at 1538
4 [1914] 1 Ch 856
5 F Hoffmann-La Roche & Co AG v DDSA Pharmaceuticals Ltd [1972] RPC at 21
6 [1973] RPC 473
7 [1974] 1 All ER at 533, [1973] 1 WLR at 1539
8 [1974] 1 All ER at 534, [1973] 1 WLR at 1539
9 (1886) 33 Ch D 392
10 [1972] RPC 1

scheme of colouring involves a representation or description of the whole get-up, the whole external appearance, I do not agree that those cases lead to that conclusion; for it was in that sense that it was said that to be a mark there must be something separate from the goods. The judge criticised the opponents' contention that the woven threads in the hose in *Reddaway's* case[1] must be regarded as a representation in practice of the use of the mark rather than as the mark itself. I think that the distinction was a perfectly valid one, though it does not, I think, assist.

The judge then dealt with the decision in the Australian case[2], first by agreeing in general terms with Mr Moorby's approach to it in his decision[3]. The judge thought (incorrectly as it transpired in this court from a full transcript of argument) that *Re James's Trade-Mark*[4] had not been cited to Windeyer J. In referring to the remarks of Lindley LJ in that case, Graham J said[5]:

'He was not as I understand it saying, as counsel for the [opponents] logically must say if he is right, that if the mark is part of the article it can never be a mark within the Act.'

Here again I detect the possibility that before Graham J the true question, as I see it, did not fully emerge. Graham J finally sought to distinguish the decision of Windeyer J on the ground that the applications before the latter were not in the finally amended form of the United Kingdom applications: but, as I have indicated, it appears from the judgment of Windeyer J[6] that he was dealing with the problem on the footing of those finally amended forms.

Mr Moorby, in his decision, did not follow Windeyer J, relying on *Reddaway's* case[1] as indicating that colour woven into an article could be a mark. He was unable to find a difference between the application of a colour pattern in the present applications and the wrapping of the capsule in multi-coloured wrappings or labels. The relevance of the comparison depends of course on the validity of the assumption that a description or representation of the whole of colour patterned wrapping— the whole of the get-up—could qualify as a mark.

Here then is the problem. In *Reddaway's* case[1] the stripes made a mark; it was not the whole external appearance of the article; the decision of the Comptroller-General was scotched insofar as it proceeded on the hypothesis that the fact that a mark was proposed to be incorporated with the goods in the course of manufacture deprived it of the title of a relevant mark. His wider proposition that the peculiar pattern or construction which characterises an article could not be a 'mark' was not criticised, but it was not necessary to the decision to do so. The *James* case[4] *did* decide that the mere description in terms of shape of the article or goods could not be relevantly a mark or trade mark so as to prevent production by others of goods in that shape: but of course it was clear in that case that the shape of the article per se was, or was no longer, distinctive of blacklead as having a trade connection with the proprietor of the mark. In the present case the evidence shows that the colour pattern of, for example, application no 849769 is distinctive in fact of a product of the applicants.

There is established as a registrable mark, the Parke Davis monocoloured band around the middle of a pharmaceutical capsule. Suppose in the present case the mark sought to be registered was a band round the middle of the capsule of speckled or stippled appearance, would that (granted distinctiveness) not be a 'mark', whether or not the effect were produced by a speckled band superimposed on the capsule,

---

1   [1914] 1 Ch 856
2   *Smith Kline and French Laboratories (Australia) Ltd v Registrar of Trade Marks* [1972] RPC 519
3   [1972] RPC 247
4   (1886) 33 Ch D 392
5   [1974] 1 All ER at 535, [1973] 1 WLR at 1540
6   [1972] RPC at 527

a or by a similar effect produced by multicoloured pellets viewed through a transparent uncoloured centre band in the capsule? Suppose further that the mark sought to be registered was one half of the capsule of speckled or stippled appearance, would that (granted distinctiveness) not be a 'mark', however the effect was produced? Take no 849769: could it not, the argument proceeded, have been application for a mark (of course granted distinctiveness) in which one half of the capsule exhibits a

b speckled or stippled pattern of grey/red/white? If that were so, why should it be disqualified as a 'mark' because it is also insisted that the other half of the capsule be coloured opaque grey?

I see the force of those contentions, but in the end I do not consider that the ordinary meaning of 'mark' in relation to goods extends to something which amounts to an entire and complete description or representation of the external appearance of the

c goods in question—the entire get-up. A mark, to be registered as a trade mark in respect of goods, must be something which can be represented or described separately from the goods in relation to which it is to be used in the sense that it is not merely a description of the goods as they appear to the eye. Of any of the capsules to which the present applications are related, it would seem to me that in ordinary parlance it would be said to be recognisable by its whole appearance rather than by the fact that it bears an indicative mark.

d Having formed the view that there is not here a mark or a trade mark, I do not express any view whether, if there were one, it would be inherently adapted to distinguish, etc.

Accordingly, I would allow the appeal.

e **BUCKLEY LJ.** In this case we are concerned with ten applications for registration of trade marks made by the applicants, Smith Kline & French Laboratories Ltd, in 1963. All ten applications were substantially in the same form, differing only in the colour schemes involved. I can take as an example application no 849766, which was in the following terms:

f 'The trade mark consists of a maroon colour applied to one half of the capsule at one end, the other half being colourless and transparent, and yellow, blue and white colours being each applied to a substantial number of pellets so that each pellet is of one colour only.'

This language is identical, mutatis mutandis, with the language of the example selected by Russell LJ. The application was made in respect of pharmaceutical substances sold in pellet form within capsules. No representation of the mark claimed was included in the advertisement in the Trade Marks Journal, nor apparently was one included in the application form in its final state. A specimen of the mark, consisting of a capsule answering to the description which I have read, was deposited at the registry.

Three points have been argued in this court. The first is whether the subject-matter of the application is capable of being a trade mark; the second, whether it possesses the necessary degree of distinctiveness; and the third, whether it would be likely to deceive or cause confusion, so as to be disentitled to registration by reason of s 11 of the Trade Marks Act 1938. The assistant registrar[1] answered the first and last of these questions in the applicants' favour but answered the second question adversely to them. On appeal, Graham J[2] answered all three questions in favour of the applicants, and he accordingly directed registration for all ten marks, but with the limitation that none of them should be registered in respect of pharmaceutical

1   [1972] RPC 247
2   [1974] 1 All ER 529, [1973] 1 WLR 1534

substances sold in pellet form within capsules generally, as the application sought, but that each should be registered only in respect of a particular drug.

I will deal first with the question whether the subject-matter of the application is capable of constituting a trade mark. The Trade Marks Act 1938, s 68(1), provides that 'trade mark' means a mark used or proposed to be used in relation to goods for the purpose of indicating, or so as to indicate, a connection in the course of trade between the goods and some person having the right either as proprietor or as registered user to use the mark. The same subsection also provides that 'mark' includes a device, brand, heading, label, ticket, name, signature, word, letter, numeral, or any combination thereof. It will be observed that this is not a definitive exposition of the meaning for the purposes of the Act of the word 'mark': it does not say what a mark is but what it includes. It has been common ground in this case that the subject-matter of the application does not fall within any of the specific descriptions contained in the definition of 'mark'. We have therefore to consider whether it falls within such wider meaning as the word 'mark' may be properly capable of sustaining in the context of the Act as a whole.

That word is susceptible in the English language of a surprisingly large number of varied meanings. From the primary meaning of a boundary, which it seems to have had in the Germanic languages from which it is derived, it has acquired such diverse meanings as a target or goal, a sign, a symbol, a brand or badge, a token, a symptom, a distinctive feature, a standard of quality, an influence, a distinction or reputation, and a point awarded for merit, to mention but a selection of the meanings given in the dictionaries. Many of these meanings, particularly those having abstract significancies, would clearly be inappropriate to the present case. The argument in this appeal has revolved round the question whether the appearance of the product itself can constitute a mark for the purposes of the 1938 Act, or whether the mark must be something distinct from the product itself.

I turn to the Act to see what assistance it offers in determining the sense in which the word 'mark' is used in it. First, it appears to me that all the types of mark specifically mentioned in s 68(1) in relation to the meaning of the word 'mark' are primarily graphic in character, either pictorial or in writing, although they may also be capable of extending to marks reproduced in plastic forms. Certain kinds of mark are recognised by the Act as marks but are disentitled to registration as trade marks (see s 39(5), which relates to line headings on cloth, and rr 15 to 19 of the Trade Marks Rules 1938[1], which relate to certain words, names and pictorial or armorial representations). These all relate to marks of a written or pictorial character. Secondly, a trade mark (the only kind of mark with which we are concerned) must be a mark capable of use 'in relation to goods' as an indication of origin. A get-up or the appearance of the product itself might perform this function as effectively as a symbol of some kind imprinted on the goods or otherwise connected with them. Section 68(2), however, provides that references in the Act to the use of a mark shall be construed as references to the use of a printed or other visual representation of the mark. So a trade mark must be susceptible of being represented in a printed or other visual form. The subsection also provides that references to the use of a mark 'in relation to goods' shall be construed as references to the use thereof on, or in physical or other relation to, goods. This language does not seem very appropriate to be applied to the appearance of the product itself.

The monopoly conferred by registration in Part A of the register consists of 'the exclusive right to the use of the trade mark in relation to' the goods in respect of which it is registered (see s 4), that is, for the use of the mark on the goods or in physical or other relation to them (see s 68(2)). Can it reasonably be said that the appearance of the product itself can be sensibly described as a result of the use of a mark on the product or in physical relation to it?

---

1   SR & O 1938 No 661

a   It is clear that the particular application under consideration is limited to specified colours. The only provision of the 1938 Act relevant to this is s 16, which provides that a trade mark may be limited in whole or in part to one or more specified colours, and in any such case the fact that it is so limited shall be taken into consideration by any tribunal having to decide on the distinctive character of the trade mark. This relates colour to distinctiveness, but does not lend support to the view that a colour scheme affecting the appearance of the product itself can constitute a mark.

b   The rules made under the 1938 Act have statutory effect as if contained in the Act (s 40(2)). Rules 23 to 25 of the Trade Marks Rules 1938 require every application for registration to contain, and to be accompanied by, representations of the mark. It is apparent from r 28 that such a representation may take the form of a drawing or other representation (which I take to mean a pictorial or an alphabetical representation) or a specimen (an example of which might be a piece of cloth with a particular

c   mark woven into its heading or selvage). This rule also provides that the registrar may also, in exceptional cases, deposit in the office a specimen or copy of any trade mark which cannot be conveniently shown by representation. So a trade mark must normally be something which can be represented pictorially or in writing but may exceptionally be something which can conveniently be demonstrated only by a

d   physical sample or copy.

     I have been unsuccessful in finding any other context in the statute having at all a direct bearing on the meaning in the 1938 Act of the word 'mark'. These contexts all seem to me to be readily understood consistently with a 'mark' meaning a graphic or plastic symbol or device of some kind, including a written name, word or phrase, in whatever kind of script it may be reproduced. They may not be absolutely

e   irreconcilable with a meaning extending to a get-up or the appearance of the product itself, but I find it very difficult to fit such a meaning to them. The learned judge, for whose experience in these matters I have the greatest respect, does not seem to have felt this difficulty. After referring to a remark of Harman LJ in *F Hoffmann-La Roche & Co AG v DDSA Pharmaceuticals Ltd*[1], which was a passing-off case and did not relate in any way to trade marks, the learned judge said[2]:

> 'If, as it normally is, get-up is something which can be registered as a trade mark there can be no difference in principle between the nature of the indication of origin in that case and in the present case. Clearly Harman LJ was regarding the colour applied to the capsule as a mark indicating origin.'

Counsel, however, were unable to bring to our attention any case in which a get-up as such has been registered as a trade mark. It was suggested that the distinctive dimple bottle in which Haig's whisky is sold might be such a trade mark, but on investigation it became apparent that the registered mark consists of a picture of such a bottle with some letterpress and a facsimile signature beneath it. It may well be the case that a get-up may be based on, or may make use of some prominent feature of, a trade mark; but, with deference to the learned judge, I have not been satisfied that it is accurate to say that a get-up is normally, or can ever be, registrable as a trade mark.

     Apart from contexts, what meaning can one reasonably attach to the word 'mark', in connection with trade marks? If a red pillar box was painted blue, no one could, in my opinion, reasonably say that it bore a blue mark or that it had been marked in blue. If, on the other hand, a blue band, of perhaps two inches wide, were painted round its waist, one might very reasonably say that it had been marked with a blue mark. In the one case it has ceased to be a red pillar box; in the other it remains a red pillar box but distinguished by a blue mark on it. A mark in this sense must, in my opinion, be something sufficiently superficial to be distinguishable from the thing marked. The difference between the two examples I have given may perhaps

---

1   [1972] RPC at 21
2   [1974] 1 All ER 529 at 533, [1973] 1 WLR 1534 at 1539

be a matter of degree, in which case difficult borderline examples could be imagined, *a*
but nevertheless the difference is, I think, a clearly intelligible one. Lindley LJ
seems to me to have stated the matter succinctly and persuasively in *Re James's
Trade-Mark*[1], saying:

> 'A mark must be something distinct from the thing marked. The thing
> itself cannot be a mark of itself, but here we have got the thing and we have got
> a mark on the thing, and the question is whether that mark on the thing is or is *b*
> not a distinctive mark within the meaning of the Act[2].'

This does not mean that a trade mark must always be physically distinct from the
product in relation to which it is used. It may be incorporated in the physical substance of the product, as in the case of a watermark in a sheet of paper or of the three
coloured lines woven into the fabric of a hose in *Re F Reddaway & Co Ltd's Applica-* *c*
tion[3]. It may be impressed or embossed on the actual substance of the product, as
in *Re James's Trade-Mark*[4]. These are merely methods of using the mark, that is, of
displaying the mark on the product to which it relates. The point of the decision in
Re James's Trade-Mark[4], as Cotton LJ made clear, was that the applicant was not
claiming a monopoly of the production of blocks of blacklead of a particular shape,
that is of a particular appearance, but a monopoly of the right to use a particular *d*
device as a mark on their blacklead in whatever shape they might fashion the product.
In *Re F Reddaway & Co Ltd's Application*[3] the registered mark was not a hose with
three coloured lines running along it, but three coloured lines extended (that is,
used) along the length of a hose; it was not the product, but a mark on the product.
Counsel for the applicants accepted that the goods, that is the product itself, cannot
be a trade mark, and that the mark must be something added to the product. They *e*
contend that in this case the mark is the pattern of colour (half opaque and coloured
and half having a stippled appearance on account of the variously coloured pellets
seen through the transparency) imparted to the capsule in the course of manufacture.
They say, and I think rightly, that the fact that the mark, if it be one, is imparted in
the course of manufacture is of no significance (*Re F Reddaway & Co Ltd's Application*[3].)
They say that this pattern of colours is put on the capsule for the purpose of indicating
that the product is their product. It seems to me that the policy of using different
colour schemes for different drugs may also serve another purpose, quite as important, of distinguishing one product of the applicants from another (that is, one drug
from another) in use; but for the present purpose I am prepared to accept that the
colour schemes are designed to indicate manufacturing origin. This does not, however, answer the question whether the colour scheme is a trade mark. It must still *f*
be shown to be a mark within the meaning of the 1938 Act. A get-up might quite
well acquire an association with the goods of a particular producer so as to sustain
a good cause of action in passing-off without being a trade mark. So I return to what
seems to me to be the crucial question, whether what is here sought to be registered
is a 'mark'.
The description of the mark contained in the application for registration is, in my
opinion, a description of the capsule itself. What was deposited at the registry as a
specimen of the mark was such a capsule. It seems to me that the application is for
registration of the capsule as a trade mark relating to itself. I find it impossible to
regard the colour scheme as a mark distinct from the capsule. For reasons which I
have already indicated, I do not think that this application can properly be regarded
as an application for the registration of a 'mark' within the meaning of the 1938 Act.

1   (1886) 33 Ch D 392 at 395
2   Trade Marks Registration Act 1875
3   [1914] 1 Ch 856
4   (1886) 33 Ch D 392

a Accordingly, in my judgment, none of these applications can succeed, and the appeal should be allowed.

This makes it unnecessary to discuss the question of distinctiveness or s 11 of the 1938 Act. In any case, the point under the section was scarcely pursued in this court.

b **LAWTON LJ.** I too would allow this appeal. In my judgment, what the applicants have sought to register are not marks at all within the meaning of the Trade Marks Act 1938.

Section 68 of the 1938 Act assigns meanings to both 'trade mark' and 'mark'. If what was sought to be registered were marks at all, there was ample evidence to establish that they were trade marks. The problem then is whether the colour patterns formed by the appearance of the capsules themselves were marks. Section 68 does not define c 'mark'. It is said to include 'a device, brand, heading, label, ticket, name, signature, word, letter, numeral, or any combination thereof'. The applicants accepted in argument that the colour patterns were not covered by any of the specific statutory examples of marks. All these examples are capable of representation and of being applied to goods. It follows, so it seems to me, that the applicants must show that their colour patterns come within the ordinary meaning of the word 'mark'. The examples d must have been intended to cover any strained or unusual meaning of the word. The residual meaning must have been intended to be that in the ordinary usage of English. The question then is whether as a matter of the ordinary meaning of the word the colour patterns could be said to be 'marks'. In my judgment, they could not. I find support for this opinion first in the dictionary meanings given in Chambers Dictionary (1901 and 1952 editions), Murray's Oxford Dictionary and the Shorter Oxford Dictionary, and secondly in the decided cases.

e The word 'mark' has many meanings: Murray's Oxford Dictionary has nearly five pages dealing with them. In relation to 'trade mark', the relevant meanings given in Murray's Dictionary are—

f 'a device, stamp, seal, label, or the like, placed upon an article as an indication of ownership or origin, as an attestation of quality, as a means of identification, etc.'

The appearance of an article is something different from a mark on it. A mark on an article may be large or small; but if it becomes so large that it represents the appearance of the article, it is no longer a mark. To attempt to state in words when a mark on an article ceases to be such and becomes the appearance of the article itself is to attempt g to solve the semantic problem which is typified by the question when does a heap become a pile. Herein, I think, lies the solution to the problem discussed in argument whether a repetition all around the fire hose of the stripes which were adjudged to be a 'mark' in *Reddaway's* case[1] would still have been a mark. In my judgment, such repetition would not have been a mark, as it would have amounted to the appearance of the hose itself.

h The construction which I would put on the word 'mark' seems to accord with that which was put on it in *Re James's Trade-Mark*[2]. All the relevant cases have been reviewed by Russell LJ. There is nothing I can usefully add.

Appeal allowed. Order of Graham J set aside and order of registrar restored. Leave to appeal to the House of Lords granted.

j Solicitors: *McKenna & Co* (for the opponents); *Woodham Smith & Greenwood* (for the applicants).

Mary Rose Plummer   Barrister.

1   [1914] 1 Ch 856
2   (1886) 33 Ch D 392

Director of Public Prosecutions v Brooks   a

PRIVY COUNCIL
LORD WILBERFORCE, LORD DIPLOCK, LORD CROSS OF CHELSEA, LORD SALMON AND SIR
ERIC SACHS
19th, 20th FEBRUARY, 3rd APRIL 1974

b

*Drugs – Dangerous drugs – Possession – Unauthorised possession – Meaning of possession –
Custody or control – Servant having custody or control of goods belonging to master – Evidence
from which it could be inferred that servant knew goods were dangerous drug – Whether
servant in 'possession' of dangerous drug – Dangerous Drugs Law (Jamaica), s 7(c).*

Some police officers saw a van parked, with its engine running, in a lay-by at Braco,   c
Jamaica.   The respondent was occupying the driver's seat and there were several
other people in the cab.   When the officers hurried towards the van, the occupants
scrambled out and ran off.   The respondent was caught by the officers.   Inside the
body of the van, which was neither visible nor accessible from the cab itself, the police
found 19 sacks containing a total of more than 1,000 lbs of ganja.   When questioned
by the officers, the respondent said that he had been employed by R and had been   d
told to drive the van, loaded as it was, to Braco.   When asked whether he knew
what was in the sacks, the respondent made no reply.   The respondent was charged
with, and convicted of, unlawfully having in his possession ganja, contrary to s 7(c)
of the Dangerous Drugs Law of Jamaica.   He appealed to the Court of Appeal of
Jamaica, which quashed the conviction on the ground that he, as R's servant, merely
had custody of the van and the contents, and that was not enough to constitute   e
'possession'.

Held – The appeal would be allowed and the conviction restored, for (i) a person
had possession of a dangerous drug, within s 7(c), if, to his knowledge, he had the
drug in his physical custody or under his physical control, and (ii) on the evidence
the respondent had in his physical custody and control the 19 sacks of ganja and from   f
the evidence it could be inferred that he knew what he was carrying in the van (see
p 842 j and p 843 c d h, post).

Notes
For possession of dangerous drugs, see 26 Halsbury's Laws (3rd Edn) 200, para 458,
and for cases on the subject, see Digest (Cont Vol B) 522, 243b, and Digest (Cont Vol C)   g
670, 243bca-243bcf.

Cases referred to in opinion
R v Livingston (1952) 6 JLR 95.
Warner v Metropolitan Police Comr [1968] 2 All ER 356, [1969] 2 AC 256, [1968] 2 WLR
1303, 132 JP 378, 52 Cr App Rep 373, HL, Digest (Cont Vol C) 182, 95d.   h

Appeal
The Director of Public Prosecutions of Jamaica appealed by special leave against
the judgment of the Court of Appeal of Jamaica (Luckhoo P, Smith and Graham-
Perkins JJA), dated 2nd July 1971, allowing an appeal by the respondent, Wishart
Brooks, against his conviction, by the Resident Magistrate's Court (His Honour Mr   j
Lloyd Ellis) for the parish of Trelawney, for unlawfully having in his possession ganja,
contrary to s 7(c) of the Dangerous Drugs Law, and against his sentence of 18 months
hard labour.   The facts are set out in the opinion of the Board.

J G Kerr QC (of the Jamaican Bar) and *Stuart McKinnon* for the appellant.
T O Kellock QC and *Eugene Cotran* for the respondent.

LORD DIPLOCK. This appeal is brought by special leave from a judgment of the Court of Appeal of Jamaica which quashed the conviction of the respondent by a resident magistrate for an offence under s 7(c) of the Dangerous Drugs Law of unlawfully having in his possession ganja.

The relevant facts found by the magistrate can be stated shortly. A van was seen by a number of police officers parked with its engine running on a lay-by near an airstrip at Braco. The respondent and two or three other persons were in the cab, the respondent occupying the driver's seat. When the police, who were in uniform, ran towards the car the occupants scrambled out of the door of the cab and took to their heels. Two got away into the bush but the respondent and one other (a co-defendant at the trial) were caught before they could make good their escape. In the body of the van, which was neither visible nor accessible from the cab itself, were 19 sacks containing a total of more than 1,000 lbs of ganja. When asked by Corporal Lakeman why he had run from the vehicle the respondent said that a man named Reid employed him to drive the van to Brown's Town. Reid took the van leaving him (the respondent) at Brown's Town. Reid returned with it loaded as it was and told him to drive to Braco. (Braco is some 16 miles from Brown's Town.) The respondent was also asked by the corporal whether he knew what was in the sacks, but he made no reply to this question.

At the hearing before the magistrate there was some discrepancy in the evidence of the police officer on the question whether the respondent had tried to run away. This was one of the grounds on which a submission was made at the close of the prosecution's evidence, that there was no case to answer. The other ground was that there was no evidence that the respondent was in 'possession' of the ganja. The magistrate did not find it necessary at that stage to resolve the discrepancy in the police evidence. He ruled that whether or not the respondent had tried to run away, here was a sufficient prima facie case of possession on the part of the respondent. After this ruling the respondent made an unsworn statement from the dock: 'What I told Lakeman was true. I did not run from the van. Lakeman held me around the steering wheel'. The magistrate did not accept this statement as true. He said that he believed the statements of the two constables who had deposed that the respondent had tried to run from the van. Without giving any further reasons he found the respondent guilty of the offence charged and imposed the mandatory sentence of 18 months hard labour.

The other defendant was convicted too, and his conviction was also quashed by the Court of Appeal. The evidence against him differed from the evidence against the respondent. It is unnecessary to recount it as no appeal is brought against the quashing of his conviction.

On the respondent's appeal to the Court of Appeal, that court accepted its own previous decision in R v Livingston[1] as correctly laying down the law in Jamaica as to what knowledge the accused must have of the identity of the substance as ganja, in order to amount to 'possession' of it for the purposes of an offence under s 7(c) of the Dangerous Drugs Law. The court rejected a submission by the prosecution that what was said in R v Livingston[1] as respects knowledge should be treated as having been in part overruled by the decision of the House of Lords in Warner v Metropolitan Police Commissioner[2]. This submission has not been pursued before their Lordships' Board. The question of what are the mental elements required to constitute a criminal offence of having in one's possession a prohibited substance is a finely balanced one, as Warner's case[2] itself shows. It turns on a consideration not only of the particular provision creating the offence but also of the policy of the Act disclosed by its provisions taken as a whole. The Jamaican legislation is not the same as that which was under consideration by the House of Lords in *Warner's* case[1]. Since *R v Livingston*[2] was decided more than 20 years ago, it has been treated as authoritative   *a* on the extent of the knowledge of the accused needed to constitute the offence under the Jamaican legislation, and has been frequently followed in Jamaican courts. Their Lordships would not think it right to disturb it as authority for what it did decide as to the mental element required to constitute the offence under s 7(*c*) of the Dangerous Drugs Law of having in one's possession a dangerous drug.

Since *R v Livingston*[2] was the foundation of the judgment from which the instant   *b* appeal is brought, it is however important to see what it was that that case did decide. The defendant, Livingston, was a baggageman employed by bus owners who were common carriers. He took into his custody from a consignor for carriage on the bus on which he travelled as baggageman a sack which was found to contain ganja. It was argued that there could not be 'possession' within the meaning of s 7(*c*) without knowledge of the thing possessed. The Court of Appeal formulated four questions   *c* as being those which arose for their determination: '(1) Could the temporary dominion or control which the appellant had over the ganja as baggageman on the bus amount to possession within the meaning of section 7(*c*) or was it merely custody or charge? (2) Does "possession" in section 7(*c*) of the Dangerous Drugs Law require that a defendant before he can be convicted, must be shown to have had knowledge that he had the thing in question? (3) If so, must a defendant, before he can be con-   *d* victed, be further shown to have had knowledge that the thing he had was ganja? (4) If the answers to questions (1), (2) and (3) are in the affirmative, was there evidence of knowledge by the appellant in this case on which the learned magistrate could properly find him guilty of the offence charged?'

Their Lordships would observe that questions (1) and (4) are special to the facts of *Livingston's* case[2], and that question (1) is not about the knowledge that a person   *e* has about a thing that is in his physical custody or control. That is dealt with separately in questions (2) and (3). These two questions are not special to the facts of *Livingston's* case[2] but deal with principles of law of general application as to the extent of the two different requirements of knowledge on the part of a defendant needed to constitute the mental element in the *criminal* offence of having in one's possession   *f* a dangerous drug.

All four questions were answered in the affirmative. Their Lordships need not deal further with the answers to the general questions (2) and (3). They accept the affirmative answers as correctly stating the law applicable to this offence in Jamaica.

The affirmative answer to question (1) was clearly right on the particular facts of *Livingston's* case[2]; but in their Lordships' view, the way in which the question was framed and the brief reason given for the answer are liable to mislead and have led   *g* the Court of Appeal in error in the instant case. The reason given was:

'As regards question (1) above, we think that the appellant's position was that of a common carrier or the agent of a common carrier and that, as such, he had possession, and not merely custody or charge, of the ganja. (Pollock and Wright on *Possession In The Common Law*[3].)'   *h*

In the ordinary use of the word 'possession', one has in one's possession whatever is, to one's own knowledge, physically in one's custody or under one's physical control. This is obviously what was intended to be prohibited in the case of dangerous drugs. Question (1) and the reason given for the answer, however, suggest that, in addition to the mental element of knowledge on the part of the accused, which the Court of

---

1   [1968] 2 All ER 356, [1969] 2 AC 256
2   (1952) 6 JLR 95
3   (1888), pp 130, 131, 166

a Appeal had chosen to deal with separately in questions (2) and (3), the word 'possession' imported into this criminal statute as a necessary ingredient of an offence against public health the highly technical doctrines of the civil law about physical custody without ownership as a source of legal rights in the actual custodian against third parties and about the legal relationships between owner and custodian which bring about the separation of proprietary and possessory rights in chattels. If this is the

b implication to be drawn from this part of the judgment in *R v Livingston*[1] it is, in their Lordships' view, wrong. These technical doctrines of the civil law about possession are irrelevant to this field of criminal law. The only actus reus required to constitute an offence under s 7(c) is that the dangerous drug should be physically in the custody or under the control of the accused. The mens rea by which the actus reus must be accompanied is the kind of knowledge on the part of the accused that

c is postulated in questions (2) and (3).

On the evidence, including his own statement to the police, the 19 sacks of ganja were clearly in the physical custody of the respondent and under his physical control. The only remaining issue was whether the inference should be drawn that the respondent knew that his load consisted of ganja. On all the evidence and in particular the fact that he and the other occupant of the van attempted to run away as soon as

d they saw the uniformed police approaching, the magistrate was, in their Lordships' view, fully entitled to draw the inference that the respondent knew what he was carrying in the van.

Although the judgment of the Court of Appeal includes an elaborate discussion of the speeches in the House of Lords in *Warner's* case[2], which were concerned with the accused's knowledge of the identity of what was in his physical custody or control,

e the Court of Appeal, as their Lordships understand the judgment, did not find it necessary to reach a final conclusion whether the magistrate's inference as to the respondent's knowledge was justified or not. They quashed the conviction on a different ground.

Misled, as their Lordships think, by the apparent distinction drawn in question (1) in *Livingston's* case[1] between physical custody and control, and possession in the

f technical sense in which that expression is used in civil law to connote a source of legal rights against third parties, they held that the respondent 'was not . . . shown to have anything more than mere custody or charge of both the van and its contents' and that this was not enough to constitute 'possession' in the meaning attributed to that word in *Livingston's* case[1]. This conclusion they reached on the ground that the respondent was in charge of the van in the capacity of servant to the man Reid referred to in the respondent's statement to the police; and relying on the authority of Pollock

g and Wright on Possession in the Common Law[3], they held that the 'possession' of the van and its contents remained in Reid as the master and never passed to the respondent as his servant. Accordingly they held that he could not be convicted whether or not he knew the contents of the van to be ganja. In so holding the Court of Appeal fell into error.

Their Lordships will humbly advise Her Majesty that this appeal should be allowed

h and the conviction of the respondent restored. The case should be remitted to the Court of Appeal for consideration of the respondent's appeal against sentence.

Appeal allowed.

j Solicitors: *Charles Russell & Co* (for the appellant); *Wilson Freeman* (for the respondent).

Christine Ivamy   Barrister.

---

1   (1952) 6 JLR 95
2   [1968] 2 All ER 356, [1969] 2 AC 256
3   (1888) pp 59, 60, 138–140

Woodward v Docherty and another

COURT OF APPEAL, CIVIL DIVISION

DAVIES, STEPHENSON AND SCARMAN LJJ

28th, 29th MARCH, 24th APRIL 1974

Rent restriction – Furnished letting – Amount of rent attributable to use of furniture – Value of furniture to tenant – Substantial part of whole rent attributable to use of furniture – Determination whether part substantial – Approach of court – Changing social and economic conditions – Value of furniture on secondhand market – Shortage of housing accommodation – Rent Act 1968, s 2(3).

By an agreement dated 24th June 1972 the landlord let to the tenants a fully-furnished flat for a term of six months which, on 19th November, was renewed for a further six months expiring on 31st May 1973. The rent was £10 per week payable monthly. At the date of the agreement the furniture had been in the flat and in use for some 12 years. The obligation to repair, renew or replace furniture was on the tenants. At the expiry of the term the tenants refused to give up possession. The landlord brought an action for possession in the county court. At the trial the tenant called a secondhand furniture dealer who gave evidence that the furniture in the flat could be acquired for about £50 and stated that he could provide similar furniture for that figure; the landlord alleged that the furniture was worth £300 to £400. The judge found that in June 1972 the furniture was worth £100 and that the use of furniture was worth £70 a year to the tenants, made up of £50 special value to the tenants and £20 per year attributable annually to its capital value. Accordingly he granted the order sought by the landlord, holding that, by virtue of s 2[a] of the Rent Act 1968, the tenancy was not a protected tenancy under the 1968 Act since the flat was bona fide let at a rent which included payments in respect of the use of furniture in that the amount of rent fairly attributable to the use of the furniture was about 14 per cent of the annual rent and therefore formed 'a substantial part of the whole rent', within s 2(3). The tenants appealed.

Held – In applying s 2(3) of the 1968 Act the court should adopt a broad approach and bear in mind changing social and economic conditions, such as the shortage of housing accommodation and the fact that furniture of a sort, capable of furnishing flats and rooms, was available at junk shops and other emporia at no very great price. Adopting that approach, and in the light of the evidence as to the market in secondhand furniture, £40 a year rather than £70 was the most that ought to be attributed on a fair assessment of the evidence to the value of the use of the furniture to the tenant. That sum was not a 'substantial part' of the annual rent of £520. Accordingly the tenancy was a protected tenancy and the appeal would therefore be allowed (see p 846 h to p 847 a and h and p 848 a to f, post).

Notes

For exemption of furnished premises from protection of the Rent Acts, see 23 Halsbury's Laws (3rd Edn) 748-751, paras 1503, 1505, 1506, and for cases on the subject, see 31(2) Digest (Reissue) 1018-1023, 8089-8113.

For the Rent Act 1968, s 2, see 18 Halsbury's Statutes (3rd Edn) 784.

---

[a] Section 2, so far as material, provides:

    '(1) A tenancy is not a protected tenancy if . . . (b) under the tenancy the dwelling-house is bona fide let at a rent which includes payments in respect of . . . use of furniture . . .

    '(3) For the purposes of paragraph (b) of subsection (1) above, a dwelling-house shall not be taken to be bona fide let at a rent which includes payments in respect of . . . the use of furniture unless the amount of the rent which is fairly attributable to . . . use of furniture, having regard to the value of . . . the use to the tenant, forms a substantial part of the whole rent.'

Case referred to in judgment

Palser v Grinling, Property Holding Co Ltd v Mischeff [1948] 1 All ER 1, [1948] AC 291,
[1948] LJR 600, HL, 31(2) Digest (Reissue) 1017, 8072.

Cases also cited

Bwllfa and Merthyr Dare Steam Collieries (1891) Ltd v Pontypridd Waterworks Co [1903]
AC 426, [1900-3] All ER Rep 600, HL.
Christodoulou v Umeh (8th May 1973) unreported; [1973] Bar Library transcript 185, CA.
Egert v Seaward (19th July 1973) unreported; [1973] Bar Library transcript 296, CA.
Goel v Sagoo [1969] 1 All ER 378, [1970] 1 QB 1, CA.
Hern v Palmer [1955] 1 All ER 396, [1955] 1 WLR 123, CA.
Roppel v Bennett [1948] 2 All ER 627, [1949] 1 KB 115, CA.

Appeal

Michael William Woodward ('the landlord') brought an action in the Wandsworth
County Court against Gordon Docherty and his wife ('the tenants') in which he
alleged that he was the owner of a furnished flat situate in the basement of premises
known as 41 Montague Road, Richmond, Surrey, that the tenants occupied the
flat under a tenancy agreement which had expired on 31st May 1973, and that the
tenants had failed or refused to yield up vacant possession of the flat, despite a notice
served on Mr Docherty on 29th April 1973 requiring the tenants to vacate the flat
on 31st May. The landlord claimed, inter alia, possession of the flat. By their defence
the tenants alleged that the tenancy of the flat was a regulated tenancy within the
meaning of the Rent Act 1968, that the tenants were holding over under the provisions of that Act, and that the landlord was not entitled to possession. At the trial
of the action on 9th August 1973 his Honour Judge Noakes ordered that the landlord should recover possession of the flat. The tenants appealed against that order.
The facts are set out in the judgment of Scarman LJ.

Stephen Sedley for the tenants.
Austin Allison for the landlord.

Cur adv vult

24th April. **SCARMAN LJ** read the first judgment at the invitation of Stephenson
LJ. I am authorised by Davies LJ to say that he agrees with the judgment about to
be delivered. Perhaps I should also add that he very much regrets that he cannot
be present in court for judgment in this case.

This is an appeal by a tenant and his wife against an order of the county court
requiring them to give possession of their flat to their landlord, the plaintiff. The
landlord, Mr Woodward, asserts that the letting is furnished; the tenant, Mr
Docherty, says that the landlord has failed to prove that the flat was 'bona fide let
at a rent which includes payments in respect of . . . the use of furniture'. The county
court judge found that the landlord had proved such a tenancy: the tenant in this
appeal challenges that finding.

Not for the first time, this court is faced with the problem of the true meaning and
effect of s 2 of the Rent Act 1968, which excepts certain tenancies from the protection of the Act. In the present case, unless the landlord can show that this flat
is bona fide let at a rent which includes payments in respect of the use of furniture,
it is a protected tenancy, and Mr and Mrs Docherty cannot be evicted. The problem
arises on s 2(3), which provides :

'. . . a dwelling house shall not be taken to be bona fide let at a rent which
includes payments in respect of . . . the use of furniture unless the amount of

rent which is fairly attributable to ... use of furniture, having regard to the
value of ... the use to the tenant, forms a substantial part of the whole rent.'

The subsection is a safeguard for tenants. Landlords are not to be able to exclude
a tenancy from the protection of the Act unless they can go all the way required by
it; any shortfall, and the tenancy is protected. The subsection puts on a landlord
the burden of proving a case involving a number of stages: first, the rent must include
payments in respect of the use of furniture; secondly, the amount of rent fairly
attributable to the use of furniture must form a substantial part of the whole rent;
thirdly, in determining the amount of rent fairly attributable to this use, regard
must be had to the use to the tenant. These stages are no mere sequence in an arith-
metical process: each calls for the exercise of judgment outside the field of
mathematics. Does the rent include payments in respect of the use of furniture? This
is a question the answer to which depends on the particular circumstances of the
letting. How much of the rent is fairly attributable to the use of the furniture, having
regard to the value of its use to the tenant? What is fair, and what is the value of
the use to the tenant, are questions to which arithmetic can give no conclusive
answer. Finally, what is a substantial part of the whole rent? Here, arithmetic can
help a lot; but even so it is not capable of answering the question, what is 'substantial'? In applying the subsection, arithmetic is a handy tool, a useful check,
but not, in my judgment, the determining factor. Counsel for the tenants contended otherwise: he submitted that the judge was primarily required to do his
sums, and could use, he said, 'the broad approach of judgment' only as a check.

For the reasons I have given, I think it is the other way round; furthermore, I
believe this has been settled law ever since *Palser v Grinling, Property Holding Co Ltd v
Mischeff*[1], decided by the House of Lords. Two passages in the speech of Viscount
Simon are directly relevant. In the first he said[2]:

'... the governing consideration is the word "fairly". The questions involved
are to be answered by common-sense considerations rather than by any formula
... It is the value to the tenant of the landlord's covenant to provide furniture
which mainly controls the figure to be arrived at ...'

And in the second he said[3] of the phrase 'substantial portion' (in the 1968 Act this is
now 'substantial part'):

'"Substantial" in this connection is not the same as "not unsubstantial," *i.e.,*
just enough to avoid the *de minimis* principle. One of the primary meanings
of the word is equivalent to considerable, solid, or big ... Applying the word
in this sense, it must be left to the discretion of the judge of fact to decide as best
he can according to the circumstances in each case, the onus being on the landlord ... Aristotle long ago pointed out that the degree of precision that is
attainable depends on the subject-matter.'

Common sense considerations require the court to exercise its knowledge of the
world. Today there is, as there has been since 1914, a shortage of dwelling-houses;
a landlord who can on the expiry of a contractual tenancy evict his tenant has an asset
incomparably more valuable than has the landlord who cannot; a man with a
wife, or wife and family, who is seeking a home will accept furniture he does not
really want in order to obtain accommodation he desperately needs, even though
by accepting it he loses security of tenure which he would dearly like to have. Further,
in 1973 and 1974, unlike the immediate post-war years of *Palser v Grinling*[1], furniture
of a sort, capable in a way of furnishing flats and rooms, is available at junk shops

---

1 [1948] 1 All ER 1, [1948] AC 291
2 [1948] 1 All ER at 10, 11, [1948] AC at 315, 316
3 [1948] 1 All ER at 11, [1948] AC at 317

a and other emporia at no very great price: witness the evidence of Mr Spencer, the valuer in this case. In applying the subsection, county court judges must bear in mind general considerations such as these—considerations which can and will change with social and economic changes in our society.

I now turn to the facts of the present case, The furniture had been in the flat—the basement floor flat—at 41 Montague Road, Richmond—since 1960, when some of it was new, some of it secondhand. There had been a succession of tenancies: perhaps b the landlord believed that he was better able to obtain vacant possession when he wanted it, if he let on fixed term tenancies rather than on periodic ones. Be that as it may, Mr Docherty's tenancy was created by a written agreement of 24th June 1972, by which time the furniture had been in situ and in use for some 12 years. His term was for six months, which on 19th November was renewed for a further period expiring on 31st May 1973. Thus the value of the use of the furniture to the tenant c and the amount of the rent fairly attributable to its use to him have to be assessed as at 24th June 1972. The rent was £10 a week (£43·30 per month) payable monthly in advance. The landlord was under no obligation to repair, renew or replace furniture: the tenant agreed 'to replace breakages, to restore anything lost ... and to make good any damage'.

The flat was let fully furnished, the judge finding that 'the flat contained almost d everything that Mr and Mrs Docherty would require', though some items were not of the standard they would like and did not work as well as they might have expected. The landlord led no evidence as to the value of the furniture, relying on the fact that the flat was let fully furnished. The tenant called Mr Spencer, a secondhand furniture dealer, who said that the furniture could be acquired for about £50 and that he could provide furniture such as was in the flat for that figure. The judge e allowed the landlord to be recalled to say that the worth of the furniture was £300 to £400: he found as a fact, however, that its value in June 1972 was £100.

On a 'broad approach' I find it hard to accept that the provision of £100 worth of furniture for the use of a tenant of a flat the rent of which is £10 per week enables the landlord to establish that the amount of rent fairly attributable to the use of that furniture is a substantial part of the rent. Nevertheless the judge so found. f He thought that the value of £100 should be depreciated over a period of five years, that is to say £20 per year attributable annually to its capital value. He attached a special 'value to the tenant' of £50 per year, and so reached the surprising conclusion that the use of furniture which it would have cost the tenant £100 to buy was worth to him £70 a year. He concluded that £70 represented slightly under 14 per cent of the annual rent and was a substantial part of it.

g I do not think this court could reverse his finding that £70 a year was a substantial part of a rent of about £520 per year—though it was, I think, very near the borderline and may have been influenced by the judge's mistake of law in believing, contrary to the opinion of Viscount Simon in *Palser v Grinling*[1], that 'substantial' meant 'not unsubstantial'.

Neither do I think this court can upset the judge's finding that £20 per annum h is a fair rate of depreciation. But I believe he fell into error when he accepted that £50 a year was fairly attributable as the furniture's special value to this tenant. The judge gave his reasons for this attribution. They are unconvincing, and in one important respect wrong. He went wrong in thinking that the landlord had to pay for replacements, and for cleaning and looking after the furniture. Nothing of the sort: the obligation was on the tenant. He brought into account the inconvenience j to the tenant in having to buy furniture, the loss of interest on the purchase price of £100, the chance that the furniture would not suit if he had to move, and removal expenses. Loss of interest on the £100 which he would have had to pay if he had bought the furniture is certainly a factor of some significance: perhaps today it is as

---

1 [1948] 1 All ER at 11, [1948] AC at 317

much as £14 per year. But the other matters, though relevant, are slight: they
could have little more than marginal significance. If one disregards the judge's error, a
attaches a value of £14 per year to loss of interest, and takes note of the other
marginal considerations, it becomes impossible to say that the use of this furniture,
valued at £100 in June 1972 was worth to the tenant £70 per year. An annual sum
of £20 plus £14 plus something, not much, for the other matters is the most that in
my judgment can or ought to be attributed from the annual rent to the value of b
the use of this furniture to the tenant. And in the light of Mr Spencer's evidence
as to the market I would have thought such an attribution high. A fair assessment
of the evidence leaves one far short of £70 per annum—much nearer £40 per annum.
The judge never considered whether £40 or indeed any sum less than £70 was a
'substantial part' of the rent of £520 per annum. In my judgment it is not; and I
would reverse his decision and find that this flat was not bona fide let at a rent which c
included payments for the use of furniture. The landlord fails because he has not
established that the amount of rent fairly attributable to the use of furniture is a
substantial part of it. I think the judge attached too much importance to the fact
that the flat was fully furnished. This is, of course, an important matter; but today,
there being, as Mr Spencer told the court, a flourishing market for the sale of furniture
suitable for furnished lettings, it is necessary to remember how easy it is for a person d
like Mr Docherty to buy furniture of the sort provided. The difficulty that faces
people in search of accommodation is to find a flat without the furniture. It costs
landlords little to ensure that they do not. There may well be cases where the use
of furniture that the landlord requires the tenant to have is more of a burden than a
benefit. I do not suggest that this is such a case. Yet in every case it is necessary to
bear in mind that calculations of market value, depreciation, loss of interest and so
forth should be made in the light of all the circumstances: those circumstances e
include the state of affairs of which an illuminating glimpse was given the court by
Mr Spencer.

I would allow the appeal.

STEPHENSON LJ. I agree. f

Appeal allowed.

Solicitors: *Seifert, Sedley & Co* (for the tenants); *Dixon, Ward & Co*, Richmond (for
the landlord).

Mary Rose Plummer Barrister. g

a

Lord Advocate v de Rosa and another

HOUSE OF LORDS
VISCOUNT DILHORNE, LORD HAILSHAM OF ST MARYLEBONE, LORD SIMON OF GLAISDALE,
b LORD KILBRANDON AND LORD SALMON
23rd, 24th APRIL, 13th JUNE 1974

*Employment – Period of continuous employment – Transfer of trade, business or under-
taking – Employee in trade, business or undertaking at time of transfer – Dismissal of employee
by transferors on transfer taking place – Employee entering new contract of employment with
c transferees – New contract containing different provisions as to capacity and place of work –
Employee subsequently dismissed by transferees by reason of redundancy – Dismissal after
lapse of requisite period of employment with transferees to qualify for redundancy payment –
Computation of amount of payment – Whether period of employment with transferors to be
taken into account – Contracts of Employment Act 1963, Sch 1, para 10(2) – Redundancy
d Payments Act 1965, ss 1(1), 3(2), 13(2), Sch 1, para 1(1).*

From 1950 until 24th April 1967 D was employed by a company ('the transferors').
At the end of that period he was employed as transport manager. On 24th April
the business was transferred to another company ('the transferees'). There was no
interruption in D's employment for, on the transfer taking place, D became employed
by the transferees; the nature of his employment changed, however, for instead
e of working mainly in an office, he was employed at the docks as a dock foreman,
and subsequently as a store foreman. On 31st December 1971 D was dismissed by
the transferees by reason of redundancy. Since D had been continuously employed
by the transferees for a period exceeding 104 weeks it was common ground that,
under s 8(1)[a] of the Redundancy Payments Act 1965, he was entitled to receive a
redundancy payment of £132 in respect of his period of employment with the trans-
f ferees. He claimed however to be entitled in addition to a further £451 on the
ground that his period of employment with the transferors was, by virtue of s 1(1)[b]
of, and Sch 1, para 1(1)[c], to, the 1965 Act and Sch 1, para 10(2)[d], to the Contracts of
Employment Act 1963, to be taken into account in computing the amount due to
him. The National Industrial Relations Court and, on appeal, the Court of Session
rejected that claim holding that, since the terms of D's employment with the trans-
g ferees differed from those under his contract with the transferors, the effect of ss 3(2)[e]

---

a   Section 8 is set out at p 854 *b* to *e*, post
b   Section 1(1), so far as material, provides: 'Where ... an employee who has been continu-
    ously employed for the requisite period—(*a*) is dismissed by his employer by reason of
    redundancy ... then ... the employer shall be liable to pay to him a sum (in this Act
    referred to as a "redundancy payment") calculated in accordance with Schedule 1 to
    this Act.'
c   Paragraph 1(1), so far as material, is set out at p 858 *j*, post
d   Paragraph 10(2) is set out at p 851 *j*, post
e   Section 3(2), so far as material, provides: 'An employee shall not be taken for the purposes
    of this Part of this Act to be dismissed by his employer if his contract of employment is
    renewed, or he is re-engaged by the same employer under a new contract of employment,
    and—(*a*) in a case where the provisions of the contract as renewed, or of the new contract,
    as the case may be, as to the capacity and place in which he is employed, and as to the
    other terms and conditions of his employment, do not differ from the corresponding
    provisions of the previous contract, the renewal or re-engagement takes effect immediately
    on the ending of his employment under the previous contract ...'

and 13(2)*f* of the 1965 Act was that D was to be deemed to have been dismissed
by the transferors with the result that the continuity of his employment had been   *a*
broken by that dismissal so that he was only entitled to a redundancy payment in
respect of his period of employment with the transferees.   On appeal,

Held – Sections 3(2) and 13(2) of the 1965 Act had no relevance to the computation
of the period of continuous employment under Sch 1 to the 1963 Act.   Since at the
date of his dismissal D had been employed by the transferees for the requisite period   *b*
under s 8(1) of the 1965 Act he was entitled to a redundancy payment which, by virtue
of s 1(1) of, and para 1(1) of Sch 1 to, the 1965 Act, was to be calculated in accordance
with Sch 1 to the 1963 Act. As D had been employed in the business of the transferors
at the time of the transfer of the business it followed that, by virtue of para 10(2) of
Sch 1 to the 1963 Act, the period of his employment with the transferors counted as
a period of employment with the transferees and it was irrelevant that D had been,   *c*
or was to be deemed to have been, dismissed by the transferors on the transfer
taking place.   He was therefore entitled to the full claim of £583 and the appeal
would be allowed accordingly (see p 852 *d* and *e*, p 855 *d e* and *g*, p 858 *f* to *h*, p 859 *h*
and *j* to p 860 *a* and *e*, p 862 *a f* and *j* to p 863 *a g* and *h*, p 864 *f* and *g*, p 865 *a b h*
and *j* and p 866 *h* and *j*, post).

d

Notes
For redundancy payments after a change of ownership of a business, see Supplement
to 25 Halsbury's Laws (3rd Edn) para 945A, 7, and for cases on the subject, see Digest
(Cont Vol C) 687-689, 692, 816Aa-Adf, 816Afd.
     For the Contracts of Employment Act 1963, Sch 1, para 10, see 12 Halsbury's Statutes
(3rd Edn) 214.   *e*
     For the Redundancy Payments Act 1965, ss 1,3, 8, 13, Sch 1, para 1, see 12 Halsbury's
Statutes (3rd Edn) 238, 240, 245, 249, 287.
     As from 27th July 1972, para 10 of Sch 1 to the 1963 Act has been replaced by the
Contracts of Employment Act 1972, Sch 1, para 9.

Cases referred to in opinions
Fitzgerald v Hall, Russell & Co Ltd [1969] 3 All ER 1140, [1970] AC 984, [1969] 3 WLR   *f*
     868, 5 ITR 1, 7 KIR 263, [1969] 2 Lloyd's Rep 514, HL; *rvsg* 1969 SC 50, 4 ITR 32,
     Digest (Cont Vol C) 691, 816Aee.
Grey v Pearson (1857) 6 HL Cas 61, 26 LJCh 473, 29 LTOS 67, 3 Jur NS 823, 10 ER 1216,
     HL; *affg* sub nom *Pearson v Rutter* (1853) 2 De GM & G 398, 43 ER 156, LC, 44
     Digest (Repl) 214, 286.
Woodhouse v Peter Brotherhood Ltd [1972] 3 All ER 91, [1972] 2 QB 520, [1972] 3 WLR 215,   *g*
     [1972] ICR 186, 13 KIR 45, CA; *rvsg* [1972] 1 All ER 1047, [1972] 1 WLR 401, 12 KIR
     213, NIRC.

Appeal
On 31st December 1971 the first respondent, Louis de Rosa, was dismissed from
his employment by the second respondents, John Barrie (Contractors) Ltd, from   *h*

---

f   Section 13, so far as material, provides:
     '(1) The provisions of this section shall have effect where—(a) a change occurs (whether
     by virtue of a sale or other disposition or by operation of law) in the ownership of a business
     for the purposes of which a person is employed, or of a part of such a business, and (b) in
     connection with that change the person by whom the employee is employed immediately
     before the change occurs (in this section referred to as "the previous owner") terminates
     the employee's contract of employment, whether by notice or without notice.
     '(2) If, by agreement with the employee, the person who immediately after the change
     occurs is the owner of the business or of the part of the business in question, as the case
     may be (in this section referred to as "the new owner") renews the employee's contract
     of employment (with the substitution of the new owner for the previous owner) or re-
     engages him under a new contract of employment, section 3(2) of this Act shall have effect
     as if the renewal or re-engagement had been a renewal or re-engagement by the previous
     owner (without any substitution of the new owner for the previous owner) . . .'

a whom he received a redundancy payment of £132. The first respondent applied to an industrial tribunal claiming that he was entitled to a redundancy payment of £583. On 21st February 1972 the tribunal dismissed the application and the first respondent appealed against that decision to the National Industrial Relations Court (sitting in Scotland). On 19th June 1972 the court dismissed the appeal and the appellant, the Lord Advocate, as representing the Secretary of State for Employment,
b appealed against that decision. On 26th September 1973 the Second Division of the Inner House of the Court of Session (the Lord Justice-Clerk (Wheatley), Lord Milligan and Lord Kissen) dismissed the appeal and the appellant appealed to the House of Lords. The facts are set out in the opinion of Viscount Dilhorne.

C K Davidson QC and *D R B Cay* (both of the Scottish Bar) and *Brian Davenport* for the appellant.
c *I C Kirkwood QC* and *A Lothian* (both of the Scottish Bar) for the second respondents.
The first respondent did not appear and was not represented.

Their Lordships took time for consideration.

d 13th June. The following opinions were delivered.

VISCOUNT DILHORNE. My Lords, the first respondent, Mr de Rosa, was employed by the second respondents, John Barrie (Contractors) Ltd, first as a dock foreman and then as a store foreman from 24th April 1967 to 31st December 1971 when he was dismissed by reason of redundancy. Having been continuously employed
e by them for the requisite period, he thereupon became entitled to a redundancy payment calculated in accordance with Sch 1 to the Redundancy Payments Act 1965, para 1 of which requires it to be computed in accordance with Sch 1 to the Contracts of Employment Act 1963.

From 1950 until 24th April 1967 Mr de Rosa had been employed by Issac Barrie (Transport) Ltd (hereafter referred to as 'Isaac Barrie') at the end of that period as
f transport manager. While there was no interruption in his employment, for directly he ceased to be employed by Isaac Barrie he became employed by the second respondents, the nature of his employment changed for, instead of working mainly in an office, he worked at the docks. He was paid the same wages but, when employed by the second respondents, became eligible for new insurance benefits.

It is not disputed that Mr de Rosa became entitled to receive a redundancy payment
g from the second respondents of £132 in respect of the period of his employment by them. He claimed to be entitled also to receive from them payment in respect of the period he worked for Isaac Barrie, that is to say, a further £451 making his total claim £583 for he contends that under the Act the period of his employment by Isaac Barrie must, by virtue of Sch 1 to the Redundancy Payments Act 1965 and Sch 1 to the Contracts of Employment Act 1963, be taken into account in computing
h the amount due to him.
Paragraph 10(2) of Sch 1 to the 1963 Act reads as follows:

'If a trade or business or an undertaking (whether or not it be an undertaking established by or under an Act of Parliament) is transferred from one person to another, the period of employment of an employee in the trade or business or undertaking at the time of the transfer shall count as a period of employment with the transferee, and the transfer shall not break the continuity of the period of employment.'

If the terms of this paragraph are to be applied without any qualification and if Isaac Barrie's trade or business or undertaking was transferred to the second respondents, Mr de Rosa's claim is well founded. It was, however, rejected by the

industrial tribunal which heard it, on appeal by the National Industrial Relations *a*
Court, and by the unanimous decision of the Inner House of the Court of Session,
to whom an appeal was taken by the Lord Advocate representing the Secretary of
State for Employment who had a locus standi by virtue of the Industrial Tribunal
(Redundancy Payments) (Scotland) Regulations 1967[1].

In the course of giving their decision the industrial tribunal said that certain assets
of Isaac Barrie had been taken over by the second respondents under an agreement *b*
dated 1st March 1967. In the appellant's case it is said that under that agreement
the second respondents 'acquired the whole undertaking of Isaac Barrie'. We have
not seen the agreement and so are unable to say whether this statement is correct.
Taking over certain assets of a business may or may not include the taking over of
the business. Twice in the course of their decision the industrial tribunal referred
to the second respondents taking over the business of Isaac Barrie and, as the second *c*
respondents did not in the argument before the House seek to assert that they had
not done so, I am prepared to assume that they did. As Mr de Rosa's claim depends
on Isaac Barrie's trade or business or undertaking having been taken over by the
second respondents, it is unfortunate that the industrial tribunal made no precise
finding on the matter.

That tribunal held that as Mr de Rosa's terms and conditions of employment *d*
with the second respondents differed from those of his contract of employment
with Isaac Barrie, the effect of ss 13(2) and 3(2) of the Redundancy Payments Act
1965 was that Mr de Rosa was to be deemed to have been dismissed by Isaac Barrie.
The National Industrial Relations Court agreed with this and the Lord Justice-Clerk,
with whose judgment the other members of the Inner House agreed, also appears
to have accepted it. Having reached this conclusion, they held that the continuity *e*
of his employment had been broken by that dismissal and so that Mr de Rosa was
only entitled to a redundancy payment in respect of the period of his employment
by the second respondents.

I regret to have to disagree with that conclusion but, in my opinion, it is clear that
ss 13(2) and 3(2) of the 1965 Act do not have that effect. The first matter that the
1965 Act deals with is the right to a redundancy payment. That only arises under s 1(1) *f*
where an employee is dismissed by his employer by reason of redundancy or is
laid off or kept on short-time to the extent specified in the Act after having been
continuously employed for the requisite period. Section 1(2) provides:

'For the purposes of this Act an employee who is dismissed shall be taken to
be dismissed by reason of redundancy if the dismissal is attributable wholly
or mainly to—(a) the fact that his employer has ceased, or intends to cease, to *g*
carry on the business for the purposes of which the employee was employed
by him, or has ceased, or intends to cease, to carry on that business in the place
where the employee was so employed, or (b) the fact that the requirements
of that business for employees to carry out work of a particular kind, or for
employees to carry out work of a particular kind in the place where he was so
employed, have ceased or diminished or are expected to cease or diminish.'

The industrial tribunal and the National Industrial Relations Court were both of *h*
the opinion that Mr de Rosa would have had a valid claim for a redundancy payment
against Isaac Barrie if he had made it in time, but it is not stated on what ground
they held that his deemed dismissal was by reason of redundancy. Presumably it
was on the basis that Isaac Barrie ceased or intended to cease to carry on the business
in which Mr de Rosa was employed.

Section 3(1) of the 1965 Act provides that an employee shall be taken to be dismissed
by his employer—

1   SI 1967 No 360

a
'if, but only if,—(a) the contract under which he is employed by the employer is terminated by the employer, whether it is so terminated by notice or without notice, or (b) where under that contract he is employed for a fixed term, that term expires without being renewed under the same contract, or (c) the employee terminates that contract without notice in circumstances (not falling within section 10(4) of this Act) such that he is entitled so to terminate it by reason of the employer's conduct.'

b
Paragraphs (b) and (c) above do not apply in this case, so Mr de Rosa could only be entitled to a redundancy payment from Isaac Barrie if they terminated his employment. On the transfer of a business from A to B, those employed by A before the transfer will cease to be employed by him but it does not necessarily follow that their employment was terminated by him. It may have been agreed that an em-

c
ployee's contract will continue with the contract varied by the substitution of B for A as the employer. It might be that A did nothing with regard to the contracts of employment and that the employee just carried on as before with B. Again the decision of the industrial tribunal does not disclose what, if anything, was done by Isaac Barrie with regard to Mr de Rosa's contract of employment with them. So the transfer of a business to which para 10(2) of Sch 1 to the Contracts of Employment

d
Act 1963 applies, while it must necessarily involve a change of employers, does not necessarily involve a termination by the transferor of the contract of employment with him.

Section 3(2) of the 1965 Act does not provide that in certain circumstances an employee shall be deemed to be dismissed. It provides the opposite, that, subject to the prescribed conditions being fulfilled, a dismissal is not to count as a dismissal.

e
Section 13(2) applies s 3(2) to where there has been a change in the ownership of the business for the purposes of which a person is employed, or of part of such a business and the transferor of the business immediately before the change occurs, terminates the employee's contract of employment. Section 13(2) does not apply unless there is such a termination and this express requirement for termination is an indication that for the purposes of this section a transfer of ownership is not of

f
itself to be regarded as effecting a termination by the transferor.

Section 22(1) provides:

'Where in accordance with any enactment or rule of law—(a) any act on the part of an employer, or (b) any event affecting an employer (including, in the case of an individual, his death), operates so as to terminate a contract under which an employee is employed by him, that act or event shall for the purposes

g
of this Act be treated as a termination of the contract by the employer, if apart from this subsection it would not constitute a termination of the contract by him.'

No reliance was placed on this provision in the course of the argument and I do not therefore propose to consider its impact on s 13 of the 1965 Act, but it may be that the transfer of a business is by virtue of this subsection to be treated as a termina-

h
tion of the contract of employment by the transferor. However this may be, the operation of s 13 depends on there having been a termination by the employer. If there had been in this case by reason of redundancy, then, as Mr de Rosa's contract with the second respondents differed from that with Isaac Barrie, it would have been right to hold that his dismissal by Isaac Barrie was not nullified by ss 13(2) and 3(2).

Section 13(6) of the 1965 Act reads:

j
'Nothing in this section shall be construed as requiring any variation of a contract of employment by agreement between the parties to be treated as constituting a termination of the contract.'

I find the inclusion of this subsection puzzling for, if it was not there, I do not see that there is anything in the section which would require a variation by agreement between the parties to be treated as a termination of the contract. It may be that, as s 13(2) refers to the renewal of a contract of employment with the substitution of the new employer for the old, the subsection was intended to make it clear that that was not to be treated as a termination of the old contract.

Section 8 of the 1965 Act is in the following terms:

'(1) For the purposes of section 1(1) of this Act the requisite period is the period of one hundred and four weeks ending with the relevant date, excluding any week which began before the employee attained the age of eighteen.

'(2) Subject to the preceding subsection, and to the following provisions of this section, the provisions of Schedule 1 to the Contracts of Employment Act 1963 (computation of period of employment), and the provisions of any order for the time being in force under section 7 of that Act in so far as it modifies that Schedule, shall have effect for the purposes of this Part of this Act in determining whether an employee has been continuously employed for the requisite period.

'(3) Where by virtue of section 3(2) of this Act an employee is treated as not having been dismissed by reason of a renewal or re-engagement taking effect after an interval, then in determining for the purposes of section 1(1) of this Act whether he has been continuously employed for the requisite period, the period of that interval shall count as a period of employment, notwithstanding that it does not count under that Schedule.

'(4) The preceding provisions of this section shall have effect subject to sections 17 and 24 of this Act in cases to which those sections apply respectively.'

If Mr de Rosa had not been employed by the second respondents for 104 weeks, he could, therefore, by virtue of para 10(2) of Sch 1 to the Contracts of Employment Act 1963, for the purpose of establishing his right to a redundancy payment by the second respondents, having included sufficient weeks of his employment by Isaac Barrie to have made up the 104 weeks. If, for instance, he had been dismissed on account of redundancy four weeks after his employment by the second respondents began, he could have established his right to a redundancy payment by counting 100 weeks of his employment by Isaac Barrie.

If he had been dismissed by reason of redundancy by Isaac Barrie, then as that dismissal was not nullified by ss 13(2) and 3(2), he would have been entitled to a redundancy payment from Isaac Barrie if he made his claim within six months of his dismissal as prescribed by s 21. Mr de Rosa did prefer a claim against Isaac Barrie but it was dismissed as it was not made within six months.

If he had succeeded on that claim he would have received from Isaac Barrie payment in respect of the weeks which he could count, if he required to do so, to show that he had been continuously employed for 104 weeks for the purpose of establishing his right to a redundancy payment from the second respondents. He might thus have secured a redundancy payment from Isaac Barrie and, if he had been dismissed by the second respondents after four weeks, have obtained a second redundancy payment from them.

Section 8 of the 1965 Act is made subject to s 24 which, so far as material, reads as follows:

'(1) The provisions of this section shall have effect where—(a) a redundancy payment is paid to an employee, whether in respect of dismissal or in respect of lay-off or short-time; (b) the contract of employment under which he was employed (in this section referred to as "the previous contract") is renewed, whether by the same or another employer, or he is re-engaged under a new contract of employment, whether by the same or another employer; and (c) the circumstances of the renewal or re-engagement are such that, in determining

a   for the purposes of section 1(1) of, or Schedule 1 to, this Act whether at any
subsequent time he has been continuously employed for the requisite period,
or for what period he has been continuously employed, the continuity of his
period of employment would, apart from this section, be treated as not having
been broken by the termination of the previous contract and the renewal or
re-engagement.

b   '(2) Where the conditions mentioned in the preceding subsection are fulfilled,
then in determining, for the purposes of section 1(1) of, or Schedule 1 to, this
Act, whether at any subsequent time he has been continuously employed for
the requisite period, or for what period he has been continuously employed, the
continuity of the period of employment shall be treated as having been broken
at the date which was the relevant date in relation to the redundancy payment
mentioned in paragraph (a) of the preceding subsection, and accordingly no
c   account shall be taken of any time before that date . . .'

Section 24 does not apply in this case, for Mr de Rosa did not receive a redundancy
payment from Isaac Barrie and it is a payment and not entitlement to payment
that the section stipulates as a condition to be fulfilled for the section to operate.
d   The industrial tribunal, the National Industrial Relations Court and the Inner
House of the Court of Session were all of the opinion that Mr de Rosa's dismissal,
which they deemed to have taken place by virtue of ss 13 (2) and 3(2) of the 1965 Act,
interrupted the continuity of his employment.   While one might have expected
Parliament so to provide and to have avoided imposing on his new employer liability
to make payments to Mr de Rosa in respect of his employment by Isaac Barrie, I
can find no ground in the provisions of the Act for so concluding.
e   Dismissal by reason of redundancy is an essential element in a claim to a redundancy
payment.   Sections 13(2) and 3(2), if they apply, operate to deprive an employee
of a right he might otherwise have had to redundancy payment, but they do not
affect the computation of his continuous employment.   That is governed by para
10(2) of Sch 1 to the Contracts of Employment Act 1963. If, for the purpose of determining whether an employee has been continuously employed for 104 weeks for
f   the purposes of entitlement, there was any justification for reading para 10(2) as
qualified in its operation by virtue of the dismissal of the employee by his
old employer so that the period of his continuous employment began to run from
the time he began to be employed by his new employer, then it might have been
possible to come to the conclusion that, in computing the amount of the payment
to be made to him, para 10(2) must be similarly qualified.   I can find nothing in
g   the Act to warrant any such conclusion and, in my opinion, full effect must be given
to the clear and unambiguous language of para 10(2), even though the consequence
is that, where a transfer of a business takes place and the other conditions are satisfied,
an employee dismissed by reason of redundancy by his new employer, after having
been employed by him for less than 104 weeks, can still be entitled to a redundancy
payment from his new employer and even though, if entitled to a redundancy
h   payment, its amount will be calculated taking into account his weeks of continuous
employment with his old employer.
It is, I think, unfortunate that the Redundancy Payments Act 1965, which gives
rights to a great many people, was not more clearly drafted so as to make it easy
for them to ascertain their rights.   It contains complicated provisions dealing with
dismissal and, when one wants to find out how much should be paid to a person for
i   redundancy, one is referred to Sch 1 to the Act.   That does not provide the answer.
For that one has to turn to Sch 1 to the Contracts of Employment Act 1963.   This is
a bad example of legislation by reference, and while I feel no doubt about its effect,
I have some doubt whether, when the bill was being enacted, the extent of the
financial burden being placed on the new employer was fully appreciated.   In this it
is £451 to be paid in respect of service with Isaac Barrie.

In my opinion, for the reasons I have given, this appeal should be allowed. Mr de *a*
Rosa was entitled to a redundancy payment of £583 of which £132 has been paid
to him.

LORD HAILSHAM OF ST MARYLEBONE. My Lords, the appellant in the
present proceedings is the Lord Advocate, representing the Secretary of State for
Employment. The Secretary of State, being entitled under the Industrial Tribunals *b*
(Redundancy Payments) (Scotland) Regulations 1967 to appear in proceedings of
this nature, has elected to take up the cudgels on the same side as the first respondent, the original claimant, who was unrepresented here as he had been in the
Court of Session from whose decision this is an appeal. The proceedings consisted in a
claim by the first respondent against the second respondents for a redundancy
payment under the Redundancy Payments Act 1965. *c*
    Before 31st December 1971 the first respondent had been in the employment of
the second respondents at first as a docks foreman and later as a stores foreman.
On 31st December 1971 he was dismissed by the second respondents by reason of
redundancy, and, as he had been employed continuously by the second respondents
for more than 104 weeks, he became thereby entitled to a redundancy payment
under the Redundancy Payments Act 1965. The second respondents paid him £132, *d*
basing their calculation on a period of continuous employment going back to 24th
April 1967. But this, so the first respondent contended, and the appellant now
contends, was inadequate. He was entitled, so the contention runs, to £583, a sum
calculated on the assumption that the true period of continuous employment in
respect of which the calculation should be made is not the four years between 24th
April 1967 and 31st December 1971, on which the second respondents had based their *e*
calculation, but a period of 21 years dating from 1950. This longer period is based
on the assumption that the first respondent is entitled to take into account not merely
the period of four years during which he was employed by the second respondents,
but a further period of 17 years prior to that during which he was employed by a
company with a somewhat similar name, namely, Isaac Barrie (Transport) Ltd,
whose business was wholly or in part taken over by the second respondents in 1967. *f*
This difference of opinion resulted in the present proceedings. Before the industrial
tribunal and the National Industrial Relations Court, to whom he appealed, the first
respondent lost the day and then dropped out of the case. The Lord Advocate
intervened before the Court of Session, but similarly failed. Having agreed to
indemnify the second respondents in costs whatever the result of the appeal, the Lord
Advocate now appeals to your Lordships' House by leave of the Court of Session. *g*
He claims that a point of law is involved of general importance in the administration
of the Redundancy Payments Act 1965. This point of law involved the construction
of various sections of that Act and of the Contracts of Employment Act 1963.
    The facts on which the appeal is based are somewhat inadequately stated in the
courts below. This is partly because this particular claim was only one of a series
of claims affecting a number of former employees of Isaac Barrie (Transport) Ltd *h*
who, after the take-over of the former company by the second respondents, had
entered the second respondents' services. The exact form, date and circumstances
surrounding the take-over were apparently already familar to the industrial tribunal
when they decided the present case and, for this reason, perhaps they did not fully
state them in their decision. In particular they described the take-over variously
as 'a transfer of certain assets' in Isaac Barrie (Transport) Ltd and the taking-over of *j*
the 'business' of Isaac Barrie (Transport) Ltd. That these two phrases are not, in
fact, synonymous for this purpose is obvious (see, for instance, *Woodhouse v Peter
Brotherhood Ltd*[1]) and I was at one time concerned lest the outcome of this appeal

---

1   [1972] 3 All ER 91, [1972] 2 QB 520

a might be a remission to the tribunal to find further facts, as happened in *Fitzgerald v Hall, Russell & Co Ltd*[1]. I am, however, satisfied that this is not necessary.

As I have already said, it is common ground that the first respondent was employed continuously by the second respondents first as a docks foreman, and then as a stores foreman, between 24th April 1967 and 31st December 1971. Prior to 1st March 1967 he had been employed by Isaac Barrie (Transport) Ltd as a transport manager.

b By an agreement dated 1st March 1967 the second respondents acquired some of the assets of Isaac Barrie (Transport) Ltd and, from the language of the decision of the industrial tribunal, we are entitled to assume that the nature of the take-over involved or resulted in a transfer of the relevant portion of the business. What exactly happened between 1st March and 24th April 1967 is not at all clear, but, again from the language of the decision, we are entitled to assume that, without any temporal interval in the continuity of his period of employment, on 24th April 1967 the

c first respondent entered the service if the second respondents at the same wage, but in a new and different capacity (docks foreman as distinct from transport manager) involving different work (work on a dock as distinct from work in an office) with additional insurance benefits and, of course, a new and different employer. It is, thus, that the second respondents base their contention that the redundancy payment

d must be calculated by reference to a period of four years and the appellant that it must be based on a calculation of 21 years of continuous employment.

I must now turn to the statutory provisions. The right to a redundancy payment on dismissal for redundancy is conferred by the Redundancy Payments Act 1965. It contains two quite distinct stages in the enquiry. The first consists in ascertaining whether the conditions establishing entitlement are fulfilled. The second stage,

e which arises only when an affirmative conclusion has been reached on the first, involves the calculation of the amount of the payment.

By s 1(1) of the 1965 Act, the right to a payment is conferred on 'an employee' who after the appointed day (6th December 1965) has been (1) 'continuously employed for the requisite period' (i e, 104 weeks ending with the 'relevant date') and is thereafter (2) 'dismissed by his employer' (3) 'by reason of redundancy'. I ignore for this

f purpose the provisions relating to temporary lay-off and short-time working as irrelevant to this appeal. Each of the expressions I have put in inverted commas is given a specialised definition by later provisions of the Act and must be construed in accordance with its statutory definition rather than by reference to its dictionary meaning. 'Employee', 'employer' and 'relevant date' are defined in s 25. 'Requisite period' and 'continuous employment' are defined in s 8. 'Dismissal' is defined in s 3 of the Act with certain exceptions in s 3(2); which are extended by s 13 to cases where there

g has been a change of ownership of the business for the purposes of which the employee has been employed. Section 9 of the Act applies certain presumptions in favour of continuity of employment, and, where dismissal has taken place, in favour of redundancy as the reason for dismissal.

Since both became material at a later period of the discussion, I must here explain

h that both ss 3(2) and 13 (which for certain purposes must be read with s 3(2)) are deeming provisions. Section 3(1) provides that an employee must be taken to have been dismissed by his employer if, but only if, the contract under which he is employed by his employer is terminated by that employer whether with or without notice (and in two other sets of circumstances not material to this appeal). Section 3(2) provides in effect that this is not to count as a dismissal where an employee is continued after termination by his employer without intermission on the same job,

j or where, if the job is different or there is an interval, the employee is re-engaged in pursuance of a written offer. Section 13(2) in effect applies the provisions of s 3(2) on a change of ownership if (with the exception of the identity of the employer) the provisions of s 3(2) would otherwise apply. The effect of this is that wherever s 3(2) is applied there is no dismissal and therefore no entitlement to a redundancy

---

1 [1969] 3 All ER 1140, [1970] AC 984

payment. The section does not per se operate to enlarge or diminish the period of
continuous employment for the requisite period as defined in s 8. It simply provides
that what would otherwise be a dismissal under s 3(1) is not to be treated as a dismissal. The period of continuous employment for the requisite period is defined
by s 8 as 104 weeks, in effect to be ascertained under Sch 1 to the Contracts of Employment Act 1963 (to be considered later) as modified by ss 17 and 24 of the Redundancy
Payments Act 1965 and further by the provision that, notwithstanding anything in
Sch 1 to the 1963 Act, if circumstances have arisen which, under s 3(2) prevent what
would otherwise be a dismissal from being treated as dismissal, any interval between
original engagement and re-engagement should count as part of the period of continuous employment. Section 8 does not make a dismissal anything which apart from
s 8 would not be a dismissal, but, as will be seen, it may operate to extend the period
of continuous employment of 104 weeks behind the engagement of the employer who
dismissed the employee at the relevant date and to disregard any discontinuity in
the employment caused only by a re-engagement to which s 3(2) applies. Section 8
of the 1965 Act does not affect the period of continuous employment which
is necessary to be ascertained for the purposes of calculating the amount of redundancy payment. As will be seen, the calculation of this amount falls to be ascertained
under a different part of the Act and under a slightly different code.

From the above analysis it can readily be seen that the ascertainment of entitlement may well involve a technical, to some extent artificial and, at least potentially,
elaborate and difficult enquiry where doubts are raised either as to the fact or reason
of dismissal at the relevant date or as to the continuity of employment for the requisite period prior to that date if, but only if, dismissal at the relevant date is established to have taken place and to have taken place by reason of redundancy. But,
in the particular case we are now considering, it is accepted that the relevant date is
31st December 1971 and, since the first respondent was admittedly continuously
employed by the second respondents for more than 104 weeks prior to the relevant
date and was admittedly dismissed on that date by reason of redundancy, none of
these difficulties arises directly here.

They arise only if and to the extent that these difficult questions are imported into
the discussion of the second stage of the enquiry, that is, into the discussion of the
period of time by reference to which the amount of the payment is to be calculated.
The second respondents contend, and the courts below have decided, that they are
to be so imported. The appellant disputes this. In essence his contention is that,
though these questions can be relevant and essential to the ascertainment of entitlement, they do not arise where entitlement is admitted and when the only question
for consideration is the calculation of the amount.

At first sight the appellant's contention is correct. Section 1(1) of the 1965 Act
provides that, once an employee is entitled to a redundancy payment the amount is
to be 'calculated in accordance with Schedule 1 to this Act'. In other words, the first
stage of the enquiry is concluded by reference to the operative sections of the Act but
the second stage of the enquiry is concluded by reference to the schedule.

Murmuring 'How convenient' and, no doubt, full of optimism, the earnest seeker
after truth must therefore look at Sch 1 to see how the calculation is made. But when
he gets there he is due for a disappointment, for para 1(1) of the schedule provides
that subject to its other provisions the amount to which an employee is entitled in
any given case is to be—

'calculated by reference to the period, ending with the relevant date, during
which he has been continuously employed; and for the purpose of this Schedule
that period shall be computed in accordance with Schedule 1 to the Contracts
of Employment Act 1963 . . .'

but with certain modifications spelled out in the same paragraph of Sch 1 to the
1965 Act.

a   Thus, having set out to discover the treasure in Sch 1 to the 1965 Act, the earnest seeker after truth, instead of being given what he is looking for, is given another clue and is sent scurrying after another schedule in another Act for the computation of the relevant period of employment and then back to the schedule of the Redundancy Payments Act 1965 to see if the modifications apply. As if this were not enough the expression 'period during which he has been continuously employed' (which is

b   here defined for the purpose of defining the quantum) for the purposes of the earlier stage in the enquiry, that is for the purpose of ascertaining the entitlement, is defined in s 8(2) of the Act by sending the enquirer back to the same schedule of the same earlier Act but with slightly different modifications.

At this stage, however, I am only pursuing the question of quantum and with that solely in view I approach Sch 1 to the 1963 Act. I pause to point out that that Act

c   was concerned not with redundancy payments following dismissal, but with minimum periods of notice prior to dismissal to which the employee is entitled irrespective of the terms of his contract of employment. It is not, of course, self-evident that what is appropriate for the one purpose is necessarily appropriate to the other. Nevertheless, Parliament has sent the enquirer back to that Act, but with slightly different terms of reference, for two separate purposes, first, for the purpose of

d   ascertaining whether an employee dismissed at the relevant date has been continuously employed for the requisite period—and that is relevant only to entitlement—and, second, for the purpose of the ascertainment of the period of continuous employment by reference to which the amount of the payment is to be calculated, and that is relevant only to quantum. In each case the modifications are spelled out in the appropriate parts of the 1965 Act, for the earlier stage of the enquiry in s 8 and for the

e   later stage of the enquiry in the first sub-paragraph of Sch 1.

It is, however, to the 1963 Act that it is now necessary to turn, bearing in mind that it is for the second and not for the first purpose that it is necessary to turn to it at the present stage of the discussion.

For the purposes of this appeal the most relevant paragraph of Sch 1 to the 1963 Act is para 10. So far as is relevant this paragraph provides as follows:

f   '(1) Subject to this paragraph ... the foregoing provisions of this Schedule relate only to employment by the one employer.

    '(2) If a trade or business or an undertaking (whether or not it be an undertaking established by or under an Act of Parliament) is transferred from one person to another, the period of employment of an employee in the trade or business or undertaking at the time of the transfer shall count as a period of employment

g   with the transferee, and the transfer shall not break the continuity of the period of employment.'

(Sub-paragraphs (3), (4) and (5) are not relevant.)

Not unnaturally, the appellant founds his contention on the clear terms of

h   para 10(2). The 1965 Act says clearly that, whatever may be true of entitlement, the amount of the redundancy payment is to be calculated by reference to Sch 1. The schedule refers us back to Sch 1 to the earlier Act, and Sch 1 to the earlier Act clearly states that in the case of the transfer of a business from one person to another (which is this case) the period of employment at the time of the transfer shall count as part of the period of employment with the transferee (in this case the second respondents)

j   and that the fact of the transfer shall not break the continuity of the employment. True, there are certain modifications to adapt the 1963 Act to the purposes of the 1965 Act. But these modifications, which are clearly spelled out in Sch 1 to the 1965 Act, do nothing to modify the conclusion to be drawn from Sch 1 to the 1963 Act. More than that they exclude the importation into Sch 1 to the 1963 Act for the purpose of calculating quantum any of the provisions of the 1965 Act other than those specified. Expressio unius, exclusio alterius.

I personally can see no answer to this contention. How then, one may ask, can *a*
the industrial tribunal, the National Industrial Relations Court and the Court of
Session all come unanimously to a contrary conclusion? Although all the assumptions of fact are not absolutely identical, the answer appears to be as follows. They
appear, first, to have asked themselves the question whether, in 1964, there had been
a dismissal of the first respondent by Isaac Barrie (Transport) Ltd. This question
did not arise because entitlement was accepted. As the relevant date was 31st *b*
December 1971 the question of dismissal in 1967 would only arise directly if the
period of continuous employment for the purpose of ascertaining the requisite period
was in dispute; but it was not in dispute since on any view the first respondent had
been employed by the second respondents for more than 104 weeks. In my view,
Lord Upjohn was right when in *Fitzgerald v Hall, Russell & Co Ltd*[1] he said, in discussing
the effect of para 5 of Sch 1 to the 1963 Act on the computation of redundancy *c*
payments:

> 'That dismissal is not conclusive against the employee's claim is, I think, clear
> having regard to the whole structure of the Schedule to the Act of 1963.'

However, the courts below asked the question and answered it affirmatively, on the
ground that Isaac Barrie (Transport) Ltd had terminated their contract with the *d*
first respondent either automatically on going out of business or by giving some sort
of notice in anticipation of going out of business. (The judgments do not say which,
but we were led by counsel to believe that the latter was the true alternative.) They
then asked the question whether the dismissal could be disregarded under the
combined effect of ss 3(2) and 13(2) of the 1965 Act and this question, which equally
did not arise, they answered in the negative because, although the new engagement *e*
was continuous with the old, the work was different and the re-engagement was not
in pursuance of a written offer. This question also did not arise since, like the other,
it was only relevant to entitlement and then only on the question whether there had
been a dismisssal. Even if the question had been whether for the purposes of s 8
of the Act there had been a requisite period of continuous employment, which itself
is not relevant for the second stage of the enquiry, the question could only have *f*
arisen, so far as I can see, if the employment had not, in fact, been continuous, since,
although the terms of reference back to Sch 1 to the 1963 Act for the purposes of s 8
are not identical with those relevant to the second stage of the enquiry, they do
apply para 10(2) of the earlier schedule without modification, and the question to
be considered is whether the employment was, in fact, continuous in point of time,
and not whether the contract of employment had been broken. For this purpose *g*
we are told that the change in the identity of the employer on transfer of the business
is to be disregarded and we are not told to look at the history of the relationship
of the employer to the employee unless this shows that the period of employment
was not in time continuous (when paras 3 to 6 of Sch 1 to the 1963 Act have to be
looked at).

Of course, it may seem odd that virtually the same expression should be used *h*
for the purpose of ascertaining the requisite period of employment under s 1(1) of
the 1965 Act and the period of continuous employment under para 1 of the schedule
by reference to which the calculation of quantum must be made and that the two
do not exactly coincide. It may also be that in certain fairly rare cases anomalies
may arise. But s 24, which is incorporated with both sets of criteria, prevents double
payments being received, and in the ordinary case the criteria would be the same, *j*
since in neither case is s 3(2) directly incorporated so as to make it applicable to the
periods of continuous employment. Where there has been dismissal within s 3(1),
ordinarily the transferor employer, if either, will be liable for any redundancy payment unless the employee is continued in the same job by the transferee or given

---

1 [1969] 3 All ER at 1150, [1970] AC at 1001

a another job on a written offer. Under s 21, the right against the transferor employer will be lost if a claim is not made within six months. What, however, will happen in such a case will be that, should the transferee employer subsequently, and after the requisite period of continuous service, dismiss the same employee for redundancy, the amount of the payment for which the transferee employer will be liable will be calculated by reference to the joint period of employment under both masters and not by reference to the shorter period in which the employee was employed

b by the transferee. Such a situation is not correctly described, as it was during the argument, as a revival of the earlier right. It is a new right; it is a different redundancy payment from a different employer calculated by reference to a different period. Nevertheless, the result is said to be so bizarre that Parliament could not have intended it. I am not sure that this is so, and, in any event, it seems to me that this is what Parliament has said. Modern Parliaments have, in fact, made quite a number

c of fairly rough provisions in favour of employees overriding the original freedom of contract and based, at least to some extent, on administrative convenience. The employer on Monday of a part-time employee may be responsible for the whole of the employer's social security contribution which, over a period of years, can be very large, to the exclusion of employers later in the week. There does not seem to me to be anything inherently unlikely that a modern Parliament should have decided

d that a transferee employer takes over a contingent liability to pay a higher redundancy payment in respect of an employee with a long period of continuous service behind him in the same way that he undoubtedly does take over the contingent liability if he dismisses the same employee to give him a comparably longer period of notice under the earlier Act.

Faced with the difficulties in the way of supporting the judgments, counsel for

e the second respondents made two alternative bold submissions. The first was that, on the true construction of the 1963 Act, a continuous period of employment was inevitably broken, even for the purposes of that Act, when, during the period of employment it could be shown that there was a successive series of contracts by a single employer or by a succession of employers under a transfer. This contention I understood him ultimately to abandon in the light not only of the plain language

f of the Act but of the ease with which such an interpretation would give rise to an evasion of the policies of the Act with regard to minimum periods of notice. The second contention was that, on a true interpretation of the 1963 Act, for the purposes of redundancy payments the schedule must be read in the light of the 1965 Act and not alone in the light of its own language. I was never able fully to understand this argument but, in putting it forward, counsel placed reliance on a passage in Lord

g Upjohn's judgment in *Fitzgerald v Hall, Russell & Co Ltd*[1]. However the contention were put it must involve the provision either (1) that the 1963 Act altered in meaning for all purposes in 1965 when the Redundancy Payments Act was passed, or (2) that it bore two inconsistent meanings, one for the purposes of minimum periods of notice and one for the purposes of the 1965 Act. The former view I regard as unarguable; the second as possible only to the extent of the modifications to Sch 1 to the 1963 Act

h which were directly imported by the 1965 Act. In the absence of some indications in the later Act that the 1963 Act is to be interpreted in a special sense for the purposes of the later Act, I do not feel able to read it in any sense different from that which it had always borne. The short passage in Lord Upjohn's opinion cited by counsel is quite incapable of bearing the meaning attributed to it. In that passage Lord Upjohn was simply referring to two sections of the 1965 Act to illustrate the meaning

j which he was saying the 1963 Act had always borne.

For the above reasons, and despite doubts generated by the complicated and peculiar drafting of the 1965 Act, and by the unanimity in a contrary sense of the courts below, I come to the conclusion that this appeal should be allowed.

---

1 [1969] 3 All ER at 1150, [1970] AC at 1001

LORD SIMON OF GLAISDALE. My Lords, I have had the advantage of *a* reading in draft the speech prepared by my noble and learned friend, Lord Hailsham of St Marylebone, with which I agree. I would accordingly allow the appeal.

In *Grey v Pearson*[1] Lord Wensleydale said, in words which have frequently been quoted and applied and which have indeed come to be called 'the golden rule':

> 'In construing . . . statutes . . . the grammatical and ordinary sense of the words is to be adhered to, unless that would lead to some absurdity, or some repugnance *b* or inconsistency with the rest of the instrument, in which case the grammatical and ordinary sense of the words may be modified, so as to avoid that absurdity and inconsistency, but no farther.'

The sense of the words used in the statutes with which your Lordships are concerned is, to my mind, plain beyond any question. The first respondent admittedly satisfied *c* the statutory conditions for a redundancy payment from the second respondents. By s 1(1) of the Redundancy Payments Act 1965 the amount of such redundancy payment was to be calculated in accordance with Sch 1 to the Act. Paragraph 1(1) of that schedule in turn provides that, subject to its other provisions and to some modifications thereby (all irrelevant in the instant case), the amount was to be—

d

> 'calculated by reference to the period, ending with the relevant date, during which he has been continuously employed; and for the purposes of this Schedule that period shall be computed in accordance with Schedule 1 to the Contracts of Employment Act 1963 . . .'

The relevant provision of Sch 1 to the Contracts of Employment Act 1963 is para *e* 10(2):

> 'If a trade or business or an undertaking . . . is transferred from one person to another, the period of employment of an employee in the trade or business or undertaking at the time of the transfer shall count as a period of employment with the transferee, and the transfer shall not break the continuity of the period of employment.'
>
> *f*

That precisely and clearly covers the present case; and entitles the first respondent to have his period of service with Isaac Barrie (Transport) Ltd (the transferors) to count as a period of service with the second respondents (the transferees) for the purpose of computing the amount of his redundancy payment.

I see no reason to think that Parliament did not intend effect to be given to the *g* palpable meaning of these plain words. Section 24 of the 1965 Act obviates the possibility of a double payment to the employee (i e from both the transferor and the transferee); and there is nothing extraordinary in a transferee assuming a transferor's liability to make redundancy payments along with all the other liabilities and assets involved in the taking over of a business. Certainly, I can discern no absurdity, repugnance or inconsistency which would justify your Lordships in modifying the *h* ordinary meaning of the statutory words used, or in adding some rider on the assumption that Parliament could not possibly have meant what she said.

I venture, moreover, to emphasise the last words of Lord Wensleydale's 'golden rule'[1]: '. . . the grammatical and ordinary sense of the words may be modified so as to avoid that absurdity or inconsistency, *but no farther.*' Even were there some discrepancy between s 8(2) of the 1965 Act and para 10(2) of Sch 1 to the 1963 *j* Act, so that it were necessary to modify the meaning of para 10(2) to bring it into line, this would only apply as regards the period of service required to establish *entitlement to redundancy payment;* and there would be no justification in going on

---

1 (1857) 6 HL Cas 61 at 106

a to make the same modification in para 10(2) as regards the period to be considered for the purpose of *computing the amount* of redundancy payment. This would be so even if the statute did not (as it does) stipulate different modifications of the operation of para 10(2) for the two respective purposes.

My Lords, it is of the utmost importance that courts should adhere to 'the golden rule', if we are ever to have statutes couched in plain and intelligible language. Parlia-
b ment and her draftsmen are entitled to assume that the language of a statute will be given its natural and ordinary meaning unless it is clear from the purpose of the statute (as collected from its setting and its provisions) that some other meaning must have been intended; the most usual circumstances for this would be where there arises some forensic situation which Parliament is unlikely to have contemplated. If the courts are unwilling to construe plain words in their natural and ordinary sense the prospect will be like one of those distressing scenes in a neurological
c ward: a patient has a 'crisis', which provokes some different idiosyncratic symptom in another patient, which in turn brings on fresh disorders in the first, and so on in a reciprocal and accumulating train of tribulation. So, if courts claim to discover tortuous and remote anomalies arising from the plain words of a statutory provision, and to modify those words accordingly, the draftsman will reciprocate by attempting to meet such cases in a way which will throw up yet more labyrinthine anomalies.
d Forensic ingenuity will be matched by statutory anfractuosity; and the hapless citizen will be sucked down in a vortex of verbiage. Ever since Plato it has been recog-
nised that legal rules were meant to do justice in the generality of situations; that since the rules were framed by fallible humankind—in courts as well as legislatures —there will inevitably be peculiar circumstances where the general rule will fail to do justice; but that to attempt to strain the rule to deal with such particular situations
e is liable to distort it so that it fails to do justice in the general and ordinary situations for which it was meant. In statutory interpretation, no less than in legislation (parliamentary or judicial), hard cases are apt to make bad law. Justice is more likely to be served, as well as constitutional propriety to be observed, if Parliament is given the credit for meaning what she has said.

f
LORD KILBRANDON. My Lords, once the Redundancy Payments Act 1965 has been completely analysed, as has been done by my noble and learned friend, Viscount Dilhorne, the manner in which this appeal must be disposed of becomes clear; no purpose would be served by my making another analysis, and arriving at the same result. Mr de Rosa became entitled to a redundancy payment on his dismissal on
g 31st December 1971. Schedule 1 to the 1965 Act requires the amount of payment to be calculated in accordance with Sch 1 to the Contracts of Employment Act 1963. It is provided by para 10(2) of that schedule that if a trade or business is transferred from one person to another, the period of employment of an employee in that business at the time of the transfer shall count as a period of employment with the transferee, and the transfer shall not break the continuity of the period of employment—that
h is the basis of the calculation. The case has been conducted on the footing that in fact the circumstances of Mr de Rosa's employment with the successive businesses exactly fall within that provision. It follows that the view of the appellant is correct.

It seems probable that there could arise cases in which the provisions of the Act are not easy to explain as matter of policy or to justify a priori. But this is not, in my opinion, such a case. The words which have been used to express the intention
j of Parliament in relation to such a case as the present appear to admit of only one interpretation. I would allow the appeal.

LORD SALMON. My Lords, Isaac Barrie (Transport) Ltd ('the transferors') ceased to trade and transferred the whole of their business to the second respondents ('the transferees') on 24th April 1967. At the date of the transfer the first respondent,

Mr de Rosa, was and had been continuously employed by the transferors since 1950. *a*
On 24th April 1967 he entered the employment of the transferees in a substantially
different capacity from that in which he had served the transferors. He served the
former as a transport manager in their head office and the latter as a foreman on
the docks. He remained in the transferees' employment until 31st December 1971,
when he was dismissed for redundancy.

It is not disputed that he is entitled to a redundancy payment by the transferees. *b*
The question is whether that payment is to be computed on the basis that his relevant
employment commenced on 24th April 1967, or on the date in 1950 when he was
first employed by the transferors. Section 1(1) of the Redundancy Payments Act
1965 provides that the payment is to be 'calculated in accordance with Schedule 1
to this Act'. Paragraph 1(1) of that schedule, following the fashionable but, to my
mind, highly objectionable practice of legislation by reference, laid down:

c

> 'The amount of a redundancy payment to which an employee is entitled in
> any case shall . . . be calculated by reference to the period, ending with the
> relevant date, during which he has been continuously employed; and for the
> purposes of this Schedule that period shall be computed in accordance with
> Schedule 1 to the Contracts of Employment Act 1963 . . .'

d

The schedule to the 1963 Act was an odd choice. That Act had been passed before
redundancy payments had come into existence and accordingly had nothing to do
with redundancy. It was concerned chiefly with the minimum length of notice which
could lawfully be given to terminate employment. The length of notice depended
on the length of service with any one employer or successive employers and nothing
else. The nature and terms of successive employments with the same employers *e*
or successive employers were irrelevant under the 1963 Act but vital for the purpose
of establishing liability to make redundancy payments under the 1965 Act.

Paragraph 10(2) of Sch 1 to the 1963 Act, so far as material, reads as follows:

> 'If a . . . business . . . is transferred from one person to another, the period
> of employment of an employee in the . . . business . . . at the time of the
> transfer shall count as a period of employment with the transferee, and the *f*
> transfer shall not break the continuity of the period of employment.'

Mr de Rosa having been in the employ of the transferors at the time of the transfer
and being indisputably entitled in 1971 to a redundancy payment by the transferees,
it appears to me to be an inescapable conclusion that for the purpose of computing
the amount of that payment, the period of his employment with the transferors must
count as a period of employment with the transferees and therefore the transferees *g*
are liable to have an award made against them on a computation not merely for the
period 1967-1971 but for the whole period from 1950-1971.

By going out of business an employer automatically terminates the contracts of
employment between himself and all those then in his employ. Section 3(1) of the
1965 Act provides, amongst other things, that an employee must be taken to have
been dismissed by his employer, if, but only if, the contract under which he is em- *h*
ployed by his employer is terminated by that employer whether with or without
notice. Section 1(2) provides that for the purposes of the Act, an employee shall be
taken to be dismissed for redundancy if his dismissal is attributable to his employers
ceasing to carry on business. Section 3(2) provides that if, in effect, the employer
continues the employee in substantially the same job and in certain other circumstances also inapplicable to the facts of the present case, the termination of a contract *j*
of employment shall not constitute a dismissal by the employers for the purposes of
the Act.

It is apparent from the foregoing that Mr de Rosa was dismissed by the transferors
when they ceased to trade on transferring their business to the transferees and that he
then became entitled to a red undancy payment from the transferors. He, however

a lost that claim against them because he failed to bring it within the time limit (fixed by s 21 of the 1965 Act) of six months from the date of his dismissal. Section 13(2) of the Act provides that if the transferees employ anyone in the employment of the transferors at the date of transfer in the same circumstances as those postulated in s 3(2), such person shall be taken not to have been dismissed by the transferors. This of course means that in such circumstances (which do not apply in the present

b case) the employee would have no claim for a redundancy payment against the transferors. By itself s 13(2), however, does not cast any obligation on the transferees even when it does apply. It merely relieves the transferors from liability. When s 13(2) does apply, liability is cast on the transferees by s 8(2) which reads:

'... the provisions of Schedule 1 to the Contracts of Employment Act 1963 (computation of period of employment) ... shall have effect for the purposes of

c this Part of this Act in determining whether an employee has been continuously employed for the requisite period.'

The 'requisite period' during which an employee must have been in continuous employment before qualifying under s 1(1) for any redundancy payment is 104 weeks; see s 8(1) of the 1965 Act. The language of s 8(2) which I have quoted says, somewhat indirectly, that para 10(2) of Sch 1 to the 1963 Act must apply not only for com-

d puting the amount of any redundancy payment which may be due but also for discovering whether the employee has enough continuous employment to his credit in order to qualify for any redundancy payment at all. It follows that if an employee engaged by the transferors at the time of the transfer is then engaged by the transferees and, say, three or four weeks later dismissed for redundancy, his period of employment with the transferors shall count as a period of employment with the

e transferees for the purpose of ascertaining whether he has sufficient continuous service to qualify for a redundancy payment as well as for the purpose of computing the amount of redundancy payment to which he is entitled. This, no doubt, produces a fair and sensible result when s 13(2) applies, but hardly does so when in a case such as the present the employee is engaged in entirely different employment by the transferees from that in which he served the transferors. In the present case—and there

f must be many other cases in which the disparity between the old employment and the new is even greater—it is most unlikely that the transferors had any inkling of the liabilities for redundancy payments which they were undertaking. Even had they pored over all the obscurities of the 1965 Act and darted from Sch 1 to that Act to Sch 1 to the 1963 Act, they might well have concluded that, since s 13(2) did not apply, the continuity of Mr de Rosa's employment had been broken by his dismissal by the trans-

g ferors when they went out of business and that accordingly they (the transferees) could be liable under the 1965 Act only in respect of the entirely new and different employment which began on 24th April 1967. And in this they would have been in very good company, for that is the conclusion at which the industrial tribunal, the National Industrial Relations Court and the Court of Session arrived.

For my part, I have no doubt but that the transferors by ceasing to trade, ter-

h minated their contract of employment with Mr de Rosa and are deemed thereby to have dismissed him for redundancy. The fact that he was taken on by the transferees and entered into a contract of employment with them cannot, in my view, be regarded as a mere variation of the contract with the transferors. Nor was it argued that the new contract was only a variation of the old. Nevertheless qua the transferees, the period of Mr de Rosa's employment with the transferors counted as a

j period of employment with the transferees: see para 10(2) of Sch 1 to the 1963 Act.

It follows, therefore, that although the termination of the old contract constituted a dismissal on account of redundancy in respect of which Mr de Rosa could have claimed a redundancy payment against the transferors, he could also have claimed a redundancy payment covering the same period against the transferees. Although he could have claimed redundancy payments from both employers in respect of the same period this apparent anomaly would have been cured by s 24 of the 1965 Act which prevents any employee from receiving more than one redundancy payment in *a* respect of the same period of employment.

The Act, however, produces other anomalies for which it provides no cure. Suppose, e g, that there had been no transfer by the old employers but they had closed down the transport side of their business on 24th April 1967, this would have brought Mr de Rosa's job as transport manager to an end, and would have constituted dismissal under the Act. He would have become redundant. Suppose the old employers *b* then (on 24th April 1967) employed him as their docks foreman—the very job in which he in fact was employed by the transferees—s 3(2) would not have applied. He would have had a valid claim for redundancy payment on 24th April 1967, but he would have lost it because he brought it out of time. Suppose that in 1971 he had been dismissed by his old employers as docks foreman on account of redundancy, his claim for redundancy payment could then have been computed only on the basis of *c* four years continuous employment and would have amounted to £132. If, however, he can now compute his redundancy payment on the basis of 20 years continuous employment, as, in my view, he can, he is entitled to £583. It follows, therefore, that, although the circumstances of his employments after 24th April 1967 would have been precisely the same, he is now more than four times better off than he would have been solely because of the transfer of the business and the consequent alteration in *d* the identity of his employers.

It seems odd, too, that if the transferors had given due notice to determine Mr de Rosa's employment with them expiring on the day before the transfer, he probably could not have received more than £132 because he would not have been 'an employee in the ... business ... at the time of the transfer ...'; accordingly para 10(2) of Sch 1 to the 1963 Act would have had no application to his case. I do not wish, *e* however, to express any concluded view on this point because it has not been argued. We have been told that there may have been a notice, but we do not know when it expired nor any of its terms. There is no mention of a notice in the record and this appeal must I think be decided without regard to any notice which may possibly have been given.

I have earlier ventured to express the view that legislation by reference is, as a rule, *f* most objectionable. A statute should contain within itself, stated with reasonable clarity, the measures which it enacts. Important measures should not be tucked away in one of the schedules with which modern statutes abound—particularly if they do not harmonise with what appears in the main body of the statute. Still less should they be introduced by a reference in one of the schedules to a schedule of another Act. With the plethora of modern legislation it is impossible when bills are passing through Parliament for schedules to receive the same meticulous scrutiny *g* as that accorded to the body of the bill. The practice to which I refer creates a real danger that Parliament, through no fault of its own, may enact a measure which it does not understand and which it would not have enacted if it had.

I have considerable doubt whether Parliament realised or intended the bizarre results which might follow from incorporating by reference para 10(2) into the 1965 *h* Act for the purposes of ss 1(1) and 8(2) of that Act. Nevertheless Parliament certainly did incorporate that paragraph into the 1965 Act for those purposes and the language of the paragraph is clear and unambiguous so far as its impact on s 1(1) is concerned. It lays down that the amount of the redundancy payment to which Mr de Rosa is entitled must be calculated on the basis that the period of his employment with the transferors counts as a period of his employment with the transferees. My Lords, *j* for these reasons I would allow the appeal.

Appeal allowed.

Solicitors: *The Solicitor, Department of Employment*, agent for *Shepherd & Wedderburn WS*, Edinburgh (for the appellant); *Slaughter & May*, agents for *Downie, Aiton, Farrell & Co*, Glasgow, and *D G McGregor WS*, Edinburgh (for the second respondents).

Christine Ivamy   Barrister.

a   # Worcestershire County Council v Newman

QUEEN'S BENCH DIVISION

LORD WIDGERY CJ, ASHWORTH AND PHILLIPS JJ

4th, 24th APRIL 1974

Reversed in part CA [1975] 2 All
ER 673

b

Highways – Maintenance – Enforcement of liability to maintain – Highway out of repair – Complaint to justices – Meaning of 'out of repair' – Obstruction on highway – Circumstances in which existence of obstruction rendering highway 'out of repair' – Obstruction attributable to failure of highway authority to carry out duty of maintenance – Obstruction which could have been prevented or remedied in course of routine maintenance – Footpath – Footpaths
c *obstructed by hedges and wire – Footpath blocked by cesspool effluent – Whether footpaths 'out of repair' – Highways Act 1959, s 59(2)(4).*

Highway – Obstruction – Removal – Duty of highway authority – Complaint to justices – Order to remove obstruction within 24 hours – Obstruction arising from accumulation of snow, falling down of banks or from any other cause – Words 'or any other cause' to be construed
d *ejusdem generis – Peremptory order for removal of obstruction limited to cases of emergency – Order not appropriate for removal of hedge – Highways Act 1959, s 129(1)(2) (as substituted by the Highways (Amendment) Act 1965, s 1).*

The respondent served a notice on the appellant, the county council, under s 59(2)[a]
e of the Highways Act 1959 alleging that certain footpaths were out of repair. The appellant gave notice under s 59(4) admitting that the footpaths were highways and that it was responsible for maintaining them. The respondent applied under s 59(4) for orders requiring the appellant to put the footpaths in proper repair, and under s 129[b] for orders requiring it to remove obstructions on those footpaths. The justices found that one of the footpaths, footpath 19, had a seven foot hawthorn hedge in the middle of it making passage along it impossible; that another, footpath
f 20, was overgrown by a hedge and blocked by wire; that at a point where footpaths 73 and 75 joined, the path was blocked by wire, and that footpath 123 was blocked by cesspool effluent. The appellant contended that, although the impediments on the footpaths were 'obstructions' in respect of which it could, under s 116 of the 1959 Act, take action or not as it thought fit, the existence of an obstruction on a highway did not justify a finding that the highway was 'out of repair' within s 59. The justices,
g however, held that the condition of the footpaths was such that they were 'out of repair' and accordingly they made orders under s 59(4) requiring the appellant to put them in proper repair. The justices also made an order under s 129 requiring the appellant to remove the obstruction on footpath 19. On appeal,

h **Held** – (i) The fact that a footpath was obstructed could justify an allegation that the footpath was 'out of repair' but in the context of the 1959 Act the two expressions were not wholly synonymous although they might sometimes overlap. A highway which was obstructed could be regarded as being 'out of repair' for the purposes of s 59 if its condition could fairly be attributed to a failure on the part of the highway authority to carry out its duty of maintenance under s 44 of the 1959 Act. If the
j obstruction was such that it ought to have been prevented or remedied in the course of normal routine maintenance, its existence resulted in the highway being out of repair (see p 873 *d* to *f* and p 874 *c*, post); dicta of Cockburn CJ and Crompton J in

---

a   Section 59, so far as material, is set out at p 872 *a* to *d*, post

b   Section 129, as amended and so far as material, is set out at p 873 *j*, post

R v Heath (1865) 12 LT at 493 and of du Parcq J in *Bishop v Consolidated London Properties*   a
Ltd [1933] All ER Rep at 968 applied.

   (ii) Accordingly, in respect of footpaths 19, 20 and 73 and 75, the justices had not
erred in law for they were entitled to take the view that cutting back undergrowth
and cutting wire with the simple tools available to a labourer were all incidents of
maintenance. The appeals in respect of those orders would therefore be dismissed.
However, although the effluent on footpath 123 might have been a result of a failure   b
of maintenance, on the facts found that was not necessarily so; thus if someone
had built a cesspit in such a way that effluent flooded the footpath it could not be
regarded as being 'out of repair'. Accordingly the appeal in respect of footpath 123
would be allowed and the case remitted to the justices for reconsideration (see
p 873 g and h, post).

   (iii) A peremptory order under s 129(2) of the 1959 Act requiring removal of an   c
obstruction within 24 hours should be confined to a sudden and substantial obstruction
which occurred without warning and which had to be removed with equal urgency.
Accordingly an order under s 129 was not appropriate for the removal of the hedge
on footpath 19. The appeal against that order would therefore be allowed and the
order quashed (see p 874 a to c, post).

Notes   d
For complaint to justices that highway is out of repair, see 19 Halsbury's Laws (3rd
Edn) 145, 146, para 223; for the extent of the duty to repair, see ibid, 115, 116, para
173, and for cases on the subject, see 26 Digest (Repl) 470-473, 1587-1617.

   For the duty of highway authorities to remove impediments and obstructions
arising from accumulations of snow etc, see 19 Halsbury's Laws (3rd Edn) 283,
284, para 448, and for cases on the subject, see 26 Digest (Repl) 503, 1845-1850.   e

   For the Highways Act 1959, ss 44, 59, 116, 129, 295, see 15 Halsbury's Statutes (3rd
Edn) 195, 208, 261, 272, 413.

Cases referred to in judgment
Bishop v Consolidated London Properties Ltd [1933] All ER Rep 963, 102 LJKB 257, 148
   LT 407, 31(2) Digest (Reissue) 600, 4883.   f
Inglis v Buttery (1878) 3 App Cas 552, HL, 7 Digest (Repl) 341, 18.
R v Heath (1865) 6 B & S 578, 12 LT 492, 122 ER 1309, DC.

Case stated
This was an appeal by way of a case stated by justices for the county of Worcester
acting in and for the petty sessional division of Redditch in respect of their adjudi-
cation as a magistrates' court sitting at Redditch on 31st May May 1973.
                                                                                       g
   On 24th November 1972 four complaints were preferred by the respondent, Peter
John Newman, against the appellant, Worcester County Council, under s 59(4) of the
Highways Act 1959. (a) The first complaint alleged that a certain way, namely footpath
19 in the parish of Inkberrow (national grid reference SP010593; ordnance survey map
SP05 NW), was a highway maintainable at the public expense and was out of repair
in that it was overgrown by a hedge. (b) A further complaint alleged that a certain   h
way, namely footpath 20 in the parish of Inkberrow (national grid reference SP009599;
ordnance survey map SP05 NW), was a highway maintainable at the public expense
and was out of repair in that it was overgrown by a hedge and blocked by wire. (c)
A further complaint alleged that a certain way, namely the junction of footpaths
73 and 75 in the parish of Inkberrow (national grid reference SP0044576; ordnance
survey map SP05 NW), was a highway maintainable at the public expense and was   j
out of repair in that it was blocked by a wire fence. (d) A further complaint alleged
that a certain way, namely footpath 123 in the parish of Inkberrow (national grid
reference SP014594; ordnance survey map SP05 NW), was a highway maintainable
at the public expense and was out of repair in that it was blocked by a cesspit outlet.
By each complaint the respondent applied for an order requiring the appellant to
put the highway in proper repair within such reasonable period as may be specified.

a   Two complaints were also preferred by the respondent against the appellant under
s 129 of the Highways Act 1959.

The first complaint alleged that an obstruction had arisen in a highway, namely,
footpath 20 in the parish of Inkberrow, in that it was overgrown by a hedge and
blocked by wire and that the appellant, being the highway authority for that highway,
had failed to remove it. The second complaint alleged that an obstruction had arisen

b   in a certain highway, namely, footpath 123 in the parish of Inkberrow, that it was
blocked by a cesspit outlet and that the appellant, being the highway authority for
the highway, had failed to remove it. On 18th January 1973 two further complaints
were preferred by the respondent against the appellant under s 129 of the 1959
Act. The first complaint alleged that an obstruction had arisen in a highway, namely
footpath 19 in the parish of Inkberrow (national grid reference SP010593; ordnance

c   survey map no SP05 NW), in that it was overgrown by a hedge and that the appellant,
being the highway authority for the highway, had failed to remove it. A further
complaint alleged that an obstruction had arisen in a highway, namely the junction
of footpath 73 and 75 in the parish of Inkberrow (national grid reference no SP004576;
ordnance survey map no SP05 NW), in that the junction of the footpaths was blocked
by a wire fence and that the appellant, being the highway authority for the highway,

d   had failed to remove it. By each of the complaints preferred under s 129 of the 1959
Act, the respondent applied for a order requiring the appellant to remove each of
the obstructions.

The justices heard the complaints on 31st May 1973.   Not less than 21 days prior
to the hearing the appellant had given notice under s 61(3) of the 1959 Act to two
persons liable to maintain certain of the footpaths by virtue of the Inkberrow Inclosure
Award of 1818 and the Inclosure Act 1801 and those persons were heard on the question

e   whether the highways for which they were liable were in proper repair. The justices
found the following facts. (a) On 3rd November 1972 the appellant served on the
respondent a notice admitting both that the paths in question were highways and
that the appellant was liable to maintain them. (b) At the time of the hearing there
was a hawthorn hedge approximately seven feet high growing in the middle of

f   footpath 19, and passage along that footpath was impossible. (c) At the time of the
hearing there was a barbed wire fence and thick undergrowth across footpath 20.
Passage along that footpath could only be effected by negotiating that fence; a way
could be forced through the undergrowth but that would result in the scratching
of the clothes of the walker. (d) At the time of the hearing there was a barbed wire
fence consisting of several strands of wire at the junction of footpaths 73 and 75.

g   Passage at that junction could only be effected by negotiating the fence. (e) At the
time of the hearing there was a cesspit outlet on footpath 123. The effluent at the
point extended for about six feet along the length of the path and was at least one
foot deep. Passage along the footpath was impossible.

It was contended by the appellant (in relation to the complaints preferred under
s 59): (a) that the respondent had laid one complaint under s 59 and one under s 129

h   in respect of each of the four paths; it was clear from the terms of all those complaints
that the true nature of the respondent's complaints was that the paths were
obstructed; s 59 did not provide a remedy in respect of obstructed paths; it dealt
only with paths which were 'out of repair'; (b) that it was important to distinguish
between the obstruction of a path on the one hand and a path becoming 'out of
repair' on the other; the distinction could be clearly seen in the imaginary case of a

j   normal county road; such a road might be in an exemplary state of repair, as the
term was commonly understood, being well metalled, curbed and drained etc;
if a person were unlawfully to erect a barrier across it, then nobody coming on the
barrier would think to himself 'this road is out of repair' and seek a remedy under
s 59; on the contrary, he would regard the barrier as an unlawful obstruction and
would expect it to be dealt with on that basis; (c) that the distinction of fact between
an obstruction on the one hand, and lack of repair on the other hand, was recognised

by the 1959 Act; each was treated by a separate section of the Act; the present pro- *a*
ceedings were concerned with the enforcement of duties; whilst the 1959 Act gave
a highway authority several *powers* to effect the removal of obstructions from footpaths which they might exercise at their discretion having regard to all material
considerations—the important point was to see on whom the *duty* so to do was
ultimately laid; the duty to maintain was contained in s 44 of the 1959 Act; that
section cast on the highway authority, in this case the appellant, the duty to maintain *b*
all publicly maintainable highways in its area; s 295 defined the word 'maintain'
so as to include 'repair'; on the other hand, the duty to secure the removal of
obstructions was contained in s 116; that section by sub-s (3) cast a duty on district
councils, in this case the rural district council, to assert and protect the rights of the
public to the use and enjoyment of all highways in their district and to prevent,
as far as possible, the stopping-up or obstruction of those highways; by sub-s (5) *c*
district councils were empowered to institute legal proceedings to that end, and
since the passing of the Highways Act 1971 they could do that in their own name;
the section went on to provide that if the district council were to default in carrying
out that duty, the parish council or parish meeting might petition the county council,
and if the latter so resolved, the functions of the district council under that section
were transferred to the county council; if all kinds of obstructions could be brought *d*
within the compass of s 59 and any individual were able to compel the highway
authority to remove an obstruction from a footpath by securing the order of a
magistrates' court under s 59, then the detailed default machinery embodied in s 116
would be otiose; the respondent was seeking to secure the removal of the obstructions
under the wrong section; (d) that the best known former remedy for failure to
repair a highway was by indictment at common law; that remedy was abolished by *e*
s 59(1) of the 1959 Act; it was significant that none of the reported cases of indictment
were concerned with the removal of obstructions. The appellant contended in relation
to the complaints preferred under s 129 that the words 'any other cause' in s 129
were to be construed ejusdem generis with 'accumulation of snow or from the falling
down of banks on the side of the highway'; the specific words mentioned in the
section confined the kinds of obstructions dealt with in two ways; first, the *f*
obstructions had to arise from natural causes. Consequently man-made obstructions
such as a cesspit outlet or fences were not caught by s 129; secondly, the obstructions
had to emanate from a source which was external to the highway.
   It was contended by the respondent: (a) that the word 'repair' in s 59 should be
given its natural meaning which was to put back into its original condition; (b) that
even if s 116 placed a duty on district councils that did not exclude the operation of s 59
against county councils; and (c) that s 129 did not read 'any other natural cause' and *g*
the word 'obstruction' in that section was not qualified in any way.
   The justices were of the opinion: (a) that the words 'out of repair' in s 59 referred
not only to the condition of the surface of the highway but also to its fitness for the
purpose for which it was intended to be used; the four highways in question were
footpaths and in each case their condition was such as to impede the passage of pedes-
trians along them; (b) that although s 116 placed certain duties on the district council *h*
that did not exclude proceedings against the appellant under s 59; (c) that the words
'any other cause' in s 129 were to be construed ejusdem generis with 'accumulation of
snow or from the falling down of banks on the side of a highway'; footpath 19 was
obstructed by a natural cause, i e a hawthorn hedge; the justices considered it immaterial that that obstruction was not external to the highway: and accordingly they
made four orders under s 59 requiring the appellant to put the highways in proper re- *j*
pair within three months; the justices made a further order under s 129 requiring the
appellant to remove the obstruction arising in footpath 19 within three months.
However, they dismissed the remaining complaints preferred under s 129 as revealing
no case to answer.
   The questions for the opinion of the High Court were: (a) whether the justices

a had correctly interpreted and applied the words 'out of repair' and 'obstructions' in ss 59 and 129 of the 1959 Act respectively; (b) in particular was a highway 'out of repair' within the meaning of s 59 of the 1959 Act by reason only of its being obstructed? (c) did s 59 of the 1959 Act lay an enforceable duty on the appellant as highway authority to secure the removal of obstructions from footpaths, notwithstanding the provisions of s 116 of the 1959 Act?

b

Patrick Freeman QC and *Konrad Schiemann* for the appellant.
Harry Wolton for the respondent.

Cur adv vult

c
24th April. **LORD WIDGERY CJ** read the following judgment. This is an appeal by case stated by justices for the county of Worcester in respect of their adjudication as a magistrates' court sitting at Redditch on 31st May 1973. On that occasion the justices made four orders as the suit of the respondent and against the appellant county council under s 59(4) of the Highways Act 1959, in each case requiring the
d appellant to put a specified highway in proper repair. A further order was made in respect of one of the same highways under s 129 of the Act requiring the appellant to remove an obstruction on the highway.

Each of the highways is a footpath and the appellant admits that it is liable for the maintenance of each such path.

The case gives only brief details of the particular respects in which each of these
e highways was said to be out of repair or obstructed, but the substance of the matters found by the justices appear to be as follows. Footpath 19 in the parish of Inkberrow was alleged to be out of repair in that it was overgrown by a hedge. Later in the case the justices say that a hawthorn hedge approximately seven feet high was growing in the middle of this footpath so that passage along the footpath was impossible. The second highway is footpath 20 in the same parish alleged to be out of repair
f in that it was overgrown by a hedge and blocked by wire. The justices observed that there was a barbed-wire fence and thick undergrowth across this footpath. Passage along the footpath could only be effected by negotiating the fence. A way could be forced through the undergrowth but this would result in a scratching of the clothes of the walker. The third highway referred to was said to be out of repair at a point where footpaths 73 and 75 in the same parish joined. The nature of the lack of repair
g was alleged to be that the path was blocked by a wire fence. Apparently this fence was a barbed-wire fence consisting of several strands of wire. Passage at the junction between these paths could be effected only by negotiating the fence. Finally, in regard to footpath 123 in the same parish, it was alleged that the footpath was out of repair in that it was blocked by a cesspit outlet. The justices say that the effluent from this cesspit outlet at the point where it crossed the footpath extended along
h the path for about six feet and was at least one foot deep. Passage along the footpath was impossible. The justices made an order under s 59 against the appellants in respect of each of these four paths, and in addition in regard to footpath 19 a further order was made under s 129 of the Act.

The scheme of the Act appears to be as follows. By s 44(1):

j   'The authority who are for the time being the highway authority for a highway maintainable at the public expense shall, subject to the following subsection, be under a duty to maintain the highway.'

By s 295, ' "maintenance" includes repair, and "maintain" and "maintainable" shall be construed accordingly'. Section 59 contains provisions for the enforcement of the obligation of the highway authority to keep the highway in repair. By s 59(2) it is provided:

'A person . . . who alleges that a way or bridge—(a) is a highway maintainable
at the public expense or a highway which a person is liable to maintain under a
special enactment or by reason of tenure, enclosure or prescription, and (b) is
out of repair, may serve a notice on the highway authority or other person alleged
to be liable to maintain the way or bridge (in this and the next following section
referred to as "the respondent") requiring the respondent to state whether he
admits that the way or bridge is a highway and that he is liable to maintain it.'

It is further provided by s 59(4):

'If, within one month from the date of service on him of a notice under subsection (2) of this section, the respondent serves on the complainant a notice
admitting both that the way . . . in question is a highway and that the respondent
is liable to maintain it, the complainant may, within six months from the date
of service on him of that notice, apply to a magistrates' court for an order requiring the respondent, if the court finds that the highway is out of repair, to put
it in proper repair, within such reasonable periods may be specified in the
order.'

The appellants having duly served notice under s 59(4) admitting their responsibility to maintain the highway, the complainant, who is the respondent in this court,
applied to the justices who made an order requiring in each instance that the highway
be put in proper repair.

Returning to the general scheme of the Act, one finds in s 116 that wide powers
are given to a variety of public authorities to enable them to secure the removal of
obstructions on a highway. So far as a county council is concerned, these powers
are discretionary.

The contest both below, and in this court, has been between the appellant which
alleges that the impediments found in these four highways are obstructions in respect
of which it can take action or not as in its discretion it thinks right, and the respondent
who alleges that the impediments cause the highway to be out of repair so as to enable
him to obtain an order from the justices requiring the appellant to take the
appropriate action.

The justices' opinion was that the words 'out of repair' in s 59 refer not only to the
condition of the surface of the highway, but also to its fitness for the purpose for which
it was intended for use. Accordingly they found that the condition of the four highways in question was such that they were out of repair.

Historically, the question whether a highway is out of repair is one for the jury,
which may explain why counsel have found so little authority on it. 'Repair' can
mean to make good defects including renewal where necessary (Inglis v Buttery[1])
but the word can extend to defects which affect the functioning of the subject-
matter as well as to those which affect its physical condition. Thus in Bishop v Consolidated London Properties Ltd[2], a covenant to keep a drainage system in repair was
held to be broken when a dead pigeon was washed into the system and obstructed it.
Du Parcq J said[3]:

'I have come to the conclusion that a pipe which is choked and not able to do
its duty as a pipe is out of repair, and that the [defendants] are none the less
liable as for a breach of their covenant though they may show that the cause
of the defect in the pipe is fortuitous and beyond their control. I think one must
remember that "to repair" after all merely means to prepare or make fit again
to perform its functions; it means to put in order, and, I think, means no more.'

1 (1878) 3 App Cas 552
2 [1933] All ER Rep 963
3 [1933] All ER Rep at 968

a Again, in *R v Heath*[1], where a similar question arose under different legislation, Cockburn CJ said:

b
'Now the main purpose of the Act is the repair of the highway, and the keeping of the highway in a proper condition; but the existence of an obstruction which is a nuisance on a highway is manifestly inconsistent with the highway being kept in a proper state of repair, and therefore I think, on a wise and liberal construction of the Act, they might have been fairly and legitimately included in the purposes of the Act, in carrying the purposes out.'

Crompton J said[1]:

c
'Mr. McIntyre put his case very shortly and simply, and on two very short and simple propositions. He said, "Here is this body bound to keep in repair from time to time the roads. It is impossible to do that without removing obstructions. It is impossible in many cases that obstructions can properly be removed without having recourse to the arm of the law." He says those are repairs under one or both of these Acts. I have not heard a word that has been said during the whole course of the case that seems to meet that argument,

d and I think those propositions are correct, and the inference drawn from them is correct.'

Accordingly it seems to me that the justices were right in thinking that the fact that a footpath was obstructed could also justify an allegation that it was 'out of repair', but in the context of the 1959 Act I do not think that the two expressions are wholly synonymous although on occasion they overlap.

e In my opinion a highway which is obstructed can be regarded as being out of repair for the purposes of s 59 if its condition can be fairly attributed to a failure of the highway authority to carry out its duty of maintenance under s 44. I do not think that Parliament intended that enforcement action under s 59 should impose a higher duty on the highway authority than that imposed by s 44. If the obstruction is such that it ought to have been prevented or remedied in the course of normal routine

f maintenance, its existence caused the highway to be out of repair. If, however, a builder chose to dump tons of rubble on a footpath thus rendering it impassable, it would, I think, be an abuse of language to say that the highway authority had allowed the footpath to become out of repair.

Applying this principle to the present case I do not think that the justices can be said to have erred in law in their judgment in the first three orders referred to.

g They were entitled to take the view that cutting back undergrowth and cutting wire with the simple tools available to a labourer were all incidents of maintenance. I would accordingly dismiss this appeal so far as it relates to the first three orders under s 59.

The fourth case I find more difficult because the facts found are so limited. If the effluent was originally carried under the footpath in a culvert which has collapsed

h or become obstructed, this may well be a failure in maintenance. If, however, someone has built a cesspit in such a way that the effluent floods the footpath, I do not think that the result is to make the footpath out of repair. In regard to the fourth case under s 59 I would allow the appeal to the extent of sending the matter back to the justices for reconsideration in the light of this judgment.

I must now deal with the order under s 129. Section 129(1) provides:

j
'If an obstruction arises in a highway from accumulation of snow or from the falling down of banks on the side of the highway, or from any other cause, the highway authority for the highway shall remove the obstruction.'

---

1 (1865) 12 LT 492 at 493

Section 129(2) enables the court to make a peremptory order for the removal of *a* the obstruction within a period of not less than 24 hours.

The justices rightly considered that the words 'or for any other cause' should be construed ejusdem generis with accumulation of snow and falling banks and thus confined to obstructions attributable to natural causes. In my view, however, the construction of these words is even more limited and should be confined to sudden and substantial obstructions occurring without warning and requiring to be removed *b* with equal urgency. The seven foot hedge obstructing footpath 19 was natural in origin but lacked the sudden onset and urgent requirement of removal which is characteristic of the mischief at which s 129 is aimed.

Accordingly, I would further allow the appeal to the extent of quashing the order under s 129.

c

ASHWORTH J. I agree.

LORD WIDGERY CJ. I am authorised by Phillips J to say that he has read this judgment and agrees with it.

Appeal dismissed. Leave to appeal granted.   *d*

Solicitors: *Sharpe, Pritchard & Co,* agents for *W R Scurfield,* Worcester (for the appellant); *Allan Jay & Co,* agents for *Cartwright & Lewis,* Birmingham (for the respondent).

N P Metcalfe Esq Barrister.

e

The Union of India v E B Aaby's Rederi A/S

HOUSE OF LORDS
LORD REID, LORD MORRIS OF BORTH-Y-GEST, VISCOUNT DILHORNE, LORD SIMON OF GLAISDALE   *f*
AND LORD SALMON
25th, 26th, 27th, 28th MARCH, 13th JUNE 1974

Shipping – Charterparty – Arbitration clause – Application – 'All disputes . . . arising out of this contract' – General average claim – Charterparty making special provision for general average – Arbitration clause providing time limit for claims – General average act occurring during voyage – Claim by owners for general average – Charterers disputing liability to make general average contribution – Whether a dispute 'arising out of' contract – Whether time limit applicable.   *g*

Shipping – Charterparty – Arbitration clause – Waiver – New contract – Arbitration clause stipulating time limit for claims – Claim by owners for general average – Charterparty giving *h* *vessel lien on cargo for average – General average act occurring during voyage – Claim submitted by owners – Charterers giving undertaking to pay general average 'legally due' and requesting release of cargo – Owners acknowledging undertaking and releasing cargo – Charterers subsequently disputing liability for general average – Whether owners' claim under new contract – Whether time limit stipulated in arbitration clause applicable.*

By a charterparty dated 16th January 1966 the Indian government chartered a vessel *j* from her owners for a voyage with a cargo of wheat in bulk from a North Pacific United States port to India. Clause 2 of the charterparty began with the words 'General average shall be payable according to York/Antwerp Rules 1950 and to be settled in London . . .' and made provision for the entitlement of the owners to general average contributions even if a general average act had resulted from

a   unseaworthiness provided that they had exercised due diligence to make the vessel in
    all respects seaworthy and to have her properly manned, equipped and supplied.
    By cl 6 the vessel was to have a lien on the cargo for all freight, dead freight, demur-
    rage and average. The charterparty incorporated the Centrocon arbitration clause
    (amended) which provided that 'All disputes from time to time arising out of this
    contract' were to be referred to arbitrators; the second sentence of the clause read:
b   'Any claim must be made in writing and Claimant's Arbitrator appointed within
    twelve (12) months of final discharge and when this provision is not complied with
    the claim shall be deemed to be waived and absolutely barred.' On 23rd January
    the vessel started her voyage. She was to call at Yokohama for bunkers. On
    12th February she ran out of fuel and it became necessary to arrange for the services
    of a tug which towed the vessel towards Yokohama. Eventually the tug was able
c   to supply her with fuel and she reached Yokohama on 18th February. Having
    refuelled there she sailed for Bombay, arriving there on 8th March. The discharge
    of the cargo was completed on 12th March. Meanwhile, on 17th February, average
    adjusters on behalf of the owners had written to the India Supply Mission ('the
    mission') in London asking for 'the usual undertaking by the Indian Government
    to pay their cargo's proportion of General Average' in respect of the expenditure
d   incurred in obtaining the services of the tug. They received a reply dated 23rd
    February giving 'an undertaking that any General Average contribution which may
    be legally due from the Government of India as cargo owners will be paid by this
    Mission' and, in view of the undertaking, requesting the release of the cargo immed-
    iately the vessel arrived at an Indian port. On 25th February the average adjusters
    acknowledged the reply and gave instructions for the cargo to be released without
    further security being obtained. In due course they produced their general average
e   adjustment, dated 24th February 1967. On 30th March the owners' agents sent a
    copy to the mission and requested the amount shown in the adjustment as being due
    from cargo. On 7th June the Indian government wrote repudiating the claim on the
    ground that the vessel had been unseaworthy before the voyage began. Correspond-
    ence followed and in April 1971 the owners renewed their claim. The Indian govern-
f   ment then raised the point that the claim was barred since no arbitrator had been
    appointed by the owners within 12 months of the discharge of the cargo.

    Held– (i) Under the provisions of the charterparty the owners' claim for general
    average contribution would have been barred by the arbitration clause since the
    dispute was one 'arising out of' the contract. Where the parties to a contract made
    provision as to their rights should certain events occur in the course of the contract
g   and a dispute arose between them as to their rights following the occurrence of
    those events that dispute was one which arose out of the contract. Furthermore
    cl 2 did not have the effect of withdrawing questions of general average from the
    scope of the arbitration clause (see p 876 f, p 879 d and e, p 880 d to f, p 884 a to c
    and f, p 885 a and e, p 886 d f and j and p 887 b and d, post).
h   (ii) The exchange of letters in February 1966 between the charterers and the average
    adjusters, however, constituted a new contract whereby, in return for the owners'
    promise to forego their right of lien on the cargo, the Indian government undertook
    to pay the cargo's proportion of general average which might be 'legally due'. The
    arbitration clause, and the time limits stipulated therein, had no application to the
    new contract and accordingly the owners were entitled to pursue their claim under
j   the contract (see p 876 f, p 882 c and d, p 886 b to d and p 888 b and g to j, post).

    ### Notes
    For conditions as to time in arbitration agreements, see 2 Halsbury's Laws (4th Edn)
    277, para 543, and for cases on the subject, see 2 Digest (Repl) 449-451, *182-188.*
    For waiver of contractual rights, see 8 Halsbury's Laws (3rd Edn) 175, para 299,
    and for cases on the subject, see 12 Digest (Reissue) 544, 545, *3796-3806.*

Cases referred to in opinions

Astraea, The, Alma Shipping Corpn v Union of India [1971] 2 Lloyd's Rep 494.

Atlantic Shipping and Trading Co v Louis Dreyfus & Co [1922] 2 AC 250, [1922] All ER Rep 250, 91 LJKB 513, 127 LT 411, 15 Asp MLC 566, 27 Com Cas 311, 10 Ll L Rep 446, 707, HL; (1921) 6 Ll L Rep 194, CA; (1920) 4 Ll L Rep 424, 2 Digest (Repl) 450, 185.

Gibraltar, Government of, v Kenney [1956] 3 All ER 22, [1956] 2 QB 410, [1956] 3 WLR 466, 2 Digest (Repl) 434, 95.

Heyman v Darwins Ltd [1942] 1 All ER 337, [1942] AC 356, 111 LJKB 241, 166 LT 306, HL, 2 Digest (Repl) 492, 435.

Morrison Steamship Co Ltd v Owners of Cargo Lately Laden on SS Greystoke Castle [1946] 2 All ER 696, [1947] AC 265, [1947] LJR 297, 176 LT 66, HL, 41 Digest (Repl) 514, 2887.

Appeal

This was an appeal by the Union of India against an order of the Court of Appeal (Lord Denning MR, Megaw and Scarman LJJ) dated 19th March 1973 dismissing the appellants' appeal against the order of Mocatta J dated 9th March 1972, in an action by the appellants against the respondents, E B Aaby's Rederi A/S, whereby he answered certain preliminary questions of law in favour of the respondents. The facts are set out in the opinion of Lord Morris of Borth-y-Gest.

R L A Goff QC and *J S Hobhouse QC* for the appellants.
C S Staughton QC and *D B Johnson* for the respondents.

Their Lordships took time for consideration.

13th June. The following opinions were delivered.

LORD REID. My Lords, for the reasons given by my noble and learned friends, Lord Morris of Borth-y-Gest and Lord Salmon, I would dismiss this appeal.

LORD MORRIS OF BORTH-Y-GEST. My Lords, the questions which arise in this appeal can best be stated after narrating the relevant facts. By a charterparty which was dated London, 14th January 1966, and which was the Form C approved Baltimore Berth Grain Charter Party, the Chief Controller of Chartering, Ministry of Transport, New Delhi, Government of India (the appellants), chartered the Norwegian motor vessel Evje from her owners (the respondents). The charter was for a voyage with a cargo of wheat in bulk. The voyage was to be from one North Pacific United States safe port to Bombay or at the charterers' option to Kandla (India).

Clause 2 of the charterparty began with the words 'General Average shall be payable according to York/Antwerp Rules 1950 and to be settled in London'. These words were followed (some words in the printed form in relation to an average bond and to security having been deleted) by words setting out the Jason clause. The clause deals, in the terms set out, with the entitlement of the owners to general average contributions even if a general average act has resulted from unseaworthiness provided that they have exercised due diligence to make the vessel seaworthy and to have her properly manned, equipped and supplied.

By cl 6 the vessel was to have a lien on the cargo for all freight, dead freight, demurrage or average. The charterparty was further to include special provisions as cll 7 to 38 inclusive. The incorporated Centrocon arbitration clause (amended) has the two following opening sentences:

'All disputes from time to time arising out of this contract shall, unless the parties agree forthwith on a single Arbitrator, be referred to the final arbitrament *a* of two Arbitrators carrying on business in London, who shall be Members of The Baltic and engaged in the Shipping and/or Grain trades, one to be appointed by each of the parties, with power to such Arbitrators to appoint an Umpire. Any claim must be made in writing and Claimant's Arbitrator appointed within twelve (12) months of final discharge and where this provision is not complied with the claim shall be deemed to be waived and absolutely barred.'

b The vessel went to Portland, Oregon, and there loaded a full cargo of wheat. It was in bulk about 17,600 tons. On 23rd January she set out to proceed to Bombay or Kandla. The owners say that when she left Portland the vessel had adequate bunkers (plus a normal surplus) to enable her to reach Yokohama. She was to call at Yokohama for bunkers. On 12th February when partly across the Pacific on her way to Yokohama she ran out of fuel oil and stopped. It is said that she had encount-
c ered severe weather and as a consequence had consumed an excessive quantity of bunkers. It became necessary to arrange by cable for the services of a tug. The vessel was presumably in a position of some peril. In due course a tug arrived (probably on 15th February) and began to tow the vessel towards Yokohama. Here was the general average act resulting in expenditure in respect of which there was a later claim for general average contribution.
d The tug towed the vessel for some period and then was able to supply her with some fuel and so enable her to reach Yokohama. That she did on 18th February 1966. Having refuelled she sailed for Bombay. She reached Bombay on 8th March 1966. The cargo was then discharged. That discharge was completed on 12th March 1966.

After the vessel had come to a stop (on 12th February) and before she reached
e Yokohama, the respondents, considering the case to be of a general average nature, communicated with their London agents and asked them to get in touch with Messrs William Richards & Son as average adjusters. The respondents desired to leave the average adjustment in Messrs Richards' hands and also wished them to make suitable arrangements which would secure the contribution of the proportion of general average attaching to the cargo. Both the respondents' agents and Messrs
f Richards knew that it was not the practice of the appellants to give either a general average bond or a cash deposit.

Having been instructed, Messrs Richards wrote to the Director-General of the India Supply Mission in London. By their letter dated 17th February 1966 Messrs Richards explained all that had happened and concluded with the words:

g 'We shall therefore be obliged if you will let us have the usual undertaking by the Indian Government to pay their cargo's proportion of General Average when this has been determined.'

A reply came dated 23rd February 1966. It was in these terms:

h 'I have for acknowledgment your letter No. G/MP dated 17th Feb. 1966 and I am to say that the High Commissioner for India in London hereby gives an undertaking that any General Average contribution which may be legally due from the Government of India as cargo owners will be paid by this Mission. In view of the above undertaking you are requested to contact the ship-owner's agents in India, by cable if necessary, to release government cargo immediately the vessel arrives at an Indian port.'

j Messrs Richards on 25th February 1966 gave instructions that the cargo was to be released to the consignee on the vessel's arrival in India without further security being obtained. On the same date they wrote to the Director-General of the India Supply Mission in these terms: 'We thank you for your letter of the 23rd February and note that we may apply to you for settlement when our Adjustment of General Average is completed.' There was in the letter also a request to be furnished in due course with particulars of the value of the Indian government cargo. Messrs Richards *a* proceeded with their work and in due course prepared their general average adjustment. It was dated 24th February 1967.

It is to be noted that a period of 12 months from the final discharge of the cargo at Bombay expired on 12th March 1967. On 30th March 1967 the owners' agents sent a copy of the general average adjustment to the Director-General of the India Supply Mission. Request was made for the sum of £5,995 4s 7d which was the amount *b* shown in the adjustment as being due from the cargo. That sum was therefore what the average adjusters considered was the appropriate contribution which was payable towards the total general average expenditure incurred which was some £12,070.

The solicitors acting on behalf of the appellants wrote in reply on 7th June 1967. No suggestion was made that any time bar operated to defeat the claim, but, while *c* reserving rights to question any other aspect of the claim it was, at least 'initially', repudiated on the ground set out in this sentence:

> 'We have examined the Average Adjustment Statement and we have come to the conclusion that the incident alleged to give rise to General Average arose due to the poor quality of the fuel oil by virtue of the presence of impurities in the same and as such we contend that the vessel was unseaworthy at or before *d* the commencement of the relevant voyage and that it was the said unseaworthiness that caused the alleged incident giving rise to General Average.'

In reply to this it was stated on 31st July 1967 on behalf of the respondents that they had ordered oil of a particular quality from reputable suppliers and that there had been no failure to exercise due diligence to provide a seaworthy vessel. *e*

Further correspondence followed in 1968 in reference to proceedings and the acceptance of service but between October 1968 and April 1971 there was a complete interval. After the claim was renewed in April 1971 the point was for the first time raised on behalf of the appellants that any claim for a contribution towards general average would be by way of arbitration in London and that as no arbitrator had been appointed within 12 months of the final discharge of the cargo the claim had *f* been waived and was absolutely barred. The fact that the point thus taken had not been raised earlier did not, in my view, in any way preclude its being raised.

On behalf of the respondents it was pointed out that the claim that was being made was made pursuant to and in order to enforce the undertaking given in the letter of 23rd February 1966. A writ was issued dated 4th June 1971 and endorsed with points of claim. The claim for the sum of £5,995 was founded on the February 1966 undertaking. In the points of defence several issues were raised. One was that the res-*g* pondents had at no time appointed an arbitrator and that under the amended Centrocon arbitration clause any claim for a general average contribution had been waived and had become barred on or about 12th March 1967. Another issue which was raised concerned the questions whether the respondents had exercised due diligence to make the vessel seaworthy and whether they had been negligent. *h*

On 16th November 1971 the learned judge (Mocatta J) ordered that there should be a preliminary trial of the following questions of law:

> '(1) Whether the [appellants] are entitled to rely on the amended Centrocon arbitration clause contained in a voyage charter party dated London the 14th January 1966 and made between the [respondents] as owners of the m.v. "EVJE" and the [appellants] as charterers thereof, in answer to the [respondents'] claim *j* and, if so,
>
> '(2) Whether under that clause the [respondents'] claim was waived and became barred on or about the 12th day of March 1967.'

In the result the learned judge (Mocatta J)[1] and the members of the Court of

---

1   [1972] 2 Lloyd's Rep 129

a   Appeal[1] all answered the questions so raised in the negative. They did so, however, for various reasons. The learned judge held that had there not been the letter of undertaking the arbitration clause and time bar would have applied to the claim for general average contribution; he held, however, that the arbitration clause did not apply to a claim based on the letter. The members of the Court of Appeal for somewhat varying reasons held that even without the letter of undertaking a claim
b   for general average contribution could have been the subject of a claim which would be unaffected by the arbitration clause and its time bar. They also all held that a claim lay under the letter of undertaking and that the arbitration clause and its time bar did not apply to such a claim.

It may here be mentioned that there was a summons before the learned judge under s 27 of the Arbitration Act 1950. In view of his decision there was no need for an extension of time but he indicated that had there been such a need he would not have
c   been disposed to allow an extension.

I propose first to express my opinion on the question whether (if there were no special undertaking) a claim for general average contribution would be a claim covered by the arbitration clause. If such a claim was made and if when made it was rebutted or denied it seems to me that a dispute would arise. Would it be a
d   dispute 'arising out of' the charterparty? In my opinion, it would. It would arise out of a charterparty which contained a clause providing that general average was to be payable according to York/Antwerp Rules 1950 and to be settled in London and which (in the terms of the Jason clause) enabled an owner, even in certain named circumstances, to recover contributions provided that he had, in defined respects, exercised due diligence. In my view, a disputed claim for a general average contri-
e   bution which might involve disputes concerning matters and questions referred to in the Jason clause would essentially and clearly arise out of the charterparty. Any such disputes would, in my view, be even more clearly within the arbitration clause than were the disputes which arose in *Heyman v Darwins Ltd*[2]. In that case there was an arbitration clause which provided that 'If any dispute shall arise between the parties hereto in respect of this agreement or any of the provisions herein contained or anything arising hereout the same shall be referred for arbitration'. A question
f   whether one party had repudiated the agreement was held to be within the terms of the arbitration clause. In his speech[3] Viscount Simon LC said:

'If, however, the parties are at one in asserting that they entered into a binding contract, but a difference has arisen between them as to whether there has been a breach by one side or the other, or as to whether circumstances have
g   arisen which have discharged one or both parties from further performance, such differences should be regarded as differences which have arisen "in respect of", or "with regard to", or "under" the contract, and an arbitration clause which uses these, or similar, expressions should be construed accordingly.'

In the same case Lord Porter said[4]:

h   'There remains the question what result follows where the original existence and efficacy of the contract is not in dispute, but one party has, or it is claimed that he has, refused to be bound by its terms and has disregarded it *in toto* and the other party has accepted his repudiation. In such a case the question of damage has still to be determined, and the question whether there has been repudiation may be still in issue. Are these disputes under the contract? I use the word "under" advisedly since expressions such as "arising out of" or "concerning" have a wider meaning. I think they are. The contract must be adverted to in order to arrive at their solution.'

1   [1973] 1 Lloyd's Rep 509
2   [1942] 1 All ER 337, [1942] AC 356
3   [1942] 1 All ER at 343, [1942] AC at 366
4   [1942] 1 All ER at 360, [1942] AC at 398, 399

Though claims for general average contribution have their origin in the common *a*
law so that they need not necessarily be the creature of contract I feel satisfied that
in the present case (leaving aside the letter of 23rd February 1966) a claim for general
average contribution relating to events during the operation of the charterparty
would have been a claim arising out of the charterparty. The term that general
average should be payable was contractual as was the further term that the York/
Antwerp Rules 1950 were to apply—as was the further term 'to be settled in London' *b*
—as was the inclusion in cl 2 of the Jason clause.

It is not necessary in the present case to express any concluded view as to the meaning of the words 'to be settled in London' but at least I think that they denote that an
adjustment is to be made in accordance, not with the law of the port of destination of
the cargo, but with the law and practice of London: the words reinforce the view
that any claim for general average contribution was to be advanced as a contractual *c*
claim. As such it would be a claim under or arising out of the charterparty contract.
The contract which contains provisions concerning general average and regulates the
circumstances under which general average contributions are to be payable also
contains the provision which requires disputes to be referred (in prescribed manner)
to arbitration and also the severe provision that unless a claim is made in writing
and unless an arbitrator is appointed within the specified time a claim is to be 'deemed *d*
to be waived' and 'absolutely barred'.

In the present case and in a recent case (*The Astraea*[1]) it has been acknowledged
that for many years experienced average adjusters thought that arbitration clauses
had generally no application to claims for general average contribution. This
circumstance coupled with the fact that distinguished judges who speak with
authority on this branch of the law have differed compels a close consideration of *e*
the questions now raised. It is pointed out that in many cases the tasks of average
adjusters are complicated and involve much investigation so that they cannot be
performed speedily or within the rigidity of a time limit. It is also pointed out that
the time limit in the Centrocon clause was formerly much shorter than 12 months.
On the other hand, it is pointed out that where there is a cargo of grain in bulk and
one consignee-owner of such cargo the tasks of an average adjuster lack the complica- *f*
tions that may arise in other and different circumstances. It is pointed out that in
the present case the adjustment statement of Messrs Richards was dated
24th February 1967 which was within the 12 months period. Doubtless it could
have been prepared earlier had the need for an earlier date been urged on the average
adjusters. So also is it pointed out that the letter of 17th February 1966 was in effect
a claim made (and made even before the 12 month period began) for a general *g*
average contribution the amount of which would later be assessed and quantified.
On the facts of the present case I think that there is little doubt that a quantified claim
could, had it been thought necessary, have been presented in ample time to enable
the appointment of an arbitrator to be made within the specified 12 months period.

Though there may be competing weight in these considerations the questions
which arise are purely questions of the interpretation of the contract which was *h*
entered into. Can it be said that by cl 2 of the charterparty questions concerning
general average are specially provided for and as a result are withdrawn from the
provision as to arbitration? In my view, this cannot be said. Clause 2 deals with
questions as to whether general average is to be payable and with questions as to the
law applicable. It does not deal with the method of settling disputes which may
arise or with the method of recovering an amount which may be disputed. Though *j*
cl 2 may contemplate that an average adjuster will be employed and though the
incorporation of the York/Antwerp rules may have the result that one will be
employed the clause certainly does not involve that the decision or assessment of an

1   [1971] 2 Lloyd's Rep 494

a average adjuster is to command or compel acceptance on the part of the parties to the contract. An average adjuster is not by cl 2 made an arbitrator.

In argument it was submitted and in two of the judgments in the Court of Appeal[1] the view is expressed that the second sentence of the Centrocon clause (the sentence imposing the time limit for a claim and a waiver and barring of any claim not time-ously presented) does not apply to a claim for general average contribution. This *b* view may or may not involve that the first sentence of the clause would apply but without the second. With every respect I do not find myself able to share either view. In my opinion the second sentence cannot be divorced from the first.

It was pointed out that the arbitration clause begins by referring disputes to arbitra-tion. It was contended that in the present case there was a claim made within 12 months but that the claim was not disputed until after the 12 months period and *c* that as no dispute had arisen within the 12 months period the arbitration clause did not apply. The clause only applied, so it was contended, to disputes arising within the 12 months period. The second sentence, it was contended, should be interpreted as though the words were that any claim must be in writing and if disputed the claimant's arbitrator appointed within the 12 months time limit; or as though there was an exception for a claim for a general average contribution. I cannot accept these *d* contentions. The arbitration clause must be read as a whole without severing or excluding any part of it or without making additions to it. The words are imperative and decisive which say that unless a provision is complied with any claim 'shall be deemed to be waived and absolutely barred'. What, then, is the provision? It is two-fold, viz, (a) a claim in writing must be made within the 12 months period and (b) the claimant must appoint his arbitrator within the 12 months period. His arbitrator *e* must have the qualification or description set out in the first sentence. It seems to me to follow that, being subject to a compelling time bar and time limit, a claimant must take all such steps as may be necessary to ensure not only that his claim in writing is in time but also that within time he has appointed his chosen and qualified arbitrator to be one of two arbitrators to settle a disputed claim. In the case of a voyage charter for the carriage of a cargo of wheat in bulk a time limit expiring *f* 12 months after the date of final discharge of the cargo may not be thought to be oppressive. In certain circumstances and in a proper case the powers of the court under s 27 of the Arbitration Act 1950 could possibly be invoked. For the reasons which I have set out I agree with the conclusion of Mocatta J[2] on this part of the case and consequently with the conclusion, on the matters now under discussion, in *The Astraea*[3].

g I pass then to consider the questions arising from the letters of February 1966, to which I have earlier referred. The letters were written some time before the vessel reached Bombay. On her arrival at Bombay the respondents would have been entitled to exercise a lien on the cargo in respect of a contribution towards the general average expenditure. It was not the practice of the appellants either to give security or to give an average bond in a customary form under which in consideration of a *h* promise by a shipowner to deliver goods a promise is made to pay a general average contribution. So the letters were exchanged. There was a request for the 'usual undertaking' to be given by the appellants that they would pay their cargo's propor-tion of general average when that had been determined. In reply the promise was made to pay the legally due amount of such general average contribution. That amount was to be paid 'by this Mission'—which was the India Supply Mission in *j* London. The promise was given so that the cargo would not be made the subject of any lien but would be released immediately the vessel arrived at an Indian port. The clear expectation was that there would be an adjustment of general average, which would be followed by a claim for contribution from the appellants, which as a

---

1   [1973] 1 Lloyd's Rep 509
2   [1972] 2 Lloyd's Rep 129
3   [1971] 2 Lloyd's Rep 494

result of the promise given would result in payment being made by the India Supply   *a*
Mission of such amount as was legally due. Both parties understood that they
were then to wait until the average adjusters had completed their task and made
their adjustment and that a request for payment of the contribution amount would
then be made. If when payment was demanded it was asserted that payment was
being demanded of a sum that was not legally due then for a determination of the
issue so raised it would of course be necessary to refer to the provisions of the charter-   *b*
party. But would the question fall to be determined by the ordinary processes of
law or would the question be a dispute within the arbitration clause of the charterparty, as the appellants contend, with the result that any claim for payment would
be deemed to be waived and barred in default of compliance with the terms of the
arbitration clause? This is by no means an easy question but I have come to the
conclusion in agreement with Mocatta J[1] and the Court of Appeal[2] that there was   *c*
a new promise for which there was clearly good consideration. There was a new
contractual obligation. Rights of lien were given up in exchange for it. It did not
contain an arbitration clause. A claim under it would be resolved by the ordinary
processes of law. I consider that Mocatta J[3] was right in distinguishing the present
case from *Atlantic Shipping and Trading Co v Louis Dreyfus & Co*[4]. In that case a letter
was relied on as being a waiver. In the present case the claim arises out of a new   *d*
contract. It was on that basis that the claim was formulated, pleaded and presented.
I would dismiss the appeal.

VISCOUNT DILHORNE. My Lords, by a charterparty dated 14th January
1966 the appellants chartered the Evje from the respondents to carry a cargo of
wheat from the west coast of America to India. The vessel was to call at Yokohama   *e*
for bunkers and on her way there she ran out of fuel and, it appears, was in consequence in some peril. A tug was hired to tow her to Yokohama. After a few days
of towing, fuel was transferred from the tug to the Evje and she was then able to
complete her journey to Yokohama under her own power. She ran out of fuel on
12th February 1966 and on 17th February 1966 William Richards & Son, who had
been appointed by the respondents general average adjusters, wrote to the Director-   *f*
General of the India Supply Mission saying that the extra expenses in hiring the tug
appeared to give rise to general average and asking that they should be given the
usual undertaking by the Indian government to pay their cargo's proportion of
general average when that had been determined. On 23rd February 1966 the reply
came that—

> 'the High Commissioner for India in London hereby gives an undertaking that   *g*
> any General Average contribution which may be legally due from the Government
> of India as cargo owners will be paid by this Mission. In view of the above
> undertaking you are requested to contact the ship-owner's agents in India, by
> cable if necessary, to release government cargo immediately the vessel arrives
> at an Indian port.'
                                                                                       h
Relying on this undertaking, instructions were given by William Richards & Son
for the release of the cargo to the consignee on arrival in India without further
security being obtained. The same day William Richards & Son wrote to the Director-
General saying that they noted they might apply to him for settlement when the
adjustment of general average was completed.
    The vessel arrived in India and her cargo was finally discharged on 12th March   *ʲ*
1966. But for the undertaking the respondents would have been able to exercise a

1 [1972] 2 Lloyd's Rep 129
2 [1973] 1 Lloyd's Rep 509
3 [1972] 2 Lloyd's Rep at 137
4 [1922] 2 AC 250, [1922] All ER Rep 250

a lien on the cargo for the appellants' general average contribution. To do so is a tiresome business and to avoid it an average bond and security are usually given. The Government of India instead of giving such a bond and security normally give an undertaking such as that given in this case.

William Richards & Son completed their average adjustment on 24th February 1967. It showed that the cargo's proportion of general average was £5,995 4s 7d.
b Over a month later, on 30th March 1967 the appellants were asked for their cheque for this sum. On 7th June 1967 they repudiated liability on the ground that it was unseaworthiness of the Evje at the commencement of the voyage which caused her to run out of fuel. It was then, and only then, that, in my opinion, a dispute can be said to have arisen between the appellants and the respondents.

It was not, however, until 4th June 1971 that a writ was issued by the respondents claiming the £5,995·23. After the pleadings were completed, Mocatta J ordered that
c the following two questions should be tried as a preliminary issue:

'(1) Whether the [appellants] are entitled to rely on the amended Centrocon arbitration clause contained in a voyage charter party dated London the 14th January 1966 and made between the [respondents] as Owners of the m.v. "EVJE" and the [appellants] as charterers thereof, in answer to the [respondents']
d claim and, if so,
'(2) Whether under that clause the [respondents'] claim was waived and became barred on or about the 12th March 1967.'

The amended Centrocon arbitration clause was in the following terms:

'All disputes from time to time arising out of this contract shall, unless the
e parties agree forthwith on a single Arbitrator, be referred to the final arbitrament of two Arbitrators carrying on business in London, who shall be Members of The Baltic and engaged in the shipping and/or Grain trades, one to be appointed by each of the parties, with power to such Arbitrators to appoint an Umpire. Any claim must be made in writing and Claimant's Arbitrator appointed within twelve (12) months of final discharge and where this provision is not complied
f with the claim shall be deemed to be waived and absolutely barred. No award shall be questioned or invalidated on the ground that any of the Arbitrators is not qualified as above, unless objection to his acting be taken before the award is made.'

The unamended Centrocon arbitration clause provided that the claim must be made and the claimant's arbitrator appointed within three months of final discharge.
g So if the dispute between the appellants and the respondents arose out of the charterparty, the respondents' claim had to be made and they had to appoint their arbitrator by 12th March 1967. A dispute may arise without a claim being preferred. The claim may be formulated only after a dispute has arisen. From the way in which this clause is drafted, it seems likely that the claim referred to is the one made in the arbitration and so after the dispute has arisen. In this case, one has fortunately
h not to decide to what kind of claim the clause refers, as the claim for £5,995·23 was not made until after 12th March 1967 and no arbitrator was appointed by the respondents before then. The appellants consequently contend that, by virtue of this clause, their claim is to be deemed to have been waived and to be absolutely barred.

The making of an average adjustment usually takes a considerable time and the Centrocon arbitration clause makes no provision for a case where a dispute arises,
j as it did in this case, more than 12 months after final discharge. The parties in this case must have known that average adjustment frequently takes more than a year to complete and that a dispute with regard thereto, either as to liability or quantum or both, might not arise until after 12 months after final discharge. They chose to agree that all claims should be deemed to be waived and absolutely barred if not made and the claimant's arbitrator appointed within 12 months of final discharge

and effect must be given to that provision. I see nothing in the clause or in any other a
part of the charterparty to justify the conclusion that when the clause refers to
'All disputes', those words are to be read as meaning 'All disputes save disputes as
to general average arising after twelve months from final discharge' and, in my view,
it is not the function of the courts to rewrite a contract to insert provisions to which
the parties could have agreed to deal with a situation which might arise.

I do not think, as Scarman LJ[1] appears to have thought, that it is possible to b
sever the second sentence of the arbitration clause from the first and to hold that
while a dispute as to general average is a dispute arising out of the contract, it is not
one to which the second sentence need necessarily apply, for, as a matter of construction, I do not think that the second sentence can be divorced from the first.
It was, in my opinion, intended to and does apply to all disputes covered by the
first sentence.

So if the dispute in this case as to the general average contribution is a dispute c
arising out of the contract, if there had been no undertaking by the appellants, in
my opinion it follows that the respondents claim was by virtue of the Centrocon
arbitration clause to be deemed waived and absolutely barred.

I now turn to the question whether the dispute was one arising out of the contract.
Lord Denning MR[2] held that it did not, saying: d

> 'It arises "in the course of it". It arises in the course of the voyage. It arises
> out of the perils encountered in carrying out the contract, and not out of the
> contract itself.'

I respectfully agree that the dispute in this case had its origin in events in the
course of the voyage out of perils encountered in carrying out the contract but I e
do not myself see that that precludes the dispute being one which arises out of
the contract. If the parties to a contract make provision in it as to their rights should
certain events occur in the course of the contract and a dispute arises between them
as to their rights following the occurrence of those events, then, in my opinion,
that dispute as to their rights arises out of the contract.

It was agreed that cl 2 which the charterparty provided should be contained in f
the bills of lading is to be treated as applying to the appellants and the respondents.
It reads as follows:

> 'General average shall be payable according to York/Antwerp Rules 1950
> and to be settled in London. If the owner shall have exercised due diligence
> to make the Steamer in all respects seaworthy and to have her properly manned,
> equipped and supplied, it is hereby agreed that in case of danger, damage or g
> disaster, resulting from faults or errors in navigation, or in the management of
> the steamer, or from any latent defect in the steamer, her machinery or appurten-
> ances, or from unseaworthiness, whether existing at the time of shipment or
> at the beginning of the voyage (provided the latent defect or the unseaworthiness
> was not discoverable by the exercise of due diligence), the consignees or owners
> of the cargo ... shall contribute with the shipowner in General Average to the h
> payment of any sacrifices, losses or expenses of a General Average nature that
> may be made or incurred for the common benefit, or to relieve the adventure
> from any common peril ...'

The printed form of the charterparty contained the following sentence which
appeared after the words 'York/Antwerp Rules': 'Average Bond with values declared j
thereon to be signed, also sufficient security to be given as required by master or
agents'. These words were struck out and '1950 and to be settled in London' typed
in their place.

---

1 [1973] 1 Lloyd's Rep 509
2 [1973] 1 Lloyd's Rep at 513

a   It is thus clear that to determine whether the respondents were entitled to a general average contribution from the appellants, recourse has to be made to this clause and that its terms govern the matter. The respondents seek to rely not on their rights at common law but on their rights under this clause. And in my opinion any dispute as to the their rights under the clause is a dispute arising out of the contract and so covered by the arbitration clause.

b   In *Heyman v Darwins Ltd*[1] Lord Porter said that the words 'arising out of a contract' have a wider meaning than the words 'under a contract', a view which was repeated by Sellers LJ in *Government of Gibraltar v Kenney*[2]. Although the words are different, I must confess my inability to discern any difference in their content.

All the members of the Court of Appeal[3] were agreed that disputes about general average did not come within the arbitration clause as provision for dealing with them was made by cl 2. I do not consider that agreement that general average should c   be payable according to York/Antwerp Rules leads to the conclusion that a dispute with regard thereto is excluded from the arbitration clause; nor do I consider that the words 'to be settled in London' have that effect. At first sight those words appear to me to mean no more and no less than that the contributions to be made have to be determined in London and paid there and that implies determined in accordance d   with English law. The clause does not prescribe machinery for the determination and is silent on whether in default of agreement it is to be a litigation or arbitration. I see no conflict between this clause and the arbitration clause which provides for arbitration in London. The words in question may have been inserted to secure that the law applicable should be that of England and not that of the port of discharge. Determination of the amount payable according to the York/Antwerp Rules and whether there is liability to pay under the clause can be made in an arbitration.

e   In my opinion Roskill J in *Alma Shipping Corporation v Union of India (The Astraea)*[4] and Mocatta J[5] in this case were right in holding that the arbitration clause applied, so if the India Supply Mission had not given the undertaking, in my opinion this appeal should be allowed.

Average adjusters have long held the view that the Centrocon arbitration clause did not apply to general average claims. If the charterparty was in the printed f   form used in this case unamended, the explanation may be that the charterparty which provided that the bills of lading signed pursuant to the charterparty should supersede the contract contained in the charterparty, required the bills of lading to contain the clause set out above. In the absence of any express stipulation, the bills of lading would not incorporate the Centrocon arbitration clause in the charter-party. In this case the bill of lading was, however, overstamped with a provision g   stating that all the terms and conditions of the charterparty were incorporated therein.

It was not until 23rd April 1971 that the appellants took the point that the res-pondents' claim was absolutely barred, the undertaking having been given on 23rd February 1966 and the appellants' repudiation of liability prior to 23rd April 1971 being based on alleged unseaworthiness of the vessel.

h   In a note of a judgment given in chambers by McNair J in an unreported case[6], he is reported to have said:

'... where the person who signs [a Lloyd's average bond] turns out to be the consignee, new obligations are created for a valid consideration. The shipowner gives up valuable rights of lien and gives them up in exchange for the obligations j   in Lloyd's average bond. I accept Mr Phillips' submission that one of the purposes

---

1   [1942] 1 All ER 337 at 343, [1942] AC 356 at 366
2   [1956] 3 All ER 22, [1956] 2 QB 410
3   [1973] 1 Lloyd's Rep 509
4   [1971] 2 Lloyd's Rep 494
5   [1972] 2 Lloyd's Rep 129
6   6th October 1965

of the Lloyd's average bond procedure is to crystallise the situation and so that   *a*
the parties need not have regard to time limit provisions in other documents.'

In this case the undertaking took the place of a Lloyd's average bond and the
acceptance of that undertaking in my opinion constituted a fresh contract which did
not contain or import the Centrocon arbitration clause. If the words 'Average
Bond with value declared therein to be signed, also sufficient security to be given as
required by master or agents' had not been struck out and a bond and security   *b*
had been given, it might perhaps have been possible to contend that, as the giving of
the bond and security was in performance of the contract, the giving and acceptance
of it did not constitute a fresh contract. However, that is not this case and, in my
opinion, the Court of Appeal[1] and Mocatta J[2] were right in the conclusion to which
they came on this question.

For these reasons I would dismiss the appeal.   *c*

LORD SIMON OF GLAISDALE. My Lords, I have had the advantage of
reading in draft the speeches prepared by my noble and learned friends, with which I
agree. I would therefore dismiss the appeal.

LORD SALMON. My Lords, if this appeal turned solely on the true construction of   *d*
the charterparty, I would hold that the claim for general average contribution
arises out of the charterparty and is barred by the Centrocon arbitration clause
which the charterparty incorporates and that the appeal should, therefore, succeed.
I respectfully prefer the reasons given by Roskill J in *The Astraea*[3] and adopted by
Mocatta J[2] in the present case for so construing the charterparty to the diverse reasons
which commended themselves to the Court of Appeal[1] for construing it in a contrary   *e*
sense. I think that but for the correspondence to which I shall later refer, the claim
for general average contribution would arise solely out of or under the charterparty
and it would follow from the Centrocon clause that since the respondents' arbitrator
was not appointed within 12 months of final discharge, the claim for contribution
would be 'absolutely barred'.

I recognise that even if the charterparty had made no reference to general average,   *f*
general average would still be payable under the common law in the event of a
general average act occurring. The charterparty does, however, provide by cl 2 that
'General Average shall be payable according to York/Antwerp Rules 1950 and to be
settled in London'. There are many differences between the liability to pay general
average contribution under the common law and the liability to pay such contribution under the charterparty which incorporates the York/Antwerp Rules. At   *g*
common law, e g, no general average would be payable by the charterers if the
general average expenditure had been due to a breach of the shipowners' warranty
of seaworthiness. Under the York/Antwerp Rules, however, even if the expenditure
had been incurred by reason of the ship's unseaworthiness, general average contribution would nevertheless be payable by the charterers unless the unseaworthiness
was caused by lack of due diligence on the part of the shipowners. Indeed, in the   *h*
present case, the real dispute between the parties seems to be whether or not the
general average expenditure has been so caused.

The respondents' claim for general average contribution no doubt arose in the
course of the voyage, as such claims always do, but this does not prevent it from arising
out of or under the charterparty.

We have been referred to a statement by Lord Porter in *Heyman v Darwins Ltd*[4]   *j*
to the effect that the words 'arising out of' a contract have a wider meaning than the

1   [1973] 1 Lloyd's Rep 509
2   [1972] 2 Lloyd's Rep 129
3   [1971] 2 Lloyd's Rep 494
4   [1942] 1 All ER 337 at 360, [1942] AC 356 at 398, 399

a words 'arising under' a contract. Lord Porter did not, however, define this difference, and I confess that I find difficulty in understanding what it is. Nor do I think that it has any significance for the purposes of the present appeal.

In addition to applying the York/Antwerp Rules to general average, cl 2 of the charterparty provides for general average to be settled in London. At common law it would be settled at the port of final discharge. This is an additional reason b for concluding that claims for general average are governed by and arise out of or under the charterparty. It is not seriously disputed that the words 'to be settled in London' mean to be adjusted in accordance with an adjustment prepared in London and conforming with normal English practice. It is unnecessary to express any final view whether these words also mean 'to be paid in London' although, as at present advised, I am inclined to think that they do.

c Neither party is bound by an average adjustment whether or not it is made by a professional average adjuster. Disputes can and often do arise both before and after an adjustment has been made. I am afraid that I cannot accept the view expressed by Lord Denning MR[1] that cl 2 provides the means by which such disputes are to be decided when they arise. If it did, no doubt the maxim generalia specialibus non derogant would apply and such disputes would implicitly be excluded from d the Centrocon arbitration clause. As it is, however, in my respectful view, that clause alone provides the means of resolving all disputes and claims arising out of the charterparty. In my opinion, claims and disputes relating to general average, for the reasons I have already indicated, fall squarely within the clause. No doubt it may not seem sensible that a general average claim should be barred unless the claimant appoints his arbitrator within 12 months of final discharge when the odds are that the adjustment will not be completed until after this period has expired. No doubt e there may also be other sound commercial reasons (referred to by Megaw LJ) why parties might well exclude general average claims from the Centrocon arbitration clause or modify that clause in its relation to such claims. The parties, however, have not done so; and there is no power in the courts to do so for them.

I recognise that prior to *The Astraea*[2] the general view was that clauses such as the f Centrocon arbitration clause had no application to claims for general average contribution. I doubt whether this view was based on any consideration of the language of charterparties in general or the Centrocon clause in particular. I think that the general view is more likely to have been based on the language of the Lloyd's general average bond which, when applicable, may have afforded it a much firmer foundation. However this may be, whilst I have the same respect for the experience of the distinguished average adjusters who gave evidence in *The Astraea*[2] as had Roskill J, g like him, I cannot think that their views are relevant on a point concerned solely with the true construction of a charterparty. It must be remembered that in the report of *The Astraea*[2] there is no mention of any general average bond. That case turned on the construction of the charterparty alone.

I find difficulty in agreeing with Scarman LJ that, even if the arbitration clause applied, as I think it does, to claims for general average, it does not follow that the h time limit stipulated in the second sentence of the clause need apply to such claims. In my view, there is nothing in the charterparty which would justify the exclusion or modification of the second sentence in the arbitration clause. That sentence reads as follows:

j 'Any claim must be made in writing and Claimant's Arbitrator appointed within twelve (12) months of final discharge and where this provision is not complied with the claim shall be deemed to be waived and absolutely barred.'

The words 'any claim' are very wide and, in my view, clearly cover general average claims. Had the parties intended to exclude such claims from the ambit of the

1   [1973] 1 Lloyd's Rep at 513
2   [1971] 2 Lloyd's Rep 494

second sentence of that clause or to modify the time limit for the appointment of the *a*
claimant's arbitrator nothing would have been easier than for them to have done so.
They have not, however, made any alteration to the clause. The courts cannot
rewrite their contract for them, even if to do so may appear to be reasonable and to
make far better commercial sense.

Accordingly, had this appeal depended solely on the construction of the charterparty, I should have concluded that it ought to be allowed. There is, however, *b*
the letter from the Supply Mission of the High Commission of India in London
dated 23rd February 1966 and addressed to the respondents' agents, William Richards
& Son. This letter contains the clearest undertaking that 'any General Average
contribution which may be legally due from the Government of India as cargo
owners will be paid by this Mission'. The letter goes on to say:

> 'In view of the above undertaking you are requested to contact the ship- *c*
> owner's agents in India . . . to release government cargo immediately the vessel
> arrives at an Indian port.'

This letter clearly offered the undertaking in consideration of the shipowners
releasing the lien which they undoubtedly could have lawfully exercised over the
cargo until the appellants had given security for general average contribution. Since
it is not the normal practice of the appellants to give a general average bond or any *d*
other security, they offered the undertaking instead. The shipowners accepted that
offer (a) by a letter from their agents dated 25th February 1966 in the following terms:

> 'We thank you for your letter of the 23rd February and note that we may
> apply to you for settlement when our Adjustment of General Average
> is completed.' *e*

and (b) by releasing the cargo in reliance on the undertaking after the vessel had
completed her voyage to India and the cargo had been finally discharged on 12th
March 1966.

The general average expenditure had been incurred when the vessel, being short
of bunkers, was towed into Yokohama on 15th February 1966. Thereupon the
general average contribution became legally due from the appellants: see *Morrison* *f*
Steamship Co Ltd v SS Greystoke Castle[1]. This liability was, of course, subject to the
expenditure not having been caused by any negligence on the part of the owners.
The appellants' contingent liability to contribute was therefore in existence, to their
knowledge, when they wrote their letter of 23rd February 1966. This letter contained a clear undertaking to pay unconditionally 'any General Average contribution
which may be legally due'. The contract which came into existence on the *g*
acceptance of the undertaking was a fresh contract which varied the charterparty.
The charterparty imposed an obligation on the appellants to pay any general average
contribution which might be legally due conditionally on the claim being made and
the claimants' arbitrator being appointed within 12 months of final discharge. The
fresh contract imposed an unconditional obligation on the appellants to pay any
general average contribution which might be legally due. Under the fresh contract *h*
the respondents' claim to any general average contribution due to them was subject
to no time limit for bringing proceedings save such as may be imposed by statute.
I am inclined to think that these are the only respects in which the fresh contract
altered the rights and obligations arising under the charterparty in relation to general
average.

My Lords, for these reasons I would dismiss the appeal.

Appeal dismissed.

Solicitors: *Stocken & Co* (for the appellants); *William A Crump & Son* (for the
respondents).

Christine Ivamy Barrister.

---

1 [1946] 2 All ER 696 at 701, 718, [1947] AC 265 at 283, 312

a

L Lucas Ltd and another v Export Credits Guarantee Department

HOUSE OF LORDS

LORD REID, LORD MORRIS OF BORTH-Y-GEST, VISCOUNT DILHORNE, LORD SIMON OF GLAISDALE

b AND LORD SALMON

19th, 20th, 21st MARCH, 13th JUNE 1974

Guarantee – Payment under – Loss – Recovery – Guarantors entitled to 90 per cent of 'sums recovered ... in respect of a loss to which this Guarantee applies' – Guarantee relating to export contract between merchant and foreign buyer – Occurrences covered including delay
c *in payment by foreign buyer – Guarantors undertaking to pay 90 per cent of loss – Amount of loss – Payment under contract in foreign currency – Rate of exchange – Loss to be calculated according to rate of exchange at date of export – Delay in payment caused by exchange control restrictions imposed by buyer's country – Payment by guarantors in respect of loss – Subsequent payment by buyers – Sterling proceeds of payment exceeding loss calculated under guarantee because of devaluation of sterling – Whether guarantors entitled to recover sum in*
d *excess of amount paid in respect of loss.*

A company ('the merchant') sold flour to Egyptian buyers and the contracts with them provided that payment therefor should be made in US dollars. The contracts were covered by a 'guarantee' given by the Export Credits Guarantee Department acting for the Board of Trade ('the guarantors') in return for the payment of a premium. By cl 1 of that guarantee the guarantors agreed to pay the merchant
e a percentage of the amount of any loss sustained in connection with the export of any goods under such contracts caused, inter alia, by the prevention of or delay in the transfer of payment from the buyer's country to the United Kingdom in circumstances outside the control of both the merchant and the buyer. The guarantors undertook to pay to the merchant 90 per cent of 'the loss' immediately after it had
f been ascertained, which, under the terms of the guarantee, would be four months after the due date of payment by the buyer. The amount of the loss was defined in cl 9 as being the gross invoice value of the goods the subject of the contract of sale, delivered and accepted by the buyer. Under an endorsement added to the contract, where the currency of payment was other than in sterling, the amount of the loss was to be calculated in sterling by converting the foreign currency into sterling at the buying rate of exchange in the foreign exchange market on the date when the
g goods were exported under the contract of sale. Clause 17 of the contract provided: 'Any sums recovered by the Merchant or the Guarantors in respect of a loss to which this Guarantee applies, after the date at which the loss is ascertained, whether from the buyer or any other source shall ... be divided between the Guarantors and the Merchant in the proportions of 90 and 10; The Merchant shall pay all sums recovered to the Guarantors forthwith upon their being received by him or any
h person on his behalf, the Merchant hereby acknowledging and declaring that until such payment is made to the Guarantors, he receives and holds such sums in trust for the Guarantors'. Six drafts in US dollars given by the Egyptian buyers to the merchant in respect of goods exported under the contract of sale were not paid on maturity because certain restrictions on the transfer of currency were imposed by the United Arab Republic. The drafts were for a total of US$1,155,181·26. The
j merchant made a claim under the guarantee in respect of the delay in payment. The guarantors examined the claim and paid to the merchant £372,071 6s 10d, i e 90 per cent of £413,412 12s, which was the sterling equivalent of the gross invoice value of the goods (US$1,155,181·26) at the date when the loss fell to be ascertained. Subsequently the currency restrictions of the United Arab Republic were removed and the amounts due on the drafts in US dollars were paid in four instalments to

the merchant's bankers who converted the dollars into sterling at the prevailing *a*
rate of exchange for payment to the merchant. After the first instalment had been
paid, the rate of exchange altered and in consequence the total sum received by the
merchant as payment, when converted into sterling, amounted to £443,032 8s 1d.
The merchant repaid the guarantors the £372,071 6s 10d that they had paid (i e the
90 per cent of £413,412 12s). The guarantors contended that they were entitled to
be paid £398,729 3s 3d, i e 90 per cent of the sum received (£443,032 8s 1d). *b*

Held – The merchant's liability to the guarantors was limited to £372,071 6s 10d
for, on the true construction of cl 17, (i) 'the loss to which this Guarantee applies'
was the sum of money (i e the £413,412 12s) which the merchant did not receive
from the buyer at the time which he should have received it, and 'the sum recovered
in respect of' the loss was the sum, calculated in accordance with the contract,
recovered in recoupment of the loss as defined; (ii) the word 'recovered' in the second *c*
sentence of the clause related back to the opening words of the clause and meant
recovered in respect of a loss to which the guarantee applied. It followed that once
the sum recovered in respect of a loss covered by the guarantee reached the amount
of the loss, cl 17 ceased to apply and any further sum received was not received in
respect of the loss (see p 891 *b*, p 895 *a c f* to *h* and *j* to p 896 *a*, p 898 *e* and *f* and
p 899 *b* to *d*, post). *d*
    Decision of the Court of Appeal [1973] 2 All ER 984 reversed.

Note
For export credit guarantee insurance, see 22 Halsbury's Laws (3rd Edn) 399, para 815.

Case referred to in opinion *e*
Miller, Gibb & Co Ltd, Re [1957] 2 All ER 266, [1957] 1 WLR 703, [1957] 1 Lloyd's Rep
    258, 29 Digest (Repl) 551, 3745.

Appeal
By an originating summons dated 26th March 1971 the appellants, L Lucas Ltd and
Lamet Trading Ltd, sought (1) the determination of the court on the question *f*
whether the first appellants were obliged to pay the sum of £26,651·57 claimed
by the respondents, Export Credits Guarantee Department, as a sum recovered in
respect of a loss paid by the respondents under a policy dated 15th April 1964, and
(2) an order that the respondents pay to the first appellants the sum of £8,634·49
being the proportion of interest in respect of late payment of the price of certain
goods sold and delivered to La Société Misr pour la Commerce Exterieur by the
first appellants to which the first appellants were entitled under the terms of the *g*
policy and under an agreement whereby the first appellants paid over to the respondents the whole of the interest paid to the first appellants in respect of such late
payment on terms that the respondents would account to the first appellants for
the first appellants' due proportion thereof. The respondents counterclaimed for
an order that both appellants pay the sum of £26,651·27 under the contract dated
15th April 1964 together with interest on that sum from the date at which recoveries *h*
were effected; they further claimed against the appellants the right to set off the sum
of £8,639·49 (sic) against the sum of £26,651·27. On 23rd June 1972 Cooke J ordered
that judgment be entered for the first appellants and that the respondents pay
£11,105·02 (£8,640·74 judgment debt and £2,464·28 interest thereon at the rate of
one per cent over bank rate from 1st October 1968 to 1st June 1972). Cooke J dismissed the respondents' counterclaim. The respondents appealed. On 5th April *j*
1973 the Court of Appeal[1] (Davies, Megaw LJJ and Sir Gordon Willmer) allowed
the appeal and ordered the judgment of Cooke J to be set aside and judgment entered
for the respondents on the claim and the counterclaim for £24,403·01, being the

---

1 [1973] 2 All ER 984, [1973] 1 WLR 914

a sum of £18,017·08 together with interest thereon at one per cent over the bank rate from 1st October 1968 to 4th April 1973 amounting to £6,385·93. The appellants appealed, with the leave of the Court of Appeal, to the House of Lords. The facts are set out in the opinion of Lord Morris of Borth-y-Gest.

R A MacCrindle QC and *Stewart Boyd* for the appellants.
b *Andrew J Bateson* QC and *Brian Davenport* for the respondents

LORD REID. My Lords, for the reasons given by your Lordships I would allow this appeal.

c **LORD MORRIS OF BORTH-Y-GEST.** My Lords, the determination of this appeal depends on the construction of the terms of a contract entered into between the parties. The contract is called a guarantee. In the submissions it was contended that it has many of the features either of a contract of insurance or of a contract of indemnity. No occasion arises, in my view, to assign to it its appropriate legal description. Its terms are self-sufficient both for an understanding of them and for d an application of them.

The nature of the contract is at once apparent when it is seen that it was a contract between two companies, the appellants (called 'the merchant'), and the respondents, the Export Credits Guarantee Department acting for the Board of Trade (called 'the guarantors'). Those who export goods to purchasers in other countries must inevitably encounter problems which differ from the problems of those who e sell in a home market. Particularly is this so if for any reason there are difficulties in obtaining payment from a purchaser. As international trade is to be encouraged it has been felt to be desirable to provide some measure of safeguard for exporters. Since 1945 a department of the Board of Trade, i e the Export Credits Guarantee Department, has entered into contracts to that end. The purpose of the contracts has been to assist exporters in circumstances in which ordinary insurance would not f normally be available.

The contract now under consideration was entered into on 15th April 1964. It recited that the merchant had made a proposal (dated 14th February 1964), that the guarantors 'should give to the Merchant a guarantee in connection with certain contracts for the sale of goods' and that the proposal was accepted on the terms and conditions of the contract. The merchant was to pay a premium for the benefit that g he obtained. In broad outline the arrangement was that if for various specified reasons the merchant did not receive payment from his buyer the Board of Trade would make a payment to the merchant of a certain percentage of the sum that he should have received. Naturally there were provisions in regard to recovery from the buyer of what he owed and the present case involves a consideration of the terms of such provisions.

h The contract is long and detailed and contains many conditions and stipulations and definitions but it is only necessary to give special attention to some of its provisions. The early part of cl 1 which is headed 'RISKS COVERED' and has at its side the words 'CAUSES OF LOSS' is in the following terms:

> 'The Guarantors, in consideration of the premium paid and to be paid by the
j Merchant as specified in Paragraph 18 hereof, agree, subject to the terms hereof, to pay to the Merchant a percentage of the amount of any loss as hereinafter defined which he may sustain in connection with the export between 1st March 1964 and 28th February 1965 of any goods under a contract to which this Guarantee applies by reason of the occurrence on or after the export of such goods of any of the following causes: (i) The insolvency of the buyer as hereinafter defined, or (ii) The prevention of or delay in the transfer of payment from the buyer's

country to the United Kingdom in circumstances outside the control of both
the Merchant and the buyer, or (iii) The occurrence of any war which prevents *a*
in whole or in part the delivery of the goods the subject of the contract to the
buyer's country, or (iv) The occurrence of war, hostilities, civil war, rebellion,
revolution, insurrection, or other disturbance in the buyer's country ...'

Then follows one further 'cause' and a number of provisos. The particular cause
which occurred in the present case was that set out under (ii) above.   *b*
    Clause 2 specified the contracts for the sale of goods made by the merchant to which
the 'guarantee' applied and under cl 5 the merchant had to make declarations setting
out the relevant exports made by him and amounts remaining unpaid. Clause 3
enabled the guarantors to give notice 'suspending cover' in respect of certain contracts.
    Clause 7 relating to 'ASCERTAINMENT AND PAYMENT OF LOSS' and to 'DATE FOR PAYMENT
OF LOSS' provided as follows: *c*

    'The Guarantors will pay to the Merchant the sum hereby guaranteed immedi-
    ately after the loss has been ascertained, and such loss shall be ascertained:—
    (i) where the loss is due to the buyer's insolvency as hereinafter defined, immedi-
    ately after the occurrence of such insolvency; (ii) where the loss is due to the
    prevention of or delay in the transfer of payments from the buyer's country to *d*
    the United Kingdom in circumstances outside the control of both the Merchant
    and the buyer, four months after the due date of payment by the buyer, or, if
    the buyer has made an irrevocable deposit for transfer to the Merchant, four
    months after the making of such deposit, if the expiry of this period shall be
    later; (iii) in all other cases four months after the occurrence of the event which
    is the cause of loss ...'   *e*

There followed certain provisos. Clause 8 provided as follows:

    'The percentage of the amount of any loss which the Guarantors hereby agree
    to pay shall be:—(i) 85% where the loss is due to the occurrence of the cause
    specified in sub-paragraph (i) of Paragraph 1 of this Guarantee; (ii) 90% where *f*
    the loss is due to the occurrence of any other cause specified in Paragraph 1 of
    this Guarantee.'

On the facts of the present case the applicable percentage was 90 per cent.
    By the material part of cl 9 it was provided that 'The amount of loss shall (i) as
regards goods the subject of the contract delivered to and accepted by the buyer be
the gross invoice value of those goods' less certain amounts not applicable in the *g*
present case.
    Clause 15 obliged the merchant to take all reasonable steps to prevent or minimise
loss, and cl 16 provided as follows:

    'Upon payment by the Guarantors the Merchant shall:—(a) take all steps
    which may be necessary or expedient or which the Guarantors may at any time *h*
    require, to effect recoveries, whether from the buyer or from any other guarantor
    or other person from whom such recoveries may be made, including (if so
    required) the institution of proceedings; (b) upon request assign and transfer
    to the Guarantors his rights under any contract in respect of which such payment
    has been made including his right to receive any monies payable under such
    contract or his right to damages from any breach thereof; (c) upon request to *j*
    deliver up to the Guarantors any goods in respect of which such payment has
    been made and any documents relating thereto and assign and transfer to the
    Guarantors his rights and interest in any such goods and documents; (d) upon
    request assign, deliver up or otherwise transfer to the Guarantors any negotiable
    instruments, guarantees or other securities relating to such goods or such contract.'

a Clause 17 dealt with recoveries in the following terms:

'Any sums recovered by the Merchant or the Guarantors in respect of a loss to which this Guarantee applies, after the date at which the loss is ascertained, whether from the buyer or any other source shall:—(i) if the ground of the claim is the occurrence of the cause specified in sub-paragraph (i) of Paragraph 1 of this Guarantee, be divided between the Guarantors and the Merchant in the

b proportions of 85 and 15; (ii) in any other case be divided between the Guarantors and the Merchant in the proportions of 90 and 10; the Merchant shall pay all sums recovered to the Guarantors forthwith upon their being received by him or any person on his behalf, the Merchant hereby acknowledging and declaring that until such payment is made to the Guarantors, he receives and holds such sums in trust for the Guarantors.'

c
Before relating the provisions of the contract to the facts of the present case—which are conveniently recorded in an agreed statement—it is necessary to mention that an endorsement dated 27th November 1964 was added to the contract. It has particular relevance to the facts of the case. Its effect was that if a contract made with a buyer in the United Arab Republic specified that payment was to be made

d direct from the buyer's country to the United Kingdom in United States dollars the guarantors gave their approval provided that for the purposes of para 5 of the contract any amount in a currency other than sterling had to be declared as sterling amounts calculated at the buying rate of exchange for telegraphic transfer of that currency quoted at the close of business in the London Foreign Exchange Market on the date when the goods were exported: also for the purpose of para 9 of the contract the

e amount of loss was to be calculated in sterling by converting any amounts in a currency other than sterling to sterling amounts as above set out.
The merchant exported goods (which consisted of wheat and flour) to a concern carrying on business in the United Arab Republic. By way of payment that concern drew six drafts in United States dollars which represented the gross invoice value of the goods. The above mentioned endorsement applied and there is no dispute as

f to what were the sterling equivalents of the drafts. The figures were as follows:

'Number	Amount U.S. $	Sterling equivalent £ s d
1	246,600·00	88,150 2 8
2	92,475·00	33,063 14 11
3	322,635·00	115,510 8 2
4	316,470·00	113,328 11 2
5	168,016·80	60,140 4 10
6	8,984·46	3,219 10 3
	1,155,181·26	413,412 12 0'

On maturity the drafts were not paid. That was because certain restrictions had been imposed by the government of the United Arab Republic. That was an occurrence which fell within the provisions of cl 1(ii) of the contract as set out above. So the merchant was able to make a claim under the contract. The claim was made on 17th March 1966. It was examined by the guarantors and the loss was ascertained at the above-mentioned figure of £413,412 12s. That sum was 'the amount of any loss as hereinafter defined' (within the words of cl 1 of the contract) for it was the 'gross invoice value' (converted to sterling) of the goods delivered to and accepted by the buyer and was therefore 'the amount of loss' as laid down by cl 9.
As the appropriate relevant percentage (see cl 8) was 90 per cent the guarantors admitted liability for 90 per cent of £413,412 12s. They paid such percentage amount (i e £372,071 6s 10d) to the merchant on 31st August 1966. The guarantors

did not make any request under cl 16 and there was no assignment or delivery or transfer within that clause.

At the time that restrictions were imposed by the government of the United Arab Republic the buyers made an irrevocable deposit (to the order of the merchant) in Egyptian currency in a bank of the United Arab Republic. It was equal to the amount due for payment under the contract. This was done with the approval of the guarantors.

At a later date the restrictions were removed and on varying dates payments of the drafts above mentioned were made in United States dollars. The payments were received by the bankers (Rea Brothers Ltd) of the merchant. The bankers then converted the dollars into sterling for payment to the merchant. Such conversions were naturally made at the rate of exchange which prevailed at the time the bankers received the payments. But before the later payments were received the rate of exchange of United States dollars into pounds sterling had changed. The result was that the United States dollars, for which the drafts were drawn, produced in 1968 a greater number of pounds sterling than would have been the case earlier.

The dates when the drafts were paid and received by Rea Brothers Ltd and the rates of exchange at those dates and the resultant numbers of pounds sterling were as follows:

'No(s) of drafts		$	$	£	s	d
1, 2 and 3	12th May 1967	661,710·00	2·79$\frac{13}{16}$	236,483	7	3
4	20th June 1968	316,470·00	2·38$\frac{5}{8}$	132,622	6	4
5	22nd July 1968	168,016·80	2·39$\frac{7}{16}$	70,171	9	4
6	23rd July 1968	8,984·46	2·39$\frac{1}{4}$	3,755	5	2
		1,155,181·26		443,032	8	1'

The merchant made the following payments to the guarantors:

	£	s	d
12th May 1967	212,828	15	6
30th June 1968	113,328	11	2
22nd July 1968	45,914	0	2
	372,071	6	10

In the result, therefore, the guarantors having in 1966 paid 90 per cent of the figure of £413,412 12s (i e £372,071 6s 10d) received back the amount which it had paid. The difference between the parties is that the guarantors claim that they should also receive 90 per cent of the additional pounds that resulted from the variation in the rate of exchange.

It should here be mentioned that interest was payable by the buyers on the overdue drafts. That interest was received by Rea Brothers Ltd and was paid in full to the guarantors. The parties agreed in regard to the entitlement to the interest paid and as to a minor adjustment: they agreed that if the merchant succeeded in the litigation £8,640·74 was to be paid by the guarantors and that if the guarantors succeeded they were to be paid £18,017·08 by the merchant. Those sums were agreed without prejudice to the right of either party to claim interest thereon at such rate and for such period as the court should direct. The merchant succeeded before Cooke J and were given judgment for £11,105·02 (being £8,640·74 and £2,464·28 being interest thereon as awarded by the learned judge at one per cent over bank rate from 1st October 1968 to 1st June 1972). The guarantors succeeded in the Court of Appeal[1]

---

1 [1973] 2 All ER 984, [1974] 1 WLR 914

a and were given judgment for £24,403·01 (being £18,017·08 and £6,385·93 being interest thereon at one per cent over bank rate from 1st October 1968 to 4th April 1973). The merchant now appeals.

I return to a consideration of cl 17 of the contract. The clause provides for a division of 'any sums recovered by the Merchant or the Guarantors in respect of a loss to which this Guarantee applies'. The loss in the present case was £413,412 12s. The agreed statement of facts records that the claim of the merchant was examined

b and the loss ascertained by the guarantors at the figure of £413,412 12s. Under cl 7 of the agreement the department was to make payment immediately after the loss was ascertained and such loss was to be ascertained (in a case where the cause of the loss came within cl 1(ii)) four months after the date when payment was due by the buyer. In amount the loss was (see cl 9) the gross invoice value of the goods sold and exported by the merchant. What, then, in the present case was the loss to which

c the contract applied? It was £413,412 12s. Where a 'loss' is a loss of a sum of money the words 'loss' and 'amount of loss' are really interchangeable terms. In the present and in similar cases the term 'loss' is used to denote the sum of money which an exporter of goods does not receive at the time when he should have received it.

d   Where in cl 15(ii) an obligation is imposed on the merchant to notify the guarantors 'of any event likely to cause a loss within 30 days of his becoming aware of any such occurrence' the distinction is made apparent between an event which is a cause (as to which see cl 1) and a loss. The loss is different from the 'event' or the 'cause' or the 'occurrence'. The loss is always a sum of money the amount of which is specified (see cl 9). The loss and the amount of it are really indistinguishable. The view taken by the Court of Appeal[1] seems to me with all respect to involve reading cl 17 as though

e instead of the words 'any sums recovered in respect of a loss' there were words referring to any sums received following on an event or occurrence which was the cause of a loss. It was said in the Court of Appeal that the loss covered by the contract was the delay in the payment for the goods. I do not agree. The delay was the cause or event or occurrence which caused the loss. The loss was the loss of £413,412 12s. That sum was the loss.

f   If a sum is recovered (whether by a merchant or by the guarantors) in respect of a loss to which the 'guarantee' applied then naturally it should be divided in the proportions applicable to the transaction. If the guarantors had to make a payment of 90 per cent of the £413,412 12s (the loss) then if there was recovery in respect of the £413,412 12s the sum recovered ought to be divided so that the guarantors received 90 per cent of it. So the question arises—what sum was recovered in respect

g of the £413,412 12s? The answer is that all the £413,412 12s was recovered. The loss was adeemed. The guarantors became entitled to 90 per cent of the amount recovered in respect of the loss. Clause 17 is really the counterpart of cl 8. But once a sum recovered in respect of a loss covered by the 'guarantee' reaches the amount of that loss then cl 17 has, in my view, no further application. Any further sum received is not received in respect of the loss.

h   If pursuant to cl 16 of the contract there had been a request to the merchant to assign and transfer under (b) or a request to assign, deliver up or transfer securities under (d) and if the guarantors had later received more than the amount of the loss certain problems might have arisen. Clauses 16 and 17 are, in my view, linked: this is so because cl 17 refers to sums recovered in respect of a loss either by the merchant or by the 'Guarantors'. The contract does not in terms provide for what is to

j happen if it is the guarantors who receive a sum of money over and above what they recover in respect of a loss. The problem that might arise does not call for present determination.

Some reliance was placed on behalf of the guarantors on the opening words of the second sentence of cl 17, viz, 'The Merchant shall pay all sums recovered to the

1 [1973] 2 All ER 984, [1974] 1 WLR 914

Guarantors forthwith upon their being received by him or any person on his behalf . . .' *a*
In my view, that sentence merely follows on on the first sentence so that the reference
to all sums recovered is a reference to all sums which are recovered in respect of a
loss.

It is to be observed that the word 'loss' appears both in the second line of cl 17
and also in the third line. It must have the same meaning in both places. The second
mention is in the words 'the date at which the loss is ascertained'. That refers to *b*
cl 7 and, in my view, cl 7 (which provides for payment being made to the merchant)
denotes a money sum as being ascertained: the amount of such sum being determined
according to cl 9. This reinforces the view that no valid distinction can be drawn
between a sum of money which is called a loss and the amount of such sum of money.

For the reasons which I have given I would allow the appeal. I would, therefore,
restore the judgment of Cooke J and I would follow his decision as to the appropriate *c*
rate of interest. The result would be that there would be judgment in favour of
the merchant for £8,640·74 together with interest on that sum at one per cent over
bank rate from 1st October 1968 to the present date.

VISCOUNT DILHORNE. My Lords, the first appellants, L Lucas Ltd, sold
flour to Egyptian buyers and the contracts with them provided that payment therefor
should be made in United States dollars. Six of the drafts given by the buyers in *d*
payment were not paid on maturity in consequence of restrictions imposed by the
United Arab Republic which prevented or delayed the transfer to the United Kingdom
of the necessary currency. The buyers made an irrevocable deposit to the order of
the first appellants with a bank in the United Arab Republic of an amount in
Egyptian currency equal to the amount due to the first appellants.

The contracts were covered by a 'guarantee' given by the respondents on 15th *e*
April 1964 to the appellants in return for the payment of a premium. By cl 1 of the
'guarantee' the respondents agreed to pay the appellants 'a percentage of the amount
of any loss as hereinafter defined' which they might sustain in connection with the
export between 1st March 1964 and 28th February 1965 of any goods under a contract
to which the guarantee applied by reason of one of the causes specified in the
paragraph. One specified cause was: *f*

'(ii) The prevention of or delay in the transfer of payment from the buyer's
country to the United Kingdom in circumstances outside the control of both
the Merchant [the appellants] and the buyer.'

So, if the failure to pay the drafts on maturity caused a loss as defined in the guarantee,
the respondents were obliged to pay the agreed percentage of it which was in this *g*
case 90 per cent (cl 8(ii)).

Clause 7 of the 'guarantee' provided that the respondents would pay to the appellants the sum guaranteed immediately after the loss was acertained and that the loss
should be ascertained—

'(ii) where the loss is due to the prevention of or delay in the transfer of payments from the buyer's country to the United Kingdom in circumstances outside *h*
the control of both the [appellants] and the buyer, four months after the due
date of payment by the buyer, or, if the buyer has made an irrevocable deposit
for transfer to the [appellants], four months after the making of such deposit,
if the expiry of this period shall be later . . .'

Clause 9 provided that the amount of the loss should 'as regards goods the subject *j*
of the contract delivered to and accepted by the buyer be the gross invoice value
of those goods' less certain deductions which do not apply in this case. With this
clause there has to be read the following stipulation contained in an endorsement
annexed to the guarantee:

'(2) For the purpose of Paragraph 9 of the Guarantee, the amount of loss shall
be calculated in sterling by converting any amounts in a currency other than
sterling to sterling amounts as hereinbefore provided.'

a The six drafts which were not paid on maturity were for a total of $1,155,181·26 of which the sterling equivalent, at the date when the loss fell to be ascertained in accordance with cl 7 of the guarantee, was £413,412 12s and the respondents being liable for 90 per cent of the loss ascertained in accordance with the guarantee paid 90 per cent thereof, £372,071 6s 10d to the appellants on 31st August 1966.

Clause 16 of the guarantee made provision for action after payment of a claim.
b It read as follows:

'Upon payment by the [respondents] the [appellants] shall:—(a) take all steps which may be necessary or expedient or which the [respondents] may at any time require, to effect recoveries, whether from the buyer or from any other guarantor or other person from whom such recoveries may be made, including (if so required) the institution of proceedings; (b) upon request assign and transfer
c to the [respondents their] rights under any contract in respect of which such payment has been made including [their] right to receive any monies payable under such contract or [their] right to damages from any breach thereof; (c) upon request deliver up to the [respondents] any goods in respect of which such payment has been made and any documents relating thereto and assign and transfer to the [respondents their] rights and interest in any such goods and
d documents; (d) upon request assign, deliver up or otherwise transfer to the [respondents] any negotiable instruments, guarantees or other securities relating to such goods or such contract.'

Clause 17 reads as follows:

'Any sums recovered by the [appellants] or the [respondents] in respect
e of a loss to which this Guarantee applies, after the date at which the loss is ascertained, whether from the buyer or any other source shall:—(i) if the ground of the claim is [the insolvency of the buyer] be divided between the [respondents] and the [appellants] in the proportions of 85 and 15; (ii) in any other case be divided between the [respondents] and the [appellants] in the proportions of 90 and 10; The [appellants] shall pay all sums recovered to the [respondents]
f forthwith upon their being received by [them] or any person on [their] behalf, the [appellants] hereby acknowledging and declaring that until such payment is made to the [respondents they receive] and [hold] such sums in trust for the [respondents].'

After payment by the respondents of the £372,071 6s 10d the restrictions on the transfer of currency were lifted and the amounts due on the drafts in United States
g dollars were paid to the first appellants in four instalments. After the first three drafts had been met by the first instalment, the pound was devalued, with the result that the conversion of the US $1,155,181·26 paid by the buyers into sterling produced £443,032 8s 1d whereas the loss calculated in accordance with the guarantee amounted to £413,412 12s.

The first appellants have repaid to the respondents the £372,071 6s 10d and main-
h tain that no more is payable to them. The respondents, on the other hand, say that they are entitled to receive 90 per cent of the £443,032 8s 1d, that is to say, £398,729 3s 3d, £26,657 15s 5d more than they had paid to the first appellants.

An originating summons was taken out for the determination of this question and on 23rd June 1972 Cooke J decided it in favour of the appellants. His decision was reversed on appeal. In the Court of Appeal[1] Megaw LJ said that in his opinion
j the correct approach to this question was—

'to consider this contract—the policy of insurance, for that is its nature—by reference to its terms. If, but only if, there should emerge some real doubt or ambiguity in the construction of the policy, would it be right to invoke the general principles of subrogation as a guide or a controlling authority.'

---

1 [1973] 2 All ER 984 at 989, [1973] 1 WLR 914 at 922

I too think that this is the correct approach and I agree that the document issued *a*
by the respondents in return for the payment of a premium would be more aptly
described as a policy of insurance, a policy to indemnify the appellants against a
percentage of a loss in sterling which might be sustained on the contracts covered
by the policy from one of the specified causes.

Cooke J thought that cl 16 of the policy was concerned merely with matters of
machinery. I agree. In order to recover the sum they had paid out, it is not surprising *b*
that the respondents should be able to require the appellants to undertake to take
all necessary steps to 'effect recoveries' and, on request, to assign all their rights
under a contract in respect of which a payment had been made by the respondents.
In this case no such request was made. If it had been and had been complied with,
it might well be that the respondents would have been entitled to receive and to
keep all the dollars and not only sufficient of them to repay to them on conversion *c*
to sterling the sum that they had paid to the appellants. But the consequences of
such an assignment do not, in my opinion, assist in determining whether or not,
where there has been no assignment by the appellants of their rights against the
buyers, the respondents are entitled under the contract with the appellants to obtain
more than the sum they paid in respect of the loss.

The answer to that question, in my opinion, depends on the meaning of the words *d*
at the beginning of cl 17 'Any sums recovered by the [appellants] or the [respondents]
in respect of a loss to which this Guarantee applies'.

What was the loss to which the guarantee applied? By cl 1 of the contract the
respondents undertook to pay 'a percentage of the amount of any loss as hereinafter
defined'. The endorsement required the amount of loss to be calculated in sterling
by converting any amounts in any other currency into sterling. The amount of the *e*
loss for the purposes of the contract was consequently the sum of £413,412 12s.

What, then, is the meaning of 'recovered in respect of' that £413,412 12s? Recovered
in respect of a loss to me signifies recovered in recoupment of the loss. I cannot
interpret those words as entitling the respondents to require payment to them of
sums in excess of the loss calculated in accordance with the contract.

The last sentence of cl 17 required the appellants to pay all sums recovered to the *f*
respondents, although under that clause the respondents were only entitled to retain
90 per cent thereof. 'Recovered' in this sentence relates back to the opening words
of the clause and, in my view, means recovered in respect of a loss to which the
guarantee applies.

If the amount of the loss calculated in accordance with the contract had been the
US $1,155,181·26, then the respondents would have been entitled to receive that
sum, whatever might be its sterling equivalent. But the contract did not so provide. *g*

That a policy of this kind should contain provisions designed to secure that the
respondents would recover the percentage of the loss which they had paid if later
the appellants received payment for their goods, is to be expected. But I doubt if
it was ever contemplated that delay in payment by the buyer would lead in the end
to the vendor getting more than the sterling value of the dollars at the time they fell *h*
to be converted into pounds in order to calculate the amount of a loss in accordance
with the terms of the policy. If it had been intended that the respondents should
be entitled to 90 per cent of any such fortuitous profits, I would have expected that
to have been made explicit. The contract would then not have been one indemnifying against a percentage of a loss and containing provisions enabling recoupment
of that loss but also one providing for sharing of any profit there might be as a result
of devaluation.

I feel no doubt that the language of the contract does not permit of interpretation
in accordance with the respondents' contention, for I cannot see that any part of it
supports the conclusion that the respondents were under it entitled to receive back
more than they had paid in respect of a loss.

The parties have agreed that, after making some adjustment in the event of the a appellants succeeding, the sum for which judgment should be given is £8,640·74. In the courts below interest was awarded to the successful party at one per cent over bank rate.

In my opinion, for the reasons I have stated this appeal should be allowed and judgment entered for the appellants with interest at the rate of one per cent over bank rate from 1st October 1968 to the date of the decision of this appeal with costs here and below.

b

LORD SIMON OF GLAISDALE. My Lords, I have had the advantage of reading in draft the speeches prepared by my noble and learned friends, Lord Morris of Borth-y-Gest and Viscount Dilhorne, with which I agree. The contract with which your Lordships are concerned is a contract of indemnity (*Re Miller, Gibb & Co Ltd*[1]). There is nothing either in the public scheme out of which it arises or in the terms of this agreement itself which suggests in any way a profit-sharing venture.

c

I would allow the appeal.

LORD SALMON. My Lords, I have had the advantage of reading the speech of my noble and learned friend, Lord Morris of Borth-y-Gest. I agree with it, and I would, therefore, allow the appeal.

d

Appeal allowed.

Solicitors: *Coward, Chance & Co* (for the appellants); *Treasury Solicitor* (for the respondents).

Christine Ivamy   Barrister.

e

Re Attorney-General's Reference (No 1 of 1974)

COURT OF APPEAL, CRIMINAL DIVISION
LORD WIDGERY CJ, ASHWORTH AND MOCATTA JJ
f 25th APRIL 1974

Criminal law – Handling stolen goods – Stolen goods – Goods ceasing to be stolen goods once restored to lawful possession or custody – Taking into possession or custody – What amounts to – Relevance of intention – Discovery of goods by police officer – Officer suspecting goods stolen and taking steps to prevent removal – Officer keeping goods under observation
g *– Whether conduct of officer amounting to taking of possession or custody of goods – Theft Act 1968, s 24(3).*

A constable found an unattended car. He saw that it contained packages of new clothing which he suspected, and which subsequently proved, to be stolen. He removed the rotor arm from the car to immobilise it and kept observation. After
h about ten minutes the accused appeared, got into the car and attempted to start the engine. When questioned by the constable, he gave an implausible explanation and was arrested. The accused was charged, inter alia, with handling stolen goods, contrary to s 22(1) of the Theft Act 1968. At his trial his counsel submitted that there was no case to answer in that the goods had been 'restored to . . . lawful possession or custody' within the meaning of s 24(3)[a] of the 1968 Act before the accused arrived
j and attempted to drive the car away. The judge accepted that submission and directed the jury to acquit the accused. The Attorney-General referred to the Court of Appeal, under s 36(1)[b] of the Criminal Justice Act 1972, the question whether in those

---

1 [1957] 2 ALL ER 266, [1957] 1 WLR 703
a Section 24(3), so far as material, is set out at p 901 *h*, post
b Section 36(1) is set out at p 901 *a* and *b*, post

circumstances the stolen goods had been restored to lawful possession or custody
within s 24(3) of the 1968 Act.

a

Held – The question whether the constable's conduct in examining the goods, removing the rotor arm of the car and keeping the goods under observation, amounted
to taking possession of the goods depended primarily on the constable's intention.
The judge was not entitled to conclude from the facts that the goods had been taken
into possession by the constable but should have left it to the jury to determine
whether the constable had made up his mind to take possession of the goods so that
they could not be removed and he would have the disposal of them, or whether he
was at that stage of an open mind whether to take possession of them or not and was
merely concerned to ensure that the driver did not get away without being questioned
(see p 905 *b* to *j*, post).

b

 R v Dolan (1855) 6 Cox CC 449, *R v Schmidt* (1865) LR 1 CCR 15 and *R v Villensky*
[1892] 2 QB 597 applied.

c

Notes
For handling stolen goods, see Supplement to 10 Halsbury's Laws (3rd Edn) para
1565A, and for cases on what is receiving, see 15 Digest (Repl) 1140-1142, *11,474-11,496*.
 For the Theft Act 1968, ss 22, 24, see 8 Halsbury's Statutes (3rd Edn) 796, 797.
 For the Criminal Justice Act 1972, s 36, see 42 Halsbury's Statutes (3rd Edn) 129.

d

Cases referred to in judgment
Haughton v Smith [1973] 3 All ER 1109, [1974] 2 WLR 1, HL; *affg* sub nom *R v Smith*
 (*Roger Daniel*) [1973] 2 All ER 896, [1973] 2 WLR 942, 57 Cr App Rep 666, CA.
R v Dolan (1855) Dears CC 436, 24 LJMC 59, 24 LTOS 279, 19 JP 55, 1 Jur NS 72, 6 Cox
 CC 449, CCR, 15 Digest (Repl) 1141, *11,490*.
R v King [1938] 2 All ER 662, CCA, 15 Digest (Repl) 1141, *11,494*.
R v Schmidt (1866) LR 1 CCR 15, 35 LJMC 94, 13 LT 679, 30 JP 100, 12 Jur NS 149,
 10 Cox CC 172, CCR, 15 Digest (Repl) 1141, *11,491*.
R v Villensky [1892] 2 QB 597, 61 LJMC 218, 56 JP 824, CCR, 15 Digest (Repl) 1141,
 11,493.

e

f

Cases also cited
R v Hancock & Baker (1878) 38 LT 787, 14 Cox CC 119, CCR.
Hobson v Impett (1957) 41 Cr App Rep 138, DC.
R v Lyons (1841) Car & M 217.

g

Reference
On 24th October 1973 the respondent was tried on indictment in the Crown Court
at Liverpool before his Honour Judge Lawton and a jury. He was charged (count 1)
with theft, contrary to s 1(1) of the Theft Act 1968, and, alternatively (count 2), with
handling stolen goods, contrary to s 22(1) of the 1968 Act. He was acquitted on both
counts. The Attorney-General referred a point of law which had arisen in the case
to the Court of Appeal under s 36 of the Criminal Justice Act 1972. The facts are
set out in the judgment of the court.

h

C M Clothier QC and *Christopher Carus* for the Attorney-General.
John Leonard QC and *Ann Curnow* as amici curiae.
The respondent did not appear and was not represented.

j

LORD WIDGERY CJ. This is a reference to the court by the Attorney-General
of a point of law seeking the opinion of the court pursuant to s 36 of the Criminal
Justice Act 1972. It is in fact the first occasion on which the Attorney-General has

a exercised his power under this section to refer a question for our opinion. Section
36(1) provides:

> 'Where a person tried on indictment has been acquitted (whether in respect
> of the whole or part of the indictment) the Attorney General may, if he desires
> the opinion of the Court of Appeal on a point of law which has arisen in the case,
> refer that point to the court, and the court shall, in accordance with this section,
b> consider the point and give their opinion on it.'

Again one observes that for the first time the prosecution is given a limited right of
appeal on a point of law following an acquittal on indictment, a right which the
prosecution has enjoyed in magistrates' courts for many years, but it is a novelty
in the Crown Court. The Act and the rules made under it go to great lengths to
c ensure that the accused in the court below, who on this hypothesis has been acquitted,
shall not be prejudiced by the fact that the Attorney-General seeks the opinion of
this court on a point of law. The accused below, who is conveniently to be called
the respondent, is given the opportunity if he wishes to appear in this court by counsel;
provision is made for the payment of his costs, and perhaps most significant of all,
r 6 of the Criminal Appeal (Reference of Points of Law) Rules 1973[1] provides that
d the court shall ensure that the identity of the respondent is not disclosed during the
proceedings on a reference except where the respondent has given his consent for the
use of his name in the proceedings. Accordingly, there is little if any prospect of
the respondent being prejudiced by a reference of this kind, and in the instant case,
although served with the appropriate notices, the respondent has not been concerned
to come here and make representations.

e The facts of the present case, which I take from the terms of the reference itself,
are these:

> 'A Police Constable found an unlocked unattended car containing packages of
> new clothing which he suspected, and which in fact subsequently proved to be,
> stolen. The Officer removed the rotor arm from the vehicle to immobilise
> it, and kept observation. After about ten minutes, the accused appeared, got
f> into the van and attempted to start the engine. When questioned by the Officer,
> he gave an implausible explanation, and was arrested.'

On those facts two charges were brought against the respondent: one of stealing
the woollen goods, the new clothing, which was in the back of the car in question, and
secondly and alternatively of receiving those goods knowing them to be stolen.
g The trial judge quite properly ruled that there was no evidence to support the first
charge, and that he would not leave that to the jury, but an argument developed
whether the second count should be left to the jury or not. Counsel for the
respondent in the court below had submitted at the close of the prosecution case
that there was no case to answer, relying on s 24(3) of the Theft Act 1968. Section
24(3) provides:

h> '... no goods shall be regarded as having continued to be stolen goods after
> they have been restored to the person from whom they were stolen or to other
> lawful possession or custody ...'

The rest of the subsection is not relevant and I do not read it. It was therefore
contended in the court below on the facts to which I have already referred that by
j virtue of s 24(3) the goods had been restored to other lawful possession or custody,
namely the custody or possession of the police officer, before the respondent appeared
on the scene and sought to drive the car away. If that argument was sound, of
course it would follow that there was no case for the respondent to answer, because

---

1 SI 1973 No 1114

if in fact the police constable had restored the stolen goods to his own lawful posses-   *a*
sion or custody before the act relied on as an act of receiving occurred, it would
follow that they would not be stolen goods at the material time.

After hearing argument, the judge accepted the submission of the respondent
and directed the jury that they should acquit on the receiving count. That has
resulted in the Attorney-General referring the following point of law to us for an
opinion under s 36 of the 1972 Act. He expresses the point in this way: *b*

> 'Whether stolen goods are restored to lawful custody within the meaning of
> Section 24(3) of the Theft Act 1968 when a Police Officer, suspecting them to be
> stolen, examines and keeps observation on them with a view to tracing the thief
> or a handler.'

One could put the question perhaps in a somewhat different way by asking whether
on the facts set out in the reference the conclusion as a matter of law was clear to the   *c*
effect that the goods had ceased to be stolen goods. In other words, the question
which is really in issue in this reference is whether the trial judge acted correctly in
law in saying that those facts disclosed a defence within s 24(3) of the 1968 Act.

Section 24(3) is not perhaps entirely happily worded. It has been pointed out in
the course of argument that in the sentence which I have read there is only one relevant verb, and that is 'restore'. The section contemplates that the stolen goods   *d*
should be restored to the person from whom they were stolen or to other lawful
possession or custody. It is pointed out that the word 'restore', although it is entirely
appropriate when applied to restoration of the goods to the true owner, is not really
an appropriate verb to employ if one is talking about a police officer stumbling on
stolen goods and taking them into his own lawful custody or possession.

We are satisfied that despite the absence of another and perhaps more appropriate   *e*
verb, the effect of s 24(3) is to enable a defendant to plead that the goods had ceased
to be stolen goods if the facts are that they were taken by a police officer in the course
of his duty and reduced into possession by him.

Whether or not s 24(3) is intended to be a codification of the common law or not,
it certainly deals with a topic on which the common law provides a large number
of authorities. I shall refer to some of them in a moment, although perhaps not   *f*
all, and it will be observed that from the earliest times it has been recognised that
if the owner of stolen goods resumed possession of them, reduced them into his
possession again, that they thereupon ceased to be stolen goods for present purposes
and could certainly not be the subject of a later charge of receiving based on events
after they had been reduced into possession. It is to be observed that in common
law nothing short of a reduction into possession, either by the true owner or by a   *g*
police officer acting in the execution of his duty, was regarded as sufficient to change
the character of the goods from stolen goods into goods which were no longer to be
so regarded.

I make that assertion true by a brief reference from the cases to which we have
been referred. The first is R v Dolan[1]. The facts there were that stolen goods were
found in the pocket of a thief by the owner. The owner sent for a policeman, and   *h*
the evidence given at the subsequent trial showed that after the policeman had taken
the goods from the thief, the thief, the policeman and the employer went towards
the shop owned and occupied by the prisoner at which the thief had asserted that he
was hoping to sell the stolen goods. When they got near the shop the policeman
gave the goods to the thief, who then went on ahead into the shop with a view to
selling the goods, closely followed by the owner and the policeman, who proceeded   *j*
to arrest the shopkeeper. It was held there—

> 'that the prisoner was not guilty of feloniously receiving stolen goods; inas-
> much as they were delivered to him under the authority of the owner by a
> person to whom the owner had bailed them for that purpose.'

1 (1855) 6 Cox CC 449

a   Put another way, one can explain that decision on the broad principle to which I have already referred: the goods had already been returned to the possession of the owner before they were then released by him into the hands of the thief in order that the thief might approach the receiver with a view to the receiver being arrested. The principle thus enunciated is one which, as I have already said, is to be found in the other authorities to which we have been referred.

b   The next case which is similar is *R v Schmidt*[1]. The reference in the headnote suffices:

> 'Four thieves stole goods from the custody of a railway company, and afterwards sent them in a parcel by the same company's line addressed to the prisoner. During the transit the theft was discovered; and, on the arrival of the parcel at the station for its delivery, a policeman in the employ of the company opened it, and then returned it to the porter whose duty it was to deliver it, *c*   with instructions to keep it until further orders. On the following day the policeman directed the porter to take the parcel to its address, when it was received by the prisoner, who was afterwards convicted of receiving goods knowing them to be stolen . . .'

And it was held by the Court of Crown Cases Reserved—

d   'that the goods had got back into the possession of the owner, so as to be no longer stolen goods, and that the conviction was wrong.'

Again unquestionably they had been reduced into the possession of the owner by the hand of the police officer acting on his behalf. They had not been allowed to continue their course unaffected. They had been taken out of circulation by the police officer, reduced into the possession of the owner or of the officer, and it matters not which, *e*   and thus had ceased to be stolen goods for present purposes. Mellor J, in giving a brief judgment, said[2]:

> 'The property is rightly laid in the company [that is the railway company] because at the time of the larceny there was a bailment to them by the true owners. I concur in the propriety of the decision in *Reg. v. Dolan*[3]; but there the goods got back into the possession of the true owner. In this case *f*   the policeman merely looked at the goods, and did not take possession of them.'

It is to be observed that he was taking a different view of the effect of the acts of the police officer, but the principle as far as we can see is unaffected by that decision.

Then there is a helpful case, *R v Villensky*[4]. Again it is a case of a parcel in the hands of carriers. This parcel was handed to the carriers in question for conveyance to the consignees, and whilst in the carriers' depot it was stolen by a servant of the *g*   carriers who removed the parcel to a different part of the premises and placed on it a label addressed to the prisoners by a name by which they were known and at a house where they resided. The superintendent of the carriers, on receipt of information as to this and after inspection of the parcel, directed it to be replaced in the place from which the thief had removed it and to be sent with a special delivery receipt in a van accompanied by two detectives to the address shown on the label. At that *h*   address it was received by the prisoners under circumstances which clearly showed knowledge on their part that it had been stolen. The property in the parcel was laid in the indictment in the carriers and an offer to amend the indictment by substituting the names of the consignees was declined. The carriers' servant pleaded guilty to a count for larceny in the same indictment. It was there held by the Court of Crown Cases Reserved—

j   'that as the person in which the property was laid [ie the carriers] had resumed possession of the stolen property before its receipt by the prisoners, it

1 (1866) LR 1 CCR 15
2 LR 1 CCR at 19
3 (1855) 6 Cox CC 449
4 [1892] 2 QB 597

had then ceased to be stolen property, and the prisoners could not be convicted
of receiving it knowing it to have been stolen.'
In the same report there is a brief and valuable judgment by Pollock B in these
terms[1]:

'The decisions in *Reg. v. Dolan*[2] and *Reg. v. Schmidt*[3] are, in my judgment,
founded on law and on solid good sense, and they should not be frittered away.
It is, of course, frequently the case that when it is found that a person has stolen
property he is watched; but the owner of the property, if he wishes to catch
the receiver, does not resume possession of the stolen goods; here the owners
have done so, and the result is that the conviction must be quashed.'

We refer to that brief judgment because it illustrates in a few clear words what is
really the issue in the present case. When the police officer discovered these goods
and acted as he did, was the situation that he had taken possession of the goods, in
which event, of course, they ceased to be stolen goods, or was it merely that he was
watching the goods with a view to the possibility of catching the receiver at a later
stage? I will turn later to a consideration of those two alternatives.

Two other cases should, I think, be mentioned at this stage. The next one is *R v
King*[4]. We are now getting to far more recent times because the report is published
in 1938. The appellant here was convicted with another man of receiving stolen
goods knowing them to have been stolen. A fur coat had been stolen and shortly
afterwards the police went to a flat where they found the man Burns and told him
they were enquiring about some stolen property. He at first denied that there was
anything there, but finally admitted the theft and produced a parcel from a ward-
robe. While the policeman was in the act of examining the contents of the parcel,
the telephone bell rang. Burns answered it and the police heard him say: 'Come
along as arranged'. The police then suspended operations and about 20 minutes
later the appellant arrived, and, being admitted by Burns, said: 'I have come for the
coat. Harry sent me.' This was heard by the police, who were in hiding at the
time. The coat was handed to the appellant by Burns, so that he was actually in
possession of it. It was contended that the possession by the police amounted to
possession by the owner of the coat, and that, therefore, the coat was not stolen
property at the time the appellant received it. It was held by the Court of Criminal
Appeal that 'the coat had not been in the possession of the police, and it was therefore
still stolen property when the appellant received it'.

Counsel for the Attorney-General, appearing in support of this reference, showed
some hesitation in relying on this case, because he clearly took the view that it was
perhaps a rather unlikely decision, the policemen having started to examine the coat
and then stopped for 20 minutes until the prisoner arrived and then claiming that the
coat was not in their possession. It might be thought to be a rather bold decision to
say that the police action in that case had not reduced the coat into their possession.
But nevertheless that was the view of this court in the judgment of Humphreys J.
All the authorities, as I say, point in the same direction.

The most recent case on the present topic, but of little value in the present problems, is *Haughton v Smith*[5]. The case being of little value to us in our present problems, I will deal with it quite briefly. It is a case where a lorry-load of stolen meat
was intercepted by police, somewhere in the north of England, who discovered that
the lorry was in fact full of stolen goods. After a brief conference they decided to
take the lorry on to its destination with a view to catching the receivers at the London
end of the affair. So the lorry set off for London with detectives both in the passenger
seat and in the back of the vehicle, and in due course was met by the defendant at its
destination in London. In that case before this court it was conceded, as it had been
conceded below, that the goods had been reduced into the possession of the police

1 [1892] 2 QB at 599   3 (1866) LR 1 CCR 15   5 [1973] 3 All ER 1109, [1974] 2 WLR 1
2 (1855) 6 Cox CC 449   4 [1938] 2 All ER 662

a when they took possession of the lorry in the north of England, so no dispute in this court or later in the House of Lords was raised on that issue. It is, however, to be noted that three of their Lordships, when the matter got to the House of Lords, expressed some hesitation as to the propriety of the prosecution conceding in that case that the goods had been reduced to the possession of the police when the lorry was first intercepted. Since we cannot discover on what ground those doubts were expressed either from the report of the speeches or from the report of the argument,

b we cannot take advantage of that case in the present problem.

Now to return to the present problem again with those authorities in the background: did the conduct of the police officer, as already briefly recounted, amount to a taking of possession of the woollen goods in the back seat of the motor car? What he did, to repeat the essential facts, was: seeing these goods in the car and being suspicious of them because they were brand new goods and in an unlikely position,

c he removed the rotor arm and stood by in cover to interrogate any driver of the car who might subsequently appear. Did that amount to a taking possession of the goods in the back of the car? In our judgment it depended primarily on the intentions of the police officer. If the police officer seeing these goods in the back of the car had made up his mind that he would take them into custody, that he would

d reduce them into his possession or control, take charge of them so that they could not be removed and so that he would have the disposal of them, then it would be a perfectly proper conclusion to say that he had taken possession of the goods. On the other hand, if the truth of the matter is that he was of an entirely open mind at that stage as to whether the goods were to be seized or not and was of an entirely open mind as to whether he should take possession of them or not, but merely stood by

e so that when the driver of the car appeared he could ask certain questions of that driver as to the nature of the goods and why they were there, then there is no reason whatever to suggest that he had taken the goods into his possession or control. It may be, of course, that he had both objects in mind. It is possible in a case like this that the police officer may have intended by removing the rotor arm both to prevent the car from being driven away and to enable him to assert control over

f the woollen goods as such. But if the jury came to the conclusion that the proper explanation of what had happened was that the police officer had not intended at that stage to reduce the goods into his possession or to assume the control of them, and at that stage was merely concerned to ensure that the driver, if he appeared, could not get away without answering questions, then in that case the proper conclusion of the jury would have been to the effect that the goods had not been reduced

g into the possession of the police and therefore a defence under s 24(3) of the 1968 Act would not be of use to this particular defendant.

In the light of those considerations it has become quite obvious that the trial judge was wrong in withdrawing the issue from the jury. As a matter of law he was not entitled to conclude from the facts which I have set out more than once that these goods were reduced into the possession of the police officer. What he should have

h done in our opinion would have been to have left that issue to the jury for decision, directing the jury that they should find that the prosecution case was without substance if they thought that the police officer had assumed control of the goods as such and reduced them into his possession. Whereas, on the other hand, they should have found the case proved, assuming that they were satisfied about its other elements, if they were of the opinion that the police officer in removing the rotor arm and standing by and watching was doing no more than ensure that the driver should not

j get away without interrogation and was not at that stage seeking to assume possession of the goods as such at all. That is our opinion.

Determination accordingly.

Solicitors: *Director of Public Prosecutions* (for the Attorney-General); *Treasury Solicitor.*

N P Metcalfe Esq Barrister.

The Albazero

Owners of cargo lately laden on board the ship or vessel Albacruz v Owners of the ship or vessel Albazero

QUEEN'S BENCH DIVISION (ADMIRALTY COURT)

BRANDON J

19th, 20th, 21st, 22nd, 23rd, 26th NOVEMBER 1973, 14th JANUARY 1974

Shipping – Carriage by sea – Breach of contract – Damages – Substantial damages – Action by consignor – Loss of or damage to cargo – Consignor no longer having interest in cargo at date of loss or damage – Agreement between consignor and carrier for carriage of cargo – Agreement that cargo being carried for consignor and cost of carriage to be paid by him – Ship sinking on voyage with loss of cargo – Property in and right to possession of cargo having passed to consignee at date of loss – Whether carrier precluded from denying that consignor had sufficient interest in cargo to maintain action for substantial damages.

Sale of goods – Passing of property – Reservation of right of disposal – Bill of lading – Goods deliverable to order of seller – Presumption that right of disposal reserved – Delivery of goods to carrier for shipment – Fulfilment of conditions imposed by seller – C i f contract between associated companies – Sale on credit terms – Presumption that right of disposal reserved to secure payment rebutted – Seller's agents despatching endorsed bills of lading to buyer by post during voyage – Power of seller to divert goods before despatch of bills of lading – Whether property passing on date bill of lading posted – Sale of Goods Act 1893, s 19(1)(2).

By a contract in writing dated 27th May 1968 ('the purchase contract') an oil company ('Esso') agreed to sell and deliver, or cause to be sold and delivered, to the plaintiffs large quantities of crude oil to be delivered in bulk fob La Salina, Venezuela, in consecutive cargo lots over a period of a little over three years. The plaintiffs were a wholly owned subsidiary of a company ('Occidental') which also had two other subsidiaries: a French company ('Courtage') centred in Paris, and a Belgian company ('RBP') which operated a refinery in Antwerp. By a contract in writing dated 23rd December 1968 ('the sale contract') the plaintiffs agreed to sell and deliver to RBP large quantities of crude oil. Under that contract delivery was to be made c i f Antwerp by tank vessels to be supplied by the plaintiffs and payment was to be made not later than 180 days after the date of invoice. Under cl A.7 of Incoterms 1953, which were incorporated in the sale contract, the plaintiffs undertook to furnish RBP with a bill of lading for the agreed port of destination, i e Antwerp. Under a time charterparty dated 9th May 1969 the plaintiffs hired a tank vessel from the defendants. Clause 2 of the charterparty imposed on the defendants obligations of due diligence with regard to the seaworthiness of the vessel at delivery and the maintenance of seaworthiness during service. Clause 3 provided that the vessel was to be at the service of the plaintiffs for a period of five years for the carriage of all lawful merchandise. Clauses 7 and 8 provided for the payment of hire monthly in advance and cl 13 provided that the master should be under the orders and directions of the plaintiffs as regards the employment of the vessel and that bills of lading should be signed as the plaintiffs or their agents might direct without prejudice to the charter. The vessel was nominated by Courtage, on behalf of the plaintiffs, to carry one of the consecutive shipments of oil to be supplied by Esso to the plaintiffs under the purchase contract and by the plaintiffs to RBP under the sale contract. Courtage notified Esso that the vessel would arrive at La Salina on 2nd January 1970 to load 20,000 tons of oil and notified RBP that the vessel would arrive at Antwerp at the latest on *a* 16th/17th January. Appropriate orders were also given by Courtage to the master of the vessel. In accordance with the sale contract, Esso caused the cargo of oil to be supplied by another oil company ('Creole') at La Salina. Creole were also appointed charterers' agents for the vessel at La Salina. The vessel arrived at La Salina on 2nd January and loading was completed on the following day. A bill of lading was issued and signed by the master in respect of the cargo naming Creole

b as shippers and the plaintiffs as consignees, the vessel to proceed to Gibraltar for orders. Accordingly, under the bill of lading, the goods were deliverable to the order of the plaintiffs. The bill of lading did not therefore comply with the terms of the sale contract but was made up in that form on instructions given on behalf of the plaintiffs in accordance with the policy of the Occidental group that bills of lading in relation to shipments by the plaintiffs to RBP should be taken in that form

c so that, if necessary or desirable, the ship could be diverted to another port of discharge or the cargo to another customer at another port, without the necessity of new shipping documents being issued. The vessel sailed from La Salina on 3rd January. On 6th January Creole airmailed to Courtage a number of documents including two original bills of lading. They were received by Courtage on 12th January. Courtage endorsed the bills of lading generally and posted them to RBP

d on 13th January. On 14th January the vessel sank and the cargo was lost. On 15th January the endorsed bills of lading were received by RBP in Antwerp. Payment for the cargo against invoice was later made by RBP to the plaintiffs. In an action in rem the plaintiffs claimed damages from the defendants for the loss of the cargo, alleging that the defendants had been in breach of cl 2 of the charterparty. A preliminary issue was ordered to be tried whether, on the assumption that the defendants

e had been in breach of cl 2, the plaintiffs were entitled to claim substantial, or merely nominal, damages for the loss of the cargo.

Held – (1) The property in the cargo had passed from the plaintiffs to RBP before the date of the loss for the following reasons—

f (i) Although, under s 19(2)[a] of the Sale of Goods Act 1893 there was a presumption that, since by the bill of lading the cargo was deliverable to the order of the plaintiffs, the plaintiffs had reserved the right of disposal of the goods, that presumption was rebuttable. Since the plaintiffs and RBP were associated companies, and the goods had been sold on credit, it was unnecessary for the plaintiffs to reserve the right of disposal to secure payment of the price by RBP; nor was there any desire or intention on the part of the plaintiffs to raise money by a pledge of the shipping documents;

g the presumption that the plaintiffs had reserved the right of disposal in order to secure payment, or to raise money on the shipping documents, had therefore been rebutted (see p 925 *d* to *f* and p 926 *d*, post).

(ii) The proper inference to be drawn from the evidence was that the plaintiffs had reserved the right of disposal of the goods until all possibility of diverting the cargo to another customer at another port had disappeared and that it was the intention

h of the parties that the property in the cargo should not pass until that situation had arisen. In the circumstances all possibility of diversion disappeared when Courtage,

---

a Section 19, so far as material, provides:

  '(1) Where there is a contract for the sale of specific goods or where goods are subsequently

j appropriated to the contract, the seller may, by the terms of the contract or appropriation, reserve the right of disposal of the goods until certain conditions are fulfilled. In such case, notwithstanding the delivery of the goods to the buyer, or to a carrier or other bailee or custodier for the purpose of transmission to the buyer, the property in the goods does not pass to the buyer until the conditions imposed by the seller are fulfilled.

  '(2) Where goods are shipped, and by the bill of lading the goods are deliverable to the order of the seller or his agent, the seller is prima facie deemed to reserve the right of disposal ...'

having endorsed the bills of lading, posted them to RBP on 13th January 1970. *a*
Accordingly the property in the cargo passed to RBP on that date (see p 926 *f g* and
h, post).

(2) At the date of the loss the plaintiffs no longer had the right to possession of the
cargo. Although under an ordinary cif contract, where delivery of the shipping
documents was to be made only against payment, it was an implied term that the
documents should be tendered at the place of business or residence of the buyer, no *b*
such term could be implied in a contract where delivery of the bill of lading was
entirely independent of payment. The bills of lading having been committed to
the post on 13th January, and neither the plaintiffs nor Courtage as their agents
having any control over them thereafter, it followed that they had ceased to retain
possession of the bills of lading, and with it the right to possession of the cargo, on
that date (see p 928 *b* to *f*, post). *c*

(3) It followed that the plaintiffs were not entitled to claim substantial damages
on the ground that, at the date when the cargo was lost, they had the property in,
or the right to possession of, the cargo (see p 926 *j* and p 928 *f*, post).

(4) The plaintiffs were nevertheless entitled to recover substantial damages for
the loss of the cargo for the following reasons—

(i) In certain circumstances a consignor could sue for and recover substantial *d*
damages from a carrier for loss of, or damage to, goods even though, at the material
time, he had neither the property nor the risk in the goods. Those circumstances
existed where there was a special contract between the consignor and the carrier,
i e an agreement that the goods were being carried for the consignor and that the
cost of the carriage was to be paid by him. From such an agreement an estoppel
arose which precluded the carrier from disputing that the consignor had a sufficient *e*
interest in the goods to maintain an action for substantial damages for loss or damage
(see p 921 *b* to *h* and p 922 *a*, post); *Davis and Jordan v James* (1770) 5 Burr 2680,
Moore v Wilson (1787) 1 Term Rep 659, *Joseph v Knox* (1813) 3 Camp 320, *Dunlop
v Lambert* (1839) 6 Cl & Fin 600 and *Mead v South Eastern Railway Co* (1870) 18 WR
735 applied.

(ii) A 'special contract' existed between the plaintiffs and the defendants by virtue *f*
of the charterparty and the bill of lading. By that contract the defendants agreed
to carry the cargo as the plaintiffs' cargo and to be paid for the carriage by them, for
the defendants had a contractual obligation to carry the cargo and, by issuing at
the request of Creole (acting as agents for the plaintiffs) a bill of lading which named
Creole as shippers and the plaintiffs as consignees, they had acknowledged that they
were to carry the cargo as the plaintiffs' cargo; further carriage was to be paid for *g*
by the plaintiffs by way of hire. The defendants were therefore precluded from
denying that the plaintiffs had a sufficient interest in the cargo to claim substantial
damages (see p 922 *j* to p 923 *a d e* and *h*, post); *Gardano & Giampari v Greek Petroleum
George Mamidakis & Co* [1961] 3 All ER 919 applied; dictum of Bramwell LJ in *Hayn,
Roman & Co v Culliford* (1879) 4 CPD at 185, 186 doubted.

Per Brandon J. (i) A right to possession of goods is sufficient to enable a person to *h*
sue for and recover substantial damages in contract for loss of the goods (see p 927 *a*,
post); *Margarine Union GmbH v Cambay Prince Steamship Co Ltd* [1967] 3 All ER 775
applied.

(ii) Where a consignor who no longer has an interest in the goods recovers substantial damages for the loss of, or damage to, them, he holds the amount recovered
on a constructive trust for the person who has suffered the loss or damage (see *j*
p 922 *c* and *d*, post); dictum of Lord Ellenborough in *Joseph v Knox* (1813) 3 Camp
at 321, 322 applied.

Notes

For remedies against carriers, see 5 Halsbury's Laws (4th Edn) 234, 235, paras 452-455,
and for cases on the subject, see 8 Digest (Repl) 166-168, 1074-1094.

a For the passing of property and reservation of rights of disposal under a c i f contract,
   see 34 Halsbury's Laws (3rd Edn) 173, 174, para 295.
   For the Sale of Goods Act 1893, s 19, see 30 Halsbury's Laws (3rd Edn) 19.

Cases referred to in judgment

Badische Anilin und Soda Fabrik, The v The Basle Chemical Works, Bindschedler [1898]
b   AC 200, 67 LJCh 141, 77 LT 573, HL, 39 Digest (Repl) 609, 1223.
Brown v Hodgson (1809) 2 Camp 36, 170 ER 1073, 8 Digest (Repl) 168, 1090.
Coats v Chaplin (1842) 3 QB 483, 11 LJQB 315, 2 Gal & Dav 552, 6 Jur 1123, 114 ER
    592, 8 Digest (Repl) 168, 1092.
Comptoir D'Achat et de Vente du Boerenbond Belge SA v Luis de Ridder, Limitada [1949]
    1 All ER 269, [1949] AC 293, [1949] LJR 513, HL, 39 Digest (Repl) 640, 1488.
c *Davis and Jordan v James* (1770) 5 Burr 2680, 98 ER 407, 8 Digest (Repl) 167, 1080.
Dawes v Peck (1799) 8 Term Rep 330, 3 Esp 12, 101 ER 1417, 8 Digest (Repl) 167, 1078.
Dunlop v Lambert (1839) 6 Cl & Fin 600, Macl & Rob 663, 7 ER 824, HL, 8 Digest (Repl)
    166, 1074.
Fragano v Long (1825) 4 B & C 219, [1824-34] All ER Rep 171, 6 Dow & Ry KB 283,
    3 LJOSKB 177, 107 ER 1040, 8 Digest (Repl) 168, 1091.
d *Gardano & Giampari v Greek Petroleum George Mamidakis & Co* [1961] 3 All ER 919,
    [1962] 1 WLR 40, [1961] 2 Lloyd's Rep 259, 41 Digest (Repl) 271, 876.
Hayn, Roman & Co v Culliford (1879) 4 CPD 182, 48 LJQB 372, 40 LT 536, 4 Asp MLC
    128, CA, 41 Digest (Repl) 309, 1166.
Johnson v Taylor Bros & Co Ltd [1920] AC 144, 89 LJKB 227, 122 LT 130, 25 Com Cas
    69, HL, 39 Digest (Repl) 799, 2691.
e *Joseph v Knox* (1813) 3 Camp 320, 170 ER 1397, 41 Digest (Repl) 458, 2380.
Margarine Union GmbH v Cambay Prince Steamship Co Ltd [1967] 3 All ER 775, [1969]
    1 QB 219, [1967] 3 WLR 1569, [1967] 2 Lloyd's Rep 315, Digest (Cont Vol C) 857,
    1539a.
Mead v South Eastern Railway Co (1870) 18 WR 735, 8 Digest (Repl) 167, 1079.
Moore v Wilson (1787) 1 Term Rep 659, 99 ER 1306, 8 Digest (Repl) 168, 1089.
f *Sargent v Morris* (1820) 3 B & Ald 277, 106 ER 665, 8 Digest (Repl) 167, 1082.
Sewell v Burdick (1884) 10 App Cas 74, [1881-85] All ER Rep 223, 54 LJQB 156, 52 LT
    445, 5 Asp MLC 376, HL, 41 Digest (Repl) 240, 621.
Smyth (Ross T) & Co Ltd v T D Bailey, Son & Co [1940] 3 All ER 60, 164 LT 102, 45 Com
    Cas 292, HL, 39 Digest (Repl) 611, 1239.
Steamship Den of Airlie Co Ltd v Mitsui and Co Ltd and British Oil and Cake Mills Ltd (1912)
g   106 LT 451, 12 Asp MLC 169, 17 Com Cas 116, CA; *affg on other grounds* (1911)
    105 LT 823, 12 Asp MLC 97, 2 Digest (Repl) 499, 472.
Swain v Shepherd (1832) 1 Mood & R 223, 8 Digest (Repl) 167, 1083.
Tronson v Dent (1853) 8 Moo PCC 419, 14 ER 159, PC, 41 Digest (Repl) 413, 1997.

Cases also cited
h *Blanchard v Page* (1857) 74 Mass 281.
Browne v Hare (1858) 3 H & N 484.
Calcutta & Burmah Steam Navigation Co v De Mattos (1863) 32 LJQB 322.
Carlos Federspiel & Co SA v Charles Twigg & Co [1957] 1 Lloyd's Rep 240.
Clemens (E) Horst Co v Biddell Brothers [1912] AC 18, [1911-13] All ER Rep 93, HL.
Coombs v Bristol & Exeter Railway Co (1858) 3 H & N 510.
j *Cork Distilleries Co v Great Southern and Western Railway Co (Ireland)* (1874) LR 7 HL
    269, HL.
Dutton v Solomonson (1803) 3 Bos & P 582.
Freeman v Birch (1833) 3 QB 492.
Furby v Hoey [1947] 1 All ER 236, DC.
Parchim, The [1918] AC 157, PC.

Shaw B & J and John Tullock v Cox's Shipping Agency Ltd and Keighley Shipping Co (Third   a
Parties) (1923) 16 Lloyd LR 216, CA.
Wilmshurst v Bowker (1843) 7 Man & G 882.

Preliminary issue
The plaintiffs, Concord Petroleum Corporation, the owners of cargo lately laden on
board the ship or vessel Albacruz, issued a writ in rem against the ship or vessel   b
Albazero, a sister ship of the Albacruz, claiming damages against the defendants,
Gosford Marine Panama SA, the owners of the Albazero, for the loss of the cargo
on board the Albacruz by reason of the defendants' breach of cl 2 of a time charterparty dated 9th May 1969 whereby the defendants agreed to let and the plaintiffs
agreed to hire the Albacruz for a period of five years from the time and date of
delivery.   On 2nd October 1973 Brandon J ordered the following preliminary issue   c
to be tried: whether, on the assumption that the loss of the cargo had been caused
by the defendants' breach of cl 2 of the charterparty, the plaintiffs were entitled to
recover from the defendants substantial, as distinct from nominal, damages for such
loss under the charterparty.   The facts are set out in the judgment.

J S Hobhouse QC and *Andrew Longmore* for the plaintiffs.   d
Michael Mustill QC and *Jonathan Gilman* for the defendants.

Cur adv vult

14th January. **BRANDON J** read the following judgment. This is a preliminary issue in an action by plaintiff charterers against defendant shipowners for   e
loss of cargo. The cargo concerned was crude oil in bulk which was being carried
from La Salina, in Venezuela, to Antwerp in the defendants' ship Albacruz. During
the voyage, which was in January 1970, the ship sank and the cargo, valued at about
£137,000, was lost.   There is a dispute whether the loss was caused by the defendants'
breach of charterparty. This does not, however, fall to be decided now, for the
parties have agreed to have tried first the question whether, assuming that the loss   f
was so caused, the plaintiffs are entitled to recover substantial, as distinct from
merely nominal, damages in respect of it.
    The plaintiffs bought the cargo fob La Salina and resold it cif Antwerp. Questions
arise as to when, in relation to the time of the loss, the property and risk in the cargo,
and the right to possession of it, passed from the plaintiffs to their cif buyers.   The
plaintiffs say, first, that these questions are irrelevant, because the defendants   g
agreed to carry the cargo for them and are therefore precluded from disputing their
title to sue for substantial damages in respect of its loss.   The plaintiffs say, secondly,
that in any case the property in the cargo, or at least the right to possession of it,
was still in them at the time of the loss, and that either of these matters entitles them
to recover substantial damages.
    The defendants dispute each element of the plaintiffs' case. They say, first, that   h
both the property in the cargo, and the right to possession of it, had passed from the
plaintiffs to their cif buyers by the time of the loss; secondly, that, since the property
and the right to possession had passed, the plaintiffs suffered no damage by reason
of the loss and can only recover nominal damages for it; and, thirdly, that, even if
the right to possession (as distinct from the property) in the cargo was still in the
plaintiffs, such right would not by itself entitle them to recover substantial damages.   j
    Before considering the questions so raised it is necessary to set out the primary
facts in some detail.   These appear from the agreed bundles of documents, supplemented by the written and oral evidence of one witness called for the plaintiffs, and
are not for the most part in dispute. It will be convenient to consider the facts
under eight headings as follows: first, the companies concerned and their relationship to each other; second, the fob contract of sale to the plaintiffs (which I shall

a call 'the purchase contract'); third, the cif contract of resale by the plaintiffs (which I shall call 'the sale contract'); fourth, the charterparty; fifth, the arrangements for the shipment of the cargo; sixth, the sale and shipping documents; seventh, the insurance of the cargo; and, eighth, the claim on cargo underwriters.

First, as to the companies concerned and their relationship. The defendants are a Panamanian company, Gosford Marine Panama SA, who were at all material times the owners of the Liberian steam tanker Albacruz. The plaintiffs are Concord

b Petroleum Corporation, described in the charterparty as being of Nassau in the Bahamas, but apparently also having offices and carrying on business in Bermuda. They are a wholly owned subsidiary of the Occidental Petroleum Corporation. That company has two other wholly owned subsidiaries in Europe: first, a French company, Courtage Occidental, centred in Paris; and, second, a Belgian company, Raffinerie Belge de Petroles SA, operating and having a refinery in Antwerp. I shall refer to

c these three companies as 'Occidental', 'Courtage' and 'RBP' respectively.

Second, as to the purchase contract. The plaintiffs bought the cargo under a written contract with Esso International Inc (which I shall call 'Esso') dated 27th May 1968. This contract provided that Esso would sell and deliver, or cause to be sold and delivered, to the plaintiffs large quantities of Bachaquero crude oil in bulk fob La Salina in consecutive cargo lots over a period of a little over three years.

d Part I of the contract, after dealing with quantity, quality and fob prices, provided:

'D. PAYMENT
'Payment of the price of each cargo shall be made to Seller to a Bank designated by Seller in U.S. Dollars . . . ninety (90) days after the date of the bill of lading for such cargo . . .

e 'E. DELIVERY
'Delivery shall be made in accordance with the following schedule: in cargo lots of substantially even quantities to be lifted at evenly spread intervals during the period of this Agreement . . .

'G. DURATION
f 'This Agreement shall be and remain in force for a term of three years plus ninety days commencing on January 1, 1969 and ending on March 31, 1972.'

Part II of the contract, as amended by cl H of Part I, provided:

'DELIVERY
'Section 5.1. Delivery of Oil hereunder shall be made in bulk to Buyer free on board (FOB) tank vessel to be provided by Buyer at the place of delivery . . .

g 'Section 5.3. Title to the Oil delivered hereunder, and risk of loss thereof, shall pass to Buyer when the Oil passes the flange connection between the delivery hose and the vessel's cargo intake . . .

'VESSEL NOMINATION
'Section 6.1. Buyer shall nominate each vessel by notice to Seller given in

h writing at least 30 days in advance of its arrival at loading port . . . stating the following: (a) name and size of vessel to be loaded, (b) scheduled date of arrival, (c) quantity of Oil to be delivered to vessel, and (d) full instructions regarding vessel, the makeup and disposition of bills of lading and other documents—all of which shall be acceptable to Seller and may only be changed with Seller's consent at any time . . .'

j Third, as to the resale contract. The plaintiffs resold the cargo to RBP under a written contract dated 23rd December 1968. This contract provided that the plaintiffs would sell and deliver, or cause to be sold and delivered, to RBP large quantities of asphaltic crude oil, including Bachaquero crude, by consecutive shipments during 1969. This particular cargo was shipped, and but for its loss would have arrived at destination, in January 1970, outside the contract period. The new contract for 1970 had not,

however, by then been made, and it was agreed by counsel on either side that the
shipment here concerned should be regarded as a belated shipment under the   *a*
contract for 1969 referred to above.

That contract, after dealing with the nature, quality and quantity of the oil to be
supplied, provided as follows:

'4.   Price: The CIF price will be the sum of the following components: (a)
FOB price: . . .—*Bachaquero Crude Oil*: The price posted at La Salina on date of *b*
actual commencement of loading by Creole Petroleum Corporation . . . (b)
Freight: From loading port to Antwerp on the gross Bill of lading quantities
at the US Dollar rate as published by Intascale . . . prior to November 18, 1967,
less 35% . . . (c) *Marine and War Risk Insurance*: at cost.

'5.   *Delivery*: Delivery will be made CIF Antwerp by tank-vessels to be supplied by SELLER, evenly spread over 1969, in accordance with a delivery schedule *c*
to be mutually agreed.

'6.   *Payment*: In US Dollars, not later than 180 days after the date of invoice,
by bank transfer to the Banque de Commerce S.A. . . . Antwerp . . . for credit
to Concord Petroleum Corporation's US Dollars account, or to any other bank
which may be designated by SELLER to BUYER.

'7.   *Insurance*: SELLER will provide for Marine Insurance subject to Standard *d*
Bulk Oil clauses including war risks, issued by a reputable Insurance Company
of SELLER's choice . . .

'9.   *Destination*: The Crude Oil delivered under the present agreement will
be processed in BUYER's refinery in Belgium . . .

'11.   *General Terms and Conditions*: SELLER's General Terms and Conditions,
attached hereto as Exhibit II, shall be applicable.'   *e*

The plaintiffs' general terms and conditions, incorporated into the contract by
cl 11 above, provide, so far as material:

'9.   . . . Where products are sold C.I.F., Seller will only pay for putting on
board, freight . . . and insurance against marine risks. For such C.I.F. sales,
Seller will provide and pay for marine insurance . . . for the full C.I.F. invoice *f*
value . . . In all cases, Seller's responsibility will cease after the products have
been put on board . . .

'13.   Whenever the provisions of the Contract are not contrary to Incoterms
1953, the latter shall be applicable to the Contract.'

Incoterms 1953 cover various types of contract, including cif contracts of sale. *g*
In relation to these they provide, among other things:

'A.   *Seller must*: . . . 2. Contract on usual terms at his own expense for the
carriage of the goods to the agreed port of destination by the usual route in a sea-
going vessel . . . 4. Load the goods at his own expense on board the vessel at the
port of shipment . . . and notify the buyer . . . that the goods have been loaded . . .
5. Procure, at his own cost and in a transferable form, a policy of marine insurance *h*
against the risks of the carriage involved in the contract . . . 6. . . . bear all risks of
the goods until such time as they shall have effectively passed the ship's rail
at the port of shipment. 7. At his own expense furnish to the buyer without
delay a clean negotiable bill of lading for the agreed port of destination, as well
as the invoice of the goods shipped and the insurance policy or . . . a certificate
of insurance . . . The bill of lading must cover the contract goods . . . and provide *j*
by endorsement or otherwise for delivery to the order of the buyer . . .

'B.   *Buyer must*: 1. Accept the documents when tendered by the seller, if
they are in conformity with the contract of sale, and pay the price as provided
in the contract . . . 3. Bear all risks of the goods from the time when they shall
have effectively passed the ship's rail at the port of shipment.'

a Fourth, as to the charterparty. The plaintiffs hired the Albacruz from the defendants under a time charterparty on the 'Shelltime B' form made in Paris on 9th May 1969. Clause 2 imposed on the defendants obligations of due diligence with regard to the seaworthiness of the vessel at delivery and the maintenance of seaworthiness during service. It is on the alleged failure of the defendants to comply with these obligations that the plaintiffs' case on breach of charterparty is based. Clause 3 provided that the ship would be at the service of the charterers for a period of five *b* years from the date of delivery for the carriage of all lawful merchandise in any part of the world subject to certain limits. Clauses 7 and 8 provided that the charterers should pay hire for the use of the ship monthly in advance, subject to certain deductions, at the rate of US \$2·25 per ton on the ship's total deadweight. Clause 13 provided that the master should be under the orders and directions of the plaintiffs as regards employment of the vessel, agency and other arrangements, and that bills of lading *c* should be signed as the plaintiffs or their agents might direct without prejudice to the charter. Clause 39 provided that all bills of lading issued under the charterparty should contain a paramount clause incorporating the Hague Rules as enacted in the Carriage of Goods by Sea Act 1924 or similar legislation. Clause 40 provided that English law should govern.

d Fifth, as to the arrangements for the shipment of the cargo. The cargo which was lost constituted one of the consecutive shipments of oil supplied or caused to be supplied firstly by Esso to the plaintiffs under the purchase contract, and secondly by the plaintiffs to RBP under the sale contract. It was the plaintiffs' duty under the purchase contract to nominate the ship into which the oil was to be loaded, and under the sale contract to supply the ship in which it was to be carried to Antwerp. The nomination and provision of the Albacruz for these purposes were dealt with *e* on behalf of the plaintiffs by Courtage in Paris. Courtage was in communication about these matters during November and December 1969, mainly by telex, with both Esso (either direct or through Occidental in New York) and RBP. After various preliminary exchanges the matter was finalised in this way. First, by a telex dated 22nd December 1969, as varied by a further telex dated about 29th December 1969. Courtage notified Esso through Occidental that the Albacruz would arrive at La Salina *f* on 2nd January 1970 to load about 20,000 tons of Bachaquero crude. Secondly, by telex dated 24th December 1969, as modified by further telexes dated 26th and 30th December 1969, Courtage notified RBP that the Albacruz would arrive at Antwerp at the latest on the 16th to 17th January 1970 with about 19,000 tons of Bachaquero crude.

g These final notifications followed on orders given by Courtage on behalf of the plaintiffs as charterers to the master of the Albacruz, by telegram dated 29th December, to load a full cargo of Bachaquero crude at La Salina for discharge at Antwerp.

Esso did not themselves supply the cargo for the Albacruz but caused it to be supplied (as the purchase contract entitled them to do) by a Venezuelan company operating at La Salina, Creole Petroleum Corporation (whom I shall call 'Creole'). *h* Creole were also, by a letter from Courtage dated 23rd December 1969, appointed as charterers' agents for the Albacruz at La Salina.

The Albacruz arrived at La Salina on 2nd January 1970, and Creole there shipped on board her, as one of the shipments due under the purchase contract, a full cargo of 19,013 long tons (net) or 19,317 metric tons of Bachaquero crude. Loading was completed on 3rd January 1970.

j A bill of lading was issued and signed by the master in respect of the cargo. It was on an Esso printed form and dated 3rd January 1970. It contained the following particulars: shippers, Creole Petroleum Corpn; ship, Albacruz; loading port, La Salina; cargo, 19,317 metric tons of Bachaquero heavy crude oil; port of delivery, Gibraltar for orders; consignees, Concord Petroleum Corpn.

Later on 3rd January 1970, the Albacruz sailed from La Salina bound, in accordance

with Courtage's orders to the master, for Antwerp. Telegrams reporting the loading
of the cargo and the sailing of the ship were sent on the same day by Creole to Esso
and by the master to Courtage. Subsequently, on 5th January 1970, Courtage sent
a further telex to RBP stating that the Albacruz was expected to arrive at Antwerp
with 19,013 long tons of Bachaquero crude on 17th January 1970.

Sixth, as to the sale and shipping documents. So far as the purchase contract is
concerned, Esso sent to the plaintiffs an invoice dated 8th January 1970 for
US $159,986·93, the fob price of the cargo, and this was paid by the plaintiffs by
transfer through the Chase Manhattan Bank in London on 3rd April 1970.

So far as shipping documents under the sale contract are concerned, Creole airmailed to Courtage, under cover of a letter dated 6th January 1970, a large number of
documents relating to the shipment of the cargo, including in particular two original
bills of lading and two non-negotiable copies of them. These were received by
Courtage on 12th January 1970. Courtage then endorsed the two original bills of
lading generally, and posted them, under cover of a letter dated 13th January, to
RBP. On 14th January the Albacruz sank with her cargo, and on 15th January
Courtage's letter, with the endorsed bills of lading enclosed, was received by RBP
in Antwerp. Payment for the cargo against invoice was later made by RBP to the
plaintiffs, but it will be convenient to deal with this under a later heading.

Seventh, as to the insurance of the cargo. The evidence with regard to this was
incomplete. It appears, however, that there was in existence an open ocean cargo
policy issued in London which covered, for the benefit of companies in the Occidental
group, including RBP, whatever cargoes might be declared under it from time to
time, and that insurance of the cargo here concerned was effected by a declaration
made by Courtage under that policy.

Eighth, as to the claim on cargo underwriters. Following the loss of the cargo
discussions took place between Courtage and RBP with regard to claiming on underwriters. In order to facilitate such claim two fresh documents, not in existence at
the time of the loss, were brought into being. These were, first, a written contract
of sale between the plaintiffs and RBP relating specifically to this particular cargo, and,
secondly, an invoice from the plaintiffs to RBP in respect of it.

The first document, the contract of sale, was dated retrospectively 7th November
1969. While relating to only one shipment of 20,000 long tons plus or minus ten per
cent at buyer's option, it contained many terms the same as or similar to those of the
sale contract for 1969 dated 23rd December 1968. There was, however, a difference
in the terms as to price and payment. The cif price was stated simply as US $15·50
per metric ton, and payment was required to be made not 180 days but only 30 days
after date of invoice.

The second document, the invoice, was dated, again retrospectively, 3rd January
1970. It described the goods as 19,317 metric tons of Bachaquero crude oil at US $15·50
per metric ton c i f Antwerp, and stated the total price as US $299,413·50. Under
the heading 'terms' appeared the words 'no later than February 2nd, 1970'.

One at least of the purposes of bringing these fresh documents into being after the
loss, and of backdating them in the way which I have described, becomes apparent
from a confidential letter from Courtage to RBP dated 20th January 1970. It was to
provide sale documents in support of a claim on underwriters which would not
disclose the 180 days credit facilities accorded by the plaintiffs to RBP under the sale
contract for 1969 dated 23rd December 1968, but would instead show an obligation
on RBP to pay the price of the goods by 2nd February 1970. It seems to have been
thought by Courtage that, unless this was done, underwriters might delay settlement
of the claim until the expiry of the 180 day credit period. RBP accepted these new
documents as effective between the plaintiffs and themselves and paid the amount of
the invoice to the plaintiffs by two transfers to the Chase Manhattan Bank in London
made on 6th and 10th February 1970 respectively.

Following these transfers Courtage, as agents for RBP, notified the claim for loss of a cargo by a letter to brokers dated 16th February 1970, and this claim was later settled by cargo underwriters.

These being the primary facts, I shall examine first the question whether, assuming against the plaintiffs that the property and risk in the cargo, and the right to possession of it, had passed to RBP before the loss occurred, the plaintiffs are nevertheless entitled to recover substantial damages from the defendants for such loss. On this

b I was referred to a large number of authorities going back many years, in which the question of title to sue a carrier for loss of or damage to goods arose. Most of these were cases relating to land carriers or to carriers by sea before the passing of the Bills of Lading Act 1855.

The earlier cases fall, as it seems to me, into three categories. The first category of cases comprise those in which it was held that the consignee rather than the consignor was the proper person to sue. The ground of decision in those cases was that

c the consignor, in delivering the goods to the carrier, was acting as agent for the consignee and that the property and risk in the goods were either in the consignee before such delivery or passed to him on its taking place. Examples of such cases are: *Dawes v Peck*[1] and *Brown v Hodgson*[2] (actions on the case), and *Fragano v Long*[3] and *Tronson v Dent*[4] (actions in assumpsit).

d The second category of cases comprise those in which it was held that the consignor rather than the consignee was the proper person to sue. The ground of decision in those cases was that the consignor, in delivering the goods to the carrier, was acting as principal on his own account, and that the property and risk in them remained in him during the carriage. Examples of such cases are: *Swain v Shepherd*[5] and *Coats v Chaplin*[6] (actions on the case), and *Sargent v Morris*[7] (an action in assumpsit).

e The third category of cases comprise those in which it was held that the consignor was entitled to sue, whether the property and the risk in the goods was in him at any material time or not. The ground of decision in those cases was that the consignor had made a 'special contract' with the carrier, and that, because of this, the carrier could not dispute the consignor's title to sue. Examples of such cases are: *Davis and Jordan v James*[8], *Moore v Wilson*[9], *Joseph v Knox*[10], *Dunlop v Lambert*[11] and *Mead v South Eastern Railway Co*[12].

f It is to be observed generally, with regard to all three categories of cases, that, while the distinction between substantial and nominal damages is not raised in terms (it could not have been in the actions on the case and does not seem to have been in the actions in assumpsit), nevertheless what is being discussed and decided in all the cases is the right to sue for, and to recover, substantial damages.

g It is on the third category of cases that the plaintiffs rely in support of their contentions on the question now under consideration, and I shall therefore examine those cases in detail in order to establish, so far as I can, the principle of law on which they are founded.

Davis and Jordan v James[8] is a decision of the Court of King's Bench in an action in assumpsit against a common carrier for non-delivery. The plaintiffs were cloth manufacturers of Shipton-Mallet, and their declaration stated that they, being

h

---

1   (1799) 8 Term Rep 330
2   (1809) 2 Camp 36
3   (1825) 4 B & C 219, [1824-34] All ER Rep 171
4   (1853) 8 Moo PCC 419
5   (1832) 1 Mood & R 223
j 6   (1842) 3 QB 483
7   (1820) 3 B & Ald 277
8   (1770) 5 Burr 2680
9   (1787) 1 Term Rep 659
10   (1813) 3 Camp 320
11   (1839) 6 Cl & Fin 600
12   (1870) 18 WR 735

possessed of cloth which belonged to them, delivered it to the defendant and asked
him to deliver it, safely and securely, for them, to one Elizabeth Bowman at the Three
Nuns at Whitechapel, which he undertook to do, for a reasonable price payable
and paid by the plaintiffs to the defendant, but the goods were lost and never
delivered. The defendant pleaded not guilty but the plaintiffs got the verdict. The
defendant then moved for a new trial, objecting that the action should have been
brought in the name of the consignee and not that of the consignor, because the
property in the goods had passed from the consignor to the consignee on their
delivery by the consignor to the carrier. The plaintiffs argued that the question of
title to sue did not turn on the strict property in the goods. The carrier had nothing
to do with the vesting of the property, and it did not lie in his mouth to say that the
consignor was not the owner. He was the owner, with respect to the carrier, who
had undertaken to him, and was paid by him. Lord Mansfield, with whom Willes
and Ashhurst JJ, agreed, said[1]:

> 'There was neither law nor conscience in the objection. The vesting of the
> property may differ according to the circumstances of cases: but it does not enter
> into the present question. This is an action upon the agreement between the
> plaintiffs and the carrier. The plaintiffs were to pay him. Therefore the action
> is properly brought by the persons who agreed with him and were to pay him.'

Moore v Wilson[2] is a decision of the same court in an action in assumpsit against
a common carrier for failing safely to carry and deliver goods sent by the plaintiffs.
The declaration stated that the defendant undertook to carry the goods for a certain
hire and reward to be paid by the plaintiffs. The evidence showed that the consignee
had agreed with the plaintiffs to pay for the carriage, and it was then contended for
the defendant that the declaration had not been proved. Buller J, before whom the
action came at the Guildhall, non-suited the plaintiffs. Later, however, after the
plaintiffs had obtained a rule to show cause why the non-suit should not be set aside,
and *Davis and Jordan v James*[3] had been cited to him, Buller J reversed his previous
opinion, saying[4]:

> '... on considering the question he found he had been mistaken in point of
> law; for that, whatever might be the contract between the vendor and the
> vendee, the agreement for the carriage was between the carrier and the vendor,
> the latter of whom was by law liable.'

The other two judges agreed with Buller J and the non-suit was set aside.
Joseph v Knox[5] was a decision of the same court in an action in assumpsit against
a shipowner for failure to carry goods. The plaintiffs had shipped goods on board
the defendant's ship in London for carriage to Surinam. The plaintiffs had received
the goods as agents from principals in Amsterdam to be forwarded to one Davids
in Surinam, and the shipment was made under a bill of lading signed by the master
and providing for delivery of the goods in Surinam to Davids or his assigns. The
bill of lading freight was paid by the plaintiffs. It was contended for the defendant
that the plaintiffs could not maintain the action, because the goods were the property
of Davids and the plaintiffs had no interest in them. Lord Ellenborough rejected this
contention, saying[6]:

> 'I am of opinion that this action well lies. There is a privity of contract estab-
> lished between these parties by means of the bill of lading. That states that the

1   (1770) 5 Burr at 2680, 2681
2   (1787) 1 Term Rep 659
3   5 Burr 2680
4   1 Term Rep at 659, 660
5   (1813) 3 Camp 320
6   3 Camp at 321, 322

a   goods were shipped by the plaintiffs, and that the freight for them was paid by
the plaintiffs in London. To the plaintiffs, therefore, from whom the consideration
moves, and to whom the promise is made, the defendant is liable for the non-
delivery of the goods. After such a bill of lading has been signed by his agent,
he cannot say to the shippers they have no interest in the goods, and are not
damnified by his breach of contract. I think the plaintiffs are entitled to recover
the value of the goods, and they will hold the sum recovered as trustees for

b   the real owner.'

Dunlop v Lambert[1] was an appeal to the House of Lords from the Court of Session
in Scotland. The appellants, who were the pursuers in the Court of Session, were
wine and spirit merchants in Edinburgh. The respondents, who were the defenders
in the Court of Session and most of whom resided in Newcastle, were the owners of
c   the Ardincaple, a steamer carrying passengers and goods between Leith and Newcastle. On 31st August 1833 the appellants shipped on board the Ardincaple at Leith
a puncheon of whisky addressed to one Robson at an address in Houston-le-Spring
care of one Lattimer in Newcastle. A bill of lading was issued by the respondents'
agents in Leith, dated the day of shipment and stating the goods to be deliverable
to Robson or his assigns, freight being paid by the appellants. On the same day
d   the appellants sent a letter to Robson advising him of the shipment, and enclosed
with it the bill of lading and an invoice for the goods. The letter further stated that
they had drawn on him by bill for three months, payable in London. The appellants'
charges, which made up part of the sum for which the bill was drawn, included
10s for freight to Newcastle and 8s for insurance. In fact, however, the appellants
had no instructions or authority to insure the goods and did not do so.

e   During the passage from Leith to Newcastle the ship ran into very severe weather,
and, after nine of those on board had been washed overboard and lost, the remainder jettisoned part of the cargo, including the puncheon of whisky, in order to
save the ship and themselves. This they succeeded in doing and the ship reached
harbour at Shields on 2nd September.

The ship having failed to deliver the puncheon of whisky, the appellants began
f   an action against the respondents in the Court of Session to recover its value. At the
trial the Lord President directed the jury that, as it appeared that the appellants,
at the time of supplying the puncheon of whisky, had sent an invoice to Robson,
the buyer, in which the latter had been charged for the freight and insurance, the
appellants were not entitled in law to recover the value of the goods from the
respondents. The jury, acting on this direction, while finding for the appellants
g   on other issues, found against them on the issue of title to sue, on the ground that they
were not, at the time of the loss, the owners of the goods, their right in them having
ceased on shipment.

The appellants took an exception to the direction referred to, and their bill of
exceptions was later heard by the First Division of the Court of Session, which by a
majority disallowed it. The appellants then took an appeal to the House of Lords,
h   which succeeded.

Lord Cottenham LC, after stating that there was no difference between the law
of Scotland and the law of England on the subject, and referring to the English
authorities, including Davis and Jordan v James[2], Moore v Wilson[3] and Joseph v Knox[4],
said[5]:

j   'These authorities, therefore, establish in my mind the propositions which are
necessary to be adopted, in order, to overrule this direction of the Lord President.

1   (1839) 6 Cl & Fin 600
2   (1770) 5 Burr 2680
3   (1787) 1 Term Rep 659
4   (1813) 3 Camp 320
5   6 Cl & Fin at 626, 627

I am of opinion, that although, generally speaking, where there is a delivery to a carrier to deliver to a consignee, he is the proper person to bring the action against the carrier should the goods be lost; yet that if the consignor make a special contract with the carrier, and the carrier agreed to take the goods from him, and to deliver them to any particular person at any particular place, the special contract supersedes the necessity of showing the ownership in the goods; and that, by the authority of the cases of *Davis* v. *James*[1] and *Joseph* v. *Knox*[2], the consignor, the person making the contract with the carrier, may maintain the action, though the goods may be the goods of the consignee.'

Lord Cottenham LC went on to hold[3] that the direction of the Lord President to the jury was wrong on two grounds. The first ground, which is not relevant to the matter immediately under discussion, was that the Lord President had not left to the jury the question whether the risk in the goods had in fact passed from the appellants to Robson. The second ground, which is directly relevant, was that the Lord President had not left to the jury the further question whether there was a special contract between the consignor and the consignee, which might have enabled the appellants to recover in the action.

Mead v South Eastern Railway Co[4] is a decision of the Court of Common Pleas in an action against railway carriers for damage to goods. The plaintiff, a miller at Bromley, in Kent, bought from one Buckmaster, another miller at Framlingham, in Suffolk, 16 sacks of flour. The contract was oral and the price was over £10. The contract was based on the previous course of dealing between the parties. Under this Buckmaster would select the flour from the bulk in his possession, consign it to the plaintiff in Bromley, and send it by the Great Eastern Railway from Framlingham to the Brick Lane goods station in London, paying for the carriage up to that point. The Great Eastern Railway would then forward the flour to the Bricklayers Arms goods station in London of the South Eastern Railway, which would on-carry the goods to Bromley, the carriage from London to Bromley being paid for by the plaintiff. This practice was followed in the particular case, but, owing to the South Eastern Railway loading the flour into wagons previously used for carrying tar, the flour arrived in tainted condition.

At the trial the jury found for the plaintiff on the facts. The defendants moved for a non-suit, and on their behalf it was argued that, since the contract of sale did not satisfy s 17 of the Statute of Frauds 1677, the property in the flour had not passed from Buckmaster to the plaintiff under it, but had remained in Buckmaster; and that, in those circumstances, the plaintiff could not sue the defendants for the loss. This argument was rejected. Bovill CJ said[5]:

'If the case depended on whether the property in the flour had passed to the consignee, a rule ought to be granted to have that point discussed. But the point does not arise; for here, under the circumstances, there was a contract for carriage between the plaintiff and the South Eastern Railway Company.'

Then, after referring to the course of dealing between the parties, he continued[5]:

'There was therefore evidence for the jury of a special contract between the plaintiff and the defendants for the carriage of the goods, and on that ground the verdict must be sustained.'

Keating, Smith and Brett JJ agreed. Brett J said that it was unnecessary to go into the question whether the property had passed or not, because there was evidence of

1 (1770) 5 Burr 2680
2 (1813) 3 Camp 320
3 (1839) 6 Cl & Fin at 627
4 (1870) 18 WR 735
5 18 WR at 735

a   a contract between the plaintiff and the defendants for the carriage of the goods on
    the defendants' line. He went on[1]:

    'If so, it is not open to the defendants to say they have not contracted with the
    plaintiff to carry for him.'

    I have so far referred only to authorities dating from 1770 to 1870, and it remains
    to consider what more modern authorities there are which bear on the subject.
b   The passing of the Bills of Lading Act 1855 obviously made it much less likely for
    disputes about title to sue to arise in relation to carriage by sea, and this no doubt
    accounts, in part at least, for the paucity of later authorities. Three more recent
    cases were, however, cited to me, and it is necessary that I should examine them
    also. They are *Hayn, Roman & Co v Culliford*[2], *Steamship Den of Airlie Co Ltd v Mitsui
    and Co Ltd*[3], and *Gardano and Giampari v Greek Petroleum George Mamidakis & Co*[4].
c   *Hayn, Roman & Co v Culliford*[2] is a decision of the Court of Appeal in an action
    against shipowners for negligent damage to goods, The plaintiffs had shipped on
    board the defendants' ship at Hamburg 280 bags of sugar for carriage to London.
    The ship was operating under a voyage charter and the charterers, having put her
    up as a general ship at Hamburg, had signed as agents a bill of lading which con-
    tained an exception for negligent navigation but no exception for negligent stowage.
d   The sugar was negligently stowed and arrived damaged in consequence. There
    was no evidence to show with whom the plaintiffs had made the contract of carriage.
    It was held that the plaintiffs were entitled to recover for the damage to the sugar,
    either in contract under the bill of lading, if the contract of carriage was made with
    the defendants, or in tort for negligence if it was not. The judgment of the court
    was given by Bramwell LJ and the actual decision is not in point. At the end of the
e   judgment, however, Bramwell LJ observed[5]:

    'It is certain that if the charterers sued on the charter in respect of the com-
    plaint in this action there would be no defence, and it is certain that they ought
    to sue if necessary for the benefit of the plaintiffs.'

f   *Steamship Den of Airlie v Mitsui*[6] is a decision of Bray J and the Court of Appeal
    on an application made by plaintiff shipowners against defendant charterers for
    an injunction restraining the charterers from proceeding with an arbitration or
    alternatively for leave to the shipowners to revoke their submission to arbitration.
    The plaintiffs had chartered the ship, the Den of Mains, from the first defendants to
    carry a cargo of beans from Vladivostok to the United Kingdom under a charterparty
    containing a London arbitration clause. In April 1911 the first defendants sold 6,000
g   tons of beans to the second defendants and in June 1911 these were shipped on board
    the Den of Mains at Vladivostok for carriage to Liverpool under two bills of lading
    signed by the master and providing for delivery to the first defendants or their assigns.
    Subsequently the first defendants declared to the second defendants that the beans
    had been shipped by the Den of Mains. On the arrival of the ship at Liverpool the
    first defendants transferred the bill of lading after endorsement to the second defen-
h   dants against payment for the goods. On completion of discharge there was alleged
    to be a shortage of 171 bags, The second defendants paid only on the basis of the
    quantity delivered and the first defendants, in view of this, instructed the second de-
    fendants to deduct from the freight a sum of £103 1s 6d, the value of the bags not
    delivered, and this was done.

j
    1   (1870) 18 WR at 735
    2   (1879) 4 CPD 182
    3   (1912) 106 LT 451
    4   [1961] 3 All ER 919, [1962] 1 WLR 40
    5   4 CPD at 185, 186
    6   (1912) 106 LT 451, CA; (1911) 105 LT 823

The plaintiffs disputed the short delivery and the first defendants claimed arbitration under the charterparty and gave notice of appointment of their arbitrator. *a* The plaintiffs did not appoint their own arbitrator and the first defendants then appointed their arbitrator as sole arbitrator. Shortly afterwards the plaintiffs began an action in the Commercial Court[1] claiming the balance of freight and other relief relating to the arbitration, and in that action made the application for an injunction or for leave to revoke their submission to which I referred earlier.

On the hearing of the application before Bray J[1] three points were argued for *b* the plaintiffs. The third of these was that the plaintiffs' obligation to deliver the beans under the charterparty had ceased. In relation to this point, which he described as the main point, Bray J said[2]:

> 'Nor can I see any sufficient reason why the shipowner should ask that his liability should cease. He cannot in any event be liable for more than the value *c* of the goods short delivered. If the charterer has parted with his interest in all the goods shipped, he can only recover, at most, nominal damages. If, as here, he has not parted with his interest in any goods that do not arrive, the holder of the bill of lading can at most recover nominal damages. I doubt if he would have any cause of action.'

Bray J decided all three points against the plaintiffs and dismissed the application. *d* The Court of Appeal[3] upheld his decision but did so without dealing with the third point which, unlike Bray J, they thought it was unnecessary to decide at that stage.

Gardano & Giampari v Greek Petroleum George Mamidakis & Co[4] is a decision of McNair J in the Commercial Court on a case stated in an arbitration in which charterers claimed against shipowners for damage to cargo. The claimants had voyage chartered *e* the respondents' ship to carry kerosene from Constanza to Piraeus under a charterparty which contained a London arbitration clause. In March 1958 Russian exporters, as agents for the claimants, shipped on board the ship at Constanza a full cargo of kerosene for carriage to Piraeus, and a bill of lading was issued in which the Russian exporters were named as shippers and the Greek government, to which the claimants had agreed to sell the kerosene, was named as consignee. On discharge at Piraeus *f* there were allegations of shortage and contamination of the cargo, and the claimants accordingly withheld part of the charterparty freight against their claim for such shortage and contamination. The dispute went to arbitration and in the arbitration the respondents contended that the claimants had no right of suit under the charterparty on the ground that, pursuant to the contract of sale, the property in the cargo had passed from the claimants to the Greek government on or by reason of the consignment by the bill of lading, and that accordingly, under s 1 of the Bills of *g* Lading Act 1855, all rights of suit in respect of the cargo had been vested solely not the Greek government.

McNair J, after examining the terms of the contract of sale between the claimants and the Greek government, was not satisfied that the property in the goods had passed to the Greek government on or by reason of the consignment made by the *h* bill of lading, and said that, on this ground alone, he would decide the case against the respondents. He went on, however, to consider the alternative argument put forward by counsel for the claimants that, even if the property had passed, the charterers were still entitled to recover. As to this he said[5]:

> 'I think that it is quite clear on the facts that, although this bill of lading was taken out in the name of the Soviet authorities as shippers, they were shipping *j*

---

1 (1911) 105 LT 823
2 105 LT at 825
3 (1912) 106 LT 451
4 [1961] 3 All ER 919, [1962] 1 WLR 40
5 [1961] 3 All ER at 925, [1962] 1 WLR at 53

a   as agents for the charterers in the performance of their sale contract, and the property must have passed from the Soviet authorities to the charterers. It seems to me, on the authority of the cases to which I was referred by counsel for the charterers, namely *Davis* v. *James*[1], *Joseph* v. *Knox*[2], and *Dunlop* v. *Lambert*[3], that the charterer, on the assumption that he is the original party to the bill of lading, is entitled to sue for substantial damages whether or not

b   the property and the risk remained in him.'

I do not think that there can be any doubt that the earlier cases dated from 1770 to 1870 which I have examined establish a principle of law under which a consignor can, in certain circumstances, sue for and recover substantial damages from a carrier for loss of or damage to goods, whether the property or the risk in the goods was at the material time in him or not. The difficulty is to ascertain precisely what is the

c   basis of the principle, and what are the precise circumstances which are necessary in order to bring it into operation.

As regards the basis of the principle, I think it is clear that it is based on an estoppel, which has the effect, as between the consignor and the carrier, of precluding the carrier from disputing that the consignor has a sufficient interest in the goods to maintain an action for substantial damages for loss of or damage to them. That this is so appears,

d   in my view, from the authorities which I have examined, and in particular from the passages which I have quoted from the judgments of Lord Mansfield in *Davis and Jordan v James*[4] (when read with the argument of counsel for the plaintiffs), Lord Ellenborough in *Joseph v Knox*[5] and Brett J in *Mead v South Eastern Railway Co*[6], and from the speech of Lord Cottenham LC in *Dunlop v Lambert*[7].

As regards the circumstances which are necessary in order to bring the principle

e   into operation, it is clear that the essential circumstance is the existence of a contract, described in the authorities as a 'special contract', between the consignor as principal and the carrier for the carriage of the goods. The expression 'special contract', as used in the authorities, does not appear to have meant a contract with special or unusual terms in it. It appears rather to have been used to distinguish the ordinary type of situation, where goods were delivered to a common carrier without anything

f   being agreed as to the identity of the person for whom they were being carried and who would pay for the carriage, and the special type of situation, where there was an agreement that the goods were being carried for the consignor and that the cost of the carriage would be paid for by him.

It is this agreement between the parties, that the goods are being carried for the consignor and that he is to pay for the carriage which is, as I understand the authorities,

g   the essence of the matter. It is from that agreement that the estoppel to which I have referred arises, and the foundation of the estoppel is, I think, this, that a carrier who agrees to carry goods for a person as if that person had an interest in them, and who accepts payment or the promise of payment by that person for the carriage on that footing, cannot afterwards be heard to say, when he is sued for loss of or damage to the goods, that that person in fact had no interest in them.

h   It was argued strongly for the defendants that, if the suggested principle of law existed, it would conflict with the general and wider rule that a party to a contract, who has suffered no loss by breach of it, can only recover nominal damages for such breach. This consideration it was said, tended to show that the suggested principle of law did not exist.

j   1 (1770) 5 Burr 2680
     2 (1813) 3 Camp 320
     3 (1839) 6 Cl & Fin 600
     4 5 Burr at 2680, 2681
     5 3 Camp at 321, 322
     6 (1870) 18 WR at 735
     7 6 Cl & Fin at 626, 627

I cannot accept this argument. It seems to me that the suggested principle, when properly viewed, involves no departure from the general and wider rule relied on by *a* the defendants. This is because the principle depends, as I have said, on an estoppel, which has the effect of preventing the carrier from denying that the goods were the consignor's goods, and that he has therefore suffered loss by reason of loss of or damage to them.

It is no doubt true that the result of the estoppel may be that a person who has no interest in goods can recover for loss of or damage to them as if he had. All estoppels, *b* however, by their nature involve, potentially at least, a notional view of the facts instead of a real view, and because of this, when they operate, disputes may have to be decided by applying the law to the notional facts rather than the real facts. The justification for such estoppels, and the consequences which flow from them, is that it is more just, as between the parties concerned in the particular circumstances of the case, to decide the dispute on the basis of the notional facts than it would be *c* to decide it on the basis of the real facts.

It was further argued for the defendants that, if a person was entitled to recover, in circumstances like those under discussion, for a loss which he had not in fact suffered, he could make a profit out of it, because there was no further principle of law which required him to hold the amount recovered as trustee for the person who had suffered the loss. I do not accept this argument either, for I think that, in a situation *d* of that kind, a constructive trust in favour of the second person would arise. This appears from the passage in the judgment of Lord Ellenborough in *Joseph v Knox*[1] quoted earlier.

On the footing that I have correctly stated the principle of law established by the earlier cases, it remains to consider whether it applies to the claim of the plaintiffs in the present case. This depends on whether there was a 'special contract' between *e* the plaintiffs and the defendants within the meaning of that expression as I have defined it: in other words, whether there was a contract under which the defendants agreed to carry the cargo for the plaintiffs and to look to the plaintiffs for the payment of the carriage.

It was common ground that the charterparty was the only contract between the parties. This is on the basis that Creole took the bill of lading as agents for the *f* plaintiffs, and that the document was therefore, as between the plaintiffs and the defendants, no more than a receipt for the goods. The earlier authorities, from which I have derived the principle of law under discussion, do not include any case of goods carried under a charterparty, and are not therefore of direct assistance on the question whether the principle is applicable to such a case. The three later cases to which I referred, however, are all charterparty cases, and I shall consider *g* shortly what guidance can be got from them.

I have already set out earlier the main terms of the charterparty. By cl 3 the ship was put at the service of the plaintiffs to carry lawful merchandise, including oil, during the period of the charterparty. By cll 7 and 8 the plaintiffs were to pay hire for the use of the ship monthly in advance. By cl 13 the master was to be under the directions of the plaintiffs as regards the employment of the ship, and bills of lading *h* were to be signed for the defendants as the plaintiffs might direct without prejudice to the charter. It was pursuant to their rights under cll 3 and 13 that the plaintiffs on this occasion ordered the master to load at La Salina the cargo of Bachaquero crude which was subsequently lost, and that Creole as their agents asked for and were given a bill of lading naming them as shippers and providing for delivery of the cargo to the plaintiffs. It was further the obligation of the plaintiffs under *i* cll 7 and 8 to pay, by way of monthly hire in advance, for the use of the ship for the carriage of this cargo.

In these circumstances, looking at the matter unaided by any authority on charterparty cases, I should have thought it clear that there was here a 'special contract'

[1] (1813) 3 Camp at 321, 322

a for the carriage of the cargo within the meaning of the principle under discussion; that is to say, a contract under which the defendants agreed to carry the cargo as the plaintiffs' cargo and to be paid for the carriage by them. The defendants had a contractual obligation to carry the cargo, and, by issuing at Creole's request a bill of lading in the form in which they did, which named Creole (for this purpose agents of the plaintiffs) as shippers and the plaintiffs as consignees, they acknowledged that b they were to carry the cargo as the plaintiffs' cargo. Further the carriage was to be paid for by the plaintiffs by way of hire.

It was argued for the defendants that it was not legitimate to combine the contract contained in the charterparty and the receipt contained in the bill of lading together in this way, and to spell out of the two documents when so combined a 'special contract' for the purposes of the rule. I do not, however, see the objection to this. c The object is to ascertain the terms and basis on which the goods were carried by the plaintiffs, and to achieve this it seems to me not only right but necessary to look both at the underlying contract, the charterparty, and at the receipt given for this particular cargo shipped pursuant to it, the bill of lading.

This view, which I should form unaided by direct authority on charterparty cases, is supported by *Gardano & Giampari v Greek Petroleum George Mamidakis & Co*[1]. d In this connection it is to be observed that McNair J did not say that the charterers were entitled to sue for substantial damages merely because the cargo was carried in the ship under the charterparty. He added the further requirement that they should have been the original party to the bill of lading. That requirement was satisfied in the case which he had before him, and it is also satisfied in the present case.

e *Hayn, Roman & Co v Culliford*[2] goes further, for it suggests that charterers can sue for substantial damages in respect of any cargo carried in a ship chartered by them, whether they were the shippers under the relevant bill of lading or not. It does not decide the point, however, and I think, with respect, that the observations of Bramwell LJ[3] in that case may in this respect go too far.

Finally, there is *Steamship Den of Airlie v Mitsui*[4]. The defendants relied on the f judgment of Bray J[5] as showing that, where a charterer-shipper has parted with his interest in the goods shipped, he can only recover nominal damages for loss of the goods by the breach of charterparty of the shipowners. While the opinion of Bray J on the matter is entitled to respect, it is to be noted that, in the way in which the case was ultimately decided by the Court of Appeal, the point in relation to which the opinion was expressed ceased to be a relevant one. It is further to be observed that Bray J does not appear to have been referred to, or to have had present to his mind, the g line of earlier authorities which I have examined in this case. In these circumstances, if and in so far as the judgment of Bray J is inconsistent with the conclusions which I have reached on the basis of those earlier authorities and of the *Gardano* case[1], I do not feel able to follow it.

For the reasons which I have given I decide the first question in favour of the plain- h tiffs. I hold that the plaintiffs are entitled to sue for and recover substantial damages for loss of the cargo by the defendants' breach of charterparty, even on the assumption that they no longer had any interest (whether property, risk or right to possession) in the cargo at the time of the loss.

If I am right in the conclusion which I have reached in the first question, it is not necessary for me to decide the other questions raised, namely whether the plaintiffs j still had the property in, or the right to possession of, the cargo at the time of the loss,

---

1   [1961] 3 All ER 919, [1962] 1 WLR 40
2   (1879) 4 CPD 182
3   4 CPD at 185, 186
4   (1912) 106 LT 451
5   (1911) 105 LT 823

and are entitled to sue for and recover substantial damages on one or other or both   *a*
those grounds also.   Since, however, I may be wrong in that conclusion, and as I
have had the benefit of full argument by counsel on these other matters, I think
it right that I should go on and deal with them.

I consider first the question of the passing of the property.   This depends on the
application of the Sale of Goods Act 1893 to the facts of the case.   The relevant
provisions are in ss 16-19, and, in relation to the contract here concerned, which is a   *b*
contract for the sale of unascertained or future goods by description, I can summarise
the effect of those provisions in this way.   First, the property cannot pass until the
goods are ascertained (s 16).   Second, the property passes when the parties intend it
to pass, and their intention is to be ascertained from the terms of the contract, the
conduct of the parties, and the circumstances of the case (s 17, which has been held to
apply equally to contracts for the sale of unascertained goods).   Third, unless a   *c*
contrary intention appears, where goods of the contractual description in a deliverable
condition are delivered to a carrier for transmission to the buyer, then, unless the
seller reserves the right of disposal, he is deemed to have appropriated the goods
unconditionally to the contract and the property passes to the buyer (s 18, r 5(1) and
(2)).   Fourth, where goods are appropriated to the contract, the seller may, by the
terms of the appropriation, reserve the right of disposal until certain conditions are   *d*
fulfilled, and, if he does so, the property in the goods does not pass to the buyer until
such fulfilment occurs (s 19(1)).   Fifth, where the goods are shipped and the seller
takes a bill of lading by which the goods are deliverable to his order, there is a presumption, which is rebuttable, that he has reserved the right of disposal (s 19 (2)).

Applying these provisions to the present case the crucial question is whether the
plaintiffs reserved the right of disposal of the goods, and, if so, until the fulfilment   *e*
of what condition.

In approaching this question counsel for the plaintiffs laid great stress on the fact
that the contract of sale was a cif contract, and that, under many contracts of this
kind, the property does not pass until the shipping documents are taken up and
paid for by the buyers.   In this connection he relied strongly on the decision of the
House of Lords in *Ross T Smyth & Co Ltd v Bailey Son & Co*[1].

In that case Lord Wright analysed what might be called the ordinary or typical   *f*
cif contract.   As appears from what he said, the essential characteristic of such a
contract is that the seller reserves the right of disposal of the goods for at least one,
and often two, commercial purposes.   The first purpose is to secure the payment of
the price of the goods by the buyer.   The second purpose, which often also applies,
is to enable the seller to raise money by a pledge of the shipping documents so as to
bridge the time between shipment and payment.   The seller achieves these purposes   *g*
by taking a bill of lading by which the goods are deliverable to him or his order, and
so arranging matters that the shipping documents, including the bill of lading, are
only transferred to the buyer against payment of the price of the goods in cash or by
the acceptance of a bill of exchange drawn on him.   When this procedure is followed,
it is well settled that there is no unconditional appropriation of the goods, and no   *h*
passing of the property in them, unless and until the shipping documents are taken up
and paid for by the buyer.

This is not, however, by any means always the situation under a c i f contract, for
there are also cases of such contracts where the right of disposal is not reserved and
the property accordingly passes on shipment.   That this is so appears from the
speech of Lord Porter in *Comptoir D'Achat et de Vente du Boerenbond Belge SA v Luis*   *.*
de Ridder Limitada[2].   The earlier case of *Ross T Smyth v Bailey*[1] had been cited in   *j*
argument and Lord Porter must have been well aware of that decision.   Nevertheless
he said[3]:

---

1   [1940] 3 All ER 60
2   [1949] 1 All ER 269, [1949] AC 293
3   [1949] 1 All ER at 274, [1949] AC at 309

a

'... the obligations imposed on a seller under a c.i.f. contract are well known, and in the ordinary case include the tender of a bill of lading covering the goods contracted to be sold and no others, coupled with an insurance policy in the normal form and accompanied by an invoice which shows the price ... Against tender of these documents the purchaser must pay the price. In such a case the property may pass either on shipment or on tender, the risk generally passes on shipment ... but possession does not pass until the documents which represent the goods are handed over in exchange for the price.'

b

It is true that Lord Simonds, at the end of his speech[1] in the same case, said that the salient characteristic of a c i f contract was that the property in the goods not only may but must pass by delivery of the documents against which payment is made. I think, however, that, in the context of the facts of the case before him, he meant only that

c the property must at least pass then if it has not passed at some earlier time.

I do not find it particularly helpful to approach the present case by reference to what has been decided with regard to the passing of property under an ordinary or typical cif contract of the kind discussed in *Ross T Smyth v Bailey*[2]. The reason why I do not find that approach particularly helpful is that the sale contract in this case, though certainly described, and I think rightly described, as a c i f contract, is not a cif

d contract of the same kind. The essential difference is that, because the plaintiffs and RBP are associated companies, both being wholly owned and controlled subsidiaries of Occidental, it was not necessary for the plaintiffs to reserve the right of disposal in order to secure payment of the price of the goods by RBP. On the contrary the oil was expressly sold on credit terms under which payment was not due until 180 days from date of invoice. I say this on the basis, agreed by counsel on both sides as correct,

e that the shipment should be treated as a belated shipment under the sale contract for 1969. But, even if the retrospective contract made after the loss is regarded, the sale was still on credit terms, the time for payment being 30 days from date of invoice instead of 180 days.

Not only was it not necessary for the plaintiffs to reserve the right of disposal in order to secure payment, but it also seems clear from the circumstances of the case

f that there was never any desire or intention on the part of the plaintiffs to be able to raise money by a pledge of the shipping documents. Indeed there were no shipping documents in the ordinary sense, the bill of lading being forwarded by Courtage to RBP without any accompanying policy or certificate of insurance, and without any invoice, which it seems it was intended should be sent later.

There remain, however, two important facts with regard to the form of the bill

g of lading. The first fact is that Creole (as agents for the plaintiffs) are named as shippers and the plaintiffs as consignees. It was therefore a bill of lading by which the goods were deliverable to the order of the seller. The second fact is that the port of delivery is given not as Antwerp, but as Gibraltar for orders. Such a bill of lading did not, as it seems to me, comply with the sale contract. This is because by cl A7 of the Incoterms 1953, which were incorporated into the sale contract, and the material parts of which

h I set out earlier, the seller had to furnish the buyer with a bill of lading for the agreed port of destination, which was Antwerp. Nevertheless that was the form in which the bill of lading was taken.

The purchase contract, under the heading 'Vessel Nomination' in Part II, required the plaintiffs to give instructions to Esso regarding the make-up of bills of lading, subject to their being acceptable to Esso. It seems right therefore to infer that the

j form of the bill of lading taken by Creole in this case was the result of instructions given by the plaintiffs. The question is what was the purpose of these instructions, and in particular whether it was to reserve the right of disposal of the goods until some, and if so what, condition was fulfilled.

---

1   [1949] 1 All ER at 279, [1949] AC at 317
2   [1940] 3 All ER 60

The only evidence bearing on these matters was that given by the plaintiffs' witness, Mr De Korver. He was the shipping co-ordinator of Courtage in Paris at the material *a* time, and was responsible for the co-ordination of the marketing, supply and transportation of oil for various companies in the Occidental group, including the plaintiffs and RBP. As regards the bill of lading naming the plaintiffs as consignees he said, in effect, that it was and had been for a number of years standard practice for bills of lading relating to shipments by the plaintiffs to RBP to be taken in this form. As *b* regards the description of the port of delivery as Gibraltar for orders he said that this was done for flexibility, so that, if it became necessary to change the port of discharge, the ship could be diverted without the necessity of new shipping documents being issued. Asked further about this in the witness-box he said that Courtage wished to have the possibility of diverting a cargo to another customer at another port of discharge in certain circumstances, for instance if there was a shutdown or change of refining requirements at RBP's Antwerp refinery, but that they would only do this at *c* the request of RBP themselves.

Since by the bill of lading the goods were deliverable to the order of the plaintiffs there is, as already indicated, a presumption, under s 19(2) of the 1893 Act, that the plaintiffs reserved the right of disposal. That presumption, however, is rebuttable, and the question is whether there is material in this case sufficient to rebut it.

For the reasons which I have given I think that there is ample material to rebut *d* any presumption that the plaintiffs reserved the right of disposal in order to secure payment, or in order to be able to raise money on the shipping documents. There is material, however, which tends to suggest that they had another purpose for reserving the right of disposal, namely the preservation, for reasons of commercial flexibility, of the ability to divert the cargo to another customer at another port of discharge without the need for the issue of fresh shipping documents. This material consists of *e* the description of the port of discharge in the bill of lading as Gibraltar for orders, and the reasons given by Mr De Korver in his written and oral evidence for the use of such description.

Bearing in mind the presumption, and the material to which I have just referred, the inference which I draw is that the plaintiffs reserved the right of disposal until all possibility of diversion of the cargo to another customer at another port had dis- *f* appeared, and that it was the intention of the parties that the property in the cargo should not pass until that situation had arisen. While there is no evidence that diversion of the cargo was ever contemplated in this case, it seems to me that all possibility of it disappeared when Courtage, having endorsed the bill of lading, posted it to RBP on 13th January 1970. I therefore hold that the property was intended by the parties to pass, and did pass, at that time. *g*

If I am wrong about that, then I think that the alternative view is that the plaintiffs did not reserve the right of disposal at all, in which case, under s 18, r 5(1) and (2), the property passed on shipment. I certainly cannot see any material for inferring, as counsel for the plaintiffs invited me to do, that the property was not intended to pass until RBP received the bill of lading in Antwerp.

Both on the first view of the matter, which I prefer, and on the alternative view, *h* which I would fall back on if the first view were held to be wrong, the property in the cargo passed to RBP before the loss. It follows that I decide the second question, namely whether the plaintiffs still had the property in the cargo at the time of its loss, and are entitled to sue for and recover substantial damages on that ground, against the plaintiffs.

I consider finally the question of the right to possession. There are two points here. *i* The first point is whether the right to possession of the cargo, if it was still in the plaintiffs at the time of loss, would be sufficient of itself to enable them to sue for and recover substantial damages. The second point is whether, on the facts, the right to possession was still in them at the time of the loss.

As regards the first point, it seems to be accepted that a right to possession of goods *a* is sufficient to found an action for damages in negligence: *Margarine Union GmbH v Cambay Prince Steamship Co Ltd*[1]. That being so, I see no reason why it should not also be sufficient to enable a person to sue for and recover substantial damages in contract. No authority for any distinction between the two situations was cited to me, and I can see no logical ground for making any such distinction.

b As regards the second point, it is not in doubt that the endorsement and delivery of a bill of lading transfers the right to possession of the goods to which it relates: *Sewell v Burdick*[2]. It is equally not in doubt, on the facts of the present case, that the bill of lading relating to the cargo was, after endorsement, delivered by Courtage, as agents for the plaintiffs, to RBP. The question to be determined, however, is whether the transfer of the right to possession from the plaintiffs to RBP took place when the endorsed bill of lading was posted in Paris on 13th January, the day before the loss, or

c when it reached RBP in Antwerp on 15th January, the day after the loss.

For the plaintiffs it was argued that, under an ordinary cif contract, the obligation of the seller is to tender the shipping documents to the buyer at his place of business or residence: *Johnson v Taylor Bros & Co Ltd*[3]. The bill of lading in the present case should, therefore, it was said, be regarded as not having been delivered until it reached RBP in Antwerp in the ordinary course of the post and was accepted by them there.

d For the defendants it was argued that delivery of the bill of lading was effected when it was posted by Courtage to RBP in Paris, and reliance was placed on *Badische Anilin und Soda Fabrik v Basle Chemical Works, Bindschedler*[4]. In that case, which concerned a claim for infringement of patent, it was held by the House of Lords that, where an English trader ordered goods from a Swiss manufacturer to be sent by post, the delivery of the goods took place when the goods were handed to the Post Office in Switzerland, the Post Office being the agent of the buyer and not the seller.

e I do not find either argument wholly convincing. As regards the argument for the plaintiffs, it seems to me that, once again, too much stress is being laid on the incidents of the ordinary cif contract, and too little regard bring paid to the special features of the contract here concerned. It seems to me clear that, under the ordinary cif contract, where the shipping documents, including the bill of lading, are only delivered to the

f buyer against payment, and where tender of the documents has to be made at the place of business or residence of the buyer, that the delivery of the bill of lading, and the consequent transfer of the right to possession of the goods, will take place at the time when and the place where the documents are tendered and taken up. In that case, however, it would be unusual for the shipping documents to be posted direct to the buyer. They would normally be sent either to the seller's agent for presentation to the buyer, or delivered to a banker against a confirmed credit, leaving the banker to

g forward them to his agent at the place of payment for collection of the price.

Under the contract here concerned, however, the bill of lading was not to be delivered to the buyer only against payment. On the contrary it was to be delivered irrespective of payment, which was not required until 180 days (or, if the retrospective contract is regarded, 30 days) after the date of invoice. It is, therefore, in the light of that circumstance that the question, when and where delivery of the bill of lading

h took place, has to be considered.

As regards the argument for the defendants, I do not regard the *Badische Anilin und Soda Fabrik* case[4] as affording more than limited guidance because of the wide difference in subject-matter between it and the present case. I recognise, however, that it can be argued with some force that, if the handing of the goods by the seller to the

j post pursuant to a contract of sale constitutes delivery of the goods to the buyer, then equally the handing to the post of a bill of lading which represents goods, should constitute a delivery of the bill of lading.

1 [1967] 3 All ER 775, [1969] 1 QB 219
2 (1884) 10 App Cas 74, [1881-85] All ER Rep 223
3 [1920] AC 144
4 [1898] AC 200

The question must in the end, I think, be solved by a consideration of the terms of, and the conduct of the parties under, this particular sale contract. By cl A7 of the a Incoterms 1953, to which I have already referred earlier, it was the obligation of the plaintiffs to furnish the bill of lading to the buyer without delay. It was further the evidence of Mr De Korver that it was the practice of the plaintiffs, in order to speed up the transmission of the bills of lading, to have the shipping documents sent direct by Creole to Courtage, and to authorise Courtage to endorse two of the original bills of lading and forward them to RBP. b

I fully accept the proposition that, under the ordinary cif contract, where the delivery of the shipping documents is to be made only against payment, it is an implied term of the contract, in the absence of any express term relating to the matter, that the documents should be tendered at the place of business or residence of the buyer. I do not see, however, that there is any need to imply such a term in a contract like the present one, where the delivery of the bill of lading was entirely independent of c payment. On the contrary I should have thought that, if it were necessary to imply any term on the subject at all, it would be a term that the bill of lading should be forwarded by any usual and commercially recognised method, including sending by post.

I have already held, on the question of the passing of the property, that the property in the cargo passed when the endorsed bill of lading was posted by Courtage in Paris. d It would, I think, be illogical and inconsistent to hold that, although the property itself passed then, the right to possession of the cargo only passed when the bill of lading reached RBP in Antwerp. The bill of lading having been committed to the post in an envelope addressed to RBP, and neither the plaintiffs nor Courtage as their agents having or intending to have thereafter any control or possibility of control over it, I think that it would be artificial and unrealistic to hold that the plaintiffs still e retained possession of the bill of lading and with it the right to the possession of the cargo.

For the reasons which I have given, I have reached the conclusion that the right to possession of the cargo, like the property in it, had passed from the plaintiffs to RBP before the loss. It follows that, in my view, while the right to possession would in principle entitle the plaintiffs to sue for substantial damages, they cannot rely on that f ground of entitlement in this case.

I have now, I think, decided all the questions raised before me. I have decided the first question in the plaintiffs' favour and the second and third questions in the defendants' favour. The plaintiffs, however, only needed to succeed on one question, and the result is therefore that there must be a judgment for them on the preliminary issue in this case. I will hear counsel on the form which that judgment should take, g and on costs.

Declaration that, on the assumption that the loss of the cargo was caused by the defendants' breach of the charterparty, the plaintiffs are entitled to recover substantial damages for the loss.

h

Solicitors: *Clyde & Co* (for the plaintiffs); *Ince & Co* (for the defendants).

N P Metcalfe Esq Barrister.

a
Banbury Borough Council v Oxfordshire and District Water Board

COURT OF APPEAL, CIVIL DIVISION
EDMUND DAVIES, STEPHENSON LJJ AND SIR GORDON WILLMER
b   6th, 7th MARCH, 8th MAY 1974

Water supply – Duty of statutory water undertakers – Duty to provide domestic supply to new buildings – Duty on request by owner of land on which buildings to be erected – Power of undertakers to require owner to make contribution to cost of laying the necessary mains – Necessary mains – Meaning – Request by landowner for supply of water to serve new dwell-
c *ings – Construction of trunk main necessary to bring water to dwellings – Right of undertakers to require landowner to make contribution to cost of laying trunk main – Whether 'necessary mains' including trunk main – Water Act 1945, s 37(1) (as amended by the Housing Act 1949, s 46).*

A local authority proposed to erect a number of houses on land which they owned
d   in Banbury and, pursuant to s 37(1)[a] of the Water Act 1945, as amended, requested the statutory water undertakers for the area ('the board') to supply water to the proposed dwellings. The board, in purported exercise of their power under proviso (a) to s 37(1) to require a landowner in such circumstances to pay a contribution in respect of 'laying the necessary mains', required the local authority to make a financial contribution to the cost of construction of a 27 inch diameter trunk main to Banbury
e   from a point 20 miles away. The construction of that main was necessary to bring sufficient water to, inter alia, the local authority's proposed buildings. The local authority disputed the board's right to make that demand on them, contending that the phrase 'necessary mains' in s 37(1) did not include a trunk main.

Held (Sir Gordon Willmer dissenting) – The board were entitled to require the
f   local authority to make a contribution towards the cost of the 27 inch trunk main for (i) on the true construction of s 37(1) a trunk main was capable of being a necessary main within the meaning of that subsection and (ii) the particular trunk main to be constructed at Banbury came within the words 'necessary mains' in s 37(1) (see p 934 f and p 937 d, post).
Decision of Mocatta J [1973] 3 All ER 257 reversed.
g

Notes
For the duty of statutory water undertakers to provide domestic supply of water for new buildings, see 39 Halsbury's Laws (3rd Edn) 402, 403, para 618.
For the Water Act 1945, s 37, see 39 Halsbury's Statutes (3rd Edn) 108. Section 37 has been further amended by the Water Act 1973, s 11(7), and Sch 8, para 53(4),
h   as from 1st April 1974.

Cases referred to in judgments
River Wear Comrs v Adamson (1877) 2 App Cas 743, [1874-80] All ER Rep 1, 47 LJQB 193, 37 LT 543, 42 JP 244, 3 Asp MLC 521, HL, 44 Digest (Repl) 198, *109.*
St Aubyn (LM) v Attorney-General (No 2) [1951] 2 All ER 473, [1952] AC 15, 30 ATC 193,
j   HL, 21 Digest (Repl) 49, *199.*

Case also cited
Matthews v Strachan [1901] 2 KB 540, DC.

---

a   Section 37(1), as amended, is set out at p 930 j and p 931 a to d, post

Appeal

By an originating summons dated 21st December 1971, as amended pursuant to an order of Master Lubbock dated 16th October 1972, the plaintiffs, Banbury Borough Council, sought the determination of the court on the following question, namely, whether on a request by the plaintiffs that supplies of water be provided by the defendants, Oxfordshire and District Water Board, to serve certain houses to be erected by the plaintiffs at Penrose Close off Penrose Drive and at Rustcote within the borough of Banbury, the defendants could lawfully demand the payment by the plaintiffs of financial contributions towards the cost of constructing a 27 inch diameter trunk main between the outskirts of Woodstock and Banbury. On 11th May 1973 Mocatta J[1] held that the defendants had no power under s 37(1) of the Water Act 1945, as amended, to require the plaintiffs to make the contribution and made a declaration accordingly. The defendants appealed. The facts are set out in the judgment of Edmund Davies LJ.

Michael Mann QC and *H D Donovan* for the defendants.
G E Moriarty for the plaintiffs.

Cur adv vult

8th May. The following judgments were read.

EDMUND DAVIES LJ. This is a defendants' appeal from the judgment of Mocatta J[1], who made a declaration in favour of the plaintiffs in proceedings which they instituted by way of originating summons. The question thereby raised related to the construction of s 37(1) of the Water Act 1945.

In 1971 the plaintiffs were minded to erect, pursuant to their power under the Housing Acts 1957 to 1969, a number of houses on land which they owned within their borough. At Penrose Close they planned to erect four bungalows, 12 flats and warden's accommodation, and at Rustcote 16 bungalows. The defendants are the statutory body empowered by the Water Acts 1945 and 1948 to supply water to the area known as Oxfordshire and District, which includes the borough of Banbury. In June 1971 the plaintiffs enquired of them regarding the supply of water to their two proposed development sites, as this would involve the laying of the mains necessary for that purpose. In July the defendants stated that the estimated cost of laying the mains required to serve the Penrose Drive development was £1,434, made up as to £1,060 in respect of a main from the development to the existing mains network in the borough, and £374 in respect of a contribution towards a 27 inch diameter trunk main between Woodstock and Banbury; they also informed the plaintiffs that the corresponding estimated cost in respect of the Rustcote development was £1,227, made up by the sums of £875 and £352. No dispute arises as to the defendants' entitlement to demand the sums of £1,060 and £875. By the originating summons, however, a declaration was sought whether the defendants could lawfully demand the sums of £374 and £352, but it is agreed that Mocatta J was misled thereby and that the dispute relates to sums of £46·75 and £44·00 only, being one-eighth of the sums indicated by the defendants. The items involved thus total a mere £90·75, but it is common ground that the issue raised is of considerable importance to water authorities generally.

Whether the plaintiffs were entitled to a declaration that the defendants could not lawfully demand payment of either of these two sums depends on the construction of s 37(1), which, as amended, provides:

> 'Where an owner of land proposes to erect thereon buildings for which a supply of water for domestic purposes will be needed, he may require any statutory water undertakers within whose limits of supply that land is situated to construct

---

1 [1973] 3 All ER 257, [1973] 1 WLR 984

a any necessary service reservoirs, to lay the necessary mains to such point or points
as will enable the buildings to be connected thereto at a reasonable cost and to
bring water to that point or those points, and thereupon the undertakers shall,
subject as hereinafter provided, comply with that requisition: Provided that the
undertakers before complying with a requisition under this subsection—(a) may
require the owner to undertake to pay in respect of each year a sum amounting to
one-eighth of the expense of providing and constructing the necessary service
b reservoirs and providing and laying the necessary mains (less any amounts
received by the undertakers in respect of water supplied, whether for domestic
or non-domestic purposes, in that year from those mains) until the aggregate
amount of water rates payable annually in respect of the buildings when erected
and in respect of any other premises connected with the said mains at the rates for
the time being charged by the undertakers equals or exceeds such sum as afore-
c said or until the expiration of a period of twelve years, whichever first occurs; and
(b) except where the owner is a local or public authority, may also require him to
deposit with the undertakers as security for payments of the said annual sums,
such sum, not exceeding the total expense of constructing the service reservoirs
and providing and laying the mains, as the undertakers may require.'

d Certainly not later than February 1970 the defendants had planned to construct a
27 inch diameter trunk main from the outskirts of Woodstock to an existing service
reservoir at Banbury, the distance being 20 miles and the cost £940,000, and by the
time the matter came before Mocatta J[1] the construction works were already under
way. This was because, although the Banbury service reservoir and its general pipe
distribution system are adequate, provided the corporation has sufficient water to
e distribute, the Cherwell, from which it at present draws its water, is an insufficient
source to meet growing demands in the borough. The supply had to be sufficient to
cope with the sort of drought conditions which may statistically be expected to occur
once in every 50 years, due regard being paid not only to the needs of existing developments but also to the needs of such other developments as may be expected to occur
between the present time and the year 2001. It is important to note that, as Mocatta J
f said[2]:

'It was agreed that construction of the trunk main was necessary in order, with
water from the Cherwell, to bring sufficient water to Banbury to maintain at all
times a proper supply of domestic water to Banbury users existing in 1971 and also
to the plaintiffs' two proposed developments. However the size of the trunk main
g under construction is such that it will be capable of conveying to Banbury additional quantities of water far in excess of the needs of 1971 users supplemented by
the plaintiffs' proposed developments: in other words it will be able to cater for
greatly increased demands for water in the borough. It was also agreed that the
figures of £374 and £352 relate solely to the cost of constructing the trunk main,
and include no element in respect of finding a source of water, or winning or
h pumping it.'

We were told that at the present time water is in fact being supplied to the two
developments, but this cannot be ensured for the future until the 27 inch trunk
main is completed.

The question for decision is whether a trunk main can as a matter of law be a
j 'necessary main' within the meaning of s 37(1), for if it cannot the defendants may not
require an undertaking from the plaintiffs to pay the £90·75. The plaintiffs submit
that their liability is limited to the sums of £1,060 and £875, since these represent the

---

1 [1973] 3 All ER 257, [1973] 1 WLR 984
2 [1973] 3 All ER at 258, 259, [1973] 1 WLR at 985, 986

cost of the only 'necessary main' required to be laid to connect up their two develop- *a*
ments to the existing mains network, and that no part of the cost of such construction
works as are required in order that water may be brought to that network can be
recovered from them.

The Waterworks Clauses Acts 1847 and 1863 were repealed by the 1945 Act, which
substituted therefor its lengthy Sch 3 which can be incorporated in orders relating to
water undertakers. Section 3 of the Oxfordshire and District Water Board Order 1966[1] *b*
provides (with certain exceptions irrelevant to this appeal) that Sch 3 'shall apply to the
undertaking of the board and is hereby incorporated with this order . . .' Section 1 of
the schedule contains a long list of definitions, of which the following are material:

> '. . ."main" means a pipe laid by the undertakers for the purpose of giving a
> *general* supply of water as distinct from a supply to *individual* consumers . . . [the
> emphasis is mine] "trunk main" means a *main* constructed for the purpose of *c*
> conveying water from a source of supply to a filter or reservoir, or from one filter
> or reservoir to another filter or reservoir, or for the purpose of conveying water in
> bulk from one part of the limits of supply to another part of those limits, or for
> the purpose of giving or taking a supply of water in bulk'.

It may here be parenthetically noted (a) that the Woodstock/Banbury trunk main *d*
would appear to fall certainly within the first of these four categories—and maybe
within others; and (b) that, for the sake of convenience, counsel before us and below
divided the genus 'main' into two species only, namely (1) 'trunk main' and (2)
'distributing main'.

> ' "service pipe" means so much of any pipe for supplying water from a main to
> any premises as is subject to water pressure from that main, or would be so *e*
> subject but for the closing of some tap'.

Neither the Act nor the schedule defines 'necessary main'. Mocatta J[2] upheld the plaintiffs' contention that, while a 'main' could be either a 'trunk main' or a 'distributing
main', dependent on the context in which the word 'main' is used, a 'trunk main' can
never be a 'necessary main' for the purpose of s 37. *f*

It was submitted that, in construing the provision in s 37(1) that a developer may, in
circumstances such as the present, require the undertaker 'to lay the necessary mains
to such point or points as will enable the buildings to be connected *thereto* . . .',
regard should be had to the evolution of the present form of that subsection. Originally it enabled the developer to require the undertaker 'to lay any necessary mains
and bring water thereto', that is, to the buildings proposed to be erected and for *g*
which a water supply for domestic purposes would be needed. Section 14(4) of the
Water Act 1948[3] provided that s 37 of the principal Act—

> 'shall have effect as if references therein to the laying or providing of mains
> included references to the construction of service reservoirs'.

Finally, s 46(2) of the Housing Act 1949 substituted for the words 'to lay any necessary *h*
mains and so bring water thereto' the words—

> 'to construct any necessary service reservoirs, to lay the necessary mains to such
> a point or points as will enable the buildings to be connected thereto at a reason-
> able cost and to bring water to that point or those points.'

Mocatta J attached importance to these last words, saying[4]: *j*

1   SI 1966 No 1163
2   [1973] 3 All ER 257, [1973] 1 WLR 984
3   Repealed by the Housing Act 1949, s 51, Sch 3, Part II
4   [1973] 3 All ER at 261, [1973] 1 WLR at 989

a   '. . . the phrase "to construct any necessary service reservoirs" is placed before
       the new and greatly extended phrase about the mains. I agree with counsel for
       the plaintiffs that this positioning suggests that the draftsman was not, so far as
       dealing with the cost of the requisition was concerned, considering construction
       work further up stream from the consumer than a service reservoir. This argu-
       ment is in my opinion greatly strengthened by the newly introduced words "to
b   lay the necessary mains to such a point or points as will enable the buildings to be
       connected thereto at a reasonable cost and to bring water to that point or those
       points".'

       But counsel for the defendants will have none of this. He makes the following points:
       (a) Mocatta J himself observed[1] that the 1945 Act itself placed no limitation on the
       phrase 'necessary mains'; (b) neither did the 1948 Act, which merely provided that if a
c   service reservoir was necessary for the purpose of supplying the new development it
       was to be provided and its cost included when calculating the amount of the developer's
       undertaking; being thus a simple addition, it ought not to be invoked so as to limit the
       meaning of 'the necessary mains' to which it was being added; (c) the sole purpose of
       the 1949 Act was to remove ambiguity as to where the necessary mains had to go to,
       by providing that they had to be laid to such point 'as will enable the buildings to be
d   connected thereto at a reasonable cost . . .', sub-s (3) providing that any dispute as to
       where this point should, in default of agreement, be determined by the Minister
       of Health. In other words, the terminus having been left undefined by the earlier
       statutes, all the 1945 Act did was to indicate where the place was, while leaving the
       point of commencement untouched; it effected no conversion of the genus 'main' to
       some specific form thereof, and the point of commencement of a 'necessary main' is
e   therefore as far back as is necessary to afford to the developer the supply which he
       requires.
            On the other hand, counsel for the plaintiffs submits that s 37, as amended, makes it
       perfectly clear that the phrase 'necessary mains' excludes a trunk main and includes
       merely distributing mains. Although, apparently contrary to their agreement below,
       counsel now agree that a trunk main is physically 'tappable', counsel for the plaintiffs
f   continues to regard as significant and relevant the fact that the proviso to s 30(1) of
       Sch 3 prevents a developer from demanding a supply of water 'from a trunk main', and
       the further fact that, although the developer may require the undertaker 'to bring
       water to' the necessary point or points, the proviso to s 37(1) enacts that the expense
       incurred thereby is not recoverable in any proportion from the developer.
            It is clear that the undertaking dealt with by the proviso cannot exceed a proportion-
g   ate part of such works as the developer may lawfully require the undertaker to carry
       out for the purpose of ensuring 'a supply of water for domestic purposes . . . needed'
       by the proposed buildings. Then can a developer ever require an undertaker to lay a
       trunk main? It is unsatisfactory to answer merely that, if such were the intention, the
       subsection would have said so. It could, I think, be argued with more force that, as a
       trunk main undoubtedly falls within the Sch 3 definition of a 'main', whenever the
h   statute was intended to exclude trunk mains this would have been made clear.
       Equally unsatisfactory, to my way of thinking, is the stress laid by counsel for the
       plaintiffs on the fact that the reference in s 37(1) to the laying of 'the necessary mains'
       is immediately preceded by a reference to the construction of 'any necessary service
       reservoirs'. This leads him to submit that the undertaking required of a developer
       cannot relate to the cost of any works further back than a service reservoir, and even to
j   make the unqualified submission that 'if there is no service reservoir, there can be no
       trunk main'. As a general proposition this is, with respect, unacceptable. We know
       that in the present case there already exists a service reservoir, but the fourfold
       definition of 'trunk main' makes clear the untenable nature of the proposition. Then

       _____

       1   [1973] 3 All ER at 261, [1973] 1 WLR at 989

in a case where no service reservoir exists, how far back may one go for the purpose of   a
determining what works are relevant in calculating the undertaking which may be
exacted from the developer? One answer which may be suggested is that one should
not go beyond the point where the distributing mains leading to the point where the
development can be connected thereto are themselves connected to the undertaker's
bulk supply. But, as counsel for the defendants pointed out, a new developer might
require water to be brought in bulk and any main constructed for this purpose would   b
be within the Sch 3 definition of a 'trunk main'. For my part, I am also impressed by
his reference to s 29 of Sch 3 which (in supplementation of s 36 of the Act) deals with the
duty of undertakers on certain conditions to lay any necessary mains and bring water
for domestic purposes to *existing* buildings. Counsel for the defendants submits (and,
to my mind, convincingly) that the phrase 'necessary mains' for the purpose of s 29
must include all species of mains and embraces both trunk and distributing mains,   c
and I did not understand counsel for the plaintiffs to challenge that submission. The definitions of 'main' and 'trunk main' in s 1 of the schedule make clear that the latter is but
a species of the former, and, elsewhere in the schedule, where a 'main' is not intended
to include a 'trunk main', this is specifically provided: see, for example, s 32, with its
reference to 'mains (other than trunk mains)'. It therefore appears to follow that the
reference in s 36(2) of the Act to 'the necessary mains' may also include a trunk main,   d
and, that being so, it seems indefensible to give the phrase a different meaning when
construing s 37(1). In this context it is noteworthy that, although Mocatta J[1] held that
the exact meaning of 'mains' must depend on the context, ss 36 and 37 belong to the
same fasciculus of 'Miscellaneous' provisions in Part IV of the Act. In relation to
both situations counsel for the defendants submits that the underlying 'philosophy' is
that those requiring water should not be entitled to impose on existing consumers   e
(and at no cost to themselves) the burden of laying any 'necessary mains', and
that for the purposes of s 37, as for s 29, one needs to look at the necessity for the main
and not at its species.

For my part, I prefer the submission of counsel for the defendants, and I would
answer in the affirmative the question submitted to this court, namely: can a 'trunk
main' as a matter of law be a 'necessary main' within the meaning of s 37(1) of the   f
1945 Act? Counsel intimated to us that if the proper answer to that question is 'Yes',
as I think it is, no further question arises either whether the Woodstock/Banbury
trunk main is in fact a necessary main or whether the proportion of the cost attributable to the plaintiffs' development is correct. I would therefore be for allowing the
appeal and making the consequent declaration.

STEPHENSON LJ. Proviso (a) to s 37(1) of the Water Act 1945 provides for an   g
owner of land on which he proposes to erect buildings undertaking to pay in respect of
each year one-eighth of the expense of providing and constructing the necessary mains
to such point or points as will enable the buildings to be connected thereto at a reasonable cost (less any amounts received by the undertakers in respect of water supplied
from those mains).   h

The real question we are asked to decide is not: is this particular main in course of
being laid from Woodstock to Banbury a necessary main within the subsection for
these particular buildings which the council proposes to erect? but, is any trunk main
capable of being a necessary main within the subsection for any buildings which any
landowner may propose to erect? For, as counsel have informed us, our answer to the
latter question determines our answer to the former and decides this appeal.   j

At first sight, the material words of sub-s (1) seem to have no application to a main
already laid, or to a reservoir already constructed, whether or not applicable to a main
partly laid or a service reservoir in course of construction. But it was not argued that

---

1   [1973] 3 All ER at 260, [1973] 1 WLR at 988

a they applied only to mains to be laid, or service reservoirs to be constructed. No reliance was placed on the additional word 'providing' which now occurs in both provisos (a) and (b) in every place where mains and service reservoirs are mentioned, except where service reservoirs are mentioned at the end of proviso (b). The omission there may indicate that the addition elsewhere is insignificant—as insignificant as the apparently haphazard transposition of 'providing' and 'laying' in proviso (b) as originally drawn in the 1945 Act. What was argued was that if undertakers could
b charge a landowner for new works only, they would be reduced to laying expensive new mains instead of making use of existing mains, and such an uneconomical proliferation of small mains could not be intended by the statute. We have therefore to read the owner's requirement from the undertakers as a requisition to lay the necessary mains if and insofar as they are not already laid, and to construct any necessary service reservoirs if and insofar as they are not already constructed; and to read the under-
c takers' requirement from the owner as an undertaking to contribute to the expense of providing and laying such mains, and of providing and constructing such service reservoirs.

Another possible reading of the material words, which we are not, as I understand the arguments, asked to adopt, is that the necessary mains are those mains which are directly connected to the buildings; in other words, the last link in the chain of mains
d which is connected to the service pipes bringing water to the buildings. For this would exclude intermediate mains distributing water between a trunk main, or service reservoir, and the last main in the chain of distribution, even where an intermediate main and the last main could be connected to the service pipe or pipes at a reasonable cost. How then do we give the material words in their context a meaning which excludes this trunk main because it is a trunk main and for no other reason?
e A trunk main is in name and nature a main; in name because it is so described, in nature because it is defined in s 1(1) of Sch 3 to the 1945 Act as a main of four different species or sub-species. It is not defined in s 59 of the Act; but it is not suggested that its definition in the schedule differs from what any instructed person of intelligence would understand it to mean, or that the definitions of 'main' and 'trunk main' in the schedule can be ignored when interpreting s 37 of the Act. It is a species of main. It
f does not differ from other mains as a trunk from branches, or a sewer from drains, because it shares the same name. So when the Act refers to a main or mains it refers to all species of the genus, including trunk mains, unless they are excluded expressly by clear words or unless we are convinced, when we take the whole statute together, by some great inconsistency, absurdity or inconvenience, that the legislature could not have intended to use the relevant words in their ordinary signification: *River Wear*
g *Comrs v Adamson*[1]. If trunk mains were intended to be excluded they could have been, and I think would have been, by plain words as they were in s 32 of Sch 3 which requires undertakers to 'fix fire-hydrants on their mains (other than trunk mains)': compare s 35. But the judge has held that the context compels their exclusion because a trunk main cannot be a necessary main in the sense in which those words are used in s 37.
h It cannot be denied that a trunk main is a main or, I should have thought, that it may be a necessary main in the sense that it is necessary to use it to bring water from a source of supply on part of its way to its ultimate destination, the buildings, whether they are already erected (s 29 of Sch 3 and s 36 of the Act) or only proposed (s 37). But it is said that a trunk main is not the sort of main which undertakers are required to lay to such point or points as will enable the buildings to be connected
j thereto at a reasonable cost and to bring water to that point or points. The mains which are necessary for that purpose are distributing (or branch) mains only, and that is confirmed by the introduction of service reservoirs into the subsection, first by the Water Act 1948, s 14(4), and then by the Housing Act 1949, s 46(1) and (2), by the

---

1 (1877) 2 App Cas 743 at 764, 765, [1874-80] All ER Rep 1 at 12, per Lord Blackburn

additional words defining the points to which mains are to be laid and water brought *a*
which the same section of the 1949 Act introduces, by the difficulty of crediting amounts
received in respect of water supplied from trunk mains and by the unfairness of
saddling the building owner with the cost, albeit only a fraction of his share of it, of
providing and laying a trunk main it may be at great length and expense and many
miles away. I do not regard either that difficulty or that unfairness as great enough to
justify the judge's interpretation of Parliament's language.   *b*
The history of s 37 is prayed in aid by both sides, and it is a double-edged weapon, as
is counsel for the plaintiffs' argument from the contrast between amending s 37
of the Act and leaving s 29 of Sch 3 unamended. Counsel for the defendant is, I
think, right in contending that 'the necessary mains' in the unamended s 37 included a
trunk main; and I do not regard the two amendments—first, the introduction of
necessary service reservoirs, and then the addition of the point or points which will   *c*
enable the buildings to be connected to the mains, and to which the undertakers can
be required to bring water—as clearly cutting down 'the necessary mains' by cutting
out trunk mains. If Parliament intended to absolve owners from their liability to pay
for necessary trunk mains, I would have expected them to do so in express terms and
not by making them liable to pay for necessary service reservoirs.
Nor can I regard the additional words introduced by the second amendment as   *d*
having any such effect. I accept the argument that they define the terminus or termini
to which mains must be taken: compare the language of s 37(3). Undertakers cannot
stop their mains at such a distance from the buildings that the owner can only get his
water from the mains at an unreasonable cost. But the 1949 words do not help to
determine the point where the necessary mains are to begin, and consequently the
owner's financial contribution is to begin. That 'cut-out' point, as it was called, must   *e*
be derived from the language of the subsection in its ordinary meaning. If a trunk
main is necessary for the purpose of satisfying the owner's need, which is a supply of
water for his proposed buildings for domestic purposes, then it is one of the necessary
mains which the undertakers can be required to pay for, and the cut-out point cannot
be fixed where the branch (or the service reservoir) joins the trunk.
That disposes of this appeal, and it is not relevant that the trunk main was already   *f*
necessary for supplying others, or that some other means of supply might have been
provided instead of this trunk main for supplying the plaintiffs' need, or that though
'tappable' it could not be connected directly with the buildings which the plaintiffs'
proposed to erect because of the pressure involved, or that the owner could not
demand a supply of water from it because of the proviso to s 30(1) of Sch 3.
I would add three things. (1) Once the section is held to cover mains already laid in
whole or in part there is difficulty in imposing a restrictive view of what mains may be   *g*
necessary. On the one hand, it might appear ridiculous to suppose that an owner
could require the undertakers to lay a trunk main and monstrous that he should be
required to pay for a part of its cost. On the other hand, his share of its cost might be
surprisingly small (as in this case) and it would be unreasonable that the undertakers
should not be able to perform their duty to lay necessary mains for bringing water to   *h*
his buildings by taking account of existing and future developments and requirements,
by making use of existing mains and by charging a proportion of their cost. Perhaps
the words 'at a reasonable cost' provide a restriction on what is necessary and deserve
more attention than they have received in argument. As proviso (a) makes the cost of
connecting the buildings to the necessary mains a matter of interest to the owner as
well as to the undertakers, I would read those words as meaning at a cost which is
reasonable for both. So read they might exclude trunk mains so large or long or so   *j*
distant as to be unreasonably expensive for the owner. (2) What the owner wants,
and what the undertakers have to bring to his buildings, is water for domestic purposes. That may have to be pumped and filtered; but the fact that the owner cannot be
required under proviso (a) to contribute to the expense of such things as pumping and
filtering does not help me, with all respect to those who think differently, to determine

a the question whether he can be required thereunder to contribute to the expense of providing a trunk main. (3) An extensive building programme proposed by a developer might, I should have thought in the absence of evidence to the contrary, be so located as to be most cheaply supplied with domestic water by the construction of a new trunk main. That trunk main would then be a necessary main, however narrow the definition of necessity within s 37. That instance is enough to answer the question raised b by the plaintiffs' summons and appeal: a trunk main is, however rarely, capable of being a necessary main.

Applying Lord Wensleydale's golden rule, which Lord Blackburn quoted in the passage in his speech in *River Wear Comrs v Adamson*[1], to which reference has been made, I find nothing in the context of the section and the Act to indicate clearly that Parliament intended to exclude trunk mains from the necessary mains referred to in c s 37(1). If mains other than trunk mains was the aim of the legislature in enacting this section—and I am not convinced that it was—it was mains including trunk mains that it fairly and squarely hit: see *L M St Aubyn v Attorney-General (No 2)*[2].

For these reasons, as well as those given by Edmund Davies LJ, I differ with reluctance from the learned judge and from Sir Gordon Willmer, whose judgment I have had the advantage of reading, and I agree with Edmund Davies LJ in holding that on d the true construction of the subsection a trunk main is in law capable of being a necessary main, and that on the agreed facts this trunk main in fact was one. I would therefore allow the appeal and declare that the defendants can lawfully demand the two (reduced) sums as contributions in respect of the 27 inch trunk main.

SIR GORDON WILLMER. In this difficult case it is my misfortune to find myself e unable to agree with the conclusions at which Edmund Davies and Stephenson LJJ have arrived. For my part, I am by no means persuaded that the learned judge below came to the wrong conclusion.

In the first place, I cannot agree with counsel's formulation of the question for decision with which Edmund Davies and Stephenson LJJ have dealt. With all respect, the question is not whether a trunk main can as a matter of law be a 'necessary main' f within the meaning of s 37(1). The question as formulated in para 9 of the originating summons is—

'whether the Defendants can lawfully demand the said sums £374 and £352 [or rather, as now agreed, one-eighth thereof] as contributions in respect of the said 27-inch diameter trunk main, or at all'.

g In other words, the question actually to be decided is restricted to the particular trunk main relevant to this case. It may well be that the decision in this case will effectively, though indirectly, determine the wider question as formulated by Edmund Davies and Stephenson LJJ, namely, whether a trunk main can ever be a 'necessary main' within s 37(1). But I still think it is important to observe that this is not the question submitted to the court by the originating summons.

h We are all, I think, agreed that, however it is formulated, the question to be decided depends on the true construction, in its context, of s 37 of the Water Act 1945, as amended in 1948 and 1949. Furthermore, I accept that the code set out in Sch 3 to the Act (to which I shall refer hereafter as 'the code') must be treated as one with the rest of the Act, and that its provisions, where relevant, may be taken into consideration in construing s 37 of the Act. Section 1 of the code includes definitions of 'main' and 'trunk j main'. I will refer hereafter to the four types of 'trunk main' set out as coming within the definition thereof. For the moment it is sufficient to say that a 'trunk main' is undoubtedly a 'main'. But, in my judgment, it does not follow that whenever the Act

---

1   (1877) 2 App Cas at 764, 765, [1874-80] All ER Rep at 12
2   [1951] 2 All ER 473 at 485, [1952] AC 15 at 32 per, Lord Simonds

refers to a 'main' that word necessarily includes a 'trunk main'. In every case regard
must be had to the context in which the word 'main' is used.

I do not think it is particularly helpful to consider the past history of s 37, or the
form which it took at various times prior to its final amendment in 1949. It is to be
presumed that the amendment was introduced because Parliament considered that in
its previous form the section did not adequately give effect to what was intended.
The section should, therefore, be construed as it stands without regard to past history.

What an owner of land who proposes to erect buildings thereon may 'require' under
s 37(1) of the Act must be related to the need therein defined, that is, the need for
a supply of water for domestic purposes. To this end he may 'require' the relevant
water undertakers: (a) to construct any necessary service reservoirs; (b) to lay the
necessary mains to such point or points as will enable the buildings to be connected
thereto at a reasonable cost; and (c) to bring water to that point or those points. For
purposes of brevity I will refer hereafter to such a point as a 'delivery point'. The word
'thereto' may be thought ambiguous, in that it could grammatically refer to connecting the buildings either to the service reservoirs or to the mains themselves. But I do
not think it matters for the purposes of the present case which of the two alternatives
was intended.

The service reservoirs and the mains which the undertakers can be 'required' to
construct or lay must be 'necessary' to meet the need referred to above. The laying of
mains from a service reservoir to the delivery point is clearly necessary to meet that
need. But I can find no words in the subsection which enable the owner of the land to
require the laying of mains or any other constructional work beyond the service
reservoir, or (if there is no service reservoir) beyond the point where the mains
leading to the delivery point can themselves be connected to the undertakers' bulk
supply. On the contrary, the obligation of the undertakers to bring water to the
delivery point would appear to assume the pre-existence of a bulk supply of water. If
it were intended that the owner of the land could require the laying of a trunk main in
order to create such bulk supply, the subsection must surely have so provided in
terms.

What the owner of the land can be required to pay is governed by proviso (a) to
sub-s (1). It is to be a contribution towards: (a) the expense of providing and constructing the necessary service reservoirs; and (b) the expense of providing and laying
the necessary mains. Such service reservoirs and mains must clearly be the same reservoirs and mains as the owner of the land is entitled to 'require' under the earlier part
of the subsection. In other words, he must be prepared to pay his contribution towards
the cost of the work which he can 'require' the undertakers to carry out. But it is
noteworthy that the proviso does not entitle the undertakers to require a contribution in respect of bringing water to the delivery point. This again appears to assume
the pre-existence of a bulk supply of water. In any event, it must be clear that, if the
owner of the land is not entitled to 'require' the laying of a trunk main, equally the
undertakers cannot require him to contribute to its cost. It would appear that it is the
undertakers' responsibility, and theirs alone, to meet the expense of creating the bulk
supply of water, whether by laying a trunk main or otherwise.

I do not find it possible to attach the same degree of importance as Edmund Davies
and Stephenson LJJ have expressed to the agreement between counsel, recorded by
the learned judge, to the effect that construction of the trunk main was necessary in
order, with water from the Cherwell, to bring sufficient water to Banbury to maintain
at all times a proper supply of domestic water to Banbury users existing in 1971 and
also to the plaintiffs' two proposed developments. Of course it was necessary in one
sense, namely, in the sense that without it Banbury users (including the plaintiffs' two
proposed developments) would have been in danger of suffering at times from a
deficiency in bulk supply of water on which to draw for domestic purposes. But, with
respect, this goes no distance towards showing that the 'necessary mains' to enable the
buildings with which we are concerned to be connected to the delivery point must be

construed, within s 37(1) of the Act, as including, in the absence of express words to that effect, whatever trunk main may be necessary to ensure the bulk supply of water on which to draw.

Nor do I find that much assistance is to be derived by analogy from the provisions contained in s 29 of the code as modified by s 36 of the Act. These provisions relate to a wholly different problem, and deal with it in a different way. They relate to the terms on which water is to be supplied to already existing buildings, as opposed to new buildings which an owner of land proposes to erect. Under s 29 of the code the cost of the necessary works to supply already existing buildings is relevant only for the purpose of ascertaining whether the owners of the buildings qualify for the right to a supply of water for domestic purposes. In order to qualify, their aggregate annual water rates must amount to not less than one-eighth of the cost of the works. But the combined effect of s 29 of the code and s 36 of the Act is such that, if the water rates payable annually by the owners of the buildings fall below the specified proportion of the expenses of providing and laying the necessary mains, the local authority may make up the deficiency. The effect is that the owners of the buildings, if they qualify, with or without the assistance of the local authority, and if they pay their water rates, are not under any further liability, and can hardly be said to be contributing to the cost of laying the necessary mains as such.

The argument on behalf of the undertakers, as I understood it, was that, inasmuch as s 29 appears in the code, which itself defines 'main' and 'trunk main', the expression 'necessary mains' must be construed as including trunk mains unless there is a specific provision to the contrary. This strikes me as a non sequitur. However, the argument goes on to the effect that s 36 of the Act, in that it covers the same ground as s 29 of the code, must consequently be construed in the same sense as s 29. If so, it would be absurd to suppose that ss 36 and 37 of the Act, appearing in juxtaposition, are to be interpreted differently insofar as they deal with the cost incurred by the undertakers in carrying out the necessary works. I do not find this argument very helpful, much less convincing.

The definition of 'trunk main' contained in s 1 of the code includes four types of main, namely: (a) a main constructed for the purpose of carrying water from a source of supply to a filter or reservoir; or (b) from one filter or reservoir to another filter or reservoir; or (c) for the purpose of conveying water in bulk from one part of the limits of supply to another part of those limits; or (d) for the purpose of giving or taking a supply of water in bulk. I am quite unable to see how the laying of 'the necessary mains to such point or points as will enable the proposed buildings to be connected thereto', as envisaged by s 37(1) of the Act, can be fitted into any one of these four categories of trunk main. A contrary conclusion could lead to quite absurd results utterly repugnant to common sense. The owner of land desiring to erect a building a few yards away from where a trunk main is in course of being laid could be required to contribute not only to the expense of laying the necessary main to the point where his proposed building could be connected thereto, but also to the expense of laying the whole trunk main, whatever its size and however long it might be. Any ordinary person would require a good deal of persuasion that Parliament ever intended such a bizarre result.

For these reasons, I do not see any ground on which, on the true construction of sub-s (1) of s 37 of the Act, the plaintiff council can be required to contribute to the cost of laying the 27 inch main in question in this case. It follows that in my view the learned judge came to a correct conclusion in answering the question raised by the originating summons as he did, and for my part I would dismiss the appeal.

I think I should conclude by adding a word on the wider question formulated by Edmund Davies and Stephenson LJJ, namely, whether a 'trunk main' could ever in any circumstances amount to a 'necessary main' within the meaning of s 37 of the Act. Edmund Davies and Stephenson LJJ evidently think that it can. For my part, I think it would be difficult, on such a question, to give a ruling which would be conclusive in all circumstances. I content myself with saying that, as at present advised, I find it *a* difficult to envisage circumstances in which a trunk main could properly be regarded as a 'necessary main' within what I regard as the somewhat limited purview of s 37 of the Act.

Appeal allowed. Leave to appeal to House of Lords granted.

Solicitors: *Lewin, Gregory, Mead & Sons* (for the defendants); *Jaques & Co* (for the *b* plaintiffs).

Mary Rose Plummer   Barrister.

Cruse v Chittum (formerly Cruse)   *c*

FAMILY DIVISION
LANE J
14th MARCH 1974

Divorce – Foreign decree – Recognition by English court – Grounds for recognition – Residence d – Spouse habitually resident in country in which decree obtained – Requisites of habitual residence – Elements of intention and quality rather than period of residence – 'Habitually' denoting physical presence enduring for some time – Finding by foreign court that spouse actual bona fide resident of that country for more than one year – Whether equivalent to finding that spouse habitually resident there – Recognition of Divorces and Legal Separations Act 1971, s 3(1)(a).   *e*

The parties were married in September 1950. There were no children of the marriage. In July 1961 the wife, in the company of a United States serviceman, left the husband. Thereafter the husband lost touch with her. In August 1964 the wife wrote from Mississippi informing the husband that she had obtained a divorce there in July 1963 and that he was a free man. The husband took no further steps in the matter until 1971 when *f* he formed a wish to remarry. His solicitors obtained from the Chancery Court of Harrison County, Mississippi, two documents: a 'Bill of Complaint for Divorce' filed by the wife and a 'Final Decree' dated 17th July 1963. The decree recited that the wife 'is an actual bona fide resident citizen of Harrison County, Mississippi and has been for more than one year next immediately preceding the filing' of the bill. The husband sought a declaration that the validity of the Mississippi decree should be recognised *g* under s 3(1)(a)[a] of the Recognition of Divorces and Legal Separations Act 1971 since at the date when the wife had instituted proceedings in the state she was 'habitually resident' there.

Held – The husband was entitled to the declaration sought for the following reasons—
   (i) The expression 'habitually resident' indicated the quality of the residence rather *h* than its duration and required an element of intention to reside in the country in question. It was necessary that the residence should not be temporary or of a secondary nature. The word 'habitually' denoted a regular physical presence which had to endure for some time. Habitual residence was to be distinguished from ordinary residence and was equivalent to the residence required to establish domicile without the element of animus necessary for the purpose of domicile (see p 942 g to j to p 943 *j* *a* and *b*, post).
   (ii) The finding of fact that at the date when the wife's proceedings were instituted that she had been an actual bona fide resident of Mississippi for a period of one year was equivalent to a finding that at that date she was 'habitually resident' in that

---
a   Section 3(1), so far as material, is set out at p 942 *f* post

a state and, in the absence of evidence to the contrary, was to be treated as sufficient proof of that fact by virtue of s 5[b] of the 1971 Act (see p 943 *g* to *j*, post).

Notes
For the recognition of foreign decree of divorce, see Supplement to 7 Halsbury's Laws (3rd Edn) para 200A, 2, 4.

b For the Recognition of Divorces and Legal Separations Act 1971, ss 3, 5, see 41 Halsbury's Statutes (3rd Edn) 219, 221.

Cases referred to in judgment
Indyka v Indyka [1967] 2 All ER 689, [1969] 1 AC 33, [1967] 3 WLR 510, HL; *affg* [1966] 3 All ER 583, [1967] P 233, [1966] 3 WLR 603, CA; *rvsg* [1966] 1 All ER 781, [1967]
c P 233, [1966] 2 WLR 892, DC, Digest (Cont Vol C) 149, *1094c*.
Travers v Holley and Holley [1953] 2 All ER 794, [1953] P 246, [1953] 3 WLR 507, CA, Digest (Cont Vol A) 240, *1023a*.

Petition
The husband petitioned for a declaration that his marriage to the respondent had
d been validly dissolved by a decree of the Chancery Court in Biloxi, Harrison County, in the state of Mississippi, on 17th July 1963. The facts are set out in the judgment.

Thomas Coningsby for the petitioner.
The respondent did not appear and was not represented.

e

LANE J. This is a petition for a declaration that the marriage of the petitioner was validly dissolved by a decree of a foreign court. The facts are these. The petitioner, a domiciled Englishman, was married on 7th September 1950 to the respondent at the Register Office at Luton in Bedfordshire. There are no children of that marriage or family, and so far as the petitioner knows the respondent has never had any
f children. They lived together in Bedfordshire until 17th July 1961, when the respondent left the petitioner. She left in the company of a sergeant in the American forces whose name the petitioner can no longer recall. The petitioner understood that she went immediately to live with her parents in England. Thereafter he lost touch with her completely and knew nothing of her whereabouts or situation until August 1964 when he received a letter from her saying:

g
'I think it only right to tell you I have got a divorce so you are a free man now. I should have told you before as it has been final for a year now. It is quite easy to obtain a divorce here.'

'Here' was presumably the state of Mississippi, the address given at the head of that letter being a street in a town called Biloxi, in that state. The petitioner at that time
h was not interested remarrying and took no steps in the matter. As far as I am aware he did not even acknowledge the letter. But in 1971 he formed a wish to remarry and he applied to a registrar of marriages in Wales, where he was then living, in respect of remarriage. Not unexpectedly the registrar required satisfactory proof that his former marriage had been validly dissolved. The petitioner therefore consulted solicitors, who made enquiries which were facilitated by the fact that the
j petitioner had received information from a friend that the respondent was then in England. Her name and address were obtained and discovered to be, according to a document emanating from her, Mrs Chittum, c/o T/Sergeant C B Chittum, Hillview, Upton, Huntingdonshire. She furnished the petitioner's solicitors with sufficient

---

b Section 5 is set out at p 943 *c*, to *e*, post

information to enable them to obtain from the Chancery Court of Harrison County, *a*
Mississippi, legal documents relating to the divorce which she had obtained there.
Those documents are now before the court and are in two parts, the first being described as a 'Bill of Complaint for Divorce', which is the equivalent of our petition
for divorce, as is apparent from its contents. Towards the end of that first document
is a statement by a notary public that the present respondent, as complainant in
the American proceedings, personally appeared before him and on oath stated that the
allegations in her bill of complaint were true. That I take to resemble the old affidavit *b*
in verification of the petition which used to be a requirement of the English divorce
law. The second document before me is entitled 'Final Decree'. It is signed by someone called William G Hughes who is described as 'chancellor'. This being in the
Chancery Court in Mississippi, I think it reasonable to assume that a chancellor is
the equivalent of a judge for the purpose of making a final decree.

The decree, which is dated 17th July 1963, is the document on which the petitioner *c*
must rely for the purposes of satisfying this court that his marriage was validly dissolved and that the decree should be recognised here. It recites, inter alia, that it
appeared to the court that—

> 'the Complainant is an actual bona fide resident citizen of Harrison County,
> Mississippi, and has been for more than one year next immediately preceding *d*
> the filing of the Bill of Complaint for Divorce'.

The document ends:

> 'IT IS THEREFORE ORDERED, ADJUDGED, AND DECREED that the bonds of matrimony
> now and heretofore existing between the Complainant . . . and the Defendant . . .
> be, and the same are hereby dissolved and cancelled, and the Complainant is hereby *e*
> awarded an absolute Divorce from the Defendant.'

The question is: will this court recognise the Mississippi decree? The relevant
statutory provision to which I am referred by counsel for the petitioner is s 3 of the
Recognition of Divorces and Legal Separations Act 1971, and in particular sub-s (1)
of that section. This reads: *f*

> 'The validity of an overseas divorce or legal separation shall be recognised if,
> at the date of the institution of the proceedings in the country in which it was
> obtained—(a) either spouse was habitually resident in that country . . .'

Paragraph (b) refers to either spouse being a national of that country and is of no
application or interest to this case. *g*
The first question which arises in determining whether or not this court should
recognise that decree is what is meant by the phrase 'habitually resident in that
country'. Counsel for the petitioner submits that habitual residence requires an
element of intention, an intention to reside in that country. He further submits that
'habitual' must indicate a quality of residence rather than a period of residence.
He argues that as no period of residence is specified in the 1971 Act, this of itself points *h*
to the importance of the quality of residence in order to make it habitual. This
submission derives support from the fact that in s 5(2) of the Domicile and Matrimonial Proceedings Act 1973, the same phrase 'habitually resident' appears, but for
the purposes of that subsection is required to be one year's duration. Counsel draws
a comparison with the wording used in the well-known case of *Indyka v Indyka*[1], the
effect of which is, of course, superseded by the 1971 Act, and draws a distinction
between the wording of the Act and the principles set forth in, for example, *Travers v
Holley*[2]. He says further that one may point to characteristics of residence which

1   [1967] 2 All ER 689, [1969] 1 AC 33
2   [1953] 2 All ER 794, [1953] P 246

a will not make it habitual but other than habitual. For example the residence must not be temporary or of a secondary nature. He urges that the phrase in the decree of the American court that the residence was 'actual' and 'bona fide' really defines what is meant by 'habitual' in this context, and denotes a regular physical presence which must endure for some time. He further submits that ordinary residence is different from habitual residence in that the latter is something more than the former and is similar to the residence normally required as part of domicile, although *b* in habitual residence there is no need for the element of animus which is necessary in domicile. I accept those submissions.

Section 5 of the 1971 Act reads in this way:

> *c* '(1) For the purpose of deciding whether an overseas divorce or legal separation is entitled to recognition by virtue of the foregoing provisions of this Act, any finding of fact made (whether expressly or by implication) in the proceedings by means of which the divorce or legal separation was obtained and on the basis of which jurisdiction was assumed in those proceedings shall—(a) if both spouses took part in the proceedings, be conclusive evidence of the fact found [that does not apply here; (b) applies here:]; and (b) in any other case be sufficient proof of that fact unless the contrary is shown.
>
> *d* '(2) In this section "finding of fact" includes a finding that either spouse was habitually resident or domiciled in, or a national of, the country in which the divorce or legal separation was obtained; and for the purposes of subsection (1) (a) of this section, a spouse who has appeared in judicial proceedings shall be treated as having taken part in them.'

e Counsel submits that the finding of 'actual and bona fide residence of a year and upwards' is equivalent to a finding that the spouse was habitually resident or domiciled in the country where the decree was granted.

As to further evidence of such residence or domicile he points to the first letter from the wife, received in August 1964, which showed that she was then still resident in the state which granted the decree, as she had been for at least a year before the decree *f* was granted on 17th July 1963.

During the hearing there was reference to s 8 of the 1971 Act, but on the facts as they are before me, particularly as the final decree of the Mississippi divorce recites that there had been the equivalent of substituted service, I think there is no need for me to consider that section.

I am satisfied that a valid decree of dissolution of the petitioner's marriage was *g* pronounced in the Mississippi court on 17th July 1963, and that sufficient facts are apparent therefrom and from other evidence before me to show that the respondent at the time she instituted the proceedings in that court was habitually resident in the country where the decree was pronounced. I am fortified in my view by the fact that under s 5(2) of the Domicile and Matrimonial Proceedings Act 1973 the court has jurisdiction to entertain proceedings for divorce if either party to the marriage has *h* been habitually resident here throughout a period of one year ending with the date when divorce proceedings are begun. It would therefore be somewhat anomalous if habitual residence in a foreign country granting a decree were required to be of more than a year's duration in order that the decree should be recognised here.

These being my conclusions, I grant the declaration sought that the petitioner's marriage was validly dissolved and that the decree may be recognised here.

j
Declaration granted.

Solicitors: *Peacock & Goddard*, agents for *W J Williams & Davies*, Cardigan (for the petitioner).

R C T Habesch Esq   Barrister.

Applied in Re Bailey (A Bankrupt)
[1977] 2 All ER 26

Burke v Burke

COURT OF APPEAL, CIVIL DIVISION

DAVIES, BUCKLEY AND LAWTON LJJ

9th NOVEMBER 1973

Husband and wife – Property – Matrimonial home – Sale under trust for sale – Power to postpone sale – Power of court to order sale – Discretion – Declaration as to property rights – Declaration that husband holding property in trust for himself and wife in equal shares – Husband and wife divorced – Wife living in house with two children of marriage – Factors to be taken into consideration by court when determining whether to order sale – Duty of husband to provide for children – Whether relevant consideration – Married Women's Property Act 1882, s 17.

The parties were married in 1962 and had two children, born in 1964 and 1966 respectively. In 1966 the parties acquired a house which became the matrimonial home. The house was transferred into the husband's sole name. In November 1967 the husband left the matrimonial home, leaving the children with their mother. In October 1971 the husband was granted a decree nisi based on two years separation, with the wife's consent. Custody of the children was granted to the wife and by consent no maintenance was ordered for the wife but the husband was ordered to pay £3 a week in respect of each child. It was contemplated that the wife would purchase the husband's share in the equity of redemption in the matrimonial home but nothing came of it. Consequently, in April 1972 the husband applied under s 17 of the Married Women's Property Act 1882 for a declaration as to the parties' beneficial interests in the home. The registrar made an order declaring that the husband held the property in trust for himself and the wife in equal shares. The property was accordingly held on the statutory trusts for sale subject to the statutory power to postpone sale. In July 1972 the husband applied for an order that the trust for sale should be carried out. No order was made on that application until March 1973 when the registrar ordered that the house should be put up for sale before 1st May 1973 but gave liberty to the wife to apply for a further postponement of the sale on filing an affidavit setting out what further attempts she had made to find alternative accommodation, to raise money to buy out the husband's interest or to find work for herself. The wife filed an affidavit stating that she had had difficulty in raising money with which to buy her husband's interest and also gave reasons why she found it difficult to find part-time employment suitable for her to engage in while caring for the children. The husband also filed an affidavit stating, inter alia, that he wished to obtain his share of the proceeds of sale in order to set up in business. On 17th May 1973 the registrar refused the wife's application for a further postponement of the sale. The wife appealed contending (i) that the property had been acquired to serve as a matrimonial home not only for the parents but also for the children; (ii) that, so long as the children had no other home available, the purposes for which the acquisition had been made still subsisted, and (iii) that, in consequence, the court ought not, in the exercise of its discretion, to order a sale.

Held – Since the husband's application had been made under s 17 of the 1882 Act the matter had to be looked at having regard only to the legal and equitable interests which had been declared to subsist in the property. Accordingly, in exercising its discretion whether or not the husband as trustee should or should not continue to postpone the execution of the trust for sale, the court had to have regard to all the relevant circumstances of the case and to the situation of the beneficial owners. Although personal problems which affected those beneficiaries were matters which fell to be taken into account, since the beneficial interests in the home belonged to a   the husband and wife alone the interests of the children were to be taken into consideration only insofar as they affected the equities as between the husband and wife. Accordingly, it was not appropriate to consider the matter on the footing that the husband was obliged to make provision for his children by agreeing to retain the property unsold, for to do so was to introduce into the exercise of a discretion relating to property rights considerations which were relevant only to maintenance.

b   It followed that the registrar had not exercised his discretion on any wrong principle and the appeal should therefore be dismissed (see p 947 *f g h* and *j* to p 948 *a d e* and *h* and p 949 *b*, post).

Dictum of Salmon LJ in *Rawlings v Rawlings* [1964] 2 All ER at 814 disapproved.

Notes

c   For the orders which may be made in summary proceedings between husband and wife as to property, see 19 Halsbury's Laws (3rd Edn) 900, 901, para 1492, and for cases on the subject, see 27(1) Digest (Reissue) 305-315, 2267-2330.

For the Married Women's Property Act 1882, s 17, see 17 Halsbury's Statutes (3rd Edn) 120.

d   ### Case referred to in judgment

Rawlings v Rawlings [1964] 2 All ER 804, [1964] P 398, [1964] 3 WLR 294, CA, 27(1) Digest (Reissue) 94, 680.

Cases also cited

Jackson v Jackson [1971] 3 All ER 774, [1971] 1 WLR 1539, CA.
e   *Jones v Challenger* [1960] 1 All ER 785, [1961] 1 QB 176, CA.
Mesher v Mesher [1973] The Times, 13th February, [1973] Bar Library transcript 59, CA.

Appeal

This was an appeal by the wife, Marie Joan Burke, against an order of Mr Registrar
f   Stranger-Jones dated 17th May 1973 whereby he refused the wife's application for a further postponement of the sale of the former matrimonial home which on 2nd March 1973, on an application by the husband, Terence Burke, he had ordered to be sold with vacant possession. At all material times the wife was living in the home with the two children of the marriage. The facts are set out in the judgment of Buckley LJ.

g
Paul Hampton for the wife.
Duncan Matheson for the husband.

BUCKLEY LJ delivered the first judgment at the invitation of Davies LJ. This
h   is an appeal from a decision of Mr Registrar Stranger-Jones on 17th May 1973 when he refused further to postpone the sale of the former matrimonial home of the parties (who were previously husband and wife but as between whom a decree nisi has now been granted), that matrimonial home being owned by them in equal shares. The history of the matter is this. The parties were married in 1962. They had two children, born in 1964 and 1966 respectively. At some date in 1966 they bought the house
j   which is in dispute in the present proceedings, 22 Rochford Avenue, Chadwell Heath, in Essex. A separation took place in November 1967, when the husband left the matrimonial home, leaving the children of the marriage with their mother. In October 1971 Mrs Justice Lane granted a decree nisi on the husband's prayer on the ground of two years separation, with the wife's consent. There had previously been cross-allegations of cruelty, but those were not proceeded with and the decree was made on the ground I have stated. Custody of the children was granted to the wife

and by consent no maintenance was ordered for the wife but the husband was ordered *a*
to pay £3 a week in respect of each of the two children. We have been told that that
order was made as the result of negotiations between the parties which contemplated
(and we were informed that the learned judge was told this) that the wife would
pay the husband £2,250 for his share in the equity of redemption in the house, the
house being subject to a mortgage which has not yet been fully discharged. But
it seems that she was not able to find that money, or at any rate did not find the *b*
money, and in consequence in April 1972 proceedings which the husband had commenced by originating summons issued on 25th February 1970 under s 17 of the
Married Women's Property Act 1882 were brought on before the learned registrar,
who on 13th April 1972 made an order declaring that the husband, into whose sole
name the property had been conveyed, held the property in trust for himself and
the wife in equal shares. It appears that the husband had, at an earlier stage, been *c*
asserting that he had the sole beneficial interest, but he did not press that claim and
the matter stands that those are the equitable interests in the property. Consequently
the property is, under the Law of Property Act 1925, held on the statutory trust for
sale, with the ordinary statutory power to postpone sale; and the beneficiaries under
the trust are the husband and the wife.

The question of an immediate sale was not considered at the time of that order; *d*
but the matter was brought back before the learned registrar in July 1972 on an
application by the husband (as I will continue to call him) for an order that the trust
for sale should be carried out. On that application the registrar made no order on
the question of the sale of the property save that both parties should have leave to
file affidavits on the question of whether there should be a sale or not. The husband
filed an affidavit; the wife filed an affidavit. On 30th October the application was *e*
restored, but it was adjourned not to come on again until the end of February 1973.
On 2nd March 1973 the matter came again before the registrar, at which time he had
the two affidavits before him. He ordered that the house be put up for sale with
vacant possession on or before 1st May 1973, but he gave liberty to the wife to apply
for further postponement of the sale on filing an affidavit at least ten days before the
hearing of the further application, if any, setting out what further attempts she had *f*
made to try to find alternative accommodation or to raise money to buy out the
husband, and to find work for herself and, if unable to work due to illness, to exhibit
a full medical report containing a prognosis; and in the event of a further application
the registrar ordered that the wife should attend to give oral evidence. The husband
was given leave to file a further affidavit if he wished to do so. The wife did file an
affidavit, in which she made certain allegations against her husband to the effect that
he was an improvident man and that he had not bothered about the children; she *g*
explained why, as she said, she had difficulty in raising money with which to buy
out her husband's interest, and also gave reasons why she found it difficult to find
part-time employment suitable for her to engage in while she was also caring for
the children. But I must say that I myself find it a little odd that the only kind of
part-time employment that she seems to have investigated at all was work as a
lunch-time waitress in a restaurant or as a counter-hand in one of Lyons's stores. She *h*
then goes on to say that it was difficult for her to work as a waitress because she
suffers from varicose veins, and indeed she exhibits a medical certificate which says
that she cannot follow any occupation which involves standing. That, I can quite see,
may make it difficult for her to find part-time employment; but it does not make
her enquiries about work as a waitress really very helpful.

The matter came back before the registrar on 17th May, when the registrar ordered *j*
that the wife's application for a further postponement of the sale should be refused;
but a stay of the earlier order for sale was granted for six weeks from that date.
That was to enable the wife to consider whether she wished to appeal. The learned
registrar gave reasons for his decision to which I will refer later.

The application is one made solely under s 17 of the Married Women's Property a   Act 1882. That section, as has been held by the House of Lords[1], is a machinery section only, enabling the court to entertain in a summary way disputes between husband and wife, or a former husband and wife, with regard to their interests in property. It is not a section which enables the court to do otherwise than to give effect to the legal and equitable interests of the parties as they arise on the facts of the case. It is not a section which enables the court in any way to modify those rights

b   or interests. In the present case, as I have indicated, the property is held on the statutory trust for sale, subject to the statutory power to postpone the sale, the beneficial interest in the proceeds of sale and in the rents and profits, if any, until sale being in the husband and wife in equal shares.

     The argument that has been presented persuasively to us in this case by counsel for the wife is that the court will not in such a case direct that the property shall be

c   sold so long as the purpose for which the property was acquired subsists, and he says that in this case the proper inference to draw from the fact that the purchase was made in 1966, at a time when I think both the children were born, certainly the elder child was born, is that the property was to serve as the matrimonial home and as a home not only for the parents but also for the children, and that so long as the children have no other home available the purposes of that purchase are sub-

d   sisting and the court ought not, in the exercise of its discretion, to order a sale. He has relied on a dictum of Salmon LJ in *Rawlings v Rawlings*[2], where, having discussed the general principles applicable to such a case, he said:

e   'If there were young children the position would be different. One of the purposes of the trust would no doubt have been to provide a home for them, and whilst that purpose still existed a sale would not generally be ordered. But when those children are grown up and the marriage is dead, the purposes of the trust have failed.'

     That was a case in which the marriage was still subsisting, there having been no divorce; the wife had deserted the husband, and the husband remained in the matrimonial home with one son who was living with him but he was of age and

f   there were no young children involved.

     Section 17 being a section such as I have mentioned, one must, I think, look at the matter having regard to the legal and equitable interests subsisting in the property: that is to say, one must regard it as property the legal estate in which is vested in the husband on a statutory trust for sale and the beneficial interests in the proceeds of sale being the interests of the husband and the wife equally; and the court, in the

g   exercise of its discretion, in considering whether or not the trustee should or should not continue to postpone the execution of the trust for sale, which, subject to that discretionary power, is an immediate, binding trust, must have regard to all the relevant circumstances of the case and must have regard to the situation of both the beneficial owners. I think it is right to say that personal problems which affect those beneficiaries connected with the question of whether or not the property should be

h   retained unsold are matters which fall to be taken into account. For instance, to part from the facts of this case altogether, if one had property held by two persons in undivided shares, one of whom was in occupation of the property and the other was claiming a sale, and the one who was in occupation had some infirm and aged relative living with him or her who might have to be rehoused somehow and whom there was great difficulty in rehousing, the court would not order a sale instanter in such a way

j   as to cause great difficulty in making proper arrangements to rehouse that person. But the interests of the children in the present case, it seems to me, with due respect to Salmon LJ, are interests which are only incidentally to be taken into consideration in that sort of way. They are, as I say, proper to be taken into consideration so far as

---

1   *Pettitt v Pettitt* [1969] 2 All ER 385, [1970] AC 777
2   [1964] 2 All ER 804 at 814, [1964] P 398 at 419

they affect the equities in the matter as between the two persons entitled to the bene- a
ficial interests in the property. But it is not, I think, right to treat this case as though
the husband was obliged to make provision for his children by agreeing to retain the
property unsold. To do this is, as I think, and as was urged on us by counsel for the
husband, to confuse with a problem relating to property, considerations which are
relevant to maintenance. Those are two different things. If the property is sold and
the means available to the husband in the present case are enhanced by his receiving b
his share of the proceeds of sale, it may well be that he may find himself exposed to an
application for an order for increased maintenance; but that does not seem to me to
be a good ground for refusing to give effect to the trust for sale which is the primary
provision applicable to this property.

The learned registrar in his reasons for his decision evidently took into consideration the interests of the children, for he said in the course of his judgment: c

> 'The actual selling was postponed because I was conscious of the children—I
> knew it would be wrong to keep the husband out of his money indefinitely but I
> wanted to give the wife and children a good long opportunity to find somewhere
> else.'

In my judgment that was a very proper approach. The learned registrar here was d
exercising the discretion of the court. He did not, in my judgment, exercise it on any
wrong principle. He did not fail to take into account any matters that he ought to
have taken into account or give consideration to any matter which he ought not to
have taken into account; and in my judgment we ought not to interfere with his
exercise of his discretion. I would dismiss the appeal.

e

DAVIES LJ. I entirely agree, and would only add a few sentences.

If the order further to postpone the sale sought by the wife had been granted, it
would mean that the husband would, for an unascertained period, be out of his
capital, some £2,500, or perhaps more now, which he said in his affidavit he would like
to use to set up a business of some kind. By the same token of course, he would
lose the interest that he might derive from that capital being invested. In all the f
circumstances, I do not think it would be right that that should happen.

The only other thing that I would suggest is this. Counsel for the husband has
explained to us the circumstances in which the wife was not cross-examined on the
last appearance before the learned registrar. I should have thought that in a case of
this kind it would have been advantageous both to the registrar and to us to have had
the wife, and possibly the husband as well, cross-examined on this question of means g
and the future prospects of the wife and the children and the husband.

Apart from that, I have nothing to add. I entirely agree with what Buckley LJ has
said.

LAWTON LJ. I agree that this appeal should be dismissed; and I wish to add a
comment for one purpose only, to show the limits of the reasoning which has led me to h
agree.

During the course of the argument a question arose as to what was meant by the
term 'matrimonial home', which was used in all three cases to which the court
was referred[1]. I asked counsel whether the term 'matrimonial home' might not
mean, when there are children either in being or in contemplation, a home for them.
If the circumstances are such that the parents buy a house in which to accommodate j
themselves and any children of the marriage, for my part I cannot see why the
children should not be beneficiaries under any implied trust which may come into
existence on the purchase of the home; and, if that is the position on the evidence in

---

1 *Jones v Challenger* [1960] 1 All ER 785, [1961] 1 QB 176; *Rawlings v Rawlings* [1964] 2 All ER
804, [1964] P 398, and *Jackson v Jackson* [1971] 3 All ER 774, [1971] 1 WLR 1539

a any particular case, then it may well be that the position of the children has to be considered. But when I raised this question Buckley LJ pointed out that the order of the registrar dated 13th April 1972 had in fact decided what the trust was in this case. It is pertinent to bear in mind that the registrar had heard the evidence of the parties and of such witnesses as they called. He then adjudged and declared that the property was held in trust for the husband and the wife in equal shares. It follows from that moment onwards (the order not having been appealed) that the learned registrar was

b concerned with the position of a trust for the spouses, and in those circumstances I agree with what has been said already, that the personal problems were factors to be taken into consideration but nothing more.

Appeal dismissed.

c Solicitors: *S S Bookatz & Co* (for the wife); *Duthie, Hart & Duthie* (for the husband).

Mary Rose Plummer Barrister.

d
Lincoln Corporation v Parker and another

Applied in LEICESTERSHIRE CC v
CROSS [1976] 2 All ER 491

e

Criminal law – Compensation – Compensation order – Children and young persons – Court's power to order parent or guardian to pay compensation instead of child or young person – Guardian – Person having charge of or control over child or young person – Young person placed in care of local authority pursuant to care order – Local authority allowing young person to be under charge and control of parents – Young person committing offences while residing
f *with parents – Whether local authority having 'charge of or control over' young person when offences committed – Children and Young Persons Act 1933, s 55(1) (as amended by the Children and Young Persons Act 1969, s 72(3), Sch 5, para 5, and the Criminal Justice Act 1972, s 64(1), Sch 5), s 107(1) – Children Act 1948, s 13(2) (as substituted by the Children and Young Persons Act 1969, s 49).*

g
The defendant, a young person, was found guilty of certain offences. He was made the subject of a care order and was committed to the care of a local authority which placed him in a community home. Subsequently the local authority, in exercise of its powers under s 13(2)[a] of the Children Act 1948, allowed the defendant to return home to live with his parents for a trial period. While living at home the defendant
h committed further offences. He was brought before a juvenile court which conditionally discharged him. In purported exercise of its power under s 55(1)[b] of the Children and Young Persons Act 1933 the court ordered the local authority to pay compensation to the victims of the offences on the basis that, at the material time, it was, within s 107[c] of the 1933 Act, 'the guardian' of the defendant in that it had 'charge of or control over' him. The local authority appealed.

j
Held – Where a local authority made an order under s 13(2) of the 1948 Act, the charge of or control over the child left the authority in whose favour the care order

a Section 13(2), as substituted, is set out at p 953 *h*, post
b Section 55(1), as amended, is set out at p 952 *d* to *f*, post
c Section 107(1), so far as material, is set out at p 952 *h* and *j*, post

had been made, and vested for the time being in the parents. Accordingly, when *a* that happened the liability of the local authority as guardian for the purposes of s 55 of the 1933 Act ceased for the time being and the natural parents took on that onus with the responsibility which it entailed. It followed that at the material time the defendant was not in the charge, or under the control, of the local authority, and the justices had no power to make an order for the payment of compensation against the authority. The appeal would therefore be allowed and the compensation *b* order quashed (see p 954 *b c d f* and *g*, post).

Somerset County Council v Brice [1973] 3 All ER 438 applied.

R v Croydon Juvenile Court Justices, ex parte Croydon London Borough Council [1973] All ER 476 distinguished.

Notes

For the court's power to order a 'guardian' to pay compensation instead of a child or *c* young person, see 10 Halsbury's Laws (3rd Edn) 516, para 940.

For the Children and Young Persons Act 1933, ss 55, 107, see 17 Halsbury's Statutes (3rd Edn) 473, 515.

For the Children Act 1948, s 13, see 17 Halsbury's Statutes (3rd Edn) 550.

For the Chidren and Young Persons Act 1969, ss 49, 72, Sch 5, para 5, see 40 Halsbury's *d* Statutes (3rd Edn) 909, 929, 947.

For the Criminal Justice Act 1972, s 64, Sch 5, see 42 Halsbury's Statutes (3rd Edn) 139, 148.

Cases referred to in judgments

R v Croydon Juvenile Court Justices, ex parte Croydon London Borough Council [1973] 1 *e* All ER 476, [1973] QB 426, [1973] 2 WLR 61, 137 JP 283, DC.

Somerset County Council v Brice [1973] 3 All ER 438, [1973] 1 WLR 1169, 137 JP 645, DC.

Case stated

This was an appeal by way of a case stated by justices for the county borough of Lincoln, acting in and for the petty sessional division of the city of Lincoln, in respect *f* of their adjudication as a juvenile court sitting at Lincoln on 26th March 1973.

On 8th January 1973 an information was preferred by the respondent Cecil Ernest Muxlow against Brian Andrew Hopkins ('the defendant') that he with others on or about 20th November 1972 stole lead value £2·75, contrary to ss 1 and 7 of the Theft Act 1968. On 8th February 1973 informations were preferred by the respondent Gerald David Parker against the defendant that he on 13th December 1972 (i) with *g* others entered a dwelling-house as a trespasser and stole property value £9·07; (ii) with others entered a dwelling-house as a trespasser and stole property value £5·54, both contrary to s 9(1)(b) of the Theft Act 1968. On 14th March 1973 informations were preferred by the respondent Parker against the defendant that he (i) on 6th January 1973 with others stole a moped; (ii) on 9th January 1973 with others stole a motor cycle, both contrary to ss 1 and 7 of the Theft Act 1968.

At the hearing of the information the defendant pleaded guilty to all five charges, *h* and asked for seven similar offences to be taken into consideration. The justices found the following facts. The defendant was a young person, having been born on 11th March 1959. As a result of previous findings of guilt on 8th March 1971 he had been made the subject of a care order and committed to the care of the appellant, Lincoln Corporation ('the local authority'). From 10th May 1971 until 22nd August 1972 he resided at Skegby Hall community school, Nottinghamshire. On 22nd August *j* 1972 the local authority allowed him to return home to reside with his parents for a trial period. In November 1972 he began to absent himself from school and resumed association with a delinquent peer group. He was to have appeared in court in January 1973 to answer the charge of stealing lead but prior to that appearance took a quantity of paracetamol tablets and was admitted to hospital. On his release from hospital a the local authority took him into a children's home where he continued to reside at the date of hearing.

The justices considered it inexpedient to impose a penalty and ordered that the defendant be discharged conditionally for a period of two years, pursuant to the provisions of s 7 of the Criminal Justice Act 1948. Having regard to the provisions of s 24(1) and (2) of the Children and Young Persons Act 1969 the justices were of opinion that the local authority stood in loco parentis to the defendant and that by virtue of
b the definition of 'guardian' in s 107(1) of the Children and Young Persons Act 1933 the local authority was also his guardian. Section 5(8) of the 1969 Act required a person who laid an information in respect of a young person to give notice to the appropriate local authority. The justices were satisfied that that provision had been complied with because they had before them a report prepared by Mr R R Hogarth, a social worker employed by the local authority. Mr Hogarth was present in the court.
c The local authority had not been required to be present in court, pursuant to the provisions of s 34 of the 1933 Act. The defendant's mother had been served with a summons requiring her to be present, and she was so present.

The justices considered that the notice on the local authority in accordance with s 5(8) of the 1969 Act was sufficient notice that a young person in the care of the local authority was to appear before the court and then considered that that afforded the
d local authority an opportunity to appear before the court to be heard on the question whether an order should be made under s 55 of the 1933 Act. The local authority was not present by solicitor or counsel and the justices were not satisfied that the local authority had not conduced to the commission of the offences by neglecting to exercise due care and control of the defendant. In their opinion he should not have been allowed to remain with his natural parents after it had become clear to the local
e authority that he was absenting himself from school and associating with known delinquents. In forming that opinion they were mindful of the report of Mr Hogarth but heard no evidence or argument as to the reasons for the local authority's decision not to remove the defendant from the home of his parents since the local authority did not appear.
f Having indicated that they were making a compensation order against the local authority, the justices were informed by Mr Hogarth that he had no power to accept such an order on behalf of the local authority. They consulted their clerk and decided that the compensation order would stand. They therefore ordered, pursuant to the provisions of s 55 of the 1933 Act, that the local authority should pay sums totalling £36·62 by way of compensation in respect of the charges set out in the informations and in respect of the offences taken into consideration.
g The questions for the opinion of the High Court were: (a) were the justices correct in their opinion that the, local authority was a guardian of the defendant for the purpose of s 55 of the 1933 Act? (b) in the absence of any formal requirement for the local authority to attend or the appearance of the local authority did the justices afford the local authority a sufficient opportunity of being heard? (c) were the justices correct in making the compensation order against the local authority?
h

F B Smedley for the local authority.
The respondents did not appear and were not represented.

LORD WIDGERY CJ. This is an appeal by case stated by justices for the county borough of Lincoln sitting at Lincoln as a juvenile court. On 26th March 1973 they
j had before them a charge against the defendant, a young person, that on a date in November he stole goods to the value of £2·75. There was a further information against the same young man of entering a dwelling-house as a trespasser and stealing, in December 1972, and further informations in regard to acts of dishonesty in January 1973.

The juvenile court before whom these matters came decided to award a conditional discharge in respect of the three cases, but made a further order, purporting to be under s 55 of the Children and Young Persons Act 1933, to the effect that the local authority should pay £36·62 by way of compensation to the victims in respect of the offences of which the young man had been guilty. The appeal is brought by the local authority, saying that in the circumstances of this case the order for payment of compensation was bad in law.

I should deal with the history of the defendant as set out in the case. He was born on 11th March 1959, so he was about 14 years of age at the material time. As a result of previous findings of guilt reached on 8th March 1971 he was made the subject of a care order and committed to the care of the local authority. From May 1971 until 22nd August 1972 he resided at a community school in Nottingham and nothing arises on that period. But on 22nd August 1972 the local authority, exercising powers under the care order, allowed the defendant to return home to reside with his parents for a trial period. It was whilst he was living at home with his parents by virtue of that trial period that he became associated with delinquents and became involved in the offences to which I have referred.

The justification for ordering the payment of compensation by the local authority was that the young person at the relevant time was within their care and control. Section 55(1) of the Children and Young Persons Act 1933, as amended, is the basic legislation on this subject:

'Where a child or young person is found guilty of any offence for the commission of which a fine or costs may be imposed or a compensation order may be made under section 1 of the Criminal Justice Act 1972, if the court is of opinion that the case would be best met by the imposition of a fine or costs or the making of such an order,whether with or without any other punishment, the court may in any case, and shall if the offender is a child, order that the fine, compensation or costs awarded be paid by the parent or guardian of the child or young person instead of by the child or young person, unless the court is satisfied that the parent or guardian cannot be found or that he has not conduced to the commission of the offence by neglecting to exercise due care or control of the child or young person.'

The words 'or control' were added by subsequent legislation.

The basis, therefore, of the claim to make the local authority pay the amount of compensation for damage was that by virtue of the care order the authority had become the guardian of the defendant. It certainly had not become the parent of the defendant, but it was said that it had become the guardian of the defendant, whereupon, if that assumption was right, it was open to the juvenile court to order the payment of this sum by the local authority unless it could show that it had not conduced to the commission of the offence by neglecting to exercise due care or control over the child.

It is evident that the juvenile court took that view. They were supported no doubt by the definition of 'guardian' in the 1933 Act, which provides in s 107(1):

' "Guardian", in relation to a child or young person, includes any person who, in the opinion of the court having cognisance of any case in relation to the child or young person or in which the child or young person is concerned, has for the time being the charge of or control over the child or young person'.

Hence one sees the link in the reasoning. It is said that by virtue of the care order the local authority has the charge of or control over the young person, and that, it is said, makes the local authority the young person's guardian, and that is authority under s 55 for the making of the present order.

There is some support for that view in the first of the cases which have come before this court in similar circumstances, R v Croydon Juvenile Court Justices, ex parte Croydon London Borough Council[1]. I do not find it necessary to go into the facts in detail;

1   [1973] 1 All ER 476, [1973] QB 426

a it suffices to say that in that case the local authority, in whose care the child was, had chosen, from the various options open to it, to put the child in a home owned and run by that selfsame local authority. There was really, therefore, no room for argument in the *Croydon* case[1] bar that at the material time the child was in the care and control of that local authority, because he was in a home owned and run by that very authority. Accordingly an order for payment of a fine in that case by the local authority was upheld.

b A significantly different situation can arise where the local authority having the care of the child has chosen to put it in an institution which is not directly run by the local authority. This was a point which came to light in *Somerset County Council v Brice*[2]. I take the facts from the headnote[3]:

c 'A county council, in whose care a boy aged 15 was placed under a care order, sent him to reside in an independent community home in another county. They were not entitled to interfere with the day-to-day running of the home or to order that he should be kept or confined in any particular part of it. He absconded from the home and committed an offence. Justices before whom he was brought decided to award compensation to the victim, and they ordered that the compensation be paid by the county council as the boy's guardian as *d* defined by section 107 (1) of the Children and Young Persons Act 1933. On appeal by the county council:—*Held*, allowing the appeal, that, in determining who had for the time being the charge of or control over the boy for the purposes of section 107(1) of the Children and Young Persons Act 1933, the material time for consideration was the moment when he absconded from the home; that the boy ceased to be in the charge or under the control of the county council when *e* they placed him as a resident in the de facto control of the independent home; and that no form of joint charge or control existed to establish a residuary responsibility in the county council for the boy's activities . . .'

So there we are; the local authority in exercise of its powers had put the boy physically into the control of an independent home which the local authority itself did not *f* control, and it was held that it had ceased to be the guardian of the child and thus ceased to be liable to have made against it orders under s 55.

Today one has a further variation on the same theme because from the facts which I have already recited, at the material time when this young man got into bad company and committed these offences, the local authority had sent him to reside with his parents for a trial period. The authority is s 13(2) of the Children Act 1948, as *g* amended by s 49 of the Children and Young Persons Act 1969. Section 13, having set out a number of alternatives which are open to local authorities in whose care the child is from time to time, adds a further option in sub-s (2) in these terms:

'Without prejudice to the generality of subsection (1) of this section, a local authority may allow a child in their care, either for a fixed period or until the *h* local authority otherwise determine, to be under the charge and control of a parent, guardian, relative or friend.'

I would say at once in considering the effect of that subsection that I agree with the submission made by counsel for the local authority that 'guardian' in that context really means legal guardian, and I take that view because we are dealing here with a provision of the Children Act 1948, and in that Act the definition of 'guardian' is *j* equivalent to the definition of 'legal guardian'. So that the power of the local authority is to allow the child to be under the charge and control of a parent, legal

---

1   [1973] 1 All ER 476, [1973] QB 426
2   [1973] 3 All ER 438, [1973] 1 WLR 1169
3   [1973] 1 WLR at 1170

guardian, relative or friend. It is to be observed at once that the words in the definition of 'guardian' in the 1933 Act which resulted in the Croydon Borough Council being held to be a guardian were a 'person who . . . has for the time being the charge of or control over the child or young person'. Those words are virtually identical with the words used in s 13(2) of the 1948 Act. That cannot be an accident. Parliament must have used the same phrase in order that it shall have the same meaning, so we find under s 13 of the 1948 Act that that which the local authority can surrender for the time being to the parents is the charge of or control over the child or young person. It was the retention of those very functions, namely, having the charge of or control over the young person which in the *Croydon* case[1] had caused the local authority to be the guardian and to be responsible for the activities of the child.

In my judgment when an order is made under s 13(2) of the 1948 Act, the charge of or control over the child for the present purpose leaves the authority in whose favour the care order was made and vests for the time being in the parents. Accordingly, when that happens the liability of the local authority as guardian for the purposes of s 55 of the 1933 Act ceases for the time being and the natural parents take on that onus with the responsibility it entails. In the result it seems to me in the particular circumstances of this case that at the material time the young person was not in the charge of or control of the local authority and that the argument of counsel for the local authority is right when he submits that the juvenile court had no power to make the order for the payment of compensation by the local authority. I would allow the appeal and quash the order for payment of compensation by the local authority.

Before leaving this case altogether, it might be proper to point out that a further argument which might have arisen in favour of the local authority had it not succeeded on the argument to which I have referred, would have been that it had not been given due notice of the proceedings as required by s 55(3) of the 1933 Act. I had occasion in the *Somerset* case[2] to draw attention to the importance of seeing that local authorities are given proper notice when this kind of consideration is going to arise, and I hope that case having now been reported, although it was not reported when the present case was before the juvenile court, that due regard will be paid to it in future and that the appropriate notice will be given to the local authority when an order of this kind is in contemplation.

ASHWORTH J. I agree.

MELFORD STEVENSON J. I agree.

Appeal allowed.

Solicitors: *Sharpe, Pritchard & Co*, agents for *H B Hodgson*, Lincoln (for the local authority).

N P Metcalfe Esq Barrister.

1 [1973] 1 All ER 476, [1973] QB 426
2 [1973] 3 All ER at 446, [1973] 1 WLR at 1178

R v Woodman

COURT OF APPEAL, CRIMINAL DIVISION
LORD WIDGERY CJ, ASHWORTH AND MOCATTA JJ
26th APRIL 1974

Criminal law – Theft – Property belonging to another – Property in possession or control of another person – Control – Articles on premises under the control of other person – Other person ignorant that articles on premises – Whether articles in 'control' of other person – Theft Act 1968, s 5(1).

The owners of a disused factory sold all the scrap metal remaining on the premises. The purchasers entered the factory and removed most of the scrap but, unknown to the owners, left a small quantity which was too inaccessible to be worthwhile removing. After the factory had been cleared the owners erected a barbed wire fence round it with the intention of excluding trespassers. At no time were the owners aware that remnants of scrap metal still remained in the factory. Subsequently the appellant took a van to the factory and removed a quantity of scrap metal. He was charged on indictment with theft and convicted. He appealed, contending that the scrap was not 'property belonging to another' within ss 1(1)^a and 5(1)^b of the Theft Act 1968 since the owners, having sold it, had no proprietary interest in it and, being ignorant of its presence in the factory, had neither possession nor control of it.

Held – Where a person was in control of a site it followed that he was also prima facie in control of articles on the site even though he was ignorant that those articles were there. Since the owners had taken steps to exclude trespassers from the factory there was evidence from which the jury could properly find that they were in control of the factory and accordingly had control of the scrap metal there. The appeal would therefore be dismissed (see p 957 *d e g* to *j* to p 958 *a*, post).

Notes
For the meaning of property belonging to another, see Supplement to 10 Halsbury's Laws (3rd Edn) para 1475A, 7.

For the Theft Act 1968, ss 1, 5, see 8 Halsbury's Statutes (3rd Edn) 783, 785.

Case referred to in judgment
R v Rowe (1859) 8 Cox CC 139, Bell CC 93, 28 LJMC 128, 32 LTOS 339, 23 JP 117, CCR, 15 Digest (Repl) 1086, *10,751*.

Cases also cited
Hibbert v McKiernan [1948] 1 All ER 860, [1948] 2 KB 142, DC.
Warner v Metropolitan Police Comr [1968] 2 All ER 356, [1969] 2 AC 256, HL.

Appeal
On 4th October 1973 in the Crown Court at Bristol before Mr Recorder Tyrell the appellant, George Eli Woodman, was convicted of the theft of certain scrap metal. On 5th October he was sentenced to a fine of £40 and ordered to pay £50 towards his legal aid costs, or four months imprisonment in default. He appealed against conviction by leave of Bristow J. The facts appear in the judgment of the court.

J D Foley for the appellant.
Stephen Lowry for the Crown.

---

a   Section 1(1), so far as material, is set out at p 956 *j*, post
b   Section 5(1), so far as material, is set out at p 956 *j*, post

LORD WIDGERY CJ. On 4th October 1973 at Bristol Crown Court the appellant, *a* George Eli Woodman, together with Terence George Woodman, were convicted of theft. The appellant was fined and sentenced to a term of imprisonment in default of payment. Terence George Woodman was sentenced to imprisonment to run concurrently with an existing term which he was serving. Both appealed against their conviction, but Terence George Woodman has since abandoned his appeal, and this court is only concerned with the appellant, George Eli Woodman.

The facts of the case were these. On 20th March 1973 the appellant and his son, and *b* another man called Davey who was acquitted, took a van to some premises at Wick near Bristol and loaded on to the van one ton six cwt of scrap metal, which they proceeded to drive away.

The premises from which they took this scrap metal were a disused factory belonging to English China Clays, and the indictment alleged that the scrap metal in question *c* was the property of English China Clays. Whether that was entirely true or not depends on the view one takes of the events immediately preceding this taking of scrap metal, because what had happened, according to the prosecution evidence, was that the business run by English China Clays at this point had been run down. In August 1970 the business had ceased. There was at that time a great deal of miscellaneous scrap metal on the site, and English China Clays, wishing to dispose of this, sold the *d* scrap metal to the Bird Group of companies, who thereupon had the right and title to enter on the site and remove the scrap metal which they had bought. They or their sub-contractor went on to the site. They took out the bulk of the scrap metal left there by English China Clays, but a certain quantity of scrap was too inaccessible to be removed to be attractive to the Bird Group of companies so that it was left on the site and so it seems to have remained for perhaps a couple of years until the appellant *e* and his son came to take it away, as I have already recounted.

Also in the history of the matter, and important in it, is the fact that when the site had been cleared by the Bird Group of companies a barbed wire fence was erected around it obviously to exclude trespassers. The site was still in the ownership of the English China Clays and their occupation, and the barbed wire fence was no doubt erected by them. Within the barbed wire fence were these remnants of scrap which *f* the Bird Group had not taken away.

English China Clays took further steps to protect their property because a number of notices giving such information as 'Private Property. Keep Out' and 'Trespassers will be prosecuted' were exhibited around the perimeter of the site. A Mr Brooksbank, who was an employee of English China Clays, gave evidence that he had visited the site about half a dozen times over a period of two or three years, and indeed he had *g* visited it once as recently as between January and March 1973. He did not notice that any scrap metal had been left behind, and it is perfectly clear that there is no reason to suppose that English China Clays or their representatives appreciated that there was any scrap remaining on the site after the Bird Group had done their work.

When this matter came on before the Bristol Crown Court, at the close of the prosecution case when evidence had been led to deal with the facts I have referred to, a *h* submission was made to the recorder that there was no case to answer, because it was said that on that evidence there was no ground in law for saying that the theft had been committed.

By now of course it is the Theft Act 1968 which governs the matter, and so one must turn to see what it says. Section 1(1) provides: 'A person is guilty of theft if he dishonestly appropriates property belonging to another . . .' I need not go further *j* because the whole of the debate turns on the phrase 'belonging to another'.

Section 5(1) of the 1968 Act expands the meaning of the phrase in these terms:

'Property shall be regarded as belonging to any person having possession or control of it, or having it in any proprietary right or interest . . .'

a   The recorder took the view that the contract of sale between English China Clays and the Bird Group had divested English China Clays of any proprietary right to any scrap on the site. It is unnecessary to express a firm view on that point, but the court are not disposed to disagree with that conclusion that the proprietary interest in the scrap had passed.

b   The recorder also took the view on the relevant facts that it was not possible to say that English China Clays were in possession of the residue of the scrap. It is not quite clear why he took that view. It may have been because he took the view that difficulties arose by reason of the fact that English China Clays had no knowledge of the existence of this particular scrap at any particular time. But the recorder did take the view that so far as control was concerned there was a case to go to the jury on whether or not this scrap was in the control of English China Clays, because if it was, then it was to be regarded as their property for the purposes of a larceny charge even if they

c   were not entitled to any proprietary interest.

The contention before us today is that the recorder was wrong in law in allowing this issue to go to the jury. Put another way, it is said that as a matter of law English China Clays could not on these facts have been said to be in control of the scrap.

We have formed the view without difficulty that the recorder was perfectly entitled

d   to do what he did, that there was ample evidence that English China Clays were in control of the site and had taken considerable steps to exclude trespassers as demonstrating the fact that they were in control of the site, and we think that in ordinary and straightforward cases if it is once established that a particular person is in control of a site such as this, then prima facie he is in control of articles which are on the site.

The point was well put in an article written by no less a person than Oliver Wendell Holmes Jnr in his book The Common Law[1], dealing with possession. Considering

e   the very point we have to consider here, he said:

'There can be no *animus domini* unless the thing is known of; but an intent to exclude others from it may be contained in the larger intent to exclude others from the place where it is, without any knowledge of the object's existence . . . In a criminal case[2], the property in iron taken from the bottom of a canal by a stranger

f   was held well laid in the canal company, although it does not appear that the company knew of it, or had any lien upon it. The only intent concerning the thing discoverable in such instances is the general intent which the occupant of land has to exclude the public from the land, and thus, as a consequence, to exclude them from what is upon it.'

g   So far as this case is concerned, arising as it does under the Theft Act 1968, we are content to say that there was evidence of English China Clays being in control of the site and prima facie in control of articles on the site as well. The fact that it could not be shown that they were conscious of the existence of this or any particular scrap iron does not destroy the general principle that control of a site by excluding others from it is prima facie control of articles on the site as well

h   There has been some mention in argument of what would happen if, in a case like the present, a third party had come and placed some article within the barbed wire fence and thus on the site. The article might be an article of some serious criminal consequence such as explosives or drugs. It may well be that in that type of case the fact that the article has been introduced at a late stage in circumstances in which the occupier of the site had no means of knowledge would produce a different result

j   from that which arises under the general presumption to which we have referred, but in the present case there was in our view ample evidence to go to the jury on the question of whether English China Clays were in control of the scrap at the relevant

---

1   (1881), pp 222-224
2   *R v Rowe* (1859) 8 Cox CC 139

time. Accordingly the recorder's decision to allow the case to go to the jury cannot be   *a*
faulted and the appeal is dismissed.

Appeal dismissed.

Solicitors: *Registrar of Criminal Appeals; D B F P Leigh*, Gloucester (for the Crown).

N P Metcalfe Esq Barrister.   *b*

R v Boardman   *c*

COURT OF APPEAL, CRIMINAL DIVISION   Affirmed, sub nom BOARDMAN v
ORR LJ, BRABIN AND STOCKER JJ   DPP, HL [1974] 3 All ER 887
9th, 10th APRIL, 13th MAY 1974

d

*Criminal law – Evidence – Corroboration – Sexual offences – Similar fact evidence – Evidence
of other offences – Admissibility on account of probative value – No defence of innocent
association – No issue as to identity – Buggery – Accused charged with two offences involving
two different boys – Uncorroborated evidence of two boys relating to separate offences –
Evidence of each boy disclosing unusual feature of alleged offences – Whether evidence of
each boy admissible as evidence corroborating other boy's evidence in relation to other offence.*
e

The appellant was headmaster of a language school at which there were a number
of young foreign pupils. He was charged with three offences involving three different
pupils at the school. The first count charged the appellant with the offence of buggery
with a 16 year old boy, S. Count 2 charged him with inciting a 17 year old boy, H, to
commit buggery with him, and count 3 charged him with inciting another boy to   *f*
commit buggery with him. The judge in summing-up pointed out to the jury that
it was a common feature of counts 1 and 2 that the prosecution evidence involved
criminal behaviour of a particular, unusual kind, in that in each case the appellant,
a grown man, had attempted to induce acts of buggery in which an adolescent boy
would play the active, and the appellant the passive, part. On that basis, the judge
directed the jury that it was open to them to find in H's evidence with reference to
count 2, corroboration of S's evidence as to count 1, and vice versa. The appellant was   *g*
acquitted of the charge of buggery on count 1 but convicted of attempted buggery,
and was convicted on counts 2 and 3. On appeal it was contended on behalf of the
appellant that 'similar fact' evidence was admissible only to rebut a defence of
innocent association, or in relation to an issue of identity, and since the appellant
had not raised the defence of innocent association, nor had there been any issue of   *h*
identity, similar fact evidence was not, therefore, admissible.

Held – Similar fact evidence was admissible, not only to rebut the defence of innocent
association or in relation to the issue of identity, but also because of its inherent
probative value. Where, on a charge involving an allegation of homosexual conduct,
there was evidence of other acts of homosexual conduct, not related to the charge,
which bore a striking similarity to the acts of which the accused was charged, that   *j*
was a special feature which was sufficient in itself to justify the admissibility of the
evidence. The probative force of all the acts together was much greater than one
alone (see p 961 *d* to *f*, p 962 *g* and *h* and p 963 *a* to *c*, post).

R v Sims [1946] 1 All ER 697 and *Director of Public Prosecutions v Kilbourne* [1973] 1
All ER 440 applied.

Notes

a For corroboration, see 10 Halsbury's Laws (3rd Edn) 458-462, paras 843-850, and for cases on directions as to corroboration, see 14 Digest (Repl) 542-545, 5258-5304.

Cases referred to in judgment

Credland v Knowler (1951) 35 Cr App Rep 48, DC.

Director of Public Prosecutions v Kilbourne [1973] 1 All ER 440, [1973] AC 729, [1973] 2
b   WLR 254, 57 Cr App Rep 381, HL; rvsg sub nom R v Kilbourne [1973] 3 All ER 545, [1972] 1 WLR 1365, 56 Cr App Rep 828, CA.

Harris v Director of Public Prosecutions [1952] 1 All ER 1044, [1952] AC 694, 116 JP 248, 36 Cr App Rep 39, HL, 14 Digest (Repl) 423, 4118.

Makin v Attorney-General for New South Wales [1894] AC 57, [1891-94] All ER Rep 24, 63 LJPC 41, 69 LT 778, 58 JP 148, 17 Cox CC 704, PC, 14 Digest (Repl) 420, 4094.

c   R v Campbell [1956] 2 All ER 272, [1956] 2 QB 432, [1956] 3 WLR 219, 120 JP 359, 40 Cr App Rep 95, CCA, Digest (Cont Vol A) 377, 5106a.

R v Chandor [1959] 1 All ER 702, [1959] 1 QB 545, [1959] 2 WLR 522, 123 JP 131, 43 Cr App Rep 74, CCA, Digest (Cont Vol A) 367, 4204a.

R v Chapman [1973] 2 All ER 624, [1973] QB 774, [1973] 2 WLR 876, 57 Cr App Rep 511, CA.

d   R v Flack [1969] 2 All ER 784, [1969] 1 WLR 937, 133 JP 445, 53 Cr App Rep 166, CA, Digest (Cont Vol C) 195, 2238a.

R v Luisi [1964] Crim LR 605, CCA.

R v Redpath (1962) 46 Cr App Rep 319, 106 Sol Jo 412, CCA, Digest (Cont Vol A) 379, 5280a.

R v Sims [1946] 1 All ER 697, [1946] KB 531, [1947] LJR 160, 175 LT 72, 31 Cr App Rep
e   158, CCA, 14 Digest (Repl) 260, 2279.

R v Wilson (1973) 58 Cr App Rep 169, CA.

Cases also cited

R v Ailes (1918) 13 Cr App Rep 173, CCA

R v Bailey [1924] 2 KB 300, [1924] All ER Rep 466, CCA.

f   R v Ball [1911] AC 47, HL.

R v Jackson [1953] 1 All ER 872, [1953] 1 WLR 591, CCA.

Thompson v R [1918] AC 221, HL.

Appeal

Derrick Rowland Boardman appealed against his conviction on 3rd July 1973 in the
g Crown Court at Norwich before Croom-Johnson J on three counts. On count 1 he was convicted of the offence of attempted buggery, contrary to s 12(1) of the Sexual Offences Act 1956, and on counts 2 and 3 he was convicted of the offences of inciting the commission of buggery, contrary to s 12(1) of the 1956 Act. He was sentenced to three years imprisonment on the first count, and 18 months imprisonment on each of the other two counts, all those sentences to run concurrently. The appellant also
h appealed against sentence. The facts are set out in the judgment of the court.

Gerard Wright QC and A R L Ansell for the appellant.
R Ives for the Crown.

Cur adv vult

j
13th May. **ORR LJ** read the following judgment of the court. On 3rd July 1973 at the Norwich Crown Court this appellant was convicted, in each case by a majority of 11 to one, of an offence of attempted buggery (charged in count 1) and two offences of inciting the commission of buggery (counts 2 and 3). He was sentenced to three years imprisonment on the first count and 18 months imprisonment on each of the

other two counts, all those sentences to run concurrently. He now, with the leave of *a*
the full court, appeals to this court against those convictions.

At the material times the appellant was the headmaster of a language school in
Cambridge in which a number of boys from overseas were pupils and the three
offences involved three different pupils at that school. The first count charged him
with the offence of buggery with a boy S, 16 years of age at the time, and on that count
he was found not guilty of buggery but guilty of attempted buggery. The prosecution *b*
evidence was that that offence took place about mid-November 1972 in the appellant's
sitting-room at school where the appellant, after removing his own trousers and pants
and those of S, sucked S's penis until he obtained an erection and then put S's penis
against his own backside.

There was evidence of previous overtures by the appellant to S, the first in June
1972 in Tehran where S had gone home for his holidays and where the appellant *c*
was staying in an hotel. The appellant, according to S, put his hand on S's private
parts over his trousers. In September 1972, after S's return to school, according to S,
the appellant said, 'I want you to fuck me', and on a subsequent occasion in the
television room in the school the appellant made a similar request. There had also,
according to S, been occasions when the appellant pleaded with him for five minutes
of his time. *d*

The appellant was interviewed by Inspector Baker on 26th January 1973 when,
according to the inspector's evidence, S's statement was read over to him. He continually interrupted saying that it was lies and alleged that S was lying because he,
the appellant, had expelled him.

The second count of inciting the commission of buggery involved another pupil,
H, who at the time was 17 years of age. His evidence was that in January 1973 the *e*
appellant, after talking to H about his association with a girl, asked, 'Would you go
upstairs and sleep with me?' which H refused. The appellant produced some whisky,
which they drank, and, after some further talk about the girl-friend, the appellant
put his hand on H's private parts over his trousers. He again asked H to sleep with
him and said, 'If you don't want to fuck me, you can just lie on me'.

According to H there had been a previous incident when the appellant awakened *f*
him in the evening and took him in a taxi to the Taboo Disco Club where he bought
him brandy. On their return to the school from that club the appellant talked to
him about sex and touched his private parts over his trousers. The appellant said,
'Come and try it with me,' and later said, 'Come on and sleep with me, you needn't
do it if you don't like it. Just sleep only'.

The third count involved another boy, A, 18 years of age. His evidence was that in *g*
September or October 1972 he was called into the appellant's office when the appellant complained of loneliness and said, 'Let me make love with you'. When A
refused he said, 'Please, I need you, I have no friends'. The following day A was
going to telephone his father. The appellant said that if he did he, the appellant,
would tell his father that A was a 'queer'. The boy did telephone his father and the
appellant kept saying to the father, 'Don't believe him'. *h*

In January 1973, according to A, there was an occasion when the appellant was
drunk and sent for him. He said, 'You must understand that I love you'. He also
said, 'Help me, I want to make love with you. You are just as queer as I am, you
want someone to fuck you.' The boy left the room and shortly afterwards was seen
by Mr Brough, a teacher, who formed the view that he was in a distressed state.

The inspector gave evidence that on 27th March 1973 the appellant said that he *j*
was making telephone calls to the fathers of these boys and he guaranteed that he,
the inspector, would not finish up with one witness except S. He said that if there
were no witnesses, there would be no corroboration.

The appellant in his own evidence denied committing any of the alleged offences
or making any indecent overtures. He claimed that S had threatened him with a

a homosexual charge because the appellant had found S lying on a bunk in the dormitory on top of another boy. He claimed he had taken H to the Disco Club because he wanted to confront him with a bad woman with whom he was associating. He claimed that A was lying because of a row there had been over missing money from the tuck shop and another about whether A should be allowed to have a car. He denied telling the inspector that he had expelled S, but admitted that he had not in
b fact expelled him, and he denied the inspector's account of the telephone conversation.

We turn now to the grounds of appeal against conviction. In his summing-up the judge pointed out to the jury that it was a common feature of counts 1 and 2 that the prosecution evidence involved criminal behaviour 'of a particular, unusual, kind' in that in each case the appellant, a grown man, was attempting to induce acts of
c buggery in which an adolescent boy would play the active, and the appellant the passive, part, but that as respects count 3 the evidence of A fell short of establishing any suggestion of this particular kind; and on that basis he directed the jury that it was open to them to find, in H's evidence with reference to count 2, corroboration of S's evidence as to count 1 and vice versa, but that there could be no mutual corroboration between S or H and A.

d Counsel for the appellant claims that this direction, insofar as it related to counts 1 and 2, was wrong in law. He accepts that 'similar fact' evidence would have been admissible to rebut a defence of innocent association or in relation to an issue of identity, but contends, and we are prepared to accept rightly, that in the present case no defence of innocent association was set up, the appellant's evidence having been that the meetings at which the incidents were alleged to have occurred, did not in
e fact take place, and there was no issue of identity. In these circumstances he argues that 'similar fact' evidence was not admissible and that nothing in the speeches delivered in the House of Lords in *Director of Public Prosecutions v Kilbourne*[1] should be understood as involving that it was. In support of this argument he referred us to a large number of authorities beginning with *Makin v Attorney-General for New South Wales*[2] and ending with the *Kilbourne* case[1] itself. It is in our view clear that in the
f present case the judge, in framing the direction in question, was seeking to apply the decision of the House of Lords in the *Kilbourne* case[1], and that the answer to counsel's argument is to be found in the reasoning of the speeches in that case. For this reason, without intending any disrespect to counsel's able argument, we find it unnecessary to refer to many of the earlier cases, and would only mention the following matters as part of the background to the *Kilbourne*[1] decision.

g In *Makin's* case Lord Herschell LC in a well-known passage said[3]:

'It is undoubtedly not competent for the prosecution to adduce evidence tending to shew that the accused has been guilty of criminal acts other than those covered by the indictment, for the purpose of leading to the conclusion that the accused is a person likely from his criminal conduct or character to have committed the offence for which he is being tried. On the other hand, the mere
h fact that the evidence adduced tends to shew the commission of other crimes does not render it inadmissible if it be relevant to an issue before the jury, and it may be so relevant if it bears upon the question whether the acts alleged to constitute the crime charged in the indictment were designed or accidental, or to rebut a defence which would otherwise be open to the accused.'

j Counsel urged us not to put a construction on the speeches in the *Kilbourne* case[1] which would reduce the ambit of the first of these sentences, but in *Harris v Director of Public Prosecutions*[4] Viscount Simon indicated that in his view the classes of case

---

1 [1973] 1 All ER 440, [1973] AC 729
2 [1894] AC 57, [1891-94] All ER Rep 24
3 [1894] AC at 65, [1891-94] All ER Rep at 25, 26
4 [1952] 1 All ER 1044 at 1046, 1047, [1952] AC 694 at 705

mentioned in the second sentence did not constitute a closed list, and those classes
have in fact been added to since the *Makin* case[1] was decided.

In *R v Sims*[2] the judgment of the Court of Criminal Appeal includes the following
passages:

> 'The evidence of each man was that the accused invited him into the house
> and there committed the acts charged. The acts they describe bear a striking
> similarity. That is a special feature sufficient in itself to justify the admissibility
> of the evidence . . . The probative force of all the acts together is much greater
> than one alone . . . We do not think that the evidence of the men can be con-
> sidered as corroborating one another, because each may be said to be an accom-
> plice in the act to which he speaks and his evidence is to be viewed with
> caution . . .'

The second of these passages was followed in *R v Campbell*[3], where, however, the
view was expressed that, although the evidence in question could not amount to
corroboration, the jury might properly be told that a succession of similar cases
might help them to determine the truth of the matter; but in *R v Chandor*[4] and *R v
Flack*[5] it was held that such a direction was improper where the defence was that
the meeting or occasion for an incident in question did not take place at all.

In *R v Kilbourne*[6], which involved homosexual offences on boys belonging to two
different groups, this court, being satisfied that each of the accusations indicated
that the accused was a man whose homosexual proclivities took a particular form and
further that the evidence of each boy went to rebut the defence of innocent association which the accused had put forward, held that evidence from boys in either
group as to alleged offences involving them was admissible in relation to the charges
involving members of the other group but, on the authorities above referred to, was
incapable of amounting to corroboration and, because the judge's direction could
have led the jury to think that it was, they quashed the convictions.

On the second of these issues the House of Lords[7], rejecting the distinction previously drawn between evidence capable of amounting to corroboration and evidence
not so capable but as to which the jury could be directed that it might help them to
determine the truth of the matter, took a different view and restored the convictions.

In the House of Lords it appears that the issue as to the admissibility of the evidence
was (at least eventually) conceded on behalf of the accused, but it is clear from the
speeches that the House examined the relevant authorities, from *Makin*[1] onwards,
in some depth (per Lord Hailsham LC[8]) and considered it necessary to do so as a
basis for considering the issue of corroboration (per Lord Simon[9]), and it is in our
judgment clear that the House considered the evidence in question to be admissible
not only to rebut the defence of innocent association but also because of its inherent
probative value; in other words on the basis of the first passage above quoted from
the judgment in *R v Sims*[10]. We base this conclusion in particular on passages in
Lord Hailsham LC's speech[11] (with which Lord Morris agreed), in Lord Reid's[12]
and in Lord Simon's[13].

---

1 [1894] AC 57, [1891-94] All ER Rep 24
2 [1946] 1 All ER 697 at 701, 703, [1946] KB 531 at 539, 540, 544
3 [1956] 2 All ER 272, [1956] 2 QB 432
4 [1959] 1 All ER 702, [1959] 1 QB 545
5 [1969] 2 All ER 784, [1969] 1 WLR 937
6 [1972] 3 All ER 545, [1972] 1 WLR 1365
7 [1973] 1 All ER 440, [1973] AC 729
8 [1973] 1 All ER at 448, [1973] AC at 741
9 [1973] 1 All ER at 462, [1973] AC at 757, 758
10 [1946] 1 All ER at 701, [1946] KB at 539, 540
11 [1973] 1 All ER 447-452, [1973] AC at 741-746
12 [1973] 1 All ER at 456, [1973] AC at 750, 751
13 [1973] 1 All ER at 459, 462, [1973] AC at 754, 757

a   For these reasons we hold that counsel's main argument on this issue fails, but he advanced a further argument that the evidence in question was inadmissible on the basis of the view expressed by Lord Reid in the Kilbourne case[1] that only two instances would not be enough to make a system. But, with great respect to this view, we can find no support for such a restriction in any of the other speeches and indications that three of the other members of the House did not accept it, for Lord Hailsham b LC (with whose speech Lord Morris, as already mentioned, agreed, and whose citation of the Scottish cases Lord Simon considered helpful) cited[2] with approval a direction by the Lord Justice-Clerk (Lord Aitchison) in a Scottish case[3] in which the evidence of only two girls was involved. In these circumstances we do not consider that we should be justified in concluding that a majority of the House accepted Lord Reid's restriction as applying to admissibility, as distinct from weight, of evidence. c (See also, on this question, R v Wilson[4].)

Counsel next attacked a direction given by the judge with reference to certain evidence given by Inspector Baker and by the appellant at the trial. The inspector's evidence was that when he interviewed the appellant and read to him a statement by S the appellant said, 'It's all lies, he only said this because I expelled him'. In his own evidence the appellant denied saying to the inspector that he had expelled S but agreed d that he had not in fact expelled him and said that the reason why S had told lies was that the appellant had caught him in a homosexual act with another boy, and S had then threatened to implicate the appellant unless he kept quiet about it.

In relation to this evidence the judge directed the jury that if they were satisfied that the appellant had lied, either to the police before the trial or in the witness box, such lies were capable of amounting to corroboration. Counsel has attacked this e direction on the grounds that if the appellant lied to the inspector it was only on a peripheral matter and that, on the authority of R v Chapman[5], lies told by the appellant in evidence at the hearing cannot amount to corroboration. We are unable to accept the first of these arguments. In our view if the appellant lied to the inspector in saying that he had expelled S it was not a lie on a peripheral matter but, 'of such a nature, and made in such circumstances, as to lead to an inference in support of [the com- f plainant]' (see Credland v Knowler[6], citing earlier authorities[7]). As to lies by the accused in court we accept the correctness of the decision in R v Chapman[5] on the facts of that case, and that it will be applicable in most cases. Whether the judgment should be treated as authority for the proposition that a lie told by the accused in evidence can never, whatever the circumstances, be capable of amounting to corro- boration is a matter on which to feel some doubt but which does not arise for deter- mination in the present case. In our view the short answer to the present problem g is that the question of lies in court was inextricably bound up with that of lies before the hearing to Inspector Baker, for the jury could not be satisfied that the appellant had lied to the inspector unless they disbelieved his evidence at the trial that he had never mentioned expulsion of S, and in these circumstances, to the extent that there was misdirection, we have no hesitation in applying the proviso.

h With the remaining grounds of appeal we can deal very shortly. We think that there is force in the submission that as regards count 2 the evidence of Mrs Cole about a whisky bottle was too peripheral to be capable of amounting to corroboration, but the judge suggested to the jury that they might not consider this a very important matter, and here again we have no hesitation in applying the proviso.

1 [1973] 1 All ER at 456, [1973] AC at 751

j 2 [1973] 1 All ER at 451, 452, [1973] AC at 745, 746

3 HM Advocate v AE 1937 JC 96 at 98-100

4 (1973) 58 Cr App Rep 169

5 [1973] 2 All ER 624, [1973] QB 774

6 (1951) 35 Cr App Rep 48 at 55

7 Dawson v M'Kenzie (1908) 45 SLR 473 and Jones v Thomas [1934] 1 KB 323, [1933] All ER Rep 535

It was argued with reference to count 1 that the judge failed adequately to warn *a* the jury that they must be satisfied as to S's evidence before they considered corroboration and wrongly directed them that they could take into account 'similarity of behaviour in the one instance—in deciding whether you are made sure in the other instance'. But the judge had on the previous page of the summing-up directed the jury entirely properly in relation to count 2 that if they did not believe the evidence of H there was nothing to corroborate, and considering this part of the summing-up as a *b* whole, we have not been satisfied that there was any misdirection or failure to direct.

We find no substance in the arguments that the judge failed to put the defence case sufficiently before the jury or to deal in sufficient detail with the cross-examination of prosecution witnesses or sufficiently to warn the jury that they must not lump all the counts together. We also find no substance in the argument that the conviction of attempted buggery on count 1 was unsafe on the ground that S had *c* given evidence of a completed act. This matter was the subject of a very careful direction by the judge and the jury were fully entitled to convict of attempt if they otherwise believed S's evidence but were left unsure of penetration.

There remains counsel's final argument in relation to count 3. As to this count the judge directed the jury that they could find corroboration in the evidence of Mr Brough, a teacher at the school, that on a date which he put as 18th January 1973, *d* he saw A who must, he said, at that time have come out from the appellant's office, and observed that he was in a very distressed state. This was not the date of the offence charged in count 3, which was September/October 1972, but of another incident of which A gave evidence. The judge put Mr Brough's evidence to the jury as not being in any event very strong corroboration, and warned them that if they thought A was distressed because he had had a row with the appellant about some *e* other matter, his distress could not amount to corroboration, but counsel has argued that in all the circumstances this matter should not have been put to the jury as capable of being corroboration. It was pointed out in *R v Redpath*[1] that in considering observed distress as possible corroboration—

'the circumstances will vary enormously, and in some circumstances quite *f* clearly no weight, or little weight, could be attached to such evidence as corroboration.'

And in *R v Luisi*[2], where the court considered that the significance of a girl's distress had been overemphasised, it was indicated that wherever the possibility exists of the distress being feigned a careful warning should be given to the jury on that subject.

We have found this ground of appeal a difficult one. On the one hand it cannot be *g* said that the judge overemphasised the aspect of distress. On the other hand the distress was not directly associated with the incident which was the subject of count 3; it seems difficult to exclude the possibility of its being feigned; and there was no other evidence capable of supplying corroboration. We have come to the conclusion that the distress should either not have been put to the jury at all or, if put, should at least have been accompanied by a warning as to the possibility of its having been caused *h* otherwise than by an indecent suggestion made by the appellant or by a row with him, which were the two alternatives left to the jury in the summing-up; and because this count, in the respects already mentioned, stands on its own and no other corroboration was available, we do not consider it safe to apply the proviso.

In the result the conviction on count 3 will be quashed, but the appeal fails on counts 1 and 2. *j*

There remains in this case the application for leave to appeal against sentence. The appellant is a single man of 45. He has a number of previous convictions, but

1 (1962) 46 Cr App Rep 319 at 321
2 [1964] Crim LR 605

a the only relevant one for the present purpose is a conviction for an indecent assault on a male person of 11 years of age for which, in July 1954, he was sentenced to nine months imprisonment.

There was before the trial judge when he imposed sentence a prison medical report by Dr West, a consultant psychiatrist whom the appellant consulted in January 1973 after the commission of these offences, in which he concluded that the appellant was a confirmed homosexual. There was also a probation report which, through no *b* fault of the probation officer, was not a particularly helpful one. Before this court there is also a letter from the appellant's mother.

The quashing by this court of the conviction on count 3 makes no difference, in itself, to the sentences imposed because the sentences imposed were concurrent. But counsel before this court has renewed the argument which he put before the judge as to the sentence of three years on count 1. He has in addition asked us to have in mind the *c* very difficult circumstances, apparent from her letter, in which the appellant's mother is placed by reason of the niece.

This court has considered carefully all the matters that have been put forward in mitigation and gives what weight it can to all those matters, but we find it quite impossible to say that the sentence in this case was either wrong in principle or excessive. The subject-matter of the first count was a grave matter involving the *d* relationship of master and pupil and it was an offence committed by a man who had already had this previous conviction. We find it impossible to take the view that the sentence was excessive, and accordingly the application for leave to appeal against sentence must be refused.

e *Appeal against conviction on counts 1 and 2 dismissed; appeal against conviction on count 3 allowed, and that conviction quashed; appeal against sentence dismissed. Leave to appeal to the House of Lords refused but the following point of law was certified as being of general public importance: 'Whether on a charge involving an allegation of homosexual conduct, where there is evidence that the accused person is a man whose homosexual proclivities take a particular form, that evidence is thereby admissible although it tends to show that the accused* *f* *has been guilty of criminal acts other than those charged?'*

20th June 1974. The appeal committee of the House of Lords gave leave to appeal.

Solicitors: *Bobbetts, Harvey & Grove*, Bristol (for the appellant); *Director of Public Prosecutions.*

Lea Josse   Barrister.

Practice Direction   *a*

QUEEN'S BENCH DIVISION

Practice – Summons for directions – Hearing – Application for leave to call expert evidence – Disclosure of reports – Procedure – RSC Ord 25 (as amended by the Rules of the Supreme Court (Amendment) 1974, SI 1974 No 295) – RSC Ord 38, rr 35-44 (as added by the Rules of the Supreme Court (Amendment) 1974, SI 1974 No 295).   *b*

1. RSC Ord 38, rr 35-44, came into force on 1st June 1974 and apply to all actions set down since that date.

2. It is provided by Ord 25, as now amended, that consideration must be given at the hearing of the summons for directions to whether orders under these rules should be made and that all parties must, where practicable, make any application for leave to call expert evidence and as to the disclosure of reports, at that hearing.   *c*

3. For the guidance of the profession and to provide uniformity, it is notified that the practice at the hearing of the summons for directions, with such variations as the circumstances may require, will be as follows:

    (a) *Agreement of the parties.* If the parties have agreed as to adducing expert evidence or disclosure of reports this fact will be recorded.   *d*

Otherwise

    (b) *Medical reports.* Mutual disclosure (i e exchange of reports) will normally be ordered within a specified period; if any further medical examination is necessary, the period asked for should allow for this, but should not materially extend beyond setting down. Reciprocity will be the normal practice, but in exceptional circumstances, and to save costs, disclosure by one party only may be ordered and the other party permitted to defer disclosure of any report, e g where a defendant has not had a medical examination and it is likely that the plaintiff's report will be agreed.   *e*

    (c) *Non-medical experts.* If both parties have instructed, or are likely to instruct, experts the question of disclosure of reports will be dealt with at the hearing of the summons for directions; any order for disclosure will normally be by way of exchange. In other cases, disclosure of one party's report only may be ordered in exceptional circumstances (see (b), foregoing), or the parties may be given leave to call expert witnesses without disclosure of reports; liberty to apply subsequently for disclosure may be given.   *f*

    (d) *Engineers' reports in collision cases.* If any party wishes to call an expert in a case of collision on land and has not yet disclosed his report, that party must ask for an extension of time for so doing.   *g*

4. Practice form PF 51A, replacing paras 23 and 24 of PF 51 (summons for directions), will be used for short forms of order in straightforward cases. Extended forms of order may be used wherever necessary.   *h*

W RUSSELL LAWRENCE
Senior Master

18th June 1974

a   Fairline Shipping Corporation v Adamson

QUEEN'S BENCH DIVISION AT WINCHESTER
KERR J
18th, 19th OCTOBER, 8th NOVEMBER 1973

b

*Contract – Offer and acceptance – Acceptance – Acceptance by silence – Offer by defendant to
plaintiffs – Novation of contract – Offer by defendant to take over third party's contract with
plaintiffs – Acquiescence but no response to offer by plaintiffs – Whether defendant bound by
contract – Whether defendant liable for breach.*

c   *Negligence – Duty to take care – Circumstances in which duty arising – Bailment of goods –
Assumption of duty of care by third party – Bailment of goods to company – Director of
company – Assumption of duty of care by director with respect to goods – Personal liability
of director for damage to goods.*

d
A company ('GM Ltd') operated a cold store as part of its business of buying and
reselling game and meat products. Only on very rare occasions did GM Ltd use the
premises to store goods which did not belong to it. In September 1971 the defendant
bought the freehold of the store, it being a term of the agreement that he would
grant a lease of the store to GM Ltd. The defendant also acquired a 50 per cent holding
in GM Ltd, which was in financial difficulties, and became its managing director.
e
The business of buying and selling the company's products remained under the
management of other directors. By January 1972 it was clear that GM Ltd was in
serious financial difficulty and probably could not be saved. From that time on
the defendant was only concerned with the liquidation of the business. No lease
of the cold store to GM Ltd was executed although in January GM Ltd paid some
£3,000 to the defendant, representing a year's rent in advance. A typist employed by
f
GM Ltd at the store was discharged in January and thereafter, apart from the directors,
the only person on its payroll was an assistant employed by the defendant to look
after his interests. From January onwards the financial and secretarial side of the
business was conducted by the defendant and his assistant, with the help of the
defendant's secretary who did the necessary typing, from other premises owned by
the defendant. Correspondence on behalf of GM Ltd was, however, typed on that
company's headed notepaper and not on the defendant's personal notepaper. At
g
the beginning of March the plaintiffs' agent contacted V, a director of GM Ltd, and
arranged with him, on behalf of GM Ltd, for a consignment of meat, vegetable
and fat products to be stored at the cold store. V informed the defendant who raised
no objection to the arrangement. The consignment was delivered into the store
on 14th March. Subsequently the defendant realised that there was nothing in writing
to confirm the arrangement and on 23rd March a letter was written to the plaintiffs'
h
agents on paper carrying the defendant's letterhead and signed by his secretary
'for' him. The letter read: 'I confirm the arrangement regarding the storage of goods
in my premises . . . I understand there is a 12·1/5 ton involved and the rent per calendar
month as agreed with your Representative is £5 per ton per month and £5 per ton
per part month. My invoice for £61·00 being the first months rental due will be sent
to you on or around the 14th April, 1972'. The plaintiffs' agents received the letter
j
and accepted it without querying why it had not come from GM Ltd; the defendant
was known to them as a businessman of substance. An invoice was sent to the
plaintiffs' agents by the defendant on 14th April. While the plaintiffs' consignment
was in the store no steps were taken to check on the temperature of the chamber
in which the goods were stored. On occasion the defendant visited the store to show
round prospective purchasers of the premises; he heard the refrigeration machinery

working and assumed all was well. On 16th April it was discovered that one of the *a*
fans distributing cold air into the chamber had broken down and the contents of the
chamber had thawed. The plaintiffs brought an action against the defendant for
breach of contract and/or negligence, alleging (i) that the defendant's letter of 23rd
March and the plaintiffs' acquiescence operated as a novation between the defendant
and the plaintiffs' agents of the original contract with GM Ltd, and (ii) that the defendant was a bailee of the goods or liable in negligence in the same way as a bailee. *b*

Held – (i) In order to constitute a contract the acceptance of an offer had to be communicated to the offeror and the uncommunicated acceptance of the offer could
not have the effect of binding the offeror. Accordingly, if the defendant's letter of
23rd March constituted an offer by the defendant to take over the contract from
GM Ltd, the absence of any response by the plaintiffs' agents to that offer could not *c*
be construed as an acceptance capable of binding the defendant. Such a result could
only flow from an estoppel operating against the offeror and the plaintiffs' cause
of action could not be founded on estoppel. Accordingly the claim in contract failed
(see p 974 *h* and *j* to p 975 *a*, post); *Felthouse v Bindley* (1862) 11 CBNS 869 applied.
   (ii) Although the evidence was insufficient to establish that the defendant was a
bailee of the goods, his liability to the plaintiffs in negligence was not necessarily *d*
excluded as a matter of law on the ground that there was no contract with him and
that he was not a bailee having a right to the legal possession of the goods. In the
circumstances the defendant owed a duty of care to the plaintiffs since, at the
relevant time, GM Ltd could only perform its duties in relation to the goods through
its directors and the only director who had concerned himself in any way with the
goods after delivery was the defendant. The letter of 23rd March showed that the *e*
defendant regarded himself, and not the company, as concerned with the storage of
the goods. The defendant had therefore assumed a duty of care to the plaintiffs in
respect of the storage of their goods in his premises and, in consequence of his breach
of that duty, the goods had been damaged. The plaintiffs were therefore entitled
to judgment (see p 975 *h* and p 976 *e* to *g*, post); *Adler v Dickson* [1954] 3 All ER 397
and *Morris v C W Martin & Sons Ltd* [1965] 2 All ER 725 applied. *f*

Notes
For the mode of acceptance so as to constitute a contract, see 8 Halsbury's Laws
(3rd Edn) 72, 73, para 126, and for cases on the subject, see 12 Digest (Reissue) 81-86,
419-444.
   For cases in which a duty of care arises, see 28 Halsbury's Laws (3rd Edn) 7, para 4, *g*
and for cases on the duty to take care, see 36 Digest (Repl) 12-22, *34-89.*

Cases referred to in judgment
Adler v Dickson [1954] 3 All ER 397, [1955] 1 QB 158, [1954] 3 WLR 696, [1954] 2 Lloyd's
   Rep 267, CA, 12 Digest (Reissue) 50, 259.
Felthouse v Bindley (1862) 11 CBNS 869, 31 LJCP 204, 6 LT 157, 142 ER 1037; *affd* (1863) *h*
   1 New Rep 401, 7 LT 835, Ex Ch, 39 Digest (Repl) 482, 307.
Morris v C W Martin & Sons Ltd [1965] 2 All ER 725, [1966] 1 QB 716, [1965] 3 WLR
   276, [1965] 2 Lloyd's Rep 63, CA, Digest (Cont Vol B) 30, *151a.*

Action
By a writ issued on 4th August 1972 the plaintiffs, Fairline Shipping Corporation,
brought an action against the defendant, Brian Adamson, claiming damages for breach *j*
of contract and, in the alternative, negligence. The facts are set out in the judgment
of Kerr J.

Martin Tucker for the plaintiffs.
John Spokes QC for the defendant.

a   *Cur adv vult*

8th November. **KERR J** read the following judgment. In this action the plaintiffs claim damages for negligence or breach of contract due to damage suffered by a large quantity of ship's provisions owned by them which were not kept under adequate refrigeration. The consignment was stored in the defendant's cold store at 36 Castle Way, Southampton, from 14th March 1972. By 17th April it had become

b apparent that due to the machinery not working properly a large part of the consignment, which consisted mostly of meat, vegetable and fat products, had gone bad. The quantum of the plaintiffs' loss has been agreed at £3,143·78 and is not in issue. The defendant denies liability on two grounds. First and foremost, he contends that he was not the bailee or otherwise responsible for the goods, but that the sole responsibility in contract and tort lay with a company called Game & Meat Products Ltd

c (to which I will refer as 'Game & Meat') of which he was the managing director. Secondly, he denies that the damage occurred as the result of breach of contract or negligence by anyone.

The main issue in the case concerns the position of Game & Meat in relation to these goods and to the defendant. For this purpose it is necessary to set out certain background material and events which occurred some time before the goods arrived

d in the store.

The defendant has a number of different business and property interests in Southampton. His private address was originally 74 London Road, but he subsequently moved into a private hotel operated by him at 15 Lawn Road, Southampton. His main business interest appears at all times to have been that he owned and operated a club know as the Silhouette Club at St Michael's Square, which is just

e round the corner from the cold store in Castle Way. Until September 1971 the freehold of the club and of the cold store had been owned by a company called Vernon & Tear Ltd. This was one of the companies in what was referred to in the evidence as 'the Vernon Group'. The moving spirits of the Vernon Group for present purposes were Messrs Vernon senior and junior, one of the companies in the group of which they were both directors being Game & Meat. As the name indicates,

f the business of Game & Meat was the buying and reselling, largely to the Continent, of game and meat products. This required the storage of such products under refrigeration between their purchase and resale, and Game & Meat used the cold store in Castle Way for this purpose. There does not appear to have been any lease of the cold store by Vernon & Tear Ltd to Game & Meat at any time. Since both companies were in the same group the matter was evidently dealt with informally,

g and I understand that no rent was ever paid by Game & Meat, though certain entries were made in the accounts of the two companies reflecting the right of Game & Meat to use the premises. On only rare occasions had the premises been used for the storage of goods which did not belong to Game & Meat, and until the arrival of the consignment in question this had not happened for many months and was not part of the ordinary business of the company.

h The Vernons were evidently members of the Silhouette Club and friends of the defendant. By September 1971 it had been agreed that certain business transactions should be carried out between them and the defendant. The defendant bought the freehold of the Silhouette Club from Vernon & Tear Ltd, and by a contract dated 16th September 1971 he also bought from this company the freehold of the cold store in Castle Way, together with the refrigerating units in it. It was a term of this

j contract that on completion the defendant was to grant a lease of the cold store to Game & Meat for two years at the yearly rent of £3,000, either party having the right to determine the lease by a three months notice given on or after 31st March 1973. However, for reasons to which I must refer in a moment no such lease was ever granted. At the same time it was also decided that the defendant should acquire an interest in Game & Meat. It was then already known that Game & Meat was in financial difficulty; the company ultimately went into voluntary liquidation on

24th April 1972, shortly after the discovery of the damage to the consignment in
question. The defendant evidently agreed to attempt to procure additional finance
for Game & Meat, but I understand that this did not materialise, or at any rate not
to a sufficient extent. In return he acquired a 50 per cent shareholding in Game &
Meat, and from September 1971 he became its managing director. The business of
buying and selling the products of the company however remained under the
management of the Vernons. From the autumn of 1971 onwards the defendant
began to concern himself actively with the financial affairs of Game & Meat and
asked his accountant to carry out an investigation. He also asked an employee of
his, a Mr Buckingham, to concern himself with the accounts and records of Game &
Meat which had got into a confused state. Mr Buckingham described himself as a
company administrator and had considerable experience in the keeping of books
and records and general accountancy matters. Until some time in December 1971
Mr Buckingham had been employed by the defendant or by one of his companies
at the Silhouette Club. From December 1971 until the end of March 1972, when he
also concerned himself with the affairs of Game & Meat on behalf of the defendant,
his salary was paid by Game & Meat. I am however satisfied that this was little
more than a convenient financial arrangement between the defendant and the
Vernons, and that the bulk of Mr Buckingham's time and work continued to be
devoted to the personal interests of the defendant. He agreed in evidence that his
position in Game & Meat was in reality that of a watchdog on behalf of the defendant's
interests. By about January 1972 it had become clear that Game & Meat was in serious
financial difficulty and could probably not be saved. I do not accept that this was not
appreciated until late March or April 1972. In January 1972 the typist employed by
Game & Meat in the cold store was discharged. Apart from the directors (one of
whom was also the company secretary) and Mr Buckingham, Game & Meat then
had no other person on its payroll. When goods were brought in or taken out of the
cold store this was done by outside labour. From about January onwards the business
of Game & Meat consisted solely in the acquisition and disposal of the season's stocks,
and this was dealt with by the Vernons. Mr Buckingham's functions were limited
to trying to chase up debtors and to deal with the increasing pressures from creditors,
but this only occupied him for a short period on each day. Insofar as correspondence
was necessary for this purpose I conclude on balance that this was carried out under
the letterhead of Game & Meat, as one would expect. For this purpose Mr Buckingham spent a short period of each day in the office accommodation at the cold store;
for the remainder of the day he worked in the Silhouette Club round the corner in
the same way as before. After the dismissal of the typist employed by Game & Meat,
a Mrs Hawkins, who was employed by the defendant as his secretary in the Silhouette
Club, used to do whatever typing was necessary on behalf of Game & Meat. Having
seen her, the defendant and Mr Buckingham in the witness box I conclude that for
this purpose she also used the letterhead of Game & Meat and not the defendant's
personal letterhead. Both she and Mr Buckingham had considerable experience in
commercial correspondence and fully appreciated the difference between writing
on the company's notepaper and on the defendant's personal notepaper. I do not
accept the evidence that the latter was used indiscriminately because the company's
notepaper was often unavailable. The evidence relating to this aspect was scanty
and unsatisfactory but it does show that the company still used its own letterhead,
with its registered address at Canute Road, Southampton, in April 1972. Although
Mrs Hawkins said that she kept a Game & Meat file of correspondence at the
Silhouette Club, this was not produced either on discovery or in evidence; nor were
any of the accounts of Game & Meat produced. I do not accept the evidence on behalf
of the defendant suggesting that the company's notepaper was not readily available
or was not used for the company's business in the normal way. I think that this was
a distortion of the facts in an attempt to explain away the use of the defendant's
personal notepaper in relation to these goods, as mentioned hereafter.

a   As I have already mentioned, the proposed lease from the defendant to Game &
Meat was never executed; nor were any steps ever taken to put this in train. Mr
Martin Vernon, who gave evidence, said that this was merely an administrative
oversight, but I do not accept this. The defendant virtually admitted in evidence
that the reason why no lease was ever executed was because Game & Meat's financial
position was such that it was doubtful whether it was really in his own interest,
b   and possibly also in the interest of Game & Meat, to pursue this proposal. But if
Game & Meat was heading for disaster, then it was clearly in the defendant's interest
to salvage as much as he could for himself, and I think that in view of his close
association with the Vernons, and the efforts which he had made on behalf of the
company, they raised no objection to this. I think that it was in these circumstances
and against this background that Game & Meat paid two sums of £1,560 each to
c   the defendant by means of two cheques, respectively dated 4th and 20th January
1972, signed by one of the Vernons and the defendant himself. This total sum of
£3,120 was intended to include the rent said to be payable by Game & Meat for
the cold store in respect of the first year, presumably up to 16th September 1972,
the balance of £120 being irrelevant for present purposes. It was said on behalf of
the defendant that although no lease had ever been executed or set in train, it had
d   been orally agreed that the whole of each year's rent was to be payable in advance.
I do not believe that any such agreement was ever made. I think that this payment
was made because Game & Meat undoubtedly had the use of the cold store for the
company's business, and because the proposal that the defendant should grant a
formal lease to the company provided some justification for a payment of £3,000 at
a time when the company was still able to make such a payment but when the
e   likelihood of its being able to do so in the future was more than doubtful.
    I am satisfied that by January 1972 neither the defendant nor the Vernons nor
Mr Buckingham expected Game & Meat to survive more than a few months, and
that they were thereafter only concerned with the liquidation of the season's business.
    This is my assessment of the background position, and one then comes to the events
relating to the plaintiffs' consignment of provisions in March and April 1972. This
f   had been discharged from a vessel in Southampton and was due to be loaded on
another vessel about six weeks later. Pending such reloading it was necessary to
find refrigerated storage for the consignment. The plaintiffs' agents who took
delivery of the consignment were a company of ship's agents named Keller Bryant
& Co Ltd. It was not disputed that Keller Bryant acted in all respects as agents for
the plaintiffs, and the plaintiffs' right to sue as principals both in contract and in tort
g   was admitted. The refrigerated stores normally used by Keller Bryant were unavailable at the time, and Keller Bryant accordingly enquired from the port health
authority whether they could suggest some other store. The port health authority
mentioned the name of Game & Meat and the cold store in Castle Way, and a Mr
Stafford, the stores superintendent of Keller Bryant, accordingly telephoned to Game
& Meat on about 3rd March to enquire whether they could store this consignment.
h   This call was received by Mr Martin Vernon at the offices of the cold store in Castle
Way. In the course of this telephone conversation Mr Vernon was speaking on behalf
of Game & Meat and Mr Stafford also understood him to be speaking on behalf
of the company. No one in Keller Bryant had dealt with Game & Meat before or
had until then known anything about the company; nor did anyone concerned in
Keller Bryant know anything about any connection between the defendant and
j   Game & Meat or that the defendant was the owner of the cold store in Castle Way.
Mr Stafford explained that storage was required for about five to six weeks and
described the general nature of the consignment. Mr Vernon agreed to store the
goods in Castle Way at a rate of £5 per ton per month and on the basis that Keller
Bryant would provide the necessary labour for the movement of the consignment
into and out of the cold store. Mr Vernon also informed Mr Stafford that the key
to the cold store could be obtained from the Silhouette Club, and I am satisfied that
this is where it was normally kept.

On 14th March the goods were delivered into the cold store. The person in charge
on behalf of Keller Bryant was a Mr Broom who arrived at the cold store with one *a*
of the lorries transporting the goods. I accept Mr Broom's evidence as to what then
happened. He found the store locked, but obtained the key from someone who
got it from the Silhouette Club, probably Mr Buckingham. The labour engaged by
Keller Bryant arrived a little later and the goods were then moved into one of the
refrigerated chambers in the store. Mr Buckingham was in the cold store while this *b*
was being done, but no receipt for the goods was issued, and on the evidence no one
can be said formally to have taken delivery of the goods, either on behalf of Game
& Meat or on behalf of the defendant. However, Mr Broom certainly considered that
the goods were being delivered to Game & Meat. The refrigerated chamber had two
doors, one through which the goods were moved in and the other leading into an
adjoining refrigerated chamber. One or more representatives of the port health *c*
authority were also present, and when all the goods had been moved in, the door
through which they had been moved in was sealed by the port health authority.
The other door was not sealed. I am satisfied that this was done so that people could
not walk through the refrigerated storage space and so that its contents should only
be exposed to the refrigerated atmosphere of that and the adjoining chamber. Mr
Broom and the lorries then left.

Prior to the arrival of the goods Mr Martin Vernon had informed the defendant *d*
about the arrangements which he had made relating to their storage and the defendant had raised no objection. Mr Vernon knew about the unsealed entrance to the
chamber, and by looking at the goods he was able to form an approximate estimate
of their weight, amounting to a little over 12 tons, of which he informed the defendant
or Mr Buckingham shortly thereafter. It was then realised by the defendant or
Mr Buckingham, or both, that there was still nothing in writing to confirm the arrange- *e*
ments under which the goods had been stored. It was in these circumstances that
a significant letter was written to Keller Bryant on 23rd March. I am satisfied that
this was dictated to Mrs Hawkins either by the defendant or by Mr Buckingham
with the knowledge and approval of the defendant. Having considered the evidence
of these witnesses and seen them in the witness box I do not accept that the defendant
knew nothing about this letter. It was typed by Mrs Hawkins on the defendant's *f*
personal and business notepaper, with his name printed at the top, after she had
altered his printed address from 74 London Road to 15 Lawn Road. It bore the
defendant's and her dictation codes and was in the following terms:

'Dear Sirs, I confirm the arrangement regarding the storage of goods in my
premises at 36, Castle Way; I understand there is a 12.1/5 ton involved and the *g*
rent per calendar month as agreed with your Representative is £5 per ton
per month and £5 per ton per part month. My invoice for £61·00 being the
first months rental due will be sent to you on or around the 14th April, 1972.
Yours faithfully, [signed:] A. Hawkins (Mrs) for [the defendant].'

Neither of the Vernons had anything to do with the writing of this letter and there *h*
was no evidence that they knew about it. I am satisfied that it meant exactly what
it said. I do not accept that it was due to an oversight that it came to be written in
the first person singular and on the defendant's notepaper, instead of emanating from
Game & Meat and under their letterhead. The defendant, Mr Buckingham and Mrs
Hawkins were all experienced in the writing of business letters and appreciated
perfectly well the difference between a letter from the defendant personally, such *j*
as this, and a letter from the company. I think that the reason why the letter was
written in these terms and on the defendant's notepaper was that the affairs of Game
& Meat had by then reached a stage when the defendant wanted to treat the storage
of these goods in his cold store as his own venture. Whether Mr Martin Vernon so
regarded this transaction when Mr Stafford spoke to him on the telephone on or
about 3rd March I do not know, but I doubt it. It may well be that he came to

a acquiesce in this arrangement between that date and 23rd March, by which time it must have been even clearer that the company's days were numbered. Alternatively it may be that Mr Martin Vernon never gave any real thought to the matter. There was no evidence, and certainly none that I accept, that either of the Vernons took any interest in the storage of these goods after the telephone call on or about 3rd March, apart from Mr Martin Vernon informing the defendant that the goods were

b due to arrive and thereafter informing the defendant or Mr Buckingham of their approximate weight for the purpose of computing the storage charges.

The letter of 23rd March in due course arrived on the desk of Mr Miller, an assistant director of Keller Bryant. He knew the defendant as the owner of the Silhouette Club and as a businessman of substance. He was quite content with the defendant's letter of 23rd March and it did not occur to him to query it in any way or to wonder

c why it did not come from Game & Meat. He merely concluded, rightly, that the goods were stored in the defendant's cold store and not in one owned by Game & Meat, but he was quite content with this arrangement because the cold store itself had been suggested by the port health authority.

When the defendant or Mr Buckingham on his behalf dictated the letter of 23rd March to Mrs Hawkins they also wished to ensure that the invoice for the first month's

d storage should be sent to Keller Bryant on or about 14th April. Mrs Hawkins was therefore instructed to make this out at the same time as she typed the letter of 23rd March. In accordance with the terms of that letter, she therefore also typed an invoice dated 14th April from the defendant on his own notepaper in the same way as the letter, asking for a cheque for £61 to be sent to his address at St Michael's Square.

e On or about 31st March Mr Buckingham drew his last wages from Game & Meat and the company thereafter had no employees apart from its directors. No one appears to have taken any interest in the plaintiffs' goods in the cold store. There was evidence that Mr Martin Vernon had been there very little in March and only occasionally thereafter; there was no evidence that Mr Vernon senior or Mr Tear, the other directors on the notepaper of Game & Meat, ever went there during this

f period. The defendant went into the cold store from time to time for the purpose of showing it to prospective purchasers. I think that he said that he hoped to sell the cold store for conversion as an office block. Whenever he went there he heard refrigeration machinery running, apparently normally, and therefore assumed that all was well. There were no thermometers indicating the temperature inside the chamber in which the plaintiffs' goods were stored, and no attempt was made to

g check on their temperature by means of any portable thermometers which may have been available. I am satisfied that it is part of the ordinary precautions to be taken in a refrigerated store from time to time to carry out checks to ensure that the goods stored in it are maintained at a proper temperature; but no attempt to do so was made in the present case. The defendant did not even know that there was a second unsealed door giving access to the chamber. But even if all means of access

h had been sealed, I am satisfied that in any properly run refrigerated store the temperature inside a sealed chamber can and should be verified by means of fixed thermometers on the outside, indicating the temperature inside the chamber. Reliance on the noise made by the running machinery alone is not sufficient, as was shown by the events in this case.

The defendant had been showing a prospective purchaser around the cold store

j on Friday, 14th April, and all then seemed to him to be normal. On the same day Mrs Hawkins sent off the invoice for the first month's storage and this reached Mr Miller of Keller Bryant on the following day. I accept his evidence that if payment of this invoice had not been overtaken by events, Keller Bryant's cheque would have been made out in favour of the defendant personally, pursuant to its terms and those of the letter of 23rd March. The defendant and Mr Buckingham said that if this had happened the cheque would have been endorsed over to Game & Meat or

the proceeds paid over to the company. I am very doubtful about this, but it is my   *a*
view in any event irrelevant to the issue of liability between the parties to this action.
On Sunday, 16th April, the defendant noticed a large quantity of liquid fat and blood
oozing into Castle Way from under the door of the cold store. He managed to get
hold of an engineer, and it was then discovered that there had been a breakdown
of one of the fans distributing cold air into the chamber, with the result that the contents had thawed. The machinery of the unit was still running, but the fan was frozen   *b*
to such an extent that it was going to take about three days to thaw it out. I am
satisfied that the fan must have broken down about a week before the damage was
discovered and that the damage to the goods was due to negligence in failing to
maintain any check at any time on the temperature within the chamber. On Monday,
17th April, the defendant telephoned Mr Miller of Keller Bryant and informed him
of what he had discovered. He also told him that any claim would have to be addressed   *c*
to Game & Meat but that this company was about to go into liquidation, as happened
on 24th April. Mr Miller did not accept this, but contended that the contract was
with the defendant personally, having in mind the letter of 23rd March. On the
following day Mr Miller himself typed and sent a letter to the defendant and had
it delivered to him by hand, informing him that any part of the goods not condemned
by the port health authority would be removed from his premises at Castle Way on   *d*
that day. I am satisfied that this was sent in an envelope addressed to the defendant
personally. On 20th April the plaintiffs' solicitors sent a letter of claim, again in an
envelope addressed to the defendant personally. The defendant subsequently contended that this letter had arrived in an envelope addressed to Game & Meat, which
he purported to produce. When this was refuted by the plaintiffs' solicitors, he
contended that Mr Miller's letter of 17th April had arrived in this envelope. Neither   *e*
of these statements was true, and this episode, though not directly relevant to the
issues, added nothing to the defendant's general credibility as a witness.
    These are the facts and I now turn to the question of liability, first in contract
and then in tort. The plaintiffs' contention that the defendant is liable in contract
was put on two grounds. They contended, first, that they oral contract made on the
telephone on or about 3rd March between Mr Stafford and Mr Martin Vernon had   *f*
been made by the latter on behalf of the defendant as undisclosed principal. I reject
this because there is no evidence to suggest that Mr Martin Vernon then intended
to contract otherwise than as a director of Game & Meat. Alternatively and mainly,
the plaintiffs contended that the letter of 23rd March, together with the invoice of
14th April, and Keller Bryant's acquiescence in their terms, operated as a novation
between the defendant and Keller Bryant as agents for the plaintiffs of the original   *g*
contract concluded with Game & Meat. Faced with the difficulty of showing any
acceptance of the terms of these documents by Keller Bryant, and the decision in
Felthouse v Bindley[1], that silence cannot amount to an acceptance, they sought to overcome this in the following manner. The submitted that the letter of 23rd March,
followed by the despatch of the invoice on 14th April, showed that the defendant
intended or was content to treat Keller Bryant's silence as an acceptance of his having   *h*
taken over the original contract with Game & Meat, and that this contract was
accordingly thereafter binding on him. In this connection they relied on the comment
on *Felthouse v Bindley*[1] in Chitty on Contracts[2], where it is suggested, as I understand
it, that in such circumstances the offeror (the defendant) may be bound to the offeree
(Keller Bryant as agents for the plaintiffs) even though he himself might not be
able to hold the offeree to any contract. It seems to me, however, that such a result   *j*
can only flow from an estoppel operating against the offeror and that such facts
cannot give rise to any contract or fit into the settled law governing offer and acceptance. The plaintiffs' cause of action against the defendant cannot be founded on

1   (1862) 11 CBNS 869
2   23rd Edn (1968), vol 1, p 30, art 57

a estoppel, and there is in any event no or no sufficient evidence of any reliance by Keller Bryant to give rise to an estoppel in the plaintiffs' favour. There is also no evidence of any tripartite agreement capable of supporting a novation of the original contract. I therefore hold that the plaintiffs' claim in contract fails.

In the alternative, the plaintiffs contended that they are entitled to succeed against the defendant in tort on the basis that he was either a bailee of the goods or liable
b in negligence in the same way as a bailee. Their submission can be summarised by saying that on the facts, supported or confirmed by the terms of the letter of 23rd March and the invoice of 14th April, the defendant was in all the circumstances to be regarded as having accepted responsiblity for the goods or as the person responsible for ensuring that care was taken in their storage. The defendant countered all these submissions on the basis that the only contract was with Game & Meat, that only the company could therefore be held to be the bailee, and that the defendant
c could accordingly not be under any personal liability.

I do not think that the defendant's contentions operate in law as a bar to the plaintiffs' claim. Let me take first the question of bailment. A defendant can be in the position of a bailee without any contract between him and the owner of the goods. On the facts of this case it is by no means clear whether Game & Meat or
d the defendant is to be regarded as the bailee of these goods by the time when the damage occurred in April. I do not think that Game & Meat ever had exclusive possession of the cold store and of its contents as against the defendant, except as regards goods owned by the company itself. Such exclusive possession would have resulted if a lease to this effect had been granted by the defendant to the company. But this did not happen, in my view as a matter of deliberate policy. Such exclusive possession is also inconsistent with the terms of the defendant's letter of 23rd March which
e in my view meant what it said, as already mentioned. It is quite possible, for instance, that at the time of the telephone conversation of 3rd March, and even at the time of the delivery of the goods on 14th March, Game & Meat was not only the intended bailee (as it obviously was) but also initially the actual bailee, but that afterwards there was a deliberate change in the arrangement as between the company and the defendant, which resulted and was reflected in the letter of 23rd March. The financial
f position of the company at this time and the letter of 23rd March would certainly be consistent with such an inference. But in my view the evidence is insufficiently clear to support the conclusion that the defendant had exclusive possession of the goods at the time when the damage occurred. I am also not persuaded by the proposition of counsel for the plaintiffs that by that time the case is to be regarded as one of a joint bailment of the company and the defendant. I do not think that the
g refinements of the concepts of legal possession and bailment are or should be determinitive of liability in the tort of negligence.

The real answer to the submission made on behalf of the defendant is in my judgment that the question of his liability in negligence to the plaintiffs is not necessarily excluded as a matter of law on the ground that there was no contract with him and that he is also not to be regarded as a bailee with a right to the legal
h possession of the goods. Depending on the facts, he may nonetheless owe a duty of care to the plaintiffs and be liable in negligence for breach of that duty. The fact that he was a director of Game & Meat and that the company was the contracting party does not necessarily exclude his personal liability. The legal position in this connection can be conveniently illustrated by reference to two cases, but such examples could easily be multiplied. In *Adler v Dickson*[1] the plaintiff's contract with the
j defendant's employers, although excluding all liability for negligence, nevertheless did not preclude her from recovering damages in negligence from the defendant, a servant of the company with which she had contracted, because he owed her a personal duty of care apart from his contractual obligations to his employers, and

---

1   [1954] 3 All ER 397, [1955] 1 QB 158

because he was held to be in breach of that duty. That was a case of personal injury, *a*
but I do not see why a case of damage to the plaintiff's property must be regarded
differently in law. Take the facts of *Morris v C W Martin & Sons Ltd*[1]. In that case
the plaintiff's fur coat was stolen by a servant of the defendants, who were sub-
contractors and sub-bailees of the coat without any contractual or other nexus
existing between the plaintiff and the defendants. The plaintiff recovered damages
against the defendants for the loss of her coat because they were held responsible *b*
for the act of their servant. It is however clear that if she had chosen to sue the
servant personally in the tort of conversion she would equally have succeeded, indeed
with less difficulty. But would the position on this basis have been any different if
instead of stealing the coat the servant had negligently caused or allowed it to be
ruined in the process of cleaning it. If he had carelessly plunged it into a vat of green
dye or left it in cleaning fluid for so long that it became destroyed by some foreseeable *c*
chemical action, could he not have been made liable in negligence as well as his
employers? I do not see why it should follow as a matter of law that in such cases an
action could only be maintained against his employers. A duty of care by somebody
else's servant to the owner of goods, and a breach of that duty by a particular servant,
may of course be much more difficult to establish than a wrongful conversion of
the goods by such a servant. But this depends on the facts. Generally speaking, *d*
if an employer is liable to a plaintiff in tort on the basis of the doctrine respondeat
superior, the servant can also be held personally liable, though in practice it is of
course usually much more convenient and worthwhile to sue his employers. If this
is the law as regards servants it cannot logically be more favourable to company
directors.

    It follows that in my view the crucial question in the present case is whether or *e*
not, on the facts, the defendant owed a duty of care to the plaintiffs in respect of their
goods which were stored in his cold store, and, if so, whether he was in breach of
that duty. In my view both limbs of this question are to be answered in the affirmative on the special facts of this case which I have already reviewed. Game & Meat
could only perform its duties in relation to these goods through its human servants
and agents. At the relevant time the only persons through whom these duties *f*
could be performed were the directors. The only one of these who concerned himself with these goods in any way after their delivery was the defendant. The letter
of 23rd March dictated by him or on his behalf in my view reflected the true position,
in that he regarded himself, and not Game & Meat, as concerned with the storage
of these goods. On the facts of this case the defendant in my view assumed and
owed a duty of care to the plaintiffs in respect of the storage of their goods in his
premises and was in breach of that duty with the result that the plaintiffs' goods *g*
were damaged. I therefore give judgment for the plaintiffs against the defendant
in the agreed amount of £3,143·78.

Judgment for the plaintiffs.

Solicitors: *Hepherd, Winstanley & Pugh*, Southampton (for the plaintiffs); *Lamport,* *h*
Bassitt & Hiscock, Southampton (for the defendant).

                                                        Deirdre McKinney Barrister.

1   [1965] 2 All ER 725, [1966] 1 QB 716

Explained in RE GONIN (DEC'D)
[1977] 2 All ER 720

a
Steadman v Steadman

HOUSE OF LORDS

LORD REID, LORD MORRIS OF BORTH-Y-GEST, VISCOUNT DILHORNE, LORD SIMON OF GLAISDALE
AND LORD SALMON

b   1st, 2nd, 3rd, 4th APRIL, 19th JUNE 1974

*Sale of land – Contract – Part performance – Acts constituting part performance – Acts as
evidence of existence of contract – Acts as evidence of nature of contract – Payment of sum of
money – Circumstances in which payment capable of constituting part performance – Compromise of proceedings – Husband and wife – Agreement to variation of maintenance order –*
c   *Husband to pay lump sum in respect of arrears – Balance of arrears to be discharged – Wife
to transfer interest in matrimonial home for agreed sum – Agreement approved by justices –
Sum in respect of arrears paid by husband – Form of transfer prepared by husband's solicitors
and sent to wife for signature – Whether sufficient acts of part performance – Law of Property
Act 1925, s 40.*

d   The husband and wife were registered as the joint proprietors of the house in which
they lived with their child. In July 1968 the wife left the husband and in November,
on application to the magistrates' court, she obtained a maintenance order of £2 a
week for herself and £2·50 a week for the child. In April 1970 the wife obtained a
decree nisi of divorce and in June she applied to the county court for an order under
s 17 of the Married Women's Property Act 1882 that the house be sold and the pro-
e   ceeds divided between herself and the husband. Following considerable correspondence a tentative agreement was reached in February 1972 whereby the wife would
transfer to the husband her interest in the house for £1,500. At that time the husband
was in arrears in paying the wife's maintenance in a sum of £194. On 2nd March
the matter came before the magistrates' court in proceedings by the husband for
variation of the maintenance order and by the wife for enforcement of payment of
f   the arrears. Before the hearing the parties met and came to an oral agreement,
subject so far as necessary to the approval of the justices, that the wife would surrender
her interest in the property for £1,500, that the wife would consent to the discharge
of the maintenance order in her favour, that the parties would consent to the continuance of the maintenance order in favour of the child, that the husband would,
before 30th March, pay £100 in part discharge of the arrears and that the wife would
g   consent to the remission of the balance of the arrears. At the hearing the husband's
solicitor explained to the justices what had been agreed and the clerk obtained the
wife's confirmation of the terms. The justices thereupon approved the agreement
and, so far as it lay within their jurisdiction, implemented it by varying the maintenance order and adjourning the proceedings with regard to the arrears. The court
notified the husband in writing that: 'The proceedings have been adjourned for you
h   to pay the sum of £100 not later than the 30th March, 1972, as all the arrears except
that amount have today been remitted. If you fail to pay as directed, further proceedings will be commenced to recover the amount due.' The husband paid the
£100 by 30th March. The husband's solicitors prepared a form of transfer and sent
it to the wife's solicitors for signature. They returned the transfer unsigned stating
that the wife did not find the terms acceptable. The proceedings under s 17 of the
j   1882 Act were restored for hearing, the wife contending that the agreement of 2nd
March, being an agreement for the disposition of an interest in land, was unenforceable under s 40[a] of the Law of Property Act 1925 in that there was no note or
memorandum in writing and no act of part performance.

---

a Section 40, so far as material, is set out at p 980 *d*, post

Held (Lord Morris of Borth-y-Gest dissenting) – The agreement of 2nd March was   *a*
enforceable against the wife for the following reasons—

(i) In order to establish facts amounting to part performance it was necessary for
a plaintiff to show that he had acted to his detriment and that the acts in question
were such as to indicate on a balance of probabilities that they had been performed
in reliance on a contract with the defendant which was consistent with the contract
alleged. There was no general rule that the payment of a sum of money could never   *b*
constitute part performance (see p 981 *d e* and *h*, p 982 *b*, p 994 *d* and *e*, p 999 *d* and *e*,
p 1000 *g* and *h* to p 1001 *a* to *d*, p 1002 *c* to *j*, p 1003 *d* and *e*, p 1006 *e* to *g* and p 1007 *b*,
post).

(ii) Although the payment by the husband to the wife of £100 would, by itself,
have been insufficient to constitute part performance, that payment taken in conjunction with the announcement of the oral agreement to the justices, the abandon-   *c*
ment by the husband of his right to claim full remission of arrears of maintenance
and the preparation and delivery to the wife of a form of transfer for her signature
amounted to acts of part performance by the husband in that the acts were such as
to indicate that they had been carried by him in reliance on a contract with the wife
of the nature alleged. In the circumstances it would therefore be inequitable to allow
the wife to rely on the defence under s 40(1) of the 1925 Act and oral and affidavit   *d*
evidence was admissible to prove the contract (see p 980 *f* to *h*, p 983 *b*, p 991 *d*, p 992
b to *e*, p 993 *f* to *j*, p 1001 *h*, p 1002 *g* to *j*, p 1007 *e* to *g* and p 1008 *f* to *j*, post).

Dicta of the Earl of Selborne LC in *Maddison v Alderson* (1883) 8 App Cas at 475,
476 and of Upjohn LJ in *Kingswood Estate Co Ltd v Anderson* [1962] 3 All ER at 604
applied.

Quaere. Whether, to constitute part performance, the acts in question must be   *e*
such as to indicate the nature of the contract and in particular that it was a contract
for the sale or other disposition of land or an interest in land (see p 982 *b* and *c*, p 999
f to *j*, p 1000 *a* and *b*, p 1005 *a* to *c* and p 1006 *e*, post).

Decision of the Court of Appeal [1973] 3 All ER 977 affirmed.

Notes   *f*
For part performance, see 34 Halsbury's Laws (3rd Edn) 209, 210, para 348, and for
cases on the subject, see 40 Digest (Repl) 39-44, 218-264.

For the Married Women's Property Act 1882, s 17, see 17 Halsbury's Statutes (3rd
Edn) 120.

For the Law of Property Act 1925, s 40, see 27 Halsbury's Statutes (3rd Edn) 399.

  g

Cases referred to in opinions
Bannister v Bannister [1948] 2 All ER 133, CA, 47 Digest (Repl) 101, 733.
Brough v Nettleton [1921] 2 Ch 25, 90 LJCh 373, 124 LT 823, 31(1) Digest (Reissue) 67,
   494.
Chaproniere v Lambert [1917] 2 Ch 356, [1916-17] All ER Rep 1089, 86 LJCh 726, 117
   LT 353, CA, 12 Digest (Reissue) 178, 1060.   *h*
Dysart Peerage Case (1881) 6 App Cas 489, HL, 22 Digest (Reissue) 129, 1023.
Fowler v Fowler (1859) 4 De G & J 250, 45 ER 97, LC, 24 Digest (Repl) 1135, 164.
Hill v Hill [1959] 1 All ER 281, [1959] 1 WLR 127, PC, 27(1) Digest (Reissue) 67, 479.
Joscelyne v Nissen [1970] 1 All ER 1213, [1970] 2 QB 86, [1970] 2 WLR 509, CA, 35 Digest
   (Repl) 706, 68a.
Kingswood Estate Co Ltd v Anderson [1962] 3 All ER 593, [1963] 2 QB 169, [1962] 3 WLR   *j*
   1102, CA, Digest (Cont Vol A) 318, 250a.
Lacon v Mertins (1743) 3 Atk 1, Dick 39, 21 ER 430, LC, 12 Digest (Reissue) 205, 1303.
Maddison v Alderson (1883) 8 App Cas 467, 52 LJQB 737, 49 LT 303, HL, 40 Digest
   (Repl) 38, 210.
Morris v Davies (1837) 5 Cl & Fin 163, [1835-42] All ER Rep 270, 1 Jur 911, 7 ER 365,
   HL, 3 Digest (Repl) 399, 14.
Ottaway v Norman [1971] 3 All ER 1325, [1972] Ch 698, [1972] 2 WLR 50.

a   *Owen v Davies* (1748) 1 Ves Sen 82, 27 ER 905, LC, 33 Digest (Repl) 669, *1150*.
    Piers v Piers (1849) 2 HL Cas 331, [1843-60] All ER Rep 159, 13 LTOS 41, 13 Jur 569,
       9 ER 1118, HL, 27(1) Digest (Reissue) 76, *576*.
    Pilcher v Pilcher (No 2) [1956] 1 All ER 463, [1956] 1 WLR 298, 120 JP 127, DC, 27(2)
       Digest (Reissue) 1003, *8005*.
    Ratten v Reginam [1971] 3 All ER 801, [1972] AC 378, [1971] 3 WLR 930, PC.
b   *Rochefoucauld v Boustead* [1897] 1 Ch 196, 66 LJCh 74, 75 LT 502, CA; *subsequent pro-*
       ceedings [1898] 1 Ch 550, CA, 12 Digest (Reissue) 211, *1352*.
    Shelburne (Countess Dowager of) v Earl of Inchiquin (1784) 1 Bro CC 338, 28 ER 1166, LC;
       on appeal sub nom Earl of Inchiquin v Fitzmaurice (1785) 5 Bro Parl Cas 166, 2 ER 603,
       HL, 35 Digest (Repl) 148, *372*.
    Smallman v Smallman [1971] 3 All ER 717, [1972] Fam 25, [1971] 3 WLR 588, CA, 27(1)
c   Digest (Reissue) 315, *2330*.
    Somerset (Duke of) v Cookson (1735) 3 P Wms 390, 24 ER 1114, 45 Digest (Repl) 528,
       709.
    Teper v Reginam [1952] 2 All ER 447, [1952] AC 480, 116 JP 502, PC, 14 Digest (Repl)
       451, *4377*.
    Wakeham v Mackenzie [1968] 2 All ER 783, [1968] 1 WLR 1175, 19 P & CR 565, 12
d   Digest (Reissue) 61, *323*.
    Winans v Attorney-General [1904] AC 287, [1904-7] All ER Rep 410, 73 LJKB 613, 90
       LT 721, HL, 11 Digest (Repl) 329, *41*.

Appeal
Sylvia Emily Lila Steadman ('the wife') appealed against an order of the Court of
Appeal[1] (Roskill and Scarman LJJ, Edmund Davies LJ dissenting) dated 30th July
e   1973 allowing an appeal by Norman Leslie Steadman ('the husband') against so
much of the order of his Honour Judge Fife given on 24th May 1973 at Bromley
County Court as allowed the wife's appeal against the interlocutory order of Mr
Registrar Miller at Bromley County Court dated 23rd January 1973 on a preliminary
point adjourning generally, with liberty to restore, the wife's application under s 17
of the Married Women's Property Act 1882. The facts are set out in the opinion of
f   Viscount Dilhorne.

Michael Morland QC and *Mark Lennox-Boyd* for the wife.
Conrad Dehn QC and *J R Playford* for the husband.

Their Lordships took time for consideration.
g

19th June. The following opinions were delivered.

LORD REID. My Lords, the marriage of the appellant, the wife, and the respondent, the husband, was dissolved in 1970. They were then joint owners of a house
h   which had been bought in 1963 for £3,600. Prior to the divorce the husband had been
ordered to pay maintenance of £2 per week to the wife and £2 10s per week for
their child. The husband remained in occupation of the house.
    In 1970 the wife applied under s 17 of the Married Women's Property Act 1882
for, inter alia, an order for the sale of the house and division of the proceeds but no
further steps were taken until 1972. At that time the husband was in arrears in paying
j   the wife's maintenance in a sum of £194. There were long negotiations between the
parties' solicitors, and ultimately on 2nd March 1972 the matter came before the
magistrates' court. The husband's solicitor met the wife before the hearing. Unfortunately her solicitor was not present but there is no suggestion that the husband's
solicitor took advantage of his absence.

---

1   [1973] 3 All ER 977, [1974] QB 161

The parties then reached an oral agreement with regard to both the maintenance *a* and the house. The court were to be asked to authorise discharge of the maintenance order against the husband and continuation of the order with regard to the child, to order the husband to pay £100 of the arrears of her maintenance and to order remission of the balance. In addition the court were to be informed of the agreement with regard to the house that the husband should pay £1,500 to the wife and the wife would transfer to the husband her interest in the house. The justices made *b* orders in accordance with the agreement and the husband paid £100 to the wife.

The husband then borrowed £1,500 from a building society and paid that sum to his solicitor and the solicitor prepared a deed of transfer of the wife's interest in the house and sent it for her signature. But the wife refused to sign thinking that £1,500 was less than she ought to have. She renewed her application under s 17 to have the house sold. The husband pleaded the parties' agreement as a binding compromise *c* but the wife pleaded that the agreement was unenforceable.

She relied on s 40 of the Law of Property Act 1925 which provides:

'(1) No action may be brought upon any contract for the sale or other disposition of land or any interest in land, unless the agreement upon which such action is brought, or some memorandum or note thereof, is in writing, and signed by the party to be charged or by some other person thereunto by him lawfully *d* authorised.

'(2) This section . . . does not affect the law relating to part performance . . .'

The husband relied on sub-s (2) and the registrar held that there had been part performance so that sub-s (1) did not apply. His decision was reversed by the county court judge but an appeal to the Court of Appeal[1] was allowed by a majority *e* (Roskill and Scarman LJJ, Edmund Davies LJ dissenting).

The first point taken by the husband was that s 40 does not apply to an agreement compromising a litigation or to an agreement dealing with other matters besides the transfer of land. We did not find it necessary to hear argument on this matter and I therefore express no opinion about it.

The sole question for your Lordships' decision is whether the admitted facts amount *f* to part performance within the meaning of s 40(2). In my view it is clear that the oral agreement of 2nd March 1972 is indivisible and not severable. The whole must stand or fall. Indeed the contrary was not seriously argued. And it is clear that the payment of £100 to the wife as ordered by the magistrates' court was, taking the words in their ordinary sense, in part performance of the agreement. The husband also relies on the following other acts by him or his solicitor as being further part *g* performance: (1) the intimation of the agreement to the justices and his abandonment of his attempts to have all arrears of maintenance remitted, and (2) sending to the wife the transfer which she refused to sign and incurring the cost of its preparation. I am very doubtful about the first of these but I am inclined to think that the second could be regarded as part performance. It is the universal custom that a deed of transfer of an interest in land is prepared by the solicitor of the transferee *h* so the wife or her solicitor as her agent must have known that the husband would incur the cost of preparation of the deed in carrying out the agreement.

But the wife's case is that we must take 'part performance' in its ordinary meaning because the phrase has acquired a highly technical meaning over the centuries.

This matter has a very long history. Section 40 replaced a part of s 4 of the Statute of Frauds (1677)[2] and very soon after the passing of that Act authorities on this *j* matter began to accumulate. It is now very difficult to find from them any clear guidance of general application. But it is not difficult to see at least one principle behind them. If one party to an agreement stands by and lets the other party

---

1   [1973] 3 All ER 977, [1974] QB 161
2   29 Car 2 c 3

a incur expense or prejudice his position on the faith of the agreement being valid he will not then be allowed to turn round and assert that the agreement is unenforceable. Using fraud in its older and less precise sense, that would be fraudulent on his part and it has become proverbial that courts of equity will not permit the state to be made an instrument of fraud.

b It must be remembered that this legislation did not and does not make oral contracts relating to land void: it only makes them unenforceable. And the statutory provision must be pleaded; otherwise the court does not apply it. So it is in keeping with equitable principles that in proper circumstances a person will not be allowed 'fraudulently' to take advantage of a defence of this kind. There is nothing about part performance in the Statute of Frauds. It is an invention of the Court of Chancery and in deciding any case not clearly covered by authority I think that the equitable nature of the remedy must be kept in mind.

c A large number of the authorities are cases where a purchaser under an oral agreement has been permitted to take possession of or to do things on the land which he has agreed to buy. But sometimes rules appropriate to that situation have been sought to be applied to other cases of part performance where they are not appropriate. Indeed the courts have sometimes seemed disinclined to apply the principle at all to such other cases.

d Normally the consideration for the purchase of land is a sum of money and there are statements that a sum of money can never be treated as part performance. Such statements would be reasonable if the person pleading the statute tendered repayment of any part of the price which he had received and was able thus to make restitutio in integrum. That would remove any 'fraud' or any equity on which the purchaser could properly rely. But to make a general rule that payment of money can never be part performance would seem to me to defeat the whole purpose of the doctrine and I do not think that we are compelled by authority to do that.

e The argument for the wife, for which there is a good deal of authority, is that no act can be relied on as an act of part performance unless it relates to the land to be acquired and can only be explained by the existence of a contract relating to the land. But let me suppose a case of an oral contract where the consideration for the transfer of the land was not money but the transfer of some personal property or the performance of some obligation. The personal property is then transferred or the obligation is performed to the knowledge of the owner of the land in circumstances where there can be no restitutio in integrum. On what rational principle could it be said that the doctrine of part performance is not to apply? And we were not referred to any case of that kind where the court had refused to apply it. The transfer of the personal property or the performance of the obligation would indicate the existence of a contract but it would not indicate that that contract related to that or any other land.

h I think that there has been some confusion between this supposed rule and another perfectly good rule. You must not first look at the oral contract and then see whether the alleged acts of part performance are consistent with it. You must first look at the alleged acts of part performance and see whether they prove that there must have been a contract and it is only if they do so prove that you can bring in the oral contract.

j A thing is proved in civil litigation by shewing that it is more probably true than not; and I see no reason why there should be any different standard of proof here. If there were what would the standard be? The only other recognised standard of proof is beyond reasonable doubt but why should that apply here?

I am aware that it has often been said that the acts relied on must necessarily or unequivocally indicate the existence of a contract. It may well be that we should consider whether any prudent reasonable man would have done those acts if there had not been a contract but many people are neither prudent nor reasonable and they might often spend money or prejudice their position not in reliance on a contract

but in the optimistic expectation that a contract would follow. So if there were a
rule that acts relied on as part performance must of their own nature unequivocally
shew that there was a contract, it would be only in the rarest case that all other possible
explanations could be excluded.

In my view, unless the law is to be divorced from reason and principle, the rule
must be that you take the whole circumstances, leaving aside evidence about the
oral contract, and see whether it is proved that the acts relied on were done in reliance
on a contract: that will be proved if it is shewn to be more probable than not.

Authorities which seem to require more than that appear to be based on an idea,
never clearly defined, to the effect that the law of part performance is a rule of evidence rather than an application of an equitable principle. I do not know on what
ground any court could say that, although you cannot produce the evidence required
by the Statute of Frauds, some other kind of evidence will do instead. But I can see that
if part performance is simply regarded as evidence then it would be reasonable to
hold not only that the acts of part performance must relate to the land but that they
must indicate the nature of the oral contract with regard to the land. But that appears
to me to be a fundamental departure from the true doctrine of part performance,
and it is not supported by recent authorities such as *Kingswood Estate Co Ltd v Anderson*[1].

But it was strenuously argued that such a view is inconsistent with the decision of
this House in *Maddison v Alderson*[2]. That decision is now so embedded in the law
that I would not depart from it even if I thought it wrong: it would be impracticable
to foresee all the consequences of tampering with it. The case for the unsuccessful
appellant was that her deceased employer had induced her to serve him down to
his death without wages by promising to leave to her by his will an estate in land.
But as the Earl of Selborne LC pointed out[3] there was no contract that she should continue in his service: she could have left or he could have dismissed her at any time.
So her continuing to work for him without wages could not be part performance of
any contract.

Nevertheless their Lordships made an extensive examination of the law of part
performance and I think that the general view was best expressed by Lord Selborne
LC[4]:

> 'The matter has advanced beyond the stage of contract; and the equities
> which arise out of the stage which it has reached cannot be administered unless
> the contract is regarded. The choice is between undoing what has been done
> (which is not always possible, or, if possible, just) and completing what has been
> left undone. The line may not always be capable of being so clearly drawn as
> in the case which I have supposed; but it is not arbitrary or unreasonable to hold
> that when the statute says that no action is to be brought to charge any person
> upon a contract concerning land, it has in view the simple case in which he is
> charged upon the contract only, and not in which there are equities resulting
> from res gestae subsequent to and arising out of the contract. So long as the
> connection of those res gestae with the alleged contract does not depend upon
> mere parol testimony, but is reasonably to be inferred from the res gestae them-
> selves, justice seems to require some such limitation of the scope of the statute...'

There are some expressions of opinion by Lord O'Hagan and Lord FitzGerald which
may go farther but I do not think that we are bound by them. Lord Blackburn took
a rather different line but he said[5]:

---

1   [1962] 3 All ER 593, [1963] 2 QB 169
2   (1883) 8 App Cas 467
3   8 App Cas at 472
4   8 App Cas at 476
5   8 App Cas at 489

a   'The conduct of the parties may be such as to make it inequitable to refuse to complete a contract partly performed. Wherever that is the case, I agree that the contract may be enforced on the ground of an equity arising from the conduct of the party.'

So in my judgment I am in no way precluded from acting on the views which I expressed earlier and I would therefore dismiss this appeal.

b

LORD MORRIS OF BORTH-Y-GEST. My Lords, this case furnishes a striking example of the desirability of ensuring that agreements which may be within the ambit of s 40 of the Law of Property Act 1925 should be in writing. If there are then the risks of doubt and disagreement as to what was agreed will be avoided or c   minimised.

As the facts are so fully and clearly set out in the judgment of Edmund Davies LJ[1] I do not find it necessary to recount them. The matter with which we are concerned was tried as a preliminary point in proceedings in the Bromley County Court on an originating application under s 17 of the Married Women's Property Act 1882. Under that application, which was dated 5th June 1970, one of the main orders sought by the d   wife was that a house which was jointly owned by her and by her husband should be sold and the net proceeds of sale divided equally between them. The house had been bought in their joint names in June 1963 for £3,600. It had been bought with the aid of a mortgage from a building society. By his answer dated 27th October 1970 the husband disputed her entitlement and the extent of her interest. The application came on for hearing or was restored for hearing on 18th January 1973. e   But before that date an oral agreement comprising certain terms had undoubtedly been made between husband and wife. The husband said that the terms included one as a result of which he was to become the sole owner of the house and would pay a sum of money to his wife. The wife said that such a term was not included. The agreement had been made on 2nd March 1972. Those present on that occasion were the husband, the wife, and the husband's solicitor. It has been firmly stated that no f   suggestion is made that advantage was taken of the circumstances that the wife's solicitor was not present. But most unhappily and unfortunately the terms of the agreement made were not reduced to writing and signed by the parties. Had they been there would have been no room for differences of recollection and lengthy proceedings would have been avoided.

As it was when the hearing of 18th January 1973 began counsel for the husband g   took the point that under the circumstances the court could not order a sale of the house or make an order as to the division of the proceeds. Counsel for the wife contended that there had never been any agreement as to the house and that the registrar could make an order for its sale. Affidavits had been sworn before 18th January 1973 by the husband (on 3rd January) and by his solicitor (on 8th January) and by the wife (on 16th January) setting out their recollections as to what had h   happened on 2nd March 1972. In her affidavit the wife swore that on 2nd March 1972 she had said that she was not prepared to discuss matters concerning the house in the absence of her solicitor: she furthermore swore that she did not remember mention being made of the house in the magistrates' court.

In that sorry state of affairs what happened was that the learned registrar proceeded in effect to try an action for specific performance but to call it 'the question of compro-
j   mise' and to try it as a preliminary point. So he was called on to hear the evidence of the parties who were cross-examined on their affidavits and to decide what it was that they had agreed on 2nd March 1972 and if he concluded that their oral agreement had covered the house then to decide whether there had been part performance.

---

1   [1973] 3 All ER 977 at 979-981, [1974] QB 161 at 166-169

On the facts his conclusion was that the oral agreement did cover the house. His
conclusion on that matter stands and was not challenged on the hearing of the appeal   *a*
to the judge in the Bromley County Court. The learned registrar further held that
there had been part performance. I think that this finding was on the basis that, if
the husband claimed specific performance and if the wife pleaded s 40, he (the
learned registrar) would hold that there had been part performance within s 40(2) of
the Law of Property Act 1925. The actual order that he made was that the action   *b*
be adjourned generally with liberty to restore. The order was made because there
might have been some outstanding matters in relation to chattels to be dealt with
under the s 17 application. If the husband lost this appeal with the result that the
matter proceeded under s 17 the husband has reserved his right to contend that
the agreement he made though unenforceable could be relied on by him by way of
defence. I express no opinion whether he could do so.

On appeal to the learned judge in the Bromley County Court he held that there   *c*
had been no part performance. A different conclusion was reached by the majority
in the Court of Appeal[1], though the view formed as to what constituted part
performance was not that which had appealed to the learned registrar.

The finding of fact of the learned registrar was that was an oral agreement made
on 2nd March 1972 which was in these terms: (a) that the wife would surrender her
interest in the property for £1,500, (b) that the wife's maintenance order should   *d*
be discharged, (c) that the child's maintenance order would continue, and (d) that
the arrears would be remitted except as to £100. Those were arrears under the
maintenance order in favour of the wife. The learned registrar held that the oral
agreement was made before the matrimonial case was called on in the magistrates'
court and that after it was made the parties went into court. He found that the
solicitor 'explained to the magistrates what had been agreed and that the clerk   *e*
obtained [the wife's] confirmation of the terms': the learned registrar said that the
solicitor did not say that he remembered a figure in regard to the house being mentioned in court but said that the husband did say that the sum was mentioned in
court. Once the justices were assured that both husband and wife were agreed in
regard to the only matters within their jurisdiction (i e the maintenance orders) it   *f*
may be that they would not be interested to know much about any other term of
agreement.

In the magistrates' court on 2nd March 1972 two orders were made. One order
recited that the parties had agreed to delete from a previous order payments in respect
of the wife and made the required deletion. That was an order made on an application to the court by the husband. The other order was in proceedings brought against
the husband on the wife's application. The order stated: *g*

> 'The proceedings have been so adjourned for you [the husband] to pay the
> sum of £100·00 not later than 30th March, 1972, as all the arrears except that
> amount have today been remitted. If you fail to pay as directed, further pro-
> ceedings will be commenced to recover the amount due.'

h

It appears than in fact the arrears amounted to £194.

On the findings it must be accepted that there was one oral 'package' agreement
containing the above four terms and not four separate agreements. Involved in
the agreement was an understanding that the magistrates' court would be invited
to make certain orders on the basis of being told that the parties had come to an
agreement. Three of the terms, when analysed, could only mean that the parties   *j*
would invite the magistrates' court to make certain orders. Those three terms were
not such as to need a reduction to writing. Presumably if the justices had not seen
fit to make the orders which the husband and the wife invited them to make the

---

1   [1973] 3 All ER 977, [1974] QB 161

a   term as to the surrendering by the wife of her interest in the property for £1,500 would lapse. What, then, was the term of the oral agreement which related to an interest in land? In effect it was that if the justices on the invitation of the parties discharged the maintenance order in favour of the wife while continuing the maintenance order in favour of the child and if the justices remitted arrears of maintenance owed by the husband to the wife provided that he made payment to his wife of £100 in respect of such arrears then the wife would surrender her interest in the property for £1,500.

b

When the £100 was received by the wife the contract was still an oral contract which was 'a contract for the sale or other disposition of land or any interest in land'. It was a contract on which, under s 40(1), if pleaded, no action could be brought, in the absence of writing. That subsection does not, however 'affect the law relating to part performance' (see sub-s (2)). That law, now given statutory recognition, is the law which was developed in courts of equity. 'The law relating to part performance' mentioned in sub-s (2) must in the context refer to the law relating to part performance of oral contracts for the sale or other disposition of land or any interest in land.

c

The problem that is raised in this case is whether there was any act which qualified to be regarded as an act of part performance of the contract. The view of the learned registrar was that being released from the maintenance order was not such an act nor was the arrangement regarding the arrears nor was the making of arrangements with the building society. The only act of part performance held by the learned registrar was the incurring by the husband of solicitors' costs of about £25 in connection with the contemplated transfer. That view did not find favour with any member of the Court of Appeal[1].

d

The learned judge in the county court considered that there was no act of part performance. On appeal to the Court of Appeal, the notice of appeal set out five acts which it was submitted were sufficient acts of part performance. In the result the act that appealed to the majority in the Court of Appeal was the payment of £100. They found it unnecessary to discuss certain other suggested acts.

e

It is difficult out of the richness of learning and authority to make selection, but the theme running through the speech of Lord Selborne LC in *Maddison v Alderson*[2] is, I think, made clear. He drew[3] the line between the simple case where a person is charged on a contract only and the case in which 'there are equities resulting from res gestae subsequent to and arising out of the contract'. Lord Selborne LC said: 'So long as the connection of those res gestae with the alleged contract does not depend upon the mere parol testimony, but is reasonably to be inferred from the res gestae themselves' then justice seemed to require some limitation on the scope of the Statute of Frauds. He also added[4]:

f

g

> 'It is not enough that an act done should be a condition of, or good consideration for, a contract, unless it is, as between the parties, such a part execution as to change their relative positions as to the subject-matter of the contract.'

h   Lord FitzGerald thus expressed himself[5]:

> '... the acts relied on as performance to take the case out of the statute must be unequivocally and in their own nature referable to some such agreement as that alleged, and I may add must necessarily relate to and affect the land the subject of that agreement.'

i

---

1   [1973] 3 All ER 977, [1974] QB 161
2   (1883) 8 App Cas 467
3   8 App Cas at 476
4   8 App Cas at 478
5   8 App Cas at 491

A passage in Fry on Specific Performance reads[1]:

a

'The true principle, however, of the operation of acts of part performance seems only to require that the acts in question be such as must be referred to some contract, and may be referred to the alleged one; that they prove the existence of some contract, and are consistent with the contract alleged.'

That I take to be in full accord with the first of the four circumstances which Fry states[2] must concur to withdraw a contract from the operation of the statute. The acts of part performance must be such that they point unmistakeably and can only point to the existence of some contract such as the oral contract alleged. But of course the acts of part performance need not show the precise terms of the oral contract (see *Kingswood Estate Co Ltd v Anderson*[3]). The terms of the |oral contract must be proved by acceptable evidence but effect to them can only be given if and when acts of part performance establish that there must have been some such contract. Until then a door is, so to speak, closed against them.

b

c

In his speech in *Maddison v Alderson*, Lord O'Hagan[4] thus spoke of part performance:

'But there is no conflict of judicial opinion, and in my mind no ground for reasonable controversy as to the essential character of the act which shall amount to a part performance, in one particular. It must be unequivocal. It must have relation to the one agreement relied upon, and to no other. It must be such, in Lord Hardwicke's words[5], "as could be done with no other view or design than to perform that agreement." It must be sufficient of itself, and without any other information or evidence, to satisfy a Court, from the circumstances it has created and the relations it has formed, that they are only consistent with the assumption of the existence of a contract the terms of which equity requires, if possible, to be ascertained and enforced.'

d

e

When examining the alleged acts of part performance the evidence, if already given, of the terms of the oral contract which it is sought to enforce must be disregarded. Thus, in the present case it will not suffice to determine what were the terms which were orally agreed on 2nd March 1972 and then to examine whether any one of them was carried out. The law has not developed in such way as to permit that approach. In the judgment of the Court of Appeal[6] expressing the majority view the question is examined as to what would be the layman's answer if he were asked why the husband paid £100 to the wife and it is suggested that the answer would be that it was as a first step to the performance of the oral agreement of 2nd March 1972 of which one term was that he should make that payment in addition to paying the £1,500 for his wife's interest in the house.

f

g

With every respect the tests which courts of equity have evolved do not warrant any such approach. Courts of equity did not set out to make the terms of an Act of Parliament virtually nugatory. What the courts did was to consider the alleged acts of part performance and to decide whether the reasonable explanation of them was that the parties must have made (or stated otherwise had made) some contract such as the contract alleged. As the whole area of the law of part performance relates to contracts 'for the sale or other disposition of land or any interest in land' I would have thought that it followed that on a consideration of alleged acts of part performance it has to be decided whether their reasonable explanation is that the parties

f

1 6th Edn (1921), p 278, para 582
2 Ibid, p 276, para 580
3 [1962] 3 All ER 593, [1963] 2 QB 169
4 (1883) 8 App Cas at 485
5 In *Gunter v Halsey* (1739) Amb at 586, 587
6 [1973] 3 All ER at 992, [1974] QB at 181

a   must have made some contract in relation to land such as the contract alleged. I read the speeches in *Maddison v Alderson*[1] as having proceeded on that basis. Thus, in that part of his speech in which he said that it was settled that part payment of purchase price was not enough to amount to part performance, Lord Selborne LC said[2] that the best explanation of that was that the payment of money is an equivocal act, not (in itself) until the connection is established by parol testimony, 'indicative

b   of a contract concerning land'. It is because of this that the taking of possession of land will often be considered to be an act having strong claims to be regarded as an act of part performance indicative of a contract concerning the land.

I turn then to the question whether the payment of £100 by the husband can be regarded as an act of part performance. In my view, it cannot possibly be. The money was paid by the husband to the petty sessional division court in Bromley. It was

c   paid after that court had made the order of 2nd March 1972 in the terms which I have set out. The payment into court by a husband of a sum of money to be sent by the court to his wife does not, in my view, prove that there had been some contract between them: even more emphatically it does not prove that there had been any contract concerning land. The only inference that would be drawn from the payment of £100 into court by a husband in matrimonial proceedings would be that he was

d   in arrears in regard to some payments that he had been ordered to make. Without a connection established by parol testimony the payment of the money would not begin to suggest or to establish either the existence of a contract or of a contract in relation to land.

The other suggested acts relied on on behalf of the husband do not, in my view, possess any greater merit. Nor, in my view, if they fail to qualify as acts of part

e   performance do they have an accrual of merit by being linked with other suggested acts which also fail to qualify. It was submitted that the fact of mentioning the agreed terms to the justices and inviting them to make orders can be regarded as an act of part performance. But in agreement with Edmund Davies LJ[3] I consider that an act of part performance, in order to be such, must be an act in relation to that term of a contract (in a case where there are other terms) which alone is required

f   to be in writing if it is to be enforceable as satisfying s 40. In the present litigation what is being considered is whether an oral and prima facie unenforceable contract in relation to land has been made enforceable by reason of there being some act of part performance which shows that there must have been a contract in relation to land. An oral statement (or concurrence in an oral statement) that there was such an oral contract cannot, in my view, suffice.

g   Nor do I consider that any abandonment on the part of the husband of any attempt to ask the justices to remit the whole amount of the arrears of maintenance he owed to his wife can qualify as an act of part performance in relation to land. The fact that he incurred legal costs and then caused a draft conveyance to be sent to his wife's solicitors (which she ignored after receiving it—indicating to her solicitors that she was very reluctant to agree the terms) could certainly indicate a belief on his part

h   that there had been an oral contract or it could indicate a hope or expectation that agreement would in the future be reached. Without more I do not think that an act of part performance was established.

This is most unfortunate litigation. Having regard to the findings of fact which must be accepted I much regret that I am reaching a different conclusion from that of your Lordships. The case is a very special one but even so I consider that the

j   decision of the majority in the Court of Appeal[4] involves extending the law relating to part performance in a way which I do not consider to be warranted.

I would allow the appeal.

---

1   (1883) 8 App Cas 467
2   8 App Cas at 479
3   [1973] 3 All ER at 986, [1974] QB at 174
4   [1973] 3 All ER 977, [1974] QB 161

VISCOUNT DILHORNE. My Lords, the wife and the husband were married
on 4th August 1962. In 1963 they bought 9 Brookmead Close, Orpington, and were
registered as joint proprietors. In July 1968 the wife left the husband and on 6th
November 1968 she made an application to the magistrates' court as a result of which
an order was made for the payment to her of £2 a week maintenance and £2 10s
a week for their child. On 30th July 1969 she commenced proceedings for divorce
and on 28th April 1970 she obtained a decree nisi. On 5th June 1970 she made an
application under s 17 of the Married Women's Property Act 1882 to Bromley County
Court seeking, inter alia, an order that the house should be sold and the proceeds
divided between her and the husband. On 30th July 1970 the decree nisi was made
absolute.

Between May 1969 and March 1972 considerable correspondence took place between
the wife's and the husband's solicitors with a view to reaching an agreement about
what should be done about the house. This culminated in the wife's solicitor writing
on 17th February 1972 to say that the wife was not prepared to compromise her
claim in respect of the house for less than a lump sum payment of £1,500, and
in the husband's solicitor writing on 21st February 1972 to say that the husband was
prepared to pay that sum on condition that: (1) the wife would transfer to him her
interest in the property; (2) the £1,500 was in full and final settlement of the
wife's claims under the Married Women's Property Act 1882; (3) the wife would
consent to the order for maintenance in her favour being revoked or discharged and
all arrears under that order remitted; (4) the order for the payment of £2·50 a week
for the maintenance of their daughter should continue, and (5) an application would
be made by the wife to the county court to settle the action on these terms and on
the understanding that, as both parties were legally aided, there should be no order
as to costs.

On 2nd March 1972 there were further proceedings in the magistrates' court. On
27th February 1972 the husband's solicitor had written to the wife's suggesting that
they should meet early on that day to 'finalise the final terms of the settlement and
then explain them to the Magistrates'.

The wife's solicitors replied on 1st March 1972 pointing out that the arrears of
maintenance were £194 and that the husband had made no effort to reduce them
or to pay the weekly sum payable for his wife's maintenance. They said that they
felt great difficulty in advising the wife that 'the claim should include the arrears
of maintenance' for as the value of the house increased, the value of the proposed
settlement to the wife decreased. They said that they did not intend to attend
the magistrates' court.

Before the registrar of the county court there was a dispute about what had happened at the magistrates' court. He found as a fact that: (1) there was no written
agreement to pay £1,500; but (2) there was an oral agreement on 2nd March (a) that
the wife would surrender her interest in the property for £1,500; (b) that the wife's
maintenance order should be discharged; (c) that the child's maintenance order
would continue and (d) that the arrears would be remitted except as to £100. He
said that he was completely satisfied that there was this oral agreement made outside
the magistrates' court. Mr Boyd-White, the husband's solicitor, said in evidence that
he had explained to the justices what had been agreed and that the clerk of the
court had obtained the wife's confirmation of the terms.

On the husband's application for variation of the maintenance order, the magistrates ordered that it should be varied and that the husband should pay £2·50 weekly
in respect of the child so the husband was relieved of the obligation to pay the wife
£2 a week. Their order recited that the application for variation had been made
on the ground that it had been agreed between the parties 'to delete payments in
respect of the Defendant'.

The court adjourned the proceedings with regard to the arrears of maintenance
and notified the husband in writing of the grounds on which they had done so, saying:

a
'The proceedings have been adjourned for you to pay the sum of £100 not later than the 30th March, 1972, as all the arrears except that amount have today been remitted. If you fail to pay as directed, further proceedings will be commenced to recover the amount due.'

The justices thus accepted that an agreement had been made as the husband alleged. Insofar as it lays in their power to do so, they implemented all its terms.
b But for the agreement it is unlikely that they would have required the husband to pay the £100 within 28 days. The husband paid the £100 by 30th March 1972. The husband's solicitors obtained the consent of the building society, which had a mortgage on the house, to the transfer of the house into the husband's name and to the release of the wife from her covenants under the mortgage deed. The transfer was then sent to the wife's solicitors for her to sign. On 11th May 1972 they wrote saying
c that she was—

'very reluctant to agree the present terms having regard to the very much increased prices of property and her own personal circumstances',

and on 5th June 1972 they returned the transfer unsigned saying that the wife did not find the terms acceptable.
d The wife's application to the county court was then restored for hearing. There were no pleadings but the husband filed an affidavit in answer to the wife's claim to half the proceeds of the sale of the house, asserting that a binding agreement had been made between her and him that she would accept £1,500 for her interest. The wife filed an affidavit in answer denying that there had been such an agreement. So the first matter the registrar had to decide was whether there was such an agree-
e ment and, if so, whether it was binding on the wife. It was agreed that this should be decided as a preliminary point.

When the evidence had been heard, junior counsel for the wife submitted that, if there was an agreement, it was one to which s 40 of the Law of Property Act 1925 applied and so was unenforceable in the absence of part performance. He submitted that there had been no act of part performance. Section 40 of the 1925 Act is in the
f following terms:

'(1) No action may be brought upon any contract for the sale or other disposition of land or any interest in land, unless the agreement upon which such action is brought, or some memorandum or note thereof, is in writing, and signed by the party to be charged or by some other person thereunto by him lawfully
g authorised.
'(2) This section . . . does not effect the law relating to part performance . . .'

This section replaced that part of s 4 of the Statute of Frauds (1677) relating to interests in land. That section began with the words 'No action shall be brought . . .'

The agreement alleged by the husband and held by the registrar to have been
h made was described by the registrar as an 'oral package deal'. It was one which dealt not only with an interest in land but also the wife's maintenance and with the arrears of maintenance. Although it dealt with these three matters, it was one agreement, not divisible into separate parts, for if the husband had not agreed to pay the £100, presumably the wife would not have agreed to sell her interest in the house, and if the wife had not agreed to sell her interest, the husband would not have been prepared to pay £100 more than was offered by his solicitor in their letter
j of 21st February 1972.

The registrar, on appeal from him, his Honour Judge Fife and all members of the Court of Appeal[1] (Edmund Davies, Roskill and Scarman LJJ) held that it was a contract to which the section applied. I agree. It was a contract for the disposition

1   [1973] 3 All ER 977, [1974] QB 161

of an interest in land and it did not cease to be that on account of the inclusion in it *a*
of terms relating to maintenance.

The question whether, if not enforceable, the contract can nevertheless be relied on
by the husband as an answer to the wife's claim, does not arise for decision now.
Edmund Davies LJ referred to it in the course of his judgment. While s 40 of the Law
of Property Act 1925 and s 4 of the Statute of Frauds both prohibit the bringing of an
action on such a contract, neither Act prohibits it being relied on in defence. If this *b*
appeal is allowed, then the husband can put forward this contention at the resumed
hearing in the registrar's court. If successful on it, the wife will not succeed on her
claim and in the absence of part performance the husband will be unable to enforce
the agreement. The determination of the preliminary point now before the House
which has already been considered by three courts, with both parties legally aided,
will not necessarily therefore conclude this litigation at the public expense. The *c*
temptation to try and take a short cut by the decision of a preliminary point should,
I think, be resisted unless it is clear that its determination, whichever way the decision
goes, will finally resolve the case. It will not do so if this appeal succeeds.

While the wife is, of course, entitled to rely on s 40 of the Law of Property Act 1925
I cannot but regard her appeal as devoid of all merit. Soon after the enactment of
the Statute of Frauds, the courts began to grant relief against its operation, as the Earl *d*
of Selborne LC pointed out in *Maddison v Alderson*[1], on the principle, summarily
stated, that the Act passed 'For Prevention of many fraudulent practices, which are
commonly endeavoured to be upheld by perjury and subornation of perjury' will
not be allowed to be made 'an instrument of fraud'.

Despite the absence of merits, as there was no sufficient memorandum or note of
the agreement in writing to satisfy the section, this appeal must succeed unless there
was such part performance of it as to render it binding on and enforceable against *e*
the wife.

Where it is contended that there has been such part performance[2]—

    'the defendant is really "charged" upon the equities resulting from the acts
    done in execution of the contract, and not (within the meaning of the statute)
    upon the contract itself. If such equities were excluded, injustice of a kind *f*
    which the statute cannot be thought to have had in contemplation would follow.
    Let the case be supposed of a parol contract to sell land, completely performed
    on both sides, as to everything except conveyance; the whole purchase-money
    paid; the purchaser put into possession; expenditure by him (say in costly
    buildings) upon the property; leases granted by him to tenants. The contract
    is not a nullity; there is nothing in the statute to estop any Court which may *g*
    have to exercise jurisdiction in the matter from inquiring into and taking notice
    of the truth of the facts. All the acts done must be referred to the actual contract,
    which is the measure and test of their legal and equitable character and conse-
    quences. If, therefore, in such a case a conveyance were refused, and an action
    of ejectment brought by the vendor or his heir against the purchaser, nothing
    could be done towards ascertaining and adjusting the equitable rights and liabilities *h*
    of the parties, without taking the contract into account. The matter has ad-
    vanced beyond the stage of contract; and the equities which arise out of the
    stage which it has reached cannot be administered unless the contract is regarded.
    The choice is between undoing what has been done (which is not always possible,
    or, if possible, just) and completing what has been left undone. The line may not
    always be capable of being so clearly drawn as in the case which I have supposed; *j*
    but it is not arbitrary or unreasonable to hold that when the statute says that no
    action is to be brought to charge any person upon a contract concerning land,

1 (1883) 8 App Cas 467 at 474
2 8 App Cas at 475, 476

a it has in view the simple case in which he is charged upon the contract only, and not that in which there are equities resulting from res gestae subsequent to and arising out of the contract. So long as the connection of those res gestae with the alleged contract does not depend upon mere parol testimony, but is reasonably to be inferred from the res gestae themselves, justice seems to require some such limitation of the scope of the statute, which might otherwise interpose an

b obstacle even to the rectification of material errors, however clearly proved, in an executed conveyance, founded upon an unsigned agreement.'

Per Lord Selborne LC in *Maddison v Alderson*[1]. Later Lord Selborne LC said[2]:

'All the authorities shew that the acts relied upon as part performance must be unequivocally, and in their own nature, referable to some such agreement as that alleged . . .'

c

The res gestae subsequent to and arising out of the contract were (1) the announcement by the husband's solicitor to the justices of the terms of the agreement made outside the court; (2) the payment by the husband of the sum of £100 in respect of arrears of maintenance by 30th March 1972 and (3) the despatch to the wife's solicitor of the transfer of her interest in the house to the husband for her to execute.

d In ordinary parlance these acts could properly be described as acts of part performance of the agreement by the husband or his solicitor on his behalf. Counsel for the wife, however, submitted that they were not, either collectively or individually, part performance such as the law requires. He submitted that none of them, looked at without regard to the agreement, was unequivocally and in its own nature referable to some such agreement as that alleged and he also submitted that, to constitute

e part performance of an agreement relating to an interest in land, the act or acts relied on must be referable to the disposition of an interest in land.

In *Chaproniere v Lambert*[3] Warrington LJ cited a passage from Fry on Specific Performance[4] (repeated in the sixth edition[5]) which stated four conditions which had to be satisfied for there to be part performance: (1) the acts of part performance must be such as not only to be referable to a contract such as alleged but to be refer-

f able to no other title; (2) they must be such as to render it a fraud in the defendant to take advantage of the contract not being in writing; (3) the contract to which they refer must be such as in its own nature is enforceable by the court; and (4) there must be proper parol evidence of the contract which is let in by the acts of part performance, and Warrington LJ added[6]:

g 'Every one of those four conditions is essential to enable the act relied on to be treated as part performance. It is not sufficient to prove acts referable only to the contract alleged and no other. They must be such as to render it a fraud in the defendant to take advantage of the contract not being in writing.'

In *Kingswood Estate Co Ltd v Anderson*[7] the point was taken that the act of part

h performance was as referable to a weekly tenancy as to a tenancy for life, the defendant asserting an oral agreement for a tenancy for life. In the Court of Appeal it was unanimously held that the tenant's acts in quitting her rent controlled premises and moving into the flat offered her by the plaintiffs were sufficient part performance to make the oral agreement for a tenancy for life enforceable. Upjohn LJ rejected the

1   (1883) 8 App Cas at 475, 476
2   8 App Cas at 479
3   [1917] 2 Ch 356 at 361, [1916-17] All ER Rep 1089 at 1092
4   5th Edn (1911), p 291, para 580
5   (1921), pp 276, 277, para 580
6   [1917] 2 Ch at 361, [1916-17] All ER Rep at 1092
7   [1962] 3 All ER 593, [1963] 2 QB 169

contention that the acts of part performance had to be referable to no other title than
that alleged, saying that that was 'a long exploded idea' and[1]:

'The true rule is, in my view, stated in FRY ON SPECIFIC PERFORMANCE[2]: "The
true principle, however, of the operation of acts of part performance seems only
to require that the acts in question be such as must be referred to some contract,
and may be referred to the alleged one; that they prove the exsitence of some
contract, and are consistent with the contract alleged." '

In my opinion, the res gestae to which I have referred show exclusively the existence of a contract between the wife and the husband. If there had been no contract,
there would have been no announcement to the justices with the clearly implied
request that they should act in accordance with it, there would not have been the
undertaking to pay and the payment of the £100, and no transfer would have been
sent for execution by the wife. One does not send to a person a document for execution which transfers title to property unless there has been some prior agreement
with regard thereto. While an oral statement made by a party or his solicitor will
not ordinarily be an act of part performance, in this case the making of the statement
to the justices was an essential part in the performance of the contract. Without it,
and the justices' co-operation, the agreement could not have been implemented.

It follows that, in my view, all these acts suffice in law to constitute part performance. I do not think that the contention of counsel for the wife that the sending of
the transfer for execution was an act preparatory to the performance of the contract
and not in performance of it is well founded. It is well established that preparatory
acts such as instructing a solicitor to prepare a lease or conveyance do not constitute
sufficient part performance (see Williams on the Statute of Frauds[3]). But here it
went beyond mere preparation. In the absence of conditions it was the husband's
duty to send the transfer for execution by the wife (see Williams on Title[4]). The
transfer was thus sent in discharge of an obligation that rested on the husband by
virtue of the contract.

Nor do I think that counsel's contention that there will only be a sufficient act
of part performance if the act is referable to the disposition of the interest in land
is well founded. Most of the reported cases relate to what one might call single
term contracts for the disposition of land. It is not, therefore, surprising that one
finds in the judgments dicta relating the part performance to the stipulation relating
to land. In *Brough v Nettleton*[5] the oral agreement alleged was the grant of a lease
of a house with the option to purchase it during the tenancy. The option was exercised but the landlord sought to rely on the Statute of Frauds. On his behalf it was
contended that the tenant could not succeed unless he could prove some act of part
performance unequivocally referable to the contract of sale made by the exercise
of the option. The obligation to sell should the option be exercised was held by
P O Lawrence J[6] to be—

'an essential term of the agreement upon the faith of which the plaintiff entered
into possession, and can, in my judgment, be enforced without the necessity of
proving any further act of part performance just as much as any other term of
the agreement could have been so enforced.'

So in that case it was not necessary to prove part performance of the contract of
sale. In this case it was an essential term of the agreement that the wife should sell her

1 [1962] 3 All ER at 604, [1963] 2 QB at 189
2 6th Edn (1921), p 278, para 582
3 The Statute of Frauds, Section IV, in the Light of its Judicial Interpretation (1932), p 245
4 3rd Edn (1966), p 709
5 [1921] 2 Ch 25
6 [1921] 2 Ch at 29

a interest in the house, but provided there was part performance of that agreement, it is not in my opinion necessary that there should be part performance of the term as to transfer of title. In *Brough v Nettleton*[1] the contract contained two provisions both relating to an interest in land, but I do not think that the decision in that case would have been different if the other provision to the option had not related to land and it would indeed be odd if a contract, wholly unenforceable because of one

b of its terms related to land, could only be enforced, even though the party seeking performance had fulfilled its obligations in respect of the other terms completely, if there was part performance of the term relating to the land. If equity has power to prevent the statute operating to facilitate fraud, I can see no justification either on principle or in logic for concluding that its power to do so is restricted to when the part performance is of the provision relating to land. Indeed in this case if the act to which I have referred were not part performance, I have difficulty in seeing what other

c acts of the husband could have been. He was in possession of the property throughout. If he paid the £1,500 there is well-established authority for saying that that could not be part performance. We have not in this case to consider whether that is right, though I find it difficult to discern on what principle that conclusion has been reached.

If, however, contrary to my view, it is necessary that the act of part performance should relate to the disposition of an interest in land, then, in my opinion, the act

d of sending the transfer and the announcement in the magistrates' court both did so.

The registrar found that there had been sufficient part performance. He took the view that the incurring of solicitors' costs by the husband in connection with the transfer was an act to the husband's detriment and therefore was sufficient part performance. The mere fact that a party has acted to his detriment does not, in my view, establish that his act was in part performance of the contract and I doubt very

e much the correctness of his view that just to incur solicitors' costs amounted to part performance. Roskill and Scarman LJJ in the Court of Appeal[2] based their conclusion that there had been part performance on a different ground. They both were of opinion that the payment of £100 by itself was sufficient part performance. I do not think that it is possible to sever this payment from what preceded it and, as I have said, this payment, following on the announcement made to the justices, taken with that,

f does in my view suffice.

I now turn to the second of the conditions stated in Fry on Specific Performance[3] to to which Warrington LJ[4] referred, namely, were the acts of part performance such as to render it a fraud in the wife to take advantage of the contract not being in writing? or, to apply the words of Lord Selborne LC in *Maddison v Alderson*[5], did such equities arise from the acts done in execution of the contract as to make it an injustice which the

g section cannot be thought to have had in contemplation if specific performance was not ordered? In my opinion, it would be most unjust if this agreement was not, owing to the absence of writing, held to be enforceable. If there had been no part performance, that would have been the position, but there having been, in my opinion, part performance of it, it would now be wrong and inequitable, in my view, if the wife was held not to be bound by the agreement. She was present in the magis-

h trates' court. She heard the terms of the agreement announced. She made no objection. She received £100 from the husband which she has retained and then, in the hope no doubt that she would get more than the £1,500 for her share of the house, she gave, more than two months later, on 7th May 1972, her first intimation of her intention to resile from the agreement. I think that to allow her to do so and to retain the £100 she obtained on the faith of the agreement would indeed be to allow s 40 of the Law of

j Property Act 1925 to be an instrument of injustice.

---

1 [1921] 2 Ch 25
2 [1973] 3 All ER 977, [1974] QB 161
3 5th Edn (1911) p 291, para 580
4 [1917] 2 Ch at 361, [1916-17] All ER Rep at 1092
5 (1883) 8 App Cas at 475, 476

As to the third condition stated in Fry[1], that the contract to which the acts of part
performance refer must be such as is in its own nature is enforceable by the courts,
counsel for the wife conceded that if the agreement had been in writing the specific
performance of it could have been ordered. But,

As to the fourth condition stated in Fry[1], that there must be proper parol evidence
of the contract which is let in by the acts of part performance, there was here proper
parol evidence of the contract. I think that in the statement of this condition the use of
the words 'let in' was a little unfortunate for it lends some support to the argument
advanced by counsel for the wife that acts of part performance are the key which opens
the door to the contract. I do not think that that is so. They are the key to rendering
the contract enforceable. But, as Lord Selborne LC said[2], a court is not estopped
'from inquiring into and taking notice of the truth of the facts.' The contract is not a
nullity. The acts of part performance must be of part performance of that contract and
whether they are or not, cannot be determined without regard to the contract. The
party seeking to rely on such a contract has to prove it and to prove such acts. But
at a trial the matters are not dealt with separately. Such a party does not first have
to prove such acts and the court has first to decide whether they can be so regarded
and then, if the court holds that they can, the party does not have to produce evidence
of the contract and determine whether or not there is any contract. The court is
not required to operate in blinkers. If the contract is proved, it does not prevent
the court from considering and deciding whether the alleged acts of part performance
are unequivocally and of their own nature referable to a contract of the character
alleged. In the course of the argument some discussion took place as to the interpretation of the word 'unequivocal' as used by Lord Selborne LC. I think it does not mean
any more than that the acts of part performance which are alleged to have taken
place must point to the existence of some such contract as alleged.

In my opinion, for the reasons stated, there was sufficient part performance in this
case to render the contract enforceable. It follows that the conclusions of the registrar
and of the majority of the Court of Appeal[3] were right and I am of opinion that
this appeal should be dismissed.

LORD SIMON OF GLAISDALE. My Lords, the facts which lie behind the
issues here have been stated by Edmund Davies LJ in the Court of Appeal[3] and by my
noble and learned friends who have preceded me. The respondent ('the husband') in
effect is seeking to enforce that term of what the learned registrar called 'an oral
package deal' (by which is meant an indivisible contract consisting of a number of
obligations on each side) which relates to the disposition of an interest in land. The
contract (of 2nd March 1972) disposed of the various issues raised by three legal
processes: (i) a summons under s 17 of the Married Women's Property Act 1882
taken out by the appellant ('the wife'); (ii) a summons under the Matrimonial Proceedings (Magistrates' Courts) Act 1960 taken out by the husband for variation of a
maintenance order which had been made in favour of the wife and the child of the
marriage; (iii) a summons by the wife for enforcement of payment of arrears of £194
which had accrued under the maintenance order. The terms of the contract were
necessarily conditional on approval by the justices at the hearing which would
immediately ensue. They were in effect as follows: (1) the wife would consent to the
discharge of the maintenance order of £1·75 weekly in her favour; (2) the husband and
the wife would consent to the continuance of the maintenance order of £2·50 weekly
in respect of the child; (3) the husband would, before 30th March 1972, pay £100 in
part discharge of the arrears; (4) the wife would consent to the remission of the

---

1   Fry on Specific Performance (6th Edn, 1921), p 277, para 580
2   (1883) 8 App Cas at 475
3   [1973] 3 All ER 977, [1974] QB 161

a balance of the arrears; (5) the wife would surrender to the husband the interest which
she claimed in the former matrimonial home; (6) the husband would pay her £1,500
for such interest.

As will appear hereafter, it is only the obligations incumbent on the husband which
are relevant to the doctrine of part performance, with which your Lordships are concerned. But, in addition to his positive obligations set out under heads (2), (3) and (6)
b above, which would on execution involve detriment to him, there were some tacit
forbearances by the husband: (a) it was open to him, on his complaint for variation of
the maintenance order, to ask the justices to reduce the maintenance order in respect
of the child; (b) it would be unusual, to say the least, for justices to order the discharge of maintenance arrears otherwise than by a weekly instalment order; before
ordering a payment of £100 within 28 days they would require positive proof that the
c husband had such a sum at his immediate disposal; the husband forbore from putting
the wife to proof; (c) the enforcement of arrears of maintenance is a matter of judicial
discretion, so that it was open to the husband to ask the court to discharge the entire
arrears; (d) it is the practice not to enforce more than a year's arrears of maintenance
(Pilcher v Pilcher (No 2)[1]); the evidence does not show how long the arrears had been
accumulating (this would depend mainly but not exclusively on whether the husband
d had been keeping up the maintenance payments in respect of the child); and it might
be that the justices would have refused to enforce arrears of £100, even by instalments.

I would emphasise that the agreement generally, and various terms of it specifically,
provided for the justices to be informed as to what had been agreed and to be asked to
implement the matters which lay within their jurisdiction.

The justices, on being informed of the agreement between the parties and on being
e satisfied that the wife was a freely and knowledgeable consenting party, approved it,
and implemented so much of it as lay within their jurisdiction, by varying the maintenance order on the husband's complaint and by adjourning the wife's complaint
for variation, in order that the husband might pay the £100 not later than 30th March
1972; they remitted the balance of the arrears. This adjournment and remission were
the only positive orders that the justices made on the wife's complaint; they did not
f actually order the husband to pay the £100, though the order states: 'If you fail to
pay as directed, further proceedings will be commenced to recover the amount due.'
There was, in other words, no merger of the husband's contractual obligation to pay
£100 in a subsequent judgment debt. On the justices' approval the agreement
between the parties became contractually binding (Smallman v Smallman[2]), subject to
any question of enforceability in view of the want of writing and signature to evidence
it.
g This is one of the most difficult situations where two legal principles are in
competition. The first legal principle is embodied in s 40(1) of the Law of Property Act
1925 which states:

h 'No action may be brought upon any contract for the sale or other disposition
of land or any interest in land, unless the agreement upon which such action is
brought, or some memorandum or note thereof, is in writing, and signed by the
party to be charged or by some other person thereunto by him lawfully
authorised.'

This provision replaced that part of s 4 of the Statute of Frauds (1677) which related
to interests in land. The preamble to the Statute of Frauds explained its object:
j 'For prevention of many fraudulent Practices, which are commonly endeavoured to
be upheld by Perjury or Subornation of Perjury . . .' The 'mischief' for which the
statute was providing a remedy was, therefore, that some transactions were being
conducted orally in such a way that important interests were liable to be adversely

---

1 [1956] 1 All ER 463, [1956] 1 WLR 298
2 [1971] 3 All ER 717, [1972] Fam 25

affected by a mode of operation that invited forensic mendacity. The remedy was to require some greater formality in the record of such transaction than mere word of mouth if it was to be enforced. The continuing need for such a remedy for such a mischief was apparently recognised as subsisting when the law of landed property was recast in 1925.

The second, competing, legal principle was evoked when, almost from the moment of passing of the Statute of Frauds, it was appreciated that it was being used for a variant of unconscionable dealing, which the statute itself was designed to remedy. A party to an oral contract for the disposition of an interest in land could, despite performance of the reciprocal terms by the other party, by virtue of the statute disclaim liability for his own performance on the ground that the contract had not been in writing. Common law was helpless. But equity, with its purpose of vindicating good faith and with its remedies of injunction and specific performance, could deal with the situation. The Statute of Frauds did not make such contracts void but merely unenforceable; and, if the statute was to be relied on as a defence, it had to be specifically pleaded. Where, therefore, a party to a contract unenforceable under the Statute of Frauds stood by while the other party acted to his detriment in performance of his own contractual obligations, the first party would be precluded by the Court of Chancery from claiming exoneration, on the ground that the contract was unenforceable, from performance of his reciprocal obligations; and the court would, if required, decree specific performance of the contract. Equity would not, as it was put, allow the Statute of Frauds 'to be used as an engine of fraud'. This became known as the doctrine of part performance—the 'part' performance being that of the party who had, to the knowledge of the other party, acted to his detriment in carrying out irremediably his own obligations (or some significant part of them) under the otherwise unenforceable contract. This competing principle has also received statutory recognition, as regards contracts affecting interests in land, in s 40(2) of the Law of Property Act 1925.

But what was in origin a rule of substantive law designed to vindicate conscientious dealing seems to have come in time sometimes to have been considered somewhat as a rule of evidence. It is easy to appreciate how this happened. Part performance could be viewed as a way of proving an agreement falling within s 4 notwithstanding the absence of writing. Seen as such it was no doubt considered necessary to frame stringent requirements to prevent the doctrine from carting a sedan chair through the provision of the statute. If part performance was to be evidence of a contract which could not otherwise and directly be proved, the acts of part performance should themselves intrinsically be capable of proving some such contract as that alleged. Oral evidence was not admissible to connect them with the alleged contract: otherwise, it was held, the statutory object would be defeated by allowing an interest in land to pass on mere oral testimony. As the Earl of Selborne LC put it in *Maddison v Alderson*[1] (in a passage I label '(A)' for ease of reference later):

> (A) 'The doctrine . . . has been confined . . . within limits intended to prevent a recurrence of the mischief which the statute was passed to suppress . . . All the authorities shew that the acts relied upon as part performance must be unequivocally, and in their own nature, referable to some such agreement as that alleged . . . '

It may be questionable whether it was direct respect for the statute which led to such confinement of the doctrine, or whether it was not rather because part performance seems sometimes to have been regarded as an alternative way of proving an oral agreement; for equity allowed a person to prove by parol evidence that land conveyed to another was so conveyed on trust for himself, notwithstanding s 7 of the

---

1 (1883) 8 App Cas 467 at 478, 479

a Statute of Frauds: *Rochefoucauld v Boustead*[1]; *Bannister v Bannister*[2]—the passages show that here, too, the guiding rule was that the court would not allow the statute to be used as a cloak for fraud. However that may be, the speech of the Earl of Selborne LC has always been regarded as authoratative, notwithstanding that what he said about part performance was, strictly, obiter.

b But Lord Selborne LC went on to effect a complete reconciliation between the provisions of the statute and the doctrine of part performance in a passage[3] which is of crucial importance to the instant appeal, and which I have labelled '(B)':

c (B) 'In a suit founded on such part performance, the defendant is really "charged" upon the equities resulting from the acts done in execution of the contract, and not (within the meaning of the statute) upon the contract itself. If such equities were excluded, injustice of a kind which the statute cannot be thought to have had in contemplation would follow ... All the acts done must be referred to the actual contract, which is the measure and test of their legal and equitable character and consequences ... The matter has advanced beyond the stage of contract; and the equities which arise out of the stage which it has reached cannot be administered unless the contract is regarded. The choice is between undoing what has been done (which is not always possible

d or, if possible, just) and completing what has been left undone ... it is not arbitrary or unreasonable to hold that when the statute says that no action is to be brought to charge any person upon a contract concerning land, it has in view the simple case in which he is charged upon the contract only, and not that in which there are equities resulting from res gestae subsequent to and arising out of the contract. So long as the connection of those res gestae with the

e alleged contract does not depend upon the mere parol testimony, but is reasonably to be inferred from the res gestae themselves, justice seems to require some such limitation of the scope of the statute ...'

The following questions arise for determination in relation to the facts of the nstant case: (1) what is meant by res gestae in passage (B)? Are they different

f from acts of part performance of the alleged contract? If so, do they impose some limitation—e g contemporaneity? Or are they words of extension—permitting, for example, evidence of explanatory acts antecedent to the alleged contract (such as the correspondence between the solicitors in the instant case)? (2) In passage (A) Lord Selborne LC says 'referable to *some such agreement* as that alleged': in passage (B), 'referred to the *actual contract*'. Is there a discrepancy here? What

g must be the relationship between the acts of part performance and/or the res gestae (if there is a distinction), on the one hand, and the alleged contract, on the other, in order to raise an equity precluding the other party from relying on the statute? (3) Must the alleged act(s) of part performance indicate specifically the term of the alleged contract to which the statute is pleaded as a defence (e g the term relating to the disposition of an interest in land), or is it sufficient that the

h alleged act(s) indicate *some* contract? (4) What does 'unequivocally' in passage (A) mean in this connection? What is the standard of proof required? (5) What does 'of their own nature' in passage (A) mean? Must each act of alleged part performance 'of its own nature' be separately referable to the alleged, or 'some such', contract, or can they be regarded cumulatively—reinforcing each other, so to speak? (6) For what purpose, if at all, is oral evidence admissible? (7) Can payment of a sum of money

j ever be a relevant act of part performance? (8) What issues arise at the trial and how are they to be resolved?

These questions to some extent overlap. I do not think that it is possible to reconcile

---

1 [1897] 1 Ch 196 at 206
2 [1948] 2 All ER 133 at 136
3 (1883) 8 App Cas at 475, 476

all the authorities and dicta. There seems to be an uneasy oscillation between regard- *a*
ing the doctrine as a principle vindicating conscientious dealing and as a rule of
evidence. Concurrently with this, and reinforcing the latter view, there seems to have
been a hardening of equity's arteries, an increasing technicality until quite recent
times. The chancellor's foot evolves into the vice-chancellor's footrule.

(1) *Res gestae* (i e things done). The concept is more familiar in the law of evidence,
where it relates to the admissibility of acts, declarations and incidents which either are *b*
constituents of, or accompany and explain, the fact or transaction in question (see
Phipson on Evidence[1]). Lord Selborne LC probably had two reasons for using the
words in preference to 'acts of part performance of the alleged contract': (i) they are
sometimes used in the law of evidence to mark the distinction between the principal
fact or transaction in question, on the one hand (as to which evidence is always
admissible), and ancillary facts, on the other (as to which evidence is only admissible *c*
if they are so closely connected with the principal fact as either to form one continuous
transaction with it or to be necessary to give meaning to it): Lord Selborne LC was
emphasising that what gave rise to the equity was, not the contract itself, but what was
done ancillary to it; (ii) one rationale for the res gestae rule of evidence is that the
probability of an occurrence may often be tested by considering its attendant circumstances (*Dysart Peerage Case*[2]): so here, once it was considered incumbent to do equity *d*
without undermining the statute, it was reasonable to look for attendant circumstances which inherently rendered it probable that there had been an antecedent contract the obligations of which it would be inequitable to allow a party to escape. But I
do not think that Lord Selborne LC intended to import generally the rules of the law
of evidence relating to res gestae. Those rules often extend to admitting acts and declarations antecedent to the principal fact where they either form one continuous
transaction with it or are necessary to explain it. But an act or declaration antecedent *e*
to a contract cannot be part performance of it; and it was the doctrine part of part
performance which Lord Selborne LC was concerned with. He speaks[3] of 'res gestae
subsequent to and arising out of the contract'. I do not think, therefore, that the
correspondence between the solicitors before 2nd March 1972 can avail the husband
in obviating the plea of s 40(1) (though it is available to aid him in establishing the *f*
alleged agreement of 2nd March 1972, once the plea of the statute is obviated). Then
there is authority that acts preparatory, not merely to the contract, but to the performance of a term of the contract (such as compiling an abstract of title or making a
valuation) are not sufficient acts of part performance: but these certainly would seem
to be res gestae pursuant to the contract involving detriment to the plaintiff. Did the
preparation of the conveyance on behalf of the husband in the instant case stand alone,
it might be necessary to give consideration to this line of authority: however, on the *g*
view I take of other matters it is not called for. Again, I do not think that Lord Selborne LC's description of acts of part performance as res gestae under the contract
imports from the law of evidence into this branch of the law the requirement of
substantial contemporaneity: equity's doctrine of laches and the requirement of
referability provide superior and less technical safeguards against injustice. On the
other hand, the fact that Lord Selborne LC used the term res gestae throws some light *h*
on the admissibility of oral testimony in this branch of the law, since in the law of
evidence the doctrine of res gestae is very largely concerned with the question of
admissibility of oral declarations.

(2) '*Some such agreement*'/'*the actual agreement*'. I think that the discrepancy in expression foreshadows Upjohn LJ's formulation of the rule—the acts must be such as
'prove the existence of some contract, and are consistent with the contract alleged' *i*

---

1   11th Edn (1970), p 70, para 171
2   (1881) 6 App Cas 489
3   (1883) 8 App Cas at 476

a (*Kingswood Estate Co Ltd v Anderson*[1], citing Fry on Specific Performance[2]; see also *Wakeham v Mackenzie*[3]). Alternatively, Lord Selborne LC might have been drawing a distinction between the stage of part performance giving rise to equities in favour of the plaintiff which preclude the defendant from pleading the statute, and the next state where the plaintiff may lead evidence of the oral contract with sufficient particularity that equity will enforce it. Both must now be accepted as valid ways of considering the rule.

b   The law here is not logical: it represents the compromise of the two principles to which I referred near the outset of this speech. If the contract alleged is such that it ought not to depend on oral testimony, it is *this* contract, not merely *some* contract, that the acts should prove. If the plaintiff has so performed his obligations under the contract that it would be unconscionable for the defendant to plead the statute, it is immaterial whether or not the plaintiff's acts prove the contract—let alone some other

c contract. But it is the sort of illogical compromise, doing some deference to each of two competing and inconsistent principles, in which English law abounds. There is no reason to disturb it so long as it does substantial justice, as it seems to have done in all the recent reported cases. However, I have already ventured to point out that equity did not find it necessary to create the same difficulties as regards s 7 of the

d statute—unembarrassed by a long line of authority, it took the direct route to oral evidence.

     But the law as stated by Upjohn LJ is juridically justifiable. If the plaintiff proves that he carried out acts in part performance of *some contract* to which the defendant was a party while the latter stood by, it becomes inequitable that the latter should be allowed to plead, in exoneration of reciprocal obligations, that *any such contract*

e was unenforceable by reason of the statute—particularly when it is borne in mind that few acts of performance point exclusively to a particular contract, least of all a particular multi-term contract. But 'some such contract' must be a contract with the defendant—otherwise no equity arises against him to preclude his pleading the statute.

     (3) *Must the act of part performance indicate that term of the contract which concerns the*

f *disposition of an interest in land?* This question has often been answered in the affirmative. Snell's Principles of Equity[4] for example states: '... the acts must indicate the land concerned'. But where, as so often, the only term to be performed by the defendant is the transfer of the interest in land, the fulfilment of the other conditions stipulated by equity will generally involve that the effective act of part performance indicates the land concerned. The Earl of Selborne LC's 'referable to some such agreement as that alleged' is not so specific; and it has now, in any event, received

g Upjohn LJ's gloss. In *Wakeham v Mackenzie*[5] a woman agreed to surrender her rent-restricted flat and keep house for an elderly widower in consideration of his oral promise to leave her his house by will: her action was held to be sufficient part performance to make the widower's oral promise binding on his personal representative. The case must be compared with *Maddison v Alderson*[6], where the only material distinction was that woman had no house of her own to give up. This distinction

h might be sufficient to justify the inference in the later case that the housekeeper's actions implied a quid pro quo, a bargain, which had not been a justifiable inference in the earlier case (see Lord Blackburn in *Maddison v Alderson*[7]); but they could hardly be said to have indicated a bargain a term of which related to the widower's house.

---

j 1 [1962] 3 All ER at 604, [1963] 2 QB at 189
   2 6th Edn (1921), p 278, para 582
   3 [1968] 2 All ER 783 at 786, 787, [1968] 1 WLR 1175 at 1180
   4 27th Edn (1973), p 587
   5 [1968] 2 All ER 783, [1968] 1 WLR 1175
   6 (1883) 8 App Cas 467
   7 8 App Cas at 487

It is unnecessary to determine the point in the instant case. The husband's acts of part performance included two which specifically indicated the land in question: (i) procuring his solicitor to inform the justices of the entire bargain and to invite them to implement such of its terms as concerned them; (ii) procuring his solicitor to carry out the obligation which, under the bargain, the husband had assumed of drafting the conveyance and sending it to the wife (see Williams on Title[1])—this was the performance of an obligation arising from the contract, not preparation for performance.

Other acts of part performance by the husband proved that there had been *some* contract with the wife, though without specifically indicating those terms which concerned the house. The consent to the justices' orders and the payment of £100 are, in my view, only reasonably intelligible on the hypothesis that the issues raised by the cross-summonses in the magistrates' court had been settled by agreement. As for the other limb of Upjohn LJ's formulation of the rule, the husband's acts were consistent with the contract alleged by him.

(4) *'Unequivocally'*. This could bear three meanings: (i) referable to the alleged contract and no other; (ii) clearly, on more than a mere balance of probabilities; (iii) not equally referable to the hypothesis of a contract or some other hypothesis, i e on the preponderance of probability.

The first view was apparently held at one time—in logical consistency with the principle that the doctrine of part performance should not be allowed to undermine the statutory insistence that the contract must not be proved by oral testimony. It would seem, indeed, to be a reflection of the tendency to regard the doctrine of part performance as a rule of evidence. But it must often have led to a failure of justice, to equity helplessly standing by while the statute was used as an engine of fraud; since, as Snell[2] puts it 'Few acts of part performance are so eloquent as to point to one particular contract alone'. This idea is therefore now to be regarded as 'long exploded', to use Upjohn LJ's expression in *Kingswood Estate Co Ltd v Anderson*[3].

As for the second view, there would be nothing unique in equity requiring that the act of part performance should indicate beyond doubt that it was in pursuance of a contractual obligation. For example, for rectification, there must be 'strong irrefragable evidence' of mistake (*Countess of Shelburne v Earl of Inchiquin*[4]): it must 'leave no fair and reasonable doubt upon the mind' (*Fowler v Fowler*[5]); there must be 'convincing proof' (*Joscelyne v Nissen*[6]). A similar standard is probably required to establish a secret trust (*Ottaway v Norman*[7]). Or that persons who have lived together purporting to be husband and wife were not married, especially if there had been *some* ceremony (*Morris v Davies*[8]; *Piers v Piers*[9]; *Hill v Hill*[10]). Or to prove the abandonment of a domicile of origin (*Winans v Attorney-General*[11]).

Nevertheless, the general standard of proof in civil proceedings is proof on a balance of probabilities. In some of the situations referred to in the preceding paragraph justice may call for a higher standard of proof; but I can see no reason why it should here—though no doubt, here as elsewhere, the evidence (and the nexus) will be more jealously scrutinised where the other party to the alleged contract is deceased. In

---

1   3rd Edn (1966), p 709
2   Principles of Equity (27th Edn, 1973), p 587
3   [1962] 3 All ER at 604, [1963] 2 QB at 189
4   (1784) 1 Bro CC 338 at 341
5   (1859) 4 De G & J 250 at 265
6   [1970] 1 All ER 1213 at 1222, [1970] 2 QB 86 at 98
7   [1971] 3 All ER 1325 at 1332, [1972] Ch 698 at 712
8   (1837) 5 Cl & Fin 163, [1875-42] All ER Rep 270
9   (1849) 2 HL Cas 331, [1843-60] All ER Rep 159
10   [1959] 1 All ER 281, [1959] 1 WLR 127
11   [1904] AC 287, [1904-7] All ER Rep 410

a passage (B)[1] the Earl of Selborne LC used the words 'reasonably to be inferred'. In *Wakeham v Mackenzie*[2] the alleged acts of part performance can only on a balance of probability have been more likely to have been in pursuance of some contract than otherwise. I am therefore of opinion not only that the facts relied on to prove acts of part performance must be established merely on a balance of probability, but that it is sufficient if it be shown that it was more likely than not that those acts were in

b performance of some contract to which the defendant was a party.

(5) *'Of their own nature'.* This means merely that oral testimony is not admissible to show that the acts relied on were in part performance of a contract: the acts must themselves on a balance of probability indicate this. But it does not mean that each act must be considered seriatim by itself. The acts may throw light on each other; and there is no reason to exclude light. In the instant case, for example, the payment

c of £100 would, standing by itself, have been equivocal: it would not even marginally have been more suggestive of performance of a contractual term than otherwise. But taken together with the other acts and forbearances of the husband in relation to the summary matrimonial proceedings it becomes strongly indicative of a bargain. So, too, the preparation of the draft conveyance when taken together with the statements made to the justices—provided that the latter were admissible in evidence.

d (6) *Oral evidence.* The extent of the exclusionary rule is to preclude oral evidence to establish that the acts relied on were in part performance of a contract; in other words, the nexus between the acts and the alleged contract, or some such, cannot be established by oral testimony at the trial. But the acts themselves may be, and generally are, proved orally. Moreover, spoken words may themselves be part performance of a contract.

e   'Words spoken are facts just as much as any other action by a human being. If the speaking of the words is a relevant fact, a witness may give evidence that they were spoken.'

(Lord Wilberforce in *Ratten v Reginam*[3], in relation to the evidentiary rule of res gestae). As such they are to be considered as of the nature of real evidence (see Lord
f Normand in *Teper v Reginam*[4]). So, in the instant case, the bargain between the parties necessitated the justices being informed of what had been agreed, as a preliminary to the invitation to them to implement part of the agreement. The statement to the justices was part performance of the bargain, including those terms adverse to the husband; and oral evidence is admissible as to what was said to them. But 'human utterance is both a fact and a means of communication' (Lord Normand
g in *Teper v Reginam*[5]). When it comes to determining whether acts of part performance of their own nature indicate the contract alleged, or some such, words inevitably speak more specifically than deeds; but that is no reason for excluding them either as facts or as means of communication. The statement to the justices as an act of part performance indicated in terms that there had been an agreement between the parties and what were its provisions. Moreover, the ensuing actions of the husband (in inviting
h the order of the justices, instructing his solicitor to prepare the conveyance, and paying the £100) must be viewed in the light of the statement to the justices—they were integral res gestae in every sense of that expression.

(7) *Payment of money.* It has sometimes been said that payment of money can never be a sufficient act of part performance to raise the required equity in favour of the plaintiff—or, more narrowly, that payment of part or even the whole of the purchase
j price for an interest in land is not a sufficient act of part performance. But neither of

---

1   (1883) 8 App Cas at 475, 476
2   [1968] 2 All ER 783, [1968] 1 WLR 1175
3   [1971] 3 All ER 801 at 805, [1972] AC 378 at 387
4   [1952] 2 All ER 447 at 449, 450, [1952] AC 480 at 487
5   [1952] 2 All ER at 449, [1952] AC at 486

the reasons put forward for the rule justifies it as framed so absolutely. The first was
that a plaintiff seeking to enforce an oral agreement to which the statute relates needs   a
the aid of equity; and equity would not lend its aid if there was an adequate remedy
at law. It was argued that a payment could be recovered at law, so there was no call
for the intervention of equity. But the payee might not be able to repay the money
(he might have gone bankrupt), or the land might have a particular significance for
the plaintiff (cf the equitable order for specific delivery of a chattel of particular   b
value to the owner: *Duke of Somerset v Cookson*[1]), or it might have greatly risen in
value since the payment, or money may have lost some of its value. So it was sought
to justify the rule, alternatively, on the ground that payment of money is always an
equivocal act: it need not imply a pre-existing contract, but is equally consistent with
many other hypotheses. This may be so in many cases, but it is not so in all cases.
Oral testimony may not be given to connect the payment with a contract; but cir-   c
cumstances established by admissible evidence (other acts of part performance, for
example) may make a nexus with a contract the probable hypothesis. In the instant
case, for example, what was said (i e done) in the magistrates' court in part performance of the agreement makes it plain that the payment of the £100 was also in part
performance of the agreement and not a spontaneous act of generosity or discharge
of a legal obligation or attributable to any other hypothesis.

(8) *The issues at the trial.* A plaintiff alleges an oral agreement. If the defendant   d
does not plead the statute, the plaintiff may prove the agreement by any relevant
evidence, including oral testimony. But if the defendant does plead the statute, the
plaintiff is barred unless he can establish that the defendant's plea of the statute should
not be admitted because its maintenance would be unconscionable. To do this the
plaintiff has to prove that: (i) on balance of probability he acted to his detriment;
(ii) it was more probable than not he so acted because he was contractually obliged   e
to the defendant to do so; (iii) such actions were consistent with the oral agreement
which he alleges. As regards (i), the plaintiff's detrimental actions can include words;
and he can prove them by any relevant evidence, including oral testimony. But he
cannot lead oral or any testimony (other than a written confession by the defendant
which satisfies the requirements of the statute) as to (ii) and (iii); the facts proved   f
under (i) must themselves answer (ii) and (iii) in his favour. But if all three requirements are satisfied, an equity arises in his favour which precludes the defendant from
relying on the statute; and the plaintiff can then lead evidence (including oral
evidence) to establish the oral agreement on which he bases his claim for relief, as if
the statute had never been pleaded. He still, of course, has to prove such oral agreement on a balance of probability; and if the other party is dead the evidence will be   g
rigorously scrutinised.

In the instant case the husband proved to the satisfaction of the registrar the following acts which were to his detriment: (i) procuring his solicitor to consent an order
by the justices which placed him under a continuing legal obligation; (ii) procuring
his solicitor to forbear from seeking from the justices orders which might have been
more advantageous to himself; (iii) paying £100 to the wife before 30th March 1972;   h
(iv) procuring his solicitor to draft a conveyance for execution by the wife. Even if,
contrary to my view, these matters could be considered in isolation from the statements inviting the justices to play their part in implementing them, they still, in my
opinion, make it more probable than not that the husband acted as he did because
he had contracted with the wife to do so; and they are consistent with the agreement
which the husband alleges. This makes it inequitable for the wife to allege that the
agreement was unenforceable because the formalities required by s 40(1) were not
complied with. The registrar, therefore, rightly admitted oral and affidavit evidence
to establish the agreement alleged by the husband, which he found proved.

I would therefore dismiss the appeal.

---

1   (1735) 3 P Wms 390

LORD SALMON. My Lords, soon after the Statute of Frauds was enacted, the Court
a of Chancery laid down the principle that should A be sued by B on a parol contract
disposing of an interest in land, A could not be allowed to rely on the absence of a
written memorandum of the contract in order to defeat B's claim if there had been
part performance of the contract. This was because it would be unconscionable in
such circumstances for A to seek to take advantage of the statute. For example, if
b B had performed his obligations under the parol contract, the benefit of which had
been accepted by A, it would clearly be an abuse of the statute if A were then allowed
to take the point that the contract was unenforceable against him when sued by B
to perform his corresponding contractual obligations.

This appeal turns on a consideration of the true nature of part performance which
is, of course, the same for the purposes of s 40 of the Law of Property Act 1925, as it
was for that part of s 4 of the Statute of Frauds which s 40 replaced.

c During the last 300 years there has been a mass of authority on this topic. Unfortunately many of the cases are irreconcilable with each other and it is by no means
easy to discover the true answer to the question with which we are faced, namely,
what are the essential elements of part performance in relation to contracts disposing
of an interest in land. One rule, however, emerges clearly; a parol contract relating
to land cannot be enforced unless the acts relied on as part performance, of them-
d selves, establish a prima facie case that they were done in the performance of a
contract. Then, but only then, may parol evidence of the contract be accepted. In
order to discover the significance of the alleged acts of part performance, the circumstances in which they were performed must, I think, clearly be relevant. What is
perhaps not so clear is whether the acts are sufficient to constitute part performance
if they establish only that they were done in the performance of some contract which
e might but equally well might not be a contract disposing of an interest in land.
There is certainly powerful authority for the view that this is not enough but that the
acts relied on must of themselves show prima facie that they were done in
performance of a contract disposing of such an interest.

It is perhaps not very difficult to see the reason for this view. Acts relied on as part
performance which show that a parol contract of the kind referred to in the statute
f was probably made and that it has been partly performed by the party who seeks to
enforce it, raises a substantially stronger equity in his favour than acts which are
equally consistent with the existence and part performance of a contract having
nothing to do with land. The object of the statute was to prevent a dishonest person
from fraudulently inventing a parol contract under which someone is supposed to
have disposed of an interest in land to him and then bringing perjured evidence in
g support of his claim under the spurious contract. An act which proves that probably
a contract for the disposal of an interest in land had been concluded and that the
person seeking to enforce it had done his part under it goes further to obviate the
mischief at which the statute was aimed than an act which shows merely the existence
of some contract which may equally well have nothing to do with land.

The celebrated but perhaps somewhat delphic passage in the speech of the Earl of
h Selborne LC in *Maddison v Alderson*[1] which has been cited by my noble and learned
friend, Viscount Dilhorne, is not inconsistent with either view. I think, however, that
it is plain from other passages in the Earl of Selborne LC's speech that he took the
view, generally held in his time, that for an act of alleged part performance to preclude
a defendant from relying on the statute it must be an act 'indicative of a contract
concerning land'. For example, he says[2]:
j

'. . . and it may be taken as now settled that part payment of purchase-
money is not enough; and judges of high authority have said the same even of

---

1   (1883) 8 App Cas 467 at 475
2   8 App Cas at 478, 479

payment in full . . . Some of the reasons which have been given for that *a*
conclusion are not satisfactory; the best explanation of it seems to be, that the
payment of money is an equivocal act, not (in itself), until the connection is
established by parol testimony, indicative of a contract concerning land . . .
All the authorities shew that the acts relied upon as part performance must be
unequivocally, and in their own nature, referable to some such agreement as
that alleged . . .'   *b*

Then, having reviewed many cases, he says[1]:

'The law deducible from these authorities is . . . fatal to the appellant's case.
Her mere continuance in Thomas Alderson's service, though without any actual
payment of wages, was not such an act as to be in itself evidence of a new contract, much less of a contract concerning her master's land.'   *c*

To my mind, Lord Blackburn clearly agreed with the Earl of Selborne LC that, to
take a case out of the statute, the act of part performance must show the existence
of a contract concerning land. Indeed, he went a good deal further. Lord Blackburn
said[2]:

' . . . there are cases that for the purpose of enforcing a specific performance *d*
of a contract for the purchase of an interest in land, a delivery of possession of
the land will take the case out of the statute. This is I think in effect to construe
the 4th section of the Statute of Frauds as if it contained these words, "or unless
possession of the land shall be given and accepted." Notwithstanding the very high
authority of those who have decided those cases, I should not hesitate if it was res
integra in refusing to interpolate such words . . . But it is not res integra and *e*
I think that the cases are so numerous that this anomaly, if as I think it is an
anomaly, must be taken as to some extent at least established. If it was originally
an error it is now I think communis error and so makes the law . . . But I do
not think this anomaly should be extended; and it is not a little remarkable that
there is no case . . . in which there has not been a change in the possession of
the land . . .'   *f*

Immediately after the passages to which I have referred the following sentences
appear in Lord Blackburn's speech[2]:

'The conduct of the parties may be such as to make it inequitable to refuse to
complete a contract partly performed. Wherever that is the case, I agree that
the contract may be enforced on the ground of an equity arising out of the *g*
conduct of the party.'

Those sentences, however, cannot be read in isolation; they must be read in conjunction with the passage which preceded them, and also with the passage which
follows them[3]:

'But the cases where this is given as the ground of decision are all cases in *h*
which there has been a change of possession, and I do not think that, as far as
they are anomalous, they should be extended to a case where there has not been
such a change.'

Lord O'Hagan and Lord FitzGerald both said plainly that in order to take the case
out of the statute there must be testimony of an act of part performance showing *j*
the existence of a contract concerning land, and they say nothing which could be
understood in any different sense.

---

1   (1883) 8 App Cas at 480, 481
2   8 App Cas at 489
3   8 App Cas at 490

a   I respectfully consider that Lord Blackburn went too far in limiting part performance to a change of possession but, in my opinion, all the speeches in *Maddison v Alderson*[1] laid down that acts which prima facie establish the existence of some contract no more likely to be concerned with land than with anything else cannot be sufficient part performance for the purpose of taking a case out of the statute. This expression of opinion may have been obiter because the House concluded that no
b   contract of any kind had been established. Nevertheless, it is a highly persuasive authority and for the reasons I have already indicated, I am not prepared to reject it.

We have certainly been referred to no reported case, and I have found none, in which an act of part performance which did not point to the existence of a contract concerning land has been held sufficient to take the case out of the statute. *Kingswood Estate Co Ltd v Anderson*[2] did not explode the idea accepted in *Maddison v Alderson*[1]
c   and a host of other cases. It exploded only the idea which had been expressed in some of the older authorities that, in order to take a case out of the statute, the act of part performance had to show not only the existence of a contract concerning land but also the very terms of the contract on which the party seeking to enforce it relied. In the *Kingswood Estate*[2] case a widow had for 45 years resided in premises of which she had become the statutory tenant. Her landlords were anxious to obtain posses-
d   sion of these premises in order to redevelop them. They acquired other premises to which they asked her to move. Having regard to the value of these premises, the Rent Acts did not apply to them, and she would, therefore, have had no security of tenure except by agreement. She entered into a parol agreement with the landlords under which she agreed to move on the terms that she would be left in possession of the new premises for the rest of her life. After she had moved the landlords served her with a notice to quit. She set up the parol agreement. The landlords relied on the
e   statute, arguing, unsuccessfully, that although the facts established a contract between them and the tenant relating to land, they did not take the case out of the statute because they did not show that the contract was for a life tenancy; they were equally consistent with a weekly tenancy. In his judgment, Upjohn LJ cited[3] a passage from Fry on Specific Performance[4] to which I shall presently return. That passage
f   in its context does not, in my view, mean more than that if the acts or part performance relate prima facie to some contract concerning land, then parol evidence may be given to show what the terms of that contract are. I think that Upjohn LJ would have been surprised if anything which he said in that case were to be construed as throwing any doubt on the long-established principle that the only acts which can take a case out of the statute are acts which establish prima facie that they were done in part performance of a contract concerning land—especially as the point did not
g   arise for decision since it was there necessarily conceded that the acts relied on did raise such a prima facie case. Moreover, he cited without dissenting from it, a passage in the judgment of Warrington LJ in *Chaproniere v Lambert*[5] restating the principle to which I have referred.

The passage from Fry on Specific Performance[4], to which I have referred, reads as
h   follows:

> 'The true principle, however, of the operation of acts of part performance seems only to require that the acts in question be such as must be referred to some contract, and may be referred to the alleged one; that they prove the existence of some contract, and are consistent with the contract alleged.'

Taken in isolation, that passage appears to support the husband's contention that it is
j   unnecessary for the act to show a connection with a contract concerning land. But the

---

1   (1883) 8 App Cas 467
2   [1962] 3 All ER 593, [1963] 2 QB 169
3   [1962] 3 All ER at 604, [1963] 2 QB at 189
4   6th Edn (1921), p 278, para 582
5   [1917] 2 Ch 356 at 361, [1916-17] All ER Rep 1089 at 1092

passage must be read in its context. If it means what the husband suggests, it is in
flat contradiction of what appears on the two pages immediately preceding it. The
learned author says[1]:   *a*

> 'In order thus to withdraw a contract from the operation of the Statute several
> circumstances must occur: first, the acts of part performance must be such as
> not only to be referable to a contract such as that alleged but to be referable to
> no other title . . .'   *b*

Later he says[2]:

> 'First, "the acts relied upon as part performance must be unequivocally and
> in their own nature referable to some such agreement as alleged", but if the
> acts go so far as this they are admissible, for it seems evident that all that can be
> gathered from the acts of part performance is the existence of some contract in   *c*
> pursuance of which they are done and the general character of the contract.'

Moreover, the words immediately following the passage relied on by the husband
make it plain that the same principle applied to contracts within s 17 of the Statute of
Frauds; e g providing the acts of part performance showed that they were done in
performance of a contract for the sale of goods, for instance by acceptance of delivery,   *d*
parol evidence might be given of the contractual terms; it is unnecessary and usually
impossible for the precise terms of the contract to be ascertained from acts of part
performance.

It has never been held nor, so far as I can discover, ever before the present case
suggested, that acts alleged to be in part performance of a parol contract take the
contract out of the statute unless they make plain the general nature of the contract.   *e*
I can find no reason for departing from that principle.

This, however, by no means concludes the appeal. Although I accept the authorities which show that acts of part performance if they are to take a parol contract out
of the statute must be acts from which the nature of the contract can be deduced, I
do not accept the line of authority which, overruling Lord Hardwicke in *Lacon v Mer-*
tins[3] and *Owen v Davies*[4], laid down that payment can never constitute such an act   *f*
because it is impossible to deduce from payment the nature of the contract in respect
of which the payment is made. It is no doubt true that often it is impossible to deduce
even the existence of any contract from payment. For example, a payment by a
parent to his child or a husband to his wife is in general no evidence of a contract;
indeed, the presumption is to the contrary. Nevertheless the circumstances surrounding a payment may be such that the payment becomes evidence not only of the
existence of the contract under which it was made but also of the nature of that con-   *g*
tract. What the payment proves in the light of its surroundings circumstances is not a
matter of law but a matter of fact. There is no rule of law which excludes evidence of
the relevant circumstances surrounding the payment—save parol evidence of the
contract on behalf of the person seeking to enforce the contract under which the payment is alleged to have been made.

My Lords, let us assume evidence of the following facts: A is anxious to sell an   *h*
attractive house at a reasonable price of, say, £20,000. Full particulars of the house
are sent to B by A's estate agents. The estate agents tell B, truthfully, that there are
several people anxious to buy the house for the price asked but that owing to present
economic conditions they have not yet been able to complete the necessary financial
arrangements. They are expecting to do so at any moment. The estate agent, at B's
request, makes an immediate appointment for B to inspect the house and meet A.   *j*
B keeps the appointment. No written contract of sale comes into existence. B's cheque

1   6th Edn (1921), p 276, para 580
2   6th Edn (1921), p 277, para 581
3   (1743) 3 Atk 1
4   (1748) 1 Ves Sen 82

a in favour of A for £20,000 is specially cleared by A the day after the appointment. A then refuses to convey the house to B and there is good reason to suppose that he is unable to repay the £20,000. Can anyone doubt that this evidence, unexplained, establishes a strong prima facie case that A orally agreed with B to sell him the house for £20,000 and that B performed his part of the contract by paying A the purchase price? If B sues A for specific performance of the parol agreement and applies

b for an interlocutory injunction to restrain A from parting with the house pending the trial of the action, it is surely inconceivable that our law can be so defective that it would allow A to shelter behind the statute. Yet A could succeed in doing so if the authorities which hold that payment can never constitute part performance for the purpose of taking a contract out of the statute were correctly decided. In my opinion, they were not.

c   Suppose another set of facts. B sues A for specific performance of a parol contract for the sale of A's house to him for £X,000 and alleges that he has paid A the £X,000. B gives evidence of the payment. A pleads the statute. A would have no case to answer because there would be no evidence of any circumstances surrounding the payment to connect it with the parol agreement. Suppose, however, that B, who is unrepresented, says to the judge at the trial: 'Of course I agreed with A to sell him my house for

d £X,000 and he has certainly paid me that sum which unfortunately I cannot repay.' A's admission would, in my view, be sufficient to connect the payment with the parol contract, establish part performance and deprive A of his defence under the statute. Once a party to a parol contract relating to land admits to any court the existence of the contract and that he has received a benefit under it which he is unable or unwilling to restore, the mischief aimed at by the statute disappears. It would be most unreason-

e able and unjust that, in such circumstances, he should be able to rely on the statute in order to break his word and evade performing his part under the contract. There is certainly no authority binding on this House which would enable him to do so.

In the present case, the payment of £100 by the husband to his wife who had divorced him—looked at without regard to its surrounding circumstances—would not be any evidence of any contract, let alone of a contract concerning land. If the

f proposition that payment in part or even in full can never be part performance is correct, which, in my view, it is not, then the circumstances surrounding the payment must be irrelevant. I think, however, that the Court of Appeal[1] were bound to accept this proposition by the authorities referred to with approval by the Earl of Selborne LC in *Maddison v Alderson*[2]. On this basis, the reasons given by Edmund Davies LJ for reluctantly dismissing the appeal appear to me to be impeccable. The proposition

g has, however, never yet been debated before this House. In *Maddison v Alderson*[3] it was assumed, without argument, to be correct: in any event it was wholly un-necessary for the decision of that appeal. This House is, therefore, not bound to accept the proposition and, for my part, I am unable to do so. I believe that the analysis of the proposition which I have attempted demonstrates that the proposition is funda-mentally unsound and would lead to grave injustice.

h   If, in the present case, the payment of the £100 is looked at in the light of its sur-roundings circumstances, it is, in my opinion, quite plain that that sum was paid in part performance of a parol contract concerning land. The correspondence prior to 2nd March 1972 shows that the only outstanding differences between the husband and the wife were then (a) the amount which he was to pay to her for transferring to him the interest which she claimed in the former matrimonial home and (b) what was

j to be done about the amount of arrears of maintenance to the wife which were then outstanding.

The husband had applied for the whole of these arrears to be remitted, and for an order for the wife's maintenance to be discharged. She had agreed to the discharge

---

1 [1973] 3 All ER 977, [1974] QB 161
2 (1883) 8 App Cas at 479
3 8 App Cas 467

of that order. It is plain that the parties had very nearly reached agreement under
which the wife should accept a total of £1,250 in full discharge of both her claims.   *a*
Her solicitors then wrote on 17th February 1972, 'Our client feels that she cannot
compromise her claims for less than £1,500'. The husband's solicitors wrote on 21st
February 1972, stating that he would pay the £1,500 providing it was accepted in full
discharge of both claims and asking the wife's solicitors to confirm that this was
finally agreed. Having had no answer to that letter, the solicitor wrote on 29th Feb-   *b*
ruary, 'Perhaps we could meet you at the court to finalise the final terms of settlement
and then explain them to the magistrates'. The next day the wife's solicitors wrote to
say that they did not propose to attend the court and that they found difficulty in
advising their client that the £1,500 should cover the arrears of maintenance as well
as the purchase of the wife's interests in the house.

On 2nd March the husband's solicitor met the wife outside the magistrates' court.
There is no suggestion that he put any pressure on her or behaved otherwise than with   *c*
complete propriety. He and the wife came into court and he told the justices
that they had come to an agreement settling all differences between the wife and the
husband as follows: (1) She was to transfer her interests in the house to the husband for
£1,500. 2. The husband was to pay her £100 not later than 30th March 1972 in full
discharge of the arrears of maintenance, the balance of such arrears to be remitted.   *d*
3. The order for her maintenance was to be discharged but he was to continue paying
maintenance (as previously ordered) in respect of the child of the marriage.

The clerk then asked the wife if she had indeed come to this agreement. She replied
that she had. The justices made an order implementing the agreement so far as they
were able to do so. They also adjourned the proceedings until 30th March with an
intimation that if the husband did not then pay the £100, further proceedings might
be taken against him. He did pay the wife that sum on 30th March.   *e*

It is plain from the registrar's finding that the wife admitted in open court the
parol agreement which she had made. It was a composite indivisible agreement, the
integral parts of which were that she was to receive £100 within one month and that
she was to transfer her interest in the house for £1,500.

The wife's admission in open court plainly connected the payment of the £100 with   *f*
the parol agreement relating to the disposition of an interest in land and showed that
the payment was in part performance of that agreement. She has not repaid or ever
offered to repay any part of the £100. This payment, in my opinion, bars the wife from
relying on the statute and she is accordingly bound to perform her part of the agreement.

I had some doubt whether incurring the costs incidental to the preparation of the
deed of transfer and the transmission of that deed to the wife's solicitors also consti-   *g*
tuted part performance. A deed could well be prepared and transmitted in contemplation of a concluded agreement so as to save time. This clearly could not constitute
part performance. The unchallenged evidence, however, shows that the deed in fact
was not prepared until after 2nd March 1972, the date on which the wife admitted
before the magistrates that the parol agreement was made. According to established
practice, such an agreement calls for the transferee to incur the expense of preparing   *h*
the deed and forwarding it to the transferor for approval. I am, therefore, inclined to
think that in the circumstances of this case the preparation and transmission of the
deed of transfer also amounted to part performance of the parol agreement.

My Lords, for these reasons I would dismiss the appeal.

Appeal dismissed.   *j*

Solicitors: *Dowding & Dowding*, Orpington (for the wife); *Thomas Boyd Whyte*, Bexley-
heath (for the husband).

                                                            Christine Ivamy   Barrister.

a

R v Shannon

Applied in R v WHITEHOUSE [1977]
3 All ER 737

COURT OF APPEAL

ROSKILL, JAMES LJJ AND TALBOT J

25th OCTOBER, 8th NOVEMBER, 21st DECEMBER 1973

b   HOUSE OF LORDS

LORD REID, LORD MORRIS OF BORTH-Y-GEST, VISCOUNT DILHORNE, LORD SIMON OF GLAISDALE

AND LORD SALMON

28th FEBRUARY, 1st, 4th, 12th, 13th, 14th MARCH, 19th JUNE 1974

Criminal law – Conspiracy – Separate trials – Different verdicts – Effect – Two accused
c   charged with conspiring with each other and with no one else – First accused pleading guilty
– Second accused pleading not guilty – Second accused subsequently tried and acquitted –
Whether conviction of first accused invalidated by subsequent acquittal of second accused.

Criminal law – Appeal – Court of Appeal – Appeal against conviction – Jurisdiction – Ground
of appeal – Plea of guilty – No decision on question of law – Accused indicted with one other
d   person for conspiracy – Accused pleading guilty – Co-accused pleading not guilty – Co-accused
subsequently tried and acquitted – Accused appealing on ground that his conviction invalidated
by subsequent acquittal of co-accused – Jurisdiction of Court of Appeal to allow appeal –
Criminal Appeal Act 1968, s 2(1).

On 22nd March 1973 the respondent and T were charged on indictment, inter alia,
e   with having conspired together dishonestly to handle stolen goods. The respondent,
who was advised by solicitor and counsel, pleaded guilty to the charge. There was
no evidence that he did not appreciate and understand what he was doing when he
did so. He was sentenced to four years imprisonment. T pleaded not guilty (i) to
the conspiracy charge and (ii) to a count charging him with handling stolen goods.
The jury were unable to agree on their verdict and T was retried a few days later.
f   T was found not guilty of handling stolen goods. The prosecution offered no evidence
against him on the conspiracy charge and a formal verdict of not guilty was entered
on that count. The respondent thereupon appealed, contending that as T had been
found not guilty of conspiring with him, his own conviction and sentence following
on his plea of guilty to conspiring with T could not stand. The Court of Appeal,
in purported exercise of its power under s 2(1)[a] of the Criminal Appeal Act 1968,
allowed the appeal and quashed the respondent's conviction. The Crown appealed.
g

Held – The appeal would be allowed and the respondent's conviction restored for
the following reasons—
    (i) Where one of two alleged conspirators had been fairly and properly tried and,
on the evidence adduced, rightly convicted, there was no reason why his conviction
h   should be invalidated if for any reason the other alleged conspirator was acquitted
at a subsequent trial. Accordingly, just as the respondent's conviction on his plea
of guilty was not relevant to (and therefore not admissible evidence to prove) T's
guilt, so T's acquittal was not relevant to the respondent's conviction (see p 1025 *j*,
p 1034 *c* to *g*, p 1039 *b* to *d*, p 1040 *e*, p 1042 *b* and *c*, p 1043 *b* to *d*, p 1045 *d*, p 1047 *d* and
p 1048 *h* to p 1049 *f*, post); dictum of Eveleigh J in *R v Andrews Weatherfoil Ltd* [1972]
j   1 All ER at 71, 72 approved; *Dharmasena v The King* [1951] AC 1 disapproved; *R v*
Plummer [1900-3] All ER Rep 613 overruled.
    (ii) In any event the Court of Appeal had no jurisdiction under s 2(1) of the 1968
Act to quash the conviction since (a) there had been no verdict of a jury to set aside,
(b) no decision on any question of law, and therefore no wrong decision, and (c) no

---

a   Section 2(1) is set out at p 1027 *g* and *h*, post

material irregularity in the course of the trial (see p 1025 *j*, p 1028 *a b d* and *g*, p 1029 *a* *c* and *d*, p 1037 *b* and *c*, p 1041 *f* and *g* and p 1050 *j* to p 1051 *a*, post).

Observations on the directions to be given by a judge to a jury where A and B are tried together on a charge of conspiring with each other and with no one else (see p 1034 *h* and *j*, p 1035 *b* to *e*, p 1040 *f* to p 1041 *b*, p 1046 *b* to *h* and p 1049 *j* to p 1050 *c*, post).

Notes

For conspiracy, see 10 Halsbury's Laws (3rd Edn) 310-315, paras 569-573, and for cases on the subject, see 14 Digest (Repl) 121-136, 851-1005.

For grounds for allowing appeal against conviction, see 10 Halsbury's Laws (3rd Edn) 535, 536, para 985, and for cases on the subject, see 14 Digest (Repl) 629-657, 6364-6685.

For the Criminal Appeal Act 1968, s 2, see 8 Halsbury's Statutes (3rd Edn) 690.

Cases referred to in judgments

Admiralty Comrs v Owners of Steamship Amerika [1917] AC 38, [1916-17] All ER Rep 177, 86 LJP 58, 116 LT 34, 13 Asp MLC 558, HL, 1 Digest (Repl) 40, 290.

Anon (circa 1435) YB 14 Hen 6, 25b; cited 5 B & C at 541, 108 ER at 202.

Dharmasena (Kannangara Aratchige) v The King [1951] AC 1, 66 (pt 2) TLR 365, PC, 14 Digest (Repl) 679, 6949.

Director of Public Prosecutions v Doot [1973] 1 All ER 940, [1973] AC 807, [1973] 2 WLR 532, 57 Cr App Rep 600, HL.

Director of Public Prosecutions v Schildkamp [1969] 3 All ER 1640, [1971] AC 1, [1970] 2 WLR 279, 54 Cr App Rep 90, HL.

Federal Steam Navigation Co Ltd v Department of Trade and Industry [1974] 2 All ER 97, [1974] 1 WLR 505, HL.

Harison v Errington (1627) Poph 202, 79 ER 1292, 14 Digest (Repl) 126, 878.

Haughton v Smith [1973] 3 All ER 1109, [1974] 2 WLR 1, HL.

Kamara v Director of Public Prosecutions [1973] 2 All ER 1242, [1974] AC 104, [1973] 3 WLR 198, HL.

Marsh v Vauhan (1599) Cro Eliz 701, 78 ER 937, 14 Digest (Repl) 131, 943.

Mulcahy v R (1868) LR 3 HL 306, HL, 14 Digest (Repl) 360, 3506.

O'Connell v R (1844) 11 Cl & Fin 155, 3 LTOS 429, 9 Jur 25, 1 Cox CC 413, 8 ER 1061, HL, 14 Digest (Repl) 131, 941.

Platt v State (1943) 8 NW (2d) 849.

R v Ahearne (1852) 6 Cox CC 6, 14 Digest (Repl) 132, *540.

R v Andrews Weatherfoil Ltd [1972] 1 All ER 65, [1972] 1 WLR 118, 56 Cr App Rep 31, CA.

R v Cooke (1826) 5 B & C 538, 7 Dow & Ry KB 673, 3 Dow & Ry MC 510, 108 ER 201, CCR, 14 Digest (Repl) 132, 958.

R v Doyle [1963] Crim LR 37, CCA.

R v Forde [1923] 2 KB 400, [1923] All ER Rep 477, 92 LJKB 501, 128 LT 798, 87 JP 76, 27 Cox CC 406, 17 Cr App Rep 99, CCA, 14 Digest (Repl) 606, 5998.

R v Griffiths [1965] 2 All ER 448, [1966] 1 QB 589, [1965] 3 WLR 405, 129 JP 380, 49 Cr App Rep 279, CCA, Digest (Cont Vol B) 157, 942a.

R v Grimes and Thompson (1688) 3 Mod Rep 220, 87 ER 142, 14 Digest (Repl) 131, 946.

R v Heaps (1699) 2 Salk 593, 1 Ld Raym 484, 12 Mod Rep 262, 91 ER 502, 14 Digest (Repl) 360, 3506.

R v Kenrick (1843) 5 QBD 49, 1 Dav & Mer 208, 12 LJMC 135, 1 LTOS 336, 7 JP 463, 7 Jur 848, 114 ER 1166, CCR, 14 Digest (Repl) 130, 934.

R v Kinnersley and Moore (1719) 1 Stra 193, 93 ER 467, 14 Digest (Repl) 112, 777.

R v Mandeville (1968) unreported, CA.

R v Manning (1883) 12 QBD 241, [1881-85] All ER Rep 852, 53 LJMC 85, 51 LT 121, 48 JP 536, DC, 14 Digest (Repl) 131, 947.

a
R v Nichols (1742) 13 East 412, 2 Stra 1227, 104 ER 429, 16 Digest (Repl) 486, *3043*.
R v Plummer [1902] 2 KB 339, [1900-3] All ER Rep 613, 71 LJKB 805, 86 LT 836, 66 JP 647, 20 Cox CC 269, CCR, 14 Digest (Repl) 131, *951*.
R v Rowley [1948] 1 All ER 570, 112 JP 207, 32 Cr App Rep 147, 46 LGR 244, CCA, 14 Digest (Repl) 112, *775*.
R v Scott and Hams (1761) 3 Burr 1262, 1 Wm Bl 291, 350, 97 ER 822, 15 Digest (Repl) 794, *7481*.

b
R v Starling (1663) 1 Sid 174, 1 Lev 125, 82 ER 1039, 14 Digest (Repl) 125, *871*.
R v Thompson (1851) 16 QB 832, 20 LJMC 183, 17 LTOS 72, 15 JP 484, 15 Jur 654, 5 Cox CC 166, 117 ER 1100, CCR, 14 Digest (Repl) 128, *894*.
R v Verney (1909) 2 Cr App Rep 107, 73 JP 288, CCA, 14 Digest (Repl) 605, *5995*.
Robinson v Robinson and Lane (1859) 1 Sw & Tr 362, 29 LJPM & A 178, 31 LTOS 268, 5 Jur NS 392, 164 ER 767, 22 Digest (Reissue) 94, *635*.

c
Rutherford v Richardson [1923] AC 1, [1922] All ER Rep 13, 92 LJP 1, 128 LT 399, HL, 27(2) Digest (Reissue) 787, *6330*.
Thody's Case (1674) 1 Vent 234, 86 ER 157, 1 Freem KB 514, 89 ER 386, 14 Digest (Repl) 93, *557*.

Appeal

d
On 22nd March 1973 at the Crown Court at Warwick before Mr Recorder De Piro the accused, David Charles Shannon, was convicted, inter alia, of conspiring with one Tracey to handle dishonestly stolen goods, and was sentenced to four years imprisonment. He appealed against his conviction with leave of the single judge. The facts are set out in the judgment of the court.

e
C A Coode for the accused.
H C Tayler for the Crown.

Cur adv vult

21st December. **ROSKILL LJ** read the following judgment of the court. The accused, Shannon, was one of a number of defendants charged on an indictment containing 22 counts at Warwick Crown Court before Mr Recorder de Piro QC on
f
22nd March 1973. Of those 22, five concerned the accused, counts 8, 11, 16, 20 and 22. Counts 8, 11 and 16 charged him with the dishonest handling of stolen goods contrary to s 22(1) of the Theft Act 1968. Counts 20 and 22 charged him with conspiring dishonestly to handle stolen goods. Count 20 charged him, one Paul Joseph Wood, and three co-accused of conspiring together. But count 22, which is the all-important count for the purposes of this appeal, charged only the accused and Ronald Gordon
g
Tracey, a co-accused, with so conspiring together, and referred to no other alleged conspirator known or unknown. The accused pleaded guilty to counts 11, 16 and 22. He pleaded not guilty to counts 8 and 20 and those pleas were accepted by the Crown with the leave of the recorder. He was sentenced to three years imprisonment on counts 11 and 16 and four years on count 22, all sentences to run concurrently.

h
Tracey in addition to being charged with conspiracy under count 22 was charged with dishonest handling on count 17. His trial was adjourned to a later date. On what is recorded as having been 27th March 1973 leave was given to amend count 17 by dividing it into two counts thereafter known as counts 17(a) and 17(b). To all three counts, as they thus became, he pleaded not guilty. He was tried at Warwick Crown Court on 26th and 27th March 1973 before a different judge. The counts were severed and the trial proceeded on counts 17(a) and 17(b) only. The jury disagreed.
i
A retrial was ordered to take place at Coventry Crown Court and the severed conspiracy count was also sent to that court for trial. The dishonest handling counts (now renumbered counts 1 and 2 for the convenience of the jury at Coventry Crown Court) were retried at Coventry on 3rd and 4th April before yet another recorder. Acquittal on those two charges followed. Thereupon Mr Tayler, who has at all times appeared for the Crown in these cases, offered no evidence on the conspiracy

count and invited the recorder concerned to enter a verdict of not guilty. This was   *a*
duly done.

We thought it right, in view of the importance of this case, to send for the original
indictment and the formal record of all the pleas, verdicts and sentences. In Tracey's
case the formal record regarding count 22 was entered up as follows:

Count	Offence	Plea	Verdict	Sentence or order	
22	Conspiracy	Not guilty	Formal verdict, not guilty	No evidence offered. Formal verdict of not guilty entered.	*b*

In the case of the accused the formal record regarding count 22 was entered up as
follows:

Count	Offence	Plea	Verdict	Sentence or order	
22	Conspiracy	Guilty	—	4 years imprisonment concurrent.	*c*

Following Tracey's acquittal, the accused sought leave to appeal against his conviction for conspiracy notwithstanding his plea of guilty to count 22 made when
represented by experienced counsel and with full appreciation of what he was doing.   *d*
Waller J, as single judge, granted leave to appeal stating for the information of counsel
and the full court:

> 'I have reluctantly granted leave to appeal against the conviction for conspiracy,
> because there are authorities, which may give it some support. In my opinion,
> these authorities are distinguishable. I suggest that if a man pleads guilty,
> knowing what he is doing, that is the end of the matter, and the fact that a jury at   *e*
> a later date is not satisfied that the guilt of his co-accused has been established,
> does not affect the matter.'

Technically the accused did not require leave to appeal his ground being a point of
law.

The submission for the accused was this. The crime of conspiracy cannot be com-   *f*
mitted by one person. Two persons at least must be proved to be guilty before
anyone can be convicted of conspiracy. In this case two persons have not been proved
to be guilty. One admitted he was guilty. One has been found to be not guilty. The
verdict of acquittal of Tracey shows that there was no proof that both were guilty—
indeed it proves that both cannot have been guilty. The 'record' on a count which
charged only the two men (and no others, known or unknown) with conspiracy   *g*
contains mutually inconsistent entries, namely that one man, the accused, is guilty
but that the other, Tracey, is not guilty. The record is the same record even though
the plea of guilty and verdict of not guilty were arrived at on separate occasions and
the accused and Tracey were not tried together. Those entries are repugnant and
cannot be allowed to stand. Since Tracey's acquittal must stand on the record, that
repugnancy can only now be avoided by quashing the accused's conviction notwith-   *h*
standing his plea of guilty.

The starting point of the submission is that the common law offence of conspiracy
cannot be committed by a single person. That this is and has always been the law
is beyond question. Sir William Holdsworth[1] summarises the history of what he calls
the 'two divergent streams of doctrine' which have gone to the making of the law
of conspiracy and adds[2]:   *j*

> 'The modern crime of conspiracy is almost entirely the result of the manner
> in which conspiracy was treated by the court of Star Chamber. Almost the only

1   History of English Law, vol 8, p 378
2   Ibid, pp 379, 380

a   idea which it has borrowed from the common law is the rule, taken from the
     statutory writ of conspiracy, that the crime (like the crime of riot) cannot be
     committed by one person, though the other persons need not be specified, and
     may indeed be unknown.'

     He cites as authority for that proposition *R v Starling*[1] which reports the judges of
     the King's Bench as stating in 1664 'ne poit estre conspiracy sans ascun overt act de
b   plusors'. The oft quoted passage in the advice of the judges to the House of Lords in
     Mulcahy v The Queen[2] delivered by Willes J treated as axiomatic the view that a single
     person could not conspire. That view had been accepted by the time of the publica-
     tion of the first edition of Hawkins's Pleas of the Crown in 1716 as is clear from the
     passage[3] referred to by Lord Hailsham of St Marylebone LC in his speech in the
     recent case of *Kamara v Director of Public Prosecutions*[4].
c   It was, we think, the fundamental principle that a single person could not be guilty
     of conspiracy which led to the acceptance at least towards the end of the 19th century
     of the conclusion, that if A and B alone were indicted together and 'tried together'
     for conspiracy a jury must be directed either that 'both must be convicted or both
     must be acquitted'. These last two quotations are from the judgment of Lord
     Coleridge CJ in *R v Manning*[5]. We shall return to consider this decision. It may,
d   however, be pointed out at this juncture that the conclusion of the court was reached
     'with great reluctance' and that Lord Coleridge CJ himself had otherwise directed
     the jury at the trial, namely that they might find Manning guilty (as they did) but
     acquit his co-accused; in fact they were unable to agree as to the co-accused's guilt.
     On further consideration in the Queen's Bench Division, Lord Coleridge CJ said[5]
     that he was satisfied he had misdirected the jury and that the law as the court held it
e   to be, seemed to him 'to have been determined, or, if not determined, taken for
     granted from very early times'. It is also to be observed Lord Coleridge CJ expressly
     limited his judgment to a case 'when two people are indicted and are tried together'.
     He added in parenthesis: 'because different considerations arise where people are
     not tried together'. Lord Coleridge CJ's reference to what had been determined or
     taken for granted from 'very early times' makes it necessary to trace the complex
f   history of this question and consider whether if that be so, why it was so.
         The first reported case to which counsel drew our attention (other than one[6]
     referred to in a footnote to *R v Cooke*[7] and in *R v Manning*[5]) is *Marsh v Vauhan*[8].
     The two defendants pleaded not guilty to conspiracy. They were tried together.
     One was found guilty: the other not guilty. It was argued that the bill must abate
     for 'one cannot conspire alone'. The court accepted that view and the defendant
g   secured judgment. Some 30 years later in *Harison v Errington*[9] three men were
     indicted and tried for riot. Only one was found guilty. The verdict was held to
     be void because one man cannot make a riot. The argument was that as in conspiracy,
     if one only one of two is found guilty the verdict is void 'for one alone cannot conspire'.
     About half a century later, in *Thody's Case*[10], Thody and two others were indicted
     for conspiracy. Thody pleaded not guilty and was convicted. The others did not
h   appear. On a motion to arrest judgment for that reason, Lord Hale said[11]:

---

1   (1663) 1 Sid 174
2   (1868) LR 3 HL 306 at 317
3   Book 1, c 72, s 2
4   [1973] 2 All ER 1242 at 1253, [1974] AC 104 at 121
j   5   (1883) 12 QBD 241 at 245, [1881-85] All ER Rep 852 at 855
6   *Anon* (circa 1435) YB 14 Hen 6, 25b
7   (1826) 5 B & C 538 at 541
8   (1599) Cro Eliz 701
9   (1627) Poph 202
10 (1674) 1 Vent 234
11 1 Vent at 234

'If one be acquitted in an action of conspiracy, the other cannot be guilty: *a*
but where one is found guilty and the other comes not in upon process, or if
he dies hanging the suit, yet judgment shall be upon the verdict against the
other.'

In *Thody's Case*[1] a distinction is drawn between the case of conspirators charged and
tried together and the case of one conspirator tried alone, the others not answering
to the charge. In *R v Grimes and Thompson*[2] the indictment was that Grimes had *b*
unlawfully obtained certain goods and that he 'per conferationem' with Thompson
detained the goods. Thompson was acquitted and Grimes convicted. It was held
that the verdict could not stand for the reason that 'the acquittal of one is the acquittal
of both upon this indictment'. *R v Heaps*[3] is another riot case wherein the conviction of two and the acquittal of the rest, all being charged and tried together, was
held to be bad since two cannot make a riot. Apart from *Thody*[1] these are all, if we *c*
correctly read the reports—often extremely brief and sometimes obscure—cases
where the persons concerned were indicted and tried together. They seem to
support Lord Coleridge CJ's statement in *R v Manning*[4] that in such cases of joint
indictment and joint trial both must be convicted or both must be acquitted.

We next turn to the cases where the alleged conspirators though indicted together
were not tried together. The first after *Thody's Case*[1] is *R v Kinnersley and Moore*[5]. *d*
Both men were charged with conspiracy. Only Kinnersley 'appeared'. He was
tried and convicted. He moved in arrest of judgment. It is the third exception
taken in arrest of judgment which is presently relevant[6]:

'To every conspiracy there must be two persons at least, whereas here is only
one brought in and found guilty. If hereafter the other should be found not *e*
guilty, that will consequently be an acquittal of Kinnersley. If three be indicted
for a riot and an assault, and one only found guilty, and the others acquitted;
this discharges them all, because the riot is the foundation, and the assault only
the consequence. Salk 593[7]. And one person alone cannot be guilty of committing a riot: so in this case one cannot be guilty of conspiracy, though he
may of the overt act, and yet the foundation (which is the conspiracy) being *f*
removed, the other part, which is only the consequence, falls of course.'

In answer to this exception counsel for the Crown argued[8]:

'Say they, no judgment shall be given against Kinnersley, because possibly
Moore may be acquitted, and that will be an acquittal of both. This is arguing
from what has not happened, and probably never will; for though Moore may *g*
have an opportunity to acquit himself, and is not concluded by the verdict as
Kinnersley is; yet as the matter now stands Moore himself is found guilty, for
the conspiracy is found as it is laid, and therefore judgment may be given against
one before the trial of the other.'

The exception was overruled. The court proceeded to sentence Kinnersley. *h*
The report shows that Moore was later tried, convicted and sentenced so that ultimately both alleged conspirators were tried albeit on separate occasions and convicted. The argument for the Crown is interesting for it postulates that the conviction of Kinnersley ranks as a finding of guilt against Moore 'for the conspiracy is found

1   (1674) 1 Vent 234
2   (1688) 3 Mod Rep 220
3   (1699) 2 Salk 593
4   (1883) 12 QBD 241 at 245, [1881-85] All ER Rep 852 at 855
5   (1719) 1 Stra 193
6   1 Stra at 193
7   *R v Heaps* (1699) 2 Salk 593
8   1 Stra at 195

a as laid'. In other words the record is, on the face of it, in order. *R v Kinnersley*[1] was followed in *R v Nichols*[2]. There the co-accused had died before Nichols was arraigned. Nichols was convicted. The court upheld the conviction on the authority of *R v Kinnersley*[1] which would appear to have been regarded as a stronger case than *Nichols*[2] since in the former case the conviction had been upheld notwithstanding that the possibility existed of inconsistent verdicts at a future date whereas in the *b* latter case there was no such possibility, the co-accused being already dead.

It is, however, to be noted that in both these cases it appears to have been accepted without argument to the contrary that had the other alleged conspirator been tried separately and acquitted after the first had been convicted, the conviction of the first would not be allowed to stand.

We move into the 19th century. In *R v Cooke*[3] four men were indicted together for conspiracy. J S S Cooke and Jenkinson pleaded not guilty. A third, Miles, *c* disappeared. The fourth, R S Cooke, pleaded in abatement to which plea there was both a demurrer and a joinder. While the demurrer was pending, J S S Cooke and Jenkinson were tried. J S S Cooke was convicted and Jenkinson acquitted. The verdict was recorded[4] as follows: 'J. S. S. Cooke guilty of conspiring with his brother, Richard Stafford Cooke; Jenkinson not guilty'.

d J S S Cooke obtained a rule nisi to stay judgment on his conviction[4]—

> 'on the ground that the verdict of the jury negatived all the conspiracy charged, except with R. S. Cooke, who was still to be presumed innocent, who had pleaded not guilty, and whose acquittal, if he should be tried hereafter, would be a virtual acquittal of J. S. S. Cooke, and render any judgment passed on him erroneous.'

e The arguments of counsel show that some of the cases already referred to were cited at length. Counsel's argument for Cooke shows that the foundation of the submission rested on the possibility of repugnancy on the record and the court would not presume that repugnancy would arise. The importance attached to the record can be seen from the way in which Abbott CJ[5] dealt with the history of the *f* proceedings:

> 'There is an indictment against the defendant now before the Court, and R. S. Cooke for a conspiracy; it is said that the latter has pleaded not guilty, and that this case is by that circumstance distinguished from all those which have been cited. But he first pleaded in abatement, to which plea there was a demurrer, and he did not plead not guilty until Trinity term 1824. In the mean time, *g* at the Spring Assizes in that year, the record was taken down to trial, and J. S. S. Cooke was convicted. At that time there was no plea of not guilty by R. S. Cooke upon the record, nor had judgment of respondeat ouster been given upon the demurrer. Then the jury found that J. S. S. Cooke was guilty of conspiring with R. S. Cooke. It is said, that peradventure R. S. Cooke may be acquitted, and that then there will be a repugnancy upon the record if judgment is pro-*h* nounced against the other defendant. That is certainly possible, but are we to presume that it will be so against the verdict that has been found? I think that the Court would not be warranted in coming to such a conclusion, or in forbearing to pronounce judgment upon the defendant who has been found guilty.'

j Bayley J drew an analogy between an accessory tried by his consent before the

1   (1719) 1 Stra 193
2   (1742) 13 East 412
3   (1826) 5 B & C 538
4   5 B & C at 539
5   5 B & C at 543, 544

principal and convicted. If the principal were later acquitted the conviction of the
accessory falls to the ground, but that did not prevent judgment against the accessory   *a*
meanwhile. Here again it appears implicit both from the arguments and the reasoning of the judgments (except that of Littledale J) that, were R S Cooke later to be
acquitted, the verdict against J S S Cooke could not stand, the reason being repugnancy upon the record in that one of two alleged conspirators would there be recorded as guilty and the other as not guilty. Littledale J[1] introduced a note of
doubt in the words 'If the other defendant R. S. Cooke shall hereafter be acquitted,   *b*
perhaps this judgment [shall not stand].'

We were referred briefly to *R v Kenrick*[2]. There a father and son were jointly
indicted with others (unnamed) for conspiracy. The son died before trial. The
father was convicted. A rule was obtained arresting the judgment on grounds
including one that it was misdirection to try the father after the death of the co-
accused. The point we have already discussed was canvassed in argument[3] but the   *c*
court in discharging the rule to quash the conviction did not pronounce on that
aspect.

We turn next to *O'Connell v R*[4]. This famous case is massively reported almost
verbatim in several contemporary law reports. Since it is relied on in later 19th
century cases and in particular in *R v Manning*[5] we have examined it with especial
care, for it is the only decision of the House of Lords to which we were referred and   *d*
is of course binding on this court in respect of what was there decided.

The first count[6] was lengthy. It charged the appellants with conspiracy to do
five different acts. There were ten other related conspiracy counts. By the finding
of the jury eight of the accused were found guilty of one conspiracy alleged in counts
1 and 2, seven of the accused were found guilty of a different conspiracy in the same
counts and three were found guilty of yet a third conspiracy in the same counts.   *e*
It was argued[7] that though there was only one conspiracy charge, yet the jury had
convicted of several different conspiracies. A similar situation existed in relation
to the third count. We turn to the judgment of Tindal CJ. Answering the second
question put to the judges, Tindal CJ said[8] that all the judges were of opinion
that the verdicts on the first four counts were not supportable in law because
each count charged one conspiracy and no more than one, yet a number of the   *f*
defendants had been found guilty of separate and distinct conpiracies under the
same counts. There is some uncertainty arising from the report in relation to
the fourth count on which all except one were convicted of one conspiracy and the one
exception was acquitted. In short the point was that there was a finding of several
conspiracies on a count charging one. This view was accepted and the convictions
quashed. A modern illustration of the same principle can be found in *R v Griffiths*[9].   *g*
But we do not find anything in the lengthy opinions and speeches which touch on
the point presently under consideration. As will appear later in this judgment we
have difficulty in extracting from that case the support derived from it on the issue
in *Manning*[5].

This question did, however, arise for consideration a few years later in *R v Thomp-*
son[10]. There were three named conspirators, Thompson, Tillotson and Maddock,   *h*

---

1   (1826) 5 B & C at 545, 546
2   (1843) 5 QBD 49
3   5 QBD at 54, 58
4   (1844) 1 Cox CC 413
5   (1883) 12 QBD 241, [1881-85] All ER Rep 852
6   See 1 Cox CC at 416
7   1 Cox CC at 426, 427
8   1 Cox at 473, 474
9   [1965] 2 All ER 448, [1966] 1 QB 589
10 (1851) 16 QB 832

j

a who were charged with conspiracy together and with others unknown. The jury convicted Thompson, saying that he was guilty of conspiracy with either Tillotson or Maddock but they did not know which. The judge directed a verdict of not guilty in the case of the last two but of guilty in the case of Thompson, but gave leave to move to enter a verdict of not guilty in his case also. The rule was made absolute (Erle J dissenting) on the broad ground that on an indictment for conspiracy the acquittal of the two must involve the acquittal of the third. When one looks at the b report of the Attorney-General's argument[1] against the rule it seems clear that, since the verdict excluded (in the view of the majority of the court) the possibility of Thompson having conspired with persons unknown, the reason for the decision was repugnancy on the face of the record.

The following year the Irish Court of Criminal Appeal considered the question in *R v Ahearne*[2]. Ahearne was indicted for conspiracy with two named co-accused c and others unknown to murder one Power. He was tried alone, convicted and sentenced to death. He appealed on the ground that if he were executed and later the others were acquitted, he would have been executed for conspiracy with himself, 'which was absurd'. But the court refused to respite or arrest judgment. Lefroy CJ, after hearing argument founded on a number of the cases to which we have referred, refused to regard the possibility of the subsequent acquittal of the other two as d justifying the postponement of Ahearne's execution. It is, however, to be observed that once again it seems to have been taken for granted without argument that the latter acquittal of the other two, had it occurred timeously, would have involved the posthumous quashing of Ahearne's conviction.

We turn next to the only case in this series which was not a criminal case, *Robinson v Robinson and Lane*[3]. The petitioner's case depended on the uncorroborated e evidence of the respondent's diary entries which were (as the law then stood) no evidence against the co-respondent who was dismissed from the suit. The question then arose whether the suit against the wife must fail. In giving the judgment of the full court, Cockburn CJ said[4]:

f 'The case of an indictment against two persons for conspiracy suggested an apparent analogy; and as, in such a case, a plea of guilty by the one, if followed by the acquittal of the other, would not have supported a judgment of guilty against the delinquent confessing and pleading guilty, so it might be said that here, as the offence of adultery necessarily implied the joint delinquency of two, if one of the parties was acquitted, the other could not properly be condemned. We were however of opinion that a principle of so purely technical a nature g should be confined to the cases in the criminal law in which it had hitherto been applied, and that it ought not to be extended to a proceeding in which the addition of the co-delinquent to the suit had been made compulsory by the Legislature with a view to his own protection, and in which but for this special provision of the Act of Parliament, the suit would have been against the wife alone.'

h Thus Cockburn CJ regarded it as clear, although the principle involved was one of a purely technical nature, that a plea of guilty by one alleged conspirator followed by an acquittal of the other would not support a judgment of guilty against him who had confessed and pleaded guilty.

This passage is obiter but it has all the authority of Cockburn CJ and it seems plain that he drew no distinction in principle between the cases of (a) conviction by j verdict of a jury of one conspirator tried separately followed by the subsequent

1 (1851) 16 QB at 838, 839
2 (1852) 6 Cox CC 6
3 (1859) 1 Sw & Tr 362
4 1 Sw & Tr at 392, 393

trial and acquittal of a co-accused and (b) the conviction of one conspirator on his *a*
own confession followed by the subsequent acquittal of the co-conspirator on a trial
conducted either immediately thereafter or on some subsequent occasion. He
regarded the inevitable subsequent quashing of the conviction of the self-confessed
conspirator as due to a technical rule. Though he does not say so in terms, it seems a
fair inference that he used the word 'technical' because of the by then well established
rule that repugnant verdicts could not be allowed to appear on the record. *b*

We come back in chronological sequence to *R v Manning*[1]. *Manning*[1] does not
decide that when A pleads guilty and B is subsequently acquitted, A's conviction cannot stand. There, two people had been indicted for a conspiracy and at the trial
before Lord Coleridge CJ he directed the jury that the evidence might satisfy them
as to one prisoner and not as to the other and that they might on the indictment
find one of the defendants guilty and acquit the other. When the case came before *c*
the Queen's Bench Division comprising Lord Coleridge CJ, Stephen and Mathew JJ,
it was held that that was a misdirection and that there must be a retrial. The court
relied on the decision in *Cooke*[2] and on other authorities to show what Mathew J
described as an imperative rule of law, a rule that where there is a charge of conspiracy against two persons jointly indicted and tried together the question for the
jury is whether both of them are or are not guilty and that if the jury are not satisfied *d*
as to the guilt of both of them then both must be acquitted. It was held that it was
impossible on such a charge to convict one of them and to acquit the other. Mathew J
expressed his opinion only after considerable doubt and Stephen J said that it was
with the greatest possible reluctance that he had come to the same conclusion.

What is interesting and relevant for the purposes of the present case is a dictum
of Lord Coleridge CJ[3]:
e

> 'The earlier cases, it is true, are stated shortly and without much particularity
> of detail. It may be, if we had all the facts of those cases, they might turn out
> to be less in point than they appear to be at present, but still from the time
> of 14 Hen. 4[4], it has been taken for granted by the judges of these Courts, that
> in cases of an indictment for conspiracy, when two people are indicted and tried
> together (because different considerations arise where people are not tried *f*
> together), either both must be convicted or both must be acquitted.'

One of the difficulties in considering *Manning*[1] is that each of the learned judges
relied in support of the existence of the main principle on the authority of the House
of Lords in *O'Connell*[5].

We turn next to *R v Plummer*[6], a decision of the full Court of Crown Cases Reserved.
Plummer and two others were charged with conspiracy together. Plummer pleaded *g*
guilty and was sentenced. He was called as a witness against the other two who
were tried immediately afterwards and acquitted. Counsel for Plummer then objected
that his client could not be convicted and punished but the objection was overruled.
The case was submitted to the full court who quashed the conviction. Wright J
said there was no previous *decision* (our italics) precisely in point. We think he was
right in so stating. He referred to many of the cases already discussed in this judgment. *h*
We respectfully agree with his criticism of the passages in the judgments of Mathew
and Stephen JJ which are founded on the decision in *O'Connell*[5]. The learned judge
was, however, much influenced by the opinion of Cockburn CJ in *Robinson v Robinson
and Lane*[7] already quoted, which he felt ought not to be disregarded. He was, we

---

1 (1883) 12 QBD 241, [1881-85] All ER Rep 852   *j*
2 (1826) 5 B & C 538
3 12 QBD at 245, [1881-85] All ER Rep at 855
4 *Anon* (circa 1435) YB 14 Hen 6, 25b
5 (1844) 11 Cl & Fin 155
6 [1902] 2 KB 339, [1900-3] All ER Rep 613
7 (1859) 1 Sw & Tr at 392, 393

a think, right in saying that it was the analogy in that case which had to be adopted or rejected by the court concerned. But it is important to observe that while as late as 1902 the learned judge and indeed the whole court clearly treated this question as not then concluded by authority, they thought that the underlying principles of the long line of the cases cited supported Cockburn CJ's view. It is also clear that both Wright and Bruce JJ were much influenced by the repugnancy argument. Lord Alverstone CJ and Jelf J agreed but with marked reluctance.

b We are driven to say that if the reasoning in *Plummer*[1] is to be followed in 1973, the accused's conviction cannot be sustained. It is to be observed that counsel for the prosecution (which seems to have been initiated privately) did not take part in the argument and the court did not therefore have the benefit of argument in support of the conviction.

c *Plummer*[1] is the last relevant decision to which reference was made in argument before the passing of the Criminal Appeal Act 1907. Section 20(1) of that Act provided:

'Writs of error, and the powers and practice now existing in the High Court in respect of motions for new trials or the granting thereof in criminal cases, are hereby abolished.'

d Sections 3 and 5 of the Crown Cases Act 1848 were repealed but by s 20(4) 'All jurisdiction and authority' under that Act in relation to questions of law arising in criminal trials' (already transferred to judges of the High Court) was vested in the new Court of Criminal Appeal. Section 3 of the 1907 Act permitted an appeal against conviction on any ground which involved a question of law or with the leave of the court or e on a certificate of the trial judge on any question of fact or of mixed fact and law or on any other ground which appeared to the court to be a sufficient ground of appeal. Section 4 made provision for allowing appeals on the various grounds there set out.

The 1907 Act (subject to certain changes) continued to operate until the passing of the Criminal Appeal Act 1968 which repealed the whole of the 1907 Act. Section f 1 of the 1968 Act, broadly speaking, replaced s 3 of the 1907 Act, and s 2 the former s 4. Section 2 re-enacted the 'unsafe or unsatisfactory' test first introduced by the Criminal Appeal Act 1966 in relation to appeals against conviction by verdict of a jury.

It is not necessary to consider the details of these sections. The relevant point is that since 1907 the entire appellate jurisdiction in criminal cases has been founded g on statute. The procedures which had obtained before 1907 were expressly abolished by statute. *Manning*[2] was an example of review by the contemporary complex procedure which managed to survive the reforms of the 1870s while *Plummer*[1], as already pointed out, was a decision of the Court of Crown Cases Reserved, which followed and applied the previously current practice and procedure.

The history of this earlier criminal practice and procedure is usefully summarised h in Thompson and Wollaston's The Court of Appeal, Criminal Division[3]. It will be found more elaborately explained in Holdsworth's History of English Law[4]. What was all important for the successful invocation of the writ of error was the state of the record. An error not on the record could not in general be reviewed by writ of error. The record did not show the evidence of the judge's direction to the jury. However much the Court of King's Bench might seek to extend its jurisdiction at the j expense of other courts, the ability of the writ of error to correct errors of substance rather than of technicality was always limited though this very fact seems to have

---

1 [1902] 2 KB 339, [1900-3] All ER Rep 613
2 (1883) 12 QBD 241, [1881-85] All ER Rep 852
3 (1969), pp 105, 106, paras 8. 1 1—8. 1 5
4 Volume 1, pp 212 et seq

led that court to adopt a strict and technical approach to errors on the record as a
means of widening the process of review.   A writ of certiorari was also used in cases   *a*
of misdemeanour but not of felony and then only when misdemeanour was tried
before the Queen's Bench Division in the exercise of its original jurisdiction (now
abolished) or sent by it to be tried at assizes.   It was not available in the case of
ordinary trials at quarter sessions or assizes.   A study of the report in R v Manning[1]
suggests that this was an example of the use of this machinery.   See also Holdsworth[2].
     We emphasise this part of our legal history since it explains much which underlies   *b*
the many decisions we have quoted.   But from 1907 onwards all was changed.
Although the Court of Crown Cases Reserved was not finally abolished until 1966,
the old limited powers of review disappeared.   The much wider powers replaced
them, which powers were still further extended by the provisions of the Criminal
Appeal Acts 1966 and 1968.
     Before we consider what effect, if any, these changes have on the authority to be   *c*
accorded to the earlier decisions, it is necessary to consider the cases since 1907 in
which the present question or questions akin to it have arisen.
     In R v Rowley[3] the Court of Criminal Appeal, consisting of Lord Goddard CJ,
Humphreys and Singleton JJ, held that where an accessory was indicted with an
alleged principal offender it was wrong to accept a plea of guilty from the accessory
before the issue of guilt of the alleged principal offender had been determined.   The   *d*
former had pleaded guilty.   The latter was acquitted.   The former appealed.
No attempt was made to support the conviction.   In giving judgment Humphreys J
said[4]:

     'As a result, there is error on the record which cannot be cured by amendment.
     Writs of error . . . have been abolished since 1908 by the Criminal Appeal Act,   *e*
     1907, but this court has the power which the Court of King's Bench used to
     exercise in dealing with error on the record.   Where there are no means of
     amending the record so as to make it consonant with the proved facts of the
     case and where it is inconsistent with itself, as the record is here, the only course
     which this court can take is to quash the conviction, and that must be done in
     this case.'   *f*

He ended his judgment by saying[5]:

     'If the other person is awaiting trial, it is wrong to accept a plea of guilty from
     a prisoner who is indicted for an offence which involves his knowledge of the
     guilt of another person who is protesting his innocence and is about to be tried by
     a jury.   The same observation would apply to a case of conspiracy.'   *g*

     Three observations fall to be made about that case.   First, the Court of Criminal
Appeal regarded the record, which showed the conviction of an accessory and acquittal
of the principal, as being inconsistent with itself and contrary to proved facts and
therefore one which must be corrected by way of quashing the conviction.   Secondly,
that court regarded the position in a conspiracy case as the same and inferentially   *h*
as still untouched by the change in appellate procedure in 1907.   Thirdly, it appears
that the matters argued in the present appeal were not then argued, and in relation
to the offence of conspiracy the observation was obiter.   With respect to that court,
it would seem to be wrong in principle to say that a plea of guilty by one of two
conspirators should never be accepted in the absence of a plea of guilty or prior
                                                                            j

1   (1883) 12 QBD 241, [1881-85] All ER Rep 852
2   History of the English Law, vol 1, p 217
3   [1948] 1 All ER 570
4   [1948] 1 All ER at 571, 32 Cr App Rep at 149
5   See 32 Cr App Rep at 151; cf [1948] 1 All ER at 571

a   conviction of the other, and there is no logic in distinguishing the situation in which one pleads guilty and the other has not been arrested or even found.

The next relevant authority is *Dharmasena v The King*[1], an appeal from Ceylon, the Criminal Appeal Ordinance 1938 of which country permitted the ordering of a new trial in certain circumstances: see s 5(2) and (4). Two accused to whom we will refer as S and D were charged with conspiracy to murder and murder. S was also

b   charged with aiding and abetting murder by D. Both were convicted of conspiracy to murder and D of murder. S's conviction was quashed on appeal and a new trial ordered. At the new trial S was acquitted of conspiracy. D's appeal against both convictions was dismissed. D then appealed to the Privy Council. Lord Porter said[2]:

c   'After this verdict the position was that of two conspirators one had been found guilty by one jury and the other acquitted by another. In their Lordships' opinion this is an impossible result where conspiracy is concerned. It is well-established law that if two persons are accused of conspiracy and one is acquitted the other must also escape condemnation. Two at least are required to commit the crime of conspiracy; one alone cannot do so. In the present case the only conspirators suggested were the two accused persons, and there were no others,

d   known or unknown, who might have participated in the crime. It is true that one conspirator may be tried and convicted in the absence of his companions in crime: *Reg. v. Ahearne*[3], but where two have been tried together so that the only possible verdict is either that both are, or neither is, guilty, an order for the retrial of one makes it imperative that the other should also be retried. In their Lordships' opinion, therefore, if two persons are accused of a criminal conspiracy and convicted, and on appeal one can be, and is, sent for retrial, the other should

e   be sent at the same time for retrial also on that charge so that both may be convicted or acquitted together. In the present case in as much as Mrs. Seneviratne has been found not guilty of conspiracy, their Lordships think the proper course is to treat her acquittal as a disposal of the charge of conspiracy and as involving the acquittal of the appellant also on that charge. The appeal against

f   conviction on that count should accordingly be allowed.'

That decision does not of course bind this court but it is of the highest persuasive authority. It treats as clear law (i) that if A and B are tried together for conspiracy between them alone, the verdict must be the same for each, and (ii) if for any reason A's conviction in such a case is later quashed and, on any new trial, he is acquitted, then B's conviction cannot stand. It is argued with force that unless a distinction can be drawn between a case where before A's ultimate acquittal B pleads guilty,

g   and a case where B is convicted by verdict of one jury and A is acquitted by verdict of another, the decision of the Privy Council strongly supports the present accused. The arguments are not reported and there is nothing to show whether *R v Plummer*[4] was referred to. The decision in *R v Ahearne*[3] was not doubted. But the words of Lord Porter already cited emphasise that the case was one of a joint trial of con-

h   spirators and that in such a case a retrial of one after conviction of both is not the proper procedure.

We were also referred to *R v Doyle*[5] and were supplied with a copy of the transcript of the judgment of Lord Parker CJ in that case. Doyle was charged on two counts of conspiracy of which the second charged him together with three other men with

j   conspiracy to rob. Doyle and two of the others were tried together and convicted.

---

1   [1951] AC 1
2   [1951] AC at 5, 6
3   (1852) 6 Cox CC 6
4   [1902] 2 KB 339, [1900-3] All ER Rep 613
5   [1963] Crim LR 37

The fourth was brought up subsequently at another assize and the Crown accepted   *a*
his plea of not guilty on this count. He was not put in charge of a jury. There was
then no power to record a verdict of not guilty. The convictions of the other two
were quashed. Doyle's conviction was then referred to the Court of Criminal Appeal
by the Secretary of State. It was quashed. The court referred to and followed
R v Plummer[1] saying: 'That entirely covers this case save for one possible complication.' The complication was the position of the fourth named conspirator. The   *b*
court adopted a broad approach saying:

> 'This is a case of four men ... three of whom in one form or another have been
> acquitted and accordingly it does not seem to this court that this conviction can
> stand.'

The Criminal Law Review[2] commented that the rule applied by the court was
illogical but well established and referred to certain other criticisms of it, including   *c*
the dissenting judgment of Erle J in *R v Thompson*[3] to which we have already referred.
The actual decision in *Doyle*[2] was dependent on the court treating an acceptance of a
plea of not guilty as equivalent to a verdict of not guilty.
    There is also an unreported decision of this court in *R v Mandeville*[4]. The court,
in a judgment delivered by Phillimore LJ, treated as axiomatic that the quashing of
the conviction of one conspirator must lead to the quashing of the conviction of the   *d*
co-accused however strong the evidence against the latter, who though not pleading
guilty had made a statement admitting his guilt and had not given evidence and
whose counsel had felt unable to address the jury.
    The only other recent case to which we ought to refer is not a conspiracy case. In
R v Andrews Weatherfoil Ltd[5] Sporle was charged on a number of counts including
count 10 which charged that he had corruptly received money from one Smith.   *e*
Smith had been charged with corruptly offering that money and had been granted
a separate trial. Sporle was convicted on count 10. Smith was later acquitted by
another jury. It was argued that the verdicts were inconsistent and that it was
unsafe and unsatisfactory to allow Sporle's conviction to stand. This court rejected
this argument and dismissed the appeal. In giving the judgment of the court,
Eveleigh J said that the fact of different verdicts by different juries did not of itself   *f*
indicate inconsistency. 'Very often', he said[6]—

> 'an apparent inconsistency reflects no more than the jury's strict adherence
> to the judge's direction that they must consider each case separately and that
> evidence against one may not be admissible against the other; e g where there is
> a signed confession.'
                                                                                       g
    Counsel for the Crown on the present appeal relied strongly on that decision.
The verdicts of those two juries involved that Sporle had corruptly received the
money though Smith had not offered the money corruptly. If this were right then
equally Sporle's conviction would have stood had he pleaded guilty notwithstanding
Smith's subsequent acquittal, And if that were right, why should not the accused's
conviction on his own confession stand notwithstanding Tracey's subsequent acquittal,   *h*
a result to be explained on the ground that the evidence against the accused was,
inter alia, his own confession but the evidence against Tracey was insufficient to justify
the jury in his case in convicting him?
    We think that the conspiracy cases decided before 1907 support the following
propositions of law as at that date. (1) If A and B alone (that is with no other person
                                                                                       j

1 [1902] 2 KB 339, [1900-3] All ER Rep 613
2 [1963] Crim LR 37
3 (1851) 16 QB 832
4 (7th October 1968) unreported
5 [1972] 1 All ER 65, [1972] 1 WLR 118
6 [1972] 1 All ER at 71, [1972] 1 WLR at 126

named or unnamed) are indicted and tried together for conspiracy together, the jury
a must be told that both must be convicted or both must be acquitted, and if one is
convicted and the other acquitted, the conviction must be quashed. (2) If A and B
alone (that is with no other person named or unnamed) are indicted but only A is
tried, either because B is dead or has disappeared and A is convicted of conspiracy
with B, that conviction is in no way vitiated by B's death or absence. (3) If A and B
alone (that is with no other person known or unknown) are indicted for conspiracy
b and only A is tried and convicted, and subsequently B is tried and acquitted, A's
conviction must be quashed. (4) If A and B alone (that is with no other person known
or unknown) are indicted for conspiracy together and A pleads guilty and B not
guilty and B is tried and is acquitted, A's conviction must be quashed.

We further think it clear that since 1907 not only have the cases on which the foregoing propositions of law are founded been consistently followed and applied, but
c that they and the later cases (if the latter be correctly decided) support the further
propositions. (5) If A and B alone (that is with no other person named or unnamed)
are indicted for conspiracy together and both plead not guilty and both are tried and
convicted, either together or on separate occasions, and B's conviction is later quashed
for any reason, whether for misdirection or insufficient evidence to justify conviction
or (since 1966) because the verdict against B is unsafe and unsatisfactory, A's conviction
d must be quashed. (6) If A and B alone (that is with no other person named or unnamed) are indicted for conspiracy together and A pleads guilty, and B is tried
either on the same occasion or on a later occasion and is convicted but B's conviction
is later quashed for any reason, A's conviction must be quashed.

It is worth observing that the recent report of the Law Commission's Working
Party on the Law of Conspiracy[1] does not suggest that the law today is otherwise
e than as stated in the above propositions or that *Plummer*[2] can no longer be regarded
as good law. It refers to the many criticisms which have been made of the present
state of the law, both in the past and more recently in Smith and Hogan's Criminal
Law[3] and Glanville Williams's Criminal Law[4]. It suggests changes in the law to
overcome certain of the anomalies, to which the propositions of law we have sought to
state lead.
f If we have correctly stated the law as we believe it to have been up to 1907 and if
the later cases together with the earlier cases justify the two further propositions,
this court can only depart from them if it is convinced, first that the changes in the law
applicable to criminal appeals wrought in 1907 and the later changes in 1966 and 1968
justify departure from the earlier decisions, and, secondly, that the cases since 1907,
which followed the earlier cases either expressly or by implication, overlooked the
g suggested effect of these changes to which the attention of the courts concerned
was not drawn and must therefore be treated as having been wrongly decided.

The argument is that the earlier cases were founded on repugnant entries on the
record, the need to establish errors on the record before any power of review was
available, and the necessity for quashing a conviction which resulted in error or
inconsistency on the record. Once the old powers of review were abolished, errors
h on the face of the record no longer mattered, and the Court of Criminal Appeal
and this court, as its successor, exercised and exercise a jurisdiction not dependent
on such errors being shown. The argument put so far is of course sound. But it
does not provide the complete answer to the question. The reason why, in a case of
conspiracy comprising only two persons, a record on the face of which one was
guilty and the other not guilty was held to be bad and could not be allowed to stand
i on the ground of repugnancy, was not merely that inconsistent results were recorded

1 (July 1973) Law Com 50
2 [1902] 2 KB 339, [1900-3] All ER Rep 613
3 3rd Edn (1973), p 181
4 2nd Edn (1961), pp 669-671, para 213

but that different results are recorded in respect of an offence which could not be committed by either without the other; in other words the record showed on its face guilt of an offence the ingredients of which were not established.

We readily accept the force of the criticisms which have been made of the position and which lead to the anomalies mentioned, especially that A's ultimate liability to conviction should depend not on the strength of the evidence against him nor on his own solemn confession (if any) in the presence of the court, but on the decision whether B should be charged, or if B is charged, on the appearance or non-appearance of B or on whether if B appears, he is convicted or acquitted on what may be wholly different evidence, or on whether if B is convicted his conviction may subsequently be quashed for any one or more of a number of possible reasons not related to the case against A; all matters totally irrelevant to proof of A's guilt, some or all of the evidence against whom (for example A's confession) may be inadmissible against B.

But we take to be clear law beyond the power of judicial review at least in this court that if A and B are indicted and tried together (there being no other alleged conspirators known or unknown) however strong the evidence against A and however weak it be against B, both must be convicted or both acquitted. A jury may and perhaps does receive this oft-given direction with dismay and act on it with reluctance in a case where they are also told to consider the cases of the two accused separately and the evidence against one is overwhelming and against the other slight. A jury who successively tried A and B together for conspiracy and received this direction and acted loyally on it and then in the next case tried C for offering a bribe and D for receiving it and were told that these were separate offences and that in legal theory they might convict one and acquit the other, might well be forgiven if they thought that the law was indeed curious and might ponder on Lord Reid's recent observation in *Haughton v Smith*[1]: 'The law may sometimes be an ass but it cannot be so asinine as that.'

We do not think that the changes introduced in 1907 altered the law in this respect. The Court of Criminal Appeal in *Rowley*[2] clearly did not think so. It was suggested at one point in the argument that the introduction in 1966 of the 'unsafe or unsatisfactory' provisions in relation to jury verdicts as a new ground for quashing a conviction affected the position because where an accused person has pleaded guilty it cannot be said that his conviction was 'unsafe or unsatisfactory'. But the short answer is that that statutory provision is related to verdicts of juries and we are not here concerned with a verdict of a jury against the accused. The provisions of s 2(1)(b) of the Criminal Appeal Act 1968 are appropriate to this case:

'... the Court of Appeal shall allow an appeal against conviction if they think ... (b) that the judgment of the court of trial should be set aside on the ground of a wrong decision of any question of law ...'

It has always been accepted since 1907 that, subject to well defined limits, an accused person who pleaded guilty might nevertheless appeal against his conviction if (inter alia) on the admitted facts he could not in law have been convicted of the offence charged (see *R v Forde*[3] and *Thompson and Wollaston*[4]).

One therefore comes back to the same point. Can A's conviction on his own confession of conspiracy solely with B stand when B is for any reason subsequently acquitted of that conspiracy with A? The submission for the accused is that it cannot because on the admitted facts (namely A's confession and B's subsequent acquittal) A cannot in law be guilty of conspiracy. The question does not depend only on criminal procedure of former times although the cases arise from the repugnancy of entries

1   [1973] 3 All ER 1109 at 1121, [1974] 2 WLR 1 at 14
2   [1948] 1 All ER 570
3   [1923] 2 KB 400, [1923] All ER Rep 477
4   The Court of Appeal Criminal Division, (1969), pp 130-132, para 9. 5

a on the record. The reason why those entries were repugnant is that they showed A
as guilty and B as not guilty of the same conspiracy and since there cannot in law be
a conviction for conspiracy unless two or more persons are proved to be guilty of
that conspiracy, once B is for any reason acquitted of conspiracy with A, A in law
cannot be guilty of conspiracy with B even though, apart from B's acquittal, A was
prepared to admit and did admit his guilt. B's acquittal is a finding of no conspiracy
b not merely a finding of no proof of conspiracy against B. The long line of cases shows
that the principle derives from the nature of the offence or conspiracy.

The contrary argument for the Crown is that A may be independently proved to
be guilty of conspiracy irrespective of proof of B's guilt of the same offence. If A
can (in legal theory) be guilty of corruptly receiving a bribe while B can be acquitted
of offering it, or if A (in like theory) can be guilty of adultery with B but B not guilty
of adultery with A why, it is asked, should the same position not obtain in conspiracy?
c To hold otherwise produces results which are illogical and, in the light of facts proved
against A, in some cases absurd.

The answer we think (on the authorities which have stood through the centuries)
lies in the nature of the offence of conspiracy. If we were not constrained by long
established if not technically binding authority to hold that where A and B alone
are charged together with conspiracy, both must be convicted of conspiracy or both
d acquitted, a different result must logically have followed in the present appeal.
But as the authorities stand the question is not one of proof but of the nature in law
of the offence of conspiracy. The nearest analogy is that a plea of guilty by an accessory
cannot be allowed to stand if the principal offender is later acquitted. This is not
because of any question of proof but because in law a man cannot be guilty of being
an accessory if the alleged principal offender has been found not guilty.
e Accordingly we feel reluctantly obliged to allow this appeal and quash the
accused's conviction. We indicated at the close of the argument that, subject to agreement on the terms of the certificate, we would be willing to certify that a question
of law of general public importance arose and give leave to appeal in order that the
issues we have discussed at length might receive final and authoritative determination
in the House of Lords.
f

*Appeal allowed. The court certified the following point of law to be of general public importance:
'If two persons alone (that is to say with no other persons named or unnamed) are indicted
for conspiracy together and the first pleads guilty but the second pleads not guilty and is
subsequently tried and acquitted, must the conviction of the first upon his own confession
thereupon be quashed?' and gave leave to appeal to the House of Lords.*
g

A S Virdi Esq Barrister.

Appeal

h The Crown appealed against the decision of the Court of Appeal.

Andrew Leggatt QC and *H C Tayler* for the Crown.
Douglas Draycott QC and *C A Coode* for the respondent.

Their Lordships took time for consideration.
j
19th June. The following opinions were delivered.

LORD REID. My Lords, I have had an opportunity of reading the speech of my
noble and learned friend, Lord Morris of Borth-y-Gest. I agree with it. I would
allow the appeal.

LORD MORRIS OF BORTH-Y-GEST. My Lords, the law of conspiracy *a* has been fertile in producing many problems for lawyers. The question raised in this appeal is whether it should yield an apparent bonus for the respondent, Shannon. On 22nd March 1973 he pleaded guilty in the Crown Court at Warwick to a count of an indictment which charged him and a man named Tracey with having conspired together dishonestly to handle stolen goods. There has been no suggestion that he did not appreciate and understand what he was doing when he pleaded guilty. He *b* was represented by counsel. Counsel made a plea in mitigation covering both the conspiracy count and two other counts which were of handling stolen goods and to which counts the respondent also pleaded guilty. Sentences were passed on 22nd March.

Tracey pleaded not guilty to the charge of conspiring with the respondent and not guilty to a count charging him separately with handling stolen goods. Tracey *c* was not tried on that date (22nd March). He came up for trial at Warwick Crown Court on 26th and 27th March. By leave, the count against him of handling stolen goods was amended so that it became divided into two counts. The trial proceeded on those two counts, the trial on the charges against him being severed so that the outstanding charge against him on the conspiracy count was left to be later separately tried. At that trial on the two counts the jury disagreed. *d*

The next step was that Tracey was retried on the two counts of handling stolen goods. That took place at the Crown Court in Coventry. Incidentally the presiding recorder at Coventry was not the recorder who had presided at Warwick on 26th and 27th March who, in turn, was not the recorder who had presided at Warwick on 22nd March. The new trial took place on 3rd and 4th April. The severed conspiracy count against Tracey was also sent to the Coventry court though at first *e* Tracey was tried (by way of retrial) only on the two counts of handling stolen goods. The result was that the jury acquitted Tracey on those counts.

The next step was that the prosecution decided to offer no evidence against Tracey on the outstanding conspiracy count. Being invited to do so, the recorder entered a verdict of not guilty. Section 17 of the Criminal Justice Act 1967 became operative. That section provides as follows: *f*

'Where a defendant arraigned on an indictment or inquisition pleads not guilty and the prosecutor proposes to offer no evidence against him, the court before which the defendant is arraigned may, if it thinks fit, order that a verdict of not guilty shall be recorded without the defendant being given in charge to a jury, and the verdict shall have the same effect as if the defendant had been tried and acquitted on the verdict of a jury.' *g*

The next step was that the respondent, having heard of what had happened in Tracey's case, applied for leave to appeal to the Court of Appeal first in regard to his conviction on the conspiracy count and secondly in regard to his sentences. We are only concerned with the first of these. We have not had to consider the facts or the extent of the respondent's involvement. Leave was asked for on the ground and contention that though there had been a plea of guilty by the respondent the *h* consequence of Tracey's acquittal (the count having named as conspirators only the respondent and Tracey) was that the conviction of the respondent could not stand.

In the result the Court of Appeal held, for the reasons given in a most helpful and illuminating judgment in which the authorities are carefully marshalled and considered, that the respondent's appeal against conviction succeeded. The court felt 'reluctantly' obliged to allow the appeal but gave leave to appeal to this House *j* and certified the following point of law of general public importance:

'If two persons alone (that is to say with no other persons named or unnamed) are indicted for conspiracy together and the first pleads guilty but the second pleads not guilty and is subsequently tried and acquitted, must the conviction of the first upon his own confession thereupon be quashed?'

a   So the question arises whether if A and B (but no others) are charged with conspiracy and if A, with full intention, pleads guilty and if B pleads not guilty and if B's trial is postponed, but, taking place at some subsequent time, results in his acquittal, the law requires that the conviction of A (on his own confession) must be set aside. If it must, the law will be producing a strange result.   No one could know better than A whether he did or did not agree with B to do something wrongful and if, fully under-
b   standing what he was doing, and having skilled advice to guide or assist him, he acknowledged by way of confession to the court that he had so agreed, the law might seem to be artificial and contrarywise which required that because the charge against B failed A must be held to be not guilty when he himself knew and had admitted that he was guilty.

Before examining the matter more deeply the question arises whether, in the circumstances of this case, the Court of Appeal was possessed of statutory power
c   to set aside the conviction of the respondent.   I do not find it necessary to set out the legislative history which has culminated in the endowment of the Court of Appeal (Criminal Division) with its statutory powers.   This is because, irrespective of question as to jurisdiction to entertain an appeal, the powers of the court on the hearing of an appeal are now to be found in and are contained in s 2 of the Criminal Appeal
d   Act 1968.   For an appreciation of many of the older authorities it has to be remembered that writs of error (abolished by the Criminal Appeal Act 1907, s 20(1)) only enabled errors to be corrected if they were errors on the record.   Under the Crown Cases Act 1848 (now repealed), the court itself could reserve and state a case on a point of law for the consideration of the Court for the Consideration of Crown Cases Reserved.   The jurisdiction of that court in relation to such questions of law became vested in the Court of Criminal Appeal (see the Criminal Appeal Act 1907, s 20(4)).
e   After the establishment of that court the determination of appeals in ordinary cases was governed by s 4 of the 1907 Act.   On the transfer by the Criminal Appeal Act 1966 of the jurisdiction of the Court of Criminal Appeal to the Court of Appeal, s 4 of the 1966 Act amended the provisions of s 4 of the 1907 Act.   It is to be observed that whereas in s 4 of the 1907 Act one available ground for allowing an appeal was 'that on any ground there was a miscarriage of justice' one amendment made in 1966
f   was that for those words there was a substitution of the words 'there was a material irregularity in the course of the trial'.   Now the provisions of s 2 of the 1968 Act are as follows:

'(1) Except as provided by this Act, the Court of Appeal shall allow an appeal against conviction if they think—(a) that the verdict of the jury should be set
g   aside on the ground that under all the circumstances of the case it is unsafe or unsatisfactory; or (b) that the judgment of the court of trial should be set aside on the ground of a wrong decision of any question of law; or (c) that there was a material irregularity in the course of the trial, and in any other case shall dismiss the appeal: Provided that the Court may, notwithstanding that they are of opinion that the point raised in the appeal might be decided in favour of the
h   appellant, dismiss the appeal if they consider that no miscarriage of justice has actually occurred.

'(2) In the case of an appeal against conviction the Court shall, if they allow the appeal, quash the conviction.

'(3) An order of the Court of Appeal quashing a conviction shall, except when under section 7 below the appellant is ordered to be retried, operate as a direction
j   to the court of trial to enter, instead of the record of conviction, a judgment and verdict of acquittal.'

The wording in s 2 is precise.   In certain cases (except as provided by the Act) the court 'shall' allow an appeal against conviction.   In any other case the court 'shall' dismiss the appeal.   It is not suggested that any denoted exception applied in the respondent's case.   It followed that the court could only allow his appeal if the case came within either (a) or (b) or (c). There was no verdict of a jury and so (a) did not apply. It is perhaps to be considered whether under (a) the limitation to cases where there has been the verdict of a jury is not unduly restrictive. Was there (see (c)) a material irregularity in the course of his trial? Can it be said that the respondent should not have been sentenced before the guilt or innocence of Tracey had been established? The court could have postponed passing sentence and the court might have decided that that would be the best course to adopt. But I do not think that the decision to pass sentence on 22nd March 1973 should be regarded as a 'material irregularity'. The Court of Appeal while considering what was said in *R v Rowley*[1] did not say or suggest that there had been any such irregularity. It may often, or, perhaps, generally be desirable to avoid accepting a plea of guilty by one of two persons charged with conspiracy until or so that both can be tried or dealt with together but it has not been suggested that there was a material irregularity when the court at Warwick (on 22nd March) accepted the respondent's plea of guilty.

It follows that there only was power to allow the respondent's appeal if the judgment of the court of trial could be set aside 'on the ground of a wrong decision of any question of law'. This raises the enquiry—did the court of trial give or make a decision on some question of law which was a wrong decision? Stated otherwise—did the learned recorder on 22nd March have a question of law before him which called for his decision and did he decide the question wrongly? The answer I think must be in the negative. No question of law arose. He gave no decision on any question of law.

The Court of Appeal[2] thus expressed their reason for invoking s 2(1)(b):

'It has always been accepted since 1907 that, subject to well defined limits, an accused person who pleaded guilty might nevertheless appeal against his conviction if (inter alia) on the admitted facts he could not in law have been convicted of the offence charged . . .'

The words used in *R v Forde*[3] were cited. That may well be so. If certain facts are admitted and if on the basis of them there is a plea of guilty and if the facts do not warrant such a plea it may be that the acceptance by the court of the plea could amount to a wrong decision of a question of law. It is to be remembered that a similar provision to that contained in s 2(1)(b) as to setting aside a conviction on the ground of a wrong decision of a question of law was contained in the 1907 Act. Furthermore, it may often happen that a ruling by a judge on a question of law is followed by a plea of guilty which is made on the basis of such ruling: the accused will thereafter be entitled to appeal against his conviction on the ground that there was a wrong decision on the question of law.

In the present case not only was there on 22nd March no question of law and no decision on any question of law; there were no facts which made an acceptance of the plea of guilty unwarranted or which involved that such acceptance constituted a wrong decision on a question of law.

It was contended on behalf of the respondent that regard should be had to 'the circumstances appertaining to the indictment' and that that entails looking at events subsequent to the plea of guilty on 22nd March; and that if the indictment is now looked at and the formal record of all pleas, verdicts and sentences it will be seen that on the conspiracy count it is recorded that the respondent pleaded guilty and that after a plea of not guilty by Tracey there was a formal verdict of not guilty. On this basis it was contended that 'that which was provisionally correct at the court of trial can now be shown to be wrong on the record'.

There was, however, nothing provisional about the proceedings concerning the respondent on 22nd March. There was no irregularity. The contention seems to

1 [1948] 1 All ER 570
2 Page 1024, ante
3 [1923] 2 KB 400, [1923] All ER Rep 477

a suggest that there could be some sort of relation back which transformed the proceedings of 22nd March and make them other than they had been and really were. The contention cannot, in my view, create or bring into being a decision on a question of law when there was in fact no such question of law and no such decision.

b I will proceed to examine some of the older cases but they will not throw any light in regard to the construction of the statutory provision that now governs the functions of the Court of Appeal. Under s 2(1)(b) the only question that arises is this: should the judgment of the court of trial (i e the judgment of the Crown Court on 22nd March 1973 passing a sentence of imprisonment on the respondent after he had confessed his guilt) be set aside on the ground of a wrong decision of any question of law? If no question of law arose and if, therefore, there was no decision of any question of law the court could not set the judgment aside on that ground. There cannot be attributed to the court of trial some notional decision on a non-existence question.

c As none of the grounds under paras (a) and (b) and (c) of s 2(1) applied in the respondent's case the concluding words applied, viz, 'and in any other case shall dismiss the appeal'.

For the reasons which I have set out, the present appeal must, in my view, on the above-mentioned ground be allowed and the conviction restored. This brings me to

d the next question which is whether the appeal should also be allowed on the ground that the conviction of the respondent was not invalidated by the subsequent acquittal of Tracey. The issue is raised whether there is as a matter of law any intrinsic or fundamental objection or bar to the conviction of one only of two persons who are charged with conspiring with each other.

It must be a self-evident proposition that one man acting alone cannot conspire and therefore cannot be guilty of conspiring. It is the very essence of a conspiracy

e that a person agrees with some other person or persons. For present purposes I need not refer to the other elements which comprise the crime of conspiracy. It follows that if there is a charge that A and B conspired together unlawfully there cannot be a conviction of A unless it is proved that he did conspire with B (and of course did so with the unlawful elements). Likewise B cannot be convicted unless it is proved that he did conspire with A (also of course with the unlawful elements).

f Both A and B are separate persons. If A is tried separately on a charge of conspiring with B evidence can only be given which is admissible evidence to prove the case against A. Similarly if B is tried separately the evidence which is given must be evidence which is admissible against B to prove the charge against him. If A and B are tried together the rules of evidence are no different. If all the evidence that is given is evidence which is equally admissible both against A and against B I think it would

g follow that there would be something wrong if a jury returned different verdicts in the two cases. If, however, the evidence against A was strong while the evidence against B was weak would it be objectionable in law (assuming that the trial was in every way correctly conducted) if the jury convicted A and acquitted B? I will return to a consideration of this question.

h In days when any review of convictions in criminal cases involved bringing the record before the court it was assumed that if there was an apparent inconsistency on the face of the record then that must have been the reflection or the consequence of some error. The error could then be corrected. I say apparent inconsistency because if the charge was that A and B (and no others) conspired together and if the record showed that one was found guilty and the other not guilty it need not logically

j have been inferred that there necessarily was inconsistency. The case against A might have been proved while the case against B had not. On the other hand, when only the record was available and when the apparent inconsistency very probably or possibly reflected a real inconsistency the fair course was to decide that there was error which called for correction. Holdsworth[1] points out that the common

---

1　History of English Law, vol 1, pp 212-217

law knew nothing of an appeal by way of a rehearing of a criminal case. It only
knew a procedure in error in which only errors which appeared on the record could
be alleged. It was 'a most inadequate procedure'. The procedure on a writ of
error was cumbersome because though on the record there was the formal history
of the case (the arraignment, the plea, the issue and the verdict) it took no account
of some of the most material parts of the trial where error was most likely to occur—
viz the evidence and the direction of the judge to the jury. So the writ could do
nothing to remedy the only errors that were really substantial. Holdsworth traced
the old practice under which if a judge, where there was a conviction, felt a doubt as
to the law he would respite judgment or sentence and thereafter discuss the matter
with other judges. If they thought that the accused had been improperly convicted
a pardon would follow. This practice led to the establishment in 1848 of what came
to be called the Court for the Consideration of Crown Cases Reserved. But under
the 1848 Act it was only by leave of the court of trial and in the discretion of the
court of trial that on a conviction a question of law which had arisen on the trial
could be reserved for the consideration of the court.

It is in the setting of and against the background of the legal procedures available
before the 1907 Act that the many decided cases concerning charges of conspiracy
must be viewed.

In the various decisions there are distinctions between the cases where alleged conspirators are tried together and cases where they are tried separately. Thus, if the
charge was that A and B conspired together it could be that they were tried together
or it could be that A was tried separately and that B was later tried separately or it
could be that A was tried separately and that B was never tried.

I take the last-mentioned situation. If the charge was that A and B (and no others)
had conspired and if A was separately tried—could the point be taken that he could
not be convicted because it might be that B would later be tried and perhaps
acquitted? The cases show that the answer was No. *R v Kinnersley and Moore*[1] is
one example. On the separate trial of Kinnersley he was found guilty and it was
then unsuccessfully argued in arrest of judgment that because every conspiracy
requires that there must be two persons at least judgment ought not to be given
against Kinnersley before the trial of Moore. In the argument it was assumed that
if Moore were later tried and acquitted there would 'consequently' be an acquittal
of Kinnersley. In the argument for the Crown it was pointed out that Moore would
have every opportunity, at his trial, to secure his acquittal which would not be precluded by the conviction of Kinnersley but that at the trial of Kinnersley it had been
proved against Kinnersley that he had in fact conspired with Moore. (In fact Moore
was later convicted.)

So in *R v Nichols*[2] it was held that on a charge against Nichols of conspiring with
Bygrave the court could give judgment against Nichols though Bygrave was dead
at the time of the indictment.

R v Kenrick[3] showed that where A and B pleaded not guilty to an indictment for
conspiracy there was no mistrial when, B having died, the trial proceeded of A alone
and led to his conviction.

In *R v Cooke*[4] it was held that there was no reason why judgment should not
be pronounced on J S S Cooke who had been found guilty of conspiring with R S
Cooke even though R S Cooke might at a later time be acquitted of conspiring.

I take the next situation. Suppose that A is first tried and is convicted and that B
at a later date is tried and is acquitted. Will the court then set aside A's conviction?
These are cases now calling for consideration which show that in such circumstances
A's conviction should be set aside. In *R v Cooke*[4] where it was held, as referred to

1 (1719) 1 Stra 193
2 (1742) 13 East 412
3 (1843) 5 QBD 49
4 (1826) 5 B & C 538

a above, that judgment could be pronounced on J S S Cooke after he was found guilty of conspiring with R S Cooke and was so found guilty though R S Cooke might later be acquitted, Littledale J said[1]:

b
'It was for the jury to consider whether the defendant, who was upon his trial, was guilty of the charge contained in the indictment. They have found that he was guilty of conspiring with R. S. Cooke, and that is sufficient to prevent the application of the rule of law that one cannot be guilty of a conspiracy. If the other defendant R. S. Cooke shall hereafter be acquitted, perhaps this judgment may be reversed.'

c This case was referred to in an Irish case in 1852 (*R v Ahearne*[2]) and it is interesting to note that as far back as 1865 the rule was challenged that if A and B are charged with conspiracy and if A is convicted and if B is subsequently acquitted the conviction of A must be set aside. The challenge came from the editor (Mr C S Greaves QC) of Russell on Crime[3]. Referring to what Littledale J had said in *R v Cooke*[1] he wrote a note as follows:

d
'*Sed quaere* for such acquittal would not *necessarily* show that the verdict of guilty on the former trial was wrong, as witnesses might be dead or absent who were examined on the former trial, or the one defendant might have been convicted on his own confession, which would not be admissible against the other defendant.'

In *Robinson v Robinson and Lane*[4] Cockburn CJ using the law of conspiracy as an analogy said:

e
'. . . a plea of guilty by one, if followed by the acquittal of the other; would not have supported a judgment of guilty against the delinquent confessing and pleading guilty . . .'

I take the situation where A and B are tried together. If one is convicted and the other acquitted what has been the result? The cases show that the conviction *f* of A has not been allowed to stand. In *Harison v Errington*[5], which was a case 'In error to reverse an indictment of rescous and riot', one error assigned was that the indictment of riot was against three and that the jury found only one of them guilty with the result that the verdict was 'void' for 'one alone cannot make a riot'. It was said that if there was a charge of conspiracy against two and only one was found guilty 'it is void, for one alone cannot conspire'.

g No one could question the obvious truth of the proposition that 'one alone cannot conspire'. But equally is it true that proof that two people did in fact conspire together may only be available against one of them.

In *Thody's Case*[6] Thody and two others were indicted for conspiracy. Thody pleaded and was found guilty—the others not having pleaded. It was then moved that judgment should not be entered against Thody, 'until the others came in; for *h* being laid by way of conspiracy, if the rest should chance to be acquitted, no judgment could be given against him: and so is 14 H. 6, 25.' The report proceeds[7]:

'Hale said, If one be acquitted in an action of conspiracy, the other cannot be guilty: but where one is found guilty and the other comes not in upon process,

j 1 (1826) 5 B & C at 545, 546
2 6 Cox CC 6
3 4th Edn (1865), vol 3, p 146, note *u*
4 (1859) 1 Sw & Tr 362 at 392, 393
5 (1627) Poph 202
6 (1674) 1 Vent 234
7 1 Vent at 234

of if he dies hanging the suit, yet judgment shall be upon the verdict against
the other. And so is 18 E. 3, 1, and 24 E. 3, 34.'   *a*

In *R v Grimes and Thompson*[1] it was assumed that if two persons were tried for
conspiracy and if one was convicted and the other acquitted the conviction of the one
must be quashed.

A difficult problem arose in *R v Thompson*[2]. Effectively there was a charge of
conspiracy against A and Y and Z and all three were tried together. The jury stated *b*
their opinion on the evidence to be that A had conspired with either Y or Z but that
they did not know with which. Thereupon the judge directed that a verdict of
not guilty should be taken in respect of Y and Z. I think that that must have been
correct. He further directed that a verdict of guilty be taken against A. He reserved
leave to move to enter a verdict of not guilty. In the result, Erle J dissenting, the
rule was made absolute. Lord Campbell CJ in the course of his judgment said[3]:   *c*

> 'It cannot be denied that, where the indictment is only that two defendants
> conspired together, the acquittal of one involves the acquittal of the other.'

Erle J with much force expressed the view that the jury had clearly found that A
had conspired with someone, that person being either Y or Z, and that it mattered
not, so far as A's offence was concerned, that they could not say whether it was with *d*
Y or with Z that A had conspired.

The matter came up for consideration in *R v Manning*[4], in which case a charge
of conspiracy against A and B was removed by certiorari and was tried on the civil
side at Winchester Assizes. The trial was before Lord Coleridge CJ and a special
jury. Lord Coleridge CJ directed the jury that they could find one prisoner guilty
and acquit the other. The jury convicted A but could not agree as to B. A was put *e*
under recognizance to surrender to receive judgment and the trial of B was postponed. A rule was obtained on the ground of misdirection. Though it was argued
that the application was premature because it might be that B would be convicted
when put on trial it was held that there had been misdirection and the rule was made
absolute for a new trial. In argument[5] on behalf of A reference was made to Chitty's
Treatise on the Criminal Law[6] where it was stated: *f*

> 'And it is holden, that if all the defendants mentioned in the indictment,
> except one, are acquitted, and it is not stated as a conspiracy with certain persons
> unknown, the conviction of the single defendant will be invalid, and no judgment
> can be passed upon him[7]. But one conspirator may be tried singly: as if the others
> had escaped or died before the time of trial, or the finding of the bill, he may *g*
> be rightly convicted alone[8].'

In giving the first judgment in the case Mathew J[9] expressed himself as satisfied
that there was 'an imperative rule of law' which should have prevented the giving
of a direction that it was possible on the joint trial to convict one and to acquit the
other. He further said[9]:   *h*

> 'The rule appears to be this. In a charge for conspiracy in a case like this where
> there are two defendants, the issue raised is whether or not both the men are

1 (1688) 3 Mod Rep 220
2 (1851) 16 QB 832
3 16 QB at 843
4 (1883) 12 QBD 241, [1881-85] All ER Rep 852
5 12 QBD at 242
6 2nd Edn (1826), vol III, p 1141
7 *Harison v Errington* (1627) Poph 202; *R v Scott and Hams* (1761) 3 Burr 1262; *R v Heaps* (1699) 2 Salk 593
8 *R v Kinnersley and Moore* (1719) 1 Stra 193; *R v Nichols* (1742) 13 East 412
9 12 QBD at 243, [1881-85] All ER Rep at 853

a guilty, and if the jury are not satisfied as to the guilt of either, then both must be acquitted.'

Though there is authority supporting the existence of a 'rule' to that effect the reasoning on which it was based calls for examination.

Lord Coleridge CJ with possibly some reluctance agreed that he had misdirected the jury though he said that having regard to the principles and practice that had
b obtained in the divorce court (see *Robinson v Robinson and Lane*[1]), it seemed sound to say that where there is a joint offence which has to be proved against each person separately the evidence which was sufficient to convict one person of the offence might not be sufficient to convict the other. However, he felt bound by what he understood to be 'the established rule of practice'.

In *R v Plummer*[2] there were three defendants in one arraignment. In regard to a
c count charging the three of them with conspiracy one pleaded guilty and was called as a witness against the other two. They were found not guilty. On a case being reserved by the chairman of quarter sessions for the opinion of the Court for the Consideration of Crown Cases Reserved it was held that the conviction of the one who had pleaded guilty should be quashed and that the judgment passed against him could not stand. Wright J regarded the case as intermediate between the case of a
d wholly joint trial and the case of separate trials of alleged co-conspirators. In learned judgments Wright and Bruce JJ based their decision partly on authority and partly on the ground that there ought not to be a conviction which would make the record inconsistent and contradictory and so bad on its face. Bruce J protested at the suggestion that a verdict of not guilty was not to be taken as establishing the innocence of the person acquitted on the ground that the verdict might have been arrived at
e simply in consequence of the absence of evidence to prove his guilt.

Dharmasena v The King[3] in the Privy Council calls for mention. D and S were tried together in Ceylon. One count in the indictment against them charged them both with conspiring to murder the husband of S. Another count charged D alone with murdering the husband of S. The jury convicted both on the first count and convicted D on the second. On appeal the conviction of S was set aside and a new trial in
f her case was ordered: the convictions of D on both counts were upheld. On the retrial of S she was acquitted. D appealed. In giving the reasons of the Board Lord Porter referred to the fact that one of two alleged conspirators had been found guilty by one jury and the other acquitted by another: that was felt to be 'an impossible result'. Lord Porter added[4]:

g 'It is well-established law that if two persons are accused of conspiracy and one is acquitted the other must also escape condemnation. Two at least are required to commit the crime of conspiracy; one alone cannot do so. In the present case the only conspirators suggested were the two accused persons, and there were no others, known or unknown, who might have participated in the crime. It is true that one conspirator may be tried and convicted in the absence of his companions in crime: *Reg v. Ahearne*[5], but where two have been tried together so that the
h only possible verdict is either that both are, or neither is, guilty, an order for the retrial of one makes it imperative that the other should also be retried. In their Lordships' opinion, therefore, if two persons are accused of a criminal conspiracy and convicted, and on appeal one can be, and is, sent for retrial, the other should be sent at the same time for retrial also on that charge so that both may be convicted or acquitted together. In the present case in as much as Mrs. Seneviratne

---

1   (1859) 1 Sw & Tr 362
2   [1902] 2 KB 339, [1900-3] All ER Rep 613
3   [1951] AC 1
4   [1951] AC at 6
5   (1852) 6 Cox CC 6

has been found not guilty of conspiracy, their Lordships think the proper course
is to treat her acquittal as a disposal of the charge of conspiracy and as involving   *a*
the acquittal of the appellant also on that charge.'

In the result D's appeal on the conspiracy count was allowed but his appeal against
his conviction for murder was dismissed.

Having referred to many of the relevant cases (and being relieved from referring to
them all by the thoroughness of the review of the cases in the judgment of the Court   *b*
of Appeal), I can now return to a closer examination of the problems which arise.
It seems to be clear that in its development during the period when it was by the
procedure in error that the validity of a conviction could be tested the law became
dominated by the consideration that an inconsistency on the record pointed to the
conclusion that a conviction was wrong. If, however, on a charge that A and B
conspired with each other there are separate trials it may well happen that the   *c*
available evidence at the trial of one of them is not the same as the available evidence
at the trial of the other. If A is first tried the jury cannot convict unless on the
evidence they are satisfied that he did conspire with B. That necessarily involves
that the jury are satisfied that B conspired with A. But that conclusion of the jury
for the purposes of that trial cannot affect B or be evidence against B if and when he
is later separately tried. If A had been fairly and properly tried with the result that *d*
on the evidence adduced he was properly convicted I see no reason why his conviction
should be invalidated if for any reason B on his subsequent trial is acquitted. The
reasons for the acquittal of B may have nothing to do with A. The circumstances
that B's acquittal will result from the absence of proof of the case against him does
not diminish the fact that he can fully assert that he has been cleared of the charge
against him.   *e*

As I have earlier indicated I think that it is very desirable, where there is a charge
of conspiracy against A and B, that they should be tried together. If however for
any reasons this cannot be, then if A pleads guilty or is found guilty I see no reason
why his conviction must be set aside if B on his later separate trial is acquitted.

Having regard to the state of the previous authorities, it would have been difficult
for the Court of Appeal to decide the question of law otherwise than as they did.   *f*
But for the reasons which I have given and departing from much of what was said
in such cases as R v Manning[1] and R v Plummer[2] and Dharmasena v The King[3] I consider that the conviction of the respondent Shannon was not invalidated by the
subsequent acquittal of Tracey.

If, as in Dharmasena's case[3], two people are tried together for conspiring with each
other and are convicted and if they can and do appeal and if for any reason a new   *g*
trial can be ordered I express no disagreement with the view expressed in Dharmasena's
case[3] that the order for a new trial should be of both.

If A is charged with conspiring with a named person who has died or who has not
been apprehended or cannot be found or if the charge is of conspiring with some
unknown person there is of course no reason why the trial of A should not proceed.

The difficult situation is that which arises where A and B, charged with conspiring   *h*
with each other, are tried together and where there is evidence which is admissible
against one but not against the other, or where the evidence against one seems
stronger than the evidence against the other. In that situation can one be convicted
and the other acquitted? If the only evidence on a joint trial is evidence which is
admissible against both and equally of force against both then clearly both could be
convicted or both acquitted but no other result could be valid.   *j*

If I am right in my view that, where there is a charge of conspiracy against A and B

---

1 (1883) 12 QBD 241, [1881-85] All ER Rep 852
2 [1902] 2 KB 339, [1900-3] All ER Rep 613
3 [1951] AC 1

a (the charge not alleging any conspiracy with anyone else) and where A is first separately tried and pleads or is found guilty and where B is later separately tried and acquitted, such acquittal does not of itself warrant setting aside the conviction of A—should the same reasoning which supports this view also lead to the conclusion that if A and B are tried together but if the evidence is strong against one but weak or lacking in the case of the other a permisssible result could be that one would be convicted and the other acquitted?

b Here the force in logic comes into collision with what Mathew J called 'an imperative rule of law' and with what Lord Coleridge CJ called an 'established rule of practice'. Though the 'rule', whether it be called a rule of law or of practice, came into existence with the historical background to which I have alluded, I think that the rule has much to commend it where it is related to a case where a jury has to consider (in the circumstances under consideration) whether to return similar verdicts

c in the cases of A and B or whether to return different verdicts. Though by a clear direction a jury could have explained to them the processes of thought that they should apply in their deliberations, any jury might feel embarrassed and might well be perplexed in sorting out the reasoning that would enable them to say that they were fully satisfied in A's case that A conspired with B (with its corollary that in A's case they were fully satisfied that B conspired with A) and yet also to say that in B's

d case they were not satisfied that B conspired with A. In the administration of the criminal law it is particularly desirable that complications and subtleties should if possible be avoided. A 'rule' which at least at first sight would appeal to many as having the backing of common sense ought not lightly to be jettisoned. I consider, therefore, that in the situation posed it would be wiser to adhere to the 'rule' and that summings-up should give effect to it.

e For the reasons which I have given I would allow the appeal, with the result that on the count in question the conviction of the respondent should be restored.

VISCOUNT DILHORNE. My Lords, on 22nd March 1973 the respondent and ten other persons appeared at the Crown Court at Warwick to answer an indictment containing 22 counts. Twenty of the counts charged theft or handling stolen

f goods, some of the defendants being charged with theft and the others with handling stolen goods. The respondent was charged in the 11th and 16th counts with handling stolen goods and in the 20th and 22nd counts with conspiracy. He pleaded guilty to the 11th and 16th counts, not guilty to the 20th count, and his plea on that was accepted by the prosecution, and guilty on the 22nd count which charged him and man named Tracey with conspiring to handle stolen goods.

g Tracey pleaded not guilty to this count and also not guilty to a count charging him with handling stolen goods. The jury at Warwick were unable to agree on their verdict on the charge of handling stolen goods, so his trial was adjourned to the Crown Court at Coventry. At that court on 4th April 1973 Tracey was found not guilty of handling stolen goods and the prosecution then offered no evidence against him on the conspiracy charge so a formal verdict of not guilty was entered on that

h count.
  The respondent appealed successfully to the Court of Appeal (Criminal Division) on the ground that Tracey, having been found not guilty of conspiring with him, his conviction and sentence following on his plea of guilty to conspiring with Tracey could not stand. That court granted leave to appeal to this House, certifying that the following question, namely:

j 'If two persons alone (that is to say with no other persons named or unnamed) are indicted for conspiracy together and the first pleads guilty but the second pleads not guilty and is subsequently tried and acquitted, must the conviction of the first fall upon his own confession thereupon be quashed?'

was of general public importance.

Counsel for the Crown submitted that the answer was No and he also submitted *a* that the Court of Appeal had not power to allow the respondent's appeal. I propose to consider this submission first.

The Court of Criminal Appeal was created by the Criminal Appeal Act 1907 with the powers specified in that Act. By s 4(1) of that Act it was provided that the court should allow the appeal if they thought that 'the verdict of the jury should be set aside on the ground that it is unreasonable or' could 'not be supported having regard *b* to the evidence' or that 'the judgment of the court before whom the appellant was convicted should be set aside on the ground of a wrong decision of any question of law' or that: 'on any ground there was a miscarriage of justice' and in every other case should dismiss the appeal.

In *R v Forde*[1] Avory J said:

c
'A plea of Guilty having been recorded, this Court can only entertain an appeal against conviction if it appears (1.) that the appellant did not appreciate the nature of the charge or did not intend to admit he was guilty of it, or (2.) that upon the admitted facts he could not in law have been convicted of the offence charged.'

d
In such circumstances the court presumably entertained the appeal on the ground that there had been a miscarriage of justice, for ordinarily no question of law arises for decision by the court of trial on a plea of guilty, though that can happen, as it did in *Director of Public Prosecutions v Doot*[2], where the pleas of guilty followed the judge's decision on a question of law.

Avory J, when he made these observations in *R v Forde*[1], cannot have had in mind *e* circumstances such as those in the present case. If the conviction of one conspirator could not in law stand if the only person or persons with whom he is charged is or are subsequently acquitted, there can be no doubt that the Court of Criminal Appeal had power to quash the conviction on the ground that there had been a miscarriage of justice.

In the light of the recommendations of the Interdepartmental Committee on the *f* Court of Criminal Appeal presided over by Lord Donovan, the jurisdiction of the Court of Criminal Appeal was transferred to the Court of Appeal by s 1(1) of the Criminal Appeal Act 1966. Section 1(8) repealed the Crown Cases Act 1848 but provided that that repeal should not affect the jurisdiction to order the issue of writs of venire de novo vested by s 2 of that Act and s 20(4) of the 1907 Act in the Court of Criminal Appeal and that: 'that jurisdiction is transferred with the other jurisdiction of the court to the Court of Appeal by subsection (1) of this section.' The other *g* jurisdiction transferred by sub-s (1) was the other jurisdiction of the Court of Criminal Appeal.

Section 4(1) of the Criminal Appeal Act 1966 replaced the provision that the court should allow the appeal if they thought that the verdict was unreasonable and could not be supported having regard to the evidence by the provision that they should do *h* so if under all the circumstances of the case the verdict was unsafe or unsatisfactory. It also repealed the power of the court to allow an appeal on the ground that there was a miscarriage of justice, and in place thereof provided that the court might allow the appeal on the ground that there was a material irregularity in the course of the trial. Why this change was made I do not know. By the first amendment above referred to it was clearly the intention of Parliament to enlarge the power of the *j* Court of Appeal to quash verdicts. It may have been thought that in view of this enlargement it was not necessary to retain the wide power of the Court of Criminal

1 [1923] 2 KB 400 at 403, [1923] All ER Rep 477 at 479
2 [1973] 1 All ER 940, [1973] AC 807

a Appeal to quash a conviction on the ground that there had been a miscarriage of justice. Whether or not this was the case, the power substituted, namely, to quash a conviction on the ground of a material irregularity in the course of a trial is a narrower power and the change was not one recommended by the Donovan Committee.

b Section 4(1) of the 1907 Act, as amended by the 1966 Act, is now replaced by s 2 of the Criminal Appeal Act 1968, a consolidation Act. It follows that the Court of Appeal in this case, the respondent having pleaded guilty, had only power to quash his conviction if either there had been a wrong decision on a question of law or a material irregularity in the course of the trial. It was not and could not have been suggested that there was a material irregularity in the course of the trial. The Court of Appeal thought they had power to quash on the ground that there had been a wrong decision on the question of law. They did not, however, say what that wrong decision was, and I must confess my inability to discern that the judge at the trial at Warwick in the proceedings on the conspiracy count made any decision on any question of law, and, if that be so, he could not have made a wrong decision. I, therefore, conclude that the Court of Appeal had no power to quash the conviction.

c I recognise that it cannot have been the intention of Parliament to narrow the powers of the Court of Appeal, but our task is to construe and give effect to the language of the enactment, and I cannot myself reach the conclusion that the meaning to be given to 'a material irregularity in the course of the trial' can be construed as the same as that of the words 'miscarriage of justice', though, of course, a material irregularity may lead to a miscarriage of justice. We are only entitled to infer what was the intention of Parliament from the language used in the enactment. It is, indeed, regrettable that this should be the consequence of the amendment made in 1966 and I hope that Parliament will put the matter right without delay.

e For there to be a conspiracy there must be an agreement between two or more persons and where two persons only are charged with conspiring together and are tried together, it has from the time of 14 Hen IV until the present day been held that they must either both be convicted or both acquitted. Where two are charged with conspiring together and tried together, the conviction of one will not be allowed to stand if the other is not found guilty. Where a number of persons are charged with conspiring together and with no one else, the conviction of one will be quashed, if none of the others charged are convicted (see *Marsh v Vauhan*[1]; *R v Grimes and Thompson*[2]; *R v Thompson*[3]; *R v Manning*[4]; *R v Plummer*[5]; *Dharmasena v The King*[6]; *R v Doyle*[7]; *R v Mandeville*[8]).

g This rule appears to have been based on the ground that the conviction of only one of two charged with conspiring together or of only one of a number of persons charged with conspiring together in the same indictment meant that there was a repugnancy on the record which could only be corrected by quashing the conviction. In olden days it was not possible to go behind the record and to examine whether the evidence justified a finding that one conspirator alone was guilty. Proceedings by way of writ of error were taken to correct the record. Since the Criminal Appeal Act 1907, which abolished proceedings by writ of error, it has been possible for the appellate court to examine and to consider the evidence against each conspirator tried. Under the Crown Cases Act 1848 a trial judge could reserve a question for the Court of Crown Cases Reserved and to state a case for that court but neither the

1 (1599) Cro Eliz 701
j 2 (1688) 3 Mod Rep 220
3 (1851) 16 QB 832
4 (1883) 12 QBD 241, [1881-85] All ER Rep 852
5 [1902] 2 KB 339, [1900-3] All ER Rep 613
6 [1951] AC 1
7 [1963] Crim LR 37
8 (1968) unreported

passage of that Act nor of the Criminal Appeal Act 1907 nor any subsequent Act
affected the application of the rule. At the same time it was recognised that if one
conspirator was tried alone and convicted, his conviction was not invalidated by the
possibility that his co-conspirator or co-conspirators might later be brought to trial
and acquitted (*Thody's Case*[1];   *R v Kinnersley and Moore*[2];   *R v Cooke*[3];   *R v Ahearne*[4]).

In *Robinson v Robinson*[5] an attempt was made to apply this rule to divorce cases
but the conclusion that if a charge of adultery against a co-respondent was dismissed
that against the respondent charging adultery with the co-respondent must also fail
was rejected and in *Rutherford v Richardson*[6] Lord Birkenhead said that the conclusion,
that the respondent might be found guilty of adultery with the co-respondent and
the co-respondent not found guilty of adultery with the respondent 'which has
sometimes been ignorantly derided' was 'both logical and defensible' for a court[7]—

'may quite reasonably conclude that it is proved that B. has committed
adultery with C., but not that C. has committed adultery with B. The law of
England does not technically recognize a verdict of "not proven," but substantially this is the nature of the verdict which in the circumstances supposed
exculpates C.'

It was with great reluctance that the court in *R v Manning*[7] decided that this logical
and defensible conclusion could not be reached in cases of conspiracy. In the course
of his judgment Lord Coleridge CJ said[8]:

'. . . in cases of an indictment for conspiracy, when two people are indicted
and are tried together (*because different considerations arise where people are not
tried together*), either both must be convicted or both must be acquitted.'

And in *Robinson v Robinson*[9] Cockburn CJ said that the court were 'of opinion that
a principle of so . . . technical a nature should be confined to the cases in the criminal
law to which it has hitherto been applied . . .'

In *R v Plummer*[10] Plummer had pleaded guilty to conspiracy. The two persons
with whom he was charged with conspiring were tried at the same quarter sessions
and acquitted. The chairman despite objection then sentenced Plummer. On
appeal his conviction was quashed, Wright J saying[11]:

'So far as we have been able to discover, there is no reported precedent which
on the facts is exactly in point . . . It is, however, not clearly settled whether
in such a case of separate trials a subsequent acquittal of the other would not
avoid the effect of the previous conviction of the appellant.'

He thought that as the appellant and his co-defendants were jointly indicted and
arraigned together there would have been one record, the trial should be regarded
as joint, and so the plea of guilty could not stand.

In the present case the respondent and Tracey were indicted and arraigned together
and although the respondent pleaded guilty and was sentenced at the Crown Court

1   (1674) 1 Vent 234
2   (1719) 1 Stra 193
3   (1826) 5 B & C 538
4   (1852) 6 Cox CC 6
5   (1859) 1 Sw & Tr 362
6   [1923] AC 1 at 6, [1922] All ER Rep 13 at 14, 15
7   (1883) 12 QBD 241, [1881-85] All ER Rep 852
8   12 QBD at 245, [1881-85] All ER Rep at 855
9   1 Sw & Tr at 393
10 [1902] 2 KB 339, [1900-3] All ER Rep 613
11 [1902] 2 KB at 343, 344, [1900-3] All ER Rep at 614, 615

a at Warwick on 22nd March 1973 and a verdict of not guilty entered in respect of Tracey at the Crown Court at Coventry on 4th April 1973, there was presumably only one record. As the plea of guilty and the recording of the verdict of not guilty did not take place at the same court on the same occasion, it can be said that the technical rule that where two are charged with conspiring together and are tried together both must be convicted or both acquitted does not apply, and so that it is

b not necessary, in order to decide this case, to decide whether or not the long-established rule applicable to joint trials no longer applies.

Where an accused person pleads guilty to a charge of conspiracy and it cannot be said that he has done so mistakenly, it cannot, in my view, be right that his conviction should be quashed if his co-conspirator or conspirators are tried subsequently—and it might be after the man who had pleaded guilty had served a sentence of imprison-

c ment—and he or they are found not guilty or on appeal have their convictions quashed. It may be that owing to lapse of time important witnesses may not have been available at the subsequent trial. It may be that owing to lapse of time their recollection of events has faded. While the non-availability of witnesses who were available at the first trial or the failure of witnesses to recollect events might account for the acquittal of the co-conspirator or conspirators, it is no ground for saying that the conviction of the man who pleaded guilty was wrong.

d The only case in which a contrary view has been expressed appears to be *Dharmasena v The King*[1] where the conviction of one of two persons tried together and found guilty was quashed on appeal and a new trial ordered. At the new trial he was acquitted and it was held that the conviction of the other conspirator must be quashed, Lord Porter saying that where two are charged with conspiracy it is an impossible result for one to be found guilty and the other acquitted. The rule

e applicable to joint trials was thus in this instance applied to separate trials.

In *R v Andrews Weatherfoil Ltd*[2] one of the accused, Sporle, was convicted of corruptly accepting emoluments. At a separate trial later a Mr T Dan Smith was acquitted of corruptly offering emoluments to the convicted man. Sporle appealed on the ground that in consequence of this acquittal his conviction was unsafe and

f unsatisfactory. Eveleigh J, delivering the judgment of the Court of Appeal, said[3]:

'As long as it is possible for persons concerned in a single offence to be tried separately, it is inevitable that the verdicts returned by the two juries will on occasion appear to be inconsistent with one another. Such a result may be due to differences in the evidence presented at the two trials or simply to the different views which the juries separately take of the witnesses. That the result produced

g by such inconsistency is "unsatisfactory" cannot be disputed but it is the unsatisfactory character of the guilty verdict to which s 13 [sic: ? s 2] of the Criminal Justice Act 1968 is directed, rather than an unsatisfactory result of the two trials as a whole. When inconsistent verdicts are returned by the same jury, the position is usually more simple. If the inconsistency shows that that single jury was confused, or self-contradictory, its conclusions are unsatisfactory or unsafe

h and neither verdict is reliable. Very often, however, an apparent inconsistency reflects no more than the jury's strict adherence to the judge's direction that they must consider each case separately and that evidence against one may not be admissible against the other; e g where there is a signed confession. So, too, where the verdicts are returned by different juries, the inconsistency does not, of itself, indicate that the jury which returned the verdict was confused or

j misled or reached an incorrect conclusion on the evidence before it. The verdict "not guilty" includes "not proven". We do not, therefore, accept the submission

---

1 [1951] AC 1
2 [1972] 1 All ER 65, [1972] 1 WLR 118
3 [1972] 1 All ER at 71, 72, [1972] 1 WLR at 125, 126

of counsel for the appellant Sporle that inconsistent verdicts from different *a* juries ipso facto render the guilty verdict unsafe. If, as usually will be the case, evidence at the two trials was significantly different this not only explains the different verdicts but also defeats the claim that inconsistency alone renders the guilty verdict unsafe.'

Sporle's appeal was consequently dismissed. It does not appear from the report of the case that any of the cases to which I have referred were cited. Both Sporle *b* and Smith were charged in the same indictment but were not jointly charged. This may account for the fact that, so far as one can determine from the judgment, no argument was advanced based on repugnancy on the record or by analogy with conspiracy. However this may be, the reasoning of the passage cited above is equally applicable to and equally compelling with regard to the separate trials of two persons charged with conspiring together. In *Dharmasena v The King*[1] no significance appears *c* to have been attached to the fact that the trials were separate, and it seems to have been assumed by Lord Porter that the ancient rule applicable in the case of joint trials also applied to separate trials. In my view, it is no more an impossible result where two are charged with conspiring together and tried separately that one should be found guilty and the other acquitted than where A is charged with corruptly offering emoluments and is acquitted after B has been convicted of corruptly receiv- *d* ing them. I do not think that where there are separate trials for conspiracy the decision in *Dharmasena v The King*[1] should be followed.

Where only the record could be looked at, it was no doubt right to give great weight to repugnancy but now since 1907 as the evidence can be examined and regard had to what actually took place at the trial, there seems no valid reason why such importance should be attached to the appearance of repugnancy on the record. *e*

So where conspirators are tried separately, it is, in my opinion, no ground for quashing the conviction of one of the two, whether following his plea of guilty or after verdict by a jury, that later his co-conspirator is acquitted or has his conviction quashed. Similarly, where a conspiracy is charged between a number of named persons and one pleads guilty or is found guilty, the fact that at a separate trial the others are acquitted is, in my opinion, no ground for quashing the conviction. *f*

Ordinarily where two persons are tried together when charged with conspiring together and with no one else and there is no material difference in the evidence admissible against each, the result will be that either both will be convicted or both acquitted. In such cases there is really no need for, and no need to question, the long-established rule.

In some cases, however, the weight of the evidence admissible against conspirator A *g* may be far greater than that admissible against conspirator B. A, for instance, may have made a statement admissible against him and not against B, which goes a long way to proving his guilt and B may have made no such statement. In every case, before a man charged with others is convicted, a judge must direct the jury to con- sider the evidence admissible against him separately for surely it is a fundamental principle of English law that no man is to be convicted save on proof of his guilt *h* beyond reasonable doubt by evidence admissible against him. I see no justification for any departure from this, I think, well-established practice in cases of conspiracy where only two are charged with that offence. It is adhered to where there are a greater number of conspirators and I think that it would be highly undesirable that a departure from it should be approved where two only are so charged.

If a jury are not satisfied of B's guilt but are satisfied of A's, has a judge to direct *j* them that even though satisfied of A's guilt, they must acquit him if they acquit B? It is said that a jury would not be able to understand a direction that they could find one conspirator guilty and also acquit the man with whom he is charged with conspiring. Whether or not that be so—and I doubt it—I do not think that a jury

---

1   [1951] AC 1

a would think the law was anything but a nonsense if after they have been told that they must consider the evidence against each of the accused separately, they must, even though satisfied of A's guilt, acquit him if they think that the evidence is insufficient to convict B.

If it were necessary in this case to decide whether or not the long established rule was now obsolete, it is these considerations which would incline me to holding that b it was, the foundation for it having gone and the court now being able to ascertain what happened at the trial. I feel, however, considerable reluctance to expressing a firm conclusion on a question that does not arise for decision in this case and on which anything that is said is clearly obiter. Here we have not to consider what is to happen at a joint trial of two conspirators charged with conspiring together and with no one else, and who have both pleaded not guilty. Here the plea of guilty by one was c followed days later by the acquittal at a separate trial of the other. There is no long line of authority deciding that in such cases the rule that both must be acquitted or both convicted should be applied. As Lord Coleridge CJ said in *R v Manning*[1] different considerations arise where people are not tried together.

Where two are arraigned together and one pleads guilty and the other not, their trials are from that moment separate and not joint. The trial of the one who pleaded d not guilty may follow immediately after the plea of guilty but that does not mean that they are jointly tried. It follows from what I have said, in my opinion, *R v Plummer*[2] was wrongly decided. It should have been held that there were separate trials and that the acquittal of those charged with Plummer should not have been held to invalidate his conviction on his plea of guilty.

In my opinion, this appeal should be allowed.

e

LORD SIMON OF GLAISDALE. My Lords, I would allow this appeal on two grounds: first ('substantive'), that the rule of law which the Court of Appeal felt bound to apply should be recognised as and declared to be of no subsisting validity; and, secondly ('procedural'), that, owing to an apparent slip in the drafting of the Criminal Appeal Act 1966, s 4(1) (now the Criminal Appeal Act 1968, s 2), the respon- f dent had no access to the Court of Appeal by way of appeal against his conviction. The facts which lie behind these two issues have been stated by my noble and learned friends who have preceded me; and I beg to take advantage of their narration. Moreover, I have had the advantage of reading their speeches in draft: and I agree with what they have said on the procedural issue. I venture, however, to add some words of my own on the substantive issue.

g The relevant law has been fully set out in the masterly judgment of the Court of Appeal and by my noble and learned friends; and I can, therefore, state summarily what it seems to me to establish. The essence of a conspiracy is an unlawful agree- ment. A must agree with B, and therefore B with A: A's agreement with B is mirrored by B's agreement with A. In consequence, it was held, if the record showed that A had been convicted of conspiracy with B, and B acquitted of conspiracy with A, the h record disclosed an inherent contradiction; and this could only be resolved by quash- ing A's conviction. It further followed that, if A and B were tried together, it was a misdirection to tell the jury that they should consider the evidence separately against each defendant, and could convict A and acquit B, or vice versa. A general rule of law developed that the acquittal of B on a charge of conspiracy with A involved automatically that A could not be convicted of conspiracy with B, and if so convicted j his conviction would be quashed. The rule was applied even though A's conviction was based on a plea of guilty. But if B were dead, or for any other reason could not be or had not been brought to trial, his presumption of innocence did not serve to

---

1   (1883) 12 QBD 241, [1881-85] All ER Rep 852
2   [1902] 2 KB 339, [1900-3] All ER Rep 613

exculpate A; for there was then no inconsistency on the face of the record, and the *a* court would not speculate that one might arise.

A comparable rule was applied to the offence of riot, and cross-analogies between riot and conspiracy were drawn in this regard. It takes at least three persons to constitute a riot. If, therefore, A, B and C were charged with rioting together, the acquittal of B or C precluded the conviction of A.

The foundations of this legal superstructure contained, however, a flaw. The law *b* in action is not concerned with absolute truth, but with proof before a fallible human tribunal to a requisite standard of probability in accordance with formal rules of evidence (in particular, rules relating to admissibility of evidence). No doubt, in the realm of the absolute, A could not conspire with B without B also conspiring with A. But it by no means follows that it cannot be proved forensically that A conspired with B (necessarily involving that it is also proved, as against A, that B conspired *c* with him) notwithstanding a total failure of forensic proof, as against B, that B conspired with A (necessarily involving a failure of proof, as against B, that A conspired with him). This flaw has, indeed, been recognised. The rules have been subjected to cogent criticism by eminent criminal lawyers—by C S Greaves (a 19th century editor of Russell on Crime), for example, and by Professor Glanville Williams and Professor J C Smith in our own days. The fallacious basis of the old rule was also *d* forcibly demonstrated in the judgment of the Supreme Court of Nebraska in *Platt v State*[1].

Then, adultery is an unlawful meeting of bodies as conspiracy is an unlawful meeting of minds. In the realm of the absolute A cannot commit adultery with B without B also committing adultery with A. But it may well be proved forensically that A committed adultery with B (necessarily involving that it is also proved, as against A, that B committed adultery with her), notwithstanding a total failure of *e* forensic proof, as against B, that B committed adultery with A (necessarily involving a failure of proof, as against B, that A committed adultery with him). So in *Robinson v Robinson and Lane*[2], the full Court of Divorce and Matrimonial Causes refused to extend the 'technical' rule of conspiracy to the strictly analogous case of adultery ('technical', in this sense, meaning a rule, based on a requirement of adjective law, which is recognised as juridically anomalous, but is nevertheless considered to be *f* binding). In *Rutherford v Richardson*[3] Viscount Birkenhead said:

> '. . . the Court may quite reasonably conclude that it is proved that B. has committed adultery with C., but not that C. has committed adultery with B. The law of England does not technically recognize a verdict of "not proven," but substantially this is the nature of the verdict which in the circumstances supposed *g* exculpates C.'

Viscount Birkenhead explained how verdicts of this sort, sometimes 'ignorantly derided' as inconsistent, are in fact 'both logical and defensible', being based on differential admissibility of evidence.

Again, in *R v Andrews Weatherfoil Ltd*[4], Sporle was charged with (inter alia) corruptly receiving a certain sum of money from Smith, and was convicted. Smith was charged *h* with corruptly offering that money to Sporle. These were 'mirror offences'; in an absolute sense Sporle could not be guilty and Smith innocent, or vice versa. Smith was granted a separate trial, and was later acquitted by a different jury. Sporle appealed. It was argued on his behalf that the two verdicts were inconsistent, and that in consequence Sporle's conviction was unsafe. The Court of Appeal dismissed the appeal. Eveleigh J, giving the judgment of the court, said[5]: *j*

---

1 (1943) 8 NW (2d) 849
2 (1859) 1 Sw & Tr 362 at 392, 393
3 [1923] AC 1 at 6, [1922] All ER Rep 13 at 15
4 [1972] 1 All ER 65, [1972] 1 WLR 118
5 [1972] 1 All ER at 71, 72, [1972] 1 WLR at 125, 126

a   'As long as it is possible for persons concerned in a single offence to be tried
separately, it is inevitable that the verdicts returned by the two juries will on
occasion appear to be inconsistent with one another. Such a result may be due to
differences in the evidence presented at the two trials or simply to the different
views which the juries separately take of the witnesses ... When inconsistent
verdicts are returned by the same jury, the position is usually more simple. If
b   the inconsistency shows that that single jury was confused, or self-contradictory,
its conclusions are unsatisfactory or unsafe and neither verdict is reliable. Very
often, however, an apparent inconsistency reflects no more than the jury's strict
adherence to the judge's direction that they must consider each case separately
and that evidence against one may not be admissible against the other; e g where
there is a signed confession. So, too, where the verdicts are returned by different
c   juries, the inconsistency does not, of itself, indicate that the jury which returned
the verdict was confused or misled or reached an incorrect conclusion on the
evidence before it. The verdict "not guilty" includes "not proven".'

I respectfully agree; and would merely emphasise the implication that the same
principles govern joint and separate trials, even though they may operate differently,
since discrepant verdicts from the same jury *may* indicate that it has fallen into
d   confusion. But 'guilty/not guilty' are not synonymous with 'guilty/innocent'; they
are no more than the mundane, forensic counterparts of those ethical absolutes.

However, the faulty foundation for the rule that B's acquittal of conspiracy with A
involves also the acquittal (or the quashing of the conviction) of A for conspiracy
with B was not glaringly obvious so long as the court could not consider the evidence
e   against A and B respectively. This was certainly the position of courts of review
until 1848, and possibly as late as 1907 (since case stated, made available by the Crown
Cases Act 1848, is at best an inapt instrument for review of evidence and summing-
up). Nor, even if the illogicality had been egregious, would it have constituted an
unsuperable objection. Logic must play an important part in every jurisprudence,
since it is the means by which the tribunal determines whether circumstances are so
f   similar that it would be inequitable to apply different rules. But English law has
not allowed logic to take command of a legal situation in such a way as to defeat
justice; and the rule your Lordships have been considering was probably for most of
our legal history the only way that justice could be done in the generality of cases.
In the majority of cases the evidence of conspiracy would have been the same against
both A and B; so that B's acquittal would raise serious doubt whether (as we would
put it today) A's conviction was unsafe or unsatisfactory or (to use the terminology
g   of the 1907 Act) there was a miscarriage of justice in A's conviction. Thus, even
though the rule that B's acquittal invalidated A's conviction was based on a foundation
juristically unsound, and therefore meant that, in the odd case, a conviction of A
which could not be faulted on the evidence would nevertheless be quashed, yet it
was the only means by which, in the generality of cases, doubts could be resolved
which B's acquittal had raised as to whether A had been properly convicted. The
h   quashing of A's conviction based on an inconsistency on the face of the record probably
did general justice, and for long was the only available way of doing so.

But the Criminal Appeal Act 1907 abolished the system of review by writ of error
(based on some fault apparent on the face of the record), and substituted a system
of review by way of examination of the evidence and of the summing-up. The court
of review was no longer confined to scrutiny of the formal record only or what it
j   could glean from the occasional case stated. Justice, therefore, no longer required
so clumsy and indiscriminate a rule as that B's acquittal involves automatically the
quashing of A's conviction. Today the Court of Appeal can unblinkeredly determine
whether B's acquittal in truth renders A's conviction unsafe or unsatisfactory, or
whether, on the other hand, the evidence of the same conspiracy was significantly
stronger as against A than as against B.

If, therefore, the maxim cessante ratione cessat ipsa lex expressed a legal principle   *a*
of comprehensive effect, the rule would be abrogated whereby B's acquittal
of the conspiracy involved automatically that A's conviction of it must be quashed.
With the rule as to the quashing of A's conviction would also go the concomitant
rule that at a joint trial the jury must not be told to consider the evidence against
each accused separately, but rather told to convict or acquit both. The maxim
cessante ratione cessat ipsa lex is not, however, a universal legal talisman. As Lord   *b*
Sumner said in *Admiralty Comrs v SS Amerika*[1]:

> ' . . . an established rule does not become questionable merely because
> different conjectural justifications of it have been offered, or because none is
> forthcoming that is not fanciful.'

A rule may have become so embedded in the law, so often acted on, as to have   *c*
acquired a validity independent of the reason which led to its original formulation.
It may well, too, have developed juridical adhesions, so that it cannot be modified
without dislocations elsewhere. In such circumstances any modification is better
left to other organs of the constitution than the law courts. When an executive
decision is taken, all foreseeable repercussions are carefully weighed—often a
decisive repercussion was never envisaged at all when the relevant proposal was   *d*
originally made. Of course, courts of law, too, weigh repercussions before formulating
or modifying a rule—much of legal argument is concerned precisely with this. But
it is only in the field of 'lawyers' law' that a court can feel anything approaching the
sort of confidence that, say, a Cabinet committee properly feels that all reactions to a
decision have been taken into account.

May I try to explain what I mean by adhesions, repercussions and reactions?   *e*
Maitland was wont to observe how rules of substantive law have seemed to grow
in the interstices of procedure. Not only can the substantive rule acquire a life of
its own, but the rebuilding of its roothold is apt to endanger that life. Again, what I
have called 'the procedural issue' in the instant case illustrates how unfortunate
consequence can ensue from what was proffered as beneficial reform. What Avory J
said in *R v Forde*[2] was in the context of the terminology of the 1907 Act. The amend-   *f*
ment of that terminology in 1966 cannot have been desired to preclude an appeal
by an appellant who has pleaded guilty without appreciating the nature of the charge
against him or without intending to admit that he was guilty of it; and yet, as my
noble and learned friends have shown, such is its plain effect. If an executive and
legislative reform can go awry in this way, how much more may judicial law-making,
without the benefit of official advice. Finally, by way of example, a few years ago   *g*
it was modish to scoff at a Division of the High Court with so heterogeneous a
jurisdiction as admiralty, probate and matrimonial causes; and such mockery proceeded in complacent ignorance of the sound reasons for grouping these jurisdictions
together in 1873 Nevertheless, those reasons had in time lost all cogency—just as
the conspiracy rule has by now lost its raison d'être. But when an attempt was made
to implement proposals for a more functionally rational structure of jurisdictions,   *h*
it was found that to sunder uncontentious probate business from interlocutory and
ancillary jurisdiction in matrimonial causes would involve quite unacceptable expense
and loss of expertise—so closely and economically had the two jurisdictions become
integrated over the years—and the extraordinary course had to be taken of transferring contentious probate jurisdiction to the Chancery Division, while leaving uncontentious business (the vast submerged mass of the iceberg) still part of the   *j*
responsibilities of the President of the Family Division (even though the extremely
important uncontentious probate business has no functional or logical relationship
with the jurisdiction of the Family Division). It is a characteristic of our way of life

---

1   [1917] AC 38 at 56, [1916-17] All ER Rep 177 at 187
2   [1923] 2 KB 400 at 403, 404, [1923] All ER Rep 477 at 479

a to make virtues of illogicalities: it is for this reason that rationalisation sometimes involves loss of virtue. But it is only within a limited sphere that courts of law are capable of the sort of realistic appraisal of consequences that is habitually made when an administrative decision is taken—the sort of appraisal which prevented the full implementation in 1970 of the reconstruction of the High Court that had been so confidently proposed in the name of reason and reform. The proposal for the reform of the jurisdiction of the High Court had been made by lawyers: yet even they had

b failed to appreciate the adverse repercussions which became apparent on a balanced and penetrating administrative scrutiny. It is essential that courts of law should recognise their limitations, and preserve a decent reticence when invited to undertake bold innovations in the law.

The instant seems to me very much a borderline case. The rule with which your Lordships are concerned is so deeply embedded as to have compelled the obviously

c reluctant adherence of the Court of Appeal. It has continued to be acted on after 1907 and was taken for granted by the Privy Council in *Dharmasena v The King*[1]. On the other hand, your Lordships are concerned here with 'lawyers' law'. The technical foundation of the rule is apparent, and so is the purpose which it served for so many years. But its irrationality and practical inexpediency are also apparent; and so is the fact that it is no longer needed to serve its former purpose. On the

d contrary, the present case illustrates its absurdity, inconvenience and injustice. The respondent pleaded guilty, fully understanding the situation and professionally advised. His conviction was not relevant to (and therefore not admissible evidence to prove) Tracey's guilt: why should Tracey's acquittal be relevant to the respondent's conviction? B's trial might take place years after A was convicted, and much of the evidence of the conspiracy might no longer be available. If B cannot be brought

e to trial he is presumed to be innocent, and yet A's conviction stands. A may have made a full written confession which is evidence against himself but not against B; and yet, according to the rule as heretofore applied, B's acquittal exculpates A too. Such absurdities bring the law into discredit, and mean that rogues escape society's sanctions. This is only to be borne if necessary to ensure that no one is unsafely or unsatisfactorily convicted; but the rule is no longer required for that purpose.

f In the instant case the respondent and Tracey were charged in the same indictment, so that there was an 'inconsistency on the face of the record' in the old technical sense. But the indictment against Tracey was afterwards redrawn for the convenience of the jury (though not severed in the technical sense), and there were separate trials. It would be enough to dispose of this appeal for your Lordships to declare that the old rule has no subsisting validity where an indictment is redrawn and/or

g where there are separate trials. This would accord with the judicial caution in modification of the prevailing law which I have suggested as desirable. It would also accord with the line that seems to have commended itself in *Platt v State*[2] (though the Supreme Court of Nebraska was not there in fact faced with 'inconsistent' verdicts in joint trials). But it would not be satisfactory. To declare that the old rule has no subsisting validity only where the indictment does not remain in its original form and/

h or where there are separate trials would be both illogical and practically inexpedient.

The objections to the old rule are equally valid whether or not the indictment remains in its original form and whether there are joint or separate trials. To affirm the old rule where there are joint trials would leave it in anomaly with the dicta in *Robinson v Robinson and Lane*[3] (which have been acted on without difficulty in matrimonial cases for over a century) and with the reasoning in *R v Andrews Weather-*

j *foil Ltd*[4] (which was plainly correct). But I am less concerned with the illogicality

---

1 [1951] AC 1
2 (1943) 8 NW (2d) 849
3 (1859) 1 Sw & Tr 362
4 [1972] 1 All ER 65, [1972] 1 WLR 118

of stopping short of declaring that the entire and integral body of rules has no subsisting validity, and with the consequent inconsistencies in our criminal law (though
its rules should, unless justice requires the tolerance of anomalies, desirably be
comprehensive and consistent), than with the fact that the illogicality is of the sort
which, through producing anomaly, produces injustice. Whether A's conviction
stands would depend on whether, fortuitously and irrelevantly, B can be brought to
trial at the same time as A. This would sometimes lie within the discretion of the
prosecution, and it is contrary to constitutional propriety that a person's guilt should
be at the choice of the Crown (see *Federal Steam Navigation Co Ltd v Department of
Trade and Industry*[1]).

As for the practical disadvantages of affirming, where there are joint trials, the
old, irrational and anachronistic rule, in the majority of joint trials for conspiracy
the evidence will be substantially the same against both accused. The judge must
of course, as in all joint trials, tell the jury that they should consider the evidence
separately against each accused—that 'this means that you must consider first and
separately the evidence against A, and then and separately the evidence against B.
But in this case there is not sufficient difference in the evidence as against A and B
respectively for you to find one guilty and the other not guilty. Unless, therefore,
after separate consideration, you are sure that *both* A *and* B are guilty, you should
acquit both A and B. However, if you are sure that the prosecution has proved that
A and B each is guilty, you will, of course, return a verdict of guilty against them
both'. In other words, the practice in such a situation will be as heretofore; but it
will be founded on common sense and general principle, and no longer on a
technicality.

But in the case where there is a significant difference in the evidence as against
A and B—which will generally be a case where A has made a confession which is
not admissible evidence against B—the judge will again tell the jury that they must
consider first and separately the evidence against A, and then and separately the
evidence against B. In his review of the evidence against each he will, in the usual
way, emphasise that the confession (or other significantly different evidence) is
evidence against A only, and that the jury must put it out of their minds when
considering the case against B. He will conclude by telling the jury that, in view of
the difference in the evidence against each (if they accept it), it is open to them to
convict A and acquit B. All this follows the normal practice in a joint trial where
the evidence against one accused is significantly different from that against a co-
accused. I can see no reason why there should be any different sort of direction in
a joint trial for conspiracy. On the contrary, it seems to me most undesirable that
the jury should either have to shut its eyes to part of the evidence or to run the risk
of convicting B on evidence which is not admissible against him. It seems to me
almost equally undesirable, and inherently likely to confuse a jury, for them to be
told to consider the evidence separately as against A and B (having such evidence
summarised to them), and then in effect to be told that, even though the evidence
admissible against A leaves them sure of his guilt, they should nevertheless acquit
A if the different evidence against B, considered separately, leaves them less than
sure of B's guilt.

Again, *R v Thompson*[2] provides a useful touchstone. A, B, and C were charged
with a conspiracy together and with others unknown which involved A in having
obtained the use of a key of which both B and C had duplicates. The jury convicted
A, saying that he was guilty of conspiracy with either B or C but they did not know
which. The judge directed a verdict of not guilty in favour of B and C, but guilty in the
case of A. A's conviction was, however, quashed. This was, no doubt, correct as the
law stood at that time; but it was based on the technicality of an inconsistency on

1   [1974] 2 All ER 97, [1974] 1 WLR 505
2   (1851) 16 QB 832

a the face of the record; and it seems to me to be quite absurd that it should be approved as representing subsisting law.

Then, take another case of a joint trial for conspiracy. A, after being put in charge of the jury, changes his plea to guilty (say, at the end of the prosecutor's opening speech). He then gives evidence for the Crown against B. The judge gives the proper direction as to the desirability of the jury finding corroboration of A's evidence. The *b* jury acquits B. This in itself implies no doubt as to A's guilt: it merely means (faithfully following the judge's warning) that they think a self-confessed criminal provides an unsafe foundation for the conviction of an accused in whose favour there is a strong presumption of innocence. Or it may be—who is to know?—that they are not convinced of evidence which, if accepted, was capable of being corroborated. There would be something seriously wrong with a rule that, in such circumstances, A's conviction must be quashed or a verdict of not guilty directed.

c Finally, consider the analogous rule in riot as applied to a joint trial. A, B and C are jointly indicted for riot. The jury, convinced that A took part in the riot, find him guilty; but, not being sure that B and C have been correctly identified as his fellow-rioters, acquit them. It affronts common sense and justice that a verdict of not guilty must therefore be entered in respect of A.

d I would therefore be in favour of a declaration that the whole body of rules whereby the acquittal of B of conspiracy with A must of itself be held to be inconsistent with A's conviction of conspiracy with B has no subsisting validity.

I venture to add a word on forensic technique. At the conclusion of their respective arguments leading counsel for the appellant and the respondent handed in written summaries of the submissions. This was of great assistance and convenience— particularly as there were no formal cases on each side—and is a practice which, in *e* my view, might well be followed generally.

LORD SALMON. My Lords, the respondent, together with a number of other defendants, was charged on 22nd March 1973 on an indictment containing 22 counts. *f* This appeal is concerned only with the last count charging the respondent and a man called Tracey with conspiring with each other (and no one else) to handle stolen goods. The respondent, who was advised by solicitor and counsel, pleaded guilty to this count and to a number of others concerned with handling stolen goods. There is no suggestion that he did not understand what he was doing when he confessed his guilt by pleading guilty. A plea of guilt is equivalent to a conviction: *R v Verney*[1]. The respondent was sentenced to four years imprisonment on count *g* 22 to run concurrently with concurrent sentences of three years imprisonment which he received on each of the other counts to which he had pleaded guilty.

Tracey pleaded not guilty to handling stolen goods and not guilty to conspiracy under count 22. After a jury had disagreed on 27th March Tracey was retried and on 4th April was found not guilty of the substantive offences. The Crown then offered no evidence in respect of the conspiracy charge under count 22. The recorder entered *h* a formal verdict of not guilty on that count.

The respondent appealed on the ground that his conviction on the conspiracy count, following on his plea of guilty, must be quashed owing to Tracey's subsequent acquittal on that count. The Court of Appeal reluctantly came to the conclusion that a stream of authority stretching back for some 300 years compelled them to allow the appeal.

j The judgment of the Court of Appeal delivered by Roskill LJ contains a masterly analysis, which I adopt and will not repeat, of all the relevant authorities. I agree with Roskill LJ that having regard to this long line of authority, it was virtually impossible for the Court of Appeal to do other than quash the conviction. This

---

1   (1909) 2 Cr App Rep 107

is the first occasion, however, on which the point has ever come before your Lordships' House for consideration. I agree with the Court of Appeal that nothing said in this House in *O'Connell v R*[1] even remotely touches this point. Your Lordships are, therefore, free to redirect the common law on to its true course if your Lordships are convinced that in the past it has diverged from it.

By the beginning of the 19th century it was accepted by the courts as a firmly established legal principle that where A and B are indicted together for conspiring with each other and no one else, then, whether they are tried together or separately, the conviction of one cannot stand if the other is acquitted (*R v Grimes and Thompson*[2]; *R v Nichols*[3]; *R v Cooke*[4]). The root of a conspiracy is an agreement between two or more persons to do an unlawful act or a lawful act by unlawful means. No man can conspire with himself. Accordingly, if in the case postulated, nothing is known save that A has been convicted and B acquitted, the result would appear to be inconsistent with and repugnant to justice. And so, sometimes, it may be even when all the true facts are known.

In the early days when there was no appeal in criminal cases, the sole method of challenging a conviction was by writ of error, which gave the courts power to intervene only if there was some apparent inconsistency or repugnancy on the face of the record. The courts could not look at the evidence, nor the summing-up: all that they could look at was the record. It was for this reason that the rule was established from very early times that, if the record disclosed an apparent inconsistency or repugnancy on its face, the court must intervene and quash the conviction. This rule, no doubt, had much to commend it when the court could look only at the record to discover whether any injustice had been done. The rule, which involved a strictly technical approach to the record, offered, in early times, the only means by which the injustice of a seemingly wrongful conviction could be remedied. This rule became so firmly established that even after all reason for its existence had long since disappeared, it continued to survive. Even after a case could be stated for the opinion of the court, and still later, after the Court of Criminal Appeal was set up and invested with its very wide powers and writs of error were abolished, the continued existence of the rule was assumed and has been accepted by our courts, without question, ever since. This appeal turns on whether this acceptance of the rule was justifiable.

My Lords, for my part, I am convinced, that although there was originally a sound reason for the existence of the rule, it had probably disappeared by the middle of the last century and certainly by 1907, when any convicted person was given an absolute right of appeal on any question of law and, by leave of the court, or on the certificate of the trial judge, a right of appeal on any question of fact or mixed fact and law or on any other ground which appeared to the court to be a sufficient ground of appeal.

The old rule undoubtedly lead to anomalies and absurdities, some of which were commented on by C S Greaves as long ago as 1865 and all by Professor J C Smith very recently. The old rule was, however, better than nothing; and for many hundreds of years there was nothing else on which anyone could rely for relief against a wrongful conviction. Today, things are, and have for a very long time, been very different. The courts are no longer obliged to approach a conviction in blinkers with their eyes directed to nothing but the record. The old Court of Criminal Appeal had, and the present Court of Appeal (Criminal Division) has, the most ample powers thoroughly to investigate the trial and to correct injustice without resorting to arid technicalities. It seems to me that the old rule has long

---

1   (1844) 11 Cl & Fin 155
2   (1688) 3 Mod Rep 220
3   (1742) 13 East 412
4   (1826) 5 B & C 538

a since outlived its usefulness and should now be swept away, together with the anomalies and absurdities from which it is inseparable. I will give but two examples. A and B are indicted together for conspiring with each other and with no one else. B disappears. A, having received the best legal advice and understanding all the facts, pleads guilty, or A is convicted by the jury on overwhelming evidence, and properly sentenced to a long term of imprisonment. Later, perhaps years later, B is caught

b and brought to trial. By then, most of the evidence which had been available against A is no longer available against B, who accordingly is acquitted. It is surely absurd that in such circumstances, A's conviction should automatically become bad in law and that he should accordingly be entitled to have it quashed. Suppose the same facts, save that B disappears before A is caught and indicted and A is accordingly indicted alone for conspiring with B. When B is caught, he is necessarily indicted

c separately. His acquittal would not then affect A's conviction because the rule depends on A and B being indicted together. Under the rule it was the record, i e the one indictment and the entries on it (whenever made), which had to be consistent in order for A's conviction to stand. This technicality which depends on the mere chance of whether or not A and B are indicted together, surely piles absurdity on absurdity. The rule was, no doubt, acceptable when the writ of error afforded a

d wrongly convicted man his only remedy. That writ was however, abolished, because its preservation was no longer necessary. Indeed, long before it died it had become moribund. The rule which drew its life's breath from the writ naturally expired with it. It was, however, perhaps impossible for the courts to notice its demise until this House pronounced it to be dead. My Lords, I suggest that this pronouncement should now be made.

e It follows that, in my view, *R v Plummer*[1] should be overruled and many of the dicta in *R v Rowley*[2], *Dharmasena v The King*[3] and *R v Doyle*[4] can longer be accepted.

In the case which I have postulated, B's acquittal will no longer, of itself, give A the right in law to have his own conviction quashed. A should however (subject to a procedural point to which I shall presently refer) be able to seek leave to appeal against his conviction on the ground that B's acquittal makes A's conviction unsafe

f or unsatisfactory. Whether or not A would succeed would depend not on technicalities but on all the relevant facts and circumstances which the Court of Appeal would be in a position fully to investigate.

Interesting questions have been debated before your Lordships as to the true effect of an acquittal. An accused is entitled to be acquitted unless the evidence satisfies the jury beyond reasonable doubt that he is guilty. A verdict of not guilty may mean that the jury is certain that the accused is innocent, or it may mean that,

g although the evidence arouses considerable suspicion, it is insufficient to convince the jury of the accused's guilt beyond reasonable doubt. The verdict of not guilty is consistent with the jury having taken either view. The only effect of an acquittal, in law, is that the accused can never again be brought before a criminal court and tried for the same offence. So far as the Crown is concerned, the accused is deemed, in law, to be innocent. His acquittal cannot, however, affect anyone but himself

h and indeed would not be admissible in evidence on behalf of or against anyone else. Anyone acquitted of a criminal conspiracy may still be sued in damages for the conspiracy of which he has been acquitted at his trial.

If A and B are tried together for conspiring with each other and with no one else, the judge should nevertheless, in all save the most exceptional cases, continue to

j direct the jury that they should convict or acquit both, that is to say, they cannot convict the one and acquit the other. This may not accord with strict logic. The

---

1   [1902] 2 KB 339, [1900-3] All ER Rep 613
2   [1948] 1 All ER 570
3   [1951] AC 1
4   [1963] Crim LR 37

law does not, however, rest wholly on logic but more on experience and common *a* sense. Theoretically it is, no doubt, possible that the evidence in respect of A might be so different from the evidence affecting B that a verdict against A of conspiring with B might be justified whilst a verdict against B of conspiring with A would not be justified. In practice, however, this does not happen save in the rarest of cases. Accordingly when A and B are charged with conspiring with each other and no one else it would, as a general rule, be highly undesirable for the trial judge to recite *b* the usual formula about the jury's duty of considering the evidence against each of the accused separately. In such a case it would be particularly difficult for a jury to perform this intellectual feat. Even if there were a confession by A and only slight evidence against B, I doubt whether, whatever the judge might tell them, the jury would convict A and acquit B. They would still convict or acquit both. In such a case, however, it would be the duty of the judge to direct the jury that A's *c* confession was no evidence at all against B.

The only other kind of case I can imagine in which the evidence against the alleged conspirators might differ in any important particular, is where, for example, A, B and C are charged with conspiring to rob a bank. There might be a great deal of evidence that three men had been observed doing acts which were consistent only with a conspiracy to rob the bank. There might be very strong evidence identifying *d* A as one of the men, but comparatively weak evidence identifying the others. If all three were indicted and tried together for conspiring with each other and no one else it would obviously be impossible to convict A if B and C were acquitted. If, however, they were charged with conspiring with each other and with persons unknown, A could, in my view, properly be convicted although the others were acquitted. Although it is unnecessary to express any concluded opinion on the point, *e* I incline to the view that even in 1851 when it was delivered the majority judgment of the court in *R v Thompson*[1] was wrong and that the dissenting judgment of Erle J is to be preferred.

My Lords, I must now deal briefly with the procedural point to which I earlier referred. There is a lacuna in the Criminal Appeal Act 1968, which apparently has gone unnoticed until the hearing of this appeal. Section 2(1) of the Act lays down *f* when appeals against conviction shall be allowed and reads as follows:

> 'Except as provided by this Act, the Court of Appeal shall allow an appeal against conviction if they think—(a) that the verdict of the jury should be set aside on the ground that under all the circumstances of the case it is unsafe or unsatisfactory; or (b) that the judgment of the court of trial should be set aside on the ground of a wrong decision of any question of law; or (c) that there was *g* a material irregularity in the course of the trial, and in any other case shall dismiss the appeal . . .'

The 1968 Act was, I think, intended to extend the powers conferred by the Criminal Appeal Act 1907. It was certainly not intended to diminish them. Section 4(1) of the 1907 Act, amongst other things required the Court of Criminal Appeal to allow *h* an appeal (subject to the proviso) if they thought 'that on any ground there was a miscarriage of justice'. Under that provision the court had ample power to allow an appeal against a conviction following on a plea of guilty if the plea had been made (1) without the accused understanding what he was doing or (2) prior to some subsequent event such as an acquittal of a co-conspirator. Such cases are not covered by para (a) of s 2(1) of the 1968 Act which applies only to the verdict of a jury, nor *j* by para (b) of that subsection which is wide enough to cover cases in which the accused has pleaded guilty but only if the count to which he has pleaded discloses no offence known to the law (see e g *Director of Public Prosecutions v Schildkamp*[2])

---

1 (1851) 16 QB 832
2 [1969] 3 All ER 1640, [1971] AC 1

a
nor by para (c) of that subsection which, I think, refers only to procedural irregularities. For many years prior to 1968, it was the law that an accused might have a
conviction following on a plea of guilty quashed and a new trial ordered if he could
establish that he had pleaded guilty without understanding the nature of the charge
or intending to admit that he was guilty of what he had done (R v Forde[1]). In my view
an accused should certainly still have this right. Although a conspirator who has
pleaded guilty no longer has the right to have his conviction quashed if his sole co-
b
conspirator is found not guilty, he should still, in my view, have the right to apply
for leave to appeal on the ground that his conviction, in all the circumstances, constituted a miscarriage of justice or was unsafe or unsatisfactory. It seems to me,
therefore, that the 1968 Act should be amended to preserve these rights. This could
be accomplished by a short amendment of the Act, e g by substituting the words
'the conviction' for the words 'the verdict of the jury' in para (a) of s 2(1) of the 1968
c
Act. In the present case, however, there are no grounds for supposing that the accused
did not fully understand what he was doing when he pleaded guilty nor that his
conviction was unsafe or unsatisfactory.

My Lords, for the reasons I have indicated, I would allow the appeal and restore
the conviction.

d
Appeal allowed.

Solicitors: *Director of Public Prosecutions; Bosworth, Bailey, Cox & Co*, Birmingham
(for the respondent).

e
Christine Ivamy Barrister.

---

1 [1923] 2 KB 400, [1923] All ER Rep 477

R v Denbigh Justices, ex parte Williams   a
R v Denbigh Justices, ex parte Evans

QUEEN'S BENCH DIVISION
LORD WIDGERY CJ, ASHWORTH AND BRISTOW JJ
30th APRIL, 1st MAY 1974

b

Magistrates – Court – Open court – Petty sessional or occasional court-house – Requirement that sitting be in open court – Accused arriving at court-house with over 20 supporters – Only seats for five members of the public in courtroom – Five supporters occupying the five seats – Five supporters interrupting proceedings shortly after start of hearing – Five having to leave courtroom as a result – Five seats remaining empty for rest of hearing – Member of press present during hearing – Whether hearing in 'open court' – Magistrates' Courts Act c *1952, s 98(4).*

The two applicants refused, for political reasons, to provide themselves with television licences. They were charged with unlawfully using a television set without a licence, contrary to s 1 of the Wireless Telegraphy Act 1949. When they arrived at the magistrates' court for the hearing, they were accompanied by 20 to 30 friends or d supporters. The courtroom allocated for the hearing was a small one and once the accommodation for the press, the parties and their advocates had been taken, there were only five seats available for members of the public. The justices gave each of the applicants the opportunity, which each accepted, of nominating two or three of his friends to occupy those five seats. The remainder of their supporters had to stay outside the courtroom. Shortly after the start of the hearing the five e spectators in the courtroom interrupted the proceedings and they then left the court-room, either voluntarily or by direction of the court. Their five seats remained empty for the rest of the hearing. The applicants were convicted and fined. An accurate report of the proceedings, prepared by the representative of the press who was present at the hearing, appeared in the local paper the following day. Each appli-cant moved for an order of certiorari to bring up and quash the decision of the justices f on the ground that there had been a breach of s 98(4)ᵃ of the Magistrates' Courts Act 1952 in that the hearing had not been in 'open court'.

Held – The applications would be refused for a presiding judge or magistrate, in performing his obligation to see that members of the public who wished to be present at the proceeedings to be held in open court were admitted, had to have due regard g to the facilities that were available, to the possibility of disorder, to the danger from fire risks in an overcrowded courtroom and to the problem of security, etc. In the circumstances, the justices had acted reasonably and in accordance with their duty in deciding to admit only five spectators to fill the available seats and it had not been established that, once the five had left, any member of the public who wished to be present had been refused admission (see p 1055 h and j, p 1056 c and f to j and p 1057 h *e g* and *h*, post).
Daubney v Cooper (1829) 10 B & C 237 applied.
Per Curiam. The fact that the press are present does not conclusively show that proceedings are in open court but, conversely, it would be difficult to hold that a case was held publicly if the press were actively excluded (see p 1056 *d* and *e* and p 1057 *g*, post).   j

Notes
For the requirement to hear cases in open court, see 25 Halsbury's Laws (3rd Edn) 163, para 296.

---

a Section 98(4), so far as material, provides: '. . . where a magistrates' court is required by this section to sit in a petty sessional or occasional court-house, it shall sit in open court.'

a For the Wireless Telegraphy Act 1949, s 1, see 35 Halsbury's Statutes (3rd Edn) 94.
For the Magistrates' Courts Act 1952, s 98, see 21 Halsbury's Statutes (3rd Edn) 268.

Cases referred to in judgment
Daubney v Cooper (1829) 10 B & C 237, 5 Man & Ry KB 314, 3 Man & Ry MC 23, 8
LJOSKB 21, 109 ER 438, 33 Digest (Repl) 215, *509*.
b *People v Hartman* (1894) 37 Pac 153.

Cases also cited
Hawksley v Fewtrell [1953] 2 All ER 1486, [1954] 1 QB 228, CA.
Kenyon v Eastwood (1888) 57 LJQB 455.
McPherson v McPherson [1936] AC 177, PC.
R v Governor of Lewes Prison, ex parte Doyle [1917] 2 KB 254.
c

Motions for certiorari
David Charles Williams and Robert John Evans each applied to the Divisional Court
of the Queen's Bench Division for an order of certiorari to remove into the court
and quash an order made in respect of each of the applicants by the Denbigh justices,
sitting as a magistrates' court for the petty sessional division of Uwchdulas and
d Uwchaled at Llanrwst, on 15th January 1973, whereby each applicant was convicted of unlawfully using a television set without a licence, contrary to s 1 of the
Wireless Telegraphy Act 1949, and fined £15. The facts are set out in the judgment
of Lord Widgery CJ.

John Blofeld for the applicants.
e *Gordon Slynn* for the respondents.

LORD WIDGERY CJ. These two applications arise out of the same facts, and with
one exception are subject to exactly the same considerations; accordingly, by consent
of the parties the two applications have been heard together, and I can confine myself
in the main to the case of Mr Evans.
f Each applicant moves through counsel for an order of certiorari to remove into this
court with a view to its being quashed two decisions of justices sitting at Llanrwst
on 15th January 1973, where in each case it was adjudged that the applicant should
pay a fine of £15 and £5 costs in respect of a conviction by the court for unlawfully
using an apparatus for wireless telegraphy, to wit a television set, without a licence,
contrary to s 1 of the Wireless Telegraphy Act 1949—in brief they were convicted of
g having television sets without a licence.
The reasons why the two applicants had not provided themselves with television
licences were political ones; they were both members of the Welsh Language Society,
and indeed there had been previous proceedings of a similar character in 1972 when
each of these applicants had been summoned for having a television set without a
licence and where similar convictions had been recorded. The earlier proceedings
h are only of brief relevance, but they should be mentioned to this extent.
Prior to the hearing in 1972 the applicants had requested the court that the
hearing should be a hearing in the Welsh language, and the court had assented to
that and a hearing in the Welsh language had in fact taken place. On that occasion
in 1972 the applicants had attended with a substantial number of friends or supporters,
and at the end of the case there had been a disturbance—we are not told the details
j and I am anxious not to be unfair to the applicants by overstating it, but there had
been some kind of disturbance on the part of those attending in support of the
applicants. This undoubtedly had some influence on the Bench, because in 1973
with these two further prosecutions in prospect, when the applicants again requested
in writing that there should be a trial in the Welsh language, the justices declined
and said they were going to conduct the proceedings in a perfectly ordinary fashion.

On the day in question, 15th January 1973, there were two magistrates' courts sitting *a*
at Llanrwst. Apparently in a modern purpose-built building in that town there is
accommodation for two courts. Court 1 I understand to be a magistrates' court of
normal size and with normal fittings and equipment, and court 2 is a very much
smaller court designed primarily for the juvenile court, because in modern times,
as everybody has accepted, juveniles should be tried in rather less formal surroundings
than the normal formal court. So court 2 at Llanrwst was designed as a juvenile *b*
court; it was very small, but it was used from time to time when the first court was
occupied, and on this day the list of cases for hearing provided that the two applicants'
cases should be heard in court 2 in company with other cases concerned with the
absence of television licences, minor speeding offences and the like—just the sort
of case one should say one would expect to be sent to the smaller court in the situation
which presented itself here.
   When the applicants arrived for the hearing, they were accompanied by some 20 *c*
or 30 friends or supporters, and they moved down the corridor to the entrance of
court 2; it was obvious at once that they would not all be able to get in. The size of
court 2 is best exemplified by the fact that when accommodation is provided for the
press, the parties and advocates there is only accommodation for five members of
the public, and that was the situation that morning.
   It seems clear to me, although there are many instances when one cannot achieve *d*
certainty as to the facts, that in one instance, if not more, one of the police officers
who was on duty in court 2 told one of the applicants or one of the supporters that
no one was to be allowed in except the parties to the proceedings themselves.
   In fact that did not happen, because the prosecuting solicitor, and if I may say so
all credit to him, realising that the five seats for the public were unoccupied, and *e*
realising that there were 20 or 30 people outside who wanted to come in, stood up
and raised the point with the Bench, and the chairman of the justices at once responded
by saying: 'Very well, the five seats can be filled.' Each of the two applicants was
given the opportunity, which he accepted, of nominating two or three of his friends
to come and fill these five seats. Accordingly, when the case against Mr Evans was
called on, the public seats were filled; there was also a representative of the press, *f*
who produced an accurate and really entirely excellent report of the affair in the
local paper next morning, and there were these five members of the public in the
public parts.
   As soon as Mr Evans's case was called on, he again asked for a trial in the Welsh
language. He was refused. In the course of the discussion arising out of that point,
two of the five members of the public who had come in on the nomination of Mr
Evans made some kind of interruption, and by direction of the chairman of the *g*
Bench left the court. So now we have three members of the public in the five seats,
two seats unoccupied.
   Mr Evans, having failed to persuade the court that the trial should be in the Welsh
language, then left the court and the remainder of the proceedings against him were
conducted in his absence, and the conviction and fine to which I have referred were *h*
arrived at and imposed respectively.
   Then it came to Mr Williams's turn. When Mr Williams's case was called on a
very similar passage took place. He also requested a trial in the Welsh language;
he was refused; at least one of the three remaining occupants of the five public seats
addressed the court and there was some interruption or intervention and she was
invited to leave. In fact all five of the original spectators had left, either of their own *j*
volition or by direction of the court within really a few moments of the hearing
beginning and before the completion of the case against Mr Williams. In Mr
Williams's case, as in the case of Mr Evans, he having left the court, the adjudication
took place in his absence, and he was convicted and fined.
   Just what was happening outside the court door at this time is not altogether clear
on the affidavits. There were, as I have said, a large number of people present.

There was a certain amount of noise generated by the presence of these people, and
a the police officers, sensibly enough, shut the court door, so at one time the door was
closed. Considerable controversy has been raised whether, when the five seats began
to become vacant, an opportunity was or was not given to the other supporters of
the applicants outside the court to come in and occupy them. The affidavit of the
police officer is to the effect that no one sought to replace the original five. His
version of the matter is that as the applicants and their supporters began to come
b out of the courtroom, those outside clustered around them to ask what had happened,
and showed no desire themselves to go in and occupy the five seats.

On the other hand, there is evidence filed by the applicants to the effect that one
or more of their supporters outside, observing that space must now be available
within the courtroom, had asked to be admitted and had been refused.

Those, as far as I can detect them with any accuracy from the affidavits before us,
c are the basic facts of this case. The applications for certiorari are supported by the
following reasons: first, that the case was heard and determined in circumstances
that the general public were excluded or severely limited in the numbers allowed to
attend thereby resulting in justice not being seen to be done and contrary to natural
justice; secondly, that the court did not sit in open court, contrary to s 98(4) of the
Magistrates' Courts Act 1952. We have had no argument on the first of those grounds,
d and I say no more about it other than to observe that it is conceded by counsel that
there is no case in the books in which it has been said to be a breach of the rules of
natural justice to exclude members of the public from the courtroom. The point
is not important in the present case because the substance of the applicants' complaint
can be fully raised and dealt with on the second ground, it being perfectly clear that
the statute requires these proceedings to be in open court, and thus as a matter of
e law it is open to the applicants to argue that the statute was breached because the
hearing was not in open court.

I am not going to take time in reciting again the importance which English law
has always attached to justice being administered in public. The authorities are
strong, compelling and well known, and nothing I say today is to be taken in any
sense as indicating a whittling down of the importance which the courts attach to
f that absolutely fundamental principle of the administration of justice in this country.

But although it is easy enough to say that a hearing must be in open court, and
although the conception of an open court as opposed to one which is in camera is
easy enough to understand, it is not altogether easy to define in terms the characteristics which make a court open, as opposed to one which is conducted in private.
I get assistance from two authorities to which counsel for the respondents has referred,
g giving some observations on this question. The first is *Daubney v Cooper*[1]. It is unnecessary to deal with the circumstances of the particular case, but Bayley J, dealing with
the question which is before us, said[2]:

h   '. . . we are all of opinion, that it is one of the essential qualities of a Court of
      Justice that its proceedings should be in public, and that all the parties who
      may be desirous of hearing what is going on, if there be room in the place for the
      purpose,—provided they do not interrupt the proceedings, and provided there
      is no specific reason why they should be removed,—have a right to be present
      for the purpose of hearing what is going on.'

I would commend those words to any presiding judge or magistrate who is asking
j himself what was his duty with regard to keeping the court open to the public for
present purposes.

---

1   (1829) 10 B & C 237
2   10 B & C at 240

There is a transatlantic authority which counsel for the respondents put before us, *a* People v Hartman[1], a case in the Supreme Court of California in 1894. Again the facts do not matter and I refer to it for the statement of principle which appears in this observation of the judge[2]:

'The trial should be "public," in the ordinary commonsense acceptation of the term. The doors of the court room are expected to be kept open, the public are entitled to be admitted, and the trial is to be public in all respects . . . with due *b* regard to the size of the court room, the conveniences of the court, the right to exclude objectionable characters and youth of tender years, and to do other things which may facilitate the proper conduct of the trial.'

Again, one may say, the injunction to the presiding judge or magistrate is: do your best to enable the public to come in and see what is happening, having a proper *c* common sense regard for the facilities available and the facility for keeping order, security and the like. I start by accepting those two explanations of the significance of the phrase 'open court', but I would at once add to them a comment based on the fact that since those cases were decided, the press has assumed a very much greater importance in these matters. Today, as everybody knows, the great body of the British public get their news of how justice is administered through the press or other *d* mass media, and the presence or absence of the press is a vital factor in deciding whether a particular hearing was or was not in open court. I find it difficult to imagine a case which can be said to be held publicly if the press have been actively excluded. On the other hand, the fact that the press is present is not conclusive the other way, because one must not overlook the other factor of an open and public proceeding, namely one to which individual members of the public can come if they have *e* sufficient interest in the proceedings to make it worth their while so to do.

How one deals with individual members of the public who want to come in must, of course, depend on the circumstances of the case. It is the duty of a presiding judge or magistrate, as I have already said, to fulfil the obligations expressed in the extracts which I have read to the best of his ability having regard to all the prevailing circumstances: the number of seats available, the desirability or undesirability of allowing *f* people to stand, the possibility of disorder, the possibility of fire risk in a small overcrowded court, overcrowded by too many people being allowed to enter it, and so on.

In my judgment the method by which this duty is to be performed in a particular case is primarily for determination by the presiding judge or magistrate on the spot. If he has shown himself conscious of his duty in this regard, and has reached a conclusion which a reasonable magistrate might reach, then I do not think it is for us in this *g* court to substitute our own views whether the facilities offered to the public were or were not sufficient.

In the present case at the beginning of the proceedings, when Mr Evans's case was called on, it seems to me quite unarguable that the court was other than an open court. True it was a small court; true there were 20 or so people outside who wanted to come in, but all the available seats were full, and it was a perfectly proper decision *h* for the chairman of the Bench to say that he would not have people standing, either from the danger of disorder or from fire risks, or for any other reason. There were actually in the court at that time five members of the public selected by the two applicants; there was also incidentally a defendant and his solicitor concerned in a later case who happened to be in court waiting their turn, and who I suppose for present purposes were members of the public, and I do not think really in the end *j* counsel for the applicants seeks to persuade us that when the proceedings began the court could be described as otherwise than open.

1 (1894) 37 Pac 153
2 37 Pac at 154

a He has to concentrate his attack on what happened when the five seats began to empty. In substance his contention before us is that even if the proceedings were initially in open court, they ceased to be in open court when space for further spectators became available and those further spectators were not admitted.

Of course, on that point the controversy between the police officer's evidence and that filed by the applicants is of the utmost importance, because if the police officer
b is right there was never any question of others being excluded; they just did not try to come in. If the applicants' witnesses are right, the converse is true: others wanted to come in and failed.

It seems to me quite clear, at the end of the day, that following the well-settled practice of this court, it will not pursue disputed issues of fact on the affidavits. We cannot approach this problem other than on the footing that no further requests to
c fill the five public seats were made, and if that is the explanation of why they were not filled, the applicants' case it seems to me is at an end.

But I would say one other thing which may be of some consequence to the applicants and others who are concerned with these problems in Wales. I would have taken the same view even if I had come to the conclusion that there had been a request to fill the vacant seats. I would have come to the same conclusion because
d I do not think that the question: open court or no? can depend on such minutiae as to whether at a particular moment there was a particular member of the public anxious to come in who was wrongly refused.

Here the question: open court or no? has to be answered by a broad consideration of all the circumstances of the case, and I would have come to the conclusion in this case that the applicants' case was not made out even if I felt that some request to fill one or more of the vacant seats had been in fact made.
e A further point I must mention is that in the case of a discretionary remedy, of which certiorari is one, I should have great hesitation in allowing certiorari to go in this case if only because there seems to have been every possible justification for the chairman, if the matter had been referred to him, to refuse to have the five seats filled. Having regard to the conduct of those who filled the seats initially, and the
f apprehension of similar conduct by those who might fill them later, it would have been entirely right for him had he taken that view to have said that he would not have any more of the spectators obstructing his court.

However, I would base my conclusion on the first proposition—that it was not established that any member of the public who wished to go in when there was room was refused admission. On that footing it seems to me the application must be
g refused.

ASHWORTH J. I agree.

BRISTOW J. I agree.

h *Applications dismissed.*

Solicitors: *Barlow, Lyde & Gilbert*, agents for *William George & Son*, Portmadoc (for the applicants); *Treasury Solicitor* (for the respondents).

Jacqueline Charles Barrister.

Gunn and others v Sharpe and others

QUEEN'S BENCH DIVISION
WILLIS AND O'CONNOR JJ
27th, 28th MARCH, 10th APRIL 1974

Explained in MORGAN v SIMPSON
[1974] 3 All ER 722

Elections – Local government – Validity – Election conducted substantially in accordance with law as to elections – Irregularities affecting result of election – Ballot papers not bearing official mark – Rejection – Substantial irregularities likely to affect result – Rejected ballot papers almost all issued at one polling station – Officers at polling station in question failing to stamp 98 out of 189 ballot papers issued – Rejection of ballot papers affecting result of election – Whether election conducted substantially in accordance with law as to elections – Whether election void – Representation of the People Act 1949, s 37(1).

At a local government election the returning officer, in accordance with the requirements of the law, gave clear instructions to the staff at each of the ten polling stations to ensure that ballot papers were stamped with the official mark as required by rr 16(1)[a] and 33(1)[b] of the Local Elections (Principal Areas) Rules 1973[c]. Appropriate notices were displayed at the polling stations. In the event 102 ballot papers were rejected under r 43(1)[d] of the 1973 rules because they did not bear the official mark. Of the rejected papers 98 came from one polling station, constituting more than half of the 189 papers issued at that station. If the votes on the rejected papers had been counted, the two petitioning candidates would have been successful instead of the respondents who had in fact been elected. The petitioners sought a declaration that the election of the respondents was void on the grounds (i) that the election had not been conducted 'substantially in accordance with the law as to elections', within s 37(1)[e] of the Representation of the People Act 1949, and (ii) that the errors had affected the result of the election.

Held – The errors which had occurred at the polling station in question were of such a nature that they went beyond the trivial errors that inevitably occurred at all elections. They were substantial and such as to be likely to affect the result of the election, since they had resulted in more than half the voters who had sought to vote at the polling station being disfranchised and thus prevented from voting for the petitioners. It followed that the election could not be said to have been conducted 'substantially in accordance with the law as to elections'. Since the errors had in fact affected the result, the election of the respondents should therefore be declared void (see p 1063 *h* and *j* and p 1064 *b* to *e*, post).

Dictum of Grove J in *Hackney Case, Gill v Reed and Holms* (1874) 31 LT at 71, 72 applied.

Birmingham Case, Woodward v Sarsons [1874-80] All ER Rep 262 and *Morgan v Simpson* [1974] 1 All ER 241 distinguished.

Notes

For irregularities at elections, see 14 Halsbury's Laws (3rd Edn) 149-151, para 261, and for cases on the subject, see 20 Digest (Repl) 115, 116, 940-942.

For the Representation of the People Act 1949, s 37, see 11 Halsbury's Statutes (3rd Edn) 582.

---

a Rule 16(1) is set out at p 1062 *a*, post
b Rule 33(1), so far as material is, set out at p 1062 *b* and *c*, post
c SI 1973 No 79
d Rule 43(1) is set out at p 1062 *d*, post
e Section 37(1) is set out at p 1061 *j*, post

Cases referred to in judgment

Birmingham Case, Woodward v Sarsons (1875) LR 10 CP 733, [1874-80] All ER Rep 262, 44 LJCP 293, 32 LT 867, 39 JP 766, 20 Digest (Repl) 112, 918.

Hackney Case, Gill v Reed & Holms (1874), 31 LT 69, 39 JP 151, 2 O'M & H 77, 20 Digest (Repl) 104, 859.

Morgan v Simpson [1974] 1 All ER 241, [1974] QB 344, [1973] 3 WLR 893, DC.

Cases also cited

Levers v Morris [1971] 3 All ER 1300, [1972] 1 QB 221, DC.

Wigtown District Burgh Case (1874) 2 O'M & H 215.

Petition

By a petition presented under s 113 of the Representation of the People Act 1949, the petitioners, (1) Edith Mary Jane Gunn, (2) Leslie William Carter and (3) Ronald Wilfred Avenell, questioned the local government election for the Langley Ward of the West Midlands Metropolitan District of Sandwell, held on 10th May 1973. The respondents were (1) Thomas Charles Sharpe, (2) Joseph William Cutler, (3) Doreen Keeling, the successful candidates, and (4) Kenneth Pearce, the returning officer. Notice of the petition was served on the Director of Public Prosecutions in accordance with r 5(1) of the Election Petition Rules 1960[1]. By order of O'Connor J it was directed that the petition be stated as a special case for the determination of the High Court pursuant to s 126(1) of the 1949 Act. An agreed special case was stated and by agreement between all the parties the hearing of the special case was treated as the hearing of the petition. The facts are set out in the judgment of the court.

Barry Payton for the petitioners.
David Keene for the returning officer.
Anthony Hidden for the Director of Public Prosecutions.

28th March. **WILLIS J.** The court understands that it will be convenient to the parties if our decision were given at once, the reasons to be expressed in the judgment to be delivered at a later date.

We come to a clear conclusion as to what our decision should be and we have been greatly assisted by counsel appearing, as it were, as amicus curiae for the Director of Public Prosecutions and counsel for the petitioners' acceptance of the arguments of counsel as amicus curiae as to the correct approach to s 37 of the Representation of the People Act 1949, namely that it is the election of the three respondents separately with which this court is concerned. This enables us to take the course which we would have wished in any event to take if we could properly do so in the event that we felt that the election should be declared void.

We have come to the conclusion that the election was not conducted substantially in accordance with the law as to elections and that the acts or omissions complained of do affect the result of the election of the second and third respondents but not of the first respondent. We hold, therefore, that the second and third respondents were not duly elected.

In order to achieve this result formally we understand that the proceedings must be amended and I think we have already given leave, but if not, we do give leave for the appropriate amendments to be made to the form of the agreed case in order that on the pleadings it is open for that decision to be reached which we have reached, and we leave it to counsel to make the appropriate amendments.

---

1 SI 1960 No 543

Cur adv vult *a*

10th April. **WILLIS J** read the following judgment of the court. This is an election petition presented under the Representation of the People Act 1949 arising out of the local government election for the Langley Ward of the West Midlands Metropolitan District of Sandwell, held on 10th May 1973. The three petitioners were candidates at the election, the first three respondents were the successful candi- *b* dates, and the fourth respondent was the returning officer. The petition (as amended) prayed that it be determined that the second and third respondents were not duly elected and that their election should be declared void. The effect of the amendments to the petition is that the petitioners do not challenge the due election of the first respondent.

The basis of the petitioners' case is that of 102 ballot papers which were rejected *c* for want of the official mark, no less than 98 came from one polling station out of a total of 189 ballot papers issued from that station, namely 52 per cent of the total issued; that the failure to stamp the papers before issue to the voters was in breach of r 33 of the Local Elections (Principal Areas) Rules[1]; that the result of the election was affected thereby and that in consequence the second and third respondents were not duly elected and their election should be declared void.

At one stage the petitioners desired that there should be a local inquiry into the *d* circumstances of the election, but it was ultimately decided that an agreed special case should be stated and by agreement between all parties the hearing of the special case has been treated as the hearing of the petition.

On 10th May 1973 the poll was declared as follows:

First petitioner	1016 votes
Second petitioner	1009 votes
Third petitioner	978 votes
First respondent	1097 votes
Second respondent	1033 votes
Third respondent	1032 votes

e

f

The three respondents were declared elected. 2,295 ballot papers were issued according to the accounts and 2,294 were found in the ballot boxes.

In the report dated 24th September 1973 made by Master W Russell Lawrence QC, the Senior Master, the following matters were established: (1) 102 ballot papers were rejected for want of the official mark. (2) The number of votes in respect of individual candidates rejected for want of the official mark were: *g*

First petitioner	66
Second petitioner	68
Third petitioner	63
First respondent	30
Second respondent	33
Third respondent	28

h

(3) If these votes had not been rejected but had been counted, the result of the election would have been:

(a) First respondent	1097 + 30 = 1127
(b) First petitioner	1016 + 66 = 1082
(c) Second petitioner	1009 + 68 = 1077
(d) Second respondent	1033 + 33 = 1066
(e) Third respondent	1032 + 28 = 1060
(f) Third petitioner	978 + 63 = 1041

j

1 SI 1973 No 79

a   (4) Whether or not the ballot papers rejected were valid, the first respondent would have been elected. If the rejected ballot papers are admitted, the second and third respondents presently elected would have been fourth and fifth and so unsuccessful at the election.

    The ward had ten polling stations, each staffed by one presiding officer and one poll clerk during the 13 hours of polling. Two ladies filled these positions at polling *b* station 56. The 102 rejected papers were divided as follows:

Polling Station 53	1
Polling Station 54	1
Polling Station 56	98
Polling Station 61	2

c   At polling station 56 what happened was this: two books each containing 100 papers were used; from the first book came numbers 3070, 3084 to 3092 inclusive, and 3100, namely 11 papers; from the second book came numbers 3101 to 3164 inclusive, 3166, 3167, 3169 to 3189 inclusive, namely, 87 papers. The four rejected papers at three stations are of no consequence: the issue in this case centres on the very high proportion rejected for want of the official mark at polling station 56. *d* Although we accept that the individual voter, if properly notified, must bear some responsibility for seeing that his paper is properly marked before recording his vote, we think that the overriding responsibility for the serious omissions in polling station 56 must be borne by the presiding officer, Mrs Worton.

    It is accepted by counsel for the petitioners that the returning officer performed his duties exactly in accordance with the requirements of the law, that the appro-*e* priate instructions were given to the polling station staffs, that the presiding officers were, to the best of his understanding, competent and qualified to perform their duties, that the appropriate notices were exhibited in the polling stations and that no blame at all can be attributed to him for what happened in polling station 56.

    It is contended by the petitioners that the election was not conducted substantially in accordance with the law as to elections in that the presiding officer and poll clerk *f* at polling station 56 failed to apply the official mark to 98 out of 189 ballot papers issued at that station.

    The first three respondents take no part in these proceedings but the returning officer contends that: (1) the election was conducted substantially in accordance with the law as to elections; (2) even if it be found that the election was not so conducted and that the result of the election was affected, the Representation of the People Act 1949 does not require that the election should be declared invalid and *g* that in the circumstances it should not be declared invalid. The relevant statutory provisions and statutory rules are as follows:

(1) *Representation of the People Act 1949*
   Section 23(1) provides:

h   'All persons voting as electors at a local government election shall do so in person at the polling station allotted to them under the local elections rules, except in so far as this section makes exceptions . . .'

The exceptions are then set out and it is immaterial to refer to them. Section 37(1) reads:

j   'No local government election shall be declared invalid by reason of any act or omission of the returning officer or any other person in breach of his official duty in connection with the election or otherwise of the local elections rules if it appears to the tribunal having cognizance of the question that the election was so conducted as to be substantially in accordance with the law as to elections and that the act or omission did not affect its result.'

(2) *The Local Elections (Principal Areas) Rules 1973*
Schedule 2 provides as follows:

'16.—(1) Every ballot paper shall be marked with an official mark, which shall be either embossed or perforated . . .
'33.—(1) A ballot paper shall be delivered to a voter who applies therefor, and immediately before delivery—(a) the ballot paper shall be stamped with the official mark, either embossed or perforated; (b) the number, name and description of the elector as stated in the copy of the register of electors shall be called out; (c) the number of the elector shall be marked on the counterfoil; (d) a mark shall be placed in the register of electors against the number of the elector to denote that a ballot paper had been received but without showing the particular ballot paper which has been received; and (e) in the case of a person applying for a ballot paper as proxy, a mark shall also be placed against his name in the list of proxies . . .
'43.—(1) Any ballot paper—(a) which does not bear the official mark; or (b) on which votes are given for more candidates than the voter is entitled to vote for; or (c) on which anything is written or marked by which the voter can be identified except the printed number on the back; or (d) which is unmarked or void for uncertainty; shall, subject to the provisions of this rule, be void and not counted . . .

Finally, reg 54 provides for the general duty of the returning officer:

'It shall be the general duty of the returning officer to do any act or thing that may be necessary for effectually conducting the election under these rules.'

We do not find it necessary to refer to the written instructions which were given to presiding officers and poll clerks or to the notices to voters which were displayed inside and outside the polling stations. They were in common form and are set out in the case. It is sufficient to say that counsel for the petitioners accepts that the returning officer did all that was required of him to ensure that the election was conducted in accordance with the rules, and in particular saw to it that all presiding officers and poll clerks were made aware, as were the voters, of the great importance of making sure that the ballot paper was impressed with the official mark before being handed to the voter. We agree with counsel for the petitioners that no criticism can be made of the returning officer. The question, nevertheless, remains whether, in the events which happened, this court should declare the election of the second and third respondents void.

We have been greatly assisted by the recent decision of a Divisional Court, *Morgan v Simpson*[1], which is binding on us. In that case 82 ballot papers out of a total of 23,691 were rejected, of which 44 were rejected for not bearing the official mark. The 44 papers were spread over 18 polling stations, the highest number at any one station being seven. The court was satisfied[2] that the failure to stamp the papers was due to the sort of inevitable human error 'which cannot be wholly eliminated in an operation of this kind'. Nevertheless, had the rejected papers been counted the narrow win of the respondent of 11 votes at the election would have been converted into an even narrower win of seven votes for the petitioner, so that the result of the election was affected by the errors. After considering the decision in *Woodward v Sarsons*[3], when the judgment of the Court of Common Pleas was given by Lord Coleridge CJ, a case under s 13 of the Ballot Act 1872, Milmo J said[4]:

'In the opinion of this court the passages cited from the judgment of the Court of Common Pleas remain true statements of the law as it is today. This

---

1 [1974] 1 All ER 241, [1974] QB 344
2 [1974] 1 All ER at 243, [1974] QB at 349
3 (1875) LR 10 CP 733, [1874-80] All ER Rep 262
4 [1974] 1 All ER at 247, [1974] QB at 353, 354

a election was conducted "substantially in accordance with the law as to elections" and although there were a modest number of errors which in the event did affect the result, this is not a sufficient reason for declaring the election invalid. The court is not disturbed by the conclusion that it has reached. Were the contentions of the petitioner well founded the consequences would have been far-reaching and hardly in the public interest. It is reasonably clear that a small percentage of ballot papers not bearing the official stamp is something which is b apt to occur at all elections. In any election in which the majority of the winning candidate is a small one there would appear to be a substantial chance that it will be exceeded by the number of voting papers rejected for want of the official mark. If the contentions of the petitioners are right an election petition will probably result and there would be something like an even chance of a fresh election having to be ordered. This would be largely attributable to the fault c of the supporters of the petitioning candidate who had failed to check that their ballot papers were stamped before they were put in the ballot box.'

It is to be observed that in *Woodward's* case[1] at one of the polling stations the presiding officer marked every ballot paper issued—294 in all—with the number of the voter appearing on the burgess roll. This was an admitted error which invali-
d dated the papers and effectively disfranchised all those who wanted to exercise their vote at the polling station in question. Nevertheless, the result of the election was not affected. Unlike the *Hackney* case[2], when the court was unable to assess the effect on the result of the failure to open two polling stations and the limited opening of others, and declined to speculate, the court in *Woodward's* case[1] was able to ascertain the resultant figure if the 294 votes had been counted. In the circumstances the court
e took the view that the majority of the electors had not been prevented from effectively exercising their votes in favour of the candidate they preferred. If the error had been shown to have affected the result we incline to the view that the election of Mr Sarsons would have been declared void.

The facts of the *Hackney* case[2], of course, show errors so extensive that the court invalidated the election irrespective of whether or not the result of the election would
f have been affected. A possibility, albeit remote, was a 50/50 division of the lost votes. In declaring the election void, Grove J said[3]:

'Among the principles of the [Ballot Act 1872] is one that there should be districts arranged for the convenience of the electors at which they might have on the polling day suitable machinery for giving their votes to the candidate to whom they choose . . . to give their votes . . . An election is not to be upset for
g an informality or for a triviality. . . The objection must be something substantial, something calculated really to affect the result of the election . . . the judge is to look to the substance of the case and to see whether the informality is of such a nature as to be fairly calculated in a rational mind to produce a substantial effect upon the election.'

h We find the observations of Grove J provide us with a valuable guide to our approach to this case. The voters in the district of polling station 56 were required in accordance with s 23 of the 1949 Act to vote at that station, except for any who might have been within the exceptions; more than half of those who sought to vote were effectively disfranchised, and in this way the majority of the voters in this ward were, in our view, so far as the first and second petitioners are concerned, prevented from voting
j for the candidate of their choice, and the election result would have been otherwise had this not occurred. We are very conscious of the importance of the principle which

---

1   (1875) LR 10 CP 733, [1874-80] All ER Rep 262
2   (1874) 31 LT 69
3   31 LT at 71, 72

occurs throughout the cases to which we have been referred that elections should   *a*
not be lightly set aside, simply because there have been informalities and errors,
and that both s 13 of the 1872 Act and s 37 of the 1949 Act were framed with this
principle in mind. If we are right in taking the view that *Woodward's* case[1] would
probably have been decided differently if it could have been demonstrated, as it has
in this case, that the errors had affected the result, then the facts would have been
virtually indistinguishable from the present case and the respondents' case really   *b*
unarguable. But whether or not we are right in taking that view, we think the scale
of errors in polling station 56 went far beyond the mistakes spread over 18 polling
stations in the *Morgan* case[2] which were regarded as it were as 'all in the day's work'
and no more than the sort of informalities which, according to Grove J, should not
be allowed to upset an election.

   The only issue before us under s 37 is whether the election was so conducted as to   *c*
be substantially in accordance with the law as to elections. That law requires at
least that electors should be able to record their votes at the polling station where
they are required to vote in the way which ensures that the votes they register are
effectively cast for the candidate of their choice. We, of course, bear in mind that
for some reason none of the 94 voters at polling station 56 seems to have noticed,
as strictly they should, that they were voting on unmarked papers, but after making   *d*
allowance for that matter we think that this case is clearly distinguishable on its
facts from *Morgan's* case[2], and that the errors which were concentrated at polling
station 56 compared with the trivial few spread over the remaining stations were so
great as to amount to conduct of the election which was not substantially in accordance
with law. These are the reasons why we have already declared the election of the
second and third respondents void.

   We only add that we accept the submission made by counsel for the Director of   *e*
Public Prosecutions, with which counsel for the petitioners agreed, that a reference
to ss 112-118 of the 1949 Act suggests that it is the election of an individual which is
called in question by an election petition and that s 37 should be construed accordingly
and not as necessarily involving the avoidance of all those elected in the ward election,
irrespective of whether the election result of a particular candidate would have been   *f*
affected or not. This is certainly a construction which seems to us to avoid unfairness
in the present case and leaves the election of the first respondent undisturbed.

   In the event of any party desiring to take this matter further, we give leave. The
security will be fixed by the learned senior master.

Petition granted. Election of second and third respondents declared void. Leave to appeal.
                                                                                        g

Solicitors: *Clinton Davis & Co* (for the petitioners); *Sherwood & Co* (for the returning
officer); *Director of Public Prosecutions*.

                                                     F K Anklesaria Esq Barrister.

---

1 (1875) LR 10 CP 733, [1874-80] All ER Rep 262   *h*
2 [1974] 1 All ER 241, [1974] QB 344

a

Rose v Epstein and another

CHANCERY DIVISION   Affirmed CA [1974] 3 All ER 745
PENNYCUICK V-C
14th MARCH 1974

b

Costs – Security for costs – Plaintiff – Person in position of plaintiff – Probate proceedings – Caveator – Executor issuing writ to establish will – Caveator joined as defendant to writ – Caveator resident abroad – Caveator counterclaiming for pronouncement against will – Allegation of undue influence – Beneficiary under will joining at own election as defendant – Burden of upsetting will on caveator – Whether caveator 'in the position of plaintiff' – RSC Ord 23, r 1(3).

c

By his will the testator devised his residuary estate to the applicant. On the testator's death the caveator, who was resident in Israel, lodged a caveat against probate of the will. In consequence the executor of the will issued a writ which joined the caveator as defendant. By the writ the executor claimed that he was the sole executor named in the testator's true last will and to have the will established. The applicant on her own

d

application was added as a defendant to the writ. The caveator delivered her defence in which she alleged that the execution of the will had been obtained by the undue influence of the applicant and she counterclaimed that the court should pronounce against the will. The applicant delivered a defence denying the allegation of undue influence and counterclaimed that the court should pronounce for the will in solemn form. By summons the applicant applied for an order, under RSC Ord 23, r 1[a], that

e

the caveator give security for costs on the ground that the caveator was 'in the position of plaintiff' within RSC Ord 23, r 1(3), in that when the action came to be heard the matters in dispute would have to be fought out between the caveator and the applicant and the burden of upsetting the will would fall on the caveator.

f

Held – For the purposes of RSC Ord 23, r 1(3), a caveator could not, as between himself and the executor, be regarded as being in the position of a plaintiff and the position of the executor and the caveator in the proceedings could not be altered by the election of a beneficiary under the will to be joined as a co-defendant. Nor was a caveator placed in the position of a plaintiff merely because he delivered a counter-claim. Accordingly the application would be dismissed (see p 1070 *d* to *g*, post).

Re Emery [1923] P 184 applied.

g

Notes
For order for security for costs when plaintiff is ordinarily out of jurisdiction, see 30 Halsbury's Laws (3rd Edn) 378-380, para 706, and for cases on the subject, see 51 Digest (Repl) 973, 974, 5091-5104.

h

Cases referred to in judgment
Emery, Re, Emery v Emery [1923] P 184, 92 LJP 138, 130 LT 127, 1 Digest (Repl) 12, 98.
Freeman (deceased), Re, Nicholson v Street (11th April 1973) unreported.
Lambert v Bassett (1877) 11 Ir R Eq 291, 23 Digest (Repl) 284, *792.
Moran v Place [1896] P 214, 65 LJP 83, 74 LT 661, CA, 1 Digest (Repl) 11, 96.
Robson v Robson (1864) 3 Sw & Tr 568, 34 LJPM & A 6, 11 LT 459, 10 Jur NS 1243, 164

j

ER 1396, 23 Digest (Repl) 284 3473.
Salter v Salter [1896] P 291, 65 LJP 117, 75 LT 7, CA, 23 Digest (Repl) 209, 2473.

Case also cited
Visco v Minter [1969] 2 All ER 714, [1969] P 82.

---

a Rule 1, so far as material, is set out at p 1067 *b* and *c*, post

Procedure summons

By a summons dated 9th July 1973, Frieda Kafka ('Mrs Kafka'), being the residuary
legatee under the will of Paul Portman who died on 3rd July 1971 and the second
defendant to a writ issued on 9th November 1971 by the plaintiff, Philip Charles
Rose ('the executor'), whereby he claimed to be the sole executor named in the will
and to have the will established, applied for an order that Emma Epstein ('Mrs Epstein'), who was resident in Israel and the first defendant to the writ, give security for
costs. The facts are set out in the judgment.

F J Cridlan for Mrs Kafka.
Dennis G Rice for Mrs Epstein.
J A P Hazel for the executor.

PENNYCUICK V-C. I have before me an application in this action for an order
for security for costs. The application raises an issue of principle which may be of
some importance, and I think that for that reason I ought to give a full judgment.

The matter arises in certain probate proceedings in the estate of Paul Portman,
deceased. The facts may be summarised for the present purpose as follows. The
testator, Paul Portman, made a will dated 29th August 1969, whereby he appointed
one Philip C Rose to be his sole executor and gave his residuary estate to Mrs Frieda
Kafka. The testator died on 3rd July 1971. Mrs Epstein, who is the sister of the
testator and claims to be the sole next-of-kin, lodged a caveat. That caveat resulted in
the issue by the executor of the writ in this present action on 9th November 1971.
The only defendant joined in the first place was Mrs Epstein. The writ is in common
form and reads:

'THE PLAINTIFF CLAIMS to be the sole executor named in the true last will, dated
the 29th August 1969, of Paul Portman, Late of 34, The Ridgeway, Kenton, In the
County of Middlesex, who died on the 3rd day of July 1971, and to have the said
will established. This is the Plaintiff's Statement of Claim.'

Then comes the note:

'This Writ is issued against you as the lawful sister of the whole blood of the
said Paul Portman deceased, and the only person entitled to his estate in the
event of an intestacy, and because you have entered a Caveat and have appeared
to the warning thereto.'

Mrs Epstein's ground of opposition to probate of the will is, summarily, undue
influence by Mrs Kafka. Mrs Kafka, on her own application, was added as a defendant
on 3rd November 1972. Then, on 13th December, Mrs Epstein served her defence,
setting out particulars of the undue influence, which are of a far-reaching nature, and
there is a counterclaim that the court shall pronounce against the alleged will propounded by the plaintiff. Mrs Kafka in due course also put in a defence by which she
denies that the execution of the will was obtained by the undue influence of herself
and does not admit that Mrs Epstein is the lawful sister or that she is the only
person entitled to the estate on intestacy. I do not think that anything turns on that
last point. There is a counterclaim that the court shall pronounce for the will in
solemn form of law. It is unnecessary for the purpose of this application to go into
the particulars of 'undue influence'.

Mrs Epstein resides in Israel, and on that ground Mrs Kafka now applies for security
for costs. There is also before the court an application for security against Mrs
Epstein by the executor, but that has not been pursued before me although all
parties are separately represented by counsel.

Summarily, the question is this, whether Mrs Epstein is to be treated as a person in
the position of plaintiff in these proceedings so as to warrant an order for security for

a costs. Before elaborating on this matter, I would say at once that apart from authority I should have thought that this was, for all practical purposes, an action in which Mrs Epstein is seeking to set aside the will, and Mrs Kafka is opposing that application, while the executor is neutral. However, it appears that I am not at liberty to take that perhaps oversimplified view of the matter.

The order which regulates this matter today is RSC Ord 23. That order states:

b '1.—(1) Where, on the application of a defendant to an action or other pro-ceeding in the High Court, it appears to the Court—(a) that the plaintiff is ordi-narily resident outside the jurisdiction . . . then if, having regard to all the circum-stances of the case, the Court thinks it just to do so, it may order the plaintiff to give such security for the defendant's costs of the action or other proceedings as it thinks just . . .

c '(3) The references in the foregoing paragraphs to a plaintiff and a defendant shall be construed as references to the person (howsoever described on the record) who is in the position of plaintiff or defendant, as the case may be, in the proceed-ing in question, including a proceeding on a counterclaim.'

In the notes[1] to RSC Ord 23 it is stated:

d 'This Order is taken from R.S.C. (Rev.), 1962, O.23, which replaced the former O.65, rr. 6, 6A, 6B and 7, and embodied the previous case law dealing with the power of the Court to order security for costs.'

That appears to be a correct statement.

The case law begins with two decisions of the Court of Appeal in 1896. The more *e* important is *Moran v Place*[2]. The headnote is as follows:

'An executor's probate action, brought in consequence of a caveat entered by a married woman who was made defendant to the action, resulted in a verdict for the plaintiff with costs against the defendant. Upon an application by the plaintiff under the Married Women's Property Act, 1893, s.2, for an order for *f* payment of the costs out of property to which the defendant was entitled subject to a restraint on anticipation:—*Held*, by the Court of Appeal, affirming the de-cision of Gorell Barnes J., that the proceedings in the probate action were "instituted" within the meaning of the Act of 1893 by the issue of the writ by the plaintiff, and not by the entry of the caveat, or the appearance of the caveator in answer to the warning; and accordingly that the order applied for could not be *g* made.'

It will be seen that that case turns on the construction of a different set of provisions, but it contains statements by the Lords Justices as to the position of a party in a probate action which have subsequently been adopted and applied. Lindley LJ said[3]:

'A caveat is not a notice to any opponent in particular. It is a notice to the *h* registrar or officer of the Court not to let anything be done by anybody in the matter of the will, or the goods of the deceased, without notice to the person who lodges the caveat. It is impossible to look at it as commencing any litigation —it merely requests the registrar to tell the caveator if anybody stirs in this mat-ter. That caveat having been entered and there being an address so that the person entering it can be found, the next thing is that somebody does begin to *j* stir in the matter. That is the present plaintiff, who is the executor of the will and wishes to prove it. When a caveat has been entered the person who wishes to prove the will has to warn the person who entered the caveat, and if such person,

1 Supreme Court Practice 1973, p 376, para 23/1-3/1
2 [1896] P 214
3 [1896] P at 216, 217

i.e. the caveator, intends to make any real objection, he enters an appearance.
Then, if the litigation goes on, the person who wants to prove the will issues a *a*
writ and serves it on the caveator. Then, and not before, there is litigation between the person propounding the will on the one side, and the person opposing
it on the other. Now, if we look at the state of things quite apart from all technicalities, who is the person who institutes the proceeding? I should say that it is
the person who is the actor from the beginning, namely, the plaintiff. It is per- *b*
fectly true that the person who entered the caveat caused the litigation, but she
did not institute the proceeding by herself or anybody acting as her agent. What
she did was to force somebody else to institute proceedings against her.'

Later on he said[1]: 'I confess I am rather sorry for the conclusion at which I have
arrived . . .'

The other case in the same year is *Salter v Salter*[2], again in the Court of Appeal. The *c*
headnote reads:

'A. entered a caveat against probate of a will. B., the executor named in the will,
warned it, and A. appeared. Before anything further had been done A. moved
for an order for a receiver and administrator pendente lite:—*Held* (affirming
the decision of the President), that there was no jurisdiction to make the order, *d*
for the caveat proceedings did not constitute a lis pendens, and, as no writ had
been issued, there was no application to the Court on which the Court could act.'

I do not think that that case takes the matter any further.

Then comes what I think is the critical authority in the present action, *Re Emery*[3],
before Sir Henry Duke P. Before citing from his judgment, I should mention that as
the law then stood the provision in the Rules of the Supreme Court with regard to *e*
security for costs, RSC Ord LXV, r 6, was in general terms, namely:

'In any cause or matter in which security for costs is required, the security shall
be of such amount, and be given at such times, and in such manner and form, as
the Court or a Judge shall direct.'

The headnote in *Re Emery*[3] is as follows: *f*

'A person who has lodged a caveat against probate of a will is not, though his
action compels the executors to take proceedings, so much the actor in the proceedings as to be liable to give security for costs. The bankruptcy or insolvency
of a defendant is not per se a ground for ordering him to give security for costs.
Lambert v. *Bassett*[4] not followed. *Moran* v. *Place*[5] applied.' *g*

Sir Henry Duke P quotes[6] the Irish case of *Lambert v Bassett*[4] and proceeds:

'It was founded in some particulars upon a judgment of Lord Penzance in *Robson*
v. *Robson*[7] in 1864, where, in fact, no order for security for costs was made against
the defendant who had interposed in a probate suit under circumstances which
were alleged to entitle the plaintiffs in the suit to security for costs against him, he *h*
being out of the jurisdiction. But the learned judge laid it down that, in questions
relating to the right for security for costs in proceedings in probate, the Court
would have regard, not to the technical situation of the parties in relation to the
suit, but to their substantial position and to the question whether, in truth, the

1   [1896] P at 217, 218   *j*
2   [1896] P 291
3   [1923] P 184
4   (1877) 11 Ir R Eq 291
5   [1896] P 214
6   [1923] P at 186, 187
7   3 Sw & Tr 568

a party against whom security for costs was demanded was the actor in the proceedings. It is upon that view of the matter that the Court will have regard to the question of who is, in fact, the actor in the proceedings, and upon the application of that principle in the case of *Lambert* v. *Basset*[1] the plaintiffs in the present action claimed to have security against the defendant.'

b Robson v Robson[2] is shortly reported in Swabey and Tristram's Reports. Sir J P Wilde stated[3]:

'In this suit the plaintiff is really the plaintiff, as she is seeking to obtain a sum of money, which she cannot obtain without the assistance of the Court, and the defendant is really the defendant, as he is brought into the court by the citation issued by her.'

c To continue Sir Henry Duke P's judgment[4]:

'The position of the matter is that the defendant is the caveator at whose instance proceedings which might otherwise have been non-contentious proceedings have become contentious proceedings, and he was at all material times and is an undischarged bankrupt. The appeal is founded upon the proposition that, given the concurrence of those facts, there is, subject to the discretion of the Court, a right on the part of the plaintiffs to require security for costs against such a defendant. First, with regard to the position of the defendant as being, as he is alleged to be, the actor in these proceedings, that is, the party by whom law is set in motion with the result of entailing cost upon other parties, I am not able to take the view that a caveator is an actor in probate proceedings in the sense which is contended for. He is not the person who institutes the suit. It is quite true that his conduct gives cause for the institution of the suit, but he is not in substance and in fact the actor in the proceedings. Regard must be had to the nature of a caveat. It is a warning put upon the file of the Court in the Probate Registry which prevents proceedings to obtain probate or administration except after notice to the caveator. The question whether the filing of a caveat is the institution of a suit, or whether it makes the caveator the actor in the subsequent probate proceedings, was considered in *Moran* v. *Place*[5] . . .'

He then cites a passage from the judgment of Lindley LJ[6] in that case which I have already cited. He concludes[7], so far as now in point:

'I do not intend to go beyond what is necessary to be said upon the question of what state of facts, either in the High Court generally or in this Division, will put a person who is nominally a defendant under the liability to give security for costs . . . Any lawyer needs only to look at the authorities upon the subject in the High Court (where the rule is as equitable as it ever was in the Probate Court) to discover what are the various circumstances under which a person who is nominally a defendant may be treated as being in truth a plaintiff. But the conclusion at which I arrive is that the caveator in this case, with the caveat filed under the ordinary circumstances which entitle a party claiming interest or having an interest to file a caveat, is not the actor in these proceedings in such a way as requires that he, the present party, should give security for costs.'

It is important to observe not only the result of that case, but the fact that the learned judge, on his reading of *Robson v Robson*[2] and also of *Moran v Place*[5], was of the view

j 1 (1877) 11 Ir R Eq 291
   2 (1864) 3 Sw & Tr 568
   3 3 Sw & Tr at 571
   4 [1923] P at 187
   5 [1896] P 214
   6 [1896] P at 216, 217
   7 [1923] P at 188, 189

that, even looking at the substance of the matter and not the mere form of the *a* action, the caveator could not be regarded as the actor in the proceedings, and consequently could not be regarded as being in the position of a plaintiff in those proceedings.

That decision[1] was given before the introduction of the new RSC Ord 23, but I think that I am bound to hold, for the purposes of r 1(3) of RSC Ord 23, that a caveator cannot be regarded as being in the position of a plaintiff as between himself and the *b* executor. A comparable point came before me in *Re Freeman*[2]. That case was not reported, but I have been able to find a note of my judgment. I went through the same authorities then as I have gone through today and reached the conclusion that I was not able to order security for costs against the defendant caveator. In that action, as in *Re Emery*[1], the only parties were the executor as plaintiff and the caveator as defendant.

Coming back to the present case, the position is certainly different, in this sense, *c* that Mrs Kafka has now been added as a second defendant. One has an action, not between the executor and the caveator alone, but between the executor on the one hand and the caveator and the residuary legatee under the will on the other hand. That is the form of the action. No doubt, when the action comes to be heard, counsel for the executor, having opened the case, will step aside and leave the case to be fought *d* out between Mrs Epstein and Mrs Kafka, and the burden of upsetting the will will undoubtedly lie on Mrs Epstein.

I would much like to hold, in those circumstances, that Mrs Epstein is in the position of plaintiff in these proceedings, but, bearing in mind the way in which this matter has been approached in *Re Emery*[1] and the earlier cases, I am unable to reach that conclusion. It is difficult to see how it can be said that the executor's position as the *e* actor has been altered by the addition of Mrs Kafka as a defendant. It would be anomalous that so long as Mrs Epstein was the only defendant, security for costs could not be ordered against her; yet she can be rendered liable to give security for costs by reason of a fact entirely outside her control, namely, the election of Mrs Kafka to be joined as a party and to take on the role of opposing Mrs Epstein. I do not think that I have really any logical ground on which I could distinguish the present *f* case from that of *Re Emery*[1] and the principle on which that case was decided. The truth of the matter, it seems to me, is that the caveator is neither more nor less in the position of a plaintiff by reason of the fact that the beneficiary under the will is joined as a co-defendant.

It is not suggested that Mrs Epstein is in the position of plaintiff merely by reason that she has delivered a counterclaim (see the notes under RSC Ord 23[3]). I must *g* accordingly dismiss this application.

Application dismissed.

Solicitors: *Belmont & Co* (for Mrs Kafka); *E Duchin* (for Mrs Epstein) ; *John Wood & Co* (for the executor). *h*

Evelyn Budd Barrister.

---

1 [1923] P 184
2 (11th April 1973)
3 Supreme Court Practice 1973, p 379, para 23/1-3/7

a Oxfam v City of Birmingham District Council

CHANCERY DIVISION

Affirmed HL [1975] 2 All ER 289

TEMPLEMAN J

13th, 14th MAY, 10th JUNE 1974

b Rates – Relief – Charitable and other organisation – Hereditaments wholly or mainly used for charitable purposes – Fund raising activities – Charity for relief of poverty – Shops occupied by charity – Shops used for reception and sorting of articles given to charity and for subsequent sale – Whether shops 'used for charitable purposes' – General Rate Act 1967, s 40(1).

The plaintiffs were a charitable organisation whose main purpose was the relief *c* of poverty, distress and suffering. The plaintiffs ran 'gift shops' in the United Kingdom which were mainly used for the reception and sorting of articles given to the plaintiffs, and for the retail sale of most of those articles. Those activities promoted the plaintiffs' objects by raising funds for them. The shops were also used to a much less extent for the sale of village handicraft articles made by poor people and the sale of articles made by a subsidiary company of the plaintiffs, which publicised the *d* plaintiffs and made profits for them. The shops, some of which were occupied rent free or at a low rent, were manned by local groups of the plaintiffs' supporters on a voluntary basis. The plaintiffs claimed relief under s 40(1)*a* of the General Rate Act 1967 against rates chargeable in respect of certain of the shops.

Held – Fund raising was not a charitable activity and accordingly premises used for *e* the purposes of fund raising were not premises 'used for charitable purposes' within s 40(1). The reception and sorting of articles at the plaintiffs' shops and their subsequent sale could not be regarded as constituting a form of management and administration of charitable property; they were simply fund raising activities. Accordingly, since the shops in question were mainly used for the purposes of fund raising, it followed that they were not 'wholly or mainly used for charitable purposes', *f* within s 40(1), and the plaintiffs' claim failed (see p 1073 *f* to *h*, post).

Aldous v Southwark Corpn [1968] 3 All ER 498 distinguished.

Notes

For reduction of rates payable by charitable organisations, see Supplement to 32 Halsbury's Laws (3rd Edn) para 210A.

g For the General Rate Act 1967, s 40, see 27 Halsbury's Statutes (3rd Edn) 131.

Cases referred to in judgment

Aldous v Southwark Corpn [1968] 3 All ER 498, [1968] 1 WLR 1671, 15 RRC 269, 132 JP 564, 67 LGR 62, [1968] RA 484, CA, Digest (Cont Vol C) 821, 346*b*.

Belfast Association for Employment of Industrious Blind v Comr of Valuation for Northern *h* *Ireland* [1968] NI 21, Digest (Cont Vol C) 821, *368a*.

Glasgow City Corpn v Johnstone [1965] 1 All ER 730, [1965] AC 609, [1965] 2 WLR 657, 11 RRC 127, 129 JP 250, 63 LGR 171, [1965] RVR 111, [1965] RA 49, sub nom *Belhaven-Westbourne Church Congregation Board v Glasgow Corpn* 1965 SLT 133, HL, Digest (Cont Vol B) 613, *343a*.

a Section 40(1), so far as material, provides: 'If notice in writing is given to the rating authority *j* that—(*a*) any hereditament occupied by, or by trustees for, a charity and wholly or mainly used for charitable purposes . . . is one falling within this subsection, then, subject to the provisions of this section, the amount of any rates chargeable in respect of the hereditament for any period during which the hereditament is one falling within . . . paragraph (*a*) . . . of this subsection, being a period beginning not earlier than the rate period in which the notice is given, shall not exceed one-half of the amount which would be chargeable apart from the provisions of this subsection . . .'

Cases also cited

Bromley v Tryon [1951] 2 All ER 1058, [1952] AC 265, HL.
Fawcett Properties Ltd v Buckingham City Council [1960] 3 All ER 503, [1961] AC 636, HL.
Northern Ireland Comr of Valuation v Fermanagh Protestant Board of Education [1969]
    3 All ER 352, [1969] 1 WLR 1708, HL.
Polish Historical Institution Ltd v Hove Corpn (1963) 10 RRC 73.
Wynn v Skegness Urban District Council [1966] 3 All ER 336, [1967] 1 WLR 52.

Adjourned summons

By an originating summons dated 17th November 1972, and amended by order dated
27th June 1973, the plaintiffs, Oxfam, claimed (1) a declaration that, on the true construction of s 40(1) of the General Rate Act 1967, the plaintiffs were entitled to relief
thereunder in respect of each of their hereditaments at 372 Coventry Road, Small
Heath; 11 Suffolk Street, Queensway; 171 High Street, Harborne; 150A Alcester
Road, Moseley; 44 Grosvenor Shopping Centre, Northfield; 89 Villa Road, Hands-
worth; 1100 Warwick Road, Acocks Green; 880 Bristol Road South, Birmingham 31;
and 4 (formerly 5) Fox and Goose Centre, Washwood Heath, all in the city of Birmingham; (2) a declaration that, on the true construction of s 40(5) of the 1967 Act, the
plaintiffs were eligible for relief thereunder in respect of each of those hereditaments.
The defendants were the City of Birmingham District Council, the rating authority.
The facts are set out in the judgment.

David Widdicombe QC and *Charles Fay* for the plaintiffs.
N C H Browne-Wilkinson QC and *Elizabeth Appleby* for the defendants.

Cur adv vult

10th June. **TEMPLEMAN J** read the following judgment. The plaintiffs, Oxfam,
claim under s 40 of the General Rate Act 1967 relief against rates chargeable in respect
of certain of their shops. The defendants as the rating authority resist the claim.
    Relief under s 40 is accorded to premises occupied by a charity and wholly or mainly
used for charitable purposes. There are two conditions to be fulfilled, first occup-
tion and secondly user. A charity which occupies property necessarily uses the
property for charitable purposes in the sense that all activities of a charity must
have as an ultimate objective the achievement of charitable aims. But for s 40 there
must be something more than lawful occupation by a charity; the purposes for which
the premises are used must be 'wholly ancillary' to or must 'directly ... facilitate
the carrying out of its main charitable purposes': per Lord Reid in *Glasgow City Corpn
v Johnstone*[1]. In that case the residence of a church officer in a house for the purpose
of looking after the adjoining church and assisting the minister constituted occupation
and user of the house by the church board which 'directly facilitated' the advancement
of religion.
    The main charitable purpose of Oxfam is the relief of poverty, distress and suffer-
ing. The Oxfam shops are used for four purposes, first the reception and sorting of
articles given to Oxfam, secondly the sale of most of the articles given to Oxfam,
thirdly the sale of village handicraft articles made as a result of the Oxfam 'Helping
by Selling' programme and fourthly the sale of articles made by Oxfam Activities
Ltd, a subsidiary of Oxfam which publicises Oxfam and makes profits for Oxfam.
The shops, some of which are occupied rent free or at a low rent, are an effective
form of fund raising, and are manned by local groups of Oxfam supporters on a voluntary basis. The shops give opportunities to the old and poor, but also to the not so

---

1   [1965] 1 All ER 730 at 735, [1965] AC 609 at 622

a old and not so poor, to acquire clothes at modest prices and to establish links with the local groups.

The activities carried on at the shops promote the activities of Oxfam and help to extend the ambit and usefulness of the operations of Oxfam, but none of the activities carried on in the shops directly assists in the relief of poverty save the third activity. Under the 'Helping by Selling' programme the poor are relieved by employment on

b village handicrafts provided the articles they make are sold; the shops provide a necessary outlet for that sale. This activity 'directly facilitates' the relief of poverty: see the judgments of Lord Macdermott CJ and McVeigh LJ in *Belfast Association for Employment of Industrious Blind v Comrs of Valuation for Northern Ireland*[1]. But in the present instance the sales of village handicraft articles only account for 7 per cent of the sales of the shops. I propose therefore to ignore this third activity. I also propose to ignore the fourth activity, namely the sales of articles for Oxfam produced

c by Oxfam Activities Ltd. It was not contended that this activity ranked as user of the premises for charitable purposes; it only represented 13 per cent of the sales.

Argument ranged largely round the first and second activities, namely the collection and sorting of gifted articles and the sale of most of the gifted articles. These activities appear to be, or to be analogous to, the carrying on of a retail shop for the purpose of fund raising. Such activities are not more relevant to the relief of poverty

d than they are to any other charitable or benevolent purpose. They are not wholly ancillary to the relief of poverty.

Counsel for Oxfam relied on *Aldous v Southwark Corpn*[2]. In that case an estate office and other premises occupied and used for the management of the Dulwich Estate which forms an endowment of Dulwich College were held by the Court of Appeal to attract rate relief. The Court of Appeal decided that the management

e and administration of a charitable endowment is itself a charitable purpose. Counsel for Oxfam commended the result and the reasoning of the decision, both of which are binding on me. Counsel for the rating authority reserved the right of criticism elsewhere.

Counsel for Oxfam urged that the articles given to Oxfam are charitable property, that the receipt and sorting and sale of the gifted articles constitute a form of manage-

f ment and administration of charitable property and that the purpose of the sales was to convert the gifted articles into usable form, that is to say, money. But the Court of Appeal in *Aldous v Southwark Corpn*[2] recoiled from the suggestion that premises used for fund raising are used for charitable purposes within s 40 of the 1967 Act, and in truth and in substance the Oxfam shops are used for fund raising and very little else. The elaborate analysis to which counsel subjected the activities of an

g Oxfam shop served to disguise but failed to hide the difference between management and fund raising which, as the law now stands, distinguishes the Dulwich Estate office from the Oxfam shop. In my judgment the Oxfam shops do not qualify for rate relief.

h *Summons dismissed. Certificate granted under s 12 of the Administration of Justice Act 1969 on the plaintiffs' application to present a petition of appeal to the House of Lords.*

Solicitors: *Waterhouse & Co* (for the plaintiffs); *Sharpe, Pritchard & Co*, agents for Town Clerk, Birmingham.

Jacqueline Metcalfe Barrister.

j

1 [1968] NI 21
2 [1968] 3 All ER 498, [1968] 1 WLR 1671

Re Downer Enterprises Ltd

CHANCERY DIVISION
PENNYCUICK V-C
23rd, 24th APRIL 1974

Company – Winding-up – Lease – Rent – Retention of possession after winding-up – Rights of landlord – Subrogation of rights – Rent accruing after commencement of winding-up – Retention of possession for purpose of disposing of lease advantageously – Company assignee of lease – Assignor liable to landlord for payment of rent – Company ultimately liable for rent – Assignor paying rent to landlord – Assignor claiming rent from company – Whether assignor entitled to claim rent in full as expense of winding-up.

The landlord let property to GP Ltd for a term of 21 years from 1964. In 1969 GP Ltd assigned the lease to SI Inc and therefore, while GP Ltd remained liable as the original lessee for the payment of the rent to the landlord, GP Ltd was entitled to be indemnified by SI Inc which was thus ultimately liable for the payment of the rent. In 1970 SI Inc assigned the lease to DE Ltd with the result that DE Ltd in turn became ultimately liable for the rent. In November 1971 DE Ltd went into a creditors' voluntary winding-up and a liquidator was appointed. From the commencement of the winding-up DE Ltd ceased to pay the rent. The liquidator decided that the obligations of DE Ltd under the lease were onerous and ought to be terminated, but he was advised that an application for leave to disclaim the lease would be unsuccessful. Accordingly, at some date in the early spring of 1972, before 30th April, he instructed estate agents to sell the residue of the lease as soon as possible. It took some time to find a suitable purchaser and it was not until March 1973 that the residue of the lease was assigned to M. The landlord demanded and recovered payment from GP Ltd of the arrears of rent which had accrued for the period between the commencement of the winding-up and the assignment to M. GP Ltd in turn demanded payment from SI Inc, who paid in full the arrears of rent and fire insurance premiums amounting to £4,552·84. That payment by SI Inc was made without the knowledge or approval of the liquidator. SI Inc proved for £4,552·84 as an ordinary debt and for part of the sum, namely £1,927·38, which was the gross amount of the price realised on the assignment to M, as an expense in the winding-up. The liquidator accepted SI Inc's proof for £4,552·84 as an ordinary debt but rejected their proof for £1,927·38 as an expense in the winding-up. By summons SI Inc applied for an order against the liquidator that they were entitled to be paid, as an expense in the winding-up, the sum of £1,340, the net amount realised on the assignment to M and the sum to which, for the purposes of the summons, they limited their claim.

Held – (i) From the date when the liquidator gave the estate agents instructions to find a suitable purchaser he was to be treated as having remained in possession of the property with a view to realising it to the best possible advantage. Accordingly, if the landlord had not been put in funds by GP Ltd, or by SI Inc through GP Ltd, it would have been entitled to be paid four quarters rent, i e £2,000, as an expense in the winding-up (see p 1081 *b* to *d* and *h* to p 1082 *b*, post); *Re Lundy Granite Co* (1871) 6 Ch App 462, *Re Oak Pits Colliery* (1882) 21 Ch D 322 and *Re ABC Coupler and Engineering Co Ltd (No 3)* [1970] 1 All ER 650 applied.

(ii) Where A and B were liable to a creditor for the same debt in such circumstances that the ultimate liability fell on A, and if B in fact paid the debt to the creditor, B was entitled to take over by subrogation any securities or rights which the creditor might have had against A, including, in the circumstances where A was a company in liquidation, the right to be paid rent in full. Accordingly SI Inc, having paid the arrears of rent for which DE Ltd was ultimately liable, was entitled by subrogation *a* to be paid in full the rent which had accrued from the date when the liquidator gave the estate agents instructions to find a purchaser, that being the moment from which he had retained the property for the purposes of the winding-up. It followed that SI Inc was entitled to be paid the sum of £1,340 (being the maximum sum claimed by SI Inc) out of the assets of DE Ltd as an expense in the winding-up (see p 1082 *b c* and *h* to p 1083 *a* and p 1084 *d* and *h*, post); *Duncan, Fox & Co v North and South Wales* *b* *Bank* (1880) 6 App Cas 1 applied; *Baynton v Morgan* (1888) 22 QBD 74 explained.

Notes

For distress for rent after commencement of winding-up, see 7 Halsbury's Laws (4th Edn) 771, 772, 835, paras 1361, 1362, 1502, and for cases on the subject, see 10 Digest (Repl) 1022-1024, 7029-7054.

c For doctrine of subrogation, see 14 Halsbury's Laws (3rd Edn), 618, para 1141, and for a case on the subject, see 20 Digest (Repl) 542, 2521.

Cases referred to in judgment

ABC Coupler and Engineering Co Ltd (No 3), Re [1970] 1 All ER 650, [1970] 1 WLR 702, DC, Digest (Cont Vol C) 117, 6734a.

d *Barleycorn Enterprises Ltd, Re, Mathias and Davies (a firm) v Down (liquidator of Barleycorn Enterprises Ltd)* [1970] 2 All ER 155, [1970] Ch 465, [1970] 2 WLR 898, CA, Digest (Cont Vol C) 119, 6927a.

Baynton v Morgan (1888) 22 QBD 74, 58 LJQB 139, 53 JP 166, CA, 31(1) Digest (Reissue) 531, 4455.

Craythorne v Swinburne (1807) 14 Ves 160, 33 ER 482, [1803-13] All ER Rep 181, LC, 26 Digest (Repl) 145, 1063.

e *Dering v Winchelsea (Earl)* (1787) 1 Cox Eq Cas 318, 29 ER 1184, sub nom *Deering v Winchelsea (Earl)* 2 Bos & P 270, [1775-1802] All ER Rep 140, 26 Digest (Repl) 145, 1065.

Duncan, Fox & Co and Robinson & Co v The North and South Wales Bank, S C Radford, Radford & Sons and Balfour, Williamson & Co (1880) 6 App Cas 1, 50 LJCh 355, 43 LT 706, 26 Digest (Repl) 118, 829.

f *Lundy Granite Co, Re, ex parte Heavan* (1871) 6 Ch App 462, 40 LJCh 588, 24 LT 922, 10 Digest (Repl) 1023, 7047.

Oak Pits Colliery Co, Re, (1882) 21 Ch D 322, [1881-85] All ER Rep 1157, 51 LJCh 768, 47 LT 7, CA, 10 Digest (Repl) 1023, 7050.

Stirling v Forrester (1821) 3 Bli 575, 4 ER 712, 26 Digest (Repl) 143, 1048.

g **Cases also cited**

Anglo-Austrian Printing and Publishing Union, Re, Brabourne v Same [1895] 2 Ch 891.

Arnal, ex parte, Witton, Re (1883) 24 Ch D 26, [1881-85] All ER Rep 975, CA.

Congresbury Motors Ltd v Anglo-Belge Finance Co Ltd [1970] 3 All ER 385, [1971] Ch 81, CA.

h *Coptic Ltd v Bailey* [1972] 1 All ER 1242, [1972] Ch 446.

Dressler, ex parte, Solomon, Re (1878) 9 Ch D 252, [1874-80] All ER Rep 1194, CA.

Progress Assurance Co, Re, Liverpool Exchange Co, ex parte (1870) LR 9 Eq 370.

Silkstone and Dodworth Coal and Iron Co, Re (1881) 17 Ch D 158.

Slough Estates Ltd v Slough Borough Council (No 2) [1969] 2 All ER 988, [1969] 2 Ch 305, CA.

j *Wilson v Wallani* (1880) 5 Ex D 155.

Adjourned summons

By an originating summons dated the 16th May 1973, Schick International Inc ('Schick'), a creditor of Downer Enterprises Ltd ('the company'), applied for an order that the decision of the respondent, Martin Pollins, who had been appointed the liquidator of the company under a creditors' voluntary winding-up, to reject the

proof of Schick for £4,552·84 being as to £1,927·38 a preferential claim be reversed
and that the proof be ordered to be admitted in full. The facts are set out in the
judgment.

J H G Sunnucks for Schick.
John G C Phillips for the liquidator.

PENNYCUICK V-C. I have before me a summons in the matter of Downer
Enterprises Ltd (to which I will refer as 'the company'). The company is in liquidation
under a creditors' voluntary winding-up. The respondent on this summons is the
liquidator of the company, and the applicant is Schick International Inc, an American
company (to which I will refer as 'Schick'). Although it is not expressed in quite
those terms in the summons, the effective question before the court is whether
Schick is entitled to be paid in full out of the assets of the company a sum representing
rent accrued after the commencement of the winding-up owing by the company
to Prudential Assurance Co Ltd ('Prudential'), the landlord of certain premises,
and paid by Schick, Schick having been an intermediate lessee of those premises.

The facts are contained in affidavits sworn by Mr Vincent, a director of Schick,
Mr Flavell, a partner in the firm of Pollins, Flavell, Powell, in which the liquidator
is another partner, a much fuller affidavit sworn by the liquidator himself, and
finally an affidavit in reply by Mr Vincent. There are also a number of exhibits to
those affidavits. I understand that it was originally intended that the various deponents should be tendered for cross-examination, but, in the event, neither party has
insisted on cross-examining any of the deponents.

The history of the matter is as follows. The property concerned is 17 London Road,
Croydon. That property formed the subject-matter of a lease dated 17th May 1964.
The term under the lease was 21 years from 8th April 1964, the rent, so far as now
material, being £2,000 per annum. The lease contains a number of usual covenants,
including a covenant against assignment without the consent of the landlords. The
original tenant was a company known as Granada Properties Ltd ('Granada'), the
original lessor being a company known as Combined Properties Ltd. The freehold
reversion has at all material times been vested in Prudential. So far as the leasehold
interest is concerned, Granada assigned the leasehold interest to Schick on 29th January
1969. The effect of that assignment was, by virtue of the provisions in the Law of
Property Act 1925 and the general law, that Schick became liable to Prudential
for the rent under the lease, Granada remained liable as the original tenant, but,
as between Granada and Schick, Granada was entitled to be indemnified by Schick.
Then, on a date in 1970, Schick in its turn assigned the lease to the company, producing a corresponding result to that produced by the assignment from Granada
to Schick. The date is left blank in the assignment.

On 8th November 1971 the company went into a creditors' voluntary winding-up
and the liquidator was appointed. Summarily, the liquidator made some enquiries
as to the possibility of disclaiming the tenancy, but was advised that he would be
unable to do so. He then retained this asset, consisting of the leasehold interest under
the lease, with a view to selling it as soon as practicable. It took some time to find
a purchaser, and finally the lease was assigned to one Mentesh Mustafa on 5th March
1973. Although it is not in evidence, it has now been ascertained and is not in dispute
that the liquidator gave instructions to agents to find a purchaser for the property
at some time before 30th April 1972. One cannot place the date more precisely.
Throughout this period from the commencement of the winding-up until the assignment to Mr Mustafa, rent continued to accrue due under the lease. The company,
in liquidation, failed to pay that rent. Prudential, as it was entitled to do, demanded
payment from Granada, which in turn demanded payment from Schick, and Schick
paid the rent in full.

a At the commencement of the winding-up the amount owing for arrears of rent and fire insurance premiums was £2,526·42. With those arrears I am not directly concerned on this summons because there is no doubt that they only form the subject-matter of proof. The amount which had accrued since the date of the liquidation was £2,026·42 at the time when Mr Flavell swore his affidavit on 25th July 1973. Presumably Mr Mustafa has since duly paid the rent; with that again I am not concerned.

b The precise amount realised on the sale to Mr Mustafa is not directly relevant and its amount has not been agreed with precision for various reasons, but I am invited for the purposes of this summons to treat the net amount realised as being £1,340.

The question then arises whether Schick, having paid the amount of the rent which had accrued since the commencement of the winding-up to Prudential, is
c entitled to recover in full the amount so paid as an expense in the winding-up, or is merely entitled to prove for this amount, presumably on the basis that it had a prospective and contingent liability to pay the rent at the commencement of the winding-up and would have a corresponding prospective and contingent claim against the company. It is conceded on behalf of the liquidator that Schick has such
d a right of proof and, for a reason which is not wholly apparent, Schick has limited its claim to be paid in full in respect of the rent to the net amount of the price realised on the sale to Mrs Mustafa.

I will next refer to certain passages in the affidavits, particularly that of the liquidator. The first affidavit is by Mr Vincent. He states that the liquidator is the liquidator of the company and has accepted Schick's proof of debt in the sum of £4,552·84 as an ordinary debt, but has rejected its claim that a part of this debt, namely £1,927·38
e —that I think is the gross amount received by way of purchase price from Mr Mustafa—has preferential status. The words 'preferential status' are, I think, not strictly accurate; what Schick is claiming is to be paid the sum in question in full as an expense in the winding-up. Mr Vincent then sets out the chain of assignments whereby the company became entitled to the lease. Then he says:

f '. . . [Prudential] became entitled to claim rent and rent arrears from [Granada] which company in turn became entitled to claim against [Schick]. [Schick] accordingly under pressure of proceedings paid arrears of rent and fire insurance due to [Prudential] in the sum of £4552·84 which payment enabled the respondent liquidator to secure the consent of [Prudential] under clause 29 of the fourth Schedule to the said lease to a sale of the said leasehold interest . . . the [liquidator]
g has been able to sell the said leasehold interest in the sum of £1750 and to retain for the benefit of creditors the sum of £177·38 in rent paid by a subtenant making a total sum of £1927·38 preserved realised or got in by the liquidator as a direct result of [Schick's] payment to the landlord of £4552·84.'

Then he says that Schick contends that it is entitled to preferential payment of
h £1927·38. It is common ground that the figures may require adjustment in various respects. I am not invited to go into those matters of adjustment, and, for the purpose of this summons, as I have said, I am treating the net amount realised from the sale as £1,340.

Mr Flavell swore a very short holding affidavit. I think I have already summarised the only material statements in that affidavit, namely, that £2,026·42 accrued after the date of the liquidation and that the lease was disposed of to Mr Mustafa on 5th
j March 1973; and then he goes into figures with which I am not concerned.

As I have said, the liquidator made the most important affidavit, because that goes to the course he took with regard to this asset and the reasons why he took that course. The relevance of that will be apparent when I refer to certain cases which have been decided in this connection. He says in the affidavit: 'When I became liquidator of [the company] I discovered that the company was tenant of property

at 17 London Road, Croydon . . .' He sets out the chain of assignments and he says
that he further discovered the amount of arrears of rent. He continues:

> '4. I decided that the company's obligations under this lease were onerous and
> ought to be terminated as soon as possible. I had no clear idea of the value of
> the residue of the lease as an asset and sought the advice of my Solicitors, Messrs.
> Donne, Mileham & Haddock of Ship Street Brighton as to whether I would be
> able to disclaim the lease. I was advised by them and verily believed that an
> application for leave to disclaim would be unsuccessful.'

That statement has been somewhat elaborated or explained by counsel for the
liquidator. It appears—I say no more than that—that what he was really advised
was that he would only be given leave to disclaim on terms that he made a substantial payment of rent to Prudential. He continues:

> 'I therefore attempted to dispose of the residue of the lease as quickly as
> possible. I instructed Messrs. Fox & Son of Brighton, Estate Agents, to dispose
> of the lease and they informed me and I verily believe that they appointed sub
> agents in Croydon in order to assist them. Unfortunately it took a long time to
> find a suitable purchaser for the residue of the lease and it was only finally dis-
> posed of to one Mentesh Mustafa on the 5th January 1973. [That I suppose was
> the date of contract, the March date being the date of assignment.]
> '5. It is true that during the period between the commencement of the liquida-
> tion and the date when I was finally able to dispose of the lease rent continued
> to accrue due to the freehold reversioners, the Prudential Assurance Co. Ltd.,
> and I accept that during this period the Prudential Assurance Co. Ltd. recovered
> the arrears of rent from their immediate tenants, Granada Properties Limited,
> and that that company in turn recovered £4452 [·84] from Schick . . . But the
> payment of this sum by Schick . . . was part of no agreement to which I was a
> party and was not done at my request or at my instance. In so far as Schick . . .
> rely upon their payment of the said sum as being an act done for the benefit of
> creditors of [the company], I can only say that they made the payment volun-
> tarily and not at my instigation or with my knowledge or approval.
> '6. As I said in my letter [which is exhibited] . . . I did not hold onto the
> property in the hope of obtaining a better deal for the creditors in general.
> I would have sought to disclaim the lease had I not been advised that an applica-
> for leave to disclaim would be unsuccessful. I did not retain the property volun-
> tarily. I had to retain it because of the lease and I disposed of it as soon as I
> possibly could. My reason for being desirous of disposing of the property as
> soon as I possibly could was of course to end as soon as possible the liability of
> [the company] to pay rent under the lease. At no time subsequent to the com-
> mencement of the litigation did I or the company carry on the business of the
> company or make use of the leased premises.'

That last sentence is accepted. Then he submits that the claim is misconceived and
refers to *Re Barleycorn Enterprises Ltd*[1], which in the end, as the issue has developed,
has proved to be rather beside the point on this summons. Then he says finally:

> '9. I should add with reference to Mr. Vincent's affidavit:—(a) If the second
> sentence of paragraph 5 of the affidavit is intended to state or infer that the
> payment was made by Schick . . . in order to enable the liquidator to secure
> the consent of [Prudential] to a sale of the leasehold interest, this is incorrect.
> In the early stages of liquidation the solicitors acting for [Prudential] were seek-
> ing some agreement with the other parties concerned whereby they should be
> paid the arrears of rent in return for a consent to assign, but no such agreement

---

1 [1970] 2 All ER 155, [1970] Ch 465

a   was made and [Prudential] therefore proceeded to recover the monies due
to them from their immediate tenant [Granada which] similarly proceeded
against Schick . . .'

Then he deals with rents received from a subtenant, with which I am not concerned.
Finally, Mr Vincent in his affidavit in reply says:

b   '3. I accept the evidence in paragraphs 1 to 5 of [the liquidator's] said affidavit
in so far as I am in a position to know the facts there stated . .
'4. With reference to paragraph 6 [that is the paragraph in which the liquidator
sets out his retention of the property for some 15 months and his reasons for so
doing] I fully accept what is stated . . .'

He adds a comment not now material. I do not think I need read anything more of
c Mr Vincent's affidavit.
It is on those facts that I have to consider the issue of law raised by counsel for
Schick which may be stated in the following terms. Was Prudential entitled, as
against the company, to be paid in full arrears of rent due after the commencement
of the winding-up, or, perhaps more accurately, would the court, in the exercise of
its discretion and applying certain established principles, have so directed? Secondly,
d assuming that Prudential would have been so entitled, then is Schick, having paid
the arrears to Granada and Granada having paid them to Prudential, entitled to the
same right by way of subrogation, or again perhaps more accurately, should the
court in the exercise of its discretion make a similar direction in favour of Schick?
The first question then which has to be determined is whether, if Prudential had
not been paid these arrears by Granada, and ultimately by Schick through Granada,
e Prudential would have been entitled to have the arrears paid in full as an
expense in the winding-up. By 'arrears' I mean, of course, the arrears which have
accrued since the commencement of the liquidation. I say 'entitled'. Strictly, the
court has a discretion whether to allow arrears to be paid in full in such circumstances, but that is a judicial discretion which the court exercises on well established
principles.
f   The law on this point has been the subject of a number of judicial decisions, most
of the leading cases having been decided just about a century ago, i e in the 1870s.
I do not propose to go directly to the earlier cases, because the law on this point was
fully reviewed recently by Plowman J in *Re ABC Coupler and Engineering Co Ltd
(No 3)*[1].
The effect of the earlier decisions may be gathered from two quotations contained
g in Plowman J's judgment, first from *Re Lundy Granite Co*[2], in which James LJ said[3]:

'But in some cases between the landlord and the company, if the company for
its own purposes, and with a view to the realization of the property to better
advantage, remains in possession of the estate, which the lessor is therefore not
able to obtain possession of, common sense and ordinary justice require the
h   Court to see that the landlord receives the full value of the property.'

Mellish LJ said[4]:

'If the official liquidator, for the convenience of the winding-up, does not
surrender the lease, but continues to keep possession for the purpose of obtaining
a better price for the goods, the landlord should not be deprived of his right to
j   recover his rent.'

---

1   [1970] 1 All ER 650, [1970] 1 WLR 702
2   (1871) 6 Ch App 462
3   6 Ch App at 466
4   6 Ch App at 467

Then in *Re Oak Pits Colliery*[1] Lindley LJ, delivering the judgment of the Court of
Appeal, said: *a*

> 'Secondly as to rent accruing after the commencement of the winding-up.
> 1. If the liquidator has retained possession for the purposes of the winding-up,
> or if he has used the property for carrying on the company's business, or has
> kept the property in order to sell it or to do the best he can with it, the landlord
> will be allowed to distrain for rent which has become due since the winding-up *b*
> . . .'

He then cites a number of cases. Counsel for the liquidator pointed out what I have
no doubt is true, that none of the earlier cases directly warrants the words 'or to do the
best he can with it', but those are the words used by the Court of Appeal and
must, I think, be treated as part of the principle established by the decision. *c*
Lindley LJ continued[2]:

> '2. But if he has kept possession by arrangement with the landlord and for his
> benefit as well as for the benefit of the company, and there is no agreement
> with the liquidator that he shall pay rent, the landlord is not allowed to
> distrain . . .
> 'But no authority has yet gone the length of deciding that a landlord is entitled *d*
> to distrain for or be paid in full rent accruing since the commencement of the
> winding-up, where the liquidator has done nothing except abstain from trying
> to get rid of the property which the company holds as lessee'.

There is no relevant distinction between a landlord's right to distrain and a land-
lord's right to receive payment of the rent in full.   *e*
Applying all the passages dealt with in a review taken from Buckley on the
Companies Acts[3], Plowman J said in *Re ABC Coupler and Engineering Co Ltd (No 3)*[4]:

> '. . . it appears that, apart from the question of some special equity (which,
> in my judgment, does not arise in the present case) the test of liability for pay-
> ment in full of rent accrued since the winding-up is whether the liquidator has
> retained possession "for the convenience of the winding-up", and that whether *f*
> he has done so or not, depends on his purpose in retaining possession—on what
> counsel for the official receiver called his motivation.'

Plowman J proceeded to apply those principles to the facts in the case before him
and held that the landlord was entitled to payment of rent in full as from the date
when the liquidator put the property in question on the market.   *g*
I confess that I am not entirely happy at the expression 'motivation'. That seems
to make the right of a landlord dependent on the subjective processes in the mind
of a liquidator. However, the difficulty is perhaps not a very real one in most
ordinary cases and there is nothing extraordinary about the case before me because
the motivation of Prudential will be found or will be inferred from what they in
fact did.   *h*
Turning to the present case, what happened, as appears from the evidence, as
supplemented by one statement to which I have already referred, and made by
counsel on instructions, was that for a short time, certainly a matter of weeks
but probably a matter of a few months, after the commencement of the winding-up
on 8th November 1971, the liquidator cast about by way of taking legal advice and
so forth to ascertain what he should do with this property and, in particular, whether *j*

---

1 (1882) 21 Ch D 322 at 330, [1881-85] All ER Rep 1157 at 1161
2 21 Ch D at 330, 331, [1881-85] All ER Rep at 1161, 1162
3 13th Edn (1957), pp 483, 484, 485, 487, 488
4 [1970] 1 All ER at 657, [1970] 1 WLR at 709

a he should disclaim it. However, having, for one reason or another, decided on advice not to disclaim it, he then gave instructions to agents to find a purchaser. Those instructions were certainly given, as appears from the letter which has been found, before 30th April 1972 and, in the absence of any more precise evidence, one must, I think, treat the instructions as having been given at some time in the early spring of 1972. It is immaterial for this purpose that the ultimate purchaser was apparently in fact found by Schick.

b Given those facts, it seems to me that from the date when he gave instructions to find a purchaser—that is some date in the early spring of 1972—the liquidator must be treated as having remained in possession of this property with a view to the realisation of the property to the best available advantage, or, in other words, he must be treated as having kept the property in order to sell it or do the best he *c* could with it. It is immaterial, I think, in considering the purpose for which the liquidator retained the property that, having regard to the amount of the rent and the amount which he expected to realise on a sale of the property, it might have been more advantageous to him and to his trust estate to have realised it at an earlier date.

Given those facts, it seems to me that, applying well established principles, I must *d* hold that Prudential, if they had not been put in funds by Granada, or by Schick through Granada, would have been entitled to be paid, as an expense of the winding-up, rent for approximately one year. That would cover the four quarter days at the end of March, June, September and December. That involves a sum of £2,000 which is rather larger than the sum actually claimed by Schick in this case.

I have not disregarded the evidence given by the liquidator as to his own motivation, if I may quote the word used by Plowman J[1]. In para 4 of the *e* liquidator's affidavit, which I have read, he states that he was—

> 'advised . . . and verily believed that an application for leave to disclaim would be unsuccessful. I therefore attempted to dispose of the residue of the lease as quickly as possible. I instructed Messrs. Fox & Son . . . to dispose of the lease . . .'

f
So far no difficulty arises, but then in para 6 he does say:

> 'I did not hold onto the property in the hope of obtaining a better deal for the creditors in general. I would have sought to disclaim the lease had I not been advised that an application for leave to disclaim would be unsuccessful. I did not *g* retain the property voluntarily. I had to retain it because of the lease and I disposed of it as soon as I possibly could. My reason for being desirous of disposing of the property as soon as I possibly could was of course to end as soon as possible the liability of [the company] to pay the rent under the lease.'

That statement is accepted by Mr Vincent as true. For all that analysis of his own *h* mental processes, the fact remains that from the date when he gave instructions to Messrs Fox & Son to sell until the actual sale the liquidator was holding this property with a view to its realisation at the best available price, and I do not think that there is anything in this analysis of his own mental processes which justifies one in reaching any other conclusion as to his purpose in retaining the property. He did in fact retain it and he retained it with a view to disposal as soon as he possibly could, which *i* clearly means (as he says in the earlier paragraph) as soon as he could find a suitable purchaser, which means, I suppose, a purchaser to whom leave to assign would be granted and who was willing to pay what he regarded as a fair price. I do not feel able to interpret the liquidator's evidence as establishing any motivation on his part

---

1   [1970] 1 All ER at 657, [1970] 1 WLR at 709

which would take the case out of the principle laid down in *Re Lundy Granite Co*[1] *a*
and *Re Oak Pits Colliery*[2].

So far as that issue is concerned then, I conclude that the court, applying a judicial
discretion in accordance with established principles, would have directed that
Prudential was entitled to receive four quarters rent in full as an expense of the
winding-up.

Then comes the next question, namely, whether Schick is entitled by subrogation *b*
to have the judicial discretion exercised in its favour in the same way as Prudential
would have been. The general principle here, I think, is not in doubt, namely that
if A and B are liable to a creditor for the same debt in such circumstances that the
ultimate liability falls on A, and if B in fact pays the debt to the creditor, then B is
entitled to be reimbursed by A, and likewise is entitled to take over by subrogation
any securities or rights which the creditor may have against A, and I can see no reason
why such rights should not include the right to be paid rent in full in circumstances *c*
such as the present, i e the circumstances of a company in liquidation.

The general principle is clearly stated in *Duncan, Fox & Co v North and South Wales
Bank*[3], by Lord Selborne LC:

'In examining the principles and authorities applicable to this question, it *d*
seems to me to be important to distinguish between three kinds of cases: (1.)
Those in which there is an agreement to constitute, for a particular purpose, the
relation of principal and surety, to which agreement the creditor thereby secured
is a party; (2.) Those in which there is a similar agreement between the principal
and surety only, to which the creditor is a stranger; and (3.) Those in which,
without any such contract of suretyship, there is a primary and a secondary
liability of two persons for one and the same debt, the debt being, as between *e*
the two, that of one of those persons only, and not equally of both, so that the
other, if he should be compelled to pay it, would be entitled to reimbursement
from the person by whom (as between the two) it ought to have been paid.'

Lord Selborne LC in that passage makes it perfectly clear that this right of reimbursement, which carries with it the right of subrogation, is not confined to the case of a *f*
guarantee, but applies in any case where there is a primary and secondary liability
for the same debt. Lord Blackburn ultimately puts the same principle in rather
different terms[4]:

'I think it is established by the case of *Deering* v. *Lord Winchelsea*[5], and the
observations on that case by Lord *Eldon* in *Craythorne* v. *Swinburne*[6], and Lord
Redesdale in *Stirling* v. *Forrester*[7], that where a creditor has a right to come upon *g*
more than one person or fund for the payment of a debt, there is an equity
between the persons interested in the different funds that each shall bear no
more than its due proportion. This is quite independent of any contract between
the parties thus liable.'

Clearly that principle applies equally where ultimately one person is primarily *h*
liable for the whole debt and the other is ultimately liable for none of it.

Unless there is any more to it, it seems to me that the principle laid down in that
case is plainly applicable in the present case; that is to say, Granada, Schick and the
company were each of them liable to Prudential for the rent accruing after the

---

1   (1871) 6 Ch App 462
2   (1882) 21 Ch D 322, [1881-85] All ER Rep 1157
3   (1880) 6 App Cas 1 at 10, 11
4   6 App Cas at 19
5   (1787) 1 Cox Eq Cas 318, [1775-1802] All ER Rep 140
6   (1807) 14 Ves 160, [1803-13] All ER Rep 181
7   (1821) 3 Bli 575

a commencement of the winding-up   The company was unable to pay; Schick in fact paid, and, that being so, Schick is entitled to recoupment from the company and is entitled to take over by subrogation whatever rights Prudential had against the company, including, it seems to me, the right to be paid in full in the winding-up.

Counsel have been unable to find any case directly in point, but there appears to me to be no reason why the principle (which is not in dispute) should not apply in b circumstances such as the present one, and, indeed, it would be a great injustice if it did not do so.

Great reliance was placed by counsel for the liquidator on *Baynton v Morgan*[1] in the Court of Appeal, where the headnote runs as follows:

> 'The plaintiff demised premises to the defendant for a term of years by deed containing a covenant by the defendant for the payment of the rent reserved. c   The defendant assigned the term, and his assignee surrendered a portion of the premises to the plaintiff. In an action on the covenant the plaintiff claimed to recover the amount of the apportioned rent for the part of the premises not surrendered:—*Held*, that the liability of the defendant on the covenant was not extinguished by the surrender of part of the demised premises, but he still remained liable thereon, at any rate to the amount claimed.'

d
It will be seen that the issue in that case was whether the defendant was in the position of a guarantor whose liability to the creditor had been discharged by some arrangement made between the creditor and the principal debtor.   Lord Esher MR said[2]:

> 'One of the grounds relied on by the defendant is that this covenant, after an assignment, is merely one of suretyship, by which the lessee guarantees the e   payment of the rent by his assignee of the lease; and, that being so, that, the assignee and the lessor having altered the original contract without the consent or knowledge of the guarantor, he is released from further liability on the covenant. The true answer to this contention seems to me to be that this is not a contract of guarantee. We must construe this contract, which is in writing, in accordance with its terms. There is not a word in it about a guarantee. It is a f   direct promise that certain sums of money shall be paid as rent on certain days during a certain period. Such being its express terms, it could only be contended to be a contract of suretyship by virtue of some implication. I see nothing that authorizes us to make any such implication. It was suggested that, unless the contract were treated as one of suretyship, some hardship might arise. I do not think that such considerations afford any ground for altering the effect of the g   plain words of the covenant. If there were any hardship, it would be one arising out of the terms of the contract which the parties have chosen to make.'

He then goes not to deal with the position which would arise if this were a contract of guarantee, but comes back to his former point later[3]:

> 'The true answer, however, to the argument appears to me to be that the h   contract is not one of suretyship, but one creating a primary liability. The covenant for payment of the rent is a covenant which has been usually inserted in leases for a very long time, I think I may safely say for at least a hundred years, and it has never been suggested before that it is a contract of guarantee.'

Now, that is a decision that the relation of the original lessee under a lease and his j assignee is not that of guarantor and principal debtor. So be it. But that takes, it seems to me, the liquidator no further in the present case because, as clearly appears

---

1   (1888) 22 QBD 74
2   22 QBD at 77, 78
3   22 QBD at 78

from the speeches in the House of Lords in *Duncan, Fox & Co v North and South Wales Bank*[1], this principle of subrogation is not confined to cases of guarantee.

Counsel for the liquidator placed great stress on the expression 'primary liability'. I venture to think that here there is some ambiguity in the expression 'primary liability' and likewise the expression 'secondary liability'. The expression 'primary liability' may mean, as it is used in *Baynton v Morgan*[2], direct liability, that is, the liability of the covenantor towards his convenantee. On the other hand, the expression 'primary liability' may mean something quite different; it may mean ultimate liability; that is to say, it may indicate the person on whom the liability ultimately falls as between two or more individuals each of whom is liable to the creditor and another of whom may well be primarily liable in the other sense of the word. It is with this sense of the word 'primary'—i e 'ultimate'—'liability' that one is concerned in the context of subrogation, and that is, I think, quite clear from the speeches in *Duncan, Fox & Co v North and South Wales Bank*[1] which I have quoted. Lord Selborne LC[3] referred to 'primary and secondary liability', and by 'primary' there he meant the person who would ultimately be liable for the debt and would have to reimburse the other person if the other person paid.

I conclude, then, that Schick is entitled by subrogation to the right which Prudential would have had on an exercise of judicial discretion on established principles, namely, the right to be paid in full the rent accrued as from the date when the liquidator gave instructions to the estate agents to find a purchaser for the property, that being the moment from which he was retaining the property for the purposes of the winding-up. As I have said, one may take four quarter days as included in that period, which would give a figure of £2,000. In fact, the figure which Schick has claimed is less than that, and it follows that Schick is entitled to be paid in full the sum of £1,340, that being the sum to which, for the purposes of this application, Schick's claim is limited.

Counsel for Schick advanced one or two other contentions on which, so he said, Schick ought to be entitled to payment in full of either these arrears of rent or this sum of £1,340. Very broadly, I think it is a fair paraphrase to say that the contentions came to this: that by paying the rent, Schick had preserved this asset for the benefit of the company in liquidation and, accordingly, Schick ought to be recouped its expense in so preserving the asset. The answer to that attractive argument, I think, is that there was no arrangement at all to that effect between Schick and the liquidator. Schick paid this sum not by arrangement with the liquidator, but because Schick was bound to pay it under the general law, first by way of indemnifying Granada against liability to Prudential. It has not been contended that there was anything in the nature of an arrangement between Prudential and the liquidator which would have prevented Prudential from claiming payment of the arrears of rent in full if Prudential were otherwise entitled to payment.

I propose then, in answer to the summons, to make an order the effect of which will be that Schick is entitled to be paid the sum of £1,340 out of the assets of the company as an expense in the winding-up of the company.

Order accordingly.

Solicitors: *Monro, Pennefather & Co* (for the applicant); *Donne, Mileham & Haddock* (for the liquidator).

Evelyn Budd   Barrister.

---

1   (1880) 6 App Cas 1
2   (1888) 22 QBD 74
3   6 App Cas at 10

a
R v Edwards

COURT OF APPEAL, CRIMINAL DIVISION
LORD WIDGERY CJ, LAWTON LJ AND ASHWORTH J
24th APRIL, 21st MAY 1974

b

Criminal law – Burden of proof – Negative averment – Prohibition of act subject to proviso, exception, excuse or qualification – Burden of proving that proviso etc applicable – Intoxicating liquor – Sale by retail without holding justices' licence – Grant of licence not peculiarly within knowledge of accused – Whether burden on prosecution to establish prima facie case that no licence granted – Whether burden on accused to prove grant of licence – Licensing Act
c *1964, s 160(1)(a).*

The appellant was charged on indictment with selling by retail intoxicating liquor without holding a justices' licence authorising the sale, contrary to s 160(1)(a)[a] of the Licensing Act 1964. At the trial the prosecution proved that the appellant had sold intoxicating liquor on the occasion in question but did not adduce any evidence
d that he was not in possession of a justices' licence. The appellant was convicted and appealed, contending that, since the clerk to the licensing justices was required by s 30(1) of the 1964 Act to keep a register giving particulars of justices' licences granted in the district, the question whether a licence had been granted to him was not one peculiarly within his own knowledge and accordingly the onus was on the prosecution to prove that no licence had been granted to him.

e

Held – Where an enactment made the doing of a particular act an offence, save in specified circumstances, or by persons of specified classes or with special qualifications or with the permission or licence of specified authorities, and, on its true construction, the effect of the enactment was to prohibit the doing of the act in question subject to a proviso, exception, excuse or qualification, there was no need for the
f prosecution to establish a prima facie case that the proviso etc did not apply. In those circumstances, whether or not the matter was peculiarly within the knowledge of the accused, it was sufficient for the prosecution to prove the act in question and the burden, in the sense of the legal or persuasive burden, then lay on the accused to prove that the proviso etc applied. It followed that the onus lay on the appellant to prove that a justices' licence had been granted to him. The appeal would therefore
g be dismissed (see p 1095 *b* to *f*, post).

R v Scott (1921) 86 JP 69 and *R v Oliver* [1943] 2 All ER 800 applied.

R v Stone (1801) 1 East 639 and dictum of Bayley J in *R v Turner* (1816) 5 M & S at 211 explained.

h
Notes
For the burden of proof in criminal proceedings, see 10 Halsbury's Laws (3rd Edn) 436, 437, paras 808-811, and for cases on the subject, see 14 Digest (Repl) 493-495, 4767-4791.

For sale of intoxicating liquor without a justices' licence, see 22 Halsbury's Laws (3rd Edn) 663, 664, para 1393, and for cases on the subject, see 30 Digest (Reissue) 90-96, 668-706.
j
For the Licensing Act 1964, ss 30, 160, see 17 Halsbury's Statutes (3rd Edn) 1095, 1193.

---

a Section 160(1), so far as material, provides: '... if any person—(a) sells or exposes for sale by retail any intoxicating liquor without holding a justices' licence ... authorising the sale of that liquor ... he shall be guilty of an offence under this section.'

Cases referred to in judgment

Apothecaries' Co v Bentley (1824) Ry & M 159, 1 C & P 528, 171 ER 978, 14 Digest (Repl) 495, 4782.

Buchanan v Moore [1963] NI 194, CA, Digest (Cont Vol B) 670, *772a.

Davis v Scrace (1849) LR 4 CP 172.

John v Humphreys [1955] 1 All ER 793, [1955] 1 WLR 325, 119 JP 309, 53 LGR 321, DC, 45 Digest (Repl) 80, 258.

Jones v Axen (1696) 1 Ld Raym 119, 91 ER 976.

McGowan v Carville [1960] IR 330, DC.

Nimmo v Alexander Cowan & Sons Ltd [1967] 3 All ER 187, [1968] AC 107, [1967] 3 WLR 1169, 1967 SLT 277, 1967 SC (HL) 79, HL, Digest (Cont Vol C) 375, 277e.

R v James [1902] 1 KB 540, 71 LJKB 211, 86 LT 202, 66 JP 217, 20 Cox CC 156, CCR, 44 Digest (Repl) 330, 1621.

R v Jarvis (1756) 1 East 643n, 1 Burr 148, 102 ER 249, 44 Digest (Repl) 330, 1629.

R v Oliver [1943] 2 All ER 800, [1944] KB 68, 113 LJKB 119, 170 LT 110, 108 JP 30, 29 Cr App Rep 137, 42 LGR 37, CCA, 17 Digest (Repl) 475, 265.

R v Putland & Sorrell [1946] 1 All ER 85, 110 JP 115, 44 LGR 73, 31 Cr App Rep 27, sub nom *R v Sorrell & Putland* 174 LT 148, CCA, 17 Digest (Repl) 473, 254.

R v Scott (1921) 86 JP 69, 14 Digest (Repl) 495, 4784.

R v Stone (1801) 1 East 639, 102 ER 247, 14 Digest (Repl) 494, 4779.

R v Turner (1816) 5 M & S 206, [1814-23] All ER Rep 713, 105 ER 1026, 14 Digest (Repl) 494, 4781.

Southwell's Case (1595) Poph 93, 79 ER 1204.

Spicers v Parker (1786) 1 Term Rep 141, 99 ER 1019.

Taylor v Humphries (1864) 34 LJMC 1.

Cases also cited

R v Ewens [1966] 2 All ER 470, [1967] 1 QB 322, CCA.

R v Spurge [1961] 2 All ER 688, [1961] 2 QB 205, CCA.

Robertson v Bannister [1973] RTR 109, DC.

Williams v Russell (1933) 149 LT 190, DC.

Appeal

On 15th October 1973 in the Crown Court sitting at Sessions House, Newington Causeway, London, SE1, (before his Honour Judge Friend) the appellant, Errington Edwards, was convicted on an indictment which charged him with selling intoxicating liquor without a justices' licence, contrary to s 160(1)(*a*) of the Licensing Act 1964. He was sentenced to six months imprisonment which was ordered to run consecutively to a term of 21 months imprisonment which he was already serving and which sentence had been imposed by the same court on 23rd May 1973 for, inter alia, similar offences. He was also ordered to pay £400 towards the prosecution costs. He appealed against conviction. The facts are set out in the judgment of the court.

Michael Underhill QC and *Henry Boyd* for the appellant.
H J Leonard QC and *J J Walker-Smith* for the Crown.

24th April. At the conclusion of argument the court dismissed the appeal and stated that its reasons for doing so would be given at a later date.

21st May. **LAWTON LJ** read the following judgment of the court at the invitation of Lord Widgery CJ. On 15th October 1973 the appellant was convicted at the Inner London Crown Court of selling by retail intoxicating liquor without holding a justices' licence authorising such a sale, contrary to s 160(1)(*a*) of the Licensing Act a 1964. He was sentenced to six months imprisonment to run consecutively to sentences totalling 21 months imprisonment which had been imposed on him on 23rd May 1973 for unlawfully gaming and for no less than three offences of selling by retail intoxicating liquor without a justices' licence.

He appealed against his conviction. His appeal was heard on 24th April 1974 and dismissed. The court decided to give its reasons later as the main point in the
b appeal seemed to raise a question of importance, namely, whether on a charge under s 160(1)(a) the prosecution should call evidence to prove that the appellant did not hold a justices' licence. The prosecution, following the practice of many years in the metropolitan police district and probably one followed generally throughout England and Wales, did not call any such evidence, leaving the appellant to prove, if he could, that he did hold a justices' licence. As a further ground, the appellant
c submitted that there was no evidence, or no sufficient evidence, to prove that he had sold intoxicating liquor at all.

At all material times since September 1967 the appellant had been the lessee of premises at 7 and 7a Railton Road, Brixton. On 6th October 1972 he went to Brixton police station to report that someone had smashed his windows at no 7. From 13th October until 16th October 1972 two police officers kept observation on these
d premises between 8 p m and 4 a m each day. During this period they saw 323 people enter no 7, mostly late at night after the public houses had closed. On 15th October 1972 at 8.10 p m these officers saw the appellant go to no 7 and unlock the door. He went in and came out again at 8.57 p m, going to 13 Railton Road. On 21st October 1972 shortly after midnight a number of police officers went to no 7, being in possession of a warrant given under s 187 of the Licensing Act 1964. In the basement they found about 70 people, most of whom were drinking beer. The basement was
e fitted up as a bar. The appellant was not present when the warrant was executed. He was seen by a police officer on 1st November 1972 and told he would be reported for the offence in respect of which he has been convicted. He said: 'Haven't you had enough money out of me already' and walked away. At his trial he was unrepresented. He did not give evidence but made an unsworn statement, the effect of which
f was to suggest that he had not been in occupation of the premises. The appellant made no submission based on the prosecution's omission to call any evidence to prove that no justices' licence had been granted to him.

When a submission based on this omission was first made to this court it seemed a surprising one as those who practise and sit in criminal courts have long thought that the burden of proving that a licence has been granted to authorise the doing of an act which is prohibited by statute unless a licence to do it is held rests on the
g defendant: see R v Oliver[1] and John v Humphreys[2]. Stone's Justices' Manual[3], which is, of course, the textbook used in magistrates' courts, where most cases of this kind are dealt with, states the law as follows:

'... where a person is charged with doing an act except under and in accordance with the terms of a licence, permit or other authority granted by or on behalf
h of a Government department, the burden of proving the possession of a licence, permit or other authority rests on the defendant, and there is no obligation on the prosecution to establish a prima facie case on this issue ...'

So far as magistrates' courts are concerned this statement of the law is founded on s 81 of the Magistrates' Courts Act 1952 which provides that on the hearing of an
j information or complaint in those courts the onus of proving exceptions, exemptions, provisos, excuses and qualifications shifts from the prosecution to the accused. Counsel

---

1   [1943] 2 All ER 800, [1944] KB 68
2   [1955] 1 All ER 793, [1955] 1 WLR 325
3   106th Edn (1974), vol 1 p 89, note (n)

for the Crown submitted that s 81 is a statutory statement of a common law rule applicable in all criminal courts. If it were not the law would be in an unsatisfactory state, because the burden of proof in summary trials would be different from that in trials on indictment.

Counsel for the appellant submitted, however, that at common law the burden of proving an exception, exemption, proviso, excuse or qualification only shifts when the facts constituting it are peculiarly within the accused's own knowledge and that they were not in this case because the Licensing Act 1964 requires the clerk to the licensing justices for a licensing district to keep a register of licences, containing particulars of all justices' licences granted in the district, the premises for which they were granted, the names of the owners of those premises, and the names of the holders of the licences (see s 30(1)). It follows, submitted counsel for the appellant, that the Brixton police had available to them in their own area a public source of knowledge which they could go to at any reasonable time (see s 34(2)). If the rule about shifting the onus of proof only applies when the facts initiating the operation of the exception are peculiarly in the accused's own knowledge, there is much to be said for the appellant's submission.

Counsel accepted that there are three exceptions to the fundamental rule of our criminal law that the prosecution must prove every element of the alleged offence. The first relates to insanity and the second to those cases in which a statute expressly imposes a burden of proof on an accused. The third exception has been under consideration in this appeal and questions have arisen as to its nature and the circumstances in which it applies.

The phrase which counsel for the appellant used in making his submission, namely, 'facts peculiarly within the accused's own knowledge' has been used many times in textbooks and judgments: for examples, see *John v Humphreys*[1] per Lord Goddard CJ; Phipson on Evidence[2]; and Cross on Evidence[3]. It has been taken from the judgment of Bayley J in *R v Turner*[4]. If the rule only applies when the facts constituting exculpation are peculiarly within the defendant's own knowledge, we would have expected to have found reported cases giving some help as to how the courts were to decide this. If a query arises, should the judge or the jury decide who had what knowledge? Should evidence be called on this issue? If not, why not? In the century and a half since 1816 this appellant is unlikely to have been the first defendant wishing to query the extent of the prosecution's knowledge. Counsel brought no such cases to our attention and we have found none for ourselves.

Despite the many times in the cases and textbooks reference has been made to the words used by Bayley J in *R v Turner*[4], we thought it necessary to examine that case carefully in its historical setting. For many decades before *R v Turner* there had been much discussion amongst lawyers how negative averments were to be pleaded in informations and indictments.

By the end of the 17th century a pleading distinction was drawn between a proviso in a statute and an exception: see Hale's Pleas of the Crown[5] (which was written about 1650) and *Jones v Axen*[6]. Exceptions had to be pleaded and disproved whereas there was no need to plead or disprove provisos. In *R v Jarvis*[7] (referred to in a note to the report of *R v Stone*[8]) Lord Mansfield CJ stated the rule as follows:

---

1   [1955] 1 All ER at 794, [1955] 1 WLR at 327
2   11th Edn (1970), p 108
3   3rd Edn (1967), p 81
4   (1816) 5 M & S 206 at 211, [1814-23] All ER Rep 713 at 715
5   1800 edition, vol 2, pp 170, 171
6   (1696) 1 Ld Raym 119
7   (1754) 1 East 643, note (e)
8   (1801) 1 East 639

a
'For it is a known distinction that what comes by way of proviso in a statute must be insisted on by way of defence by the party accused; but where exceptions are in the enacting part of a law, it must appear in the charge that the defendant does not fall within any of them.'

In some cases, however, it was difficult to decide whether provisions in the enacting part of a statute were in the nature of a proviso. This is shown by the cases arising
b on certiorari out of the notorious game laws. These laws, which were statutory, prohibited those without certain qualifications (some ten in number set out in the statute 22 & 23 Car 2 c 25) from keeping a gun or being in possession of game. The problem for those drafting informations under these laws and conducting prosecutions was whether the defendant's alleged lack of qualification should be pleaded and proved. By the end of the 18th century it seems to have been accepted
c that in actions for penalties under the game laws lack of qualifications did not have to be proved (see R v Stone[1]). The problem of what had to be proved in a criminal case came before the King's Bench on certiorari in R v Stone[1]. Before the justices the prosecution had not proved the defendant's lack of qualification. The court was equally divided, two of the judges (Lord Kenyon CJ and Grose J) being strongly of the opinion that the prosecution had to prove lack of qualification, whereas the
d other two (Lawrence and Le Blanc JJ) were of the contrary view. The court being equally divided the conviction stood.

The approach to the problem by all four judges was substantially the same: to wit, their understanding of the rules of pleading. In the course of argument counsel adverted to the difficulty of proving negative averments and there was some discussion about this. Lord Kenyon CJ thought that some general evidence should be
e given from which lack of qualification could be inferred whereas Lawrence J thought that proof of the act forbidden by the statute was enough to place the burden on the accused to show that he was qualified to do it. Lord Kenyon CJ's judgment is the foundation of the submissions which have been made in recent years that even when the prosecution seeks to rely on the exception to the burden of proof rule which is said to derive from R v Turner[2], it can only do so after having given some
f evidence, albeit slight, from which no lawful excuse can be inferred: see R v Putland & Sorrell[3] and Buchanan v Moore[4]; both these cases will be discussed later in this judgment.

The opinion of Lawrence and Le Blanc JJ were in accord with what was said in Hawkins' Pleas of the Crown[5] where the rule was stated as follows:

g
'It seems agreed, that there is no need to alledge in an indictment, that the defendant is not within the benefit of the provisoes of a statute whereon it is founded; and this hath been adjudged, even as to those statutes which in their purview expressly take notice of the provisoes; as by saying, that none shall do the thing prohibited, otherwise than in such special cases, & as are expressed in this act.'

h
He cites a number of authorities starting with Southwell's Case[6], where, in the enacting clause, the wording was 'otherwise than in such special cases . . . expressed in this Act'. An illustration of how Serjeant Hawkins envisaged this rule would apply appears from a passage to be found in the same edition[7], which was noted and

j 1   (1801) 1 East at 646, 650, 654
2   (1816) 5 M & S 206, [1814-23] All ER Rep 713
3   [1946] 1 All ER 85
4   [1963] NI 194
5   7th Edn (1795), vol 4, bk 2, c 25, s 113, pp 68, 69
6   (1595) Poph 93
7   7th Edn (1795), vol 2, bk 1, c 89, s 17, p 460

approved in *R v Oliver*[1]. He was commenting on the form of indictment alleging
an offence under the statute 9 & 10 Will 3 c 41 which enacted that no warlike naval
stores should be made by any person 'other than Persons authorized by contracting
with his Majesty's principal Officers or Commissioners of the Navy, Ordnance, or
Victuallying Office for His Majesty's use'. It was his opinion that the indictment
should allege that the prisoner was not an authorised person but he went on to say:

> '. . . yet it is not incumbent on the prosecutors to prove this *negative averment*,
> but that it is incumbent on the defendant to shew, if the truth be so, that he is
> within the exception in the statute.'

These passages indicate first that by Serjeant Hawkins's time the old distinction
between provisos and exceptions was becoming blurred, secondly that he, like the
judges, based his opinion on rules of pleading, and thirdly that he did not associate
the rule with the fact that the positive of a negative averment would, or might be,
peculiarly within the defendant's own knowledge.

In our judgment *R v Turner*[2] must be considered against this historical background. The point for discussion was the same as in *R v Stone*[3]. The information
had alleged that the defendant, a carrier, not being a person 'qualified or authorised
by the laws of this realm to kill game', had had in his custody and possession pheasants
and hares 'the same not being sent up or placed in [his] hands . . . by any person or
persons qualified to kill game'. No evidence was called by the prosecution to prove
want of qualification. The defendant's case on certiorari was argued by Scarlett,
probably the most able advocate of his generation. He took two points: the first
was technical as to the way the conviction had been drawn up; the second was an
echo of what Lord Kenyon CJ had said in *R v Stone*[4] about the need for prima facie
evidence. The leading judgment was delivered by Lord Ellenborough CJ. He
commented on the difficulty which would rest on the prosecution of proving the lack
of qualification and the ease with which the defendant could show he was qualified;
but towards the end of his judgment he referred to Lord Mansfield CJ's opinion
expressed in *Spieres v Parker*[5] as to the burden of proof resting on the defendant in
actions on the game laws and gave his own which was that he saw no reason why the
same rule should not be applied to informations as well as actions. He ended as
follows[6]:

> 'I am, therefore, of opinion, that this conviction, which specifies negatively in
> the information the several qualifications mentioned in the statute, is sufficient,
> without going on to negative, by the evidence, those qualifications.'

We read Lord Ellenborough CJ's judgment as being based on common law concepts of pleading, rather than on difficulties of proof, such difficulties being the
reason why the rule of pleading had developed as it had.

The second judgment was delivered by Bayley J. He started by referring to rules
of pleading[6]:

> 'I have always understood it to be a general rule, that if a negative averment
> be made by any one party, which is peculiarly within the knowledge of the
> other, the party within whose knowledge it lies, and who asserts the affirmative
> is to prove it, and not he who avers the negative.'

---

1   [1943] 2 All ER 800, [1944] KB 68
2   (1816) 5 M & S 206, [1814-23] All ER Rep 713
3   (1801) 1 East 639
4   1 East at 649
5   (1786) 1 Term Rep 141
6   5 M & S at 211, [1814-23] All ER Rep at 715

a As far as we have been able to discover from our researches this was the first time the rules of pleading which had been applied for so long were qualified in this way. The qualification cannot apply to all negative averments. There is not, and never has been, a general rule of law that the mere fact that a matter lies peculiarly within the knowledge of the defendant is sufficient to cast the onus on him. If there was any such rule, anyone charged with doing an unlawful act with a specified intent would find himself having to prove his innocence because if there ever was a matter which

b could be said to be peculiarly within a person's knowledge it is the state of his own mind. Such rule as there is relating to negative averments in informations and indictments developed from the rules for pleading provisos and exceptions in statutes and is limited in its application. No doubt the reason why the rules developed as they did was the common sense of the matter to which Lord Ellenborough CJ referred. In our judgment what Bayley J was doing was to state the reason for the rule

c as if it was the rule. The third judge, Holroyd J[1], used the phrase 'peculiarly within the knowledge of the party' but did so in order to demolish the argument that this case was an exception to the general rule of pleading.

It seems likely that practitioners in the decades which followed R v Turner[2] did not regard Bayley J's words of qualification as a limitation on an established rule.

d Thus in Apothecaries' Co v Bentley[3], which was an action for penalties under the statute[4] for practising as an apothecary without having obtained a certificate from the Society of Apothecaries of the City of London as required by that Act, no evidence was called by Scarlett, who appeared for the plaintiffs, to prove that they had not issued the defendant with a certificate or that he was exempted from the statute by the fact that he had been in practice before August 1815. Brougham, who was to become Lord Chancellor six years later, is reported[5] as having put his argument as

e follows:

'The distinction he conceived was this, that where an exception was created by a distinct clause, the burthen of shewing that he was within it lay upon the defendant; but here the exception was introduced to qualify the penal clause in its very body, the negative therefore must be both stated and proved by the

f plaintiffs.'

There was no submission that as a statutory corporation charged with the duty of examining apothecaries and issuing certificates to those qualified to practise, the plaintiffs would have known whether the defendant had obtained a certificate from them or had been in practice before the commencement of the Act so that the necessary qualification, or lack of it, was not peculiarly within his knowledge. R v Turner[2]

g was cited to the court by Scarlett in answer to Brougham's submission. Abbott CJ's ruling was that the onus was on the defendant to prove he had a certificate and was based on concepts of pleading, not on the plaintiffs' opportunities of knowing. In our judgment it is most unlikely that an experienced advocate such as Brougham would have failed to appreciate that R v Turner[2] only applied when the facts showing

h exception were peculiarly within the defendant's knowledge. Starkie's Law of Evidence[6] states the rule in these terms:

'And in general, where it has been shown that the case falls within the scope of any general principle or rule of law, or the provision of any statute, whether remedial or even penal, it then lies on the opposite party to show by evidence that the case falls within an exception or proviso.'

j

1 (1816) 5 M & S at 213, [1814-23] All ER Rep at 715
2 5 M & S 206, [1814] All ER Rep 713
3 (1824) Ry & M 159
4 55 Geo 3 c 194
5 Ry & Mat 160
6 3rd Edn (1842), vol 1, p 422

In 1848 by Jervis's Act[1] Parliament consolidated, amended and extended various
statutes which had conferred summary jurisdiction on justices. The modern courts   *a*
of summary jurisdiction came into being. The Act provided a statutory framework
for the conduct of proceedings in those courts at all stages. Section 14 dealt with
proceedings at the trial stage. It is clear that what Parliament was trying to do by this
section was to adapt proceedings on indictment to the new type of court. The section
had a proviso to the effect that if the information or complaint should negative 'any
exception, proviso or condition' the prosecutor or complainant need not prove such   *b*
negative, but the defendant might prove the affirmative. In our judgment the object
of the proviso to s 14 was to apply the common law relating to exceptions and provisos
to the new courts.   After 1848 the courts put a restricted meaning on the word
'exception' in this proviso. See *Taylor v Humphries*[2] and *Davis v Scrace*[3].   Parliament
stopped this restricting tendency by the terms of s 39(2) of the Summary Jurisdiction
Act 1879, 'the object of which was to widen the provision and to direct attention to the   *c*
substance and effect rather than the form of the enactment to which it is to be
applied': see the speech of Lord Pearson in *Nimmo v Alexander Cowan and Sons Ltd*[4].
Section 39(2) of the 1879 Act was repealed by the Magistrates' Courts Act 1952 and replaced by s 81 of that Act. In our judgment s 81 sets out the common law rule in
statutory form.

Paragraph 5(2) of Sch I to the Indictments Act 1915 contained a similar provision   *d*
relating to the form of an indictment. This is now r 6(c) of the Indictment Rules 1971,
which provides as follows:

> 'It shall not be necessary (when charging an offence created by or under any
> enactment) to specify or negative an exception, proviso, excuse or qualification.'

e

If it is not necessary to specify or negative exceptions and the like in a count, it is
difficult to see on principle why it should be necessary to prove an element in the
offence charged which has not been set out in the count.

Since 1816 there are a number of cases in the reports illustrating the shifting of the
onus of proof on to the defendant to prove either that he held a licence to do an act
which was otherwise prohibited by a statute or that he was exempted in some way.   *f*
Thus in *R v Scott*[5] the question arose whether the prosecution should have proved,
which they did not, that the defendant, who was charged with an offence under the
Dangerous Drugs Act 1920, was not authorised to supply specified drugs. That Act
provided that no person should supply any of the specified drugs unless he was
licensed by the Secretary of State to do so. Swift J held that if the defendant was
licensed, it was a fact which was peculiarly within his own knowledge and there was   *g*
no hardship on him in being put to the proof. We can see no difference between that
case (which was approved by the Court of Criminal Appeal in *R v Oliver*[6] and cited by
Lord Pearson with approval in *Nimmo v Alexander Cowan and Sons Ltd*[7]) and this.
There would have been no difficulty whatsoever in calling someone on the Secretary
of State's staff to say that the defendant had not been licensed to supply the drugs.

The statutory prohibition of acts otherwise than under licence granted by a govern-   *h*
ment department was a commonplace of life during the war years 1939 to 1945 and for
some time afterwards. The problem of who was to prove lack of licence was considered
fully in *R v Oliver*[6]. The appellant had been convicted on an indictment charging him
with supplying sugar otherwise than under the terms of a licence, permit or other

---

1   11 & 12 Vict c 43   *j*
2   (1864) 34 LJMC 1
3   (1869) LR 4 CP 172
4   [1967] 3 All ER 187 at 202, [1968] AC 107 at 135
5   (1921) 86 JP 69
6   [1943] 2 All ER 800, [1944] KB 68
7   [1967] 3 All ER at 201, [1968] AC at 133, 134

a   authority granted by the Ministry of Food, contrary to the Defence (General) Regulations and art 2 of the Sugar Control Order 1940[1]. The prosecution did not prove that he had not been granted a licence and he appealed on that ground. Counsel for the appellant submitted[2] that the rule shifting the onus to the defendant to prove he came within an exception did not apply 'as the information could easily have been obtained by the prosecution from official sources'. The Solicitor-General, who
b   appeared for the prosecution, put his case in these terms[3]:

'If a statute lays down that an act is prohibited except in the case of persons who are excepted, the onus is on the defendant to prove that he is within the excepted class.'

c   The Court of Criminal Appeal accepted this submission; and in his judgment Viscount Caldecote CJ dealt with two points which counsel for the appellant had put forward in support of his main submission. Both had been canvassed in the 18th century and had echoed through the courts in the 19th century; first, that although there was no need for the prosecution to prove that a proviso in a statute did not apply, this was not so with an exception; and secondly, the prosecution should have given prima facie evidence of the non-existence of a licence. As we have sought to show in this judgment
d   the old distinction between provisos and exceptions had been moribund, if not dead, for well over a century, although some life had been injected into it by Lord Alverstone CJ in R v James[4]. As to this, Viscount Caldecote CJ said[5]:

'With the greatest respect to the judgment of LORD ALVERSTONE, L.C.J., in R. v. James[6], it seems to us to be difficult to make the result depend on the question whether the negative is of a proviso or of an exception. We think it makes
e   no difference at all that the Order was drafted as it now appears instead of being in a form which absolutely prohibits the supply of sugar except as thereinafter provided, with a later clause providing that if a person is supplied under a licence, he should be excused.'

As to the second point Viscount Caldecote CJ said plainly that the prosecution was
f   under no necessity of giving prima facie evidence of the non-existence of a licence. As this point had been raised we infer that the court did not consider that the availability of evidence to the prosecution was a relevant factor in shifting the burden of proof.

R v Oliver[7] was cited to the House of Lords in Nimmo v Alexander Cowan and Sons Ltd[8], which was concerned with the onus of pleading and proving, in cases under
g   s 29(1) of the Factories Act 1961, that it was not reasonably practical to make and keep working places safe. Where the onus lay would, of course, be the same in both civil and criminal cases brought under that Act, although the standard of proof would be higher in criminal cases than in civil. None of their Lordships criticised R v Oliver[7]; Lord Pearson clearly approved it. Not everyone has done so; for an example, see Glanville Williams, Criminal Law[9]. In R v Putland & Sorrell[10] some judicial doubt
h   was expressed as to how far R v Oliver[7] went. The appellants were charged with having conspired to acquire, and having acquired, rationed goods (namely, silk stockings)

1 S R & O 1940 No 1068
2 [1944] 1 KB at 69
3 [1944] 1 KB at 70
j 4 [1902] 1 KB 540 at 545
5 [1943] 2 All ER at 802, 803, [1944] 1 KB at 73, 74
6 [1902] 1 KB 540
7 [1943] 2 All ER 800, [1944] KB 68
8 [1967] 3All ER 187, [1968] AC 107
9 2nd Edn (1961), pp 901-904
10 [1946] 1 All ER 85

without surrendering the appropriate number of coupons, in contravention of the
Consumer Rationing Order 1944. No evidence was called by the prosecution to prove
that coupons had not been surrendered. *R v Oliver*[1] was cited, but Humphreys J,
who delivered the judgment of the court, distinguished that case by stating that there
was a very broad distinction between a statutory prohibition against doing an act, in
which case it was for the defendant to prove that he might do it lawfully, and a statutory prohibition against doing an act otherwise than in a particular way, as for example
by surrendering coupons, in which case it was for the prosecution to give prima facie
evidence that the specified lawful way had not been followed. We have been unable
to appreciate the difference between the two types of case. The court had clearly
been impressed, as had Lord Kenyon CJ 150 years before in *R v Stone*[2], by the argument
that the shifting of the onus of proof could be oppressive; but under the Defence
(General) Regulations the only difference between a wholesaler of sugar called on to
justify his trade in that commodity and a man wearing a new shirt (one of the examples
given by Humphreys J) called on to prove that he had acquired it lawfully might be
that one could do so more easily than the other. We find this difference not
substantial enough to justify distinguishing *R v Oliver*[1].

In *John v Humphreys*[3] the Divisional Court had to consider the problem of the
onus of proof in a case of a defendant who had been charged with driving a motor
vehicle on a road without being the holder of a licence. He did not appear at the
hearing before the justices and no evidence was called other than to prove that he had
driven a motor vehicle along a road. The justices were of the opinion that mere proof
of driving (that not being in itself an unlawful act) was not enough to support the
charge and that before the burden of proving that he was the holder of a licence
passed to the defendant the prosecution should have established a prima facie case.
They dismissed the information. The prosecutor appealed. Before the justices he had
argued that the burden of proving the holding of a licence lay on the defendant
since it was a fact peculiarly within his knowledge; as indeed it was. It would have
been impracticable for the prosecution to have proved that no licensing authority
had issued a licence. It follows that this case is of little help on the question whether
R v Turner[4] applies when the prosecution can prove a defendant's lack of qualification
or lawful excuse. The court decided that there was no need for the prosecution to
establish a prima facie case. Ormerod J expressed some hesitation on this point but
concluded that the court was bound by the decision in *R v Oliver*[1].

On much the same kind of facts as in *John v Humphreys*[3] the problem was considered
by both the High Court and the Supreme Court in Eire: see *McGowan v Carville*[5].
Both courts ruled to the contrary effect to *John v Humphreys*[3] but Maguire CJ dissented. In *Buchanan v Moore*[7] the Divisional Court in Northern Ireland had much
the same problem to consider; but this time the charges were of using a motor vehicle
without insurance and failing to produce a certificate of insurance. The driver had
been asked to produce his certificate of insurance and had failed to do so. Proving that
a driver has no certificate of insurance may be even more difficult than proving that
he has no driving licence. Most of the relevant modern English authorities were cited
in argument. Lord MacDermott CJ[7] based his judgment on the proposition that—

'where one of the elements of a criminal charge consists of an averment of a
negative nature, and where the averment relates to a fact which is peculiarly
within the knowledge of the defendant, then the burden of disproving that
averment falls upon the defendant.'

1　[1943] 2 All ER 800, [1944] KB 68
2　(1801) 1 East 639
3　[1955] 1 All ER 793, [1955] 1 WLR 325
4　(1816) 5 M & S 206, [1814-23] All ER Rep 713
5　[1960] IR 330
6　[1963] NI 194
7　[1963] NI at 196

a He was doubtful about the validity of the prosecution's submission that with charges of this kind there was no need to establish a prima facie case. The court did not rule on this point because the prosecution had proved a sufficient prima facie case to shift the burden of proof on to the defendant.

b In our judgment this line of authority establishes that over the centuries the common law, as a result of experience and the need to ensure that justice is done both to the community and to defendants, has evolved an exception to the fundamental rule of our criminal law that the prosecution must prove every element of the offence charged. This exception, like so much else in the common law, was hammered out on the anvil of pleading. It is limited to offences arising under enactments which prohibit the doing of an act save in specified circumstances or by persons of specified classes or with specified qualifications or with the licence or permission of specified authorities. Whenever the prosecution seeks to rely on this exception, the court must

c construe the enactment under which the charge is laid. If the true construction is that the enactment prohibits the doing of acts, subject to provisos, exemptions and the like, then the prosecution can rely on the exception.

In our judgment its application does not depend on either the fact, or the presumption, that the defendant has peculiar knowledge enabling him to prove the positive of any negative averment. As Wigmore pointed out in his great treatise on

d evidence[1] this concept of peculiar knowledge furnishes no working rule. If it did, defendants would have to prove lack of intent. What does provide a working rule is what the common law evolved from a rule of pleading. We have striven to identify it in this judgment. Like nearly all rules it could be applied oppressively; but the courts have ample powers to curb and discourage oppressive prosecutors and do not hesitate to use them.

e Two consequences follow from the view we have taken as to the evolution and nature of this exception. First, as it comes into operation on an enactment being construed in a particular way, there is no need for the prosecution to prove a prima facie case of lack of excuse, qualification or the like; and secondly, what shifts is the onus: it is for the defendant to prove that he was entitled to do the prohibited act. What rests on him is the legal or, as it is sometimes called, the persuasive burden of proof. It is

f not the evidential burden.

When the exception as we have adjudged it to be is applied to this case it was for the appellant to prove that he was the holder of a justices' licence, not the prosecution.

In conclusion we turn to the appellant's second ground of appeal, namely, that there was no evidence, or no sufficient evidence, to prove that he had sold intoxicating liquor at all. We are sure there was. He was the lessee of the premises where selling

g on a large scale was taking place. He took an interest in the condition of the premises as was shown by his complaining to the police about windows being broken. He had and used a key to the premises. He went to them at a time they were fitted with a bar. He used premises nearby, no 13, at a time when large numbers of people late at night were going to no 7. When he was told he would be reported for the offence of which he was subsequently convicted, he made no denial but gave an equivocal answer.

h There was no substance in this ground of appeal.

It was for these reasons that we dismissed the appeal.

Appeal dismissed. Application for leave to appeal to the House of Lords adjourned.

j Solicitors: *Robert Thompson & Partners* (for the appellant); *Solicitor, Metropolitan Police* (for the Crown).

N P Metcalfe Esq   Barrister.

---

1 A Treatise on the System of Evidence in Trials at Common Law (1905), vol 4, p 3525

Myers v Milton Keynes Development Corporation

COURT OF APPEAL, CIVIL DIVISION

LORD DENNING MR, BUCKLEY AND ROSKILL LJJ

11th, 12th, 13th, 14th FEBRUARY, 8th MARCH, 3rd MAY 1974

Compulsory purchase – Compensation – Assessment – Development scheme – Compulsory purchase in pursuance of scheme – Method of assessment of compensation – Planning permission for development not in force at date of service of notice to treat – Statutory assumption to be made in such circumstances – Assumption that planning permission would be granted such as would permit development in accordance with proposals of acquiring authority – Apparent conflict between statutory assumption and principle that compensation cannot include increase in value entirely due to scheme underlying acquisition – Land Compensation Act 1961, s 15(1).

In 1966 the Minister of Housing and Local Government made an order under the New Towns Act 1965 designating a 22,000 acre site in north Buckinghamshire as the site of a new town. The site included the whole of the Walton Manor estate ('the estate') which was owned by the appellant. On 17th March 1970 the development corporation, which had been established under the 1966 order and had power to acquire land compulsorily, published a master plan containing its proposals for the development of the area. Those included the compulsory acquisition of the estate. The master plan showed that the estate would remain untouched during the first ten years of the development, but that after the ten year period the estate would become a residential area. On 18th March the development corporation gave a notice to treat to the appellant for the purchase of the estate and on the same day vacant possession was given. The appellant and the development corporation made a joint reference to the Lands Tribunal to determine the amount of compensation to be paid to the appellant. The tribunal considered that there was a conflict in the principles it had to apply in that it was bound to disregard the scheme for the new town by virtue of the well established principle that compensation for the compulsory acquisition of land could not include an increase in value which was entirely due to the scheme underlying the acquisition ('the *Pointe Gourde*[a] principle') but compelled to have regard to the scheme by virtue of the provision in s 15(1)[b] of the Land Compensation Act 1961 that it was to be assumed that planning permission would be granted in respect of the relevant land, such as would permit development thereof in accordance with the proposals of the acquiring authority. The tribunal attempted to resolve the conflict by posing two questions: (i) was the assumed planning permission derived directly from the scheme? (ii) if so, could planning permission for the proposals have reasonably been expected to be granted in the absence of the scheme? The first question it answered in the affirmative and the second in the negative. On that basis it found that the estate was deemed to be without the benefit of a planning permission for development and that the value of the land was therefore to be assessed at its existing use value only. On appeal,

Held – The appeal would be allowed and the case remitted to the tribunal for reconsideration as it had misdirected itself as to the law and applied the wrong principles in determining the compensation to be paid. There was no conflict between the *Pointe Gourde*[a] principle and s 15(1) of the 1961 Act; the tribunal had first to determine the nature and extent of the interest to be valued, which would, where relevant, include the benefit of planning permission assumed under s 15(1), and then ascertain the value of that interest; it was only at that stage, in evaluating the interest,

---

a   See *Pointe Gourde Quarrying and Transport Co Ltd v Sub-Intendent of Crown Lands* [1947] AC 565

b   Section 15(1), is set out at p 1101 h, post

a that the *Pointe Gourde* principle applied to ensure that any increase in value due to
the scheme was left out of account. It followed that the tribunal should, pursuant
to s 15, have assumed that, after ten years, planning permission would have been
available for the development of the estate as a residential area 'in accordance with
the proposals of the acquiring authority' and then determined the purchase price
for the land in March 1970 by assessing what price the land with that deferred plan-
b ning permission would fetch leaving out of account the scheme for the development
of the new town (see p 1100 *f* to *h*, p 1101 *j* to p 1102 *c* and p 1103 *c* to *h*, post).

Notes

For the valuation of freeholds and leaseholds for compensation purposes, see 10
Halsbury's Laws (3rd Edn) 113, 114, para 187, and for cases on the subject, see 11
Digest (Repl) 282-292, *1947-1977*.
c   For the Land Compensation Act 1961, s 15, see 6 Halsbury's Statutes (3rd Edn) 254.

Cases referred to in judgment

Birmingham City Corpn v West Midland Baptist (Trust) Association (Inc) [1969] 3 All ER
172, [1970] AC 874, [1969] 3 WLR 389, 133 JP 524, 67 LGR 571, 20 P & CR 1052,
[1969] RVR 484, HL, Digest (Cont Vol C) 133, *192d.*
d *Camrose (Viscount) v Basingstoke Corpn* [1966] 3 All ER 161, [1966] 1 WLR 1100, 130
JP 368, 64 LGR 337, [1966] RVR 459, CA, Digest (Cont Vol B) 698, *176b.*
Devotwill Investments Ltd v Margate Corpn [1969] 2 All ER 97, 20 P & CR 150, 67 LGR
764, CA; rvsd sub nom *Margate Corpn v Devotwill Investments Ltd* [1970] 3 All ER 864,
22 P & CR 328, 69 LGR 271, HL.
Horn v Sunderland Corpn [1941] 1 All ER 480, [1941] 2 KB 26, 110 LJKB 353, 165 LT 298,
e 105 JP 223, 39 LGR 367, CA, 11 Digest (Repl) 127, *167.*
*Jelson Ltd v Minister of Housing & Local Government, George Wimpey & Co Ltd v Minister
of Housing & Local Government* [1969] 3 All ER 147, [1970] 1 QB 243, [1969] 3 WLR 282,
133 JP 564, 67 LGR 543, 20 P & CR 663, [1969] RVR 391, CA, Digest (Cont Vol C)
979, *164b.*
Pointe Gourde Quarrying & Transport Co Ltd v Sub-Intendent of Crown Lands [1947]
f   AC 565, PC, 11 Digest (Repl) 131, *149.*
Provincial Properties (London) Ltd v Caterham and Warlingham Urban District Council
[1972] 1 All ER 60, [1972] 1 QB 453, [1972] 2 WLR 44, 136 JP 93, 23 P & CR 8, CA.
Rugby Joint Water Board v Foottit, Rugby Joint Water Board v Shaw-Fox [1972] 1 All
ER 1057, [1973] AC 202, [1972] 2 WLR 757, 136 JP 317, HL.

Appeal

g Under an agreement dated 20th March 1970 the appellant, Bernard Myers, agreed
to sell to the respondents, Milton Keynes Development Corporation, a freehold
property known as Walton Manor estate in the parishes of Walton and Milton
Keynes near Bletchley in Buckinghamshire, the purchase price to be—

h 'such sum as shall be agreed between the parties as compensation for the
compulsory acquisition of the property including if appropriate compensation
for disturbance assessed on the basis that a notice to treat was served by the
[respondents] pursuant to Section 7(1) of the New Towns Act 1965 on the [appel-
lant] and vacant possession was given one day after the publication of the Plan
for Milton Keynes by the [respondents] on 17th March 1970 and in accordance
with the provisions of the Land Compensation Act 1961 ... and failing agree-
j ment as shall be determined by an award of the Lands Tribunal consequent
upon a reference by consent of the parties ... to the Lands Tribunal for the
determination of the amount of such compensation ... with such variations
... upon the application of either party as any Court upon Appeal from such
award may determine'.

The parties failed to reach agreement and on 18th June 1970 there was a joint reference
to the Lands Tribunal to determine the compensation to be paid. The tribunal

(R C Walmsley Esq) gave its decision on 4th December 1972. The tribunal deter- *a*
mined the purchase price of the acquisition of the land at the sum of £230,700. The
tribunal stated that, had it decided differently the question of law that arose in
the course of proceedings, it would have made an award of £636,070. The appellant
appealed by way of a case stated, pursuant to s 3(4) of the Lands Tribunal Act 1949,
and the respondents cross-appealed. The facts are set out in the judgment of the
court.   *b*

George Dobry QC and *Michael Barnes* for the appellant.
Alan de Piro QC and *Crawford Lindsay* for the respondents.

Cur adv vult

8th March. **LORD DENNING MR** read the following judgment of the court.

1 *The facts*   *c*
In 1962 life was peaceful in Buckinghamshire. We mean in the northern part of
it. It retained its old attractive qualities. Bletchley was the little market town
serving the villages and farms round about. Two miles north of Bletchley there was
the little hamlet of Walton. It had a manor house built in Tudor times, and a few
cottages. Ten years ago it was bought by the appellant, Mr Bernard Myers, together
with over 300 acres round about. He made it a place to be envied. He modernised *d*
the manor house into a well appointed home. He restored the Elizabethan barn
with fine care. He made a stud farm with a head groom's house, extensive stabling
and an exercise yard. He had a dairy farm with buildings of the highest quality.
All in the midst of large fields. But the peace was doomed. The population of
London was spilling out all over the country. The planners fixed their eyes on this
area north of Bletchley. They thought it was a most suitable site for a new town. *e*
It was to have its centre at the hamlet of Milton Keynes. It was halfway between
London and Birmingham. Halfway between Oxford and Cambridge. Next to the
electrified railway, the M1 motorway, the A5 trunk road, and the Grand Union
Canal. So the planners produced a 'scheme'. It started in January 1962. Mr
Pooley, the county planning officer, made a report called 'The Overspill Problem
in Bucks. A new city?' That report proposed a new town centred on Milton *f*
Keynes, with a population of a quarter of a million.
The scheme grew apace. In April 1966 the Minister was satisfied that it was
expedient in the national interest that the area should be developed as a new town.
He made an order designating it as the site of a new town under the New Towns
Act 1965. Under it a development corporation was established with powers to
acquire land compulsorily. It was called the Milton Keynes Development Corpora- *g*
tion. The designated area covered 22,000 acres. It included the towns of Bletchley,
Wolverton and Stony Stratford. Also many villages. In particular it included the
whole of the Walton Manor estate owned by Mr Myers.
On 17th March 1970 the development corporation published a master plan which
contained its proposals for the development of the area. It included the compulsory
acquisition of the Walton Manor estate. On the next day, 18th March 1970, the *h*
corporation gave a notice to treat to Mr Myers for the purchase of the estate; or
rather, by agreement, a notice to treat was deemed to be served on that day. On
the same day, 18th March 1970, vacant possession was given. The value is to be
assessed as at that date: see *Birmingham City Corpn v West Midland Baptist (Trust)
Association (Inc)*[1].
In assessing the value, it is important to consider what would have happened if *j*
there had been *no scheme*, but instead the area had been allowed to develop without
it. This was a matter of controversy. But it would seem likely that Bletchley would
have developed as the major town in the area, and that the surrounding villages
would have developed into modest satellite towns around Bletchley. But that
there would be stretches of open countryside in between. The Walton Manor

---

1 [1969] 3 All ER 172, [1970] AC 874

a estate would have been fortunately placed. It would have been in an open stretch of land between the two villages of Wavendon and Simpson. 'The foregone outcome', said the Lands Tribunal, 'would have been to remain as it is, as open countryside'.

In contrast, however, we must see what had really happened by 18th March 1970. The new corporation had already done, or allowed to be done, considerable develop-
b ment in Bletchley itself. But nothing much in the neighbourhood of Walton. It had, however, prepared the master plan which it showed on two maps. One map showed 'The First Ten Years plan'. This showed that during the first ten years the development corporation proposed to develop a strip about eight miles long and two miles wide from Bletchley northwards; but to leave the whole of the Walton Manor estate untouched. The estate was situate next to the Open University, and
c it was proposed to be kept as open countryside for ten years. The other map showed 'The Strategic Plan'. This showed the final development, when completed, more than ten years hence, of the whole of the 22,000 acres of the new town. In this map it was proposed that the Walton Manor estate would become a residential area between the Open University and the further education colleges.

Those maps, of course, showed only the proposals at 18th March 1970. A year or
d so later things changed. A big pharmaceutical company, called Hoechst Ltd, controlled from West Germany, spotted Walton Manor estate. They acquired the house and 35 acres round it. They got all the necessary permissions. They erected buildings for pharmaceutical research, and made the place a centre of their activities. This development made the land of much value. An attempt was made to bring this value into the award, but the Lands Tribunal rejected it because the material time was March 1970, and at that time a prospective purchaser could not have foreseen
e the Hoechst development, or anything like it, or even anticipating anyone seeking permission for industrial development. That decision was not challenged before us.

Such being the facts, the question for the Lands Tribunal was: what was the compensation payable by the Milton Keynes Development Corporation for the Walton Manor estate?
f The case was heard by Mr R C Walmsley, a member of the Lands Tribunal, who was not a lawyer but a surveyor. No doubt when the case was allotted to him it was not anticipated that any serious point of law would arise. But Mr Walmsley thought that the case raised an acute conflict as to the law. On one basis of law (as he conceived it) the compensation would be £230,000. On the other basis (as he conceived it) it would be £636,070. He decided in favour of £230,700. The land-
g owner appeals to this court. The development corporation cross-appeal. At the request of both parties, we heard the appeal only, because each side thought they might want to test our decision on that part of the case in the House of Lords.

2 *The conflict as seen by the Lands Tribunal*
The Lands Tribunal stated:

h '. . . a conflict *does* arise in the instant case, between the *Pointe Gourde*[1] principle and the assumed planning permission, and this conflict has to be resolved.'

What is this conflict? The *Pointe Gourde*[1] principle was stated by Lord Macdermott[2] in these words:

j 'It is well settled that compensation for the compulsory acquisition of land cannot include an increase in value which is entirely due to the scheme underlying the acquisition.'

In applying that principle, the member of the Lands Tribunal thought that he had to *disregard* altogether the scheme for the new town.

---

1 *Pointe Gourde Quarrying and Transport Co Ltd v Sub-Intendent of Crown Lands* [1947] AC 565
2 [1947] AC at 572

The assumed planning permission is given by s 15(1) of the Land Compensation   *a*
Act 1961 which says:

> '... it shall be assumed that planning permission would be granted, in
> respect of the relevant land ... such as would permit development thereof in
> accordance with the proposals of the acquiring authority.'

In applying that assumption, the member of the Lands Tribunal thought that he
had to have regard to the scheme so as to see what were the proposals of the acquiring   *b*
authority. So there was the conflict as the member saw it. The *Pointe Gourde*[1]
principle required him to *disregard* the scheme. Section 15 required him to *have
regard* to it by making an assumption in accordance with it.

Faced with this conflict, the member thought that it was to be resolved by asking
these two questions and answering them in this way: (1) Was the assumed planning
permission derived directly from the scheme? To which the answer was clearly: *c*
yes, it was. (2) If so, could planning permission for the proposals have reasonably
been expected to be granted in the absence of the scheme? If it could have been
expected, then planning permission was to be assumed. If it could not have been,
then planning permission was not to be assumed.

The member answered the second question by finding that planning permission
could not reasonably have been expected to be granted in the absence of the scheme.   *d*
So he held that planning permission was not to be assumed. He found in terms—

> 'that the subject land is deemed to be without the benefit of a planning
> permission for development, and therefore as having an existing use value only.'

I am afraid that the member of the Lands Tribunal misdirected himself about the
law. Both counsel before us agreed that it was so. He read s 15 as if there were   *e*
written into it the words about 'reasonably expected to be granted'. Those words
are to be found in other places in the statute, such as ss 14(3), 16(2) and 17(4). But
they are not in s 15. And there is no justification for writing them into that section.

Furthermore, both counsel agreed that there was no conflict, such as the member
thought, between the *Pointe Gourde*[1] principle and s 15. The two can and should be
reconciled by tackling the valuation in this way. (1) Determine what was the nature of   *f*
the property to be valued. In this case it was the freehold of the Walton Manor estate.
(2) Determine the extent of the interest to be valued. In this case it was the freehold of
the Walton Manor estate, with the benefit of the planning permission assumed under
s 15. (3) Ascertain the value of that interest. It is at this stage, in evaluating the
interest, that the *Pointe Gourde*[1] principle applies. '[That] principle', said Lord Cross
of Chelsea, '. . . does not affect the interest to be valued, but only its value when
ascertained' (see *Rugby Joint Water Board v Foottit*[2]). It applies so as to ensure that any   *g*
increase in value due to the scheme is to be left out of account. The result is that the
assumed planning permission is to be taken into account. It is not to be ignored, as the
Lands Tribunal thought. It is a way in which the landowner can be compensated for
the potentialities of his land.

3 *The principles to be applied*   *h*

Before planning permission was thought of, the value of the land was always assessed
at its value to the owner. It was not merely the existing use value, but the value
of the land with all its potentialities. Thus, if it was used as agricultural land, but was
dead-ripe for the building of houses, the compensation was increased accordingly. In
those days front land, that is, land with a frontage to roads, was worth more than
back land, and so forth. This was commonplace: see *Horn v Sunderland Corpn*[3] by Sir   *j*
Wilfrid Greene MR[4], and Scott LJ[5].

1 [1947] AC 565
2 [1972] 1 All ER 1057 at 1095, [1973] AC 202 at 253
3 [1941] 1 All ER 480, [1941] 2 KB 26
4 [1941] 1 All ER at 486, [1941] 2 KB at 35
5 [1941] 1 All ER at 495, 496, [1941] 1 KB at 48, 49

a In 1947 there came the Town and Country Planning Act 1947 with all its great changes. No one was allowed to develop his land by building on it, or by making any material change in the use of it, unless he obtained permission from the planning authority: see s 12. If his land was acquired compulsorily, he only received compensation for its existing use value. He got nothing for its potentiality as building land. Even if it was dead-ripe land, he got nothing for it except existing use value: see s 51 (2) (4).

b This gave rise to no end of difficulties. So in the Town and Country Planning Act 1959 the basis of compensation was altogether changed by provisions which were soon afterwards embodied in the Land Compensation Act 1961.

These new provisions recognised this basic fact: land with planning permission may be worth far more than the same land without it. Its value may be multiplied tenfold, or even a hundredfold. In March 1970 the 300 acres at Walton for agricultural purposes would have fetched £300 to £350 an acre. Sold for residential purposes with planning permission for immediate development, it might have fetched £10,000 or £11,000 an acre.

c Under the new provisions, Parliament enacted that land should be credited with the benefit of planning permission in various situations. These provisions are very complicated, so we will only take some illustrations. If there was planning permission

d actually in force, the land should be credited with the benefit of that planning permission: see s 14 (2) of the 1961 Act. If there was no planning permission actually in force, but the land was in a zone allocated for residential or industrial use, the land should be credited with the benefit of whatever planning permission might reasonably be expected to be granted: see s 16(2) of the 1961 Act; Margate Corpn v Devotwill Investments Ltd[1]; and Provincial Properties (London) Ltd v Caterham and Warlingham Urban District Council[2]. If it was in a zone allocated for a reservoir or playing fields, or

e roads, but might, as an alternative, appropriately be developed for residential or industrial use, the land might be credited with planning permission for that alternative development, if it was such as might reasonably have been expected to be granted: see s 17 of the 1961 Act, and Jelson Ltd v Ministry of Housing & Local Government[3].

The present case is different from any of the instances we have given, because the

f Walton Manor estate did not have any actual permission. It was not in a zone that was allocated for residential use in any development plan. So it did not come within s 16(2). It was in an area where nothing was zoned or allocated: but where proposals had been made by the acquiring authority. These proposals had been made by the development corporation under s 6 of the New Towns Act 1965, and approved by the Minister. So far as Walton Manor estate is concerned, the proposals were not for immediate development, but for it to be a residential area after ten years.

g That is the setting in which we have to interpret s 15(1) of the Land Compensation Act 1961, which says:

'In a case where—(a) the relevant interest is to be acquired for purposes which involve the carrying out of proposals of the acquiring authority for development of the relevant land or part thereof, and (b) on the date of service of the notice to

h treat there is not in force planning permission for that development, it shall be assumed that planning permission would be granted, in respect of the relevant land or that part thereof, as the case may be, such as would permit development thereof in accordance with the proposals of the acquiring authority.'

That section gives rise to these questions. First: what is to be assumed about the rest of the designated area of the new town of Milton Keynes? One thing is quite clear.

j You are not to assume that it would have been developed in the way it had already been developed by the development corporation, or that there was the prospect of it being developed in the future in the way proposed by the development corporation.

---

1   [1970] 3 All ER 864, HL, rvsg [1969] 2 All ER 97, CA
2   [1972] 1 All ER 60, [1972] 1 QB 453
3   [1969] 3 All ER 147, [1970] 1 QB 243

You are only to assume such development as would have been likely to take place if
the development corporation had *never* come into being: see s 6(1) of the 1961 Act and   *a*
Sch 1, Part I, Case 3. *Second*: what is to be assumed about the Walton Manor estate
itself? Here again one thing is clear. You are not to assume that it would have been
developed in accordance with the proposals of the development corporation. You are
to disregard any increase by reason of the estate itself being developed in accordance
with their proposals: see *Viscount Camrose v Basingstoke Corpn*[1]. But you are to assume
that after ten years planning permission would be available for development as a   *b*
residential area.

It comes to this: in valuing the estate, you are to disregard the effect of the scheme.
but you are to assume the availability of planning permission. This is best explained
by taking an imaginary instance. A scheme is proposed for building a motorway
across Dartmoor with a service station every five miles. Suppose that land is taken on
which a service station is to be built as soon as possible. In assessing compensation,   *c*
you are to disregard any increase due to the proposed motorway, or service stations.
But, if the landowner had already been granted *actual* permission for that piece of
land for commercial purposes (e g as a café), you are to have regard to it: see s 14(2).
Even if he had no such permission already, you are to assume that he would have
been granted planning permission for a service station: see s 15(1). And you are to
value that land with that permission in the setting in which it would have been if   *d*
there had been no scheme. If it would have been a good site for a service station, there
would be a great increase in value. If it would have been in an inaccessible spot on the
wild moor, there would be little, if any, increase in value, because there would be no
demand for it. A further complication arises when the proposals are not to be put
into effect for ten years. Planning permissions are not in practice granted so far ahead.
They are only granted for immediate development. In the illustration you are, there-   *e*
fore, to assume that, after ten years, planning permission would be granted for
development of a service station—in a setting where there had been no scheme.

4 Application in this case

It is apparent, therefore, that the valuation has to be done in an imaginary state of
affairs in which there is no scheme. The valuer must cast aside his knowledge of what   *f*
has in fact happened in the past eight years due to the scheme. He must ignore the
developments which will in all probability take place in the future ten years owing to
the scheme. Instead, he must let his imagination take flight to the clouds. He must
conjure up a land of make-believe, where there has not been, nor will be, a brave new
town, but where there is to be supposed the old order of things continuing—a county
planning authority which will grant planning permission of various kinds at such   *g*
times and in such parcels as it thinks best, but with an assurance that in March 1980
planning permission would be available for the residential development of the Walton
Manor estate.

In this imaginary state of affairs, the valuer has then to ask himself: what is the
appropriate way of valuing the land with this assumed planning permission? He
would do well, we think, to follow the course set by Mr Hobbs, that most experienced   *h*
member of the Lands Tribunal, in *Viscount Camrose v Basingstoke Corpn*[1]. If the land,
apart from the scheme, would be virtually certain to be developed in a reasonable
time, then it would be appropriate to take the present value of the land with planning
permission now, but then make a deduction for the period during which the development would be deferred and also for the risk that it might not take place. That is the
method Mr Hobbs adopted for the 150 acres. But, if the land, apart from the scheme,   *j*
was unlikely to be developed for a long time (indeed so far ahead that it would not be
realistic to use a method of deferring a present value), then it would be appropriate
to value it at a 'hope' value. That is the value which it has for its existing use as agricultural land, but with an addition on account of the 'hope' that it would at some time
in the foreseeable future be profitable to develop it—in accordance with the assumed

1   [1966] 3 All ER 161, [1966] 1 WLR 1100

a planning permission. That is the method Mr Hobbs adopted for the 233 acres. Perhaps we may quote what was said there[1]:

'Even though the 233 acres are assumed to have planning permission, it does not follow that there would be a demand for it. It is not planning permission by itself which increases value. It is planning permission coupled with demand. The tribunal thought that the demand for these 233 acres was so far distant as to
b warrant only a "hope" of development, and valued them accordingly. I see nothing wrong with this method of calculation.'

But these are valuation questions, not questions of law. Different valuers may take different views about the best method of valuing the land in the hypothetical circumstances which have to be imagined. In the event of any divergence of views of
c valuers called to give expert evidence, the tribunal must decide whose evidence it prefers and determine the value as a question of fact.

In the present case the question of fact to be answered can, we think, be best formulated in this way: on 18th March 1970 what price would a willing seller be prepared to accept, and a willing purchaser to pay, for the Walton Manor estate, if there had been no proposal for a new town at Milton Keynes; and if the prospects of development on
d and in the neighbourhood of the Walton Manor estate had then been such as they would have been if there had been no proposals for a new town; but with this one additional circumstance, that the purchaser had an assurance that in March 1980 or thereafter, if he applied for planning permission to develop the Walton Manor estate or any part of it for residential purposes—in a manner not inconsistent with the development corporation's proposals—he would be granted it.

In the present case the member of the tribunal asked himself the question: 'Would
e 318 acres of land at Walton, offered for sale in March 1970 with planning permission for residential development deferred ten years, have fetched £1,750 per acre in the absence of the scheme?' His answer was: '[Yes], a price of £1,750 per acre would not be excessive.' He rejected that figure because he thought it was formed on a wrong basis in law. We think the question was the right question, but, having regard to the
f way in which the case developed in the Lands Tribunal, we are not sure that the evidence supporting the figure of £1,750 per acre was based on the proper assumptions. Counsel for the development corporation suggested that, in giving that figure, the valuer for the landowner may have proceeded on the assumption that the scheme originated in February 1964, whereas the tribunal held that it originated in 1962. Furthermore, that the roads giving access to the estate would be provided by the
g highway authorities free of expense to the developer. Likewise the infrastructure. Such assumptions may be mistaken and may have led to error.

In the circumstances, we think that the case must go back to the Lands Tribunal for reconsideration in the light of the law as we have tried to expound it. It will be for the member of the Lands Tribunal to decide whether he wants further evidence or argument.
h We would, therefore, allow the appeal and remit the case to the Lands Tribunal for reconsideration.

Appeal allowed: case remitted to the Lands Tribunal for reconsideration in accordance with the principles stated by the Court of Appeal.

Summons for directions
The parties applied to the Lands Tribunal for directions as to how the inquiry should
j proceed.
26th March. The tribunal (R C Walmsley Esq) stated that there was no need for further evidence or argument, but after hearing counsel's submissions in respect of the assumptions mentioned at the end of the Court of Appeal's judgment, gave the following direction:

1 [1966] 3 All ER at 164, [1966] 1 WLR at 1106

'I direct (1) that the [appellant] do tender his expert witness on value for further
cross-examination by counsel for the [respondents] (and re-examination by   *a*
counsel for the [appellant]) and that counsel for the [respondents] be permitted to
cross-examine the said witness (a) as to whether his valuation of £1,750 per acre
previously given in evidence by him proceeded on one or two or all and if so
which of the following assumptions: A. That the scheme originated in February
1964, whereas the tribunal held that it originated in 1962. B. That the roads   *b*
giving access to the estate would be provided by the highway authorities free of
expense to the developer. C. Likewise the infrastructure. (b) If the said valuation
proceeded on one or two or all of the said assumptions as to the value-effect, in
the context of said valuation, of the assumption or assumptions so relied on.
(2) That insofar as the valuation proceeded on assumption B and/or assumption
C aforesaid, counsel for the parties be permitted to address the Tribunal on the
question whether the assumption or, as the case may be, each assumption relied   *c*
upon was a proper assumption. (3) That insofar as the valuation proceeded on one
or two or all of the said assumptions, counsel for the [respondents] be permitted
to call evidence rebutting such value effect of the same as may be contended for
by the said expert witness.'

Application   *d*
By notice of motion dated 30th April 1974 the respondents applied ex parte for
elucidation of the Court of Appeal's judgment.

3rd May. **LORD DENNING MR.** I think I should say first a few words so as
to get it clear on the detail.

We gave judgment in this case on 8th March 1974. The parties went before the   *e*
Lands Tribunal on 26th March 1974 asking for directions as to how the inquiry should
proceed. At first the member of the Lands Tribunal thought that there was no need
for further evidence or argument but that he could make an award for the higher
alternative award. After some discussion he was ready to allow Mr Caws, the owner's
valuer, to be cross-examined on the 'assumptions' mentioned at the end of our
judgment. Counsel for the appellant submitted that those 'assumptions' were   *f*
exhaustive and that no other matters were to be inquired into. The member accepted
that submission. He gave directions limiting the inquiry accordingly.

I am sorry to find that our judgment has given rise to such misunderstanding. We
cannot have expressed ourselves as clearly as we should. We did not intend that the
'assumptions' were to be exhaustive. They were only illustrations of some of the
ways in which the higher alternative award might have been erroneous. If I remem-   *g*
ber rightly, the member found that, if there had been no scheme, this land would
probably have remained open countryside. So far from endorsing that higher alternative award, we contemplated that the member of the Lands Tribunal might find
that his original award was correct, or that he might find a figure in between. We
felt that the member had misdirected himself in principle on the main issue in the
case and that it was necessary for him to consider it afresh in the light of the principles   *h*
which we had stated. We stated the correct principle. Both parties have today
before us accepted that the member should direct himself in accordance with that
principle. In those circumstances we will direct that each party should be at liberty to
adduce further evidence—one expert on each side—on the value to be placed on the
property on the footing as we stated it. Each party should be at liberty to cross-
examine. It might be convenient for proofs to be exchanged beforehand. The parties   *j*
will, of course, be able to address the member on all the circumstances which they
wish to put to him. I hope that the matter can be dealt with in the two or three days
that have been allotted to it.

Application granted.

Solicitors: *Stones, Porter & Co* (for the appellant); *Frere, Cholmeley & Co* (for the
respondent corporation). L J Kovats Esq Barrister.

Easy v Universal Anchorage Co Ltd

COURT OF APPEAL, CIVIL DIVISION
LORD DENNING MR, ORR AND ROSKILL LJJ
1ST MAY 1974

Writ – Extension of validity – Good and sufficient reason for extension – Negotiations for settlement – Negotiations proceeding when application made to extend validity of writ – Whether negotiations affording sufficient reason for not serving writ within time or for renewal of writ – RSC Ord 6, r 8(2).

The plaintiff was injured at work. He instructed a solicitor in Ipswich who wrote to his employers, the defendants, claiming damages. There were negotiations with insurers for a settlement, the only question being as to the quantum of damages. The plaintiff moved about a good deal so that the Ipswich solicitor had difficulty in getting instructions from him and nothing further was done in the matter save that, to prevent the claim from becoming statute-barred, the Ipswich solicitor issued a writ on the plaintiff's behalf on 17th August 1972 claiming damages for personal injuries. As he had no instructions for the purpose the solicitor did not serve the writ. During the year following the issue of the writ it was arranged that solicitors in Bolton, where the plaintiff was then living, should act as intermediaries to get instructions from him regarding his claim for damages. The Ipswich solicitor again took up the claim with the insurers and further negotiations took place which continued during July 1973 when the insurers increased their offer to £3,000. The Ipswich solicitor put that figure to the Bolton solicitors who took instructions from the plaintiff that he would not settle for less than £3,500. Those instructions were not passed on to the Ipswich solicitor until 23rd August 1973. On 17th August the validity of the writ expired but the Ipswich solicitor had overlooked the necessity of serving the writ by that date and had gone on holiday. On his return in September he sought to renew the writ, relying on the fact that negotiations for a settlement were in progress.

Held – The fact that negotiations for a settlement were in progress did not afford a sufficient reason for not serving the writ within 12 months of its issue, nor did it afford sufficient reason for the court to exercise its discretion under RSC Ord 6, r 8(2)[a], to renew the writ; it was the duty of the plaintiff's solicitor to serve the writ in time even though negotiations were in progress. Accordingly, the writ would not be renewed (see p 1107 e to h and p 1108 a and g, post).

Dictum of Karminski LJ in *Jones v Jones* [1970] 3 All ER at 56 approved.
The Prins Bernhard [1963] 3 All ER 735 explained.

Notes
For renewal of a writ of summons, see 30 Halsbury's Laws (3rd Edn) 303, para 558, and for cases on the subject, see 50 Digest (Repl) 292, 293, *331-338*, and Digest (Cont Vol C) 1080, 1081, *331a-339*.

Cases referred to in judgments
Baker v Bowketts Cakes Ltd [1966] 2 All ER 290, [1966] 1 WLR 861, CA, Digest (Cont Vol B) 502, *2022Aa*.

---

a   RSC Ord 6, r 8(2), provides: 'Where a writ has not been served on a defendant, the Court may by order extend the validity of the writ from time to time for such period, not exceeding twelve months at any one time, beginning with the day next following that on which it would otherwise expire, as may be specified in the order, if an application for extension is made to the Court before that day or such later day (if any) as the Court may allow.'

Chittenden Re, Chittenden v Doe [1970] 3 All ER 562, [1970] 1 WLR 1618, Digest (Cont Vol C) 1079, 80a. *a*

Heaven v Road and Rail Wagons Ltd [1965] 2 All ER 409, [1965] 2 QB 355, [1965] 2 WLR 1249, 50 Digest (Repl) 292, *337*.

Jones v Jones [1970] 3 All ER 47, [1970] 2 QB 576, [1970] 3 WLR 20, CA, Digest (Cont Vol C) 1080, *331a*.

North v Kirk (1967) 111 Sol Jo 793, CA, Digest (Cont Vol C) 1080, *329a*.

Prins Bernhard, The, Rolimpex Centrala Handlu Zagranicznego v Owners of Motorship or *b* *Vessel Prins Bernhard* [1963] 3 All ER 735, [1964] P 117, [1963] 3 WLR 1043, [1963] 2 Lloyd's Rep 236, Digest (Cont Vol A) 5, *738a*.

Cases also cited
Liberian Shipping Corpn v A King & Sons Ltd [1967] 1 All ER 934, [1967] 2 QB 86, CA.
Ruttie (deceased), Re, Ruttie v Saul [1969] 3 All ER 1633, [1970] 1 WLR 89. *c*

Interlocutory appeal
This was an appeal by the plaintiff, William John Easy, against the order of Cusack J, made on 22nd January 1974, allowing an appeal by the defendants, Universal Anchorage Co Ltd, against the order of Mr District Registrar Lamb, made on 3rd January 1974, renewing the plaintiff's writ against the defendants for three months from *d* 17th August 1973, the date on which its validity expired. The facts are set out in the judgment of Lord Denning MR.

Margaret Puxon for the plaintiff.
Patrick Phillips for the defendants.

e

LORD DENNING MR. On 18th August 1969 the plaintiff, Mr William John Easy, suffered an accident. The head of a rig fell from the top and caught his foot as it fell. He instructed solicitors, Josselyn & Sons, Ipswich, who wrote to the defendants, his employers, making a claim for damages. The insurers replied and there were negotiations for a settlement. It would appear that liability would be admitted. The only question was how much. But the plaintiff moved about a good deal and *f* did not give his solicitors his address. They had difficulty in getting instructions from him. So nothing was done; save that, in order that the claim should not become statute-barred, his solicitors issued a writ on his behalf just within the three years on 17th August 1972. But they did not serve it then. They had no instructions for the purpose. Under the Rules of the Supreme Court they had a further year in which to serve the writ. Within that year the plaintiff did get in touch with them. *g* He was by this time living at Bolton in Lancashire. He had instructed solicitors there, Messrs Russell & Russell, in divorce proceedings. It was arranged that Russell & Russell should act as intermediaries to get instructions from him about his claim for damages.

So the Ipswich solicitors took up the claim again with the insurance company for the defendants. There were negotiations as to the figure to be paid in settlement. *h* The Ipswich solicitors knew that the time was running on. On 9th July 1973 they wrote to the insurers, saying, 'If we do not hear from you within a short time, we must obviously file a Statement of Claim ...' They could not, of course, serve a statement of claim unless they first served the writ. So they must have known that they had to serve the writ by 17th August 1973. During the month of July 1973 there were further negotiations. Counsel's opinion was taken. The insurers made an *j* increased offer of £3,000. The Ipswich solicitors put that figure to the Bolton solicitors, Messrs Russell & Russell, for them to get the plaintiff's instructions. On 31st July 1973 the plaintiff said he would not take less than £3,500. But Russell & Russell unfortunately did not pass that information on to the Ipswich solicitors until 23rd August 1973. By that time the crucial date, 17th August 1973, had passed and the

a writ had not been served. And the Ipswich solicitor, Mr Scorer, had gone on holiday. He eventually got back on 12th September. He spoke to the insurers on the telephone. Then the truth appeared. The insurers said: 'You did not serve the writ by 17th August 1973 as you ought to have done: you are out of time'. So there it was. The four years had gone by and they had not served the writ. Mr Scorer tried to remedy the position. He sought to renew the writ. He went to the district registry. He made

b an affidavit setting out the position, asking that the failure should be excused. The affidavit was not accurate. In para 8 he said, 'On my return from holiday on the 12th day of September I found awaiting me instructions to accept the offer'. That was not correct. The instructions were not to accept less than £3,500. But at all events the district registrar did allow it to be renewed. The defendants appealed to the judge. He allowed the appeal and held that the writ was not to be renewed. Now there is an appeal to us.

c Counsel for the plaintiff admitted that the solicitors had made a mistake in not serving the writ, but she urged that it was excusable, and that the defendants have not suffered any prejudice. She relied on the negotiations for a settlement and urged that they afforded a sufficient reason for renewal. She referred us to the notes to RSC Ord 6, r 8, in the White Book[1] in which it is said:

d 'Thus, it is a sufficient reason that the defendant's insurers have stated that there is no need to serve the writ of summons pending negotiations ... or [and these are the important words] there are negotiations for a settlement between the parties proceeding at the time of the application for renewal ...'

The Prins Bernhard[2] is cited, but it does not support that proposition. I do not think that note is correct. The plaintiff's solicitors are under a duty to their client to serve

e the writ in time, even though negotiations are in progress. This is quite unlike the cases when an action is struck out for want of prosecution. In those cases there is much discussion whether the delay has been such as to prejudice a fair trial. But that does not enter into the renewal of a writ. The only principle is that a writ is not to be renewed except for good reason. That appears from the cases starting with the judgment of Megaw J in Heaven v Road and Rail Wagons Ltd[3]; and going on to the

f judgments of this court in Baker v Bowketts Cakes Ltd[4] and Jones v Jones[5]. In Jones v Jones[6] Salmon LJ helpfully summarised all the authorities; and Karminski LJ went out of his way to say[7]:

'We were told in the course of argument that sometimes writs are not served because, rightly or wrongly, it is thought that it might prejudice the possibilities of a settlement of a claim with the insurance company or underwriters concerned.

g I find this most difficult to accept as a valid reason. Negotiations for a settlement remain a matter of commercial judgment, and I find it very difficult to accept that the susceptibilities of those who undertake this kind of insurance would be upset by the mere service of a writ on their assured.'

That is right. Negotiations for a settlement do not afford any excuse for failing to serve a writ in time or to renew it.

h I am afraid that the solicitors for the plaintiff made a mistake: they knew perfectly well that they ought to have served the writ by 17th August 1973. They did not do it. It was an unfortunate oversight by the Bolton solicitors—who did not write promptly to Ipswich—and by the Ipswich solicitors themselves. They overlooked the necessity of serving the writ by 17th August 1973. It is true that negotiations were in progress for a settlement; but that is not a sufficient reason for not serving the writ.

j 1 The Supreme Court Practice 1973, vol 1, p 55, para 6/8/3A
2 [1963] 3 All ER 735, [1964] P 117
3 [1965] 2 All ER 409, [1965] 2 QB 355
4 [1966] 2 All ER 290, [1966] 1 WLR 861
5 [1970] 3 All ER 47, [1970] 2 QB 576
6 [1970] 3 All ER at 51 et seq, [1970] 2 QB at 582 et seq
7 [1970] 3 All ER at 56, [1970] 2 QB at 588

I would add that this does not mean that the plaintiff will suffer. He has a *a* remedy against the solicitors. I think the judge was right not to renew the writ. I would dismiss the appeal.

ORR LJ. I agree that this appeal should be dismissed and I also agree with the observations Lord Denning MR has made with reference to *The Prins Bernhard*[1].

ROSKILL LJ. I agree with both judgments. I would only add one or two words *b* on that last point. The note to RSC Ord 6, r 8, in the White Book[2] is, with great respect to the editors, inaccurate in one respect. After setting out the well-known passage in the judgment of Megaw J in *Heaven v Road and Rail Wagons Ltd*[3] the note goes on: 'Thus, it is a sufficient reason that the defendant's insurers have stated that there is no need to serve the writ of summons pending negotiations . . .'. Pausing there, the authority given is *North v Kirk*[4]. That statement is accurate. The note *c* continues:

> '. . . or there are negotiations for a settlement between the parties proceeding at the time of the application for renewal (*The Prins Bernhard*[1]; *Re Chittenden, deceased*[5] . . .)'

With great respect, that sentence as respects *The Prins Bernhard*[1] is inaccurate. When *d* one looks at the report Hewson J said[6]:

> 'It seems to me that if parties wish to negotiate such negotiations should not be prejudiced while still active. The evidence is all one way in this case, that the plaintiffs thought that the service of the writ would, or might, prejudice those negotiations. I have always understood it to be the attitude of this court to encourage parties to negotiate and, as we all know, they commonly do so in *e* commercial cases. Counsel for the defendants, under some pressure, agreed that if the parties were locked in negotiations and the defendants knew that the writ was issued that might be a good reason. In my view, and it is my discretion which I must exercise, after fully considering this case, as the negotiations were proceeding and as the application to extend the time was made during the currency of the writ, there was, and still is, a good reason why the extension should *f* be granted.'

There are two points to be made on that passage. The note, with great respect, does not accurately represent what the judge said. Secondly, even if it had, I would, with great respect, not agree with that passage. I think, although *The Prins Bernhard*[1] was not referred to by name in *Jones v Jones*[7], the comment made by Karminski LJ in the passage Lord Denning MR has cited is entirely correct. The law is correctly *g* stated by Megaw J in *Heaven v Road and Rail Wagons Ltd*[8], as expanded in one or two of the later cases. In my judgment Cusack J in the present case manifestly reached the right conclusion in setting aside service. The registrar ought not to have made the ex parte order which he made; and therefore I would dismiss this appeal.

h

Appeal dismissed.

Solicitors: *Field, Fisher & Martineau*, agents for *Josselyn & Sons*, Ipswich (for the plaintiff); *L Bingham & Co* (for the defendants).

Wendy Shockett Barrister.

1 [1963] 3 All ER 735, [1964] P 117
2 The Supreme Court Practice 1973, vol 1, p 55, note 6/8/3A   *j*
3 [1965] 2 All ER at 415, [1965] 2 QB at 365
4 (1967) 111 Sol Jo 793
5 [1970] 3 All ER 562, [1970] 1 WLR 1618
6 [1963] 3 All ER at 744, [1964] P at 130
7 [1970] 3 All ER at 56, [1970] 2 QB at 588
8 [1965] 2 All ER 409, [1965] 2 QB 355

Coenen v Payne and another
Payne v Coenen

COURT OF APPEAL, CIVIL DIVISION

LORD DENNING MR, STAMP AND STEPHENSON LJJ

3rd, 4th APRIL 1974

Practice – Trial – Separate trials – Action begun by writ – Different questions – Trial of one or more questions before others – Liability and damages – Claim for personal injuries – Trial of issue of liability before trial of issue of damages – Circumstances in which order for separate trials should be made – Just and convenient – Time and expense involved in trying issue of damages – RSC Ord 33, r 4(2).

The plaintiff was a veterinary surgeon and was employed by a firm in West Germany, where he resided. He was injured in a collision which took place in England between the car he was driving and a car driven by the defendant. The defendant was also injured. The plaintiff brought an action for negligence against the defendant claiming damages for personal injuries, and putting his loss of earnings at three months. The defendant denied liability and counterclaimed damages for negligence against the plaintiff. Subsequently the plaintiff amended his statement of claim. By his amendment he claimed damages for future loss of earnings at the rate of some £8,000 a year on the footing that before the accident he had intended entering private practice in Germany in which he would have earned large sums but, because of his injuries, he would have to remain in employment with his existing employers. The length of the trial had been estimated at three days but because of the new issue as to damages it was estimated that it would take a further four or five days and would entail much expense, e g on discovery of documents, obtaining evidence from Germany on the plaintiff's professional prospects and on deciding the effect of German tax laws on the claim. The defendant applied for an order under RSC Ord 33, r 4(2)[a], for separate trials of the issues of liability and damages. The plaintiff opposed the application. Being resident abroad he had given security for the costs of the trial of the action and was prepared to give additional security if the issues of liability and damages were tried together. The judge refused the application and the defendant appealed.

Held – (i) Although it should be the normal practice for issues of liability and damages to be tried together, the courts had power under RSC Ord 33, r 4(2), to order separate trials of those issues in personal injury cases, and should be ready to do so wherever it was just and convenient (see p 1112 c and d, p 1113 d and p 1114 c and d, post); dicta of Jessel MR in *Piercy v Young* (1880) 15 ChD at 480 and *Emma Silver Mining Co v Grant* (1879) 11 ChD at 927 explained.

(ii) Having regard to the time and expense which would be involved in trying the issue of damages, the case was a proper one for separate trials, the issue of liability being tried first and the issue of damages afterwards. The appeal would be allowed accordingly (see p 1112 e and g, p 1113 h and j and p 1114 d, post).

Per Stephenson LJ. The plaintiff has no right to choose the normal method of trying liability and quantum at the same time, and cannot claim any such right by agreeing to pay for the extra expense of his choice (see p 1114 b, post).

Notes

For the power to order separate trials in actions commenced by writ, see 30 Halsbury's

---

a Rule 4(2) is set out at p 1112 c, post

Laws (3rd Edn) 375, 376, para 699, and for cases on the trial of one issue before another, *a* see 51 Digest (Repl) 645-648, 2544-2555.

Cases referred to in judgments

Emma Silver Mining Co v Grant (1879) 11 ChD 918, 40 LT 804; *subsequent proceedings* (1880) 17 ChD 122, 51 Digest (Repl) 646, 2546.

Hawkins v New Mendip Engineering Ltd [1966] 3 All ER 228, [1966] 1 WLR 1341, CA, Digest (Cont Vol B) 567, 1062e. *b*

Piercy v Young (1880) 15 Ch D 475, 42 LT 292, 51 Digest (Repl) 645, 2544.

Stevens v William Nash Ltd [1966] 3 All ER 156, [1966] 1 WLR 1550, CA, 17 Digest (Reissue) 224, 972.

Cases also cited

Gold v Patman and Fotheringham Ltd [1958] 2 All ER 497, [1958] 1 WLR 697, CA.

Polskie Towarzystwo Handlu Zagranicznego Dla Elektrotechniki "Elektrim" Spolka Z *c* *Ograniczona Odpowiadziolnoscia v Electric Furnace Co Ltd* [1956] 2 All ER 306, [1956] 1 WLR 562, CA.

Interlocutory appeals

The respondent, Hans Dieter Coenen, brought an action for damages for personal injuries caused by negligent driving against the appellants, Barrie Coburn Payne and *d* Bristol Metal Spraying and Welding Co Ltd, in which the appellants counterclaimed for damages for personal injuries against the respondent. In a second action, the first appellant sued the respondent for damages for personal injuries caused by negligence. In each action the appellants applied for a separate trial of the questions or issues of liability and damages. In the first action Mr District Registrar Cameron, and in the second action Mr District Registrar Parmiter, ordered that the issue of liability should *e* be tried as a preliminary issue before the issue of damages. The respondent appealed against those orders, and on 11th January 1974 Bridge J allowed both appeals and ordered that each action should be tried as one trial, the second action to be tried immediately after the trial of the first action. The appellants appealed against the order of Bridge J. The grounds of the appeal in the first action were: (1) that the judge had been wrong in law in deciding that the respondent was entitled to have *f* the issues of liability and quantum tried together if he was prepared to accept the financial consequences which that course involved; (2) that the district registrar had been right in ordering the issues of liability to be tried as preliminary issues before the issues of quantum because (a) the issues were quite separate; (b) the issue of the quantum of the respondent's claim involved (i) complicated questions of fact and law including the earning capacity of veterinary surgeons in Germany and matters relat- *g* ing of the tax laws of Germany and their application to the respondent's claim for loss of earnings; (ii) calling about eight witnesses from Germany all of whom were professional men; (iii) calling two surgeons from London to give evidence about the respondent's injuries; (iv) calling two other expert witnesses from London to give evidence regarding German law; (v) consideration of a large number of documents relating to the respondent's claim for loss of earnings and the incidence of German *h* income tax thereon; (vi) very great expense, far in excess of the issue of liability; (c) apart from the respondent, all witnesses in the issue of liability resided in England; (d) trial of the issue of liability would probably take about three days whereas the issue of quantum would probably occupy a further six days; (e) if, as the appellants contended, the accident concerned was caused solely by the respondent's negligence, the time, trouble and expense of trying the issue of quantum would be saved by *j* trying liability as a preliminary issue; but if the respondent's claim was well-founded little or no extra expense would be incurred by the issues being tried separately. The facts are set out in the judgment of Lord Denning MR.

C S Rawlins for the appellants.

John Loyd for the respondent.

LORD DENNING MR. The question here is whether liability should be tried

a before damages. In December 1969 there was a conference at Langford in Somerset. It was attended by veterinary surgeons from many countries. The conference came to an end on 9th December 1969. They had a celebration. Afterwards Dr Coenen, a veterinary surgeon from Germany, with other veterinary surgeons from Spain and Turkey, went to a few hotels for drinks. Dr Coenen was driving them in his Volks-

b wagen along the A38 road at Langford towards Bridgwater. Coming in the opposite direction was Mr Payne, a director of the Bristol Metal Spraying and Welding Co Ltd, driving the company's car, an Alfa Romeo. Unfortunately they came head-on into collision. The surgeon from Spain was killed. Dr Coenen was seriously injured. So was the surgeon from Turkey. Mr Payne, in the other car, was also seriously injured. Actions have been brought for damages. Dr Coenen is suing Mr Payne. Mr Payne is suing Dr Coenen. The drivers, Dr Coenen and Mr Payne, remem-

c ber very little. A great deal will depend on the position of the cars, the marks on the road, and so forth. In the beginning Dr Coenen's action against Mr Payne followed simple lines. He put his loss of earnings at three months, because he went back to his firm in Germany—to his previous employment. The defence of Mr Payne included a charge that Dr Coenen was driving on the wrong side of the road and that his ability to drive was impaired through drink. The case was all ready for trial. It was

d to take place in Bristol before a judge alone, and the length was estimated to be three days.

Then there was a new development. In March 1973 Dr Coenen proposed to put in an amended statement of claim. The amendment was as to the damages. He had put his loss of earnings at a very high sum. He says that before the accident it was his intention to enter into private practice in Germany; that in that type of practice

e he would have made very large sums; that because of the accident he will not be going into private practice, but will have to remain in his employment with his present firm. He says he will have an ever-increasing loss on that account. He gives particulars, which, put into English money, are in the region of £8,000 a year or more and continuing. At his age of 34, the claim might come to £100,000.

f That proposed amendment changes the whole aspect of the case. The proposed amendment will entail the discovery of many more documents. Evidence will have to be obtained from Germany as to the prospects in the profession. Further, there is a serious question of law as to the effect of tax. It was suggested that in Germany the damages are assessed on the gross amount of earnings (on which the plaintiff will have to account to the tax authorities for the tax on it). That is, of course, different from the English rule. Other points will have to be considered in the case. So that it is

g quite plain that as a result of this amendment, the trial is going to be a great deal longer than was originally anticipated. Whereas originally the whole trial was esti-mated at three days, the new issue of damages alone will take four to six days.

In those circumstances the defendants make application for separate trials as to liability and damages. The registrar ordered separate trials. Dr Coenen appealed

h to Bridge J. Seeing that Dr Coenen is resident out of the jurisdiction, he has given security for costs. He is prepared to give additional security. In these circumstances the judge refused separate trials. He said:

'I see the force of the contention for split trials. The submission that allowing the appeals will involve a substantial risk that a great deal of time and money would be wasted is deprived of a lot of its force by the argument that the plain-

j tiff himself is prepared to accept the financial consequences. There is really no answer to [counsel's] submission that whether for good reason or bad the plaintiff is entitled to choose the normal method of trying liability and quantum at the same time.'

The defendants appeal to this court.

As the judge said, the normal method hitherto has been to try liability and quantum

at the same time. It has been the practice not to make an order for separate trials *a*
save in exceptional circumstances and on special grounds. Winn LJ's committee
said in their report[1]:

> 'In practice this power has hitherto been exercised only in "extraordinary and
> exceptional cases" or where "the Judge has serious reason to believe that the
> trial of the issue will put an end to the action".'
>
> *b*

Winn LJ's committee did not like that practice. They thought[2] 'a more robust and less
restrictive approach' should be approved. They recommended[3] that a new rule
should be made to alter it. In addition to the committee's recommendation, Winn
LJ in two cases indicated that separate trials might well have been ordered with
advantage. Those were *Hawkins v New Mendip Engineering Ltd*[4] and *Stevens v William
Nash Ltd*[5]. I think the time has come to adopt a new approach. There is no need to *c*
order a new rule. The practice can be altered without it. The courts already have
power to do it. RSC Ord 33, r 4(2), says:

> 'In any [action begun by writ] different questions or issues may be ordered to
> be tried at different places or by different modes of trial and one or more
> questions or issues may be ordered to be tried before the others.'
>
> *d*

In future the courts should be more ready to grant separate trials than they used to
do. The normal practice should still be that liability and damages should be tried
together. But the courts should be ready to order separate trials wherever it is just
and convenient to do so.

In this case there is this strong point to be made in favour of separate trials. It is the *e*
time and expense which will be involved in trying the issue of damages. It will take
four or five days to try; witnesses will have to come from Germany and surgeons
and experts from London. All will be unnecessary if Dr Coenen should fail. As
against that, counsel for Dr Coenen stressed the point of credibility. It was mentioned by Winn LJ's committee[6]. A man's credibility on one issue may be affected
by his credibility on the other. For instance, if he puts a claim for inflated damages *f*
which the judge disbelieves, it may affect his credibility on liability. Vice versa, if
he is moderate and restrained on damages, the judge may be impressed by it in
deciding on liability. In the present case counsel for Dr Coenen said the judge would
have a better opportunity of assessing the credibility of Dr Coenen if he was two
days in the witness box rather than two hours. I doubt it. I should think a judge
could assess his credibility pretty well in two hours anyway.

At any rate, this seems to me to be a case where the new practice should prevail. *g*
It is a proper case for separate trials, the issue of liability being decided first and then
afterwards damages. I would allow the appeal accordingly.

STAMP LJ. By RSC Ord 33, r 4, the court may, on the hearing of a summons for
directions, order different questions, whether of fact or law, to be tried at different *h*
places or by different modes of trial, and one or more questions or issues may be
ordered to be tried before the others.

In the Report of the Committee on Personal Injuries Litigation[7], presided over by
Winn LJ, it was remarked in relation to this rule:

1 Report of the Committee on Personal Injuries Litigation (Cmnd 3691), p 139, para 494(*b*)   *j*
2 Ibid, pp 139, 140, para 494(*b*)
3 Ibid, p 143, recommendation (2)
4 [1966] 3 All ER 228 at 232, 233, [1966] 1 WLR 1341 at 1347
5 [1966] 3 All ER 156 at 160, [1966] 1 WLR 1550 at 1554
6 Page 137, para 490(*a*)
7 Report of the Committee on Personal Injuries Litigation (Cmnd 3691) p 139, para 494 (*b*)

a

'In practice this power has hitherto been exercised only in "extraordinary and exceptional cases" or where "the Judge has serious reason to believe that the trial of the issue will put an end to the action".'

And for this proposition two judgments or two remarks by Jessel MR in *Piercey v Young*[1] and *Emma Silver Mining Co v Grant*[2] were cited. The committee went on to suggest[3]—

b

'that a more robust and less restrictive approach to the rule would be likely to solve most of the present problems'

to which the report was directed; and it was indicated[4] that if necessary the decisions —and I think the committee was referring to the two decisions to which I have just referred—which had been regarded as inhibiting wider use of the rule, should be

c reversed so far as personal injury litigation was concerned; and it recommended[5] a new rule in terms set out in the appendix[6] to the report. The recommendation was not adopted by the Rules Committee, perhaps because it was thought that in the generality of personal injuries cases the objections to separate trials outweighed the advantages; or perhaps because it was thought, as I think to be the case, that RSC Ord 33, r 4, was wide enough in its terms to enable the court to separate the trial

d as to liability from a subsequent enquiry as to damages in a case where such a course was desirable in the interests of justice. I would not for a moment question the unde-sirability of ordering separate trials of separate issues of fact where both issues of fact have to be determined in favour of the plaintiff before the liability of the defendant can be ascertained. But I cannot accept that the remarks of Jessel MR were directed in the least degree to cases where what was sought to be dealt with as two separate

e issues were liability and the ascertainment of quantum of damages. What he was speaking of, I think, was a process by which one issue of facts is to be tried in advance of another issue of fact both of which have to be determined in favour of the plaintiff before he can get judgment for damages at all. The sort of case with which he was dealing was a case such as where someone claimed to be a next-of-kin and claimed accounts and enquiries on this basis; and he took the view that in only

f very exceptional circumstances should you first of all have a trial as to whether the plaintiff was the next-of-kin; and, having determined that question, then have a separate trial of the question whether the plaintiff was entitled to the accounts and enquiries which he sought. I do not think that the question of separating the question of liability and the question of damages was within the mind of Jessel MR when he made those remarks. What he was speaking of was quite a different kind of process.

g It is the commonest thing in the world in the Division with the practice of which I am most familiar for the question of liability to be determined before the quantum of damages: it is a regular practice to determine liability and then have an enquiry as to damages. RSC Ord 37, r 1, accepts this practice as being a completely normal one. In my judgment therefore the court ought not to be inhibited by the remarks referred to in the report of the committee from ordering what was called—I think

h perhaps somewhat unfortunately—a split trial in a case where this is in the interests of justice.

I have found some difficulty in coming to a conclusion whether on the facts of this particular case it would be right to order a separation of the two questions. But on the whole and with some hesitation, I agree that separate issues ought to be ordered for the reasons given by Lord Denning MR, and I would allow the appeal.

j
_____

1   (1880) 15 Ch D 475 at 480
2   (1879) 11 Ch D 918 at 927
3   Pages 139, 140, para 494(*b*)
4   Page 140, para 494(*c*)
5   Page 143, recommendation (2)
6   Page 229, appendix 21

STEPHENSON LJ. I agree with all that Lord Denning MR and Stamp LJ have said and I too would allow this appeal.

In most personal injury cases the issues of liability and damages, though clearly separate, are rightly tried together. That is so, even where the issue of damages, perhaps because of complicated medical evidence, takes longer to try than the issue of liability. The reason is, I think, that it is usually most convenient for the parties to have all the issues between them decided together and that it helps the judge to assess the credibility of the plaintiff if he can hear what the plaintiff has to say not only about his accident but also about his injuries and his financial loss. I would not disturb that general practice. But the plaintiff has, in my judgment, no right to choose the normal method of trying liability and quantum at the same time, as the judge appears to have thought, and cannot claim any such right by agreeing to pay for the extra expense of his choice. The court has inherent jurisdiction to make any use of the relevant provisions in the Rules of the Supreme Court which are now RSC Ord 33, rr 2, 3, 4, and RSC Ord 37, rr 1 and 4. If the court thinks it just and convenient to order separate trials of separate issues or to give judgment for damages to be assessed by another court, the court can and should do so without treating ancient decisions as limiting its powers. In a personal injuries case the courts will not depart from the normal practice except for good reason; but though I appreciate the plaintiff's desire to be heard on liability and damages by the same judge, I think that in this special case the issue of damages is likely to take so much time and expense to try that it could more conveniently, and without injustice, be tried after liability has been decided, it may be in such a way as to make a trial on the issue of damages unnecessary.

Appeals allowed. Orders of district registrars restored.

Solicitors: *Stanleys & Simpson, North*, agents for *Stanley, Wasbrough & Co*, Bristol (for the appellants); *Cartwrights*, Cardiff (for the respondent).

Wendy Shockett Barrister.

Lake v Bayliss and another

CHANCERY DIVISION
WALTON J
18th MARCH 1974

Sale of land – Vendor – Duty to purchaser – Trust – Vendor as trustee for purchaser – Trust of property pending completion – Sale of property by vendor to third party before completion – Whether vendor holding proceeds of sale on trust for original purchaser.

M issued a writ against B claiming specific performance of an alleged agreement whereby B had agreed to sell certain land to M in consideration of M's withdrawing writs he had issued against her and of his assuming liability in respect of a planning application. B, however, sold the land to a third party for approximately £50,000 before the contract had been completed. The plaintiff, B's solicitor, received the proceeds of sale, and took out an interpleader summons whereby he applied for directions as to what he ought to do with the money. The master ordered that the proceeds of sale be paid into court and that B and M should proceed to the trial of the question whether the proceeds of sale should be paid forthwith to B or should remain in court pending the determination of the action started by M.

Held – A vendor who, after entering into a contract for the sale of property, sold that property to another person for valuable consideration, was accountable as a *a* trustee to the original purchaser for the proceeds of sale. Accordingly, if M were able to prove in the action which he had started that there was a contract as alleged, B would be bound to hold the proceeds of sale on trust to transfer them to M on M's completing the obligations on his part. The money should, therefore, remain in court to abide the outcome of M's action (see p 1118 *a* and *c*, post).

Dictum of Lord Eldon LC in *Daniels v Davison* [1803-13] All ER Rep at 435 applied.

b **Notes**

For payment into court in an action for specific performance, see 36 Halsbury's Laws (3rd Edn) 343, 344, para 507.

For contractual and other relations creating constructive trusts, see 38 Halsbury's Laws (3rd Edn) 855, 856, para 1441, and for cases on the subject, see 47 Digest (Repl) *c* 180-192, 1493-1609.

Cases referred to in judgment

Daniels v Davison (1809) 16 Ves 249, [1803-13] All ER Rep 432, 33 ER 978, 44 Digest (Repl) 37, 260.

Shaw v Foster and Pooley (1872) LR 5 HL 321, 42 LJCh 49, 27 LT 281, HL, 47 Digest (Repl) 182, 1508.

d **Case also cited**

Hamilton-Snowballs' Conveyance, Re [1958] 2 All ER 319, [1959] Ch 308.

Procedure summons

On 13th June 1969 the second defendant, Henry Andrew Mullen ('Dr Mullen'), *e* issued a writ in the Cardiff District Registry against the first defendant, Mervyn Victoria Bayliss ('Miss Bayliss'), seeking specific performance of an agreement which he alleged had been entered into on 27th December 1968 whereby Miss Bayliss agreed to sell 3¼ acres of land in Overndale Road, Mangotsfield, Bristol, to him in consideration of his not proceeding with his existing legal actions against her and of his assuming liability in respect of a certain planning application. Miss Bayliss *f* sold the land for approximately £50,000 to a third party and the proceeds were received by the plaintiff, Joel Seth Lake, who was her solicitor. By an interpleader originating summons dated 5th September 1972, the plaintiff applied for directions as to the disposal of the proceeds of sale, Miss Bayliss and Dr Mullen being the defendants to the summons. On 17th January 1973 in those proceedings, Master Ball ordered, inter alia, that the plaintiff lodge the proceeds of sale amounting to £45,230·29 with interest less costs to be taxed to the account of the Accountant-*g* General of the Supreme Court, and that Miss Bayliss and Dr Mullen proceed to the trial of an issue in the High Court in which Dr Mullen should be the plaintiff and Miss Bayliss the defendant and that the question to be tried should be whether the funds to be paid into court pursuant to the order should be paid forthwith to the defendant in the issue or should remain in court pending the determination of *h* the action proceeding in the Cardiff District Registry. By summons dated 9th November 1973 Miss Bayliss applied for the following relief: (1) that the issue which Master Ball had directed to be tried should be dismissed for want of prosecution, Dr Mullen having failed to set the issue down for trial; (2) alternatively, that the issue be dismissed on the ground that it disclosed no cause of action, and (3) that, in any event, the funds paid into court should be paid out to Miss Bayliss less only such sum as should in the opinion of the court be sufficient to answer the costs of the *j* plaintiff. The master having refused the relief claimed, the matter then came before Walton J. By consent, both parties treated the issue as being before the judge, and accordingly Miss Bayliss's summons was not proceeded with.

Sarah Cockburn for Miss Bayliss.
Peter Millett QC and *C I Howells* for Dr Mullen.

WALTON J. In this matter the allegation is that Miss Mervyn Victoria Bayliss on 27th December 1968 entered into a written agreement to sell to Dr Henry Andrew Mullen a certain parcel of land. The consideration for the transfer of that piece of land was a rather unusual one, and it is in a sense the very unusual nature of that consideration which has given rise to the present proceedings in front of me. The consideration was primarily to withdraw a couple of writs which Dr Mullen had issued against Miss Bayliss and to assume certain liability in respect of a certain planning application.

What happened was that, having entered into that agreement on 27th December 1968 Miss Bayliss proceeded to dispose of the land elsewhere. That happened notwithstanding that Dr Mullen had issued a writ on 13th June 1969 claiming specific performance of that very agreement. There appears to have been either a muddle in a proper search by the purchaser, who is as far as I am aware completely blameless in this matter, or alternatively it may be that the purchaser described the land in a slightly different way from the way it was described in the application for the registration of the estate contract. Be that as it may, Miss Bayliss sold the land for the sum of approximately £50,000. The proceeds were received by her solicitor, Mr Joel Seth Lake, who immediately he had received the proceeds began to have qualms about accounting to Miss Bayliss for the money. Ultimately, by an interpleader originating summons dated 5th September 1972, to which Mr Lake was plaintiff and Miss Bayliss and Dr Mullen were defendants—which are in fact the proceedings now in front of me—he applied for directions as to what he ought to do with the money.

On 17th January 1973 in those proceedings it was ordered that—

'the Defendants proceed to the trial of an issue in the High Court of Justice in which the Defendant Henry Andrew Mullen shall be the Plaintiff and the Defendant Mervyn Victoria Bayliss shall be the Defendant and that the question to be tried shall be whether the funds to be paid into Court pursuant to the foregoing provisions of this Order should be paid forthwith to the Defendant in the issue or should remain in Court pending the determination of the Action now proceeding in the Cardiff District Registry of the Chancery Division of this Court between the parties to the issue the short title and reference to the record of which Action is Mullen v Bayliss [and the number is then given].

It is apparent from the fact that the order was made on 17th January 1973 that the matter has not been proceeding exactly with expedition. Now it comes in front of me, and the parties are agreed that I should proceed to the trial of that issue which is an issue which must in fact arise: what ought to be done with the money?

I take first the way it is presented from the point of view of Dr Mullen. On his behalf counsel has urged that although the relief which he is seeking is unusual, one has to go back to first principles, and if one goes back to first principles there is really no difficulty in the matter. He says that it is one of the standing doctrines of the court that on a contract for the transfer of property being entered into the vendor or intending transferor becomes a trustee for the purchaser or transferee. Admittedly, it is a qualified trusteeship. It does not have all the usual incidents of a bare trusteeship for a cestui que trust, and of course the most glaring and most obvious departure from such normal incidents is that the trustee has his own interest, in the shape of the receipt of the purchase money, to protect. Of course he has a lien on the property until he has been paid his purchase money in the normal course of events. But, says counsel, as to the basic relationship in regard to the land contracted to be sold or transferred, no matter what may be the case in relation to other collateral matters, such as moneys paid under a contract of insurance or receipts under derequisitioning procedures, there is no doubt at all that the property itself is held as by a trustee. He says, that being the case, if in fact before the contract comes to be completed the vendor wrongfully—as is the allegation here—sells the property then *a* the purchaser is entitled, if he is so minded, to say that what has happened is that the vendor has sold trust property, and he is entitled under those circumstances to follow the trust property and say when it comes to the final performance of the contract that he will take the proceeds of sale instead of the property.

There is certainly a dearth of authority in the books on this point, and counsel for Dr Mullen points out that the reason is, in his view, that no less than four matters *b* must concur before it is worthwhile for a purchaser to pursue this remedy. The first is that the vendor must have sold the property twice over, and that in itself is rare because most people honourably fulfil their obligations. Secondly, for some reason the registration of an estate contract by the purchaser must either not have taken place, or if it has taken place it must have been for some rare reason, such as an error in searching, of no effect. Thirdly—and of course this is most vital—the *c* purchaser must be in time to intercept the purchase money, to trace the purchase money. Once it has been paid into an overdrawn bank account or something of that nature, which is the only likely occasion on which these prior circumstances would concur, it is too late to follow it. Lastly, for some reason the purchaser must prefer to pursue the tracing of the purchase money rather than to pursue his remedy in damages. Where the vendor is solvent, of course there is really very little in it. *d* Again, where the vendor has a lien on the trust property for a purchase price, which will normally be very roughly the amount of the sale price, there is not much in it, and probably it is hardly worthwhile in these days seeking to trace the proceeds of sale rather than simply taking the remedy in damages. But of course in the present case the consideration to be provided by Dr Mullen is rather special, and if he cannot in fact trace the purchase money in the way suggested, he will of necessity be forced *e* into a completely different contract from the one which he intended to enter into, because he will be left with the rights which he was going to give up in exchange for the land, and he will get nothing but damages. That will be a very extraordinary result as far as he is concerned.

Authority appears to be silent on this save for one case which the industry of counsel for Dr Mullen has unearthed, a decision of Lord Eldon LC in *Daniels v Davison*[1]. *f* I can go, I think, straightaway to the passage in the judgment of Lord Eldon LC on this point where he says[2]:

'My judgment on that point [after dealing with other points in the case] lays out of consideration the question, whether, taking Cole not to be affected with notice, Davison, the vendor, is to be considered in equity as holding the money, derived from the second purchase, viz. the difference between the prices, *g* in trust for the person, to whom he had first agreed to sell the estate. The estate by the first contract becoming the property of the vendee, the effect is, that the vendor was seised as a trustee for him; and the question then would be, whether the vendor should be permitted to sell for his own advantage the estate, of which he was so seised in trust; or should not be considered as selling it for the benefit of that person, for whom by the first agreement he became *h* trustee; and therefore liable to account. It is not however necessary to decide that point.'

It is perfectly true that Lord Eldon LC there puts it in the form of a query, but I think that it is to be understood in the sense that he would have given, if pressed, the answer to that query that that indeed represented the law.

j Again, the industry of counsel for Dr Mullen has found out that Sir George Jessel, when solicitor-general, arguing the leading case of *Shaw v Foster*[3] in the House of Lords, stated flatly:

1 (1809) 16 Ves 249, [1803-13] All ER Rep 432
2 16 Ves at 254, [1803-13] All ER Rep at 435
3 (1872) LR 5 HL 321 at 327

'*Daniels* v. *Davison*[1] shews that after a contract for the sale of an estate, if
the vendor sells to another person for valuable consideration, he is accountable
for the money as a trust.'

a

In my opinion that is absolutely in line with authority, and entirely represents the
law.

Counsel for Miss Bayliss has taken a number of points on her behalf, and really
her main point was that in the sort of circumstances where the vendor enters into *b*
one contract and then resells the property elsewhere, the purchaser is restricted to
damages. The trusteeship, she says, is as if it never had been and the purchaser
must accept that accordingly. In my view it would be pessimi exempli if a vendor
was entitled to shed the character of a trustee by a wholly wrongful act on his or
her part. Once one has undertaken the role of trustee then it is a role which, unless
discharged by some external circumstance, one must carry out to the bitter end if *c*
so required by the other party to the contract. The vendor cannot be heard to say
that because of her wrongful act in reselling the property she never was a trustee.
She remained a trustee right down to the moment of resale, and accordingly is
bound to hold the purchase price as trust property to transfer to the purchaser on
the purchaser completing the obligations on the purchaser's part.

Counsel for Miss Bayliss did raise a very good point, that is to say, how far does *d*
this concept of trusteeship go? Does it follow, for example, if counsel for Dr Mullen
is right, that if a vendor obtained better offers for the property after having entered
into a contract for sale, he would be under an obligation to pass them on? If so,
she said, that would be an extraordinary result. I do not think it is such an extraordinary result, but I do not think that that is the sort of question—good question
though it is—that can be asked in vacuo. I think one must have a concrete case in *e*
which that sort of thing happens before one knows what the duty of the vendor is.
After all, in most cases one will know that the purchaser is purchasing the property
for his own occupation. Under those circumstances, quite clearly, unless the subsequent offer was astronomical, there would be no real reason for thinking that it
would be of any interest to the purchaser. In other cases it may be that the vendor
well knows that the purchaser is merely buying for speculation and, although I do *f*
not say that it will necessarily be the case, I can see that under certain circumstances
it might very well be the case that the vendor ought to pass the offers on.

Another point that counsel for Miss Bayliss took was on the pleadings in the action
for specific performance—which we have referred to as 'the Cardiff action' because
it was commenced in the Cardiff District Registry. She says that Dr Mullen ought
not to be allowed, and would not be allowed, to amend the pleadings in that action *g*
because the amendment relating to the following of the proceeds of sale would be
something entirely new and something entirely different which has happened subsequent to the issue of the writ, and therefore a new writ and a new proceeding would
be called.

I should be very sorry indeed to think that the Rules of the Supreme Court were
so ossified and stylised that it was impossible to pursue the action when it is changed *h*
somewhat into a protean shape by reason of some action of the defendant. But it
seems to me that, although of course not so stated in so many words, there is the
implied term, as it were, in the statement of claim following on the allegation of the
written agreement, 'and thereby the defendant became a trustee of the property
for the plaintiff'; and if one reads that in—which is implied anyway—the transition,
if the defendant has wrongfully disposed of the trust property in exchange for much *j*
fine gold which Dr Mullen seeks to trace, becomes a simple and quite obviously
clearly allowable amendment as to which I do not think there would be any difficulty
whatsoever.

Of course, one must remember that the Cardiff action is still being very bitterly

1   (1809) 16 Ves 249, [1803-13] All ER Rep 432

a fought, and it may very well turn out at the end of the day that there is no such contract as is alleged by Dr Mullen. But on the basis that there is, it seems to me that it is quite clear that the money should remain in court to abide the outcome of the Cardiff action. In saying that it is to remain in court to abide the outcome of the Cardiff action, of course one must, I think, understand that that means when Dr Mullen finally obtains in the Cardiff action, as amended, a declaration that he is
b entitled, on fulfilling his part of the contract, to the moneys now standing in court. There can, as far as I can see, be no grounds for an order, as was suggested in argument that Miss Bayliss pay the money over to him, because in fact she has not got it. It is a trust fund on the hypothesis that he succeeds in the action; it is a trust fund which is now under the jurisdiction of this court, and all he will require—he personally—is a declaration that he is or has become entitled to it.

c
Order accordingly.

Solicitors: *Seifert, Sedley & Co* (for Miss Bayliss); *Field, Fisher & Martineau,* agents for *Hallinan, Blackburn, Gittings & Hambleton,* Cardiff (for Dr Mullen).

d
Jacqueline Metcalfe Barrister.

Practice Direction

e
FAMILY DIVISION

Injunction – Husband and wife – Application – High Court – Divorce county court – Procedure.

f Following the general practice of the Chancery Division, although not that of the Queen's Bench Division, applications for injunctions in matrimonial cases in the Family Division and divorce county courts have hitherto been heard in open court. Experience of the present divorce law has led to the conclusion that in the interests of the parties and the better administration of justice this practice should be changed. Accordingly, as from 1st October 1974, a summons or notice of application to a judge
g for an injunction in a matrimonial cause in the High Court or a divorce county court should be issued for hearing in chambers. Where the case is one of such urgency that even two days' notice in accordance with the President's direction of 10th July 1972[1] is impracticable and the application has to be made ex parte it should likewise be made to a judge in chambers.

The judge's discretion to hear any particular application in open court is not
h affected by this direction.

The registrar's direction of 5th March 1957 (application for injunction prohibiting removal of child from jurisdiction to be made in open court) is hereby cancelled.

Issued by the President of the Family Division with the concurrence of the Lord Chancellor.

D NEWTON
j 24th June 1974   Senior Registrar

---

1 [1972] 2 All ER 1360, [1972] 1 WLR 1047

Practice Direction

FAMILY DIVISION

Divorce – Consent applications – Divorce Registry – Procedure.

In the Divorce Registry the present practice on consent applications to a registrar (on summons in High Court cases and on notice of application in cases treated as pending in a divorce county court) is to require attendance thereon. It has been decided on an experimental basis to change this practice.

As from 1st May 1974 it will no longer be necessary for such attendance, unless it is subsequently required by the registrar, provided that at the time of issue of the summons or notice there is lodged the written consent of the opposite party to an order in the terms sought. This can either be endorsed on the summons or notice or contained in a separate letter. In such cases a return date will be fixed and the copy summons or notice which is returned to the issuing solicitor will be stamped: 'No attendance necessary unless required by court.' This should be reproduced on the copy served.

If on the date on which the application comes before the registrar he finds that there are minor matters which require clarification or explanation he will note them on the summons or notice and return it to the issuing solicitor by post. Where the registrar so indicates, such queries can be dealt with without the need for attendance. However there will be some cases in which the registrar will require assistance from the solicitor which can only be given by personal attendance. In such cases the registry will fix a new date and communicate it to the issuing solicitors with a request that they attend on that day. The solicitors must give notice of the new date to the other party.

It has been found that the most common type of consent application in which queries have to be raised is in connection with financial provision. Practitioners are reminded that they should specifically deal with, inter alia, the following points on such applications: (1) what is the commencement date for the order? (2) to whom are payments under the order to be made? (3) if they are for a wife and child, how are payments to be apportioned? (4) if the order relates to a child what is to be the date on which payments are to terminate? (Unless otherwise agreed, the order ceases to have effect on the child's 17th birthday.)

In all cases in which an order for costs is required, an application for costs must be contained in the summons or notice.

This new practice applies only to cases proceeding in the Divorce Registry. It is in no way intended to disturb the practice in divorce county courts. It will be reviewed in due course to determine whether it should continue.

D NEWTON
Senior Registrar

10th April 1974

R v Orpin

COURT OF APPEAL, CRIMINAL DIVISION
LORD WIDGERY CJ, PARK AND FORBES JJ
11th JUNE 1974

b

Crown Court – Justices as judges – Judge or recorder sitting with justices – Decisions of court – Justices to play full part in decisions of court – Majority decisions – Questions of law – Ruling of judge on law to be followed – Decision on admissibility of evidence – Proper for judge to retire with justices to consider decision – Courts Act 1971, ss 4(2), 5(8).

c

Where a judge or recorder is sitting in the Crown Court with justices of the peace, the justices are, by virtue of s 4(2)[a] of the Courts Act 1971, themselves judges of the Crown Court and must play a full part in all decisions of the court, whether on interlocutory matters or on sentence. In the event of a difference of opinion, under s 5(8)[b] of the 1971 Act the decision of the majority of the members of the court prevails even if the judge alone is in the minority (see p 1122 *j* and p 1123 *d* and *e*, post). The charge to the jury must, however, be given by the judge (see p 1123 *g* and *h*, post).

d

Where a decision of the court so constituted involves a question of law the judge alone must give a ruling on the law and the court must then come to a decision on the basis of that ruling (see p 1123 *j* to p 1124 *a*, post).

Accordingly where, in the course of a trial, the issue is raised whether a confession obtained in breach of the Judges' Rules is admissible, it is perfectly proper for the judge to retire with the justices to consider and come to a decision on the point (see p 1123 *f* and p 1124 *a* and *b*, post).

e

Notes

For justices of the peace as judges of the Crown Courts, see Supplement to 9 Halsbury's Laws (3rd Edn), para 963A, 2, 5.

f   For the Courts Act 1971, ss 4, 5, see 41 Halsbury's Statutes (3rd Edn) 291, 293.

Case cited

R v Prager [1972] 1 All ER 1114, [1972] 1 WLR 260, CA.

Appeal

g

This was an appeal by Michael John Orpin against his conviction in the Crown Court at York on 6th February 1974, before his Honour Judge McKee, sitting with justices, and a jury, on three charges of arson. The appellant was sentenced to four years imprisonment on each count, the sentences to run concurrently. He appealed by leave of the single judge. The facts are set out in the judgment of the court.

h

P H Bowers for the appellant.
P Worsley for the Crown.

LORD WIDGERY CJ. On 6th February 1974 at York Crown Court, before his Honour Judge McKee, this appellant pleaded not guilty to three offences of arson. He was convicted and sentenced to four years imprisonment on each count. He

j

appeals against his conviction by leave of the single judge, who granted legal aid, and who indicated that his motive in giving leave to appeal was so that the third ground put forward by the appellant might be considered by the full court. The third ground is expressed in these terms:

---

a   Section 4(2) is set out at p 1122 *h*, post
b   Section 5(8), so far as material, is set out at p 1123 *c*, post

'The learned Judge was wrong in retiring with two Justices in order to decide *a* and rule on the admissibility of the said evidence and/or whether to exercise his discretion to exclude the said evidence.'

The background of the case is simple enough. There were three separate fires. The police suspected the appellant of being involved in each of them. On 10th November 1973 the appellant went voluntarily to the police station to discuss some matter concerned with these fires. He was seen later in the day by two police officers. *b* He was cautioned at the outset, and then there followed a lengthy interview in which the police were putting to the appellant that he had some knowledge of the fires, and he was giving somewhat evasive answers. He was, as I say, cautioned at the very start and on occasion in the course of the conversation which went on he indicated that he did not want to say anything more at that time. The police nevertheless persisted and in the end he made a written statement, which was made again *c* under caution and which contained a statement by the appellant that he had made the confession voluntarily.

Nevertheless at the trial the point was taken by counsel for the defence that the admission should be excluded on the ground that it was obtained in breach of the Judges' Rules and was not voluntary. The judge retired with the two justices who were sitting with him to consider this, and on returning he gave a brief judgment on *d* the issues which had been raised, a judgment which recognises that at one point there was what one can fairly describe as a minor breach of the Judges' Rules, but a decision which goes on to say that, looking at the matter in the round, the court was satisfied that the statement was voluntary and, therefore, admissible.

There has been brief argument before us today on the merits of the ruling but we are quite satisfied that there is nothing in it and that this experienced judge had in *e* fact approached the problem perfectly properly. He had not been deterred by a minor breach of the Judges' Rules, which in the judgment of the court was not sufficient to exclude the statement, and he had applied his mind to the question of whether the statement was proved to have been voluntary. It is not necessary, therefore, to say any more about that ground of appeal.

The ground of appeal which the single judge had approved of for consideration *f* by this court is based on the provisions of the Courts Act 1971. The question quite shortly is whether, on a trial within a trial being held, or some other situation arising in the course of a trial on indictment which involves some interlocutory decision by the court, the lay justices, who may be sitting with the professional judge, if I may so describe him, should accompany the judge if he retires to consider the point, or should in any event have a vote on issues of that kind which fall for decision by the *g* court.

The point has not been raised before, and not surprisingly because the Courts Act 1971 is still a relatively new invention. Under s 4(1) of the Act it is provided: 'There shall be a Crown Court in England and Wales...' Subsection (2) is important:

'The jurisdiction and powers of the Crown Court shall be exercised by— (a) any judge of the High Court, or (b) any Circuit judge or Recorder, or (c) subject *h* to and in accordance with the provisions of the next following section, a judge of the High Court, Circuit judge or Recorder sitting with justices of the peace, and any such persons when exercising the jurisdiction and powers of the Crown Court shall be judges of the Crown Court.'

That seems to us to mark, at the beginning, the fact that justices of the peace *j* sitting with the judge in the Crown Court are themselves judges of the Crown Court, subject of course to the other provisions of the 1971 Act which may exclude them from certain powers possessed by a professional judge.

In s 5 is the more detailed provision for the introduction of lay justices into the Crown Court. Subsection (1) requires the presence of justices in the Crown Court in certain circumstances, and sub-s (3) provides:

a   'Without prejudice to the provisions of subsection (1) above, any jurisdiction
      or power of the Crown Court may be exercised by a judge of the High Court,
      Circuit judge or Recorder sitting with not more than four justices of the peace.'

      That is a very wide provision enabling any jurisdiction or power of the Crown Court
      to be exercised by a judge sitting with justices of the peace. It is perfectly true that under
b   sub-s (4) there is a requirement for the Lord Chief Justice with the concurrence of the
      Lord Chancellor to indicate what type of trial by indictment is suitable for trial
      before a court consisting of a judge and justices of the peace. But the jurisdiction,
      subject to any such directions by the Lord Chief Justice, is clear and wide, and the
      intention of the Act is, in our judgment, that the judge in question should sit with
      justices of the peace; that in view of s 4(2), which I have already read, those justices
c   shall be treated as judges of the Crown Court, and if there is a difference between
      them, we find the provision making that difference in s 5(8):

          'When a judge of the High Court, Circuit judge or Recorder sits with justices
          of the peace he shall preside, and—(a) the decision of the Crown Court may be
          a majority decision . . .'

d
      That again clearly provides, in our judgment, that the justices are to take part in the
      decision making, and indeed that they are to take part in the decision making on the
      footing equal to that of a Crown Court judge. In the event of a difference the majority
      prevails, whether the majority contains the professional judge, or whether he is
      alone in the minority.
e   In view of those provisions, what is the proper course when a trial within a trial is
      required to be held because the defence wish to take objection to certain evidence
      as being obtained as a result of pressure? The decision which results from a trial
      within a trial is a decision of the court. The decision is one which the court as then
      constituted must reach. The court as then constituted must include for decision-
      making purposes any justices who are sitting with the judge.
f   Accordingly, in our judgment, in the circumstances of this case it was perfectly
      proper for the judge to consult with the lay justices on the question of whether
      the evidence was admissible or not. Whether he chose to retire for the purpose, or
      whether he chose to consult with them briefly and informally on the Bench, is
      another matter, but that they should be given an opportunity of taking part in the
      decision, we think, is clear enough.
g   It has been suggested to us that such a view will give rise to practical problems.
      What, says counsel in his helpful argument for the appellant, are we going to do
      about the summing-up? Who is going to give that? The answer, of course, must
      be clear that the judge, and the judge alone, is to deliver the charge to the jury. It
      is argued that in deciding how to put his summing-up certain decisions have to be
      taken. The judge has to decide whether to refer to the bad character of the defen-
h   dant and so on. But that, in our judgment, makes no difference to the principle
      that the delivery of the summing-up is not a decision, and therefore both in law and
      in common sense is not a function of the court in which anyone other than the
      professional judge should take part.
          But any decisions properly so-called, be they decisions on sentence or interlocutory
      decisions delivered in the course of the hearing, are matters on which the full court
j   must play its part. All one need add today is really a glimpse of the obvious, so
      obvious that no doubt the draftsman did not think it necessary to put it in the Act,
      namely, that in matters of law the lay justices must take a ruling from the presiding
      judge in precisely the same way as the jury is required to take his ruling when it
      considers its verdict. No sort of difficulty, we believe, will be created for the circuit
      judges and those justices who sit with them if it is clearly understood: first, that
      decisions are the product of all members of the court, but secondly that any question

of law is a question on which the lay members of the court must defer to the views *a*
of the qualified presiding judge.

That being the position, no valid objection to the conviction can be taken in this
case by reason of the fact that the lay justices retired with the judge. For them to do
so was entirely correct, and when they retired, the judge should, and no doubt did,
explain the law to them, and then the decision on the facts which followed should
have been the product of all the members of the court. In those circumstances *b*
the appeal is dismissed.

Appeal dismissed.

Solicitors: *Hague, Dixon and Burn,* York (for the appellant); *Drury's,* Scarborough
(for the Crown). *c*

Jacqueline Charles   Barrister.

Cooke v Head (No 2) *d*

COURT OF APPEAL, CIVIL DIVISION
LORD DENNING MR, ORR LJ AND SIR SEYMOUR KARMINSKI
10th MAY 1974

Legal aid – Costs – Charge on property recovered for deficiency of costs – Property recovered *e*
or preserved in proceedings – Priority of charge – Order for payment of costs – Declaration
that plaintiff entitled to share in proceeds of sale of property – Defendant ordered to pay
plaintiff's costs of proceedings – Both parties legally aided – Charge on sum preserved by
defendant – Whether charge attaching to whole sum or to balance remaining after effect given
to court's order to pay plaintiff's costs – Legal Aid and Advice Act 1949, s 3(4).

f

C, a young woman, and H, a married man, formed an association. H purchased a
piece of land and together they built a bungalow on it. Subsequently they separated
and the bungalow was sold. C claimed to be entitled to a share in the proceeds of
sale, which, with interest, amounted to £2,546, and to £75 which she had contributed
to the deposit. She obtained legal aid and started proceedings against H. He also
obtained legal aid and resisted the claim. In the High Court the judge ordered H to *g*
pay C £75 and awarded her one-twelfth of the proceeds of sale. He also ordered H
to pay C all her costs. C appealed and the Court of Appeal[a] held that, in addition
to the £75, she was entitled to a one-third share, i e £849, leaving H with £1,697.
H was ordered to pay the costs of the appeal. C's costs on a common fund basis
came to £1,419 and H's costs to £1,166. H contended that since the Legal Aid and
Advice Act 1949, s 3(4)[b], gave the legal aid fund a first charge on property 'recovered *h*
or preserved', that charge fell on the property as soon as it had been recovered or
preserved before any question of costs was dealt with; and that, in consequence,
the amount which H had recovered in excess of his costs, i e £531, should be paid
to the legal aid fund in reduction of the amount by which C's costs exceeded the
amount which she had recovered.

j

---

a [1972] 2 All ER 38

b Section 3(4) provides: 'Except so far as regulations otherwise provide, any sums remaining
unpaid on account of a person's contribution to the legal aid fund in respect of any proceedings and, if the total contribution is less than the net liability of that fund on his account,
a sum equal to the deficiency shall be a first charge for the benefit of the legal aid fund on
any property (wherever situate) which is recovered or preserved for him in the proceedings.'

a **Held** – The court had power to deal with the money recovered or preserved and to make orders for payment out to one party or the other before the legal aid charge attached at all; that charge attached to such moneys as were left to the parties after the court's order had been fulfilled. Accordingly C was entitled to recover from H her party and party costs, and the legal aid charge for the difference between her party and party costs and common fund costs, estimated at £219, attached to the amount recovered from H, i e £849 plus £75, leaving an estimated balance of £704
b in C's hands (see p 1127 c d and h, post).

Notes

For charges for the benefit of the legal aid fund on property recovered or preserved, see 30 Halsbury's Laws (3rd Edn) 506, 507, paras 940, 941.

c   For the Legal Aid and Advice Act 1949, s 3, see 25 Halsbury's Statutes (3rd Edn) 762.

As from 8th May 1974, s 3(4) of the 1949 Act has been replaced by the Legal Aid Act 1974, s 9(6).

Cases referred to in judgments

d *Carr v Boxall* [1960] 1 All ER 495, [1960] 1 WLR 314, Digest (Cont Vol A) 976, *504a*.
Cooke v Head [1972] 2 All ER 38, [1972] 1 WLR 518, CA.
Nolan v C & C Marshall Ltd [1954] 1 All ER 328, [1954] 2 QB 42, [1954] 2 WLR 285, CA, 50 Digest (Repl) 497, *1766*.
Pettitt v Pettitt [1968] 1 All ER 1053, [1968] 1 WLR 443, 19 P & CR 245, CA; *rvsd on other grounds* [1969] 2 All ER 385, [1970] AC 777, [1969] 2 WLR 966, 20 P & CR 991,
e HL, Digest (Cont Vol C) 1088, *1753a*.
Till v Till [1974] 1 All ER 1096, [1974] 2 WLR 447, CA.

Application

On 21st December 1970, at the trial of an action by the plaintiff, Jacqueline Cooke, against the defendant, Dennis Head, Plowman J declared that the plaintiff was
f entitled to one-twelfth of the moneys standing to the credit of a deposit account in the joint names of the parties' solicitors and ordered the defendant to pay the plaintiff the sum of £75. His Lordship further ordered that the defendant pay to the plaintiff her costs of the action, the payment of those costs to be suspended until further order, and that the costs of the parties to which the Legal Aid Acts 1949 to 1964 applied be referred to the taxing master to be taxed on the common fund basis. On 19th January 1972 the Court of Appeal[1] (Lord Denning MR, Karminski
g and Orr LJJ) allowed an appeal by the plaintiff and varied the order below by declaring that the plaintiff was entitled to one-third of the moneys standing to the credit of the deposit account. The court further ordered that the defendant pay to the plaintiff the costs of the appeal, payment to be suspended until further order and that the parties' costs to which the 1949 to 1964 Acts applied be referred to the taxing master to be taxed on the common fund basis. The plaintiff applied to the
h court for directions as to the liability of the defendant for payment of the plaintiff's costs. The facts are set out in the judgment of Lord Denning MR.

Anthony Scrivener for the plaintiff.
Geoffrey Dearbergh for the defendant.

j
LORD DENNING MR. In January 1972 we decided the case of *Cooke v Head*[1]. Miss Cooke was a young woman of 20. Mr Head was much older. He was a married man with a wife and two children. He was in a good way of business at Bexhill.

---

1   [1972] 2 All ER 38, [1972] 1 WLR 518

He took Miss Cooke out and gave her driving lessons. An attachment grew up   *a*
between them and she had a child. For three or four years they associated together.
He said he was going to get a divorce from his wife and marry her. He bought a
piece of land. Together they built a bungalow on it. But then their association
ended. They separated in 1966. His divorce eventually went through. He married
another woman. He now has a four year old child by her and he is working as a
carpet fitter at some £30 a week. Miss Cooke has remained unmarried. She has a   *b*
child and is working in a household. Meanwhile the bungalow was sold. She claimed
a share in it. Also £75 which she contributed to the deposit. She got legal aid and
brought proceedings against Mr Head. He resisted the claim altogether. He too
was legally aided. The case was heard by Plowman J on 21st December 1970. Miss
Cooke had some partial success. The judge ordered Mr Head to pay her £75 and he
awarded her one-twelfth of the value of the bungalow. Further, he ordered Mr   *c*
Head to pay her all her costs; but, as he was legally aided, the judge said it was not
to be enforced except on further order. Miss Cooke appealed to this court[1]. She
succeeded in that the one-twelfth awarded by the judge was increased to one-third.
This court held that she was to have one-third of the proceeds of the bungalow.
Again Mr Head was ordered to pay the costs of the appeal. But that order in turn
was suspended until further application.   *d*
     The question now is as to the proceeds of sale of the bungalow. Are they to be
applied in payment of costs? Or is Miss Cooke to have any of them, or Mr Head?
The difficulty is shown by taking the actual figures. The net proceeds of sale were
£1,946. That sum was put on deposit in the joint names of the solicitors. It has
earned interest, so that the sum has increased to £2,546. If that sum is divided
according to the order of this court—one-third and two-thirds—Miss Cooke would   *e*
get £849 and Mr Head £1,697. What is to be done with those moneys? Are they
to go in payment of costs? Both Miss Cooke and Mr Head were legally aided. Under
the Legal Aid and Advice Act 1949 and the Legal Aid (General) Regulations 1971[2],
the legal aid fund have a charge for their costs on the 'property recovered or preserved'. The property 'recovered' for Miss Cooke was £849. Her costs on a common
fund basis come to £1,419. If the legal aid fund are entitled to a charge for £1,419   *f*
on her £849, she will get nothing out of the litigation. The property 'preserved'
for Mr Head may be said to be £1,697. His costs taxed on the common fund basis
come to £1,166. If the legal aid fund are entitled to a charge for that sum on his
£1,697, they would get their costs in full and he would receive the balance of £531,
but that would go in payment of the balance of Miss Cooke's costs.
     So if the charges and the legal aid fund are given full effect—without the court
being able to interfere—neither Miss Cooke nor Mr Head could get anything out of   *g*
the proceeds of the £2,546. The legal aid fund would sweep it all up for costs.
     Now counsel for Miss Cooke comes to this court. He asks that the order for costs
made in her favour should take priority over the charges to the legal aid fund.
Taking the actual figures, he says that Miss Cooke has an order on Mr Head requiring
him to pay the party and party costs both before Plowman J and this court. Those
costs on a common fund basis come to £1,419, but on a party and party basis come   *h*
to about £1,200. Mr Head's two-thirds share of the proceeds of the bungalow come
to £1,697. Counsel suggests that the £1,200 party and party costs payable to Miss
Cooke should come out of that £1,697. That would leave Mr Head with £497, which
has been 'preserved' for him and on which the legal aid fund may be said to have a
charge for their costs incurred on his behalf. If this is done, Miss Cooke's one-third
share of the proceeds of the bungalow, £849, will come to her intact without having   *j*
to bear any of the party and party costs, because £1,200 will have been recovered
from Mr Head. Her £849 will only have to bear the £219, being the difference
between £1,419 on the common fund basis and £1,200 on the party and party basis.

1 [1972] 2 All ER 38, [1972] 1 WLR 518
2 SI 1971 No 62

a So Miss Cooke should receive £849 less £219, that is £630, plus the £75 for deposit. In support of his contention, counsel for Miss Cooke has referred us to three cases in which the courts have made orders for the payment of costs without any regard to the charge to the legal aid fund. So that the court's order takes priority over the charge to the legal aid fund. Those cases are *Nolan v C & C Marshall Ltd*[1]; *Carr v Boxall*[2], and *Pettitt v Pettitt*[3].

b On the other hand, in answer to that, counsel for Mr Head points to s 3(4) of the Legal Aid Act 1949 and reg 18 of the Legal Aid (General) Regulations 1971. These are effective to give the legal aid fund a first charge for their costs on the property recovered or preserved: see *Till v Till*[4]. Counsel for Mr Head suggests that this charge falls on the property as soon as it is recovered or preserved, before any question of costs is dealt with.

c As between those two arguments, I think that counsel for Miss Cooke is right. The court has power to deal with the money recovered or preserved and to make orders for payment out to one party or the other before the legal aid charge attaches at all. The legal aid charge only attaches to such moneys as are left to the parties after the court's order is fulfilled.

d Applied to this case, it seems to me then, that out of the £2,546 which is now available as the proceeds of the bungalow, Miss Cooke should get her £849. She should also get out of Mr Head's £1,697 her party and party costs, which are estimated to be £1,200. She should also have the £75 awarded to her for her contribution to the deposit. So she gets the £849 plus the £75, that is £924. But on that sum which she has recovered, the legal aid fund will have a charge for the difference between the party and party costs and the common fund costs. It looks as if it may be £219.

e So far as Mr Head's position is concerned, he starts with £1,697 out of the proceeds of the bungalow. Out of that there will be deducted the party and party costs which are payable to Miss Cooke, which are estimated at £1,200. He will also have to pay the £75 out of it. This leaves a balance of £422. On that sum the legal aid fund will have a charge for so much as is properly due to them.

f There is an argument as to how much the charge against Mr Head should be. It depends on the amount of property which has been 'recovered or preserved' for him. It is said to be very small, because Miss Cooke only claimed a share of one-half. So that only one-half of one-third, and that is one-sixth, was preserved for him. One sixth of £1,946 is £324. If that is right, the legal aid charge will be only on £324 and Mr Head will get £98. But that is a matter between him and the fund. It does not come up for our consideration today.

g The net result is therefore that out of the £2,546, Miss Cooke will get about £705 and Mr Head will get about £98. The balance will go in costs to the legal aid fund. This shows that when the sole asset is the proceeds of a house, it is much better for the disputing parties to settle at the outset; because, if they go to law, much of those proceeds will be eaten up in law costs, even though the parties are both legally aided with a nil contribution.

h **ORR LJ.** I agree.

SIR SEYMOUR KARMINSKI. I also agree.

Order accordingly.

j Solicitors: *Bridges, Sawtell & A J Adams*, agents for *Pead, Ash, Fynmore & Pembroke*, Bexhill (for the plaintiff); *Blyth, Dutton, Robins, Hay*, agents for *Menneer, Idle & Brackett*, St Leonards-on-Sea (for the defendant).

L J Kovats Esq Barrister.

1 [1954] 1 All ER 328, [1954] 2 QB 42
2 [1960] 1 All ER 495, [1960] 1 WLR 314
3 [1968] 1 All ER 1053, [1968] 1 WLR 443
4 [1974] 1 All ER 1096 [1974] 2 WLR 447

a

F Hoffmann-La Roche & Co AG and others v Secretary of State for Trade and Industry

HOUSE OF LORDS

LORD REID, LORD MORRIS OF BORTH-Y-GEST, LORD WILBERFORCE, LORD DIPLOCK AND LORD *b*
CROSS OF CHELSEA

23rd, 24th, 25th, 29th APRIL, 3rd JULY 1974

Injunction – Interlocutory – Undertaking as to damages – Crown – Undertaking by Crown or government department – Propriety – Proceedings by Crown to enforce law – Secretary of State commencing proceedings under statutory duty – Proceedings against companies for c injunction to enforce compliance with statutory order – Order made by Secretary of State regulating prices at which companies permitted to sell drugs – Companies alleging order invalid and ultra vires – Secretary of State applying for interlocutory injunction – Whether companies entitled to undertaking as to damages as condition of submitting to interlocutory injunction – Monopolies and Restrictive Practices (Inquiry and Control) Act 1948, ss 10(1) d (as amended by the Monopolies and Mergers Act 1965, ss 3(2), 11(5), Sch 3), 11(2) – Monopolies and Mergers Act 1965, s 3(1)(4).

Certain companies were members of a group which manufactured pharmaceutical products. The companies held a patent for two tranquillising drugs known as 'Librium' and 'Valium'. Those drugs had been very successful and were widely e used in the United Kingdom. They could only be obtained on a doctor's prescription. Since the great majority of patients who used the drugs were within the National Health Service a large proportion of the drugs sold were paid for by the Department of Health and Social Security. For some years the department had been of the view that the selling price of the drugs was too high. In consequence the Secretary of State for Trade and Industry, acting under s 2(1)[a] of the Monopolies and Restrictive f Practices (Inquiry and Control) Act 1948, referred the matter to the Monopolies Commission for investigation and report. In their report the commission found that the conditions to which the 1948 Act applied, as defined by s 3(1)[b] of the 1948 Act, prevailed, that the prices charged by the companies had been excessive and recommended that they should be substantially reduced. The report was laid before Parliament in accordance with s 9[c] of the 1948 Act. Subsequently the Secretary of g State made an order[d] in the form of a statutory instrument under s 10(1)[e] of the

---

a Section 2(1), so far as material, provides: 'Where it appears to the Board of Trade that it is or may be the fact that conditions to which this Act applies prevail as respects . . . (*a*) the supply of goods of any description . . . the Board may, if they think fit, refer the matter h to the Commission for investigation and report . . .'

b Section 3(1), so far as material, is set out at p 1136 *h*, post

c Section 9, so far as material, is set out at p 1136 *b*, post

d Regulation of Prices (Tranquillising Drugs) Order 1973 (SI 1973 No 720)

e Section 10(1), as amended, provides: 'The provisions of this section shall have effect where —(*a*) the Board of Trade have referred a matter to the Commission under the preceding j provisions of this Act for investigation and report; and (*b*) the reference is not so framed as to limit the investigation and report to the facts; and (*c*) the report of the Commission has been laid before Parliament, with or without omissions; and (*d*) according to the report of the Commission, as laid before Parliament, conditions to which this Act applies prevail; and (*e*) (i) according to the report, as laid before Parliament, those conditions, or any things done by the parties concerned as a result of, or for the purpose of preserving, those conditions, operate or may be expected to operate against the public interest.'

a 1948 Act and s 3*f* of the Monopolies and Mergers Act 1965, the effect of which was to reduce the prices that could lawfully be charged for Librium and Valium to the figures recommended by the commission. The order expired after 28 days and two further orders*g* to the same effect were made in succession. The third order became permanent when it was approved by both Houses of Parliament. The companies wrote to the Secretary of State alleging that the commission's report *b* was vitiated by a failure to observe the requirements of natural justice with the result that there was no valid report which, under s 10(1) of the 1948 Act and s 3 of the 1965 Act, was a prerequisite to the exercise of the Secretary of State's powers to make the orders and further that the orders were ultra vires and invalid because the price levels fixed were arbitrary and penalising. They stated that they would accordingly disregard the third order and restore the prices of the drugs to their original level but would pay the difference between the two prices into a special *c* bank account to await the decision of the courts on the validity of the orders. The companies then issued a writ against the Secretary of State claiming that the orders were ultra vires. The Secretary of State issued a writ against the companies seeking an injunction, under s 11(2)*h* of the 1948 Act, restraining the companies from charging prices in excess of those specified in the order. The Secretary of State applied for an interlocutory injunction to the same effect but stated that he was not prepared to *d* give the companies an undertaking as to damages. The companies were only prepared to submit to an interlocutory injunction on condition that such an undertaking was given.

Held (Lord Wilberforce dissenting) – The Secretary of State was entitled to the interlocutory injunction sought for the following reasons—
e
(i) Where the Crown was engaged in litigation for the purpose of asserting a proprietary or contractual right the ordinary rule applied and on a motion by the Crown the courts would not grant an interlocutory injunction unless the Crown chose to give the usual undertaking as to damages. Where however the Crown had commenced proceedings for an injunction for the purpose of enforcing the law in *f* the manner prescribed by statute, it was for the person against whom an interlocutory injunction was sought to show special reason why justice required that it should not be granted or should only be granted on terms. Unless and until a statutory instrument had been declared to be ultra vires by a final judgment in an action in the courts, the instrument was to be treated as part of the law and enforced accordingly (see p 1134 *b* to *f*, p 1141 *e*, p 1142 *e* and *h*, p 1143 *a* and *g h*, p 1151 *j* to p 1152 *b* and *j*,

g ────────────────────────────────

f Section 3, so far as material, provides:
'(1) In the circumstances described in section 10(1) of the [Monopolies and Restrictive Practices (Inquiry and Control) Act 1948, as amended, the Board of Trade, for the purpose of remedying or preventing any mischiefs which in their opinion result or may be expected to result from the conditions or things which, according to the report of the Commission *h* as laid before Parliament, operate or may be expected to operate against the public interest, may by order (whatever the recommendation, if any, made by the Commission) exercise all or any of the powers conferred by subsections (3) to (7) below . . .
'(4) The Board may . . .
(c) regulate to such extent and in such circumstances as may be provided by or under the order the prices to be charged for any goods or services so specified or described,
but the Board shall not, in relation to goods or services of any class to which the report re-
j lates, exercise the power conferred by virtue of paragraph (c) above unless it appears to the Board on the facts found by the Commission as stated in the report that prices charged in the case of goods or services of that class are, or have been, such as to operate, or to be expected to operate, against the public interest . . .'
g Regulation of Prices (Tranquillising Drugs) (No 2) Order 1973 (SI 1973 No 925); Regulation of Prices (Tranquillising Drugs) (No 3) Order 1973 (SI 1973 No 1093)
h Section 11 is set out at p 1133 *e* and *f*, post

p 1153 c, p 1155 b to d and p 1158 c d and g to j, post); *Attorney-General v Albany Hotel* a
Co [1896] c Ch 696 and *Post Office v Estuary Radio Ltd* [1967] 3 All ER 663 distinguished.

(ii) It could not be argued that, because the Crown itself was a substantial purchaser
of the companies' drugs, the dispute was to be regarded as essentially a private one
between the companies and the Crown for to do so would be to overlook the special
interest that private purchasers of the drugs had in seeing that the law was enforced.
Accordingly the Secretary of State was entitled to an interlocutory injunction without b
giving any undertaking as to damages unless the companies could show a strong
prima facie case that the order sought to be enforced by the injunction was ultra
vires. It was not for the Secretary of State to show that the companies' case could
not possibly succeed but for the companies to show that their defence that the order
was ultra vires was likely to be successful. That they had failed to do (see p 1134 g
to p 1135 b, p 1144 d to f, p 1155 h and j, p 1156 f, p 1157 g to p 1158 b and p 1159 a c
to e, post).

Per Lord Diplock and Lord Cross of Chelsea. The courts have jurisdiction to
declare an order made by statutory instrument to be invalid even though, in accordance with the requirements of the enabling legislation, it has been approved by both
Houses of Parliament (see p 1153 g and h and p 1159 f, post).

Decision of the Court of Appeal sub nom *Secretary of State for Trade and Industry* d
v F Hoffmann-La Roche & Co AG [1973] 3 All ER 945 affirmed.

Notes

For proceedings by the Attorney-General for an injunction to protect public rights,
see 21 Halsbury's Laws (3rd Edn) 403, 404, paras 844, 845.

For undertakings as to damages on the grant of an interlocutory injunction, see
21 Halsbury's Laws (3rd Edn) 422, 423, paras 887-890, and for cases on the subject, e
see 28(2) Digest (Reissue) 1133-1136, 1328-1377.

For the Monopolies and Restrictive Practices (Inquiry and Control) Act 1948, ss 2,
3, 9, 10, 11, see 37 Halsbury's Statutes (3rd Edn) 60, 62, 67, 68, 70.

For the Monopolies and Mergers Act 1965, s 3, see ibid 180.

Cases referred to in opinions

Anisminic Ltd v The Foreign Compensation Commission [1969] 1 All ER 208, [1969] 2 AC
147, [1969] 2 WLR 163, HL; rvsg [1967] 2 All ER 986, [1968] 2 QB 862, [1967] 3 WLR
382, CA, Digest (Cont Vol C) 590, 280ac.

Attorney-General v Albany Hotel Co [1896] 2 Ch 696, 65 LJCh 885, 75 LT 195, CA, 28(2)
Digest (Reissue) 1134, 1350.

Attorney-General v Cockermouth Local Board (1874) LR 18 Eq 172, 30 LT 590, 38 JP 660, g
16 Digest (Repl) 542, 3827.

Attorney-General v Oxford, Worcester and Wolverhampton Railway Co (1854) 2 WR 330,
38 Digest (Repl) 283, 7.

Durayappah v Fernando [1967] 2 All ER 152, [1967] 2 AC 337, [1967] 2 WLR 289, PC,
Digest (Cont Vol C) 811, *420b.

Pergamon Press Ltd, Re [1970] 3 All ER 535, [1971] Ch 388, [1970] 3 WLR 792, CA, h
Digest (Cont Vol C) 107, 4188e.

Post Office v Estuary Radio Ltd [1967] 3 All ER 663, [1968] 2 QB 740, [1967] 1 WLR 1396,
[1967] 2 Lloyd's Rep 299, CA, Digest (Cont Vol C) 189, 1174b.

Ridge v Baldwin [1963] 2 All ER 66, [1964] AC 40, [1963] 2 WLR 935, 127 JP 295, 61
LGR 369, HL; rvsg [1962] 1 All ER 834, [1963] 1 QB 539, [1962] 2 WLR 716, CA,
37 Digest (Repl) 195, 32.

Secretary of State for War v Cope [1919] 2 Ch 339, 88 LJCh 522, 121 LT 547, 36 RPC 223, j
28(2) Digest (Reissue) 1135, 1351.

Smith v Day (1882) 21 Ch D 421, 48 LT 54, 28(2) Digest (Reissue) 1133, 1332.

Smith v East Elloe Rural District Council [1956] 1 All ER 855, [1956] AC 736, 120 JP 263,
54 LGR 233, HL; varying [1955] 2 All ER 19, 119 JP 325, 53 LGR 299, CA, 26 Digest
(Repl) 703 135.

Interlocutory appeal

a   By notice of motion dated 28th June 1973, the Department for Trade and Industry, the plaintiffs in an action commenced by a writ issued on 28th June 1973 against F Hoffmann-La Roche & Co AG, SAPAC Corporation Ltd and Roche Products Ltd ('the Roche Group'), sought an order that each of the companies in the Roche Group be restrained whether by the directors, officers, servants or agents, or any of them, of the respective companies or otherwise howsoever during the currency of the

b   Regulation of Prices (Tranquillising Drugs) (No 3) Order 1973[1] ('the no 3 order') until judgment in the action or until further order from charging or from causing or permitting any body corporate (wherever incorporated) in which the companies of the Roche Group had or any of them had a controlling interest for the purposes of the no 3 order to charge prices for the pharmaceutical preparations known as Librium, Valium, Brontrium, Libraxin, Pantrium and Limbritol or any of them on

c   the sale thereof in the United Kingdom (other than on a sale of goods which were to be exported from the United Kingdom) in excess of the relevant prices specified in the no 3 order and from doing any other act declared to be unlawful by the no 3 order. By an order made on 13th July Walton J ordered that the motion be treated as if it had been brought in an action commenced by the Roche Group against the Secretary of State for Trade and Industry by a writ issued on 25th June and that all

d   further proceedings in the action commenced by the Department of Trade and Industry be stayed. On the Roche Group undertaking until further order (i) that any sums charged by or paid to the Roche Group or any of the companies of the Roche Group for any of the drugs specified in the no 3 order in excess of the relevant prices specified in the no 3 order should be placed and kept deposited in a joint banking account to be opened and maintained for the purpose in the joint names of the Roche Group's

e   solicitors and the Treasury Solicitor; and (ii) that they would forthwith adopt all necessary measures to ensure that any moneys which should ultimately become refundable should reach the proper destination, Walton J dismissed the motion. On 30th July 1973 the Court of Appeal[2] (Lord Denning MR, Buckley and Lawton LJJ) allowed an appeal by the Secretary of State for Trade and Industry, and discharged the order of Walton J but, on the Roche Group giving an undertaking in the terms of

f   the injunction asked for in the notice of motion, made no further order. The Roche Group appealed to the House of Lords. The facts are set out in the opinion of Lord Morris of Borth-y-Gest.

R A MacCrindle QC, Richard Yorke QC, A R Barrowclough and Genevra Caws for the Roche Group.

g   Sir Peter Rawlinson QC, Kenneth Jupp QC, Gordon Slynn and Peter Gibson for the Secretary of State.

Their Lordships took time for consideration.

3rd July. The following opinions were delivered.

h

LORD REID. My Lords, in recent years a number of very successful new drugs have been discovered and put on the market. The discovery of a new drug is generally unpredictable. Several large international companies have engaged in extensive research. Most of it is unproductive but occasionally a valuable discovery is made. The practice of these companies is to recover the cost of their unproductive

j   research by increasing the selling price of their successful products. No one objects to that system in principle but obviously there is room for much difference of opinion as to how far it can fairly be carried. And there is also the question of what is a fair profit on such sales.

---

1   SI 1973 No 1093
2   [1973] 3 All ER 945, [1973] 3 WLR 805

The appellants ('the Roche Group') are related companies, some of which spend
very large sums on such research. They discovered and have marketed since about
1963 two new tranquillisers which they sell under the names Librium and Valium.
These drugs are obtainable from chemists on doctors' prescriptions. They became
very popular and we are informed that before the proceedings to which I shall
later refer sales in this country brought in some £10,000 per day. A very large
proportion of these sales is under the National Health Service. The patient is only
charged a small fee by the chemist and he recovers from the Department of Health
and Social Security the balance of what he has to pay for the drugs plus his profit.
So if the manufacturer overcharges for his drugs the department is the loser.

For years before 1971 the department thought the selling price of these drugs
much too high but they were unsuccessful in getting a sufficient reduction. So the
machinery of the Monopolies and Mergers Acts 1948 and 1965 was set in motion.
There was a reference to the Monopolies Commission in September 1971 and after
long enquiries the commission reported in February 1973. In para 217 of their report
the commission say:

'We conclude, therefore, that the determination of the level of prices at which
chlordiazepoxide and diazepam are supplied (which we have found in paragraph
205 to be a thing done by Roche Products as a result of, and for the purpose
of preserving, the conditions) operates and may be expected to operate against
the public interest.'

In para 235 they say:

'Among the points we bear in mind in reaching a conclusion on the
appropriate level of prices in future are the following:
'(a) Even if we could accept the cost figures in appendix 5, table 2, fair prices
based upon these costs might have been lower than those actually charged
in 1970 by at least 40 per cent for Librium and at least 50 per cent for Valium
(paragraph 230).
'(b) For reasons we have given in detail (paragraphs 219 to 227) we are satisfied
that some of the cost figures referred to—in particular those for research
and promotion costs—grossly exceed the levels that should be taken into
account to arrive at fair prices. It follows that fair prices should in any case
be substantially below the levels indicated in (a).
(c) There are no grounds for maintaining the particular price differential
between Valium and Librium which existed in 1970 (paragraph 228).
'(d) The excessive prices charged up to the present have already produced
excessive profits on a very large scale (paragraph 234).
'Although we have made a number of calculations in an attempt to quantify
the effects of (b) and (c) above, none has proved entirely satisfactory having
regard to our incomplete knowledge of the business of the Roche Group. But
in the event this scarcely matters in the light of (d).'

In paragraph 237 they say:

'We recommend that Roche Products' selling prices for the reference drugs
should be reduced (i) as regards Librium, to not more than 40 per cent of the
selling prices in 1970, (ii) as regards Valium, to not more than 25 per cent of the
selling prices in 1970, (iii) as regards other drugs covered by the reference, by
corresponding proportions as may be determined by DHSS.'

The Acts provide for orders being made consequent on a report of the Monopolies
Commission and accordingly the Regulation of Prices (Tranquillising Drugs) Order
1973[1] was made and came into operation on 23rd April 1973. By virtue of provisions

1   SI 1973 No 720

a   in the Acts such an order ceases to have effect after 28 days unless there have been affirmative resolutions of both Houses of Parliament. The order was sent to the Special Orders Committee of this House and the Roche Group were heard at some length. So the order ceased to have effect for want of an affirmative resolution in due time and so did a second order[1]. But a third order[2], which came into operation on 25th June 1973, was duly approved by both Houses.

b   The no 3 order narrated, as did the earlier order, that it appeared to the Secretary of State on facts found by the Monopolies Commission that the prices charged are or have been such as to operate against the public interest. It then adopted the recommendation of the Monopolies Commission and prohibited the Roche Group from charging more than the prices set out in the schedule.

On 25th June 1973 the Roche Group brought the present action against the Secretary of State claiming declarations that the Monopolies Commission had proceeded un-
c   fairly and in a way contrary to natural justice, that the findings, conclusions and recommendations in their report were invalid and of no effect and that the order to which I have referred was ultra vires invalid and of no effect. On 28th June 1973 the Secretary of State sought an injunction restraining the Roche Group from charging prices in excess of those specified in the no 3 order and they also sought an interim
d   injunction. Walton J, on an undertaking given by the Roche Group, refused to grant an interim injunction but the Court of Appeal[3] allowed an appeal by the Secretary of State.

Section 11 of the Monopolies and Restrictive Practices (Inquiry and Control) Act 1948 provides for the enforcement of orders made under this legislation:

e   '(1) No criminal proceedings shall lie against any person by virtue of the making of any order under the last preceding section on the ground that he has committed, or aided, abetted, counselled or procured the commission of, or conspired or attempted to commit, or incited others to commit, any contravention of the order.

'(2) Nothing in subsection (1) of this section shall limit any right of any person to bring civil proceedings in respect of any contravention or apprehended contra-
f   vention of any such order, and, without prejudice to the generality of the preceding words, compliance with any such order shall be enforceable by civil proceedings by the Crown for an injunction or for any other appropriate relief...'

It will be seen that there is no reference in this section to interim injunctions, but it is not disputed that the court has power to grant interim injunctions. The question in this appeal is in what terms such an injunction should be granted.
g   An interim injunction against a party to a litigation may cause him great loss if in the end he is successful. In the present case it is common ground that a long time—it may be years—will elapse before a decision can be given. During that period, if an interim injunction is granted, the Roche Group will only be able to make the charges permitted by the order. So if in the end the order is annulled that loss will
h   be the difference between those charges and those which they could have made if the order had never been made. And they may not be able to recover any part of that loss from anyone. It is said that the loss might amount to £8 million. The Roche Group's case is that justice requires that such an injunction should not be granted without an undertaking by the Secretary of State to make good that loss to them if they are ultimately successful.
j   The Secretary of State's first answer is that when an interim injunction is granted to the Crown no undertaking can be required as a condition of granting it. It is not in doubt that in an ordinary litigation the general rule has long been that no interim

1   Regulation of Prices (Tranquillising Drugs) (No 2) Order 1973 (SI 1973 No 925)
2   Regulation of Prices (Tranquillising Drugs) (No 3) Order 1973 (SI 1973 No 1093)
3   [1973] 3 All ER 945, [1973] 3 WLR 805

injunction likely to cause loss to a party will be granted unless the party seeking the *a*
injunction undertakes to make good that loss if in the end it appears that the injunction was unwarranted. He cannot be compelled to give an undertaking but if he will
not give it he will not get the injunction. But there is much authority to show that
the Crown was in a different position. In general no undertaking was required of
it. But whatever justification there may have been for that before 1947 I agree with
your Lordships that the old rule or practice cannot be justified since the passing of *b*
the Crown Proceedings Act 1947. So if this had been a case where the Crown were
asserting a proprietary right I would hold that the ordinary rule should apply and
there should be no interlocutory injunction unless the Crown chose to give the usual
undertaking.

But this is a case in a different and novel field. No doubt it was thought that
criminal penalties were inappropriate as a means of enforcing orders of this kind, *c*
and the only method of enforcement is by injunction. Dealing with alleged breaches
of the law is a function of the Crown (or of a department of the executive) entirely
different in character from its function in protecting its proprietary right. It has
more resemblance to the function of prosecuting those who are alleged to have
committed an offence. A person who is prosecuted and found not guilty may have
suffered serious loss by reason of the prosecution, but in general he has no legal *d*
claim against the prosecutor. In the absence of special circumstances I see no reason
why the Crown, in seeking to enforce orders of this kind, should have to incur legal
liability to the person alleged to be in breach of the order.

It must be borne in mind that an order made under statutory authority is as much
the law of the land as an Act of Parliament unless and until it has been found to be
ultra vires. No doubt procedure by way of injunction is more flexible than procedure *e*
by prosecution and there may well be cases when a court ought to refuse an interim
injunction or only to grant it on terms. But I think that it is for the person against
whom the interim injunction is sought to show special reason why justice requires
that the injunction should not be granted or should only be granted on terms.

The present case has a special feature which requires anxious consideration. As I
have already indicated the Crown has a very large financial interest in obtaining an *f*
interim injunction. The Department of Health and Social Security will reap a large
immediate benefit from the lower prices set out in the order at the expense of the
Roche Group. If in the end it were decided that the order is ultra vires those prices
ought never to have been enforced, the department ought never to have had that
benefit and the Roche Group would have suffered a large loss. So why should the
Secretary of State not be required to give the undertaking which the Roche Group *g*
seek as a condition of getting the interim injunction?

But, on the other hand, the order which the Roche Group seeks to annul is the law
at present and if an interim injunction is refused that means that the law is not to
be enforced and the Roche Group are to be at liberty to disregard it by charging
forbidden prices. And the matter does not stop there. Doctors will continue to
prescribe these drugs. Chemists will have to pay the forbidden prices if the public *h*
are to be provided with drugs which doctors think they ought to have. And chemists
cannot be expected to pay the Roche Group's prices unless the department is willing
to reimburse them. So the department will have to acquiesce in and indeed aid and
abet the Roche Group's breaches of the law if the medical profession and the public
are to get what they are entitled to.

It is true that the Roche Group have proposed an ingenious scheme which they *j*
would undertake to operate if an interim injunction is refused. The effect of it would
be that they would continue to charge the forbidden prices but that if the order were
ultimately held to be ultra vires they would repay the difference between the forbidden charges which they had made and the lower charges which they ought to
have made. The scheme would involve considerable practical difficulties and would
probably not be fully effective, but I shall not discuss those difficulties because the

serious objection would remain that the law laid down in the order is to be disregarded
a   until the case is decided.

My Lords, if I thought that the Roche Group had a strong case on the merits I
would try to stretch a point in their favour to protect them from obvious injustice,
though I would find difficulty in doing so. It is true that although we heard a good
deal of argument on the merits we are not in a position to express any firm opinion
as to the Roche Group's prospects of success. But if it is for them to show us at this
b   stage that their case is so strong that they are entitled to some special consideration,
I can say that they have completely failed to convince me that they have a strong
prima facie case.

I would therefore dismiss this appeal.

c   **LORD MORRIS OF BORTH-Y-GEST.** My Lords, we are concerned in this
case with an application which was made by the Crown for an injunction to enforce
an order made by a Secretary of State which recited that it had been made in the
exercise of statutory powers vested in him. The order was one which had received
the approval by resolution of each House of Parliament. Contravention of the order
did not attract criminal proceedings but civil proceedings could be brought by any
d   person in respect of a contravention or apprehended contravention of the order.
In particular, as was provided by statute, the order was enforceable by civil proceedings
by the Crown for an injunction or for any other appropriate relief.

The order which the Crown sought to enforce made it unlawful to sell certain
goods at prices exceeding those laid down. The order was made because it appeared
to the Secretary of State (on the basis of certain facts found) that the prices previously
e   charged for the goods had been such as to operate against the public interest. The
Secretary of State made the order with a view to remedying or preventing certain
mischiefs. They were the mischiefs which 'in his opinion' resulted or might be expected to result 'from the things' which, according to a report of the Monopolies
Commission, operated or might be expected to operate against the public interest.

The function of the Secretary of State was to promote the public interest by dealing
f   with the mischiefs which may arise if there are conditions of monopoly or restriction.
The plan adopted by Parliament was to set up machinery to enquire whether such
conditions existed. If the supply of certain goods (or the application of processes)
is considerably under the control of one person there is the risk that prices may be
charged which exceed those which purchasers or others ought fairly to be expected
to pay. Such a state of things may operate against the public interest.

g   The legislative scheme adopted by Parliament to deal with the 'mischiefs' which
may arise from monopoly conditions resulted in the passing of the Monopolies and
Restrictive Practices (Inquiry and Control) Act 1948 and of the Monopolies and
Mergers Act 1965. The first of these, under which the Monopolies and Restrictive
Practices Commission was constituted, was an Act—

h   'to make provision for inquiry into the existence and effects of, and for dealing
        with mischiefs resulting from, or arising in connection with, any conditions of
        monopoly or restriction or other analogous conditions prevailing as respects the
        supply of, or the application of any process to, goods, buildings or structures, or
        as respects exports.'

The 1965 Act made further provision in regard to the constitution and proceedings
j   of the Monopolies Commission and in regard to matters dealt with in the 1948 Act,
and furthermore made provision for preventing or remedying 'mischiefs' which
may result from mergers of businesses or similar transactions.

The 1948 Act laid down the meaning of the phrase 'conditions to which this Act
applies'. Section 3 laid down its meaning in relation to supply, s 4 in relation to
processing and s 5 in relation to exports. Under s 2(1), if it appeared to the Board

of Trade that it was or might be the fact that the 'conditions' prevailed, there could   *a*
be a reference to the commission. Section 6 dealt with the scope of references to the
commission and s 7 with the duties of the commission on a reference. The opening
words of s 9 provide as follows:

> 'When the Commission report to the Board of Trade on any matter referred
> to them under the preceding provisions of this Act for investigation and report,
> the Board may, and, unless the reference was so framed as to limit the investi-   *b*
> gation and report to the facts, shall, lay the report before each House of
> Parliament . . .'

The powers of the competent authority thereafter to make orders derive from various
provisions in s 10 of the 1948 Act and s 3 of the 1965 Act.

For an appreciation of the issues raised in the appeal it will be helpful to refer to   *c*
the sequence of dates and events which preceded the making of the order, compliance
with which the Crown sought to enforce. The order is the Regulation of Prices
(Tranquillising Drugs) (No 3) Order 1973[1].

The reference to the Monopolies Commission to which this case relates was made
on 14th September 1971. It was made in exercise of the powers given by s 2(1) of the
1948 Act. It referred to the commission for investigation and report the supply in   *d*
the United Kingdom of two descriptions of goods, which consisted of tranquillising
drugs. The drugs in question were manufactured by the Roche organisation and
were sold under the trade marks 'Librium' and 'Valium'. The active ingredients of
these are manufactured by Roche Group companies outside the United Kingdom.
The ingredients are imported in bulk by Roche Products Ltd, who make them up
into tablets or capsules or in some other suitable form. The drugs are protected   *e*
in this country by United Kingdom patents which expire in one case in 1975 and in
the other in 1976.

The drugs are only obtainable on a doctor's prescription. As most people in this
country (over 90 per cent) are within the National Health Service, the result is that
retail chemists who buy from wholesalers are reimbursed by the Department of
Health and Social Security. It is not necessary to set out the precise details of the   *f*
arrangements, but it is apparent that if excessive prices have been charged in the past
that will have been to the detriment of that department and that if for the remainder
of the patent periods and for the future the prices are very considerably reduced the
result will be to the benefit of that department.

The reference directed the commission to investigate and report whether the
'conditions' (see in particular s 3 of the 1948 Act) in fact prevailed. Section 3(1) of   *g*
the 1948 Act is in the following terms:

> 'Conditions to which this Act applies shall be deemed for the purposes of
> this Act to prevail as respects the supply of goods of any description if either—
> (a) at least one-third of all the goods of that description which are supplied in
> the United Kingdom or any substantial part thereof are supplied by or to any   *h*
> one person, or by or to any two or more persons, being interconnected bodies
> corporate, or by or to any such two or more persons as are described in
> subsection (2) of this section; or . . .'

If the commission found that such conditions did so prevail they were instructed
thereafter to confine their investigations to the question whether and to what extent
'the following thing' was done by the parties concerned as a result of or for the pur-   *j*
poses of preserving the 'conditions'. 'The following thing' was defined as being
'the determination of the level of the prices at which each of the two descriptions
of goods hereinbefore specified are supplied'. If the commission so held they

---

1   SI 1973 No 1093

a were to consider whether 'such thing' operated or might be expected to operate against the public interest.

Shortly and broadly stated it appears, therefore, that the commission in the reference now in question were directed to report (after investigation) as to three questions, viz, (a) did what might be called monopoly conditions prevail in regard to the supply of drugs in question? (b) if so, were the price levels on the supply of the

b drugs determined as a result of or for the purposes of preserving the monopoly conditions? and (c) if so, did that operate against the public interest or might it be expected so to operate?

It is to be observed that if the commission answered those questions affirmatively they were under no obligation to make recommendations as to how a Minister should deal with the situation. If they made recommendations the Minister was in

c no way obliged to accept them. It would be entirely for the Minister to form his own opinion as to what course to follow.

Section 8 of the 1948 Act deals with the procedure and powers of the commission on references. Subsection (1) is in the following terms:

'The procedure of the Commission in carrying out any investigation where a matter has been referred to them under the preceding provisions of this Act

d for investigation and report shall be such as the Commission may determine, and in particular the Commission shall have power to determine the extent, if any, to which persons interested or claiming to be interested in the subject matter of the reference are allowed to be present or to be heard, either by themselves or by their representatives, or to cross-examine witnesses or otherwise take part in the investigation of the Commission, and the extent, if any, to which the

e sittings of the Commission are held in public:

'Provided that where any person appearing to the Commission to be substantially interested, or to any body appearing to the Commission to represent substantial numbers of persons substantially interested, submits to the Commission any representations relating to the subject matter of the reference, the Commission shall consider those representations and shall, unless in all the

f circumstances they consider that it is not reasonably necessary or is not reasonably practicable so to do, permit that person or body to be heard orally by the Commission or by a member of the Commission nominated by the Commission for that purpose.'

Seven members of the commission (including the chairman) discharged the func-

g tions of the commission in relation to the investigations under the reference. No suggestion has been made that the commission was not properly constituted. The report of the commission in its introduction records as follows:

'3. We received written and oral evidence from Roche Products Limited. Written and oral evidence was also given by the Department of Health and Social Security, Berk Pharmaceuticals Limited and DDSA Pharmaceuticals Limited.

h We received written evidence from the Association of the British Pharmaceutical Industry and several other witnesses.'

The introduction further records that on 19th May 1972 the commission informed Roche Products Ltd of their provisional conclusions that conditions to which the 1948 Act (as amended) applied prevailed in respect of the supply in the United Kingdom

j of the drugs in question. They informed the company of the issues that required consideration in deciding whether and to what extent the determination of the level of prices was a thing done as a result of or for the purposes of preserving the conditions, and, if so, whether it operated or might be expected to operate against the public interest. With the letter of 19th May 1972 there were three annexes extending in all to over 20 pages: the first contained a summary of the facts which might be relevant concerning Roche Products Ltd and the reference goods; the second set

out points for consideration arising out of annex 1; the third set out a list of com- *a*
plaints and criticisms which might be taken into account by the commission. Roche
Products Ltd made certain representations in writing to the commission. The
report also records that later (i e in October 1972) representatives of that company and
the Roche Group attended a hearing for the purpose of discussing those matters.
The company was also represented by counsel at that meeting. At the meeting
the chairman of the commission called attention to and specified various considerations
of which account would have to be taken. *b*

The report of the Monopolies Commission (in a document of some 80 pages of
print) was signed in the following year. It was signed on 13th February 1973. To each
of the three questions which I have summarised above the commission gave an
affirmative answer. Thus in regard to (a) they reported (in para 195) as follows:

> 'We conclude, therefore, that conditions to which the Act applies prevail as
> respects the supply of (i) chlordiazepoxide and salts thereof, and (ii) diazepam *c*
> and salts thereof, because Roche Products supplies at least one third of the refer-
> ence goods of each of these two classes which are supplied in the United Kingdom.'

In regard to (b) they reported (in para 205) as follows:

> 'We therefore conclude that the determination of the level of prices at which
> chlordiazepoxide and diazepam are supplied is a thing done by Roche Products *d*
> as a result of, and for the purpose of preserving, the conditions which we have
> found to prevail as respects the supply of each of these products.'

In regard to (c) they reported (in para 217) as follows:

> 'We conclude, therefore, that the determination of the level of prices at which
> chlordiazepoxide and diazepam are supplied (which we have found in paragraph *e*
> 205 to be a thing done by Roche Products as a result of, and for the purpose of
> preserving, the conditions) operates and may be expected to operate against the
> public interest.'

Having set out that their principal reason for finding that the determination of
price levels by Roche Products was against the public interest was that prices for *f*
some years had been 'manifestly too high', they said that the principal remedy for
consideration was one which would establish fair maximum price levels. They
recorded that the problems involved in such consideration were threefold. The
first was concerned with the questions as to what costs should be taken into account.
They examined costs such as those involved in sales promotion and those referable
to central overheads and in particular they examined and gave consideration to *g*
research costs. Their conclusion in regard to research costs was that they were substantially higher than could be accepted as reasonable in relation to fair selling prices;
and that the Roche Group's current research expenditure had been inflated by the
use of excess profits to a point at which it ceased to be reasonable to regard the
expenditure as fully recoverable from current sales. The second problem was concerned with the level of profit that could be regarded as reasonable if the commission *h*
were determining what should have been fair prices up to the date of the investigation.
The third problem was concerned with the extent to which the excessive prices
hitherto charged must be brought into the reckoning. In regard to the last of these
they said that it could only be a matter of judgment as to what was the stage when
undue exploitation of success could be said to begin. They had no doubt that such
stage had long been passed. *j*

Having considered all these matters they recommended that the selling prices
for the reference drugs should be very considerably reduced: in one case to not
more than 40 per cent of the selling price in 1970 and in another case to not more
than 25 per cent of the selling price in 1970. In making these recommendations they
said in para 236:

a
'No future price which it is practicable to recommend for the reference drugs could take full acount of the excessive profits which have been made on them at the expense of the NHS in the past and will continue to be made until the prices are reduced. This damage could be remedied by the repayment of large sums to DHSS. Such repayment could be made as a result of negotiations between DHSS and the Roche Group and we think it desirable that negotiations to this

b
end should take place. The prices we are recommending could be considered more than adequate in the light of the facts revealed in our report and particularly so were there to be no repayment of past profits. We certainly see no room for argument that in recommending what may appear to be drastic reductions we are being unduly severe.'

The commission having reported on 13th February 1973, it became a matter for
c
the Minister to form his opinions. It became a matter for him to decide whether to take any action that was within his powers. Under s 3(1) of the 1965 Act it is provided that if there are the circumstances described in s 10(1) of the 1948 Act (as amended) then—

d
'the Board of Trade, for the purpose of remedying or preventing any mischiefs which in their opinion result or may be expected to result from the conditions or things which, according to the report of the Commission as laid before Parliament, operate or may be expected to operate against the public interest, may by order, (whatever the recommendation, if any, made by the Commission) exercise all or any of the powers conferred by subsections (3) to (7) below.'

It seems to me to be clear that it was for the Board of Trade to form opinions and to
e
make decisions.

The report of the commission was laid before Parliament on 11th April 1973. The circumstances described in s 10(1) of the 1948 Act (as amended) applied. There had been a reference to the commission for investigation and report; the reference was not so framed as to limit the investigation and report to the facts; the report had been laid before Parliament; according to that report conditions prevailed to which
f
the 1948 Act applied; according to the report those conditions operated or might be expected to operate against the public interest. So it was open to the Minister to form his opinions and to decide whether to exercise any of his powers, one of which (see s 3(4)(c) of the 1965 Act) was to regulate the prices to be charged for goods. That power was, however, not to be exercised 'unless it appears to the Board on the facts found by the Commission as stated in the report' that prices charged have been
g
such as to operate or to be expected to operate against the public interest.

An order was made on 12th April 1973[1]. The opinion formed by the Minister is set out in the opening paragraphs of the order which read:

'Whereas it appears to the Secretary of State on the facts found by the Mono- polies Commission as stated in their report entitled "A report on the supply of
h
chlordiazepoxide and diazepam" that the prices charged in the case of goods of the classes to which the report relates, being goods to which this Order applies, are or have been such as to operate against the public interest:

'Now, therefore, the Secretary of State in exercise of the powers conferred by section 3(3)(a), (b) and (d) and (4)(c) of the Monopolies and Mergers Act 1965 and section 10(3) of the Monopolies and Restrictive Practices (Inquiry and Control) Act
j
1948 and now in him vested and of all other powers enabling him in that behalf and with a view to remedying or preventing mischiefs which in his opinion result or may be expected to result from the things which according to the said report as laid before Parliament on 11th April 1973 operate or may be expected to operate against the public interest hereby orders as follows . . .'

1   Regulation of Prices (Tranquillising Drugs) Order 1973 (SI 1973 No 720)

The order regulated the prices to be charged. The limitations were in fact in accord *a* with the recommendations which the commission had made. The order was laid before Parliament on 12th April and came into operation on 23rd April 1973. Pursuant to the provision contained in s 3(11)(*b*) of the 1965 Act the order would cease to have effect if not approved by resolution of each House of Parliament within 28 days. The order was approved by an affirmative resolution of the House of Commons on 3rd May.

The Roche Group, to whom the terms of the commission report and of the order *b* came as a disappointment, presented (on 1st May) a petition to the House of Lords asking that the order should not be approved but should be referred to a select committee for a further enquiry. That petition was referred to the Special Orders Committee of the House of Lords. Written representations were received by the committee and the committee heard oral arguments from counsel on 14th, 15th, *c* 21st, 29th and 30th May 1973. Meanwhile a second order[1] (in the terms of that of 12th April) was laid before Parliament on 18th May. That order was made because of the statutory provision to which I have referred (see s 3(11)(*b*) of the 1965 Act) pursuant to which an order would lapse if not approved within 28 days. The Special Orders Committee of the House of Lords, having reserved its decision, announced (on 8th June) that it recommended that there ought to be a further enquiry by a *d* select committee limited to the issue whether in the prices recommended by the Monopolies Commission adequate provision was made for a proper allocation of group research and development expenditure in the sales of the drugs and if not what (if any) upward adjustment should be made.

After a debate in the House of Lords the recommendation of the Special Orders Committee was on 22nd June rejected. A third order[2] (again in the terms of the *e* first) was made on 21st June and was laid before Parliament on 22nd June. It was made for the reason previously mentioned. On 4th July that order was approved by affirmative resolution of the House of Commons. On 5th July it was approved by affirmative resolution of the House of Lords.

The order then undoubtedly had the force of law. Obedience to it was just as obligatory as would be obedience to an Act of Parliament. There was only the *f* difference that whereas the courts of law could not declare that an Act of Parliament was ultra vires it might be possible for the courts of law to declare that the making of the order (even though affirmatively approved by Parliament) was not warranted within the terms of the statutory enactments from which it purported to derive its validity. In the statutes to which I have referred, Parliament gave the power to the executive to make certain orders: any order made must, however, be within the *g* mandate given by Parliament.

The Roche Group then (by letter to the Secretary of State dated 25th June 1973) stated that they claimed that the successive orders had been ultra vires and were invalid and that they felt obliged to adopt what they called 'a posture of apparent defiance'. While threatening to continue to charge prices as before they stated that they were commencing proceedings and would seek a declaration that the orders *h* were invalid; if they did charge the higher prices they would set aside in a bank account the difference between the higher prices and the prices permitted by the order; if an injunction were sought against them they would contend that only on the giving of a satisfactory undertaking in damages ought an injunction to be granted. The grounds of their discontent were broadly stated to have been (a) that the commission's report was vitiated by a failure to observe the requirements of natural *j* justice with the result that there was no valid report which was a prerequisite to the exercise of powers by the Secretary of State and (b) that the orders were ultra vires and valid because the price levels which were fixed were arbitrary and penalising.

1 Regulation of Prices (Tranquillising Drugs) (No 2) Order 1973 (SI 1973 No 925)
2 Regulation of Prices (Tranquillising Drugs) (No 3) Order 1973 (SI 1973 No 1093)

a   The writ of the Roche Group of 25th June 1973 was followed by the writ against them on 28th June 1973 and the matter came before the court in July 1973 on the application for an injunction against the Roche Group to restrain them from charging prices above those permitted by the order.   The Roche Group had been informed that the Secretary of State was not in a position to give any undertaking of the nature suggested by the Roche Group.

b   Questions as to the methods of enforcing the law are for Parliament to decide.   In the sphere with which we are now concerned the decision of Parliament was embodied in s 11 of the 1948 Act.   Parliament decided that enforcement was not to be by the sanction of the criminal law (see s 11(1)).   It was laid down in s 11(2) as follows:

c   'Nothing in subsection (1) of this section shall limit any right of any person to bring civil proceedings in respect of any contravention or apprehended contravention of any such order, and, without prejudice to the generality of the preceding words, compliance with any such order shall be enforceable by civil proceedings by the Crown for an injunction or for any other appropriate relief.'

d   On the application for an injunction the position was that there was an order made on 21st June 1973 after all the procedures which I have described which followed on the investigation and report of the statutory commission which had been directed in September 1971.   The order had effectively the full force of law unless and until it could be shown to be ultra vires.   It is in the public interest that the law should be obeyed.   It is in the public interest that resistance to it should be suppressed.   Unless some very good reason could be shown a court would, therefore, accede to an application to enforce the law and to enforce it in the way in which Parliament had prescribed as the appropriate way.   So in the present case the question which, in my

e   view, arises is whether there was any valid and sufficient reason why an injunction should not have been granted.

The reason suggested was that the order was to be attacked as being ultra vires and, furthermore, that the lower prices laid down by the order would result in a very considerable saving of money for one branch of the public service (the Department of

f   Health and Social Security).   So it was urged that unless means were found to enable the Roche Group to be recouped (to the extent of the difference between the former prices and the lower prices) in the event of their succeeding in setting aside the order, the court ought not to insist on the observance of the law pending the trial.

It is to be observed that there has been no suggestion that the seeking of an injunction was inspired by any improper motive.   What has been said is that if the Roche

g   Group succeed at a later date in showing that the order was ultra vires they will in the meantime have been prevented from receiving sums that they would have been entitled to receive and that in the absence of an undertaking in suitable form the court would be justified in refusing to give an injunction.

The invidious position that would arise if a court of law declined to enforce a law in the manner directed by Parliament was fully in the mind of the trial judge.   He

h   said:

'If it were a simple choice between granting an injunction even without an undertaking and refusing an injunction tout court (which would present this court with a very invidious choice indeed, since the adoption of either course could then lead to possible injustice at the conclusion of the case) I think I would probably at the end of the day have decided that the sanctity of the apparent law

j   must prevail, and that the injunction should go, there being no other real remedy for this apparent defiance of the terms of the order.'

One question which arises is whether the way out of the dilemma which appealed to the judge was appropriate.

The High Court has power to grant an injunction (see s 45 of the Supreme Court of Judicature (Consolidation) Act 1925) by an interlocutory order in all cases in which it appears to the court to be just or convenient to do so. An injunction may, of *a* course, be granted either unconditionally or on such terms and conditions as the court thinks just. In cases where a plaintiff considers that a defendant is doing or is threatening to do something that he ought not to do, a plaintiff may be able to persuade a court that it is just or convenient to compel the defendant to desist pending a decision whether the plaintiff has the law on his side. But if the plaintiff proves to have been wrong the defendant may have suffered loss by having been ordered *b* to desist. In disputes between private parties a plaintiff in ordinary circumstances would only secure the order he sought if in suitable form he gave an undertaking to the court that he would abide by any order as to damages which the court might make in case the court should afterwards be of opinion that the defendant had sustained damage by reason of the order and which damage was damage for which the plaintiff ought to pay. Matters would be left on that footing until the rights of *c* the parties were determined.

The position of the Crown, in times before the Crown Proceedings Act 1947, may be illustrated by a study of *Attorney-General v Albany Hotel Co*[1]. In circumstances in which, had the litigation been between two citizens (e g as between a lessor and lessee) it would have been virtually a matter of course to require an undertaking as the condition of the granting of an injunction, the general practice appears to have been *d* not to expect or to require such an undertaking from the Crown. That was probably for the reason that the Crown was not liable in damages in the ordinary way and that relief against the Crown could only be obtained by a petition of right. Today, if the Crown as lessor or in some proprietary capacity were seeking interlocutory relief, there would seem to be no reason for any differentiation from what would be the position if relief were being sought by an ordinary plaintiff litigant. But *e* even in 1896 the Crown was not placed in an isolated position of privilege. North J, in the case cited, said[2]:

'... and even the Crown may find an injunction refused by the Court when the defendant might be exposed to serious injury if the interlocutory injunction was granted, but not made perpetual, and no protection against that injury was forthcoming.'   *f*

In the same case, in the Court of Appeal, Lindley LJ said[3]:

'Of course, if the case presented to the Court on the motion for injunction were doubtful, the Court might say, even to the Attorney-General, "We shall not grant you an injunction"; and if the case were very near the line, the Court might say, "If you like to give an undertaking, or find somebody to do so, we *g* will then grant an injunction." That is possible. But if the case for an injunction is sufficiently plain, as, in my opinion, this is, the practice is entirely against imposing any such condition.'

The above passages show that in such a case as the *Albany Hotel* case[1] the court would be obliged even at the stage of an application for an interlocutory injunction to *h* consider whether the case for an injunction was 'doubtful' or whether it was 'sufficiently plain'. In the present case we are concerned with law enforcement and with law enforcement by the one and only method decreed by Parliament. The proceedings do not in any way lose the character of being law enforcement proceedings merely because the law to be enforced will result in a reduction of sums to be paid by one limb of the public service. What the court is asked to enforce is a statutory instrument *j* which each House of Parliament has had the opportunity to reject but which each

---

1   [1896] 2 Ch 696
2   [1896] 2 Ch at 702
3   [1896] 2 Ch at 703

a   House has positively affirmed. Accepting for present purposes that in certain events the court could declare that what had been laid before Parliament was something which was laid before it in excess of a Minister's powers, it must remain true that unless and until that is shown the statutory instrument is part of the law of the land. The approach of the court must be that the law is to be enforced.

b   It is not suggested that the court can compel the Crown to give an undertaking, though it is open to the court to say that unless one is given there will be no injunction. In the present case the Crown has stated that it does not propose to give an undertaking. The reasons for this standpoint seem to be twofold. In the first place, there is the consideration that where an injunction is being sought as the statutory method of law enforcement, it is in the nature of things inapposite to expect that an undertaking will be given. In the second place, there is the consideration that it is purely fortuitous that in the present case there will be a very considerable saving of money

c   for one limb of the public service by reason of the operation of the order; that there will be other cases in which the enforcement of some order prohibiting sales at above certain prices may have far less or even minimal effect on the public purse and may primarily and extensively concern many private purses; and that the general approach of the court in enforcing the law should be the same whatever may be divergent benefits or detriments resulting from the making of an order.

d   In the present case the court had to accept the fact that no undertaking was forthcoming. The reasons why no undertaking would be given were reasons which the Crown regarded as reasonable and adequate. It was, in the first place, for the advisers of the Crown and not for the court to consider them and to decide as to them. The problem for the court was to decide whether, there being no question of the giving of an undertaking, an injunction should be refused in a case in which the law was

e   being deliberately challenged. By this I do not mean that there was any contumacious attitude but rather that the validity of what was prima facie the law was being questioned.

From my brief review of the statutory provisions it will have been seen that it was for the Minister to form certain opinions and for the Minister to decide what, if any, action to take. Questions of policy were for him subject to the control of Parliament.

f   Matters of judgment were matters for his judgment subject to the control of Parliament. The only questions for a court are those based on suggestions that he acted unlawfully because he exceeded his powers or lacked powers.

On an application for an interlocutory injunction the court must consider whether it is just or expedient to accede to the application. All considerations appertaining to the justice of the matter become within the purview of the court. All the circum

g   stances of the case must be weighed. But where the situation is that the applicant can point to a definite law in definite terms which prima facie should be enforced, and where the defendant asserts that that which bears all the indicia of authentic law should be declared to be no law at all, the issue is very much narrowed and concentrated. Clearly the defendant must of necessity say why he so asserts. When he does, the court cannot avoid forming some view or estimate in regard to the strength

h   and merits of his assertion. Herein lies a situation of difficulty. The court cannot then decide the points which are to be raised at the trial. Neither will the court restrict the full freedom of decision of the trial judge. But, on the other hand, the court will not refrain from enforcing a law merely because a challenge to it can in terms be formulated or expressed. In the decision cited above, Lindley LJ[1] spoke of situations where the case for an injunction was 'doubtful' or 'very near the line'.

j   In such a case as the present, where enforcement of an affirmed statutory instrument is being sought, the measure of the strength of the attack on the statutory instrument must inevitably call for some consideration.

For obvious reasons I desire to say as little as possible in regard to this. One limb

---

1   [1896] 2 Ch at 703

of the attack on the order required an attack through the order on the validity of the *a* report of the commission. It involved an attack on the report at first remove. Any suggestion that if some violation of some principle of natural justice could be proved the result would be that the whole report would be void, with the consequence that the Minister must be held to have acted without having any report at all before him and so to have acted ultra vires, would not appear to me to be warranted. On any view some of the findings of the report are accepted as being beyond assail. The *b* strength of a much more limited attack on the validity of some particular findings must be a matter of assessment. Another limb of the attack was on the lines that the prices set out in the order (in adoption of, or in agreement with, the recommendations of the commission) were invalidly fixed because they were penalising and because they were fixed with the object of exacting sums referable to past periods during which no law regulated or limited prices being charged. How far *c* such attack relates to validity and how far it relates to opinions formed as a matter of judgment cannot now be decided.

In a very careful argument on behalf of the Roche Group we were introduced as fully as was reasonable to the lines of the contentions that the Roche Group will wish to advance and to expand at the trial. Being anxious to limit myself to present necessity, and while remembering the extent of the dealings involved and the mone- *d* tary sums mentioned, I confine myself to expressing the conclusion that, in my view, no sufficient reason has been shown why the law should not now be enforced. I was not attracted by the proposal involved in the course of action which the Roche Group offered to follow. Shortly stated it was to the effect that if the court would tolerate their defiance of the order they would in reference to purchasers within the National Health Service place the sums received in excess of the order prices to a *e* special joint account to await the result of the action, and that in reference to others who purchased the goods they would devise some system under which purchasers would be given some variety of stamps which it was hoped could result in a return of money to them in the future if the Roche Group failed to invalidate the statutory instruments. In that event the purchasers would all along have been charged more than a valid order permitted them to be charged. As, in my view, no compelling *f* or sufficient reason has been shown why the law should not at this stage be enforced the proposal need not be further explored.

I would dismiss the appeal.

LORD WILBERFORCE. My Lords, this appeal is concerned with a motion by the Secretary of State for Trade and Industry (the 'DTI') for an interim injunction *g* restraining the appellants ('the Roche Group') until trial of an action between the Roche Group and the DTI from selling the tranquillisers, Librium and Valium, which the Roche Group manufacture or distribute at more than the prices fixed by the Monopolies Commission. The interlocutory nature of the proceedings must be emphasised, but in order to decide the limited issue it is necessary to say something, however skeletally, about the main action. *h*

The DTI, acting on and implementing a report of the Monopolies Commission, which said that the Roche Group's monopoly prices were much too high, made an order, in the form of a statutory instrument[1], that the Roche Group could only charge in the United Kingdom the prices fixed by the Monopolies Commission's report. These were, as to Librium, 40 per cent, and as to Valium, 25 per cent of the prices charged in 1970. The order was made purportedly under powers given by *j* the Monopolies and Mergers Act 1965, s 3. It was (I omit some skirmishing detail), as the Act requires, laid before each House of Parliament and approved.

The action, in which the motion is treated as being brought, is by the Roche Group against the DTI seeking a declaration that the order is invalid and of no effect. It

1   Regulation of Prices (Tranquillising Drugs) (No 3) Order 1973 (SI 1973 No 1093)

a does so on a number of grounds mainly founded on contentions as to administrative law. Two may be mentioned: first, that the DTI has exceeded its powers because it is seeking to control, viz, to reduce, prices in the future in order to redress overcharging in the past—an illegitimate purpose according to the Roche Group; secondly, that the Monopolies Commission's report, on which the order is based, is invalid for failure to observe the requirements of 'natural justice'—an English port-

b manteau expression which includes the more precise infringement of important procedural rules (EEC Treaty, art 173).

That an attack can be made on a statutory instrument for want of power needs no demonstration, and I agree with your Lordships that it makes no difference, for this purpose, that the instrument has been laid before and approved by the two Houses of Parliament. That a report of such a body as the Monopolies Commission can be

c attacked for failure to observe requirements of 'natural justice' is shown by *Re Pergamon Press Ltd*[1]. The Roche Group have clearly a locus standi to assert both claims in the courts.

The action so commenced by the Roche Group is in its initial stages; a statement of claim voluminous but not necessarily insubstantial has been delivered. We were told that proceedings to strike it out have been started, a step which helps to crystallise

d the situation, since if they succeed the present question falls, and if they fail, the action is established as viable. Apart from this, it is, at the present stage, impossible for the courts to form more than a most general impression as to the strength of the Roche Group's case or its ultimate prospect of success. No attempt at this kind of appraisal is ever made in interlocutory proceedings. All that we are entitled to say is that the DTI relies on a statutory instrument enacted in the correct manner; that this is

e challenged as to its validity by the Roche Group; that the issue so joined awaits trial.

So far I have referred only to action taken by the Roche Group. I must now describe the counter-action by the DTI. It issued a writ, on 28th June 1973, against the Roche Group for an injunction restraining them from charging prices in excess of those specified in the statutory order. This it did acting under s 11 of the Monopolies and Restrictive Practices (Inquiry and Control) Act 1948 ('the 1948 Act'). Subsections (1)

f and (2) are important:

'(1) No criminal proceedings shall lie against any person by virtue of the making of any order under the last preceding section on the ground that he has committed, or aided, abetted, counselled or procured the commission of, or conspired or attempted to commit, or incited others to commit, any contravention of the order.

g '(2) Nothing in subsection (1) of this section shall limit any right of any person to bring civil proceedings in respect of any contravention or apprehended contravention of any such order, and, without prejudice to the generality of the preceding words, compliance with any such order shall be enforceable by civil proceedings by the Crown for an injunction or for any other appropriate relief.'

h The position under s 11(2) is clear: civil proceedings may be brought, in the ordinary way, and, if a case is made out, an injunction may follow. The defendant against whom the proceedings are brought, correspondingly, has the right to defend himself and, if he does so, an ordinary civil trial in the courts takes place.

The section says nothing about interim relief, so any right to it must depend on normal principles applied by the civil courts. The DTI, on the same day that it

j issued the writ, gave notice of a motion for an injunction until trial or further order, and it is its right to this which we are now considering.

The present jurisdiction of the courts to grant interim injunctions is derived from the Supreme Court of Judicature (Consolidation) Act 1925, s 45; it arises 'in all cases in which it appears to the court to be just or convenient to do so' and an injunction

---

1 [1970] 3 All ER 535, [1971] Ch 388

may be granted on such terms or conditions as the court thinks fit. Motions for interim
injunctions are everyday fare in the courts: the terms of s 45, which reflect earlier
judicial invention, provide a flexible and most useful tool in aid of justice. The object
is to prevent a litigant, who must necessarily suffer the law's delay, from losing by
that delay the fruit of his litigation; this is called 'irreparable' damage, meaning that
money obtained at the trial may not compensate him. Since the injunction by its
nature freezes the situation, it is necessary also to think of the other party's position
and rights; he, too, by being stopped in what may be some lawful action, may suffer
serious damage. So the procedure has been evolved—and it is over 100 years old—
of matching the injunction with an undertaking to pay any damage which it is just
should be paid if it should turn out that the injunction was unjustified. Precisely
because this procedure is so obviously just, it is almost universal; no interim injunction
is given unless accompanied by the undertaking.

The courts have considerable liberty of action, described as discretion, in adapting
both injunctions and undertakings in their form and content to the individual requirements of each case. It is, or ought to be, well established that Courts of Appeal do
not interfere with their arrangements unless they are wrong in law.

The present bears the appearance of a typical case for an undertaking in damages.
If the Roche Group are prevented from charging their previous or other market
prices until the trial, and if at the trial they are proved to have rightly protested that
the order against them was invalid, they will have lost the difference between their
price and the DTI price for possibly two years. The figure of £8 million has been
mentioned as the amount of their possible loss. It has not been contended that this
loss would be recoverable in law from the DTI. The most that is said is that the
Roche Group may have a moral claim for some ex gratia payment.

Correspondingly, and this is the unique feature of the present case, the executive,
though it may be proved wrong, i e to have made an invalid order, will, if the interim
injunction is granted, have made a profit of some £8 million. This arises from the
fact that 90 per cent of the sales of the products goes to the National Health Service
and is paid for by the Department of Health and Social Security ('the DHSS'). Thus
the DHSS will have bought the products too cheaply by some £8 million. (I am aware
that the DHSS is a different department from the DTI and no doubt this is disturbing
to the finance officers in either department. But constitutionally both are just the
executive, and any money paid or received is public money.) So justice seems clearly
to call for some undertaking to prevent this.

The trial judge, Walton J, who considered all the circumstances and the relevant
law, approved a plan by which an interim injunction should be granted, provided
that the DTI gives the usual undertaking in damages; and, moreover, to cover the
possibility that the DTI might refuse or feel unable to give the undertaking—and
so disentitle itself to the injunction—he accepted from the Roche Group an undertaking to pay the difference between the two prices into a special banking account
in the joint names of the parties' solicitors. Thus everyone would be safeguarded.

My Lords, a discretion so exercised seems to be well within the area permitted to
the judge and should not be displaced except for some error in law. The result
appears both 'just and convenient'. The contrary course, approved by the Court
of Appeal, of granting an injunction tout court (as if the DTI had already won the
action) potentially creates a serious injustice.

The position so stated—and there is, I believe, no oversimplification about it—
is for me decisive of this appeal: I think that the judge's approach was right. There
I am tempted to leave the matter, without discussion of other arguments we have
heard on which my opinion is to be of no authority. But perhaps some observations
are called for in support of the judge and also in view of the relevance of this case
to others which may arise. It implies no disrespect if I make them brief.

   1.   The point on which this case really comes to this House is the important one,
whether an undertaking in damages can be required of 'the Crown'. It is said in

a The Supreme Court Practice[1], and has been said for 50 years or more, that it cannot. Although there is not much authority for the proposition—essentially it rests on *Attorney-General v Albany Hotel Co*[2]—I think that it can be accepted that such was, before 1947, the generally accepted rule, though even then not an absolute rule, since both North J[3] and Lindley LJ[4] in the *Albany Hotel* case contemplated that there might be exceptions. Whatever the precise reasons for it may have been, one of them,

b I would think the most powerful, must have lain in the impossibility before 1947 of suing the Crown for damages. This immunity was removed by the Crown Proceedings Act 1947, s 21 of which provides that, subject to some exceptions, in civil proceedings by or against the Crown the court may make all such orders as it has power to make in proceedings between subjects. It seems to me significant that the procedure first embodied in s 11 of the 1948 Act and later embodied in other Acts in

c pari materia which substituted for criminal sanctions civil proceedings for an injunction, was introduced so soon after the change in the Crown's procedural status. If one reads s 11 of the 1948 Act together with s 21 of the Crown Proceedings Act 1947, the inference can only be that the Crown, in seeking injunctions, including interim injunctions, is to be in the same position as other litigants. The position seems clear. Indeed I did not understand the DTI to contend that the old rule, as such, now sur-

d vived. The power, which would certainly exist if subjects only were involved, to make it a condition of granting an injunction that there should be an undertaking in damages clearly now applies when the injunction is sought by or on behalf of the Crown.

2. It does not, of course, follow that because there is power to impose the condition, it ought to be imposed in this case, or similar cases. Regard must be had to

e the nature of the dispute and the position of the disputants. In a case such as the present, the fact that the effective plaintiff is a government department, acting in the public interest and responsible for public money, is important. The real issue is how far this difference is to be carried. The main argument relied on for preserving, in the present case, a special right for the Crown to obtain injunctions without offering an undertaking, is that the Crown is 'enforcing the law', and—so I understood the

f argument—should not be hampered by being put on terms. Or, putting it another way, the company, being in breach of the law, is not in a position to ask for protective terms. My Lords, I am afraid that I regard this argument as fallacious. To say that the Crown is enforcing the law is a petitio principii, since the very issue in the action is whether what is alleged to be law (and denied to be law by the Roche Group) is law or not. The answer given to this is, I understand, that there is a presumption of validity until the contrary is shown. The consequence drawn from this is that

g unconditional obedience must be required by the court: '. . . obey first and argue afterwards' in Lord Denning MR's graphic phrase[5]. I think that there is a confusion here. It is true enough that a piece of subordinate legislation is presumed to be valid against persons who have no locus standi to challenge it; the puzzling case of *Durayappah v Fernando*[6] can be understood as exemplifying this. But it is quite

h another matter to say, and I know of no supporting authority, that such a presumption exists when the validity of the subordinate legislation is legitimately in question before a court and is challenged by a person who has locus standi to challenge it. Certainly no support for any such proposition is to be found in the passage, so often partially quoted, from the speech of Lord Radcliffe in *Smith v East Elloe Rural District Council*[7]. One has only to read what he said:

j 1 (1973) vol 1, p 455, para 29/1/20
2 [1896] 2 Ch 696
3 [1896] 2 Ch at 702
4 [1896] 2 Ch at 703
5 [1973] 3 All ER at 953, [1973] 3 WLR at 821
6 [1967] 2 All ER 152, [1967] 2 AC 337
7 [1956] 1 All ER 855 at 871, [1956] AC 736 at 769

'At one time the argument was shaped into the form of saying that an order *a* made in bad faith was in law a nullity and that, consequently, all references to compulsory purchase orders in para. 15 and para. 16 must be treated as references to such orders only as had been made in good faith. But this argument is, in reality, a play on the meaning of the word nullity. An order, even if not made in good faith, is still an act capable of legal consequences. It bears no brand of invalidity on its forehead. Unless the necessary proceedings are taken at law *b* to establish the cause of invalidity and to get it quashed or otherwise upset, it will remain as effective for its ostensible purpose as the most impeccable of orders.'

How can this be said to support an argument that when proceedings *are* taken at law, the impugned order must be given full legal effect against the challenger before the proceedings are decided, I am unable to comprehend. *c*

In any event the argument proves too much, for if it were right, the court would have no discretion to refuse an injunction whatever the consequences, however irreparably disastrous, to the subject. Such rigidity of power seems to be contrary to s 45 of the Supreme Court of Judicature (Consolidation) Act 1925. Further, if one considers some of the orders which can be made under s 3 of the Monopolies and Mergers Act 1965, the injustice of this can be easily perceived. And as an example *d* in practice there is *Post Office v Estuary Radio Ltd*[1], which I discuss shortly, a case where an interim injunction was refused—no doubt just because to grant it would cause irreparable damage. If, then, it is said that there must always remain a residual discretion the argument vanishes. We are back on discretion.

3. It is said that no undertaking should be insisted on, unless the effect of the Roche Group's eventual success were to make the order 'void ab initio'—the argu- *e* ment being that otherwise no injustice would result. Buckley LJ[2] made this the conclusion of a judgment with the rest of which I respectfully concur. This phrase 'void ab initio' has engendered many learned distinctions and much confused thinking —unnecessarily, in my opinion. There can be no doubt in the first place that an ultra vires act is simply void: see in confirmation *Ridge v Baldwin*[3]. In truth when the court says that an act of administration is voidable or void but not ab initio this is *f* simply a reflection of a conclusion, already reached on unexpressed grounds, that the court is not willing in casu to give compensation or other redress to the person who establishes the nullity. Underlying the use of the phrase in the present case, and I suspect underlying most of the reasoning in the Court of Appeal, is an unwillingness to accept that a subject should be indemnified for loss sustained by invalid adminis-trative action. It is this which requires examination rather than some supposed *g* visible quality of the order itself.

In more developed legal systems this particular difficulty does not arise. Such systems give indemnity to persons injured by illegal acts of the administration. Consequently, where the prospective loss which may be caused by an order is pecuniary, there is no need to suspend the impugned administrative act; it can take effect (in our language an injunction can be given) and at the end of the day the sub- *h* ject can, if necessary, be compensated. On the other hand, if the prospective loss is not pecuniary (in our language 'irreparable') the act may be suspended pending decision—in our language, interim enforcement may be refused.

There is clearly an important principle here which has not been elucidated by English law, or even brought into the open. But there are traces of it in some areas. I have referred to *Post Office v Estuary Radio Ltd*[1], which arose on a section in the *j* Wireless Telegraphy Act 1949 similar to s 11 of the 1948 Act. In that case the Post

---

1   [1967] 3 All ER 663, [1968] 2 QB 740
2   [1973] 3 All ER 945 at 958, [1973] 3 WLR 805 at 827
3   [1963] 2 All ER 66, [1964] AC 40

a Office applied for an injunction and also moved for interim relief.   This was refused, no doubt partly for the reason that to grant it at the interim stage would cause the defendants irreparable damage.   We are not bound by the decision, but I suggest that it is based on sound principle.

Secondly, there are instances of statutes which themselves provide for the interim suspension of impugned orders.   One such is the Acquisition of Land (Authorisation *b* Procedure) Act 1946, Sch 1, Part IV.   This provides that if any person desires to question the validity of a compulsory purchase order the court may ad interim suspend the effect of the order.   These are examples of at least a partial recognition in our law that the subject requires protection against action taken against him or his property under administrative orders which may turn out to be invalid.   How far this principle goes need not, and cannot, be decided in the present case.   But what can be said is *c* that the combination of s 11 of the 1948 Act with s 45 of the Judicature Act 1925 gives to the court a practical instrument by which injustice to private individuals, faced with possibly invalid action, may be avoided.   If this is not possible in every case, it should not be rejected in a case, however special, where justice to both sides can be done.

In the present case there is the feature, special and possibly unique, that the execu-*d* tive, seeking to enforce the order, has itself a pecuniary interest; it is a monopoly buyer confronting a monopoly seller.   It stands to make a large profit at the Roche Group's expense if they are right.   So even if one thinks that in general there is no right of compensation for illegal action, that is not a belief which need, or should, influence the present decision.   The potentiality of large loss on one side and large profit on the other are factors which are relevant to the court's discretion.

e 4.   Some criticisms were made in argument of the Roche Group's offer to under-take to place the price difference aside in a joint banking account.   This is an argu-ment which goes to the 'convenience' of the order made by the judge.   It was said that this would not meet every case (e g that of private patients) or provide for the retail chemists' percentage.   Apart from the fact that, in relation to the huge sum generally involved, these matters were almost trivial (it appears that the trade *f* price for 100 tablets (10 m g) of Librium is £1, and Valium is cheaper), the Roche Group offered, in the most explicit terms, and I have no doubt in good faith, to add to their undertaking any other protective measures which might be necessary. This offer was not taken up or fully canvassed in this House, the fact being that the executive's objections were founded on principle rather than detail.   For myself I would have been satisfied with the Roche Group's offer, in the absence of agreement, *g* to refer this aspect of the case back to the judge, confident in the latter's ability to reach a practical solution.   Comparable problems arise frequently in the courts and, within what is a very flexible procedure, are satisfactorily resolved.   Subject to this I would restore the judgment of Walton J.

h **LORD DIPLOCK.**   My Lords, the question in this appeal is whether Walton J exercised his discretion rightly when he refused to grant an interlocutory injunction restraining the Roche Group from acting in breach of the Regulation of Prices (Tran-quillising Drugs) (No 3) Order 1973[1], except on terms that the Secretary of State should give an undertaking as to damages in the usual form.   The Secretary of State was unwilling to do this.   So Walton J refused the injunction, on an undertaking being given by the Roche Group in the terms which have already been mentioned *j* by your Lordships.

The practice of exacting an undertaking as to damages from a plaintiff to whom an interim injunction is granted originated during the Vice-Chancellorship of Sir James Knight Bruce who held that office from 1841 to 1851.   At first it applied only to

1   SI 1973 No 1093

injunctions granted ex parte, but after 1860 the practice was extended to all inter-   *a*
locutory injunctions. By the end of the century the insertion of such an undertaking
in all orders for interim injunctions granted in litigation between subject and subject
had become a matter of course.

The advantages of this practice in any suit for the protection or enforcement of
personal or proprietary rights are plain enough. An interim injunction is a temporary and exceptional remedy which is available before the rights of the parties   *b*
have been finally determined and, in the case of an ex parte injunction even before
the court had been apprised of the nature of the defendant's case. To justify the
grant of such a remedy the plaintiff must satisfy the court first that there is a strong
prima facie case that he will be entitled to a final order restraining the defendant
from doing what he is threatening to do, and secondly that he will suffer irreparable
injury which cannot be compensated by a subsequent award of damages in the action,   *c*
if the defendant is not prevented from doing it between the date of the application
for the interim injunction and the date of the final order made on trial of the action.
Nevertheless, at the time of the application it is not possible for the court to be
absolutely certain that the plaintiff will succeed at the trial in establishing his legal
right to restrain the defendant from doing what he is threatening to do. If he should
fail to do so the defendant may have suffered loss as a result of having been prevented   *d*
from doing it while the interim injunction was in force; and any loss is likely to
be damnum absque injuria for which he could not recover damages from the plaintiff
at common law. So unless some other means is provided in this event for compensating the defendant for his loss there is a risk that injustice may be done.

It is to mitigate this risk that the court refuses to grant an interim injunction unless
the plaintiff is willing to furnish an undertaking by himself or by some other willing   *e*
and responsible person—

> 'to abide by any order the Court may make as to damages in case the Court
> shall hereafter be of opinion that the Defendant shall have sustained any damages
> by reason of this order [sc the interim injunction] which the Plaintiff ought to
> pay.'
>
>   *f*

The court has no power to compel an applicant for an interim injunction to furnish
an undertaking as to damages. All it can do is to refuse the application if he declines
to do so. The undertaking is not given to the defendant but to the court itself.
Non-performance of it is contempt of court, not breach of contract, and attracts the
remedies available for contempts; but the court exacts the undertaking for the
defendant's benefit. It retains a discretion not to enforce the undertaking if it con-   *g*
siders that the conduct of the defendant in relation to the obtaining or continuing
of the injunction or the enforcement of the undertaking makes it inequitable to do so;
but if the undertaking is enforced the measure of the damages payable under it is
not discretionary. It is assessed on an enquiry into damages at which principles to
be applied are fixed and clear. The assessment is made on the same basis as damages
for breach of contract would be assessed if the undertaking had been a contract   *h*
between the plaintiff and the defendant, that the plaintiff would *not* prevent the
defendant from doing that which he was restrained from doing by the terms of the
injunction. (See *Smith v Day*[1] per Brett LJ.)

Besides mitigating the risk of injustice to the defendant the practice of exacting an
undertaking as to damages facilitates the conduct of the business of the courts. It
relieves the court of the necessity to embark at an interlocutory stage on an enquiry   *j*
as to the likelihood of the defendant's being able to establish facts to destroy the
strong prima facie case which ex hypothesi will have been made out by the plaintiff.
The procedure on motions is unsuited to inquiries into disputed facts. This is best
left to the trial of the action; and if the plaintiff then succeeds in establishing his claim

---

1   (1882) 21 Ch D 421 at 427

a he suffers no harm from having given the undertaking; while if he fails to do so, the defendant is compensated for any loss he may have suffered by being temporarily prevented from doing what he was legally entitled to do.

The practice of insisting on an undertaking as to damages was not extended to cases where the Crown sought an interim injunction in suits brought to protect or to enforce its proprietary or contractual rights (jus privatum). That the Crown ought

b not to be required to give an undertaking was laid down authoritatively by the Court of Appeal when it upheld the judgment of North J in *Attorney-General v Albany Hotel Co*[1], a case in which the Crown was seeking to assert its proprietary rights as lessor of Crown land. In his judgment North J dealt with the history of the practice as respects the Crown but he did not explain its rationale; nor is this dealt with in the judgments of Lindley and Lopes LJJ in the Court of Appeal.

c Since the practice of requiring an undertaking as to damages in suits between subjects was itself of comparatively recent origin, the exemption of the Crown from this requirement cannot be accounted for as one of the ancient procedural privileges of the Crown when litigating in its own courts. It would appear likely, however, that both North J and the Court of Appeal accepted the argument advanced by the Attorney-General, Sir Richard Webster, that since the Crown was not liable for damages in the ordinary way and the only mode of obtaining relief against the Crown was by

d petition of right, to require from the Crown an undertaking as to damages would involve an encroachment on its immunity from liability except in those limited categories of cases in which relief could be obtained by the special procedure of petition of right.

If this is the true rationale of the decision in *Attorney-General v Albany Hotel Co*[1]— and it is difficult to think of any other—with the passing of the Crown Proceedings

e Act 1947 it ceased to justify the differentiation between what should be required of the Crown and what should be required of the subject on the grant of an interim injunction. Subject to the specific exceptions provided for by the 1947 Act, the Crown is now 'liable for damages in the ordinary way' and the special procedure by petition of right has been abolished. It is expressly provided by s 21(1) of the Crown Proceed-

f ings Act 1947:

'In any civil proceedings by or against the Crown the court shall, subject to the provisions of this Act, have power to make all such orders as it has power to make in proceedings between subjects, and otherwise to give such appropriate relief as the case may require . . .'

g While some former privileges of the Crown in relation to litigation are expressly preserved either in their previous or a modified form as, for instance, in respect to venue and to discovery, there is no express preservation of the Crown's former right to obtain an interim injunction without giving any undertaking in damages.

I conclude, therefore, that the reason for the former practice in favour of the Crown in not requiring an undertaking as to damages as a condition of the grant of an in-

h terim injunction disappeared with the passing of the Crown Proceedings Act 1947, and that it is open to your Lordships to consider afresh, in the light of the changes brought about by that Act, the principles on which the court ought now to exercise its discretion whether or not to do so.

My Lords, now that the Crown no longer enjoys its former general immunity from legal liability for damages apart from those which were recoverable by and in accor-

j dance with the special procedure of petition of right, I see no reason why, when the Crown applies for an interlocutory injunction in an action brought against a subject to enforce or to protect its proprietary or contractual rights (jus privatum), the Crown should not be put on the same terms as a subject as respects the usual undertaking as to damages.

---

1 [1896] 2 Ch 696

The instant case, however, is not an action to enforce a jus privatum of the Crown. *a*
It falls into another category that has no counterpart in ordinary litigation between
subject and subject. It is what may conveniently be called a 'law enforcement
action', in which civil proceedings are brought by the Crown to restrain a subject
from breaking a law where the breach is harmful to the public or some section of it
but does not necessarily affect any proprietary or contractual rights of the Crown.
Its purpose is to enforce or to protect jus publicum. *b*

The right of the Attorney-General, acting on behalf of the Crown as parens patriae,
to apply to the court for an injunction to restrain the commission of illegal acts which
affect the public was recognised in the 19th century. It was not, however, the practice
for the Attorney-General to act on his own initiative. Although this type of action was
brought in his name as nominal plaintiff it was brought 'on the relation' of a subject
and the conduct of the case was undertaken by the 'relator'. The Attorney-General's *c*
function in a relator action was in effect limited to determining, when consent to the
use of his name was sought, whether the breach of law alleged by the relator was
sufficiently injurious to the public interest to justify its being restrained by injunction.
The reason for adopting this device appears to have been that at that time orders for
costs could not be made for or against the Crown. The Attorney-General had an
undoubted right to sue alone ex officio in a law enforcement action (*Attorney-General* *d*
v Oxford, Worcester and Wolverhampton Railway Co[1]), but in that event the expense
incurred by him in doing so would have to be met from public funds win or lose;
while the defendant if he lost was out of pocket for the costs of his successful defence.
So instead of suing ex officio it became the practice for the Attorney-General to sue
on the relation of a subject so that orders for costs could be made for and against the
relator (*Attorney-General v Cockermouth Local Board*[2]). For practical purposes, once the *e*
Attorney-General's consent had been obtained the relator stood in the shoes of a
plaintiff in an ordinary suit between subject and subject; and it appears that when
the practice was introduced in ordinary suits of making an undertaking as to damages a
condition of the grants of interim injunctions, a similar undertaking was required in
relator actions from the relator; but it was never required from the Attorney-General.

The special position of the Crown with regard to costs was abolished by s 7 of the *f*
Administration of Justice (Miscellaneous Provisions) Act 1933, but in spite of this the
practice of bringing law enforcement actions only on the relation of a subject remained
unchanged. So did the practice of requiring undertakings as to damages to be given
by relators. Both practices have continued to be followed since the passing of the
Crown Proceedings Act 1947. This Act, indeed, expressly excludes relator actions from
its procedural provisions. It is only in law enforcement actions brought under recent
statutes which provide expressly that compliance with some provision of the Act *g*
shall be enforceable by civil proceedings by the Crown for an injunction, that the
Crown sues directly and not by way of a relator action. Three statutes which contain
provisions of this kind are the Monopolies and Restrictive Practices (Inquiry and Control) Act 1948, the Wireless Telegraphy Act 1949, and the Resale Prices Act 1964.

So even before the passing of the Crown Proceedings Act 1947 the fact that the suit *h*
was brought to enforce jus publicum was not of itself sufficient to displace the ordinary
rule that a defendant was entitled to the usual undertaking in damages as a condition
of the grant of any interlocutory injunction against him; though the undertaking
was exacted from the relator and not from the Crown on whose behalf the Attorney-
General was the nominal plaintiff in the suit. I see no reason since the passing of the
1947 Act why a rigid rule that the Crown itself should *never* be required to give the *j*
usual undertaking in damages should be retained in those law enforcement actions
where the Crown now sues without a relator.

Nevertheless, the converse does not follow that in this type of action the court, in
granting an interim injunction, ought *always* to require an undertaking as to damages

1 (1854) 2 WR 330
2 (1874) LR 18 Eq 172

a   from the Crown. A relator owes no duty to the public to initiate any law enforcement action. He does not usually do so unless he or a section of the public that he represents has some special interest to protect in enforcing that particular law, that is not shared by the public at large. Even if he has no special interest—and it is not essential that he should—his action nevertheless is that of an officious, though well-meaning, bystander who is content merely to stand by. When, however, a statute provides

b   that compliance with its provisions shall be enforceable by civil proceedings by the Crown for an injunction, and particularly if this is the only method of enforcement for which it provides, the Crown does owe a duty to the public at large to initiate proceedings to secure that the law is not flouted, and not simply to leave it to the chance that some relator may be willing to incur the expense and trouble of doing so.

    I agree, therefore, with all your Lordships that the practice of exacting an undertaking in damages from the Crown as a condition of the grant of an interlocutory

c   injunction in this type of law enforcement action ought not to be applied as a matter of course, as it should in actions between subject and subject, in relator actions, and in actions by the Crown to enforce or to protect its proprietary or contractual rights. On the contrary, the propriety of requiring such an undertaking from the Crown should be considered in the light of the particular circumstances of the case.

    In the instant case, the circumstances which, to my mind, are crucial to the exercise

d   of the discretion whether to grant an interim injunction to the Crown without requiring an undertaking as to damages are: *first*, that the law the Crown is seeking to enforce by the only means available under the governing statute is an order made by statutory instrument which has been approved by affirmative resolution of each House of Parliament and is valid on its face; *secondly*, that the Roche Group threaten to act in a way which they admit would contravene the terms of this order and claim

e   to be entitled to do so on the ground that the order itself is ultra vires (a) because of unfair conduct by the Monopolies Commission in the course of the investigations which led to their report on which the order was based, and (b) because of the inclusion in that report of recommendations (which the Minister adopted in the order) for the purpose of remedying a mischief to which they were not entitled to have

f   regard; and *thirdly*, that the Crown itself through the Department of Health and Social Security had a substantial financial interest in enforcing the order.

The legal status of the order

    My Lords, in constitutional law a clear distinction can be drawn between an Act of Parliament and subordinate legislation, even though the latter is contained in an order made by statutory instrument approved by resolutions of both Houses of

g   Parliament. Despite this indication that the majority of members of both houses of the contemporary Parliament regard the order as being for the common weal, I entertain no doubt that the courts have jurisdiction to declare it to be invalid if they are satisfied that in making it the Minister who did so acted outwith the legislative powers conferred on him by the previous Act of Parliament under which the order purported to be made; and this is so whether the order is ultra vires by reason of its

h   contents (patent defects) or by reason of defects in the procedure followed prior to its being made (latent defects). Insofar as there are passages[1] in the judgment of Lord Denning MR in the instant case which may appear to suggest the contrary, I think that they are wrong.

    Under our legal system, however, the courts as the judicial arm of government do not act on their own initiative. Their jurisdiction to determine that a statutory instru-

j   ment is ultra vires does not arise until its validity is challenged in proceedings inter partes, either brought by one party to enforce the law declared by the instrument against another party, or brought by a party whose interests are affected by the law so declared sufficiently directly to give him locus standi to initiate proceedings to challenge the validity of the instrument. Unless there is such challenge and, if there

---

1   See [1973] 3 All ER 945 at 954, 955, [1973] 3 WLR 805 at 823

is, until it has been upheld by a judgment of the court, the validity of the statutory *a*
instrument and the legality of acts done pursuant to the law declared by it, are presumed. It would, however, be inconsistent with the doctrine of ultra vires as it has
been developed in English law as a means of controlling abuse of power by the
executive arm of government if the judgment of a court in proceedings properly
constituted that a statutory instrument was ultra vires were to have any lesser consequence in law than to render the instrument incapable of ever having had any legal *b*
effect on the rights or duties of the parties to the proceedings (cf *Ridge v Baldwin*[1]).
Although such a decision is directly binding only as between the parties to the proceedings in which it was made, the application of the doctrine of precedent has the
consequence of enabling the benefit of it to accrue to all other persons whose legal
rights have been interfered with in reliance on the law which the statutory instrument
purported to declare.   *c*

The presumption of validity of the order

My Lords, I think it leads to confusion to use such terms as 'voidable', 'voidable ab
initio', 'void' or 'a nullity' as descriptive of the legal status of subordinate legislation
alleged to be ultra vires for patent or latent defects, before its validity has been pronounced on by a court of competent jurisdiction. These are concepts developed in *d*
the private law of contract which are ill-adapted to the field of public law. All that
can usefully be said is that the presumption that subordinate legislation is intra vires
prevails in the absence of rebuttal, and that it cannot be rebutted except by a party
to legal proceedings in a court of competent jurisdiction who has locus standi to
challenge the validity of the subordinate legislation in question.   *e*

All locus standi on the part of anyone to rebut the presumption of validity may be
taken away completely or may be limited in point of time or otherwise by the express
terms of the Act of Parliament which conferred the subordinate legislative power;
though the courts lean heavily against a construction of the Act which would have this
effect (cf *Anisminic Ltd v The Foreign Compensation Commission*[2]). Such was the case,
however, in the view of the majority of this House in *Smith v East Elloe Rural District
Council*[3], at any rate as respects invalidity on the ground of latent defects; so the *f*
compulsory purchase order sought to be challenged in the action had legal effect
notwithstanding its potential invalidity. Furthermore, apart from express provision
in the governing statute, locus standi to challenge the validity of subordinate legislation may be restricted, under the court's inherent power to control its own procedure,
to a particular category of persons affected by the subordinate legislation, and if none
of these persons chooses to challenge it the presumption of validity prevails. Such was *g*
the case in *Durayappah v Fernando*[4] where, on an appeal from Ceylon, although the
Privy Council was of opinion that an order of the Minister was ultra vires owing to a
latent defect in the procedure prior to its being made, they nevertheless treated it as
having legal effect because the party who sought to challenge it had, in their view, no
locus standi to do so.

The legal status of the Regulation of Prices (Tranquillising Drugs) (No 3) Order 1973[5], *h*
which the Roche Group seek to challenge in the instant case, is aptly stated in the
words of Lord Radcliffe in *Smith v East Elloe Rural District Council*[6]:

'An order . . . is still an act capable of legal consequences. It bears no brand of
invalidity on its forehead. Unless the necessary proceedings are taken at law to

          j

1   [1963] 2 All ER 66, [1964] AC 40
2   [1969] 1 All ER 208, [1969] 2 AC 147
3   [1956] 1 All ER 855, [1956] AC 736
4   [1967] 2 All ER 152, [1967] 2 AC 337
5   SI 1973 No 1093
6   [1956] 1 All ER at 871, [1956] AC at 769

a   establish the cause of invalidity and to get it quashed or otherwise upset, it will remain as effective for its ostensible purpose as the most impeccable of orders.'

The instant case is not one where the Roche Group contend that what they are threatening to do would not be a contravention of the order—as was the case in *Post Office v Estuary Radio Ltd*[1]. Different considerations would apply to that. Their only answer to the application for an interim injunction to enforce the order against them
b   is that they intend to challenge its validity. It is not disputed that they have locus standi to do so, but this does not absolve them from their obligation to obey the order while the presumption in favour of its validity prevails—as it must so long as there has been no final judgment in the action to the contrary.

So in this type of law enforcement action, if the only defence is an attack on the validity of the statutory instrument sought to be enforced, the ordinary position of the
c   parties as respects the grant of interim injunctions is reversed. The duty of the Crown to see that the law declared by the statutory instrument is obeyed is not suspended by the commencement of proceedings in which the validity of the instrument is challenged. Prima facie the Crown is entitled as of right to an interim injunction to enforce obedience to it. To displace this right or to fetter it by the imposition of conditions, it is for the defendant to show a strong prima facie case that the statutory
d   instrument is ultra vires.

Even where a strong prima facie case of invalidity has been shown on the application for an interim injunction it may still be inappropriate for the court to impose as a condition of the grant of the injunction a requirement that the Crown should enter into the usual undertaking as to damages. For if the undertaking falls to be implemented, the cost of implementing it will be met from public funds raised by taxation
e   and the interests of the members of the public who are not parties to the action may be affected by it. The instant case has the exceptional feature that the greater part of the drugs supplied by the Roche Group that are the subject of the order are supplied through the National Health Service and paid for ultimately out of public funds. To the effect of this on the Crown's claim for an interim injunction I shall revert later; but the balance that is bought by private patients out of their own pockets affords an
f   example of how the interest of members of the public who are not parties to the action could be affected by an undertaking as to damages if it fell to be implemented. As a result of the interim injunction this section of the public would have been able to purchase the drugs at the prices prescribed by the order; but if the undertaking as to damages had to be fulfilled because the order was ultimately held to be ultra vires, their purchases would, in effect, have been subsidised out of public funds to the
g   extent of the difference between the prescribed prices and the higher prices which the Roche Group would have been able to charge had they not been restrained by the injunction. It was not the intention of Parliament when it passed the governing statute or of the Commons House of Parliament when it approved the order, that a subsidy to this section of the public should be paid for out of moneys raised by taxation; and the constitutional propriety of a voluntary undertaking by the executive
h   government that might have this effect is, in my view, questionable.

Accordingly, I agree with the majority of your Lordships that the Secretary of State is entitled to the interim injunction that he claimed without giving any undertaking as to damages unless the Roche Group have succeeded in showing a strong prima facie case that the order sought to be enforced by the injunction is ultra vires. It is not for the Secretary of State to show that the Roche Group's case cannot possibly
j   succeed, as Walton J thought it was. It is for the Roche Group to show that their defence of ultra vires is likely to be successful.

I agree with the majority of your Lordships that they have signally failed to do this. The basic issue in the investigation by the Monopolies Commission into the prices charged by the Roche Group in the United Kingdom for Librium and Valium and their

1   [1967] 3 All ER 663, [1968] 2 QB 740

derivatives ('the reference drugs') was the extent to which, consistently with the public
interest, they should be permitted to recover from the proceeds of sale of these
outstandingly successful products contributions to the cost of current research undertaken by the Roche Group with a view to the discovery of new products and also a
high profit margin to compensate for losses or profits at a lower level on world-wide
sales by the group of current or future less successful drugs. It was for the commission to arrive at its own conclusion whether the way in which the Roche Group
took account of these two factors in determining the level of the prices at which the
reference drugs were supplied in the United Kingdom operated or might be expected
to operate against the public interest. The commission makes its own investigation
into facts. It does not adjudicate on a lis between contending parties. The adversary
procedure followed in a court of law is not appropriate to its investigations. It has a
wide discretion as to how they should be conducted. Nevertheless, I would accept
that it is the duty of the commissioners to observe the rules of natural justice in the
course of their investigation—which means no more than that they must act fairly by
giving to the person whose activities are being investigated a reasonable opportunity
to put forward facts and arguments in justification of his conduct of these activities
before they reach a conclusion which may affect him adversely.

The case which the Roche Group sought to make before Walton J and the Court of
Appeal was that the commission had failed to do this. The argument ran: (1) that this
failure to observe the rules of natural justice made null and void the conclusion embodied in the commission's report that the Roche Group's determination of the level
of the prices of the reference drugs operated or might be expected to operate against
the public interest; (2) that the report must accordingly be treated in law as not containing this conclusion; (3) that the presence of such a conclusion in the report was a
condition precedent to the power of the Secretary of State to make any order under s 3
of the Monopolies and Mergers Act 1965; and (4) the condition precedent not having
been fulfilled the order which the Secretary of State had purported to make was also
a nullity.

My Lords, I do not find it necessary to express any view as to the prospects of success
of this ingenious argument if the factual promise on which it is based could be established, viz, that the commission reached the relevant conclusion in its report in breach
of the rules of natural justice. Whether the argument is sound does not arise at the
present stage because the Roche Group have, in my view, failed to show any prima
facie case, let alone a strong one, for the existence of the factual premise.

On the facts presented to your Lordships' House all that their case amounts
to is that after an investigation into the facts about which no complaint can plausibly
be made, the Roche Group were informed by the chairman of the commission at an
oral hearing that the commission were considering recommending a level of prices
which did not allow for the group to continue to recover out of the proceeds of sale
of the reference drugs in the United Kingdom the same proportion of its current research costs directed to the discovery of new drugs or the same level of profit margin
as it had done in previous years. The chairman invited the Roche Group to suggest
some alternative standard by which an appropriate allowance for current research
costs and for profit might be arrived at. The Roche Group, for what no doubt appeared
to them to be good tactical reasons, declined to do so. Their real complaint is that
having adopted and persisted in this attitude, they were not subsequently informed by
the commission of its intention to recommend that no further allowance should be
made in the future prices of the reference drugs for current research costs and that a
much lower level of profit on the sale of the reference drugs in the United Kingdom
should be allowed for.

My Lords, on the only evidence that is before your Lordships the Roche Group
were given every opportunity to put their case before the commission both orally and
in writing. Their case was that it was in the public interest that they should go on
fixing prices on the same basis as they had done before; that any other basis would be

unfair to them: and that they were not going to help the commission to find one.

a   The commission, for reasons that are set out in its report, rejected the Roche Group's arguments. Even in judicial proceedings in a court of law, once a fair hearing has been given to the rival cases presented by the parties, the rules of natural justice do not require the decision-maker to disclose what he is minded to decide so that the parties may have a further opportunity of criticising his mental processes before he reaches a final decision. If this were a rule of natural justice only the most talkative of judges

b   would satisfy it and trial by jury would have to be abolished.

In your Lordships' House, however, the Roche Group developed for the first time an alternative argument. What it amounted to was this. (1) In its report the commission had expressed the view that the Roche Group had made excessive profits from the sale of reference drugs in previous years. (2) It was to be inferred that in making its recommendations as to future prices the purpose of the commission was to penalise

c   the Roche Group in the future for what they had done in the past. (3) Although the Secretary of State is required by s 3(1) of the 1965 Act to form an independent judgment as to the appropriate order to make, it was to be inferred from the fact that his order followed the recommendations of the commission as to the future prices that the purpose of his order was the same as the inferred purpose of the commission.

d   (4) The only permissible purpose of an order under s 3(1) of the 1965 Act is to remedy or to prevent mischiefs occurring after the report of the commission was laid before Parliament. (5) Inasmuch as the purpose of the order (as inferred under (2) and (3)) was in part to remedy the mischief which had resulted from excessive prices which had been charged before the commission had reported, the order was ultra vires.

My Lords, I will not burden this speech with an examination of the detailed wording of the relevant provisions of the statutes which, in my view, make implausible any

e   argument that past mischiefs resulting from the state of affairs found by the commission are to be left out of account by the Secretary of State when he makes an order specifying prices to be charged in the future for goods that were the subject of the reference. In any event on a fair reading of the commission's report, from which this argument of the Roche Group starts, the view that the commission expressed was that the Roche Group had already recovered out of the proceeds of sale of the ref-

f   erence drugs in the United Kingdom more of the cost of current research and a higher margin of profit than was justified in the public interest, and that accordingly it was not in the public interest that they should recover in the prices to be charged in the future any further costs of current research or anything like so high a profit margin as in the past. If the purpose of the Secretary of State when he made the order—and it is his purpose that matters—was to prevent the Roche Group doing this it was, in

g   my view, a legitimate purpose.

So the Roche Group have, in my opinion, failed to make out any prima facie case that the order is ultra vires. It therefore follows that in the ordinary course the Secretary of State would be entitled to an interim injunction to restrain the Roche Group from contravening its provisions. It only remains to consider whether the fact that the Crown itself has a substantial financial interest in the enforcement of the

h   order takes this case sufficiently out of the ordinary course of law enforcement actions to justify refusing an injunction against the Roche Group and accepting instead an undertaking given by them in the terms approved by Walton J.

My Lords, although the scheme embodied in that undertaking would protect the Department of Health and Social Security from financial loss resulting from the Roche Group's refusal to obey what must be presumed to be the law until the final hearing

j   of the action, the consequence of the scheme would be that other people, wholesale and retail chemists and private patients, pending the hearing of the action which may take two years, would be compelled to lend their assistance to the Roche Group in their disobedience to the order and, in the case of private patients, would be out of pocket for the difference between the permitted prices and those actually charged by the Roche Group. The practical difficulties of adjusting the position of private patients in particular would appear to be insuperable if the Roche Group fail at the hearing of the action to rebut the presumption of validity of the order. The sum involved in sales to private patients may be trivial to the Roche Group. It is not trivial to the individual private patients. I do not think that it can be brushed aside as de minimis.

In common with the majority of your Lordships, I cannot regard this undertaking as a satisfactory alternative to an interim injunction. I would dismiss this appeal.

LORD CROSS OF CHELSEA. My Lords, when the Crown is seeking to protect some property to which it claims to be entitled, such as a house, as in the case of *Attorney-General v Albany Hotel Co*[1], or a registered design as in *Secretary of State for War v Cope*[2], I think—in common, I believe, with all your Lordships—that nowadays, in the light of the Crown Proceedings Act 1947, the courts should only grant it an interim injunction subject to the condition on which such injunctions are granted to private litigants—namely the giving of the common form undertaking in damages. But if the Crown is taking proceedings under a statutory provision such as that contained in s 11 of the Monopolies and Restrictive Practices (Inquiry and Control) Act 1948, the court, in considering whether or not to make the grant of an interim injunction conditional on the giving of an undertaking in damages, has to bear in mind the interest which the public—and in particular any section of it which will benefit directly thereby—has in seeing that the law in question is enforced.

To make the granting of an interim injunction conditional on the giving of an undertaking in damages may deter the Crown from asking for one. The Attorney-General may say to himself: 'I think that we are right—but one never knows; and if we get an interim injunction and it turns out that we are wrong we may be held liable to pay very heavy damages. The Crown has not much direct interest in this dispute and it would be wrong to hazard public money to obtain interim relief which will not benefit the public at large.' If the case advanced by the defendant is—as it was in *Post Office v Estuary Radio Ltd*[3]—that what he is doing or proposing to do is not prohibited by the order in question then there may well be no objection to the advisers of the Crown being placed in this sort of dilemma. In such a case there is no prima facie presumption that the defendant is breaking the law—and if the Crown wishes to prevent him from acting or continuing to act in a certain way before the case comes to trial it may be fair enough that it should have to back its view with an undertaking in damages. But where—as here—the defence is that what is on the face of it the law of the land is not in fact the law, I agree with Lord Diplock that the position is quite different. In such a case what the defendant is doing or proposing to do is, prima facie, a breach of the law, and if he is allowed to continue his course of conduct pending the trial because the Crown is deterred from applying for an interim injunction by the necessity of giving an undertaking in damages the result will be—if the defendant loses at the trial—that those for whose benefit the order was made will be deprived of the benefit of it for the period, which may be considerable, between the starting of proceedings and the eventual decision—a period during which the defendant will have been pursuing a course of conduct which contravenes what throughout appears to be and is eventually shown always to have been the law. It is, I think, only in exceptional circumstances that the courts should countenance the possibility of such a result. One can, of course, imagine a case where the argument for saying that the order was invalid appeared prima facie to be so strong that the judge might think that the Crown ought not to be granted an interim injunction unless it gave an undertaking in damages; but no one could suggest for a moment that this case is a case of that sort.

---

1 [1896] 2 Ch 696
2 [1919] 2 Ch 339
3 [1967] 3 All ER 633, [1968] 2 QB 740

a
So if the Crown had not been itself by far the largest purchaser of these drugs I would have had no hesitation in holding that the judge was wrong to have refused to grant an interim injunction without an undertaking in damages. But as 90 per cent of the drugs sold are bought by the Department of Health and Social Security the Roche Group can argue with some force that in substance this is simply a private dispute between the Crown as purchasers and the Roche Group as vendors in which the pub-

b
lic has only that indirect interest which the general body of taxpayers inevitably has in any dispute in which the Crown is seeking to establish a right to some property or to reduce some liability to which it is said to be subject. But this line of argument involves overlooking the special interest which the ten per cent of private purchasers have in seeing that this order is enforced. The Roche Group have, indeed, suggested a way—by the issue of stamps which could be cashed if the Roche Group lose—by which

c
these private purchasers might be protected. But as a practical matter such a protection would be largely illusory since having regard to the small sums involved many purchasers would undoubtedly lose or forget to cash their stamps. The court has, therefore, to face the fact that if no interim injunction is granted because the Secretary of State will not give an undertaking, then in the event which is, certainly, not imtherefore, to face the fact that if no interim injunction is granted because the Attorney-General will not give an undertaking, then in the event which is, certainly, not im-

d
probable of the Roche Group losing at the trial, an appreciable number of people will have reaped no benefit from an order which was intended to benefit them during the period which may well be substantial over which the Roche Group will have been allowed to defy what always appeared to be and was eventually held to have been the law. Although I have no particular sympathy with the attitutde adopted by the Crown in refusing to give an undertaking in this case, I can equally see no such merits

e
in the Roche Group as would disentitle the Crown to shelter behind the group of private purchasers who might be injured if no interim injunction were granted. Accordingly, I would dismiss the appeal—though my approach to the problem is somewhat different from that of the Court of Appeal and in particular I am not, any more than Lord Diplock, prepared to agree with the view apparently expressed by Lord Denning MR[1] that an order made by statutory instrument acquires the status

f
of an Act of Parliament if it is approved by resolutions of both Houses of Parliament.

Appeal dismissed.

Solicitors: *Herbert Smith & Co* (for the Roche Group); *Treasury Solicitor.*

g
Christine Ivamy Barrister.

---

1 [1973] 3 All ER 945 at 954, 955, [1973] 3 WLR 805 at 823

Earl Bathurst v Fine

COURT OF APPEAL, CIVIL DIVISION
LORD DENNING MR, ORR AND ROSKILL LJJ
25th APRIL 1974

Landlord and tenant – Lease – Forfeiture – Relief – Refusal of relief – Grounds for refusal –
Personal qualifications of tenant – Circumstances in which personal qualifications of tenant
a relevant consideration – Personal qualifications of importance for preservation of value
and character of property – Lease of country house to American citizen – Tenant banned
from re-entering United Kingdom.

In May 1971 the landlord let a large country house to the tenant, an American citizen,
for a term of 20 years. The rent was comparatively small but the lease contained
stipulations that the tenant should put the property in good order and make considerable improvements to it over the period of the lease. Letters passed stating
that the tenant was to employ a regular gardener and household staff necessary to
maintain the property to the high standard befitting the character of the property.
The lease stipulated that the tenant was not to assign or underlet it or part with
possession of any part of it, except for a cottage for an employee. There was also
an express covenant that the tenant would not carry on, or permit to be carried on,
any trade or business on the premises or permit them 'to be occupied or used in any
other manner than as a private dwelling-house and parkland'. The lease also contained a provision that if the tenant suffered any distress or execution to be levied on
his goods it should be lawful for the landlord to re-enter. In the late summer of
1973 the tenant went abroad and was subsequently banned by the Home Office from
re-entering the United Kingdom. Because of his absence he failed to pay promptly
two debts, one to a store for food supplied and the other a quarter's rent under the
lease. The store obtained judgment for the amount owing to them and in November
execution was levied on the premises. The tenant thereupon suffered a forfeiture.
The landlord served a notice under s 146 of the Law of Property Act 1925 and obtained
an order for possession in the county court. The tenant, who had since discharged
his debts, applied for relief against forfeiture. He had spent some £5,000 on improvements to the property and there was no suggestion that he could not meet his financial
obligations under the lease.

Held – In a case where the personal qualifications of the tenant were of importance for
the preservation of the value or character of the property, those qualifications were a
legitimate consideration for the court to take into account in determining whether
to exercise its discretion to grant relief against forfeiture. The stipulations in the
lease clearly showed that the personal qualifications and suitability of the tenant
were very much at the heart of the lease; it was fundamental that he would reside
there himself and keep the house in a character befitting the estate. In the circumstances the tenant had shown himself to be unsuitable personally and accordingly
relief should be refused (see p 1162 c and p 1163 b to d, post).

Notes

For the tenant's right to relief against forfeiture, see 23 Halsbury's Laws (3rd Edn)
677, para 1403, and for cases on the subject, see 31(2) Digest (Reissue) 827, 828, 6863-
6869.

For the Law of Property Act 1925, s 146, see 27 Halsbury's Statutes (3rd Edn) 563.

Case referred to in judgment

Hyman v Rose [1912] AC 623, [1911-13] All ER Rep 238, 81 LJKB 1062, 106 LT 907, HL; *rvsg* [1911] 2 KB 234, 80 LJKB 1011, 104 LT 619, CA, 31(2) Digest (Reissue) 827, 6865.

Appeal

By a lease made on 11th April 1972 the plaintiff, the Rt Hon Henry Allen John, Earl Bathurst ('the landlord'), demised to the defendant, Herman Fine ('the tenant'), premises known as Daneway House, Sapperton, Gloucestershire, for a term of 20 years from 1st May 1971 at the yearly rent of £450 payable be equal quarterly payments in arrear on the usual quarter days. The lease contained a proviso for re-entry if, inter alia, the rent should be unpaid for 21 days after becoming payable (whether legally demanded or not) or if the tenant should suffer any execution to be levied on his goods. The tenant failed to pay the instalment of rent payable on 29th September 1973 and on 7th November he suffered an execution to be levied on his goods at the premises. On 8th November the landlord served a notice in writing under s 146 of the Law of Property Act 1925 specifying the execution levied on the tenant's goods as the breach of condition of the lease. On 14th November the landlord commenced an action for possession of the premises in Stroud County Court and on 11th December his Honour Judge Elder Jones granted the order sought. On 18th January 1974 the judge dismissed an application by the tenant for relief against the forfeiture and the tenant appealed against that decision on the following grounds: (i) the judge in exercising his discretion whether or not to grant to the tenant relief from forfeiture had taken into account matters which ought not to have been taken into account or alternatively had in the circumstances given too much weight to such matters: the matters referred to being the fact that the Home Office had refused the tenant entry into the United Kingdom and the fact that the tenant had at one stage been in arrear with the rent falling due under the lease on 29th September 1973; (ii) the judge had erred in law in that when exercising his discretion whether or not to grant the tenant relief from forfeiture he had not given any or any sufficient weight to the following facts or matters: (a) that the tenant had never been in breach of any provision in the lease except in relation to the payment of one rental instalment on 29th September 1973; (b) that it was not suggested on behalf of the landlord that there was any likelihood or possibility that the tenant would be in breach of any provision of the lease in the future were relief to be granted; (c) that since the date of the demise the tenant had properly maintained and run the premises; (d) that the event giving rise to the forfeiture was not in the circumstances a serious matter or in any way prejudicial to the interests of the landlord; (e) that the tenant had discharged the debt, which was the subject-matter of the execution, before 11th December 1973; (f) that at the date of his application the tenant was not in arrears with rent in respect of the lease; (g) that the tenant had expended substantial moneys in improving the premises; and (iii) that the judge ought in the exercise of his discretion to have granted to the tenant relief from forfeiture.

Roger Ellis for the tenant.
Christopher Priday for the landlord.

LORD DENNING MR. This case concerns a large country house known as Daneway, Sapperton, in Gloucestershire. It is scheduled as of architectural and historic interest. It is on the Bathurst estate belonging to the landlord, Lord Bathurst. In 1971 it was let to the tenant, Mr Herman Fine, an American citizen, for a term of 20 years running from 1st May 1971. The rent was comparatively small, £450 a year, but that was because there were stipulations that the tenant should put the place in good order and make very considerable improvements to it over the period of the lease. The Bathurst estate were very anxious that the standing of the property should be kept up. Letters passed saying that Mr Fine was to employ a regular gardener and household staff necessary to maintain the property to the high standard befitting a property of that character. Furthermore, in the lease itself there were special terms providing that Mr Fine was not to assign or underlet it or part with possession of it or any part of it, except for a cottage for an employee. Furthermore, there was an express covenant—

'Not at any time during the term to carry on or permit to be carried on any trade or business upon the premises or permit the same to be occupied or used in any other manner than as a private dwelling-house and parkland ...'

Those stipulations seem to me to show very clearly that the personal qualifications and suitability of Mr Fine as a tenant were very much at the heart of this lease. It was fundamental that he would be there himself and that he would reside there himself and keep the house in a character fitting the estate. That was in May 1971.

In August or September 1973 Mr Herman Fine went to France. He must have done something very wrong, because he was banned by the Home Office from re-entering this country. Owing to his absence, he did not pay promptly two debts. One of them was to Messrs Fortnum and Mason, no doubt for high quality food, of some £89 and costs. The other was the quarter's rent due on 29th September 1973 of £110 or thereabouts. Judgment was obtained by Fortnum and Mason for the amount owing to them. On 7th November 1973 execution was levied on the premises. Walking possession was taken.

Thereupon there came into operation the proviso for re-entry in this lease. It included a provision that if the tenant suffered any distress or execution to be levied on his goods it should be lawful for the landlord at any time to re-enter. So he suffered a forfeiture then. On the very next day, 8th November, the landlord served a notice under s 146 of the Law of Property Act 1925. The notice was affixed to the premises, as Mr Fine was not there. Afterwards, on 14th November, the landlord took proceedings in the county court for possession. In due course judgment was obtained for possession. The lawyers for Mr Fine admitted that this breach (suffering execution to be levied) was incapable of remedy and therefore there was no answer to the claim for forfeiture as such.

But thereafter Mr Fine, although abroad, instructed his lawyers to apply for relief against forfeiture; and they did apply. He did not give any evidence himself or make any affidavit, but he arranged that someone who looks after his interests, a Mr Frank Duggan, should make an affidavit. By this time Mr Fine had discharged his debt to Fortnum and Mason and had paid the rent. So he had made good his financial obligations. It was proved also that Mr Fine had spent a lot of money on the premises in improving them in the two years when he had been there. Some £5,000 at least he has paid. It is said that it would be a shame if, in the circumstances, he was not given relief from forfeiture. The learned judge, nevertheless, decided that he would not grant relief. Mr Fine appeals to this court.

It is quite plain that the two money matters were of minor importance. They were remedied at once. There is no suggestion whatever that Mr Fine could not fulfil any financial obligations under the tenancy or do any repairs which were required of him. In the ordinary way relief is almost always granted to a person who makes good the breach of covenant and is able and willing to fulfil his obligations in the future. That has been the position since *Hyman v Rose*[1].

This case is unusual because it concerns the personal qualifications of the tenant. How far are those to be taken into account in granting or refusing relief from forfeiture? In many cases it would not be a ground for refusing relief, but in some cases it is. For instance, we have been referred to s 146(9) of the 1925 Act which shows

---

1   [1912] AC 623, [1911-13] All ER Rep 238

a   that there are leases, such as leases of agricultural land, where the personal qualifications of the tenant are of importance. It says:

'This section does not apply to a condition for forfeiture on the bankruptcy of the lessee or on taking in execution of the lessee's interest [in the case of five classes of lease, including a lease of:] (e) Any property with respect to which the the personal qualifications of the tenant are of importance for the preservation

b   of the value or character of the property . . .'

That applies to forfeiture for bankruptcy or execution, but it seems to me that it is a legitimate consideration in other cases when relief is being considered. It applies in any case where the personal qualifications of the tenant are of importance for the preservation of the value or character of the property. This is essentially such a case.

c   If the tenant is shown to be unsuitable personally, then relief can be refused. Here we have a man who is not a subject of this country but an American citizen. He has behaved in such a way that he is banned from entering this country and he is not a fit person to be a tenant of this property. The judge was quite right in refusing relief.

I would therefore dismiss this appeal.

d   **ORR LJ.** I agree.

ROSKILL LJ. I also agree.

Appeal dismissed.

e   Solicitors: *Bernard Sheridan & Co* (for the tenant); *Mullings, Ellet & Co*, Cirencester (for the landlord).

L J Kovats Esq Barrister.

f
Durston v O'Keeffe
Durston Plant Contractors Ltd v Tivoli Contractors Ltd

QUEEN'S BENCH DIVISION

FORBES J

g   6th, 19th DECEMBER 1973

Practice – Reference to referee – Order by district registrar – Jurisdiction of registrar – Registrar assigning business to circuit judge as official referee – Registrar reserving interlocutory applications to himself – Registrar subsequently making orders in respect of interlocutory matters – Extent of registrar's jurisdiction – Courts Act 1971, s 25(4).

h   Two related actions were started in the Bristol District Registry of the High Court. On 26th October 1972 the district registrar made an order in each action that the business be assigned to the circuit judge as official referee, in accordance with the Lord Chancellor's directions under s 25(4)ᵃ of the Courts Act 1971; the orders reserved interlocutory applications to the registrar. On 15th January 1973 the registrar

j   made orders in each action relating to certain interlocutory matters. The defendants in each action appealed against the orders of 26th October and 15th January.

Held – Once the district registrar had made an order referring a cause as official referees' business, he had no further jurisdiction in the cause. The circuit judge

---
a   Section 25(4) is set out at p 1166 a, post

thereupon became seised of the matter and any application for directions had to be   *a*
made, in accordance with RSC Ord 36, r 6, to the circuit judge to whom the cause
had been allocated. It followed that all four orders had been made by the registrar
without jurisdiction. The appeal would therefore be allowed and the orders set
aside (see p 1167 *a* and *b* and p 1168 *d* and *j* to p 1169 *a*, post).

Notes   *b*
For references to official referees, see 30 Halsbury's Laws (3rd Edn) 440-442, paras
824-830, and for cases on the subject, see 51 Digest (Repl) 680-684, 2823-2872.
   For the Courts Act 1971, s 25, see 41 Halsbury's Statutes (3rd Edn) 312.

Interlocutory appeals
Frank James Durston brought an action in the Bristol District Registry against Patrick   *c*
Joseph O'Keeffe, and Durston Plant Contractors brought an action in the same registry
against Tivoli Contractors Ltd (formerly trading as Durston Contractors Ltd).
On 26th October 1972 Mr District Registrar Parmiter made an order in each action
assigning the business of each to his Honour Judge Forrest as official referee but
reserving interlocutory applications to the registrar. On 15th January 1973, on
further summonses for directions, the district registrar made orders in each action   *d*
relating to setting down, certificates of readiness etc. The defendants appealed
against the orders of 26th October 1972 and 15th January 1973. The facts are set out
in the judgment of Forbes J.

S E Brodie for the defendants.
C A J Gosland for the plaintiffs.

                                                      Cur adv vult   *e*

19th December.   **FORBES J** read the following judgment. This is an interesting
case concerned with the procedure to be followed for the transfer of cases to be
tried as official referees' business outside London. Because the provisions are new
and have only recently fallen to be dealt with in district registries, I have been asked   *f*
to adjourn these four appeals into open court for judgment.
   The two actions with which these appeals are concerned relate to the affairs of
two companies of building contractors. The plaintiff is the first action—which I
shall call 'the personal action', that is *Durston v O'Keeffe*—sold to the defendant
certain shares in Durston Contractors Ltd, a company now called Tivoli Contractors
Ltd. He claims the balance of the agreed price. The defendant avers that he was
induced to agree too high a price for the shares on the face of a misrepresentation   *g*
by the plaintiff as to the state of the account between Tivoli Contractors Ltd and
another company—Durston Plant Contractors Ltd, of which the plaintiff was a
director and major shareholder. These two companies are respectively defendants
and plaintiffs in the second action, which I shall call 'the company action'. That
action is concerned with a complicated series of transactions between the two companies relating to contracts for plant hire and various services, the plaintiffs claiming   *h*
some £22,000 for these; the defendants claim a set-off against certain details and
have a series of counterclaims for various goods supplied, services provided, and
indemnities said to be implied in the contracts for plant hire. The state of account
between the two companies thus forms the substance of the company action and
until this dispute is determined the personal action, depending as it does on whether
there has been a misrepresentation as to the state of that account, cannot be   *j*
determined either.
   There is no dispute that the company action ought properly to be regarded as
official referees' business and that, as the personal action must depend on the
company action, the two actions should either be tried together or one immediately
after the other.

a   Both actions started in the Bristol District Registry of the High Court, and on 27th
April 1972 the district registrar had before him a number of summonses in each
action asking for directions as to mode of trial and discovery and other interlocutory
matters.   Due to want of time these summonses were in effect adjourned without
any order and by 26th October 1972, the time they came to be heard again, all parties
had agreed that both actions should be treated as official referees' business.   The
b district registrar thereupon made an order in each action in these terms: that the
business be assigned to his Honour Judge Forrest as official referee, reserving interlocutory applications to the registrar.   On 15th January 1973, on further summonses
for directions, the district registrar made orders in each action relating to setting
down, certificates of readiness, and mode of trial, and in the company action for a
Scott schedule and subsequent pleadings.
       The defendants in each action now appeal against the two orders of 26th October
c 1972 and the two orders of 15th January 1973 on the grounds that the district registrar
had no power to make any of these orders.
       The procedure relating to official referees' business is governed by RSC Ord 36,
but this order now has to by read in conjunction with the provisions of the Courts Act
1971.   I shall attempt to set out the procedure laid down in RSC Ord 36, before the
d alterations made by the 1971 Act, and then consider the effect of those alterations.
       We are only really concerned with three of the rules under RSC Ord 36, namely
rr 1, 5 and 6.   Rule 1, which I need not set out in full provides: '... in any cause ..
the Court may ... order that the cause ... shall be tried before an official referee
    ..'   Such an order, referring business to an official referee, is made by a master or
by a district registrar, usually on a summons for directions.   Rule 5 provides for
the allocation of the business, which has been referred, between official referees, of
e whom, before the 1971 Act, there were three.   Rule 5(1) provides: 'No order referring
any business to an official referee ... shall specify any particular referee'.   The
business is allocated to a particular referee in rotation by the rota clerk to the senior
official referee, when the order of reference, which has been made by the master or
district registrar is produced to him.   Rule 6 takes the matter along the next step:
f once the rota clerk has allocated the matter to a particular referee it must be entered
forthwith with that referee's clerk, and within 14 days of entry the party which
produced the reference to the rota clerk must apply for directions to the official
referee to whom the business has been assigned.   If he does not do so, then any other
interested party may do so.
       This was the position before the Courts Act 1971 came into force, and official
referees would, in accordance with directions which they gave, sit sometimes in
g London and sometimes outside London; but wherever they sat, the same procedure
for the allocation of the matter to a particular official referee and for that referee
to give the necessary directions was followed; and once the district registrar outside
London had made an order referring any cause to an official referee, that registrar
had no further jurisdiction in the cause.
       The Courts Act 1971, s 25, made a profound change.   Its provisions are as follows:
h

'(1) After the appointed day no person shall be appointed to the office of
official referee and on and after that day functions conferred on official referees
by provisions of rules of the Supreme Court, or by any other provision, shall be
discharged in accordance with the provisions of this section.
'(2) Such of the Circuit judges as the Lord Chancellor may from time to time
j determine shall discharge the said functions conferred on official referees.
'(3) The cases in which jurisdiction or powers of the High Court or a judge of
the High Court may be exercised by official referees, whether by virtue of rules
of court made under section 15 of the Administration of Justice Act 1956 or
otherwise, shall be known as "official referees' business", and except where the
context otherwise requires, any reference in any enactment, in rules of court

or in any other document to an official referee shall, in accordance with this
section, be construed as, or where the context requires as including, a reference *a*
to a Circuit judge discharging the functions of an official referee.

'(4) Subject to rules of court, the distribution of official referees' business,
performed in accordance with this section, shall be determined in accordance
with directions given by or on behalf of the Lord Chancellor.'

Now, under s 25(2), the Lord Chancellor has made a determination, appointing *b*
those circuit judges, who were the official referees in office at the time the Act came
into operation, to discharge the functions of official referees; and he has made a further
determination, appointing certain other circuit judges in each of the five circuits,
other than the south-eastern, to discharge such functions in their respective circuits.
Notwithstanding these last appointments, the circuit judges taking the official
referees' business in London—whom I might call the 'old' official referees—are still *c*
available to deal with such business outside London if it is referred to them.   A choice
is thus open to the district registrar who desires to transfer a cause to a circuit judge
discharging the functions of an official referee.   He can either transfer it to the London
circuit judges discharging these functions (when the judge dealing with it may sit
either in London or outside), or to one of the circuit judges appointed to discharge
these functions on the appropriate circuit.   If he transfers the cause to the London *d*
circuit judges, the procedure laid down in RSC Ord 36, r 5, and which has already
been described, will be followed; that is the procedure for allocation.   But this
procedure is inappropriate in the case of circuit judges outside London.   There is no
rota clerk, and the assignment of the business to a particular circuit judge must
therefore be made by the district registrar himself.

The Lord Chancellor has made a determination under s 25(4) of the Courts Act *e*
1971 in these terms: the matter is set out in the supplement to the White Book[1],
under the heading 'Official Referees'.   It points out that the Lord Chancellor has
made the determination appointing circuit judges, to which I have already referred,
and goes on:

'Notwithstanding such appointments, the Circuit judges taking official referee *f*
business in London will continue to be available to take cases referred to them
by District Registries, and to sit, if desirable, outside London; and in such cases,
the procedure laid down in O. 36, r 5 . . . will continue to be followed. Moreover,
in cases where the London Circuit judges are taking Official Referee cases outside
London, the Solicitors to the parties should notify the appropriate Circuit Administrator of the names of counsel retained as soon as the dates are fixed so as to *g*
avoid clashes of dates.   On the other hand, where a reference is contemplated
by one of the Circuit judges taking official referee business outside London, the
following procedure should be followed: (a) Before the reference is made the
District Registrar should inquire of the courts administrator whether the particular Circuit judge is likely to be available to take the reference.   (b) If he is,
the reference should be made to the Circuit judge by name, but this is without *h*
prejudice to the power of that judge to order the transfer of the case to the other
judge taking official referee business on the same circuit or to one of the judges
taking official referee business in London, if that judge consents.   (c) The District
Registrar should also ascertain where the Circuit judge is likely to sit for the
purpose of taking the business referred to him.   An officer of the District Registry
for the town of sitting should act as the Circuit judge's clerk for the purpose of *j*
O. 36, r. 6 . . . as if the business had been allocated to him under r. 5 . . .'

It will be noticed from the procedure described above that, broadly, RSC Ord 35,
r 5, provides the machinery for allocating the cause to a particular London circuit

---

1 Supreme Court Practice 1973, 3rd Cumulative Supplement, para 36/1/1

a   judge who is dealing with official referees' business, while RSC Ord 36, r 6, contains
the procedure for the conduct of the cause once it has been so allocated.   It is only
the allocation procedure under r 5 which cannot be followed outside London, and
for which new arrangements have had to be made.   Once the cause is allocated to a
particular circuit judge, whether in London or outside, the procedure described in
r 6 must be followed. Thus, once the district registrar has made an order referring the
cause as official referees' business, there is nothing further for him to do.   The circuit
b   judge then becomes seised of the matter and under RSC Ord 36, r 6, the cause must be
entered with that circuit judge's clerk.   For the circuit judges outside London the
district registrar will have to appoint the appropriate officer to act as such clerk, in
accordance with the Lord Chancellor's determination. Any application for directions must then be made, in accordance with r 6, to the circuit judge to whom the
cause has been allocated.   I should add that there is good reason for the provision of
c   r 6 in this class of case.   One of the great advantages of the procedure adopted in
cases designated as official referees' business is that, as in the Commercial Court cases,
the judge who will try the case has charge of it from the moment of transfer.   In
dealing with the interlocutory matters he is able to propose the procedures to be
adopted and the steps to be followed to meet the needs of each case with a view to
d   minimising costs in a class of litigation which, by virtue of its complexity, is potentially
expensive.

I have described this procedure at some length because I have been told that it has
not been followed universally in district registries.   In the causes now before me, the
orders of the district registrar on 26th October 1972 were that the matters should be
assigned to his Honour Judge Forrest, as official referee, reserving interlocutory
applications to the registrar.   The reasons for this order became clear during the
e   argument on these appeals when I was shown a copy of a note from the district
registrar in Bristol to other registrars on the Western Circuit, which is in these terms:

'Official Referee Business.   I have discussed the situation with his Honour
Judge Forrest.   (1) All official referee business should now be dealt with within
the circuit unless there is good reason for it to be transferred elsewhere.   (2)
f   Whereas previously official referees dealt with all interlocutory work themselves,
on cases kept within the circuit, registrars should deal with all interlocutory
matters.   (3) In consequence, instead of an order for a transfer to an official
referee, there should only be an order assigning the matter to his Honour Judge
Forrest as official referee business.   (4) He has directed that all interlocutory
applications in business so assigned should be issued before the registrar.'

g   Counsel, in these cases for both the defendants, first asks for an extension of time in
which to appeal against these orders and also the subsequent orders of 15th January
1973 giving directions in both matters. Counsel for the plaintiffs accepts that it would be
right for such an extension to be granted.   Accordingly I grant the necessary exten-
sions of time.   Counsel for the defendants then says that the district registrar had no
jurisdiction to make any order reserving interlocutory applications to himself and
h   that, accordingly, both the original orders of 26th October 1972 are nullities, as are also
the orders giving directions on 15th January 1973. Counsel for the plaintiffs accepts,
as I understand it, that the proper procedure is that which I earlier set out at some
length.   He contends, however, that the original orders are not nullities because it is
clear from the registrar's note that the learned circuit judge gave the district registrar
a general direction that all interlocutory applications and business assigned to him
j   should be issued before the registrar; or alternatively, since the note to which I have
referred, is not strictly in evidence before me, that I should make the usual presumption omnia praesumuntur rite esse acta that such a direction had been given by the
learned judge.   He then contends that the learned judge had jurisdiction to give such
general directions.   He admits that the power to do so cannot be found in RSC Ord 36
but suggests that it can be found elsewhere. His first suggestion was that such a power

can be found in the County Court Rules, but he was constrained to accept that, although the district registrar of the High Court in Bristol happens to be the same person as the county court registrar for that area, he could have no jurisdiction as a county court registrar to deal with an action in the High Court—nor could the circuit judge, clothed only with his county court jurisdiction, purport to give directions in a matter proceeding in the High Court. Counsel for the plaintiffs' second suggestion, therefore, was that a power of a different character can be found elsewhere in the rules of the Supreme Court, namely in RSC Ord 32, r 11. That is a rule which confers on masters of the Queen's Bench Division, which term for this purpose includes district registrars, power 'to transact all such business and exercise all such authority and jurisdiction as under . . . these rules may be transacted and exercised by a judge in chambers', and the last three words mean, and must mean, a High Court judge in chambers; but RSC Ord 36, r 6, is not dealing with the transaction of business by a High Court judge in chambers—it is dealing with the transaction of business by a circuit judge discharging the functions of an official referee. Accordingly, in my judgment, this point has no validity and RSC Ord 32, r 11, does not apply to the discharge of business by those circuit judges.

Counsel for the plaintiffs argues, lastly, that this is a failure to comply with the requirement of the rules of the Supreme Court, which under RSC Ord 2, r 1, should be treated as a mere irregularity and not a matter nullifying the orders. Counsel for the defendants contends that this is not a mere irregularity but a question of want of jurisdiction and I consider that he is right. It follows that all four orders were made by the district registrar without jurisdiction. Since 15th January 1973 there have been further interlocutory orders made by the district registrar, in the company action on 6th April and on 26th September 1973, and in the personal action on the latter date, 26th September. Strictly, there is no appeal before me against these orders, but in the circumstances, counsel for the defendants applies to amend his notice of appeal to include them, and counsel for the plaintiffs waives all objections. Accordingly, I give leave to amend it to include appeals against these three orders.

On 22nd November 1973 his Honour Judge Forrest himself gave directions in both actions, transferring both causes to London. These orders are not before me, and indeed could not be. Any appeal would lie to the Court of Appeal. I have been told that these latter orders came to be made by the learned judge in this way: both actions were listed for hearing before the judge on 22nd November; they were not, in fact, heard in court; instead, he made, in his private room, the interlocutory orders to which I have referred. There had been no summons or other application by either party for directions. Of course, any circuit judge, discharging the functions of an official referee, must be free—if for some reason he cannot take the case—to transfer it to some other circuit judge discharging those functions, provided that judge consents, and this is obviously what this learned judge did on this occasion. Indeed, I should add, the power to do so is expressly provided in para (b) of the Lord Chancellor's determination under s 25(4) of the Courts Act 1971.

At one time, in the course of the argument, I canvassed the possibility of striking out only so much of the district registrar's original orders as reserved interlocutory matters to himself, leaving intact that part which referred the matter to Judge Forrest, but both counsel have asked me not to sever the orders in that way. I should only add that if, as I propose to do, I set aside the district registrar's orders, transferring the business to the circuit judge in Bristol, then presumably that judge's orders transferring the matters to London, will fall. Both parties, however, agree that the matter should proceed in the High Court in London, rather than in Bristol, and I propose to make an order to that effect.

Both parties agree also that the costs of this appeal and of all the interlocutory applications, save, of course, the proceedings before Judge Forrest, over which I have no jurisdiction, should be costs in the cause.

These appeals will, therefore, be allowed. The orders of the district registrar in the

a company action on 26th October 1972 and on 15th January, 6th April, and 26th September 1973 will be set aside, as will his orders in the personal action on 26th October 1972 and 15th January and 26th September 1973. There will be an order that both actions should be tried in London as official referees' business, and the costs both here and of all the orders set aside will be costs in the cause. There will be a certificate for two counsel for the defendants in each action.

b *Appeals allowed; orders set aside.*

Solicitors: *Sacker & Partners* (for the defendants); *Seager & Co*, Bristol (for the plaintiffs).

E H Hunter Esq Barrister.

c

Rightside Properties Ltd v Gray

CHANCERY DIVISION
d WALTON J
23rd, 24th, 25th APRIL, 10th MAY 1974

Applied in Country and Metropolitan Homes Surrey Ltd v Topclaim Ltd [1997] 1 All ER 254

Sale of land – Contract – Repudiation – Effect – Other party in default – Failure to complete on date fixed for completion – Time not of essence – Other party not in unreasonable delay – Need for other party to prove ability to complete as condition of claim for damages for wrongful
e *repudiation – Failure by purchaser to complete on date fixed – Vendor purporting to terminate contract – Purchaser not in unreasonable delay – Right of purchaser to treat purported termination as wrongful repudiation – Whether purchaser required to fulfil obligations under contract following repudiation in order to bring action based on repudiation – Whether purchaser required to prove he is ready willing and able to complete – Law of Property Act 1925, s 41.*

f *Sale of land – Contract – Completion – Notice to complete – Failure of purchaser to complete on date fixed for completion – Power of vendor to resell after notice – Rights of vendor conditional on giving notice – Whether failure of purchaser to complete capable of amounting to fundamental breach entitling vendor to rescind contract – Statutory Form of Conditions of Sale 1925 (SR & O 1925 No 779), condition 9.*

g *Sale of land – Contract – Completion – Notice to complete – Period of notice – Right of vendor to give to purchaser 'at least twenty-one days' notice' – Vendor giving notice to complete 'within 21 days' – Whether notice valid – Statutory Form of Conditions of Sale 1925 (SR & O 1925 No 779), condition 9.*

h In April 1972 the plaintiffs contracted to buy the defendant's freehold property for £50,000. The date fixed for completion was 19th June. The contract incorporated the statutory conditions of sale[a], condition 9[b] of which provided (i) that if the purchaser should neglect or fail to perform his part of the contract, the vendor might give to the purchaser or to his solicitor 'at least twenty-one days notice in writing specifying the breach and requiring the purchaser to make good the default before
j the expiration of the notice' and (ii) that if the purchaser did not comply with the terms of the notice, the vendor might resell the property. The plaintiffs failed to complete on 19th June. On 23rd June, a Friday, the defendant's solicitors posted a letter to the plaintiffs' solicitors, enclosing 'a notice to complete the transaction in

---

a See the Statutory Form of Conditions of Sale 1925
b Condition 9 is set out at p 1173 h and j, post

accordance with No. 9 of the Statutory Conditions of Sale'. The notice stated that if *a* the plaintiffs failed to comply with notice 'within 21 days from the date hereof' the defendant would either rescind the contract or resell the property. The plaintiffs did not comply with that notice. Accordingly, on 20th July, the defendant's solicitors wrote to the plaintiffs' solicitors making it clear that the defendant regarded the contract as no longer in existence; the letter purported to accept a repudiation by the plaintiffs of the contract, and maintained that it had accordingly come to an end. *b* In an action by the plaintiffs for specific performance or, alternatively, damages for breach of contract, the defendant contended (i) that the plaintiffs had failed to complete on 19th June and failed to comply with the notice under condition 9, and (ii) that, apart from the notice, by their failure to complete on 19th June the plaintiffs were, at law, in fundamental breach of, and had therefore repudiated, the contract and that the defendant's acceptance of that repudiation by his letter of 20th July *c* had brought the contract to an end unless, by virtue of s 41^c of the Law of Property Act 1925, the plaintiffs could show that, either on 19th June or within a reasonable time thereafter, they were ready, willing and able to perform their part of the contract. At the hearing the plaintiffs elected to accept the defendant's letter of 20th July as a repudiation of the contract and did not therefore press their claim for specific performance.

d

Held – (i) The defendant's notice enclosed with the letter of 23rd June was invalid for, even on the assumption that it had been delivered on 24th June, a condition requiring a period of 'at least twenty-one days' was not satisfied by giving notice that something was to be done 'within 21 days' from the date of service of the notice; the words 'at least' indicated that the period allowed was to be exclusive of the day *e* of service and the day of expiry of the notice (see p 1175 *f* and *g* and p 1176 *j* to p 1177 *a* and *e*, post); dictum of Alderson B in *Young v Higgon* (1840) 6 M & W at 54 applied.

(ii) It followed that the defendant's letter of 20th July was a wrongful repudiation of the contract and the plaintiffs were entitled to damages for the following reasons—

(a) Since under s 41 of the 1925 Act the date fixed for completion was not to be taken as of the essence, a party who could not or did not complete on the day fixed for *f* completion was not in fundamental breach of the contract provided he was ready to complete within a reasonable time thereafter. Where a vendor repudiated a contract at any time before the purchaser became in unreasonable delay beyond the date fixed for completion, the purchaser was entitled to accept that repudiation as discharging him from all further performance under the contract including that of taking any further steps to prepare for a completion which, ex hypothesi, would *g* not take place. Equity did not impose on the purchaser a burden of showing that, at a time after the vendor's repudiation, he was in a position to complete a contract which never would be completed. In such circumstances, therefore, repudiation discharged the purchaser from performing any condition precedent which it would otherwise fall on him to discharge. Although the plaintiffs had failed to comply with the date for completion before the defendant repudiated the contract, they were *h* not in unreasonable delay. It followed that, in consequence of the repudiation, the plaintiffs were not at any time under an obligation to show that they were 'able' to complete the contract (see p 1179 *c* and *d*, p 1182 *a b* and *h* and p 1183 *e*, post); dicta of Lord Campbell CJ in *Cort v Ambergate etc Railway Co* (1851) 17 QB at 143, 144, of Parker J in *Re Bayley-Worthington and Cohen's Contract* [1909] 1 Ch at 664, 665 and of Lord Parker of Waddington in *Stickney v Keeble* [1914-15] All ER Rep at 81 applied; dicta *j* of Fry LJ in *Howe v Smith* [1881-5] All ER Rep at 209 and of Lord Atkinson in *Stickney v Keeble* [1914-15] All ER Rep at 79 explained.

(b) In any event, on the true construction of the contract, condition 9 was only intelligible on the basis that failure to complete on the date fixed for completion was not in any sense fundamental. Condition 9 did no more than provide for the

---

c Section 41 is set out at p 1178 *g*, post

a consequences of a fundamental breach after—and hence *only* after—the service of the appropriate notice. Accordingly there had been no breach of contract by the plaintiffs which amounted to a fundamental breach (see p 1184 *d* and *e*, post).

Notes

For repudiation of contract, see 8 Halsbury's Laws (3rd Edn) 203–205, paras 344, 345, and for cases on the subject, see 12 Digest (Reissue) 411-416, *3032-3049*.

b   For the time for completion of a contract for the sale of land, see 34 Halsbury's Laws (3rd Edn) 256, 257, para 426, and for cases on the subject, see 40 Digest (Repl) 117-121, 910-949.

For the Law of Property Act 1925, s 41, see 27 Halsbury's Statutes (3rd Edn) 405.

For the Statutory Form of Conditions of Sale 1925, condition 9, see 18 Halsbury's Statutory Instruments (2nd Reissue) 310.

c

Cases referred to in judgment

Bayley-Worthington and Cohen's Contract, Re [1909] 1 Ch 648, 78 LJ Ch 351, 100 LT 650, 40 Digest (Repl) 128, *982*.

British and Beningtons Ltd v North Western Cachar Tea Co Ltd [1923] AC 48, [1922] All ER Rep 224, 92 LJKB 62, 128 LT 422, HL, 12 Digest (Reissue) 440, *3185*.

d *Cort v Ambergate etc Railway Co* (1851) 17 QB 127, 20 LJQB 460, 17 LTOS 179, 15 Jur 877, 117 ER 1229, 12 Digest (Reissue) 543, *3788*.

Hector Whaling Ltd, Re [1936] Ch 208, [1935] All ER Rep 302, 105 LJ Ch 117, 154 LT 342, 9 Digest (Repl) 618, *4114*.

Howe v Smith (1884) 27 Ch D 89, [1881-85] All ER Rep 201, 53 LJ Ch 1055, 50 LT 573, 48 JP 773, CA, 44 Digest (Repl) 98, *792*.

e *Papillon v Brunton* (1860) 5 H & N 518, 29 LJ Ex 265, 2 LT 326, 157 ER 1285, 31(2) Digest (Reissue) 782, *6490*.

Railway Sleepers Supply Co, Re (1885) 29 Ch D 204, 54 LJCh 720, 52 LT 731, 9 Digest (Repl) 618, *4120*.

Schnabel v Allard [1966] 3 All ER 816, [1967] 1 QB 627, [1966] 3 WLR 1295, CA, 31(2) Digest (Reissue) 760, *6290*.

f *Stickney v Keeble* [1915] AC 386, [1914-15] All ER Rep 73, 84 LJCh 259, 112 LT 664, HL, 44 Digest (Repl) 96, *783*.

Young v Higgon (1840) 6 M & W 49, [1835-42] All ER Rep 278, 8 Dowl 212, 9 LJMC 29, 4 JP 88, 4 Jur 125, 151 ER 317, 45 Digest (Repl) 254, *214*.

Cases also cited

g *Gresham House Estate Co v Rossa Grande Gold Mining Co* [1870] WN 119.

Holt v Heatherfield Trust Ltd [1942] 1 All ER 404, [1942] 2 KB 1.

Action

By a writ issued on 15th December 1972, the plaintiffs, Rightside Properties Ltd ('Rightside'), brought an action against the defendant, Bernard Gray ('Mr Gray'), in which they claimed (i) specific performance of a contract made by correspondence in April 1972 between Rightside and Mr Gray whereby Mr Gray agreed to sell, and Rightside agreed to buy, freehold property known as 53 Bassett Road, London, W10, for £50,000, and (ii) further, or alternatively, damages for breach of contract. By his amended defence and counterclaim, Mr Gray denied that he had acted in breach of contract or wrongfully neglected and refused to complete the contract and alleged that Rightside had wrongfully failed to complete the contract on 19th June 1972, and had wrongfully failed to comply with a notice sent to them by letter dated 23rd June 1972 pursuant to condition 9 of the Statutory Form of Conditions of Sale 1925[1] (which applied to the contract) requiring them to complete the contract within 21 days, and accordingly denied that Rightside were entitled to the relief claimed,

1   SR & O 1925 No 779

or, alternatively, to equitable relief. Mr Gray counterclaimed for a declaration that he was entitled to resell the property. By their amended reply and defence to *a* counterclaim Rightside alleged, inter alia, that the notice did not give them 21 days as required by condition 9, and that further, or alternatively, the period of 21 days was in the circumstances, unreasonably short. The facts are set out in the judgment.

Roger Ellis for Rightside.   *b*
N C H Browne-Wilkinson QC and *Mark Blythe* for Mr Gray.

Cur adv vult

10th May. **WALTON J** read the following judgment. On 25th April 1972, in consideration of the sum of £50, the defendant, Mr Gray, gave to the plaintiffs, Rightside Properties Ltd ('Rightside'), an option to purchase the property known as *c* 53 Bassett Road, London, W10, for the sum of £50,000. This option was duly exercised by a letter from Rightside to Mr Gray of 30th April 1972. It is accordingly common ground between the parties that the contract thereby constituted was a contract by correspondence, within the meaning of s 46 of the Law of Property Act 1925, and that it is therefore governed by the statutory conditions of sale.

By condition 1 of such conditions the date for completion was accordingly fixed *d* at the first day after the expiration of seven weeks from 30th April 1972 or (since such day was, in fact, a Sunday) the next following working day, namely, 19th June 1972. Completion did not in fact take place on that date, and by letter dated 23rd June 1972, enclosing a notice therewith, Mr Gray's solicitors wrote to Rightside's then solicitors as follows: *e*

'... We have discussed this matter with our client and in the circumstances have agreed that your clients should, despite their actions so far, be given the opportunity to complete the contract. Accordingly we enclose herewith by way of service upon you a notice to complete the transaction in accordance with No. 9 of the Statutory Conditions of Sale. Please acknowledge receipt. We should be grateful if you would request your clients to cease telephoning and calling on *f* our client, who has no desire to discuss the matter. Would you also kindly inform your clients that they are not entitled to have free access to the premises to show prospective sub-purchasers round, and that they should not continue to disturb the tenants of the premises.'

The notice enclosed therewith was in the following terms: *g*

'TO: Rightside Properties Ltd. of 56 Haymarket London SW1 and Messrs. Michael Freeman & Co. of 18 Grosvenor Street London SW1. We the under-signed as solicitors for and on behalf of Bernard Gray of 5 Salem Road London W2 (hereinafter called "the Vendor") hereby give you notice as follows: 1. The Vendor is willing and ready to execute and deliver a transfer to yourselves of *h* the title to the property known as 53 Bassett Road London W10 registered at H.M. Land Registry with Title Absolute under title number LN 156647 which property was contracted to be purchased by you by an agreement made on the 30th day of April 1972 and made between the Vendor of the one part and your-selves of the other part. 2. The said agreement being formed by correspondence between the Vendor and yourselves the Statutory Form of Conditions of Sale 1925 are applicable thereto. 3. You have failed to perform your part of the said agreement in that you have failed to complete the purchase of the said property and the completion date fixed by Condition No. 1 of the said statutory form of Conditions of Sale has passed. 4. The Vendor requires you forthwith to pay the balance of the purchase money together with interest thereon in accordance with the terms of the said agreement. 5. If you fail to comply with this notice

a
within 21 days from the date hereof the Vendor will either rescind the contract or resell the property in accordance with the provisions of the said agreement.'

Then the notice is 'Dated the 23rd day of June 1972' and signed by Mr Gray's solicitors. Rightside did not complete in accordance with the terms of such notice, and after the expiration of the period thereby limited, namely on 20th July 1972, Mr Gray's solicitors wrote to Rightside's then solicitors, making it perfectly clear that Mr Gray

b
regarded contract as no longer in existence. In substance, Mr Gray purported to accept a repudiation by Rightside of the contract between them, and maintained that the contract had accordingly come to an end. For good measure his solicitors added that in view of their actions and omissions so far, it was not reasonable for Rightside to expect the date for completion to be extended beyond the expiry of the notice to complete.

c
If, of course, the notice given by Mr Gray to Rightside to which I have already referred was for any reason bad, this letter of 20th July 1972 was, prima facie, itself a wrongful repudiation of the contract by Mr Gray, which Rightside was entitled, if they were so minded, to accept. They did not, however, do so at once. Indeed, they had, on 29th June 1972, entered into a contract to resell the property to one Leslie Ratcliffe for the sum of £53,000. By a coincidence, on the same 20th July 1972,

d
Mr Ratcliffe's solicitors had written to Rightside's then solicitors asking for authority to inspect the register—the land is, of course, held with a registered title—and such request was one which placed Rightside's solicitors, in the circumstances, in a near inpossible position.

Mr Gray himself was also placed in a difficult situation; he had been counting on receiving the proceeds of sale of 53 Bassett Road in time to enable him to complete

e
a subsequent auction purchase into which he had entered, and the delay in completion had embarrassed him. Neither side, however, at this juncture, knew of the difficulties in which the other had been placed.

Ultimately the present proceedings were commenced by Rightside on 15th December 1972, claiming specific performance of the contract or, alternatively, damages for breach of contract. It is right to record that the statement of claim was only

f
delivered after there had been an application to strike out the action for want of prosecution; but thereafter matters have progressed normally. There is nothing remarkable in the statement of claim, beyond: (a) the usual allegation that Rightside have at all material times been and then were ready and willing to fulfil their obligations under the contract; and (b) an allegation of a collateral oral contract, relating to the affording of access by potential sub-purchasers to 53 Bassett Road, and a breach

g
of that agreement for which damages were claimed.

Mr Gray's defence and counterclaim, as finally amended, pleaded the terms of condition 9 of the statutory conditions of sale, which is in the following form:

h
'(1) If the purchaser shall neglect or fail to perform his part of the contract the vendor may give to the purchaser or to his solicitor at least twenty-one days' notice in writing specifying the breach and requiring the purchaser to make good the default before the expiration of the notice.

'(2) If the purchaser does not comply with the terms of the said notice (a) the deposit money, if any, shall, unless the court otherwise directs, be forfeited to the vendor, or, in the case of settled land, to his Settled Land Act trustees;

j
(b) the vendor may resell the property without previously tendering a conveyance or instrument of transfer to the purchaser; and the following provisions shall apply.

'(3) Any resale may be made, by auction or private contract, at such time, subject to such conditions, and in such manner generally, as the vendor may think proper, and the defaulting purchaser shall have no right to any part of the purchase money thereby arising.'

The defence and counterclaim then continued:

'By letter dated 23 June 1972 [Mr Gray's] solicitors gave notice to [Rightside] pursuant to the said Condition 9 requiring [Rightside] to complete the said contract within 21 days. Wrongfully and in breach of contract [Rightside] failed to comply with the said notice.'

There is then a remarkable plea, as follows:

'6A. Alternatively, [Rightside] are not entitled to equitable relief by reason of the following facts and matters—(a) Notwithstanding that [Rightside] were contractually obliged to purchase 53 Bassett Road London W.10 for the sum of £50,000 [Rightside] by a letter sent to [Mr Gray] and dated 17 June 1972 stated that "we are interested in considering the purchase of your property [meaning the said property]. We would appreciate your writing to us quoting the price required by you . . ." By this letter [Rightside] intended to suggest to [Mr Gray] that no binding contract for the purchase of the said property existed. (b) Notwithstanding that [Rightside] failed to complete the said contract on 19 June 1972 [Rightside] (acting by their agents Arthur Lawrence Agencies Ltd.) wrongfully attempted on 23 June 1972 to collect the rents payable to [Mr Gray] on that day by the tenants of the said property.'

And the conclusion is stated that Rightside are not entitled to the relief claimed or alternatively to equitable relief.

Rightside's reply and defence to counterclaim, as finally amended pursuant to leave given at the hearing, was basically to the effect that the notice actually given did not give Rightside 21 days notice as required by condition 9; and that further or alternatively the period of 21 days thereby limited was, in all the circumstances, unreasonably short. The letter complained of in the defence was admitted, but stated to have been sent in error, and the alleged attempt to collect the rent was denied.

On opening the case for Rightside, counsel at once elected to accept the repudiation of the contract contained in the letter of 20th July 1972 and stated that he was not pressing for specific performance. He also indicated that he was going to take his stand in relation to the disputed condition 9 notice on the simple point that the requirements of that condition had not been complied with, and did not intend to pursue the allegation that in any event a 21 days notice was in all the circumstances of the case too short. The announcement of his intentions came as a surprise to those representing Mr Gray, who had naturally come prepared to deal with all the allegations which were, on the pleadings, in issue. The fact that they had no prior intimation of the course which counsel was proposing to take may well have some effect on the question of costs; counsel for Mr Gray could not, and did not, pretend that any surprise they may have felt put them at any disadvantage in meeting the case which counsel actually presented.

As the case proceeded, therefore, counsel called only one witness, Rightside's former solicitor, Mr Freeman, who was a cautious and impressive witness. The original of the letter of 23rd June 1972 bore his firm's date stamp of '26th June 1972': it was entirely typical of Mr Freeman's caution that he would not swear positively that it did bear his firm's date stamp, since it was a common form of stamp, but only that it bore a stamp in the same form. 26th June 1972 (which was a Monday) was indeed the date which his firm's acknowledgment of the receipt of the notice bore. Mr Freeman deposed to the fact that there were, during the normal working weekdays of Monday to Friday, two posts per day received by his firm. On Saturdays, however, there was only one post, which was markedly smaller than any other post, and which consisted in the main of second class post. He was unable to say whether the notice was received by his firm in the course of the sole Saturday post, or by the Monday's post.

Counsel for Mr Gray called his solicitor, Mr Lavender, who had actually signed, and whose staff were responsible for posting, the letter. Mr Lavender's firm kept no postbook, so it was only possible for him to rely on the general practice of his firm. He undoubtedly proved that the letter was signed by him on Friday, 23rd June, and that, had the settled routine of his firm been followed, the letter would have been put in the post with a first-class stamp late on Friday evening.

It appears to me that the onus of showing that Rightside's solicitor received the notice at any earlier date than 26th June rests fairly and squarely on Mr Gray, and that that onus has not been discharged. Even if I make the assumption most favourable to him that the letter was indeed posted on the Friday night—and it appears to me that when the precise time of delivery and hence of posting is in issue the person who actually put the letter into the pillar box ought to be called—I have no evidence before me as to when in the ordinary course of post the letter would have been delivered. Counsel for Mr Gray indeed urged on me that I could see from Mr Freeman's date stamp on other letters in the bundle before me that letters posted one night were delivered the following day. I entirely accept this, but in all such cases one is dealing with letters posted Monday to Thursday, with delivery Tuesday to Friday. There was no evidence before me as to which post carried these letters —the first or second. Moreover, such evidence as I did have in relation to the ordinary course of post came from Mr Freeman who said, inter alia, that the post on Saturday (on the few occasions when he went into the office on a Saturday, always for specific purposes) was markedly smaller than that on a weekday and differently constituted. Since it can hardly be supposed that the volume of local letters posted on a Friday, and of out-of-town letters posted on a Thursday, differs markedly from the volume of such letters posted on other working days during the week, it appears to me that the only proper inference to be drawn as to the course of post is that the letter in question, with its enclosure, would not have been delivered on the Saturday morning in the ordinary course of post, and was therefore delivered on the Monday.

If this was so, then, of course, there could be no pretence that the notice was a valid notice. But even if I am wrong on the whole of this, it appears to me—and I think was really eventually conceded sub silentio by counsel for Mr Gray—that it makes little difference to the result. The notice of 23rd June 1972 limited a period of 'within 21 days from the date hereof'. If, making the assumption most favourable to Mr Gray, it was in fact delivered on 24th June, the length of the same period, reckoned from 24th June, could only have been 20 days. Hence the notice was, on any footing, too short by at least one day.

I should add that counsel for Rightside made two additional submissions on this point. He first of all submitted that it did not matter at all when the letter enclosing the notice was delivered; what mattered was when, as a matter of ordinary routine, it could be expected that it would be opened by the solicitor. It would, he suggested, be absurd in the extreme if service on a solicitor (as expressly envisaged by condition 9) could be validly effected out of normal working hours; and, whatever may have been the case in the past, Saturday nowadays was not a normal working day for most solicitors. Counsel did not quite put it in this way, but I think he would have drawn a contrast between service on an individual at his own home (permitted, of course, by condition 9) and service on a businessman at his business address, as is the normal case with a solicitor, at which he does not reside.

I am inclined to think that counsel's submission is correct. It is interesting to observe that in *Papillon v Brunton*[1], which was one of the only two cases on this point cited to me, Martin B left it to the jury to say whether the letter there in question arrived at the chambers of the plaintiff's solicitors on 25th March *after business hours,* or on the morning of the 26th. In effect the jury replied that it arrived after the

---

1 (1860) 5 H & N 518

solicitor had left his office, but during business hours. This was the point on which
I think all the judges seized in their judgments. Thus Pollock CB said[1]:

> 'The agent of the landlord said that he was at his chambers until six or seven
> o'clock in the evening of that day, and he did not receive the letter, but he found
> it the next morning when he went there. The jury found that the letter arrived
> on the 25th, after the agent had left; and they said that they thought he ought
> to have had somebody there to receive it. The agent, not having received the
> letter until the morning of the 26th, treated the notice as too late, and this action
> was brought as if the tenancy continued. The question arises whether, under
> these circumstances, the notice was sufficient to determine the tenancy. Now,
> without entering upon a larger discussion than is necessary to dispose of the point
> before us, or saying whether the doctrine with respect to notice of dishonour
> of bills of exchange applies (upon which we give no opinion), we think that in
> the case of a notice to quit the putting it into the post office is sufficient, and
> that the party sending it is not responsible for its miscarriage. As this letter was
> posted in London between nine and ten o'clock in the morning, the probability
> is that it arrived immediately after the agent left his chambers. Indeed it is
> possible that it may have arrived in the due course of post, but by some accident
> was overlooked—either not delivered by the servant to the clerk or in some way
> mislaid. Besides it did not appear that it was not delivered before seven o'clock
> in the evening; and the jury considered that the agent ought to have had some one
> in his chambers at that time. A notice so sent must be considered as having
> reached the agent in due time, and the same consequences must result as if he
> had actually been there and received it. In my opinion the finding of the jury
> was right, and the notice was delivered at the agent's place of business in sufficient
> time to inform him, if he had been there, that the tenancy was to be determined
> at the time specified.'

Bramwell B said[2]:

> 'When the jury say that in their judgment the agent should have had someone
> in his chambers at the time the notice arrived, they in effect say it arrived within
> the ordinary business hours.'

It is true that he adds[2]:

> 'I doubt whether, in the absence of any express limitation by the agent, it is
> necessary that the notice should be given within the hours of business.'

but that is no more than a glancing expression of opinion, not, I think, accepted by
Wilde B, who said[2]:

> 'I am also of opinion that there ought to be no rule. I take the same view as
> my brother Bramwell. The jury have found that the notice arrived at the agent's
> place of business at a time when some one ought to have been there to receive it.'

Martin B concurred.

It would seem to me to be the height of absurdity if a notice, whose function is
always to draw some fact to the attention of another party, for action or information,
could be served at a time when it would, as a matter of ordinary routine, be utterly
impossible for it to convey any information to anyone.

Counsel for Rightside's second point here was that condition 9 requires a period
of 'at least 21 days' and that this was not in any event satisfied by giving a notice
requiring something to be done 'within 21 days' from the date of the service of the

---

1 (1860) 5 H & N at 521, 522
2 5 H & N at 522

a notice, as the formula 'at least' indicated that the period allowed must be exclusive of both the day of service and the day of expiry of the notice. Here he relied on *Re Hector Whaling Ltd*[1], and distinguished the case cited by counsel for Mr Gray, *Schnabel v Allard*[2], on two grounds. First, that that case was exclusively concerned with the law of landlord and tenant, where the law as to length of notice had been fixed for a very long time, and, second, on the ground that where the notice required an act

b to be performed—here completion—unless the first and the last day were both excluded, the person to whom notice was given would not have the full period in question within which to perform the act, since nobody would suppose, as a matter of business, that it could be performed at, literally, the 23rd hour of the day. I am only putting, I think, in less felicitous language the words of Alderson B in *Young v Higgon*[3], where he says:

c 'I am of the same opinion, that the rule ought to be made absolute; on the simple principle, that where there is given to a party a certain space of time to do some act, which space of time is included between two other acts to be done by another person, both the days of doing those acts ought to be excluded, in order to ensure to him *the whole* [and those two words are italicised in the report] of that space of time.'

d In *Re Railway Sleepers Supply Co*[4], a case which itself adopts the same approach, these words were approved.

For all the foregoing reasons I think it is plain that the notice enclosed with the letter of 23rd June 1972 was wholly invalid for any purpose. Counsel for Mr Gray, after I had intimated that, in my view, having regard to the terms of para 6 of his

e defence and counterclaim, it was not open to him to take the point without amendment, initially applied for leave to amend his pleadings so as to plead in the alternative that the notice enclosed with that letter was given under the general law, and not under condition 9 at all. Counsel for Rightside thereupon, in my view correctly, urged that if leave was given it could only be on terms involving an adjournment to be paid for by Mr Gray, in that Rightside was not prepared with any evidence as to

f what would have been a reasonable time for such a notice, since such a point did not arise on the pleadings in view of the way he had presented his case. When I intimated that I agreed with this submission, counsel for Mr Gray, after taking time to consider, ultimately did not make any such application for amendment.

I would, however, make it clear that, so far as I can see, such amendment, even if allowed, would have done his case no conceivable good whatsoever. In the first

g place, it is to be observed that the covering letter of 23rd June speaks of the enclosed notice as 'a notice to complete the transaction in accordance with No. 9 of the Statutory Conditions of Sale'. I think Mr Gray must be bound by his own solicitors' description of the notice they were serving on his behalf; if not, the notice was a 'tricky' notice, and effect would not be given to it in equity at all. Secondly, the contractual time for completion was 19th June, and the notice was sent only four days thereafter.

h I am wholly unaware of any case in which a notice under the general law served such a short time after the expiration of the contractual date for completion has ever been held to be good. It is not merely delay in performing the obligation of completion, but unreasonable delay therein which entitles the other party to make time of the essence of the contract. I do not consider four days delay to have been unreasonable delay on any view of the case. Thirdly, the submission of counsel for Mr Gray involves the proposition that in spite of the terms of condition 9 it was

j nevertheless open to Mr Gray to serve, under the general law, a notice having the

---

1 [1936] Ch 208, [1935] All ER Rep 302
2 [1966] 3 All ER 816, [1967] 1 QB 627
3 (1840) 6 M & W 49 at 54, cf [1835-42] All ER Rep 278 at 280
4 (1885) 29 Ch D 204

like effect to a notice under condition 9, but of shorter length. This appears to me
a totally astonishing proposition, and one which only has to be stated at length to be
seen to be wrong.

Accordingly, putting the service of this notice entirely on one side, counsel for Rightside says that the position here is simple. This is a case in which time never became
of the essence of the contract, nor was there ever any such unreasonable delay on
the part of Rightside as would amount to repudiative dealy on their part. Hence,
the contract was still in being when, on 20th July, Mr Gray repudiated it; such
repudiation discharged Rightside from any obligation which might otherwise have
rested on them to perform any conditions precedent on their part, such as proving
their ability and readiness to pay the purchase money; they have finally accepted
the repudiation, which has not been, as it might have been, withdrawn in the meantime, and they are accordingly entitled to damages for fundamental breach by Mr
Gray of the contract.

Counsel for Mr Gray, however, says that this is far too simple a way of looking at
the matter. He starts from the fundamental proposition that, at law—as distinct
from the position in equity—time is of the essence of the date for completion. I
should here add straightaway that this proposition is, on the specific terms of this
contract, denied by counsel for Rightside, and to this I shall have to return later; for
the moment I shall assume that the general proposition does apply to this contract.

The result is, says counsel for Mr Gray, that when Rightside failed to complete on
19th June 1972 they fundamentally breached the contract. Of course, in equity the
position was somewhat different. They could still obtain, in effect, relief from their
fundamental breach if they had not disentitled themselves from claiming the equitable remedy of specific performance. But it was only if they were in a position to
claim this remedy that they could obtain any relief. Accordingly, his analysis of the
position was that: (a) by failure to complete on 19th June Rightside had repudiated
their obligations under the contract; (b) by the terms of his letter of 20th July Mr
Gray accepted that repudiation, and this brought the contract to an end; but (c)
subject to Rightside being able to show that they were entitled to specific performance
—presumably as at the date when the letter of 20th July was sent—in which case
it would be Mr Gray and not Rightside who had repudiated the contract. And that
involved, said counsel for Mr Gray, Rightside showing that, either on 19th June
or within a reasonable time thereafter, it was ready, willing and able to perform its
part of the contract.

Counsel for Mr Gray conceded that at first sight that was not the effect of the
Law of Property Act 1925, s 41, which reads as follows:

'Stipulations in a contract, as to time or otherwise, which according to rules
of equity are not deemed to be or to have become of the essence of the contract,
are also construed and have effect at law in accordance with the same rules.'

But he said that that proposition as the law of the land was established by the
decision in two cases, one in the House of Lords, to which I must now turn. They
were both decisions on s 25 of the Supreme Court of Judicature Act 1873 but nothing
turns on this as the language is virtually identical to s 41 of the 1925 Act.

The first is *Howe v Smith*[1]. This was an action brought originally for specific
performance of an agreement to sell certain property and, by later amendment,
for a return of the deposit in the alternative. It was found as a fact that the purchaser,
by his persistent delay, had precluded himself from insisting on the completion
of the contract, i e he had, by his delay, repudiated it. In the present case there is
not, and so far as I can see could not possibly have been, any such allegation on the
part of Mr Gray. Fry LJ said this[2]:

---

1   (1884) 27 Ch D 89, [1881-85] All ER Rep 201
2   27 Ch D at 103, [1881-85] All ER Rep at 209

a

'The 25th section of the *Judicature Act, 1873*, enacted that stipulations in contracts as to time, which would not before the passing of the Act have been deemed to be of the essence of such contracts in a Court of Equity, should receive in all Courts the same construction and effect as they would theretofore have received in equity. The effect of this clause is, in my opinion, that the purchaser seeking damages is no longer obliged to prove his willingness and readiness to complete

b

on the day named, but may still recover if he can prove such readiness and willingness within a reasonable time after the stipulated day; and the inquiry therefore arises whether the purchaser in the present case could aver and prove such readiness and willingness within a reasonable time.'

Now as I read those words, with which it would be presumptuous of me to say I entirely agree, it appears to me that they fit in exactly and precisely with my own

c

understanding of s 41. If I expand s 41, as I understand it, in relation to a case such as the present, it would read something along the following lines: 'The date fixed for completion by the contract is not to be taken to be one of which time is of the essence; it is to be taken to mean that completion is to take place by that date, or within a reasonable time thereafter. Accordingly, there is no fundamental breach by a party who cannot or does not complete on the day fixed for completion, pro-

d

vided he completes or is ready to complete within a reasonable time thereafter.' In a case, therefore, where there has been no repudiation by the vendor, but, on the contrary, by the purchaser, the words of Fry LJ in my opinion follow quite logically and consistently from the provisions of s 41.

Fry LJ's words, however, were approved by Lord Atkinson in *Stickney v Keeble*[1]. This case was one for the return of a deposit by a purchaser who, after intolerable

e

delays on the part of the vendor, had given a fairly peremptory notice to complete. It was held that, given the preceding conduct of the vendor, the notice to complete was not too short, and on that ground there was no answer to his claim. But the vendor had, after the action for the return of the deposit had been commenced, sold the property, so that he could not have given specific performance of the contract if requested. It is to be noted that it was not requested. Now as I read the speeches

f

in the House, the only Law Lord who dealt with Fry LJ's judgment was Lord Atkinson, and he dealt with it as follows[2]:

'Fry L.J. alone amongst the learned Lords Justices dealt with the question whether under s. 25 sub-s. (7), of the Judicature Act, 1873, the rule of law, as distinguished from the rule in equity, still prevails, and came to the conclusion[3]

g

that the effect of the sub-section is that a purchaser seeking damages need no longer prove his readiness and willingness to complete on the day named, but may still recover if he can prove his readiness and willingness to complete within a reasonable time after that day. The same rule would, of course, apply to the case of a vendor suing for damages. If this decision be right, as I am inclined to think it is, the law laid down in [two cases[4] to which he refers] is to this extent

h

modified.'

Again, it appears to me that this is all fully in line with what I venture to call the plain meaning of s 41. Apart from various expressions of approval of his judgment generally, by Earl Loreburn and Lord Mersey, the only lord who adopted a different approach, as an alternative, was Lord Parker of Waddington, and he said this[5]:

j

---

1 [1915] AC 386 at 404, [1914-15] All ER Rep 73 at 79
2 [1915] AC at 404, [1914-15] All ER Rep at 79
3 (1884) 27 Ch D at 103, [1881-85] All ER Rep at 209
4 *Tilley v Thomas* (1867) 3 Ch App 61; *Noble v Edwardes* (1877) 5 Ch D 378
5 [1915] AC at 415-417, [1914-15] All ER Rep at 80-82

'My Lords, in a contract for the sale and purchase of real estate, the time fixed *a*
by the parties for completion has at law always been regarded as essential. In
other words, Courts of law have always held the parties to their bargain in this
respect, with the result that if the vendor is unable to make a title by the day
fixed for completion, the purchaser can treat the contract as at an end and recover
his deposit with interest and the costs of investigating the title. In such cases,
however, equity having a concurrent jurisdiction did not look upon the stipula- *b*
tion as to time in precisely the same light. Where it could do so without injustice
to the contracting parties it decreed specific performance notwithstanding failure
to observe the time fixed by the contract for completion, and as an incident
of specific performance relieved the party in default by restraining proceedings
at law based on such failure. This is really all that is meant by and involved in the
maxim that in equity the time fixed for completion is not of the essence of the *c*
contract, but this maxim never had any application to cases in which the stipulation as to time could not be disregarded without injustice to the parties, when,
for example, the parties, for reasons best known to themselves, had stipulated
that the time fixed should be essential, or where there was something in the
nature of the property or the surrounding circumstances which would render it
inequitable to treat it as a non-essential term of the contract. It should be observed, *d*
too, that it was only for the purposes of granting specific performance that equity
in this class of case interfered with the remedy at law. A vendor who had put
it out of his own power to complete the contract, or had by his conduct lost the
right to specific performance, had no equity to restrain proceedings at law
based on the non-observance of the stipulation as to time. My Lords, this is an
action by a purchaser for return of his deposit and other relief, based upon the *e*
failure by the vendor to observe the stipulation as to the date of completion,
and it will, I think, tend to simplicity if the matter be first considered irrespective
of the changes introduced by the Judicature Acts. Prior to these Acts the vendor
could have only obtained relief from the consequences of his failure by filing
a bill for specific performance and for an injunction restraining the action. On
such a bill he could have obtained no relief unless he were himself able and *f*
willing to make a title to the purchaser. It appears, however, that almost immediately after the institution of the action the vendor had put it out of his power to
complete the sale by reselling the property to a third party, and under these
circumstances there could be no question of specific performance, and, therefore,
no injunction restraining the action. It seems to me that on this ground alone
the bill must have failed. An injunction, if granted, would not have been incident
to, and in aid of, the equitable remedy of specific performance, but a means of *g*
enabling the vendor to forfeit the purchaser's deposit, in other words, to exercise
a right which, if it existed at all, was a legal right, and this would be contrary
to the principles upon which the Court of Chancery has always acted. Counsel for
the respondents in effect admitted this, but relied on s. 25, sub-s. 7, of the Judicature Act, 1873, [which he then quotes.] They argued that under this section it is
only necessary to consider whether, at the date of the institution of the action, time *h*
would in equity have been considered of the essence, and that the subsequent
act of the vendor, whereby he put it out of his power specifically to perform the
contract, was immaterial. My Lords, I cannot give to the section in question the
interpretation for which the respondents contend. It means, in my opinion, that
where equity would prior to the Act have, for the purposes of decreeing its own
remedies, disregarded a stipulation as to time and restrained an action at law *j*
based on the breach thereof, the Courts constituted by the Act are for the purpose
of giving common law relief to disregard it in like manner. In considering whether
it would give relief by restraining proceedings at law the Court of Chancery
took cognizance of everything which had happened up to the date of the decree,
and in applying s. 25, sub-s. 7, of the Act, everything up to the date of judgment,

ought, in my opinion, to be similarly taken into account. The section cannot in my opinion mean that the rules as to time laid down by Courts of Equity in certain cases, for certain purposes, and under certain circumstances only, shall be applied generally and without inquiry whether the particular case, purpose, or circumstances are such that equity would have applied the rules. If since the Judicature Acts the Court is asked to disregard a stipulation as to time in an action for common law relief, and it be established that equity would not under the then existing circumstances have prior to the Act granted specific performance or restrained the action, the section can, in my opinion, have no application, otherwise the stipulation in question would not, as provided in the section, receive the same effect as it would prior to the Act have received in equity.'

Now it is to be observed that Lord Parker[1] stated very clearly what the nature of the action with which he was dealing was, in these words:

'... this is an action by a purchaser for return of his deposit and other relief, based upon the failure by the vendor to observe the stipulation as to the date of completion ...'

In these circumstances, the vendor being himself in default and having put it out of his power to perform the contract, Lord Parker says that he cannot offer any resistance to the claim for a return of the deposit. In the circumstances of that case, the statement appears quite sensible and straightforward. What the vendor was saying to the purchaser was: 'You must wait for completion, which will take place later, but because you have not been prepared to wait you must suffer the forfeiture of your deposit, even although, after you sued for the return of your deposit, I put it completely out of my power to complete—ever.' It is not surprising that Lord Parker says that equity would not countenance such procedure on the part of the vendor, and that it is certainly not to be presumed to be authorised by s 41 of the Law of Property Act 1925.

If, however, this doctrine is to be wrenched out of context, and sought to be applied to any kind of case other than the precise case before their Lordships, I think considerable caution has to be exercised, and I think that in consequence the law reporter's cautious 'semble' in the headnote is fully justified. Let us go back to *Howe v Smith*[2] and imagine that all the facts were the same, save and except that there had been an initial failure by the vendor to complete on the day fixed—but no more than a temporary delay, of which he had given the purchaser notice, so that he was in fact unaware that even if he himself had been willing to complete on that day the purchaser would not have been. Could it nevertheless have made any difference to the result of that case? The vendor had there (i) fundamentally breached the contract at law, and (ii) had disposed of the property after the commencement of an action which became an action for the return of the deposit. But I venture to think that the result would have been precisely the same.

I think, therefore, that, in any case in which the facts are not on all fours with those in *Stickney v Keeble*[3], what must be applied is the wide principle laid down by Lord Parker[4], which I will read once more:

'My Lords, I cannot give to the section in question the interpretation for which the respondents contend. It means, in my opinion, that where equity would prior to the Act have, for the purposes of decreeing its own remedies, disregarded a stipulation as to time and restrained an action at law based on the breach thereof, the Courts constituted by the Act are for the purpose of giving common law relief to disregard it in like manner.'

---

1 [1915] AC at 416, [1914-15] All ER at 81
2 (1884) 27 Ch D 89, [1881-85] All ER Rep 210
3 [1915] AC 386, [1914-15] All ER Rep 73
4 [1915] AC at 417, [1914-15] All ER Rep at 81

Applying this principle, can there be any equitable reason why, in a case where, at
a time before the purchaser becomes in unreasonable delay beyond the date fixed
for completion—for that is the case here—the vendor repudiates the contract, the
purchaser should not simply accept such repudiation as discharging him from all
further performance under the contract, including that of preparing for completion,
which ex hypothesi will now never take place? I think that in such a case equity
must simply follow the law, and cannot be so esoteric as to place on the purchaser the
burden of showing that, ex hypothesi at a time after repudiation, he was in a position
to complete the contract which it was then quite certain would never be completed.

Indeed, I think that this accords with what Lord Parker himself, when a judge at
first instance, had said expressly in relation to a contract for the sale of land in *Re
Bayley-Worthington and Cohen's Contract*[1]:

> 'The next question is whether the delay in completion was due to this default.
> The purchaser points out that the vendors were under the contract bound to
> commute or discharge certain duties before the day fixed for completion, and
> that admittedly they had not commuted or discharged those duties by February
> 28, 1908. He therefore contends that even if he had raised no objection to title he
> would not have been bound to complete at any time prior to February 28, 1908.
> The vendors, on the other hand, argue that when the purchaser on July 20, 1907,
> issued his originating summons he, in effect, repudiated the contract and relieved
> them from proceeding with the commutation and discharge of the duties until
> January 30, 1908, the date of the judgment of the House of Lords, and that after
> that date they were entitled to the same period during which they could commute
> or discharge the duties as they would have had if the contract had never been
> repudiated, that, is a period equal to the interval between July 20 and September
> 2, 1907. The question is as to the real cause of the delay, and if the conduct of the
> vendors in not proceeding with the commutation or the discharge of the duties
> was the natural consequence of the default of the purchaser in insisting on an
> untenable objection to title, it cannot lie in the purchaser's mouth to say that such
> conduct was the real cause of the delay. In my opinion the repudiation of the con-
> tract by the purchaser relieved the vendors during such time as the purchaser
> insisted on repudiation from proceeding with their part of the bargain . . . In
> other words, the conduct of the vendors in this respect was the natural consequence
> of the repudiation and cannot prevent me from holding that the repudiation was
> the real cause of the delay in completion. It was said, however, that by no possi-
> bility could the vendors have commuted the duties by September 2, seeing that
> they actually took from January 30, 1908, till September in the same year in
> arranging for such commutation. I do not consider that it is open to the Court
> to speculate on what would have happened if the purchaser had not been guilty
> of default . . .'

That passage was, indeed, expressly approved by Lord Atkinson in *British and Beningtons Ltd v North Western Cachar Tea Co Ltd*[2] in the House of Lords.

In my judgment, in equity as well as at common law, the wrongful repudiation by
one party of his obligations under the contract entitles the other to accept such
repudiation, and thereby put an end to the contract, and such other is, as a
consequence, discharged from performing any conditions precedent which it would
otherwise fall on him to discharge. I think this is made perfectly clear in the speech
of Lord Campbell CJ in *Cort v Ambergate etc Railway Co*[3]. This is a case in which there
was a contract in relation to the supply of railway chairs. Lord Campbell CJ says[4]:

---

1 [1909] 1 Ch 648 at 664, 665
2 [1923] AC 48 at 66, [1922] All ER Rep 224 at 232
3 (1851) 17 QB 127
4 17 QB at 143, 144

a   'The defendants contend that, as the plaintiffs did not make and tender the residue of the chairs, they cannot be said to have been ready and willing to perform the contract; that the defendants cannot be charged with a breach of it; that, after the notice from the defendants, which in truth amounted to a declaration that they had broken and thenceforward renounced the contract, the plaintiffs, if they wished to have any redress, were bound to buy the requisite quantity

b   of the peculiar sort of iron suited for these railway chairs, to make the whole of them according to the pattern, with the name of the Company upon them, and to bring them to the appointed places of delivery and tender them to the defendants, who, from insolvency, had abandoned the completion of the line for which the chairs were intended, desiring that no more chairs might be made, and declaring, in effect, that no more should be accepted or paid for. We are of opinion,

c   however, that the jury were fully justified upon the evidence in finding that the plaintiffs were ready and willing to perform the contract, although they never made and tendered the residue of the chairs. In common sense the meaning of such an averment of *readiness and willingness* must be that the noncompletion of the contract was not the fault of the plaintiffs, and that they were disposed and able to complete it if it had not been renounced by the defendants. What more

d   can reasonably be required by the parties for whom the goods are to be manufactured? If, having accepted a part, they are unable to pay for the residue, and have resolved not to accept them, no benefit can accrue to them from a useless waste of materials and labour, which might possibly enhance the amount of damages to be awarded against them.'

e   This again is a passage approved in the speech of Lord Atkinson in *British and Beningtons Ltd v North Western Cachar Tea Co Ltd*[1].

Of course, in the present case the repudiation was not accepted at once: Rightside kept the contract open. Equally, however, there was at all times until, and there was persisted in during, the trial, a wrongful repudiation. It appears to me that in consequence Rightside was never at any time under any obligation to show that it was

f   'able' to perform its part of the contract. 'Ability', in this connection, means arranging the finance, which, under modern conditions, could be done either by arranging a mortgage or a sub-sale, and doubtless there are other methods as well. But they all involve some form of preparation on the part of the person raising the finance; and it appears to me pessimi exempli if the vendor was in a position to say: 'Because you were not on a particular day ready with your finance, you cannot claim damages against me. True it is that it would have been perfectly useless for you to make the

g   preparations because I told you I was not going to complete, but I can now huff you for having failed to carry out this perfectly useless exercise'. This is the morality of a game, not of a serious legal contest.

But even if I am wrong in my conclusions on this point, it is surely only at the 'material' time(s) that the purchaser must be ready with his finance. One of such times

h   must have been the time when completion ought to have taken place. It appears to me that it is sufficient for Rightside to point to the fact that they had entered into a valid contract for the sub-sale of the property, whose time for completion in fact spanned the time for completion of the contract actually here in question. It is perfectly true that no evidence has been given as to the purchaser's financial position, but the solicitor who dealt with the contract on behalf of Rightside gave evidence,

j   and no single question challenging the effectiveness of the contract was put to him.

Had Rightside claimed specific performance, I think the trial would then have been another 'material time' and Rightside might have had to show their financial ability to complete at that date. But, as they elected the other way, the date of the trial cannot, in my judgment, be material for this purpose.

---

1   [1923] AC 48, [1922] All ER Rep 224

It is, I think, interesting to observe that the only grounds pleaded in the defence as
justifying the refusal of equitable relief to Rightside are those contained in para 6A
which I have already read. The allegation in sub-para (a) that the letter was sent was,
of course, admitted: but how what was quite obviously on the face of it a stupid error,
however disturbing to Mr Gray, could justify a denial of the relief of specific performance was never—wisely as I think—attempted to be explained to me by counsel
for Mr Gray. Some evidence was tendered with regard to the allegation in relation
to the attempted collection of rents under para 6A(b), but whatever the true explanation of the incident proved may be (and counsel for Rightside, correctly from his
standpoint, did not attempt to proffer one), it certainly involved no element of
dishonesty, concealment, deception, or anything else which could be classed as
inequitable conduct leading to a court of equity refusing such relief.

This is not quite the end of the matter, because, as I indicated above, counsel for
Rightside submitted that, even at common law, time was not of the essence of the
date for completion. That is simply to say that, on the true construction of the co-
tract, the date for completion was not of the essence. The true enquiry—since construction as distinct from the effect given to a stipulation does not differ at law and in
equity—is as to the effect which the parties have agreed a failure to complete on the
day fixed for completion is to have. Is it a fundamental term of the contract, subject
to the saving hand of equity, or is it to be a merely venial breach, not in any sense
fundamental? In my judgment, counsel for Rightside was correct in submitting that
it is the latter. The provisions of condition 9 are, in my judgment, only intelligible on
such a basis, for they do no more than provide for the consequences of a fundamental
breach after—and hence *only* after—the service of such a notice as is thereby envisaged.
I therefore come to the conclusion that there never was here such a breach by Rightside as would have been equivalent to a fundamental breach of the contract, even
apart from the doctrines of equity, so that in any event the doctrine enunciated by
Lord Parker would never be applicable until at any rate after service of the appropriate
notice.

Accordingly, I conclude that Rightside are entitled to the damages they claim for
Mr Gray's wrongful fundamental breach of contract by repudiation. As I understand
the position with regard to the calculation of damages in an action in the Chancery
Division, the rule is that the plaintiff (or counterclaiming defendant) must show *some*
damage arising to him from whatever it is he is complaining of. Thereupon, the
damages will automatically be referred to an enquiry. In a very plain and simple
case, the judge may deal with the matter then and there. In an exceedingly complicated case he may reserve the enquiry to himself. Normally, however, the question of
damages will be referred to an enquiry before the master. The main virtue of this
general procedure is, of course, that it absolves both parties from the necessity of
coming armed with elaborate evidence which, in the event, may be unnecessary.

I accordingly propose to refer the question of quantum of damages for enquiry by
the master. I propose to say no more on this matter than that it was apparent from
exchanges between counsel that the question of the proper measure of damages in
the present case, including the question of possible mitigation, is far from simple, and
it may well be that the master will think fit that the rival contentions should be properly pleaded before he commences his enquiry. That, however, is no more than a
suggestion: I do not intend to fetter his hands in any way.

Judgment for Rightside; enquiry into damages ordered.

Solicitors: *Randall, Rose & Co* (for Rightside); *Allen & Son* (for Mr Gray).

Jacqueline Metcalfe　Barrister.

a

Shaw v Vauxhall Motors Ltd

COURT OF APPEAL, CIVIL DIVISION
LORD DENNING MR, BUCKLEY AND ORMROD LJJ
13th MAY 1974

b
Discovery – Production of documents – Production before commencement of proceedings – Claim in respect of personal injuries – Discretion – Circumstances in which discovery should be ordered – Duty of proposed plaintiff to set out in writing nature of allegation so as to show documents might be material to claim – Legally aided plaintiff – Desirability of early disclosure which might affect continuance of claim – Likelihood of documents showing whether substantial prospect of success – Discovery likely to assist in disposing fairly of dispute or
c
result in saving of costs – Administration of Justice Act 1970, s 31 – RSC Ord 24, r 8.

While the applicant was driving a truck at work his foot came off the pedal, a braking device. The truck should have stopped but did not do so and in consequence the applicant was crushed against a wall. The applicant instructed solicitors to write to
d
his employers on his behalf. The solicitors made general allegations that there was an unsafe system of work, that the employers had failed to provide safe machinery etc, but in a later telephone conversation with the employers the solicitors gave a general description of the nature of the accident alleging that the truck was defective and that a number of men had complained of difficulty in operating it. The applicant obtained legal aid limited to getting an engineer's report on the truck, and counsel's opinion. The engineer inspected the truck but could not detect any defect. Counsel advised
e
that before further legal aid was sought records of complaints made about the truck and relating to its inspection, maintenance and repair should be disclosed by the employers. The employers refused to disclose those records and the applicant applied for discovery under s 31[a] of the Administration of Justice Act 1970. The affidavit in support of the application alleged that one of the causes of the accident was the defective condition of the pedal braking device. The registrar ordered discovery
f
under s 31 but on appeal the judge refused to order discovery thereunder on the ground that the affidavit had indicated that there might be complaints other than that the truck was defective which would have to be investigated and that therefore RSC Ord 24, r 8, applied, since discovery of the records was not necessary for disposing of the cause or matter or for saving costs. The applicant appealed to the Court of Appeal. That court was informed that there was only one cause of complaint, i e that
g
the truck was defective; and that if the records showed that the truck was in good condition and had been properly maintained the proceedings would be discontinued with the consequent saving of costs. It was common ground that the application fell within the scope of s 31. On appeal,

h
Held – In the exercise of its discretion under s 31 the court should order discovery of the records before commencement of the proceedings for the following reasons—
(i) Discovery of documents might properly be ordered under s 31 provided that the proposed plaintiff had set out in writing the nature of his allegations and that information showed that the documents might be material to his claim, and (per Buckley LJ) provided also that he satisfied the court, in accordance with RSC Ord
j
24, r 8 (which applied to applications under s 31), that the discovery would, or would be likely to, assist in disposing fairly of the dispute or would result in the saving of costs (see p 1188 *b* and *j* to p 1189 *a* and *g h*, post).
(ii) Where the proposed plaintiff was legally aided the court should bear in mind that it was in the public interest that there should be early disclosure under s 31

---

a Section 31 is set out at p 1187 *e* to *g*, post

of documents which might affect the bringing or continuance of proceedings with   *a*
legal aid for it was undesirable that proceedings should be brought or continued
with legal aid beyond the point at which it was reasonably clear that the plaintiff
had got no substantial prospect of success (see p 1188 *c* and *f*, p 1189 *a* to *c* and p 1190 *b*,
post).

(iii) So far as the applicant's case was concerned, the information given to the court,
and in the telephone conversation, had sufficiently indicated the nature of the appli-   *b*
cant's allegation. On the information given to the court it was proper that an order
should be made under s 31 having regard to the fact that there would be a substantial
saving of costs if the records showed that the truck was in good condition and properly
maintained, and that the applicant was legally aided. Accordingly the appeal would
be allowed (see p 1188 *f* and *g*, p 1189 *c* to *f*, and p 1190 *a* to *c*, post).

Notes   *c*
For discovery before commencement of proceedings, see Supplement to 12 Halsbury's
Laws (3rd Edn) para 2A.

For the Administration of Justice Act 1970, s 31, see 40 Halsbury's Statutes (3rd
Edn) 1101.

Case referred to in judgments   *d*
Dunning v Board of Governors of the United Liverpool Hospitals [1973] 2 All ER 454,
  [1973] 1 WLR 586, CA.

Case also cited
Probatina Shipping Co Ltd v Sun Insurance Office Ltd [1974] 2 All ER 478, [1974] 2 WLR
  666, CA.   *e*

Interlocutory appeal
The applicant, Raymond Peter Shaw, pursuant to leave of Kilner Brown J, appealed
against an order made by the judge on 7th December 1973, whereby he refused to
make an order for the discovery of documents under s 31 of the Administration of
Justice Act 1970, and allowed the appeal of the respondents, Vauxhall Motors Ltd,   *f*
against the order of Mr District Registrar O T Williams made on 31st October 1973
in the Chester District Registry. The applicant asked for an order restoring the registrar's order that, pursuant to RSC Ord 24, r 7A, the respondents should disclose (a)
all those documents known as 'AVO forms' relating to a Clark Electric Fork Lift
Truck Model NR 70 (numbered CR 74 by the respondents) made between 13th
January 1969 and 13th January 1972; (b) all documents, books or records made from,   *g*
of, or with the aid of the AVO forms relating to the fork lift truck between those
dates, and (c) all documents, books or records made by the respondents, their servants
or agents relating to the inspection, overhaul, maintenance and other work performed
on the fork lift truck between those dates. The facts are set out in the judgment
of Lord Denning MR.

   h

T P Russell QC and *Michael Kershaw* for the applicant.
Piers Ashworth QC and *Ronald Livesey* for the respondents.

LORD DENNING MR. Section 31 of the Administration of Justice Act 1970 gives
a new power to the courts. It enables a person, before he brings an action, to apply
to the court for discovery of documents.   *j*

This is an ordinary personal injury case. The applicant, Mr Shaw, on 30th January
1971 was driving a fork lift truck at the works of the respondents, Vauxhall Motors
Ltd ('the employers'). He says that the braking system of the truck was defective
and as a result the truck crushed him against a wall of the factory. The truck has
'a dead man's pedal'. It is so designed that, if the driver takes his foot off the pedal,
or by some mischance, his foot comes off the pedal, the truck should stop at once.

a It only goes at six miles an hour. So if the device works, a man is in no danger. In the present case Mr Shaw said that, by some mischance, his foot came off the 'dead man's pedal'; but the truck did not stop and he got crushed against the wall.

He instructed solicitors to write on his behalf. The insurance company asked for particulars. His solicitors made general allegations of unsafe system of work, failure to provide safe machinery, and so forth. But they gave no details in the beginning.
b Later in a telephone conversation on 8th December 1971 his solicitors did give a general description of the nature of the accident. They said that the machine was defective and that a number of men had complained of difficulty in operating it.

The plaintiff sought legal aid. It was granted so as to authorise getting an engineer's report on the machine; and also an opinion. There was no difficulty as to the engineer's inspection. That is expressly authorised to be had before action brought:
c see s 21 of the Administration of Justice Act 1969. So the engineer had an inspection and made a report[1]. But counsel advised something more. He wanted to see the various reports which had been made about this machine. The solicitors accordingly asked the employers to disclose the 'AVO forms'[2]. Those are forms in which complaints are recorded. They asked the employers to disclose their records as to the inspection of the machine, and maintenance and repairs done to it, or any records
d relating to it. They asked for those documents for the two years before the accident and the one year after it. The employers declined. The solicitors applied to the district registrar under s 31 of the 1970 Act. They wanted to see these documents before they went again to the legal aid committee. They say—and it has now been confirmed by counsel before us today—that if the records show that this machine was well inspected and maintained and repaired, it may well mean that the action
e will not proceed. Section 31 provides:

'On the application, in accordance with rules of court, of a person who appears to the High Court to be likely to be a party to subsequent proceedings in that court in which a claim in respect of personal injuries to a person or in respect of a person's death is likely to be made, the High Court shall, in such circumstances as may be specified in the rules, have power to order a person who appears
f to the court to be likely to be a party to the proceedings and to be likely to have or to have had in his possession, custody or power any documents which are relevant to an issue arising or likely to arise out of that claim—(*a*) to disclose whether those documents are in his possession, custody or power; and (*b*) to produce to the applicant such of those documents as are in his possession, custody or power.'

We have already had one case on that section. It was *Dunning v Board of Governors*
g *of the United Liverpool Hospitals*[3]. It concerned the words 'likely to be made'. It was held that they meant 'may' or 'may well be made', dependent on the outcome of the discovery. One of the objects of the section is to enable the plaintiff to find out before he starts proceedings whether he has a good cause of action or not. That object would be defeated if he had to show in advance that he already had a good cause of action before he saw the documents. That reasoning applies to the present
h case. If the reports did show a want of proper maintenance or repair of this truck, an action would no doubt be brought. Whereas if they show that there was proper maintenance and repair, an action would not be brought.

But Winn LJ's Committee[4] seem to have taken the view that such reports as those sought here should not be disclosed before action brought. In para 366 of their report they said:

j '*After, but not before, delivery of a statement of claim* all records in the possession or control of a defendant, which reveal what repairs or modifications may have

---

1 The engineer reported that he could not detect any defect in the truck
2 'Avoid verbal orders' forms
3 [1973] 2 All ER 454, [1973] 1 WLR 586
4 Report of the Committee on Personal Injuries Litigation, July 1968, Cmnd 3691, p 103

been made to machinery or other plant or premises involved in the relevant   *a*
accident and any earlier accidents, should be disclosed voluntarily or under an
order.'

So the committee thought the disclosure should not be until *after* writ issued and
statement of claim delivered. I can understand why the committee took that view.
They did not want a plaintiff to have a free run over the reports before he set out his
case. But I would not myself postpone the disclosure to so late a time. All that should   *b*
be required is that the potential plaintiff should set out in an open letter in general
terms his own knowledge, however vague, of how his accident happened. If he does
so, and gives information which shows that the reports may well be material, then
I think the court may properly order disclosure of them before action brought.
That should I think be the general practice. It enables each side to know the strength
or weakness of the case before embarking on litigation. It is particularly useful in   *c*
a legal aid case, because it gives the solicitors and counsel better material on which
to advise.

In this case the letters did not give all the particulars that could be desired; but
the affidavit in support of the application did give a considerable amount of
information. On it the registrar made an order for discovery under s 31.

On appeal Kilner Brown J refused to order discovery. He thought the case came   *d*
within RSC Ord 24, r 8, which states the principle that the court—

'shall in any case refuse to make such an order if and so far as it is of opinion
that discovery is not necessary either for disposing fairly of the cause or matter
or for saving costs.'
                                                                                          e
The judge thought that rule applied in this case. He did it because it was indicated
in an affidavit that Mr Shaw might make other causes of complaint which would
have to be investigated anyway. So the judge thought that discovery should take
place in the ordinary course. But the position has been made clear before us. Counsel
for Mr Shaw has told us that Mr Shaw has only one cause of complaint, namely,
that this machine was defective; and furthermore that, if the reports show that the   *f*
machine was in good condition and that it was properly maintained, the legal
advisers would not feel able to recommend to the legal aid fund a continuance of
the proceedings. The claim would no longer be proceeded with. That would be a
great saving in costs. On this new information which has been given to us, it does
seem proper that an order should be made under s 31 for further discovery of the
documents in the application. I would allow the appeal accordingly.   *g*

BUCKLEY LJ. It is common ground between the parties that this is a case which
falls within the scope of s 31 of the Administration of Justice Act 1970; and that
section confers on the court a discretion which is not fettered by the terms of the
section by any conditions whatever. It is, of course, however a discretion which must   *h*
be exercised with the proper considerations in mind and must not be exercised in
an arbitrary manner. This power to order discovery before proceedings are commenced is certainly not one which should be used to encourage fishing expeditions
to enable a prospective plaintiff to discover whether he has in fact got a case at all.
I fully agree with what Lord Denning MR has said with regard to the desirability
of a prospective plaintiff who proposes to make application for discovery under s 31   *j*
of the 1970 Act to formulate the nature of his allegations and his claims in writing
before discovery and before launching any application under the section; and when
he brings his application before the court, it seems to me that it must still be for him
to satisfy the court that the order he is seeking will, or at least is likely to, assist in
disposing of the dispute between the parties fairly or result in the saving of costs.
In that way it seems to me that r 8 of RSC Ord 24 is applicable to applications under

a this section of the Act as it is to other applications for discovery of particular documents under Ord 24. But there is an important aspect of the matter which I think it is right for any court before whom such an application comes to bear in mind. That is the public interest where the plaintiff is qualified for legal aid. Where the plaintiff is qualified for legal aid, his advisers are under a duty to inform the legal aid committee of their view of his prospects of succeeding in the action and to keep

b the committee informed from time to time throughout the progress of the proceedings of any change in that respect; it is undesirable that proceedings should be brought or continued with legal aid beyond the point at which it is reasonably clear that the plaintiff has got no substantial prospect of success; and therefore there is a special ground for saying that it is desirable that the advisers of legally aided parties should have as early information as possible on matters which may affect that aspect of a legally aided party's position in the litigation. In the present case it has now been made

c clear by counsel for the applicant that the applicant's case rests wholly on the allegation that the truck which the applicant was driving when the accident occurred is said to have been defective; and counsel for the applicant concedes that if disclosure of the documents which are sought to be disclosed shows that in fact the machine was not defective, the applicant could not succeed in the action; and the disclosure of the documents may therefore result in the action being abandoned before it is

d even commenced, the dispute never reaching the stage of litigation at all. This seems to me to make this case clearly one in which it is right for the court to exercise its discretion in favour of ordering early disclosure—pre-proceeding disclosure—of the documents in question, and on that ground I agree that the appeal should be allowed.

e **ORMROD LJ.** I agree. This is to my mind particularly a case in which s 31 should be used by the court, because, having been told by counsel for the applicant that the production of the documents which are sought will virtually decide whether to go on with the action or to stop, it makes it plain that there could be in this case substantial saving in costs. In my judgment the more general matters require to be looked at a little more carefully than that. It is clear that the Administration of

f Justice Acts 1969 and 1970 are both intended to enable inspection, in one case, and discovery, in the other, to take place at an earlier stage than has been customary.

Discovery always seems to sensitise lawyers one way or the other. This seems to me to be clearly such a case. But it cuts both ways, and if the prospective plaintiffs are to obtain discovery at an earlier stage than the old fashioned way, then it is clear that defendants should be able to know at an early stage—at a corresponding stage

g —what the plaintiff's case really is. And accordingly I think the observations in para 366 of the Winn report[1], which Lord Denning MR has read, are extremely important, and if a plaintiff or prospective plaintiff proposes to take advantage of s 31, then he ought to set out the substance of his case either by letter or affidavit or in some other way; but it should be set out in a document which can, if necessary, be used at the subsequent trial, if any. In my experience in recent years of trying this kind of case,

h the letter before action, which used to be a useful document, which could sometimes be a very helpful yardstick in assessing the credibility and so on of a witness, has now become what I would describe as an empty formality. It merely sets out the cause of action expressed in the widest possible terms. One understands the object perfectly —to leave the matter open as far as possible so that the plaintiff does not have to commit himself at that stage to an account of the accident. I see the advantages from

j the point of view of the plaintiff; but if he is going to ask the court to exercise its discretion in his favour to get earlier discovery, it is only fair, in my judgment, that he should commit himself to at least either a description of the accident and how it happened, or a statement that he does not know how it happened. His evidence

---

1   Report of the Committee on Personal Injuries Litigation, July 1968, Cmnd 3691

can then be examined in relation to the account which he put forward at that early stage. In this particular case I gather that an account has been given to the respondents partly in telephone conversations, and partly in court, before the learned judge and before this court. I think in the circumstances so far as this particular case is concerned, that will do; but in other cases I would be reluctant to make an order under the section unless the information was given in a form which could be used at the subsequent trial. I entirely agree with what Buckley LJ has just said about the legally aided plaintiff. It seems to me that that is a very important factor in these cases, when applicants have to satisfy the legal aid committee that they have a prima facie case before they can start proceedings. Often that will require earlier discovery without which they may be unable to make out a prima facie case. I think, therefore, that this is another reason in this case for ordering discovery at this stage. I accordingly agree that the appeal should be allowed.

Appeal allowed; order for discovery of records 12 months before and 12 months after the accident.

Solicitors: *Lovell Son & Pitfield*, agents for *Walker, Smith & Way*, Chester (for the applicant); *Davis Campbell & Co*, Liverpool (for the respondents).

Wendy Shockett Barrister.

R v Middleton

COURT OF APPEAL, CRIMINAL DIVISION
EDMUND DAVIES, JAMES LJJ AND BOREHAM J
22nd JANUARY 1974

Criminal law – Evidence – Admissibility – Confession – Threat or inducement – Threat relating to person other than accused or immediate family – Threat relating to acquaintance of accused – Whether threat rendering confession inadmissible.

Criminal law – Evidence – Admissibility – Confession – Evidence relating to admissibility – Allegation that confession made involuntarily – Duty of judge to hear evidence as to circumstances in which confession obtained – Discretion of judge to reject confession even though voluntary.

The accused was charged with burglary and handling stolen goods. The goods in question had been found at the house of Mrs B, a prosecution witness. Mrs B was known to the accused. She said that she had been out with him on one occasion and that he had also visited her house on a few occasions over a short period when he and her sister were going about together. After his arrest, and when Mrs B was herself in custody, the accused made a confession which the Crown proposed to adduce in evidence at the trial. The accused objected to the admission of the confession on the ground that he had made it only because of a threat by the police that if he did not do so Mrs B would be kept in custody and her children would have to go into care. At the trial the judge was informed, in the absence of the jury, of the circumstances in which it was alleged that the confession had been made but, without any evidence being called, he ruled that, even if the facts were as alleged, the confession was admissible since the threat by the police did not relate to the accused or his immediate family but to Mrs B. The accused was convicted of handling and appealed.

Held – The appeal would be allowed for the following reasons—

(i) Where a confession had been extorted from an accused person by means of a threat or inducement, that was sufficient to render the confession inadmissible. Although the relation to the accused of the person who was the subject of the threat or inducement was a consideration going to the weight of the evidence that the confession had been made in consequence of the threat or inducement, the relationship was irrelevant once it had been established that the confession had been made in those circumstances. It followed that, if the facts were as alleged by the accused, the confession was inadmissible and therefore the judge's ruling was incorrect (see p 1194 *e* to *j* and p 1195 *f* to *h*, post).

(ii) In any event, even if the confession had been made voluntarily, the judge had a discretion to exclude it, if it had been obtained in circumstances that rendered its reception unfair to the accused. By ruling as he did without hearing evidence as to the circumstances in which the accused had made the confession, the judge had deprived himself of the opportunity of exercising that discretion (see p 1195 *c* to *h*, post).

Per Curiam. In most cases where the admissibility of a confession is challenged the proper course is for a 'trial within a trial' to take place on that issue (see p 1195 *b*, post).

Notes

For confessions and statements by a defendant, see 10 Halsbury's Laws (3rd Edn) 469, 470, paras 860-863, and for cases on the subject, see 14 Digest (Repl) 468, 469, 4508-4526.

Cases referred to in judgment

R v Smith [1959] 2 All ER 193, [1959] 2 QB 35, [1959] 2 WLR 623, 123 JP 295, 43 Cr App Rep 121, C-MAC, Digest (Cont Vol A) 369, 4517a.

R v Thompson [1893] 2 QB 12, [1891-4] All ER Rep 376, 62 LJMC 93, 69 LT 22, 57 JP 312, 17 Cox CC 641, 5 R 392, CCR, 14 Digest (Repl) 468, 4521.

Appeal

On 28th June 1973 in the Crown Court at Burnley (before Mr Recorder Tetley) the appellant, William Middleton, and a co-accused, John Peter Berry, were convicted of handling stolen goods (count 2), and acquitted on alternative charges of burglary and assisting in the unlawful retention of the goods (counts 1 and 3). The appellant was sentenced to 2½ years imprisonment. He appealed against conviction with leave of the single judge. The facts are set out in the judgment of the court.

Harold Singer for the appellant.

R G Mundy for the Crown.

EDMUND DAVIES LJ delivered the following judgment of the court. This appeal of William Middleton against his conviction at Burnley Crown Court in June 1973, together with a man named Berry, of handling by receiving, contrary to s 22 of the Theft Act 1968, comes before this court by leave of the single judge.

The short facts are that on 9th April 1973 factory premises in Burnley were broken into and a quantity of suede leather clothing and other goods were stolen. The value was just under £900. Mrs Birkett, who lived near the factory, said that on 9th April just before midnight she saw a man run from the factory to a green van which drove off at speed as soon as he entered it. She further gave evidence that some three weeks later she toured the district with two police officers and then indicated to them a green van similar to the one she had seen. It turned out to be owned by the co-accused, Berry, a man whom she identified in court for the first time (and that point was understandably stressed by the defence counsel) 'as being as near as possible' like the man she had seen running from the factory on 9th April.

Mrs Bentley said that at 8 am on 10th April the appellant, whom she already knew, and Berry, who had hitherto been a stranger to her, came to her house and the

appellant asked if he could store some goods there. She agreed and the two men then
carried a number of leather coats and anoraks into the house and put them into her   *a*
pantry. She said that later, because she felt 'a bit nervous', she moved all the clothing
into a bedroom upstairs and when she later met the appellant at a public house she
twice demanded that he remove all the goods. But on each of these two occasions, so
she testified, he said that he was unable to find anyone who would remove the goods,
but promised that he would do his best to have them taken away.

She said that on Friday, 13th April, when she saw the appellant again at a public   *b*
house and threatened to 'dump' the goods if he did not collect them, he said to her:
'Yes, dump them', but when she got back to her house later that evening she found
that 'the law' had arrived in the shape of a police officer who was awaiting her arrival.
In cross-examination she said that she had been out with the appellant on one occasion. He had also visited her home on a few occasions over a short period when he and
her sister were going about together. Mrs Bentley was herself taken into custody.   *c*
She said that during the 3½ hours that she was detained the police said nothing to her
about the possibility of her children being put into care. She also denied another
suggestion put by defence counsel that it was she who had approached the appellant
in the first place and asked him if he could find a buyer for the goods which were
already in her possession.

A Mr Ratcliffe was living with Mrs Bentley and he testified that he told the appellant   *d*
on several occasions to remove the goods from the house and that the appellant had
made the reply that he would do so as soon as a 'fence' from Preston arrived. He also
said that the appellant on several occasions boasted that he was responsible for the
actual burglary and went on to give details as to how it had been effected. He said
that there was no truth in the suggestion put to him in cross-examination that the goods
were already in Mrs Bentley's house and that the only roles of the appellant and Berry   *e*
were to seek a buyer.

When the appellant and Berry were arrested they emphatically denied any involvement in the burglary, but when discussing the goods found at Mrs Bentley's house
it was said that the appellant gave an evasive answer such as: 'I am saying nothing
at the moment' and a little later, 'I can't say any more yet. I want to think about it'.
Berry, for his part, said: *f*

> 'I don't want to say anything about it. Just let me tell you that that girl June
> [i e Mrs Bentley] doesn't know anything about it. I can't tell you any more yet.'

The police evidence was that when formally charged with burglary both the appellant and Berry said: 'Not guilty.' But—and here comes the most important matter
in relation to this appeal against conviction—it was said that when Berry's finger   *g*
prints were being taken he said that he had been thinking matters over, that he had
decided to tell the truth and admit that he and the appellant had taken the goods
to Mrs Bentley's house. He also said: 'I knew it was hot stuff, but what can you
do when a mate wants a lift?' That was Berry, it must be emphasised, and not the
appellant.

What did the appellant say when his fingerprints were being taken? He did not   *h*
say what Berry had said. But he was like Berry in that he also volunteered to tell
the truth, whatever that was, but added that he first wished to have a word with
Berry. The two men were then put into a cell together. A few minutes later when
two officers entered the cell both men, after being cautioned, admitted that they
had taken the property to Mrs Bentley's house but insisted that they were not the
burglars and had merely helped to 'stash' the goods away for a man who promised   *j*
to see them right later on. They each added that Mrs Bentley had nothing at all
to do with the 'job'.

The evidence for the Crown was also that the appellant was alleged to have said
that all the best clothing seemed to have disappeared from Mrs Bentley's house
and that he then offered to try and recover the missing property. The officers were

a challenged on that evidence. They insisted that it was both accurate and truthful and that they had invented and added nothing to the replies which the two men had made. They also denied the suggestion that they had told the appellant and Berry that, if they did not make a statement regarding their guilt and exculpating Mrs Bentley, she would remain in custody and her three children would be placed in care.

b The case for the defence was that the two men had spent the night of 9th April at a public house and then went straight to their respective homes and remained there in the company of their wives until late the following morning. Each of them met again at the same public house at about 12.30 p m. They then went in Berry's van to Mrs Bentley's house. The appellant said in evidence that he had known Mrs Bentley since childhood, that he had been going out with her sister for some time and that it was in the hope of contacting the sister once more that he had gone on

c 10th April to Mrs Bentley's house. When he got there Mrs Bentley had asked him if he could find a buyer for some leather coats. Having fetched Berry, the two of them inspected the goods and then left, saying that if they learned of a buyer they would contact Mrs Bentley. He denied at any time saying he would get a 'fence' to collect the clothing.

d He described as pure invention most of the police evidence and also that of Mrs Bentley and Mr Ratcliffe. He alleged that he had not at any time made any of the alleged incriminating replies and that he had certainly not made any admission whilst he was being fingerprinted. He said that he had from the outset protested his innocence but that the police would not accept his denials. He said that on several occasions they told him that unless he confessed 'to handling or summat like that' they would keep Mrs Bentley in custody and put her three children into care. He

e denied having asked to see Berry in private but testified that when the police of their own volition put the two of them together in the cell they made up a story, in the five or ten minutes that they were on their own, about taking the goods to Mrs Bentley's house and this they did simply so that Mrs Bentley would be released and her children would not be put into care. Berry's evidence was on similar lines.

f This trial took an unusual and, as the result demonstrated, unfortunate course. When the case was called on, defence counsel having already intimated to the prosecution that he was going to object to the admissibility of the alleged confessions of the appellant and Berry, counsel for the Crown rightly did not initially open either confession. In the absence of the jury, the recorder was told what the point was which counsel for the appellant had in mind, namely that the appellant's assertion was that he had been induced to make the oral confession to the police because of the threat

g made to each of the men by the police before they entered the cell that, unless they gave a confession, Mrs Bentley would be kept in custody and her children would accordingly have to go into care; and that it was concern for her and the consequent impact on her family if Mrs Bentley was kept in custody that induced him to say what he did to the police. Counsel for the appellant submitted that if this was true or if the judge thought that it might be true and was not completely satisfied that it

h was untrue, his duty was to exclude the confession. We should here add that counsel for the Crown has told us that this confession was of vital importance to the prosecution, who, without it, might well have been in difficulty in bringing guilt home to the two accused.

j The customary trial within a trial was never conducted. Nobody is to be blamed for that, though on reflection I dare say everyone concerned may now consider it would have been prudent to follow that customary course. The defence founded their submission on the long established rule of law that in order to be admissible a confession must be free and voluntary, and, as was said by Cave J, giving the written judgment of the court in *R v Thompson*[1]: 'If it flows from hope or fear excited by a person in authority, it is inadmissible'.

---

1 [1893] 2 QB 12 at 15, [1891-4] All ER Rep 376 at 378

Over the years it has been held that, in order to vitiate a confession, the inducement   *a*
or threat must relate to some temporal advantage. But what we understand to
have been the answer of the Crown to counsel for the appellant's submission was,
in effect, this: 'It really does not matter whether or not the appellant is truthful
when he asserts that the police said what he alleges. It constituted no inducement
to the accused person or to any member of his family circle or even to any intimate
of his. It did not threaten him or any member of his family or intimate circle. It   *b*
related at most to a woman whom he had known for years, maybe, but no more
than that—a mere acquaintance. That will not do. To render the confession inadmissible, the inducement or threat must concern either the accused himself or a member
of his family, and what merely concerned Mrs Bentley could be of no moment.'

R v Smith[1] was referred to by counsel for the appellant. That was a case where,
an offence having been committed in the Army, the company sergeant said to the   *c*
parade that it would not be dismissed unless and until one of them owned up. The
Courts-Martial Appeal Court held that there was in those circumstances both a threat
to the guilty man on parade that he would be kept there until he owned up and also
an inducement to own up for the sake of his comrades. But the recorder distinguished
that case from the present one in that there the threat impinged on the person of the
man who ultimately confessed, whereas the inducement or threat here alleged had   *d*
reference to matters which could not be said to be the concern of either the appellant
or Berry.   He accordingly ruled that, as a matter of law, the confessions were
admissible.

The question that arises in this appeal is whether there is any authority for the
proposition that the inducement or threat is relevant only if it impinges on the small
circle embracing the alleged offender and members of his family and *possibly* his   *e*
very close intimates. Counsel for the Crown has told the court today frankly he can
cite no authority for having so submitted below. We have to ask ourselves accordingly:
is it the law? Each member of this court (who, if we may say so, combine between
us an extremely long experience of the criminal law and practice) does not so regard
it. We do not think it accords with our own experience, nor do we think it accords
with principle, for underlying the basic rules about the admissibility of confessions   *f*
is the need for fairness to an accused person.

The courts reprehend the resorting to threats or inducements in order to extort
a confession.   But if such extortion *is* used, what does it matter to whom the inducement or the threat relates?   As a matter of common sense, of course, the more
remote the person involved in the inducement or threat is from the person or close
circle of the accused man the more difficult it may be to establish that the confession
was improperly obtained; but that is a consideration which goes to the weight of   *g*
the evidence that a threat was made and not to the admissibility of a confession if
the threat is, in fact, established. To take a possibly absurd and far-fetched example,
if a person suspected of a crime is told that someone who is a stranger to him will
be grievously harmed unless he 'comes clean' and makes a confession and he accordingly complies, is it the law that in those circumstances the admissibility of the
confession is unimpaired?   In a civilised country we think that question has only to   *h*
be asked to answer itself.   In our judgment it demands a negative answer.

The law, as we understand it, is not confined in the way submitted to and accepted
by the recorder.   The categories of inducement are not closed.   But the effect of the
Crown's submission to the contrary was that the recorder heard no evidence, but
said:
                                                                            j
    'I cannot agree that if a threat or inducement was made relating to putting
    Mrs Bentley's children in care this would be sufficient to render the statement
    subsequently made by the accused inadmissible.   The facts of the case in R v
    Smith[1] are not the same as the present case.   The threat or inducement referred

---

1   [1959] 2 All ER 193, [1959] 2 QB 35

a to the accused himself as well as other comrades, in that he was told that he would be kept on the parade ground as well until someone confessed. To that extent the principles regarding threats or inducements not to the accused and his immediate family, but to someone else not related, do not I think extend this principle. In my opinion it is within the limits and I reject your submission.'

b Then what are the 'limits'? The recorder did not answer that question, nor (with all deference to counsel for the Crown) has it been made clear to us today. Whenever the admissibility of a confession is challenged, it is wise that the presiding judge should, if the phrase may be allowed, keep his options open, and in most cases a trial within a trial should ensue. If that customary course is followed, the judge has the advantage (if the accused alleging inducement or threat gives evidence, as he usually does) of seeing and hearing and judging the sort of person who is making allegations
c of threats or inducements. He can then form an impression of considerable value which, whatever be his ruling on the strict question of admissibility, may well afford a useful guide when he comes to discharge the yet further duty resting on the court, even where there is no doubt that the alleged confession was voluntary and, therefore, admissible. That is by no means necessarily the end of the matter, for it is not every voluntary confession that should go before a jury. To quote from Professor
d Cross[1]:

> 'Even though a confession was voluntary ... the judge has a discretion to reject it if he considers that it was obtained in circumstances which would render its reception unfair to the accused.'

e A little later he writes of a confession being 'liable to rejection at discretion because it was obtained in some other circumstances which would render its reception unfair to the accused'.

In the present case, having regard to the course that the trial took at its earliest stage, the judge came to no decision on fact, but he made the assumption that the facts were as the accused asserted. He then wrongly ruled that, even making such assumption, the confessions of both men were admissible. Furthermore, having so
f ruled without any evidence being called, he deprived himself of the opportunity of gathering material relevant to the exercise of his discretion even were his ruling correct. In these circumstances, in our judgment the admissibility of these confessions was not established by the Crown and the recorder prematurely ruled that nothing that the defence alleged affected their admissibility. If he had proceeded to conduct a trial within a trial it might have been that he would have unimpeachably
g arrived at the same conclusion, but he did not. There is no doubt about the cogency and compelling quality of the confessions, there is no doubt that the Crown understandably attached importance to them, and it is impossible for us to say that, had those confessions been excluded, the appellant must nevertheless have been convicted. Accordingly this appeal against conviction is allowed and the conviction is quashed.
h

Appeal allowed. Conviction quashed.

Solicitors: *Registrar of Criminal Appeals* (for the appellant); *A Hacking*, Burnley (for the Crown).

N P Metcalfe Esq Barrister.

j _____

1 Evidence (3rd Edn, 1967), p 446

Leake (formerly Bruzzi) v Bruzzi

COURT OF APPEAL, CIVIL DIVISION
STEPHENSON, ORMROD LJJ AND SIR SEYMOUR KARMINSKI
26th APRIL 1974

Husband and wife – Property – Matrimonial home – Beneficial interests – Declaration of trust – Conveyance to husband in sole name – Execution of trust deed – Husband and wife possessed of property as 'joint tenants beneficially' – Terms of trust deed conclusive of parties' beneficial interests.

Husband and wife – Property – Matrimonial home – Mortgage repayments – Capital and interest repayments – Home in beneficial ownership of both parties – Wife leaving home – Husband thereafter making mortgage repayments – Husband in sole occupation – Wife obtaining divorce based on husband's behaviour – Petition undefended – Sale of home – Parties entitled to equal shares in proceeds of sale – Husband entitled to credit for mortgage repayments in respect of capital – Husband not entitled to credit for interest payments.

In June 1967 the husband and wife, who were then engaged to be married, acquired a house on mortgage. The wife was a minor and the house was conveyed into the sole name of the husband. On the same date a trust deed was executed by the parties which declared that the husband held the property in trust for both parties in fee simple and that the parties were possessed of the property on trust for sale and would stand possessed of the proceeds of sale in trust for themselves 'as joint tenants beneficially'. The parties were married in July 1967 and the house became the matrimonial home. The parties each contributed towards the mortgage repayments. In February 1971 the wife left the husband. Thereafter the husband alone paid the mortgage instalments and had sole use of the house. On 13th March 1972, on an undefended petition under s 2(1)(b) of the Divorce Reform Act 1969 based on the husband's behaviour, the wife obtained a decree nisi of divorce which was made absolute on 15th June. On an application by the wife under s 17 of the Married Women's Property Act 1882 for the determination of her beneficial interest in the matrimonial home, the registrar declared, in effect, that the wife was entitled to one-third and the husband to two-thirds of the proceeds of sale of the home, taking into account the parties' respective financial contributions towards the purchase. The wife appealed contending, inter alia, that the husband should not be given credit for the mortgage repayments which he had made after she had left him in view of the fact that the marriage had irretrievably broken down because of his behaviour.

Held – The appeal would be allowed for the following reasons—
(i) The court was not entitled to go behind the terms of the trust deed which were conclusive of the parties' respective beneficial interests in the home. The wife was therefore entitled to a beneficial interest in one-half of the proceeds of sale (see p 1199 *c e* and *f*, p 1200 *g* and p 1201 *b*, post); *Wilson v Wilson* [1963] 2 All ER 447 followed.

(ii) It was undesirable that matters of conduct should be considered on an application under s 17 and, since there had been no investigation of the parties' conduct, that was not a factor which could be taken into account. Since the husband had had sole use of the home following the wife's departure he was not entitled to credit for mortgage repayments in respect of interest but was entitled to credit for half of the repayments which he had made in respect of capital (see p 1200 *a* to *d* and *j* to p 1201 *c*, post); *Cracknell v Cracknell* [1971] 3 All ER 552 considered.

Notes
For the determination of property rights between husband and wife, see 19 Halsbury's

a Laws (3rd Edn) 898-901, paras 1488-1492, and for cases on the beneficial ownership of the matrimonial home, see 27(1) Digest (Reissue) 89-104, 662-715.

For the Married Women's Property Act 1882, s 17, see 17 Halsbury's Statutes (3rd Edn) 120.

For the Divorce Reform Act 1969, s 2, see 40 Halsbury's Statutes (3rd Edn) 770.

As from 1st January 1974, s 2(1) of the Divorce Reform Act 1969 has been replaced
b by the Matrimonial Causes Act 1973, s 1(2).

Cases referred to in judgments

Cracknell v Cracknell [1971] 3 All ER 552, [1971] P 356, [1971] 3 WLR 490, CA, 27(1) Digest (Reissue) 314, *2318*.

Pettitt v Pettitt [1969] 2 All ER 385, [1970] AC 777, [1969] 2 WLR 966, 20 P & CR 991, HL, 27(1) Digest (Reissue) 102, 707.
c
Wilson v Wilson [1963] 2 All ER 447, [1963] 1 WLR 601, CA, 27(1) Digest (Reissue) 93, *676*.

Appeal

This was an appeal by Jill Leake, formerly Jill Bruzzi ('the wife'), against an order
d of Mr Registrar Holloway, made on 1st October 1973 on an application under s 17 of the Married Women's Property Act 1882, whereby, inter alia, it was declared that the wife was entitled to one-third, and her former husband, Mario Bruzzi ('the husband'), was entitled to two-thirds of the proceeds of sale of property known as 162a Bellingham Road, Catford, London, SE6. The facts are set out in the judgment of Stephenson LJ.

e
Sheila Cameron for the wife.
Geoffrey Grigson for the husband.

STEPHENSON LJ. This is an appeal by the wife against an order of Mr Registrar
f Holloway made on 1st October 1973. By that order he—

'ADJUDGED AND DECLARED that the [husband] holds the beneficial interest in the property 162A Bellingham Road Catford London SE6, in trust for himself and the [wife] as tenants in common.'

He ordered that the husband pay to the wife within three months of the date of the order a sum representing the value of her interest 'calculated in the following
g manner'—and then he set out the detailed calculation. What it really comes to, as set out in para 4 of that order, is that the wife's share of the sum resulting from the sale of this property on the exercise of the power of sale was to be one-third and the husband was to have two-thirds. Then there was a direction that if the property was sold (and so on) various other payments should be made.

It is a long and complicated (I will not say unnecessarily complicated) order, but
h the appeal has really turned on a short point. This couple married on 15th July 1967, the husband being an Italian aged 28 and the wife English and (then) a minor aged 19; she did not become 21 until 12th March 1969. By that time they were both living in London in this house, both working; and since June 1968 they have had a joint bank account. Both of them were contributing repayments towards the mortgage which had been raised on this house. The wife left the husband in February 1971;
j and since that date he has been making all the mortgage repayments and he has been living in the house. On her petition (undefended) under s 2(1)(*b*) of the Divorce Reform Act 1969 the wife got a decree nisi on 13th March 1972 which was made absolute on 15th June; and on 6th January 1973 she remarried. On 26th January she took out a summons under s 17 of the Married Women's Property Act 1882. The husband apparently goes back to Italy from time to time and was absent from

the first hearing of the wife's summons on 1st September but was present when the *a*
registrar made his order on 1st October. He is not in this country at the moment,
and that has understandably put counsel, who has appeared for him on the hearing
of this appeal but did not appear for him in the court below, in some difficulty. But
we have been able to dispose of this appeal today on really a short point of law,
on which counsel for the husband has very properly told us he does not feel able to
ask the court to take a different view from that which counsel for the wife asks us *b*
to take.

The property with which we are concerned (and of course, these being proceedings
under s 17 of the 1882 Act, we are only concerned with the legal and beneficial title
to it; we are not dealing with a property under s 4 of the Matrimonial Proceedings
and Property Act 1970 or its successor) was conveyed into the sole name of the husband
on 9th June 1967. On the same day there was executed a trust deed, which really *c*
(counsel for the wife argues) concludes this appeal in favour of the wife and compels
this court, as it should have compelled the registrar, to decide that the wife is entitled
not to one-third only of the proceeds of the sale of this house, but to one-half, subject
to a possible deduction crediting the husband with part of the mortgage repayments
which he has made since February 1971.

That trust deed was between the husband, described as 'nominee', that was *d*
nominee for the purchasers, and himself and his future wife, who were described in
it as 'the purchasers'. It was necessary to execute this deed in that way because she
was, as I have said, still an infant. The material parts of that deed read as follows. It
begins with a recital:

> 'WHEREAS: (1) This declaration is supplemental to a Transfer dated the 9th
> day of June 1967 and made BETWEEN [a man named Jones, who was the vendor] *e*
> of the one part and the nominee [i e the husband] of the other part whereby
> certain freehold property . . . was transferred to the nominee in fee simple [for
> £4,950]'.

Recital (2) stated that the consideration—

> 'was provided (a) as to Three thousand five hundred pounds advanced by the *f*
> Greater London Council upon security of a Legal Charge and which the pur-
> chasers agree shall be repaid from their joint monies; (b) as to remainder by the
> purchasers in equal shares and the said property was conveyed to the nominee
> as the nominee of the purchasers as the nominee hereby acknowledges'.

The deed continues:
g
> '(3) The said JILL RAYNSFORD [that is the future wife] is under the age of
> twenty-one years and does not attain her majority until the Twelfth day of March
> 1969
> 'Now THIS DEED WITNESSETH as follows:
> '1. THE nominee hereby declares that he holds the said property in trust for
> the purchasers in fee simple [I need not read the rest of that clause.] *h*
> '2. IT is hereby agreed and declared that the Purchasers shall stand possessed
> of the premises hereby transferred upon trust to sell the same with power at
> discretion to postpone any sale and shall stand possessed of the net proceeds of
> sale (after payment of expenses and of rates taxes costs of insurance repairs and
> other outgoings) in trust for the purchasers as joint tenants beneficially'.

I need not trouble with cl 3. Clause 4 emphasises what I may call the equality of *j*
beneficial interest between these two spouses, as they were shortly to become, by
providing:

> 'THE nominee shall not be required to incur any expenditure in respect of the
> said property except in so far as moneys in respect thereof shall have been
> provided by the purchasers . . . and any purchaser or his personal representatives

a providing more than one equal share of such expenditure shall be entitled to contribution from the other purchasers or their respective personal representatives on the footing that such expenditure is to be borne equally by all the purchasers'.

The effect of that declaration of trust is, says counsel for the wife, that which is stated in the current edition of Rayden on Divorce[1] where the learned editors say:

b 'It has been said that where the conveyance or lease of the land declares not merely in whom the legal title is to vest but in whom the beneficial title is to vest, that necessarily concludes the question of title as between the spouses for all time, and in the absence of fraud or mistake at the time of the transaction the parties cannot go behind it at any time thereafter, even on death or break-up of the marriage.'

c And that, counsel for the wife says, is what the husband here is seeking to do.

Here, although the wife is an infant, it cannot be suggested that this trust was not a trust for her benefit (it has not been so suggested) and therefore the beneficial interest that she has in the terms of this trust deed is an interest in one-half, and it cannot be reduced to one-third, as the registrar reduced it, without going behind the declaration of trust, which is something that a court of law is forbidden to do.

d One of the authorities which is given for that statement in Rayden on Divorce[1] is the decision of this court in Wilson v Wilson[2], a decision which has not been questioned, which was referred to by counsel in arguing the case of Pettitt v Pettitt[3] in the House of Lords and which exactly covers this case. There, a registrar had awarded a wife a very much smaller share than this registrar has awarded this wife, and that for what appeared to be at first sight the good reason that in that case the husband e had put up all the purchase price except that which was raised on mortgage and had made all the mortgage repayments. But this court said that that was quite wrong because the trust deed (which was in very similar terms to this) prevented that being done on an application under s 17 of the Married Women's Property Act 1882. It is not necessary to read the passage which sets out the law most clearly from the judgment of Russell LJ[4] in that case, because counsel for the husband has not felt f able to challenge that authority.

It follows therefore that, subject to the remaining point, this appeal must be allowed and it must be declared that on sale the wife is entitled to one-half of the proceeds of the sale.

Two further questions have arisen. The first is the question whether there should be deducted from the wife's half-share of the proceeds of the sale on this house part g of the mortgage repayments which the husband has made since she left. That is a course which was taken in Cracknell v Cracknell[5] as well as in Wilson v Wilson[2], to which I have referred. In giving the first judgment in this court in Cracknell's case[5] Lord Denning MR stated that in Cracknell's case[5], as in Wilson's case[2], the wife had left the house of her own accord; and he stated that where the position was different and where she had been driven out of the house by the conduct of the husband it h would be wrong for the expelling party (to call him that) to be given any credit for his mortgage repayments. It is said by counsel for the wife that this case falls within that latter category because the wife petitioning under s 2(1)(b) of the 1969 Act, the marriage having irretrievably broken down because of the unreasonable behaviour of the husband, ought not to have to deduct anything in favour of the husband in respect of his mortgage repayments.

j
1 11th Edn (1971), p 637, para 6
2 [1963] 2 All ER 447, [1963] 1 WLR 601
3 [1969] 2 All ER 315, [1970] AC 777
4 [1963] 2 All ER at 452, 453, [1963] 1 WLR at 608, 609
5 [1971] 3 All ER 552, [1971] P 356

It seems unfortunate if the conduct of the parties, perhaps including the allegations that the husband made about adultery on the wife's part which were not proved or persisted in, have to be considered when we are dealing with a s 17 application. We do not have to say whether there may not be cases in which the husband should be given no credit for any mortgage repayments such as the husband has made in this case since the wife left the matrimonial home.   But my conclusion in this case is that the wife should give the husband credit for half that part of the mortgage repayments which he has made in respect of capital.   We are told that the total amount of mortgage repayments which he has made, or at any rate should have made, in the three years since they separated, would be of the order of £900, and it may be, therefore, that the wife will have to credit him with about £450. It may be that there are arrears.   But £450 will be the maximum, because some part—no doubt not a large part but perhaps an increasing part—of those repayments which he has made will have been repayments in respect of capital. Though the distinction between repayments in respect of capital and repayments in respect of interest does not appear to have been drawn in any of the cases to which we have been referred, nonetheless it seems to me that it is proper to draw a distinction between the two and to credit the husband with half of the payments which he has made in respect of capital only. I would incorporate in the order of this court a direction that that deduction should be made.

There is one other point which counsel for the wife challenges in the order of the learned registrar, and that is the direction that the sale of the property should be in the hands of the husband's solicitors. She asks in her notice of appeal and in her submissions to this court that it should be in the hands of the wife's solicitors. Counsel for the husband, being without instructions, finds difficulty in dealing with that application; but for myself I would have thought that we ought to grant the wife's application and allow the appeal on that matter.

Finally, the learned registrar ordered the husband to pay three-quarters only and not the full amount of the wife's costs. I think it follows (and counsel for the husband again has quite properly conceded that it follows) from the order which I would make allowing the appeal that the appeal should be allowed with full costs to the wife, both here and below; and that is the order which I would make in dismissing the appeal with the credit provisions which I have already indicated.

ORMROD LJ. I agree. In my judgment, the question of the respective interests of these parties is concluded by the authority of *Wilson v Wilson*[1], in this court, to which Stephenson LJ has already referred, and there is nothing more to be said on that aspect of the case.

In relation to the accounting to be taken on the sale of the house, it does seem to me in these days increasingly unfortunate that the issue of conduct should be creeping in through the back door, even into a Married Women's Property Act 1882 summons under s 17, because increasingly in these days the court is trying to avoid making judgments about conduct and it will become increasingly difficult to ascertain where the rights and wrongs of the situation lie on the conduct question and where (as in this case) the wife says that prima facie she was justified in leaving because she got a decree under s 2(1)(b) of the Divorce Reform Act 1969 and her husband replies by saying that he thought he had reason to suspect adultery before she left. None of these matters has been investigated, and it would therefore seem to me undesirable, if it is possible to avoid it, to link these matters with costs. On the other hand, when one comes to take account, it seems to me reasonable that the husband in this case, who has paid some of the mortgage repayments, should get credit for half the capital repayments that he has made, but not for half the interest repayments, for the reason

---

1   [1963] 2 All ER 447, [1963] 1 WLR 601

a that he has had the use and enjoyment of the house for himself and it is not at all unrealistic to regard the interest under the mortgage as something equivalent to rent or payment for use and occupation. I agree with the order proposed by Stephenson LJ in that and in all other respects.

b **SIR SEYMOUR KARMINSKI.** I agree, and would only add this. Some reference has been made to the wife's conduct So far as I am concerned, there is nothing before the court which might affect, as a result of the wife's conduct, the proportion of the share which she ought to have in this property. Otherwise I have nothing to add to the judgments which have been delivered by Stephenson and Ormrod LJJ. I have come to the same conclusion, and for the same reasons.

c *Appeal allowed; declaration that property held by parties as tenants in common in equal shares; husband to be given credit for half mortgage repayments made by him in respect of capital.*

Solicitors: *Rodgers, Horsley & Burton* (for the wife); *Ellis, Wood, Bickersteth & Hazel* (for the husband).

d   A S Virdi Esq Barrister.

Harrison and another v Battye and others

e CHANCERY DIVISION AT LEEDS   Affirmed on another ground CA
   BLACKETT-ORD V-C   [1974] 3 All ER 830
   6th NOVEMBER 1973

Sale of land – Contract – Formation – Exchange of contracts – Constructive exchange –
f *Purchasers' part returned by vendor to purchasers in mistake for vendor's part – Whether binding contract created.*

The plaintiffs agreed subject to contract to purchase the defendant's house. It was contemplated that the contract would be subject to the Law Society's Conditions of Sale (1970 Edn) and that it would come into being on exchange of contracts. The plaintiffs' solicitors sent their part of the contract signed by the plaintiffs to the
g defendant's solicitors and requested the defendant's solicitors to send them the defendant's part of the contract signed by him. The defendant signed his part of the contract but his solicitors in error despatched to the plaintiffs' solicitors the plaintiffs' part of the contract with a letter stating: 'We enclose part contract signed by our client to complete the exchange.' Thereafter the defendant refused to proceed with the transaction and the plaintiffs sought specific performance of the alleged contract
h and an order that the defendant's solicitors deliver up the defendant's part of the contract, contending that the defendant's solicitors' attempt to effect an exchange was equivalent to an exchange.

Held – The parties contemplated entering into a contract by exchange and exchange only, and as no exchange had in fact taken place, no contract had come into existence.
j Accordingly the plaintiffs' claim failed (see p 1204 g and p 1205 f and g, post).
   Eccles v Bryant [1947] 2 All ER 865 applied.

Notes
For the formation of contracts for the sale of land, see 34 Halsbury's Laws (3rd Edn) 205, para 342, and for cases on the subject, see 40 Digest (Repl) 11-14, 1-38

For agreements subject to the exchange of formal contracts, see 8 Halsbury's Laws (3rd Edn) 76, 77, para 130, and for cases on the subject, see 12 Digest (Reissue) 78, *a* 416-417.

Cases referred to in judgment

Eccles v Bryant [1947] 2 All ER 865, [1948] Ch 93, [1948] LJR 418, CA, 12 Digest (Reissue) 78, 416.

Walsh v Lonsdale (1882) 21 Ch D 9, 52 LJCh 2, 46 LT 858, CA, 31(1) Digest (Reissue) *b* 78, 594.

Cases also cited

Griffin v Wetherby (1868) LR 3 QB 753.
Griffiths v Young [1970] 3 All ER 601, [1970] Ch 675, CA.
Law v Jones [1973] 2 All ER 437, [1974] Ch 112, CA.   *c*
Shamia v Joory [1958] 1 All ER 111, [1958] 1 QB 448, DC.
Walker v Rostron (1842) 9 M & W 411.

Action

On or about 18th September 1972 the plaintiffs, Douglas Charles Harrison and his wife, Jennifer Lindsay Harrison ('the purchasers'), agreed subject to contract to *d* purchase and the first defendant, Roy Battye ('the vendor'), to sell property known as 27 West End Drive, Horsforth, Yorkshire ('the property'). Both parties contemplated that a formal agreement in writing should be agreed and prepared in two parts by their respective solicitors, signed by the respective parties, and that thereafter the parts should be exchanged. On 29th September the second defendants, Walker, Morris & Coles, who were the vendor's solicitors, sent to the pur- *e* chasers' solicitors a draft contract for approval on the Law Society's form[1] with a copy and added: 'We look forward to hearing from you as to exchange of contracts as soon as possible.' There followed a discussion as to the date of completion and amount of deposit. On 4th October the purchasers' solicitors wrote: 'We ... enclose the contract approved for signature by the Vendor. Please let us know when you are ready to exchange.' On 5th October the second defendants replied that they would *f* let the purchasers' solicitors know when they were ready to exchange. On 6th October the purchasers' solicitors sent their part of the contract, signed by Mr Harrison on behalf of himself and his wife, on which the amount of the deposit had been altered from '£825' to '£100', together with a cheque for £100, which the solicitors had agreed by telephone would be acceptable. The purchasers' solicitors in their accompanying letter wrote: 'We would be pleased to receive part Contract *g* signed by the Vendors.' That letter was received by the second defendants on 9th October. On the same day they wrote:

'We enclose part contract signed by our client to complete the exchange and we confirm that your draft Transfer is approved and one copy of it is returned herewith.'
      h
With the letter they inadvertently enclosed not the part contract signed by the vendor but that signed by Mr Harrison. (The vendor had signed his part but it recorded the amount of the deposit unamended.) On receiving that letter on 10th October the purchasers' solicitors sent back their part with a letter which read:

'We return the contract as you have returned the part which was signed by *j* our client. No doubt you will let us have the part signed by your client in due course.'

The vendor's own contract to purchase another property having fallen through, he

---

1 Law Society's Form of Contract for Sale and General Conditions of Sale (1970 Edn)

a declined to proceed further. On 23rd October the purchasers served a notice to complete but the vendors refused to do so.

By a writ issued on 30th April 1973 the purchasers brought an action against the vendor and the second defendants, claiming (i) against the vendor damages for breach of contract and specific performance of an alleged agreement in writing for the sale of the property, and (ii) against the second defendants an order that they deliver up the vendor's part of that agreement to the purchasers. By their statement of claim

b the purchasers averred that the contracts had been effectively exchanged and that after the exchange the vendor's part became the property of the purchasers. By their joint defence the defendants contended that no contract for the sale of the property had ever come into existence, and relied on condition 5(2) of the Law Society's Conditions of Sale: 'Where exchange of contracts is effected by post the contract shall be made when the last part is actually posted.'

c

Matthew Caswell for the purchasers.
John M Collins for the defendants.

BLACKETT-ORD V-C. In 1972 Mr and Mrs Harrison were disposed to pur-
d chase a house, 27 West End Drive, Horsforth, Yorkshire, from Mr Roy Battye for £8,250. The matter was subject to the Law Society's Conditions of Sale (1970 Edn) and proceeded in the usual way—solicitors being instructed on each side. A draft contract which embodied the Law Society's Conditions of Sale was submitted on behalf of the vendor and approved on behalf of the purchasers, and I need only refer to a letter from the purchasers' solicitors of 4th October 1972 saying:

e   'We . . . enclose the contract approved for signature by the Vendor. Please let us know when you are ready to exchange.'

On 5th October the vendor's solicitors replied: 'We will let you know when we are ready to exchange'. On 6th October the purchasers' solicitors wrote:

f   'Further to your telephone conversation with us today, we now enclose Contract signed by our client together with cheque for £100 the deposit.'

There are other parts of the letter which I need not read, but it says: 'We would be pleased to receive part Contract signed by the Vendors.' (There is only one vendor but nothing turns on that.) With the letter of 6th October was duly sent the purchasers' part of the contract together with a cheque for £100, and that was
g acknowledged by the vendor's solicitors in a postscript to a letter of 9th October saying: 'Your letter enclosing contract received since dictating above.' Then the vendor's solicitors wrote a more formal letter replying to certain outstanding enquiries—it is also dated 9th October 1972—and ending:

'We enclose part contract signed by our client to complete the exchange and
h   we confirm that your draft Transfer is approved and one copy of it is returned herewith.'

The vital words are: 'We enclose part contract signed by our client to complete the exchange'. With that letter they did not send the part contract signed by their client but, presumably in error, they returned the part signed by the purchasers, retaining in their own office the vendor's part of the contract which had indeed
j been signed by him. After that the vendor refused to proceed and this is an action by the purchasers for specific performance of the contract which they allege has come into existence and for certain relief against the vendor's solicitors.

Now it is not disputed that the matter was originally intended to proceed in the usual way   Counsel for the purchasers conceded that up to the time of the letter of 5th October there was no contract and the parties contemplated exchange of

contracts in the usual way before they could be legally bound. The Law Society's *a*
Conditions of Sale, as is mentioned in the pleadings, though it has not been mentioned
in argument, do say in cl 5(2) that where exchange of contracts is effected by post
the contract shall be made when the last part is actually posted. Perhaps it could
be said that that was somehow not incorporated, though I think it must be an indication of what was in the contemplation of the parties. And although that might be
sufficient to dispose of the case, I will go on and consider the law more generally. *b*

The leading case of course is *Eccles v Bryant*[1]. There Lord Greene MR, after dealing
with the matter of exchange of contracts and expressing the view that where a transaction is subject to contract initially, as was the case in the present matter, the parties
are not bound until the contracts are actually exchanged, said[2]:

> 'I am prepared to assume that their intention was that the exchange should *c*
> take place by post. When an exchange takes place by post and a contract comes
> into existence through the fact of exchange, the earliest date at which such a
> contract can come into existence would be the date when the later of the two
> documents to be put in the post is actually put in the post.'

That has been accepted ever since, I think, as laying down the general rule. Where
it appears that the parties contemplate an exchange of contracts in the usual way, *d*
as was in my judgment the present case, then they are not bound usually until the
second contract, the second part, is actually posted.

Counsel for the purchasers accepts that, but he seeks to distinguish this case from
the run of cases because of this accident whereby the vendor's part of the contract
was not actually posted although the vendor's solicitors wrote the letter saying:
'We enclose part contract signed by our client to complete the exchange'. He said *e*
first that equity regards that as done that ought to have been done and that on the
principle in *Walsh v Lonsdale*[3] (which is broadly to the effect that an agreement for a
lease can be treated in equity as an actual lease) I should treat the intention to exchange
as an actual exchange; that the omission to put the right part in the envelope is
simply a matter of form and does not interfere with the creation of the contract,
because that clearly was intended. Or, putting the matter another way, he said *f*
that the attempt by the vendor's solicitors to exchange is equivalent to an actual
exchange; or anyway creates a contract because it is an unequivocal act or declaration
on their part authorised by their client and communicated to the other side. Well
that, I think, as far as it goes, is true. It was an unequivocal act and the letter of
course was sent to the purchasers' solicitors. But that is not, in my judgment,
sufficient to effect the creation of a contract in these circumstances. *g*

This is the mischief that the rule laid down in *Eccles v Bryant*[1] is intended to meet.
Thus, referring again to Lord Greene MR's judgment[4]:

> 'It was argued that exchange is a mere matter of machinery, having in itself
> no particular importance or significance. So far as significance is concerned, it
> appears to me that not only is it not right to say of exchange that it has no sig- *h*
> nificance, but it is the crucial and vital fact which brings the contract into exis-
> tence. As for importance, it is of the greatest importance, and that is why in
> past ages this procedure came to be adopted by everybody as the proper pro-
> cedure. In dealing with contracts for the sale of land, it is of the greatest impor-
> tance to the vendor that he should have a document signed by the purchaser
> and to the purchaser that he should have a document signed by the vendor.
> It is of the greatest importance that there should be no dispute whether a contract *j*

1 [1947] 2 All ER 865, [1948] Ch 93
2 [1947] 2 All ER at 866, [1948] Ch at 97
3 (1882) 21 Ch D 9
4 [1947] 2 All ER at 867, [1948] Ch at 99

a has or has not been made, and that there should be no dispute as to the terms of it. This procedure of exchange ensures that none of those difficulties will arise. Each party has got a document of title, because directly a contract is entered into, and that contract is in writing relating to land, it is a document of title. That can be illustrated by the simple case where a purchaser makes a sub-sale. The contract is a vital document for the purpose of the sub-sale. If he had not got the vendors' part, signed by the vendors, to show to the sub-purchaser, the
b purchaser would not be able to make a good title. If the argument for the purchaser is right and the contract comes into existence before exchange takes place, it would mean that neither party could call on the other to hand over his part. The non-exchanged part would remain the property of the party who signed it, because exchange would be no element in the contract, and, therefore, should the purchaser wish to resell he would have no right to obtain from the
c vendor the vendor's signed part.'

Later he said[1]:

'It is of the greatest importance, it appears to me, that these principles should be upheld. The inconvenience and chaos into which these matters would be
d thrown by the adoption of any other rules appear to me to be very great, but ultimately the matter comes down to this. Parties become bound by contract when and in the manner in which they intend and contemplate becoming bound. That is a question of the facts of each case, but in this case the manner of becoming bound which the parties and their solicitors must have contemplated from the very beginning was the ordinary customary convenient method of
e exchange. From that contemplation neither side and neither of the solicitors ever resiled, and there is no justification for taking the view that some new method of making the contract was ever contemplated by anybody.'

I think that last paragraph applies to this present case. It is a question of fact as to what method of entering into the contract the parties had in contemplation. In my judgment it was exchange and exchange only, and that is confirmed indeed by the
f letter of 9th October itself which says: 'We enclose part contract signed by our client to complete the exchange.'

So although one must have sympathy with the purchasers in the circumstances, I am satisfied that no contract came into existence and the result is that the action must be dismissed with costs. As regards the second defendants, the vendor's solicitors, they have been brought in to meet perhaps the passage in *Eccles v Bryant*[2] which
g I read a few moments ago about the difficulties if contracts come into existence otherwise than by way of exchange, because a purchaser would not have a part signed by the vendor and would not be able to get it. Counsel for the purchasers put forward a claim based really on trust, to the effect that the letter of 9th October constituted the vendor's solicitors trustees of the vendor's part of the contract for the purchaser. But that is not an argument which I could accept, and anyway it does not in the
h circumstances become relevant. And so as regards both defendants the action is dismissed with the consequences which I have mentioned.

Action dismissed. Judgment for defendants.

Solicitors: *Gibbs, Pollard & Co*, Horsforth (for the purchasers); *Walker, Morris & Coles*,
j Bradford (for the defendants).

John M Collins Esq Barrister.

1 [1947] 2 All ER at 869, [1948] Ch at 104
2 [1947] 2 All ER at 867, [1948] Ch at 100

a

R v Bishop

COURT OF APPEAL, CRIMINAL DIVISION
STEPHENSON LJ, MACKENNA AND O'CONNOR JJ
20th, 21st MAY, 13th JUNE 1974

b

Criminal law – Evidence – Character of accused – Imputation on character of prosecution witness – Accused making allegation against prosecution witness of homosexual conduct – Homosexual practices between consenting adults in private not criminal offence – Whether accused impugning character of prosecution witness – Criminal Evidence Act 1898, s 1(f)(ii).

c

When P returned to his flat one evening he discovered that certain articles, including two packets of after-shave lotion, belonging to him were missing from his bedroom. The appellant's fingerprints were found on a medicine cabinet and after-shave lotion container in P's bedroom. The appellant was charged with burglary by stealing. He denied committing the offence and when he gave evidence at the trial he explained the presence of the fingerprints by saying that he had a homosexual relationship *d* with P and was in the habit of visiting him for that purpose and using the after-shave lotion. The prosecution applied for leave to ask the appellant questions to show that he had been convicted of other offences on the ground that the nature and conduct of the defence was such as to involve imputations on the character of P, within the meaning of proviso (f)(ii)*ᵃ* to s 1 of the Criminal Evidence Act 1898. The trial judge directed that the appellant could be cross-examined as to his previous convictions, *e* of which the appellant had seven, involving 25 offences, ten for dishonesty. He appealed contending that evidence of those convictions should not have been admitted for it was not an imputation on P's character to say that he practised homosexuality in private.

Held – The evidence had been rightly admitted and the appeal would accordingly *f* be dismissed for the following reasons—

(i) An imputation on character, within the meaning of proviso (f)(ii) to s 1 of the 1898 Act, included charges of faults or vices, whether reputed or real, which were not criminal offences and an allegation of homosexual conduct was such a charge in that it still carried with it a certain stigma (see p 1209 *b* to *e* and p 1210 *e*, post).

(ii) Although the evidence was gravely prejudicial to the appellant, the judge had *g* not erred in the exercise of his discretion in deciding to admit it, for the evidence was relevant to the jury's consideration of the case for the defence (see p 1210 *f* and *g*, post).

Notes
For cross-examination of defendant as to character, see 10 Halsbury's Laws (3rd Edn) *h* 449-451, para 828, and for cases on the subject, see 14 Digest (Repl) 511-518, 4942-5016.

For the Criminal Evidence Act 1898, s 1, see 12 Halsbury's Statutes (3rd Edn) 865.

---

a Section 1, so far as material, provides: 'Every person charged with an offence . . . shall be *j* a competent witness for the defence at every stage of the proceedings . . . Provided . . . (f) A person charged and called as a witness in pursuance of this Act shall not be asked, and if asked shall not be required to answer, any question tending to show that he has committed or been convicted of or been charged with any offence other than wherewith he is then charged, or is of bad character, unless . . . (ii) . . . the nature or conduct of the defence is such as to involve imputations on the character of the prosecutor or the witnesses for the prosecution . . .'

Cases referred to in judgment

a *Knuller (Publishing, Printing and Promotions) Ltd v Director of Public Prosecutions* [1972]
2 All ER 898, [1973] AC 435, [1972] 3 WLR 143, 136 JP 728, 56 Cr App Rep 633, HL;
affg in part, rvsg in part sub nom R v Knuller (Publishing, Printing and Promotions) Ltd
[1971] 3 All ER 314, [1972] 2 QB 179, [1971] 2 WLR 633, 135 JP 569, CA.
R v Cook [1959] 2 All ER 97, [1959] 2 QB 340, [1959] 2 WLR 616, 123 JP 271, 43 Cr App
Rep 138, CCA, Digest (Cont Vol A) 374, 4942a.

b *R v Preston* [1909] 1 KB 568, 78 LJKB 335, 100 LT 303, 73 JP 173, 21 Cox CC 773, 2 Cr
App Rep 24, CCA, 14 Digest (Repl) 517, 5007.
Selvey v Director of Public Prosecutions [1968] 2 All ER 497, [1970] AC 304, [1968] 2 WLR
1494, 132 JP 430, 52 Cr App Rep 443, HL; *affg sub nom* R v Selvey [1968] 1 All ER
94, [1968] 1 QB 706, [1967] 3 WLR 1637, CA, Digest (Cont Vol C) 217, 5016b.

c **Cases also cited**

R v Brown (No 2) (1960) 44 Cr App Rep 181, CCA.
R v Clark [1955] 3 All ER 29, [1955] 2 QB 469, CCA.
R v Cunningham [1958] 3 All ER 711, [1959] 1 QB 288, CCA.
R v Horwood [1969] 3 All ER 1156, [1970] 1 QB 133, CA.
d *R v Hudson* [1912] 2 KB 464, CCA.
R v Jenkins (1945) 31 Cr App Rep 1, CCA.
R v Jones (1923) 17 Cr App Rep 117, CCA.
R v King (Dennis Arthur) [1967] 1 All ER 379, [1967] 2 QB 338, CA.
R v Morgan (1910) 5 Cr App Rep 157, CCA.
R v Morris (1959) 43 Cr App Rep 206, CCA.
R v Rappolt (1911) 6 Cr App Rep 156, CCA.
e *R v Rouse* [1904] 1 KB 184, CCR.
R v Sargvon (1967) 51 Cr App Rep 394, CCA.
R v Weldon [1963] Crim LR 439, CCA.
R v Westfall (1912) 7 Cr App Rep 176, CCA.
R v Wood [1951] 2 All ER 112, 35 Cr App Rep 61.
f *R v Wright* (1910) 5 Cr App Rep 131, CCA.

Appeal

This was an appeal by Roger Anthony Bishop against his conviction for burglary at
the Central Criminal Court on 11th February 1974, before Judge Honig and a jury,
when he was sentenced to nine months imprisonment. The facts are set out in the
judgment of the court.
g
David Bate for the appellant.
Michael Worsley for the Crown.

Cur adv vult

h 13th June. **STEPHENSON LJ** read the judgment of the court. The appellant
was convicted at the Central Criminal Court on 11th February 1974 of burglary
and sentenced to nine months imprisonment. Against that conviction he appeals
on the ground that the jury were wrongly allowed to hear evidence from the
appellant in cross-examination of his previous convictions.
He had been for 12 days the tenant of a Mr Price's first floor back room in a house
j in North London on the introduction of a lady in a local public house where the
appellant worked as a barman. He was convicted of entering as a trespasser the ground
floor flat which Mr Price himself occupied in the same house and stealing therein
two packets of after-shave lotion and other property, including clothing and £10
belonging to Mr Price, on 30th June 1972. Mr Price left him in the house when he
went to work at 7.15 a m and on his return about 5.30 p m he found that the lock on

his bedroom door had been interfered with, the door forced open, the property
was missing from his bedroom, and the appellant missing from the house. The
appellant had left without notice or leaving any address but with his two keys, his
key to the front door and his key to his room. His fingerprints were found on a portable medicine cabinet and an after-shave lotion container in Mr Price's bedroom.
A second after-shave lotion container, which had also been in his bedroom, was
found in the appellant's room.

When the appellant was traced by the police to Blackpool in March 1973 he denied
committing any offence. He said that he had been into Mr Price's bedroom a number
of times at his invitation and had also taken aspirins from his medicine cabinet.
He had never seen an after-shave lotion container and someone must have put in
his room the one that was found there. When he gave evidence at his trial he repeated
his denial and explained the presence of his fingerprints by the fact that he had a
homosexual relationship with Mr Price and was in the habit of going into his bedroom
at his invitation on many nights during his short stay in the house in order to have
homosexual relations with him, of using his after-shave lotion and of taking aspirins
from his medicine cabinet, where he said the after-shave lotion was also kept.
He repeated his allegation that the after-shave container found in his own room
must have been left there without his knowledge by somebody else. He had mentioned to Mr Price that he would be leaving but admitted that he had not told
him that he was going to leave that day. He claimed that he had left his two keys
on the bottom step opposite the door of his flat for Mr Price to pick up, and he
suggested two other men living in the house as possibly responsible for the burglary.

Mr Price, in his evidence, emphatically denied that he had had homosexual relations
with the appellant. He said that the appellant had only once come to his bedroom,
on the evening before he left; on that occasion he had not gone further than four
feet inside the bedroom and he had never touched anything in the bedroom;
further the medicine cabinet was empty and there were no aspirins in it.

After the appellant had given his evidence-in-chief, prosecuting counsel asked leave
in the absence of the jury to ask him questions tending to show (in the words of
s 1(f) of the Criminal Evidence Act 1898) that he had been convicted of offences other
than that wherewith he was there charged on the ground that, in the words of
proviso (ii) to s 1(f), 'the nature and conduct of the defence is such as to involve
imputations on the character of' Mr Price. Relying on *Selvey v Director of Public
Prosecutions*[1], counsel submitted that the appellant had made a very serious allegation
against Mr Price's character, that he was having homosexual relations with the
appellant, which made it right that the jury should know what sort of person the
appellant was in order to decide fairly who was telling the truth.

The appellant had seven previous convictions since 1966 involving 25 offences, ten
for dishonesty. Evidence of them was therefore gravely prejudicial—so prejudicial
as perhaps to excuse the appellant's recorded comment on the judge's ruling, after
strenuous objection by his counsel, that his convictions could be given in evidence:
'I have no chance now.' No complaint is made of the judge's direction that they did
not mean that he must be disbelieved, far less that he must be guilty of the offence
with which the jury were concerned.

Defending counsel's objection to the evidence before the trial judge and before
this court was twofold. First, the allegation of homosexual relations between Mr
Price and the appellant was not an imputation on Mr Price's character or at least not
an imputation on his character in the sense in which character is used in s 1(f)(ii) of the
1898 Act. Second, if it was, the evidence of the appellant's own character and convictions
was so prejudicial that the judge should have exercised his discretion in favour of
the appellant to exclude it. In our opinion, the judge rightly rejected both submissions
and this appeal fails.

1 [1968] 2 All ER 497, [1970] AC 304

a Counsel for the appellant submitted that in these progessive (or permissive) days it was no longer an imputation on a man's character to say of him that he was a homo-sexual or that he practised homosexuality. Since 1967, when s 1 of the Sexual Offences Act 1967 became law, it was no longer an offence to commit a homosexual act with another man of full age in private. No reasonable person would now think the worse of a man who committed such acts; he might not wish to associate with him but he
b would not condemn him. We think that this argument goes too far and that the gap between what is declared by Parliament to be illegal and punishable and what the common man or woman still regards as immoral or wrong is not wide enough to support it. We respectfully agree with the opinion of Lord Reid in *Knuller v Director of Public Prosecutions*[1] that—

c   'there is a material difference between merely exempting certain conduct from criminal penalties and making it lawful in the full sense',

and with him we read the 1967 Act as saying that, even though homosexual acts between consenting adults in private may be corrupting, if people choose to corrupt themselves in this way, that is their affair and the law will not interfere. If Mr Price were to sue the appellant in respect of his allegation if repeated outside a court of law,
d we venture to think that a submission that the words were incapable of a defamatory meaning would be bound to fail and a jury would generally be likely to find them defamatory. Most men would be anxious to keep from a jury in any case the know-ledge that they practised such acts and many would be debarred from going to the police to charge another with any offence if they thought that he might defend himself by making such an allegation, whether baseless or not. If this is still true,
e we are not behind the times in holding that Mr Price's character was clearly impugned by the allegation of homosexual conduct made against him by the appellant.

   Then it is contended that even if the allegation reflects on his character, it does not reflect on his integrity, his honesty or his reliability so that he is thereby rendered less likely to be a truthful witness, or if in fact it has that effect it was not made with
f that intention. This contention, particularly the second part of it, is based on older authorities, particularly the well-known judgment given by Channell J in *R v Preston*[2], where he said this of s 1(*f*)(ii) of the 1898 Act:

g   '... if the defence is so conducted, or the nature of the defence is such, as to involve the proposition that the jury ought not to believe the prosecutor or one of the witnesses for the prosecution upon the ground that his conduct—not his evidence in the case, but his conduct outside the evidence given by him—makes him an unreliable witness, then the jury ought also to know the character of the prisoner who either gives that evidence or makes that charge, and it then becomes admissible to cross-examine the prisoner as to his antecedents and character with the view of shewing that he has such a bad character that the jury ought not to rely upon his evidence. That is the general nature of the enactment and
h   the general principle underlying it.'

And the court went on to hold[3]:

      'The statement in the present case was a mere unconsidered remark made by the prisoner without giving any serious attention to it, and in our opinion it does not come within s. 1, sub-s. (*f*)(ii.), of the Act as being an imputation made
j   upon the character of a witness for the prosecution for the purpose of discrediting his testimony,'

---

1 [1972] 2 All ER 898 at 904, [1973] AC 435 at 457
2 [1909] 1 KB 568 at 575
3 [1909] 1 KB at 576

Counsel says that the appellant's allegation against Mr Price was made not for the
purpose of discrediting his testimony but for the purpose of explaining his presence *a*
in Mr Price's room. We do not consider that this argument can succeed against the
plain words of s 1(*f*)(ii) given their natural and ordinary meaning. If we give them
that meaning, as we are now required to do by the House of Lords in *Selvey's* case[1] (see
for instance what Viscount Dilhorne said[2]), they cannot be restricted in the way suggested by the words of the judgment which we have just quoted. Though we agree *b*
that the general nature of the 1898 Act and the general principle underlying it are as
there stated, we do not accept the submission that an imputation of homosexual
immorality against a witness may not reflect on his reliability—generally or in the
witness box; nor do we accept the submission that a defendant can attack the character
of a witness without risk of the jury's learning that his own character is bad by disclaiming any intention to discredit the witness's testimony. Such a construction of the
section would enable many guilty men to resort to variations of 'the Portsmouth *c*
defence' with success by unfairly keeping the jury in ignorance of their true character
and would fly in the face of the decision in *Selvey's* case[1] to strip the plain words of
proviso (ii) of the gloss put on them in earlier cases.
    Counsel for the appellant referred us to numerous earlier authorities, but with
no disrespect to him we do not find it necessary or helpful to refer to them because, *d*
as counsel for the Crown pointed out, many of them are difficult to reconcile and
were given on a construction of the statute strained in the defendant's favour through
a failure to appreciate that the trial judge had a discretion: see *R v Cook*[3], approved
in *Selvey's* case[1].
    Once it is conceded, as counsel for the appellant rightly conceded, that an
imputation on character covers charges of faults or vices, whether reputed or real,
which are not criminal offences, it is difficult to restrict the statutory exception of *e*
proviso (ii) in any such way as has been suggested on behalf of the appellant.
    Being clearly of opinion that the appellant's allegation against Mr Price brought
him within proviso (ii), we have to ask whether the judge exercised his discretion
wrongly in admitting the appellant's previous convictions. Counsel for the appellant
began his appeal by abandoning this ground but on second thoughts returned to *f*
it. In our judgment his first thoughts were best. This court will not readily interfere
with the exercise of this discretion by the trial judge, and even if we thought that
we might ourselves have excluded the evidence, we would not decide that he was
wrong to admit it. In this case we do not find ourselves able to say that we would
have excluded it. Though, as we have said, gravely prejudicial, it was relevant to
the jury's consideration of the only escape route suggested by the appellant from
the conclusion to which all the evidence pointed in what was a strong case against *g*
him. We think that we would probably have admitted it.
    For these reasons the appeal has been dismissed.

Appeal dismissed.

The court certified under s 33 of the Criminal Appeal Act 1968 that the following point of law of *h*
general public importance was involved: 'Whether in law an allegation of homosexual practices
between consenting adults in private is incapable of being an imputation on the character of
the prosecutor or a witness for the prosecution within s 1(f)(ii) of the Criminal Evidence Act
1898', but refused leave to appeal to the House of Lords.

Solicitors: *Registrar of Criminal Appeals* (for the appellant); *Solicitor, Metropolitan* *j*
Police.

                                                          N P Metcalfe Esq Barrister.

1   [1968] 2 All ER 497, [1970] AC 304
2   [1968] 2 All ER at 508, [1970] AC at 339
3   [1959] 2 All ER 97, [1959] 2 QB 340

a

Brent v Brent

Dictum of DUNN J at 1215 disapproved in HALE v HALE [1975] 2 All
ER 1090

FAMILY DIVISION

DUNN J

23rd MAY 1974

b

Injunction – Husband and wife – Matrimonial home – Exclusion of spouse from home – Jurisdiction – Decree nisi granted – Applicant having no proprietary interest in home – Council dwelling – Tenancy in husband's name – Wife granted decree in consequence of husband's behaviour – Parties living together in home with grown-up children – Husband and wife not on speaking terms – Application by wife for injunction to exclude husband from
c *home – Whether court having jurisdiction to grant injunction.*

The husband and wife were married in 1950. There were two children of the marriage, a son and a daughter. The family lived in a council flat of which the husband was tenant. In 1969 the husband suffered a heart attack, and since October 1973 had been unable to work. He received sickness benefit at the rate of £14 per week. The wife
d and the two children, who were both over 18, were all working and between them earned £55 per week after deductions. In May 1974 the wife was granted a decree nisi of divorce under s 1(2)(*b*) of the Matrimonial Causes Act 1973 by reason of her husband's behaviour. At the time of the decree the situation in the flat was unhappy since the wife and daughter were not on speaking terms with the husband. The wife applied for an injunction excluding the husband from the flat.

e

Held – (i) The wife's right to occupy the matrimonial home during marriage did not continue after marriage and so could not thereafter be protected by injunction in the absence of any proprietary right of the wife in the premises. Furthermore the right of a wife to apply for a transfer of property order under s 24 of the 1973 Act was not a proprietary right which could be protected by a mandatory injunction. Accordingly
f the court had no jurisdiction after decree absolute to grant an injunction excluding the husband from premises wholly owned by him, or to grant an injunction before decree absolute calculated to produce such a result (see p 1214 *g* and p 1215 *a* and *c*, post); *Montgomery v Montgomery* [1964] 2 All ER 22 followed; *Gurasz v Gurasz* [1969] 3 All ER 822 distinguished.

(ii) Even if the court had jurisdiction, the case was not one in which an injunction
g should be granted for the real purpose of the application was to confirm the wife's occupancy of the flat in the hope that the housing authority would, by reason of the husband's illness, give him rehousing priority. The court would not, however, cut across the housing authority's practices by itself creating priorities. Furthermore the case was not one in which a wife on social security was having to look after small children, and the situation in the flat was such that it was not impossible for the parties
h to live there together (see p 1213 *j*, p 1215 *f* to *j* and p 1216 *a* and *b*, post).

Notes

For injunctions in matrimonial proceedings, see 12 Halsbury's Laws (3rd Edn) 477, 478, paras 1067-1069, and for cases on the subject, see 27(2) Digest (Reissue) 935, 936,
j 7543-7565.

For the Matrimonial Causes Act 1973, ss 1, 24, see 43 Halsbury's Statutes (3rd Edn) 541, 566.

Cases referred to in judgment

Gurasz v Gurasz [1969] 3 All ER 822, [1970] P 11, [1969] 3 WLR 482, CA, 27(1) Digest (Reissue) 97, 697.

Jones v Jones [1971] 2 All ER 737, [1971] 1 WLR 396, CA, 27(1) Digest (Reissue) 103, 710.
Montgomery v Montgomery [1964] 2 All ER 22, [1965] P 46, [1964] 2 WLR 1036, 27(2) *a*
    Digest (Reissue) 936, 7555.
Stewart v Stewart [1973] 1 All ER 31, [1973] Fam 21, [1972] 3 WLR 907.
Tarr v Tarr [1972] 2 All ER 295, [1973] AC 254 [1972] 2 WLR 1068, 136 JP 484, HL.

Cases cited in argument   *b*
Hall v Hall [1971] 1 All ER 762, [1971] 1 WLR 404, CA.
Morris v Tarrant [1971] 2 All ER 920, [1971] 2 QB 143.
Phillips v Phillips [1973] 2 All ER 423, [1973] 1 WLR 615, CA.
Vaughan v Vaughan [1953] 1 All ER 209, [1953] 1 QB 762, CA.

Summons   *c*
On 22nd May 1974 the wife, Josephine Mary Frances Brent, obtained a decree nisi of
divorce having satisfied the court that the husband, James Henry Brent, had behaved
in such a way that she could not reasonably be expected to live with him. By a summons of the same date the wife sought an injunction ordering the husband to vacate
the matrimonial home, 36 Horton House, Field Road, London, W6, and restraining
him from coming to or entering the premises. The facts are set out in the judgment.   *d*

Alan Ward for the wife.
Jonathan Sofer for the husband.

DUNN J. This is an application by a wife for an injunction ordering the husband to
vacate the matrimonial home, which is a flat, 36 Horton House, London, W6. The   *e*
background to the application is that the parties were married in 1950. They themselves
are now both in their late forties. They have two grown-up children, a boy, James, of
20 and a girl, Christine, of 18. Yesterday, as the result of a defended divorce suit, I
granted the wife a decree nisi on the prayer of her petition, on the ground of irretrievable breakdown under s 1(2)(*b*) of the Matrimonial Causes Act 1973, and I rejected
the prayer of the answer, which prayed for dissolution under that same section.   *f*
The flat in question is a three-bedroomed flat owned by the Hammersmith Borough
Council, of which the husband is the tenant. The family have occupied the flat for
about the last seven years and the rent is now about £9 a week.
    Until 1969 both husband and wife were working, the husband earning between £50
and £60 a week as a foreman. In 1969 the husband had the misfortune to suffer a heart
attack. He suffers from angina pectoris and an atrial flutter. He returned to light   *g*
work in February 1970, but has been unable to do more than light work since. He has
had a recurrence of heart trouble more than once. Since October 1973 he has been
unable to work at all. His employers, who obviously regarded him as a good workman, paid his wages until January 1974, when they said they were unable to continue
to do so and, moreover, were unable to employ him again unless he was passed fit
for work by their own doctor. So he is now unable to work, maybe permanently.   *h*
    He is living on sickness benefit, which is at the rate of about £14 a week, and it is at
that figure because he is still living in the same household as his wife, who is herself fit
to work and working. If he were not living in those circumstances he would
receive about £18 a week by way of sickness benefit. The wife herself is a hard-
working woman. She works full time and she earns about £20 a week; that is her
take home pay after all deductions. The daughter, Christine, brings home about £15   *j*
a week. The son, James, works as a mate to a lorry driver and he brings home about
£20 a week, although at the present time he is also ill in hospital; but there is no
suggestion that his illness is chronic. It is conceded by counsel for the wife that on
those figures she would not be entitled to any financial provision under Part II of the
1973 Act, either by way of periodical payments or otherwise.

a   The husband told me, and I accept, that if he were to leave the flat, leave the
furniture in the flat and take furnished accommodation, it would cost him about £14
a week. He told me that he would be willing, if the wife and children left the flat, to
surrender his tenancy and hope that he would be granted by the council a tenancy of
one room for himself. His counsel, on his behalf, submits that the wife and the two
children between them, if they wish to live together, can, with some £55 a week net
b   which the three of them are earning, well afford alternative accommodation.

The present position in the flat is plainly an unhappy one. I referred to it in my judgment in the divorce suit. The husband excluded the wife and children from the flat in
August 1973 by changing the locks, but in October 1973 Watkins J made an order that
the wife was to return to the flat, on cross-undertakings by husband and wife not to
molest one another. Apart from one incident in November, to which I referred in my
c   judgment, there have been no major incidents since then. The situation now is that
the husband and wife are not on speaking terms. The husband and daughter do not
get on together, but the husband and son, James, as the result of a reconciliation
some months ago, are now on good terms. They go out together and they find
pleasure in one another's company.

The wife and daughter say that the situation in the flat is impossible so long as all
d   four of them are living there. The husband says that the situation, though not happy,
is not impossible, particularly having regard to his relations with his son. But from a
human and social point of view it is obviously undesirable that the situation should
continue longer than is necessary. The wife told me that when she applied to the
council for rehousing they told her to reapply after the decision in the divorce case
was known.

e   The basis of the wife's application is, first, that this court has held that the husband
has behaved in such a way that the wife could not reasonably be expected to live with
him, and that he, by his behaviour, has brought the present situation on himself. It is
also said, and said rightly, that there is medical evidence to the effect that for some
years past—certainly since 1972—the wife has been consulting a doctor for anxiety
and depressive problems and has been prescribed sedation and tranquillisation. And
f   it is said that the wife and the two children together form a family unit, and that the
court should protect that family unit by making the order which is asked for. Finally,
it is said that, in reality, it is a pure accident that the husband is the sole tenant of this
house; that if the house were freehold the wife, having worked all her life and having
contributed to the welfare of the family, would undoubtedly be held by the court to
have a share in the equity of the house, and that the court should not take too strict a
view of the proprietary rights of the parties.
g   It is well established that this court will, in a proper case pending suit, control the
occupation of the matrimonial home and will, if the situation warrants it, on well-
established principles even make an order, the effect of which is to exclude a husband
from his own property. And strictly, these parties being still married, it might be
said that at any rate until decree absolute those well-established principles should
h   apply.

But the real reason for this application is not to control the situation pending suit,
but to create a situation which will exist after the dissolution of the marriage by decree
absolute, because the real purpose of this application is that the court should order the
husband to vacate the matrimonial home so that the wife may apply for the tenancy
to be transferred to her, and that she may continue to live there with the children
j   even after the marriage has been dissolved, in the hope that because of his medical
condition the housing authority will give the husband sufficiently high priority to
rehouse him in some other accommodation.

So I approach this application looking ahead—only a matter of six weeks—to the
time when these parties are no longer husband and wife. Nothing that I say in this
judgment is to be taken as in any way affecting the principle that this court will
protect the interests of infant children to remain in occupation of the matrimonial

home, as was done in *Stewart v Stewart*[1]. But this is not a case of infant children. *a*
This is a case of a wage-earning mother and two grown-up wage-earning children
on the one hand, and on the other of a man who, through no fault of his own,
is living on sickness benefit; and a case in which, on the basis that I approach it,
husband and wife will no longer be husband and wife.

The first question that I have to decide is whether I have the jurisdiction to make the
order which is prayed. In *Montgomery v Montgomery*[2] Ormrod J held that where a wife *b*
had no proprietary right in the premises in which the parties were living, the court
had no jurisdiction to make a mandatory order to exclude the husband from those
premises. The basis of his judgment was that the wife had no legal right to exclude her
husband from the premises and therefore, there being no legal right, the court had
no jurisdiction to grant her an injunction.

Counsel for the wife submitted that I should not follow that case, firstly because it *c*
was wrongly decided. He referred me to *Jones v Jones*[3] in which Karminski LJ expressed
some doubts about the decision in *Montgomery v Montgomery*[2] He submitted that a
wife, as was held in *Montgomery v Montgomery*[2], even after decree absolute has a right
not to be molested by her former husband, and that she also has a right, at common
law, to be provided with a roof over her head. In support of that submission counsel
referred me to *Gurasz v Gurasz*[4] in which Lord Denning MR dealt with the position at *d*
common law, and said[5]:

> 'Some features of family life are elemental in our society. One is that it is the
> husband's duty to provide his wife with a roof over her head; and the children too.
> So long as the wife behaves herself, she is entitled to remain in the matrimonial
> home . . . This right is a personal right which belongs to her as a wife. It is not a
> proprietary right . . . It is only available against the husband.' *e*

Counsel for the wife submitted that that right was overlooked by Ormrod J in
Montgomery v Montgomery[2], and that it constituted a right which the courts had
jurisdiction to protect by the grant of an injunction in a proper case.

Counsel for the wife also submitted that the law had changed since *Montgomery v
Montgomery*[2], because, as a result of the provisions of what is now Part II of the *f*
Matrimonial Causes Act 1973, the wife has a right to apply for the transfer of the
matrimonial home to her, and that, says counsel, is a right which this court also has
jurisdiction to protect by injunction; so that even if *Montgomery v Montgomery*[2] was
rightly decided in 1964, it should be differently decided today.

I do not accept that the right to remain in occupation of the matrimonial home
during marriage is a right which continues after marriage so that it can thereafter *g*
be protected by injunction, in the absence of any proprietary right of the wife in the
premises. It is relevant that in *Gurasz v Gurasz*[4] the matrimonial home was owned
by the parties jointly, and as Lord Denning MR said[6]:

> 'In the first place, the wife has a proprietary right in the house. She is joint
> owner with her husband. By virtue of her joint ownership, she has a right to *h*
> occupy the house by herself and her children. The courts can certainly enforce
> that right by allowing her to re-enter the house and by preventing the husband
> from interfering with her exercise of that right . . . If his conduct is so out-
> rageous as to make it impossible for them to live together, the court can restrain
> him from using the house, even though he is a joint owner.'

j

---

1 [1973] 1 All ER 31, [1973] Fam 21
2 [1964] 2 All ER 22, [1965] P 46
3 [1971] 2 All ER 737, [1971] 1 WLR 396
4 [1969] 3 All ER 822, [1970] P 11
5 [1969] 3 All ER at 823, [1970] P at 16
6 [1969] 3 All ER at 824, [1970] P at 17

a   No such proprietary right exists in the wife in this case. And, in *Gurasz v Gurasz*[1] the parties were still husband and wife.

Nor do I agree that the undoubted right of the wife to apply under s 24 of the Matrimonial Causes Act 1973 for transfer of property is a proprietary right which can be protected by a mandatory injunction ordering the husband to leave the house. No such application is before me. If the wife were to make such an application, the
b   court would have ample powers under the relevant statutory provision to make orders protecting the property and restraining the husband from disposing of it. But I am doubtful whether a mere tenancy from a council—which is the only interest which this husband has in this property—could be said to be property in respect of which the court would ever make a transfer order under s 24 of the Matrimonial Causes Act 1973.

c   For those reasons I follow *Montgomery v Montgomery*[2] and hold that after decree absolute this court has no jurisdiction to make an injunction excluding the husband from premises wholly owned by him nor, as is the fact in this case, before decree absolute to make such an order, the purpose and effect of which is to produce that result.

Counsel for the husband referred me to *Tarr v Tarr*[3], a case in which the House
d   of Lords held that on an application under s 1(2) of the Matrimonial Homes Act 1967 the court had no power to prohibit the exercise by the property-owning spouse of his right to occupy his home. Counsel commented that it was surprising that that case should have gone right through the courts without apparently it ever having been suggested that the wife could have achieved the same result by applying to the court under its inherent jurisdiction for an injunction prohibiting the husband from occupying the matrimonial home.
e   I think it right, notwithstanding the decision which I have reached on the question of jurisdiction, to consider the matter on the basis that in fact I have jurisdiction to make the order which is asked for. I have already indicated that this is not a case in which infant children are involved, so I do not pause to consider the special principles which apply to them. Having heard a great deal of evidence as to the circumstances
f   in the house, I do not find that it is impossible or intolerable for the parties to continue living there. The state of health of the wife is nowhere approaching the state of health of the wife in cases in which it has been held that it is impossible for the family to continue living in the home. I saw her in the witness box at some length. No doubt she is anxious and depressed, but she is a robust, strong-minded woman, perfectly capable of coping with the situation.

g   I agree with counsel for the husband that this application is really an attempt to force the hand of the local authority. Not only that, but it is an attempt to do so in the absence of the local authority. It is to be observed that in the private sector—which is the only sector of housing covered by the Matrimonial Homes Act 1967—notice must be served on the landlord of any application in relation to occupation by a tenant. Similarly, if application is made for transfer of property under the Matrimonial Causes
h   Act 1973, notice must be served on the mortgagees, if there are any. But this is council property. Counsel for the husband submits that the effect of this order would be to dispose of part of the council's housing stock without hearing the council.

I also agree with counsel for the husband that the court should not lend itself to any extension of attempts to influence the housing priorities of the local authority by itself creating priorities. There is no evidence before me and I do not know the various
j   priorities and the various matters which are taken into consideration by the Hammersmith Borough Council in offering council accommodation to different classes of persons. It seems to me that those are matters exclusively for them. They have their statutory duties and they must perform them in accordance with their own practice.

1   [1969] 3 All ER 822, [1970] P 11
2   [1964] 2 All ER 22, [1965] P 46
3   [1972] 2 All ER 295, [1973] AC 254

It is not for this court to step in and present them with a situation which may or may   a
not cut right across their accepted procedures and practices.

This is not, like so many of the cases, the case of a wife living on social security with
small children to bring up, and a wage-earning husband. It is the case of a wage-
earning wife and two adult wage-earning children, and a sick husband. It is, as I see
it, a housing problem which is for the local authority to solve and not for this court.
It is a housing problem involving the housing of four independent adults, and accord-   b
ingly, even if I had held that I had jurisdiction to make the order asked for, I would
not make it. This application accordingly must be refused.

Application dismissed.

Solicitors: *Watson, Marshal & Co* (for the wife); *Myers, Ebner & Deaner* (for the   c
husband).

R C T Habesch Esq Barrister.

d

R v Marquis   <small>Applied in R v WEHNER [1977]
3 All ER 553</small>

COURT OF APPEAL, CRIMINAL DIVISION
LORD WIDGERY CJ, PARK AND FORBES JJ
10th JUNE 1974

e

*Criminal law – Sentence – Probation order – Willingness of offender to comply with order –
Probation order ineffective unless offender expresses his willingness to comply – Offender to
be given a fair opportunity to make choice whether to be bound by order – Offender given
impression custodial sentence only alternative to order – Whether order valid – Criminal
Justice Act 1948, s 3(5) (as amended by the Children and Young Persons Act 1969, s 72(4),*   f
Sch 6).

*Criminal law – Appeal – Sentence – Probation order – Right of appeal against order – Order
invalid.*

The appellant, who was aged 19 and had no previous convictions, was convicted in
the Crown Court of handling stolen goods. Following her conviction the trial judge   g
asked whether she wished to be put on probation. The appellant made it clear that
she did not. Further discussion took place, as a result of which the appellant was
given the impression that the only alternative to probation was a custodial sentence.
The judge then asked again whether she was prepared to be put on probation, to
which she replied: 'I will agree to be put on probation only because the court offers
an alternative of a custodial sentence'. Accordingly, the judge ordered that she be put   h
on probation for three years. On appeal,

Held – Under s 3(5)[a] of the Criminal Justice Act 1948 a probation order could not
effectively be made unless the defendant had expressed his willingness to be bound
by the requirements thereof. For that purpose the defendant had to be given a fair
opportunity to make his choice whether to agree to the terms of the order. Since   j
the appellant had been given the false impression that the only alternative to probation was a custodial sentence, she had not been given a fair chance to decide for
herself whether she was willing to be bound by the terms of the order or not. It

---

a Section 3(5), as amended and so far as material, is set out at p 1218 *j*, post

t has been submitted here, and is accepted by the prosecution, however, is *a*
a person has had imposed on him or her in the Crown Court a probation order,
pen to that person to appeal to this court if the ground of appeal is that the
g of the order was defective, and that therefore no probation order was made
. If the matter is argued on that basis, it is said, and accepted by the Crown in
present argument, that it is open for the accused to complain to this court, because
is then a person who has been convicted and who is complaining of a sentence *b*
known to the law, namely a purported probation order which for one reason
another could not be such. That is the basis of the present case.

The appellant having been convicted, the question arose as to her disposal, and a
somewhat lengthy discussion took place between the trial judge, counsel, the appel-
nt at times and her father on occasions as well, whether a probation order was
to be made. To anyone who reads the transcript, it is clear that the appellant did not *c*
want to be put on probation; she seems to have been a young woman with a mind
of her own. Further it is quite clear to this court that there were good arguments
against the making of a probation order; she did not seem to need the supervision
thus involved. For the reasons already mentioned based on *R v Tucker*[1], she could
not come and complain of the probation order on its merits merely by arguing it was
not necessary. It is the other approach, that the probation order ultimately purporting *d*
to be made was ineffective, which is relevant in this case.

There was a somewhat protracted discussion about what was to happen to her.
There is no doubt whatever that she was given the impression that if the probation
order was not made, the only alternative was a custodial sentence. That was not an
impression which she ought to have been given because, on the facts of this case, a
custodial sentence, far from being the only alternative, was an exceedingly remote *e*
alternative.

It is possible in a case of this kind that a court might send a juvenile to a detention
centre, but at the material time the detention centres for girls had all been closed,
so that was not possible. She could of course have been given a sentence of up to
six months imprisonment, but that for a girl of good character was not appropriate,
and borstal equally seems unsuitable, so it really is not right to assess the alternatives *f*
in the way in which it was, either a probation order or a custodial sentence. However,
through the course of the discussions that went on there seems to be little doubt
that the appellant had got it into her mind that those were the only two alternatives.

When she was asked by the judge the commonplace if not particularly accurate
question: 'Are you willing to be put on probation?' she said: 'I don't want to be
put on probation.' The judge said: 'You don't want to be put on probation?' The *g*
appellant: 'What am I meant to do? They tell me if I don't want probation you are
going to lock me up.' Then she showed signs of distress, and the judge told her father
to take her out and give her a glass of water. In due course she came back to the dock.
The judge said: 'Have you had a chance to talk it over with your father?' The appellant:
'Yes, your Honour.' The judge: 'If we are prepared to make a probation order, are
you prepared to be put on probation?' Answer: 'I will agree to be put on probation *h*
only because the court offers an alternative of a custodial sentence.'

Whether the court regarded itself as offering only those two alternatives is very
hard to say, but what was going through the girl's mind was very clear. She was
saying: I consent but only because I understand the alternative is a custodial sentence.

The question is: was that an adequate consent from the proposed probationer to
make the probation order subsequently imposed a valid order? This depends on *j*
s 3(5) of the Criminal Justice Act 1948 which provides:

> 'Before making a probation order, the court shall explain to the offender in
> ordinary language the effect of the order ... and that if he fails to comply therewith
> or commits another offence he will be liable to be sentenced for the original

1 Page 639, ante, [1974] 1 WLR 615

followed that the order had been made in contraven
a sentence known to the law. Accordingly, as a perso
subject to a sentence unknown to the law, she was en
would be allowed and a conditional discharge for tw
'probation order' (see p 1219 *a* to *d*, post).

R v Tucker p 639, ante, distinguished.

Notes

For the making of a probation order, see 10 Halsbury's Lav
para 912, and for cases on the subject, see 14 Digest (Repl) 573,

For the Criminal Justice Act 1948, s 3, see 8 Halsbury's Statu

As from 1st July 1974, s 3(5) of the 1948 Act has been replacec
Criminal Courts Act 1973, s 2(6).

Case referred to in judgment

R v Tucker p 639, ante, [1974] 1 WLR 615, CA.

Case also cited

R v Clarke [1972] 1 All ER 219, CA.

Appeal

On 15th January 1974 in the Crown Court at Norwich before his Honour Juc
the appellant, Yvonne Marquis, was convicted of handling stolen goods.
put on probation for a period of three years and ordered to pay the sum of £
value of the goods in question, to the firm from which they had been stolen.
was also ordered to pay £200 towards the legal aid costs of her defence. She appe
against sentence with leave of the single judge. The facts are set out in the judgm
of the court.

Colin Lamb for the appellant.
Gerald Draycott for the Crown.

LORD WIDGERY CJ delivered the following judgment of the court. On 14th January 1974 at the Norwich Crown Court the appellant, together with a man known as
Hale, was charged on a count of theft, and later an alternative count of handling
was added. The basis of these charges was that she and Hale worked together in a
shop; he was responsible for a department, or it may have been a counter, on which
curtain material and the like was sold. The prosecution case was that the appellant
came into the shop, went through the motions of buying a portion of curtain material,
but that which was charged up to her comprised very much less than the price which
ought to have been paid; the basis of the complaint was that that was something
which had been arranged between the appellant and Hale. Hale pleaded guilty to
theft, the appellant pleaded not guilty to both charges, but she was eventually convicted of handling and received a probation order for three years. It is arising out of
that probation order that the matter comes before this court.

In the ordinary way, as was decided by this court in R v Tucker[1], there is no appeal
under the Criminal Appeal Act 1968 against the merits of a probation order; that
is because a person who has been convicted by a jury and subsequently put on probation is not to be regarded for present purposes as having been convicted at all,
and since she is not regarded as having been convicted at all, that means that she does
not satisfy the requirements of the Criminal Appeal Act 1968 of being a person
convicted and thus entitled to appeal against sentence.

---

1   Page 639, ante, [1974] 1 WLR 615

a offence; and the court shall not make the order unless he expresses his willingness to comply with the requirements thereof.'

So a probation order cannot effectively be made unless the intended probationer expresses his willingness to be bound by the requirements thereof.

That means, in our judgment, that the probationer must be given a fair opportunity to make his choice, and if the probationer apparently agrees to comply with the *b* terms of the probation order, but has not really been given a fair choice, that agreement should not be adhered to by the courts, and an opportunity should be taken if possible to have the matter reviewed.

In this case, if the appellant thought, as we have no doubt she did think, that it was a probation order or a custodial sentence, when in fact those are not the only possible alternatives, or even the probable alternatives, we take the view that she *c* was not given a fair chance to decide for herself whether she was willing to be bound by the terms of the order or not, and that accordingly we should regard the order as having been made without the consent of the probationer as required by s 3(5) of the 1948 Act. Once one reaches that point, the purported probation order was not a probation order at all; accordingly it was a sentence unknown to the law, and from that it is possible to go to s 9 of the Criminal Appeal Act 1968 and say that the appel-*d* lant, having been convicted by the jury, was subject to a sentence which this court regards as being a sentence which requires review. It is for us to decide under s 11(3) of the 1968 Act whether she ought to be sentenced differently. We think she ought to be sentenced differently not merely because of her personal choice, but because she was not a girl who needed a probation order; so we shall allow the appeal and substitute for the probation order a conditional discharge for two years.

e

Appeal allowed. Sentence varied.

Solicitors: *Registrar of Criminal Appeals* (for the appellant); *J V Bates*, Norwich (for the Crown).

N P Metcalfe Esq Barrister.

f

R v Thames Magistrates' Court, ex parte Polemis

QUEEN'S BENCH DIVISION
g LORD WIDGERY CJ, ASHWORTH AND BRISTOW JJ
8th MAY 1974

Natural justice – Hearing – Duty to hear parties etc – Opportunity to prepare case – Party allocated time for case to be heard – Party not given reasonable opportunity to prepare case – Whether breach of rules of natural justice.
h

Certiorari – Ground of complaint – Failure to grant adjournment – Magistrates' court – Application by defendant for adjournment – Purpose of adjournment to enable defendant to have reasonable time to prepare his case – Failure to give defendant reasonable opportunity to prepare case breach of rules of natural justice – Whether failure to grant adjournment ground for certiorari.
j

The applicant, a Greek who had little knowledge of English, was the master of a vessel which, on 1st July 1973 arrived at a berth in the London docks. The berth was clean and no oil was seen in the neighbourhood of the vessel over the next seven or eight days. On 9th July a large patch of oil appeared close to the vessel. Analysts' reports were obtained by the authorities on samples of the oil and of the oil

in the vessel's bunkers. At 10.30 a m on 11th July a summons was served on the applicant charging that he was the master of a vessel from which oil or a mixture containing
oil had been discharged into navigable waters, contrary to s 2(1)^a of the Prevention of
Oil Pollution Act 1971. The applicant's vessel was due to sail at 9.00 p m on 11th
July and the summons was returnable at the magistrates' court at 2.00 p m on that
day. The owners of the vessel obtained the services of solicitors who immediately took
steps to obtain samples of the oil, to find eye-witnesses and to obtain other evidence.
They had, however, made little progress before 2.00 p m. At 2.30 p m the case came
before a bench of lay justices who rejected an application for an adjournment, being
impressed by the fact that the applicant's vessel was due to sail that evening. As
a concession to the difficulties of the defence, however, they stood over the hearing
until 4.00 p m on the same day. At 4.00 p m the justices were still occupied with their
own list and so the case was transferred to a stipendiary magistrate then sitting in the
same building. No new application for an adjournment was made to the magistrate,
although he knew that an earlier application had been made and refused. He heard
the case out and convicted the applicant, fining him £5,000. On a motion by the
applicant for an order of certiorari to quash the conviction, it was contended, inter
alia, by the respondents that it was not the practice of the court to allow an order of
certiorari to go where the complaint was that the inferior court had failed to grant an
adjournment when it should have done.

Held – An order of certiorari would be granted for the following reasons—
    (i) It was a requirement of the rules of natural justice that a party to proceedings,
and particularly the defendant in a criminal case, should be given a reasonable
opportunity to present his case, and that included a reasonable opportunity to prepare
his case before being called on to present it. On the facts the applicant had not
been given such an opportunity (see p 1223 *a* to *f* and p 1225 *j*, post); dictum of Viscount
Haldane LC in *Local Government Board v Arlidge* [1914-15] All ER Rep at 6 applied.
    (ii) There was no general rule that certiorari could never be used to correct a breach
of the rules of natural justice when the manifestation of that breach took the form
of a refusal to grant an adjournment. When the central allegation was that the
applicant had not been given a reasonable time to prepare his case, the mere fact that
that had become apparent as the result of a refusal of an adjournment did not prevent
the court from treating the basic cause of complaint, i e the failure to provide the
applicant with adequate time, as being a ground on which certiorari should be granted
(see p 1224 *g* and p 1225 *b c* and *j*, post).
    Per Curiam. When the court cannot conduct a trial in accordance with the rules
of natural justice in the time available before the defendant's ship sails, the court
should ensure that some sensible provision is made for security for the appropriate
penalty in the event of a conviction, bearing in mind that, in the absence of security
being offered, the court has power, as a last resort, to remand the defendant in custody
(see p 1225 *e* to *j*, post).

Notes
For orders of prohibition or certiorari when there has been a breach in the rules of
natural justice in judicial proceedings, see 11 Halsbury's Laws (3rd Edn), 64-66, para
122, and for cases on the circumstances in which certiorari may be granted, see 16
Digest (Repl) 466-470, 2862-2904.
    For the requirement of natural justice that a party should be given an opportunity
to be heard, see 1 Halsbury's Laws (4th Edn) 93, 94, para 76.
    For the Prevention of Oil Pollution Act 1971, s 2, see 41 Halsbury's Statutes (3rd
Edn) 1364.

Cases referred to in judgment
Ekins, Re (1953) 117 JP Jo 705, DC, 16 Digest (Repl) 484, 3029.

---

a Section 2(1), so far as material, is set out at p 1221 *j*, post

a   *Local Government Board v Arlidge* [1915] AC 120, [1914-15] All ER Rep 1, 84 LJKB 72, 111 LT 905, 79 JP 97, 12 LGR 1109, HL; *rvsg* [1914] 1 KB 160, 83 LJKB 86, 109 LT 651, 78 JP 25, 11 LGR 1186, CA, 51 Digest (Repl) 644, *2532*.
R (Harrington) v Clare County Court Judge and County Justices [1918] 2 IR 116, 580, 33 Digest (Repl) 166, *145*.

b   **Motion for certiorari**
This was an application by way of motion by Andreas Polemis, of the Greek Merchant Navy, employed by Portland Shipping Corporation of Panama, for an order of certiorari to bring up and quash an order made by the respondents, Thames Magistrates' Court, on 11th July 1973 whereby it was adjudged that the applicant had been guilty of an offence against s 2(1) of the Prevention of Oil Pollution Act 1971, and the applicant was ordered to pay a fine of £5,000, plus court and analysts' costs within
c   28 days, or be committed to prison in default. The facts are set out in the judgment of Lord Widgery CJ.

Conrad Dehn QC and *Mark Potter* for the applicant.
Alan Campbell QC and *Ami Feder* for the respondents.

d   **LORD WIDGERY CJ.** In these proceedings counsel moves on behalf of the applicant for an order of certiorari to bring up into this court with a view to its being quashed an order made by the Thames Magistrates' Court on 11th July 1973 whereby it was adjudged that the applicant was guilty of the following offence, namely, that on 9th July 1973 at no 17 shed, West India Dock, he was the master of the motor vessel
e   Corinthic from which oil or a mixture containing oil was discharged into navigable waters, namely, West India Dock waters, contrary to s 2(1) of the Prevention of Oil Pollution Act 1971.
On 1st July 1973 the motor vessel Corinthic came up the Thames and berthed at no 17 shed in the West India Dock. The applicant was the master of the vessel, and she was due to sail again from the Port of London on 11th July after a stay of
f   approximately ten days.
Evidence for the prosecution given at the hearing before the justices was that she went into a clean berth and that no oil was observed in her neighbourhood in the dock over the seven or eight days following her arrival on 1st July. It was, however, testified by witnesses called for the prosecution that on 9th July there became apparent a large patch of oil on the water close to the Corinthic, a patch of oil which those seeing
g   it considered or suspected to have come from her bilges and to have been discharged into the dock contrary to the section to which I have referred.
Accordingly, analysts' reports having been obtained by the prosecution in respect of samples obtained of the oil and of oil in the ship's bunkers and bilges, on 11th July, the day she was due to sail, at 10.30 a m her captain was served with a summons alleging the discharge of oil into the waters of the West India Dock in the terms to
h   which I have referred. The summons was returnable at the Thames Magistrates' Court at 2.00 p m that very afternoon, some 3½ hours after it had been served on him.
The offence under the section in question is not a trivial matter by any means. Section 2(1) of the Prevention of Oil Pollution Act 1971 provides:

j   'If any oil or mixture containing oil is discharged as mentioned in the following paragraphs into waters to which this section applies, then, subject to the provisions of this Act, the following shall be guilty of an offence . . .'

and we find that the owner or master of the vessel may be held guilty of an offence if the discharge is from a vessel.
When we come to look at s 3(3), where the penalty for this offence is given, it is stated:

'A person guilty of an offence under this section shall be liable on summary
conviction to a fine not exceeding £50,000 or on conviction on indictment to a
fine.'

In fact the justices awarded a fine of £5,000 in this case. I cite the figure to show this
is a matter of significance, and at 10.30 a m this Greek-speaking captain was served
with this summons, returnable at 2.00 p m.

No one, I venture to think, would criticise the speed with which the prosecution
obtained the issue of the summons and served it. It was obviously necessary for
them to get the summons issued and served before the ship sailed, and the speed
with which they acted up to that point is commendable in my judgment and certainly
not open to criticism. But one only has to pause for a moment and visualise the
situation of the applicant, who knows nothing of the complaint until 10.30 a m and
who finds himself summoned to appear and defend himself at 2.00 p m that same
afternoon.

The representatives of the owners of the ship instructed solicitors. A considerable
amount of energy was expended by those solicitors in the morning of 11th July to
see what could be done to prepare for a hearing at 2.00 p m. It was apparent to them
that they would have to consider the obtaining of samples of the oil, because at that
stage they had not had any information about the prosecution samples. It was also
apparent to them that they might have to look for factual evidence of when the oil
first appeared, the state of the wind and weather which might affect the accumulation
of oil in the vicinity of the ship and, to put it briefly, to find eye-witnesses who might
speak to an oil situation different from that spoken to by the witnesses called for the
Crown.

Needless to say, by 2.00 p m, when everybody gathered at the Thames Magistrates'
Court, the defence had not made a great deal of progress on any of those matters.
The court did not sit until 2.30 p m because it had had a rather heavy morning and no
doubt adjourned late. When it sat at 2.30 p m the solicitor appearing for the applicant, the captain of the ship, asked for an adjournment. One ventures to think he
asked for it with some confidence from the short interval of time since the summons
had been served. He made his application to a bench of lay justices, who considered
it rapidly, one gathers from the evidence, and determined that the matter must
be heard that day.

I have no doubt, in fairness to them, that they were much impressed by the fact
that this ship was going to sail at 9.00 p m that night, which was a practical aspect
of this matter which clearly could not be overlooked. But be that as it may, the
decision of the four lay justices was that there should be no adjournment, but as a
concession to the defence difficulties they said that the case could stand over until
4.00 p m, which would give the applicant's solicitor just that much extra time to find
out what he could about the affair.

At 4.00 p m the lay justices, who had adjourned the case for 1½ hours, were still
occupied on their own list, and so the case was transferred to a stipendiary magistrate
sitting in the same building. He heard the case out. I think on balance on the
evidence no further application was made to him, although he knew that an
application for adjournment had been made and refused. He heard the case out and
found the case proved. He imposed a fine of £5,000.

The ship sailed that night and has not been back to the Port of London since, and
all that happened since the date of the hearing is that, on request from the applicant's
solicitors, the prosecution have supplied samples of the oil which the applicant has
been able to have independently analysed. Although we have not seen the analyst's
report, we are told that it was not favourable to the applicant. Therefore, so far as
these matters are of materiality, we would have to proceed on the footing that there
was considerable evidence to identify the oil in the water as being the kind of oil
which might have been found in the Corinthic's bilges.

a However, the matter in fact comes to us on a motion for certiorari on the footing that in the circumstances which I have outlined, and which are not really subject to dispute, there has here been a breach of the rules of natural justice.

To start with, nothing is clearer today than that a breach of the rules of natural justice is said to occur if a party to proceedings, and more especially the defendant in a criminal case, is not given a reasonable chance to present his case. It is so elemen-
b tary and so basic it hardly needs to be said. But of the versions of breach of the rules of natural justice with which in this court we are dealing constantly, perhaps the most common today is the allegation that the defence were prejudiced because they were not given a fair and reasonable opportunity to present their case to the court, and of course the opportunity to present a case to the court is not confined to being given an opportunity to stand up and say what you want to say; it necessarily extends to a reasonable opportunity to prepare your case before you are called on to present it.
c A mere allocation of court time is of no value if the party in question is deprived of the opportunity of getting his tackle in order and being able to present his case in the fullest sense. I have said one hardly needs authority for that, but in *Local Government Board v Arlidge*[1] the point was well made by Viscount Haldane LC when he said:

d   'My Lords, when the duty of deciding an appeal is imposed, those whose duty it is to decide it must act judicially. They must deal with the question referred to them without bias, and they must give to each of the parties the opportunity of adequately presenting the case made.'

In this instance, on the brief and simple facts that I have related, can it be said that
e the applicant was given a reasonable opportunity to present his case? It seems to me to be totally unarguable that he was given such a reasonable opportunity. He had no time to take samples, no time to see a report of the samples taken by the prose-cution, no time to look for witnesses, no time to prepare any supporting evidence supportive to his own, and that too when he was a man with a very rudimentary knowledge of the English language in a country foreign to his own. When one just
f looks at those facts it seems to me to be a case in which any suggestion that he had a reasonable chance to prepare his defence is completely unarguable.

What is said on the other side? Counsel for the respondents, who has said every-thing possible, has made three points. He says first of all that the relief of certiorari is discretionary, and so it is. No one can come to this court and demand an order of certiorari as of right. No such order goes unless the court in its discretion thinks that the situation is appropriate.
g Counsel for the respondents says that in this case, when one looks at the whole history of the matter right up to today, it becomes only too obvious that the applicant has no merit in his case. Counsel relies on the fact that the analyst's report supplied to the applicant was unfavourable, and that there has been no sort of suggestion over the period which has elapsed since the hearing that the applicant could call any evidence in regard to the state of the weather, which would support his own
h theory which was that the oil had been there when he came in to berth. So, says counsel for the respondents, looking back now with hindsight on all these events, it is apparent that there is no merit in the applicant's case, and therefore the court in its discretion should refuse him an order of certiorari.

I reject that submission. It is again absolutely basic to our system that justice
j must not only be done but must manifestly be seen to be done. If justice was so clearly not seen to be done, as on the afternoon in question here, it seems to me that it is no answer to the applicant to say, 'Well, even if the case had been properly con-ducted, the result would have been the same'. That is mixing up doing justice with seeing that justice is done, so I reject that argument.

---

1   [1915] AC 120 at 132, [1914-15] All ER Rep 1 at 6

Counsel's second submission is a technical one, but none the worse for that. He
submits that the fault which is alleged by the applicant was the refusal of an adjournment. He says correctly that the adjournment was refused by the court of lay justices
who considered the matter at 2.30 p m. He says that, that being the case, it cannot be a
foundation for an order of certiorari to go and quash the decision of the stipendiary
magistrate when he took over at 4.00 p m that afternoon.

Again in my judgment there is no substance in that argument. In deciding whether
an accused has been treated in accordance with the rules of natural justice, one must,
I think, look at the way in which he was treated on the occasion in question and on
the charge in question, and I see no reason whatever to distinguish between what
happened before the lay justices and what happened before the stipendiary magistrate. The overall picture is that when the applicant went to that court at 2.00 p m
and eventually came out at, I suppose, about 5.00 p m, he had not been treated in
accordance with the rules of natural justice. It seems to me to be totally unimportant
to decide what contribution towards that unhappy result was made by one bench
of magistrates as compared with the other.

Then, thirdly, counsel for the respondent says that it is not the practice, and never
has been the practice in this court, to allow an order of certiorari to go where the
complaint is that the inferior court declined to order an adjournment when it should.
Surprisingly enough, despite his industry, there is only one case cited in support of
this proposition, although for myself I do not hesitate to accept it as being generally
correct. The case cited is *Re Ekins*[1]. It was, if one may be permitted to say so, a
rather cheeky application for an adjournment because the accused had been charged
with riding a motor cycle uninsured. When he came to answer the charge he put
up the defence that he had sold the motor cycle before the date in question and
therefore could not have ridden it. He produced some documents representing a
receipt for the deposit on the sale of the cycle and an IOU for the balance. When
the prosecution saw those documents they cross-examined the accused on the basis
that they were forgeries, and it was then that the accused's counsel asked for an
adjournment in order that he could call rebutting evidence to show that they were
not forgeries. I do not think any of us would have had much hesitation in saying
that that was not a case in which an adjournment should have been granted, but
Lord Goddard CJ, in the very brief report, puts the matter in very general terms.
He is reported as saying[2]:

'... to make an order of *certiorari* because justices had refused to grant an
adjournment would be to extend the ambit of the remedy beyond all authority
and that the application must be refused.'

It is a very short report. It may not entirely reflect what Lord Goddard CJ said,
but I do not read it, or accept it, as authority for the fact that one can never use certiorari to correct a breach of the rules of natural justice when the manifestation of
that breach took the form of a refusal to grant an adjournment.

Indeed I think the matter is put in balance by one of the reports to which counsel
for the applicant referred us, *R (Harrington) v Clare County Court Judge and County
Justices*[3], where a case not unlike the present was under consideration. Campbell
CJ, in giving the judgment of the court, said[4]:

'We are asked to quash the order of conviction made at the Petty Sessions on
three grounds. 1, that the defendant was not given a reasonable time for
defence; 2, that the defendant was refused an adjournment, which the justices
should have granted; and, 3, bias on the part of the tribunal which heard the
case. In my opinion the first two grounds overlap, because, in all the cases I

1 (1953) 117 JP Jo 705
2 117 JP Jo at 706
3 [1918] 2 IR 116
4 [1918] 2 IR at 124

a have been able to find, the discretion of the justices to refuse to grant an adjournment arose in connexion with the consideration by the Court of whether the
defendant had had reasonable time. In almost all these cases where the question
of reasonable time has been discussed the question of the refusal by the justices
to adjourn the case has been part of the matter for consideration. That is the
reason why Mr. O'Connor was able to state that there appeared to be no case
reported in which the Court had been asked to interfere with the discretion of
b the justices as to granting or refusing adjournments.'

I think that that is probably the explanation of the position. I would hold that
where the central allegation on which an order of certiorari is sought is that the
applicant was not given a reasonable time to prepare his case, the mere fact that the
matter became apparent as a result of a refusal of an adjournment does not prevent
the court from treating the basic cause of complaint, namely the failure to provide
c the applicant with adequate time, as being a ground on which certiorari should go.

For those reasons I have come to the conclusion that this is a case in which the
conviction must be quashed. But we have been told, and I think no doubt correctly,
that some guidance in this situation would be welcome if the court could give it. I
come back now to the four lay justices who refused the adjournment. As I have
d already said, I have not the slightest doubt that what was in their minds was that the
applicant's ship would be liable to sail with the tide that night, and if they adjourned
the case, it was equivalent to forgetting all about it and saying goodbye to the applicant
and to any fine which might be imposed. I think they weighed the considerations
for and against conducting the enquiry that afternoon and came to the view that the
considerations in favour of conducting it prevailed.

e I think they were wrong in that approach. I think they should have asked themselves, first, whether the enquiry could be conducted having due regard to the rules
of natural justice that afternoon, and if the answer was No, then that would be
the end of the matter; they would then have to make up their minds that they were
not going to conduct that enquiry that afternoon at all. Of course it would then be
for their consideration as to what steps could properly be taken to make sure that the
f captain, the fine and all other trace of the affair did not slip away with the tide. But
they would have no difficulty within the powers open to them in taking appropriate
steps to that end. One bears in mind to start with that they had the power to remand
the captain in custody, which would most effectively ensure that he was still available
for disposal on the adjourned hearing date. One does not imagine that in practice
such an extreme course would be necessary, but the possibility of that being available
g as a last resort would no doubt stimulate the shipowners in cases of this kind to make
some useful alternative suggestion, either by the provision of sureties for bail, or the
deposit of a sum of money for any potential fine or otherwise. Indeed on that hurried
day, 11th July 1973, the solicitors for the applicant did make an attempt to provide
some kind of security of that sort. The practical answer, as I see it, is that if the court
cannot conduct a trial in accordance with the rules of natural justice before the ship
h sails, then the justices must adjourn the matter because the rules of natural justice
are paramount, but they have adequate powers to see that some sensible provision
is made whereby there would be some security for the appropriate penalty in the
event of a subsequent conviction.

So far as this court today is concerned, all that I need say is that in my opinion
certiorari should go to quash the conviction.

j **ASHWORTH J.** I agree.

BRISTOW J. I agree.

Certiorari granted. Leave to appeal to House of Lords refused.

Solicitors: *Richards, Butler & Co* (for the applicant); *T V Edwards & Co* (for the
respondents).

N P Metcalfe Esq Barrister.

H P Bulmer Ltd and another v J Bollinger SA and others

COURT OF APPEAL, CIVIL DIVISION

LORD DENNING MR, STAMP AND STEPHENSON LJJ

4th, 5th, 8th, 9th APRIL, 22nd MAY 1974

European Economic Community – Reference to European Court – Request for preliminary ruling concerning interpretation of treaty – Power of national court to refer question it considers necessary to enable it to give judgment – Discretionary power of trial judge – Factors to be considered in deciding whether reference should be made – European Communities Act 1972, s 3(1) – EEC Treaty, art 177.

For many years certain producers of cider in England when marketing their products used the words 'champagne cider' and 'champagne perry' to describe them. Producers of the sparkling wine produced in the Champagne district of France and known as 'champagne' took no steps to prevent the English producers using those words until 1970 when they brought an action against an English firm claiming an injunction to restrain them using the name champagne. Two of the biggest producers of cider in England thereupon brought an action against the French producers claiming declarations that the English producers were entitled to use the expression 'champagne cider' and 'champagne perry'. The French producers counterclaimed for an injunction to stop the English producers from using the word 'champagne' in connection with any beverage not being a wine produced in the Champagne district of France. After the entry of the United Kingdom into the European Economic Community on 1st January 1973, the French producers amended their pleadings so as to include a claim for a declaration that the use by English producers of the expressions 'champagne cider' and 'champagne perry' in relation to beverages other than wine produced in the Champagne district of France was contrary to EEC Regulation 816/70, art 30[a], and EEC Regulation 817/70, arts 12[b] and 13[c]. The French producers then moved for an order under RSC Ord 114 referring the two following questions to the Court of Justice of the European Communities for a preliminary ruling in accordance with art 177[d] of the EEC Treaty: '[A] Whether upon the true interpretation of the Regulations [relied on] or any other relevant provisions of European Community Law the use of the word "Champagne" in connection with any beverage other than champagne is a contravention of the . . . Regulations or other provisions of European Community law. [B] Whether upon the true interpretation of Article 177 of the Treaty a national court of a member State should where there is no earlier decision of the Court of Justice of the European Communities refer to the Court of Justice such a question as has been raised herein, even though the court is not compelled to do so under the . . . Article.' The judge refused to make the order sought. The French producers appealed.

Held – The appeal would be dismissed for the following reasons—

(1) A High Court judge was not bound to refer a question of law, within the meaning of s 3(1)[e] of the European Communities Act 1972, to the European Court; under art 177(2) he had a discretion whether to refer any such question (involving the interpretation of the treaty and the regulations) to that court or to decide it himself. In deciding it himself he would apply the principles of interpretation applied by that court. The ruling on the request for such a reference could be given at any time before judgment. The judge

---

a   Article 30, so far as material, is set out at p 1230 *h*, post

b   Article 12, so far as material, is set out at p 1230 *j* to p 1231 *a*, post

c   Article 13, so far as material, is set out at p 1231 *b*, post

d   Article 177 is set out at p 1232 *h* and *j*, post

e   Section 3(1) is set out at p 1232 *f*, post

a   was only entitled to refer questions on which he considered a decision was *necessary* to enable him to give judgment. Generally it would not be possible to ascertain whether it was 'necessary' to decide a point until all the facts were ascertained. In considering whether to exercise his discretion in favour of referring a point, he should take account of the time that it would take to get a ruling from the European Court, the expense that would be involved, the wishes of the parties, and the difficulty and importance of

b   the point. References should be made sparingly and only if serious problems of interpretation arose (see p 1233 *d* and *e*, p 1234 *g* and *h*, p 1235 *d e* and *g*, p 1236 *d* to p 1237 *b*, p 1238 *b* and *j*, p 1239 *b e* and *f* and p 1241 *b* to *d*, post).

(2) The judge had considered all the relevant matters and exercised his discretion correctly in refusing to refer either question A or question B because (i) it was too early for him to say whether it would be 'necessary' for him to have a decision on

c   question A to enable him to give judgment, and (ii) question B was outside the scope of art 177; it was not the province of the European Court to give any guidance or advice to a national court as to when it should refer a question; that was a matter for the national court itself (see p 1238 *c* to *f* and *h j*, p 1239 *h* to p 1240 *d* and *g* to p 1241 *a* and p 1242 *d*, post).

Notes

d   For reference of questions of law to the Court of Justice of the European Communities, see 39A Halsbury's Laws (3rd Edn) para 38.

For the European Communities Act 1972, s 3, see 42 Halsbury's Statutes (3rd Edn) 84.

Cases referred to in judgments

Adjustment Tax on Petrol, Re [1966] CMLR 409, Finanzgericht, Hamburg.

e   *Albatros SARL v Société des Pétroles et des Combustibles Liquides (SOPECO) (No 2)* [1965] CMLR 159, CJEC.

Baker, Re, Nichols v Baker (1890) 44 Ch D 262, 59 LJCh 661, 62 LT 817, CA, 44 Digest (Repl) 311, 1422.

Bellenden (formerly Satterthwaite) v Satterthwaite [1948] 1 All ER 343, CA, 27(2) Digest (Reissue) 845, 6731.

f   *Bollinger (J) v Costa Brava Wine Co Ltd* [1959] 3 All ER 800, [1960] Ch 262, [1959] 3 WLR 966, [1960] RPC 16, DC, 46 Digest (Repl) 227, 1485.

Da Costa en Schaake NV v Nederlandse Belastingadministratie [1963] CMLR 224, CJEC.

Deutsche Grammophon Gesellschaft mbH v Metro-SB-Grossmärkte GmbH & Co KG [1971] CMLR 631, CJEC.

Esso Petroleum Co Ltd v Kingswood Motors (Addlestone) Ltd [1973] 3 All ER 1057, [1973]

g   3 WLR 780, [1973] CMLR 665, DC.

Evans v Bartlam [1937] 2 All ER 646, [1937] AC 473, 106 LJKB 568, sub nom *Bartlam v Evans* 157 LT 311, HL, 50 Digest (Repl) 401, 1113.

Export of Oat Flakes, Re [1969] CMLR 85, Verwaltungsgericht, Frankfurt am Main.

Firma Rheinmühlen Düsseldorf v German Intervention Agency for Cereals and Feeding-stuffs [1974] The Times, 18th February, CJEC.

h   *Fratelli Grassi v Amministrazione delle Finanze* [1973] CMLR 322, CJEC.

French Widow's Pension Settlement, Re [1971] CMLR 530, Bundessozialgericht.

Hessische Knappschaft v Maison Singer et Fils [1966] CMLR 82, CJEC.

Ibenewka v Egbuna [1964] 1 WLR 219, 108 Sol Jo 114, PC, Digest (Cont Vol B) 469, 241a.

Import Licence for Oats, Re [1968] CMLR 103, Verwaltungsgericht, Frankfurt am Main.

Import of Powdered Milk (No 3), Re [1967] CMLR 326, Bundesfinanzhof.

j   *John Walker & Sons v Henry Ost & Co Ltd* [1970] 2 All ER 106, [1970] 1 WLR 917, Digest (Cont Vol C) 143, 892b.

Lapeyre v Administration des Douanes [1967] CMLR 362, French Cour de Cassation (Criminal Chamber).

Lerose Ltd v Hawick Jersey International Ltd [1973] CMLR 83.

Löwenbräu München v Grunhalle Lager International Ltd [1974] CMLR 1.

Magor and St Mellons Rural District Council v Newport Corporation [1951] 2 All ER 839,
[1952] AC 189, 115 JP 613, [1951] 2 TLR 935, 50 LGR 133, HL; *affg* [1950] 2 All ER
1226, CA, 44 Digest (Repl) 267, 932.
*Milchwerke Heinz Wöhrmann & Sohn KG v EEC Commission, Alfons Lütticke GmbH v
EEC Commission* [1963] CMLR 152, CJEC.
Minnesota Mining & Manufacturing Co v Geerpres Europe Ltd [1973] CMLR 259.
*NV Algemene Transport-en Expeditie Onderneming Van Gend en Loos v Nederlandse Tarief-
commissie* [1963] CMLR 105, CJEC.
Osenton (Charles) & Co v Johnston [1941] 2 All ER 245, [1942] AC 130, 110 LJKB 420, 165
LT 235, HL, 51 Digest (Repl) 681, 2840.
Potato Flour Tax, Re [1964] CMLR 96, Finanzgericht, Nuremberg.
Processed Vegetable Growers Association Ltd v Commissioners of Customs and Excise [1974]
CMLR 113, Leeds VAT Tribunal.
Russian Commercial and Industrial Bank v British Bank for Foreign Trade Ltd [1921] 2 AC
438, [1921] All ER Rep 329, 90 LJKB 1089, 126 LT 35, HL, 30 Digest (Reissue) 192, 225.
Salgoil SpA v Foreign Trade Ministry of the Italian Republic [1969] CMLR 181, CJEC.
Sirena SRL v Eda SRL [1971] CMLR 260, CJEC.
Sociale Verzekeringsbank v H J van der Vecht [1968] CMLR 151, CJEC.
Société des Pétroles Shell-Berre, Re [1964] CMLR 462, French Conseil d'Etat.
State v Cornet [1967] CMLR 351, French Cour de Cassation (Criminal Chambers).
Tax on Imported Lemons, Re [1968] CMLR 1, Finanzgericht, Hamburg.
Van Duyn (Yvonne) v Home Office [1974] CMLR 347.
Vereniging van Fabrikanten en Importeurs van Verbruiksartikelen (FIVA) v Mertens [1963]
CMLR 141, District Court, Amsterdam.
Vine Products Ltd v Mackenzie & Co Ltd [1969] RPC 1, Digest (Cont Vol C) 1025, 1560a.
Ward v James [1965] 1 All ER 563, [1966] 1 QB 273, [1965] 2 WLR 455, [1965] 1 Lloyd's
Rep 145, CA, Digest (Cont Vol B) 219, 783a.

Interlocutory appeal
H P Bulmer Ltd and Showerings Ltd brought an action against J Bollinger SA and
Champagne Lanson Père et Fils (sued on their own behalf and on behalf of all persons
who produced wine in the district of France known as the Champagne district and
shipped such wine to England and Wales) claiming (i) a declaration that they were
entitled to use the expressions 'champagne cider' and 'champagne cyder' on and in
relation to cider provided that such use was not contrary to any government regulation in force at the relevant time; (ii) a declaration that they were entitled to use the
expression 'champagne perry' on and in relation to perry provided that such use was
not contrary to any government regulation in force at the relevant time; and (iii)
further or other relief. By their amended defence and counterclaim the defendants
counterclaimed, inter alia, for (i) a declaration that the use by the plaintiffs of the
expressions 'champagne cider' and 'champagne perry' in relation to beverages other
than wine produced in the Champagne district of France was contrary to European
Community law; and (ii) an injunction restraining the plaintiffs and each of them
(whether by their respective directors, officers, servants or agents or any of them or
otherwise howsoever) from using in the course of trade the word 'champagne' in
connection with any beverage not being a wine produced in the Champagne district
of France. By notice of motion dated 30th November 1973 the defendants applied,
under RSC Ord 114, for (i) an order that the following question be referred to the
Court of Justice of the European Communities for a preliminary ruling in accordance
with art 177 of the EEC Treaty: 'Whether upon the true interpretation of the
Regulations particularised . . . or any other relevant provisions of European Community Law the use of the word "Champagne" in connection with any beverage
other than champagne is a contravention of the said Regulations or other provisions
of European Community Law'; and (ii) an order that all further proceedings in the
action be stayed until the Court of Justice of the European Communities had given

a   its ruling or until further order. By notice of motion dated 11th December 1973 the defendants applied, under RSC Ord 114, for (i) an order that the following question be referred to the Court of Justice of the European Communities for a preliminary ruling in accordance with art 177 of the EEC Treaty: 'Whether upon the true interpretation of Article 177 of the Treaty a national court of a member State should where there is no earlier decision of the Court of Justice of the European Communities refer to the Court of Justice such a question as has been raised herein, even though

b   the national court is not compelled to do so under the said Article'; and (ii) for such further or other order as the court might think fit. On 14th December 1973 Whitford J refused to make an order on the two motions for reference to the European Court for preliminary rulings. The defendants appealed. The facts are set out in the judgment of Lord Denning MR.

c   *Charles Sparrow QC* and *John Burrell QC* for the defendants.
David Hirst QC, William Aldous and *Simon Thorley* for the plaintiffs.

Cur adv vult

22nd May. The following judgments were read.

d   **LORD DENNING MR.** In France the name 'champagne' is well protected by law. It denotes a sparkling wine produced in a well favoured district of France, called the Champagne district. The vineyards are about 100 miles east of Paris, around Rheims and Epernay. The wine has a high reputation all the world over.

In England, too, the name champagne is well protected by law when used for wine.
As far back as 1956 some intruders brought into England a somewhat similar wine.

e   It had been produced in the Costa Brava district of Spain. They marketed it under the name 'Spanish champagne'. The French growers and shippers brought an action to stop it. They succeeded. Danckwerts J held that the French growers had a goodwill connected with the word champagne, and that the Spanish intruders had been guilty of dishonest trading: see *J Bollinger v Costa Brava Wine Co Ltd*[1]. That case opened up a new field of English law. It gave a remedy for unfair competition. It was applied in

f   *Vine Products v Mackenzie & Co Ltd*[2] when Cross J said: ' . . . the decision went beyond the well-trodden paths of passing-off into the unmapped area of "unfair trading" or "unfair competition".' It was followed recently by Foster J in *John Walker & Sons Ltd v Henry Ost & Co Ltd*[3].

The 1959 *Bollinger* case[1] concerned wine—wine made from grapes—for which the French are so famous. Now we are concerned with cider and perry. Cider from

g   apples. Perry from pears. We English do know something about these; at any rate, those who come up from Somerset or Herefordshire.

For many years now some producers of cider in England have been marketing some of their drinks as 'champagne cider' and 'champagne perry'. When it started the French producers of champagne took no steps to stop it. It went on for a long time. But in 1970 the French producers brought an action against an English firm,

h   claiming an injunction. They sought to stop the use of the name champagne on these drinks. To counter this, two of the biggest producers of cider in England on 8th October 1970 brought an action against the French producers. They claimed declarations that they were entitled to use the expression 'champagne cider' and 'champagne perry'. They said that they had used those expressions for 70 or 80 years in England; that many millions of bottles had been marketed under those descriptions;

j   and that the government of the United Kingdom had recognised it in the various regulations. They said further that the French producers had acquiesced in the use

---

1   [1959] 3 All ER 800, [1960] Ch 262
2   [1969] RPC 1 at 23
3   [1970] 2 All ER 106, [1970] 1 WLR 917

and were estopped from complaining. In answer the French producers of champagne   *a*
claimed that the use of the word 'champagne' in connection with any beverage other
than champagne was likely to lead to the belief that such beverage was or resembled
champagne, or was a substitute for it, or was in some way connected with champagne. They claimed an injunction to stop the English producers from using the
word 'champagne' in connection with any beverage not being a wine produced in the
Champagne district of France.   *b*

1 *After England joined the Common Market*
   Thus far it was a straightforward action for passing-off. It was to be determined by
well-known principles of English law. But on 1st January 1973 England joined the
Common Market. On 26th March 1973 the French producers amended their pleading
so as to add these claims: *c*

> '9A. Following the adhesion of the United Kingdom to the European Economic
> Community the use of the word "Champagne" in connection with any beverage
> other than champagne will contravene European Community Law.'

They relied on EEC Regulation 816/70, art 30, and EEC Regulation 817/70, arts 12 and
13. By a further amendment the counterclaimed for: *d*

> 'A declaration that the use by the [English producers] of the expression
> "Champagne Cider" and "Champagne Perry" in relation to beverages other
> than wine produced in the Champagne District of France is contrary to European
> Community Law.'

2 *Reference to Luxembourg*   *e*
   Now the French producers ask that two points of European Community law should
be referred to the European Court at Luxembourg. Shortened they are:

> (A) 'Whether . . . the use of the word "Champagne" in connection with any
> beverage other than Champagne is a contravention of . . . the provisions of
> European Community Law.'
> (B) 'Whether . . . a national court of a member state should . . . refer to the   *f*
> Court of Justice [of the European Community] such a question as has been raised
> herein . . .'

The judge at first instance refused to refer either question at this stage. He said that
he would try the whole case out before he came to a decision on it. The French
producers appeal to this court.   *g*

3 *The Regulations*
   The Community regulations relied on by the French producers are these:

EEC Regulation 816/70, art 30:

> '. . . . 2. Member States may subject the use of a geographical mark for
> describing a table wine to this condition, in particular, that that wine is obtained *h*
> wholly from certain wine-producing areas expressly designated and that it
> comes exclusively from the territory marked out in an exact manner, whose
> name it bears . . .'

'Wine' means[1] 'the product obtained exclusively from whole or partial alcoholic
fermentation of fresh grapes, whether or not crushed, or of grape must.'   *j*

EEC Regulation 817/70, art 12:

> 'The Community reference q.w.p.s.r. [quality wine produced in a specific
> region] or a traditional specific reference used in member States to describe

---

1   See EEC Regulation 816/70, Annex II (7)

a certain wines, may only be used for wines complying with the provisions of this Regulation and with those adopted in application of this Regulation . . .'

The specific traditional reference for France is: 'Appellation d'origine controlée. Champagne et vin délimité de qualité supérieure.'

Article 13:

b '1. Each Member State shall ensure the inspection and protection of q.w.p.s.r marketed in accordance with this Regulation . . .'

The French producers claim that, under those regulations, the name champagne is their own special property. It must not be applied to any *wine* which is not produced in the Champagne district of France. So much the English producers concede. But c the French producers go further. They say that the name 'champagne' must not be applied to any *beverage* other than their champagne. It must not, therefore, be applied to cider or perry, even though they are not wines at all. The English producers deny this. They say that the regulations apply only to *wines*—the product of grapes —and not to cider or perry—the product of apples and pears.

This is obviously a point of the first importance to the French wine trade and to d the English cider trade. It depends no doubt on the true interpretation of the regulations. It seems that three points of principle arise: First, by which court should these regulations be interpreted? By the European Court at Luxembourg or by the national courts of England? Second, at what stage should the task of interpretation be done? Should it be done now *before* the case is tried out in the English court or at a later stage *after* the other issues have been determined? Third, in any case, e whichever be the court to interpret them, what are the principles to be applied in the interpretation of the regulations? If we were to interpret the regulations as if they were an English statute, I should think they would apply only to wines, not to cider or perry. But, if other principles were to be applied, the result might be different. That is indeed what the French producers say. They contend that the European Court can fill in any gaps in the regulations. So that the words can be f extended so as to forbid the use of the word 'champagne' on cider or perry. That is, no doubt, the reason why the French producers want the point to be referred here and now to the European Court.

To answer these questions, we must consider several points of fundamental importance. To make the discussion easier to understand, I will speak only of the interpretation of 'the treaty', but this must be regarded as including the regulations g and directions under it. I will make reference to the English courts because I am specially concerned with them; but this must be regarded as including the national courts of any member state.

4 *The impact of the treaty on English law*
The first and fundamental point is that the treaty concerns only those matters h which have a European element, that is to say, matters which affect people or property in the nine countries of the Common Market besides ourselves. The treaty does not touch any of the matters which concern solely the mainland of England and the people in it. These are still governed by English law. They are not affected by the treaty. But when we come to matters with a European element, the treaty is like an incoming tide. It flows into the estuaries and up the rivers. It cannot be held back. j Parliament has decreed that the treaty is henceforward to be part of our law. It is equal in force to any statute. The governing provision is s 2(1) of the European Communities Act 1972. It says:

'All such rights, powers, liabilities, obligations and restrictions from time to time created by or arising under the Treaties, and all such remedies and procedures from time to time provided for by or under the Treaties, as in accordance

with the Treaties are without further enactment to be given legal effect or used   *a*
in the United Kingdom shall be recognised and available in law, and be enforced,
allowed and followed accordingly; and the expression "enforceable Community
right" and similar expressions shall be read as referring to one to which this
subsection applies.'

The statute is expressed in forthright terms which are absolute and all-embracing.
Any rights or obligations created by the treaty are to be given legal effect in England   *b*
without more ado. Any remedies or procedures provided by the treaty are to be
made available here without being open to question. In future, in transactions which
cross the frontiers, we must no longer speak or think of English law as something
on its own. We must speak and think of Community law, of Community rights and
obligations, and we must give effect to them. This means a great effort for the
lawyers. We have to learn a new system. The treaty, with the regulations and   *c*
directives, covers many volumes. The case law is contained in hundreds of reported
cases both in the European Court of Justice and in the national courts of the nine.
Many must be studied before the right result can be reached. We must get down to it.

5 *By what courts is the treaty to be interpreted?*
It is important to distinguish between the task of interpreting the treaty—to see   *d*
what it means—and the task of *applying* it—to apply its provisions to the case in hand.
Let me put on one side the task of *applying* the treaty. On this matter in our courts
the English judges have the final word. They are the only judges who are empowered
to decide the case itself. They have to find the facts, to state the issues, to give judgment for one side or the other, and to see that the judgment is enforced.
Before the English judges can apply the treaty, they have to see what it means and   *e*
what is its effect. In the task of *interpreting* the treaty, the English judges are no longer
the final authority. They no longer carry the law in their breasts. They are no longer
in a position to give rulings which are of binding force. The supreme tribunal for
interpreting the treaty is the European Court of Justice at Luxembourg. Our Parliament has so decreed. Section 3 of the European Communities Act 1972 says:
                                                                                   f
'(1) For the purposes of all legal proceedings any question as to the meaning or
effect of any of the Treaties, or as to the validity, meaning or effect of any Community instrument, shall be treated as a question of law (and, if not referred to
the European Court, be for determination as such in accordance with the
principles laid down by and any relevant decision of the European Court).
'(2) Judicial notice shall be taken of the Treaties, of the Official Journal of the   *g*
Communities and of any decision of, or expression of opinion by, the European
Court on any such question as aforesaid . . .'

Coupled with that section, we must read art 177 of the treaty. It says:

'[1] The Court of Justice [i e the European Court of Justice] shall have jurisdiction to give preliminary rulings concerning: (*a*) the interpretation of this   *h*
Treaty; (*b*) the validity and interpretation of acts of the institutions of the Community; (*c*) the interpretation of the statutes of bodies established by an act of the
Council, where those statutes so provide.
'[2] Where such a question is raised before any court or tribunal of a Member
State, that court or tribunal *may*, if it considers that a decision on the question is
necessary to enable it to give judgment, request the Court of Justice to give a   *j*
ruling thereon.
'[3] Where any such question is raised in a case pending before a Court or
tribunal of a Member State, against whose decisions there is no judicial remedy
under national law, that court or tribunal shall bring the matter before the
Court of Justice.'

a That article shows that, if a question of interpretation or validity is raised, the European Court is supreme. It is the ultimate authority. Even the House of Lords has to bow down to it. If a question is raised before the House of Lords on the interpretation of the treaty—on which it is necessary to give a ruling—the House of Lords is bound to refer it to the European Court. Article 171(3) of the treaty uses that emphatic word 'shall'. The House has no option. It must refer the matter to the European Court and,

b having done so, it is bound to follow the ruling in that *particular* case in which the point arises. But the ruling in that case does not bind *other* cases. The European Court is not absolutely bound by its previous decisions: see *Da Costa en Schaake NV v Nederlandse Belastingadministrie*[1]. It has no doctrine of stare decisis. Its decisions are much influenced by considerations of policy and economics; and, as these change, so may their rulings change. It follows from this that, if the House of Lords in a *subsequent* case thinks that a previous ruling of the European Court was wrong—or should not be followed—it can

c refer the point again to the European Court, and the European Court can reconsider it. On reconsideration it can make a ruling which will bind that *particular* case. But not subsequent cases. And so on.

6 *The discretion to refer or not to refer*

d But short of the House of Lords, no other English court is bound to refer a question to the European Court at Luxembourg. Not even a question on the *interpretation* of the treaty. Article 177(2) uses the permissive word 'may' in contrast to 'shall' in Art 177(3). In England the trial judge has complete *discretion*. If a question arises on the interpretation of the treaty, an English judge can decide it for himself. He need not refer it to the court at Luxembourg unless he wishes. He can say: 'It will be too costly', or 'It will take too long to get an answer', or 'I am well able to decide it myself'.

e If he does decide it himself, the European Court cannot interfere. None of the parties can go off to the European Court and complain. The European Court would not listen to any party who went moaning to them. The European Court take the view that the trial judge has a complete discretion to refer or not to refer (see *Firma Rheinmühlen Düsseldorf v German Intervention Agency for Cereals and Feeding-stuffs*[2]) with which they

f cannot interfere (see *Milchwerke Heinz Wöhrmann & Sohn KG v EEC Commission, Alfons Lütticke GmbH v EEC Commission*[3]). If a party wishes to challenge the decision of the trial judge in England—to refer or not to refer—he must appeal to the Court of Appeal in England. (If the judge makes an order referring the question to Luxembourg, the party can appeal *without leave*: see RSC Ord 114. If the judge refuses to make an order, he needs leave, because it is an interlocutory order: see the Supreme Court of

g Judicature (Consolidation) Act 1925, s 31.) The judges of the Court of Appeal, in their turn, have complete discretion. They can interpret the treaty themselves if they think fit. If the Court of Appeal do interpret it themselves, the European Court will not rebuke them for doing so. If a party wishes to challenge the decision of the Court of Appeal—to refer or not to refer—he must get leave to go to the House of Lords and go there. It is only in that august place that there is no discretion. If the point of

h interpretation is one which is 'necessary' to give a ruling, the House *must* refer it to the European Court at Luxembourg. The reason behind this imperative is this. The cases which get to the House of Lords are substantial cases of the first importance. If a point of interpretation arises there, it is assumed to be worthy of reference to the European Court at Luxembourg. Whereas the points in the lower courts may not be worth troubling the European Court about. See the judgment of the German Court of

j Appeal at Frankfurt in *Re Export of Oat Flakes*[4].

1 [1963] CMLR 224
2 [1974] The Times, 18th February
3 [1963] CMLR 152
4 [1969] CMLR 85 at 97

7   *The condition precedent to a reference: it must be 'necessary'*

Whenever any English court thinks it would be helpful to get the view of the European Court—on the interpretation of the treaty—there is a *condition precedent* to be fulfilled. It is a condition which applies to the House of Lords as well as to the lower courts. It is contained in the same paragraph of art 177(2) of the treaty and applies in art 177(3) as well. It is this. An English court can only refer the matter to the European Court *'if it considers* that a decision on the question is necessary to enable it to give judgment'. Note the words 'if *it* considers'. That is, 'if the *English court* considers'. On this point again the opinion of the English courts is final, just as it is on the matter of discretion. An English judge can say either: 'I consider it necessary', or 'I do not consider it necessary'. His discretion in that respect is final. Let me take the two in order.

(i) If the English judge considers it *necessary* to refer the matter, no one can gainsay it save the Court of Appeal. The European Court will accept his opinion. It will not go into the grounds on which he based it. The European Court so held in *NV Algemene Transport-en Expeditie Onderneming Van Gend en Loos v Nederlandse Tarief-commissie*[1] and *Albatros v Sopeco*[2]. It will accept the question as he formulates it: *Fratelli Grassi v Amministrazione delle Finanze*[3]. It will not alter it or send it back. Even if it is a faulty question, it will do the best it can with it: see *Deutsche Grammophon Gesellschaft mbH v Metro-SB-Grossmärkte GmbH & Co KG*[4]. The European Court treats it as a matter between the English courts and themselves—to be dealt with in a spirit of co-operation—in which the parties have no place save that they are invited to be heard. It was so held in *Hessische Knappschaft v Maison Singer et Fils*[5].

(ii) If the English judge considers it *not necessary* to refer a question of interpretation to the European Court—but instead decides it itself—that is the end of the matter. It is no good a party going off to the European Court. They would not listen to him. They are conscious that the treaty gives the final word in this respect to the English courts. From all I have read of their cases, they are very careful not to exceed their jurisdiction. They never do anything to trespass on any ground which is properly the province of the national courts.

8   *The guidelines*

Seeing that these matters of 'necessary' and 'discretion' are the concern of the English courts, it will fall to the English judges to rule on them. Likewise the national courts of other member states have to rule on them. They are matters on which guidance is needed. It may not be out of place, therefore, to draw attention to the way in which other national courts have dealt with them.

(1) *Guidelines as to whether a decision is necessary*

(i) *The point must be conclusive.* The English court has to consider whether 'a decision of the question is *necessary* to enable it to give *judgment*'. That means judgment in the very case which is before the court. The judge must have got to the stage when he says to himself: 'This clause of the treaty is capable of two or more meanings. If it means *this*, I give judgment for the plaintiff. If it means *that*, I give judgment for the defendant.' In short, the point must be such that, whichever way the point is decided, it is conclusive of the case. Nothing more remains but to give judgment. The Hamburg court stressed the necessity in *Re Adjustment of Tax on Petrol*[6]. In *Van Duyn v Home Office*[7] Pennycuick V-C said: 'It would be quite impossible to give judgment without such a decision.'

1   [1963] CMLR 105 at 128
2   [1966] CMLR 159 at 177
3   [1973] CMLR 322 at 335
4   [1971] CMLR 631 at 656
5   [1966] CMLR 82 at 94
6   [1966] CMLR 409 at 416
7   [1974] CMLR 347

a
(ii) *Previous ruling.* In some cases, however, it may be found that the same point—or substantially the same point—has already been decided by the European Court in a previous case. In that event it is not necessary for the English court to decide it. It can follow the previous decision without troubling the European Court. But, as I have said, the European Court is *not* bound by its previous decisions. So if the English court thinks that a previous decision of the European Court may have been wrong—or if there are new factors which ought to be brought to the notice of the

b
European Court—the English court may consider it *necessary* to re-submit the point to the European Court. In that event, the European Court will consider the point again. It was so held by the European Court itself in the *Da Costa* case[1], in Holland in *Vereniging van Fabrikanten en Importeurs van Verbruiksartikelen (FIVA) v Mertens*[2], and in Germany in *Re Import of Powdered Milk*[3].

c
(iii) *Acte claire.* In other cases the English court may consider the point is reasonably clear and free from doubt. In that event there is no need to interpret the treaty but only to apply it, and that is the task of the English court. It was so submitted by the Advocate-General to the European Court in the *Da Costa* case[4]. It has been so held by the highest courts in France: by the Conseil d'Etat in *Re Société des Pétroles Shell-Berre*[5], by the Cour de Cassation in *State v Cornet*[6], and *Lapeyre Administration des Douanes*[7]; also by a superior court in Germany in *Re French Widow's Pension Settlement*[8].

d
(iv) *Decide the facts first.* It is to be noticed, too, that the word is 'necessary'. This is much stronger than 'desirable' or 'convenient'. There are some cases where the point, if decided one way, would shorten the trial greatly. But, if decided the other way, it would mean that the trial would have to go its full length. In such a case it might be 'convenient' or 'desirable' to take it as a preliminary point because it might save much time and expense. But it would not be 'necessary' at that stage. When the facts were

e
investigated, it might turn out to have been quite unnecessary. The case would be determined on another ground altogether. As a rule you cannot tell whether it is necessary to decide a point until all the facts are ascertained. So in general it is best to decide the facts first.

f
(2) *Guidelines as to the exercise of discretion*
Assuming that the condition about 'necessary' is fulfilled, there remains the matter of discretion. This only applies to the trial judge or the Court of Appeal, not to the House of Lords. The English court has a discretion either to decide the point itself or to refer it to the European Court. The national courts of the various member countries have had to consider how to exercise this discretion. The cases show that they have taken into account such matters as the following.

g
(i) *The time to get a ruling.* The length of time which may elapse before a ruling can be obtained from the European court. This may take months and months. The lawyers have to prepare their briefs; the advocate-general has to prepare his submissions; the case has to be argued; the court has to give its decision. The average length of time at present seems to be between six and nine months. Meanwhile, the whole action in the English court is stayed until the ruling is obtained. This may be very unfortunate,

h
especially in a case where an injunction is sought or there are other reasons for expedition. This was very much in the mind of the German Court of Appeal of Frankfurt in *Re Export of Oat Flakes*[9]. It is said that it was important 'to prevent undue protraction

---

j
1 [1963] CMLR 224
2 [1963] CMLR 141
3 [1967] CMLR 326
4 [1963] CMLR at 234
5 [1964] CMLR 462
6 [1967] CMLR 351
7 [1967] CMLR 362 at 368
8 [1971] CMLR 530
9 [1969] CMLR 85 at 97

of both the proceedings before the European Court and trial before the national
courts'. On that ground it decided a point of interpretation itself, rather than submit it
to the European Court.

(ii) *Do not overload the court.* The importance of not overwhelming the European
Court by references to it. If it were overloaded, it could not get through its work.
There are nine judges of that court. All nine must sit in plenary sessions on these cases,
as well as many other important cases: see art 165. They cannot split up into divisions
of three or five judges. All nine must sit. So do not put too much on them. The Court
of Appeal in Frankfurt took this view pointedly in *Re Import Licence for Oats*[1]:

'The European Court must not be overwhelmed by requests for rulings . . .
Courts should exercise their rights sparingly. A reference to the European Court
must not become an automatic reaction and ought only to be made if serious
difficulties of interpretation arise.'

(iii) *Formulate the question clearly.* It must be a question of *interpretation only* of the
treaty. It must not be mixed up with the facts. It is the task of the national courts to
find the facts and apply the treaty. The European Court must not take that task on
themselves. In fairness to them, it is desirable to find the facts and state them clearly
before referring the question. That appears from *Salgoil SpA v Foreign Trade Ministry
of the Italian Republic*[2] and *Sirena SRL v Eda SRL*[3]. In any case, the task of interpretation is better done with the facts in mind rather than in ignorance of them.

(iv) *Difficulty and importance.* Unless the point is really difficult and important, it
would seem better for the English judge to decide it himself. For in so doing, much
delay and expense will be saved. So far the English judges have not shirked their
responsibilities. They have decided several points of interpretation on the treaty to
the satisfaction, I hope, of the parties. At any rate, there has been no appeal from them.
I refer to the decisions of Whitford J in *Lerose Ltd v Hawick Jersey International Ltd*[4],
Graham J in *Minnesota Mining and Manufacturing Co v Geerpres Europe Ltd*[5]; Bridge J
in *Esso Petroleum Co Ltd v Kingswood Motors*[6]; Graham J in *Löwenbräu München v
Grunhalle Lager International Ltd*[7]; the Hon Kenneth Suenson-Taylor QC in *Processed
Vegetable Growers Association Ltd v Commissioners of Customs and Excise*[8].

(v) *Expense.* The expense to the parties of getting a ruling from the European Court.
That influenced a Nuremberg Court in *Re Potato Flour Tax*[9]. On a request for interpretation, the European Court does not as a rule award costs, and for a simple reason.
It does not decide the case. It only gives advice on the meaning of the treaty. If either
party wishes to get the costs of the reference, he must get it from the English court,
when it eventually decides the case: see *Sociale Verzekeringsbank v H J van der Vecht*[10].

(vi) *Wishes of the parties.* If both parties want the point to be referred to the European
Court, the English court should have regard to their wishes, but it should not give them
undue weight. The English court should hesitate before making a reference against
the wishes of one of the parties, seeing the expense and delay which it involves.

9   *The principles of interpretation*

In view of these considerations, it is apparent that in very many cases the English
courts will interpret the treaty themselves. They will not refer the question to the

1   [1968] CMLR 103 at 117
2   [1969] CMLR 181 at 193
3   [1971] CMLR 260 at 263
4   [1973] CMLR 83
5   [1973] CMLR 259
6   [1973] 3 All ER 1057, [1973] CMLR 665
7   [1974] CMLR 1
8   [1974] CMLR 113
9   [1964] CMLR 96 at 106
10 [1968] CMLR 151

a   European Court at Luxembourg. What then are the principles of interpretation to be applied? Beyond doubt the English courts must follow the same principles as the European Court. Otherwise there would be differences between the countries of the nine. That would never do. All the courts of all nine countries should interpret the treaty in the same way. They should all apply the same principles. It is enjoined on the English courts by s 3 of the European Communities Act 1972, which I have read.

b   What a task is thus set before us! The treaty is quite unlike any of the enactments to which we have become accustomed. The draftsmen of our statutes have striven to express themselves with the utmost exactness. They have tried to foresee all possible circumstances that may arise and to provide for them. They have sacrificed style and simplicity. They have foregone brevity. They have become long and involved. In consequence, the judges have followed suit. They interpret a statute as applying only to the circumstances covered by the very words. They give them a

c   literal interpretation. If the words of the statute do not cover a new situation—which was not foreseen—the judges hold that they have no power to fill the gap. To do so would be a 'naked usurpation of the legislative function': see *Magor and St Mellons Rural District Council v Newport Corporation*[1]. The gap must remain open until Parliament finds time to fill it.

d   How different is this treaty. It lays down general principles. It expresses its aims and purposes. All in sentences of moderate length and commendable style. But it lacks precision. It uses words and phrases without defining what they mean. An English lawyer would look for an interpretation clause, but he would look in vain. There is none. All the way through the treaty there are gaps and lacunae. These have to be filled in by the judges, or by regulations or directives. It is the European way. That appears from the decision of the Hamburg court in *Re Tax on*

e   *Imported Lemons*[2].

Likewise the regulations and directives. They are enacted by the Council of Ministers sitting in Brussels for everyone to obey. They are quite unlike our statutory instruments. They have to give the reasons on which they are based: see art 190 of the EEC Treaty. So they start off with pages of preambles, 'whereas' and 'where-as' and 'whereas'. These show the purpose and intent of the regulations and direc-

f   tives. Then follow the provisions which are to be obeyed. Here again words and phrases are used without defining their import. Such as 'personal conduct' in the EEC Directive 64/221, which was considered by Pennycuick V-C in *Van Duyn v Home Office*[3]. In case of difficulty, recourse is had to the preambles. These are useful to show the purpose and intent behind it all. But much is left to the judges. The enactments give only an outline plan. The details are to be filled in by the judges.

g   Seeing these differences, what are the English courts to do when they are faced with a problem of interpretation? They must follow the European pattern. No longer must they examine the words in meticulous detail. No longer must they argue about the precise grammatical sense. They must look to the purpose or intent. To quote the words of the European Court in the *Da Costa* case[4]; they must limit themselves to deducing from 'the wording and the spirit of the treaty the meaning of

h   the Community rules ...' They must not confine themselves to the English text. They must consider, if need be, all the authentic texts, of which there are now eight: see the *Sociale Verzekeringsbank* case[5]. They must divine the spirit of the treaty and gain inspiration from it. If they find a gap, they must fill it as best they can. They must do what the framers of the instrument would have done if they had thought about it. So

j
1 [1951] 2 All ER 839 at 841, [1952] AC 189 at 191, per Lord Simonds
2 [1968] CMLR 1
3 [1974] CMLR 347
4 [1963] CMLR at 237
5 [1968] CMLR 151

we must do the same.   Those are the principles, as I understand it, on which the   *a*
European Court acts.

10 *Applied to the present case*

To return to the three questions I asked at the beginning: first, I think these regulations should be interpreted by the High Court and the Court of Appeal in England.
But if the cases should reach the House of Lords they must be interpreted by the
European Court; second, the task of interpretation should be done at the time of the   *b*
trial or the appeal, together with the other issues in the case; third, the English court
should apply the same principles of interpretation as the European Court would
do if it had to decide the point.

I come now to the two specific questions sought to be referred.   The first question
raised is:

> 'Whether . . . the use of the word "Champagne" in connection with any   *c*
> beverage other than Champagne is a contravention of the provisions of European
> Community law.'

I do not think it is *necessary* at this stage to decide that question.   Take the claim in
passing-off.   If the French growers succeeded in this claim for passing-off in English
law—for an injunction and damages—it would not be necessary to decide the point   *d*
under the regulations.   So the facts must be found before it can be said that a
reference is 'necessary'.

Next take the claim of the French growers for a declaration that the use of the
expression 'champagne cider' and 'champagne perry' was contrary to European Community law.   Counsel for the French producers said that it would be necessary on this
issue to decide the point on the regulations. I do not agree. It is always a matter for the   *e*
discretion of the judge whether to grant a declaration or not.   He could very properly
say in the present case: whatever the true interpretation of the regulations, it is not a
case in which I would make any declaration on the point.   Taking that view, it would
not be necessary to decide the point.

Even if it could be said to be necessary to decide the point, I think that an English
court (short of the House of Lords) should not, as matter of discretion, refer it to the   *f*
European Court.   It should decide the point itself.   It would take much time and
money to get a ruling from the European Court.   Meanwhile the whole action would
be held up. It is, no doubt, an important point, but not a difficult one to decide.
I think it would be better to deal with it as part of the whole case, both by the trial
judge and by the Court of Appeal.   If it should then go to the House of Lords, it
will by that time have become clear whether it is a 'necessary' point or not.   If it is,   *g*
then the House of Lords will refer it.

The second point is: 'Whether a national court should . . . refer to the Court of
Justice such a question as has been raised herein'.   The object of this question is
to get a ruling from the European Court as to the circumstances in which a national
court should refer a question of interpretation to the European Court.   I am
quite clear that it is unnecessary to ask this question.   The answer is clear.   It is not   *h*
the province of the European Court to give any guidance or advice to the national
court when it should, or should not, refer a question.   That is a matter for the
national court itself.   It is no concern of the European Court.

In my opinion Whitford J was right in refusing to refer either of the questions.
I would dismiss the appeal.

i

STAMP LJ.   I have had the advantage of reading, in draft, the judgment which is
about to be delivered by Stephenson LJ.   I wholly agree with it, and because I would
be reluctant to express any views which might be said to go outside the confines of
this case, I am content gratefully to adopt that judgment as if it were my own.

I too would dismiss the appeal.

STEPHENSON LJ. Three things are clear—so clear that they scarcely need
a   saying—about art 177 of the EEC Treaty which Lord Denning MR has read, numbering its three sentences according to the convenient practice of the community
law reporters: (i) The rulings which the European Court has jurisdiction to give
under art 177(1) are not strictly 'preliminary'. They do not have to be given 'in
limine', before the court of the member state crosses the threshold and begins to
hear a dispute, but they can be given at any time before the court finishes hearing
b   the dispute by giving judgment. The ruling is in that sense 'prejudicial', not necessarily
preliminary, though it may be. (ii) Article 177(2) confers a power, whereas art
177(3) imposes an obligation. A lower court of a member state 'may' request a
ruling, a final court 'shall'. The contrast in the language is as clear as in the section
of the English statute[1] which this court construed in *Re Baker*[2] and has the same
effect: the lower court is trusted with a discretion, the final court is not. All attempts
c   to blur the distinction between the power of the one and the duty of the other when
a question is raised under art 177(1) of the treaty break down on the different wording
of art 177(2) and (3). Section 2(1) of the European Communities Act 1972 distinguishes
powers from obligations, and so by this wording does art 177, by whatever canon of
construction it is interpreted. The European Court has always recognised that
distinction, e g in *Da Costa en Schaake NV v Nederlandse Belastingadministratie*[3], and has
d   recently emphasised it and described the power given to the national courts by art
177(2) as conferring on them 'the widest discretion', which no domestic Court of
Appeal can fetter: *Firma Rheinmühlen Düsseldorf v German Intervention Agency for Cereals
and Feeding-stuffs*[4], shortly reported in The Times newspaper, to which Lord Denning MR has already referred. (iii) The only questions which the courts of a member
state can, or in some cases must, refer to the European Court are questions of law
e   within art 177(1) on which decisions are necessary to enable them to give judgment.
If they consider that they can give judgment in the dispute in which the question is
raised without deciding the question, they need not and indeed must not trouble
the European Court by requesting a ruling or bringing the matter before it. Section 3(1) of the 1972 Act recognises that questions within art 177(1) of the treaty are
questions of law and may be for determination by our courts without referring them
f   to the European Court. That is how the courts of member states have rightly proceeded, including English judges, Whitford J among them: see *Lerose Ltd v Hawick
Jersey International Ltd*[5].

The appellants, by their amendments to paras 9, 18 and 21 of their defence and
counterclaim, have raised the question whether the use of the word 'champagne'
in connection with any beverage other than champagne, in particular the use of the
g   expressions 'champagne cider' and 'champagne perry' will contravene or be contrary
to European Community law, in particular EEC Regulation 816/70, art 30, and EEC
Regulation 817/70, arts 12 and 13, and other regulations subsequently particularised.
By re-amendment they counterclaim a declaration that the use of those expressions in
relation to beverages other than wine produced in the Champagne district of France
is contrary to European Community law. Question A, which Lord Denning MR
h   has read, is therefore, in my judgment, a question within art 177(1)(b) of the treaty
which was clearly raised before Whitford J in the Chancery Division of the High
Court. But he did not consider a decision on it necessary to enable him to give
judgment. So he refused to request the European Court to give a ruling on it. In
that I am of opinion he was right. If he intended to refuse ever to request a ruling
on it he would have been wrong. It is too early to say whether it will become neces-
j   sary and whether he should request a ruling on it later. When he has heard the

1   Bankruptcy Act 1883, s 125(4)
2   (1890) 44 Ch D 262
3   [1963] CMLR 224 at 237
4   [1974] The Times, 18th **February**
5   [1973] CMLR 83

evidence he may reject the respondents' claim. He may find that the appellants
have a right to restrain the respondents from using the expressions 'champagne
cider' and 'champagne perry', and from supplying beverages so described, without
recourse to European law or becoming involved in any law but the law of England
as it was before the adherence of the United Kingdom to the European Economic
Community added anything to it. If so, it will not be necessary for him to decide
any question concerning the interpretation of the Community's regulations. It
was argued for the appellants that a decision of question A might shorten proceedings
and enable the judge to give judgment without going into evidence of passing-off
or acquiescence. But art 177 does not provide for a court considering that a decision
on the question is expedient or convenient or necessary to enable it to give judgment
shortly, or more shortly, or more cheaply and conveniently, but necessary to enable
it to give it—justly of course but with no other implication or qualification.

It was also argued that the declaration counterclaimed could not be granted without deciding question A. That is true and would be relevant if it were possible to
say at this stage whether it will be necessary for the court to grant the declaration.
But if the appellants succeed on other grounds, the declaration will not be necessary
and the judge in his discretion might refuse to grant it, however helpful it might be to
the appellants in other litigation: see *Russian Commercial and Industrial Bank v British
Bank for Foreign Trade*[1] and *Ibeneweka v Egbuna*[2]. So by counterclaiming a declaration
the appellants have not made an unnecessary decision necessary. They must wait
and see how the case goes.

I do not read anything which judges of the European Court, Judge Sorensen[3] or
Lord Mackenzie Stuart[4], have said as encouraging courts of member states to refer
questions under art 177 before they know whether a decision of them will be necessary
to enable them to give judgment or before they have ascertained the relevant facts
or the best formulation of the question or questions. Lower courts are rightly discouraged from postponing a simple request for a ruling in plain cases, cases where a
decision of a question within art 177 will plainly be necessary on assumed or admitted
facts. Nothing I have said is intended to throw doubt on such an interpretation or
application of art 177 or on such decisions as that of Pennycuick V-C in *Van Duyn
v Home Office*[5]. But this is an altogether different case, and all experience in our
courts of attempts to take short cuts by obtaining preliminary decisions on points of
law shows how difficult it is to isolate an issue and the relevant facts and to avoid
going back to the beginning and taking the ordinary route.

Question B, which Lord Denning MR has read, seems to me to fall outside art 177.
The question borrows some words of the District Court of Amsterdam in giving
judgment in *Vereniging van Fabrikanten en Importeurs van Verbruiksartikelen (FIVA) v
Mertens*[6] in a case where the question raised under art 177 had already been the subject of a decision by the European Court, and seeks to derive from them general
guidance in situations to which they were not addressed and to turn into a question
concerning the interpretation of art 177 of the treaty what is really a question how its
provisions should be applied in practice. Whether art 177(2) gives a lower court of
a member state a discretion is a question concerning the interpretation of the article;
how it should exercise that discretion is not. To concede that on its true interpretation art 177(2) gives a discretion and to contend that the width or extent of the discretion is a question of interpretation confuses a question of construction, which is

1   [1921] 2 AC 438, [1921] All ER Rep 329
2   [1964] 1 WLR 219
3   See 'General introduction, jurisdiction, organisation and procedure and Article 177 (pre-
     liminary rulings)', address to visiting judges from the nine member states, Court of Justice
     of the European Communities, 8th-12th October 1973
4   See 'The European Court and the British Lawyer', address to meeting of the Law Society
     Solicitors' European Group, 25th January 1974
5   [1974] CMLR 347
6   [1963] CMLR 141 at 144

a for the European Court, with a question of performance, which is for the courts of the member states.

It is significant, and not surprising, that the European Court does not yet appear to have been asked to lay down guidelines for the exercise of the national courts' discretion under art 177(2). If any guidelines are to be laid down, they should, in my judgment, be laid down by national courts, in this country by this court, which is accustomed to doing so in such matters as costs, interest, mode of trial or disposition

b of matrimonial property. But, in my opinion, the guidelines should be few and firmly related to the basic requirement that the decision of the question raised must be necessary at the time the reference is requested to enable the court to give judgment at the end of the case. The best judge of that in any particular case is the court to which the treaty submits the discretion, the judge who will have to give that judgment. If he does not consider that he needs a ruling from the European Court,

c an appellate court should be slow to consider that he does. He must bear in mind that art 177, as the European Court has said, 'provides a procedure to safeguard the uniform judicial interpretation of Community law' (*Sociale Verzekeringsbank v H J van der Vecht*[1], to which Lord Denning MR has referred) and exercise his right to refer sparingly and in cases of serious doubt or difficulty only, as the Verwaltungsgericht, Frankfurt am Main, said in *Re Import Licence for Oats*[2]; compare the judg-

d ment of the same court in *Re Export of Oat Flakes*[3]. He should also bear in mind the other considerations which Lord Denning MR has set out, but beyond that I would not go to guide the court of trial.

The ordinary jurisdiction of an appellate court is entirely unaffected by art 177 except in one respect: art 177(3) (paraphrased but not I hope misinterpreted) imposes on it if it is a final court of appeal a duty in a case pending before it to bring a 'neces-

e sary' question before the European Court. We do not have to decide whether art 177(3) applies to a final court before which an appeal against refusal to refer is brought at a preliminary or interlocutory stage, because neither question A nor question B is a necessary question; but I would be wary of so construing art 177(3) as to make nonsense of art 177(2), or reduce it to a dead letter. Nor do we have to decide whether the absence of any right of appeal from this court without leave would ever

f bring it within art 177(3); but without further argument I would not feel able either to assume that this court is under the same duty as the House of Lords or to agree with Lord Denning MR that in the hierarchy of our courts that House is the only court 'against whose decisions there is no judicial remedy' under our law. What we do have to decide is whether to uphold or upset the judge's refusal to request a ruling now.

g It is not and cannot be disputed that we have jurisdiction to hear an appeal from such a refusal. It is curious that new rules of the Supreme Court—RSC Ord 114, rr 1 to 6—deal with references to the European Court under art 177 (and under articles of two other treaties) but, perhaps by an oversight, RSC Ord 114, r 6, which deals with appeals, does not deal with refusals to make an order referring to the

h European Court. By RSC Ord 114, r 6, an appeal lies against an order referring without leave, but that special provision cannot affect the general power of the judge or this court to grant leave against a refusal to make such an order just as against any other interlocutory exercise of judicial discretion. The special provision cannot give a party dissatisfied with a judge's refusal to refer a corresponding right to appeal, nor can it take way his right to apply for leave to appeal—which the judge appears

j to have given here. And it cannot alter this court's duty to interfere with an exercise of judicial discretion when and only when the judge's decision 'exceeds the generous

1 [1968] CMLR 151 at 161
2 [1968] CMLR 103 at 117
3 [1969] CMLR 85 at 97

ambit within which reasonable disagreement is possible and is, in fact, plainly wrong'; for I respectfully agree with Asquith LJ that that is the principle which emerges from the decisions of the House of Lords in *Evans v Bartlam*[1] and *Charles Osenton & Co v Johnston*[2]; see *Bellenden (formerly Satterthwaite) v Satterthwaite*[3], and compare *Ward v James*[4].

One other thing the rule cannot do, and that is to fetter the judge's discretion to refer or refuse. If it did, I would agree that it would be invalid: *Firma Rheinmühlen Düsseldorf v German Intervention Agency for Cereals and Feeding-stuffs*[5] to which I have already referred. But it does not. I find it hard to follow the argument that a rule which gives a right of appeal to a party dissatisfied with a judge's exercise of his discretion one way restricts in some manner the judge's power to exercise it. It may facilitate appeals against one way of exercising it; it does nothing thereby to prevent its exercise either way. The judge is left as free to exercise this discretion as any judicial discretion and this court has its customary freedom to correct its exercise if unjudicial, unjust or wrong.

In my judgment the judge considered all the matters which he should have considered and no others, exercised the discretion given him by art 177(2) of the treaty rightly, and was correct in refusing to refer either question. He may later consider it necessary to obtain a decision from the European Court on question A to enable him to give judgment in this action. Before he gives judgment the answer may have become obvious or have been already given by a ruling of the European Court in another case. The question may or may not have to be referred. But I cannot, as at present advised, see how question B can ever become a question for decision by the European Court.

I agree that this appeal fails.

Appeal dismissed. Leave to appeal refused.

Solicitors: *Monier-Williams & Keeling* (for the defendants); *Ashurst, Morris, Crisp & Co* (for the plaintiffs).

L J Kovats Esq Barrister.

1 [1937] 2 All ER 646, [1937] AC 473
2 [1941] 2 All ER 245, [1942] AC 130
3 [1948] 1 All ER 343 at 345
4 [1965] 1 All ER 563 at 570, [1966] 1 QB 273 at 293
5 [1974] The Times, 18th February

a

Fletcher v Budgen

QUEEN'S BENCH DIVISION
LORD WIDGERY CJ, PARK AND FORBES JJ
11th JUNE 1974

b   *Trade description – False trade description – Buyer of goods – Application of false trade description to goods by buyer – Application in course of trade or business carried on by buyer – Whether an offence – Trade Descriptions Act 1968, s 1(1)(a).*

Section 1(1)[a] of the Trade Descriptions Act 1968 is not limited to false trade descriptions applied by a seller of goods. Accordingly a person who, in the course of a trade or
c   business, applies a false trade description to goods which he is buying is guilty of an offence under s 1(1)(a) of the 1968 Act (see p 1246 *b*, p 1247 *f* to *j* and p 1248 *a* to *c*, post)

Notes
For the prohibition of false trade descriptions, see Supplement to 10 Halsbury's Laws (3rd Edn) para 1314A, 1.
d   For the Trade Descriptions Act 1968, s 1, see 37 Halsbury's Statutes (3rd Edn) 949.

Cases referred to in judgments
Fletcher v Stedmore [1973] RTR 371, 71 LGR 179, DC.
Wickens Motors (Gloucester) Ltd v Hall [1972] 3 All ER 759, [1972] 1 WLR 1418, [1972] RTR 519, 137 JP 8, DC.
e   *Wycombe Marsh Garages Ltd v Fowler* [1972] 3 All ER 248, [1972] 1 WLR 1156, [1972] RTR 503, DC.

Cases also cited
Kensington and Chelsea (Royal) London Borough Council v Riley [1973] RTR 122, DC.
Preston v Albuery [1963] 3 All ER 897, [1964] 2 QB 769.
f   *Taylor v Smith* [1974] The Times, 23rd January.

Case stated
This was an appeal by way of a case stated by justices for the City of York in respect of their adjudication as a magistrates' court sitting at York on 25th September and 12th October 1973.
g   On 25th May 1973 three informations were preferred by the appellant, Herbert Edward Fletcher, against the respondent, Howard Anthony Budgen, that he on 9th December 1972, in the course of a trade or business, namely, a dealer in motor cars, applied by means of an oral statement false trade descriptions to a Fiat 500 motor car, registration number AVY 281B, namely, (1) that there was 'No possibility of repairing' the motor car; (2) that 'Repairs would not make the car safe', and (3) that
h   'The only possible course of action with this car would be for the car to be scrapped', contrary to s 1(1)(a) of the Trade Descriptions Act 1968.
    The following facts were found. (1) The respondent was in business as a dealer in motor cars. (2) In July 1971 Mr Keith John Durkin purchased a Fiat 500 motor car, registration number AVY 281B, for the sum of £165 and he used it thereafter. (3) Between August and October 1972 Mr Durkin spent some £56·44 on repairs to the
j   motor car in an effort to put it in a sufficiently good state of repair for it to pass the Ministry of Transport test but it failed to pass the test. (4) Some time shortly before 9th December, at the invitation of Mr Durkin's father-in-law, the respondent called to see the motor car. A discussion took place during which Mr Durkin told the respondent of the work he had had done to the motor car. The respondent said he would

---

a   Section 1(1), so far as material, is set out at p 1245 *c*, post

have to examine the car more thoroughly before offering a price for it and it was
arranged for the car to be taken to the respondent's business premises. (5) Pursuant to
that arrangement Mr Durkin took the car to the respondent's business premises on 9th
December. (6) On that occasion the respondent and a colleague examined the car,
both the bodywork and underneath, using a hydraulic jack. (7) After the examination
the respondent said to Mr Durkin (a) that there was no possibility of repairing the
car because the floor and the floor supports were too weak; (b) that repairs would
not make the car safe; (c) that the only possible course of action with the car would
be for it to be scrapped. (8) As a result of those statements Mr Durkin said that he
would dispose of the vehicle to a local scrap dealer but later agreed to sell the car to
the respondent for £2 as scrap value. He handed over both the car and the log book
to the respondent. (9) Subsequently in February 1973 the respondent advertised the
car for sale at a price of £135. A Ministry of Transport certificate was issued for the
car in early February 1973. (10) After purchasing the car the respondent had carried
out repairs to the car to the value of about £56. (11) The statements made by the
respondent and referred to in (7) above were false to the knowledge of the respondent
when he made them.

It was contended by the appellant that the statements made by the respondent
were false trade descriptions which he had applied to the car in the course of his
business during negotiations for the purchase of the car.

It was contended by the respondent : (a) that the 1968 Act had no application to
representations made by a buyer in the course of acquiring goods and that its application was confined exclusively to the situation where a seller made representations
about goods in the course of disposal of those goods; (b) that in any event the statements were not 'trade descriptions', within s 2(1)(d) of the 1968 Act, because they
amounted to negative representations about the goods whereas to be a trade
description there had to be a positive representation about the goods.

The justices were of the opinion that each of the statements amounted to a false
trade description within s 2(1)(d) of the 1968 Act but that the Act had no application
to circumstances where the descriptions were applied to goods by a purchaser in the
course of his acquisition of those goods. Accordingly they dismissed the informations.

Anthony Scrivener for the appellant.
The respondent did not appear and was not represented.

LORD WIDGERY CJ. This is an appeal by case stated by justices for the city of
York in respect of their adjudication in the magistrates' court in York on 12th October
1973. Before them on that occasion were three informations preferred by the appellant prosecutor against the respondent. Each related to 9th December 1972. Each
was concerned with a Fiat 500 motor car, which at that time the respondent was
considering buying from its then owner. The respondent was engaged in the trade
or business of a dealer in motor cars. When this Fiat was brought to him by its
potential seller for him to consider its purchase, and he examined it in the course
of his trade or business as a dealer in cars, he made three disparaging remarks about
the car. First of all, he said there was no possibility of repairing it. Secondly, he said
the repairs would not make the car safe, and, thirdly, summing up the whole
situation, he said the only possible course of action with regard to the car would be
for the car to be scrapped. The then owner of the car, a Mr Durkin, discouraged,
and accepting that the car was good for scrap only, sold it to the respondent for £2.

To his astonishment no doubt he discovered very shortly afterwards that the car
was being advertised for sale by the respondent at a price of £135. The justices found
that the respondent had done repairs to the car to the value of about £56 and thus
had managed to make the car sufficiently roadworthy for it to obtain its Ministry
of Transport certificate. It was duly offered for sale, as I have said. The justices

a also found that the statements made by the respondent in regard to the car were false to his knowledge when he made the statements.

In other words, on its facts this is a very strong case. You have the non-trader who is selling the car; the motor trader who is buying it; an examination made by the potential buyer, jacking up the car and going underneath it; three extremely positive and unequivocal comments about the unsuitability of the car for any further use, and the ultimate result of the respondent having acquired the car for £2, being *b* able apparently to sell it for a substantial profit.

Arising out of those facts there were, as I have said, three informations laid by the prosecutor against the respondent, alleging in each case that he had applied a false trade description to the car and thus committed an offence contrary to s 1 of the Trade Descriptions Act 1968.

One must look again at the first four sections, although in this court we seem to *c* refer to them very frequently. Section 1(1) provides:

> 'Any person who, in the course of a trade or business,—(a) applies a false trade description to any goods ... shall, subject to the provisions of this Act, guilty of an offence.'

d It is important to bear in mind throughout that the offence is created by a person who, in the course of a trade or business, applies a false trade description to the goods in question. Section 2 tells us what is meant by the expression 'trade description', and it is in the widest possible words. It is 'an indication, direct or indirect, and by whatever means given, of any of the following matters with respect to any goods or parts of goods, that is to say', and then there are listed a number of descriptions. The relevant one in the present case is (e): 'any physical characteristics not included *e* in the preceding paragraphs.' The case for the prosecution was that when the respondent used these three derogatory observations in relation to the motor car, the observations amounted to a trade description because they were an indication of the physical characteristics of the car.

Then the Act goes on to define 'false trade description' in s 3(1), and that not surprisingly describes or defines a false trade description as 'a trade description which *f* is false to a material degree'. This is somewhat further developed in sub-ss (2) and (3) in a manner which I do not find it necessary to pursue in this case because if the remarks passed on this motor car were trade descriptions, as the prosecution contended, there is no doubt whatever that they were not only false to a material degree, but, for good measure, they were known by the respondent to be false, which is not in itself an essential of the offence charged.

g In s 4 one has the important provisions dealing with what amounts to an applying of a trade description, it being remembered again that the offence in sub-s (1) is created by applying a false trade description to any goods. Section 4(1) provides:

> 'A person applies a trade description to goods if he—(a) affixes or annexes it to or in any manner marks it on or incorporates it with—(i) the goods themselves ... (c) uses the trade description in any manner likely to be taken as referring *h* to the goods.'

Subsection (2) provides: 'An oral statement may amount to the use of a trade description', so it is not necessary for the description to be contained in writing; an oral statement will do.

Again looking at the facts of this case, it cannot be doubted that if these words *j* amounted to a trade description they would certainly be likely to be taken as referring to the goods, namely, the car; indeed, they could not have referred to anything else.

So at first blush one looks at the four sections and observes the wide ambit which they enjoy, and if when construing the statute, one looks at the words and sees what their natural meaning is, it seems that they cover this case.

But why? Because, according to s 1(1), the respondent was carrying on a trade or business, and it was in the course of his trade or business that he made the observations. Further, the trade description was applied to the goods because it was used in a manner likely to be taken as referring to the goods. That it was a false description is really beyond doubt, as I have already sought to demonstrate.

There is, therefore, on the face of it only one reason why the prosecution might be held unsuccessful in this case, and that would be on the fundamental proposition that, although the Act does not condescend in terms to say so, yet the scheme of ss 1 to 4 is restricted to false trade descriptions made by a seller of goods and cannot apply to a buyer of goods. If on a proper consideration of the Act it can be said with confidence that Parliament must have intended that it should not have been, so be it. If one cannot, on a consideration of the sections of the Act, conclude that buyers are necessarily excluded from its terms, then it would seem to me that a buyer is as much liable to be convicted as a seller under the terms of the sections to which I have referred.

Oddly enough, this is a point which has not arisen before. Perhaps the nearest to it is *Fletcher v Stedmore*[1]. That was a case with rather unusual facts in which the owner of a motor car had agreed to sell and, being a repairer of cars, had agreed to undertake certain repairs before the car was delivered to the buyer. The buyer was contemplating reselling it to a sub-purchaser. He brought the sub-purchaser along to see the car in the state in which it was, partly dismantled for repair purposes, and the respondent, who was the original seller of the car, was present. On enquiry being made by the prospective sub-purchaser as to the quality of the car, the respondent volunteered the information that it was all right, it was a good little engine, and he had driven it himself.

That case raised a number of points not relevant in the instant case, but in the judgment of Eveleigh J there are some useful observations as to the scope of this Act, and I find them of assistance in the present problem. Having looked at the same sections to which I have already referred, he said[2]:

'Reading the words of the section, one sees no limitation which specifies the nature of the transaction in which the description of the goods is made. Counsel for the prosecutor has very properly drawn the court's attention to *Hall v Wickens Motors (Gloucester) Ltd*[3]. In that case the defendants, who were car dealers, sold a car, and some 40 days later received an oral complaint from the purchaser about the steering. The defendants replied "There is nothing wrong with the car". Examination of the car revealed in fact that it was defective. The defendants were charged with applying a false trade description to the car, namely, an oral statement that there was nothing wrong with it. They were convicted and appealed to quarter sessions, where the recorder accepted their submission that no offence had been committed under section 1(1)(a) of the Act of 1968.'

Then Eveleigh J goes on to deal with certain other aspects of that case, and he continued[4]:

'However, on the facts of this particular case it would not be right to say that the statement was unconnected with the supply or the sale of goods. There are no qualifications in section 1 as to the time when the representation is to be made. The only qualification there specifically to be seen is that it should be in the course of trade or business, in other words should be made as part of the business activities of the person charged. There is no reason to introduce any time qualification.

---

1   [1973] RTR 371
2   [1973] RTR at 375
3   [1972] 3 All ER 759, [1972] 1 WLR 1418
4   [1973] RTR at 376

a   The question then remains whether or not there is reason to introduce the quali-
cation that the person charged should himself be a contracting party in the
matters in which the representation is made. No such limitation appears in
the section itself, and I see no reason why such a limitation should be implied.'

I cite that case because, as I have said, it indicates the attitude of this court towards
b suggestions made from time to time that the clear language of the statute should
be restricted on some assumed basis that Parliament must have so intended.

A case in which such a submission was made and upheld in this court is, however,
Wycombe Marsh Garages Ltd v Fowler[1]. This was a case in which the owner of a car had
taken the car to a garage to obtain a Ministry of Transport certificate. The accused
in that case examined the car and came to the conclusion that the nearside tyres were
c defective to such a degree as to make it impossible to issue a certificate. He, therefore,
refused the certificate, certifying that the tyres suffered from this particular defect.
He was wrong. He was honestly wrong, but he was wrong, and eventually it was
shown that the tyres suffered from no such defect.

Somewhat to the surprise of the members of the court sitting on that occasion,
the authorities then proceeded to prosecute him with a criminal offence under s 1 of
d the 1968 Act. It was held that he had committed no such offence, and the value of
the case, I think, is that it emphasises that the Act is only concerned with false trade
descriptions applied to goods in association with a contract for the sale or supply of
the goods. In other words, *Wycombe Marsh Garages Ltd v Fowler*[1] is valuable for the
proposition that a person who merely makes an inspection of goods as a service to
its owner, and who honestly certifies his findings, is not to be convicted of an offence
e under s 1 because, although he may be said to have applied a trade description to
the goods, he has not done so in a transaction associated with sale or supply of the
goods.

There one has an example of this court imposing certain limitations on the wide
words of the section, but in general we must take the Act as it stands. We must look
at the language used and we must give it its natural consequences.

f   I confess to being surprised at the conclusion to which I have ultimately come
because I confess that in considering this Act in the past I have subconsciously thought
that it could only apply to false trade descriptions applied by the seller. I suppose
that I had never before been required to think about the circumstances in which
the public need to apply these restrictions to a buyer is every bit as much as is the
public need to apply them to a seller. If one visualises the present case where the
g potential buyer of the goods is engaged in the trade or business of buying cars, and
if one reminds oneself that this Act only applies to people who apply false trade
descriptions in the course of a trade or business, then I think it becomes apparent
that to allow the Act to operate according to its terms in the present case is not in
any sense illogical and is not likely to run counter to any intention which Parliament
may have had.

h   It seems to me that it is perfectly reasonable when the buyer is the expert and the
seller may be the amateur, where the buyer makes an examination of the goods in
his capacity as an expert and then proceeds to pronounce on the qualities or otherwise,
that he should be as much liable to be restrained in his language as is a seller, who in
the normal course of events is the man who knows all about the goods and who
is to be restricted in any temptation to make false and misleading statements about
j them.

I do not believe that upholding the prosecution in the present case is going
to mean that every buyer of goods runs the risk of committing a criminal offence
merely because he deprecates or makes some derogatory remarks about the goods
which are offered to him. It would be a sad thing if such a situation arose.

---

1   [1972] 3 All ER 248, [1972] 1 WLR 1156

But when one remembers that it is only a buyer who is conducting a trade or business, and who, therefore, in most instances will himself be the expert on this subject, who can fall foul of this Act, it seems to me that a decision in favour of the prosecution in this case will not only accord with the language of the Act and be consistent with what we have said about it in the past, but also make very good sense in view of the fact that its effect is restricted to those who carry on a trade or business.

For those reasons I am persuaded that the justices were wrong, and I would allow the appeal and send the case back with a direction to continue the hearing in the light of this court's judgment.

PARK J. I agree.

FORBES J. I agree.

Appeal allowed.

Solicitors: *Sharpe Pritchard & Co*, agents for *W A Harrison*, Northallerton, Yorkshire (for the appellant).

Jacqueline Charles   Barrister.

Practice Direction

SUPREME COURT TAXING OFFICE

Costs – Taxation – Bill of costs – Lodging of bill when reference taken – Procedure – RSC Ord 62, rr 21, 23.

1.   The purpose of the amendment to RSC Ord 62, rr 21 and 23, which extended the time for taking a reference from seven days to three months, was to assist solicitors who were having difficulty in drawing bills within the prescribed time and to reduce the work devolving on the chambers of the Supreme Court Taxing Office in sending out numerous reminders to solicitors to lodge bills.

2.   In a number of cases, as a result of the amendment, parties having the conduct of a taxation have delayed taking a reference, to the detriment of other parties entitled to costs in the same proceedings, as well as to paying parties who are anxious to know the extent of their liability.

3.   Henceforth any party to a taxation, whether he is entitled to costs or is a paying party, may take a reference at any time after the entry of the judgment or order or service of other document authorising the taxation.

4.   When such a party desires to take a reference he must, before doing so, inform the party having carriage of the relevant order or other document in writing of his intention, and, if he thereafter takes a reference, produce to the rota clerk when taking the reference a copy of such notice.

5.   In all other respects the practice direction of 30th November 1972[1] is confirmed.

GRAHAM GRAHAM-GREEN
Chief Master

4th July 1974

---

1   [1973] 1 All ER 52, [1973] 1 WLR 43